CAMPERSTOP EUROPE 2017

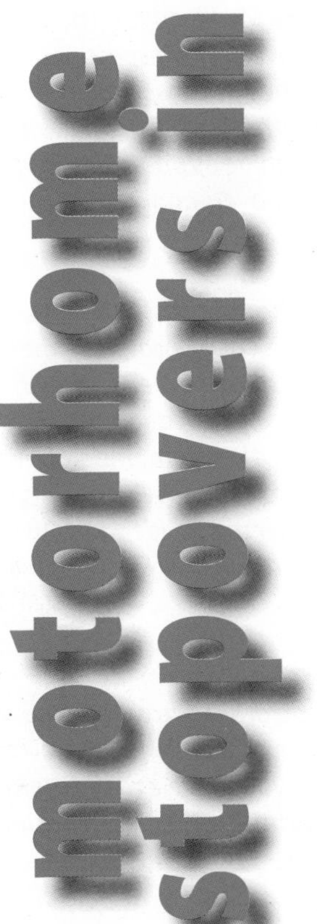

Albania
Austria
Belgium
Bosnia-Herzegovina
Croatia
Czech Republic
Denmark
Finland
France
Germany
Greece
Hungary
Ireland
Italy
Luxemburg
Montenegro
Netherlands
Norway
United Kingdom
Poland
Portugal
Romania
Slovenia
Slovakia
Spain
Sweden
Switzerland

Publisher - Herausgeber - Éditeur - Editore Facile Media

Reliable information

Every summer, 50 teams of Facile Media drive all across Europe to inspect the motorhome stopovers. The inspections take place according to predefined guidelines. The inspections by these specially trained motorhome enthusiasts have made it possible to make the information in the guide as up-to-date as possible. More than 9000 motorhome stopovers and 7099 illustrative photos are the result.

Unique way to find the motorhome sites

The motorhome stopovers can be easily located on the 40 maps. Below each map, you'll find a location name index with map referral and a page number where the location can be found in the guide. In addition, the type of motorhome stopover is indicated. In a glance, you'll be able to see whether it is the type of stopover you had in mind. In order to provide you with additional information, the location is described extensively on the relevant page, usually with a picture.

GPS-data sets on your navigation system

In addition to this guide, you can order datasets online, which you can download. The sets can be uploaded to the most common navigation systems. This allows you to drive to the motorhome stopovers listed in this guide without any effort. More information about this is available on *page 8.*

Follow us on Facebook for the latest news:
facebook.com/CamperstopEurope

For more information: camperstop.com/app

COLOPHON

A publication of:

Facile Media b.v., Oss
Landweerstraat-Zuid 109
5349 AK Oss
Postbus 555
NL-5340 AN Oss
tel: +31 412 65 68 85
E-mail: info@camperstop.com
Internet: www.camperstop.com

Chief editor
Anne van den Dobbelsteen

The draft of this version is saved in October 2016

Comments or suggestions can be sent to the publisher:

Facile Media
Postbus 555, NL-5340 AN Oss
Tel.: +31 412 65 68 85
E-mail: info@camperstop.com

ISBN 978-90-76080-50-5

20 YEARS MOTORHOME GUIDE DUTCH EDITION

The 2017 edition of the Dutch publication of this guide is 20 years old. What began in 1997 as a 336-page Dutch book of information on the Benelux countries and France has now become a voluminous guide with 27 countries in 5 languages.

Our Camperstop-app has been available in the stores since the spring of 2016. The app is easy to use, but the underlying technology is very complicated. After a start with teething problems the app now works to our full satisfaction. This digital path is a new experience for us. Your help is therefore very welcome, please give us feedback and write reviews about motorhome stopovers you have visited. In this way the app together with this guide will become the most useful and reliable travel companion during each motorhome trip.

A number of our inspectors checked motorhome stopovers in Scandinavia in 2016. I hope that the photos that now accompany the stopovers in Finland, Sweden and Norway, will be an inspiration to plan a memorable trip to one of these countries.

Like every year I am making you a partaker on one of our trips. In June 2016 we travelled to Corsica and Sardinia. An amazing experience! Island hopping with the motorhome, the overnight ferry from Genoa to Bastia, then from Bonifacio to Santa Teresa Gallura in 50 minutes and another overnight ferry from Golfo Aranci to Livorno. Unfortunately it was not possible to sleep in our motorhome during the crossing, but staying in a cabin is also comfortable and in the morning you drive off the boat fully rested.

Corsica: a memory of wonderful scents and narrow roads. The Cap Corse coastal road leads you along narrow roads and past deep precipices, but is breathtakingly beautiful. The pass that leads straight across the island is stunning, but pay attention here as well. The former mule track is different widths and you meet all kinds of animals on the road. The beautiful 'bounty' beaches south of Porto Vecchio and wonderful Bonifacio with its picturesque harbour and the walled fortress high above the water are well worth a visit. The weather in Corsica was disappointing so we shortened our stay in the hope that the weather gods in Sardinia would be better disposed towards us.

The ferry in Bonifacio takes you to Sardinia in 50 minutes. After a slight hesitation, the sun appeared more often and the mercury rose to a comfortable temperature. No crowds, varied landscapes, stunning beaches and delicious food. This makes Sardinia a great motorhome destination. The rugged west coast where you can watch the sunset in the evening, high above the sea, with a glass of wine in your hand. The east coast with long sandy beaches and an azure blue sea invites you to wonderfully relax. The whole island is gorgeous but you must not skip a visit to Orgosolo, a town with many wall murals and authentic Bosa, where you can stay overnight in your motorhome in the centre of town.

I hope this guide inspires you to take beautiful motorhome journeys throughout Europe.

Anne van den Dobbelsteen
Chief editor

Table of contents

Table of contents

How to use the guide

Searching in a region
In the table of contents, at the beginning of the guide, one can search a region in preferred country. On the page of the region a map indicates the different departments/provinces with a reference to the pages.

Maps
On pages 12-13 the countries are divided into sections. The number in each box is the number of the map. On the map the red dots indicate the location of the town. Next to each map an index is published with the places on maps. The index shows the name, type of stopover, map code and page number of each location. This way the description of the motorhome stopover can be found quickly and easy.

Searching for a town
Places identified in this guide can be found under the name of the local town in the alphabetical index at the back. Use the index like a dictionary to look for specific towns, the facilities offered, map references and relevant page numbers.

Country specific rules
When travelling you have to take into account that each country has its own rules and regulations. These rules are written on the first page of each countries section.

Advise
It is recommended not to wait to long to look for an overnight stop. It could be that chosen motorhome stopover is already full and you have to go looking for an alternative.

Other symbols

Motorhome stopover, number of pitches and rate

- Signposted on the spot
- Signposted in town
- No signs to indicate the motorhome stopover

Payment
- Collector parking fee
- Parking meter
- Payment only with a credit/debit card
- Payment with cash and credit/debit card

S Service facilities
This symbol indicates that there are service facilities available.
- drinking water
- grey water dump
- Ch chemical toilet disposal point
- charging battery
- electricity available
- WC toilets
- showers
- washing machine/ dryer on the spot
- wifi access point

Description motorhome stopover

The information per motorhome stopover always begins with a colored block containing the type of stopover, town name and reference to the map. Directly below the name, address, GPS coordinates mostly followed by a picture. Beneath the picture you find the following information: number of pitches, rate, facilities and opening period. After that, if known, distances to city centre, shop, restaurant etc. Specific information of the motorhome stopover and a brief route description.

Motorhome facilities

MOTORHOME PARK
This symbol indicates a motorhome park, a park designed for motorhomes with a range of facilities.

OFFICIAL MOTORHOME STOPOVER
This symbol indicates an area suitable for overnight parking

OVERNIGHT PARKING TOLERATED
In some countries tolerated places are mentioned. This means that it is officially prohibited but is being tolerated by local authorities. Therefore the local or national situation may change at any time. Nevertheless these places are listed because they were frequently being used by motorhomes at the time of writing.

OVERNIGHT STAY IN HARBOUR/MARINA
Motorhome stopover in or near harbour or marina, often with a beautiful view.

OVERNIGHT STAY AT FARM/VINEYARD
Farms and vineyards that welcome motorhomes, you may be encouraged to sample and buy their fare.

OVERNIGHT STAY AT RESTAURANT
Motorhomes are allowed to stopover on the car park of a hotel, restaurant or bar. You should expect to dine or drink in the bar. Some restaurants insist on you having dinner. Sometimes a nominal charge is asked for the overnight stay.

OVERNIGHT STAY AT SPA
A growing number of spas and thermal baths offer stopovers to motorhomes.

OVERNIGHT STAY AT ZOO/MUSEUM/AMUSEMENT PARK
Motorhomes are allowed to stopover on the car park of a zoo, museum or amusement park. Entrance is not always obligated.

OVERNIGHT STAY AT COMPANY/ENTERPRISE
Overnight stay, mostly inside the gates, at companies/enterprises.

OVERNIGHT STAY OUTSIDE THE CAMPSITE
Motorhomes are allowed to stopover on the parking place outside the gate of a campsite.

CAMPSITE
Overnight stay on a campsite.

P CAR-PARK
Motorhome parking bays, suitable for daytime use only. Often in large cities and/or tourist towns, charges may apply.

GPS - convenience

Downloading GPS-coordinates

Downloads of the gps-coordinates for the motorhome stopovers listed in this guide are available from www.camperstop.com. The files are suitable for most navigation systems. The data that appears on the screen gives the town name and page number in this guide so you can look up the details of the facilities very easily.

The downloadable files list the stopovers and most of the other facilities mentioned in the guide. Therefore it could be a stopover with or without service facilities, a place with service facilities only, but also a tourist information office or a campsite.

You can easily check for your nearest stopover, the navigation system will list the stopovers by distance. Use the guide to see what facilities are available. Once a choice has been made you can navigate to there without a problem.

The costs for downloading are € 3.25 per country/dataset. The Netherlands/ Belgium/Luxembourg are sold as one country, also Austria/Switzerland and Spain/Portugal are treated the same.

Full downloading instructions are found on at camperstop.com. There are different downloads of several navigation systems.

Traveling in England - South West Coast

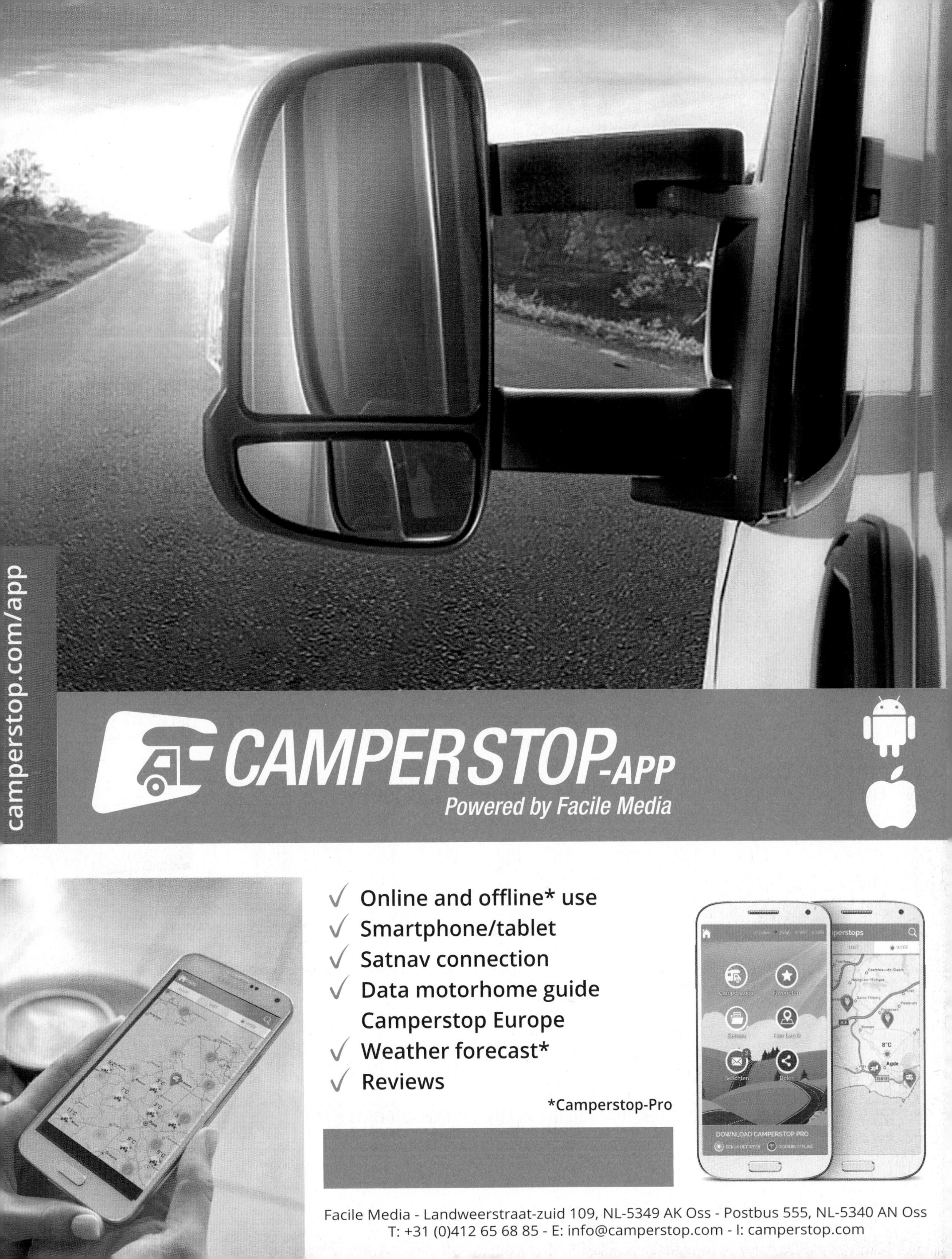

Driving regulations in Europe

Each country has different driving rules. For motorhomes sometimes there are different regulations. Here below an overview with maximum speed limits for motorhomes.

Per country there are also different rules as for warning triangles, security vests or driving with daily lights. Here below this information at a glance.

	within towns	single carriageway		expressway		motorway		compulsory in your vehicle:
		<3,5T	>3,5T	<3,5T	>3,5T	<3,5T	>3,5T	
AL Albania	40	80	70	90	70	110	80	
A Austria	50	100	70			130	80	A10-A12-A13-en A14 : 22-05h max. 110km/h.
B Belgium	50	90				120	90	
BIH Bosnia and Herzegovina	50	80		100	80	130	80	
CH Switzerland	50	80		100	80	120	80	
CZ Czech Republic	50	90	80	120	80	130	80	
D Germany	50	100	80	130	100	130	100	130km/h is a recommended speed limit.
DK Denmark	50	80	70	110	80	130	80	
ES Spain	50	80		90	80	100	90	
FIN Finland	50	80		100	80	100	80	
F France	50	90	80	110	100	130	110	Speed limits on a dry road. Safety vest also for bicycles.
GB Great Britain	30	60	50	70	60	70		30mph=48km 50mph=80km 60mph=96km 70mph=112km Speed limits in mph.
GR Greece	50	90		110	90	120	90	
HR Croatia	50	90	80	110	80	130	90	Set of spare bulbs.
HU Hungary	50	90	70	110	70	130	80	

	within towns	single carriageway		expressway		motorway		compulsory in your vehicle:
IRL Ireland	50	80		100 <3,5T	80 >3,5T	120 <3,5T	80 >3,5T	
I Italy	50	90 <3,5T	80 >3,5T	110 <3,5T	80 >3,5T	130 <3,5T	100 >3,5T	* Speed limits on a dry road. * Suburban.
L Luxemburg	50	90 <3,5T	75 >3,5T			130 <3,5T	90 >3,5T	Speed limits on a dry road.
MNE Montenegro	50	80		100 <3,5T	80 >3,5T	100 <3,5T	80 >3,5T	
NL The Netherlands	50	80		100 <3,5T	80 >3,5T	130 <3,5T	80 >3,5T	>3,5 ton = motorhome on truck basis.
N Norway	50	80		90 <3,5T	80 >3,5T	100 <3,5T	80 >3,5T	
PL Poland	50	90 <3,5T	70 >3,5T	120 <3,5T	80 >3,5T	140 <3,5T	80 >3,5T	
P Portugal	50	90 <3,5T	80 >3,5T	100 <3,5T	80 >3,5T	120 <3,5T	90 >3,5T	
RO Romania	50	80		90 <3,5T	80 >3,5T	120 <3,5T	110 >3,5T	
S Sweden	50	70		100 <3,5T	70 >3,5T	120 <3,5T	80 >3,5T	
SLO Slovenia	50	90 <3,5T	80 >3,5T	100 <3,5T	80 >3,5T	130 <3,5T	80 >3,5T	Set of spare bulbs.
SK Slovakia	60	90		90 <3,5T	80 >3,5T	130 <3,5T	90 >3,5T	

warning triangle

security vest

fire extinguisher

first aid kit

daily lights

recommended

Information is based on information available in November 2016.

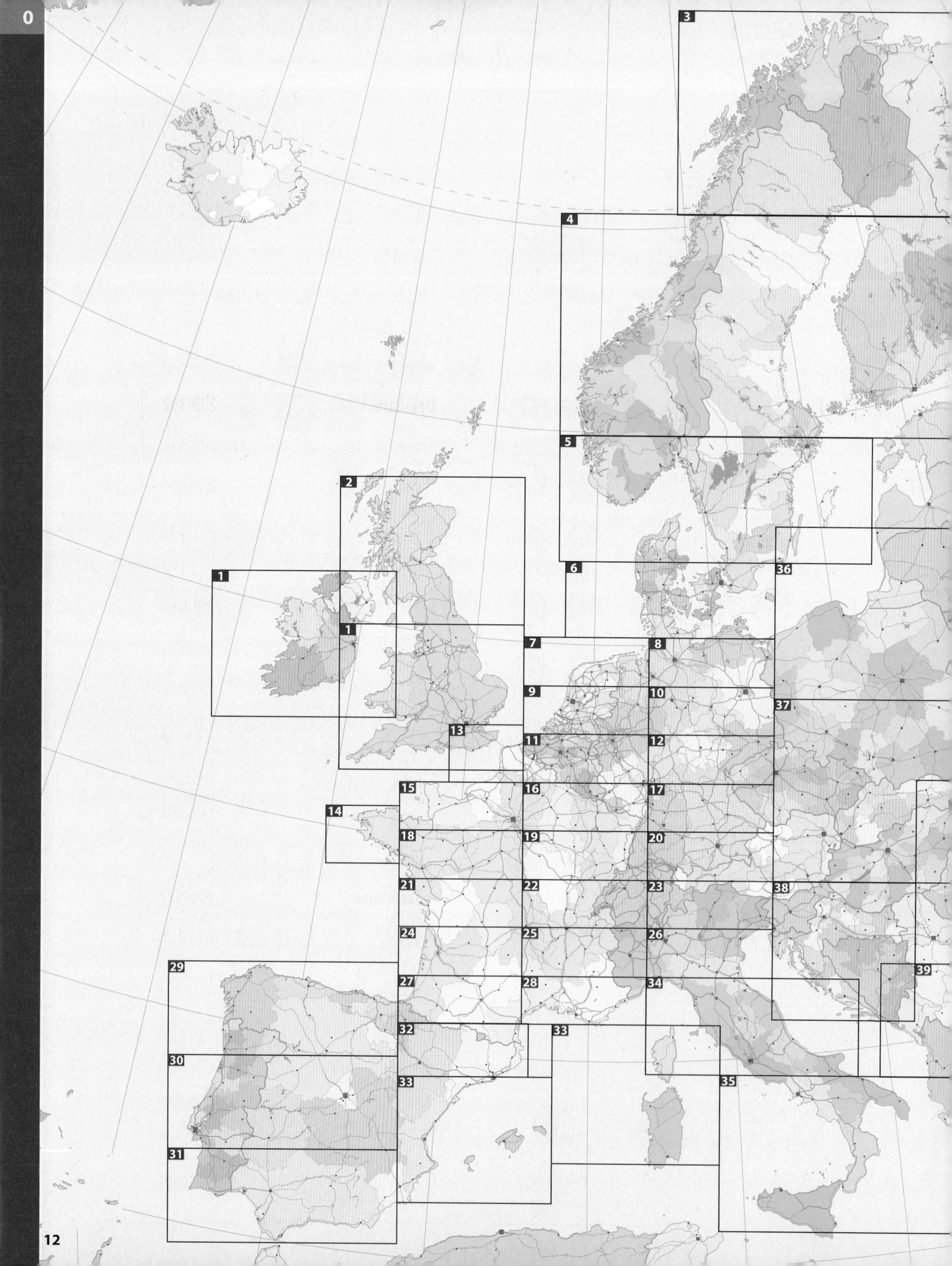
3
4
5
2
6
36
1
1
7
8
9
10
37
13
11
12
15
16
17
14
18
19
20
21
22
23
38
24
25
26
29
27
28
34
39
32
33
30
33
35
31

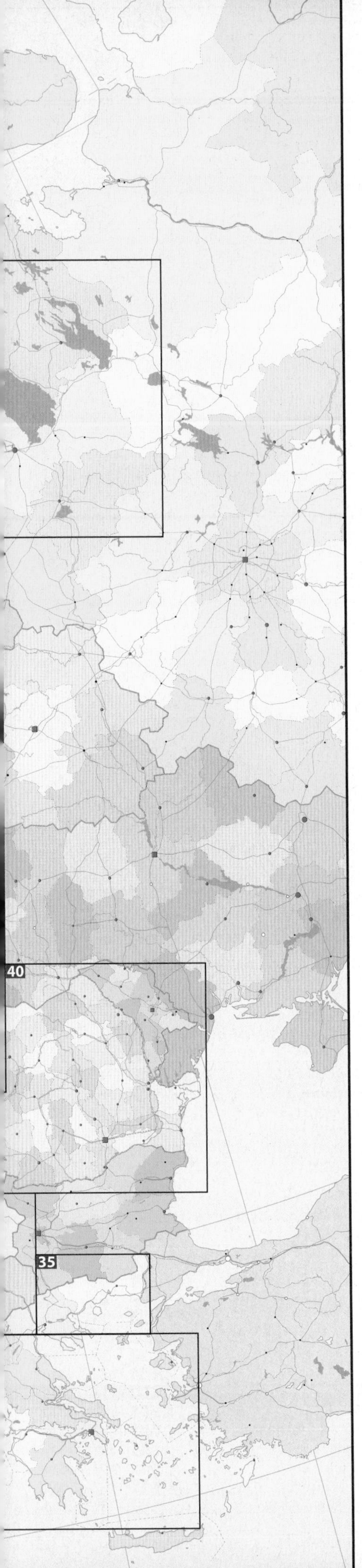

Overview map

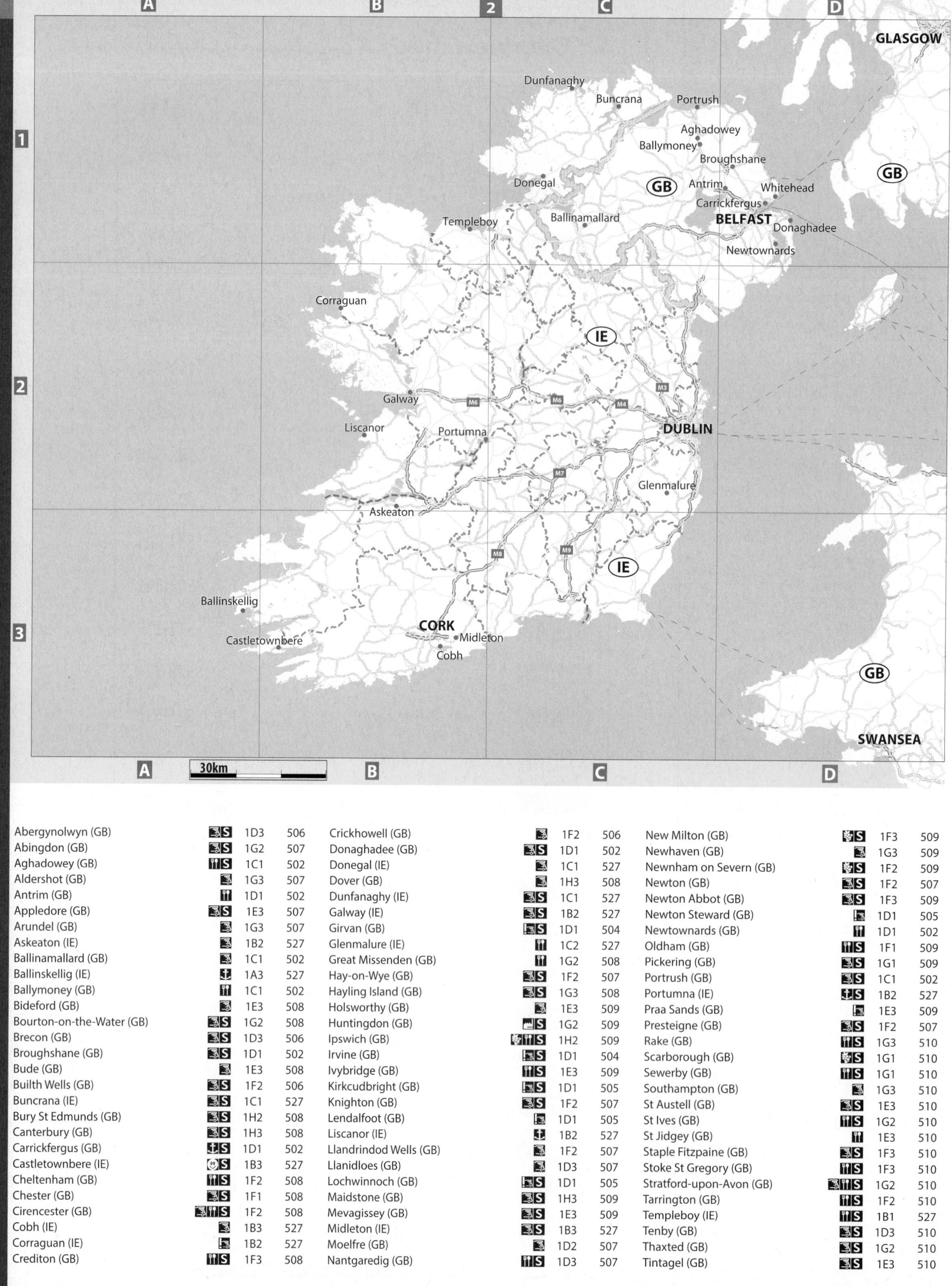

Place	Map	Page
Abergynolwyn (GB)	1D3	506
Abingdon (GB)	1G2	507
Aghadowey (GB)	1C1	502
Aldershot (GB)	1G3	507
Antrim (GB)	1D1	502
Appledore (GB)	1E3	507
Arundel (GB)	1G3	507
Askeaton (IE)	1B2	527
Ballinamallard (GB)	1C1	502
Ballinskellig (IE)	1A3	527
Ballymoney (GB)	1C1	502
Bideford (GB)	1E3	508
Bourton-on-the-Water (GB)	1G2	508
Brecon (GB)	1D3	506
Broughshane (GB)	1D1	502
Bude (GB)	1E3	508
Builth Wells (GB)	1F2	506
Buncrana (IE)	1C1	527
Bury St Edmunds (GB)	1H2	508
Canterbury (GB)	1H3	508
Carrickfergus (GB)	1D1	502
Castletownbere (IE)	1B3	527
Cheltenham (GB)	1F2	508
Chester (GB)	1F1	508
Cirencester (GB)	1F2	508
Cobh (IE)	1B3	527
Corraguan (IE)	1B2	527
Crediton (GB)	1F3	508
Crickhowell (GB)	1F2	506
Donaghadee (GB)	1D1	502
Donegal (IE)	1C1	527
Dover (GB)	1H3	508
Dunfanaghy (IE)	1C1	527
Galway (IE)	1B2	527
Girvan (GB)	1D1	504
Glenmalure (IE)	1C2	527
Great Missenden (GB)	1G2	508
Hay-on-Wye (GB)	1F2	507
Hayling Island (GB)	1G3	508
Holsworthy (GB)	1E3	509
Huntingdon (GB)	1G2	509
Ipswich (GB)	1H2	509
Irvine (GB)	1D1	504
Ivybridge (GB)	1E3	509
Kirkcudbright (GB)	1D1	505
Knighton (GB)	1F2	507
Lendalfoot (GB)	1D1	505
Liscanor (IE)	1B2	527
Llandrindod Wells (GB)	1F2	507
Llanidloes (GB)	1D3	507
Lochwinnoch (GB)	1D1	505
Maidstone (GB)	1H3	509
Mevagissey (GB)	1E3	509
Midleton (IE)	1B3	527
Moelfre (GB)	1D2	507
Nantgaredig (GB)	1D3	507
New Milton (GB)	1F3	509
Newhaven (GB)	1G3	509
Newnham on Severn (GB)	1F2	509
Newton (GB)	1F2	507
Newton Abbot (GB)	1F3	509
Newton Steward (GB)	1D1	505
Newtownards (GB)	1D1	502
Oldham (GB)	1F1	509
Pickering (GB)	1G1	509
Portrush (GB)	1C1	502
Portumna (IE)	1B2	527
Praa Sands (GB)	1E3	509
Presteigne (GB)	1F2	507
Rake (GB)	1G3	510
Scarborough (GB)	1G1	510
Sewerby (GB)	1G1	510
Southampton (GB)	1G3	510
St Austell (GB)	1E3	510
St Ives (GB)	1G2	510
St Jidgey (GB)	1E3	510
Staple Fitzpaine (GB)	1F3	510
Stoke St Gregory (GB)	1F3	510
Stratford-upon-Avon (GB)	1G2	510
Tarrington (GB)	1F2	510
Templeboy (IE)	1B1	527
Tenby (GB)	1D3	510
Thaxted (GB)	1G2	510
Tintagel (GB)	1E3	510

Torrington (GB)		1E3	511
Welshpool (GB)	S	1F2	507
Westward Ho! (GB)		1E3	511
Whaplode St Catherines (GB)	S	1G2	511
Whitehead (GB)	S	1D1	502
Winchester (GB)		1G3	511
Yeovil (GB)	S	1F3	511

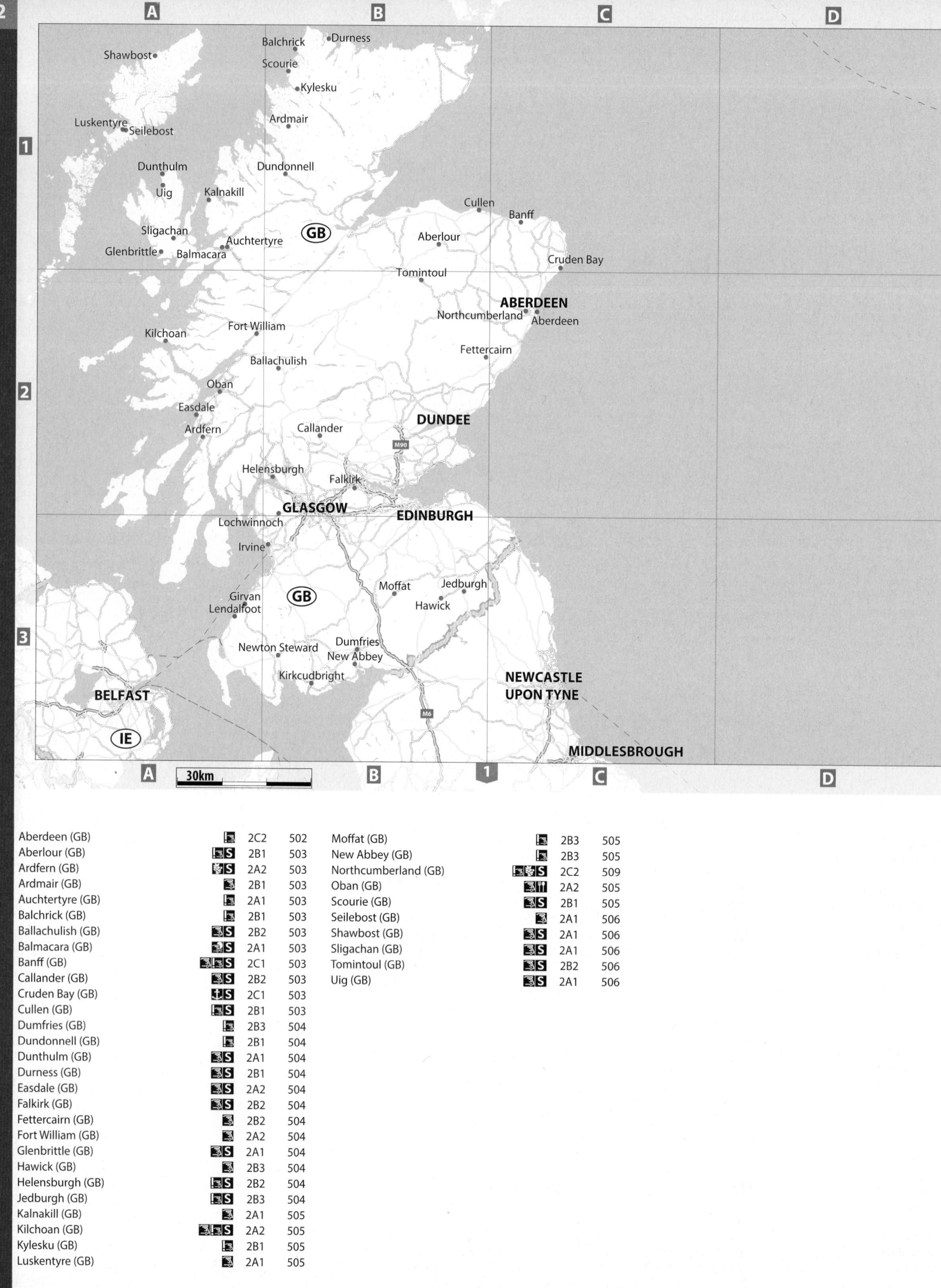

Aberdeen (GB)	2C2	502
Aberlour (GB)	2B1	503
Ardfern (GB)	2A2	503
Ardmair (GB)	2B1	503
Auchtertyre (GB)	2A1	503
Balchrick (GB)	2B1	503
Ballachulish (GB)	2B2	503
Balmacara (GB)	2A1	503
Banff (GB)	2C1	503
Callander (GB)	2B2	503
Cruden Bay (GB)	2C1	503
Cullen (GB)	2B1	503
Dumfries (GB)	2B3	504
Dundonnell (GB)	2B1	504
Dunthulm (GB)	2A1	504
Durness (GB)	2B1	504
Easdale (GB)	2A2	504
Falkirk (GB)	2B2	504
Fettercairn (GB)	2B2	504
Fort William (GB)	2A2	504
Glenbrittle (GB)	2A1	504
Hawick (GB)	2B3	504
Helensburgh (GB)	2B2	504
Jedburgh (GB)	2B3	504
Kalnakill (GB)	2A1	505
Kilchoan (GB)	2A2	505
Kylesku (GB)	2B1	505
Luskentyre (GB)	2A1	505
Moffat (GB)	2B3	505
New Abbey (GB)	2B3	505
Northcumberland (GB)	2C2	509
Oban (GB)	2A2	505
Scourie (GB)	2B1	505
Seilebost (GB)	2A1	506
Shawbost (GB)	2A1	506
Sligachan (GB)	2A1	506
Tomintoul (GB)	2B2	506
Uig (GB)	2A1	506

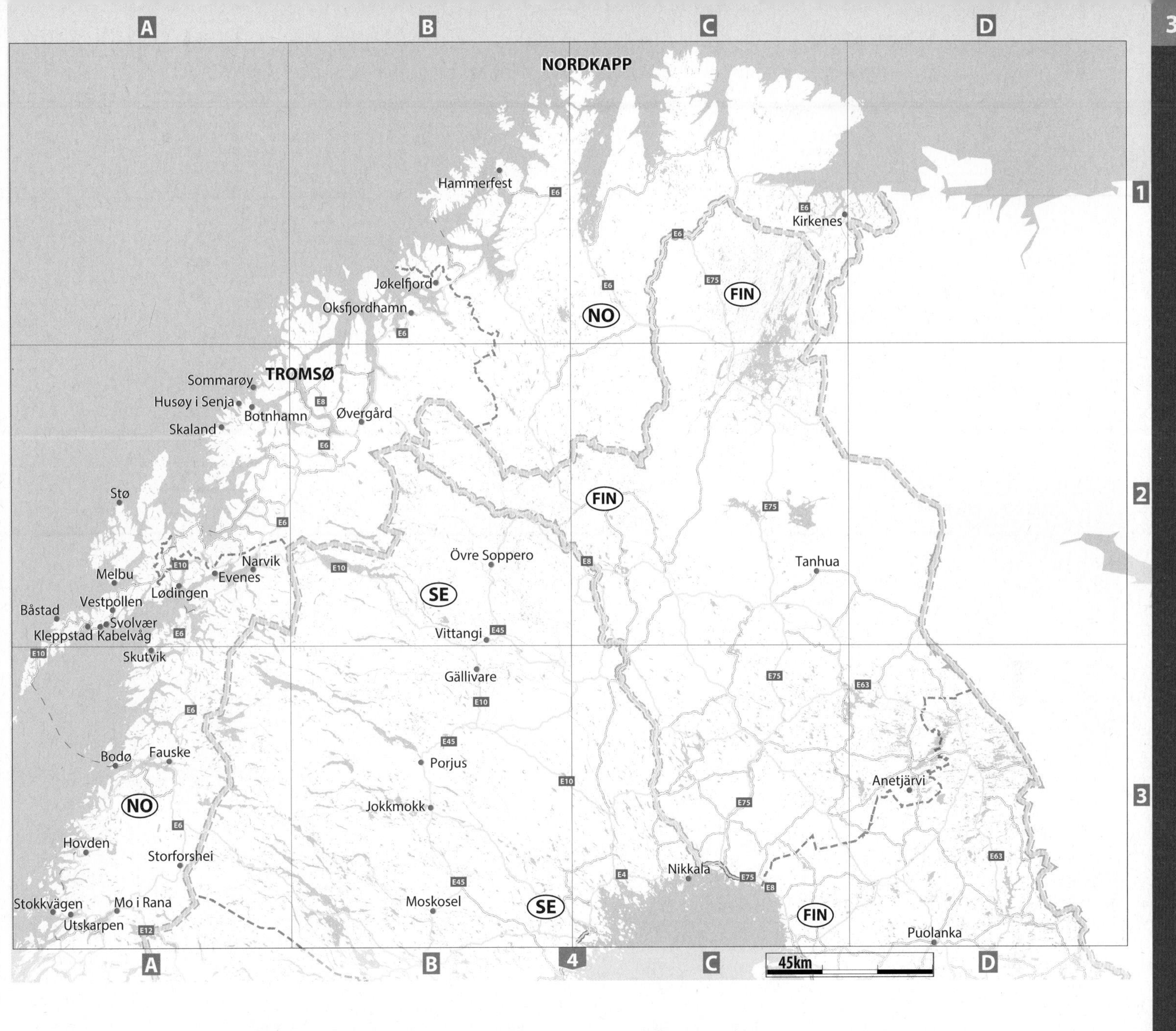

Place	Grid	Page
Anetjärvi (FI)	3D3	330
Båstad (NO)	3A2	628
Bodø (NO)	3A3	628
Botnhamn (NO)	3A2	628
Evenes (NO)	3A2	628
Fauske (NO)	3A3	628
Gällivare (SE)	3B3	659
Hammerfest (NO)	3A2	628
Hovden (NO)	3A3	628
Husøy i Senja (NO)	3A2	629
Innhavet (NO)	3A2	629
Jokkmokk (SE)	3B3	660
Jøkelfjord (NO)	3B1	629
Kabelvåg (NO)	3A2	629
Kirkenes (NO)	3C1	629
Kleppstad (NO)	3A2	629
Lødingen (NO)	3A2	629
Melbu (NO)	3A2	629
Mo i Rana (NO)	3A3	629
Moskosel (SE)	3B3	660
Narvik (NO)	3A2	629
Nikkala (SE)	3C3	660
Oksfjordhamn (NO)	3B1	629
Övre Soppero (SE)	3B2	660
Porjus (SE)	3B3	660
Puolanka (FI)	3D3	329
Skaland (NO)	3A2	629
Skutvik (NO)	3A3	629
Sommarøy (NO)	3A2	629
Stokkvägen (NO)	3A3	629
Storforshei (NO)	3A3	629
Stø (NO)	3A2	629
Svolvær (NO)	3A2	629
Tanhua (FI)	3C2	330
Utskarpen (NO)	3A3	629
Vestpollen (NO)	3A2	629
Vittangi (SE)	3B2	660
Øvergård (NO)	3B2	629

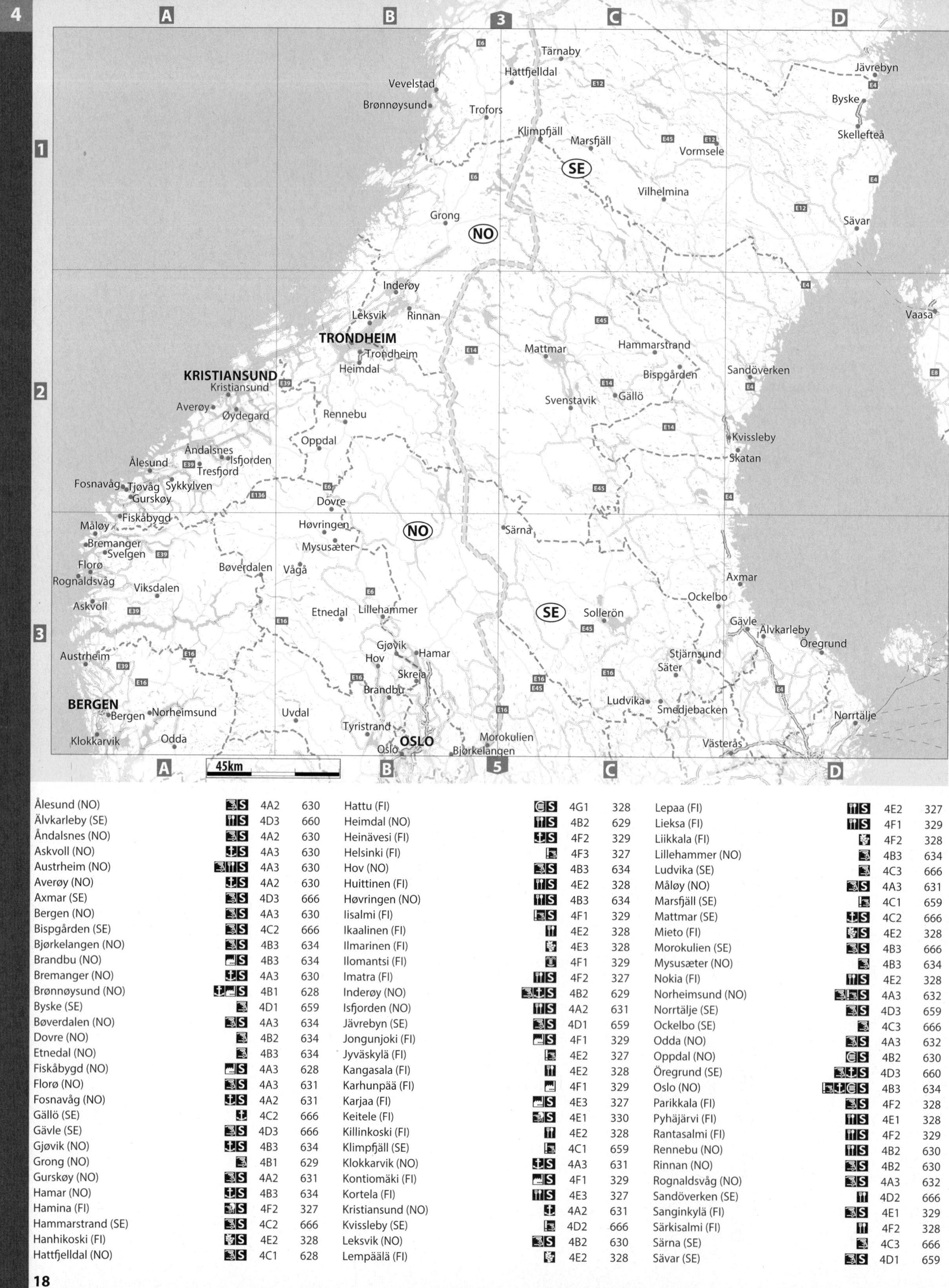
A
B
3
C
D
1
2
3
Tärnaby
Hattfjelldal
Jävrebyn
Vevelstad
Brønnøysund
Trofors
Byske
Klimpfjäll
Marsfjäll
Vormsele
Skellefteå
SE
Vilhelmina
Grong
NO
Sävar
Inderøy
Leksvik
Rinnan
Vaasa
TRONDHEIM
Trondheim
Heimdal
Mattmar
Hammarstrand
Bispgården
Sandöverken
KRISTIANSUND
Kristiansund
Averøy
Øydegard
Rennebu
Svenstavik
Gällö
Oppdal
Kvissleby
Åndalsnes
Isfjorden
Ålesund
Tresfjord
Skatan
Fosnavåg
Tjøvåg
Sykkylven
Gurskøy
Dovre
Fiskåbygd
Måløy
Høvringen
NO
Särna
Bremanger
Svelgen
Mysusæter
Florø
Bøverdalen
Vågå
Rognaldsvåg
Viksdalen
Axmar
Ockelbo
Askvoll
Etnedal
Lillehammer
SE
Sollerön
Gävle
Älvkarleby
Öregrund
Gjøvik
Hamar
Austrheim
Hov
Stjärnsund
Säter
Skreia
Brandbu
BERGEN
Bergen
Norheimsund
Uvdal
Ludvika
Smedjebacken
Norrtälje
Tyristrand
Klokkarvik
Odda
OSLO
Oslo
Morokulien
Bjørkelangen
Västerås
A
45km
B
5
C
D

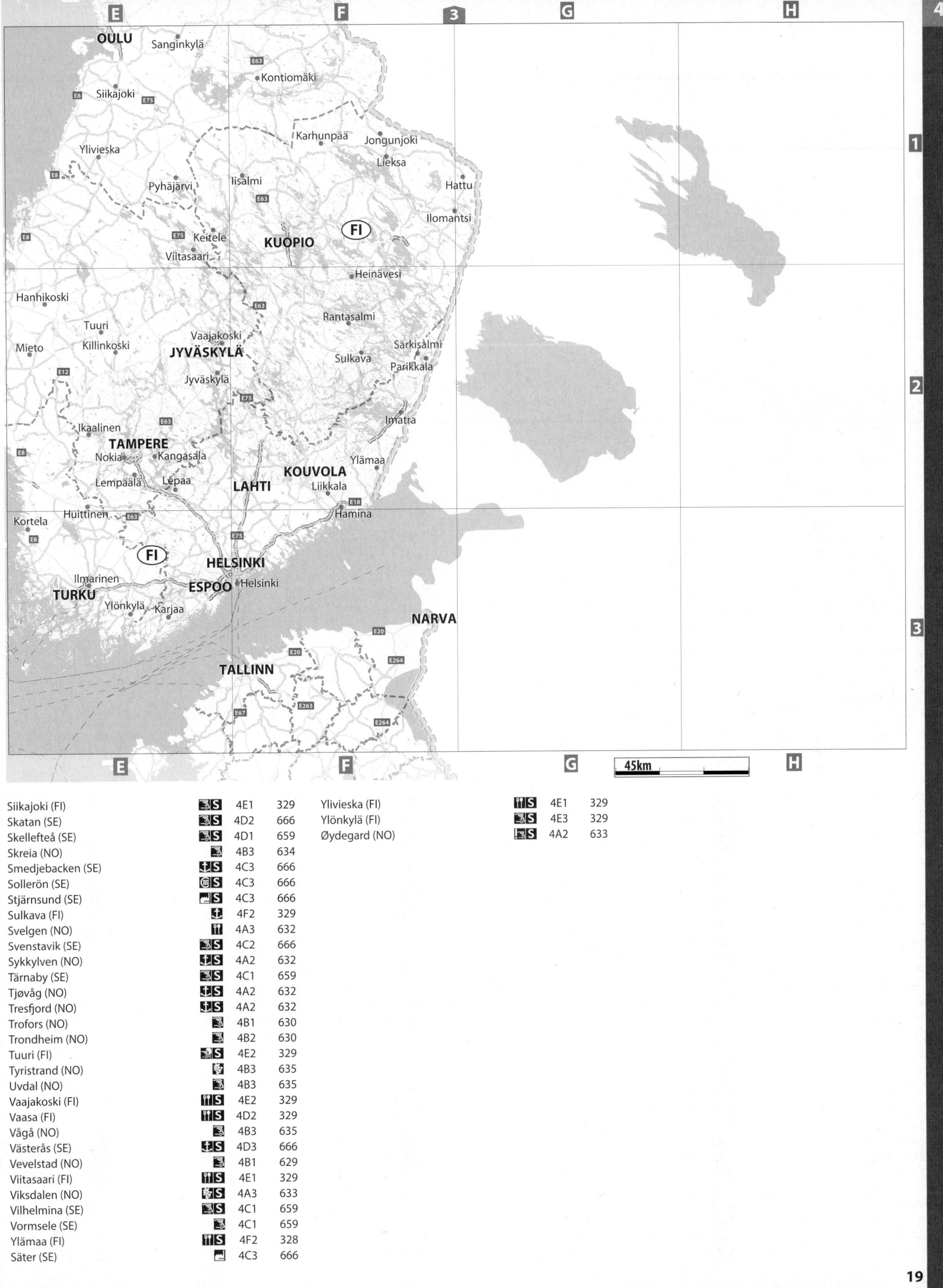
E
F
3
G
H
OULU
Sanginkylä
E63
Kontiomäki
E8
Siikajoki
E75
Karhunpää
Jongunjoki
Ylivieska
Lieksa
E8
Pyhäjärvi
Iisalmi
Hattu
E63
Ilomantsi
FI
E8
E75
Keitele
KUOPIO
Viitasaari
Heinävesi
Hanhikoski
E63
Rantasalmi
Tuuri
Vaajakoski
Mieto
Killinkoski
JYVÄSKYLÄ
Särkisalmi
Sulkava
Parikkala
E12
Jyväskylä
E75
E63
Imatra
Ikaalinen
TAMPERE
E8
Nokia
Kangasala
Ylämaa
Lempäälä
Lepaa
LAHTI
KOUVOLA
Liikkala
E18
Huittinen
Hamina
Kortela
E63
E8
E75
FI
HELSINKI
Ilmarinen
ESPOO
Helsinki
TURKU
Ylönkylä
Karjaa
NARVA
E20
E20
E264
TALLINN
E67
E263
E264
1
2
3
45km

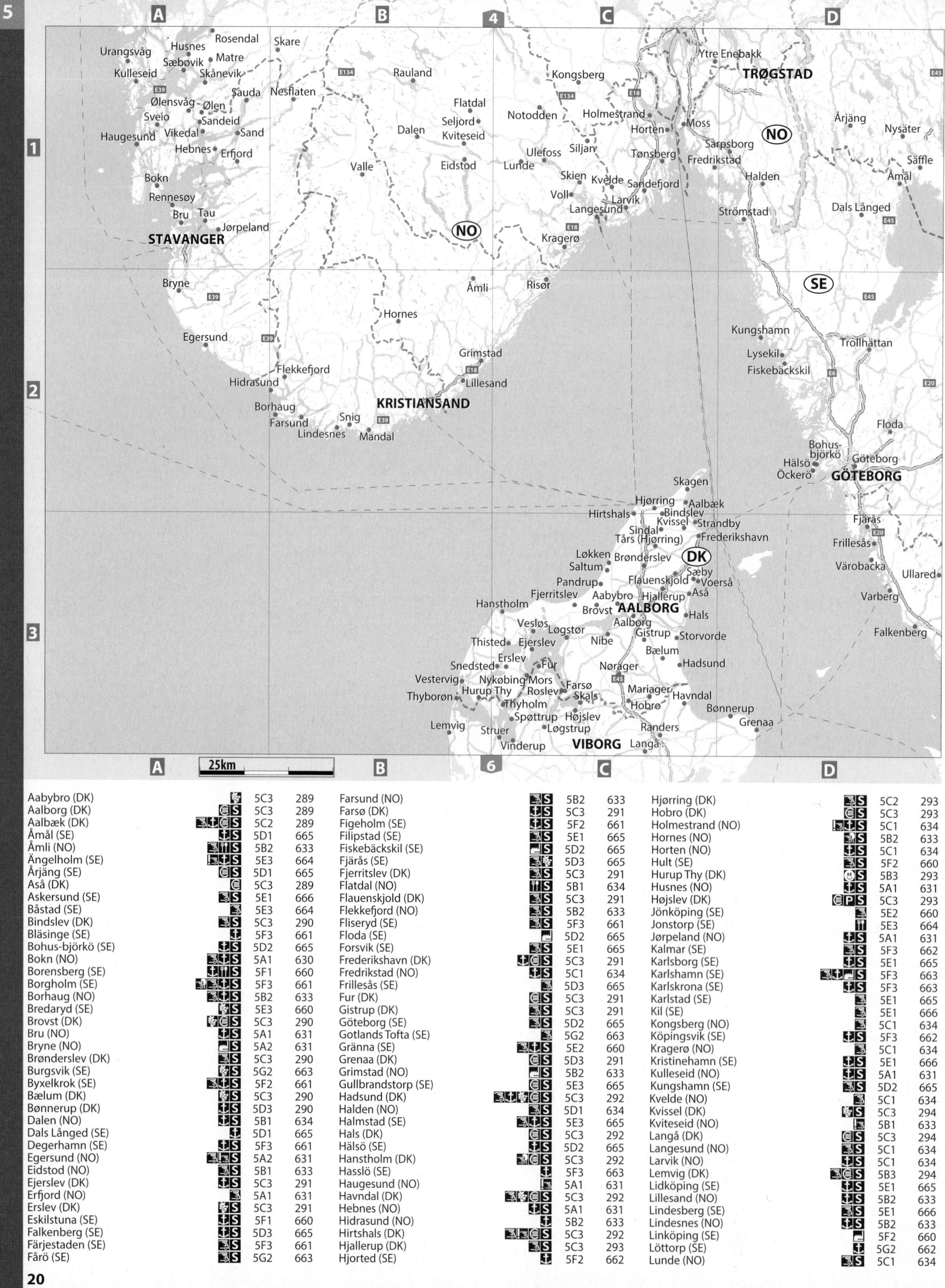

Aabybro (DK)	5C3	289
Aalborg (DK)	5C3	289
Aalbæk (DK)	5C2	289
Åmål (SE)	5D1	665
Åmli (NO)	5B2	633
Ängelholm (SE)	5E3	664
Årjäng (SE)	5D1	665
Aså (DK)	5C3	289
Askersund (SE)	5E1	666
Båstad (SE)	5E3	664
Bindslev (DK)	5C3	290
Bläsinge (SE)	5F3	661
Bohus-björkö (SE)	5D2	665
Bokn (NO)	5A1	630
Borensberg (SE)	5F1	660
Borgholm (SE)	5F3	661
Borhaug (NO)	5B2	633
Bredaryd (SE)	5E3	660
Brovst (DK)	5C3	290
Bru (NO)	5A1	631
Bryne (NO)	5A2	631
Brønderslev (DK)	5C3	290
Burgsvik (SE)	5G2	663
Byxelkrok (SE)	5F2	661
Bælum (DK)	5C3	290
Bønnerup (DK)	5D3	290
Dalen (NO)	5B1	634
Dals Långed (SE)	5D1	665
Degerhamn (SE)	5F3	661
Egersund (NO)	5A2	631
Eidstod (NO)	5B1	633
Ejerslev (DK)	5C3	291
Erfjord (NO)	5A1	631
Erslev (DK)	5C3	291
Eskilstuna (SE)	5F1	660
Falkenberg (SE)	5D3	665
Färjestaden (SE)	5F3	661
Fårö (SE)	5G2	663

Farsund (NO)	5B2	633
Farsø (DK)	5C3	291
Figeholm (SE)	5F2	661
Filipstad (SE)	5E1	665
Fiskebäckskil (SE)	5D2	665
Fjärås (SE)	5D3	665
Fjerritslev (DK)	5C3	291
Flatdal (NO)	5B1	634
Flauenskjold (DK)	5C3	291
Flekkefjord (NO)	5B2	633
Fliseryd (SE)	5F3	661
Floda (SE)	5D2	665
Forsvik (SE)	5E1	665
Frederikshavn (DK)	5C3	291
Fredrikstad (NO)	5C1	634
Frillesås (SE)	5D3	665
Fur (DK)	5C3	291
Gistrup (DK)	5C3	291
Göteborg (SE)	5D2	665
Gotlands Tofta (SE)	5G2	663
Gränna (SE)	5E2	660
Grenaa (DK)	5D3	291
Grimstad (NO)	5B2	633
Gullbrandstorp (SE)	5E3	665
Hadsund (DK)	5C3	292
Halden (NO)	5D1	634
Halmstad (SE)	5E3	665
Hals (DK)	5C3	292
Hälsö (SE)	5D2	665
Hanstholm (DK)	5C3	292
Hasslö (SE)	5F3	663
Haugesund (NO)	5A1	631
Havndal (DK)	5C3	292
Hebnes (NO)	5A1	631
Hidrasund (NO)	5B2	633
Hirtshals (DK)	5C3	292
Hjallerup (DK)	5C3	293
Hjorted (SE)	5F2	662

Hjørring (DK)	5C2	293
Hobro (DK)	5C3	293
Holmestrand (NO)	5C1	634
Hornes (NO)	5B2	633
Horten (NO)	5C1	634
Hult (SE)	5F2	660
Hurup Thy (DK)	5B3	293
Husnes (NO)	5A1	631
Højslev (DK)	5C3	293
Jönköping (SE)	5E2	660
Jonstorp (SE)	5E3	664
Jørpeland (NO)	5A1	631
Kalmar (SE)	5F3	662
Karlsborg (SE)	5E1	665
Karlshamn (SE)	5F3	663
Karlskrona (SE)	5F3	663
Karlstad (SE)	5E1	665
Kil (SE)	5E1	666
Kongsberg (NO)	5C1	634
Köpingsvik (SE)	5F3	662
Kragerø (NO)	5C1	634
Kristinehamn (SE)	5E1	666
Kulleseid (NO)	5A1	631
Kungshamn (SE)	5D2	665
Kvelde (NO)	5C1	634
Kvissel (DK)	5C3	294
Kviteseid (NO)	5B1	633
Langå (DK)	5C3	294
Langesund (NO)	5C1	634
Larvik (NO)	5C1	634
Lemvig (DK)	5B3	294
Lidköping (SE)	5E1	665
Lillesand (NO)	5B2	633
Lindesberg (SE)	5E1	666
Lindesnes (NO)	5B2	633
Linköping (SE)	5F2	660
Löttorp (SE)	5G2	662
Lunde (NO)	5C1	634

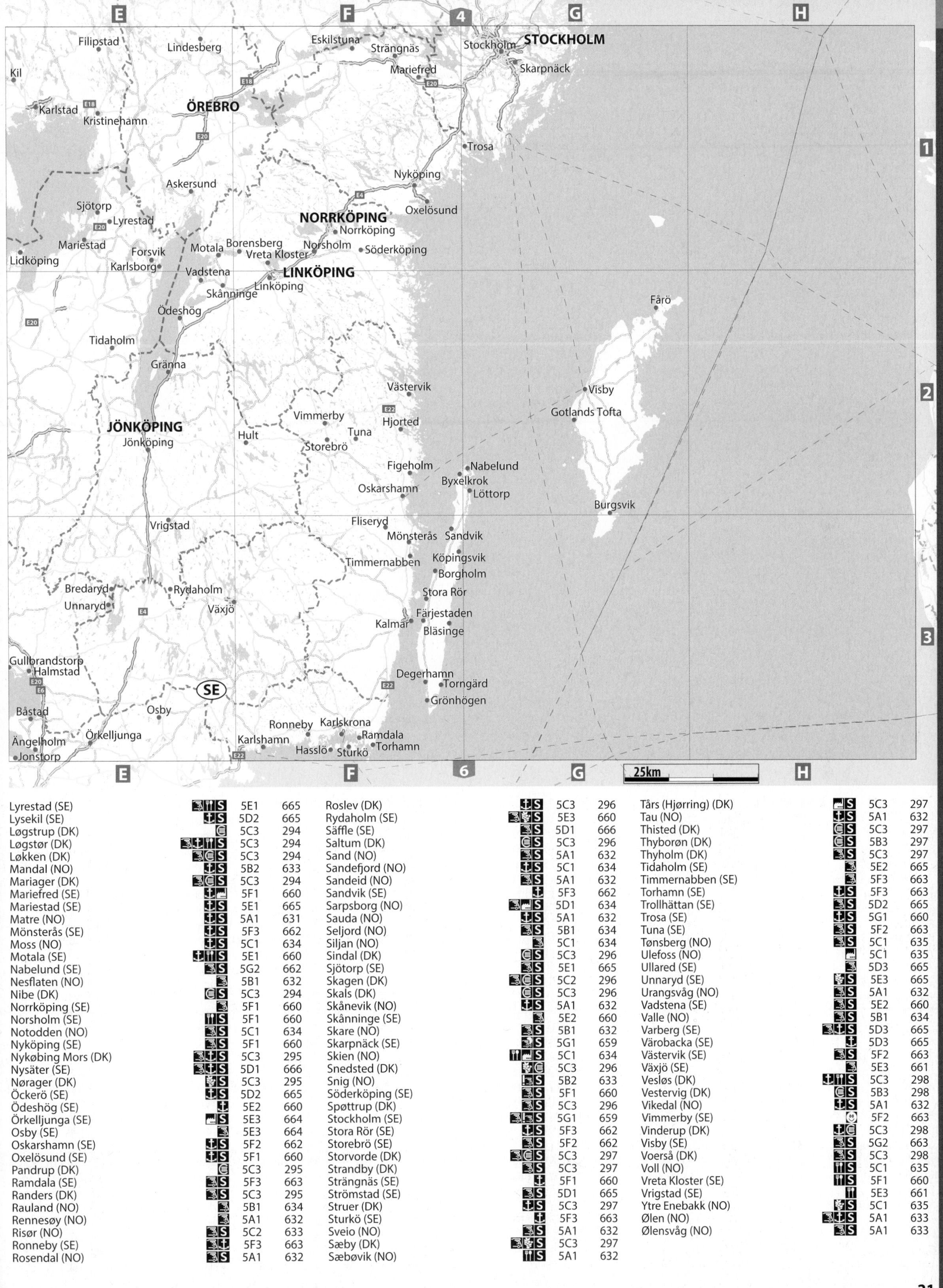

E
F
4
G
H
STOCKHOLM
Stockholm
Skarpnäck
Filipstad
Lindesberg
Eskilstuna
Strängnäs
Mariefred
Kil
Karlstad
Kristinehamn
ÖREBRO
Trosa
Nyköping
Askersund
Oxelösund
Sjötorp
Lyrestad
NORRKÖPING
Norrköping
Mariestad
Forsvik
Motala
Borensberg
Norsholm
Söderköping
Lidköping
Karlsborg
Vreta Kloster
Vadstena
LINKÖPING
Linköping
Skänninge
Fårö
Ödeshög
Tidaholm
Gränna
Västervik
Visby
Gotlands Tofta
Vimmerby
Hjorted
JÖNKÖPING
Jönköping
Hult
Tuna
Storebrö
Figeholm
Nabelund
Byxelkrok
Oskarshamn
Löttorp
Burgsvik
Vrigstad
Fliseryd
Mönsterås
Sandvik
Timmernabben
Köpingsvik
Borgholm
Bredaryd
Rydaholm
Unnaryd
Växjö
Stora Rör
Färjestaden
Kalmar
Bläsinge
Gullbrandstorp
Halmstad
Degerhamn
Torngård
SE
Grönhögen
Båstad
Osby
Ronneby
Karlskrona
Ramdala
Ängelholm
Örkelljunga
Karlshamn
Hasslö
Sturkö
Torhamn
Jonstorp
E
F
6
G
25km
H
1
2
3
E18
E20
E4
E22
E6

Place	Grid	Page
Aarhus (DK)	6D1	289
Aarup (DK)	6D2	298
Åbenrå (DK)	6D2	289
Achtrup (DE)	6C3	119
Ahrenshoop (DE)	6F3	158
Åhus (SE)	6G1	663
Altenhof (DE)	6D3	119
Anderslöv (SE)	6G2	664
Asperup (DK)	6D2	298
Assens (DK)	6D2	298
Augustenborg (DK)	6D2	289
Aventoft (DE)	6C3	119
Bad Malente (DE)	6E3	120
Bagenkop (DK)	6E3	298
Bansin (DE)	6H3	158
Barkenholm (DE)	6C3	120
Barth (DE)	6F3	158
Behrensdorf (DE)	6E3	120
Bergen/Rügen (DE)	6G3	158
Billund (DK)	6C1	290
Binz (DE)	6G3	158
Bistensee (DE)	6D3	120
Bjert (DK)	6D2	290
Blekendorf (DE)	6E3	120
Boeslunde (DK)	6E2	299
Bogense (DK)	6D2	298
Bogø By (DK)	6F2	299
Borgdorf-Seedorf (DE)	6D3	120
Borrby (SE)	6G1	664
Bredstedt (DE)	6C3	120
Bredsten (DK)	6C1	290
Breiholz (DE)	6D3	121
Broager (DK)	6D3	290
Broby (DK)	6D2	298
Brodersby (DE)	6D3	121
Bromölla (SE)	6H1	664
Brædstrup (DK)	6D1	290
Büdelsdorf (DE)	6D3	121
Busdorf (DE)	6D3	121
Bylderup-Bov (DK)	6C2	290
Børkop (DK)	6D1	290
Copenhagen (DK)	6F1	299
Dabitz (DE)	6F3	159
Dalby (DK)	6E2	300
Damp (DE)	6D3	121
Dannemare (DK)	6E3	300
Dranske/Bakenberg (DE)	6G3	160
Drelsdorf (DE)	6C3	121
Dronningsmølle (DK)	6F1	300
Ebeltoft (DK)	6D1	290
Eckernförde (DE)	6D3	121
Egå (DK)	6D1	291
Elmenhorst (DE)	6F3	160
Emmelsbüll-Horsbüll (DE)	6C3	121
Engesvan (DK)	6C1	291
Esbjerg (DK)	6C2	291
Faaborg (DK)	6D2	298
Fakse (DK)	6F2	300
Fanø (DK)	6C2	291
Farum (DK)	6F1	300
Farø (DK)	6F2	300
Fehmarn (DE)	6E3	121
Ferritslev (DK)	6D2	298
Fjälkinge (SE)	6G1	664
Flensburg (DE)	6D3	122
Fockbek (DE)	6D3	122
Fredericia (DK)	6D2	291
Frederikssund (DK)	6F1	300
Frederiksværk (DK)	6F1	300
Friedrichstadt (DE)	6C3	122
Frørup (DK)	6E2	299
Føllenslev (DK)	6E1	300
Gedser (DK)	6F3	300
Gelting (DE)	6D3	122
Gilleleje (DK)	6F1	300
Give (DK)	6C1	291
Glejbjerg (DK)	6C2	291
Graal-Müritz (DE)	6F3	160
Gram (DK)	6C2	299
Greifswald (DE)	6G3	160
Greve (DK)	6F1	300
Grödersby (DE)	6D3	122
Grömitz (DE)	6E3	122
Großenbrode (DE)	6E3	123
Großsolt (DE)	6D3	123
Gørlev (DK)	6E2	300
Haderslev (DK)	6D2	292
Handewitt (DE)	6C3	123
Harrislee (DE)	6D3	123
Hasselberg (DE)	6D3	123
Heiligenhafen (DE)	6E3	124
Hejls (DK)	6D2	292
Helsinge (DK)	6F1	300
Hemmet (DK)	6C1	292
Heringsdorf (DE)	6H3	161
Herning (DK)	6C1	292
Hillerød (DK)	6F1	300
Hinrichshagen (DE)	6G3	161
Hohenfelde (DE)	6D3	124
Hohn (DE)	6D3	124
Hohwacht (DE)	6E3	124
Höllviken (SE)	6F2	664
Holsted (DK)	6C2	293
Hörnum (DE)	6C3	124
Horsens (DK)	6D1	293
Hörsten (DE)	6D3	124
Hovborg (DK)	6C2	293
Hoven (DK)	6C1	293
Humble (DK)	6E3	299
Hundested (DK)	6E1	300
Husum (DE)	6C3	124
Hvide Sande (DK)	6B1	293
Jagel (DE)	6D3	124
Jelling (DK)	6C1	293
Juelsminde (DK)	6D1	293
Kalundborg (DK)	6E1	300
Kalvehave (DK)	6F2	300
Kappeln (DE)	6D3	124
Karise (DK)	6F2	300
Karrebæksminde (DK)	6E2	300
Karup (DK)	6C1	293
Kerteminde (DK)	6E2	299
Kiel (DE)	6D3	124
Kirke Hyllinge (DK)	6F1	300
Knebel (DK)	6D1	294
Kolding (DK)	6D2	294
Korsør (DK)	6E2	300
Kristianstad (SE)	6G1	664

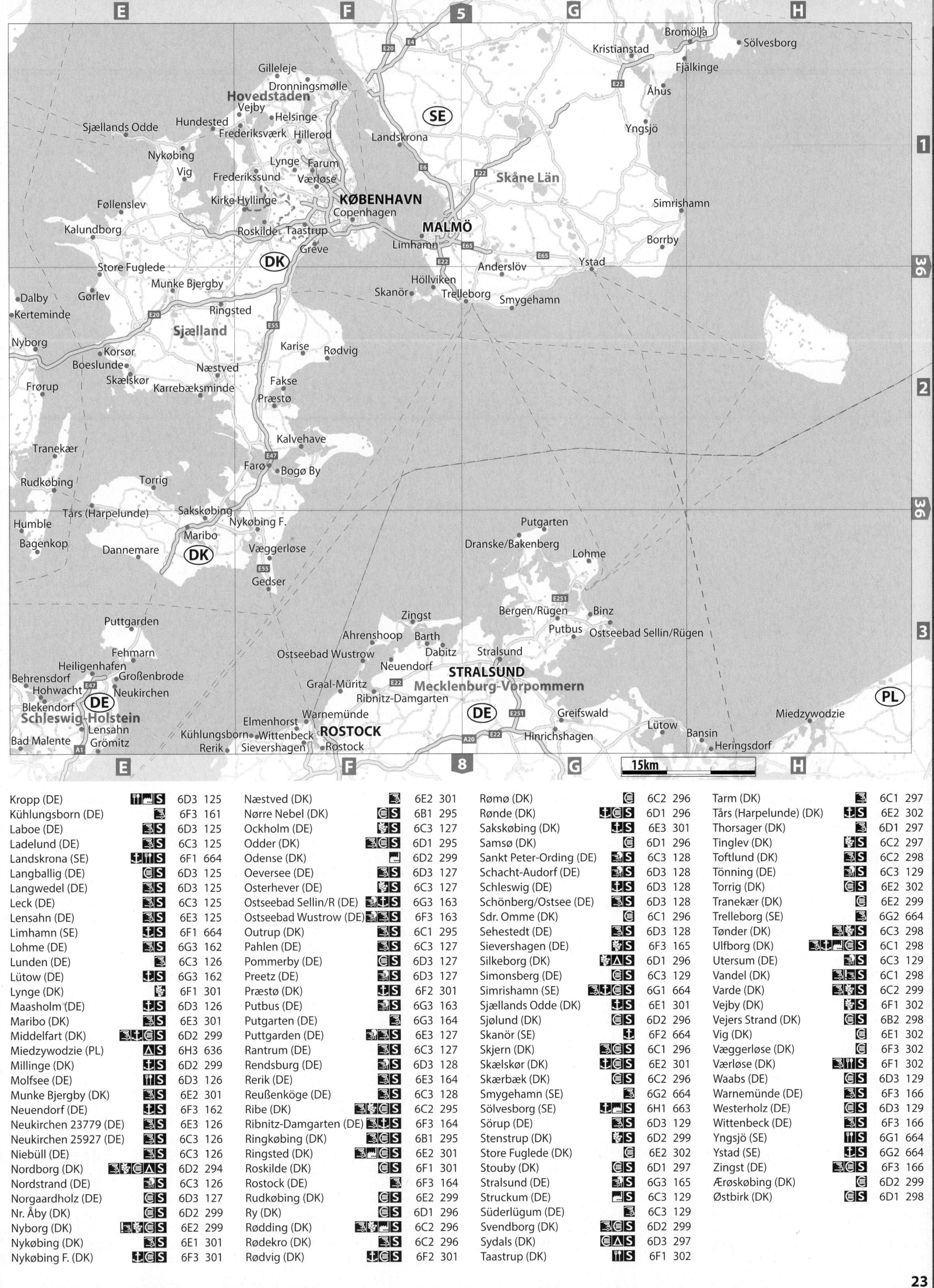

E
F
G
H
5
8
1
2
3
36
Bromölla
Sölvesborg
Kristianstad
Fjälkinge
Åhus
Yngsjö
Gilleleje
Dronningsmølle
Hovedstaden
Vejby
Helsinge
Sjællands Odde
Hundested
Frederiksværk
Hillerød
Landskrona
SE
Nykøbing
Vig
Lynge
Farum
Frederikssund
Værløse
Skåne Län
Følllenslev
Kirke Hyllinge
KØBENHAVN
Copenhagen
Simrishamn
Kalundborg
Roskilde
Taastrup
MALMÖ
Limhamn
Borrby
Greve
DK
Store Fuglede
Anderslöv
Ystad
Munke Bjergby
Höllviken
Skanör
Trelleborg
Smygehamn
Dalby
Gørlev
Kerteminde
Ringsted
Sjælland
Nyborg
Korsør
Karise
Rødvig
Boeslunde
Næstved
Skælskør
Fakse
Frørup
Karrebæksminde
Præstø
Kalvehave
Tranekær
Farø
Bogø By
Rudkøbing
Torrig
Sakskøbing
Tårs (Harpelunde)
Humble
Nykøbing F.
Putgarten
Maribo
Bagenkop
Dannemare
Væggerløse
Dranske/Bakenberg
Lohme
Gedser
Zingst
Bergen/Rügen
Binz
Puttgarden
Putbus
Ostseebad Sellin/Rügen
Ahrenshoop
Barth
Fehmarn
Ostseebad Wustrow
Dabitz
Stralsund
Heiligenhafen
Neuendorf
STRALSUND
Behrensdorf
Großenbrode
Graal-Müritz
Mecklenburg-Vorpommern
Hohwacht
Neukirchen
Ribnitz-Damgarten
DE
PL
Blekendorf
Schleswig-Holstein
Warnemünde
Greifswald
Miedzywodzie
Elmenhorst
Lütow
Lensahn
Kühlungsborn
Wittenbeck
ROSTOCK
Bansin
Bad Malente
Grömitz
Hinrichshagen
Rerik
Sievershagen
Rostock
Heringsdorf
E20
E4
E22
E6
E65
E55
E47
E251
A20
A1
15km

A
B
C
D
1
2
3
Hogebeintum
Sint Jacobiparochie
Friesland
Sexbierum
Ried
NL
Leeuwarden
A31
Texel/De Cocksdorp
Harlingen
Winsum
Zurich
Lollum
A32
Wommels
Tersoal
E22
Bolsward
Akkrum
Noord-Holland
A7
Makkum
Sneek
IJlst
Workum
A7
Joure
Den Helder
Den Oever
Woudsend
Langweer
Ypecolsga
Molkwerum
Koudum
Rohel
Balk
E22
Sloten
Stavoren
Oudemirdum
Slootdorp
Het Zand
Mirns
Lemmer
A6
10km
9

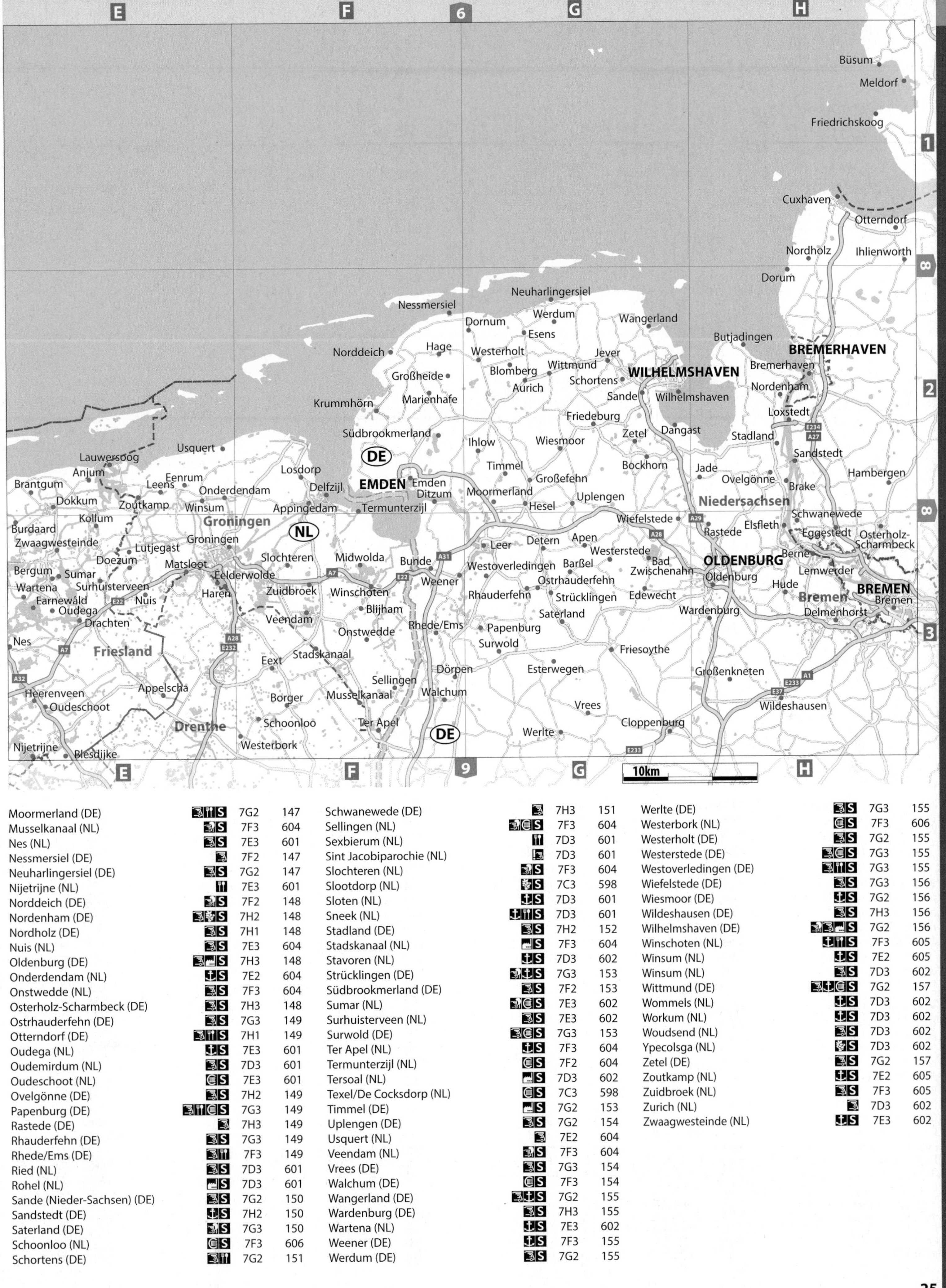
E
F
6
G
H
Büsum
Meldorf
Friedrichskoog
1
Cuxhaven
Otterndorf
Nordholz
Ihlienworth
Dorum
8
Neuharlingersiel
Nessmersiel
Werdum
Dornum
Wangerland
Esens
Butjadingen
Norddeich
Hage
Westerholt
Jever
BREMERHAVEN
Großheide
Blomberg
Wittmund
WILHELMSHAVEN
Bremerhaven
Aurich
Schortens
Nordenham
Krummhörn
Marienhafe
Sande
Wilhelmshaven
2
Friedeburg
Loxstedt
Südbrookmerland
Dangast
Stadland
Zetel
Ihlow
Wiesmoor
Usquert
DE
Sandstedt
Lauwersoog
Timmel
Bockhorn
Hambergen
Anjum
Losdorp
Jade
Eenrum
Ovelgönne
Brantgum
Leens
Delfzijl
EMDEN
Emden
Großefehn
Brake
Onderdendam
Ditzum
Moormerland
Uplengen
Dokkum
Zoutkamp
Winsum
Appingedam
Termunterzijl
Hesel
Niedersachsen
Kollum
Groningen
Wiefelstede
Schwanewede
Burdaard
NL
Elsfleth
Rastede
Eggestedt
Osterholz-Scharmbeck
Zwaagwesteinde
Groningen
Leer
Detern
Apen
Lutjegast
Slochteren
Midwolda
Westerstede
Berne
Bunde
Bad Zwischenahn
OLDENBURG
Doezum
Bergum
Matsloot
Westoverledingen
Barßel
Lemwerder
Sumar
Eelderwolde
Weener
Oldenburg
Wartena
Surhuisterveen
Zuidbroek
Winschoten
Ostrhauderfehn
Hude
BREMEN
Haren
Rhauderfehn
Strücklingen
Edewecht
Bremen
Earnewâld
Nuis
Bremen
Oudega
Blijham
Wardenburg
Delmenhorst
Saterland
Drachten
Veendam
Rhede/Ems
Papenburg
3
Onstwedde
Nes
Friesland
Surwold
Friesoythe
Stadskanaal
Eext
Dörpen
Esterwegen
Großenknoten
Sellingen
Heerenveen
Appelscha
Borger
Musselkanaal
Walchum
Oudeschoot
Wildeshausen
Vrees
Schoonloo
Ter Apel
Cloppenburg
Drenthe
DE
Werlte
Nijetrijne
Westerbork
Blesdijke
E
F
9
G
10km
H

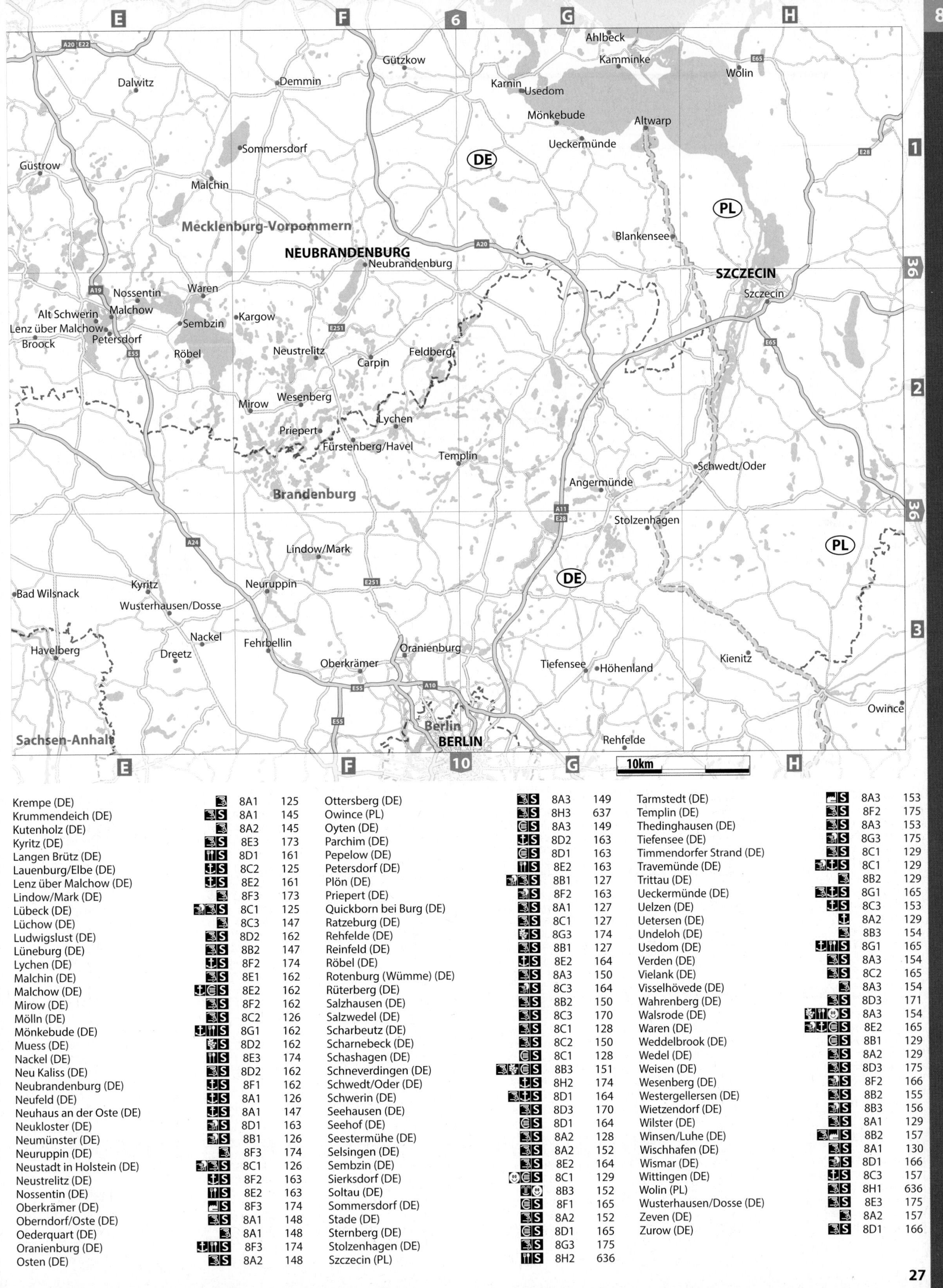
E
F
6
G
H
A20 E22
Ahlbeck
Kamminke
Gützkow
E65
Wolin
Dalwitz
Demmin
Karnin
Usedom
Mönkebude
Altwarp
Ueckermünde
Sommersdorf
DE
E28
1
Güstrow
Malchin
PL
Mecklenburg-Vorpommern
Blankensee
A20
NEUBRANDENBURG
Neubrandenburg
SZCZECIN
36
Szczecin
A19
Nossentin
Waren
Alt Schwerin
Malchow
Lenz über Malchow
Sembzin
Kargow
E251
Broock
Petersdorf
E55
Röbel
Neustrelitz
Carpin
Feldberg
E65
2
Mirow
Wesenberg
Lychen
Priepert
Fürstenberg/Havel
Templin
Schwedt/Oder
Angermünde
Brandenburg
A11
E28
Stolzenhagen
36
PL
A24
Lindow/Mark
DE
Kyritz
Bad Wilsnack
Neuruppin
E251
Wusterhausen/Dosse
3
Nackel
Havelberg
Dreetz
Fehrbellin
Oranienburg
Oberkrämer
Tiefensee
Höhenland
Kienitz
A10
E55
Owince
E55
Berlin
BERLIN
Sachsen-Anhalt
Rehfelde
E
F
10
G
10km
H

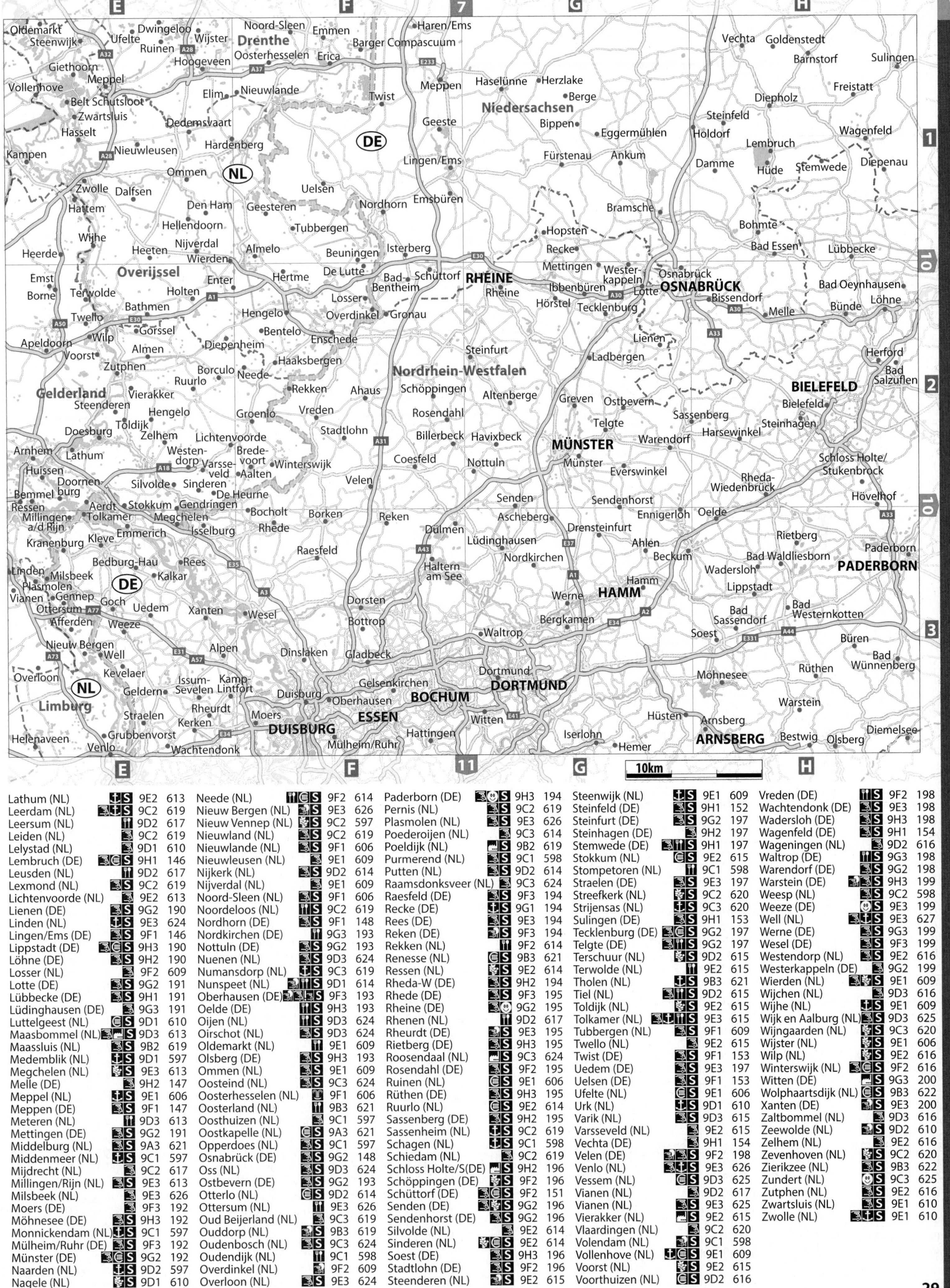

Place	Grid	Page
Lathum (NL)	9E2	613
Leerdam (NL)	9C2	619
Leersum (NL)	9D2	617
Leiden (NL)	9C2	619
Lelystad (NL)	9D1	610
Lembruch (DE)	9H1	146
Leusden (NL)	9D2	617
Lexmond (NL)	9C2	619
Lichtenvoorde (NL)	9E2	613
Lienen (DE)	9G2	190
Linden (NL)	9E3	624
Lingen/Ems (DE)	9F1	146
Lippstadt (DE)	9H3	190
Löhne (DE)	9H2	190
Losser (NL)	9F2	609
Lotte (DE)	9G2	191
Lübbecke (DE)	9H1	191
Lüdinghausen (DE)	9G3	191
Luttelgeest (NL)	9D1	610
Maasbommel (NL)	9D3	613
Maassluis (NL)	9B2	619
Medemblik (NL)	9D1	597
Megchelen (NL)	9E3	613
Melle (DE)	9H2	147
Meppel (NL)	9E1	606
Meppen (DE)	9F1	147
Meteren (NL)	9D3	613
Mettingen (DE)	9G2	191
Middelburg (NL)	9A3	621
Middenmeer (NL)	9C1	597
Mijdrecht (NL)	9C2	617
Millingen/Rijn (NL)	9E3	613
Milsbeek (NL)	9E3	626
Moers (DE)	9F3	192
Möhnesee (DE)	9H3	192
Monnickendam (NL)	9C1	597
Mülheim/Ruhr (DE)	9F3	192
Münster (DE)	9G2	192
Naarden (NL)	9D2	597
Nagele (NL)	9D1	610
Neede (NL)	9F2	614
Nieuw Bergen (NL)	9E3	626
Nieuw Vennep (NL)	9C2	597
Nieuwland (NL)	9C2	619
Nieuwlande (NL)	9F1	606
Nieuwleusen (NL)	9E1	609
Nijkerk (NL)	9D2	614
Nijverdal (NL)	9E1	609
Noord-Sleen (NL)	9F1	606
Noordeloos (NL)	9C2	619
Nordhorn (DE)	9F1	148
Nordkirchen (DE)	9G3	193
Nottuln (DE)	9G2	193
Nuenen (NL)	9D3	624
Numansdorp (NL)	9C3	619
Nunspeet (NL)	9D1	614
Oberhausen (DE)	9F3	193
Oelde (DE)	9H3	193
Oijen (NL)	9D3	624
Oirschot (NL)	9D3	624
Oldemarkt (NL)	9E1	609
Olsberg (DE)	9H3	193
Ommen (NL)	9E1	609
Oosteind (NL)	9C3	624
Oosterhesselen (NL)	9F1	606
Oosterland (NL)	9B3	621
Oosthuizen (NL)	9C1	597
Oostkapelle (NL)	9A3	621
Opperdoes (NL)	9C1	597
Osnabrück (DE)	9G2	148
Oss (NL)	9D3	624
Ostbevern (DE)	9G2	193
Otterlo (NL)	9D2	614
Ottersum (NL)	9E3	626
Oud Beijerland (NL)	9C3	619
Ouddorp (NL)	9B3	619
Oudenbosch (NL)	9C3	624
Oudendijk (NL)	9C1	598
Overdinkel (NL)	9F2	609
Overloon (NL)	9E3	624
Paderborn (DE)	9H3	194
Pernis (NL)	9C2	619
Plasmolen (NL)	9E3	626
Poederoijen (NL)	9C3	614
Poeldijk (NL)	9B2	619
Purmerend (NL)	9C1	598
Putten (NL)	9D2	614
Raamsdonksveer (NL)	9C3	624
Raesfeld (DE)	9F3	194
Recke (DE)	9G1	194
Rees (DE)	9E3	194
Reken (DE)	9F3	194
Rekken (NL)	9F2	614
Renesse (NL)	9B3	621
Ressen (NL)	9E2	614
Rheda-W (DE)	9H2	194
Rhede (DE)	9F3	195
Rheine (DE)	9G2	195
Rhenen (NL)	9D2	617
Rheurdt (DE)	9E3	195
Rietberg (DE)	9H3	195
Roosendaal (NL)	9C3	624
Rosendahl (DE)	9F2	195
Ruinen (NL)	9E1	606
Rüthen (DE)	9H3	195
Ruurlo (NL)	9E2	614
Sassenberg (DE)	9H2	195
Sassenheim (NL)	9C2	619
Schagen (NL)	9C1	598
Schiedam (NL)	9C2	619
Schloss Holte/S(DE)	9H2	196
Schöppingen (DE)	9F2	196
Schüttorf (DE)	9F2	151
Senden (DE)	9G2	196
Sendenhorst (DE)	9G2	196
Silvolde (NL)	9E2	614
Sinderen (NL)	9E2	614
Soest (DE)	9H3	196
Stadtlohn (DE)	9F2	196
Steenderen (NL)	9E2	615
Steenwijk (NL)	9E1	609
Steinfeld (DE)	9H1	152
Steinfurt (DE)	9G2	197
Steinhagen (DE)	9H2	197
Stemwede (DE)	9H1	197
Stokkum (NL)	9E2	615
Stompetoren (NL)	9C1	598
Straelen (DE)	9E3	197
Streefkerk (NL)	9C2	620
Strijensas (NL)	9C3	620
Sulingen (DE)	9H1	153
Tecklenburg (DE)	9G2	197
Telgte (DE)	9G2	197
Terschuur (NL)	9D2	615
Terwolde (NL)	9E2	615
Tholen (NL)	9B3	621
Tiel (NL)	9D2	615
Toldijk (NL)	9E2	615
Tolkamer (NL)	9E3	615
Tubbergen (NL)	9F1	609
Twello (NL)	9E2	615
Twist (DE)	9F1	153
Uedem (DE)	9E3	197
Uelsen (DE)	9F1	153
Ufelte (NL)	9E1	606
Urk (NL)	9D1	610
Varik (NL)	9D3	615
Varsseveld (NL)	9E2	615
Vechta (DE)	9H1	154
Velen (DE)	9F2	198
Venlo (NL)	9E3	626
Vessem (NL)	9D3	625
Vianen (NL)	9D2	617
Vianen (NL)	9E3	625
Vierakker (NL)	9E2	615
Vlaardingen (NL)	9C2	620
Volendam (NL)	9C1	598
Vollenhove (NL)	9E1	609
Voorst (NL)	9E2	615
Voorthuizen (NL)	9D2	616
Vreden (DE)	9F2	198
Wachtendonk (DE)	9E3	198
Wadersloh (DE)	9H3	198
Wagenfeld (DE)	9H1	154
Wageningen (NL)	9D2	616
Waltrop (DE)	9G3	198
Warendorf (DE)	9G2	198
Warstein (DE)	9H3	199
Weesp (NL)	9C2	598
Weeze (DE)	9E3	199
Well (NL)	9E3	627
Werne (DE)	9G3	199
Wesel (DE)	9F3	199
Westendorp (NL)	9E2	616
Westerkappeln (DE)	9G2	199
Wierden (NL)	9E1	609
Wijchen (NL)	9D3	616
Wijhe (NL)	9E1	609
Wijk en Aalburg (NL)	9D3	625
Wijngaarden (NL)	9C3	620
Wijster (NL)	9E1	606
Wilp (NL)	9E2	616
Winterswijk (NL)	9F2	616
Witten (DE)	9G3	200
Wolphaartsdijk (NL)	9B3	622
Xanten (DE)	9E3	200
Zaltbommel (NL)	9D3	616
Zeewolde (NL)	9D2	610
Zelhem (NL)	9E2	616
Zevenhoven (NL)	9C2	620
Zierikzee (NL)	9B3	622
Zundert (NL)	9C3	625
Zutphen (NL)	9E2	616
Zwartsluis (NL)	9E1	610
Zwolle (NL)	9E1	610

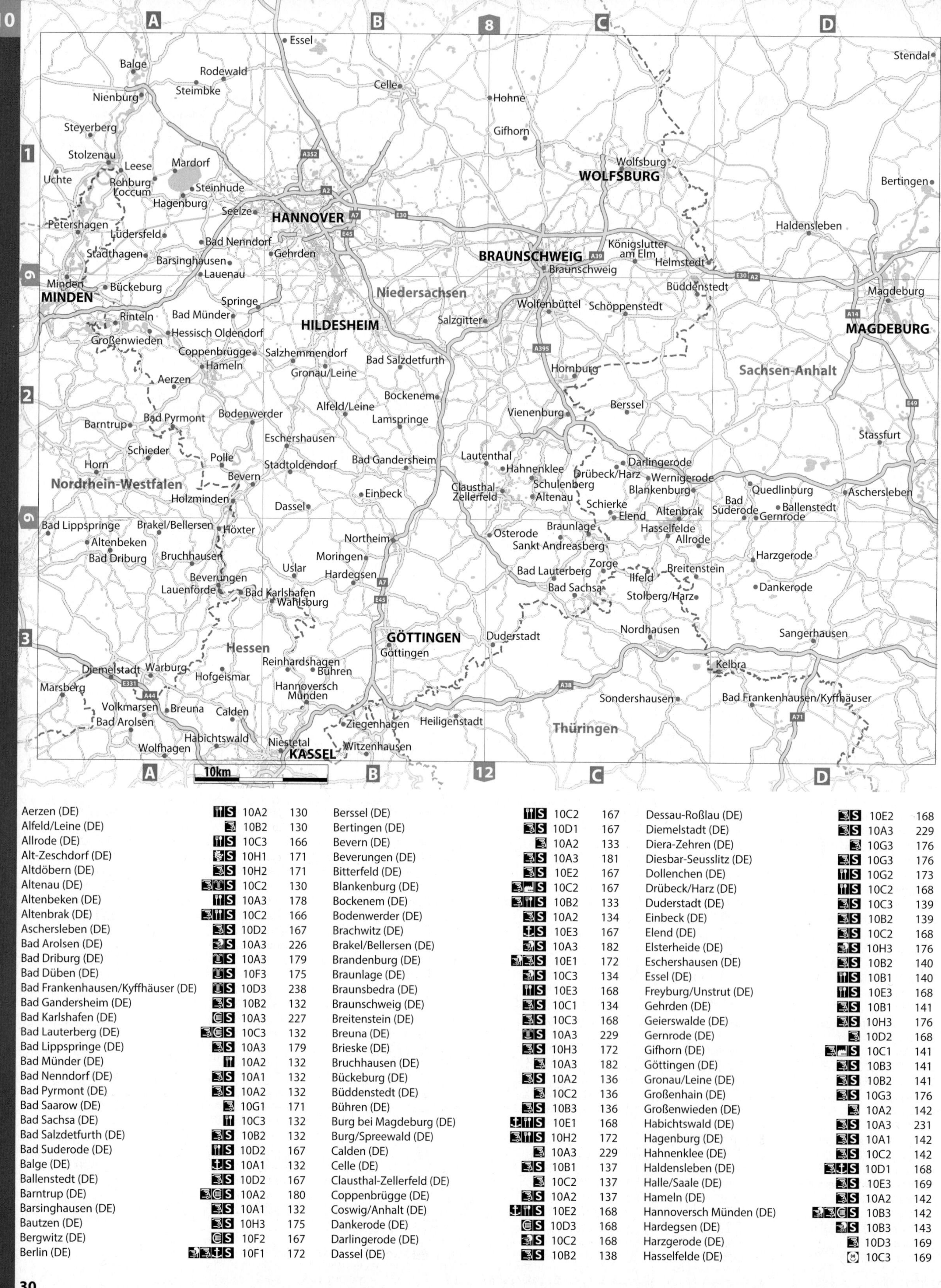

A
B
8
C
D
Essel
Stendal
Balge
Rodewald
Celle
Nienburg
Steimbke
Hohne
Steyerberg
Gifhorn
1
Stolzenau
A352
Wolfsburg
WOLFSBURG
Uchte
Leese
Mardorf
Bertingen
Rehburg-Loccum
Steinhude
A2
Hagenburg
Seelze
HANNOVER
A7
E30
Petershagen
Haldensleben
Lüdersfeld
E45
Bad Nenndorf
Königslutter am Elm
Stadthagen
Gehrden
BRAUNSCHWEIG
A39
Helmstedt
Barsinghausen
Braunschweig
Lauenau
E30
A2
Minden
Bückeburg
Büddenstedt
Magdeburg
MINDEN
Niedersachsen
Springe
Wolfenbüttel
Schöppenstedt
Rinteln
Bad Münder
A14
HILDESHEIM
Salzgitter
MAGDEBURG
Großenwieden
Hessisch Oldendorf
Coppenbrügge
Salzhemmendorf
A395
Hameln
Bad Salzdetfurth
Gronau/Leine
Hornburg
Sachsen-Anhalt
Aerzen
2
Bockenem
Berssel
Alfeld/Leine
E49
Barntrup
Bad Pyrmont
Bodenwerder
Vienenburg
Lamspringe
Stassfurt
Eschershausen
Schieder
Lautenthal
Darlingerode
Horn
Polle
Stadtoldendorf
Bad Gandersheim
Hahnenklee
Drübeck/Harz
Wernigerode
Bevern
Schulenberg
Blankenburg
Quedlinburg
Nordrhein-Westfalen
Clausthal-Zellerfeld
Aschersleben
Einbeck
Altenau
Bad Suderode
Holzminden
Schierke
Ballenstedt
Dassel
Altenbrak
Gernrode
Elend
Bad Lippspringe
Brakel/Bellersen
Höxter
Braunlage
Hasselfelde
Northeim
Osterode
Allrode
Altenbeken
Sankt Andreasberg
Bad Driburg
Bruchhausen
Moringen
Harzgerode
Uslar
Zorge
Breitenstein
Beverungen
Hardegsen
Bad Lauterberg
Ilfeld
A7
Lauenförde
Bad Karlshafen
Bad Sachsa
Dankerode
Wahlsburg
Stolberg/Harz
E45
Nordhausen
3
GÖTTINGEN
Duderstadt
Sangerhausen
Hessen
Göttingen
Reinhardshagen
Kelbra
Diemelstadt
Warburg
Bühren
Hofgeismar
E331
A38
Marsberg
A44
Hannoversch Münden
Sondershausen
Bad Frankenhausen/Kyffhäuser
Volkmarsen
Breuna
Calden
A71
Bad Arolsen
Ziegenhagen
Heiligenstadt
Thüringen
Habichtswald
Niestetal
Wolfhagen
KASSEL
Witzenhausen
A
10km
B
12
C
D

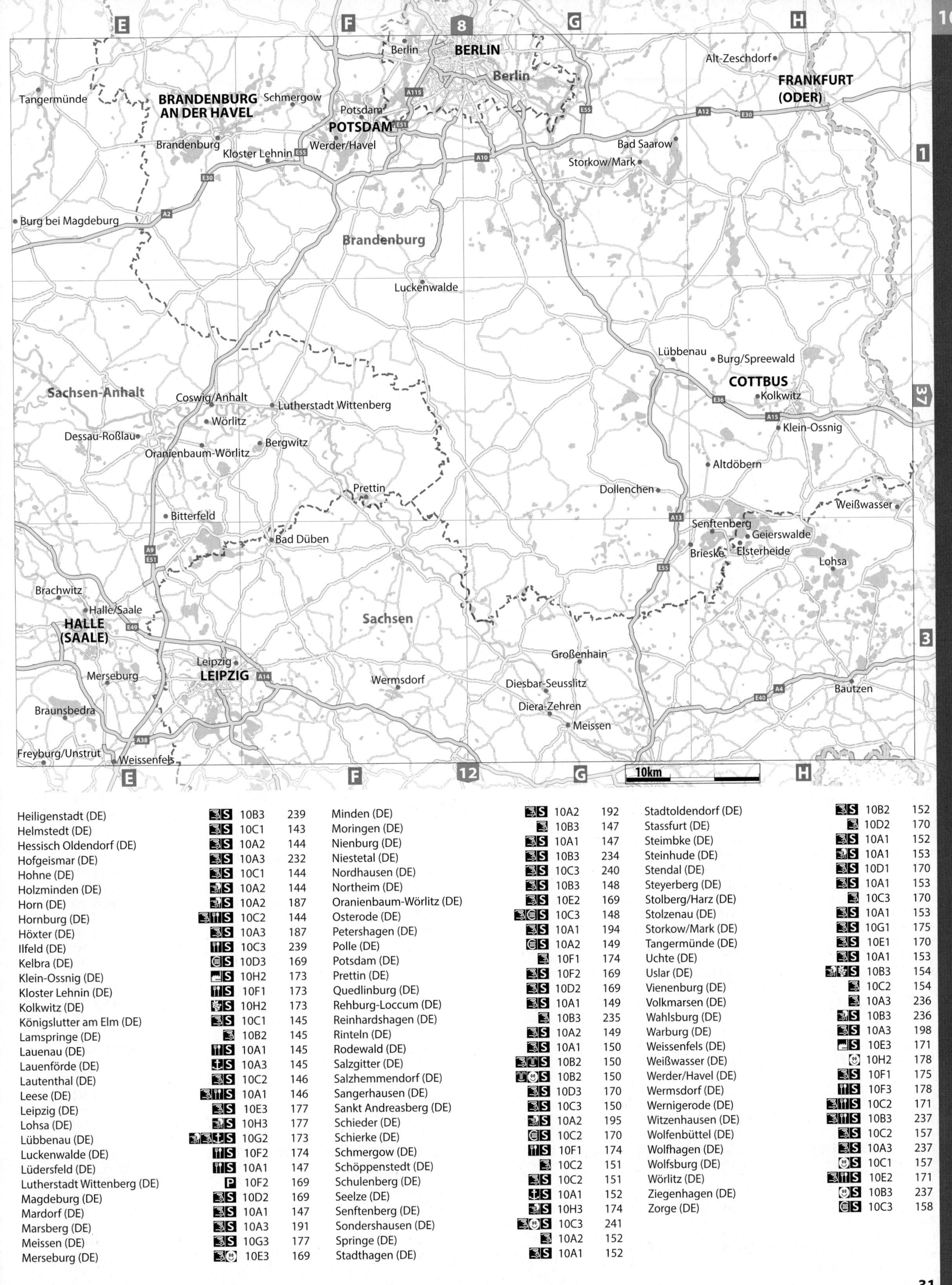

E
F
8
G
H
Berlin
BERLIN
Berlin
Alt-Zeschdorf
FRANKFURT (ODER)
Tangermünde
BRANDENBURG AN DER HAVEL
Schmergow
Potsdam
POTSDAM
Brandenburg
Kloster Lehnin
Werder/Havel
Bad Saarow
Storkow/Mark
A115
E51
E55
A12
E30
A10
A2
1
Burg bei Magdeburg
Brandenburg
Luckenwalde
Lübbenau
Burg/Spreewald
COTTBUS
Kolkwitz
37
Sachsen-Anhalt
Coswig/Anhalt
Lutherstadt Wittenberg
Wörlitz
E36
A15
Klein-Ossnig
Dessau-Roßlau
Oranienbaum-Wörlitz
Bergwitz
Altdöbern
Prettin
Dollenchen
Weißwasser
Bitterfeld
A13
Senftenberg
Geierswalde
Bad Düben
A9
E51
Brieske
Elsterheide
Lohsa
Brachwitz
Halle/Saale
HALLE (SAALE)
Sachsen
E49
3
Leipzig
LEIPZIG
Großenhain
Merseburg
A14
Wermsdorf
Diesbar-Seusslitz
A4
E40
Bautzen
Braunsbedra
Diera-Zehren
Meissen
A38
Freyburg/Unstrut
Weissenfels
12
10km

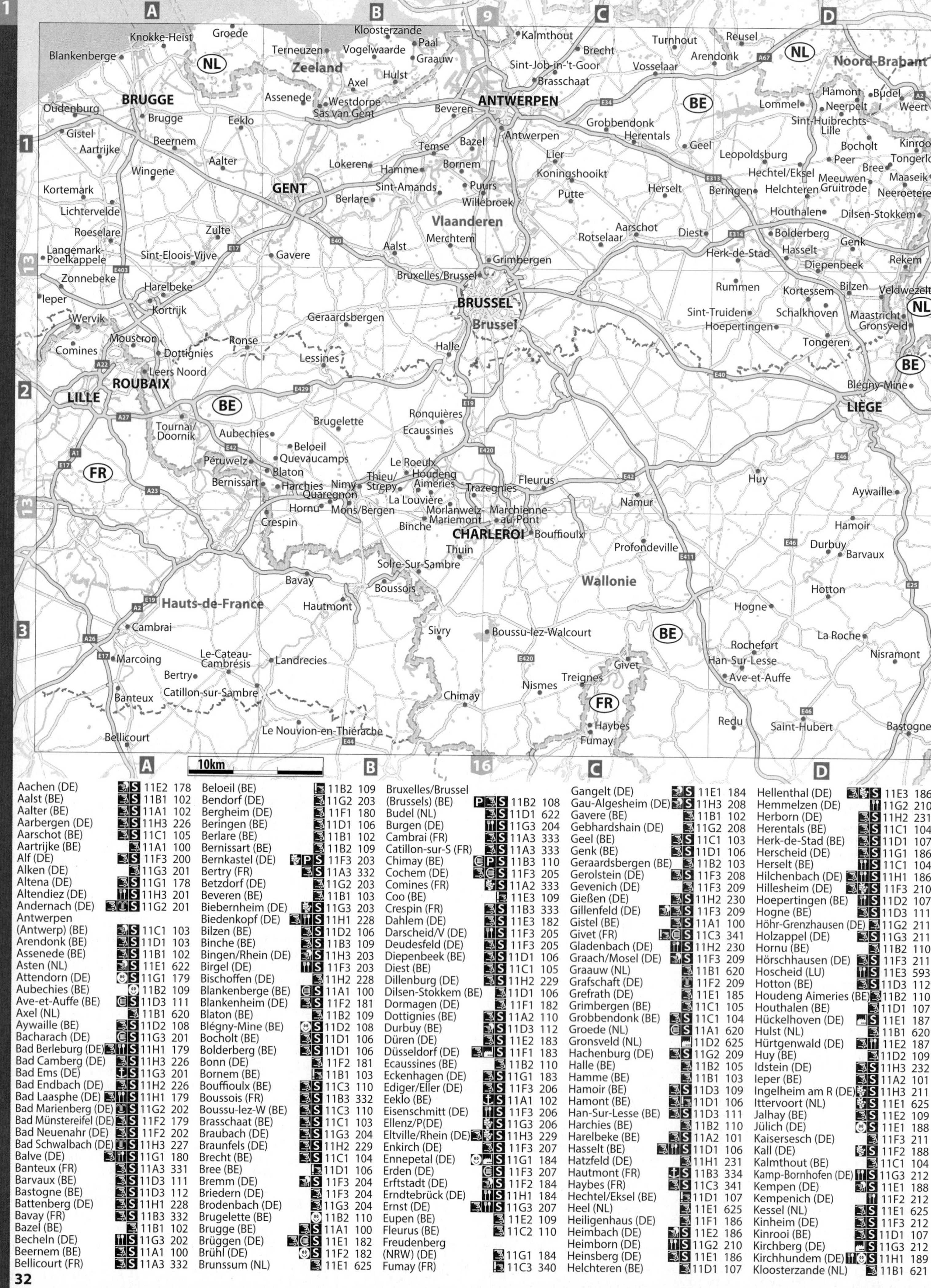

A
B
9
C
D
Knokke-Heist
Groede
Kloosterzande
Kalmthout
Turnhout
Reusel
Blankenberge
NL
Terneuzen
Vogelwaarde
Paal
Graauw
Brecht
Arendonk
Noord-Brabant
Zeeland
Hulst
Sint-Job-in-'t-Goor
Vosselaar
Axel
Brasschaat
BRUGGE
Assenede
Westdorpe
Sas van Gent
Beveren
ANTWERPEN
BE
Hamont
Budel
Oudenburg
Brugge
Eeklo
Grobbendonk
Lommel
Neerpelt
Weert
Gistel
Antwerpen
Herentals
Sint-Huibrechts-Lille
Aartrijke
Beernem
Temse
Bazel
Geel
Leopoldsburg
Bocholt
Kinrooi
Aalter
Lokeren
Hamme
Bornem
Lier
Peer
Tongerlo
Wingene
Bree
Koningshooikt
Hechtel/Eksel
Meeuwen-Gruitrode
Maaseik
Kortemark
GENT
Sint-Amands
Puurs
Putte
Herselt
Beringen
Helchteren
Neeroeteren
Lichtervelde
Berlare
Willebroek
Houthalen
Dilsen-Stokkem
Vlaanderen
Roeselare
Zulte
Aarschot
Diest
Bolderberg
Rotselaar
Genk
Langemark-Poelkappele
Sint-Eloois-Vijve
Gavere
Aalst
Merchtem
Herk-de-Stad
Hasselt
Grimbergen
Diepenbeek
Rekem
Zonnebeke
Bruxelles/Brussel
Harelbeke
Rummen
Kortessem
Bilzen
Veldwezelt
Ieper
BRUSSEL
Kortrijk
Wervik
Geraardsbergen
Sint-Truiden
Schalkhoven
Maastricht
Brussel
Hoepertingen
Gronsveld
Mouscron
Ronse
Comines
Dottignies
Halle
Tongeren
Lessines
Leers Noord
ROUBAIX
Blégny-Mine
LILLE
LIÈGE
Ronquières
Tournai/Doornik
Brugelette
Aubechies
Ecaussines
Beloeil
Quevaucamps
Péruwelz
Le Roeulx
Blaton
Houdeng Aimeries
FR
Bernissart
Harchies
Nimy
Thieu/Strepy
Trazegnies
Fleurus
Huy
Quaregnon
Aywaille
La Louvière
Namur
Hornu
Mons/Bergen
Morlanwelz-Mariemont
Marchienne-au-Pont
Crespin
Binche
CHARLEROI
Bouffioulx
Hamoir
Durbuy
Thuin
Profondeville
Barvaux
Solre-Sur-Sambre
Wallonie
Bavay
Boussois
Hotton
Hauts-de-France
Hautmont
Hogne
Cambrai
Sivry
Boussu-lez-Walcourt
La Roche
Rochefort
Le-Cateau-Cambrésis
Landrecies
Han-Sur-Lesse
Nisramont
Marcoing
Givet
Ave-et-Auffe
Bertry
Treignes
Nismes
Banteux
Catillon-sur-Sambre
Chimay
Haybes
Redu
Saint-Hubert
Bastogne
Le Nouvion-en-Thiérache
Fumay
Bellicourt
16
10km

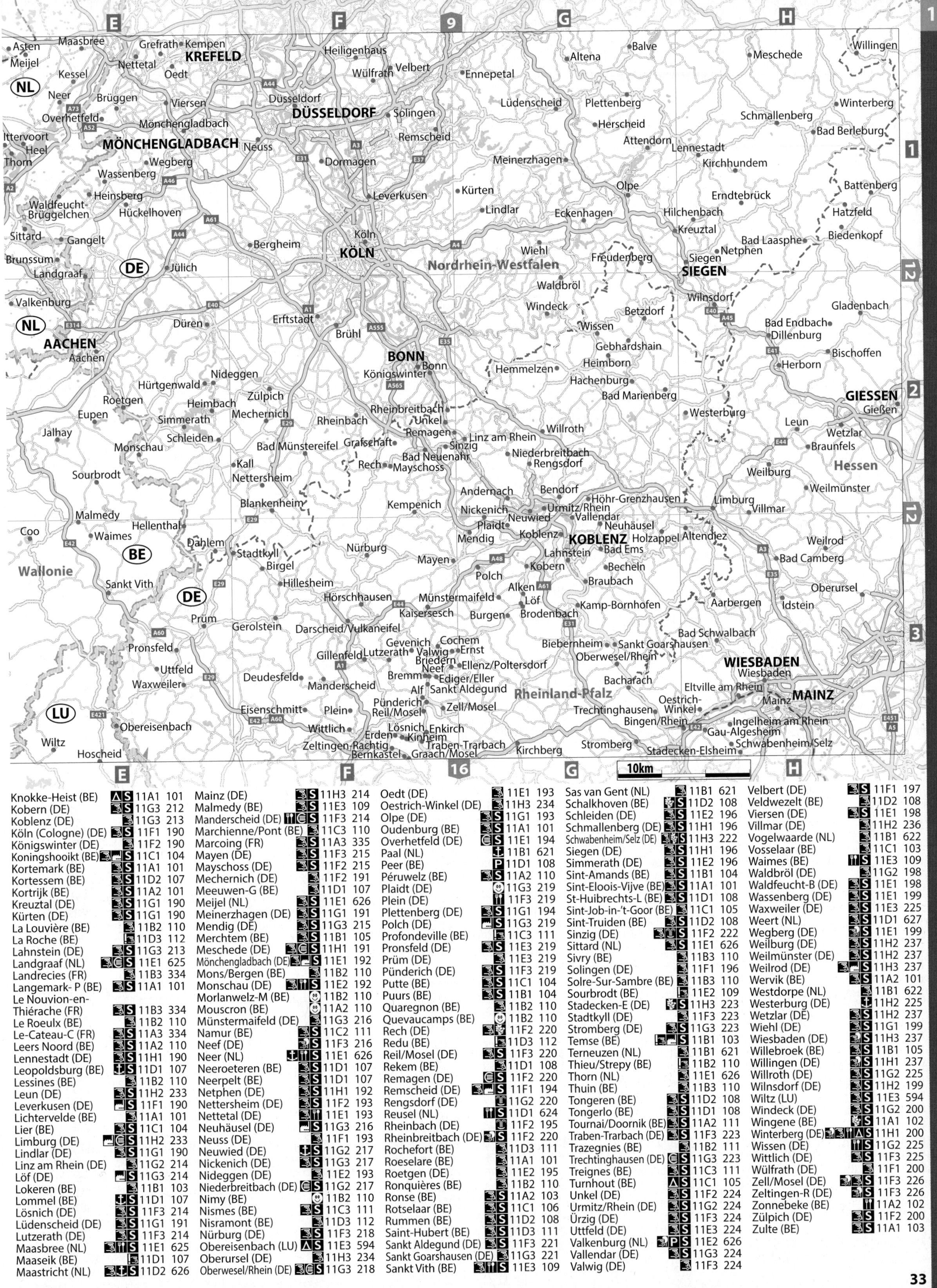

Place	Grid	Page
Knokke-Heist (BE)	11A1	101
Kobern (DE)	11G3	212
Koblenz (DE)	11G3	213
Köln (Cologne) (DE)	11F1	190
Königswinter (DE)	11F2	190
Koningshooikt (BE)	11C1	104
Kortemark (BE)	11A1	101
Kortessem (BE)	11D2	107
Kortrijk (BE)	11A2	101
Kreuztal (DE)	11G1	190
Kürten (DE)	11G1	190
La Louvière (BE)	11B2	110
La Roche (BE)	11D3	112
Lahnstein (DE)	11G3	213
Landgraaf (NL)	11E1	625
Landrecies (FR)	11B3	334
Langemark- P (BE)	11A1	101
Le Nouvion-en-Thiérache (FR)	11B3	334
Le Roeulx (BE)	11B2	110
Le-Cateau-C (FR)	11A3	334
Leers Noord (BE)	11A2	110
Lennestadt (DE)	11H1	190
Leopoldsburg (BE)	11D1	107
Lessines (BE)	11B2	110
Leun (DE)	11H2	233
Leverkusen (DE)	11F1	190
Lichtervelde (BE)	11A1	101
Lier (BE)	11C1	104
Limburg (DE)	11H2	233
Lindlar (DE)	11G1	190
Linz am Rhein (DE)	11G2	214
Löf (DE)	11G3	214
Lokeren (BE)	11B1	103
Lommel (BE)	11D1	107
Lösnich (DE)	11F3	214
Lüdenscheid (DE)	11G1	191
Lutzerath (DE)	11F3	214
Maasbree (NL)	11E1	625
Maaseik (BE)	11D1	107
Maastricht (NL)	11D2	626
Mainz (DE)	11H3	214
Malmedy (BE)	11E3	109
Manderscheid (DE)	11F3	214
Marchienne/Pont (BE)	11C3	110
Marcoing (FR)	11A3	335
Mayen (DE)	11F3	215
Mayschoss (DE)	11F2	215
Mechernich (DE)	11F2	191
Meeuwen-G (BE)	11D1	107
Meijel (NL)	11E1	626
Meinerzhagen (DE)	11G1	191
Mendig (DE)	11G3	215
Merchtem (BE)	11B1	105
Meschede (DE)	11H1	191
Mönchengladbach (DE)	11E1	192
Mons/Bergen (BE)	11B2	110
Monschau (DE)	11E2	192
Morlanwelz-M (BE)	11B2	110
Mouscron (BE)	11A2	110
Münstermaifeld (DE)	11G3	216
Namur (BE)	11C2	111
Neef (DE)	11F3	216
Neer (NL)	11E1	626
Neeroeteren (BE)	11D1	107
Neerpelt (BE)	11D1	107
Netphen (DE)	11H1	192
Nettersheim (DE)	11F2	193
Nettetal (DE)	11E1	193
Neuhäusel (DE)	11G3	216
Neuss (DE)	11F1	193
Neuwied (DE)	11G2	217
Nickenich (DE)	11G3	217
Nideggen (DE)	11E2	193
Niederbreitbach (DE)	11G2	217
Nimy (BE)	11B2	110
Nismes (BE)	11C3	111
Nisramont (BE)	11D3	112
Nürburg (DE)	11F3	218
Obereisenbach (LU)	11E3	594
Oberursel (DE)	11H3	234
Oberwesel/Rhein (DE)	11G3	218
Oedt (DE)	11E1	193
Oestrich-Winkel (DE)	11H3	234
Olpe (DE)	11G1	193
Oudenburg (BE)	11A1	101
Overhetfeld (DE)	11E1	194
Paal (NL)	11B1	621
Peer (BE)	11D1	108
Péruwelz (BE)	11A2	110
Plaidt (DE)	11G3	219
Plein (DE)	11F3	219
Plettenberg (DE)	11G1	194
Polch (DE)	11G3	219
Profondeville (BE)	11C3	111
Pronsfeld (DE)	11E3	219
Prüm (DE)	11E3	219
Pünderich (DE)	11F3	219
Putte (BE)	11C1	104
Puurs (BE)	11B1	104
Quaregnon (BE)	11B2	110
Quevaucamps (BE)	11B2	110
Rech (DE)	11F2	220
Redu (BE)	11D3	112
Reil/Mosel (DE)	11F3	220
Rekem (BE)	11D1	108
Remagen (DE)	11F2	220
Remscheid (DE)	11F1	194
Rengsdorf (DE)	11G2	220
Reusel (NL)	11D1	624
Rheinbach (DE)	11F2	195
Rheinbreitbach (DE)	11F2	220
Rochefort (BE)	11D3	111
Roeselare (BE)	11A1	101
Roetgen (DE)	11E2	195
Ronquières (BE)	11B2	110
Ronse (BE)	11A2	103
Rotselaar (BE)	11C1	106
Rummen (BE)	11D2	108
Saint-Hubert (BE)	11D3	111
Sankt Aldegund (DE)	11F3	221
Sankt Goarshausen (DE)	11G3	221
Sankt Vith (BE)	11E3	109
Sas van Gent (NL)	11B1	621
Schalkhoven (BE)	11D2	108
Schleiden (DE)	11E2	196
Schmallenberg (DE)	11H1	196
Schwabenheim/Selz (DE)	11H3	222
Siegen (DE)	11H1	196
Simmerath (DE)	11E2	196
Sint-Amands (BE)	11B1	104
Sint-Eloois-Vijve (BE)	11A1	101
St-Huibrechts-L (BE)	11D1	108
Sint-Job-in-'t-Goor (BE)	11C1	105
Sint-Truiden (BE)	11D2	108
Sinzig (DE)	11F2	222
Sittard (NL)	11E1	626
Sivry (BE)	11B3	110
Solingen (DE)	11F1	196
Solre-Sur-Sambre (BE)	11B3	110
Sourbrodt (BE)	11E2	109
Stadecken-E (DE)	11H3	223
Stadtkyll (DE)	11F3	223
Stromberg (DE)	11G3	223
Temse (BE)	11B1	103
Terneuzen (NL)	11B1	621
Thieu/Strepy (BE)	11B2	110
Thorn (NL)	11E1	626
Thuin (BE)	11B3	110
Tongeren (BE)	11D2	108
Tongerlo (BE)	11D1	108
Tournai/Doornik (BE)	11A2	111
Traben-Trarbach (DE)	11F3	223
Trazegnies (BE)	11B2	111
Trechtinghausen (DE)	11G3	223
Treignes (BE)	11C3	111
Turnhout (BE)	11C1	105
Unkel (DE)	11F2	224
Urmitz/Rhein (DE)	11G2	224
Ürzig (DE)	11F3	224
Uttfeld (DE)	11E3	224
Valkenburg (NL)	11E2	626
Vallendar (DE)	11G3	224
Valwig (DE)	11F3	224
Velbert (DE)	11F1	197
Veldwezelt (BE)	11D2	108
Viersen (DE)	11E1	198
Villmar (DE)	11H2	236
Vogelwaarde (NL)	11B1	622
Vosselaar (BE)	11C1	103
Waimes (BE)	11E3	109
Waldbröl (DE)	11G2	198
Waldfeucht-B (DE)	11E1	198
Wassenberg (DE)	11E1	199
Waxweiler (DE)	11E3	225
Weert (NL)	11D1	627
Wegberg (DE)	11E1	199
Weilburg (DE)	11H2	237
Weilmünster (DE)	11H2	237
Weilrod (DE)	11H3	237
Wervik (BE)	11A2	101
Westdorpe (NL)	11B1	622
Westerburg (DE)	11H2	225
Wetzlar (DE)	11H2	237
Wiehl (DE)	11G1	199
Wiesbaden (DE)	11H3	237
Willebroek (BE)	11B1	105
Willingen (DE)	11H1	237
Willroth (DE)	11G2	225
Wilnsdorf (DE)	11H2	199
Wiltz (LU)	11E3	594
Windeck (DE)	11G2	200
Wingene (BE)	11A1	102
Winterberg (DE)	11H1	200
Wissen (DE)	11G2	225
Wittlich (DE)	11F3	225
Wülfrath (DE)	11F1	200
Zell/Mosel (DE)	11F3	226
Zeltingen-R (DE)	11F3	226
Zonnebeke (BE)	11A2	102
Zülpich (DE)	11F2	200
Zulte (BE)	11A1	103

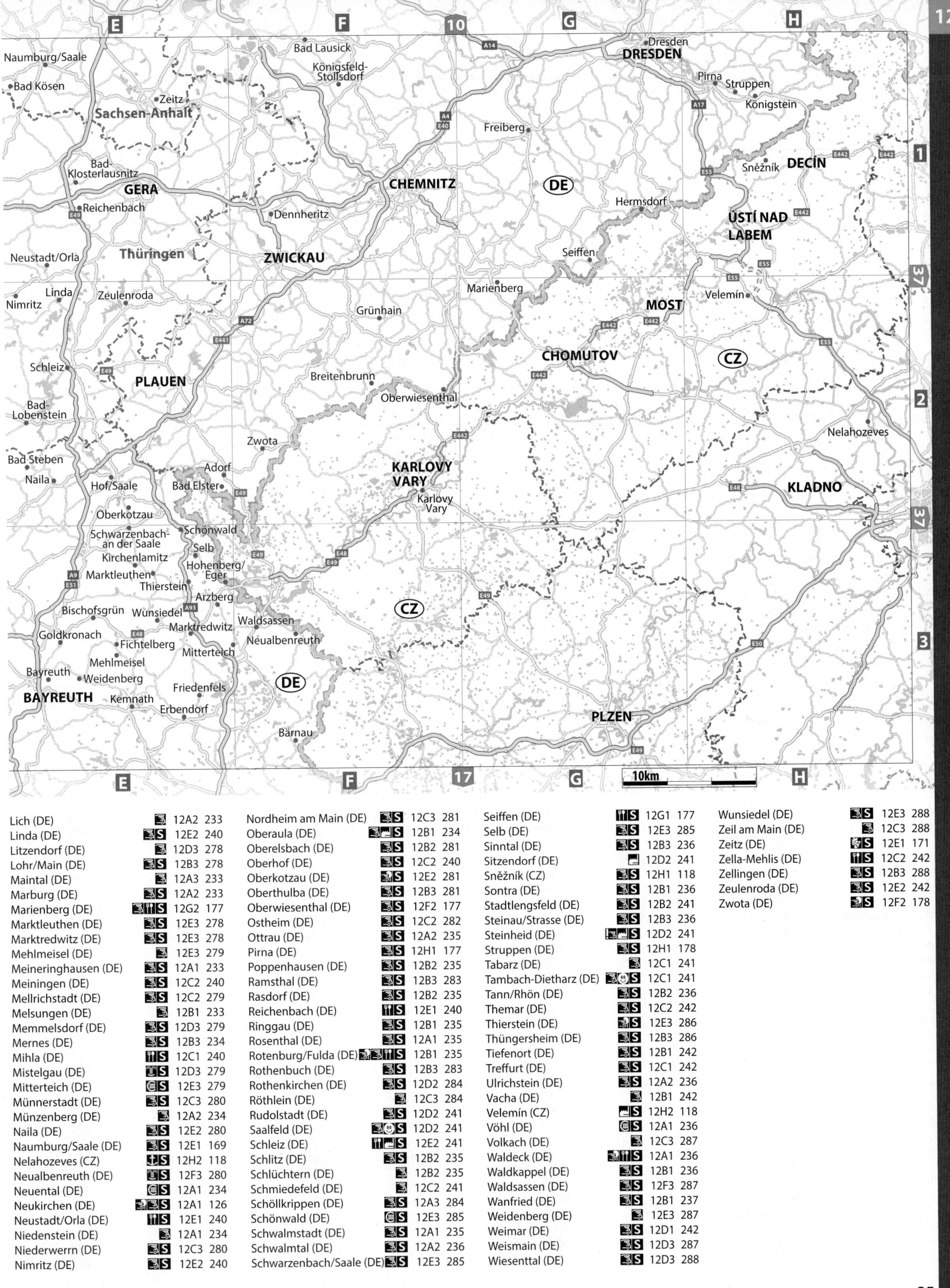
E
F
10
G
H
Naumburg/Saale
Bad Lausick
Königsfeld-Stollsdorf
Dresden
DRESDEN
Bad Kösen
Zeitz
Sachsen-Anhalt
Pirna
Struppen
Königstein
Freiberg
Bad-Klosterlausnitz
GERA
CHEMNITZ
DE
Sněžník
DECÍN
Reichenbach
Dennheritz
Hermsdorf
ÚSTÍ NAD LABEM
Neustadt/Orla
Thüringen
ZWICKAU
Seiffen
Linda
Nimritz
Zeulenroda
Marienberg
MOST
Velemín
Grünhain
CHOMUTOV
CZ
Schleiz
PLAUEN
Breitenbrunn
Oberwiesenthal
Bad-Lobenstein
Zwota
Nelahozeves
Bad Steben
Naila
Hof/Saale
Adorf
Bad Elster
KARLOVY VARY
Karlovy Vary
KLADNO
Oberkotzau
Schwarzenbach-an der Saale
Schönwald
Kirchenlamitz
Selb
Marktleuthen
Hohenberg/Eger
Thierstein
Arzberg
Bischofsgrün
Wunsiedel
Marktredwitz
Waldsassen
Goldkronach
Neualbenreuth
Fichtelberg
Mitterteich
Mehlmeisel
Bayreuth
Weidenberg
BAYREUTH
Kemnath
Friedenfels
Erbendorf
PLZEN
Bärnau
17
10km
1
2
3
37

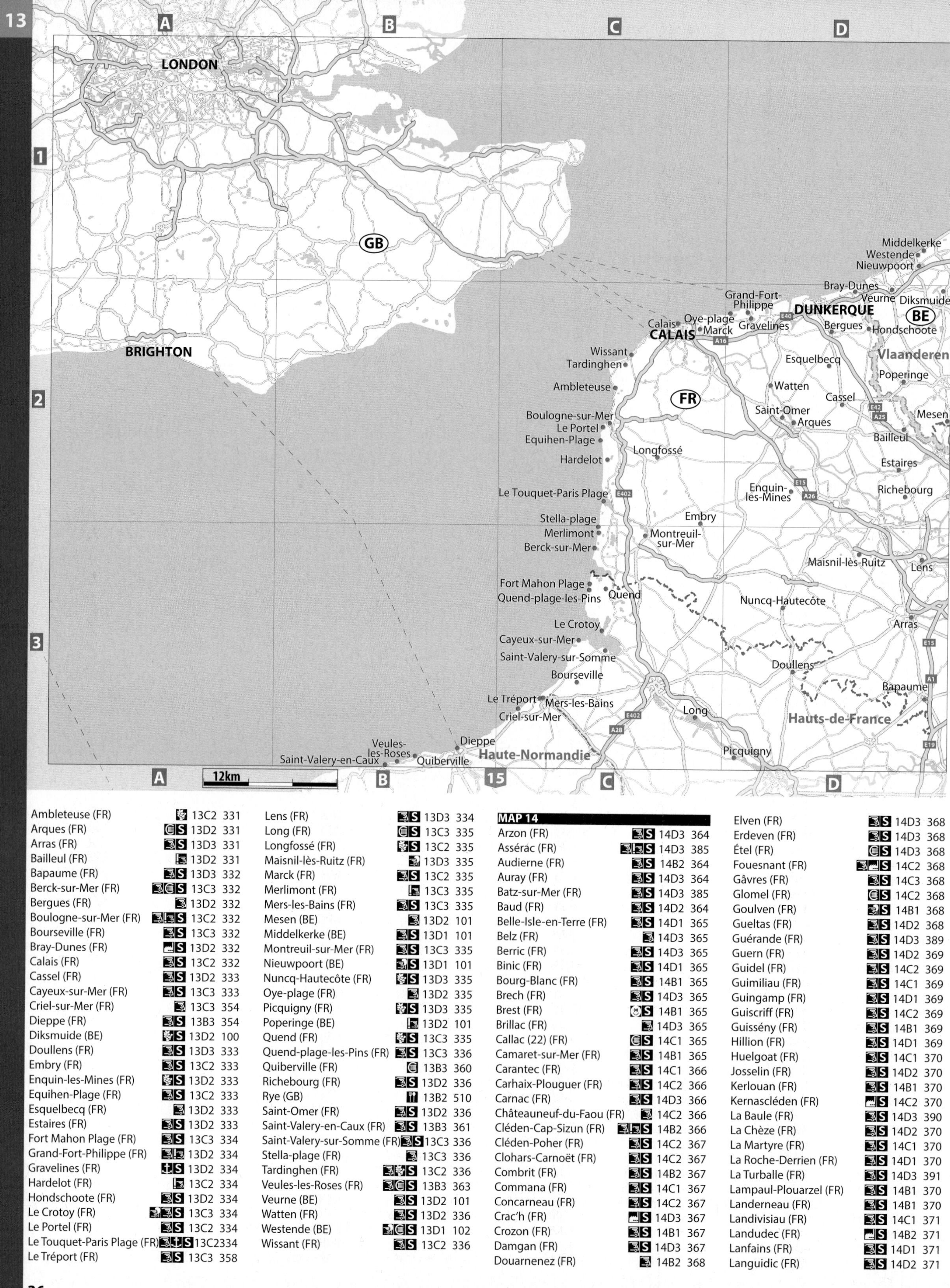

A
B
C
D
1
2
3
LONDON
BRIGHTON
GB
FR
BE
Middelkerke
Westende
Nieuwpoort
Bray-Dunes
Veurne
Diksmuide
Grand-Fort-Philippe
DUNKERQUE
Calais
Oye-plage
Marck
Gravelines
Bergues
Hondschoote
CALAIS
Wissant
Tardinghen
Esquelbecq
Vlaanderen
Poperinge
Ambleteuse
Watten
Cassel
Saint-Omer
Arques
Mesen
Boulogne-sur-Mer
Le Portel
Equihen-Plage
Bailleul
Hardelot
Longfossé
Estaires
Le Touquet-Paris Plage
Enquin-les-Mines
Richebourg
Stella-plage
Embry
Merlimont
Montreuil-sur-Mer
Berck-sur-Mer
Maisnil-lès-Ruitz
Lens
Fort Mahon Plage
Quend-plage-les-Pins
Quend
Nuncq-Hautecôte
Le Crotoy
Arras
Cayeux-sur-Mer
Saint-Valery-sur-Somme
Doullens
Bourseville
Bapaume
Le Tréport
Mers-les-Bains
Long
Criel-sur-Mer
Hauts-de-France
Dieppe
Veules-les-Roses
Saint-Valery-en-Caux
Quiberville
Haute-Normandie
Picquigny
E40
A16
E42
A25
E15
A26
E402
A28
A1
E19
12km
15

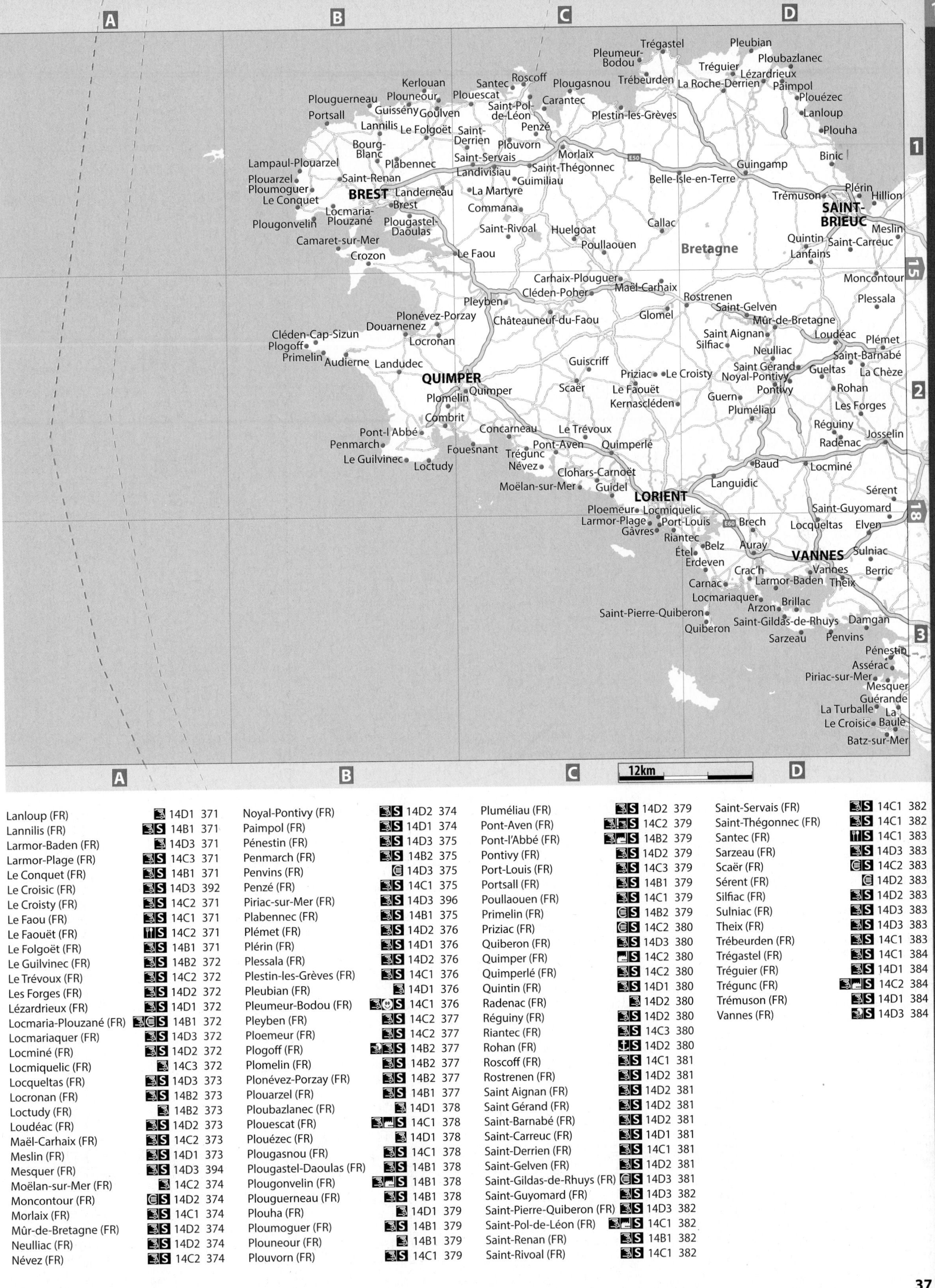
A
B
C
D
1
2
3
15
18
Trégastel
Pleubian
Pleumeur-Bodou
Ploubazlanec
Tréguier
Lézardrieux
Kerlouan
Santec
Roscoff
Plougasnou
Trébeurden
La Roche-Derrien
Paimpol
Plouézec
Plouguerneau
Plouneour
Plouescat
Carantec
Lanloup
Portsall
Guissény
Goulven
Saint-Pol-de-Léon
Plestin-les-Grèves
Plouha
Lannilis
Le Folgoët
Saint-Derrien
Penzé
Bourg-Blanc
Plouvorn
Morlaix
Binic
Lampaul-Plouarzel
Plabennec
Saint-Servais
Saint-Thégonnec
Guingamp
Plouarzel
Saint-Renan
Landivisiau
Guimiliau
Belle-Isle-en-Terre
Plérin
Ploumoguer
Le Conquet
BREST
Landerneau
Brest
La Martyre
Trémuson
Hillion
SAINT-BRIEUC
Locmaria-Plouzané
Commana
Plougonvelin
Plougastel-Daoulas
Saint-Rivoal
Huelgoat
Callac
Meslin
Camaret-sur-Mer
Poullaouen
Bretagne
Quintin
Saint-Carreuc
Lanfains
Crozon
Le Faou
Carhaix-Plouguer
Moncontour
Cléden-Poher
Maël-Carhaix
Pleyben
Rostrenen
Saint-Gelven
Plessala
Plonévez-Porzay
Châteauneuf-du-Faou
Glomel
Mûr-de-Bretagne
Douarnenez
Cléden-Cap-Sizun
Saint Aignan
Loudéac
Plémet
Plogoff
Locronan
Silfiac
Primelin
Audierne
Landudec
Neulliac
Saint-Barnabé
Guiscriff
Saint Gérand
Gueltas
La Chèze
QUIMPER
Priziac
Le Croisty
Noyal-Pontivy
Quimper
Scaër
Le Faouët
Pontivy
Rohan
Plomelin
Kernascléden
Guern
Pluméliau
Les Forges
Combrit
Réguiny
Pont-l'Abbé
Concarneau
Le Trévoux
Josselin
Penmarch
Pont-Aven
Quimperlé
Radenac
Fouesnant
Trégunc
Le Guilvinec
Loctudy
Névez
Baud
Locminé
Clohars-Carnoët
Moëlan-sur-Mer
Guidel
Languidic
Sérent
LORIENT
Ploemeur
Locmiquelic
Saint-Guyomard
Larmor-Plage
Port-Louis
E60
Brech
Locqueltas
Elven
Gâvres
Riantec
Étel
Belz
Auray
VANNES
Sulniac
Erdeven
Crac'h
Vannes
Berric
Carnac
Larmor-Baden
Theix
Locmariaquer
Brillac
Arzon
Saint-Pierre-Quiberon
Saint-Gildas-de-Rhuys
Damgan
Quiberon
Sarzeau
Penvins
Pénestin
Assérac
Piriac-sur-Mer
Mesquer
Guérande
La Turballe
La Baule
Le Croisic
Batz-sur-Mer
E50
12km

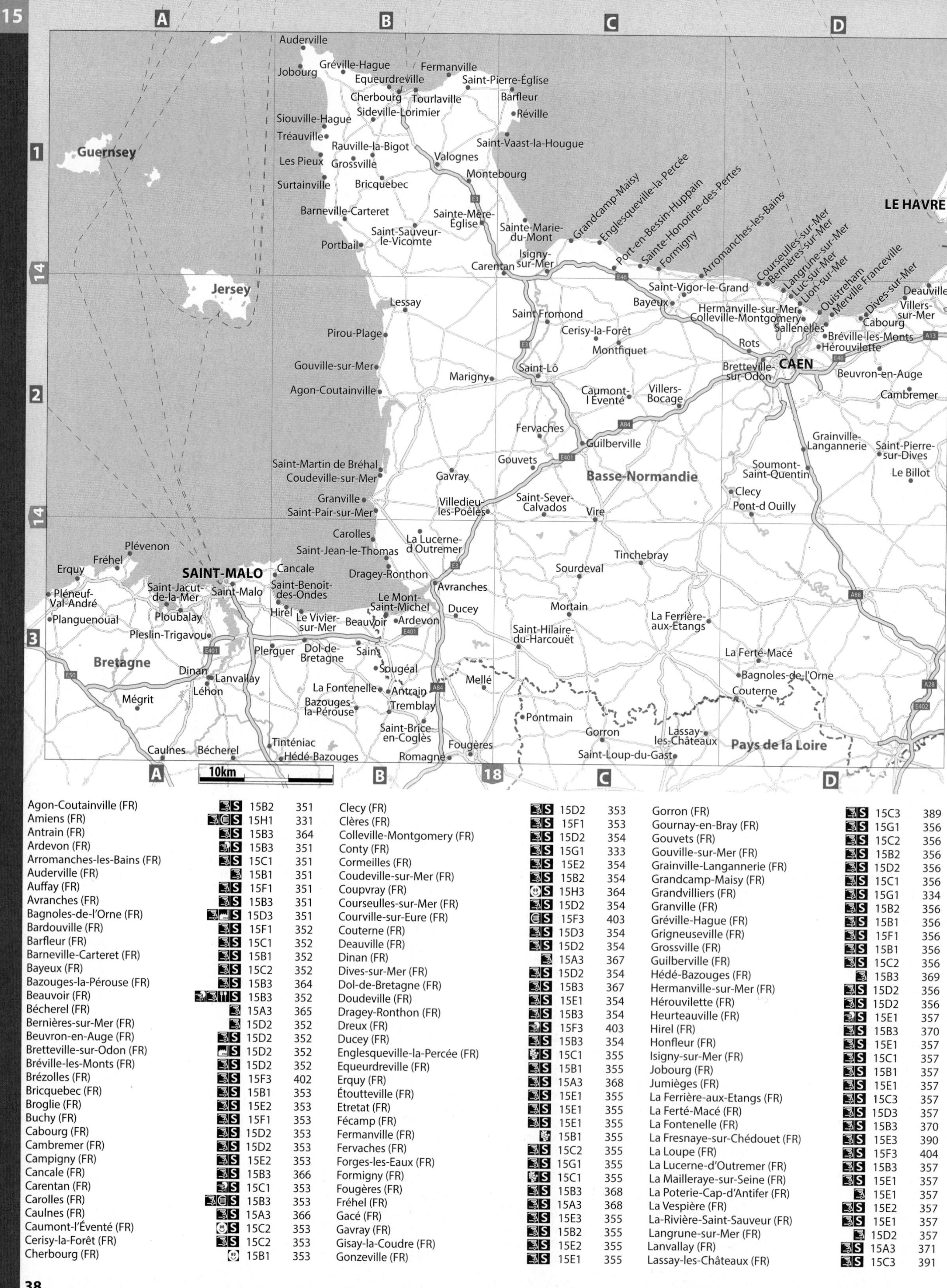

A
B
C
D
1
2
3
14
14
18
Auderville
Jobourg
Gréville-Hague
Fermanville
Equeurdreville
Saint-Pierre-Église
Cherbourg
Tourlaville
Barfleur
Sideville-Lorimier
Réville
Siouville-Hague
Tréauville
Saint-Vaast-la-Hougue
Guernsey
Rauville-la-Bigot
Valognes
Les Pieux
Grossville
Montebourg
Surtainville
Bricquebec
LE HAVRE
Barneville-Carteret
Sainte-Mère-Église
Saint-Sauveur-le-Vicomte
Sainte-Marie-du-Mont
Portbail
Grandcamp-Maisy
Englesqueville-la-Percée
Port-en-Bessin-Huppain
Sainte-Honorine-des-Pertes
Formigny
Arromanches-les-Bains
Courseulles-sur-Mer
Bernières-sur-Mer
Langrune-sur-Mer
Luc-sur-Mer
Lion-sur-Mer
Ouistreham
Merville Franceville
Dives-sur-Mer
Isigny-sur-Mer
Carentan
Jersey
Saint-Vigor-le-Grand
Deauville
Bayeux
Villers-sur-Mer
Lessay
Hermanville-sur-Mer
Colleville-Montgomery
Cabourg
Saint Fromond
Sallenelles
Cerisy-la-Forêt
Bréville-les-Monts
Pirou-Plage
Hérouvilette
Montfiquet
Rots
Gouville-sur-Mer
Saint-Lô
Bretteville-sur-Odon
CAEN
Beuvron-en-Auge
Marigny
Agon-Coutainville
Caumont-l'Eventé
Villers-Bocage
Cambremer
Fervaches
Guilberville
Grainville-Langannerie
Saint-Pierre-sur-Dives
Gouvets
Saint-Martin de Bréhal
Soumont-Saint-Quentin
Coudeville-sur-Mer
Gavray
Basse-Normandie
Le Billot
Clecy
Granville
Saint-Sever-Calvados
Villedieu-les-Poêles
Pont-d Ouilly
Vire
Saint-Pair-sur-Mer
Carolles
La Lucerne-d Outremer
Plévenon
Saint-Jean-le-Thomas
Tinchebray
Fréhel
Erquy
SAINT-MALO
Cancale
Dragey-Ronthon
Sourdeval
Saint-Benoit-des-Ondes
Avranches
Saint-Jacut-de-la-Mer
Pléneuf-Val-André
Saint-Malo
Le Mont-Saint-Michel
Mortain
Ducey
Hirel
Le Vivier-sur-Mer
Beauvoir
Ardevon
La Ferrière-aux-Etangs
Planguenoual
Ploubalay
Saint-Hilaire-du-Harcouët
Pleslin-Trigavou
Plerguer
Dol-de-Bretagne
Sains
La Ferté-Macé
Bretagne
Dinan
Sougéal
Lanvallay
Bagnoles-de-l'Orne
Mellé
Léhon
La Fontenelle
Antrain
Couterne
Mégrit
Bazouges-la-Pérouse
Tremblay
Pontmain
Saint-Brice-en-Coglès
Lassay-les-Châteaux
Gorron
Tinténiac
Pays de la Loire
Fougères
Caulnes
Bécherel
Hédé-Bazouges
Romagné
Saint-Loup-du-Gast
10km

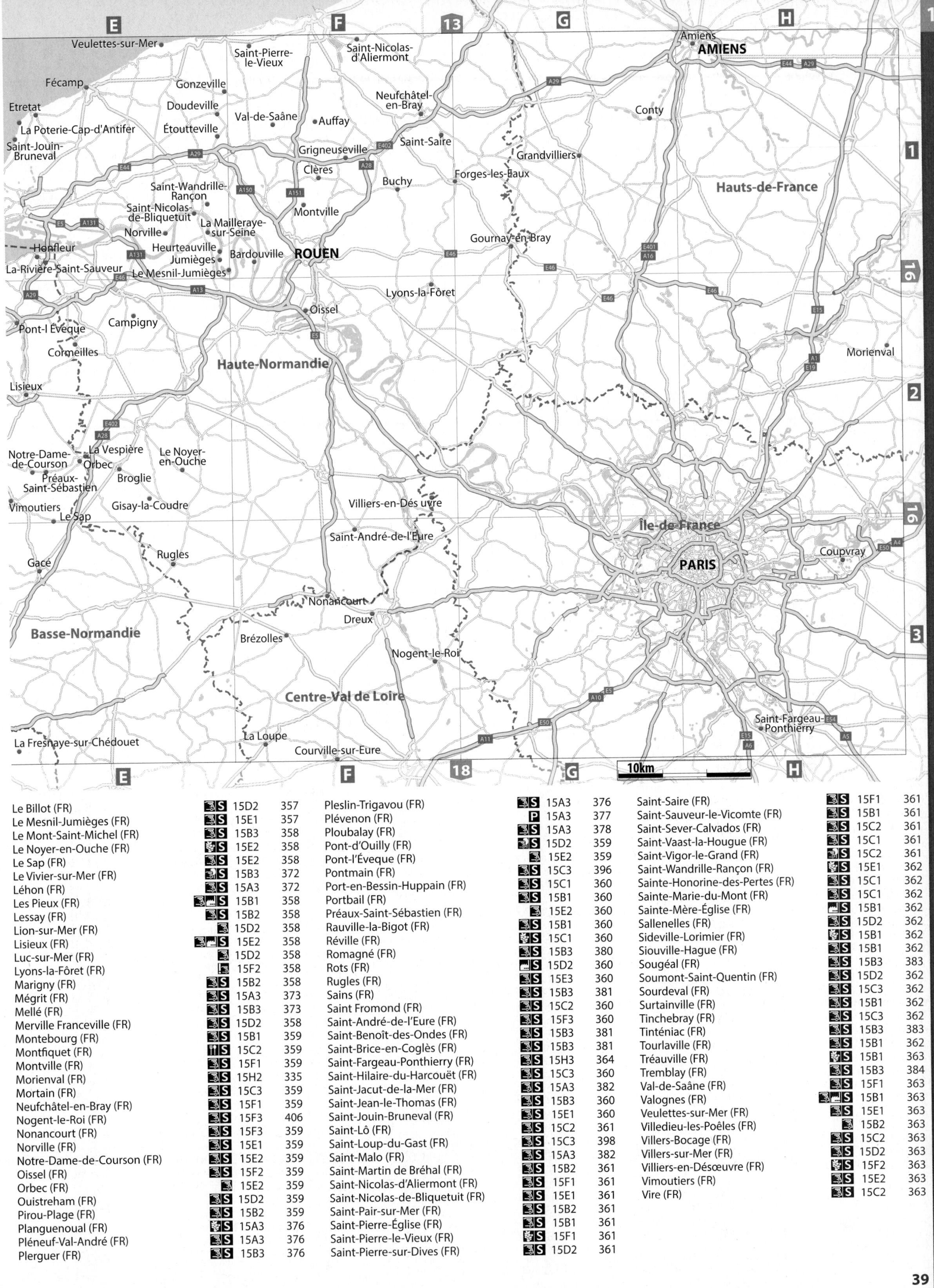

E
F
13
G
H
Veulettes-sur-Mer
Saint-Pierre-le-Vieux
Saint-Nicolas-d'Aliermont
Amiens
AMIENS
Fécamp
Gonzeville
Neufchâtel-en-Bray
Etretat
Doudeville
Val-de-Saâne
Auffay
Conty
La Poterie-Cap-d'Antifer
Étoutteville
Saint-Jouin-Bruneval
Grigneuseville
Saint-Saire
Grandvilliers
Clères
Buchy
Forges-les-Eaux
Hauts-de-France
Saint-Wandrille-Rançon
Saint-Nicolas-de-Bliquetuit
Montville
La Mailleraye-sur-Seine
Norville
Gournay-en-Bray
Honfleur
Heurteauville
Jumièges
Bardouville
ROUEN
La Rivière-Saint-Sauveur
Le Mesnil-Jumièges
Lyons-la-Fôret
Oissel
Pont-l Évêque
Campigny
Cormeilles
Morienval
Haute-Normandie
Lisieux
Notre-Dame-de-Courson
La Vespière
Orbec
Le Noyer-en-Ouche
Préaux-Saint-Sébastien
Broglie
Vimoutiers
Le Sap
Gisay-la-Coudre
Villiers-en-Dés uvre
Saint-André-de-l'Eure
Île-de-France
Rugles
Coupvray
Gacé
PARIS
Nonancourt
Dreux
Basse-Normandie
Brézolles
Nogent-le-Roi
Centre-Val de Loire
Saint-Fargeau-Ponthierry
La Fresnaye-sur-Chédouet
La Loupe
Courville-sur-Eure
18
10km
1
2
3
16

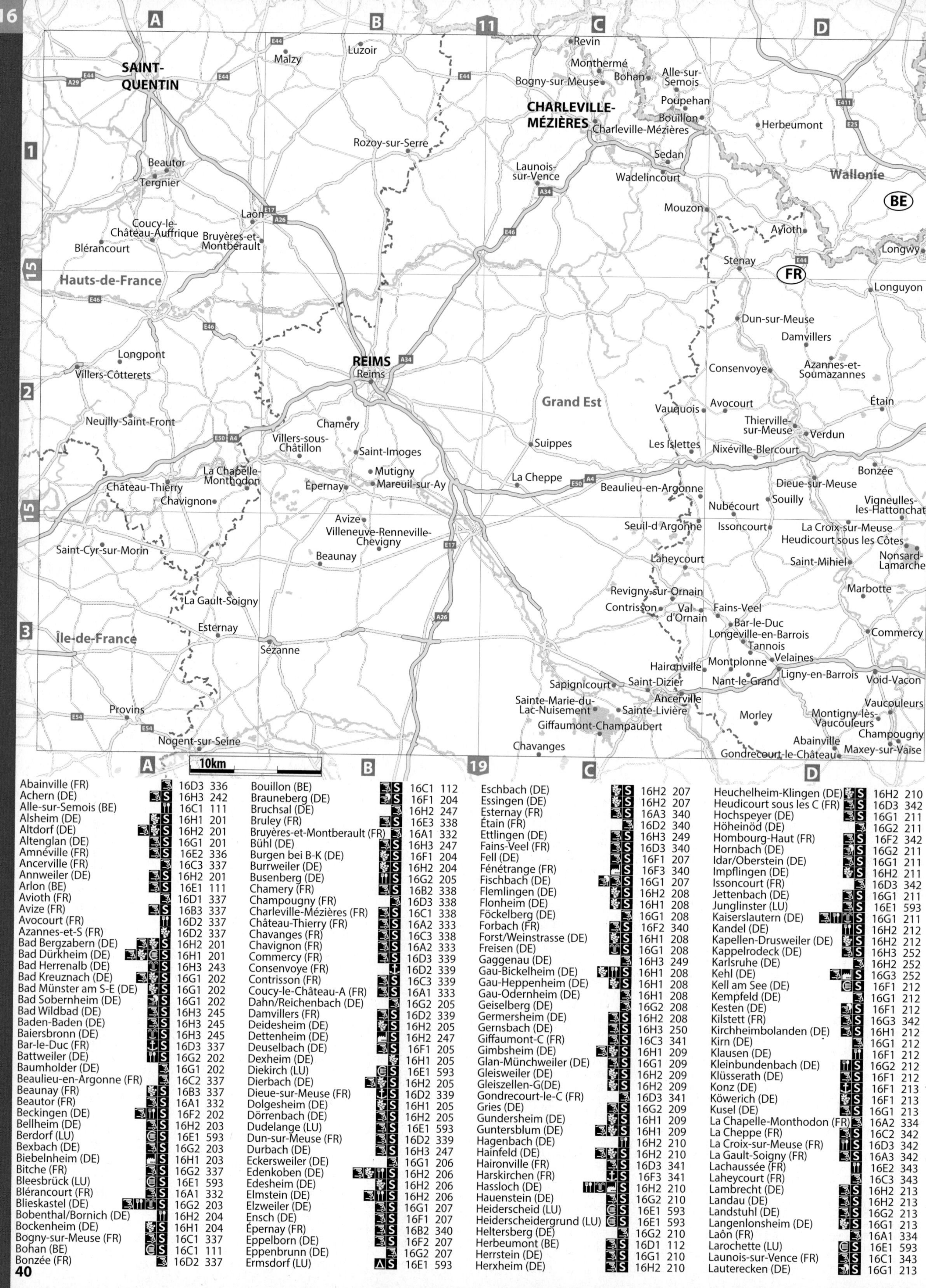
A
B
11
C
D
1
2
3
15
15
SAINT-QUENTIN
Malzy
Luzoir
Revin
Monthermé
Bogny-sur-Meuse
Bohan
Alle-sur-Semois
Poupehan
CHARLEVILLE-MÉZIÈRES
Charleville-Mézières
Bouillon
Herbeumont
Rozoy-sur-Serre
Beautor
Tergnier
Launois-sur-Vence
Sedan
Wadelincourt
Wallonie
BE
Mouzon
Laon
Coucy-le-Château-Auffrique
Bruyères-et-Montbérault
Blérancourt
Avioth
Stenay
Longwy
FR
Hauts-de-France
Longuyon
Dun-sur-Meuse
Damvillers
Longpont
Villers-Côtterets
REIMS
Reims
Consenvoye
Azannes-et-Soumazannes
Grand Est
Vauquois
Avocourt
Étain
Neuilly-Saint-Front
Chamery
Thierville-sur-Meuse
Verdun
Villers-sous-Châtillon
Saint-Imoges
Suippes
Les Islettes
Nixéville-Blercourt
La Chapelle-Monthodon
Mutigny
Bonzée
Château-Thierry
Épernay
Mareuil-sur-Ay
La Cheppe
Beaulieu-en-Argonne
Dieue-sur-Meuse
Chavignon
Souilly
Nubécourt
Vigneulles-les-Hattonchat
Avize
Seuil-d Argonne
Issoncourt
La Croix-sur-Meuse
Villeneuve-Renneville-Chevigny
Heudicourt sous les Côtes
Saint-Cyr-sur-Morin
Beaunay
Laheycourt
Saint-Mihiel
Nonsard-Lamarche
Revigny-sur-Ornain
Marbotte
La Gault-Soigny
Contrisson
Val-d'Ornain
Fains-Veel
Bar-le-Duc
Esternay
Île-de-France
Longeville-en-Barrois
Commercy
Sézanne
Tannois
Velaines
Haironville
Montplonne
Ligny-en-Barrois
Sapignicourt
Saint-Dizier
Nant-le-Grand
Void-Vacon
Provins
Ancerville
Sainte-Marie-du-Lac-Nuisement
Sainte-Livière
Morley
Vaucouleurs
Montigny-lès-Vaucouleurs
Giffaumont-Champaubert
Champougny
Abainville
Chavanges
Maxey-sur-Vaise
Nogent-sur-Seine
Gondrecourt-le-Château
10km
19
E44
A29
E17
A26
A34
E46
E50
A4
E54
E411
E25

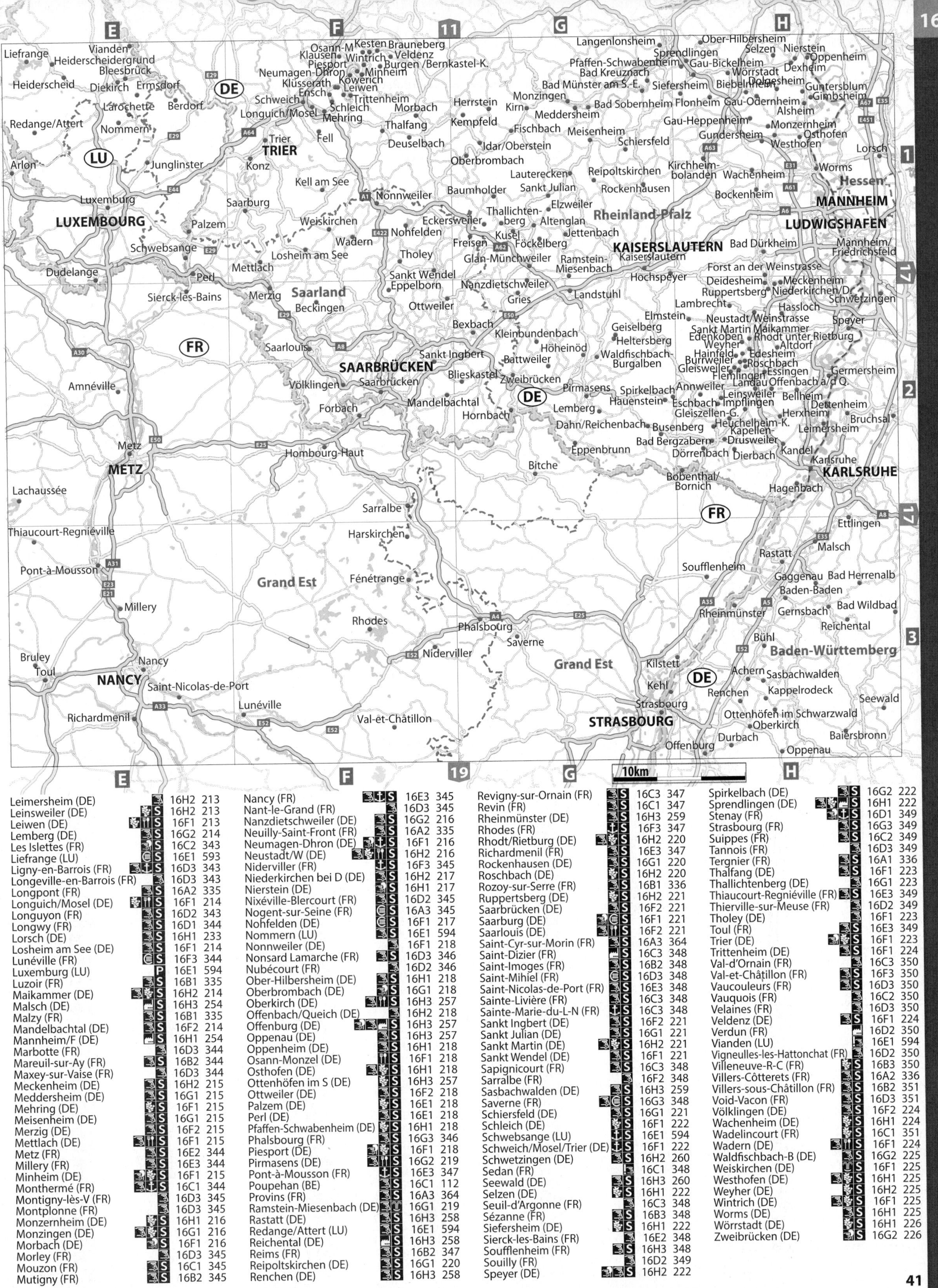

E
F
11
G
H
Liefrange
Vianden
Heiderscheidergrund
Bleesbrück
Heiderscheid
Diekirch
Ermsdorf
DE
Larochette
Berdorf
Redange/Attert
Nommern
LU
Arlon
Junglinster
Luxemburg
LUXEMBOURG
Palzem
Schwebsange
Dudelange
Perl
Sierck-les-Bains
FR
Amnéville
Metz
METZ
Lachaussée
Thiaucourt-Regniéville
Pont-à-Mousson
Millery
Bruley
Toul
NANCY
Nancy
Saint-Nicolas-de-Port
Richardmenil
Lunéville
Osann-M
Kesten
Brauneberg
Klausen
Wintrich
Veldenz
Piesport
Burgen /Bernkastel-K.
Neumagen-Dhron
Minheim
Klüsserath
Kowerich
Leiwen
Ensch
Trittenheim
Schweich
Schleich
Morbach
Longuich/Mosel
Mehring
Thalfang
Fell
Trier
TRIER
Deuselbach
Konz
Kell am See
Saarburg
Nonnweiler
Weiskirchen
Wadern
Nohfelden
Losheim am See
Mettlach
Tholey
Sankt Wendel
Eppelborn
Merzig
Saarland
Beckingen
Ottweiler
Saarlouis
SAARBRÜCKEN
Saarbrücken
Völklingen
Forbach
Mandelbachtal
Hornbach
Homburg-Haut
Sarralbe
Harskirchen
Grand Est
Fénétrange
Rhodes
Phalsbourg
Saverne
Niderviller
Val-et-Châtillon
Herrstein
Kirn
Monzingen
Kempfeld
Fischbach
Meddersheim
Idar/Oberstein
Oberbrombach
Baumholder
Bad Münster am S.-E.
Bad Sobernheim
Meisenheim
Schiersfeld
Lauterecken
Sankt Julian
Reipoltskirchen
Rockenhausen
Elzweiler
Thallichtenberg
Altenglan
Eckersweiler
Kusel
Jettenbach
Freisen
Föckelberg
Glan-Münchweiler
Ramstein-Miesenbach
Rheinland-Pfalz
KAISERSLAUTERN
Kaiserslautern
Nanzdietschweiler
Gries
Landstuhl
Bexbach
Kleinbundenbach
Höheinöd
Sankt Ingbert
Battweiler
Blieskastel
Zweibrücken
Pirmasens
Lemberg
Dahn/Reichenbach
Eppenbrunn
Bitche
Langenlonsheim
Sprendlingen
Ober-Hilbersheim
Selzen
Nierstein
Oppenheim
Pfaffen-Schwabenheim
Bad Kreuznach
Gau-Bickelheim
Wörrstadt
Dexheim
Siefersheim
Biebelnheim
Dolgesheim
Guntersblum
Gimbsheim
Flonheim
Gau-Odernheim
Alsheim
Gau-Heppenheim
Monzernheim
Gundersheim
Osthofen
Westhofen
Lorsch
Kirchheim-bolanden
Wachenheim
Worms
Hessen
Bockenheim
MANNHEIM
LUDWIGSHAFEN
Bad Dürkheim
Mannheim/Friedrichsfeld
Forst an der Weinstrasse
Deidesheim
Meckenheim
Ruppertsberg
Niederkirchen/D.
Schwetzingen
Hochspeyer
Lambrecht
Hassloch
Elmstein
Neustadt/Weinstrasse
Speyer
Geiselberg
Heltersberg
Sankt Martin
Maikammer
Edenkoben
Rhodt unter Rietburg
Weyher
Altdorf
Waldfischbach-Burgalben
Hainfeld
Edesheim
Burrweiler
Roschbach
Gleisweiler
Flemlingen
Essingen
Germersheim
Annweiler
Landau
Offenbach a/d Q.
Spirkelbach
Hauenstein
Leinsweiler
Bellheim
Eschbach
Impflingen
Gleiszellen-G.
Herxheim
Dettenheim
Busenberg
Heuchelheim-K.
Bruchsal
Kapellen-Drusweiler
Leimersheim
Bad Bergzabern
Dörrenbach
Dierbach
Kandel
Karlsruhe
KARLSRUHE
Bobenthal/Bornich
Hagenbach
Ettlingen
Malsch
Rastatt
Soufflenheim
Gaggenau
Bad Herrenalb
Baden-Baden
Rheinmünster
Gernsbach
Bad Wildbad
Reichental
Bühl
Baden-Württemberg
Kilstett
Achern
Sasbachwalden
Kehl
Renchen
Kappelrodeck
Seewald
Strasbourg
STRASBOURG
Ottenhöfen im Schwarzwald
Oberkirch
Durbach
Offenburg
Baiersbronn
Oppenau
1
2
3
17
19
10km

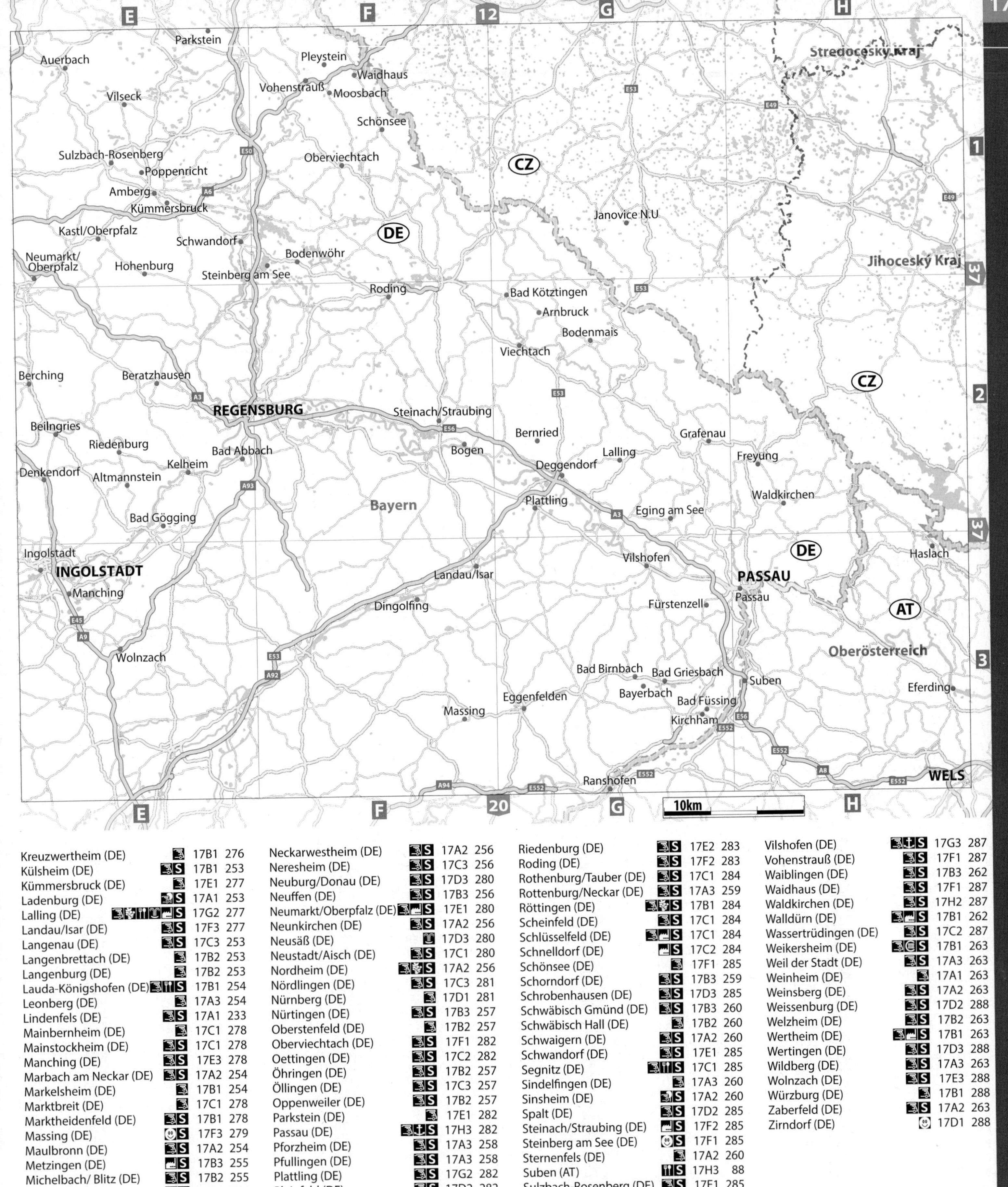

E
F
12
G
H
Parkstein
Auerbach
Pleystein
Waidhaus
Vohenstrauß
Moosbach
Vilseck
Schönsee
Stredočeský Kraj
Sulzbach-Rosenberg
Poppenricht
Oberviechtach
CZ
Amberg
Kümmersbruck
Janovice N.U
Kastl/Oberpfalz
DE
Schwandorf
Neumarkt/Oberpfalz
Hohenburg
Bodenwöhr
Steinberg am See
Jihočeský Kraj
Roding
Bad Kötztingen
Arnbruck
Bodenmais
Viechtach
Berching
Beratzhausen
CZ
REGENSBURG
Steinach/Straubing
Beilngries
Bernried
Grafenau
Riedenburg
Bogen
Bad Abbach
Lalling
Freyung
Kelheim
Deggendorf
Denkendorf
Altmannstein
Waldkirchen
Bayern
Plattling
Eging am See
Bad Gögging
DE
Haslach
Ingolstadt
Vilshofen
INGOLSTADT
Landau/Isar
PASSAU
Manching
Passau
Fürstenzell
AT
Dingolfing
Oberösterreich
Wolnzach
Bad Birnbach
Bad Griesbach
Suben
Eferding
Bayerbach
Eggenfelden
Bad Füssing
Massing
Kirchham
Ranshofen
WELS
E
F
20
G
10km
H
1
2
3
37
E53
E49
E50
A6
A3
E56
A93
E45
A9
A92
A94
E552
A8

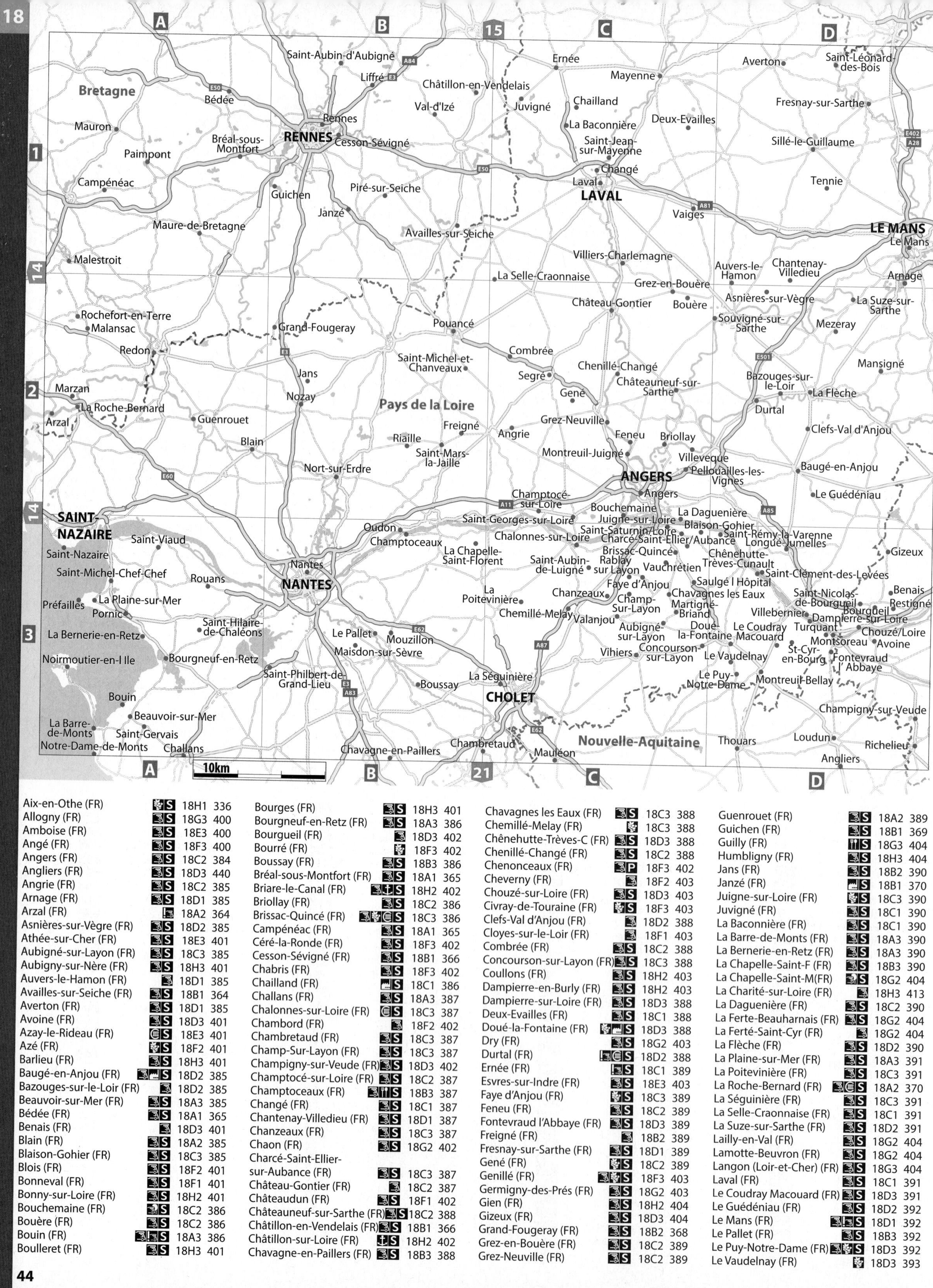
A
B
15
C
D
Saint-Aubin-d'Aubigné
Liffré
Châtillon-en-Vendelais
Ernée
Mayenne
Averton
Saint-Léonard-des-Bois
Bretagne
Bédée
Val-d'Izé
Juvigné
Chailland
Fresnay-sur-Sarthe
Mauron
Rennes
La Baconnière
Deux-Evailles
RENNES
Bréal-sous-Montfort
Cesson-Sévigné
Saint-Jean-sur-Mayenne
Sillé-le-Guillaume
Paimpont
Changé
Campénéac
Laval
LAVAL
Tennie
Guichen
Piré-sur-Seiche
Janzé
Vaiges
Maure-de-Bretagne
Availles-sur-Seiche
LE MANS
Le Mans
Malestroit
Villiers-Charlemagne
Auvers-le-Hamon
Chantenay-Villedieu
La Selle-Craonnaise
Grez-en-Bouère
Arnage
Château-Gontier
Bouère
Asnières-sur-Vègre
La Suze-sur-Sarthe
Rochefort-en-Terre
Malansac
Grand-Fougeray
Pouancé
Souvigné-sur-Sarthe
Mezeray
Redon
Combrée
Saint-Michel-et-Chanveaux
Chenillé-Changé
Mansigné
Jans
Segré
Châteauneuf-sur-Sarthe
Bazouges-sur-le-Loir
Marzan
Nozay
Gené
La Flèche
La Roche-Bernard
Pays de la Loire
Durtal
Arzal
Guenrouet
Freigné
Grez-Neuville
Clefs-Val d'Anjou
Riaille
Angrie
Feneu
Briollay
Blain
Saint-Mars-la-Jaille
Montreuil-Juigné
Villevêque
Nort-sur-Erdre
ANGERS
Pellouailles-les-Vignes
Baugé-en-Anjou
Angers
Champtocé-sur-Loire
Le Guédéniau
Bouchemaine
La Daguenière
SAINT-NAZAIRE
Saint-Georges-sur-Loire
Juigné-sur-Loire
Blaison-Gohier
Oudon
Saint-Saturnin/Loire
Saint-Rémy-la-Varenne
Saint-Viaud
Champtoceaux
Chalonnes-sur-Loire
Charcé-Saint-Ellier/Aubance
Longué-Jumelles
Saint-Nazaire
La Chapelle-Saint-Florent
Brissac-Quincé
Chênehutte-Trèves-Cunault
Gizeux
Nantes
Saint-Aubin-de-Luigné
Rablay sur Layon
Vauchrétien
Saint-Michel-Chef-Chef
Saint-Clément-des-Levées
Rouans
NANTES
Faye d'Anjou
Saulgé l Hôpital
La Poitevinière
Chanzeaux
Chavagnes les Eaux
Saint-Nicolas-de-Bourgueil
Benais
Préfailles
La Plaine-sur-Mer
Champ-Sur-Layon
Martigné-Briand
Bourgueil
Restigné
Pornic
Chemillé-Melay
Valanjou
Villebernier
Dampierre-sur-Loire
Saint-Hilaire-de-Chaléons
Aubigné-sur-Layon
Doué-la-Fontaine
Le Coudray Macouard
Turquant
Chouzé/Loire
La Bernerie-en-Retz
Le Pallet
Mouzillon
Montsoreau
Avoine
Maisdon-sur-Sèvre
Vihiers
Concourson-sur-Layon
Le Vaudelnay
St-Cyr-en-Bourg
Fontevraud l' Abbaye
Noirmoutier-en-l Ile
Bourgneuf-en-Retz
Saint-Philbert-de-Grand-Lieu
La Séguinière
Le Puy-Notre-Dame
Montreuil-Bellay
Boussay
CHOLET
Bouin
Champigny-sur-Veude
Beauvoir-sur-Mer
La Barre-de-Monts
Saint-Gervais
Nouvelle-Aquitaine
Thouars
Loudun
Notre-Dame-de-Monts
Challans
Chavagne-en-Paillers
Chambretaud
Mauléon
Richelieu
Angliers
10km
21

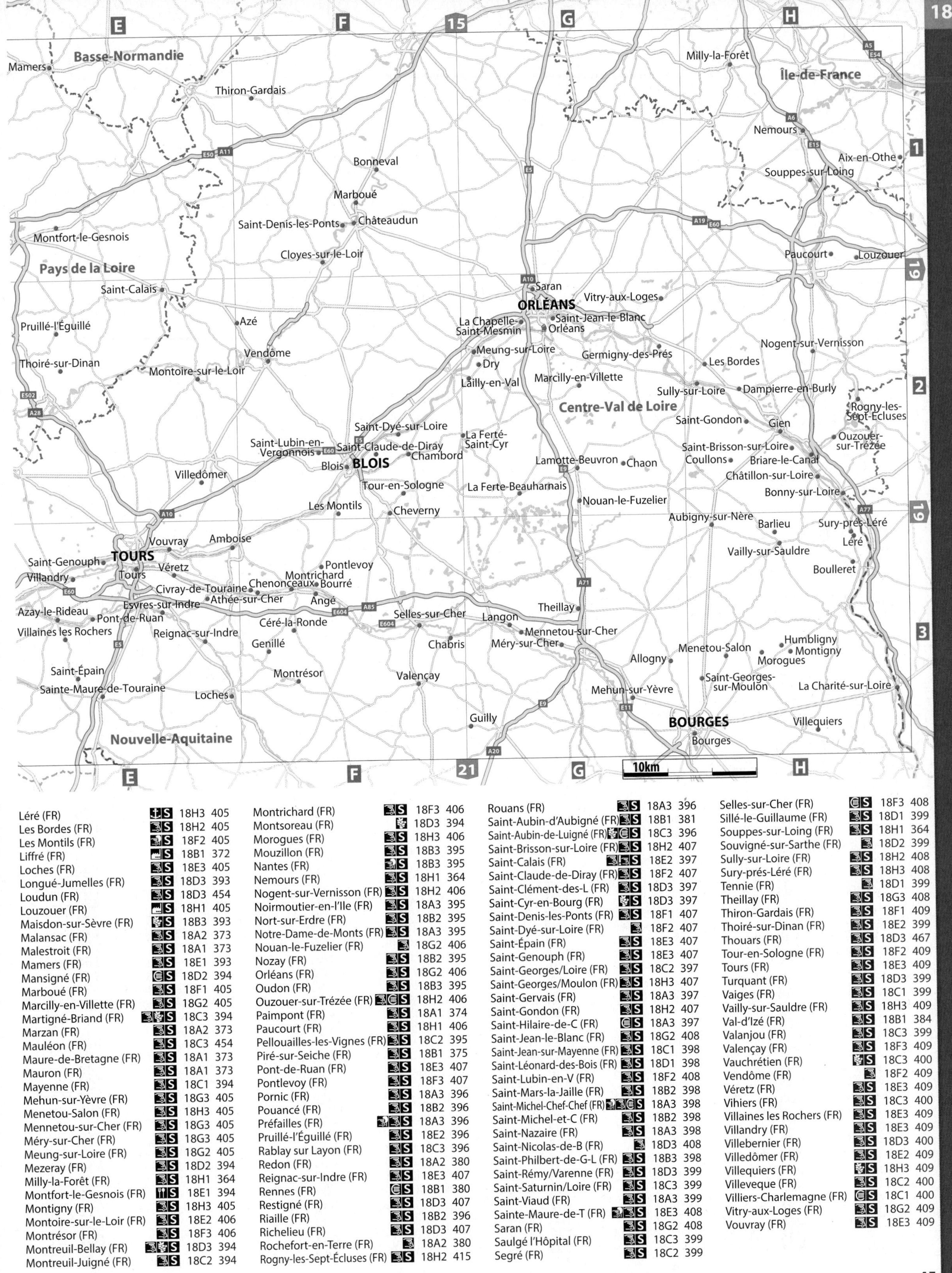

E
F
15
G
H
Basse-Normandie
Mamers
Thiron-Gardais
Milly-la-Forêt
Île-de-France
Nemours
Aix-en-Othe
Souppes-sur-Loing
Bonneval
Marboué
Saint-Denis-les-Ponts
Châteaudun
Montfort-le-Gesnois
Cloyes-sur-le-Loir
Paucourt
Louzouer
Pays de la Loire
Saint-Calais
Saran
ORLÉANS
Vitry-aux-Loges
Pruillé-l'Éguillé
Azé
La Chapelle-Saint-Mesmin
Saint-Jean-le-Blanc
Orléans
Nogent-sur-Vernisson
Vendôme
Meung-sur-Loire
Germigny-des-Prés
Les Bordes
Thoiré-sur-Dinan
Montoire-sur-le-Loir
Dry
Lailly-en-Val
Marcilly-en-Villette
Sully-sur-Loire
Dampierre-en-Burly
Centre-Val de Loire
Rogny-les-Sept-Écluses
Saint-Gondon
Gien
Saint-Dyé-sur-Loire
La Ferté-Saint-Cyr
Ouzouer-sur-Trézée
Saint-Lubin-en-Vergonnois
Saint-Claude-de-Diray
Chambord
Saint-Brisson-sur-Loire
Coullons
Briare-le-Canal
Blois
BLOIS
Lamotte-Beuvron
Chaon
Châtillon-sur-Loire
Villedômer
Tour-en-Sologne
La Ferte-Beauharnais
Bonny-sur-Loire
Nouan-le-Fuzelier
Les Montils
Cheverny
Aubigny-sur-Nère
Barlieu
Sury-près-Léré
Léré
Vouvray
Amboise
Vailly-sur-Sauldre
Saint-Genouph
TOURS
Tours
Véretz
Pontlevoy
Montrichard
Boulleret
Villandry
Chenonceaux
Bourré
Civray-de-Touraine
Athée-sur-Cher
Angé
Theillay
Azay-le-Rideau
Esvres-sur-Indre
Pont-de-Ruan
Selles-sur-Cher
Langon
Céré-la-Ronde
Mennetou-sur-Cher
Villaines les Rochers
Reignac-sur-Indre
Genillé
Chabris
Méry-sur-Cher
Menetou-Salon
Humbligny
Montigny
Allogny
Morogues
Saint-Épain
Montrésor
Valençay
Saint-Georges-sur-Moulon
La Charité-sur-Loire
Sainte-Maure-de-Touraine
Loches
Mehun-sur-Yèvre
Guilly
BOURGES
Villequiers
Bourges
Nouvelle-Aquitaine
21
10km
1
2
3
19

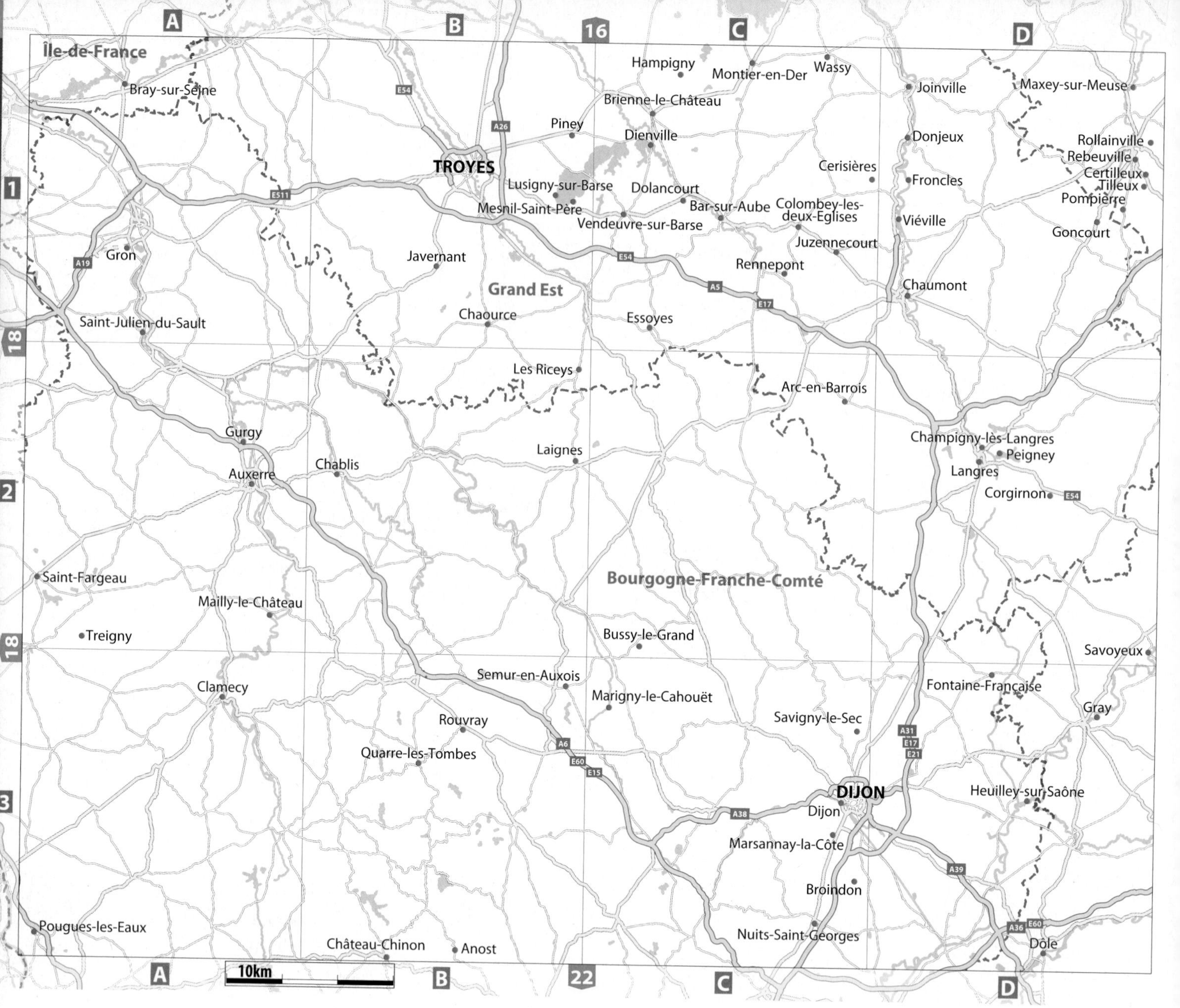

A B 16 C D

Île-de-France
Bray-sur-Seine
Hampigny
Montier-en-Der
Wassy
Joinville
Maxey-sur-Meuse
Brienne-le-Château
Piney
Dienville
Donjeux
Rollainville
Rebeuville
Certilleux
Tilleux
TROYES
Cerisières
Froncles
Lusigny-sur-Barse
Dolancourt
Pompierre
Mesnil-Saint-Père
Bar-sur-Aube
Colombey-les-deux-Eglises
Vendeuvre-sur-Barse
Viéville
Goncourt
Gron
Javernant
Juzennecourt
Rennepont
Grand Est
Chaumont
Saint-Julien-du-Sault
Chaource
Essoyes
Les Riceys
Arc-en-Barrois
Gurgy
Champigny-lès-Langres
Peigney
Laignes
Auxerre
Chablis
Langres
Corgirnon
Bourgogne-Franche-Comté
Saint-Fargeau
Mailly-le-Château
Treigny
Bussy-le-Grand
Savoyeux
Semur-en-Auxois
Fontaine-Française
Clamecy
Marigny-le-Cahouët
Gray
Rouvray
Savigny-le-Sec
Quarre-les-Tombes
DIJON
Dijon
Heuilley-sur-Saône
Marsannay-la-Côte
Broindon
Pougues-les-Eaux
Nuits-Saint-Georges
Château-Chinon
Anost
Dôle
10km
A B 22 C D

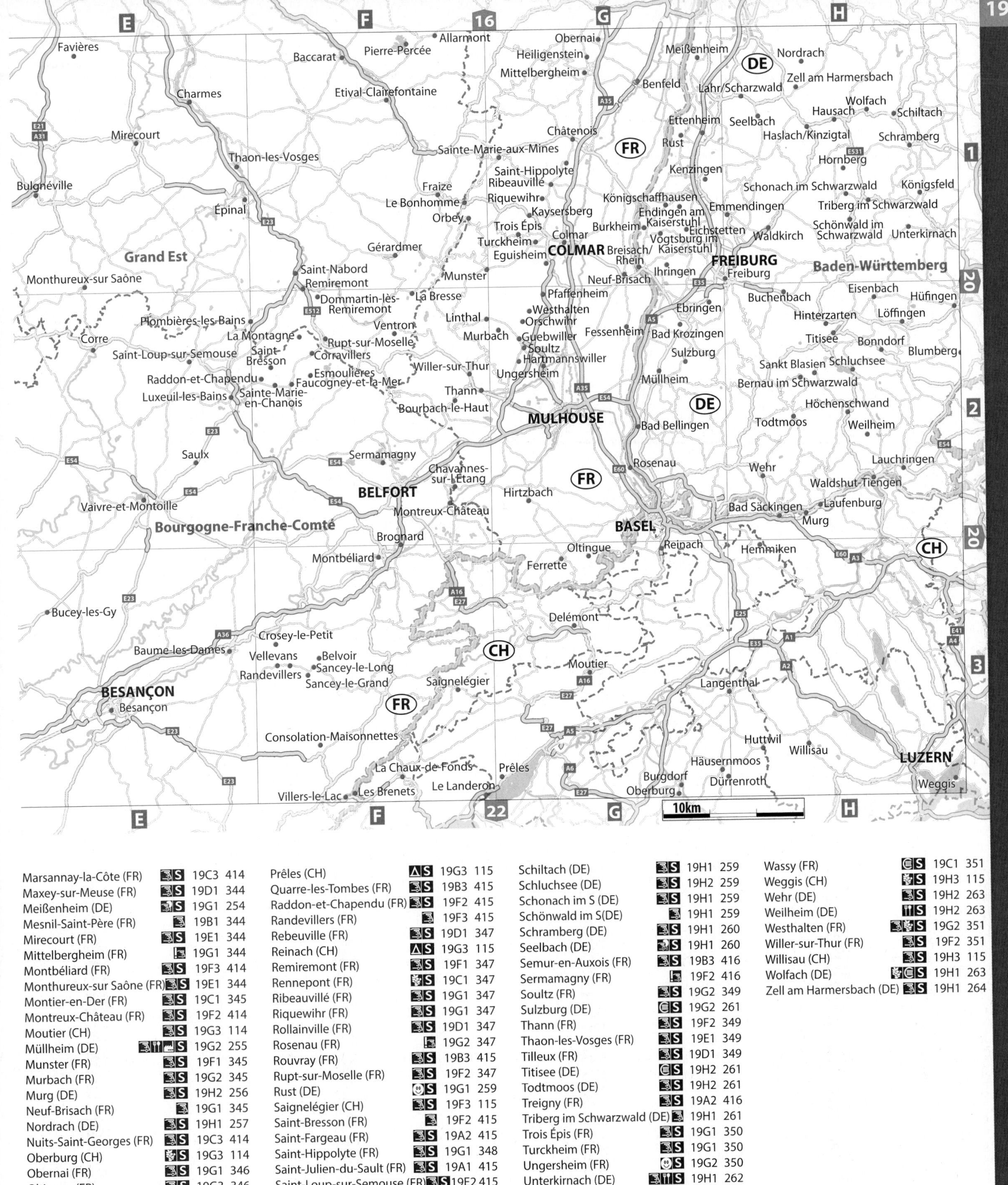
E
F
16
G
H
Favières
Baccarat
Pierre-Percée
Allarmont
Obernai
Heiligenstein
Mittelbergheim
Meißenheim
DE
Nordrach
Zell am Harmersbach
Benfeld
Lahr/Schwarzwald
Wolfach
Hausach
Schiltach
Charmes
Etival-Clairefontaine
Ettenheim
Seelbach
Haslach/Kinzigtal
Schramberg
Mirecourt
Châtenois
FR
Rust
Hornberg
Sainte-Marie-aux-Mines
Thaon-les-Vosges
Saint-Hippolyte
Kenzingen
1
Bulgnéville
Fraize
Ribeauvillé
Schonach im Schwarzwald
Königsfeld
Le Bonhomme
Riquewihr
Königschaffhausen
Épinal
Orbey
Kaysersberg
Endingen am Kaiserstuhl
Emmendingen
Triberg im Schwarzwald
Trois Épis
Colmar
Burkheim
Eichstetten
Schönwald im Schwarzwald
Unterkirnach
Gérardmer
Turckheim
Vogtsburg im Kaiserstuhl
Waldkirch
Grand Est
Eguisheim
COLMAR
Breisach/Rhein
FREIBURG
Freiburg
Baden-Württemberg
Saint-Nabord
Ihringen
Monthureux-sur Saône
Remiremont
Munster
Neuf-Brisach
20
Dommartin-lès-Remiremont
La Bresse
Pfaffenheim
Eisenbach
Hüfingen
Buchenbach
Westhalten
Ebringen
Plombières-les-Bains
Linthal
Orschwihr
Hinterzarten
Löffingen
Ventron
Fessenheim
Bad Krozingen
Corre
La Montagne
Rupt-sur-Moselle
Murbach
Guebwiller
Titisee
Bonndorf
Saint-Loup-sur-Semouse
Saint-Bresson
Corravillers
Soultz
Sulzburg
Blumberg
Hartmannswiller
Sankt Blasien
Schluchsee
Raddon-et-Chapendu
Esmoulières
Willer-sur-Thur
Faucogney-et-la-Mer
Ungersheim
Müllheim
Bernau im Schwarzwald
Luxeuil-les-Bains
Sainte-Marie-en-Chanois
Thann
Höchenschwand
Bourbach-le-Haut
MULHOUSE
Todtmoos
Weilheim
2
Bad Bellingen
Saulx
Sermamagny
Lauchringen
Rosenau
Chavannes-sur-l'Etang
Wehr
FR
Waldshut-Tiengen
BELFORT
Hirtzbach
Vaivre-et-Montoille
Montreux-Château
Bad Säckingen
Laufenburg
Bourgogne-Franche-Comté
BASEL
Murg
Brognard
Oltingue
Reinach
Hemmiken
CH
Montbéliard
Ferrette
Bucey-les-Gy
Delémont
Crosey-le-Petit
Baume-les-Dames
Vellevans
Belvoir
CH
Sancey-le-Long
Randevillers
Moutier
Sancey-le-Grand
Saignelégier
Langenthal
3
BESANÇON
Besançon
FR
Consolation-Maisonnettes
Huttwil
Willisau
Häusernmoos
LUZERN
La Chaux-de-Fonds
Prêles
Burgdorf
Dürrenroth
Villers-le-Lac
Les Brenets
Le Landeron
Oberburg
Weggis
22
10km

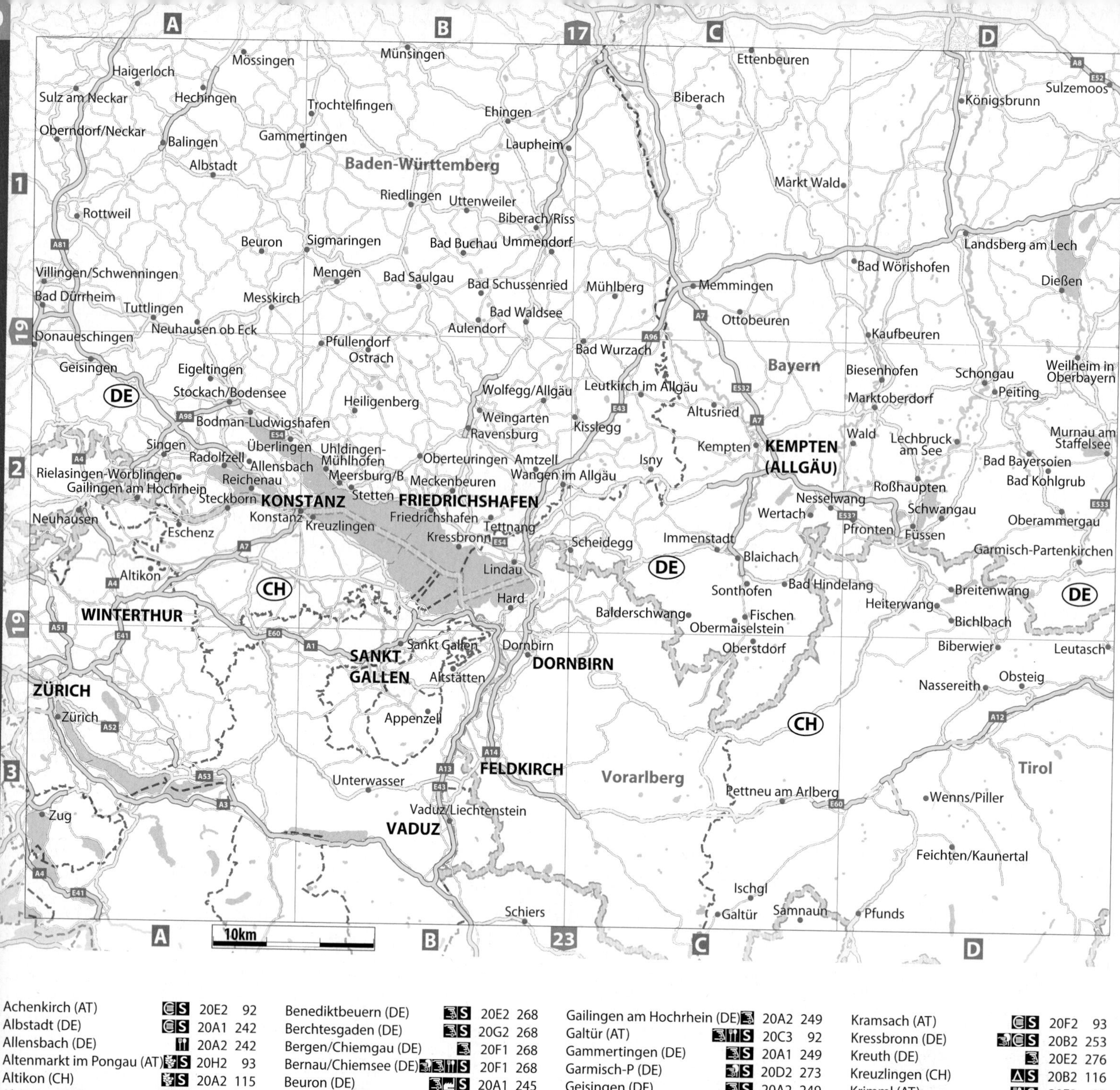
A
B
17
C
D
1
2
3
19
23
Haigerloch
Mössingen
Münsingen
Ettenbeuren
Sulz am Neckar
Hechingen
Trochtelfingen
Ehingen
Biberach
Königsbrunn
Sulzemoos
Oberndorf/Neckar
Balingen
Gammertingen
Laupheim
Albstadt
Baden-Württemberg
Markt Wald
Riedlingen
Uttenweiler
Biberach/Riss
Rottweil
Beuron
Sigmaringen
Bad Buchau
Ummendorf
Landsberg am Lech
Villingen/Schwenningen
Mengen
Bad Saulgau
Bad Schussenried
Mühlberg
Memmingen
Bad Wörishofen
Bad Dürrheim
Messkirch
Dießen
Tuttlingen
Bad Waldsee
Ottobeuren
Donaueschingen
Neuhausen ob Eck
Aulendorf
Kaufbeuren
Pfullendorf
Ostrach
Bad Wurzach
Geisingen
Eigeltingen
Bayern
Biesenhofen
Schongau
Weilheim in Oberbayern
DE
Stockach/Bodensee
Heiligenberg
Wolfegg/Allgäu
Leutkirch im Allgäu
Marktoberdorf
Peiting
Bodman-Ludwigshafen
Weingarten
Altusried
Ravensburg
Kisslegg
Murnau am Staffelsee
Singen
Überlingen
Uhldingen-Mühlhofen
Wald
Lechbruck am See
Radolfzell
Allensbach
Oberteuringen
Amtzell
Isny
Kempten
KEMPTEN (ALLGÄU)
Bad Bayersoien
Rielasingen-Worblingen
Meersburg/B
Meckenbeuren
Wangen im Allgäu
Bad Kohlgrub
Gailingen am Hochrhein
Reichenau
Stetten
Roßhaupten
Steckborn
KONSTANZ
FRIEDRICHSHAFEN
Nesselwang
Schwangau
Neuhausen
Konstanz
Friedrichshafen
Wertach
Oberammergau
Kreuzlingen
Tettnang
Pfronten
Füssen
Eschenz
Kressbronn
Scheidegg
Immenstadt
Garmisch-Partenkirchen
Blaichach
Altikon
Lindau
CH
Sonthofen
Bad Hindelang
Breitenwang
Hard
Heiterwang
WINTERTHUR
Balderschwang
Fischen
Obermaiselstein
Bichlbach
Sankt Gallen
Dornbirn
Oberstdorf
Biberwier
Leutasch
SANKT GALLEN
DORNBIRN
Altstätten
Obsteig
ZÜRICH
Nassereith
Zürich
Appenzell
FELDKIRCH
Vorarlberg
Tirol
Unterwasser
Pettneu am Arlberg
Wenns/Piller
Zug
Vaduz/Liechtenstein
VADUZ
Feichten/Kaunertal
Ischgl
Schiers
Galtür
Samnaun
Pfunds
10km

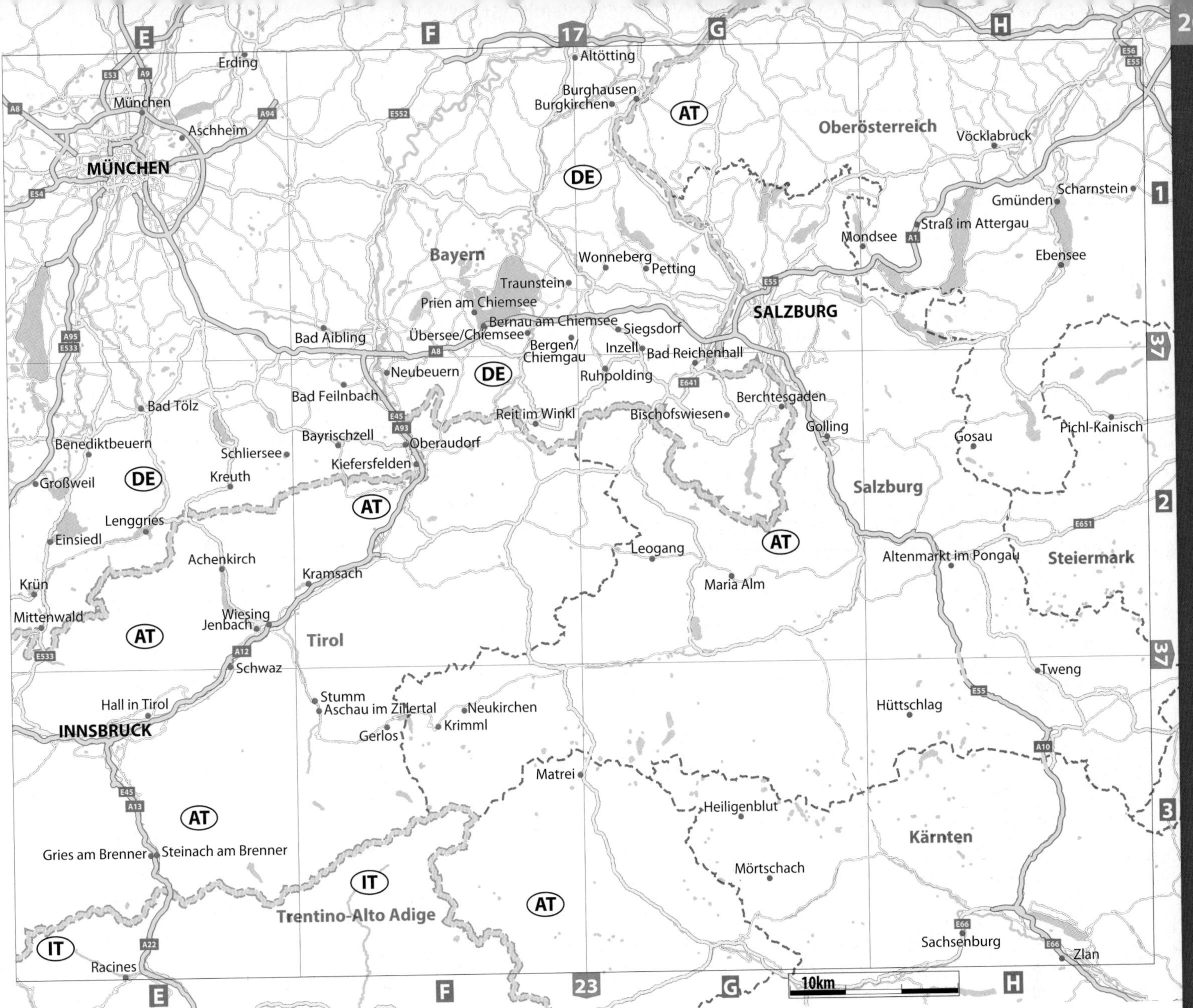
E
F
17
G
H
Erding
Altötting
München
Aschheim
MÜNCHEN
Burghausen
Burgkirchen
AT
Oberösterreich
Vöcklabruck
DE
Scharnstein
Gmünden
Straß im Attergau
Mondsee
Ebensee
Bayern
Wonneberg
Petting
Traunstein
Prien am Chiemsee
Bernau am Chiemsee
Siegsdorf
SALZBURG
Bad Aibling
Übersee/Chiemsee
Bergen/ Chiemgau
Inzell
Bad Reichenhall
Neubeuern
DE
Ruhpolding
Bad Feilnbach
Berchtesgaden
Bad Tölz
Reit im Winkl
Bischofswiesen
Golling
Bayrischzell
Oberaudorf
Gosau
Pichl-Kainisch
Benediktbeuern
Schliersee
Kiefersfelden
Großweil
DE
Kreuth
Salzburg
AT
Lenggries
Einsiedl
Leogang
AT
Achenkirch
Kramsach
Altenmarkt im Pongau
Steiermark
Krün
Maria Alm
Mittenwald
Wiesing
Jenbach
AT
Tirol
Schwaz
Tweng
Stumm
Aschau im Zillertal
Neukirchen
Hall in Tirol
Krimml
Hüttschlag
INNSBRUCK
Gerlos
Matrei
Heiligenblut
AT
Gries am Brenner
Steinach am Brenner
Kärnten
Mörtschach
IT
AT
Trentino-Alto Adige
IT
Sachsenburg
Zlan
Racines
E
F
23
G
10km
H
1
2
3
37
37

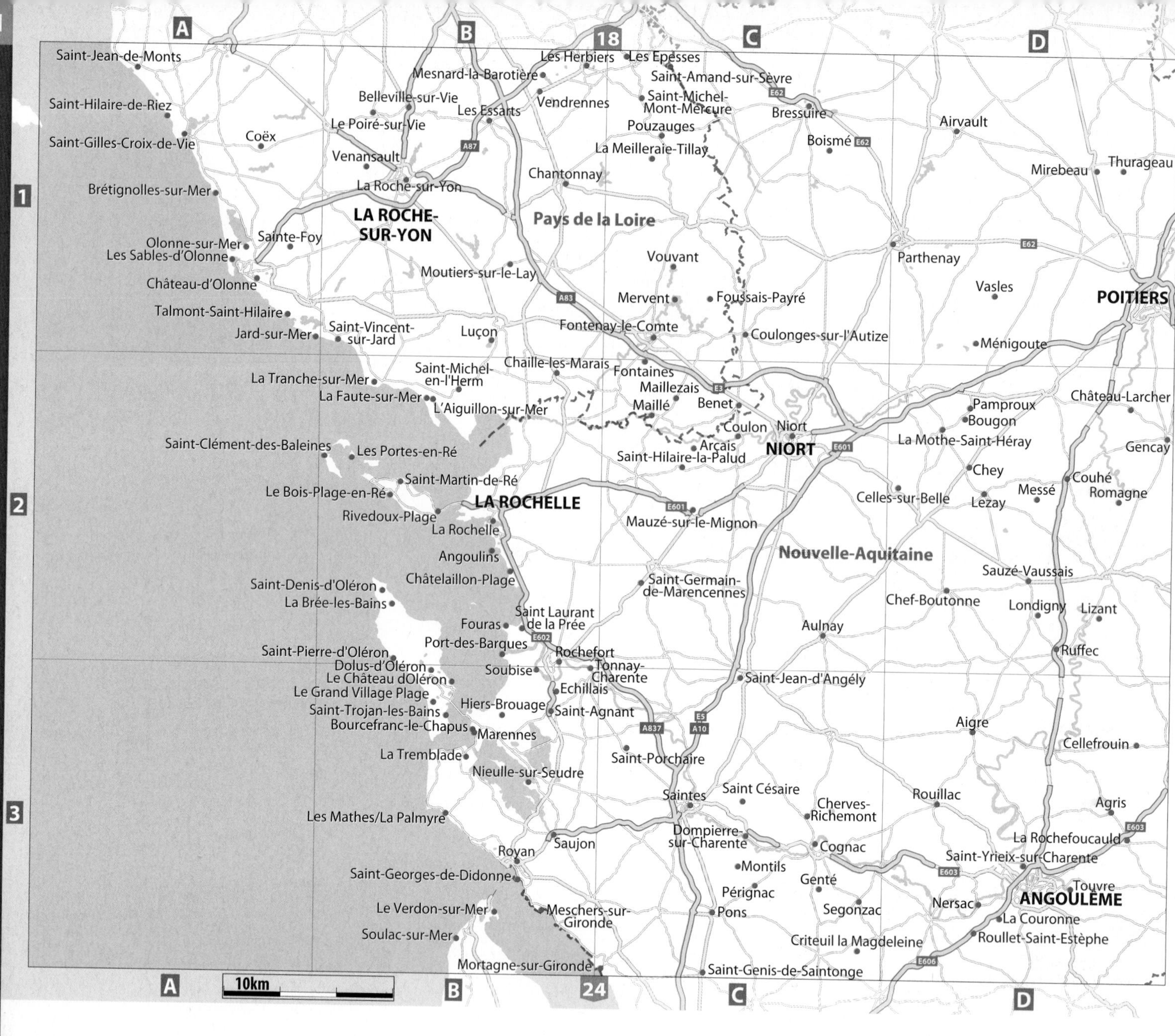
A
B
18
C
D
Saint-Jean-de-Monts
Les Herbiers
Les Epesses
Mesnard-la-Barotière
Saint-Amand-sur-Sèvre
Saint-Hilaire-de-Riez
Belleville-sur-Vie
Les Essarts
Vendrennes
Saint-Michel-Mont-Mercure
Bressuire
Airvault
Le Poiré-sur-Vie
Pouzauges
Saint-Gilles-Croix-de-Vie
Coëx
Boismé
Venansault
La Meilleraie-Tillay
Mirebeau
Thurageau
Brétignolles-sur-Mer
La Roche-sur-Yon
Chantonnay
1
LA ROCHE-SUR-YON
Pays de la Loire
Sainte-Foy
Olonne-sur-Mer
Les Sables-d'Olonne
Parthenay
Vouvant
Moutiers-sur-le-Lay
Château-d'Olonne
Vasles
Mervent
Foussais-Payré
POITIERS
Talmont-Saint-Hilaire
Fontenay-le-Comte
Jard-sur-Mer
Saint-Vincent-sur-Jard
Luçon
Coulonges-sur-l'Autize
Ménigoute
Saint-Michel-en-l'Herm
Chaille-les-Marais
Fontaines
La Tranche-sur-Mer
Maillezais
Château-Larcher
La Faute-sur-Mer
L'Aiguillon-sur-Mer
Maillé
Benet
Pamproux
Bougon
Coulon
Niort
Saint-Clément-des-Baleines
Arçais
La Mothe-Saint-Héray
Gencay
Les Portes-en-Ré
Saint-Hilaire-la-Palud
NIORT
Chey
Saint-Martin-de-Ré
Couhé
Le Bois-Plage-en-Ré
Messé
Romagne
2
LA ROCHELLE
Celles-sur-Belle
Lezay
Rivedoux-Plage
Mauzé-sur-le-Mignon
La Rochelle
Nouvelle-Aquitaine
Angoulins
Saint-Germain-de-Marencennes
Sauzé-Vaussais
Saint-Denis-d'Oléron
Châtelaillon-Plage
La Brée-les-Bains
Chef-Boutonne
Londigny
Lizant
Saint Laurant de la Prée
Fouras
Aulnay
Port-des-Barques
Saint-Pierre-d'Oléron
Rochefort
Ruffec
Dolus-d'Oléron
Tonnay-Charente
Soubise
Le Château dOléron
Saint-Jean-d'Angély
Echillais
Le Grand Village Plage
Hiers-Brouage
Saint-Agnant
Saint-Trojan-les-Bains
Aigre
Bourcefranc-le-Chapus
Marennes
Cellefrouin
La Tremblade
Saint-Porchaire
Nieulle-sur-Seudre
Saint Césaire
Rouillac
Saintes
Cherves-Richemont
Agris
3
Les Mathes/La Palmyre
Dompierre-sur-Charente
La Rochefoucauld
Saujon
Cognac
Royan
Saint-Yrieix-sur-Charente
Montils
Saint-Georges-de-Didonne
Genté
Touvre
Pérignac
ANGOULÊME
Nersac
Le Verdon-sur-Mer
Meschers-sur-Gironde
Pons
Segonzac
La Couronne
Soulac-sur-Mer
Criteuil la Magdeleine
Roullet-Saint-Estèphe
Mortagne-sur-Gironde
Saint-Genis-de-Saintonge
A
10km
B
24
C
D

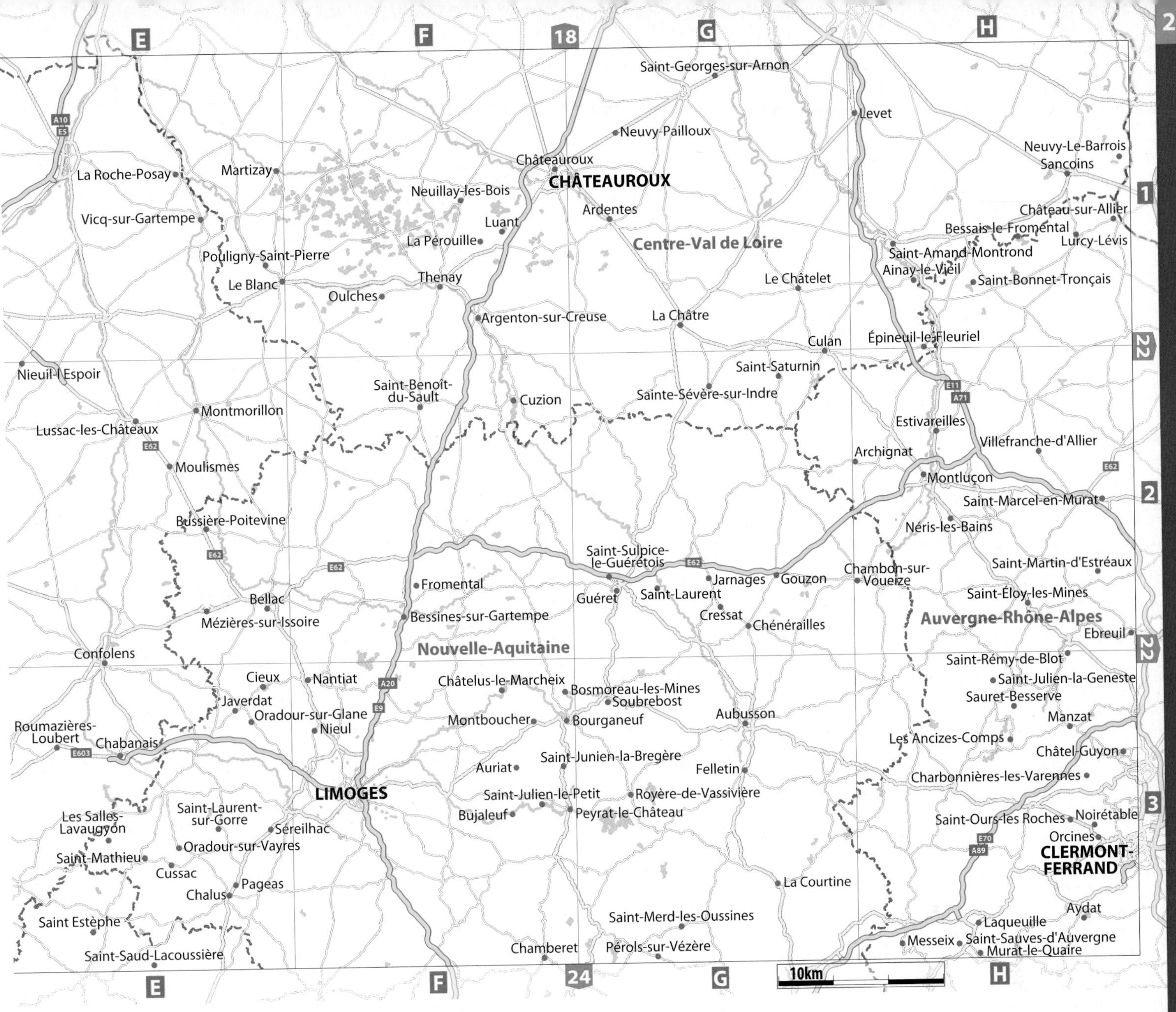
E
F
18
G
H
Saint-Georges-sur-Arnon
Levet
Neuvy-Pailloux
Neuvy-Le-Barrois
Sancoins
Châteauroux
CHÂTEAUROUX
La Roche-Posay
Martizay
Neuillay-les-Bois
Ardentes
Château-sur-Allier
Vicq-sur-Gartempe
Luant
Bessais-le-Fromental
Lurcy-Lévis
La Pérouille
Centre-Val de Loire
Saint-Amand-Montrond
Pouligny-Saint-Pierre
Ainay-le-Vieil
Thenay
Le Châtelet
Saint-Bonnet-Tronçais
Le Blanc
Oulches
Argenton-sur-Creuse
La Châtre
Culan
Épineuil-le-Fleuriel
Saint-Saturnin
Nieuil-l'Espoir
Saint-Benoît-du-Sault
Cuzion
Sainte-Sévère-sur-Indre
Montmorillon
Lussac-les-Châteaux
Estivareilles
Villefranche-d'Allier
Archignat
Moulismes
Montluçon
Saint-Marcel-en-Murat
Néris-les-Bains
Bussière-Poitevine
Saint-Sulpice-le-Guérétois
Saint-Martin-d'Estréaux
Chambon-sur-Voueize
Jarnages
Gouzon
Fromental
Guéret
Saint-Laurent
Saint-Éloy-les-Mines
Bellac
Cressat
Mézières-sur-Issoire
Bessines-sur-Gartempe
Chénérailles
Auvergne-Rhône-Alpes
Ebreuil
Nouvelle-Aquitaine
Confolens
Saint-Rémy-de-Blot
Cieux
Nantiat
Châtelus-le-Marcheix
Saint-Julien-la-Geneste
Bosmoreau-les-Mines
Sauret-Besserve
Javerdat
Soubrebost
Oradour-sur-Glane
Montboucher
Bourganeuf
Aubusson
Manzat
Roumazières-Loubert
Nieul
Les Ancizes-Comps
Chabanais
Châtel-Guyon
Saint-Junien-la-Bregère
Auriat
Felletin
Charbonnières-les-Varennes
LIMOGES
Saint-Julien-le-Petit
Royère-de-Vassivière
Les Salles-Lavauguyon
Saint-Laurent-sur-Gorre
Bujaleuf
Peyrat-le-Château
Saint-Ours-les Roches
Noirétable
Séreilhac
Orcines
Saint-Mathieu
Oradour-sur-Vayres
CLERMONT-FERRAND
Cussac
Pageas
La Courtine
Chalus
Aydat
Saint Estèphe
Saint-Merd-les-Oussines
Laqueuille
Messeix
Saint-Sauves-d'Auvergne
Murat-le-Quaire
Chamberet
Pérols-sur-Vézère
Saint-Saud-Lacoussière
24
10km
1
2
3
22

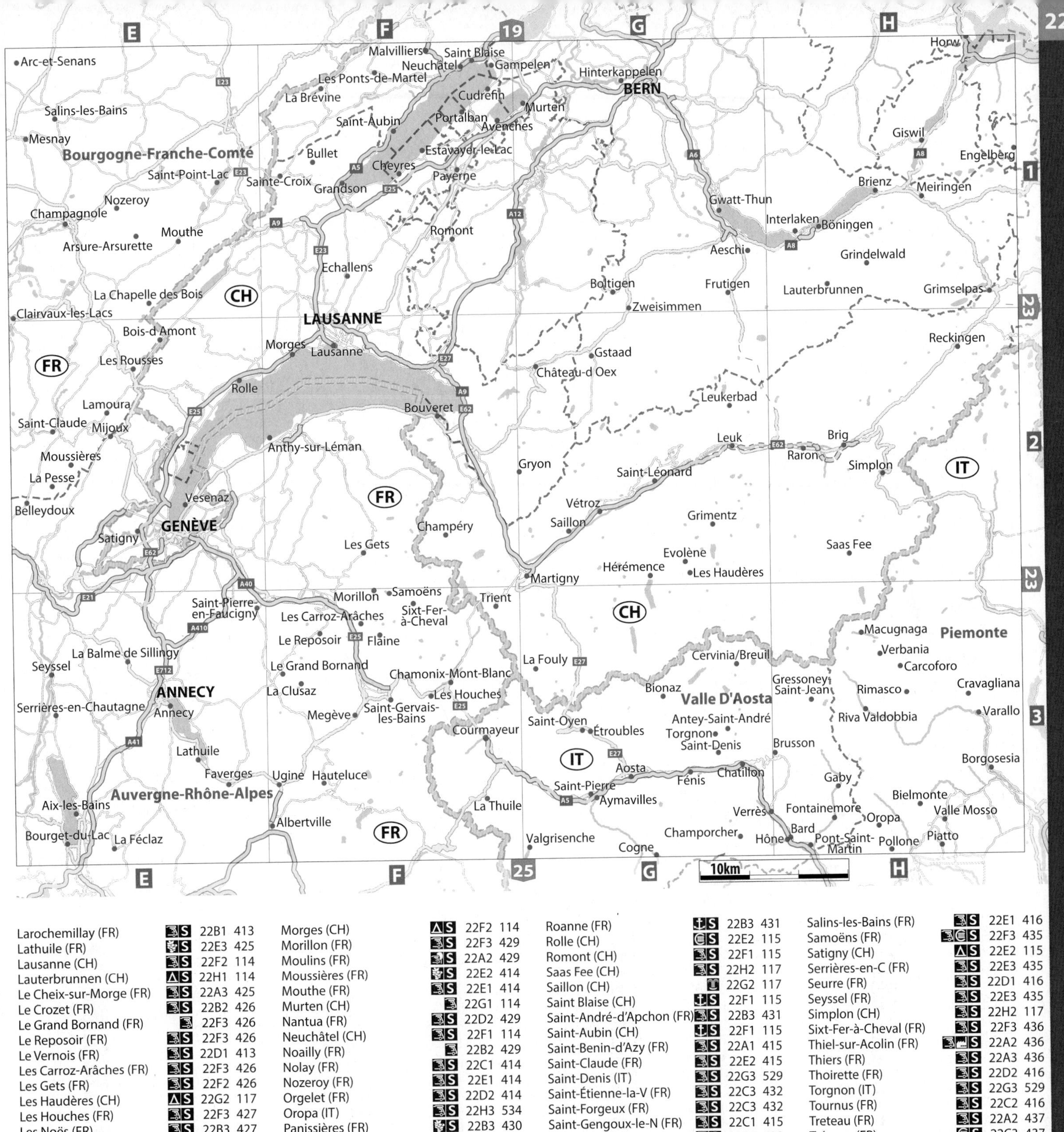
E
F
19
G
H
Arc-et-Senans
Salins-les-Bains
Mesnay
Bourgogne-Franche-Comté
Saint-Point-Lac
Nozeroy
Champagnole
Mouthe
Arsure-Arsurette
La Chapelle des Bois
Clairvaux-les-Lacs
Bois-d'Amont
Les Rousses
FR
CH
Lamoura
Saint-Claude
Mijoux
Moussières
La Pesse
Belleydoux
Malvilliers
Saint Blaise
Neuchâtel
Gampelen
Les Ponts-de-Martel
La Brévine
Cudrefin
Murten
Saint-Aubin
Portalban
Avenches
Bullet
Estavayer-le-Lac
Cheyres
Payerne
Sainte-Croix
Grandson
Romont
Echallens
LAUSANNE
Morges
Lausanne
Rolle
Bouveret
Anthy-sur-Léman
Vesenaz
GENÈVE
Satigny
Hinterkappelen
BERN
Gwatt-Thun
Interlaken
Böningen
Aeschi
Grindelwald
Boltigen
Frutigen
Lauterbrunnen
Zweisimmen
Gstaad
Château-d Oex
Leukerbad
Horw
Giswil
Engelberg
Brienz
Meiringen
Grimselpass
Reckingen
Leuk
Brig
Raron
Simplon
IT
Gryon
Saint-Léonard
Vétroz
Saillon
Grimentz
Champéry
Les Gets
Saas Fee
Evolène
Hérémence
Les Haudères
Martigny
Morillon
Samoëns
Trient
Saint-Pierre-en-Faucigny
Les Carroz-Arâches
Sixt-Fer-à-Cheval
Le Reposoir
Flaine
La Balme de Sillingy
Seyssel
Le Grand Bornand
Chamonix-Mont-Blanc
La Fouly
Cervinia/Breuil
Macugnaga
Piemonte
Verbania
Carcoforo
ANNECY
La Clusaz
Les Houches
Bionaz
Valle D'Aosta
Gressoney-Saint-Jean
Rimasco
Cravagliana
Serrières-en-Chautagne
Annecy
Megève
Saint-Gervais-les-Bains
Saint-Oyen
Étroubles
Antey-Saint-André
Torgnon
Riva Valdobbia
Varallo
Courmayeur
Saint-Denis
Brusson
Lathuile
Faverges
Ugine
Hauteluce
Aosta
Fénis
Chatillon
Gaby
Borgosesia
Auvergne-Rhône-Alpes
Saint-Pierre
Aymavilles
La Thuile
Bielmonte
Aix-les-Bains
Albertville
Verrès
Fontainemore
Oropa
Valle Mosso
Bourget-du-Lac
La Féclaz
Valgrisenche
Cogne
Champorcher
Hône
Bard
Pont-Saint-Martin
Pollone
Piatto
25
10km
1
2
3
23

A · B · 20 · C · D — 1 · 22 · 2 · 22 · 3 — A · B · 26 · C · D

Brunnen · Elm · Zizers · Chur · AT · Tirol · AT · Breil/Brigels · Churwalden · Sent · IT · Davos · Glorenza · Silandro · Vals · Andeer · Savognin · CH · Solda · Splügen · Sankt Moritz · Livigno · Bormio · Rabbi · Caldes · Bivio · Pontresina · Santa Caterina Valfurva · Dimaro · Folgarida · Sonogno · Stampa · Chiavenna · Chiesa in Valmalenco · Trentino-Alto Adige · CH · IT · Novate Mezzola · Tirano · Andalo · Gordevio · Bellinzona · Colico · Morbegno · Sondrio · Molveno · Avegno · Tenero · Vezzano · IT · Locarno · Rivera · Santa Maria Maggiore · Piemonte · Capo di Ponte · Arco · Cannobio · Maccagno · LUGANO · Menaggio · Lombardia · Niardo · Bezzecca · Riva del Garda · Oggebbio · Germignaga · Muzzano·Lugano · Esine · Torbole · Mergozzo · Luino · Molinazzo di Montegio · Agno · Rovetta · Clusone · Brentonico · Baveno · Mandello del Lario · Costa Volpino · Malcesine · Omegna · Meride · Gavirate · Gandino · Campione · Avio · Orta San Giulio · Ternate · Como · Lecco · Olginate · Carenno · Lodrino · Ferrara di Monte Baldo · Madonna del Sasso · Arona · Monte Marenzo · Alzano Lombardo · Molina · Pombia · Merate · BERGAMO · Sulzano · Garda · Saronno · Biassono · Stezzano · Iseo · Bardolino · Veneto · Nova Milanese · Lazise · BRESCIA · Brescia · Treviglio · Desenzano del Garda · Sirmione · Colà di Lazise

10km

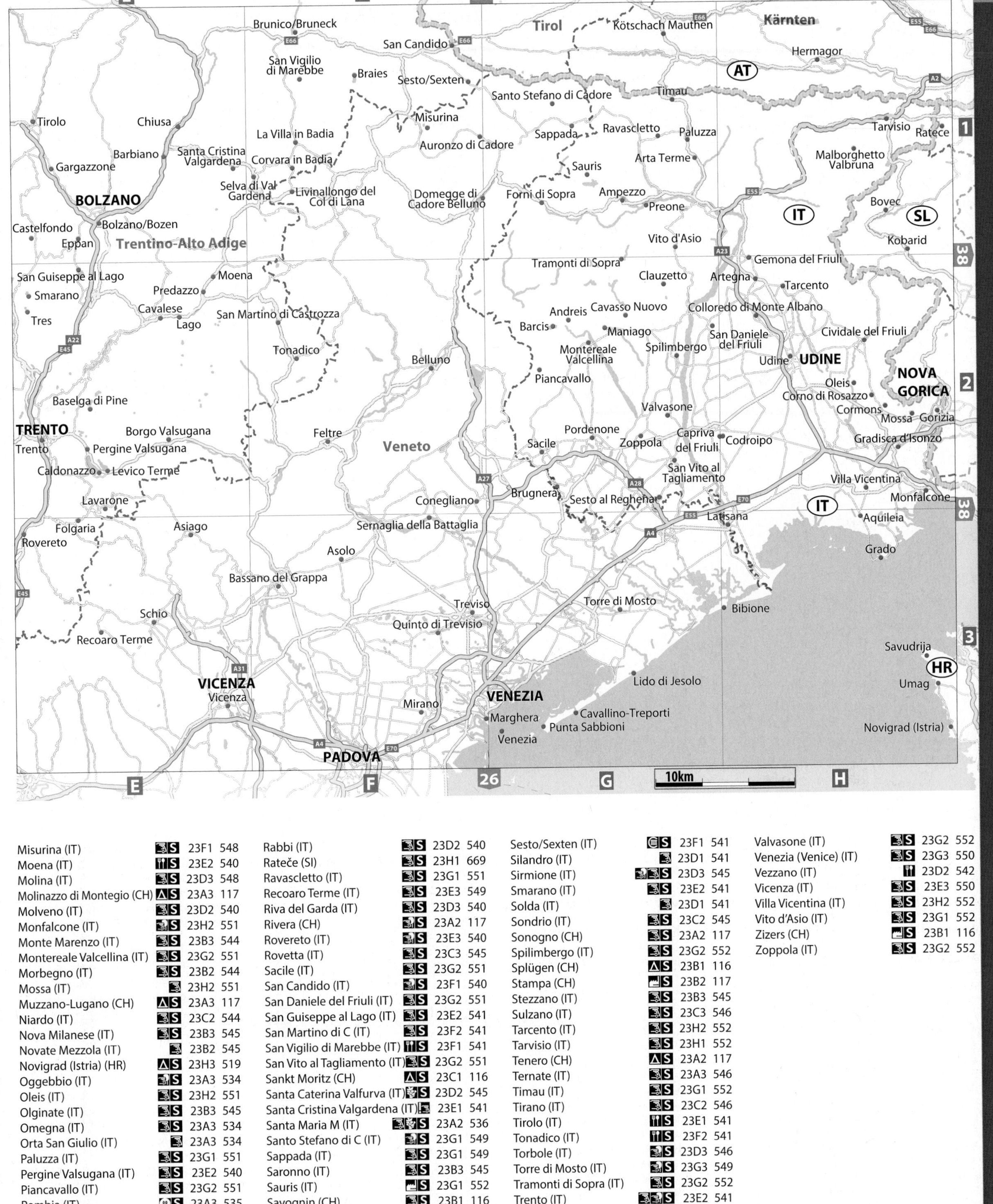

E
F
20
G
H
Brunico/Bruneck
San Candido
Tirol
Kötschach Mauthen
Kärnten
Hermagor
San Vigilio di Marebbe
Braies
Sesto/Sexten
AT
Santo Stefano di Cadore
Timau
Tirolo
Chiusa
Misurina
La Villa in Badia
Auronzo di Cadore
Sappada
Ravascletto
Paluzza
Tarvisio
Ratece
1
Barbiano
Santa Cristina Valgardena
Corvara in Badia
Gargazzone
Sauris
Arta Terme
Malborghetto Valbruna
BOLZANO
Selva di Val Gardena
Livinallongo del Col di Lana
Domegge di Cadore Belluno
Forni di Sopra
Ampezzo
Preone
Bovec
IT
SL
Castelfondo
Bolzano/Bozen
Eppan
Trentino-Alto Adige
Vito d'Asio
Kobarid
38
Tramonti di Sopra
Gemona del Friuli
San Guiseppe al Lago
Moena
Clauzetto
Artegna
Tarcento
Smarano
Predazzo
Cavalese
Andreis
Cavasso Nuovo
Colloredo di Monte Albano
Tres
Lago
San Martino di Castrozza
Barcis
Maniago
San Daniele del Friuli
Cividale del Friuli
Montereale Valcellina
Spilimbergo
Tonadico
Belluno
Udine
UDINE
NOVA GORICA
2
Piancavallo
Oleis
Corno di Rosazzo
Baselga di Pine
Valvasone
Cormons
Mossa
Gorizia
TRENTO
Trento
Borgo Valsugana
Pergine Valsugana
Feltre
Veneto
Pordenone
Sacile
Zoppola
Capriva del Friuli
Codroipo
Gradisca d'Isonzo
Caldonazzo
Levico Terme
San Vito al Tagliamento
Villa Vicentina
Lavarone
Conegliano
Brugnera
Sesto al Reghena
Monfalcone
Folgaria
Asiago
Sernaglia della Battaglia
Latisana
Aquileia
Rovereto
Asolo
Grado
Bassano del Grappa
Treviso
Torre di Mosto
Bibione
Schio
Quinto di Trevisio
Recoaro Terme
3
Savudrija
HR
Lido di Jesolo
Umag
VICENZA
Vicenza
VENEZIA
Mirano
Cavallino-Treporti
Marghera
Punta Sabbioni
Venezia
Novigrad (Istria)
PADOVA
26
10km

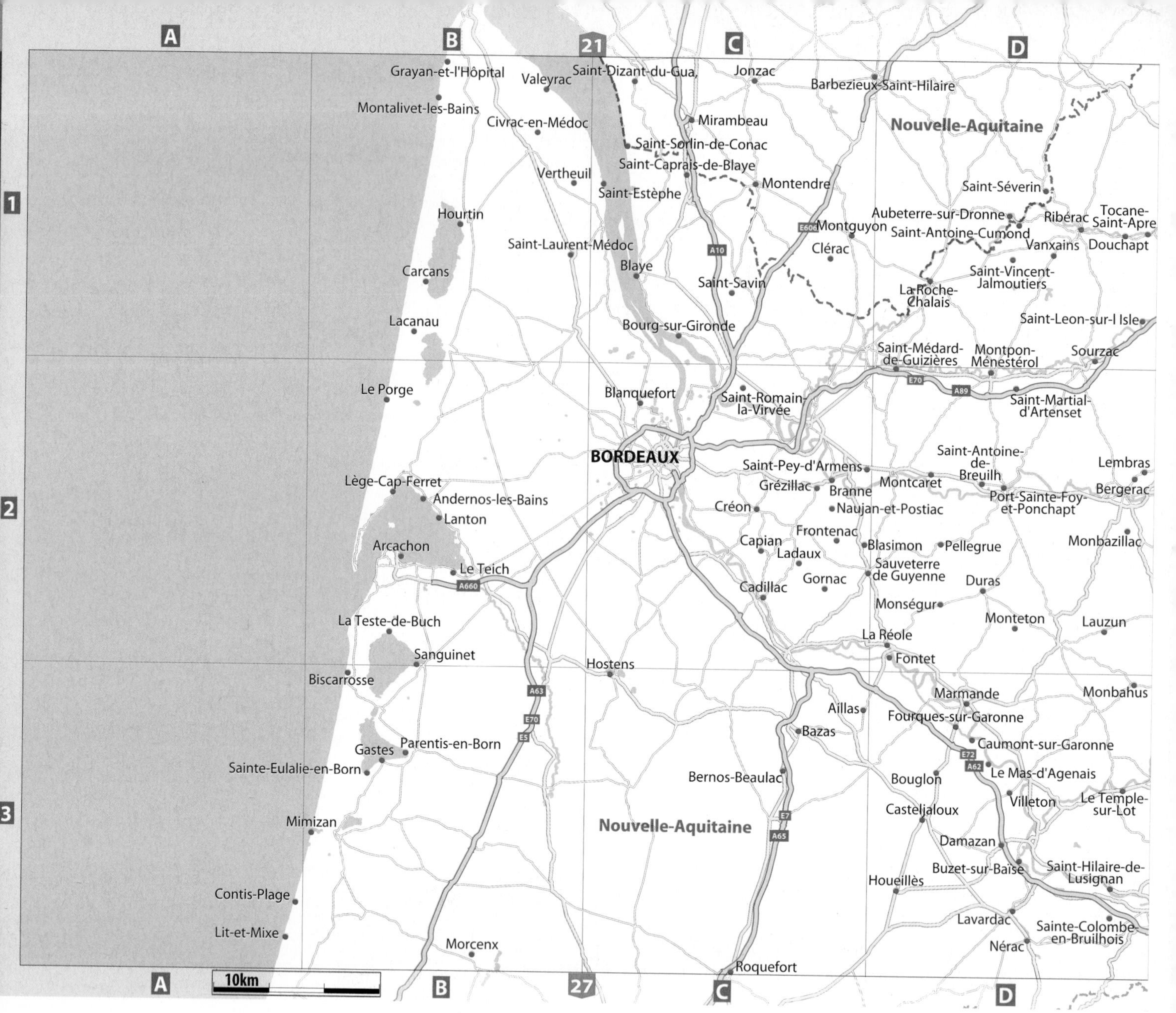

A B 21 C D

Grayan-et-l'Hôpital
Valeyrac
Saint-Dizant-du-Gua
Jonzac
Barbezieux-Saint-Hilaire
Montalivet-les-Bains
Civrac-en-Médoc
Mirambeau
Nouvelle-Aquitaine
Saint-Sorlin-de-Conac
Saint-Caprais-de-Blaye
Vertheuil
Montendre
Saint-Estèphe
Saint-Séverin
Hourtin
Montguyon
Aubeterre-sur-Dronne
Ribérac
Tocane-Saint-Apre
Saint-Antoine-Cumond
Saint-Laurent-Médoc
Clérac
Vanxains
Douchapt
Blaye
Saint-Vincent-Jalmoutiers
Carcans
Saint-Savin
La Roche-Chalais
Lacanau
Bourg-sur-Gironde
Saint-Leon-sur-l Isle
Saint-Médard-de-Guizières
Montpon-Ménestérol
Sourzac
Le Porge
Blanquefort
Saint-Romain-la-Virvée
Saint-Martial-d'Artenset
BORDEAUX
Saint-Pey-d'Armens
Saint-Antoine-de-Breuilh
Lembras
Lège-Cap-Ferret
Grézillac
Branne
Montcaret
Port-Sainte-Foy-et-Ponchapt
Bergerac
Andernos-les-Bains
Créon
Naujan-et-Postiac
Lanton
Frontenac
Arcachon
Capian
Ladaux
Blasimon
Pellegrue
Monbazillac
Le Teich
Gornac
Sauveterre de Guyenne
Duras
Cadillac
Monségur
La Teste-de-Buch
Monteton
Lauzun
La Réole
Sanguinet
Fontet
Hostens
Biscarrosse
Marmande
Monbahus
Aillas
Fourques-sur-Garonne
Bazas
Caumont-sur-Garonne
Gastes
Parentis-en-Born
Sainte-Eulalie-en-Born
Le Mas-d'Agenais
Bernos-Beaulac
Bouglon
Villeton
Le Temple-sur-Lot
Casteljaloux
Mimizan
Nouvelle-Aquitaine
Damazan
Buzet-sur-Baïse
Saint-Hilaire-de-Lusignan
Houeillès
Contis-Plage
Lavardac
Sainte-Colombe-en-Bruilhois
Lit-et-Mixe
Nérac
Morcenx
Roquefort

1 2 3

A 10km B 27 C D

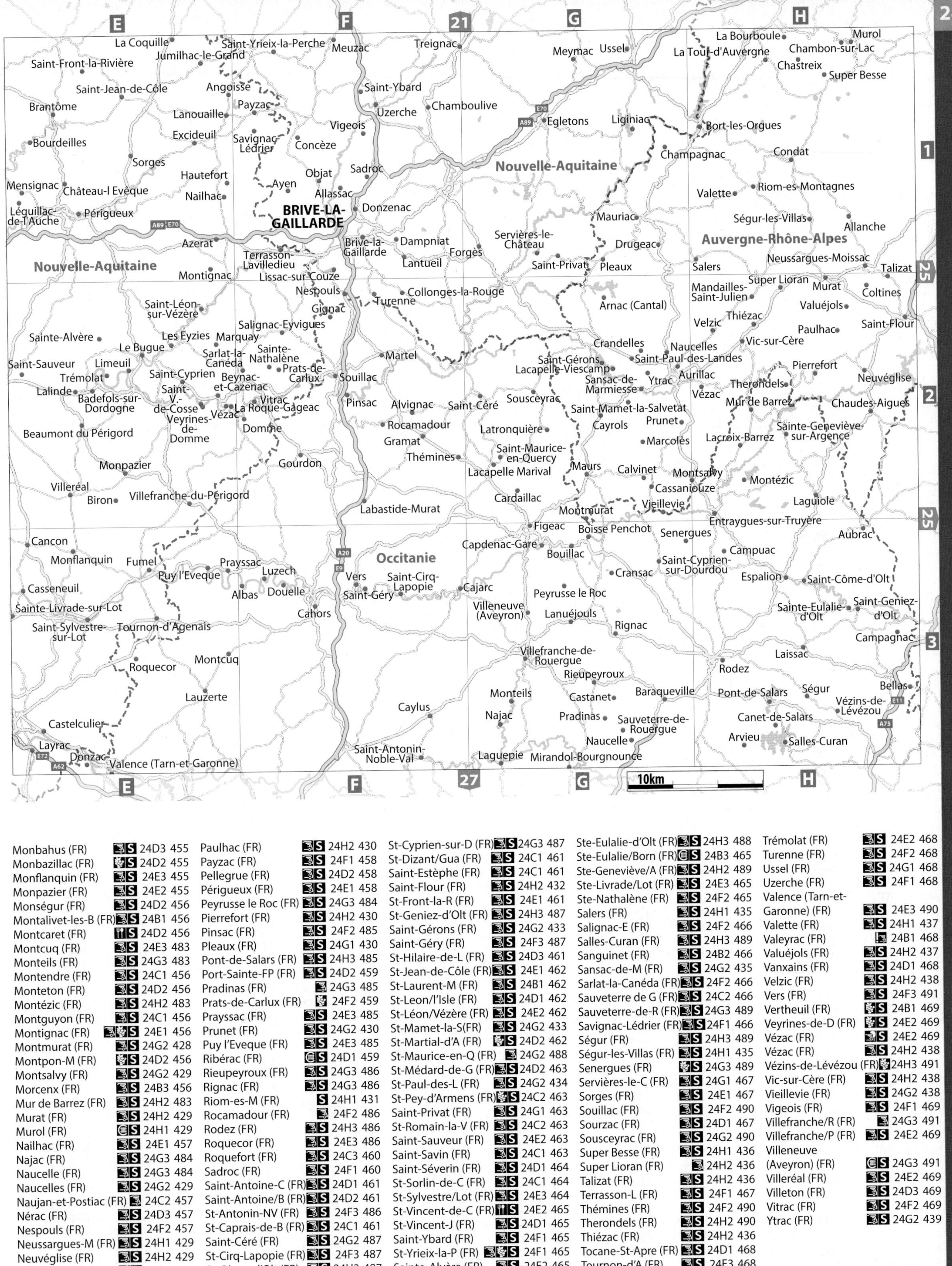

E
F
21
G
H
La Coquille
Saint-Yrieix-la-Perche
Meuzac
Treignac
Meymac
Ussel
La Bourboule
Murol
La Tour-d'Auvergne
Chambon-sur-Lac
Chastreix
Super Besse
Saint-Front-la-Rivière
Jumilhac-le-Grand
Saint-Jean-de-Côle
Angoisse
Saint-Ybard
Brantôme
Lanouaille
Payzac
Uzerche
Chamboulive
Egletons
Liginiac
Bort-les-Orgues
Excideuil
Vigeois
Bourdeilles
Savignac-Lédrier
Concèze
Champagnac
Condat
Sorges
Hautefort
Objat
Sadroc
Nouvelle-Aquitaine
Mensignac
Château-l Evêque
Ayen
Allassac
Valette
Riom-es-Montagnes
Nailhac
Léguillac-de-l'Auche
Périgueux
BRIVE-LA-GAILLARDE
Donzenac
Mauriac
Ségur-les-Villas
Allanche
Azerat
Brive-la-Gaillarde
Dampniat
Servières-le-Château
Drugeac
Auvergne-Rhône-Alpes
Terrasson-Lavilledieu
Forgès
Neussargues-Moissac
Nouvelle-Aquitaine
Lantueil
Saint-Privat
Pleaux
Salers
Talizat
Montignac
Lissac-sur-Couze
Super Lioran
Nespouls
Collonges-la-Rouge
Mandailles-Saint-Julien
Murat
Coltines
Saint-Léon-sur-Vézère
Turenne
Arnac (Cantal)
Valuéjols
Gignac
Thiézac
Velzic
Paulhac
Salignac-Eyvigues
Saint-Flour
Sainte-Alvère
Les Eyzies
Marquay
Crandelles
Naucelles
Vic-sur-Cère
Le Bugue
Sarlat-la-Canéda
Sainte-Nathalène
Martel
Saint-Gérons
Saint-Paul-des-Landes
Saint-Sauveur
Limeuil
Prats-de-Carlux
Lacapelle-Viescamp
Pierrefort
Trémolat
Saint-Cyprien
Beynac-et-Cazenac
Souillac
Sansac-de-Marmiesse
Ytrac
Aurillac
Neuvéglise
Lalinde
Badefols-sur-Dordogne
Saint-V.-de-Cosse
Vitrac
Thérondels
Vézac
Pinsac
Alvignac
Saint-Céré
Sousceyrac
Mur de Barrez
Chaudes-Aigues
Vézac
La Roque-Gageac
Saint-Mamet-la-Salvetat
Veyrines-de-Domme
Prunet
Domme
Rocamadour
Cayrols
Sainte-Geneviève-sur-Argence
Beaumont du Périgord
Latronquière
Gramat
Saint-Maurice-en-Quercy
Marcolès
Lacroix-Barrez
Thémines
Monpazier
Gourdon
Maurs
Lacapelle Marival
Calvinet
Montsalvy
Villeréal
Cassaniouze
Montézic
Biron
Villefranche-du-Périgord
Cardaillac
Vieillevie
Laguiole
Labastide-Murat
Montmurat
Figeac
Entraygues-sur-Truyère
Boisse Penchot
Senergues
Aubrac
Cancon
Capdenac-Gare
Bouillac
Campuac
Monflanquin
Fumel
Occitanie
Saint-Cyprien-sur-Dourdou
Prayssac
Luzech
Cransac
Espalion
Saint-Côme-d'Olt
Puy l'Eveque
Vers
Saint-Cirq-Lapopie
Cajarc
Casseneuil
Albas
Douelle
Saint-Géry
Peyrusse le Roc
Saint-Geniez-d'Olt
Sainte-Livrade-sur-Lot
Cahors
Villeneuve (Aveyron)
Lanuéjouls
Sainte-Eulalie-d'Olt
Saint-Sylvestre-sur-Lot
Tournon-d'Agenais
Rignac
Campagnac
Villefranche-de-Rouergue
Laissac
Roquecor
Montcuq
Rieupeyroux
Rodez
Monteils
Castanet
Baraqueville
Pont-de-Salars
Ségur
Bellas
Lauzerte
Vézins-de-Lévézou
Caylus
Najac
Pradinas
Sauveterre-de-Rouergue
Canet-de-Salars
Castelculier
Naucelle
Arvieu
Salles-Curan
Layrac
Saint-Antonin-Noble-Val
Donzac
Laguepie
Mirandol-Bourgnounce
Valence (Tarn-et-Garonne)
E
F
27
G
10km
H
1
2
3
25
25

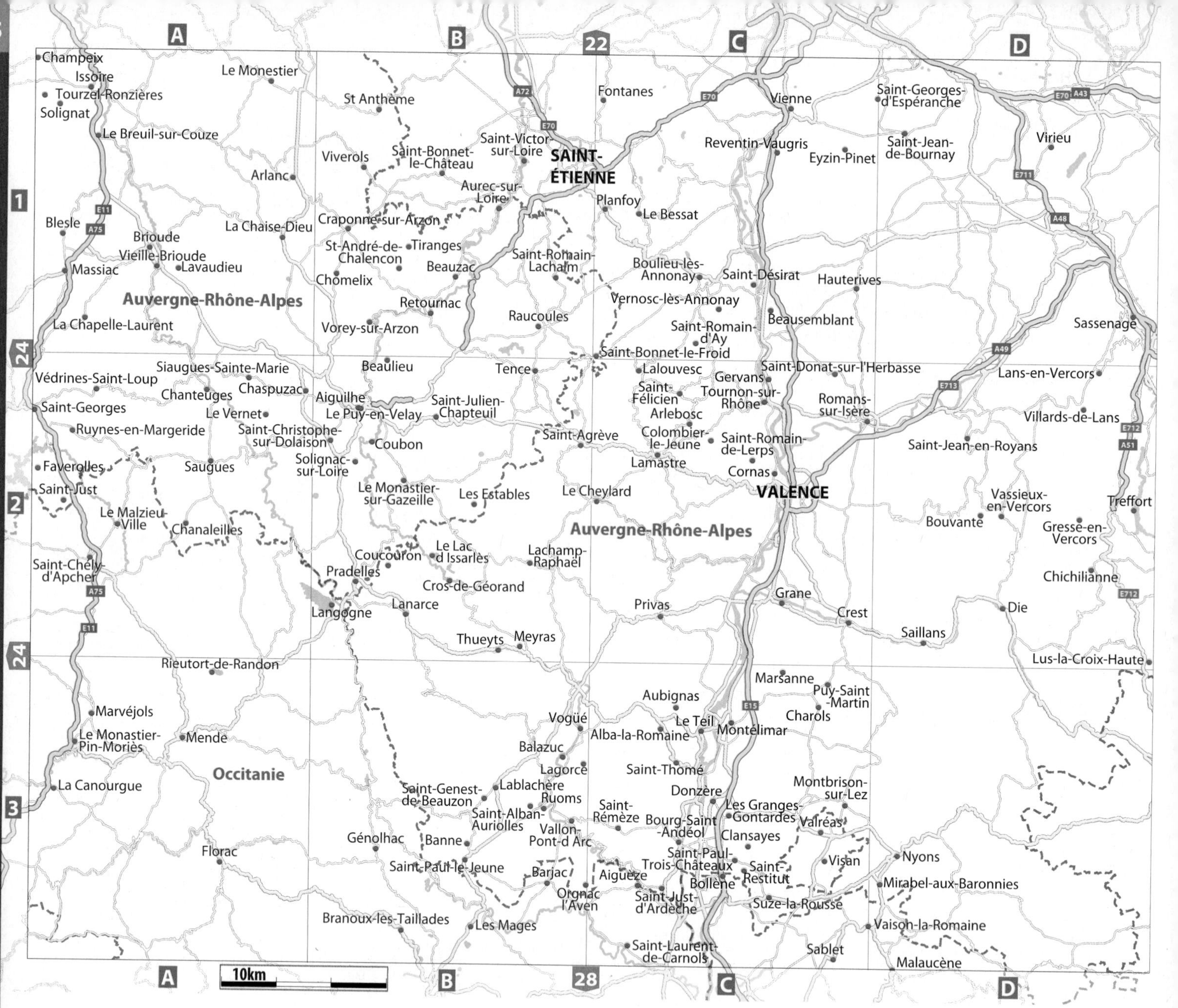

A B 22 C D

Champeix
Issoire
Tourzel-Ronzières
Solignat
Le Monestier
St Anthème
Fontanes
Vienne
Saint-Georges-d'Espéranche
Le Breuil-sur-Couze
Viverols
Saint-Bonnet-le-Château
Saint-Victor-sur-Loire
SAINT-ÉTIENNE
Reventin-Vaugris
Eyzin-Pinet
Saint-Jean-de-Bournay
Virieu
Arlanc
Aurec-sur-Loire
Planfoy
Le Bessat
Blesle
Brioude
La Chaise-Dieu
Craponne-sur-Arzon
St-André-de-Chalencon
Tiranges
Saint-Romain-Lachalm
Vieille-Brioude
Lavaudieu
Massiac
Beauzac
Boulieu-lès-Annonay
Saint-Désirat
Hauterives
Chomelix
Auvergne-Rhône-Alpes
Retournac
Vernosc-lès-Annonay
Raucoules
Beausemblant
La Chapelle-Laurent
Vorey-sur-Arzon
Saint-Romain-d'Ay
Sassenage
Saint-Bonnet-le-Froid
Védrines-Saint-Loup
Siaugues-Sainte-Marie
Beaulieu
Tence
Lalouvesc
Gervans
Saint-Donat-sur-l'Herbasse
Lans-en-Vercors
Chanteuges
Chaspuzac
Aiguilhe
Saint-Félicien
Tournon-sur-Rhône
Saint-Georges
Le Vernet
Le Puy-en-Velay
Saint-Julien-Chapteuil
Arlebosc
Romans-sur-Isère
Villards-de-Lans
Ruynes-en-Margeride
Saint-Christophe-sur-Dolaison
Saint-Agrève
Colombier-le-Jeune
Saint-Romain-de-Lerps
Coubon
Saint-Jean-en-Royans
Faverolles
Saugues
Solignac-sur-Loire
Lamastre
Cornas
Saint-Just
Le Monastier-sur-Gazeille
Les Estables
Le Cheylard
VALENCE
Vassieux-en-Vercors
Treffort
Le Malzieu-Ville
Chanaleilles
Bouvante
Gresse-en-Vercors
Auvergne-Rhône-Alpes
Le Lac d'Issarlès
Lachamp-Raphaël
Coucouron
Saint-Chely-d'Apcher
Pradelles
Chichilianne
Cros-de-Géorand
Grane
Langogne
Lanarce
Privas
Crest
Die
Thueyts
Meyras
Saillans
Rieutort-de-Randon
Lus-la-Croix-Haute
Marsanne
Aubignas
Puy-Saint-Martin
Marvéjols
Vogüé
Le Teil
Charols
Le Monastier-Pin-Moriès
Mende
Alba-la-Romaine
Montélimar
Balazuc
Occitanie
Lagorce
Saint-Thomé
La Canourgue
Saint-Genest-de-Beauzon
Lablachère
Donzère
Montbrison-sur-Lez
Ruoms
Saint-Remèze
Les Granges-Gontardes
Saint-Alban-Auriolles
Bourg-Saint-Andéol
Valréas
Génolhac
Banne
Vallon-Pont-d'Arc
Clansayes
Florac
Saint-Paul-Trois-Châteaux
Nyons
Visan
Saint-Paul-le-Jeune
Barjac
Aiguèze
Saint-Restitut
Bollène
Mirabel-aux-Baronnies
Orgnac-l'Aven
Saint-Just-d'Ardèche
Suze-la-Rousse
Branoux-les-Taillades
Les Mages
Vaison-la-Romaine
Saint-Laurent-de-Carnols
Sablet
Malaucène

A 10km B 28 C D

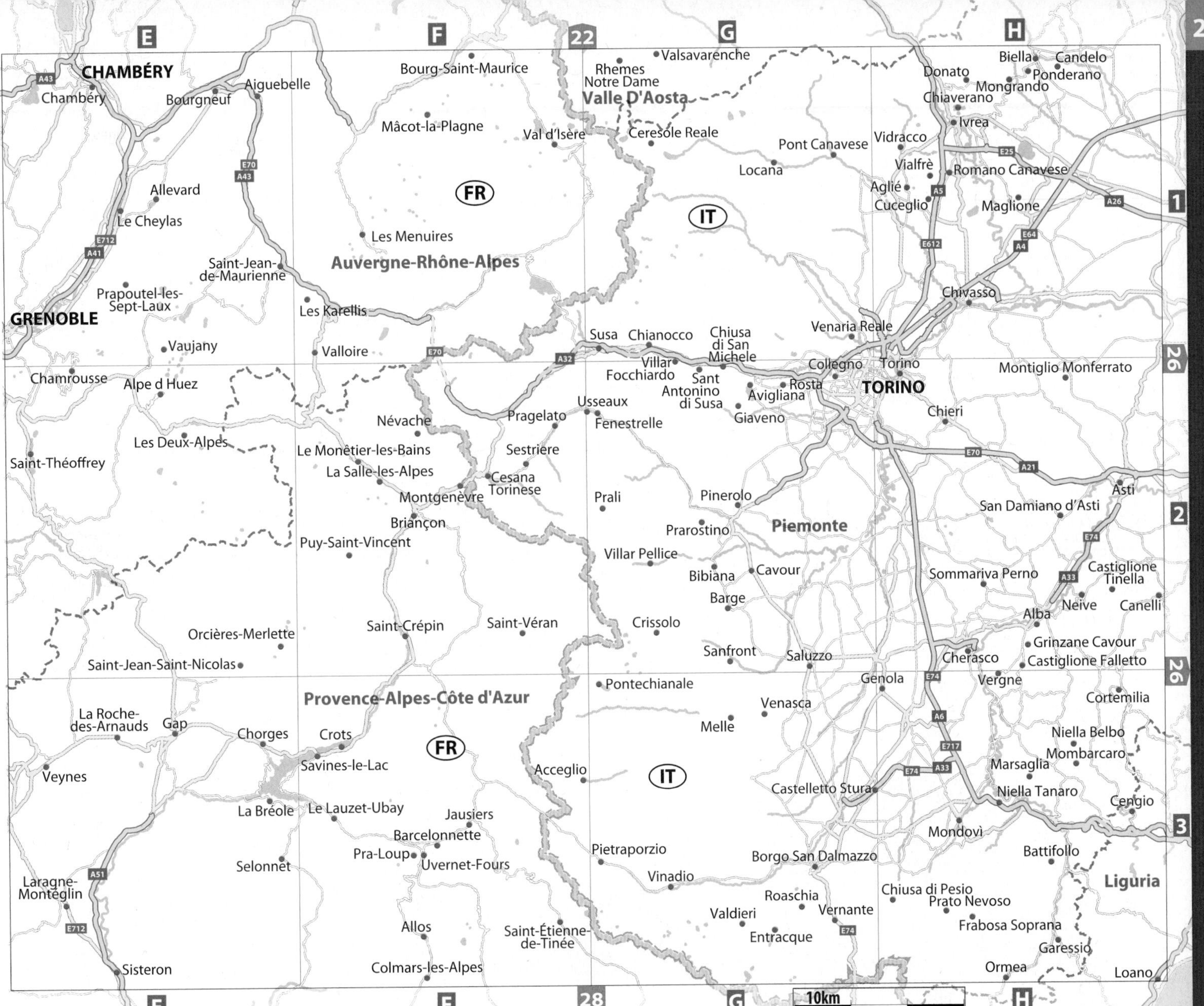
E
F
22
G
H
CHAMBÉRY
Chambéry
Bourgneuf
Aiguebelle
Bourg-Saint-Maurice
Rhemes Notre Dame
Valsavarenche
Valle D'Aosta
Donato
Biella
Candelo
Ponderano
Mongrando
Chiaverano
Ivrea
Mâcot-la-Plagne
Val d'Isère
Ceresole Reale
Pont Canavese
Vidracco
Locana
Vialfrè
Romano Canavese
Agliè
Cuceglio
Maglione
Allevard
FR
IT
Le Cheylas
Les Menuires
Saint-Jean-de-Maurienne
Auvergne-Rhône-Alpes
Prapoutel-les-Sept-Laux
Chivasso
GRENOBLE
Les Karellis
Vaujany
Valloire
Susa
Chianocco
Chiusa di San Michele
Venaria Reale
Villar Focchiardo
Sant Antonino di Susa
Collegno
Torino
TORINO
Rosta
Avigliana
Montiglio Monferrato
Chamrousse
Alpe d Huez
Usseaux
Pragelato
Fenestrelle
Giaveno
Chieri
Névache
Saint-Théoffrey
Les Deux-Alpes
Le Monêtier-les-Bains
La Salle-les-Alpes
Sestriere
Cesana Torinese
Montgenèvre
Prali
Pinerolo
Asti
San Damiano d'Asti
Briançon
Prarostino
Piemonte
Puy-Saint-Vincent
Villar Pellice
Bibiana
Cavour
Sommariva Perno
Castiglione Tinella
Barge
Alba
Neive
Canelli
Orcières-Merlette
Saint-Crépin
Saint-Véran
Crissolo
Grinzane Cavour
Sanfront
Saluzzo
Cherasco
Castiglione Falletto
Saint-Jean-Saint-Nicolas
Pontechianale
Genola
Vergne
Provence-Alpes-Côte d'Azur
Cortemilia
La Roche-des-Arnauds
Gap
Venasca
Chorges
Crots
Melle
Niella Belbo
Veynes
Savines-le-Lac
Mombarcaro
Marsaglia
Acceglio
Castelletto Stura
Niella Tanaro
Cengio
La Bréole
Le Lauzet-Ubay
Jausiers
Barcelonnette
Mondovì
Pra-Loup
Uvernet-Fours
Selonnet
Pietraporzio
Battifollo
Borgo San Dalmazzo
Vinadio
Liguria
Laragne-Montéglin
Roaschia
Chiusa di Pesio
Prato Nevoso
Vernante
Valdieri
Entracque
Frabosa Soprana
Allos
Saint-Étienne-de-Tinée
Garessio
Sisteron
Colmars-les-Alpes
Ormea
Loano
28
10km
1
2
3
26

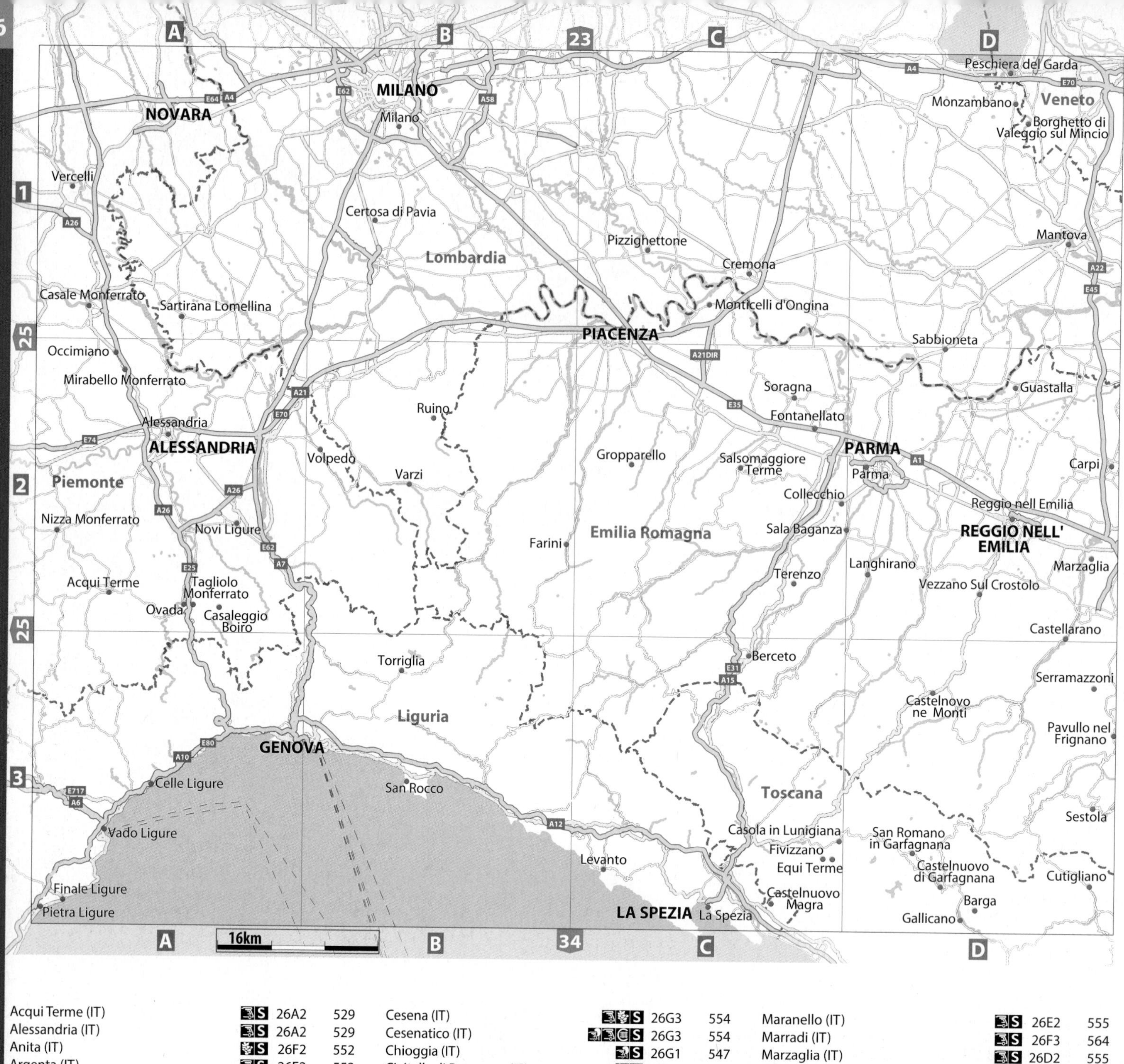

Place	Grid	Page
Acqui Terme (IT)	26A2	529
Alessandria (IT)	26A2	529
Anita (IT)	26F2	552
Argenta (IT)	26F2	552
Arquà Polesine (IT)	26F1	546
Barbarano Vicentino (IT)	26E1	546
Barberino di Mugello (IT)	26E3	560
Barga (IT)	26D3	560
Bellaria-Igea Marina (IT)	26G3	553
Berceto (IT)	26C3	553
Bertinoro (IT)	26G3	553
Bomporto (IT)	26E2	553
Borghetto di Valeggio sul Mincio (IT)	26D1	547
Borgofranco sul Po (IT)	26E1	542
Brisighella (IT)	26F3	553
Carpi (IT)	26D2	553
Casal Borsetti (IT)	26G2	553
Casale Monferrato (IT)	26A1	531
Casaleggio Boiro (IT)	26A2	531
Casola in Lunigiana (IT)	26C3	561
Casola Valsenio (IT)	26F3	553
Castel San Pietro Terme (IT)	26F3	553
Castelguglielmo (IT)	26E1	547
Castellarano (IT)	26D2	553
Castelnovo ne' Monti (IT)	26D3	554
Castelnuovo di Garfagnana (IT)	26D3	561
Castelnuovo Magra (IT)	26C3	558
Celle Ligure (IT)	26A3	558
Certosa di Pavia (IT)	26B1	542
Cervia (IT)	26G3	554
Cesena (IT)	26G3	554
Cesenatico (IT)	26G3	554
Chioggia (IT)	26G1	547
Civitella di Romagna (IT)	26F3	554
Collecchio (IT)	26C2	554
Comacchio (IT)	26F2	554
Conselice (IT)	26F2	554
Cremona (IT)	26C1	543
Cutigliano (IT)	26D3	562
Equi Terme (IT)	26C3	562
Faenza (IT)	26F3	554
Farini (IT)	26B2	555
Ferrara (IT)	26F2	555
Finale Ligure (IT)	26A3	559
Firenzuola (IT)	26E3	562
Fivizzano (IT)	26C3	563
Fontanellato (IT)	26C2	555
Forlimpopoli (IT)	26G3	555
Gallicano (IT)	26D3	563
Gradara (IT)	26H3	572
Gropparello (IT)	26C2	555
Guastalla (IT)	26D2	555
Imola (IT)	26F3	555
La Spezia (IT)	26C3	559
Lagosanto (IT)	26F2	555
Langhirano (IT)	26D2	555
Levanto (IT)	26C3	559
Lido di Dante (IT)	26G3	555
Magnacavallo (IT)	26E1	544
Mantova (IT)	26D1	544
Maranello (IT)	26E2	555
Marradi (IT)	26F3	564
Marzaglia (IT)	26D2	555
Mesola (IT)	26G2	555
Milano (Milan) (IT)	26B1	544
Mirabello Monferrato (IT)	26A2	533
Mirandola (IT)	26E2	556
Misano Adriatico (IT)	26G3	556
Modena (IT)	26E2	556
Moglia (IT)	26E2	544
Montagnana (IT)	26E1	548
Monticelli d'Ongina (IT)	26C1	556
Monzambano (IT)	26D1	544
Nizza Monferrato (IT)	26A2	534
Novi Ligure (IT)	26A2	534
Occimiano (IT)	26A2	534
Ovada (IT)	26A2	534
Padova (Padua) (IT)	26F1	548
Palazzuolo sul Senio (IT)	26F3	565
Parma (IT)	26D2	556
Pavullo nel Frignano (IT)	26D3	556
Pesaro (IT)	26H3	573
Peschiera del Garda (IT)	26D1	548
Pietra Ligure (IT)	26A3	559
Pizzighettone (IT)	26C1	545
Porto Corsini (IT)	26G2	556
Porto Tolle (IT)	26G2	549
Portomaggiore (IT)	26F2	556
Premilcuore (IT)	26F3	556
Ravenna (IT)	26G3	556

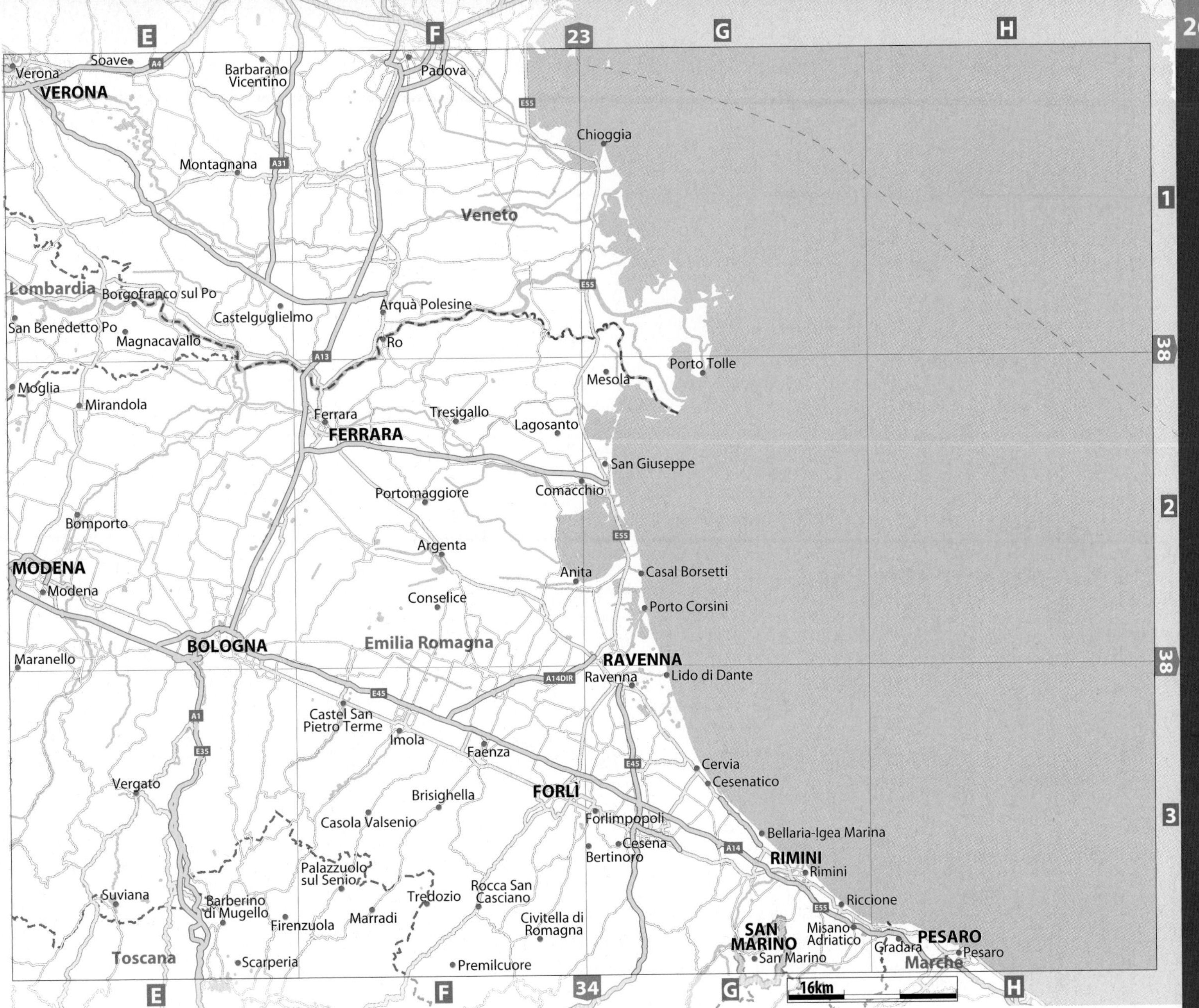
E
F
23
G
H
1
2
3
38
34
Verona
VERONA
Soave
Barbarano Vicentino
Padova
Chioggia
Montagnana
Veneto
Lombardia
Borgofranco sul Po
Castelguglielmo
Arquà Polesine
San Benedetto Po
Magnacavallo
Ro
Porto Tolle
Mesola
Moglia
Mirandola
Ferrara
FERRARA
Tresigallo
Lagosanto
San Giuseppe
Portomaggiore
Comacchio
Bomporto
Argenta
MODENA
Modena
Anita
Casal Borsetti
Conselice
Porto Corsini
Emilia Romagna
BOLOGNA
Maranello
RAVENNA
Ravenna
Lido di Dante
Castel San Pietro Terme
Imola
Faenza
Cervia
Cesenatico
Vergato
Brisighella
FORLÌ
Casola Valsenio
Forlimpopoli
Bellaria-Igea Marina
Cesena
Bertinoro
RIMINI
Rimini
Palazzuolo sul Senio
Rocca San Casciano
Suviana
Barberino di Mugello
Tredozio
Riccione
Firenzuola
Marradi
Civitella di Romagna
SAN MARINO
San Marino
Misano Adriatico
Gradara
PESARO
Pesaro
Marche
Toscana
Scarperia
Premilcuore
16km

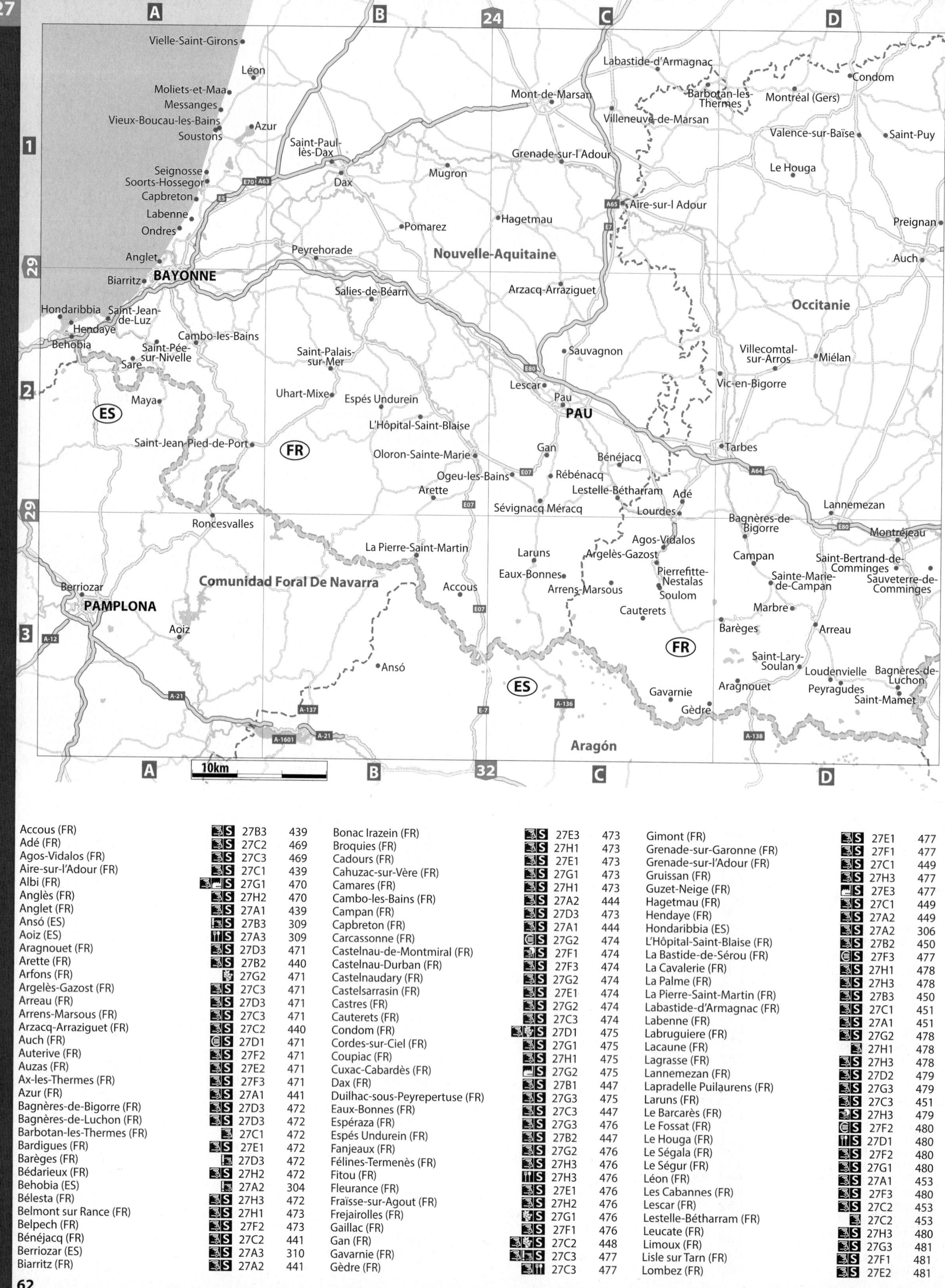

A
B
24
C
D
1
2
3
29
29
32
10km
Vielle-Saint-Girons
Léon
Moliets-et-Maa
Messanges
Vieux-Boucau-les-Bains
Azur
Soustons
Saint-Paul-lès-Dax
Seignosse
Soorts-Hossegor
Capbreton
Labenne
Ondres
Dax
Mugron
Pomarez
Anglet
Biarritz
BAYONNE
Peyrehorade
Hondaribbia
Saint-Jean-de-Luz
Hendaye
Behobia
Cambo-les-Bains
Saint-Pée-sur-Nivelle
Sare
Maya
ES
Saint-Jean-Pied-de-Port
Salies-de-Béarn
Saint-Palais-sur-Mer
Uhart-Mixe
Espés Undurein
L'Hôpital-Saint-Blaise
FR
Oloron-Sainte-Marie
Ogeu-les-Bains
Arette
Roncesvalles
La Pierre-Saint-Martin
Comunidad Foral De Navarra
Berriozar
PAMPLONA
Aoiz
Accous
Ansó
Mont-de-Marsan
Labastide-d'Armagnac
Barbotan-les-Thermes
Villeneuve-de-Marsan
Grenade-sur-l'Adour
Hagetmau
Aire-sur-l'Adour
Nouvelle-Aquitaine
Arzacq-Arraziguet
Sauvagnon
Lescar
Pau
PAU
Gan
Bénéjacq
Rébénacq
Lestelle-Bétharram
Adé
Sévignacq Méracq
Lourdes
Laruns
Eaux-Bonnes
Arrens-Marsous
Argelès-Gazost
Agos-Vidalos
Pierrefitte-Nestalas
Soulom
Cauterets
ES
Aragón
Gavarnie
Gèdre
Condom
Montréal (Gers)
Valence-sur-Baïse
Saint-Puy
Le Houga
Preignan
Auch
Occitanie
Villecomtal-sur-Arros
Miélan
Vic-en-Bigorre
Tarbes
Lannemezan
Bagnères-de-Bigorre
Montréjeau
Campan
Saint-Bertrand-de-Comminges
Sainte-Marie-de-Campan
Sauveterre-de-Comminges
Marbre
Barèges
Arreau
FR
Saint-Lary-Soulan
Loudenvielle
Bagnères-de-Luchon
Aragnouet
Peyragudes
Saint-Mamet
E70
A63
E5
A65
E7
E80
E07
A64
A-12
A-21
A-137
A-1601
E-7
A-136
A-138

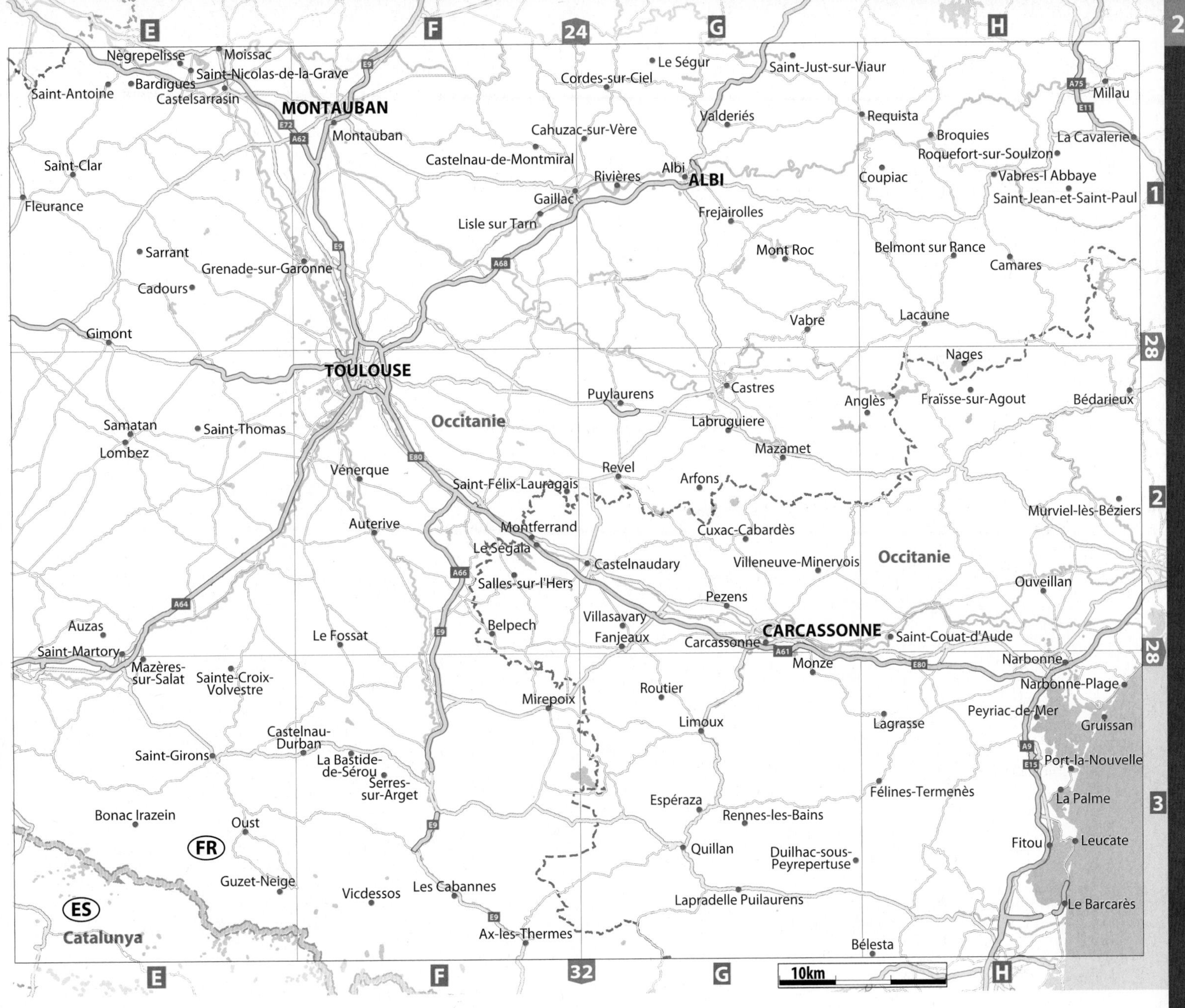
E
F
24
G
H
E
F
32
G
H
1
2
3
28
28
Nègrepelisse
Moissac
Saint-Nicolas-de-la-Grave
Saint-Antoine
Bardigues
Castelsarrasin
MONTAUBAN
Montauban
Saint-Clar
Fleurance
Sarrant
Grenade-sur-Garonne
Cadours
Gimont
TOULOUSE
Samatan
Lombez
Saint-Thomas
Vénerque
Auterive
Auzas
Saint-Martory
Mazères-sur-Salat
Sainte-Croix-Volvestre
Le Fossat
Castelnau-Durban
Saint-Girons
La Bastide-de-Sérou
Serres-sur-Arget
Bonac Irazein
Oust
FR
Guzet-Neige
ES
Catalunya
Vicdessos
Les Cabannes
Ax-les-Thermes
Le Ségur
Cordes-sur-Ciel
Cahuzac-sur-Vère
Castelnau-de-Montmiral
Rivières
Gaillac
Lisle sur Tarn
Albi
ALBI
Valderiés
Saint-Just-sur-Viaur
Requista
Broquies
Roquefort-sur-Soulzon
Coupiac
Vabres-l Abbaye
Saint-Jean-et-Saint-Paul
Millau
La Cavalerie
Frejairolles
Mont Roc
Belmont sur Rance
Camares
Vabre
Lacaune
Nages
Castres
Puylaurens
Anglès
Fraïsse-sur-Agout
Bédarieux
Occitanie
Labruguière
Mazamet
Revel
Arfons
Saint-Félix-Lauragais
Montferrand
Le Ségala
Cuxac-Cabardès
Murviel-lès-Béziers
Castelnaudary
Villeneuve-Minervois
Occitanie
Ouveillan
Salles-sur-l'Hers
Pezens
Belpech
Villasavary
Fanjeaux
Carcassonne
CARCASSONNE
Saint-Couat-d'Aude
Monze
Narbonne
Narbonne-Plage
Routier
Mirepoix
Limoux
Lagrasse
Peyriac-de-Mer
Gruissan
Port-la-Nouvelle
Espéraza
Rennes-les-Bains
Félines-Termenès
La Palme
Quillan
Duilhac-sous-Peyrepertuse
Fitou
Leucate
Lapradelle Puilaurens
Le Barcarès
Bélesta
10km
A75
E11
E9
E72
A62
A68
E80
A66
A64
A61
A9
E15

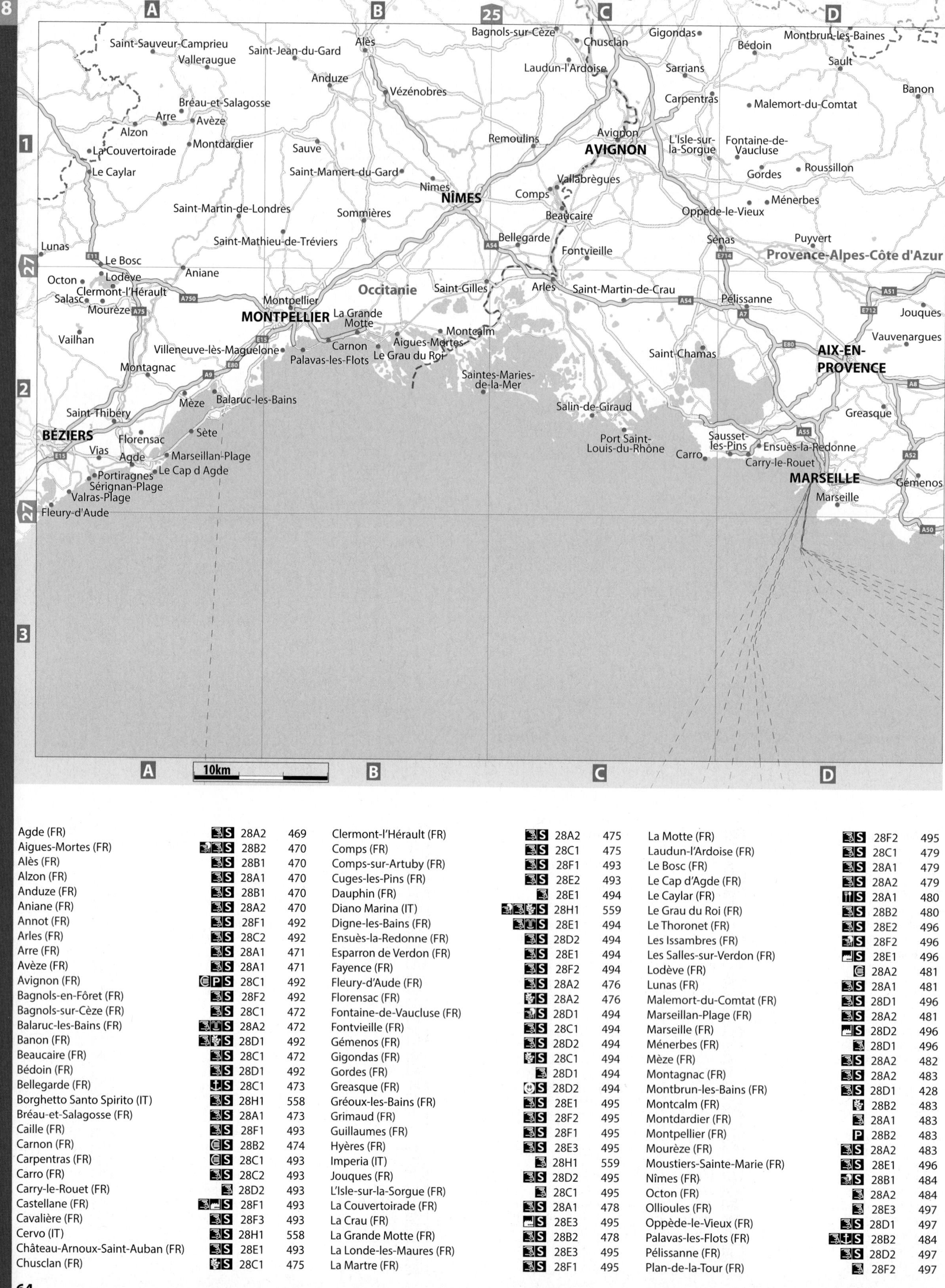
A
B
25
C
D
1
2
3
27
Saint-Sauveur-Camprieu
Valleraugue
Saint-Jean-du-Gard
Alès
Anduze
Vézénobres
Bagnols-sur-Cèze
Chusclan
Laudun-l'Ardoise
Gigondas
Sarrians
Carpentras
Bédoin
Montbrun-les-Baines
Sault
Banon
Malemort-du-Comtat
Bréau-et-Salagosse
Arre
Avèze
Alzon
La Couvertoirade
Montdardier
Le Caylar
Sauve
Remoulins
Avignon
AVIGNON
L'Isle-sur-la-Sorgue
Fontaine-de-Vaucluse
Gordes
Roussillon
Saint-Mamert-du-Gard
Nîmes
NÎMES
Comps
Vallabrègues
Beaucaire
Ménerbes
Oppède-le-Vieux
Saint-Martin-de-Londres
Sommières
Saint-Mathieu-de-Tréviers
Bellegarde
Fontvieille
Sénas
Puyvert
Provence-Alpes-Côte d'Azur
Lunas
Le Bosc
Lodève
Aniane
Octon
Clermont-l'Hérault
Salasc
Mourèze
Occitanie
Saint-Gilles
Arles
Saint-Martin-de-Crau
Pélissanne
Jouques
Vauvenargues
Montpellier
MONTPELLIER
La Grande Motte
Montcalm
Aigues-Mortes
Vailhan
Villeneuve-lès-Maguelone
Carnon
Palavas-les-Flots
Le Grau du Roi
Saint-Chamas
AIX-EN-PROVENCE
Montagnac
Saintes-Maries-de-la-Mer
Mèze
Balaruc-les-Bains
Salin-de-Giraud
Greasque
Saint-Thibéry
BÉZIERS
Florensac
Sète
Port Saint-Louis-du-Rhône
Sausset-les-Pins
Ensuès-la-Redonne
Vias
Agde
Marseillan-Plage
Carro
Carry-le-Rouet
Portiragnes
Le Cap d Agde
Sérignan-Plage
Valras-Plage
MARSEILLE
Marseille
Gémenos
Fleury-d'Aude
10km

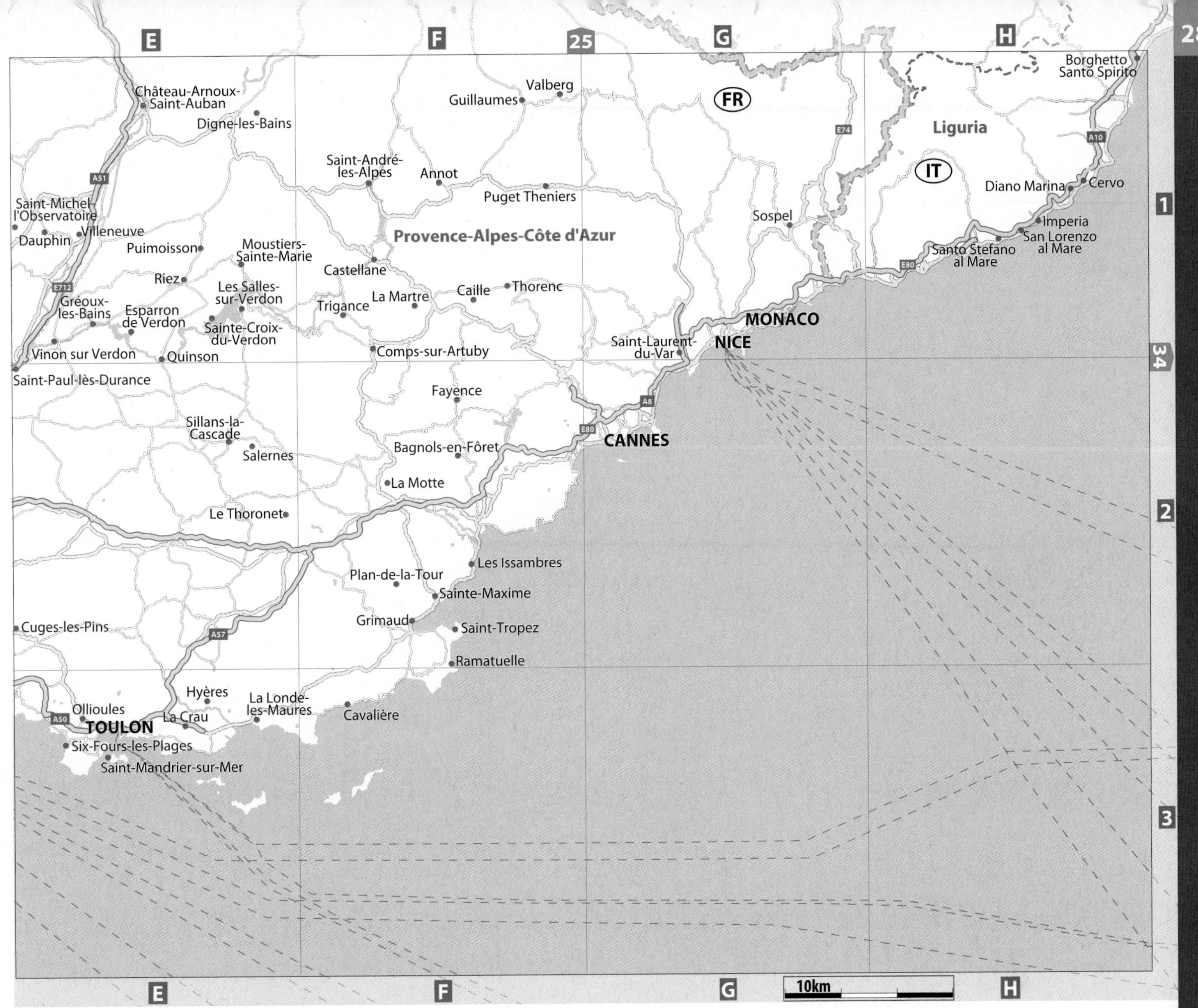

E
F
25
G
H
Château-Arnoux-Saint-Auban
Digne-les-Bains
Guillaumes
Valberg
FR
Liguria
Borghetto Santo Spirito
Saint-André-les-Alpes
Annot
Puget Theniers
IT
Diano Marina
Cervo
1
Saint-Michel-l'Observatoire
Dauphin
Villeneuve
Puimoisson
Moustiers-Sainte-Marie
Provence-Alpes-Côte d'Azur
Sospel
Imperia
San Lorenzo al Mare
Santo Stefano al Mare
Riez
Castellane
Les Salles-sur-Verdon
La Martre
Caille
Thorenc
Gréoux-les-Bains
Esparron de Verdon
Trigance
Sainte-Croix-du-Verdon
MONACO
Saint-Laurent-du-Var
NICE
Vinon sur Verdon
Quinson
Comps-sur-Artuby
34
Saint-Paul-lès-Durance
Fayence
Sillans-la-Cascade
CANNES
Salernes
Bagnols-en-Fôret
La Motte
2
Le Thoronet
Les Issambres
Plan-de-la-Tour
Sainte-Maxime
Cuges-les-Pins
Grimaud
Saint-Tropez
Ramatuelle
Hyères
La Londe-les-Maures
Cavalière
Ollioules
La Crau
TOULON
Six-Fours-les-Plages
Saint-Mandrier-sur-Mer
3
10km
A51
E712
A57
A50
A8
E80
E74
A10

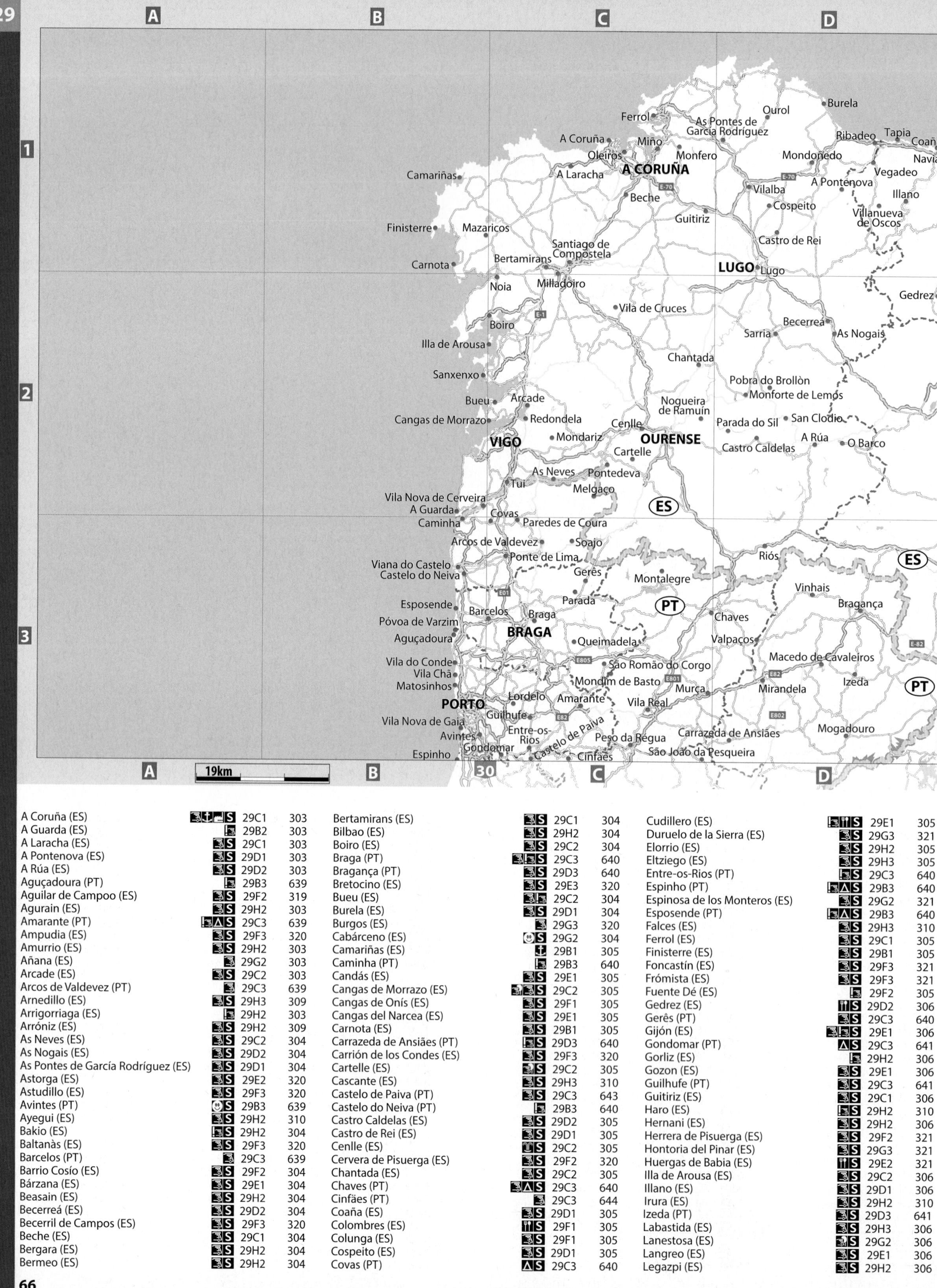

A Coruña (ES)	29C1	303
A Guarda (ES)	29B2	303
A Laracha (ES)	29C1	303
A Pontenova (ES)	29D1	303
A Rúa (ES)	29D2	303
Aguçadoura (PT)	29B3	639
Aguilar de Campoo (ES)	29F2	319
Agurain (ES)	29H2	303
Amarante (PT)	29C3	639
Ampudia (ES)	29F3	320
Amurrio (ES)	29H2	303
Añana (ES)	29G2	303
Arcade (ES)	29C2	303
Arcos de Valdevez (PT)	29C3	639
Arnedillo (ES)	29H3	309
Arrigorriaga (ES)	29H2	303
Arróniz (ES)	29H2	309
As Neves (ES)	29C2	304
As Nogais (ES)	29D2	304
As Pontes de García Rodríguez (ES)	29D1	304
Astorga (ES)	29E2	320
Astudillo (ES)	29F3	320
Avintes (PT)	29B3	639
Ayegui (ES)	29H2	310
Bakio (ES)	29H2	304
Baltanàs (ES)	29F3	320
Barcelos (PT)	29C3	639
Barrio Cosío (ES)	29F2	304
Bárzana (ES)	29E1	304
Beasain (ES)	29H2	304
Becerreá (ES)	29D2	304
Becerril de Campos (ES)	29F3	320
Beche (ES)	29C1	304
Bergara (ES)	29H2	304
Bermeo (ES)	29H2	304
Bertamirans (ES)	29C1	304
Bilbao (ES)	29H2	304
Boiro (ES)	29C2	304
Braga (PT)	29C3	640
Bragança (PT)	29D3	640
Bretocino (ES)	29E3	320
Bueu (ES)	29C2	304
Burela (ES)	29D1	304
Burgos (ES)	29G3	320
Cabárceno (ES)	29G2	304
Camariñas (ES)	29B1	305
Caminha (PT)	29B3	640
Candás (ES)	29E1	305
Cangas de Morrazo (ES)	29C2	305
Cangas de Onís (ES)	29F1	305
Cangas del Narcea (ES)	29E1	305
Carnota (ES)	29B1	305
Carrazeda de Ansiães (PT)	29D3	640
Carrión de los Condes (ES)	29F3	320
Cartelle (ES)	29C2	305
Cascante (ES)	29H3	310
Castelo de Paiva (PT)	29C3	643
Castelo do Neiva (PT)	29B3	640
Castro Caldelas (ES)	29D2	305
Castro de Rei (ES)	29D1	305
Cenlle (ES)	29C2	305
Cervera de Pisuerga (ES)	29F2	320
Chantada (ES)	29C2	305
Chaves (PT)	29C3	640
Cinfães (PT)	29C3	644
Coaña (ES)	29D1	305
Colombres (ES)	29F1	305
Colunga (ES)	29F1	305
Cospeito (ES)	29D1	305
Covas (PT)	29C3	640
Cudillero (ES)	29E1	305
Duruelo de la Sierra (ES)	29G3	321
Elorrio (ES)	29H2	305
Eltziego (ES)	29H3	305
Entre-os-Rios (PT)	29C3	640
Espinho (PT)	29B3	640
Espinosa de los Monteros (ES)	29G2	321
Esposende (PT)	29B3	640
Falces (ES)	29H3	310
Ferrol (ES)	29C1	305
Finisterre (ES)	29B1	305
Foncastín (ES)	29F3	321
Frómista (ES)	29F3	321
Fuente Dé (ES)	29F2	305
Gedrez (ES)	29D2	306
Gerês (PT)	29C3	640
Gijón (ES)	29E1	306
Gondomar (PT)	29C3	641
Gorliz (ES)	29H2	306
Gozon (ES)	29E1	306
Guilhufe (PT)	29C3	641
Guitiriz (ES)	29C1	306
Haro (ES)	29H2	310
Hernani (ES)	29H2	306
Herrera de Pisuerga (ES)	29F2	321
Hontoria del Pinar (ES)	29G3	321
Huergas de Babia (ES)	29E2	321
Illa de Arousa (ES)	29C2	306
Illano (ES)	29D1	306
Irura (ES)	29H2	310
Izeda (PT)	29D3	641
Labastida (ES)	29H3	306
Lanestosa (ES)	29G2	306
Langreo (ES)	29E1	306
Legazpi (ES)	29H2	306

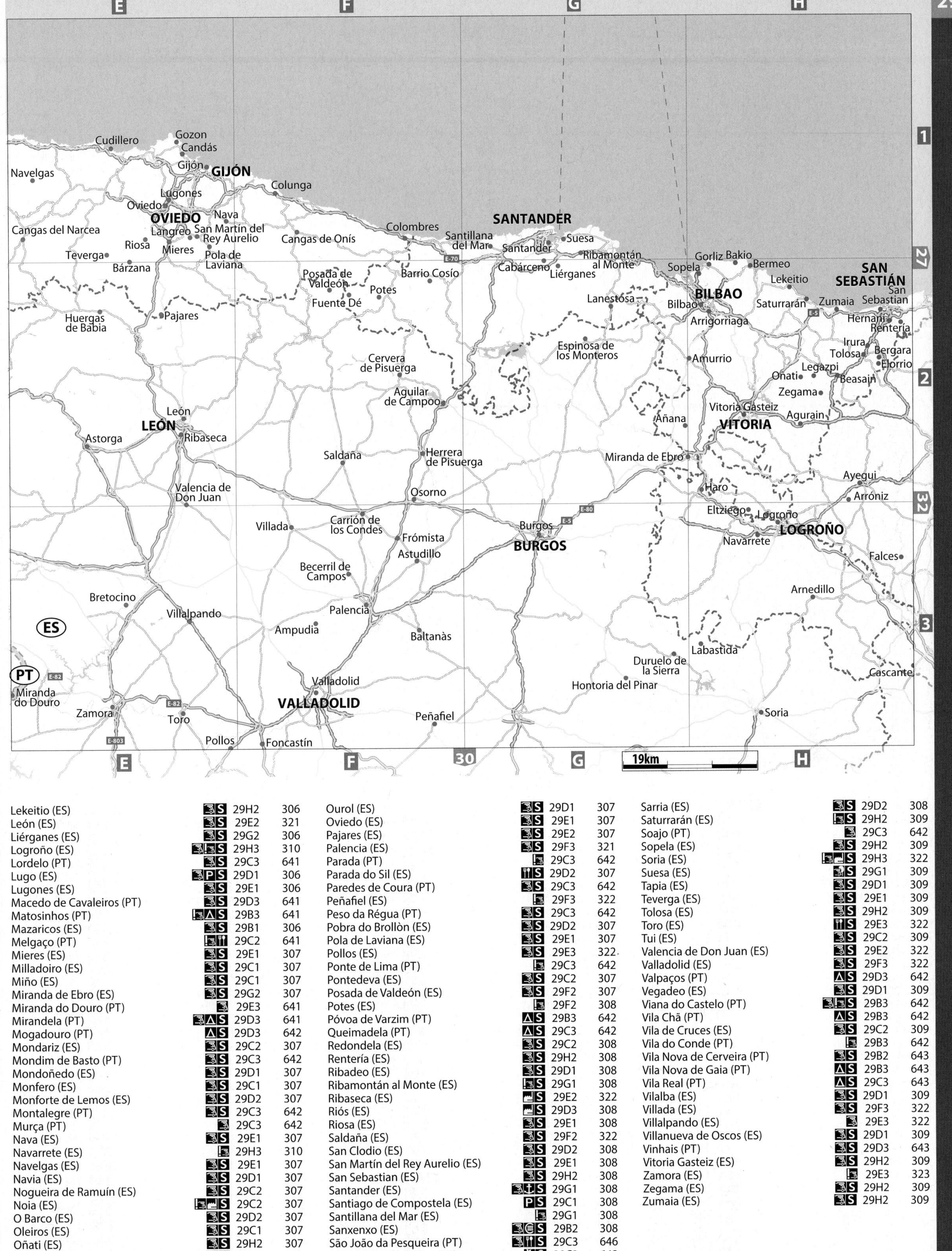
E
F
G
H
1
2
3
27
32
30
Cudillero
Gozon
Candás
Navelgas
Gijón
GIJÓN
Colunga
Lugones
Oviedo
OVIEDO
Nava
Cangas del Narcea
Langreo
San Martín del Rey Aurelio
Riosa
Mieres
Pola de Laviana
Teverga
Bárzana
Cangas de Onís
Colombres
Santillana del Mar
SANTANDER
Santander
Suesa
Ribamontán al Monte
Cabárceno
Liérganes
Posada de Valdeón
Barrio Cosío
Potes
Fuente Dé
Huergas de Babia
Pajares
Cervera de Pisuerga
Aguilar de Campoo
Espinosa de los Monteros
Lanestosa
Gorliz
Bakio
Bermeo
Sopela
BILBAO
Bilbao
Arrigorriaga
Lekeitio
Saturrarán
Zumaia
SAN SEBASTIÁN
San Sebastian
Hernani
Rentería
Irura
Tolosa
Bergara
Elorrio
Legazpi
Oñati
Beasain
Zegama
Amurrio
Vitoria Gasteiz
VITORIA
Agurain
Añana
León
LEÓN
Ribaseca
Astorga
Saldaña
Herrera de Pisuerga
Miranda de Ebro
Haro
Ayegui
Arróniz
Valencia de Don Juan
Osorno
Elztiego
Logroño
LOGROÑO
Navarrete
Villada
Carrión de los Condes
Frómista
Astudillo
Burgos
BURGOS
Falces
Becerril de Campos
Arnedillo
Bretocino
Villalpando
Palencia
Ampudia
Baltanàs
ES
PT
Labastida
Duruelo de la Sierra
Hontoria del Pinar
Cascante
Miranda do Douro
Zamora
Toro
Valladolid
VALLADOLID
Peñafiel
Soria
Pollos
Foncastín
E-70
E-80
E-5
E-82
E-803
19km

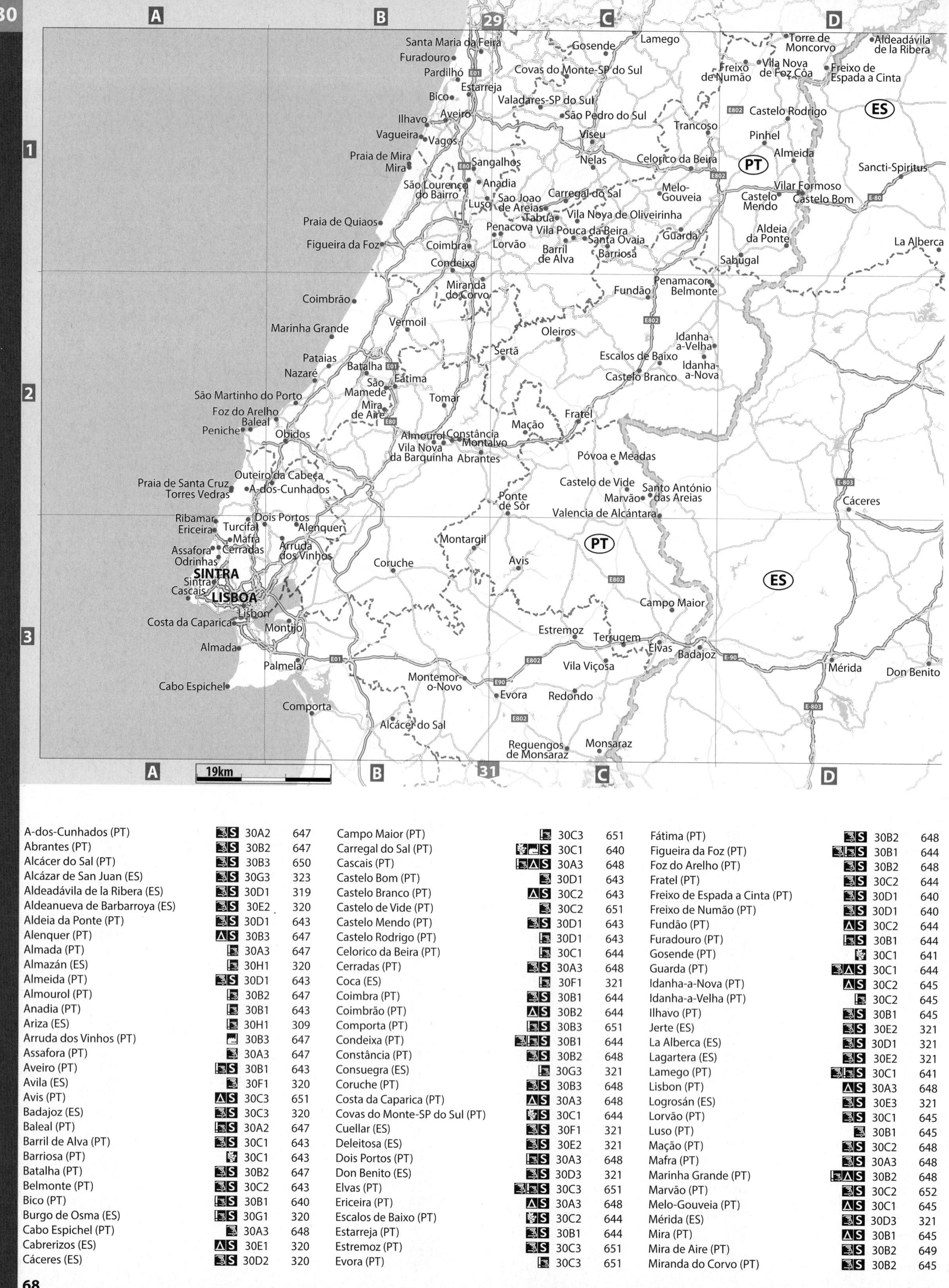

A-dos-Cunhados (PT)	30A2	647
Abrantes (PT)	30B2	647
Alcácer do Sal (PT)	30B3	650
Alcázar de San Juan (ES)	30G3	323
Aldeadávila de la Ribera (ES)	30D1	319
Aldeanueva de Barbarroya (ES)	30E2	320
Aldeia da Ponte (PT)	30D1	643
Alenquer (PT)	30B3	647
Almada (PT)	30A3	647
Almazán (ES)	30H1	320
Almeida (PT)	30D1	643
Almourol (PT)	30B2	647
Anadia (PT)	30B1	643
Ariza (ES)	30H1	309
Arruda dos Vinhos (PT)	30B3	647
Assafora (PT)	30A3	647
Aveiro (PT)	30B1	643
Avila (ES)	30F1	320
Avis (PT)	30C3	651
Badajoz (ES)	30C3	320
Baleal (PT)	30A2	647
Barril de Alva (PT)	30C1	643
Barriosa (PT)	30C1	643
Batalha (PT)	30B2	647
Belmonte (PT)	30C2	643
Bico (PT)	30B1	640
Burgo de Osma (ES)	30G1	320
Cabo Espichel (PT)	30A3	648
Cabrerizos (ES)	30E1	320
Cáceres (ES)	30D2	320
Campo Maior (PT)	30C3	651
Carregal do Sal (PT)	30C1	640
Cascais (PT)	30A3	648
Castelo Bom (PT)	30D1	643
Castelo Branco (PT)	30C2	643
Castelo de Vide (PT)	30C2	651
Castelo Mendo (PT)	30D1	643
Castelo Rodrigo (PT)	30D1	643
Celorico da Beira (PT)	30C1	644
Cerradas (PT)	30A3	648
Coca (ES)	30F1	321
Coimbra (PT)	30B1	644
Coimbrão (PT)	30B2	644
Comporta (PT)	30B3	651
Condeixa (PT)	30B1	644
Constância (PT)	30B2	648
Consuegra (ES)	30G3	321
Coruche (PT)	30B3	648
Costa da Caparica (PT)	30A3	648
Covas do Monte-SP do Sul (PT)	30C1	644
Cuellar (ES)	30F1	321
Deleitosa (ES)	30E2	321
Dois Portos (PT)	30A3	648
Don Benito (ES)	30D3	321
Elvas (PT)	30C3	651
Ericeira (PT)	30A3	648
Escalos de Baixo (PT)	30C2	644
Estarreja (PT)	30B1	644
Estremoz (PT)	30C3	651
Evora (PT)	30C3	651
Fátima (PT)	30B2	648
Figueira da Foz (PT)	30B1	644
Foz do Arelho (PT)	30B2	648
Fratel (PT)	30C2	644
Freixo de Espada a Cinta (PT)	30D1	640
Freixo de Numão (PT)	30D1	640
Fundão (PT)	30C2	644
Furadouro (PT)	30B1	644
Gosende (PT)	30C1	641
Guarda (PT)	30C1	644
Idanha-a-Nova (PT)	30C2	645
Idanha-a-Velha (PT)	30C2	645
Ilhavo (PT)	30B1	645
Jerte (ES)	30E2	321
La Alberca (ES)	30D1	321
Lagartera (ES)	30E2	321
Lamego (PT)	30C1	641
Lisbon (PT)	30A3	648
Logrosán (ES)	30E3	321
Lorvão (PT)	30C1	645
Luso (PT)	30B1	645
Mação (PT)	30C2	648
Mafra (PT)	30A3	648
Marinha Grande (PT)	30B2	648
Marvão (PT)	30C2	652
Melo-Gouveia (PT)	30C1	645
Mérida (ES)	30D3	321
Mira (PT)	30B1	645
Mira de Aire (PT)	30B2	649
Miranda do Corvo (PT)	30B2	645

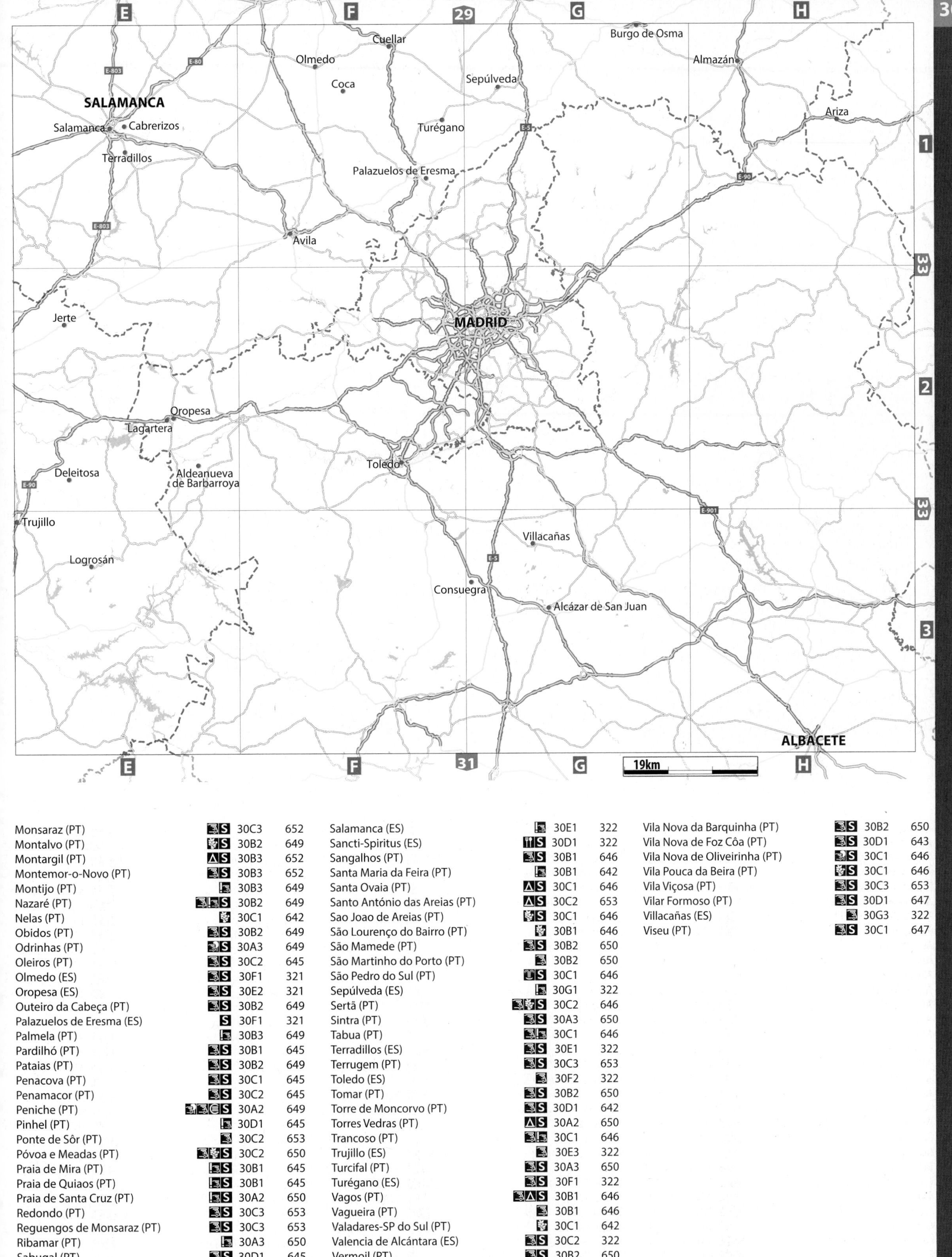

E
F
29
G
H
Burgo de Osma
Cuellar
Olmedo
Almazán
E-803
E-80
Coca
Sepúlveda
SALAMANCA
Salamanca
Cabrerizos
Turégano
Ariza
Terradillos
Palazuelos de Eresma
E-5
E-90
1
Avila
33
Jerte
MADRID
2
Oropesa
Lagartera
Toledo
Deleitosa
Aldeanueva de Barbarroya
E-90
Trujillo
E-901
Villacañas
Logrosán
E-5
Consuegra
Alcázar de San Juan
3
ALBACETE
E
F
31
G
19km
H

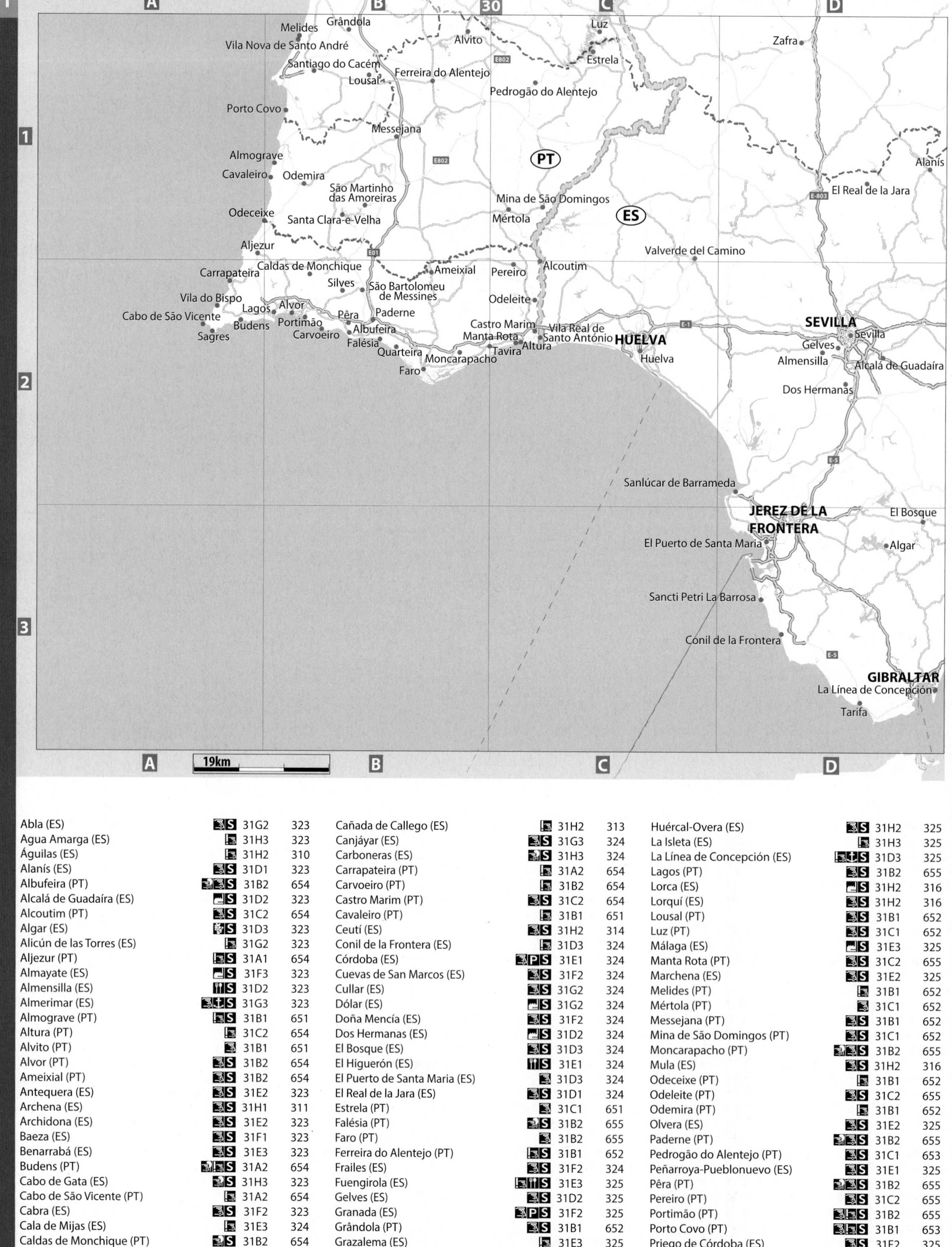

A
B
30
C
D
1
2
3
Melides
Grândola
Vila Nova de Santo André
Alvito
Luz
Estrela
Zafra
Santiago do Cacém
Lousal
Ferreira do Alentejo
Pedrogão do Alentejo
Porto Covo
Messejana
Almograve
Cavaleiro
Odemira
PT
Alanís
São Martinho das Amoreiras
El Real de la Jara
Mina de São Domingos
Odeceixe
Santa Clara-e-Velha
Mértola
ES
Aljezur
Valverde del Camino
Carrapateira
Caldas de Monchique
Ameixial
Pereiro
Alcoutim
Silves
São Bartolomeu de Messines
Vila do Bispo
Odeleite
Lagos
Alvor
Paderne
Cabo de São Vicente
Portimão
Pêra
Castro Marim
Vila Real de Santo António
HUELVA
SEVILLA
Sevilla
Budens
Albufeira
Manta Rota
Sagres
Carvoeiro
Falésia
Tavira
Altura
Gelves
Quarteira
Moncarapacho
Huelva
Almensilla
Alcalá de Guadaíra
Faro
Dos Hermanas
Sanlúcar de Barrameda
JEREZ DE LA FRONTERA
El Bosque
El Puerto de Santa Maria
Algar
Sancti Petri La Barrosa
Conil de la Frontera
GIBRALTAR
La Línea de Concepción
Tarifa
19km

E
F
30
G
H
1
2
3
33
Peñarroya-Pueblonuevo
Córdoba
El Higuerón
CÓRDOBA
Baeza
Úbeda
JAÉN
E-902
Doña Mencía
Cabra
Frailes
Priego de Córdoba
Marchena
Rute
Villanueva de Algaidas
Cuevas de San Marcos
Archidona
GRANADA
Granada
Olvera
Antequera
Sierra Nevada
Grazalema
MÁLAGA
Málaga
Torre de Benagalbón
Almayate
Benarrabá
MARBELLA
Fuengirola
Cala de Mijas
E-15
Alicún de las Torres
Cullar
Dólar
Abla
Canjáyar
ALMERÍA
Almerimar
Cabo de Gata
La Isleta
Carboneras
Agua Amarga
Vera
Huércal-Overa
San Juan de los Terreros
Águilas
Taberno
Vélez-Rubio
Lorca
Totana
Ramonete
Cañada de Callego
Calnegre
Ricote
Archena
Ceutí
Lorquí
Mula
19km

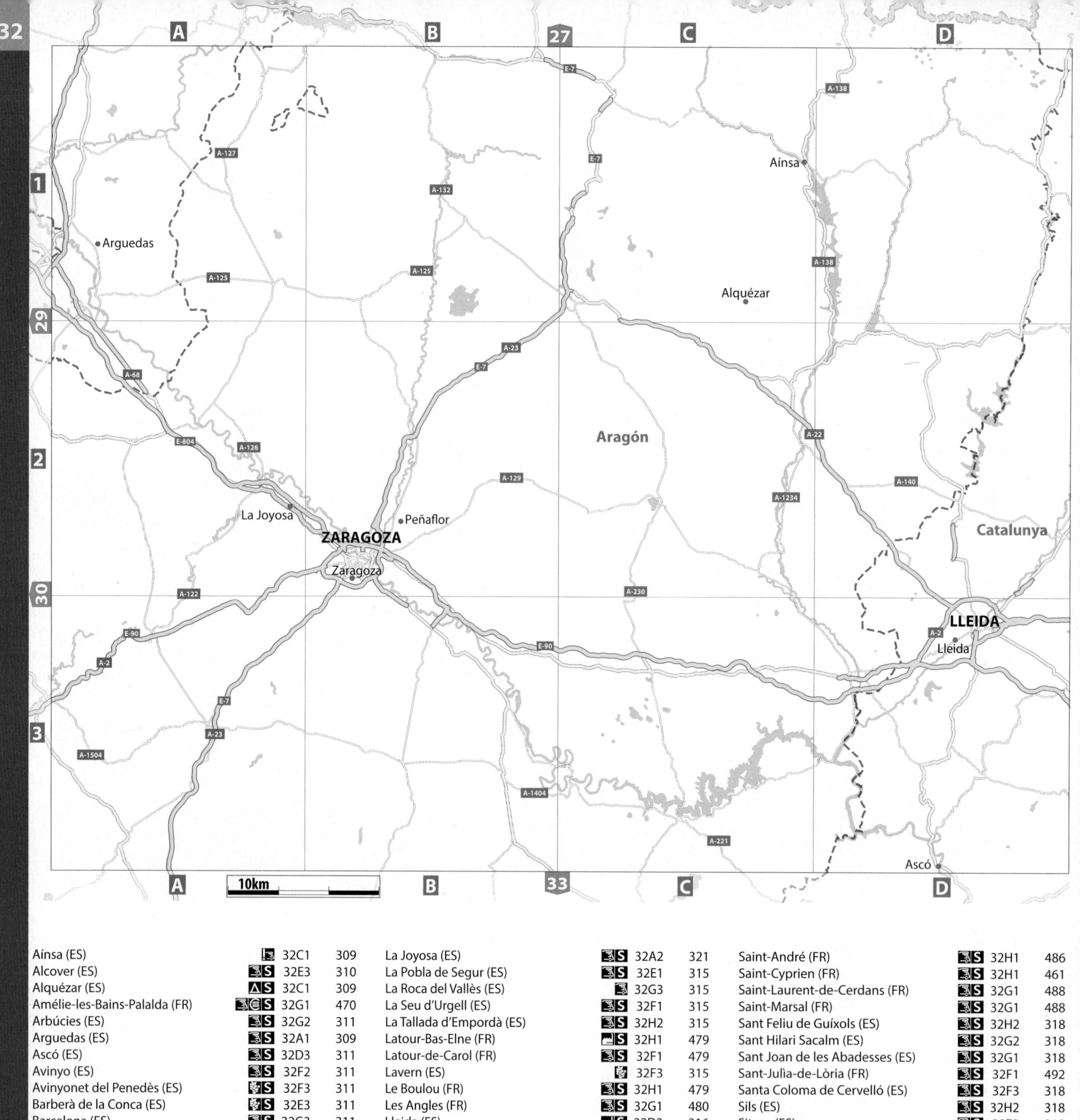
A
B
27
C
D
1
2
3
29
30
E-7
A-138
A-127
A-132
Aínsa
Arguedas
A-125
A-125
Alquézar
A-23
E-7
A-68
Aragón
A-22
E-804
A-126
A-129
A-140
A-1234
La Joyosa
Peñaflor
ZARAGOZA
Catalunya
Zaragoza
A-122
A-230
LLEIDA
E-90
A-2
Lleida
E-90
A-2
E-7
A-23
A-1504
A-1404
A-221
Ascó
A
10km
B
33
C
D

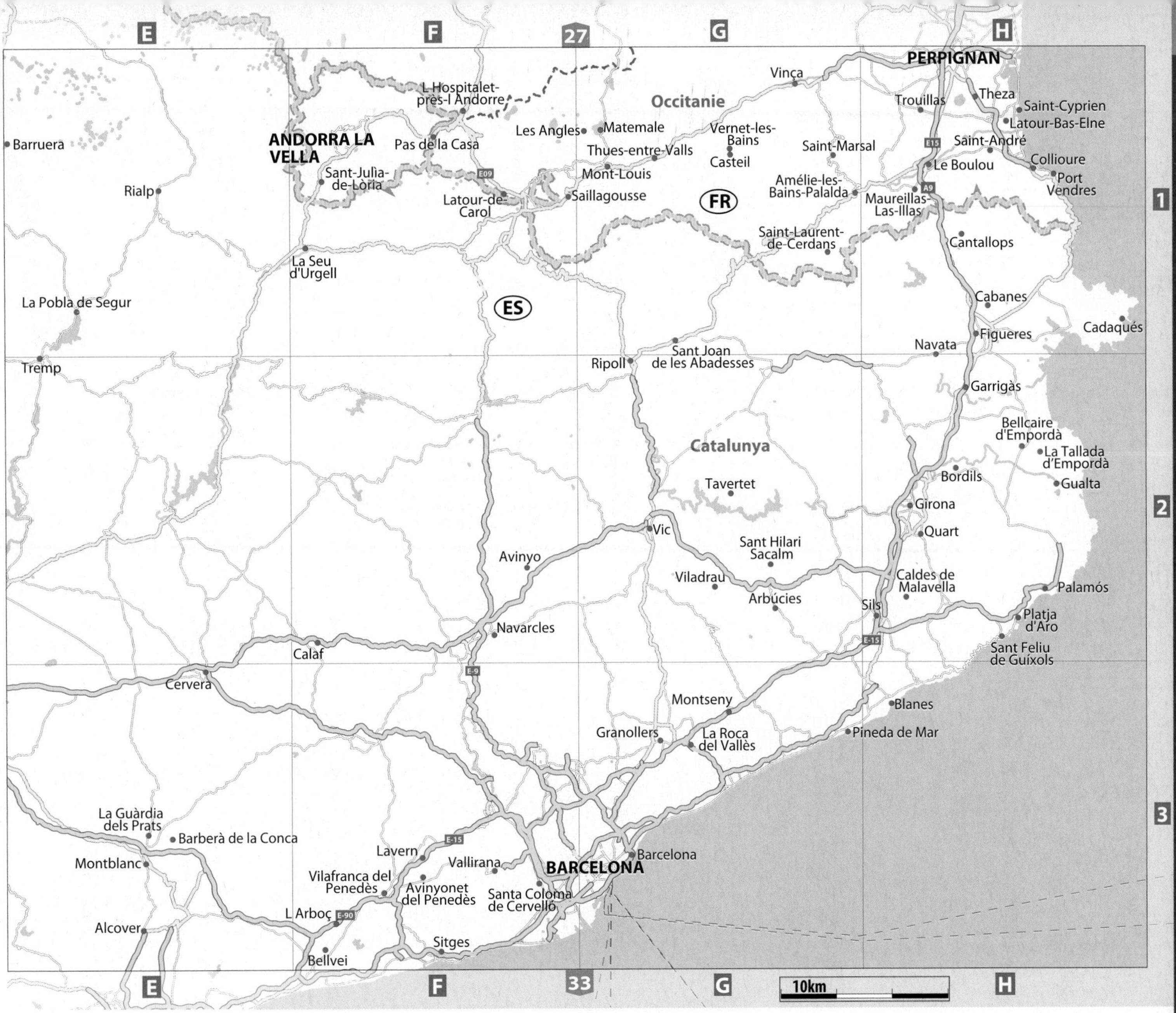

E F 27 G H

PERPIGNAN
Vinça
Occitanie
L'Hospitalet-près-l'Andorre
Trouillas
Theza
Saint-Cyprien
Latour-Bas-Elne
Barruera
ANDORRA LA VELLA
Pas de la Casa
Les Angles
Matemale
Vernet-les-Bains
Saint-Marsal
Saint-André
Thues-entre-Valls
Casteil
Le Boulou
Collioure
Sant-Julià-de-Lòria
Mont-Louis
Amélie-les-Bains-Palalda
Port Vendres
Rialp
Latour-de-Carol
Saillagousse
FR
Maureillas-Las-Illas
Saint-Laurent-de-Cerdans
Cantallops
La Seu d'Urgell
ES
Cabanes
La Pobla de Segur
Cadaqués
Figueres
Navata
Tremp
Ripoll
Sant Joan de les Abadesses
Garrigàs
Bellcaire d'Empordà
Catalunya
La Tallada d'Empordà
Bordils
Tavertet
Gualta
Girona
Vic
Quart
Avinyo
Sant Hilari Sacalm
Viladrau
Caldes de Malavella
Palamós
Arbúcies
Sils
Navarcles
Platja d'Aro
Sant Feliu de Guíxols
Calaf
Cervera
Montseny
Blanes
Granollers
La Roca del Vallès
Pineda de Mar
La Guàrdia dels Prats
Barberà de la Conca
Lavern
Montblanc
Vallirana
Barcelona
BARCELONA
Vilafranca del Penedès
Avinyonet del Penedès
Santa Coloma de Cervelló
L'Arboç
Alcover
Sitges
Bellvei

E F 33 G 10km H

1 2 3

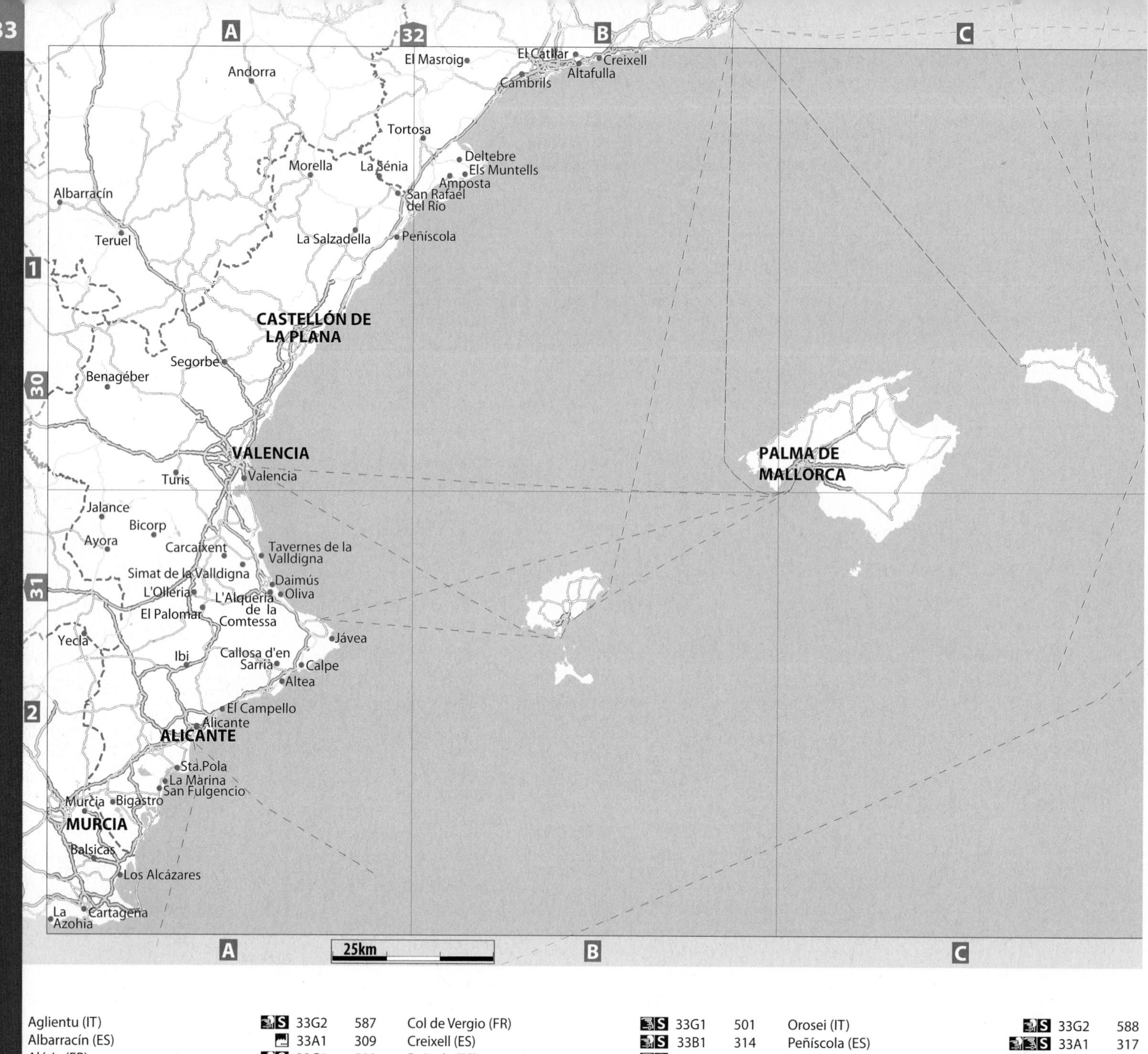
A
32
B
C
1
30
31
2
El Masroig
El Catllar
Creixell
Altafulla
Cambrils
Andorra
Tortosa
Deltebre
Els Muntells
Morella
La Sénia
Amposta
San Rafael del Rio
Albarracín
Teruel
La Salzadella
Peñíscola
CASTELLÓN DE LA PLANA
Segorbe
Benagéber
VALENCIA
Valencia
Turis
PALMA DE MALLORCA
Jalance
Bicorp
Ayora
Carcaixent
Tavernes de la Valldigna
Simat de la Valldigna
Daimús
L'Olleria
L'Alqueria de la Comtessa
Oliva
El Palomar
Jávea
Yecla
Ibi
Callosa d'en Sarrià
Calpe
Altea
El Campello
Alicante
ALICANTE
Sta.Pola
La Marina
San Fulgencio
Murcia
Bigastro
MURCIA
Balsicas
Los Alcázares
La Azohia
Cartagena
25km

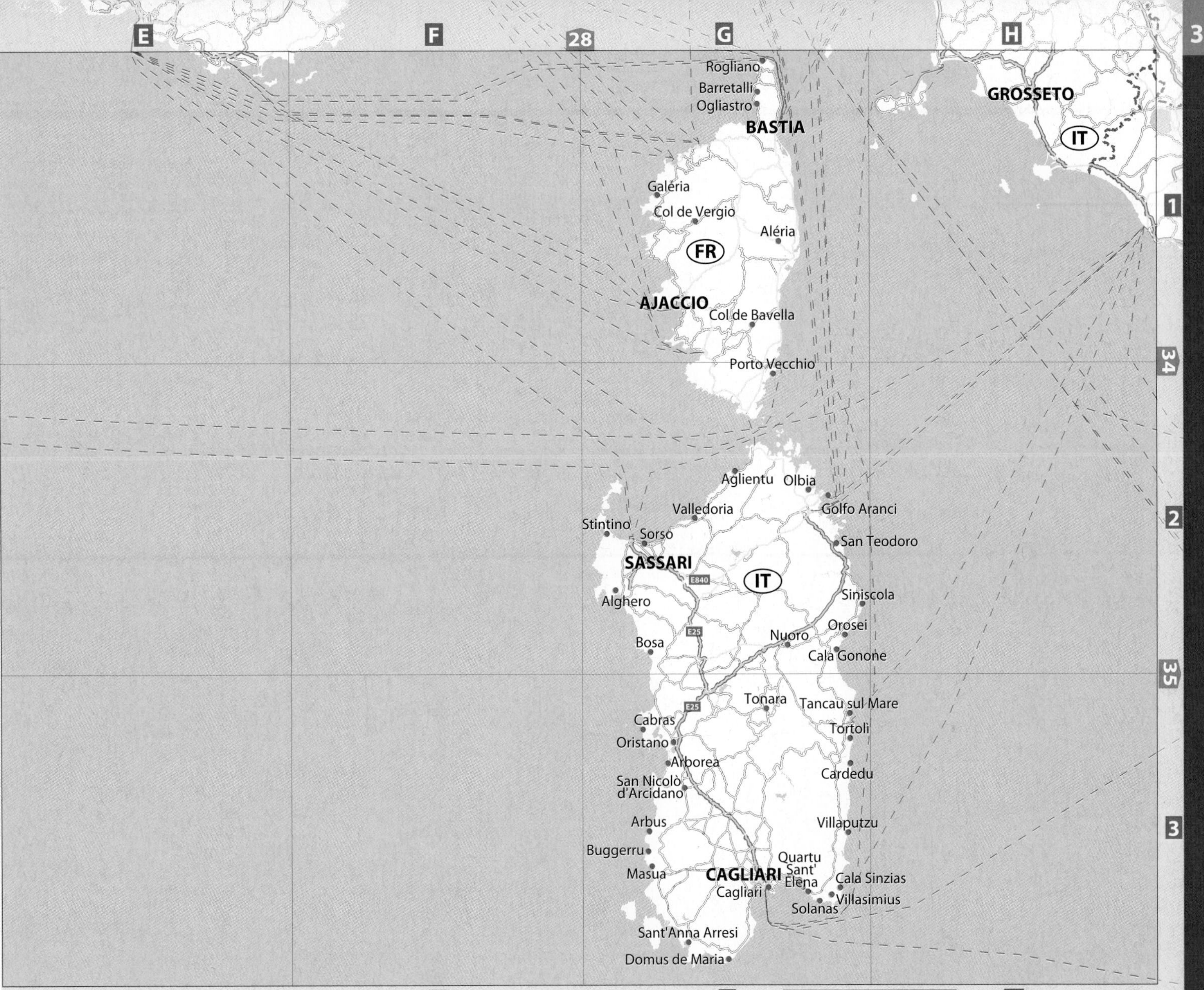
E
F
28
G
H
Rogliano
Barretalli
Ogliastro
BASTIA
GROSSETO
IT
Galéria
Col de Vergio
Aléria
FR
AJACCIO
Col de Bavella
Porto Vecchio
1
34
Aglientu
Olbia
Valledoria
Golfo Aranci
Stintino
Sorso
San Teodoro
SASSARI
E840
IT
2
Alghero
Siniscola
Orosei
E25
Nuoro
Bosa
Cala Gonone
35
Tonara
Tancau sul Mare
E25
Cabras
Oristano
Tortolì
Arborea
Cardedu
San Nicolò d'Arcidano
Arbus
Villaputzu
3
Buggerru
Quartu Sant' Elena
Masua
CAGLIARI
Cagliari
Cala Sinzias
Villasimius
Solanas
Sant'Anna Arresi
Domus de Maria
E
F
G
25km
H

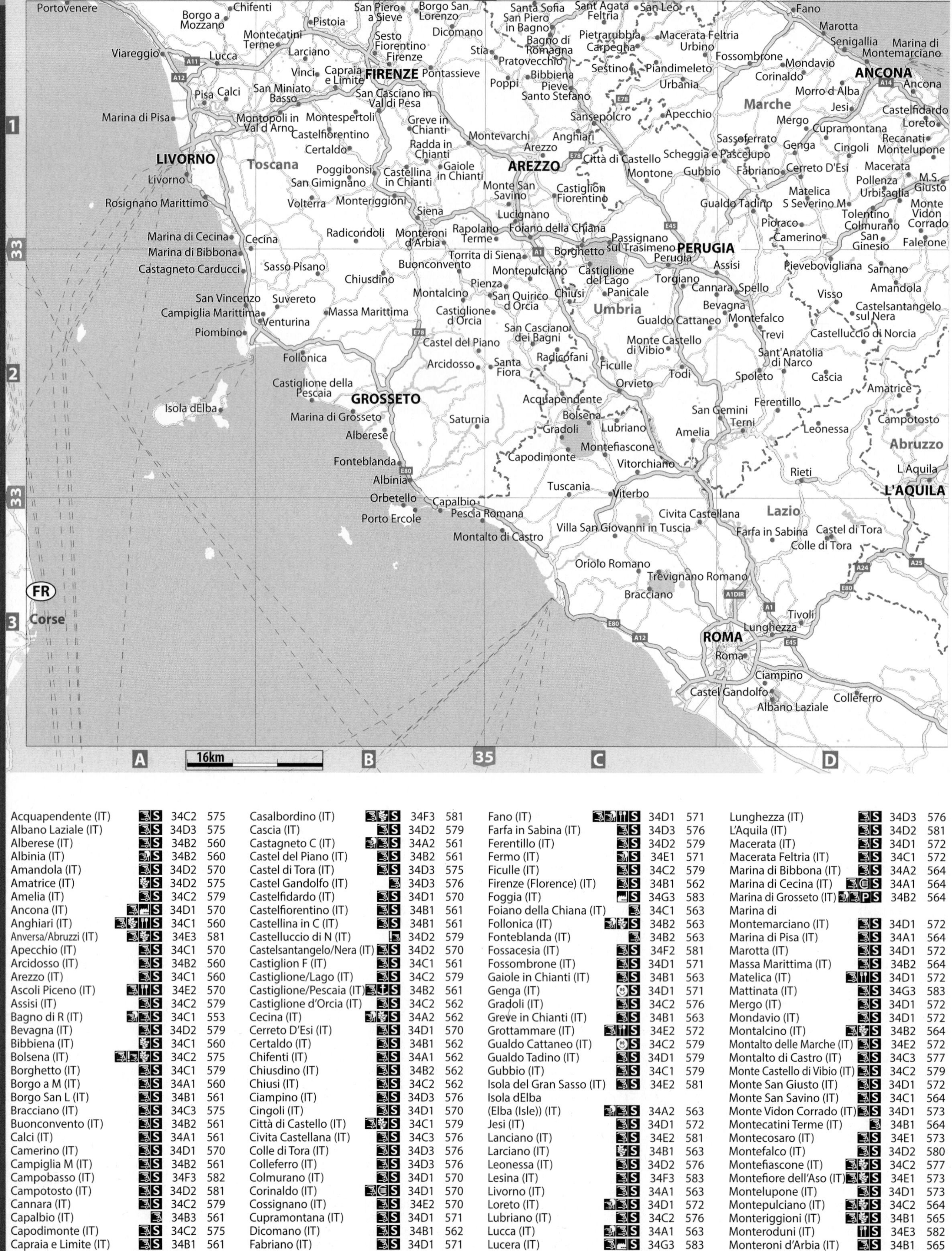
A
B
26
C
D
Portovenere
Borgo a Mozzano
Chifenti
Pistoia
San Piero a Sieve
Borgo San Lorenzo
Santa Sofia
San Piero in Bagno
Sant Agata Feltria
San Leo
Fano
Marotta
Viareggio
Lucca
Montecatini Terme
Larciano
Sesto Fiorentino
Firenze
Dicomano
Stia
Bagno di Romagna
Pratovecchio
Pietrarubbia
Carpegna
Macerata Feltria
Urbino
Fossombrone
Senigallia
Marina di Montemarciano
Mondavio
Vinci
Capraia e Limite
FIRENZE
Pontassieve
Bibbiena
Poppi
Pieve Santo Stefano
Sestino
Piandimeleto
Urbania
Corinaldo
ANCONA
Ancona
Pisa
Calci
San Miniato Basso
San Casciano in Val di Pesa
Morro d Alba
Marche
Jesi
Castelfidardo
Loreto
Marina di Pisa
Montopoli in Val d Arno
Montespertoli
Greve in Chianti
Sansepolcro
Apecchio
Mergo
Cupramontana
Castelfiorentino
Certaldo
Montevarchi
Anghiari
Sassoferrato
Genga
Cingoli
Recanati
Montelupone
Radda in Chianti
Arezzo
LIVORNO
Toscana
Poggibonsi
Castellina in Chianti
Gaiole in Chianti
AREZZO
Città di Castello
Scheggia e Pascelupo
Montone
Gubbio
Fabriano
Cerreto D'Esi
Macerata
Livorno
San Gimignano
Monte San Savino
Castiglion Fiorentino
Pollenza
Urbisaglia
M.S. Giusto
Rosignano Marittimo
Volterra
Monteriggioni
Siena
Lucignano
Gualdo Tadino
Matelica
S Severino M
Monte Vidon Corrado
Tolentino
Colmurano
Marina di Cecina
Cecina
Radicondoli
Monteroni d'Arbia
Rapolano Terme
Foiano della Chiana
Passignano sul Trasimeno
Pioraco
Camerino
San Ginesio
Falerone
Marina di Bibbona
Torrita di Siena
Borghetto
PERUGIA
Perugia
Castagneto Carducci
Sasso Pisano
Buonconvento
Montepulciano
Castiglione del Lago
Assisi
Pievebovigliana
Sarnano
Chiusdino
Pienza
Torgiano
Cannara
Spello
Amandola
San Vincenzo
Suvereto
Montalcino
San Quirico d Orcia
Chiusi
Panicale
Visso
Campiglia Marittima
Massa Marittima
Castiglione d Orcia
Umbria
Bevagna
Castelsantangelo sul Nera
Venturina
Gualdo Cattaneo
Montefalco
Piombino
San Casciano dei Bagni
Trevi
Castelluccio di Norcia
Castel del Piano
Monte Castello di Vibio
Follonica
Arcidosso
Santa Fiora
Radicofani
Ficulle
Sant'Anatolia di Narco
Castiglione della Pescaia
Orvieto
Todi
Spoleto
Cascia
Amatrice
GROSSETO
Acquapendente
Isola dElba
Ferentillo
San Gemini
Marina di Grosseto
Saturnia
Bolsena
Terni
Campotosto
Alberese
Gradoli
Lubriano
Amelia
Leonessa
Montefiascone
Abruzzo
Capodimonte
Fonteblanda
Vitorchiano
Rieti
L Aquila
Albinia
Tuscania
L'AQUILA
Orbetello
Capalbio
Viterbo
Porto Ercole
Pescia Romana
Civita Castellana
Lazio
Villa San Giovanni in Tuscia
Farfa in Sabina
Castel di Tora
Montalto di Castro
Colle di Tora
Oriolo Romano
Trevignano Romano
FR
Bracciano
Corse
Tivoli
Lunghezza
ROMA
Roma
Ciampino
Castel Gandolfo
Colleferro
Albano Laziale
1
2
3
33
A
16km
B
35
C
D

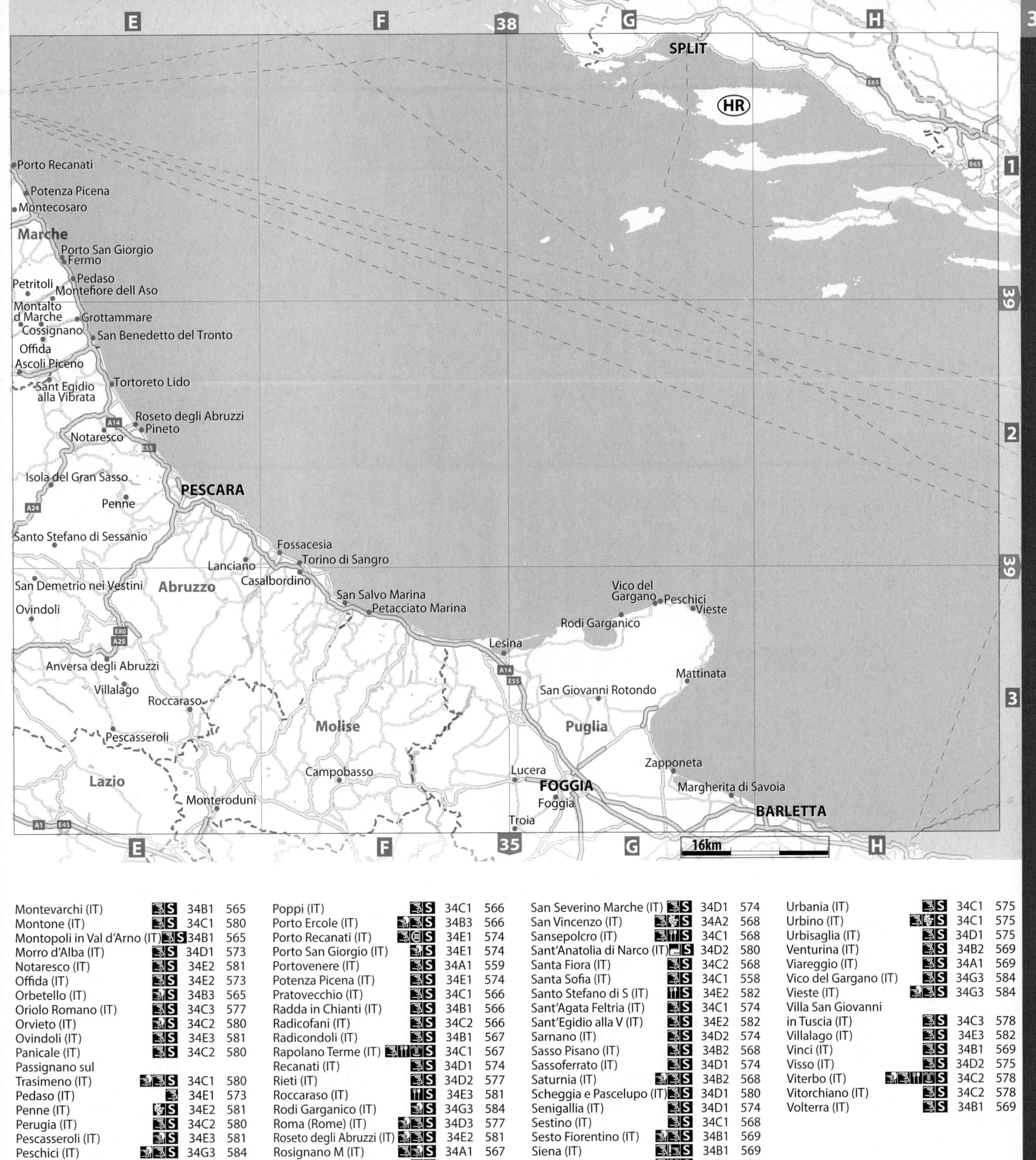

E
F
38
G
H
SPLIT
HR
E65
1
Porto Recanati
Potenza Picena
Montecosaro
Marche
Porto San Giorgio
Fermo
Pedaso
Petritoli
Montefiore dell Aso
Montalto d Marche
Grottammare
Cossignano
San Benedetto del Tronto
Offida
Ascoli Piceno
Sant Egidio alla Vibrata
Tortoreto Lido
39
Roseto degli Abruzzi
Pineto
A14
Notaresco
E55
2
Isola del Gran Sasso
PESCARA
Penne
A24
Santo Stefano di Sessanio
Fossacesia
Lanciano
Torino di Sangro
Casalbordino
San Demetrio nei Vestini
Abruzzo
San Salvo Marina
Petacciato Marina
Ovindoli
Vico del Gargano
Peschici
Vieste
Rodi Garganico
Lesina
E80
A25
Anversa degli Abruzzi
Mattinata
Villalago
Roccaraso
San Giovanni Rotondo
3
Molise
Puglia
Pescasseroli
Zapponeta
Campobasso
Lucera
Lazio
FOGGIA
Margherita di Savoia
Foggia
Monteroduni
BARLETTA
Troia
A1
E45
35
16km

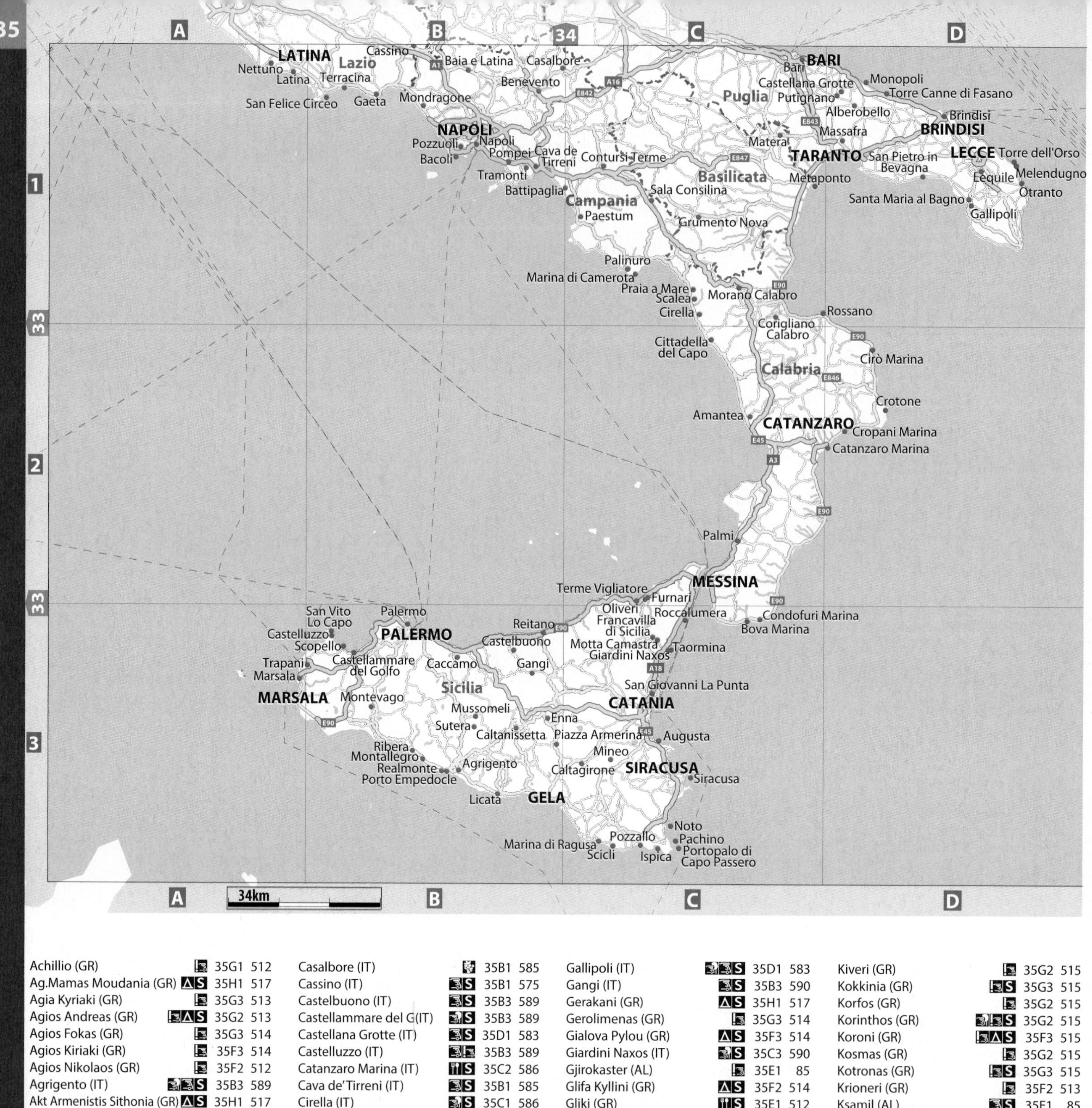
A
B
34
C
D
1
2
3
33
A
B
C
D
34km
LATINA
Lazio
Cassino
Nettuno
Latina
Terracina
San Felice Circeo
Gaeta
Mondragone
Baia e Latina
Casalbore
Benevento
NAPOLI
Pozzuoli
Napoli
Bacoli
Pompei
Cava de Tirreni
Tramonti
Battipaglia
Contursi Terme
Campania
Paestum
Sala Consilina
Basilicata
Grumento Nova
BARI
Bari
Castellana Grotte
Monopoli
Torre Canne di Fasano
Puglia
Putignano
Alberobello
Brindisi
BRINDISI
Massafra
Matera
TARANTO
San Pietro in Bevagna
LECCE
Torre dell'Orso
Melendugno
Lequile
Otranto
Metaponto
Santa Maria al Bagno
Gallipoli
Palinuro
Marina di Camerota
Praia a Mare
Scalea
Morano Calabro
Cirella
Rossano
Corigliano Calabro
Cittadella del Capo
Cirò Marina
Calabria
Crotone
Amantea
CATANZARO
Cropani Marina
Catanzaro Marina
Palmi
Terme Vigliatore
Furnari
MESSINA
Oliveri
Francavilla di Sicilia
Roccalumera
Condofuri Marina
Bova Marina
San Vito Lo Capo
Palermo
Castelluzzo
PALERMO
Reitano
Scopello
Castelbuono
Motta Camastra
Giardini Naxos
Taormina
Trapani
Marsala
Castellammare del Golfo
Caccamo
Gangi
Sicilia
San Giovanni La Punta
MARSALA
Montevago
Mussomeli
CATANIA
Enna
Sutera
Caltanissetta
Piazza Armerina
Augusta
Ribera
Montallegro
Mineo
Realmonte
Porto Empedocle
Agrigento
Caltagirone
SIRACUSA
Siracusa
Licata
GELA
Noto
Pachino
Marina di Ragusa
Pozzallo
Scicli
Ispica
Portopalo di Capo Passero
A1
A16
A3
A18
E842
E843
E847
E846
E45
E90

Place	Map	Page
Mineo (IT)	35C3	590
Mondragone (IT)	35B1	585
Monemvasía (GR)	35G3	515
Monopoli (IT)	35D1	583
Montallegro (IT)	35B3	590
Montevago (IT)	35B3	590
Morano Calabro (IT)	35C1	586
Motta Camastra (IT)	35C3	590
Moustheni (GR)	35H1	517
Mussomeli (IT)	35B3	590
Mycenae (GR)	35G2	515
Nafpaktos (GR)	35F2	513
Nafplio (GR)	35G2	516
Napoli (Naples) (IT)	35B1	585
Neo Itylo (GR)	35G3	516
Nettuno (IT)	35A1	577
Noto (IT)	35C3	590
Oliveri (IT)	35C2	591
Olympia (GR)	35F2	516
Orikum (AL)	35E1	85
Otranto (IT)	35D1	583
Ouranoupoli (GR)	35H1	517
Pachino (IT)	35C3	591
Paestum (IT)	35C1	585
Palermo (IT)	35B3	591
Palinuro (IT)	35C1	585
Palmi (IT)	35C2	586
Paralia Astros (GR)	35G2	516
Paralia Epanomi (GR)	35G1	517
Paralia Platanou (GR)	35F2	516
Paralia Rizomilos (GR)	35F2	516
Parga (GR)	35E1	513
Pátra (GR)	35F2	516
Perahóra (GR)	35G2	516
Perdika (GR)	35E1	513
Petalidi (GR)	35F3	516
Piazza Armerina (IT)	35B3	591
Pilion (GR)	35G1	513
Pírgos Dhiroú (GR)	35G3	516
Plataria (GR)	35E1	513
Pompei (IT)	35B1	585
Porto Empedocle (IT)	35B3	591
Porto Kagio (GR)	35G3	516
Porto Lagos (GR)	35H1	517
Portopalo di Capo P (IT)	35C3	591
Pozzallo (IT)	35C3	591
Pozzuoli (IT)	35B1	585
Praia a Mare (IT)	35C1	586
Préveza (GR)	35F1	513
Putignano (IT)	35D1	584
Radhimë (AL)	35E1	86
Rafina (GR)	35G2	516
Realmonte (IT)	35B3	591
Reitano (IT)	35B3	592
Ribera (IT)	35B3	592
Roccalumera (IT)	35C3	592
Rossano (IT)	35C1	586
Sala Consilina (IT)	35C1	585
Salandi (GR)	35G2	516
San Felice Circeo (IT)	35B1	578
San Giovanni La Punta (IT)	35C3	592
San Pietro in Bevagna (IT)	35D1	584
San Vito Lo Capo (IT)	35B3	592
Santa Maria al Bagno (IT)	35D1	584
Sarandë (AL)	35E1	86
Savalia (GR)	35F2	516
Scalea (IT)	35C1	587
Scicli (IT)	35C3	592
Scopello (IT)	35B3	592
Siracusa (IT)	35C3	592
Sivota (GR)	35E1	513
Skoutari (GR)	35G3	516
Sounion (GR)	35G2	516
Sutera (IT)	35B3	592
Taormina (IT)	35C3	592
Terme Vigliatore (IT)	35C2	592
Terracina (IT)	35B1	578
Tolo (GR)	35G2	516
Torre Canne di F (IT)	35D1	584
Torre dell'Orso (IT)	35D1	584
Tramonti (IT)	35B1	585
Trapani (IT)	35A3	592
Tyrchu (GR)	35G2	516
Vagia (GR)	35G2	513
Vergina (GR)	35G1	517
Vonitsa (GR)	35F2	513
Zacharo (GR)	35F2	517

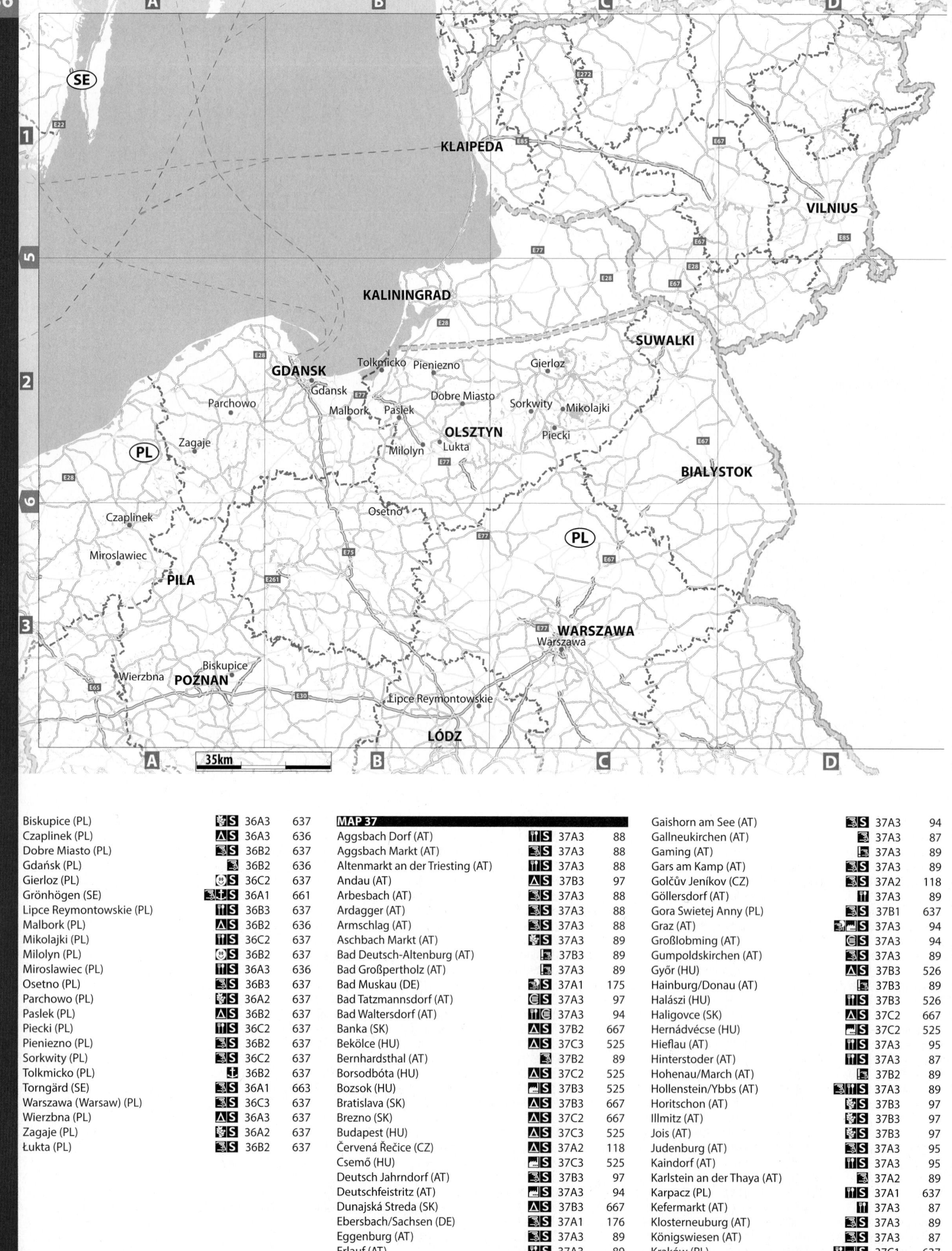
A
B
C
D
1
5
2
6
3
SE
E22
KLAIPEDA
E85
E272
E67
VILNIUS
E85
E67
E77
E28
E67
E28
KALININGRAD
E28
SUWALKI
E28
GDANSK
Tolkmicko
Pieniezno
Gierloz
Gdansk
E77
Dobre Miasto
Sorkwity
Mikolajki
Parchowo
Malbork
Paslek
OLSZTYN
Piecki
Zagaje
Milolyn
Lukta
E67
PL
E28
E77
BIALYSTOK
Czaplinek
Osetno
E77
PL
E75
Miroslawiec
E67
PILA
E261
E77
WARSZAWA
Warszawa
Biskupice
Wierzbna
POZNAN
E65
E30
Lipce Reymontowskie
LÓDZ
A
35km
B
C
D

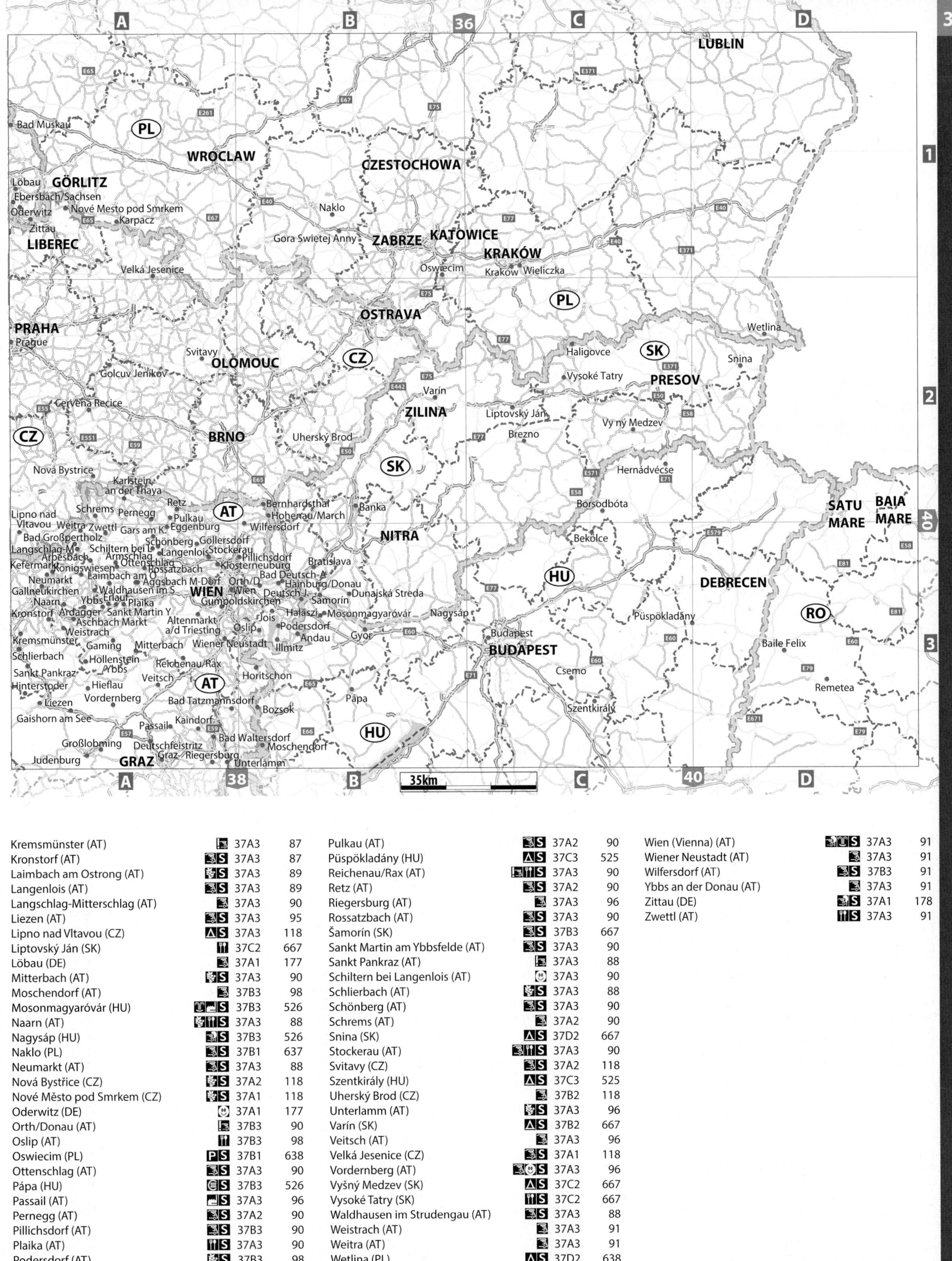

A
B
36
C
D
LUBLIN
Bad Muskau
PL
WROCLAW
CZESTOCHOWA
Löbau GÖRLITZ
Ebersbach/Sachsen
Oderwitz
Nové Mesto pod Smrkem
Karpacz
Zittau
LIBEREC
Naklo
Gora Swietej Anny
ZABRZE
KATOWICE
KRAKÓW
Oswiecim
Kraków
Wieliczka
Velká Jesenice
PL
OSTRAVA
Wetlina
PRAHA
Prague
Svitavy
OLOMOUC
CZ
Haligovce
SK
Snina
Vysoké Tatry
PRESOV
Golcuv Jenikov
Varín
Cervená Recice
ZILINA
Liptovský Ján
Brezno
Vy ný Medzev
CZ
BRNO
Uherský Brod
SK
Nová Bystrice
Karlstein an der Thaya
Hernádvécse
Retz
Schrems
Pernegg
AT
Bernhardsthal
Hohenau/March
Banka
Borsodbóta
SATU MARE
BAIA MARE
Lipno nad Vltavou
Weitra
Zwettl
Gars am K.
Pulkau
Eggenburg
Wilfersdorf
NITRA
Bad Großpertholz
Schönberg
Göllersdorf
Bekölce
Langschlag-M
Schiltern bei L
Langenlois
Stockerau
Arbesbach
Armschlag
Pillichsdorf
Bratislava
Kefermarkt
Königswiesen
Ottenschlag
Klosterneuburg
Rossatzbach
Neumarkt
Laimbach am O
Bad Deutsch-A
HU
Gallneukirchen
Waldhausen im S
Aggsbach M-Dorf
Orth/D
Hainburg/Donau
Naarn
Ybbs
Erlauf
Plaika
WIEN
Wien
Deutsch-J.
Dunajská Streda
DEBRECEN
Kronstorf
Ardagger
Sankt Martin Y
Gumpoldskirchen
Samorín
Aschbach Markt
Altenmarkt a/d Triesting
Halászi
Mosonmagyaróvár
Nagysáp
RO
Weistrach
Oslip
Jois
Podersdorf
Püspökladány
Kremsmünster
Gaming
Mitterbach
Wiener Neustadt
Illmitz
Andau
Gyor
Budapest
Baile Felix
Schlierbach
Hollenstein
Ybbs
Reichenau/Rax
BUDAPEST
Sankt Pankraz
Hinterstoder
Veitsch
Horitschon
Csemo
Hieflau
AT
Remetea
Liezen
Vordernberg
Bad Tatzmannsdorf
Pápa
Gaishorn am See
Bozsok
Szentkirály
Passail
Kaindorf
Großlobming
Deutschfeistritz
Bad Waltersdorf
Moschendorf
HU
Judenburg
GRAZ
Graz
Riegersburg
Unterlamm
A
38
B
35km
C
40
D
1
2
40
3

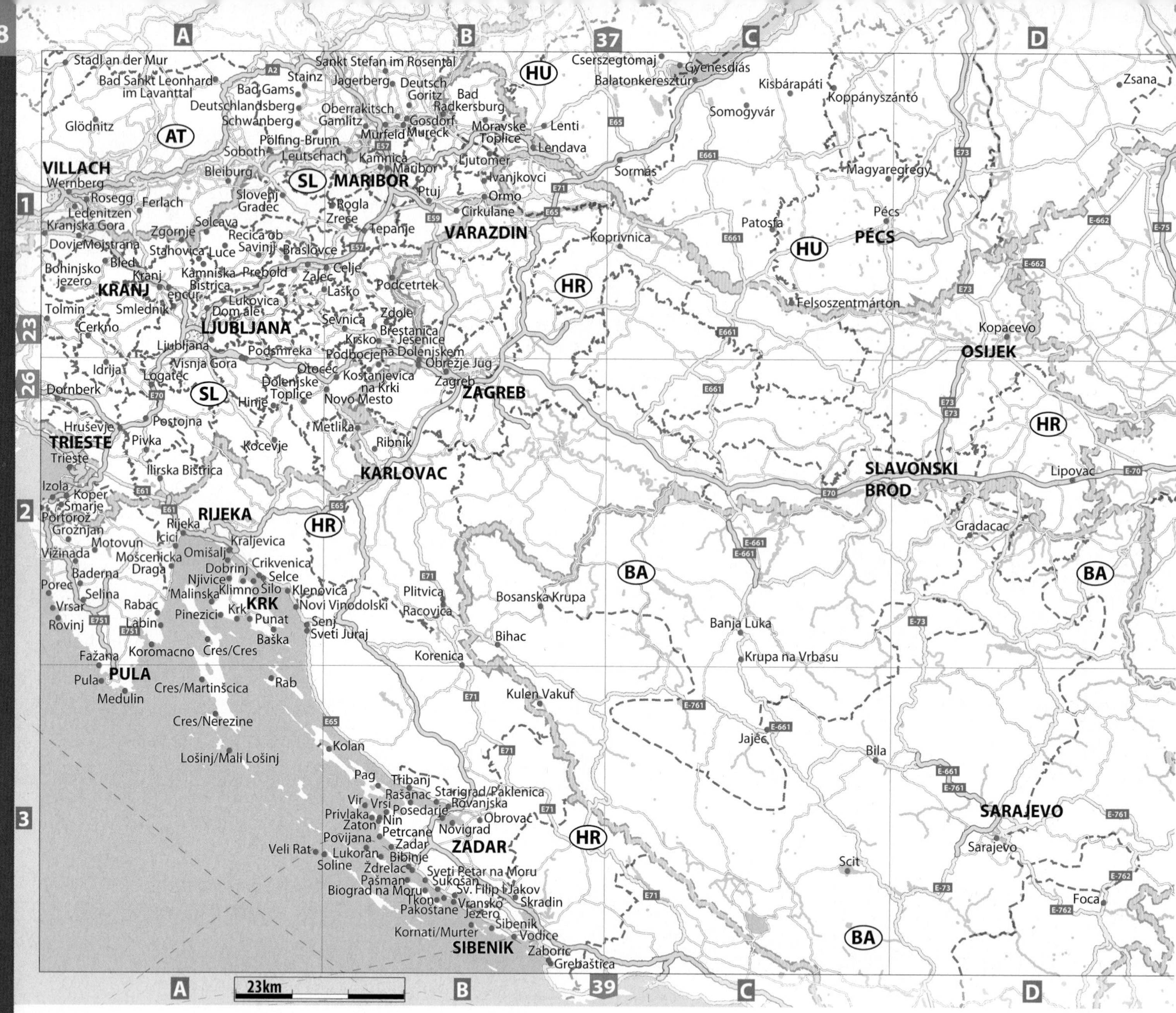

Place	Grid	Page
Bad Gams (AT)	38A1	94
Bad Radkersburg (AT)	38B1	94
Bad Sankt Leonhard im Lavanttal (AT)	38A1	96
Baderna (HR)	38A2	518
Balatonkeresztúr (HU)	38C1	525
Banja Luka (BA)	38C2	99
Bibinje (HR)	38B3	520
Bihać (BA)	38B2	99
Bila (BA)	38C3	99
Biograd na Moru (HR)	38B3	520
Bled (SI)	38A1	668
Bleiburg (AT)	38A1	96
Bohinjsko jezero (SI)	38A1	668
Bosanska Krupa (BA)	38B2	99
Braslovče (SI)	38A1	670
Brestanica (SI)	38B1	670
Celje (SI)	38B1	670
Cerkno (SI)	38A1	668
Cirkulane (SI)	38B1	670
Cres/Cres (HR)	38A2	518
Cres/Martinščica (HR)	38A3	518
Cres/Nerezine (HR)	38A3	518
Crikvenica (HR)	38A2	518
Cserszegtomaj (HU)	38C1	525
Deutsch Goritz (AT)	38B1	94
Deutschlandsberg (AT)	38A1	94
Dobrinj (HR)	38A2	518
Dolenjske Toplice (SI)	38A2	670
Domžale (SI)	38A1	668
Dornberk (SI)	38A2	668
DovjeMojstrana (SI)	38A1	668
Fažana (HR)	38A3	518
Felsőszentmárton (HU)	38C1	526
Ferlach (AT)	38A1	97
Gamlitz (AT)	38B1	94
Glödnitz (AT)	38A1	97
Gosdorf (AT)	38B1	94
Gradačac (BA)	38D2	99
Grožnjan (HR)	38A2	518
Gyenesdiás (HU)	38C1	525
Hinje (SI)	38A2	670
Hruševje (SI)	38A2	668
Ičiči (HR)	38A2	518
Idrija (SI)	38A2	668
Ilirska Bistrica (SI)	38A2	668
Ivanjkovci (SI)	38B1	670
Izola (SI)	38A2	668
Jagerberg (AT)	38B1	95
Jajec (BA)	38C3	99
Jesenice na Dolenjskem (SI)	38B2	670
Kamnica (SI)	38B1	670
Kamniška Bistrica (SI)	38A1	668
Kisbárapáti (HU)	38C1	525
Klenovica (HR)	38A2	518
Kocevje (SI)	38A2	670
Kolan (HR)	38B3	521
Kopačevo (HR)	38D1	524
Koper (SI)	38A2	669
Koppányszántó (HU)	38C1	525
Koprivnica (HR)	38C1	524
Korenica (HR)	38B2	521
Kornati/Murter (HR)	38B3	521
Koromačno (HR)	38A2	518
Kostanjevica na Krki (SI)	38B2	670
Kraljevica (HR)	38A2	518
Kranj (SI)	38A1	669
Kranjska Gora (SI)	38A1	669
Krk/Baška (HR)	38A2	518
Krk/Klimno (HR)	38A2	518
Krk/Krk (HR)	38A2	518
Krk/Malinska (HR)	38A2	519
Krk/Njivice (HR)	38A2	519
Krk/Omišalj (HR)	38A2	519
Krk/Pinezici (HR)	38A2	519
Krk/Punat (HR)	38A2	519
Krk/Šilo (HR)	38A2	519
Krško (SI)	38B1	670
Krupa na Vrbasu (BA)	38C2	99
Kulen Vakuf (BA)	38B3	99
Labin (HR)	38A2	519
Laško (SI)	38A1	671
Ledenitzen (AT)	38A1	97
Lendava (SI)	38B1	671
Lenti (HU)	38B1	526
Leutschach (AT)	38B1	95
Lipovac (HR)	38D2	524
Ljubljana (SI)	38A1	669
Ljutomer (SI)	38B1	671
Logatec (SI)	38A2	669
Lošinj/Mali Lošinj (HR)	38A3	519
Luče (SI)	38A1	669
Lukoran (HR)	38B3	521
Lukovica (SI)	38A1	669
Magyaregregy (HU)	38C1	526
Maribor (SI)	38B1	671
Medulin (HR)	38A3	519
Metlika (SI)	38B2	671
Moravske Toplice (SI)	38B1	671
Moščenička Draga (HR)	38A2	519
Motovun (HR)	38A2	519
Mureck (AT)	38B1	95
Murfeld (AT)	38B1	96
Nin (HR)	38B3	521
Novi Vinodolski (HR)	38A2	519
Novigrad (Dalmatia) (HR)	38B3	521
Novo Mesto (SI)	38B2	671
Oberrakitsch (AT)	38B1	96
Obrežje Jug (SI)	38B2	671
Obrovac (HR)	38B3	521
Ormož (SI)	38B1	671
Otočec (SI)	38B2	671
Pag (HR)	38B3	521
Pakoštane (HR)	38B3	521
Pašman (HR)	38B3	522
Patosfa (HU)	38C1	526
Pécs (HU)	38C1	525
Petrcane (HR)	38B3	522
Pivka (SI)	38A2	671
Plitviča (HR)	38B2	524
Podbočje (SI)	38B2	671
Podčetrtek (SI)	38B1	672
Podsmreka (SI)	38A2	672
Pölfing-Brunn (AT)	38A1	96
Poreč (HR)	38A2	519
Portorož (SI)	38A2	669
Posedarje (HR)	38B3	522
Postojna (SI)	38A2	669
Povijana (HR)	38B3	522
Prebold (SI)	38A1	672
Privlaka (HR)	38B3	522
Ptuj (SI)	38B1	672

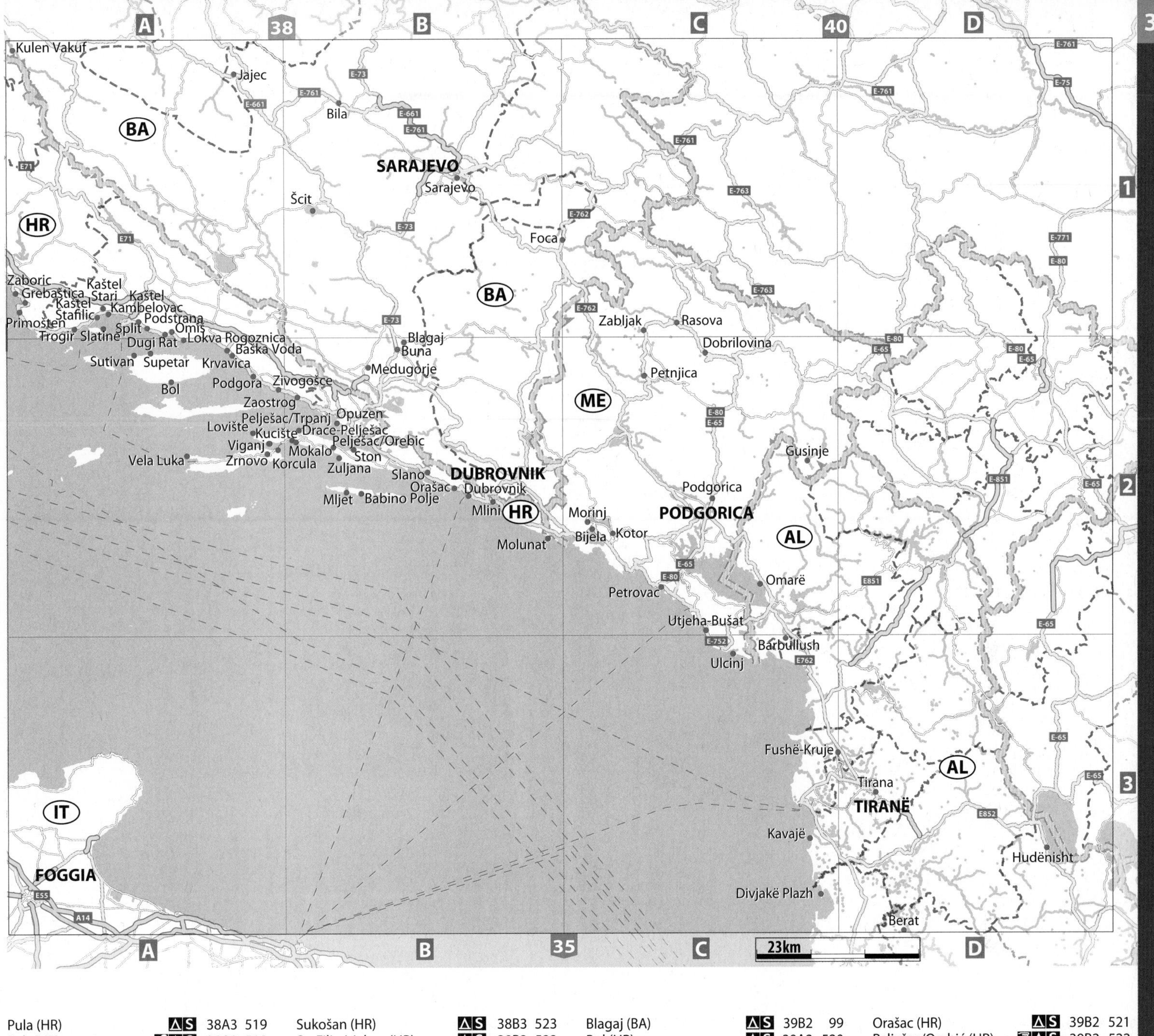
A
38
B
C
40
D
1
2
3
Kulen Vakuf
Jajec
Bila
(BA)
SARAJEVO
Sarajevo
Šcit
(HR)
Foca
(BA)
Zaboric
Kaštel
Grebaštica
Stari
Kaštel
Kaštel
Kambelovac
Štafilic
Primošten
Podstrana
Split
Omiš
Trogir
Slatine
Dugi Rat
Lokva Rogoznica
Baška Voda
Sutivan
Supetar
Krvavica
Bol
Podgora
Zivogošće
Blagaj
Buna
Medugorje
Zaostrog
Peljesac/Trpanj
Opuzen
Lovište
Kucište
Drace-Peljesac
Viganj
Mokalo
Peljesac/Orebic
Vela Luka
Zrnovo
Korcula
Ston
Zuljana
Slano
DUBROVNIK
Orašac
Dubrovnik
Mljet
Babino Polje
Mlini
(HR)
Molunat
Zabljak
Rasova
Dobrilovina
Petnjica
(ME)
Gusinje
Podgorica
Morinj
PODGORICA
Bijela
Kotor
(AL)
Omarë
Petrovac
Utjeha-Bušat
Barbullush
Ulcinj
Fushë-Kruje
Tirana
(AL)
TIRANË
(IT)
Kavajë
Hudënisht
FOGGIA
Divjakë Plazh
Berat
35
23km

MAP 39

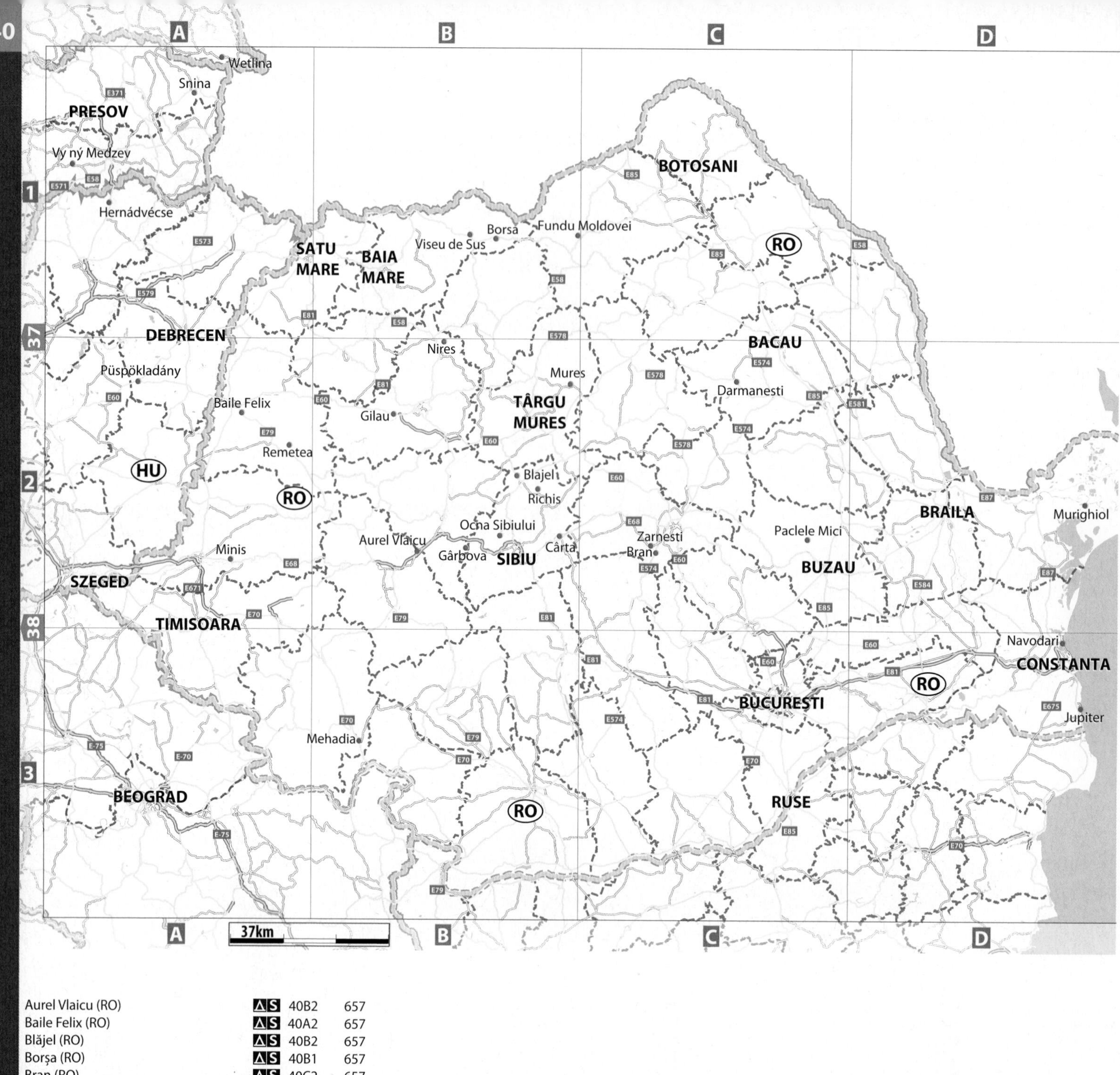
A
B
C
D
1
2
3
37
38
Wetlina
Snina
PRESOV
Vy ný Medzev
Hernádvécse
SATU MARE
BAIA MARE
Viseu de Sus
Borsa
Fundu Moldovei
BOTOSANI
RO
DEBRECEN
Püspökladány
Nires
BACAU
Mures
Darmanesti
Baile Felix
Gilau
TÂRGU MURES
Remetea
HU
RO
Blajel
Richis
BRAILA
Murighiol
Ocna Sibiului
Aurel Vlaicu
Gârbova
SIBIU
Cârta
Zarnesti
Bran
Paclele Mici
Minis
SZEGED
BUZAU
TIMISOARA
Navodari
CONSTANTA
RO
BUCURESTI
Jupiter
Mehadia
BEOGRAD
RO
RUSE
37km

Albania

Capital: Tirana
Government: parliamentarian republic
Official Language: Albanian
Population: 3.029.000 (2015)
Area: 28.748 Km^2

General information
Dialling code: 0355
General emergency: 112
Currency: Lek (ALL) € 1 = 136 ALL, 10 ALL = € 0,07
£1 = 158 ALL, 10 ALL = £0.06 (November 2016)
Credit cards are accepted in the main cities.

Regulations for overnight stays
Wild camping is allowed with permission from land owner/manager or local government.

Additional public holidays 2017
March 14 Summer Day
March 21 Nowruz
April 14 Good Friday
October 19 Mother Teresa Day
November 28 Independence Day
November 29 Liberation Day

Time Zone
Winter (Standard Time) GMT+1
Summer (DST) GMT+2

Tirana

Albania
page: 85-86

Barbullush 39C3

Restaurant/Camping Albania, Barbullush 4022.
GPS: n41,92386 e19,54186.

€ 12 Ch WC €3,50 included.
Location: Rural. **Surface:** grassy. 01/01-31/12.
Distance: Skodër 20km.

Berat 39D3

Berat Caravan Camping, Ura Vajgurore. **GPS**: n40,77914 e19,85848.

30 € 17 Ch WC included.
Surface: grassy. 01/01-31/12.
Distance: city centre Berat 18km on the spot on the spot.

Divjakë Plazh 39C3

Bar/Rest/Hotel Adrian Satka. **GPS**: n40,97156 e19,48036.

Fushë-Kruje 39D3

Hotel Nordpark. **GPS**: n41,47078 e19,69875.

€ 19 Ch WC included.
Remarks: Incl. access swimming pool.

Gjirokaster 35E1

Viroi, SH4. **GPS**: n40,10308 e20,12289.

2 free.
Distance: 3km on the spot.

Himarë 35E1

Camping Kranea, Livadh Beach. **GPS**: n40,10734 e19,72739.

€ 14 €2 €3.

Hudënisht 39D3

Peshku, SH3.
GPS: n40,96725 e20,64274.
€ 5-12 Ch WC included €2.
Surface: grassy. 01/01-31/12.
Distance: 100m.
Remarks: Lake Ohrid, free use of sun beds and beach chairs.

Kavajë 39C3

Camp Pa Emer, Rrakull-Karpen. **GPS**: n41,18138 e19,47750.

34 € 18 Ch WC included.
Surface: grassy/gravel. 01/04-01/11.
Distance: 1km on the spot on the spot.

Ksamil 35E1

Sunset, SH81. **GPS**: n39,77908 e20,00831.
20 € 10 Ch included.
Surface: unpaved. 01/01-31/12.
Distance: Sarandë 10km on the spot on the spot.

Leskovik 35E1

Farma Sotira, SH75, Leskovik > Erseké 15km.
GPS: n40,21477 e20,64611.

20 € 10 Ch WC included.
Location: Rural, isolated. **Surface:** grassy. 01/04-01/11.
Distance: on the spot on the spot on the spot on the spot.

Llogara 35E1

Hotel Hamiti, SH8. **GPS**: n40,21035 e19,57924.
€ 5.

Omarë 39C2

Lake Shkodra Resort, Rruga E Liqenit.
GPS: n42,13836 e19,46562.
€ 12, Jul/Aug € 14 Ch €2 WC €3,95 included.
Surface: grassy. 01/04-15/11.
Distance: Skodër 10km lake with sandy beach on the spot on the spot.
Remarks: Free use of sun beds and beach chairs, canoe and bicycle rental.

Orikum 35E1

Camping Dion. **GPS**: n40,34407 e19,48280.

AL

12 € 10 Ch WC included.
Surface: metalled. 01/01-31/12.
Distance: 500m on the spot on the spot.
Remarks: S 148.

S Radhimë 35E1

Rezidenca Cekodhima, SH8. **GPS**: n40,37706 e19,47872.

20 € 20 Ch WC .
Surface: gravel. 01/01-31/12.
Distance: pebbled beach on the spot.

S Sarandë 35E1

Hotel Mediterrane, Rruga Skënderbeu. **GPS**: n39,87041 e20,01854.

10 € 15 included WC .
Location: Urban. **Surface:** asphalted. 01/01-31/12.
Distance: city centre 1km 600m on the spot.

S Tirana 39D3

Hotel Baron, Rruga e Elbasanit. **GPS**: n41,29947 e19,85012.

6 € 15 Ch WC included.
Surface: metalled.
Distance: centre 4km on the spot.

AL

Austria

Capital: Vienna
Government: federal, parliamentarian, democratic republic
Official Language: German
Population: 8,665,000 (2015)
Area: 83,857 km^2

General information
Dialling code: 0043
General emergency: 112
Currency: Euro

Regulations for overnight stays
In general overnight parking is allowed, except: Tyrol, Vienna, nature reserves and in areas where locally prohibited. No "camping" activities allowed and disposal wastewater must be at official places.

Additional public holidays 2017
January 6 Epiphany
May 1 Labor Day
June 15 Corpus Christi
August 15 Assumption of the Virgin Mary
October 26 National Holiday
November 1 All Saints' Day
December 8 Immaculate Conception

Time Zone
Winter (Standard Time) GMT+1
Summer (DST) GMT+2

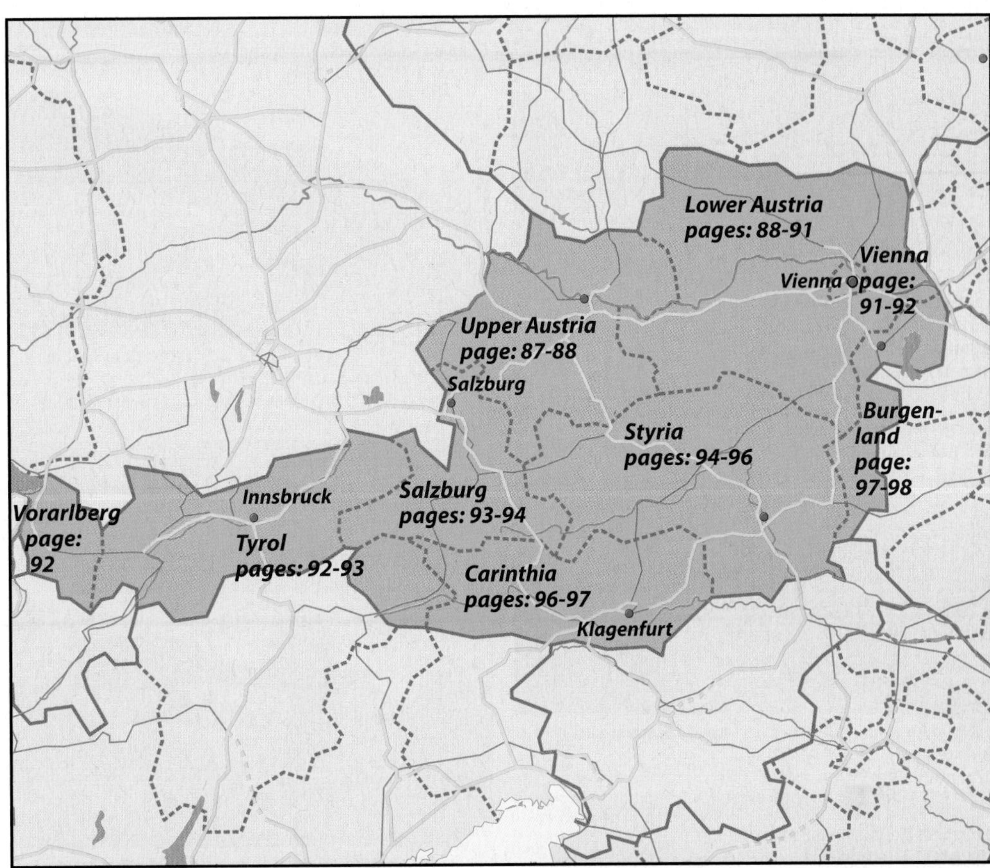

Upper Austria

S Ebensee 20H1

Am Traunsee, Trauneck. **GPS**: n47,81283 e13,77730.

5 € 12/24h €0,50/50liter Ch (12x)€3 WC.
Location: Rural, simple, quiet. **Surface:** asphalted.
Distance: 500m on the spot 300m.
Remarks: At lake.

S Ebensee 20H1

Freizeitanlage Rindbach, Strandbadstraße.
GPS: n47,80934 e13,79002.

30 € 12 €1/25liter (4x)€1/h. **Location:** Rural, simple, quiet. **Surface:** grassy. 01/04-31/10.
Distance: 1,4km.
Remarks: At lake.

Eferding 17H3

Brandstatt, Pupping. **GPS**: n48,33503 e14,02698.
.
Remarks: On the Danube river.

Gallneukirchen 37A3

Freizeitcentrum, Veitsdorfer Weg 10. **GPS**: n48,36045 e14,40797.

10 free.
Location: Rural, simple. **Surface:** asphalted. 01/01-31/12.
Distance: 1km on the spot 1km.

Gmünden 20H1

Parkplatz des Toscanapark, Scharnsteiner Straße.
GPS: n47,91186 e13,78708.
5 free. **Surface:** asphalted. 01/01-31/12.
Distance: 1km 200m.

S Gosau 20H2

Gasthaus Echo, Gosau 614. **GPS**: n47,55171 e13,51345.
10 free €5 . **Location:** Rural, simple, isolated, quiet.
Surface: asphalted. 01/05-31/10.
Distance: 400m on the spot.

S Gosau 20H2

Hotel Gosauschmied, Gosau 57. **GPS**: n47,55072 e13,51607.
10 € 10 Ch on demand.
Surface: asphalted. 01/01-31/12.
Distance: 3km on the spot 3km on the spot 500m on the spot.

S Haslach 17H3

Gasthof Furtmühle, Schwackerreith 20, St.Oswald.
GPS: n48,60497 e14,01967.
15 free against payment. 01/01-31/12 Tue.
Distance: on the spot.

S Hinterstoder 37A3

Gasthof Baumschlagerreith. **GPS**: n47,64525 e14,09632.
10 € 8, guests free .
Location: Rural, simple, isolated, quiet. 01/01-31/12.
Distance: 9km on the spot.

Kefermarkt 37A3

Schloßbrauerei Weinberg, Weinberg 2. **GPS**: n48,44856 e14,53957.

5 guests free. **Location:** Rural, simple. **Surface:** asphalted.
01/01-31/12.
Distance: 800m on the spot.

S Königswiesen 37A3

Freibad, Badgasse 4. **GPS**: n48,40450 e14,84080.

3 € 2 + € 2/pp Ch WC free. **Location:** Rural, simple, quiet.
Surface: asphalted. 01/04-31/10.
Distance: 500m 10m Freibadbuffet 300m.
Remarks: Parking swimming pool.

Kremsmünster 37A3

Parkplatz Benediktiner Stift, Fuxjägerstraße.
GPS: n48,05407 e14,12607.
.
Distance: 500m 500m.

S Kronstorf 37A3

Stellplatz Metzenhof, Dörfling 2. **GPS**: n48,12828 e14,43432.

AT

10 € 18, 2 pers.incl WC included.
Location: Rural, comfortable, isolated, quiet.
Surface: gravel/metalled. 01/03-30/11.
Distance: on the spot on the spot.
Remarks: At golf court.

Mondsee 20H1

Geflügelhof Schweighofer, Schwand 10.
GPS: n47,88186 e13,31105.

5 € 13, 2 pers.incl Ch included. **Location:** Rural, quiet.
Surface: grassy. 01/01-31/12.
Distance: 3km 2km 3km.

Naarn 37A3

Bauernhof Mostschenke, Dirnwagram 1.
GPS: n48,21750 e14,61972.

5 € 10 Ch €2/day WC included.
Location: Rural, simple. **Surface:** asphalted.
Distance: 2km on the spot 2km.
Remarks: Arrival <19.30h, max. 4 days.

Naarn 37A3

Gasthof zur Post, Marktplatz 1. **GPS**: n48,22579 e14,60662.

5 € 6, 2 pers.incl.
Location: Simple, noisy. **Surface:** asphalted. Thu.
Distance: on the spot on the spot.

Neumarkt 37A3

Stellplatz Einfach Ausspannen, Seisenbachweg 12.
GPS: n48,43457 e14,47739.
2 € 10 WC included. **Location:** Rural, isolated, quiet.
Surface: grassy.
Distance: 1km on the spot 1km.

Ranshofen 17G3

Vereinslokal, Scheuhub 2. **GPS**: n48,23228 e12,99893.
10 free Ch. **Surface:** grassy. 01/01-31/12.
Distance: 2km on the spot 2km 2km.

Sankt Pankraz 37A3

Parkplatz Klauser Stausee, Klaus an der Pyhmbahn.
GPS: n47,82733 e14,15703.
.
Remarks: Along river.

Scharnstein 20H1

Camping Schatzlmühle, Viechtwang 1A.
GPS: n47,91578 e13,97353.

5 € 10 Ch included €3 €2 €2. **Location:** Rural, quiet.
Surface: grassy/gravel. 01/05-31/10.
Distance: 2km on the spot 600m on the spot on the spot on the spot.

Schlierbach 37A3

Bauernhof Eisterer, Föhrenweg 7. **GPS**: n47,95083 e14,08639.
3 € 6 + € 4/pp Ch €2,50/day . **Location:** Rural, comfortable. **Surface:** grassy.

Straß im Attergau 20H1

Landgasthof Rosslwirt, Halt 4. **GPS**: n47,90488 e13,44677.

6 guests free free. **Location:** Rural, simple, quiet.
Surface: grassy/gravel. 01/01-31/12.
Distance: on the spot.

Suben 17H3

Hotel Suben, Etzelshofen 125. **GPS**: n48,40149 e13,42582.
40 € 10 Ch included. **Location:** Motorway, simple, noisy.
01/01-31/12.
Distance: on the spot on the spot.

Vöcklabruck 20H1

Hallenbad am Freizeitgelände, Hausruckstraße.
GPS: n48,01107 e13,65299.

6 free Ch. **Location:** Rural, simple. **Surface:** metalled.
01/01-31/12.
Distance: 500m.
Remarks: Max. 48h.

Waldhausen im Strudengau 37A3

Badesee, Schloßberg. **GPS**: n48,28420 e14,95883.

6 voluntary contribution €1/10minutes Ch €1/8h.
Location: Rural, isolated, quiet. **Surface:** gravel.
01/01-31/12.
Distance: 2km on the spot on the spot 2km 2km.

Lower Austria

Aggsbach Dorf 37A3

Gasthof Pension zur Kartause, Aggsbach-Dorf 38.
GPS: n48,29638 e15,42604.
10 free . **Location:** Rural, isolated, quiet. **Surface:** grassy.
01/01-31/12.
Distance: on the spot.

Aggsbach Markt 37A3

Badestrand. **GPS**: n48,29814 e15,40497.

26 € 11,50 Ch €1/24h WC . **Location:** Comfortable.
Surface: gravel. 01/03-31/10.
Distance: 500m 50m Donaustüberl 500m.
Remarks: On the Danube river.

Altenmarkt an der Triesting 37A3

Gasthof Zum Kleinen Semmering, Hafnerberg 15.
GPS: n48,01762 e16,01383.

10 free WC. **Location:** Rural, simple.
Surface: gravel.
Distance: 2,3km on the spot 2,3km.

Arbesbach 37A3

Am Ganser. **GPS**: n48,49123 e14,95683.

15 € 5 Ch included. **Location:** Rural, simple.
Surface: gravel. 01/01-31/12.
Distance: 500m on the spot 500m 500m 500m.
Remarks: Check in at town hall.

Ardagger 37A3

Stellplatz am Donauwellenpark, Markt 39.
GPS: n48,17981 e14,82579.

10 free €2 Ch (6x)€1/kWh. **Location:** Rural, simple.
01/01-31/12.
Distance: 100m 7km 100m 100m on the spot.
Remarks: At Danube cycle route.

Armschlag 37A3

Mohndorf. **GPS**: n48,45222 e15,21944.

AT

5 €7, 2 pers.incl. Ch included. **Location:** Rural, simple. **Surface:** asphalted. 01/01-31/12.
Distance: on the spot on the spot 2km Mohnstrudelwandernetz.

S Aschbach Markt 37A3

Fam. Edtbauer, Auckental 1 u. 2. **GPS**: n48,10682 e14,69988.

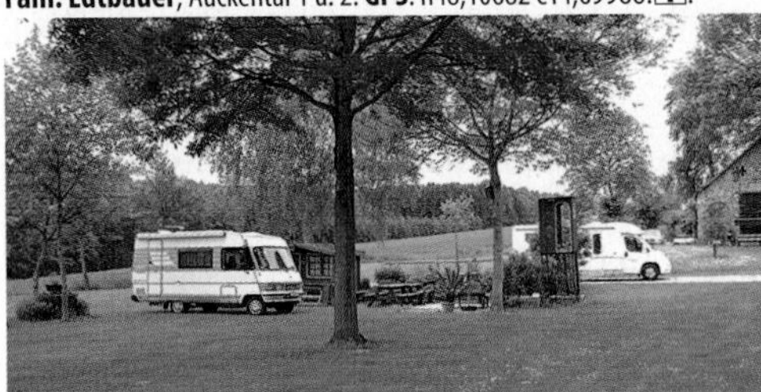

8 free €2. **Location:** Rural, quiet. 15/04-30/10.
Distance: 7km 3km 7km.

Bad Deutsch-Altenburg 37B3

Parking Donaupromenade, Donaupromenade.
GPS: n48,14110 e16,90090.

. **Location:** Rural, simple. **Surface:** asphalted.
01/01-31/12.
Distance: 500m on the spot 1km 1km.

Bad Großpertholz 37A3

Busparkplatz Naturpark Nordwald, Scheiben.
GPS: n48,61765 e14,81548.
. **Location:** Rural. **Surface:** asphalted.

Bernhardsthal 37B2

Am Bernhardsthaler Teich, Schulstrasse.
GPS: n48,69402 e16,87481.

5 free. **Surface:** grassy.
01/01-31/12.
Distance: 500m on the spot on the spot weekends only.

S Eggenburg 37A3

Stellplatz an der Stadtmauer, Erzherzog-Karl-Ring 19.
GPS: n48,64513 e15,81745.

8 €4 €1/10minutes Ch (8x)€1/8h. **Location:** Rural, comfortable. **Surface:** gravel. 01/04-31/10.
Distance: on the spot 4km creek 300m 200m 500m on the spot 300m.

S Erlauf 37A3

Plaikawirt, Plaika 1, Bergland. **GPS**: n48,16866 e15,16436.

10 guests free €2/100liter €2/24h. **Location:** Rural, quiet.
Surface: asphalted. Mo.
Distance: 2km on the spot on the spot.

Gaming 37A3

Kartause. **GPS**: n47,92463 e15,08223.
.

S Gars am Kamp 37A3

Sport- und Erlebnisbad, Gföhler Strasse/Strandgasse, Thunau am Kamp. **GPS**: n48,59300 e15,65723.

5 €16 Ch WC included. **Location:** Comfortable.
01/01-31/12.
Distance: 200m on the spot 200m.
Remarks: At swimming pool.

Göllersdorf 37A3

Parkplatz Barbara Heuriger, Spitalgasse 467.
GPS: n48,49667 e16,11171.

10 free. **Location:** Rural, simple. **Surface:** gravel.
Distance: 500m 1km on the spot 1km.

Gumpoldskirchen 37A3

Brunngasse. **GPS**: n48,04212 e16,27820.

10 free. **Location:** Rural, simple. **Surface:** asphalted.
Distance: 500m 500m.
Remarks: Max. 8M.

S Gumpoldskirchen 37A3

Neustiftgasse. **GPS**: n48,04423 e16,27552.
Ch.

Hainburg/Donau 37B3

Parkplatz an der Donau, Donaulande 4.
GPS: n48,15110 e16,94440.

. **Location:** Rural, simple. **Surface:** asphalted.
01/01-31/12.
Distance: 500m on the spot on the spot 500m.

Hohenau/March 37B2

Freizeitzentrum, Kindergartenstrasse. **GPS**: n48,61095 e16,91010.

free. **Surface:** asphalted. 01/01-31/12.
Remarks: Swimming pool 200m.

S Hollenstein/Ybbs 37A3

Naturpark Hollenstein, Wenten 1. **GPS**: n47,76884 e14,77270.
3 €5 Ch. **Location:** Rural, isolated, quiet.
01/01-31/12.
Distance: 4km.

S Hollenstein/Ybbs 37A3

Gasthof Staudach, Walcherbauer 5. **GPS**: n47,80703 e14,76687.
4 €14, 4 pers.incl Ch.
Distance: 200m 10m 200m on the spot.

Karlstein an der Thaya 37A2

Sieghartser Straße. **GPS**: n48,88186 e15,40442.
. **Surface:** grassy. 01/01-31/12.
Distance: 200m 200m.
Remarks: At tennis-court.

S Klosterneuburg 37A3

Euromobil Campers, Bahnhofplatz 16, Kritzendorf.
GPS: n48,33582 e16,29863.

4 free Ch. **Location:** Simple. **Surface:** asphalted.
01/01-31/12.
Distance: 12,5km 300m 500m.
Remarks: Lock-up parking, guarded.

S Laimbach am Ostrong 37A3

Bauernhof Stoiber, Wagmühle 34. **GPS**: n48,31711 e15,12565.

5 €12 Ch included. **Location:** Rural, simple.
Surface: grassy.
Distance: 300m 300m 300m.

S Langenlois 37A3

Reisemobilstellplatz Langenlois, Krumpöckallee 21.
GPS: n48,47063 e15,69782.

7 €8 + €1,50/pp €1/10minutes Ch (7x)€1/8h.
Location: Rural, simple, quiet. **Surface:** metalled.
Distance: 1,5km 1km 1km.

AT

Langschlag-Mitterschlag 37A3

Freizeitanlage Frauenwieserteich, Böhmerwald-Bundesstraße. **GPS**: n48,58038 e14,83507.

10 free.
Location: Rural, simple, isolated, quiet. **Surface:** grassy/gravel.
01/01-31/12.
Distance: 5km on the spot on the spot on the spot 5km.

Mitterbach 37A3

Biobauernhof Sepplbauer, Bergstraße 11. **GPS**: n47,83216 e15,30648.
10 € 6 €2. **Location:** Rural, isolated, quiet. **Surface:** grassy.
01/05-30/09.
Distance: 4km.

Orth/Donau 37B3

P2, Am Rosenhügel. **GPS**: n48,14523 e16,70383.

4 free. **Location:** Urban, simple. **Surface:** grasstiles.
01/01-31/12.
Distance: on the spot 3km 250m 1,2km.

Ottenschlag 37A3

Florianigasse. **GPS**: n48,42361 e15,22750.

8-10 € 5 €1/10minutes Ch €1/8h. **Location:** Rural, simple.
Surface: gravel.
Distance: 500m Gaststätte 500m.

Pernegg 37A2

Freizeitanlage Gallien, Gallien 1. **GPS**: n48,71333 e15,66139.
20 € 15 + € 5/pp Ch WC included. **Location:** Rural, comfortable.
Distance: on the spot on the spot.

Pillichsdorf 37B3

Am Tennisclub, Bahnstraße 8A. **GPS**: n48,36167 e16,53750.

8 free, use facilities € 10 Ch WC. **Location:** Simple.
01/01-31/12.
Distance: 500m, Vienna 15km 300m 500m on the spot.
Remarks: Use facilities clubhouse possible.

Plaika 37A3

Gasthaus zum Plaikawirt, Plaika 1. **GPS**: n48,16878 e15,16416.
5 free . 01/01-31/12.
Distance: 5km on the spot.

Pulkau 37A2

Rat-Cumfe Straße. **GPS**: n48,70430 e15,86637.

8 € 5 €1/10minutes Ch €1/6h. **Location:** Urban, simple.
Surface: gravel. 01/01-31/12.
Distance: 500m 300m on the spot on the spot.

Reichenau/Rax 37A3

Kaiserbrunn, Bundesstraße Höllental 27. **GPS**: n47,73480 e15,79188.

free. **Surface:** metalled.

Reichenau/Rax 37A3

Gasthof Flackl Wirt, Hinterleiten 12. **GPS**: n47,69056 e15,82778.

5 € 14 breakfest incl according consumption WC at restaurant.
Distance: 1,5km on the spot.

Retz 37A2

Parkplatz Alter Sportplatz, Jahnstraße. **GPS**: n48,75382 e15,95105.

2 € 3 €1/10minutes Ch €1/8h. **Location:** Simple.
Surface: asphalted. 01/04-31/10 last weekend of Sep.
Distance: 500m 500m.

Rossatzbach 37A3

Wohnmobilplatz Artner, Aggsteiner-Bundesstraße.
GPS: n48,38750 e15,51722.

12 € 10 Ch (12x) WC included. **Location:** Rural, comfortable. **Surface:** gravel. 01/01-31/12.
Distance: 300m on the spot 100m 1,5km.
Remarks: Vinotheek 300m.

Sankt Martin am Ybbsfelde 37A3

Gemeindeparkplatz, St. Martin. **GPS**: n48,16465 e15,01995.

free (2x) €1/8h. **Location:** Rural, simple, quiet.
Surface: grasstiles. 01/01-31/12.
Distance: on the spot.
Remarks: Parking in front of church.

Schiltern bei Langenlois 37A3

Erlebnisgärtner Kittenberger, Laabergstraße 15.
GPS: n48,51180 e15,63277.

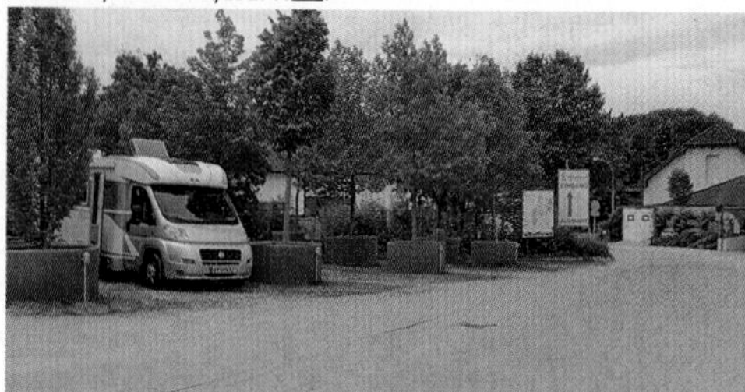

3 free. **Location:** Simple, isolated. 01/01-31/12.
Distance: 500m.

Schönberg 37A3

Freizeitzentrum, Badgasse. **GPS**: n48,52063 e15,69377.

5 € 5, first night free WC. **Location:** Rural, simple.
Surface: asphalted. 15/05-31/08.
Distance: 200m 300m 200m Kamptalradweg.
Remarks: Along river, use sanitary only during opening hours swimming pool.

Schrems 37A2

Parkplatz Stadthalle, Doktor-Karl-Renner-Straße.
GPS: n48,79167 e15,07120.

3 free. **Location:** Urban, simple, central. **Surface:** asphalted.
01/01-31/12.
Distance: on the spot on the spot 100m.

Stockerau 37A3

Hallenbad Wellness Oase, Pestalozzigasse.
GPS: n48,39385 e16,21912.

6 free €2 Ch WC sanitary in swimming pool.
Location: Comfortable. **Surface:** gravel. 01/01-31/12.
Distance: 1,5km 500m 50m.

AT

Stockerau 37A3

Alte Au, Zum Spitzgarten. **GPS**: n48,38366 e16,20394.

3 free.
Location: Urban, simple. **Surface:** asphalted. 01/01-31/12.
Distance: 1km 50m.
Remarks: At sports centre.

Weistrach 37A3

Parkplatz Sportplatz. **GPS**: n48,05475 e14,58167.

10 free. **Location:** Rural, simple. **Surface:** asphalted.
01/01-31/12.
Distance: 200m on the spot 200m.
Remarks: Near sports fields.

Weitra 37A3

Freizeitzentrum Hausschachen, Promenade.
GPS: n48,70414 e14,89343.

10 free. **Location:** Simple, quiet. **Surface:** gravel.
01/01-31/12. **Distance:** 600m 600m.
Remarks: Max. 1 night.

Wiener Neustadt 37A3

Parkplatz Stadion, Stadionstrasse. **GPS**: n47,82156 e16,25629.

20. **Location:** Urban. **Surface:** asphalted. 01/01-31/12.
Distance: 500m on the spot.

Wilfersdorf 37B3

Schloss Wilfersdorf, Parkplatz am Schloss.
GPS: n48,58600 e16,64514.

3 €4 WC. 01/01-31/12.
Distance: 100m 300m on the spot.
Remarks: Check in at Schloss, 10-16h tue/su.

Ybbs an der Donau 37A3

Donauufer, Donaulände. **GPS**: n48,17979 e15,08387.
5 free. **Surface:** metalled. 01/01-31/12.
Distance: 700m 700m.

Zwettl 37A3

Wirtshaus zur Minidampfbahn, 47, Teichhäuser bei Zwettl.
GPS: n48,66278 e15,15444.

10 €5 Ch €2,50. **Location:** Rural, simple, quiet.
Surface: grassy. 01/01-31/12.
Distance: 2km 200m on the spot 2,5km.

Vienna

Wien 37A3

Reisemobilstellplatz Wien, Perfektastraße 49-53, Vienna (Wien).
GPS: n48,13698 e16,31582.

167 €19 Ch (167x)€2/24h WC included
Location: Urban, comfortable. **Surface:** grassy/gravel.

AT

01/01-31/12.
Distance: city centre 12km 4km 30m 30m metro 150m, bus 50m 100m.

Wien 37A3

Kurpark Oberlaa, Filmteichstrasse 5, Vienna (Wien).
GPS: n48,15215 e16,40363.

free. **Location:** Urban, simple. **Surface:** grasstiles. 01/01-31/12.
Distance: centre > bus 68A Reumannplatz > tram U1 Stefansdom.
Remarks: No camping activities.

Tourist information Vienna (Wien):
Overnight parking prohibited.
Tourist-Info, Albertinaplatz 1, info.wien.at/. Imperial city, many curiosities, capital of the classic music.
Wien-Karte. Card gives 72h entrance to public transport and discounts on museums, curiosities. Available at Tourist-Info and hotels. € 24,90.
Spanische Hofreitschule, Michaelerplatz 1. Spanish Riding School, morning-training can be visited without reservation. 10-12.
Kunsthistorisches Museum, Maria Theresien-Platz. Important painting collection. Tue-Su 10-18h, Thu 10-21h. € 15.
Wurstelprater. Amusement park. 15/03-15/10 10-24h.

Vorarlberg

Dornbirn 20B3

Stellplatz Mathis, Obere Härte 27. **GPS**: n47,40577 e9,72492.
3 (7-8-10m) € 15 + tourist tax € 1/pp Ch included.
Location: Comfortable. **Surface:** grasstiles.
01/01-31/12.
Distance: on the spot 2km on the spot on the spot.

Hard 20B2

Gasthaus Sternen, Landstraße 49. **GPS**: n47,48442 e9,68698.
8 customers free . **Surface:** asphalted. Mo.
Distance: Bregenz 4,5km on the spot.

Tyrol

Achenkirch 20E2

Wohnmobilhafen Achensee, Achenkirch 17.
GPS: n47,49947 e11,70655.

10 from € 14 + € 1,50/pp tourist tax, € 1 Umwelttaxe Ch €3,50/24h WC included. **Location:** Rural, comfortable, luxurious, quiet. **Surface:** grasstiles/metalled. 01/01-31/12.
Distance: on the spot on the spot.
Remarks: Max. 1 night, dog € 4,50, extra pers € 7, electricity winter € 0,70/kWh.

Aschau im Zillertal 20F3

Reisemobilhafen Aufenfeld, Aufenfeldweg.
GPS: n47,26318 e11,90063.

10 € 17 Ch WC . **Location:** Rural. **Surface:** grassy.

01/01-31/12.
Remarks: Quick-Stop: >19h - <9h.

Biberwier 20D3

Wohnmobilhafen Arienberg, Marienbergstrasse 15.
GPS: n47,37472 e10,89223.

18 € 15, 2 pers.incl, tourist tax € 2/pp Ch €2,50/24 included. **Location:** Rural, comfortable. **Surface:** grassy/gravel.
01/01-31/12.
Distance: on the spot 2km on the spot on the spot.

Bichlbach 20D2

Almkopfbahn. **GPS**: n47,42367 e10,78116.

15 . 01/01-31/12.
Distance: 5km on the spot on the spot on the spot.
Remarks: Parking next to valley station.

Breitenwang 20D2

Seespitze. **GPS**: n47,47438 e10,78515.
€ 22,50-31 Ch WC . 01/01-31/12.

Breitenwang 20D2

Sennalpe. **GPS**: n47,48639 e10,83972.
€ 14. 15/12-15/10.

Feichten/Kaunertal 20D3

Kaunertal. **GPS**: n47,05333 e10,75056.
60 € 20,50 Ch WC . 01/05-30/09.

Galtür 20C3

Bergbahnen, Silvretta-Bundesstraße, B188, Wirl.
GPS: n46,96570 e10,16390.

€ 20, summer free Ch.
Location: Rural. **Surface:** gravel. winter.
Distance: 100m on the spot on the spot on the spot.
Remarks: Free skibus to Ischgl.

Galtür 20C3

Zeinissee, Zeinisjochstrasse. **GPS**: n46,97824 e10,12738.

€ 23-25,50 incl. 2 pers, dog € 3 €0,70/kWh WC included against payment. **Location:** Rural. **Surface:** grassy/gravel.
Whitsuntide-05/10.
Distance: Galtür 8,5km on the spot.
Remarks: Silvrettacard incl., one night stay + € 5.

Gerlos 20F3

Bauernhof Schönachhof, Schönachtal 242. **GPS**: n47,22639 e12,05476.

24 € 20, winter € 30 + tourist tax, dog € 4 Ch WC .
Location: Isolated. 01/01-31/12.

Tourist information Gerlos:
Activ Wellness. Free wellness program. 01/07-30/09.

Gries am Brenner 20E3

Gasthof Humler-Hof, Nößlach 483. **GPS**: n47,06660 e11,47187.
50 free WC free. 01/01-31/12.
Distance: Gries 5km 1km.

Hall in Tirol 20E3

Wohnmobilpark, Scheidensteinstraße 24.
GPS: n47,28444 e11,49665.

10 € 10-15 + € 1/pp + tourist tax Ch included.
Location: Urban. **Surface:** metalled. 01/01-31/12.
Distance: 400m 200m Gaststätte 300m.
Remarks: Max. 1 night.

Heiterwang 20D2

Ferienhof Sunnawirt, Mühle 4. **GPS**: n47,44951 e10,74812.

30 € 7 + tourist tax € 2/pp Ch €3 .
Surface: grassy/gravel.
Distance: 200m Heiterwanger See 1,6km 200m 200m on the spot 3km on the spot.
Remarks: Bread-service.

Ischgl 20C3

Mathoner Straße 5, Ischgl-Mathon. **GPS**: n46,98967 e10,24751.

8 € 15 + tourist tax Ch (8x) .
Location: Rural, simple. **Surface:** gravel. 01/01-31/12.
Distance: 1km 100m.
Remarks: Free skibus to Ischgl and Galtür.

Jenbach 20E2

Gasthof Rieder, Fischl 3. **GPS**: n47,40131 e11,77500.

3 free. **Location:** Rural, simple, isolated.
Surface: asphalted.
Remarks: Guests only.

S Kramsach 20F2

Camping Seehof, Moosen 42. **GPS**: n47,46206 e11,90733.

10 € 18-25 2 pers.incl, dog € 3-3,50 Ch (10x)€3/4kWh WC included €4/4 €3/day. **Location:** Rural.
Surface: asphalted. 01/01-31/12.
Distance: 3km Reintalersee on the spot on the spot free on the spot on the spot on the spot.
Remarks: 10 overnight pitches outside side + 10 special motorhome pitches on campsite (same price).

S Leutasch 20D3

Am Kreithlift, Weidach 381. **GPS**: n47,36392 e11,16657.
20 € 26, 2 pers.incl Ch WC included.
Surface: asphalted/gravel. 15/12-15/03.
Distance: 1,5km on the spot on the spot on the spot.
Remarks: Loipenplakette, drying room for skis and sauna included.

Matrei 20F3

Matreier Tauernhaus, Nähe Tauer 22. **GPS**: n47,11833 e12,49778.
20 € 5/24h. **Surface:** gravel. 01/05-30/11.
Distance: on the spot.

S Nassereith 20D3

Roßbach, Roßbach 325. **GPS**: n47,31046 e10,85524.

€ 20,50 Ch WC. **Surface:** grassy. 01/01-31/12.
Distance: 500m.

S Obsteig 20D3

Gasthof zum Lenz, Gschwent 282. **GPS**: n47,30930 e10,94482.

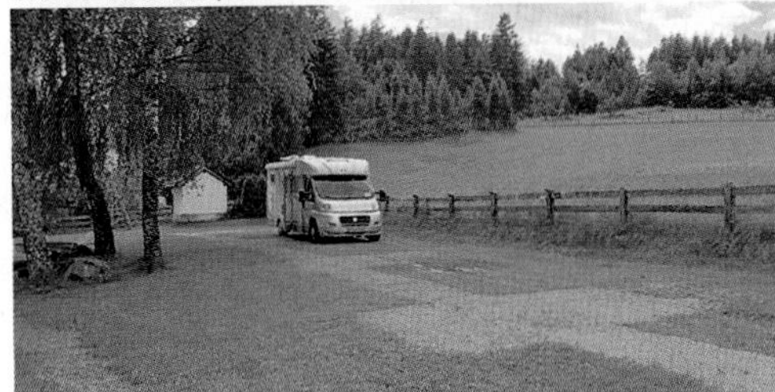

6 € 15 Ch included. **Location:** Rural, simple, isolated.
Surface: grassy/gravel. 01/01-31/12.
Distance: on the spot on the spot.

S Pettneu am Arlberg 20C3

Camping Arlberg, Pettneu am Arlberg 235. **GPS**: n47,14506 e10,33816.

54 € 15, winter € 23 + tourist tax, dog € 3 Ch included €1/2kWh. **Location:** Luxurious. **Surface:** grassy/metalled.
01/01-31/12.
Distance: 1km 250m on the spot.
Remarks: Bread-service, winter: skibus, summer: hiking bus.

S Pfunds 20D3

Wohnmobilplatz Via Claudiasee, Rauth 714.
GPS: n46,95429 e10,51171.

10 € 10 + € 1,50/pp tourist tax, dog € 1,50 €1/80liter Ch €0,60/kWh WC sanitary€3/pp from€0,50. **Location:** Rural, comfortable.
Surface: grassy/metalled.
01/01-31/12.
Distance: 2km on the spot 200m on the spot on the spot.
Remarks: Bread-service.

S Schwaz 20E2

Wohnmobilstellplatz Königfeld, Königfeldweg.
GPS: n47,34655 e11,70436.

10 € 4 €2 Ch. **Location:** Urban, simple, central.
Surface: asphalted. 01/01-31/12.
Distance: 500m 1,9km Gaststätte 50m 50m.

Tourist information Schwaz:
Schwazer Silberbergwerk. 01/05-30/09 9-17, 01/10-30/04 10-16h.

S Steinach am Brenner 20E3

Gasthaus Wolf, Brennerstraße 36. **GPS**: n47,06704 e11,48574.
5 guests free. **Surface:** asphalted.
Distance: 2km on the spot.
Remarks: At the old Brennerstraße.

Stumm 20F3

Gasthof Rißbacher Hof, Ahrnbachstraße 37.
GPS: n47,27951 e11,89347.

3 € 15 WC.
Location: Rural, simple. **Surface:** asphalted. Wed.

S Wenns/Piller 20D3

Gasthof Sonne, Piller 41. **GPS**: n47,13581 e10,69390.

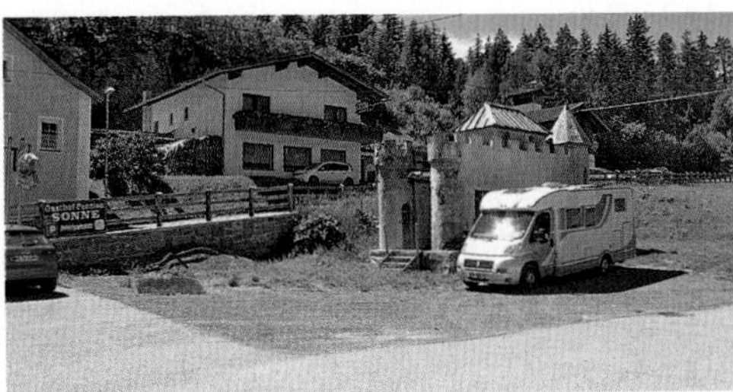

3 € 5, guests free. **Location:** Rural, simple, isolated. **Surface:** gravel.
01/01-31/12.
Distance: on the spot 50m.
Remarks: Altitude 1350m.

S Wiesing 20E2

Inntal. **GPS**: n47,40585 e11,80536.

€ 20-24,50 Ch WC. 01/01-31/12.

Salzburg

S Altenmarkt im Pongau 20H2

Stellplatz Kellerbauer, Kellerdörfl 18. **GPS**: n47,37043 e13,42903.
10 € 11 Ch (15x)€3/24h,16Amp WC €2/2 included.
Location: Comfortable, isolated, quiet. **Surface:** grassy/gravel.
01/01-31/12.
Distance: 1,2km 4km 2km 1,2km on the spot 1km.

S Golling 20G2

Wohnmobil-Park Aqua Salza, Möslstraße 199.
GPS: n47,59543 e13,17222.

15 € 9,90 + € 1/pp tourist tax €1/80liter Ch €0,50/kWh.
Location: Rural, quiet. **Surface:** asphalted. 01/01-31/12.
Distance: 500m 300m 300m 200m.
Remarks: Max. 5 days, check in on arrival.

S Hüttschlag 20H3

Bauernhof Stockham-Camping, See 5. **GPS**: n47,14775 e13,28947.
5 € 15,60, 2 pers.incl Ch €1,50 WC €1. 01/04-31/10.
Distance: 6km 150m 6km.

S Krimml 20F3

Hotel Krimmlerfälle, Wasserfallstraße 42.
GPS: n47,21827 e12,17543.

AT

10 € 20, dog € 4 Ch included (4x). **Location:** Rural, simple.
Surface: grassy/gravel. 15/05-25/10.
Distance: 500m on the spot.

Leogang 20G2

Leoganger Bergbahnen, Hütten 39. **GPS:** n47,43963 e12,72040.

50 € 8 + € 1,50/pp tourist tax Ch (50x)€2/24h WC.
Location: Rural, comfortable, quiet. **Surface:** grassy/gravel.
Distance: 3,5km on the spot on the spot.

Maria Alm 20G2

Wohnmobilstellplatz Stegerbauer, Stegen 16.
GPS: n47,39765 e12,90350.

10 € 10-12 + tourist tax € 1/pp Ch (10x)€2,50.
Surface: gravel. 01/01-31/12.
Distance: 1km on the spot 500m 1km 200m on the spot 1km on the spot.

Neukirchen 20F3

Panoramastellplatz, Scheffau 96. **GPS:** n47,23862 e12,24083.

17 € 7, guests free Ch €2 WC.
Location: Rural, isolated, quiet. **Surface:** gravel.
01/01-31/12.
Distance: 4km on the spot Tauernradweg on the spot on the spot on the spot.
Remarks: Bread-service.

Tweng 20H3

Landhotel Postgut, Tweng 2. **GPS:** n47,19058 e13,60210.

5 € 10. **Surface:** metalled. 01/01-31/12.
Distance: on the spot on the spot.

Styria

Bad Gams 38A1

Freizeitzentrums GamsBad, Bad Gams 2.
GPS: n46,86730 e15,22743.

6 € 5 Ch. **Surface:** grasstiles/metalled. 01/01-31/12.
Distance: 200m on the spot 200m 100m 200m.
Remarks: Check in at Gamsbad.

Bad Radkersburg 38B1

Camping Alt-Weindörfl, Altneudörfl 144. **GPS:** n46,69444 e15,98991.
€ 4 + € 3/pp WC included. **Surface:** gravel.
Distance: 750m on the spot 750m.

Bad Waltersdorf 37A3

Gasthof Erhardt, Am Waltersdorfberg 99.
GPS: n47,16687 e15,98921.

4 € 8, guests free. **Location:** Rural, simple. **Surface:** grasstiles.
01/01-31/12.
Distance: 1,8km 3,2km on the spot.

Bad Waltersdorf 37A3

Thermenland Camping, Campingplatzweg 316.
GPS: n47,16246 e16,02296.
10 Mondscheinplätze € 9,50/18-9h, 2 pers. incl. + tourist tax.
01/01-31/12.
Distance: 1,6km 3km Stüberl.

Deutsch Goritz 38B1

Pechmann's Alte Ölmühle, Ratschendorf 188.
GPS: n46,75072 e15,81337.
15 customers free according consumption. **Surface:** metalled.
Distance: 850m on the spot.

Deutschfeistritz 37A3

Sportclub Union. GPS: n47,20116 e15,32710.

20 € 11, 2 pers.incl Ch €2 WC included.
Surface: grassy. 01/04-01/11.
Remarks: At manege, check in on arrival, bread-service.

Deutschlandsberg 38A1

Koralmhalle, Höhe Frauentalerstraße 51.
GPS: n46,81783 e15,22248.

2 free. **Surface:** asphalted. 01/01-31/12.
Distance: 200m on the spot 100m on the spot.

Remarks: Max. 3 days.

Gaishorn am See 37A3

Sportzentrum, Sieberer Weg, B113. **GPS:** n47,48583 e14,54803.
10 € 10 + € 1,20/pp Ch (6x)€1 WC included.
Surface: gravel. 15/04-30/09.
Distance: 500m 4,6km Gaishorner See 100m 150m 500m.

Gamlitz 38B1

Wohnmobilstellplatz Gamlitz, Untere Hauptstraße 455.
GPS: n46,72028 e15,56833.

30 € 20 €1/100liter Ch €1/2kWh WC. **Location:** Rural, comfortable. **Surface:** gravel.
01/04-31/10.
Distance: 1km 5km on the spot on the spot on the spot.
Remarks: Parking at Motorikpark.

Gamlitz 38B1

Buschenschank Loar-Moar, Untere Hauptstraße 21.
GPS: n46,72196 e15,56495.

9 € 22 Ch WC included. **Location:** Rural.
Surface: grassy. 01/05-31/10.
Distance: 900m 5,5km.

Gosdorf 38B1

Hof Schönwetter, Haus 5. **GPS:** n46,72630 e15,79652.
6 € 10 . **Surface:** grassy. 01/01-31/12.
Distance: 500m 2km.

Graz 37A3

Reisemobil Stellplatz Graz, Martinhofstraße 3.
GPS: n47,02472 e15,39694.

160 € 21 Ch (160x) WC included €2/2 €2/day.
Location: Urban. **Surface:** grassy/gravel. 01/01-31/12.
Distance: on the spot 3,5km on the spot on the spot 200m 250m 200m on the spot on the spot.
Remarks: Video surveillance.

Graz 37A3

Stellplatz Wölfl, Steinfeldgasse 47. **GPS:** n47,06527 e15,42046.
5 € 12 €2/day. **Location:** Simple. **Surface:** asphalted.
01/01-31/12 Sa-Su.
Distance: 1,5km 3,7km.
Remarks: At motorhome dealer, check in during opening hours.

Tourist information Graz:
Freilichtmuseum, Stübing. Open air museum. 18/03-31/10.
Schloß Eggenberg, Eggenberger Allee 90.
01/04-31/10 Tue-Su 10-17h. € 11,50.
Schlossbergbahn, Kaiser-Franz-Josef-Kai. Mountain railway, gradient 61%.

Großlobming 37A3

Murinsel, Teichweg 1. **GPS:** n47,19326 e14,80422.
16 € 9/18-10h 2 pers.incl, 1 hour € 1 Ch included.
Surface: grassy. 01/01-31/12.
Remarks: Reservation in winter peak season.

AT

Hieflau 37A3

Gasthaus zum Harmonika Wald, Wandau 9.
GPS: n47,62255 e14,75411.
5 guests free included.
Surface: asphalted. 01/01-31/12 Wed.
Distance: 1,8km on the spot.

Jagerberg 38B1

Am Freibad. **GPS:** n46,85152 e15,74655.

6 free €0,50/60liter Ch. **Location:** Rural, simple.
Surface: asphalted/gravel.
Distance: 500m 500m 500m.

Jagerberg 38B1

Kindergarten Vorplatz, Jagerberg 98.
GPS: n46,85692 e15,74292.

15 free (1x).
Location: Rural, simple. **Surface:** gravel. 01/01-31/12.
Distance: 400m 400m 400m 400m.

Judenburg 37A3

Erlebnisbad, Fichtenhainstraße. **GPS:** n47,16407 e14,65308.

5 €5 ChWCfree. **Surface:** gravel. 01/01-31/12.
Distance: 500m 200m 200m.
Remarks: Check in at swimming pool.

Kaindorf 37A3

Buschenschank Schleiss, Obertiefenbach 42.
GPS: n47,23839 e15,84498.

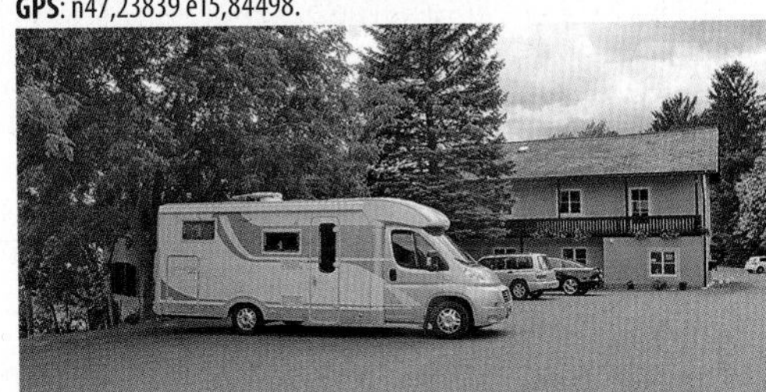

4 €6, guests free Ch.
Location: Rural, simple. **Surface:** asphalted. 01/03-15/12.
Distance: on the spot.

Leutschach 38B1

Buschenschank Krampl, Schloßberg 9. **GPS:** n46,63898 e15,45872.
10 Ch . 01/03-30/11.
Distance: 6km.

Leutschach 38B1

Ölpresse Resch, Schlossberg 89. **GPS:** n46,65170 e15,47114.
6 €13 WC included. **Location:** Rural, simple.
Surface: asphalted. 01/04-30/11.
Distance: 2km.

Leutschach 38B1

Weinbau Peter Grill, Kranach 48. **GPS:** n46,68478 e15,47191.
4 free included €3. **Surface:** grassy. Easter-01/11.
Distance: 4,5km.

Liezen 37A3

Sportzentrum, Friedau. **GPS:** n47,56500 e14,23333.

3 free €1. **Surface:** gravel. 01/01-31/12.
Distance: 1km 5,3km 300m 1km on the spot.

Mureck 38B1

Ölmühle Sixt, Oberrakitsch 115. **GPS:** n46,73818 e15,74574.
10 €10 Ch WCincluded. **Surface:** gravel.
Distance: 600m.
Remarks: Bread-service.

Mureck 38B1

Wohnmobilstellplätze Mureck, Hauptplatz 30.
GPS: n46,70489 e15,77240.

5 €12,40-19. **Location:** Urban, simple. **Surface:** metalled.
01/04-03/11.
Distance: 350m 10km.

AT

Remarks: Max. 5 days.

S **Murfeld** 38B1

Gasthof Dorfheuriger Rom Thomas, Dorfstrasse 1, Unterschwarza. **GPS**: n46,71557 e15,67624.

40 € 10 Ch WC included. **Location:** Comfortable. **Surface:** grassy. 01/01-31/12.
Distance: 200m 2,5km on the spot.
Remarks: Check in at restaurant, bread-service, wifi code: Camping01, entrance code: camp1.

S **Oberrakitsch** 38B1

Ölmühle Sixt, Oberrakitsch 115. **GPS**: n46,73863 e15,74605.

10 € 10 Ch WC included. **Location:** Rural, simple. **Surface:** gravel. 01/01-31/12.
Distance: 1km on the spot 1km 3km 4km.
Remarks: Bread-service.

S **Passail** 37A3

Almenland Stellplatz, Auen 61. **GPS**: n47,28217 e15,55711.

4 free €0,50/60liter Ch €0,50/kWh. **Location:** Rural, comfortable. **Surface:** asphalted. 01/01-31/12.
Distance: Passail 3,5km.

Pichl-Kainisch 20H2

Sportstüberl Andrea, Pichl 57. **GPS**: n47,56711 e13,85207.
3 guests free. **Surface:** metalled. 01/01-31/12 Wed.

Pölfing-Brunn 38A1

Kipferlbad, Badstraße 13. **GPS**: n46,72422 e15,29268.

10 free. **Location:** Rural, simple. **Surface:** grassy. 01/01-31/12.
Distance: 1km on the spot on the spot 1km 1km.

Riegersburg 37A3

P Seebad. **GPS**: n46,99677 e15,94107.

10 free. **Location:** Rural, simple. **Surface:** asphalted. 01/01-31/12.
Distance: 500m on the spot 500m.
Remarks: Swimming pool available.

S **Sankt Stefan im Rosental** 38B1

Schichenauerstraße 6. **GPS**: n46,90634 e15,71431.

15 free €1/100liter Ch (6x)€0,50/kWh. **Location:** Rural, comfortable. **Surface:** gravel. 01/01-31/12.
Distance: 200m 200m 200m.

S **Schwanberg** 38A1

Freibad, Badstraße. **GPS**: n46,76361 e15,20639.

4 free, 16/05-14/09 € 6 Ch included. **Surface:** gravel. 01/01-31/12.
Distance: 500m on the spot on the spot 500m 500m.

Soboth 38A1

Parkplatz Soboth-Stausee. **GPS**: n46,68142 e15,03805.

free. **Location:** Rural, simple. **Surface:** asphalted.
Distance: 5km on the spot 200m on the spot.
Remarks: Parking at artificial lake.

S **Stadl an der Mur** 38A1

Da' Bräuhauser, Steindorf 23. **GPS**: n47,08885 e13,98824.
15 € 14-18, 2 pers.incl, tourist tax € 1/pp Ch included €0,60/kWh. **Surface:** grassy. 01/01-31/12.
Distance: 500m.

Stainz 38A1

Ettendorfer Straße 3. **GPS**: n46,89377 e15,26823.

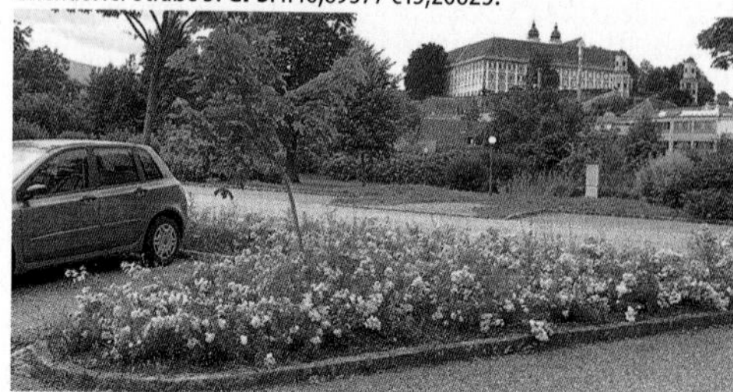

10 free. **Surface:** metalled. 01/01-31/12.
Distance: 100m 100m 100m.

Tourist information Stainz:
Region Süd-Weststeiermark, Hauptplatz 34, www.stainz.at. Das Land des Schilcher, country of the Austrian rosé wine.
Der Stainzer Flascherlzug. Narrow-gauge steam train.
01/05-31/10 Sa/Su/holidays 15h.
Ren(nt)t a Traktor, Anton Nettwall, Sommereben 95, St. Stefan ob Stainz.
With a tractor through Schilcherland. € 58 1/2 day.

S **Unterlamm** 37A3

Sieghof, Magland 44. **GPS**: n46,98152 e16,09172.

10 € 5 on demand. **Location:** Rural, simple. **Surface:** grassy/gravel. 01/01-31/12 Tue + Wed.
Distance: 4km on the spot 1,5km on the spot.

Veitsch 37A3

Marktgemeindeamt, Obere Hauptstraße 18. **GPS**: n47,57896 e15,48961.

2 free. **Surface:** asphalted. 01/01-31/12.
Distance: 300m 100m 100m 100m.

S **Vordernberg** 37A3

Hauptplatz 2. **GPS**: n47,48617 e14,99202.

6 €1/10minutes Ch €1/8h. **Surface:** gravel. 01/04-31/10.
Distance: 500m 500m 500m on the spot.

S **Vordernberg** 37A3

Traktormuseum, Böhlerstraße 8. **GPS**: n47,47364 e14,98741.
5 € 5, free with a meal.
Surface: grassy. 01/01-31/12 Restaurant: Mo-Tue.
Distance: 13km on the spot.
Remarks: Parking nearby museum.

Carinthia

Bad Sankt Leonhard im Lavanttal 38A1

Bachwegbrücke. **GPS**: n46,96037 e14,79358.

8 free. 01/01-31/12.
Remarks: Parking behind Spar-supermarket.

Bleiburg 38A1

Grabenstraße. **GPS**: n46,59095 e14,79550.

AT

4 free. **Surface:** grasstiles. 01/01-31/12.
Distance: 100m on the spot 200m.

Ferlach 38A1

Messeparkplatz Schloß Ferlach. GPS: n46,52633 e14,29750.

30 € 4/24h €1/10minutes Ch (10x)€1/10h.
Location: Urban, simple. **Surface:** metalled. 01/01-31/12.
Distance: 500m on the spot 300m 300m 300m.
Remarks: Max. 24h, no camping activities.

Glödnitz 38A1

Gasthof Hochsteiner, Laas Straß2 9. **GPS:** n46,87226 e14,11655.
20 € 3, guests free.
Surface: asphalted. 01/01-31/12 Restaurant: Mo.
Distance: on the spot.

Heiligenblut 20G3

Möllfluss-Camping, Pockhorn 30. **GPS:** n47,02371 e12,86180.
€ 16 2p incl. + tourist tax. **Surface:** asphalted.
15/06-01/09.

Hermagor 23H1

Schluga, Vellach 15. **GPS:** n46,63147 e13,39532.

6 € 14 2 pers.incl, dog € 3,10 Ch (6x)€2,72 WC included.
Surface: gravel. 01/01-31/12.
Distance: winter free shuttle to piste.
Remarks: Peak season max. 3 days, max. 7 days.

Tourist information Hermagor:
Presseggersee. Nature reserve, no motor boats allowed.

Kötschach-Mauthen 23G1

Gasthof Gailberghöhe, Gailberg 3. **GPS:** n46,71525 e12,96753.

70 € 14,50, 2 pers.incl. Ch WCincluded.
Surface: asphalted/gravel. 01/05-15/11, 15/12-15/03.
Distance: 7km on the spot 7km 2km 7km.

Ledenitzen 38A1

Ferien am Walde. GPS: n46,57000 e13,95242.
220 € 13-18 Ch WC . 01/05-01/10.

Mörtschach 20G3

Gasthaus Schwaiger, Mörtschach 35. **GPS:** n46,92287 e12,91348.

4 guests free . **Surface:** grassy.

Rosegg 38A1

Gasthof Roseggerhof, Schulweg 4. **GPS:** n46,59026 e14,02037.

30 € 10,50-12 + € 1,20/pp tourist tax included €2.
Location: Rural, simple. **Surface:** grassy.
01/04-01/11.
Distance: 8km on the spot bakery 150m.

Sachsenburg 20H3

Restaurant Auszeit, Obergottesfeld 79. **GPS:** n46,79959 e13,35137.

10 guests free.
Location: Rural, simple. **Surface:** gravel.
01/01-31/12 week after Easter, week after All Saints' Day.
Distance: 9km on the spot.

Wernberg 38A1

Landgasthof Fruhmann, Triester Straße 1.
GPS: n46,62501 e13,92933.

5 guests free. **Location:** Rural, simple. **Surface:** gravel.
01/01-31/12.
Distance: Villach 6,5km 1,2km on the spot bakery + butcher.

Zlan 20H3

Nagelerhof, Ziebl 4. **GPS:** n46,74042 e13,57707.

8 € 17,20 + € 1,50/pp tourist tax Ch €1,50 WC included.
Location: Simple. **Surface:** grassy.
01/03-31/10.
Distance: 8km.
Remarks: Not suitable for motorhomes +7m.

Burgenland

Andau 37B3

Pusztasee. GPS: n47,77426 e17,01307.
150 € 19-23 Ch . 15/04-15/10.

Bad Tatzmannsdorf 37A3

Thermencamping, Am Campingplatz 1, Oberschützen.
GPS: n47,33912 e16,21892.

15 € 13-20,20 + € 1,50/pp tourist tax Ch €0,52/kWh WC included . **Location:** Rural, comfortable. **Surface:** gravel.
01/01-31/12.
Distance: 1,5km 500m 450m.

Deutsch Jahrndorf 37B3

Deutsch Jahrndorf, Söldnergasse 19. **GPS:** n48,00777 e17,11073.

17 voluntary contribution Ch. **Location:** Rural, simple.
Surface: grassy. 01/04-31/10.
Distance: 500m 500m 500m.
Remarks: Max. 3 nights.

Horitschon 37B3

Weingut Duschanek, Hauptstraße 104. **GPS:** n47,59162 e16,53493.

10 € 5, guests free included €3/24h WC. **Location:** Simple.
Surface: metalled. 01/01-31/12.
Distance: 600m on the spot 600m on the spot.

Illmitz 37B3

Wohnmobilstellplatz Pustablick, Ufergasse 42.
GPS: n47,75851 e16,79606.

5 voluntary contribution €2. **Location:** Rural, simple.
Surface: grassy. 01/04-01/11.
Distance: 900m 900m bakery 500m.

Jois 37B3

Bioweingut Edelhof, Hauptplatz 6. **GPS:** n47,95922 e16,79012.

AT

3 €15 Ch included. **Location:** Rural, simple.
Surface: grassy/gravel. 01/03-31/10.
Remarks: In the courtyard of a medieval farmstead.

Moschendorf 37B3

P Weinmuseum-Kulturverein Moschendorf, Moschendorf 95.
GPS: n47,05784 e16,47713.

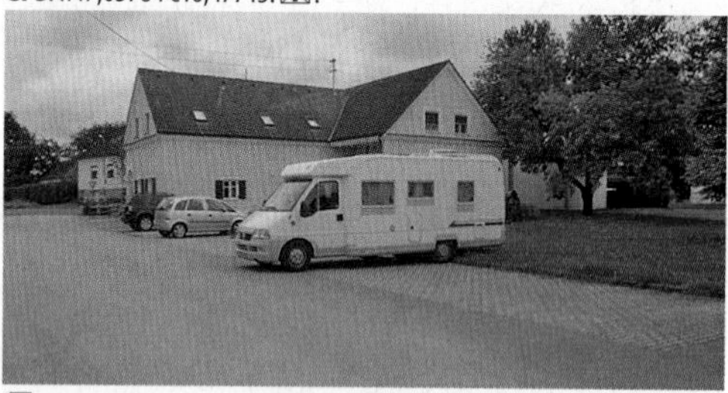

free. **Location:** Urban, simple. **Surface:** asphalted.
01/01-31/12.
Distance: on the spot.

Oslip 37B3

Kulturzentrum Gasthof Cselly Mühle, Sachsenweg 63.
GPS: n47,84119 e16,62510.

10 free. **Location:** Rural, simple, isolated. **Surface:** grassy.
01/01-31/12.
Distance: 1,2km on the spot.
Remarks: Check in on arrival.

S Podersdorf 37B3

Weingut Schaller, Frauenkirchnerstraße 20.
GPS: n47,85032 e16,83934.

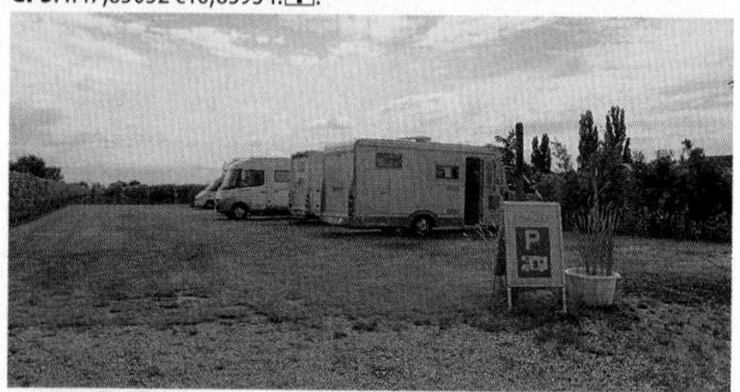

8 €8 Chincluded €2/24h. **Location:** Rural, simple.
Surface: grassy.
Distance: 300m.
Remarks: When buying wine 1 night free.

S Podersdorf 37B3

Weingut Sloboda, Alte Satz 1. **GPS:** n47,85020 e16,83091.

11 €10 Ch WCincluded. **Location:** Rural, comfortable, quiet. **Surface:** grassy. 01/03-31/10.
Distance: 500m 13,5km 500m Neusiedler See on the spot 1km.
Remarks: When buying wine 1 night free.

Bosnia and Herzegovina

Capital: Sarajevo
Government: Federation
Official Language: Bosnien, Croatien and Serbian
Population: 3,867,000 (2015)
Area: 51,209 Km²

General information
Dialling code: 0387
General emergency: 112
Currency: convertible Mark (BAM) also the Euro is accepted as currency.
Credit cards are accepted in the main cities.

Regulations for overnight stays
Wild camping is not allowed.

Additional public holidays 2017
March 1 Independence Day
May 1 Labour Day
May 9 Victory Day
November 25 Statehood Day

Time Zone
Winter (Standard Time) GMT+1
Summer (DST) GMT+2

Banja Luka 38C2
Kamp Olimp. GPS: n44,71114 e17,16642.
10 € 15 Ch included. **Surface:** grassy. 01/01-31/12.
Distance: 8km on the spot on the spot.

Bihać 38B2
Kamp Orljani. GPS: n44,80145 e15,90643.
120 € 18,50 Ch included .
Surface: grassy/gravel. 01/05-01/11.
Distance: 3,5km on the spot 100m.

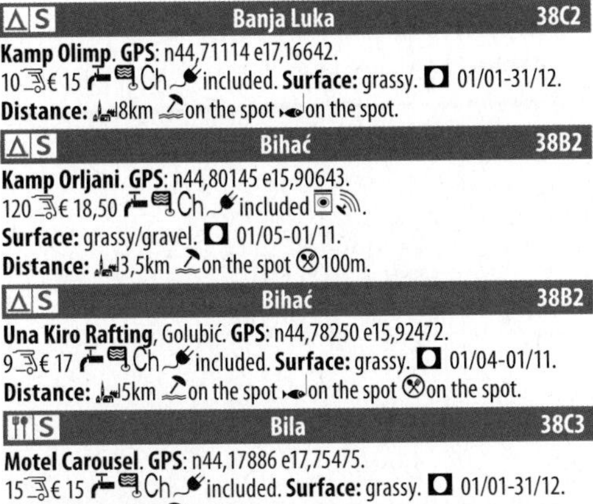

Bihać 38B2
Una Kiro Rafting, Golubić. **GPS:** n44,78250 e15,92472.
9 € 17 Ch included. **Surface:** grassy. 01/04-01/11.
Distance: 5km on the spot on the spot on the spot.

Bila 38C3
Motel Carousel. GPS: n44,17886 e17,75475.
15 € 15 Ch included. **Surface:** grassy. 01/01-31/12.
Distance: 1km on the spot.

Blagaj 39B2
Autocam Blagaj. GPS: n43,25682 e17,87936.
25 € 20 Ch included. **Surface:** grassy.
01/04-01/10.
Distance: Mostar 12km on the spot.

Blagaj 39B2
Mail Wimbledon. GPS: n43,26317 e17,87799.
60 € 18 Ch €3 included. **Surface:** grassy/gravel.
01/01-31/12.
Distance: Mostar 10km 150m 100m.

Blagaj 39B2
River Camp Aganovac. GPS: n43,25724 e17,88774.
8 € 20 Ch included. **Surface:** grassy/sand.
01/01-31/12.
Distance: on the spot on the spot 200m 150m.

Bosanska Krupa 38B2
Una Camping. GPS: n44,91484 e16,15696.
€ 16 Ch included. **Surface:** grassy. 01/05-01/10.
Distance: on the spot on the spot.

Buna 39B2
River Camp Half Island. GPS: n43,24166 e17,83861.

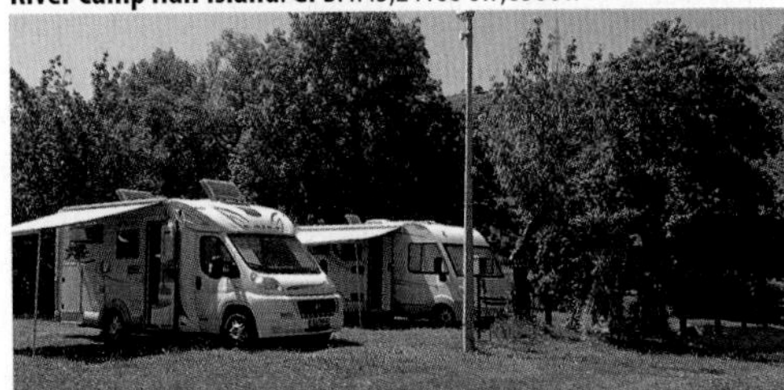

20 € 17 Ch included.
Surface: grassy. 01/04-01/10.
Distance: on the spot on the spot 500m 500m.
Remarks: Only cash payment.

Foča 39C1
Auto Camp Drina. GPS: n43,52948 e18,78254.
15 € 17 Ch included. **Surface:** grassy.
01/05-15/09.
Distance: 3km on the spot on the spot on the spot.

Gradačac 38D2
Hipodrom Vuković. GPS: n44,91860 e18,41893.
€ 20 Ch included.
Location: Rural. **Surface:** grassy/sand. 01/04-01/11.
Distance: on the spot.

Jajec 38C3
Autocamp Plivsko Jezero. GPS: n44,35103 e17,22682.

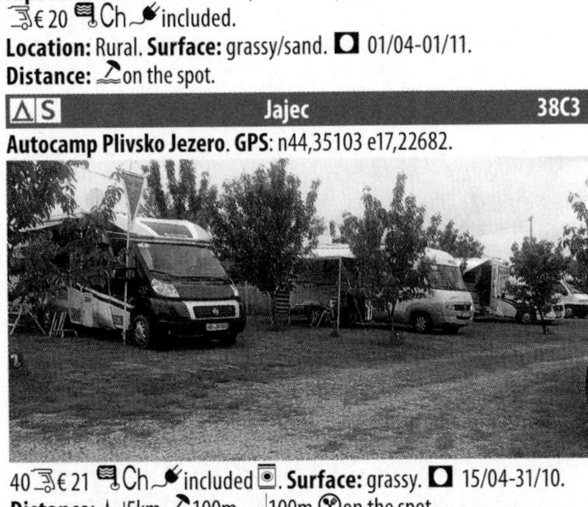

40 € 21 Ch included . **Surface:** grassy. 15/04-31/10.
Distance: 5km 100m 100m on the spot.

Krupa na Vrbasu 38C2
Camp Krupa. GPS: n44,61616 e17,14837.
80 € 12 Ch included. **Surface:** grassy. 01/05-01/10.
Distance: on the spot on the spot 200m.

Kulen Vakuf 38B3
RC Discover Bihac. GPS: n44,56909 e16,08338.

25 € 5 + € 5/pp Ch WC included.
Surface: grassy/gravel. 01/04-30/10.
Distance: on the spot on the spot on the spot.

Medugorje 39B2
Camp Zemo. GPS: n43,19432 e17,67612.
45 € 10 Ch included. **Surface:** gravel. 01/01-31/12.
Distance: 100m 100m.

Sarajevo 39B1
Oaza. GPS: n43,82799 e18,29659.

350 € 20,90 Chincluded €2,60.
Surface: grassy. 01/01-31/12.
Distance: 10km 100m 800m.

Šćit 39B1
Konoba Gaj. GPS: n43,80230 e17,52560.
5 € 10 Ch included.
Location: Rural. 01/01-31/12.
Distance: on the spot on the spot on the spot.

BA

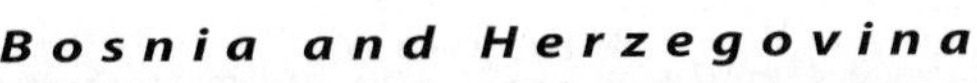

Belgium

Capital: Brussels
Government: Constitutional monarchy
Official Language: Dutch/Flemish, French and German
Population: 11,324,000 (2015)
Area: 30,518 km²

General information
Dialling code: 0032
General emergency: 112
Currency: Euro

Regulations for overnight stays
Wild camping is forbidden.

Additional public holidays 2017
May 1 Labour Day
July 11 Feast Flemish Community
July 21 National Day
August 15 Assumption Day
September 27 Feast of the Walloon Region
November 1 All Saints' Day
November 11 Armistice Day 1918

Time Zone
Winter (Standard Time) GMT+1
Summer (DST) GMT+2

Antwerp pages: 103-105
Antwerp
East Flanders pages: 102-103
West Flanders pages: 100-102
Limburg pages: 106-108
Flemish Brabant pages: 105-106
Brussels pages: 108
Brussels
Hainaut pages: 109-111
Liège pages: 108-109
Namur pages: 111
Luxembourg pages: 111-112

BE

West Flanders

Aartrijke 11A1
Sint-Aarnoutstraat. **GPS**: n51,11341 e3,08983.

3 free. **Surface:** asphalted. 01/01-31/12.
Distance: 400m 80m 50m.

Beernem 11A1
Kanaaloever Beernem, Oude Vaartstraat.
GPS: n51,13482 e3,33427.

6 € 10/24h Ch (4x) WC included, sanitary at harbour building.
Location: Rural. **Surface:** metalled. 01/01-31/12.
Distance: 1,9km.
Remarks: Max. 72h, only exact change.

Blankenberge 11A1
Kampeerautoterrein De Wielen, Zeebruggelaan 135.
GPS: n51,31106 e3,15154.
26 € 20-23 Ch included €0,50 €4/3.
Surface: grassy/metalled. 01/01-31/12.
Distance: 2km 2km.

Tourist information Blankenberge:
Dienst Toerisme, Koning Leopold III-plein. Lively bathing resort.
Sea Life Centre, Koning Albert I Laan 116. Underwaterworld. 10-18h.
Serpentarium, Zeedijk 147. World of the reptiles. Easter-Oct 10-18h, 01/07-31/08 10-21h.

Brugge 11A1
Bargeweg. **GPS**: n51,19633 e3,22544.

59 € 15, € 22,50 01/04-30/09 €0,50 Ch included.
Location: Urban, simple, central. **Surface:** metalled. 01/01-31/12.
Distance: within walking distance on the spot.
Remarks: Max 3,5t, monitored parking.

Tourist information Brugge:
Brugge City Card gives for free entrance on among other things 27 museums, boat trips and many discounts on purchases. € 47.
Toerisme Brugge, 't Zand 34, www.brugge.be. City with medieval character, hiking itinerary available at Tourist office.
Brouwerij Halve Maan, Walplein 26. Town brewery. 11-16u. € 8,50.
Lamme Goedzak, Noorweegsekaai 31. Boat excursion from Bruges to Damme with the 'Lamme Goedzak', departure Noorweegse Kaai. 01/04-30/09 10-16.
Diamantmuseum, Katelijnestraat 43. Diamond museum. 10.30-17.30h.
Boudewijn Seapark, Alfons De Baeckerstraat 12, Sint-Michiels. Attractions park with dolphinarium, seal island etc., in winter large skating rink covered. 01/07-31/08 10-18h.

Diksmuide 13D2
't Nesthof, Zijdelingstraat 2a. **GPS**: n51,07178 e2,86422.

14 € 9/night Ch €2.
Location: Rural, isolated, quiet. **Surface:** grassy. 01/04-01/10.
Distance: 5km.
Remarks: Bread-service.

Gistel 11A1
Sportstraat. **GPS**: n51,16112 e2,96495.

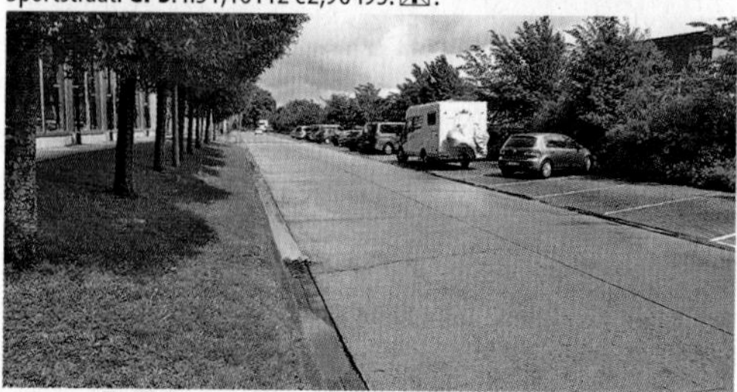

2 free Ch free. **Surface:** metalled.
Distance: 1km 3,3km on the spot on the spot.
Remarks: Parking behind swimming pool, key service at swimming pool, many walking and bicycle area.

Harelbeke 11A2

Kampeerautoterrein De Dageraad, Stasegemsesteenweg 21.
GPS: n50,84396 e3,31057.

8 € 5/24h Ch included WC €1,25 free.
Surface: metalled. 01/01-31/12.
Distance: 1,6km 4,5km 700m 100m.
Remarks: Parking next to midget golf, service during opening hours: 8-20h.

Ieper 11A2

Kampeerautoterrein Zillebekevijver, Zillebekevijverdreef.
GPS: n50,83578 e2,90504.

17 € 8/24h €1/100liter Ch included.
Location: Rural, comfortable. **Surface:** grasstiles/metalled.
01/01-31/12.
Distance: 2,5km 500m 1,5km 1km on the spot on the spot.
Remarks: Max. 48h.

Knokke-Heist 11A1

Holiday, Natiënlaan 72. **GPS**: n51,33612 e3,28866.
10 € 16-23 Ch WC . **Surface:** metalled. 01/01-31/12.
Distance: 1km.

Kortemark 11A1

Sporthal Kortemark, Ichtegemstraat 2a. **GPS**: n51,03201 e3,04168.

2 free €2 €2 Ch. **Surface:** metalled. 01/01-31/12.
Distance: 500m on the spot.
Remarks: Max. 48h.

Kortrijk 11A2

Kampeerautoterrein Broeltorens, Damkaai.
GPS: n50,83120 e3,26818.

8 € 10/24h Ch included. **Location:** Urban.
Surface: metalled. 01/01-31/12.
Distance: centre 400m 100m.

Tourist information Kortrijk:
Dienst Toerisme, Begijnhofpark, www.kortrijk.be. Historical little town with Beguine convent.

Langemark- Poelkappele 11A1

Boezingestraat 51a. **GPS**: n50,90944 e2,91763.

8 € 12/24h Ch (4x)included €1. **Location:** Urban, simple. **Surface:** grasstiles. 01/01-31/12.
Distance: on the spot on the spot.
Remarks: Max. 72h, check in at reception sports centre.

Lichtervelde 11A1

O.C. De Schouw, Twee Lindenstraat. **GPS**: n51,02389 e3,13493.
2 free. **Surface:** metalled. 01/01-31/12.
Distance: 600m 600m 300m on the spot on the spot.
Remarks: Max. 48h.

Mesen 13D2

Kerkstraat. **GPS**: n50,76391 e2,89825.

3 free. **Surface:** metalled. 01/01-31/12.
Distance: on the spot frituur 200m 100m.
Remarks: In front of church, max. 24h.

Middelkerke 13D1

Camperpark Poldervallei, Westendelaan 178.
GPS: n51,16684 e2,78246.
16 € 15-22 Ch included. **Surface:** asphalted.
01/01-31/12.
Remarks: Nearby camp site.

Nieuwpoort 13D1

De Zwerver, Brugsesteenweg 29, N367. **GPS**: n51,12988 e2,76576.

28 € 0,50/h €0,50/50liter Ch included,10Amp WC €4.
Surface: grassy. 01/01-31/12.
Distance: within walking distance 3,3km.

Oudenburg 11A1

Carpool, Stationsstraat. **GPS**: n51,19387 e3,00567.

free €2 €2 Ch. **Surface:** metalled.
Distance: 800m.
Remarks: P service max. 30 min.

Tourist information Oudenburg:
Wed-afternoon.

Poperinge 13D2

Oudstrijdersplein. **GPS**: n50,85333 e2,72332.

. Fri.
Distance: 500m 50m.

Roeselare 11A1

O.L. Vrouwenmarkt. **GPS**: n50,94786 e3,13450.

1 free. **Surface:** metalled. 18-9h, 01/01-31/12h.
Distance: 200m on the spot.
Remarks: Max. 1 night.

Roeselare 11A1

Trakelweg. **GPS**: n50,94438 e3,13320.

10 free. **Location:** Urban. **Surface:** asphalted. 01/01-31/12.
Distance: 1km on the spot on the spot.
Remarks: No camping activities.

Sint-Eloois-Vijve 11A1

Kampeerautoterrein Leiekamper, Leiesas 15.
GPS: n50,90879 e3,40468.

8 € 5 €1/100liter included,16Amp. 01/01-31/12.
Distance: 400m 400m 1km on the spot on the spot.
Remarks: Max. 72h.

Veurne 13D2

Kaaiplaats/Lindendreef. **GPS**: n51,07052 e2,66484.

6 free WC €0,50 €1,50,sanitary at harbour building.
Surface: metalled.
Distance: on the spot 2km.
Remarks: Max. 6,5m.

Wervik 11A2

Kampeerautoterrein De Balokken, De Balokken.
GPS: n50,77456 e3,03705.

BE

8 € 10/72h €1/100liter Ch included. 01/01-31/12.
Distance: 1km on the spot on the spot cafetaria 700m bakery.
Remarks: On leisure island, max. 72h.

S Westende 13D1

Camperpark Westende, Heidestraat 18. **GPS**: n51,15597 e2,76623.

30 € 18, 2 pers.incl Ch WC included. 01/01-31/12.
Distance: on the spot 1km on the spot.
Remarks: Discount longer stays, swimming pool.

S Westende 13D1

Kompas kampeerautoterrein, Strandjuttersdreef.
GPS: n51,15594 e2,76019.

35 20h € 12,50-19, 44h € 21-29 Ch included.
Surface: grasstiles/metalled. 01/01-31/12.
Distance: on the spot 1km Taverne, Frituur on the spot.

S Westende 13D1

Polervallei, Westendelaan 178. **GPS**: n51,16675 e2,78242.
15 € 16-25 Ch included. **Surface:** asphalted.
01/01-31/12.
Distance: 1km.

S Wingene 11A1

Smart - ijs, Noordakkerstraat 1a. **GPS**: n51,07377 e3,26515.

6 € 8, discount for clients Ch included.
Location: Rural. **Surface:** gravel. 01/01-31/12.
Distance: 2km 1,5km bike junction on the spot.
Remarks: Max. 72h.

Zonnebeke 11A2

Café De Dreve, Lange Dreef 16. **GPS**: n50,85410 e2,97924.

free. **Surface:** gravel. 01/01-31/12.
Distance: Zonnebeke 2,7km 3,5km A19 snacks on the spot on the spot.
Remarks: Passendalemuseum-Zonnebeke.

East Flanders

S Aalst 11B1

Zwembadlaan 2. **GPS**: n50,93825 e4,05829.

2 free Ch included1h €5.
Surface: metalled.
Distance: city centre ± 1km 3,8km on the spot on the spot on the spot.
Remarks: Only 2 plots indicated, more plots permitted.

Tourist information Aalst:
Thu-morning.

Aalter 11A1

Vaart-Zuid, Bellem. **GPS**: n51,09821 e3,49365.

25 free. **Surface:** asphalted.
Distance: Canal.

Aalter 11A1

Vaart-Noord, Bellem. **GPS**: n51,09875 e3,49468.

25 free. **Surface:** asphalted.
Distance: 600m 500m.

Aalter 11A1

Bellemdorpweg, Bellem. **GPS**: n51,09323 e3,48308.

2 free. **Surface:** asphalted.
Distance: 500m.
Remarks: At football ground.

S Aalter 11A1

Wingenestraat, Maria Aalter. **GPS**: n51,09915 e3,37141.
2 free €1 . **Surface:** metalled. 01/01-31/12.
Distance: on the spot.
Remarks: Near church.

Tourist information Aalter:
Kasteel Poeke, Kasteelstraat 26, Poeke. weekend, holidays, 01/04-31/10 Su 14-17h.
Wed-morning.

S Assenede 11B1

Kapelledreef. **GPS**: n51,23067 e3,74891.

5 € 10/72h €1/60 Ch WC free €1/1. **Location:** Urban, comfortable, quiet. **Surface:** grassy. 01/01-31/12 Service: winter.
Distance: 500m 600m on the spot on the spot.
Remarks: Behind gymnasium, max. 72h, sanitary during opening hours gymnasium.

Bazel 11B1

Sporthal De Dulpop, Beekdam 1. **GPS**: n51,14778 e4,30583.

10 free. **Location:** Rural, simple. **Surface:** asphalted.
Distance: 200m 6km 3km 500m 500m on the spot on the spot.
Remarks: Barn-museum 200m.

Berlare 11B1

Donklaan, Berlare-Overmere. **GPS**: n51,04258 e3,98293.

4 free. **Surface:** grasstiles. 01/01-31/12.
Distance: 9km Donkmeer on the spot.

S Eeklo 11A1

Jachthaven Eeklo, Nijverheidskaai. **GPS**: n51,17884 e3,54959.

12 € 10/24h €0,50/130liter Ch €5/24h,6Amp WC .
Surface: grasstiles/metalled. 01/01-31/12.
Distance: 1,5km 1,5km 800m.
Remarks: Check in at harbourmaster, use sanitary only during opening hours.

Tourist information Eeklo:
Provinciaal Domein "Het Leen", Gentsesteenweg 80. Nature reserve. 9-12h, 13-17h Mo.

Gavere 11B1

Sportdreef. **GPS**: n50,92823 e3,65810.

12 free. **Surface:** asphalted. 01/01-31/12.

Distance: on the spot.
Remarks: Behind sports complex.

S Geel 11C1

Parking Pas, Diestseweg. **GPS**: n51,15828 e4,99158.
3 €5 Ch €1/kWh.
Surface: metalled. 01/01-31/12.
Distance: city centre 200m 400m.
Remarks: Service 100m.

Geraardsbergen 11B2

Jeugherberg 't Schipken, Kampstraat 59, N460, dir Ninove.
GPS: n50,79500 e3,90412.

4 free. **Surface:** grassy. 01/01-31/12.
Distance: Geraardsbergen 3,7km on the spot.
Remarks: Max. 1 night.

Tourist information Geraardsbergen:
Provinciaal Domein "de Gavers", Onkelzelestraat 280. Recreation area; swimming, watersports, fishing, boat trips and tennis.Free entrance, payment per attraction.

Hamme 11B1

Camperplaats Hamme, Mirabrug, Hamveer.
GPS: n51,10418 e4,14246.

2 free. **Location:** Rural, simple, quiet.
Surface: metalled.
Distance: 1km 400m 500m on the spot on the spot.
Remarks: Max. 48h.

Lokeren 11B1

Veerstraat. **GPS**: n51,11013 e3,97163.

5 free. **Location:** Urban, noisy.
Surface: metalled. 01/01-31/12.
Distance: 1,5km, bakery 500m.
Remarks: Parking in front of church, max. 48h.

Lokeren 11B1

Verloren Bos, Aardeken. **GPS**: n51,10981 e3,99525.

2 free. **Location:** Rural, simple.
Surface: unpaved. 01/01-31/12.
Distance: 500m 600m.

Tourist information Lokeren:
Stationsplein. Flea market. Su 7-12h.
Molsbroek. Protected European Nature Reserve, 80ha marsh area with many birds, asphalted hiking trail.
Su 14-17h, 01/07-31/08 Wed-Su 14-17h.

S Ronse 11A2

Engelsenlaan/Boulevard des Anglais. **GPS**: n50,74447 e3,58794.

4 free free. **Surface:** asphalted.
Distance: 1km 200m on the spot. **Remarks:** Behind swimming pool, entrance code available at swimming pool.

Temse 11B1

De Zaat, Nagelheetmakerslaan1. **GPS**: n51,12466 e4,21007.

free. **Location:** Urban. **Surface:** asphalted. 01/01-31/12.
Distance: 400m 250m.
Remarks: Behind police station, temporary stopover.

S Temse 11B1

Camperbedrijf Alpha Motorhomes, Kapelanielaan 13a, N16.
GPS: n51,13699 e4,18017.

free Chfree. **Surface:** metalled.
Distance: city centre 3km.

Tourist information Temse:
Grote Markt. Fri-morning.

Vosselaar 11C1

Sportcentrum Diepvenneke, Diepvenneke 43.
GPS: n51,30142 e4,89418.
2 free. **Surface:** metalled. 01/01-31/12.
Distance: city centre 1,5km.

S Zulte 11A1

Leihoekstraat, Machelen. **GPS**: n50,96103 e3,48352.

8 €8/72h €1 Ch included. **Surface:** metalled.
01/01-31/12.
Distance: 150m 50m 150m on the spot.
Remarks: Max. 72h.

Antwerp

S Antwerpen 11C1

Vogelzang, Vogelzanglaan 7-9, Antwerp (Antwerpen).
GPS: n51,18983 e4,40074.

115 €8, Jun/Jul/Aug €10 €1 Chincluded (30x)€1/kWh.
Location: Simple.
Surface: grassy/metalled. 01/01-31/12 31/10-11/11, 04/01-19/01.
Distance: city centre 3km 1km 3km 500m 1km 3km 150m.

Tourist information Antwerp (Antwerpen):
Antwerp City Card. Antwerp City Card gives free City tour, entrance to museums, churches and many discounts on purchases. from € 27.
Toerisme Antwerpen, Grote Markt, 13, www.visitantwerpen.be. Large port city, worth seeing is the city centre.
Dageraadsplaats. Thu 8-13h.
Lijnwaadmarkt. Antiques market. Easter-Oct Sa 9-17h.
St. Andriesplaats. Tue 8-13h.
St. Jansplein. Wed, Fri 8-13h.
St. Jansvliet. Bric-a-brac market. Su 9-17h.
Theaterplein. Exotic market. Sa.
Vogelenmarkt, Theaterplein. Famous flea market. Su-morning.

S Arendonk 11D1

De Vloed. **GPS**: n51,32253 e5,08610.

free.
Distance: 400m on the spot 100m.
Remarks: Parking in front of swimming pool, max. 24h, water during openinghours swimming pool.

Beveren 11B1

De Meerminnen, Klapperstraat. **GPS**: n51,21201 e4,24377.
2 free. **Location:** Urban. **Surface:** asphalted. 01/01-31/12.

Bornem 11B1

Kasteel d'Ursel, Koningin Astridlaan. **GPS**: n51,10294 e4,27261.

5 free. **Location:** Rural.
Surface: unpaved. 01/01-31/12.
Remarks: Parking next to castle, open 8-21h.

S Brasschaat 11C1

P5b, Elshoutbaan 17. **GPS**: n51,28555 e4,50325.

15 free €1/100liter Chfree €0,50/kWh.
Location: Rural. **Surface:** metalled/sand. 01/01-31/12.
Distance: 1,7km 6km 500m 500m on the spot on the spot.
Remarks: Parking sports and recreation centre, max. 72h.

Tourist information Brasschaat:

BE

Armand Reusensplein. Mo 8-13h.

Brecht 11C1

Mudeausstraat. **GPS**: n51,34814 e4,64123.

2 free Attownhall. **Location:** Urban. **Surface:** metalled.
01/01-31/12.
Distance: on the spot 1,2km 150m 150m.
Remarks: Max. 48h.

Brecht 11C1

Schoolstraat. **GPS**: n51,34992 e4,64577.

10 free. **Surface:** grassy.
Distance: 800m 1,5km.

Essen 9C3

Kerkeneind, N133. **GPS**: n51,47086 e4,46401.

2 free Chfree. **Location:** Urban, simple, central, quiet.
Surface: metalled. 01/01-31/12.
Distance: 500m 150m on the spot on the spot.
Remarks: Max. 24h.

Grobbendonk 11C1

Vaartkom. **GPS**: n51,18954 e4,73638.

6 free €1/5minutes Ch€1 (6x)€1.
Surface: asphalted. 01/01-31/12.
Distance: 200m 3,6km frituur 200m.

Herentals 11C1

Herenhoutseweg. **GPS**: n51,16586 e4,82664.

. **Surface:** asphalted.
Distance: 1,5km 2,8km bakery 200m.
Remarks: Parking multipurpose area, next to footballstadium VC Herentals.

Herentals 11C1

Jachthaven, Noordervaart 45. **GPS**: n51,17666 e4,85694.
€ 10 €0,50/kWh. **Surface:** metalled. 01/01-31/12.
Distance: 3,9km on the spot.

Herentals 11C1

BLOSO centrum Netepark, Vorselaarsebaan. **GPS**: n51,18937 e4,82899.
15 free. **Surface:** asphalted.

Tourist information Herentals:
Augustijnenlaan. Su-morning.
Grote Markt. Fri-morning.

Herselt 11C1

Taverne Herberg Mie Maan, Diestsebaan 28.
GPS: n51,06025 e4,92897.

6 free . **Surface:** gravel. 01/01-31/12.
Distance: 3km on the spot 3km.
Remarks: Restaurant visit appreciated, intersection hiking and biking trails.

Kalmthout 11C1

Kalmthoutse Heide, Heibloemlaan. **GPS**: n51,37688 e4,44911.

2 free. **Location:** Rural, simple, isolated, quiet. **Surface:** grasstiles.
01/01-31/12.
Distance: city centre 2km 50m on the spot on the spot.
Remarks: Parking nature reserve, max. 24h.

Koningshooikt 11C1

Donderheide. **GPS**: n51,08439 e4,56541.

free. **Surface:** unpaved.
Distance: on the spot.
Remarks: In front of 'Het Fort'.

Koningshooikt 11C1

Motorhomes Konings, Sander de Vosstraat 141.
GPS: n51,08774 e4,62816.

€ 2,50 €2 €2,50. **Surface:** asphalted.
Remarks: Apply during openinghours.

Lier 11C1

Parking Mol Poort, Aarschotsesteenweg. **GPS**: n51,12525 e4,57332.

7 €1 Ch . 01/01-31/12.
Distance: 1km.

Lier 11C1

Zaat, Leuvense Poort. **GPS**: n51,13020 e4,58212.

2 free. **Surface:** metalled.
01/01-31/12.

Tourist information Lier:
Dienst Toerisme, Grote Markt 57. City with old centre worth a visit.
City walls, prison tower and Zimmertoren.
10-12h, 14-17/18h.
Grote Markt/Eikelstraat. Sa 8-13h.
Kerststallentocht. Dec.

Putte 11C1

Ixenheuvel, Heuvel. **GPS**: n51,04678 e4,62564.

2 free Chfree.
Location: Simple. **Surface:** asphalted. 01/01-31/12.
Distance: 1,5km.
Remarks: Max. 48h.

Puurs 11B1

Eeuwfeeststraat/ Kerkhofstraat. **GPS**: n51,07476 e4,28337.

2 free Chfree. **Surface:** metalled. 01/01-31/12.
Distance: 5,3km.
Remarks: Max. 48h, intersection hiking and biking trails.

Sint-Amands 11B1

Parking Noord, Emile Verhaerenstraat. **GPS**: n51,05906 e4,20206.

2 free Chfree. **Surface:** metalled. 01/01-31/12.
Distance: 200m 200m on the spot on the spot.

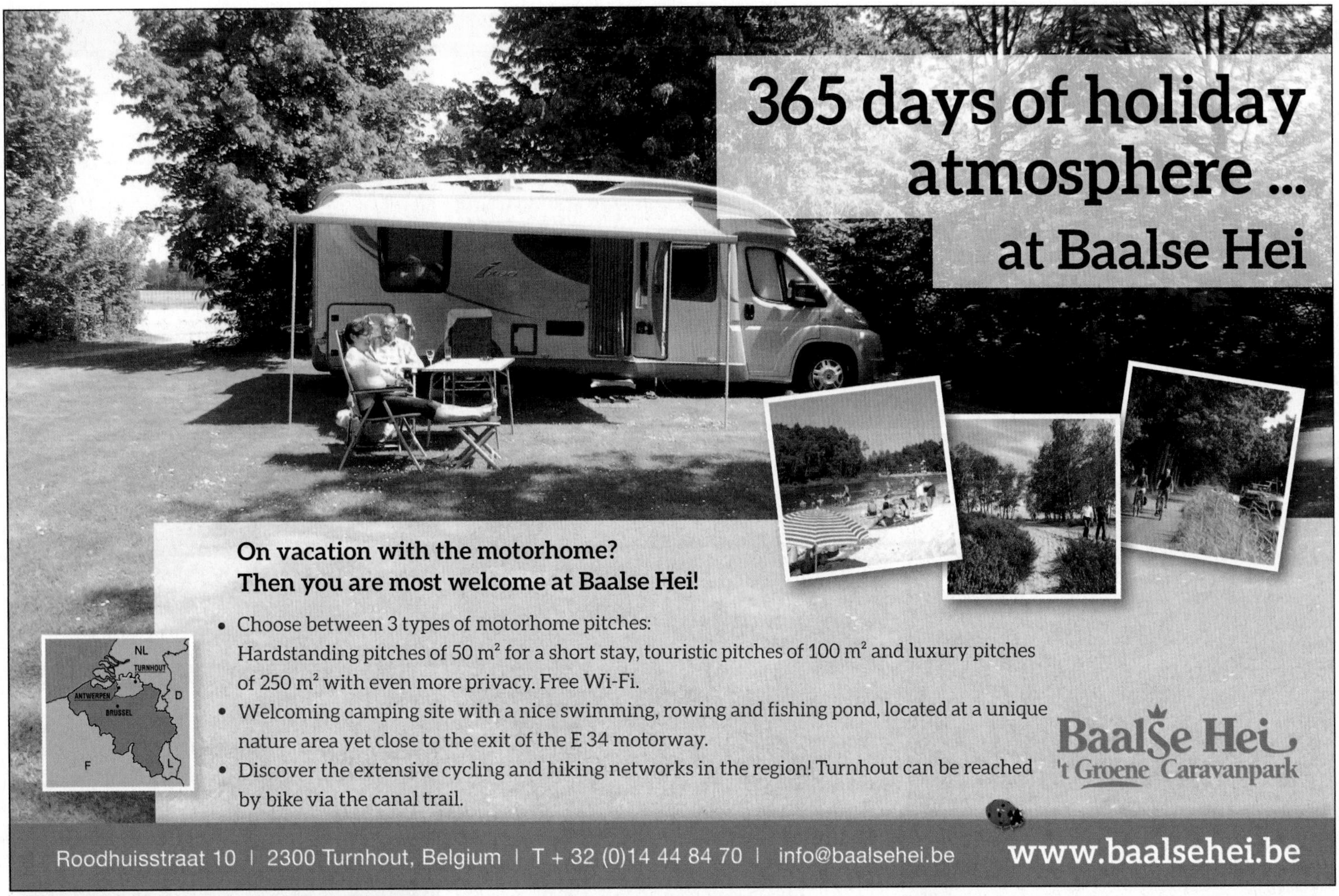

Sint-Job-in-'t-Goor 11C1

Vaartlaan. **GPS**: n51,30151 e4,56888.

2 free. **Location:** Urban. **Surface:** metalled. 01/01-31/12.
Distance: on the spot 50m 50m.
Remarks: Max. 48h.

Turnhout 11C1

Baalse Hei, Roodhuisstraat. **GPS**: n51,35385 e4,95591.
7 € 16-28 Ch €1,20 WC free. **Location:** Rural. 15/01-15/12. **Distance:** 3km on the spot on the spot on the spot. **Tourist information Turnhout:**
M Begijnhof. Beguine convent. Tue-Sa 14-17h, Su 11-17h Christmas.

Willebroek 11B1

Dijlelaan. **GPS**: n51,06028 e4,34472.

3 free €1 €1 Ch. **Surface:** metalled. 01/01-31/12.
Distance: 300m.
Remarks: Max. 2 nights.

Flemish Brabant

Aarschot 11C1

Demervallei. **GPS**: n50,98285 e4,83809.
free free.
Distance: on the spot on the spot.
Remarks: Max. 48h.

Diest 11C1

De Halve Maan, Omer Vanaudenhovelaan 48.
GPS: n50,98607 e5,06373.

4 € 15 Ch (4x)included WC. **Location:** Comfortable, quiet. **Surface:** grassy/gravel. 01/11-28/02.
Distance: 1,2km, beguine convent 350m 20m 200m 100m 100m.
Remarks: Check in at pay desk recreation centre, max. 72h.
Tourist information Diest:
Begijnhof. Beguine convent. Art studios open: sa/so afternoon and in july/aug each afternoon. Beguine convent daily, Angel convent Sa/Su 14.30-17h, church Easter-Oct Su 14-17h.

Grimbergen 11C1

K.S.C. Grimbergen, Brusselsesteenweg. **GPS**: n50,92787 e4,36610.

10 free. **Location:** Simple. **Surface:** asphalted. 01/01-31/12.
Distance: 1km 1km > Brussels.
Tourist information Grimbergen:
Gemeentelijke Dienst voor Toerisme, Prinsenstraat 22. Well-known for the Abbey beer, info at the beer museum.
Abdijkerk. Abbey-church. 10-12h, 13-17h.
Jaarmarkt. Village festival with among other things fair, cattle market. 1st weekend Sep.

Halle 11B2

Jean Laroystraat 12. **GPS**: n50,73945 e4,24203.
free. 01/01-31/12.
Distance: centre 600m.

Merchtem 11B1

Brusselsesteenweg. **GPS**: n50,95553 e4,24011.

4 free.
Surface: metalled.
Distance: 300m Good bus connection for Brussels.
Remarks: Next to cemetery and sports fields, no camping activities.

BE

Rotselaar 11C1

Recreatiedomein Sportoase Ter Heide, Vakenstraat 18.
GPS: n50,96217 e4,72288.

4 free €1/100liter Chfree €1/kWh WC.
Surface: gravel. 01/01-31/12.
Distance: 2km 100m 100m 500m 2km 200m on the spot on the spot.

Limburg

Beringen 11D1

P Koolmijnmuseum, Koolmijnlaan. **GPS**: n51,07048 e5,22097.
2 free. **Surface:** metalled. 01/01-31/12 events.
Distance: 2,3km.
Remarks: Max. 24h.

Bilzen 11D2

Parking Lanakerdij, Lanakerdij. **GPS**: n50,86985 e5,52215.

7 free €2/4minutes Ch (5x).
Surface: asphalted. 01/01-31/12.
Distance: 300m 3km 300m 300m on the spot on the spot.**Remarks:** Max. 24h.

Tourist information Bilzen:
Landcommanderij Alden Biesen, Kasteelstraat 6. Tue-Su 10-17h. €3.
Zuivelhoeve 't Wanthof. Dairy farm. Tue-Fri 10-22h, Sa-Su 9-23h.
Markt. Wed.

Bocholt 11D1

Heuvelzicht, Schipperstraat 1. **GPS**: n51,17722 e5,58500.

7 € 6,50/24h Ch WCincluded €1.
Surface: metalled.
01/01-31/12.
Distance: on the spot 50m 100m 50m 50m.
Remarks: Parking marina at Zuidwillemsvaart, max. 48h.

Bolderberg 11D1

Domein Bovy, Galgeneinde. **GPS**: n50,98690 e5,27048.

3 free €2 Ch €2/1h.
Location: Rural.
Surface: metalled.
Distance: 500m 150m 500m on the spot.

Remarks: Estate with i.e. restaurant, bar, brasserie, marked hiking trails, herb garden, petting zoo, old tools.

Bree 11D1

N721, Opitter. **GPS**: n51,11788 e5,64524.

5 free. **Surface:** metalled. 01/01-31/12.
Distance: on the spot on the spot.
Remarks: Parking next to church, in front of petrol station, max. 48h.

Tourist information Bree:
Vrijthof. Fri.
Sint-Antoniuskapel, Opitter.

Diepenbeek 11D1

Demerstrand, Stationsstraat. **GPS**: n50,91323 e5,42189.

4 free €2/100liter Ch €2/8h. **Surface:** asphalted.
01/01-31/12.
Distance: 500m 250m 1km.
Remarks: At gymnasium, video surveillance.

Dilsen-Stokkem 11D1

De Wissen, Maaspark 3. **GPS**: n51,02361 e5,74945.

3 free. **Location:** Rural. **Surface:** gravel. 01/01-31/12.
Distance: 500m on the spot on the spot Taverne Maascentrum 500m on the spot on the spot on the spot.
Remarks: Parking at tourist office De Wissen, starting point of cycle routes.

Genk 11D1

Parking Kattevennen, Kattevennen. **GPS**: n50,95728 e5,53337.

8 €5 Ch.
Surface: asphalted. 01/01-31/12.
Distance: 3km taverne on the spot on the spot on the spot.
Remarks: Max. 24h, mountainbike and hiking trails, national park Hoge Kempen.

Tourist information Genk:
Zondagsmarkten. Flea market. 01/06-31/08 9-13h.

Hamont 11D1

Michielsplein, Achel. **GPS**: n51,25421 e5,48128.

4 free. **Location:** Urban. **Surface:** metalled.
Distance: on the spot on the spot on the spot.
Remarks: At bicycle trail Limburgse Kempen, behind church of Achel, max. 24h, market Tuesday 8-13h.

Hamont 11D1

Kerkplein. **GPS**: n51,25152 e5,54612.

5 free. **Location:** Urban. **Surface:** metalled. 01/01-31/12.
Distance: on the spot 50m 50m 50m on the spot.
Remarks: Behind church, max. 24h.

Hamont 11D1

Stadpark. **GPS**: n51,25085 e5,55200.

5 free. **Location:** Rural.
Surface: grasstiles/grassy.
Distance: 200m.
Remarks: Large parking in the centre behind tennis-courts, max. 24h.

Tourist information Hamont:
VVV, Generaal Dempseylaan 1, www.hamontachel.com. Historical little town. Mo-Fri 9-12h, 13-16h, Sa 9-12h.

Hasselt 11D1

Sporthal Alverberg, Herkenrodesingel. **GPS**: n50,93871 e5,32081.

>5 free €2 Ch. **Surface:** asphalted. 01/01-31/12.
Distance: city centre 3km Carrefour on the spot.

Hasselt 11D1

Bakkerslaan. **GPS**: n50,92141 e5,32562.

3 free. **Location:** Urban, simple. **Surface:** grasstiles/grassy.
01/01-31/12.
Distance: 2km 600m 500m 500m on the spot.

BE

Hasselt 11D1

Restaurant Aan het Water, Overdemerstraat 20, Kuringen.
GPS: n50,94663 e5,30877.

8 guests free. **Surface:** grassy. 01/01-31/12 Tue, Wed, 26/09-06/10.
Distance: on the spot bakery 50m.

Hechtel/Eksel 11D1

Parking CC De Schans, Rode Kruisplein 10, Hechtel.
GPS: n51,12391 e5,36271.

3 free. **Surface:** asphalted.
Distance: 400m.

Hechtel/Eksel 11D1

Pijnven, Bosmuseum, Kiefhoekstraat. **GPS**: n51,16133 e5,31091.

5 free. **Location:** Rural. **Surface:** asphalted.
Distance: 4km.
Remarks: Parking forest.

Helchteren 11D1

Parking de Dool, Sportstraat. **GPS**: n51,06087 e5,38650.

10 free. **Surface:** asphalted. 01/01-31/12.
Distance: 1km 500m 500m.
Remarks: Next to castle.

Herk-de-Stad 11D1

Park Olmenhof, Pikkeleerstraat. **GPS**: n50,93361 e5,16654.

7 free €1/100liter Ch €0,60/kWh WC. **Location:** Rural, simple. **Surface:** asphalted. 01/01-31/12.
Distance: 400m 7km 50m 300m.
Remarks: At football ground, max. 48h.

Hoepertingen 11D2

De Verborgen Parel, Hoenshovenstraat 5.
GPS: n50,80224 e5,29073.
6 €7,50 Ch included.
Location: Simple. **Surface:** grassy. 01/01-31/12.
Distance: 1,5km on the spot 1,5km on the spot on the spot.
Remarks: Bread-service, use of sauna against payment.

Houthalen 11D1

Parking Kelchterhoef, Kelchterhoefstraat.
GPS: n51,03015 e5,44063.

4 free. **Location:** Rural. **Surface:** grasstiles/metalled. 01/01-31/12.
Distance: 6km on the spot on the spot.
Remarks: In front of abbey farm.

Kinrooi 11D1

Bomerhof, Bomerstraat 13. **GPS**: n51,15201 e5,74064.

25 € 10 Ch WC included.
Surface: grassy. 01/01-31/12.
Distance: 800m 800m on the spot on the spot.
Remarks: Check in on arrival.

Kortessem 11D2

Kapittelstraat. **GPS**: n50,85724 e5,39126.

5 free (10x). **Surface:** asphalted. 01/01-31/12.
Distance: 200m 200m bakery 200m on the spot.
Remarks: At gymnasium, max. 2 nights.

Tourist information Kortessem:
't Rood Kasteel, Guigoven. Former medieval water castle.

Leopoldsburg 11D1

Jachthaven, Antwerpsesteenweg 129. **GPS**: n51,12892 e5,25028.

22 € 10 included WC €1.
Surface: asphalted. 01/01-31/12.
Distance: 2km on the spot on the spot 2km.
Remarks: Check in at harbourmaster.

Lommel 11D1

Taverne Haven de Meerpaal, Boskantstraat 60.
GPS: n51,24266 e5,36891.

10 € 10 €0,50 Ch (6x)€1 WC €1. **Surface:** asphalted.
Distance: 500m on the spot.
Remarks: Near marina.

Maaseik 11D1

Sportlaan P4. **GPS**: n51,10108 e5,78964.

20 free. **Surface:** asphalted. 01/01-31/12.
Distance: historical centre 200m.

Tourist information Maaseik:
Marktplein. Wed 9-12h.

Meeuwen-Gruitrode 11D1

CC Gruitrode, Royerplein 1, Gruitrode. **GPS**: n51,08939 e5,58949.

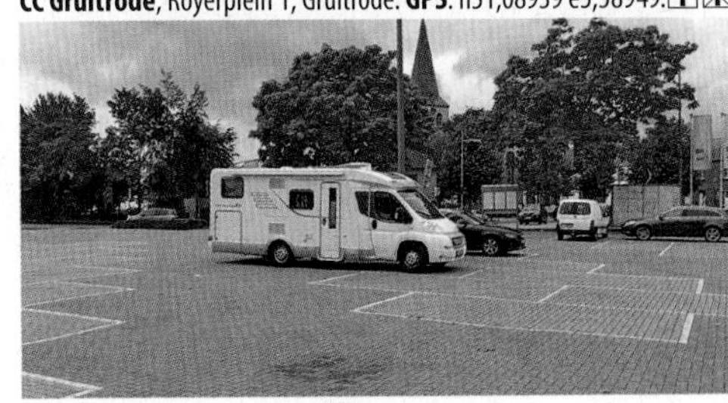

8 free. **Surface:** metalled. 01/01-31/12.
Distance: 200m on the spot 200m 200m on the spot.
Remarks: Max. 24h.

Neeroeteren 11D1

Komweg. **GPS**: n51,08375 e5,70284.

6 € 8 €1/150liter Ch.
Surface: metalled. 01/01-31/12.
Remarks: At football ground.

Neerpelt 11D1

De Welvaart, Jaak Tassetstraat. **GPS**: n51,23333 e5,43164.

BE

8 € 6/24h Ch free. Surface: metalled.
01/01-31/12.
Distance: 500m.
Remarks: At the canal, parking marina, max. 48h, checked, coin waste dump € 1.

P Peer 11D1
P1 Aan den Boogaard. GPS: n51,13193 e5,45741.
free.
Distance: 100m.
Remarks: Max. 24h.

P Peer 11D1
P2 Noordervest. GPS: n51,13422 e5,45511.
free.
Distance: 150m.
Remarks: Max. 24h.

Rekem 11D1
Kanaalstraat. **GPS:** n50,92177 e5,70493.

13 free. **Location:** Rural. **Surface:** gravel. 01/01-31/12.
Distance: 1km on the spot on the spot 500m 1km 100m on the spot.
Remarks: Max. 48h, walking and bicycle area.

Tourist information Rekem:
Oud-Rekem with museum-church, city walls and castle, marked walking route 2km.

S Rummen 11D2
Ketelstraat. **GPS:** n50,89285 e5,16037.

4 free. **Surface:** grasstiles/metalled. 01/01-31/12.
Distance: on the spot 300m 250m on the spot on the spot.
Remarks: At gymnasium.

S Schalkhoven 11D2
Nollekes Winning, Schalkhovenstraat 79. **GPS:** n50,84531 e5,44687.

9 voluntary contribution Ch WC.
Surface: grasstiles/metalled. 01/01-31/12.
Distance: 200m on the spot.
Remarks: Sale of wines.

S Sint-Huibrechts-Lille 11D1
De Bosuil, Bosuilstraat 4. **GPS:** n51,22371 e5,49502.

32 € 6 Ch included. **Location:** Quiet. **Surface:** grassy.
01/01-31/12.
Distance: 1,5km on the spot on the spot on the spot.
Remarks: Check in on arrival.

S Sint-Truiden 11D2
Scouting, Hasseltsesteenweg. **GPS:** n50,82946 e5,20547.
5 free Ch. **Surface:** metalled. 01/01-31/12.
Distance: city centre 2km.
Remarks: Max. 72h.

Tourist information Sint-Truiden:
Toerisme Sint-Truiden, Stadhuis, Grote Markt, www.sint-truiden.be. Abbey-town.
Grote Markt, Groenmarkt, Trudoplein, Minderbroedersplein. Sa 7.30-13h.
Veemarkt, Speelhoflaan. Antiques and flea market. Sa 6-12h.

S Tongeren 11D2
Pliniuspark, Fonteindreef. **GPS:** n50,78626 e5,45256.

25 € 10/24h €0,50/100liter free Ch €0,50/kWh.
Location: Rural. **Surface:** grasstiles/metalled. 01/01-31/12.
Distance: 2km on the spot on the spot.
Remarks: At swimming pool, max. 24h.

Tourist information Tongeren:
Dienst Toerisme, Stadhuisplein 9, www.tongeren.be. Oldest city of Belgium with numerous historico-cultural heritage.
Maastrichterstraat, Schiervelstraat, Clarissenstraat. Biggest antique market in the Benelux, also all antique stores open. Su 6-13h.

S Tongerlo 11D1
De Kieper, Keyartstraat. **GPS:** n51,12397 e5,65449.

4 free €1/100liter €1.
Location: Rural. **Surface:** metalled. 01/01-31/12.
Distance: 10 min walking on the spot on the spot.

Veldwezelt 11D2
Omstraat 20. **GPS:** n50,86195 e5,62696.

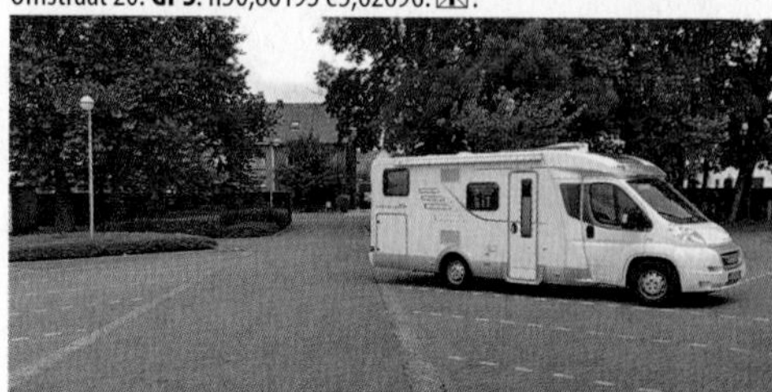

5 free. **Surface:** metalled. 01/01-31/12.
Distance: 800m 200m 500m.
Remarks: Parking gymnasium.

Brussels

P Bruxelles/Brussel 11B2
Bruparck, Wemmel/Heizel, Brussels (Bruxelles/Brussel).
GPS: n50,89745 e4,33826.
Remarks: Max. 24h. Ring road Brussels exit 8.

S Bruxelles/Brussel 11B2
Jeugdherberg Génération Europe, Rue de l'Eléphant 4, Brussels (Bruxelles/Brussel). **GPS:** n50,85317 e4,33479.
5 € 30 Ch WC. 01/01-31/12.
Distance: on the spot.

P Bruxelles/Brussel 11B2
Heizel/Heysel Metro, Brussels (Bruxelles/Brussel).
GPS: n50,89736 e4,33827.
Remarks: Nearby Bruparck.

Tourist information Brussels (Bruxelles/Brussel):
Brussels City Card gives for free entrance on public transport and museums and many discounts on purchases. T € 22.
Bureau van Toerisme, Office de Tourisme, Grote Markt 1, Grand Place, visit.brussels. Capital of Belgium, with a history of more than 1000 years. A lot of buildings worth seeing and historical places.
Koninklijke Serres van Laken, Les serres royales à Laeken. Park, garden, nature area.
M Basiliek van Koekelberg, basilique de Koekelberg. The fifth largest church of the world. Wed, Thu, Sa, Su 14-16h. T € 5.
M Autoworld, Jubelpark 11, Parc du Cinquantenaire. Motorcar history from 1886 up to 1970s. 01/04-30/09 10-18, 01/10-31/03 10-17.
M Museum van de stad Brussel Broodhuis, Musée de la ville Bruxelles, Grote Markt 44, Grand Place. History of the city. Tue-Su 10-17h.
Grote Zavel, Place du Grand Sablon. Antiques and book market. Sa 9-17h, Su 9-14h.
Vossenplein. Flea market. 6-14h.
Grote Markt, Grand place. Flowers and plant market. 8-18h.
Kunstmarkt, marché d'art, Boterstraat, rue au Beurre. Painters and portraitists. 11-18h.
Atomium, Bruparck, Boulevard du Centenaire, Laeken. Built for the occasion of the 1958 Brussels World Fair, symbolising a crystallised iron molecule to the scale of its atoms enlarged 160 thousand million times. 10-18h.
Bruparck, Boulevard du Centenaire 20, Laeken. Family park with among other things Mini-Europe, paradise pool and The Village with restaurants, cafés and shops. 01/01-31/12.
Mini-Europe, Bruparck, Boulevard du Centenaire, Laeken. Europe in miniature, 350 monuments.
Oceade, Bruparck, Boulevard du Centenaire, Laeken. Subtropical leisure pool park. holidays, Sa-Su 10-22h.

Liège

S Aywaille 11D2
Esplanade du Fair-Play, Rue de la Heid. **GPS:** n50,47583 e5,67809.

8 € 8/48h, incl. 1 coin (water or 2h electricity) €2 Ch (4x) €2/h. **Surface:** metalled. 01/01-31/12.
Distance: 300m 200m.
Remarks: At recreation area.

S Blégny-Mine 11D2
Domaine de Blégny-Mine, Rue Lambert Marlet.
GPS: n50,68617 e5,72367.

8 free Chfree (8x)€2/12h. **Location:** Rural, comfortable,

BE

isolated, quiet. **Surface:** gravel. 01/01-31/12.
Distance: 4,6km on the spot on the spot on the spot.
Remarks: At former coalmine, UNESCO World Heritage, access € 9,30, 1 day all inclusive € 29,50, coins electricity at reception park.

Coo 11E3
Petit Coo. **GPS**: n50,39222 e5,87531.
€ 5. **Location:** Simple. **Surface:** asphalted. 01/01-31/12.
Distance: 150m 150m.

Eupen 11E2
Langesthal 164. **GPS**: n50,62180 e6,09148.

free. **Surface:** asphalted. 18-10h.
Distance: Eupen 4km 150m Taverne.
Remarks: At weir, isolated.

Tourist information Eupen:
Benedenstad. Wed 7-12.30h.
Eupen/Keltenis. Flea market. Su 7-16h.

Hamoir 11D3
Complexe Sportif, Quai du Batty. **GPS**: n50,42463 e5,53522.

10 € 8/24h Chfree. **Location:** Urban, comfortable.
Surface: grassy/gravel. 01/01-31/12.
Distance: 200m on the spot on the spot 200m 200m.
Remarks: Along the Ourthe river, max. 24h.

Huy 11D2
Avenue Godin Parnajon. **GPS**: n50,52379 e5,24310.

2 free. **Location:** Urban, central, noisy. **Surface:** asphalted.
01/01-31/12.
Distance: 500m on the spot 500m.
Remarks: Parking in front of restaurant Quick.

Huy 11D2
Quai de Namur. **GPS**: n50,51673 e5,23453.

2 free. **Location:** Urban, central, noisy. **Surface:** asphalted.
01/01-31/12.
Distance: 500m on the spot on the spot 500m.
Remarks: Under the citadel, along the Meuse River, in front of Hôtel du Fort to the right to the quay.

Tourist information Huy:
Office du Tourisme, Quai de Namur,1, www.huy.be. Tourist town, citadel above the city.
Fort en museum. Easter-Sep 10-17/18/19h.

Jalhay 11E2
Baraque de La Gileppe. **GPS**: n50,58759 e5,96980.
4 free free.
Distance: 3,5km.
Remarks: At artificial lake.

Malmedy 11E3
Avenue de la Gare, N62. **GPS**: n50,42282 e6,03080.

30 € 5/24h Ch (8x).
Surface: gravel/metalled. 01/01-31/12.
Distance: 300m 300m bakery 100m, supermarket 800m on the spot on the spot on the spot Waimes 5km.
Remarks: At cycle route (former railroad).

Tourist information Malmedy:
Place St. Géréon. Fri 7-13h.
Hautes Fagnes. Nature reserve Hautes Fagnes.

Sankt Vith 11E3
An den Weyern, Rodter Strasse 9a. **GPS**: n50,28091 e6,12240.

20 free € 1/4minutes . **Location:** Urban, simple.
Surface: asphalted. 01/01-31/12.
Distance: 500m on the spot on the spot.
Remarks: At sports centre.

Sankt Vith 11E3
Skihütte-Biermuseum, Rodt 89/A. **GPS**: n50,29720 e6,06193.

10 free. **Location:** Rural, isolated, quiet. **Surface:** asphalted/gravel.
01/01-31/12.
Distance: 5km 3km on the spot 5km on the spot on the spot.

Sourbrodt 11E2
Signal de Botrange, Rue de Botrange. **GPS**: n50,50148 e6,09312.

20 free. **Location:** Rural, simple, noisy. **Surface:** gravel.
01/01-31/12.
Distance: on the spot on the spot on the spot.

Waimes 11E3
La Faitafondue, Rue de Merkem 4. **GPS**: n50,39532 e6,07024.

10 € 9, free with a meal WC . **Location:** Rural, comfortable. **Surface:** gravel. 01/01-31/12 Wed.
Distance: 4km 6km on the spot on the spot 200m.

Hainaut

Aubechies 11B2
Parking Archéosite, Rue de l'Abbaye 1Y. **GPS**: n50,57419 e3,67546.
Remarks: At museum.

Tourist information Aubechies:
Archéosite d'Aubechies. Archeological open air museum. Mo-Fri 9-17h, 01/04-31/10 9-18h.

Beloeil 11B2
Château Beloeil, Rue de la Hunelle. **GPS**: n50,55128 e3,73280.
free. **Surface:** unpaved. 01/01-31/12.
Remarks: Parking castle.

Tourist information Beloeil:
Château de Beloeil, www.beloeil.be/. 01/06-30/09 10-19h, 01/04-31/05 Sa/Su/holidays 10-19h.

Bernissart 11B2
Musée de l'Iguanodon, Ruelle des Médecins. **GPS**: n50,47530 e3,64958.

free.
Distance: 6km.
Remarks: Parking 100m of dinosaur museum.

Binche 11B3
Pastures, Rue des Pastures. **GPS**: n50,41413 e4,17070.

50 free Ch (2x). **Surface:** asphalted. 01/01-31/12.
Distance: on the spot.
Remarks: Parking just outside centre.

Tourist information Binche:
Office du Tourisme, Parc communal, rue des Promenades, 2, www.binche.be. Medieval city with ramparts.

Blaton 11B2
Place de Feignies. **GPS**: n50,50179 e3,66135.

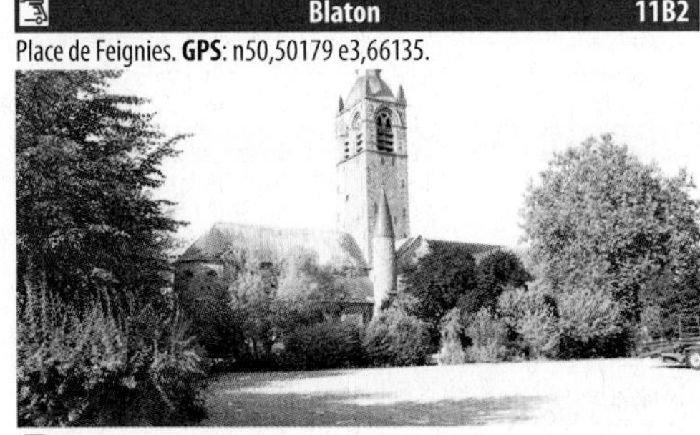

free.
Distance: 200m.
Remarks: Nearby Romanesque church.

BE

S Bouffioulx 11C3

Maison de la Poterie, Rue du Général Jacques.
GPS: n50,39024 e4,51406.
3 €0,50 Ch. **Surface:** metalled. 01/01-31/12.
Remarks: Next to Centre d'Interprétation de la Poterie, coins at Maison de la Poterie.

S Boussu-lez-Walcourt 11C3

Les Lacs de l'Eau d'Heure, Route de la Plate Taille.
GPS: n50,19265 e4,37958.

20 free Chfree. **Surface:** asphalted. 01/01-31/12.
Distance: on the spot on the spot on the spot on the spot.

Brugelette 11B2

Pairi Daiza, Domaine de Cambron. **GPS**: n50,58892 e3,88670.
€ 7. **Surface:** gravel/sand. 01/04-31/10.

Tourist information Brugelette:
Parc Paradisio, Domaine de Cambron. Park with bird paradise and monkey island. 26/03-06/11 10-18.

S Chimay 11B3

Communal de Chimay, Allée des Princes 1. **GPS**: n50,04557 e4,30956.
7 € 5 Ch. included. **Surface:** grassy/metalled.
01/01-31/12.
Distance: on the spot 300m 200m.

P Chimay 11B3

Place Froissart. **GPS**: n50,04728 e4,31307.

P Chimay 11B3

Place Léopold. **GPS**: n50,04747 e4,31784.
. Fri.

S Dottignies 11A2

Rue des Écoles 75b. **GPS**: n50,72821 e3,30011.
4 free free. 01/01-31/12.
Distance: 500m 1,3km.
Remarks: Square behind fire-station.

Ecaussines 11B2

Château de la Folie, Rue de la Folie. **GPS**: n50,57443 e4,17851.
free.
Distance: 800m.

Ecaussines 11B2

Eglise Sainte Aldegonde, Rue Jacquemart Boulle 28, Ecaussines-Lalaing. **GPS**: n50,57085 e4,18107.
free.
Distance: 500m.

Fleurus 11C2

Parking Gare, Avenue de la Gare. **GPS**: n50,48215 e4,54433.

Fleurus 11C2

Stade Communal, Rue de Fleurjoux. **GPS**: n50,47852 e4,55237.
free.

Harchies 11B2

Place du Rivage. **GPS**: n50,47106 e3,69619.

Hornu 11B2

Le Site du Grand Hornu, Rue Sainte-Louise 82.
GPS: n50,43488 e3,83707.

free.
Distance: 1km.

Tourist information Hornu:
Grand-Hornu. Old industrial mining complex, a remarkable reminder of the Industrial Revolution.
Tue-Fri 10-18h. € 8.

Houdeng Aimeries 11B2

Musée de la Mine de Bois-du-Luc, Rue Saint-Patrice.
GPS: n50,47081 e4,14952.
free.

La Louvière 11B2

Boulevard de Roi Baudouin. **GPS**: n50,46619 e4,19055.
free.
Remarks: P Station Sud.

Tourist information La Louvière:
M Ascenseur Funiculaire de Strépy-Thieu, Strépy-Bracquegnies. Draw-works, 19th century. 01/02-27/11 9.30-18.30.
Rue du Marché. Sa 8-13h.

Le Roeulx 11B2

Grand Place. **GPS**: n50,50019 e4,10919.

Le Roeulx 11B2

Place de la Chapelle. **GPS**: n50,50294 e4,10874.
Distance: 100m.
Remarks: Next to church.

Le Roeulx 11B2

Place de la Tannée. **GPS**: n50,50339 e4,10819.

Le Roeulx 11B2

Place du Château. **GPS**: n50,50406 e4,11024.
Remarks: Parking at castle.

S Leers Noord 11A2

La Maison du Canal, Rue du Canal 6. **GPS**: n50,69089 e3,25728.

3 free Chfree. **Location:** Rural, quiet. **Surface:** gravel.
01/01-31/12.
Distance: on the spot on the spot on the spot on the spot.
Remarks: Tarerne closed on Monday.

Lessines 11B2

Rue des 4 fils Aymon. **GPS**: n50,71280 e3,83403.
free.
Distance: 400m.

Marchienne-au-Pont 11C3

Musée d'Histoire et d'Archéologie Industrielle, 134 rue de la Providence. **GPS**: n50,41301 e4,40450.
free.
Remarks: In front of museum.

Mons/Bergen 11B2

Maison Van Gogh, Rue de Pavillon 3, Cuesmes, Mons (Mons/Bergen).
GPS: n50,44174 e3,92630.
free.
Remarks: In case of city-visit use parking nearby station or bypass.

Tourist information Mons (Mons/Bergen):
M Maison Van Gogh, Rue du Pavillon 3, Cuesmes. Former place of residence of painter Van Gogh 1879/80, exhibition of reproductions.
10-18h Mo.
Château Havré, Havré. Castle, 12-13th century.

Morlanwelz-Mariemont 11B2

Musée Alex Louis Martin, Place de Carnières, 52, Carnières.
GPS: n50,44402 e4,25416.
10 free.

Mouscron 11A2

Musée du Folklore, Rue des Brasseurs, 3.
GPS: n50,74217 e3,21795.
free.
Remarks: Possibility make a reservation tel 02.56.33.23.36.

Nimy 11B2

Musée de la Pipe et du Vieux Nimy, Rue Mouzin.
GPS: n50,47499 e3,95853.
free. **Surface:** metalled.
Remarks: Museum closed: Nov-Mar.

S Péruwelz 11A2

Port de plaisance, Rue de la Boitérie. **GPS**: n50,51864 e3,60904.
10 € 5 WC . **Surface:** asphalted/gravel. 01/02-30/11.

Quaregnon 11B2

La Grand Place. **GPS**: n50,44369 e3,86428.
2.

Quevaucamps 11B2

Musée de la Bonneterie, Rue Paul Pastur.
GPS: n50,52671 e3,68776.

2 free. 01/01-31/12.
Remarks: Parking in front of museum, via N527.

Ronquières 11B2

Grande tour et promenade en Bateau Mouche, Rue Rosemont.
GPS: n50,60636 e4,22249.

20 free. 01/01-31/12.
Distance: on the spot on the spot.

Sivry 11B3

Observatoire de Sivry, Route de Mons 52. **GPS**: n50,17897 e4,22646.
2.
Remarks: Centre for nature studies.

Solre-Sur-Sambre 11B3

Château-Fort, Rue du Chateau Fort. **GPS**: n50,30918 e4,15585.
free.
Remarks: At castle.

Thieu/Strepy 11B2

Rue Saint-Géry. **GPS**: n50,47156 e4,09069.
+10 free. **Surface:** metalled. 01/01-31/12.

Thuin 11B3

Drève des Alliés. **GPS**: n50,33951 e4,29860.
Remarks: Max. 24h.

Thuin 11B3

L'Abbaye d'Aulnes, Rue Vandervelde. **GPS**: n50,36592 e4,33324.
free.
Remarks: Near abbey, max. 24h.

Thuin 11B3

Place du Chapitre. **GPS**: n50,33980 e4,28724.

Remarks: Max. 24h.

Tournai/Doornik 11A2

Maison de la Culture, Boulevard Frère Rimbaud, Tournai (Tournai/Doornik). **GPS**: n50,60432 e3,38199.

15-20 free Ch free.
Surface: metalled. 01/01-31/12.
Distance: 5 min walking 5 min walking 5 min walking on the spot.

Trazegnies 11B2

Place Albert I 32. **GPS**: n50,46248 e4,33025.
Distance: 1,5km.
Remarks: Parking at castle.

Namur

Alle-sur-Semois 16C1

Recreatiecentrum Recrealle, restaurant les Pierres du Diable, Rue Léon Henrard 16. **GPS**: n49,84648 e4,97579.

10 free. **Location:** Rural, simple. **Surface:** unpaved.
01/01-31/12.
Distance: 700m on the spot fishing permit obligatory on the spot 700m.

Tourist information Alle-sur-Semois:
Recrealle. Canoe rent; departures for canoe and kayaks, fishing and swimming possibilities, bowling, tennis, play ground, restaurant.

Ave-et-Auffe 11D3

Le Roptai, Rue du Roptai 34. **GPS**: n50,11144 e5,13373.

10 € 15-20 Ch (10x)€3/24h WC included €1 €4 €1/3h. **Location:** Rural, comfortable, quiet. **Surface:** grassy/gravel.
08/01-31/12.
Distance: 4km 2km 1km 5km 1km on the spot.
Remarks: Bread-service, Han 5km.

Bohan 16C1

Rue de Monts les Champs. **GPS**: n49,86918 e4,88628.
4 Ch . **Surface:** metalled. 01/01-31/12.
Distance: 600m 600m.

Han-Sur-Lesse 11D3

Rue de la Lesse. **GPS**: n50,12751 e5,18819.

40 € 7,50, Jul/Aug € 10 Ch WC included.
Location: Urban. **Surface:** asphalted. 01/01-31/12.
Distance: 200m 200m 200m on the spot. **Remarks:** Parking nearby caves and centre. **Tourist information Han-Sur-Lesse:**
Tourist centre around the caves.
Grottes de Han. Caves, son-et-lumière and boat trip on underground river. 01/04-31/10 10-16/18h, 01/11-31/03 11.30-16h.
Réserve d'Animaux. European animals alive today and those which lived previously in this area. 01/03-31/12 10-17h, 01/07-31/08 9.30-18h.

Hogne 11D3

Aire del Foy, 16 rue de Serinchamps. **GPS**: n50,24981 e5,27933.
25 € 5-10 16Amp WC . **Surface:** grassy.
Distance: on the spot.

Namur 11C2

Tabora, Place André Ryckmans.
GPS: n50,46770 e4,85056.

8 free Ch €7,50. **Surface:** asphalted. 01/01-31/12.
Distance: 1km 1km 1km 200m.
Remarks: Behind gymnasium.

Nismes 11C3

Rue Longue. **GPS**: n50,07387 e4,54863.

± 8 € 5 €2/100liter Ch €2/h . **Surface:** asphalted.
01/01-31/12.
Distance: on the spot 100m bakery 100m on the spot on the spot.
Remarks: Coins at tourist info.

Profondeville 11C3

Chaussée de Namur. **GPS**: n50,37644 e4,87106.

4 free. **Surface:** asphalted. 01/01-31/12.
Distance: 50m 150m 50m.
Remarks: Max. 24h.

Rochefort 11D3

Route de Marche. **GPS**: n50,15800 e5,22639.

10 free. **Location:** Urban, simple. **Surface:** metalled.
01/01-31/12.
Distance: 200m 200m 200m.

Saint-Hubert 11D3

Chemin des Etangs/ Rue de Lavaux. **GPS**: n50,02689 e5,38088.

3 free free. **Location:** Urban, simple. **Surface:** gravel.
01/01-31/12.
Distance: 500m 500m 500m on the spot on the spot.
Remarks: Max. 48h, 10 parking places tolerated, European campital of hunting, events: 1st weekend September and November 1st Saint Hubert.

Saint-Hubert 11D3

Fourneau Saint Michel, Rue Saint Hubert.
GPS: n50,08480 e5,33902.

10 free Ch free (4x)€1/h. **Location:** Rural, simple.
Surface: asphalted/grassy. 01/01-31/12.
Distance: St Hubert 9km 200m on the spot.
Remarks: At open air museum from Fourneau Saint-Michel.

Treignes 11C3

Rue de la Gare. **GPS**: n50,09085 e4,68182.

3 free €2 Ch €2. **Surface:** gravel. 01/01-31/12.
Distance: 900m.
Remarks: At former station, coins at tourist info Nismes, steam train museum.

Luxembourg

Arlon 16E1

Casserne Callemeyn, Drève des Espagnols, N882.
GPS: n49,68990 e5,81929.

5 free free. **Location:** Urban, simple. **Surface:** asphalted.
01/01-31/12.
Distance: 600m 5,8km.
Remarks: At fire-station.

Tourist information Arlon:
Parc Archéologique, Rue des Thermes. Archeological site. 9-12h, 14-17h.
Flea market. 01/03-31/10 1st Su of the month 7-19h.

Barvaux 11D3

Petit Barvaux. **GPS**: n50,35223 e5,49501.

BE

20 € 10/24h €2 Ch.
Surface: grasstiles.
01/01-31/12.
Distance: 300m Delhaize 50m Ravel-route on the spot.
Remarks: Along the Ourthe river, max. 24h, coins at tourist info.

Tourist information Barvaux:
Labyrinthus, Rue Basse Commene. Labyrinth park. Jul/Aug 10-19h, Sep 11-17h.
Domaine de Hottemme. Nature reserve with visitor centre.
10.30-17h, summer 10.30-18h. € 2.

S Bastogne 11D3

Avenue Albert I. **GPS**: n49,99825 e5,71526.

10 free free. **Location:** Urban, simple, central.
Surface: asphalted. 01/01-31/12.
Distance: 300m 3km 300m 300m.

S Bouillon 16C1

Parking du stade, Rue de la Poulie. **GPS**: n49,79106 e5,05767.

10 free Ch €1/kWh. **Surface:** gravel.
01/01-31/12.
Distance: 1,3km 1,3km 1,5km.
Remarks: Coins at tourist info.

S Durbuy 11D3

P Mobilhome Le Vedeur, Rue Fond de Vedeur.
GPS: n50,35780 e5,45672.

50 € 21, 2 pers.incl Ch WC included.
Location: Comfortable. **Surface:** gravel. 01/01-31/12.
Distance: 750m on the spot fishing permit obligatory 750m 750m on the spot.

Tourist information Durbuy:
Confiturerie Saint Amour, Rue St Amour 13. Production of traditional products. 10-18h 01/10-31/03 Mo. free.
Diamour, Rue de la Prevoté 2. Centre of diamonds and goldsmithing. 10.30-19.30h Tue-Wed. free.
Parc des Topiaires, Rue Haie Himbe. Model garden. 10-18h 01/01-31/01. € 4,50.
Antiques and flea market. 01/03-30/09, 9-17h, 2nd Sa of the month.

S Herbeumont 16D1

Avenue de Combattants. **GPS**: n49,77729 e5,23700.

50 free Chfree.
Location: Rural. **Surface:** asphalted/grassy.
Distance: 500m 500m.
Remarks: Parking of old station.

Tourist information Herbeumont:
Royal Syndicat d'Initiative, Avenue des Combattants, 7, www.herbeumont.be. Beautiful position in the Ardennes landscape. Ruins of medieval castle, free entry.
Au cœur de l'Ardoise, Rue du Babinay 1, Bertrix. Slate mine. sa-su 10-18h, wed 14h. € 9,50.

S Hotton 11D3

Haie Notre Dame. **GPS**: n50,26937 e5,45738.
6 € 10 Ch. **Surface:** asphalted. 01/01-31/12.
Distance: 800m 800m RAVeL.
Remarks: At cemetery.

Tourist information Hotton:
Grottes de Hotton, Chemin du spéléoclub 1. Caves. 01/04-31/10 10-17h, 01/07-31/08 10-18h.

La Roche 11D3

Rue du Harzé. **GPS**: n50,19075 e5,57432.

5 free. **Location:** Urban, simple. **Surface:** asphalted.
01/01-31/12. **Distance:** 500m 500m 500m on the spot.
Remarks: Parking at sports park.

Tourist information La Roche:
Syndicat d'Initiative, Place du Marché, 15, www.la-roche-tourisme.com. Small town totally destroyed during the battle of the Ardennes, 1944/45.
Medieval citadel. 10-12h, 14-17h, 01/07-31/08 10-19h, winter Sa-Su frost.

Nisramont 11D3

Barrage de Nisramont, Rue de barrage. **GPS**: n50,14089 e5,67118.

10 free. **Location:** Simple, isolated, quiet. **Surface:** metalled.
01/01-31/12.
Distance: 3,7km 15km on the spot on the spot on the spot on the spot.
Remarks: At artificial lake.

S Poupehan 16C1

Rue du Pont. **GPS**: n49,80886 e5,00418.

20 free Chfree. **Location:** Rural, simple, quiet.
Surface: gravel. 01/01-31/12.
Distance: on the spot on the spot 200m 300m.
Remarks: Along the Semois river, next to sports fields, max. 24h, canoe rental.

Redu 11D3

Rue de Saint Hubert. **GPS**: n50,00877 e5,16348.

10 free. **Location:** Rural, simple. **Surface:** gravel. 01/01-31/12.
Distance: on the spot.

BE

Switzerland

Capital: Bern
Government: Direct democracy, Federal republic
Official Language: German, French, Italian, Romansh
Population: 8,120,000 (2015)
Area: 41,284 km²

General information
Dialling code: 0041
General emergency: 112
Currency: Swiss franc (CHF)
1 CHF = € 0,93, € 1 = 1,07 CHF
1 CHF = £0.80, £1 = CHF 1,25 (November 2016)

Regulations for overnight stays
Overnight parking is allowed, max 15 hours.

Additional public holidays 2017
August 1National Day

Time Zone
Winter (Standard Time) GMT+1
Summer (DST) GMT+2

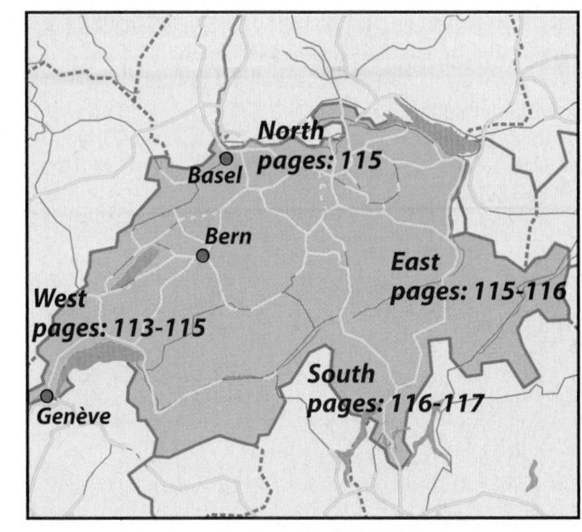

Switzerland West

Aeschi 22G1
Panorama, Scheidgasse 272. **GPS**: n46,65399 e7,70070.
50 CHF 22,40-31,20 Ch WC. 15/05-15/10.

Avenches 22F1
Port-Plage. **GPS**: n46,90351 e7,04918.
300 CHF 45 Ch WC. 01/04-01/10.

Boltigen 22G1
Jaunpass. **GPS**: n46,59208 e7,33758.
117 Ch WC. 01/01-31/12.

Böningen 22H1
Seeblick, Campingstrasse 14. **GPS**: n46,68987 e7,89398.
105 CHF 41,80 Ch WC. Easter-01/10.

Brienz 22H1
Aaregg. **GPS**: n46,74859 e8,04957.
180 CHF 30-45 Ch WC.
24/03-31/10.
Tourist information Brienz:
Alpen Region Brienz-Meiringen-Hasliberg, Bahnhofstrasse 22, Meiringen, www.alpenregion.ch. Village of wood-cutters.
during school hours 01/07-31/08.
Brienz Rothorn Bahn. Steam rack-railway.
01/06-31/10 8.45h. CHF 57-88.
Freilichtmuseum Ballenberg. Open air museum.
15/04-31/10 10-17h.

Bullet 22F1
Restaurant Les Cluds, Les Cluds. **GPS**: n46,84248 e6,55991.

4 CHF 10 Ch (4x)included. **Location:** Rural, simple, isolated, quiet. **Surface:** asphalted.
01/01-31/12 Restaurant: Mo.
Distance: on the spot.
Remarks: Max. 2 nights, pay at restaurant.

Burgdorf 19G3
Waldegg, Waldeggweg. **GPS**: n47,05407 e7,62895.
CHF 28-31,50 Ch WC. 01/04-31/10.

Château-d'Oex 22G2
Le Berceau. **GPS**: n46,46673 e7,12529.
70 CHF 38,50 Ch WC. 01/01-31/12.

Cheyres 22F1
Route de Crevel. **GPS**: n46,81651 e6,78501.
10minutes Ch (2x)against payment h. **Location:** Simple.
01/01-31/12.
Tourist information Cheyres:
Fête de vendanges. Wine festivals. beginning Oct.

Cudrefin 22F1
Route de Neuchâtel. **GPS**: n46,96000 e7,02750.
Chfree. 15/03-01/11.

Remarks: In front of camping Le Chablais.

Delémont 19G3
Place de Parc Gros-Pré Monsieur, Route de Porrentruy.
GPS: n47,36289 e7,34008.

10 free Ch free. **Surface:** gravel. 01/01-31/12.
Distance: 200m.

Dürrenroth 19G3
Reisemobilstellplatz Blueberry Hill, Brunnen 54.
GPS: n47,06563 e7,76553.

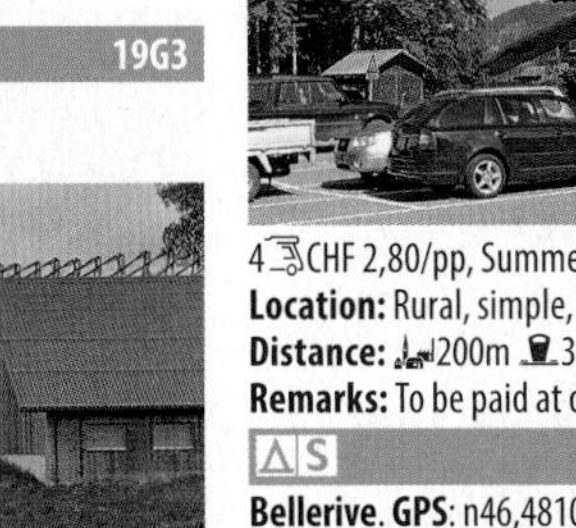

5 CHF 10 CHF 2. **Location:** Rural, comfortable, quiet.
Surface: gravel. 01/01-31/12.
Distance: Dürrenroth 3,5km on the spot on the spot.
Remarks: Panoramic view.

Echallens 22F1
Chemin du Pont. **GPS**: n46,63945 e6,64096.

5 free Ch free. **Location:** Rural, simple. **Surface:** asphalted.
01/01-31/12.
Distance: 700m 300m 700m.

Estavayer-le-Lac 22F1
Nouvelle-Plage. **GPS**: n46,85602 e6,84801.
30 CHF 27-46,60 Ch WC. 01/04-01/11.

Frutigen 22G1
Grassi. **GPS**: n46,58178 e7,64213.
68 CHF 26 Ch. 01/01-31/12.

Gampelen 22F1
Fanel, Seestraße. **GPS**: n47,00154 e7,03957.
CHF 42-52 Ch. 24/03-09/10.

Grandson 22F1
Le Pécos, Rue du Pécos. **GPS**: n46,80371 e6,63575.
4 CHF 26 Ch WC. 01/04-01/10.
Remarks: Next to campsite.

Grindelwald 22H1
Eigernordwand. **GPS**: n46,62135 e8,01683.
CHF 34 Ch.
01/01-31/12.
Tourist information Grindelwald:
Jungfraubahn. Train journey to the highest train station of Europe.

Gryon 22G2
Place de la Barboleuse. **GPS**: n46,28222 e7,07028.

4 CHF 2,80/pp, Summer CHF 5,30/pp Ch (4x)CHF 5.
Location: Rural, simple, quiet. **Surface:** asphalted.
Distance: 200m 3,5km on the spot 100m.
Remarks: To be paid at office de tourisme.

Gstaad 22G2
Bellerive. **GPS**: n46,48106 e7,27328.
CHF 27,50-30 Ch. 01/01-31/12.

Gwatt-Thun 22G1
Betlereiche. **GPS**: n46,72749 e7,62760.
CHF 42-62 Ch WC. 24/03-09/10.

Häusernmoos 19G3
Restaurant Koi-Gartenteich, Huttwilstrasse 22.
GPS: n47,07890 e7,74935.
4 CHF 10, overnight stay free Ch CHF 4 included,at restaurant. 01/01-31/12 Restaurant: Mo-Tue.
Distance: on the spot 2km.

Hinterkappelen 22G1
Kappelenbrucke, Wohlenstrasse 62. **GPS**: n46,96433 e7,38361.
70 Ch WC. 01/01-31/12.

Huttwil 19H3
Firma Flyer E-Bike, Luzernstrasse. **GPS**: n47,11527 e7,86795.

16 free Ch free. **Location:** Rural. **Surface:** gravel.
01/01-31/12.
Distance: 500m.
Remarks: E-bike factory, guided tour Tuesdays 14.30h.

Interlaken 22H1
Hobby, Lehnweg 16. **GPS**: n46,68424 e7,83022.
80 CHF 29,40-40 Ch WC. 01/04-30/09.

CH

Interlaken 22H1

Lazy-Rancho, Lehnweg 6. **GPS**: n46,68583 e7,83095.
90 CHF 33-51 Ch WC . Easter-01/10.

Tourist information Interlaken:
Heimwehfluhbahn. Telpher carrier from 1906. 24/03-23/10 10-17.
JungfrauPark. Attractions and themepark. 01/05-23/10 11-18u 25/12-01/01.

La Brévine 22F1

Les Varodes. **GPS**: n46,97195 e6,58860.

10 free Ch (2x)WCfree. **Location:** Rural, simple, isolated, quiet. **Surface:** asphalted. 01/01-31/12.
Distance: 3km on the spot 1,5km on the spot on the spot on the spot.
Remarks: Parking at Lac des Tailleres.

La Chaux-de-Fonds 19F3

Bois du Couvent. **GPS**: n47,09334 e6,83593.

2 free Ch (4x)free. **Location:** Rural, simple.
Surface: gravel. 01/05-30/09.
Distance: 1,3km 350m 700m on the spot.
Remarks: In front of campsite du Bois du Couvent.

Tourist information La Chaux-de-Fonds:
Tourisme neuchâtelois - Montagnes, Espacité 1, Place Le Corbusier. Capital of the clock industry.
Musée International d'Horlogerie, Rue des Musée 29. Watch museum. 10-17h Mo, 25/12-01/01.
Musée paysan et artisanal, Rue des Crêtets 148. The farmers' life and old crafts industry. 01/04-31/10 14-17h, 01/11-28/02 Wed, Sa, Su 14-17h Mo, 01/03-31/03.

Langenthal 19G3

Lexa-Wohnmobile, Bern-Zürichstrasse 49b.
GPS: n47,22461 e7,77944.

5 free Ch free. **Surface:** asphalted. 01/01-31/12.
Distance: 2km.
Remarks: At motorhome dealer.

Lausanne 22F2

Vidy, Chemin du Camping 3. **GPS**: n46,51734 e6,59777.

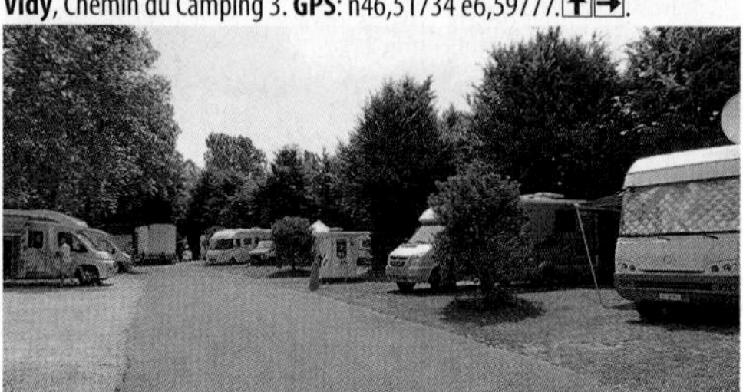

10 CHF 23,10 or € 20 Ch WC included CHF 4,35/4h. **Location:** Urban, simple, central. **Surface:** grassy/metalled. 01/01-31/12.
Distance: on the spot on the spot.
Remarks: Next to campsite the Vidy, pay at reception, service passerby CHF 3, free bus to centre.

Tourist information Lausanne:
Lausanne Tourisme, Avenue de Rhodanie 2, www.lausanne-tourisme.ch. Parking at the port, rack-railway to city centre.
Musée Olympique, Quai d'Ouchy 1. All about the Olympic games. 01/05-14/10 9-18h, 14/10-30/04 10-18h Mo, 01/10-30/04.

Lauterbrunnen 22H1

Jungfrau. **GPS**: n46,58834 e7,90882.
CHF 42,80 Ch WC . 01/01-31/12.

Lauterbrunnen 22H1

Schützenbach. **GPS**: n46,59047 e7,91194.
Ch WC .
01/01-31/12.

Tourist information Lauterbrunnen:
Jungfraubahn, Grindelwald. Train journey to the highest train station of Europe.
Klöppelstube, Altes Schulhaus. Making of bobbin lace. Fri 13.30-16.30h. free.
Trümmelbachfälle, Lauterbrunnen dir Stechelberg. Underground waterfalls. 01/04-30/11 9-17h.

Le Landeron 19F3

Camp des Pêches. **GPS**: n47,05257 e7,06993.
CHF 38 Ch WC . 01/04-15/10.

Tourist information Le Landeron:
Restaurant Le Carnotzet, Rue de la Gare 22. Restaurant with regional specialities. Tue-Sa 11-14h, 17-23h Mo, Su.

Les Brenets 19F3

Champ de la Fontaine. **GPS**: n47,06588 e6,69898.
CHF 5 Ch . 01/01-31/12.
Remarks: Nearby campsite Lac de Brenets.

Les Ponts-de-Martel 22F1

Rue du Bugnon. **GPS**: n46,99644 e6,73065.

3 free Ch (2x)free. **Location:** Rural, simple.
Surface: asphalted.
Distance: 600m 700m.
Remarks: At community centre.

Malvilliers 22F1

Hotel-Restaurant La Croisée, Route de Neuchâtel.
GPS: n47,03200 e6,86779.

5 CHF5 Ch (4x)included. **Location:** Simple, noisy.
Surface: asphalted. 01/01-31/12.
Distance: 100m on the spot.

Meiringen 22H1

Alpencamping, Brüningstrasse 46. **GPS**: n46,73448 e8,17122.
8 CHF 27,90 Ch WC included. **Surface:** grassy.
Distance: 1km 1km.
Remarks: Max. 3 nights.

Morges 22F2

Le Petit Bois. **GPS**: n46,50446 e6,48894.
170 CHF 56 Ch WC . 01/04-01/10.
Remarks: Service at entrance campsite.

Moutier 19G3

Chemin de la Piscine. **GPS**: n47,27365 e7,37923.

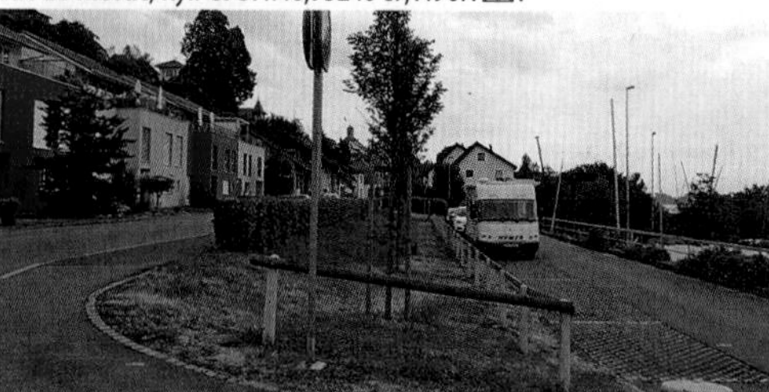

5 free Ch free. **Location:** Urban, simple, quiet.
Surface: asphalted.
Distance: 1km.
Remarks: At swimming pool.

Murten 22G1

Lac de Morat, Ryf. **GPS**: n46,93240 e7,11967.

30 CHF 1/h, overnight stay free. **Location:** Urban, simple, central.
Surface: grasstiles. 01/01-31/12.
Distance: on the spot on the spot on the spot.

Neuchâtel 22F1

Route des Falaises. **GPS**: n47,00145 e6,95735.

8 free Ch (4x)free.
Location: Simple, noisy.
Surface: grasstiles.
Distance: city centre 2km 300m 100m.
Remarks: Max. 2 days, max. 7m.

Tourist information Neuchâtel:
Le Creux-du-Van, Val-de-Travers. Nature reserve. 01/01-31/12.

Oberburg 19G3

Reisemobilstellplätze Kürbishof, Krauchthalstrasse 40.
GPS: n47,03807 e7,62079.
5 CHF 13 or € 9 Ch WC against payment.
01/01-31/12.
Distance: 600m 300m. **Remarks:** Payment also in euros.

Payerne 22F1

Place de la Concorde. **GPS**: n46,81976 e6,93757.

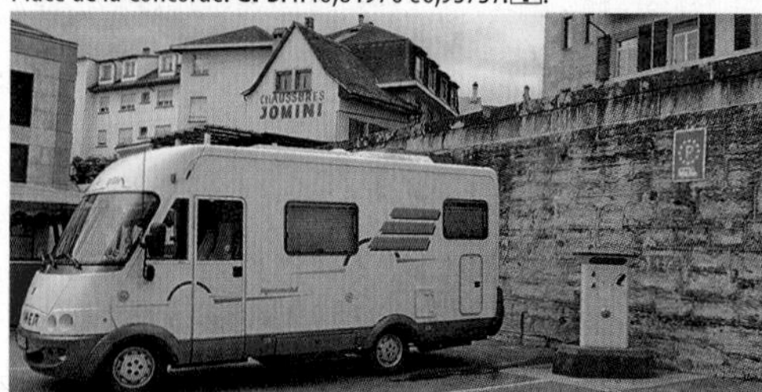

2 free Ch (2x)free. **Location:** Urban, simple, central, noisy. **Surface:** asphalted. 01/01-31/12.
Distance: on the spot on the spot on the spot.

Portalban 22F1

Route du Port. **GPS**: n46,92131 e6,95614.

CH

25 CHF 20, 2 pers.incl Ch (30x)WC included.
Location: Rural, simple. **Surface:** grasstiles.
01/01-31/12.
Distance: on the spot 200m on the spot on the spot.
Remarks: In harbour, near campsite, check in at reception.

Prêles 19G3

Prêles, Route de la Neuveville 61. **GPS**: n47,08569 e7,11714.
CHF 37,50 Ch WC . 01/04-15/10.

Rolle 22E2

Camping de Rolle Aux Vernes, Chemin de la Plage.
GPS: n46,46191 e6,34630.
5 CHF 18-30 + CHF 8,50-10/pp tourist tax CHF 3.
Surface: asphalted. 01/03-01/10.
Distance: 500m.
Remarks: Max. 48h.

Romont 22F1

Promenade des Avoines. **GPS**: n46,69753 e6,91774.

2 free Ch (4x)free. **Location:** Rural, simple, noisy.
Surface: grasstiles. 01/01-31/12.
Distance: on the spot 100m 700m.
Remarks: Max. 24h.

Saignelégier 19F3

Chemin de la Tuilerie. **GPS**: n47,25223 e7,00347.

10 free Ch free. **Location:** Rural, simple, noisy.
Surface: grasstiles. 01/01-31/12.
Distance: 700m on the spot 200m.

Saint Blaise 22F1

Chemin des Pêcheurs. **GPS**: n47,01139 e6,98778.

12 CHF 16/24h Ch (4x)WC included.
Location: Urban, simple, central, noisy.
Surface: asphalted.
Distance: Neuchâtel 5km 300m 250m 500m 600m.

Saint-Aubin 22F1

Port de St-Aubin-Sauges. GPS: n46,89181 e6,77427.

10 CHF 20 Ch (6x)WC included. **Location:** Simple, quiet. **Surface:** asphalted. 01/01-31/12.
Distance: 600m on the spot on the spot 400m 400m.
Remarks: Parking port, nearby the capitainerie.

Sainte-Croix 22F1

Grand-Rue, L'Auberson. **GPS**: n46,82019 e6,47230.

4 free Ch (4x)free. **Location:** Rural, simple.
Surface: asphalted.
Distance: 2km on the spot 3km.

Satigny 22E2

Bois de Bay, Route du Bois-de-Bay 19. **GPS**: n46,20087 e6,06619.
Ch WC. 01/01-31/12.

Vesenaz 22E2

Pointe a la Bise. GPS: n46,24517 e6,19331.
105 CHF 62 Ch WC . 28/03-05/10.

Zweisimmen 22G1

Vermeille, Eygässli 2. **GPS**: n46,56265 e7,37766.
25 CHF 24,80-30,30 Ch . 01/01-31/12.

Switzerland North

Altikon 20A2

Stellplatz auf dem Bauernhof, Feldistrasse 18.
GPS: n47,57337 e8,78391.
3 CHF 10 CHF 1 Ch CHF 4 CHF 2. **Surface:** metalled.
01/01-31/12.
Distance: 200m 200m.
Remarks: Max. 48h.

Brunnen 23A1

Hopfraeben. GPS: n46,99700 e8,59300.
40 CHF 23-39 Ch WC . 01/05-01/10.

Engelberg 22H1

Eienwäldli, Wasserfallstraße 108. **GPS**: n46,81009 e8,42243.
130 CHF 28-36 Ch WC . 01/01-31/12.

Giswil 22H1

Stellplatz an der Kirche, Panoramastrasse. **GPS**: n46,83230 e8,17900.
3 free. **Surface:** asphalted. 01/01-31/12.
Distance: on the spot on the spot on the spot.
Remarks: Max. 1 night.

Hemmiken 19H3

Stellplatz Bauernhof, Asphof 50. **GPS**: n47,49682 e7,88749.
3 CHF 20 Ch . **Location:** Isolated. **Surface:** unpaved.
01/01-31/12.
Distance: 1,4km.

Horw 22H1

Steinibachried. GPS: n47,01100 e8,31100.
CHF 38-50 Ch . 24/03-09/10.

Reinach 19G3

Waldhort, Heideweg 16. **GPS**: n47,49923 e7,60296.
CHF 36 Ch WC . 01/03-01/10.

Weggis 19H3

Bauernhof Gerberweid, Eichistrasse 2. **GPS**: n47,03888 e8,41446.

15 CHF 6-10 + CHF 6/pp + CHF 2,70/pp tourist tax CHF 1 Ch CHF 3 CHF 2. **Surface:** grassy. 01/04-15/10.
Distance: 2km 1km 1km 500m on the spot.

Willisau 19H3

Bisangmatt. **GPS**: n47,11937 e7,99829.

4 CHF 5 (4x)included. **Surface:** metalled. 01/01-31/12.
Distance: 800m 800m 800m.
Remarks: At fire-station.

Zug 20A3

Zugersee, Chamer Fussweg 36. **GPS**: n47,17758 e8,49358.
CHF 40 Ch WC. 24/03-09/10.
Remarks: Max. ^3.17m.

Switzerland East

Altstätten 20B3

Gasthausziel, Trogenerstrasse 99. **GPS**: n47,38892 e9,53457.
6 CHF 10, guests free Ch CHF 5/day. 01/01-31/12
Wed-Thu.
Distance: 3km on the spot.

Andeer 23B1

Sut Baselgia. GPS: n46,60651 e9,42630.
CHF 30 Ch WC . 01/01-31/12.

Appenzell 20B3

Restaurant Eggli, Egglistrasse. **GPS**: n47,32104 e9,46565.
10 Ch guests free. **Surface:** asphalted.
01/01-31/12.
Remarks: The most beautiful panorama of Appenzell.

Bivio 23B2

Wohnmobil-Stellplatz Tua. GPS: n46,46304 e9,65597.

20 CHF 10-15 + CHF 2,50/pp tourist tax Ch CHF 7/day.
Surface: grasstiles. 01/01-31/12.
Distance: Savognin 18km on the spot Savognin 18km on the spot.
Remarks: Parking ski-lifts.

Breil/Brigels 23A1

Parkplatz der Bergbahnen. GPS: n46,77104 e9,06770.

20 CHF 7 + CHF 3/pp tourist tax CHF 2/50liter Ch CHF 3/day.
Surface: metalled. 01/04-30/11.
Distance: 600m on the spot Imbiss on the spot, restaurants

CH

600m 600m on the spot nearby.
Remarks: At Brigeler See.

Chur 23B1

Stellplätze Camp Au, Felsenaustrasse 61. **GPS**: n46,86187 e9,50756.
CHF 15 + CHF 1,20/pp tourist tax Ch WC.
01/01-31/12.
Distance: 3km 2km on the spot on the spot.
Remarks: Max. 1 night, oldest city of Switzerland.

Churwalden 23B1

Pradafenz, Girabodawag 34. **GPS**: n46,77690 e9,54121.
50 CHF 35,60 Ch WC. 01/01-31/12.

Davos 23C1

Rinerlodge Talstation, Landwasserstrasse. **GPS**: n46,74150 e9,77814.
10 CHF 26-32 Ch CHF 2.
Surface: gravel.
01/01-31/12.
Distance: 1km on the spot on the spot on the spot on the spot.
Remarks: Max. 24h.

Tourist information Davos:
Davos Alpengarten. Botanical garden.
01/05-30/09 9-17h.
Berghaus Stafelalp, Frauenkirch. 250 Year old inn where they still cook on a wood oven and shimmer paraffin lamps are lit.

Elm 23B1

Sportbahnen Elm, Schiesserblock. **GPS**: n46,91332 e9,16228.
50 free. **Surface:** asphalted. 01/03-30/11.
Distance: 650m 650m on the spot on the spot.

Eschenz 20A2

Hüttenberg. GPS: n47,64436 e8,85935.
8 CHF 20 Ch WC included.
Location: Rural. **Surface:** grassy/metalled.
01/01-31/12.
Remarks: 01/04-31/10 Quickstop >19h <10h, payment also in euros.

Kreuzlingen 20B2

Fischerhaus, Promenadestraße 52. **GPS**: n47,64745 e9,19898.
CHF 41-51 Ch WC. 23/03-16/10.

Neuhausen 20A2

Parkplatz Fischacker, Nohlstrasse. **GPS**: n47,67373 e8,60866.

50 € 15 Ch WC. **Surface:** grassy/metalled.
Distance: 200m on the spot 200m 1km.

Tourist information Neuhausen:
Der Rheinfall. Water falls.

Pontresina 23C2

Plauns. GPS: n46,46200 e9,93400.
Ch. 01/06-15/10, 15/12-15/04.

Samnaun 20C3

Wohnmobilstellplatz Samnaun-Ravaisch, Sportplatzweg 13.
GPS: n46,94906 e10,36705.

18 CHF 18-39/day, CHF 6,20/pp Ch WC included.
01/01-31/12.
Distance: 750m 200m on the spot.
Remarks: At football ground.

Sankt Gallen 20B3

Paul-Grüninger-Stadion, Grütlistrasse. **GPS**: n47,43361 e9,40464.
2 CHF 2/9-19h, CHF 1/19-8h CHF 1/100liter CHF 0,50/kWh.
Surface: asphalted. 01/01-31/12.
Distance: 2km 300m.
Remarks: Next to sports fields.

Sankt Moritz 23C1

Olympiaschanze. GPS: n46,47800 e9,82600.
125 CHF 45 Ch WC. 20/05-03/10.

Tourist information Sankt Moritz:
Clean Energy Tour. Hiking trail, nature, energy, climate and weather adventure. Sign up at Kur- und Verkehrsverein St. Moritz. 15/06-01/10 Wed 13.45h duration 2,5 hours.

Savognin 23B1

Veia Sandeilas. **GPS**: n46,59660 e9,59226.
15 CHF 15 + CHF 8/pp CHF 1 Ch CHF 2,50. **Surface:** gravel.
01/01-31/12.
Distance: 500m.
Remarks: Near the chair-lift, summer: parking at campsite Julia.

Schiers 20B3

Restaurant Prättigauerhof, Flurystrasse 19. **GPS**: n46,97034 e9,68752.
2 free, use of a meal obligated. **Surface:** metalled.
01/01-31/12 Sa + Su.
Distance: 300m on the spot 100m.

Sent 23C1

Camping Sur En. GPS: n46,81852 e10,36596.
10 CHF 15 + CHF 2,50/pp tourist tax CHF 3.
01/01-31/12.
Distance: on the spot.
Remarks: Max. 1 night, 17-10h.

Splügen 23B1

Auf dem Sand. GPS: n46,54922 e9,31399.
CHF 40 Ch WC. 01/01-31/12.

Steckborn 20A2

Wohnmobilplatz Steckborn, Schützengraben.
GPS: n47,66813 e8,98462.

8 CHF 12/24h Ch (8x)included. **Surface:** gravel.
01/01-31/12.
Distance: 400m 200m 400m 300m.

Unterwasser 20B3

Hotel Restaurant Post, Postplatz. **GPS**: n47,19673 e9,30949.
6 CHF 15 + CHF 3/pp tourist tax, guests free (6x).
01/01-31/12.
Distance: 300m on the spot 300m on the spot.

Vaduz/Liechtenstein 20B3

Rheinparkstadion, Rheindamm. **GPS**: n47,14022 e9,50945.

10 CHF 4,50, 19-07h free Ch WC free. **Surface:** asphalted.
01/01-31/12.
Distance: 1,8km on the spot.
Remarks: Along the Rhine river, parking near stadium, max. 24h.

Tourist information Vaduz/Liechtenstein:
Liechtenstein Tourismus, Städtle 37, www.vaduz.li. Monarchy on the Austrian-Swiss border.
Kunstmuseum Lichtenstein, Städtle 32. Tue-Su 10-17h.
Erlebniswelt Neuguthof, Neugutweg 30. Maize labyrinth with wild-west city. 15/06-30/09 Wed 13-18h, Sa-Su 10-20h, holidays Mo-Fri 10-20h, Sa-Su 10-22h.

Vals 23B1

Stellplatz Vals, Vallée. **GPS**: n46,60891 e9,17438.

10 CHF 17 + CHF 2,80/pp tourist tax WC. **Surface:** metalled.
summer.
Distance: 300m on the spot 300m 300m on the spot.
Remarks: Parking funicular railway.

Zizers 23B1

K. Lüthi, Rappagugg. **GPS**: n46,91937 e9,56270.
5 free Ch. **Surface:** metalled.
Distance: 1,6km on the spot.
Remarks: At motorhome dealer.

Zürich 20A3

Camping Zürich, Seestrasse 559. **GPS**: n47,33641 e8,53960.
01/01-31/12.

Tourist information Zürich:
Zürich Tourismus, Im Hauptbahnhof, www.zuerich.com. Historical city with large pedestrian area.

Switzerland South

Agno 23A3

Eurocampo, Via di Molinnazzo. **GPS**: n45,99556 e8,90621.
CHF 30-34 Ch WC. 01/04-31/10.

Avegno 23A2

Piccolo Paradiso, Via Cantonale 13. **GPS**: n46,20100 e8,74300.
280 CHF 27-46 Ch WC. 20/03-25/10.

Bellinzona 23A2

Centro Sportivo, Viale Giuseppe Motta. **GPS**: n46,20116 e9,01729.

7 CHF 20 CHF 1/20liter Ch. **Surface:** asphalted.
01/01-31/12.
Distance: 1,5km 4km.
Remarks: Max. 48h.

Tourist information Bellinzona:
Castelgrande, Via Salita Castelgrande 18. 11-16h, Apr/Jun/Sep/Oct 10-18h, Jul/Aug 10-19h.
Castello di Montebello, Via Artore 4. 01/03-30/11 10-18h.
Castello di Sasso Corbaro. 01/04-30/11 10-18h.
Palestra di Roccia San Paolo, Palazo Civico. Climbing garden for beginners and experienced, 30.000m^2, 23 climbing trails.

Bouveret 22F2

Rive Bleue. GPS: n46,38645 e6,86041.
CHF 28,20-37,20 Ch WC. 25/03-16/10.

Brig 22H2

Brigerbad. GPS: n46,30209 e7,93102.
400 CHF 29-33 Ch WC. 30/04-02/11.

Champéry 22F2

Route de la Fin. **GPS**: n46,17592 e6,87076.

6 CHF 18 + CHF 2,20/pp Ch (4x)included. **Location:** Rural, simple. **Surface:** asphalted. 01/01-31/12.
Distance: 100m on the spot 200m 200m.
Remarks: Parking supermarket, nearby the télépherique.

CH

Evolène 22G2

Evolène. **GPS**: n46,11075 e7,49654.
CHF 29,40 Ch WC. 01/01-31/12.

Gordevio 23A2

Bella Riva. **GPS**: n46,22159 e8,74194.
Ch WC. 01/04-01/10.

Grimentz 22G2

Aire camping-car l'Illôt Bosquet, Route de Moiry.
GPS: n46,17432 e7,57271.

20 CHF 15 Ch CHF 3. **Location:** Rural, simple, quiet.
Surface: asphalted. 01/01-31/12.
Distance: on the spot on the spot on the spot on the spot nearby nearby.
Remarks: Pay and coins at tourist office, public transport, free entrance swimming pool (summer).

Tourist information Grimentz:
Grimentz/St.Jean Tourisme, www.grimentz.ch. Many signposted cycle and hiking routes.
La Maison bourgeoisiale. Life of the citizens of Grimentz. guided tour Mo. free.

Grimselpas 22H1

Hotel Grimselblick, Totensee. **GPS**: n46,56115 e8,33673.
20 CHF 10. **Surface:** asphalted.
Distance: on the spot.
Remarks: Service at hotel.

Hérémence 22G2

Val des Hérémence, Parking B,C,D en E, Le Chargeur.
GPS: n46,08882 e7,40362.

15 free. **Surface:** unpaved. 01/01-31/12.
Remarks: At artificial lake.

La Fouly 22G3

Les Glaciers. **GPS**: n45,93351 e7,09361.
Ch WC. 15/05-30/09.

Les Haudères 22G2

Molignon. **GPS**: n46,09061 e7,50776.
CHF 14,50-30,60 Ch WC. 01/01-31/12.

Leuk 22G2

Hexenplatzstrasse. **GPS**: n46,31082 e7,63436.
4 CHF 15/24h Ch. **Surface:** asphalted. 01/01-31/12.
Distance: 400m on the spot on the spot 400m 400m.

Leukerbad 22G2

Winterstellplatz, Parkplatz Fischweiher. **GPS**: n46,38215 e7,63232.

30 CHF 10/24h.
Location: Rural, simple. **Surface:** gravel/sand.
01/11-15/04.
Distance: 150m 600m 100m.
Remarks: Payment only with coins.

Locarno 23A2

Parco della Pace, Via Gioacchino Respini.
GPS: n46,16011 e8,80255.

50 CHF 5/6h. **Surface:** gravel. 01/01-31/12.
Distance: 900m 100m 100m.
Remarks: Max. 24h.

Tourist information Locarno:
Rasa. Touristic car-free miniature village, can be reached by first taking the Centrovall-track, till Verdasio, then the small telpher carrier to Rasa.
Tenero-Locarno-Tenero. Free boat service. 31/05-30/09.

Martigny 22G2

Les Neuvilles, Rue du Levant 68. **GPS**: n46,09787 e7,07930.
70 CHF 44 Ch WC. 24/03-16/10.

Tourist information Martigny:
Gorges du Durnand. Hiking trail through the gorge of the river Durnand.

Meride 23A3

Parco al Sole. **GPS**: n45,88806 e8,94944.
CHF 38-56 Ch WC. 15/04-25/09.

Molinazzo di Montegio 23A3

Tresiana. **GPS**: n45,98990 e8,81576.
95 CHF 26-46 Ch WC. 19/03-23/10.

Muzzano-Lugano 23A3

Piodella di Agnuzzo. **GPS**: n45,99463 e8,90857.
200 CHF 45 Ch WC. 01/01-31/12.

Raron 22H2

Santa Monica, Kantonstrasse 56. **GPS**: n46,30007 e7,82374.
CHF 23-29 Ch WC. 01/01-31/12.

Reckingen 22H2

Camping Augenstern, Im Ellbogen 21. **GPS**: n46,46500 e8,24500.
50 CHF 29-35 Ch WC. 01/05-18/10 and 15/12-15/03.

Rivera 23A2

Area Camper Tamaro, Monte Ceneri 19. **GPS**: n46,13926 e8,90675.
80 3-72h CHF 1/h Ch included.
Surface: grassy/gravel. 01/01-31/12, 24/24h.
Distance: on the spot.
Remarks: Video surveillance.

Saas Fee 22H2

Parkplatz P4. **GPS**: n46,11090 e7,93208.

50 CHF 26/24h Ch included CHF 2 WC. **Location:** Rural, simple, isolated, quiet. **Surface:** grassy/gravel.
01/01-31/12 service in winter.
Distance: 100m 200m 900m 200m.

Saillon 22G2

Bains de Saillon, Route du Centre Thermal 16. **GPS**: n46,17353 e7,19372.
12 free. **Surface:** grassy.
01/01-31/12.
Distance: 4km.
Remarks: Max. 48h.

Tourist information Saillon:
Sentier des Vitraux. Hiking trail, 45 minutes, through wine region.

Saint-Léonard 22G2

Place du Lac Souterrain. **GPS**: n46,25564 e7,42600.

15 CHF 10/night Ch (4x) WC included. **Location:** Rural, simple, central, quiet. **Surface:** asphalted/grassy.
service: 01/11-19/03.
Distance: 5,5km 300m.
Remarks: Pay in at kiosk.

Simplon 22H2

Col du Simplon, Simplonstrasse. **GPS**: n46,24944 e8,03056.

18 free Ch WC free. **Location:** Rural, simple, isolated.
Surface: asphalted.
Distance: 200m.

Sonogno 23A2

Camper Area Sonogno, Cioss. **GPS**: n46,35058 e8,78846.
15 € 16/night Ch included. **Location:** Rural, isolated, quiet.
Surface: grassy. 01/01-31/12.
Distance: 200m 200m 200m.

Stampa 23B2

Tankstelle Esso, Strada Principale. **GPS**: n46,34593 e9,59660.
8 CHF 8 CHF 3 Ch CHF 3. 01/01-31/12.
Distance: on the spot.
Remarks: Max. 24h.

Tenero 23A2

Lido Mappo, Via Mappo. **GPS**: n46,17692 e8,84433.
CHF 36-56 Ch. 18/03-23/10.

Tenero 23A2

Tamaro, Via Mappo 32. **GPS**: n46,17525 e8,84779.
CHF 36 Ch WC. 15/03-01/11.

Trient 22F3

Place de Repos Du Peuty, Le Peuty. **GPS**: n46,04645 e6,99499.

6 CHF 3/pp free. **Location:** Rural, simple, isolated, quiet.
Surface: grassy.
Distance: 1,5km on the spot.

Vétroz 22G2

Restaurant As de Pique. **GPS**: n46,20556 e7,27833.
Ch CHF 15, guests free. 01/01-31/12.

CH

Czech Republic

Capital: Prague
Government: parliamentary constitutional republic
Official Language: Czech
Population: 10.645.000 (2015)
Area: 78,866 Km²

General information
Dialling code: 00420
General emergency: 112
Currency: Koruna(CZK)
€ 1 = 27 CZK, 1 CZK = € 0,04 (October 2016)
£1 = 30,20 CZK, 10 CZK = £0.33 (October 2016)
Credit cards are accepted almost everywhere.

Regulations for overnight stays
Wild camping is not allowed.

Additional public holidays 2017
May 1 Labour Day
May 8 Liberation Day
July 5 St. Cyril & St. Methodius Day
July 6 Jan Hus Day
September 28 St. Wenceslas Day
October 28 Independent Czechoslavak State Day
November 17 Freedom and Democracy Day

Time Zone
Winter (Standard Time) GMT+1
Summer (DST) GMT+2

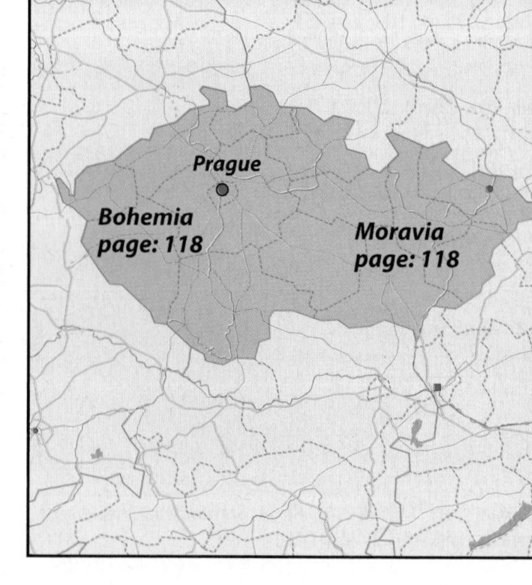

Bohemia

Golčův Jeníkov 37A2
Mamolina, Římovice 9. **GPS**: n49,80428 e15,44581.
20 Ch . 01/01-31/12.

Janovice N.U 17G1
Camping U Dvou Orechu, Splz 13- Strzov. **GPS**: n49,28137 e13,24008.
10 € 19/22 Ch WC included. **Surface:** grassy/metalled.
01/05-15/09.
Distance: 3km 3km 500m on the spot on the spot.

Karlovy Vary 12F2
Nakladni. **GPS**: n50,23438 e12,86782.
15 € 20 Ch included €1. **Surface:** metalled.
01/03-01/11.
Distance: 500m 200m 600m.

Karlovy Vary 12F2
U. Podjezdu 1616/5. **GPS**: n50,21992 e12,83688.
10 Chincluded €2,50. **Surface:** grassy.
01/03-01/11.
Distance: 400m.

Lipno nad Vltavou 37A3
Camping Hotel Panorama, Lipno nad Vltavou 22.
GPS: n48,63869 e14,22484.
40 € 10,50-17,50 Ch WC included.
Location: Rural. **Surface:** grassy/metalled. 01/04-01/10.
Distance: on the spot on the spot on the spot on the spot.
Remarks: Bread-service.

Nelahozeves 12H2
Marina Vltava, Dvořákova stezka. **GPS**: n50,25898 e14,30230.
15 € 6 €2/100liter €2 €2 . **Surface:** grasstiles.
01/01-31/12.
Distance: on the spot on the spot 300m.

Nová Bystřice 37A2
Farma Alpaka, Dobrá Voda čp 20. **GPS**: n49,06400 e15,10481.
10 € 8 Ch . **Location:** Rural. **Surface:** gravel.
01/01-31/12.
Distance: 6km.
Remarks: Bread-service.

Nové Město pod Smrkem 37A1
Ludvikov Horses&Holiday, Ludvikov pod Smrkem 9.
GPS: n50,91579 e15,20486.
15 € 13 Ch included WC . **Location:** Rural.
Surface: grassy. 01/01-31/12.
Distance: on the spot on the spot 10km.

Prague 37A2
Camp Herzog, Trojská 602/161. **GPS**: n50,11719 e14,42717.
20 € 14 Ch €3,50 WC included.
Location: Urban. **Surface:** grassy.
01/01-31/12.
Distance: 4,2km 500m.

Prague 37A2
Caravan Camping Císařská Louka, Císařská louka 16.
GPS: n50,05584 e14,41336.
40 € 16,50 ChWC €3,50 included. **Location:** Urban.
Surface: grassy. 01/01-31/12.
Distance: 4km 750m.

Prague 37A2
Dana Troja, Trojská 357/129. **GPS**: n50,11716 e14,43176.
15 € 19 Ch €3 WC €2,50 included.
Location: Urban. **Surface:** grassy.
01/01-31/12.
Distance: 4km 200m.

Sněžník 12H1
Stellplatz Sněžník, Jílové. **GPS**: n50,79647 e14,08425.

15 € 5/5h, then € 0,60/h €0,10/10liter Ch €0,60/kWh.
01/01-31/12.
Distance: 50m.

Svitavy 37A2
U Stadion, U Stadionu. **GPS**: n49,75146 e16,46521.
6 free Chfree €0,25/kWh. **Location:** Urban.
Surface: metalled. 01/01-31/12.
Distance: on the spot.
Remarks: At stadium.

Velemín 12H2
Finaso, Velemin 198. **GPS**: n50,53639 e13,97333.

6 free Chfree €0,50/kWh. **Location:** Simple.
Surface: metalled. 01/01-31/12.

Velká Jesenice 37A1
Stellplatz Rozkoš, Vodní nádrž Rozkoš . **GPS**: n50,36444 e16,05944.
16 € 11 Ch included. **Location:** Rural.
01/01-31/12.
Distance: on the spot on the spot.

Moravia

Červená Řečice 37A2
Camping Kovarna, Červená Řečice 63. **GPS**: n49,51922 e15,15661.
39 € 15 Ch €3,75 WC included. **Location:** Rural.
Surface: grassy. 01/06-26/08.
Distance: on the spot 5km 2km on the spot on the spot.
Remarks: Bread-service.

Uherský Brod 37B2
Aquapark Delfin, Slovácké náměstí 2377.
GPS: n49,01960 e17,64828.
2 free. **Location:** Urban. **Surface:** metalled. 01/01-31/12.
Distance: 100m 150m.

CZ

Germany

Capital: Berlin
Government: Federal republic
Official Language: Germany
Population: 81,000,000 (2015)
Area: 356,970 km²

General information
Dialling code: 0049
General emergency: 112
Currency: Euro

Regulations for overnight stays
Overnight stays on the public highway are allowed, if there is no local prohibition, but no "camping" activities are allowed.

Additional public holidays 2017
January 6 Epiphany
April 14 Good Friday
April 17 Eastermonday
May 1 Labor Day
June 5 White Monday
June 15 Corpus Christi
August 15 Assumption of the Virgin Mary
October 3 Day of German Unity
November 1 All Saints' Day

Time Zone
Winter (Standard Time) GMT+1
Summer (DST) GMT+2

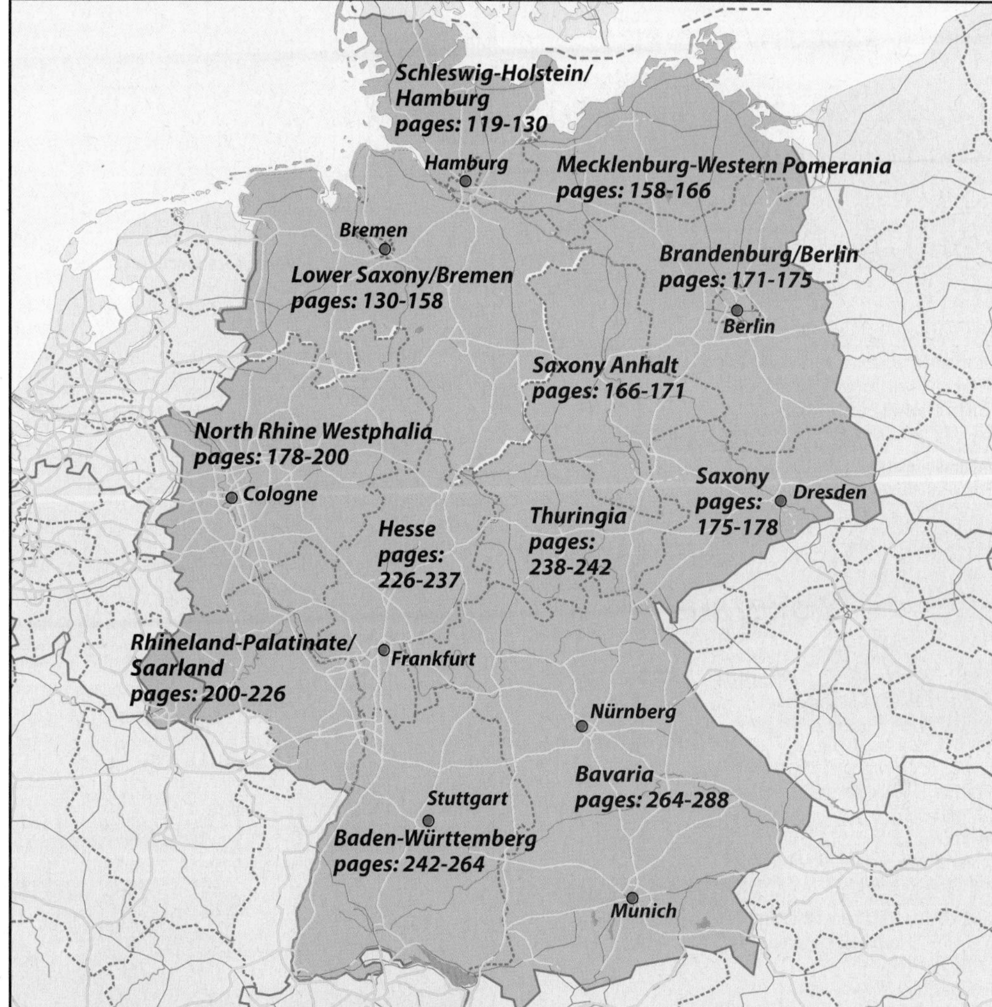

DE

Schleswig-Holstein/ Hamburg

Achtrup 6C3

Landgasthof Achtruper Stuben, Ladelunderstrasse 24.
GPS: n54,79337 e9,02676.

3 free, free. **Location:** Simple.
01/01-31/12, Mo-Tue.
Distance: 5km, on the spot, 5km.
Remarks: Along through road.

Albersdorf 8A1

Freitzeitbad Albersdorf, Weg zur Badeanstalt 18.
GPS: n54,15135 e9,28055.

6 € 15 swimming pool incl Ch (6x)included.
Location: Rural, isolated, quiet. **Surface:** grassy.
01/05-31/08.
Distance: 1km, 100m, 300m, on the spot, on the spot.
Remarks: Parking at swimming pool, max. 3 days.

Altenhof 6D3

Wohnmobilpark Ostsee 'Grüner Jäger', Grünen Jäger.
GPS: n54,44392 e9,90526.

80 €8 Chincluded (40x)€4/24h WC €1.
Location: Rural, simple, isolated, quiet. **Surface:** grassy.
01/01-31/12.
Distance: Eckernförde 6km, 2km, on the spot, 6km, 200m busstop -> Kiel, on the spot, on the spot.
Remarks: Check in at restaurant Grüner, bread-service.

Aukrug 8B1

Parkplatz am Freibad, Zum Sportplatz 1.
GPS: n54,07441 e9,79160.

10 €8 Ch (10x)included. **Location:** Rural.
Surface: grassy/metalled. 01/01-31/12.
Distance: 1km, 800m, 1km, on the spot, on the spot.
Remarks: Max. 5 days, check in and key service at pay-desk of swimming pool.

Aventoft 6C3

Wohnmobillstellplatz Zu den Fuchswiesen, Revtoftweg 1.
GPS: n54,87661 e8,84562.

15 €5 €1,50/24h. **Location:** Rural, simple, isolated, quiet. **Surface:** asphalted/grassy. 01/01-31/12.
Distance: 3km, 3km, 3km, on the spot.
Remarks: Bread-service.

Bad Bramstedt 8B1

Parkplatz P7, Am Bahnhof, König Christian Strasse.
GPS: n53,92167 e9,88967.

5 free. **Location:** Urban, simple, central, noisy. **Surface:** metalled.
01/01-31/12.
Distance: centre 500m, 500m, 500m, on the spot.
Remarks: At station, max. 1 night, service at camping Roland, Kielerstrasse.

S Bad Malente 6E3

Parkplatz Krützen, Sebastian-Kneipp-Straße.
GPS: n54,17198 e10,54919.

4 € 5 + € 2/pp tourist tax €1 €1 Ch.
Location: Rural, simple. **Surface:** metalled. 01/01-31/12.
Distance: on the spot 500m 1km.
Remarks: Max. 24h.

S Bad Oldesloe 8B1

Wohnmobilplatz Exer, Am Bürgerpark.
GPS: n53,81101 e10,36915.

8 free €1/10minutes Ch (8x)€2/10h WC.
Location: Urban, simple, quiet. **Surface:** metalled.
01/01-31/12.
Distance: on the spot 3km on the spot 400m.
Remarks: Max. 3 nights, bread-service.

S Bad Schwartau 8C1

Landschaftsschutzgebiet Riesebusch. **GPS**: n53,92405 e10,69795.
15 € 5/24h, tourist tax € 1,65/pp €1/90liter Ch €1/8h.
01/01-31/12.
Distance: 1,5km 1,5km.
Remarks: Max. 72h.

S Bad Segeberg 8B1

Kalkbergblick, Kastanienweg 1b. **GPS**: n53,93872 e10,31423.

25 € 8 Chincluded (15x)€2/12h,6Amp.
Location: Rural, comfortable, quiet. **Surface:** gravel.
01/01-31/12.
Distance: 500m A7 3km 600m Segerberger See 600m 500m 500m on the spot on the spot.
Remarks: Jun/Aug Karl May Spiele, open air theater.

S Barkenholm 6C3

Gaststätte Jägerstuben, Dorfstraße 28. **GPS**: n54,23497 e9,17484.

6 € 5, free with a meal free €1/day. **Location:** Rural, simple, isolated. **Surface:** grasstiles.
01/01-31/12 Wed.
Distance: 8km on the spot.
Remarks: Wifi at restaurant.

S Barmstedt 8B1

Parkplatz am Rondeel, Platz Roissy-en-Brie.
GPS: n53,78640 e9,76420.

5 € 5 Ch WC included. **Location:** Urban, simple.
Surface: metalled. 01/01-31/12.
Distance: on the spot on the spot 500m on the spot on the spot.
Remarks: To be paid at swimming pool, key electricity at pool.

S Behrensdorf 6E3

Campingpark Waldesruh, Neuland. **GPS**: n54,35754 e10,60216.

23 € 11-13, 2 pers. incl., dog € 1,50 Ch €0,40/kWh WC. **Location:** Rural, comfortable. **Surface:** grassy.
01/04-31/10.
Distance: 2km on the spot on the spot on the spot on the spot.
Remarks: Dog € 1,50/night.

S Bistensee 6D3

Ferienplatz bei Matz, Mühlenweg 1. **GPS**: n54,39538 e9,71386.

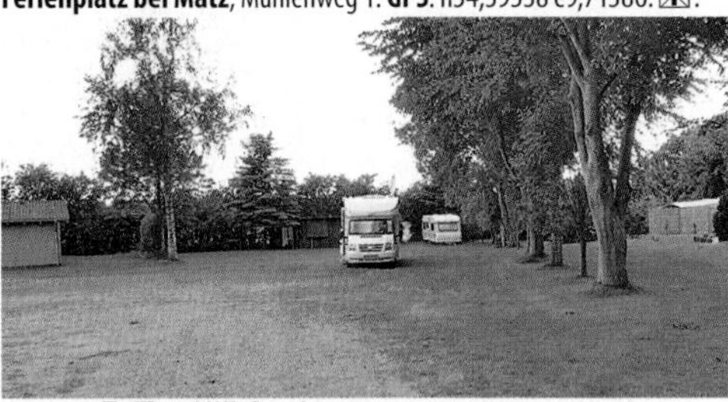

4 € 10 WC €1 included. **Location:** Rural, simple, isolated, quiet. **Surface:** grassy. 01/01-31/12.
Distance: 500m 600m Bistensee on the spot 2km 1km on the spot on the spot.
Remarks: Dog € 2/day.

S Blekendorf 6E3

Am Sehlendorfer Strand, Strandstrasse 24.
GPS: n54,30571 e10,69358.

40 € 15,50 €1 Ch included WC.
Location: Rural, comfortable. **Surface:** grassy.
01/01-31/12.
Distance: 1km on the spot on the spot on the spot 5km.

Bordesholm 8B1

Festplatz, Kielerstrasse. **GPS**: n54,18389 e10,02667.

6 free. **Location:** Rural, simple, quiet. **Surface:** grassy/sand.
01/01-31/12.
Distance: 1,5km 4km.
Remarks: Max. 18h, service at petrol station.

S Bordesholm 8B1

Shell tankstelle, Bahnofstrasse 78. **GPS**: n54,17343 e10,03497.
Ch. 01/01-31/12.

S Borgdorf-Seedorf 6D3

Seecampingplatz BUM, Hauptstrasse 99. **GPS**: n54,18256 e9,88422.
12 € 13,50 Ch €3,50.
Distance: 3km.

S Bosau 8B1

Dat Gröne Huus, Stadtbeker Strasse 97. **GPS**: n54,09198 e10,42886.

3 € 5, guests free €3. **Location:** Rural, simple, quiet.
Surface: gravel. 01/04-30/11.
Distance: 100m Großer Plöner See on the spot on the spot 1km.
Remarks: Bread-service.

S Bösdorf 8B1

Wohnmobilcamp Augustfelde, Vierer See, Augustfelde.
GPS: n54,12898 e10,45506.

16 € 11,50-13,50 Ch (16x)WCincluded €0,75.
Surface: grassy. 01/04-25/10.
Distance: on the spot on the spot on the spot on the spot.

S Bösdorf 8B1

Landhaus zur Tenne, Hörn 6. **GPS**: n54,12792 e10,50194.
10 € 6 Chincluded €2/day. **Surface:** grassy/gravel.
Distance: on the spot on the spot.

S Bösdorf 8B1

Campingpark Gut Ruhleben, Missionsweg 2, Ruhleben.
GPS: n54,14308 e10,45021.

10 € 11-13 Ch €2,50 included.
Location: Rural, simple. **Surface:** grassy/gravel. 01/04-30/09.
Remarks: Max. 3 nights.

Bredstedt 6C3

Süderstraße. **GPS**: n54,61307 e8,97082.

15 free. **Location:** Rural, simple, quiet. **Surface:** asphalted.
01/01-31/12.
Distance: 900m Aldi 650m.

Remarks: Nearby sports complex, nearby swimming pool.

Breiholz 6D3

Campingplatz Eidertal, Fährstraße 1. **GPS**: n54,21502 e9,53157.
12 € 12 Ch WC included.
Distance: on the spot.

Brodersby 6D3

Ferienhof Lassen, Grossbrodersbyer weg 5.
GPS: n54,53829 e9,71443.

3 € 10 Ch included.
Location: Rural, simple, quiet. **Surface:** grassy.
Distance: 500m 2km 500m.

Brokdorf 8A1

Stellplatz Brokdorf, Dorfstrasse 53. **GPS**: n53,86417 e9,31667.

30 € 5, 01/03-31/10 € 10 €1/70liter €1 Ch (30x)€0,50/kWh WC free €1.
Location: Rural, comfortable. **Surface:** metalled. 01/01-31/12.
Distance: 800m 400m on the spot 500m on the spot on the spot.
Remarks: Max. 3 days.

Brunsbüttel 8A1

An der Braake, Am Freizeitbad. **GPS**: n53,89832 e9,13138.

12 € 3 €2 Ch. **Location:** Rural, comfortable, central, quiet.
Surface: grassy/metalled. 01/01-31/12.
Distance: 500m 500m 500m on the spot.
Remarks: To pay at swimming pool.

Büdelsdorf 6D3

Hermann-Ehlers-Platz, Agnes Miegel Strasse.
GPS: n54,31583 e9,69306.

10 free. **Location:** Simple, central. **Surface:** metalled.
01/01-31/12.
Distance: on the spot 1km 1,5km.
Remarks: Max. 1 night.

Busdorf 6D3

Autohof Wikingerland, Wittgenstein 2. **GPS**: n54,47736 e9,54454.
free Ch (6x) WC. **Location:** Motorway.
Distance: on the spot.
Remarks: At petrol station, special part for motor homes.

Büsum 7H1

Wohnmobilstellplatz Nordsee, Dr. Martin Bahr Strasse.
GPS: n54,12889 e8,86889.

100 € 11, 01/03-31/10 € 15 €0,50/50liter Ch (100x) included WC €0,50 €1/4minutes €0,50/day. **Location:** Rural, comfortable, isolated, quiet. **Surface:** grassy. 01/01-31/12.
Distance: 1km 500m 300m on the spot on the spot.
Remarks: Key shower at Imbiss.

Damp 6D3

Wohnmobilpark Damp, Parkstrasse 2.
GPS: n54,57750 e10,01667.

70 € 14 €1/100liter Ch (60x)€0,60/kWh WC €1/4minutes . **Location:** Rural, comfortable, quiet. **Surface:** grassy/gravel.
01/01-31/12.
Distance: on the spot on the spot on the spot 150m.

Drelsdorf 6C3

Drelsdörper Krog, Dorfstrasse 23. **GPS**: n54,60555 e9,03555.

10 € 5, guests free €2 WC. **Location:** Rural, central, noisy.
Surface: grassy. 01/01-31/12.
Distance: 200m on the spot 2km.
Remarks: Along through road.

Eckernförde 6D3

Wohnmobilstellplatz am Noor, Kakabellenweg.
GPS: n54,46443 e9,83402.
49 € 13 + € 2/pp tourist tax €1/100liter Ch €0,50/kWh WC €2/2 included. 01/01-31/12.
Distance: 1km on the spot on the spot 500m on the spot.

Elmshorn 8A1

Stellplatz Elmshorn, Nordufer. **GPS**: n53,75157 e9,65268.

4 free €1/80liter Ch WC. **Location:** Urban, simple, central, quiet. **Surface:** metalled. 01/01-31/12.
Distance: 800m on the spot on the spot on the spot.

Emmelsbüll-Horsbüll 6C3

Stellplatz am Badedeich, Südwesthörner Strasse.
GPS: n54,79686 e8,66075.

3 free €1. **Location:** Rural, simple, isolated, quiet.
Surface: grassy/gravel. 01/01-31/12.
Distance: on the spot on the spot.
Remarks: Max. 5 days.

Eutin 8C1

Elisabethstrasse. **GPS**: n54,13507 e10,60935.

6 free. **Location:** Urban. **Surface:** asphalted. 01/01-31/12.
Distance: on the spot 300m.
Remarks: Parking at station.

Eutin 8C1

Forsthaus am Ukleisee, Zum Ukleisee 23, Sielbeck.
GPS: n54,18181 e10,64137.
€ 5. **Surface:** grassy/gravel.

Fehmarn 6E3

Wohnmobilpark Wulfener Hals, Wulfener-Hals-Weg 16, Wulfen.
GPS: n54,40687 e11,17489.

100 from € 12,90-49 Ch €4,20 WC €0,90 .
Location: Rural, luxurious. **Surface:** grassy. 01/01-31/12.
Distance: on the spot.
Remarks: Bike/car rental.

Fehmarn 6E3

Wohnmobilplatz Johannisberg, Johannisberg 4, Burg.
GPS: n54,50081 e11,17865.
50 € 10-15 €0,10/10liter €2 Ch €0,50 €1 €3,50/2,00.
Surface: grassy. 01/01-31/12.
Distance: 800m on the spot.
Remarks: Bread-service.

Fehmarn 6E3

Hintz-Heizungsbau, Landkirchenerweg 1b, Burg.
GPS: n54,44228 e11,18967.

16 € 10 €1 Ch (16x)€5. **Location:** Simple, quiet.
Surface: metalled. 01/01-31/12.
Distance: on the spot.

Fehmarn 6E3

Parkplatz Ost, Osterstrasse, Burg. **GPS**: n54,43754 e11,19990.

DE

30 € 8 (21-8h). **Location:** Urban, simple. **Surface:** metalled.
01/01-31/12.
Distance: 100m.

Fehmarn 6E3

Kommunal- und Yachthafen Burgstaaken, Burgstaaken/Am Binnensee. **GPS**: n54,42028 e11,19224.

15 € 10 21-08h. **Location:** Rural, simple. **Surface:** metalled.
01/01-31/12.
Distance: 100m 100m.

Fehmarn 6E3

Ferienhof Wachtelberg. GPS: n54,44653 e11,26039.
4 € 13, 2 pers.incl, extra pers € 5 WC included.
Surface: grassy. 01/01-31/12.
Distance: 1km.

Fehmarn 6E3

Camping Strukkamphuk, Strukkamp. **GPS**: n54,41239 e11,10223.

21 € 14,50-31 Ch WC included.
Location: Rural. **Surface:** grassy. 01/01-31/12.
Distance: 10m.

Flensburg 6D3

Am Industriehafen, dir Flensburg Mürwick. **GPS**: n54,80444 e9,44388.

20 free.
Location: Urban, simple, isolated, quiet. **Surface:** gravel.
Distance: 1,5km on the spot on the spot.

Fockbek 6D3

Am Freibad, Grosse Rheie 17. **GPS**: n54,30190 e9,60331.

3 free ChWC. **Location:** Rural, quiet. **Surface:** grassy/sand.
01/01-31/12.
Distance: 800m 800m 800m on the spot on the spot.

Remarks: Parking swimming pool, max. 24h.

Friedrichskoog 7H1

P2, Nordseestrasse. **GPS**: n54,03272 e8,84833.

30 € 10/24h Chincluded.
Location: Rural, comfortable, isolated, quiet.
Surface: asphalted/grassy. 01/03-31/10.
Distance: 1km 550m 800m on the spot.
Remarks: Bread-service.

Friedrichstadt 6C3

Friedrichstädter Wohnmobilstellplatz, Halbmond 5.
GPS: n54,37256 e9,08868.

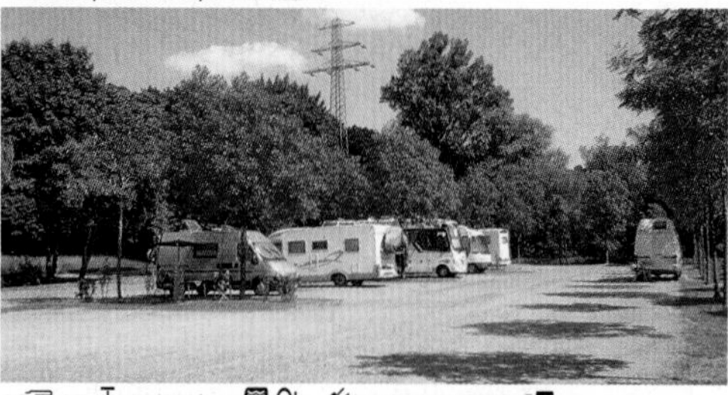

65 € 13 €0,10/10liter Ch €0,60/kWh WCfree
€1 €3,50/3,50 €1/1h. **Location:** Rural, luxurious.
Surface: grassy/gravel. 01/01-31/12.
Distance: 300m on the spot 300m.

Geesthacht 8B2

Alter Schiffsanleger 777, Elbuferstrasse.
GPS: n53,42574 e10,37907.

16 € 7 €1/100liter Ch (12x)€0,50/kWh.
Location: Rural, simple. **Surface:** grasstiles/metalled.
01/01-31/12.
Distance: 1,5km on the spot on the spot 1,5km 2km on the spot on the spot on the spot.
Remarks: Along the river Elbe, max. 3 days.

Gelting 6D3

Hafen Wackerballig, Strandweg, Wackerballig.
GPS: n54,75564 e9,87842.

12 € 8 Chincluded €1,50/day WC €0,50.
Location: Rural, simple. **Surface:** grassy/gravel.
01/04-31/10.
Distance: 1,5km on the spot 2km.
Remarks: Key sanitary building/waste dump at harbour master, caution € 20.

Glückstadt 8A1

Park & Ride platz, Pentzstrasse. **GPS**: n53,78776 e9,43145.

10 free. **Location:** Urban, simple. **Surface:** asphalted.
01/01-31/12.
Distance: 900m 200m on the spot on the spot.

Glückstadt 8A1

Am Außenhafen, Am Hafen. **GPS**: n53,78560 e9,41088.

16 € 10. **Location:** Rural, comfortable. **Surface:** metalled.
01/01-31/12 high water.
Distance: 1km on the spot on the spot on the spot on the spot on the spot.
Remarks: Along the river Elbe, money in envelope in mail box.

Grödersby 6D3

WSG Arin/Grödersby, Friedenshöher Straße 21.
GPS: n54,63444 e9,92944.

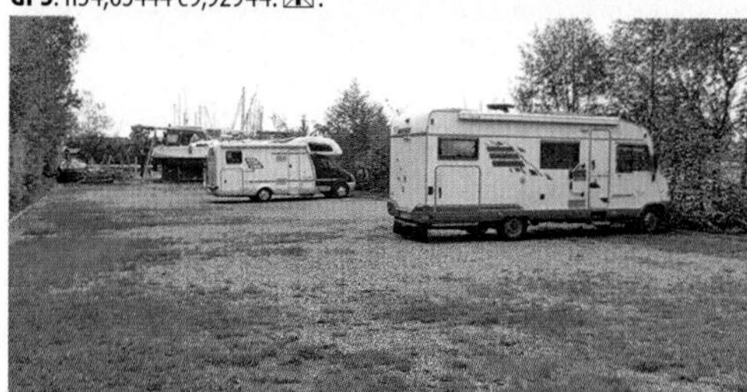

20 € 15 Ch WC €3/2 included.
Location: Rural, simple, quiet. **Surface:** gravel/metalled.
01/05-30/09.
Distance: 200m on the spot on the spot 200m on the spot.

Grömitz 6E3

Großraumparkplatz, Gildestraße 14. **GPS**: n54,14490 e10,95262.

60 15/03-31/10 € 15, 01/11-14/03 € 6 €0,50 Ch (20x)€1/kWh. **Location:** Rural, comfortable. **Surface:** metalled.
01/01-31/12 water disconnected in winter.
Distance: 200m on the spot 200m 500m.

Grömitz 6E3

Wohnmobilstellplatz am Lensterstrand, Blankwasserweg.
GPS: n54,15650 e10,99134.

50 free, 15/03-31/10 € 10 WC. **Location:** Rural.
Surface: grassy. 01/01-31/12 water disconnected in winter.

DE

Distance: on the spot on the spot.
Remarks: Max. 24h.

S **Grömitz** 6E3

Wohnmobilplatz Kattenberg/Cismar, Kattenberg 8, Cismar.
GPS: n54,18637 e10,96541.
5 € 8 Ch €2. **Surface:** grassy.
Distance: Grömitz 5km 1,3km.

Großenaspe 8B1

Wildpark Eekholt, Eekhol 1. **GPS**: n53,94819 e10,02916.

10 free. **Location:** Rural, simple, isolated, quiet.
Surface: grassy/sand. 01/01-31/12.
Distance: 4km Grossenaspe Kiek ut Stuben, Game preserve > Wildpark.

S **Großenbrode** 6E3

Wassersportzentrum, Am Kai 29. **GPS**: n54,35583 e11,07798.

50 € 10-12 €0,50/100liter Ch €1/kWh WC €0,50 .
Location: Rural. **Surface:** grassy/metalled. 01/01-31/12.
Distance: 300m on the spot 2km.

S **Großenbrode** 6E3

Wohnmobilhafen Reise, Südstrand 1.
GPS: n54,36170 e11,08567.

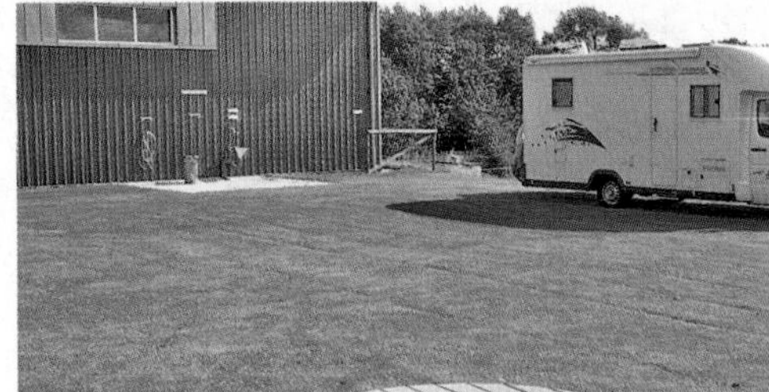

36 € 10-14 Ch WC included €0,50 €3/day.
Location: Rural, comfortable. **Surface:** gravel. 01/01-31/12.
Distance: 300m on the spot 500m on the spot.
Remarks: Bread-service.

S **Großsolt** 6D3

Stellplatz Mühlenbrück, Flensburger strasse, Mühlenbrück.
GPS: n54,70853 e9,52243.

13 € 10 Ch (13x)€2/day WC €0,50.
Location: Rural, comfortable, quiet. **Surface:** gravel.
01/03-01/10.
Distance: 200m.

S **Hamburg** 8B2

Elbepark-Bunthaus, Moorwerder Hauptdeich 33.
GPS: n53,46194 e10,06265.

80 € 12-19 Ch (70x)WC included €0,50 €1 .
Location: Rural, comfortable, quiet.
Surface: asphalted.
15/03-05/10.
Distance: 15km on the spot on the spot.
Remarks: Several locations, bread-service, possibility for reservation.

S **Hamburg** 8B2

Wohnmobilhafen Hamburg, Grüner Deich 8, Hammerbrook.
GPS: n53,54360 e10,02570.

60 € 19 Ch WC included.
Location: Urban, simple, central, noisy. **Surface:** gravel.
01/01-31/12.
Distance: 4km 200m.

S **Hamburg** 8B2

Heiligengeistfeld. **GPS**: n53,55523 e9,97361.

30 € 18 €5/day €5/day included.
Location: Urban, simple. **Surface:** gravel/sand. during event.
Distance: on the spot 300m 300m.
Remarks: Accessible via entrance C, max. 3 nights, possibility for reservation, special part for motor homes.

Hamburg 8B2

Am Strand Pauli, St. Pauli Hafenstraße. **GPS**: n53,54598 e9,96099.
20 € 12,50, weekend € 19,50.
Surface: asphalted.
01/01-31/12.
Distance: Hamburg Altstadt 2,4km on the spot many restaurant 100m 600m.

Tourist information Hamburg:
Hamburg-card. Card offers free entrance to public transport and museums, discounts on boat trips, zoo etc. Available at Tourist Information.
€ 9,90 1 day, € 25,50/3 days, 1 adult max. 3 childeren.
Sankt Pauli. City district with well-known Reeperbahn.
Flohschanze, Rinderschlachthalle St Pauli. Antiques and flea market.
Sa 8-16h.
Tierpark Hagenbeck, Stellingen. Zoo.
Antikpassage, Klosterwall 9-21. Arcade with 39 antique stores.
Tue-Fri 12-18h, Sa 10-16h.

S **Handewitt** 6C3

Scandinavian Park. **GPS**: n54,77826 e9,33445.
€ 10 Ch WC .
Distance: on the spot on the spot.
Remarks: At shopping centre.

S **Hanerau-Hademarschen** 8A1

Ferienhof Sievers, Wilhelmsburg. **GPS**: n54,12360 e9,38627.

5 € 10 Ch (6x)WC included.
Location: Rural, comfortable, isolated, quiet.
Surface: grasstiles/grassy. 01/01-31/12.
Distance: 2km 500m on the spot on the spot.

S **Harrislee** 6D3

Skandic Camping, Am Oxer 17a. **GPS**: n54,79800 e9,36960.

5 € 5 Ch included WC €1.
Location: Urban, simple, isolated. **Surface:** metalled. 01/01-31/12.
Distance: 6km.
Remarks: Motorhome dealer, accessory shop.

S **Hasloh** 8B2

Stellplatz Tante Henni, Garstedter Weg 36a.
GPS: n53,69251 e9,92608.

21 € 17 Ch (21x)WC €1 included.
Location: Rural, comfortable, quiet. **Surface:** grassy. 01/01-31/12.
Distance: on the spot on the spot 4km 1,5km 1,5km 800m on the spot on the spot.
Remarks: Check in on arrival.

S **Hasselberg** 6D3

Camping Oehe-Draecht, Drecht. **GPS**: n54,71590 e9,99030.

10 € 11 Ch €3 WC included.
Location: Rural, simple, quiet. **Surface:** grassy. 01/04-30/09.
Distance: 3km on the spot on the spot.

S **Heide** 8A1

Wohnmobilplatz Heide, Langvogt-Johannsen-strasse.
GPS: n54,20181 e9,11319.

16 € 7 €1/100liter €1 Ch €1/2kWh .
Location: Urban, comfortable, central, noisy.
Surface: grasstiles/metalled. 01/01-31/12.

DE

Distance: 800m 5,5km 100m 300m.
Remarks: At swimming pool, use of sauna against payment.

Heiligenhafen 6E3

Reisemobilstellplatz Binnensee, Eichholzweg.
GPS: n54,37721 e10,95548.

20 € 7,50-10. **Location:** Urban. **Surface:** metalled.
01/01-31/12.
Distance: 1km on the spot.
Remarks: Max. 24h.

Hohenfelde 6D3

Campingpark Ostseestrand, Strandstraße.
GPS: n54,38588 e10,49152.

25 € 15-21, dog € 2 Ch WC included. **Location:** Rural, luxurious. **Surface:** grassy. 01/04-15/10.
Distance: 1km beach 150m 150m on the spot on the spot.

Hohenfelde 6D3

Wohnmobilplatz Radeland, Strandstraße 18.
GPS: n54,38278 e10,49295.

20 € 6, dog € 1,50 €2 Ch €0,70/kWh WC €3/day.
Location: Rural. **Surface:** grassy/sand. 01/04-30/09.
Distance: 300m.

Hohn 6D3

Rosenhof Hohn, Westende 12. **GPS:** n54,29980 e9,49485.
5 € 10 Ch. **Surface:** grassy. 01/04-31/10.
Distance: on the spot.

Hohwacht 6E3

Parkplatz Alt-Hohwacht, Strandstrasse.
GPS: n54,31902 e10,67529.

19 € 10 €1/80liter €1 Ch (20x)€1/kWh.
Location: Urban. **Surface:** metalled. 01/01-31/12.
Distance: on the spot on the spot.

Hörnum 6C3

Zeltplatz. **GPS:** n54,76385 e8,28335.
30 € 18 Ch €0,45/kWh WC.
Distance: on the spot on the spot 750m.

Hörsten 6D3

Reisemobilstellplatz NOK, Schachtholm 1.
GPS: n54,22472 e9,60194.

49 € 10 WC included.
Distance: on the spot on the spot.
Remarks: Bread-service.

Husum 6C3

Loof's Wohnmobilhafen, Dockkoogstrasse 7.
GPS: n54,47451 e9,04249.

30 € 12 €1 €2 Ch€2 (30x)€3 WC included €0,50.
Location: Urban, simple, central, quiet. **Surface:** gravel.
01/01-31/12.
Distance: 200m 200m 200m 200m 200m on the spot on the spot.

Husum 6C3

Wohnmobilplatz Am Dockkoog, Dockoogstrasse 17.
GPS: n54,47888 e9,01138.

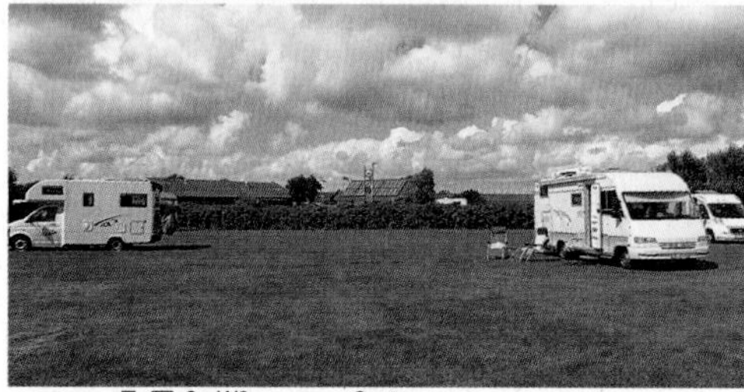

25 € 13 Ch WC included. **Location:** Rural, simple, quiet.
Surface: grassy. Easter-15/10.
Distance: 500m 200m 200m on the spot on the spot on the spot.
Remarks: Max. 3 nights, sanitary at campsite.

Itzehoe 8A1

Malzmüllerwiesen, Schuhmacherallee.
GPS: n53,91970 e9,51815.

5 free (4x)€0,50/kWh.
Location: Rural, simple, central, quiet. **Surface:** metalled/sand.
01/01-31/12 during event.
Distance: 600m 20m on the spot on the spot.

Jagel 6D3

Wohnmobilhafen Jagel, Bundesstrasse 13.
GPS: n54,45388 e9,53416.

31 € 10 Ch €2/day WC. **Location:** Rural, comfortable, quiet. **Surface:** grassy. 01/01-31/12.
Distance: 250m 4,5km.

Kaltenkirchen 8B1

Reisemobilstellplatz Holstentherme, Norderstrasse 8.
GPS: n53,84056 e9,94650.

20 free €1/80liter €1 Ch€1 €0,50/kWh.
Location: Urban, quiet. **Surface:** grassy/gravel. 01/01-31/12.
Distance: 1,5km 1km on the spot 1,5km on the spot.
Remarks: Coins available at pay-desk of theTherme.

Kappeln 6D3

Aral-Tankstelle, Eckernförder Strasse 9/B. **GPS:** n54,65688 e9,94480.

10 free Ch €5/day. **Location:** Urban, simple.
Surface: metalled. 01/01-31/12.
Distance: 300m 2km on the spot.
Remarks: Caution key electricity € 25.

Kappeln 6D3

Anker Yachting, Am Hafen. **GPS:** n54,66715 e9,93718.
50 € 10-14 Ch €0,50/kWh €1. 15/02-15/11.
Distance: 1km 1km 100m.
Remarks: Near marina.

Kellinghusen 8A1

Am Freibad, Jacob-Fleischer-Strasse 6. **GPS:** n53,94715 e9,71035.

6 free €0,50/100liter Ch€0,50 (4x)€1/h WC use sanitary facilities at swimming pool.
Location: Rural, simple, quiet. **Surface:** gravel. 01/01-31/12.
Distance: centre 500m 500m 500m on the spot.
Remarks: Check in at swimming pool.

Kiel 6D3

Wohnmobilstellplatz Kiel, Förde und Kanalblick, Mecklenburgstrasse 58. Kiel-Wik. **GPS:** n54,36362 e10,14705.

32 € 12-15 Ch (33x)€3,50/24h WC €1/5minutes €3/1.
Location: Urban, simple, central, noisy.
Surface: metalled.
01/01-31/12.
Distance: 6,5km Imbiss on the spot 1,5km on the spot on the spot.
Remarks: Check in and pay at reception, bread-service.

Kiel 6D3

Olympiahafen Schilksee, Soling 26. **GPS:** n54,43033 e10,16634.

DE

20 € 10 €0,50/3minutes €1 Ch. WC.
Surface: metalled.
01/01-31/12 last 2 weeks of Jun.
Distance: 13km 400m 400m.
Remarks: Check in and coins service at harbourmaster.

Tourist information Kiel:
M Schleswig-Holsteinisches Freilichtmuseum, Hamburger Landstraße 97, Molfsee. Open air museum. 01/04-31/10 daily 9-18h, 01/11-31/03 Su/holidays 11-16h. T € 8, family card € 17.

Krempe 8A1
Am Schul- und Sportzentrum, Am Freibad.
GPS: n53,83356 e9,49447.

3 free. **Location:** Rural, simple, quiet. **Surface:** gravel.
01/01-31/12.
Distance: 200m.

Kropp 6D3
Hotel Wikingerhof, Tetenhusener Chaussee 1.
GPS: n54,40638 e9,51055.

8 € 5, guests free WC. **Location:** Urban, simple, quiet.
Surface: metalled. 01/01-31/12.
Distance: 300m on the spot 300m.

Kropp 6D3
Restaurant Rosengarten, Rheiderweg 7.
GPS: n54,41388 e9,50138.

5 € 5 WC. **Location:** Urban, simple, quiet. **Surface:** metalled.
01/01-31/12.
Distance: 200m on the spot 200m.

Kropp 6D3
Garage Audi-VW Thomsen, Werkstrasse 2. **GPS**: n54,41361 e9,52833.

5 € 5 Ch. **Location:** Urban, simple, noisy.
Surface: metalled. 01/01-31/12.
Distance: 300m 300m 300m.

Laboe 6D3
Ostseebad Laboe Ehrenmal, Steinerweg/Prof. Munzerring.
GPS: n54,41029 e10,23289.

18 € 12 €1/5minutes €1 Ch. **Location:** Urban, simple.
Surface: grassy. 01/01-31/12.
Distance: 1km 400m 400m on the spot 1km.

Ladelund 6C3
Am Naturbad, Stato. **GPS**: n54,84919 e9,03629.

5 € 10 Ch. WC included. **Location:** Rural, comfortable, isolated, quiet. **Surface:** grassy. 01/01-31/12.
Distance: 1km on the spot.

Langballig 6D3
Campingplatz Langballigau, Strandweg 3, Langballigau.
GPS: n54,82234 e9,65969.

50 € 10, dog € 1 Ch. €2,50/night WC included €1.
Location: Rural, simple. **Surface:** grassy/gravel.
01/01-31/12.
Distance: 100m on the spot.

Langwedel 6D3
Caravanpark am Brahmsee, Mühlenstraße 30a.
GPS: n54,21462 e9,91943.

20 € 15 €1/80liter Ch. €2,50/24h,6 Amp WC sanitary at campsite. **Location:** Rural, comfortable, quiet. **Surface:** grassy/gravel.
01/01-31/12.
Distance: 600m 3km Brahmsee 500m 500m 7km.
Remarks: Check in at reception campsite, bread-service.

Lauenburg/Elbe 8C2
Marina Lauenburg/Yachthafen, Hafenstrasse 14.
GPS: n53,37156 e10,56527.

20 € 10 €1/100liter (8x)€1/kWh WC €0,50 €1 €4/4.
Location: Rural, comfortable.
Surface: metalled.
01/01-31/12.
Distance: 10 min walking on the spot 10 min walking.

Leck 6C3
Reisemobilhafen Leck, Am Stadion 3. **GPS**: n54,76704 e8,98123.

20 € 5 €1/80liter Ch. (16x)€0,50/kWh.
Location: Comfortable, central, quiet. **Surface:** grassy/gravel.
01/01-31/12.
Distance: 850m on the spot.
Remarks: At swimming pool, to be paid at swimming pool.

Lensahn 6E3
Reisemobilplatz Lensahn, Dr. Julius-Stinde strasse.
GPS: n54,21446 e10,87745.

15 € 8 €1/80liter €1 Ch. (4x)€2. **Location:** Rural, simple. **Surface:** grasstiles. 01/01-31/12.
Distance: 1,5km on the spot 200m 2,5km.

Lübeck 8C1
Wohnmobil Treff Lübeck, An der Hülshorst 11.
GPS: n53,89510 e10,71088.

40 € 9/day Ch. included WC €1/5minutes €1,50.
Location: Urban, luxurious, quiet. **Surface:** gravel. 02/01-31/10.
Distance: 4,5km 5km on the spot 50m.

Lübeck 8C1
Wohnmobilstellplatz Lübeck Marienbrücke P4, Lastadie.
GPS: n53,87147 e10,67904.

16 free, 18-10h.
Location: Urban, simple. **Surface:** asphalted.

DE

01/01-31/12.
Distance: 500m 2km on the spot on the spot.
Remarks: Max. 24h.

Tourist information Lübeck:
Museum Holstentor, Holstentorplatz. Historical museum.
10-16/17h. € 7, family card € 15.
Niederegger Einkaufserlebnis, Café und Marzipan-Museum, Breite strasse 89. Marzipan, Lübecker speciality, museum, café and shop.

Lunden 6C3

Wollersumer Straße. **GPS**: n54,33280 e8,99697.

10 free. **Location:** Rural, simple. **Surface:** grassy/gravel.
01/01-31/12 high water.
Distance: 1,7km on the spot.

Maasholm 6D3

Stellplatz am Yachthafen, Uleweg 31. **GPS**: n54,68334 e9,99436.

40 € 10 Ch €2/day WC €0,50 €2
Location: Rural, comfortable, quiet. **Surface:** grassy/gravel.
01/01-31/12.
Distance: 100m 5km on the spot on the spot 100m.
Remarks: Parking marina.

Meldorf 7H1

Reisemobil-Stellplatz am Deich, Deichstraße 2.
GPS: n54,09409 e8,95070.

80 € 8 (18x)€3 WC €2.
Location: Rural, comfortable, isolated, quiet.
Surface: grassy/metalled. Easter-31/10.
Distance: 7km on the spot Imbiss 10-18 uur on the spot on the spot.

Molfsee 6D3

Freilichtmuseum/Restaurant Drathenhof, Hamburger Landstrasse 99. **GPS**: n54,27411 e10,07571.

20 free, use of a meal desired WC at restaurant.
Location: Central. **Surface:** gravel. 01/01-31/12.
Distance: on the spot on the spot on the spot on the spot on the spot.
Remarks: At open air museum.

Mölln 8C2

Alt Möllner strasse. **GPS**: n53,62564 e10,68314.

24 € 7 (20x)included.
Location: Rural. **Surface:** gravel. 01/01-31/12.
Distance: 1km 250m 300m.
Remarks: Service: Vorkamp 19, GPS N53,62024, E10,67701.

Neufeld 8A1

SBC Neufeld, An'n Hoven. **GPS**: n53,90677 e9,02042.

20 € 8 (20x)€2/day WC included. **Location:** Rural, comfortable, quiet. **Surface:** grassy. 01/04-31/10.
Distance: on the spot on the spot on the spot.

Neukirchen 23779 6E3

Wohnmobilhafen Seepark Sütel, Sütel.
GPS: n54,33359 e11,06620.
30 € 12-14, 2 pers. incl included. **Surface:** grassy.
Distance: 500m 750m on the spot on the spot.
Remarks: Bread-service in summer period.

Neukirchen 25927 6C3

Sportzentrum, Kirchenweg 2. **GPS**: n54,86602 e8,73304.

4 free . **Location:** Rural, simple, quiet. **Surface:** concrete.
01/01-31/12.
Distance: 500m 500m 350m.
Remarks: Max. 4 days.

Neumünster 8B1

Bad am Stadtwald, Hansaring 177. **GPS**: n54,08078 e9,96064.

22 € 10 €0,50/100liter €0,50 Ch (22x)€0,50/kWh WC €1 . **Location:** Rural, comfortable, central, quiet.
Surface: grassy/gravel. 01/01-31/12.
Distance: 2km A7 1 km on the spot 300m on the spot.
Remarks: Check in at swimming pool.

Neustadt in Holstein 8C1

Wohnmobilstellplatz Ostsee, Auf der Pelzer Wiese 45, Pelzerhaken.
GPS: n54,08889 e10,87250.

90 € 14 + tourist tax (summer) €1/100liter €1 Ch (90x)€1/2kWh WC €2. **Location:** Rural, luxurious, noisy.
Surface: grassy. 05/01-03/03.
Distance: 900m 150m 900m 400m on the spot.

Neustadt in Holstein 8C1

P5, Am Binnenwasser. **GPS**: n54,11096 e10,81496.

10 Mo-Fr € 5/24h, Sa-Su free (2x)€0,50/kWh.
Location: Urban, simple. **Surface:** metalled. 01/01-31/12.
Distance: on the spot.

Niebüll 6C3

Parkplatz, Lornsenstrasse 19. **GPS**: n54,78901 e8,82546.

25 € 5 €1/5minutes €1 Ch (12x)€1/8h free.
Location: Urban, simple, central, quiet. **Surface:** grassy.
01/01-31/12 1st week in June.
Distance: on the spot 200m 300m.
Remarks: Parking swimming pool, max. 24h.

Nordstrand 6C3

Wohnmobilplatz Margarethenruh, Süderhafen 8.
GPS: n54,46944 e8,91000.

21 € 20,50, 2 pers. incl Ch €3,20/24h WC included €3/3 . **Location:** Rural, comfortable, central, quiet.
Surface: grassy/gravel. 01/01-31/12.
Distance: 3km 300m 150m 3km.

Nordstrand 6C3

Womoland, Norderquerweg 2. **GPS**: n54,51736 e8,93012.

44 € 7 + € 4/pp Ch €0,60/kWh WC included.
Location: Comfortable, isolated, quiet.
Surface: grassy/gravel.
15/03-31/10.

DE

Distance: 10km 6km on the spot on the spot 6km.
Remarks: Bread-service.

Tourist information Nordstrand:
Former Wadden island.

Norgaardholz 6D3

Campingplatz Nordstern, Nordstern 1. **GPS**: n54,78528 e9,79889.

10 € 8, dog € 1 Ch €2/day WC €1, use sanitary €4/night free. **Location:** Rural, simple, quiet. **Surface:** gravel/metalled. 01/04-30/09.
Distance: on the spot on the spot.

Ockholm 6C3

Wohnmobilstellplätze Altes Pastorat Ockholm, Baderstrasse 5/6. **GPS**: n54,66517 e8,82940.

5 €9 Ch (5x)€2/24h WC included €5/5. **Location:** Rural, simple, isolated, quiet. **Surface:** grassy/gravel. 01/01-31/12.
Distance: 100m on the spot.
Remarks: Along through road, bread-service.

Oeversee 6D3

Kranzbinderei Schnell, Frörupsand 2. **GPS**: n54,69134 e9,43602.

9 €6 Ch €1/night free. **Location:** Rural, simple, quiet. **Surface:** grassy. 01/01-31/12.
Distance: 500m.

Osterhever 6C3

Stellplatz Norderheverkoog, Norderheverkoogstraße 12, Norderheverkoog. **GPS**: n54,39656 e8,76163.

10 € 10 Ch (10x) WC included €1. **Location:** Rural, isolated, quiet. **Surface:** grassy. 01/04-31/10.
Distance: 1km 2km 1km on the spot on the spot.
Remarks: Bread-service, bicycle rental.

Pahlen 6C3

Fischerstrasse 17. **GPS**: n54,27101 e9,30015.

12 €6 + €1/pp (12x) WC included. **Location:** Rural, comfortable, quiet. **Surface:** grassy. 01/01-31/12.
Distance: 200m 50m 50m 200m 200m.

Plön 8B1

Wohnmobilhafen Plön, Ascheberger straße 76. **GPS**: n54,14709 e10,39841.

14 € 17, dog € 3 Ch WC included.
Location: Comfortable, noisy. **Surface:** grassy/gravel. 01/04-15/12.
Distance: 1,5km on the spot.
Remarks: Max. 4 nights.

Plön 8B1

Womo-Stop Kleinen Plöner See, Hamburgerstrasse/Aschenberg strasse, B430. **GPS**: n54,15278 e10,40417.

11 € 5 €1/1 €0,50 Ch. **Location:** Simple. **Surface:** asphalted. 01/01-31/12.
Distance: on the spot.
Remarks: In front of passage to beach, max. 24h.

Pommerby 6D3

Campingplatz Seehof, Gammeldam 5. **GPS**: n54,76495 e9,96782.

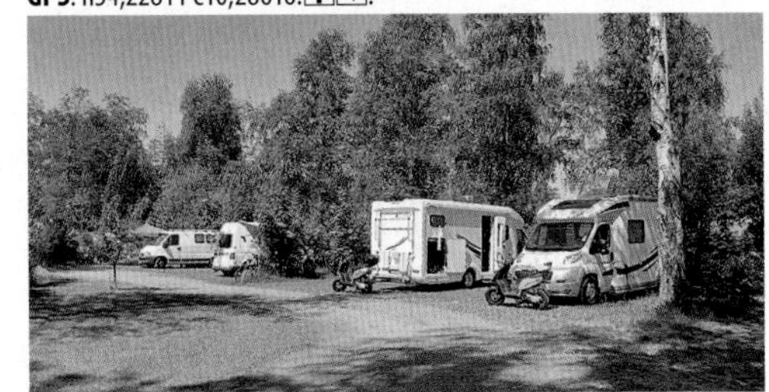

5 €3,75 + €4,50/pp, child €2, dog €2 Ch €2/day WC €0,50/5 €2,50. **Location:** Rural, simple, quiet. **Surface:** grassy/gravel. 01/04-31/10.
Distance: on the spot on the spot.

Preetz 6D3

Wohnmobilpark Preetz, Kahlbrook 25a. **GPS**: n54,22811 e10,28616.

10 € 15 included WC . **Surface:** gravel. 01/01-31/12 service 01/11-31/03.
Distance: 10min on the spot on the spot.
Remarks: Bread-service, canoe and bicycle rental.

Puttgarden 6E3

Wohnmobilplatz Johannisberg, Johannisbergstrasse. **GPS**: n54,50054 e11,17938.

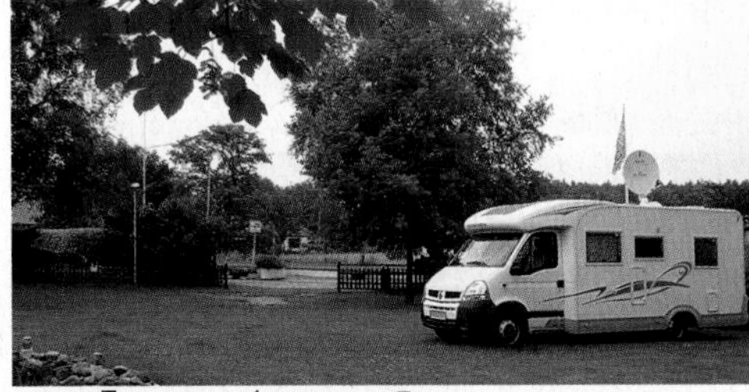

50 € 10-15 €0,10/10liter €2 Ch €0,50/kWh WC €1 €3,50/2,00. **Location:** Rural, simple, quiet. **Surface:** grassy/metalled. 01/01-31/12.
Distance: 2,5km 800m 800m on the spot.
Remarks: In nature reserve Am Grüner Brink, bread-service.

Puttgarden 6E3

Bade- und Surfstrand Grüner Brink, Krögenweg. **GPS**: n54,51174 e11,18285.
30 € 9 €2,50 Ch. **Surface:** gravel. 01/01-31/12.
Distance: on the spot.

Quickborn bei Burg 8A1

Am Helmschen-Bach, Hauptstraße 2. **GPS**: n54,01165 e9,21648.

5 € 6 included €0,50/kWh. **Location:** Rural, comfortable, quiet. **Surface:** grassy. 01/04-30/09.
Distance: 300m on the spot.

Rantrum 6C3

Reisemobilhafen Rantrum, Bannony. **GPS**: n54,43369 e9,12743.

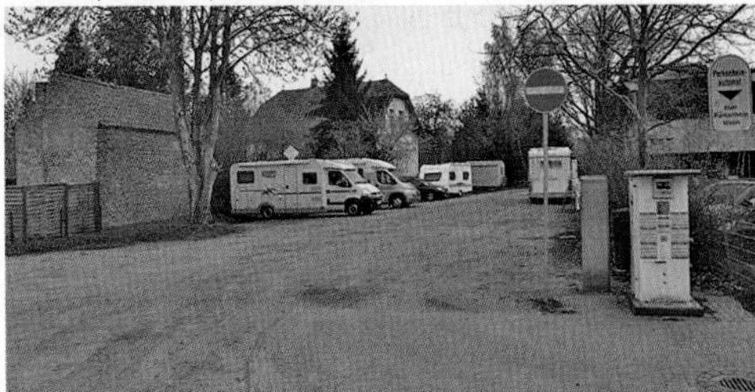

13 € 10 Ch (12x) WC included. **Location:** Rural, simple, isolated, quiet. **Surface:** gravel. 01/01-31/12.
Distance: 8km 30km 300m.
Remarks: At swimming pool.

Ratzeburg 8C1

Hallenbad Aqua Siwa, Fischerstrasse 43. **GPS**: n53,69567 e10,77598.

12 € 8/24h €1/80liter Ch €0,50/kWh. **Location:** Urban, simple, central, noisy. **Surface:** gravel. 01/01-31/12.
Distance: 500m on the spot on the spot on the spot.

Reinfeld 8B1

Am Herrenteich, Karpfenplatz. **GPS**: n53,83024 e10,48362.

DE

5 free €0,50/70liter €0,50 Ch €0,50/kWh.
Location: Urban, simple, quiet. **Surface:** metalled.
01/01-31/12.
Distance: 500m 200m 400m.

S Rendsburg 6D3

Wohnmobil-Hafen Eiderblick, An der Untereider 9.
GPS: n54,30406 e9,65610.

40 € 15 €1/75liter Ch (45x)€0,50/kWh WC included against payment . **Location:** Urban, luxurious, central, quiet.
Surface: gravel. 01/01-31/12.
Distance: 800m on the spot 800m on the spot on the spot on the spot.
Remarks: Bread-service, internetcafé.

Tourist information Rendsburg:
Eiserne Lady. Train-bridge North Sea-Baltic Canal, 42m high.
Blue Line. City walk 3 km.
Hausbrauerei Niewarker, Paradeplatz. Guided tour and tastery.

S Reußenköge 6C3

Amsinck Haus, Sönke Nissenkoog 36a. **GPS**: n54,61666 e8,87027.

11 €7 (6x)€2/24h WC included €3.
Location: Rural, comfortable, isolated, quiet. **Surface:** asphalted.
01/04-31/10.
Distance: 4km 4km.
Remarks: Bicycle rental.

S Sankt Peter-Ording 6C3

Reisemobilhafen St.Peter-Ording, Am Ketelskoog.
GPS: n54,30881 e8,63522.

70 € 16 €2/50liter Ch (70x)€0,60/kWh WC €0,20 €1 €1/h.
Location: Rural, comfortable. **Surface:** gravel. 01/01-31/12.
Distance: 300m 1km 300m 300m.
Remarks: Arrival <22h, market Wednesday.

Tourist information Sankt Peter-Ording:
Westküstenpark, Wohldweg 6. Animal park. summer 9.30-18h, winter 11h-sunset.

S Schacht-Audorf 6D3

WohnmobilPark Schacht-Audorf, K76. **GPS**: n54,30611 e9,71250.

41 € 10 €0,50/100liter Ch (33x)€0,60/kWh WC €0,50 €1 . **Location:** Rural, comfortable. **Surface:** gravel.
01/01-31/12.
Distance: 700m A7 2km 800m 800m on the spot.
Remarks: Max. 3 nights.

S Scharbeutz 8C1

Reisemobilplatz Hamburger Ring, Hamburgerring/Trelleborg Strasse.
GPS: n54,03028 e10,75222.

58 € 15,60/24h, beach tax incl €1/100liter Ch (2x)€1.
Location: Rural. **Surface:** sand. 01/01-31/12.
Distance: 300m 300m, dog friendly beach 1km 400m.

S Schashagen 8C1

Ostsee-Campingplatz Kagelbusch, Strandweg/Kagelbusch.
GPS: n54,12570 e10,92789.
€ 10 €1.
Distance: 500m.

S Schashagen 8C1

Wohnmobilpark Ostseeblick, Biesdorf.
GPS: n54,11934 e10,92108.

30 € 7, 01/04-30/09 € 14,50-16,50, 2 pers. incl., dog € 2,50-3,50 €1/80liter Ch €0,50/kWh WC . **Location:** Rural, comfortable, quiet. **Surface:** grasstiles. 01/01-31/12 Service: winter.
Distance: 300m.

S Schleswig 6D3

Am Schleswig Stadthafen, Am Hafen 5. **GPS**: n54,51167 e9,56917.

45 € 16/24h Ch WC €2,50/2,50 included.
Location: Urban, comfortable, central. **Surface:** gravel/metalled.
01/04-01/11.
Distance: 150m 5km on the spot on the spot 50m 500m nearby 50m.
Remarks: Max. 48h, check in at harbourmaster.

S Schleswig 6D3

Wiking-Yachthafen, Wikingeck 11. **GPS**: n54,50670 e9,54733.
8 € 12 €1 €1 Ch €0,40/kWh WC €2 .
Surface: metalled.
01/05-30/09.
Distance: 2km on the spot on the spot on the spot on the spot.
Remarks: Check in at harbourmaster.

Tourist information Schleswig:
Tourist Information Schleswig, Plessenstrasse 7. Historical city, founded by the Vikings, Haithabu.
Schloß Gottorf. Regional museum, archeological museum and museum for art and culture.
Museum am Danewerk, Ochsenweg 5, Dannewerk. Fortifications, 650-1200. winter 10-16h, 01/04-31/10 Tue-Fri 9-17h, Sa-Su 10-18h.
Wikinger Museum Haithabu, Haddeby-Busdorf. All about the life of the Vikings. 01/04-31/10 9-17h, 01/11-31/03 Tue-Su 10-16h.

S Schönberg/Ostsee 6D3

Brasilien, Seesternweg. **GPS**: n54,42408 e10,39116.

40 € 9, 15/05-15/09 € 11 Ch included. **Location:** Rural, simple. **Surface:** grassy. 01/01-31/12.
Distance: 200m 200m.

S Schönberg/Ostsee 6D3

Stellplatz Mittelstrand, Mittelstrand.
GPS: n54,42233 e10,39573.

50 € 9, 01/05-30/09 € 11 Ch €2 WC included.
Location: Rural. **Surface:** grassy. 01/01-31/12.
Distance: 200m 200m on the spot.
Remarks: Bread-service in summer period.

S Seestermühe 8A2

Achtern Diek. **GPS**: n53,70333 e9,56232.

4 € 2 €2 €2 Ch €2 €2/day €1,50.
Location: Rural. **Surface:** metalled. 01/01-31/12.
Distance: 200m.

S Sehestedt 6D3

Wohnmobilstellplatz Sehestedt, Fährstrasse 1.
GPS: n54,36466 e9,81973.

13 € 7/24h €0,50/80liter Ch. **Surface:** gravel.
01/01-31/12.
Distance: 750m A7 13km on the spot 200m.
Remarks: Directly at North Sea-Baltic canal.

DE

Sierksdorf 8C1

Hansa-Park, Am Fahrenkrog 1. **GPS**: n54,07417 e10,77522.
200 € 4/24h.

Sierksdorf 8C1

Wohnmobilstellplatz Hof Sierksdorf, Altonaer Straße.
GPS: n54,06013 e10,75737.
15 € 11 excl. tourist tax €1 €1 Ch €0,50/kWh WC.
Surface: gravel. 01/04-30/09.
Distance: beach 100m.

Simonsberg 6C3

Nordsee Camping Zum Seehund, Lundenbergweg 4.
GPS: n54,45515 e8,96958.

15 € 15-21 Ch WC included €3/time free.
Location: Rural, comfortable, isolated, quiet. **Surface:** gravel.
Easter-31/10.
Distance: 3km 500m on the spot on the spot on camp site on the spot on the spot.
Remarks: Use steam bath, sauna, fitness-studio incl.

Sörup 6D3

Südensee, Seeblick. **GPS**: n54,71216 e9,66611.

5 € 4 Ch €2/night WC.
Location: Rural, simple, quiet. **Surface:** grassy. 01/04-31/10.
Distance: on the spot on the spot kiosk.
Remarks: Parking at small lake.

Struckum 6C3

Marschblick, Kennedy Weg 3. **GPS**: n54,58597 e8,99117.

30 € 10 Ch WC included €3.
Location: Rural, simple, quiet. **Surface:** asphalted.
01/01-31/12.
Distance: 100m 8km 750m 1,5km 100m on the spot.
Remarks: Money in envelope in mail box.

Süderlügum 6C3

Wohnmobilplatz Mehrzweckhalle, Jahnstrasse.
GPS: n54,87472 e8,90306.

5 free. **Location:** Rural, simple, central, quiet. **Surface:** metalled.
01/01-31/12.
Distance: 500m 300m.
Remarks: Max. 7m.

Timmendorfer Strand 8C1

Am Vogelpark, P4, Bäderrandstraße, B76.
GPS: n53,99136 e10,81439.

50 € 7,50 + € 3/pp tourist tax €0,50/120liter Ch €1/kWh.
Location: Rural. **Surface:** grassy/sand.
01/01-31/12.
Distance: 180m.
Remarks: Max. 1 night.

Tönning 6C3

Wohnmobilplatz Eiderblick - Kapitänshaus, Am Strandweg.
GPS: n54,30920 e8,93684.

50 € 12 2p incl. + tourist tax €1/100liter Ch €0,60/kWh included €4/3 €1/2h.
Location: Rural, luxurious, isolated, quiet. **Surface:** grassy.
01/01-31/12.
Distance: 500m on the spot on the spot on the spot.
Remarks: Along the Eider river, swimming pool 200m.

Travemünde 8C1

Wohnmobilparkplatz Kowitzberg, Kowitzberg.
GPS: n53,97598 e10,87830.

49 15/5-14/9 € 12, 15/9-14/5 € 8 €1/100liter Ch (48x)€1/5kWh. **Location:** Urban. **Surface:** grassy. 01/01-31/12.
Distance: 2,5km 800m 800m 300m 250m 50m.

Travemünde 8C1

Parkplatz am Fischerreihafen, Auf dem Baggersand 15.
GPS: n53,95556 e10,86139.

90 € 12-15 €1/35liter Ch (5x)€3/kWh WC €2.
Location: Urban, simple. **Surface:** grassy/gravel.
01/01-31/12.
Distance: beach 800m max. 500m express bus Altstadt Lubeck.
Remarks: Parking fishing port, bicycle rental.

Trittau 8B2

Zum Schützenplatz. **GPS**: n53,61063 e10,40843.
5 free. 01/01-31/12.
Distance: on the spot 500m.
Remarks: Next to swimming pool.

Uetersen 8A2

Am Stichhafen, Ziegelei. **GPS**: n53,67977 e9,66861.

4 free. **Location:** Urban, simple. **Surface:** metalled.
01/01-31/12.
Distance: 400m 7,4km 300m.

Utersum 6C3

Wohnmobilstellplatz Föhr, Strunwai 14. **GPS**: n54,71593 e8,40117.
€ 15 €0,50/100liter Ch WC €0,50. **Surface:** grassy.
Distance: 400m.

Waabs 6D3

Gut Ludwigsburg. **GPS**: n54,50350 e9,95767.
10 € 11 Ch WC €4.

Weddelbrook 8B1

Campingplatz Vogelzunge, Schulstraße 19.
GPS: n53,89995 e9,82657.

6 € 10 Ch included €0,50/4h WC €1/4minutes.
Location: Rural, simple, quiet. **Surface:** grassy.
01/01-31/12.
Distance: 300m on the spot.
Remarks: At lake, check-in and key at reception.

Wedel 8A2

Am Freibad. **GPS**: n53,57860 e9,69520.

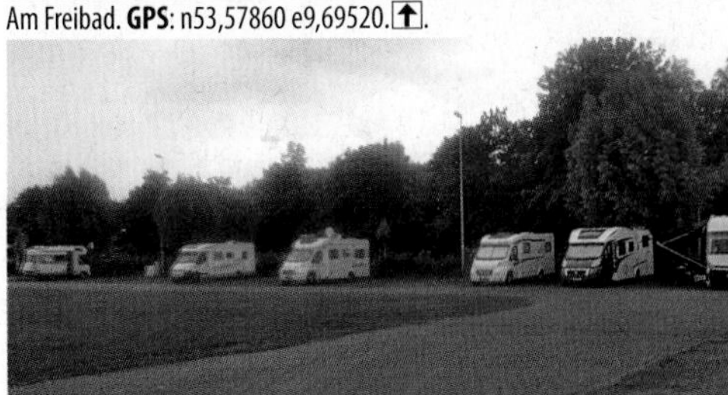

20 € 10 €1/10minutes Ch (14x)€1/8h WC.
Location: Rural, simple, quiet. **Surface:** grassy/metalled.
01/01-31/12 during event.
Distance: 800m.
Remarks: Max. 3 days, to be paid at swimming pool.

Westerholz 6D3

Campingplatz Fördeblick, Kummle 1. **GPS**: n54,81998 e9,66686.
45 € 10 Ch €3/night,6Amp WC €1 included **Location:** Rural, simple, quiet. **Surface:** grassy/gravel.
01/04-30/09.
Distance: 2,5km 100m 1,5km 2,5km on the spot.
Remarks: At Flensborg Fjord, max. 24h.

Wilster 8A1

Colosseumplatz, Etatsrätin-doos-strasse 14-17.
GPS: n53,92419 e9,37449.

15 free €1/5minutes Ch €1 (4x)€0,50/kWh.
Location: Urban, simple, central, quiet. **Surface:** grassy/gravel.
01/01-31/12 fair.
Distance: 200m 100m on the spot on the spot.

DE

S Wischhafen 8A1

Alter Hafen, Hafenstraße 10. **GPS**: n53,77278 e9,32278.

8 free (6x)€1/kWh. **Location:** Rural, simple.
Surface: grassy/gravel. 01/01-31/12.
Distance: 500m 1km.

S Wischhafen 8A1

Ziegelstraße, Gewerbegebiet Wischhafen.
GPS: n53,76417 e9,32111.

3 free Chfree.
Location: Rural, simple. **Surface:** gravel. 01/01-31/12.
Distance: 1km 200m.

Wischhafen 8A1

Süder-Elbe, Glückstädter Straße. **GPS**: n53,78678 e9,34017.

15 free. **Location:** Rural, simple, isolated. **Surface:** gravel.
01/01-31/12.
Distance: 3km 150m.
Remarks: Parking at ferry-boat.

Wischhafen 8A1

Unterm Deich 7. **GPS**: n53,77528 e9,32111.

6 free. **Location:** Rural, simple. **Surface:** grassy.
01/01-31/12.
Distance: 300m on the spot 1km.

Lower Saxony/Bremen

S Adendorf 8C2

Freizeitzentrum, Scharnebecker Weg. **GPS**: n53,28925 e10,45398.

30 € 8 €1/10minutes Ch (4x)€1/8h,01/10-30/04€2/8h.
Location: Rural, simple, noisy. 01/01-31/12.
Distance: 500m.

Remarks: Parking sports centre, max. 3 days, swimming pool and sauna on site.

S Aerzen 10A2

Restaurant Waldquelle, Waldquelle 1.
GPS: n52,05952 e9,26146.

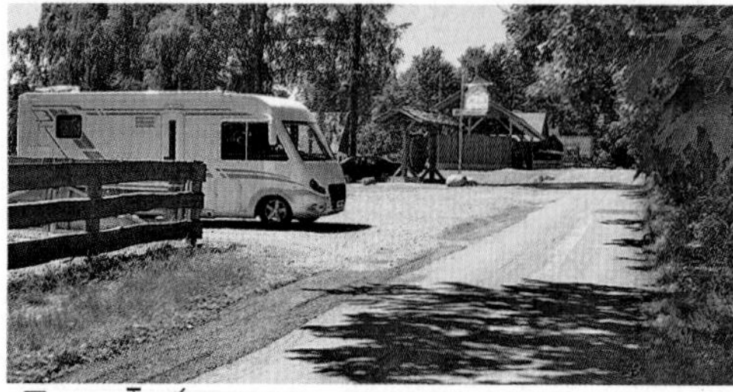

4 € 4,50 (1x)€1,50/day. **Location:** Rural, isolated.
Surface: gravel. 01/01-31/12 Tue.
Distance: 2km 1km 500m on the spot.
Remarks: Check in at hotel.

S Ahlerstedt 8A2

Ahlerstedt Ottendorf, Rickstücken 2. **GPS**: n53,38908 e9,41017.

25 € 8 Ch included. **Location:** Rural, simple.
Surface: metalled. 01/01-31/12.
Distance: 3km 3km.

Alfeld/Leine 10B2

Bornstrasse. **GPS**: n51,98586 e9,82769.

4 free. **Location:** Simple. **Surface:** metalled.
01/01-31/12.
Distance: on the spot 80m 200m.
Remarks: Parking in city centre behind the evangelical church.

S Altenau 10C2

Alter Bahnhof Altenau, Rothenbergerstrasse 52.
GPS: n51,79879 e10,43320.

20 € 13, tourist tax incl €1/50liter €1 Ch (10x)€2,50/day WC. **Location:** Quiet. **Surface:** gravel.
01/01-31/12.
Distance: 1km 2km 1km on the spot on the spot 2km on the spot.

S Altenau 10C2

Kristall-Saunatherme Heißer Brocken, Karl-Reinecke-Weg 35.
GPS: n51,79836 e10,44408.

20 € 10 + € 2/pp tourist tax €0,50/40liter Ch €0,50/kWh €1,50/time. **Location:** Rural, quiet. **Surface:** metalled.
01/01-31/12.
Distance: 1,5km on the spot on the spot on the spot.
Remarks: Pay at pay-desk of theTherme.

S Amelinghausen 8B3

Lopausee, Auf der Kalten Hude. **GPS**: n53,13324 e10,23441.

50 € 5, 1/9-1/7 € 3,50 Chincluded. **Location:** Simple, isolated, quiet. **Surface:** gravel/sand. 01/01-31/12.
Distance: 1km 100m 100m 1km 1km on the spot on the spot.
Remarks: Bread-service in summer period, ticket available at petrol stations, kiosk Lopausee, pay-desk Waldbad and tourist office.

S Amelinghausen 8B3

Waldbad, Zum Lopautal. **GPS**: n53,12402 e10,23018.

40 € 8 Ch included.
Location: Comfortable. 01/01-31/12.
Distance: 1km 500m 1km 1km on the spot on the spot.
Remarks: Bread-service in summer period, incl. access swimming pool.

Amelinghausen 8B3

Kronsbergheide, Hochseilgarten. **GPS**: n53,13500 e10,23389.

10 € 5, 1/9-1/7 € 3,50.
Location: Rural, simple, isolated, quiet. 01/01-31/12.
Distance: 1km 500m on the spot 1km 1km on the spot on the spot.
Remarks: Ticket available at petrol stations, kiosk Lopausee, pay-desk Waldbad and tourist office.

Amelinghausen 8B3

Schwindbeckerheide, Steinbeckerstrasse, Soderstorf.
GPS: n53,12247 e10,09934.

DE

15 € 5, 1/9-1/7 € 3,50. **Location:** Rural, simple, isolated.
Surface: metalled/sand. 01/01-31/12.
Distance: 6km on the spot on the spot.
Remarks: Ticket available at petrol stations, kiosk Lopausee, pay-desk Waldbad and tourist office.

Amelinghausen 8B3

Landgasthaus Eichenkrug, Unter den Eichen 10, Dehnsen.
GPS: n53,12804 e10,16817.

4 € 6 included. **Location:** Simple, isolated.
Surface: metalled. 01/01-31/12.
Distance: 4km on the spot 4km on the spot on the spot.
Remarks: Max. 3 nights.

Amelinghausen 8B3

Schenck's Hotel & Gasthaus, Lüneburgerstrasse 48.
GPS: n53,12568 e10,21426.

15 € 10 €0,80/kWh,+€1,50 WC included.
Location: Simple, central. **Surface:** metalled.
Distance: on the spot on the spot on the spot on the spot on the spot.

Tourist information Amelinghausen:
Oldendorfer Totenstatt. Hunnebed cineraria from the ice-age.
guided tour 01/05-30/09.

Ankum 9G1

Ferienhof Buse-Glass, Tütingen 5. **GPS**: n52,51431 e7,86842.

5 € 15 WC included. **Location:** Quiet. **Surface:** grassy.
01/01-31/12.
Distance: 2,5km 500m 2,5km.

Apen 7G3

Am Drahkamp, Edewechter Strasse, Godensholt.
GPS: n53,16999 e7,83356.
free. **Location:** Rural.
Distance: Apen 6km 900m.

Apen 7G3

Am Freibad, Hauptstraße, Hengstforde. **GPS**: n53,21795 e7,78706.

10 free. **Location:** Rural, simple. **Surface:** metalled.
01/05-15/09.
Distance: 5,8km 50m.
Remarks: Along railwayline, swimming pool Hengstforde.

Apen 7G3

Viehmarktplatz, Hauptstraße. **GPS**: n53,21820 e7,80221.

10 free.
Location: Simple. **Surface:** metalled. 01/01-31/12.
Distance: 100m 5km on the spot.
Remarks: Max. 2 days.

Artlenburg 8C2

Am Sportboothafen, Am Deich 9. **GPS**: n53,37680 e10,48550.

30 € 10-15 Ch WC.
Location: Comfortable, quiet. **Surface:** grassy. 15/04-15/10.
Distance: 500m on the spot on the spot 500m 500m 500m.
Remarks: Along the river Elbe.

Aurich 7G2

Familienbad De Baalje, Tannenbergstraße.
GPS: n53,46540 e7,47568.
20 € 9 €1/100liter Ch (24x)€1/kWh €1.
Surface: metalled. 01/01-31/12.
Distance: 500m 100m.
Remarks: Check in and pay at pay desk swimming pool.

Aurich 7G2

An den Kiesgruben, Tannenhausen. **GPS**: n53,52173 e7,47834.

free. **Surface:** unpaved.
Distance: 10m on the spot.
Remarks: At the lake of Tannenhausen.

Aurich 7G2

Landgasthof Alte Post, Essenerstrasse. **GPS**: n53,54573 e7,60736.

6 € 6, guests € 3 €1 Ch WC.
Surface: metalled. 01/01-31/12.
Distance: on the spot.
Remarks: Caution key electricity € 10.

Bad Bentheim 9F2

Am Mühlenberg, Mühlenberg. **GPS**: n52,29360 e7,10095.

10 € 8 €1/80liter Ch €0,50/kWh WC.
Location: Rural. **Surface:** metalled. 01/01-31/12.
Distance: 200m 50m 200m on the spot on the spot.

Bad Bentheim 9F2

Am Schloßpark, Funkenstiege. **GPS**: n52,30328 e7,15448.

35 € 8 €1/80liter Ch (36x)€0,50/kWh WC.
Surface: metalled. 01/01-31/12.
Distance: 200m 100m.

Bad Bevensen 8C3

Am Waagekai. **GPS**: n53,07417 e10,60139.

30 € 5,40 + € 3/pp tourist tax Ch included €1.
Location: Rural, simple, quiet. **Surface:** gravel/sand.
01/01-31/12.
Distance: 1km on the spot 1km 600m on the spot on the spot.

Bad Essen 9H1

Wohnmobilstellplatz Falkenburg, Falkenburg 3.
GPS: n52,32352 e8,36384.

50 € 7 €1/100liter Ch €2/4kWh WC €0,50.
Location: Rural, comfortable, quiet. **Surface:** grassy/metalled.
01/03-30/10.
Distance: 1,2km 900m 300m.
Remarks: At the Mittelland canal, near marina, bread-service

DE

(weekend).

Bad Gandersheim 10B2

Wohnmobil-Stellplatz Rio Gande, An der Wiek.
GPS: n51,87191 e10,01881.

24 € 7/24h, tourist tax incl € 1/100liter Ch (14x)€ 0,50/kWh.
Location: Rural, simple. **Surface:** gravel.
01/01-31/12.
Distance: 400m 100m 200m on the spot on the spot.
Remarks: Max. 3 nights, bread-service only in summer.

Bad Lauterberg 10C3

Erlebnisbad Vitamar, Mast Tal 1. **GPS**: n51,63358 e10,48661.

5 free € 1 € 1 Ch € 1. **Location:** Simple, quiet.
Surface: metalled. 01/01-31/12.
Distance: 1,5km 30km on the spot 1,5km on the spot.

Bad Lauterberg 10C3

Wiesenbeker Teich, Wiesenbek 75. **GPS**: n51,61719 e10,49074.

4 € 13 Ch included.
Location: Isolated, quiet. **Surface:** gravel.
01/01-31/12.
Distance: 2km 30km on the spot on the spot on the spot 2km 2km on the spot.
Remarks: Check in and pay at reception campsite, max. 1 night.

Bad Münder 10A2

Rhomelbad, Lindenallee. **GPS**: n52,19305 e9,47111.

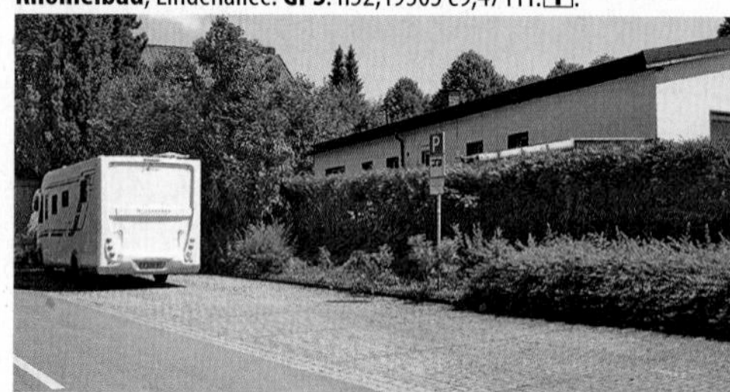

5 free. **Location:** Simple. **Surface:** metalled.
01/01-31/12.
Distance: 400m on the spot 400m 200m.

Bad Nenndorf 10A1

Wohnmobilstellplatz am Schulzentrum, Bahnhofstrasse 77.
GPS: n52,34294 e9,37666.

15 free € 2/45liter Ch (8x)€ 1/6h WC.
Location: Simple. **Surface:** gravel/metalled. 01/01-31/12.
Distance: 700m 3,4km on the spot on the spot on the spot.

Bad Pyrmont 10A2

Reisemobilhafen in den Emmerauen, Hauptmann Boelke-Weg.
GPS: n51,98092 e9,25108.
65 € 9 + € 2,30-3,20/pp tourist tax € 0,10/10liter Ch (44x)€ 0,60/kWh WC free.
Location: Urban, central. **Surface:** grassy/gravel.
01/01-31/12.
Distance: historical centre 400m 200m 400m 100m.
Remarks: Bread-service, free swimming < 9AM, e-bike rental, free shuttle to spa resort.

Tourist information Bad Pyrmont:
Bad Pyrmont Tourismus GmbH, Europa-Platz 1, www.badpyrmont.de. Health resort.

Bad Sachsa 10C3

Harzer Schnitzelhaus & Waffelbäckerei, Schützenstrasse 13.
GPS: n51,59778 e10,55056.

2 guests free. **Location:** Rural, simple, central. **Surface:** asphalted.
01/01-31/12.
Distance: on the spot on the spot 100m.
Remarks: Max. 2 days.

Bad Salzdetfurth 10B2

Am Solebad, Solebadstraße, Detfurth.
GPS: n52,07193 e10,01859.

10 € 5/24h € 1/50liter Ch € 1/6h.
Location: Rural. **Surface:** asphalted.
01/01-31/12.
Distance: 2km Bistro 50m 100m on the spot on the spot.
Remarks: Market Friday-morning.

Bad Zwischenahn 7G3

Wohnmobilstellplatz Am Badepark, Am Badepark.
GPS: n53,18722 e8,00021.

50 € 14 tourist tax incl € 0,50/100liter Ch (35x)€ 0,60/kWh WC (spa resort) included. **Location:** Urban, simple.
Surface: metalled. 01/01-31/12.
Distance: on the spot 6,8km on the spot on the spot 100m 500m on the spot.

Balge 10A1

Stellplatz Marina Mehlbergen, Werderstraße.
GPS: n52,68788 e9,17779.
20 € 10 Ch (16x)€ 0,50/kWh WC included.
Surface: metalled. 01/01-31/12.
Distance: 2km on the spot on the spot 2km 2km 1km on the spot on the spot.
Remarks: Check in on arrival.

Balje 8A1

Am Natureum, Neuenhof 8, Neuhaus. **GPS**: n53,81958 e9,03867.

6 free. **Location:** Rural, simple, isolated. **Surface:** grassy.
01/01-31/12.
Distance: 4km on the spot 4km 4km.

Barnstorf 9H1

Wohnmobilstellplatz Midden int Dörp, Rathausweg/Brinkstraße.
GPS: n52,71170 e8,50780.
3 free Ch. **Surface:** metalled. 01/01-31/12.
Distance: on the spot 100m 300m.

Barßel 7G3

Am Bootshafen, Deichstrasse. **GPS**: n53,16754 e7,73441.

18 € 6 Ch (34x)€ 2/24h WC € 1 included.
Location: Urban, simple. **Surface:** grasstiles.
01/01-31/12.
Distance: 500m on the spot on the spot 500m.

Barsinghausen 10A1

Wohnmobilstellplatz am Besucherbergwerk Klosterstollen, Conrad-Bühreweg. **GPS**: n52,29858 e9,46943.

5 € 6,50 (5x)included. **Location:** Rural, simple.
Surface: gravel. 01/01-31/12.
Distance: 300m nearby 300m.
Remarks: Max. 3 days, visit coalmine possible.

Berge 9G1

Stift Börstel, Börstel 5. **GPS**: n52,64957 e7,69438.
2 € 5, in envelope in mail box € 2 € 2. **Surface:** metalled.
01/01-31/12.
Distance: city centre Haselünne 7km 3km 7km 150m.
Remarks: Near abbey, max. 2 nights.

Berge 9G1

Dorfteich Berge, Schienenweg 19. **GPS**: n52,62011 e7,75099.
2 free. 01/01-31/12.
Distance: 400m 400m 300m 150m.

Bergen 8B3

Stellplatz am Ziegeleiweg, Ziegeleiweg. **GPS**: n52,81273 e9,96457.

DE

6 €3,50 €1 Ch included.
Surface: gravel.
01/01-31/12.
Distance: nearby 300m 450m 250m.
Remarks: Caution key € 20 at town hall.

Tourist information Bergen:
Wildpark Lüneburger Heide, Nindorf. Game preserve. 01/03-31/10 8-19h, 01/11-28/02 9.30-16.30h.

S Berne 7H3

Fähranleger Motzen, Motzener Strasse. **GPS**: n53,17972 e8,55778.

4 free €1/60liter Ch (4x)€1/6h.
Location: Urban, simple, isolated, noisy. **Surface:** gravel/sand.
01/01-31/12.
Distance: 3,5km on the spot 1km 100m 100m.
Remarks: Parking at ferry-boat at river Weser.

Bevern 10A2

Schwimm- und Freizeitzentrum, Jahnstrasse.
GPS: n51,85750 e9,50805.

5 free. **Location:** Rural, simple. **Surface:** asphalted.
01/01-31/12.
Distance: 1,2km 500m 500m.

S Bienenbüttel 8C3

Wohnmobilstellplatz Ilmenauwiese, Niendorfer strasse, K42.
GPS: n53,14514 e10,49051.

12 €6 €1/8minutes Ch (12x)€1/8h WC €1.
Location: Rural, comfortable, quiet. **Surface:** metalled.
01/01-31/12.
Distance: 500m on the spot on the spot 500m 500m
special sculpture route.

Bippen 9G1

Dorfteich, Hauptstrasse. **GPS**: n52,58209 e7,73887.
2 free. 01/01-31/12.

S Bippen 9G1

Ferienhof Nyenhuis, Hallweg 8. **GPS**: n52,59360 e7,73005.

20 €13 WC €2,50. **Location:** Rural, simple, quiet.
Surface: grassy. 01/01-31/12.
Distance: 1km.

S Bippen 9G1

Gasthof Mol, Einigkeitsstraße 20, Lonnerbecke.
GPS: n52,54337 e7,67118.
10 free Service €7/day.
Distance: on the spot.

S Bippen 9G1

Hotel-Restaurant-Café Sülte Mühle, Ölmühle 1, Lonnerbecke.
GPS: n52,54972 e7,69594.
2 free €2.

S Bispingen 8B3

Parkplatz Oberhaverbeck, Oberhaverbeck. **GPS**: n53,14281 e9,91998.

30 € 3/day, € 6/night €1/10minutes Ch (8x)€1/10h.
Location: Rural, simple, isolated. **Surface:** grassy/gravel.
01/01-31/12 Service: winter.
Distance: 6km 350m 6km 100m on the spot
on the spot.
Remarks: In nature reserve the the Lüneburg Heide (heath).

Bispingen 8B3

Parking Rathaus, Borsteler Straße 4-6. **GPS**: n53,08499 e9,99789.

5 free. **Location:** Simple, central. **Surface:** metalled.
01/01-31/12.
Distance: on the spot 1km 100m 100m on the spot on the spot.

S Bispingen 8B3

Reiter- und Ferienhof Cohrs, Volkwardingen 1, Moorweg.
GPS: n53,13409 e10,00047.

10 €14 Ch included WC €3.
Location: Comfortable, isolated, quiet. **Surface:** grassy.
01/01-31/12.
Distance: 3km 5,5km 500m 5km on the spot.
Remarks: Bread-service.

S Bissendorf 9H2

Reisemobil-Center Veregge & Welz, Gewerbepark 14, A30 Abfahrt Bissendorf. **GPS**: n52,24026 e8,13977.

6 free €1/5minutes Ch (4x)€1/6h. **Location:** Urban, simple, quiet. **Surface:** metalled. 01/01-31/12.
Distance: 1km 650m 800m 800m.

S Bleckede 8C2

Campingpark Elbtalaue, Am Waldbad 23.
GPS: n53,25948 e10,80526.

15 € 14, 2 pers incl €1 Ch €3,50/night,or€0,50/0,8kWh WC included €3,50/3 €4/day,€9/3 days. **Location:** Rural, luxurious, isolated, quiet. **Surface:** grassy. 01/01-31/12.
Distance: 2km 300m 800m 6km 50m.

S Blomberg 7G2

Dorfplatz Blomberg, Hauptstrasse. **GPS**: n53,57718 e7,55815.

20 free €1 Ch€1 €0,50/kWh WC.
Surface: grassy/metalled. 01/01-31/12.
Distance: on the spot 200m 200m 50m.

Bockenem 10B2

Am Freibad, In den Reesen. **GPS**: n52,00787 e10,13610.

5 free. **Location:** Rural, simple, quiet. **Surface:** gravel.
01/01-31/12.
Distance: 800m 200m 300m.

S Bockenem 10B2

Hotel Sauer am Aral Autohof, Allensteiner strasse 7.
GPS: n52,00224 e10,13379.

20 guests free €1,50 Ch (8x)€2,50 WC €1,50.
Location: Rural, simple. **Surface:** metalled. 01/01-31/12.
Distance: 300m on the spot 500m.

S Bockhorn 7G2

Reisemobilplatz Germer, Am Geeschendamm 1.
GPS: n53,38575 e8,00857.

DE

30 €6 €1,50 Ch (30x)€0,50/kWh WC €2. Location: Comfortable. 01/01-31/12.

Bockhorn 7G2

Erlebnisbad, Urwaldstrasse 35a. **GPS**: n53,39876 e7,99410.

5 free. **Location:** Rural. **Surface:** metalled. 01/01-31/12.
Distance: on the spot.
Remarks: Parking swimming pool, max. 1 day.

Bockhorn 7G2

Gaststätte Altdeutsche Diele, Landesstrasse 11, Steinhausen.
GPS: n53,41539 e8,03622.

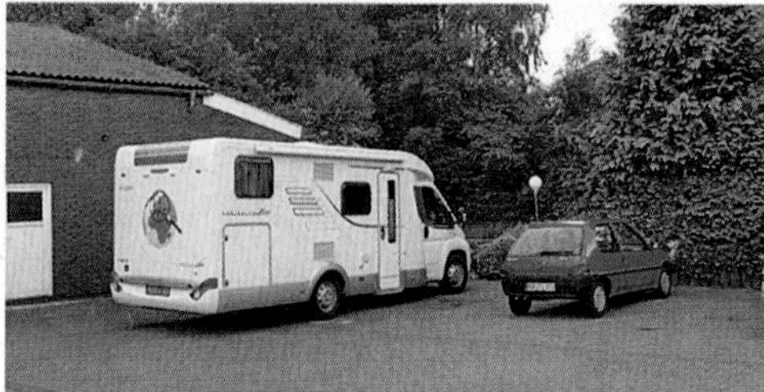

3 free (3x)against payment. **Location:** Simple.
Surface: metalled. 01/01-31/12.

Bockhorn 7G2

Zum Sandkrug, Sandkrugsweg 21,Grabstede.
GPS: n53,35893 e8,00186.

4 free. **Location:** Rural, simple, quiet. **Surface:** grassy.
01/01-31/12.
Distance: on the spot.

Bodenwerder 10A2

Wohnmobilstellplatz Bodenwerder, Am Mühlentor.
GPS: n51,98037 e9,51795.

25 €6, tourist tax €1/pp €2/10minutes Ch €2,50/day WC €1,50. **Location:** Urban, simple. **Surface:** grassy.
01/01-31/12.
Distance: 200m Weser 200m 200m 500m 200m.
Remarks: Check in and pay at pay desk swimming pool.

Bohmte 9H1

Golfclub Arenshorst, Arenshorster Kirchweg 2.
GPS: n52,35651 e8,28450.

3 guests free. **Location:** Rural, simple. **Surface:** grassy/metalled.
01/01-31/12.
Distance: 3km on the spot 3km.

Bohmte 9H1

Landgasthaus Gieseke-Asshorn, Bremer strasse 55.
GPS: n52,36674 e8,31261.

4 guests free free. **Location:** Urban, quiet.
Surface: metalled. 01/01-31/12.
Distance: 50m on the spot 200m.

Bohmte 9H1

VARIOmobil Fahrzeugbau GmbH, Bremer strasse.
GPS: n52,38623 e8,30761.

2 free Ch free. **Location:** Rural, quiet. **Surface:** metalled.
01/01-31/12.
Distance: 500m 1km 1km.
Remarks: Service only during opening hours.

Brake 7H2

City-Parkplatz, Breite Strasse. **GPS**: n53,32534 e8,47982.

2 free. **Location:** Urban, simple, central, noisy. **Surface:** metalled.
01/01-31/12.
Distance: on the spot on the spot 200m 200m on the spot.
Remarks: Key at aparthotel Panorama (50m).

Brake 7H2

Am Binnenhafen, Hafenstrasse. **GPS**: n53,32802 e8,48296.

4 free €1/10minutes Ch (4x)€0,50/6h. **Location:** Urban, simple, central, noisy. **Surface:** grasstiles.
01/01-31/12.
Distance: on the spot 1km 100m 200m 200m on the spot.

Bramsche 9G1

Wohnmobilstellplatz Waldwinkel, Zum Dreschhaus 4.
GPS: n52,39591 e8,10244.

60 €7 €0,10/10liter Ch (80x)€2 WC €1.
Location: Rural, comfortable, quiet. **Surface:** grassy.
01/01-31/12.
Distance: 3,5km 100m 3,5km on the spot on the spot.
Remarks: Next to campsite Waldwinkel.

Bramsche 9G1

Hasebad, Malgartener strasse 49. **GPS**: n52,41493 e7,99423.

6 free. **Location:** Urban, simple, quiet. **Surface:** metalled.
01/01-31/12.
Distance: 500m.

Bramsche 9G1

Reisemobile Lewandowsky, Am Kanal 1b.
GPS: n52,38524 e7,92958.

2 free Chfree €2/day. **Location:** Rural, simple.
Surface: gravel. 01/01-31/12.
Distance: 1km 1km 1km.
Remarks: Also repairs possible, service during opening hours, walking and bicycle area.

Braunlage 10C3

Schützenplatz, Schützenstrasse 21. **GPS**: n51,71658 e10,60847.

85 €10 + €2,20/pp tourist tax €1/80liter Ch €0,50/kWh WCincluded €1,50 €3. **Location:** Rural, luxurious, quiet.
Surface: gravel. 01/01-31/12.
Distance: 400m Café Restaurant Hubertushöhe on the spot on the spot on the spot.
Remarks: Bread-service.

Braunschweig 10C1

Theodor-Heuss-Straße. **GPS**: n52,24964 e10,51835.

DE

16 free €1/10minutes Ch (16x)€1/8h.
Location: Urban, simple, noisy. **Surface:** asphalted.
01/01-31/12.
Distance: 2km 400m 200m on the spot.
Remarks: Max. 2 nights.

S Bremen 7H3

Wohnmobil Oase Bremen, Schoster born, via Emil von Behringstrasse. **GPS:** n53,06778 e8,86333.

8 € 15 + tourist tax € 1/pp €2 Ch WCincluded €1,50,use luxurious bathroom €5, sauna €5 €6.
Location: Urban, comfortable, central. **Surface:** gravel.
01/01-31/12.
Distance: 4km on the spot 50m Tram on the spot.
Remarks: Motorhome < 7m.

S Bremen 7H3

Am Kuhhirten, Kurhirtenweg. **GPS:** n53,06500 e8,81871.

70 € 15 €1/100liter Ch (70x)€0,50/kWh WC€1/24h €1/5minutes. **Location:** Urban, comfortable, central.
Surface: gravel. 01/01-31/12.
Distance: Old city centre 1,3km 500m on the spot 800m Tram 700m on the spot.
Remarks: Bread-service.

S Bremen 7H3

Bremer Schweiz, Im Pohl, Lesum. **GPS:** n53,16765 e8,69560.

7 € 5/24h €1/10minutes Ch (8x)€1/8h.
Location: Urban, comfortable, quiet. **Surface:** gravel.
01/01-31/12.
Distance: on the spot 2,4km on the spot 300m on the spot on the spot.

S Bremen 7H3

Maritime Meile, Schulkenstrasse. **GPS:** n53,17298 e8,60906.

5 € 5 + tourist tax €1/80liter Ch (4x)€1/8h.
Location: Urban, comfortable, central, quiet. **Surface:** asphalted.
01/01-31/12.
Distance: Bremen 20km 100m 200m on the spot.

S Bremen 7H3

Camping Stadtwaldsee, Hochschulring 1.
GPS: n53,11381 e8,84389.

20 € 12-15 €1/80liter Ch (20x)€1/5h WC included.
Location: Rural, luxurious.
Surface: grasstiles.
01/01-31/12.
Distance: 5,5km 3km on the spot on the spot on the spot 100m on the spot.

Tourist information Bremen:
Tourist Information, Obernstrasse en Hauptbahnhof, www.bremen-tourism.de. Hanseatic city and second harbour of Germany.
Böttcherstrasse. Pedestrian passage.
Weserpromenade Schlachte. Antiques and flea market. Sa 8-14h.

S Bremerhaven 7H2

Reisemobil-Parkplatz Doppelschleuse, An der Neuen Schleuse. **GPS:** n53,53230 e8,57607.

63 € 10 €1/80liter Ch (40x)€0,50/kWh WC€0,50 €0,50. **Location:** Urban, comfortable, luxurious, central, quiet.
Surface: asphalted. 01/01-31/12.
Distance: 1km 8km 1km 1,5km 1,2km on the spot.
Remarks: Bread-service.

S Bremerhaven 7H2

Reisemobil-Parkplatz Fischereihafen, Hoebelstrasse, Fischereihafen 1. **GPS:** n53,52634 e8,57610.

47 € 10, tourist tax incl €1/100liter Ch (36x)€0,50/kWh WCincluded €0,50. **Location:** Urban, luxurious, central, quiet.
Surface: asphalted/metalled. 01/01-31/12.
Distance: 4km on the spot on the spot 500m 500m 200m 200m.
Remarks: At harbour, caution key sanitary € 5.

S Bremerhaven 7H2

Havenhostel Bremerhaven, Bürgermeister-Smidt-Straße 209.
GPS: n53,55932 e8,56793.
20 € 15 Ch included WC €2/2. **Surface:** grassy.
01/01-31/12.
Distance: 1km on the spot.
Remarks: Check in at reception, breakfast-service.

S Bremervörde 8A2

Wohnmobilstation Bremervörde, Kiebitzweg 1.
GPS: n53,49453 e9,15576.
40 € 9,50, 01/11-28/02 € 6,50 Ch (21x)€3/day,10Amp WC €1 included. **Location:** Rural, comfortable, quiet.
Surface: metalled. 01/01-31/12.
Distance: 1,5km 100m 100m 300m 1km 1,5km on the spot on the spot.

S Brietlingen 8B2

Reihersee, Grosse strabe. **GPS:** n53,34344 e10,45844.

50 € 8 €2,50. **Location:** Rural, simple, isolated.
Surface: grassy. 01/03-31/10.
Distance: on the spot.

S Brietlingen 8B2

Landhotel Franck, Bundesstrasse 31b. **GPS:** n53,32951 e10,44491.

5 guests free (1x)€5/night.
Location: Rural, simple, quiet.
Distance: on the spot on the spot 500m.

S Bruchhausen-Vilsen 8A3

Reisemobilstellplatz Bruchhausen-Vilsen, Bollenstrasse.
GPS: n52,82671 e8,99536.

40 € 6 €1/100liter Ch (24x)WCincluded.
Surface: gravel. 01/01-31/12.
Distance: 200m 200m 200m.
Remarks: Max. 3 days.

Buchholz/Nordheide 8B2

Campingplatz Nordheide, Weg zum Badeteich 20. **GPS**: n53,28202 e9,87495.

12 € 12-15 Ch (6x)€2 WC included.
Location: Rural, comfortable. **Surface:** metalled/sand.
01/01-31/12.
Distance: 200m on the spot on the spot 200m.

Bückeburg 10A2

Am Schloss, Georgstrasse/Liebesallee. **GPS**: n52,25777 e9,04583.

20 €5 €1 Ch (24x)€1/12h **Location:** Urban, quiet. **Surface:** gravel/metalled. 01/01-31/12.
Distance: 500m 500m 500m 200m on the spot.

Bückeburg 10A2

Neumarktplatz, Unterwallweg 5c. **GPS**: n52,26326 e9,05040.

15 free €1/80liter Ch (6x)€0,50/kWh.
Location: Urban, simple. **Surface:** gravel. 01/01-31/12.
Distance: 250m 250m 250m.

Büddenstedt 10C2

Am Sportplatz. **GPS**: n52,17567 e11,01843.

3 free. **Location:** Rural, simple, quiet. **Surface:** asphalted.
01/01-31/12.
Distance: 1km on the spot 2km.
Remarks: Parking swimming pool.

Büddenstedt 10C2

Parking K22, Barneberger Straße, Offleben. **GPS**: n52,13738 e11,04409.

2 free. **Location:** Rural, simple. **Surface:** asphalted.
01/01-31/12.
Distance: 500m 500m 500m.

Bühren 10B3

Alter Festplatz, Im Teich. **GPS**: n51,48378 e9,67451.

20 €2 €2. **Location:** Rural, isolated. **Surface:** grassy.
01/01-31/12.
Distance: 700m 5km on the spot on the spot.

Bunde 7F3

Am Friedhofsweg. **GPS**: n53,18500 e7,26639.

15 €5 €1 €1 Ch €1/10h. **Surface:** grasstiles.
01/01-31/12.
Distance: 100m 2,3km 350m 200m.
Remarks: At townhall, max. 3 days.

Bunde 7F3

Freizeitgelände, Denkmalstrasse 11, Ditzumerverlaat. **GPS**: n53,26028 e7,26861.

10 €3/24h €0,50 Ch (8x)€1/8h. **Surface:** metalled.
01/01-31/12 during event.
Distance: 250m on the spot on the spot 350m 250m.
Remarks: Max. 3 days.

Bunde 7F3

Möhlenlandbad, Kellingwold 25. **GPS**: n53,18683 e7,27418.
10 €3. **Surface:** metalled. 01/01-31/12.
Distance: 500m.

Butjadingen 7H2

Henken's Stellplatz, Am Hafen 6, Fedderwardersiel. **GPS**: n53,59581 e8,35669.

80 €5 + €1,10-2,20/pp tourist tax €0,01/1liter Ch €1/24h (48x)€2,50/day. **Location:** Rural, comfortable, central, quiet.
Surface: grassy. 01/01-31/12.
Distance: 500m on the spot on the spot on the spot on the spot 500m on the spot on the spot.
Remarks: Bread-service.

Butjadingen 7H2

Jachthaven Fedderwardersiel. **GPS**: n53,59518 e8,35700.

30 € 10 excl. tourist tax Ch€1,50 (20x)€2,50/day WC 4minutes €6. **Location:** Rural, comfortable, isolated, quiet.
Surface: grassy. 01/01-31/12.
Distance: 800m on the spot on the spot 800m 800m on the spot on the spot on the spot.

Butjadingen 7H2

Hof Iggewarden, Iggewarden 1. **GPS**: n53,58622 e8,32653.

20 €8 €1/100liter Ch (2x)€2/day WC.
Location: Rural, comfortable, isolated, quiet. **Surface:** gravel.
01/01-31/12.
Distance: 2km 2km on the spot on the spot 300m on the spot on the spot.

Butjadingen 7H2

Knaus Campingpark Burhave, Strand Allee, Burhave. **GPS**: n53,58306 e8,37000.

50 €9,80 + €2,20/pp tourist tax €2,20 Ch €0,70/kWh WC €3,30. **Surface:** grassy. 15/04-15/10.
Distance: 1km on the spot 200m 1km.

Buxtehude 8A2

Pfingstmarktplatz, Cuxhavenerstrasse, Neukloster, B73. **GPS**: n53,47974 e9,63528.

40 free €1/100liter Ch €2. **Location:** Rural, simple.
Surface: asphalted. 01/01-31/12 week before/after Whitsuntide. **Distance:** 3km Imbiss bakery 200m.
Remarks: Key shower at Imbiss.

Buxtehude 8A2

Stellplatz am Schützenplatz, Genslerweg. **GPS**: n53,47139 e9,69528.

30 €5 €1/100liter Ch (18x)€1/kWh. **Location:** Urban,

central. **Surface:** gravel. 01/01-31/12.
Distance: nearby Old city centre 50m bakery 50m on the spot on the spot.

Tourist information Buxtehude:
Das Fleth. Old inland-port.

S Cadenberge 8A1

Reisemobilvermietung Hennig, Alter Postweg 1.
GPS: n53,76686 e9,05681.

4 € 5 €0,50/100liter €1,50/24h. **Location:** Rural, simple.
Surface: grassy. 01/01-31/12.
Distance: 50m on the spot 50m.

S Celle 10B1

Schützenplatz, Hafenstraße. **GPS**: n52,62794 e10,07348.

35 free €1 Ch WC.
Surface: grassy/metalled. 01/01-31/12.
Distance: 150m 100m.

Celle 10B1

Langensalzaplatz. **GPS**: n52,61842 e10,08052.

3 free. **Surface:** metalled. 01/01-31/12.
Distance: on the spot.

Clausthal-Zellerfeld 10C2

Busbahnhof, Bahnhofstraß2 5. **GPS**: n51,81360 e10,33602.

4 tourist tax € 1,50. **Location:** Rural, simple. **Surface:** metalled.
01/01-31/12.
Distance: on the spot 200m 600m on the spot on the spot on the spot.

S Clenze 8C3

Regenbogen-Hof, Mützen. **GPS**: n52,94079 e10,93899.

5 € 7/pp Ch WC included. **Location:** Rural, simple, isolated, quiet. **Surface:** grassy. 01/01-31/12.
Distance: 3km on the spot 3km on the spot.
Remarks: Arrival <22h.

S Cloppenburg 7G3

Am Stadtpark, Hagenweg. **GPS**: n52,84649 e8,04687.

3 € 5, tourist tax incl €1/80liter Ch free €0,50/kWh.
Location: Urban, simple. **Surface:** metalled.
01/01-31/12.
Distance: 100m 2km 100m 300m.
Remarks: Max. 3 days.

Cloppenburg 7G3

Museumsdorf Cloppenburg, Bether Straße.
GPS: n52,85197 e8,05335.

20 free. **Location:** Rural, simple. **Surface:** metalled.
01/01-31/12.
Distance: 900m 1km.
Remarks: Parking in front of museum village, max. 24h.

S Coppenbrügge 10A2

Parkplatz am Frei- und Hallenbad, Felsenkellerweg.
GPS: n52,11613 e9,53676.

12 € 3,50 €2,50 Ch (12x)€1. **Location:** Rural, simple.
Surface: grassy/gravel. 01/01-31/12.
Distance: 1,5km 500m 500m on the spot on the spot.
Remarks: Check in at campsite.

S Cuxhaven 7H1

Duhner Allee, Duhnen. **GPS**: n53,88284 e8,64814.

60 € 8, peak season € 10 Ch €2/day WC €0,50 €1.
Location: Simple. **Surface:** asphalted. 01/01-31/12.
Remarks: Beach parking, in front of campsite am Bäderring.

S Cuxhaven 7H1

Elbe-Ferry, Am Fährhafen. **GPS**: n53,87508 e8,70315.

100 € 10-13, tourist tax incl Ch.
Location: Urban, simple. **Surface:** asphalted. 01/01-31/12.
Distance: 1km 500m.
Remarks: Bread-service.

S Cuxhaven 7H1

Privatparkplatz Kugelbake Halle, Nordfeldstraße.
GPS: n53,89033 e8,67703.

80 € 8 Ch WC. **Location:** Urban, simple.
Surface: metalled. 01/01-31/12.
Distance: 200m 100m.

S Cuxhaven 7H1

Campingplatz Finck, Am Sahlenburger Strand 25.
GPS: n53,86039 e8,59167.

16 € 17, tourist tax incl Ch (16x)included WC €0,50 .
Location: Comfortable. 15/03-31/10.
Distance: 3km on the spot on the spot on camp site 100m.
Remarks: Sanitary at campsite.

S Damme 9H1

Stellplatz am Flugplatz, Am Flugplatz 8.
GPS: n52,49055 e8,17925.

12 € 10 €0,50/80liter Ch (12x)€0,50/kWh WC €1.
Location: Luxurious. **Surface:** grassy/gravel. 01/01-31/12.
Distance: 1.4km on the spot 100m.
Remarks: Parking airport Damme.

Damme 9H1

Parkplatz Altes Amtsgericht, Ohlkensbergweg 10.
GPS: n52,52389 e8,19488.
5 free. **Surface:** metalled. 01/01-31/12.
Distance: 300m 400m 100m 150m.

S Damme 9H1

Olgahafen, Dümmerstrasse, Dümmerlohausen.
GPS: n52,52917 e8,31098.

DE

12 free €1 Ch €1. **Location:** Rural, simple, quiet. **Surface:** gravel. 01/01-31/12.
Distance: 100m 100m on the spot bakery.
Remarks: At lake Dümmer, max. 3 days.

Dangast 7G2

Sielstrasse 30. **GPS:** n53,44539 e8,10979.
40 € 9 included. **Location:** Simple. **Surface:** grassy. 15/04-15/10.
Distance: on the spot on the spot on the spot.

Dannenberg 8C3

Bäckergrund 32. **GPS:** n53,10062 e11,10903.
4 Ch. 01/04-30/09.
Distance: 300m 850m.

Dassel 10B2

Am Badesee in der Ortschaft, Lauenberg.
GPS: n51,75750 e9,76389.

8 free, 01/05-01/10 € 5 €1/80liter Ch €1/8h included,01/05-30/09. **Location:** Rural, isolated, quiet. **Surface:** asphalted. 01/01-31/12.
Distance: 8,5km on the spot 300m 300m 300m on the spot on the spot.

Dassel 10B2

Am Sollingbad, An der Badeanstalt. **GPS:** n51,80722 e9,68917.

5 free. **Location:** Rural, isolated. 01/01-31/12.
Distance: Old city centre 500m 1km on the spot on the spot.

Deinste 8A2

Gut Deinster Mühle, Im Mühlenfeld 30. **GPS:** n53,53132 e9,43301.
15 free. **Surface:** grassy. 01/01-31/12.
Distance: on the spot 400m bakery on the spot on the spot.
Remarks: Golf court.

Delmenhorst 7H3

Reisemobilhafen Delmenhorst, An den Graften.
GPS: n53,04722 e8,62278.

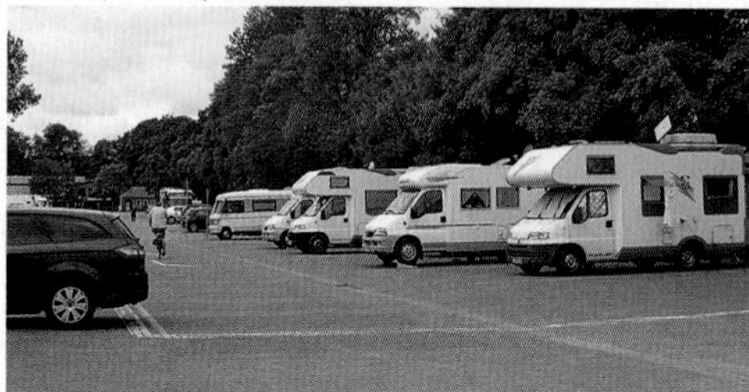

8 free Chfree €1/kWh. **Location:** Urban, simple, central, quiet. **Surface:** gravel/sand. 01/01-31/12 during event.
Distance: on the spot 2,8km on the spot 200m.
Remarks: Max. 7 days.

Detern 7G3

Reisemobilhafen Detern, Alte Heerstrasse 6, Stickhausen.
GPS: n53,21560 e7,64743.

40 € 8 €1/100liter Ch (44x)€2/24h WC €1/6minutes €0,50. **Location:** Urban, luxurious.
Surface: asphalted/gravel. 01/01-31/12.
Distance: on the spot 6km on the spot on the spot on the spot on the spot on the spot.
Remarks: Behind tourist info, bread-service.

Diepenau 9H1

Stellplatz am Bahnhof, Am Bahnhof. **GPS:** n52,42470 e8,74106.

5 free €1 Ch (5x)€1/8h. **Surface:** metalled. 01/01-31/12.
Distance: 500m 500m 500m.

Diepenau 9H1

Wohnmobilstellplatz Am Tor zum Moor, Steinbrinkerstrasse 8.
GPS: n52,47664 e8,74016.

30 € 8 Ch included. **Surface:** grassy/metalled. 01/04-31/10.
Distance: on the spot on the spot 1km.

Diepholz 9H1

Parkplatz Am Heldenhain, Am Heldenhaim (B69).
GPS: n52,61250 e8,37056.

20 free €1/80liter Ch (20x)€0,50/kWh free.
Location: Urban. **Surface:** grassy. 01/01-31/12.
Distance: 500m 500m 500m.
Remarks: Max. 3 days.

Ditzum 7F2

Ankerplatz Blank, Pogumer Straße. **GPS:** n53,31489 e7,27619.

14 € 7/24h €1/100liter Ch (10x)€1/2kWh WC €0,50.
Surface: metalled. 01/01-31/12.
Distance: 100m 300m 300m 100m on the spot.

Ditzum 7F2

Reisemobilstellplatz Ditzum, Am Deich.
GPS: n53,31555 e7,28666.

45 € 7/night €1/100liter Ch (45x)€1/2kWh.
Surface: metalled.
01/01-31/12.
Distance: 100m 100m 100m 100m 300m.
Remarks: Bread-service, waste dump € 1, shower € 1.

Dornum 7G2

Schöpfwerkstraße, Dornumersiel. **GPS:** n53,67272 e7,48092.
30 € 9, Nordsee-ServiceCard incl €1/8h. **Surface:** metalled. 01/01-31/12.
Distance: 500m 100m 100m.

Dornum 7G2

Schützenplatz. **GPS:** n53,64850 e7,42365.

30 € 9, Nordsee-ServiceCard incl €1/65liter Ch €1/8h.
Surface: grassy. 01/01-31/12.
Distance: on the spot 300m 50m.
Remarks: Max. 1 night.

Dornum 7G2

Wohnmobilstellplatz Nordseeblick. GPS: n53,67912 e7,47767.
38 € 13 Nordsee-ServiceCard incl €2/100liter Ch €1/kWh WC. **Surface:** grasstiles. 24/03-03/10.
Distance: 200m 200m 500m 500m.
Remarks: Swimming pool.

Dornum 7G2

Am Nordseestrand, Hafenstraße 7. **GPS:** n53,68063 e7,48294.
10 € 17 Nordsee-ServiceCard incl Ch included. 01/04-30/09.
Distance: on the spot 300m 500m.
Remarks: Bread-service.

Dörpen 7F3

Festplatz, Veeneweg. **GPS:** n52,97115 e7,33425.

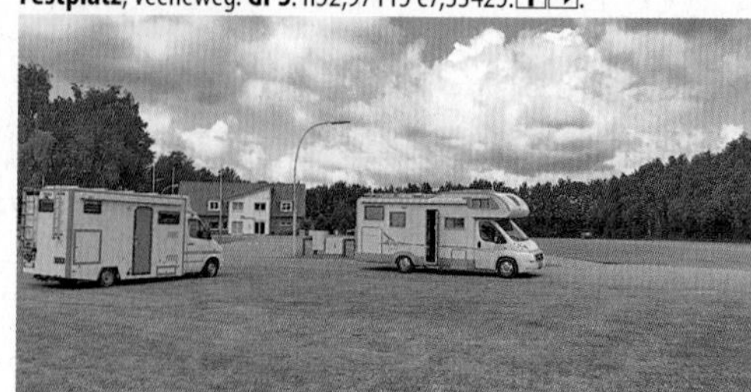

5 free. **Location:** Simple. **Surface:** grassy/metalled. 01/01-31/12 1st week in June: fair.
Distance: 500m on the spot 500m on the spot.
Remarks: Max. 4 nights.

Dorum 7H2

Wohnmobilhafen Grube-Petrat, Am Neuen Deich 2a.
GPS: n53,73838 e8,51966.

DE

20 € 12,50 + € 2 tourist tax, 01/05-15/09 € 14 + € 3,40 tourist tax Ch included WC €1 **Location:** Simple.
Surface: metalled. 01/01-31/12.
Distance: on the spot on the spot on the spot.
Remarks: Check in at Deichhotel, bread-service.

S Dörverden 8A3

In der Worth. **GPS**: n52,84529 e9,22568.

5 free €1/80liter (5x)€1/8h. **Location:** Urban, simple, quiet.
Surface: gravel. 01/01-31/12.
Distance: 200m 200m 200m Bremen/Hanover 100m 1km.
Remarks: Behind town hall, max. 3 nights.

Dörverden 8A3

Wolfcenter, Kasernenstraße, Barme. **GPS**: n52,82635 e9,21417.
10 free.
Location: Simple. **Surface:** concrete. 01/01-31/12.
Distance: Dörverden 3km on the spot Aldi 3km.
Remarks: Parking wolf park.

S Drage/Elbe 8B2

Reisemobilplatz Stover Strand, Stover Strand 10.
GPS: n53,42467 e10,29213.

100 € 13, dog € 2 €1/80liter Ch (100x)€0,50/kWh WC €0,50/4minutes €4/4 €2/h.
Location: Comfortable. **Surface:** grassy. 01/01-31/12.
Distance: on the spot on the spot on the spot on the spot 500m on the spot on the spot.
Remarks: Next to campsite.

S Drochtersen 8A2

Wohnmobilstellplatz Krautsand, Hinterm Elbdeich, Krautsand.
GPS: n53,75167 e9,39028.

10 € 10 WC included. **Location:** Rural, simple.
Surface: grassy/metalled. 15/04-03/10.
Distance: Elbestrand 300m.

Drochtersen 8A2

Hallenbad Drochtersen, Am Sportplatz. **GPS**: n53,70548 e9,38215.

6 free.
Location: Simple. **Surface:** metalled. 01/01-31/12.
Distance: 1km 1km.
Remarks: Parking at swimming pool.

Drochtersen 8A2

Am Alten Hafen, Asseler Sand. **GPS**: n53,69418 e9,43928.

6 free.
Location: Rural, simple. **Surface:** gravel. 01/01-31/12.
Distance: 500m 1km.

S Duderstadt 10C3

P&R Parkplatz, Adenauerring. **GPS**: n51,51043 e10,27278.

50 free €1/120liter €1 Ch€1 (4x)€0,50/kWh.
Location: Rural, quiet. **Surface:** gravel. 01/01-31/12.
Distance: 800m 17km 800m 200m 100m.

Duderstadt 10C3

Eichsfeldhalle, August Werner Allee. **GPS**: n51,50662 e10,25890.

5 free.
Location: Rural, simple. **Surface:** gravel.
01/01-31/12.
Distance: 900m 17km 900m 900m 700m.
Remarks: Max. 1 night.

Tourist information Duderstadt:
Gästeinformation der Stadt Duderstadt, Marktstrasse 66, www.duderstadt.de. Old part of town with half-timbered houses.

S Edewecht 7G3

Am Marktplatz, Rathhausstrasse. **GPS**: n53,12834 e7,98201.

20 € 5/24h €1/80liter Ch (8x)€1/6h. **Location:** Urban, simple. **Surface:** grassy. 01/01-31/12.
Distance: on the spot 400m Aldi 50m.

S Egestorf 8B3

Naturerlebnisbad Acquadies, Ahornweg 5.
GPS: n53,19796 e10,05455.

30 € 8 €1 Ch (20x)€2/10h WC €2.
Location: Simple, quiet. **Surface:** gravel/metalled.
01/01-31/12.
Distance: 1km 2,2km on the spot 700m 1km.
Remarks: At swimming pool, shower during opening hours.

S Eggermühlen 9G1

Reiterhotel Vox, OT Bockraden 1. **GPS**: n52,57278 e7,79553.

8 € 25, clients € 7,50 Ch WC included. **Location:** Rural.
Surface: grassy. 01/01-31/12.
Distance: 3km 3km.

Eggestedt 7H3

Eggestedt, Betonstrasse/Habichthorsterweg.
GPS: n53,22819 e8,63902.

8 free. **Location:** Simple, isolated, noisy. **Surface:** metalled/sand.
01/01-31/12.
Distance: 4km 400m.

S Einbeck 10B2

Am Schwimmbad, Ochsenhofweg. **GPS**: n51,82433 e9,86464.

30 free €1/60liter €1 Ch (18x)€0,50/kWh.
Location: Simple. **Surface:** gravel. 01/01-31/12.
Distance: 800m 500m 500m on the spot on the spot.
Remarks: Parking at swimming pool.

Tourist information Einbeck:
Alte Marktplatz. Wed + Sa morning.

S Elsfleth 7H3

Im Hafen, An der Kaje. **GPS**: n53,23771 e8,46545.

DE

20 €8/24h €1/80liter Ch (16x)€2/8h WC €2.
Location: Urban, comfortable, central, noisy. **Surface:** concrete.
01/01-31/12.
Distance: 150m 900m on the spot 100m 500m on the spot on the spot.

Emden 7F2

Alter Binnenhafen, Am Eisenbahndock. **GPS**: n53,36306 e7,20778.

29 €9 €0,50/100liter €0,50 Ch (36x)€0,50/kWh WC €0,50 €1 €3/1. **Surface:** metalled. 01/01-31/12.
Distance: 500m 500m 500m.
Remarks: Pay at harbourmaster.

Emden 7F2

Wohnmobilstellplatz Knock, Jannes Ohling Strasse.
GPS: n53,35559 e7,00367.

25 €4,50. **Surface:** metalled. 01/01-31/12.
Distance: 13km 500m on the spot 13km.
Remarks: Beautiful view.

Emden 7F2

Außenhafen Emden, An der Nesserlanderschleuse.
GPS: n53,34571 e7,19132.
10 €5. **Surface:** asphalted. 01/01-31/12.
Distance: 3,5km on the spot on the spot.

Emden 7F2

Nordkai, Zum Nordkai 6. **GPS**: n53,35037 e7,21712.
9 €8. **Surface:** metalled. 01/01-31/12.
Distance: centre 2,5km Hafenbistro on the spot.

Emsbüren 9F1

Landgasthof Elberger Schlipse, Elbergen 1, Elbergen.
GPS: n52,46825 e7,30103.

30 €4 Chincluded (15x)€2,50/24h WC.
Location: Rural, quiet. **Surface:** grassy. 01/01-31/12.
Distance: 2km 100m 2km on the spot on the spot.

Eschershausen 10B2

Reisemobil-Stellplatz am Angerplatz, Angerweg.
GPS: n51,92965 e9,62806.

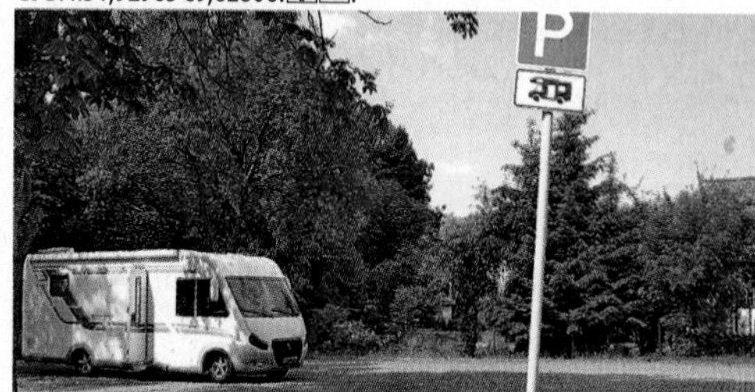

10 free €1/100liter €1 Ch €0,50/kWh. **Surface:** metalled.
01/01-31/12.
Distance: 1km.

Esens 7G2

Wohnmobil-Stellplatz Esens, Schützenplatz.
GPS: n53,63921 e7,61077.

20 €2 + €2,80/pp tourist tax Ch included.
Surface: grassy. 01/01-31/12.
Distance: 500m 50m 200m.
Remarks: Max. 2 nights.

Essel 10B1

Hotel Heide-Kröpke, Esseler Damm 1. **GPS**: n52,73240 e9,69419.

5 free (3x).
Surface: grassy. 01/01-31/12.
Distance: on the spot 9km.
Remarks: Use of a meal desired, bird reserve Ostenholzer-Moor.

Esterwegen 7G3

Am Erikasee. **GPS**: n52,99366 e7,66768.

6 free €1/100liter Ch (8x)€1/2kWh WC.
Location: Rural, simple, isolated. **Surface:** gravel/metalled.
01/01-31/12.
Distance: 2km 100m Imbiss 80m.
Remarks: Walking and bicycle area.

Estorf 8A2

Wohnmobilstellplatz Gräpel - An der Prahmfähre, Zum Hafen 21.
GPS: n53,56596 e9,17315.
3 free. **Surface:** gravel.
Distance: on the spot.
Remarks: Along the Oste river.

Eystrup 8A3

Bahnhofstrasse 21. **GPS**: n52,78004 e9,21840.

5 free. **Surface:** grassy. 01/01-31/12.
Distance: 100m.
Remarks: Max. 5 days.

Faßberg 8B3

Am Schützenplatz, Moorweg. **GPS**: n52,90518 e10,16991.

50 €2 €1 ChWC. **Surface:** grassy. 01/01-31/12.
Distance: 700m.

Faßberg 8B3

Parkplatz Heidesee, Unterlüßerstraße, L280, Müden.
GPS: n52,87889 e10,12472.

20 €2 €1 Ch €1. **Surface:** grassy. 01/01-31/12 end Sep.
Distance: 500m 1km.

Faßberg 8B3

Parkplatz am Wildpark, Willinghäuser Kirchweg, Müden.
GPS: n52,87222 e10,10861.

20 €2. **Surface:** grassy. 01/01-31/12.
Distance: 1km 1km.

Fredenbeck 8A2

Dinghornerstraße 21. **GPS**: n53,52146 e9,39598.
5 free. **Surface:** grassy/gravel. 01/01-31/12.
Distance: on the spot on the spot on the spot.

Fredenbeck 8A2

Restaurant Niedersachsenschänke, Schwingestraße 33.
GPS: n53,52646 e9,39314.
5 free. **Surface:** grassy. 01/01-31/12.
Distance: 300m on the spot 300m on the spot on the spot.

Freiburg/Elbe 8A1

Stellplatz am Freizeitcentrum, Am Bassin 25.
GPS: n53,82285 e9,29305.

30 €8 Ch WCincluded €1.
Location: Rural, simple. **Surface:** metalled.
01/01-31/12.
Distance: 200m 50m 300m 400m.
Remarks: Find more possibilities on the city plan.

Freistatt 9H1

Freistätter Feldbahn, Badeweg. **GPS**: n52,62613 e8,65147.
6 €9 Ch included. 01/01-31/12.
Distance: 1km 400m.

Friedeburg 7G2

Schützenplatz. **GPS**: n53,45488 e7,83349.

DE

20 free Ch (6x)€1/8h. **Location:** Rural, simple.
Surface: grassy. 01/01-31/12.
Distance: 15/05-15/09 400m.
Remarks: Max. 3 days.

Friedeburg 7G2

Gasthaus Wilken am See, Friedeburger Straße 19.
GPS: n53,45794 e7,88265.
10 € 5 . **Surface:** grassy.
Distance: on the spot.
Remarks: At lake.

Friesoythe 7G3

Am Aquaferrum, Thüler Straße 28A. **GPS:** n53,01149 e7,86152.

5 free €1/100liter Ch€3 (8x)€6/24h. 01/01-31/12.
Distance: 900m 900m 800m.
Remarks: At swimming pool.

Fürstenau 9G1

Schlossinsel Fürstenau, Schlossplatz 1. **GPS:** n52,51638 e7,67333.

2 free €3 Ch €2/day.
Location: Quiet. **Surface:** metalled. 01/01-31/12.
Distance: 100m 100m 100m on the spot on the spot.
Remarks: Next to castle.

Gartow 8D3

Imbiss am See, Springstraße 88. **GPS:** n53,02944 e11,44944.

20 € 5 WC. **Surface:** gravel/metalled. 01/04-30/10.
Distance: 1km on the spot on the spot on the spot.
Remarks: Imbiss 11-21h.

Geeste 9F1

Am Speicherbecken, Biener Straße 13. **GPS:** n52,59407 e7,27417.

10 free WC. **Location:** Quiet. **Surface:** metalled.
01/01-31/12.
Distance: 2km 100m.
Remarks: Max. 1 night.

Geeste 9F1

P Biotop/Ausblick, Osterbrocker Strasse. **GPS:** n52,59840 e7,29279.

4 free. **Surface:** metalled. 01/01-31/12.
Distance: 1,5km 1,5km on the spot on the spot.
Remarks: Max. 1 night, hiking area.

Gehrden 10B1

An den Sporthallen, Lange Feldstraße 12.
GPS: n52,31197 e9,60971.

2 free (2x)€0,50/kWh. **Location:** Simple. **Surface:** metalled.
01/01-31/12.
Distance: centre 700m 200m.

Gifhorn 10C1

Frei- und Hallenbad Allerwelle, Konrad Adenauerstrasse.
GPS: n52,48437 e10,55407.
12 free €1/stay Ch (12x)€1/8h WC. **Location:** Rural, comfortable, quiet. **Surface:** grasstiles.
01/01-31/12.
Distance: 200m 100m 250m 200m 200m on the spot on the spot.
Remarks: Max. 3 days.

Gifhorn 10C1

Fischer Camping + Gas, Schmiedeweg 4, Wische.
GPS: n52,50863 e10,48462.

8 free €0,50/50liter Ch (8x). **Location:** Rural, simple, isolated. **Surface:** grassy. 01/01-31/12.
Distance: 3km 500m 3km.
Remarks: Accessory shop.

Gnarrenburg 8A2

Parkplatz Brillit, Alte Strasse, Brillit. **GPS:** n53,41390 e9,00007.

15 free Chfree. **Location:** Rural, simple. **Surface:** gravel.
01/01-31/12.
Distance: 1km 3km 1km on the spot on the spot.
Remarks: At community centre.

Gnarrenburg 8A2

Schulzentrum, Brilliterweg. **GPS:** n53,39000 e9,00028.

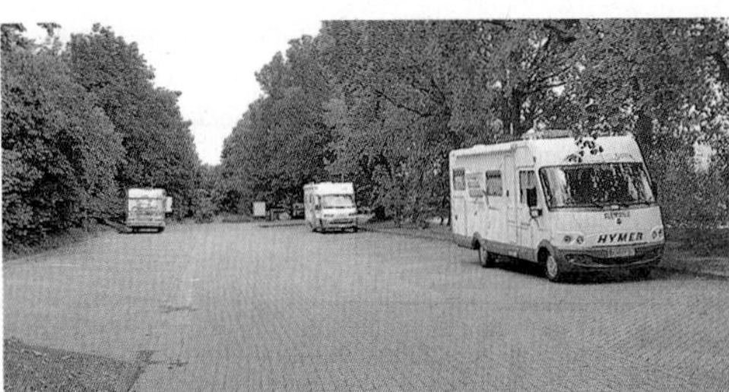

15 free Chfree. **Surface:** metalled. 01/01-31/12.
Distance: 1km 500m.
Remarks: Sports centre.

Goldenstedt 9H1

Haus im Moor, Arkeburger Straße 22. **GPS:** n52,72777 e8,39120.
6 free.
Distance: 8,5km.

Gorleben 8D3

Am Sportboothafen, Ringstraße. **GPS:** n53,04972 e11,35111.

5 € 5 €1/10minutes (4x)€1/10h WC .
Location: Rural, comfortable, quiet. **Surface:** grasstiles.
01/01-31/12.
Distance: on the spot on the spot 500m.
Remarks: Bakery 500m.

Göttingen 10B3

Reisemobilhafen Eiswiese, Windausweg 6.
GPS: n51,52320 e9,92965.

28 € 9 €1/100liter Ch (24x)€0,50/kWh WC €1/15h.
Location: Comfortable. **Surface:** gravel. 01/01-31/12.
Distance: 500m 5,2km 100m 20-400m 100m 500m 100m.
Remarks: Max. 3 nights.

Grasberg 8A3

P&R, Wörpedorfer Straße. **GPS:** n53,18411 e8,98433.

10 free €1 Ch (8x)€1/6h. **Location:** Simple.
Surface: gravel. 01/01-31/12.
Distance: on the spot on the spot on the spot > Bremen.

Gronau/Leine 10B2

Kuhmasch. **GPS:** n52,08265 e9,77034.

DE

4 €5 €1,50 WC. **Location:** Rural, simple. **Surface:** grassy.
01/01-31/12.
Distance: 200m 300m 300m on the spot.
Remarks: Check in at swimming pool, caution key electricity € 10.

S Großefehn 7G2

Ostfriesen-Bräu Bagband, Voerstad 8, Badband.
GPS: n53,35034 e7,61060.

4 € 5,70, after consumption € 7/pp free 16Amp WC.
Surface: metalled. 01/01-31/12.
Distance: 10km 4km on the spot 600m.

Großenkneten 7H3

Dorfplatz, Bahnhofstrasse, Huntlosen. **GPS:** n52,99145 e8,28658.

6 free. **Location:** Rural, simple. **Surface:** grasstiles.
01/01-31/12.
Distance: on the spot 50m 1km.

Großenkneten 7H3

Wilhelm-Wellman-Platz, Ahlhorner Strasse/markt.
GPS: n52,94274 e8,25751.

6 free. **Location:** Rural, simple. **Surface:** grasstiles.
01/01-31/12.
Distance: 200m 200m on the spot.

Großenwieden 10A2

Am Steinbrink, Hessisch Oldendorf. **GPS:** n52,17191 e9,18982.

4 free. **Location:** Rural. **Surface:** gravel. 01/01-31/12.
Distance: 3,8km Gasthaus/Biergarten 300m Weserradweg on the spot.

S Großenwörden 8A2

Deichstraße 21. **GPS:** n53,67757 e9,25769.
3 €5 €1 €1/kWh. **Surface:** grasstiles. 01/01-31/12.
Distance: 200m.
Remarks: Along the Oste river.

Großheide 7F2

Kirchweg, Berumerfehn. **GPS:** n53,56040 e7,34713.

6 free. **Surface:** metalled. 01/01-31/12.
Distance: on the spot on the spot 2km.
Remarks: Max. 2 nights.

Großheide 7F2

P Freizeitanlage Am Kiessee, Doornkaatsweg.
GPS: n53,58656 e7,35787.
free.
Distance: on the spot.

S Großheide 7F2

AC Dehne, Dorfstraße 86. **GPS:** n53,56254 e7,36077.
€4 €1 €1. **Surface:** grassy.

S Hage 7F2

Kurzentrum, Wichter Weg, Blandorf-Wichte.
GPS: n53,60373 e7,31998.
12 €9 €0,50/80liter Ch €1/2kWh included.
Surface: metalled. 01/01-31/12.

S Hagenburg 10A1

Grillplatz, Steinhuder-Meer-Straße. **GPS:** n52,43684 e9,32388.

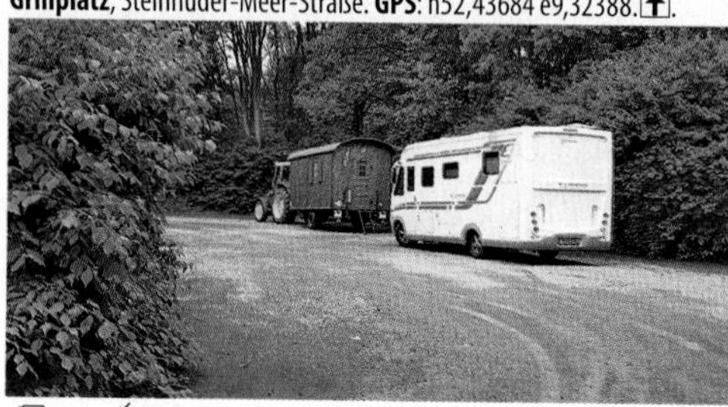

8 free (8x)€1/6h. **Location:** Rural, isolated. **Surface:** gravel.
01/01-31/12.
Distance: 500m Lake Steinhude 1,1km 200m.
Remarks: At sports park.

S Hahnenklee 10C2

Am Bocksberg. **GPS:** n51,85757 e10,34176.
free €2/60liter Ch. **Location:** Rural, comfortable, quiet.
Surface: concrete. 01/01-31/12.
Distance: 500m 1km 500m on the spot on the spot on the spot.

S Hambergen 7H2

Festplatz, Kirchweg/Am Langenend. **GPS:** n53,31050 e8,82389.

20 €3,50 Ch . **Location:** Urban, simple.
Surface: gravel/sand. 01/01-31/12.
Distance: on the spot 50m 50m 1km on the spot on the spot.
Remarks: Caution key service € 25.

S Hameln 10A2

Hannes Weserblick, Ruthenstrasse 14.
GPS: n52,09623 e9,35853.

27 €8/24h €1/100liter Ch (27x)€1/8h. **Location:** Urban, simple. **Surface:** metalled. 01/01-31/12.
Distance: 1km 600m 600m 800m Weser-Radweg.

S Hankensbüttel 8C3

Parkplatz Am Boldhamm, Wiesenweg.
GPS: n52,73111 e10,61417.

10 €6 Ch included.
Location: Rural. **Surface:** grassy.
01/04-30/09.
Distance: 900m 1km 1km.
Remarks: Service: Mo/Fr 6-12h, Sa/Su 8-10h.

Tourist information Hankensbüttel:
Otter-Zentrum. Zoo. 15/03-31/10 9.30-18h, 01/11-14/03 9.30-17h 15/12-15/01.

S Hannoversch Münden 10B3

Am Weserstein, Tanzwerder. **GPS:** n51,42000 e9,64888.

30 €6/24h €1 Ch (16x)€1/8h.
Location: Central. **Surface:** metalled.
01/01-31/12 Easter Market, service: 01/11-31/03.
Distance: 900m 100m on the spot on the spot.
Remarks: 01/11/- 31/03 no service.

Hannoversch Münden 10B3

Am Hochbad, Rattwerder. **GPS:** n51,40595 e9,64643.

15 free. **Location:** Rural. **Surface:** asphalted. 01/01-31/12.
Distance: 1,7km on the spot.

Hannoversch Münden 10B3

Am Werraweg, Werraweg. **GPS:** n51,41701 e9,66176.

10 free. **Location:** Simple. **Surface:** gravel. 01/01-31/12.
Distance: 700m on the spot.
Remarks: Along the Werra river.

S Hannoversch Münden 10B3

Grüne Insel Tanzwerder, Tanzwerder 1. **GPS:** n51,41694 e9,64751.

DE

20 €6 + €3,50/pp, dog €2 €1/80 Ch. (6x)€0,60/kWh,+€2 WC €3/h.
Location: Simple. **Surface:** grassy.
01/01-31/12.
Distance: 100m 150m 150m on the spot on the spot.
Remarks: Max. 3t.

Tourist information Hannoversch Münden:
Touristik Naturpark Münden e.V, Rathaus, www.hann-muenden.net/spontan. Old city centre with 430 half-timbered houses.

Hardegsen 10B3

Wohnmobilhafen Steinbreite, Alte Uslarer Straße 1. **GPS**: n51,65093 e9,82267.

15 €6 €1/100 Ch. (16x)€1/8h WC €2/day €2/day €2,50/day. **Location:** Comfortable. **Surface:** grasstiles.
01/01-31/12.
Distance: 500m on the spot on the spot.

Haren/Ems 9F1

Am Schloss Danken, Am Tiergarten. **GPS**: n52,79724 e7,20530.

22 € 12/24h Ch. (18x) WC €1. **Location:** Rural, simple. **Surface:** grassy/gravel. 21/03-25/10.
Distance: 1km 2,8km on the spot on the spot on the spot on the spot.

Haren/Ems 9F1

Stellplatz an der Ems, Schleusenstraße. **GPS**: n52,78890 e7,24744.
15 free. **Surface:** grasstiles. 01/01-31/12.
Distance: 500m 550m.

Harsefeld 8A2

Klosterpark, Kirchenstrasse. **GPS**: n53,45384 e9,50344.

5 free (10x).
Location: Rural, simple. 01/01-31/12.
Distance: 100m 100m 100m 100m on the spot on the spot.
Remarks: Caution key electricity € 10 at hotel, parking park of monastery, max. 5 days.

Haselünne 9G1

Erholungsgebiet am See. GPS: n52,67060 e7,49907.
free Ch. **Surface:** metalled. 01/01-31/12.
Distance: centre 1,2km on the spot on the spot 1,2km.

Haselünne 9G1

Sportzentrum, Lingener Strasse 28. **GPS**: n52,66778 e7,48222.

4 free Ch. **Location:** Simple, quiet. **Surface:** metalled.
01/01-31/12.
Distance: 400m 400m 400m 100m on the spot.
Remarks: Parking swimming pool.

Haselünne 9G1

Dröge-Polle, Poller Straße 19. **GPS**: n52,65123 e7,49849.
Ch. .

Helmstedt 10C1

Am Maschweg, Maschweg. **GPS**: n52,23535 e11,01128.

25 free €1/3minutes €1/4h.
Location: Rural, simple. **Surface:** metalled. 01/01-31/12.
Distance: 500m 800m 50m 200m on the spot on the spot.
Remarks: Other parking in case of festivities.

Helmstedt 10C1

Brunnentheater, Brunnenweg 6A, Bad Helmstedt. **GPS**: n52,23676 e11,06411.

5 free. **Location:** Rural, simple, isolated, quiet. **Surface:** asphalted.
01/01-31/12.
Distance: 4km 500m 4km on the spot on the spot.

Hermannsburg 8B3

Parkplatz Waldschwimmbad, Lotharstrasse 66. **GPS**: n52,82718 e10,10807.

6 free €1 €1 Ch. **Surface:** metalled. 01/01-31/12.
Distance: 500m.
Remarks: Parking at swimming pool.

Hermannsburg 8B3

Schützenplatz, Lotharstraße 75. **GPS**: n52,82787 e10,10963.

40 €2 Ch. **Surface:** grassy. 01/01-31/12.
Distance: 500m on the spot.
Remarks: Max. 1 night, service at Waldbad (50m).

Hermannsburg 8B3

Grillplatz Bonstorf, Schulstrasse. **GPS**: n52,86492 e10,05134.

4 free. **Surface:** grassy. 01/01-31/12.
Distance: 5km.
Remarks: Parking sports park.

Hermannsburg 8B3

Parkplatz am Feuerwehrhaus, Weesenerstrasse, Weesen. **GPS**: n52,83645 e10,13692.

3 free. **Surface:** grassy. 01/01-31/12.
Distance: 500m.
Remarks: Parking fire-station.

Hermannsburg 8B3

Parkplatz Örtzetal- Halle, Lutterweg. **GPS**: n52,83363 e10,09579.

5 free. **Surface:** metalled. 01/01-31/12.
Distance: 100m.

Hermannsburg 8B3

Lutter Hof, Waldstrasse, Lutter. **GPS**: n52,84188 e10,09894.

5 €5 included. **Surface:** grassy. 01/01-31/12.

Herzlake 9G1

Hasetal, Im Mersch. **GPS**: n52,68211 e7,60780.

DE

30 free Ch WC free. **Surface:** grassy. 15/03-15/11.
Distance: 700m 200m.
Remarks: Parking sports centre.

S Hesel 7G2

Dorfplatz, Kirchstrasse. **GPS:** n53,30497 e7,59174.

12 €4 €1 Ch €1/8h €1, at swimming pool Hesel.
Surface: metalled. 01/01-31/12.
Distance: on the spot 1km on the spot on the spot.

S Hessisch Oldendorf 10A2

Südwall P1, Weserstraße. **GPS:** n52,16693 e9,25049.

4 free €0,50/5minutes €0,50 Ch€0,50. **Location:** Rural, simple. **Surface:** grassy/gravel. 01/01-31/12.
Distance: 400m 500m 500m Weserradweg 1km.
Remarks: Max. 5 days.

S Hitzacker 8C3

Bleichwiesen, K36, Elbufferstrasse. **GPS:** n53,15074 e11,04941.

40 free €2/70liter Ch (17x)€2/6h WC.
Location: Rural, comfortable. **Surface:** metalled.
01/01-31/12.
Distance: 200m 450m.
Remarks: Max. 2 nights.

S Hohne 10C1

Am Waldbad, Am Schwimmbad 23. **GPS:** n52,59340 e10,37398.

4 €5 Ch (4x) WC included. **Location:** Rural, comfortable, quiet. **Surface:** gravel. 01/01-31/12.
Distance: 1km 50m 200m.
Remarks: Max. 7 days, caution key € 50, use sanitary only during opening hours swimming pool.

S Hohnstorf/Elbe 8C2

Wohnmobilstellplatz Hohnstorf, Schulstraße 1.
GPS: n53,36234 e10,56223.

9 €8/24h €1/100liter Ch (3x)€1/10h.
Location: Comfortable. **Surface:** metalled. 01/01-31/12.
Distance: on the spot 500m 500m.
Remarks: Along the river Elbe.

S Holdorf 9H1

Zeltplatz Heidesee, Zum Heidesee 53. **GPS:** n52,57788 e8,11424.

60 €9 Ch included €2 against payment.
Surface: grasstiles.
01/03-15/10.
Distance: 1,5km 3,4km Sandy beach on the spot 1,5km.
Remarks: At tennis-courts, bread-service.

Hollern 8A2

Am Deich, Twielenfleth. **GPS:** n53,60417 e9,55917.

15 €5/24h. **Location:** Rural, simple. **Surface:** metalled.
01/01-31/12.
Distance: 200m Imbiss 300m.
Remarks: Along the river Elbe.

S Holzminden 10A2

Mobilcamping Holzminden, Stahler Ufer 16.
GPS: n51,82681 e9,43909.

145 €7,50 €1/100liter Ch €0,60/kWh WC €0,50.
Location: Comfortable. **Surface:** grassy. 01/01-31/12.
Distance: 550m 100m 100m 100m 200m on the spot on the spot.
Remarks: Bread-service.

Hornburg 10C2

Am Freibad, Bgm. Löhdenstrasse. **GPS:** n53,10350 e9,56874.
8 free. **Location:** Urban. **Surface:** metalled. 01/01-31/12.

S Hornburg 10C2

Iberg-Gaststätte, Schützenallee 1. **GPS:** n52,03133 e10,59677.

20 €2 (6x)€1/night. **Location:** Rural, simple, quiet.
Surface: grassy/metalled. 01/01-31/12.
Distance: 600m 5,6km on the spot 1km on the spot.

S Hoya/Weser 8A3

Reisemobilstellplatz Weserblick, Stettiner Straße.
GPS: n52,80106 e9,13987.

10 voluntary contribution €1/150liter Ch.
Surface: grassy/gravel. 01/01-31/12.
Distance: 500m 100m 500m.

S Hude 7H3

Wohnmobilstellplatz Hude, Schützenstrasse.
GPS: n53,10758 e8,45867.

10 €5 €1 Ch (12x)€0,50/kWh.
Location: Urban, quiet. **Surface:** gravel. 01/01-31/12.
Distance: on the spot on the spot 400m on the spot on the spot 1km.

S Hüde (49448) 9H1

Freizeitarena Dümmer See, Rohrdommelweg 33.
GPS: n52,50176 e8,35425.

50 € 10 Ch €3/day WC included. **Location:** Rural, quiet.
Surface: grassy. 15/04-01/11.
Distance: 150m 150m bakery 300m on the spot.

S Ihlienworth 7H1

Auf der Schöpfwerkinsel, Hauptstrasse 40.
GPS: n53,74539 e8,91831.
9 free €1 free Ch€1 €1/kWh. **Location:** Rural, simple.
Surface: grassy/metalled. 01/03-30/10.
Distance: on the spot on the spot 500m.

S Ihlow 7G2

Straub's Bürgerstuben, 1.Kompanieweg 3, Ihlowerfehn.
GPS: n53,41153 e7,44013.
free Ch against payment. **Surface:** metalled.
01/01-31/12 Wed.
Distance: on the spot on the spot on the spot.

S Isterberg 9F1

Am Isterberger Waldhaus, Lehmstrasse. **GPS:** n52,35167 e7,14906.
30 €7 €2 Ch €1.
Distance: on the spot.

DE

Jade 7H2

Quittenweg, Süderschweiburg. **GPS**: n53,39139 e8,26639.

8 free €1 Ch (8x)€1/8h. **Location:** Rural, comfortable, isolated. **Surface:** gravel/metalled. 01/01-31/12.
Distance: 800m 500m 1km 800m on the spot on the spot.

Jade 7H2

Drei Eichen, Kreuzmoorstrasse 28. **GPS**: n53,31531 e8,23084.

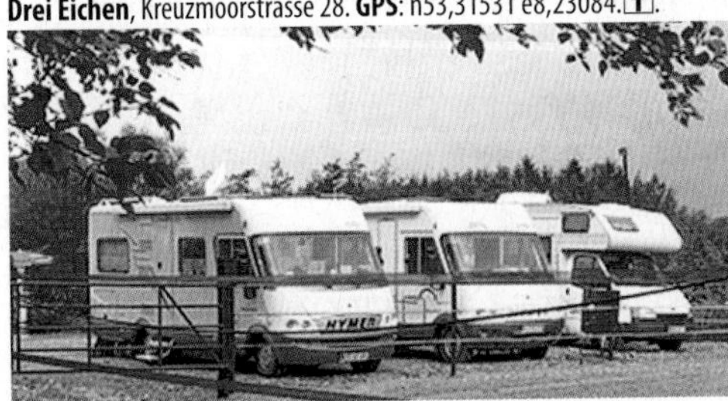

10 € 10 Ch (3x) WC included against payment.
Location: Rural, simple, quiet. **Surface:** grassy/gravel.
01/01-31/12.
Distance: 4km.
Remarks: At manege.

Jade 7H2

Schützenhof, Am Schützenplatz, Vareler Strasse.
GPS: n53,34111 e8,18667.

10 guests free on demand (3x)€2/night.
Location: Simple. **Surface:** metalled. 01/01-31/12.
Distance: on the spot on the spot on the spot.
Remarks: Parking of Shooting Club.

Jade 7H2

Jaderpark, Tiergartenstrasse 69, Jaderberg.
GPS: n53,32679 e8,18521.

20 free.
Location: Simple. **Surface:** gravel. 01/01-31/12.
Distance: on the spot on the spot.
Remarks: Parking Jarderpark, zoo and adventure park, max. 1 night.

Jever 7G2

Jahnstrasse. **GPS**: n53,57733 e7,89074.

20 € 8 €2 Ch (20x)€2.
Surface: metalled. 01/01-31/12.
Distance: Old city centre 750m 100m.
Remarks: Sports centre, max. 3 days, coins at petrol station Henn.

Tourist information Jever:
Schloßmuseum. Castle, English gardens and museum. Tue-Su 10-18h, 01/07-31/08 Mo-Su 10-18h.
Frisiesches Brauhaus. Brewery with museum. Guided tour 2 hours, 2 drinks included. Mo-Fri 9.30-16.30h, Sa 9.30-12.30h.

Jork 8A2

Festplatz, Schützenhofstrasse/Festplatzweg.
GPS: n53,53100 e9,68336.

80 € 7 €1/100liter Ch WC €0,50.
Location: Rural, simple. **Surface:** metalled. 01/01-31/12.
Distance: 200m 200m 200m.
Remarks: Parking event ground, max. 24h.

Jork 8A2

Stellplatz Lühe-Anleger, Fährstraße, Grünendeich.
GPS: n53,57271 e9,63129.
10 € 10/24h. **Surface:** gravel. 01/01-31/12.

Jork 8A2

Am Yachthafen, Neuenschleuse. **GPS**: n53,55375 e9,66858.

18 € 7 €1/90liter Ch (18x)€0,50/kWh WC €2.
Location: Urban, simple. **Surface:** unpaved.
01/01-31/12.
Distance: Jork 3km on the spot on the spot on the spot.
Remarks: Along the river Elbe.

Jork 8A2

Stubbe's Gasthaus, Lühe 46. **GPS**: n53,56861 e9,63333.

14 € 10 €2 . **Location:** Rural, comfortable.
Surface: grassy. 01/01-31/12.
Distance: on the spot.
Remarks: Bread-service, picnic area Am Gartenteich.

Königslutter am Elm 10C1

P1 Niedernhof, Amtsgarten. **GPS**: n52,25009 e10,81996.

5 free €1/5minutes €1 Ch €1 (4x)€1/8h.
Location: Urban, comfortable, central, noisy. **Surface:** grasstiles.
01/01-31/12.
Distance: on the spot on the spot on the spot.

Krummendeich 8A1

Stellplatz Krummendeich, Osterwechtern.
GPS: n53,83145 e9,20231.

6 free WC €0,50 €0,50. **Location:** Rural, simple. **Surface:** gravel.
01/01-31/12.
Distance: 100m 300m.

Krummhörn 7F2

Reisemobilhafen Greetsiel, Mühlenstrasse 3, Greetsiel.
GPS: n53,49711 e7,10181.

55 € 11, 2 pers.incl €2/90liter Ch (40x)€1/8h.
Surface: gravel. 01/01-31/12.
Distance: 250m.

Kutenholz 8A2

Festhalle, Bürgermeister-Schmetjen-Platz. **GPS**: n53,48163 e9,31486.
10 free. 01/01-31/12.
Distance: 800m 500m on the spot on the spot.

Lamspringe 10B2

Am Bahnhof. **GPS**: n51,95404 e10,00656.

3 free. **Location:** Rural, isolated. **Surface:** gravel.
01/01-31/12.
Distance: 750m 1km 400m 250m Radweg zur Kunst on the spot.
Remarks: Max. 3 days.

Lauenau 10A1

Brauhaus Felsenkeller, Feggendorfer Straße 10.
GPS: n52,27914 e9,36906.

10 free free.
Location: Rural, simple. **Surface:** gravel. 01/01-31/12.
Distance: 500m 2,4km on the spot.
Remarks: Check in at restaurant.

Lauenförde 10A3

Yachthafen Dreiländereck, Würgasser Straße.
GPS: n51,65045 e9,37983.

DE

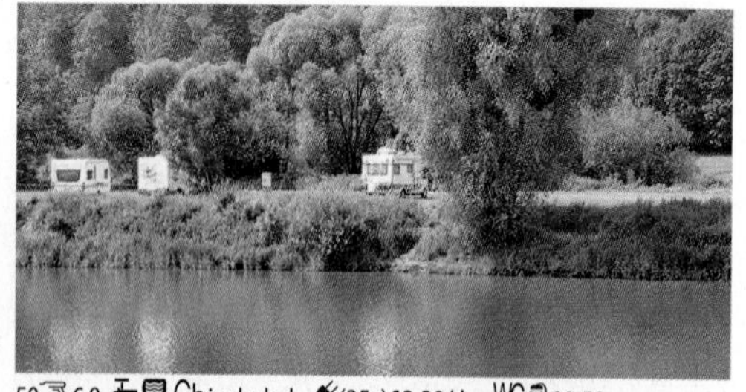

50 € 8 Chincluded (35x)€2,20/day WC €0,50 €2,50 €4,95. **Location:** Rural, comfortable. **Surface:** gravel. 01/04-01/11.
Distance: 3km on the spot 3km on the spot on the spot.
Remarks: Bread-service.

S Lautenthal 10C2

Kaspar Bitter Strasse 7b. **GPS**: n51,87020 e10,28729.

25 € 4 + € 1/pp tourist tax €1/60liter €2 Ch€2 (8x)€1/6h.
Location: Rural, comfortable, quiet. **Surface:** gravel.
01/01-31/12.
Distance: 300m 300m 500m 50m.

S Leer 7G3

P9, Große Bleiche. **GPS**: n53,22577 e7,44686.

6 free €1/100liter €1 Ch (6x)€1/24h WC€0,50 €1.
Location: Urban, simple. **Surface:** metalled. 01/01-31/12.
Distance: 200m on the spot 2km.
Remarks: Max. 3 nights, caution key sanitary € 30, sanitary at offices Bruchbrücke.

Leer 7G3

Hallen- und Freibad, Burfehnerweg 32. **GPS**: n53,23927 e7,44998.

10 free. **Location:** Urban, simple. **Surface:** metalled.
01/01-31/12.
Distance: on the spot on the spot 1km.
Remarks: Max. 3 nights.

S Leer 7G3

Am Hafen, Nessestrasse. **GPS**: n53,22527 e7,45472.

10 free WC€0,50 €1. **Location:** Urban, simple.
Surface: asphalted/gravel. 01/01-31/12.
Distance: 500m 300m 2km.

Remarks: Max. 3 nights, caution key sanitary € 30, sanitary at offices Bruchbrücke.

S Leer 7G3

Segelnverein, Segelerweg 3. **GPS**: n53,21907 e7,44793.
3 € 8 Chincluded €0,30/kWh WC €1. 01/01-31/12.

S Leer 7G3

Landgaststätte zur Jümme-Fähre, Amdorfer Straße 101.
GPS: n53,22429 e7,52593.

Distance: on the spot on the spot on the spot.
Remarks: Along river.

S Leer 7G3

Windmühlenhof Eiklenborg, Logabirumer Straße, Logabirum.
GPS: n53,24745 e7,51582.
5 € 12 Ch WC €2,50. **Surface:** grassy/metalled.
01/01-31/12.
Remarks: Near old Dutch windmill.

S Leese 10A1

Wohnmobilhafen Leeser See, Mühlenberg. **GPS**: n52,50616 e9,10360.
free €1/6h.
Distance: bakery 500m.

Leese 10A1

Loccumer Straße. **GPS**: n52,50272 e9,11733.

4 free. **Surface:** metalled. 01/01-31/12.
Distance: 200m on the spot 200m.

S Leese 10A1

Rasthaus Leeser Tanger, Bahlweg. **GPS**: n52,49372 e9,12055.

8 € 15, discount for clients included. **Surface:** metalled.
01/01-31/12.
Distance: 800m on the spot.

Lembruch 9H1

Stellplatz Dümmer-See Lembruch, Seestraße.
GPS: n52,52439 e8,36703.

20 free. **Location:** Rural. **Surface:** grassy. 01/01-31/12.
Distance: 300m 100m.

S Lembruch 9H1

Campingplatz Seeblick, Birkenallee. **GPS**: n52,52583 e8,36056.

20 € 9 Chon campsite €5,50. **Location:** Rural.

Surface: grassy. 01/01-31/12.
Distance: 50m 50m.
Remarks: Max. 1 night.

S Lemwerder 7H3

Reisemobilhafen Peter-Baxmann-Platz, Schulstrasse 44.
GPS: n53,15784 e8,61783.

50 € 3/24h Chincluded (40x)€1/8h.
Location: Urban, comfortable, isolated, quiet. **Surface:** gravel.
Distance: on the spot 200m 500m 500m 300m.
Remarks: Nearby swimming pool.

Lemwerder 7H3

Vulkanparkplatz an der Weser, Uferweg.
GPS: n53,17000 e8,60028.

5 free. **Location:** Urban, simple, quiet. **Surface:** asphalted/metalled.
01/01-31/12.
Distance: 2km on the spot 2km 2km on the spot on the spot.

S Lingen/Ems 9F1

Linus Bad, Teichstrasse. **GPS**: n52,51863 e7,30606.

30 € 5 €1 Ch (16x)€0,50/kWh.
Location: Rural. **Surface:** gravel. 01/01-31/12.
Distance: 1km on the spot on the spot.
Remarks: Max. 3 days.

Loxstedt 7H2

Stotel, Alte Schulstraße 75. **GPS**: n53,44067 e8,59356.

4 free. **Location:** Urban, simple, quiet. **Surface:** grassy.
01/01-31/12.
Distance: 600m 1km Stoteler See 100m on the spot.

S Loxstedt 7H2

Am Bootshafen, Fährstrasse. **GPS**: n53,44438 e8,49942.

DE

5 free (6x)€0,50/kWh. **Location:** Rural, simple.
Surface: gravel/sand. 01/04-15/10.
Distance: 300m on the spot on the spot on the spot.
Remarks: Along the Weser river.

Lüchow 8C3

Parkstraße. **GPS:** n52,96983 e11,14594.

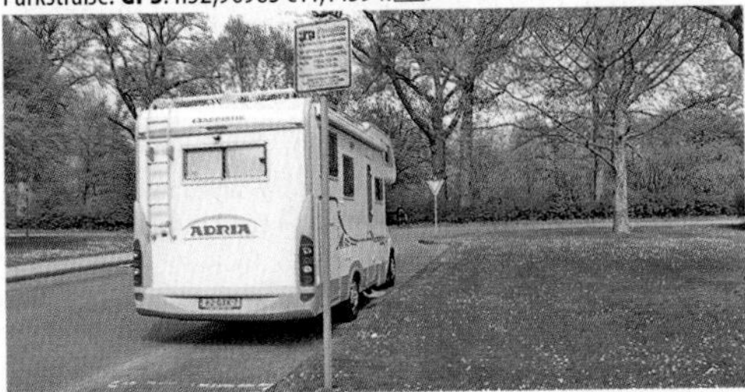

2 free. **Location:** Urban, simple. **Surface:** asphalted/metalled.
01/01-31/12.
Distance: 900m 900m 1,7km.
Remarks: Max. 3 nights.

Lüdersfeld 10A1

Heinrichs'Reisemobil Stellplatz, Am Hülsebrink 10+11.
GPS: n52,35972 e9,25512.

30+15 € 6 Ch (8x)included. **Location:** Rural, simple.
Surface: gravel. 01/01-31/12.
Distance: 500m on the spot.
Remarks: Check in at hotel, bread-service.

Lüneburg 8B2

Am Sülzwiesen, Pieperweg. **GPS:** n53,24556 e10,39694.

53 € 10 €1/10minutes Ch (40x)€1/8h,01/10-30/04 €2/8h.
Location: Rural, comfortable, isolated, quiet. **Surface:** metalled.
01/01-31/12.
Distance: 1km 300m.
Remarks: Max. 1 night.

Mardorf 10A1

Wohnmobilstellplatz Steinhuder Meer, Rote-Kreuz-Strasse 16.
GPS: n52,48704 e9,30065.

60 € 7 €1/100liter Ch (60x)€3. **Surface:** grassy.
01/01-31/12.

Distance: 1km 300m 1km.
Remarks: Bread-service.

Marienhafe 7F2

Rechtsupweg, Poststrasse. **GPS:** n53,52658 e7,32550.
20 free against payment. **Surface:** gravel. 01/01-31/12.
Distance: 150m 150m.

Marienhafe 7F2

Tjücher Moortun. **GPS:** n53,52835 e7,28168.
5 € 5 €1/100liter Ch €1/24h. **Location:** Rural, comfortable. **Surface:** gravel. 01/01-31/12.
Distance: 400m on the spot Lidl 400m.

Marienhafe 7F2

Dorfplatz Leezdorf, Sträkweg. **GPS:** n53,54802 e7,29354.
. 01/01-31/12.
Distance: 150m.

Melle 9H2

Am Wellenbad 43. **GPS:** n52,20497 e8,32368.

10 free. **Location:** Simple, quiet. **Surface:** metalled.
01/01-31/12.
Distance: on the spot 1,2km nearby 300m.
Remarks: Parking swimming pool.

Meppen 9F1

Reisemobilplatz am Hallenbad, An der Bleiche.
GPS: n52,69107 e7,28399.

10 € 8, swimming pool incl. 1 pers €2/100liter Ch (4x)€2/24h. **Surface:** metalled. 01/01-31/12.
Distance: 200m on the spot 300m.
Remarks: Parking swimming pool, max. 2 nights.

Tourist information Meppen:
Tue-Sa morning.

Moormerland 7G2

Am Rathaus, Theodor Heussstrasse 12, Warsingsfehn.
GPS: n53,31062 e7,48618.

4 free. **Surface:** metalled. 01/01-31/12.
Distance: 50m 250m 50m 50m.
Remarks: Parking townhall, max. 3 nights.

Moormerland 7G2

Bei Cassi, Deichlandstraße 10, Rorinchem.
GPS: n53,32010 e7,35473.

15 € 5, free with a meal €1 Ch €2 €1.
Surface: gravel. 01/04-31/10 Restaurant: Mo.
Distance: on the spot.

Moringen 10B3

Domänenhof, Amtsfreiheit. **GPS:** n51,69833 e9,86861.

3 free. **Location:** Rural, simple. **Surface:** gravel.
01/01-31/12.
Distance: on the spot 5,5km 300m.
Remarks: At city park.

Nessmersiel 7F2

Strandstrasse. **GPS:** n53,68369 e7,35963.
€ 10. **Location:** Rural, simple. **Surface:** grassy/gravel.
01/01-31/12.
Distance: 2km on the spot.

Neuharlingersiel 7G2

Wohnmobilstellplatz am Ostanleger, Am Hafen Ost.
GPS: n53,70173 e7,70741.

23 € 12 included WC. **Location:** Rural, comfortable, quiet.
Surface: metalled. 01/01-31/12.
Distance: 500m 800m 1km.
Remarks: Max. 3 nights.

Neuhaus an der Oste 8A1

Am Yachthafen. **GPS:** n53,80348 e9,04013.
13 € 9 Ch €2/day €2 €7,50. **Location:** Rural.
Surface: grassy. 01/03-30/10.
Distance: on the spot on the spot.

Nienburg 10A1

Reisemobilstellplatz Nienburg/Weser, Oyler Straße.
GPS: n52,64094 e9,20137.

25 € 5 €1/120liter Ch (12x)€1/8h.
Surface: gravel. 01/01-31/12.
Distance: 10 min walking on the spot on the spot 300m 500m.
Remarks: Along the river Weser.

Nienburg 10A1

Am Theaterparkplatz, Mühlenstraße. **GPS:** n52,63651 e9,20563.
. **Surface:** metalled. 01/01-31/12.
Distance: on the spot.

DE

DE

S Norddeich 7F2

Wohnmobilhafen Norddeich, Itzendorferstrasse.
GPS: n53,61073 e7,15649.

100 € 11/24h, 2 pers. + tourist tax, incl. 30% discount Erlebnisbad Ocean Wave Ch (96x)€1/2kWh WC €1. **Surface:** metalled.
01/01-31/12.
Distance: 100m 100m 100m 500m 100m.

S Norddeich 7F2

Womo Park Norddeich, Deichstraße 24. **GPS**: n53,60166 e7,13527.

44 € 11, tourist tax excl., dog € 2 €1/100liter Ch €1/kWh WC €1 €3/1,50.
Surface: gravel. 01/01-31/12.
Distance: 2km beach 1,5km, beach (dog allowed) 1km on the spot 500m 100m.
Remarks: Bread-service.

S Nordenham 7H2

Freizeitbad Störtebeker, Atenser Allee.
GPS: n53,49478 e8,47368.

15 € 6 €1/liter Chfree (16x)€1/8h €2,at sauna.
Location: Urban, comfortable, noisy. **Surface:** grasstiles.
01/01-31/12.
Distance: 1km 2km on the spot 400m on the spot on the spot.
Remarks: Max. 3 days, bread-service.

S Nordenham 7H2

Volkers, Deichstrasse 158. **GPS**: n53,54003 e8,50905.

6 € 5 €1/100 Ch (6x)€2/day WC on demand.
Location: Rural, comfortable, quiet. **Surface:** gravel.
01/01-31/12.
Distance: 2km 100m 500m on the spot.

S Nordholz 7H1

Wuster Strasse 12, Spieka. **GPS**: n53,75772 e8,59409.

5 € 5 + tourist tax €1/100liter €1 Ch (5x)€1/2kWh.
Location: Rural, simple. **Surface:** metalled.
Distance: on the spot 100m.

S Nordhorn 9F1

Vechtesee, Heseperweg. **GPS**: n52,43683 e7,08190.

35 € 5 €1/80liter Ch €1/5h. **Location:** Rural.
Surface: grassy/metalled. 01/01-31/12.
Distance: 400m 300m 300m on the spot on the spot.

S Northeim 10B3

Grosser Freizeitsee, Am Nordhafen. **GPS**: n51,72920 e9,96286.

10 € 6 €0,50/50liter Ch (8x)€1/kWh.
Location: Rural, simple, noisy. **Surface:** gravel.
01/01-31/12.
Distance: 5km 3km on the spot 2km.

S Oberndorf/Oste 8A1

Wohnmobilplatz Bentwisch, Hoffmann-von-Fallersleben-Straße 10.
GPS: n53,75398 e9,15054.

8 € 5 €2/100liter Ch (6x)€2/8h WC €0,50 €0,50.
Location: Rural, comfortable. **Surface:** grassy/gravel.
01/01-31/12.
Distance: 2km 100m 100m on the spot.

Oederquart 8A1

Am Sportplatz. **GPS**: n53,80411 e9,24485.
6 free. **Surface:** metalled.
Remarks: At sports centre.

Oldenburg 7H3

Am Küstenkanal, Westfalendamm. **GPS**: n53,12927 e8,21465.

3 voluntary contribution. **Location:** Rural, simple. **Surface:** gravel.
01/01-31/12.
Distance: on the spot 1km on the spot 100m 400m.
Remarks: Alternative: in front of campsite Am Flötenteich, 53,166944 8,235, 2 pitches free.

S Oldenburg 7H3

Hymer Zentrum Fassbender, Sieben Berge. **GPS**: n53,19187 e8,22574.
4 free €0,50 Chfree €1. **Location:** Simple.
Surface: metalled.
Distance: 50m.

S Osnabrück 9G2

Wohnmobilplatz Netebad, Im Haseesch 6.
GPS: n52,30470 e8,05413.

5 € 5 €1/100liter Ch €1/10h. **Location:** Urban, simple, quiet. **Surface:** grassy/metalled. 01/01-31/12.
Distance: on the spot.
Remarks: Max. 48h.

S Osten 8A2

Festhalle, Altendorf 13. **GPS**: n53,69602 e9,18813.

10 € 8 Ch (2x)included. **Location:** Rural, simple.
Surface: metalled. 01/01-31/12.
Distance: on the spot on the spot 500m.
Remarks: Pay at Hotel Fährkrug.

S Osterholz-Scharmbeck 7H3

August-Schlüter-Turnhalle, Lange Strasse 28.
GPS: n53,22562 e8,79000.

4 free €1/100liter . **Location:** Urban, simple, central.
Surface: metalled. 01/01-31/12.
Distance: on the spot on the spot on the spot.

S Osterode 10C3

Aloha-Aqualand, Schwimmbadstraße.
GPS: n51,72263 e10,24998.

7 € 8-10 €1/75liter €1 Ch (7x)€1,50/8h.
Location: Rural, noisy. **Surface:** metalled. 01/01-31/12.
Distance: 1km 200m 500m.
Remarks: Max. 2 nights.

S Osterode 10C3

Campingplatz Eulenburg, Scheerenberger Straße 100.
GPS: n51,72766 e10,28347.

13 € 8, 2 pers.incl €1/100liter Ch (12x)€1/kWh WC €0,70/4minutes €4/day. **Location:** Rural, comfortable, quiet. **Surface:** gravel. 01/01-31/12.
Distance: 2km on the spot 2,5km on the spot.
Remarks: Bread-service, swimming pool incl.

Ostrhauderfehn 7G3

Reisemobilhafen Ostrhauderfehn, Hauptstrasse 115. **GPS:** n53,13872 e7,62318.

32 € 5 Ch (12x)€1/2kWh WC €0,50 €2 included.
Surface: grassy/metalled.
01/01-31/12 during fair in June.
Distance: 100m 100m 100m.
Remarks: Caution key € 10, sanitary at bar.

Otterndorf 7H1

Schützenplatz, Fröbelweg. **GPS:** n53,80861 e8,89444.

8 free. **Location:** Rural, simple. **Surface:** metalled.
01/01-31/12.
Distance: on the spot 200m.

Otterndorf 7H1

Seglertreff, Schleuse 5. **GPS:** n53,82250 e8,89472.

12 free, 01/04-31/10 € 7 + tourist taks Ch €2,50/24h WC €1,50. **Location:** Rural, comfortable. **Surface:** metalled.
01/01-31/12.
Distance: 2km 50m on the spot on the spot 2km on the spot on the spot.

Ottersberg 8A3

Am Sportzentrum, Fährwisch. **GPS:** n53,10721 e9,13558.

8 free €1 Ch €1/8h. **Location:** Simple.
Surface: gravel/sand. 01/01-31/12.
Distance: 500m 200m.

Ovelgönne 7H2

Burgdorf Ovelgönne, Am Sportplatz. **GPS:** n53,34333 e8,42750.

5 free €1/100liter Ch free. **Location:** Urban, simple, isolated, quiet. **Surface:** grassy. 01/01-31/12.
Distance: 700m 700m 700m on the spot.

Oyten 8A3

KNAUS Reisemobilpark, Oyter See 1. **GPS:** n53,04645 e9,00396.

28 € 22 Ch €3,50 WC included €1
Location: Rural, comfortable. **Surface:** metalled.
01/03-01/11.
Distance: 2,5km 3km Oyter See 150m.
Remarks: Caution key € 5, service passerby € 4.

Papenburg 7G3

Roten Kreuz, Rathausstraße. **GPS:** n53,07646 e7,39266.
30 free. **Surface:** gravel. 01/01-31/12.
Distance: on the spot 300m.

Papenburg 7G3

Hotel-Restaurant Hilling, Mittelkanal links 94.
GPS: n53,07879 e7,43894.
22 € 8 €1 €1 Ch €0,50/kWh. **Surface:** grassy.
Distance: on the spot.

Papenburg 7G3

Hotel-Restaurant Hilling, Mittelkanal links 94.
GPS: n53,07879 e7,43894.
22 € 8 €1 €1 Ch €0,50/kWh. **Surface:** grassy.
01/01-31/12.
Distance: on the spot.

Papenburg 7G3

Poggenpoel, Zum Poggenpoel. **GPS:** n53,06526 e7,42630.

20 € 10 €3/100liter €3 Ch (8x)€2,50/24h WC €2
Location: Rural, simple. **Surface:** gravel. 01/01-31/12.
Distance: 3,5km Badesee.
Remarks: At lake, max. 3 nights.

Polle 10A2

Weserpromenade, Mühlenweg 2. **GPS:** n51,89871 e9,40830.

15 € 8 + € 1/pp tourist tax, 01/10-31/05 free Ch included
Location: Rural, simple. **Surface:** grassy. 01/01-31/12.
Distance: 100m on the spot on the spot 100m 100m Weser-Radweg.
Remarks: Along the Weser river, check in at campsite.

Rastede 7H3

Mühlenstraße. **GPS:** n53,24806 e8,20944.

4 free. **Location:** Urban, simple. **Surface:** metalled.
01/01-31/12.
Distance: 1km 2,7km 1km 2km.

Rehburg-Loccum 10A1

Wohnmobilstellplatz Rehburg, Auf der Bleiche.
GPS: n52,47370 e9,23227.

8 € 5 €1/100liter €1/12h.
Surface: gravel. 01/01-31/12.
Distance: 400m on the spot on the spot.

Tourist information Rehburg-Loccum:
Dinosaurierpark Münchehagen. Attractions park around the dinosaur. 12/03-30/10 9-18.

Rhauderfehn 7G3

Paddel- und Pedalstation, Am Siel 8. **GPS:** n53,13878 e7,58689.

16 € 5 €1/100liter Ch (16x)€1/8h WC €1,50.
Location: Rural, luxurious, quiet. **Surface:** grassy. 01/01-31/12.
Distance: 500m on the spot on the spot 50m.
Remarks: Caution key sanitary € 10, canoe and bicycle rental.

Rhede/Ems 7F3

Emspark, Am Sportplatz 6. **GPS:** n53,05853 e7,27621.

5 free.
Location: Simple. **Surface:** metalled. 01/01-31/12.
Distance: 500m 500m 500m.
Remarks: Parking in front of sports park.

Rhede/Ems 7F3

Gasthof Prangen, Kirchstraße 25. **GPS:** n53,05943 e7,26923.
10 guests free.
Distance: on the spot.

Rinteln 10A2

Reisemobilplatz am Weseranger, Dankerser strasse.
GPS: n52,19226 e9,07842.

DE

40 free €2/100liter €2 Ch€2 (36x)€0,50/kWh.
Location: Rural, simple. **Surface:** grassy/gravel.
01/01-31/12.
Distance: 600m on the spot on the spot 100m 400m 400m Weserradweg on the spot.
Remarks: Max. 3 days.

Rodewald 10A1

Am Freibad, Im Zentrum. **GPS:** n52,66369 e9,48020.

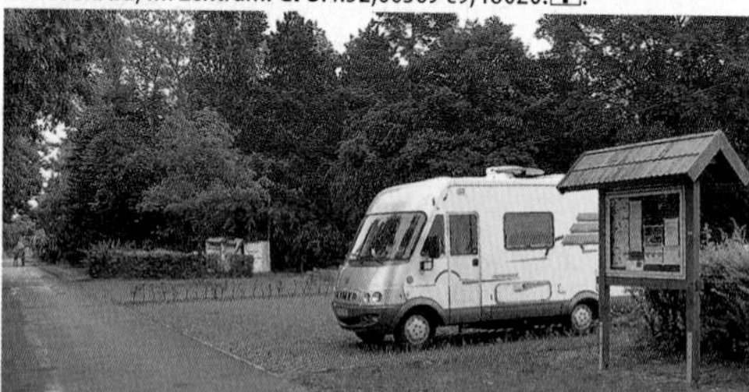

6 voluntary contribution €0,50/100liter (10x)€0,50/kWh.
Surface: grasstiles. 01/01-31/12.
Distance: 200m on the spot on the spot.

Rotenburg (Wümme) 8A3

Am Weichelsee, Bremer Straße. **GPS:** n53,11960 e9,38230.

20 €5 Ch (20x)€3 .
Location: Rural, simple. **Surface:** metalled.
01/01-31/12.
Distance: 2km on the spot Strandhaus 2km on the spot.
Remarks: Check in at StrandHouse.

Salzgitter 10B2

Reisemobilstellplatz am Salzgittersee, Zum Salzgittersee.
GPS: n52,15222 e10,31306.

18 free €2/100liter Ch (14x)€1/6h. **Location:** Rural, comfortable. **Surface:** grassy/metalled. 01/01-31/12.
Distance: 1km on the spot 500m 1km on the spot on the spot on the spot.
Remarks: Max. 4 days, boat rental.

Salzgitter 10B2

Thermalsolebad, Parkallee 3, Salzgitter-Bad.
GPS: n52,03724 e10,38351.

6 free. **Location:** Rural, simple, quiet. **Surface:** metalled.
01/01-31/12.
Distance: 1,5km on the spot 1,5km on the spot on the spot on the spot.
Remarks: Max. 4 days, no camping activities.

Salzhausen 8B2

Am Waldbad, Schwienbrink. **GPS:** n53,22199 e10,17841.

6 free €1/10minutes Chfree (4x)€1/8h. **Location:** Rural, simple. **Surface:** gravel. 01/01-31/12.
Distance: 1km 500m.

Salzhemmendorf 10B2

Ith-Sole-Therme, In der Saale-Aue. **GPS:** n52,07093 e9,58564.

20 €7,50 €0,20/20liter €1 Ch (20x)€1/kWh.
Location: Rural, quiet. **Surface:** grassy/gravel. 01/01-31/12.
Distance: 400m on the spot.
Remarks: Check in at pay-desk of the Therme.

Salzhemmendorf 10B2

Rasti-land, Quanthofer strasse 9. **GPS:** n52,09706 e9,66451.

5 free. **Location:** Isolated. **Surface:** gravel/sand.
Distance: 1km.
Remarks: Bus parking amusement park.

Tourist information Salzhemmendorf:
Rasti-Land, Quanthofer strasse 9. Amusement park. 01/04-31/10 10-17/18h, Apr, Sep: Sa, Su.

Sande (Nieder-Sachsen) 7G2

Am Markt. **GPS:** n53,50251 e8,01113.

4 free. **Location:** Urban, simple. **Surface:** metalled.
01/01-31/12.
Distance: 100m 100m 100m.

Sande (Nieder-Sachsen) 7G2

Jade Weser Airport, Mariensielerstrasse. **GPS:** n53,50788 e8,05245.
4 free. **Location:** Simple. **Surface:** grassy/metalled.

Sande (Nieder-Sachsen) 7G2

Paddel- und Pedalstation, Altmarienhausen.
GPS: n53,51174 e8,01076.
4 free. **Surface:** gravel. 01/01-31/12.
Distance: 1km Sander See 50m.

Sande (Nieder-Sachsen) 7G2

Sander See, Loppelter Weg. **GPS:** n53,51162 e8,00206.

4 free. **Surface:** metalled. 01/01-31/12.
Distance: 2km on the spot.

Sande (Nieder-Sachsen) 7G2

Freizeitmobile von der Kammer, Huntestraße 1.
GPS: n53,49076 e8,02292.
Ch on demand. winter.

Sandstedt 7H2

Wohnmobilstellplatz Sandstedt, Am Radarturm 5.
GPS: n53,36317 e8,51231.

10 free €1/100liter €1 Ch€1 (9x)€1 WC 150m on campsite. **Location:** Rural, comfortable, isolated, quiet.
Surface: grassy/gravel. 01/04-30/09.
Distance: 500m 3km 100m 950m 3km 500m on the spot on the spot.

Sankt Andreasberg 10C3

Silbererzgrube Samson, Am Samson 4. **GPS:** n51,71398 e10,51625.

20 €11 (20x)included. **Location:** Rural, simple, quiet.
Surface: gravel. 01/01-31/12.
Distance: 1km 400m 1km on the spot.
Remarks: At Historical Mine of SIlver Ores.

Saterland 7G3

Reisemobilhafen am Maiglöckchensee, Am Sportplatz, Scharrel.
GPS: n53,07060 e7,70116.

28+7 €5 €1/100liter €1 Ch€1 (28x)€2/24h WC €0,50 €2. **Location:** Rural, luxurious, quiet. **Surface:** grassy.
01/01-31/12.
Distance: 300m 50m 50m 1km 500m 500m.

Scharnebeck 8C2

Wohnmobilstellplatz Am Schiffshebewerk, Adendorfer Straße 40.
GPS: n53,29196 e10,49320.

DE

15 € 6/24h, park € 2 € 1/10minutes Ch (8x)€ 1/8h.
Location: Rural, comfortable, isolated, quiet. **Surface:** metalled.
01/01-31/12.
Distance: 1km 200m Aldi 400m.
Remarks: Climbing wall 100m, boat lift Scharnebeck.

S **Schneverdingen** 8B3

Wohnmobil-Park Lüneburger Heide, Badeweg 3, Heber.
GPS: n53,07104 e9,86481.
44 € 16 € 1/80liter Ch (40x),10Amp WC included . **Location:** Rural, comfortable. **Surface:** grassy/metalled.
01/04-31/10.
Distance: 7km 5km on the spot on the spot on camp site on the spot on the spot.
Remarks: Use sanitary facilities at campsite, car rental, shuttle bus.

S **Schneverdingen** 8B3

Am Quellenbad, Inseler Straße. **GPS:** n53,13110 e9,77280.

10 free € 2 Ch WC € 1. **Location:** Urban, simple.
Surface: grassy. 01/01-31/12.
Distance: 2km on the spot on the spot on the spot.
Remarks: Max. 2 nights, use sanitary only during opening hours swimming pool.

Schneverdingen 8B3

Parkplatz Festhalle, Im Osterwald. **GPS:** n53,11893 e9,80681.

10 free. **Location:** Simple. **Surface:** metalled.
01/01-31/12.
Distance: 2km 2km.
Remarks: Max. 2 nights, entrance via Festhalle.

Schneverdingen 8B3

Walter-Peters-Park, Verdener Straße. **GPS:** n53,11307 e9,78799.
2 free.

Distance: 100m.
Remarks: Nearby police station.

S **Schneverdingen** 8B3

Mariechens Hoff, Voßbarg 15, Reinsehlen.
GPS: n53,17122 e9,83316.

8 € 8 Ch included (8x)€0,40/kWh. **Location:** Rural, simple, isolated, quiet. **Surface:** grassy. 01/01-31/12.
Distance: 7km 15km 3km 4km on the spot on the spot.

S **Schneverdingen** 8B3

Reisemobilhafen Lüneburgerheide, Badeweg 3, Heber.
GPS: n53,07108 e9,86464.

5 € 12 Ch (5x)included WC € 2,50.
Location: Rural, luxurious, quiet. **Surface:** grasstiles/metalled.
01/04-31/10.
Distance: 5km on camp site on the spot on the spot.
Remarks: Sanitary at campsite.

Schöppenstedt 10C2

Elm-Asse-Platz, Schützenplatz am Berge.
GPS: n52,14756 e10,77737.

15 free. **Location:** Rural, simple, noisy. **Surface:** asphalted.
01/01-31/12.
Distance: 600m 1km 1km.
Remarks: Next to sports fields.

Tourist information Schöppenstedt:
The region of Till Eulenspiegel. Tills-Tauf-Tour: cycle and hiking routesin the country of Jester Till, start at the Till Eulenspiegel museum.
Tue-Fri 14-17h, Sa/Su/holidays 11-17h.
Till Eulenspiegelmuseum, Nordstrasse 4a. Tue-Fri 14-17h, Sa/Su/holidays 11-17h Mo.

Schortens 7G2

Aqua-toll, Beethovenstrasse. **GPS:** n53,53961 e7,93780.

2 free. **Surface:** metalled. 01/01-31/12.
Distance: 200m 25m.
Remarks: Parking swimming pool, max. 6,5m.

Schortens 7G2

Reisemobilstellplatz Fair-Cafe, Birkenstraße.
GPS: n53,55281 e7,97650.

6 guests free. **Surface:** unpaved. 01/01-31/12.
Distance: 3km 100m.

S **Schulenberg** 10C2

Wiesenbergstrasse. **GPS:** n51,83535 e10,43464.

20 € 5 + € 1,50/pp tourist tax € 1/80liter Ch (6x)€0,60/kWh WC. **Location:** Rural, comfortable, quiet. **Surface:** gravel.
01/01-31/12.
Distance: on the spot on the spot 6km on the spot on the spot.
Remarks: Check in at tourist office, view at Okerstausee.

S **Schüttorf** 9F2

Am Kuhmplatz, Graf-Egbert-Straße. **GPS:** n52,32123 e7,22642.

10 free Ch free. **Location:** Rural, simple. **Surface:** gravel.
01/01-31/12.
Distance: 2,4km 100m.
Remarks: Parking swimming pool.

S **Schüttorf** 9F2

Quendorfer See, Weiße Riete 3. **GPS:** n52,33892 e7,22665.
€ 5 Ch included. **Surface:** gravel. 01/04-31/10.
Distance: 450m 450m.

Schwanewede 7H3

Am Markt, Am Markt. **GPS:** n53,22412 e8,59644.

3 free. **Location:** Simple, central. **Surface:** metalled.
01/01-31/12.
Distance: on the spot on the spot on the spot.

Schwanewede 7H3

Brücke zu Harriersand, Inselstraße. **GPS:** n53,26489 e8,49762.

5 free. **Location:** Rural, simple, isolated. **Surface:** grassy.
01/01-31/12.

DE

Distance: 7km.

Schwanewede 7H3

Löhnhorst, Hammersbeckerweg/Am Fosshall.
GPS: n53,20355 e8,62453.

2 free. **Location:** Rural, simple, isolated, quiet. **Surface:** metalled.
01/01-31/12.
Distance: 6km 6km 6km.

Schwanewede 7H3

Wohnmobilstellplatz, Klint, Neuenkirchen.
GPS: n53,23670 e8,50919.

5 free. **Location:** Rural, simple, quiet. **Surface:** unpaved.
01/01-31/12.
Distance: 500m.
Remarks: Dead end street.

Seelze 10A1

Marina Rasche Werft, Werftstraße 10. **GPS:** n52,39560 e9,56435.

13 € 6,50 Chincluded (13x)€3 WC €2.
01/04-15/10.
Distance: 2km 4,5km on the spot.
Remarks: Bread-service.

Selsingen 8A2

Wohnmobilstation, Im Sick. **GPS:** n53,37573 e9,20681.

25 free Chfree. **Location:** Rural, simple. **Surface:** metalled.
01/01-31/12.
Distance: 500m 100m.

Soltau 8B3

Soltau Therme, Stubbendorffweg. **GPS:** n52,99301 e9,84443.

10 free. **Location:** Simple, central, quiet. **Surface:** metalled.
01/01-31/12.
Distance: 1km on the spot on the spot on the spot.
Remarks: Max. 1 night.

Soltau 8B3

Heidepark. **GPS:** n53,02166 e9,87370.

100 € 6.
Location: Rural, simple, isolated. **Surface:** grasstiles.
19/03-30/10.
Remarks: Parking amusement park.
Tourist information Soltau:
Heidepark. Amusement park. 01/03-31/10 9-18h, 01/07-15/08 Sa 9-21h.

Springe 10A2

Auf dem Burghof. **GPS:** n52,20765 e9,55717.

5 free. **Location:** Simple. **Surface:** asphalted. 01/01-31/12.
Distance: Old city centre 200m 300m.

Stade 8A2

Wohnmobilstellplatz Am Schiffertor, Schiffertorsstrasse 21.
GPS: n53,60278 e9,46667.

79 € 9,50/24h €1/80liter Ch €0,50/kWh WC.
Location: Urban, central. **Surface:** gravel.
01/01-31/12.
Distance: 500m 700m on the spot.
Remarks: Bread-service in summer period.

Stadland 7H2

Am Sportplatz, Hauptstrasse, Seefeld. **GPS:** n53,45639 e8,35778.

5 free €1/10minutes (4x)€1/8h.
Location: Urban, simple, quiet. **Surface:** asphalted. 01/01-31/12.
Distance: on the spot on the spot on the spot on the spot on the spot.
Remarks: Next to sports fields.

Stadland 7H2

Deichparkplatz, Fährstrasse, Kleinensiel. **GPS:** n53,44250 e8,47833.

5 free €1/100liter (4x)€1. **Location:** Rural, simple, isolated, quiet. **Surface:** gravel. 01/01-31/12.
Distance: 500m 200m Weserstrand 300m on the spot.

Stadland 7H2

Rathausplatz, Am Markt, Rodenkirchen. **GPS:** n53,39944 e8,45444.

10 free €1/10minutes Ch (4x)€1/8h.
Location: Urban, simple, central, quiet.
Surface: grasstiles/metalled.
01/01-31/12 Thu 5-13h market.
Distance: on the spot 500m 500m on the spot on the spot.

Stadland 7H2

Birkenweg, Kleinensiel. **GPS:** n53,44194 e8,47444.
Chfree. **Location:** Urban. 01/01-31/12.

Stadthagen 10A1

Reisemobilplatz am Tropicana, Jahnstraße 2.
GPS: n52,32236 e9,18896.

15 free €1/100liter Ch (4x)€1/2kWh WC.
Location: Rural, quiet. **Surface:** gravel. 01/01-31/12.
Distance: 2km 1km 1km on the spot on the spot.
Remarks: Max. 3 days, service at Tropicana.

Stadtoldendorf 10B2

Mobilcamping unter den Homburg, Linnenkämper Strasse 33.
GPS: n51,87777 e9,63500.

30 € 5/day €1 €1 Ch (25x)€2/day.
Location: Simple. **Surface:** grassy. 01/01-31/12.
Distance: 1km 1km.
Remarks: Check in at restaurant.

Steimbke 10A1

Klostergarten. **GPS:** n52,65989 e9,38707.
8 voluntary contribution (8x). 01/01-31/12.
Distance: 400m on the spot.

Steinfeld 9H1

Zur Schemder Bergmark, Dammer Strasse.
GPS: n52,58308 e8,21476.

DE

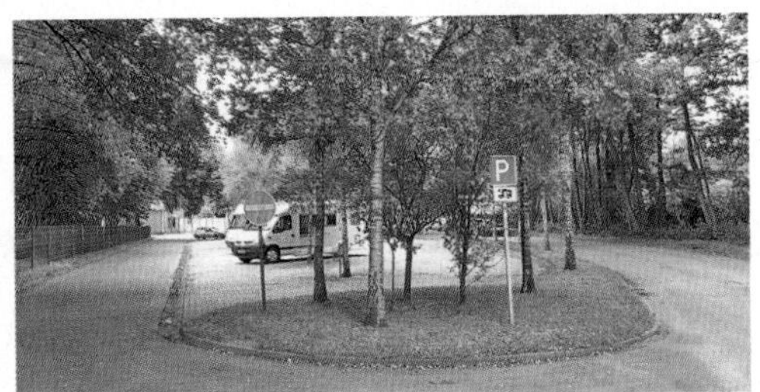

10 free €1/100liter €0,50 Ch€0,50. **Location:** Rural, quiet.
Surface: metalled. 01/01-31/12.
Distance: 500m 500m.
Remarks: Parking swimming pool, max. 3 days.

S Steinhude 10A1

Wohnmobilstellplatz Steinhude, Am Bruchdamm.
GPS: n52,44874 e9,35478.

180 € 7,50 €1 Ch (60x)€3/day WC €1 €2,50/2,50.
Surface: grassy.
01/01-31/12.
Distance: 500m 500m 500m 500m.
Remarks: Max. 3 nights, bread-service.

Tourist information Steinhude:
Marina on lake of the same name.

S Steyerberg 10A1

Wohnmobilstellplatz Steyerberg, Kleine Straße 7.
GPS: n52,56655 e9,02505.
4 free €1 Ch€1 (8x)€1/8h.
Surface: gravel. 01/01-31/12.
Distance: on the spot.

S Stolzenau 10A1

Reisemobilstellplatz Stolzenau, Weserstrasse.
GPS: n52,51021 e9,08104.

33 € 4 €1/60liter Ch (24x)€2/12h.
Surface: grasstiles. 01/01-31/12 service 01/11-31/03.
Distance: 250m on the spot on the spot 300m 300m.
Remarks: Along the Weser river.

S Strücklingen 7G3

Reisemobilpark Sagter Ems, Haupstrasse.
GPS: n53,12166 e7,66761.
55 € 7 €1/100liter Ch €0,50/kWh €1/10minutes against payment . **Location:** Rural, comfortable.
Surface: grassy/gravel. 01/01-31/12.
Distance: on the spot.

S Strücklingen 7G3

Reisemobilplatz Am Bootshafen, Hauptstrasse 640, Strücklingen.
GPS: n53,12819 e7,66762.

15 € 3 €1/100liter €1 Ch €1,50/24h WC€1 €0,50.
Location: Rural, simple. **Surface:** grassy/gravel.
01/01-31/12.
Distance: 100m on the spot on the spot on the spot on the spot 100m.

S Südbrookmerland 7F2

Grosses Meer, Langerweg. **GPS**: n53,44454 e7,30808.
30 € 9 €0,50/100liter €0,50 Ch€0,50 €1/2kWh WC .
Location: Rural, comfortable. **Surface:** metalled.
01/01-31/12.
Distance: on the spot on the spot.

S Sulingen 9H1

Am Stadtsee, Kornstraße. **GPS**: n52,67653 e8,80127.

20 free €1/5minutes €1 Ch€1. **Surface:** metalled.
01/01-31/12.
Distance: 600m 300m.

S Surwold 7G3

Privatplatz Klapper, Papenburgerstrasse 57.
GPS: n53,01774 e7,48470.

10 € 10 Ch (4x)€2/24h WC €2. **Location:** Rural, simple. **Surface:** grassy. 01/01-31/12.
Distance: 1km 1,5km 1km 1km.
Remarks: Swimming pool and picnic area available.

S Surwold 7G3

Erholungsgebiet Surwolds Wald, Waldstrasse.
GPS: n52,96743 e7,51535.

20 € 8 €1/100liter Ch €3 WC €2.
Surface: grassy. 01/01-31/12.
Distance: 800m 250m.

S Tarmstedt 8A3

Landtechniek Grabau, Bahnhofstraße.
GPS: n53,22421 e9,08728.

15 € 6 Chincluded according consumption.
Location: Simple. **Surface:** metalled. 01/01-31/12.
Distance: on the spot 500m on the spot.

S Thedinghausen 8A3

Reisemobilstellplatz Erbhof, Braunschweiger Straße 45.
GPS: n52,96188 e9,03020.

8 € 5 €1/10minutes Ch (8x)€1/6h WC.
Surface: grasstiles. 01/01-31/12.
Distance: 500m on the spot on the spot.

S Timmel 7G2

Ferienhof Welsch, Ulbagrgerstrasse 17. **GPS**: n53,36492 e7,52840.
6 € 6 €1 Ch €0,50/kWh . **Location:** Comfortable.
Surface: grassy/metalled. 01/01-31/12.
Distance: 1,1km 250m 1km.

S Twist 9F1

Am Hallenbad. **GPS**: n52,64719 e7,08918.

6 free €1/100liter Ch (8x)€1/2kWh.
Surface: metalled. 01/01-31/12.
Distance: on the spot on the spot.
Remarks: Barefoot path.

S Uchte 10A1

Balkenkamp. **GPS**: n52,49761 e8,90618.

3 free €1 Ch €1/8h.
Surface: metalled. 01/01-31/12.
Distance: 100m 500m 100m.

S Uelsen 9F1

Festplatz, Hardinghauserstrasse. **GPS**: n52,49575 e6,88840.

10 free €2 ChWC. **Surface:** asphalted. 01/01-31/12.

S Uelzen 8C3

Im Sportboothafen, Riedweg 7. **GPS**: n52,95722 e10,59444.

8 € 8 + € 1/pp €1/70liter €1 Ch (8x)€1/6h WC included €2,50/2,50.
Location: Rural, simple, quiet. **Surface:** metalled. 01/01-31/12.
Distance: on the spot on the spot on the spot 1,9km on the spot on the spot.

DE

Remarks: Max. 3 nights, free bicycles available, playground.

Undeloh 8B3

Am Naturschutzpark, Wilseder Straße. **GPS**: n53,19253 e9,97709.

30 € 3/day, € 6/night. **Location:** Rural, simple.
Surface: unpaved. 01/01-31/12.
Distance: 500m 100m on the spot.
Remarks: In nature reserve the the Lüneburg Heide (heath).

Uplengen 7G2

Remelser Paddel- & Pedalstation, Uferstrasse.
GPS: n53,30123 e7,75151.

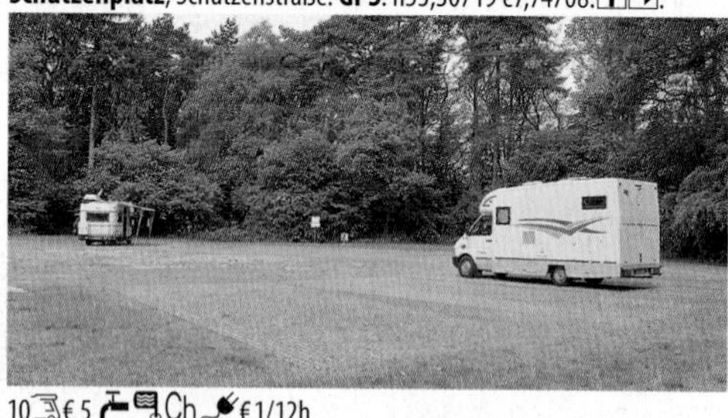

5 € 5 Ch (4x)€ 1/12h.
Surface: metalled. 01/01-31/12.
Distance: 500m 50m 500m.
Remarks: Max. 3 days, canoe and bicycle rental.

Uplengen 7G2

Schützenplatz, Schützenstraße. **GPS**: n53,30719 e7,74708.

10 € 5 Ch € 1/12h.
Surface: grasstiles. 01/01-31/12 10/06-15/06.
Distance: 500m.
Remarks: Max. 3 nights.

Uslar 10B3

Reisemobilpark am Badeland, Zur Schwarzen Erde.
GPS: n51,66753 e9,62831.

20 € 6 + reduction swimming pool € 1/10minutes Ch € 1/8h WC € 0,50. **Location:** Quiet. **Surface:** grasstiles.
01/01-31/12.
Distance: 1km on the spot 500m on the spot.

Uslar 10B3

Am Lindenhof, Lindenhof 1. **GPS**: n51,67213 e9,62952.

5 first night € 8, € 2 each additional night Ch included € 0,50/kWh.
Location: Rural, simple. **Surface:** grassy/gravel.
01/01-31/12.
Distance: 2,5km 2,5km 2,5km on the spot.

Tourist information Uslar:
Market, city centre. Fri 9-13h.
Alaris Schmetterlingspark. Butterfly park in tropical rain forest.
18/03-01/10 9.30-17.30, 02/10-01/11 9.30-16.30.
Uslarer Badeland. Swimming pool complex. Sa 13-19h, Su 10-18h, Tue-Fri 15-20h.

Vechta 9H1

Am Hallenwellen- und Freibad, Dornbusch.
GPS: n52,74000 e8,29639.

10 free. **Location:** Urban, simple. **Surface:** grassy/metalled.
01/01-31/12.
Distance: 1km 1km 1km.
Remarks: Parking swimming pool, max. 3 days, service Bokenerddamm 40.

Vechta 9H1

Oldenburgerstraße. **GPS**: n52,73245 e8,28833.

5 free. **Location:** Urban, simple. **Surface:** metalled.
01/01-31/12.
Distance: on the spot on the spot on the spot.

Verden 8A3

Conrad-Wode-Straße. **GPS**: n52,92572 e9,22738.
14 € 6/24h € 1/90liter Ch € 1/8h.
Location: Urban, comfortable, central.
Surface: grassy.
01/01-31/12 26/05-05/06.
Distance: 350m 300m 300m 300m.

Tourist information Verden:
Reiterstadt, horse city of international reputation.
Deutsches Pferdemuseum, Holzmarkt 9 . Horse museum. Tue-Su 10-17h.
Verdener Bauernmarkt. Sa 8-13h.

Vienenburg 10C2

Schacht I. **GPS**: n51,95705 e10,56772.

4 free. **Location:** Rural, simple, quiet. **Surface:** metalled.
01/01-31/12.
Distance: 700m 700m 600m on the spot on the spot.
Remarks: At Vienenburg Lake, max. 24h.

Visselhövede 8A3

Zu den Visselwiesen, Wüstenhof 1. **GPS**: n52,98530 e9,57772.

8 free. **Location:** Urban, simple. **Surface:** metalled.
01/01-31/12.
Distance: on the spot 100m 200m.

Vrees 7G3

Herzog-Arenberg-Straße 5. **GPS**: n52,88972 e7,77488.
6 free € 1/100liter Ch € 1/2kWh. 01/01-31/12.
Distance: on the spot 350m.

Wagenfeld 9H1

Hallen-Freibad, Schulstraße 12. **GPS**: n52,54531 e8,59634.
20 € 7 Ch included. 01/01-31/12.
Distance: 300m 300m.
Remarks: At swimming pool.

Wagenfeld 9H1

Ströher Lokschuppen, Bahnhofstraße 29, Ströhen.
GPS: n52,53954 e8,68465.
25 € 4 € 1,50 € 1,50 Ch € 1 € 3 . **Surface:** grassy.
01/01-31/12.
Distance: on the spot bakery.

Walchum 7F3

Marinapark Emstal, Steinbilder Straße. **GPS**: n52,92680 e7,29624.

10 € 10 Ch (6x) WC € 1,50.
Location: Rural. **Surface:** grassy. 01/01-31/12.
Distance: fishing permit obligatory 300m on the spot on the spot on the spot.

Walsrode 8A3

Ferienhof Wiechers, Klein Eilstorf 6. **GPS**: n52,81462 e9,47898.
3 € 15 + € 3/pp. **Surface:** grassy.

Walsrode 8A3

Forellenhof, Hünzingen 3. **GPS**: n52,89855 e9,59122.

10 € 15 (2x)included. **Location:** Rural, simple, isolated, quiet. **Surface:** grasstiles/grassy.
Distance: 3km on the spot 3km.
Remarks: Free with a meal.

Walsrode 8A3

Weltvogelpark, Am Vogelpark. **GPS**: n52,88425 e9,59720.

20 free (12x)€ 1/8h. **Location:** Rural, simple, central.
Surface: grassy. 01/01-31/12.
Distance: 2,5km on the spot 2,5km.
Remarks: Max. 1 night.

DE

Tourist information Walsrode:
Weltvogelpark. Bird park and botanical garden. 01/03-31/10 10-17h.

S Wangerland 7G2

Am Hallenwellenbad, Hooksiel. **GPS**: n53,63435 e8,03532.
18 € 10, dog € 3 € 1/100liter Ch €0,50/kWh included.
01/01-31/12.
Distance: 1km 100m.
Remarks: At swimming pool.

S Wangerland 7G2

An der Ostdüne, Bäderstrasse, Hooksiel.
GPS: n53,64103 e8,03514.

75 € 12 + € 2,90/pp tourist tax, dog € 3,10 Ch WC included. **Surface:** gravel. 01/04-30/10.
Distance: 1,7km beach ±250m.

S Wangerland 7G2

Nordsee-Camping-Schillig, Jadestraße, Schillig.
GPS: n53,69986 e8,02338.

80 € 12 + € 2,90/pp tourist tax, dog € 3,10 Ch (80x) WC included. **Surface:** grassy. 01/04-31/10.
Distance: 200m.

S Wangerland 7G2

Wangermeer, Jelliestede. **GPS**: n53,66962 e7,90975.
10 free against payment. **Location:** Simple.
Surface: grassy/sand.
Distance: 800m 100m Lidl.

S Wangerland 7G2

Am Yachthafen, Zum Hafen, Horumersiel.
GPS: n53,68293 e8,02091.

22 € 12 € 1 Ch WC included.
Surface: concrete. 01/04-30/10.
Distance: 600m on the spot.

S Wardenburg 7H3

Keilstrasse, Astrup. **GPS**: n53,04770 e8,21197.

5 free (3x). **Location:** Urban, simple. **Surface:** grassy.
01/01-31/12.
Distance: 2,5km.

Wardenburg 7H3

Marktplatz, Huntestraße. **GPS**: n53,06401 e8,19832.

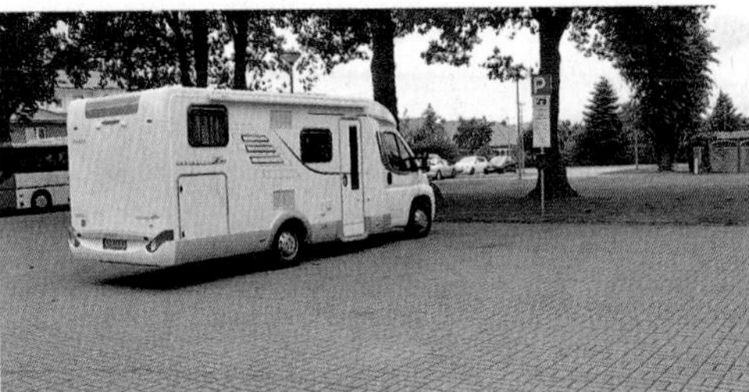

3 free. **Location:** Urban, simple. **Surface:** metalled.
01/01-31/12.
Distance: on the spot 3,6km.

S Weener 7F3

Am Alten Hafen, Panneborgstrasse. **GPS**: n53,16953 e7,36167.

45 € 7,50/24h € 1/100liter Ch (45x)€ 2,50/24h WC € 1.
Location: Urban, comfortable. **Surface:** asphalted. 01/01-31/12
during harbor festival 3rd week of June.
Distance: on the spot on the spot on the spot.
Remarks: Max. 3 days.

S Weener 7F3

Am Yachthafen, Am Marina-Park. **GPS**: n53,16570 e7,36480.
24 € 7,50 € 2,50 € 2. **Surface:** metalled. 01/04-30/09.
Distance: centre 1,2km 50m.

S Werdum 7G2

Raiffeisenplatz. **GPS**: n53,65823 e7,71515.
15 € 10 €0,50 Ch €0,50/kWh. **Location:** Simple.
Surface: gravel. 01/01-31/12.
Distance: on the spot on the spot.

S Werlte 7G3

Kreutzmanns Mühle, Kirchstraße 28. **GPS**: n52,85463 e7,68155.

6 free € 1/100liter Ch (8x)€ 1/2kWh. **Location:** Urban, comfortable. **Surface:** metalled. 01/01-31/12.
Distance: 200m 200m 200m.

S Westergellersen 8B2

Turniergelände Luhmühlen, Westergellerser Heide.
GPS: n53,23306 e10,21623.

35 € 8 € 1 Ch (35x)€ 1/8h WC . **Location:** Rural, comfortable, isolated, quiet. **Surface:** grassy. 01/01-31/12.
Distance: 4km 1,5km 4km 4km 2km.
Remarks: Key sanitary building at Autohaus.

S Westerholt 7G2

Schützenplatz, Nordener Straße. **GPS**: n53,58918 e7,45327.

6 free € 1/5minutes € 1 Ch€ 1 € 1/2kWh.
Location: Rural. 01/01-31/12.
Distance: 400m 400m on the spot on the spot.
Remarks: Max. 3 days.

S Westerholt 7G2

Sportzentrum. **GPS**: n53,59120 e7,44852.
free Ch. 01/01-31/12.
Distance: 750m 800m.

Westerstede 7G3

Albert-Post-Platz, Auf der Lohe. **GPS**: n53,25883 e7,92685.

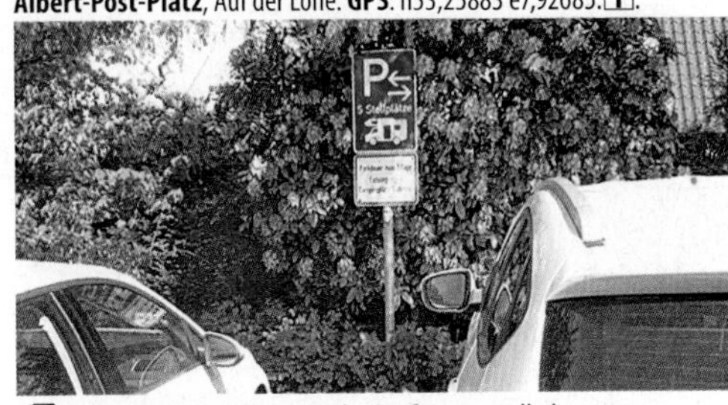

5 free. **Location:** Urban, simple. **Surface:** metalled.
01/01-31/12.
Distance: 100m 2km 250m.
Remarks: Max. 3 days.

Westerstede 7G3

Badesee Karlshof, Bekassinenweg. **GPS**: n53,18811 e7,86954.

5 free. **Location:** Rural, simple, isolated. **Surface:** gravel.
01/01-31/12.
Distance: Badesee.
Remarks: Max. 3 days.

Westerstede 7G3

Hössensportanlage, Jahnallee. **GPS**: n53,25369 e7,91229.
5 free. **Surface:** grasstiles. 01/01-31/12.
Distance: 1km 500m 500m.
Remarks: At swimming pool, max. 3 days.

S Westerstede 7G3

Wohnmobilhafen Westerstede, Süderstraße 2.
GPS: n53,24968 e7,93438.

50 € 9 Ch WC included. **Location:** Urban, comfortable, quiet. **Surface:** grassy/gravel. 01/01-31/12.
Distance: 800m 1,4km McDonalds 200m.

S Westoverledingen 7G3

Rathausplatz, Bahnhofstrasse 18, Ihrhove.
GPS: n53,16634 e7,45173.

DE

3 free €1/100liter Ch. **Location:** Urban, simple.
Surface: grassy. 01/01-31/12 last week Jun.
Distance: on the spot 50m.
Remarks: At townhall.

Westoverledingen 7G3

Reisemobilhafen zur Mühle, Mühlenstrasse 214, Steenfelderfehn.
GPS: n53,12944 e7,44051.

30 €5 Ch (18x)WC included. **Location:** Rural, simple.
Surface: grassy/metalled. 01/01-31/12.
Distance: on the spot 1km.

Westoverledingen 7G3

Schützenplatz Flachsmeer, Papenburger strasse 74, Flachsmeer.
GPS: n53,12700 e7,46367.

10 €5 (10x)included. **Location:** Rural, simple.
Surface: grassy. 01/01-31/12.
Distance: on the spot on the spot 100m.

Wiefelstede 7G3

Wohnmobilstellplatz am Bernsteinsee, Dorfstrasse 11, Conneforde.
GPS: n53,32657 e8,06362.

30 €6 €1 €2 Ch (25x)€0,50/kWh WC €0,50 on campsite. **Location:** Rural, comfortable. **Surface:** grassy.
01/01-31/12.
Distance: on the spot on the spot.
Remarks: In front of campsite, caution sepkey €5.

Wiefelstede 7G3

Freibad Wiefelstede, Alter Damm 11. **GPS:** n53,26146 e8,10713.

10 free. **Location:** Rural, simple, quiet. **Surface:** metalled.
01/01-31/12.
Distance: 500m on the spot 1,5km.

Wiesmoor 7G2

Bootshafen Ottermeer, Am Stadion. **GPS:** n53,40951 e7,71841.

14 €5,50 Ch included. **Surface:** grassy/metalled.
01/01-31/12.
Distance: 1,5km.
Remarks: Key service at Gastätte (12-19h).

Wietzendorf 8B3

Übernachtungsoase Südsee Camp, Südsee camp 1, K41.
GPS: n52,93120 e9,96474.

40 €15 €1/100liter €0,50/kWh WC.
Location: Comfortable. **Surface:** metalled.
Distance: 2km 100m on the spot.
Remarks: Caution key service €3.

Wildeshausen 7H3

Am Krandel, Krandelstrasse. **GPS:** n52,90042 e8,42728.

19 €5/24h €1/80liter Ch (20x)included €2.
Location: Rural, simple. **Surface:** grassy/metalled.
01/01-31/12.
Distance: 500m 4,4km 400m 700m.
Remarks: Parking at swimming pool.

Wilhelmshaven 7G2

Wohnmobilhafen Nautimo, Friedenstrasse 99.
GPS: n53,53546 e8,10104.

26 €8 €1/100liter Ch (26x)€1/6h,10Amp WC €1 €2/h.
Surface: metalled. 01/01-31/12.
Distance: 2km 3km 4km 1,5km on the spot 200m 1,5km 100m on the spot on the spot.
Remarks: Max. 7 days.

Wilhelmshaven 7G2

Wohnmobilstellplatz Schleuseninsel, Schleussenstrasse 37.
GPS: n53,51478 e8,15218.

30 €10, trailer €5 €1/100liter Ch (28x)€3/24h WC.
Surface: gravel. 01/01-31/12.
Distance: 250m Jadebus.

Wilhelmshaven 7G2

Am Freibad Nord, Möwenstraße 30. **GPS:** n53,57032 e8,10368.

6 €6, free with use of swimming pool Ch €1/6h WC.
Surface: gravel. 01/05-31/08.
Distance: 1,5km.
Remarks: Use sanitary only during opening hours swimming pool.

Wilhelmshaven 7G2

Reisemobilstellplatz Wilhelmshaven Südstadt, Banterweg 12.
GPS: n53,51559 e8,09072.

16 €10 Ch (16x)included. **Surface:** gravel.
01/01-31/12.

Wilhelmshaven 7G2

Fliegerdeich West, Fliegerdeich. **GPS:** n53,50996 e8,12718.

40 €0,75/h, €12/day. **Location:** Rural. **Surface:** metalled.
01/01-31/12.
Distance: 2,5km sea nearby.
Remarks: No camping activities.

Wilhelmshaven 7G2

Wohnmobilstellplatz Jade, Bunsenstraße 10.
GPS: n53,51110 e8,08153.

10 €10 included.
Surface: asphalted. 01/01-31/12 water: 01/11-31/03.

Tourist information Wilhelmshaven:

Aquarium Wilhelmshaven, Südstrand 123. Sea aquarium. 10-18h.

Winsen/Luhe 8B2

Festplatz Bleiche, Tönnhäuserweg. **GPS**: n53,36452 e10,21228.

10 free. **Location:** Simple, central. **Surface:** asphalted. 01/01-31/12.
Distance: 100m 100m 100m.

Winsen/Luhe 8B2

GreenEagle Golf, Radbrucher Straße 200. **GPS**: n53,32278 e10,22778.
15 free, playing golf obligatory. **Location:** Simple. **Surface:** gravel.
01/01-31/12.
Distance: 6km 2,2km on the spot.

Winsen/Luhe 8B2

Freizeit Center Albrecht, Porchestrasse 15, Gewerbegebiet Lühdorf.
GPS: n53,33750 e10,21947.

10 free €1 €2 Ch (11x) WC. **Location:** Rural, simple.
Surface: metalled. 01/01-31/12.
Distance: 4,5km on the spot.

Wittingen 8C3

Wittinger Sporthafen, Am Sporthafen 1.
GPS: n52,72706 e10,66187.

20 € 9 + € 0,50/pp Ch (20x) WC included €2,50/2,50.
Location: Rural, comfortable. **Surface:** grassy. 01/04-01/10.
Distance: 4km on the spot on the spot on the spot 4km 200m on the spot.
Remarks: Near marina.

Wittmund 7G2

Am Gulfhof, Funnixer Riege 11. **GPS**: n53,64202 e7,78566.
8 € 9 Ch included. **Location:** Simple. **Surface:** grassy.
01/01-31/12.

Wittmund 7G2

Schützenplatz, Auricherstrasse. **GPS**: n53,55763 e7,69156.
15 free. **Surface:** grassy. 01/01-31/12.
Distance: 800m bakery 200m.

Wittmund 7G2

Wohnmobilstellplatz an der Mole, Am Harlesiel 20.
GPS: n53,70941 e7,80839.

54 € 12 + € 2,50/pp tourist tax, dog € 2 Ch €3 WC.
Surface: metalled. 15/03-31/10.
Distance: on the spot.
Remarks: Caution key electricity € 10.

Wittmund 7G2

Campingplatz Harlesiel, Am Harlesiel, Carolinensiel-Harlesiel.
GPS: n53,70797 e7,80649.
€ 12 + € 2,50/pp tourist tax, dog € 2 Ch €3 WC.
Surface: asphalted. 15/03-31/10.
Distance: 100m 100m.

Wolfenbüttel 10C2

Alte Spinnerei, Am Seeligerpark. **GPS**: n52,16228 e10,52632.
10 free €1 (3x)€1. **Surface:** metalled. 01/01-31/12.
Distance: 800m 300m.
Remarks: Max. 3 days, quiet at night, crowdy during the day.

Wolfenbüttel 10C2

Sporthalleninsel, Vor dem Wehre. **GPS**: n52,16168 e10,52646.

2 free €1/80liter (4x)€1/8h. **Location:** Urban, central, noisy.
Surface: metalled. 01/01-31/12.
Distance: 250m 500m 500m 200m.
Remarks: Along railwayline.

Wolfenbüttel 10C2

Wohnmobilpark Stadtbad Okeraue, Harztorwall 21.
GPS: n52,15689 e10,50411.
44 € 12, 2 pers.incl Ch (44x)included WC.
Surface: grassy. 01/01-31/12.
Remarks: Next to swimming pool.

Wolfsburg 10C1

Autostadt P2, Berliner Brücke. **GPS**: n52,43485 e10,79716.

9 € 3/day, € 6/24h included. **Location:** Urban, noisy.
Surface: asphalted. 01/01-31/12.
Distance: 2km on the spot 2km.

Tourist information Wolfsburg:
Autostadt. Of the Volkswagen-concern; with pavilion of several car makes, car tower of 20 floors, test driving. 9-20h.

Zetel 7G2

Johann Quathamer, Fuhrenkampstrasse 60.
GPS: n53,40084 e7,91893.

15 € 7 €1/100liter Ch (15x) WC included €0,50.
Location: Rural, comfortable, quiet. **Surface:** grassy.
01/01-31/12.
Distance: 4km.

Zetel 7G2

Markthamm, Neuenburger Strasse. **GPS**: n53,41706 e7,97000.

40 free Ch free (6x)€1/kWh.
Location: Urban, simple, central. **Surface:** grasstiles.
01/01-31/12.
Distance: on the spot Imbiss.
Remarks: Parking centre, max. 2 days, service Kläranlage open: Mo/Tue 11-23h, Thu/Sa 11-23h, Su 16-23h.

Zetel 7G2

Driefeler Esch. **GPS**: n53,41835 e7,98445.

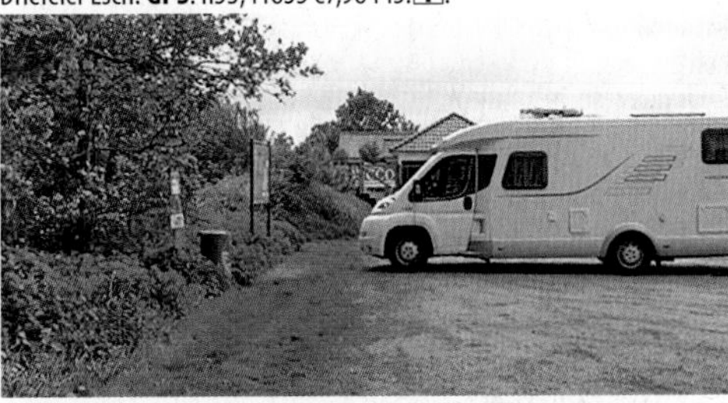

10 free. **Location:** Simple. **Surface:** gravel. 01/01-31/12.
Remarks: Parking swimming pool, max. 48h.

Zetel 7G2

Schulmuseum Bohlenbergerfeld, Wehdestrasse.
GPS: n53,41322 e7,92143.

25 free. **Location:** Rural, simple, isolated. **Surface:** grassy/gravel.
01/01-31/12.
Distance: 2,5km.
Remarks: At museum.

Zetel 7G2

Urwald, Urwaldstrasse, Neuenburg. **GPS**: n53,39293 e7,96547.

20 free. **Location:** Rural, simple, quiet. 01/01-31/12.
Remarks: Max. 1 day.

Zetel 7G2

Kläranlage, Moorstraße. **GPS**: n53,42302 e7,97937.
Ch free. 01/01-31/12.
Remarks: Mo/Thu 7-16h, Fri 7-13h, Sa/Su 9-9.30h.

Zeven 8A2

Viehmarktplatz, Meyerstrasse/Godenstedterstrasse.
GPS: n53,29764 e9,27514.

4 free. **Location:** Simple. **Surface:** metalled.

DE

01/01-31/12.
Distance: 500m.

Zorge 10C3

Campingplatz im Waldwinkel, Kunzental 2.
GPS: n51,64188 e10,64881.

30 € 9,50, 2 pers.incl €0,20/10liter Ch (15x)€2/day WC €1/pp. **Location:** Rural, simple, quiet. **Surface:** grassy/gravel.
01/01-31/12.
Distance: 1,5km on the spot 6km 300m on the spot on the spot.
Remarks: Max. 2 nights.

Mecklenburg-Western Pomerania

Ahlbeck 8G1

Caravanplatz Am Wiesenrand, Gothenweg 5a.
GPS: n53,94100 e14,17600.

27 € 11-13,50 Ch €0,50/kWh WC included €1 €3/2 €3,50/3h.
Location: Rural, comfortable, quiet. **Surface:** grassy. 01/03-31/10.
Distance: 10min 10min 500m 200m.
Remarks: Bread-service, possibility for reservation.

Ahlbeck 8G1

Wohnmobilstellplatz Rauthe, Waldstrasse 7.
GPS: n53,93660 e14,18660.

30 € 16 Ch (30x) WC included €2 €4.
Location: Urban, central. **Surface:** grassy.
01/01-31/12.
Distance: on the spot 5 min 200m 200m.

Ahlbeck 8G1

Parkplatz an der Grenze, Swinemüdestrasse.
GPS: n53,92380 e14,21280.

30 € 5 + € 2,50/pp. **Location:** Urban, simple. **Surface:** metalled.
01/01-31/12.
Distance: 3km.
Remarks: Max. 24h.

Ahrenshoop 6F3

Dorfstraße. **GPS:** n54,39155 e12,43914.

10 € 6/day, € 25/night. **Location:** Rural, simple, isolated, noisy.
Surface: gravel. 01/01-31/12.
Distance: 2km beach 50m.

Alt Schwerin 8E2

Insel Camping Werder, Wendorf 8. **GPS:** n53,48696 e12,31833.

13 € 15,80 €0,50/40liter Ch €2 WC €1 €3/3 included. **Location:** Rural, luxurious, quiet. **Surface:** grassy.
01/01-31/12.
Distance: 4km on the spot on the spot 1km 3,5km.
Remarks: Max. 9m, dog € 2/day.

Altwarp 8G1

Hafen, Seestrasse. **GPS:** n53,73905 e14,27147.

40 € 9,50 Ch €2/24h WC included €1 €2/1.
Location: Rural, luxurious, quiet. **Surface:** grassy/metalled.
01/01-31/12.
Distance: 500m 300m on the spot 300m 400m 300m on the spot.
Remarks: At tourist office.

Bansin 6H3

Waldparkplatz Bansin, Am Heuberg 1. **GPS:** n53,98834 e14,11291.

100 € 5-6 + € 3-3,50/pp, dog € 1,50 Ch €2,70/24h WC included €1 €4,50/3. **Location:** Rural, comfortable, isolated.
Surface: grassy/metalled. 01/05-30/09.
Distance: 3km 400m on the spot.

Barth 6F3

Segelverein, Am Westhafen. **GPS:** n54,37130 e12,72510.

20 € 10 Ch €2 WC €1.
Surface: grassy. 01/05-01/10.
Distance: on the spot on the spot on the spot.

Remarks: Caution key sanitary € 20.

Barth 6F3

Wohnmobilparkplatz Barth, Am Osthafen.
GPS: n54,36965 e12,73251.

10 € 7 (8x)€0,50/kWh. **Location:** Urban, simple, noisy.
Surface: metalled. 01/01-31/12.
Distance: 300m 300m 300m on the spot on the spot.

Beckerwitz 8D1

Ostseecamping Beckerwitzer Strand, Ostseestrasse 10.
GPS: n53,94137 e11,31682.

12 € 6-8 €1 Ch €2,60/night WC €0,50 €3,50/3,50.
Location: Rural, comfortable. **Surface:** grassy. 01/04-10/10.
Distance: on the spot on the spot on the spot 4km on the spot on the spot.

Bergen/Rügen 6G3

Wohnmobilstellplatz Rügen, Tilzower Weg 32a.
GPS: n54,40281 e13,42781.
20 € 14 €1/60liter Ch (16x)€2/24h,25Amp WC €2/6minutes €4/4 included.
Location: Comfortable. **Surface:** metalled. 01/01-31/12.
Distance: 1km 400m 500m, bakery 300m 100m on the spot.
Remarks: Car rental.

Binz 6G3

Wohnmobil-Oase Rügen, Proraer Chaussee 60.
GPS: n54,44819 e13,56181.

150 € 13-16 €1/50liter €1 Ch €0,50 €1/kWh WC €0,20 €0,50/minutes €4/4 according consumption.
Location: Luxurious, isolated, quiet. **Surface:** grassy/gravel.
15/04-15/10.

DE

Distance: Binz 6km 1,5km on the spot 6km on the spot.
Remarks: Bread-service.

Binz 6G3

Parkplatz Zentrum, Proraer Chaussee 5.
GPS: n54,40278 e13,60194.

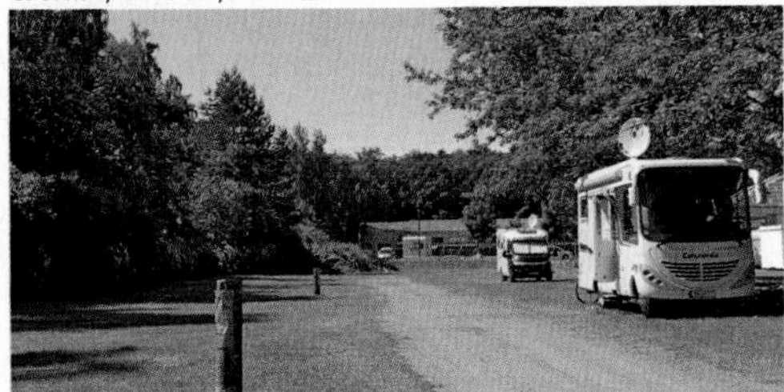

60 € 17/24h. **Location:** Urban, simple. **Surface:** grassy/metalled.
01/01-31/12.
Distance: on the spot 50m on the spot.
Remarks: Next to petrol station.

Blankensee 8G1

Reisemobilplatz Lühn, Am Achterfeld 1.
GPS: n53,51787 e14,31844.
4 € 4 €2 €2 Ch €0,50/kWh WC. **Location:** Quiet.
Surface: grassy.
Distance: 800m 600m 5km.

Boiensdorf 8D1

Am Strand, Bungalowsiedlung. **GPS**: n54,02412 e11,54744.

35 € 8/24h €0,20/10liter €2 Ch €2/day WC €0,50.
Location: Rural, comfortable, quiet. **Surface:** grassy.
01/01-31/12.
Distance: on the spot on the spot 50m on the spot on the spot.

Boltenhagen 8C1

Krämer's Wohnmobilhafen, Ostsee-allee 58b.
GPS: n53,98122 e11,21908.

45 € 10-14, 2 pers.incl €0,20/20liter Ch €2,50/day WC €0,50. **Location:** Urban, comfortable, central, noisy.
Surface: grassy/gravel. 01/01-31/12.
Distance: 800m 200m 200m 100m 700m on the spot on the spot on the spot.
Remarks: Bread-service in summer period, bicycle rental.

Boltenhagen 8C1

Wohnmobilpark Boltenhagen, Ostsee-allee 58.
GPS: n53,98133 e11,21854.

50 € 9-13 + € 2,10/pp tourist tax €2,50 Ch €2,50/day WC €1 €5 . **Location:** Urban, simple, noisy. **Surface:** grassy.
01/01-31/12.
Distance: 700m 200m 200m on the spot 700m on the spot on the spot.

Boltenhagen 8C1

Swin Golf Boltenhagen, Ausbau 15, Redewisch.
GPS: n54,00851 e11,17180.

10 € 13-15 €2/day. **Location:** Rural, comfortable, quiet. **Surface:** grassy. 01/04-31/10.
Distance: on the spot on the spot on the spot.
Remarks: At golf court.

Boltenhagen 8C1

Regenbogen Boltenhagen, Ostseeallee 54.
GPS: n53,98196 e11,21714.

20 € 20 WC included €4/3 €1/h.
Location: Urban, comfortable, central, noisy.
Surface: grassy/metalled. 01/01-31/12.
Distance: 600m 200m 200m on the spot 100m on the spot on the spot on the spot.
Remarks: Max. 1 night, check in at reception.

Brenz 8D2

Landhaus Böttcher, Parchimer strasse 11.
GPS: n53,38688 e11,67103.

5 € 10, guests free €1,50 (4x)€2/day WC included.
Location: Rural, simple. **Surface:** grassy/metalled.
01/01-31/12.
Distance: on the spot 3km on the spot 5km 200m.

Broock 8E2

Hotel-Restaurant Am Worns-Berg, Am Worns-Berg 1.
GPS: n53,46734 e12,10698.

6 € 5, free with a meal Ch €2 WC €1,50.
Surface: gravel.
01/01-31/12.
Distance: 5km 1,5km 1,5km on the spot 5km 500m.

Carpin 8F2

Landgasthof Am Schlesersee, Hauptstrasse 25.
GPS: n53,35424 e13,24028.

10 € 5, guests free WC included. **Surface:** metalled.
01/01-31/12.
Distance: 500m on the spot on the spot on the spot 4km.

Dabitz 6F3

Hafen Dabitz, Boddenstraße. **GPS**: n54,36217 e12,80610.

5 € 6/night. **Location:** Rural, simple, quiet. **Surface:** concrete.
01/01-31/12.
Distance: 500m on the spot on the spot on the spot on the spot.

Dalwitz 8E1

Ferien Gut Dalwitz, Dalwitz 46. **GPS**: n53,93484 e12,53830.

2 € 10 €1 WC €3/3 .
Surface: grassy. 01/01-31/12.
Distance: 15km on the spot on the spot.
Remarks: Parking estate.

Dassow 8C1

Reisemobilplatz Ostseestrand, Straße des Friedens 14, Rosenhagen.
GPS: n53,96040 e10,94430.

10 € 10 Ch €3 WC €3. **Location:** Rural, comfortable, quiet. **Surface:** grassy. 01/01-31/12.
Distance: 1km 500m.
Remarks: At Café Strandgut.

Demmin 8F1

Kanuhaus Demmin, Meyenkrebs 15. **GPS**: n53,91806 e13,02833.

2 € 6-8,40 WC included €1/3minutes. **Location:** Simple.
Surface: grassy. 01/04-31/10.
Distance: 1km on the spot 400m 500m.

DE

S Dömitz 8D3

WasserWanderZentrum Dömitz, An der Schleuse 1.
GPS: n53,14078 e11,25908.

30 € 10 €1,50/150liter Ch €2/day WC €1.
Location: Rural, comfortable, quiet. **Surface:** grassy.
01/01-31/12.
Distance: 400m on the spot on the spot 100m 800m.

S Dömitz 8D3

Dömitzer Hafen, Hafenplatz 3. **GPS**: n53,13724 e11,26034.

22 € 8 €1/50liter (10x)€2/day WC €1. **Location:** Rural, comfortable, quiet. **Surface:** grassy. 01/01-31/12.
Distance: 1km 10m 10m 200m 800m 600m.
Remarks: Bread-service.

S Dranske/Bakenberg 6G3

MC Burgstaedt Wohnmobilstellplatz, Nonnevitz 23a.
GPS: n54,67139 e13,29278.

12 € 19-25 €3/day WC included. **Location:** Rural, simple, isolated, quiet. **Surface:** grassy. 15/05-31/10.
Distance: 6km 100m 300m 300m.
Remarks: Dog € 2/day.

S Dranske/Bakenberg 6G3

Küstencamp, Nonnevitz 23. **GPS**: n54,66288 e13,26929.

15 € 13,50-15 Ch €3,20/day WC included €1/2minutes €3/3. **Location:** Rural, comfortable, isolated, quiet.
Surface: metalled. 01/01-31/12.
Distance: 7km 400m 400m 500m.
Remarks: Bread-service, car rental.

S Eldena 8D2

Bootshafen und Campingplatz Eldena, Am Bootshafen 1.
GPS: n53,23163 e11,42422.

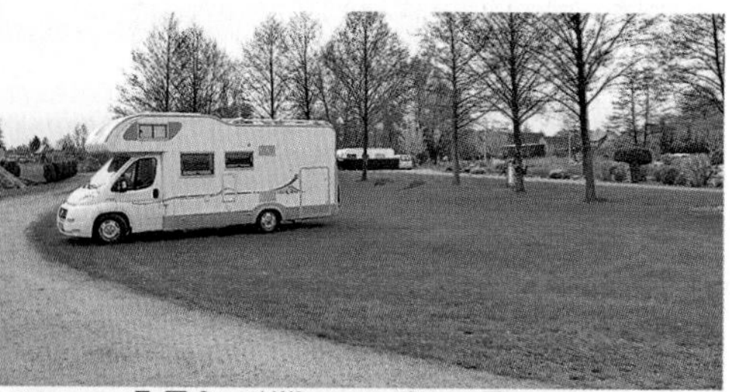

12 € 10,50 Ch WC included €1,10 €3,50/3,50.
Location: Rural, comfortable, quiet. **Surface:** grassy.
01/04-31/10.
Distance: 400m 10m 10m 50m 400m on the spot.

S Elmenhorst 6F3

Stellplatz Elmenhorst, Gewerbeallee 3a.
GPS: n54,15321 e12,01584.
24 € 10 €0,10/10liter Ch included €0,50/kWh free.
Surface: metalled. 01/01-31/12.

S Elmenhorst 6F3

Firma Stuhr, Haupstrasse 47. **GPS**: n54,15882 e12,00464.

20 € 8 Ch €2 WC. **Location:** Rural, simple, quiet.
Surface: grassy. 01/01-31/12.
Distance: 1km 1,3km 1km 500m 200m.
Remarks: Use sanitary € 2/pp per day.

S Elmenhorst 6F3

Stellplatz Elmenhorst, Gewerbeallee 3a.
GPS: n54,15250 e12,01667.

24 € 10 €1/100liter Ch €0,50/kWh free.
Location: Quiet. **Surface:** metalled. 01/01-31/12.
Distance: 300m.

Feldberg 8F2

Weidendamm 1. **GPS**: n53,33583 e13,44176.

10 € 10. **Location:** Urban, simple. **Surface:** grassy/metalled.
01/01-31/12.
Distance: on the spot 150m 400m.

S Fresenbrügge 8D2

Wohnmobilhafen an der Edle, Eldeufer 1.
GPS: n53,26355 e11,54243.

23 € 10 Ch included €2/day WC €1/pp.
Location: Rural, comfortable, isolated, quiet. **Surface:** grassy.
01/01-31/12.
Distance: on the spot on the spot 2km 2km on the spot on the spot.

S Graal-Müritz 6F3

Strandmitte, Buchenkampweg. **GPS**: n54,25663 e12,25005.

20 € 15/24h, tourist tax € 2/pp €1/100liter.
Location: Rural, simple, quiet. **Surface:** grassy/metalled.
01/01-31/12.
Distance: 500m on the spot on the spot 500m 500m on the spot on the spot.
Remarks: Max. 3 days.

S Grabow 8D2

Stadthafen, Canalstrasse. **GPS**: n53,27738 e11,55949.

18 free €0,50 Ch€0,50 WC€0,50 €1.
Surface: metalled. 01/01-31/12, service: 8-9.30h and 18.30-20h.
Distance: 200m 10m 10m 100m 50m.

S Greifswald 6G3

Am Museumhafen, Marienstraße 10. **GPS**: n54,09887 e13,38945.

20 € 15 Ch WC included.
Location: Urban, simple. **Surface:** metalled.
01/03-30/11.
Distance: 300m 300m 1km.

Tourist information Greifswald:

Fischerdorf Greifswald-Wieck. Fishermen's village worth seeing.

Güstrow 8E1

Gleviner Platz. **GPS**: n53,79117 e12,18054.

3 free. **Location:** Urban. **Surface:** asphalted. 01/01-31/12.
Distance: 400m 5km 5km 100m 100m.

S Güstrow 8E1

Hotel Am Tierpark, Verbindungschaussee 7.
GPS: n53,79159 e12,21577.
30 € 10, 2 pers.incl Ch €2,50 WC use sanitary €2,50/pp.
Surface: grassy. 01/01-31/12.
Distance: 5km on the spot 5km.

S Gützkow 8F1

Rittergut Schloss Pentin, Zum Bollwerk 11.
GPS: n53,91824 e13,46763.

DE

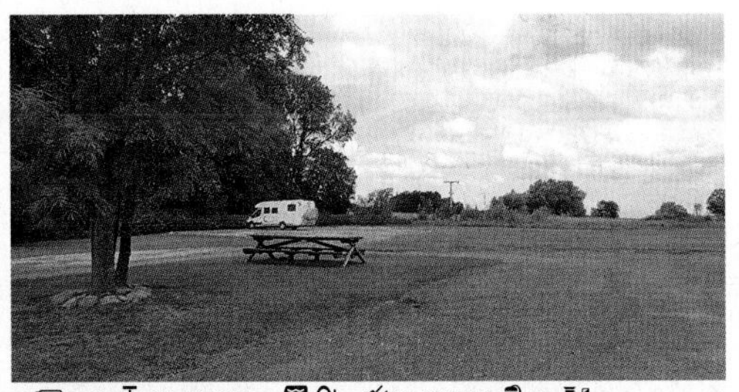

10 € 10 €0,50/80liter Ch €0,50/kWh €1.
Location: Rural, simple. **Surface:** grassy/gravel.
01/01-31/12.
Distance: 1km 400m.
Remarks: Bread-service, nature reserve.

S Heringsdorf 6H3

Blasendorff, Labahnstrasse 10. **GPS:** n53,95940 e14,15680.

3 € 10 €0,50/40liter €1,50 €1,80. **Location:** Urban, simple. **Surface:** grassy. 01/01-31/12.
Distance: 10min 300m 300m 300m.

S Heringsdorf 6H3

P An der Kirche, Rudolf-Breitscheid-Straße.
GPS: n53,95762 e14,16219.

30 € 10,50, 2,50 pers.incl, tourist tax € 2,50/pp Ch €1,50 WCincluded €1. **Location:** Urban, central. **Surface:** grassy/sand.
01/01-31/12.
Distance: on the spot beach 500m 250m 250m.

S Hinrichshagen 6G3

Reisemobilstellplatz Wöller, Chausseestraße 12.
GPS: n54,07450 e13,35230.

50 € 10 Ch included WC. **Location:** Comfortable.
Surface: grassy/gravel. 01/01-31/12.
Distance: 3,5km 1,8km 800m.
Remarks: Use sanitary € 5/motorhome, in winter limited services, service passerby € 5.

S Hornstorf 8D1

Gartencenter Offermann, Dorfstraße 1. **GPS:** n53,89473 e11,54159.

20 € 10 Ch included. **Location:** Rural, simple, noisy.
Surface: concrete. 01/01-31/12.

S Insel Poel 8D1

Strandparkplatz Timmendorf, Tau n Lüchttorm.
GPS: n53,99287 e11,38058.

60 € 5/day, € 4/night + € 2/pp tourist tax €0,50/80liter Ch (64x)€2/2kWh €1. **Location:** Rural, simple, quiet.
Surface: grassy. 01/01-31/12.
Distance: 150m 500m 200m 300m on the spot on the spot.
Remarks: Check in at kosk, caution key sanitary € 10.

S Insel Poel 8D1

Poeler Forellenhof, Niendorf 13. **GPS:** n53,99454 e11,44714.

16 € 13, 2 pers.incl €2/100liter WC included €2,60/2,60.
Location: Rural, simple. **Surface:** concrete. 01/01-31/12.
Distance: 1,5km on the spot on the spot on the spot 1,5km on the spot on the spot.
Remarks: Check in at restaurant, steam bath and sauna, fish smokehouse.

Kamminke 8G1

Ortstraße. **GPS:** n53,86750 e14,20480.

15 € 8. **Surface:** grassy. 01/01-31/12.
Distance: on the spot on the spot.

S Karenz 8D2

Reiterhof am Steinberg, Grebserstrasse 1. **GPS:** n53,23638 e11,34836.

3 € 10 €1 Ch €1,50 WC. **Location:** Rural, simple, isolated. **Surface:** grassy. 01/01-31/12.
Distance: 1km 1km 300m.
Remarks: Parking at manege.

S Kargow 8F2

Reisemobilstellplatz Ziegenwiese, Schwarzenhof 7.
GPS: n53,46433 e12,79925.

10 € 7,50 €3 Ch €1,50. **Location:** Rural, quiet.
Surface: grassy. 01/01-31/12.
Distance: 1km 1km 200m 4km.

S Karnin 8G1

Hafen, Karnin 14a. **GPS:** n53,84450 e13,85860.

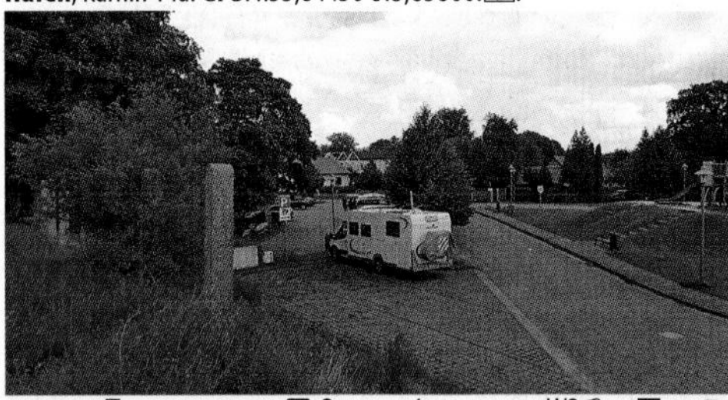

3 € 10 €0,50/100liter Ch€1 €0,50/kWh WC €1 €4.
Location: Rural, quiet. **Surface:** metalled. 01/01-31/12.
Distance: 6km 500m 6km on the spot on the spot on the spot.
Remarks: Intersection hiking and biking trails.

Kühlungsborn 6F3

Hafenstrasse. **GPS:** n54,15051 e11,76329.

20 € 8/24h.
Location: Urban, simple, noisy. **Surface:** concrete. 01/01-31/12.
Distance: 500m on the spot on the spot on the spot.

S Langen Brütz 8D1

Landhaus Bondzio, Hauptstrasse 21a. **GPS:** n53,65722 e11,55737.

4 € 12 WCincluded €2. **Location:** Rural, simple.
Surface: asphalted/grassy. 01/01-31/12 Restaurant: Mo.
Distance: 150m on the spot 50m.

S Lenz über Malchow 8E2

Lenzer Hafen, Zum Hafen 1. **GPS:** n53,46793 e12,34929.

25 € 13,30-16,30 €2 Ch€0,50 €1/2kWh WC €1,50 €3 included. **Location:** Rural, quiet. **Surface:** grasstiles.
01/03-31/10.
Distance: 5km on the spot on the spot on the spot 5km.
Remarks: Parking eastern bank Plauersee.

DE

S Lohme 6G3

Wohnmobilstellplatz Dorfladen, Arkonastrasse 4.
GPS: n54,58300 e13,61150.

35 € 14 - € 17,50 €1/90liter Ch€2 €1/2kWh WC €2/5minutes €3/3 included.
Location: Rural, comfortable. **Surface:** grassy/metalled.
01/01-31/12.
Distance: on the spot 200m on the spot on the spot on the spot.
Remarks: Dog € 1,50/night, breakfast-service, discount longer stays.

S Lohme 6G3

Zum Königsstuhl, Stubbenkammerstraße 57, Hagen.
GPS: n54,56220 e13,62590.

40 € 10,50 + € 1/pp tourist tax €1/100liter Ch €2,50/24h WC €0,50 €1/4minutes. **Location:** Rural.
Surface: grassy/metalled. 01/01-31/12.
Distance: on the spot 600m on the spot.

S Ludwigslust 8D2

Am Schloss, Friedrich-Naumann-Allee. **GPS**: n53,32735 e11,49080.

20 € 7/24h €1/100liter €1 Ch€1 WC.
Location: Rural, simple, quiet. **Surface:** gravel/sand.
01/01-31/12.
Distance: 600m 500m 600m.
Remarks: Coins at the shops.

S Lütow 6G3

Yachtlieger Achterwasser, Netzelkow. **GPS**: n54,02690 e13,90950.

22 € 1/m + € 1/pp Ch (20x)€0,25/kWh WC €2.
Surface: grassy. 01/01-31/12.
Distance: on the spot on the spot on the spot.
Remarks: Bread-service, bike/car rental.

S Malchin 8E1

Malchiner Kanu-club, Am Kanal 2. **GPS**: n53,74417 e12,76611.

8 € 10 Ch €1 WC included €0,50 €3/2.
Location: Comfortable, quiet. **Surface:** grassy. 01/05-30/09.
Distance: 500m on the spot on the spot 500m 500m.
Remarks: Dog € 3.

S Malchow 8E2

Marina Malchow, Ziegeleiweg 5. **GPS**: n53,46432 e12,42417.

20 € 10-20 excl. tourist tax Ch €2,50 WC included €2,50.
Location: Rural, comfortable, quiet. **Surface:** grassy.
01/05-30/09.
Distance: 2km 4km on the spot on the spot 2km 4km 250m.
Remarks: Bread-service.

S Malchow 8E2

Wohnmobilstellplatz Am Plauer See, Zum Plauer See 1.
GPS: n53,49192 e12,37268.

5 € 10-12, 2 pers.incl Ch (5x)€3,30 WC stay included. **Location:** Rural, quiet. **Surface:** grassy.
01/01-31/12.
Distance: 5km on the spot on the spot on the spot on the spot.
Remarks: Use sanitary € 2/pp per day.

S Mirow 8F2

Schloßstraße 1A. **GPS**: n53,27623 e12,81348.

8 free €1 €1 Ch€1 (8x) WC€0,50.
Location: Simple. **Surface:** grasstiles/metalled. 01/01-31/12.
Distance: 400m 200m 400m.

S Mönkebude 8G1

Stettinger Haff, Am Hafen. **GPS**: n53,77174 e13,96868.

25+15 € 8,50-10, tourist tax € 1/pp €0,50/100liter Ch €2/24h WC included €1/4minutes €3,50 €4/4h.
Location: Rural, comfortable. **Surface:** grassy. 01/01-31/12.
Distance: 50m on the spot 50m.
Remarks: Dog € 2/day, peak season: sanitary installation, nov/apr service only on demand.

Mönkebude 8G1

Gastätte Kregelin's Bistro, Hauptstrasse.
GPS: n53,76663 e13,97614.

4 guests free. **Surface:** metalled.
Distance: on the spot.

S Muess 8D2

Feriendorf Muess, Alte Crivitzer Landstrasse 6.
GPS: n53,59995 e11,47940.

15 € 10, 01/03-30/09 € 20, dog € 1 Ch WC included,winterfeenoshower €2/1,70.
Location: Rural, comfortable. **Surface:** grassy.
01/01-31/12.
Distance: 100m 100m 100m 100m 100m on the spot.
Remarks: At open air museum, check in at reception, bicycle rental.

S Neu Kaliss 8D2

Find 's Hier, An der Elde 2. **GPS**: n53,17810 e11,29720.

13 € 9 Ch included €2/night WC €1.
Location: Rural, simple, isolated, quiet. **Surface:** grassy.
01/01-31/12.
Distance: on the spot on the spot on the spot 400m 400m.

S Neubrandenburg 8F1

Wassersportzentrum Tollensesee, Augustastrasse 7.
GPS: n53,53861 e13,25665.

30 € 10 €1 Ch€1 €0,50/kWh WC €1 €2/day.
Location: Quiet. **Surface:** grassy/metalled. 15/03-31/10.
Distance: 2km on the spot on the spot 200m 500m.
Remarks: Water sports centre.

S Neuendorf 6F3

Wohnmobilstellplatz Saal Neuendorf, Am Hafen.
GPS: n54,33516 e12,52812.

DE

36 € 10 included WC€0,20 €1 on demand.
Location: Rural, simple, quiet. **Surface:** grassy.
01/04-31/10.
Distance: 100m on the spot on the spot Imbiss kiosk 400m on the spot on the spot.

S Neukloster 8D1

Wohnmobilpark Neuklostersee, Alte Gärtnerei 3.
GPS: n53,86121 e11,69536.

69 € 9,50 €1,50 Ch €1/2kWh WC €2 €4/2.
Location: Rural, comfortable, luxurious, quiet. **Surface:** gravel.
16/03-31/10.
Distance: 500m on the spot 50m 500m 1,2km 500m on the spot on the spot.

S Neustrelitz 8F2

Parkplatz Am Stadthafen, Zierker Nebenstrasse 6.
GPS: n53,36568 e13,05551.

25 € 8 €0,50/80liter €0,50 Ch€0,50 €0,50/kWh WC€0,20 €0,50 €2.
Location: Urban, comfortable, quiet. **Surface:** metalled.
01/01-31/12.
Distance: on the spot 100m, swimming 1km 200m 100m 200m 200m on the spot on the spot.
Remarks: Coins at harbourmaster (200m), historical centre.

S Nossentin 8E2

Am Fleesensee, Am Park 33. **GPS**: n53,51866 e12,46766.

5 € 8 Ch WCincluded . **Surface:** grassy.
01/04-31/10.
Distance: 5km 100m 100m on the spot 5km.

S Ostseebad Sellin/Rügen 6G3

Reisemobilhafen Sellin, Kiefernweg 4b. **GPS**: n54,37170 e13,70165.

50 € 13-15 €0,50/60liter Ch (50x)€0,50/kWh WCincluded €0,50/2minutes. **Surface:** grassy/metalled. 15/03-15/11.
Distance: 300m 1km 1km 200m 300m 300m.

S Ostseebad Sellin/Rügen 6G3

Hafen Seedorf, Seedorf 8. **GPS**: n54,35410 e13,65359.

5 € 10 on demand €0,50/kWh €0,50/2minutes.
Location: Rural, simple, quiet. **Surface:** metalled.
01/05-15/10.
Distance: 250m 250m 250m.

S Ostseebad Wustrow 6F3

Surfcenter Wustrow, An der Nebelstation 2.
GPS: n54,34080 e12,38040.

30 € 16-29, dog € 2,50-5 Ch €2,50/day WC€0,50 €1/2minutes included.
Location: Rural, simple, quiet. **Surface:** asphalted. 01/04-31/10.
Distance: 1km 50m on the spot on the spot on the spot.

Ostseebad Wustrow 6F3

Hafenstraße. **GPS**: n54,34363 e12,40053.

30 € 4/day, € 10/night. **Location:** Rural, simple, quiet.
Surface: grassy/sand. 01/01-31/12.
Distance: 400m 1,5km on the spot on the spot on the spot on the spot.
Remarks: Max. 1 night.

S Parchim 8D2

Yachthafen, Am Fischerdamm. **GPS**: n53,42594 e11,84494.

10 € 6 €0,50/50liter Ch€0,50 €0,50/kWh WC€0,50 €0,50. **Location:** Urban, comfortable, central. **Surface:** metalled.
01/01-31/12.
Distance: 100m on the spot on the spot 100m 100m.

S Pepelow 8D1

Wohnmobilpark Am Salzhaff, Seeweg 1.
GPS: n54,03805 e11,58441.

39 € 8-12, 2 pers.incl Ch €3,30/night WC €2,50/pp €3/3 included. **Location:** Rural, comfortable, luxurious, quiet.
Surface: grassy. 01/01-31/12.
Distance: 700m on the spot on the spot on the spot on the spot on the spot on the spot.

S Petersdorf 8E2

Hotel Haus Waldesruh, Lenzerstrasse 19.
GPS: n53,45892 e12,36060.

10 € 7,50 €1 Ch €2 WC €1,50 €1,50/1,50.
Surface: grassy. 01/01-31/12.
Distance: 7km 600m 600m on the spot 7km.

S Priepert 8F2

Wohnmobilpark Am Großen Priepertsee, An der Freiheit 8.
GPS: n53,22043 e13,04201.

30 € 7 Chincluded €2,25 WC€3/day €1 €5.
Location: Rural, comfortable, quiet. **Surface:** grassy.
01/01-31/12.
Distance: on the spot 70m 70m 500m 12km.

S Putbus 6G3

Im-Jaich OHG, Am Yachthafen 1, Lauterbach.
GPS: n54,34278 e13,50167.

14 € 16-18 €0,50/50liter WC €0,50 €4/3 included.
Location: Luxurious. **Surface:** gravel. 01/01-31/12.
Distance: 500m on the spot on the spot on the spot 800m.
Remarks: Bread kiosk, seaview.

S Putbus 6G3

Wohnmobilstellplatz Lauterbach, Chausseestrasse 14.
GPS: n54,34639 e13,49889.

DE

26 € 13-15 €0,60/50liter Ch €0,70/kWh WC €0,30 €2/5minutes €4/4 €1/day. **Location:** Rural, luxurious, quiet. **Surface:** grassy/metalled. 15/03-15/10.
Distance: 1km 400m 400m 100m.
Remarks: Max. 8M.

Putbus 6G3

Wohnmobilstellplatz Lauterbach, Chausseestrasse 14.
GPS: n54,34639 e13,49889.
26 € 13-15 €0,60/50liter Ch €0,70/kWh WC €0,30 €2/5minutes €4/4 €1/day. **Location:** Rural, luxurious, quiet. **Surface:** grassy/metalled. 15/03-15/10.
Distance: 1km 400m 400m 100m.
Remarks: Max. 8M.

Putgarten 6G3

Kap Arkona, Varnkevitzer Weg. **GPS**: n54,67190 e13,40800.

30 € 5, ^3,10m € 15. **Location:** Simple. **Surface:** asphalted.
01/01-31/12.
Distance: 100m Imbiss 6km.

Rerik 6E3

Wohnmobilhafen Ostseebad Rerik, Straße am Zeltplatz 8.
GPS: n54,11332 e11,63037.

35 € 13, Jul/Aug € 23 Ch WC €0,30 €3/3 included. **Location:** Rural, comfortable, quiet. **Surface:** grassy.
01/01-31/12.
Distance: sandy beach 600m on the spot on the spot on the spot on the spot on the spot.
Remarks: Check in at reception.

Ribnitz-Damgarten 6F3

Gänsewiese, Am See 50. **GPS**: n54,24513 e12,42265.

25 free, night € 8 €0,50/100liter Ch €0,50/12h WC.
Location: Rural, simple, quiet. **Surface:** grasstiles/grassy.
01/01-31/12.
Distance: 500m on the spot on the spot 500m 500m on the spot on the spot.

Ribnitz-Damgarten 6F3

Hafen Ribnitz, Am See 44. **GPS**: n54,24536 e12,42921.

10 free, night € 10 WC €1/3minutes.
Location: Urban, simple, quiet. **Surface:** concrete.
01/01-31/12.
Distance: 100m on the spot on the spot on the spot 200m on the spot on the spot.

Röbel 8E2

Am Seglerhafen, Müritzpromenade 20. **GPS**: n53,38734 e12,61755.

40 € 12 Ch €2 WC included €1 €2/day.
Location: Comfortable. **Surface:** grasstiles/metalled.
01/04-31/10.
Distance: 2km on the spot on the spot 300m 1km.

Rostock 6F3

Am Stadthafen, Warnowuffer. **GPS**: n54,09297 e12,12878.

25 € 12. **Location:** Urban, simple. **Surface:** asphalted/metalled.
01/01-31/12.
Distance: on the spot on the spot on the spot.

Tourist information Rostock:
www.rostock.de. Hanseatic city with historical centre.

Rüterberg 8C3

Wohmobilparkplatz Dorfrepublik Rüterberg, Ringstraße 2.
GPS: n53,15294 e11,18511.

10 € 5/24h+ € 0,50/pp €1/50liter €1 Ch €1 €1,50/kWh WC €1. **Location:** Rural, simple, central, quiet. **Surface:** grassy.
01/01-31/12.
Distance: 10m 50m.
Remarks: Bread-service.

Schwerin 8D1

Am Hauptbahnhof, Wismarsche Straße. **GPS**: n53,63692 e11,40893.

4 € 8/24h €1/80liter Ch (4x)€1/2kWh.
Location: Urban, simple, central, noisy. **Surface:** metalled.
01/01-31/12.
Distance: on the spot on the spot on the spot on the spot.

Schwerin 8D1

Am Stadthafen, Schliemannstraße. **GPS**: n53,62977 e11,41966.

10 € 16/24h (8x)€0,50/kWh.
Location: Urban, simple, central, noisy. **Surface:** metalled.
01/01-31/12.
Distance: on the spot 8km on the spot on the spot on the spot on the spot on the spot.
Remarks: No camping activities.

Schwerin 8D1

Marina-Nord Schwerin, Buchenweg 19.
GPS: n53,64584 e11,43264.

16 € 10 + € 1/pp Ch (14x)€0,50/kWh WC €1,50 €1/24h. **Location:** Rural, comfortable, quiet. **Surface:** grassy.
15/04-15/10.
Distance: 4km 5km on the spot on the spot on the spot 1km 100m on the spot on the spot.
Remarks: Check in at reception, bread-service.

Schwerin 8D1

Sportbootzentrum Ziegelsee, Güstrower Straße 88.
GPS: n53,64823 e11,43004.

10 € 12/24h €0,50/70liter Ch €1/24h WC €1/6minutes €5/5. **Location:** Rural, comfortable, quiet. **Surface:** concrete.
01/04-30/10.
Distance: 2km 8km on the spot on the spot 2km 300m on the spot on the spot on the spot.

Seehof 8D1

Campingplatz Seehof, Am Zeltplatz 1. **GPS**: n53,69676 e11,43658.

10 € 15-24, 2 pers.incl Ch WC included €1 €3,50/3,50. **Location:** Rural, comfortable. **Surface:** grassy.
01/01-31/10.
Distance: 1,2km on the spot on the spot on the spot on the spot on the spot on the spot.
Remarks: Bike/boat rental.

Sembzin 8E2

Rasthof Sembzin, Dorfstrasse 2. **GPS**: n53,46445 e12,60386.

DE

16 € 8 Ch included WC €1/24h. **Location:** Noisy.
Surface: grassy/gravel. 01/04-31/10.
Distance: 8km on the spot 1,5km.
Remarks: € 8 voucher restaurant, use sanitary € 2/pp per day, swimming pool incl.

S Sievershagen 6F3

Ferienhof Dubberke, Alt Sievershagen 16.
GPS: n54,11480 e12,03481.

7 € 10 Ch WCincluded €1. **Location:** Rural, comfortable, quiet. **Surface:** grassy. 01/01-31/10.
Distance: 500m, Rostock 5km 2km 800m 800m on the spot on the spot.

S Sommersdorf 8F1

Wohnmobilpark Sommersdorf, Am Kummerower See.
GPS: n53,79824 e12,87576.

28 € 8-12, 2 pers. incl Ch €3/day WC €1 included.
Location: Rural, comfortable, isolated, quiet. **Surface:** grassy.
01/01-31/12.
Distance: 1km on the spot on the spot 1km.
Remarks: Use sanitary € 2/pp per day.

S Sternberg 8D1

Sternberger, Maikamp 11. **GPS**: n53,71318 e11,81236.

15 € 14-18 Ch €3/day WC included €2.
Location: Rural. **Surface:** grassy. 01/04-31/10.
Distance: 1km on the spot on the spot on the spot 500m 500m.

S Stralsund 6G3

An der Rügenbrücke, Werftstraße 9a. **GPS**: n54,30222 e13,09889.

40 € 15, 2 pers.incl €1/50liter €1 Ch€1 (40x)€0,50/kWh
WCincluded €1 €3/3 €4,95/day. **Location:** Comfortable, noisy.
Surface: grassy/gravel. 01/01-31/12.
Distance: 1,8km 1,8km 200m on the spot.
Remarks: Bread-service.

S Ueckermünde 8G1

An der Uecker, Ueckerstrasse 125. **GPS**: n53,73470 e14,04930.

13 € 8 + € 1/pp tourist tax Ch included.
Location: Urban, simple. **Surface:** grassy/metalled.
01/01-31/12.
Distance: Old city centre 200m 200m 100m.

Ueckermünde 8G1

See Sport, Grabenstrasse. **GPS**: n53,73917 e14,04944.
€ 6 €0,50/100liter €0,50/kWh WC €0,50/2minutes.
Location: Urban, central. **Surface:** grassy.
01-01/31/12.
Distance: 200m on the spot 200m 500m.

Ueckermünde 8G1

See Sport, Grabenstrasse. **GPS**: n53,73917 e14,04944.

€ 6 €0,50/100liter €0,50/kWh WC €0,50/2minutes.
Location: Urban, central. **Surface:** grassy.
01-01/31/12.
Distance: 200m on the spot 200m 500m.

S Usedom 8G1

Am Hafen Usedom, Peenestraße. **GPS**: n53,87099 e13,92679.

20 € 10 €0,50/50liter Ch €0,50/kWh WC€0,50 €2.
Location: Rural, simple. **Surface:** metalled.
01/01-31/12.
Distance: 600m on the spot on the spot 1,3km.
Remarks: At former fishing-port.

S Usedom 8G1

Gaststätte Haffschänke, Dorfstraße 19, Karnin.
GPS: n53,84348 e13,86537.

20 €7 Ch €3 WC €2,50.
Surface: grassy. 01/01-31/12.
Distance: on the spot on the spot on the spot.

S Vielank 8C2

Vielanker Brauhaus, Lindenplatz 1. **GPS**: n53,23443 e11,14023.

12 free €3 WC. **Location:** Rural, simple, quiet. **Surface:** grassy.
01/01-31/12.
Distance: 20m on the spot.
Remarks: Check in at reception.

S Waren 8E2

Blumen und Parken, Mecklenburgerstrasse.
GPS: n53,51363 e12,69431.

40 € 9,50 + € 1,50/pp tourist tax Ch €0,50/kWh WCincluded € 1/5minutes. **Location:** Urban, simple.
Surface: grassy/gravel. 01/01-31/12.
Distance: 100m 1km 1km 1km 1km on the spot.

S Waren 8E2

Wohnmobilpark Kamerun, Zur Stillen Bucht 3, Müritz.
GPS: n53,51175 e12,65174.

60 € 10-15,50 + tourist tax Ch €3,30 WC €0,75 included. **Location:** Rural, comfortable, quiet. **Surface:** grassy.
01/01-31/12.
Distance: 3km on the spot on the spot on the spot on the spot 500m.
Remarks: Use sanitary € 2,50/pp per day.

S Waren 8E2

Parkplatz Am Hafen, Strandstrasse 3b. **GPS**: n53,51194 e12,68583.

20 € 13 Ch included.
Location: Urban. **Surface:** metalled. 01/01-31/12.
Distance: on the spot on the spot on the spot on the spot on the spot.

S Waren 8E2

Campingplatz Ecktannen, Fontanestraße 66.
GPS: n53,49944 e12,66361.

DE

17 € 14-18, 2 pers. incl Ch WC €2,60/2,60 included. **Location:** Comfortable, quiet.
Surface: grasstiles/metalled.
01/01-31/12.
Distance: 3,5km 500m 500m Bistro 3km on the spot.

S Warnemünde 6F3

Am Bahnhof. **GPS:** n54,17762 e12,09002.

100 € 6/3h, € 12/12h, € 16/24h €0,50/100liter.
Location: Urban, simple, central, noisy. **Surface:** grassy/metalled.
01/01-31/12.
Distance: on the spot on the spot on the spot on the spot on the spot on the spot on the spot.

Warnemünde 6F3

Parkplatz Strand-Mitte, Parkstrasse 46. **GPS:** n54,17643 e12,05765.

100 € 10/24h. **Location:** Urban, simple, noisy.
Surface: metalled. 01/01-31/12.
Distance: 2,5km 100m 400m 2km on the spot on the spot on the spot.

S Wesenberg 8F2

Stellplatz Marina Wesenberg, Ahrensberger Weg 11.
GPS: n53,27666 e12,98694.

34 € 16, 2 pers.incl Ch WC included.
Surface: grassy. 01/04-30/09.
Distance: 1km on the spot on the spot 1,5km 2,5km 1km.

S Wismar 8D1

Wohnmobilpark Westhafen Wismar, Schiffbauerdamm 12.
GPS: n53,89430 e11,45151.

65 € 7/12h, € 10/24h €1/100liter Ch €1/8h WC €1.
Location: Urban, simple, central, noisy. **Surface:** asphalted/gravel.
01/01-31/12.
Distance: 800m 500m 300m, Burger King 400m 300m 800m 100m.
Remarks: Caution key sanitary € 10.

S Wittenbeck 6F3

Sanddornstrand, Bäderweg. **GPS:** n54,14513 e11,79277.

150 € 12-14 Ch (60x)€0,60/kWh WC €0,50 included.
Location: Rural, simple, quiet. **Surface:** grassy/metalled.
01/03-31/10.
Distance: 1km on the spot on the spot on the spot 2,5km 50m on the spot on the spot.
Remarks: Bread-service.

S Zingst 6F3

Strandübergang 6, Straminke. **GPS:** n54,44070 e12,70750.

40 € 10/15 + € 2/pp tourist tax €1/100liter €3 WC included €1. **Location:** Rural, simple, quiet. **Surface:** grassy.
01/01-31/12.
Distance: 500m on the spot 500m 500m 1km 1km on the spot on the spot.

S Zingst 6F3

Wohnmobilhafen Am Freesenbruch, Am Bahndamm 1.
GPS: n54,44060 e12,66058.

40 € 12 + € 9/pp, dog € 4 Ch €2,30/day WC included €3/3. **Location:** Rural, comfortable, noisy. **Surface:** grassy.
01/01-31/12.
Distance: 1,5km 50m on the spot on the spot on the spot on the spot.
Remarks: Bread-service.

S Zurow 8D1

Urlaub am Schloss, Kastanienallee 56, Krassow.
GPS: n53,87379 e11,56618.

10 € 5 €1 Ch €2/day WC €2 . **Location:** Rural, simple, quiet. **Surface:** grassy/metalled. 01/01-31/12.
Distance: 1,5km 1km 3km 100m on the spot on the spot.
Remarks: Caution key sanitary € 10.

Saxony Anhalt

S Ahlum 8C3

Fischerhütte Ahlumer See, Am Mühlenberg 63.
GPS: n52,69541 e11,00583.

100 € 10, 2 pers.incl Ch €3 WC included.
Surface: grassy. 01/01-31/12.
Distance: on the spot on the spot on the spot.
Remarks: Bread-service.

S Allrode 10C3

Hotel Harzer Land, Teichstraße 28. **GPS:** n51,67774 e10,96478.

25 € 15,50 Ch WC included.
Surface: grassy. 01/01-31/12.
Distance: on the spot on the spot.

Altenbrak 10C2

Bodewiese, Am Bielstein. **GPS:** n51,72569 e10,94196.

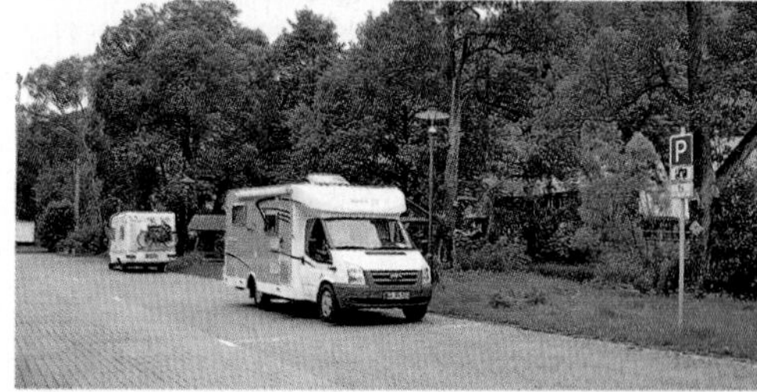

8 € 5, overnight stay free. **Location:** Rural, simple.
Surface: metalled. 01/01-31/12.
Distance: 100m on the spot 100m 200m on the spot.

S Altenbrak 10C2

Hotel Zur Talsperre, Oberbecken 1, Wendefurth.
GPS: n51,73434 e10,90690.

20 € 10 excl. tourist tax (20x)€0,50/kWh WC included.
Location: Rural, simple, isolated. **Surface:** asphalted/grassy.
01/01-31/12.
Distance: on the spot.

S Arendsee 8D3

Im kleinen Elsebusch, Lüchower strasse 6a.
GPS: n52,87656 e11,46121.

10 € 13 €1,50 €1,50 Ch . **Surface:** grassy.
01/01-31/12.
Distance: 2,5km on the spot 2,5km.

DE

S Aschersleben 10D2

Sport- und Freizeitzentrum Ballhaus, Seegraben.
GPS: n51,76101 e11,45760.

8 free €1/15minutes €2 Ch€2 (12x)€1/6h.
Location: Urban, comfortable, central, quiet. **Surface:** asphalted.
01/01-31/12.
Distance: 1km 200m 200m on the spot on the spot on the spot.
Remarks: Caution key € 15, key at reception desk BallHaus.

Bad Bibra 12D1

Parkplatz am Schwimmbad. **GPS**: n51,21214 e11,60002.

20 € 3. **Location:** Rural, simple, isolated, quiet.
Surface: gravel/metalled. 01/01-31/12.
Distance: 1,5km 200m 1,5km.
Remarks: At swimming pool.

Bad Bibra 12D1

Parkplatz Bürgergarten, Haus des Gastes.
GPS: n51,20526 e11,57929.

10 € 3. **Location:** Urban, simple, central, quiet.
Surface: gravel/metalled. 01/01-31/12.
Distance: 200m 500m.

S Bad Kösen 12E1

Am Saalebogen, Stendorf 14. **GPS**: n51,11356 e11,69609.

15 € 8 Ch (15x)€2/day WC included €1.
Location: Rural, comfortable, quiet. **Surface:** grasstiles/metalled.
01/01-31/12.
Distance: 3km 200m bakery 200m on the spot on the spot.

S Bad Suderode 10D2

Restaurant Am Kurpark, Jägerstrasse 7. **GPS**: n51,72685 e11,12078.

4 € 10, € 13 service incl Ch €5/day.
Location: Urban, comfortable, central, quiet.
Surface: grasstiles/grassy. 01/01-31/12.
Distance: 100m on the spot 200m 200m on the spot on the spot.

S Ballenstedt 10D2

Verkehrslandeplatz Ballenstedt/Quedlinburg, Asmusstedt 13.
GPS: n51,74190 e11,23427.

32 € 9 Ch (16x) WC included. **Location:** Rural, simple, quiet. **Surface:** grasstiles/metalled. 01/01-31/12.
Distance: 2km on the spot 2km 200m.

S Bergwitz 10F2

Camping Bergwitzsee, Strandweg. **GPS**: n51,79439 e12,57773.

20 € 6 €3 Ch. **Location:** Rural, simple, isolated, quiet.
Surface: grassy/sand. 01/01-31/12.
Distance: 1km 50m 50m 300m 1,5km.
Remarks: Check in at reception campsite, service on campsite.

S Berssel 10C2

Gasthof Zum Schloß, Am Schloß 1. **GPS**: n51,95266 e10,76027.

5 free on demand. **Location:** Rural, simple, quiet.
Surface: metalled. 01/01-31/12.
Distance: 200m on the spot on the spot on the spot.

S Bertingen 10D1

Hotel La Porte, Im Wald 2. **GPS**: n52,35994 e11,82264.

30 € 7,50 Ch included. **Surface:** grassy. 01/01-31/12.
Distance: on the spot 5km.
Remarks: Bread-service.

S Bitterfeld 10E2

Spaßbad Woliday, Reudener Straße, Bitterfeld-Wolfen.
GPS: n51,67102 e12,24842.

10 € 13 WC included.
Surface: grasstiles. 01/01-31/12.
Distance: 1,2km on the spot 900m.
Remarks: Incl. access swimming pool.

S Blankenburg 10C2

Am Schnappelberg, Schnappelberg 2. **GPS**: n51,78862 e10,96036.

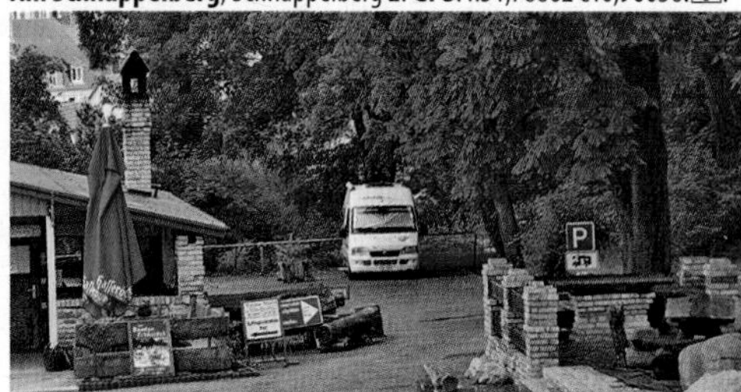

4 € 6 €1 €2/night WC. **Location:** Urban, simple, central, quiet. **Surface:** asphalted. 01/01-31/12.
Distance: 500m 300m on the spot.

S Blankenburg 10C2

Busparkplatz, Am Schnappelberg. **GPS**: n51,78884 e10,96076.

6 € 4/24h (6x)€1/kWh. **Location:** Urban, simple, quiet.
Surface: metalled. 01/01-31/12.
Distance: 400m 300m 200m on the spot on the spot.

S Blankenburg 10C2

Teichwirtschaft, Harzstraße 31a, Timmenrode.
GPS: n51,76874 e10,99134.

10 € 9 €1 Ch €1 €1. **Location:** Rural, simple, quiet.
Surface: grassy/metalled. 01/01-31/12.
Distance: Blankenburg 5km on the spot on the spot.
Remarks: Fishpond.

S Brachwitz 10E3

Marina Saale-Ufer, An der Fähre. **GPS**: n51,53270 e11,87059.

30 € 5 (4x)€0,50/kWh WC. **Location:** Rural, comfortable, quiet. **Surface:** grassy. 01/01-31/12.
Distance: 500m on the spot 500m.

DE

Braunsbedra 10E3

Mobilpark am Geiseltalsee, Schortauer Weg.
GPS: n51,29421 e11,85346.

25 € 10 Ch WC included €2 against payment.
Location: Urban, comfortable, quiet. **Surface:** grassy/metalled.
01/01-31/12.
Distance: 700m 500m.

Breitenstein 10C3

Hauptstrasse, L236. **GPS**: n51,61756 e10,94957.

8 free (4x)€1/8h. **Location:** Rural, simple, quiet. **Surface:** gravel.
01/01-31/12.
Distance: 400m Sportgaststätte.

Burg bei Magdeburg 10E1

Wassersportfreunde Burg, Am Kanal 20a.
GPS: n52,28329 e11,84808.

6 € 18 €1/100liter WC included. **Surface:** grassy.
01/05-30/09.
Distance: 1km on the spot.

Burg bei Magdeburg 10E1

Eschenhof, Parchauer Chaussee 5. **GPS**: n52,28718 e11,86583.

15 € 12 2 pers.incl, dog € 1 Ch WC included.
Surface: grassy. 01/01-31/12.
Distance: 2km on the spot 1km.

Coswig/Anhalt 10E2

Marina Coswig, Post Elbstrasse 22. **GPS**: n51,88071 e12,43552.

40 € 12 2 pers.incl, dog € 1 €1/100liter Ch €0,60/kWh WC €1/4minutes. **Location:** Comfortable, quiet. **Surface:** gravel.
01/01-31/12.
Distance: 750m on the spot on the spot 150m on the spot.

Coswig/Anhalt 10E2

Hotel Zur Fichtenbreite, Fichtenbreite 5.
GPS: n51,88723 e12,40749.

15 € 5 Ch included (4x)€2,50/day €3,50.
Location: Rural, simple, noisy. **Surface:** grassy.
01/01-31/12.
Distance: 2km 500m on the spot 2km.
Remarks: Bread-service, bicycle rental.

Dankerode 10D3

Campingplatz Panoramablick, Hinterdorf 79.
GPS: n51,58832 e11,14189.

12 € 10 excl. tourist tax €1 €1 Ch €1 (6x)€2,50 WC.
Location: Rural, simple, isolated, quiet. **Surface:** grassy.
01/04-30/10.
Distance: 500m on the spot 500m on the spot on the spot.

Darlingerode 10C2

Wohnmobilpark Harzblick, Hinter den Gärten 11.
GPS: n51,85278 e10,73667.

25 € 8 €1/80liter Ch (12x)€0,60/kWh €1/day.
Location: Rural, comfortable, quiet. **Surface:** grassy/gravel.
01/01-31/12.
Distance: 600m 500m 500m 500m on the spot on the spot.

Dessau-Roßlau 10E2

Flugplatz Hugo Junkers, Alte Landesbahn 27.
GPS: n51,83447 e12,18289.

8 € 9 Ch WC included.
Location: Rural, comfortable, isolated, quiet.
Surface: grassy/metalled. 01/01-31/12.
Distance: 5km.
Remarks: Arrival < 19h, max. 8M.

Drübeck/Harz 10C2

Zur Waldschänke, Tänntalstraße 6. **GPS**: n51,84564 e10,71415.

8 first day € 10, then € 5 Ch included.
Location: Rural, simple, quiet. **Surface:** grassy/gravel.
01/01-31/12 Restaurant: Mo-Tue.
Distance: 1,5km on the spot.

Elend 10C2

Waldbad Schenke, Am Waldbad 1. **GPS**: n51,74612 e10,69531.

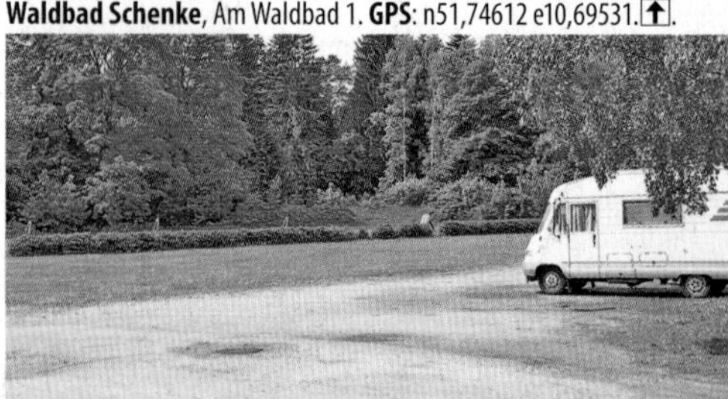

10 € 5-10 + € 1,50/pp tourist tax (5x)€1.
Location: Rural, simple, quiet. **Surface:** grassy/metalled.
01/01-31/12.
Distance: 600m on the spot 500m on the spot on the spot.

Freyburg/Unstrut 10E3

Stellplatz Schleusenblick, Wasserstraße 22.
GPS: n51,21049 e11,76979.

8 € 10 + € 1/pp tourist tax Ch WC included €2/day.
Location: Urban, comfortable, central, quiet. **Surface:** metalled.
01/01-31/12.
Distance: 100m 50m 300m.
Remarks: Along the Unstrut river.

Gernrode 10D2

Osterteich, Osterallee. **GPS**: n51,72449 e11,16007.

20 free. **Location:** Rural, simple, isolated, quiet. **Surface:** metalled.
01/01-31/12.
Distance: 1,5km 300m 1,5km on the spot.
Remarks: Next to train stop Selketalbahn.

Haldensleben 10D1

Am Stendaler Turm, Bornsche Strasse. **GPS**: n52,29291 e11,41342.

10 free. **Surface:** concrete. 01/01-31/12.
Distance: 200m 250m 150m Aldi.

DE

Haldensleben 10D1

Am Sportboothafen, Kronesruhe. **GPS**: n52,27933 e11,40240.

15 € 10 Ch included €0,50/kWh WC €1. **Location:** Rural. **Surface:** grassy. 15/04-31/10.
Distance: 2km 14km on the spot on the spot 200m.
Remarks: Bread-service.

Halle/Saale 10E3

Parkplatz, Fährstraße. **GPS**: n51,50210 e11,95397.

3 € 5 €1/80liter Ch stay WC against payment.
Location: Urban, simple, central, noisy. **Surface:** metalled.
01/01-31/12.
Distance: 2km 7km 200m 500m on the spot.
Remarks: Max. 5 days, green zone: environmental badge obligatory.

Halle/Saale 10E3

P25, An der Stadtschleuse. **GPS**: n51,48065 e11,96183.

10 free. **Location:** Urban, simple, central, noisy. **Surface:** metalled.
01/01-31/12. **Distance:** Old city centre 500m on the spot.
Remarks: Along railwayline, green zone: environmental badge obligatory.

Harzgerode 10D3

Parkplatz Wallgarten, Wallstrasse. **GPS**: n51,64210 e11,13983.

5 free. **Location:** Urban, simple, quiet. **Surface:** metalled.
01/01-31/12.
Distance: 100m 1km 3km 100m 100m 100m 1km.

Hasselfelde 10C3

P Pullman City/Westernstadt, Im Rosentale.
GPS: n51,70179 e10,86604.

10 free. **Location:** Rural, simple, quiet. **Surface:** gravel.
15/04-31/10.

Havelberg 8E3

Campinginsel. **GPS**: n52,82830 e12,06853.

€ 6 €1 €3 Ch (24x)€1/kWh. **Surface:** metalled.

Kelbra 10D3

Seecamping Südharz, L1040. **GPS**: n51,42583 e11,00287.

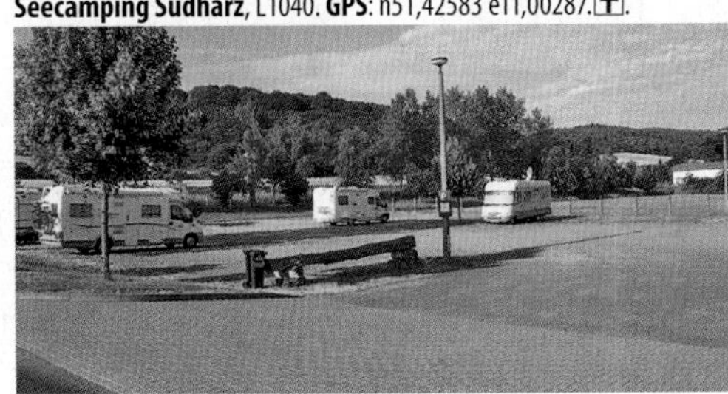

15 € 10-12 Ch included against payment.
Location: Rural. **Surface:** gravel. 01/01-31/12.
Distance: 2,5km on the spot on the spot on the spot.

Lutherstadt Wittenberg 10F2

Platz der Jugend. **GPS**: n51,86712 e12,63120.

5 free. **Location:** Urban, simple, noisy. **Surface:** metalled.
01/01-31/12.
Distance: centre 500m 150m 150m.
Remarks: Max. 8h, overnight stay allowed.

Magdeburg 10D2

Stellplatz Petriförde, Petriförder 1. **GPS**: n52,13289 e11,64714.

50 € 8 €1 €1 Ch €1. **Surface:** metalled. 01/01-31/12.
Distance: on the spot.
Remarks: Along the river Elbe.

Merseburg 10E3

Am Saaleufer, Brühl. **GPS**: n51,35491 e12,00234.

3 free. **Location:** Urban, simple. **Surface:** metalled.
01/01-31/12.
Distance: 500m.

Merseburg 10E3

Luftfahrt und Technik-museum Merseburg, Kastanienpromenade 50. **GPS**: n51,36004 e11,97044.

6 € 3, guests free. **Location:** Rural, simple, quiet.
Surface: gravel/metalled. 01/01-31/12.
Distance: 1km 1,5km.

Naumburg/Saale 12E1

Altstadtparkplatz Vogelwiese, Luisenstraße.
GPS: n51,14861 e11,81391.

15 € 10 €0,50/80liter Ch (6x)€0,50/kWh WC.
Surface: gravel. 01/01-31/12.
Distance: 500m 50m 500m 50m.
Remarks: Max. 3 days.

Oranienbaum-Wörlitz 10E2

Jugendverkehrsschule Oranienbaum, Dessauer Strasse 47.
GPS: n51,80279 e12,39023.

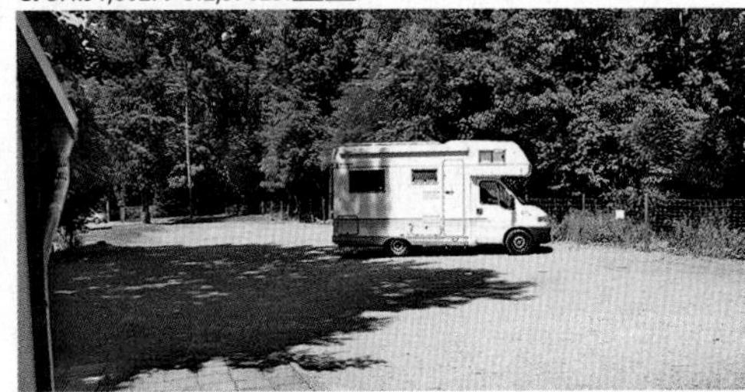

6 € 7,50 Ch (6x) WC included €1/day.
Location: Rural, comfortable, quiet. **Surface:** gravel/metalled.
01/01-31/12.
Distance: 1km.

Oranienbaum-Wörlitz 10E2

Seespitze 25. **GPS**: n51,84729 e12,41301.
24 € 10 (24x)€2. **Surface:** metalled. 01/01-31/12.
Distance: 600m 7,5km on the spot 600m.

Prettin 10F2

Bade- und Angelsee, Hinterfährstraße. **GPS**: n51,66485 e12,90551.

5 € 6 + € 2,80/pp Ch included €0,30/kWh.
Surface: gravel. 01/04-31/10.
Distance: 1,2km.

Quedlinburg 10D2

An den Fischteichen. **GPS**: n51,79308 e11,14863.

20 € 10 + € 5/pp tourist tax €1/80liter

DE

(8x)€1/6h. **Location:** Urban, comfortable, central, quiet.
Surface: grasstiles/metalled. 01/01-31/12.
Distance: 350m 300m 250m 150m.

Quedlinburg 10D2

Marschlinger Hof. **GPS**: n51,79138 e11,13965.

6 € 15/24h €1/80liter Ch (4x)€1/6h WC.
Location: Urban, comfortable, central, quiet. **Surface:** metalled.
01/01-31/12.
Distance: 100m 50m 400m 200m.
Remarks: Max. 7m.

Quedlinburg 10D2

Schloßparkplatz, Schenkgasse. **GPS**: n51,78755 e11,13507.

6 € 6/24h €1/80liter Ch (4x)€1/6h.
Location: Urban, comfortable, quiet. **Surface:** metalled.
01/01-31/12.
Distance: on the spot 100m.

Quedlinburg 10D2

Wohnmobilparkplatz Familie Jahnke, Feldmark links der Bode 17.
GPS: n51,80373 e11,17548.

10 € 10 €2/day WCincluded. **Location:** Rural, simple, quiet. **Surface:** concrete. 01/01-31/12.
Distance: 2,5km.

Salzwedel 8C3

Stellplatz der Hansestadt Salzwedel, Dämmchenweg 41.
GPS: n52,85049 e11,13911.

6 €3 Ch €2 WC sanitary€2. **Surface:** metalled.
01/01-31/12.
Distance: historical centre 1km 100m.

Sangerhausen 10D3

An der Walkmühle, Taubenberg. **GPS**: n51,49056 e11,31127.

50 free. **Surface:** sand. 01/01-31/12.
Distance: 2km on the spot.

Sangerhausen 10D3

P7, An der Probstmühle. **GPS**: n51,47707 e11,30798.

20 free. **Surface:** unpaved. 01/01-31/12.
Distance: 500m 200m 100m.

Sangerhausen 10D3

Rosarium, Sotterhäuser Weg. **GPS**: n51,47245 e11,31798.
€2 Ch. 15/04-15/10.
Remarks: Check in at shop.

Schierke 10C2

Campingplatz Am Schierker Stern, Hagenstrasse.
GPS: n51,75696 e10,68398.

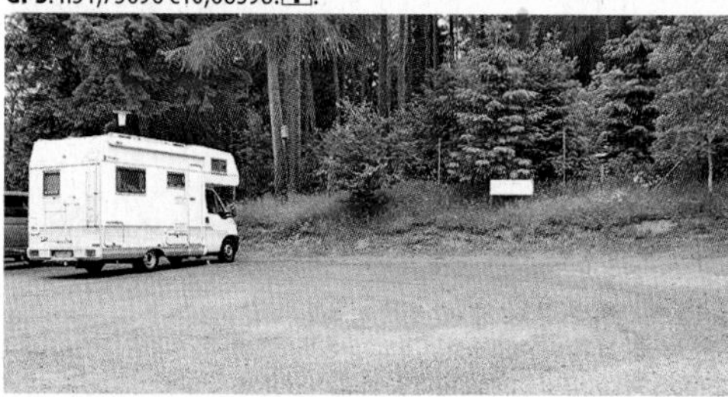

6 € 10 excl. tourist tax Chincluded (6x)against payment.
Location: Rural, simple, quiet. **Surface:** gravel/metalled.
01/01-31/12.
Distance: 1km on the spot on the spot on the spot on the spot on the spot.

Seehausen 8D3

Stellplatz Seehausen, Schulstrasse 6. **GPS**: n52,89068 e11,75119.

12 €5 €2 Ch (3x)€2.
Surface: metalled. 01/01-31/12.
Distance: 100m 200m.
Remarks: Check in at tourist office.

Stassfurt 10D2

Neumarkt, Lehrter Straße. **GPS**: n51,85424 e11,58284.

6 free. **Location:** Urban, simple, central, quiet. **Surface:** gravel.
01/01-31/12.
Distance: 500m 100m.

Remarks: Along the Bode river.

Stendal 10D1

Nordwall-Schützenplatz. **GPS**: n52,61116 e11,86121.

20 free €1/80liter €1 Ch.
Surface: grassy/metalled. 01/01-31/12.
Distance: on the spot bakery 50m.

Stolberg/Harz 10C3

Am Bahnhof. **GPS**: n51,56727 e10,95696.

5 free. **Location:** Rural, simple, quiet. **Surface:** asphalted.
01/01-31/12.
Distance: centre 800m.
Remarks: Max. 2 days.

Stolberg/Harz 10C3

Am Rittertor, Rittergasse. **GPS**: n51,57655 e10,94539.

5 free. **Location:** Rural, simple, quiet. **Surface:** asphalted.
01/01-31/12.
Distance: 1km.
Remarks: Max. 2 days.

Stolberg/Harz 10C3

Freizeitbad Thyragrotte, Thyratal 5. **GPS**: n51,56378 e10,95796.

3 free. **Location:** Rural, simple. **Surface:** asphalted.
01/01-31/12.
Distance: city centre 1km 1km on the spot.

Tangermünde 10E1

Tangerplatz, Klosterberg. **GPS**: n52,53774 e11,96803.

30 €5 Ch included. **Surface:** metalled. 01/01-31/12.
Distance: 700m 150m.

DE

S Wahrenberg 8D3

Stellplatz Storchenwiese, Eichenwinkel 34.
GPS: n52,98342 e11,67362.

8 €5 €1/100liter Ch€2 (6x)€3. **Surface:** grassy.
01/01-31/12.

S Weissenfels 10E3

Caravan- und Freizeitmarkt Gerth, Drei Wege.
GPS: n51,19822 e11,99875.

7 free €1/80liter Ch (4x)€1/stay. **Location:** Urban, simple, noisy. **Surface:** asphalted. 01/01-31/12.
Distance: 4km on the spot on the spot.

S Wernigerode 10C2

Am Katzenteich. GPS: n51,83882 e10,78168.

20 € 5/stay €1/40liter Ch (20x)€1/kWh WC€0,50.
Location: Comfortable, quiet. **Surface:** metalled. 01/01-31/12.
Distance: 500m 200m 500m on the spot on the spot on the spot.

S Wernigerode 10C2

Schlossparkplatz am Anger, Halberstädler strasse 1.
GPS: n51,83807 e10,79535.

24 €5, overnight stay free €2 ChWC€0,50.
Location: Urban, simple, central, quiet. **Surface:** metalled.
01/01-31/12, service 9-18h.
Distance: 300m 200m 600m on the spot on the spot.

S Wernigerode 10C2

Harzpension Familie Mann, Mühlental 76, B244.
GPS: n51,81902 e10,81430.

6 € 10 excl. tourist tax €0,50 Chincluded €0,50/kWh WC €0,50. **Location:** Rural, simple, quiet. **Surface:** gravel.

01/04-10/11.
Distance: 4km on the spot.
Remarks: Arrival <21h, check in at restaurant.

S Wörlitz 10E2

Seeparke, Seespitze, K2376. **GPS**: n51,84899 e12,41296.

24 €5 day/€5 night free (24x)€2 WC€0,50 €0,50.
Location: Rural, comfortable, quiet. **Surface:** metalled.
01/01-31/12.
Distance: 800m 500m 800m 800m on the spot on the spot.
Remarks: Parking at the edge the Wörlitzer park, max. 24h, caution key sanitary € 15.

Wörlitz 10E2

Hotel Coswiger Elbterrasse, Elbterrasse 1.
GPS: n51,87750 e12,45097.

10 €5, guests free. **Location:** Simple, quiet. **Surface:** grassy.
01/01-31/12.
Distance: 1,5km on the spot 4km.
Remarks: Check in at hotel, guests free.

S Zeitz 12E1

Obsthof Martin, Kloster Posa 1. **GPS**: n51,05836 e12,15797.

20 €5 Ch (4x)€3/day. **Location:** Rural, comfortable, quiet. **Surface:** grassy. 01/01-31/12.
Distance: 1,5km 200m 1km.

Brandenburg/Berlin

S Abbendorf 8D3

Gasthaus Dörpkrog an Diek, Am Deich 7.
GPS: n52,89663 e11,90975.

6 €5 Ch WCincluded. 01/01-31/12.
Distance: on the spot.
Remarks: Bread-service.

S Alt-Zeschdorf 10H1

Reiterhof Blumrich, Falkenhagerweg 11.
GPS: n52,42649 e14,42328.

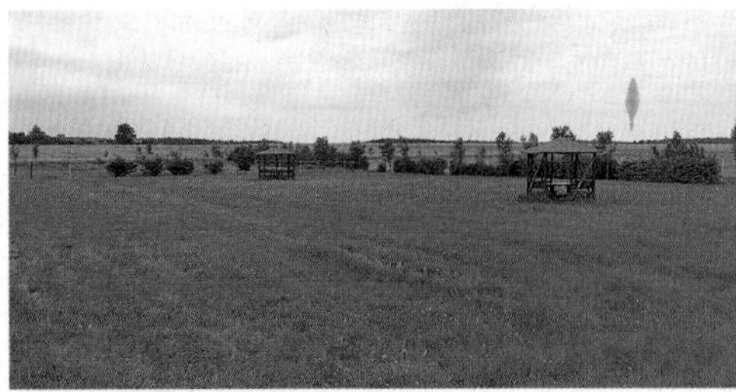

30 € 10 Ch included. **Surface:** grassy.
01/01-31/12 winter Mo.
Distance: 1,5km.
Remarks: At manege, bread-service.

S Altdöbern 10H2

Q1 Rasthof Altdöbern, Senftenberger strasse 11.
GPS: n51,64523 e14,03544.

20 € 10 WCincluded.
Surface: metalled. 01/01-31/12.
Distance: 500m on the spot 500m.

S Angermünde 8G2

Parkplatz Am Oberwall, Oberwall 5. **GPS**: n53,01501 e14,00371.

5 free €1/100liter €1/2kWh. **Location:** Urban, simple, central.
Surface: metalled. 01/04-31/10.
Distance: on the spot on the spot on the spot Historische Stadtkerne Märkischer Landweg.
Remarks: Near city wall.

Angermünde 8G2

NABU-Erlebniszentrum Blumberger Mühle, Blumberger Mühle 2.
GPS: n53,03572 e13,96806.

10 free. **Location:** Rural, simple, isolated, quiet.
Surface: grassy/metalled. 01/01-31/12.
Distance: 4km near fish pond on the spot on the spot on the spot.
Remarks: At biosphere reserve.

Bad Saarow 10G1

Parkplatz Strolin, Silberbergerstrasse. **GPS**: n52,28726 e14,03895.

4 free. **Surface:** metalled. 01/01-31/12.
Distance: 100m 100m.

DE

Bad Saarow 10G1

Saarow-Therme, Ringstrasse. **GPS:** n52,29399 e14,06243.

6 free. **Surface:** metalled. 01/01-31/12.
Distance: on the spot 300m 400m.

Bad Wilsnack 8E3

Kur- und Gradier-Therme Bad Wilsnack, Am Kähling.
GPS: n52,96316 e11,95007.

43 € 13,50 + € 1/pp tourist tax Ch (43x) WC included.
Surface: sand. 01/01-31/12.
Distance: 500m 200m 500m.
Remarks: Check in at pay-desk of the Therme, bread-service.

Berlin 10F1

Historisches Fährhaus Berlin, Muggelbergallee 1, Berlin-Köpenick.
GPS: n52,41851 e13,58734.

15 € 19-23 incl. 2 pers, dog € 3 Ch (15x) €5/24h WC included €1/5minutes €5/stay. **Location:** Urban, luxurious, quiet.
Surface: grassy/gravel. 01/01-31/12.
Distance: on the spot 8km on the spot on the spot on the spot 100m, supermarket 750m 1km tram 100m.
Remarks: Possibility for reservation, sauna € 5.

Berlin 10F1

WohnmobilPark Berlin, Waidmannsluster Damm 12-14.
GPS: n52,59559 e13,28910.

90 € 10-22, 2 pers.incl, tourist tax € 1/pp, dog € 2 €1/100liter Ch €3,50/24h WC €1, €4/4 .
Location: Urban, central. **Surface:** grassy/metalled.
01/01-31/12.
Distance: centre Berlin 16km 600m on the spot on the spot metro 1km.
Remarks: Key sanitary building € 4/day, hotline-Nr.: 0176 – 99 55 25 00.

Berlin 10F1

Reisemobilhafen Berlin Spandau, Askanierring 70.
GPS: n52,55309 e13,20050.

180 € 15, 2 pers.incl, tourist tax € 1/pp €0,10/10liter Ch WC included €1/5minutes €2/24h.
Location: Urban, simple, central, noisy. **Surface:** grassy/gravel.
01/01-31/12.
Distance: on the spot 100m on the spot 300m.
Remarks: Near approach route of airport, 23-5h quiet, check in at kosk, outside environmental zone. In area of the former English barracks 'Alexander Barracks', A10 exit Berlin-Spandau, follow road till cross roads Heerstraße/Gatowerstraße,here to the left, at Flakenseerplatz straight on, Neuendorferstraße, before Hohenzollernring to the left.

Berlin 10F1

Köpenicker Hof, Stellingdamm 15, Berlin-Köpenick.
GPS: n52,45929 e13,58532.

40 € 12-20 incl. 2 pers, dog € 3 Ch €0,50/kWh WC included . **Location:** Simple, quiet.
Surface: grassy/metalled. 01/01-31/12.
Distance: on the spot on the spot Tram (centre 300m).
Remarks: Caution key sanitary building € 20, bread-service, dog € 1,50/night.

Berlin 10F1

Marina Lanke Berlin, Scharfe Lanke 109-131.
GPS: n52,50344 e13,18801.

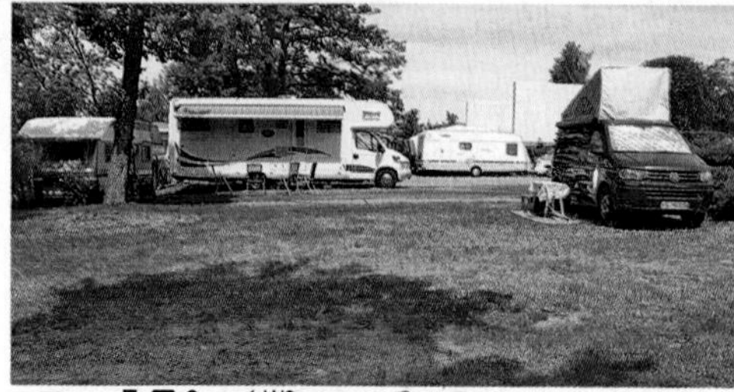

20 € 1,50/m + € 3,50/pp, dog €2 Ch WC included €3/2 . **Location:** Urban. **Surface:** asphalted.
01/05-15/10.
Distance: centre Berlin 16km on the spot on the spot 1km.
Remarks: Check in at harbourmaster.

Berlin 10F1

Marina Wendenschloss, Wendenschlossstrasse 350-354.
GPS: n52,42558 e13,58384.

10 € 15 Ch WC included €1.
Location: Simple, quiet. **Surface:** grassy/metalled.
01/04-31/10.
Distance: 18km city centre on the spot 100m Tram 200m.
Remarks: Outside environmental zone.

Tourist information Berlin:

Berlin Card gives for free entrance on public transport and museums and many discounts on purchases.
from € 42.

Tourist Info, Europacenter, Eingang Budapester strasse 3; Brandenburgertor, Südflügel; Fernsehturm, Alexanderplatz, http://www.visitberlin.de/. Documentation available, via Internet.

Haus am Checkpoint Charly, Friedrichstrasse 44. At the former border crossing. History of the Wall is told with photographs. 9-22h.

Zeughaus. German historical museum.

Alexanderplatz. The old historical centre of Berlin.

Brandenburger Tor. Built in 1791 as a triumphal arch after the construction of the Berlin Wall the arch remained as a symbol of the German separation. free.

Schloß Charlottenburg, Spandauer Damm 10-22. Summer residence of the Prussian kings. Tue-Su 10-18h 01/11-31/03. € 10.

Arkonaplatz. Flea market. Su 10-16h.

Ostbahnhof. Antiques and flea market. Su 9-17h.

Strasse des 17. Juni. Arts and fleamarket. Sa-Su 10-17h.

Zoologischer Garten, Hardenbergplatz 8. City-zoo. 01/04-30/09 9-18.30h, 01/10-31/10 9-18h, 01/11-28/02 9-17h.

Brandenburg 10E1

Am Brandenburger Dom, Grillendamm.
GPS: n52,41724 e12,56576.

60 € 10 €1/100liter Ch (26x) €1/kWh WC €1/4minutes.
Location: Urban, simple, noisy. **Surface:** asphalted.
01/01-31/12.
Distance: Neustadt 15min, Altstadt 15min on the spot Imbiss on the spot on the spot on the spot.

Brandenburg 10E1

Wassersportzentrum Alte Feuerwache, Franz Zieglerstrasse 27.
GPS: n52,40485 e12,54868.

30 € 12 Ch €1/day WC €1 included.
Location: Urban, simple, central, noisy. **Surface:** grassy/metalled.
01/01-31/12.
Distance: 500m on the spot 500m on the spot on the spot on the spot.
Remarks: Bread-service, boat rental, bike and e-bike rental.

Brieske 10H3

Reimann, Brieske Dorf 27. **GPS:** n51,49203 e13,94743.

20 € 6 Ch (12x) €2 WC included.
Surface: grassy. 01/01-31/12.
Distance: 200m 9,3km 2km.

Burg/Spreewald 10H2

Hagens Insel - Wasserwanderrastplatz, Weidenweg 4.
GPS: n51,86138 e14,11527.

10 € 10 Ch WC included. **Surface:** grassy.

Burg/Spreewald 10H2

Landgasthof zur Wildbahn, Wildbahnweg 20.
GPS: n51,85104 e14,09384.

9 € 20, 2 pers. incl., dog € 2 WC included.
Surface: metalled. 01/03-30/10.

Dollenchen 10G2

Gasthaus Stuckatz, Hauptstrasse 29. **GPS:** n51,60745 e13,86226.

20 € 8 Ch WC included. **Surface:** grassy.
01/01-31/12.
Distance: on the spot on the spot 3km.

Dreetz 8E3

Reiterhof Müller, Schulstrasse 61. **GPS:** n52,79796 e12,46874.

10 € 14 Ch included WC. **Location:** Rural, simple, isolated, quiet. **Surface:** grassy. 01/01-31/12.
Distance: 800m 300m 500m 500m.

Fehrbellin 8F3

FF Freizeitmobile, Gewerbepark 29. **GPS:** n52,79770 e12,78624.

10 € 7,50 Ch included € 2,50/day free.
Location: Urban, simple, quiet.
Surface: grassy.
01/01-31/12.
Distance: 1km 2km 1km 1km on the spot on the spot.
Remarks: Accessory shop.

Fürstenberg/Havel 8F2

Marina Fürstenberg, Ravensbrücker Dorfstrasse 26.
GPS: n53,19489 e13,14895.

50 € 9 Ch included € 2,50/day WC € 1,50 free.
Location: Rural, comfortable, quiet. **Surface:** grassy.
01/01-31/12.
Distance: 1km on the spot on the spot on the spot 1km on the spot on the spot.
Remarks: Wifi code at harbour master, boat rental, near the former women's concentration camp Ravensbrück.

Höhenland 8G3

Das Forsthaus, Bahnhofstraße 13. **GPS:** n52,68433 e13,88171.

8 € 10,50 Ch WC included € 5/day.
Location: Rural, comfortable, quiet. **Surface:** grasstiles.
01/01-31/12.
Distance: 3km on the spot on the spot.
Remarks: Bread-service.

Kienitz 8H3

Ferienhaus Marth, Kienitzeroderstrasse 20.
GPS: n52,67616 e14,39890.

8 € 10 Ch € 1,50 WC € 1,50. **Surface:** grassy.
01/04-30/09.
Distance: 3km 3km.

Klein-Ossnig 10H2

Caravan-Krokor, Hauptstrasse 12/a, B169.
GPS: n51,69962 e14,27917.

15 € 7 Ch included.
Surface: grassy. 01/01-31/12.
Distance: on the spot 3km 50m 2km on the spot on the spot.
Remarks: Arrival only during opening hours: Mo-Fr 8-18, Sa 8-13h.

Kloster Lehnin 10F1

Hotel Seehof, Am See 51. **GPS:** n52,34924 e12,70374.

15 € 10, guests free € 2/day WC € 2.
Location: Rural, simple, comfortable. **Surface:** grassy.
01/01-31/12.
Distance: 1,8km on the spot on the spot on the spot on the spot.
Remarks: Check in at hotel.

Kolkwitz 10H2

Bauernhof Korreng, Papitzerstrasse 48. **GPS:** n51,76676 e14,22410.

3 € 10 Ch WC included.
Surface: grassy. 01/03-31/10.
Distance: 2,5km.

Kyritz 8E3

Parkplatz Wässering, Graf-von-der-Schulenburg-Straße.
GPS: n52,94044 e12,40053.

15 free € 1/100liter Ch € 1/8h WC € 0,50 € 1.
Location: Urban, comfortable, noisy. **Surface:** grasstiles.
01/01-31/12.
Distance: city centre 100m on the spot 250m 250m.

Lindow/Mark 8F3

Am Wutzsee. **GPS:** n52,97205 e12,98924.

3 free, tourist tax € 0,50/pp. **Location:** Urban, simple, noisy.
Surface: metalled. 01/01-31/12.
Distance: on the spot on the spot 150m 150m on the spot on the spot.
Remarks: Max. 1 night, pay at tourist office.

Lübbenau 10G2

Autocamping im Spreewald, Chausseestrasse 17a, Lübbenau-Zerkwitz.
GPS: n51,86559 e13,93324.

6 € 14/24h, tourist tax € 1,50/pp, dog € 1 € 1,50

DE

Ch WC included. **Surface:** grasstiles. Easter-31/10.
Distance: 2,5km 500m.

Lübbenau 10G2

Am Bahnhof, Bahnhofstraße (B115). **GPS**: n51,86139 e13,96361.

10 € 8 €1/80liter Ch €0,50/kWh.
Surface: asphalted. 01/01-31/12.
Distance: 800m 3,3km 350m 50m.
Remarks: Along railwayline, max. 2 days.

Lübbenau 10G2

Kahnfährhafen Leipe, Dorfstrasse 34, Leipe.
GPS: n51,85301 e14,05023.

4 € 5. **Surface:** metalled. 01/01-31/12.
Distance: 11,6km.

Luckenwalde 10F2

Waldidyll im Elsthal, Elsthal 6. **GPS**: n52,07511 e13,16908.
10 € 10 Ch WC included.
Surface: sand. 01/01-31/12.
Distance: on the spot.
Remarks: Max. <>2.35m.

Lychen 8F2

Marina-Yachthafen Lychensee, Schlüssstrasse 7.
GPS: n53,21187 e13,29686.

6 € 10 Ch €2,50/day WC €1. **Location:** Rural, simple, quiet. **Surface:** grassy. 15/04-15/10.
Distance: 700m 650m.
Remarks: Check in at harbourmaster, boat rental.

Nackel 8E3

Gaststätte Birkenhof, Segeletzerstrasse 2.
GPS: n52,82503 e12,56528.

3 € 3 €3 Ch included WC.
Location: Rural, simple, isolated, quiet. **Surface:** metalled.
01/01-31/12 Tue.
Distance: 5km on the spot on the spot on the spot.

Neuruppin 8F3

Sportcenter Neuruppin, Trenckmannstraße 14.
GPS: n52,91573 e12,80365.

30 € 6 WC €2,50 . **Location:** Urban, simple, quiet.
Surface: grasstiles. 01/01-31/12.
Distance: on the spot Neuruppiner See 500m on the spot 200m, bakery 400m on the spot on the spot.
Remarks: Check in at sport centre.

Oberkrämer 8F3

Bäckerei Plentz, Dorfstraße 43. **GPS**: n52,73643 e13,08540.

4 € 8 Ch WC included. **Location:** Rural, simple, quiet.
Surface: metalled. 01/01-31/12.
Distance: on the spot 1km 500m train 500m on the spot on the spot.
Remarks: Along railwayline, in front of bakery.

Oranienburg 8F3

Am Schlosshafen, Rungestrasse 47. **GPS**: n52,75760 e13,23879.

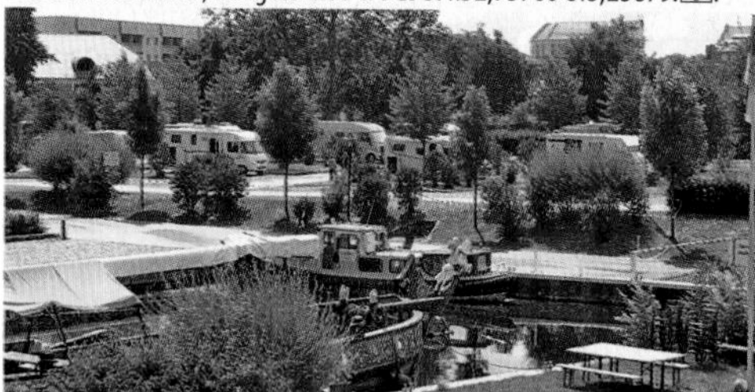

26 € 10 €1/80liter Ch (16x)€1/kWh WC €0,50 €1/5minutes €5.
Location: Rural, comfortable, central, quiet. **Surface:** metalled.
01/01-31/12.
Distance: 600m on the spot 600m 600m on the spot on the spot.
Remarks: Tallycard: service, electricity, sanitary building, caution € 10.

Oranienburg 8F3

Motel Havelidyll, Havelhausener Brücke 1, Havelhausen.
GPS: n52,72161 e13,25047.

10 € 15 Ch WC included. **Location:** Rural, simple, isolated, quiet. **Surface:** grassy. 01/04-15/11.
Distance: 10km 4km on the spot on the spot.

Potsdam 10F1

Am Krongut, Potsdamer Straße 196. **GPS**: n52,41332 e13,02905.

11 € 10/24h. **Location:** Urban, simple. **Surface:** concrete.
01/01-31/12.
Distance: city centre 2km 100m Tram 300m.

Potsdam 10F1

P historische Mühle, Zur Historischen Mühlen.
GPS: n52,40562 e13,03453.

5 € 2/h, max. € 20/24h. **Location:** Urban, simple.
Surface: metalled. 01/01-31/12.
Distance: 2km on the spot.

Tourist information Potsdam:
Filmpark Babelsberg, Großbeerenstrasse 200. Attractions park concerning the film. 23/03-31/10 10-18.

Rehfelde 8G3

Campershof, Alt Werder 8. **GPS**: n52,52093 e13,94080.

12 € 8,50 Ch included €1/day WC €2,50.
Location: Rural, comfortable, quiet. **Surface:** grassy.
01/01-31/12.
Distance: 2km 2km 2km on the spot on the spot.
Remarks: Bread-service.

Schmergow 10F1

Zum fröhlichen Landmann, Ziegeleiweg 17.
GPS: n52,45416 e12,80553.

30 € 7,50 Ch €1/2kWh included.
Location: Rural, simple, isolated. **Surface:** grassy. 01/04-31/10.
Distance: 500m on the spot 500m 400m.

Schwedt/Oder 8H2

Wassersportzentrum Schwedt, Wasserplatz 4.
GPS: n53,05759 e14,29861.

30 € 10 Ch WC included.
Surface: grassy. 01/01-31/12.
Distance: 1km on the spot on the spot 500m.
Remarks: Check in at harbourmaster or bar.

Senftenberg 10H3

Wohnmobilstellplatz Buchwalde, Buchwalder Straße 52.
GPS: n51,51256 e14,02278.
12 € 11-14 Ch included €2 WC €0,50. **Surface:** grasstiles.
01/04-01/11.
Distance: 2km Senftenberger See on the spot on the spot.
Remarks: Max. 4 nights, caution key sanitary € 20.

DE

Stolzenhagen 8G3

Am Kietz, Kietz 9. **GPS**: n52,94916 e14,10833.

20 € 7,50 Ch (10x)€ 2,50/day WC included € 2,50/pp.
Location: Rural, comfortable, quiet. **Surface:** grassy/metalled.
01/01-31/12.
Distance: on the spot Imbiss Oder-Neiße-Radweg on the spot.
Remarks: Directly on the canal, check in at Imbiss, bread-service.

Storkow/Mark 10G1

An der Schleuse, Kirchstrasse. **GPS**: n52,25792 e13,93178.
5 € 10 included. **Surface:** grasstiles. 01/01-31/12.
Distance: 200m 300m 500m.
Remarks: At the Storkower Canal, max. 36h.

Templin 8F2

Alter Knehdenerstrasse. **GPS**: n53,12359 e13,49423.

40 free € 1/60liter Ch. **Location:** Urban, simple, quiet.
Surface: asphalted/metalled. 01/01-31/12.
Distance: 300m 300m 300m on the spot on the spot.

Tiefensee 8G3

Reisemobilplatz, Country Camping Tiefensee, Schmiedeweg 1.
GPS: n52,68302 e13,84292.

64 € 16,50 incl. 2 pers, dog € 1,50 Ch (51x) WC included € 0,50 € 2,50 . **Location:** Rural, comfortable, quiet.
Surface: grassy. 01/01-31/12.
Distance: on the spot on the spot on the spot on the spot on the spot on the spot on the spot on the spot.
Remarks: Check in at reception campsite.

Weisen 8D3

Wohnmobilstellplatz Am Biotop, Heinrich-Heine-Strasse 4.
GPS: n53,02062 e11,78086.

8 € 5 Ch included. **Surface:** gravel. 01/01-31/12.
Distance: 300m 200m 300m.

Werder/Havel 10F1

An der Föhse. **GPS**: n52,37807 e12,93704.

25 € 7 + € 1,50/pp tourist tax € 0,50/80liter Ch (8x)€ 0,50/kWh,(8x)€ 0,50/kWh WC € 0,50. **Location:** Urban, simple.
Surface: gravel. 01/01-31/12.
Distance: on the spot on the spot on the spot on the spot 100m on the spot.
Remarks: Check in at harbourmaster.

Wusterhausen/Dosse 8E3

Dossehalle, Zur Dossehalle 6. **GPS**: n52,89337 e12,46537.

3 free € 1/25liter Ch € 1/8h. **Location:** Urban, simple, quiet. **Surface:** asphalted. 01/01-31/12.
Distance: centre 500m 450m.

Saxony

Adorf 12E2

Waldbad, Waldbadstrasse 5. **GPS**: n50,30778 e12,25056.

3 free. **Surface:** metalled. 01/03-30/11.
Distance: 1km 500m.
Remarks: Max. 24h.

Tourist information Adorf:
TouristInfo, Freiberger Str. 8.

Bad Düben 10F3

Im Kurgebiet, Parkstraße 1. **GPS**: n51,60139 e12,58247.

4 free, tourist tax € 1,20-1,50/pp € 1/80liter € 1 Ch € 1 WC.
Location: Rural, simple, isolated. **Surface:** metalled.
01/01-31/12.
Distance: 750m 1,4km 1,4km.

Bad Elster 12E2

Albertbad, Austus-Klingner Straße. **GPS**: n50,28545 e12,24034.
5 € 8 + € 2,20/pp tourist tax € 1/100liter included.
Surface: asphalted. 01/01-31/12.
Distance: 1km 250m.
Remarks: Check in at pay desk swimming pool, caution € 20.

Bad Lausick 12F1

Freizetbad Am Riff, Am Riff 3. **GPS**: n51,14321 e12,65383.

10 free. **Location:** Rural, simple, central, quiet. **Surface:** grasstiles.
01/01-31/12.
Distance: 100m 100m on the spot on the spot.
Remarks: At swimming pool.

Bad Muskau 37A1

Am Fürst-Pückler-Park, Bautzener Straße 39.
GPS: n51,53382 e14,71838.

25 € 8, € 12 service incl. + € 1,25/pp tourist tax Ch (25x) WC . **Location:** Urban, comfortable, central, quiet.
Surface: grasstiles/metalled. 01/01-28/12.
Distance: 400m 4km 2km on the spot on the spot.

Bautzen 10H3

Schliebenstraße. **GPS**: n51,18168 e14,41482.

4 free € 1 € 1 (4x)€ 0,50/kWh.
Surface: metalled. 01/01-31/12.
Distance: 1,2km 1km.
Remarks: Max. 2 nights.

Breitenbrunn 12F2

Sportpark Rabenberg, Rabenbergweg. **GPS**: n50,45556 e12,74417.

15 € 8,50 + € 8,50/pp Ch included € 2/day WC € 1.
Surface: metalled. 01/01-31/12.
Distance: 5km 5km 5km.
Remarks: Arrival <22h, dog € 2/day.

Dennheritz 12F1

Caravan Service Bressler, Zwickauerstrasse 78.
GPS: n50,80889 e12,48667.

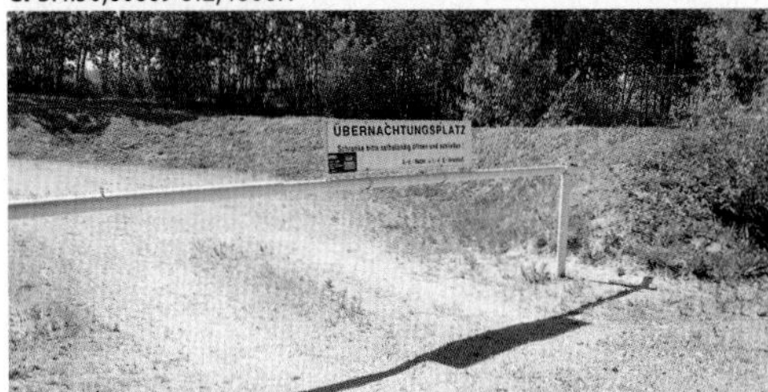

6 € 4/night € 1 Ch € 2. **Surface:** metalled. 01/01-31/12.
Distance: 2,1km.

DE

Diera-Zehren 10G3

Zum Zuessenhaus, Elbstraße 10. **GPS**: n51,19500 e13,41917.

10 € 5. **Location:** Rural, simple. **Surface:** grassy/metalled.
01/01-31/12.

Diesbar-Seusslitz 10G3

Parkplatz Am Schloss, An der Weinstraße.
GPS: n51,24111 e13,41575.

6 € 4 (9-19h), overnight stay free (6x)€ 1/6h.
Location: Rural, simple, quiet. **Surface:** metalled.
01/01-31/12.
Distance: 100m 200m on the spot on the spot.

Dresden 12G1

Parkplatz Grosse Meissner, Wiesentor Strasse.
GPS: n51,05639 e13,74306.

60 € 18/24h €2/100liter Ch€2 (14x)€5/day WC.
Location: Urban, simple, central. **Surface:** asphalted.
01/01-31/12.
Distance: 100m on the spot on the spot on the spot.

Dresden 12G1

Sachsenplatz Dresden, Käthe-Kollwitz-Ufer 4.
GPS: n51,05700 e13,75990.
150 € 10 (25x)€5/24h. **Location:** Urban, central.
01/01-31/12.
Distance: Old city centre 2,2km 300m Aldi 700m 500m.

Dresden 12G1

Werner Knopf, B6, Meissner Landstrasse.
GPS: n51,08131 e13,65563.

7 € 5/6m + € 1/m €2 (8x)€2/night €1,50.
Location: Urban, simple, quiet. **Surface:** grasstiles.
01/03-30/10.
Distance: 6km 500m on the spot.
Remarks: Gate closes at 22h.

Dresden 12G1

Wohnmobilstellplatz am Blüherpark, Zinzendorfstraße 7.
GPS: n51,04426 e13,74371.

50 € 14 €1 €1 €3/night,16Amp €2/day.
Location: Urban, comfortable, central. **Surface:** grassy/metalled.
01/01-31/12.
Distance: 1km 5km 500m 450m.
Remarks: Check in at Cityherberge, Lingnerallee 3, 24/24.

Dresden 12G1

Wohnmobilstellplatz Dresden, Kesselsdorfer Straße 153.
GPS: n51,03988 e13,66949.

5 € 12 Ch (5x)€2,50/night €2/pppd.
Location: Urban, comfortable, central. **Surface:** gravel/metalled.
01/01-31/12.
Distance: centre Dresden 4km 4km on the spot 200m 800m.
Remarks: At Wellnesshotel Landlust.

Dresden 12G1

CaravaningPark Schaffer, Kötzschenbroderstrasse 125.
GPS: n51,08639 e13,68222.

100 € 15 €0,50/60liter €0,50 Ch€0,50 €0,50/kWh WC €0,50.
Location: Urban, comfortable.
Surface: grassy.
01/01-31/12.
Distance: Dresden 5km 2km 200m 500m 200m 500m.
Remarks: Bread-service, repair possibilities motorhome, access <19h.

Tourist information Dresden:
Dresden-City-Card. Card gives among other things for free public transport, entrance to many museums, discounts on boat trips, restaurants etc.
01/01-31/12. € 35/48h.
Tourist Information, Prager strasse; Schinkelwache/Theaterplatz, www.dresden.de. Former residence city with many curiosities.
Striezelmarkt, Altstadt. Christmas fair. advent season.

Ebersbach/Sachsen 37A1

Fest- und Parkplatz am Freibad, Kottmarsdorfer Strasse 1.
GPS: n51,00972 e14,59806.

7 € 5, € 10 service incl Ch WC. **Location:** Rural, simple, isolated, quiet. **Surface:** metalled. 01/01-31/12.
Distance: 1km 500m 1km on the spot.

Elsterheide 10H3

Wohnmobilstellplatz Lothar Meusel, Am Hochwald 27, Tätzschwitz.
GPS: n51,48304 e14,10750.

14 € 8,50 €1 Ch included WC€2,50/day . **Location:** Rural, comfortable, isolated, quiet.
Surface: grasstiles/grassy. Easter-31/10.
Distance: 3km 8-10km on the spot.

Freiberg 12G1

Am Johannisbad, Lessingstraße. **GPS**: n50,91461 e13,33368.

10 first night € 10, € 7,50 second night €1/80liter €1 Ch€1 (10x)€0,50/kWh WC.
Location: Urban, simple, central, quiet. **Surface:** metalled.
01/01-31/12.
Distance: Altstadt 900m 150m Kaufland 500m on the spot.

Geierswalde 10H3

Ferien- und Freizeitpark Geierswalde See, Promenadeweg 1-3.
GPS: n51,49372 e14,13481.

100+ € 6 €2/day Ch €3 WC. **Location:** Rural, simple, isolated, quiet. **Surface:** grassy. 01/01-31/12.
Distance: 500m Geierswaldesee 300m 1km 5km on the spot.

Großenhain 10G3

Carl-Maria-von-Weber-Allee. **GPS**: n51,29032 e13,53584.
5 € 5, 15/09-15/05 free €1/70liter €1 €1/4h.
Surface: metalled. 01/01-31/12.
Distance: 500m 100m.
Remarks: To pay at swimming pool.

Grünhain 12F2

Freizeitpark, Auer Strasse 82, Haus des Gastes, Grünhain-Beierfeld.
GPS: n50,58139 e12,79167.

6 € 10 €1 €1,customers free Ch €1,50/day WC €1.
Surface: metalled. 01/01-31/12.
Distance: 1km on the spot 3km.

Hermsdorf 12G1

Ski- & Sporthotel SWF, Bahnhofstraße 7.
GPS: n50,73241 e13,66400.

DE

8 € 5, tourist tax € 0,50/pp €2 €2 Ch €0,50/kWh.
Location: Rural, simple, isolated, quiet. **Surface:** gravel/metalled.
01/01-31/12.
Distance: on the spot on the spot on the spot on the spot.

S Königsfeld-Stollsdorf 12F1

Spreer's Ferienhaus, Hauptstrasse 28. **GPS**: n51,04861 e12,74500.

4 € 8 Ch €2. 01/01-31/12.
Distance: 4km 4km.

S Königstein 12H1

Panoramhotel Lilienstein, Ebenheit 7. **GPS**: n50,92505 e14,07546.

10 € 22 included €5. **Location:** Rural, simple, isolated, quiet. **Surface:** grassy/gravel. Easter-15/11.
Distance: on the spot on the spot.
Remarks: Bread-service and breakfast buffet.

S Leipzig 10E3

Reisemobilhafen Leipzig „Parc Fermé", Im Dölitzer Holz 20.
GPS: n51,28525 e12,38352.

30 € 11,50 €1 Ch (12x)€3,50/day free.
Location: Rural, comfortable, quiet. **Surface:** gravel/metalled.
01/01-31/12.
Distance: 5,5km 2,5km 100m Tram 850m.
Remarks: Can be reached without environmental: from the direction Goethesteig.

S Leipzig 10E3

Stellplatz Melinenburg, Stöhrerstraße 3.
GPS: n51,36648 e12,42717.

20 € 10, 2 pers.incl, extra pers € 1, dog € 1 €1 €1 Ch€1 (8x)€2/day. **Location:** Urban, comfortable, central, quiet.
Surface: concrete. 01/01-31/12.

Distance: 4,5km 1,2km 200m.
Remarks: Bread-service, outside environmental zone.

Löbau 37A1

Am Löbauer Berg, Beethovenstraße. **GPS**: n51,09508 e14,68088.

3 free (3x)against paymentkWh. **Location:** Rural, simple, isolated, quiet. **Surface:** grasstiles/metalled. 01/01-31/12.
Distance: 1km.

S Lohsa 10H3

Dreiweibern See, Am strand Weißkollm 1.
GPS: n51,40782 e14,40008.

14 € 10 €1/80liter Ch (14x)WCincluded.
Location: Rural, comfortable, isolated, quiet.
Surface: grasstiles/grassy. 01/01-31/12.
Distance: 1,5km on the spot Imbiss on the spot.

S Marienberg 12G2

Ratsseite-Wiesenweg, Pobershau. **GPS**: n50,63250 e13,20896.
10 € 3 + € 1/pp tourist tax €1 €1. 01/04-31/10.
Distance: Marienberg 5km 200m.

S Marienberg 12G2

Tourismuszentrum Rätzteich, Gelobtland 27c.
GPS: n50,62417 e13,17861.

4 € 3 €1 €1 Ch€1 €1.
Surface: metalled. 01/01-31/12.
Distance: 5km on the spot 500m 5km on the spot on the spot 3km on the spot.
Remarks: Recreation area.

S Marienberg 12G2

Drei Brüder Höhe. **GPS**: n50,65660 e13,12437.
10 € 6/pp WC included. **Location:** Isolated.
01/04-31/10.
Distance: on the spot.

S Meissen 10G3

Wellenspiel, Berghausstraße 2. **GPS**: n51,17444 e13,49861.
19 € 5 €2/day. **Location:** Rural, simple, quiet.
Surface: grassy/metalled. 01/01-31/12.
Distance: 900m.
Remarks: At swimming pool, caution key € 20.

Meissen 10G3

An der Elbe, Hochuferstraße. **GPS**: n51,16806 e13,47361.

20 € 5. **Location:** Urban, simple, central. **Surface:** metalled.
01/01-31/12.
Distance: 800m on the spot 800m 300m on the spot.

S Oberwiesenthal 12F2

OTG Tennishalle, Vieren Strasse 1a. **GPS**: n50,42722 e12,96944.

20 € 18, 01/11-31/03 € 25, tourist tax excl Ch WCincluded €1. **Surface:** metalled.
01/01-31/12.
Distance: on the spot 250m.
Remarks: Check in at reception tennishall < 22h, bread-service.

Oderwitz 37A1

Rodelpark Oberoderwitz, Spitzbergstraße 4a.
GPS: n50,96528 e14,70111.

5 free. **Location:** Rural, simple, isolated, quiet.
Surface: gravel/metalled. 01/01-31/12.
Distance: 600m on the spot.

S Pirna 12H1

Schloßpark Pirna, Schloßpark 13a. **GPS**: n50,95998 e13,95232.

8 € 12 Chincluded €1/kWh.
Location: Quiet. **Surface:** metalled. 01/01-31/12.
Distance: 2,5km 500m.

Pirna 12H1

Elbeparkplatz, Hauptplatz 14. **GPS**: n50,96654 e13,93775.

15 free. **Surface:** asphalted. 01/01-31/12.
Distance: 650m on the spot 350m on the spot.
Remarks: Along the river Elbe, max. 24h.

S Seiffen 12G1

Berghof, Kurhausstrasse 36. **GPS**: n50,64605 e13,48114.

20 guests free . 01/01-31/12.

DE

Distance: 2,5km on the spot 300m.

S Struppen 12H1

Camping-Stellplatz Struppen, Kirchberg 20.
GPS: n50,93814 e14,01307.

30 € 10, 25/03-05/11 € 13 + € 0,75/pp tourist tax €1/100liter Ch (30x)€0,60/kWh €1 €3/3. **Location:** Luxurious. **Surface:** grassy/metalled. 01/01-31/12.
Distance: 500m 500m.

Weißwasser 10H2

Am Tierpark, Teichstraße 56. **GPS:** n51,51205 e14,63665.

10 free. **Location:** Urban, simple, central. **Surface:** metalled. 01/01-31/12.
Distance: 500m on the spot 500m 500m on the spot.

S Wermsdorf 10F3

Zum Goldnen Hirsch, Hirschplatz 2. **GPS:** n51,28300 e12,94065.

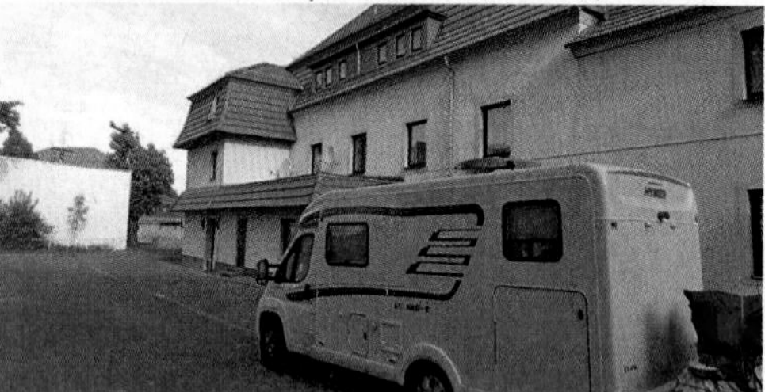

4 € 5 €1 (4x) WC. **Location:** Urban, simple. **Surface:** metalled. 01/01-31/12.
Distance: on the spot on the spot on the spot.

S Zittau 37A1

Zittau Am Dreiländereck, Brückenstrasse 23.
GPS: n50,89457 e14,82143.

100 € 7 €1/10minutes Ch (32x)€1/6h WC.
Location: Urban, comfortable, central, quiet. **Surface:** grassy. 01/01-31/12.
Distance: 1,5km 200m 100m on the spot.
Remarks: Three Countries' Corner Germany-Czech Republic-Poland.

S Zwota 12F2

Natur Camping Platz, Merkneukirchner Strasse 79.
GPS: n50,35111 e12,38111.

40 € 10 €1,50 €1 Ch (16x) WC included. **Surface:** gravel. 01/01-31/12.
Distance: Klingenthal 6km 6km.

North Rhine Westphalia

S Aachen 11E2

Aachen-Camping, Branderhofer Weg 11.
GPS: n50,76111 e6,10306.

46 € 15 Ch WC included €1. **Location:** Urban, luxurious, central, quiet. **Surface:** metalled. 01/01-31/12.
Distance: 1,7km 700m 700m 300m.
Remarks: Baker 8.30-09.00.

S Ahaus 9F2

Am Aquahaus, Vredener Dyk. **GPS:** n52,07778 e6,98361.

8 €0,50/40liter Ch (8x)€0,50/kWh,16Amp WC.
Location: Rural, simple, isolated. **Surface:** metalled. 01/01-31/12.
Distance: 2km 1,5km on the spot.
Remarks: Max. 3 days.

S Ahaus 9F2

Kirmesplatz, Schlossstrasse. **GPS:** n52,07450 e7,00299.

8 free €0,50/80liter Ch (6x)€0,50,16Amp WC.
Location: Rural, simple, isolated. **Surface:** metalled. 01/01-31/12 during event.
Distance: on the spot 600m 600m.
Remarks: Parking centre, max. 3 nights.

S Ahlen 9G3

Parkbad Ahlen, Dolbergerstrasse 66. **GPS:** n51,75559 e7,89694.

4 € 8/24h Ch included. **Location:** Rural, comfortable, quiet. **Surface:** metalled. 01/01-31/12.
Distance: centre 300m 100m 300m on the spot on the spot.
Remarks: Max. 3 nights, caution key service € 10, 50% discount at swimming pool.

S Alpen 9E3

An der Motte, Burgstrasse 66. **GPS:** n51,57985 e6,51846.

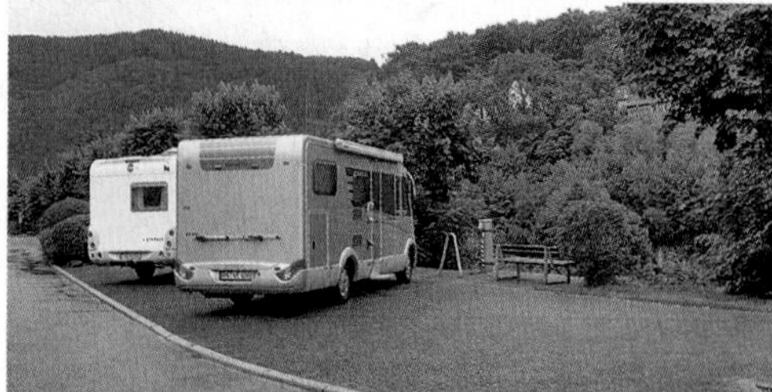

11 € 7,50 Ch included.
Location: Rural, comfortable. **Surface:** gravel. 01/01-31/12.
Distance: 500m 2,5km 700m 500m.
Remarks: At tennis-courts.

S Altena 11G1

Sauerlandhalle Pragpaul, Hermann Vossstrasse 14.
GPS: n51,30861 e7,66056.

8 free €1 €1 Ch (6x)€1/kWh. **Location:** Rural, simple, quiet. **Surface:** asphalted/gravel. 01/01-31/12.
Distance: 2km 10km nearby 2km on the spot on the spot.

S Altenbeken 10A3

Landhaus Friedenstal, Hüttenstrasse 42. **GPS:** n51,75992 e8,95111.

5 € 5 (5x)€2,50/24h WC on demand, at restaurant.
Location: Simple, central. **Surface:** grassy/gravel. 01/01-31/12.
Distance: 200m on the spot 200m.

S Altenberge 9G2

Sportpark Grosseberg, Sportzentrum. **GPS:** n52,05528 e7,47056.

15 free €0,50/60liter Ch. **Location:** Rural, isolated, quiet. **Surface:** metalled. 01/01-31/12 water disconnected in winter.
Distance: 1,6km nearby 1,5km.
Remarks: Parking sports centre.

Arnsberg 9H3

An der Schlacht. **GPS:** n51,40174 e8,06574.
4 free. **Location:** Simple. **Surface:** gravel.
Distance: 3,3km Lidl 50m.

Arnsberg 9H3

Wohnmobilstandort Neheim Jahnallee, Jahnallee 38, Neheim.
GPS: n51,44855 e7,95105.
free.
Distance: city centre 1km on the spot 3km.

Ascheberg 9G3

Appelhof, Appelhofstraße. **GPS:** n51,79003 e7,61902.

DE

4 free. **Location:** Rural, simple, central, quiet. **Surface:** metalled.
01/01-31/12.
Distance: on the spot on the spot on the spot.

Ascheberg 9G3

Gasthaus Eickholt, Frieport 22, Davensberg. **GPS:** n51,82619 e7,59391.

6 € 5, free with a meal €3/24h WC free.
Location: Simple. **Surface:** grassy. 01/01-31/12 Mo.
Distance: 800m 1km on the spot 1km 800m on the spot.
Remarks: Swingolf.

Attendorn 11G1

Atta Höhle, Finnentroper Straße 39. **GPS:** n51,12489 e7,91421.
8 € 7,50 Ch included.
Surface: metalled. 01/01-31/12.
Distance: 500m Lidl 400m.

Bad Berleburg 11H1

Bismarckstraße. **GPS:** n51,04986 e8,39406.
3 free €2/80liter Ch €1/6h. **Surface:** metalled.
01/01-31/12.
Distance: 500m 500m.

Bad Berleburg 11H1

Hotel-Restaurant Erholung - Laibach, Auf dem Laibach 1.
GPS: n51,06776 e8,44527.

5 free with a meal (1x)€5/day WC.
Surface: asphalted. 01/01-31/12.
Distance: 5km on the spot 5km on the spot on the spot on the spot 1,5km.

Bad Berleburg 11H1

Pension-Bauernladen Schmelzhütte, K52 Hoheleye.
GPS: n51,13874 e8,45742.

6 € 10 Ch €2.
Surface: asphalted. 01/01-31/12 Mo.
Distance: 1km on the spot 1km.
Remarks: Bread-service.

Bad Driburg 10A3

P Driburg Therme, Georg-Nave-Strasse 24.
GPS: n51,74194 e9,02542.

10 € 5 + tourist tax (10x)€3/24h WC.
Location: Rural, simple, quiet. **Surface:** asphalted.
01/01-31/12.
Distance: 1km on the spot 1km on the spot on the spot on the spot.
Remarks: Max. 7m, caution € 10, key electricity at pay-desk.

Bad Laasphe 11H1

Mühlenstrasse. **GPS:** n50,92412 e8,41146.

7 € 9/24h €0,50/80liter Ch (6x)€0,50/kWh.
Surface: asphalted. 01/01-31/12.
Distance: 500m 500m 500m.
Remarks: Parking at town hall.

Bad Laasphe 11H1

Hotel Jagdhof Glashütte, Glashütterstrasse 20, Volkholz.
GPS: n50,92008 e8,28070.

6 € 13,80, guests free WC. **Location:** Rural. **Surface:** grassy.
01/01-31/12 23-24/12.
Distance: 4km on the spot on the spot 4km 1,5km.

Bad Laasphe 11H1

Restaurant-Café Marburger, Hesselbacher Straße 21.
GPS: n50,88558 e8,36338.
6 guests free. Mo.
Distance: on the spot.

Bad Lippspringe 10A3

Arminiuspark, Burgstraße 10. **GPS:** n51,78124 e8,82447.

11 € 6,50 Ch. **Location:** Urban, quiet. **Surface:** metalled.
01/01-31/12.
Distance: 300m 350m on the spot on the spot.
Remarks: Pay at tourist office.

Bad Münstereifel 11F2

Wohnmobilpark Bad Münstereifel, Dr.-Greve-Straße 16.
GPS: n50,54600 e6,76514.

26 € 7, tourist tax € 1/pp €1/100liter €1 Ch (30x)included WC €1,80.
Location: Rural, comfortable, quiet. **Surface:** grassy/metalled.
01/01-31/12.
Distance: 350m on the spot 100m.
Remarks: Pay and coins at swimming pool, 20% discount pool.

Bad Oeynhausen 9H2

Südbahnstraße/Detmolder Straße. **GPS:** n52,19680 e8,80038.
3 free. **Surface:** asphalted. 01/01-31/12.
Remarks: Max. 2 days.

Bad Oeynhausen 9H2

Siekmeiers Hof, Volmerdingsener strasse 111.
GPS: n52,24679 e8,78394.

10 guests free. **Location:** Urban, quiet. **Surface:** gravel.
01/01-31/12 Mon, Tue.
Distance: on the spot on the spot 1km.

Bad Salzuflen 9H2

Wohnmobil-Park Flachsheide, Forsthausweg.
GPS: n52,09868 e8,74569.

25 € 7, tourist tax € 2,90/pp Ch WC included.
Location: Rural, quiet. 01/01-31/12.
Distance: 1,5km 5,5km on the spot 500m 1,5km free.

Bad Sassendorf 9H3

Kurcamping Rumkerhof, Weslarnerstrasse 30.
GPS: n51,59581 e8,17909.

90 € 9, tourist tax excl Ch (93x)€0,50/kWh included.
Surface: gravel. 01/01-31/12.
Distance: 1,3km 1,3km.
Remarks: Waste dump € 0,50, bread-service.

Bad Waldliesborn 9H3

Wohnmobilpoint, Quellenstraße. **GPS:** n51,71759 e8,33587.

DE

10 € 4,40 + € 7,55/pp €2/100liter Ch (8x)€2/24h.
Location: Rural, quiet. **Surface:** gravel. 01/01-31/12.
Distance: 400m 200m 400m 400m.
Remarks: Discount on access terme.

S Bad Westernkotten 9H3

Wohnmobilplatz An den Sole-Thermen, Mühlenweg 1.
GPS: n51,63126 e8,35195.

46 € 7, tourist tax € 2/pp €1/100liter Ch €0,50/kWh.
Surface: grassy. 01/01-31/12.
Distance: bakery 300m.
Remarks: Bread-service.

S Bad Wünnenberg 9H3

Wohnmobilhafen, In den Erlen. **GPS**: n51,52058 e8,70133.

12 € 5 €1/100liter Ch (12x)€1/24h.
Location: Urban, central. **Surface:** gravel.
01/01-31/12.
Distance: 100m 400m 100m 400m on the spot on the spot.

S Balve 11G1

Am Hallenbad, In der Murmke 9. **GPS**: n51,32729 e7,86920.

3 free €1/80liter €1/kWh. **Location:** Urban, simple.
Surface: metalled. 01/01-31/12.
Distance: 600m 600m 600m on the spot on the spot.

S Balve 11G1

Haus Recke Hönnetal, Binolen 1. **GPS**: n51,37037 e7,86108.
3 Ch.
Distance: on the spot on the spot.

S Barntrup 10A2

Badeanstaltsweg. **GPS**: n51,98790 e9,10990.

4 € 6 €1/100liter Ch €0,50/kWh. **Location:** Rural, simple.
Surface: asphalted. 01/01-31/12.
Distance: 450m 450m 450m 450m.
Remarks: To be paid at campsite Teutoburger Wald.

S Barntrup 10A2

Ferienpark Teutoburger Wald, Badeanstaltsweg 4.
GPS: n51,98768 e9,11027.

9 € 20,50 Ch €5/5 included. **Location:** Rural, luxurious, quiet. **Surface:** grassy/metalled. 01/04-31/10.
Distance: 450m 450m 450m 450m on the spot on the spot.

S Beckum 9G3

Am Hallenbad, Paterweg 4. **GPS**: n51,75129 e8,03585.

3 free €0,50/100liter Ch (2x)€0,50/kWh.
Location: Urban, simple, noisy. **Surface:** metalled.
01/01-31/12.
Distance: 1km 4km 1km 1km.

S Bedburg-Hau 9E3

Womo-Moyland, Moyländer Allee 3a, Moyland.
GPS: n51,75562 e6,24381.

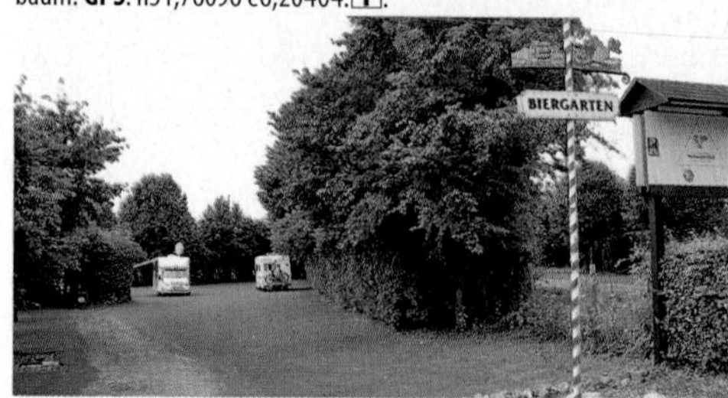

50 € 7 €0,50/100liter Ch (40x)€3/24h included.
Location: Rural, comfortable, isolated, quiet. **Surface:** forest soil.
01/01-31/12.
Distance: Kleve 8km 2,5km 300m on the spot.
Remarks: Golf court 500m, Schloss Moyland 300m.

S Bedburg-Hau 9E3

Landgasthaus Schwanenhof, Mühlenstraße 71, Ortsteil Schneppenbaum. **GPS**: n51,76096 e6,20404.

25 € 5 €1,50 Ch (18x)€1,50 included.
Location: Rural, comfortable, isolated, quiet. **Surface:** grassy.
01/01-31/12.
Distance: 500m on the spot 1km.

Tourist information Bedburg-Hau:
Schloß Moyland, Am Schloss 4. Castle. Tue-Fri 11-18h, Sa-Su 10-18h, 01/04-30/09 Tue-Su 11-17h Mon.

Bergheim 11F1

Stellplatz Paffendorf, Königsstrasse/Kastanienallee.
GPS: n50,96389 e6,61194.

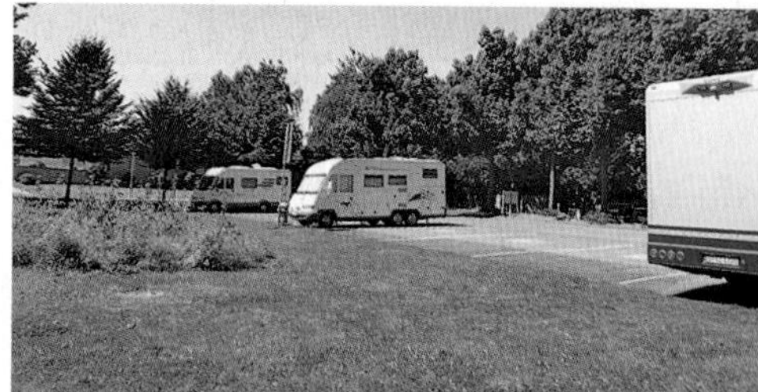

8 free. **Location:** Rural, simple, quiet. **Surface:** asphalted.
01/01-31/12.
Distance: Bergheim 2km 2,3km 300m 500m.
Remarks: Max. 2 days, castle Paffendorf 100m.

S Bergkamen 9G3

Wohnmobilhafen Marina Rünthe, Hafenweg, Rünthe.
GPS: n51,64106 e7,64309.

18 € 7/24h €1/80liter Ch (12x)€0,50/kWh.
Surface: grassy/gravel. 01/01-31/12.
Distance: 500m 3,8km.
Remarks: Max. 3 days, only exact change.

Bergkamen 9G3

Freizeitzentrum Im Häupen, Häupenweg 29.
GPS: n51,61300 e7,63075.

5 free. **Surface:** metalled. 01/01-31/12.
Distance: 500m 3,4km 500m 500m.
Remarks: Max. 72h.

Bestwig 9H3

Besucherbergwerk, Ziegelwiese, Ramsbeck.
GPS: n51,31821 e8,40318.

10 free.
Location: Simple. **Surface:** metalled. 01/01-31/12.
Distance: 800m.

Bestwig 9H3

Ludwigstrasse. **GPS**: n51,36064 e8,40165.

4 free. **Location:** Simple, simple. **Surface:** metalled.
01/01-31/12.
Distance: on the spot 300m 200m.

DE

S Beverungen 10A3

Wohnmobilhafen Weser, Am Hakel. **GPS**: n51,66167 e9,37639.

10 free €1/100liter Ch€1 (12x)€1/6h.
Location: Urban, simple. **Surface:** grassy/metalled.
01/01-31/12 service: 01/11-01/03.
Distance: on the spot on the spot on the spot on the spot on the spot.
Remarks: Next to Festplatz.

S Bielefeld 9H2

Am Johannisberg, Dornbergerstrasse. **GPS**: n52,02270 e8,51155.

10 € 5/24h €0,50/40liter Ch (10x)€1/2kWh.
Location: Rural, comfortable, quiet. **Surface:** metalled.
01/01-31/12.
Distance: 2km Imbiss 2km 2km.
Remarks: Max. 5 days.

S Billerbeck 9F2

Am Freibad, Osterwickerstrasse. **GPS**: n51,97928 e7,28190.

11 € 5 €1/100liter Ch (8x)€1/2kWh,16Amp.
Location: Urban, simple. **Surface:** gravel. 01/01-31/12.
Distance: 500m 500m.
Remarks: At swimming pool.

S Billerbeck 9F2

Am Konzert Theater, Osterwicker Straße 39.
GPS: n51,95322 e7,17390.

12 free €1/100liter Chfree (12x)€1/2kWh €1.
Location: Rural, simple. **Surface:** gravel/metalled.
01/01-31/12.
Distance: 800m 800m 100m.

S Blankenheim 11F2

An der Weiherhalle, Koblenzerstrasse. **GPS**: n50,43499 e6,65439.

15 € 5/24h €1/80liter Ch (12x)€2/10h.
Location: Rural, simple. **Surface:** metalled. 01/01-31/12.
Distance: 150m.

S Bocholt 9F3

WoMo Park am Aasee, Uhlandstraße 39.
GPS: n51,83496 e6,63146.

50 € 6 €0,50/50liter Ch€0,50 (44x)€0,50/kWh WC€0,50 €1 €3,50/2,50 €1/24h. **Location:** Rural, comfortable, noisy.
Surface: metalled. 01/01-31/12.
Distance: 800m 300m 300m 300m 300m 200m on the spot on the spot.
Remarks: Service passerby € 2.

S Bocholt 9F3

Inselbad Bahia, Hemdenerweg 169. **GPS**: n51,86265 e6,61002.

10 free €1/72liter €1 Ch€1.
Location: Rural, simple, quiet. **Surface:** grasstiles.
01/01-31/12.
Distance: 2,5km 450m 1km on the spot.
Remarks: Max. 72h, coins at swimming pool, first coin € 3, next € 0,50.

Bocholt 9F3

Euregio-Gymnasium, Unter den Eichen, Blücherstrasse.
GPS: n51,84884 e6,63700.

10 free. **Location:** Urban, simple, noisy. **Surface:** metalled.
01/01-31/12.
Distance: 1km 700m on the spot.
Remarks: Parking 'Stadtswald', max. 3 nights.

Tourist information Bocholt:
Rathaus - Gasthausplatz. Thu-evening.

Bonn 11F2

An der Rheinaue, Ludwig-Erhard-Allee. **GPS**: n50,70981 e7,13904.
18 free.
Surface: asphalted. 01/01-31/12.
Distance: centre 4km A565 4,6km 300m line 66 > Bonn centre.

S Borken 9F3

Reisemobilstellplatz am Aquarius-Freizeitbad, Parkstraße.
GPS: n51,83618 e6,86074.

15 € 6 Ch .
Location: Rural, simple. **Surface:** grasstiles. 01/01-31/12.
Distance: 1km 1km 800m 500m on the spot on the spot.
Remarks: Parking swimming pool, max. 72h.

Borken 9F3

Festplatz Weseke, Borkenwirther strasse, Weseke.
GPS: n51,90529 e6,85210.

10 free. **Location:** Rural, simple. **Surface:** metalled.
01/01-31/12.
Distance: 500m 500m 500m.
Remarks: Max. 3 nights.

Borken 9F3

Schlossklinik Pröbsting, Pröbstinger Allee.
GPS: n51,83861 e6,80556.

10 free.
Location: Rural, noisy. **Surface:** metalled. 01/01-31/12.
Distance: Badesee 150m 300m on the spot on the spot.

Borken 9F3

Wasserburg Gemen, Coesfelderstrasse, Gemen.
GPS: n51,86172 e6,86909.

5 free.
Location: Rural, simple. **Surface:** metalled. 01/01-31/12.
Distance: 1km 500m 500m 1km 1km.
Remarks: Parking sports park, max. 3 nights.

S Borken 9F3

Gestüt Forellenhof Wolter, Zum Homborn 9.
GPS: n51,86245 e6,89797.

15 € 10 Ch (7x)included. **Location:** Rural. **Surface:** gravel.

DE

01/01-31/12.
Distance: Borken 3,5km fish pond on the spot.
Remarks: Check in at Gaststätte, € 5 euro discount coupon.

Borken 9F3

Camping Pröbstingersee, Dirkshof 11, Hoxfeld.
GPS: n51,83237 e6,78764.

10 free Ch.
Surface: metalled. 01/01-31/12.
Distance: 6,5km 100m 100m.
Remarks: Max. 3 nights, service against payment on campsite.

Bottrop 9F3

Movie Park, Kirchhellen, Warner Allee 1. **GPS:** n51,62400 e6,97096.

100 € 5. **Surface:** metalled. 01/04-31/10.
Distance: 2,7km 100m 2,7km.

Tourist information Bottrop:
Alpincenter, Prosperstrasse. Indoor ski centre. 9-24h. day ticket from € 49, <18h € 25.
Warner Bros Movie World, Kirchhellen. Attractions park concerning the film.

Brakel/Bellersen 10A3

Wohnmobilhafen Mühlengrund, Meinolfussstrasse 6.
GPS: n51,77217 e9,18804.

23 € 9,50 €0,50 Ch (23x)included. **Location:** Rural, comfortable, isolated. **Surface:** grasstiles. 01/01-31/12.
Distance: 800m 400m 800m 800m on the spot on the spot.

Bruchhausen 10A3

Bruchhäuserstrasse. **GPS:** n51,70714 e9,29192.

4 free. **Location:** Rural, simple. **Surface:** grassy/gravel.
01/01-31/12.
Distance: 200m 200m 200m.

Brüggen 11E1

Wohnmobilhafen Brüggen, Bornerstraße 48.
GPS: n51,24264 e6,18955.

30 € 4 Chincluded €2/24h. **Surface:** gravel.
01/01-31/12.
Distance: 500m 100m 50m 50m.
Remarks: Behind Aldi-süd.

Brüggen 11E1

Freizeitplatz Brachter Wald, St.-Barbara-Straße 40-42, Bracht.
GPS: n51,25713 e6,17022.

14 € 9, 2 pers.incl Ch €2/day WC €1. **Surface:** grasstiles.
01/01-31/12.
Distance: 2km on the spot on the spot.

Brühl 11F2

Phantasialand P1, Berggeiststrasse 31-41.
GPS: n50,79919 e6,87875.

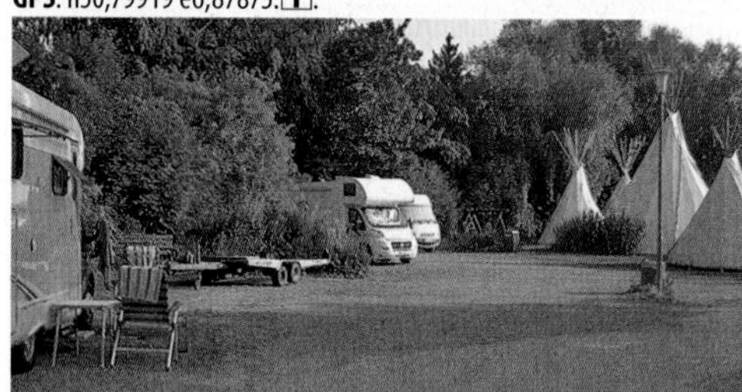

10 € 12,50/night WC.
Location: Comfortable, quiet. **Surface:** metalled.
04/04-31/10.
Distance: 100m on the spot.

Tourist information Brühl:
Phantasialand. Large amusement park. 19/03-01/11 9-18h, winter changing visiting hours.

Bünde 9H2

Stadthallen, Steinmeisterstrasse. **GPS:** n52,19869 e8,58986.

5 free. **Location:** Urban, simple. **Surface:** metalled.
01/01-31/12.
Distance: 50m 50m 50m.
Remarks: Max. 72h.

Büren 9H3

Wohnmobilparkplatz Netz - Bürener Land, Fürstenberger Strasse.
GPS: n51,54969 e8,56356.

8 free €1/10minutes Ch €1/8h. **Location:** Urban, simple.
01/01-31/12.
Distance: on the spot 500m 200m.
Remarks: Parking nearby swimming pool, coins at petrol station.

Büren 9H3

Dorfhalle, Niederhagen, Wewelsburg. **GPS:** n51,60947 e8,65544.
free.
Distance: 600m.

Büren 9H3

Ringelsteiner Wald, Eichenweg, Ringelstein.
GPS: n51,50097 e8,56999.
free. 01/01-31/12.
Distance: 1km 1km on the spot.

Coesfeld 9F2

Brauhaus Stephanus, Overhagenweg 1. **GPS:** n51,93719 e7,15617.

4 guests free.
Location: Urban, simple, noisy. **Surface:** metalled. 01/01-31/12.
Distance: on the spot 100m on the spot.

Dahlem 11E3

Flugplatz Dahlemer Binz, Dahlemer Binz.
GPS: n50,40663 e6,53700.

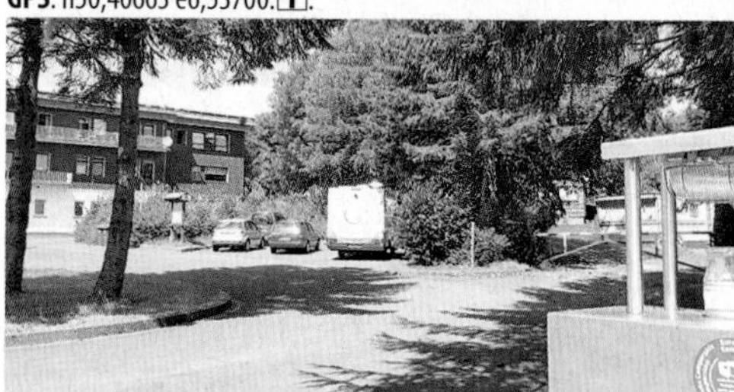

3 free €1/80liter Ch. **Location:** Rural, simple.
Surface: asphalted. 01/01-31/12.
Distance: on the spot.
Remarks: Airport Dahlemer Binz.

Dahlem 11E3

Wohnmobilstellplatz Kronenburger See, Seeuferstrasse 6.
GPS: n50,35785 e6,46989.

12 € 8/24h €1/120liter Ch (12x)included.
Location: Rural, simple, quiet. **Surface:** grassy.
01/01-31/12.
Remarks: At artificial lake.

Dinslaken 9F3

Am Rotbachsee, Am Freibad. **GPS:** n51,56707 e6,77807.

10 free. **Surface:** sand. 01/01-31/12.
Distance: 100m 100m 100m on the spot on the spot.

Dormagen 11F1

Parkplatz Flügeldeich, Herrenweg, Feste Zons.
GPS: n51,12553 e6,85001.

DE

3 € 5. **Surface:** metalled. 01/01-31/12.
Distance: 400m on the spot on the spot 100m 500m.
Remarks: Near the Rhine river, max. 3 days.

S Dorsten 9F3

Reisemobilhafen An der Lippe, Zur Lippe.
GPS: n51,66550 e6,96744.

38 € 8/24h Ch included (34x)€ 1/8h € 2.
Surface: metalled/sand. 01/01-31/12.
Distance: 300m 300m 300m.
Remarks: Bread-service in summer period, charging point for electric bicycles.

Tourist information Dorsten:
Marler Str.. Flea market. 2nd Su of the month, 11-18h.

S Dortmund 9G3

Mobil-Camp Wischlingen, Wischlinger Weg 50-61, Wischlingen.
GPS: n51,52001 e7,39868.

50 € 8, 2 pers.incl € 1/80liter Ch (30x)€ 0,50/kWh WC € 1.
Surface: asphalted. 01/01-31/12.
Distance: 1km Rewe 1km 200m.
Remarks: Former tennis-court in recreation area.

S Drensteinfurt 9G3

Am Erlbad, Im Erlfeld 2. **GPS**: n51,78972 e7,74778.

3 € 3/pp Ch € 3/24h WC included € 3.
Location: Rural, simple, noisy. **Surface:** asphalted/metalled.
01/05-15/09.
Distance: 800m 9km 800m.
Remarks: Max. 3 nights, max. 8M, check in at swimming pool, swimming pool incl.

S Duisburg 9F3

Landschaftspark Duisburg-Nord, Emscherstraße 71, Meiderich.
GPS: n51,48413 e6,78077.
5 free Ch. **Surface:** asphalted. 01/01-31/12.
Distance: 1,6km on the spot on the spot.

S Dülmen 9F3

Reisemobilstellplatz Hüttendyk, Ecke Halterner Strasse.
GPS: n51,82606 e7,27228.

8 free € 1/80liter Ch (8x)€ 2/8h. **Location:** Rural, simple.
Surface: metalled. 01/01-31/12.
Distance: 500m 200m 100m.
Remarks: Max. 72h.

S Dülmen 9F3

Reisemobilstellplatz Kapellenweg, Kapellenweg.
GPS: n51,82331 e7,27945.

7 free Ch. **Location:** Rural, simple. **Surface:** metalled.
01/01-31/12.
Distance: 500m 600m on the spot on the spot.
Remarks: Max. 72h.

Dülmen 9F3

Reisemobilstellplatz Düb, Nordlandwehr 99.
GPS: n51,84408 e7,27300.

7 free. **Location:** Rural, simple. **Surface:** grasstiles/metalled.
01/01-31/12.
Distance: 2km 1km.
Remarks: Max. 72h.

Dülmen 9F3

Reisemobilstellplatz Hausdulmen, Sandstrasse.
GPS: n51,80707 e7,24746.

20 free. **Location:** Rural, simple, quiet. **Surface:** grassy.
01/01-31/12.
Distance: 2,5km 500m 400m on the spot.
Remarks: Max. 72h.

S Düren 11E2

IG Reisemobilhafen Düren, Rurstrasse 188. **GPS**: n50,80861 e6,46556.

20 € 7 Ch included (18x)€ 2.
Location: Rural, simple, quiet. **Surface:** gravel.
Distance: 900m Bistro 100m Lidl 500m.
Remarks: Service passerby € 2.

Düsseldorf 11F1

P Rheinterasse/Tonhalle, Robert-Lehr-Ufer.
GPS: n51,23710 e6,77029.

30 € 2/h, max. € 12/24h. **Surface:** metalled. 01/01-31/12.
Distance: Old city centre 1km 50m 1,3km.

S Düsseldorf 11F1

Wohnmobilstellplatz Düsseldorf/Erkrath, Heinrich-Hertz-Straße 18, Unterfeldhaus, Düsseldorf/Erkrath. **GPS**: n51,19825 e6,91679.

6 € 6 € 1/100liter Ch included.
Location: Urban, simple, quiet. **Surface:** metalled. 01/01-31/12.
Distance: 500m 5,5km 300m 50m.111

Tourist information Düsseldorf:
Tourist Info, Immermannstrasse, Gegenüber Station; Kö-Galerie/Finanzhaus, Berliner Alee; Burgplatz, Berliner Allee, www.duesseldorf-tourismus.de. Historical centre, important city of fashion, all large marks established in the Königsallee, Umweltzone: the green environmental badge is required.
During the Caravan Salon (by the end of August/beginning September) there is a large area for motorhomes available. Free shuttlebus to the exhibition and Old city centre. Also several events on the exhibition grounds.

S Eckenhagen 11G1

Rodener Festplatz, Rodener Platz. **GPS**: n50,98667 e7,69361.

20 free Ch free. **Location:** Urban, simple, quiet.
Surface: asphalted/gravel. 01/01-31/12.
Distance: 200m 4km 300m 300m on the spot on the spot.

Emmerich 9E3

Auf dem Eltenberg Hoch Elten, Luitgardisstraße.
GPS: n51,86559 e6,17265.

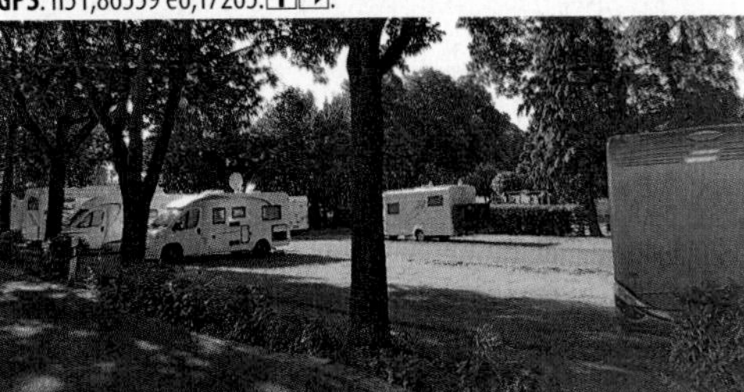

25 free.
Location: Rural, simple. **Surface:** grassy. 01/01-31/12.
Distance: 1km 100m 1km on the spot.
Remarks: Service at marina.

Emmerich 9E3

P6, Kleiner Wall, Rheinpromenade. **GPS**: n51,83229 e6,23594.

DE

5 free. **Location:** Urban, simple, central, noisy. **Surface:** gravel.
15/03-01/11.
Distance: on the spot on the spot on the spot on the spot.

Emmerich 9E3

Yachthafen, Fackeldeystrasse 15-65. **GPS:** n51,83693 e6,21948.

75 € 12 Ch (80x)4,. WC €0,50 included.
Location: Rural, luxurious, isolated. **Surface:** grassy.
01/03-30/11.
Distance: 2,5km on the spot on the spot 1,5km on the spot on the spot.
Remarks: Arrival <22h, max. 9m.

Ennepetal 11G1

Am Platsch, Mittelstraße 108. **GPS:** n51,29295 e7,37668.

4 € 3 included. **Surface:** gravel. 01/01-31/12.
Distance: 10,8km 5km 5km on the spot on the spot routes for nordic walking.
Remarks: Check in at pay-desk of swimming pool, on the spot: bistro, pool, sauna and golf court.

Ennepetal 11G1

Firma Möller-Elektronic, Königstrasse 17, Oelkinghausen.
GPS: n51,29086 e7,32050.

5 free Ch €3. **Location:** Urban, simple, quiet.
Surface: metalled. 01/01-31/12.
Distance: 2km 1km 200m on the spot on the spot.

Ennigerloh 9G3

Am Freibad 3. **GPS:** n51,83304 e8,01629.

2 free €0,50/50liter Ch €0,50/kWh. **Location:** Rural, simple, noisy. **Surface:** metalled. 01/01-31/12.
Distance: 600m 600m 600m on the spot on the spot.

Erftstadt 11F2

Mobilcamp am Ville-Express, Carl-Schurz-strasse 1a, Liblar.
GPS: n50,81781 e6,81986.

11 € 6 €1/80liter Ch (11x)€0,50/kWh.
Location: Urban, comfortable. **Surface:** metalled.
01/01-31/12.
Distance: 1km 4,4km 500m 200m 1km.

Erndtebrück 11H1

Pension Hofius, Hilchenbachterweg 2, Zinse.
GPS: n51,00599 e8,21224.

3 € 6/24h Ch included. 01/01-31/12.
Distance: 5km on the spot on the spot.
Remarks: Max. 8M.

Everswinkel 9G2

Vitus-Bad, Alverkirchenerstrasse 29. **GPS:** n51,92309 e7,83776.

3 free €0,50/50liter Ch €0,50/kWh. **Location:** Rural, simple, noisy. **Surface:** metalled. 01/01-31/12.
Distance: 500m on the spot 100m on the spot 100-Schlösser-Route on the spot.
Remarks: Parking swimming pool.

Freudenberg (NRW) 11G1

Lohmühle, P5. **GPS:** n50,89625 e7,87636.

5 free. **Surface:** metalled. 01/01-31/12.
Distance: on the spot 100m 200m.
Remarks: Max. 3 days.

Gangelt 11E1

Rodebachtal, Am Freibad 13. **GPS:** n50,98583 e5,99806.

40 € 10 Ch €0,40/kWh WC €0,60/4minutes €2,40.
Location: Rural, luxurious, quiet. **Surface:** metalled.
01/01-31/12.
Distance: on the spot on the spot on the spot 1,5km on the spot on the spot.
Remarks: Arrival <18h, caution key € 10.

Geldern 9E3

Am Holländer See, Am Holländer See 19.
GPS: n51,51131 e6,32867.

50 € 8/24h, 3 days € 19 €1/80liter Ch €0,50/kWh.
Surface: grassy/metalled. 01/01-31/12.
Distance: 1km 1km 1km.
Remarks: Parking centre.

Geldern 9E3

Reisemobilhafen Am Freibad, Am Freibad 6, Walbeck.
GPS: n51,49461 e6,22666.

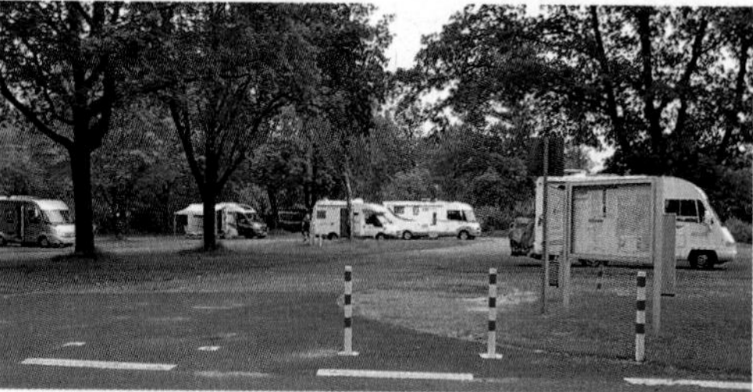

50 € 8/24h €1/80liter Ch (36x)€0,50/kWh.
Surface: grassy/sand. 01/01-31/12.
Distance: city centre Walbeck 1km, city centre Geldern 6km 1km 1km.
Remarks: At swimming pool.

Geldern 9E3

Reisemobilstellplatz Am Sportplatz, Hülspassweg 20, Veert.
GPS: n51,52960 e6,30347.

30 free. **Surface:** gravel. 01/01-31/12.
Distance: city centre Veert 200m, city centre Geldern 2km 500m.
Remarks: Parking at sports park.

Geldern 9E3

Freizeit-Store Diepers, Liebligstrasse 33. **GPS:** n51,52971 e6,35456.
€1 €1 Ch. 01/01-31/12, during opening hours.

Tourist information Geldern:

Internationaler Wettbewerb der strassenmaler und strassenmusikanten und -theatergruppen, Centrum. International street painting competition, street musicians and theater groups. beginning Sep.

Internationales Reisemobilfest. International festival for motorcaravanners with vast tourist program. Not necessary to book in advance,. last weekend April. free.

Gelsenkirchen 9F3

Stellplatz Nienhausen, Feldmarkstraße 201.
GPS: n51,50167 e7,06333.

20 € 7, 2 pers.incl. €1/90liter Ch €1/2kWh €3.

DE

Surface: metalled. 01/01-31/12.
Distance: 2,8km 3,2km 100m 2km Tram 700m.
Remarks: Bread-service.

S Gladbeck 9F3

Freitzeitstätte Wittringer Wald, Bohmertstrasse 277.
GPS: n51,55912 e6,98403.

20 free Ch. **Surface:** grasstiles/grassy. 01/01-31/12.
Distance: 2km 1km 200m 1km.
Remarks: Green zone: environmental badge obligatory, Wasserschloß Wittringen 450m.

S Goch 9E3

Friedensplatz, Thielenstrasse. **GPS:** n51,67556 e6,16639.

70 € 5/24h €1/100liter Chincluded (60x)€0,50/kWh.
Location: Urban, comfortable, quiet. **Surface:** grassy.
01/01-31/12.
Distance: 700m on the spot 700m 700m 100m.
Remarks: Along the Niers river.

Goch 9E3

Reisemobilstellplatz GochNess, Kranenburger Strasse 20, Kessel.
GPS: n51,70291 e6,08915.

6 free.
Location: Rural, simple, isolated, quiet.
Surface: grassy.
01/01-31/12.
Distance: 1km 1km 1km.
Remarks: At swimming pool.

Tourist information Goch:
Pilgrimage for motorhomes. last weekend Jun.
Museumscafé Edison, Museum Goch. Collection of gramophones.
Su 15-17h.
Herrensitz-Route. Cycle route along the Meuse and the Niers, available at Kultourbühne Goch. T € 7,90.

Grefrath 11E1

Eissportzentrum Grefrath, Stadionstrasse. **GPS:** n51,34889 e6,33972.

50 free. **Surface:** grasstiles.
Distance: 2km 500m 300m 2km.
Remarks: Niederrheinisches Freilichtmuseum, Open air museum 650m.

S Greven 9G2

Reisemobilhafen Camp Marina, Fuestruperstrasse 37, Fuestrup.
GPS: n52,04449 e7,68328.

90 € 11 €0,50/50liter Ch €2,50 WC €1 €3/2,50.
Location: Comfortable. **Surface:** grassy.
01/01-31/12.
Distance: on the spot Restaurant/Biergarten 3km on the spot on the spot.
Remarks: Marina at canal, bread-service, shopping service.

S Gronau 9F2

Erholungsgebiet Dreiländersee, Brechterweg.
GPS: n52,23716 e7,08006.

80 € 8/24, only exact change €0,50/130liter Ch (32x)€1/4h WC. **Location:** Rural, simple, isolated. **Surface:** grassy/metalled.
01/01-31/12.
Distance: 3km 100m on the spot 200m 50m (camping) on the spot.
Remarks: Near the lake, max. 48h.

S Haltern am See 9F3

Wohnmobilpark Haltern am See, Hullerner Straße 45-49.
GPS: n51,74186 e7,20179.
20 € 10 €1/100liter Ch (20x)€0,50/kWh WC.
Surface: grasstiles.
Distance: 1km 300m on the spot.
Remarks: At swimming pool.

S Haltern am See 9F3

RMS ReisemobileSpezialist, Hellweg 252.
GPS: n51,75589 e7,20127.

4 € 7 €1/70liter Ch €3,50. **Location:** Rural, simple, isolated. **Surface:** grassy/gravel. 01/01-31/12.
Distance: Old city centre 1km 800m 800m.

Hamm 9G3

Freizeitpark Maximilian Park, Alter Grenzweg 2.
GPS: n51,68392 e7,88395.

10 free.
Location: Rural, simple. **Surface:** grassy.
01/01-31/12.
Distance: 300m 300m 300m 200m on the spot on the spot.

Harsewinkel 9H2

Frei- und Hallenbad, Prozessionsweg 8. **GPS:** n51,96556 e8,21935.

6 free. **Location:** Rural, simple, quiet. **Surface:** grassy.
01/01-31/12.
Distance: 200m 100m 200m 200m on the spot.
Remarks: Parking next to swimming pool, max. 48h.

S Hattingen 9F3

Roonstrasse. **GPS:** n51,40167 e7,18389.

2 € 4 . **Location:** Urban, simple, quiet.
Surface: asphalted/metalled. 01/01-31/12.
Distance: 300m 5km 300m 300m.

S Hattingen 9F3

Wohnmobilstellplatz Ruhrtal, Ruhrdeich 24.
GPS: n51,40839 e7,18091.

15 € 7 €1/90liter Ch (12x)€1/2kWh free.
Location: Rural, comfortable, quiet. **Surface:** gravel.
01/01-31/12.
Distance: 2,5km 5km on the spot on the spot 500m 1km.
Remarks: Along the Ruhr river, next to midget golf, bread-service.

Hattingen 9F3

August-Bebel strasse. **GPS:** n51,39833 e7,18028.

2 € 3. **Location:** Urban, simple, central, noisy. **Surface:** metalled.
01/01-31/12.
Distance: on the spot 5km on the spot on the spot on the spot.
Remarks: At shopping centre Carré.

Hattingen 9F3

Ruhrgasse, Bahnhofstrasse. **GPS:** n51,40127 e7,17700.

DE

3 free. **Location:** Urban, simple, quiet. **Surface:** gravel.
01/01-31/12.
Distance: 500m 5km 500m 500m.
Remarks: Parking behind the Amtshäusern, only on Sa and Su.

Hattingen 9F3

Wanderparkplatz, Isenbergstrasse. **GPS:** n51,38969 e7,15340.

3 free. **Location:** Rural, simple. **Surface:** gravel.
Mo-Fri, 01/01-31/12.
Distance: 2km 5km 300m 1km on the spot on the spot on the spot.
Remarks: Parking along the Ruhr, max. 2 days.

Havixbeck 9G2

Am Freibad, Kardinal-von-Hartmann-Straße.
GPS: n51,97507 e7,42092.

8 free €1/80liter Ch (8x)against payment WC.
Location: Simple, quiet. **Surface:** metalled. 01/01-31/12.
Distance: 1km 1km 800m 800m on the spot.
Remarks: Parking at swimming pool, small pitches.

Havixbeck 9G2

Klute's Historischem Brauhaus, Poppenbeck 28.
GPS: n51,98938 e7,39291.

15 guests free (8x)€5 . **Location:** Rural, simple, isolated. **Surface:** metalled. 01/01-31/12.
Distance: 2km on the spot 2km.

Heiligenhaus 11F1

Westfalenstrasse. **GPS:** n51,32853 e6,97327.
3 free.
Location: Simple. **Surface:** metalled. 01/01-31/12.
Distance: 200m 200m 200m.

Heimbach 11E2

Wohnmobilhafen am Nationalpark-Tor, An der Laag 4.
GPS: n50,63683 e6,47265.

19 €7,50/24h, €0,45/pp tourist tax €1/100liter Ch (20x)€0,50/kWh. **Location:** Rural, simple, noisy. **Surface:** gravel.
01/01-31/12.
Distance: 200m 100m on the spot.
Remarks: Nearby Regioshuttle Rurtallbahn.

Heinsberg 11E1

Heinsberg am Lago, Fritz-Bauer-Strasse 3.
GPS: n51,07333 e6,09278.

44 P1 € 10/day, P2 € 10/2 days €1/100liter Ch (31x)€0,50/kWh.
Location: Rural, luxurious, quiet. **Surface:** grasstiles.
Distance: 1km Bagger See on the spot 800m.

Hellenthal 11E3

Europa-Wohnmobilhafen, Am Weissen Stein, Udenbreth, B265.
GPS: n50,40896 e6,37220.

28 € 10 €2 Ch (28x)included.
Location: Rural, simple. **Surface:** metalled.
01/01-31/12.
Distance: on the spot on the spot.
Remarks: Service on campsite, winter sports area Hellenthal am Wald.

Hellenthal 11E3

Grenzlandhalle Hellenthal, Aachenerstrasse.
GPS: n50,49251 e6,43651.

15 free. **Location:** Rural, simple. **Surface:** grasstiles.
01/01-31/12.
Distance: 500m on the spot 200m.
Remarks: Service on campsite.

Hellenthal 11E3

Breuerhof, Zum Wilsamtal 39, Udenbreth.
GPS: n50,41081 e6,38992.

2 € 10 Ch (2x).
Location: Rural, comfortable, quiet. **Surface:** metalled.
Distance: 2km on the spot.
Remarks: Check in at nr. 35.

Tourist information Hellenthal:

Greifvogelstation, Wildfreigehege 1. Predatory bird station.
01/11-31/03 10-17h, 01/04-31/10 9-18h.

Hemer 9G3

Wohnmobilstellplatz Hemer, Hönnetalstraße.
GPS: n51,37841 e7,77151.

20 € 2/8-20h €1/100liter Ch€1 (12x)€0,50/kWh.
Location: Urban, comfortable, quiet. **Surface:** asphalted/grassy.
01/01-31/12.
Distance: 1km 6km 300m bakery 500m on the spot.

Herford 9H2

H2O, Wiessenstrasse 90. **GPS:** n52,10750 e8,68534.

22 € 5 Ch . **Location:** Rural, comfortable.
Surface: metalled. 01/01-31/12.
Distance: on the spot 2km 200m.
Remarks: At swimming pool.

Herford 9H2

Am Stadion, Dennewitzstrasse 15. **GPS:** n52,10474 e8,68931.

10 free. **Location:** Rural, simple. 01/01-31/12.
Distance: 2,5km 3km 350m 350m.

Herscheid 11G1

Am Warmwasserfreibad, Unterdorfstraße.
GPS: n51,17567 e7,74368.

3 free €1/10minutes Ch (4x)€1/8h.
Location: Rural, comfortable, quiet. **Surface:** gravel.
01/01-31/12.
Distance: 1,2km 10km 400m 650m on the spot.

Hilchenbach 11H1

Hallenbad Dahlbruch, Bernhard-Weiss-Platz, Dahlbruch.
GPS: n50,97792 e8,05343.

3 free €1/10minutes . **Surface:** asphalted/metalled.
01/01-31/12.
Distance: 400m 400m.
Remarks: Parking behind swimming pool, max. 48h.

DE

Hilchenbach 11H1

Bürgerhaus, Merklinghäuser weg, Müsen.
GPS: n50,99267 e8,04497.

3 free. **Surface:** asphalted. 01/01-31/12.
Remarks: Max. 48h.

Hilchenbach 11H1

Parkplatz P4, Rothenberger strasse, L728.
GPS: n50,99702 e8,11103.

3 free.
Surface: metalled. 01/01-31/12.
Distance: 100m 200m 100m.
Remarks: Parking in front of shopping centre Gerberpark, max. 48h.

Hilchenbach 11H1

Landhotel Steubers Siebelnhof, Siebelnhoferstrasse, Vormwald.
GPS: n50,98658 e8,13173.
6 € 20,50, use sanitary facilities/swimming pool sauna incl WC included. 01/01-31/12.
Distance: on the spot.

Hopsten 9G1

Dreifachturnhalle, Rüschendorfer strasse 4.
GPS: n52,38544 e7,60490.

6 free Ch free. **Location:** Rural, simple.
Surface: grassy/metalled. 01/01-31/12.
Distance: 100m 100m 100m on the spot on the spot.
Remarks: Parking at gymnasium, max. 3 days.

Horn 10A2

Wohnmobilhafen am Bad Meinberger Badehaus, Wällenweg, Bad Meinberg. **GPS**: n51,89818 e8,99249.

24 € 7,50 + € 2,60/pp tourist tax €1/100liter €0,50 Ch €0,50/kWh WC €2,50.
Location: Rural, quiet. **Surface:** grassy/metalled.
01/01-31/12.
Distance: 200m on the spot 200m 100m.
Remarks: Behind spa, bread-service, discount at swimming pool.

Hörstel 9G2

Wohnmobilhafen Riesenbeck, Postdamm-Lazarusbrücke.
GPS: n52,25574 e7,63387.

20 free €1/2kWh. **Location:** Rural, comfortable, central, noisy.
Surface: grassy/gravel. 01/01-31/12.
Distance: 700m on the spot on the spot 300m on the spot 100-Schlösser-Route on the spot.
Remarks: Max. 3 nights.

Hövelhof 9H2

P Bahnhof, Westfalenstrasse. **GPS**: n51,82417 e8,66099.

6 free free (6x)€1/kWh. **Location:** Urban. **Surface:** gravel.
01/01-31/12.
Distance: 500m 4,2km 500m 700m 50m on the spot on the spot.

Hövelhof 9H2

Wohnmobil-stellplatz Apelhof, Paderborner Straße 172.
GPS: n51,80166 e8,67697.
8 € 8 . **Surface:** grassy.
Distance: 3km 250m 3km.

Höxter 10A3

Freizeitanlage Godelheimer See, Godelheimer Strasse, Höxter-Godelheim. **GPS**: n51,75787 e9,37557.

50 € 7/24h ChWC included. **Location:** Comfortable.
Surface: grasstiles. 01/01-31/12 service: 01/10-01/04.
Distance: 2km on the spot river 500m on the spot 2km on the spot on the spot.
Remarks: Bread-service, recreation area.

Höxter 10A3

Wohnmobilhafen Floßplatz, Milchweg.
GPS: n51,77325 e9,38781.

50 € 7/24h €1/100liter Ch (18x)€1/2kWh.
Location: Rural, comfortable, central, quiet.
Surface: grassy/gravel.
01/01-31/12.
Distance: 300m on the spot fishing permit available 100m 300m 500m on camp site 50m on the spot.
Remarks: Parking beside river Weser, bread-service in summer period.

Hückelhoven 11E1

Hückelhovener Ruraue, Rheinstraße 4b. **GPS**: n51,05146 e6,21208.

6 € 4,50 €0,50/100liter Ch €0,50/kWh.
Location: Rural, simple, isolated, quiet. **Surface:** metalled.
01/01-31/12 With snow.
Distance: 1,5km.

Hürtgenwald 11E2

Einmünding Kall-Rur, Zerkall. **GPS**: n50,69156 e6,45212.

10 free.
Location: Rural, simple. **Surface:** gravel. 01/01-31/12.
Distance: 100m on the spot on the spot 200m.
Remarks: Along the river Kall/Rur.

Hürtgenwald 11E2

Parkplatz Burgstrasse, Burgstrasse, Bergstein.
GPS: n50,69582 e6,43848.

5 free. **Location:** Simple. **Surface:** metalled.
01/01-31/12.

Hürtgenwald 11E2

Soldatenfriedhof, Höhenstrasse, Hürtgen.
GPS: n50,70552 e6,36063.

9 free. **Location:** Rural, simple, noisy. **Surface:** asphalted.
01/01-31/12.

Hürtgenwald 11E2

Landhotel Kallbach, Kallweg 24, Simonskall. **GPS**: n50,66716 e6,35395.

5 € 12. **Location:** Rural, comfortable, quiet. **Surface:** metalled.
01/01-31/12.
Distance: 200m on the spot.
Remarks: Discount at restaurant.

Hüsten 9G3

Parkplatz Große Wiese. **GPS**: n51,43151 e8,00475.
4 free. **Surface:** asphalted.

DE

Distance: 2km on the spot on the spot.
Remarks: Next to the Sole-Bad.

Ibbenbüren 9G2

Aseebad, An der Umfluth 99. **GPS**: n52,26181 e7,73171.

30 € 3.
Location: Comfortable, central, quiet. **Surface:** grassy.
Distance: 2,3km.
Remarks: Parking next to swimming pool, max. 4 nights.

Iserlohn 9G3

Parkplatz Seilerblick, Friesenstraße. **GPS**: n51,38456 e7,71128.

5 free €1 Ch€1 (4x)€0,50. **Location:** Urban, simple, noisy. **Surface:** asphalted. 01/01-31/12.
Distance: 2km 2,5km on the spot on the spot.
Remarks: Next to tennis-court.

Isselburg 9E3

Stellplatz am Stadtturm, Münsterdeich. **GPS**: n51,83452 e6,46477.

6 € 5 €1/100liter Chincluded (6x)€1/day.
Location: Rural, simple, quiet. **Surface:** grassy.
01/01-31/12.
Distance: on the spot on the spot 300m 100m.
Remarks: At the Issel, parking centre, max. 72h.

Isselburg 9E3

Hotel Restaurant Brüggenhütte, Hahnerfeld 23, Anholt.
GPS: n51,85301 e6,47187.

5 free.
Location: Rural, simple, noisy. **Surface:** grassy.
01/01-31/12.
Distance: 200m on the spot 2km on the spot.
Remarks: Along through road, behind restaurant, max. 3 days.

Isselburg 9E3

Bürgerhaus, Anholter strasse, Vehlingen. **GPS**: n51,83089 e6,42297.

5 free. **Location:** Rural, simple. **Surface:** gravel.
01/01-31/12.
Distance: 1km on the spot.
Remarks: Max. 2 nights.

Isselburg 9E3

Biotopwildpark Anholter Schweiz, Pferdehorster Str. 1.
GPS: n51,83225 e6,43013.

6 € 7 (6x)included. **Location:** Rural, simple.
Surface: gravel/metalled. 15/03-25/10.
Distance: 1km.
Remarks: Max. 3 days, check in at pay-desk, caution key electricity € 20.

Isselburg 9E3

Ponyhof Leiting, Alte Bundesstrasse 3, Werth.
GPS: n51,81332 e6,49258.

20 free. **Location:** Rural, simple, quiet. **Surface:** grassy.
01/01-31/12.
Distance: on the spot.
Remarks: Max. 72h.

Issum-Sevelen 9E3

Wohnmobilpark Hexenland-Sevelen, Koetherdyck 18.
GPS: n51,49926 e6,43676.

20 € 9 Ch €3/24h WC €1/10minutes. **Surface:** gravel.
01/01-31/12.
Distance: Sevelen 1km 200m 100m 1km.

Jülich 11E1

Brückenkopf-Park, Rurauenstrasse 11. **GPS**: n50,92345 e6,34029.

22 € 9,50 €1/100liter Ch WC .
Location: Simple, noisy. **Surface:** grassy.
01/01-31/12 sanitary building: 1/11-31/3.
Remarks: Parking at the Rur.

Tourist information Jülich:
Old fortress city.

Kalkar 9E3

Reisemobilstellplatz Kalkar, Waysche strasse.
GPS: n51,74008 e6,30101.

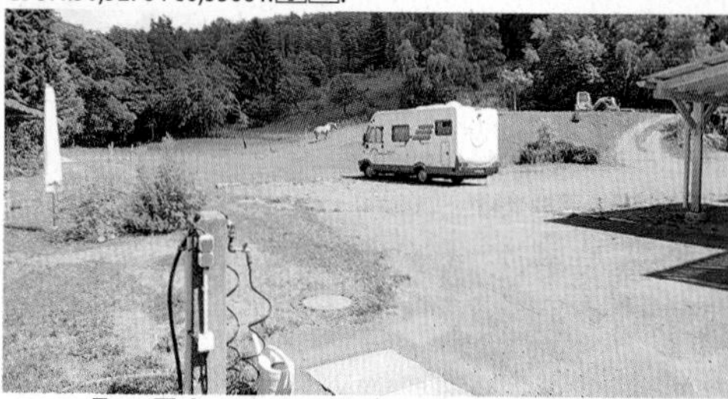

35 € 4/24h €1/30liter €1 Ch (24x)€1/2kWh.
Location: Rural, comfortable, central. **Surface:** grassy/gravel.
01/01-31/12.
Distance: 500m 400m 700m on the spot.
Remarks: Max. 3 nights.

Tourist information Kalkar:
KernWasser Wunderland. Amusement park.

Kall 11F2

Im Kallbachtal, Kapellenstrasse 25, Golbach.
GPS: n50,52784 e6,53681.

6 € 6 €1 Ch (8x)€0,50/kWh. **Location:** Rural, simple, quiet. **Surface:** gravel. 01/01-31/12.

Kamp-Lintfort 9E3

Pappelsee, Berthastraße 74. **GPS**: n51,50026 e6,53861.

20 free. **Surface:** asphalted. 01/01-31/12.
Distance: 1,5km 1km 1,5km.
Remarks: Caution € 2,50 to pay-desk of the park.

Tourist information Kamp-Lintfort:
Marktplatz, Eberstrasse. Thu, Sa.
Rathausplatz. Tue 7.30-13h.
Mittelalterlicher Markt, Abteiplatz. Medieval market. 3rd weekend Sep.

Kempen 11E1

Reisemobilpark Kempen am Aqua-sol, Berliner Allee.
GPS: n51,36719 e6,40910.

29 € 8/24h €1/100liter Ch €0,50/kWh. **Surface:** metalled.
01/01-31/12.
Distance: 1,5km on the spot 1,5km.

Kerken 9E3

Wohnmobilpark Aldekerker Platte, Kempener Straße 9, Aldekerk.
GPS: n51,43551 e6,41902.

DE

30 € 9 Ch €3. **Surface:** grassy/gravel. 01/01-31/12.
Distance: 600m ⊗600m 600m.

Kevelaer 9E3

Den Heyberg, Im Auwelt 45, Twisteden. **GPS**: n51,56345 e6,19418.

150 € 9 Ch (150x)included.
Surface: asphalted/metalled. 01/01-31/12.
Distance: 2km ⊗100m 2km 100m.
Remarks: Bread-service (weekend), barbecue place.

Kevelaer 9E3

Sporthotel Schravelsche Heide, Grotendonkerstrasse 54-58.
GPS: n51,59556 e6,25306.

80 € 9,50 Ch WC €0,50/time included.
Location: Comfortable, quiet. **Surface:** grassy. 01/01-31/12.
Distance: 1,5km ⊗100m 1km.

Kevelaer 9E3

Europaplatz, Bahnhof/Geldernstrasse, B9.
GPS: n51,57904 e6,25192.

3 free. **Surface:** asphalted.
Distance: 500m ⊗500m on the spot.

Tourist information Kevelaer:
Fr 14-18h.

Kirchhundem 11H1

Restaurant Rhein-Weser-Turm, Rhein-Weser-Turm 2.
GPS: n51,07109 e8,19791.

10 € 15 Ch included. 01/01-31/12.
Distance: ⊗on the spot.

Kirchhundem 11H1

Restaurant Zur Hahnenquelle, Rhein-Weser-Turm.
GPS: n51,07198 e8,19792.
10 € 8 Chincluded. 01/01-31/12.
Distance: ⊗on the spot.

Kirchhundem 11H1

PanoramaPark Sauerland Wildpark, Rinsecker Straße 100.
GPS: n51,06972 e8,17417.
10 € 2. 01/01-31/12.

Kleve 9E3

Stellplatz van-den-Bergh-Straße, Van-den-Bergh-Straße.
GPS: n51,78917 e6,14836.

60 € 4 Ch (30x)€0,50/kWh.
Location: Urban, simple, noisy. **Surface:** metalled. 01/01-31/12.
Distance: 500m ⊗400m 200m.
Remarks: Behind railway station, max. 72h.

Kleve 9E3

Reisemobilpark Kleve, Landwehr/Spyckstraße.
GPS: n51,80083 e6,13222.

75 € 6,50 €1 Ch (45x)€2,50 WC €0,50 €1 .
Location: Comfortable. **Surface:** grassy/metalled. 01/01-31/12.
Distance: Kleve-zentrum 1,5km ⊗300m 400m.

Kleve 9E3

Am Willisee, Zyfflicherstrasse 33, Keeken.
GPS: n51,84013 e6,08307.

25 € 10 Ch (25x)€2/day WC included.
Location: Luxurious, isolated, quiet. **Surface:** grassy/gravel.
01/01-31/12.
Distance: 900m, Kleve city centre 7km on the spot ⊗400m 4,2km 150m on the spot on the spot.
Remarks: Fishing permit available.

Kleve 9E3

Parkplatz Sporthalle Kleve-Kellen, Postdeich, Kellen.
GPS: n51,80463 e6,16378.

20 free. **Location:** Rural, simple, quiet. **Surface:** metalled.
01/01-31/12.
Distance: 2,5km ⊗Steakhaus 350m 300m on the spot.

Kleve 9E3

Schenkenschanz. **GPS**: n51,83526 e6,11205.

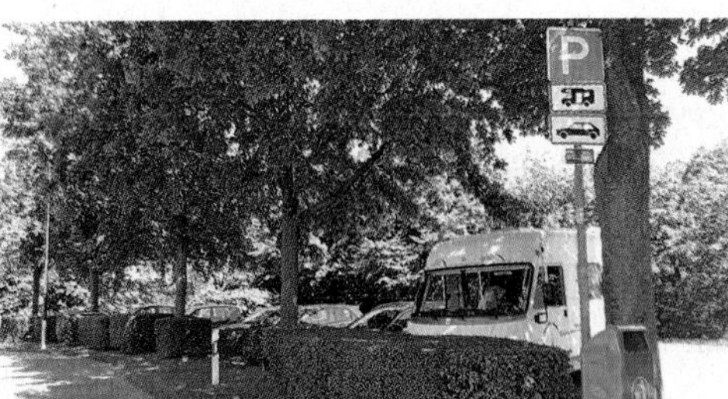

5 free. **Location:** Rural, simple, isolated, quiet. **Surface:** metalled.
01/01-31/12.
Distance: Kleve 6,5km ⊗1km 2,5km.

Kleve 9E3

Stellplatz Reichswalde, Dorfanger, Reichswalde.
GPS: n51,75985 e6,10243.

10 free. **Location:** Urban, simple, quiet. **Surface:** asphalted.
01/01-31/12.
Distance: Kleve 3km ⊗200m 500m on the spot on the spot on the spot.

Kleve 9E3

Stellplatz Rindern, Drususdeich, Rindern.
GPS: n51,81212 e6,12884.

5 free. **Location:** Rural, simple, quiet. **Surface:** metalled.
01/01-31/12.
Distance: Kleve-zentrum 2,3km ⊗450m 400m on the spot on the spot.
Remarks: Behind church.

Kleve 9E3

Tiergarten, Tiergartenstrasse, B9 dir Nijmegen.
GPS: n51,79784 e6,12059.

5 free. **Location:** Motorway, simple. **Surface:** metalled.
01/01-31/12.
Distance: 800m ⊗250m.

Kleve 9E3

Wehrpöhl, Griethausen. **GPS**: n51,82476 e6,16448.

5 free. **Location:** Rural, simple, quiet. **Surface:** asphalted.
01/01-31/12.
Distance: 2,5km ⊗300m 300m on the spot.

DE

Remarks: Access via Brienen.

Tourist information Kleve:

Lichterfest. City celebration. 2nd Sa of the month.

Tiergarten Kleve, Tiergartenstrasse. Animal park.

Köln 11F1

Reisemobilhafen Köln, An der Schanz, Cologne (Köln). **GPS:** n50,96265 e6,98254.

65 € 10/24h €1 Ch (30x)€0,50/kWh.
Location: Urban, comfortable, quiet. **Surface:** asphalted.
Distance: on the spot 5km metro 10 min walking.
Remarks: Along the Rhine river.

Königswinter 11F2

Hauptstrasse, Niederdollendorf. **GPS:** n50,69697 e7,17641.

30 free. **Location:** Urban, simple. **Surface:** asphalted/metalled. 01/01-31/12.
Distance: 400m 9km 800m on the spot on the spot.

Kranenburg 9E3

Am Sportzentrum, Großen Haag. **GPS:** n51,79242 e6,01033.

30 €4 €0,20/liter Ch (12x)€0,50/kWh.
Location: Rural, simple. **Surface:** grassy. 01/01-31/12.
Distance: 500m 1km 1km 500m 500m.
Remarks: Service 500m.

Kreuztal 11G1

Heugraben. **GPS:** n50,95778 e7,99167.

2 free €1/100liter Ch €1/2kWh. **Surface:** metalled.
Distance: 300m 7,5km 300m 300m station 100m.
Remarks: Max. 3 days.

Kürten 11G1

Wohnmobilpark am Splash, Broch 8. **GPS:** n51,05586 e7,28943.

20 €8 €2 Ch €2.
Location: Rural, simple, quiet. **Surface:** gravel. 01/01-31/12.
Distance: 2km 17km on the spot on the spot on the spot.
Remarks: Behind Sauna-/Badeland Splash.

Ladbergen 9G2

Rathauspark, Jahnstrasse. **GPS:** n52,13652 e7,74009.

8 free. **Location:** Rural, simple, quiet. **Surface:** grassy. 01/01-31/12.
Distance: 200m 200m 300m 200m on the spot.
Remarks: Parking behind town hall.

Lennestadt 11H1

Naturerlebnisbad, Fasanenweg 10. **GPS:** n51,11814 e8,16990.
3 free . 01/01-31/12.
Distance: 300m 300m.
Remarks: At swimming pool.

Lennestadt 11H1

Parkplatz P4, An der Sauerlandhalle. **GPS:** n51,10557 e8,08017.

4 free (4x)€0,50/4h. **Surface:** asphalted. 01/01-31/12.
Distance: 700m 700m 100m.

Leverkusen 11F1

Camping-Caravaning Meier, Adolf-Kaschny-Straße 9, Küppersteg. **GPS:** n51,05211 e7,00003.

10 free €0,50 Ch€0,50. **Location:** Urban. **Surface:** gravel. 01/01-31/12.
Distance: 3,2km.
Remarks: Motorhome dealer, accessory shop, repairs.

Lienen 9G2

Hallenfreibad, Holperdorperstrasse 37/39. **GPS:** n52,15575 e7,97392.

3 free €5 Ch WC €3. **Location:** Simple, quiet.
Surface: metalled. 01/01-31/12.
Distance: 1km 100m 2km on the spot on the spot.
Remarks: Parking in front of swimming pool, max. 3 nights, service to be paid at swimming pool.

Lindlar 11G1

Am Freizeitpark, Brionner Straße. **GPS:** n51,01550 e7,36645.

2 free €1 Ch (4x)€1/6h. **Location:** Urban, simple.
Surface: metalled. 01/01-31/12.
Distance: 1km 16km 1km 1km on the spot on the spot.

Lippstadt 9H3

Bückeburger Straße. **GPS:** n51,67348 e8,33336.

11 free €1/10minutes Chfree €1.
Location: Urban, comfortable, quiet. 01/01-31/12.
Distance: 1,2km 500m 600m on the spot on the spot.
Remarks: At swimming pool, max. 4 days.

Lippstadt 9H3

Camping Lippstadt, Seeuferstraße 16. **GPS:** n51,70194 e8,40789.
18 € 11, 2 pers. incl., dog € 2,50 €0,50 Ch €0,50 WC.
Surface: grassy/gravel.
Distance: 200m 200m.

Lippstadt 9H3

Campingoase Lange, Dorfstraße 47, Benninghausen. **GPS:** n51,66103 e8,24435.

15 € 10, 2 pers.incl Ch included. **Location:** Rural, simple.
Surface: metalled. 01/01-31/12.
Distance: 300m on the spot.

Löhne 9H2

Reisemobilstellplatz, Albert-Schweitzer-strasse 12. **GPS:** n52,20399 e8,71892.

DE

18 €8 Chincluded (18x)€1/2kWh. **Location:** Rural, quiet. **Surface:** metalled. 01/01-31/12.
Distance: 500m 1km 100m 500m 500m.

S Lotte 9G2

Fam. Arendröwer, Am Nordberg 4. **GPS:** n52,26306 e7,89833.

4 €4 €2/24 included. **Location:** Simple, isolated, noisy. **Surface:** grassy/metalled. 01/03-01/10.
Distance: 3km 500m 3km.

Lotte 9G2

Tennishalle Lotte, Kornweg 3. **GPS:** n52,27192 e7,92275.

10 free. **Location:** Simple, quiet. **Surface:** gravel/metalled. 01/01-31/12.
Distance: 900m 3,5km 1km 300m.

S Lübbecke 9H1

Stellplatz Lübbecke, Rahdener Straße. **GPS:** n52,31019 e8,61839.

4 €6 €3 Ch €3. **Location:** Urban, central. **Surface:** metalled. 01/01-31/12.
Distance: 600m 500m.
Remarks: Max. 3 days.

S Lüdenscheid 11G1

Familienbades Nattenberg, Talstraße 59. **GPS:** n51,21042 e7,61803.

4 free €1/100liter Ch (4x)€1/6h. **Location:** Urban, simple. **Surface:** metalled. 01/01-31/12.
Distance: city centre 1,6km 4km Burger King 450m Aldi 900m on the spot.

Lüdinghausen 9G3

Parkplatz Aqua-See, Rohrkamp 23. **GPS:** n51,77229 e7,42731.

10 free. **Location:** Rural, simple, quiet. **Surface:** metalled. 01/01-31/12.
Distance: 1,5km 1km on the spot.
Remarks: Parking swimming pool.

Lüdinghausen 9G3

Parkplatz Rosengarten, Am Rosengarten, Seppenrade. **GPS:** n51,76407 e7,39728.

2 free. **Location:** Simple, quiet. **Surface:** asphalted. 01/01-31/12.
Distance: 200m 200m 800m.

S Marsberg 10A3

Wohnmobilhafen, Am Sportplatz. **GPS:** n51,45974 e8,84864.

4 €5/24h Ch (4x)included.
Location: Urban. **Surface:** asphalted. 01/01-31/12.
Distance: 100m 200m 200m.
Remarks: Max. 5 days, caution key € 20 (pay-desk of theTherme).

Mechernich 11F2

Mühlental, Elisabethhütte, B477. **GPS:** n50,59686 e6,63207.

20 free. **Location:** Rural, simple, noisy. **Surface:** asphalted. 01/01-31/12.
Distance: 500m.

Mechernich 11F2

Parkplatz Essensgasse, Am Kirchberg, Kommern. **GPS:** n50,61376 e6,64479.

8 free. **Location:** Rural, simple, noisy. **Surface:** metalled. 01/01-31/12.
Distance: historical centre 200m.
Remarks: Via B266.

S Meinerzhagen 11G1

An der Musikschule, Schulplatz. **GPS:** n51,10865 e7,64329.

3 free (4x)€0,50/kWh. **Location:** Urban, simple, quiet. **Surface:** asphalted. 01/01-31/12.
Distance: 400m 3km 400m 400m on the spot on the spot.

S Meschede 11H1

Am Wofibad, Im Ohl 13, Freienohl. **GPS:** n51,37574 e8,17664.

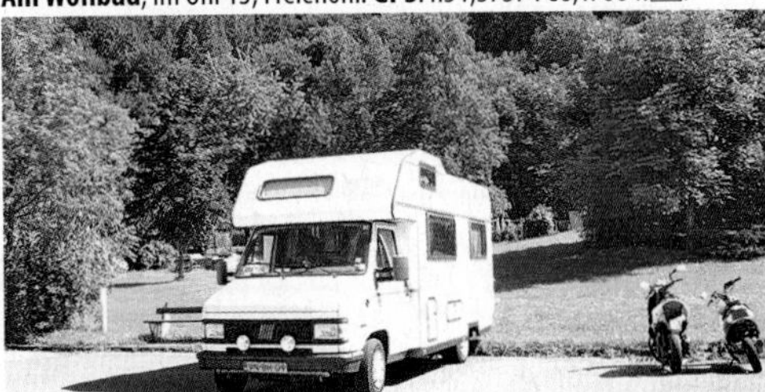

3 free against payment. **Location:** Simple. **Surface:** metalled. 01/01-31/12.

Meschede 11H1

An der Ruhr, Arnsberger Strasse. **GPS:** n51,34897 e8,27356.

10 free.
Location: Simple. **Surface:** metalled. 18.30-9.30h.
Distance: 500m on the spot on the spot 500m 500m.
Remarks: At swimming pool.

S Meschede 11H1

Knaus Campingpark Hennesee, Mielinghausen 7. **GPS:** n51,29846 e8,26366.

17 €8-10 €1/60liter €0,50 Ch€0,50 (16x)€0,70/kWh WC sanitary€2,30-3,50 .
Surface: grassy/metalled. 01/01-31/12.
Distance: 5km 100m 100m on the spot on the spot on the spot on the spot.

S Mettingen 9G2

Hallenbad, Bahnhofstrasse 18-20. **GPS:** n52,31738 e7,78312.

2 free WC. **Location:** Simple. **Surface:** metalled. 01/01-31/12.
Distance: on the spot 200m 200m on the spot on the

DE

spot on the spot.
Remarks: Parking swimming pool, service: Kläranlage, Neuenkirchenerstrasse 208, bicycle rental.

S Minden 10A2
Reisemobilstellplatz Kanzlers Weide, Hausbergerstrasse. **GPS**: n52,28750 e8,92551.

100 € 5 €1/100liter Ch (18x)€0,50/kWh,6Amp.
Location: Urban, simple, quiet. **Surface:** metalled.
01/01-31/12.
Distance: 200m 50m 50m 200m 200m 200m.
Remarks: Max. 3 nights, not during big events.

Moers 9F3
Freizeitpark Schoßpark, Krefelder straße. **GPS**: n51,44659 e6,61642.

4 free. **Surface:** grasstiles. 01/01-31/12.
Distance: 700m 700m 500m.

S Möhnesee 9H3
Freizeitanlage Möhnesee-Körbecke, Börnigeweg. **GPS**: n51,49160 e8,12555.

20 € 6/24h (8x)€2/24h.
Location: Simple. **Surface:** metalled. 01/01-31/12.
Distance: 1km on the spot on the spot 1km on the spot on the spot.
Remarks: Max. 24h.

S Möhnesee 9H3
Strandbad, Linkstraße 20, Delecke. **GPS**: n51,49177 e8,08255.
50 € 12 Ch (16x)WC included. **Location:** Rural, comfortable, quiet. **Surface:** gravel. 01/03-01/11.
Distance: Möhnesee 3,5km 7,3km A44 Möhnesee.

Möhnesee 9H3
Völlinghausen, Kettelbötel. **GPS**: n51,47360 e8,19831.

10 free. **Surface:** grassy/gravel. 01/01-31/12.
Distance: 1,5km on the spot on the spot.

Mönchengladbach 11E1
Schloß Wickrath, Neukircherweg, Wickrath.
GPS: n51,12889 e6,42258.

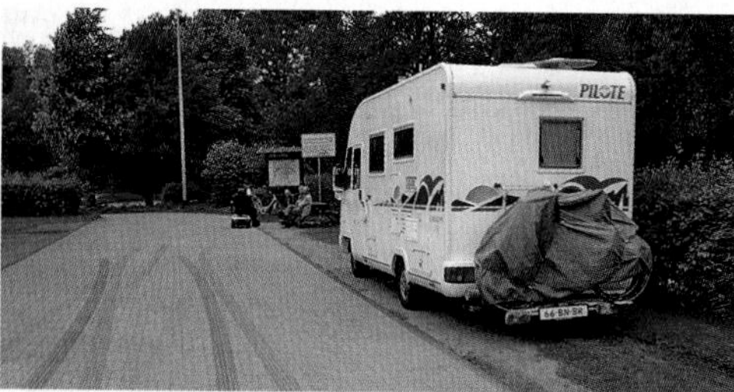

10 free. **Surface:** asphalted. 01/01-31/12.
Distance: 2km 2km 500m.
Remarks: Parking behind castle (500m), max. 2 days.

S Mönchengladbach 11E1
Camping-Center Krings, Monschauerstrasse 10/32.
GPS: n51,19454 e6,40884.

15 free Ch free. **Surface:** metalled. 01/01-31/12.
Distance: 3km 1km 500m.
Remarks: Max. 2 nights, service during opening hours.

S Monschau 11E2
Biesweg, B258. **GPS**: n50,55389 e6,23194.

4 € 12 €5/7minutes Ch (4x)€5/10h.
Location: Simple, noisy. **Surface:** asphalted. 01/01-31/12.
Distance: 600m 600m 600m.
Remarks: Max. 1 night.

Monschau 11E2
Haus Vennblick, Hauptstrasse 24, Höfen. **GPS**: n50,53934 e6,25292.

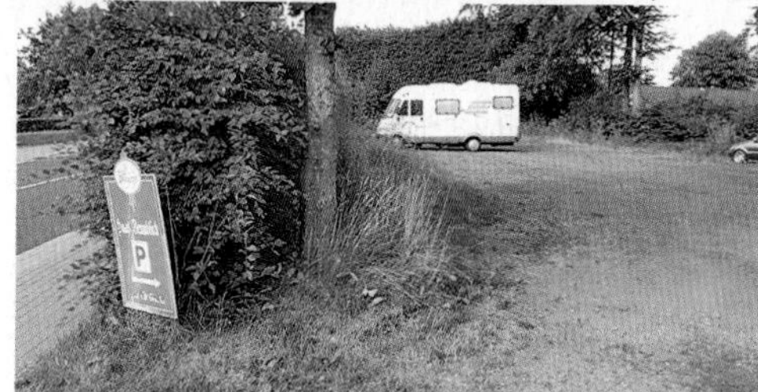

8 € 10, guests free. **Location:** Rural, simple, noisy. **Surface:** gravel.
Wed.
Distance: 300m on the spot 4km on the spot 4km.

Mülheim/Ruhr 9F3
Mintarder Straße 4. **GPS**: n51,41462 e6,86934.

6 free. **Surface:** metalled. 01/01-31/12.
Distance: 2,7km 50m 100m on the spot on the spot.
Remarks: Max. 72h.

S Mülheim/Ruhr 9F3
Hymer Zentrum, Kölner Strasse 35-37. **GPS**: n51,39985 e6,87700.
€0,50/80liter Ch.

Münster 9G2
Am Ostbad, Mauritz-Lindenweg. **GPS**: n51,95922 e7,65879.

6 free. **Location:** Urban, simple. **Surface:** metalled.
01/01-31/12.
Distance: 2,5km 100m 300m 300m on the spot.
Remarks: At swimming pool, max. 8M.

Münster 9G2
Hafenstraße/Albersloher Weg. **GPS**: n51,95199 e7,63600.

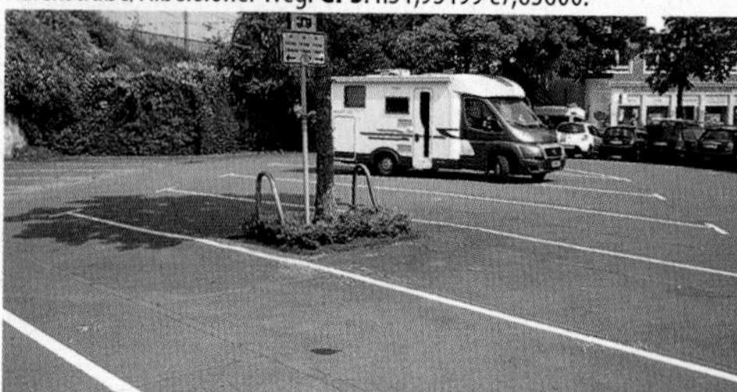

6 € 2/h, overnight stay free. **Location:** Urban, simple, central, noisy.
Surface: asphalted. 01/01-31/12.
Distance: Old city centre 1km on the spot on the spot on the spot.
Remarks: Along railwayline.

S Münster 9G2
Campingplatz Münster, Laerer Werseufer. **GPS**: n51,94583 e7,69082.

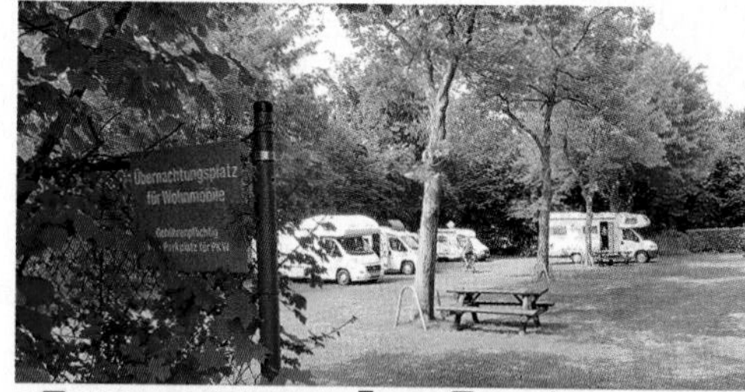

24 € 15 2 pers.incl, dog € 3,50 €0,50 €0,50 Ch€0,50 WCincluded €0,50/3 €3/day. **Location:** Rural, simple.
Surface: gravel. 01/01-31/12.
Distance: Münster 4,5km 100m on the spot 100m on the spot on the spot.
Remarks: Pay at reception campsite.

S Netphen 11H1
Freitzeitpark Netphen, P3, Brauersdorferstrasse. **GPS**: n50,91250 e8,12567.

3 € 3,50/day €1/70liter Ch. **Surface:** metalled.
01/01-31/12.
Distance: 2km 2km.
Remarks: Max. 3 nights, coins at swimming pool.

DE

Wohnmobilhafen Nettersheim, Urftstraße.
GPS: n50,48606 e6,62627.
25 € 8,50/24h €1 Ch (25x)included.
Location: Rural, simple, quiet. **Surface:** metalled.
01/01-31/12.
Distance: 500m 7,5km on the spot 500m 1,5km 700m on the spot on the spot on the spot.
Remarks: Bread-service.

Nettetal 11E1

Am Nettebruch, Flothender straße/Flothend.
GPS: n51,30188 e6,26715.

5 free. **Surface:** grassy/gravel. 01/01-31/12.
Distance: 1km on the spot on the spot 1km.

Nettetal 11E1

Am Krickenbeck See, Krickenbecker Allee 38. **GPS**: n51,34460 e6,25793.

50 Free, use of a meal desired. **Surface:** asphalted. 01/01-31/12.
Distance: 2km on the spot 2km.

Neuss 11F1

Allrounder Winterworld/Skihalle, An der Skihalle 1.
GPS: n51,17316 e6,64862.

30 free. **Surface:** metalled. 01/01-31/12.
Distance: on the spot indoor ski.

Nideggen 11E2

Parkplatz Danzley, Bahnhofstrasse. **GPS**: n50,69247 e6,47952.

14 free. **Location:** Rural, simple. **Surface:** metalled.
01/01-31/12.
Distance: 500m 500m.

Nordkirchen 9G3

Hotel Plettenberger Hof, Schlossstrasse 28.
GPS: n51,73659 e7,52819.

2 guests free. **Surface:** asphalted. 01/01-31/12.
Distance: 200m on the spot.

Nottuln 9G2

Wellenfreibad/Hallenbad, Rudolf-Harbigstrasse.
GPS: n51,92410 e7,34514.

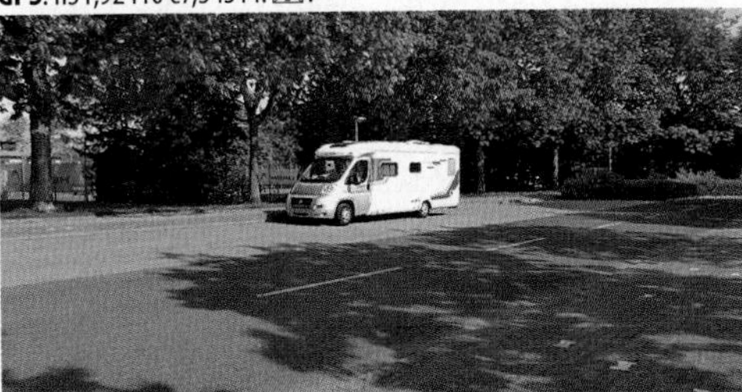

5 free. **Location:** Rural, simple. **Surface:** metalled.
01/01-31/12.
Distance: 1,5km bakery 800m on the spot.
Remarks: Parking swimming pool, service during opening hours.

Oberhausen 9F3

Stellplatz Kaisergaten, Am Kaisergarten 28.
GPS: n51,48743 e6,85519.

60 € 7 €1/100liter Ch (24x)€0,50/2h.
Surface: grassy. 01/01-31/12.
Distance: Oberhausen City 30 min walking 1,6km 1,7km 1,7km.

Oberhausen 9F3

Stellplatz Marina, Heinz-Schleußer-Straße 1.
GPS: n51,49444 e6,88417.
18 € 1,25/meter €2/day WC €1.
Surface: gravel/metalled. 01/01-31/12.
Distance: 1km 200m on the spot 250m 800m.

Oberhausen 9F3

Parking 10 - CentrO, Arenastraße. **GPS**: n51,48930 e6,87063.

40 free. **Surface:** metalled. 01/01-31/12.
Distance: 100m on the spot on the spot.
Remarks: At CentrO.

Tourist information Oberhausen:
CentrO. Large shopping centre, 250 shops, 100 restaurants/bars and a market. 10-20h restaurants till 22h, thu 10-21h.

Oedt 11E1

Wohnmobile-Stellplatz Niers-Perle-Oedt, Mühlengasse.
GPS: n51,32327 e6,37650.

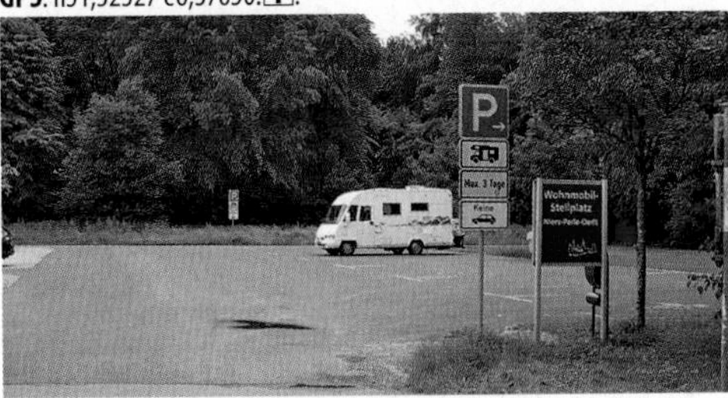

7 free. **Surface:** asphalted. 01/01-31/12.
Distance: 800m 500m 500m.

Oelde 9H3

Pott's Brau und Backhaus, In der Geist 120.
GPS: n51,81192 e8,13103.

6 € 5 €1/60liter Ch included. **Location:** Simple, noisy.
Surface: grassy/metalled. 02/01-23/12.
Distance: 500m on the spot.
Remarks: Caution key € 35.

Olpe 11G1

Freizeitbad Olpe, Seeweg 5. **GPS**: n51,03242 e7,84163.

10 € 5 €0,20/liter Ch (4x)€1/2kWh WC included, at swimming pool 7-22h. **Location:** Urban. **Surface:** asphalted.
01/01-31/12.
Distance: 500m 2km 250m.
Remarks: On the banks of the Biggesee, max. 3 days.

Olsberg 9H3

Wohnmobilplatz am AquaOlsberg, Zur Sauerlandtherme 1.
GPS: n51,35637 e8,48487.
10 € 8,50/24h, tourist tax € 1,50/pp €1/80liter €1/8h.
Surface: grassy.
Distance: on the spot 250m 250m.
Remarks: Discount at swimming pool.

Ostbevern 9G2

Bever Bad, Am Hanfgarten 22. **GPS**: n52,03673 e7,84392.

DE

6+10 € 10, overnight stay only 20-9h free Ch WC included.
Location: Luxurious, quiet. **Surface:** grassy.
01/01-31/12.
Distance: 400m 300m 300m 300m.
Remarks: Parking swimming pool, caution key service € 10, incl. access swimming pool.

Overhetfeld 11E1

Camp Graskamp, Graskamp 19. **GPS:** n51,22259 e6,13977.

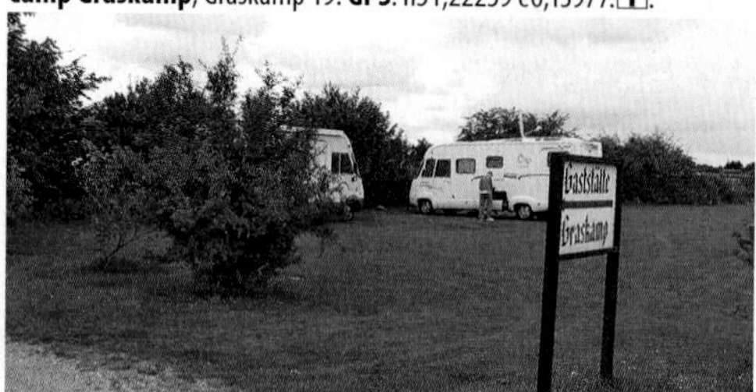

5 € 8 Ch WC included.
Surface: grassy. 01/01-31/12.
Distance: 200m 200m on the spot.

Paderborn 9H3

Maspernplatz, P4, Hathumarstrasse. **GPS:** n51,72278 e8,75417.

7 day € 6, weekend free (4x)€0,50/h. **Location:** Urban, central, noisy. **Surface:** metalled. 01/01-31/12.
Distance: 500m 4km 100m 500m on the spot.

Paderborn 9H3

Rolandsbad, Fürstenweg. **GPS:** n51,72825 e8,74509.

16 € 5/24h €0,50/60liter Ch (16x)€0,50/kWh.
Surface: asphalted. 01/01-31/12.
Distance: centre 700m on the spot on the spot on the spot on the spot.
Remarks: Max. 72h.

Paderborn 9H3

Lippesee-Nordufer, Sennelagerstraße 58, Sande.
GPS: n51,76087 e8,67756.

10 free. **Location:** Rural, simple. **Surface:** grassy.
01/01-31/12.
Distance: city centre Paderborn 9km 150m 150m 1km 500m on the spot on the spot.

Paderborn 9H3

Heinz Nixdorf MuseumsForum, Fürstenallee 7.
GPS: n51,73193 e8,73592.
3 free. **Surface:** metalled. 01/01-31/12.
Distance: centre 2,5km on the spot.
Remarks: At museum.

Petershagen 10A1

Am Sportplatz, Hohoffstraße 15. **GPS:** n52,37532 e8,96875.

10 free €1/90liter (8x)€1/kWh. **Location:** Urban, quiet.
Surface: metalled. 01/01-31/12.
Distance: 100m 100m 100m on the spot.
Remarks: Nearby football ground, max. 3 days, check in at tourist office.

Plettenberg 11G1

Aqua Magis, Albert Schweizerstrasse, Böddinghausen.
GPS: n51,23220 e7,85308.

12 free €1/40liter Ch (8x)€0,50 WC.
Location: Rural, comfortable, quiet. **Surface:** metalled.
01/01-31/12.
Distance: on the spot 11km on the spot 200m on the spot on the spot.
Remarks: At paradise pool, max. 48h.

Raesfeld 9F3

Wohnmobilstellplatz Graf Alexander, Südring.
GPS: n51,76523 e6,83035.

8 € 8 €1/8minutes Ch (8x)€1/12h WC.
Location: Rural, simple, quiet. **Surface:** gravel.
01/01-31/12.
Distance: 1km 150m on the spot on the spot.
Remarks: At historic moated castle, max. 2 nights.

Recke 9G1

Yackthafen Marina Recke, Auf der Haar 23.
GPS: n52,35082 e7,71174.

40 € 7 Ch (10x)€1,50 WC €1,50.
Surface: grassy/metalled. 01/01-31/12.
Distance: 1km, Recke 3,5km on the spot on the spot on the spot 900m 400m on the spot on the spot.
Remarks: At the Mittelland canal, check in at harbourmaster.

Rees 9E3

Stellplatz Rees am Niederrhein, Ebentalstrasse.
GPS: n51,76428 e6,38829.

46 € 6/day Ch included. **Location:** Urban, comfortable, central. **Surface:** grassy. 01/01-31/12.
Distance: 400m.
Remarks: Behind swimming pool, bread-service.

Reken 9F3

Wohnmobilstellplatz Reken, Bergen 2a.
GPS: n51,82864 e7,05895.

20 € 6 €1/200liter Ch (20x)€0,50/kWh.
Location: Rural, comfortable, quiet. **Surface:** grassy.
01/01-31/12.
Distance: 1km 1km 1km on the spot.
Remarks: Max. 2 days, friday market.

Remscheid 11F1

Brückenpark Müngsten, Mügstener Brückenweg.
GPS: n51,16833 e7,13750.

4 free. **Location:** Rural, simple, quiet. **Surface:** gravel.
01/01-31/12.
Distance: 5km 4km 100m 100m on the spot.
Remarks: Max. 1 night.

Remscheid 11F1

Dörperhöhe, Bei Haus nr. 15, Lennep. **GPS:** n51,17986 e7,30205.
4 free. **Surface:** asphalted. 01/01-31/12.
Remarks: Max. 1 night.

Remscheid 11F1

Jahnplatz, Am Stadion, Lennep. **GPS:** n51,19052 e7,26110.
4 free. **Surface:** asphalted. 01/01-31/12.
Distance: historical centre of Lennep 300m.
Remarks: Max. 1 night.

Remscheid 11F1

Garage Pauli GmbH, Lenneperstrasse 152 (Bundesstrasse 229).
GPS: n51,18020 e7,22591.
3 free Ch free. **Surface:** grasstiles. 01/01-31/12.
Remarks: At motorhome dealer, max. 1 night.

Rheda-Wiedenbrück 9H2

Am Werl, Güterslöherstrasse. **GPS:** n51,85456 e8,29768.

4 free Ch WC. **Location:** Urban. **Surface:** metalled.

DE

01/01-31/12.
Distance: 300m 300m.
Remarks: Max. 3 days.

Rheda-Wiedenbrück 9H2

P Hallenbad, Ostring/Am Hallenbad, Wiederbrück.
GPS: n51,83188 e8,32350.

4 free. **Location:** Urban, quiet. **Surface:** metalled.
01/01-31/12.
Distance: 1km 200m bakery 200m on the spot on the spot.
Remarks: Parking swimming pool.

Rhede 9F3

Reisemobilstellplatz Kettelerplatz, Kettelerstrasse 9.
GPS: n51,83677 e6,69346.

15 free €1/3minutes Ch (6x)€1/stay.
Location: Urban, simple, quiet. **Surface:** grassy.
01/01-31/12.
Distance: 750m 750m 500m.
Remarks: At fire-station.

Rhede 9F3

Hallen- und Freibad, Heideweg 59. **GPS**: n51,83164 e6,68635.

2 free. **Location:** Urban, simple, quiet. **Surface:** metalled.
01/01-31/12.
Distance: 1,5km 600m 1,2km.
Remarks: Parking swimming pool, max. 3 days.

Rheinbach 11F2

Freizeitpark Monte Mare, Münstereifelerstraße 69.
GPS: n50,61883 e6,93262.

4 free. **Location:** Rural, simple. **Surface:** metalled.
01/01-31/12.
Distance: 1,5km on the spot 1,5km.
Remarks: Max. 3 days.

Rheine 9G2

Im Stadtpark, Kopernikusstrasse. **GPS**: n52,28137 e7,45478.

2 free. **Location:** Urban, simple. **Surface:** metalled.
01/01-31/12.
Distance: 500m on the spot 500m 300m on the spot on the spot.

Rheine 9G2

Am Naturzoo, Weihbishof-Dalhaus-strasse.
GPS: n52,29526 e7,41645.

10 free. **Location:** Rural, simple. **Surface:** grasstiles.
01/01-31/12.
Distance: 1,5km 5km on the spot 100m.

Rheurdt 9E3

Wohnmobilhafen Ökodorf, St. Nikolausweg 15.
GPS: n51,46382 e6,46780.

21 € 10 Ch included WC.
Surface: metalled. 01/01-31/12.
Distance: 500m 500m 500m on the spot on the spot.

Rietberg 9H3

Jakobistrasse, Mastholte. **GPS**: n51,75667 e8,39111.

6 free €0,50/80liter Ch. **Location:** Rural, central.
Surface: asphalted. 01/01-31/12.
Distance: 100m 100m 100m.

Rietberg 9H3

Parkplatz Rottwiese, Jerusalemer Straße.
GPS: n51,80999 e8,41203.
free Ch. **Surface:** gravel. 01/01-31/12.
Distance: centre 1,2km.
Remarks: At museum.

Rietberg 9H3

Am Heimathaus, Langenberger Strasse, Mastholte.
GPS: n51,75765 e8,38945.

2 free. **Location:** Urban. **Surface:** asphalted. 01/01-31/12.
Distance: 100m 100m 100m.

Roetgen 11E2

Am Bahnhof, Bahnhofstrasse. **GPS**: n50,64868 e6,18506.

10 free. **Location:** Rural, simple, noisy. **Surface:** gravel/metalled.
01/01-31/12.
Distance: 300m 300m.

Rosendahl 9F2

Wohnmobilplatz Darfeld, Sudetenstrasse, Darfeld.
GPS: n52,02696 e7,26501.

20 free €1/100liter Ch (12x)€1/6h. **Location:** Rural, simple. **Surface:** grassy/metalled. 01/01-31/12.
Distance: 500m on the spot 500m 1km.

Rüthen 9H3

Auf der Kamp. GPS: n51,49523 e8,43293.

12 €5 €1 Ch €1/8h. **Surface:** asphalted.
Distance: on the spot 200m.

Sassenberg 9H2

Parkplatz Feldmark, Feldmark. **GPS**: n52,00370 e8,06528.

3 free €1/80liter Ch. **Location:** Rural, simple.
Surface: metalled.
Distance: 2,5km 100m on the spot on the spot on the spot on the spot.

Schieder 10A2

Freizeitzentrum Schiedersee, Kronenbruch.
GPS: n51,92073 e9,16471.

DE

300 € 10 €1/100liter Ch €0,50/kWh WC €0,50 €2.
Location: Rural, comfortable, quiet. **Surface:** grassy/metalled.
01/01-31/12.
Distance: 1,3km 50m 50m on the spot on the spot on the spot on the spot.

S Schleiden 11E2

Wohnmobilhafen am Nationalpark-Eifel, Pfarrer-Kneipp-Straße, Gemünd. **GPS**: n50,57855 e6,49107.

55 € 8, tourist tax € 1/pp Ch included €1,100m.
Location: Rural, comfortable, quiet. **Surface:** gravel/metalled.
01/01-31/12.
Distance: within walking distance 500m 500m on the spot on the spot.
Remarks: Bread-service.

Schleiden 11E2

Erlebnisfreibad, Im Wiesengrund. **GPS**: n50,52993 e6,47022.

3 free. **Location:** Rural, simple, quiet. **Surface:** asphalted.
01/01-31/12.
Remarks: Max. 24h.

S Schloss Holte/Stukenbrock 9H2

Reisemobilstellplatz Am Sennebach, Liemkerstrasse 27, Liemke. **GPS**: n51,86979 e8,61531.

20 € 5 €2 Ch (18x)included. **Location:** Rural, isolated, quiet. **Surface:** grasstiles. 01/01-31/12 service: sa/su.
Distance: 1km 1km.
Remarks: Behind Froli Kunstoffwerk Fromme.

S Schmallenberg 11H1

Im Sorpetal, Winkhausen 21. **GPS**: n51,16083 e8,34056.

11 € 9 + € 1,25/pp tourist tax €0,50/60liter Ch (12x)€0,50/kWh. **Surface:** grassy. 01/01-31/12.
Distance: on the spot 100m 2km 500m 1km on the spot.
Remarks: Trout pond, golf court 500m, playground.

S Schöppingen 9F2

Schulze Althoff, Heven 48. **GPS**: n52,07361 e7,22361.

30 € 14/night, 3 pers. Incl, 4th pers. € 4 Ch (12x) included,6Amp WC sanitary €2/pp €5. **Location:** Rural, simple.
Surface: grassy.
Distance: 2,5km on the spot on the spot 2,5km on the spot.
Remarks: Swimming pool available.

Senden 9G2

Sportpark Senden, Buldenerstrasse 13b. **GPS**: n51,85419 e7,47433.

10 free. **Location:** Simple, noisy. **Surface:** grasstiles.
01/01-31/12.
Distance: on the spot 200m 300m on the spot.
Remarks: Parking at sports park.

S Senden 9G2

Wohnmobilstellplatz Steinhoff, Gettrup 37.
GPS: n51,83305 e7,46878.

10 € 6 Ch (6x)€0,50/kWh. **Location:** Rural, isolated.
Surface: grassy/metalled. 01/01-31/12.
Distance: Senden 4km 2,5km 2,5km.

S Sendenhorst 9G2

Westor 31. **GPS**: n51,84286 e7,81849.

3 free €0,50/40liter Ch €0,50.
Location: Urban, simple, central, noisy. **Surface:** metalled.
01/01-31/12.
Distance: on the spot 300m 1km on the spot.
Remarks: Max. 3 nights.

S Siegen 11H1

An der Alche, Freudenbergerstraße 67. **GPS**: n50,88073 e8,00764.
4 free €0,50/40liter Ch (4x)€0,50/kWh. 01/01-31/12.
Distance: 1km 5km 200m 1km.
Remarks: Max. 3 days.

S Siegen 11H1

Hallenbad Weidenau, Poststraße 27. **GPS**: n50,89463 e8,02405.

3 free €1/10minutes Ch (2x)€1/8h. **Location:** Urban.
Surface: metalled. 01/01-31/12.
Distance: 200m 200m 200m 250m on the spot on the spot.
Remarks: Max. 3 days.

S Simmerath 11E2

Wohnmobilhafen Rurseezentrum, Seeufer 1, Rurberg.
GPS: n50,60658 e6,38177.

10 € 8/24h €2 Ch. **Location:** Rural, comfortable.
Surface: grasstiles. 01/01-31/12.
Distance: 100m 50m.

S Soest 9H3

City Motel, Altes Stellwerk 9. **GPS**: n51,57503 e8,11478.

14 € 8 Ch (14x) €2 €3 included.
Location: Urban, comfortable, central, quiet. **Surface:** gravel.
01/01-31/12.
Distance: 200m 200m 200m 200m on the spot on the spot.

Solingen 11F1

Am Brandteich, Gräfrath. **GPS**: n51,21151 e7,07217.

10 free. **Location:** Urban, simple, quiet. **Surface:** concrete.
01/01-31/12.
Distance: on the spot 2,7km on the spot 300m.
Remarks: Parking fire-station.

S Stadtlohn 9F2

Freizeit- und Hallenbad, Uferstrasse 29.
GPS: n51,99792 e6,93019.

4 free €0,50/100liter Ch (4x)€1/kWh WC.
Location: Rural, simple, isolated. **Surface:** metalled. 01/01-31/12

water disconnected in winter.
Distance: 800m 1km 800m.
Remarks: Parking swimming pool.

S Steinfurt 9G2

Wohnmobilstellplatz Steinfurt, Liedekerkerstrasse 70, Burgsteinfurt.
GPS: n52,14738 e7,34746.

20 free €1/100liter Ch €1/2kWh. **Location:** Rural, simple.
Surface: gravel. 01/01-31/12.
Distance: 1km 500m 200m.
Remarks: Parking behind police station, max. 3 nights, voluntary contribution.

Steinfurt 9G2

Am Rathaus, Emsdettener Strasse 40. **GPS**: n52,12822 e7,39356.

6 free. **Location:** Urban, simple. **Surface:** asphalted.
01/01-31/12.
Distance: 400m 200m 400m 400m 200m.

Steinhagen 9H2

Am Cronsbach. **GPS**: n51,99998 e8,42351.

2 free. **Location:** Urban, simple. **Surface:** metalled.
01/01-31/12.
Distance: 100m 100m 100m.
Remarks: Max. 2 days.

S Stemwede 9H1

Stellplatz Hollenmühle, Hinterm Teich 3, Levern.
GPS: n52,36783 e8,43833.

36 € 14 Ch WC included. **Location:** Rural, comfortable. **Surface:** grassy/gravel. 01/01-31/12.
Distance: on the spot 3,2km.
Remarks: Bread-service.

Stemwede 9H1

Park Stemwederberg, Stemwederbergstrasse/Freudeneck, Westrup.
GPS: n52,43246 e8,43973.

8 free. **Location:** Rural, comfortable. **Surface:** grassy.
01/01-31/12.
Distance: 2km 2km 2km on the spot.

S Stemwede 9H1

Hotel-Gasthof Moorhof, Wagenfelderstrasse 34, Oppenwehe.
GPS: n52,49979 e8,53507.

20 € 7, free with a meal included €2,16Amp.
Location: Rural, quiet. **Surface:** grassy.
01/01-31/12 Mo, Thu.
Distance: on the spot.

S Straelen 9E3

Fitnessbad Wasserstraelen, Lingsforterstraße 100.
GPS: n51,45201 e6,25708.

27 € 8 €1/80liter Ch (30x)€0,50/kWh included.
Surface: asphalted. 01/01-31/12.
Distance: 1,2km 1km 1km.
Remarks: Max. 3 days.

Tecklenburg 9G2

Parkplatz Bismarckturm, Am Weingarten.
GPS: n52,22129 e7,79905.

5 € 4. **Location:** Simple, quiet. **Surface:** asphalted.
01/01-31/12.
Distance: 800m 200m.

S Tecklenburg 9G2

Regenbogen-Camp, Grafenstraße. **GPS**: n52,22941 e7,89052.
4 € 10 > 17h < 13h Ch included. **Location:** Urban, simple, noisy. **Surface:** asphalted. 01/01-31/12.
Distance: Tecklenburg 7km.

S Telgte 9G2

Am Dümmert, Emstor. **GPS**: n51,98497 e7,79151.
3 free €1/100liter Ch €1/kWh. **Location:** Simple.
Surface: gravel. 01/01-31/12.
Distance: 600m 600m 600m on the spot.

S Telgte 9G2

Waldschwimmbad Klatenberge, Waldweg.
GPS: n51,99459 e7,78328.

20 free. **Location:** Rural, simple. **Surface:** asphalted.
01/01-31/12.
Distance: 1km 300m 900m on the spot.
Remarks: Parking swimming pool, recreation area.

S Telgte 9G2

Altes Gasthus Lauheide, Lauheide 3, K17.
GPS: n51,99862 e7,75319.

80 € 10 Ch included. **Location:** Quiet. **Surface:** grassy.
01/01-31/12 Restaurant: Wed.
Distance: 4km on the spot Bus 300m on the spot on the spot.

S Uedem 9E3

Reisemobilstellplatz Uedem, Bergstraße 99.
GPS: n51,66173 e6,28734.

26 € 9 Ch WC included. **Location:** Rural, comfortable.
Surface: grassy. 01/01-31/12.
Distance: 1,5km 1,3km on the spot on the spot.

S Velbert 11F1

Unter der Saubrücke, Parkstraße, Velbert-Mitte.
GPS: n51,34097 e7,03050.

6 € 5/24h €1/100liter Ch €0,50/kWh.
Location: Urban, simple, quiet. **Surface:** gravel.
01/01-31/12.
Distance: 800m 1,6km 250m on the spot.

S Velbert 11F1

Panoramabad Velbert-Neviges, Wiesenweg.
GPS: n51,30582 e7,08546.

4 free €1/80liter Ch. **Location:** Urban, simple, quiet.
Surface: concrete. 01/01-31/12.

DE

Distance: 800m nearby 500m.
Remarks: Parking swimming pool, max. 3 nights.

Velbert 11F1

Domparkplatz, Bernsaustrasse Schloss Hardenberg.
GPS: n51,31565 e7,08724.

4 free.
Location: Urban. **Surface:** gravel. 01/01-31/12.
Distance: 600m on the spot.
Remarks: Max. 3 nights.

Velbert 11F1

Nizzabad, Nizzatal 4, Langenberg. **GPS**: n51,34362 e7,13766.

3 free. **Location:** Simple, quiet. **Surface:** metalled.
01/01-31/12.
Distance: Langenberg 2,5km on the spot.
Remarks: Max. 3 nights.

Velen 9F2

Stellplatz Erholungsgebied, Klyer Damm 8-10.
GPS: n51,90167 e7,01167.

30 € 15, 2 pers.incl Ch (50x) WC €1/4minutes.
Location: Rural, luxurious. **Surface:** gravel.
01/01-31/12.
Distance: 2km 8,5km on the spot on the spot on the spot.
Remarks: Bread-service (weekend).

Velen 9F2

Freibad Ramsdorf, Velener Straße, Ramsdorf.
GPS: n51,88955 e6,92503.

5 free. **Location:** Rural, simple, noisy. **Surface:** asphalted.
01/01-31/12.
Distance: Ramsdorf 300m 200m on the spot on the spot.
Remarks: At swimming pool.

Viersen 11E1

Am Familienbad Ransberg, Heesstraße 80, Viersen-Dülken.
GPS: n51,25083 e6,35291.

9 € 10 €0,50/100liter Ch (9x)included.
Surface: metalled. 01/01-31/12.
Distance: Dülken 400m, Viersen 3km 400m 2km 100m.
Remarks: Max. 3 days, to be paid at swimming pool.

Vreden 9F2

Hotel Zum Möwenparadies, Zwillbrockerstrasse 39.
GPS: n52,05305 e6,70733.

10 € 10 Ch WC included. **Location:** Simple, isolated.
Surface: grassy. 01/01-31/12.
Distance: 4km on the spot on the spot on the spot 200m.
Remarks: Trout pond.

Vreden 9F2

Wohnmobilpark Vreden, Ottensteiner Strasse 59.
GPS: n52,03962 e6,84136.

50 € 8, 4 pers.incl Ch (14x)included WC €2 €3/h.
Location: Rural, simple, quiet. **Surface:** grassy.
01/01-31/12.
Distance: 500m on the spot.
Remarks: Breakfast-service, swimming pool € 2/pp.

Wachtendonk 9E3

Bleiche P4, Achter de Stadt. **GPS**: n51,40601 e6,33170.

24 € 7 €0,50/60liter €0,50 Ch (12x)€0,50/kWh.
Surface: gravel. 01/01-31/12.
Distance: 400m 100m 400m.
Remarks: Money in envelope in mail box.

Wadersloh 9H3

Im Klostergarten 18, Liesborn. **GPS**: n51,71414 e8,25960.

4 free €0,50/80liter Ch (4x)€0,50/12h. **Location:** Rural.
Surface: metalled. 01/01-31/12.
Distance: 400m 100m 400m on the spot on the spot.
Remarks: Behind gymnasium.

Waldbröl 11G2

Am Hallenbad, Vennstrassse. **GPS**: n50,87511 e7,60987.

5 free. **Location:** Rural, simple, quiet. **Surface:** metalled.
01/01-31/12.
Distance: on the spot 350m 300m on the spot on the spot.
Remarks: Max. 2 days.

Waldfeucht-Brüggelchen 11E1

Reisemobilstellplatz Tilder Weg, Tilderweg.
GPS: n51,07076 e5,99454.

18 € 5 €1/80liter Ch (10x)€0,50/kWh.
Location: Rural, simple, quiet. **Surface:** metalled.
01/01-31/12.
Distance: 1km on the spot 500m 100m on the spot.
Remarks: Max. 4 nights, money in envelope in mail box.

Waltrop 9G3

Restaurant Zur Lohburg, Lohburgerstrass 105, A2 Ausfahrt henreichenburg, Schiffshebewerk. **GPS**: n51,60613 e7,34882.

10 € 5 €3. **Surface:** grassy. 01/01-31/12.
Distance: 1km on the spot 1km.

Warburg 10A3

Schützenplatz, Paderborner Tor 134. **GPS**: n51,48993 e9,13810.
5 € 5 Ch included. **Surface:** metalled.
15/09-15/10.
Distance: 500m 100m 200m.
Remarks: Max. 3 days.

Warendorf 9G2

DE

Parkplatz am Emsseepark, Sassenberger Strasse.
GPS: n51,95447 e7,99904.
14 free €1/50liter Ch (14x)€1/kWh.
Location: Rural, simple, central, quiet. **Surface:** metalled.
01/01-31/12.
Distance: 500m on the spot 100m 800m 100m on the spot on the spot.

Warendorf 9G2

Parkplatz Zwischen den Emsbrücken, Am Emswehr.
GPS: n51,95426 e7,99164.

2 free. 01/01-31/12.
Distance: 100m.

S Warstein 9H3

Camperpark zum Bayernstadl, Enkerbruch 12a.
GPS: n51,43041 e8,37432.

40 € 8 €1/100liter Ch (18x)€2/day . **Surface:** gravel.
01/01-31/12.
Distance: 1,5km on the spot 1,5km 1,5km.
Remarks: Bread-service.

S Warstein 9H3

Vans in Paradise, Zu Hause im Waldpark. **GPS**: n51,42615 e8,35525.

40 € 15 Ch (76x),16Amp WC included €2/2.
Location: Isolated, quiet. **Surface:** grassy/gravel. 01/01-31/12.
Distance: 2km small menu 2km 2km.
Remarks: At Warstein brewery, bread-service + breakfast-service.

S Warstein 9H3

Schützenhalle, Schützenstraße 30, Hirschberg.
GPS: n51,43398 e8,27477.
3 free . 01/01-31/12 Whitsuntide.
Distance: 500m, Warstein 12km 500m.

Warstein 9H3

Wohnmobilstellplatz, Dammweg. **GPS**: n51,45103 e8,34750.

5 free.
Location: Simple. **Surface:** gravel/metalled.
01/01-31/12.
Distance: 2km 500m 1km 1km.
Remarks: At sports park.

Tourist information Warstein:
Warsteiner Brauerei, Zu Hause im Waldpark. Guided tour 1.45h, 2 drinks included. daily 12-17, Su 13-15h.

S Wassenberg 11E1

Parkbad Wassenberg, Auf dem Taubenkamp 2.
GPS: n51,09833 e6,14364.

11 € 5/day, € 20/week €1/100 €1 Ch €0,50/kWh.
Location: Rural, comfortable, quiet. **Surface:** metalled.
01/01-31/12.
Distance: 1,5km.
Remarks: To be paid at swimming pool.

S Weeze 9E3

Tierpark Fährsteg, L5 Fährsteg. **GPS**: n51,63074 e6,20086.

13 € 5 €0,50/kWh. **Location:** Simple. 01/01-31/12.
Distance: 500m 500m.

S Weeze 9E3

Aral, Industriestraße. **GPS**: n51,62029 e6,20972.
€1 Ch.

S Wegberg 11E1

Wegberger Reisemobilstellplatz, Schul- und Sportzentrum, Maaseiker Strasse 67. **GPS**: n51,13389 e6,28266.

10 € 8 Ch included.
Surface: grassy/gravel. 01/01-31/12.
Distance: 400m 400m 400m on the spot.
Remarks: To be paid at swimming pool, caution key € 20.

S Werne 9G3

Natur Solebad, Am Hagen. **GPS**: n51,65910 e7,63414.

12 € 5/24h €1/80liter Ch €0,50/kWh.
Surface: metalled. 01/01-31/12.
Distance: 400m 200m 400m.
Remarks: Tuesday and Friday market.

S Wesel 9F3

Reisemobilstellplatz Römerwardt, Rheinpromenade.
GPS: n51,66116 e6,59256.

45 € 7, 01/04-31/10 € 9 €1/80liter Ch included €1/kWh €1,50/time. **Location:** Rural, comfortable, quiet.
Surface: grassy/metalled. 01/01-31/12.
Distance: 1,5km 100m 1,5km on the spot on the spot.
Remarks: Check in on arrival, bread-service, bicycle rental, market Wednesday and Saturday.

Westerkappeln 9G2

Am Freibad, Bullerteichstraße 12. **GPS**: n52,31556 e7,88070.

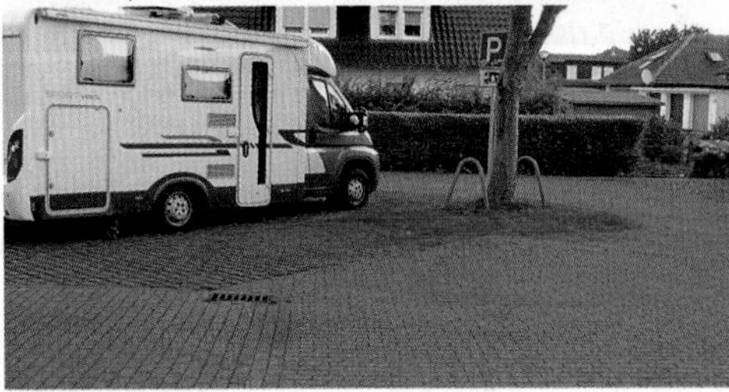

2 free. **Location:** Urban, simple. **Surface:** grasstiles.
01/01-31/12.
Distance: 600m 400m 50m.

S Wiehl 11G1

Freizeitpark Wiehl, Brüchnerstrasse. **GPS**: n50,94716 e7,54585.

5 free €1/80liter Ch.
Location: Simple, central.
Surface: metalled.
Distance: 300m 5,4km 400m.
Remarks: Parking next to recreation park and disco, max. 3 nights.

Wiehl 11G1

Sportplatz Eichhardt, Friedhofstrasse.
GPS: n50,95110 e7,54482.

3 free.
Location: Urban. **Surface:** metalled.
01/01-31/12.
Distance: 1km 5,3km 1km 1km.
Remarks: Parking sports park, max. 3 nights.

Tourist information Wiehl:
www.wiehl.de. Small town in the green hills. 180 kilometres marked hiking routes.
Wiehler Dahlienschau. 150 varieties of dahlias. 01/08-31/10 daily 9-19h. free.
Wiehler Trofsteinhöhle. Caves Temperature is approx. 8ºC.
15/03-31/10 10-17h, 01/11-14/03 Sa-Su 11-16h.
Bergische Postkutsche, Nümrecht Post. Ride by mail-coach between Wiehl and Nümbrecht. 01/05-30/09 Fri-Su 10-16h.

S Wilnsdorf 11H2

Wielandshof, Bauhofstraße 5. **GPS**: n50,80692 e8,10896.

DE

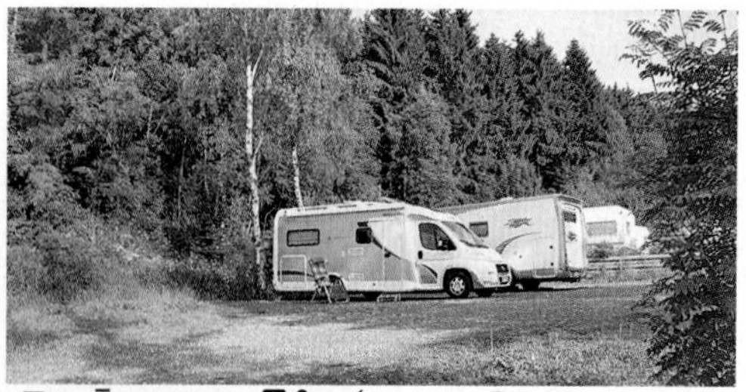

5 €5 €0,50/60liter Ch (4x)€1/12h. **Surface:** gravel.
01/01-31/12.
Distance: 900m 900m.
Remarks: Check in at farm.

S Windeck 11G2

Am Sportplatz, Im Bungert, Herchen. **GPS:** n50,78025 e7,51308.

5 free (10x)€0,50/kWh. **Location:** Rural, simple, quiet.
Surface: gravel. 01/01-31/12.
Distance: 200m 8,5km 200m 200m on the spot on the spot.
Remarks: Parking sports park.

S Windeck 11G2

Hallenbad, Bergische strasse 21, Dattenfeld.
GPS: n50,80754 e7,56105.

4 free €2 €2 Ch€2. **Location:** Rural, simple, quiet.
Surface: metalled. 01/01-31/12.
Distance: 8,5km on the spot on the spot.

Windeck 11G2

Auf dem Greent, Dattenfeld. **GPS:** n50,80697 e7,55495.

50 free. **Location:** Rural, simple, quiet. **Surface:** asphalted/grassy.
01/01-31/12.
Distance: 500m 8,5km 500m 500m.
Remarks: Fair ground.

Windeck 11G2

Brunnenweg, Dattenfeld. **GPS:** n50,80486 e7,56087.

5 free. **Location:** Simple, quiet. **Surface:** grassy/gravel.
01/01-31/12.
Distance: 200m 8km 200m 150m on the spot on the spot.

Remarks: Recreation park.

Windeck 11G2

Museumsdorf Altwindeck, Im Thal Windeck 17, Alt-Windeck.
GPS: n50,81276 e7,57554.

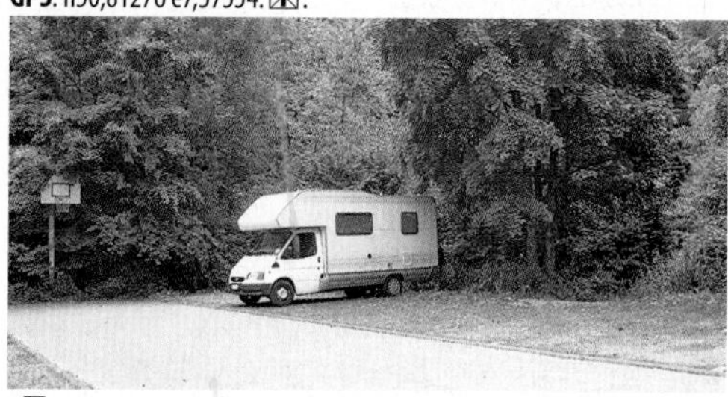

4 free. **Location:** Rural, simple, quiet. **Surface:** gravel.
01/01-31/12.
Distance: 2km 8,5km on the spot 2km on the spot on the spot.
Remarks: Parking museum, max. 3 days.

S Winterberg 11H1

Wohnmobilpark Winterberg, Neuastenberger Straße 4a, OT Neuastenberg. **GPS:** n51,15974 e8,48383.
70 €7,50-13,50 + € 1,95/pp tourist tax €1/100liter Ch €0,60/kWh €1 €2,50/2,50. **Surface:** gravel.
01/01-31/12.
Distance: on the spot on the spot.
Remarks: Bread-service.

S Winterberg 11H1

Parkplatz Stadthalle, Schulstrasse. **GPS:** n51,19163 e8,53810.

20 €8/24h €0,50/50liter Ch (10x)€0,50/3h.
Surface: metalled. 01/01-31/12.
Distance: 1km 1km.

Winterberg 11H1

Bergrestaurant Bobhaus, Auf der Kappe 1. **GPS:** n51,18493 e8,50559.

8 € 12, free with a meal.
Location: Rural. **Surface:** asphalted.
Distance: 2km on the spot on the spot on the spot on the spot on the spot.
Remarks: Parking ski-lift, check in at restaurant.

S Winterberg 11H1

Campingplatz Winterberg. **GPS:** n51,18632 e8,50445.

€ 18,50-20,50 Ch (25x)€0,55/kWh WC €1 €0,50.
Location: Rural, luxurious. **Surface:** metalled. 01/01-31/12.
Distance: 2km on the spot 2km 20m on the spot on the spot on the spot on the spot.
Remarks: Parking at skipistes.

S Witten 9G3

Reisemobil-Center, Pferdebachstrasse 150.
GPS: n51,45411 e7,35246.

8 free €1/80liter Ch. **Surface:** gravel. 01/01-31/12.
Distance: 3km 3km 3km.

Wülfrath 11F1

Parkplatz, Mettmanner Straße 42. **GPS:** n51,28188 e7,02741.

6 free. **Location:** Urban, simple, quiet. **Surface:** concrete.
01/01-31/12.
Distance: on the spot 500m 800m.

S Xanten 9E3

Womopark Xanten, Fürstenberg 6. **GPS:** n51,65413 e6,46389.

60+20 € 10 + tourist tax € 2,50/motorhome Ch included €3 €1. **Location:** Rural, luxurious, quiet. **Surface:** grassy.
01/01-31/12.
Distance: 1,7km 300m 200m.
Remarks: Check in on arrival.

S Zülpich 11F2

Wohnmobilpark Seepark, Eichenallee.
GPS: n50,67660 e6,65867.

40 €9 €1 Ch included. **Location:** Rural, simple, isolated. **Surface:** grassy. 01/01-31/12.
Distance: 100m.
Remarks: Service nearby tenniscourt 100m.

Rhineland-Palatinate/Saarland

S Alf 11F3

Freizeitbad Arrastal, Mühlenstraße. **GPS:** n50,05273 e7,11326.

100 €6 Ch included €2,50/day . **Location:** Rural, simple. **Surface:** asphalted/grassy. 01/01-31/12.
Distance: 800m.

DE

Alken 11G3

Moselstraße 1. **GPS**: n50,25090 e7,44590.

5 free. **Location:** Rural, simple. **Surface:** gravel.
01/01-31/12.
Distance: 200m 100m 200m on the spot.

Alsheim 16H1

Weingut Elisabethenhof, In den Weingärten 10.
GPS: n49,76563 e8,34748.

4 € 10 included €2/24h. **Location:** Rural, simple, quiet.
Surface: concrete. 01/01-31/12.
Distance: 300m 500m.

Altdorf 16H2

Schulstraße. **GPS**: n49,28426 e8,22035.
free. **Surface:** metalled.
Distance: 300m 300m.

Altdorf 16H2

Spelzenhof, Hauptstrasse 77. **GPS**: n49,28869 e8,22028.

6 € 7,50 included. **Location:** Simple. **Surface:** grassy.
01/01-31/12 Mon, Tue.
Distance: nearby 7km 150m 400m nearby.

Altendiez 11H3

Restaurant Bimbes-Stubb, Lahnblick 4.
GPS: n50,36612 e7,98041.

6 € 8 included. **Location:** Simple. **Surface:** gravel.
01/01-31/12 Mo.
Distance: on the spot on the spot 500m.

Altenglan 16G1

Draisine, Austrasse. **GPS**: n49,55001 e7,46465.

4 free €1/80liter Ch (6x)€1. **Location:** Rural, simple, quiet.
Surface: gravel. 01/04-31/10.
Distance: 100m 100m on the spot on the spot.

Andernach 11G2

Wohnmobilstellplatz Andernach, Scheidsgasse/Uferstrasse.
GPS: n50,44176 e7,40796.

70 € 7 €1/100liter Ch (40x)€1/2kWh WC €0,50.
Surface: metalled. 01/01-31/12.
Distance: on the spot Rhine river 200m 400m.
Remarks: Max. 3 nights.

Andernach 11G2

Wohnmobilstellplatz Monte Mare, Klingelswiese 1.
GPS: n50,42633 e7,38492.

12 € 3 €1/100liter Ch (12x)€0,50/kWh WC.
Surface: concrete. 01/01-31/12.
Distance: 2km.
Remarks: Bread-service.

Tourist information Andernach:
Sa 7-13h.

Annweiler 16H2

Am Kurpark, Bindersbacherstrasse. **GPS**: n49,19624 e7,96817.

10 free €1/80liter Ch free. **Location:** Rural, quiet.
Surface: asphalted. 01/01-31/12.
Distance: 1km 600m.
Remarks: Max. 3 days.

Bacharach 11G3

Reisemobilplatz Sonnenstrand, B9 Leinpfad.
GPS: n50,05487 e7,77123.

30 € 8 €1 Ch (12x)€2,50/24h €1 €3/3.
Location: Comfortable, central, quiet. **Surface:** gravel.
01/01-31/12 high water.
Distance: on the spot Rhine river 300m 300m.
Remarks: Bread-service.

Bad Bergzabern 16H2

Schloßgärten, Weinbergstrasse 7. **GPS**: n49,10322 e7,99737.

10 € 4 €1/80liter €1 Ch €1.
Location: Urban, simple, central, noisy. **Surface:** metalled.
01/01-31/12 water disconnected in winter.
Distance: on the spot on the spot 200m.

Bad Bergzabern 16H2

Weingut Hitziger, Liebrauenbergweg 3. **GPS**: n49,10667 e7,99611.

8 € 5 Ch included €1/kWh.
Location: Rural, simple, quiet. **Surface:** grassy. 01/01-31/12.
Distance: 1km 2km 2km.

Bad Dürkheim 16H1

In der Silz, Leistadterstrasse. **GPS**: n49,46944 e8,16722.

170 € 6 €1/80liter Ch €1/kWh.
Location: Urban, simple. **Surface:** grassy/gravel. 01/01-31/12.
Distance: 300m 100m 300m 200m.
Remarks: Servicepoint at Knaus Park.

Bad Dürkheim 16H1

Katharinenhof, In den Kornwiesen 1. **GPS**: n49,46633 e8,20144.
10 € 10 Ch. **Surface:** grassy. 01/01-31/12.
Remarks: Bread-service.

Bad Dürkheim 16H1

Knaus park, In den Almen 3. **GPS**: n49,47472 e8,19167.

16 € 9,50 €1/70liter Ch €0,70/kWh €3,30/pp.
Surface: gravel/metalled. 01/01-31/12.

Bad Ems 11G3

Yachthafen Kutscher's Marina, Nievernerstrasse 20.
GPS: n50,33278 e7,70167.

16 € 10 Ch €1/kWh WC €1. **Location:** Comfortable, quiet. **Surface:** gravel. 01/03-15/11.
Distance: on the spot on the spot 1km 300m.

DE

S Bad Kreuznach 16G1

Wohnmobilstellplatz Salinental, Karlshalle 11, Saline.
GPS: n49,82778 e7,85001.

40 € 13 €0,50/60liter Ch €3/night WC €1.
Surface: gravel. 01/01-31/12.
Distance: 2km on the spot on the spot 200m 2km on the spot.

S Bad Kreuznach 16G1

Weingut Desoi, Am Darmstädter Hof. **GPS**: n49,82803 e7,88934.

3 € 5 included. **Location:** Rural, simple, quiet.
Surface: concrete. 01/01-31/12.
Distance: 1,5km 10km 500m.

S Bad Kreuznach 16G1

Weingut Gut Neuhof, Gut Neuhof. **GPS**: n49,86923 e7,85924.

4 € 10 included. **Location:** Rural, simple, quiet.
Surface: grassy. 01/01-31/12.
Distance: 3km 2,5km.

S Bad Marienberg 11G2

Marienbad, Bismarckstrasse 65. **GPS**: n50,64321 e7,93515.

40 € 10 €1/80liter Ch (40x)€0,50/kWh included.
Location: Luxurious, quiet. **Surface:** metalled. 01/01-31/12.
Distance: 2km Bistro.
Remarks: 10 days € 78, bread-service, free use of sun beds and beach chairs.

S Bad Münster am Stein-Ebernburg 16G1

Reisemobilstellplatz Weingut Rapp, Schlossgartenstrasse 74.
GPS: n49,80800 e7,83208.

3 € 9,50 €1/100liter . **Location:** Rural, simple, quiet.
Surface: gravel. 01/01-31/12.
Distance: 15km.

S Bad Neuenahr 11F2

Am Schwimmbad. **GPS**: n50,53806 e7,10139.

25 € 7 €0,50 Ch €1/2kWh €0,50.
Location: Urban, central. **Surface:** metalled. 01/01-31/12.
Distance: 400m 300m bakery 500m.
Remarks: Along the Ahr river, max. 24h.

S Bad Neuenahr 11F2

Apolinaris-Stadion, Kreuzstrasse. **GPS**: n50,54456 e7,15132.

20 € 5/24h €1/80liter Ch. **Surface:** asphalted.
01/01-31/12.
Distance: 3km.

Bad Neuenahr 11F2

Wohnmobilstellplatz Bachem, St.-Pius-Straße.
GPS: n50,53962 e7,10775.

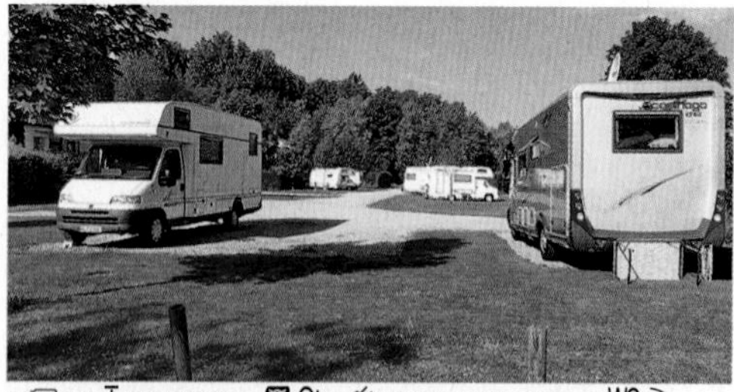

20 € 5/24h. **Location:** Urban, simple. **Surface:** asphalted.
01/01-31/12.
Distance: 700m 700m.
Remarks: Parking at the Ahr.

S Bad Sobernheim 16G1

Reisemobilstellplatz am Nohfels, Hömigweg 1.
GPS: n49,77993 e7,65702.

39 € 9 €0,10/10liter Ch (48x)€2,50/day,16Amp WC .
Location: Rural, comfortable, quiet. **Surface:** metalled.
01/01-31/12.
Distance: 500m 100m 100m 200m 500m 300m on the spot on the spot.
Remarks: Bread-service.

S Battweiler 16G2

Flugplatz Pottschütthöhe, Pottschütthöhe.
GPS: n49,26761 e7,49096.

10 € 15 Ch (10x)included. **Location:** Simple, isolated, quiet. **Surface:** grassy/gravel. 01/01-31/12 Mo.
Distance: 2km 10km on the spot.
Remarks: At airfield.

Baumholder 16G1

Freizeitzentrum Am Weiher, Ringstrasse.
GPS: n49,61111 e7,33917.

3 free. **Location:** Rural, simple. **Surface:** asphalted.
01/04-31/10.
Distance: 2km on the spot McDonalds 250m 250m.

S Becheln 11G3

Restaurant Zum Wolfsbusch, Emser strasse 1.
GPS: n50,29609 e7,71503.

5 € 2, guests free €2. **Location:** Simple, quiet.
Surface: gravel/metalled.
Distance: on the spot on the spot 300m.

S Beckingen 16F2

Wohnmobilstellplatz Düppenweiler, Brunnenstrasse 11, Düppenweiler. **GPS**: n49,41414 e6,76973.

20 € 4 €1/100liter Ch (6x)€1/day. **Location:** Simple, quiet. **Surface:** metalled. 01/01-31/12.
Distance: on the spot 300m.

S Beckingen 16F2

Landgasthaus Wilscheider Hof, Zum Wilscheider Hof, Düppenweiler.
GPS: n49,42562 e6,76422.

15 € 5 Ch (7x)€1/day WC €1,50 . **Location:** Rural, comfortable, isolated, quiet. **Surface:** grassy. 01/01-31/12.
Distance: 1,5km on the spot 1,5km.

DE

S Bellheim 16H2

Wohnmobilstellplatz Bellheim, Auchtweide.
GPS: n49,19552 e8,27466.

8 € 5 WC included €1/pp. **Location:** Simple, isolated, quiet. **Surface:** grassy/gravel. 01/05-31/10.
Distance: 700m 3km 750m 1km 200m.
Remarks: At tennis-courts, max. 24h.

Bendorf 11G2

Wohnmobilstellplatz Bendorf, Koblenz Olper Strasse.
GPS: n50,43998 e7,57486.
6 free. 01/01-31/12.
Distance: 4km.

S Bernkastel 11F3

Weingut Studert-Prüm im Maximin Hof, Hauptstrasse 150, Wehlen.
GPS: n49,93771 e7,04811.

43 € 10-12 Ch WC included. **Location:** Rural, comfortable, quiet. **Surface:** grassy. 01/04-31/10.
Distance: on the spot on the spot on the spot on the spot 2km, bakery 300m on the spot on the spot.

P S Bernkastel 11F3

Nikolausufer. **GPS**: n49,91119 e7,06721.

40 Ch. **Location:** Urban. **Surface:** grasstiles. 01/01-31/12, 10-18h.
Distance: on the spot.
Remarks: Max. 6h.

Betzdorf 11G2

Friedrichstrasse. **GPS**: n50,78636 e7,87781.

1 free. **Location:** Urban, simple, noisy. **Surface:** asphalted. 01/01-31/12.
Distance: 500m.
Remarks: Max. 24h.

Betzdorf 11G2

Schützenplatz, Martin-Luther-Strasse. **GPS**: n50,79323 e7,86793.

1 free. **Location:** Urban, simple. **Surface:** gravel. 01/01-31/12.
Distance: on the spot on the spot.
Remarks: Max. 1 night.

Betzdorf 11G2

Vor dem Stadion, Eberhardystrasse. **GPS**: n50,78524 e7,86507.

1 free. **Location:** Urban, simple, central. **Surface:** gravel. 01/01-31/12.
Distance: 1km 50m on the spot on the spot.
Remarks: Max. 1 night.

S Bexbach 16G2

Bexbacher Reisemobilhafen, Im Blumengarten.
GPS: n49,34161 e7,25698.

35 € 7 €1/80liter Ch (36x)€2,50/night WC.
Location: Rural, luxurious, quiet. **Surface:** grassy. 01/01-31/12.
Distance: 900m 5km on the spot 500m 200m on the spot on the spot.
Remarks: Bread-service.

S Biebelnheim 16H1

Wohnmobilpark am Petersberg, Flonheimer Strasse 34.
GPS: n49,79432 e8,16236.

20 € 5 €2 Ch €2. **Surface:** metalled. 01/01-31/12.
Distance: 1km 1,5km Bistro Am Petersberg 1km.
Remarks: Max. 2 nights.

S Biebernheim 11G3

Reiterhof Pabst, Auf dem Flürchen. **GPS**: n50,14127 e7,70828.

20 € 6, 2 pers.incl Ch (6x)€2. **Location:** Rural, simple, isolated, quiet. **Surface:** grassy. 01/01-31/12.
Distance: 10km.

Remarks: Bread-service.

S Bingen/Rhein 11H3

Wohnmobilpark Bingen, Mainzer Straße, Bingen/Kempten.
GPS: n49,96860 e7,94417.

39 € 6,50/night Ch €2,50/24h €3/3 included stay.
Location: Comfortable, quiet. **Surface:** grassy/metalled. 01/01-31/12.
Distance: 2,5km 1,5km 800m 2,7km.
Remarks: Bread-service.

S Birgel 11F3

Historische Wassermühle, Bahnhofstrasse 16.
GPS: n50,32033 e6,61764.

10 € 15, free with a meal > € 15 Ch (2x)included.
Location: Simple, quiet. **Surface:** gravel. 01/01-31/12.
Distance: 500m 25km on the spot 1km.

S Blieskastel 16G2

Freizeitanlage Würzbacher Weiher, Marxstraße, Niederwürzbach.
GPS: n49,24674 e7,19226.

10 € 4,50 €1/10minutes €1 Ch €1/4h.
Location: Rural, simple, quiet. **Surface:** grassy/gravel. 01/01-31/12.
Distance: 500m on the spot on the spot 100m 600m 600m.
Remarks: At lake, Würzbacher Weiher.

S Blieskastel 16G2

Hotel Restaurant Hubertushof, Kirschendell 32.
GPS: n49,24456 e7,21573.

8 € 5, free with a meal.
Surface: asphalted. 01/01-31/12.
Distance: on the spot on the spot 1km.
Remarks: Arrival < 19h, max. 2 nights, bread-service.

Blieskastel 16G2

Freizeitzentrum Blieskastel, Bliesaue 1, Webenheim.
GPS: n49,23527 e7,26946.

DE

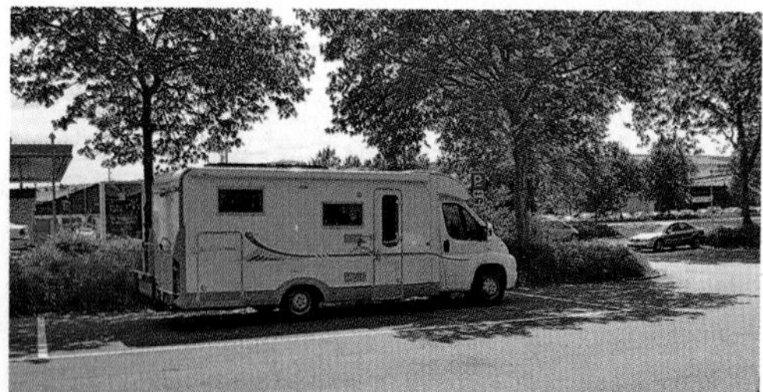

3 free. **Location:** Urban, simple, noisy. **Surface:** metalled.
01/01-31/12.
Distance: on the spot 5km on the spot.

Bobenthal/Bornich 16H2

Hotel-Restaurant St. Germanshof, Hauptstrasse 10.
GPS: n49,04749 e7,89985.

4 guests free. **Surface:** metalled. 01/01-31/12 Mo.
Distance: 5km on the spot 7km.

Bockenheim 16H1

Weingut Benss, Am Spiegelpfad 10. **GPS:** n49,59959 e8,17823.

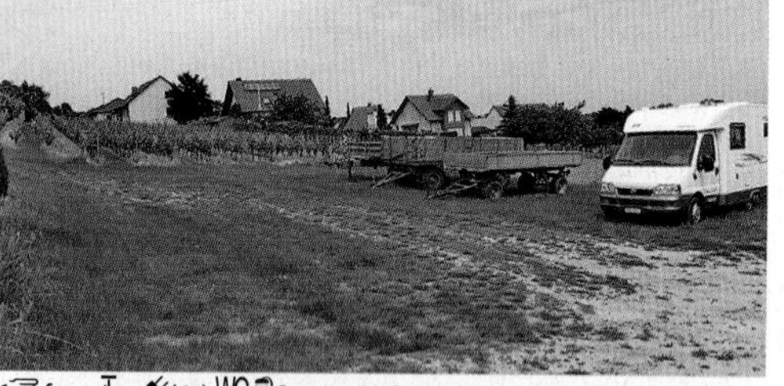

6 free (6x) WC Service€5. **Location:** Rural, simple, quiet.
Surface: grassy. 01/01-31/12.
Distance: 7km 500m 3km.

Bockenheim 16H1

Weingut W. Kohl, Am Sonnenberg 3. **GPS:** n49,59902 e8,17925.

6 € 8/night WC included. **Surface:** metalled.
01/01-31/12.
Distance: 500m 500m 3km.

Braubach 11G3

Braubacher Rheintreff, Rheinuferstrasse, B42.
GPS: n50,26972 e7,64750.

30 € 10 liter Ch kWh WC included €3.
Location: Comfortable, quiet. **Surface:** asphalted. 01/01-31/12.
Distance: 300m on the spot on the spot 300m 300m 300m.
Remarks: Bread-service.

Brauneberg 16F1

Wohnmobilplatz Juffer, Moselweinstrasse.
GPS: n49,90518 e6,97760.

25 € 8 Ch. **Surface:** metalled. 01/01-31/12.
Distance: 100m on the spot 300m 300m 100m.

Bremm 11F3

Weingut Oster-Franzen, Calmontstrasse 96.
GPS: n50,09593 e7,12383.

16 € 14, 2 pers incl €0,50/60liter Ch €0,60/kWh WC €2/6minutes €3,50. **Location:** Rural, comfortable.
Surface: gravel. 01/03-30/11.
Distance: on the spot 800m on the spot on the spot.

Briedern 11F3

Wohnmobilstellplatz Briedern, Moselstrasse.
GPS: n50,11165 e7,20867.

15 € 6,50.
Location: Rural, simple. **Surface:** grassy/gravel.
Distance: on the spot 300m 200m on the spot.

Brodenbach 11G3

Moselufer. **GPS:** n50,22471 e7,43930.

2 free. **Location:** Urban, simple. **Surface:** metalled.
01/01-31/12.
Distance: 500m 500m on the spot.

Brodenbach 11G3

Salzwiese 9. **GPS:** n50,22519 e7,44291.

4 free. **Location:** Urban. **Surface:** concrete. 01/01-31/12.
Distance: 400m Moselle river 200m 400m.

Burgen 11G3

Hotel Schmause Mühle, Baybachstrasse 50.
GPS: n50,20859 e7,39365.

20 € 8 Ch €2,50/day WC €1.
Location: Quiet. 01/01-31/12.
Distance: on the spot on the spot 300m.

Burgen bei Bernkastel-Kues 16F1

Weingut Bohn-Leimbrock, Lindenstrasse 6.
GPS: n49,87986 e6,99967.

4 € 8 WC. **Surface:** grassy. 01/01-31/12.
Distance: 150m 50m 2km 50m on the spot on the spot.

Burrweiler 16H2

Wein- und Sektgut Hermann-Bruno Eberle, Böchingerstrasse 1a.
GPS: n49,24649 e8,07989.

3 € 6 WC included. **Location:** Rural, quiet.
Surface: metalled. 01/01-31/12.
Distance: 100m 200m.
Remarks: Arrival <21h.

Burrweiler 16H2

Weingut Diether Bauer, Weinstrasse 52. **GPS:** n49,21982 e8,03059.

3 € 5 WC included. **Location:** Rural, quiet.
Surface: metalled. 01/01-31/12.
Distance: on the spot 300m.

Burrweiler 16H2

Weingut Hertel, Raiffeisenstrasse 2. **GPS:** n49,24861 e8,07705.

3 € 5 free WC on demand. **Location:** Rural, simple, quiet.
Surface: metalled. 01/04-31/10.

Burrweiler 16H2

Weingut Winzerhof, Am Schlossberg 3. **GPS:** n49,25147 e8,07902.

DE

4 € 8 WC included. **Location:** Rural, quiet.
Surface: metalled. 01/01-31/12.
Distance: 1km 300m.

Busenberg 16G2

Weißensteiner Hof, An der B427. **GPS**: n49,12152 e7,83943.

3 guests free on demand. **Location:** Rural, simple.
Surface: asphalted. 01/01-31/12 Mon + Fri.

Cochem 11F3

Bergstrasse, K59. **GPS**: n50,15028 e7,17083.

4 € 2,50 9-19h, overnight stay free.
Surface: grasstiles/metalled.
Distance: 300m 300m.

Cochem 11F3

Moselpromenade, B49. **GPS**: n50,14108 e7,16936.

4 € 1/h 8-19h, overnight stay free. **Surface:** metalled.
01/01-31/12.

Cochem 11F3

Wohnmobil-Stellplatz an der Nordbrücke, Moselstrasse, B49.
GPS: n50,15329 e7,16828.

16 € 1/h 8-19h, overnight stay free. **Location:** Urban, simple.
Surface: metalled. 01/01-31/12.
Distance: 700m 200m 200m on the spot.

Cochem 11F3

Wohnmobil-Stellplatz am Freizeitzentrum, Stadionstrasse.
GPS: n50,16051 e7,17956.

50 € 0,50/h . **Surface:** gravel/sand. 01/01-31/12.
Distance: 2,5km 400m on the spot.
Remarks: Along the Moselle river, max. 24h.

Dahn/Reichenbach 16G2

Altes Bahnhöf'l, An der Reichenbahn 6. **GPS**: n49,13890 e7,79908.

10 free. **Location:** Rural, simple, quiet. **Surface:** gravel.
01/01-31/12 Mo.
Distance: on the spot on the spot 100m.

Darscheid/Vulkaneifel 11F3

Kucher's Landhotel, Karl-Kaufmann-Strasse 2.
GPS: n50,21060 e6,88270.
3 guests free . 01/01-31/12 Tue.

Deidesheim 16H2

Weinhaus Villa Giessen, Weinstrasse 3. **GPS**: n49,41210 e8,19105.
3 € 7,50 . 01/01-31/12.
Distance: 5km.

Deudesfeld 11F3

Meisburgerstrasse. **GPS**: n50,10084 e6,72932.

8 free € 1/120liter € 1 Ch € 0,50/kWh. **Location:** Rural, simple, quiet. **Surface:** grassy. 01/01-31/12.
Distance: 300m.

Deudesfeld 11F3

Leyendecker Platz, Mandertscheider Strasse.
GPS: n50,10164 e6,73217.

4 free. **Location:** Rural, simple, quiet. **Surface:** gravel.
01/01-31/12.
Distance: 200m.

Deuselbach 16F1

Wohnmobilstellplatz Erbeskopf, K130. **GPS**: n49,73589 e7,08327.

50 € 4 Ch (5x)€ 3/day WC included € 0,50/5minutes.
Location: Rural, simple, quiet. **Surface:** metalled.
01/01-31/12.
Distance: 10km.

Dexheim 16H1

Weingut Bacchushof, Wörrstädter Strasse 14.
GPS: n49,84812 e8,31144.

5 free.
Location: Rural, simple. **Surface:** concrete. 01/01-31/12.
Distance: 12km.

Dierbach 16H2

Jahnstrasse. **GPS**: n49,08177 e8,06201.

10 € 5 Ch (5x)free. **Location:** Simple, quiet.
Surface: asphalted. 01/01-31/12.
Distance: 700m 12km 1km 3km 50m.
Remarks: At sports centre.

Dierbach 16H2

Weingut Geiger, Hauptstrasse 21. **GPS**: n49,08344 e8,06673.

30 € 10 Ch WC included € 2/day. **Location:** Rural, comfortable, luxurious, quiet. **Surface:** grassy. 01/03-31/12.
Distance: on the spot 12km 500m.
Remarks: Bread-service.

Dolgesheim 16H1

Weingut Seck, Weinolsheimer Strasse 12. **GPS**: n49,79752 e8,26154.

3 € 5 included. **Location:** Rural, simple, quiet.
Surface: grassy. 01/01-31/12.
Distance: 200m 13km 300m 2km.

Dörrenbach 16H2

Übergasse. **GPS**: n49,08840 e7,96921.

DE

10 €6 Ch included. **Location:** Rural, quiet.
Surface: gravel/sand. 01/01-31/12.
Distance: 500m 700m.
Remarks: Next to sports fields.

Eckersweiler 16G1

Am Sportplatz. GPS: n49,55646 e7,30577.

4 free. **Location:** Rural, simple, isolated. **Surface:** grassy.
01/01-31/12.
Distance: 1,3km on the spot on the spot.

Edenkoben 16H2

Wohnmobilstellplatz Kirchbergplatz, Bahnhofstraße.
GPS: n49,28234 e8,13116.

40 €5 €1/100liter Ch (8x)€1/kWh. **Surface:** asphalted.
01/01-31/12.
Distance: on the spot 2km 300m Aldi 800m.
Remarks: Max. 3 nights.

Edenkoben 16H2

Obstgut & Brennerei Göring, Blücherstrasse 45.
GPS: n49,27792 e8,13487.

5 €10 Ch included WC.
Surface: grassy. 01/01-31/12.
Distance: 3km.

Edenkoben 16H2

Weingut Bernd und Herbert Schäfer, Rhodter Strasse 24.
GPS: n49,27844 e8,12572.
3 free €5. 01/01-31/12.
Distance: 3,5km.

Edenkoben 16H2

Weingut Edel Brauch, St.-Martiner-Strasse 30.
GPS: n49,28901 e8,12236.
4 free €2 Ch €2. 01/01-31/12.
Distance: 3km.

Edenkoben 16H2

Gasthof Ziegelhütte, Luitpoldstrasse 75-79. **GPS:** n49,28539 e8,13872.

3 €5/night . **Surface:** metalled. 01/01-31/12.
Distance: on the spot 1km on the spot on the spot.

Edesheim 16H2

Weingut Boos, Ludwigstrasse 150. **GPS:** n49,25785 e8,11673.

3 €6 Ch (3x)included. **Location:** Rural, simple, quiet.
Surface: grassy. 01/01-31/12.
Distance: 500m 300m 1km.
Remarks: Bread-service.

Edesheim 16H2

Weingut Braun & Sohn, Ludwigsstrasse 151.
GPS: n49,25761 e8,11587.

3 €5 Ch included. **Location:** Rural, simple, quiet.
Surface: grassy. 01/01-31/12.
Distance: 300m 300m.

Edesheim 16H2

Weingut Erlenmühle, Erlenmühle 1. **GPS:** n49,25865 e8,11417.

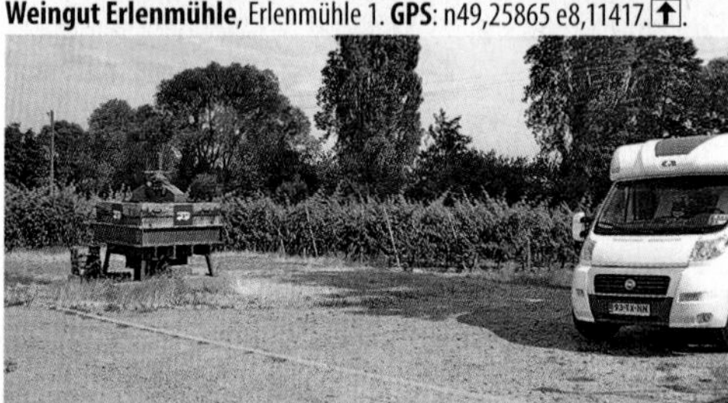

5 €5 Ch included on demand.
Location: Rural, simple, quiet. **Surface:** gravel. 01/01-31/12.
Distance: 500m on the spot 1km.
Remarks: Arrival <22h.

Edesheim 16H2

Weingut Rehm, Ludwigstrasse 36. **GPS:** n49,26015 e8,12734.

6 €5 included (6x)€2,50/day WC €2,50. **Location:** Rural, simple, quiet. **Surface:** grassy. 01/01-31/12.

Ediger/Eller 11F3

Stellplatz Ediger, Moselweinstrasse. **GPS:** n50,09320 e7,15942.

18 €5 Ch included. **Location:** Rural, simple.
Surface: gravel/metalled. 01/04-30/11.
Distance: 100m on the spot on the spot on the spot on the spot on the spot.
Remarks: Along the Moselle river in Ediger.

Ediger/Eller 11F3

Stellplatz Moselufer, Eller. **GPS:** n50,09915 e7,14370.

10 €5.
Location: Rural, simple. **Surface:** metalled. 01/04-30/11.
Distance: on the spot on the spot on the spot 200m on the spot.
Remarks: Along the Moselle river in Eller.

Eisenschmitt 11F3

Hotel-Restaurant Molitors Mühle, Eichelhütte.
GPS: n50,03681 e6,73766.

5 guests free WC included.
Location: Rural, simple. **Surface:** gravel. 01/01-31/12.
Distance: 1km 6km on the spot on the spot on the spot 1km 300m on the spot.
Remarks: Arrival <23h.

Ellenz/Poltersdorf 11G3

Weingut Loosen, Im Goldbäumchen 4. **GPS:** n50,11389 e7,23528.

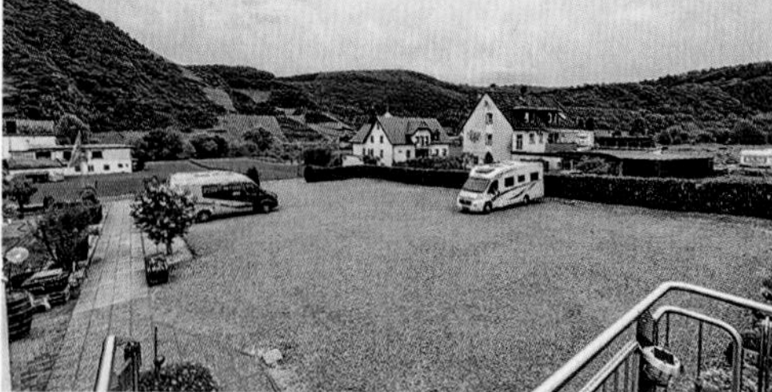

12 €9 WC included. **Location:** Rural, comfortable, quiet.
Surface: gravel. 01/01-31/12.
Distance: on the spot 150m 500m 1km on the spot.

Tourist information Ellenz/Poltersdorf:
Strassenweinfest. Wine-growers and - houses open their doors, wine-tastery. end Sep.
Wein- und Heimatfeste. Traditional wine celebration. last weekend Jul, 1st weekend Aug.

Elmstein 16H2

NaturFreundeHaus Elmstein, Esthaler Strasse 63.
GPS: n49,36133 e7,95123.

DE

12 €3 €1 €2 €1/pp. **Location:** Rural, simple, central, quiet. **Surface:** gravel. 01/01-31/12.
Remarks: Bread-service.

S Elmstein 16H2

Stellplatz Elmstein, Bahnhofstrasse 88. **GPS**: n49,34803 e7,94337.

4 free (4x)€0,50/kWh. **Location:** Rural. **Surface:** gravel. 01/01-31/12.
Distance: 500m 100m 500m.

Elmstein 16H2

Wohnmobilplatz Waldesruhe, Schwarzbach 36.
GPS: n49,34037 e7,83397.

10 €5, free with a meal. **Location:** Rural, simple, isolated, quiet. **Surface:** grassy. 01/01-31/12.
Remarks: To be paid at restaurant.

S Elzweiler 16G1

Stellplatz Elzweiler, Hauptstraße 7. **GPS**: n49,58036 e7,51393.

2 free €1 Ch €1. **Location:** Rural. **Surface:** metalled. 01/01-31/12.
Distance: on the spot on the spot on the spot on the spot.
Remarks: Small pitches.

S Enkirch 11F3

Wohnmobilplatz an der Mosel, Moselvorgelände, B53.
GPS: n49,98396 e7,12157.

200 €7 €1/80liter Ch (90x)€1/2kWh WC €1 €1,50/30minutes **Location:** Rural, comfortable, quiet.
Surface: grassy. Easter-31/10.
Distance: on the spot on the spot.
Remarks: Along the Moselle river.

S Ensch 16F1

Reisemobilplatz An den 2 Pappeln, Am Moselufer/ B53.
GPS: n49,82760 e6,83549.

45 €5 Ch (45x)€2.
Surface: grassy. 01/04-31/10.
Distance: 200m 300m 500m 100m.
Remarks: Bread-service.

S Eppelborn 16F2

Wohnmobilstellplatz Finkenrech, L303.
GPS: n49,43285 e6,99986.
3 €5 €0,50. **Location:** Rural, simple, quiet. **Surface:** gravel. 01/01-31/12.
Distance: 3km on the spot.

Eppenbrunn 16G2

Im Sportzentrum. **GPS**: n49,11179 e7,56512.

6 free. **Location:** Rural, simple, quiet. **Surface:** metalled. 01/01-31/12.
Distance: 500m on the spot 1km.
Remarks: Parking sports centre in nature reserve Pfälzer Wald.

Eppenbrunn 16G2

Neudorfstrasse. **GPS**: n49,11531 e7,55360.

5 free. **Location:** Rural, simple, noisy. **Surface:** metalled. 01/01-31/12.
Distance: on the spot on the spot on the spot on the spot.

S Erden 11F3

Wohnmobilstellplatz Erden, An Moselufer 1.
GPS: n49,97989 e7,02120.

21 €10 Ch included (21x)€3 €0,30/minutes on demand. **Location:** Rural. **Surface:** grassy. 01/04-31/10.
Distance: 15km 300m on the spot on the spot.

S Ernst 11G3

Wohnmobilstellplatz im Weinberg, Weingartenstrasse 106.
GPS: n50,14339 e7,23237.

30 €9 Ch included €5/10h. **Location:** Rural, comfortable. **Surface:** gravel. 01/01-31/12.
Distance: 300m on the spot 200m 100m.

S Ernst 11G3

Mosella Schinkenstube, Weingatenstrasse 97.
GPS: n50,14382 e7,23071.

18 €8 Ch included. **Surface:** grassy.
Distance: on the spot.

S Eschbach 16H2

Weingut Wind, Weinstrasse 3-5. **GPS**: n49,17594 e8,02171.

3 €5, discount for clients €1/100liter €3 WC included.
Location: Rural, simple, quiet. **Surface:** gravel. 01/01-31/12.
Distance: on the spot on the spot 250m.
Remarks: Check in on arrival.

S Essingen 16H2

Weingut Schweikart Dalberghof, Kirchstrasse 16.
GPS: n49,23478 e8,17524.

3 €5 €1/100liter (3x)€1/night WC €1.
Location: Simple, quiet. **Surface:** grassy. 01/01-31/12.
Distance: on the spot 3km 1km 3km 7km 30m.
Remarks: Sale of wines.

S Fell 16F1

Besucherbergwerk, Auf den Schiefergruben, K82.
GPS: n49,75440 e6,79731.

30 €4 €2. **Location:** Isolated, quiet. **Surface:** concrete. 01/01-31/12.

S Fischbach 16G1

Wohnmobilpark, Marktstraße 1. **GPS**: n49,74046 e7,40444.

DE

40 €7 Chincluded (40x)€2,50,. **Location:** Rural, simple, central. **Surface:** grassy. 01/01-31/12.
Distance: 800m on the spot 300m 1,5km.
Remarks: Bread-service, service passerby € 3.

Fischbach 16G1

Historisches Kupferbergwerk, Hosenbachstraße. **GPS:** n49,75398 e7,38287.

15 free. **Location:** Rural, simple, isolated, quiet. **Surface:** gravel. 01/01-31/12.
Distance: 1,7km on the spot.
Remarks: Visitors' center former copper mine.

Flemlingen 16H2

Weingut Eichhorn, Maxstrasse 21. **GPS:** n49,24122 e8,09341.

10 €5 (10x)€2 WCincluded €2/pp. **Location:** Rural, simple, quiet. **Surface:** grassy. 01/01-31/12.
Distance: 6km 400m.

Flonheim 16H1

Weingut Meyerhof, Aussiedlerhof. **GPS:** n49,78836 e8,04531.

4 €8 (4x)included. **Location:** Rural, simple, quiet. **Surface:** concrete. 01/01-31/12.
Distance: 700m 4km 100m 100m.
Remarks: Bread-service.

Föckelberg 16G1

Wildpark Potzberg, Auf dem Potzberg. **GPS:** n49,52240 e7,48079.

4 free. **Location:** Rural, simple, quiet. **Surface:** asphalted/sand. 01/01-31/12.
Distance: 1km.

Forst an der Weinstrasse 16H1

Weingut Margarethenhof, Wiesenweg 4. **GPS:** n49,42814 e8,19219.

3 €8 WC. 01/01-31/12.
Distance: 1km 7km 1km.

Freisen 16G1

Weiselbergbad, Zum Schwimmbad. **GPS:** n49,53324 e7,26048.

3 €5 €2/day. **Location:** Rural, simple, noisy. **Surface:** metalled. 01/01-31/12.
Distance: 1km 3km.
Remarks: Check in at swimming pool.

Gau-Algesheim 11H3

Reimo Gau-Algesheim, Bingerstrasse 8. **GPS:** n49,96331 e8,01213.

38 €4/night Chincluded (40x)€2/24h.
Location: Comfortable, quiet. **Surface:** metalled. 01/01-31/12.
Distance: 800m 2,5km 500m 200m.

Gau-Bickelheim 16H1

Winzerhof Schnabel, Bahnhofstrasse 31. **GPS:** n49,83941 e8,02116.

15 €5 included (8x)€3/day. **Location:** Rural. **Surface:** grassy. 01/01-31/12.
Distance: 3km 5km 1km.

Gau-Bickelheim 16H1

Am Autohof, B50. **GPS:** n49,83461 e7,99664.

15 free. **Location:** Rural, simple, noisy. **Surface:** asphalted. 01/01-31/12.
Distance: on the spot.

Gau-Heppenheim 16H1

Weingut Gustavshof, Hauptstrasse 53. **GPS:** n49,74138 e8,17082.

3 €8 (3x)included. **Location:** Rural, simple, quiet. **Surface:** concrete. 01/04-31/10.
Distance: 4km 2km 3km.

Gau-Odernheim 16H1

Petersberghalle, Mühlstraße. **GPS:** n49,78528 e8,19575.

3 free. **Surface:** metalled. 01/01-31/12.
Distance: 200m 400m 200m.
Remarks: Max. 3 days.

Gebhardshain 11G2

Festwiese, Steinebacherstrasse. **GPS:** n50,74412 e7,82079.

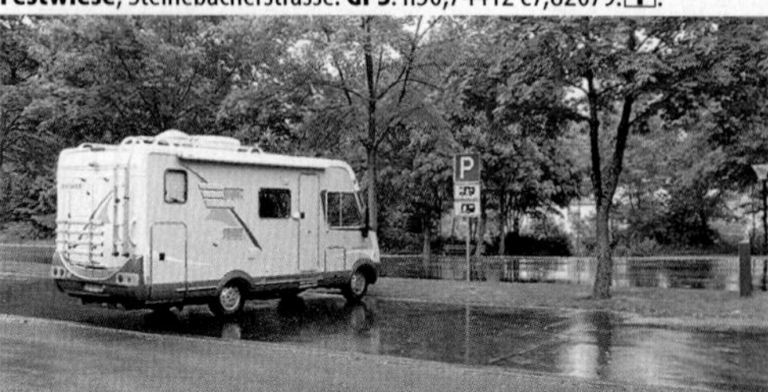

5 free. **Location:** Urban, simple, central, quiet. **Surface:** asphalted. 01/01-31/12.
Distance: 500m 500m 500m.

Geiselberg 16G2

Grillplatz Geiselberg, Hauptstrasse, K31. **GPS:** n49,32381 e7,70957.

10 free. **Location:** Rural, simple, quiet. **Surface:** gravel. 01/01-31/12.
Remarks: Max. 2 days.

Germersheim 16H2

Carnot'sche Mauer, Rüdolf von Habsburgstrasse. **GPS:** n49,22004 e8,37906.

8 €3/24h €1/100liter Ch (8x)€1/5kWh.
Location: Simple, central.
Surface: grassy.
01/01-31/12.
Distance: 300m 2km 500m 300m 100m on the spot.

Gerolstein 11F3

Am Hallen- und Freibad, Raderstrasse 22. **GPS:** n50,22096 e6,65387.

25 €10/24h €1/100liter Ch (12x)€1/day.
Location: Urban, simple. **Surface:** grassy/metalled.

15/03-15/11.
Distance: nearby 25km 500m 1km.
Remarks: At swimming pool.

Gevenich 11F3

Am Sportplatz. **GPS**: n50,14727 e7,08385.

5 free. **Location:** Rural, simple, isolated. **Surface:** grassy.
01/01-31/12.
Distance: 1km on the spot.

Gillenfeld 11F3

Wohnmobilhafen Pulvermaar, K14. **GPS**: n50,13294 e6,93218.

30 € 7, 2 pers. incl., dog € 1 €1/50liter Ch €0,50/kWh WC €2. **Location:** Simple. **Surface:** gravel. 01/01-31/12.
Distance: 3km on the spot on the spot 200m 200m 300m.

Gillenfeld 11F3

Feriendorf Pulvermaar, Vulkanstrasse. **GPS**: n50,13000 e6,93194.

40 € 7, 2 pers.incl. €1/50liter Chincluded €0,50/kWh WCfree €2/stay. **Location:** Rural, comfortable, quiet.
Surface: grassy/gravel. 01/03-30/11.
Distance: 3km 7km on the spot on the spot 150m 150m 200m.

Gimbsheim 16H1

Schwimbadstrasse. **GPS**: n49,77806 e8,38278.

8 € 4/night. **Surface:** asphalted/grassy. 15/05-15/09.
Distance: 500m 300m.

Gimbsheim 16H1

Weingut Falger-Baier, Alsheimerstrasse 25. **GPS**: n49,77733 e8,36959.
3 € 5 . 01/01-31/12.
Distance: 3km Pizzeria 50m 500m.

Glan-Münchweiler 16G1

Am Bahnhof, Bahnhofstraße. **GPS**: n49,46935 e7,44420.

3 free €1 Ch (4x)€1/2h. **Location:** Urban, simple, central, noisy. **Surface:** metalled. 01/01-31/12.
Distance: 750m 150m on the spot.

Gleisweiler 16H2

Weingut Kost, Hainbachtalstrasse 3. **GPS**: n49,23862 e8,06737.

3 free free. **Location:** Rural, quiet. **Surface:** grassy.
01/01-31/12.
Distance: 8km on the spot.

Gleiszellen-Gleishorbach 16H2

Weingut Schoenlaub, Bergstrasse 14. **GPS**: n49,13131 e8,00465.

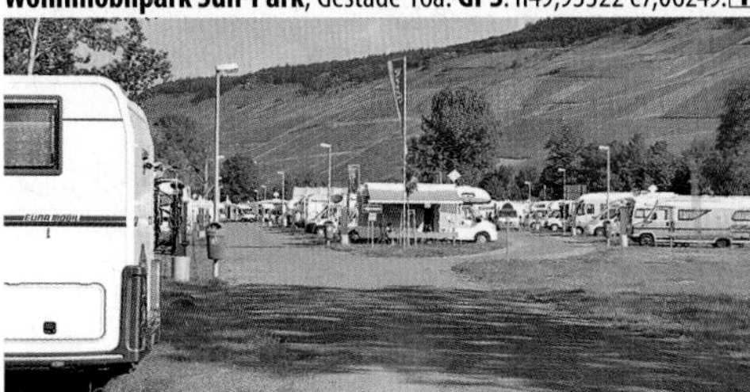

2 free free. **Location:** Rural, simple, quiet. **Surface:** grassy.
01/01-31/12.
Distance: 15km 500m.
Remarks: Check in at Weingut.

Graach/Mosel 11F3

Wohnmobilpark Sun-Park, Gestade 16a. **GPS**: n49,93322 e7,06249.

140 € 10/day liter Ch (132x)€3/day WCincluded €1,50/pp €2,50. **Location:** Rural, simple. **Surface:** grassy/gravel.
27/03-03/11.
Distance: 200m on the spot 200m 2km on the spot on the spot on the spot.
Remarks: Bread-service, video surveillance.

Grafschaft 11F2

Panorama Sauna, Panoramaweg 2. **GPS**: n50,56029 e7,05368.

20 free. **Surface:** gravel. 01/01-31/12.
Distance: 5km 300m 300m.

Gries 16G2

Seestube am Ohmbachsee, Bahnhofstrasse 17b.
GPS: n49,41664 e7,40377.

12 € 6 €1/80liter Ch (12x)€0,60/kWh.
Location: Rural, simple, quiet. **Surface:** grassy.
01/01-31/12.
Distance: 6km on the spot on the spot.
Remarks: Bread-service.

Gundersheim 16H1

Huppert's Wohnmobile Wingert, Untere Grabenstraße 21.
GPS: n49,69499 e8,20465.

12 € 5 €3. **Surface:** gravel/sand. 01/01-31/12.
Distance: 1km on the spot 300m.
Remarks: Max. 3 nights.

Guntersblum 16H1

Am Sportanlage, Alsheimerstrasse 85. **GPS**: n49,78974 e8,34373.

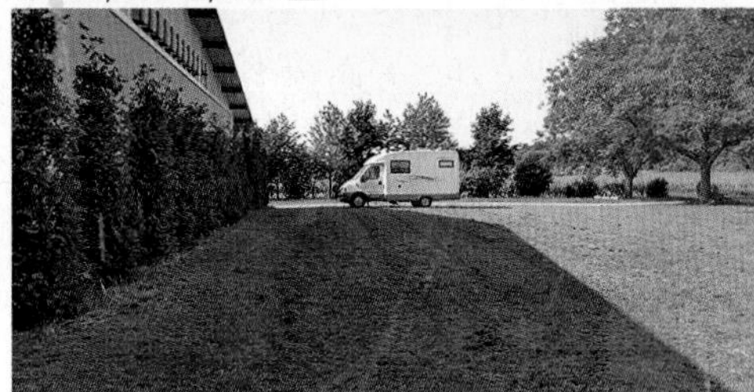

16 € 5 €1/80liter Ch (12x)€0,50/kWh. **Location:** Rural.
Surface: gravel. 01/01-31/12.
Distance: 500m 500m 500m.

Guntersblum 16H1

Weingut Katharinenhof, Alsheimerstrasse 95.
GPS: n49,78667 e8,34324.

10 € 5 included (7x)€2/24h.
Location: Rural, simple, quiet. **Surface:** grassy. 01/01-31/12.
Distance: 1km 1km 1km.

Hachenburg 11G2

P4 - Burggarten, Alexanderring. **GPS**: n50,66250 e7,82694.

8 free €1/70liter Ch €1/6h WC. **Location:** Urban, simple, quiet. **Surface:** grasstiles. 01/01-31/12.
Distance: 300m 300m 300m on the spot on the spot.
Remarks: June 2014 during inspection service out of order, just electricity, historical centre.

DE

Hagenbach 16H2

Stadtbrauhaus Hagenbach, Stixwörthstrasse 2-4.
GPS: n49,00884 e8,25902.

10 free. 01/01-31/12 Mon, Tue.
Distance: 5km on the spot.

Hainfeld 16H2

Modenbach. **GPS**: n49,25730 e8,10328.

20 free. **Location:** Simple, quiet. **Surface:** gravel.
Distance: 150m 3km 250m 1km on the spot.

Hainfeld 16H2

Weingut Edgar und Andreas Lutz, Weinstrasse 57.
GPS: n49,25696 e8,09882.
4 € 6, € 8 service incl WC. **Location:** Simple.
Surface: metalled.
Distance: on the spot 100m.

Hassloch 16H2

Hotel Sägmühle, Sägmühlweg 140. **GPS**: n49,34674 e8,25491.

2 € 12, guests free (2x) WC included. **Location:** Simple, isolated, quiet. 01/01-31/12.
Distance: 10km.
Remarks: Bicycle rental.

Hassloch 16H2

Badepark Hassloch, Lachener Weg 175. **GPS**: n49,34804 e8,24677.

9 free free. **Location:** Simple, quiet. 01/01-31/12.
Distance: 2km 10km 50m 200m 100m.

Hassloch 16H2

Magin Reisemobile, Hans-Böckler-Strasse 52.
GPS: n49,34968 e8,23935.

8 € 12,50, 2 pers.incl Ch (8x)included.
Location: Urban, simple, quiet.
Surface: gravel/metalled.
01/01-31/12.
Distance: 2km 7km 50m 200m.

Tourist information Hassloch:
Holiday Park. Attractions park with shows. 01/03-31/10 10-18h.

Hauenstein 16G2

Stellplatz am Deutschen Schumuseum Hauenstein, Turnstrasse 5.
GPS: n49,18896 e7,85669.

16 € 7 80liter Chfree €0,55/kWh. **Location:** Rural, simple, quiet. **Surface:** gravel. 01/01-31/12.
Distance: on the spot 200m 300m.
Remarks: Check in on arrival, pay at pay-desk of the museum.

Heimborn 11G2

Gasthaus zum Nisterstrand, Vor der Hardt.
GPS: n50,71609 e7,75322.

6 guests free Ch. **Location:** Rural, simple, quiet.
Surface: asphalted. 01/01-31/12.
Distance: on the spot on the spot on the spot.

Heltersberg 16G2

Am Bergbad, Bergstrasse. **GPS**: n49,31654 e7,70380.

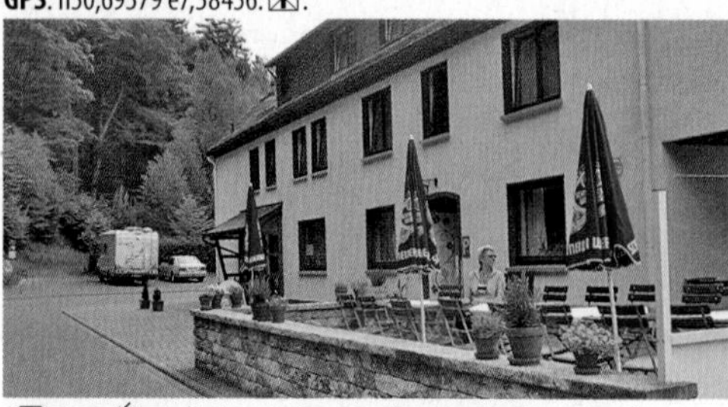

5 free. **Location:** Rural, simple, quiet. **Surface:** grassy.
01/01-31/12.
Distance: 900m.
Remarks: Parking swimming pool.

Hemmelzen 11G2

Hotel Im Heisterholz, Heisterholzstrasse 10.
GPS: n50,69579 e7,58456.

4 € 12 included. **Location:** Rural, quiet. **Surface:** gravel.
01/01-31/12 Mo.
Distance: 200m on the spot 100m on the spot on the spot.
Remarks: € 2 reduction in restaurant.

Herrstein 16G1

Wohnmobilstellplatz Herrstein, Brühlstrasse.
GPS: n49,77963 e7,33569.

3 free €1/80liter €0,50/kWh WC.
Location: Rural, simple. **Surface:** metalled.
01/01-31/12.
Distance: 300m on the spot.
Remarks: Max. 48h.

Tourist information Herrstein:
Touristinformation Deutsche Edelsteinstraße, Brühlstrasse 16. Renovated mall half-timbered city. 01/05-01/10.

Herxheim 16H2

Festhalle, Bonifatiusstraße. **GPS**: n49,14463 e8,21656.

8 free Chfree. **Location:** Simple, central. **Surface:** grasstiles.
01/01-31/12.
Distance: on the spot 4km 150m 200m 75m.

Heuchelheim-Klingen 16H2

Gästehaus am Fürstweg, Hauptstrasse 2. **GPS**: n49,14511 e8,05788.
3 € 5 Ch. 01/01-31/12.
Distance: 14km.

Heuchelheim-Klingen 16H2

Weingut Junghof, Hauptstrasse 21. **GPS**: n49,14572 e8,05580.

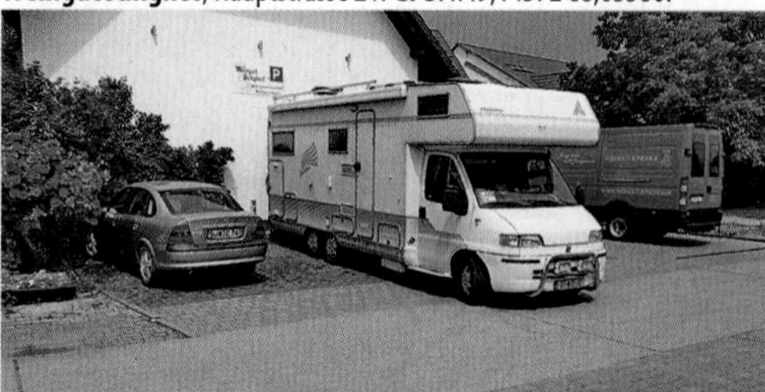

4 € 5, free with a meal €2/100liter €2/night.
Location: Simple. **Surface:** grassy/metalled. 01/01-31/12.
Distance: on the spot 14km 500m 2km 500m.

Hillesheim 11F3

Markt- und Messeplatz, Am Viehmarkt.
GPS: n50,28895 e6,67239.

6 € 7 Ch (6x) WC included. **Location:** Urban, simple, central. **Surface:** gravel. 01/01-31/12.
Distance: on the spot on the spot 200m.

Hillesheim 11F3

Wohnmobilstellplatz Birkenhof, Birkenhof 1.
GPS: n50,28639 e6,69083.

DE

8 € 10 (6x)included free. **Location:** Rural, simple, quiet. **Surface:** gravel. 01/01-31/12.
Distance: 1,5km 1,5km.
Remarks: Bread-service.

S Hochspeyer 16G1

Am Schwimmbad, Mühlhofstraße. **GPS:** n49,44108 e7,89333.

6 € 5 €1/80liter Ch (12x)€0,50/kWh.
Location: Simple, central, quiet. **Surface:** asphalted.
01/01-31/12 01/08-15/08.
Distance: 400m 5km 400m bakery.
Remarks: Max. 3 days.

Höheinöd 16G2

Am Haus des Bürgers, Hauptstrasse 24. **GPS:** n49,28691 e7,60468.

3 free. **Location:** Rural, simple, quiet. **Surface:** metalled.
01/01-31/12.
Distance: on the spot 8km.
Remarks: Max. 2 nights.

Höhr-Grenzhausen 11G2

Ferbachstraße. **GPS:** n50,43330 e7,66833.

8 free. 01/01-31/12.
Distance: on the spot 2km 100m.

S Holzappel 11G3

Stellplatz am Herthasee, Am Herthasee. **GPS:** n50,36135 e7,90274.

12 € 6/24h, € 11/48h, € 15/72h €1/90liter Ch (12x)€1/2kWh. **Location:** Rural, comfortable, quiet.
Surface: grassy. 01/01-31/12.
Distance: 1km on the spot on the spot on the spot.

S Hornbach 16G2

Wohnmobilpark Hornbach, Bahnhofstraße.
GPS: n49,18382 e7,36560.

26 € 7 €1/60liter Ch (30x)€1/2kWh included.
Location: Rural, comfortable, quiet. **Surface:** gravel.
01/01-31/12.
Distance: on the spot 8km on the spot 300m on the spot on the spot.
Remarks: Barbecue place.

S Hörschhausen 11F3

Mechels Hof, Dauner Straße 24. **GPS:** n50,24248 e6,92770.

3 € 5 + € 4/pp, dog € 1 Ch (3x)€2/24h.
Location: Rural, simple. **Surface:** gravel. 01/01-31/12.
Distance: 9km.
Remarks: Bread-service.

S Idar/Oberstein 16G1

Parking Börse, Hauptstrasse 100. **GPS:** n49,71932 e7,30313.

12 € 6/day, first 24h free €1/100liter Ch WC.
Location: Urban, simple. **Surface:** asphalted. 01/01-31/12.
Distance: 300m on the spot 300m.

Tourist information Idar/Oberstein:
Edelsteinminen des Steinkaulenberges. Gem mine. 15/03-15/11 10-18h.
M Deutsches Edelsteinmuseum. Gem museum. 01/05-31/10 9.30-17.30h, 01/11-30/04 10-17h 14/01-01/02.

S Impflingen 16H2

Weingut Junker, Sonnenberghof 1. **GPS:** n49,16242 e8,10728.

3 € 5 (4x)€2 WC. **Location:** Simple, quiet.
Surface: gravel. 01/01-31/12.
Distance: 1km 7km on the spot 3km 200m on the spot on the spot.

S Ingelheim am Rhein 11H3

Weingut Menk, Außenliegend 143. **GPS:** n49,97190 e8,09295.

6 € 10 Ch WC included. **Location:** Rural, comfortable, quiet. **Surface:** grassy. 01/01-31/12.
Distance: 2km 9km on the spot.

S Jettenbach 16G1

Freizeitgelände Schwimmbad, Austrasse.
GPS: n49,52919 e7,56453.

6 free Ch. **Location:** Simple, quiet. **Surface:** asphalted.
01/01-31/12.
Distance: 500m 800m.
Remarks: Service on demand.

Kaisersesch 11F3

Am Markt. **GPS:** n50,23223 e7,14044.
4 free. 01/01-31/12.
Distance: 1km.

S Kaiserslautern 16G1

Daennerplatz. **GPS:** n49,44300 e7,80230.

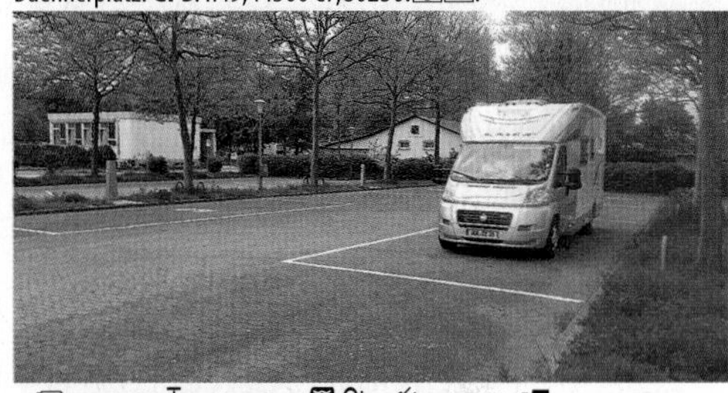

11 € 10/24h €1/100liter Ch €2/2kWh.
Location: Urban. **Surface:** metalled.
Distance: 2,5km on the spot on the spot.
Remarks: Free bus to centre.

S Kaiserslautern 16G1

Gasthaus Licht Luft, Entersweilerstraße 51.
GPS: n49,43828 e7,80338.

14 free Ch on demand. **Location:** Urban, central, quiet.
Surface: gravel. 01/01-31/12.
Distance: 5km on the spot on the spot on the spot on the spot.

Kaiserslautern 16G1

Am Monte Mare, Mailänder Straße 6. **GPS:** n49,45387 e7,81203.

DE

10 free. **Location:** Rural, simple, quiet. **Surface:** metalled.
01/01-31/12.
Distance: 1km.

Kamp-Bornhofen 11G3

Bistro Rheinufer, Rheinuferstrasse 66 A.
GPS: n50,22305 e7,61888.
7 € 8 €1 €2,50 WC.
Surface: metalled. 01/01-31/12.
Distance: on the spot on the spot 300m on the spot.
Remarks: Along the Rhine river, toilets only during opening hours restaurant.

Kandel 16H2

Adams Hof, Rheinzaberner Strasse 1. **GPS:** n49,08902 e8,22194.

30 € 10/night €2,50 (20x)€2,50/12h WC.
Location: Simple, quiet. **Surface:** grassy. 01/01-31/12.
Distance: 1,5km on the spot on the spot 1,5km 1,5km.
Remarks: € 5 voucher Biergarten.

Kapellen-Drusweiler 16H2

Weingut Manderschied, Dorfstrasse 4. **GPS:** n49,10482 e8,03723.

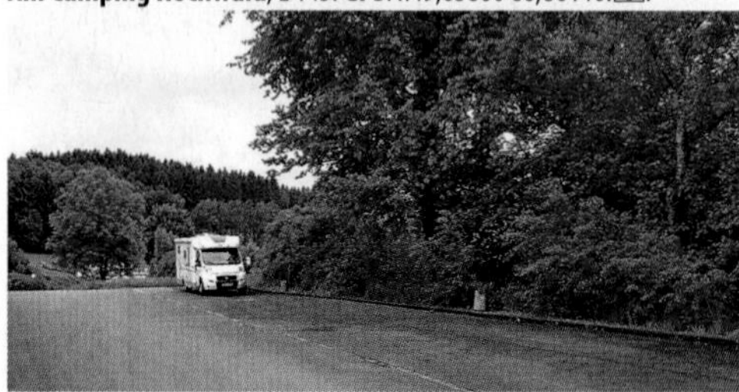

10 free (3x)free. **Location:** Rural, simple, quiet.
Surface: grassy. 01/01-31/12.
Distance: 500m 500m 2km.

Kell am See 16F1

Am Camping Hochwald, L 143. **GPS:** n49,63800 e6,80140.

10 € 20, 2 pers.incl Ch WC included. **Location:** Rural, quiet.
Surface: metalled. 01/06-30/08.
Distance: 2km 2km.
Remarks: Free entrance swimming pool.

Kempenich 11F2

Eifel-Gasthof Kleefuß, In der Hardt 1. **GPS:** n50,42209 e7,10951.

4 guests free. **Location:** Rural. **Surface:** gravel. 01/01-31/12
Mon, Tue.
Distance: 500m.

Kempfeld 16G1

An der Wildenburg, Wildenburgstraße.
GPS: n49,77588 e7,25423.

3 free. **Location:** Rural. **Surface:** metalled. 01/01-31/12.
Distance: 2km 2km.

Kesten 16F1

Wohnmobilpark Kesten/Mosel, Urmetzgasse/K134.
GPS: n49,90306 e6,96232.

100 € 6/24h €0,50/50liter Ch included (100x)€2/24h,6Amp.
Surface: grassy/metalled. 01/04-31/10.
Distance: 300m 10m 10m 300m 1km 300m on the spot on the spot.
Remarks: Parking at the Moselle River, bread-service.

Kinheim 11F3

Am Moselufer, Moselweinstraße, B53. **GPS:** n49,97218 e7,05706.

50 € 8 Ch €2/day included.
Location: Rural, simple, quiet. **Surface:** grassy. 01/01-31/12.
Distance: 100m on the spot on the spot 150m on the spot on the spot.
Remarks: Parking at the Moselle River.

Tourist information Kinheim:
Tag den offenen Weinkeller. Open wine-cellars. 2nd Thu after Whitsuntide.
Wein- und Frülingsfest. Wine and spring celebration. Whitsuntide.
Winzerfest. Wine festival. 2nd weekend Sep.

Kirchberg 11G3

AMB-Reisemobile, Herbert-Kühn-Straße 10.
GPS: n49,95400 e7,40829.

15 € 6 Ch included. **Location:** Rural, simple.
Surface: grassy. 01/01-31/12.
Distance: 700m 700m 700m 600m on the spot.

Kirchheimbolanden 16H1

Festplatz Herrengarten, Hitzfeldstrasse. **GPS:** n49,66667 e8,01501.

20 free €1/70liter Ch €0,50. **Surface:** metalled.
01/01-31/12 2nd weekend May-Aug-Oct.
Distance: 300m 300m on the spot.

Kirn 16G1

Wohnmobilstellplatz Auf der Kiesel, Fontaine-les-Dijon-Strasse.
GPS: n49,78406 e7,45798.

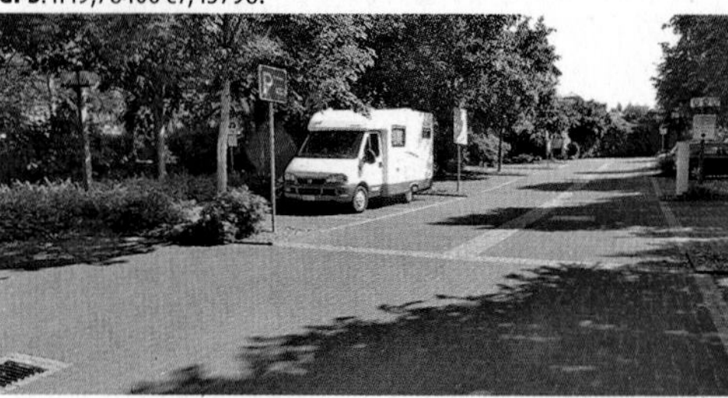

3 € 1,25/day. **Location:** Urban, comfortable, quiet, noisy.
Surface: concrete. 01/01-31/12.
Distance: 300m on the spot on the spot.
Remarks: Monday market.

Klausen 16F1

Zentralparkplatz, Eberhardstrasse/ K51. **GPS:** n49,90550 e6,88104.

5 free. 01/01-31/12.
Distance: 2km.

Kleinbundenbach 16G2

Auf der Stampermühle, Stampermühle 1.
GPS: n49,31778 e7,45694.

10 € 7 included. **Location:** Rural, simple, isolated.
Surface: gravel.
Distance: on the spot.

Klüsserath 16F1

Reisemobilpark Klüsserath, B53. **GPS:** n49,84170 e6,85475.

400 € 6,50 €1/90liter Ch €1,50/24h. **Surface:** grassy.
Easter-31/10.
Remarks: Along the Moselle river, bread-service.

Kobern 11G3

Am Kalkofen B416, Kobern-Gondorf. **GPS:** n50,30524 e7,46064.

DE

50 € 5/24h €1/80liter €0,10 Ch€0,10. **Surface:** metalled.
01/01-31/12.
Distance: 300m 8km on the spot on the spot 300m 300m.

Koblenz 11G3

Busparkplatz, Pastor-Klein-Straße. **GPS**: n50,36557 e7,57417.

50 free. **Location:** Simple. **Surface:** gravel. 01/01-31/12.
Distance: Old city centre 2km 600m Aldi 500m.

Konz 16F1

An der Saarmündung, Am Moselufer 1. **GPS**: n49,70550 e6,57597.
3 € 8 Ch WC against payment . **Surface:** grassy.
01/03-31/10.
Distance: on the spot on the spot 100m 1km on the spot on the spot.
Remarks: Service 100m.

Köwerich 16F1

Weingut Hans Klären-Maringer 'Off'm Herrach', Beethovenstrasse 40. **GPS**: n49,84123 e6,86287.

20 € 7 Ch €0,50/kWh WC €1 €4.
Surface: grassy.
01/01-31/12.
Distance: 500m 500m 500m on the spot 2km 100m.
Remarks: Check in at restaurant, bread-service.

Kusel 16G1

Parkplatz der Tuchfabriken, Trierer Straße 61.
GPS: n49,54016 e7,39626.

3 free Ch Service €5.
Location: Urban, simple, quiet. **Surface:** asphalted.
01/04-31/10.
Distance: 500m 300m.
Remarks: Max. 3 days, key service at Touristinformation (300m).

Lahnstein 11G3

Wohnmobilstellplatz Kränchen, Johannesstraße 44.
GPS: n50,30939 e7,59833.

60 € 9,50 €1/100liter Ch €0,50/kWh WC €1.
Location: Simple. **Surface:** gravel. 01/01-31/12.
Distance: 1km 600m 600m.

Lahnstein 11G3

Wohnmobilstellplatz Blücherstraße, Blücherstraße 20.
GPS: n50,31335 e7,59331.

10 free. **Location:** Urban, simple, central. **Surface:** gravel.
01/01-31/12.
Distance: 2km on the spot on the spot on the spot.
Remarks: Max. 3 days.

Lambrecht 16H2

Blainviller-Straße 1. **GPS**: n49,37030 e8,07448.
7 free €1 Ch €1/8h.
Surface: gravel. 01/01-31/12.
Distance: on the spot on the spot.
Remarks: Near sports fields.

Landau 16H2

La Ola Das Freizeitbad, Horstring 2. **GPS**: n49,20230 e8,14270.

5 € 10/24h €4 Ch . **Location:** Simple, quiet.
Surface: metalled. 01/01-31/12.
Distance: 3km 1km 500m 100m.

Landstuhl 16G2

Bahnstraße. **GPS**: n49,41595 e7,57092.

2 free Ch free. **Location:** Urban, simple, noisy.
Surface: metalled. 01/01-31/12.
Distance: on the spot 1,3km 350m Aldi 100m.
Remarks: Max. 3 days.

Langenlonsheim 16G1

Weingut Im Zwölberich, Schützenstrasse 14.
GPS: n49,89672 e7,89466.

5 € 10 included. **Location:** Rural, simple, central, quiet.
Surface: asphalted/grassy. 01/01-31/12.
Distance: 7km.

Lauterecken 16G1

Wohnmobilstellplatz Villa Toskana, Friedhofweg 3a.
GPS: n49,65056 e7,58806.

30 € 8 €1/80liter Ch (18x)€1/8h WC €3 €1/5minutes.
Location: Comfortable, luxurious, quiet. **Surface:** gravel.
01/01-31/12.
Distance: 300m on the spot 300m on the spot on the spot on the spot.
Remarks: Bread-service.

Leimersheim 16H2

Sport- und Freizeithalle, Rheinstraße 42.
GPS: n49,12534 e8,35457.

5 free.
Location: Rural, simple, quiet. **Surface:** gravel.
01/01-31/12.
Distance: 500m 4km 100m 100m on the spot 1km.
Remarks: At tennis-courts.

Leinsweiler 16H2

Weingut Erlenswein, Wacholderhof. **GPS**: n49,18747 e8,03323.

8 € 10 Ch included. **Location:** Rural, simple, quiet.
Surface: grassy. 01/03-31/11.
Distance: 1km.
Remarks: Check in at Weingut.

Leiwen 16F1

Weingut Heinz Spieles, Schulstrasse 20. **GPS**: n49,82331 e6,87524.

4 € 8 €1 Ch €1 included. **Surface:** grassy/gravel.

DE

01/01-31/12.
Distance: 400m 400m.

Leiwen 16F1

Moselblick, Flurgartenstrasse 2/ Weinallee.
GPS: n49,82611 e6,88057.

12 €8 Ch WC €1
Surface: grassy/gravel. 01/01-31/12.
Distance: 500m on the spot on the spot on the spot 300m 500m.

Lemberg 16G2

Lemberger Weiher, Weiherstraße. **GPS**: n49,17284 e7,64731.

5 free, service/electricity incl. € 7
Location: Rural. **Surface:** grasstiles. 01/01-31/12.
Distance: 400m 600m on the spot on the spot.
Remarks: Max. 3 days.

Linz am Rhein 11G2

B42 Linzhausenstrasse. **GPS**: n50,56291 e7,27982.

6 free. **Surface:** asphalted. 01/01-31/12.
Distance: 500m on the spot 50m.
Remarks: Along the Rhine river, max. 3 days.

Löf 11G3

SOG Dahmann, In der Mark 2. **GPS**: n50,23194 e7,43750.

9 free Ch (4x)€0,50/kWh WC. **Location:** Rural.
Surface: metalled. 01/01-31/12.
Distance: 13km 1km.

Longuich/Mosel 16F1

Feiten, Rioler weg 2. **GPS**: n49,80417 e6,77899.

40 €5 €0,50/70liter Ch €3 WC €1. **Surface:** grassy.
01/01-31/12.
Distance: 300m 2km on the spot on the spot on the spot 1km.
Remarks: Playground.

Longuich/Mosel 16F1

WeinKulturgut Longen Schlöder, Kirchenweg 9.
GPS: n49,81023 e6,76427.

8 €7 €2 (3x)€2,50 WC €3.
Surface: gravel/metalled. 01/01-31/12 Tue.
Distance: 1km 150m 150m on the spot 500m.

Losheim am See 16F1

Reisemobilplatz am Stausee, Zum Stausee.
GPS: n49,51999 e6,74123.

8 €6 €0,50/70liter Ch WC included.
Location: Rural, simple. **Surface:** grassy/gravel.
01/01-31/12.
Distance: 1km 200m 200m 100m 1km on the spot on the spot.
Remarks: Parking at lake, in front of tourist office.

Lösnich 11F3

Stellplatz am Moselufer, Gestade. **GPS**: n49,97560 e7,04276.

96 €7 Ch included €2/day. **Location:** Rural, simple, quiet. **Surface:** grassy. 01/03-01/11.
Distance: on the spot on the spot on the spot on the spot 3km on the spot on the spot.
Remarks: Along the Moselle river, baker every morning.

Lutzerath 11F3

Bürgerhaus zum Üssbachtal, Trierer Strasse.
GPS: n50,13015 e7,01002.

10 €5/day €0,50 Ch (6x)€0,50/kWh. **Location:** Urban, simple. **Surface:** asphalted. 01/01-31/12.
Distance: on the spot on the spot on the spot.
Remarks: Check in at Hotel Restaurant Maas, Trierer Str. 30.

Maikammer 16H2

Sporthalle Kalmit, Johannes Dammstrasse.
GPS: n49,30307 e8,13219.

€ 4/day included. **Surface:** asphalted. 01/01-31/12.
Distance: 100m nearby nearby.

Maikammer 16H2

Weingut Gerald Groß, Bahnhofstraße 24. **GPS**: n49,30649 e8,13742.
2 € 10 WC included. **Surface:** grassy.

Maikammer 16H2

Weingut Hubert Müller, Raiffeisenstrasse 59.
GPS: n49,30737 e8,13646.
3 € 13 WC included.
Surface: gravel. 01/01-31/12.
Distance: on the spot 7km.

Maikammer 16H2

Weingut Schädler, Dieterwiesenstraße. **GPS**: n49,30848 e8,12530.
3 €7 WC included. 01/01-31/12.
Distance: 500m 1km on the spot on the spot.

Maikammer 16H2

Weingut Ziegler-Ullrich, Weinstraße Nord 46.
GPS: n49,30659 e8,13369.
2 €5 included. 01/01-31/12.
Distance: 4km.

Mainz 11H3

Wohnmobilstellplatz Mainz, Dr.-Martin-Luther-King-Weg 21.
GPS: n49,99849 e8,24638.

56 € 10 €1/90liter Ch €0,50/kWh. 01/01-31/12.
Distance: Old city centre 1,7km 150m Aldi 200m Bus 160m.

Mandelbachtal 16F2

Ommersheimer Weiher, L107. **GPS**: n49,21899 e7,16766.

2 free €1 (2x)€1/8h. **Location:** Rural, simple, isolated, quiet.
Surface: asphalted. 01/01-31/12.
Distance: on the spot on the spot.

Mandelbachtal 16F2

Kloster Gräfinthal, Gräfinthal. **GPS**: n49,15975 e7,11924.

2 free. **Location:** Rural, simple, noisy. **Surface:** metalled.
01/01-31/12.
Distance: 100m.

Manderscheid 11F3

Hotel Heidsmühle, Mosenbergstrasse 22.
GPS: n50,08504 e6,80021.

DE

20 free (4x)€2,50/day. **Location:** Rural, simple, isolated, quiet. **Surface:** grassy/gravel. 01/01-31/12.
Distance: 2km 6km on the spot on the spot on the spot on the spot.

Manderscheid 11F3

Campingplatz Vulkaneifel, Herbstwiese.
GPS: n50,09713 e6,79969.

8 € 6/pp, dog € 1,50 €0,50/100liter Ch €2,50 WC included . **Location:** Rural, simple, quiet. **Surface:** metalled. 15/03-31/10.
Distance: 800m 800m 800m on camp site on the spot on the spot.
Remarks: Bread-service.

Mayen 11F3

Wohnmobilstellplatz am Viehmarkt, Polcherstrasse.
GPS: n50,32194 e7,22806.

6 free €1/80liter ChWC.
Location: Simple. **Surface:** gravel. 01/01-31/12.
Distance: 100m 4km 100m 100m.
Remarks: Next to event ground, max. 3 nights.

Mayschoss 11F2

Ahruferplatz, Ahr-Rotweinstraße 46. **GPS:** n50,51736 e7,01948.

75 € 6 €1/100liter Ch (15x)€2,50/day WC.
Location: Rural, central. **Surface:** asphalted/gravel. 01/01-31/12.
Distance: on the spot 100m 250m bakery 50m.
Remarks: Along the Ahr river, parking at station.

Meckenheim 16H2

Sporthalle Meckenheim, Rödersheimerstraße.
GPS: n49,41167 e8,24056.
10 free €0,50/kWh. **Surface:** gravel. 01/01-31/12.
Distance: 1km.

Meddersheim 16G1

Winzergenossenschaft, Naheweinstrasse 63. **GPS:** n49,77988 e7,61347.
10 free free €3/day. **Location:** Rural, simple, quiet.
Surface: gravel. 01/01-31/12.
Distance: 800m.
Remarks: Max. 2 nights, gate can be opened manually.

Mehring 16F1

Weingut Zellerhof, Zellerhof 1. **GPS:** n49,79369 e6,81944.

43 € 6 €0,50/70liter Ch (43x)€0,50/kWh WC €1.
Surface: grassy/metalled. 01/01-31/12.
Distance: 100m on the spot on the spot on the spot 100m.

Mehring 16F1

Wohnmobilstellplatz del Mosel, Moselweinstrasse 2.
GPS: n49,79423 e6,81726.

72 € 8 €1/100liter Ch (60x)€2 WC €2.
Surface: grassy. 01/01-31/12.
Distance: 100m on the spot 200m.
Remarks: Bread-service.

Meisenheim 16G1

Schwimmbad Meisenheim, In der Heimbach.
GPS: n49,71472 e7,65750.

12 € 5 €1/100liter €1 Ch (12x)€1/kWh.
Location: Rural, simple, quiet. **Surface:** grassy/gravel. 01/01-31/12 01/07-09/07.
Distance: 1,6km on the spot 500m.

Mendig 11G3

Brauerstraße. **GPS:** n50,37678 e7,28404.

20 free €1/30liter Ch (12x)€0,50/kWh.
Location: Rural, quiet. **Surface:** gravel. 01/01-31/12.
Distance: 200m Vulkanbrauhaus&Felsenkeller 400m.
Remarks: In front of football ground, Vulkanmuseum Lava-Dome 100m.

Merzig 16F2

Das Bad, Saarwiesenring 3. **GPS:** n49,44541 e6,62418.

12 € 7,50 €1/100liter Ch included . **Location:** Rural, simple, quiet. **Surface:** grasstiles. 01/01-31/12.
Distance: 2km on the spot 2km.
Remarks: Check in at swimming pool, caution key € 50.

Mettlach 16F1

Cloef-Atrium, Alfred-Backer-strasse, Mettlach-Orscholz.
GPS: n49,50394 e6,53225.

10 € 5 WC. **Surface:** gravel.
Distance: on the spot.
Remarks: Pay with SMS, max. 24h.

Mettlach 16F1

Mettlacher Abtei-Bräu, P6, Bahnhofstrasse 32.
GPS: n49,49847 e6,59612.

10 € 5 Chfree. **Surface:** gravel. 01/01-31/12.
Distance: 500m 7km on the spot on the spot on the spot.
Remarks: Along the Saar River, pay with SMS.

Mettlach 16F1

Restaurant zum Kaltenborn, Zur Großwies 21, Orscholz.
GPS: n49,50916 e6,53030.

10 € 5. 01/01-31/12 Thu.
Distance: on the spot.

Tourist information Mettlach:
M Erlebniszentrum Villeroy&Boch. Mo-Fr: 9.30-19h, Sa 9.30-18h.
Villeroy&Boch Factory Outlet, Freiherr-vom-Stein-Strasse 4-6. Mo-Fr: 9.30-19h, Sa 9.30-18h.

Minheim 16F1

Reisemobilpark Sonneninsel, K53. **GPS:** n49,86500 e6,94111.

90 € 6,50 €1/100liter Ch €1/2kWh.
Surface: grassy/gravel. 01/01-31/12.
Distance: 10km 400m 3km.
Remarks: Along the Moselle river, next to football ground.

Minheim 16F1

Weinhaus Moselblick, In der Olk 9. **GPS:** n49,86428 e6,93294.

DE

10 €9 Ch €1,50/day.
Surface: grassy/gravel. 01/01-31/12.
Distance: 200m 200m.

Monzernheim 16H1

Weingut Helmut Geil, Am Römer 26. **GPS**: n49,72376 e8,22715.

3 €6 (3x)included. **Location:** Rural, simple, quiet.
Surface: grassy. 01/01-31/12.
Distance: 8km 4km 4km.
Remarks: Check in at Weingut.

Monzingen 16G1

Parkplatz Festhalle, Rosengartenstrasse 11.
GPS: n49,79438 e7,59075.

3 free. **Location:** Rural, simple, noisy. **Surface:** asphalted.
01/01-31/12.
Distance: on the spot 1km.

Monzingen 16G1

Weingut Axel Schramm, Soonwaldstrasse 49.
GPS: n49,81088 e7,48058.

3 free free. **Location:** Rural, simple, isolated, quiet.
Surface: concrete. 01/01-31/12.
Distance: 1,2km.

Morbach

Reisemobilhafen Morbach, Zum Camping 15, Hoxel.
GPS: n49,77855 e7,10695.

40 €5/night €1/80liter Ch (40x)€2/night. **Location:** Rural.
Surface: grassy. 16/03-15/11.
Distance: 300m 300m.

Münstermaifeld

An der Stadthalle, An den Gärten 6. **GPS**: n50,24583 e7,36778.

2 free. **Location:** Urban, simple. **Surface:** metalled.
01/01-31/12.
Distance: 800m 800m 800m.

Münstermaifeld 11G3

Erlebnisbad Maifeld, Pilligertorstrasse. **GPS**: n50,24522 e7,35831.

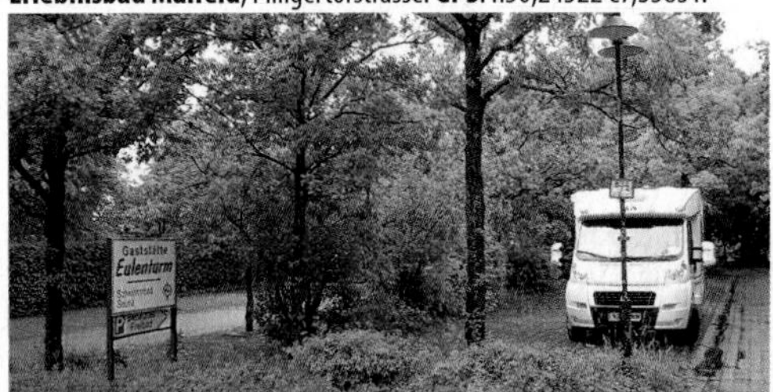

4. **Location:** Rural, simple. **Surface:** metalled.
01/09-15/05.
Distance: 700m 700m 700m.

Nanzdietschweiler 16G2

Hauptstrasse. **GPS**: n49,44083 e7,43500.

2 free €1/100liter (4x)€1/8h. **Location:** Rural, simple, isolated, quiet. **Surface:** metalled. 01/01-31/12.
Distance: 7km on the spot on the spot.

Neef 11F3

Wohnmobilstellplatz Zum Frauenberg.
GPS: n50,09455 e7,13730.

100 €6 Chincluded (42x)€2/24h,4Amp.
Location: Rural, simple. **Surface:** grassy. 01/04-01/11.
Distance: on the spot on the spot 200m.
Remarks: Along the Moselle river, nearby sports fields, bread-service.

Neuhäusel 11G3

Wohnmobilstellplatz Efferz, Im Feldchen. **GPS**: n50,38271 e7,70331.

20 €8 €1/80liter Ch (12x)€1/2kWh WC .
Surface: metalled. 01/01-31/12.
Distance: 250m 250m 250m 100m > Koblenz.
Remarks: Bread-service.

Neumagen-Dhron 16F1

Gaststatte Beim Ketsch, In der Zeil. **GPS**: n49,86449 e6,90321.

100 €6 Chincluded €1,50/day WC €2 €3 against payment. **Surface:** grassy/gravel. 01/01-31/12.
Distance: 200m on the spot 500m.
Remarks: Bread-service.

Neumagen-Dhron 16F1

Yachthafen Neumagen, Moselstrasse 21.
GPS: n49,85188 e6,89232.

40 <9m €6, >9m €8 + €2,50/pp €0,50/40liter Ch €0,60/kWh WC included €3/24h.
Surface: gravel. 01/01-31/12.
Distance: 100m on the spot on the spot on the spot 1,3km.
Remarks: Check in at harbourmaster.

Neustadt/Weinstrasse 16H2

Dammstrasse-Ost, Hambach. **GPS**: n49,33083 e8,13150.

10 free €1/100liter €1 Ch.
Surface: grassy. 01/01-31/12.
Distance: nearby nearby nearby.
Remarks: Next to swimming pool, service 500m.

Neustadt/Weinstrasse 16H2

Reisemobilstellpatz Martin-Luther-Kirche, Martin-Luther-Strasse.
GPS: n49,35485 e8,15255.

30 €4/24h €1/8minutes Ch (24x)€1/kWh.
Surface: metalled. 01/01-31/12.
Distance: 300m 250m on the spot.

Neustadt/Weinstrasse 16H2

Festplatz Neustadt-Haardt, Am Mandelring, Haardt.
GPS: n49,36731 e8,13917.
2 free. 01/01-31/12.
Distance: 5km.

Neustadt/Weinstrasse 16H2

Parkplatz am Rebenmeer, Am Falltor, Duttweiler.
GPS: n49,30148 e8,21192.

DE

10 free. **Location:** Rural, simple, quiet. **Surface:** gravel/metalled.
01/01-31/12.
Distance: 5km 300m 250m bakery.

Neustadt/Weinstrasse 16H2

Wohnmobilstellplatz Gimmeldingen, Peter-Koch-Strasse.
GPS: n49,37771 e8,15448.
2 free. 01/01-31/12.
Distance: 500m 5km on the spot on the spot.

S Neustadt/Weinstrasse 16H2

Altes Weingut Steigelmann, Lauterbachstrasse 33, Mussbach.
GPS: n49,37285 e8,17230.
5 €5 Ch €1,50. 01/01-31/12.
Distance: 3km.

S Neustadt/Weinstrasse 16H2

Rebenhof Wein- und Sektgut, Andergasse 93, Hambach.
GPS: n49,32157 e8,12241.

5 €8 included. **Surface:** grassy. 01/01-31/12.
Distance: 5km.

S Neustadt/Weinstrasse 16H2

Weingut & Weinschenke Hans Abel, Weinstrasse 103, Hambach.
GPS: n49,33784 e8,13157.
3 free €2,50. 01/01-31/12 Thu.
Distance: 4,5km.

S Neustadt/Weinstrasse 16H2

Weingut Andres, Langensteinstrasse 22, Lachen-Speyersdorf.
GPS: n49,33631 e8,20579.
3 free . 01/01-31/12.

S Neustadt/Weinstrasse 16H2

Weingut Carl Disson, Andergasse 96, Hambach.
GPS: n49,32123 e8,12220.

4 €7 WC . **Surface:** grassy. 01/01-31/12.
Distance: 5km.
Remarks: Bread-service, wine tasting.

S Neustadt/Weinstrasse 16H2

Weingut Hammer, Zum Klausental 29. **GPS**: n49,32109 e8,13251.
3 €5 . 01/01-31/12.
Distance: 5km.

S Neustadt/Weinstrasse 16H2

Weingut Klohr, An der Eselshaut 67, Mussbach.
GPS: n49,36931 e8,17414.
2 . 01/01-31/12.
Distance: 2km.

S Neustadt/Weinstrasse 16H2

Weingut Kreiselmaier, Goethestrasse 77, Lachen.
GPS: n49,32215 e8,20071.

3 €5 €2/100liter €2/night. **Location:** Simple, quiet.
Surface: grassy. 01/03-31/10.
Distance: on the spot 4,5km 250m 3km 150m.
Remarks: Sale of wines.

S Neustadt/Weinstrasse 16H2

Weingut Müller-Kern, Andergasse 38, Hambach.
GPS: n49,32266 e8,12681.

3 €6 + €3/pp WC . **Surface:** grassy. 01/01-31/12.
Distance: 4,5km 300m on the spot on the spot.
Remarks: Adjacent walking and bicycle area.

S Neustadt/Weinstrasse 16H2

Weingut Rumsauer, Von-Dalheim-Strasse 11, Diedesfeld.
GPS: n49,31978 e8,14028.
2 free . 01/01-31/12.
Distance: 5km.

S Neustadt/Weinstrasse 16H2

Weingut Schäfer, Schiessmauer 56, Mussbach.
GPS: n49,36335 e8,17111.

5 €15 Ch WC included free. 01/03-31/10.
Distance: 2km.

S Neustadt/Weinstrasse 16H2

Weingut Völcker, An der Eselshaut 15, Mussbach.
GPS: n49,36825 e8,16805.
3 €5 . **Surface:** grassy. 01/01-31/12.
Distance: 3km.

S Neustadt/Weinstrasse 16H2

Weinhaus Am Herzog, Mandelring 195, Haardt.
GPS: n49,36889 e8,14583.
2 €15 WC included. 01/01-31/12.
Distance: 4km.

S Neustadt/Weinstrasse 16H2

Weinland Königsbach-Neustadt, Deidesheimer Strasse 12, Königsbach. **GPS**: n49,38712 e8,16239.
5 . 01/01-31/12.
Distance: 6,5km.

S Neustadt/Weinstrasse 16H2

Weinland Meckenheim, An der Eselshaut 76, Mussbach.
GPS: n49,37037 e8,17479.
3 €5 €2,50. 01/01-31/12.
Distance: 2,3km.

Neustadt/Weinstrasse 16H2

Weingut Helbighof, Andergasse 40, Hambach.
GPS: n49,32256 e8,12657.
3 . 01/01-31/12.
Distance: 4,5km.

Neustadt/Weinstrasse 16H2

Hambacher Schloss, Weinstrasse 110, Hambach.
GPS: n49,33706 e8,13155.
2 free. 01/01-31/12 01/10-31/10.

Distance: 4,5km.

S Neuwied 11G2

Yachthafen Neuwied, Rheinstrasse 180. **GPS**: n50,41413 e7,47946.

40 €7, 2 pers.incl. Ch €0,50/kWh WC included.
Surface: metalled. 01/01-31/12.
Distance: 2km on the spot 2km.
Remarks: Cash payment.

S Nickenich 11G3

Wohnmobilstellplatz am Baggerado, Auf dem Teich 1.
GPS: n50,40607 e7,33299.
4 €7 Ch (4x). **Surface:** metalled. 01/01-31/12.
Distance: 800m 800m.

S Niederbreitbach 11G2

Campingplatz Neuerburg, Im Freizeitpark 1.
GPS: n50,52969 e7,41414.

8 €6 80liter Ch €1,50/day €1 €3,50.
Location: Rural, comfortable. **Surface:** gravel. 01/01-31/12.
Distance: 250m 13km on the spot on the spot on the spot on the spot on the spot.
Remarks: Bread-service.

S Niederkirchen bei Deidesheim 16H2

Wohnmobilstellplatz Niederkirchen, An de Sportanlage 1.
GPS: n49,40891 e8,22141.
6 free €1. **Surface:** gravel. 01/01-31/12.
Distance: 1km 4,5km.

S Nierstein 16H1

Mobilstellplatz auf dem Weingut Gehring, Ausserhalb 17.
GPS: n49,85621 e8,32520.

30 €9 Ch (15x)€3/day €1/6minutes included.
Location: Rural, comfortable, quiet. **Surface:** grassy.
01/01-31/12.
Distance: 1km 11km 3km 1,2km 10m 500m 1,2km 50m 10m.
Remarks: Bread-service.

S Nohfelden 16F1

Campingplatz Bostalsee, P6, L325, Bosen.
GPS: n49,56039 e7,06113.

10 €12 €0,50/60liter Ch€0,50 €1/kWh included.
Location: Rural, simple, quiet. **Surface:** metalled.

DE

01/01-31/12.
Distance: 500m 6km 200m € 8/day on the spot 800m on the spot on the spot.

Nonnweiler 16F1

Stellplatz Am Hallenbad, Triererstrasse 2.
GPS: n49,60686 e6,97216.

5 free €1/100liter (4x)€0,50. **Location:** Rural, simple, quiet.
Surface: grassy/metalled. 01/01-31/12.
Distance: on the spot 1km on the spot 800m.
Remarks: Parking swimming pool, max. 48h.

Nürburg 11F3

Wohnmobilpark Motorsporthotel, Hauptstrasse 34.
GPS: n50,33982 e6,95131.
12 € 10 included on demand. **Location:** Rural, simple.
Surface: grassy. 01/01-31/12.
Distance: on the spot.
Remarks: At racing circuit, pay at hotel.

Ober-Hilbersheim 16H1

Napoleonshöhe, Sprendlingers Straße. **GPS**: n49,89785 e8,02421.

40 free Ch. **Surface:** grassy. 01/01-31/12.
Distance: 500m 300m.

Oberbrombach 16G1

Wohnmobilstellplatz Höhenblick, Sonnenberger Strasse.
GPS: n49,69481 e7,25960.

75 €7 Chincluded (45x)€2/4kWh. **Location:** Rural, comfortable, quiet. **Surface:** grassy/gravel. 01/01-31/12.
Distance: 400m 4km 1,5km.

Oberwesel/Rhein 11G3

Stellplatz am Schiffsanleger, B9. **GPS**: n50,10816 e7,72758.
10 € 8/24h. **Surface:** metalled. 01/01-31/12.
Distance: 10km on the spot on the spot.

Oberwesel/Rhein 11G3

Camping Schönburgblick, Am Hafendamm 1.
GPS: n50,10294 e7,73663.

20 €9 Chincluded €0,60/kWh WC €2,50 €2.
Location: Comfortable, quiet. **Surface:** grassy. 15/03-31/10.
Distance: 800m on the spot on the spot on the spot 200m 400m.
Remarks: Max. 8M, possibility for reservation.

Offenbach an der Queich 16H2

Am Queichtalzentrum, Konrad-Lerch-Ring.
GPS: n49,20056 e8,19478.

2 free. **Location:** Simple. **Surface:** metalled.
01/01-31/12.
Distance: 100m 6km 500m 1km 400m.
Remarks: Max. 3 days.

Oppenheim 16H1

Womoland Oppenheim, An der Festwiese.
GPS: n49,85673 e8,36502.

20 €7 €1/50liter Ch €3/24h. **Surface:** grassy.
01/01-31/12 week before/after Whitsuntide.
Distance: 500m 500m 500m.

Osann-Monzel 16F1

Wohnmobilstellplatz Panorama, Moselstrasse 16.
GPS: n49,90904 e6,95624.

8 €5 €2 against payment.
Surface: gravel. 01/06-31/10.
Distance: 9km 50m.
Remarks: Key at aparthotel Panorama (50m).

Osthofen 16H1

Festplatz Wonnegauhalle, Herrnsheimer Strasse.
GPS: n49,69913 e8,32691.

50 free Chfree. **Surface:** gravel. 01/01-31/12.
Distance: 500m 7km 500m.
Remarks: Max. 48h.

Osthofen 16H1

Sommerried Stadion, L439. **GPS**: n49,69222 e8,32805.

10 free. **Surface:** grassy/sand. 01/01-31/12.

Distance: 6km 800m.
Remarks: Max. 48h.

Osthofen 16H1

Weingut Borntaler Hof, Alter Westhofer Weg.
GPS: n49,69985 e8,29860.

4 €5 WCincluded .
Surface: metalled. 01/01-31/12.
Distance: 9km.

Ottweiler 16F2

Stellplatz Wingertsweiher, Am Wingertsweiher.
GPS: n49,41134 e7,18076.

12 €5/24h €1/150liter €1 Ch (6x)€3/8h.
Location: Rural, simple, quiet. **Surface:** grassy/metalled.
01/01-31/12.
Distance: 1,5km on the spot on the spot on the spot 1,5km 1km.
Remarks: Max. 7 days, money in envelope in mail box.

Palzem 16E1

Weingut E. Pauly, Obermoselstrasse 5.
GPS: n49,56402 e6,37581.

3 €7 WC. **Surface:** gravel/metalled. 01/01-31/12.
Distance: 50m 4km.
Remarks: Not suitable for big motorhomes, beautiful view.

Perl 16E1

Am Perlbach, Auf dem Sabel 4. **GPS**: n49,47900 e6,38493.

6 €8, winter €5 €1/6minutes Ch €1/8h.
Surface: metalled. 01/01-31/12.
Distance: 500m 3,5km 500m 500m.

Pfaffen-Schwabenheim 16H1

Pferdepension am Sonnenhof, Brühlstraße.
GPS: n49,85224 e7,95951.
10 €10 WC included. **Location:** Rural, simple, isolated, quiet. **Surface:** concrete. 01/01-31/12.
Distance: 7km.

Piesport 16F1

Piesporter Goldtröpfchen, Moselstrasse. **GPS**: n49,87199 e6,92703.

DE

30 €6 €1/80liter Ch €2.
Surface: gravel. 01/01-31/12.
Distance: 100m 11km on the spot on the spot on the spot 500m.
Remarks: Bread-service mo-sa.

S Piesport 16F1
Altes Kelterhaus, St. Martinstrasse 33. **GPS:** n49,87872 e6,92590.

6 €7,50, guests free €2,50 Ch €2,50. **Surface:** gravel.
01/01-31/12.
Distance: 10km on the spot on the spot.

S Piesport 16F1
Weingut Heinz Kirsten, In der Noo. **GPS:** n49,88017 e6,92597.

6 €6 €1. **Surface:** gravel. 01/01-31/12.
Distance: 7,5km on the spot on the spot.
Remarks: Check in at Bahnhofstrasse 28.

S Piesport 16F1
Weingut Spang, Reisemobilplatz Rebengarten, In den Dur 11.
GPS: n49,88287 e6,92781.

3 €8 €0,70/kWh WC €2,50.
Surface: gravel.
01/01-31/12.
Distance: on the spot 8km 100m 100m 500m 500m.
Remarks: Bread-service.

S Piesport 16F1
Wohnmobilstellplatz Loreleyblick, Loreleyblick 20.
GPS: n49,87323 e6,92535.

5 €8 Ch (10x) €1.
Surface: gravel. 01/01-31/12.
Distance: on the spot 11km 1km 300m.

Remarks: Bread-service.

S Pirmasens 16G2
Am Messegelände, Zeppelinstraße. **GPS:** n49,20446 e7,60885.

8 €5/24h €1/100liter Ch €1/6h.
Location: Urban, simple, noisy. **Surface:** gravel.
01/01-31/12.
Distance: 450m 6km 450m 450m.

Pirmasens 16G2
Forsthaus Beckenhof, Beckenhofer Strasse.
GPS: n49,19604 e7,65635.

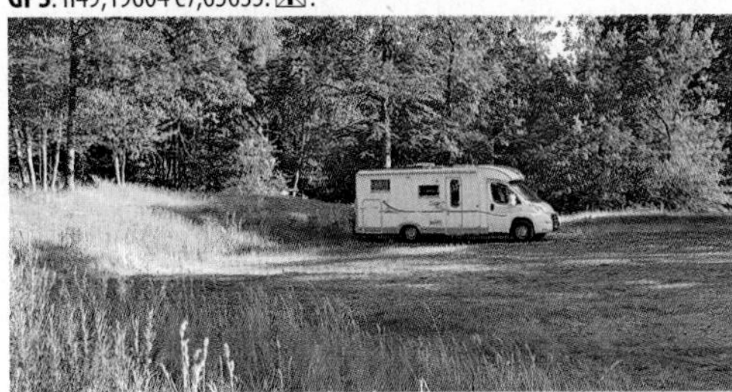

10 guests free. **Location:** Rural, simple, quiet. **Surface:** gravel.
01/01-31/12.

Plaidt 11G3
Wohnmobilstellplatz am Vulkanpark, Rauschermühle 6.
GPS: n50,38790 e7,40444.

10 free.
Location: Rural. **Surface:** metalled. 01/01-31/12.
Distance: 5km.

Plein 11F3
Hotel-Restaurant Waldschlößchen Plein, Zum Waldschlößchen 3.
GPS: n50,03223 e6,88074.
3 guests free. 01/01-31/12.
Distance: 4km on the spot.

S Polch 11G3
Niesmann&Bisschof, Clou-strasse 1. **GPS:** n50,30680 e7,30684.

25 free €0,50/80liter Ch (12x)€0,50/kWh.
Surface: metalled. 01/01-31/12.
Distance: on the spot on the spot.

S Pronsfeld 11E3
Am Alten Bahnhof, Bahnhofstrasse. **GPS:** n50,16343 e6,33669.

50 €6 €0,50/60liter Ch (24x)€0,50/kWh.
Location: Rural, comfortable, quiet. **Surface:** grassy/gravel.
01/01-31/12.
Distance: 600m 7,5km 600m 700m 500m on the spot on the spot.

Prüm 11E3
Wohnmobilstellplatz Prüm, Monthermeerstrasse 3.
GPS: n50,20956 e6,42715.

4 free. **Location:** Urban, simple. **Surface:** gravel.
01/01-31/12.
Distance: 600m 2,2km 500m 500m 200m.

S Pünderich 11F3
Wohnmobilstellplatz Pünderich, Moselallee.
GPS: n50,04355 e7,12548.

80 €6 Ch included (12x)€2/24h.
Location: Rural, simple, quiet. **Surface:** grassy. 01/04-31/10.
Distance: on the spot on the spot on the spot 300m 500m.

Ramstein-Miesenbach 16G1
City Parkplatz, Talstrasse. **GPS:** n49,45103 e7,55557.

3 free. **Location:** Urban, simple, noisy. **Surface:** gravel.
01/01-31/12.
Distance: 3,7km.

Ramstein-Miesenbach 16G1
Freizeitbad Azur, Schernauer Strasse 5. **GPS:** n49,44578 e7,56971.

30 free. **Location:** Rural, simple, noisy. **Surface:** metalled.
01/01-31/12.
Distance: 5,5km.

DE

Rech 11F2

Wohnmobilstellpark Alt Bodendorf, Rotweinstraße 13.
GPS: n50,51458 e7,03738.

15 € 4. 01/01-31/12.
Distance: 11km.

Rech 11F2

Im Bungert. **GPS**: n50,51343 e7,03865.
10 € 4. **Location:** Rural, simple. **Surface:** gravel.
01/01-31/12.
Distance: on the spot on the spot on the spot on the spot.

Reil/Mosel 11F3

Am Moselufer, Moselstrasse. **GPS**: n50,02566 e7,11493.

70 €7 Ch (48x)€2 WC included. **Location:** Rural, comfortable, quiet. **Surface:** grassy. 01/03-31/10.
Distance: 500m on the spot 450m.
Remarks: Along the Moselle river.

Reipoltskirchen 16G1

Wasserburg, Kegelbahnstrasse. **GPS**: n49,63448 e7,66373.

7 free €1/4minutes Ch (4x)€1/12h.
Location: Rural, simple, central, quiet. **Surface:** metalled.
01/01-31/12.
Distance: 150m on the spot bakery 100m on the spot.

Reipoltskirchen 16G1

Stellplatz Ausbacherhof, K42, Ausbacherhof.
GPS: n49,61307 e7,65667.

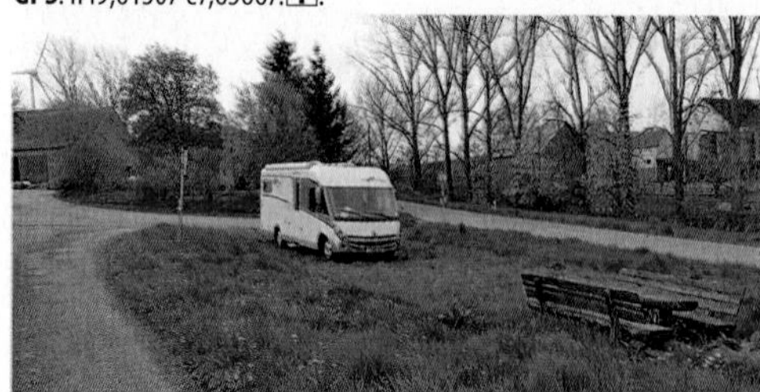

4 free. **Location:** Rural, simple, isolated, quiet.
Surface: grassy/gravel. 01/01-31/12.

Remagen 11F2

Wohnmobilhafen Goldene Meile, Simrockweg 9–13.
GPS: n50,57667 e7,24750.

30 € 12 €1/90liter Ch (18x)€1/6h. **Surface:** grassy.
01/04-31/10.
Distance: 10km on the spot on the spot.

Rengsdorf 11G2

Monte Mare, Monte-Mare-Weg 1. **GPS**: n50,50803 e7,48388.

4 free. **Location:** Rural. **Surface:** gravel. 01/01-31/12.
Distance: 600m 600m.

Rheinbreitbach 11F2

Wohnmobilstellplatz Siebengebirgsblick, Rolandsecker Weg 8.
GPS: n50,62193 e7,22812.

14 €8 €1/90liter Ch (12x)€1/2kWh.
Location: Simple. **Surface:** grassy/gravel. 01/01-31/12.
Distance: 500m.
Remarks: To be paid at Rolandsecker Weg 8.

Rhodt unter Rietburg 16H2

Theresienstraße. **GPS**: n49,27464 e8,09917.

20 €4. **Location:** Rural, simple. **Surface:** gravel.
01/01-31/12.
Distance: 100m 5km.

Rhodt unter Rietburg 16H2

Meyer Karl Herman, Edesheimerstrasse 17.
GPS: n49,26883 e8,10868.

6 €9 (6x)included. **Location:** Rural, simple, quiet.
Surface: gravel. 01/01-31/12.
Distance: 200m 200m 200m.

Rhodt unter Rietburg 16H2

Weingut Fader, Traminerweg 1. **GPS**: n49,26972 e8,11057.

12 €10 Ch (12x)included. **Location:** Rural, simple, quiet. **Surface:** gravel. 01/04-31/10.
Distance: 300m 200m 200m.

Rhodt unter Rietburg 16H2

Weingut Krieger, Edesheimerstrasse 7. **GPS**: n49,26961 e8,10803.

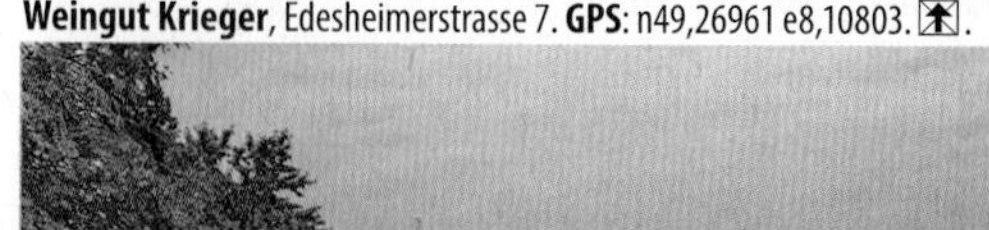

2 €5 free on demand. **Location:** Rural, simple, quiet.
Surface: grassy. 01/01-31/12.
Distance: 100m 6km 200m 200m.

Rhodt unter Rietburg 16H2

Weingut Nichterlein, Mühlgasse 15. **GPS**: n49,27349 e8,10802.

3 €6 on demand WC free. **Location:** Quiet.
Surface: metalled. 01/01-31/12.
Distance: 300m 5km.

Rhodt unter Rietburg 16H2

Weingut Jürgen Heußler, Weyherer Strasse 34/35.
GPS: n49,27052 e8,10386.

3 €3. **Location:** Simple. 01/01-31/12.
Distance: 300m 6km 100m.

Rockenhausen 16G1

Reisemobilhafen Rockenhausen, Obermühle.
GPS: n49,62136 e7,82146.

5 free €1/80liter Ch (6x)€1/6h. **Location:** Rural, simple.
Surface: gravel. 01/01-31/12.
Distance: 800m on the spot.
Remarks: At swimming pool.

Roschbach 16H2

Weingut Koch, Am Rosenkränzel 13. **GPS**: n49,24736 e8,11532.

DE

3 €5 included €2/night. **Location:** Rural, quiet.
Surface: grassy. 01/01-31/12.
Distance: 5km.

Ruppertsberg 16H2

Winzerhaus Im Linsenbusch, Hauptstrasse 70.
GPS: n49,39944 e8,20044.
2 €8 included WC €7/day. 01/01-31/12.
Distance: 3km.

Saarbrücken 16F2

Reisemobilhafen Calypso, Deutschmühlental 7.
GPS: n49,23027 e6,96222.

20 €7 + reduction swimming pool Ch included (4x)€1/24h. **Location:** Simple, noisy. **Surface:** metalled.
01/01-31/12.
Distance: 700m 100m on the spot 500m on the spot.
Remarks: To pay at swimming pool.

Saarburg 16F1

Reisemobilpark Saarburg, Am Saarufer.
GPS: n49,60158 e6,55442.

100 €9, 01/11-28/02 €6 €1/100liter Ch (70x)€0,50/kWh WC €1,50 . **Surface:** grassy/metalled. 01/01-31/12
Service: winter.
Distance: 850m on the spot on the spot 200m.
Remarks: Bread-service.

Saarburg 16F1

Reisemobilstellplatz Leukbachtal, Leukbachtal 1.
GPS: n49,59921 e6,54130.

20 €15 Ch WC included. **Location:** Comfortable, quiet. **Surface:** grassy. 01/03-31/10.
Distance: 1km 150m.

Saarlouis 16F2

In den Fliesen, St.Nazairer Allee. **GPS**: n49,32146 e6,74267.

30 free €1/80liter Ch. **Location:** Urban, simple, quiet.
Surface: metalled. 01/01-31/12.
Distance: 500m 1,5km on the spot on the spot 500m 300m.
Remarks: At sports centre, bread-service.

Saarlouis 16F2

Hotellerie Waldesruh, Siersburger Strasse 8, Wallerfangen.
GPS: n49,34440 e6,67614.

2 €10, guests free. **Location:** Rural, simple, noisy.
Surface: metalled. 01/01-31/12.
Distance: 10km on the spot.

Sankt Aldegund 11F3

Am Moselstausee. **GPS**: n50,07899 e7,13119.

40 €6 Ch included (28x)€2/24h. **Location:** Rural, simple.
Surface: grassy/metalled. 01/04-01/12.
Distance: 250m on the spot 250m.
Remarks: Bread-service.

Sankt Goarshausen 11G3

Loreley Besucherzentrum, Auf der Loreley 7.
GPS: n50,14191 e7,73303.

25 €8. **Location:** Simple, isolated.
Distance: 600m 600m.

Sankt Ingbert 16F2

Reisemobilplatz 'Das Blau', Spieser Landstraße.
GPS: n49,28652 e7,13194.

8 free €1/80liter Ch. **Location:** Simple, central, quiet.
Surface: grassy. 01/01-31/12.
Distance: 1,5km 3,5km 100m 1,7km on the spot.
Remarks: Next to parking swimming pool, service 100m.

Sankt Julian 16G1

An der Ölmühle, Mühlstraße (K26). **GPS**: n49,60758 e7,51480.

10 €5 €1 Ch €1/kWh. **Location:** Rural, simple, quiet.
Surface: grassy. 01/04-31/10.
Distance: on the spot 300m.

Sankt Martin 16H2

Edenkoperstrasse. **GPS**: n49,29702 e8,10838.

14 € 6/day. **Surface:** asphalted. 01/01-31/12.
Distance: 5km.
Remarks: Max. 1 night.

Sankt Martin 16H2

Weingut Schreieck, Friedhofstrasse 8. **GPS**: n49,30113 e8,10560.
17 €12 Ch WC included. 01/01-31/12.
Distance: 5km.

Sankt Martin 16H2

Weinkellerei Ziegler, Mühlstrasse 26. **GPS**: n49,29921 e8,10028.
3 €10 . 01/01-31/12.
Distance: 5km.

Sankt Martin 16H2

Consulat des Weines, Maikammerer strasse 44.
GPS: n49,29934 e8,10826.
10 €1/pp tourist tax. 01/01-31/12.
Distance: 4,5km.

Sankt Martin 16H2

Winzer Holger Schneider, Riedweg. **GPS**: n49,29814 e8,10824.

free for clients. **Surface:** gravel.
Distance: on the spot.

Sankt Martin 16H2

Riedweg. **GPS**: n49,29814 e8,10824.
€1 Ch.

Sankt Wendel 16F1

Am Wendelinuspark, Tholeyer Straße. **GPS**: n49,46907 e7,14267.

12 €5 Ch free. **Location:** Urban, simple.
Surface: metalled. 01/01-31/12.
Distance: 1km on the spot 100m on the spot.
Remarks: Caution key service € 10, tickets Wendelinusbad.

Schiersfeld 16G1

Sulzbachtal, Bismarkstraße. **GPS**: n49,69274 e7,76895.

DE

8-12 free €1 (8x)€1/4kWh. **Location:** Rural, simple, quiet.
Surface: gravel. 01/01-31/12.
Distance: 500m bakery 500m Moscheltalradweg on the spot.

S Schleich 16F1

Zum Moselufer, Am Moselufer. **GPS**: n49,81335 e6,84228.

6 €5 Ch €2 WC. **Surface:** grassy. 01/01-31/12.
Distance: on the spot on the spot on the spot 200m.

S Schwabenheim/Selz 11H3

Reisemobilstellplatz Schwabenheim, Ingelheimer Straße.
GPS: n49,93284 e8,09430.

10 free (12x)free. **Location:** Rural, comfortable, quiet.
Surface: grasstiles. 01/01-31/12.
Distance: 200m 8,5km 200m on the spot on the spot.
Remarks: Max. 96h free, then € 3/24h.

S Schwabenheim/Selz 11H3

Weingut Schuck Sonnenhof, Ausserhalb 6.
GPS: n49,93130 e8,09117.

3 €5 (3x)included WC. **Location:** Rural, comfortable, quiet.
Surface: grassy/gravel. 01/01-31/12.
Distance: 500m 9km.

S Schweich/Mosel bei Trier 16F1

Wohnmobilpark zum Fahrturm, Am Yachthafen.
GPS: n49,81455 e6,75038.

40 < 6m € 11 incl. 2 pers, + € 1/m, dog € 2,10 Ch €0,60/kWh,+€1 €0,50 €3 against payment. **Surface:** grassy.
01/04-31/10.
Distance: on the spot on the spot on the spot on the spot 50m on the spot on the spot.

Remarks: Boat rental.

S Selzen 16H1

Weingut Kapellenhof, Kapellenstrasse 18.
GPS: n49,86484 e8,25528.

4 €5 (4x)included. **Location:** Rural, simple, quiet.
Surface: grasstiles. 01/01-31/12.
Distance: on the spot 100m 2km.

S Siefersheim 16H1

Weingut Sommer, Mühlweg 19. **GPS**: n49,79850 e7,95245.

6 €5 (6x)included. **Location:** Rural, simple.
Surface: grassy. 01/04-31/10.
Distance: 8km 2km 2km.

S Sinzig 11F2

Wohnmobilhafen am Sportplatz, Bäderstrasse.
GPS: n50,55128 e7,21731.

10 €6/24h €1 Ch (12x)€0,50/kWh WC €1/1,at Freibad. **Location:** Rural, simple. **Surface:** gravel.
01/01-31/12.
Distance: 7km 800m on the spot on the spot.

Sinzig 11F2

Sinziger Schloß, Jahnstrasse. **GPS**: n50,54684 e7,24844.

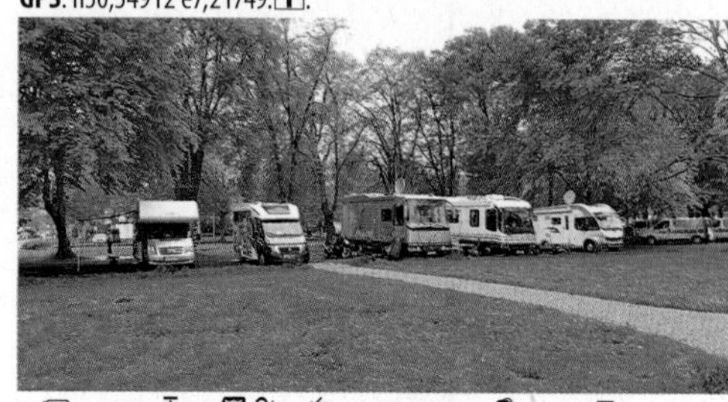

20 free. **Location:** Urban, simple. **Surface:** metalled.
01/01-31/12.
Distance: 100m on the spot.

S Sinzig 11F2

Wohnmobilhafen am Thermalfreibad, Bäderstrasse.
GPS: n50,54912 e7,21749.

50 €6/24h €1 Ch (18x)€0,50/kWh €1/pp.
Location: Rural, simple. **Surface:** metalled.

01/01-31/12.
Distance: 50m on the spot on the spot.

S Speyer 16H2

Techniek Museum Speyer, Geibstrasse. **GPS**: n49,31222 e8,45009.

90 €22 Ch WC included. **Location:** Comfortable, central, noisy. **Surface:** grassy. 01/01-31/12.
Distance: 8,5km 150m 200m on the spot on the spot on the spot.
Remarks: Bread-service, discount museum and theater.

S Speyer 16H2

An den Stadtwerken, Industriestraße 21. **GPS**: n49,30329 e8,44817.

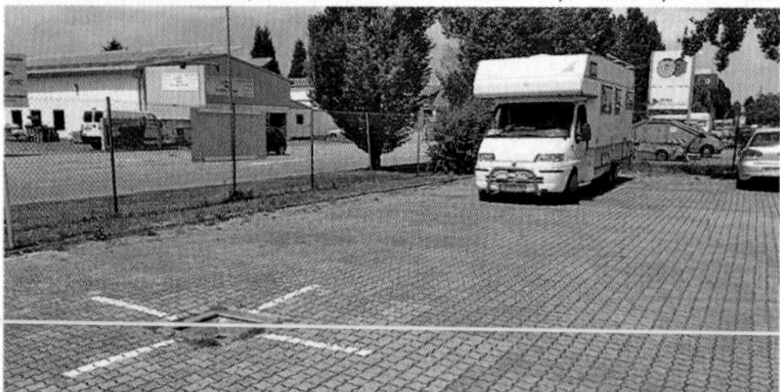

10 €5 €1 €1 Ch€1 included. **Location:** Simple.
Surface: asphalted.
Distance: 1,5km 6km 1,5km 1,6km 500m on the spot.
Remarks: Check in at Stadwerke.

Tourist information Speyer:
M Technik Museum Speyer/Imax Filmtheater, Geibstrasse. Mo-Fr 9-18h, Sa-Su 9-17h.

S Spirkelbach 16G2

Grillplatz Spirkelbach. **GPS**: n49,19454 e7,88208.

4 €7 Ch WC included. **Location:** Rural, simple, quiet.
Surface: gravel. 01/01-31/12.
Distance: 500m 500m on the spot on the spot.
Remarks: Check in on arrival, tel: 0171 3355971, nature reserve Pfalzer Wald.

S Sprendlingen 16H1

Wiesbach, Bachgasse/Bleichstrasse. **GPS**: n49,85424 e7,98538.

24 €4 €2/10minutes Ch (24x)€2/day.
Location: Rural, comfortable, quiet. **Surface:** asphalted.
01/01-31/12.
Distance: 700m 3,4km 500m 900m on the spot.
Remarks: Parking at swimming pool, bread-service, entrance swimming pool € 2/day.

S Sprendlingen 16H1

Weingut Annenhof, Außerhalb 13. **GPS**: n49,85778 e7,99278.

DE

4 free. WC free. **Location:** Rural, simple. **Surface:** concrete. 01/01-31/12.
Distance: 3km 500m 800m.

S Sprendlingen 16H1

Weingut Hembd, Karlstrasse 24a. **GPS:** n49,86422 e7,98811.

10 € 10 included. **Location:** Rural, simple.
Surface: grassy. 01/01-31/12.
Distance: 4km 500m 500m.

S Sprendlingen 16H1

Eura Mobil Stellplatz, Graf-von-Sponheimstrasse.
GPS: n49,86297 e7,97612.

38 free €1/100liter Ch (38x)free. **Location:** Rural, simple, quiet. **Surface:** asphalted/metalled. 01/01-31/12.
Distance: 600m 4,4km 300m.
Remarks: Workdays from 9h guided tours (free).

S Stadecken-Elsheim 11H3

Weingut Mengel-Eppelmann, Mühlstrasse 16.
GPS: n49,91575 e8,12107.

5 € 5, free for clients included. **Location:** Comfortable, quiet.
Surface: asphalted. 01/01-31/12.
Distance: on the spot 6km on the spot.

Stadtkyll 11F3

Kurallee. **GPS:** n50,35290 e6,52820.
6 free. 01/01-31/12.

S Stromberg 11G3

Reisemobilplatz Michelsland, Königsberger Straße.
GPS: n49,94709 e7,78818.

6 € 5 Chincluded (6x)€0,50/kWh.
Location: Comfortable, quiet. **Surface:** grassy. 01/01-31/12.

Distance: 500m 500m 50m Lidl.

S Thalfang 16F1

Festplatz Thalfang, Talstrasse 2. **GPS:** n49,75103 e6,99902.

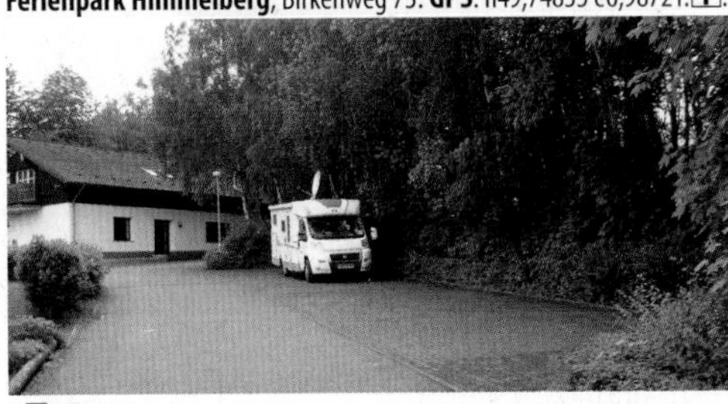

40 € 5 Ch (6x)free. **Location:** Simple, quiet.
Surface: grassy/gravel. 01/01-31/12 21/09-30/09.
Distance: 200m on the spot on the spot on the spot 200m 200m on the spot.
Remarks: Max. 4 nights, check in at swimming pool.

Thalfang 16F1

Ferienpark Himmelberg, Birkenweg 73. **GPS:** n49,74835 e6,98721.

2 free.
Location: Rural, simple. **Surface:** metalled. 01/01-31/12.
Distance: 300m.

Thallichtenberg 16G1

Burg Lichtenberg, K23. **GPS:** n49,55716 e7,35975.

4 free. **Location:** Rural, simple, quiet. **Surface:** asphalted.
01/01-31/12.
Distance: 7km 300m 1km.
Remarks: Max. 3 days.

Tholey 16F1

Parkplatz Am Schaumburg, Am Schaumberg.
GPS: n49,48965 e7,03804.

±20 free. **Location:** Rural, simple, quiet. **Surface:** metalled.
01/01-31/12.
Distance: 500m 100m on the spot on the spot.

S Traben-Trarbach 11F3

Wohnmobilstellplatz am Mosel
Traben-Trarbach
Located directly at the river
Ideal base for walking and cycling
Restaurant with regional specialties
www.moselstellplatz.de
info@moselcampingplatz.de

Wohnmobilstellplatz am Mosel, Rissbacherstraße 155.
GPS: n49,96583 e7,10583.
45 € 10 Ch (45x),6Amp WC included.
Location: Rural, comfortable. **Surface:** grassy/gravel.
01/04-31/12.
Distance: 500m on the spot on the spot 500m 200m 100m on the spot on the spot.
Remarks: Along the Moselle river.

S Trechtinghausen 11G3

Camping Marienort, Mainzer Straße. **GPS:** n50,00426 e7,85516.

20 € 7 Chincluded €2/24h WC €1.
Location: Comfortable, quiet. **Surface:** grassy.
01/01-31/12.
Distance: on the spot on the spot on the spot.
Remarks: Bread-service, sanitary at campsite, narrow entrance.

S Trier 16F1

Reisemobilpark Treviris, In den Moselauen.
GPS: n49,74092 e6,62502.

110 € 0,20/h 10-18h, € 8/18-10h €1/100liter Ch (62x)€0,70/kWh WC €1/3minutes.
Surface: grasstiles. 01/01-31/12.
Distance: 3km 6km 400m McDonald's on the spot.
Remarks: Along the Moselle river, bread-service.

S Trier 16F1

Weingut Vonnell, Im Tiergarten 12. **GPS:** n49,73840 e6,65914.

15 € 10 included.
Surface: grassy/gravel. 01/01-31/12.
Distance: 3km 7km.
Tourist information Trier:

DE

i Tourist Information, An der Porta Nigra, www.trier.de. Old Roman city with the best kept and also largest Roman gate in Europe: Porta Nigra.

i Triercard. Free city bus and discount at museums, boat trips, swimming pool etc. T € 9,90, family card € 21, 3 days.

S Trittenheim 16F1

Moselpromenade Reisemobilplatz Trittenheim, Moselstrasse. **GPS**: n49,82436 e6,90295.

50 € 6,50 €0,50/100liter Ch (30x)€3/24h.
Surface: grassy/metalled. 01/01-31/12.
Distance: 500m on the spot on the spot 300m 400m.
Remarks: Bread-service.

S Unkel 11F2

P3, Parkplatz Hallenbad, Kamenerstrasse.
GPS: n50,59776 e7,21962.

6 free €1/80liter Ch WC. **Location:** Urban.
Surface: asphalted. 01/01-31/12.
Distance: 100m 100m 150m on the spot.

S Urmitz/Rhein 11G2

Wohnmobilhafen am Rhein, Kaltenengerser Straße 3.
GPS: n50,41849 e7,52448.

24 € 7,50 €1/4minutes Ch (24x)€1/8h.
Surface: metalled. 01/01-31/12.
Distance: on the spot 5km on the spot on the spot 350m 300m.
Remarks: Along the Rhine river, bread-service.

S Ürzig 11F3

Panorama-Mobilstellplatz Ürzig, Moselufer B53.
GPS: n49,97837 e7,00700.

25 € 9,50 Ch included €1,50/day.
Location: Comfortable, quiet. **Surface:** grassy. 01/04-31/10.
Distance: 9km on the spot bakery 150m on the spot on the spot.
Remarks: Along the Moselle river.

S Uttfeld 11E3

Raiffeisenstrasse. **GPS**: n50,12740 e6,27170.
15 € 5 €0,50/80liter Ch (2x)€0,50/kWh WC.
Location: Rural, comfortable, isolated, quiet.
Surface: gravel.
01/01-31/12.
Distance: 6,5km 6,5km on the spot.

S Vallendar 11G3

Rheinufer. **GPS**: n50,39749 e7,61277.

3 free . **Location:** Urban, simple.
Surface: asphalted/metalled. 01/01-31/12.
Distance: centre 500m 3km on the spot 200m Aldi 200m.
Remarks: Along railwayline, Max. ^3m.

Valwig 11F3

Moselweinstrasse. **GPS**: n50,14271 e7,21292.

10 € 6. **Location:** Rural, simple. **Surface:** gravel.
01/01-31/12.
Distance: 100m on the spot 100m on the spot on the spot.

S Veldenz 16F1

Wohnmobilpark Veldenz, Hauptstrasse, K88.
GPS: n49,89222 e7,01944.

40 € 6 Ch (24x)included €2. **Surface:** grassy.
01/01-31/12.
Distance: 300m 300m 300m 200m.

S Völklingen 16F2

Weltkulturerbe Völklinger Hütte, Rathausstraße.
GPS: n49,24730 e6,84492.

10 free €1/80liter Ch (6x)€0,25/h.
Location: Urban, simple, central, noisy. **Surface:** asphalted.
01/01-31/12.
Distance: 500m 1,1km 400m 850m on the spot on the spot.
Remarks: Visitors centre Industrial Heritage.

S Wachenheim 16H1

Weingut Rudolf Hein, Hauptstrasse 38. **GPS**: n49,63860 e8,16832.

8 € 6 included (6x)€2/24h. **Location:** Rural, simple, quiet. **Surface:** grassy. 01/01-31/12.
Distance: 10km 1km 3km.

S Wadern 16F1

An der Stadthalle. **GPS**: n49,54188 e6,89232.

10 free €0,50 (8x)€1/day free.
Location: Urban, simple, central, quiet. **Surface:** metalled.
01/01-31/12.
Distance: on the spot 3km on the spot 100m.
Remarks: Parking in centre.

Wadern 16F1

Noswendeler See, Seestrasse. **GPS**: n49,52021 e6,86387.

5 free. **Location:** Rural, simple. **Surface:** grassy/metalled.
01/01-31/12.
Distance: on the spot on the spot 3km.

Wadern 16F1

Zum Wiesental, Nunkirchen. **GPS**: n49,48866 e6,83575.

5 free. **Location:** Rural, simple, quiet. **Surface:** metalled.
01/01-31/12.
Distance: on the spot on the spot on the spot.

Wadern 16F1

Hotel Pension Steil, Schlossstrasse 2, Lockweiler.
GPS: n49,52765 e6,90158.

4 guests free. **Surface:** metalled. 01/01-31/12.
Distance: 1km on the spot 500m.

Wadern 16F1

Hotel Restaurant Reidelbacher Hof, Reidelbach 5, Reidelbach.
GPS: n49,57706 e6,86808.
5 € 5, guests free. 01/01-31/12.

DE

Distance: 3km 9km on the spot 3km.

Tourist information Wadern:

Tourist Information, Marktplatz 13, www.wadern.de. Nature reserve Saar Hunsrück, many signposted cycle and hiking routes.

S Waldfischbach-Burgalben 16G2

In den Bruchwiesen, Carentaner Platz.
GPS: n49,28155 e7,64772.

6 free €1/80liter Ch €1/8h. **Location:** Simple, central, quiet. **Surface:** asphalted. 01/01-31/12.
Distance: 600m 100m.
Remarks: Behind gymnasium.

S Waxweiler 11E3

Wohnmobilplatz Waxweiler, Bahnhofstrasse.
GPS: n50,09401 e6,35669.

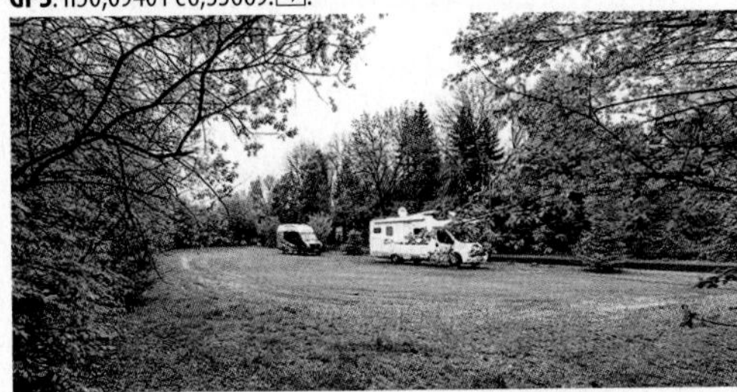

30 €5 €1 Ch €2. **Location:** Rural, simple, quiet.
Surface: metalled. 01/01-31/12.
Distance: on the spot 1km 500m.

S Weiskirchen 16F1

Am Kurpark, Burgstrasse. **GPS:** n49,55868 e6,81810.

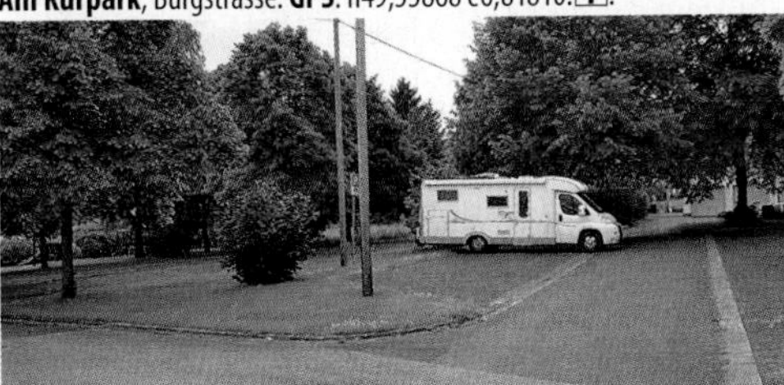

6 €1,40/pp €0,50 €0,50 Ch €0,50. **Location:** Rural.
Surface: metalled. 01/01-31/12.
Distance: on the spot 500m 300m.
Remarks: Parking at the health resort, max. 2-3 days, pay at tourist office.

Westerburg 11H2

Am Segelhafen, Seestrasse, Pottum. **GPS:** n50,59526 e7,99860.

10 free. **Location:** Rural, simple, quiet. **Surface:** metalled.
01/01-31/12.
Distance: 250m on the spot on the spot 250m.

S Westhofen 16H1

Parkplatz Nickelgarten, Am Nickelgarten.
GPS: n49,70559 e8,24672.

15 free (12x)€1/8h. **Surface:** metalled. 01/01-31/12.
Distance: 100m 4km 100m.
Remarks: Max. 3 days.

S Westhofen 16H1

Weingut Dreihornmühle, An der Brennerei.
GPS: n49,70375 e8,25288.

3 €5, guests free €1/day. **Surface:** grassy. 01/01-31/12.
Distance: 600m 600m 150m.
Remarks: Max. 24h.

S Westhofen 16H1

Tankstelle Raiffeisen. GPS: n49,70039 e8,24699.
Ch. 01/01-31/12.
Remarks: Coins at petrol station.

S Weyher 16H2

Weingut Möwes, Hübühl 10. **GPS:** n49,26982 e8,08663.

2 €8 included. **Location:** Rural, quiet. **Surface:** metalled.
01/01-31/12.
Distance: 200m 7km.

S Weyher 16H2

Weingut Valentin Ziegler Sohn, Hübühl 9.
GPS: n49,26937 e8,08609.

2 €5 included on demand. **Location:** Rural, quiet.
Surface: grassy. 01/01-31/12.
Distance: 200m 7km.

S Willroth 11G2

Steiger-Mühle, Steinstrasse. **GPS:** n50,57176 e7,52995.

15 €6 €2,50. **Location:** Rural. 01/01-31/12.
Distance: 2km on the spot.
Remarks: To be paid at Biergarten.

S Wintrich 16F1

Mosel Stellplatz Wintrich, Moselstrasse.
GPS: n49,88417 e6,94833.
90 €9 €1/100liter Ch (90x) WC €0,50 €1 included.
Surface: grassy/gravel. 01/04-31/10.
Distance: on the spot on the spot on the spot 100m 200m 200m on the spot on the spot.
Remarks: Along the Moselle river.

S Wintrich 16F1

Weingut Clemens, Kurtfürstenstrasse 11.
GPS: n49,89000 e6,95416.

20 €5 €2 Ch €2 WC. **Surface:** gravel/metalled.
01/01-31/12.
Distance: on the spot on the spot 1km.

S Wissen 11G2

Hahnhof, Nistertalstraße. **GPS:** n50,76106 e7,72083.

25 €5 Ch €1/kWh WC €1,50. **Location:** Rural, isolated, quiet. **Surface:** gravel. 01/01-31/12.
Distance: 2,5km on the spot on the spot.

S Wittlich 11F3

Zweibächen, Hasenmühlenweg. **GPS:** n49,99470 e6,87595.

30 €5/24h €1/80liter Ch. **Location:** Rural, simple.
Surface: grassy. 01/01-31/12.
Distance: 1km 4km 1km 1km.
Remarks: Max. 3 days, to be paid at swimming pool, service 50m.

S Worms 16H1

Wohnmobilhafen, Kastanienallee. **GPS:** n49,63458 e8,37513.

DE

30 € 5/24h €1 Ch (12x)€1/8h. **Surface:** gravel.
01/01-31/12.
Distance: 15 min walking 7km Rhine promenade 300m 500m on the spot.
Remarks: Along river, service at Gaststätte Hagenbräu 300m from the parking.

S Wörrstadt 16H1

Spargelhof Weinmann, Rommersheimer Strasse 105.
GPS: n49,83446 e8,10673.

3 € 6 (6x)included. **Location:** Rural, simple, central, quiet.
Surface: gravel. 01/01-31/12.
Distance: 4km 300m 300m.

S Zell/Mosel 11F3

Wohnmobilstellplatz Römerquelle, Am Freizeitzentrum, Kaimt.
GPS: n50,01632 e7,17662.

70 € 7 €1/100liter Ch €1/2kWh. **Location:** Rural, comfortable. **Surface:** grassy/metalled. 01/01-31/12.
Distance: 1km on the spot on the spot 500m 1km.
Remarks: Along the Moselle river, bread-service.

S Zell/Mosel 11F3

Am Fussgängerbrücke. GPS: n50,02991 e7,17754.

23 € 7 €0,50/90liter Ch €2,at campsite.
Location: Simple, quiet. **Surface:** asphalted. Easter-31/10.
Distance: 300m on the spot on the spot 200m 300m.

S Zeltingen-Rachtig 11F3

Wohnmobilstellplatz Zeltingen, An der Brücke.
GPS: n49,95478 e7,00942.

45 € 9 Ch (34x)included.
Location: Rural, simple, quiet. **Surface:** grasstiles.

18/03-15/11 high water.
Distance: 50m 9km on the spot 300m 700m on the spot on the spot on the spot.

S Zweibrücken 16G2

Wohnmobilplatz am Freizeitpark an der Schließ, Geschwister-Scholl-Allee 11. **GPS:** n49,25332 e7,37625.
23 € 9-12 €1/100liter Ch €0,60/kWh WC included €2/2. **Surface:** gravel.
Distance: on the spot.
Remarks: Check in at hotel.

Hesse

S Aarbergen 11H3

Im Brühl, Hauptstraße 58, Michelbach. **GPS:** n50,23099 e8,05988.

10 € 5 Ch included. **Location:** Rural. **Surface:** metalled.
01/01-31/12.

S Alsfeld 12A2

Erlenstadion, Fulder Weg. **GPS:** n50,74844 e9,27947.

20 € 5 €1 €1 Ch €0,50/kWh. **Location:** Simple.
Surface: metalled. 01/01-31/12.
Distance: 200m 1,8km.

S Alsfeld 12A2

Hotel zum Schäferhof, A20 dir Eudorf. **GPS:** n50,76742 e9,29048.

20 free €6. **Location:** Urban, simple, quiet. **Surface:** metalled.
01/01-31/12.
Distance: 2km on the spot 500m.
Remarks: Check in at hotel, use of a meal desired.

Amöneburg 12A2

In den Lückeäckern. **GPS:** n50,79554 e8,93135.

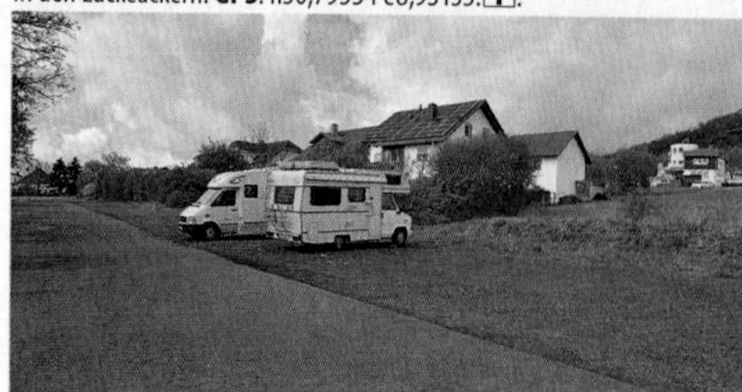

4 free. **Location:** Rural, simple. 01/01-31/12.
Distance: Old city centre 1km 500m 500m.
Remarks: Parking tennishall.

S Bad Arolsen 10A3

Reisemobilhafen Twistesee, Bericher Seeweg 1, Wetterburg.
GPS: n51,38396 e9,06546.
130 € 10, tourist tax incl €1/100liter Ch (120x)€0,50/kWh, 16Amp WC included €1. **Location:** Rural, comfortable, isolated.
Surface: grassy/gravel. 01/01-31/12.
Distance: 500m 50m 50m 800m 800m on the spot on the spot.
Remarks: Directly at lake, bread-service, dogs beach.

S Bad Camberg 11H3

Jahnstraße. **GPS:** n50,29650 e8,26660.

8 free €1 €1 Ch €1/2kWh. **Location:** Urban.
Surface: gravel. 01/01-31/12 water: 01/12-31/03.
Distance: 350m 2,5km 250m.

S Bad Emstal 12A1

Am Mineral-Thermalbad, Karlsbader Straße 4, Sand.
GPS: n51,24858 e9,24952.

8 € 7, tourist tax incl €1/100liter Ch (12x)€1/8h.
Location: Rural, comfortable. **Surface:** gravel/metalled.
01/01-31/12.
Distance: 1km on the spot on the spot on the spot.

S Bad Emstal 12A1

Erzeberg, Birkenstraße, Balhorn 21. **GPS:** n51,26927 e9,25147.

20 € 10, 2 pers.incl Ch WC €1 included.
Location: Rural, simple. **Surface:** metalled. 01/01-31/12.
Distance: 100m.
Remarks: Check in at campsite (100m), use pool incl.

S Bad Endbach 11H2

Kultur-, Sport- und Freizeitzentrum, Am Bewegungsbad 4.
GPS: n50,75669 e8,47875.

DE

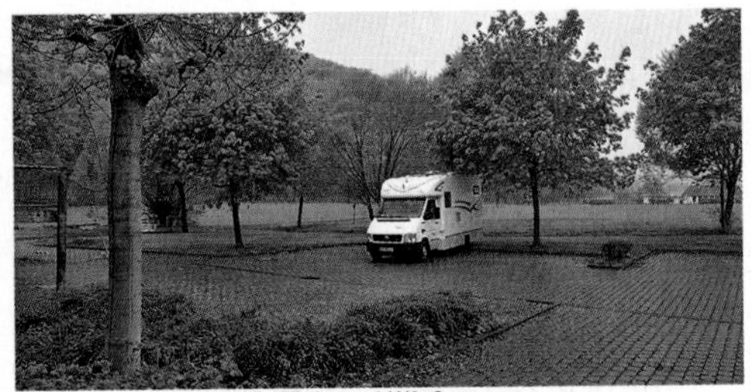

18 €5 + tourist tax Ch WC included, sanitary at sparesort. **Location:** Rural, simple, quiet. **Surface:** grasstiles. 01/01-31/12.
Distance: 1km on the spot 100m.
Remarks: Check in at Lahn-Dill-Bergland-Therme 200m.

Bad Hersfeld 12B1

Geistalbad, Am Schwimmbad. **GPS**: n50,87485 e9,70025.

6 €5 €0,50/80liter Ch (6x)€0,50/kWh. **Location:** Urban, simple. **Surface:** asphalted/metalled. 01/01-31/12 Lullusfest (Oct).
Distance: 50m 3,9km 1km.

Bad Hersfeld 12B1

Acqua-fit, Kolpingstraße 6. **GPS**: n50,86771 e9,72951.
5 free. **Surface:** asphalted. 01/01-31/12.
Distance: 2km.
Remarks: At swimming pool.

Bad Hersfeld 12B1

Auf der Unteraue. **GPS**: n50,85764 e9,69786.

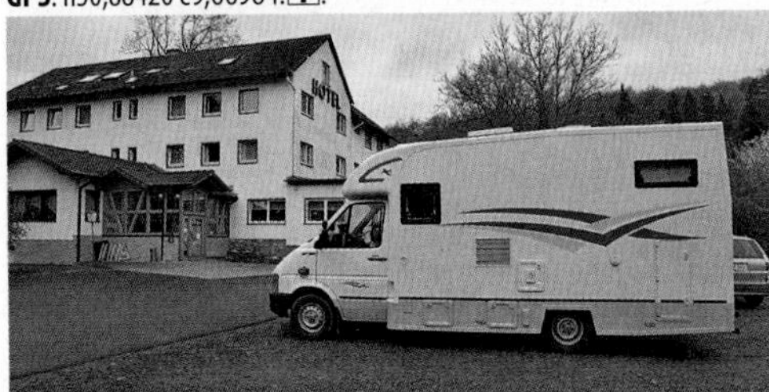

3 free. **Surface:** metalled. 01/01-31/12.
Remarks: At tennis-court.

Bad Hersfeld 12B1

Seilerweg. **GPS**: n50,87092 e9,71179.
free. 01/01-31/12.
Distance: 500m 500m.

Bad Hersfeld 12B1

Waldhotel Glimmesmühle, Hombergerstraße.
GPS: n50,88420 e9,66984.

5 free with a meal included against payment.
Location: Rural, simple. **Surface:** metalled.
01/01-31/12.
Distance: on the spot 2km.

Tourist information Bad Hersfeld:
Lullusfest. Traditional folk festival for the honour of the founder of the city. week 16/10.

Bad Karlshafen 10A3

Am Rechten Weserufer, Am Rechten Weserufer 2.
GPS: n51,64508 e9,44953.

12 €11, 2 pers.incl €0,50/100liter Ch (12x)€1/2kWh.
Location: Central. **Surface:** grasstiles/grassy.
01/01-31/12.
Distance: on the spot on the spot on the spot on the spot on the spot on the spot.
Remarks: Max. 4 days, check in at reception campsite.

Bad König 17A1

P3, Am Bahndamm. **GPS**: n49,74312 e9,00320.

9 €5 (9x)included. **Location:** Urban, simple, central, noisy.
Surface: metalled. 01/01-31/12.
Distance: 100m 100m 400m on the spot on the spot on the spot.

Bad Nauheim 12A3

Usa-Wellenbad, Friedberger Strasse 16-20.
GPS: n50,35352 e8,74305.

40 €5. **Location:** Rural, simple, isolated. **Surface:** metalled.
01/01-31/12.
Distance: 1km on the spot 300m on the spot.
Remarks: Check in at Wellenbad, 8-20h.

Bad Orb 12A3

Am Busbahnhof, Austraße. **GPS**: n50,23014 e9,34659.

4 €7, tourist tax incl Ch (4x) WC included.
Location: Urban, simple, central, noisy. **Surface:** metalled.
01/01-31/12.
Distance: 400m 450m 300m.
Remarks: Historical centre.

Bad Orb 12A3

Am Kurpark, Spessartstraße. **GPS**: n50,21700 e9,35477.

9 €7 + tourist tax €2,50/pp €1/90liter Ch €1/8h.

Location: Rural, simple, quiet. **Surface:** gravel.
01/01-31/12.
Distance: 1,1km 6km 200m on the spot.

Bad Salzschlirf 12B2

Riedstraße. **GPS**: n50,62090 e9,50304.

10 free €1 Ch €1. **Location:** Simple. **Surface:** asphalted.
01/01-31/12.
Distance: 100m 100m.

Bad Schwalbach 11H3

Wohnmobilstellplatz im Stahlbrunnental, Reitallee 21.
GPS: n50,13988 e8,06362.

4 free €0,50/50liter Ch €0,50/kWh. **Location:** Rural, simple. **Surface:** metalled. 01/01-31/12.
Distance: 500m 400m.

Bad Soden-Salmünster 12A3

Spessart Therme, Parkstraße 12, Bad Soden.
GPS: n50,28544 e9,35917.

33 €6, tourist tax incl €1/100liter Ch (33x)€1/2kWh.
Location: Rural, luxurious, quiet. **Surface:** metalled.
01/01-31/12.
Distance: 1km 300m 850m.
Remarks: Pay and coins at Spessart Therme.

Bad Sooden-Allendorf 12B1

Reisemobilhafen Franzrasen, Am Alten Festplatz, Allendorf.
GPS: n51,27149 e9,97209.

100 €8 €1/5minutes €0,50 Ch (40x)€0,50/kWh,16Amp €2,50/30minutes. **Location:** Rural, simple, isolated, quiet.
Surface: grassy/metalled. 01/01-31/12.
Distance: 200m on the spot on the spot.
Remarks: Price including tourist taxes and public transport.

Bad Wildungen 12A1

Wohnmobilstellplatz Bad Wildungen, Bahnhofstrasse.
GPS: n51,12008 e9,13631.

DE

16 € 5 €1/45liter Ch (15x)€1/2kWh.
Location: Urban, comfortable. **Surface:** grasstiles. 01/01-31/12.
Distance: 1,5km on the spot on the spot.
Remarks: Max. 3 days.

S **Bad Wildungen** 12A1

Wohnmobilstellplatz Frekot, Wiesenweg 23.
GPS: n51,11134 e9,06677.

15 € 6 Ch €0,33/kWh WC included €2.
Location: Rural, simple. **Surface:** grassy. 01/01-31/12.
Distance: 300m.
Remarks: Bread-service.

S **Bad Zwesten** 12A1

Reisemobilstellplatz, Hardtstrasse 7. **GPS**: n51,05849 e9,17613.

10 € 6 €1/100liter Ch (8x)€1/kWh.
Location: Urban, comfortable. **Surface:** gravel/metalled.
01/01-31/12.
Distance: 400m on the spot 300m.
Remarks: Max. 3 days.

S **Battenberg** 11H1

Festhalle Battenberg, Festplatzweg. **GPS**: n51,00915 e8,63643.

5 free Ch. **Location:** Rural, simple. **Surface:** gravel/metalled.
01/01-31/12.
Distance: 1km 1km 1km.
Remarks: At community centre, service: Esso-station, Battenfelderstr. 6.

S **Battenberg** 11H1

Hallen- und Freibad, Senonchesstraße. **GPS**: n51,01233 e8,63532.

3 free Ch. **Location:** Rural, simple.
Surface: asphalted.
01/01-31/12.
Distance: 300m 100m on the spot on the spot on the spot.
Remarks: Parking swimming pool, service: Esso-station, Battenfelderstr. 6.

Tourist information Battenberg:
Besucherbergwerk Burgbergstollen. 150 years old mine shaft, can be reached from Marktplatz. 01/05-30/09 1st Su of the month 14-17h.

S **Baunatal** 12A1

Parkstadion. GPS: n51,25769 e9,39851.

16 € 5/24h €1/100liter Ch (16x)€0,50/kWh.
Location: Rural, simple, simple, quiet. **Surface:** grassy/gravel.
01/01-31/12.
Distance: 500m 4km on the spot on the spot.
Remarks: Max. 3 days.

S **Bebra** 12B1

Natur- und Freizeitpark Fuldaaue Breitenbachen Seen, Hersfelder Straße. **GPS**: n50,95899 e9,78764.

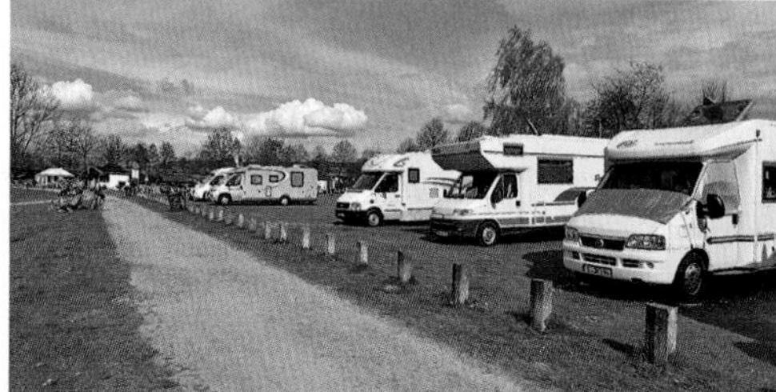

30 € 3, € 18/week €1/100liter Ch (18x)€0,50/kWh.
Location: Comfortable. **Surface:** grassy. 01/01-31/12.
Distance: 1km on the spot on the spot 1km on the spot on the spot.

Bebra 12B1

Am Schwimmbad, Annastrasse 17. **GPS**: n50,97464 e9,79836.

4 free. **Location:** Rural, simple. **Surface:** asphalted.
01/01-31/12.
Distance: 400m.
Remarks: Parking swimming pool.

Bebra 12B1

Mehrzweckparkplatz, Bei der Laupfütze/Rathausstrasse.
GPS: n50,97000 e9,79000.

10 free. **Location:** Rural, simple. **Surface:** metalled.
01/01-31/12.
Distance: on the spot.

S **Beerfelden** 17A1

Parkplatz NordicCenter, Seeweg. **GPS**: n49,56034 e8,97557.

4 free €0,50/50liter Ch (4x)€0,50/kWh.
Location: Rural, simple, quiet. **Surface:** asphalted.
01/01-31/12.
Distance: 1km on the spot on the spot.

Berkatal 12B1

Am Sportplatz. **GPS**: n51,23763 e9,91504.

3 free. **Location:** Rural, simple, isolated, quiet. **Surface:** asphalted.
01/01-31/12.
Distance: 800m 500m on the spot.

S **Biedenkopf** 11H1

Parkplatz Stadtwerke, Mühlweg 6. **GPS**: n50,90925 e8,52687.

4 € 5/24h €1/12h. **Location:** Urban. **Surface:** asphalted.
01/01-31/12.
Distance: 200m.
Remarks: Max. 3 days.

Biedenkopf 11H1

Freizeitzentrum Sackpfeife, An der Berggaststätte.
GPS: n50,94735 e8,53317.

4 € 5/24h.
Location: Rural. **Surface:** concrete. 01/01-31/12.
Distance: on the spot on the spot on the spot.
Remarks: Max. 3 days.

Biedenkopf 11H1

Halbersbacher Parkhotel Biedenkopf, Auf dem Radeköppel 2.
GPS: n50,91183 e8,53515.

5 free with a meal. **Location:** Urban. 01/01-31/12.
Distance: on the spot on the spot 500m 12km 12km.

Bischoffen 11H2

P Aartalsee, Am See. **GPS**: n50,70172 e8,46726.

DE

10 € 3/day, € 5,50/night. **Surface:** grassy/gravel. 01/01-31/12.
Distance: 1,5km.

Borken 12A1

Borkener See, Westrandstrasse. **GPS:** n51,04447 e9,27392.

2 free. **Location:** Rural, simple. **Surface:** asphalted.
01/01-31/12.
Distance: 500m 4,5km 100m 1km 500m.
Remarks: At swimming pool.

Braunfels 11H2

Wohnmobilstation Schloss Braunfels, Jahnplatz.
GPS: n50,51478 e8,38609.

4 € 5, € 7,50 service incl Ch. **Location:** Rural, simple, quiet. **Surface:** metalled. 01/01-31/12.
Distance: on the spot 350m on the spot.
Remarks: Pay and key service: Gasthof am Turm, Marktplatz 11, caution € 15.

Breuberg 17A1

Bahnhofstraße 4, Neustadt. **GPS:** n49,81576 e9,04063.

4 free €1/5minutes Ch€1 (4x)€0,50/kWh.
Location: Urban, simple, simple, central. **Surface:** asphalted.
01/01-31/12.
Distance: on the spot 300m 550m on the spot.

Breuna 10A3

Märchenlandtherme, Schulstraße. **GPS:** n51,41875 e9,18612.
3 free €3. **Surface:** gravel. 01/01-31/12.
Distance: 500m 50m.

Büdingen 12A3

Hinter der Meisterei 20. **GPS:** n50,29094 e9,12587.

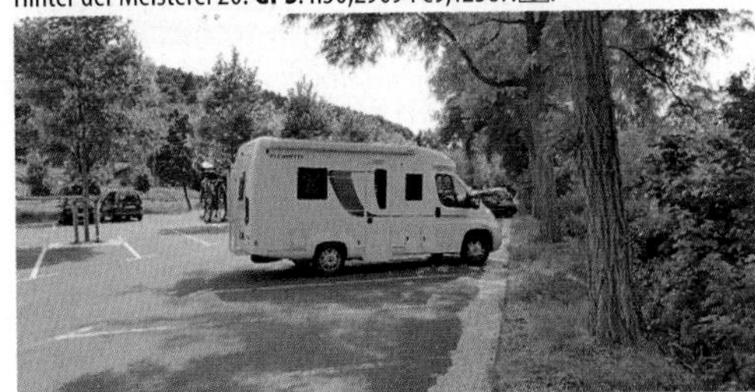

8 free. **Location:** Rural, simple, quiet. **Surface:** metalled.
01/01-31/12.
Distance: Old city centre 750m 500m.
Remarks: At swimming pool.

Büdingen 12A3

Mühltorbrücke. **GPS:** n50,29051 e9,11581.

2 € 5/5h. **Surface:** metalled. 01/01-31/12.
Distance: Old city centre 50m.

Burghaun 12B2

Oberste Straße. **GPS:** n50,69179 e9,73203.

3 free €1/100liter Ch (4x)€0,50/kWh. **Location:** Urban, simple. **Surface:** asphalted. 01/01-31/12.
Distance: 800m on the spot on the spot.

Calden 10A3

Waldschwimmbad Calden, Zum Lindenrondell.
GPS: n51,39420 e9,40064.

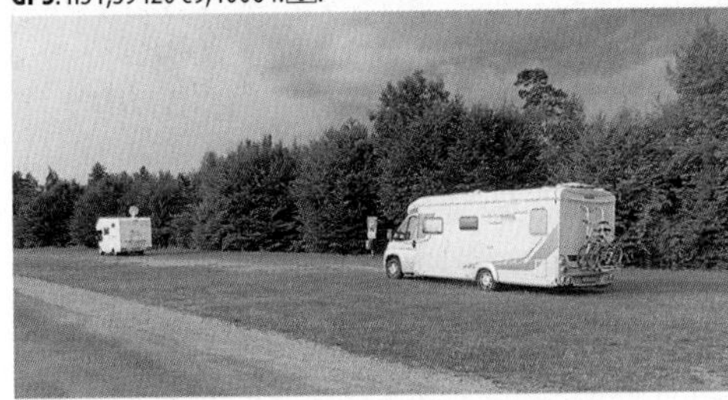

3 free. **Location:** Rural, simple, isolated. **Surface:** grassy.
01/01-31/12.
Distance: 1km 1,5km 2km.

Diemelsee 9H3

Terrassenparkplatz Hohes Rad, Hohes Rad 1.
GPS: n51,36470 e8,71935.

30 € 5 WC. **Location:** Rural, simple. **Surface:** grassy/gravel.
01/01-31/12.
Distance: Diemelsee on the spot 500m.

Diemelsee 9H3

Campingpark Hohes Rad, Hohes Rad 1. **GPS:** n51,36355 e8,71830.

5 € 5/pp Ch €0,53/kWh WC included €1/day.
Location: Rural, simple. **Surface:** grassy/gravel.
01/01-31/12.
Distance: on the spot on the spot 6km.

Diemelstadt 10A3

Autohof, Kupferkuhle. **GPS:** n51,49034 e9,00885.
10 free €1 €1 Ch €1. **Location:** Motorway.
Surface: asphalted. 01/01-31/12.
Distance: 500m 250m McDonalds.

Dillenburg 11H2

Aquarena-Bad, Stadionstrasse. **GPS:** n50,73994 e8,27815.

8 free €1/90liter Ch (6x)€1/8h. **Location:** Urban, simple.
Surface: asphalted. 01/01-31/12.
Distance: 300m.

Edermünde 12A1

Aueweg, Grifte. **GPS:** n51,21252 e9,44905.

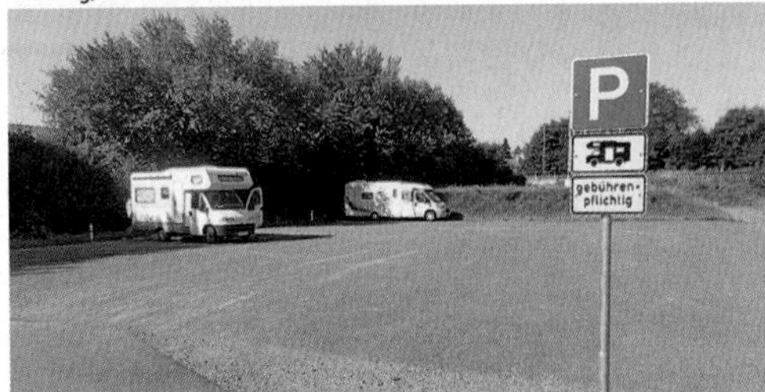

12 € 5 €1/100liter Ch (6x)included15h,then€1/3h.
Location: Rural, simple. **Surface:** asphalted.
01/01-31/12.
Distance: 300m 1,7km 300m 100m Premium-Radweg R1 on the spot.

Edertal 12A1

Wohnmobilstellplatz Hemfurth/Edersee, Kraftwerkstrasse.
GPS: n51,17022 e9,05096.

30 <8m € 6, >8m € 10 €1/100liter Ch€1. **Location:** Rural, simple. **Surface:** metalled. 01/01-31/12.
Distance: 500m on the spot 100m 500m.

Edertal 12A1

Wohnmobilstellplatz Rehbach, Am Eschelberg.
GPS: n51,18394 e9,02618.

20 <8m € 6, >8m € 10. **Location:** Rural, simple. **Surface:** gravel.
01/01-31/12.
Distance: beach 200m on the spot.

Eltville am Rhein 11H3

Parkplatz Weinhohle, Weinhohle. **GPS:** n50,02832 e8,12406.

DE

+20 € 5 €1/60liter €1 Ch.
Location: Urban, simple, central. **Surface:** metalled.
Distance: 200m 400m 50m.

Eltville am Rhein 11H3

Weingut Offenstein Erben, Wiesweg 13. **GPS**: n50,02871 e8,11728.
2 € 15 WC included. **Surface:** metalled.
Distance: 1km.

Eltville am Rhein 11H3

Weinhof Martin, Bachhöller Weg 4, Erbach im Rheingau.
GPS: n50,02365 e8,08815.
€ 10 WC. **Surface:** metalled.
Distance: 600m 400m.

Erbach 17A1

Alexanderbad, In der Stadtwiese. **GPS**: n49,66349 e8,98863.

10 free €1/70liter Ch (6x)€0,50/kWh. **Location:** Urban, simple, quiet. **Surface:** metalled. 01/01-31/12.
Distance: 800m 500m 100m 100m on the spot.
Remarks: Max. 72h.

Eschwege 12B1

Reisemobilhafen Werratalsee, Am werratalsee 2.
GPS: n51,19196 e10,06728.

20 € 10-15 €1/80liter Ch (18x)€0,70/kWh WC use sanitary €3,30/pp. **Location:** Rural, simple, central, noisy.
Surface: metalled. 01/01-31/12.
Distance: 2km on the spot on the spot.
Remarks: Pay at bistro, service passerby € 4.

Tourist information Eschwege:
Besuchbergwerk Grube Gustav, Höllethal, Meissner, Abterode. Slate mine. 15/03-31/10 Tue-Su/holidays 13-16h.

Flörsbachtal-Lohrhaupten 12B3

Am Schwimbad. **GPS**: n50,12178 e9,47258.

10 € 9 Ch €1,50/24h WC included against payment.
Location: Rural, comfortable, quiet. **Surface:** grassy/gravel.
01/01-31/12 Service: winter.
Distance: 1km 100m 1km on the spot on the spot.
Remarks: Check in at Gartenstrasse 10a.

Frankenberg/Eder 12A1

Ederberglandhalle, Teichweg 3. **GPS**: n51,05613 e8,80195.

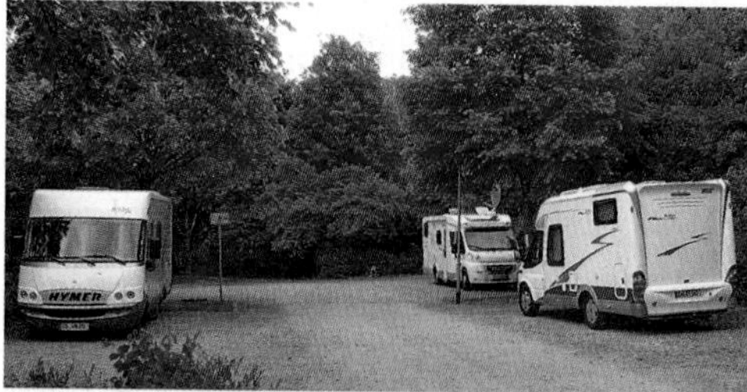

10 free €1/25liter Ch (4x)€1/kWh WC.
Location: Urban, central. **Surface:** grassy/gravel.
01/01-31/12 water disconnected in winter.
Distance: 500m 200m 100m.
Remarks: Use sanitary only during opening hours swimming pool.

Friedberg 12A3

Engel Caravaning, Dieselstraße 4. **GPS**: n50,34646 e8,75685.

2 voluntary contribution is appreciated €0,50 Ch (2x).
Location: Urban, simple, central. **Surface:** metalled.
01/01-31/12.
Distance: 800m 100m 800m.
Remarks: Motorhome dealer, accessory shop, closed at night.

Frielendorf 12A1

Wohnmobilpark Silbersee, Zum Silbersee.
GPS: n50,98389 e9,34667.

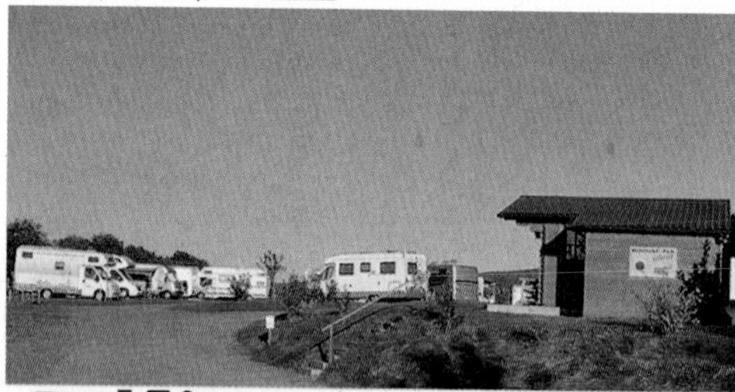

50 € 10 Ch included €2. **Location:** Rural, simple, quiet.
Surface: grassy/metalled. 01/04-01/11.
Distance: 1km 250m.

Fritzlar 12A1

Am Grauen Turm. **GPS**: n51,13221 e9,26974.

10 € 7 €1/90liter Ch €1/2kWh. **Location:** Urban, central. **Surface:** metalled. 01/01-31/12.
Distance: 100m 100m 600m.

Tourist information Fritzlar:
Stadtführingen. Guided tour around the historic city center.
15/03-31/10 Tue-Sa 10.30, Su/holidays 11h. € 4.

Fulda 12B2

Weimarerstrasse. **GPS**: n50,55685 e9,66663.

30 € 0,10/1h, € 5/24h €1 Ch €1/6h

Location: Urban, simple, central. **Surface:** asphalted.
01/01-31/12.
Distance: 400m 50m.

Gelnhausen 12A3

Am Hallenbad. **GPS**: n50,20125 e9,17795.

4 free. **Location:** Urban, simple, noisy. **Surface:** asphalted.
01/01-31/12.
Distance: 1km 100m 100m on the spot.
Remarks: Parking at swimming pool.

Gießen 11H2

Badezentrum Ringallee, Gutfleischstraße.
GPS: n50,58947 e8,68406.

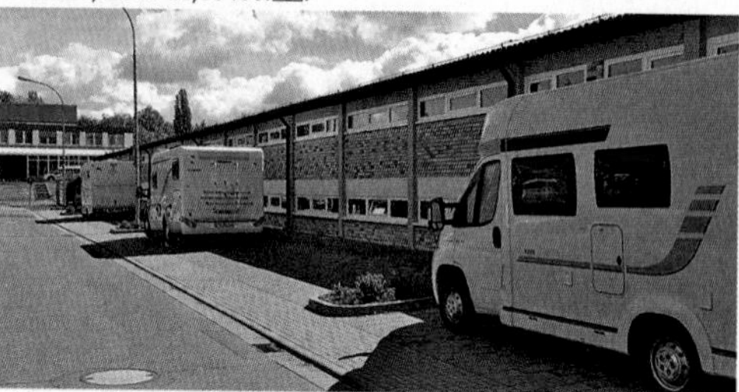

6 € 3 (6x)€0,50/kWh. **Location:** Urban, simple.
Surface: metalled. 01/01-31/12.
Distance: 600m 1,5km.

Gilserberg 12A1

Landgasthof Steller, Marburgerstrasse 3.
GPS: n50,95047 e9,06220.

4 € 5, guests € 2,50 €2,50 €2,50 WC. **Location:** Urban, simple. **Surface:** asphalted. 01/01-31/12 Wed.
Distance: 250m on the spot on the spot.

Gladenbach 11H2

Restaurant Rosengarten, Hoherainstrasse 45.
GPS: n50,77462 e8,57952.

3 € 5,50. **Location:** Urban, simple. **Surface:** grassy.
01/01-31/12.
Distance: 600m on the spot 1km.
Remarks: Pay and key at restaurant.

Grebenau 12B2

Borngasse 20. **GPS**: n50,74134 e9,47212.

4 free free. **Location:** Rural, simple. **Surface:** grassy.
01/01-31/12.
Distance: on the spot 200m 200m.
Remarks: At fire-station.

S Grebenhain 12A2

Reisemobilstellplatz am Kurpark, Hindenburgstraße, Hochwaldhausen. **GPS**: n50,51910 e9,31756.

30 € 6 Ch WC included. **Location:** Rural, simple, central.
Surface: gravel. 01/01-31/12.
Distance: 500m 500m bike-bus 200m Vulkanradweg 200m on the spot.
Remarks: Pay in at kiosk.

S Grebenhain 12A2

Gasthof Zum Felsenmeer, Jean-Berlit-Straße 1.
GPS: n50,51926 e9,31424.

10 € 5 + € 1/pp tourist tax (2x)€0,50/kWh,+€1. **Location:** Rural.
Surface: grassy. 01/01-31/12.
Distance: on the spot.

S Großalmerode 12B1

Am Mühlgraben, Oststraße. **GPS**: n51,25841 e9,79349.
20 free Ch . **Location:** Rural. **Surface:** grassy.
01/01-31/12.
Distance: 700m 150m.

Großalmerode 12B1

Panoramabad, Heinrich-Koch-Straße. **GPS**: n51,26603 e9,78452.
free. **Surface:** grassy. 01/01-31/12.
Distance: 500m 500m 500m.
Remarks: Next to swimming pool.

S Grünberg 12A2

Gallusplatz, Gerichtsstraße. **GPS**: n50,59517 e8,95593.

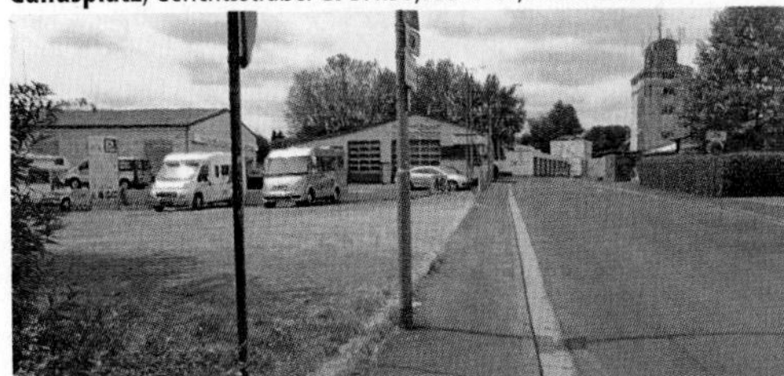

10 free €0,50 Ch (10x)€0,50/10h.
Location: Urban, simple, central. **Surface:** gravel. 01/01-31/12.
Distance: Old city centre 300m 100m Aldi 400m on the spot on the spot.

S Habichtswald 10A3

Am Kressenborn, Bergweg, Dörnberg. **GPS**: n51,34361 e9,34389.

4 free (2x)€2/24h WC. **Location:** Simple, quiet. **Surface:** gravel.
01/01-31/12.
Distance: 200m 5,5km 200m.
Remarks: Caution € 20, key electricity/toilet at petrol station.

S Habichtswald 10A3

Hasenbreite, Ehlen. **GPS**: n51,32291 e9,31961.

6 free €2/24h WC. **Location:** Rural, simple, isolated, quiet.
Surface: grassy/metalled. 01/01-31/12.
Distance: 400m 2,5km 400m 400m.
Remarks: Caution € 20, key electricity/toilet at swimming pool.

Hatzfeld 11H1

Parking Edertal strasse. **GPS**: n50,99144 e8,54817.

5 . **Location:** Urban, simple, quiet. **Surface:** grassy/gravel.
01/01-31/12.
Distance: on the spot on the spot 200m on the spot.
Remarks: Behind fire-station.

Helsa 12B1

Sportplatzweg. **GPS**: n51,25444 e9,68638.

4 free. **Surface:** metalled. 01/01-31/12.
Distance: 800m 800m 700m 400m.

S Herborn 11H2

Herborner Schießplatz, Sinner Landstraße.
GPS: n50,67950 e8,30672.

6 free €1/90liter Ch stay (6x)€1/kWh.
Location: Simple. **Surface:** metalled. 01/01-31/12.
Distance: 200m 1,8km.

S Herbstein 12A2

VulkanTherme Herbstein, Zum Thermalbad 1.
GPS: n50,56883 e9,34647.

11 € 6 + € 1,50/pp tourist tax €1/100liter Ch (11x)€1/2kWh WC €1,50. **Location:** Rural, comfortable, quiet. **Surface:** metalled.
01/01-31/12.
Distance: 1,1km 800m 300m on the spot on the spot.
Remarks: Coins available at pay-desk of theTherme.

S Hessisch Lichtenau 12B1

Alter Bahnhof/Western Rail Station, Bahnhofstrasse 5, Walburg.
GPS: n51,20055 e9,77833.

10 € 10 . **Location:** Rural, isolated, quiet.
Surface: asphalted. 01/01-31/12.
Distance: 5km 700m 1km on the spot.

S Hessisch Lichtenau 12B1

Sportcenter Fürstenhagen, Breslauer strasse 18.
GPS: n51,20672 e9,69443.

10 € 5/24h €1/80liter Ch €0,50/kWh .
Location: Rural, simple, quiet. **Surface:** metalled.
01/01-31/12.
Distance: 3km 1km 2km.
Remarks: Check in at sport centre.

Hessisch Lichtenau 12B1

Hopfelderstrasse. **GPS**: n51,19417 e9,72389.

14 free. **Location:** Urban, simple, isolated, quiet. **Surface:** metalled.
01/01-31/12.
Distance: 500m 400m 500m.

Hessisch Lichtenau 12B1

Wohnmobilstellplatz am Hallenbad, Freiherr-vom-Stein-Straße 12.
GPS: n51,20445 e9,72655.

6 free. **Location:** Rural, simple, isolated, quiet. **Surface:** metalled.
01/01-31/12.

DE

Distance: 600m.
Remarks: Parking swimming pool.

Hessisch Lichtenau 12B1

Berggasthof Hoher Meißner, Hoher Meissner 1.
GPS: n51,20376 e9,84852.

10 free WC. **Location:** Rural, simple, isolated, quiet.
Surface: metalled. 01/01-31/12.
Distance: 10km on the spot on the spot on the spot on the spot.

Hilders 12B2

Ulsterwelle, Heideweg 19. **GPS**: n50,56909 e9,99351.

5 free. **Location:** Rural. **Surface:** gravel. 01/01-31/12.
Distance: 750m 50m 800m.

Hirschhorn 17A1

Beim Ätsche, Jahnstraße 2. **GPS**: n49,44214 e8,89804.

25 € 7 €0,50/40liter Ch €2,50/day.
Location: Rural, comfortable, quiet. **Surface:** grassy.
01/01-31/12 high water.
Distance: 500m on the spot train 400m on the spot.
Remarks: Along the Neckar river.

Hirzenhain 12A2

Festplatz Hirzenhain, Robert-Eichenauerweg.
GPS: n50,39259 e9,13593.

6 free. **Location:** Urban, simple, central. **Surface:** metalled.
01/01-31/12.
Distance: 100m 100m on the spot on the spot.

Hirzenhain 12A2

Müller-Mobil, Junkernwiese 2. **GPS**: n50,40004 e9,14744.

6 free €1/130liter Ch (6x). **Location:** Rural, simple, quiet.

Surface: metalled. 01/01-31/12.
Distance: 1,5km on the spot on the spot on the spot.

Hofgeismar 10A3

Am Sälber Tor. **GPS**: n51,49521 e9,37547.

100 free €1/80liter Ch (18x)€1/2kWh.
Location: Rural, comfortable, central, quiet. **Surface:** gravel.
01/01-31/12 31/05-14/06.
Distance: on the spot 300m on the spot on the spot.

Homberg/Efze 12A1

Wassmuthshäuserstrasse, Dresdener Alee.
GPS: n51,02757 e9,41470.

7 free €1/80liter Ch free. **Location:** Urban, simple.
Surface: gravel. 01/01-31/12.
Distance: on the spot 1km 500m.

Homberg/Ohm 12A2

An der Stadthalle, Stadthallenweg 12.
GPS: n50,72626 e8,99439.

4 free €1/80liter Ch (4x)€0,50/kWh. **Location:** Rural, simple. **Surface:** metalled. 01/01-31/12.
Distance: 400m 350m 1km on the spot.

Hünfeld 12B2

Hessisches Kegelspiel, Zu den Unaben.
GPS: n50,67626 e9,77622.

18 € 5 €1/120liter Ch (12x)€1/2kWh. **Location:** Urban, simple. 01/01-31/12.
Distance: 500m 250m 500m.

Hungen 12A2

Inheiden, Am Köstgraben. **GPS**: n50,45509 e8,90049.

6 free €1/100liter Ch €2/6h WC. **Location:** Rural, comfortable, quiet. **Surface:** grasstiles. 01/01-31/12 water: 01/11-31/03.
Distance: Trais-Horloffer See 3km 500m bike-bus 1km.

Idstein 11H3

Wohnmobilhafen Idstein, Himmelsbornweg.
GPS: n50,21775 e8,27923.

12 € 10 €1/80liter Ch €1/8h. **Location:** Rural.
Surface: gravel/metalled. 01/01-31/12 water disconnected in winter. **Distance:** 500m Altstadt 3,3km.

Kassel 12A1

Wohnmobilplatz Kassel, Am Sportzentrum/Giessenallee, Kassel-süd.
GPS: n51,29250 e9,48750.

12 €12,50/day €1/100liter €0,50 Ch€0,50 (8x)€0,50/kWh.
Location: Rural, simple, isolated, quiet.
01/01-31/12.
Distance: 1,4km 500m 50m on the spot on the spot.
Remarks: With parking ticket free public transport, max. 3 nights.

Tourist information Kassel:
Treppenstrasse, shopping promenade, modern architecture.

Kaufungen 12B1

Festplatz, Am Steckkopf. **GPS**: n51,28525 e9,61956.

4 free €2/40liter Ch. **Location:** Rural, simple, quiet.
Surface: metalled. 01/01-31/12.
Distance: 800m Steinersee 300m 500m.

Kirchheim 12B2

Campingplatz Seepark, Brunnenstrasse 20.
GPS: n50,81400 e9,52000.

50 € 13, dog € 2 €1 Ch (30x)€3/day €1,50.
Location: Rural, simple. **Surface:** metalled. 01/01-31/12.
Distance: 5km 4,9km 20m on the spot 20m.

Kleinwallstadt 17A1

Fährstraße 14. **GPS**: n49,87571 e9,16378.
12 € 5 €1/100liter Ch €1/6h. **Surface:** metalled.
01/01-31/12.
Distance: 500m 500m.

Korbach 12A1

Westring. **GPS**: n51,27260 e8,85509.

5 free. **Location:** Urban, quiet. **Surface:** grasstiles/metalled.
01/01-31/12.
Distance: 1km Lidl 200m.
Remarks: Max. 3 nights.

S Laubach 12A2

Quick Camp Caravanpark Laubach, Kurze Hohl.
GPS: n50,55021 e9,00806.

30 € 6, 2 pers.incl €2 €2 Ch WC €2 .
Location: Rural, simple, isolated, quiet. **Surface:** grasstiles/grassy.
01/01-31/12.
Distance: 1,5km 1,5km 1,5km.

Lauterbach 12A2

Auf der Bleiche, Bleichstrasse. **GPS:** n50,63849 e9,40444.

5 free. **Location:** Rural, simple. **Surface:** metalled.
01/01-31/12.
Distance: 100m 150m on the spot.

Lauterbach 12A2

Freizeitzentrum Steinigsgrund, Am Sportfeld 9.
GPS: n50,62758 e9,39288.

8 free. **Location:** Urban. **Surface:** metalled. 01/01-31/12.
Distance: 800m 50m on the spot on the spot.

S Lauterbach 12A2

David-Eifertstrasse. **GPS:** n50,64288 e9,39393.
€1/80 Ch . **Location:** Urban. 01/01-31/12.

S Leun 11H2

Lahnwiese, Limburger Straße. **GPS:** n50,55089 e8,35346.

8 € 6 €2 WC. **Location:** Rural, simple. **Surface:** grassy.
01/01-31/12.
Distance: 400m 400m 400m.

Remarks: Along the Lahn river, max. 4 days.

Lich 12A2

P6, Ringstraße. **GPS:** n50,51816 e8,82257.

3 free. **Location:** Rural, simple, central, quiet.
Surface: grassy/metalled. 01/01-31/12.
Distance: 300m 400m Lidl 50m 100m.
Remarks: Max. 3 days.

S Limburg 11H2

Freizeitfalzeuge Singhof, Hoenbergstraße 2.
GPS: n50,40312 e8,07148.

3 free €3 free. **Location:** Rural, simple. **Surface:** metalled.
01/01-31/12.

S Limburg 11H2

Lahn Camping, Schleusenweg 16. **GPS:** n50,38902 e8,07387.

8 max. € 12-15/24h €0,50/50liter Ch €0,50/kWh €2/day
Location: Rural, simple, quiet. **Surface:** gravel.
01/01-31/12.
Distance: 900m 1,5km Gaststätte.
Remarks: Along the Lahn river, summer: bread-service, biergarten.

S Lindenfels 17A1

Kappstraße. **GPS:** n49,68077 e8,78304.

10 € 5 €1/80liter Ch (4x)€0,50/6h WC.
Location: Rural, comfortable, quiet. **Surface:** grassy.
01/01-31/12.
Distance: on the spot on the spot on the spot.
Remarks: Max. 3 days.

S Lorsch 16H1

Wohnmobilstellplatz Karolingerstadt Lorsch, Odenwaldallee.
GPS: n49,65206 e8,57855.

16 € 10 €1/80liter Ch (16x)€1/2kWh.
Location: Rural, comfortable, quiet. **Surface:** metalled.
01/01-31/12.
Distance: 800m 4,5km 800m 800m on the spot.
Remarks: Max. 5 days.

Maintal 12A3

Wohnmobilstellplatz Maintal, Uferpromenade, Dörnigheim.
GPS: n50,13067 e8,83920.

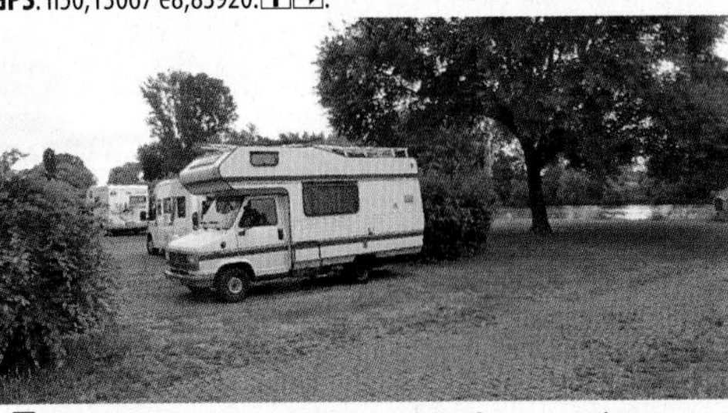

2 free. **Location:** Rural, simple, central. **Surface:** grasstiles.
01/01-31/12.
Distance: on the spot on the spot 1km on the spot on the spot.
Remarks: Along Main river.

S Marburg 12A2

Jahnstraße. **GPS:** n50,80354 e8,77544.

8 € 10/24h €1/100liter Ch (4x)€1/4h. **Location:** Urban, simple. **Surface:** gravel. 01/01-31/12.
Distance: 300m 500m.

S Meineringhausen 12A1

Hobbywiese, Walmenstrasse 25. **GPS:** n51,25945 e8,93807.

17 € 7 Ch included €0,50/kWh,or €3/day WC €1.
Location: Rural, comfortable. **Surface:** grassy/gravel.
01/01-31/12.
Distance: 2km Korbach 800m 2km on the spot on the spot.

Melsungen 12B1

Schloßbrücke, Sandstraße. **GPS:** n51,13280 e9,54502.

€ 0,30/h, overnight stay free.
Location: Urban, central. **Surface:** metalled.
01/01-31/12.
Distance: 200m 5km on the spot on the spot on the spot.
Remarks: Along the Fulda river, in front of police station.

Melsungen 12B1

Waldparkplatz, Dreuxallee. **GPS:** n51,12352 e9,55169.

DE

5 free. **Location:** Urban, simple. **Surface:** grassy/gravel.
01/01-31/12.
Distance: centre 1,1km 5km on the spot.

S Mernes 12B3

Wohnmobilstellplatz Mernes, Jossastraße, Mernes.
GPS: n50,24109 e9,47700.

6 € 5 €0,50/80liter Ch €0,50/kWh.
Location: Rural, comfortable, quiet. **Surface:** grasstiles.
01/01-31/12.
Distance: 200m 250m 200m on the spot.
Remarks: To be paid at Gasthaus Zum Jossatal, Salmünsterer Straße 15.

S Michelstadt 17A1

Parkplatz Altstadt, Wiesenweg. **GPS**: n49,68038 e9,00143.

9 free €1/90liter Ch €1/2kWh WC.
Location: Urban, simple, central, noisy. **Surface:** gravel/metalled.
01/01-31/12.
Distance: 200m 200m 50m on the spot on the spot.

Münzenberg 12A2

Sporthallenparkplatz, Am Viehtrieb. **GPS**: n50,45712 e8,77171.

5 free. **Location:** Rural, simple, quiet. **Surface:** gravel.
01/01-31/12.
Distance: 800m 2,6km 500m.
Remarks: Max. 3 days.

Münzenberg 12A2

Sportplatz, Butzbacher Straße, Gambach. **GPS**: n50,45770 e8,73412.

15 free. **Location:** Rural, simple, noisy. **Surface:** asphalted.
01/01-31/12.
Distance: 2,4km 400m on the spot.
Remarks: Max. 3 days.

S Neuental 12A1

Neuenhainer See, Seeblick 14, Neuenhain.
GPS: n50,99533 e9,26652.

12 € 4 €1 Ch €1/12h WC €0,50 . **Location:** Rural, simple. **Surface:** asphalted. 01/01-31/12.
Distance: Neuental 6km on the spot 250m.
Remarks: Use sanitary facilities at campsite.

S Neukirchen 12A1

Reisemobilpark Urbachtal, Urbachweg 1.
GPS: n50,87139 e9,34861.

49 € 10 + € 1/pp tourist tax €1/100liter Ch (52x)€0,60/kWh WC €2,80 €1,30min . **Location:** Rural, luxurious.
Surface: grassy/metalled. 01/01-31/12.
Distance: 300m 2km 300m 200m Rewe 300m 700m on the spot.

S Neukirchen 12A1

Birkenallee, Knüllgebirge. **GPS**: n50,86567 e9,34478.

5 free free. **Surface:** asphalted. 01/01-31/12.
Distance: 500m 200m.

Niedenstein 12A1

Am Hallenbad, Am Schwimmbad 2. **GPS**: n51,22739 e9,31657.

2 free.
Location: Rural, simple. **Surface:** gravel. 01/01-31/12.
Distance: 300m 300m.

S Niestetal 10B3

Spiekershäuser Straße/Fuldablick. **GPS**: n51,32686 e9,55490.
3 free €1/100liter Ch €1/2kWh. **Surface:** asphalted.
01/01-31/12.
Distance: 1,1km on the spot on the spot.
Remarks: Along the Fulda river, Kassel centre 6km.

S Oberaula 12B1

Sportplatz, Schwimmbadstraße. **GPS**: n50,85421 e9,45908.

10 free Ch free. **Location:** Rural, simple. **Surface:** asphalted.
01/01-31/12.
Distance: 800m Rewe 100m on the spot.

Oberaula 12B1

Golfplatz, Am Golfplatz 1. **GPS**: n50,83590 e9,46211.

3 free.
Location: Rural, simple, isolated, quiet. **Surface:** grassy.
01/01-31/12.
Distance: 2,5km 11km.
Remarks: Max. 4 days, follow the signs 'Golfplatz', 18-holes golf course.

Oberaula 12B1

Tennishalle, Teichstrasse. **GPS**: n50,86116 e9,47353.

10 free. **Location:** Rural, simple, isolated, quiet. **Surface:** metalled.
01/01-31/12.
Distance: 500m 500m Edeka 500m.
Remarks: Parking tennis-court, max. 4 days.

S Oberaula 12B1

Reiterhof Aumühle, Aumühle 1. **GPS**: n50,85235 e9,47794.
4 € 10 Ch included. **Location:** Rural, comfortable.
Surface: grassy/gravel. 01/01-31/12.
Distance: 1km 1km 1,5km.
Remarks: Use of sauna against payment.

Oberursel 11H3

Wanderparkplatz Taunus, Alfred-Lechler-Straße.
GPS: n50,21533 e8,53606.

5 € 7. **Location:** Simple, quiet. **Surface:** metalled.
01/01-31/12.
Distance: 4km 100m metro 100m on the spot on the spot.

Oestrich-Winkel 11H3

Am Sportzentrum, Kirchstraße 125. **GPS**: n50,00470 e7,99904.

DE

12 free. **Location:** Rural, simple, central. **Surface:** metalled.
01/01-31/12.
Distance: 1km.
Remarks: Max. 2 days.

S Ottrau 12A2

Am Schwimmbad 10. **GPS**: n50,80400 e9,38500.

4 €6 WC. **Location:** Rural, simple. **Surface:** asphalted.
01/01-31/12.
Distance: on the spot.

S Poppenhausen 12B2

Sport- und Freizeitgelände Lüttergrund, Sebastian-Kneippweg, Wasserkuppe. **GPS**: n50,49012 e9,87689.

10 €6 €1 Ch €1/6h. **Location:** Rural, simple.
Surface: metalled. 01/01-31/12.
Distance: 300m 300m 300m on the spot on the spot.

S Rasdorf 12B2

Sport- und Freizeitgelände, Setzelbacher Straße.
GPS: n50,71422 e9,90306.

4 €4 €1/120liter Ch €1/10h. **Location:** Rural, simple.
Surface: metalled. 01/01-31/12.
Distance: 850m 500m.
Remarks: Max. 3 days.

S Reichelsheim/Odenwald 17A1

Reichenbergschule, Beerfurhterstrasse.
GPS: n49,71507 e8,84234.

20 free €1/100liter Ch (8x)€0,50/kWh. **Location:** Urban, simple, central. **Surface:** asphalted. 01/01-31/12.
Distance: on the spot 100m on the spot on the spot.

Reinhardshagen 10B3

Freibad, Klinkersweg. **GPS**: n51,48694 e9,59194.

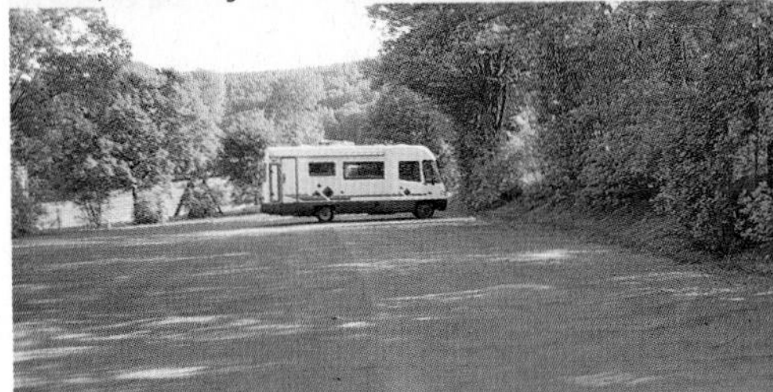

4 free. **Location:** Rural, simple, isolated. **Surface:** asphalted.
01/01-31/12.
Distance: 2km on the spot 2km 2km on the spot on the spot on the spot.
Remarks: Parking swimming pool, OT Veckerhagen, max. 3 days.

S Ringgau 12B1

Am Festplatz, In der Röste, Gandenborn. **GPS**: n51,08139 e10,04239.

20 free, service/electricity incl. €7 Ch WC.
Location: Rural, simple, quiet. **Surface:** gravel.
01/01-31/12.
Distance: 100m 200m.

S Rosenthal 12A1

Fischewosse, Willershäuser Straße 2. **GPS**: n50,97561 e8,86884.

5 free €2/day. **Location:** Urban, comfortable.
Surface: metalled. 01/01-31/12 first 2 weeks of July.
Distance: 400m on the spot 800m.
Remarks: Max. 48h.

S Rotenburg a/d Fulda 12B1

Wohnmobilpark Am Wittlich, Braacher Straße 14.
GPS: n51,00049 e9,72074.

50 €6,50 €1 Ch €0,50/kWh.
Location: Simple, quiet. **Surface:** grassy. 01/01-31/12.
Distance: Old city centre 650m 200m on the spot on the spot. **Remarks:** Along the Fulda river.

S Rotenburg a/d Fulda 12B1

Am Kuckucksmarktgelände, Braach. **GPS**: n51,00583 e9,69361.

15 free €1/50liter Ch. **Location:** Rural. **Surface:** unpaved.
01/01-31/12.
Distance: 200m on the spot on the spot 200m.
Remarks: Max. 72h.

Rotenburg a/d Fulda 12B1

Im Heienbach. **GPS**: n51,00223 e9,74141.

5 free. **Location:** Simple. 01/01-31/12.
Remarks: Parking swimming pool.

S Rotenburg a/d Fulda 12B1

Biergarten Hof Hafermas, Rotenburgerstrasse 13, Braach.
GPS: n51,00316 e9,69085.

3 free €1 Ch. **Surface:** gravel. 01/01-31/12.
Distance: on the spot on the spot.

Tourist information Rotenburg a/d Fulda:
Kuckucksmarkt, Braach. Farmers market. 01/05-30/09 last weekend of the month10-18h.

S Schlitz 12B2

Damenweg. **GPS**: n50,66909 e9,56908.

3 free €1. **Location:** Rural, simple. **Surface:** gravel.
01/01-31/12.
Distance: 2,3km.
Remarks: At swimming pool.

Schlüchtern 12B2

Ludovica-von-Stumm-Straße. **GPS**: n50,34935 e9,53023.

5 free. **Location:** Urban, simple, noisy. **Surface:** asphalted.
01/01-31/12.
Distance: 300m 4,3km on the spot.

S Schwalmstadt 12A1

Altstad Schwalmstadt-Treysa, Zwalmstraße. **GPS**: n50,91447 e9,19327.

DE

10 free Ch. 01/01-31/12.
Distance: 100m.
Remarks: Service nearby, indicated.

S Schwalmstadt 12A1

Fünftenweg, Ziegenhain. **GPS**: n50,91753 e9,24633.

5 free Ch. **Location:** Rural, simple. **Surface:** metalled.
01/01-31/12.
Distance: on the spot.
Remarks: Parking swimming pool, service nearby, indicated.

S Schwalmtal 12A2

Reisemobilplatz, Friedenstrasse, Storndorf.
GPS: n50,65579 e9,26935.

15 € 3 €1/80liter Ch (6x)€0,50/kWh. **Location:** Rural, simple. **Surface:** asphalted. 01/01-31/12.
Distance: 300m on the spot on the spot.
Remarks: Nearby sports park.

S Sinntal 12B3

Am Naturbad, Aspenweg, Altengronau.
GPS: n50,25453 e9,63316.

7 free €0,50/50liter Ch (7x)€3/24h.
Location: Rural, simple, quiet. **Surface:** metalled.
01/01-31/12.
Distance: 1,5km 1,5km 1,5km on the spot.

S Sontra 12B1

Langhelle/Jahnstrasse. **GPS**: n51,07227 e9,94673.

5 free €0,50/80liter Ch €1/12h WC.
Location: Rural, simple, isolated, quiet. **Surface:** asphalted/metalled.
01/01-31/12.
Distance: 600m on the spot.
Remarks: Parking behind swimming pool.

Sontra 12B1

Vimoutiersstrasse. **GPS**: n51,07139 e9,93306.
8 free. **Location:** Urban, simple. **Surface:** gravel/metalled.
01/01-31/12.
Distance: 400m 300m 50m.

S Steinau/Strasse 12B3

Am Steines. **GPS**: n50,31605 e9,46029.

5 free €1 Ch€1 (4x)€1/kWh. **Location:** Rural, simple, quiet. **Surface:** asphalted. 01/01-31/12.
Distance: 1km 350m.
Remarks: Parking near sports centre, max. 2 days.

S Tann/Rhön 12B2

Festplatz Tann, Am Unsbach. **GPS**: n50,64195 e10,01802.

8 € 5 €1/120liter Ch (8x)€1/6h. **Location:** Rural, simple, isolated. **Surface:** gravel. 01/01-31/12.
Distance: 1km 1km 1km.
Remarks: Max. 3 days, tickets available at tourist office, petrol station or Schreib- und Spielwaren Krenzer.

S Ulrichstein 12A2

Reisemobilstellplatz Panoramablick, Erlenweg.
GPS: n50,57588 e9,20619.

12 € 5 €1/80liter Ch (6x)€0,50/kWh.
Location: Rural, comfortable, quiet. **Surface:** asphalted.
01/01-31/12.
Distance: 1km 1km 1km on the spot on the spot on the spot.
Remarks: Beautiful view.

Villmar 11H2

P3, König-Konrad-Straße. **GPS**: n50,39102 e8,18625.

10 free. **Location:** Rural, simple. **Surface:** metalled.
01/01-31/12.
Distance: on the spot.
Remarks: Parking at the river.

S Vöhl 12A1

Camping-und Ferienpark Teichmann, Herzhausen.
GPS: n51,17472 e8,89103.

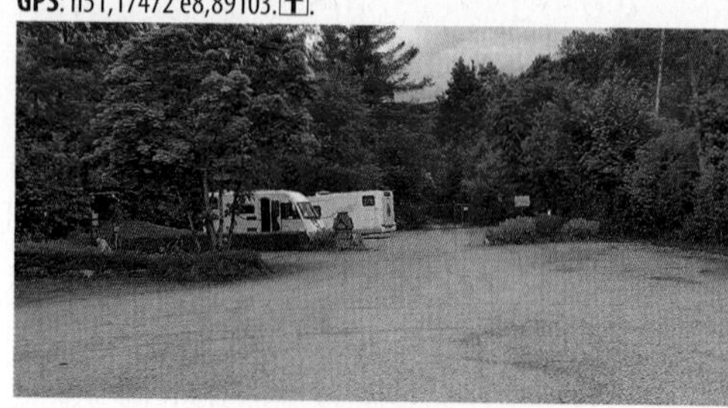

10 € 10-14 , , Ch WC included €3 €4,50.
Location: Rural, comfortable. **Surface:** metalled.
01/01-31/12.
Distance: 1km on the spot fishing permit € 8/day on the spot.
Remarks: Max. 1 night.

Volkmarsen 10A3

Schulstraße. **GPS**: n51,41249 e9,11058.
4 free. **Surface:** asphalted. 01/01-31/12.
Distance: 200m 7,8km Aldi 650m.

S Wahlsburg 10B3

Landhotel "Zum Anker", Weserstrasse 14.
GPS: n51,62447 e9,55212.

60 € 9 €0,50/50liter Ch (60x)€0,50/kWh WC .
Location: Rural, comfortable, quiet. **Surface:** grassy.
01/01-31/12.
Distance: 200m on the spot on the spot 500m on the spot on the spot.
Remarks: Along the Weser river, bread-service.

S Waldeck 12A1

Edersee Alm, Am Bettenhagen 2. **GPS**: n51,18861 e9,00944.

85 € 12 €1/100liter Chincluded €0,50/kWh WC €1/stay.
Location: Rural, luxurious. **Surface:** gravel. 01/01-31/12.
Distance: on the spot fishing permit obligatory on the spot.
Remarks: Bread-service.

S Waldeck 12A1

Seeblick Wohnmobil, Güldener Ort 12. **GPS**: n51,20309 e9,05004.

€ 11 2 pers.incl, dog € 1 Ch €3 WC included.
Location: Rural, simple. **Surface:** grasstiles.
01/01-31/12.
Distance: 50m on the spot.
Remarks: At Edersee, waste dump € 2.

S Waldkappel 12B1

Am Sportplatz. **GPS**: n51,14177 e9,87278.

4 free €1/100liter. **Location:** Rural, simple, isolated, quiet.
Surface: gravel. 01/03-31/10.
Distance: 400m 400m 400m bakery Waldpark 500m.
Remarks: At sports park.

S Wanfried 12B1

In der Werraaue, Eschweger Straße. **GPS**: n51,18722 e10,16528.

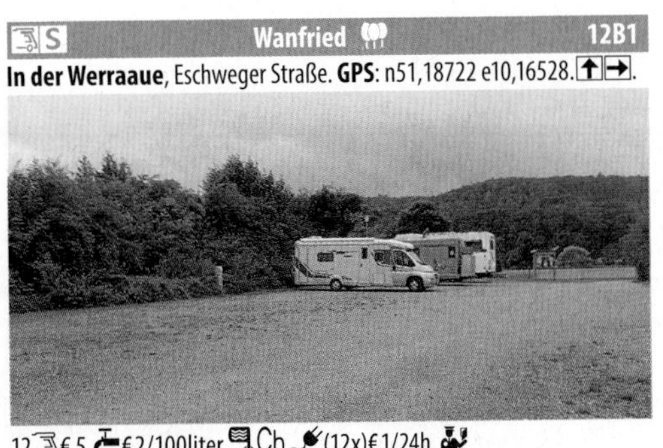

12 € 5 €2/100liter Ch (12x)€1/24h.
Location: Rural, simple, quiet. **Surface:** metalled.
01/01-31/12.
Distance: 50m 50m on the spot on the spot.

S Weilburg 11H2

Wohnmobilstation, Hainallee. **GPS**: n50,48385 e8,25848.

80 € 6 included €2 WC 10-17h. **Location:** Urban, simple. **Surface:** metalled. 01/01-31/12 events.
Distance: on the spot on the spot.
Remarks: Caution key € 15.

S Weilmünster 11H2

In der Au, Am Froschgraben, L3054. **GPS**: n50,43345 e8,37343.

12 voluntary contribution Ch free €2/16h.
Location: Rural, simple. **Surface:** metalled. 01/01-31/12.
Distance: on the spot 100m 100m.

S Weilrod 11H3

Taunus Mobilcamp, Hochtaunusstrasse. **GPS**: n50,31138 e8,42581.

30 € 7 + € 1,50/pp, dog € 1 €1/80liter Ch €0,50/kWh WC included. **Location:** Rural, simple, isolated, noisy.
Surface: metalled. 01/01-31/12.
Distance: 500m 6km.

Weilrod 11H3

Golfclub Taunus, Merzhäuser Straße 29. **GPS**: n50,32082 e8,42694.
2 free, only guest players. **Location:** Noisy. **Surface:** asphalted.
01/05-30/09.
Distance: on the spot.

S Wetzlar 11H2

An der Dill, Falkenstrasse. **GPS**: n50,55667 e8,49111.

16 € 8 Ch (16x)included. **Location:** Urban, simple.
Surface: gravel. 01/01-31/12.
Distance: 800m 3km 500m on the spot.

S Wetzlar 11H2

Parkplatz Lahninsel, Lahninsel. **GPS**: n50,55488 e8,49756.

4 € 8 (8-19h), overnight stay free Ch included WC.
Location: Urban. **Surface:** asphalted. 01/01-31/12.
Distance: 300m 1,5km 250m.

S Wiesbaden 11H3

Reisemobilhafen Wiesbaden, Wörther-See-Strasse/Saarstrasse.
GPS: n50,05583 e8,20972.

+40 € 7, overnight stay 21-9h € 3,50 €1/60liter Ch (40x)€0,50/kWh WC €1. **Location:** Urban, comfortable.
Surface: gravel. 01/01-31/12.
Distance: 150m 800m 800m 150m.
Remarks: Can be reached without environmental: A643 exit Wiesbaden Dotzheim.

S Willingen 11H1

Wohnmobilpark Willingen, Am Hagen.
GPS: n51,29050 e8,61278.

55 € 12, 2 pers.incl €1/10minutes Ch €1/2kWh WC €1,50/30minutes,at swimming pool . **Location:** Rural, comfortable. **Surface:** metalled. 01/01-31/12.
Distance: 1km 100m 1km 300m 300m.
Remarks: Discount at subtropical swimming pool and indoor skating rink.

S Witzenhausen 10B3

Reisemobilplatz Diebesturm, Oberburgstrasse.
GPS: n51,34110 e9,85435.

4 € 5 €0,50/100liter Ch (4x)€0,50.
Location: Urban, simple, central, noisy. **Surface:** gravel.
01/01-31/12.
Distance: 500m on the spot 500m.

S Witzenhausen 10B3

Reisemobilplatz Josef-Pott-Platz, Laubenweg.
GPS: n51,34477 e9,85503.

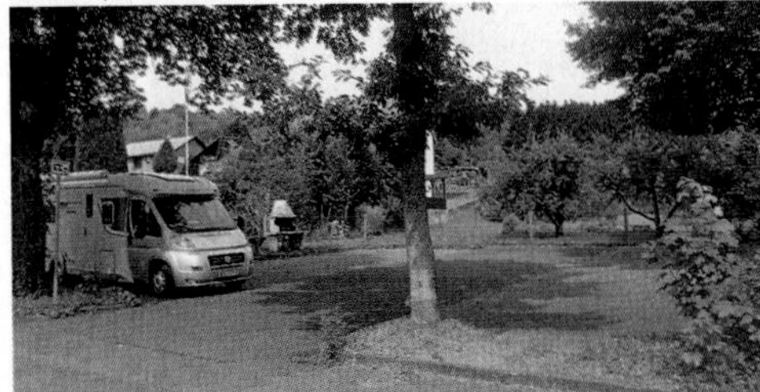

10 € 5 €1/100liter Ch (10x)€0,50/6h.
Location: Rural, simple, quiet. **Surface:** metalled.
01/01-31/12.
Distance: 800m 9km 800m Aldi 100m on the spot on the spot.

S Witzenhausen 10B3

Haus des Gastes, Ringkopfstrasse, Dohrenbach.
GPS: n51,31061 e9,83372.

8 € 4 Ch included €2/24h WC.
Location: Rural, simple, isolated, quiet. **Surface:** metalled.
01/01-31/12.
Distance: on the spot on the spot 300m on the spot.

Tourist information Witzenhausen:
Kesperkirmes. Village fair. beginning Jul.

S Wolfhagen 10A3

Freizeitanlange Bruchwiesen, Siemensstrasse.
GPS: n51,32944 e9,17083.

35 € 3/24h €1/80liter Ch (12x)€1/8h.
Location: Rural, simple, isolated, quiet. **Surface:** grassy/gravel.
01/01-31/12.
Distance: on the spot 500m 200m on the spot on the spot.

S Ziegenhagen 10B3

Erlebnispark Ziegenhagen, Ziegenberg 3.
GPS: n51,37191 e9,76472.

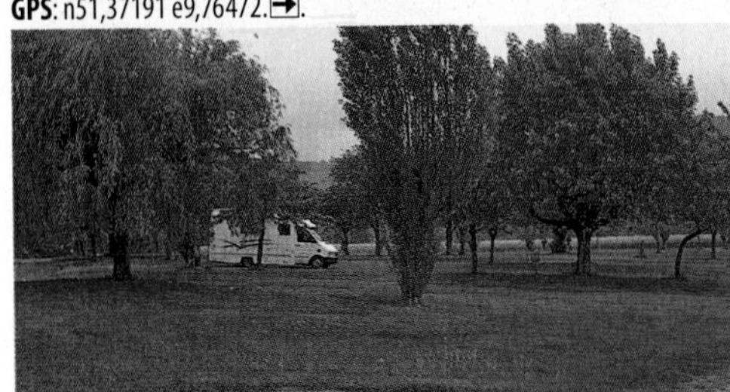

15 € 5 €1 Ch. **Location:** Simple, isolated, quiet.
01/03-31/10.
Distance: 6km.

DE

Thuringia

Asbach/Sickenberg 12B1

Grenzmuseum Schifflersgrund, Sickenberger Straße 1.
GPS: n51,28667 e10,01052.
6 € 3 Ch. **Surface:** gravel.

Bad Berka 12D1

P2, Bleichstrasse. **GPS**: n50,89969 e11,28528.

3 free €1/3minutes €1 Ch (3x)€1/3h. **Surface:** asphalted.
01/01-31/12.
Distance: 200m on the spot 200m 200m.
Remarks: 10/7/10 during inspection service out of order.

Bad Colberg/Heldburg 12C3

Rainbrünnlein. **GPS**: n50,27967 e10,73063.

5 free €1/60liter Ch €1/8h. **Location:** Simple.
Surface: grasstiles. 01/01-31/12.
Distance: 100m 200m 200m.
Remarks: At sports park.

Bad Frankenhausen/Kyffhäuser 10D3

Bornstraße, B85. **GPS**: n51,35550 e11,10333.

15 € 14 included. **Location:** Rural. **Surface:** metalled.
01/01-31/12.
Distance: 500m 200m 300m.
Remarks: Check in at pay-desk of the Therme.

Bad Klosterlausnitz 12E1

Kristall Sauna-Wellnesspark/Soletherme, Köstritzerstrasse 16.
GPS: n50,91190 e11,87242.

15 € 10 + € 1,30/pp tourist tax €1/80liter Ch €1/2kWh
WC. **Surface:** gravel. 01/01-31/12.
Distance: 800m 2,8km on the spot.

Bad Langensalza 12C1

Friederiken Therme, Böhmenstrasse.
GPS: n51,11535 e10,64440.

40 € 4, tourist tax € 1,20/pp €1 Ch (8x)€1/10h.
Surface: metalled. 01/01-31/12.
Distance: 1km on the spot 200m.
Remarks: Parking spa resort, pay at pay-desk of theTherme.

Bad Liebenstein 12C1

Villa Georg, Friedensallee 12. **GPS**: n50,81876 e10,35517.

6 € 8 €1/100liter Ch €3 WC. **Location:** Comfortable, quiet.
Surface: gravel. 01/01-31/12 Tuesday.
Distance: 500m on the spot 800m on the spot.

Bad Lobenstein 12E2

Ardesia Therme, Parkstrasse 8. **GPS**: n50,44981 e11,64294.

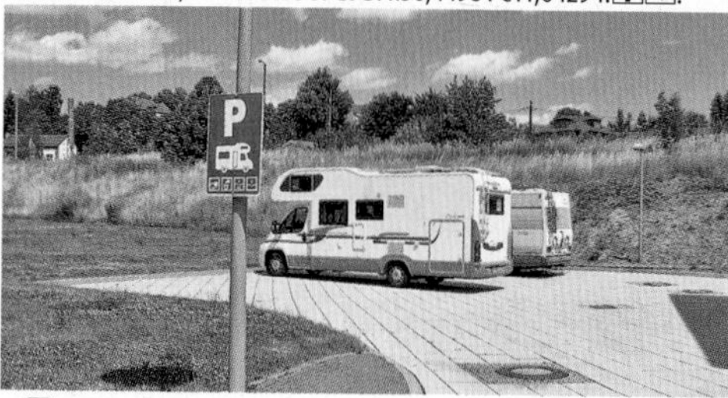

11 € 2,50 + € 1/pp tourist tax, free with use of spa €2
Ch €0,50/kWh WC €3.
Surface: metalled. 01/01-31/12.
Distance: 200m on the spot 200m on the spot.

Bad Salzungen 12C1

ErlebisINSEL Flößrasen, Flössrasen 1. **GPS**: n50,81541 e10,23748.

88 € 7,50 + € 1,50/pp tourist tax €1/60liter (88x)€1/2kWh
against payment. **Location:** Urban, comfortable.
Surface: metalled. 01/01-31/12.
Distance: 500m 400m 400m on the spot on the spot.

Bad Tennstedt 12C1

Am Swimmbad, Zweifeldersporthalle. **GPS**: n51,15994 e10,83952.
5 free. **Location:** Urban, simple. **Surface:** metalled.
01/01-31/12.
Distance: 500m 500m 500m.

Breitungen 12C2

Hotel Jagdhaus Seeblick, Seeblick. **GPS**: n50,74250 e10,32306.

15 € 5 voluntary contribution €2/day WC. **Location:** Rural,
simple, quiet. **Surface:** grassy. 01/01-31/12 Mon.
Distance: 2km 1km on the spot 2km on the spot.

Brotterode 12C1

Inselbergbad, Am Bad 1. **GPS**: n50,82290 e10,45302.

10 € 5. **Location:** Rural, simple. **Surface:** gravel.
01/01-31/12.
Distance: 500m on the spot Edeka 250m 50m.
Remarks: To be paid at swimming pool.

Dorndorf 12B1

Kultur- und Freizeitzentrum, Hardtstraße 3a.
GPS: n50,83453 e10,09087.

8 € 4 €1/90liter €1 Ch €0,50/kWh. **Location:** Urban,
simple. **Surface:** grasstiles. 01/01-31/12.
Distance: 1km 50m.
Remarks: Next to Fahrradherberge.

Eisenach 12C1

Automobilmuseum, Heinrich-Erhardt-Platz.
GPS: n50,98122 e10,32342.

3 free.
Location: Simple. **Surface:** metalled. 01/01-31/12.
Distance: 1km 400m 100m.

Eisenach 12C1

Burg Wartburg, Auf der Wartburg 1. **GPS**: n50,96775 e10,30989.

5 € 6.
Location: Urban. **Surface:** metalled. 01/01-31/12.
Distance: on the spot.
Remarks: Nearby castle Wartburg.

Eisenach 12C1

Karl-Marx-Straße. **GPS**: n50,97861 e10,32083.

DE

3 9-17h max. € 6, free overnight stay. **Surface:** gravel.
01/01-31/12.
Distance: 500m 100m 100m.

Eisenach 12C1

Wohnmobile A. Waldhelm, Ringstrasse 27.
GPS: n51,00194 e10,32667.

20 € 10 Ch included €3/day WC €0,50.
Location: Urban, simple. **Surface:** grasstiles.
01/01-31/12.
Distance: 1km 1km 1km Shuttle bus.
Remarks: Motorhome dealer, accessory shop, check in on arrival, bread-service.

Eisfeld 12D2

Festplatz, Am Volkshaus. **GPS:** n50,42615 e10,90992.

5 free. **Location:** Simple. **Surface:** grasstiles.
01/01-31/12 Whitsuntide.
Distance: 200m 200m 300m on the spot.

Eisfeld 12D2

Waldhotel Hubertus, Coburgerstrasse 501.
GPS: n50,39680 e10,92269.

20 free, use of a meal desired €2 €2.
Location: Rural, simple. **Surface:** asphalted/grassy. 01/01-31/12.
Distance: 3km on the spot 2km on the spot.

Erfurt 12D1

Wohnmobilpark Trautmann, Rottenbacherweg 11, Melchendorf.
GPS: n50,95404 e11,06654.
15 € 8,50 €1,50/150liter €1,50 Ch €1,50 (15x)€1,50/5kWh,16Amp WC €1,50 €3,50/1,50 included.
Surface: gravel. 01/01-31/12.
Distance: on the spot 1,2km 300m 200m 300m.
Remarks: Discount on access sauna/wellness, video surveillance.

Erfurt 12D1

P&R, Am Urbicher Kreuz. **GPS:** n50,94992 e11,09456.

15 free Ch.
Surface: asphalted. 01/01-31/12.
Distance: 7km Total-shop Tram till 24am.
Remarks: Service at petrol station.

Erfurt 12D1

Am kleinen Ring, Juri-Gagarin-Ring. **GPS:** n50,98111 e11,03472.

4 free. **Surface:** asphalted. 01/01-31/12.
Distance: Old city centre 1km 500m 500m.
Remarks: Max. 48h.

Erfurt 12D1

Eichenstrasse. **GPS:** n50,97327 e11,02737.

4 € 12. **Surface:** asphalted. 01/01-31/12.
Distance: 200m 200m 300m on the spot.
Remarks: Max. 48h.

Erfurt 12D1

P&R Parkplatz Messe, Gothaerstrasse. **GPS:** n50,95818 e10,98296.

4 free. **Surface:** asphalted. 01/01-31/12.
Distance: centre 4km Bus <23.00h.
Remarks: Parking exhibition ground.

Erfurt 12D1

P&R Parkplatz Thüringerhalle, Werner-Seelenbinderstrasse.
GPS: n50,95771 e11,03605.

7 free. **Surface:** gravel. 01/01-31/12.
Distance: 2,6km Tram till 23am.
Remarks: Nearby B4, south edge of the city.

Tourist information Erfurt:
Erfurt-Card. Card gives for free entrance on among other things public transport and city museums, and discount on a lot of curiosities, guided tours, swimming pools, theater, souvenirs. € 14,90.
Stadtführung, Tourist Information, Benediktsplatz 1. Guided tour around the historic city center. 01/04-31/12 Mo-Fri 13h, Sa-Su 11h, 13h, 01/01-31/03 Sa-Su 11h, 13h. € 11.

Gotha 12C1

Parkallee 1. **GPS:** n50,94402 e10,70948.
3 free. **Location:** Urban, simple. **Surface:** metalled.
Distance: 800m 800m.

Heiligenstadt 10B3

Stadthalle, Aegidienstrasse 20. **GPS:** n51,37407 e10,13715.

6 free €0,50 Ch €1/3kWh WC. **Location:** Comfortable.
Surface: asphalted. 01/01-31/12.
Distance: 150m 200m.
Remarks: At swimming pool, in front of town hall.

Tourist information Heiligenstadt:
City of churches, health resort.
Literaturmuseum Theodor Storm. Museum of important German writer. Tue-Fri 9-12h, 13-16h, Sa-Su 14-16h.

Ichtershausen 12D1

Autohof, Thöreyerstrasse. **GPS:** n50,88824 e10,93478.

20 € 6,50/24h, first hour free €0,50 Ch €0,50 WC.
Location: Motorway. **Surface:** asphalted. 01/01-31/12.
Distance: 4km on the spot Esso-shop.

Ichtershausen 12D1

Freizeitfahrzeuge Mobilease, Feldstrasse 1.
GPS: n50,86907 e10,96563.

5 € 7,50 Ch (4x)included WC during opening hours.
Surface: gravel. 01/01-31/12.
Distance: 3km 500m bakery 500m.

Ilfeld 10C3

Gasthof Brauner Hirsch, Dorfstrasse 42, Sophienhof.
GPS: n51,63467 e10,79223.

15 € 5 Ch (3x)€0,35/kWh WC €2 . **Location:** Rural.
Surface: metalled. 01/01-31/12.
Distance: on the spot 3km on the spot on the spot.

DE

S Ilmenau 12D2

Festhalle, Naumannstraße. **GPS**: n50,68139 e10,90472.

4 free €2/80liter Ch. **Surface:** asphalted. 01/01-31/12.
Distance: 1km 100m 500m.
Remarks: Max. 24h.

S Kühndorf 12C2

Flugschule Dolmar, Am Flugplatz 1. **GPS**: n50,61198 e10,47079.

20 € 6 €1 Ch€1,50 €2/day WC €1,50.
Location: Rural, isolated. **Surface:** grassy/gravel.
01/01-31/12.
Distance: 2km on the spot on the spot.
Remarks: Bread-service, parking behind the hangar.

Lauscha 12D2

Parkplatz Obermühle. **GPS**: n50,48026 e11,16795.

10 free. **Location:** Simple. **Surface:** asphalted. 01/01-31/12.
Distance: 300m 100m 1km on the spot on the spot.

Lauscha 12D2

Sommerrodelbahn, Lauschaer Straße, Ernstthal.
GPS: n50,48726 e11,17243.

10 free. **Location:** Simple. **Surface:** asphalted. 01/01-31/12.
Distance: 650m 50m 50m.

S Linda 12E2

Knappmühle, Ortsstraße. **GPS**: n50,68473 e11,78324.

10 € 6 Ch (6x)€1/kWh. **Surface:** grassy/gravel.
01/03-31/10.
Distance: 300m 5km 3km 5km.

S Meiningen 12C2

Rohrer Stirn, Frankental. **GPS**: n50,56976 e10,43477.

10 free (6x)€0,50/kWh. **Location:** Urban, simple, quiet.
Surface: asphalted. 01/01-31/12.
Distance: 2km.
Remarks: Parking at swimming pool.

Meiningen 12C2

Grossmutterwiesen, Werrastrasse. **GPS**: n50,56172 e10,41266.

5 free. **Location:** Simple. **Surface:** concrete. 01/01-31/12.
Distance: on the spot 200m 100m.
Remarks: Service possible at Kläranlage.

Meiningen 12C2

Volkshausplatz, Landsbergerstrasse. **GPS**: n50,57427 e10,41369.

5 free. **Location:** Urban, simple. **Surface:** metalled.
01/01-31/12.
Distance: 200m on the spot 200m 200m.
Remarks: Service possible at Kläranlage.

S Mihla 12C1

Graues Schloss, Thomas-Münztzer-Straße 4.
GPS: n51,07854 e10,33166.

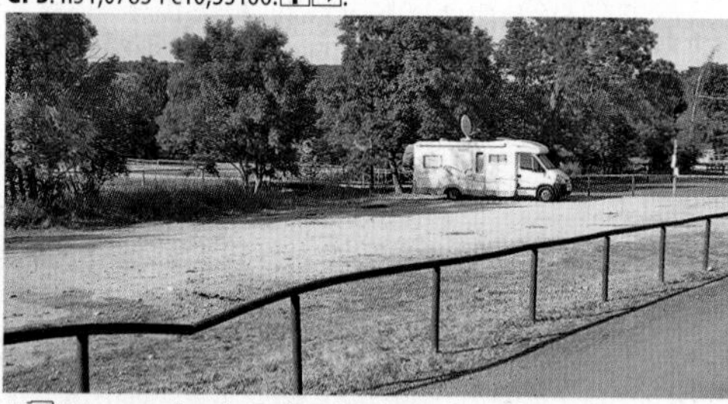

15 € 8, guests free. **Location:** Rural, simple, quiet.
Surface: unpaved. 01/01-31/12 Whitsuntide.
Distance: on the spot fishing permit obligatory on the spot 500m on the spot on the spot.

S Neustadt/Orla 12E1

Gaststätte & Pension Heinrichs-Ruhe, Heinrichsruhe 1, Rodaer Strasse. **GPS**: n50,75545 e11,75595.

10 guests free (6x)€0,50/kWh. **Surface:** grassy/gravel.
01/01-31/12 Restaurant: Mo.
Distance: 2,6km 12,2km on the spot 2,6km.

S Nimritz 12E2

Wohnmobilstellplatz Nimritz, Ortsstrasse 29.
GPS: n50,70079 e11,64858.

10 voluntary contribution €0,50 Ch (7x)€0,50/kWh.
Surface: grasstiles.
Distance: 300m 300m.

S Nordhausen 10C3

Am Badehaus, Grimmelallee 40. **GPS**: n51,50450 e10,78508.

2 € 5, € 10 service and swimming pool incl €2 €1 Ch€1 €1 €3. **Location:** Simple. **Surface:** metalled.
Distance: 800m 500m 300m.

Nordhausen 10C3

Am Kuhberg, Parkallee. **GPS**: n51,51502 e10,78492.

10 free. **Location:** Rural, isolated. **Surface:** asphalted.
01/01-31/12.
Distance: 2km on the spot 500m.

S Oberhof 12C2

Wohnmobilstellplatz Oberhof, Jahnstrasse 7.
GPS: n50,70278 e10,72694.

+60 € 10 + € 2/pp tourist tax €1/80liter Ch (50x)€0,50/kWh. **Location:** Urban, simple. **Surface:** asphalted.
01/01-31/12.
Distance: 400m 200m 500m on the spot.
Remarks: Bread-service.

Tourist information Oberhof:

Rennsteiggarten Oberhof. Botanical garden. 01/05-30/09 9-18, 01/10-31/10 9-17h.

S Reichenbach 12E1

Holzland Freizeitcenter, Rodaer Landstrasse.
GPS: n50,86118 e11,87607.

DE

50 € 8, guests free €1 Ch (15x)€2/day WC €2/pp.
Surface: concrete. 01/01-31/12.
Distance: 2km on the spot bakery 500m.

S Rudolstadt 12D2

Freizeit- und Erlebnisbad Saalemaxx, Hugo-Trinckler-Straße 6.
GPS: n50,70635 e11,31659.

9 € 7/24h €1/80liter €1 Ch €0,50/kWh.
Surface: gravel. 01/01-31/12.
Distance: 2km 100m.
Remarks: Discount at swimming pool.

Saalfeld 12D2

Reschwitzerstrasse, B281. **GPS:** n50,63720 e11,36751.

10 free. **Surface:** gravel. 01/01-31/12.
Distance: 2,8km.
Remarks: Parking at swimming pool.

S Saalfeld 12D2

Saalfelder Feengrotten, Feengrottenweg 2.
GPS: n50,63468 e11,33982.

10 € 10 €3/5minutes €3 Ch (6x)€0,50/kWh WC .
Surface: grassy. 01/01-31/12.
Distance: 2,3km on the spot bakery 500m 500m.

S Schleiz 12E2

Spitzbergs Zollhaus, Burgkerstrasse 25.
GPS: n50,55507 e11,73438.

5 € 5, free with a meal Ch (7x)€2/24h.
Surface: gravel/metalled. 01/01-31/12 Mo.
Distance: 7km 5,4km on the spot 7km.

S Schleiz 12E2

HEM-Großtankstelle, Saalburgerstrasse.
GPS: n50,55004 e11,78788.

8 € 2 €1 €1 ChWC. **Location:** Motorway. **Surface:** asphalted.
01/01-31/12.
Distance: 5km on the spot shop.
Remarks: Industrial area, max. 24h.

Schmiedefeld 12C2

Sportplatz, Sportplatzstraße. **GPS:** n50,60324 e10,81491.

20 € 3 + € 1/pp tourist tax. **Location:** Rural, simple, quiet.
Surface: grasstiles/metalled. 01/01-31/12.
Distance: 500m 400m on the spot on the spot.
Remarks: Pay at tourist office or Gasthaus Thüringer Hof.

Sitzendorf 12D2

Sitzendorfer Porzellanmanufaktur, Hauptstrasse 26.
GPS: n50,63174 e11,16788.

5 free. **Surface:** asphalted. 01/01-31/12.
Distance: on the spot 200m 200m.

S Sondershausen 10C3

P7 zur Windleite, Hospitalstrasse. **GPS:** n51,37824 e10,86234.

5 free €1 Ch (4x)€1/2h. **Surface:** metalled.
01/01-31/12.
Distance: 2,5km 500m 100m.

Sondershausen 10C3

Freizeitpark Possen, Possen 1. **GPS:** n51,33800 e10,86265.

10 € 4/stay. **Surface:** metalled. 01/01-31/12.
Distance: 5km on the spot.

S Stadtlengsfeld 12B2

Am Schwimmbad, Eisenacher Straße. **GPS:** n50,79065 e10,11373.

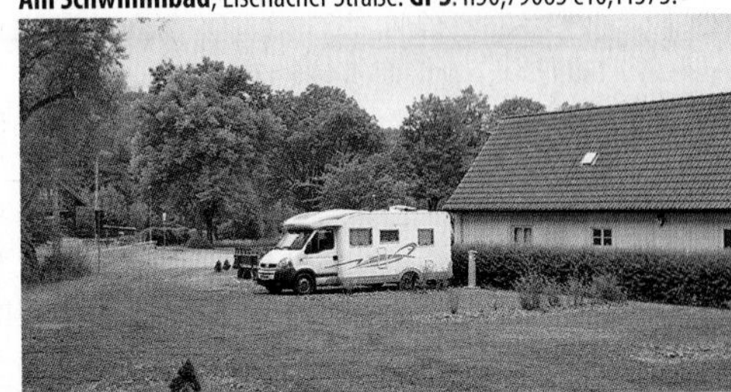

6 free €1/80liter €1/kWh. **Location:** Rural, simple.
Surface: asphalted. 01/01-31/12.
Distance: 1,5km.

Steinheid 12D2

Am Rennsteig, Eisfelder Straße, Limbach.
GPS: n50,47568 e11,06937.

4 free. **Location:** Rural, simple, noisy. **Surface:** gravel.
01/01-31/12.
Distance: 150m 10km on the spot.

S Steinheid 12D2

Thüringer Baumschmuck, Neuhäuser Strasse 8-10.
GPS: n50,47302 e11,08672.

8 € 5, free for clients €2/90liter included.
Location: Simple. **Surface:** unpaved. 01/01-31/12.
Distance: 3km, bakery 50m on the spot on the spot on the spot.
Remarks: At Christmas Balls manufacturer.

Tabarz 12C1

Karl-Kornhaß-Straße. **GPS:** n50,87782 e10,52038.

8 free, tourist tax € 1,50/pp. **Location:** Rural, simple, quiet.
Surface: metalled. 01/01-31/12.
Distance: 200m Rewe 400m.
Remarks: To be paid at TABBS sports centre.

S Tambach-Dietharz 12C1

Festplatz, Burgstallstraße. **GPS:** n50,78902 e10,60897.

4 free, tourist tax € 1/pp Ch service €6.
Location: Urban, simple. **Surface:** gravel. 01/01-31/12.

DE

Distance: on the spot ⊗on the spot.
Remarks: Key service at town hall.

Tambach-Dietharz 12C1

Freigelande Lohmühle, Lohmühle 1-5. **GPS:** n50,81056 e10,62778.

30 € 6 + € 4/pp Ch €2 WC €1 €1.
Location: Rural, simple, quiet.
Surface: grassy.
01/02-31/12 Mon.
Distance: ⊗on the spot 3km on the spot on the spot.
Remarks: Check in on arrival, barefoot park, museum.

Themar 12C2

Am Hexenturm, Mauerstrasse. **GPS:** n50,50512 e10,61194.

5 free €1/50liter Ch €1/kWh. **Location:** Urban, simple, quiet. **Surface:** grasstiles. 01/01-31/12.
Distance: 100m ⊗300m 400m on the spot on the spot.
Remarks: Along the Werra river, 01/11-31/03 water disconnected.

Tiefenort 12B1

Freizeitanlage Heerstatt, Auf der Heerstatt.
GPS: n50,83444 e10,16306.

6 free €2/day. **Location:** Rural, simple. **Surface:** concrete.
01/03-31/10.
Distance: on the spot ⊗50m bakery 900m on the spot.
Remarks: On island in the Werra river.

Treffurt 12C1

Wohnmobilstellplatz Unter den Linden.
GPS: n51,13398 e10,23659.

20 free €0,50/80liter Ch (8x)€1/kWh. **Location:** Rural, simple, quiet. **Surface:** grasstiles/grassy. 01/01-31/12 15/07-31/07.
Distance: 300m on the spot ⊗50m 500m on the spot on the spot.
Remarks: Along river, water closed during wintertime.

Tourist information Treffurt:
Small town with half-timbered houses and medival castle Normannstein.

Vacha 12B1

Frankfurter Strasse. **GPS:** n50,81856 e10,01327.
5 free. **Location:** Simple.
Distance: 1km ⊗1km.

Remarks: At swimming pool.

Weimar 12D1

Hermann Brill-Platz. **GPS:** n50,98501 e11,31701.

20 € 10/24h €1 Ch (6x)€1/6h. **Surface:** metalled.
01/01-31/12.
Distance: Weimar centre 1,2km ⊗on the spot 500m.

Zella-Mehlis 12C2

Toschis Station, An der Quelle 5. **GPS:** n50,64375 e10,68436.

10 €5 Ch (20x) . **Location:** Simple, central.
Surface: grassy/gravel. 01/01-31/12.
Distance: ⊗on the spot 300m.
Remarks: Check in at reception.

Zeulenroda 12E2

Badewelt Waikiki, Am Birkenwege 1. **GPS:** n50,66543 e11,99355.

6 € 10 Ch included,water and electricity € 10/day.
Surface: metalled. 01/01-31/12.

Baden Württemberg

Aalen 17C3

Hirschbach, Hirschbachstrasse 68. **GPS:** n48,84524 e10,10712.

12 free €1/80liter Ch €1/2kWh. **Location:** Rural.
Surface: asphalted. 01/01-31/12.
Distance: 800m ⊗100m 200m.
Remarks: At swimming pool, max. 3 days.

Aalen 17C3

Limes-Thermen, P1, Osterbucher Steige.
GPS: n48,82047 e10,07918.

12 free. **Location:** Rural. **Surface:** grasstiles.
01/01-31/12.

Distance: ⊗100m.

Achern 16H3

Wohnmobilstellplatz Achern, Kapellenstrasse/Badstrasse.
GPS: n48,62436 e8,07359.

14 €6 €1/100liter Ch (12x)€1/6h. **Location:** Urban, simple, quiet. **Surface:** gravel/metalled. 01/01-31/12.
Distance: 500m 4,8km 650m on the spot on the spot.
Remarks: Next to swimming pool, tuesday and Saturday market.

Albstadt 20A1

Sonnencamping, Beibruck 54. **GPS:** n48,21438 e8,97879.
16 €8 €0,57/kWh WC €2 .
Surface: grassy. 01/01-31/12.

Allensbach 20A2

Landgasthaus Mindelsee, Gemeinmärk 7.
GPS: n47,74279 e9,04411.

15 € 8, guests free. **Surface:** metalled. 01/01-31/12 Tue.
Distance: 5km ⊗on the spot.
Remarks: Max. 1 night, max 3,5t.

Amtzell 20B2

Wohnmobilstellplatz Büchelweisen, Büchel 3.
GPS: n47,70871 e9,76684.

36 € 10 €1/90liter Ch (36x)€0,50/kWh WC €1,50/time.
Surface: grasstiles. 01/01-31/12.
Distance: 1,5km 1km 1km ⊗on the spot 1,5km.
Remarks: Bread-service.

Aspach 17B2

Gemeindehallen, Rübengasse. **GPS:** n48,96437 e9,39706.
free.
Distance: ⊗100m.
Remarks: At gymnasium.

Aspach 17B2

Wanderparkplatz Fautenhau, Im Fautenhau, Hohrot.
GPS: n48,97823 e9,39483.

5 free. **Location:** Rural. **Surface:** metalled. 01/01-31/12.
Distance: ⊗on the spot.
Remarks: Max. 1 night, parking P0.

Aspach 17B2

Wanderparkplatz Heiligental, Heiligentalstrasse, Rietenau.
GPS: n48,99158 e9,40519.

5 free. **Location:** Rural, quiet. **Surface:** asphalted/grassy.
01/01-31/12.
Distance: on the spot.
Remarks: Max. 1 night.

S Aspach 17B2

Caravan-Service-Station, L1124. **GPS**: n48,96375 e9,37582.
Ch. 01/01-31/12.

Aulendorf 20B1

Schwaben-Therme, Ebisweilerstrasse 5. **GPS**: n47,95797 e9,63728.

20 (P3) free.
Location: Rural. **Surface:** metalled. 01/01-31/12.
Distance: 500m on the spot 500m.
Remarks: Parking swimming pool, max. 2 nights.

S Aulendorf 20B1

Carthago City, Carthago ring 1. **GPS**: n47,93156 e9,65429.
6 free €0,50 Ch €0,50/kWh. **Surface:** metalled.
01/01-31/12.
Distance: 2,5km.
Remarks: At motohome manufacturer.

S Backnang 17B2

Martin-Dietrich-Allee. **GPS**: n48,95041 e9,45281.

4 free €1/90liter Ch. **Location:** Rural, simple.
Surface: gravel. 01/01-31/12.
Distance: 1km 400m on the spot on the spot.

S Bad Bellingen 19G2

Balinea Thermen, Badstrasse 14. **GPS**: n47,72963 e7,55233.

31 € 14 + € 1,45/2,25 tourist tax €1/80liter Ch (31x)€1/kWh WC €1,50. **Location:** Urban, noisy.
Surface: asphalted/metalled. 01/01-31/12.
Distance: 500m 5,5km on the spot on the spot.

S Bad Buchau 20B1

Adelindis Therme, Am Kurpark. **GPS**: n48,06865 e9,60653.

21 € 9,50 XL-pitch € 11 €1/80liter Ch €0,50/kWh WC €1.
Surface: metalled. 01/01-31/12.
Distance: 500m.

S Bad Buchau 20B1

Seegasse. GPS: n48,06801 e9,60977.

17 € 9,50 €1/80liter Ch (17x)€0,50/kWh.
Surface: metalled. 01/01-31/12.
Distance: 500m.
Remarks: Adelindis Therme 300m.

S Bad Buchau 20B1

Federseemuseum, Wellerstraße. **GPS**: n48,07051 e9,60949.

12 € 9 (12x)€0,50/kWh WC. **Location:** Rural.
Surface: asphalted. 01/01-31/12.
Distance: 800m.
Remarks: Adelindis Therme 500m.

Bad Buchau 20B1

Am Freibad, Friedhofstrasse. **GPS**: n48,06292 e9,61714.

10 € 9. **Surface:** asphalted. 01/01-31/12.
Distance: 700m.

S Bad Ditzenbach 17B3

Vinzenz Therme, Badstraße 20. **GPS**: n48,59003 e9,70553.

10 € 5, winter € 6 Ch. **Surface:** asphalted.
01/01-31/12.
Remarks: Caution key € 50.

S Bad Dürrheim 20A1

Reisemobilhafen Bad Dürrheim, Huberstraße 34/2.
GPS: n48,01204 e8,53506.

300 € 6,50, tourist tax € 2,50/pp €1/100liter Ch €2,50/night WC €2. **Location:** Rural, comfortable. **Surface:** gravel.
01/01-31/12.
Distance: on the spot.
Remarks: Pay at reception, bread-service, special health arrangement possible.

S Bad Herrenalb 16H3

Wohnmobilstation Siebentäler Therme, Schweizer Wiese.
GPS: n48,80334 e8,44067.

9 € 5 + tourist tax € 2,50/pp €1 €1 Ch€1 (4x)€0,50/kWh.
Location: Rural, simple. **Surface:** asphalted.
01/01-31/12.
Distance: 500m 100m 200m 200m on the spot on the spot.
Remarks: Max. 2 nights, use sanitary only during opening hours, discount on access terme, friday market.

Tourist information Bad Herrenalb:
Quellenerlebnispfad, Kurpark Herrenalb. Hiking trails past 60 fountains.

S Bad Krozingen 19G2

Wohnmobilstellplatz Vita Classica, Thürachstraße.
GPS: n47,91763 e7,68821.

80 € 12, from 7th night € 10,50 Ch €3,50/day,16Amp WC €3 included.
Location: Rural, comfortable. **Surface:** gravel.
01/01-31/12.
Distance: 600m 3km 50m 600m 800m on the spot on the spot on the spot.
Remarks: Bread-service, trailer € 2,50/night, bike and e-bike rental.

S Bad Liebenzell 17A3

Campingpark Bad Liebenzell, Pforzheimer strasse 34.
GPS: n48,77850 e8,73120.

16 € 8, tourist tax € 2/pp Ch (16x) WC included €3
Location: Rural, simple, noisy. **Surface:** metalled/sand.
01/01-31/12.
Distance: on the spot 17km 500m 100m on the spot on the spot on the spot.

S Bad Mergentheim 17B1

Festplatz beim Freibad, Erlenbachweg.
GPS: n49,49194 e9,79167.

DE

20 € 5 + tourist tax €1/80liter Chfree (8x)€1/8h.
Location: Rural, simple. **Surface:** gravel.
01/01-31/12.
Distance: Old city centre 1km 200m Lidl 800m 100m.
Remarks: Max. 3 nights, check in at restaurant tennispark.

Bad Niedernau 17A3

Wohnmobilparkplatz Bad Niedernau, Blaue Brücke.
GPS: n48,45931 e8,89959.

5 free. **Location:** Rural, simple. **Surface:** gravel.
01/01-31/12.
Distance: 500m 3km on the spot.
Remarks: Along the Neckar river, max. 3 nights.

Bad Rappenau 17A2

Weinbrennerstrasse. **GPS:** n49,23517 e9,11396.

30 € 3/pp, child € 2 €1/3minutes Ch (24x)€1/kWh.
Location: Comfortable. **Surface:** metalled. 01/01-31/12.
Distance: 1km 50m 1km.
Remarks: Check in at pay-desk of the Therme, therme 400m.

Bad Rappenau 17A2

Autohof Bad Rappenau, A6, Wilhelm-Hauff-Straße 43, Fürfeld.
GPS: n49,21043 e9,06927.
15 € 10, free for clients ChWC. **Location:** Motorway, simple. **Surface:** metalled. 01/01-31/12.
Distance: 300m on the spot on the spot.
Remarks: Breakfest-service.

Bad Säckingen 19H2

Reisemobilplatz Am Rheinufer, Ausstrasse.
GPS: n47,54903 e7,94765.

40 € 12/24h, >7,8m € 16/24h €0,50/100liter €0,20 Ch (39x) WC. **Location:** Urban, comfortable, quiet. **Surface:** gravel.
01/01-31/12 beginning Mar, end Oct.
Distance: 300m 6km 50m on the spot on the spot.
Remarks: Several offers, i.e. free public transport.

Tourist information Bad Säckingen:
Nachtwächterführungen. Evening tour guided by night watch in historical cloths and with lantern. Information and booking: Kurverwaltung. € 5.

Bad Saulgau 20B1

GolfPark Bad Saulgau, Koppelweg 103. **GPS:** n47,97928 e9,48623.

30 € 10, golfers free €1/100liter Ch €1/6h.
Location: Rural, quiet. **Surface:** metalled. 01/03-31/10.
Distance: 4km on the spot 4km.

Bad Saulgau 20B1

Wonhmobilstellplatz Sonnenhof-Therme, Am Schönen Moos.
GPS: n48,01703 e9,48838.

53 € 10 + € 1,50/pp tourist tax €0,50/50liter Ch (69x)€0,50/kWh.
Location: Rural. **Surface:** metalled. 01/01-31/12.
Distance: on the spot on the spot on the spot.
Remarks: Bread-service, discount on access terme.

Bad Schönborn 17A2

Reisemobilhafen WellMobilPark, Kraichgaustraße 16.
GPS: n49,21839 e8,67144.

86 € 9, >10m € 13 €1/100liter Ch (112x)€0,50/kWh €2 €1/h. **Location:** Rural, luxurious. **Surface:** gravel.
01/01-31/12.
Distance: 800m on the spot 1km 200m.
Remarks: Bread-service, swimming pool available.

Bad Schussenried 20B1

Am Zellersee, Zellerseeweg. **GPS:** n48,00160 e9,64724.

10 € 5 + € 1,20/pp tourist tax Ch. **Surface:** asphalted.
01/01-31/12.
Distance: 900m on the spot on the spot.

Bad Schussenried 20B1

Bierkrugmuseum, Wilhelm Schussenstrasse 12.
GPS: n48,00325 e9,65902.

30 free Ch €5,reduction for guests WC. **Location:** Quiet.
Surface: metalled. 01/01-31/12.
Distance: on the spot 150m 250m.
Remarks: Brewery and brewery museum.

Tourist information Bad Schussenried:
Kloster Schussenried. History of the monastry. Easter-Oct 13.30-17.30h.

Bad Teinach 17A3

Untere talstasse 33. **GPS:** n48,68890 e8,69440.

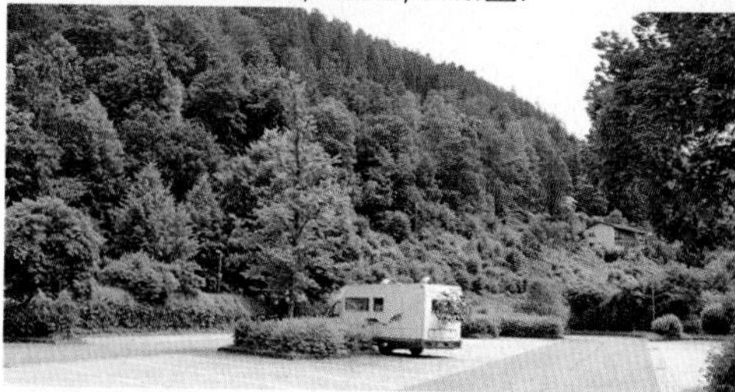

20 free. **Location:** Rural, simple. **Surface:** asphalted.
01/01-31/12.
Distance: 50m 100m 100m on the spot on the spot on the spot.
Remarks: Parking swimming pool, max. 24h.

Bad Teinach 17A3

Stellplatz am Wanderheim, Fronwaldstraße 48.
GPS: n48,69916 e8,69500.
5 free. 01/01-31/12.
Distance: centre 1,2km on the spot 1,3km 1km on the spot on the spot.
Remarks: Max. 8M.

Bad Urach 17B3

Wohnmobilstellplatz Bad Urach, Bäderstraße.
GPS: n48,50060 e9,37713.

26 € 8 €0,50/60liter €0,50 Ch included.
Location: Urban, simple. **Surface:** asphalted. 01/01-31/12.
Distance: on the spot 5km 200m 800m 200m 10km 10km.

Bad Waldsee 20B1

Bauernhof Lott, Mattenhaus 4. **GPS:** n47,95113 e9,75838.

10 € 10, 2 pers.incl, tourist tax € 2/pp Ch (10x)€0,50/kWh WC €4. 01/03-30/11.
Distance: 3,5km 3km 3km 200m 3km.
Remarks: Bread-service.

Bad Waldsee 20B1

Waldsee-Therme, Unterurbacher weg. **GPS:** n47,91441 e9,76047.

40 € 5 + € 2/pp tourist tax €1 €1 Ch €0,50/kWh.
Surface: metalled. 01/01-31/12.
Distance: 1km 1km 1km 500m 1km 500m.
Remarks: Bread-service.

DE

S Bad Wildbad 16H3

Kernerstrasse. **GPS**: n48,74132 e8,54740.

11 € 10 €1/3minutes Ch (16x)€2/8h.
Location: Rural, simple, noisy. **Surface:** asphalted.
01/01-31/12.
Distance: 500m 500m 300m on the spot on the spot on the spot.
Remarks: Max. 3 days, thursday market.

S Bad Wimpfen 17A2

An der Alten Saline 2. **GPS**: n49,23604 e9,15630.

8 € 8, tourist tax excl €1/70liter Ch (8x)€1/12h WC. **Location:** Rural, comfortable, quiet. **Surface:** asphalted.
01/01-31/12.
Distance: 800m.
Remarks: Parking at health resort.

S Bad Wurzach 20C2

Wohnmobilstellplatz Vitalium, Riedhalde, An der Thermalquelle 1.
GPS: n47,91437 e9,90363.

17 € 5,50 + € 1,50/pp tourist tax €0,50 €0,50 Ch included WC. **Location:** Rural, quiet. **Surface:** asphalted.
01/01-31/12.
Distance: 500m 300m 500m.
Remarks: Check in at pay-desk of Vitalum.

S Baden-Baden 16H3

Wohnmobilparkplatz, Hubertusstraße 2, Badenscheunern.
GPS: n48,78193 e8,20388.

28 € 12 €1/100liter Ch (28x)€0,50/kWh.
Location: Urban, comfortable, noisy. **Surface:** metalled.
01/01-31/12.
Distance: Baden-Baden 4km 1km 100m 150m on the spot on the spot on the spot.
Remarks: Max. 4 days, video surveillance.

S Baiersbronn 16H3

Schelklewiesen, Neumühleweg/Lochweg.
GPS: n48,51016 e8,37272.

15 € 10, tourist tax incl €1/80liter Ch (12x)€0,50/kWh.
Location: Rural, simple, quiet. **Surface:** metalled.
01/01-31/12.
Distance: 300m on the spot 100m 200m on the spot on the spot.
Remarks: Max. 8M.

S Balingen 20A1

Wohnmobilstellplatz an der Eyach, Heinzlerstrasse.
GPS: n48,27024 e8,85300.

10 free €1 Ch (8x)€0,50/kWh. **Location:** Urban, simple.
Surface: asphalted. 01/01-31/12.
Distance: on the spot 500m 300m 300m.
Remarks: Max. 4 days.

Benningen am Neckar 17A2

Parkplatz Gemeindehalle, Max-Eyth Strasse.
GPS: n48,94574 e9,23363.

4 free. **Location:** Rural, simple. **Surface:** metalled.
01/01-31/12.
Distance: on the spot 50m 1km.

S Bernau im Schwarzwald 19H2

Sportzentrum Spitzenberg, Sportplatzstraße.
GPS: n47,80614 e8,02803.

15 16/04-30/09 free, 01/10-15/04 € 3,50 + € 2,20/pp tourist tax €1/100liter Ch €1/8h. **Location:** Rural, simple, quiet.
Surface: grassy/gravel. 01/01-31/12.
Distance: 500m 1km 500m.
Remarks: Pay at tourist office.

S Besigheim 17A2

Wohnmobilstellplatz bei der Minigolfanlage, Auf dem Kies 32.
GPS: n48,99771 e9,14863.

9 € 5 €1/50liter Ch (6x)€0,50/kWh. **Location:** Rural, comfortable, quiet. **Surface:** metalled. 01/01-31/12.
Distance: 500m 10km 500m 200m 500m 200m on the spot on the spot.
Remarks: After 2 nights € 20/night.

S Beuren 17B3

Panorama Therme, Goethestraße. **GPS**: n48,56621 e9,39944.

4 € 6 €1/3kWh. **Location:** Urban, simple. **Surface:** metalled.
01/01-31/12.
Distance: 500m on the spot 500m 100m.

Beuron 20A1

Kloster Beuron, Abteistraße. **GPS**: n48,05306 e8,96704.

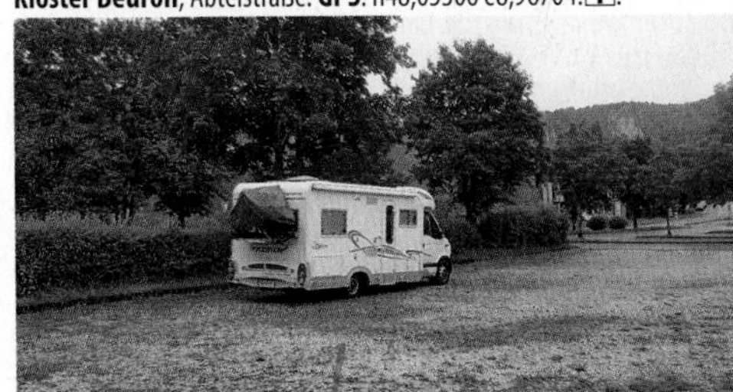

± 4 free. **Location:** Urban, simple. **Surface:** gravel.
01/01-31/12.
Distance: on the spot.
Remarks: Parking monastery.

S Beuron 20A1

Besi-Kanu-Sport, Bahnhofstrasse 29. **GPS**: n48,08597 e9,09559.

10 € 5 Ch WC included. **Location:** Rural, simple.
Surface: gravel. 01/01-31/12.
Distance: 1km 200m 5km.
Remarks: Canoe rental.

S Biberach/Riss 20B1

Rißstraße. **GPS**: n48,10401 e9,79582.

18 € 5 Ch included €0,50/kWh. **Surface:** gravel.
01/01-31/12 service: 01/11-28/02.
Distance: 700m 300m Donau-Bodensee-Radweg.
Remarks: Max. 3 days.

DE

Bietigheim-Bissingen 17A2

Wohnmobilstellplatz an der Enz, Mühlwiesenstrasse.
GPS: n48,96110 e9,13329.

9 €5 €0,50/80liter Ch (8x)€0,50/kWh.
Location: Urban. **Surface:** metalled.
01/01-31/12.
Distance: 200m 1km 1km 100m 100m 100m.
Remarks: Max. 4 days, max. 8M, check in at Lama Bar.

Blaubeuren 17B3

Parkplatz P6, Dodelweg. **GPS**: n48,41351 e9,79102.

20 €5 €1/5minutes Ch€1. **Surface:** metalled.
01/01-31/12.
Distance: 1km 1km 1km 800m.
Remarks: Parking at swimming pool, max. 2 days.

Blaustein 17B3

Freizeitbad Bad Blau, Boschstraße. **GPS**: n48,41757 e9,91630.
3 free. **Location:** Simple. **Surface:** gravel.
Distance: 6,5km 200m 500m.

Blumberg 19H2

P1, Festplatz, Oberes Ried. **GPS**: n47,83943 e8,54226.

20 €7,50, 01/11-30/04 €6,50 €1/50liter Ch (36x)€1/24h €1,50. **Location:** Comfortable, quiet. **Surface:** gravel/metalled.
01/01-31/12.
Distance: 800m 100m 80m.
Remarks: With payment: KONUS guest card with many advantages.

Blumberg 19H2

P2, Parkplatz Bahnhof Zollhaus, Achdorf.
GPS: n47,83767 e8,55777.

5 €7,50, 01/11-30/04 €6,50 . **Location:** Urban, noisy.
Surface: gravel. 01/01-31/12.
Distance: 1,5km.

Blumberg 19H2

P3, Achdorfer Tal. **GPS**: n47,83528 e8,49833.

10 €7,50, 01/11-30/04 €6,50 €1 Ch (12x)€1/night,winter €1,50. **Location:** Rural, simple, isolated, quiet. **Surface:** gravel.
01/01-31/12.
Distance: 4km.
Remarks: With payment: KONUS guest card with many advantages, caution key €10 (connection electricity), service at Kläranlage 800m.

Böblingen 17A3

Im Zimmerschlag. **GPS**: n48,67000 e9,03272.

4 free Chfree. **Location:** Urban, simple.
Surface: grasstiles/metalled. 01/01-31/10.
Distance: 3km 100m 1,5km on the spot.

Bodman-Ludwigshafen 20A2

Am Sportplatz. **GPS**: n47,82369 e9,05153.

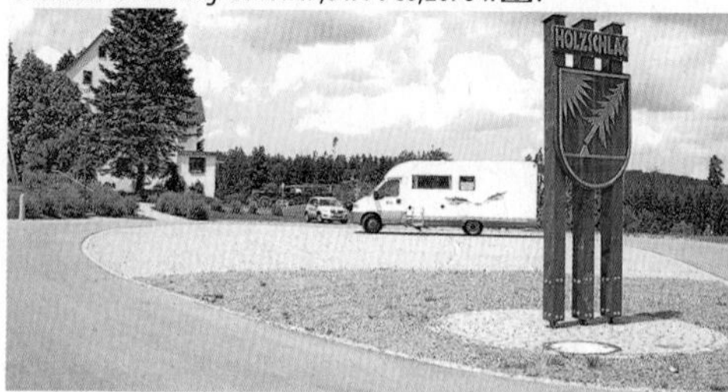

20 €8 Ch (4x)€2. **Location:** Simple.
Surface: grassy/metalled. 01/01-31/12.
Distance: 1km 3,2km 1,4km.

Bonndorf 19H2

Schwimmbad, Ob dem Tal 1. **GPS**: n47,81644 e8,33969.
€7,50 + €1/pp tourist tax WC on demand.
Distance: 450m 500m.
Remarks: Check in at swimming pool.

Bonndorf 19H2

Wohnmobilstellplatz Holzschlag, Schulstraße/Bonndorfer Straße, Bonndorf-Holzschlag. **GPS**: n47,84970 e8,26784.

€5, tourist tax €0,80/pp Chincluded. **Location:** Simple, noisy.
Distance: 100m.

Bönnigheim 17A2

Mineralfreibad Bönnigheim, Bachstrasse 40.
GPS: n49,03910 e9,08439.

4 free . **Location:** Rural, simple. **Surface:** grasstiles/metalled.
01/01-31/12.
Distance: 500m 500m 1km.
Remarks: Caution key €10 (water).

Bopfingen 17C3

Gasthof zum Bären, Nördlinger Straße 3.
GPS: n48,85715 e10,35508.

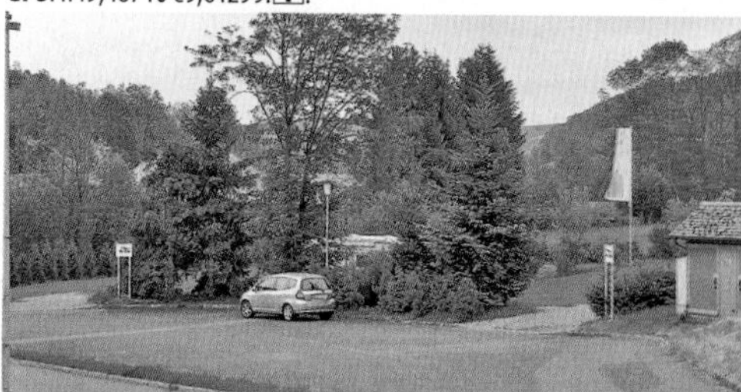

6 €6 €1 €1 Ch €1. **Surface:** asphalted. 01/01-31/12.
Distance: on the spot 16km on the spot 100m.
Remarks: Free with a meal.

Boxberg 17B1

Gasthof Hagenmühle, Uiffinger strasse 74.
GPS: n49,48710 e9,61299.

12 €5 (12x)€2,50. **Location:** Rural, simple.
Surface: grassy/gravel. 01/01-31/12 Restaurant: Mo.
Distance: 2km trout pond on the spot 1km 200m.

Brackenheim 17A2

Weingut und Besenwirtschaft 'Zum Alten Pflug', Seebergweg.
GPS: n49,10261 e9,04994.

3 €6, free for clients Ch (3x)€2 WC €2.
Surface: metalled. 01/01-31/12.
Distance: 3km 3km.
Remarks: Sunday on demand.

Brackenheim 17A2

Weingut Winkler, Stockheimer strasse 13.
GPS: n49,08001 e9,06270.

3 €5 Chincluded .
Location: Rural, simple. **Surface:** grassy/metalled.
01/01-31/12.

DE

Distance: on the spot 10km 10km 300m 1km 300m.
Remarks: When buying wine 1 night free.

S Breisach/Rhein 19G1

Wohnmobil-Parkplatz, Josef-Buebstrasse.
GPS: n48,02944 e7,57576.

80 free 8-20h, € 6/night, 2 nights € 10, 3 nights € 13, winter free €1/100liter €1 Ch€1. **Location:** Urban, simple.
Surface: asphalted. 01/01-31/12 Other parking in case of festivities.
Distance: 300m on the spot on the spot 300m 1,5km.
Remarks: Ground of wine festival, bread-service.

Breisach/Rhein 19G1

Restaurant Am Rhein, Hafenstrasse 11. **GPS**: n48,04292 e7,57378.

5 free.
Location: Simple. **Surface:** metalled. 01/01-31/12.
Distance: 2km on the spot 500m.
Remarks: Along the Rhine river, guests only.

Tourist information Breisach/Rhein:
Weinfest Kaiserstuhl Tuniberg. Wine festivals. end Aug.

S Bretten 17A2

Reisemobil-Stellplatz Bretten, Willi-Hesselbacher-Weg.
GPS: n49,02980 e8,71914.

4 free €1/100liter €1/10h. **Location:** Urban, comfortable.
Surface: metalled. 01/01-31/12.
Distance: city centre 1,5km.
Remarks: Sports centre, max. 2 days.

Bruchsal 16H2

Stellplatz am Sportzentrum, Giesgrabenweg.
GPS: n49,13227 e8,58981.

2 free. **Location:** Urban, simple, central. **Surface:** metalled.
01/01-31/12.
Distance: 1km 4km 100m 1km on the spot on the spot on the spot.
Remarks: At sports centre, max. 2 days.

S Buchen/Odenwald 17A1

Wohnmobilhafen Morretal, Mühltalstraße. **GPS**: n49,52888 e9,31020.

12 € 5/24h, 3 days € 20 €1/100liter Chincluded (12x)€0,50/kWh WC €0,20 €3/day. **Location:** Rural, comfortable, quiet. **Surface:** grassy. 01/01-31/12.
Distance: 800m on the spot. **Remarks:** Parking Waldbad, use sanitary only during opening hours swimming pool.

S Buchenbach 19H2

Wanglerhof, Vogtweg 1. **GPS**: n47,96820 e7,99269.

10 € 12 Ch (10x)includedstay €2.
Location: Rural, simple, quiet. **Surface:** grassy.
01/01-31/12.
Distance: 1km 100m 1km.

S Bühl 16H3

Wohnmobilstellplatz am SchwarzwaldbadS, Ludwig-Jahn-strasse 8.
GPS: n48,68862 e8,12995.

20 € 5 €2/100liter Ch . **Location:** Urban, simple, noisy.
Surface: gravel/metalled. 01/01-31/12.
Distance: 1km 6km 500m 1km on the spot on the spot.
Remarks: Bread-service.

S Burkheim 19G1

Am Kirchberg. **GPS**: n48,10226 e7,59656.

14 free free. **Location:** Rural, simple, quiet. **Surface:** grasstiles.
01/01-31/12.
Distance: 500m on the spot on the spot.

S Calw 17A3

Wohnmobilstellplatz Am Alten Bahnhof, Bahnhofstrasse.
GPS: n48,70592 e8,73808.

6 free €1/80liter €1 Ch€1 (4x)€0,50/7kWh.
Location: Rural, simple, noisy. **Surface:** asphalted.
01/01-31/12.
Distance: 1km 100m 200m on the spot on the spot.

Cleebronn/Tripsdrill 17A2

Erlebnispark Tripsdrill. **GPS**: n49,03102 e9,05096.

100 free.
Location: Rural, isolated, quiet.
Surface: grassy.
28/03/2015-08/11/2015.
Distance: 1km on the spot 3km 400m.
Remarks: Max. 3 days.

Tourist information Cleebronn/Tripsdrill:
Erlebnispark Tripsdrill. Amusement park. 19/03-06/11 9-18h.

S Crailsheim 17C2

Autohof Euro Rastpark, Marco-Polo-Straße 1, Satteldorf.
GPS: n49,18146 e10,06889.
10 € 10 . **Surface:** metalled. 01/01-31/12.
Distance: 600m on the spot.

S Dettenheim 16H2

Kartbahn Liedolsheim, Kartbahnring 1. **GPS**: n49,14326 e8,43118.

180 free Ch (10x)€5/day WC €2,50.
Location: Rural, simple, isolated. **Surface:** grassy/metalled.
01/01-31/12.
Distance: 3km 2km 2km on the spot 5km.
Remarks: Parking at Karting.

S Donaueschingen 20A2

Am Schlosspark, Prinz Fritz Allee. **GPS**: n47,94746 e8,51183.

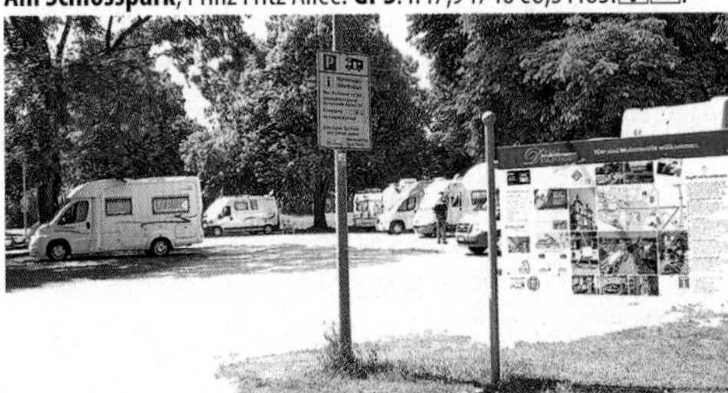

20 free €1/50liter (14x)€0,50/kWh. **Location:** Rural, simple, quiet. **Surface:** grassy. 01/01-31/12.
Distance: 1,5km Danube Bike Trail on the spot.
Remarks: Max. 2 days, service 300m.

S Donaueschingen 20A2

Kläranlage, Haberfeld. **GPS**: n47,94931 e8,52209.
€1/50liter Ch.
01/01-31/12.

Tourist information Donaueschingen:
Tourismus- und Sportamt, Karlstrasse 58, www.donaueschingen.de. Horse city, named after the source of the River danube.
Der Donau Radweg. Signposted cycle route along the Donau.

S Durbach 16H3

Grol/Festplatz, Almstrasse. **GPS**: n48,49407 e8,01105.

DE

15 € 6 €1/100liter (8x)€1/8h. **Location:** Rural, simple.
Surface: gravel. 01/01-31/12 festivities.
Distance: 500m 10km on the spot on the spot 50m on the spot.

Durbach 16H3

Wohnmobilstellplatz Ebersweier, Wiesenstraße, Ebersweier.
GPS: n48,50122 e7,98940.

6 € 6 €1/80liter Ch (6x)€1/4h. **Location:** Rural, simple.
Surface: grasstiles. 01/01-31/12.
Distance: 500m 10km 750m 200m on the spot.

Eberbach 17A1

Wohnmobilstellplatz In der Au, In der Au.
GPS: n49,46162 e8,97812.

7 free (6x)€1/2kWh WC. **Location:** Simple, isolated.
Surface: gravel. 01/01-31/12.
Distance: 1km on the spot.
Remarks: At swimming pool, max. 2 nights.

Eberbach 17A1

Wohnmobilstellplatz Neckarlauer, B37, Uferstrasse.
GPS: n49,46012 e8,98652.

7 free. **Location:** Central. **Surface:** metalled.
01/01-31/12 high water.
Distance: 300m 300m 500m.

Eberbach 17A1

In der Au. **GPS**: n49,46217 e8,97351.
€1/60liter Ch.

Ebringen 19G2

An der Schönberghalle, Schulstraße 8.
GPS: n47,95639 e7,77667.

3 free. **Location:** Rural, simple, quiet. **Surface:** grasstiles.
01/01-31/12.
Distance: 7,6km on the spot.
Remarks: Max. 2 days, max. 6,5m.

Ehingen 20B1

Wohnmobilstellplatz Ehingen, Am Stadion.
GPS: n48,28053 e9,73571.

10 free €1/50liter Ch (4x)€2/10h free.
Surface: metalled. 01/01-31/12.
Distance: 1km 1km on the spot 500m 10m Danube Bike Trail.

Eichstetten 19G1

Weingut Köbelin, Altweg 131. **GPS**: n48,09510 e7,72057.

5 € 13 Ch included.
Location: Rural, simple, comfortable, isolated, quiet.
Surface: gravel/sand. 01/01-31/12.
Distance: city centre 1,5km 1,5km 1,4km 900m on the spot on the spot.

Eigeltingen 20A2

Landgasthof Mönchhof, Mönchhof. **GPS**: n47,88094 e8,95278.

4 guests free Ch.
Surface: metalled. 01/01-31/12.
Distance: 6km on the spot 4km on the spot.

Eisenbach 19H2

Reisemobilpark Höchstberg. **GPS**: n47,94938 e8,25441.

20 € 8, tourist tax € 1,60/pp €1/100liter Ch (20x) included, only in summer. **Location:** Rural, comfortable, quiet. **Surface:** grassy/gravel. 01/01-31/12.
Distance: on the spot on the spot.
Remarks: Altitude 1033m, at sports park.

Ellwangen 17C2

Maxi-Autohof Ellwangen, Max-Eyth-Strasse 1.
GPS: n48,95628 e10,18319.

15 € 5/night Ch WC against payment.
Location: Motorway. **Surface:** asphalted. 01/01-31/12.
Distance: 3km on the spot 1km.

Emmendingen 19H1

Wohnmobilstellplatz am Sportfeld, Am Sportfeld.
GPS: n48,11869 e7,84154.

30 free €1/80liter Ch. **Location:** Urban, simple.
Surface: asphalted. 01/01-31/12.
Distance: 1km 400m 600m.
Remarks: In front of swimmingpool, max. 3 days.

Endingen am Kaiserstuhl 19G1

P2 Stadthalle, Freiburger Weg. **GPS**: n48,13830 e7,70321.

20 free. **Location:** Urban, simple, central. **Surface:** concrete.
01/01-31/12.
Distance: 200m 200m.

Eppingen 17A2

Wohnmobilhalt am Freibad, Am Altstadring.
GPS: n49,13793 e8,91402.

4 free €1/80liter €1 Ch €1 (4x)€1. **Location:** Rural, comfortable. **Surface:** metalled. 01/01-31/12.
Distance: 500m on the spot 300m 500m on the spot on the spot.

Esslingen am Neckar 17B3

Äußerer Burgplatz, Mülbergerstraße. **GPS**: n48,74713 e9,31064.

2 free. **Location:** Urban, simple. **Surface:** asphalted.
01/01-31/12.
Distance: 1km 1km on the spot 1km 300m.
Remarks: Max. 48h.

DE

S Ettenheim 19G1

Ernst Caravan und Freizeit Center, Rudolf Hell Straße 32-44.
GPS: n48,27431 e7,78161.

30 free €1 €1 Ch€1 (12x)€0,50/kWh.
Location: Motorway, simple. **Surface:** concrete. 01/01-31/12.
Distance: 500m.
Remarks: Motorhome dealer, accessory shop, repairs.

S Ettlingen 16H3

Wohnmobilstellplatz Am Freibad, Schöllbronner strasse.
GPS: n48,93561 e8,41747.

14 free €2/5minutes Ch (4x)€2/8h. **Location:** Urban, simple. **Surface:** asphalted. 01/01-31/12.
Distance: 100m 3,3km 100m 700m on the spot on the spot on the spot.
Remarks: Parking swimming pool, max. 48h, market Wednesday and Saturday.

S Filderstadt 17A3

Parkplatz P2, Tübinger Strasse 40. **GPS**: n48,67347 e9,21456.

8 € 7/24h €1/80liter Ch (8x)€0,50/kWh,16Amp.
Location: Urban. **Surface:** gravel. 01/01-31/12.
Distance: 500m 500m 500m 500m.

S Freiburg 19H1

Reisemobilplatz Freiburg, Bissierstrasse / Am Eschholzpark.
GPS: n47,99915 e7,82643.

60 € 9, motorhome >7m + € 1,00/1m €1/100liter Ch (20x)€1/kWh free. **Location:** Urban, comfortable.
Surface: asphalted/gravel.
01/01-31/12.
Distance: Old city centre 1,5km 4,3km 450m.
Remarks: Max. 72h, green zone: environmental badge obligatory.

S Freiburg 19H1

WV-Südcaravan, Hanferstrasse 30, Hochdorf.
GPS: n48,04146 e7,81473.

6 free €1/80liter Ch€2 €5/day. **Location:** Urban, simple.
Surface: asphalted/metalled. 01/01-31/12.
Distance: Old city centre 10km 3km 300m 3km.
Remarks: During opening hours.

S Freudenberg 17A1

P. Freudenberg-Süd, Hauptstrasse. **GPS**: n49,74001 e9,31938.

10 € 5/night €1/15minutes Ch (6x)€1/8h,16Amp free.
Location: Rural, comfortable. **Surface:** metalled.
01/01-31/12.
Distance: 50m 20m 20m 300m 500m.

S Friedrichshafen 20B2

Stellplatz Friedrichshafen, Lindauerstrasse 2.
GPS: n47,65025 e9,49597.

20 free, 01/04-31/10 € 12 €1/80liter ChWC .
Surface: asphalted/metalled. 01/01-31/12.
Distance: 200m 200m on the spot.
Remarks: Max. 3 nights, payment only with coins.

Gaggenau 16H3

Badstrasze 15. **GPS**: n48,80786 e8,30275.

4 free. **Location:** Rural, simple. **Surface:** grasstiles/metalled.
01/01-31/12.
Distance: 1,5km 800m on the spot on the spot.
Remarks: Parking spa resort, market Saturday.

S Gaildorf 17B2

Bleichgärten. **GPS**: n49,00224 e9,76587.

7 free Ch (4x)free,16Amp. **Location:** Simple.
Surface: metalled. 01/01-31/12.
Distance: 500m 400m 500m 500m.
Remarks: Max. 3 days.

Gailingen am Hochrhein 20A2

Rheinuferpark, Strandweg. **GPS**: n47,69051 e8,75621.
20 € 15. 01/04-31/10.
Distance: 1km on the spot.

S Gammertingen 20A1

Freizeitanlage an der Lauchert, Reutlingerstrasse.
GPS: n48,25611 e9,21056.

8 free (6x)€1/4h WC. **Location:** Simple. **Surface:** grassy/gravel.
01/01-31/12.
Distance: 1km on the spot on the spot 1km 700m on the spot.

S Geisingen 20A2

Reisemobilstellplatz Geisingen, Am Espen 8.
GPS: n47,92016 e8,65153.
37 € 9 €1/80liter Chincluded (37x)€2/4kWh.
Surface: gravel.
01/01-31/12.
Distance: 200m 1,5km 200m 200m 500m 500m 200m 100m.

DE

S Gernsbach 16H3

Am Schwimmbad 1, Oberstrot. **GPS**: n48,74239 e8,34186.

10 free (4x)€1/8h. **Location:** Rural, simple, quiet. **Surface:** grassy. 01/01-31/12.
Distance: 200m 200m on the spot on the spot.
Remarks: At swimming pool.

S Gernsbach 16H3

Parkplatz Murginsel, Schlossstrasse/Klingelstrasse.
GPS: n48,75934 e8,33900.

8 €5 €1/100liter Ch (8x)€1/12h WC. **Location:** Rural, simple. **Surface:** asphalted. 01/01-31/12.
Distance: 500m on the spot 500m 1km on the spot on the spot on the spot.
Remarks: Max. 7 days.

S Giengen 17C3

Reisemobilstation Charlottenhöhle, Lonetalstrasse 60, Hürben.
GPS: n48,58412 e10,21203.

15 € 7/night €2 Ch (6x)€2/12h,16Amp WC €2. **Location:** Rural, quiet. **Surface:** gravel. 01/01-31/12.
Remarks: At prehistoric cave, coins at Hölenhaus.

Giengen 17C3

Am Schießberg, Auf dem Schießberg. **GPS**: n48,62975 e10,25159.

8 free. **Location:** Simple. **Surface:** gravel. 01/01-31/12.
Distance: 1,5km 4,3km 1,5km 1,5km.

Tourist information Giengen:
Charlottenhöhle. Caves. 01/04-31/10 8.30-11.30 and 13.30-17h, Su/holidays 9-16.30h.

S Göppingen 17B3

Parkplatz P1, An der EWS-Arena, Lorcherstrasse.
GPS: n48,71176 e9,64816.

6 free €1/60liter Ch. **Location:** Urban. **Surface:** asphalted. 01/01-31/12.
Distance: 1km 1km 1km.
Remarks: Max. 2 nights.

S Grossbottwar 17B2

Winzerhäuser Tal, In den Frauengärten.
GPS: n49,00363 e9,28739.

5 € 10 Ch €1/2kWh.
Surface: metalled. 01/01-31/12.
Distance: 400m 400m 200m.
Remarks: At sports park, max. 5 days.

Gschwend 17B2

Naturbadesee, Frickenhofer Strasse. **GPS**: n48,93603 e9,75143.

3 free.
Location: Rural. **Surface:** forest soil. 01/01-31/12.
Distance: 1,5km.

S Gschwend 17B2

Joosenhofer Sägmühle. **GPS**: n48,92312 e9,77393.
free €1/80liter Ch. **Surface:** asphalted. 01/01-31/12.

S Güglingen 17A2

Kreuzgärten. **GPS**: n49,06492 e8,99489.

10 free €1 Ch. **Location:** Rural, simple. **Surface:** metalled. 01/01-31/12.
Distance: 700m 500m Aldi-Lidl 500m on the spot on the spot.
Remarks: At swimming pool, max. 5 nights.

S Haigerloch 20A1

Wohnmobilstellplatz Haigerloch, Weildorfer Kreuz 1.
GPS: n48,36875 e8,79384.

10 free €1/60liter Ch (10x)€1/8h. **Location:** Urban, simple. **Surface:** asphalted. 01/01-31/12.
Distance: 300m on the spot.
Remarks: Max. 4 days.

S Hardheim 17B1

Am Alten Bahnhof, Bretzinger Straße. **GPS**: n49,60245 e9,47126.

12 free €1/80liter Chfree (8x)€1/2kWh.
Location: Rural, comfortable, noisy. **Surface:** gravel. 01/01-31/12.
Distance: 1km 1km 1km.

Haslach/Kinzigtal 19H1

Eichenbachsporthalle, Strickerweg. **GPS**: n48,27854 e8,07968.

10 free. **Location:** Simple. **Surface:** metalled. 01/01-31/12.
Distance: 500m 300m.
Remarks: At gymnasium, at swimming pool.

Haslach/Kinzigtal 19H1

Waldseeparkplatz, Waldseeweg. **GPS**: n48,27161 e8,09148.

10 free. **Location:** Rural, simple. **Surface:** asphalted. 01/01-31/12.
Distance: 1km 200m 1km.

Haslach/Kinzigtal 19H1

Wanderparkplatz Klosterplatz, Klosterstraße 1.
GPS: n48,27572 e8,08509.

10 free. **Location:** Urban, simple. **Surface:** concrete. 01/01-31/12.
Distance: 50m 150m 500m 100m on the spot.
Remarks: At tourist office.

S Hausach 19H1

Waldstadion, Waldstraße. **GPS**: n48,28058 e8,17829.

DE

4 free WC. **Location:** Rural, simple, simple, quiet, noisy. **Surface:** gravel/sand. 01/01-31/12. **Distance:** 500m 100m on the spot.

Hausach 19H1

Badepark, Schanze 3. **GPS**: n48,28620 e8,16589.

6 free. **Location:** Rural, simple. **Surface:** concrete. 01/01-31/12. **Distance:** on the spot 500m on the spot on the spot. **Remarks:** Nearby swimming pool.

Hechingen 20A1

Freizeitanlage Domäne Areal, Brielhof 1. **GPS**: n48,33773 e8,94966.

18 € 18 included. **Location:** Simple. **Surface:** metalled. 01/01-31/12. **Distance:** 2km 200m on the spot. **Remarks:** Discount at restaurants and Golf Park.

Hechingen 20A1

Burg Hohenzollern, K 7110. **GPS**: n48,32579 e8,96404.

3 € 4. **Location:** Rural, simple. **Surface:** asphalted. **Distance:** Imbiss on the spot.

Hechingen 20A1

Zollernalbcamping, Niederhechingerstrasse. **GPS**: n48,35797 e8,96093.

20 € 10 €1 Ch€1 €1/kWh WC€3 €2,50. **Location:** Simple. **Surface:** metalled. 01/01-31/12 sanitary building: 01/11-01/04. **Distance:** 2km 500m on the spot on the spot. **Remarks:** Waste dump € 2/day.

Heidenheim 17C3

In den Seewiesen. **GPS**: n48,69455 e10,16410.

22 € 2/day €1/70liter €1 Ch (18x)€0,50/kWh,16Amp. **Location:** Rural, simple. **Surface:** asphalted/gravel. 01/01-31/12. **Distance:** city centre 3km 5km 1km.

Heilbronn 17A2

Wertwiesenpark, Neckarhalde. **GPS**: n49,13047 e9,20469.

20 free €1/100liter Ch (12x)€0,50/kWh. **Location:** Comfortable. **Surface:** metalled. 01/01-31/12. **Distance:** 2km 7km 100m 500m.

Heiligenberg 20B2

Sennerei Schläge, Betenbrunner strasse. **GPS**: n47,81892 e9,31445.

10 € 5/16-09h Ch. **Surface:** grassy/metalled. 01/01-31/12. **Distance:** 200m 300m 300m 200m bakery 200m on the spot. **Remarks:** Max. 2 nights.

Herbrechtingen 17C3

P7 Eselstalparkplatz, Baumschulenweg. **GPS**: n48,61758 e10,17411.

15 € 7 €2 Ch €2/24h. **Location:** Rural, quiet. **Surface:** asphalted. 01/01-31/12. **Remarks:** Check in at Hölenhaus.

Herrenberg 17A3

P Stadthalle, Stadthallenstrasse. **GPS**: n48,59832 e8,86943. 5 free €1 €1. **Location:** Simple, noisy. 01/01-31/12. **Distance:** 300m 100m 50m.

Hessigheim 17A2

Fasanenhof, Römerweg 1. **GPS**: n49,00939 e9,18877. 15 € 5 . **Location:** Rural, simple. 01/01-31/12. **Distance:** 3,5km on the spot shop with farm products on the spot on the spot. **Remarks:** Farm/restaurant/Biergarten/shop.

Hessigheim 17A2

Felsengarten Kellerei Besigheim e.G., Am Felsengarten 1. **GPS**: n48,99612 e9,18068.

5 guests free . **Surface:** asphalted. 01/01-31/12. **Distance:** 1km on the spot 1km. **Remarks:** Max. 2 nights.

Heubach 17B3

Am Freibad, Mögglinger Strasse. **GPS**: n48,79726 e9,93763.

6 € 6 €1/90liter Ch€0,50 (6x)€1/kWh. **Surface:** grasstiles. 01/01-31/12. **Distance:** 200m Lidl 400m.

Hinterzarten 19H2

Bahnhofstraße. **GPS**: n47,90441 e8,10996. free. **Surface:** grassy. 01/01-31/12. **Distance:** 300m 300m. **Remarks:** At fire-station, max. 1 night.

Höchenschwand 19H2

Natursportzentrum. **GPS**: n47,73652 e8,15990.

12 € 8 Ch (12x)€1/6h WC €3. **Location:** Rural, comfortable. **Surface:** gravel. 01/01-31/12. **Distance:** 400m 100m 600m on the spot.

Holzmaden 17B3

Urwelt-Museum Hauff, Aichelbergerstrasse 75/90. **GPS**: n48,63482 e9,52771. 6 free. **Surface:** metalled. 01/01-31/12. **Distance:** 3km 2,2km. **Remarks:** Max. 1 night.

Hornberg 19H1

Hotel Schöne Aussicht, Schöne Aussicht 1, Niederwasser. **GPS**: n48,19443 e8,18494. 4 € 8 included . **Distance:** on the spot.

Hüfingen 19H2

Wohnmobil-Stellplatz an der Breg, Bräunlinger Straße. **GPS**: n47,92361 e8,48707.

22 € 6, tourist tax € 1/pp €1,20/100liter Ch €1,20/10h WC €1,20 €3,50/3,50. **Location:** Comfortable, noisy. **Surface:** grassy. 01/01-31/12. **Distance:** 300m 300m. **Remarks:** Check in on arrival, bread-service, thursday market.

DE

Hülben 17B3

Phoenix Wohnmobihafen, Kaltentalstrasse.
GPS: n48,52620 e9,41227.

10 free €0,50/80liter Ch (6x)€0,50/kWh. **Location:** Rural, simple. **Surface:** gravel. 01/01-31/12.
Distance: 400m 400m 500m Vordere-Alb-Radweg on the spot on the spot.
Remarks: Max. 4 days.

Ihringen 19G1

Kaiserstuhl Camping, Nachtwaid 5. **GPS**: n48,03083 e7,65778.

6 € 14,60 + tourist tax Ch €1,80/3kWh WC included. **Location:** Rural, comfortable. **Surface:** asphalted/metalled. 31/03-30/10.
Distance: 600m 200m on the spot.

Isny 20C2

Parkplatz An der Untere Mühle, Seidenstrasse 43.
GPS: n47,69457 e10,03780.

16 € 7,50 + € 1,50/pp tourist tax Ch included (8x)€0,50/kWh WC. **Location:** Urban. **Surface:** asphalted/gravel. 01/01-31/12.
Distance: 300m 100m 300m 200m.
Remarks: Max. 2 nights.

Isny 20C2

Caravans Dethleffs, Rangenbergweg. **GPS**: n47,69938 e10,05490.

9 € 5 + € 1,50/pp tourist tax, clients Dethleffs free Ch (9x) included. **Surface:** metalled. 01/01-31/12.
Distance: 1km 1km 1km 1,4km 500m.
Remarks: Max. 3 nights.

Kaisersbach 17B2

Schwaben-Park, Hofwiesen 11, Gmeinweiler.
GPS: n48,90304 e9,65484.

10 free. 01/04-31/10.
Remarks: Inclining pitches.
Tourist information Kaisersbach:
Schwaben-Park. Amusement park. 19/03-06/11 9-18.

Kappelrodeck 16H3

Wohnmobileck am Heidenhof, Grüner Winkel.
GPS: n48,58370 e8,12650.

17 € 5/day, 3 days € 10, 7 days € 20 €1/100liter Ch (8x)€1/2kWh. **Location:** Rural, simple, quiet. **Surface:** gravel/metalled. 01/01-31/12.
Distance: 800m 150m 500m on the spot on the spot.
Remarks: Max. 7 nights.

Karlsruhe 16H2

Am Yachthafen Maxau, Maxau am Rhein.
GPS: n49,03720 e8,30583.

12 free. **Surface:** gravel. 01/01-31/12.
Distance: Karlsruhe 9km on the spot 2km.
Remarks: Along the Rhine river, max. 24h.

Karlsruhe 16H2

Ettlinger Allee. **GPS**: n48,98761 e8,40412.

2 free. **Surface:** asphalted. 01/01-31/12.
Distance: centre 2,5km 400m metro 400m.
Remarks: Max. 24h, small pitches.

Kehl 16G3

Am Wasserturm, Schwimbadstrasse. **GPS**: n48,56350 e7,81400.

40 € 8 €1/80liter Ch (40x)€0,50/kWh. **Location:** Urban, comfortable, quiet. **Surface:** gravel. 01/01-31/12.
Distance: 1km 100m 500m on the spot on the spot on the spot.
Remarks: Max. 3 days, friday market.

Kehl 16G3

Reisemobilstellplatz Hurst, An den Sportanlagen 1, Kehl-Auenheim.
GPS: n48,60653 e7,83146.

18 € 7 €1 Ch (12x)€3 WC €0,50 €1,50.
Location: Rural, simple, quiet. **Surface:** asphalted/grassy. 01/01-31/12.
Distance: 500m on the spot 500m on the spot on the spot.
Remarks: Check in on arrival.

Kehl 16G3

Bürstner-Service-Centrum, Elsässer strasse 80, Kehl-Neumühl.
GPS: n48,57010 e7,84042.

6 free €1/100liter (6x)€1/kWh. **Location:** Rural, simple. **Surface:** asphalted. 01/01-31/12.
Distance: 1km 100m 600m on the spot on the spot.
Remarks: Tuesday and Friday market.

Kenzingen 19G1

Ritter's Weingut, Rossleiteweg 1. **GPS**: n48,18739 e7,78343.

15 € 10, 2 pers.incl, € 2/pp €2,50/day WC included. **Location:** Rural, simple. **Surface:** grassy/gravel. 01/01-31/12.
Distance: 7,5km on the spot.

Kirchberg/Jagst 17B2

Wanderparkplatz Kirchberg-Tal, Hohen Loher Strasse.
GPS: n49,20367 e9,98344.

10 free. **Surface:** gravel. 01/01-31/12.

Kirchheim unter Teck 17B3

Ziegelwasen, Schlierbacher Straße. **GPS**: n48,64998 e9,45919.

DE

3 free.
Location: Urban, simple. **Surface:** asphalted/metalled.
01/01-31/12.
Distance: 500m Altstadt 500m 500m 100m on the spot.
Remarks: Max. 3 days.

Kisslegg 20C2

Wohnmobilhafen Kißlegg, Strandbadweg.
GPS: n47,79602 e9,87950.
24 € 5-7 €1/100liter Ch (5x)€0,50/kWh WC.
Surface: metalled. 01/01-31/12.
Distance: 800m 100m 100m 100m 1km 400m.

Kisslegg 20C2

Familiefreizeitgelände St Anna, Le Pouliguenstrasse.
GPS: n47,79119 e9,87229.

3 free. **Surface:** grassy/metalled. 01/01-31/12.
Distance: 800m 500m 500m.
Remarks: Max. 2 nights.

Kisslegg 20C2

Hotel Sonnenstrahl, Sebastian Kneipp strasse 1.
GPS: n47,78421 e9,87973.
3 free. **Surface:** asphalted/metalled. 01/01-31/12.
Distance: 800m on the spot 800m.
Remarks: Max. 2 nights.

Königschaffhausen 19G1

Wohnmobilgarten im Kirschenhof Schmidt, Königsweg 5.
GPS: n48,14277 e7,66273.

28 € 15 Ch WC included €1 . **Location:** Rural, comfortable. **Surface:** gravel/metalled. 01/01-31/12.
Distance: 500m on the spot on the spot.
Remarks: Wifi in café.

Königsfeld 19H1

Reisemobilpark Bregnitzhof, Buchenberger Strasse 34.
GPS: n48,14028 e8,40583.

21 € 10 €0,10/10liter Ch €1/2kWh.
Location: Rural, luxurious, quiet. **Surface:** gravel. 01/01-31/12.
Distance: 1km 10 min walking.
Remarks: Check in between 14-19h, 18-holes golf course, Saunalandschaft Bregnitzhof.

Konstanz 20B2

Parkplatz Döbele, Döbeleplatz. **GPS**: n47,65794 e9,16933.

12 € 1,40/h, € 14/24h Ch WC included.
Surface: asphalted/metalled. 01/01-31/12.
Distance: 1km 800m 800m 200m 800m 500m.
Remarks: Max. 24h.

Korb 17B3

Reisemobilstellplatz Unterm Korber Kopf, Brucknerstrasse 14.
GPS: n48,84597 e9,35544.

6 € 3 €0,50/80liter Ch (6x)€0,50/kWh. **Surface:** metalled.
01/01-31/12.
Distance: 400m Gaststätte 300m 500m.
Remarks: Coins at restaurant.

Kraichtal 17A2

Gochsheim, Immenstrasse, Gochsheim. **GPS**: n49,10056 e8,74084.

2 free. **Location:** Simple. **Surface:** asphalted.
Distance: 500m.
Remarks: At sports park, small pitches.

Kressbronn 20B2

Wohnmobilstellplatz Tunau, Tunau 4.
GPS: n47,58999 e9,57512.

40 € 21 Ch (40x) WC €1,50/pp included.
Surface: asphalted/grassy. 01/04-31/10.
Distance: 1km 1km 1km on the spot 1km.

Kressbronn 20B2

Gohren am See. **GPS**: n47,58818 e9,56256.
11 € 12 Ch €3/12h WC €1/day.
Surface: grassy/gravel. 01/04-15/10.
Distance: Bodensee.

Külsheim 17B1

Am Schloss Külsheim, Kirchbergweg. **GPS**: n49,67123 e9,52255.

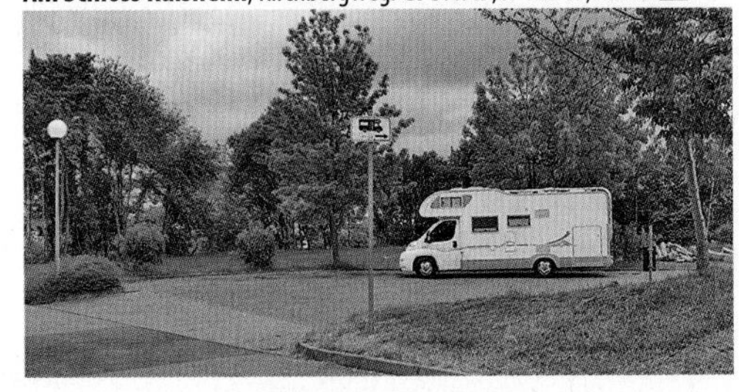

8 free €0,50/80liter Ch (12x)€0,50/kWh free.
Location: Rural. **Surface:** grasstiles.
01/01-31/12 10/09-25/09.
Distance: 300m.

Ladenburg 17A1

Wohnmobilstellplatz Ladenburg, Heidelberger Straße.
GPS: n49,46596 e8,61460.

35 € 10/24h €1/80liter Ch €1/2kWh €1/24h.
Location: Urban, comfortable, central, quiet. **Surface:** grassy.
01/01-31/12.
Distance: Altstadt 500m, Heidelberg 10km 3km 200m 200m.

Lahr/Scharzwald 19H1

Stellplatz Breitmatten, Breitmatten. **GPS**: n48,33954 e7,89885.

14 € 6 €1/100liter Ch €1/kWh. **Surface:** metalled.
01/01-31/12.
Distance: city centre 1,5km 100m 1,2km on the spot on the spot.

Langenau 17C3

Karlstraße. **GPS**: n48,50193 e10,12203.
4 € 5 €0,50/70liter €0,50/kWh. **Location:** Simple.
Surface: metalled. 01/01-31/12.
Distance: 500m 3,2km 300m 1,2km.

Langenbrettach 17B2

Freibad Langenbeutingen, Schwabbacker Strasse 24, Langenbeutingen. **GPS**: n49,21227 e9,40767.

3 free. **Location:** Rural. **Surface:** asphalted.
Remarks: Parking swimming pool.

Langenburg 17B2

Am Freibad, In der Strut 5. **GPS**: n49,24973 e9,86681.
2 free. **Surface:** gravel. 01/01-31/12.
Distance: 1km.
Remarks: Not accessible coming from the west.

Lauchringen 19H2

An der Wutach, Badstrasse. **GPS**: n47,62556 e8,31361.

19 € 8 Ch (16x)€2/24h included. **Location:** Rural, comfortable, quiet. **Surface:** gravel. 01/01-31/12 service: 01/11-01/04.
Distance: on the spot on the spot on the spot.

DE

Remarks: Pay at town hall or swimming pool, caution € 20, key electricity at pool.

Lauda-Königshofen 17B1

Badstrasse, Lauda. **GPS**: n49,55886 e9,70099.

4 free. **Location:** Rural, simple. **Surface:** asphalted. 01/01-31/12.
Distance: 1km 500m.
Remarks: Parking at swimming pool.

Lauda-Königshofen 17B1

Gasthaus Zur Lamm, St. Josefstrasse 30-32, Marbach.
GPS: n49,56568 e9,72834.

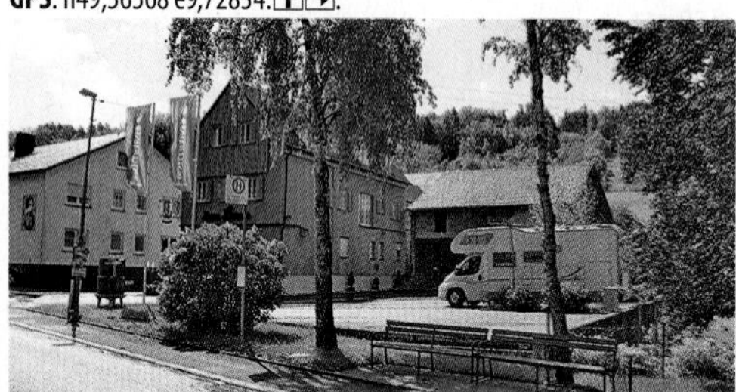

12 € 7/24h (12x)included WC free, at restaurant.
Location: Rural, simple, quiet. **Surface:** asphalted.
01/01-31/12 Restaurant: Mo.
Distance: on the spot on the spot.

Laufenburg 19H2

Laufenburg Baden P6, Andelsbachstraße.
GPS: n47,56585 e8,06677.

6 € 8 €2/5minutes Ch €2 (6x)€0,50/kWh. **Location:** Urban, quiet. **Surface:** concrete. 01/01-31/12.
Remarks: Along the Rhine river.

Laupheim 20B1

Schloß Grosslaupheim, Klaus-Graf-Stauffenberg-Strasse.
GPS: n48,23128 e9,88872.

7 € 8 €0,50 €0,50 Ch €0,50 included. **Location:** Rural.
Surface: grassy. 01/01-31/12.
Distance: on the spot.

Leonberg 17A3

Parkplatz Steinstrasse, Steinstrasse. **GPS**: n48,79705 e9,01751.

5 free, Mo-Fr 8-18h € 2,50. **Surface:** metalled. 01/01-31/12 Sa 5-13h.
Distance: 400m 150m 300m on the spot.

Leutkirch im Allgäu 20C2

Wohnmobilstellplatz Leutkirch, Kemptener Straße 62.
GPS: n47,82228 e10,03939.

14 € 6 €1/100liter Ch €0,50/kWh. **Surface:** grasstiles.
01/01-31/12.
Distance: 1km 300m.

Löffingen 19H2

Waldbad Löffingen, Am Waldbad. **GPS**: n47,90017 e8,33287.

7 € 8, tourist tax € 2/pp (4x)included €0,50, At swimming pool. **Location:** Comfortable. **Surface:** concrete. 01/01-31/12 service 01/10-01/05.
Distance: Swimming pool on the spot.
Remarks: Check in at pay-desk of swimming pool.

Tourist information Löffingen:

Schwarzwaldpark. Game preserve and summer toboggan slide (€ 1.02 a time). Easter-Oct 9-18h.

Malsch 16H3

Gast Caravanning, Daimlerstr. 20b. **GPS**: n48,89079 e8,30747.

6 free €1/80liter Ch. **Location:** Urban, simple.
Surface: asphalted/metalled. 01/01-31/12.
Distance: 7,6km.
Remarks: Motorhome dealer, accessory shop, friday market.

Mannheim/Friedrichsfeld 16H1

Güma Reisemobile, Steinzeugstrasse 21. **GPS**: n49,44570 e8,56780.

8 free Ch WC free.
Location: Simple, noisy. **Surface:** metalled.
01/01-31/12.
Distance: 10km 1km 1km 300m.
Remarks: Max. 3 nights, sanitary use during shop opening hours.

Marbach am Neckar 17A2

Parkplatz Bolzplatz, Poppenweiler/Weimarstrasse.
GPS: n48,93389 e9,26278.

5 € 5 Ch €1/2kWh. **Location:** Rural, simple.
Surface: metalled. 01/01-31/12.
Distance: 1km 6,2km 100m 600m 500m.
Remarks: Max. 2 nights, service: Gruppenklärwerk Häldenmühle, L1100.

Markelsheim 17B1

Engelbergparkplatz, Engelsbergstrasse.
GPS: n49,47537 e9,83474.

2 free. **Location:** Urban. **Surface:** asphalted.
01/01-31/12 week of Whitsuntide.
Distance: 300m 300m.
Remarks: At fire-station, max. 2 nights.

Maulbronn 17A2

Am Kloster, Hilsenbeuerstrasse. **GPS**: n48,99872 e8,80501.
8 free €1 Ch free €0,50/kWh. **Location:** Simple.
Surface: metalled. 01/01-31/12.
Distance: on the spot 50m 250m.
Remarks: Motorhome max. 7m.

Meckenbeuren 20B2

Wohnmobilplatz Besenwirtschaft Georgshof, Pfingstweiderstrasse 10-12/1, Reute. **GPS**: n47,68022 e9,55308.

9 € 9 Ch (9x)€0,50/kWh WC €1. **Surface:** grassy/gravel.
01/01-31/12.
Distance: on the spot Bodensee 5km 200m 100m.

Meersburg/Bodensee 20B2

Wohnmobilparkplatz Ergeten, Daisendorfer Strasse.
GPS: n47,70160 e9,26898.

38 € 12/24h €1/100liter €1 Ch €0,50/kWh WC .
Surface: metalled. 01/01-31/12.
Distance: 1km 100m 50m shuttle to centre.
Remarks: At edge of city, + 2x parking Allmendweg P1 n47.70211, o 9.26983, P2 n47,70159, o 9,27172.

Meißenheim 19G1

Wohnmobilpark Ortenau, Winkelstrasse 36.
GPS: n48,41616 e7,77736.

24+30 € 8 €1/100liter Chincluded (24x)€3,50/24h.
Location: Rural, comfortable. **Surface:** gravel/metalled.
01/01-31/12.
Distance: 500m 200m 800m on the spot on the spot.

Memmingen 20C1

Wohnmobil-stellplatz Memmingen, Colmarer Straße/Hemmerlesstraße. **GPS**: n47,99531 e10,18245.

20 € 1/2h, € 5/24h €0,50/100liter Ch (18x)€0,50/kWh.
Location: Urban, simple. **Surface:** metalled.
01/01-31/12.
Distance: 900m 2,2km 700m Lidl 600m.
Remarks: Max. 2 nights.

Mengen 20B1

Südsee III, Uferweg 25. **GPS**: n48,03117 e9,28265.

50 € 12 €1/80liter Ch (16x)€0,50/kWh WC included .
Location: Rural, comfortable, quiet. **Surface:** gravel.
01/01-31/12.
Distance: 500m on the spot on the spot 500m on the spot.
Remarks: Incl. access Badesee.

Messkirch 20A1

Messplatz P2, Am Stachus. **GPS**: n47,99381 e9,11514.

4 free €1/80liter ChWC. **Location:** Urban, simple.
Surface: metalled. 01/01-31/12, service 01/04-30/09.
Distance: 500m 400m 200m 500m.

Metzingen 17B3

Reisemobilplatz Outletcity Metzingen, Stetterstrasse 4.
GPS: n48,53241 e9,27574.

20 € 10 Chincluded (6x)€3,16Amp. **Location:** Urban, simple. **Surface:** gravel. 01/01-31/12.
Distance: 800m 800m 800m 800m shuttle every 15 min.
Remarks: Money in envelope in mail box.

Michelbach an der Blitz 17B2

Hagenhofweg 8. **GPS**: n49,07133 e9,76993.
2 free €1/100liter €3/24h. **Location:** Rural, quiet.
Surface: metalled. 01/01-31/12.
Distance: 300m 400m 600m 300m on the spot on the spot.

Mosbach 17A2

Wasemweg. **GPS**: n49,36139 e9,14833.

10 free €1/150liter Ch (8x)€1/12h. **Location:** Rural, comfortable, quiet. **Surface:** concrete. 01/01-31/12.
Distance: 800m 800m 600m.
Remarks: Max. 3 nights.

Mössingen 20A1

Wohnmobilstellplatz Firstwald, Firstwaldstraße, Kernstadt.
GPS: n48,41348 e9,06915.

10 free €1/50liter €1 Ch (10x)€0,50/kWh,16Amp.
Location: Urban, simple. **Surface:** grasstiles.
01/01-31/12.
Distance: 1,5km 500m 1km 100m.

Mühlberg 20C1

Ferienhof Musch, Unterer weg 7. **GPS**: n47,98534 e9,98697.

3 € 10, 2 pers.incl Ch (3x)included WC €3 €2,50/day. **Surface:** grassy/metalled. 01/01-31/12.
Distance: 10km 100m 100m 10km 10km.
Remarks: Bread-service.

Müllheim 19G2

Am Friedhof, Am Engelberg, Hügelheim.
GPS: n47,83282 e7,62320.

2 free. **Location:** Rural, simple, isolated, quiet. **Surface:** asphalted.
01/01-31/12.
Distance: 500m 300m 1,5km 400m.
Remarks: At cemetery.

Müllheim 19G2

Am Nüsslegarten, Am Nüsslegarten, Britzingen.
GPS: n47,82891 e7,67336.

2 free. **Location:** Rural, simple, quiet. **Surface:** asphalted.
01/01-31/12.
Distance: centre 700m 250m 250m on the spot on the spot.
Remarks: Next to swimming pool, max. 2 nights.

Müllheim 19G2

Freibad Müllheim, Ziegleweg 7. **GPS**: n47,80237 e7,63403.

3 free. **Location:** Urban, simple. **Surface:** asphalted.
01/01-31/12.
Distance: city centre 1km 200m 500m 600m.
Remarks: Next to swimming pool, max. 2 nights.

Müllheim 19G2

Parkplatz Nußbaumallee, Nußbaumallee.
GPS: n47,80942 e7,62985.

3 free. **Location:** Urban, simple. **Surface:** asphalted.
01/01-31/12.
Remarks: Max. 2 days.

Müllheim 19G2

Restaurant Kreuz, Bundesstrasse 3 Nr. 7. **GPS**: n47,80934 e7,60778.
5 free on demand €5. **Surface:** gravel.
Distance: on the spot on the spot.
Remarks: Breakfast-service.

Müllheim 19G2

Markgräfler Kräuterhof, Im Käppeleacker 3, Hügelheim.
GPS: n47,83237 e7,62045.

4 free. **Location:** Urban, simple. **Surface:** grasstiles.
01/01-31/12.
Distance: 500m 50m 1km 300m.
Remarks: Herbery, herb-Stube.

Münsingen 20B1

Wiesentalstadion, Grafenecker Straße. **GPS**: n48,40939 e9,48580.

DE

18 € 5/24h, 3 days € 12 €1/100liter Ch €1/6h.
Location: Urban, simple. **Surface:** gravel. 01/01-31/12.
Distance: 1km 200m within walking distance on the spot on the spot on the spot.

Murg 19H2

Am Freibad. **GPS**: n47,55196 e8,02403.

15 € 10 €1/100liter €0,50/kWh. **Location:** Rural, comfortable, quiet. **Surface:** metalled. 01/01-31/12.
Distance: 500m on the spot.

Murrhardt 17B2

Parkplatz Festhalle, Kaiser-Ludwig-Straße 25.
GPS: n48,97960 e9,57461.

3 free €1/90liter Ch. **Location:** Rural, simple.
Surface: asphalted. 01/01-31/12.
Distance: 400m 100m.

Nagold 17A3

Wohnmobilhafen am Nagoldtal-Radweg, Am Glockenrain.
GPS: n48,56389 e8,72306.

22 € 3 €1/80liter €1 Ch€1 (12x)€1/kWh.
Location: Rural, simple, quiet. **Surface:** gravel/metalled.
01/01-31/12.
Distance: 1km 25m 900m 400m on the spot on the spot.
Remarks: Market Wednesday and Saturday.

Nagold 17A3

Am Bahnhof, Bahnhofstraße. **GPS**: n48,55791 e8,72748.

4 free. **Location:** Rural, simple, noisy. **Surface:** asphalted.
01/01-31/12.
Distance: 700m 100m on the spot on the spot on the spot.
Remarks: Max. 4 nights, market Wednesday and Saturday.

Nattheim 17C3

Ramensteinbad, Dieselstrasse 22. **GPS**: n48,70261 e10,23745.

4 free Chfree €1/2kWh. **Location:** Urban, quiet.
Surface: metalled. 01/01-31/12 25/04-07/05.
Distance: 500m 300m 200m Lidl.
Remarks: Parking swimming pool, max. 3 days.

Neckarsulm 17A2

Freizeitbad Aquatoll, Reisachmühlweg. **GPS**: n49,18802 e9,24302.

25 free €1/60liter Ch. **Location:** Rural, simple.
Surface: asphalted/gravel. 01/01-31/12.
Distance: 1km 4km 450m 400m.
Remarks: Parking swimming pool, max. 24h.

Neckarwestheim 17A2

Wohnmobilstellplätze Im Bühl, Liebensteiner Strasse.
GPS: n49,04186 e9,18797.

2 free €2 Ch (4x)€2/8h. **Surface:** metalled.
01/01-31/12.
Distance: 500m 200m 500m.
Remarks: From 4th night € 25/night.

Neresheim 17C3

Stellplatz Alter Bahnhof, Dischinger Straße 11.
GPS: n48,75102 e10,33957.

5 free €1 Ch (4x)€1/4h. **Location:** Noisy.
Surface: metalled. 01/01-31/12.
Distance: on the spot 12km on the spot 300m.
Remarks: Service during opening hours.

Neuffen 17B3

Am Schützenhaus, Schützenhausweg. **GPS**: n48,54726 e9,37057.

8 free €2/8minutes Ch (7x)€2/8h. **Location:** Simple.
Surface: asphalted. 01/01-31/12.
Distance: 500m 500m 500m on the spot.

Neuhausen ob Eck 20A1

Wohnmobilstellplatz Auf der Eck, Beim Friedhof.
GPS: n47,97473 e8,92397.

8 voluntary contribution €1 €1 Ch€1 (9x).
Location: Urban, simple. **Surface:** metalled. 01/01-31/12.
Distance: 300m 500m 1km 300m 2km 2km.
Remarks: Max. 4 days.

Neunkirchen 17A2

Festplatz, Zwingenbergerstrasse. **GPS**: n49,38818 e9,01531.

8 free €1/90liter Ch. **Location:** Simple, quiet.
Surface: asphalted. 01/01-31/12.
Distance: 300m 500m.
Remarks: Service next to: Autohaus Weishaupt, Industriestrasse 3 (200m).

Nordheim 17A2

Lauffener Straße. **GPS**: n49,10461 e9,13552.

2 € 5/3 days Ch included. **Location:** Simple.
Surface: asphalted. 01/01-31/12.
Distance: on the spot on the spot.
Remarks: In front of swimmingpool, max. 3 days.

Nordheim 17A2

Müllers Weingut und Weinstube, Im Auerberg 3.
GPS: n49,10236 e9,13810.

2 € 5,with electricity and water € 8 Ch . **Location:** Rural.
Distance: 800m on the spot on the spot on the spot on the spot.

DE

Nordheim 17A2

Rolf Willy Privatkellerei, Schafhohle 26. **GPS**: n49,11212 e9,12845.
4 € 10, guests free (2x).
Distance: 350m.

Nordrach 19H1

Schwarzwald-Panorama Wohnmobilstellplatz, Im Dorf 29.
GPS: n48,39873 e8,07927.

8 free €1/10liter Ch (8x)€1/6h. **Location:** Rural, simple, central. **Surface:** metalled. 01/01-31/12.
Distance: 100m 100m.

Nürtingen 17B3

Stellplatz Plätschwiesen, B313, Plätschwiesen, Oberensingen.
GPS: n48,63645 e9,33051.

12 € 5/24h €1 Ch (8x)€1. **Location:** Urban.
Surface: metalled. 01/01-31/12.
Distance: 1km on the spot 500m.
Remarks: Max. 7 days.

Oberkirch 16H3

Am Renchtalstadion, Renchallee. **GPS**: n48,52972 e8,07250.

38 € 5, € 7/2 days + € 2 tourist tax €1/80liter €1 Ch (30x)€1/2kWh. **Location:** Rural, simple, quiet.
Surface: grassy/gravel. 01/01-31/12 week before and week after 1st weekend Sep.
Distance: 100m 100m 100m on the spot on the spot.

Oberkirch 16H3

Waldparkplatz Schauenburg, Burgstraße 29.
GPS: n48,53812 e8,09452.

4 € 8 (4x)€2 . **Location:** Simple, isolated, quiet.
Surface: grassy/sand. 01/01-31/12.
Distance: 500m.
Remarks: Max. 4 days, € 8 voucher restaurant.

Oberndorf/Neckar 20A1

Neckarhalle, Austrasse 12. **GPS**: n48,28222 e8,58472.

8 free €1/70liter Ch (4x)€1/8h.
Location: Rural, simple, noisy. **Surface:** asphalted. 01/01-31/12.
Distance: 1,5km 300m 200m 50m on the spot on the spot.
Remarks: Max. 3 days.

Oberstenfeld 17B2

Mineralfreibad, Beilsteiner Strasse 100. **GPS**: n49,03160 e9,31890.

4 free. **Surface:** asphalted. 01/01-31/12.

Oberteuringen 20B2

Ferienhof Kramer, St. Georg strasse 8. **GPS**: n47,73948 e9,47278.

8 € 16, 2 pers.incl Ch (8x)€2 WC €4.
Surface: gravel/metalled. 15/04-15/09.
Distance: 2km on the spot 300m 300m.

Offenburg 16H3

Strandbad Gifizsee, Platanenallee 15. **GPS**: n48,45785 e7,93663.

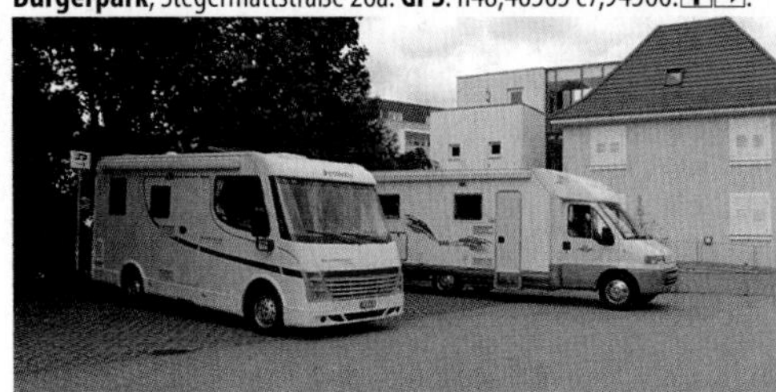

11 € 22, 2 pers.incl €1/5minutes Ch (11x)€1/kWh WC included. **Location:** Rural, simple. **Surface:** grasstiles. 01/04-31/10.
Distance: 2,5km 3,8km 100m on the spot 150m.
Remarks: Bread-service.

Offenburg 16H3

Bürgerpark, Stegermattstraße 26a. **GPS**: n48,46565 e7,94566.

2 € 2. **Location:** Urban, simple, quiet.
Surface: asphalted/metalled. 01/01-31/12.
Distance: 500m 300m.
Remarks: In front of swimmingpool, small pitches.

Offenburg 16H3

Camping Kuhn, Im Drachenacker 4. **GPS**: n48,48039 e7,92776.

10 free €0,50/50liter Ch (8x)free.
Location: Urban, simple. **Surface:** metalled. 01/01-31/12.
Distance: 2km 3,7km 500m.
Remarks: Service during opening hours.

Öhringen 17B2

Hornbergstraße 2, Cappel. **GPS**: n49,19918 e9,52610.
8 € 8 included. 01/01-31/12.
Distance: 100m 100m.
Remarks: At manege, max. 3 days.

Tourist information Öhringen:
RADius. Cycle route, 18km.

Öllingen 17C3

Parking Rathaus, Hauptstrasse. **GPS**: n48,52816 e10,14813.

4 free Ch free. **Surface:** grasstiles. 01/01-31/12.
Distance: 100m 100m on the spot.

Oppenau 16H3

Wohnmobilstellplatz Oppenau, Hauptstrasse.
GPS: n48,47639 e8,16972.

6 € 6 €1/100liter Ch (6x)€1/8h.
Location: Rural, simple, quiet. **Surface:** gravel. 01/01-31/12.
Distance: 300m 150m bakery 300m on the spot on the spot.
Remarks: Use sanitary only during opening hours swimming pool.

Oppenweiler 17B2

Caravanstation, Murrwiesenstraße 15.
GPS: n48,97999 e9,45898.

2 free €1/80liter Ch. **Surface:** asphalted. 01/01-31/12.
Distance: 600m.
Remarks: Max. 2 days.

Ostrach 20B2

Wohnmobilstellplatz Weites Ried, Burgweiler.
GPS: n47,91722 e9,35438.
€ 4 (4x)€1/8h. **Surface:** gravel. 01/01-31/12.
Distance: 5km.

Ottenhöfen im Schwarzwald 16H3

Bauernhof Murhof, Murhof 1. **GPS**: n48,56005 e8,15350.

DE

20 € 10, 2 pers.incl €1/100liter Ch (15x)€0,50/kWh WC €0,50. **Location:** Rural, simple, quiet.
Surface: grassy/metalled. 01/04-31/10.
Distance: 1km 500m 500m on the spot.
Remarks: Swimming pool 200m.

S Pforzheim 17A3

Reisemobilplatz Oststadt am Enzauenpark, Wildersinnstraße.
GPS: n48,89784 e8,72232.

15 free (6x)€1/kWh. **Location:** Urban, simple, noisy.
Surface: metalled. 01/01-31/12.
Distance: 1,5km 200m 100m on the spot on the spot on the spot.
Remarks: Max. 7 days, service 200m.

Pforzheim 17A3

Parkplatz 2&3 Wildpark, Tiefenbronnerstraße.
GPS: n48,87651 e8,71749.
€ 3-5. **Location:** Urban. 01/01-31/12.
Remarks: Max. 1 night.

S Pforzheim 17A3

Hohwiesenweg. **GPS**: n48,89750 e8,72674.
€1/80liter Ch.

S Pfullendorf 20B2

Seepark Linzgau, P-Ost, Bannholzerweg 18. **GPS**: n47,93097 e9,23728.

15 € 4/24h . **Surface:** unpaved. 01/01-31/12.

S Pfullingen 17A3

Wohnmobilplatz Schönbergbad, Klosterstraße.
GPS: n48,45537 e9,22812.

8 free €1/50liter €1 Ch €1/2kWh. **Location:** Urban, simple. **Surface:** grassy. 01/01-31/12.
Distance: 1,5km nearby on the spot.
Remarks: Max. 4 days.

S Radolfzell 20A2

Wohmobilstellplatz in den Herzen, Zeppelinstraße.
GPS: n47,73888 e8,95331.

15 € 8/24h €1/80liter Ch (12x)€0,50/kWh.
Surface: metalled. 01/01-31/12.
Distance: 1km 500m 1km BodenseeRadweg Bodensee-Rundwanderweg.
Remarks: Max. 2 nights.

S Radolfzell 20A2

Wohnmobilstellplatz Halbinsel Mettnau, Strandbadstrasse.
GPS: n47,73784 e8,98007.

12 € 8/24h €1/50liter Ch (6x)€0,50/kWh.
Surface: asphalted. 01/01-31/12.
Distance: 500m 700m 700m 500m 700m 100m.
Remarks: Max. 2 nights.

S Radolfzell 20A2

Campingplatz Böhringer See, Hindenburgstrasse.
GPS: n47,76176 e8,93488.

10 € 10-13 Ch (5x)€0,50/kWh WC €1. **Surface:** metalled. 01/01-31/12.
Distance: 1km on the spot 1km.

S Rastatt 16H3

Stellplatz am Familienbad Alohra, Leopoldring 8.
GPS: n48,85409 e8,19970.

5 € 5 €1/10minutes Ch (8x)€1/6h. **Location:** Urban, simple. **Surface:** metalled. 01/01-31/12.
Distance: 500m 3,8km.
Remarks: Check in at pay-desk of swimming pool, discount at swimming pool and sauna, tuesday, thursday and saturday market 7-13h.

S Ravensburg 20B2

Wohnmobilstellplatz Ravensburg, Mühlbruckstrasse.
GPS: n47,78196 e9,60001.

19 € 8 €1/80liter Ch €0,50/kWh.
Surface: metalled. 01/01-31/12.
Distance: centre 800m 500m 200m 250m Donau-Bodensee Radweg.
Remarks: Max. 3 nights.

Tourist information Ravensburg:

Bodensee-Erlebniskarte. Card gives free access to all boats, telpher carriers, beaches etc. Around the Lake Constance in Germany, Switzerland and Austria. € 72/3 days.

Tourist Information, Kirchstrasse 16. City of the Tore und Turme, gates and towers.

S Rechberghausen 17B3

Sportpark Lindach, Am Desenbach. **GPS**: n48,72405 e9,63594.

6 free €0,50/80liter Ch (6x)€0,50/kWh. **Location:** Rural, simple. **Surface:** grassy. 01/04-01/11.
Distance: 1km 500m 1km 1km 500m on the spot.

S Reichenau 20A2

Zum Sandseele. **GPS**: n47,69887 e9,04711.

12 € 12/24h €1/80liter Ch (8x)€1/2kWh.
Surface: asphalted/metalled. 01/01-31/12.
Distance: 1,5km on the spot on the spot 100m 2km.
Remarks: Max. 1 night.

S Reichental 16H3

Auwiesenstraze. **GPS**: n48,73166 e8,39616.

10 free Ch. **Location:** Simple, isolated, quiet. **Surface:** gravel. 01/01-31/12.
Distance: 1km on the spot.

S Renchen 16H3

Ullenburgstrasse, Ulm. **GPS**: n48,58088 e8,04556.

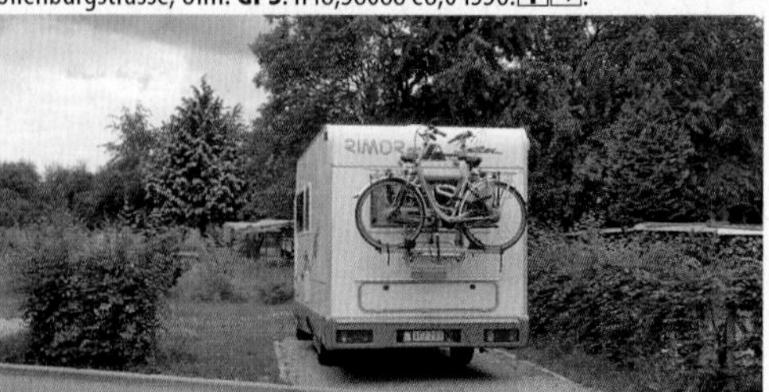

6 € 7 €1/100liter Ch included2kWh. **Location:** Rural, comfortable. 01/01-31/12.
Distance: 300m 300m on the spot on the spot.
Remarks: Friday market.

S Reutlingen 17A3

P&R Parkplatz, Am Südbahnhof/Marktstrasse.
GPS: n48,48280 e9,22982.

DE

3 free Ch. **Location:** Urban, simple, noisy. **Surface:** gravel.
01/01-31/12.
Distance: 3km on the spot on the spot.
Remarks: In front of motorhome dealer Berger, max. 48h.

S Reutlingen 17A3

Sportpark Markwasen, Hermann-Hesse-Straße.
GPS: n48,47536 e9,19377.

10 € 8 €1/80liter Ch (8x)€0,50/kWh. **Location:** Urban, simple. **Surface:** gravel. 01/01-31/12.
Distance: 3km.
Remarks: Public transport included.

S Rheinmünster 16H3

Freizeit Center Oberrhein, Am Campingpark 1.
GPS: n48,77250 e8,04240.

20 € 8/24h €1/80liter Ch (20x)€0,50/kWh.
Location: Rural, comfortable, quiet. **Surface:** grassy.
01/01-31/12.
Distance: on the spot 200m on the spot on the spot.

S Riedlingen 20B1

Stadthalle, Hindenburgstraße. **GPS**: n48,15189 e9,47766.

3 free €1/100liter Ch €1/4h. **Location:** Urban.
Surface: asphalted. 01/01-31/12.
Distance: 300m 200m 100m.
Remarks: Max. 3 days.

S Rielasingen-Worblingen 20A2

Naturbad Aachtal, Herdweg. **GPS**: n47,72127 e8,86332.
6 free, May-Sep € 4,50/day €1/100liter Ch €0,50/kWh 01/05-30/09. **Location:** Rural. **Surface:** gravel. 01/01-31/12.
Distance: 600m.

S Rottenburg/Neckar 17A3

Wohnmobilhafen Neckarufer, Ulmenweg 4.
GPS: n48,47213 e8,95010.

12 € 5 €1/80liter Ch (8x)€0,50/kWh. **Location:** Urban, simple. **Surface:** asphalted. 01/01-31/12.
Distance: 800m 800m 800m 800m on the spot.
Remarks: Max. 3 days.

S Rottweil 20A1

Parkplatz, Stadionstrasse. **GPS**: n48,15556 e8,62861.

16 € 5 €1 Ch (16x)€1/8h. **Location:** Urban, simple.
Surface: gravel. 01/01-31/12.
Distance: 1km 1km 1km 500m.
Remarks: Parking stadium.

S Rust 19G1

Europapark Rust, Europa-Parkstrasse. **GPS**: n48,27189 e7,71745.

200 8-20h € 2/h (max. € 6), 20-8h € 2,50/h (max. € 25) Ch WC 1 included.
Location: Simple. **Surface:** grasstiles.
19/03-06/11, 26/11-08/01 9-18.
Distance: on the spot on the spot.

Tourist information Rust:
Europa-park, Europa-Park-Straße 2. Large amusement and theme park with Europe as theme. 19/03-06/11 9-18, 26/11-08/01 11-19.

S Sankt Blasien 19H2

Rehbach in Menzenschwand, Rehbachweg, Sankt Blasien.
GPS: n47,81306 e8,06933.

20 € 6 Ch (16x)€3/24h.
Location: Rural, simple, quiet. **Surface:** gravel.
01/01-31/12.
Distance: St Blasien 8km bakery 500m on the spot on the spot on the spot.
Remarks: At ski-lift Rehbach, in winter time not always easy to reach.

S Sasbachwalden 16H3

Wohnmobilstellplatz Alde Gott, Talstraße 2.
GPS: n48,61945 e8,12147.

30 € 7/night €1/100liter Ch (20x)€2/24h.
Location: Rural, comfortable, quiet. **Surface:** gravel/metalled.
01/01-31/12.
Distance: centre 300m 9km 9km 100m 250m 250m 100m on the spot on the spot.
Remarks: Waterfall 1km, swimming pool 800m.

S Schiltach 19H1

Stellplatz P1 Lehwiese, Am Hirschen. **GPS**: n48,29111 e8,34250.

10 free (3x). **Location:** Urban, simple, quiet. **Surface:** gravel.
01/01-31/12.
Distance: 200m 50m 50m on the spot on the spot on the spot.
Remarks: Busy parking during the day.

S Schluchsee 19H2

P Aqua Fun, Faulenfürster Straße 18. **GPS**: n47,81569 e8,18113.

22 € 10 + € 2,60/pp tourist tax €1/100liter Ch €1/8h.
Location: Rural, comfortable, central, quiet. **Surface:** asphalted.
01/01-31/12.
Distance: 200m.
Remarks: Max. 1 night.

S Schonach im Schwarzwald 19H1

Parkplatz Obertal, Schwimmbadweg. **GPS**: n48,14573 e8,18872.

10 € 7 €1 €1 Ch (8x)€1/8h. **Location:** Rural, comfortable.
Surface: grasstiles. 01/01-31/12.
Distance: 1km 650m on the spot on the spot on the spot on the spot.
Remarks: Max. 3 nights, coins at tourist info, free entrance swimming pool, ski-lift and public transport.

Schönwald im Schwarzwald 19H1

Skilift Dobel, Franz-Schubert-Straße. **GPS**: n48,09728 e8,19588.
free. 01/01-31/12.
Distance: 600m on the spot on the spot on the spot.

S Schorndorf 17B3

Gmünder Straße 84/1. **GPS**: n48,80539 e9,54187.

DE

7 €5 + €4/pp €2 Ch€2 €0,50/kWh,+€1 WC €2 €2/2 €1.
Location: Simple. **Surface:** metalled. 01/01-31/12.
Distance: 10min.

S Schorndorf 17B3

Oskar Frech SeeBad, Lortzingstraße 56. **GPS**: n48,79645 e9,51410.
5 free €1 €1 Ch€1 €0,50/kWh.
Distance: on the spot.
Remarks: At swimming pool.

S Schramberg 19H1

Bahnhofstraße, B462. **GPS**: n48,23017 e8,38323.

2 free €1/80liter Ch. **Location:** Rural, simple, noisy.
Surface: concrete. 01/01-31/12.
Distance: on the spot 100m 50m 10m on the spot on the spot.
Remarks: Max. 7 days.

S Schwäbisch Gmünd 17B3

Schießtalplatz, Schiesstalstraße. **GPS**: n48,80543 e9,81308.

8 free €1/50liter Ch (8x)€0,50/kWh. **Location:** Rural, simple. **Surface:** gravel. 01/01-31/12.
Distance: 1km 50m 500m.
Remarks: Motorhome < 7m, max. 5 days a month.

Schwäbisch Hall 17B2

Wohnmobilstellplatz Auwiese, Spitalmühlenstraße.
GPS: n49,12218 e9,73473.

7 free. **Surface:** gravel. 01/01-31/12.
Distance: 1,5km 100m.
Remarks: Max. 48h.

S Schwaigern 17A2

Wohnmobilstellplatz Schaigern, Gemminger Straße 91.
GPS: n49,14576 e9,04529.

2 free €1/90liter Ch free. **Surface:** asphalted.
01/01-31/12.
Distance: 1km 300m on the spot on the spot.

S Schwetzingen 16H2

Ketscher Landstrasse. **GPS**: n49,37803 e8,55820.

12 free €3/80liter Ch. **Location:** Simple, noisy.
Surface: grasstiles/metalled. 01/01-31/12.
Distance: 500m on the spot on the spot 100m on the spot on the spot.
Remarks: Max. 3 nights, noisy place.

S Seelbach 19H1

Reisemobil-Wellness-Stellplatz Schwarzwälder Hof, Am Tretenbach.
GPS: n48,30042 e7,94497.

14 €20 €1/90liter Ch (14x)kWh WC .
Location: Rural, comfortable, noisy. **Surface:** grassy.
01/01-31/12.
Distance: 600m 100m.
Remarks: Including access to swimming pool, use sanitary facilities, entrance 1p wellness/sauna.

S Seewald 16H3

P4, L362. **GPS**: n48,55131 e8,49522.

17 free WCfree. **Location:** Rural, simple, quiet. **Surface:** asphalted.
01/01-31/12 service 01/11-31/03.
Distance: 1,5km 25m 600m.

S Sigmaringen 20B1

Wohnmobilplatz Sigmaringen, Georg Zimmerer Straße 4.
GPS: n48,08545 e9,21029.

20 €8 €1/80liter Ch (20x)€1/4h. **Location:** Simple.
Surface: metalled. 01/01-31/12.

Distance: 500m 500m 200m on the spot.

Sindelfingen 17A3

Badezentrum Sindelfingen, Hohenzollernstrasse.
GPS: n48,71993 e9,01779.

10 free. **Location:** Urban, simple. **Surface:** asphalted.
01/01-31/12.
Distance: on the spot on the spot on the spot on the spot.

S Singen 20A2

P Landesgartenschau, Schaffhauserstrasse.
GPS: n47,75992 e8,82766.

20 free Chfree (16x)€1/6h.
Surface: grassy/gravel. 01/01-31/12, service 15/03-15/11.
Distance: 1km on the spot 200m.
Remarks: Max. 72h.

Singen 20A2

Hallenbad, Waldeckstraße 4. **GPS**: n47,76472 e8,84781.
3 free. **Surface:** asphalted. 01/01-31/12.
Distance: 500m.
Remarks: At swimming pool.

S Sinsheim 17A2

Wohnmobilpark Sinsheim, Am Ilvesbach.
GPS: n49,25022 e8,88002.
32 €6 €1/100liter Ch €0,50/kWh included.
Surface: metalled. 01/01-31/12.
Distance: 300m.
Remarks: Discount at swimming pool.

Sternenfels 17A2

Diefenbach, Burrainstrasse, Diefenbach. **GPS**: n49,02440 e8,85535.
3 free. **Location:** Urban, simple. **Surface:** asphalted.
01/01-31/12.
Distance: 100m on the spot.

S Stetten 20B2

Alte Brennerei, Riedetsweilerstrasse 5. **GPS**: n47,69326 e9,29788.

15 €9 €1 €1 Ch (6x)€0,50/kWh. **Surface:** grassy/gravel.
01/01-31/12.
Distance: 300m 2km 2km 300m 300m 300m.

S Stockach/Bodensee 20A2

Reisemobilhafen 'Papiermühle', Johann-Glatt-strasse 3.
GPS: n47,84169 e8,99945.

DE

85 € 10 €0,50/50liter Ch (118x) WC .
Surface: gravel/metalled. 01/01-31/12.
Distance: 1,5km on the spot 700m.

Sulz am Neckar 20A1

Stellplatz Wöhrd, Ludwigstraße. **GPS**: n48,36427 e8,63681.

6 free €1/80liter €1 Ch€1 (6x)€0,50/kWh.
Location: Rural, simple, quiet. **Surface:** concrete.
01/01-31/12.
Distance: 300m 10km 100m 100m on the spot on the spot on the spot.

Sulzburg 19G2

Camping Sulzbachtal, Sonnmatt 4. **GPS**: n47,84773 e7,69868.

10 € 15 + tourist and eco tax Ch (10x)€0,70/kWh WC included. **Location:** Comfortable.
Surface: grassy/gravel. 01/01-31/12.
Distance: 500m on the spot.

Tauberbisschofsheim 17B1

P Freibad, Vittryallee. **GPS**: n49,62155 e9,66632.

3 free ChWCfree €0,50,during opening hours.
Location: Simple. **Surface:** asphalted. 01/01-31/12.
Distance: 500m 300m 100m 500m.
Remarks: Service at Kläranlage ma-do 7-16 uur.

Tettnang 20B2

Loretostrasse. **GPS**: n47,66425 e9,59175.

14 € 5 €1 €1 Ch€1 (8x)€1/8h.
Surface: grassy/metalled. 01/01-31/12.
Distance: 800m 200m 200m 200m.
Remarks: Max. 72h.

Tettnang 20B2

Gutshof Camping Badhütten, Badhütten, Laimnau.
GPS: n47,63370 e9,64668.

70 € 20 €1 Ch €1/3kWh WC €1. **Surface:** grassy.
01/01-31/12.

Titisee 19H2

Camping Bankenhof, Bruderhalde 31a, Hinterzarten.
GPS: n47,88643 e8,13046.

8 € 14, 2 pers incl Ch WC included €3/3 €0,50/h.
Location: Rural, comfortable, quiet.
Surface: gravel/sand.
01/01-31/12.
Distance: 3km Titisee 600m on the spot on the spot 3km.
Remarks: Pay at reception.

Todtmoos 19H2

Jägermatt, Vordertodtmoos. **GPS**: n47,73390 e8,00285.

30 € 5 Chincluded. **Location:** Rural, simple, noisy.
Surface: gravel/metalled. 01/01-31/12.
Distance: 1km 50m.

Triberg im Schwarzwald 19H1

Sommerauer Strasse, Nußberg. **GPS**: n48,13161 e8,25294.

20 free.
Location: Rural, simple. **Surface:** gravel. 01/01-31/12.
Distance: 2km on the spot.

Trochtelfingen 20B1

Eberhard-von Werderberg-Halle, Siemensstrasse.
GPS: n48,30811 e9,23546.

20 € 3 €1/80liter Ch (4x)free,16Amp. **Location:** Urban, simple. **Surface:** gravel. 01/01-31/12.
Distance: Old city centre 500m 500m on the spot.
Remarks: To be paid at town hall.

Trochtelfingen 20B1

Kräuter- und Erlebnisgarten Alb-Gold Nudelfabrik, Grindel 1.
GPS: n48,32838 e9,24001.

4 free. **Location:** Rural, simple, noisy. **Surface:** metalled.
01/01-31/12.
Distance: 3km on the spot on the spot on the spot.

Tuttlingen 20A1

Stellplatz Donaupark, Stuttgarter strasse.
GPS: n47,98490 e8,81316.

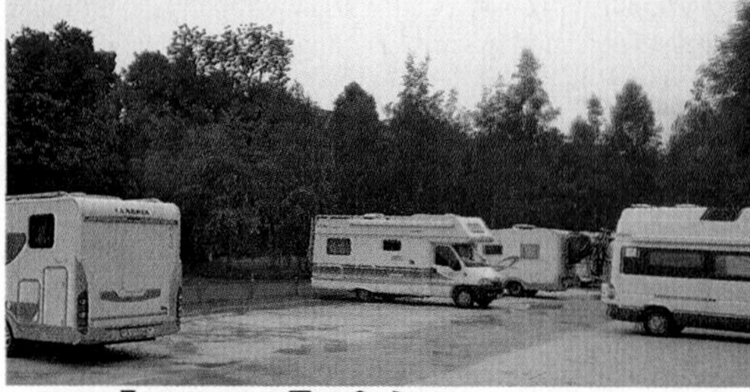

10 free €1/5minutes €1 Ch.
Location: Urban, simple. **Surface:** metalled. 01/01-31/12.
Distance: 500m 500m 500m 500m Donauradweg.
Remarks: Max. 3 nights.

Überlingen 20A2

Reisemobilhafen Überlingen, Kurt-Hahn-strasse.
GPS: n47,77617 e9,15046.

20 € 6-10 €0,50/70liter €0,50 Ch (30x)€0,50/2kWh WC.
Surface: asphalted/gravel. 01/01-31/12.
Distance: 1km 1km 1km 200m 1,5km 200m.
Remarks: Max. 3 days, price incl. bus transport (max. 5 pers) to the city centre.

Uhldingen-Mühlhofen 20B2

Ehbachstrasse. **GPS**: n47,72535 e9,23649.

21 8-18h € 1,50/h, max. € 5, night € 10 €1 €1 ChWC.
Surface: grasstiles/metalled. 01/03-31/10.
Distance: 1km 2km 2km kiosk on the spot 300m.
Remarks: Max. 24h.

Ulm 17C3

P+R Friedrichsau, Wielandstraße 74. **GPS**: n48,40774 e10,00929.

DE

50 free €1 Ch. **Location:** Urban, simple, central.
Surface: metalled. 01/01-31/12.
Distance: 200m on the spot.
Remarks: Max. 3 days, green zone: environmental badge obligatory.

S Ummendorf 20B1

Bräuhaus Ummendorf, Bachstrasse 10.
GPS: n48,06340 e9,83252.

5 free (5x)€3/day WC €3. **Surface:** metalled.
01/01-31/12.
Distance: 300m on the spot 800m 100m.
Remarks: 3 days free stay.

S Unterkirnach 19H1

Reisemobilhafen Am Rathaus, Rathausplatz.
GPS: n48,07719 e8,36707.

17 €11 Ch included,6Amp.
Location: Urban, luxurious, quiet. **Surface:** gravel.
01/01-31/12.
Distance: on the spot 400m 500m 200m 300m 200m 150m 400m.
Remarks: Pay at tourist office, alternative arrangement if full.

S Unterkirnach 19H1

Ackerloch-Grillschopf, Unteres Ackerloch 2.
GPS: n48,08473 e8,36573.

20 €5, tourist tax €2,10/pp Ch WC included.
Location: Rural, simple. **Surface:** unpaved.
Nov.
Distance: 1,5km on the spot on the spot on the spot on the spot.

S Untermünkheim 17B2

Wohnmobilpark Ostertag, Kupfer Straße 20, Übrigshausen.
GPS: n49,17603 e9,71321.

10 €8 €0,50 Ch €0,50 €1. **Location:** Rural, comfortable.
Surface: grassy/gravel. 01/03-30/11.
Distance: 50m.
Remarks: At manege.

Unteröwisheim 17A2

Muhlweg. **GPS:** n49,14306 e8,67250.

2 free.
Location: Simple, quiet. **Surface:** gravel. 01/01-31/12.
Distance: 500m on the spot.

S Uttenweiler 20B1

Naturfreibad, Weiherstrasse. **GPS:** n48,13814 e9,61962.
6 €6 Ch free €0,50/kWh. **Location:** Rural.
Surface: grassy/gravel. 01/05-01/11.
Distance: 600m on the spot 600m.

S Villingen/Schwenningen 20A1

Messegelände, Waldeckweg. **GPS:** n48,05028 e8,54056.

4 free €1 Ch. **Location:** Urban, simple, noisy.
Surface: asphalted. 01/01-31/12.
Distance: 1km 500m.

Vogtsburg im Kaiserstuhl 19G1

Hauptstraße/L115, Oberrotweil. **GPS:** n48,09000 e7,64361.

8 free.
Location: Rural, simple, isolated, quiet. 01/01-31/12.
Distance: 800m 50m on the spot on the spot.
Remarks: At swimming pool.

S Waiblingen 17B3

Parkplatz Hallenbad, An der Talaue. **GPS:** n48,83029 e9,32540.

20 €8/24h €1/80liter Ch (6x)€1/8h WC. **Location:** Urban.
Surface: gravel. 01/01-31/12.
Distance: 500m 500m 50m 300m 600m.
Remarks: Parking swimming pool, max. 3 nights, during congresses special tariff.

S Waldkirch 19H1

Wohnmobilstellplatz Waldkirch, Am Stadtrain.
GPS: n48,09023 e7,95833.

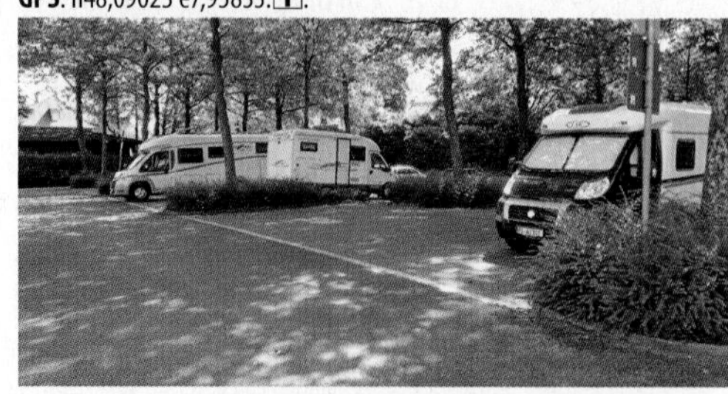

10 free €1/80liter Ch free. **Location:** Urban, simple, central.
Surface: concrete. 01/01-31/12.
Distance: 500m on the spot.
Remarks: Max. 2 days.

S Waldshut-Tiengen 19H2

Wohmobil-Park Waldshut-Tiengen, Jahnweg 22, Waldshut.
GPS: n47,61121 e8,22513.

44 €12 €1/100liter Ch €1/kWh €0,50.
Location: Urban, luxurious, quiet. **Surface:** metalled.
01/01-31/12.
Distance: on the spot.
Remarks: Along the Rhine river, bread-service.

S Walldürn 17B1

Basilikaplatz, Hauptstrasse. **GPS:** n49,58637 e9,36726.

8 free €1/80liter (4x)€0,50/kWh.
Location: Rural, simple. **Surface:** gravel. 01/01-31/12.
Distance: 250m 400m.
Remarks: Pilgrimage site.

S Walldürn 17B1

Goldschmitt Technik-Center, Industrieparkstrasse.
GPS: n49,58977 e9,39339.

30 free €1/80liter Ch (18x)€0,50/kWh.
Location: Rural, comfortable. **Surface:** asphalted/gravel.
01/01-31/12.
Distance: 2,6km 100m.
Remarks: Baker every morning.

S Wangen im Allgäu 20B2

P17, Am Klösterle. **GPS:** n47,68160 e9,83401.

40 €7 + €1,30/pp tourist tax €0,50/120liter Ch (46x) WC.
Surface: metalled. 01/01-31/12.
Distance: on the spot 500m 500m on the spot on the spot on the spot.
Remarks: Tourist tax €1.

Tourist information Wangen im Allgäu:

Tourist Information, Parkplatz 1, Rathaus. Traditional small Bavarian town. Every Thursday city walk through historical city centre, 10.30-12h. €5.
Wed.

DE

Wehr 19H2

Ludingarten. **GPS**: n47,62515 e7,90582.

7 € 10/24h € 1/100liter Ch (8x)€ 1/8h WC.
Location: Simple, quiet. **Surface:** metalled. 01/01-31/12.
Distance: nearby.
Remarks: Pay at tourist office, Hauptstr. 14 or Bistro Gleis 13, Bahnhofplatz.

Weikersheim 17B1

Parkplatz Tauberwiesen, August-Laukhuff-Straße 15.
GPS: n49,48364 e9,89706.

30 free.
Location: Rural, simple. **Surface:** gravel. 01/01-31/12.
Distance: 300m 400m.

Weikersheim 17B1

Campingplatz Schwabenmühle, Weikersheimer Strasse 21, Laudenbach. **GPS**: n49,45795 e9,92691.

6 € 19-22,50 Ch (6x)includedh . **Location:** Simple.
Surface: gravel. Easter-15/10.
Distance: 300m 200m.

Weil der Stadt 17A3

Festplatz, Jahnstrasse. **GPS**: n48,75268 e8,87453.

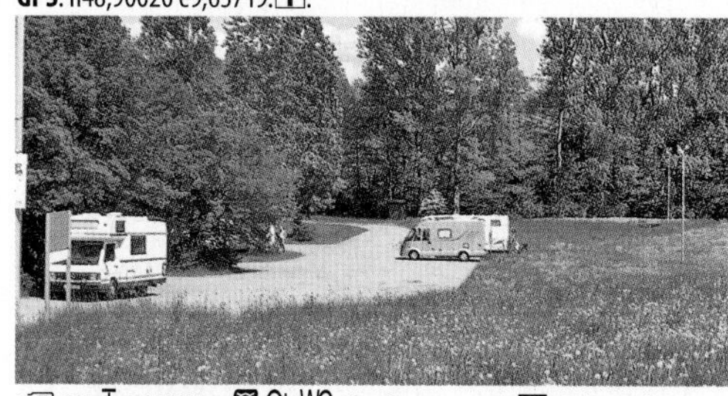

4 free € 1 € 1 Ch (4x)€ 1/4h. **Location:** Urban, simple, noisy.
Surface: asphalted. 01/01-31/12.
Distance: 300m 300m 250m on the spot on the spot.
Remarks: Max. 3 days.

Weilheim 19H2

Gret-Stube, Fohrenbachstraße 5, Nöggenschwiel.
GPS: n47,69252 e8,21349.
4 € 12 Ch included. **Location:** Rural. 01/01-31/12.
Distance: on the spot on the spot.
Remarks: Breakfast-service.

Weingarten 20B2

Festplatz, Abt Hyller Strasse 55. **GPS**: n47,81009 e9,63041.
8 € 5 € 1 € 1 Ch € 2.
Surface: metalled. 01/01-31/12.
Distance: 1km 500m on the spot on the spot.
Remarks: Max. 3 nights.

Weinheim 17A1

Am Miramar, Waidallee. **GPS**: n49,53378 e8,64473.
5 free. **Surface:** asphalted. 01/01-31/12.
Distance: 350m.
Remarks: At paradise pool.

Weinsberg 17A2

Eugen-Diez-Straße 2. **GPS**: n49,14846 e9,28464.
6 free € 1/100liter Ch (6x)€ 0,50/kWh free.
Location: Rural, quiet. **Surface:** grasstiles. 01/01-31/12.
Distance: 500m 2km 50m on the spot on the spot.

Welzheim 17B2

Aichstruter Stausee, Seiboldsweiler, Aichstrut.
GPS: n48,90020 e9,63719.

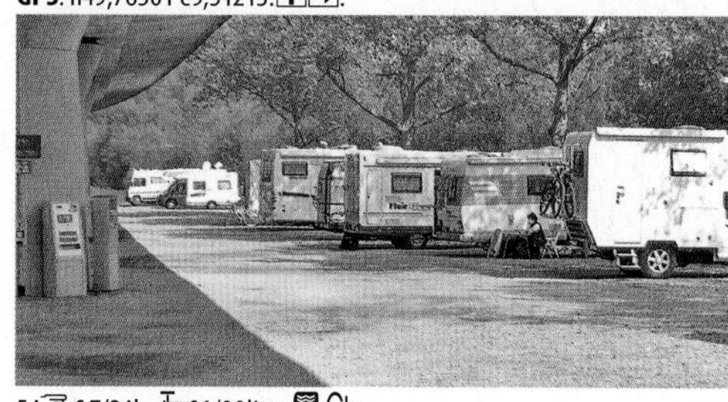

9 € 5 € 1/80liter Ch WC. **Surface:** gravel. 01/01-31/12.
Distance: 5km on the spot on the spot on the spot.
Remarks: At artificial lake, max. 1 week.

Welzheim 17B2

Am Bahnhof, Bahnhofstraße. **GPS**: n48,87256 e9,63053.
3 free. 01/01-31/12.
Distance: 400m 400m.
Remarks: Max. 3 days.

Welzheim 17B2

Am Stadtpark, Tannwaldweg. **GPS**: n48,86780 e9,63183.
2 free. 01/01-31/12.
Distance: 700m on the spot.

Wertheim 17B1

Wohnmobilstellplatz An der Taubermündung, Linke Tauberstrasse.
GPS: n49,76501 e9,51213.

54 € 7/24h € 1/90liter Ch.
Location: Simple, noisy. **Surface:** gravel.
01/01-31/12 2nd sa of the month + high water.
Distance: 500m on the spot.
Remarks: Along the Tauber river, max. 3 days.

Wertheim 17B1

Erwin Hymer World, Hymerring 1. **GPS**: n49,77368 e9,58034.

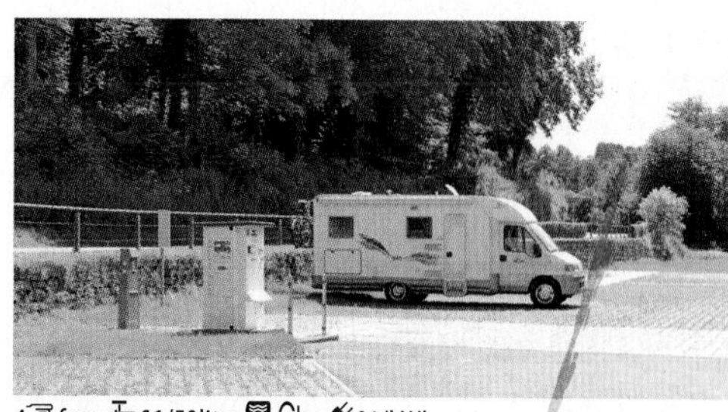

90 free € 1/90liter Ch € 1/3h WC during opening hours.
Location: Rural, comfortable. **Surface:** asphalted. 01/01-31/12.
Distance: 400m 3,7km.
Remarks: Baker at 8am, Wertheim Outletcentrum 100m.

Tourist information Wertheim:
Wertheim Village, Almosenberg. Outlet-shopping.

Wildberg 17A3

Wohnmobilstellplatz Wildberg, Klosterhof 4.
GPS: n48,62055 e8,74485.

4 free € 1/50liter Ch € 1/kWh.
Location: Quiet. **Surface:** asphalted/metalled.
01/01-31/12 service: 01/11-01/03.
Distance: historical centre 500m 700m 1km on the spot.
Remarks: Along river, nearby monastery.

Wolfach 19H1

Ferienhof Bartleshof, Ippichen 6, Ippichen.
GPS: n48,30183 e8,26264.

5 € 15 Ch (4x) € 2 € 2. **Location:** Rural, simple, quiet. **Surface:** grassy/gravel. 01/01-31/12.
Distance: on the spot on the spot.
Remarks: € 10, reduction at restaurant.

Wolfach 19H1

Trendcamping Schwarzwald, Schiltacher Straße 80, Halbmeil.
GPS: n48,29053 e8,27763.

6 € 18, 2 pers.incl Ch WC included € 3 € 2 .
Location: Rural, simple, quiet. **Surface:** grassy/sand.
10/04-15/10.
Distance: on the spot.

Wolfegg/Allgäu 20B2

Reisemobilhafen Loretopark, Rötenbacher Straße.
GPS: n47,81489 e9,79802.
12 € 5 € 1/80liter Ch € 0,50/kWh. 01/01-31/12.
Distance: 500m.

Wolfegg/Allgäu 20B2

Hofgarten, Alttaner strasse. **GPS**: n47,82105 e9,79487.

2 € 5.
Surface: gravel/metalled. 01/01-31/12.
Distance: on the spot.
Remarks: Max. 2 nights.

Tourist information Wolfegg/Allgäu:
Automobilmuseum. 200 oldtimers. 01/04-31/10 9.30-18h, 01/11-31/03 Su 10-17h.
Bauernhaus-museum. Open air museum. 01/04-31/10 Tue-Su 10-18/17h Mo Apr Oct.

Zaberfeld 17A2

An der Ehmetsklinge, Seestrasse. **GPS**: n49,05607 e8,91646.
3 free against payment Ch € 0,50/kWh. **Location:** Rural.
Surface: metalled. 01/01-31/12.

DE

Distance: 250m on the spot on the spot on the spot 250m on the spot on the spot.

S | Zell am Harmersbach | 19H1

Stellplatz Zell am Harmersbach, Nordracher Strasse.
GPS: n48,35146 e8,05942.

14 € 5 €1/10minutes Ch (8x)€2/12h. **Location:** Rural, simple, quiet. **Surface:** gravel. 01/01-31/12.
Distance: 2km 2km.

Bavaria

S | Absberg | 17D2

Badehalbinsel Brombachsee, Gunzenhausen-Pleinfeld Ausfart Absberg. **GPS**: n49,13770 e10,87389.

240 € 12/24h €0,20/60liter Ch (80x)€0,50/kWh WC €0,50. **Location:** Rural, comfortable, quiet. **Surface:** grassy. 01/04-01/10.
Distance: 1km on the spot on the spot 1km on the spot on the spot.
Remarks: Bread-service.

S | Adelsdorf | 17D1

Gasthof Niebler, Neuhauser Hauptstrasse 30.
GPS: n49,70017 e10,90221.

4 € 15, guests free .
Surface: metalled. 01/01-31/12.
Distance: on the spot on the spot.

Ahorn | 12D3

Freizeitzentrum Wittmannsberg, Badstrasse 20, Eicha.
GPS: n50,22537 e10,90252.

4 free. **Surface:** metalled. 01/01-31/12.
Distance: on the spot 5km.

S | Aichach | 17D3

Reisemobilplatz, Franz-Beck-Strasse. **GPS**: n48,45889 e11,12611.

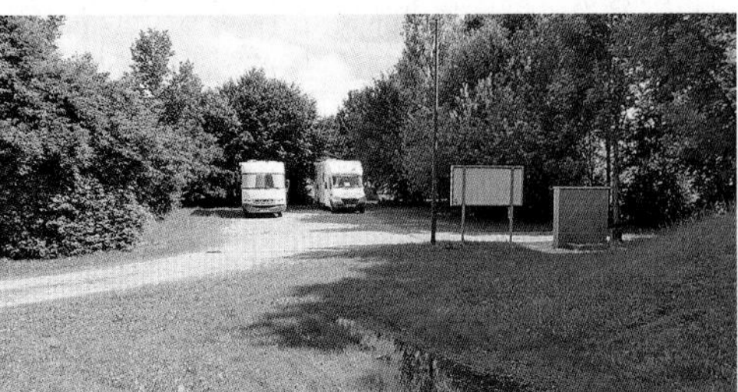

4 € 5 Chfree. **Location:** Urban, simple, quiet.
Surface: grassy/gravel. 01/01-31/12.
Distance: 500m 500m 100m.

S | Albertshofen | 17C1

An der Fähre Mainstockheim-Albertshofen, Mainstraße.
GPS: n49,77254 e10,15749.

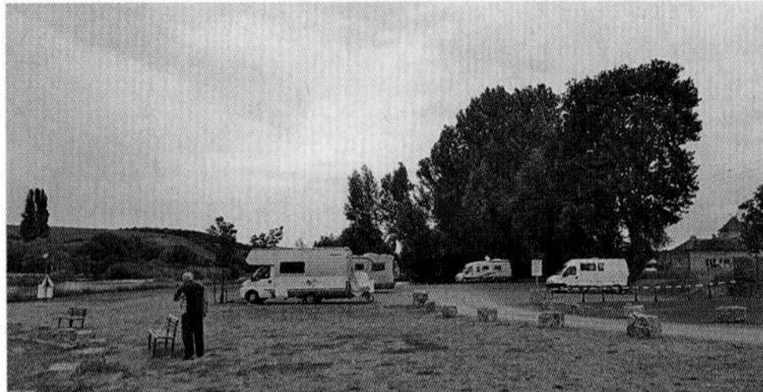

10 € 5 Ch included. **Location:** Rural, simple, quiet.
Surface: gravel. 01/01-31/12.
Distance: on the spot on the spot on the spot 50m on the spot.
Remarks: Along Main river, closed when high water.

S | Altmannstein | 17E2

Gasthof Forster, Schulstrasse 9. **GPS**: n48,90125 e11,69559.

20 guests free (4x)€2/night. **Surface:** asphalted.
01/01-31/12.
Distance: on the spot on the spot 3km.
Remarks: Bread-service, check in before 19h (Mo-Tue 16h).

S | Altötting | 20G1

P2 Dultplatz, Traunsteinerstrasse. **GPS**: n48,22287 e12,67921.

8 free €1/10liter (8x)€1/4h. **Location:** Urban, simple, central. **Surface:** gravel. 01/01-31/12.
Distance: 700m 300m 300m 250m.
Remarks: Max. 3 days.

S | Altötting | 20G1

Wohnmobilstellplatz am Parkplatz, Griesstraße.
GPS: n48,22946 e12,67493.

8 free €1/80liter Ch (8x)€1/4h WC. **Location:** Urban, simple, noisy. **Surface:** grasstiles. 01/01-31/12.
Distance: 600m 200m on the spot.

Remarks: Max. 3 days.

S | Altusried | 20C2

Am Freibad, Im Tal 4. **GPS**: n47,79915 e10,21934.

10 € 10-5 €1 Ch €0,50/kWh. **Location:** Rural, simple, quiet. **Surface:** grassy/gravel. 01/01-31/12.
Distance: 500m 700m.
Remarks: Parking at swimming pool, max. 3 days.

S | Amberg | 17E1

Gasfabrikstraße. **GPS**: n49,44043 e11,86198.

10 free (12x)€1/12h. **Location:** Urban, simple, central, quiet.
Surface: asphalted. 01/01-31/12.
Distance: 500m 50m 1km 1km 50m 50m.

Amorbach | 17A1

P Altstadt, Dr.F.A.Freundt-Straße. **GPS**: n49,64683 e9,22115.

5 free. **Location:** Urban, simple. **Surface:** asphalted.
01/01-31/12.
Distance: 500m 400m Lidl.

S | Ansbach | 17C2

Freizeitbad Aquella, Am Stadion 2. **GPS**: n49,30459 e10,55852.

12 free €0,50/50liter Ch (12x)€0,50/kWh.
Location: Simple, central. **Surface:** metalled.
01/01-31/12.
Distance: 1km 7,7km on the spot 1km on the spot.
Remarks: At swimming pool.

S | Arnbruck | 17G2

Landhotel Rappenhof, Rappendorf 5. **GPS**: n49,13517 e12,95069.

5 € 10 Ch €5 WC included. **Location:** Simple.
Surface: grassy. 01/01-31/12 15/11-15/12.
Distance: 2km on the spot 2km 10km 8km.

DE

Remarks: Use of sauna against payment.

Arnstein 12B3

Badesee, Am Alten Schwimmbad. **GPS:** n49,97667 e9,95917.

12 free €1/80liter Ch (4x)€1/2kWh.
Location: Rural, simple, quiet. **Surface:** grassy/metalled.
01/01-31/12, service 01/04-31/10.
Distance: 500m 100m 100m snack 100m 500m on the spot.
Remarks: At the old swimming pool.

Arnstein 12B3

Cancale Platz. **GPS:** n49,97637 e9,96725.

5 free. **Location:** Urban. **Surface:** metalled. 01/01-31/12.
Distance: 100m 100m 100m.
Remarks: Max. 1 night.

Arzberg 12E3

Am Rathausplatz. **GPS:** n50,05528 e12,18870.
2 free. **Surface:** metalled. 01/01-31/12.
Distance: 250m 300m 250m.

Aschaffenburg 12A3

Willigesbrücke, Grossostheimerstrasse. **GPS:** n49,97139 e9,13722.

25 € 3/24h (18x)€0,50/kWh. **Location:** Simple, quiet.
Surface: grassy/gravel. 01/01-31/12.
Distance: historical centre 500m 8km on the spot.
Remarks: Parking along the Main, near Altstadt, being indicated with small signs, max. 3 days.

Aschheim 20E1

Gasthof Zur Post, Ismaningerstrasse 11. **GPS:** n48,17433 e11,71490.

2 € 10. **Surface:** asphalted. 01/01-31/12.
Distance: on the spot on the spot 300m.

Auerbach 17E1

Franz-Josef-Strauß-Platz, Hopfenoher Straße.
GPS: n49,69171 e11,63768.

3 free. **Location:** Simple. **Surface:** grassy.
Distance: 500m 500m 500m.

Aufseß 12D3

Brauerei-Gasthof Reichold, Hochstahl 24.
GPS: n49,88389 e11,26855.

38 € 7 €1/90liter Ch (38x)€1,50 WC €1.
Location: Rural, comfortable, quiet. **Surface:** grassy/metalled.
01/01-31/12.
Distance: on the spot on the spot on the spot on the spot Brauereienweg.
Remarks: Bread-service, breakfast buffet € 8/pp.

Aufseß 12D3

Brauerei Rothenbach, Im Tal 70. **GPS:** n49,88413 e11,22781.

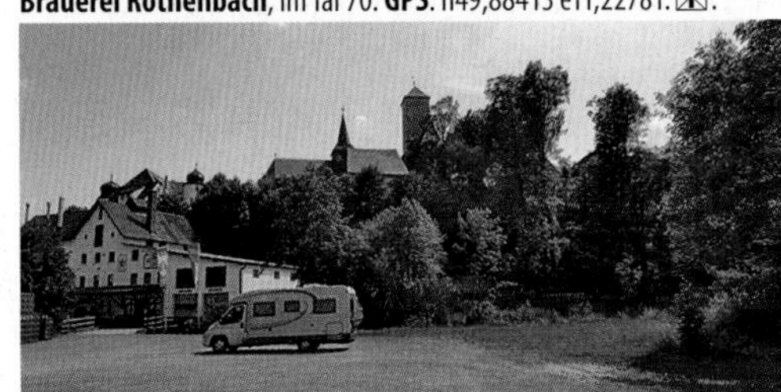

3 € 5 **Location:** Urban, simple. **Surface:** metalled.
01/03-30/10.
Distance: on the spot on the spot on the spot on the spot on the spot.

Augsburg 17D3

Schillstraße 109, Lechhausen. **GPS:** n48,38914 e10,90435.

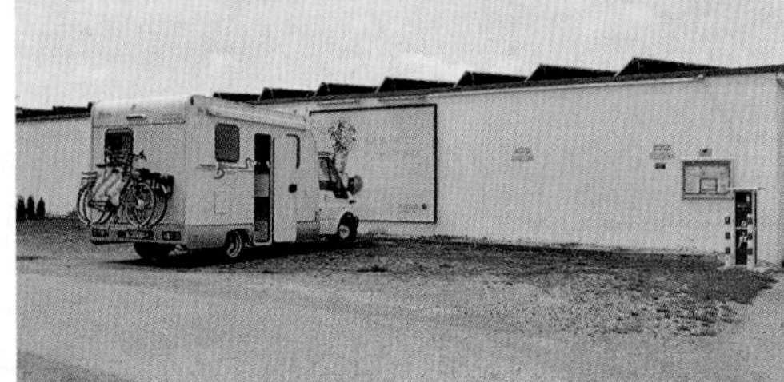

4 € 5 Ch €1/2kWh WC.
Location: Urban. **Surface:** gravel. 01/01-31/12.
Distance: 3,2km Sportgaststätte 200m on the spot on the spot.
Remarks: At sports centre.

Augsburg 17D3

Wohnmobilstellplatz Wertach, Bürgemeister Ackermann strasse 1.
GPS: n48,36944 e10,87750.

15 € 8 €1/90liter Ch €1/6h. **Location:** Urban, simple.
Surface: gravel. 01/01-31/12.

Distance: on the spot 4,5km on the spot on the spot 500m 500m on the spot on the spot.

Bad Abbach 17E2

Kaiser-Therme, Kurallee 4. **GPS:** n48,92712 e12,04044.

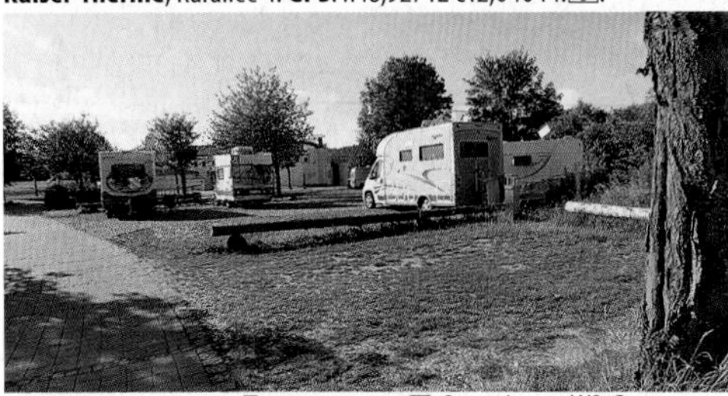

34 € 10 + € 1,80/pp €1/4minutes Ch (16x) WC.
Surface: grasstiles/grassy. 01/01-31/12.
Distance: 2km.
Remarks: Check in at pay-desk of the Therme.

Bad Aibling 20F1

Stellplatz an der Therme P13, Lindenstrasse/Heubergstrasse.
GPS: n47,85639 e12,00583.

31 € 10 €0,50/80liter Ch (20x)included.
Location: Rural, comfortable. **Surface:** grasstiles/metalled.
01/01-31/12.
Distance: 500m 400m 500m 600m 100m.
Remarks: Use sanitary only during opening hours.

Bad Bayersoien 20D2

Wohnmobilstellplatz Bad Bayersoien, Am Bahnhof 6.
GPS: n47,68798 e10,99820.

8 € 9/24h €1/90liter Ch (12x)€1/2kWh.
Location: Rural, simple, quiet. **Surface:** gravel.
01/01-31/12.
Distance: 400m 300m 300m 400m 400m.

Bad Birnbach 17G3

Camping Arterhof, Hauptstraße 3, Lengham.
GPS: n48,43512 e13,10939.

10 € 10 Ch WC included. **Location:** Rural, simple, quiet.
Surface: gravel. 01/01-31/12.
Distance: on the spot.

Bad Bocklet 12B3

Kurgarten, Aschacherstrasse. **GPS:** n50,26490 e10,07486.

DE

13 €8, tourist tax incl €1/80liter Ch (13x)€0,50/kWh.
Surface: metalled. 01/01-31/12.
Distance: 500m Free bus to Bad Kissingen.

Bad Brückenau 12B3

Schlosspark König Ludwig I, Schlüchterner Straße.
GPS: n50,30556 e9,74861.

10 €8 + €2,50/pp Gästekarte €1/100liter Ch €0,50/kWh.
Surface: asphalted. 01/01-31/12.
Distance: 4km 50m.

Bad Brückenau 12B3

Sinnflut, Industriestrasse P5. **GPS**: n50,31212 e9,79607.

8 €3 Ch (8x)€1. **Surface:** gravel. 01/01-31/12.
Distance: 250m 250m 250m.
Remarks: Parking swimming pool.

Bad Brückenau 12B3

Stellplatz Bahnhofstrasse, Buchwaldstrasse.
GPS: n50,30667 e9,78556.

20 €3 €1/8h. **Surface:** metalled. 01/01-31/12.
Distance: 300m on the spot on the spot on the spot.

Bad Feilnbach 20F2

Gasthof Tiroler Hof, Aiblinger strasse 95.
GPS: n47,76476 e12,03857.

3 guests free.
Location: Simple. **Surface:** gravel. 01/01-31/12.
Distance: on the spot on the spot 1km.

Bad Füssing 17G3

Campingplatz Holmerhof, Am Tennispark 10.
GPS: n48,35798 e13,30658.

9 €12, tourist tax incl €1/100liter Ch (8x)€0,60/kWh WC €2. **Location:** Rural, simple. **Surface:** metalled.
01/01-31/12.
Distance: 1km on the spot 1km.
Remarks: Max. 3 days, use sanitary €5/motorhome, swimming pool available.

Bad Gögging 17E2

Limes-Therme, Am Brunnenforum 1. **GPS**: n48,81857 e11,78868.

+20 €6, tourist tax €1,80/pp €0,50/50liter Ch .
Location: Simple. **Surface:** asphalted. 01/01-31/12.
Distance: 150m 150m 150m.
Remarks: Check in at pay-desk of the Therme.

Bad Griesbach 17G3

Mobilhafen Dreiquellenbad, Singham 40.
GPS: n48,42023 e13,19261.

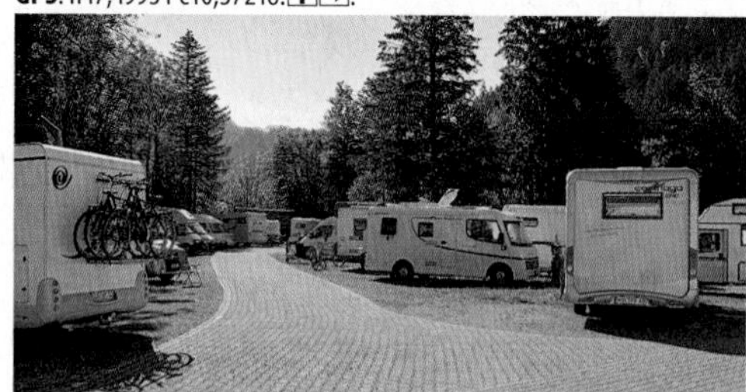

29 €16,50 + tourist tax €1/80liter Ch (29x)€0,60/kWh included €5. **Location:** Rural, simple, quiet. **Surface:** metalled.
01/01-31/12.
Distance: 2km on the spot.
Remarks: Max. 3 days, thermal-Vital-Oase incl.

Bad Hindelang 20C2

Wiesengrund Wohnmobilpark, Parkplatz Wiesengrund 1.
GPS: n47,49931 e10,37218.

30 €10-16, tourist tax €2,10/pp, child 7><16 €0,90 €1/100liter Ch €0,50/kWh WC €1 .
Location: Rural, luxurious, quiet. **Surface:** grassy/gravel.
01/01-31/12.
Distance: centre 500m on the spot 1km on the spot 3km 3km.

Bad Hindelang 20C2

Wohnmobilplatz Bergheimat, Passstraße 60, Oberjoch.
GPS: n47,51791 e10,42142.

10 €15, dog €3,50 Ch €0,80/kWh WC €1 .
Location: Rural, simple, noisy. **Surface:** grassy/gravel.
01/01-31/12.
Distance: on the spot on the spot.

Bad Kissingen 12B3

KissSalis Therme, Heilingenfelder Allee 16.
GPS: n50,18861 e10,06139.

18 €4 + €3,40/pp tourist tax €1/90liter Ch €1/8h.
Surface: asphalted. 01/01-31/12.
Distance: 500m on the spot on the spot.

Bad Kohlgrub 20D2

Kurhotel Lauter im Park, Kurhausstrasse 81.
GPS: n47,66412 e11,04315.

4 €15 . **Location:** Rural, simple, quiet. **Surface:** gravel.
01/01-31/12.
Distance: 1,5km on the spot 1,5km 1km 1km.

Bad Kohlgrub 20D2

Campingoase Reindl, Sonnen 93. **GPS**: n47,65789 e11,04393.

16 €16,40, 2 pers. incl., dog €1 Ch €0,40/kWh WC €2,50 . **Surface:** gravel. 01/01-31/12.
Distance: 1,5km 1,5km.

Bad Königshofen 12C3

Frankentherme, Am Kurzentrum 1. **GPS**: n50,30003 e10,47503.

77 €11 €1/80liter Ch (77x)€0,50/kWh WC €3/2h.
Surface: grasstiles/metalled.
01/01-31/12.
Remarks: Washing-machine/dryer available, if full 2 alternatives will be given, special health arrangement possible.
Tourist information Bad Königshofen:

Kurverwaltung Königshofen, Am Kurzentrum 1, www.bad-koenigshofen.de.
Traditional small town with half-timbered houses, cycle and hiking routes in the surroundings.

Bad Kötztingen 17G2

Aqacur, Bgm. Seidl Platz. **GPS**: n49,17539 e12,86196.

3 free €1 Ch €1/8h. **Location:** Urban, simple.
Surface: metalled. 01/01-31/12.
Distance: 50m.

Bad Neustadt 12C2

Parkplatz An der Saale. **GPS**: n50,31637 e10,22205.

60 € 8 €1/50liter Ch (48x)included.
Surface: grasstiles. 01/01-31/12.
Distance: 500m.

Bad Reichenhall 20G2

Wohnmobilpark an der RupertusTherme, Hammerschmiedweg.
GPS: n47,73466 e12,87536.

25 € 14, 2 pers incl €1/80liter Ch included.
Location: Comfortable. **Surface:** asphalted. 01/01-31/12.
Distance: 500m 5km 600m 800m on the spot on the spot on the spot.
Remarks: Bicycle rental.

Bad Rodach 12C2

ThermeNatur Bad Rodach, Thermalbadstrasse.
GPS: n50,33452 e10,77499.

24 € 4,50 + € 2/pp tourist tax €1,50 Ch (16x)€1,50 WC.
Surface: metalled. 01/01-31/12, water: 01/04-30/09.
Distance: on the spot on the spot 500m.
Remarks: Caution key service € 10, caution key electricity € 20, key service at swimming pool.

Bad Staffelstein 12D3

Stellplatz Obermain-Therme, Seestraße 3. **GPS**: n50,10766 e10,99202.

27 € 11 €0,50/40liter Ch (8x)€0,50/kWh WC included.
Surface: metalled. 01/01-31/12.
Distance: 1km 1,5km on the spot 1,5km on the spot on the spot on the spot.
Remarks: Max. 4 nights, bread-service.

Bad Steben 12E2

An der Therme, P3, Steinbacher Straße. **GPS**: n50,36250 e11,63239.

18 € 5 + € 0,50/pp tourist tax €0,50/80liter Ch €0,50/kWh. **Surface:** metalled. 01/01-31/12.
Distance: 500m 200m 500m.

Bad Tölz 20E2

Bürgermeister Stohlreiterpromenade. **GPS**: n47,76252 e11,55142.

30 € 8/24h €1/50liter Ch. **Location:** Rural, simple.
Surface: asphalted. 01/01-31/12.
Distance: 1km on the spot on the spot 500m 500m 500m.
Remarks: Max. 48h, incl. Kurkarte.

Tourist information Bad Tölz:

Alpamare. Large swimming pool complex with wave machine, Alpa, slides, sauna etc. Su-Thu 8-21h, Fri-Sa 8-22h, 24/12-01/01 8-16h.

Bad Windsheim 17C1

Phoenix Reisemobilhafen, Bad Windsheimer Strasse 7.
GPS: n49,51361 e10,41722.

100 € 10,90 €1/100liter Ch (80x)€0,50/kWh WC €1 €2,50/2,50. **Surface:** gravel. 01/01-31/12.
Distance: 1km 100m 500m.
Remarks: Bread-service.

Bad Windsheim 17C1

Fränkisches Freilandmuseum, Eisweiherweg.
GPS: n49,49705 e10,41667.

20 € 5 + € 1,60/pp tourist tax.
Surface: grassy. 01/01-31/12.
Distance: 1km 500m 500m.
Remarks: Open air museum.

Bad Wörishofen 20D1

Therme Bad Wörishofen, Thermenallee 1.
GPS: n48,02120 e10,59100.

25 € 9 €1/100liter Ch included WC. **Location:** Urban, simple. **Surface:** asphalted. 01/01-31/12.
Distance: 1,5km 4,3km on the spot 500m on the spot.
Remarks: Check in at pay-desk of the Therme, max. 3 nights, max. 8M, bread-service.

Balderschwang 20C2

Wohnmobilplatz Schwabenhof, Schwabenhof 23.
GPS: n47,45745 e10,12963.

56 € 12-17 €0,50 Ch €4/day WC €0,50/5minutes.
Location: Rural, comfortable, luxurious.
Surface: grassy/gravel.
01/01-31/12.
Distance: 3km on the spot 3km 100m 100m 100m.
Remarks: Bread-service, drying room for skis.

Bamberg 12D3

Wohnmobilplatz, Am Heinrichsdamm. **GPS**: n49,88626 e10,90296.

25 € 12 €1/100liter Ch €0,50/kWh.
Location: Urban, simple. **Surface:** gravel. 01/01-31/12.
Distance: 10 min walking on the spot on the spot on the spot.
Remarks: Max. 24h.

Bärnau 12F3

Gasthof und Wald-Pension Blei, Altglashütte 4.
GPS: n49,77222 e12,38880.

DE

30 € 10, guests free Ch WC included, customers free.
Surface: asphalted/grassy. 01/01-31/12.
Distance: 6km on the spot 6km 100m.

S Baunach 12D3

Sportplatz-Festplatz, Bahnhofstrasse 14-4.
GPS: n49,98750 e10,85444.

5 free €1 Ch €1/12h. **Surface:** grassy/metalled.
01/01-31/12.
Distance: 200m 200m 200m.
Remarks: Parking at the edge of nature reserve Haßberge, in the old part of the city, max. 2 nights.

S Bayerbach 17G3

Wohnmobilhafen Vital, Huckenham 11.
GPS: n48,41537 e13,13010.

10 € 12,50 2 pers.incl, dog € 2,50 Ch (8x)€0,60/kWh WC included €1. **Location:** Rural, simple, quiet.
Surface: metalled. 01/01-31/12.
Distance: 500m on the spot.
Remarks: Max. 3 nights, use sanitary facilities at campsite.

Bayreuth 12E3

P6 Stadthalle, Jean-Paul strasse. **GPS**: n49,94028 e11,57639.

3 € 0,60/30min, max € 10. **Location:** Urban, simple, noisy.
Surface: metalled. 01/01-31/12.
Distance: on the spot 200m 200m.

S Bayreuth 12E3

Lohengrin Therme Bayreuth, Kurpormenade 5.
GPS: n49,94204 e11,63493.

24 € 6 €1/50liter €1 Ch €1 €1/6h WC €1,50.
Location: Rural, simple, central, quiet. **Surface:** asphalted.
01/01-31/12.
Distance: 1,5km 3,5km 500m 1km on the spot on the spot on the spot.
Remarks: Bread-service.

S Bayrischzell 20F2

Wohnmobilstellplatz Bayrischzell, Seebergstraße.
GPS: n47,67189 e12,01023.

20 € 10 €0,50/80liter Ch (12x)€0,50/kWh.
Location: Comfortable, central. **Surface:** gravel.
01/01-31/12.
Distance: 400m 400m 400m 400m bus 5min on the spot.

S Beilngries 17E2

Landgasthof Euringer, Dorfstrasse 23. **GPS**: n49,01054 e11,50261.

6 guests free Ch . **Location:** Urban, simple, central.
Surface: metalled. 01/01-31/12.
Distance: 4km on the spot 4km.

S Beilngries 17E2

An der Altmühl, An der Altmühl 24. **GPS**: n49,02649 e11,47079.

20 € 14 Ch WC included. **Location:** Urban, comfortable, central, quiet. **Surface:** grassy. 01/03-31/10.
Remarks: Check in at reception campsite.

S Benediktbeuern 20E2

Wohnmobilstellplatz am Sportzentrum, Schwimmbadstraße 37.
GPS: n47,69920 e11,41556.

16 € 7 €1 €1 Ch €2/12h. **Location:** Rural, comfortable, quiet. **Surface:** asphalted. 01/04-31/10. **Distance:** 1km.
Remarks: Max. 3 nights, Alpenwarmbad 01/05-01/09 (swimming pool).

S Beratzhausen 17E2

Landgasthof Friesenmühle, Friesenmühle 1.
GPS: n49,08534 e11,81176.

10 free, use of a meal desired (2x) WC. **Surface:** grassy/gravel.
01/01-31/12 Wed.
Distance: 1km on the spot 1km.
Remarks: Motorhome service: volutary contribution, apply< 22h.

S Berching 17E2

Wohnmobilstellplatz an der Schiffsanlegestelle, Uferpromenade.
GPS: n49,10972 e11,43910.
15 free, 01/04-31/10 € 5 €1 Ch €1/8h.
Surface: grasstiles/metalled. 01/01-31/12.
Distance: 200m 50m on the spot 300m 100m.

S Berchtesgaden 20G2

Reisemobilplatz Rasp, Renothenweg 15, Oberau.
GPS: n47,65026 e13,07037.

20 € 8 + € 2,10/pp tourist tax €2 Ch €2 WC.
Location: Rural, central, quiet. **Surface:** gravel.
Easter-30/11.
Distance: 500m 500m on the spot.

Bergen/Chiemgau 20F1

Parkplatz Hochfelln-Seilbahn, Maria-Eck-Straße 8.
GPS: n47,79710 e12,59079.

10 € 4.
Location: Simple. **Surface:** metalled. 01/01-31/12.
Distance: 1,2km on the spot 500m on the spot.
Remarks: Parking ski-lift, max. 1 night.

S Bernau am Chiemsee 20F1

Am Tenniszentrum, Buchenstrasse 17.
GPS: n47,80944 e12,38222.

30 € 12 + € 1/pp tourist tax Ch €1,50/day WC €4 included. **Location:** Urban, comfortable. **Surface:** metalled.
01/01-31/12.
Distance: 800m 2km Chiemsee 3km on the spot 400m 350m on the spot on the spot 5km 5km.
Remarks: Pay at reception.

S Bernau am Chiemsee 20F1

Am See, Rasthausstrasse. **GPS**: n47,83111 e12,38528.

DE

16 € 6 ChWC €0,50 €1. Location: Noisy.
Surface: gravel/metalled. 01/01-31/12.
Distance: 2,5km 600m on the spot on the spot on the spot on the spot on the spot.
Remarks: Canoe and bicycle rental, charging point for electric bicycles.

Bernau am Chiemsee 20F1

Seiseralm & Hof, Reit 4. **GPS**: n47,79722 e12,35972.

10 € 10 Ch €5 €2 included.
Location: Simple. **Surface:** asphalted.
01/01-31/12.
Distance: 3,5km 5km on the spot on the spot on the spot.
Remarks: Sauna € 10.

Bernried 17G2

Altes Gasthaus Artmeier, Innenstetten 45.
GPS: n48,89675 e12,90262.

10 € 5 €1/100liter (4x)€1/day.
Location: Rural, simple, quiet. **Surface:** gravel/sand.
Tue, water: 01/11-31/03.
Distance: 3km on the spot on the spot.

Biberach 20C1

Brauerei Biberach, Weißenhorner Straße 24, Roggenburg.
GPS: n48,28808 e10,22047.
8 € 9 €1/80liter Chincluded €1/2kWh.
Surface: gravel/metalled. 01/01-31/12.
Distance: 400m 8km on the spot 400m 250m on the spot on the spot.
Remarks: Bike and e-bike rental.

Biesenhofen 20D2

Gasthof Stegmühle, Stegmühle 2. **GPS**: n47,82437 e10,64428.

4 € 10, guests free Ch WC . **Location:** Simple.
Surface: gravel/metalled. 01/01-31/12.
Distance: 1km 1km on the spot 1km.

Bischofsgrün 12E3

Rangenweg. **GPS**: n50,05407 e11,79292.

6 free, tourist tax € 1,50 to be paid at tourist office €1/40liter Ch (6x)€1/12h. **Surface:** metalled. 01/01-31/12.
Distance: 250m 500m nearby.

Bischofsheim an der Rhön 12B2

Viehweg 1, Haselbach. **GPS**: n50,39506 e9,99593.

12 € 5 €1/80liter Ch. **Surface:** asphalted. 01/01-31/12.
Distance: on the spot on the spot on the spot.
Remarks: Parking swimming pool in Haselbach.

Bischofswiesen 20G2

Götschen Alm, Kollertradte 21, Loipl. **GPS**: n47,64817 e12,93631.

20 € 5, tourist tax excl WC €3.
Location: Rural, simple. **Surface:** gravel. 01/05-30/10.
Distance: 2km on the spot 2km on the spot on the spot on the spot on the spot on the spot.
Remarks: Guests free.

Blaichach 20C2

Alpen-Rundblick Mobil Camping, Am Eichbichl 1.
GPS: n47,54615 e10,25917.

60 € 10,50/12,50 + € 1,70 pp €1/80liter Ch (54x)€0,60/kWh WC €1,60 €2,50. **Location:** Luxurious.
Surface: grassy/gravel. 01/01-31/12.
Distance: 300m 3,3km on the spot on the spot 500m 500m 5km 1km.

Bodenmais 17G2

Concorde-Reisemobil-Stellplatz, Kötztinger Straße.
GPS: n49,07147 e13,09273.

12 € 7 + tourist tax €0,50/100liter Ch €0,50/kWh.
Surface: asphalted.
01/01-31/12.

Distance: 800m 200m 200m.
Remarks: Use swimming pool, sauna, fitness-studio incl.

Bodenwöhr 17F1

Gasthof zum Troidlwirt, Bodenwöhrer strasse 6.
GPS: n49,28305 e12,26272.

40 € 10 Ch (12x)€1 WC €1. **Surface:** grassy/metalled.
01/01-31/12 Restaurant: Sa.
Distance: on the spot on the spot bakery 300m.

Bogen 17F2

Wohnmobilstellplätze am Volksfestplatz, Kotaustraße 12.
GPS: n48,90744 e12,68877.

5 € 10/24h €1 Ch (4x)€1/6h. **Surface:** grassy/metalled.
01/01-31/12 03/07-12/07.
Distance: 300m Edeka 100m.
Remarks: Check in at pay-desk of swiming pool.

Burgbernheim 17C1

Wohnmobilstellplatz im Gründlein, Freibadstrasse.
GPS: n49,44627 e10,31869.

12 free €1/100liter Ch (10x)€0,50/kWh.
Surface: grasstiles. 01/01-31/12.
Distance: 500m 500m 500m 500m.

Burghaslach 17C1

Hotel-Restaurant Steigerwaldhaus, Oberrimbach 2.
GPS: n49,72764 e10,53542.

10 € 10 €4 . **Surface:** grassy. 01/01-31/12.
Distance: 500m on the spot 5km.
Remarks: Breakfast-service.

Burghausen 20G1

Waldpark Lindach, Berghamer Strasse 1.
GPS: n48,15443 e12,80859.

DE

16 € 5/24h €1/80liter Ch (16x)€0,50/kWh WC .
Location: Rural, comfortable, quiet. **Surface:** gravel.
01/01-31/12 sanitary 01/11-31/03.
Distance: 1,5km 500m 1,5km.
Remarks: Check in at Bürgerhaus Marktlerstr. 15a, caution key sanitary € 20.

S Burgkirchen 20G1

Glöcklhofer, Peterhof 24. **GPS**: n48,15096 e12,75025.

3 € 15, 2 pers.incl €0,50/kWh WC included.
Location: Rural, simple, quiet. **Surface:** grassy.
01/01-31/12.
Distance: 2km 2km 2km.

S Burgkunstadt 12D3

Alter Postweg. **GPS**: n50,13965 e11,25017.

4 free €1 Ch. **Location:** Rural, simple. **Surface:** gravel.
01/01-31/12.
Distance: 100m 15km 100m 100m 300m 300m on the spot on the spot.
Remarks: Max. 48h.

S Bürgstadt 17A1

Winzerfestplatz, Josef-Ullrich-Straße. **GPS**: n49,71356 e9,26405.

25 free €1/80liter Ch (12x)€1/6h. **Location:** Rural, comfortable. **Surface:** asphalted. 01/01-31/12.
Distance: 500m 200m 200m.

S Cadolzburg 17D1

Stellplatz Am Höhbuck. **GPS**: n49,46123 e10,85188.
8 free Ch . **Surface:** metalled. 01/01-31/12.
Distance: on the spot.

Coburg 12D3

Ketschenanger, Schutzenstrasse. **GPS**: n50,25306 e10,96417.

9 free. **Surface:** asphalted.
Distance: on the spot on the spot.
Remarks: Parking next to gymnasium, max. 48h.

S Coburg 12D3

Aral-station, Bambergerstrasse. **GPS**: n50,24833 e10,96639.

3 free €1 Ch. **Surface:** metalled. 01/01-31/12.
Distance: on the spot.

Tourist information Coburg:
Die Veste Coburg. Medieval fortress.
Schloß Ehrenburg. guided tour Tue-Su.

Deggendorf 17G2

Konstantin-Bader-Straße. **GPS**: n48,82656 e12,96367.

3 free. **Location:** Simple. **Surface:** asphalted. 01/01-31/12.
Distance: centre 500m 250m.

S Deggendorf 17G2

Elypso, Sandnerhofweg 4-6. **GPS**: n48,82029 e12,91098.
4 € 6,50 €0,50/60liter €0,50/kWh. **Surface:** metalled.
01/01-31/12.
Distance: 5,3km 4km.

S Deiningen 17C2

Cowabanga, Am Sportpark. **GPS**: n48,86292 e10,58042.

10 free €2,50 WC . **Location:** Urban, simple.
Surface: asphalted. 01/01-31/12.
Distance: 2km on the spot.
Remarks: Parking sports centre.

S Denkendorf 17E2

Gasthof Lindenwirt, Hauptstrasse 43. **GPS**: n48,92806 e11,45568.

10 € 5 included. **Location:** Urban. **Surface:** gravel/sand.
01/01-31/12.
Distance: on the spot 700m on the spot 200m on the spot on the spot.

S Dettelbach 17C1

Zur Mainfähre, Mainsondheimerstrasse.
GPS: n49,80076 e10,16751.

35 € 7 €1/60liter Ch (24x)€0,50/kWh.
Surface: grassy. 01/01-31/12 Service: winter.
Distance: 100m 100m 100m.

S Dießen 20D1

Seestraße. **GPS**: n47,95220 e11,10598.
12 € 8/24h €1 €1 Ch (12x)€1/4h. **Surface:** gravel.
01/01-31/12.
Distance: 200m 200m 150m 150m.
Remarks: Max. 3 days.

S Dingolfing 17F3

Wohnmobilstellplatz Dingolfing, Wollanger/Prasserweg.
GPS: n48,62827 e12,50206.

12 free €1/80liter Ch (12x)€1/12h.
Location: Rural, comfortable, quiet. **Surface:** gravel.
01/01-31/12 01/10-31/10.
Distance: 400m 4,6km 250m.
Remarks: Nearby swimming pool.

S Dinkelsbühl 17C2

Park- & Campanlage, Dürrwanger Straße.
GPS: n49,07812 e10,32906.

12 € 12 Ch included €1,50. **Surface:** metalled.
01/01-31/12.
Distance: 1,5km 100m 500m.
Remarks: To be paid at campsite (500m).

Dittelbrunn 12C3

Gasthaus Goldene Flasche, Strohgasse 1, Hambach.
GPS: n50,09787 e10,20763.

DE

3 € 1. **Surface:** metalled. 01/01-31/12.
Distance: on the spot on the spot 200m.

S Donauwörth 17D3

Wohnmobilstellplatz am Festplatz, Neue Obermayerstraße 2.
GPS: n48,71490 e10,77874.

20 free €1/95liter Ch €1/8h. **Location:** Urban, simple.
Surface: asphalted. 01/01-31/12.
Distance: on the spot on the spot 500m on the spot.
Remarks: Max. 1 night.

Ebermannstadt 17D1

P2, Oberes Tor. **GPS:** n49,78222 e11,18946.

10 free. **Surface:** metalled. 01/01-31/12.
Distance: 750m 450m 100m.
Remarks: Max. 1 night.

S Ebern 12C3

Wohnmobilhafen Ebern, Walk-Strasser-Anlage.
GPS: n50,09312 e10,79496.

20 €6 Ch €1/2kWh WC included.
Surface: metalled.
01/01-31/12.
Distance: on the spot 1km 2km 100m 200m 100m.

S Ebern 12C3

Dietz, Bahnhofstrasse. **GPS:** n50,10167 e10,78917.

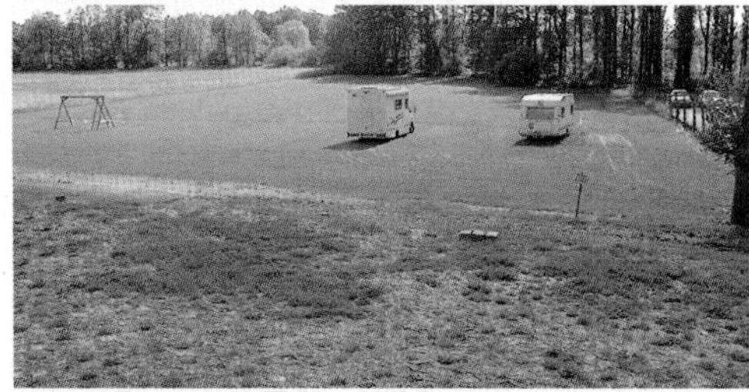

10 €5 €1/100liter Ch WC. **Surface:** asphalted/grassy.
01/01-31/12.
Distance: 400m.

S Ebrach 12C3

Naturbad, Schwimmbadweg. **GPS:** n49,84639 e10,48306.

5 free €1/80liter Ch WC.
Surface: metalled. 01/01-31/12.
Distance: 2km 2km 2km 500m.
Remarks: Parking swimming pool.

Eggenfelden 17G3

P2, Birkenallee. **GPS:** n48,40185 e12,77579.

5 free.
Location: Simple, quiet. **Surface:** grasstiles. 01/01-31/12.
Distance: 1km.
Remarks: Max. 3 days.

S Eging am See 17G2

Bavaria Kur-Sport Camping Park, Grafenauer Str. 31.
GPS: n48,72120 e13,26519.

10 €15, 2 pers.incl Ch (10x)included. **Location:** Rural, simple, quiet. **Surface:** asphalted. 01/01-31/12.
Remarks: Max. 2 days, check in at reception campsite, use sanitary facilities at campsite.

S Eibelstadt 17B1

Wassersportclub Eibelstadt, Mainparkring.
GPS: n49,73146 e9,98701.

90 €10 €1/5minutes Ch included,6Amp WC €1 €5.
Surface: grassy/gravel. 01/01-31/12.
Distance: 2km 50m 50m 500m 1km.
Remarks: Along Main river, bread-service (weekend).

S Eichstätt 17D2

Schottenwiese/Volkfestplatz. GPS: n48,88400 e11,19816.

50 €8 Ch (30x)€0,50/kWh WC €0,50.
Location: Urban, simple, central, quiet. **Surface:** metalled.
01/01-31/12 Eichstätter Volksfest.
Distance: 500m 500m on the spot on the spot.

Tourist information Eichstätt:

Volksfestplatz. Flea market. 10/05, 14/06, 12/07, 13/09, 04/10.
Altstadtfest, Innenstad. City celebration. 28/08-06/09.
Eichstätter Volksfest, Volksfestplatz. Folk festival. 02/09-11/09.
Informationszentrum Naturpark Altmühltal, Notre Dame 1, Information centre nature reserve. 01/04-31/10 Mo-Sa 9-17h, Su 10-17h, 01/11-31/03 Mo-Fr 9-12h. free.

S Einsiedl 20E2

Wohnmobilstellplatz, B11. **GPS:** n47,57000 e11,30389.

80 €6 €1/70liter €1/kWh. **Location:** Rural, comfortable, quiet. **Surface:** asphalted/gravel. 01/01-31/12.
Distance: 500m on the spot on the spot 500m 3,5km 1,5km 1,5km.
Remarks: Max. 3 nights.

S Eisenheim 12C3

Weingut Herbert Schuler, An der Mainaue, Obereisenheim.
GPS: n49,88883 e10,17942.

60 €5 €1/80liter Ch €0,50.
Surface: grassy/metalled. 01/01-31/12.
Distance: on the spot on the spot on the spot.
Remarks: Along Main river.

S Eltmann am Main 12C3

Parkplatz, Mainlände. **GPS:** n49,97306 e10,66250.

10 free €1/80liter €1/6h.
Surface: metalled. 01/01-31/12.
Distance: 500m on the spot on the spot 100m 300m.

S Enderndorf 17D2

Wohnmobilstellplatz Panorama, Kreisstraße, Spalt-Enderndorf.
GPS: n49,15028 e10,91083.

60 €8 €0,20/10liter Ch (60x)€1/kWh.
Surface: grassy. 01/04-31/10.
Distance: 400m 400m 400m 400m 3km 150m.

S Enderndorf 17D2

Reisemobilstellplatz Enderndorf-West, Zum Hafen.
GPS: n49,14777 e10,91126.

DE

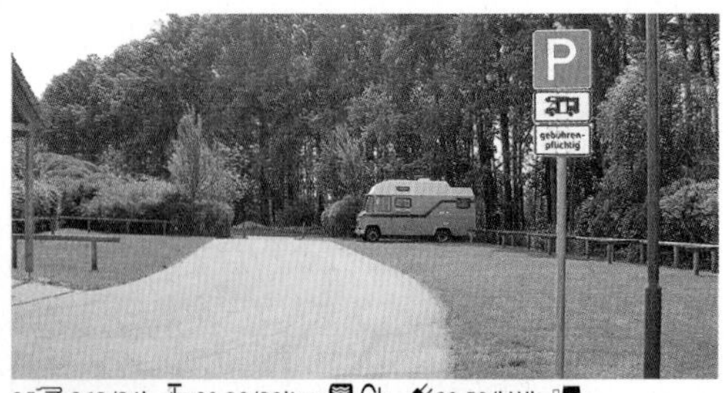

25 € 12/24h €0,20/20liter Ch €0,50/kWh.
Location: Rural, simple, isolated, quiet. **Surface:** grasstiles.
01/01-31/12.
Distance: 200m 150m 200m 200m on the spot on the spot.

S Erbendorf 12E3
Am Stadtpark, Bahnhofstraße 21. **GPS:** n49,84144 e12,04769.

10 free €1 Ch. **Surface:** gravel. 01/01-31/12.
Distance: 100m 200m 200m.
Remarks: Max. 3 days.

S Erding 20E1
Wohnmobilpark Erding, Thermenallee 1.
GPS: n48,29332 e11,88707.

55 € 10/day €1/80liter Ch €1/2kWh WC.
Surface: grasstiles/metalled. 01/01-31/12.
Distance: 2km 2km 2km 50m.
Remarks: Max. 7 nights.

S Escherndorf 12C3
Campingplatz Escherndorf, An der Güß 9a.
GPS: n49,85996 e10,17632.

22 € 9 + € 3,50/pp Ch WC. **Surface:** grassy.
01/04-31/10.
Distance: 300m 300m.

S Ettenbeuren 20C1
Wohnmobilpark Kammelaue, Zum Sportplatz 12.
GPS: n48,37565 e10,36021.

40 € 8, € 14,50 service incl Ch WC.
Location: Rural, comfortable, quiet. **Surface:** grasstiles/metalled.
01/04-31/10.
Distance: 500m on the spot 500m on the spot on the spot.

S Feucht 17D1
Am Freibad Feuchtasia, Chormantelweg. **GPS:** n49,37848 e11,22495.

9 € 7-9 €1/80liter Ch (8x)€1/2kWh. **Surface:** grasstiles.
01/01-31/12.
Distance: 1km 900m.

Fichtelberg 12E3
Automobilmuseum, Eckert Naglerweg 9.
GPS: n49,99760 e11,85820.

15 free. **Surface:** asphalted/metalled. 01/01-31/12.
Distance: 100m.
Remarks: Parking museum.

S Fischen 20C2
Wohnmobil-Stellplatz Fischen, Mühlenstraße.
GPS: n47,44950 e10,26946.

12 € 8, tourist tax € 1,95/pp €1 €1 Ch (12x)€1/12h.
Location: Rural, simple. **Surface:** asphalted.
Distance: 1,2km on the spot on the spot on the spot.
Remarks: Pay at Sportpark, Mühlenstraße 55.

S Forchheim 17D1
Sportinsel, An der Regnitzbrücke. **GPS:** n49,72120 e11,04939.

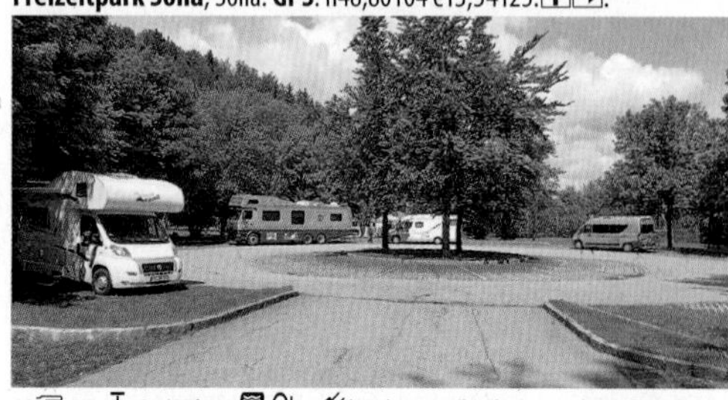

12 € 3 €3 ChWC €1. **Surface:** grasstiles.
01/01-31/12 sanitary building: 01/11-28/02.
Distance: 600m on the spot on the spot.

S Freyung 17H2
Freizeitpark Solla, Solla. **GPS:** n48,80104 e13,54125.

12 € 5 €1/50liter Ch (12x)€0,50/kWh. **Location:** Rural, simple, quiet. **Surface:** grasstiles. 01/01-31/12.
Distance: 2km 500m on the spot on the spot.

Freyung 17H2
Am Freibad, Zuppingerstraße 1. **GPS:** n48,80515 e13,54102.

12 free. **Location:** Urban, simple, quiet. **Surface:** metalled.
01/01-31/12.
Distance: 1km 1km 1km.

Friedberg 17D3
Herrgottsruhstrasse. **GPS:** n48,35765 e10,99095.

4 free. **Location:** Simple. **Surface:** gravel. 01/01-31/12.
Distance: 600m 600m 600m.

Friedberg 17D3
Seestraße. **GPS:** n48,36540 e10,96529.

4 free. **Location:** Rural, simple, quiet. **Surface:** asphalted.
01/01-31/12.
Distance: 1,8km 5km on the spot on the spot 400m on the spot on the spot.

S Friedberg 17D3
Marquardtstrasse 2/A. **GPS:** n48,34825 e10,99757.
Chfree.
Distance: on the spot.

S Friedenfels 12E3
Freibad, Badstrasse. **GPS:** n49,88639 e12,10417.

15 € 3,50 €1. **Surface:** metalled. 01/01-31/12.
Distance: 1,5km.
Remarks: Max. 3 days, service during opening hours.

S Friedenfels 12E3
Zentral, Gemmingenstraße. **GPS:** n49,88102 e12,10297.

15 € 3,50 €1/2kWh. **Surface:** metalled. 01/01-31/12.

DE

Distance: on the spot 25m.
Remarks: Max. 3 days, pay at tourist office, Café Am Steinwald, Gemmingenstr. 19.

Friedenfels 12E3

Stellplatz 'Ruhig', Weißensteiner Weg, Frauenreuth.
GPS: n49,89278 e12,08556.

5 € 3,50. **Surface:** metalled. 01/01-31/12.
Distance: 1,5km Frauenreuther Weiher.
Remarks: Max. 3 days.

Fürstenzell 17G3

Wohnmobilstellplatz bei der Waldschänke, Altenmarkt 1.
GPS: n48,55136 e13,34118.
€ 6 €1/100liter Ch €1,50. **Surface:** grassy.
01/01-31/12.
Distance: on the spot.

Füssen 20D2

Camper's Stop, Abt Hafnerstrasse 9. **GPS**: n47,58186 e10,70080.

120 € 14, trailer € 5 €0,50/150liter Ch €1/kWh WC €1 €2. **Location:** Urban, comfortable, noisy. **Surface:** gravel/metalled.
01/01-31/12.
Distance: 1,5km 600m 600m terrace 50m 250m 4km 400m.

Füssen 20D2

Wohnmobilstellplatz Füssen, Abt Hafnerstrasse 1.
GPS: n47,58224 e10,70355.

30 € 14 Chincluded (6x)€2,50 WC €0,50 €2.
Location: Noisy. **Surface:** metalled. 01/01-31/12.
Distance: 1,8km 1km 200m 300m 500m on the spot on the spot on the spot on the spot.
Remarks: Sauna, solarium.

Garmisch-Partenkirchen 20D2

Alpencamp am Wank, Wankbahnstraße 2.
GPS: n47,50573 e11,10802.

110 € 12, tourist tax > 16 € 2/pp, € 1 Umwelttaxe €1/50liter Ch (110x)€0,75/kWh WC €1 . **Location:** Rural, comfortable. **Surface:** asphalted. 01/01-31/12.
Distance: 1km 2km 50m 700m 50m 2,5km 1,5km.
Remarks: Check in on arrival.

Gerolzhofen 12C3

P3 Zur Volkach, Schallfelderstrasse. **GPS**: n49,89808 e10,35169.

6 € 5 €1 Ch (4x)€0,50/kWh WC. **Surface:** metalled.
01/01-31/12.
Distance: 100m.
Remarks: Max. 3 days.

Gerolzhofen 12C3

P1 Geomaris, Dingolshäuser Straße 2. **GPS**: n49,89980 e10,36035.

6 free. **Surface:** asphalted. 01/01-31/12.
Distance: 750m.
Remarks: Parking swimming pool.

Geslau 17C2

Bauernhof Mohrenhof, Lauterbach 3.
GPS: n49,34630 e10,32500.

20 € 10-12 Ch €0,50/kWh WC €0,50 €3 €2,50/2h.
Surface: grassy. Easter-31/10.
Distance: 500m on the spot.
Remarks: Bread-service.

Goldkronach 12E3

Festplatz, Schulstrasse. **GPS**: n50,01265 e11,68276.

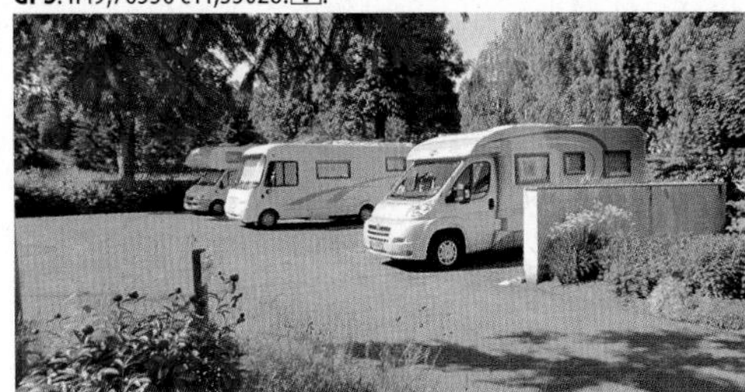

4 free €1/10minutes Ch (4x)€1/10h. **Surface:** gravel.
01/01-31/12.
Distance: 50m 500m 2km.

Gößweinstein 17D1

Alte Jugendherberge, Etzdorfer Straße 6.
GPS: n49,76556 e11,33028.

6 €7 €1/80liter Ch €1/2kWh. **Location:** Urban, simple. **Surface:** metalled.
Distance: 600m 600m 600m 300m 600m.

Grafenau 17G2

Grafenauer Kurpark, Freyunger Straße.
GPS: n48,85605 e13,40456.

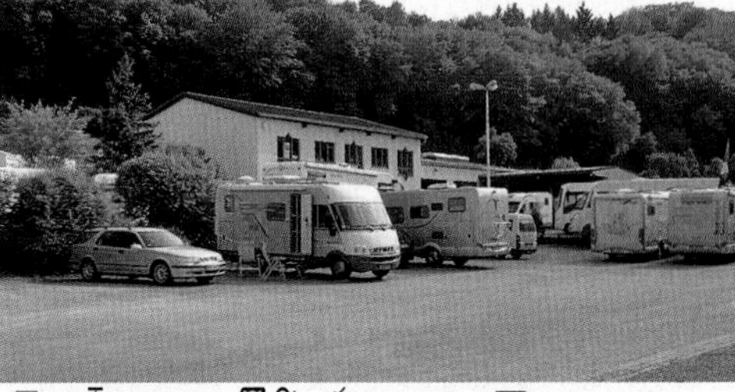

18 € 10 + € 1,95/pp tourist tax €1/80liter Ch €0,50 free.
Location: Urban, simple, quiet. **Surface:** gravel.
01/01-31/12.
Distance: 500m 600m 550m ReWe on the spot.
Remarks: Wifi in Touristinformation + 1/2h free internet in Stadtbücherei.

Gräfendorf 12B3

Volkert an der Roßmühle, Roßmühle, Weickersgrüben.
GPS: n50,10660 e9,78309.

5 € 5 €2/100liter Ch (5x)included. 01/04-31/10.
Distance: on the spot on the spot on the spot.
Remarks: At motorhome dealer, accessory shop, max. 24h, check in at shop.

Greding 17D2

Am Hallenbad. **GPS**: n49,04409 e11,35551.

20 free.
Location: Urban. **Surface:** metalled.
01/01-31/12.
Distance: Old city centre 300m 500m 250m 250m on the spot on the spot.
Remarks: Parking at city wall in front of swimming pool.

Tourist information Greding:
City wall and towers.

Großheubach 17A1

Weingut Gasthaus Zur Bretzel, Kirchstraße 1.
GPS: n49,72620 e9,22083.

25 € 17 Ch WCincluded €1. **Location:** Rural, comfortable, quiet. **Surface:** grassy/gravel. 01/11-15/11.
Distance: 100m on the spot on the spot.
Remarks: To be paid at Gasthaus, € 10 euro discount coupon (restaurant, wine).

Großweil 20E2

Berggasthof Kreut-Alm, Kreut 1. **GPS**: n47,66184 e11,28286.

DE

40 customers free. **Location:** Rural, simple, isolated, quiet. **Surface:** asphalted. 01/03-31/10.
Distance: 3,2km on the spot.

Großweil 20E2

Freilichtmuseum Glentleiten, An der Glentleiten 4.
GPS: n47,66495 e11,28506.

10 free. **Surface:** gravel.
Distance: 2km 3,5km Gaststätte - Biergarten 1km.
Remarks: Open air museum, only overnight stays.

Günzburg 17C3

Waldbad, Heidenheimer Straße. **GPS**: n48,46287 e10,26944.

24 € 5, 01/05-30/09 € 8 €1/100liter (24x)€0,50/kWh.
Location: Simple. **Surface:** gravel. 01/01-31/12.
Distance: Danube Bike Trail.
Remarks: Parking swimming pool.

Gunzenhausen 17D2

Surfzentrum Schlungenhof. **GPS**: n49,12790 e10,74559.

80 € 11/24h €1 Ch included WC €1.
Location: Rural, comfortable, quiet. **Surface:** grassy/gravel.
01/04-30/10.
Distance: 100m on the spot 1,8km.

Gunzenhausen 17D2

Altmühlsee, Seezentrum Mühr. **GPS**: n49,13145 e10,73534.

40 € 9/24h WC. **Location:** Rural, comfortable, isolated, quiet.
Surface: grassy. 01/01-31/12.
Distance: on the spot 200m on the spot on the spot.
Remarks: Max. 3 days.

Hammelburg 12B3

Am Bleichrasen, P2, Am Weiher. **GPS**: n50,11390 e9,88820.

25 € 6/24h Ch included (18x)€0,50/kWh WC.
Location: Urban, simple, quiet. **Surface:** asphalted.
01/01-31/12.
Distance: on the spot on the spot 200m 300m.

Hammelburg 12B3

Forellenhof Reuss, Am Erlich 30, Diebach.
GPS: n50,13310 e9,81917.

18 € 7 Ch included €2 €2. **Location:** Rural, comfortable, quiet. **Surface:** grassy. 01/04-31/10.
Distance: Hammelburg 7km on the spot on the spot.
Remarks: Bread-service, weekend: Gaststätte/Biergarten.

Hammelburg 12B3

Schloß Saaleck, Am Schlossberg. **GPS**: n50,10998 e9,87281.

3 free WC. **Surface:** asphalted/metalled. 01/01-31/12.
Distance: on the spot.

Hammelburg 12B3

Restaurant Nöth, Morlesauer Strasse 3. **GPS**: n50,11707 e9,80313.

5 free. **Location:** Rural, simple, quiet. **Surface:** gravel.
01/01-31/12.
Distance: on the spot on the spot on the spot on the spot on the spot.
Remarks: Check in at restaurant, use of a meal desired.

Hassfurt 12C3

Festplatz am Gries, Ringstrasse. **GPS**: n50,03068 e10,50094.

22 € 5/night €1 Ch €1 WC. **Surface:** asphalted.
01/01-31/12.
Distance: 200m 10m 200m 200m.
Remarks: Along Main river.

Herrieden 17C2

Volksfestplatz an der Altmühl, Staatsstrasse 2248.
GPS: n49,23191 e10,49588.

10 free. **Surface:** asphalted. 01/01-31/12.
Distance: 100m 200m 200m.
Remarks: Parking at the old mill bridge.

Hersbruck 17D1

Fackelmann Therme Hersbruck, Badestraße.
GPS: n49,51142 e11,44267.

6 € 6 €1/50liter Ch €1/8h. **Surface:** gravel.
01/01-31/12.
Distance: on the spot 200m 200m.
Remarks: Check in at pay-desk of the Therme.

Herzogenaurach 17D1

Freizeitbad Atlantis, Würzburger Straße 35. **GPS**: n49,57315 e10,86543.
12 € 6/24h €1 Ch (12x)€0,50/kWh.
Surface: gravel.
01/01-31/12.
Distance: on the spot.
Remarks: € 2 reduction swimming pool.

Hilpoltstein 17D2

Seezentrum Heuberg am Rothsee, Heuberg.
GPS: n49,20954 e11,18595.

50 € 8/24h Ch.
Surface: metalled. 01/01-31/12 Service: winter.
Distance: 200m 200m.

Hilpoltstein 17D2

Am Main-Donau-Kanal. **GPS**: n49,20455 e11,18813.

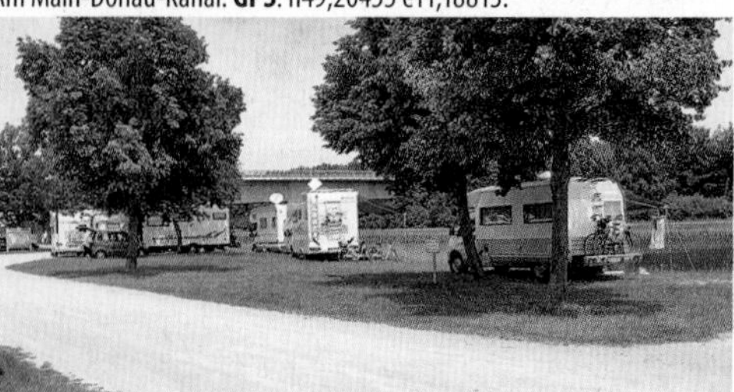

40 € 6. **Surface:** grassy. 15/04-15/10.
Distance: 1,9km Canal 1,9km 1km on the spot on the spot.

Tourist information Hilpoltstein:
Burgfeste. Festival with events. beginning Aug.

Hof/Saale 12E2

Park Theresienstein, Plauener Straße. **GPS**: n50,32956 e11,92041.

DE

10 free. **Surface:** metalled. 01/01-31/12.
Distance: 2,5km 1km.
Remarks: Max. 24h.

Hof/Saale 12E2

Utreusee, Wilhelm Löhe strasse. **GPS**: n50,28583 e11,91361.

10 free. **Surface:** asphalted/metalled. 01/01-31/12.
Distance: 100m 50m 500m.
Remarks: Max. 24h.

Hof/Saale 12E2

Clean Park, Ernst Reuterstrasse. **GPS**: n50,32641 e11,89248.

4 €5 €1 Ch . **Surface:** metalled. 01/01-31/12.
Distance: 2km 800m.
Remarks: Max. 72h.

Tourist information Hof/Saale:
Bürgerpark Theresienstein. Landscape park according English example. 9-18h, winter 9-16h.
Untreusee. Lake with water sports.

Hofheim in Unterfranken 12C3

Wohnmobilplatz Hofheim, Johannisstraße 28.
GPS: n50,14185 e10,51957.

30 €8 €1/80liter Ch €0,50/kWh WC .
Surface: grasstiles. 01/01-31/12.
Distance: 750m 750m.
Remarks: Bread-service.

Hohenberg/Eger 12E3

Wiesenfestplatz, Selberstrasse. **GPS**: n50,09762 e12,22085.

10-20 voluntary contribution Ch free WC.
Surface: metalled. 01/01-31/12.
Distance: 200m 50m.

Remarks: Beautiful view, porcelain museum.

Hohenburg 17E1

Sportplatz, Sportplatzweg 1. **GPS**: n49,29194 e11,80917.

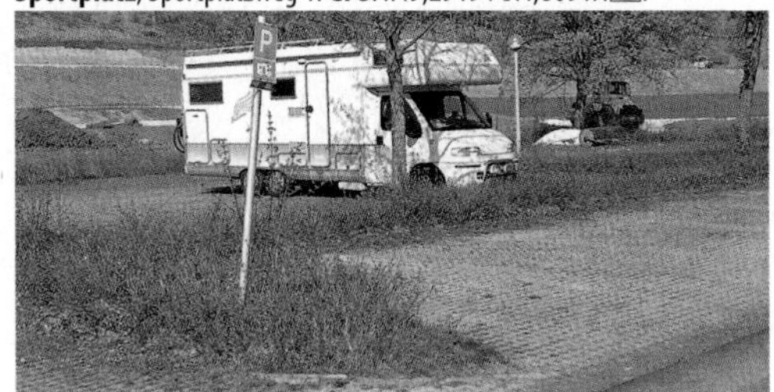

6 €7 €2 WC. **Surface:** metalled. 01/01-31/12.
Distance: 1km.
Remarks: Parking at sports park.

Huisheim 17D2

Waldparkplatz im Schwalbtal, Waldschenke 1, Gosheim.
GPS: n48,84932 e10,71530.

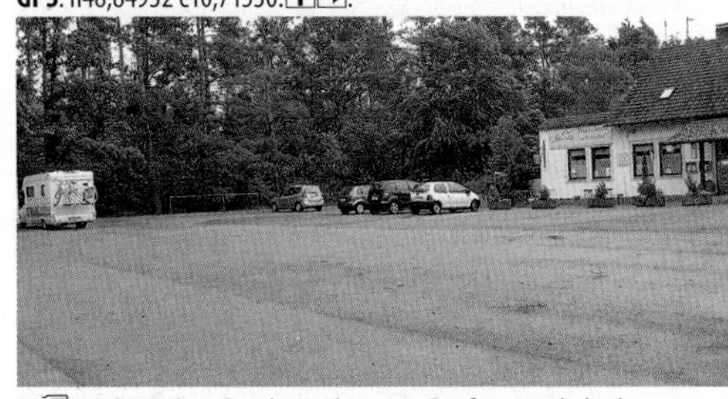

10 €5. **Location:** Rural, simple, quiet. **Surface:** asphalted. 01/01-31/12.
Distance: on the spot.

Immenstadt 20C2

P 3 Viehmarktplatz, Badeweg. **GPS**: n47,56192 e10,20857.

6 €8/24h Ch WC. **Location:** Urban, simple, comfortable.
Surface: asphalted. 01/01-31/12.
Distance: 700m.

Ingolstadt 17E3

Parkplatz Hallenbad, Jahnstrasse. **GPS**: n48,76025 e11,42038.

8 €5 (9-17h), overnight stay free €1/80liter Ch included . **Location:** Urban, comfortable. **Surface:** metalled. 01/01-31/12.
Distance: on the spot 1,6km on the spot on the spot on the spot on the spot.
Remarks: Parking at sports park, max. 3 days.

Inzell 20G1

Camping Lindlbauer, Kreuzfeldstraße 44.
GPS: n47,76717 e12,75417.

12 €16 Ch €2 WC included. **Location:** Rural, simple, quiet. **Surface:** metalled. 01/01-31/12.
Distance: 1km on the spot on the spot.
Remarks: Max. 1 night, health resort 500m.

Iphofen 17C1

Einesheimer Tor, Birklinger Straße. **GPS**: n49,70260 e10,26459.

8 free €1 Ch (6x)€1 WC. **Location:** Urban, simple.
Surface: gravel. 01/01-31/12.
Distance: 200m 200m 200m.
Remarks: Parking at city wall.

Ippesheim 17C1

Kempe's Autohof Gollhofen, Industriestraße 1.
GPS: n49,58546 e10,17579.
25 €6 WC . **Surface:** asphalted. 01/01-31/12.
Distance: on the spot.

Kastl/Oberpfalz 17E1

Wanderparkplatz Am Alten Bahnhof, Amberger Straße.
GPS: n49,36657 e11,68388.

5 free Ch WC free. **Surface:** gravel. 01/01-31/12.
Distance: 200m 200m 100m 50m on the spot on the spot.

Kaufbeuren 20D1

Wohnmobilplatz Kaufbeuren, Buronstraße.
GPS: n47,89885 e10,61650.
8 free Ch free (6x)€1/kWh. **Location:** Urban.
Surface: gravel. 01/01-31/12.
Distance: historical centre 3km.
Remarks: Max. 3 days.

Kelheim 17E2

Volksfestplatz, Am Pflegerspitz. **GPS**: n48,91331 e11,87657.

50 €6 Ch (18x)€1/2kWh WC.
Surface: metalled. 01/01-31/12 service 01/11-31/03.
Distance: 500m 500m.
Remarks: Max. 3 nights, hindmost part.

Kemnath 12E3

Wohnmobilstellplatz Kemnath, Am Eisweier 8.
GPS: n49,87219 e11,88774.

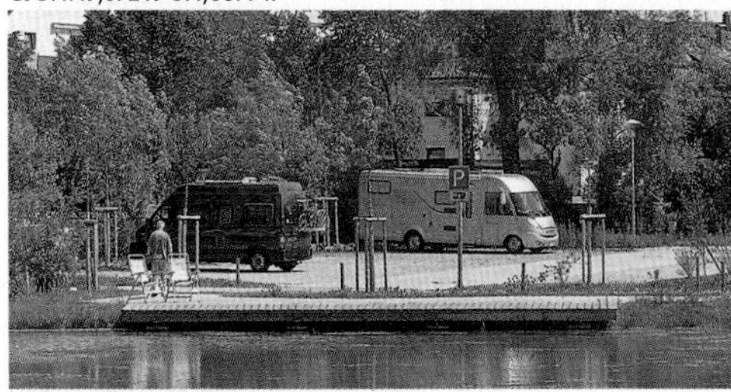

5 free €1 Ch (6x)€1/6h WC. **Surface:** grasstiles.
01/01-31/12.
Distance: 650m 650m 650m.

DE

Remarks: Max. 3 days.

Kempten 20C2

Illerstadion, Illerdamm/Jahnstrasse. **GPS**: n47,72915 e10,31940.

6 € 5 € 1. **Location:** Urban, simple, noisy. **Surface:** metalled. 01/01-31/12.
Distance: 500m 2,7km.

Kiefersfelden 20F2

Hödenauer See, Guggenauerweg 2. **GPS**: n47,62881 e12,18949.

10 € 8 WC €0,50. **Location:** Simple. **Surface:** gravel/sand. 01/01-31/12.
Distance: 2km 3km on the spot on the spot 50m 300m.
Remarks: Max. 3 days, pay at Wasserskilift Hödenauersee.

Kiefersfelden 20F2

Rathausplatz. **GPS**: n47,61303 e12,18981.

20 € 10. **Location:** Simple. **Surface:** asphalted. 01/01-31/12.
Distance: on the spot 2km 100m.
Remarks: Max. 3 days.

Kirchenlamitz 12E3

Anfahrtsskizze, Weißenstädter Straße.
GPS: n50,14905 e11,94055.

12 free Ch free voluntary contribution.
Location: Comfortable. **Surface:** asphalted. 01/01-31/12.
Distance: 500m 10m.

Kirchham 17G3

Erlebnispark Haslinger Hof, Ed 1. **GPS**: n48,34947 e13,29115.

25-30 Overnight stay € 17 (incl. € 9 voucher) € 1 Ch.
Location: Rural, simple, quiet. **Surface:** gravel.
01/01-31/12.

Distance: on the spot.

Kitzingen 17C1

Wohnmobilpark Am Main, Bleichwasen, Etwashausen.
GPS: n49,74274 e10,16491.

70 € 7/24h € 1/80liter Ch €0,50/kWh WC.
Location: Simple. **Surface:** asphalted. 01/01-31/12.
Distance: 300m on the spot on the spot 300m 300m on the spot.
Remarks: Between Alter Mainbrücke and Nordbrücke, bread-service.

Klingenberg 17A1

Sonja's Wohnmobilhafen, Zur Einladung.
GPS: n49,78370 e9,17805.

55 € 7,50 € 1 Ch (30x)€2. **Location:** Rural, comfortable, quiet. **Surface:** grassy/gravel. 01/03-29/10.
Distance: 500m on the spot 500m 2km.
Remarks: Service passerby € 2.

Königsberg 12C3

Buchweg. **GPS**: n50,08472 e10,57028.

6 € 2 Ch. **Surface:** metalled. 01/01-31/12.
Distance: 300m 300m 300m.
Remarks: Parking sports park.

Königsbrunn 20D1

Königsallee. **GPS**: n48,27243 e10,88283.

12 € 6/24h € 1/100liter Ch (12x)€0,50/kWh.
Location: Noisy. **Surface:** metalled.
Distance: 1km 1km.

Kreuth 20E2

Wildbad Kreuth, Bremerweg. **GPS**: n47,62597 e11,74681.

8 € 5. **Location:** Rural, simple. **Surface:** gravel/sand.

01/01-31/12.
Distance: 50m on the spot on the spot.

Kreuzwertheim 17B1

Am Mainufer, Fährgasse. **GPS**: n49,76251 e9,51840.

10 € 5. **Location:** Simple, quiet. **Surface:** gravel.
01/01-31/12.
Distance: Wertheim centre 1,2km on the spot 600m.
Remarks: Along Main river, max. 1 night.

Kronach 12D3

Hammermühle, Am Sand. **GPS**: n50,23195 e11,32735.

10 € 5/24h € 1 Ch (12x)€0,50/kWh. **Location:** Rural, simple. **Surface:** asphalted. 01/01-31/12.
Distance: 10min on the spot 200m 300m.

Kronach 12D3

Lucky Stable Ranch, Mostrach 1. **GPS**: n50,21840 e11,34012.

5 € 5, 2 pers.incl WC included €1,50 €1,50.
Location: Rural, simple, isolated, quiet. **Surface:** grassy/metalled.
01/01-31/12.
Distance: 2km on the spot on the spot 2km.
Remarks: At manege.

Krün 20E2

Tennsee Reisemobilhafen, Am Tennsee 1.
GPS: n47,49083 e11,25444.

37 € 14,50-17 + tourist tax € 1,50/pp, Umwelttaxe € 0,70/pp Ch €0,75/kWh WC included €3 €3/h.
Location: Rural, comfortable, luxurious, quiet. **Surface:** grassy/gravel.
01/01-31/12 07/11-15/12.
Distance: 2,5km 800m 3km on the spot on the spot 100m on the spot on the spot 5km 300m.
Remarks: Dog € 3.

Kulmbach 12D3

Wohnmobilstellplatz Kulmbach, Am Schwedensteg.
GPS: n50,11130 e11,46118.

25 € 3 €1/100liter Ch (25x)€1/2kWh.
Location: Urban, simple. **Surface:** gravel.
01/01-31/12 water disconnected in winter.
Distance: on the spot 50m 200m 500m on the spot on the spot 200m.

Kümmersbruck 17E1

Wohnmobilstellplatz Kümmersbruck, Am Butzenweg.
GPS: n49,41978 e11,89651.

8 free. **Location:** Rural, simple, quiet. **Surface:** metalled.
01/01-31/12.
Distance: 1km 1km.
Remarks: At sports centre.

S Lalling 17G2

Wohnmobilstellplatz Weber, Euschertsfurth 34.
GPS: n48,83222 e13,14444.

8 € 10 Chincluded (10x)€0,30/kWh WC €1,50.
Location: Rural, comfortable, quiet. **Surface:** grassy/metalled.
01/04-30/11.
Distance: 1,5km 100m.
Remarks: Swimming pool incl.

S Lalling 17G2

Lalling-Freizeitgelände, Waldstrasse. **GPS**: n48,84139 e13,13778.

2 free €1/80liter Ch €3/day. **Location:** Rural, simple, quiet. **Surface:** metalled/sand. 01/01-31/12.
Distance: 2km.
Remarks: At tennis-courts.

S Lalling 17G2

Ferienbauernhof Sieglinde, Obstgarten 13, Hunding.
GPS: n48,84502 e13,14939.

3 € 5 Chincluded (2x)€2/day WC. **Location:** Rural, simple, quiet. **Surface:** grassy. 01/04-31/12.
Distance: 700m.

S Lalling 17G2

Lallinger Hof, Hauptstrasse 23. **GPS**: n48,84560 e13,13851.

4 guests free against payment. **Location:** Rural, simple, quiet.
01/04-31/10.
Distance: 250m 250m.
Remarks: Check in at restaurant.

Lalling 17G2

Gasthof zur Post, Pfarrweg. **GPS**: n48,84405 e13,14064.

15 free. **Location:** Rural, simple, quiet. **Surface:** metalled.
winter.
Distance: 200m 200m.

Lalling 17G2

Feng Shui Kurpark, Euschertsfurther Straße.
GPS: n48,84137 e13,13952.

10 € 1. **Surface:** gravel. 01/01-31/12.
Remarks: Not indicated.

S Lalling 17G2

Erikas Wohlfühlplatz, Kleinfeld 6, Hunding.
GPS: n48,84333 e13,17944.

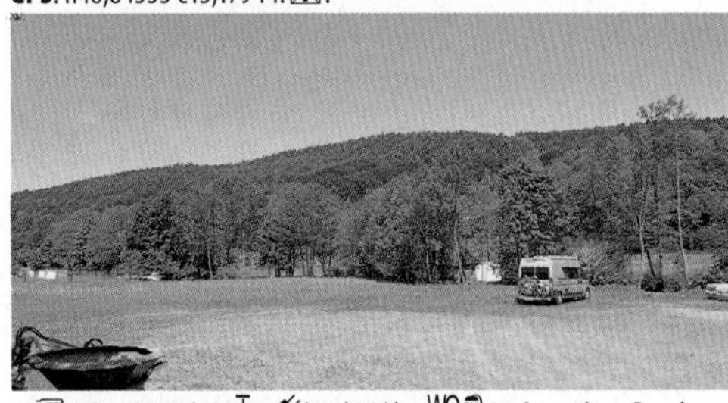

10 € 5 + €0,50/pp (10x)€1/day WC €4. **Location:** Rural, simple, quiet. **Surface:** grassy/sand. 01/04-31/10.
Distance: on the spot on the spot 3km 200m on the spot on the spot.
Remarks: Check in at Kleinfeld 6.

S Landau/Isar 17F3

Am Festplatz, Harburger Straße 20/B20.
GPS: n48,67712 e12,68323.

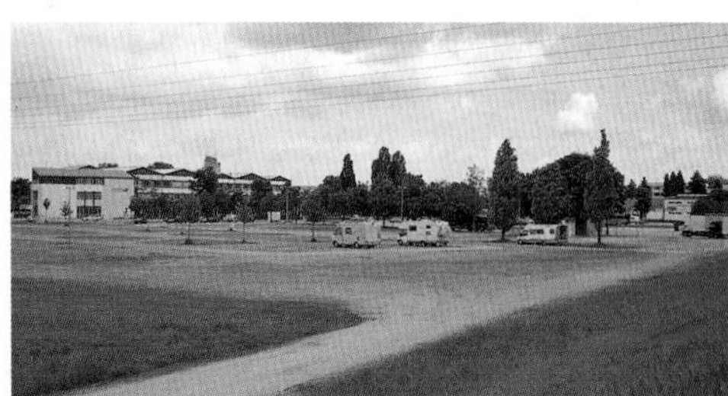

± 20 free €0,50/100liter Ch (6x)€0,50/kWh.
Surface: grassy/gravel. 01/01-31/12.
Distance: 1,5km 2,3km McDonalds 200m bakery 200m.

S Landsberg am Lech 20D1

Waitzinger Wiese, Gottesackerangerweg.
GPS: n48,05534 e10,87371.

8 € 7/24h €1/50liter Ch (8x)€1/6h WC €0,50.
Location: Urban, simple. **Surface:** metalled. 01/01-31/12.
Distance: 400m 300m.

S Lechbruck am See 20D2

Wohnmobilpark via Claudia, Via Claudia 6.
GPS: n47,71556 e10,82139.

52 € 11,50, 2 pers. incl., dog € 3-3,50 Ch included WC €1,50 €2,50 €3/24h. **Location:** Rural, comfortable, luxurious. **Surface:** gravel. 01/01-31/12.
Distance: 5km on the spot on the spot on the spot on the spot on the spot 10km on the spot.

S Lenggries 20E2

Dürrachstrasse, Fall. **GPS**: n47,57039 e11,53380.

25 € 0,50/h, € 4/24h €2 WC.
Location: Rural, isolated, quiet. **Surface:** metalled.
01/01-31/12 service: 01/11-01/04.
Distance: 250m 250m 150m 8km on the spot on the spot.
Remarks: Max. 7 days.

S Lindau 20B2

Blauwiese, P1. GPS: n47,55869 e9,70130.

30 € 1/h, € 20/24h €0,50 €0,50 ChWC. **Surface:** metalled.
01/01-31/12.

DE

Distance: on the spot 1km 1km 500m 500m on the spot.
Remarks: Max. 24h.

Lindau 20B2

Park Camping, Frauenhoferstrasse, Lindau-Zech.
GPS: n47,53764 e9,73148.

15 € 12/24h Ch WC included,on campsite.
Surface: gravel. 15/03-31/10.
Remarks: Max. 24h.

Tourist information Lindau:
Lindau Insel. Promenade along the lake with Mangturm, 700 years old lighthouse.

Litzendorf 12D3

ASV Naisa, Am Wetterkreuz. **GPS**: n49,91559 e11,00261.

8 free. **Location:** Rural, simple, quiet. **Surface:** gravel.
01/01-31/12.
Distance: 200m on the spot on the spot.

Litzendorf 12D3

Tiefenellern, Ellerbergstrasse. **GPS**: n49,91927 e11,07006.

3. **Location:** Rural, simple, isolated. **Surface:** gravel.
Distance: on the spot on the spot.

Lohr/Main 12B3

Lohr am Main, Osttangente. **GPS**: n49,99429 e9,58053.

21 € 5 € 1/100liter Ch (22x)€ 2/8h WC €2/h.
Location: Urban, noisy. **Surface:** metalled. 01/04-31/10.
Distance: 300m on the spot Aldi 800m.
Remarks: Along Main river, max. 3 days.

Mainbernheim 17C1

Goldgrubenweg. **GPS**: n49,71153 e10,22045.

10 free. **Location:** Urban, simple, quiet. **Surface:** metalled.
01/01-31/12.
Distance: on the spot 200m 200m 100m.

Mainstockheim 17C1

Wohnmobilhafen Mainstockheim, Albertshöfer straße.
GPS: n49,77173 e10,15595.

37 € 7 Ch included. **Location:** Rural, simple, quiet.
Surface: gravel. 01/01-31/12.
Distance: on the spot 5km on the spot 100m 100m on the spot.
Remarks: Along Main river.

Manching 17E3

Am Braunweiher. **GPS**: n48,71078 e11,49602.

50 free € 1/80liter Ch. **Location:** Simple.
Surface: grasstiles/metalled. 01/01-31/12.
Distance: 1,5km 1,3km Edeka 1km.

Markt Wald 20C1

Wohnmobilpark Markt Wald, Bürgle 1a.
GPS: n48,14602 e10,57517.

20 € 7 € 1/100liter Ch €0,50/kWh WC €2.
Location: Rural, comfortable, quiet. **Surface:** grassy/gravel.
01/01-31/12.
Distance: 1km on the spot on the spot on the spot 1km on the spot on the spot on the spot.
Remarks: At small lake, bread-service, use sanitary facilities at campsite.

Marktbreit 17C1

Am Kranen, Staatstraße. **GPS**: n49,66878 e10,14241.

3 free.
Location: Simple. **Surface:** metalled. 01/01-31/12.

Distance: on the spot on the spot on the spot on the spot 500m on the spot.
Remarks: Max. 1 day.

Marktheidenfeld 17B1

Martinswiese, Georg-Mayr-Straße. **GPS**: n49,84918 e9,59887.

30 € 5/24h € 1/100liter Ch (8x)€ 1/4h WC included.
Location: Rural, comfortable, quiet. **Surface:** gravel.
01/01-31/12 during event.
Distance: 600m on the spot on the spot 200m Lidl 650m.
Remarks: Along Main river, max. 3 days.

Marktheidenfeld 17B1

Georg-Mayr-Straße. **GPS**: n49,85364 e9,60025.

20 free. **Location:** Rural, simple, noisy. **Surface:** gravel.
01/01-31/12.
Distance: 1km 50m Lidl 50m.
Remarks: Max. 3 days.

Marktleuthen 12E3

Am Angerparkplatz. **GPS**: n50,12946 e11,99483.

10 free Ch (10x)free WC €0,50. **Surface:** metalled.
01/01-31/12.
Distance: 250m 150m 200m.
Remarks: Max. 7 days, bread-service.

Marktoberdorf 20D2

Parkplatz der Bayerischen Musikakademie, Kurfürstenstraße 19.
GPS: n47,78013 e10,62284.
4 free € 1/50liter Ch €0,50/kWh. **Surface:** grasstiles.
01/01-31/12.
Distance: on the spot 100m.

Marktredwitz 12E3

Wohnmobilstellplatz am Auenpark, Dörflaser Platz, Fabrikstraße.
GPS: n49,99710 e12,08640.

20 free € 0,50/150liter €0,50 Ch €0,50 (6x)€0,50/kWh.
Surface: asphalted/gravel. 01/01-31/12.
Distance: 300m 50m 150m.

Marktredwitz 12E3

Angerplatz, Egerland-Kulturhaus, Fikentscherstrasse.
GPS: n50,00379 e12,09506.

DE

6 free. **Surface:** asphalted. 01/01-31/12.
Distance: 1km 500m.

Massing 17F3

Am Freilichtmuseum, Spirknerstraße. **GPS**: n48,39528 e12,60056.
10 free on demand.
Surface: asphalted.
Distance: Museumstüberl.
Remarks: Open air museum, busy parking during the day.

Mehlmeisel 12E3

Parkplatz Am Park. **GPS**: n49,97615 e11,85471.

free. **Surface:** metalled. 01/01-31/12.
Distance: 250m bakery 100m.
Remarks: Max. 3 nights.

Mellrichstadt 12C2

Malbachweg. **GPS**: n50,43139 e10,30972.

7 free €1/80liter Ch €0,50/kWh. **Surface:** asphalted.
01/01-31/12.
Distance: 500m 750m 750m on the spot on the spot.
Remarks: Max. 3 days.

Memmelsdorf 12D3

Seehofblick, Pödeldorferstrasse 20-A. **GPS**: n49,92906 e10,95594.
4 €5 €1/80liter Ch €1/8h. **Location:** Urban, simple.
Surface: asphalted. 01/04-31/10.
Distance: on the spot 250m.

Memmelsdorf 12D3

Stocksee, Stockseestrasse. **GPS**: n49,92556 e10,93417.

5 €5 €1/80liter Chfree (4x)€1/8h. **Location:** Urban.
Surface: asphalted. 01/01-31/12.
Distance: 1,2km 500m 100m.

Miltenberg 17A1

Linkes Mainufer, Jahnstrasse/Luitpoldstrasse.
GPS: n49,70464 e9,25860.

20 free ChWCfree. **Location:** Central. **Surface:** asphalted.
01/01-31/12.
Distance: 200m 200m 200m.

Miltenberg 17A1

Am Yachthafen, Steingässerstrasse. **GPS**: n49,70446 e9,25435.

20 free. **Location:** Rural, simple. **Surface:** grassy/gravel.
01/01-31/12.
Distance: 800m on the spot 800m 500m on the spot.
Remarks: Along Main river.

Mistelgau 12D3

Therme Obernsees, An der Therme 1, Obernsees.
GPS: n49,91630 e11,37831.

40 €10 €1/50liter Ch €1/12h WC .
Location: Luxurious, quiet. **Surface:** grasstiles/metalled.
01/01-31/12.
Distance: 1km Therme-Bistro on the spot on the spot on the spot on the spot.
Remarks: Bread-service, discount on access terme.

Mittenwald 20E2

Wohnmobil-Stellplatz Karwendel, Albert-Schott-Straße.
GPS: n47,43792 e11,26411.

30 €7/24h + €4/pp tourist tax €1/80liter Ch (30x)€0,80/kWh. **Location:** Simple, noisy. **Surface:** asphalted/gravel.
01/01-31/12.
Distance: 250m on the spot.
Remarks: Along railwayline.

Mitterteich 12E3

Freizeithugl Großbüchlberg, Großbüchlberg 32.
GPS: n49,97286 e12,22496.

24 €12, 2 pers. incl., dog €1,50 Ch (16x)€0,50 WC against payment €2,50/2,50 €1/24h. **Surface:** metalled.
01/01-31/12.
Distance: 200m.
Remarks: Bread-service.

Monheim 17D2

An der Stadthalle, Schulstraße. **GPS**: n48,84503 e10,85329.

7 free €1/100liter Ch €1/8h. **Location:** Simple, central.
Surface: grasstiles. 01/01-31/12.
Distance: 400m 500m 500m.

Moosbach 17F1

Am Natur-Waldbad Tröbes, Tröbes. **GPS**: n49,55851 e12,44074.
9 €10 Ch WC . 01/03-31/10.
Distance: on the spot.

Moosbach 17F1

Bei der Wieskirche, Am Badeweiher Tröbes, Friedhofgasse.
GPS: n49,59076 e12,41193.

6 €5 Ch included. **Surface:** gravel. 01/03-31/10.
Distance: 250m 250m 250m.
Remarks: Check in at Gästeinformation.

Mörnsheim 17D2

Wohnmobilstellplatz Hammermühle, Altendorf.
GPS: n48,87455 e11,02948.

21 €10, dog €1 Chincluded €0,60/kWh €2.
Location: Rural. **Surface:** unpaved. 01/04-31/10.
Distance: Altendorf 2km Imbiss, Biergarten on the spot on the spot.
Remarks: Nature reserve Altmühltal, bread-service.

München 20E1

Allianz-Arena Wohnmobilstellplätze, Werner-Heisenberg-Allee 25, Munich (München). **GPS**: n48,22089 e11,62505.

110 €15 €0,20/20liter (10x)€1/kWh.
Surface: asphalted. during event.
Distance: Bistro-Biergarten on the spot on the spot.
Remarks: FC Bayern Erlebniswelt (Fanmuseum).

München 20E1

Oktoberfest-Camping, De-Gasperi-Bogen, München-Riem, Munich (München).
GPS: n48,13342 e11,70746.

DE

1000 € 35, 2 pers.incl, extra pers € 15 Ch WC included.
Surface: metalled.
Oktoberfest.
Distance: on the spot on the spot metro 300m.
Remarks: Opened 2 days before Oktoberfest.

Tourist information Munich (München):
München CityTourCard. Card gives for free entrance on among other things public transport and 50% discounts on curiosities.
€ 10,90/day, € 20,90/3 days.
Agustinerbräu, Neuhauserstrasse 16. Brewery from 1644.
Schloß Nymphenburg. Former summer residence of the Witelbacher monarchs.
Tue-Su 9-12.30h, 13.30-17h. € 6.
Neumarkt. Ruins of citadel dominating the city.
Oktoberfest. Beer festival, special motorhome parking.

S Münnerstadt 12C3
An der Lache, P1, Seminarstrasse. **GPS**: n50,25188 e10,19348.

4 free €1/90liter Ch (4x)€0,50/kWh,16Amp WC.
Surface: metalled. 01/01-31/12.
Distance: 350m.
Remarks: Max. 3 days.

Münnerstadt 12C3
Am Oberen Tor, P2, Dr.Engelhardt Weg. **GPS**: n50,24914 e10,19145.

3 free. **Surface:** metalled. 01/01-31/12.
Distance: on the spot on the spot.

S Murnau am Staffelsee 20D2
Am P&R Bahnof, Am Bahnhof. **GPS**: n47,68005 e11,19447.

6 € 1/day €1/100liter Ch (6x)€1/2kWh. **Location:** Rural, comfortable, central, quiet. **Surface:** grasstiles/metalled.
01/01-31/12.
Distance: 500m 10km 400m 300m on the spot.
Remarks: Max. 72h.

S Naila 12E2
Christian-Schlicht-strasse. **GPS**: n50,33071 e11,71127.

4 free Ch. **Location:** Urban, simple. **Surface:** metalled.
01/01-31/12.
Distance: 100m 50m 300m 300m on the spot on the spot.
Remarks: Parking left side of the station, thursday market.

Naila 12E2
Badstraße. **GPS**: n50,32965 e11,70108.

10 free. **Location:** Urban, simple, isolated. **Surface:** asphalted.
01/01-31/12.
Distance: 650m.
Remarks: Thursday market.

S Nesselwang 20C2
An der Riese, Altspitzbahn. **GPS**: n47,61995 e10,49830.

70 € 8 €1 Ch (62x)€1/kWh.
Location: Rural, comfortable. **Surface:** gravel/metalled.
01/01-31/12.
Distance: 500m 3,8km 1km 3km 200m 500m 500m on the spot 200m 200m.
Remarks: Baker every morning, code internet at tourist office.

S Neualbenreuth 12F3
Reisemobilhafen Sibyllenbad, Parkplatz P2, Kurallee.
GPS: n49,98099 e12,42406.

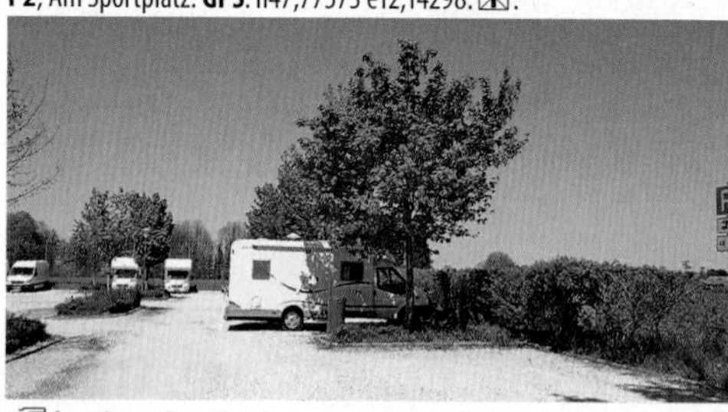

21 € 8 + € 1/pp tourist tax Ch (20x)€0,50/kWh WC.
Surface: metalled. 01/01-31/12.
Distance: 1,5km.
Remarks: Bread-service.

Neubeuern 20F2
P2, Am Sportplatz. **GPS**: n47,77573 e12,14298.

6 free. **Location:** Rural, simple, quiet. **Surface:** gravel.
Distance: 500m 500m.
Remarks: Max. 48h.

S Neuburg/Donau 17D3
Parkplatz P1, Schlösslwiese, Zur Ringmeierbucht.
GPS: n48,74022 e11,18434.

30 free €1/100liter Ch. **Location:** Urban, simple, central, quiet. **Surface:** gravel/sand. 01/01-31/12.
Distance: 100m 400m on the spot on the spot.
Remarks: On the Danube river.

Neumarkt/Oberpfalz 17E1
Volksfestplatz, Woffenbacherstrasse. **GPS**: n49,28118 e11,44528.

30 free. **Surface:** grassy. 01/01-31/12.
Distance: 600m.
Remarks: At sports centre.

S Neumarkt/Oberpfalz 17E1
Fritz Berger, Fritz-Berger-Str. 1. **GPS**: n49,30500 e11,48444.

free Chfree. **Surface:** grassy. 01/01-31/12.
Distance: 2km 2km.

Neusäß 17D3
Titania-Therme, Birkenallee 1. **GPS**: n48,40089 e10,82508.

5 free. **Location:** Urban, simple, central, quiet. **Surface:** metalled.
01/01-31/12.
Distance: 1,2km 3km 1,2km on the spot on the spot.

S Neustadt/Aisch 17C1
Am Festplatz, Bei den Sommerkeller. **GPS**: n49,58187 e10,60271.

8 free €1 Ch €1. **Surface:** gravel. 01/01-31/12.
Distance: 500m 500m 500m 500m on the spot.

Neustadt/Aisch 17C1
Am Waldwad, Eilersweg. **GPS**: n49,57462 e10,62993.

6 free. **Surface:** grasstiles. 01/01-31/12.
Distance: 3,5km 4km 4km 1km.

S Niederwerrn 12C3
Jahnstrasse. **GPS**: n50,06073 e10,17526.

35 voluntary contribution €3 Ch WC.
Surface: asphalted. 01/01-31/12.
Distance: on the spot on the spot.
Remarks: Near sports fields, max. 3 nights.

S Nordheim am Main 12C3

Zehnthofstrasse. **GPS**: n49,85952 e10,17909.

50 € 8/24h Chfree .
Surface: metalled. 01/04-31/10.
Distance: 200m.
Remarks: Along Main river, max. 3 days.

S Nördlingen 17C3

Wohnmobilstellpatz Innerer Ring, Kaiserwiese.
GPS: n48,85488 e10,48445.

30 € 3/24h €2 €2 Ch €2/24h WC. **Location:** Urban, simple, quiet. **Surface:** asphalted. 01/01-31/12.
Distance: on the spot McDonalds.
Remarks: Max. 48h.

Nürnberg 17D1

Volkspark Dutzendteich, Munchener Strasse.
GPS: n49,42403 e11,10586.

10 free. **Location:** Urban. **Surface:** asphalted. 01/01-31/12.
Distance: 4km 700m.
Remarks: Max. 3 nights.

Nürnberg 17D1

Volkspark Marienburg, Kilianstrasse.
GPS: n49,47495 e11,09606.

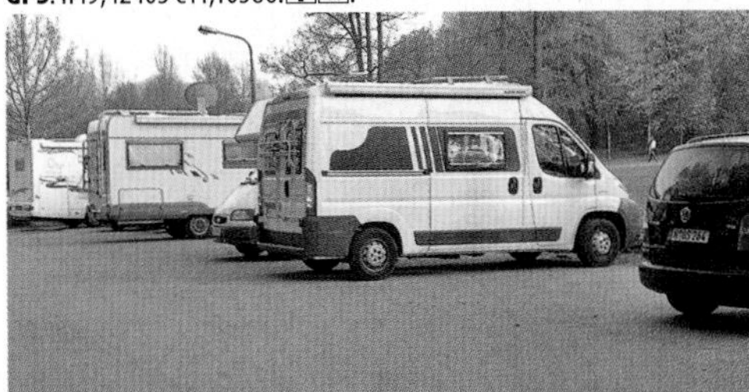

8 free. **Location:** Urban. **Surface:** grasstiles/metalled.
01/01-31/12.
Distance: centre 4km 800m 800m on the spot.

Remarks: Max. 3 nights.

Nürnberg 17D1

Wöhrder See, Rechenberganlage, Dr Gustav Heinemannstrasse.
GPS: n49,46041 e11,11548.

8 free. **Location:** Urban. **Surface:** metalled. 01/01-31/12.
Distance: 3km 500m.
Remarks: Max. 3 nights.

Tourist information Nürnberg:
City walk through old city centre, daily from Tourist Information, Hauptmarkt. 14.30h.
Nürnberg Card. Card gives for free entrance on among other things public transport and museums, discounts on purchases, boat trips, city walks etc.
Spielzeugmuseum, Karlstrasse 13-15. Toy museum. Tue-Su 10-17h.
Kaiserburg Nürnberg, Burg 13. Palace. 01/04-30/09 9-18h, 01/10-31/03 10-16h. € 7.
Tiergarten. Zoo. 8-19.30.

S Oberammergau 20D2

Campingpark Oberammergau, Ettalerstrasse 56B.
GPS: n47,59040 e11,07157.

20 € 8 Ch WC against payment. **Location:** Simple.
Surface: gravel. 01/01-31/12.
Distance: 1,2km 400m 100m 1,2km 1km.
Remarks: Max. 24h.

S Oberaudorf 20F2

Pechler Hof, Tatzlwurmstrasse 5. **GPS**: n47,66132 e12,16890.

5 € 9 included. **Location:** Rural, simple, quiet.
Surface: grassy. 01/01-31/12.
Distance: 1km 500m 200m 100m.

S Oberaudorf 20F2

Hotel Feuriger Tatzlwurm, Tatzlwurm, B307.
GPS: n47,67223 e12,08448.

10 guests free . **Location:** Rural, simple.
Surface: gravel/metalled. 01/01-31/12.
Distance: on the spot on the spot on the spot.

S Oberelsbach 12B2

Wohnmobilstellplatz Oberelsbach, Gangolfstrasse.
GPS: n50,44234 e10,11412.

6 € 5 € 1/80liter Ch (6x)€0,50/kWh. 01/01-31/12.
Distance: 500m on the spot.
Remarks: Max. 3 days.

S Oberkotzau 12E2

Wohnmobilstellplatz Am Summa-Park, Fabrikstraße.
GPS: n50,26344 e11,93849.
9 € 12 €1/100liter Ch WC included .
Surface: metalled. 01/01-31/12.
Distance: 450m.
Remarks: Max. 5 days.

S Obermaiselstein 20C2

Wohnmobilplatz Allgäu, Am Goldbach 3, Niederdorf.
GPS: n47,44422 e10,24288.

30 € 10 + € 1,30/pp tourist tax Ch (25x)€2/day WC €1 . **Location:** Rural, comfortable, luxurious.
Surface: asphalted/gravel. 01/01-31/12.
Distance: on the spot.

S Oberstdorf 20C3

Rubi-Camp, Rubinger Straße 34. **GPS**: n47,42340 e10,27772.

80 € 23-27 + € 2,60/pp tourist tax, dog € 3 Ch €0,70/kWh WC .
Surface: grassy. 01/01-31/12.
Distance: 150m (skibus) on the spot on the spot.
Remarks: Bread-service.

S Oberstdorf 20C3

Wohnmobilstellplatz Oberstdorf, Enzenspergerweg 10.
GPS: n47,40856 e10,28625.

150 € 12, tourist tax € 2,60/pp Ch €2,50/24h WC.
Location: Rural, luxurious. **Surface:** grassy/metalled.
01/01-31/12.
Distance: on the spot 250m 100m on the spot 500m 800m.

S Oberthulba 12B3

Reisemobilstellplatz Thulbatal. **GPS**: n50,17419 e9,92499.

DE

25 € 8, 2 pers.incl Chincluded €2 WC €0,80 €2,30.
Surface: grasstiles. 15/03-31/10.
Distance: 1km on the spot 150m.

Oberviechtach 17F1

Am Freibad, Im Wiesengrund. **GPS**: n49,45296 e12,42458.

+5 free Ch (3x)free. **Location:** Simple, isolated.
Surface: asphalted. 01/01-31/12.
Distance: 1km 600m.
Remarks: Max. 3 days.

Oettingen 17C2

Schießwasen. **GPS**: n48,95690 e10,60894.

4 free €1/10minutes Ch (4x)€1/8h. **Location:** Simple, quiet. **Surface:** metalled. 01/01-31/12 last weekend Jul, 1st weekend Aug.
Distance: 10 min walking 500m.

Ostheim 12C2

Streuwiesenparkplatz, Nordheimer Straße/Alexander Straße.
GPS: n50,45820 e10,22656.

6 € 3 €1/80liter Ch €0,50. **Surface:** metalled.
01/01-31/12.
Distance: 300m 300m 300m.

Ottobeuren 20C1

Parking Sportwelt, Galgenberg 4. **GPS**: n47,94907 e10,29649.

10 free €1/100liter Ch (6x)€0,50/kWh.
Location: Urban, comfortable. **Surface:** metalled.
01/01-31/12.
Distance: 1km.
Remarks: Coins at Sportwelt (9-23h), village with noteworthy cathedral.

Parkstein 17E1

Basaltkegel von Parkstein, Basaltstrasse 16.
GPS: n49,73179 e12,07127.

20 free. **Surface:** metalled. 01/01-31/12.
Distance: 200m 50m.
Remarks: Nearbij Gasthof Bergstüberl, beautiful view.

Passau 17H3

Am Parkdeck Ilzbrücke, Halser Straße. **GPS**: n48,57895 e13,47437.

13 € 1/h, max. € 8/day €1/50liter Ch €0,50/kWh.
Location: Urban, comfortable, central. **Surface:** metalled.
01/01-31/12 high water.
Distance: centre 500m 500m 500m on the spot.
Remarks: Max. 24h.

Passau 17H3

Am Parkhaus, Bahnhofstraße. **GPS**: n48,57406 e13,44495.

15 € 3/h, max. € 13/day Chincluded. **Location:** Urban, simple, noisy. **Surface:** metalled. 01/01-31/12.
Distance: 500m 500m 500m 100m.
Remarks: Price incl. bus transport to the city centre.

Passau 17H3

Winterhafen Racklau, Regensburgerstrasse/Racklau.
GPS: n48,57412 e13,42690.

30 free. **Surface:** gravel. 01/01-31/12 high water.
Distance: 2km On the Danube river on the spot 500m 500m 300m.

Peiting 20D2

Wellenfreibad, Ammergauer Strasse 22/A. **GPS**: n47,79317 e10,92227.

3 free. 01/01-31/12.
Distance: 100m.
Remarks: Parking at swimming pool, max. 48h.

Petting 20G1

Ferienhof Stubern, Stubern 1. **GPS**: n47,88988 e12,78455.

3 € 15, 2 pers.incl €2/100liter Ch €0,50/kWh WC.
Location: Rural, simple, quiet. **Surface:** grassy.
01/05-30/10.
Distance: 4km 5km 5km 3km 2km on the spot on the spot.

Petting 20G1

Stellplatz Schneiderhof, Seestrasse 11a.
GPS: n47,91375 e12,81120.

4 € 15, 2 pers.incl Ch €0,50/kWh WC included.
Location: Rural, comfortable. **Surface:** grassy. 01/05-30/10.
Distance: 300m 1km 300m 300m 500m.
Remarks: Dog € 3.

Pfronten 20D2

Wohnmobilstellplatz Wohlfahrt, Am Wiesele 7, Weißbach.
GPS: n47,59829 e10,55240.

44 € 10, 2 pers.incl €1 Ch (48x)WCincluded €0,50/3minutes €3. **Surface:** gravel.
01/01-31/12.
Distance: 400m 100m 400m Skibus 5km on the spot.

Plattling 17G2

Freizeit- und Sportzentrum Plattling, Georg-Ecklstrasse.
GPS: n48,77226 e12,87331.

20 free €1/80liter Ch (4x)€0,50/kWh.
Location: Rural, simple. **Surface:** grassy/metalled.
01/01-31/12.
Distance: 500m 500m.

Pleinfeld 17D2

Freizeitanlage Ramsberg, Leitenbuckstraße.
GPS: n49,12103 e10,93275.
28 € 12/24h €0,50/kWh WC. **Surface:** grassy.
01/01-31/12.
Distance: 800m on the spot on the spot 100m 5km.

Pleystein 17F1

Reisemobilplatz Pleystein, Vohenstraußer Straße/Galgenbergweg.
GPS: n49,64429 e12,40548.

DE

8 free WC free. **Surface:** gravel. 01/01-31/12.
Distance: 350m 200m.

Poppenricht 17E1

Wohnmobilstellplatz an der Vils, Vilsstrasse.
GPS: n49,48184 e11,83119.

20 free. **Location:** Rural, simple, quiet. **Surface:** gravel.
01/01-31/12.
Distance: 1km on the spot 2km 1km on the spot.
Remarks: Along the historic "Goldenen Straße" from Nürnberg to Prague, at sports centre.

Pottenstein 17D1

Wohnmobilpark Pottenstein, Am langen Berg.
GPS: n49,76294 e11,40826.

25 € 7 €1/80liter Ch€1 (6x)€1/kWh.
Location: Rural, simple.
Surface: grassy/metalled.
01/01-31/12 Service: winter.
Distance: 1km Aldi 200m.

Tourist information Pottenstein:
Teufelshöhle. Caves, constant temperature 9°C and atmospheric humidity 98%. 19/03-06/11 9-17.
Burg Pottenstein. 1000 Jaar oude burcht. Tue-Su 10-17h.
Sommerrodelbahn. Toboggan slide 1km. 01/04-31/10 10-17h.

Prichsenstadt 17C1

Wohnmobilstellplatz Schützengesellschaft 1752, Wiesentheider Straße 3. **GPS**: n49,81649 e10,34981.

5 € 5 €1 €2,50. **Surface:** gravel. 01/01-31/12.
Distance: 300m on the spot.

Prien am Chiemsee 20F1

Wohnmobilstellplatz Strandbad Schraml, Harrasser Strasse 39.
GPS: n47,85400 e12,36679.

20 € 10 Ch €3/day WC. **Location:** Rural, simple, isolated.
Surface: unpaved. 01/04-15/10.
Distance: 1,5km 6km on the spot 500m on the spot on the spot on the spot.
Remarks: Arrival >18h, departure <10h, pay at reception, nights closed with barrier, steep ramp.

Rain/Lech 17D3

Wohnmobilstellplatz Rain, Fasanenweg.
GPS: n48,69195 e10,90699.

8 free €1 Ch €1/6h.
Surface: metalled. 01/01-31/12.
Distance: 1km on the spot on the spot.

Ramsthal 12B3

Festplatz, Hauptstrasse, K6-4. **GPS**: n50,13750 e10,06111.

12 free €1/100liter Ch €0,50/kWh WC. **Surface:** metalled.
01/01-31/12.
Distance: on the spot Gasthof Wahler, Gaststätte zum Beck on the spot.

Reit im Winkl 20F2

Wohnmobilpark Reit im Winkl, Am Waldbahnhof 7, Groissenbach.
GPS: n47,67013 e12,48358.

250 € 12, 15/12-03/04 € 14 €0,20/10liter Ch €0,75/kWh WC use sanitary €4,50. **Location:** Rural, quiet.
Surface: grassy/metalled. 01/01-31/12.
Distance: 1km 1,5km 200m on the spot on the spot on the spot on the spot.
Remarks: Shuttle bus to ski-piste.

Reit im Winkl 20F2

Wohnmobilpark Seegatterl, Seegatterl 7.
GPS: n47,65898 e12,54213.

50 € 9, 05/12-03/04 € 13 + tourist tax €0,20/10liter Ch €0,75/kWh WC . **Location:** Rural, simple, quiet.
Surface: grassy/gravel. 05/12-10/04, 01/06-15/10.
Distance: 4km 1,5km 500m on the spot on the spot on the spot 150m on the spot.

Reit im Winkl 20F2

Gasthof Stoaner, Birnbacher Straße 34.
GPS: n47,67900 e12,44930.

15 € 10, 2 pers.incl., winter € 12 Ch (12x)WC included.
Location: Rural, quiet. **Surface:** unpaved. 01/11-20/12, Easter-30/04.
Distance: 2km on the spot on the spot on the spot on the spot.
Remarks: At golf court.

Riedenburg 17E2

Volksfestplatz, Austraße. **GPS**: n48,96446 e11,68181.

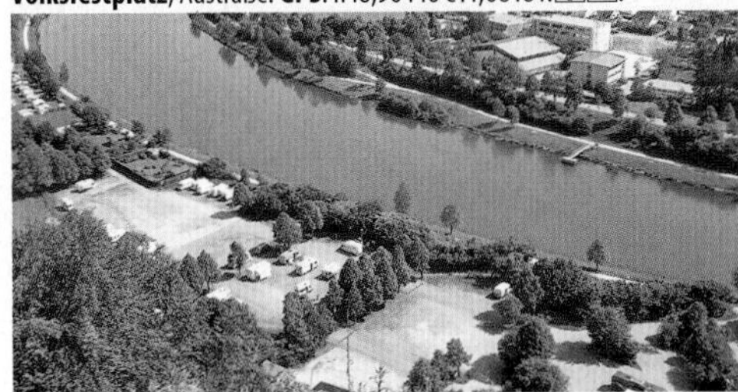

40 € 6 Ch included €1/8h.
Location: Central. **Surface:** gravel/metalled.
01/01-31/12 last week of Aug.
Distance: 450m on the spot 300m 20m.
Remarks: At the Main-Danube Canal.

Roding 17F2

Volksfestplatz, Jahnstraße 21. **GPS**: n49,19806 e12,51722.
4 free €1/70liter €1 Ch €0,50/kWh. **Location:** Urban, simple. **Surface:** asphalted/metalled. 01/01-31/12.
Distance: 150m 150m 500m.
Remarks: Max. 1 day.

Roßhaupten 20D2

Wohnmobilstellplatz Miller, Augsburger Strasse 23.
GPS: n47,65889 e10,71944.

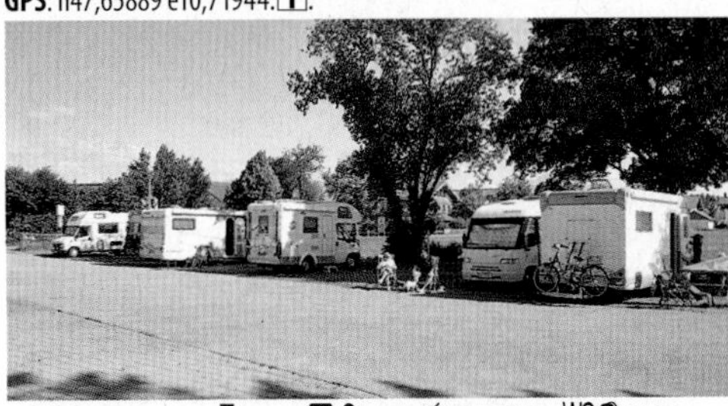

25 € 9, 4 pers.incl €1,50 Ch€2 (3x)€2/day WC €1,50.
Location: Simple. **Surface:** metalled. 01/01-31/12.
Distance: 50m 1,2km 1,2km 200m 150m 150m 1km 500m.
Remarks: Next to Camping- und Freizeitmarkt, reparation work.

Rothenbuch 12B3

Freizeitanlage, Heigenbrücker Weg. **GPS**: n49,97460 e9,39475.

DE

10 € 7 €1/80liter Ch €0,50/kWh. **Location:** Rural, simple, quiet. **Surface:** grasstiles. 01/01-31/12.
Distance: 250m.

S Rothenburg ob der Tauber 17C1

Parkplatz P2, Nördlinger Strasse. **GPS**: n49,37048 e10,18324.

25 € 10 €1/45liter Ch €0,50/kWh WC. **Surface:** metalled.
01/01-31/12.
Distance: 700m.

S Rothenburg ob der Tauber 17C1

Parkplatz P3, Schweinsdorfer Strasse. **GPS**: n49,38222 e10,18889.

30 € 10 €1/45liter Ch WC.
Surface: metalled.
01/01-31/12.
Distance: on the spot.

Tourist information Rothenburg ob der Tauber:
Mittelalterliches Kriminalmuseum, Burggasse 3. History of 1000 years of jurisdiction.
01/04-31/10 10-18h, 01/11-31/03 13-16h.
Schäfertanz. Traditional celebration.
27/03, 15/05, 04/09.

S Rothenkirchen 12D2

Waldschwimmbad. **GPS**: n50,37389 e11,31583.

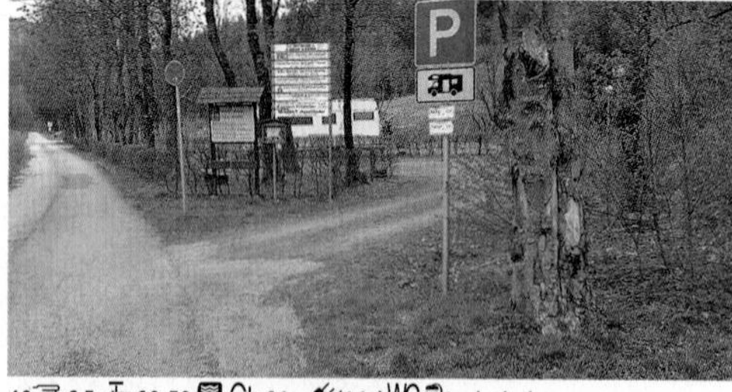

40 € 5 €0,50 Ch €1 (16x) WC included.
Surface: metalled. 01/04-31/10.
Distance: 1,5km.
Remarks: Parking swimming pool.

Röthlein 12C3

Sportanlage TSV/Bundeskegelbahn, Friedhofstrasse.
GPS: n49,98694 e10,21583.

10 free. **Surface:** unpaved.
Distance: on the spot.

S Röttingen 17B1

Wohnmobilplatz an der Tauber, Neubronner Straße.
GPS: n49,50724 e9,96995.

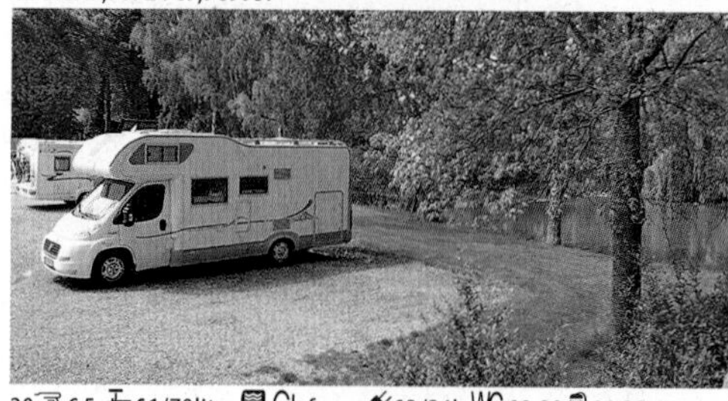

20 € 5 €1/70liter Ch free €2/24h WC €0,20 €1,20.
Location: Rural, simple. **Surface:** gravel. 01/04-31/10 last 2 weeks of August.
Distance: 300m on the spot 500m.
Remarks: Along the Tauber river.

S Röttingen 17B1

Bach, KlingerStrabe 1. **GPS**: n49,50731 e9,97368.

10 free €2,50/day WC €2,50/day. **Location:** Rural, simple.
Surface: gravel. 01/01-31/12.
Distance: 500m on the spot on the spot.
Remarks: Fishing permit available at town hall.

S Ruhpolding 20G2

Campingplatz Ortnerhof, Ortsstraße 5.
GPS: n47,74260 e12,66303.

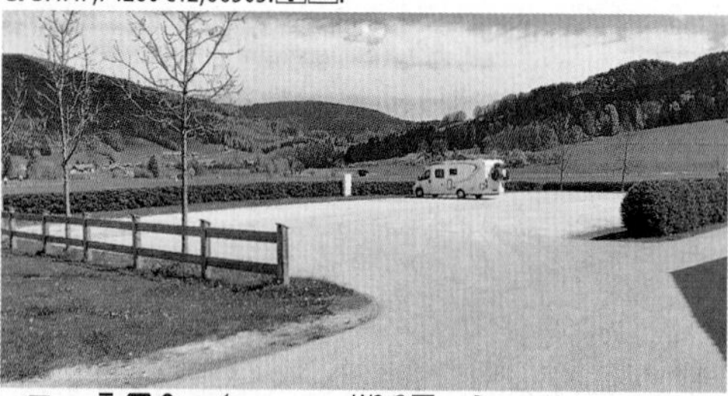

16 € 9 Ch €0,70/kWh WC €3 €3/24h.
Location: Rural, simple. **Surface:** gravel. 01/01-31/12.
Distance: 3km on the spot 2km on the spot on the spot on the spot on the spot.
Remarks: At golf court, max. 1 night.

S Scheidegg 20C2

Wohnmobilpark am Kurhaus, Am Hammerweiher 1.
GPS: n47,57351 e9,84545.
20 € 13,50 Ch (16x)included €2.
Surface: gravel/metalled. 01/01-31/12.
Distance: Minishop.
Remarks: Bread-service.

S Scheinfeld 17C1

Freibad Scheinfeld, Badstrasse 5. **GPS**: n49,67434 e10,46173.

14 € 7 Ch €1/2kWh WC. **Surface:** gravel.
01/01-31/12.
Remarks: At swimming pool.

S Schliersee 20E2

Am Spitzingsee, Spitzingstraße. **GPS**: n47,66648 e11,88851.

+10 summer € 12, winter € 9 (no service) Ch. **Location:** Rural, simple, isolated, quiet. **Surface:** gravel. 01/01-31/12 Service: winter.
Distance: 5,4km on the spot 500m on the spot on the spot on the spot.
Remarks: Altitude 1085m, at lake.

S Schlüsselfeld 17C1

Bambergerstrasse. **GPS**: n49,75572 e10,62267.

5 free €1/80liter Ch. **Location:** Urban, simple, central.
Surface: asphalted. 01/01-31/12.
Distance: on the spot on the spot on the spot 50m 50m.

S Schlüsselfeld 17C1

Concorde, Concorde-Straße 2–4. **GPS**: n49,76745 e10,56478.

20 free €1/100liter Ch €0,50/kWh.
Location: Rural, simple, quiet. **Surface:** metalled.
01/01-31/12.
Distance: 1km 1km 1km.
Remarks: At motohome manufacturer.

S Schnelldorf 17C2

BP-Truckstop Feuchtwangen, Rudolph Dieselstrasse 1.
GPS: n49,17149 e10,24124.

20 € 7 €1/80liter Ch (3x) WC €2. **Surface:** metalled.
01/01-31/12.
Distance: 300m on the spot on the spot.
Remarks: Discount at restaurant € 5, special part for motor homes.

S Schöllkrippen 12A3

Naturerlebnisbad, Häfner-Ohnhaus-Straße.
GPS: n50,08484 e9,25247.

35 € 9/24h €1/80liter Ch (24x)€0,50/kWh.

DE

Location: Rural, comfortable, quiet. **Surface:** grassy.
01/01-31/12.
Distance: 500m.
Remarks: Bread-service.

S **Schongau** 20D2

Festplatz, Lechuferstrasse. **GPS**: n47,80906 e10,89815.

70 € 5/24h €1/50liter Ch WC.
Location: Urban, simple.
Surface: asphalted.
service: 20/03-05/11 during event.
Distance: 400m 100m 400m on the spot.
Remarks: Caution key sanitary € 30, guests free.

Schönsee 17F1

Moorbad, Böhmerwaldstrasse. **GPS**: n49,51091 e12,55321.
5 free. **Location:** Simple. 01/01-31/12.
Distance: 300m.
Remarks: Max. 3 days.

S **Schönwald** 12E3

Freizeitland Schönwald, Grünhaid 4. **GPS**: n50,20958 e12,09570.
€ 10 €2,50. 01/01-31/12.
Distance: on the spot.
Remarks: Breakfast-service.

Schrobenhausen 17D3

Am Klostergarten, Rot-Kreuz-Straße.
GPS: n48,55835 e11,26234.

4 free.
Location: Simple, quiet. **Surface:** metalled. 01/01-31/12.
Distance: 400m 400m 400m.

S **Schrobenhausen** 17D3

Stadtwerke-Kläranlage, Köningslachenerweg 12.
GPS: n48,57374 e11,27519.
Ch Service € 5.
Remarks: Mo-Thu 7-12h, 13-16h, Fr 7-12h.

S **Schwandorf** 17E1

Festplatz, Angerring, Krondorf. **GPS**: n49,33230 e12,10247.

30 free Ch free.
Location: Simple. **Surface:** asphalted/grassy.
01/01-31/12 week before/after Whitsuntide.
Distance: 500m 200m 500m.
Remarks: Along the Naab river.

S **Schwangau** 20D2

Wohnmobilpark Schwangau, Münchenerstrasse 151.
GPS: n47,59167 e10,77250.

24 € 14-19, tourist tax € 1,90/pp, dog € 2 Ch (24x)€2,50 WC included. **Location:** Urban, comfortable.
Surface: grassy/gravel. 01/01-31/12.
Distance: 2km on the spot on the spot on the spot on the spot on the spot 1km on the spot.

S **Schwarzenbach an der Saale** 12E3

Fleischgasse. **GPS**: n50,22324 e11,93311.
2 free €1 Ch €1. **Location:** Central. **Surface:** metalled.
01/01-31/12.
Distance: on the spot on the spot on the spot.

Segnitz 17C1

Mainstraße 20. **GPS**: n49,67012 e10,14242.

4 free. **Location:** Urban, simple. **Surface:** metalled.
Distance: on the spot on the spot on the spot 200m.
Remarks: Max. 1 day.

S **Segnitz** 17C1

Gasthaus zum Goldenen Anker, Mainstraße 8.
GPS: n49,67063 e10,14344.

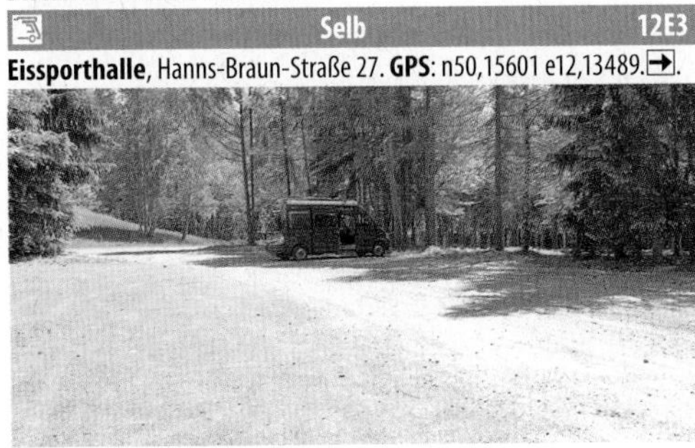

17 € 7,50 €0,50/50liter Ch €0,50. **Location:** Simple.
Surface: grassy/gravel. 01/01-31/12 Restaurant: Thu.
Distance: on the spot on the spot on the spot on the spot.
Remarks: Along Main river.

S **Selb** 12E3

Papiermühlweg 2. **GPS**: n50,16952 e12,12512.
10 € 6 €0,50/100liter Ch €0,50/kWh WC.
Surface: metalled.
Distance: 200m 400m.

Selb 12E3

Eissporthalle, Hanns-Braun-Straße 27. **GPS**: n50,15601 e12,13489.

10 free. **Surface:** gravel. 01/01-31/12.
Distance: 1km 200m 1km on the spot.
Remarks: Hiking trails.

S **Siegsdorf** 20G1

Gasthof Hörterer der Hammerwirt, Schmiedstrasse, B306, Hammer.
GPS: n47,80096 e12,70392.

10 guests free WC. **Location:** Rural, simple. **Surface:** metalled.
01/01-31/12 Wed.
Distance: 6km on the spot on the spot 100m 100m on the spot on the spot 2,5km 300m.
Remarks: Max. 3 nights.

Sonthofen 20C2

Erlebnisbad Wonnemar, Stadionweg 5.
GPS: n47,50344 e10,27883.

12 free.
Location: Urban, simple. **Surface:** gravel. 01/01-31/12.
Distance: 2,3km on the spot on the spot on the spot.
Remarks: Max. 1 night.

S **Spalt** 17D2

Wohnmobilpark Rezattal, Obeltshauserstraße 3.
GPS: n49,17512 e10,92937.
12 € 9,50 + € 1,50/pp tourist tax Ch €2,50 WC.
Surface: gravel. 01/01-31/12.
Distance: on the spot 500m 200m on the spot on the spot.

S **Steinach/Straubing** 17F2

Firma Hubert Brandl Caravantastic, Gewerbering 11.
GPS: n48,95639 e12,62250.

3 free €1 . **Location:** Simple. **Surface:** grassy.
01/01-31/12.
Distance: 1,5km 2km 1km.
Remarks: Connection electricity < 18h.

S **Steinberg am See** 17F1

Movin'G'round, Am Steinberger See. **GPS**: n49,28247 e12,17357.

25 € 7 service €2 Ch . **Location:** Rural, simple.
Surface: grassy. 01/04-31/10.
Distance: 500m on the spot on the spot.
Remarks: Check in at pay-desk.

S **Sulzbach-Rosenberg** 17E1

Großparkplatz, Bayreuther Straße. **GPS**: n49,50583 e11,74500.

DE

4 free €1/80liter Ch (4x)€0,50/kWh. **Location:** Urban, simple. **Surface:** gravel. 01/01-31/12.
Distance: 300m 500m 500m on the spot.

Sulzemoos 20D1

Der Freistaat Caravaning, Ohmstrasse. **GPS:** n48,28267 e11,26084.

40 free €1/80liter Ch (20x)€1/kWh WC.
Location: Simple. **Surface:** gravel.
01/01-31/12.
Distance: 800m 800m McDonalds 800m 800m 600m.
Remarks: Motorhome dealer.

Tauberrettersheim 17B1

Brunnenstrasse. **GPS:** n49,49635 e9,93720.

6 free.
Location: Rural, simple. **Surface:** grassy. 01/01-31/12.
Distance: on the spot on the spot on the spot.

Thierstein 12E3

Kaiserstein, Hirtweg. **GPS:** n50,10610 e12,10490.

10 €5/24h Ch included voluntary contribution.
Surface: metalled. 01/01-31/12 01/10-31/03 water disconnected. **Distance:** 500m 500m 500m.
Remarks: Max. 2 nights, beautiful view.

Thüngersheim 12B3

Parkplatz Main-Aue, Am Schwimbad. **GPS:** n49,88084 e9,83717.

20 free Chfree (16x)€0,50/kWh. **Location:** Rural, comfortable, noisy. **Surface:** grassy. 01/04-31/10.
Distance: 500m on the spot.
Remarks: Along Main river.

Traunstein 20F1

Gasthaus Jobst, Balthasar Permoserstrasse 64, Rettenbach.
GPS: n47,91188 e12,64899.

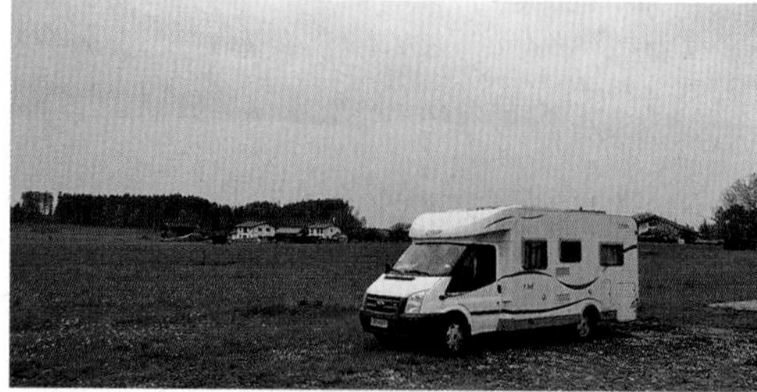

10 €3, guests free €2 €2,50 WC. **Location:** Rural, simple.
Surface: metalled. 01/01-31/12 Wed.
Distance: on the spot on the spot on the spot on the spot on the spot on the spot.

Traunstein 20F1

Firma Grüaugl, Schmidhamerstrasse 31. **GPS:** n47,88227 e12,59941.

12 €5 €1/100liter Ch €0,50/kWh. **Location:** Isolated.
Surface: metalled. 01/01-31/12.
Distance: 2,5km.
Remarks: Camping equipment store.

Treuchtlingen 17D2

Reisemobilstellplatz am Kurpark, Kästleinmühlenstrasse 20.
GPS: n48,96028 e10,91778.

56 €9,50 €1/80liter Ch (56x)€1/8h WC included .
Location: Urban, comfortable, quiet. **Surface:** grasstiles.
01/01-31/12.
Distance: 800m on the spot.
Remarks: Bread-service.

Übersee/Chiemsee 20F1

Bauernhof Steiner, Almfischer 11, Stegen.
GPS: n47,80963 e12,49136.

25 €12 Ch €0,50/kWh WC €0,50/2minutes.
Location: Rural, simple, quiet. **Surface:** gravel.
01/01-31/12.
Distance: Übersee 2km 4,6km Chiemsee 6km 1km.

Übersee/Chiemsee 20F1

Wohmobilstellplatz Schmid, Stegen 4. **GPS:** n47,81237 e12,48843.

28 € 11,50 2p incl., excl. tourist tax Ch €0,50/kWh €1,50.
Location: Rural, simple. **Surface:** grassy/gravel.
01/01-31/12.
Distance: Übersee 2km 4km Chiemsee 5km 2km 2km 1,5km on the spot.
Remarks: Bread-service.

Veitshöchheim 17B1

Parkplatz am Fußgängersteg, Am Güßgraben.
GPS: n49,83623 e9,86916.

5 free. **Location:** Rural, simple. **Surface:** metalled.
01/01-31/12.
Distance: 500m on the spot.
Remarks: Along Main river, max. 24h.

Viechtach 17G2

P1, Stadtmitte, Bierfeldstraße. **GPS:** n49,07876 e12,88235.

6 free. **Surface:** metalled. 01/01-31/12.
Distance: 400m 150m 50m.
Remarks: In front of supermarket Edeka, max. 3 nights.

Viechtach 17G2

P2, Stadthalle, Friedhofstrasse. **GPS:** n49,07722 e12,88528.

3 free. **Location:** Simple. **Surface:** metalled.
01/01-31/12.
Remarks: Max. 3 nights.

Viechtach 17G2

P5, TÜV, Karl-Gareis-Straße. **GPS:** n49,08222 e12,88306.

free. **Surface:** asphalted. 01/01-31/12.
Distance: 500m 500m.
Remarks: Max. 3 nights, small pitches.

DE

Viechtach 17G2

Berghütte 'Zum Pröller', Hinterviechtach 3, Kollnburg.
GPS: n49,02939 e12,83892.

3 € 5 included. **Surface:** gravel. 01/01-31/12.
Distance: Viechtach 7km 20m.
Remarks: Parking at skipistes.

Viechtach 17G2

Am Regenufer 1. **GPS**: n49,08303 e12,88824.
€1 €1 Ch. 01/01-31/12.

Tourist information Viechtach:
Stadtplatz. Week market. Wed 7-17h.

Vilseck 17E1

Ziegelanger. **GPS**: n49,61145 e11,80068.

20 free. **Location:** Simple, central, quiet. **Surface:** asphalted/gravel.
01/01-31/12.
Distance: 200m on the spot on the spot on the spot 200m 200m.

Vilshofen 17G3

Schiffanleger, Donaukade. **GPS**: n48,63833 e13,18000.

12 free. **Location:** Simple, noisy. **Surface:** asphalted.
01/01-31/12.
Distance: 500m On the Danube river on the spot 500m 500m.
Remarks: Max. 1 night.

Vilshofen 17G3

Yachthafen Vilshofen, Am Bootshafen.
GPS: n48,63870 e13,18785.

10 € 12 Ch (10x)€3/day WC €1. **Location:** Comfortable, quiet. **Surface:** gravel. 01/04-30/11.
Distance: 500m On the Danube river.

Vohenstrauß 17F1

Stadthalle, Neuwirtshauser Weg 11. **GPS**: n49,61872 e12,34523.

15 free Ch free WC .
Surface: gravel. 01/01-31/12.
Distance: 100m 800m 50m 100m.
Remarks: Caution key sanitary € 50.

Volkach 12C3

Mainschleife, Am Main. **GPS**: n49,86389 e10,22139.

40 € 5,50. **Surface:** gravel. 01/01-31/12.
Distance: 500m on the spot on the spot 500m 500m.

Waidhaus 17F1

Barbara Sonneschein, Pfrentsch 20. **GPS**: n49,61823 e12,49040.

10 € 5 Ch included €0,35/kWh. **Location:** Rural, simple, quiet. **Surface:** grassy. 01/01-31/12.
Distance: on the spot on the spot.

Wald 20D2

Walder Badeweiher, Am Sportplatz. **GPS**: n47,72294 e10,56348.

10 € 5 Ch.
Location: Rural, quiet. **Surface:** gravel. 01/01-31/12.
Distance: 500m on the spot 250m on the spot on the spot.

Waldkirchen 17H2

Karoli-Badepark, VDK Heimstrasse 1. **GPS**: n48,72222 e13,60278.

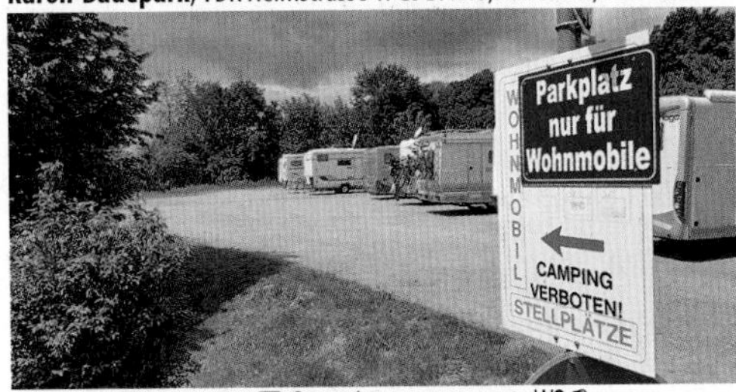

16 free €1/50liter Ch (10x)€0,50/kWh WC .
Location: Rural, simple, quiet. **Surface:** gravel.
01/01-31/12.
Distance: 1km 25m 2km on the spot on the spot.
Remarks: Parking skating rink-swimming pool, bread-service, use sanitary only during opening hours swimming pool, against payment.

Waldsassen 12F3

P2 Schwanenwiese, Schwanengasse. **GPS**: n50,00526 e12,30739.

4 € 5 (2x)€2/10h WC. **Surface:** metalled. 01/01-31/12.
Distance: 500m 500m 500m.
Remarks: Max. 3 days, pay at tourist office.

Waldsassen 12F3

P1, Joseph-Wiesnetstrasse. **GPS**: n50,00250 e12,30361.

2 free. **Surface:** metalled. 01/01-31/12.
Distance: 100m 100m 100m.
Remarks: Max. 3 days.

Wassertrüdingen 17C2

An der Wörnitz, Entengraben. **GPS**: n49,03926 e10,59494.

12 free €1/80liter Ch (6x)€2/8h €1.
Location: Urban, simple, quiet. **Surface:** metalled.
01/01-31/12.
Distance: on the spot on the spot on the spot 1km.

Weidenberg 12E3

Am Sportpark, In der Au. **GPS**: n49,93781 e11,73068.

2-3 free. **Surface:** gravel. 01/01-31/12.
Distance: 750m Chinese restaurant 100m 1,5km.

Weilheim in Oberbayern 20D2

Lohgasse. **GPS**: n47,84012 e11,13583.

8 € 6 €0,50/50liter Ch €0,50/kWh WC.
Location: Urban, simple, central. **Surface:** asphalted.
01/01-31/12.
Distance: Old city centre 500m 100m 200m.
Remarks: Along the Ammer river, max. 5 days.

Weismain 12D3

Bauhof, Burgkunstadterstrasse. **GPS**: n50,08639 e11,23872.

DE

4 free €1 €0,50 Ch€0,50 (6x)€0,50. **Location:** Urban, simple. **Surface:** asphalted. 01/01-31/12.
Distance: on the spot on the spot 200m 200m 200m.
Remarks: Parking in centre.

S Weissenburg 17D2

Kirchweihplatz, Limesbad, Badstrasse 5.
GPS: n49,02476 e10,97180.

free €1/80liter Ch. **Location:** Urban. **Surface:** metalled. 01/04-31/10.
Distance: Old city centre 300m La Fattoria, Frauentorstrasse 11; Mai Tai, Bismarckanlage 16; Wittelsbacher Hof, Fr.Ebertstrasse 21 on the spot.

S Wertach 20C2

Camping Grüntensee, Grüntenseestraße 41.
GPS: n47,61003 e10,44704.

12 €15 + tourist tax €1/pp Ch (12x)€0,50/kWh.
Location: Rural, luxurious, quiet. **Surface:** gravel. 01/01-31/12.
Distance: 2,5km 600m on the spot on the spot on the spot 1,5km 1,5km on the spot on the spot on the spot on the spot.

S Wertingen 17D3

Wohnmobilpark Wertingen, Am Bahnhof 4.
GPS: n48,55948 e10,69065.

12 €7 €0,50/50liter Ch (12x)€2/day.
Location: Urban, comfortable, central, quiet. **Surface:** grassy/gravel. 01/01-31/12.
Distance: 800m 300m.

S Wiesenttal 12D3

Wohnmobilstellplatz Streitberg, Bahnhofstrasse, B470.
GPS: n49,80782 e11,21636.

7 €2 Chfree. **Location:** Rural, simple, quiet. **Surface:** gravel. 01/01-31/12.
Distance: 500m 500m 500m 500m 300m.
Remarks: Along railwayline.

S Wolnzach 17E3

Schwimm- & Erlebnisbad Wolnzach, Hanslmühlweg 6.
GPS: n48,59718 e11,62792.

4 free €1/80liter Ch (4x)€0,50/kWh. **Location:** Simple. **Surface:** metalled. 01/01-31/12.
Distance: 600m 500m 600m.
Remarks: Service 100m.

Wonneberg 20G1

Gasthof Alpenblick, Traunsteiner Straße 21, Weibhausen.
GPS: n47,89880 e12,69123.

5 free, use of a meal desired WC against payment.
Location: Simple. **Surface:** gravel.
Distance: 5km 10km 5km on the spot on the spot on the spot.

S Wunsiedel 12E3

Wohnmobilstellplatz Festspielstadt Wunsiedel, Ludwigstraße.
GPS: n50,03638 e11,99351.

6 €5/24h Ch included.
Surface: gravel. 01/01-31/12 water: Nov-March.
Distance: 600m 300m 1km.
Remarks: Pay at tourist office.

Würzburg 17B1

Viehmarktplatz, Dreikronenstra. **GPS**: n49,79782 e9,92319.

6-20h €5, overnight stay free. **Location:** Urban, simple, noisy.
Surface: asphalted. 01/01-31/12.

Distance: 800m on the spot 50m.

Tourist information Würzburg:
Würzburger Residenz, Residenzplatz. Baroque castle, Unesco World Heritage Site. 01/04-31/10 9-18h, 01/11-31/03 10-16.30h. €7,50.

Zeil am Main 12C3

Altstadtparkplatz, Mittelweg. **GPS**: n50,00667 e10,59583.

5 free. **Surface:** metalled. 01/01-31/12.

Zeil am Main 12C3

Parkplatz Tuchanger, Oskar Winkler strasse.
GPS: n50,01083 e10,59056.

20 free. **Surface:** metalled. 01/01-31/12.
Distance: 1km 1km 1km.
Remarks: Parking gymnasium.

Tourist information Zeil am Main:
Brauereigasthof Göller "Zum alten Freyung". Brewery restaurant with regional specialities and Göller-beer. Mo-Su 9.30-01h.
Altstadt Weinfest. Wine festivals. 06/08-08/08.
Wein-Wander-Weg. Hiking trail through wine region.

S Zellingen 12B3

Am Freibad, Badstraße. **GPS**: n49,89476 e9,82680.

5 free free €3/day. **Location:** Rural, simple. **Surface:** grassy. 01/01-31/12.
Remarks: Check in at swimming pool (service).

Zirndorf 17D1

Playmobil Funpark, Brandstätterstrasse. **GPS**: n49,43087 e10,93935.
40 €4. **Surface:** metalled.
Distance: on the spot.

DE

Denmark

Capital: Copenhagen
Government: Constitutional monarchy
Official Language: Danish
Population: 5,581,500 (2015)
Area: 44,000m²

General information
Dialling code: 0045
General emergency: 112
Currency: Danish Krone (DKK), 1 DKK= 100 øre,
DKK 1 = € 0,13, € 1 = DKK 7,44,
DKK 1 = £0.12, £1 = DKK 8,64 (November 2016)
Payments by credit card are accepted at almost every shop and restaurant.

Regulations for overnight stays/campsites
Overnight parking is allowed: for 1 night, if there is no local prohibition, but no "camping" activities are allowed.

Camping Key Europe is obligatory when using Danish campsites: the card can be purchased at any campsite for DKK 110 (± € 14,80/£13.25), valid for one year.

Additional public holidays 2017
May 12 Great Prayer Day
June 5 Danisch Constitution Day
June 23 Sankt Hans Eve

Time Zone
Winter (Standard Time) GMT+1
Summer (DST) GMT+2

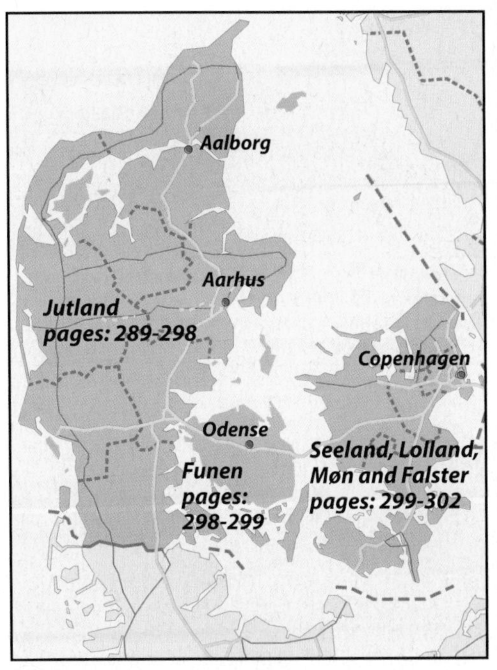

Jutland

Aabybro 5C3
Birthe&Leif Brinkmann, Kanalvej 164. **GPS**: n57,11947 e9,73156.

3 DKK 50.
Location: Simple, isolated. **Surface:** grassy. 01/01-31/12.
Distance: 5km.

Aalborg 5C3
Aalborg, Skydebanevej 50. **GPS**: n57,05379 e9,87233.
DKK 126 Ch against payment. 01/01-31/12.
Distance: on the spot.
Remarks: Quick-Stop: >20h - <10h.

Aalborg 5C3
Strandparken, Skydebanevej 20. **GPS**: n57,05502 e9,88499.
DKK 110 Ch against payment. 24/03-18/09.
Remarks: Quick-Stop: >20h - <10h.

Tourist information Aalborg:
Aalborg Tourist & Convention Bureau, østeraagade 8, www.visitaalborg.com.
Søfarts - og Marinemuseum, Vestre Fjordvej 81. Maritime museum. 01/05-31/12.
Aalborg Zoo, Mølleparkvej 63. Zoo. 01/05-30/12.

Aalbæk 5C2
Galleri & Selskabslokal Gyllegaard, Hirtshalsvej 48.
GPS: n57,60619 e10,41757.

5 DKK 100. **Location:** Simple, isolated, quiet. **Surface:** grassy. 01/01-31/12.
Distance: 4km 1km 4km 4km.

Aalbæk 5C2
Aalbæk Havn, Sønder Havnevej 69. **GPS**: n57,59306 e10,42686.

6 DKK 200 Ch (6x) WC DKK 20/20 included.
Location: Simple, quiet. **Surface:** gravel. 01/01-31/12.
Distance: 800m on the spot on the spot 800m 800m 250m.
Remarks: Pay at harbourmaster.

Aalbæk 5C2
Skiveren Camping, Niels Skiverens Vej 5-7. **GPS**: n57,61616 e10,27891.
DKK 130. 18/03-30/09.
Distance: on the spot.
Remarks: Quick-Stop: >20h - <10h.

Aarhus 6D1
Aarhus centrum parkerinsplads, Kalkværksvej 2.
GPS: n56,14815 e10,21015.

6 free free.
Location: Urban, simple, central. **Surface:** asphalted. 01/01-31/12.
Distance: 500m on the spot on the spot.
Remarks: Behind petrol station, max. 24h.

Aarhus 6D1
Marselisborg Havn, Marselisborg Havnevej 54.
GPS: n56,13927 e10,21916.
Ch WC against payment.
Distance: on the spot on the spot.

Aarhus 6D1
Aarhus Nord, Randersvej 400. **GPS**: n56,22672 e10,16335.
DKK 100 Ch against payment. 01/01-31/12.
Remarks: Quick-Stop: >20h - <10h.

Åbenrå 6D2
Camperstop Aabenraa, Sønderskovvej 104.
GPS: n55,02513 e9,41471.

34 DKK 100 DKK 20/120liter Ch DKK 4,50/kWh WC included DKK 10/5minutes DKK 25 . **Location:** Simple, central, quiet.
Surface: grassy/gravel. 01/01-31/12.
Distance: 2km 8km 400m 400m 700m 600m.
Remarks: Chip-card available at campsite.

Åbenrå 6D2
Lystbådehavn, Kystvej 55. **GPS**: n55,03434 e9,42352.

48 € 17 Ch DKK 1/24 WC included DKK 20 DKK 30 .
Location: Simple, comfortable, central. **Surface:** gravel. 01/01-31/12.
Distance: 1km on the spot on the spot on the spot 300m 200m on the spot on the spot.
Remarks: Harbour Åbenrå.

Åbenrå 6D2
Fjordlyst Camping, Sønderskovvej 100. **GPS**: n55,02466 e9,41469.
DKK 100. 19/03-23/10.
Remarks: Quick-Stop: >20h - <10h.

Åbenrå 6D2
Sandskaer Strandcamping, Sandskaervej 592.
GPS: n55,10460 e9,48481.
DKK 100. 18/03-18/09.
Distance: 100m.
Remarks: Quick-Stop: >20h - <10h.

Aså 5C3
Asaa Camping og Hytteferie, Vodbindervej 13.
GPS: n57,14560 e10,40264.
DKK 130. 19/03-25/09.
Remarks: Quick-Stop: >20h - <10h.

Augustenborg 6D2
Augustenborg Slot, Ny Stavensbøl 1. **GPS**: n54,94703 e9,85427.

DK

70 DKK 130 Ch WC . Location: Rural, comfortable. Surface: grassy. 01/01-31/12.
Distance: 1,5km on the spot on the spot.

Augustenborg 6D2

Augustenborg Yachthavn, Langdel 6. **GPS**: n54,94074 e9,86942.

19 DKK 130 Ch DKK 25 WC . Location: Luxurious, central. Surface: grassy/gravel. 01/04-31/10.
Distance: 700m 1km on the spot.

Billund 6C1

Camperpark Billund, Grenevej 5. **GPS**: n55,70480 e9,12406.

10 € 16 Ch included DKK 22. **Location:** Rural, comfortable. **Surface:** grassy. 01/01-31/12.
Distance: 3,5km 3,5km 3,5km.

Bindslev 5C3

Tannisbugt Hallen, Stadion alle 7. **GPS**: n57,54559 e10,19943.
20 € 10 Ch WC.
Location: Urban. **Surface:** metalled. 15/07-07/08.

Bjert 6D2

Stensager Strand, Oluf Ravnsvej 16. **GPS**: n55,42076 e9,58785.
DKK 180 Ch against payment. 24/03-15/09.
Remarks: Quick-Stop: >20h - <10h.

Bredsten 6C1

Naturstedet Gårdbutik, Hærvejen 96. **GPS**: n55,73927 e9,32001.
DKK 50 . **Surface:** gravel.
Distance: 6km.

Bredsten 6C1

B&B Klingsbjerggaard, Vejlevej 50. **GPS**: n55,70077 e9,40296.
DKK 100.
Distance: 1km 1km.

Broager 6D3

Broager Strand Camping, Skeldebro 32. **GPS**: n54,86780 e9,74419.
DKK 99. 01/01-31/12.
Distance: 100m.
Remarks: Quick-Stop: >20h - <10h.

Broager 6D3

Gammelmark Strand Camping, Gammelmark 20.
GPS: n54,88586 e9,72926.
DKK 150. 23/03-02/10.
Distance: 100m.
Remarks: Quick-Stop: >20h - <10h.

Brovst 5C3

Vilsbæk Rideskole ved Brovst, Kanalvej 34.
GPS: n57,11895 e9,53640.

10 DKK 60 Ch WC included. **Location:** Rural, simple, isolated, quiet. **Surface:** grassy. 01/01-31/12.
Distance: 2km.

Brovst 5C3

Tranum Klit Camping, Sandmosevej 525. **GPS**: n57,17097 e9,46312.
DKK 120. 19/03-02/10.
Remarks: Quick-Stop: >20h - <10h.

Brædstrup 6D1

Hunos Museum & Samlinger, Hallevej 7.
GPS: n55,98548 e9,50352.
DKK 100 DKK 20. **Location:** Rural. **Surface:** grassy/gravel.
Distance: 8,5km.
Remarks: At museum.

Brønderslev 5C3

Serritslev Fiskepark, Agårdsvej 35. **GPS**: n57,29750 e9,99597.

20 DKK 50 free WC. **Location:** Rural, simple, isolated, quiet. **Surface:** grassy. 01/01-31/12.
Distance: on the spot.

Bylderup-Bov 6C2

Boskov, Kvænholtvej 15. **GPS**: n54,94488 e9,06078.

10 DKK 60 Ch included. **Location:** Rural, simple, isolated, quiet. **Surface:** grassy/gravel. 01/01-31/12.
Distance: 4km 200m.

Bylderup-Bov 6C2

B&B Bredevad, Bredevadvej 5. **GPS**: n54,96885 e9,12138.

2 € 14, 2 pers incl Ch WC included.
Location: Rural, comfortable, isolated. **Surface:** grassy. 01/01-31/12.
Distance: 15km 9km 4km on the spot on the spot.

Bylderup-Bov 6C2

Kristianshåb Autocamper Park, Kristianshåbvej 5.
GPS: n54,96189 e9,06950.
25 DKK 110 Ch WC . **Location:** Comfortable, isolated. 01/01-31/12.
Distance: 6km 1km 5km.

Tourist information Bylderup-Bov:
Schackenborg Slot, Schackenborg 2, Tønder. Visit the castle garden.

Bælum 5C3

Bakgaarden, Hælskovvej 2. **GPS**: n56,83815 e10,12007.

4 DKK 75 Ch included. **Surface:** grassy. 01/01-31/12.
Distance: 1km 1km.

Bønnerup 5D3

Bønnerup Lystbådehavn, Vestre Mole 2, Glesborg.
GPS: n56,53139 e10,71139.

20 DKK 150 Ch (12x)included WC against payment. **Location:** Rural, comfortable, quiet. **Surface:** gravel. 01/01-31/12.
Distance: 500m on the spot on the spot 250m 400m.
Remarks: Parking at marina.

Børkop 6D1

Brejning Lystbådehavn, Brejning Strand.
GPS: n55,67431 e9,68920.

12 € 16 (12x) WC included . **Location:** Rural, simple, isolated, quiet. **Surface:** gravel/metalled. 01/01-31/12.
Distance: Børkop 5km 4,1km 10m 10m.
Remarks: Restaurant only in summer.

Ebeltoft 6D1

Skovgarde, Havmøllevej 5. **GPS**: n56,24475 e10,77902.

2 DKK 50. **Location:** Rural, simple, isolated, quiet. **Surface:** grassy. 01/01-31/12.
Distance: on the spot.
Remarks: Pay at Havmøllevej 5 or 20.

Ebeltoft 6D1

Blushøj, Elsegårdevej 53. **GPS**: n56,16795 e10,72943.
DKK 140 Ch against payment. 01/04-14/09.
Remarks: Quick-Stop: >20h - <10h.

Ebeltoft 6D1

Dråby Strand, Dråby Strandvej 13. **GPS**: n56,22172 e10,73778.
DKK 125 Ch against payment. 19/03-14/09.
Remarks: Quick-Stop: >20h - <10h.

Ebeltoft 6D1

Elsegårde, Kristoffenvejen 1. **GPS**: n56,16843 e10,72278.
DKK 140 Ch against payment. 01/01-31/12.
Remarks: Quick-Stop: >20h - <10h.

Ebeltoft 6D1

Krakær, Gl. Kærvej 18. **GPS**: n56,19730 e10,67426.
DKK 125 Ch against payment. 20/03-23/10.
Remarks: Quick-Stop: >20h - <10h.

Ebeltoft 6D1

Ebeltoft Strand Camping, Ndr. Strandvej 23.
GPS: n56,20983 e10,67852.
DKK 130. 01/01-31/12.
Distance: 100m.
Remarks: Quick-Stop: >20h - <10h.

Egå 6D1

Egå Marina, Egå Havvej 35. **GPS**: n56,21069 e10,28819.

7 € 19 Ch (7x) WC included .
Location: Urban, comfortable. **Surface:** asphalted. 01/01-31/12.
Distance: 2km 400m on the spot on the spot 600m 600m.
Remarks: Tallycard: service, electricity, sanitary building, caution DKK 50.

Ejerslev 5C3

Ejerslev Havn, Utkærvej 5. **GPS**: n56,91855 e8,92096.

10 DKK 110 Ch (10x) WC included .
Location: Rural, isolated, quiet.
Surface: gravel. 01/01-31/12.
Distance: 4km on the spot 4km on the spot on the spot.
Remarks: Bread-service, last 2km gravel road, borrow cycles for free.

Engesvan 6C1

Pårup Autocamperplads, Silkeborgvej 8. **GPS**: n56,13694 e9,35028.
4 DKK 50 Ch included. **Location:** Urban, simple, central. **Surface:** gravel. 01/04-01/11.
Distance: on the spot.

Erslev 5C3

Inger-Marie og Knud Erik Nielsen, Bindeleddet 4.
GPS: n56,83881 e8,68060.

4 DKK 40 . **Location:** Rural, simple, isolated, quiet.
Surface: gravel. 01/01-31/12.
Distance: 1km.

Esbjerg 6C2

Nebelso, Vestervadsvej 17 Vester Nebel.
GPS: n55,55000 e8,54361.

25 DKK 50 DKK 10 DKK 25.
Location: Rural, simple, isolated, quiet. **Surface:** grassy/gravel.
01/04-01/11.
Distance: 15km on the spot.
Remarks: Fishpond, fishing license DKK90 www.nebelsoe.dk.

Esbjerg 6C2

Esbjerg Camping, Gudenåvej 20. **GPS**: n55,51293 e8,38942.
DKK 184. 01/01-31/12.
Remarks: Quick-Stop: >20h - <10h.

Fanø 6C2

Fanø Fiskesø, Storetoft 30. **GPS**: n55,43401 e8,39294.
4 DKK 100 Ch WC against payment. **Surface:** gravel.
Distance: on the spot.
Remarks: At fish pond.

Fanø 6C2

Feldberg Familie Camping, Kirkevejen 3-5, Rindby.
GPS: n55,42894 e8,39211.
DKK 100. 18/03-23/10.
Remarks: Quick-Stop: >20h - <10h.

Farsø 5C3

Hvalpsund Autocamperplads, Fjordvej 1, Hvalpsund.
GPS: n56,70584 e9,20565.
DKK 130 Ch WC . **Surface:** grassy.
Distance: on the spot on the spot on the spot.

Fjerritslev 5C3

Erna K Nielsen, Holmsøvej 31, Haverslev. **GPS**: n57,04102 e9,39252.

6 DKK 50 included. **Location:** Rural, simple, quiet.
Surface: grassy. 01/01-31/12.
Distance: Limfjord 1,7km.

Fjerritslev 5C3

Niels Balle, Hedegardsvey 19. **GPS**: n57,12505 e9,33422.

4 DKK 70 (1x) included. **Location:** Rural, simple, isolated.
Surface: grassy. 01/01-31/12.
Distance: 7km 4km.

Flauenskjold 5C3

Markedsplad, Agertoften 4. **GPS**: n57,24854 e10,28477.

10 DKK 50 DKK 25 WC included.
Location: Rural, simple, quiet.
Surface: grassy. 01/01-31/12.
Distance: 5km.
Remarks: Money in envelope in mail box, festival and market place.

Fredericia 6D2

Lystbådehavnen, Strandvejen 115/Sanddalbakke.
GPS: n55,55246 e9,72805.

8 € 11 Ch (8x) WC included.
Location: Rural, simple, quiet.
Surface: metalled. 01/01-31/12.
Distance: 1km on the spot on the spot on the spot 1km 200m.
Remarks: Tallycard: service, electricity, sanitary building, caution DKK 50.

Fredericia 6D2

Trelde Næs, Trelde Næsvej 297. **GPS**: n55,62461 e9,83342.
DKK 135 Ch . 18/03-23/10.
Remarks: Quick-Stop: >20h - <10h.

Frederikshavn 5C3

Frederikshavn Marina, Søsportsvej 8. **GPS**: n57,42375 e10,52709.

20 DKK 150 Ch (10x) WC included.
Location: Urban, comfortable, central, quiet. **Surface:** grassy/gravel.
01/01-31/12.
Distance: 800m on the spot on the spot on the spot 700m.
Remarks: Pay at harbourmaster.

Frederikshavn 5C3

Svalereden, Frederikshavnsvej 112B.
DKK 100 Ch . 01/01-31/12.
Remarks: Quick-Stop: >20h - <10h.

Fur 5C3

Fur Camping, Råkildevej 6. **GPS**: n56,83352 e8,97739.
€ 1/h Ch service € 6 DKK 0,50/kWh DKK 3,50.
Location: Isolated, quiet. 18/03-05/09.
Distance: 650m.
Remarks: Max. 1 night.

Gistrup 5C3

Kirsten og Karl Age, Gunderupvej 164. **GPS**: n56,93476 e9,95844.

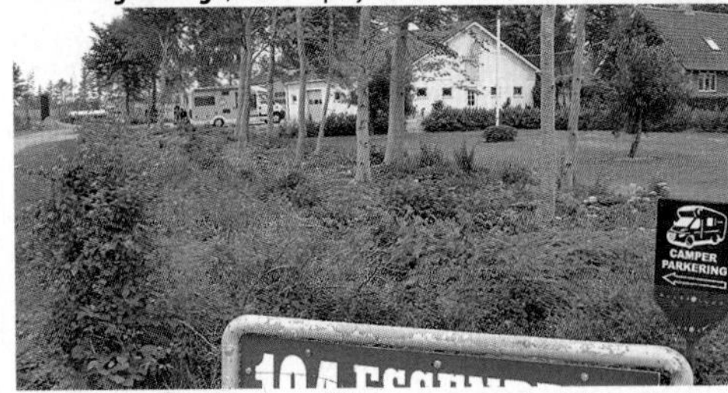

4 DKK 100 included. **Location:** Rural, simple, isolated.
Surface: gravel.

Give 6C1

Give Camping, Skovbakken 34. **GPS**: n55,85051 e9,22953.
DKK 125. 19/03-25/09.
Remarks: Quick-Stop: >20h - <10h.

Glejbjerg 6C2

Betina & Klaus Jørgensen, Gammelgårdsvej 3.
GPS: n55,55052 e8,78705.
4 free Ch free against payment WC . **Location:** Comfortable. **Surface:** grassy/gravel. 01/01-31/12.

Grenaa 5D3

Fornæs, Stensmarkvej 36. **GPS**: n56,45398 e10,94009.
DKK 125 Ch against payment. 19/03-21/09.
Remarks: Quick-Stop: >20h - <10h.

Grenaa 5D3

Grenaa Strand Camping, Fuglsangvej 58. **GPS**: n56,38976 e10,91171.
DKK 130. 23/03-04/09.

DK

Distance: 300m.
Remarks: Quick-Stop: >20h - <10h.

Tourist information Grenaa:
Kattegatcentret, Færgevej 4. The underwater world and shark centre. 10-16/17h 13/12-26/12.

S Haderslev 6D2
Fam. Nowak, Felstrupvej 37. **GPS**: n55,25488 e9,52556.
2 free Service DKK 30.
Location: Rural. **Surface:** gravel. 01/01-31/12.
Distance: 3km 100m on the spot.

S Haderslev 6D2
Haderslev Sejl Club, Sydhavnsvej 1F. **GPS**: n55,24806 e9,50028.
10 DKK 110 Ch WC included.
Surface: gravel. 15/05-30/09.
Distance: on the spot.

S Haderslev 6D2
Gåsevig Strand, Gåsevig 19. **GPS**: n55,14222 e9,49903.
DKK 109 Ch against payment. 19/03-18/09.
Remarks: Quick-Stop: >20h - <10h.

S Haderslev 6D2
Halk, Brunbjerg 105. **GPS**: n55,18599 e9,65374.
DKK 75 Ch against payment. 24/03-18/09.
Remarks: Quick-Stop: >20h - <10h.

Haderslev 6D2
Årø Camping, Årø 260. **GPS**: n55,25942 e9,75240.
DKK 100. 01/01-31/12.

Haderslev 6D2
Danhostel Haderslev, Erlevvej 34. **GPS**: n55,24431 e9,47710.
DKK 110. 18/03-23/10.
Distance: on the spot.
Remarks: Quick-Stop: >20h - <10h.

Haderslev 6D2
Sønderballe Strand Camping, Diernæsvej 218.
GPS: n55,13243 e9,47610.
DKK 130. 18/03-18/09.
Distance: on the spot.
Remarks: Quick-Stop: >20h - <10h.

Haderslev 6D2
Vikær Strand Camping, Dundelum 29. **GPS**: n55,15008 e9,49444.
DKK 125. 19/03-02/10.
Distance: on the spot.
Remarks: Quick-Stop: >20h - <10h.

Tourist information Haderslev:
Sillerup Mølle, Sillerup Møllevej 35. Mill, bake bread yourself. 01/07-31/08 Su 13-17h.
Wachman's Tour. Excursion with the night watch in the old part of the city. 01/07-31/08 Thu 21h.

S Hadsund 5C3
Hadsund Havn, Skovvej 67. **GPS**: n56,70988 e10,10428.

10 DKK 130 WC included. **Location:** Rural, comfortable, quiet. **Surface:** grassy. 01/01-31/12.
Distance: 2km 2km 2km.

S Hadsund 5C3
Hvirvelkærgård, Kystvejen 202, Als. **GPS**: n56,76414 e10,28565.

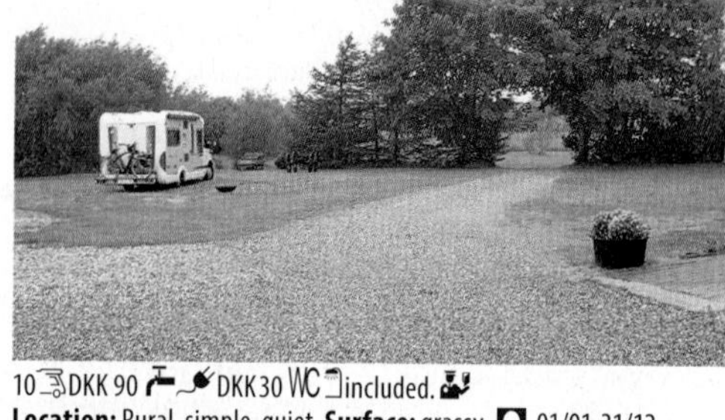

10 DKK 90 DKK 30 WC included.
Location: Rural, simple, quiet. **Surface:** grassy. 01/01-31/12.
Distance: 1km 1km.

S Hadsund 5C3
Øster Hurup Havn, Havnen 46. **GPS**: n56,80405 e10,27851.
DKK 140 Ch. **Surface:** gravel.
Distance: 500m on the spot 500m 500m.
Remarks: Tuesday market.

S Hadsund 5C3
Ingrid og Kristen Gade, Hobrovej 62. **GPS**: n56,70773 e10,07975.

4 DKK 100 (2x) WC included.
Location: Rural, simple. **Surface:** grassy. 01/01-31/12.

S Hadsund 5C3
Øster Hurup, Kystvejen 70. **GPS**: n56,79990 e10,27324.
DKK 130 Ch against payment. 19/03-25/09.
Remarks: Quick-Stop: >20h - <10h.

Hadsund 5C3
Hadsund Camping og Vandrerhjem, Stadionvej 33.
GPS: n56,72108 e10,13362.
DKK 90. 18/03-15/10.
Remarks: Quick-Stop: >20h - <10h.

S Hals 5C3
Lagunen, Lagunen 8. **GPS**: n57,04025 e10,36053.
DKK 150 Ch against payment. 23/03-13/09.
Remarks: Quick-Stop: >20h - <10h.

S Hanstholm 5C3
THy Minicamping (Rær Autocamperplads), Kærbakken 2.
GPS: n57,08945 e8,67104.

20 DKK 100 Ch WC included.
Location: Rural, comfortable. **Surface:** grassy. 01/01-31/12.
Distance: Hanstholm 4km 5km.

S Hanstholm 5C3
Hanstholm, Hamborgvej 95. **GPS**: n57,10909 e8,66724.
DKK 120 Ch against payment. 01/01-31/12.
Remarks: Quick-Stop: >20h - <10h.

Tourist information Hanstholm:
Frøstrup mini-village, Søndergade 36, Frøstrup. Miniature village.
01/05-15/10 Wed-Thu 10-12h, 01/07-31/08 daily 13.30-16.30h.

S Havndal 5C3
Udbyhøj Havn, Havnevej 62 Udbyhøj. **GPS**: n56,61111 e10,30583.
30 DKK 150 Ch included against payment WC.
Location: Rural, comfortable. **Surface:** asphalted. 01/01-31/12.
Distance: on the spot on the spot 500m.

S Havndal 5C3
Rethe og Hans Jørn Mogensen, Klattrupgade 36, Klattrup.
GPS: n56,66397 e10,21208.

4 DKK 50 Ch included. **Location:** Rural, simple, quiet.
Surface: grassy/gravel. 01/01-31/12.
Distance: 2km 2km.

S Havndal 5C3
Randers Fjord, Midtvasen 21. **GPS**: n56,60997 e10,29334.
2 DKK 125 Ch against payment. 01/01-31/12.
Remarks: Quick-Stop: >20h - <10h.

S Hejls 6D2
Hejlsminde Strand, Gendarmvej 3. **GPS**: n55,36851 e9,60095.
DKK 160 Ch against payment. 19/03-14/09.
Remarks: Quick-Stop: >20h - <10h.

S Hemmet 6C1
Bork Havn, Kirkehøjvej 9A. **GPS**: n55,84850 e8,28257.
DKK 120 Ch against payment. 18/03-24/10.
Remarks: Quick-Stop: >20h - <10h.

Herning 6C1
Møllegade. **GPS**: n56,13741 e8,96660.
4 free. 01/01/-31/12.
Distance: on the spot 100m 200m.

Hirtshals 5C3
Banegårdspladse, Banegårdspladsen 1.
GPS: n57,59119 e9,96308.

30 DKK 75.
Location: Simple, central. **Surface:** gravel. 01/01-31/12.
Distance: 600m 4,8km 600m on the spot.
Remarks: At station and ferry terminal.

Hirtshals 5C3
Willemoesvej. **GPS**: n57,59097 e9,98601.

DK

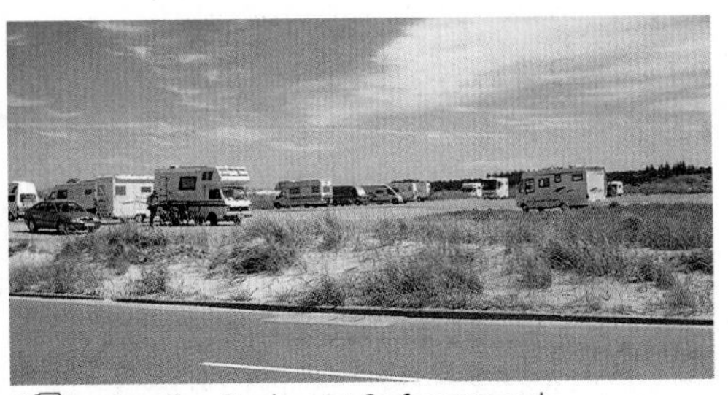

40 free. **Location:** Simple, quiet. **Surface:** unpaved.
01/01-31/12.
Distance: 1km Sandy beach 1km.
Remarks: Parking ferry to Norway.

Hirtshals 5C3

Tornby Strand, Strandvejen 13. **GPS:** n57,55540 e9,93264.
DKK 138 Ch against payment. 01/01-31/12.
Remarks: Quick-Stop: >20h - <10h.

Hirtshals 5C3

Kjul Camping, Kjulvej 12. **GPS:** n57,58279 e10,03132.
DKK 130. 18/03-30/09.
Remarks: Quick-Stop: >20h - <10h.

Tourist information Hirtshals:
M Nordsømuseet, Willemoesvej 2. Oceanarium, large aquarium.
11/01-01/12 10-17.

Hjallerup 5C3

Peter Bastholm Galleri Retro, Alborgvej 715.
GPS: n57,17919 e10,15856.

5 DKK 100 . **Location:** Rural, isolated, quiet.
Surface: gravel. 01/01-31/12.
Distance: fish pond.

Hjørring 5C2

Somo-Art, Tverstedvej 41, Uggerby. **GPS:** n57,57523 e10,12868.
6 € 16 Ch included free. **Location:** Rural, quiet.
Surface: grassy. 01/04-20/10.
Distance: 3km 3km 3km.

Hjørring 5C2

Thomas Lindrup, Tverstedvej 31. **GPS:** n57,57484 e10,12842.

6 DKK 120 Ch (6x) WC included. **Location:** Rural, comfortable, isolated, quiet. **Surface:** grassy. 01/01-31/12.

Hobro 5C3

Hobro Camping Gattenborg, Skivevej 35. **GPS:** n56,64015 e9,78265.
3 DKK 160 Ch against payment. 01/04-02/10.
Remarks: Quick-Stop: >20h - <10h.

Holsted 6C2

Holsted Golfbanen, Bergardsvej 4, Vejen-Esberg.
GPS: n55,52353 e8,93228.

15 € 10 WC. **Surface:** gravel. 01/04-30/10.

Distance: 1km.

Horsens 6D1

Lystbådehavn, Jens Hjernøes Vej 32. **GPS:** n55,85764 e9,87417.

5 DKK 160 Ch WC included . **Location:** Rural, comfortable, quiet.
Surface: gravel. 01/01-31/12.
Distance: 3km on the spot on the spot on the spot.
Remarks: Harbour Horsen, special motorhome parking, Tallycard: service, electricity, sanitary building, caution DKK 50.

Horsens 6D1

Husodde, Husoddevej 85. **GPS:** n55,86035 e9,91537.
DKK 135 Ch against payment.
01/01-31/12.
Remarks: Quick-Stop: >20h - <10h.

Tourist information Horsens:
Dolmen "Jættestuen", åbjerg Skov. Dolmen. 01/01-31/12.

Hovborg 6C2

Holme Å Camping, Torpet 6. **GPS:** n55,60919 e8,93281.
DKK 138. 01/01-31/12.
Remarks: Quick-Stop: >20h - <10h.

Hoven 6C1

Kvindehojskole, Bredgade 10, Tarm. **GPS:** n55,85065 e8,75938.

6 free WC free. **Location:** Urban, simple. **Surface:** gravel.
01/01-31/12.
Distance: on the spot.
Remarks: Parking and stay overnight possible at several places; Brugsen 2/3 campers; sport hall.

Hurup Thy 5B3

Nordisk Folkecenter, Kammersgaardsvej 16.
GPS: n56,69358 e8,41306.

8 DKK 70 WC included. **Location:** Rural, simple, isolated, quiet. **Surface:** gravel. 01/01-31/12.
Distance: on the spot 4km.
Remarks: Check in at reception, access energy-park incl.

Hvide Sande 6B1

Autocamper Fabriksvej 31, Fabriksvej 31.
GPS: n56,00245 e8,11979.
45 € 12,50. **Location:** Rural, simple. **Surface:** gravel/sand.
01/01-31/12.
Distance: 800m 500m 500m.

Hvide Sande 6B1

Autocamper Fabriksvej 42. **GPS:** n56,00475 e8,11754.
20 € 12,50.
Location: Rural, simple. **Surface:** gravel/sand.
Distance: 200m on the spot 200m.

Hvide Sande 6B1

Autocamper P, Tungevej 6. **GPS:** n55,99722 e8,12222.

40 DKK 90. **Location:** Rural, simple, quiet.
Surface: gravel/metalled. 01/01-31/12.
Distance: 200m on the spot 200m 300m on the spot.
Remarks: Beach parking, service Hvide Sande Camping, 1km, DKK 37,50.

Hvide Sande 6B1

Bjerregaard, Sdr. Klitvej 185. **GPS:** n55,90620 e8,16565.
DKK 100 Ch against payment. 15/04-01/10.
Remarks: Quick-Stop: >20h - <10h.

Hvide Sande 6B1

Hvide Sande (Beltana), Karen Brands Vej 70. **GPS:** n55,98689 e8,13478.
DKK 120 Ch against payment. 03/04-26/10.
Remarks: Quick-Stop: >20h - <10h.

Højslev 5C3

Virksund, Sundvej 14. **GPS:** n56,60785 e9,28917.
DKK 75 Ch against payment. 24/03-02/10.
Remarks: Quick-Stop: >20h - <10h.

Højslev 5C3

Virksund Lystbådehavn, Sandkrogen 10. **GPS:** n56,61014 e9,29139.
12 € 16 WC included. **Surface:** gravel.
Distance: on the spot.

Jelling 6C1

Fårup Sø Camping, Fårupvej 58. **GPS:** n55,73616 e9,41772.
DKK 130. 21/03-18/09.
Distance: on the spot.
Remarks: Quick-Stop: >20h - <10h.

Juelsminde 6D1

Havn & Marina, Havnegade 15. **GPS:** n55,71457 e10,01509.

12 € 20 Ch (12x) WC included.
Location: Rural, comfortable, central, quiet. **Surface:** gravel.
01/05-30/09.
Distance: 200m on the spot on the spot on the spot 200m.
Remarks: Tallycard: service, electricity, sanitary building, caution DKK 50.

Karup 6C1

2B Pack, Ulvedalsvej 43. **GPS:** n56,31528 e9,27361.

4 DKK 100 Ch .
Location: Isolated, quiet. 01/05-31/10.
Distance: on the spot.

Karup 6C1

Hessellund Sø, Hessellundvej 12. **GPS:** n56,32308 e9,11501.
DKK 171 Ch against payment. 27/03-29/09.
Remarks: Quick-Stop: >20h - <10h.

Karup 6C1

Hessellund Sø Camping, Hessellundvej 12. **GPS:** n56,32309 e9,11511.
DKK 171. 19/03-25/09.
Remarks: Quick-Stop: >20h - <10h.

DK

Knebel 6D1

Sølyst Gaard Strand Camping, Dragsmurvej 15, Fuglsø.
GPS: n56,17546 e10,53394.
DKK 140. 19/03-18/09.
Distance: 200m.
Remarks: Quick-Stop: >20h - <10h.

Kolding 6D2

Kolding Marina, Skamlingvejen 5. **GPS**: n55,48746 e9,50051.

15 DKK 125 Ch WC against payment.
Location: Rural, comfortable, quiet. **Surface:** grassy/gravel.
01/05-01/10.
Distance: 2,6km on the spot on the spot.
Remarks: Near marina, Tallycard: service, electricity, sanitary building, caution DKK 50.

Kvissel 5C3

Bondegård Hansen, Mejlingvej 65. **GPS**: n57,46753 e10,39556.

10 DKK 75 Ch WC included DKK 10.
Location: Rural, comfortable, quiet.
Surface: grassy. 01/01-31/12.
Distance: 1km 5km.

Langå 5C3

Langå, Skov Alle 16. **GPS**: n56,38780 e9,90439.
DKK 130 Ch against payment. 01/01-31/12.
Remarks: Quick-Stop: >20h - <10h.

Lemvig 5B3

Lemvig Havn, Toldbodgade. **GPS**: n56,55395 e8,30956.

10 free. **Surface:** gravel. 01/01-31/12.
Distance: 250m 250m.
Remarks: Max. 12h.

Lemvig 5B3

Bovbjerg, Juelsgårdvej 13. **GPS**: n56,52800 e8,12629.
DKK 110 Ch. 20/03-19/10.
Remarks: Quick-Stop: >20h - <10h.

Tourist information Lemvig:
Bovbjerg Fyr, Fyrvej 27. Lighthouse.

Løgstrup 5C3

Hjarbæk Fjord Camping, Hulager 2. **GPS**: n56,53416 e9,00000.
DKK 125. 01/01-31/12.
Remarks: Quick-Stop: >20h - <10h.

Løgstør 5C3

Løgstør Golfklub, Viborgvej 13, Ravnstrup.
GPS: n56,94689 e9,25390.

10 DKK 110 (4x)included. **Location:** Simple, isolated, quiet.
Surface: gravel.
Distance: 2km 2km 2km.

Løgstør 5C3

Løgstør Lysbadehavn, Kanalvejen 19. **GPS**: n56,96728 e9,24528.

15 DKK 130 (12x)WC included.
Location: Comfortable, central. **Surface:** grassy/metalled.
01/01-31/12.
Distance: 200m on the spot on the spot on the spot 200m.
Remarks: Pay at harbourmaster.

Løgstør 5C3

Café Bondestuen, Over Aggersund 49. **GPS**: n57,00835 e9,28776.

6 free. **Location:** Rural, simple.
Surface: gravel. 01/01-31/12.

Løkken 5C3

Galleri Munkens Klit, Munkensvej 11. **GPS**: n57,33871 e9,70522.

10 DKK 100 DKK 5 WC included. **Location:** Rural, comfortable, isolated, quiet. **Surface:** grassy. 01/01-31/12.
Distance: 3km.

Løkken 5C3

Hugo Ottesen, Kettrupvej 80. **GPS**: n57,31135 e9,67861.

5 DKK 100. **Location:** Rural, simple, isolated.
Surface: grassy. 01/01-31/12.

Løkken 5C3

Løkkensvej 875. **GPS**: n57,38972 e9,77385.
DKK 75 DKK 40 DKK 25. **Surface:** grassy. 01/01-31/12.
Distance: 4,5km.

Løkken 5C3

Camping Rolighed, Grønhoj Strandvej 35. **GPS**: n57,32143 e9,67818.
DKK 75 Ch against payment. 01/01-31/12.
Remarks: Quick-Stop: >18h - <10h.

Løkken 5C3

Gl.Klitgaard, Lyngbyvej 331. **GPS**: n57,41784 e9,76017.
DKK 140 Ch against payment. 15/04-23/10.
Remarks: Quick-Stop: >20h - <10h.

Løkken 5C3

Grønhøj Strand, Kettrupvej 125. **GPS**: n57,32127 e9,67293.
DKK 100 Ch against payment. 18/03-18/09.
Remarks: Quick-Stop: >20h - <10h.

Løkken 5C3

Løkken Campingcenter, Søndergarde 69. **GPS**: n57,36480 e9,70940.
DKK 125 Ch. 01/01-31/12.
Remarks: Quick-Stop: >20h - <10h.

Løkken 5C3

Løkken Strand, Furreby Kirkevej 97. **GPS**: n57,38533 e9,72571.
DKK 100 Ch against payment. 29/04-04/09.
Remarks: Quick-Stop: >20h - <10h.

Løkken 5C3

Gl. Klitgaard Camping og Hytteby, Lyngbyvej 331.
GPS: n57,42055 e9,76025.
DKK 169. 01/01-31/12.
Remarks: Quick-Stop: >20h - <10h.

Tourist information Løkken:
Løkken Turistbureau, Jyllandsgade 15, www.loekken.dk. Bathing resort.
Vendsyssel historiske museum "Jens Thomsens Gård", Strandfogedgården i Rubjerg, Langelinie 2. Cultural past of the coast area. Hiking-trails. 25/06-30/08 Thu-Su 11-17h.
Familiy Farm Fun Park, Lyngbyvej 86, Vittrup. Animal park. 14/05-24/10 10-18.

Mariager 5C3

Kongsdl Bådelaug, Kongsdal Havn 8. **GPS**: n56,68383 e10,07023.

24 DKK 120 Ch (24x)WC DKK 5/3minutes included. **Location:** Rural, comfortable, isolated, quiet. **Surface:** gravel.
01/01-31/12.
Distance: 7km on the spot on the spot.

Mariager 5C3

Mariager, Ny Havnevej 5A. **GPS**: n56,65399 e9,97640.
2 DKK 100 Ch against payment. 23/03-25/09.
Remarks: Quick-Stop: >20h - <10h.

Nibe 5C3

Sølyst, Løgstørvej 2. **GPS**: n56,97248 e9,62460.
DKK 140 Ch against payment. 01/01-31/12.
Remarks: Quick-Stop: >20h - <10h.

Nordborg 6D2

Kvickly, Gartnervænget. **GPS**: n55,05611 e9,74150.
10 free. **Surface:** asphalted. 01/01-31/12.
Remarks: At supermarket.

Nordborg 6D2

Lone & Henning Carlsson, Kådnervej 7. **GPS**: n55,03194 e9,73111.

5 DKK 100 DKK 20 WC. **Location:** Rural, comfortable, quiet. **Surface:** gravel. 01/01-31/12.
Distance: 5km.
Remarks: Narrow entrance.

Nordborg 6D2

Købingsmark, Købingsmarksvej 53. **GPS**: n55,07887 e9,72912.
DKK 110 Ch against payment. 01/04-25/10.
Remarks: Quick-Stop: >20h - <10h.

Nordborg 6D2

Augustenhof Strand, Augustenhofvej 30. **GPS**: n55,07767 e9,71464.
DKK 136 Ch. 01/01-31/12.
Remarks: Quick-Stop: >20h - <10h.

Nykøbing Mors 5C3

Morsø Sejlklub & Marin, Jernbanevej 3A.
GPS: n56,79282 e8,86370.

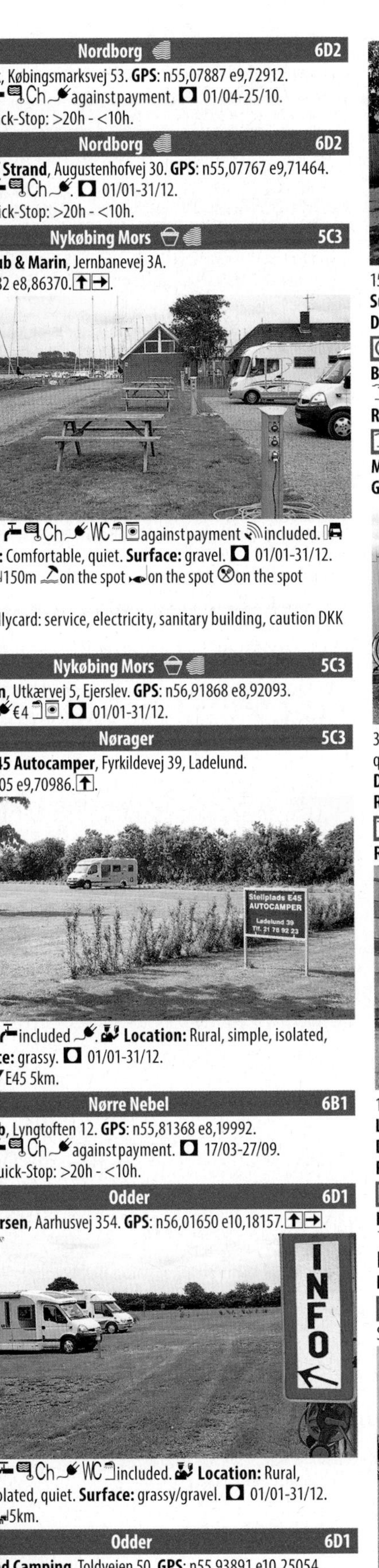

18 DKK 120 Ch WC against payment included. **Location:** Comfortable, quiet. **Surface:** gravel. 01/01-31/12.
Distance: 150m on the spot on the spot on the spot 200m.
Remarks: Tallycard: service, electricity, sanitary building, caution DKK 25.

Nykøbing Mors 5C3

Ejerslev Havn, Utkærvej 5, Ejerslev. **GPS**: n56,91868 e8,92093.
€ 11 Ch €4. 01/01-31/12.

Nørager 5C3

Stellplads E45 Autocamper, Fyrkildevej 39, Ladelund.
GPS: n56,77505 e9,70986.

15 DKK 75 included. **Location:** Rural, simple, isolated, quiet. **Surface:** grassy. 01/01-31/12.
Distance: E45 5km.

Nørre Nebel 6B1

Nymindegab, Lyngtoften 12. **GPS**: n55,81368 e8,19992.
DKK 75 Ch against payment. 17/03-27/09.
Remarks: Quick-Stop: >20h - <10h.

Odder 6D1

Jørgen Petersen, Aarhusvej 354. **GPS**: n56,01650 e10,18157.

3 DKK 75 Ch WC included. **Location:** Rural, luxurious, isolated, quiet. **Surface:** grassy/gravel. 01/01-31/12.
Distance: 5km.

Odder 6D1

Odder strand Camping, Toldvejen 50. **GPS**: n55,93891 e10,25054.
DKK 150 Ch against payment. 24/03-21/09.
Remarks: Quick-Stop: >20h - <10h.

Outrup 6C1

Autocamperplads Outrup, Gartnervænget 18.
GPS: n55,71551 e8,34654.

15 DKK 100 Ch DKK 22 WC included.
Surface: grassy/gravel. 01/01-31/12.
Distance: 500m 300m 500m on the spot.

Pandrup 5C3

Blokhus Klit Camping, Kystvejen 52. **GPS**: n57,22048 e9,58479.
DKK 100. 23/03-18/09.
Remarks: Quick-Stop: >20h - <10h.

Randers 5C3

Mellerup Bådelaug, Amtsvejen 153 Mellerup.
GPS: n56,52431 e10,22213.

3 DKK 100 WC included. **Location:** Rural, simple, quiet. **Surface:** gravel. 01/01-31/12.
Distance: Mellerup 1,2km on the spot on the spot.
Remarks: Pay at harbourmaster.

Randers 5C3

Randers havn, Toldbodgade 16. **GPS**: n56,46280 e10,05262.

10 DKK 150.
Location: Urban, simple. **Surface:** gravel. 01/01-31/12.
Distance: 500m on the spot.
Remarks: Max. 24h.

Ribe 6C2

Fabelbo, Hølleskovvej 48. **GPS**: n55,24076 e8,86077.
free WC free. **Location:** Isolated, quiet. **Surface:** grassy.
01/01-31/12.
Distance: Ribe 15km.

Ribe 6C2

Stampemøllevej. **GPS**: n55,32480 e8,75740.

25 free WC free.
Location: Urban, simple.
Surface: asphalted. 01/01-31/12.
Distance: 500m 100m 400m.
Remarks: Parking south of centre, max. 48h.

Ribe 6C2

Storkesøen, Haulundvej 164. **GPS**: n55,31703 e8,76022.

24 DKK 140 Ch WC included DKK 5. **Location:** Rural, comfortable, quiet. **Surface:** grassy. 01/01-31/12.
Distance: 1km on the spot.
Remarks: At fish pond.

Ribe 6C2

Saltgade. **GPS**: n55,33258 e8,76830.
15 free. **Surface:** asphalted. 01/01-31/12.
Distance: 200m 200m.
Remarks: Max. 48h.

Ribe 6C2

Maglegaard, Toftlundvej 6. **GPS**: n55,31067 e8,79151.

3 DKK 100 DKK 20.
Location: Rural, simple, quiet. **Surface:** grassy.
Distance: 3km.

Ribe 6C2

Ribe, Farupvej 2. **GPS**: n55,33907 e8,76940.
DKK 75 Ch.
01/01-31/12.
Remarks: Quick-Stop: >20h - <10h.

Tourist information Ribe:

Ribe Tourism Office, Torvet 3, http://www.visitribe.com/. Oldest city of Denmark to Ribeå River.
Vadehavscentret, Okholmvej 5. Wadden Sea centre. 10-16/17h 01/12-31/01.
Museet Ribes Vikinger, Odins Plads 1. Viking period in Denmark. daily 10-16h, summer 10-18h 01/11-31/03 Mo.
Ribe Vikingecenter. Open air museum. 01/05-30/06, 01/09-15/10 Mo-Fri 10-15.30h, 01/07-31/08 daily 11-17h.
Weis Stue, Torvet 2. Oldest inn of Denmark with traditional Danish kitchen.

Ringkøbing 6B1

Annemette & Svend Erik Jensen, Birkmosevej 6.
GPS: n56,08806 e8,26722.
15 free Ch against payment. **Location:** Simple.
Surface: grassy. 01/01-31/12.
Distance: 500m 500m 200m.

Ringkøbing 6B1

Lystbadenhavn, Fiskerstraede 60. **GPS**: n56,08611 e8,24056.

10 € 14 Ch (6x)DKK 2,30/kWh WC included DKK 10/3minutes. **Location:** Urban, comfortable, quiet.
Surface: gravel. 01/01-31/12.
Distance: on the spot on the spot on the spot 500m 500m.
Remarks: Parking at pier.

Ringkøbing 6B1

Autocamperplads, Vesterled 11. **GPS**: n56,09338 e8,23740.

DK

20 DKK 70.
Location: Urban, simple. **Surface:** gravel. 01/01-31/12.
Distance: 700m 400m 400m 700m 700m.
Remarks: Pay with Danish coins.

S Ringkøbing 6B1
Søndervig, Solvej 2. **GPS:** n56,11186 e8,11760.
DKK 120 Chincluded DKK2,75/kWh,+DKK19 DKK6.
04/04-25/10.
Distance: 600m.
Remarks: Quick-Stop: >20h - <10h.

S Ringkøbing 6B1
Æblehavens, Herningvej 105. **GPS:** n56,08699 e8,31642.
DKK 130 Ch against payment. 18/03-30/09.
Distance: 5km.
Remarks: Quick-Stop: >20h - <10h.

Tourist information Ringkøbing:
Fishing and Family Park West, Hovervej 56. Recreation park with swimming pool. 10h-sunset.

S Roslev 5C3
Sallingsund Sejlklub, Færgevej 7. **GPS:** n56,76333 e8,86667.
€ 16 Ch WC included.
Distance: on the spot on the spot.

S Roslev 5C3
Sundsøre Lystbådehavn, Sundsørevej. **GPS:** n56,70991 e9,17324.
€ 16 WC included. **Location:** Isolated, quiet.
Surface: grassy/gravel. 01/01-31/12.
Distance: on the spot on the spot.
Remarks: At marina and ferry-boat.

S Ry 6D1
Birkhede, Lyngvej 14. **GPS:** n56,10428 e9,74089.
DKK 150 Ch against payment. 18/03-15/09.
Remarks: Quick-Stop: >20h - <10h.

Tourist information Ry:
Ry Turistbureau, Klostervej 3.
Labyrinthia, Gamle Ryvej 2. Wooden labyrinth. 23/04-25/09 11-16.

S Rødding 6C2
JH ståldesign, Timekær 11. **GPS:** n55,33044 e9,05417.
DKK 75 Ch . **Surface:** grassy. 01/01-31/12.
Distance: 500m.

S Rødding 6C2
Inga & Ejnar Gejl, Skodborgskovvej 25, Skodborgskov.
GPS: n55,40056 e9,15722.
4 free against payment WCfree. **Location:** Rural, simple.
Surface: grassy. 01/01-31/12.
Distance: 5km.

S Rødding 6C2
Brændekilde, Haderslevvej 59. **GPS:** n55,35750 e9,18833.

13 free DKK25 Ch DKK25 WC. **Location:** Rural, simple, noisy.
Surface: gravel. 01/01-31/12.
Distance: 1km.
Remarks: Max. 1 week.

S Rødding 6C2
FB Camping Service, Industriparken 13. **GPS:** n55,42556 e9,16083.
15 free DKK10 Ch DKK40. **Location:** Urban, simple.
Surface: gravel. 01/01-31/12.

S Rødekro 6C2
Rødekro Fiskepark, østermarkvej 3-7. **GPS:** n55,08806 e9,30889.

50 DKK 100/pp Ch DKK35/24kWh WCincluded .
Location: Rural, simple, quiet.
Surface: grassy. 01/01-31/12.
Distance: 2km on the spot on the spot on the spot 2km 100m.
Remarks: At fish lake.

Rømø 6C2
Kommandørgården Camping, Havnebyvej 201.
GPS: n55,09854 e8,54292.
DKK 125. 01/01-31/12.
Remarks: Quick-Stop: >20h - <10h.

Rømø 6C2
Rømø Familie Camping, Vestervej 13. **GPS:** n55,16254 e8,54518.
DKK 110. 18/03-23/10.
Remarks: Quick-Stop: >20h - <10h.

S Rønde 6D1
Nappedam Bådelaug, Molsvej 33. **GPS:** n56,27755 e10,49529.
DKK 125 Ch WC .
Distance: 3,5km on the spot 3,5km.
Remarks: Max 3,5t.

S Rønde 6D1
Kaløvig Strandgård, Strandvejen 150. **GPS:** n56,29330 e10,40399.
DKK 140 Ch . 01/01-31/12.
Remarks: Quick-Stop: >20h - <10h.

Rønde 6D1
Kaløvig Camping, Strandvejen 150. **GPS:** n56,29338 e10,40417.
DKK 140. 01/01-31/12.
Remarks: Quick-Stop: >20h - <10h.

S Saltum 5C3
Saltum Strand, Saltum Strandvej 141. **GPS:** n57,28560 e9,65228.
DKK 140 Ch against payment. 19/03-23/10.
Remarks: Quick-Stop: >20h - <10h.

Samsø 6D1
Camping & Feriecenter Samsø, Stensbjergvej 6, Kolby.
GPS: n55,79669 e10,55146.
DKK 60. 15/03-20/12.
Remarks: Quick-Stop: >20h - <10h.

Sdr. Omme 6C1
Omme Å Camping, Sønderbro 10. **GPS:** n55,83837 e8,88872.
DKK 140. 18/03-01/10.
Remarks: Quick-Stop: >20h - <10h.

S Silkeborg 6D1
Anne & Gert Lassen, Ellinglund, Ellingvej 16, Funder Kirkeby.
GPS: n56,16546 e9,40954.
€ 14 Ch WC . **Location:** Rural, comfortable.
Surface: grassy. 01/01-31/12.
Distance: 2km.

S Silkeborg 6D1
Jørgen Engebjerg, Lemmingvej 12. **GPS:** n56,22124 e9,53991.
3 € 10 included. **Location:** Rural. **Surface:** grassy.
01/01-31/12.
Distance: 5km.

S Silkeborg 6D1
Sø-Camping, Århusvej 51. **GPS:** n56,16984 e9,57657.
DKK 99 Ch against payment.
18/03-23/10.
Remarks: Quick-Stop: >20h - <10h.

Tourist information Silkeborg:
AQUA, Vejlsøvej 55. Aquarium. 01/09-31/05 Mo-Fri 10-16h, Sa-Su 10-17h, 01/06-31/08 10-18h.

S Sindal 5C3
Sindal, Hjørringvej 125. **GPS:** n57,46849 e10,17945.
3 DKK 110 Chagainst payment DKK30 WC included.
01/01-31/12.
Remarks: Quick-Stop: >20h - <10h.

S Sjølund 6D2
Grønninghoved strand, Mosvigvej 21. **GPS:** n55,41105 e9,59220.
DKK 140 Ch against payment. 19/03-15/09.
Remarks: Quick-Stop: >20h - <10h.

Skagen 5C2
P-plads på Grenen i Skagen, Akandevej.
GPS: n57,73895 e10,63283.

20 DKK 150. **Location:** Rural, simple, isolated.
Surface: asphalted. 01/01-31/12.
Distance: 2km 100m 3km.

S Skagen 5C2
Råbjerg Mile, Kandestedvej 55. **GPS:** n57,65636 e10,45081.
DKK 130 Ch against payment. 20/03-30/09.
Remarks: Quick-Stop: >20h - <10h.

Skagen 5C2
Skagen Camping, Flagbakkevej 55. **GPS:** n57,71989 e10,53991.
DKK 120. 18/03-01/09.
Remarks: Quick-Stop: >20h - <10h.

S Skals 5C3
Ulbjerg, Skråhedevej 6. **GPS:** n56,64495 e9,33915.
€ 10,50 Ch against payment. 01/01-31/12.
Remarks: Quick-Stop: >20h - <10h.

S Skjern 6C1
Stauning Havn, Strandvejen, Stauning. **GPS:** n55,95488 e8,37352.
6, <10m € 14 Ch WC included. **Surface:** metalled.
01/01-31/12.
Distance: Skjern 8km on the spot.

S Skjern 6C1
Skjern å Camping, Birkvej 37. **GPS:** n55,93316 e8,49291.
DKK 100 Ch against payment. 01/01-31/12.
Remarks: Quick-Stop: >20h - <10h.

S Skærbæk 6C2
Skærbæk, Ullerupvej 76. **GPS:** n55,16584 e8,77909.
DKK 100 Ch against payment. 01/01-31/12.
Remarks: Quick-Stop: >20h - <10h.

Snedsted 5C3
Kaj Foget, Skyumvey 105. **GPS:** n56,84380 e8,59720.

6 DKK 50. **Location:** Rural, simple, isolated, quiet.
Surface: grassy. 01/01-31/12.

Snedsted 5C3
Krohavens familiecamping, Stenbjerg Kirkevej 21.
GPS: n56,91827 e8,36527.
DKK 135. 01/04-01/10.
Remarks: Quick-Stop: >20h - <10h.

S Spøttrup 5C3
Gyldendal hav, Vester Hærup Strandvej 34.
GPS: n56,58107 e8,71066.

15 DKK 100 Ch (4x) WC included.
Location: Rural, simple, quiet. **Surface:** gravel/sand.
01/01-31/12.
Distance: Sandy beach on the spot on the spot.

DK

Storvorde 5C3

Egense Lystbådehavan, Kystvej 1. **GPS**: n56,98270 e10,30451.

6 DKK 110 (6x) WC. **Location:** Rural, simple, quiet. **Surface:** metalled. 01/01-31/12.
Distance: on the spot on the spot 1km.
Remarks: Pay at harbourmaster.

Storvorde 5C3

Dokkedal, Kystvej 118. **GPS**: n56,93305 e10,26225.
DKK 150 Ch against payment. 01/01-31/12.
Remarks: Quick-Stop: >20h - <10h.

Storvorde 5C3

Egense, Kystvej 6. **GPS**: n56,98071 e10,30086.
DKK 100 Ch against payment. 24/03-17/09.
Remarks: Quick-Stop: >20h - <10h.

Stouby 6D1

Løgballe Autocamperplads, Løgballevej 12.
GPS: n55,70765 e9,84359.

7 DKK 75 DKK 15 Ch (7x)DKK 30 WC. **Location:** Rural, simple, isolated, quiet. **Surface:** gravel. 01/04-01/10.

Stouby 6D1

Løgballe Camping, Løgballevej 12. **GPS**: n55,70786 e9,84423.
DKK 75. 18/03-25/09.
Remarks: Quick-Stop: >20h - <10h.

Stouby 6D1

Rosenvold Strand Camping, Rosenvoldvej 19.
GPS: n55,67691 e9,81356.
DKK 100-120. 18/03-25/09.
Remarks: Quick-Stop: >20h - <10h.

Strandby 5C3

Strandby havn, Søndre Havnevej 27. **GPS**: n57,49249 e10,50245.

6 DKK 120 WC included.
Location: Urban, simple. **Surface:** metalled. 01/01-31/12.
Distance: on the spot on the spot on the spot on the spot on the spot.
Remarks: Pay at harbourmaster.

Struer 5C3

Holstebro-Struer Lystbådehavn, Fjordvejen.
GPS: n56,49380 e8,59068.

4 DKK 130 WC Access sanitary building DKK 20 included. **Location:** Urban, comfortable, quiet.
Surface: gravel. winter.
Distance: 100m 100m.
Remarks: Tallycard: service, electricity, sanitary building, caution DKK 50.

Struer 5C3

Venø Havn, Venø. **GPS**: n56,55102 e8,61622.
DKK 100 Ch WC.
Surface: gravel.
Distance: on the spot on the spot on the spot.
Tourist information Struer:
Gimsinghoved, Gimsinghoved 1. Former large Danish farm.

Sydals 6D3

Lysabildskov, Skovforten 4. **GPS**: n54,89159 e10,05268.
DKK 120 Ch against payment. 19/03-30/09.
Remarks: Quick-Stop: >20h - <10h.

Sydals 6D3

Mommark Marina Camping, Mommarkvej 380.
GPS: n54,93157 e10,04392.
DKK 120. 19/03-30/09.
Distance: on the spot.
Remarks: Quick-Stop: >20h - <10h.

Sydals 6D3

Sønderby Strand Camping, Sønderbygade 4-6, Kegnæs.
GPS: n54,86586 e9,89222.
DKK 120. 18/03-03/10.
Distance: 100m.
Remarks: Quick-Stop: >20h - <10h.

Sydals 6D3

Drejby, Kregnæsvej 85. **GPS**: n54,90530 e9,96540.
DKK 150 Ch. 18/03-02/10.
Remarks: Quick-Stop: >20h - <10h.
Tourist information Sydals:
Sydals Turistbureau, Kegnæsvej 52.
Kegnæs Fyr, Nørre Landevej 7. Lighthouse. 01/06-30/09 Mo-Su 9-19h.

Sæby 5C3

Lene en Knut Holdensgård, Holdenggårdvej 16, Sønder.
GPS: n57,21616 e10,45253.

3 DKK 50. **Location:** Rural, simple, isolated, quiet.
Surface: grassy. 01/01-31/12.

Sæby 5C3

Sæby Havn, Havnen 20. **GPS**: n57,33218 e10,53373.

20 DKK 150 (20x)included. **Location:** Urban, simple, central. **Surface:** asphalted. 01/01-31/12.
Distance: 100m 100m 100m.

Sæby 5C3

Top Plads hos Ase en Helmer, Understedvej 65, Understed.
GPS: n57,37249 e10,46447.

20 DKK 100 Ch WC. **Location:** Rural, comfortable, isolated, quiet. **Surface:** grassy. 01/01-31/12.

Sæby 5C3

Danbjerg, Hjørringvej 160. **GPS**: n57,32544 e10,36967.

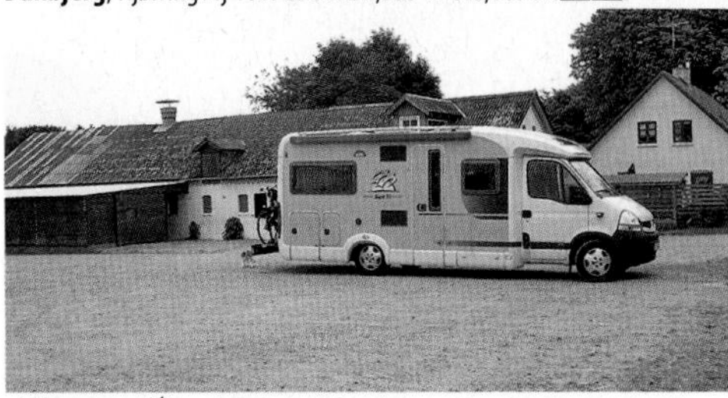

6 DKK 50. **Location:** Rural, simple, isolated, quiet.
Surface: grassy/gravel. 01/01-31/12.
Distance: 1km 1km.

Tarm 6C1

Par3Golf, Grimlundvej. **GPS**: n55,83819 e8,71321.
free. **Location:** Isolated, quiet. 01/01-31/12.
Distance: Tarm 19km.

Tårs (Hjørring) 5C3

Vendelbo Vans Autocampere, Damhusvej 23.
GPS: n57,38972 e10,11500.

8 DKK 100 Ch (8x) WC included.
Location: Urban, comfortable, central, quiet. **Surface:** grassy/gravel. 01/01-31/12.
Distance: 100m 500m 500m 300m 300m 200m.
Remarks: At motorhome dealer, max. 48h, sanitary 9-17h.

Thisted 5C3

Thisted, Iversensvej 3. **GPS**: n56,95309 e8,71249.
DKK 135 Ch against payment. 01/01-31/12.
Remarks: Quick-Stop: >20h - <10h.

Thisted 5C3

Nystrup Camping Klitmøller, Trøjborgvej 22, Klitmøller.
GPS: n57,03302 e8,47927. DKK 100. 01/03-30/10.
Remarks: Quick-Stop: >20h - <10h.
Tourist information Thisted:
Thy Turistbureau i Thisted, Store Torv 6, www.visitthy.dk. Bathing resort.
Thisted Bryghus, Bryggerivej 10. Brewery, information at Turistbureau. summer Wed 11h. DKK 50.

Thorsager 6D1

Dagli Brugsen, Thorsgade 26. **GPS**: n56,34305 e10,46286.

4 free. **Location:** Urban, simple. **Surface:** gravel/metalled. 01/01-31/12.
Distance: on the spot on the spot.
Remarks: Behind supermarket Brugsen.

Thyborøn 5B3

Thyborøn, Idrætsvej 3. **GPS**: n56,69456 e8,20456.
DKK 50 Ch. 01/01-31/12.
Remarks: Quick-Stop: >20h - <10h.

Thyholm 5C3

Jegindø Havn, Havnegade. **GPS**: n56,65219 e8,63575.
€ 15 WC included. **Surface:** gravel. 01/01-31/12.
Remarks: At harbour.

Tinglev 6C2

Stefan Christiansen, Uge Green 2. **GPS**: n54,97365 e9,34601.

DK

8 € 10 Ch (6x)DKK27/24h WC DKK 10 included.
Location: Rural, comfortable, luxurious, isolated, quiet.
Surface: grassy. 01/01-31/12.
Distance: 8km 2km on the spot on the spot 800m on the spot on the spot.
Remarks: Golf court 1km.

S Toftlund 6C2

Dahl, Lebækvej 2. **GPS**: n55,17839 e9,07768.
5 DKK 45 Ch DKK 45 included. **Surface:** grassy.

S Tønder 6C3

Tønder Sport & FritidsCenter, Sønderlandevej.
GPS: n54,93558 e8,87754.
Ch. **Surface:** gravel. 04/01-19/12.

S Tønder 6C3

Kennel Roager, Flensborg Landevej 25. **GPS**: n54,93190 e8,99793.

5 DKK 100 DKK 20/24h WC included DKK 20 DKK 30.
Location: Rural, simple, isolated, noisy. **Surface:** grassy.
01/01-31/12.
Distance: 10km 4km.

DK

Ulfborg 6C1

Tingvej. **GPS**: n56,27295 e8,00000.
4 free. **Surface:** gravel. 01/01-31/12.
Distance: on the spot 200m 300m.
Remarks: Nearby town hall.

Ulfborg 6C1

Thorsminde Havn, Vesterhavsgade. **GPS**: n56,36578 e8,12163.
DKK 75.
Distance: on the spot on the spot 200m.

Ulfborg 6C1

Tvind Skolecenter, Skorkærvej 8. **GPS**: n56,25636 e8,28110.

15 free. **Location:** Rural, simple, isolated.
01/01-31/12.
Distance: 8km 8km 8km.

S Ulfborg 6C1

Rejkjær, Ringkobingvej 24. **GPS**: n56,23319 e8,30966.
DKK 100 Ch against payment. 03/04-18/10.
Remarks: Quick-Stop: >20h - <10h.

S Ulfborg 6C1

Vedersø Klit, øhusevej 23. **GPS**: n56,25829 e8,14130.
DKK 125 Ch against payment. 18/03-23/10.
Remarks: Quick-Stop: >20h - <10h.

Vandel 6C1

Dagli' Brugsen, Hans Thomsens Vej. **GPS**: n55,71285 e9,21800.
free. **Surface:** asphalted. 01/01-31/12.
Remarks: At petrol station and supermarket, Legoland 6km.

S Vandel 6C1

Rastplads, Billundvej. **GPS**: n55,70687 e9,26709.
free WC free.

Surface: forest soil. 01/01-31/12.
Distance: on the spot 4km.
Remarks: Parking in the forest with place for campfire, Legoland 10km.

S Vejers Strand 6B2

Stjerne, Vejers Havvej 7. **GPS**: n55,61915 e8,14090.
DKK 115 Ch against payment. 01/01-31/12.
Remarks: Quick-Stop: >20h - <10h.

S Vejers Strand 6B2

Vejers Familiecamping, Vejers Havvej 15. **GPS**: n55,61950 e8,13594.
DKK 110 Ch against payment.
01/01-31/12.
Remarks: Quick-Stop: >20h - <10h.

Tourist information Vejers Strand:
Tirpitz. German bunker.

S Vesløs 5C3

Amtoft Havn, Gårdbækvej 12. **GPS**: n57,00647 e8,94068.

5 DKK 100 Ch (10x) WC included free.
Location: Rural, comfortable, quiet. **Surface:** grassy/gravel.
01/01-31/12.
Distance: on the spot on the spot on the spot on the spot.
Remarks: To be paid at supermarket.

Vesløs 5C3

Vejlernes Grill & Kiosk, Aalborgvej 219B. **GPS**: n57,02518 e9,01585.

free. **Surface:** gravel. 01/01-31/12.

S Vestervig 5B3

Krik-Vig, Krikvej 112. **GPS**: n56,77800 e8,26210.
DKK 100 Ch against payment. 19/03-23/10.
Remarks: Quick-Stop: >20h - <10h.

Vinderup 5C3

Handbjerg Marina, Strandvejen. **GPS**: n56,47568 e8,71337.
5 € 10. 01/01-31/12.
Distance: on the spot.

Vinderup 5C3

Sevel Camping, Halallé 6, Sevel.
GPS: n56,45889 e8,86950.
DKK 50.
01/01-31/12.
Remarks: Quick-Stop: >20h - <10h.

Tourist information Vinderup:
Hjerl Hedes Frilandsmuseum, Hjerl Hedevej 14. Open air museum.
01/05-30/09 10-16h, 01/07-31/07 10-17h.
Stubber Kloster, Stubbergård Sø. Ruins of former Benedictine monastery. 01/01-31/12. free.

S Voerså 5C3

Parking Havn, Havstokken 11. **GPS**: n57,20389 e10,49389.

20 DKK 120 Ch (20x) WC included.
Location: Rural, comfortable, isolated. **Surface:** gravel.
01/04-31/10.
Distance: 3km on the spot on the spot 3km 3km.

Remarks: Money in envelope in mail box.

S Østbirk 6D1

Elite Camp Vestbirk, Møllehøjvej 4. **GPS**: n55,96840 e9,75000.
DKK 140 Ch against payment. 19/03-28/09.
Remarks: Quick-Stop: >20h - <10h.

Funen

S Aarup 6D2

Annemette & Lars Mogensen, Frøbjerg Vænge 31.
GPS: n55,34907 e10,08323.
3 free free. **Surface:** gravel. 01/01-31/12.

S Aarup 6D2

Aalsbogaard Lystfiskersøer, St. Landevej 123 - 125, Billesbølle.
GPS: n55,42686 e10,01935.
DKK 100.
Distance: on the spot on the spot.
Remarks: At fish lake.

Asperup 6D2

Skovlund Camping, Kystvejen 1. **GPS**: n55,50647 e9,89967.
DKK 99. 23/03-18/09.
Remarks: Quick-Stop: >20h - <10h.

S Assens 6D2

Britta Bang, Lilletoftevej 7, Lilletofte Gamtofte.
GPS: n55,28165 e9,98850.
3 € 13,50 Ch included WC.
Location: Rural. **Surface:** metalled.
Distance: 7,5km 7km 7km.

Tourist information Assens:
Vestfyns Hjemstavnsgård, Klaregade 23, Gummerup, Glamsbjerg. Open air museum. 01/04-31/10 10-16h Mo.

Bagenkop 6E3

Koldkrigsmuseum Langelandsfor, Vognsbjergvej 4A.
GPS: n54,75306 e10,71583.
DKK 95. **Surface:** metalled. 01/04-31/10.
Remarks: Check in at museum.

S Bogense 6D2

Bogense Havn, Vestre Havnevej 29. **GPS**: n55,56806 e10,07833.

8 € 14 WC included.
Surface: gravel. 01/01-31/12.
Distance: 200m 300m 300m on the spot 200m.

S Bogense 6D2

Kyst, østre Havnevej 1. **GPS**: n55,56626 e10,08395.
DKK 210 Ch. 20/03-18/09.
Remarks: Quick-Stop: >20h - <10h.

Broby 6D2

Bakkelyet, Præsteskovvej 7. **GPS**: n55,25707 e10,19292.
DKK 50. **Location:** Isolated, quiet.
Distance: 3km on the spot 3km.

S Faaborg 6D2

Faaborg Havn, Kanalvej 19. **GPS**: n55,09658 e10,23429.
6 DKK 120 DKK 5 Ch DKK 3/kWh WC.
Surface: asphalted. 01/01-31/12.
Distance: 200m on the spot on the spot on the spot 500m 200m.
Remarks: Check in at harbourmaster.

S Faaborg 6D2

Faaborg Camping, Odensevej 140. **GPS**: n55,11667 e10,24477.
DKK 150 Ch against payment. 01/01-31/12.
Remarks: Quick-Stop: >20h - <10h.

Faaborg 6D2

Nab Strand Camping, Kildegaardsvej 8. **GPS**: n55,06428 e10,31390.
DKK 160. 29/04-28/08.
Remarks: Quick-Stop: >20h - <10h.

Ferritslev 6D2

Jørgen Christensen, Rolfvej 45. **GPS**: n55,32111 e10,56806.
47 free. **Location:** Urban, simple. **Surface:** metalled.
01/01-31/12.

Frørup 6E2

Kongshøj, Kongshøjvej 5. **GPS**: n55,22122 e10,80628.
DKK 105 Ch. 01/01-31/12.
Remarks: Quick-Stop: >20h - <10h.

Gram 6C2

Anholm Fiskesø, Folevej 11. **GPS**: n55,30564 e8,99888.

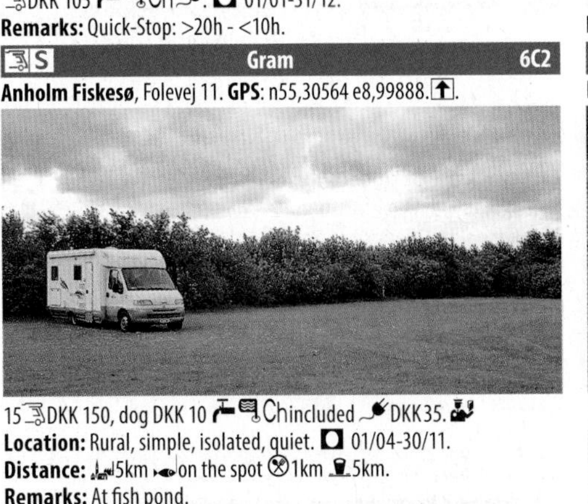

15 DKK 150, dog DKK 10 Ch included DKK 35.
Location: Rural, simple, isolated, quiet. 01/04-30/11.
Distance: 5km on the spot 1km 5km.
Remarks: At fish pond.

Gram 6C2

Gram Slot, Slotsvej 54. **GPS**: n55,29722 e9,05946.
50 DKK 75 WC included. **Surface:** grassy.
Distance: 1km.

Gram 6C2

Annemettes bondegård, Ribelandevej 18.
GPS: n55,28647 e9,00098.

3 DKK 100 Ch DKK 25. **Location:** Rural, simple, isolated, quiet. **Surface:** grassy/gravel. 03/01-01/11.

Humble 6E3

Ristinge, Ristingevej 104. **GPS**: n54,81944 e10,63988.
DKK 150 Ch against payment. 03/06-28/08.
Remarks: Quick-Stop: >20h - <10h.

Kerteminde 6E2

Color Camp Kerteminde, Hindsholmvej 80. **GPS**: n55,46409 e10,67183.
DKK 125 Ch. 21/03-18/09.
Remarks: Quick-Stop: >20h - <10h.

Middelfart 6D2

Lystbådehavn, Østre Hougvej 112. **GPS**: n55,49250 e9,73028.

13 € 17 Ch (12x) WC included.
Location: Rural, luxurious, isolated, quiet.
Surface: asphalted/metalled. 01/01-31/12.
Distance: 2km on the spot on the spot on the spot on the spot.
Remarks: Harbour Middelfahrt, Tallycard: service, electricity, sanitary building, caution DKK 50.

Middelfart 6D2

Strib Bådehavn, Strandvejen 271, Strib. **GPS**: n55,53829 e9,76387.
DKK 120 WC. **Surface:** gravel.
Distance: on the spot 350m 1km.

Middelfart 6D2

Vejlby Fed Camping, Rigelvej 1. **GPS**: n55,51949 e9,84975.
DKK 120 Ch against payment. 19/03-11/09.
Remarks: Quick-Stop: >20h - <10h.

Millinge 6D2

Fasled Havn, Fiskerstræde 1. **GPS**: n55,15347 e10,14431.
DKK 110 included. **Surface:** grassy/gravel.
Distance: on the spot 200m.
Remarks: Check in at harbourmaster, wifi code: havnen2.

Nr. Åby 6D2

Ronæs strand, Ronæsvej 10. **GPS**: n55,43975 e9,82692.
DKK 130 Ch against payment. 19/03-25/09.
Remarks: Quick-Stop: >20h - <10h.

Nyborg 6E2

Hjejlevej 107. **GPS**: n55,29734 e10,83963.

free Ch free. **Surface:** metalled.

Nyborg 6E2

Sulkendrup Vandmølle, Sulkendrupvej 1, Sulkendrup.
GPS: n55,29384 e10,71334.
3 € 10 DKK 25 Ch WC DKK 10. **Location:** Rural, comfortable.
Surface: grassy. 01/01-31/12.
Distance: 5km.

Nyborg 6E2

Grønnehave strand, Rejstrupvej 83. **GPS**: n55,35646 e10,78767.
DKK 140 Ch against payment. 24/03-25/09.
Remarks: Quick-Stop: >20h - <10h.

Tourist information Nyborg:

Borgmestergården, Slotsgade 11. Local history. 01/05-31/10 10-15/16h.

Nyborg Fæstning, Slotsgade 1. Fortress.

Nyborg Slot / Danehofslottet, Slotsgade 34. Castle, end 12th century. 01/04-31/10 10-15/16h.

Odense 6D2

Tarup Campingcenter, Agerhatten 31. **GPS**: n55,36110 e10,46722.
20 free. **Surface:** grassy. 01/01-31/12.
Distance: 6km 2km.

Rudkøbing 6E2

Færgegårdens, Spodsbjergvej 335. **GPS**: n54,93219 e10,82945.
DKK 130 Ch against payment. 01/01-31/12.
Remarks: Quick-Stop: >20h - <10h.

Stenstrup 6D2

Tronbjerggård Strandhave, Højbjergvej 13.
GPS: n55,12944 e10,58306.
3 against payment WC.

Svendborg 6D2

Mogens Nielsen, Tordensgårdevej 3. **GPS**: n55,08750 e10,55389.
10 WC included. **Location:** Rural, comfortable.
Surface: grassy/metalled. 01/01-31/12.
Distance: 5km 5km on the spot.

Svendborg 6D2

Carlsberg, Sundbrovej 19. **GPS**: n55,03344 e10,61332.
DKK 130 Ch against payment. 17/03-02/10.
Remarks: Quick-Stop: >20h - <10h.

Svendborg 6D2

Idrætshallen, Ryttervej 70. **GPS**: n55,05668 e10,57613.
DKK 100 Ch.

Tourist information Svendborg:

Egeskov Slot, Kværndrup. Citadel with park and 6 museums. 01/05-31/10 10-17/20h.

Valdemars Slot, Slotsalléen 100, Troense, Tåsinge. Castle on the island Tåsinge, fully furnished. 01/05-31/10 10-17h May, Sep, Oct: Mo.

Tranekær 6E2

Emmerbølle Strand Camping, Emmerbøllevej 24.
GPS: n55,03351 e10,84853.
DKK 170. 18/03-18/09.
Distance: on the spot.
Remarks: Quick-Stop: >20h - <10h.

Varde 6C2

Fritidscenter, Lerpøtvej 55. **GPS**: n55,63294 e8,47447.
20 DKK 100 WC against payment. **Surface:** grassy.
01/05-31/10.
Remarks: At sports centre.

Varde 6C2

Jensen, Ringkøbingvej 143. **GPS**: n55,65762 e8,48942.

4 DKK 75 WC. **Location:** Rural, comfortable, isolated, quiet. **Surface:** grassy/metalled.
Distance: 5km.

Varde 6C2

Joan & Preben Christensen, Ringkøbingvej 259, Hindsig.
GPS: n55,72077 e8,49345.

5 DKK 50 Ch.
Location: Rural, comfortable, quiet. **Surface:** grassy. 01/01-31/12.
Distance: 12km 3km.

Ærøskøbing 6D2

Ærøskøbing Camping, Sygehusvejen 40. **GPS**: n54,89408 e10,40118.
DKK 100. 01/04-23/10.
Distance: on the spot.
Remarks: Quick-Stop: >20h - <10h.

Seeland, Møn, Lolland and Falster

Boeslunde 6E2

Campinggaarden Boelunde, Rennebjergvej 110.
GPS: n55,28463 e11,26837.
DKK 140 Ch against payment. 01/04-30/09.
Remarks: Quick-Stop: >20h - <10h.

Bogø By 6F2

Grønsundvej. **GPS**: n54,94889 e11,98653.

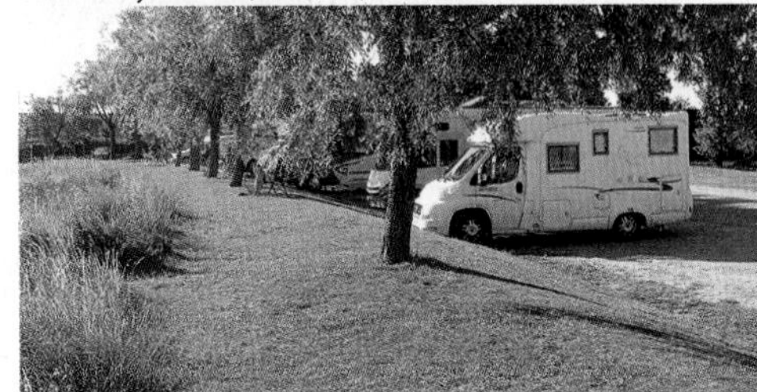

25 free Ch WC free.
Location: Rural. **Surface:** gravel.
Distance: 200m on the spot on the spot on the spot.

Bogø By 6F2

Café-Restaurant Stalden, Hougårdsbanke 5.
GPS: n54,93000 e12,02806.
4 free for clients Ch WC against payment.
Location: Rural. **Surface:** grassy. 01/01-31/12.
Distance: 1km on the spot.

Copenhagen 6F1

Copenhagen City Camp, Elvaerksvej 7-9.
GPS: n55,65440 e12,55697.

70 DKK 225 Ch WC included. **Location:** Urban, simple, quiet. **Surface:** asphalted. Whitsuntide-10/09.

DK

Distance: 4km 500m 1km 1km on the spot on the spot.

Tourist information Copenhagen:

Copenhagen Card. Card gives free entrance to public transport, 73 museums and attractions. Available at Tourist Offices, hotels, campsites.

Dyrehavsbakken, Dyrehavevej 62, Klampenborg (ten n. van Kopenhagen). Popular amusement park, oldest park of Denmark, with among other things 100 attractions and 35 restaurants.

Tivoli, Vesterbrogade 3. Large amusement park in the centre of the city with among other things 32 restaurants, 26 attractions, shows, concerts etc. DKK 110-120.

Dalby 6E2

Camp Hverringe, Blæsenborgvej 200. **GPS**: n55,50937 e10,71233.
DKK 75. 18/03-23/10.
Distance: on the spot.
Remarks: Quick-Stop: >20h - <10h.

Dannemare 6E3

Hummingen, Pumpehusvej 1. **GPS**: n54,71317 e11,24606.
DKK 140 Ch against payment. 18/03-23/10.
Remarks: Quick-Stop: >20h - <10h.

Dronningsmølle 6F1

Dronningsmølle, Strandkrogen 2b. **GPS**: n56,08393 e12,39112.
DKK 150 Ch. 15/03-14/09.
Remarks: Quick-Stop: >20h - <10h.

Fakse 6F2

Feddet, Feddet 12. **GPS**: n55,17366 e12,10118.
DKK 75, dog DKK 30 Ch against payment included.
01/01-31/12.
Remarks: Quick-Stop: >20h - <10h.

Tourist information Fakse:

Faksekystens Turistinformation, Hovedgaden 29, Fakse Ladeplads, www.faksekysten.dk. The municipality Fakse has 30 kilometres coastline, marked cycle and hiking routes.

Fortællerfestival, Fakse Lime Beach. Festival for story tellers. last weekend Jun.

Rivierafest, Fakse Ladeplads. Festival with free herring-table on Sunday. Thu-Su of week 29.

Farum 6F1

Hovedgade 32. **GPS**: n55,81222 e12,36917.

3 free. **Location:** Urban, simple, noisy. **Surface:** asphalted.
01/01-31/12.
Distance: 500m 100m on the spot 500m on the spot on the spot.

Farum 6F1

Stavnsholt Renseanlæg. GPS: n55,81278 e12,40556.
Ch free. Mo-Thu 7-15.30h, Fr 7-11.30h.

Farø 6F2

Farø, Grøsundvej. **GPS**: n54,94876 e11,98696.
20 free Ch WC free. **Location:** Noisy.
Surface: asphalted.

Frederikssund 6F1

Marbæk Lystbådehavn, Strandlystvej 26 D.
GPS: n55,82778 e12,06389.

6 125 DKK Ch WC included against payment DKK 20/20.
Location: Rural, comfortable, quiet. **Surface:** gravel. 01/01-31/12.
Distance: 1,5km on the spot on the spot 1,5km 1,5km on the spot on the spot.

Frederikssund 6F1

B&B Bybjerggaard, Sundbylillevej 42. **GPS**: n55,83579 e12,11622.
DKK 50/pp.
Distance: on the spot.

Frederiksværk 6F1

Frederiksværk Havn, Havnelinien 23. **GPS**: n55,96673 e11,99986.
4 DKK 140 included.
Distance: 2km on the spot on the spot.

Føllenslev 6E1

Vesterlyng, Ravnholtvej 3. **GPS**: n55,74278 e11,30883.
DKK 130 Ch against payment. 18/03-23/10.
Remarks: Quick-Stop: >20h - <10h.

Gedser 6F3

Gedser Lystbådehavn, Vestre Strand 3. **GPS**: n54,58194 e11,92361.
5 € 16 included. **Surface:** gravel. 01/01-31/12.
Distance: 200m.

Gilleleje 6F1

Smidstrup Farmen, Jydebjergvej 32. **GPS**: n56,10346 e12,22722.
DKK 100 . **Location:** Rural. **Surface:** grassy/gravel.
01/01-31/12.
Distance: 1,5km 2km 1,5km.
Remarks: Max. 3 days.

Greve 6F1

Copenhagen Motorhome Camp, Hundige Strandvej 72.
GPS: n55,59399 e12,34247.

42 DKK 205, 15/06-31/08 DKK 215 Ch DKK 52 included.
Surface: grassy. 01/04-31/10.
Distance: Copenhagen 19km 1km 3km 800m.

Gørlev 6E2

Reersø Havn, Strandvejen 101, Reersø. **GPS**: n55,51750 e11,11833.

5 DKK 100 WC included.
Location: Rural, simple, quiet. **Surface:** gravel. 01/04-01/11.
Distance: 300m on the spot on the spot on the spot on the spot on the spot.
Remarks: Money in envelope in mail box.

Helsinge 6F1

Anisse Vingård, Præstevej 89, Annisse. **GPS**: n55,98114 e12,17474.
DKK 75 . 01/01-31/12.

Hillerød 6F1

JOHS, Hestehavevej 24. **GPS**: n55,90221 e12,31155.
DKK 150 . **Surface:** grassy/gravel.
Distance: on the spot on the spot.

Hundested 6E1

Hundested Havn, Havnegade 8. **GPS**: n55,96557 e11,84845.

5 DKK 150 Ch WC against payment.
Location: Urban, comfortable. **Surface:** metalled. 01/01-31/12.
Distance: 500m on the spot on the spot on the spot 200m 200m on the spot.

Hundested 6E1

Lynæs Havn, Lynæs Havnevej 15 B, Lynæs.
GPS: n55,94407 e11,86507.

10 DKK 160 Ch WC included free.
Location: Rural, simple, quiet.
Surface: metalled. 01/01-31/12.
Distance: 2km 500m on the spot 2km on the spot on the spot.

Kalundborg 6E1

Debbies Bed & Breakfast, Hovvejen 114. **GPS**: n55,67564 e11,14552.
DKK 100 .
Remarks: Breakfast-service.

Kalvehave 6F2

Lystbådehavn, Kalvehave Havnevej 26. **GPS**: n54,99584 e12,16641.
2 against payment against payment. **Surface:** grassy/gravel.

Karise 6F2

Lægårdens, Vemmetoftevej 2A. **GPS**: n55,27260 e12,22306.
DKK 105 Ch. 01/01-31/12.
Remarks: Quick-Stop: >20h - <10h.

Karrebæksminde 6E2

Naestved Sjelklub, Ved Broen 29. **GPS**: n55,17706 e11,65018.

6 € 18 Ch WC DKK 50/50 included.
Location: Rural, simple, quiet.
Surface: gravel. 15/04-15/09.
Distance: on the spot on the spot on the spot on the spot on the spot.

Kirke Hyllinge 6F1

Gershøj Havn, Gershøj Havnevej 5, Gershøj.
GPS: n55,71667 e11,98000.

10 € 8 Ch against payment WC included.
Location: Rural, simple, quiet. **Surface:** gravel. 01/01-31/12.
Distance: 1,5km on the spot on the spot.

Korsør 6E2

Pit-Stop Storebælt, Storebæltsvej 85. **GPS**: n55,34833 e11,11556.

40 € 10 Ch included.
Location: Rural, simple. **Surface:** grassy. 01/01-31/12.
Distance: 1km 500m on the spot on the spot 500m on the spot on the spot on the spot.
Remarks: Along busy through road, use camp-site facilities allowed,

closed at night.

Korsør 6E2

Lystbådehavn, Sylowsvej 10. **GPS**: n55,32664 e11,13190.

20 € 17 included WC against payment.

Location: Rural, simple, quiet.

Surface: gravel. 01/01-31/12.

Distance: 300m 4km on the spot on the spot on the spot 300m on the spot on the spot.

Remarks: Harbour Åbenrå.

Korsør 6E2

Lystskov, Korsør Lystskov 2. **GPS**: n55,32219 e11,18505.

DKK 90 Ch against payment. 19/03-25/09.

Remarks: Quick-Stop: >20h - <10h.

Tourist information Korsør:

Korsør Fæstning, Korsør Coastal Battery, The Fortress, Søbatteriet 7. Fortress. 01/05-30/09 Wed-Su 11-16h.

Lynge 6F1

Irene & Aage Andersen, Stengårdsvej 12.

GPS: n55,81972 e12,27376.

3 free DKK 10/50liter. **Location:** Rural, simple, quiet.

Surface: grassy. 01/01-31/12.

Distance: 1km on the spot on the spot.

Maribo 6E3

Skelstrupgåren Bed and Breakfast, Skelstupvej 3.

GPS: n54,78774 e11,52095.

5 DKK 50 against payment. **Surface:** grassy.

Distance: 2,2km 4km.

Munke Bjergby 6E2

Dojringevej 40a. **GPS**: n55,49637 e11,55065.

10 free DKK 10/20liter DKK 10 DKK 30. **Location:** Rural, comfortable, quiet. **Surface:** grassy. 01/01-31/12.

Distance: 8km on the spot on the spot.

Remarks: Max. 48h.

Nykøbing 6E1

Lystbådehavn, Snekkevej 9. **GPS**: n55,91610 e11,67287.

10 DKK 110 Ch WC included DKK 25/20.

Location: Urban, simple, quiet. **Surface:** grassy. 01/01-31/12.

Distance: 500m 100m 100m on the spot on the spot.

Nykøbing F. 6F3

Toreby Sejlklub, Dæmningen 2, Sundby Lolland.

GPS: n54,76051 e11,86041.

5 € 14 WC included. **Surface:** gravel.

Distance: on the spot on the spot on the spot.

Nykøbing F. 6F3

Falster City Camping, østre Allé 112. **GPS**: n54,76243 e11,89479.

DKK 120 Ch against payment. 01/04-01/12.

Remarks: Quick-Stop: >20h - <10h.

Næstved 6E2

Rådmandshaven. **GPS**: n55,23166 e11,75344.

14 free. **Location:** Urban, simple, noisy. **Surface:** concrete. 01/01-31/12.

Distance: 500m 500m 500m on the spot.

Remarks: Parking in front of town hall, special part for motor homes.

Præstø 6F2

Præstø Havn, Fjordstien 1. **GPS**: n55,12444 e12,04333.

5 DKK 115 Ch WC DKK 25/25 included.

Location: Urban, simple, quiet.

Surface: asphalted. 01/01-31/12.

Distance: 500m 7km on the spot on the spot on the spot on the spot.

Ringsted 6E2

Autocamper P-plads Ringsted, Delingen.

GPS: n55,45029 e11,80077.

6 free free.

Location: Urban, simple. **Surface:** grasstiles. 01/01-31/12.

Distance: 1km 900m 900m.

Remarks: Max. 48h.

Ringsted 6E2

Mogens Madsen, Vibevej 34. **GPS**: n55,44222 e11,80667.

3 free against payment. **Location:** Urban, simple, noisy.

Surface: metalled. 01/01-31/12.

Distance: 4 km 800m.

Ringsted 6E2

Skovly Camping, Nebs Møllevej 65. **GPS**: n55,49615 e11,85768.

DKK 150. 01/01-31/12.

Remarks: Quick-Stop: >20h - <10h.

Roskilde 6F1

Camp Roskilde, Baunehøjvej 7. **GPS**: n55,67374 e12,08209.

DKK 150 DKK 45. 18/03-02/10.

Remarks: Quick-Stop: >20h - <10h.

Rødvig 6F2

Rødvig Fiskerihavn, Fiskerihavnen 8. **GPS**: n55,25417 e12,37500.

4 € 12 WC included DKK 5/4minutes.

Location: Rural, simple, quiet.

Surface: metalled. 01/01-31/12.

Distance: 200m on the spot on the spot on the spot.

Remarks: Check in at harbourmaster.

Rødvig 6F2

Rødvig Camping, Højstrupvej 2 A. **GPS**: n55,25059 e12,34970.

5 DKK 100.

Location: Rural, simple, quiet. **Surface:** grassy. 01/04-28/09.

Distance: 2km on the spot.

Remarks: Quick-Stop: >20h - <10h.

Sakskøbing 6E3

Sakskøbing Lystbådehavn, Maltrup Vænge 38.

GPS: n54,81078 e11,61957.

5 € 14 WC against payment included.

Distance: 500m.

Sjællands Odde 6E1

Sjællands Odde Havn, Østre Havnevej 42.

GPS: n55,97139 e11,36956.

2 € 16 WC included DKK 5/5minutes.

Location: Rural, simple, quiet.

Surface: gravel. 01/01-31/12.

Distance: on the spot on the spot 300m on the spot.

Skælskør 6E2

Skælskør Havn, Havnevej 20. **GPS**: n55,25223 e11,28992.

15 € 14 Ch (15x)DKK 25/kWh WC included DKK 5/5minutes DKK 25/25 free.

Location: Urban, simple, central. **Surface:** metalled. 01/01-31/12.

Distance: on the spot on the spot on the spot on the spot on the spot on the spot.

Remarks: Free bicycles available.

Skælskør 6E2

Skælskør Nor, Kildehusvej 1. **GPS**: n55,25818 e11,28395.

DK

DKK 100 Ch. 01/01-31/12.
Remarks: Quick-Stop: >20h - <10h.

Store Fuglede 6E2

Bjerge Sydstrand Camping, Osvejen 30. **GPS**: n55,56298 e11,16489.
DKK 150. 01/01-31/12.
Distance: on the spot.
Remarks: Quick-Stop: >20h - <10h.

Taastrup 6F1

Park Hotel, Brorsonsvej 3. **GPS**: n55,65389 e12,30000.

10 DKK 200 (3x)DKK25/day WC included on demand .
Location: Simple, quiet.
Surface: metalled. 01/01-31/12.
Distance: 300m 1,5km on the spot 300m on the spot on the spot.
Remarks: Breakfast buffet DKK 75, code wifi in restaurant.

Tårs (Harpelunde) 6E2

Tårs Havn Lolland, Tårsvej 215, Harpelund Lolland.
GPS: n54,87811 e11,02381.
2 DKK 125 WC included. 01/01-31/12.
Remarks: Harbour Tårs.

Torrig 6E2

Kragenæs Havn, Kragenæsvej 84. **GPS**: n54,91565 e11,35730.
DKK 135 Ch against payment. 18/03-23/10.
Remarks: Quick-Stop: >20h - <10h.

Vejby 6F1

Åmosevejen 18. **GPS**: n56,00000 e12,00000.
DKK 100 . **Location:** Rural. 01/01-31/12.
Distance: 2km.
Remarks: Max. 3 days.

DK

Vig 6E1

Kongsøre Camping, Egebjergvej 342. **GPS**: n55,82390 e11,66743.
DKK 120. 01/04-30/09.
Distance: on the spot.
Remarks: Quick-Stop: >20h - <10h.

Væggerløse 6F3

Marielyst Feriepark & Camping, Godthåbs Allé 7, Marielyst.
GPS: n54,67357 e11,94427.
DKK 100.
Remarks: Quick-Stop: >20h - <10h.

Værløse 6F1

Furesø Museer, Skovgårds alle 37. **GPS**: n55,78528 e12,37722.

4 free. **Location:** Urban, simple, noisy. **Surface:** metalled.
01/01-31/12.
Distance: on the spot 250m 250m on the spot on the spot.

Værløse 6F1

Bryggeri Skovlyst, Skovlystvej 2. **GPS**: n55,76317 e12,38365.

3 free WC. **Location:** Rural, simple, quiet. **Surface:** gravel.
01/01-31/12.
Distance: 5km on the spot on the spot on the spot.

Spain

Capital: Madrid
Government: Constitutional monarchy
Official Language: Spanish
Population: 48,146,000 (2015)
Area: 505,782 km²

General information
Dialling code: 0034
General emergency: 112
Currency: Euro

Regulations for overnight stays
Wild camping is allowed having gained permission from the municipality, olice or property owner. Along the Mediterranean coast wild camping is almost always forbidden. Parking places (P) mentioned here can be considered as tolerated places to stay overnight.

Additional public holidays 2017
January 6 Epiphany
April 14 Good Friday
May 1 Labor Day
June 15 Corpus Christi
August 15 Assumption of the Virgin Mary
October 12 National Holiday
November 1 All Saints' Day
December 6 Constitution Day
December 8 Immaculate Conception

Time Zone
Winter (Standard Time) GMT+1
Summer (DST) GMT+2

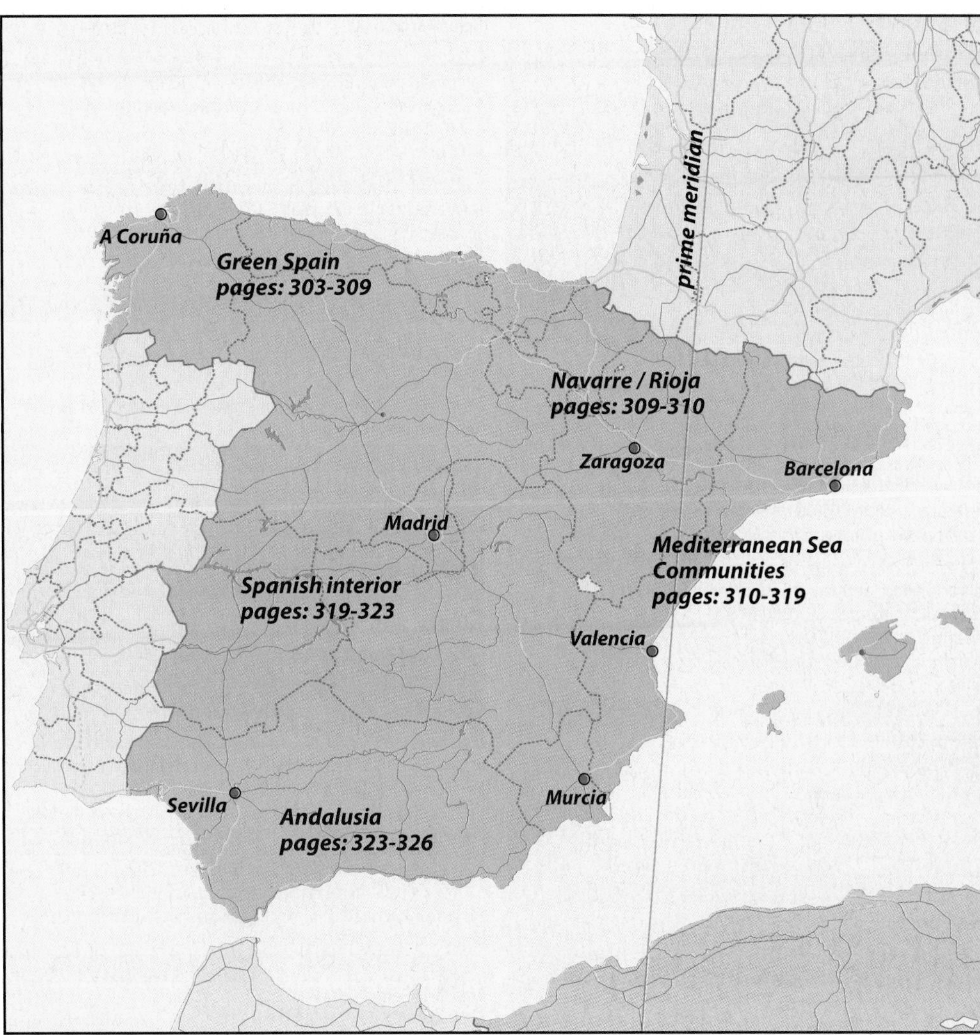

Green Spain

S A Coruña 29C1
Puerto de San Pedro de Visma, Zona de O Portiño.
GPS: n43,37167 w8,44472.

12 free Ch free. **Surface:** metalled.
Distance: 3km on the spot 50m 1km Carrefour 1km.
Remarks: Max. 48h.

A Coruña 29C1
Tore de Hercules. **GPS**: n43,38378 w8,40228.
free. **Surface:** asphalted.
Distance: on the spot 50m 50m.

S A Coruña 29C1
Parking Marina Coruña, Paseo Marítimo Francisco Vázquez s/n.
GPS: n43,36976 w8,38786.
15 € 1,50/h, € 22/24h Ch WC included.
Location: Urban. **Surface:** metalled. 01/01-31/12.
Distance: centre 800m on the spot.
Remarks: Parking marina.

S A Coruña 29C1
Yakart, Carretera de mesoiro, 63. **GPS**: n43,33228 w8,425.
15 € 10/24h Ch included. **Location:** Urban.
Surface: metalled. 01/01-31/12.
Distance: centre 4,5km 500m 70m.
Remarks: At motorhome dealer, monitored parking.

A Guarda 29B2
GPS: n41,89892 w8,87825.

5. **Location:** Urban, simple, central.
Surface: asphalted.
Distance: 1km 300m 500m.
Remarks: Parking harbour.

S A Laracha 29C1
Area de O Regado, AC-552. **GPS**: n43,24972 w8,61694.
3 free Ch free. **Surface:** asphalted.

S A Pontenova 29D1
Camiño do Antigo Ferrocarril. **GPS**: n43,35578 w7,18939.
6 free Ch free. **Surface:** asphalted. 01/01-31/12.
Distance: 800m 800m on the spot on the spot.
Remarks: Max. 48h.

S A Pontenova 29D1
Rua de la Estación. **GPS**: n43,34739 w7,19171.

8 free Ch free. **Surface:** asphalted.
Distance: 200m 100m.
Remarks: Max. 48h.

S A Rúa 29D2
Área Recreativa O Aguillón. GPS: n42,38800 w7,11459.
10 free Ch free. **Surface:** asphalted/grassy.
01/01-31/12.
Distance: 500m on the spot 500m 500m on the spot on the spot.
Remarks: Next to football ground.

S Agurain 29H2
Bizkaia Kalea. **GPS**: n42,85324 w2,38495.
7 free Ch free. **Surface:** asphalted. 01/01-31/12.
Distance: 500m 500m 350m.

S Amurrio 29H2
Araba Kalea. **GPS**: n43,05528 w2,99806.
3 free Ch free. 01/01-31/12.
Distance: 500m 500m.
Remarks: Max. 48h.

Añana 29G2
Mercado Kalea. **GPS**: n42,80344 w2,98437.
2. **Surface:** metalled. 01/01-31/12.
Distance: 300M.

S Arcade 29C2
Rúa do Peirao. **GPS**: n42,33946 w8,61329.
5 free Ch free. **Surface:** metalled. 01/01-31/12.
Distance: on the spot on the spot 100m 200m.

Arrigorriaga 29H2
Carretera Buia Etorbidea. **GPS**: n43,23772 w2,91938.

. **Location:** Urban, simple. **Surface:** asphalted.

ES

01/01-31/12.

As Neves 29C2

Camino del Emenjeric. **GPS**: n42,08726 w8,41374.

1 free Chfree. **Location:** Rural. 01/01-31/12.
Distance: 200m 200m.
Remarks: Max. 48h.

As Nogais 29D2

Calle Rosalía de Castro. **GPS**: n42,81066 w7,1069.
3 free Chfree. **Surface:** asphalted. 01/01-31/12.
Distance: 500m 500m 500m on the spot.
Remarks: Max. 48h, swimming pool and picnic area available.

As Pontes de García Rodríguez 29D1

Rúa Juan Antonio Suanzes. **GPS**: n43,45103 w7,85445.
5 free Chfree. 01/01-31/12.
Distance: 200m 200m.
Remarks: Well situated for visiting Parque Natural de las Fragas do Eume.

Bakio 29H2

Parking, BI 3101. **GPS**: n43,42783 w2,80442.

20 free WCfree.
Location: Urban, simple. **Surface:** grasstiles. 01/01-31/12.
Distance: 100m 200m 100m on the spot.
Remarks: Behind tourist info.

Barrio Cosío 29F2

Área de Autocaravanas del Valle del Nansa.
GPS: n43,23349 w4,39892.

6 first day free, then € 5 €3 Ch.
Location: Rural, simple, quiet. **Surface:** metalled.
Distance: on the spot on the spot 100m.
Remarks: Max. 24h.

Bárzana 29E1

Area de Bárzana-Quiros, El Felguere. **GPS**: n43,15611 w5,97306.
15 free Chfree. **Location:** Simple. **Surface:** asphalted.
01/01-31/12.

Bárzana 29E1

Area de Bárzana-Quirós, El Felguere. **GPS**: n43,15611 w5,97306.

15 free Chfree. **Location:** Rural, simple, quiet.
Surface: asphalted. 01/01-31/12 holidays.
Distance: 100m 100m 100m.

Remarks: Max. 48h.

Beasain 29H2

Igartza Oleta Kalea. **GPS**: n43,04682 w2,21228.
13 free Ch service€3. **Surface:** asphalted.
01/01-31/12.
Distance: city centre 1km 500m.

Becerreá 29D2

Parque Empresarial. **GPS**: n42,85283 w7,15179.
16 free Chfree. **Surface:** asphalted. 01/01-31/12.
Distance: 1km 400m.
Remarks: Max. 48h.

Beche 29C1

Lugar Beche, 6. **GPS**: n43,18318 w8,3067.
free Chfree. **Location:** Isolated, quiet. **Surface:** gravel.
01/01-31/12.
Distance: on the spot on the spot on the spot on the spot.
Remarks: Along river, max. 48h.

Behobia 27A2

N10, Calle de Aria Juncal. **GPS**: n43,34310 w1,7598.

6 € 3/2h < 19.30, overnight stay free. **Location:** Urban, simple, noisy.
Surface: asphalted. 01/01-31/12.
Distance: on the spot 500m 200m 500m on the spot.

Bergara 29H2

Telleria Kalea, Labegaraieta. **GPS**: n43,10481 w2,42265.
free Chfree. **Surface:** asphalted. 01/01-31/12.
Distance: 2km on the spot on the spot on the spot.
Remarks: Max. 48h.

Bermeo 29H2

Área de la Pérgola, Itsasoan Galdurakoen Lamera.
GPS: n43,42306 w2,72556.

10 free Chfree. **Location:** Urban, simple. **Surface:** asphalted.
01/01-31/12.
Distance: 500m 500m 500m 300m.
Remarks: Nearby football ground, max. 48h.

Bertamirans 29C1

Paseo Fluvial. **GPS**: n42,86009 w8,64838.

15 free Chfree. **Surface:** asphalted. 01/01-31/12.
Distance: 100m 50m Carrefour dir. Santiago every 30 min.
Remarks: Max. 48h.

Bilbao 29H2

Kobetamendi, Monte Kobeta, 31.
GPS: n43,25961 w2,96355.

72 € 15/day Ch included WC.
Location: Urban, comfortable, quiet.
Surface: grasstiles.
01/06-14/10.
Distance: centre 4,5km 2,8km Bilbao-bus 58.
Remarks: 16/10-14/05 free parking, asphalt, max. 72h, service passerby € 6.

Tourist information Bilbao:

Bilbao. Capital of the Basque Country and previously centre of the iron industry.

Basilica de Begoña, Virgen de Begoña, 38, Bilbao-Vizcaya. Basilica.

Boiro 29C2

Playa Jardín de Barraña. **GPS**: n42,64183 w8,89481.

10 € 3-6 Chfree. **Surface:** asphalted. 01/01-31/12.
Distance: 500m 20m 200m Bistro Prima 400m.
Remarks: Max. 48h.

Boiro 29C2

Playa Mañons, S/n 15930 Chancelas–Abanqueiro.
GPS: n42,63138 w8,85311.
8 free Chfree.
Distance: on the spot.

Bueu 29C2

PO315 dir Cabo Udra. **GPS**: n42,33460 w8,8248.
free. **Surface:** sand.
Remarks: Max. 48h.

Bueu 29C2

Puerto, Avda. de Montero Rios. **GPS**: n42,32732 w8,7838.

Burela 29D1

Area de Burela, Parque de O Campón, parking Hospital de Burela.
GPS: n43,65216 w7,35891.

4 free Chfree. **Surface:** asphalted.
Distance: 200m 300m 200m.
Remarks: Max. 48h.

Cabárceno 29G2

Área Lago del Acebo, N634> dir Parque de la naturaleze de Cabárceno.
GPS: n43,35802 w3,81959.

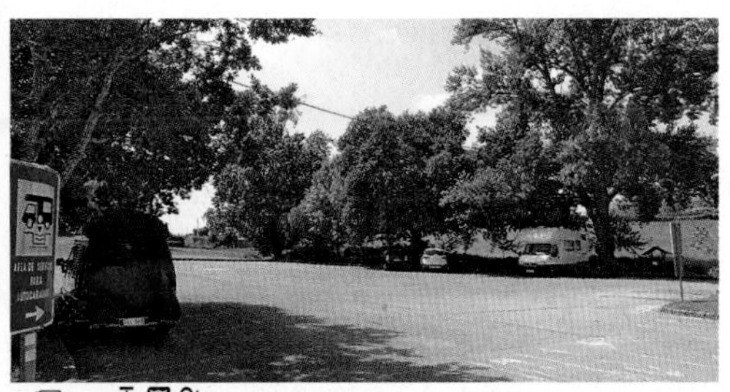

30 free Chfree. **Location:** Rural, quiet.
Surface: asphalted.
Distance: 100m 50m 50m 200m 200m.
Remarks: Max. 48h.

Camariñas 29B1

Puerto Club Nautico, Rúa Castelo. **GPS**: n43,12694 w9,18333.
5 free. **Surface:** asphalted.

Candás 29E1

Area de La Fuente de los Angeles, Calle Estacion.
GPS: n43,58495 w5,77197.

6 free ChWCfree. **Location:** Urban, simple.
Surface: asphalted. 01/01-31/12.
Distance: 500m 1km 500m 500m.
Remarks: Along railwayline.

Cangas de Morrazo 29C2

Camping Car Area Playa Arneles, Ctra Viso- Vilanova s/n.
GPS: n42,27618 w8,83399.
30 € 12 Ch €3/day WC €3 €1/day. **Surface:** grassy.
01/04-01/11.
Distance: 350m 300m 300m.

Cangas de Morrazo 29C2

Ruá Campo Morelo, Gatañal. **GPS**: n42,25546 w8,79758.
5 free Chfree. **Surface:** asphalted. 01/01-31/12.
Remarks: Behind gymnasium.

Cangas de Onís 29F1

Parking Lanzadera Picos de Europa, Calle del Llreau.
GPS: n43,35211 w5,12536.

4 free Chfree. **Location:** Urban. **Surface:** asphalted.
Distance: 100m.
Remarks: Max. 48h.

Cangas del Narcea 29E1

Av. de oviedo. **GPS**: n43,18068 w6,54848.
2 free Chfree. **Surface:** asphalted. 01/01-31/12.
Remarks: Max. 72h, no camping activities.

Carnota 29B1

Area de Mar de Lira, Calle Miñarzo s/n. **GPS**: n42,80306 w9,12944.

4 free Chfree. **Surface:** sand.
Distance: Carnota 5km 10m on the spot.
Remarks: Parking next to hatchery.

Cartelle 29C2

Camperpark O Mundil, Antigua Carretera OU-659.
GPS: n42,21444 w8,03306.

22 € 10 Ch WC free. **Surface:** gravel.
01/01-31/12.
Distance: 1km zona fluvial Río Arnoia 10m on the spot.

Castro Caldelas 29D2

Travesía da Devesa. **GPS**: n42,37479 w7,41832.
8 free Chfree. 01/01-31/12.
Distance: 850m 850m 850m.
Remarks: Max. 48h.

Castro de Rei 29D1

Castro de Ribeiras de Lea. **GPS**: n43,14663 w7,49211.
2 free Chfree. **Surface:** metalled. 01/01-31/12.
Distance: 250m.
Remarks: Max. 48h.

Cenlle 29C2

Lugar Barbantes. **GPS**: n42,33252 w8,01296.
50 free Ch WC. **Location:** Isolated, quiet.
01/01-31/12.
Distance: Cenlle 10km on the spot on the spot on the spot.
Remarks: Max. 48h, free entrance swimming pool, picnic area.

Chantada 29C2

Champ de Sangoñedo, Ctra. De Barrela o Seixo.
GPS: n42,60598 w7,77989.
5 free ChWCfree. **Surface:** gravel. 01/01-31/12.
Distance: 500m.
Remarks: At footballstadium, max. 48h.

Coaña 29D1

Area de Ortiguera, Barrio Nueva Rasa. **GPS**: n43,56082 w6,73352.
2 free Chfree. **Location:** Rural, simple.
Surface: asphalted.
Distance: on the spot on the spot.

Colombres 29F1

Area de Casa Junco, N-634. **GPS**: n43,38056 w4,55472.

15 free Chfree. **Surface:** asphalted.
Distance: on the spot.

Colunga 29F1

Area de Los Llanos, Avda de Asturias N-632.
GPS: n43,48472 w5,26491.

25 € 4 €3 €1.
Location: Simple. **Surface:** asphalted. 01/01-31/12.
Distance: 500m 2km 200m.
Remarks: Thursday market.

Cospeito 29D1

Rosalia de Castro. **GPS**: n43,23984 w7,55579.
5 free Ch free. **Surface:** asphalted. 01/01-31/12.
Distance: 300m 300m 300m.
Remarks: Bird watching, max. 48h.

Cudillero 29E1

Puerto. **GPS**: n43,56568 w6,1517.

5. **Location:** Simple. **Surface:** asphalted.
Remarks: Parking in harbour.

Cudillero 29E1

Hotel Rest. Casa Fernando II, N-632. **GPS**: n43,56028 w6,17722.

5 free Ch€3. **Location:** Simple, quiet. **Surface:** asphalted.
01/01-31/12.
Distance: on the spot.

Elorrio 29H2

San Jose Kalea. **GPS**: n43,12834 w2.
11 free Ch. **Surface:** asphalted. 01/01-31/12.
Distance: 500m 500m.

Eltziego 29H3

Área de Barrihuelo, Carr. de Laguardia. **GPS**: n42,51496 w2,61546.
14 free Chfree €2/12h. **Surface:** metalled.
01/01-31/12.
Distance: 300m 100m.
Remarks: Max. 72h.

Ferrol 29C1

Ctra. de la Malata. **GPS**: n43,49333 w8,23972.

15 free Chfree. **Surface:** asphalted. 01/01-31/12.
Distance: 700m 300m on the spot.
Remarks: Max. 48h.

Finisterre 29B1

Area El Campo, Calle de La Coruña, 53. **GPS**: n42,91110 w9,2636.
30 € 8 Chincluded €3. **Surface:** sand.
01/01-31/12.
Distance: on the spot 500m 50m.
Remarks: Private beach.

Finisterre 29B1

Praia de Langosteira. **GPS**: n42,92320 w9,26149.

5 free.
Distance: on the spot 1km 1km.
Remarks: Beach parking, max. 48h.

Fuente Dé 29F2

Picos de Europa, C621. **GPS**: n43,14433 w4,81274.
free. **Surface:** sand.

ES

Remarks: Parking funicular railway.

Gedrez 29D2

Área de Casa Funsiquín, CN-9, 42. **GPS**: n43,01344 w6,6081.
8 guests free Ch. **Location:** Rural. **Surface:** grassy.
01/01-31/12.
Distance: on the spot.

Gijón 29E1

Polígono Puerto Musel. **GPS**: n43,54467 w5,69562.

15 free free. **Location:** Urban, simple, noisy.
Surface: asphalted. 01/01-31/12.
Distance: 3km on the spot on the spot.
Remarks: Max. 48h.

Gijón 29E1

Camino de las Mimosas, El Rinconin. **GPS**: n43,54708 w5,63648.

20 free. **Location:** Urban, simple, central. **Surface:** asphalted.
01/01-31/12.
Distance: 300m.
Remarks: Baker every morning (Jul/Aug).

Gorliz 29H2

Paseo de Astondo. **GPS**: n43,41220 w2,94194.

free.
Location: Urban, simple. **Surface:** asphalted. 01/01-31/12.
Distance: 500m 50m on the spot.
Remarks: Parking beach.

Gozon 29E1

Area Autocaravanas El Molino, Ctr. Luanco-Cabo Peñas.
GPS: n43,62541 w5,81125.

25 € 10 included €4,60. **Location:** Rural, comfortable, quiet. **Surface:** grassy. 01/01-31/12.
Distance: 500m on the spot on the spot on the spot.
Remarks: To be paid at campsite.

Guitiriz 29C1

Rua do Voluntariado. **GPS**: n43,17727 w7,88062.
5 free Ch free. **Surface:** gravel. 01/01-31/12.
Distance: 800m 100m.
Remarks: Max. 48h.

Hernani 29H2

Ibaiondo Industrialdea. **GPS**: n43,26922 w1,96242.
free Ch free. **Surface:** asphalted.

Distance: 1,2km 1,5km 1,2km.
Remarks: Max. 5 nights, no camping activities.

Hondaribbia 27A2

Ramón Iribarren Pasalekua. **GPS**: n43,37929 w1,79768.

20 €12/day Ch included. **Location:** Urban, simple, quiet.
Surface: asphalted. 01/04-30/09.
Distance: 2km 8km on the spot on the spot.
Remarks: Beautiful view.

Illa de Arousa 29C2

Área de Surf Camp, Playa de Xestelas. **GPS**: n42,53565 w8,86929.
€ 10 €3. 01/06-30/09.
Distance: on the spot on the spot on the spot.
Remarks: Surf spot.

Illano 29D1

Area de Folgueirou, Area recreativa de Folgueirou.
GPS: n43,34333 w6,85116.
30 free Ch included. **Location:** Rural, simple.
Surface: grassy/gravel. 01/01-31/12.
Distance: on the spot.

Labastida 29H3

Fray Domingo Salazar Kalea. **GPS**: n42,00000 w2,79446.
4 free Ch free € 1/30minutes. **Surface:** asphalted.
01/01-31/12.
Distance: 300m 300m.

Lanestosa 29G2

Area de Lanestosa, Calle Mirabueno. **GPS**: n43,21789 w3,43878.

22 free, service € 8/24h Ch WC included.
Location: Rural, simple. **Surface:** gravel. 01/01-31/12.
Distance: 200m 400m 6km on the spot on the spot.

Langreo 29E1

Ecomuseo Minero Valle de Samuño, Calle Puente Carbón.
GPS: n43,27835 w5,67433.

11 free Ch free. **Location:** Rural, simple, quiet.
Surface: asphalted/metalled. 01/01-31/12.
Distance: on the spot.
Remarks: At Ecomuseum.

Legazpi 29H2

Parque Mirandaola de Legazpi, Carretera Legazpia, Gl 2630.
GPS: n43,03678 w2,33758.

5 free Ch free. **Location:** Urban, simple, noisy.
Surface: asphalted. 01/01-31/12.
Distance: 1,5km on the spot on the spot.
Remarks: Max. 48h.

Lekeitio 29H2

Iñigo Artieta Etorbidea. **GPS**: n43,35849 w2,50743.

14 free €3/100liter Ch. **Location:** Urban, comfortable, quiet.
Surface: asphalted. 01/01-31/12.
Distance: 500m 500m 500m 300m.
Remarks: Coins at tourist info.

Liérganes 29G2

Calle de Puente Romano. **GPS**: n43,34479 w3,74183.

10 free free. **Location:** Urban, simple, central.
Surface: asphalted. 01/01-31/12.
Distance: 200m 250m 350m.
Remarks: Parking nearby train station, max. 48h.

Lugo 29D1

Pabellón Municipal de Deportes, Avda. de Santiago.
GPS: n43,00452 w7,56144.

15 free Ch free. **Surface:** asphalted. 01/01-31/12.
Distance: 5 min 5,2km 10min.
Remarks: Parking gymnasium, max. 48h.

Lugo 29D1

Plaza de Asturias, Rúa Ánxel Fole. **GPS**: n43,00972 w7,55805.
15 € 12/24h free. **Surface:** asphalted.

Lugones 29E1

Area de Lugones, Calle Conde de Santa Bárbara.
GPS: n43,40694 w5,81139.

4 free Ch included. **Location:** Urban, simple.
Surface: asphalted/metalled. 01/01-31/12.
Distance: 9km Oviedo on the spot on the spot 200m.
Remarks: Next to sports centre.

Mazaricos 29B1

Calle Picota. **GPS**: n42,93458 w8,9906.
4 free Ch free. **Surface:** metalled. 01/01-31/12.
Distance: on the spot on the spot.
Remarks: Max. 72h.

Mazaricos 29B1

NaturMaZ, Aeródromo da Fervenza. **GPS**: n42,98398 w9,00771.

ES

€ 8 Chincluded. **Location:** Isolated, quiet.
Surface: grassy/gravel. 01/01-31/12.
Distance: 10km on the spot on the spot on the spot on the spot.
Remarks: At airfield.

S Mieres 29E1
Area de Mieres, Calle Asturias. **GPS**: n43,25194 w5,78083.

6 free Chfree. **Location:** Urban, simple. **Surface:** asphalted.
01/01-31/12.
Distance: 100m 500m on the spot on the spot.
Remarks: Along railwayline.

S Milladoiro 29C1
Traversia do Porto, Ames. **GPS**: n42,84512 w8,58079.

15 free Chfree.
Surface: asphalted.
01/01-31/12 1st week Aug.
Distance: 200m 200m dir. Santiago every 15 min.
Remarks: At swimming pool, max. 48h, monday market.

S Miño 29C1
AP-9 Coruña-Ferrol ><, km 15,5. **GPS**: n43,37404 w8,18736.
12 free ChWC free. **Surface:** asphalted.
Distance: on the spot on the spot.
Remarks: Parking nearby motorway.

S Miranda de Ebro 29G2
Calle de Burgos. **GPS**: n42,68880 w2,95403.

7 free Chfree. **Location:** Urban, simple, noisy.
Surface: metalled. 01/01-31/12.
Distance: 1km 3km river.

Tourist information Miranda de Ebro:
Medieval annual fair. around May 1.
Week market. Sa.

S Mondariz 29C2
Área recreativa da Praia do Val. **GPS**: n42,23727 w8,45943.
free free. 01/01-31/12.
Distance: 1,2km 750m on the spot.

S Mondoñedo 29D1
Calle de Vicedo. **GPS**: n43,42778 w7,37028.
10 free Chfree. **Location:** Urban. **Surface:** grasstiles.
01/01-31/12.
Distance: 500m 500m.
Remarks: Max. 48h.

S Monfero 29C1
Área de Fragas do Eume, Lugar Vilafail Nº 2.
GPS: n43,39643 w8,07621.
12 € 8 Chincluded €2 WC. **Location:** Isolated, quiet.
Surface: gravel. 01/01-31/12.
Distance: 8km 2,5km on the spot on the spot.
Remarks: In nature reserve, baker every morning.

S Monforte de Lemos 29D2
Auditorio Multiusos de Monforte, Calle de la Circuvalación / Calle de Santa Clara. **GPS**: n42,52750 w7,5119.

20 free Chfree. **Surface:** asphalted. 01/01-31/12.
Distance: 500m 550m 300m.
Remarks: Beside river, max. 48h.

S Nava 29E1
Area de Nava, Avda. de la Constitución. **GPS**: n43,35722 w5,49917.

4 free Chfree. **Surface:** asphalted/metalled.
01/01-31/12.
Distance: 900m 10km.
Remarks: At sports centre, no camping activities.

S Navelgas 29E1
Area de Navelgas, Recinto Ferial. **GPS**: n43,40402 w6,54167.
15 free Chfree. **Location:** Urban.
Surface: asphalted/metalled.
Distance: 100m.

S Navia 29D1
Area de la Granja, C/ Travesía de la Granja.
GPS: n43,54528 w6,72028.
10 free Chfree . **Location:** Urban.
Surface: gravel/metalled.
Distance: on the spot on the spot.

S Nogueira de Ramuín 29C2
Lugar Luintra. **GPS**: n42,41003 w7,72161.
8 free Chfree. **Surface:** metalled. 01/01-31/12.
Distance: 400m 400m on the spot.
Remarks: At swimming pool, max. 48h.

Noia 29C2
Rúa de Pedra Marques. **GPS**: n42,78783 w8,8906.

free. **Surface:** asphalted.
Distance: on the spot 50m 50m Bus 20m.

S Noia 29C2
Hipermercado Eroski, Carretera Puerto Abarquiña.
GPS: n42,79799 w8,88836.
+10 free Chfree. **Location:** Urban. **Surface:** asphalted.
01/01-31/12.
Distance: city centre 1,7km on the spot.
Remarks: At supermarket.

Tourist information Noia:
El Pendo, 5km S. Santander. Cave with petroglyphs.

S O Barco 29D2
Malecón Campiño. **GPS**: n42,41063 w6,97493.

10 free Chfree. **Surface:** unpaved. 01/01-31/12.
Distance: 400m 250m 250m.
Remarks: Max. 48h.

S Oleiros 29C1
Rúa Marcial del Adalid, Muíño do Vento. **GPS**: n43,33936 w8,35474.
3 free Chfree. **Surface:** asphalted. 01/01-31/12.
Distance: 650m.
Remarks: Max. 48h.

S Oñati 29H2
Area Autocaravanas Oñate, Martzelino Zelaia Kalea.
GPS: n43,02743 w2,40531.
17 free Chfree. **Location:** Rural. **Surface:** grasstiles.
01/01-31/12.
Distance: 900m.
Remarks: Max. 72h.

S Ourol 29D1
Rúa Ourol. **GPS**: n43,56485 w7,64348.
8 free Ch free. **Surface:** metalled. 01/01-31/12.
Remarks: Max. 48h.

S Oviedo 29E1
Calle Daniel Moyano. **GPS**: n43,38266 w5,82396.
16 free Chfree. **Location:** Rural. **Surface:** asphalted.
01/01-31/12.
Distance: Oviedo 10km 150m 50m 200m.

S Pajares 29E2
Valgrande-Pajares, Brañillín. **GPS**: n42,97889 w5,77194.

15 free Chfree. **Location:** Rural. **Surface:** asphalted.

S Parada do Sil 29D2
Rural Pepe, Campo da Feira 17. **GPS**: n42,38287 w7,57106.
4 guests free Ch €2. 01/01-31/12.
Distance: on the spot on the spot.

S Pobra do Brollòn 29D2
Campo Municipal de Fut. **GPS**: n42,56944 w7,39417.
8 free Chfree. **Surface:** metalled.

S Pola de Laviana 29E1
Area de Pola de Laviana, Av. Real Titánico.
GPS: n43,25478 w5,56836.

8 free Chfree.
Location: Rural, simple. **Surface:** grasstiles. 01/01-31/12.
Distance: 1,5km 1,5km 1,5km.

S Pontedeva 29C2
Aldea Valiño, Trado. **GPS**: n42,17646 w8,15477.
5 free Chfree. **Surface:** unpaved. 01/01-31/12.
Remarks: Max. 48h.

S Posada de Valdeón 29F2
Calle del General Mola. **GPS**: n43,15285 w4,91747.

ES

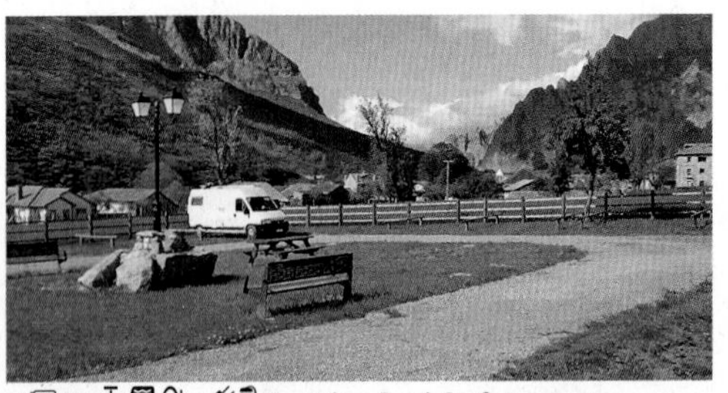

18 €8 Ch . **Location:** Rural. **Surface:** grassy.
Distance: on the spot on the spot.
Remarks: Max. 96h, in Parque Nacional de Los Picos de Europa.

Potes 29F2

Poblado Mijares. **GPS**: n43,15531 w4,61894.
+5 free. **Surface:** grassy. 01/01-31/12.
Distance: 200m 150m 50m.

Potes 29F2

Santo Toribio de Liébana, CA885. **GPS**: n43,15028 w4,65389.

free.
Location: Isolated, quiet. **Surface:** asphalted. 01/01-31/12.
Distance: Potes 3km on the spot.
Remarks: Parking monastery.

Tourist information Potes:
Local products. Mo.
Historical cattle market, since 1379.
01/08-15/08.

Redondela 29C2

Avda. de Mendiño. **GPS**: n42,28972 w8,61055.
15 free Ch.
Distance: 600m 500m 600m 600m.

Rentería 29H2

Área Rural de Listorreta-Barrengoloia.
GPS: n43,26800 w1,90135.

2 free Chfree. **Location:** Rural, simple, isolated, quiet.
Surface: asphalted. 01/01-31/12.
Distance: Renteria 7km on the spot.
Remarks: Parking nature reserve.

Ribadeo 29D1

Eroski, Camino de Vilar. **GPS**: n43,54000 w7,06055.
10 free Chfree. **Surface:** asphalted. 01/01-31/12.
Distance: 500m 1km on the spot.
Remarks: At supermarket.

Ribamontán al Monte 29G1

A8 Bilbao > Santander. **GPS**: n43,40282 w3,62877.
10 free Chfree.

Ribamontán al Monte 29G1

A8 Santander > Bilbao. **GPS**: n43,40446 w3,62476.
10 free Chfree. **Location:** Motorway. **Surface:** asphalted.

Riós 29D3

Repsol. GPS: n41,98297 w7,28602.
10 Ch WC . 01/01-31/12.
Distance: 500m.
Remarks: At petrol station.

Riosa 29E1

Area de El Angliru, Viapará s/n. **GPS**: n43,24806 w5,90667.

15 €5 Chincluded . **Location:** Rural, simple, isolated, quiet. **Surface:** metalled. 01/01-31/12.
Distance: on the spot.
Remarks: No camping activities.

San Clodio 29D2

Parque de Pena da Mula, Calle del Troque.
GPS: n42,46750 w7,28583.

3 free Chfree. **Surface:** asphalted. 01/01-31/12.
Distance: 200m Playa Fluvial 25m cafetaria.

San Martín del Rey Aurelio 29E1

Área del Pozo Entrego, Avda. de la Vega, AS17.
GPS: n43,28639 w5,63889.

3 free Chfree.
Location: Urban, simple. **Surface:** asphalted.
Distance: on the spot on the spot Alcampo 1km.
Remarks: Max. 48h.

San Sebastian 29H2

Paseo de Berio nº 2. **GPS**: n43,30797 w2,01426.

44 €6,55, 01/10-31/05 €4 Chincluded.
Location: Urban, noisy.
Surface: grasstiles.
01/01-31/12.
Distance: city centre 3km 2km 50m 100m bus city centre 33 and 5.
Remarks: Max. 48h, marked pitches, registration with licence plate number.

Tourist information San Sebastian:
Centro de Atracción y Turismo (CAT), Boulevard Alameda, 8, www.donostia.org. Old city with, Parte Vieja, historical city centre with numerous cafés, restaurants and tapa bars.
Aquarium, Plaza de Carlos Blasco Imaz, 1. Museum for oceanografics. 10-19h, Sa/Su/holidays 10-20h, 01/07-31/12 10-21h.
Su-morning.

Santander 29G1

Calle César Llamazares, Nueva Montaña. **GPS**: n43,44336 w3,83747.
10 free. **Location:** Simple, isolated. **Surface:** asphalted.
01/01-31/12.
Distance: 3,5km.
Remarks: Max. 48h.

Santander 29G1

Marina de Santander, Calle Tramo de Unión, Camargo.
GPS: n43,42736 w3,80537.

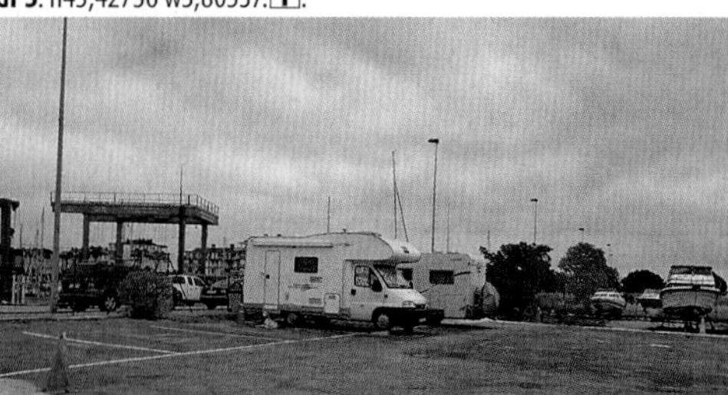

20 €6 Chincluded (2x)€3/24h €5 €4/30minutes.
Location: Simple. 01/01-31/12.
Distance: 100m 3km.

Santiago de Compostela 29C1

Rúa Manuel María.
GPS: n42,89560 w8,5317.
100 8-20h €3 €3 Ch.
Surface: asphalted.
01/01-31/12.
Distance: centre 2,5km 3km 50m line 1 > centre.
Remarks: Ticket for overnight stay € 12.

Tourist information Santiago de Compostela:
Oficina de Turismo, Rúa del Villar, 43, www.santiagoturismo.com.
City known for the termination of the pilgrime route.
Plaza de la Quintana. Impressive square.
Fiesta del Apóstol Santiago.
Most important festival of Galicia.
15/07-31/07.

Santillana del Mar 29G1

Ctra. C6316. **GPS**: n43,38895 w4,10721.

€ 2/24h. **Surface:** asphalted.

Sanxenxo 29B2

Playa Pragueira. **GPS**: n42,40967 w8,86157.

15 €8-10 Ch included €3.
Surface: grassy. 01/01-31/12.
Distance: on the spot 200m 1km.

Sanxenxo 29B2

Área de Cachadelos, PO-308. **GPS**: n42,41751 w8,86952.
65 €10 Ch included . **Surface:** grassy.
Distance: 200m 2km on the spot.
Remarks: Service passerby € 3.

Sarria 29D2

Rúa Castelao. **GPS**: n42,77194 w7,41028.

12 free Chfree. **Surface:** gravel. 01/01-31/12.
Distance: 800m on the spot 800m.

ES

S Saturrarán 29H2

GPS: n43,31968 w2,41165.

5 free WC. **Location:** Rural, simple. **Surface:** grasstiles.
01/01-31/12.
Distance: 500m on the spot 700m.
Remarks: Parking beach.

S Sopela 29H2

Polideportivo de Urko, Urgitxieta kalea. **GPS**: n43,37370 w2,9898.
24 free €1/100liter Ch.
Surface: asphalted.
01/01-31/12 service 01/10-31/05.
Distance: 300m 450m metro > Bilbao.
Remarks: Max. 48h, coins at tourist info, no camping activities.

S Suesa 29G1

Area de Autocaravanas Suesa, Mojante 25.
GPS: n43,44736 w3,72788.

66 €9 Chincluded (10x)€3 WC.
Location: Comfortable. **Surface:** grasstiles. 01/01-31/12.
Distance: 1km 1,8km 1,5km 1km 1km.
Remarks: Max. 96h, pay at reception campsite.

S Tapia 29D1

Area de Playa Grande, Av. de la Playa. **GPS**: n43,56667 w6,94639.
15 free Chfree.
Location: Rural. **Surface:** grasstiles.
Distance: 500m 500m 500m.

S Teverga 29E1

Parking Senda del Oso, Entrago. **GPS**: n43,16954 w6,09755.

20 free Chfree €3. **Location:** Simple, noisy.
Surface: asphalted. 01/01-31/12.
Distance: on the spot on the spot.
Remarks: Max. 48h.

S Tolosa 29H2

San Esteban Auzoa Auzoa. **GPS**: n43,13348 w2,08315.
€ 1/day Chincluded. **Location:** Noisy. **Surface:** asphalted.
01/01-31/12.
Distance: 700m 700m 500m.
Remarks: Along railwayline, max. 72h.

S Tui 29C2

Puente Tripes, Avenida de Portual. **GPS**: n42,04333 w8,64656.

3 free. **Location:** Urban, simple. **Surface:** asphalted.
01/01-31/12.
Distance: 1,3km 500m Lidl 1,5km.
Remarks: Max. 48h.

S Vegadeo 29D1

Area de Vegadeo, Calle Emilio Cotarelo, s/n.
GPS: n43,46667 w7,05167.
8 free Chfree. **Location:** Urban.
Surface: asphalted/metalled.
Distance: on the spot on the spot.
Remarks: Max. 72h.

S Vila de Cruces 29C2

Estrada Merza-Bodaño. **GPS**: n42,76199 w8,25602.
10 free WCfree. **Surface:** asphalted. 01/01-31/12.
Distance: Vila de Cruces 10km on the spot.
Remarks: Picnic area, recreation area.

S Vilalba 29D1

Rua da Feira. **GPS**: n43,29556 w7,67694.
15 free Chfree. **Surface:** asphalted.
Distance: 300m 300m.

S Villanueva de Oscos 29D1

Area de Villanueva, Lugar de Villanueva. **GPS**: n43,31056 w6,98583.
2 free Chfree. **Surface:** gravel.
Remarks: Max. 48h.

S Vitoria Gasteiz 29H2

Área de Lakua, Portal de Foronde. **GPS**: n42,86684 w2,68539.

10 free Chfree. **Location:** Urban, comfortable, central, quiet.
Surface: asphalted. 01/01-31/12.
Distance: 2km 5km 100m bakery 50m 50m.
Remarks: Max. 72h, market Wednesday.

S Zegama 29H2

San Bartolome. **GPS**: n42,97524 w2,29233.
8 free Chfree €3/2h. **Surface:** asphalted.
01/01-31/12.
Distance: 300m 300m 300m on the spot.

S Zumaia 29H2

Calle de la Estación. **GPS**: n43,29279 w2,24684.

25 free Chfree.
Location: Simple, noisy. **Surface:** asphalted. 01/01-31/12.
Distance: 2km 4,4km on the spot on the spot.

Navarre and Rioja

Aínsa 32C1

Plaza del Castillo.
GPS: n42,41916 e0,13515.
free.
Surface: sand.

Tourist information Aínsa:
The capital of a medieval kingdom by surrounded fortress walls.
Tue.

Albarracín 33A1

Quesería Sierra de Albarracín, Pol. Los Rubiales, 1.
GPS: n40,43286 w1,4405.

6 free. 01/01-31/12.
Distance: 1km 200m 1km 1km.

S Alquézar 32C1

Alquézar, Ctra.Barbastro,. **GPS**: n42,16456 e0,01499.
€ 16,50-19,50 Ch €5. 01/01-31/12.

Tourist information Alquézar:
Historical city.

S Ansó 27B3

Ctra. de Ansó a Fago. **GPS**: n42,75648 w0,83102.
2

S Aoiz 27A3

Hotel Ekai. **GPS**: n42,77624 w1,38536.

10 free free. **Location:** Rural, simple.
Surface: gravel/metalled. 01/01-31/12.
Distance: 3km on the spot.

S Arguedas 32A1

Aparcamiento Municipal de Autocaravanas de Arguedas, Calle Bordón. **GPS**: n42,17270 w1,5913.

9 free €2/100liter Ch. **Location:** Rural, simple, quiet.
Surface: gravel. 01/01-31/12.
Distance: 800m 800m 800m.
Remarks: At Parque de Bardenas Reales, max. 48h.

Ariza 30H1

Area de Servicios La Cadiera, A2 Madrid > Zaragoza.
GPS: n41,31210 w2,00329.
5.

S Arnedillo 29H3

Calle Miguel del Pozo. **GPS**: n42,21361 w2,23972.

40 € 10 Ch (40x)€1/4h WC, cold shower included.
Location: Rural, comfortable. **Surface:** asphalted.
01/01-31/12.
Distance: 200m 200m 200m on the spot.
Remarks: Follow the signs in the village.

S Arróniz 29H2

Carretera Barbarin 38. **GPS**: n42,58911 w2,09575.
6 free Chfree. **Surface:** asphalted. 01/01-31/12.
Distance: 300m 3km 250m.
Remarks: Max. 48h, no camping activities.

ES

S Ayegui 29H2

Plaza San Pelayo. **GPS**: n42,65436 w2,0451.
20 € 4 Ch included. **Surface**: grasstiles.
Distance: 700m 700m 700m.
Remarks: Next to swimming pool.

S Berriozar 27A3

Av. Berriozar. **GPS**: n42,84043 w1,66557.

20 free €2/100liter Ch. **Location**: Urban, simple.
Surface: concrete. 01/01-31/12.
Distance: 4km Pamplona 500m.
Remarks: Max. 72h, coins at sports centre (9-21h).

S Cascante 29H3

Av. Fuentes Dutor Parking Termolúdico. **GPS**: n41,99372 w1,68669.

40 free free.
Location: Urban, simple. **Surface**: asphalted. 01/01-31/12.
Distance: 750m 800m.

S Falces 29H3

Calle la Mota. **GPS**: n42,39295 w1,79574.
6 free Ch free. **Location**: Simple. **Surface**: metalled.
01/01-31/12.
Distance: 700m 300m.

S Haro 29H2

LR111. **GPS**: n42,57253 w2,86739.

10 free free. **Location**: Rural, simple, quiet. **Surface**: gravel.
01/01-31/12.
Distance: 1,5km 1,3km 1,5km.

S Haro 29H2

Parking centro deportivo, Av de los Ingenieros del Ministerio Obras Públicas, LR-111. **GPS**: n42,57677 w2,85222.

4 free free.
Location: Urban, simple.
Surface: asphalted.
01/01-31/12.
Distance: 500m 14km on the spot.
Remarks: At sports park, Haro, Rioja Wine Capital, wine museum, wine cellars.

Tourist information Haro:
Capital of Rioja wine.

S Irura 29H2

Area del Frontón, Calle Zilar. **GPS**: n43,16778 w2,0652.

4 free Ch free. **Location**: Urban, simple, noisy.
Surface: asphalted. 01/01-31/12.
Distance: 100m.

S Logroño 29H3

Avenue de la Sonsierra, LR132. **GPS**: n42,47916 w2,4571.

3 free Ch free. **Location**: Urban, simple, noisy.
Surface: metalled. 01/01-31/12.
Distance: 700m 100m 400m 300m 20m.
Remarks: Max. 48h.

Logroño 29H3

Emblase de la Grajera, Pontano de la Grajera.
GPS: n42,44909 w2,50189.

15 free.
Location: Rural, simple. **Surface**: concrete. 01/01-31/12.
Distance: 7km 1km on the spot.
Remarks: Parking at lake, golf court and park La Grajera.

S Maya 27A2

Otsondo, NA 4453. **GPS**: n43,23304 w1,49885.
6 free WC free. **Location**: Rural, isolated. **Surface**: gravel.
01/01-31/12.
Distance: 3km.

Navarrete 29H3

Calle de la Carretera. **GPS**: n42,42458 w2,55584.

free. **Location**: Urban, simple. **Surface**: asphalted.
01/01-31/12.
Distance: 1km 3km 600m 800m.
Remarks: Parking at sports park.

Roncesvalles 27A3

Paseo Ibaneta. **GPS**: n43,02018 w1,32401.

5. **Location**: Rural, simple. **Surface**: asphalted.
01/01-31/12.
Distance: 1,5km.
Remarks: Beautiful view.

Zaragoza 32B2

Parque de Atracciones de Zaragoza. **GPS**: n41,61994 w0,90122.
10.
Distance: 4,5km.
Remarks: Parking amusement park.

Mediterranean Sea Communities

Águilas 31H2

Playa de la Carolina. **GPS**: n37,37614 w1,62903.
free. **Location**: Isolated. 01/01-31/12.
Remarks: Beach parking.

S Alcover 32E3

Avinguda Catalunya 2. **GPS**: n41,26315 e1,17324.

5 € 5/24h Ch included. **Location**: Rural, simple, central, quiet.
Surface: concrete. 01/01-31/12.
Distance: on the spot 700m 350m 100m 280m.
Remarks: Max. 48h.

Alicante 33A2

Vía Pista. **GPS**: n38,28923 w0,52072.
. **Surface**: unpaved.
Distance: Alicante 7km on the spot on the spot 600m.
Remarks: Beach parking, max 3,5t.

S Alicante 33A2

Villafranqueza, Av. Pintor Gastón Castelló 41.
GPS: n38,37808 w0,48822.

25 € 7 Ch WC included.
Location: Noisy. 01/01-31/12.
Distance: 1km 50m 50m.
Remarks: Next to petrol station.

S Altafulla 33B1

Área de Servicio Mèdol, AP-7 km 237, Barcelona > Taragona.
GPS: n41,14157 e1,34590.
10 free Ch free.
Location: Motorway. **Surface**: asphalted. 01/01-31/12.
Distance: on the spot on the spot.

S Altafulla 33B1

Área de Servicio Mèdol, AP-7 km 237, Taragona > Barcelona.
GPS: n41,14054 e1,34746.
10 free Ch free. **Surface**: asphalted. 01/01-31/12.
Distance: on the spot on the spot.

S Altea 33A2

San Antonio Camperpark, Ctra. del Albir 5/6, CV7651.
GPS: n38,58544 w0,05989.

ES

50 € 15, 2 pers.incl Ch €0,45/kWh,10Amp WC €3 included.
Location: Comfortable. **Surface:** gravel. 30/09-30/04.
Distance: Altea > 1km < Albir 100m 500m 500m 200m, tram 1km.
Remarks: Bread-service, discount longer stays.

S Amposta 33B1

Casa de Fusta, Partida L'Encanyissada. **GPS**: n40,65851 e0,67475.

70 free €3 Ch . **Location:** Rural, comfortable, isolated, quiet. **Surface:** gravel/sand. 01/01-31/12.
Distance: on the spot on the spot on the spot on the spot on the spot.
Remarks: Bread-service.

S Arbúcies 32G2

Área de Arbúcies, Camí del Molí. **GPS**: n41,81437 e2,52076.

free Chfree. **Location:** Urban, simple, simple, central, quiet.
Surface: asphalted. 01/01-31/12.
Distance: 500m 700m 700m 250m.
Remarks: Max. 48h.

S Archena 31H1

Avendia del Río Segura. **GPS**: n38,12214 w1,29427.
30 free Chfree. **Surface:** gravel. 01/01-31/12.
Distance: 150m Mercadona 1,5km.

S Ascó 32D3

C/ Alcalde Tomas Biarnes Radua. **GPS**: n41,18673 e0,56802.

25 free Chfree. **Location:** Simple, central, noisy.
Surface: asphalted. 01/01-31/12.
Distance: 100m 200m 200m 500m 500m.

S Avinyo 32F2

Area Municipal de Avinyó, Calle Industria.
GPS: n41,86556 e1,97472.

10 free €1/50liter Ch. **Location:** Rural, simple, quiet.
Surface: gravel/sand. 01/01-31/12.
Distance: 300m 3km 300m 300m 250m.
Remarks: Nearby swimming pool, video surveillance.

S Avinyonet del Penedès 32F3

Area Cellar Can Battle - Artcava, Masia Can Batlle s/n, BV2411.
GPS: n41,36790 e1,77306.

10 free Chfree. **Location:** Rural, simple, isolated, quiet.
Surface: gravel. 01/01-31/12.
Distance: 1km 6km 1km 1km.
Remarks: Wine tasting.

S Ayora 33A2

El Nogal, Romeral 5. **GPS**: n39,05870 w1,0324.

20 € 10 Chincluded €2/day . **Location:** Rural, comfortable, isolated, quiet. **Surface:** grassy.
Distance: 2km 2km on the spot on the spot.

S Ayora 33A2

Calle Manuel Reig, N-330. **GPS**: n39,05605 w1,0526.
free Chfree. **Surface:** unpaved. 01/01-31/12.
Distance: 700m.

S Balsicas 33A2

Calle Laguna de Cifuentes, Torre-Pacheco. **GPS**: n37,82074 w0,97462.
20 € 7 €3 Ch €2 WC €5 . **Location:** Motorway.
Surface: asphalted. 01/01-31/12.
Distance: 300m.
Remarks: Industrial area, motorhome washing place.

S Barberà de la Conca 32E3

Area de la Cooperativa Barberá, Calle Comercio 40.
GPS: n41,41025 e1,22734.

10 free Chfree. **Location:** Rural, simple, central, quiet.
Surface: gravel. 01/11-31/08.
Distance: on the spot 500m.

S Barcelona 32G3

CityStop, Rambla Guipúzcoa. **GPS**: n41,42433 e2,20748.

80 € 30 Ch €4/24h WC . **Location:** Urban, comfortable. **Surface:** asphalted. 01/01-31/12.
Distance: 1km 2km 1km 400m 500m.

S Barcelona 32G3

Park & Ride del Besòs, Carrer del Taulat, B10 > salida 24 / 25, Sant Adrià del Besos. **GPS**: n41,41565 e2,22363.

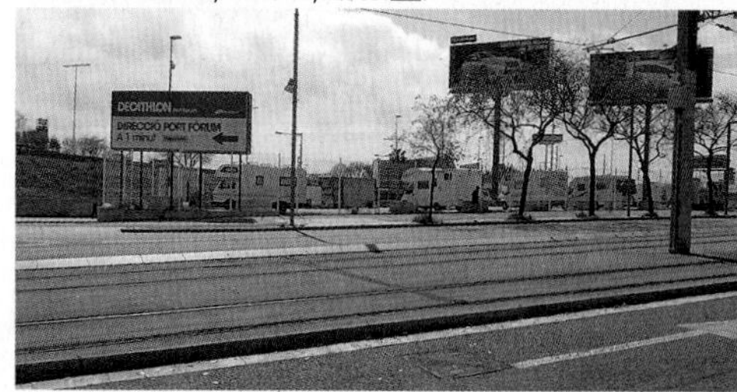

30 € 3/h, € 30/24h Ch WC included .
Location: Urban. **Surface:** metalled. 01/01-31/12.
Distance: 1km 300m 300m Tram 100m, metro 500m.
Remarks: Max. 72h, monitored parking.

Barcelona 32G3

Almogàvers, Carrer de la Llacuna. **GPS**: n41,40301 e2,19604.

7 € 2,55/h, night € 18,30. **Location:** Urban, simple.
Surface: asphalted. 01/05-31/08.
Distance: 800m 200m 400m on the spot.
Remarks: Video surveillance.

Barcelona 32G3

Garcia Fària, Carrer de Josep Pla. **GPS**: n41,40662 e2,21829.

10 € 20.
Location: Urban, simple, noisy. **Surface:** asphalted.
Distance: 1km 2km 100m 150m 400m on the spot on the spot on the spot.
Remarks: Max. ^4.50m.

Barruera 32E1

Carrer de riu. **GPS**: n42,50127 e0,79614.
free. **Location:** Rural, isolated. **Surface:** unpaved. 01/01-31/12.
Distance: 800m 800m on the spot on the spot.
Remarks: Along river.

ES

S Bellcaire d'Empordà 32H2

Àrea Massís del Montgrí, Camí Vell d'Ullà, 21.
GPS: n42,07521 e3,09748.
36 € 8, 01/06-30/09 € 10 Ch (14x)€4 WC €2/5minutes €4 included.
Location: Rural, comfortable. **Surface:** grassy. 01/01-31/12.
Distance: 500m 5km 500m 250m 100m on the spot on the spot.
Remarks: Swimming pool (summer).

S Bellvei 32F3

Bellvei del Penedès, Camino Plains. **GPS**: n41,24613 e1,56992.

30 € 6 Chincluded €3 €1/day. **Location:** Comfortable, isolated, quiet. **Surface:** grassy/gravel. 01/01-31/12.
Distance: 1km 6,5km 5km 1,2km 1km on the spot.

S Benagéber 33A1

Ctra. CV-3930. **GPS**: n39,70913 w1,10136.

70 free Chfree. **Location:** Rural, simple, isolated, quiet.
Surface: gravel/sand. 01/01-31/12.
Distance: 100m 400m on the spot on the spot.
Remarks: Max. 72h, picnic and barbecue place.

S Bicorp 33A2

Junto al Polideportivo. **GPS**: n39,13278 w0,79056.

20 € 5 Chincluded WC.
Location: Rural, isolated. **Surface:** gravel.
Distance: 200m.

S Bigastro 33A2

Camper Area La Pedrera, Calle Cañada de Andrea, 100.
GPS: n38,05116 w0,89863.
20 € 12 Ch WC included. **Location:** Rural.
Surface: gravel. 01/01-31/12.

Distance: on the spot on the spot.

Blanes 32H3

Carrer d'Antoni Gaudí. **GPS**: n41,66873 e2,78440.

free, 15/06-15/09 € 10.
01/01-31/12.
Distance: on the spot 350m 250m 450m.

Tourist information Blanes:
Oficina de Turismo, Paseo de Catalunya, 2, www.blanes.net. Bathing resort.
Jardín Botànic Mar i Murtra. Botanical garden.
Mas Enlaire. Local products.
Mo-Fri 8-14h.
Passeig de Mar. Clothing, souvenirs etc.
Mo-morning.

S Bordils 32H2

Can Carreras del Mas, Carrer Creu 34. **GPS**: n42,04580 e2,91320.

5 € 12 €2 €4 included.
Location: Rural, quiet. **Surface:** grassy.
Distance: 400m 100m.
Remarks: Narrow entrance.

S Cabanes 32H1

El Noguer, Camí de la Creu. **GPS**: n42,30594 e2,97592.

30 € 10 Ch (16x)WC included. **Location:** Rural, simple, quiet. **Surface:** grassy. 01/01-31/12.
Distance: Figueres 4km 400m 450m 300m on the spot on the spot.
Remarks: Video surveillance.

S Cadaqués 32H1

Parking SABA, Riera de Sant Vicenç. **GPS**: n42,28964 e3,27260.

€ 20,20/24h WC. **Surface:** asphalted.
Distance: 100m 1km 1,5km 100m 100m.

Tourist information Cadaqués:
La Riera. Week market. Mo 8-14h.

S Calaf 32F2

Area Calaf Barcelona, Calle Doctor Fleming, 6.
GPS: n41,72940 e1,52610.
10 € 10 Chincluded free. **Location:** Rural, simple.
Surface: asphalted. 01/01-31/12.
Distance: 500m 300m.

S Calaf 32F2

Area Municipal de Calaf, Carrer Berlin. **GPS**: n41,73500 e1,51389.

4 free Chfree. **Location:** Urban, comfortable, quiet.
Surface: gravel/metalled. 01/01-31/12.
Distance: 300m 400m 300m 400m.
Remarks: Max. 48h, market Saturday.

S Calaf 32F2

Calle de Leida-Girona. **GPS**: n41,73306 e1,52667.

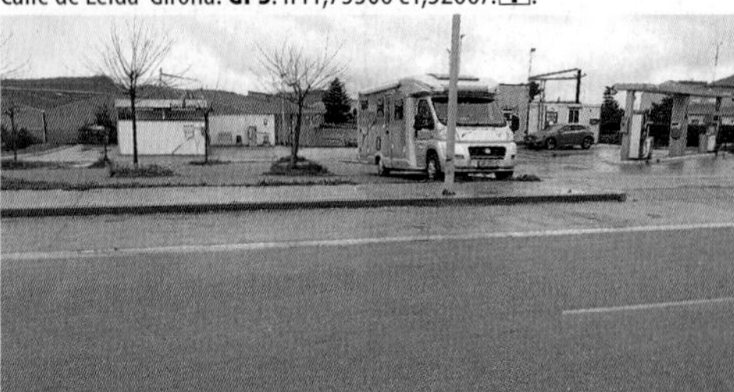

5 free Chfree. **Location:** Urban, simple. **Surface:** gravel.
01/01-31/12.
Distance: 800m 1km 800m 700m 600m.
Remarks: At petrol station, inclining pitches, video surveillance.

S Caldes de Malavella 32H2

Carrer Solei. **GPS**: n41,83873 e2,81080.

5 free Ch free. **Location:** Urban, comfortable, noisy.
Surface: gravel. 01/01-31/12.
Distance: 500m 200m 300m 100m.
Remarks: Max. 3 days.

S Callosa d'en Sarrià 33A2

Fonts de l'Algar, Partida Segarra s/n. **GPS**: n38,65430 w0,09289.

40 € 14 Ch €4 WC €2 included.
Location: Comfortable, isolated. 01/01-31/12.
Distance: 700m 700m.

S Calnegre 31H2

Camperpark Taray, RM-D21, Puntas de Calnegre.
GPS: n37,51520 w1,3985.

50 € 6 €1/100liter Ch €4. **Location:** Simple. **Surface:** sand.
01/01-31/12.
Distance: 100m 500m 500m.

ES

S Calnegre 31H2

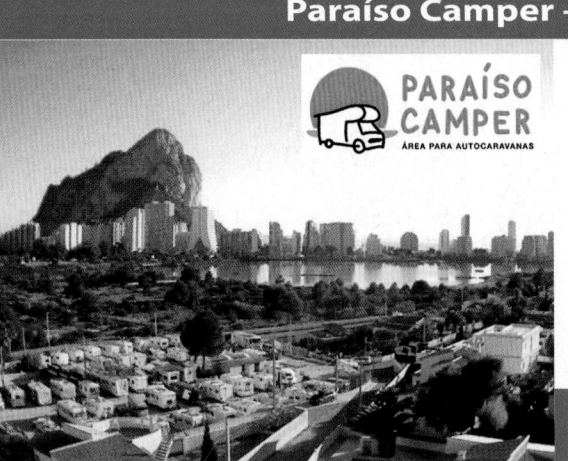

Puntas Calnegre, Ctra. Puntas de Calnegre, nº 42.
GPS: n37,51179 w1,41198.

17 € 6,50, 01/06-30/09 € 8 Ch included.
Surface: metalled. 01/01-31/12.
Distance: 600m.

S Calpe 33A2

Paraiso Camper, Urbanización Los Almendros, 9A. **GPS**: n38,64893 e0,06665.

58 € 11 (discount longer stays) Ch (58x)€0,20/kWh WC included €0,20 €3/3 €2/day.
Location: Comfortable, central. **Surface:** gravel. 01/01-31/12.
Distance: 1,8km 7km 800m 800m 400m 250m 400m 1km.

S Calpe 33A2

Mediterráneo Camper, Calle Partida Colari 7E.
GPS: n38,65126 e0,06942.

75 € 9-12, Jul/Aug € 14 Ch WC included €3/3 €2/day. **Surface:** gravel. 01/01-31/12.
Distance: beach 750m 75m Mercadona 300m.
Remarks: Discount longer stays.

S Calpe 33A2

Nautica caravanning, Ctra. N233. **GPS**: n38,65578 e0,03660.

20 € 10 Ch €2 . **Location:** Simple, central.
Surface: asphalted. 01/01-31/12 Sa-Su.
Distance: 500m 400m.
Remarks: Motorhome dealer, arrival during opening hours.

S Cambrils 33B1

Camperpark Las Moreras, Carretera N-340, Km. 1.139,1.
GPS: n41,04471 e0,99437.

120 € 11,45, Jul € 11,25 + € 6,15/pp, Aug € 11,25 + € 8,60/pp Ch WC €4/3 €1/h.
Location: Comfortable, isolated, quiet. 01/01-31/12.
Distance: 4km on the spot on the spot on the spot 4km on the spot on the spot.

S Cambrils 33B1

Area de Cambrils, A7. **GPS**: n41,08542 e1,03777.

10 free, 20-8h € 16 Ch WC included €4.
Location: Motorway, simple, central, noisy. **Surface:** asphalted.
01/01-31/12.
Distance: on the spot.

Tourist information Cambrils:
Oficina de Turismo, Paseo les Palmeres, nº 1, www.turcambrils.info. Bathing resort in traditional Mediterranean style.

Cañada de Callego 31H2

Loma de St.Antonio, Camino de Perchèles. **GPS**: n37,53542 w1,37226.

free. **Location:** Simple, isolated. **Surface:** sand.
Remarks: Parking at sea.

S Cantallops 32H1

Restaurant Can Pau, Carretera de Cantallops s/n.
GPS: n42,41863 e2,91386.
50 guests free . **Surface:** asphalted.
Distance: 1km.
Remarks: Swimming pool.

S Carcaixent 33A2

Hort de Soriano. GPS: n39,07045 w0,40918.

15 free Ch free. **Location:** Comfortable, quiet.
Surface: sand. Mo, Aug.
Distance: 7km on the spot.
Remarks: Max. 48h, picnic and barbecue place. At recreation area, first drive into Carrer Julián Ribera (39°7'19'N 00°27'04'W) ± 5km, than follow Hort de Soriano.

S Cartagena 33A2

Area Autocaravanas Cartagena. GPS: n37,65373 w1,00345.

30 € 10 Ch WC €4 included.
Surface: gravel. 01/01-31/12.
Distance: centre 5km, port 8km 400m 400m 400m on the spot on the spot.
Remarks: Bread-service, sunday market Bohio 500m, Thursday market Dolores 1km.

S Cartagena 33A2

Área Belmonte Plus, Ctra. de Tentegorra, 1.
GPS: n37,61500 w1,00555.

15 € 10 Ch included.
Location: Noisy. **Surface:** asphalted.
Distance: 500m on the spot.

S Cervera 32E3

Centre d'Accolida Turistica, Av. Francesc Macià.
GPS: n41,67815 e1,28385.

ES

10 free Ch free.
Location: Urban, quiet. **Surface:** sand. 01/01-31/12.
Distance: 2km 500m 1,5km.
Remarks: Near office de tourisme, friday market.

S Ceutí 31H2

Ceutí, Pz José Virgili 1. **GPS**: n38,08099 w1,26717.

20 free Ch WC free. **Location:** Simple.
Surface: asphalted. 01/01-31/12.
Distance: 300m 4,5km 170m 200m.

S Creixell 33B1

Area 340, Carrer Aneto. **GPS**: n41,16663 e1,45707.
25 € 10-20 Ch included. **Surface:** unpaved.
01/01-31/12.
Distance: 650m 300m.

S Daimús 33A2

Area Camper Dunes, Carrer Garbi 2a. **GPS**: n38,96981 w0,14509.

65 € 9 Ch €3 WC included €3 €1/3h.
Location: Comfortable. **Surface:** gravel/metalled.
Distance: 350m 50m 100m on the spot.

S Deltebre 33B1

Agrobotiga del Delta, Avda. Les Goles de l'Ebre, 2.
GPS: n40,72605 e0,72261.

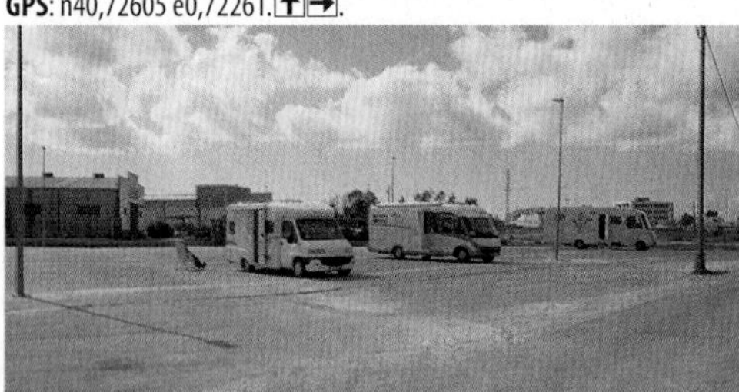

50 free Ch free. **Location:** Rural, simple, central.
Surface: concrete. 01/01-31/12.
Distance: 800m 19km 1,5km 600m on the spot.

S El Campello 33A2

Camper Area Campello Beach, Calle Juan de la Cierva.
GPS: n38,39479 w0,40985.

45 € 12, Jul-Aug € 14 Ch €2/day WC included €3 €3/3 €2.
Location: Luxurious. **Surface:** gravel/sand. 01/01-31/12.
Distance: 1km 5km 400m 500m 500m on the spot.

S El Campello 33A2

Camper Park Alicante, Carrer Llauradors 113.
GPS: n38,42599 w0,40914.

35 € 7,50 €3 Ch €2,50/day WC €2 free.
Location: Comfortable. **Surface:** gravel. 01/01-31/12.
Distance: 500m 5km 1,8km 500m 1km.

S El Campello 33A2

Bar-Restaurant, N332 km124. **GPS**: n38,45746 w0,36129.

5 € 5 WC included. **Surface:** sand.
Distance: on the spot.
Remarks: 3 days free.

El Campello 33A2

Disaminado Afueras 459. **GPS**: n38,41863 w0,39478.
20 free. **Surface:** metalled. 01/01-31/12.

S El Catllar 33B1

Area de El Catllar, Cami de la Foni. **GPS**: n41,17658 e1,32685.

10 free Ch free. **Location:** Simple, central, quiet.
Surface: metalled. 01/01-31/12.
Distance: 200m 200m on the spot on the spot.

S El Masroig 33B1

Celler El Masroig, Passeig de Arbre 3. **GPS**: n41,12658 e0,73385.

10 free Ch WC.
Location: Rural, simple. **Surface:** gravel. 01/01-31/12.
Distance: on the spot 200m 200m.
Remarks: Sale of wines.

S El Palomar 33A2

Font de Sis, Avenida Riuet. **GPS**: n38,85749 w0,5032.

17 € 5 Ch €3/day €2/day. **Location:** Isolated.
01/01-31/12.
Distance: 200m on the spot 200m.
Remarks: Picnic and barbecue place.

S Els Muntells 33B1

Carrer Major. **GPS**: n40,66852 e0,75903.

10 € 6 Ch included. **Location:** Rural, simple, isolated, quiet.
Surface: asphalted/gravel. 01/01-31/12.
Distance: 500m 1,2km 400m 600m on the spot on the spot.

Figueres 32H1

Parking Supermercado Esclat, Avda. de los Paisos Catalans, N260.
GPS: n42,26042 e2,95096.

5 free. **Surface:** asphalted.
Distance: on the spot 500m on the spot 50m.
Remarks: Max. 48h.

Tourist information Figueres:
Rambla. Antiques market. 3rd Sa of the month.
Plaza Catalunya en Plaza del Gra. Tue-Thu-Sa 9-14h.

S Garrigàs 32H2

Área del Empordà Norte, A7 km-35. **GPS**: n42,17333 e2,93194.
10 free WC free. **Surface:** metalled. 01/01-31/12.

S Garrigàs 32H2

Área del Empordà Sur, A7 km-35. **GPS**: n42,17456 e2,93074.

10 free WC free. **Surface:** metalled. 01/01-31/12.

S Girona 32H2

Vayreda la Devesa, Placa de Mela Mutermilch.
GPS: n41,98392 e2,81384.

ES

20 € 10 Ch €1/40minutes WC included.
Location: Urban, simple, central. **Surface:** metalled.
01/01-31/12.
Distance: 1km 100m 100m 200m 100m.
Remarks: Registration via intercom or phone, arrival <20h.

S Granollers 32G3
Passeig Fluvial. **GPS**: n41,59857 e2,27833.
13 free Chfree. **Surface:** asphalted. 01/01-31/12.
Distance: city centre 1,5km 500m 500m.

S Gualta 32H2
C-31. **GPS**: n42,02456 e3,13490.
58 € 12 (50x)included . 01/01/-31/12.
Distance: 8km 400m 400m.
Remarks: Bicycle rental.

S Ibi 33A2
Área Chambit, Calle Pedro Valdivia. **GPS**: n38,62222 w0,56694.

25 free Chfree.
Location: Simple. **Surface:** sand. 01/01-31/12.
Distance: 2,3km.

S Jalance 33A2
N330. **GPS**: n39,18740 w1,0761.

10 free Chfree.
Location: Isolated. **Surface:** asphalted. 01/01-31/12.
Distance: 300m.
Remarks: Parking next to swimming pool, max. 48h.

Jávea 33A2
Avda.de Nancy. **GPS**: n38,77024 e0,18945.

10 . **Surface:** unpaved.
Distance: 100m 100m.

S L'Alqueria de la Comtessa 33A2
Camperpark KM Zero, Metge Panella nº 1.
GPS: n38,93878 w0,15276.

35 €9 Ch (35x)€3/day,6Amp WC included
€3/3 €1/day. **Location:** Comfortable. **Surface:** asphalted.
01/01-31/12 01/07-31/08.
Distance: 100m 1,5km 4km 200m 200m 150m
300m 500m.
Remarks: Car rental, discount longer stays.

S L'Olleria 33A2
Carrer J Bautista Ferrere. **GPS**: n38,91572 w0,55402.

5 free Ch. **Location:** Urban. **Surface:** asphalted.
Distance: 300m 2km 250m.
Remarks: Max. 48h.

La Azohia 33A2
Carretera a La Azohía. **GPS**: n37,56332 w1,17393.

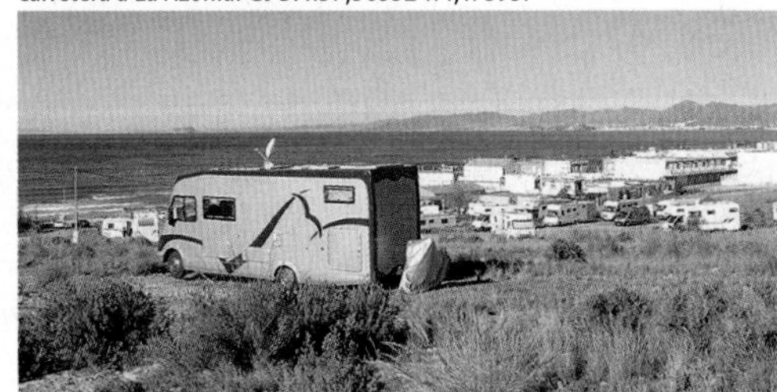

50 free. **Location:** Simple. **Surface:** unpaved.
Distance: 50m 100m 100m.

S La Guàrdia dels Prats 32E3
Heretat Masia Poblet, Carretera d'Artesa.s/C-14.
GPS: n41,41468 e1,17487.

14 € 10, guests free (14x)€3/night included.
Location: Rural, simple, isolated, quiet. **Surface:** grassy/gravel.
01/01-31/12 Tue.
Distance: on the spot 5km 5km on the spot on the spot.

S La Marina 33A2
Finca La Escuera, Escuera 300. **GPS**: n38,14360 w0,66939.

11 € 14 Ch €0,26/kWh WC €4 .
Surface: sand.
01/01-31/12.
Distance: 300m 3km 300m 300m 300m on the spot.

S La Marina 33A2
La Marina Elche, Cami del Molar o Pinet. **GPS**: n38,15628 w0,63791.

20 €8 Chincluded €0,50/kWh,16Amp. winter.

La Marina 33A2
Camino del Pinet, La Marina nord. **GPS**: n38,15087 w0,63276.

40 free. **Surface:** asphalted.

S La Pobla de Segur 32E1
Avenida Camp de la Sala. **GPS**: n42,24029 e0,96635.
12 free Ch free. **Surface:** asphalted. 01/01-31/12.
Distance: 1km 250m 550m.

La Roca del Vallès 32G3
Barri Gasuachs. **GPS**: n41,59349 e2,34521.
.
Distance: 2,2km.
Remarks: Video surveillance.

S La Salzadella 33A1
Av. Tomas Molins. **GPS**: n40,41611 e0,17305.

6 free Chfree. **Location:** Rural, simple, quiet.
Surface: asphalted.
Distance: 250m 250m 250m.
Remarks: Village of cherries: cherry soap, cherry jam.

S La Sénia 33A1
Carrer dels Domenges. **GPS**: n40,63897 e0,28502.

10 free €2 Ch. **Location:** Rural, simple, quiet.
Surface: gravel. 01/01-31/12.
Distance: 800m 200m 200m.

S La Seu d'Urgell 32F1
Parking Doctor Peiró, Avinguda del Camí Ral de Cerdanya.
GPS: n42,35871 e1,46476.
10 free €2/100liter €1/2h.
Surface: unpaved. during event.
Distance: 500m 350m.
Remarks: Max. 2 nights.

S La Tallada d'Empordà 32H2
L'Empordanet, Carretera de Marenyà, 6. **GPS**: n42,08335 e3,05734.

€ 12 €3 Ch included.
Surface: gravel/metalled. 01/01-31/12.
Distance: 1km on the spot on the spot.
Remarks: Max. 48h, swimming pool.

Lavern 32F3
Cava Guilera, Masia Ca l'Artigas. **GPS**: n41,39848 e1,77038.

ES

4 free. **Location:** Rural, simple, isolated, quiet. **Surface:** grassy.
01/01-31/12.
Distance: 1,5km 5km on the spot on the spot.
Remarks: Max. 2-3 days.

S Lleida 32D3

Autocaravanas Miguel, Ctra. N-IIa 456. **GPS**: n41,58945 e0,57591.

40 € 8 Ch (4x)€2/night WC included.
Location: Rural, simple, isolated. **Surface:** grassy/gravel.
01/01-31/12.
Distance: on the spot 4,5km 750m 2km on the spot.

S Lorca 31H2

Caravanas Lorca, P.I. Saprelorca Buzón 233. **GPS**: n37,61205 w1,75993.
20 free €2 €2 Ch. **Surface:** gravel. Su.
Distance: 7km 300m 20km 50m.
Remarks: At motorhome dealer.

S Lorquí 31H2

Parque de la Constitución. **GPS**: n38,07909 w1,25918.

15 free Chfree. **Location:** Simple, central.
Surface: asphalted/metalled. Mo 07-15h, market.
Distance: 500m 5km 300m.

S Los Alcázares 33A2

Camping Car Área Narejos, Calle Bergantín 6.
GPS: n37,76298 w0,83069.
90 € 7,90-12,90 Ch €3 WC included €3/3.
Surface: asphalted.
Distance: 700m on the spot.

S L'Arboç 32F3

Área del Penedés Norte, AP7 dir Barcelona. **GPS**: n41,28794 e1,59117.
10 Chfree. **Surface:** metalled. 01/01-31/12.
Distance: on the spot on the spot.

S L'Arboç 32F3

Área del Penedés Sur, AP7 dir Taragona. **GPS**: n41,29029 e1,59235.

10 Chfree. **Surface:** asphalted. 01/01-31/12.
Distance: on the spot on the spot.

S Montblanc 32E3

Restaurant Masia Poblet, C14, La Guardia dels Prats.
GPS: n41,41464 e1,17479.

10 € 10, guests free Chincluded €3,10Amp.
Location: Rural, comfortable, isolated, quiet.
Surface: grassy/metalled. 01/01-31/12.
Distance: 5km on the spot 5km.

S Montblanc 32E3

Area de Autocaravanas Sam, Avda. Lluis Companys.
GPS: n41,36933 e1,17180.

10 € 10 Ch WC included. **Location:** Simple.
Surface: asphalted. 01/01-31/12.
Distance: 800m 350m 800m 400m.
Remarks: At motorhome dealer.

S Montseny 32G3

Área de Montseny, AP7-Nord km-117 > Francia.
GPS: n41,64700 e2,42586.

20 free free. **Surface:** metalled. 01/01-31/12.
Distance: on the spot on the spot.

S Montseny 32G3

Área de Montseny, AP7-Sur>Barcelona. **GPS**: n41,64803 e2,42661.

20 free free. **Surface:** metalled. 01/01-31/12.
Distance: on the spot on the spot.

S Morella 33A1

N232. **GPS**: n40,62398 w0,09141.

30 free Chfree. **Location:** Rural, simple, isolated, quiet.
Surface: grassy/metalled. 01/01-31/12.
Distance: 1,5km 1,5km 1,5km on the spot.
Remarks: Max. 72h.

S Mula 31H2

Camino de las Curtis. **GPS**: n38,03972 w1,48139.

5 free Chfree. **Location:** Simple. **Surface:** asphalted.
01/01-31/12.
Distance: 500m 500m.

S Murcia 33A2

Camperpark Casablanca, F16. **GPS**: n38,00189 w1,01939.

120 € 12 Ch WC €3/3 included.
Location: Comfortable, central. **Surface:** gravel.
01/01-31/12.
Distance: Murcia 11km 500m 15km 500m on the spot on the spot on the spot.
Remarks: 24/24 surveillance.

S Murcia 33A2

Camperpark Huerta de Murcia, Carril los Cánovas, Rincón de Almodóvar, Los Ramos. **GPS**: n38,00520 w1,04229.

45 € 13 Ch WC €3/3 included.
Location: Comfortable. **Surface:** gravel. 01/01-31/12.
Distance: Alquerías 1,7km 500m 500m on the spot.
Remarks: Bread-service.

S Navarcles 32F2

Area Municipal d'Autocaravanas, Calle de la Font de la Cura.
GPS: n41,75661 e1,90833.

6 free Ch free.
Location: Urban, isolated, quiet. **Surface:** gravel. 01/01-31/12.
Distance: 500m 3km 100m 600m 200m 700m 50m.

S Navata 32H2

Restaurante Can Janot, Ctra. de Olot nº 2.
GPS: n42,22600 e2,86325.

20 guests free €5 ChWC atrestaurant. **Location:** Rural,

ES

simple, quiet. **Surface:** grassy.
01/01-31/12.
Distance: 100m on the spot 100m 150m on the spot on the spot.

Oliva 33A2

Area Camper Kikopark, C/ Assagador de Carro.
GPS: n38,93282 w0,09742.

15 € 18-26,50 Ch WC included. 01/01-31/12.
Distance: on the spot on the spot.
Remarks: Stop & Go arrival >15h, departure <15h.

Palamós 32H2

Autocaravanning Palamós, Camí Vell de la Fosca, 18.
GPS: n41,85592 e3,13535.
96 € 12, 15/07-31/08 € 17 Ch WC €3 included.
Location: Comfortable. **Surface:** gravel. 01/01-31/12.
Distance: 500m 500m.
Remarks: Motorhome washing place.

Palamós 32H2

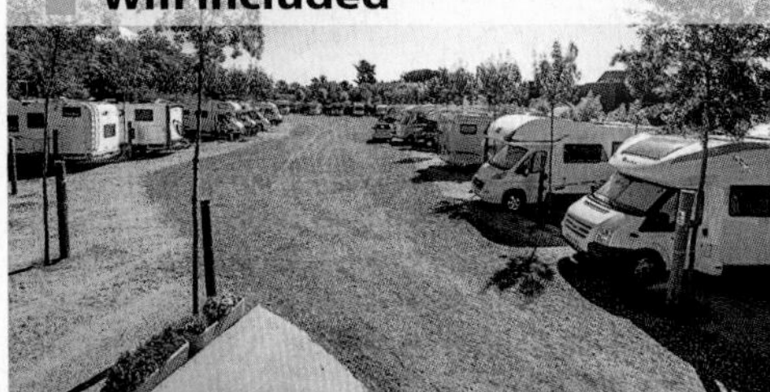

EmpordArea, C/ Pui Gorgoll s/n - C/ Pla del Llop s/n.
GPS: n41,85740 e3,11467.
40 € 12, 15/07-28/08 € 17 Ch (40x),8Amp WC €1 €4 included. **Location:** Urban, comfortable, quiet.
Surface: gravel/metalled. 01/01-31/12.
Distance: 1km 1,3km 1km 1km 700m 350m 500m 1,2km 1,2km.
Remarks: Bread-service, video surveillance, rental of electric scooters and bicycles.

Peñíscola 33A1

Area camper Vizmar, Cami de la Volta.
GPS: n40,39357 e0,40778.

25 € 7 Ch €4/day WC included €3,95/day.
Location: Rural, comfortable, quiet. **Surface:** gravel.
15/09-15/06 Semana Santa.
Distance: 3km 500m 300m 300m 300m.
Remarks: Discount longer stays.

Peñíscola 33A1

Camper Park Los Pinos, C/ Abellers, 2.
GPS: n40,37912 e0,38827.

30 15/09-15/06 € 10, 16/06-14/09 tariff camp site Ch 10Amp WC €4,50/4,50 included. **Location:** Rural, luxurious, quiet. **Surface:** gravel/metalled. 01/01-31/12.
Distance: 1,5km 2km 1,5km 800m.

Peñíscola 33A1

Stop&Go La Volta, Camino de la Volta 20.
GPS: n40,39793 e0,40316.

70 € 7, 01/07-31/08 € 10, 2 pers incl., 1 pers + € 1-2 Ch €3,6Amp WC €4/4 included.
Location: Rural, comfortable, isolated, quiet. **Surface:** grassy/gravel.
01/01-31/12.
Distance: 4km, Peñíscola 5km 1km 2km 4km 1km.

Peñíscola 33A1

Parking Els Daus, Avenida Valencia, 93. **GPS:** n40,37831 e0,40640.
130 € 6,30-12,60 Ch WC included. **Surface:** grassy.
01/01-31/12.
Distance: 2km 100m 100m 30m.
Remarks: Beach parking.

Pineda de Mar 32G3

Àrea Pineda de Mar, Carrer Tarragona, 24.
GPS: n41,62199 e2,68941.

30 € 10-12 Ch €3 WC €1 included.
01/01-31/12 9-21h.
Distance: on the spot 100m 100m.

Platja d'Aro 32H2

Calle Roma. **GPS:** n41,81028 e3,05767.

30 free Ch included. **Surface:** asphalted. 01/10-31/03.
Distance: 750m.
Remarks: Max. 2 days.

Quart 32H2

Avinguda de la Bóbila. **GPS:** n41,93944 e2,83917.

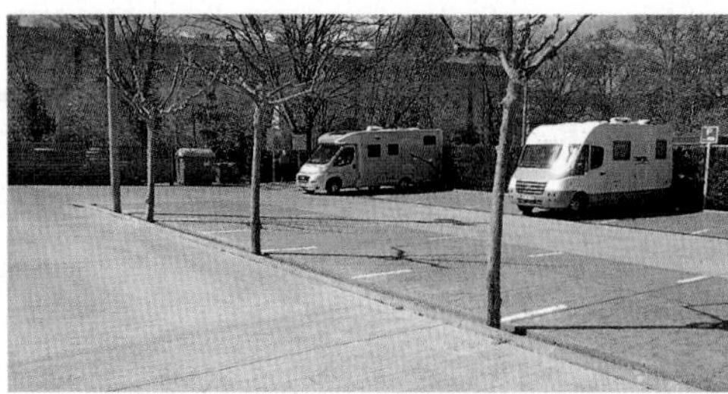

4 free Ch free. **Surface:** metalled. 01/01-31/12.
Distance: on the spot 6,5km on the spot on the spot.
Remarks: Max. 48h, max. 8M.

Ramonete 31H2

Wo-Mo Puerto Villa Brisa, Los Curas, D21, Puntas de Calnegre.
GPS: n37,52589 w1,4336.

50 € 7 €0,10/10liter Ch €0,50 €2 €4/4.
Location: Simple, isolated. **Surface:** gravel. 19/09-30/05.
Distance: 5km 5km 5km 5km.
Remarks: Bread-service.

Rialp 32E1

Paseig del Pallars. **GPS:** n42,43925 e1,13384.
5 free Ch. **Surface:** gravel.
Distance: 200m 200m 200m 100m.
Remarks: Next to football ground.

Ricote 31H1

Huerta de Rivote, Calle Alharbona. **GPS:** n38,15098 w1,36674.
30 free Ch free. **Surface:** gravel. 01/01-31/12.

Ripoll 32G2

Can Guetes, Carretera C-26 Km.126. **GPS:** n42,20267 e2,19390.

5 free Ch free. **Location:** Urban, simple, central.
Surface: asphalted. 01/01-31/12.
Distance: on the spot 500m 150m on the spot on the spot.
Remarks: Max. 24h.

Ripoll 32G2

Calle Pla D'Ordina, Raval de Barcelona. **GPS:** n42,20008 e2,18695.

5 free. **Location:** Urban, simple, noisy. **Surface:** asphalted.
01/01-31/12.
Distance: 300m 500m 500m.
Remarks: Parking next to police station, max. 24h.

Tourist information Ripoll:
Centrum. Week market. Sa-morning.

San Fulgencio 33A2

Camper Park San Fulgencio, Mar Cartabrico 7, Centro Comercial las Dunas. **GPS:** n38,12080 w0,66005.

ES

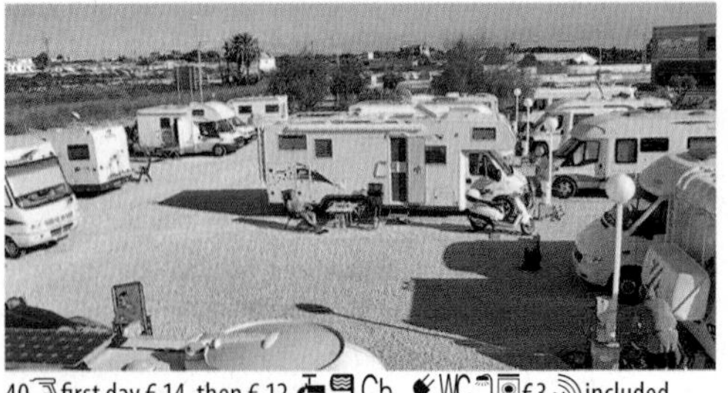

40 first day € 14, then € 12 Ch WC €3 included.
Location: Comfortable. **Surface:** gravel.
01/01-31/12.
Distance: 1,5km 200m 150m 150m.

San Fulgencio 33A2

Ghol, Calle Mar Cantabrico. **GPS**: n38,11896 w0,65614.
14 6m € 11, 9m € 12, 11m € 13 2kWh/day WC included. **Surface:** gravel. 01/01-31/12.
Distance: 2km 400m Lidl 120m.
Remarks: Next to petrol station.

San Fulgencio 33A2

Oasis, Caminal del Convenio. **GPS**: n38,11972 w0,66194.

14 € 10, 15/06-15/09 € 14 Ch €0,40/kWh,16Amp WC €3/2 included.
Location: Comfortable. **Surface:** gravel. 01/01-31/12.
Distance: San Fulgencio 7km beach 1,5km 200m 200m 300m.

San Rafael del Río 33A1

Restaurante Spätzle-Fritz, Planes del Reine, San Jorge, CV-11.
GPS: n40,57507 e0,39333.

50 € 8, guests free €2 €2 Ch €4 WC €2.
Location: Rural, comfortable, isolated, quiet. **Surface:** gravel.
01/01-31/12.
Distance: 3,5km 7km 9km on the spot.

Sant Feliu de Guíxols 32H2

Carrer de la Via del Tren. **GPS**: n41,79036 e3,04414.
15 € 10 Ch. **Surface:** sand. 01/01-31/12.
Distance: 2km 1km 800m.
Remarks: Video surveillance.

Sant Feliu de Guíxols 32H2

Parking Narcis Massanas, Ronda Narcis Massanas.
GPS: n41,78020 e3,02303.

15 free Chfree.
Location: Simple, quiet. **Surface:** unpaved. 01/01-31/12.
Distance: 200m 1,5km 200m 500m 50m.
Remarks: Max. 5 days.

Sant Hilari Sacalm 32G2

Area Autocaravana, Carretera de la Font Picant.
GPS: n41,88417 e2,50778.

30 free Chfree (2x)€1/8h. **Location:** Rural, simple, quiet.
Surface: gravel/sand. 01/01-31/12.
Distance: 300m 200m 200m 700m 10m 10m.
Remarks: Nearby swimming pool, max. 48h, key service at swimming pool.

Sant Joan de les Abadesses 32G1

Area Sant Joan de les Abadesses, Passeig de l'Estació.
GPS: n42,23535 e2,28412.

15 free Chfree.
Location: Urban, simple, central, quiet. **Surface:** unpaved.
01/01-31/12.
Distance: 500m 500m 200m on the spot on the spot.
Remarks: 5 special pitches, all parking places permitted.

Santa Coloma de Cervelló 32F3

Santa Coloma de Cervelló, Can Julià, s/n.
GPS: n41,36495 e2,02512.

6 free Chfree. **Location:** Simple, isolated, quiet.
Surface: asphalted. 01/01-31/12.
Distance: 500m 5km 400m 500m.

Segorbe 33A1

Area de Segorbe, Escalera de la Estación.
GPS: n39,84805 w0,48166.

12 free Chfree. **Location:** Simple, central, quiet.
Surface: asphalted/metalled. 01/01-31/12.
Distance: 1km 2km 800m 800m on the spot.
Remarks: Max. 48h.

Sils 32H2

Area de Sils, Carrer de l'Estany. **GPS**: n41,80751 e2,74572.

10 free Chfree. **Location:** Urban, simple, central.
Surface: gravel/sand. 01/01-31/12.
Distance: 700m on the spot on the spot 50m.
Remarks: Max. 48h.

Simat de la Valldigna 33A2

Carrer dels Brolls. **GPS**: n39,04120 w0,308.

20 free Chfree. **Surface:** sand. 01/01-31/12.
Distance: 500m 450m 500m.

Sitges 32F3

Avda. del Cami Pla. **GPS**: n41,25083 e1,81838.

10 € 5, 01/04-31/10 € 8 Ch. **Location:** Simple.
Surface: asphalted. 01/01-31/12.
Distance: 800m 2,5km 50m.
Remarks: Industrial area, max. 7 days, Barcelona 40km.

Sta.Pola 33A2

Europa-Area, Carrer dels Electricistas. **GPS**: n38,20805 w0,57416.

33 € 9 Ch €3 WC €4.
Location: Comfortable. **Surface:** gravel/metalled. 01/01-31/12.
Distance: 1,7km 1,8km 1,7km.

Tavernes de la Valldigna 33A2

Area Camper La Finca, Carrer del Carbi. **GPS**: n39,08178 w0,21245.
50 € 8 Ch €3 WC €3 included. 01/01-31/12.
Distance: 750m 50m 600m.
Remarks: Bread-service, video surveillance.

Tavertet 32G2

Carrer Jaume Balmes. **GPS**: n41,99462 e2,41572.
10 € 10 Ch included.
Surface: gravel/sand. 01/01-31/12.
Distance: 100m 450m.

Tortosa 33B1

Área de Tortosa, Cami de la Toia. **GPS**: n40,80277 e0,51388.

30 free Chfree.
Location: Simple, central, quiet. **Surface:** asphalted. 01/01-31/12.
Distance: 1,1km 10km 900m 1km.

Totana 31H2

Camperstop Sierra Espuña, Morti s/n Camino del Polideportivo.
GPS: n37,79380 w1,51139.

25 € 7 Ch €3/day WC €1 €3 included.
Location: Comfortable. **Surface:** gravel.
Distance: 2,5km 5km 450m.

S Tremp 32E2

Passeig de Conca de Tremp. **GPS**: n42,16312 e0,89043.

10 free free €1/2h. **Surface:** asphalted.
Remarks: Max. 48h.

S Turis 33A1

Carretera de Silla Tunis. **GPS**: n39,38944 w0,69777.

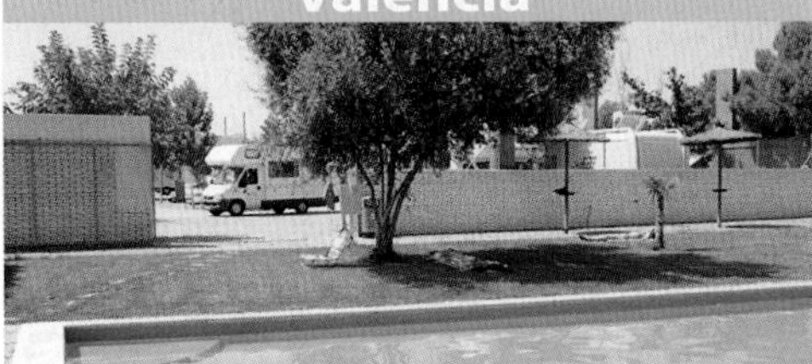

10 free Chfree.
Location: Simple. **Surface:** unpaved. 01/01-31/12.
Distance: 500m.

S Valencia 33A1

Valencia Camper Park, Calle Universo, Bétera.
GPS: n39,57958 w0,44494.
78 € 12 €0,50/40liter Ch (52x)€3/24h,4Amp,6Amp€5 WC €3 included
Location: Urban, luxurious. **Surface:** gravel. 01/01-31/12.
Distance: Valencia 12km 1,5km train 300m.
Remarks: Swimming pool (summer).

S Valencia 33A1

Area Camping-car La Marina, Carrer del Rio 556B, El Saler.
GPS: n39,38666 w0,3321.

70 € 11 ChWC . **Surface:** gravel.
Distance: Valencia 6km beach 150m 600m 500m on the spot on the spot on the spot.
Remarks: Discount longer stays.

S Valencia 33A1

Valencia Caravan Park, Camino del Tizón, 91-D, Torrent.
GPS: n39,44048 w0,52521.
15 € 8 Chincluded €2.
Location: Simple. 01/01-31/12.
Distance: 15km 150m 1km 150m.

Vallirana 32F3

Carrer Major, N340. **GPS**: n41,38239 e1,92719.

6 . **Location:** Simple, noisy. **Surface:** asphalted.
01/01-31/12.
Distance: 800m 300m 800m.

S Vic 32G2

Area Municipal de Vic, Carrer de la Fura.
GPS: n41,93444 e2,24000.

10 € 5 €2/100liter Ch €6/3h.
Location: Rural. **Surface:** grassy.
Distance: 1,8km 2km 300m 500m 400m.
Remarks: Max. 48h.

S Vic 32G2

Área de pernocta ASM, Carrer del Blat. **GPS**: n41,95688 e2,24765.

6 free Chfree.
Location: Rural, simple. **Surface:** asphalted.
Distance: 3,5km 500m 3,5km 3,5km.
Remarks: Video surveillance.

S Viladrau 32G2

Area de Viladrau, Carrer Montseny s/n. **GPS**: n41,84544 e2,38732.

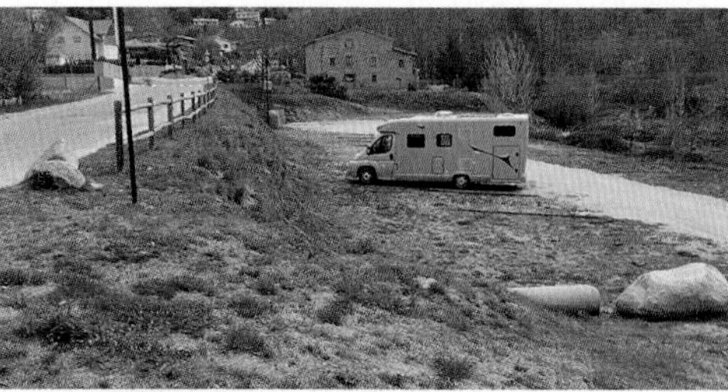

16 free Ch free. **Location:** Rural, simple, quiet.
Surface: gravel/sand. 01/01-31/12.
Distance: 500m 500m 500m.
Remarks: Max. 48h.

S Vilafranca del Penedès 32F3

Vilafranca del Penedès, Avda. Tarragona, N-340a.
GPS: n41,34001 e1,69147.

10 free Ch. **Location:** Rural, simple, central, quiet.
Surface: gravel/sand. 01/01-31/12.
Distance: 500m 1,2km 900m 850m Lidl on the spot on the spot.

S Yecla 33A2

Finca Caravana, Paraje Fuente del Pinar A-14.
GPS: n38,71443 w1,11948.

10 € 8 Chincluded. **Location:** Rural, simple, isolated.
Surface: gravel/sand. 05/06-30/06.

Spanish interior

S Aguilar de Campoo 29F2

N611, Ctra Palencia-Aguillar de Campoo.
GPS: n42,78631 w4,25757.

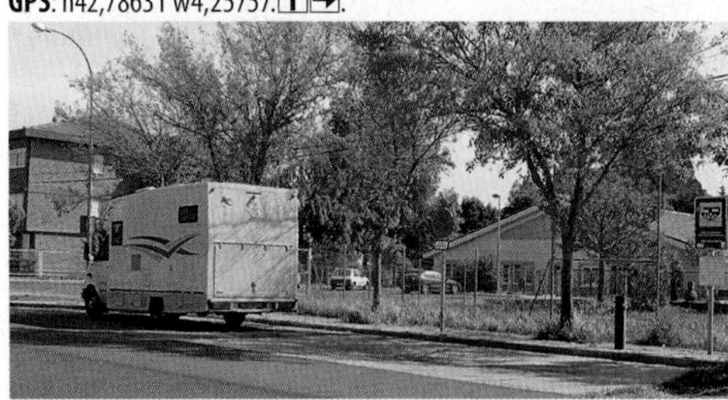

10 free Chfree.
Location: Urban, simple. **Surface:** asphalted. 01/01-31/12.
Distance: 1km 3,1km 1km 1km.
Remarks: Max. 48h.

S Aldeadávila de la Ribera 30D1

GPS: n41,22028 w6,61333.

5 free Chfree. **Surface:** asphalted. 01/01-31/12.
Distance: on the spot 200m.

Remarks: Max. 48h.

S Aldeanueva de Barbarroya 30E2

Calle Aldeanueva. **GPS:** n39,75843 w5,01482.
5 free Chfree. 01/01-31/12.
Distance: 700m 700m.
Remarks: Max. 72h.

Almazán 30H1

Camino Viejo del Cubo de la Solana. **GPS:** n41,49259 w2,53385.
Remarks: Parking at swimming pool.

S Ampudia 29F3

Area de San Martín, Glorieta. S. Martín.
GPS: n41,91130 w4,78082.

6 free Chfree. **Location:** Rural, simple.
Surface: gravel/metalled. 01/01-31/12.
Distance: 400m.
Remarks: No camping activities.

S Andorra 33A1

Area en Andorra. **GPS:** n40,98384 w0,44724.

3 free €0,20/130liter Ch. **Surface:** asphalted.
01/01-31/12.
Distance: 1km 13km 1,2km.
Remarks: Coins at petrol station.

S Astorga 29E2

Parking plaza de Toros. **GPS:** n42,45138 w6,06593.

15 free Chfree. **Surface:** metalled.
Distance: 500m 1,4km 500m 500m.
Remarks: Max. 48h.

S Astudillo 29F3

Area de la Joya, Urbanizacion de don Bosco. **GPS:** n42,18944 w4,3.

10 free Chfree.
Location: Rural, simple. **Surface:** gravel.
Distance: 1km 300m.
Remarks: No camping activities.

Avila 30F1

Parking del Palacio de Congresos, Calle Molino dell Carril.
GPS: n40,66111 w4,70472.

10 free.
Surface: asphalted.
Distance: 2,2km.

Tourist information Avila:
Small medieval town surround by ramparts.
The San Vicenta basilica is a Roman building.

S Badajoz 30C3

Parque del Guadiana, Camino Viejo de San Vicente.
GPS: n38,88481 w6,97845.

8 free Chfree. **Surface:** asphalted. 01/01-31/12.
Distance: 600m on the spot.

S Baltanàs 29F3

Area de la Ermita de Revilla, Plaza Arrañales de Revilla.
GPS: n41,93472 w4,2475.

5 free Chfree.
Location: Rural, simple. **Surface:** concrete. 01/01-31/12.
Remarks: No camping activities.

S Becerril de Campos 29F3

Carretera de Monzón. **GPS:** n42,10997 w4,64315.
free Chfree. **Surface:** metalled. 01/01-31/12.
Distance: on the spot 14km 500m 500m.
Remarks: No camping activities.

S Bretocino 29E3

Area para Autocaravanes, Cuesta de los Nogales.
GPS: n41,88654 w5,75517.

5 +25 €7 Chincluded €3,10Amp WC .
Location: Rural, comfortable, quiet. **Surface:** concrete.
20/03-20/10.
Distance: 300m 300m.
Remarks: Service passerby €3, swimming pool.

S Burgo de Osma 30G1

Calle de Santos Iruela. **GPS:** n41,58662 w3,07338.

10 free . **Location:** Rural, simple. **Surface:** metalled.
01/01-31/12.
Distance: 500m 200m 500m.

Burgos 29G3

N120, Calle de Cartuja de Miraflores. **GPS:** n42,34037 w3,69361.

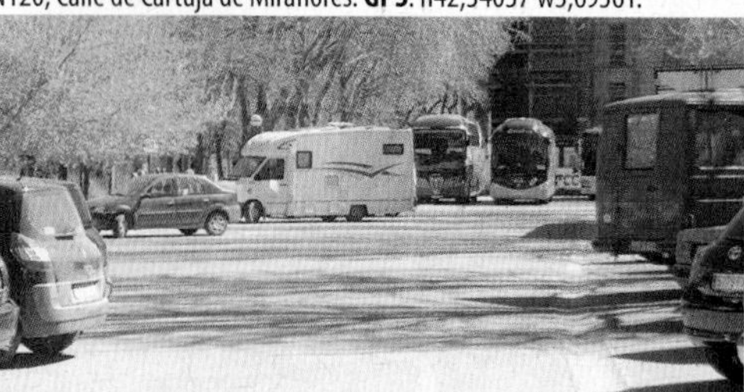

5 € 0,60/h, max. € 2,60, 20-10h free. **Surface:** asphalted.
Distance: 2,6km.
Remarks: Parking beside river.

Tourist information Burgos:
City, 8th century, with a lot of curiosities such as the cathedral, the castle and Monasterio de las Huelgas.

S Cabrerizos 30E1

Don Quijote, Ctra. Aldealengua km 4. **GPS:** n40,97500 w5,60306.
€ 17 Ch. 01/03-31/10.
Remarks: Formula Camper.

S Cáceres 30D2

Valhondo, Calle Lope de Vega. **GPS:** n39,48041 w6,36649.

15 free Ch free. **Surface:** asphalted.
Distance: 600m 6,7km.
Remarks: Max. 24h, monitored parking.

Tourist information Cáceres:
Oficina de Turismo, Plaza Mayor, nº 3, www.inedito.com/caceres/. City with historical centre.
PeroPalo. Traditional celebration. 21/02-24/02.

S Carrión de los Condes 29F3

C/ Las Huertas. **GPS:** n42,33875 w4,60808.

10 free Chfree.
Location: Rural, simple. **Surface:** metalled.
Distance: 200m 200m 200m.
Remarks: Max. 48h.

S Cervera de Pisuerga 29F2

C/ El Maderao. **GPS:** n42,87139 w4,49972.

ES

10 free Chfree. **Location:** Rural, simple, isolated.
Surface: sand.
Distance: 500m 500m 500m.
Remarks: Along river, max. 48h.

Coca 30F1

GPS: n41,21348 w4,52733.

5 free. **Location:** Urban, simple. **Surface:** metalled.
01/01-31/12.
Remarks: Parking castle.

Consuegra 30G3

GPS: n39,45339 w3,6106.
free. **Surface:** sand.
Remarks: Isolated parking at foot of hill with windmills.

Cuellar 30F1

Área El Castillo, Calle del Alamillo, 40. **GPS:** n41,40083 w4,32028.

6 free free. **Location:** Rural, simple.
Surface: metalled.
Distance: 2km.
Remarks: At castle.

Deleitosa 30E2

Área PLA Deleitosa, Calle Eras. **GPS:** n39,64041 w5,64599.
3 free €3 Ch €1/h. **Surface:** metalled.
01/01-31/12.
Distance: 500m 500m.

Don Benito 30D3

Avda. de los Deportes. **GPS:** n38,96250 w5,86305.
3 free Chfree. **Surface:** metalled. 01/01-31/12.
Distance: on the spot on the spot on the spot.

Duruelo de la Sierra 29G3

Avenida del Duero. **GPS:** n41,95242 w2,92725.
16 €4 Ch. **Surface:** metalled. 01/01-31/12.
Distance: 400m 250m.

Espinosa de los Monteros 29G2

Parking Las Cocinas, BU-570 > Bárcenas. **GPS:** n43,08556 w3,5575.

10 free Chfree. **Location:** Simple, isolated.
Surface: asphalted. 01/01-31/12.
Distance: 1km 1km 1km on the spot.
Remarks: Max. 48h, tuesday market.

Foncastín 29F3

Estación de Servicios La Loba, A6, salida 175.
GPS: n41,44131 w4,97957.

5 free Chfree. **Location:** Rural, simple. **Surface:** asphalted.
01/01-31/12.
Distance: 250m on the spot.

Frómista 29F3

Paseo de Julio Senador, P-980. **GPS:** n42,26494 w4,41198.

6 free Chfree. **Location:** Urban, simple. **Surface:** metalled.
01/01-31/12.
Distance: 600m 200m 500m 500m.
Remarks: At sports park, max. 48h, weigh bridge nearby € 0,50.

Herrera de Pisuerga 29F2

Fuente Los Caños. **GPS:** n42,59011 w4,33225.
7 Chfree. **Location:** Rural. **Surface:** gravel.
01/01-31/12.
Remarks: No camping activities.

Hontoria del Pinar 29G3

Cañon de Río Lobos, C/ De la Cuesta Herrera.
GPS: n41,84379 w3,16514.
9+24 free Chfree. **Surface:** gravel. 01/01-31/12.
Distance: 500m 450m.

Huergas de Babia 29E2

El Moriscal, CL-626. **GPS:** n42,95651 w6,09335.
10 € 5 Ch included. **Location:** Rural. **Surface:** gravel.
01/01-31/12.
Distance: on the spot on the spot.

Jerte 30E2

Area de Jerte. **GPS:** n40,20976 w5,77284.
15 €3/150liter Ch (4x). **Location:** Rural.
Surface: asphalted/metalled. 01/01-31/12.
Distance: city centre 2km 400m on the spot on the spot.
Remarks: Max. 72h, monitored parking.

La Alberca 30D1

Casa del Parque. **GPS:** n40,48833 w6,11583.
10 free Chfree. **Surface:** metalled.
Distance: 300m.
Remarks: Max. 48h.

La Joyosa 32A2

Área de Marlofa, Calle Sobradiel. **GPS:** n41,73744 w1,06664.
21 free Ch €3 WC. **Surface:** asphalted/grassy.
Distance: 9km.

Lagartera 30E2

Camino de la Estacion. **GPS:** n39,91151 w5,19978.

3 free free. **Surface:** asphalted. 01/01-31/12.
Distance: on the spot 1,4km 100m.
Remarks: Max. 48h.

León 29E2

Avenida los Peregrinos. **GPS:** n42,60471 w5,58525.

6 free Chfree. **Surface:** metalled.
Distance: 300m 300m.
Remarks: Max. 48h.

Logrosán 30E3

El Palomar, Carretera Villanueva-Seré. **GPS:** n39,33188 w5,48044.
10 free Chfree. **Location:** Isolated. **Surface:** grassy.
01/01-31/12.
Remarks: Max. 48h.

Mérida 30D3

Área Teatro Romano de Mérida, C/ Cabo Verde, s/n.
GPS: n38,91903 w6,33611.
<8m € 12/24h, >8m € 15/24h, trailer € 3 Ch €3 included.
Location: Urban. **Surface:** asphalted.
01/01-31/12.
Distance: 700m.

Tourist information Mérida:
Oficina de Turismo, Calle Santa Eulalia, 64. Also called Spanish Rome. Former stopover on the old silver trail.

Olmedo 30F1

Parque del Mudejar, N601, km 148,1. **GPS:** n41,29167 w4,68194.

9 free Chfree.
Location: Rural, simple. **Surface:** metalled. 01/01-31/12.
Distance: 100m 200m.

Oropesa 30E2

Camino de Torralba. **GPS:** n39,92124 w5,16738.
4 free Chfree. **Surface:** metalled. 01/01-31/12.
Distance: 600m.
Remarks: Max. 48h, no camping activities.

Osorno 29F2

Los Chopos, N611 Osorno > Herrera de Pisuerga.
GPS: n42,41694 w4,35111.

30 free Chfree. **Surface:** asphalted.
Distance: 700m 2,2km on the spot.
Remarks: Max. 48h, monitored parking.

Palazuelos de Eresma 30F1

Calle Cordel. **GPS:** n40,92848 w4,05529.
€1 Chfree. 01/01-31/12.
Distance: 4km.

Palencia 29F3

Parque Isla Dos Aguas, Avda. Ponce de León, 12.
GPS: n42,00389 w4,53333.

ES

23 free Chfree. **Surface:** asphalted.
Distance: on the spot 4km on the spot El Arbol 50m 100m.
Remarks: Max. 48h.

Peñafiel 29F3

Calle de Los Destiladeros. **GPS**: n41,59440 w4,11582.

5 free. **Location:** Rural, simple. **Surface:** asphalted.
01/01-31/12.
Distance: 150m.
Remarks: Parking castle.

Peñaflor 32B2

Parking Surrecreo, Urbanizacion Los Rosales Peñaflor.
GPS: n41,72777 w0,79194.
150 € 15 Ch WCincluded.
Distance: 8km.

Pollos 29E3

Estación de Servicios La Loba 2000, A62, salida 169.
GPS: n41,41004 w5,13396.

10 free Chfree. **Location:** Motorway, simple.
Surface: metalled. 01/01-31/12.
Distance: 200m on the spot on the spot.
Remarks: At petrol station.

Ribaseca 29E2

Area de Léon, Carretera la Bañeza. **GPS**: n42,54439 w5,5882.
€ 15-25 Ch WC included. **Surface:** asphalted.
01/01-31/12.
Distance: 8km 2,3km 800m.
Remarks: At motorhome dealer, car rental, motorhome washing place.

Salamanca 30E1

Antiguo Campo De Rugbi. GPS: n40,95917 w5,67464.
+10 free. **Location:** Noisy. 01/01-31/12.
Distance: 1km 100m Lidl/Mercadona.
Remarks: Next to sports fields.

Saldaña 29F2

Calle de los Sauces. **GPS**: n42,51882 w4,74125.

6 free Ch. **Location:** Rural, simple. **Surface:** concrete.
01/01-31/12.
Distance: 1km 1km.
Remarks: Next to sports fields, max. 48h.

Sancti-Spiritus 30D1

Hostal-Restaurante La Ponderosa, Carretera nacional 620 km303.
GPS: n40,73481 w6,36093.

customers free.
Distance: 3km.
Remarks: Daily menu € 8.

Sepúlveda 30G1

Calle de el Postiguillo. **GPS**: n41,29897 w3,74479.

10 free. **Surface:** asphalted.
Distance: 300m 12km 100m.

Soria 29H3

Monte de las Animas. **GPS**: n41,76769 w2,45391.

free. **Surface:** gravel.

Soria 29H3

Hypermercado E. Leclerc, Calle J, P 290. **GPS**: n41,77249 w2,48497.
6 free €2 Ch €2. **Surface:** asphalted.
01/01-31/12.
Distance: 1,8km on the spot on the spot on the spot.
Remarks: Coins at petrol station.

Terradillos 30E1

Area del Encinar, Paseo de Poniente. **GPS**: n40,88000 w5,58194.
10 free Chfree. **Location:** Simple. **Surface:** asphalted.
Distance: 200m.

Teruel 33A1

Parking Cuartel, Calle Tarazona de Aragon. **GPS**: n40,33132 w1,09273.
20 free. **Surface:** asphalted. 01/01-31/12.
Distance: 2km 300m 50m.
Remarks: In front of police station.

Toledo 30F2

Parking de la Estación, Avda. de Castilla la Mancha.
GPS: n39,86472 w4,01944.
50 free.
Surface: asphalted.
Distance:
1,3km.

Tourist information Toledo:
Catedral. Cathedral known for its richness.
El Alcázar. Roman castle ruins, 16th century.

Toro 29E3

Area de Rumbeolas, Calle Santa María de la Vega.
GPS: n41,51489 w5,39301.
10 € 4 Chincluded €3. **Location:** Rural. **Surface:** sand.
01/01-31/12.
Distance: 1,5km 5,5km on the spot.

Trujillo 30E3

Ronda de le Plaza de Toros. **GPS**: n39,45696 w5,87303.
10 free. **Surface:** asphalted. 01/01-31/12.
Distance: centre 800m 100m.

Turégano 30F1

CL603. **GPS**: n41,15241 w4,00749.

10 free Chfree. **Location:** Rural, simple. **Surface:** asphalted.
01/01-31/12.
Distance: 200m.
Remarks: Behind former grain factory, max. 48h.

Valencia de Alcántara 30C2

Area de Puerto Roque, N-521. **GPS**: n39,34104 w7,2775.
10 free €3 Ch. **Location:** Rural. **Surface:** metalled.
01/01-31/12.
Distance: 9km on the spot.

Valencia de Don Juan 29E2

Area de Coyanza, Calle Tres de Abril. **GPS**: n42,28750 w5,51333.

7 free Chfree.
Location: Urban, simple. **Surface:** concrete. 01/01-31/12.
Distance: 500m 300m.
Remarks: Max. 48h.

Valladolid 29F3

San Lorenzo, Av. Ramón Pradera. **GPS**: n41,65583 w4,73722.

15 € 2,50/24h included.
Location: Urban. **Surface:** asphalted.
Distance: city centre 1km 3,2km 400m.
Remarks: Max. 48h.

Villacañas 30G3

Calle Juan Pablo II. **GPS**: n39,62101 w3,33188.
2 free. **Surface:** asphalted.
Distance: on the spot 350m.
Remarks: Max. 48h.

Villada 29F3

C/ San Fructuoso, Calle del Ferial Nuevo 10.
GPS: n42,25533 w4,9649.

5 free Chfree. **Location:** Rural, simple, quiet.
Surface: gravel. 01/01-31/12.
Distance: 200m 200m 200m.
Remarks: Max. 48h, no camping activities.

Villalpando 29E3

Area de Servicios Villalpando, A6, salida 236.
GPS: n41,85906 w5,41993.
5 free. **Location:** Motorway, simple, isolated, noisy.

ES

Surface: asphalted. 01/01-31/12.
Distance: 200m on the spot on the spot.
Remarks: At petrol station.

Zafra 31D1
Ctra. de los Santos de Maimona, Ex101. **GPS**: n38,42527 w6,41083.

30 free Chfree. **Surface:** asphalted. 01/01-31/12.

Zafra 31D1
Ferial Zafra, Ctra. Badajoz-Granada. **GPS**: n38,42558 w6,4116.
30 free Chfree. **Location:** Urban. **Surface:** asphalted.

Zamora 29E3
Estadio Barrio 3 Arboles, Calle de los Pisones.
GPS: n41,50337 w5,75585.

18 free. **Location:** Urban, simple, central.
Surface: asphalted.
Distance: 1km 1km.
Remarks: Playground.

Andalusia

Abla 31G2
Area de Abla, A-92A. **GPS**: n37,14455 w2,77347.
7 free Chfree. **Surface:** asphalted. 01/01-31/12.
Distance: on the spot 1,5km 100m.

Abla 31G2
Area de Montagón, Carretera ALP-503.
GPS: n37,15415 w2,77716.

13 free Chfree. **Location:** Rural, simple, quiet.
Surface: asphalted. 01/01-31/12.
Distance: 1,5km 2km 1,5km 1,5km.
Remarks: Next to football ground.

Agua Amarga 31H3
Calle Ensenada. **GPS**: n36,93883 w1,93657.

20 free. **Location:** Rural, simple, quiet. **Surface:** gravel/sand.
01/01-31/12.
Distance: on the spot 100m 50m 500m 2km.
Remarks: Riverbed.

Alanís 31D1
Area de Alanís de la Sierra, Alameda del Parral.
GPS: n38,03729 w5,71057.
5 free Chfree. **Location:** Simple. **Surface:** metalled.

01/01-31/12.
Distance: on the spot 200m.

Alcalá de Guadaíra 31D2
Autocaravanas Hidalgo, A92 Sevilla><Malaga km 7.
GPS: n37,32856 w5,8056.

18 € 10 €0,50 Ch included .
Distance: 170m exit 15.
Remarks: Motorhome dealer, max. 2 nights.

Alcázar de San Juan 30G3
Area de Alcazar de San Juan. **GPS**: n39,38972 w3,21944.
10 free Ch. **Surface:** asphalted. 01/01-31/12.
Distance: on the spot 150m 300m.

Algar 31D3
Complejo Tajo del Aguila. **GPS**: n36,65111 w5,66555.
€ 20 Ch WC included. 01/01-31/12.
Distance: 1km on the spot on the spot.
Remarks: Max. 7 nights.

Alicún de las Torres 31G2
GR6104. **GPS**: n37,50836 w3,10802.

3 free. **Surface:** metalled. 01/01-31/12.
Distance: 100m 100m.
Remarks: Next to the spa resort.

Almayate 31F3
Area AMB, Carretera Nacional 340, km 266,5.
GPS: n36,72372 w4,13999.

40 € 7, 01/06-30/09 € 10 Ch included.
Location: Rural, simple. **Surface:** gravel.
Distance: 700m 100m 100m 2km 200m.
Remarks: At motorhome dealer.

Almensilla 31D2
San Diego, A-8054. **GPS**: n37,31361 w6,09333.
15 free Chfree.
Remarks: At petrol station BP and restaurant, restaurant visit appreciated.

Almerimar 31G3
Parking Almerimar, Avenida del Mar. **GPS**: n36,70803 w2,80895.
136 € 7 Ch €3/24h WC . **Location:** Urban.
Surface: metalled. 01/01-31/12.
Distance: city centre ± 1km 100m 50m 1km.

Almerimar 31G3
Area del Puerto Deportivo Almerimar, Torre del puerto.
GPS: n36,69612 w2,79425.

20 € 12,69 Ch WC included €3,50/24h.
Location: Urban, simple. **Surface:** asphalted. 01/01-31/12.
Distance: on the spot 100m 300m 100m 100m.
Remarks: Check in at harbourmaster 9-14h, 16-21h.

Antequera 31E2
Area de Antequera, Calle Miguel de Cervantes.
GPS: n37,02139 w4,57191.

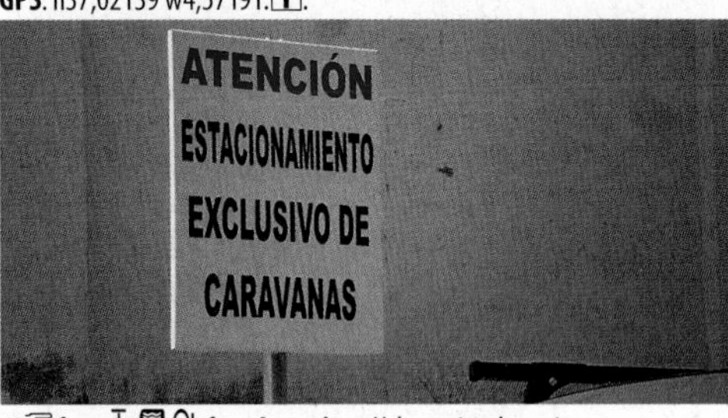

12 free Chfree. **Location:** Urban, simple, noisy.
Surface: asphalted. 01/01-31/12.
Distance: on the spot 6,5km 50m 500m.
Remarks: Next to football ground.

Archidona 31E2
A7200. **GPS**: n37,09097 w4,38879.

12 free Chfree.
Location: Rural, simple. **Surface:** concrete. 01/01-31/12.
Distance: 250m 1km 500m 1km on the spot.

Baeza 31F1
Calle Manuel Acero. **GPS**: n37,99679 w3,45923.
30 free Chfree. **Surface:** sand. 01/01-31/12.
Distance: 1km 500m bakery.
Remarks: Max. 96h, no camping activities.

Benarrabá 31E3
Area Autocaravanas Benarrabá, Carretera Comarcal MA-538.
GPS: n36,54935 w5,27901.
5 free Chfree. **Surface:** gravel. 01/01-31/12.
Distance: 500m 600m.

Cabo de Gata 31H3
Cabo de Gata Camper Park, Carrertera de San José.
GPS: n36,81639 w2,14918.

50 € 7-10 Ch (50x) WC €3,50/3,50 included.
Surface: gravel. 01/01-31/12.
Distance: 5km 7km 7km on the spot 5km on the spot on the spot on the spot.
Remarks: Service passerby € 3, bicycle rental.

Cabra 31F2
Area de Cabra II, Calle de la Libertad. **GPS**: n37,47602 w4,44271.

ES

free Chfree. **Location:** Urban. **Surface:** asphalted.
01/01-31/12 Mo 07-13h.
Distance: 600m 200m.

Cabra 31F2

Auditorio Municipal Alcalde Juan Muños, Juanita la Larga.
GPS: n37,46608 w4,42361.

4 free Chfree. **Location:** Urban, simple, quiet.
Surface: asphalted. 01/01-31/12.
Distance: 500m 300m 500m.
Remarks: Max. 48h.

Cala de Mijas 31E3

Av. del Mediterraneo. **GPS**: n36,50496 w4,68344.

50 free. **Location:** Urban, simple. **Surface:** sand.
01/01-31/12.
Distance: 500m 500m 800m 50m 100m 50m.
Remarks: Market Wednesday and Saturday.

Canjáyar 31G3

Paraje de la Alcoholera, A-348. **GPS**: n37,01400 w2,74523.

7 free Chfree. **Location:** Rural, simple, quiet.
Surface: asphalted/metalled.
Distance: 1km 450m.
Remarks: At tennis-courts.

Carboneras 31H3

El Rancho, ALP-711. **GPS**: n37,00371 w1,91127.
45 € 10 Ch WC €3,50 included. **Location:** Rural.
Surface: sand. 01/01-31/12.
Distance: 2km 2,4km Mercadona 2km.

Conil de la Frontera 31D3

Avda. del Rio. **GPS**: n36,27282 w6,08994.

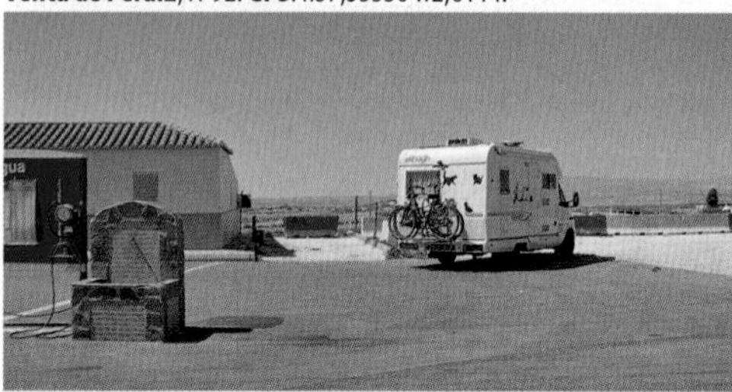

20 free. **Surface:** asphalted. 01/01-31/12.
Distance: on the spot 500m 500m.
Remarks: Parking along coast road.

Córdoba 31E1

Área del Centro Histórico, Avda. de los Custodios.
GPS: n37,87528 w4,78778.
30 € 11 Ch. **Surface:** asphalted/gravel. 01/01-31/12.
Distance: historical centre 300m 2,3km.
Remarks: In front of police station.

Córdoba 31E1

Avda. del Campo de la Verdad/Calle del Compositor Rafael Castro.
GPS: n37,87515 w4,76626.
free. **Surface:** asphalted. 01/01-31/12.
Distance: 1km.

Tourist information Córdoba:

Museo Municipal Taurino, Plaza de las Bulas. Museum about bull-fighting. Tue-Fri 8.30-20.45h, Sa 8.30-16.30h, Su 8.30-14.30h Mo. € 4.

Torre de la Calahorra. Urban museum. 10-14, 16.30-20.30. € 4,50.

Oficina de Turismo, Torrijos, 10 (Plaza del Triunfo), www.cordoba-turismo.es. Historical and culturally rich city, city of the flamenco and bull-fighting.

Palacio del Marqués de Viana. Palace with collections of leather, silverware, porcelain etc. Mo-Sa 10-19h, Su 10-15h. € 8.

Mezquita. World-famous Moorish mosque. 10-18/19u.

Cuevas de San Marcos 31F2

GPS: n37,26059 w4,40237.

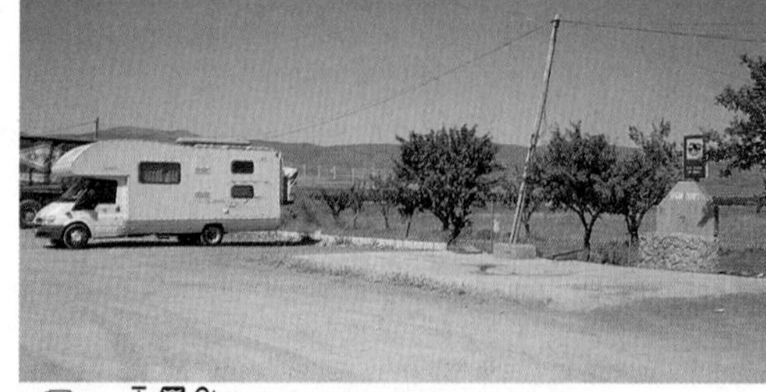

15 free free. **Location:** Rural, simple, isolated.
Surface: asphalted.
Distance: 1km 500m 1km.
Remarks: Parking at swimming pool.

Cullar 31G2

Venta de Peral2, A-92. **GPS**: n37,55336 w2,6144.

20 free WC free. **Surface:** asphalted. 01/01-31/12.
Distance: 3km 10m 10m.

Dólar 31G2

Area de Venta de Dólar, A92. **GPS**: n37,19521 w2,98397.

30 free Chfree. **Location:** Motorway, simple.
Surface: metalled. 01/01-31/12.
Distance: 2km 50m on the spot.
Remarks: At petrol station.

Doña Mencía 31F2

Area de Esparcimiento Dona Mencia. **GPS**: n37,54656 w4,35237.

7 free free. **Location:** Rural, comfortable, quiet. **Surface:** gravel.
01/01-31/12.
Distance: 500m La Cantina on the spot.

Dos Hermanas 31D2

Multiparking La Jabega, Carretera SE 9024. **GPS**: n37,21278 w5,96389.

50 € 6 Ch €3 WC included.
Surface: concrete. 01/01-31/12.
Distance: city centre Sevilla 18km.
Remarks: Video surveillance.

Dos Hermanas 31D2

Rubiales, Calle Pasadilla de Barranco. **GPS**: n37,31030 w5,9584.
20 € 12 Chincluded €3. **Surface:** gravel.
01/01-31/12.
Distance: Sevilla 10km > Sevilla 100m.

El Bosque 31D3

Calle de Juan Ramón Jiménez. **GPS**: n36,75670 w5,51056.

5 free Chfree. **Surface:** metalled. 01/01-31/12.
Distance: on the spot 100m 300m.

El Higuerón 31E1

Peter Pan, Avenida Principal. **GPS**: n37,87107 w4,85465.
10 € 6 Ch. **Surface:** concrete. 01/01-31/12.
Distance: Córdoba 7km 450m, Mercadona 2km line 54 > Córdoba.

El Puerto de Santa Maria 31D3

Parking Pasarela, Av. de Europa. **GPS**: n36,59840 w6,2212.

50 € 6. **Location:** Urban, simple. **Surface:** asphalted.
01/01-31/12.
Distance: 500m 200m Burgerking 300m 200m.

El Real de la Jara 31D1

Avenida Aguablanca. **GPS**: n37,95089 w6.
8 free Ch. **Surface:** asphalted. 01/01-31/12.
Distance: on the spot 300m.
Remarks: Max. 48h.

Frailes 31F2

Calle Mecedero. **GPS**: n37,48848 w3,8308.
10 free Ch. **Surface:** metalled. 01/01-31/12.
Distance: 500m 500m.
Remarks: Max. 48h.

ES

Fuengirola 31E3

Calle Receinto Ferial. **GPS**: n36,54843 w4,61998.
+20 free. 01/01-31/12.
Distance: on the spot 300m 100m 100m.

Fuengirola 31E3

Ristorante El Rengo, Calle Tramo de Unión.
GPS: n36,53229 w4,63844.
15 € 4,50 Chincluded €5.
Surface: gravel/sand.
01/01-31/12.
Distance: 2,5km 1,6km on the spot Centro comercial 1km.

Gelves 31D2

Puerto Gelves, Calle de Puerto Gelves. **GPS**: n37,33934 w6,02405.

20 € 12 Ch €2,80 WC **Surface:** asphalted.
01/01-31/12.
Distance: on the spot 4,3km on the spot on the spot on the spot.
Remarks: Sevilla 10km, good bus connection.

Granada 31F2

Área de Geysepark-Cármenes, Torre de Comares.
GPS: n37,15136 w3,59533.

100 € 16/day ChService €5 €2/48h.
Location: Urban, simple. **Surface:** asphalted.
01/01-31/12.
Distance: 200m 2km 200m 200m 200m.
Remarks: Covered parking, entrance motorhomes 2nd ramp, max. ^3.10m, advice: pre-order entrance tickets Alhambra.

Granada 31F2

Alhambra, P5. **GPS**: n37,17168 w3,57974.

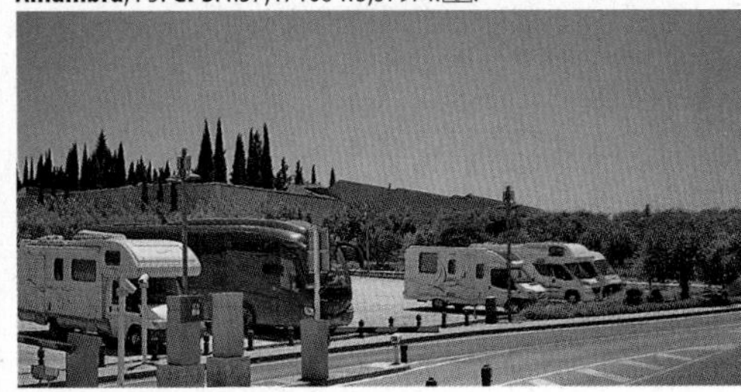

50 € 53/24h, 01/10-01/05 € 29/24h.
Location: Rural, simple.
Surface: gravel. 01/01-31/12.
Distance: 1,5km 200m 200m 100m.

Tourist information Granada:
Alhambra. Most important curiosity of the city, the best kept Arab palace. 9-20h, winter, Sa 20-22h, Su 9-18h, summer Tue,Thu, Sa 22-24h.
Cuevas del Sacromonte. Caves in Sacromonte mountain, gypsies previously lived here. Now important tourist attraction and stage of flamenco shows.
El Albaicín. Moorish district facing the Alhambra.

Grazalema 31E3

Calle Juan de la Rosa. **GPS**: n36,75807 w5,36365.

4 free. **Surface:** asphalted. 01/01-31/12.
Distance: 300m 200m 500m.

Huelva 31C2

Monumento a Colón, Avenida Francesco Montenegro.
GPS: n37,21333 w6,93972.

15 free. **Surface:** asphalted. 01/01-31/12.
Distance: 6km 50m on the spot 6km 500m.

Huércal-Overa 31H2

Travesía de la Alameda. **GPS**: n37,39823 w1,94672.

10 free €0,50/100liter Ch. **Location:** Urban, simple.
Surface: metalled. 01/01-31/12 Mo 09-14h, market.
Distance: 200m 200m 200m on the spot on the spot.
Remarks: Max. 72h, coins at El Pabellon Municipal.

La Isleta 31H3

Playa del Pénom blanca, Carreta Noria. **GPS**: n36,81670 w2,05146.

15 free. **Location:** Rural, simple. **Surface:** gravel.
Distance: 100m sandy beach 20m 150m 300m.
Remarks: Parking at sea.

La Línea de Concepción 31D3

Av. Principe de Asturias. **GPS**: n36,15583 w5,34553.

50 € 1/h, € 15/24h. **Surface:** metalled. 01/01-31/12.
Distance: 500m 1km 200m 1km.
Remarks: Market Wednesday.

La Línea de Concepción 31D3

Area de Alcaidesa Marina, Av. Principe de Asturias.
GPS: n36,15528 w5,35389.
60 € 12 Chincluded. **Surface:** metalled.
Distance: on the spot on the spot.

Málaga 31E3

Area de Los Patios, Calle Montejaque. **GPS**: n36,68706 w4,46045.

10 free €1/50liter Ch. **Location:** Urban, simple.
Surface: asphalted. 01/01-31/12.
Distance: on the spot 1,7km on the spot Carrefour 400m.

Tourist information Málaga:
Oficina de Turismo, Pasaje de Chinitas, 1, www.andalucia.org. Old sparkling port city with fine beaches.
Alcazaba. Moorish castle complex with archeological museum.
Museo casa natal de Pablo Picasso, Plaza de la Merced. House where the painter was born. Mo-Sa 10-20h Su-afternoon.
Palacio de los Condes de Buena Vista, Calle San Agustin, 6. Art-historical museum.
Su.

Marchena 31E2

Calle Sevilla s/n. **GPS**: n37,33083 w5,42416.
20 free Chfree. **Surface:** metalled.
Distance: 1km.

Olvera 31E2

Vía Verde de la Sierra. **GPS**: n36,94138 w5,25305.
48 € 5 Ch included. 01/01-31/12.
Distance: 1km.

Peñarroya-Pueblonuevo 31E1

El Pantano. **GPS**: n38,27694 w5,27722.

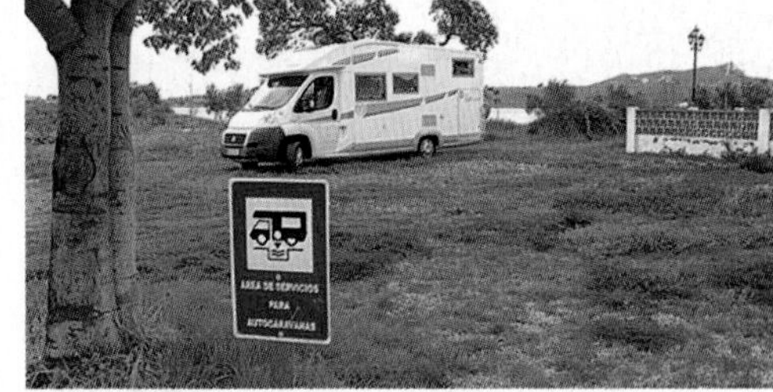

20 € 7 ChService €1,50 €2 included.
Location: Comfortable, isolated, quiet.
01/01-31/12.
Distance: 4km lake on the spot on the spot on the spot.
Remarks: Direct access to the lake, motorhome washing place € 1, swimming pool.

Priego de Córdoba 31F2

Parque Niceto Alcalá - Zamora, Calle del Carrusel s/n.
GPS: n37,44361 w4,21186.

10 free Chfree.
Location: Urban, simple. **Surface:** concrete. 01/01-31/12.
Distance: 500m 500m 500m.

Tourist information Priego de Córdoba:
Iglesia de la Aurora.

Rute 31F2

Calle de Jésus Obrero. **GPS**: n37,33113 w4,37323.

ES

6 free Chfree.
Location: Rural, simple. **Surface:** asphalted.
Distance: 500m 500m 300m.
Remarks: Parking next to police station, max. 48h.

S San Juan de los Terreros 31H2

Playa de Entrevista, A332. **GPS**: n37,35083 w1,67972.

>20 free . **Surface:** gravel/sand. 01/01-31/12.
Distance: 500m 100m 2km 2,5km.
Remarks: Parking beach.

Sancti Petri La Barrosa 31D3

Carretera de la Barossa. **GPS**: n36,38612 w6,2053.

20 free. **Surface:** metalled. 01/01-31/12.
Distance: 2km 200m 1km 5km.
Remarks: Parking beach.

S Sanlúcar de Barrameda 31D2

Sanlúcar AC Parking, Camino de la Reyerta, s/n.
GPS: n36,76195 w6,39617.

58 01/07-30/09 € 12, 01/04-30/06 € 10, 01/10-31/03 € 8 Ch (30x)€3/day,5Amp WC €3/3 included. 01/01-31/12.
Distance: 4km 100m 100m 300m 350m 400m 500m.

S Sevilla 31D2

Area Ac Sevilla Centro, Carretera de la Esclusa, Seville (Sevilla).
GPS: n37,36239 w5,99452.

100 € 15 Ch (40x)€3 WC included.
Surface: asphalted.
01/01-31/12.
Distance: 200m 200m 300m on the spot 200m 200m.

P S Sevilla 31D2

Parking Puente de los Remedios, Avenida Presidente Adolfo Suarez, Seville (Sevilla). **GPS**: n37,37235 w5,99444.
+10 € 10 €5. **Location:** Urban. **Surface:** asphalted.
01/01-31/12.
Distance: on the spot 300m 400m 400m.

P Sevilla 31D2

Parking Kansas City, Avda. de Kansas City, Seville (Sevilla).
GPS: n37,39194 w5,97333.
€ 18/24h.
Surface: asphalted.

Tourist information Seville (Sevilla):
Alcazar, Plaza del Triumfo.
Italica. Roman ruins, 9 km at north of Sevilla on N630.
Almeda de Hercules. Su-morning.
Parque de los Descubrimientos. Theme park science, in pavilion of Expo 1992. Fri-Su, summer Tue-Thu from 18h 10/01-28/02.
Calle de las Sierpes. Famous shopping street.

S Sierra Nevada 31F2

Los Peñones de San Francisco. GPS: n37,09995 w3,3947.

60 € 10/day Chincluded. **Surface:** asphalted.
Distance: 3km 1km 300m.
Remarks: Shuttle bus to village.

Tourist information Sierra Nevada:
Parc Natural de Sierra Nevada. Large nature park with Europe's most southern ski resort.

S Taberno 31H2

Área El Rancho, Los Llanos (La Carrasquilla), Santopetar.
GPS: n37,46028 w2,03833.

8 € 8 Ch (4x) WC included.
Location: Rural, simple, quiet. **Surface:** gravel. Mo.
Distance: 600m 13km on the spot.
Remarks: Entrance swimming pool € 2.

S Tarifa 31D3

Área de Tarifa centro, C/ Numancia, s/n. **GPS**: n36,01443 w5,60732.
10 <8m € 12/24h, >8m € 15/24h, trailer € 3 Chincluded €3. **Location:** Urban. **Surface:** asphalted.
01/01-31/12.
Distance: 400m 1,3km 300m.

Tarifa 31D3

GPS: n36,06804 w5,6856.

20 free. **Surface:** sand. 01/01-31/12.
Distance: 10km on the spot 50m 100m.
Remarks: Parking beach.

Tourist information Tarifa:
Tourist Office, Duke of Kent House, Cathedral Square, Gibraltar, www.gibraltar.gi. British colony at the northwest end of the Rock of Gibraltar.
Siege Tunnels, Gibraltar. Labyrinth of tunnels, ingenious defence system.

S Torre de Benagalbón 31F3

Camper Areas M&H El Rincón, Cortijo Casillas De Los Rubios.
GPS: n36,71658 w4,23799.

35 € 12/24h Chincluded €3/24h €7,50 €1/24h.
Location: Rural, comfortable, quiet. **Surface:** gravel.
01/01-31/12.
Distance: 1km 3km 700m 100m 700m 750m.

S Úbeda 31G1

Travesia Commendador Messias. **GPS**: n38,00649 w3,37953.
10 free Chfree. **Surface:** asphalted. 01/01-31/12.
Distance: centre 1km 1,8km 250m on the spot on the spot.
Remarks: Max. 48h.

S Valverde del Camino 31C1

Ctra. de Zalamea. **GPS**: n37,58111 w6,75138.

10 free Chfree. **Surface:** asphalted/sand.
01/01-31/12.
Distance: 500m.

S Vélez-Rubio 31H2

Área Puerta Oriental de Andalucía, Calle Granada.
GPS: n37,65194 w2,07555.

10 free Chfree. **Location:** Rural, simple, quiet.
Surface: metalled. 01/01-31/12 1st week Aug.
Distance: 500m 2,2km 500m 500m.

S Vera 31H2

Acvera Motorhome Park & Aire, Camino de Los Pescadores s/n.
GPS: n37,26030 w1,85347.
160 € 9 Ch (160x)€2 WC included.
Location: Rural, comfortable. **Surface:** metalled.
01/01-31/12.
Distance: Vera 2km 4,7km beach 10km on the spot.
Remarks: Tennis & padel lessons, 11 tennis courts.

S Vera 31H2

Oasis al Mar, Av del Salar. **GPS**: n37,22731 w1,82819.
50 € 7-9, trailer € 1 Ch €3/day €3 included.
Location: Rural, comfortable. **Surface:** gravel. 01/10-01/05.
Distance: centre Vera 4,4km 2km.
Remarks: Motorhome washing place € 4.

S Villanueva de Algaidas 31E2

Calle de la Archidona, A-7201. **GPS**: n37,17810 w4,45021.
20 free Chfree. **Location:** Rural, simple. **Surface:** asphalted.
Distance: 500m 50m.
Remarks: Max. 48h.

ES

Finland

Capital: Helsinki
Government: parliamentary constitutional republic
Official Language: Finnish and Swedish
Population: 5,375,000 (2015)
Area: 336,855 Km²

General information
Dialling code: 0358
General emergency: 112
Currency: Euro
Credit cards are accepted almost everywhere.

Regulations for overnight stays
Wild camping is in general allowed in the National Parks, on private land with permission of the owner.

Camping Key Europe is obligatory when using campsites: the card can be purchased at any campsite for € 16 (± £14,31), valid for one year.

Additional public holidays 2017
April 14 Good Friday
April 17 Easter Monday
May 1 Labour Day
June 24 Midsummer Eve
June 25 Midsummer
December 6 Independence Day

Time Zone
Winter (Standard Time) GMT+2
Summer (DST) GMT+3

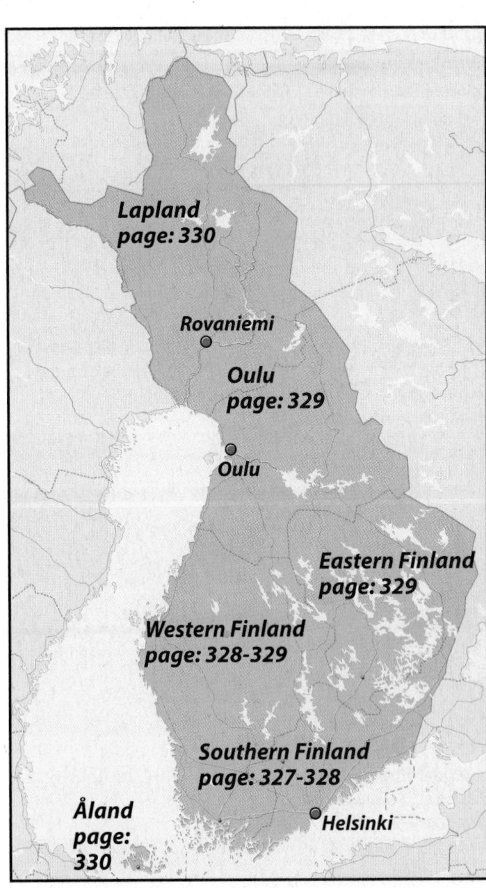

Southern Finland

S Hamina 4F2
Aallokko Caravan, Helsingintie. **GPS**: n60,56039 e27,18280.

20 € 10 + € 2,50/pp Chincluded €3/24h freeh.
Location: Rural, simple, quiet.
Surface: gravel. 01/04-31/10.
Distance: 1km on the spot on the spot 1km.
Remarks: Use of sauna against payment.

Helsinki 4F3
Mustikkanaantie / Blåbärslandsvägen. **GPS**: n60,18240 e24,99173.

10 free.
Location: Rural, simple. **Surface:** asphalted. 01/01-31/12.
Distance: 5,5km 1km on the spot on the spot on the spot 100m.

S Imatra 4F2
ABC Imatra, Tiedonkatu 2. **GPS**: n61,18466 e28,73800.

20 € 5 Ch included at restaurant.
Location: Simple, noisy. **Surface:** asphalted. 01/01-31/12.
Distance: 3km on the spot on the spot on the spot.

Jyväskylä 4E2
Parkeerplaats bij tuibrug, Vespuolentie 674.
GPS: n61,99235 e25,67093.

10 free.
Location: Rural, simple, quiet. **Surface:** asphalted. 01/01-31/12.
Distance: 10km on the spot on the spot.

Jyväskylä 4E2
Parkeerplaats bij tuibrug, Vespuolentie 674.
GPS: n61,99235 e25,67093.
10 free. **Location:** Rural, simple, quiet. **Surface:** asphalted. 01/01-31/12.
Distance: 10km on the spot on the spot.

S Karjaa 4E3
ABC Karjaa, Lepinpellonkatu 2. **GPS**: n60,05489 e23,64809.

4 € 5 Ch included WC free.
Location: Rural, simple. **Surface:** asphalted. 01/01-31/12.
Distance: 2km on the spot on the spot on the spot 10km.

S Kortela 4E3
ABC Rauma Kortela, Unajantie 2. **GPS**: n61,09888 e21,50387.

10 € 5 Chincluded €5/24h. **Location:** Motorway, simple, noisy. **Surface:** asphalted. 01/01-31/12.
Distance: 3,5km on the spot on the spot.

S Lepaa 4E2
Kyläkauppa Pikkuakka, Tyrvännöntie 576.
GPS: n61,11587 e24,34537.

12 € 20 Ch WCincluded. **Location:** Rural, simple, quiet.
Surface: grassy. 01/01-31/12.

FI

Distance: 7km 1km 1km on the spot on the spot.

Liikkala 4F2

Onnelan Tila, Hakalantie 37. **GPS**: n60,70986 e27,01708.

2 € 20 included. **Location:** Rural, simple, isolated, quiet. **Surface:** grassy. 01/01-31/12.
Distance: 2km 2km.

Parikkala 4F2

Tukkikuja. **GPS**: n61,55592 e29,49803.

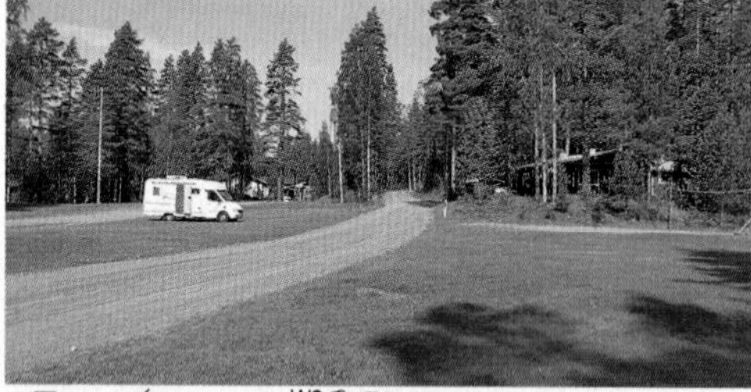

6 free € 10.
Location: Urban, simple, quiet. **Surface:** asphalted. 01/01-31/12.
Distance: 300m on the spot on the spot 300m 300m.
Remarks: At harbour.

Särkisalmi 4F2

Oronmyllyn Toimintakeskus, Oronmyllyntie 250.
GPS: n61,62059 e29,37868.

12 € 10 (4x)€ 10/24h WC. **Location:** Rural, simple, isolated, quiet. **Surface:** grassy. 01/01-31/12.
Distance: 7km 100m 100m.

Ylämaa 4F2

Korupirtti Oy Ravintola, Kikikylantie 7. **GPS**: n60,79054 e28,01026.

5 free € 1/time.
Location: Rural, simple, quiet. **Surface:** gravel. 01/01-31/12.
Distance: 1km on the spot on the spot.
Remarks: At museum.

Western Finland

Hanhikoski 4E2

Maatilamatkailu Koivusalo, Vanhatie 386.
GPS: n62,96175 e22,77427.

3 € 20 included. **Location:** Rural, simple, quiet.
Surface: grassy/gravel. 01/01-31/12.
Distance: 4km 200m.
Remarks: Sauna € 10.

Hattu 4G1

Arhipan Pirtti. **GPS**: n62,92948 e31,28065.
€ 14 € 4 WC.
Distance: 300m on the spot.

Huittinen 4E2

ABC Huittinen, Loimijoentie 89. **GPS**: n61,16713 e22,68061.

7 € 5 Ch free.
Location: Urban, simple. **Surface:** asphalted. 01/01-31/12.
Distance: 1km 1km on the spot on the spot.

Ikaalinen 4E2

Ikaalisten Kylpylä Rantasipi, Hämyläntie 2.
GPS: n61,77586 e23,01928.

20 € 12 included WC. **Location:** Rural, simple, quiet.
Surface: asphalted. 01/01-31/12.
Distance: 3km on the spot on the spot on the spot.

Ilmarinen 4E3

Ilmaristen Matkailutila, Vääntelántie 45.
GPS: n60,49801 e22,37492.

6 € 15 (4x)€5/24h WC € 2 free.
Location: Rural, simple, quiet.
Surface: gravel. 01/01-31/12.
Distance: 2km 2km 1,5km 700m.

Kangasala 4E2

Mobilan Auto Kylä, Kustaa Kolmannen tie 75.
GPS: n61,44124 e24,12997.

5 free. **Location:** Rural, simple, quiet. **Surface:** asphalted.
01/01-31/12.
Distance: 6km 100m 100m.
Remarks: At museum.

Killinkoski 4E2

Killinkosken Kyläyhdistys, Inkantie 60. **GPS**: n62,40382 e23,89105.

5 free free.
Location: Rural, simple, quiet. **Surface:** grassy. 01/01-31/12.
Distance: on the spot on the spot 400m.

Lempäälä 4E2

Kärppälän Rustholli, Kärppäläntie 50. **GPS**: n61,33448 e23,67716.

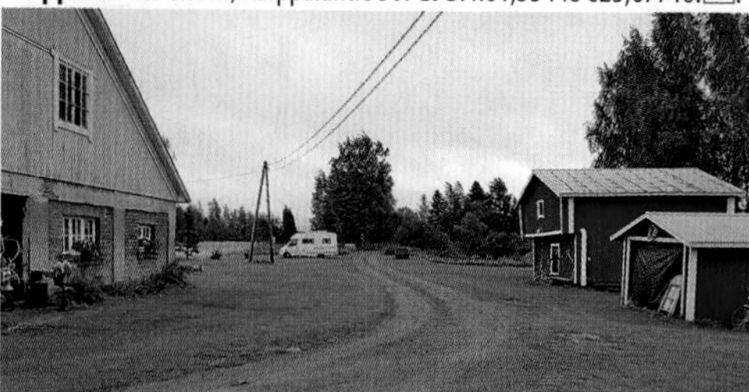

8 € 25 WC included.
Location: Rural. **Surface:** grassy. 01/01-31/12.
Distance: 6km 100m 100m.

Mieto 4E2

Hakunin kotieläintila, Hakunintie 193.
GPS: n62,57169 e22,26394.

2 € 10 included. **Location:** Rural, simple, isolated, quiet. **Surface:** grassy/gravel. 01/01-31/12.
Distance: 2km.
Remarks: Sauna € 10.

Nokia 4E2

ABC Nokia Kolmenkulma, Rounionkatu 140.
GPS: n61,50143 e23,56800.

10 € 5 Ch included (10x)€5/24h.
Location: Motorway, simple, noisy. **Surface:** asphalted.
01/01-31/12.
Distance: 2km on the spot on the spot on the spot.

Pyhäjärvi 4E1

Vaskikello Klokkenmuseum, Vaskikellontie 420.
GPS: n63,71402 e25,91985.

5 free free WC. **Location:** Motorway, simple, quiet.
Surface: asphalted.
Distance: 4km on the spot 200m.

FI

S Tuuri 4E2

Kyläkaupan Onnela Karavaanarialue, Onnelantie 45.
GPS: n62,60595 e23,71426.

243 € 20 Ch €5 WC included.
Location: Rural, luxurious, quiet. **Surface:** asphalted. 01/01-31/12.
Distance: 300m 300m.
Remarks: Swimming pool and sauna on site.

S Vaajakoski 4E2

ABC Vaajakoski, Vaajakoskentie 850. **GPS**: n62,22871 e25,90290.

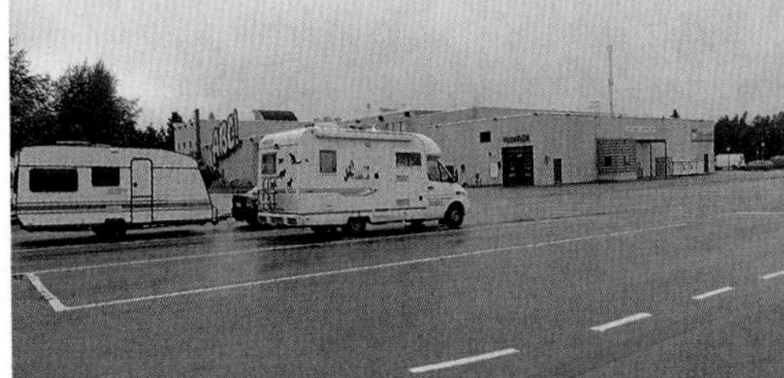

10 € 5 Ch included €5/24h at restaurant
Location: Motorway, noisy. **Surface:** asphalted. 01/01-31/12.
Distance: on the spot on the spot on the spot.

S Vaasa 4D2

ABC Kiitokaari Vaasa, Kiitokaari 2. **GPS**: n63,05239 e21,71773.

20 € 5 Ch included €5/24h at restaurant.
Location: Motorway, simple, noisy. **Surface:** asphalted.
01/01-31/12.
Distance: 8km on the spot on the spot on the spot.

S Viitasaari 4E1

ABC Viitasaari, Kokkosalmentie 78. **GPS**: n63,07527 e25,86618.

4 € 10 Ch (4x)included.
Location: Motorway, simple. **Surface:** asphalted. 01/01-31/12.
Distance: 1km on the spot on the spot on the spot on the spot on the spot.

S Ylönkylä 4E3

Katiskanmäki, Särkisalontie 2. **GPS**: n60,16479 e22,99639.

30 € 6 + € 5/pp Ch €5 WC included .
Location: Rural, simple, quiet.
Surface: gravel. 01/01-31/12.
Distance: 8km 5km 5km on the spot 8km.

Eastern Finland

S Heinävesi 4F2

Heinäveden satama, Kermarannantie 48.
GPS: n62,43835 e28,63796.

4 € 10 included WC.
Location: Rural, simple, quiet. **Surface:** asphalted. 01/01-31/12.
Distance: 2km on the spot.

S Iisalmi 4F1

Untamonkatu 6. **GPS**: n63,56465 e27,19025.

10 free. **Location:** Urban. **Surface:** asphalted. 01/01-31/12.
Distance: on the spot 800m 250m 250m.
Remarks: At gymnasium.

Iisalmi 4F1

Luuniemenkatu 11. **GPS**: n63,55102 e27,18841.

10 free. **Location:** Urban, simple, quiet. **Surface:** gravel.
01/01-31/12.
Distance: 2km 100m 100m 500m 500m.

Ilomantsi 4F1

Hyvinvointikeskus Toivonlahti, Henrikintie 4.
GPS: n62,67684 e30,91145.
12 € 10.
Distance: on the spot on the spot 200m.

S Jongunjoki 4F1

Eräkeskus Wilderness Lodge Oy, Alakylä 15.
GPS: n63,52483 e30,03822.

5 € 8 + € 4/pp Ch included €4/24h.
Location: Rural, simple, isolated, quiet, noisy. **Surface:** grassy/sand.
01/01-31/12.
Distance: 3km on the spot on the spot on the spot on the spot.

Karhunpää 4F1

Laitalan Lomat, Laitalantie 85. **GPS**: n63,61440 e28,86089.

10 € 12 stay WC included.
Location: Rural, quiet. **Surface:** grassy/gravel.
Distance: 9km on the spot on the spot on the spot.
Remarks: Sauna € 10.

S Lieksa 4F1

ABC Lieksa, Kalliokatu 8. **GPS**: n63,32240 e30,00854.
Ch . **Surface:** asphalted.
Distance: on the spot.

S Rantasalmi 4F2

Hotelli Rinssi-Eversti, Ohitustie 5. **GPS**: n62,06390 e28,30890.

6 € 10 Ch included (6x)€5/24h WC at restaurant at restaurant at restaurant. **Location:** Rural, simple, quiet.
Surface: asphalted. 01/01-31/12.
Distance: 300m 100m 100m on the spot 500m.
Remarks: Use of sauna against payment.

Sulkava 4F2

Alanteentie. **GPS**: n61,78528 e28,37769.

5 € 14 Ch WC included. **Location:** Urban, quiet.
Surface: asphalted. 01/01-31/12.
Distance: 500m on the spot on the spot 100m 500m.

Oulu

S Kontiomäki 4F1

Shell, Viitostie 2. **GPS**: n64,31988 e28,04344.
20 € 6 WC included . **Location:** Motorway.
Distance: on the spot.
Remarks: At petrol station.

S Puolanka 3D3

Pororajan Majoitus, Pudasjärventie 1. **GPS**: n64,87494 e27,64344.
8 € 12 €3 WC . **Surface:** asphalted. 01/01-31/12.
Distance: 1km 1km 1km on the spot.

S Sanginkylä 4E1

Valkeisen virkistysalueella, Puolangantie 207.
GPS: n64,86477 e26,74733.
€ 10 €2 .
Distance: on the spot on the spot.

S Siikajoki 4E1

Ruokolahden lava, Limingantie 197, Paavola.
GPS: n64,61267 e25,23947.
8 Ch €5 WC €15. **Location:** Rural. **Surface:** gravel.
23/05-06/09.
Distance: 2km on the spot on the spot.
Remarks: Key at kiosk.

S Ylivieska 4E1

Hotelli Käenpesä, Lintutie 1. **GPS**: n64,06782 e24,52621.
4 € 20 WC .
Distance: 800m on the spot.
Remarks: Check in at hotel.

FI

Lapland

S Anetjärvi 3D3

Aneen Loma, Anetjärventie 72A. **GPS**: n65,91851 e27,98786.
10 € 25 WC included. **Location:** Rural.
Distance: on the spot on the spot.
Remarks: At the beach, sauna incl..

S Tanhua 3C2

Tanhuan Erämajat, Pessijoentie 2. **GPS**: n67,52802 e27,53691.
10 € 5 Ch WC . **Surface:** grassy.
Distance: 300m.

S Tanhua 3C2

Tanhuan Erämajat, Pessijoentie 2. **GPS**: n67,52802 e27,53691.
10 € 5 Ch WC . **Surface:** grassy.
Distance: 300m.
Remarks: Use of sauna against payment.

Åland

S Keitele 4E1

Matkailukeskus Lossisaari, Sininentie 205.
GPS: n63,18941 e26,34270.

5 € 23 Ch WC included at restaurant.
Location: Rural, comfortable, quiet. **Surface:** grassy/gravel.
01/01-31/12.
Distance: 1,5km on the spot on the spot on the spot 1,5km.
Remarks: Behind petrol station, bread-service.

France

Capital: Paris
Government: Unitary republic
Official Language: French
Population: 66,300,000 (2015)
Area: 543,965 km²

General information
Dialling code: 0033
General emergency: 112
Currency: Euro
Payments by credit card are accepted almost everywhere, however chip and pin systems are non-compatible with British cards and fuel for example can only be bought at supermarkets during opening hours.

Regulations for overnight stays
Wild camping is accepted almost everywhere throughout inland France. Special regulations for motor homes you can find on signs by entering the town. It is permitted to stopover at motorway services, be aware that toll roads often issue time-constrained tickets.

Additional public holidays 2017
April 14 Good Friday
May 1 Labor Day
May 8 Liberation Day
July14 National Holiday
August15 Assumption of the Virgin Mary
November 1 All Saints Day
November 11 Armistice Day 1918

Time Zone
Winter (Standard Time) GMT+1
Summer (DST) GMT+2

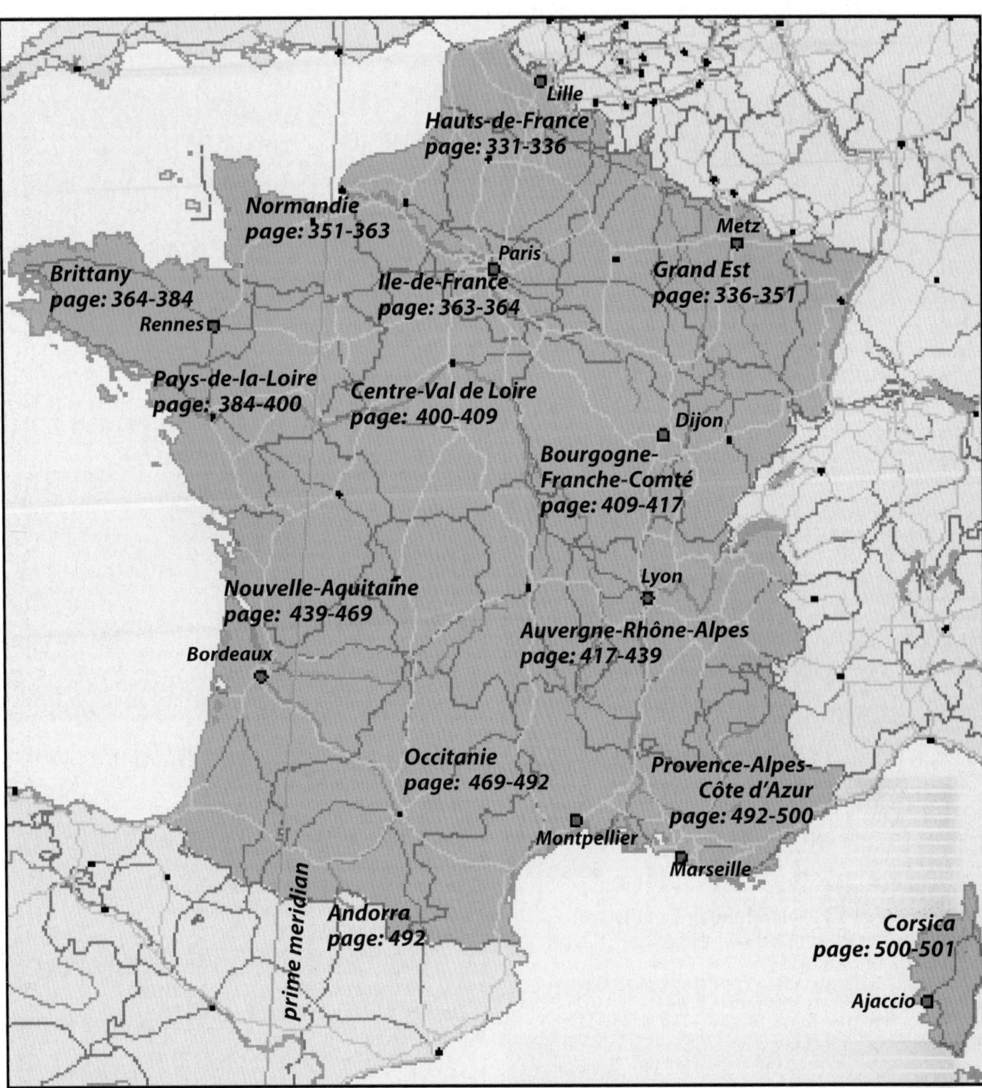

Hauts-de-France

Ambleteuse 13C2

D940 > Wimereux. **GPS**: n50,80638 e1,61484.

7 € 5. **Location:** Rural, simple, quiet. **Surface:** grassy.
Distance: 750m 1,2km.

Amiens 15H1

Boulevard Faidherbe. **GPS**: n49,89430 e2,28675.
free. **Location:** Urban, central. **Surface:** asphalted.
01/01-31/12.
Distance: centre 800m 300m 300m.

Amiens 15H1

Parc Moulin Saint-Pierre, Rue Massey. **GPS**: n49,90001 e2,31072.
free.
Location: Central. **Surface:** asphalted. 01/01-31/12.
Distance: city centre 2km.

Amiens 15H1

Parc des Cygnes, 111, Avenue des Cygnes. **GPS**: n49,92086 e2,25971.
5 € 11,70, 4 pers.incl Ch included. **Surface:** asphalted.
01/04-14/10.
Distance: city centre 5km 3km bus 50m.

Tourist information Amiens:
Office de Tourisme, 23 Place Notre Dame, www.amiens-tourisme.com. Capital of the department Somme.
St.Leu. Picturesque district.
Musée Picardie, 48, rue de la République. Archeology, Middle Ages, Fine art. Tue-Su 10-12h, 14-18h.
Zoo d'Amiens, 101, rue du Faubourg de Hem. City-zoo. 10-17h, 01/04-30/09 10-18h 16/11-31/01.

Arques 13D2

Rue Michelet. **GPS**: n50,74551 e2,30459.

20 € 3,50 €1,50 Ch €1,50. **Location:** Simple.
Surface: gravel. 01/04-31/10.
Distance: 2km 100m.
Remarks: Behind camp site Beauséjour.

Arras 13D3

Rue des Rosati. **GPS**: n50,29463 e2,78812.

10 free €2/100liter Ch €2/h.
Surface: asphalted. 01/01-31/12.
Distance: 700m 500m.

Tourist information Arras:
Hôtel de Ville. Town hall in Gothic style. Also guided tours of the subterranean passages of Arras.
Wed, Sa.

Bailleul 13D2

Rue du collège. **GPS**: n50,74010 e2,73170.

20 free. **Surface:** asphalted. 01/01-31/12.
Distance: 700m 2,8km.
Remarks: At commemorative monument.

Banteux 11A3

GPS: n50,06259 e3,20106.

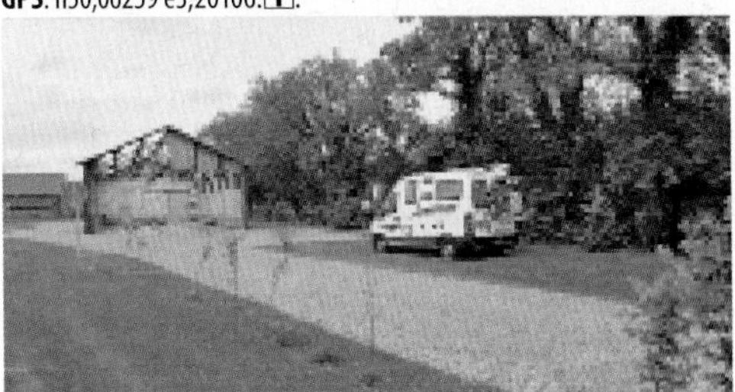

5 € 4 Ch free. **Location:** Rural, simple.
Surface: grassy/gravel. 01/01-31/12 service 01/11-31/03.
Distance: 500m 2,5km on the spot on the spot.

FR

Bapaume 13D3
Avenue Abel Guidet. **GPS**: n50,10133 e2,85045.

2 free €2 Ch.
Distance: 300m 300m.
Remarks: Coins at tourist info, town hall and bakery.

Bavay 11B3
Chemin de Ronde. **GPS**: n50,30004 e3,79551.
10 free Chfree. **Surface:** gravel. 01/01-31/12.
Distance: 200m 200m.

Beautor 16A1
Rue du Port. **GPS**: n49,66083 e3,34927.
3 free ChWC. 01/01-31/12.

Bellicourt 11A3
Hameau de Riqueval, D1044. **GPS**: n49,95156 e3,23519.

2 free Ch Service€4.
Surface: asphalted. 01/01-31/12 service: 01/10-31/03.
Distance: 300m on the spot on the spot.
Remarks: Coins at tourist info.

Berck-sur-Mer 13C3
Les Sternes, Chemin aux Raisins. **GPS**: n50,39701 e1,56431.

80 € 10 Chincluded. **Surface:** gravel. 01/01-31/12.
Distance: 1,5km 100m.
Remarks: Baker every morning.

Berck-sur-Mer 13C3
Parking Terminus, Rue Dr. Calot, Berck-Nord.
GPS: n50,42361 e1,56750.

40 € 10 Chincluded. **Location:** Simple. **Surface:** gravel.
01/01-31/12.
Distance: beach 200m.
Remarks: Beach parking.

Berck-sur-Mer 13C3
Chez Mireille, Chemin Genty. **GPS**: n50,41654 e1,57696.

80 € 8 €2 Ch (4x)€2/kWh free.
Surface: grassy. 01/04-31/10.
Distance: 600m 800m on the spot.
Remarks: To be paid at bar.

Tourist information Berck-sur-Mer:
Bagatelle, CD 940. Amusement park. Easter-Sep 10.30-18.30h.

Bergues 13D2
Rue Maurice Cornette. **GPS**: n50,96543 e2,43596.

50 free.
Location: Simple, quiet. **Surface:** gravel. 01/01-31/12.
Distance: 500m 2,2km.
Remarks: Behind football ground, max. 48h.

Bertry 11A3
Rue Victor Hugo. **GPS**: n50,09092 e3,44829.
3 free Ch . **Location:** Noisy.
Distance: on the spot 500m 700m.
Remarks: At station, max. 72h.

Blérancourt 16A1
Avenue de la Libération. **GPS**: n49,51285 e3,15035.
6 free Chfree. **Surface:** gravel. 01/01-31/12.
Distance: 750m.

Boulogne-sur-Mer 13C2
Parking Moulin Wibert, Boulevard Sainte Beuve, D940.
GPS: n50,74308 e1,59688.

40 € 6/24h €4/10minutes Ch . **Surface:** metalled.
Distance: centre 2,5km 5,5km on the spot on the spot.

Boulogne-sur-Mer 13C2
Boulevard Chanzy. **GPS**: n50,72194 e1,60027.

free. **Location:** Simple. **Surface:** asphalted.
Distance: 500m 4,5km 300m 300m.
Remarks: Nearby casino.

Tourist information Boulogne-sur-Mer:
Boulevard Clocheville. Wed-morning.
place Dalton, centre. Wed + Sa morning.
place Vignon. Su-morning.

Bourseville 13C3
Lotissement le Village. **GPS**: n50,10350 e1,52702.

35 € 5 €2 Ch €3. **Location:** Isolated, quiet.
Surface: asphalted. 01/01-31/12.
Distance: 500m 3km 500m 500m.

Boussois 11B3
Rue du Rivage. **GPS**: n50,28845 e4,04544.
4 Ch. **Surface:** gravel. 01/01-31/12.
Distance: 1km.

Bray-Dunes 13D2
Carrefour Market Bray Dunes, Rue Pierre Decock.
GPS: n51,06275 e2,52162.

6 free €2/10minutes Ch €2/h.
Location: Simple, noisy. **Surface:** grasstiles. 01/01-31/12.
Distance: on the spot.
Remarks: At supermarket Carrefour, only overnight stays 20-8.30h.

Bruyères-et-Montberault 16A1
Avenue de Verdun. **GPS**: n49,52538 e3,66080.

4 free. **Surface:** asphalted. 01/01-31/12.
Distance: 100m 100m 200m.

Calais 13C2
Digue Gaston Berthe. **GPS**: n50,96688 e1,84406.

60 free, 01/04-31/10 € 7/24h Ch WCincluded.
Location: Simple. **Surface:** asphalted.
Distance: 500m 100m 100m 100m.

Calais 13C2
Quai Edmond Pagniez. **GPS**: n50,96050 e1,84466.

100 free, 01/04-31/10 € 7/24h Ch included.
Location: Simple, noisy. **Surface:** asphalted. 01/01-31/12.
Distance: 300m 350m.
Remarks: Service: Digue Gaston Berthe.

FR

Tourist information Calais:
Centre d'Information Eurotunnel. Exhibition about the Channel tunnel.
Wed, Thu, Sa.

Cambrai 11A3
Grand Carré. **GPS**: n50,18515 e3,22587.
6 €8 Ch included. **Location:** Comfortable, quiet.
Surface: asphalted. 01/01-31/12.
Distance: 1,5km 750m.

Cassel 13D2
Route d'Oxelaere, C301. **GPS**: n50,79328 e2,48852.

5 free €2 Ch €2. **Location:** Isolated, quiet.
Surface: gravel. 01/01-31/12.
Distance: 1km.
Remarks: At sports park, coins at tourist info.

Catillon-sur-Sambre 11A3
Avenue de la Groise, N43. **GPS**: n50,07624 e3,64615.

5 €5 Ch included. **Surface:** asphalted. 01/01-31/12.
Distance: 200m on the spot.
Remarks: At the canal, max. 72h.

Catillon-sur-Sambre 11A3
Rue de la Gare. **GPS**: n50,07699 e3,64404.

20 free. **Surface:** gravel. 01/01-31/12.
Distance: 500m on the spot.
Remarks: At the canal.

Cayeux-sur-Mer 13C3
Aire de camping-cars Les Galets de la Mollière, Rue Faidherbe.
GPS: n50,20300 e1,52612.

30 €7 €3 Ch. **Surface:** gravel. 01/05-01/11.
Distance: 2km At the sea, no beach 2km 2km.
Remarks: To be paid at campsite.

Cayeux-sur-Mer 13C3
Route blanche, Le Hourdel, D102. **GPS**: n50,21448 e1,55208.

30 free. **Location:** Simple, isolated, quiet. **Surface:** gravel.
01/01-31/12.
Distance: 500m, Cayeux 6km sea 50m 500m 3km.

Château-Thierry 16A2
Aire de Château, Avenue d'Essômes. **GPS**: n49,03657 e3,38365.

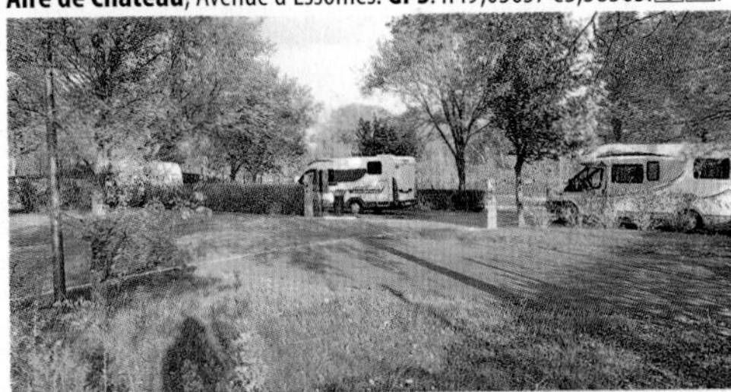

13 €7, tourist tax € 0,20/pp Ch €4/24h WC included.
Location: Urban, comfortable. **Surface:** asphalted.
01/01-31/12.
Distance: centre 1,8km on the spot on the spot on the spot on the spot on the spot on the spot.
Remarks: Along the Marne river.

Chavignon 16A2
Le domaine de ZAZA, La Fontaine Dubois.
GPS: n49,47941 e3,53396.
5 €6 Ch included €3. **Surface:** gravel.
Remarks: Check in at museum.

Comines 11A2
Ferme Hélicicole, Chemin de l'Apothicaire. **GPS**: n50,74190 e3,02322.

6 €5 €2/10minutes Ch €3/24h. **Surface:** gravel.
Distance: 3,5km on the spot on the spot.

Conty 15G1
Rue du Marais. **GPS**: n49,74333 e2,15583.

70 free €2/100liter Ch WC.
Surface: grassy. 01/01-31/12.
Distance: 200m 6,5km 300m 300m 300m.
Remarks: Coins at tourist info, town hall and bakery.

Coucy-le-Château-Auffrique 16A1
Chemin du Val Serain. **GPS**: n49,52037 e3,31150.

6 €5 Ch included. **Location:** Rural, comfortable.

Surface: gravel. 01/01-31/12.
Distance: 500m on the spot 500m.
Remarks: Castle 1km.

Crespin 11B3
Rue du Vivier. **GPS**: n50,41950 e3,66274.
3 free €2 Ch.
Remarks: At cemetery, coins at town hall.

Doullens 13D3
Rue du Pont à l'Avoine, N25-Arras-Amiens. **GPS**: n50,15390 e2,34260.

4 free €2 €2. **Surface:** asphalted. 01/01-31/12.

Embry 13C2
Les Salons de l'Embryenne, D108. **GPS**: n50,49534 e1,96610.

8 €7 €3 Ch €3/4h WC €3/12minutes
Location: Isolated, quiet. **Surface:** gravel.
01/01-31/12.
Remarks: Bread-service, video surveillance, picnic and barbecue place.

Enquin-les-Mines 13D2
La Ferme des Templiers de Flechinelle, 2 Rue des Templiers, Fléchinelle. **GPS**: n50,58175 e2,30505.
4 €7 Ch included. **Surface:** gravel. 01/01-31/12.
Distance: on the spot.

Equihen-Plage 13C2
Plage de la Crevasse, Rue du Beurre Fondu.
GPS: n50,67993 e1,56830.

20 €7 €3/10minutes Ch (6x)€6/12h
Location: Comfortable, quiet. **Surface:** grassy/gravel.
01/01-31/12.
Distance: 100m 100m 100m 100m.

Esquelbecq 13D2
Parking de la Chenaie, Rue d'Arneke. **GPS**: n50,88395 e2,43119.
free. **Surface:** asphalted.
Distance: 200m 200m.

Estaires 13D2
Rue de Merville. **GPS**: n50,64354 e2,71866.

3 free €2/10minutes Ch €2/1h (3x)€4/12h.
Distance: 200m 150m.
Remarks: Cash payment.

FR

Fort Mahon Plage 13C3

Plage Parking de la Dune, Rue de la Bistouille.
GPS: n50,33833 e1,55611.

60 €9 ChWCfree. **Surface:** gravel. 01/01-31/12.
Distance: 200m 600m 200m.

Grand-Fort-Philippe 13D2

Rue Maréchal Foch. **GPS**: n51,00249 e2,09718.
. 01/01-31/12.
Remarks: In front of campsite.

Grand-Fort-Philippe 13D2

Bd Carnot. **GPS**: n51,00142 e2,10851.
8 free. **Surface:** asphalted. 01/01-31/12.
Distance: on the spot 600m.
Remarks: At the canal, temporary stopover.

Grandvilliers 15G1

Place de la Censé. **GPS**: n49,66536 e1,93576.
3 free ChWCfree. **Surface:** asphalted. 01/01-31/12.
Distance: 100m 100m 400m.

Gravelines 13D2

Parking des Miaules, Rue des Islandais/Rue du Port.
GPS: n50,98766 e2,12232.

20 €7. **Location:** Rural, simple, quiet. **Surface:** gravel.
01/01-31/12.
Distance: 500m nearby 300m.

Gravelines 13D2

Rue de la Gendarmerie. **GPS**: n50,99342 e2,13177.
€2 Ch .

Hardelot 13C2

Place R.L. Peeters. **GPS**: n50,63500 e1,59888.

free. **Location:** Simple. **Surface:** asphalted. 01/01-31/12.
Distance: 1,7km.

Hautmont 11B3

Yacht Club Hautmont, Boulevard de l'Ecluse. **GPS**: n50,25090 e3,91206.
5 €7 Ch WC included. **Surface:** grassy.
Distance: 600m 600m 600m.
Remarks: Pay at harbourmaster, caution key € 20.

Hondschoote 13D2

Impasse Spinnewyn. **GPS**: n50,97628 e2,58033.

8 free €2/100liter Ch €2/1h. **Location:** Simple.
Surface: asphalted.
Distance: 800m 800m 800m 300m on the spot on the spot.
Remarks: Behind Moulin de la Victoire, coins available, addresses indicated on the spot.

La Chapelle-Monthodon 16A2

1 hameau de Chézy. **GPS**: n49,02904 e3,63616.
5 free. **Location:** Rural, isolated, quiet. 01/01-31/12.

Landrecies 11B3

Avenue Dumey. **GPS**: n50,12715 e3,69007.
4 . 01/01-31/12.

Laôn 16A1

Promenade de la Couloire. **GPS**: n49,56313 e3,62967.

7 free. **Surface:** metalled. 01/01-31/12.
Distance: 300m 500m.
Remarks: Near city wall.

Laôn 16A1

Rue du Maréchal Alphonse Juin. **GPS**: n49,55665 e3,16411.
6 free. **Surface:** metalled. 01/01-31/12.
Distance: on the spot on the spot.
Remarks: Medieval village.

Le Crotoy 13C3

Camping-Car Park le Tarteron, Route de Rue.
GPS: n50,22972 e1,64128.

24 € 10/24h Ch included.
Location: Noisy. **Surface:** gravel. 01/01-31/12.
Distance: 2km 2km 2km.

Le Crotoy 13C3

Aire Camping-car, Bassin des Chasses. **GPS**: n50,21800 e1,63300.

50 €7/24h €2/100liter Ch €2/1h.
Surface: sand. 01/01-31/12.
Distance: 5 min walking 15 min walking Laverie Crotelloise, 20, avenue du Gal de Gaulle.

Le Crotoy 13C3

Aire du Marais, Chemin du Marais. **GPS**: n50,22855 e1,61222.

35 €7/24h €2/10minutes Ch €2/1h.
Surface: grassy/gravel. 01/01-31/12.
Distance: 1,5km on the spot 1,5km Laverie Crotelloise, 20, avenue du Gal de Gaulle on the spot on the spot.

Le Nouvion-en-Thiérache 11B3

Allée du S/I François d'Orléans. **GPS**: n50,00542 e3,78078.
5 €3 Ch . **Location:** Rural. **Surface:** asphalted.
01/01-31/12.
Distance: 2km.
Remarks: Max. 72h, coins at campsite.

Le Portel 13C2

Rue des Champs. **GPS**: n50,71188 e1,57485.

40 €5 €2/100liter Ch €2/4h
Surface: metalled. 01/01-31/12.
Distance: 200m 300m 300m 300m.
Remarks: Next to sports fields, 300m from beach (stairs), friday market.

Le Touquet-Paris Plage 13C2

Parc International de la Canoke, Boulevard de la Canche.
GPS: n50,52648 e1,59869.

100 € 10 €2/100liter Ch €2/55minutes.
Surface: grassy/gravel. 01/01-31/12.
Distance: 10 min walking on the spot on the spot on the spot on the spot.

Le Touquet-Paris Plage 13C2

Centre Nautique du Touquet Base Nord, Avenue Jean Ruet.
GPS: n50,53588 e1,59285.

60 € 15 €2/100liter Ch €2/55minutes.
Surface: asphalted. 01/01-31/12.
Distance: 10 min walking on the spot on the spot on the spot on the spot.

Tourist information Le Touquet-Paris Plage:
Aqualud. Leisure pool park. 15/02-30/11 10-18h.

Le-Cateau-Cambrésis 11A3

Avenue du Maréchal Leclerc, N43. **GPS**: n50,10197 e3,55491.

5 free Ch free. **Surface:** asphalted. 01/01-31/12.
Distance: 1km.

Lens 13D3

Stade Bollaert-Delelis P6, Rue Maurice Fréchet.
GPS: n50,43192 e2,82057.

FR

6 free Ch free against payment. **Location:** Simple.
Surface: asphalted. 01/01-31/12.
Distance: 500m on the spot 1km on the spot.
Remarks: Max. 24h.

Long 13C3

Camping Municipal La Peupleraie, Rue de la Chasse à Vaches.
GPS: n50,03457 e1,98313.

8 €5 €2 Ch free €2/h WC. **Surface:** grassy/gravel.
01/01-31/12 service: 16/10-30/04.
Distance: on the spot on the spot.

Longfossé 13C2

Ferme du Louvet, 5, Route de Wierre, D52 Desvres > Samer.
GPS: n50,64667 e1,79062.

8 €5 €3 Ch €2/12h. **Location:** Rural, isolated, quiet.
Surface: gravel.
Remarks: Narrow entrance.

Longpont 16A2

Rue Saint-Louis, D17. **GPS**: n49,27395 e3,22129.

3 free 100liter Ch 10minutes, service €3.
Location: Rural. **Surface:** gravel. 01/01-31/12.
Distance: 100m.
Remarks: Max. 72h, abbey 150m.

Luzoir 16B1

Place de l'Église. **GPS**: n49,92520 e3,96261.
2 free. 01/01-31/12.
Remarks: Max. 48h.

Maisnil-lès-Ruitz 13D3

Parc d'Olhain, Rue de Rebreuve. **GPS**: n50,43926 e2,57826.

33 € 14,80 Ch included. **Location:** Comfortable, isolated, quiet. **Surface:** gravel. 01/01-31/12.
Remarks: Recreation park.

Malzy 16B1

Étangs des Sources, 16 rue des Marichoux.
GPS: n49,90602 e3,72153.
4 €5 €2 €2 Ch €2 €2. **Location:** Rural.
Surface: grassy. 15/03-01/11 Tue, Thu.
Distance: on the spot.
Remarks: Fishing lake (trout).

Marck 13C2

La Ferme des Aigrettes, Allée de la Découverte.
GPS: n50,95626 e1,92830.

5 €8 Ch included. **Location:** Comfortable, quiet.
Surface: asphalted.
Distance: 250m on the spot.
Remarks: Max. 48h, call for entrance code.

Marcoing 11A3

Place de la Gare. **GPS**: n50,12126 e3,18204.
6 free Ch.
Distance: 1km 1km.

Merlimont 13C3

Place de la Gare. **GPS**: n50,46026 e1,58053.

12 free. **Location:** Simple. **Surface:** gravel. 01/01-31/12.
Distance: on the spot.

Mers-les-Bains 13C3

Chemin de la Petite Allée. **GPS**: n50,06175 e1,40150.

50 €7,50 €2 Ch included. **Location:** Comfortable.
Surface: gravel. 01/01-31/12.
Distance: 1,3km sandy beach 1,5km Auchan 600m.

Montreuil-sur-Mer 13C3

Avenue des Garennes. **GPS**: n50,45944 e1,75939.

8 free €2/100liter Ch (2x)€2 WC free.
Location: Comfortable. **Surface:** asphalted. 01/01-31/12.
Distance: 500m 300m 450m.
Remarks: Max. 48h, market Saturday.

Morienval 15H2

Route de Pierrefonds 32. **GPS**: n49,30352 e2,92309.

25 €8 €2/100liter Ch (21x)€2/day. **Location:** Rural, comfortable, quiet. **Surface:** grassy/gravel. 22/03-16/11.
Distance: 500m 500m 500m on the spot on the spot.
Remarks: In case of absence, money in an envelope in mail box.

Neuilly-Saint-Front 16A2

Chemin de la Chantraine. **GPS**: n49,16713 e3,26003.
20 free €3 Ch €3/55minutes. **Surface:** grassy.
Distance: 600m.

Nuncq-Hautecôte 13D3

La Pommeraie, 13, route nationale. **GPS**: n50,30516 e2,29375.

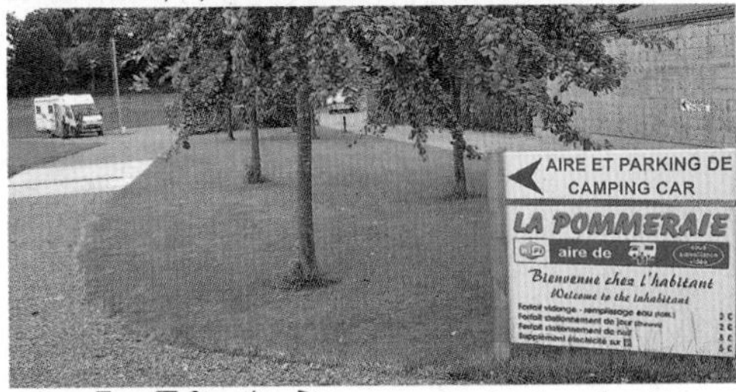

5 €5 €2 Ch €5 free. **Location:** Rural, comfortable, quiet. **Surface:** gravel. 01/01-31/12.
Distance: 50m.
Remarks: Covered pool € 3.

Oye-plage 13D2

Les Huttes d'Oye Plage. **GPS**: n50,99703 e2,04228.

10 free.
Location: Simple. **Surface:** gravel. 01/01-31/12.
Distance: on the spot 100m on the spot.
Remarks: Beach parking, service Oye-Plage: 50,97713 2,03966.

Picquigny 13D3

Rue de la Cavée d'Airaines. **GPS**: n49,94388 e2,13496.

8 €5 Ch €2 WC included.
Location: Rural. **Surface:** grassy.
Distance: 500m 500m.

Quend 13C3

Ferme de la Grande Retz. **GPS**: n50,32893 e1,61811.

10 €7 Ch €3 included. **Surface:** grassy.
01/01-31/12.

FR

Distance: 3km 9km 9km 2km.

S Quend-plage-les-Pins 13C3

Plage des Pins. GPS: n50,32410 e1,55545.

100 € 7/24h €3/10minutes Ch €3/1h.
Surface: gravel. 01/01-31/12.
Distance: 800m beach 900m on the spot.

S Richebourg 13D2

Rue de la Briqueterie. **GPS:** n50,58028 e2,74639.

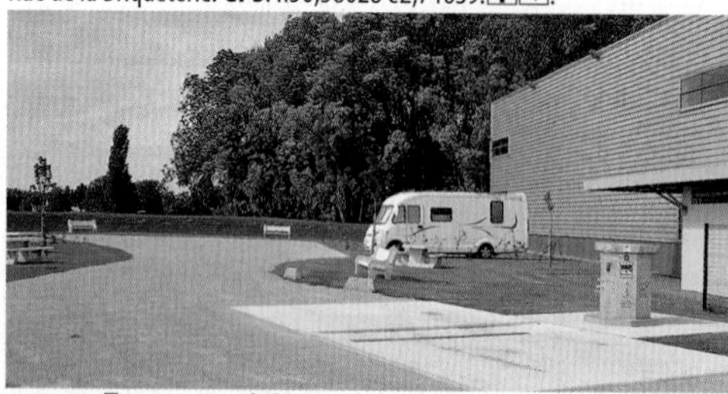

6 free €2/100liter €2/55minutes included. **Location:** Rural, comfortable. **Surface:** grassy. 01/01-31/12.
Distance: 500m on the spot on the spot.
Remarks: Max. 48h.

S Rozoy-sur-Serre 16B1

Portes de la Thiérache, Rue de la Praille. **GPS:** n49,71367 e4,12202.
5 free €2/120liter Ch. **Surface:** gravel. 01/01-31/12.
Distance: 1km 1km.

S Saint-Omer 13D2

De Haut Pont, Rue de la Gaieté. **GPS:** n50,75654 e2,25943.

13 € 5 €2 Ch €2 . **Location:** Simple, noisy.
Surface: asphalted/gravel. 01/01-31/12.
Distance: 900m 900m.
Remarks: Max. 72h.

S Saint-Valery-sur-Somme 13C3

Rue de la Croix l'Abbé. **GPS:** n50,18220 e1,62881.

180 € 9/24h Ch included.
Location: Rural. **Surface:** gravel. 01/01-31/12.
Distance: 1km nearby nearby.
Remarks: Market on Sunday.

Stella-plage 13C3

Cours des Champs Elysées. **GPS:** n50,47470 e1,57726.

30 free. **Location:** Simple, isolated. **Surface:** asphalted.
Distance: 1km on the spot 650m.
Remarks: Parking at dune.

Tardinghen 13C2

Le site des 2 caps, La Fleur des Champs.
GPS: n50,86281 e1,64907.

15 € 6/24h. **Surface:** grassy. 01/01-31/12.
Distance: 2km 2km.

S Tardinghen 13C2

Le site des 2 caps, La Ferme d'Horloge, 1615 Route d'Ausques, D249.
GPS: n50,86250 e1,64890.

30 € 6/24h €4 Ch €4/24h . **Location:** Comfortable, isolated, quiet. **Surface:** metalled. 01/01-31/12.
Distance: 1,6km.
Remarks: Swin-golf € 5.

Tardinghen 13C2

Le site des 2 caps, Le Fond de Sombre, Hervelinghen > Wissant.
GPS: n50,89361 e1,68972.

10 € 6/24h. **Location:** Simple, isolated, quiet. **Surface:** grassy.
01/01-31/12.
Distance: 1km.

S Tergnier 16A1

Base de loisirs de La Frette, Rue de la Prairie.
GPS: n49,64891 e3,31200.
20 free, 01/05-30/09 € 7 €3/100liter Ch €3/30minutes.
01/01-31/12.
Distance: 1,5km on the spot on the spot.

S Villers-Cötterets 16A2

Rue Alfred Juneaux. **GPS:** n49,26052 e3,08713.

6 free 100liter Ch 10minutes,service €3 .
Location: Urban, comfortable, quiet. **Surface:** gravel/metalled.
01/01-31/12.
Distance: on the spot 600m 600m.
Remarks: Max. 72h, service 50m.

S Watten 13D2

3 Rue Paul Mortier. **GPS:** n50,83101 e2,20887.

3 free €2 Ch €2/55minutes. **Location:** Simple, quiet.
Surface: metalled. 01/01-31/12.
Distance: 500m 500m 500m on the spot.
Remarks: Coins at tourist info, supermarket, tabac-press and cafe, max. 3 nights.

S Wissant 13C2

Parking Wissant, Avenue Georges Clémenceau.
GPS: n50,88684 e1,67064.

30 free Ch free. **Surface:** metalled. 01/01-31/12.
Distance: 700m 1,1km.
Remarks: Bread-service.

Grand Est

Abainville 16D3

Les Forges, Rue de la Dîme. **GPS:** n48,52944 e5,49556.
2 free. 01/01-31/12.
Distance: 500m.

S Aix-en-Othe 18H1

Aire du Moulin à Tan. GPS: n48,22901 e3,00000.
6 € 6 Ch included €2,50 WC . **Location:** Rural.
Surface: grassy. 01/04-15/10.
Distance: 1km 1km.

S Allarmont 19F1

Le Meix du Haut Regard, 21, rue du Haut Regard.
GPS: n48,48070 e7,01381.

2 € 5 included Ch €5/24h €4 free.
Location: Simple. **Surface:** gravel. 01/01-31/12.
Distance: 400m 400m 400m.
Remarks: Steep ramp.

S Amnéville 16E2

Rue de l'Europe. **GPS:** n49,24780 e6,13842.

10 € 9-12 Ch included. **Location:** Rural, simple, quiet.

FR

Surface: grassy. 01/01-31/12.
Distance: 1,8km.
Remarks: Max. 48h, pay at tourist office.

Ancerville 16C3

Impasse des Pransons. **GPS**: n48,63641 e5,01582.

2 free. **Location:** Urban, simple, quiet. **Surface:** grasstiles.
01/01-31/12.
Distance: on the spot 400m 400m.

Arc-en-Barrois 19C2

Camping municipal, D3/D159. **GPS**: n47,95056 e5,00528.

25 €5 Ch WC included, on campsite.
Location: Simple. **Surface:** gravel. 01/01-31/12 Whitsuntide.
Distance: 500m 500m 500m.

Avioth 16D1

Rue de l'Hôpital. **GPS**: n49,56561 e5,39067.
2 free. 01/01-31/12.

Avize 16B3

Place du Bourg Joli. **GPS**: n48,97175 e4,00999.

5 free Ch free. **Location:** Urban, simple, central, quiet.
Surface: asphalted. 01/01-31/12.
Distance: on the spot 200m bakery 50m.
Remarks: Next to town hall.

Avocourt 16D2

Restaurant La Terrasse, Rue du Moulin. **GPS**: n49,20417 e5,14227.

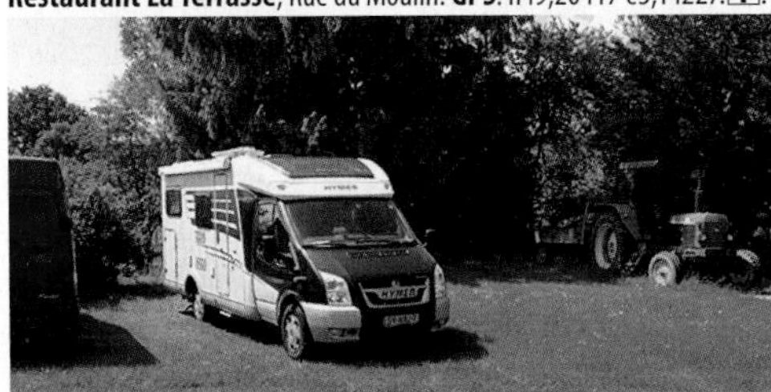

4 free.
Location: Rural, simple. **Surface:** grassy. 01/01-31/12.
Distance: on the spot on the spot.

Azannes-et-Soumazannes 16D2

Les Vieux Métiers, Domaine des Roises. **GPS**: n49,31096 e5,47714.
2 free.

Baccarat 19F1

Place du General Le'Clerc. **GPS**: n48,44667 e6,74000.

15 €4 Ch €2/3minutes WC. **Location:** Simple.
Surface: asphalted. 01/01-31/12 Fri-morning market.
Distance: 300m on the spot on the spot 300m 300m.
Remarks: Along river, max. 24h.

Tourist information Baccarat:
M Musée du Cristal. Crystal museum. Mo-Sa 10-18h.

Bar-le-Duc 16D3

Halte du port Fluvial, Rue du Débarcadère.
GPS: n48,77536 e5,16654.

7 free €2,10/100liter Ch €2,10/55minutes.
Location: Urban, simple, noisy.
Surface: asphalted.
01/01-31/12.
Distance: on the spot 150m 150m 150m on the spot.
Remarks: At the canal, coins at tourist info, 7 rue Jeanne d'Arc.

Bar-sur-Aube 19C1

7, Rue des Varennes. **GPS**: n48,23491 e4,70065.

3 free €3,50/100liter Ch €3,50/1h. **Location:** Simple.
Surface: asphalted. 01/01-31/12.
Distance: on the spot on the spot on the spot.

Beaulieu-en-Argonne 16C2

Parking Mairie, Grande Rue, D2B. **GPS**: n49,03183 e5,06665.

6 free. **Location:** Urban, simple, central, quiet. **Surface:** grassy.
01/01-31/12.
Distance: on the spot 50m on the spot on the spot.
Remarks: In front of town hall.

Beaulieu-en-Argonne 16C2

Parking St. Rouin, D2. **GPS**: n49,03554 e5,02975.

4 free.
Location: Rural, simple, isolated. **Surface:** grassy/gravel.
Distance: Beaulieu 6km.
Remarks: Isolated parking.

Beaunay 16B3

Ferme Du Bel Air, Rue Principale. **GPS**: n48,88177 e3,87475.

12 €8 Ch (6x)included . **Location:** Rural, simple, isolated, quiet. **Surface:** gravel. 01/01-31/12.
Distance: 2km 2km 2km.

Benfeld 19G1

Concessionnaire CLC Alsace, 9, Rue de Hollande, RN83 dir Strasbourg-Colmar. **GPS**: n48,37772 e7,59778.

5 free Ch free. **Location:** Motorway, simple, noisy.
Surface: asphalted. 01/01-31/12.
Distance: 2km 2km 2km.
Remarks: At motorhome dealer.

Bitche 16G2

Rue Bombelles. **GPS**: n49,05431 e7,43446.
5 free €2 Ch €2. **Location:** Comfortable, isolated, quiet.
Surface: gravel.
Distance: 750m 750m 750m.

Bogny-sur-Meuse 16C1

Rue de la Meuse. **GPS**: n49,85780 e4,74225.

6 free €2/100liter Ch €2/2h, only 2-euro coins.
Location: Rural, simple, quiet. **Surface:** asphalted.
01/01-31/12.
Distance: on the spot on the spot 250m 400m 500m.
Remarks: Along the Meuse river, service 75m.

Bonzée 16D2

Parking de la Base de Loisirs du Colvert. **GPS**: n49,09806 e5,61551.
6 . 01/01-31/12.
Distance: 1km on the spot.

Bourbach-le-Haut 19F2

Route Joffre. **GPS**: n47,79463 e7,02868.

10 €6 Ch included. **Location:** Rural, simple, quiet.
Surface: asphalted. 15/03-15/11.
Distance: 50m 100m 5km.
Remarks: In front of fire-station.

Brienne-le-Château 19C1

Rue de la Gare. **GPS**: n48,39617 e4,53130.

FR

10 free €3/10minutes Ch €3/55minutes.
Location: Simple, noisy. **Surface:** asphalted.
01/01-31/12 water disconnected in winter.
Distance: 300m 400m 300m.
Remarks: At former station, coins at tourist info, supermarket Champion.

Bruley 16E3

D118, rue Saint-Martin. **GPS**: n48,70640 e5,85554.

10 free €3/10minutes Ch (2x)€3/8h.
Location: Comfortable, quiet. **Surface:** gravel. 01/01-31/12.
Distance: 200m 300m 300m.
Remarks: Max. 48h.

Bulgnéville 19E1

Étang des Récollets, Rue des Récollets.
GPS: n48,20733 e5,83899.

10 € 3/24h Ch WC included. **Location:** Rural, luxurious, quiet.
Surface: asphalted. 15/04-31/12.
Distance: 700m 1,8km on the spot on the spot 100m 700m.

Cerisières 19C1

D186, Froideau. **GPS**: n48,29921 e5,06339.

20 free Ch free. **Location:** Rural, simple, isolated, quiet.
Surface: gravel. 01/01-31/12.
Distance: 2km.

Certilleux 19D1

Rue de l'Église. **GPS**: n48,31193 e5,72679.

8 free free. **Location:** Urban, simple. **Surface:** asphalted.
01/01-31/12.
Distance: on the spot.

Remarks: Beautiful view.

Chamery 16B2

Salle Polyvalente, Rue du Château Rouge.
GPS: n49,17475 e3,95446.

3 free €2/100liter Ch €2/2h. **Location:** Rural, simple, quiet. **Surface:** gravel. 01/01-31/12.
Distance: 300m 400m.
Remarks: In front of community centre, max. 48h.

Champigny-lès-Langres 19D2

Rue du Port, D74. **GPS**: n47,88167 e5,33861.

5 free WC. **Location:** Simple, noisy. **Surface:** gravel.
01/01-31/12.
Distance: 400m 800m.

Champougny 16D3

D145f. **GPS**: n48,54410 e5,69277.

3 free. **Location:** Rural, simple, quiet. **Surface:** grassy.
01/01-31/12.
Distance: 200m 25m.

Chaource 19B1

Chemin de Ronde/Rue des Roises. **GPS**: n48,05944 e4,13861.

10 € 2 €2/100liter Ch €2/1h.
Location: Comfortable, quiet. **Surface:** grassy.
01/01-31/12.
Distance: 100m on the spot on the spot on the spot on the spot.
Remarks: Coins at tourist info, 2, Grande rue, monday-morning market.

Charleville-Mézières 16C1

Rue des Pâquis. **GPS**: n49,78056 e4,72056.

8 free €2/100liter Ch €2/55minutes €5,40.
Surface: asphalted.
01/01-31/12 electricity: 01/11-31/03.
Distance: 800m on the spot 500m 2km 600m on the spot on the spot.
Remarks: Service only with 2-euro coins, ask for electricity at campsite.

Tourist information Charleville-Mézières:
Musée Ardennes, Place Ducale. Regional museum. 10-12, 14-18 Mo.
place Ducale. Regional products. Tue, Thu, Sa.

Charmes 19E1

Port de Plaisance. GPS: n48,37334 e6,29542.

80 € 7 included Ch (80x)€2 WC €1,50 €3/day.
Location: Urban, central. **Surface:** grassy/metalled.
01/01-31/12.
Distance: 1km 1,5km on the spot on the spot.

Tourist information Charmes:
Fri-morning.

Châtenois 19G1

Allee des Bains 10. **GPS**: n48,27476 e7,39853.

7 free €2 Ch WC free. **Location:** Urban, simple, quiet.
Surface: asphalted/grassy. 01/01-31/12.
Distance: 400m 250m.
Remarks: Max. 24h.

Chaumont 19D1

Port de la Maladière, RN74 Neufchâteau > Chaumont.
GPS: n48,11815 e5,15437.

12 € 6,95, tourist tax € 0,20/pp Ch WC €2,40 €2,35/3,35 included.
Location: Quiet. **Surface:** metalled. 02/04-31/10.
Distance: 4km Canal de la Marne 100m nearby.
Remarks: Baker every morning.

Chavanges 16C3

Ruelle du Fief Berthaux. **GPS**: n48,50691 e4,57627.

8 free €3 Ch . **Location:** Simple, quiet.
Surface: asphalted/gravel. 01/01-31/12.
Distance: 300m 400m.
Remarks: Coins at the shops.

FR

Chavannes-sur-l'Etang 19F2

Aire pique-nique La Porte d'Alsace, RD419, Rue d'Alsace.
GPS: n47,63325 e7,01858.

15 € 8 Ch WCfree. **Location:** Rural, simple, comfortable, quiet. **Surface:** asphalted. 01/01-31/12.
Distance: 900m on the spot 900m 1km on the spot on the spot.
Remarks: Parking picnic area.

Colmar 19G1

Port de Plaisance de Colmar, 6 rue du Canal.
GPS: n48,08054 e7,37599.

25 € 11-15 + € 0,22/pp tourist tax Ch WC €3/2 included. **Location:** Rural, comfortable, quiet.
Surface: asphalted/grassy. 01/01-31/12.
Distance: 1,3km 200m on the spot on the spot on the spot.
Remarks: Baker 8.30-09.00.

Colmar 19G1

Rue de la Cavalerie. **GPS**: n48,08218 e7,35990.
20 € 3/h. **Location:** Urban, simple, central, noisy.
Surface: asphalted.
Distance: 200m on the spot on the spot on the spot.
Remarks: Max. 4h.

Colmar 19G1

Rue Henry Wilhelm. **GPS**: n48,08366 e7,35527.
16 € 3/h. **Location:** Urban, simple, central.
Surface: asphalted. 01/01-31/12.
Distance: 400m 400m 400m.
Remarks: Max. 4h.

Colombey-les-deux-Eglises 19C1

Rue de Général de Gaulle. **GPS**: n48,22316 e4,88619.

10 free Ch WC free. **Location:** Simple, quiet.
Surface: asphalted/gravel. 01/01-31/12.
Distance: on the spot 50m 50m.
Remarks: Museum and Memorial Général De Gaulle 800m.

Commercy 16D3

Rue du Docteur Boyer. **GPS**: n48,76374 e5,59616.

4 free €3/15minutes Ch (4x)€3/4h free.
Location: Comfortable. **Surface:** asphalted. 01/01-31/12.
Distance: 800m on the spot on the spot 600m 100m.
Remarks: On the canal.

Commercy 16D3

Parking de la Boîte à Madeleines, Rue de la Louvière.
GPS: n48,75378 e5,59928.
3 free. **Surface:** asphalted.
Distance: 1km.

Consenvoye 16D2

Gr la Grande Rue. **GPS**: n49,28547 e5,28403.

5 free free.
Location: Urban, simple, quiet. **Surface:** asphalted.
Distance: 100m on the spot 50m.

Contrisson 16C3

Ballastière. **GPS**: n48,80530 e4,94714.

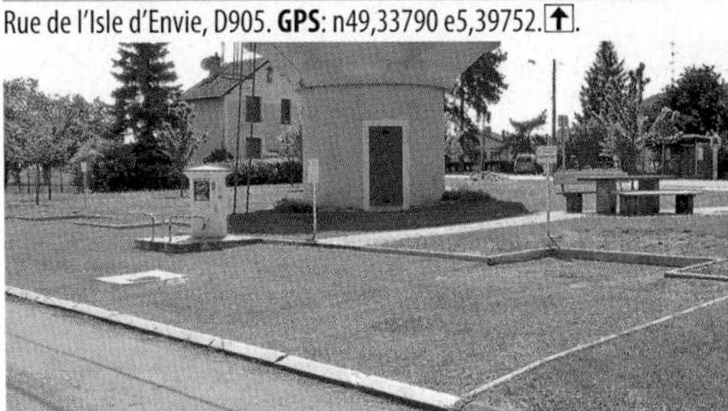

10 free WC. **Location:** Rural, simple, isolated, quiet.
Surface: grassy/sand. 01/01-31/12.
Distance: 800m on the spot on the spot 1km 1km.
Remarks: At small lake.

Corgirnon 19D2

Allée du Parc. **GPS**: n47,80681 e5,50308.

8 € 5 Ch included.
Location: Rural, comfortable, isolated, quiet. **Surface:** gravel.
01/01-31/12 water disconnected in winter.
Distance: 500m 10km 500m, baker on site (Tue-Su).
Remarks: Bread-service.

Damvillers 16D2

Rue de l'Isle d'Envie, D905. **GPS**: n49,33790 e5,39752.

4 free €2/100liter Ch €2. **Location:** Urban, simple, central.
Surface: asphalted. 01/01-31/12.
Distance: on the spot on the spot on the spot.

Damvillers 16D2

Etang, D905. **GPS**: n49,34978 e5,39970.
10 free. **Location:** Isolated. **Surface:** grassy. 01/01-31/12.
Distance: Damvillers 1km on the spot.

Dienville 19C1

Parking Autobus. **GPS**: n48,34680 e4,52806.
5 free. **Surface:** asphalted. 01/01-31/12.
Distance: 700m 300m 300m.

Dieue-sur-Meuse 16D2

Port de plaisance, Route des Dames. **GPS**: n49,07110 e5,42634.

15 free Ch free. **Location:** Rural, simple, quiet.
Surface: grassy. 01/01-31/12.
Distance: 200m on the spot 200m 200m.
Remarks: At the canal.

Dolancourt 19C1

Nigloland, RN19. **GPS**: n48,26086 e4,60945.

28 € 6/24h, free with a meal Ch included.
Location: Simple, isolated. **Surface:** asphalted. 03/04-03/11.
Distance: on the spot.
Remarks: Parking amusement park, max. 24h.

Dommartin-lès-Remiremont 19F2

Place de l'Église. **GPS**: n47,99959 e6,64401.

8 free €3/10minutes Ch €3/h.
Location: Simple, quiet. **Surface:** asphalted.
Distance: on the spot 200m.

Donjeux 19D1

Halte Nautique, D67a. **GPS**: n48,36586 e5,14891.

4 free Ch (4x)free. **Location:** Comfortable, quiet.
Surface: gravel/metalled. 01/01-31/12.
Distance: 1km Canal de la Marne on the spot 1km 800m on the spot.
Remarks: Baker every morning.

Dun-sur-Meuse 16D2

Rue du Vieux Port. **GPS**: n49,38919 e5,17787.

16 € 7 Ch WC included.
Location: Rural, comfortable, central, quiet. **Surface:** gravel.
01/01-31/12 sanitary building: 01/11-01/04.

FR

Distance: 600m on the spot on the spot 400m 600m.

Eguisheim 19G1

Bannwarth, Rue de Bruxelles 3. **GPS**: n48,04456 e7,30478.

8 free Ch WC free. **Location:** Urban, comfortable, central, quiet. **Surface:** metalled. 01/01-31/12.
Distance: 100m 100m on the spot on the spot.
Remarks: Sale of wines.

Épernay 16B2

Rue Dom Pérignon. **GPS**: n49,03602 e3,95130.

3 free €2/100liter Ch €2/1h WC €0,50.
Location: Urban, simple, central, noisy.
Surface: asphalted.
01/01-31/12.
Distance: within walking distance Avenue Jean Jaurès.
Remarks: Behind church St.Pierre-St.Paul, coins at tourist info.

Tourist information Épernay:
Cave de Catellane, 154, avenue de Verdun.
Mercier, 70, avenue de Champagne. Mo-Sa 9.30-11.30h, 14-16.30h, Su/holidays 9.30-11.30h, 14-17.30h.

Épinal 19E1

Camping-Car Park, Chemin du Petit Chaperon Rouge.
GPS: n48,17969 e6,46865.

50 € 12 Ch (20x) included.
Location: Comfortable, quiet. 01/01-31/12.
Distance: 1,5km.

Épinal 19E1

Port d'Épinal, Quai de Dogneville, D12. **GPS**: n48,18671 e6,44493.

5 summer € 5, winter € 8 Ch Service€3/15min.
Surface: asphalted.
Distance: 1km 3,5km on the spot.
Remarks: Max. 48h.

Essoyes 19C1

Impasse de la Gare. **GPS**: n48,06067 e4,53444.
3 free Ch. **Surface:** metalled. 01/01-31/12.
Distance: 600m 600m.

Esternay 16A3

Place des Tilleuls, D48, Rue de la Paix. **GPS**: n48,73245 e3,55698.

8 free free.
Location: Urban, simple, central, quiet. **Surface:** gravel.
01/01-31/12 water: 15/11-15/03.
Distance: within walking distance 200m 400m.
Remarks: Behind church, Wifi code: wifi-la-champagne.

Étain 16D2

Allée du champ de foire, D631. **GPS**: n49,20942 e5,63755.
6 free.
Location: Simple, noisy. **Surface:** metalled. 01/01-31/12.
Distance: on the spot 500m 500m.
Remarks: Next to restaurant.

Étain 16D2

Avenue Prud Homme Havette. **GPS**: n49,21025 e5,63627.
6 free.
Distance: on the spot.

Etival-Clairefontaine 19F1

Rue du Vivier. **GPS**: n48,36355 e6,86504.

20 free Ch free. **Location:** Simple, quiet. **Surface:** gravel.
01/01-31/12 water disconnected in winter.
Distance: on the spot.
Remarks: Behind town hall.

Fains-Veel 16D3

Halte Fluviale, Rue du Stade. **GPS**: n48,79276 e5,12552.
6 free free.
Location: Simple, quiet. **Surface:** asphalted.
01/01-31/12.
Distance: 300m Canal on the spot 1,5km bakery 20m.

Favières 19E1

Base de Loisirs. **GPS**: n48,46660 e5,96124.

8 free Ch WC . **Location:** Rural, comfortable, central, quiet. **Surface:** gravel/metalled.
Distance: 200m 13km on the spot on the spot on the spot bakery 300m on the spot on the spot.

Fénétrange 16F3

Wally Services, Route de Sarre Union. **GPS**: n48,85365 e7,02723.
5 free €2 Ch €2. **Surface:** grassy/metalled.
Remarks: Max. 48h.

Ferrette 19G3

Rue de Lucelle. **GPS**: n47,48882 e7,31118.

5 free €2/10minutes Ch €2/55minutes. **Location:** Rural, simple, isolated, quiet. **Surface:** asphalted.
Distance: 700m 700m 2km on the spot on the spot.

Fessenheim 19G2

Allée de la Guyane. **GPS**: n47,91833 e7,53139.

30 free €2 Ch €2. **Location:** Rural, simple, quiet.
Surface: asphalted/gravel. 01/01-31/12.
Distance: 700m 700m 200m on the spot on the spot.
Remarks: Coins available at swimming pool, supermarket.

Forbach 16F2

Avenue Saint-Rémy. **GPS**: n49,18519 e6,89252.
5 free €2/100liter Ch. **Surface:** asphalted. 01/01-31/12.
Distance: 350m 200m.

Fraize 19F1

Impasse de la Gare/ Place Jean Sonrel. **GPS**: n48,18188 e7,00360.

6 free €3 Ch €3 WC.
Surface: asphalted. 01/01-31/12.
Distance: 100m 100m 100m.
Remarks: Behind tourist info.

Froncles 19D1

Halte Nautique. **GPS**: n48,29954 e5,15246.

10 € 3 €3/day Ch (8x)€3/day €2,50 €3/3 .
Location: Comfortable. **Surface:** gravel. 01/01-31/12.
Distance: 500m river-beach on the spot on the spot 1km on the spot.
Remarks: Baker on site (Tue-Su).

Fumay 11C3

Quai des Carmélites. **GPS**: n49,99736 e4,70986.

+10 free. **Surface:** unpaved. 01/01-31/12.
Distance: 400m.
Remarks: Along the Meuse river.

Gérardmer 19F1

Chemin de la Rayée, La Mauselaine. **GPS**: n48,05846 e6,88862.

FR

100 € 5,70/24h €2/100liter Ch.
Surface: asphalted. 01/01-31/12.
Distance: Gérardmer 1,7km.
Remarks: Parking at skipistes.

S Gérardmer 19F1

Parking de la Prairie, Boulevard d' Alsace.
GPS: n48,07199 e6,87333.

100 € 5,70 €2/100liter ChWC.
Location: Simple, central, noisy. **Surface:** asphalted/gravel.
01/01-31/12.
Distance: on the spot.
Tourist information Gérardmer:
Thu, Sa.

S Giffaumont-Champaubert 16C3

Site de Chantecoq, Rue du grand Der. **GPS**: n48,56880 e4,70294.

50 free €3,80/80liter Ch €3,80/45minutes WC.
Location: Rural, simple. **Surface:** metalled.
01/01-31/12.
Distance: on the spot 900m.
Remarks: At lake Der de Chantecoq, coins at tourist info.

S Giffaumont-Champaubert 16C3

Station Nautique, P1, Rue du Port. **GPS**: n48,55358 e4,76434.

48 € 7,50 20-8h, parking free Ch included.
Location: Rural. 01/01-31/12.
Distance: on the spot 200m 8km Montier-en-Der on the spot on the spot.

S Giffaumont-Champaubert 16C3

Station Nautique, P5, La Cachotte. **GPS**: n48,55071 e4,76829.
72 € 7,50 20-8h, parking free Ch. **Surface:** grassy.
01/01-31/12.
Distance: 650m 700m.

Givet 11C3

Rue Jean Jaurès. **GPS**: n50,13593 e4,82138.

12 free. **Location:** Urban, simple, central, quiet. **Surface:** asphalted.
01/01-31/12.

S Givet 11C3

Camping Municipal, Rue Berthelot. **GPS**: n50,14291 e4,82611.

5 free €3/100liter Ch €3/h.
Location: Rural, simple. **Surface:** asphalted. 01/01-31/12.
Distance: 750m 750m 1km.
Remarks: Coins at campsite.

S Goncourt 19D1

Rue des Lottes, D74. **GPS**: n48,23685 e5,60998.

30 € 3 €3 Ch. **Location:** Rural, comfortable.
Surface: asphalted/gravel. 01/01-31/12.
Distance: 100m on the spot 100m 100m.
Remarks: Along the Meuse river, max. 48h, baker at 8am.

Gondrecourt-le-Château 16D3

Parking Musée du Cheval, Rue Saint Blaise.
GPS: n48,51390 e5,50975.

2 free. **Location:** Simple, quiet. **Surface:** gravel/metalled.
Distance: on the spot 50m 50m.

Gondrecourt-le-Château 16D3

Rue du Général Leclerc. **GPS**: n48,51373 e5,50386.

3 free Ch. **Location:** Urban. **Surface:** concrete.
01/01-31/12.
Distance: on the spot on the spot on the spot.
Remarks: Coins at town hall.

Guebwiller 19G2

Avenue Maréchal Foch. **GPS**: n47,90554 e7,21869.

20 free. **Location:** Urban, simple, central, noisy. **Surface:** gravel.
01/01-31/12.
Distance: 300m on the spot on the spot 300m 300m 300m on the spot 5km.

S Haironville 16D3

GPS: n48,68438 e5,08586.

5 free €2/10minutes Ch €2/50minutes.
Location: Rural, simple, central, quiet. **Surface:** gravel.
01/01-31/12.
Distance: 200m 200m.
Remarks: Coins at the shops in the village.

S Hampigny 19C1

La Mare, Rue de la Marcelle. **GPS**: n48,45796 e4,59707.
free €3 Ch. 01/01-31/12.
Distance: on the spot.

S Harskirchen 16F3

Port de Plaisance, Rue de Bissert. **GPS**: n48,93930 e7,02759.
2 € 10 Ch included. **Surface:** gravel.
15/03-11/11.
Distance: on the spot.
Remarks: At canal Houillères de la Sarre, max. 24h.

S Hartmannswiller 19G2

Grand Rue. **GPS**: n47,86311 e7,21494.

4 free Ch free. **Location:** Rural, simple, quiet.
Surface: asphalted. 01/01-31/12.
Distance: 200m.

S Haybes 11C3

Halte Fluviale, Quai du Docteur Adolphe Hamai.
GPS: n50,01093 e4,70762.

4 free Ch€2,05 €3,30/3,30.
Surface: metalled. 01/01-31/12.
Distance: 200m 50m bakery 200m.
Remarks: Along the Meuse river, service at camping municipal.

Heiligenstein 19G1

Lieu-dit Lindel, D35. **GPS**: n48,42780 e7,45147.

FR

3 free.
Location: Rural, simple. **Surface:** gravel. 01/01-31/12.
Distance: 800m 300m 500m on the spot.
Remarks: Hiking trails and wine tasting.

Heudicourt sous les Côtes 16D3

Ste Nautique de Madine. **GPS**: n48,93549 e5,71548.

42 € 12 Ch included WC . **Location:** Rural, comfortable, quiet. **Surface:** grassy/gravel. 01/04-31/10.
Distance: 3km on the spot on the spot on the spot.
Remarks: View on Lac de Madine.

Heudicourt sous les Côtes 16D3

Entrée 2, D133. **GPS**: n48,94035 e5,71741.

50 € 7. **Location:** Rural, simple, quiet. **Surface:** grassy.
01/04-31/10.
Distance: 3km 100m 100m.
Remarks: Next to campsite.

Hirtzbach 19G2

Place de la Gare. **GPS**: n47,60061 e7,22542.

10 free Ch free. **Location:** Simple, quiet. **Surface:** asphalted.
01/01-31/12.
Distance: 300m 200m on the spot on the spot.

Hombourg-Haut 16F2

Rue des Suédois. **GPS**: n49,12448 e6,77888.

7 free €2/100liter Ch €2/4h.
Surface: asphalted. 01/01-31/12.
Distance: 400m 200m on the spot.
Remarks: Max. 48h.

Issoncourt 16D3

Parking Relais de la Voie Sacrée, Rue de la Voie Sacrée 1.
GPS: n48,97070 e5,28776.

6 free. **Location:** Rural, simple, quiet. **Surface:** gravel.
Distance: 50m on the spot.

Javernant 19B1

Le Cheminot, N77. **GPS**: n48,14789 e4,01046.

5 free free. **Location:** Simple. **Surface:** asphalted.
01/01-31/12.
Remarks: 2013: during inspection service out of order.

Joinville 19D1

Halte Nautique, Rue des Jardins. **GPS**: n48,44583 e5,15000.

16 free €2/10minutes Ch €2/55minutes .
Location: Simple, quiet. **Surface:** gravel/metalled.
01/01-31/12.
Distance: 500m on the spot on the spot 800m 100m on the spot.

Juzennecourt 19C1

Place de la Mairie. **GPS**: n48,18429 e4,97890.

4 free Ch WC. **Location:** Simple, quiet. **Surface:** metalled.
15/04-15/11.
Distance: on the spot bakery in the village on the spot.
Remarks: Parking townhall.

Kaysersberg 19G1

Aire Camping-car P1, Place de l'Erlenbad.
GPS: n48,13565 e7,26325.

80 € 8/24h Ch WC free. **Location:** Urban, simple, quiet.
Surface: asphalted. 01/01-31/12.
Distance: 300m 300m 300m.
Remarks: Wifi at Office de Tourisme.

Tourist information Kaysersberg:
M Musée Albert Schweitzer. The life of Albert Schweitzer.

Kilstett 16G3

Place de la Mairie, Rue du Lieut de Bettignies.
GPS: n48,67501 e7,85691.

7 free. **Location:** Urban, simple, quiet. **Surface:** asphalted.
01/01-31/12.
Distance: on the spot on the spot.

Kilstett 16G3

Rue de l'Industrie. **GPS**: n48,67914 e7,84178.
Ch.

La Bresse 19F2

Camping du Haut Des Bluches, 5, route des Planches.
GPS: n47,99889 e6,91762.

17 € 11,80 Ch WC included €3,80 €5. **Location:** Quiet.
Surface: asphalted. 01/01-31/12 12/11-15/12.
Distance: 4km on camp site on the spot on the spot on the spot on the spot.
Remarks: Zone camping-car, bread-service.

La Bresse 19F2

Route de Niachamp. **GPS**: n47,99430 e6,85431.
€2/100liter Ch. 01/01-31/12.

La Cheppe 16C2

Champ d'Attila, Rue de Champo d'Attila. **GPS**: n49,04892 e4,49377.

4 free €2/100liter Ch €2/2h WC .
Location: Rural, simple, quiet. **Surface:** asphalted.
01/01-31/12.
Distance: 500m.

La Croix-sur-Meuse 16D3

Auberge de la Truite, Route de Seuzey. **GPS**: n48,98267 e5,53393.

4 € 3 (4x)€5/24h WC . **Location:** Rural, comfortable, quiet.
Surface: grassy. 01/01-31/12.
Distance: 2km on the spot on the spot.

La Gault-Soigny 16A3

Rue de la Liberté, D373. **GPS**: n48,81758 e3,59072.

FR

8 free Chfree. **Location:** Rural, simple, quiet.
Surface: asphalted. 01/01-31/12.
Distance: on the spot.
Remarks: Near Salle des Fêtes, service 50m.

Lachaussée 16E2

Domaine du Vieux Moulin, Grande Rue. **GPS**: n49,03507 e5,81735.
4. **Location:** Rural, simple. **Surface:** gravel.
Distance: 100m 50m on the spot.
Remarks: Along Étang de Lachaussée.

Laheycourt 16C3

Rue de la Gare. **GPS**: n48,88903 e5,02165.

4 free. **Location:** Rural, simple, quiet. **Surface:** grassy.
01/01-31/12.
Distance: on the spot 50m 50m.
Remarks: Along the Chée river.

Langres 19D2

Place de Bel Air. **GPS**: n47,85885 e5,33225.

free WC. **Location:** Urban, simple, noisy. **Surface:** asphalted.
01/01-31/12.
Distance: on the spot on the spot.
Remarks: Video surveillance.

Langres 19D2

Ruelle de la Poterne. **GPS**: n47,85795 e5,32989.

6 free Chfree. **Location:** Simple, quiet. **Surface:** asphalted.
01/01-31/12.
Distance: 800m.
Remarks: Max. 24h.

Langres 19D2

Parking Sous-Bie, Allée des Marronniers. **GPS**: n47,86104 e5,33674.

20 free. **Location:** Simple, quiet. **Surface:** asphalted.
01/01-31/12.
Distance: on the spot on the spot.
Remarks: Inclining pitches, video surveillance, free elevator to old town.

Tourist information Langres:
Fri.

Launois-sur-Vence 16C1

Avenue Louis Jolly. **GPS**: n49,65467 e4,54005.

10 free. **Location:** Rural, simple, quiet. **Surface:** unpaved.
01/01-31/12.
Distance: on the spot 50m.
Remarks: In front of tourist office, max. 48h.

Launois-sur-Vence 16C1

Rue du Thin. **GPS**: n49,65810 e4,53987.
€2/100liter Ch €2/1h. water: frost.
Distance: 150m.
Remarks: Coins at tourist info, coins at restaurant.

Tourist information Launois-sur-Vence:
Relais de Poste. Monthly antiques and flea market. 3rd Su of the month 9-18h.

Le Bonhomme 19F1

Col du Bonhomme, D148, route des Crètes.
GPS: n48,16495 e7,07971.

free. **Location:** Rural, simple, quiet. **Surface:** gravel.
01/01-31/12.
Distance: on the spot on the spot on the spot.

Les Islettes 16C2

Route du Lochères. **GPS**: n49,12122 e5,03684.

16 €7 Ch WC included. **Location:** Rural, comfortable, quiet. **Surface:** gravel. 01/01-31/12.
Distance: 3km 10,5km 3km 3km.

Les Riceys 19B2

D452. **GPS**: n47,99222 e4,36458.

40 free €2 Ch €2. **Location:** Simple, isolated, quiet.
Surface: asphalted. 01/01-31/12.
Distance: 500m 500m 500m.

Ligny-en-Barrois 16D3

Aire de Pilvetus, Chemin des Pains de Seigle.
GPS: n48,69262 e5,33621.

10 free. **Location:** Simple, isolated. **Surface:** gravel.
01/01-31/12.
Distance: 1,2km.

Ligny-en-Barrois 16D3

Relais Nautique, Rue Jean Willemert. **GPS**: n48,68787 e5,31943.

12 € 2 + € 0,20/pp tourist tax €2/10minutes Ch €2/55minutes WC €2 €4 free.
Location: Urban, comfortable, central, quiet. **Surface:** asphalted.
Distance: 200m on the spot 200m 200m on the spot on the spot.
Remarks: Along Canal de la Marne au Rhin, small pitches.

Linthal 19F2

Rue du Markstein, D430. **GPS**: n47,94495 e7,12783.

4 free Ch free. **Location:** Simple, quiet.
Surface: asphalted. 01/01-31/12.
Distance: 200m on the spot 200m 200m on the spot.

Longeville-en-Barrois 16D3

Gr Grande Rue. **GPS**: n48,74201 e5,20645.

6 free. **Location:** Urban, simple, quiet. **Surface:** asphalted.
Distance: on the spot on the spot 100m 100m on the spot on the spot.
Remarks: Along the Ornain river.

Longuyon 16D2

Parking Salvador Allende, N18. **GPS**: n49,44802 e5,59973.

2 free €2 Ch €2 WC.
Location: Urban, simple, central, noisy.

FR

Surface: asphalted.
Distance: on the spot on the spot 100m.
Remarks: Parking next to tourist info, not suitable for big motorhomes.

S Longwy 16D1

Stade Municipal, Avenue du 8 Mai 1945.
GPS: n49,52656 e5,76559.

7 free €2,50/20minutes Ch €2,50/4h.
Location: Urban, simple, central, noisy. **Surface:** asphalted.
01/01-31/12.
Distance: on the spot 400m 350m.
Remarks: At football ground.

S Lunéville 16F3

Les Bosquets, Quai des Petits Bosquets. **GPS**: n48,59652 e6,49865.

23 € 8 Ch included free.
Location: Comfortable, central, noisy. 01/01-31/12.
Distance: 700m 50m 600m 600m.

Tourist information Lunéville:
Château Petit Versailles. Castle, 18th century and museum.
10-12h, 14-18h Tue. € 8.

Lusigny-sur-Barse 19B1

Route du Lac. **GPS**: n48,26451 e4,29735.
free. 01/01-31/12.
Distance: 2,5km on the spot on the spot.
Remarks: At the lake, max 3,5t.

Marbotte 16D3

Parking de la Mairie, Rue Principale, D12.
GPS: n48,83445 e5,58142.

2 free. **Location:** Simple, quiet. **Surface:** unpaved.
Distance: on the spot.

S Mareuil-sur-Ay 16B2

Relais nautique, Place Charles de Gaulle. **GPS**: n49,04522 e4,03490.

8 free 150liter Ch 3h,Service€5.
Location: Urban, comfortable, central, quiet. **Surface:** asphalted.
01/01-31/12 water disconnected in winter.
Distance: on the spot on the spot on the spot on the spot on the spot.
Remarks: On the canal, in village, coins at supermarket.

S Maxey-sur-Meuse 19D1

Sous la Voie, D19A. **GPS**: n48,44861 e5,69500.

4 free (4x) free.
Location: Simple. **Surface:** gravel. 14/05-31/12.
Distance: 2km 2km 500m.

Maxey-sur-Vaise 16D3

Grande Rue. **GPS**: n48,53836 e5,66705.

6 free.
Location: Simple, central, quiet. 01/01-31/12.
Distance: on the spot.

Mesnil-Saint-Père 19B1

Rue du Lac. **GPS**: n48,25524 e4,34090.

50 free.
Location: Simple. **Surface:** asphalted. 01/01-31/12.
Distance: beach 400m.
Remarks: Nearby lake Orient.

S Metz 16E2

Allée Metz Plage. **GPS**: n49,12371 e6,16887.

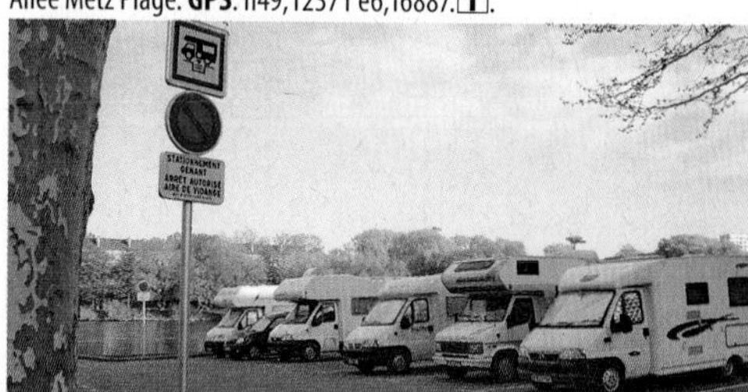

8 free Ch free.
Surface: asphalted.
Distance: 350m 1,5km 300m.
Remarks: At entrance campsite, max. 48h, inclining pitches.

Tourist information Metz:
Place St Louis. Square surrounded by houses from the 14th century.
Cathédrale St Etienne. Cathedral.

S Millery 16E3

Avenue de la Moselle, D40. **GPS**: n48,81507 e6,12716.

5 free Ch free.
Surface: asphalted. 01/04-31/10 water: 01/11-31/03.
Distance: on the spot 3,5km.
Remarks: Along Mosel.

S Mirecourt 19E1

Place Thierry. **GPS**: n48,29945 e6,13591.

20 € 6 10minutes Ch 35minutes included.
Location: Comfortable, central. **Surface:** gravel.
01/01-31/12.
Distance: on the spot.

Mittelbergheim 19G1

Parking Zotzenberg, Rue Ziegelscheuer. **GPS**: n48,39869 e7,44194.

4 free. **Location:** Rural, simple, quiet. **Surface:** asphalted.
01/01-31/12.
Distance: 300m 3km 300m 300m on the spot.
Remarks: At cemetery, wine tasting.

Monthermé 16C1

Rue du Général de Gaulle, D989. **GPS**: n49,88136 e4,72979.

6 free. **Location:** Rural, simple, quiet. **Surface:** grassy.
01/01-31/12.
Distance: 900m on the spot.
Remarks: Along the Meuse river, max. 24h.

S Monthermé 16C1

Etape fluviale, Quai A. Briand. **GPS**: n49,88608 e4,73593.

± 20 € 3 + € 0,20/pp tourist tax €2,80/day €1,50 €3,50/3,50. **Surface:** grasstiles.
Distance: 300m.
Remarks: Along the Meuse river, check in at harbourmaster.

S Monthureux-sur Saône 19E1

D460. **GPS**: n48,03199 e5,97390.

8 free Ch free €3/48h,WiÒ-Stop.
Location: Comfortable, quiet. 01/01-31/12.
Distance: on the spot on the spot 200m 75m.

FR

Remarks: At football ground.

Montier-en-Der 19C1

Rue de l'Isle. **GPS:** n48,47861 e4,76861.

6 free €2/8minutes Ch €2,80/55minutes WC.
Location: Simple. **Surface:** gravel. 01/01-31/12.
Distance: on the spot 500m 500m.
Remarks: Coins at tourist info.

Montigny-lès-Vaucouleurs 16D3

Rue de la Côte. **GPS:** n48,58875 e5,63007.

10 free. **Location:** Rural, simple, quiet. **Surface:** gravel.
01/01-31/12.
Distance: 700m.

Montplonne 16D3

Rue du Four. **GPS:** n48,68630 e5,16934.

4 free. **Location:** Rural, simple. **Surface:** gravel.
Distance: on the spot.
Remarks: Next to cemetery.

Morley 16D3

Parking Lavoir, D5A. **GPS:** n48,57848 e5,24878.

5 free.
Location: Rural, simple, central, quiet. **Surface:** grassy.
Distance: on the spot.

Mouzon 16C1

Halte fluviale. GPS: n49,60687 e5,07710.
8 € 7,80, 01/11-31/03 free Ch WC included.
Surface: asphalted. 01/01-31/12 Service: winter.
Distance: 100m.
Remarks: Along the Meuse river, sanitary and wifi code at harbour master, felt museum 100m (May-Sep).

Munster 19F1

Aire de camping-cars Munster, Rue du Dr Heid.
GPS: n48,03779 e7,13471.

54 € 6 €3 Ch €3 WC €1,50 included .
Location: Rural, comfortable, quiet. **Surface:** gravel.
01/01-31/12.
Distance: on the spot on the spot on the spot on the spot.

Murbach 19G2

Abbaye de Murbach, Rue de Guebwiller.
GPS: n47,92321 e7,16059.

20 free Ch free. **Location:** Rural, isolated, quiet.
Surface: gravel/metalled. 01/01-31/12.
Distance: 350m on the spot on the spot 5km on the spot 5km.

Mutigny 16B2

Aire de l'étang, Route de Montflambert.
GPS: n49,06894 e4,02669.

8 free 150liter Ch 3h,Service €5 . **Location:** Rural, simple, isolated, quiet. **Surface:** asphalted. 01/01-31/12.
Distance: 1km 3km 3km.

Nancy 16E3

Parking Faubourg Des III Maisons, Rue Charles Keller.
GPS: n48,70403 e6,17598.

10 € 4,50.
Location: Central. **Surface:** asphalted. 01/01-31/12.
Distance: city centre ± 1km.

Nancy 16E3

Port Saint Georges, N57, boulevard du 21ème Régiment d'Aviation.
GPS: n48,69221 e6,19318.

15 € 15,50 + € 1,50/pp Ch included WC .
Location: Central. **Surface:** asphalted.
01/05-01/11.
Distance: 500m on the spot on the spot 100m 100m 100m.
Remarks: Max. 5 nights, check in at harbourmaster.

Tourist information Nancy:
Musée Historique Lorraine, Palais Ducal. Regional museum.
15/06-15/09 Tue.
Zoo Haye, Velaine-en-Haye. Zoo with centre for wild birds.

Nant-le-Grand 16D3

Grand Rue, D169A. **GPS:** n48,67530 e5,22382.

4 free.
Location: Rural, simple, quiet. **Surface:** grassy/gravel.
Distance: on the spot.

Neuf-Brisach 19G1

Place de la Porte de Bâle. **GPS:** n48,01688 e7,53187.

free. **Surface:** asphalted. 01/01-31/12.
Distance: 300m 300m 300m.

Tourist information Neuf-Brisach:
Point I Neuf-Brisach, 6, place d'Armes, www.tourisme-rhin.com/. City worth a visit with defences of Vauban.

Niderviller 16F3

Marina Niderviller, Avenue de Lorraine. **GPS:** n48,71748 e7,09901.

12 € 12 €2/stay Ch €3/day WC .
Location: Simple, quiet. 01/03-30/10.
Distance: 200m.

Nixéville-Blercourt 16D2

Rue de la Grand. **GPS:** n49,11118 e5,24007.

4 € 6 Ch included.
Location: Rural, simple, quiet. **Surface:** concrete.
Distance: 100m.

Nogent-sur-Seine 16A3

Parking Camping/Piscine, Rue du Camping.
GPS: n48,50388 e3,50888.

FR

5 € 6,58/night, € 2,99/3h Chfree (2x)included3h.
Location: Urban, simple, quiet. **Surface:** asphalted.
01/01-31/12.
Distance: 1,5km 2km 1,5km 1,5km 2km.
Remarks: Max. 48h.

S Nonsard Lamarche 16D3

Base de Loisirs, Base de Loisirs de Madine.
GPS: n48,93064 e5,74873.

30 € 7 €3 Ch. **Location:** Rural, simple, isolated, quiet.
Surface: grassy/metalled. 01/04-31/10.
Distance: 700m on the spot on the spot on the spot.
Remarks: At lake Madine, coins at campsite.

Nubécourt 16D2

D151, Rue Raymond Poincaré. **GPS**: n48,99704 e5,17256.

8 free. **Location:** Rural, simple, central, quiet. **Surface:** gravel.
01/01-31/12.
Distance: on the spot 200m on the spot on the spot.

Obernai 19G1

Parking de l'Altau, Route d'Ottrott. **GPS**: n48,46239 e7,47369.

10 free. **Location:** Urban, simple, central. **Surface:** asphalted.
01/01-31/12.
Distance: 600m 600m 600m.
Remarks: Video surveillance.

Obernai 19G1

Parking des Remparts, Rue Poincaré. **GPS**: n48,45972 e7,48667.

50 free free. **Location:** Urban, simple. **Surface:** gravel.
01/01-31/12.
Distance: 300m 2,7km 300m 300m 200m.
Remarks: Large parking in centre, video surveillance.

S Obernai 19G1

Camping municipal Le Vallon de l'Ehn, 1, rue de Berlin.
GPS: n48,46471 e7,46757.
€2 Ch. 01/01-31/12.

S Oltingue 19G3

Place Saint Martin. **GPS**: n47,49158 e7,39068.

3 free €2/10minutes Ch €2/55minutes WCfree.
Location: Urban. **Surface:** asphalted. 01/01-31/12.
Distance: 100m on the spot 100m 200m on the spot on the spot on the spot.

S Orbey 19F1

Hôtel Restaurant Les Terrasses du Lac Blanc, Lac Blanc.
GPS: n48,13540 e7,08957.

8 € 7 included Ch (8x)€2,50.
Location: Comfortable, quiet. **Surface:** grassy/gravel.
Distance: 500m 500m on the spot.
Remarks: Guests free.

S Orschwihr 19G2

Rue de la Source. **GPS**: n47,93722 e7,23083.

4 free Chfree. **Location:** Rural, simple, quiet.
Surface: asphalted. 01/01-31/12.
Distance: 200m 200m 5km.
Remarks: Max. 48h.

S Peigney 19D2

Lac de la Liez, D284, rue Côté de Recey.
GPS: n47,87272 e5,38077.

8 € 10,50 Ch €2. **Location:** Simple.
Surface: asphalted. 01/01-31/12.
Distance: 500m on the spot on the spot on the spot on the spot.

S Pfaffenheim 19G2

Aire du Winzerhof, Rue de la Tuilerie. **GPS**: n47,98639 e7,29167.

5 € 5 Ch (5x)WCincluded. **Location:** Urban, simple, quiet. **Surface:** gravel/metalled. 01/01-31/12.
Distance: 400m 400m 3km on the spot on the spot.
Remarks: Guests free, sale of wines.

S Phalsbourg 16G3

Rue du commandant Taillant. **GPS**: n48,76545 e7,25950.
4 free €2/10minutes Ch €4/12h. **Surface:** metalled.
01/01-31/12.
Distance: 100m 100m 300m.
Remarks: Max. 48h.

S Phalsbourg 16G3

TOTAL tankstation, ZAC Louvois, Route du Luxembourg.
GPS: n48,76899 e7,24182.

free €2 Ch €2. **Surface:** asphalted. 01/01-31/12.
Distance: on the spot.
Remarks: Max. 1 night.

Pierre-Percée 19F1

D182A. **GPS**: n48,46723 e6,92911.

± 8 free.
Location: Simple, isolated, quiet. **Surface:** asphalted.
Distance: on the spot on the spot.
Remarks: Picnic area at artificial lake.

S Piney 19B1

Place des Anciens Combattants, Rue du Général de Gaulle.
GPS: n48,35878 e4,33442.

5 free €3/10minutes Ch €3/1h. **Location:** Simple.
Surface: metalled. 01/01-31/12 water: frost.
Distance: 500m 500m 500m.
Remarks: Coins at town hall and restaurant.

S Plombières-les-Bains 19E2

Allée Eugene Delacroix. **GPS**: n47,95822 e6,44966.

FR

15 free (5x). **Location:** Simple, quiet. **Surface:** asphalted. 01/01-31/12.

Pompierre 19D1

Chemin de la Corvée. **GPS**: n48,25691 e5,67188.

3 free free. **Location:** Urban, simple, noisy. **Surface:** asphalted. 01/01-31/12.
Distance: 1km 500m 500m.

Pont-à-Mousson 16E3

Port de plaisance, Avenue des Etas Unis, D910.
GPS: n48,90296 e6,06088.

42 € 9,50 Ch WC included. **Location:** Luxurious. **Surface:** asphalted. 01/04-31/10.
Distance: 400m 3,4km on the spot 400m 400m on the spot.
Remarks: Check in at reception, bread-service.

Rebeuville 19D1

Rue du Cougnot. **GPS**: n48,33530 e5,70128.

3 free Ch free. **Location:** Rural, comfortable, isolated. **Surface:** asphalted. 01/01-31/12.
Distance: 5km on the spot on the spot 5km 5km 500m.

Reims 16B2

Parc du CIS de la Comédie, Esplanade André Malraux, chaussée Bocquaine. **GPS**: n49,24881 e4,02110.

9 free Ch free. **Location:** Urban, simple, central, noisy. **Surface:** metalled.
Distance: 15 min walking 1,4km 350m 100m.
Remarks: Max. 48h, call for entrance code, noisy place.

Remiremont 19F1

Rue du Lit d'Eau. **GPS**: n48,01540 e6,60208.
31 € 6 Ch €3/24h.
Location: Comfortable. **Surface:** gravel.
Distance: 1km on the spot on the spot on the spot on the spot.
Remarks: At small lake, at station, video surveillance.

Rennepont 19C1

Domaine Rennepont, 31 Rue Principale. **GPS**: n48,14927 e4,85430. € 22, dog € 7,50 Ch included. **Location:** Isolated, quiet. **Surface:** grassy/gravel. 15/03-31/10.

Revigny-sur-Ornain 16C3

Stade/Office de Tourisme, Rue de l'Abattoir.
GPS: n48,82642 e4,98330.

2 free Ch free. **Location:** Urban, simple, central, quiet. **Surface:** asphalted. 01/01-31/12.
Distance: on the spot 100m on the spot on the spot on the spot.
Remarks: Coins at tourist info.

Revin 16C1

Rue du Port. **GPS**: n49,93962 e4,63843.
10 free €2/100liter Ch €2/1h. **Surface:** metalled. 01/01-31/12.
Distance: on the spot on the spot on the spot.
Remarks: Max. 8M.

Rhodes 16F3

Port Municipal, Rue Principale. **GPS**: n48,75784 e6,90053.

30 € 18/24h Ch WC included.
Location: Luxurious, quiet. **Surface:** grassy. 01/04-30/09.
Distance: on the spot on the spot.
Remarks: Along Etang du Stock.

Ribeauvillé 19G1

Route de Guémar. **GPS**: n48,19231 e7,32867.

15 € 1,50/5h, € 1,50/night €2 Ch.
Location: Urban, simple, noisy. **Surface:** gravel. 01/01-31/12.
Distance: 400m on the spot on the spot.
Remarks: Next to Cave de Ribeauvillé.

Tourist information Ribeauvillé:
Sa.

Richardmenil 16E3

Chemin de la Maize. **GPS**: n48,59457 e6,16078.

5 free Ch (4x)free. **Location:** Isolated, quiet. **Surface:** asphalted. 01/01-31/12.
Distance: 1km on the spot on the spot 500m 1km 1km.

Riquewihr 19G1

Avenue Jacques Preiss. **GPS**: n48,16608 e7,30175.

6 € 2/5h, € 4/night €2 Ch €2. **Location:** Simple, noisy. **Surface:** asphalted. 01/01-31/12.
Distance: 200m 200m 200m.
Remarks: Motorhomes <7m, video surveillance.

Tourist information Riquewihr:
Office de Tourisme, Rue de 1ère Armée. Picturesque street with houses of the 16th century.

Rollainville 19D1

Rue de la Cure. **GPS**: n48,36185 e5,73842.

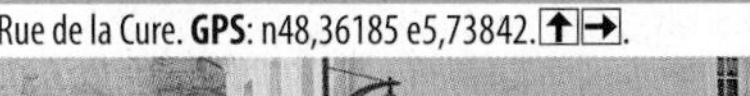

1 free €2/30minutes €2/6h. **Location:** Urban, simple, central. **Surface:** asphalted. 01/01-31/12.
Distance: on the spot.
Remarks: Baker at 8am.

Rosenau 19G2

Grand Canal d'Alsace. **GPS**: n47,65336 e7,52346.

+10 free. **Surface:** grassy. 01/01-31/12.
Distance: brasserie.
Remarks: Along the Rhine river.

Rupt-sur-Moselle 19F2

Quai de la Parelle. **GPS**: n47,92061 e6,66194.

6 free €3/10minutes Ch (4x)€3/3h WC.
Location: Simple, quiet. **Surface:** asphalted.
Distance: 350m 250m on the spot Voie Verte.

FR

Remarks: Coins at the shops and town hall.

S Saint-Dizier 16C3

Centre Loisirs Caravanning, Route de Villiers en Lieu.
GPS: n48,64255 e4,91035.

6 free Ch WCfree. **Location:** Simple. **Surface:** asphalted. 01/01-31/12.
Distance: 1,5km 400m.
Remarks: At motorhome dealer, coins during opening hours.

S Saint-Hippolyte 19G1

Rue de la 5E Division Blindée. **GPS**: n48,23084 e7,37681.

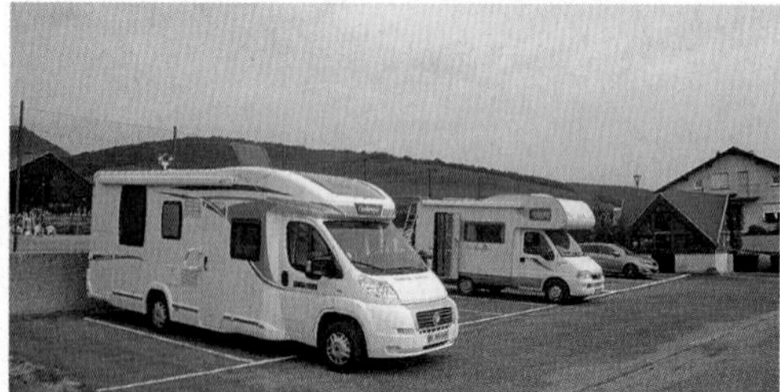

3 free €4 Ch.
Location: Urban, simple, quiet. 01/01-31/12.
Distance: on the spot 300m.
Remarks: Service 100m, 3 parking spaces Allée des Cygnes n48.23242, o7.37239, 3 parking spaces Rue Windmuehl n48.23172, e.36443.

S Saint-Imoges 16B2

Rue de la Briquetrie. **GPS**: n49,10689 e3,97903.
8 free 150liter Ch 1h,service €2. **Location:** Isolated, quiet. 01/01-31/12.

FR

S Saint-Mihiel 16D3

Chemin Gué Rapeau. **GPS**: n48,90227 e5,53960.

4 €3 Chfree €3/24h. **Location:** Rural, simple, isolated, quiet. **Surface:** asphalted. 01/01-31/12.
Distance: 1,5km 1km 1,5km.
Remarks: Directly at the river, nearby sluices, next to camping municipal, max. 24h.

S Saint-Nabord 19F1

Rue de la Croix Saint Jacques. **GPS**: n48,04527 e6,58175.

10 free €3/80liter Ch €3. **Location:** Simple, quiet.
Surface: asphalted. 01/01-31/12.
Distance: 300m 200m 50m.

S Saint-Nicolas-de-Port 16E3

Rue du jeu de Paune. **GPS**: n48,63515 e6,30048.

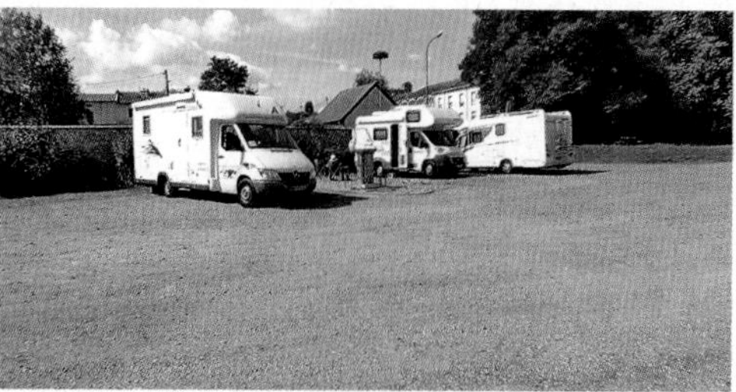

10 free €4 Ch. **Location:** Urban, simple, central, quiet.
Surface: gravel. 01/01-31/12.
Distance: on the spot 150m 200m 100m.

S Sainte-Livière 16C3

1 rue Sainte Libaire. **GPS**: n48,60133 e4,82139.
19 €8 Ch (19x) included. **Location:** Rural, isolated, quiet. **Surface:** gravel. 01/01-31/12.
Distance: 2km Lake Der-Chantecoq 2km.
Remarks: Service passerby € 3.

Sainte-Marie-aux-Mines 19G1

Place des Tisserands. **GPS**: n48,24700 e7,18322.

10 free. **Location:** Urban, simple, quiet. **Surface:** asphalted. 01/01-31/12.
Distance: 100m 100m 300m.
Remarks: Max. 24h.

Tourist information Sainte-Marie-aux-Mines:
Office de Tourisme, 86, rue Wilson, www.tourisme.fr/office-de-tourisme/sainte-marie-aux-mines-68.htm. Mineral city with silvermine, Mine d'Argent Sainte-Barthélemy.

S Sainte-Marie-du-Lac-Nuisement 16C3

Port de Nuisement, D13A. **GPS**: n48,60285 e4,74922.
6 free €3/10minutes Ch €3/55minutes.
Surface: asphalted. 01/01-31/12.
Distance: 4km on the spot.
Remarks: Coins at tourist info.

S Sapignicourt 16C3

Rue Deperthes à Larzicourt. **GPS**: n48,65111 e4,80583.

4 €2,50/10minutes Ch €2,50/55minutes.
Location: Rural, simple, isolated, quiet. **Surface:** grassy. 01/01-31/12.
Distance: 500m.
Remarks: Coins at town hall and Mr. Bauer, 14, grande rue.

Sarralbe 16F2

Rue de la Sarre. **GPS**: n49,00171 e7,03240.
4 free. **Surface:** asphalted. 01/01-31/12.
Distance: 350m 350m.
Remarks: At sports centre.

Saverne 16G3

Rue des Emouleurs. **GPS**: n48,74512 e7,36854.

€7 €2 €2/6h. **Location:** Simple, central.
Surface: gravel/sand. 01/01-31/12.
Distance: centre 650m.

S Saverne 16G3

Camping Les Portes d'Alsace, Rue du Père Liebermann.
GPS: n48,73131 e7,35504.

12 € 10-12 Ch WCincluded €2,50 €2,50. **Location:** Comfortable, quiet. **Surface:** gravel. 01/04-30/09.

Tourist information Saverne:
Château de Rohan. Museum, former summer residence of the bishops of Strasbourg.

Sedan 16C1

Rue Hue Tanton. **GPS**: n49,70145 e4,95092.
free. 01/01-31/12.
Remarks: Parking places around the castle of Sedan.

Seuil-d'Argonne 16C3

Rue du Commandant Laflotte, D2/D20. **GPS**: n48,98294 e5,06215.

5 free. **Location:** Rural, simple, quiet. **Surface:** gravel. 01/01-31/12.
Distance: 650m 650m 650m 650m.
Remarks: In fron of sports fields.

S Sézanne 16B3

Place du Champ Benoist. **GPS**: n48,72222 e3,72125.

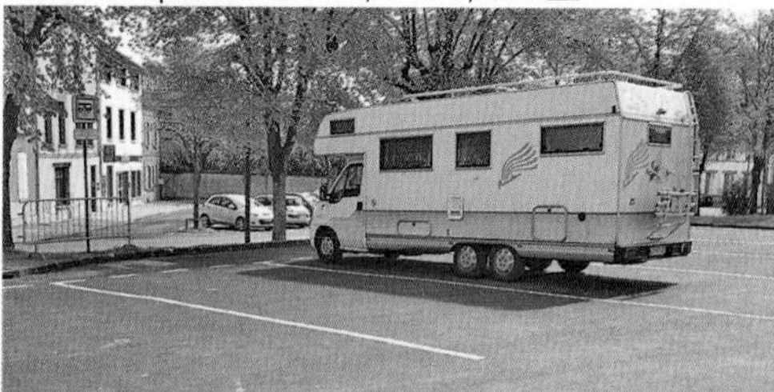

7 free €2/100liter Ch €2/1h WCfree.
Location: Urban, simple, central, noisy. **Surface:** asphalted. 01/01-31/12 Sa market.
Distance: on the spot 50m 300m 50m.

Sierck-les-Bains 16E2

Place de la Gro. **GPS**: n49,44424 e6,36217.

8 free. **Location:** Simple. **Surface:** asphalted. 01/01-31/12.
Distance: 200m 200m 350m.
Remarks: Along the Moselle river, nearby police station.

S Soufflenheim 16H3

Rue des Hirondelle. **GPS**: n48,83233 e7,96045.

13 free €2 Ch €2. **Location:** Urban, simple, quiet.
Surface: asphalted. 01/01-31/12.
Distance: 300m 200m 300m 200m.

Souilly 16D2

Route de St.André-en-Barrois, D159. **GPS**: n49,02730 e5,27985.

6 free.
Location: Rural, simple. **Surface:** gravel. 01/01-31/12.
Distance: 600m.

Soultz 19G2

Rue de la Marne. **GPS**: n47,88806 e7,23139.

30 free Ch free.
Location: Urban, simple, quiet. **Surface:** asphalted. 01/01-31/12.
Distance: 200m 200m 500m 500m.
Remarks: Payment only by bank card.

Stenay 16D1

Aire Camping-car, D947. **GPS**: n49,48979 e5,18323.

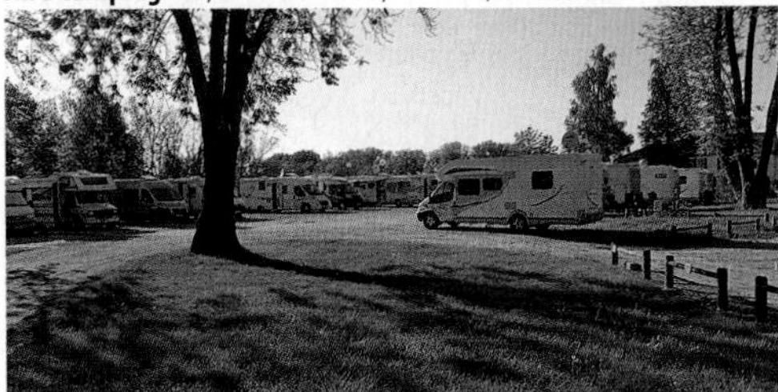

47 €8 Ch WC €4/4 included. **Location:** Rural, comfortable, quiet. **Surface:** metalled. 01/01-31/12.
Distance: 150m 150m 800m, bakery 300m.
Remarks: Pay and entrance code at harbourmaster, musée Européen de la Bière, beer museum.

Stenay 16D1

Port de plaisance, Rue du Port. **GPS**: n49,49096 e5,18312.

6 €8 Ch WC €4/4 included. **Location:** Comfortable, quiet. **Surface:** asphalted. 01/01-31/12.
Distance: on the spot 200m 500m.
Remarks: Pay at harbourmaster.

Tourist information Stenay:
Musée de la Bière. Beer museum.

Château, Louppy-sur-Loison. Renaissance castle, 17th century.

Strasbourg 16G3

Parking Auberge de Jeunesse des Deux Rives (Parc du Rhin), Rue des Cavaliers. **GPS**: n48,56659 e7,79975.

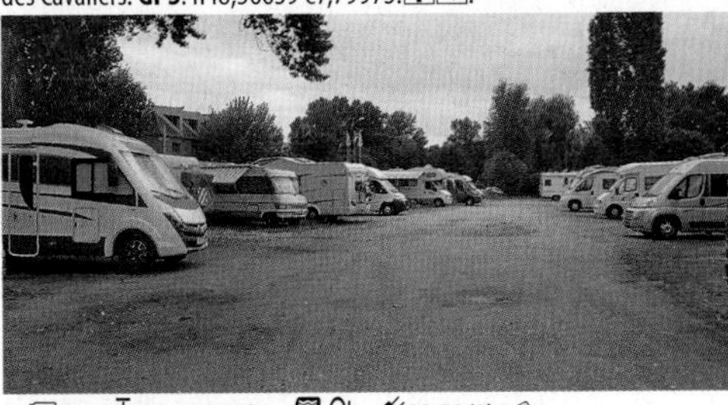

40 free €2,50/100liter Ch €2,50/1h.
Location: Rural, simple. **Surface:** asphalted/sand.
01/01-31/12.
Distance: Strasbourg centre 5km bus 21 + tram.
Remarks: Max. 7 days.

Tourist information Strasbourg:
Maison Kammerzell. Restaurant, 1467-1589, one of the most beautyfull half-timbered houses in the Alsace region.
Musée Alsacien. Folk art and handycrafts.
Cathédrale de Nôtre-Dame.

Suippes 16C2

Rue de l'Abreuvoir. **GPS**: n49,13074 e4,53419.

10 free €2/liter Ch €2/1h.
Location: Urban, simple. **Surface:** asphalted. 01/01-31/12.
Distance: on the spot 200m 200m.

Tannois 16D3

Parking du Belvédère, D169. **GPS**: n48,71977 e5,22967.

10 free. **Location:** Rural, simple, isolated, quiet. **Surface:** gravel.
01/01-31/12.
Distance: 1,3km 1,5km on the spot on the spot.

Thann 19F2

Parking du Centre, Rue du Général de Gaulle. N66.
GPS: n47,80889 e7,10460.

30 free Ch Service €4. **Location:** Urban, simple, noisy.
Surface: asphalted. 01/01-31/12.
Distance: 250m 50m 50m.

Thann 19F2

Place du Bungert, Rue des Pélerins. **GPS**: n47,81159 e7,10450.

10 free WC free.
Location: Urban, simple, central, quiet. **Surface:** asphalted.
01/01-31/12 Sa-morning market.
Distance: 200m on the spot 200m 500m on the spot on the spot.

Thaon-les-Vosges 19E1

Aire du Coignot, Rue du Coignot. **GPS**: n48,24920 e6,42520.

10 free Ch free. **Location:** Simple, quiet.
Surface: asphalted/gravel. 01/03-01/10.
Distance: 1,5km 400m.
Remarks: Next to port fluvial.

Thiaucourt-Regniéville 16E3

Rue du Stade. **GPS**: n48,95220 e5,86090.
free Ch €3/6h. **Location:** Isolated, quiet.
Surface: grassy/gravel. 01/01-31/12.
Distance: 700m 700m.
Remarks: At tennis-courts.

Thierville-sur-Meuse 16D2

Thierville sur-meuse, Avenue de l,etangbleu.
GPS: n49,17499 e5,36357.

20 free. **Location:** Rural, simple. **Surface:** asphalted.
01/01-31/12.
Distance: 100m 50m 50m on the spot on the spot.
Remarks: Along the Meuse river.

Tilleux 19D1

Grande Rue. **GPS**: n48,29300 e5,72250.

8 free free.
Location: Simple. **Surface:** gravel. 01/01-31/12.
Distance: 100m.
Remarks: Inclining pitches, entrance road max. 3,5t.

Toul 16E3

Avenue du Colonel Péchot. **GPS**: n48,67670 e5,88549.

FR

12 €7/24h Ch (8x)included. **Location:** Urban, comfortable, quiet. **Surface:** asphalted. 01/01-31/12.
Distance: 4km.
Remarks: Max. 72h.

S Trois Épis 19G1

Place des Antonins. **GPS:** n48,10101 e7,22948.

25 free €2 Ch €3/55minutes WC€0,50 €1.
Location: Urban, simple, quiet. **Surface:** asphalted.
01/01-31/12.
Distance: 150m ⊗150m 150m on the spot.

Turckheim 19G1

Quai de la gare. **GPS:** n48,08555 e7,27739.

6 €5.
Location: Urban, simple, noisy. **Surface:** metalled.
01/01-31/12.
Distance: historical centre 250m ⊗250m 300m on the spot.

S Turckheim 19G1

Camping municipal Les Cigognes, 4, quai de la Gare.
GPS: n48,08539 e7,27535.
€5,40 Ch. 15/03-31/10.

S Ungersheim 19G2

Ecomusée. GPS: n47,85200 e7,28400.

20 €6 included. **Location:** Rural, simple, quiet.
Surface: gravel/metalled. 01/01-31/12.
Distance: 6km ⊗200m.
Remarks: Check in at hotel.

Val-d'Ornain 16C3

D2. **GPS:** n48,80327 e5,07284.
6 free.
Location: Rural. **Surface:** unpaved. 01/01-31/12.

S Val-et-Châtillon 16F3

Grande Rue / D993a. **GPS:** n48,56039 e6,96525.

6 free €3 Ch €3/55minutes. **Location:** Comfortable, quiet.
Surface: gravel. 01/01-31/12.
Distance: 100m 3,5km on the spot.
Remarks: Max. 4 days, bread-service.

S Vaucouleurs 16D3

Rue du Cardinal Lépicier. **GPS:** n48,60179 e5,66737.

3 €5 €2/100liter Ch €2 WC. **Location:** Urban, simple, central. **Surface:** asphalted. 01/01-31/12.
Distance: on the spot ⊗500m 500m.

Vauquois 16C2

Parking municipal, D212. **GPS:** n49,20405 e5,07398.

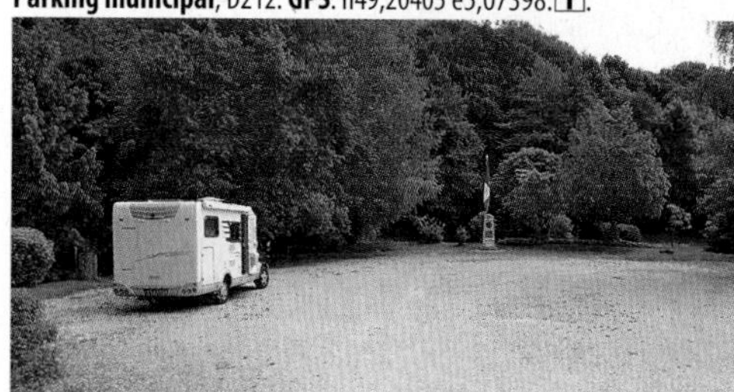

8 free. **Location:** Rural, simple. **Surface:** gravel.
Distance: on the spot.

Velaines 16D3

D120A. **GPS:** n48,70589 e5,29804.

4 free.
Location: Urban, simple, central. **Surface:** gravel.
Distance: on the spot 300m.

S Vendeuvre-sur-Barse 19C1

Place du 8 mai 1945, Rue du Pont Chevalier.
GPS: n48,23727 e4,46646.

5 free €3 Ch €3. **Location:** Urban, simple, simple.
Surface: asphalted. tue-evening, wed-morning (market).
Distance: 100m ⊗on the spot ATAC on the spot.

S Ventron 19F2

Chemin du Plain. **GPS:** n47,93906 e6,86900.

10 free €2/100liter Ch €2/55minutes. **Location:** Simple, central, quiet. **Surface:** asphalted. 01/01-31/12.
Remarks: Coins at tourist info.

Ventron 19F2

Route de Frère Joseph. **GPS:** n47,92514 e6,86223.

free. **Surface:** asphalted. 01/01-31/12.
Distance: Ventron 3,2km on the spot.
Remarks: Parking at skipistes.

Verdun 16D2

Dragées Braquir, Rue du Fort de Vaux, D112.
GPS: n49,15955 e5,39989.

10 free.
Location: Urban, simple, central. **Surface:** metalled.
Distance: on the spot.
Remarks: Max. 1 night.

S Viéville 19D1

Halte Nautique La Licorne. GPS: n48,23825 e5,12988.

6 €1,50 €1,50/day (6x)€1,50/day.
Location: Rural, simple, quiet. **Surface:** gravel.
01/01-31/12.
Distance: on the spot ⊗3km 500m on the spot on the spot.

Vigneulles-les-Hattonchat 16D2

Rue Miss Skinner. **GPS:** n48,99200 e5,70122.
5 free. **Location:** Isolated, quiet. **Surface:** gravel.
Distance: 2km.

S Villefranche-sur-Saône 22C3

Camping-car Park, 2788 Route de Riottier.
GPS: n45,97278 e4,75135.
128 €12 Ch included. **Location:** Urban, luxurious. 15/05-15/09.
Distance: A6 1,3km Station > Lyon 3,4km.
Remarks: Wifi code: 692712.

S Villeneuve-Renneville-Chevigny 16B3

Champagne Leclère-Massard, 12, rue du Plessis.
GPS: n48,91488 e4,05959.

FR

6 €5 water Ch electricity included wifi €2/day.
Location: Comfortable. **Surface:** asphalted.
Distance: 3km 2km 3km 3km on the spot.
Remarks: Tu-Su fresh bread, champagne tastery.

S Villers-sous-Châtillon 16B2

Halte camping-cars, Rue du Parc. **GPS**: n49,09642 e3,80078.

5 free water €3/100liter Ch €3/1h.
Location: Rural, simple, quiet. **Surface:** asphalted. 01/01-31/12.
Distance: 1,2km 50m 1,2km 2km.
Remarks: Coins at town hall and restaurant du Commerce.

S Void-Vacon 16D3

Rue de la Gare. **GPS**: n48,68240 e5,61960.

20 free water €2/100liter Ch €2.
Location: Rural, simple, isolated, quiet. **Surface:** grassy/gravel.
01/01-31/12.
Distance: 700m 10m 10m.
Remarks: Coins at shop/town hall.

S Wadelincourt 16C1

Ferme du Chemin de Noyers, Rue Hubert Desrousseaux.
GPS: n49,68075 e4,93553.
1 free water electricity free. 01/01-31/12.
Remarks: Regional products.

S Wassy 19C1

Lac des Leschères, Réservoir Leschères Centre.
GPS: n48,48991 e4,94924.
free water Ch. 01/01-31/12.
Distance: 1,5km on the spot on the spot 1,5km 1km.

S Westhalten 19G2

Rue St Blaise, D18, Vallée Noble, dir Soultzmatt..
GPS: n47,95626 e7,25135.

6 free water €2 Ch. **Location:** Rural, simple, noisy.
Surface: asphalted. 01/03-30/11.
Remarks: Max. 48h.

S Westhalten 19G2

Domaine du Bollenberg. **GPS**: n47,94459 e7,25652.
5 free water. 01/01-31/12.
Distance: on the spot.
Remarks: Max 3,5t.

S Willer-sur-Thur 19F2

Place de l'Eglise. **GPS**: n47,84315 e7,07292.

3 free water Ch WC free.
Location: Urban. **Surface:** asphalted. 01/01-31/12.
Distance: 250m 500m 500m, bakery 50m 500m on the spot 500m.

Normandie

S Agon-Coutainville 15B2

Flot Bleu Park, Boulevard Louis Lebel-Jéhenne.
GPS: n49,05176 w1,59123.

25 €6,30/24h water Ch electricity included
Location: Comfortable. **Surface:** grassy. 01/01-31/12.
Distance: 800m.
Remarks: Service passerby € 2,70.

S Ardevon 15B3

La Bidonnière, Route de la Rive 5. **GPS**: n48,60352 w1,47612.
60 €10, 01/11-31/03 €6 water Ch electricity (40x)€3,70/24h WC €3 wifi included.
Location: Rural, luxurious, quiet. **Surface:** grassy/gravel.
01/01-31/12.
Distance: on the spot 3km 1km 3km 1,5km on the spot on the spot.
Remarks: Bread-service, free bicycles available, view on Mt.St.Michel.

S Arromanches-les-Bains 15C1

Arromanches 360, Cinéma Circulaire, Chemin du Calvaire / D514.
GPS: n49,33924 w0,61419.

20 €6 water €2 Ch.
Location: Rural, comfortable. 01/01-31/12.
Distance: 400m 300m.

Remarks: Beautiful view.

S Arromanches-les-Bains 15C1

Rue François Carpentier. **GPS**: n49,33904 w0,62553.

14 free water €2/10minutes Ch €2/1h wifi free15minutes.
Surface: asphalted. 01/01-31/12.
Distance: 150m 100m 100m 250m.
Remarks: Next to camping municipal, max. 1 night.

Auderville 15B1

D901. **GPS**: n49,71431 w1,93481.

15 free. **Location:** Rural, simple. **Surface:** grassy/gravel.
01/01-31/12.
Distance: 300m 700m 600m.

S Auffay 15F1

Parking de la Gare. **GPS**: n49,71339 e1,09890.

4 free water €3/100liter Ch €3/1h. **Location:** Urban, simple, quiet. **Surface:** gravel. 01/01-31/12.
Distance: 800m 17km 700m 700m on the spot on the spot.

S Avranches 15B3

Centre Culturel, Boulevard Jozeau Marigné.
GPS: n48,68585 w1,367.

8 free water €2/10minutes Ch. **Location:** Urban, simple.
Surface: gravel/metalled. 01/01-31/12.
Distance: 200m 1,9km 200m 200m.
Remarks: Behind community centre, max. 1 night, attractive medieval centre.

Tourist information Avranches:
- Jardins des Plantes. Garden with exotic plants.
- Basilique St Germain. 9-12h, 14-16h.
- place des Halles. Sa + Tue-morning.

Bagnoles-de-l'Orne 15D3

Avenue du Dr Paul Lemuet. **GPS**: n48,55558 w0,40973.

FR

6 free. **Location:** Simple, noisy. **Surface:** asphalted.
01/01-31/12.
Distance: 400m 400m 900m on the spot.

Bagnoles-de-l'Orne 15D3

D235. **GPS**: n48,55821 w0,4129.

6 free.
Location: Urban, simple. **Surface:** gravel. 01/01-31/12.
Distance: on the spot 400m 400m on the spot.
Remarks: Behind tourist info, Place du Marché.

Bagnoles-de-l'Orne 15D3

D916. **GPS**: n48,55034 w0,40202.

3 Ch. **Location:** Simple. **Surface:** asphalted.
01/01-31/12.
Distance: 900m on the spot on the spot on the spot.

Bardouville 15F1

Le Grand Bois. **GPS**: n49,43027 e0,92362.

2 free Ch. **Location:** Rural, comfortable, central, quiet.
Surface: asphalted. 01/01-31/12.
Distance: 300m 15km 500m 500m.

Barfleur 15C1

Chemin de la Masse. **GPS**: n49,67368 w1,2641.

20 free ChWC. **Location:** Urban, simple. **Surface:** grassy/gravel.
01/01-31/12.
Distance: 200m.

Barneville-Carteret 15B1

Quai Émile Valmy, rue du port. **GPS**: n49,37300 w1,789.

12 free. **Location:** Urban, simple. **Surface:** asphalted.
Distance: 600m on the spot on the spot 600m.
Remarks: In front of the Gare Maritime.

Barneville-Carteret 15B1

Carrefour Market, Route du Pont Rose. **GPS**: n49,38553 w1,75239.
€2 Ch €2/1h. **Location:** Simple. 01/01-31/12.

Bayeux 15C2

Place Gauquelin-Despallières. **GPS**: n49,28044 w0,70775.

5 free ChWCfree. **Location:** Urban. **Surface:** asphalted
01/01-31/12.
Distance: on the spot 100m 100m on the spot.
Remarks: Max. 12h.

Bayeux 15C2

Voie de la Rivière. **GPS**: n49,28168 w0,69604.
free Ch. 01/01-31/12.
Distance: 850m.

Bayeux 15C2

Boulevard Fabian Ware. **GPS**: n49,27242 w0,71053.
10 overnight stay € 4. 01/01-31/12.
Distance: 900m.

Tourist information Bayeux:
Musée Mémorial de la Bataille de Normandie, Boulevard Fabian Ware. Battle of Normandy, June 6 till August 22, 1944. 9.30-17h, 01/05-30/09 9-19h.
Cathédrale Nôtre Dame. Gothic cathedral.

Beauvoir 15B3

Aire de camping-car du mont St Michel, Route de Mont St Michel.
GPS: n48,59426 w1,5122.

122 € 12,50 Ch (122x)included free.
Location: Rural, comfortable, luxurious, quiet.
Surface: grassy/gravel. 01/01-31/12.
Distance: 500m 500m.
Remarks: Service passerby € 4,50, le Mont Saint Michel 5km.

Beauvoir 15B3

Le Mont-St-Michel, Rue Au Bis. **GPS**: n48,60841 w1,50681.

220 € 20/24h .
Surface: asphalted. 01/01-31/12.
Distance: on the spot on the spot.
Remarks: Free shuttle to Le Mont-Saint-Michel 07.30-00.30h.

Beauvoir 15B3

La Ferme Saint Michel, Route du Mont Saint Michel, D976.
GPS: n48,61112 w1,50978.

35 guests free ChWC. **Location:** Simple. **Surface:** gravel.
01/01-31/12 Mo.
Distance: 600m on the spot 600m on the spot.

Bernières-sur-Mer 15D2

Rue Victor Tesnière. **GPS**: n49,33472 w0,41984.

35 free. **Location:** Urban, simple. **Surface:** gravel.
Distance: on the spot 100m 100m on the spot 100m on the spot on the spot on the spot.

Beuvron-en-Auge 15D2

Parking de la Gare, Avenue de la Gare. **GPS**: n49,18560 w0,0495.

16 € 6 Chincluded.
Location: Rural, comfortable, quiet. **Surface:** gravel.
01/01-31/12.
Distance: 200m on the spot on the spot.
Remarks: Max. 24h, pay and coins at Tabac-Presse 200m.

Bretteville-sur-Odon 15D2

Auto Camping Car Service, 4-6 Avenue des Carrières.
GPS: n49,18449 w0,41465.

6 free Chfree. **Location:** Urban, simple. **Surface:** metalled.
01/01-31/12.
Distance: 1km 500m.

Bréville-les-Monts 15D2

Rue des Dentellières. **GPS**: n49,24167 w0,228.

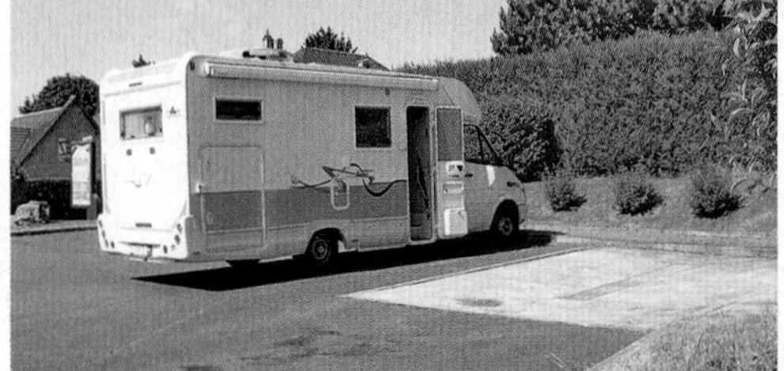

4 free €2/10minutes Ch. **Location:** Simple, comfortable.
Surface: asphalted. 01/03-15/11.
Distance: on the spot.

FR

Remarks: Max. 72h, (may-july-aug) 48h, coins at tourist info Merville and harbour.

S Bricquebec 15B1

Bas de Cattigny, D900, route de Cherbourg.
GPS: n49,47402 w1,64674.

6 free Ch (2x)free. **Location:** Comfortable, quiet.
Surface: gravel.
Distance: 1km on the spot.

S Broglie 15E2

Parc de la bibliothèque. GPS: n49,00563 e0,52948.

8 € 5/night €2,50/100liter Ch €2,50/1h.
Surface: grassy/metalled.
01/03-31/10 7-22h, 01/11-28/02 7.30-19h.
Distance: 200m 200m 200m, 7.30-19h.

Tourist information Broglie:
Fri 7-13h.

S Buchy 15F1

D919, Route de Forges. **GPS:** n49,58538 e1,36417.

8 free €2/100liter Ch €2/h.
Location: Urban. **Surface:** gravel.
01/01-31/12.
Distance: 500m 500m 500m on the spot.
Remarks: Coins at the shops in the village, monday-morning market.

S Cabourg 15D2

Avenue Michel d'Ornano. **GPS:** n49,28225 w0,11994.

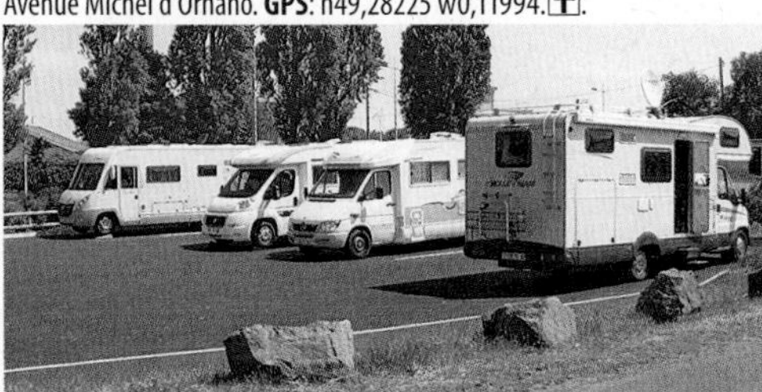

6 free €2/10minutes Ch. **Location:** Rural, comfortable, quiet. **Surface:** asphalted. 01/01-31/12.
Distance: centre 900m 7,5km 1,6km on the spot.
Remarks: Nearby Hippodrome.

S Cambremer 15D2

Place de l'Europe/Avenue des Tilleuls. **GPS:** n49,14991 e0,04729.

7 free €2/100liter Ch €2/1h.
Location: Rural, simple, central, quiet. **Surface:** gravel.
01/01-31/12.
Distance: 50m 100m bakery 100m.
Remarks: Coins at the shops and town hall.

S Campigny 15E2

Chemin de la Motte. **GPS:** n49,31139 e0,55223.

3 free Chfree. **Surface:** grassy. 01/01-31/12.
Remarks: On inner court of old presbytery, max. 24h.

S Carentan 15C1

Camping-Car Park de Carentan, Chemin du Grand Bas Pays.
GPS: n49,30937 w1,2392.

12 € 10,80 Ch included. **Location:** Comfortable, quiet. **Surface:** gravel/metalled. 01/01-31/12.
Distance: 500m 500m.
Remarks: Service passerby € 5.

S Carolles 15B3

Rue du Mont Dol. **GPS:** n48,75931 w1,57062.

15 € 8 €3/100liter Ch €3/55minutes.
Location: Comfortable. **Surface:** grassy/gravel. 01/01-31/12.
Distance: 150m on the spot on the spot.
Remarks: Only exact change.

S Carolles 15B3

La Guériniére, Residence les Jaunets. **GPS:** n48,74989 w1,55695.
5 free €2 Ch €2. **Surface:** asphalted. 01/01-31/12.
Distance: on the spot 2km.
Remarks: In front of town hall.

S Caumont-l'Éventé 15C2

Souterroscope des Ardoisières, Route de Saint Lô, D71.
GPS: n49,08868 w0,81645.

3 free €2/10minutes Ch €2/55minutes WC.
Location: Simple, isolated. **Surface:** asphalted.
01/01-31/12, service 15/02-15/11.
Distance: on the spot 500m on the spot.

S Cerisy-la-Forêt 15C2

GPS: n49,19806 w0,93389.

10 free €2 Ch €2.
Location: Rural, simple. **Surface:** gravel. 01/01-31/12.
Distance: 500m 500m.
Remarks: Near abbey.

Cherbourg 15B1

Musée Cité de la Mer, Llée du President Menut.
GPS: n49,64740 w1,61782.

40 free. **Location:** Urban, simple. **Surface:** asphalted.
Distance: 1km on the spot 1km on the spot.
Remarks: Max. 1 night.

Tourist information Cherbourg:
Musée Fort du Roule. War museum. 9.30-12h, 14-17.30h.

S Clecy 15D2

Rue du Stade. **GPS:** n48,91886 w0,48114.

5 free €2/20minutes Ch. **Location:** Simple, quiet.
Surface: gravel. 01/01-31/12.
Distance: 100m 100m 300m 200m.
Remarks: Coins at the shops in the village.

S Clères 15F1

Rue Edmond Spalikowski, Côte du Mont Blanc.
GPS: n49,60228 e1,11667.

10 free €4/100liter Ch €4/6h (8x)h.
Location: Comfortable, quiet. **Surface:** gravel.

FR

01/01-31/12 service: 01/11-28/02.
Distance: 500m 500m 500m on the spot.
Remarks: Nearby football ground, max. 72h, coins at bakery, butcher and Bar-Tabac.

Colleville-Montgomery 15D2
Rue de Saint-Aubin/Rue les Petites Rues.
GPS: n49,27166 w0,29891.

9 € 5 Ch free.
Location: Rural, simple, quiet. **Surface:** grassy. 01/01-31/12.
Distance: 200m 450m.

Tourist information Colleville-Montgomery:
Musée Omaha Beach, St.Laurent-sur-Mer. Collection of military vehicles, weapons and costumes.

Cormeilles 15E2
Route du Château de Malou, D810. **GPS**: n49,24926 e0,37371.

8 free Ch free. **Surface:** asphalted. 01/01-31/12.
Distance: 400m river 400m.

Coudeville-sur-Mer 15B2
Avenue de la Mer D351. **GPS**: n48,88707 w1,56607.

10 € 5,65/24h Ch included .
Location: Rural. **Surface:** grassy/gravel. 01/01-31/12.
Distance: 500m 200m 200m 500m 500m.

Courseulles-sur-Mer 15D2
Avenue de la Libération. **GPS**: n49,33440 w0,44551.

13 € 6,50 €2 Ch. **Location:** Urban, comfortable, central.
Surface: asphalted. 01/01-31/12.
Distance: 50m 200m pizzeria 50m.
Remarks: Nearby entrance campsite, max. 24h.

Courseulles-sur-Mer 15D2
Juno Beach, Voie des Français Libres. **GPS**: n49,33694 w0,46502.

25 free. **Location:** Central, quiet. **Surface:** metalled.
01/01-31/12.
Distance: 100m 50m.

Couterne 15D3
Place de la Mairie. **GPS**: n48,51223 w0,41417.

10 free Ch WC free. **Location:** Urban, simple.
Surface: asphalted. 01/01-31/12.
Distance: on the spot nearby nearby on the spot.
Remarks: Max. 1 night, closed when frosty.

Criel-sur-Mer 13C3
Rue de la Plage, D222. **GPS**: n50,03241 e1,31000.

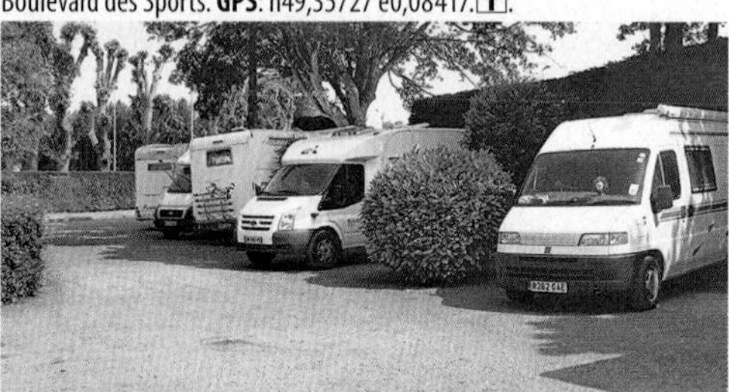

30 free. **Location:** Simple, central, quiet. **Surface:** grassy/gravel.
01/01-31/12.
Distance: 500m on the spot on the spot 500m 1km.

Deauville 15D2
Boulevard des Sports. **GPS**: n49,35727 e0,08417.

8 free Ch (6x)free. **Location:** Urban, simple, quiet.
Surface: gravel. 01/01-31/12.
Distance: on the spot 800m 500m.
Remarks: Behind stadium, max. 24h.

Dieppe 13B3
Aire d'accueil Front de Mer, Boulevard Maréchal-Foch.
GPS: n49,93188 e1,08433.

50 € 7/24h Ch (8x)included.
Location: Urban, comfortable, central, quiet. **Surface:** asphalted.
01/01-31/12.
Distance: on the spot 100m 500m 500m 100m.
Remarks: Max. 48h.

Dieppe 13B3
NEUVILLE-les-Dieppe, Quai de la Marne.
GPS: n49,93014 e1,08667.

45 € 12/24h Ch (8x)free .
Location: Urban, comfortable, quiet. **Surface:** asphalted.
01/01-31/12.
Distance: 500m on the spot on the spot 500m 500m on the spot.
Remarks: Max. 48h, wifi card available at harbour master.

Tourist information Dieppe:
Château Dieppe. Castle, 15th century, with maritime museum.
10-12h, 14-18h 01/10-31/05 Tue.
Tue, Thu 8-14h.
Normandic market. Sa 8-14h.

Dives-sur-Mer 15D2
Rue de l'avenir. **GPS**: n49,29028 w0,10345.

10 free €2/10minutes Ch . **Location:** Rural, comfortable, quiet. **Surface:** asphalted. 01/01-31/12.
Distance: 500m 900m.
Remarks: Nearby Port Guillaume.

Doudeville 15E1
Place du Mont Criquet, centre-ville. **GPS**: n49,72000 e0,78750.

20 free €2/100liter Ch. **Location:** Urban, simple, central, quiet. **Surface:** asphalted. 01/01-31/12.
Distance: 100m 100m 100m on the spot on the spot on the spot.
Remarks: Market Saturday.

Dragey-Ronthon 15B3
Route de la Plage. **GPS**: n48,70945 w1,5139.

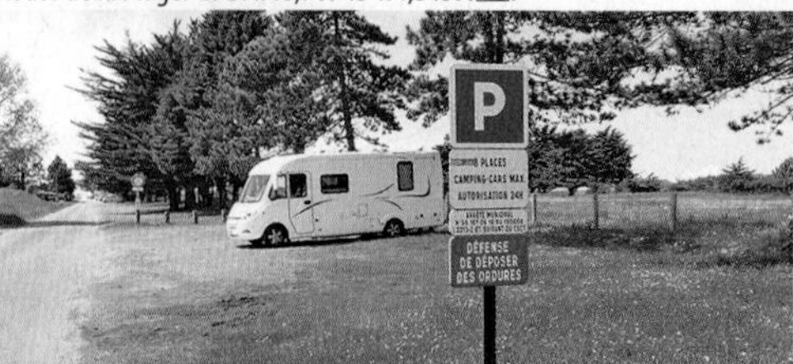

8 free. **Location:** Simple, simple, isolated. **Surface:** grassy/sand.
01/01-31/12.
Distance: 2km on the spot on the spot on the spot.
Remarks: Max. 24h.

Ducey 15B3
P du Domaine, Rue St Quentin. **GPS**: n48,62513 w1,294.

30 free €2/100liter Ch €2 WC. **Location:** Simple, noisy. **Surface:** gravel/metalled. 01/01-31/12.
Distance: 500m 500m 500m on the spot.
Remarks: Only exact change.

S Englesqueville-la-Percée 15C1

Ferme de la Rouge Fossé, D514. **GPS**: n49,38781 w0,94829.

6 € 5 Ch€3 (6x)included. **Location:** Comfortable, isolated, quiet. **Surface:** grassy/gravel. 01/01-31/12.
Distance: 500m.

S Equeurdreville 15B1

Rue Jean Bart. **GPS**: n49,65465 w1,65044.

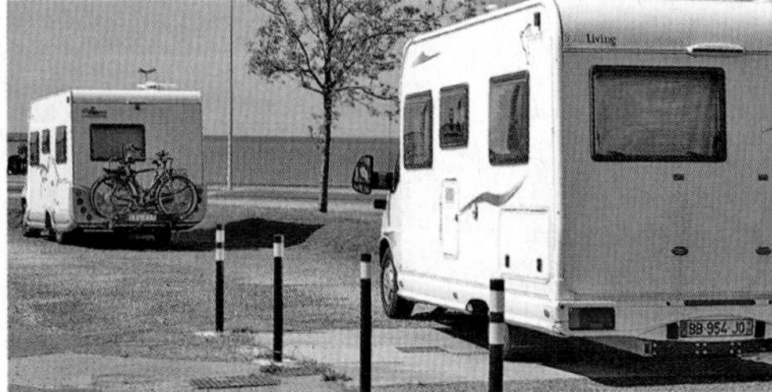

6 free Chfree. **Location:** Urban, simple.
Surface: gravel/sand.
Distance: 1km 1km on the spot.

S Étoutteville 15E1

Espace du Beau Soleil, Rue du Prieuré. **GPS**: n49,67609 e0,79073.

6 free €2/140liter Ch €2/1h.
Location: Rural, comfortable, isolated, quiet. **Surface:** concrete.
Distance: 500m 400m.

S Etretat 15E1

Aire de stationnement Maupassant, Rue Guy de Maupassant.
GPS: n49,70009 e0,21579.

30 € 8/24h €2/100liter Ch €3/55minutes .
Location: Comfortable, central, quiet. **Surface:** grassy/metalled.
01/10-31/12.
Distance: 1km 1,2km 1km 1km 350m.
Remarks: Next to camping municipal, max. 24h.

Etretat 15E1

Pl. de la Gare. **GPS**: n49,70843 e0,21524.

10 free. **Surface:** metalled. 01/01-31/12.
Distance: 900m 1km.

Tourist information Etretat:

Office de Tourisme, Place Maurice Guillard, www.etretat.net. The cliffs which have the shape of an arch are a well-known tourist attraction.

S Fécamp 15E1

Parking de la Mâture, Chaussée Gayant. **GPS**: n49,76024 e0,37412.
+10 free €3/100liter Ch. **Location:** Urban, simple, central.
Surface: asphalted.
Distance: on the spot 200m 200m 200m.

Fécamp 15E1

Quai Sadi Carnot. **GPS**: n49,76087 e0,37157.

10 free. **Location:** Urban, simple, simple, isolated.
Surface: asphalted. 01/01-31/12.
Distance: 200m on the spot on the spot 200m 500m 200m.
Remarks: Between pier and marina, max. 7m.

Tourist information Fécamp:

Office de Tourisme, Quai Sadi Carnot, www.fecamptourisme.com. City against the chalk-cliff of the Côte d'Albâtre, fishing-port is now mainly a marina.

M Palais Bénédictine, 110 rue Alexandre Le Grand. Museum with Bénédictine distillery and tasting-pub. 01/07-31/08 10-18.45h, 01/09-30/06 10.30-12.30h, 14.30-17.30h.

Fermanville 15B1

Le Cap Lévi. GPS: n49,69002.w1,4673.

6 € 3. **Location:** Rural, simple, quiet. **Surface:** grassy.
01/01-31/12.

S Fervaches 15C2

La Vallée. **GPS**: n48,99550 w1,0826.
8 € 3 ChWCincluded free. **Location:** Rural, comfortable.
Surface: grassy/gravel.
Distance: 150m 150m.
Remarks: Wifi code at grocery.

S Forges-les-Eaux 15G1

Aire de camping car de la Minière, Boulevard Nicolas Thiessé.
GPS: n49,60569 e1,54288.

35 free, 15/03-15/10 € 8 Ch (6x)included .

Location: Urban, comfortable, central, quiet. **Surface:** asphalted.
01/01-31/12.
Distance: 2km 1km 900m 300m 2km.
Remarks: Max. 48h, water closed during wintertime.

S Formigny 15C1

La Ferme du Lavoir, D517. **GPS**: n49,34041 w0,89654.

6 € 10/night Ch WC included. **Location:** Rural, comfortable, quiet. **Surface:** grassy/gravel. 01/01-31/12.
Distance: 300m 3km.
Remarks: Organic orchards, cider production.

S Gacé 15E3

Rue du Marché aux Bestiaux. **GPS**: n48,79500 e0,29583.

30 free €2 Ch. **Surface:** asphalted. 01/01-31/12.
Distance: on the spot 2,6km 50m.
Remarks: In front of tourist office, max. 24h.

S Gavray 15B2

D38. **GPS**: n48,91113 w1,34641.

8 free €4/10minutes Ch. **Location:** Urban, comfortable.
Surface: asphalted. 01/01-31/12.
Distance: 400m 200m 600m 100m.
Remarks: In front of police station.

S Gisay-la-Coudre 15E2

D35. **GPS**: n48,95001 e0,62670.

6 free €2/100liter Ch .
Surface: asphalted. 01/01-31/12.
Distance: on the spot 300m.
Remarks: Coins available at restaurant La Tortue.

S Gonzeville 15E1

La Ruette. **GPS**: n49,76590 e0,80738.

FR

4 free WC. **Location:** Rural, simple, isolated, quiet. **Surface:** asphalted/gravel. 01/01-31/12.
Distance: on the spot 7km 7km 100m on the spot on the spot.

S Gournay-en-Bray 15G1

Avenue Sadi Carnot. **GPS:** n49,48055 e1,72640.

8 free Chfree. **Location:** Urban, simple, central, quiet. **Surface:** asphalted. 01/01-31/12
Thu-morning closed because of market + 2nd weekend Sep.
Distance: on the spot on the spot on the spot on the spot on the spot on the spot.
Remarks: Max. 48h.

S Gournay-en-Bray 15G1

Route du Vieux Saint-Clair. **GPS:** n49,50106 e1,72245.

10 € 6 €1 €2.
Location: Rural, simple, isolated, quiet. 01/01-31/12.
Distance: 2,5km 3km 3km 2,5km on the spot on the spot.

S Gouvets 15C2

Le Bourg D454. **GPS:** n48,93133 w1,09492.

20 WCfree. **Location:** Rural, simple, isolated, quiet. **Surface:** asphalted/metalled. 01/01-31/12.
Distance: on the spot 6km on the spot.

S Gouville-sur-Mer 15B2

Chemin du Beau Rivage. **GPS:** n49,09970 w1,60896.

40 € 5/19-10h liter Ch minutes WCincluded.
Location: Urban. **Surface:** gravel. 01/01-31/12.
Distance: on the spot on the spot 50m.

S Grainville-Langannerie 15D2

Rue de Lapford. **GPS:** n49,01438 w0,26805.

6 free €2/10minutes Ch €2/55minutes.
Location: Rural, comfortable. **Surface:** metalled. 01/01-31/12.
Distance: 100m.
Remarks: Near Salle des Fêtes.

S Grandcamp-Maisy 15C1

Rue du Moulin Odo. **GPS:** n49,38620 w1,03782.

14 free €2 Ch. **Location:** Rural, comfortable, quiet. **Surface:** asphalted/gravel.
Distance: 500m 500m.
Remarks: Coins at tourist info, rue Aristide Briand.

S Granville 15B2

Haute Ville, Rue du Roc. **GPS:** n48,83530 w1,6095.

20 € 6 €2/10minutes Ch €2/55minutes.
Location: Simple. **Surface:** asphalted/gravel. 01/01-31/12.
Distance: 500m 500m 500m on the spot.
Remarks: Motorhome parking behind sea aquarium, upper city, Atlantic Wall 50m, max. 24h.

Tourist information Granville:
Office de Tourisme, 4, Cours Jonville, www.ville-granville.fr. The old centre, Haute-Ville, is surrounded by ramparts. The lower city is a bathing resort.
Wed, Sa.

S Gréville-Hague 15B1

D402. **GPS:** n49,67509 w1,80127.

10 free €2 Ch €2 WC.
Location: Rural, comfortable. **Surface:** metalled.
Distance: on the spot 100m.
Remarks: Next to sports fields.

S Grigneuseville 15F1

La Plaine d'Hermesnil, 7 rue de la Plaine.
GPS: n49,64427 e1,19900.

7 € 7 Ch (4x)included.
Location: Rural, comfortable, isolated, quiet. **Surface:** gravel.
Distance: 2,5km 2,5km 2,5km.
Remarks: Service passerby € 3, barbecue place, picnic area.

S Grossville 15B1

Bar-Epicerie Caladjo, Rue des Touzés. **GPS:** n49,50659 w1,74311.

15 € 6 €2 Chfree €2.
Location: Rural, simple. **Surface:** gravel. 01/01-31/12.
Distance: on the spot on the spot.

S Guilberville 15C2

D159. **GPS:** n48,98871 w0,94844.

15 free €2/100liter Ch €2/1h.
Location: Rural, simple, quiet. **Surface:** gravel.
01/01-31/12 service: 01/11-01/03.
Distance: 300m 1,5km 300m 300m.
Remarks: Coins at tourist info, Bistro and bakery.

S Hermanville-sur-Mer 15D2

Rue Verte. **GPS:** n49,28592 w0,31243.

6 free Chfree. **Location:** Simple, central, quiet. **Surface:** asphalted. 01/01-31/12.
Distance: on the spot 200m.
Remarks: Tuesday market.

Tourist information Hermanville-sur-Mer:
Tue morning.

S Hérouvillette 15D2

Place l'Aiguillon, Avenue de Caen, D 513A.
GPS: n49,21983 w0,24497.

8 free Chfree. **Location:** Rural, comfortable. **Surface:** asphalted. 01/01-31/12.

Distance: 250m 200m.

S Heurteauville 15E1

Les Cerisiers, Rue de Village. **GPS**: n49,44777 e0,81333.

20 € 5 + € 0,50/pp tourist tax €5 Ch (12x)€4/24h.
Location: Rural, comfortable, isolated, quiet. **Surface:** grassy/gravel.
01/04-30/09.
Distance: 5km 20m 20m 5km 5km on the spot on the spot.
Remarks: Along the Seine river.

S Honfleur 15E1

Bassin de l'Est, Quai de la cale. **GPS**: n49,41916 e0,24166.

120 € 10 Ch (60x)included.
Location: Urban, simple, central. **Surface:** gravel.
01/01-31/12 service in winter.
Distance: 500m 2,7km 300m 500m.

S Isigny-sur-Mer 15C1

Quai Neuf. **GPS**: n49,32150 w1,10456.

6 free €2/100liter Ch.
Location: Rural. **Surface:** asphalted.
Distance: 300m on the spot 200m.

S Jobourg 15B1

Nez de Jobourg, D202. **GPS**: n49,67722 w1,93806.

10 free WC free. **Surface:** metalled. 01/01-31/12.
Distance: 500m 500m.

S Jumièges 15E1

Rue Alphonse Callais. **GPS**: n49,43106 e0,81452.

20 free €3/100liter Ch.
Location: Rural, simple, comfortable, central. **Surface:** grassy/gravel.
01/03-30/11.

Distance: 1km 500m 200m 200m on the spot on the spot on the spot.
Remarks: Coins at Tourist Info and bakery.

S La Ferrière-aux-Etangs 15C3

Rue de l'Etang. **GPS**: n48,65931 w0,51706.

20 free €2/10minutes Ch €2/h.
Location: Simple, quiet. **Surface:** grassy/gravel.
01/01-31/12.
Distance: 400m 400m 400m on the spot.
Remarks: At lake, former campsite, only exact change.

S La Ferté-Macé 15D3

Ruelle des Fournelles, D916. **GPS**: n48,59018 w0,35528.

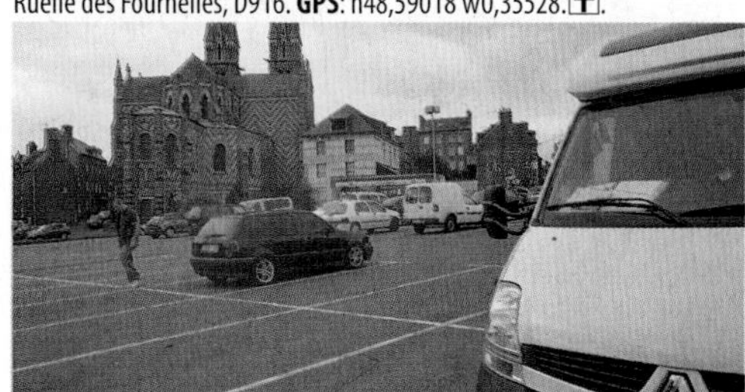

15 free Ch WC free. **Location:** Urban, simple.
Surface: asphalted. 01/01-31/12.
Distance: on the spot on the spot on the spot.
Remarks: Parking at church.

S La Lucerne-d'Outremer 15B3

D35. **GPS**: n48,78437 w1,42727.

6 free, voluntary contribution Ch voluntary contribution WC free. **Location:** Urban, simple. **Surface:** asphalted.
01/01-31/12.
Distance: on the spot 100m 100m.
Remarks: Next to castle, max. 2 days.

S La Mailleraye-sur-Seine 15E1

Quai Paul Girardeau. **GPS**: n49,48444 e0,77333.

34 € 5 + € 0,50/pp tourist taks, 01/11-31/03 free €3/10minutes Ch €3/1h.
Location: Urban, comfortable, central.
Surface: grassy.
01/01-31/12 2nd weekend April/May.
Distance: 200m on the spot on the spot on the spot 200m on the spot on the spot.
Remarks: Along the Seine river, coins at town hall and shops.

La Poterie-Cap-d'Antifer 15E1

GPS: n49,68317 e0,16480.

4 free. **Location:** Rural, simple, quiet. **Surface:** grassy/gravel.
01/01-31/12.
Distance: 2km on the spot.

S La Vespière 15E2

Chemin de la Grand Mare/Campaugé. **GPS**: n49,02763 e0,42221.

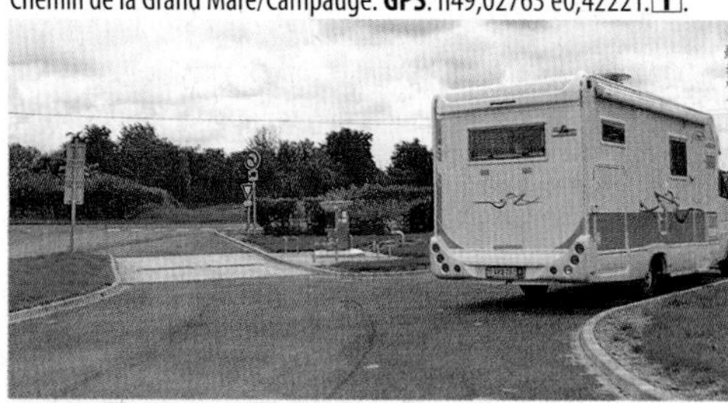

2 free €2/100liter Ch €2/1h. **Location:** Simple, comfortable. **Surface:** asphalted. 01/01-31/12.
Distance: 300m A28 2,2km Carrefour 200m.

S La-Rivière-Saint-Sauveur 15E1

Parking de l'Orange - Place Albert Harel, Chemin des Bancs, D580. **GPS**: n49,40856 e0,26926.

20 free €5/100liter Ch €5/30minutes .
Location: Rural, simple, central, quiet. **Surface:** asphalted.
01/01-31/12.
Distance: on the spot 700m supermarket + bakery 100m.
Remarks: Coins at the shops in the village.

Langrune-sur-Mer 15D2

Rue du Colonel Pierre Harivel. **GPS**: n49,32474 w0,36814.

3 free. **Location:** Comfortable, central.
Surface: asphalted/metalled. 01/01-31/12.
Distance: on the spot beach 50m 50m.

S Le Billot 15D2

D39. **GPS**: n48,96948 e0,07217.

4 free €2,50 Ch €2,50 WC. **Location:** Rural, simple.
Surface: gravel/metalled. 01/01-31/12.
Distance: 200m on the spot.
Remarks: Coins at Relais du Billot 200m, beautiful view.

S Le Mesnil-Jumièges 15E1

Base de loisirs, Route de Mesnil. **GPS**: n49,41172 e0,84494.

FR

15 €5, Jul/Aug €10 €3/100liter ChWC.
Location: Rural, comfortable, isolated. **Surface:** grassy/metalled.
01/01-31/12.
Distance: 1km 200m 200m 1km 1km on the spot on the spot on the spot.

Le Mont-Saint-Michel 15B3
Aire Camping-car du Mont-Saint-Michel. **GPS**: n48,61401 w1,50773.

€12,50/24h Ch.
Surface: grassy. 23-06h.
Distance: La Rotisserie on the spot.

Le Mont-Saint-Michel 15B3
Parking Véolia, La Jacotière Ardevon. **GPS**: n48,61388 w1,5058.

50 €20,60/24h.
Location: Rural. **Surface:** metalled. 01/01-31/12.
Distance: 100m.
Remarks: Free shuttle to Le Mont-Saint-Michel.

Tourist information Le Mont-Saint-Michel:
Office de Tourisme, Corps de Garde des Bourgeois, www.mont-saint-michel.net. Town with abbey on a cliff in the sea.

Le Noyer-en-Ouche 15E2
Ferme Lesur, La Godinière, D140. **GPS**: n49,01017 e0,72444.

5 €7,50 €3 €3. **Surface:** grassy. 01/01-31/12.

Le Sap 15E2
Les Terriers, Rue Nicolas Lesieur, D12. **GPS**: n48,89525 e0,33249.

4 free Ch free. **Surface:** gravel. 01/01-31/12.
Distance: 500m on the spot 500m 500m.
Remarks: Next to fire-station.

Le Tréport 13C3
Du Funiculaire, Route Touristique, D126E. **GPS**: n50,05777 e1,36222.

40 €6,10 €2,30/100liter Ch €2,30/55minutes.
Location: Comfortable, isolated, quiet. **Surface:** grasstiles.
Distance: Le Tréport centre 2km 2km 100m.
Remarks: Free cableway to city centre, max. 48h.

Le Tréport 13C3
Parc Sainte Croix, Rue Pierre Mendès France.
GPS: n50,05954 e1,38919.

61 €9,70, tourist tax incl Ch (61x)included €1,80.
Location: Comfortable, isolated, quiet. **Surface:** asphalted.
01/01-31/12.
Distance: 700m 700m 500m Mr.Ed.
Remarks: Industrial area, near camping municipal, max. 48h, baker every morning (Jul/Aug).

Tourist information Le Tréport:
Château d'Eu, Eu. Royal castle, 19th century. 15/03-01/11 Sa.

Les Pieux 15B1
Plage Sciotot. **GPS**: n49,50722 w1,84731.
6 free.
Location: Simple. **Surface:** metalled. 01/01-31/12.
Distance: beach 50m.
Remarks: Large parking, 50m from beach.

Les Pieux 15B1
Intermarché, Route de Cherbourg. **GPS**: n49,51736 w1,79797.

6 free €2/100liter Ch. **Surface:** asphalted.
Distance: on the spot.

Lessay 15B2
Place Saint Cloud. **GPS**: n49,21850 w1,53548.

4 free Ch WC free. **Location:** Urban, simple.
Surface: asphalted. 01/01-31/12.
Distance: on the spot 150m 200m.
Remarks: Check in at town hall (service).

Lion-sur-Mer 15D2
Rue du General Gallieni. **GPS**: n49,30174 w0,31316.

4 free.
Location: Urban, central, noisy. **Surface:** asphalted.
01/01-31/12.
Distance: on the spot on the spot 100m.
Remarks: At sea, parking townhall, only overnight stays 20-10h.

Lisieux 15E2
Basilique de Lisieux, Rue des Champs Rémouleux. **GPS**: n49,14138 .
free. **Surface:** asphalted.

Lisieux 15E2
Le Bowling de Lisieux, Rue de Paris. **GPS**: n49,14653 .
10 €8-10 Ch. 01/01-31/12.
Distance: 700m.

Lisieux 15E2
Parking du Carmel, Rue d'Alençon. **GPS**: n49,14413 e0,22788.
€2,80/100liter Ch €2,80/1h WC. 01/01-31/12.
Distance: on the spot river on the spot on the spot.

Luc-sur-Mer 15D2
Route de Lion-sur-Mer. **GPS**: n49,31430 w0,34346.

4 free. **Location:** Rural, simple. **Surface:** asphalted.
01/01-31/12.
Distance: 200m.

Lyons-la-Fôret 15F2
La Cuette. **GPS**: n49,39908 e1,47912.

8 free. **Location:** Urban, simple, central, quiet.
Distance: 100m 100m 100m 200m on the spot.

Marigny 15B2
Rue Auguste Eudeline, D53. **GPS**: n49,09911 w1,24776.

10 free €2/10minutes Ch €2/55minutes. **Location:** Urban, simple. **Surface:** metalled. 01/01-31/12.
Distance: 700m 200m 700m 700m on the spot.

Merville Franceville 15D2
Boulevard Wattier. **GPS**: n49,28483 w0,21071.

6 free €2/10minutes Ch. **Location:** Comfortable, quiet.
Surface: asphalted. 01/03-15/11.
Distance: 75m.
Remarks: Max. 48h.

S Montebourg 15B1

Parking Louis Lecacheux. GPS: n49,48486 w1,37449.

10 free Chfree. **Location:** Simple. **Surface:** metalled.
01/01-31/12.

S Montfiquet 15C2

Hotel-Restaurant Relais de la Fôret, L'Embranchement, D572.
GPS: n49,19400 w0,863.

60 € 14 Chincluded WC €2,use sanitary €2.
Surface: asphalted. 01/01-31/12.
Distance: 1km 1km.
Remarks: Pay at reception, picnic tables available.

S Montville 15F1

Place de l'Abbé Kerebel. **GPS**: n49,54710 e1,07304.

15 free €4,50/100liter Ch €4,50/1h free,(8-22.30).
Location: Urban, comfortable, central, quiet. **Surface:** gravel.
01/01-31/12.
Distance: 400m 500m 600m 400m 300m.
Remarks: Coins at mairie, restauration Hexagone, museum, market Saturday.

Tourist information Montville:
Mo-morning.

S Mortain 15C3

Place du Château. **GPS**: n48,64887 w0,94489.

6 free Ch WCfree. **Location:** Urban, simple.
Surface: asphalted. 01/01-31/12.
Distance: on the spot on the spot on the spot on the spot.
Remarks: Max. 48h.

Tourist information Mortain:
Office de Tourisme, Rue du Bourglopin, www.ville-mortain.fr. Hiking trail to the Grande and Petite Cascade, waterfalls.

S Neufchâtel-en-Bray 15F1

Aire Camping Car Sainte Claire, Rue la Grande Flandre.
GPS: n49,73725 e1,42938.

14 € 12 Ch on camp site included.
Location: Urban, comfortable, central, quiet. **Surface:** grassy/gravel.
01/01-31/12.
Distance: 1,5km 2,5km 500m 500m on camp site.
Remarks: Max. 8M.

S Nonancourt 15F3

D53, Rue Hippolyte Lozier. **GPS**: n48,77269 e1,19261.
4 free Chfree . **Surface:** asphalted.
Distance: 200m.

S Norville 15E1

Clos Saint Martin. **GPS**: n49,47859 e0,64021.

3 free €2/12minutes Ch €2/3h.
Location: Urban, comfortable, central, noisy.
Surface: asphalted/grassy. 01/01-31/12.
Distance: on the spot 500m.

S Notre-Dame-de-Courson 15E2

D4. **GPS**: n48,99021 e0,25922.

5 free €2/20minutes Ch €2/20minutes.
Location: Rural, comfortable, quiet. **Surface:** gravel.
01/01-31/12.
Distance: 200m Le Tournebroche 200m on the spot.
Remarks: Service only with 1-euro coins.

S Oissel 15F2

Île du Bras Saint-Martin. **GPS**: n49,33783 e1,09183.

2 free €2/10minutes Ch €2/55minutes.
Location: Urban, comfortable, central, quiet.
Surface: gravel.
01/01-31/12.
Distance: 200m on the spot on the spot 200m 200m 200m on the spot.
Remarks: <7m, coins at the bakery: 1, Rue du Maréchal Foch.

Orbec 15E2

Parc de Loisirs, Rue St. Pierre, D915. **GPS**: n49,01758 e0,40506.

6 free. **Surface:** unpaved. 01/01-31/12.

S Ouistreham 15D2

Rue des Dunes/Boulevard Maritime. **GPS**: n49,28716 w0,24968.

45 € 10 Chincluded. **Location:** Urban, comfortable, noisy. **Surface:** asphalted/gravel. 01/01-31/12.
Distance: 650m 150m 2km.
Remarks: Near car ferry.

S Pirou-Plage 15B2

Rue des Hublots. **GPS**: n49,16522 w1,58937.

6 free €2/10minutes Ch €2/55minutes.
Location: Simple. **Surface:** asphalted. 01/01-31/12.
Distance: 500m 500m 500m 500m.
Remarks: Coins at campsite Clos Marin and restaurant La Marée, market on Sunday.

S Pont-d'Ouilly 15D2

Rue de la Libération. **GPS**: n48,87794 w0,41304.

43 € 11/24h €2 Ch (43x)included .
Location: Rural, comfortable, quiet. **Surface:** gravel.
01/01-31/12.
Distance: 550m on the spot 550m 550m.
Remarks: Along the Orne river.

Pont-l'Évêque 15E2

Les Mouettes, Avenue de Verdun. **GPS**: n49,28563 e0,18769.

6 free.
Location: Urban, simple, central. 01/01-31/12.
Distance: on the spot 6km 100m 150m.

Port-en-Bessin-Huppain 15C1

Super U, Avenue du Général de Gaulle. **GPS**: n49,34307 w0,75212.

12 free €3 Ch €3/24h. **Location:** Simple.
Surface: gravel/metalled. 01/01-31/12.
Distance: 200m 400m 400m on the spot.

Port-en-Bessin-Huppain 15C1

Rue du 11 Novembre. **GPS**: n49,34583 w0,75861.

17 € 4,50/night.
Location: Rural, simple. **Surface:** sand. 01/01-31/12.
Distance: 300m 400m 400m 500m.

Portbail 15B1

Rue Gilles Poerier. **GPS**: n49,33776 w1,69273.

4 free €2 Ch €2/1h.
Location: Simple, quiet. **Surface:** asphalted.
Distance: 200m.
Remarks: At fire-station.

Préaux-Saint-Sébastien 15E2

Le Bourg. **GPS**: n48,98695 .
free. **Location:** Isolated, quiet. 01/01-31/12.
Distance: on the spot.

Quiberville 13B3

Camping de la Plage de Quiberville, Rue de la Saâne.
GPS: n49,90504 e0,92725.

8 free €3,80. **Location:** Urban, simple, central, quiet.
Surface: grassy/sand. 01/04-31/10.
Distance: 100m 100m 400m on the spot on the spot.
Remarks: Max. 48h, coins at campsite.

Rauville-la-Bigot 15B1

D900. **GPS**: n49,51723 w1,68368.

10 free Chfree. **Location:** Comfortable, quiet.
Surface: asphalted.
Distance: 500m.

Réville 15C1

Ferme de la Froide Rue, 165, Rue des Monts.
GPS: n49,62583 w1,25278.

6 €7 Ch . **Location:** Rural, comfortable.
Surface: grassy. 01/01-31/12.
Distance: 1km.

Rots 15D2

Centre Commercial Cora, Chemin de la Croix Vautier, RN13.
GPS: n49,19985 w0,46027.

free Chfree .
Location: Noisy. **Surface:** asphalted.
01/01-31/12.
Distance: 1km on the spot on the spot.
Remarks: Terrain with video surveillance.

Rugles 15E3

Place de la Liberté. **GPS**: n48,82230 e0,70846.

4 free Ch free. **Surface:** metalled. 01/01-31/12.
Distance: on the spot 200m 200m.
Remarks: Max. 48h.

Saint Fromond 15C2

Rue des Gabariers, D8. **GPS**: n49,22202 w1,08956.

50 free €2 Ch €2. **Location:** Rural, simple.
Surface: asphalted/gravel. 01/01-31/12.
Distance: on the spot 50m on the spot.

Tourist information Saint Fromond:
Office de Tourisme, Bd de Verdun, Carentan, www.ot-carentan.fr.
Old bishop city with Gothic cathedral.

Saint-André-de-l'Eure 15F3

Boulevard Verdun. **GPS**: n48,90644 e1,26927.

10 free Chfree. **Location:** Urban, comfortable, noisy.
Surface: metalled. 01/01-31/12.
Distance: 1km on the spot 1km on the spot.
Remarks: Along railwayline.

Saint-Hilaire-du-Harcouët 15C3

Place de la Motte. **GPS**: n48,57602 w1,09086.

10 free €2 Ch €2. **Location:** Urban, simple.
Surface: asphalted/metalled. 01/01-31/12.
Distance: on the spot on the spot on the spot.
Remarks: Behind church.

Saint-Jean-le-Thomas 15B3

Boulevard Stanislas. **GPS**: n48,72567 w1,52296.

17 € 8 €2 Ch €2 WC. **Location:** Rural, comfortable.
Surface: asphalted/grassy.
Distance: 500m 100m 100m 500m on the spot on the spot.

Saint-Jouin-Bruneval 15E1

Rue des Pruniers. **GPS**: n49,65099 e0,16322.

20 free €2/100liter Ch €2/1h. **Location:** Rural, simple, isolated, quiet. **Surface:** gravel. 01/01-31/12.
Distance: 1km 1km 1km.

Saint-Jouin-Bruneval 15E1

Plage de Bruneval, Saint Jouin plage. **GPS**: n49,64970 e0,15349.

20 free. **Location:** Simple, quiet. **Surface:** gravel/metalled.
01/01-31/12.
Distance: 4km pebbled beach on the spot 100m 4km.

FR

Saint-Lô 15C2

Place de la Vaucelle. **GPS**: n49,11351 w1,10309.

10 free €2/10minutes Ch €2/h. **Location:** Urban, comfortable. **Surface:** asphalted. 01/01-31/12.
Distance: 100m 100m 100m on the spot.
Remarks: Along river.

Tourist information Saint-Lô:
Haras National, Rue du Maréchal Juin. National Stud farm established by Napoleon in 1806. 01/06-30/09 14-18.
Musée de la Libération, Place du Champ de Mars. Invasion in 1944. 10-19h, winter 14-19h Tue. € 4.
Nôtre Dame. Renovated church 13th century.

Saint-Martin de Bréhal 15B2

Av. de l'Hippodrome. **GPS**: n48,89829 w1,56583.

20 € 4/24h free. **Location:** Urban. **Surface:** asphalted. 01/01-31/12.
Distance: 300m beach 150m 300m 400m.

Saint-Nicolas-d'Aliermont 15F1

Place du 19 Mars 1962, Rue d'Arques 88. **GPS**: n49,88045 e1,22092.

2 free €2/10minutes Ch €2/1h.
Location: Urban, simple, central, quiet.
Surface: asphalted.
01/01-31/12.
Distance: 200m 12km 200m 200m on the spot.
Remarks: Behind town hall, max. 48h, coins at town hall and library.

Saint-Nicolas-de-Bliquetuit 15E1

Route du Bac. **GPS**: n49,52083 e0,72777.

12 free €2/10minutes Ch €2/1h.
Location: Simple, quiet. **Surface:** asphalted.
01/01-31/12.
Distance: 1,4km on the spot on the spot 2km 2km on the spot.
Remarks: Along the Seine river, coins at town hall, bar and restaurant.

Saint-Pair-sur-Mer 15B2

Avenue Léon Jozeau-Marigné. **GPS**: n48,81711 w1,56988.

30 € 5 €2/10minutes Ch €2/55minutes.
Location: Urban, simple. **Surface:** asphalted/gravel.
01/01-31/12.
Distance: 500m beach 500m 500m on the spot.
Remarks: Parking at tennis-court, max. 48h.

Saint-Pierre-Église 15B1

Parking du 8 Mai 1945. **GPS**: n49,66897 w1,40387.

6 free €2/100liter Ch. **Location:** Urban. **Surface:** metalled.
01/01-31/12.
Distance: 300m on the spot.

Saint-Pierre-le-Vieux 15F1

Ferme du Moulin, Route de la Vallée du Dun.
GPS: n49,85816 e0,88000.

5 € 5 + € 1/pp €2 Ch €3. **Location:** Comfortable, isolated, quiet. **Surface:** grassy/gravel. 01/01-31/12.
Distance: 1km 1km 1km on the spot.

Saint-Pierre-sur-Dives 15D2

Aire Camping-Cars de la Halle Médiévale, Place du Marché.
GPS: n49,01713 w0,03047.

12 € 5/24h €3 Ch.
Location: Urban, simple, central. **Surface:** gravel.
01/01-31/12 Mo-morning market.
Distance: on the spot 50m 150m.
Remarks: Service passerby € 3.

Saint-Saire 15F1

Rue de la Gare, D7. **GPS**: n49,69677 e1,49476.

8 free €3/10minutes Ch €3/h.
Location: Rural, simple, comfortable, isolated, quiet. **Surface:** grassy.
01/01-31/12.
Distance: 300m on the spot on the spot on the spot.

Saint-Sauveur-le-Vicomte 15B1

Place Auguste Cousin. **GPS**: n49,38678 w1,52947.

free Chfree. **Surface:** asphalted.
Distance: on the spot.
Remarks: Next to town hall, max. 48h.

Saint-Sever-Calvados 15C2

Place de la Mairie. **GPS**: n48,84169 w1,04842.

15 free Chfree. **Location:** Urban, simple, noisy.
Surface: gravel. 01/01-31/12.
Distance: 100m 15km 100m.

Saint-Vaast-la-Hougue 15C1

Aire de la Gallouette, Rue Galouette. **GPS**: n49,58400 w1,267.

27 € 7/night €2/10minutes Ch €2/1h.
Location: Comfortable. **Surface:** metalled.
01/01-31/12.
Distance: 300m 300m.
Remarks: Near campsite Gallouette.

Tourist information Saint-Vaast-la-Hougue:
Office de Tourisme, 1, place Gen. de Gaulle, http://ot-pointedesaire.com. Important port for allied forces in 1944. Now large marina.
Île de Tatihou, Port. Island in front of the coast, maritime museum and bird hide. 01/04-30/09 10-18h.

Saint-Valery-en-Caux 13B3

Quai d'Aval. **GPS**: n49,87220 e0,70898.

40 free, weekend 01/03-31/10 € 6/day, 16/05-30/09 € 6/day + € 0,20/pp €3 Ch. **Location:** Urban, comfortable, central, quiet.
Surface: asphalted. 01/01-31/12.
Distance: 600m on the spot on the spot 500m bakery 600m on the spot.
Remarks: Max. 48h, coins at tourist info.

Saint-Vigor-le-Grand 15C2

Les Peupliers, Rue de Magny. **GPS**: n49,29949 w0,67436.

FR

7 € 6, € 9 service incl Ch included. **Location:** Rural, comfortable, isolated, quiet. **Surface:** gravel. 01/01-31/12.
Distance: 2km.
Remarks: Baker every morning, service passerby € 4, Bayeux centre 3,5km, Arromanches beaches 6,5km.

S Saint-Wandrille-Rançon 15E1

Ferme de la Mare, 20 impasse ferme de la mare.
GPS: n49,54031 e0,76800.

3 € 5 Ch (3x)€2. **Location:** Rural, comfortable, isolated, quiet. **Surface:** gravel. 01/01-31/12.
Distance: 3km 3km.

S Sainte-Honorine-des-Pertes 15C1

Garage Vally, Route d'Omaha Beach, D514, dir Colleville-sur-Mer.
GPS: n49,34868 w0,81635.

32 € 6 €1,50/100liter Ch (32x)included.
Location: Rural, comfortable, quiet. **Surface:** grassy.
01/01-31/12.
Distance: 200m 500m on the spot.
Remarks: Automatic bread distributor, service passerby € 2,50.

S Sainte-Marie-du-Mont 15C1

Camping-Car Park Utah Beach, La Madeleine, D913.
GPS: n49,41800 w1,18677.

49 € 12 Ch €4/3,50 included.
Location: Simple, quiet. **Surface:** grassy/gravel. 01/01-31/12.
Distance: 500m.
Remarks: Code wifi: f2d1941a5c.

Tourist information Sainte-Marie-du-Mont:
M Musée du Débarquement, Utah-Beach. Landing museum.

S Sainte-Mère-Église 15B1

Super U, ZA les Crutelles. **GPS**: n49,40461 w1,32223.

€2 Ch.
Surface: asphalted.
Distance: 1km on the spot.
Remarks: Motorhome washing place max. ^3.80m.

Tourist information Sainte-Mère-Église:
i Borne 0 de la voie de la Liberté. Marker 0, start of the Libery Road.
i Office de Tourisme, 2, Rue Eisenhower, www.sainte-mere-eglise.info. Village well-known for the paratrooper who landed on the church-tower.
M Musée Airborne. Exhibition about the invasion at St.-Mère-Eglise.
10-12h, 14-18h.

S Sallenelles 15D2

Boulevard Maritime D514. **GPS**: n49,26474 w0,22694.

2 free €2/10minutes Ch. **Location:** Rural, simple, quiet.
Surface: asphalted. 01/01-31/12.
Distance: 100m on the spot 300m.
Remarks: Behind town hall, max. 48h.

S Sideville-Lorimier 15B1

Camping-car l'Orimier, Route du Pont Roger, D152.
GPS: n49,58722 w1,69222.

6 € 7/night Ch (6x)included. **Location:** Comfortable, quiet. **Surface:** asphalted/grassy.
Remarks: Regional products.

S Siouville-Hague 15B1

Avenue des Peupliers. **GPS**: n49,56356 w1,8442.

30 free €2 Ch. **Surface:** grassy.
Distance: 200m.

S Soumont-Saint-Quentin 15D2

Rue de la Mine. **GPS**: n48,97840 w0,25.

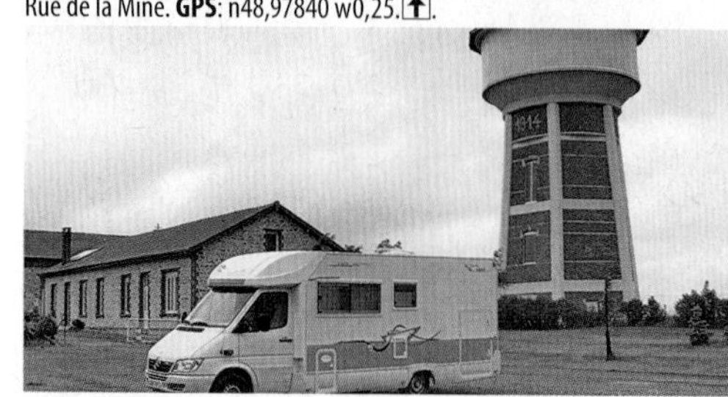

20 € 7, tourist tax € 0,20/pp €1 €2 Ch included.
Location: Simple. **Surface:** grassy. Easter-01/11.
Distance: 1km.
Remarks: Former iron mine.

S Sourdeval 15C3

Parc Saint-Lys, Rue Jean Baptiste Janin.
GPS: n48,72603 w0,92308.

8 free Ch free. **Location:** Urban, simple.
Surface: gravel/metalled. 01/01-31/12.
Distance: 100m 400m 400m.

S Surtainville 15B1

Rue des mielles. **GPS**: n49,46373 w1,82871.

10 free €4,16/10minutes Ch €4,16/55minutes .
Location: Urban. **Surface:** metalled.
Distance: on the spot 100m.
Remarks: Coins at camping municipal.

S Tinchebray 15C3

Rue André Breton, D911. **GPS**: n48,76302 w0,73753.

3 free Ch free. **Location:** Urban, simple.
Surface: asphalted. 01/01-31/12.
Distance: on the spot 300m.

S Tourlaville 15B1

Espace Loisirs Colignon, piscine-camping municipal, Rue des Algues. **GPS**: n49,65398 w1,56606.

free €2 Ch. **Location:** Simple. **Surface:** asphalted.
Remarks: Coins at campsite or swimming pool.

Tourlaville 15B1

Quai Amiral Kniskern/Boulevard Maritime. **GPS**: n49,64549 w1,59976.

free.

FR

Remarks: Parking at ferry-boat.

S **Tréauville** 15B1

1, La Chaussee, D65. **GPS**: n49,54444 w1,83472.

10 € 6,50 Ch included. **Surface:** grassy/metalled.
Distance: 2,5km.

S **Val-de-Saâne** 15F1

Rue Moulin du Traversin. **GPS**: n49,70390 e0,96506.

6 free €2/100liter Ch €2/1h.
Location: Urban, comfortable, central, quiet.
Surface: asphalted.
01/01-31/12.
Distance: 300m 300m 300m on the spot on the spot.
Remarks: Coins at town hall, bakery and restaurant, market on Sunday.

S **Valognes** 15B1

Place Félix Buhot. **GPS**: n49,51159 w1,47813.

7 free €2 Ch €2.
Location: Simple. **Surface:** asphalted.
Distance: 1km on the spot.
Remarks: Next to supermarket Champion.

S **Valognes** 15B1

Zone Artisanale d'Armanville, Chemin de la Brique.
GPS: n49,51433 w1,50004.

€ 5/24h €2 Ch €2 WC. **Location:** Simple.
Surface: asphalted. 01/01-31/12.
Distance: 1km.
Remarks: Motorhome washing place.

Veules-les-Roses 13B3

Parking des Falaises, Sentier de Four. **GPS**: n49,87508 e0,79231.

40 free. **Location:** Rural, simple, isolated, quiet. **Surface:** grassy.
01/01-31/12.
Distance: 500m on the spot on the spot 500m 500m.

S **Veules-les-Roses** 13B3

Camping des Mouettes, Avenue Jean Moulin 7.
GPS: n49,87596 e0,80289.

15 € 10/24h + € 0,40/pp tourist tax Ch.
Location: Simple, isolated, quiet. **Surface:** gravel/metalled.
01/04-30/10.
Distance: 300m 500m 500m 300m 300m on the spot on the spot.
Remarks: Max. 48h, service on campsite.

S **Veulettes-sur-Mer** 15E1

Chemin des Courses. **GPS**: n49,85233 e0,60165.

15 € 5 €3,50/100liter Ch €3,50/1h (16x).
Location: Rural, simple, central, quiet. **Surface:** asphalted.
01/01-31/12.
Distance: 200m 100m 100m 400m 400m on the spot on the spot.
Remarks: Behind Syndicat d'Initiative, coins at tourist info, campsite and supermarket.

S **Veulettes-sur-Mer** 15E1

Parking de la Plage, D10. **GPS**: n49,85488 e0,60702.

20 € 7 €3,50/10minutes Ch €3,50/1h WC.
Location: Rural, simple, quiet. **Surface:** grassy.
01/01-31/12.
Distance: 500m pebbled beach 50m 50m 500m 400m 500m.
Remarks: Beach parking.

Villedieu-les-Poêles 15B2

Parc de la Commanderie, Rue Taillemarche.
GPS: n48,83682 w1,22436.

5 free. **Location:** Urban, simple. **Surface:** asphalted.
01/01-31/12.
Distance: on the spot 2,4km 100m 100m.

S **Villers-Bocage** 15C2

Rue du Canada. **GPS**: n49,07973 w0,6609.

5 free €2/10minutes Ch €2/55minutes.
Location: Urban, simple, quiet. **Surface:** asphalted.
01/01-31/12.
Distance: 1,5km on the spot 400m on the spot.
Remarks: Max. 48h.

S **Villers-sur-Mer** 15D2

Paleospace l'Odyssee, Rue des Martois.
GPS: n49,32910 e0,01273.

14 € 10 €4 Ch included €1
Location: Urban, comfortable, quiet. **Surface:** metalled.
01/01-31/12.
Distance: 1km beach 250m bakery 1,5km.
Remarks: Max. 48h.

S **Villiers-en-Désœuvre** 15F2

Centre Equestre, La Harelle, D106. **GPS**: n48,97560 e1,50250.
4 € 10 WC included. **Location:** Isolated, quiet.
Surface: grassy.
Distance: 3,5km.
Remarks: At horse farm.

S **Vimoutiers** 15E2

D916, Avenue du Dr. Dentu. **GPS**: n48,93152 e0,19604.

6 free Ch (2x) WC free. **Location:** Urban, simple, central.
Surface: asphalted. 01/01-31/12.
Distance: 400m 500m Carrefour 200m.
Remarks: Major centre in the Camembert-region, Camembert museum.

S **Vire** 15C2

Place du champ de foire. **GPS**: n48,84084 w0,88862.

25 free Ch free. **Location:** Urban, simple, noisy.
Surface: asphalted. 01/01-31/12 Fri-Sa.
Distance: on the spot on the spot on the spot.
Remarks: Water closed during wintertime, friday-Saturday market.

Ile-de-France

S **Bray-sur-Seine** 19A1

Quai de l'Ile. **GPS**: n48,41713 e3,23745.

FR

30 free Chfree. **Surface:** asphalted.
Distance: 100m 100m.
Remarks: Along the Seine river, max. 72h, max. 7m.

Tourist information Bray-sur-Seine:
Fri 8-13h.

S Coupvray 15H3

Parking Disneyland Paris, Boulevard du Parc.
GPS: n48,87500 e2,79700.

€ 30/day ChWC included.
Surface: asphalted. 01/01-31/12.
Remarks: Motorhome area at amusement park, note: tariffs will be charged per day, even if you arrive in the evening.

Tourist information Coupvray:
Disneyland Paris, Marne-la-Vallée. Attractions and themepark.

S Milly-la-Forêt 18H1

Route de Nemours. **GPS:** n48,39798 e2,48021.
6 free Chfree. **Location:** Rural. **Surface:** asphalted.
01/01-31/12.
Distance: 1km 9,4km A6.
Remarks: In front of Conservatoire Nationale des Plantes, gate opens automatically.

S Milly-la-Forêt 18H1

Total, 49-51 Avenue de Ganay. **GPS:** n48,40720 e2,46782.

€ 3,50 Ch. **Surface:** grassy. 01/01-31/12.
Distance: centre 500m 7,7km A6.
Remarks: Behind petrol station, gate open 6-21h.

S Nemours 18H1

Les Colverts de Kabaya, Route de Moret. **GPS:** n48,27866 e2,69893.
6 € 6 €3. **Surface:** grassy. 01/01-31/12.
Distance: 1,6km 2,3km 200m 200m.

S Provins 16A3

Parking Office de Tourisme, Chemin de Villecran.
GPS: n48,56189 e3,27993.

30 € 8 €3,50 Ch €3,50
Surface: gravel. 01/01-31/12 service: frost.
Distance: 500m 500m.

Tourist information Provins:
Sa 8-14h.

S Saint-Cyr-sur-Morin 16A3

Avenue Daniel Simon. **GPS:** n48,90627 e3,18516.
4 free Chfree. **Surface:** grassy. 01/01-31/12.
Distance: on the spot.
Remarks: Behind church.

S Saint-Fargeau-Ponthierry 15H3

Base de loisirs Seine-Ecole, Avenue Max Pierrou.
GPS: n48,53610 e2,55065.
5 € 5,20 Chincluded. **Surface:** grassy.
Distance: 850m.
Remarks: Recreation park.

S Souppes-sur-Loing 18H1

GPS: n48,18083 e2,72343.

5 € 5 €2 Ch included. **Surface:** asphalted.
Remarks: Max. 72h.

Britanny

S Antrain 15B3

Route de Pontorson. **GPS:** n48,46307 w1,47938.

2 free ChWCfree. **Location:** Urban, simple, central, quiet.
Surface: asphalted.
Distance: 100m 100m 100m 100m 1km on the spot 2km.

Arzal 18A2

Barrage d'Arzal, D139. **GPS:** n47,50089 w2,38074.

15 free. **Location:** Rural, simple, quiet. **Surface:** asphalted.
01/01-31/12.
Distance: 1,5km 50m 50m 50m 50m.

S Arzon 14D3

Aire d'accueil des Camping-cars de Kermor, Avenue de Kerlun, Kerjouanno. **GPS:** n47,53886 w2,88028.

49 € 7/24h Ch (16x) included. **Location:** Rural, comfortable, quiet. **Surface:** asphalted. 01/01-31/12.
Remarks: Nearby Plage du Fageo, June/Sep max. 72h.

S Audierne 14B2

Rue Lamartine. **GPS:** n48,02733 w4,53721.

15 free €3/10minutes Ch €3/55minutes.
Location: Urban, simple. **Surface:** unpaved.
01/01-31/12.
Distance: 1,5km on the spot 500m on the spot.

S Auray 14D3

Chemin de Bellevue. **GPS:** n47,66365 w2,97393.

5 free €3/20minutes Ch €3/h WC .
Location: Simple. **Surface:** asphalted. 01/01-31/12.
Distance: 200m.
Remarks: Small pitches.

S Auray 14D3

Place du Golheres. **GPS:** n47,66524 w2,99036.

3 free €2 Ch.
Location: Urban, simple. **Surface:** asphalted. 01/01-31/12.
Distance: 500m on the spot.
Remarks: During inspection 2015 service out of order.

Tourist information Auray:
Mo.

S Availles-sur-Seiche 18B1

D106. **GPS:** n47,96248 w1,19902.
6 free Chfree. **Surface:** unpaved. 01/01-31/12.
Distance: 100m 300m.

Baud 14D2

Rue du Champ de Foire. **GPS:** n47,87375 w3,02008.

10 free.
Location: Central. **Surface:** metalled. 01/01-31/12.
Distance: on the spot 1,5km 200m on the spot.

S Baud 14D2

Rue de Pont Augan. **GPS:** n47,87580 w3,02518.
Chfree. 01/01-31/12.

S Bazouges-la-Pérouse 15B3

Boulevard de Castel Marie. **GPS:** n48,42416 w1,57408.

FR

7 free free. **Location:** Urban, simple, central, quiet. **Surface:** asphalted. 01/01-31/12.
Distance: 200m 150m 200m.

Bécherel 15A3

La Feronière. **GPS**: n48,29769 w1,93971.

40 free. **Location:** Rural, simple, simple. **Surface:** gravel. 01/01-31/12.
Distance: 700m 700m on the spot 200m.

Bédée 18A1

Rue de Dinan. **GPS**: n48,18099 w1,94416.

6 free Chfree.
Location: Urban, simple. **Surface:** asphalted.
Distance: 1km 200m 50m.
Remarks: Nearby cemetery.

Belle-Isle-en-Terre 14D1

Les Jardins du Guer, Rue Guerveur, D33.
GPS: n48,54332 w3,39417.

10 2 days free, then € 5/day Ch free.
Location: Comfortable, central, quiet. **Surface:** gravel.
01/01-31/12 service: 01/11-01/04.
Distance: 100m 10m 350m mountainbike trail.
Remarks: Narrow entrance.

Belz 14D3

Parc de Loisirs, Rue des Sports. **GPS**: n47,66940 w3,17744.

10 free. **Location:** Simple. **Surface:** gravel/metalled. 01/01-31/12.

Berric 14D3

Chemin de l'Étang. **GPS**: n47,63294 w2,52905.

6 € 5 €2/10minutes Ch €2/55minutes.
Location: Rural, comfortable, quiet. **Surface:** asphalted.
01/04-30/09.
Distance: 500m on the spot on the spot 500m 500m.
Remarks: Along river, coins at the shops in the village, access via Rue du Grand Pont.

Binic 14D1

Aire camping-car de l'Ic, Rue de l'Ic. **GPS**: n48,60059 w2,83573.

50 free Chfree. **Location:** Urban, simple, central, quiet.
Surface: gravel. 01/01-31/12.
Distance: 500m 700m 500m 500m.

Tourist information Binic:
Thu.

Bourg-Blanc 14B1

Rue de Brest. **GPS**: n48,49188 w4,50312.

6 free Chfree. **Surface:** sand. 01/01-31/12.
Distance: fish pond 100m.

Bréal-sous-Montfort 18A1

Les Jardins de Brocéliande, Les Mesnils.
GPS: n48,05384 w1,88963.

12 € 6 Ch. **Location:** Rural, simple, quiet.
Surface: unpaved. 01/01-31/12.
Distance: 2,5km 3,5km on the spot on the spot on the spot.

Brech 14D3

Rue de Pont Douar/Avenue des Pins, D768.
GPS: n47,71917 w3,00111.

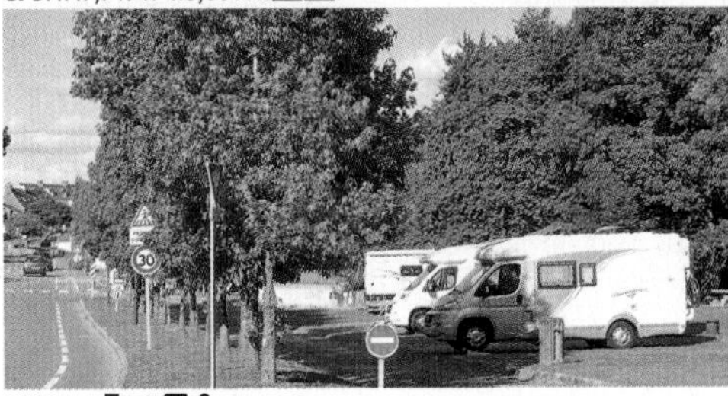

6 free €3 Ch. **Location:** Simple. **Surface:** grassy.
01/01-31/12.

Distance: 100m 200m 200m.
Remarks: Parking nearby small lake, plan d'eau, coins at the bakery.

Brest 14B1

Parking Océanopolis, Rue du Cormoran. **GPS**: n48,38893 w4,43535.

24 free. **Surface:** asphalted. 01/01-31/12.
Distance: on the spot on the spot 300m.
Remarks: Busy parking during the day, gate closes at 20h.

Brest 14B1

Port du Moulin Blanc, Rue Eugène Berest.
GPS: n48,39174 w4,43612.
Ch free. 01/01-31/12.

Tourist information Brest:
Tour Tanguy. Diorama old Brest. daily, 01/10-31/05 Wed, Su afternoon.
Océanopolis. Sea-centre, penguin and seals. 01/04-31/08 9-18h, 01/09-31/03 10-17h Mo.

Brillac 14D3

Rue Saint-Maur. **GPS**: n47,54143 w2,81748.

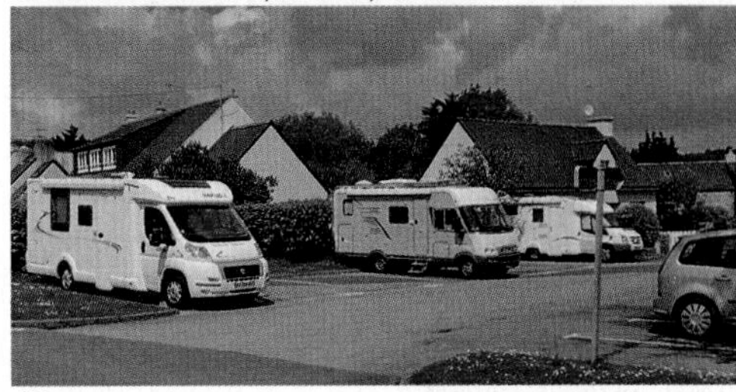

7 free. **Location:** Urban, simple, quiet. **Surface:** asphalted. 01/01-31/12.
Distance: on the spot 400m 450m on the spot on the spot.

Callac (22) 14C1

Av Ernest Renan. **GPS**: n48,40200 w3,43737.

6 free €2 Ch €2.
Location: Simple, quiet. **Surface:** gravel. 01/01-31/12.
Distance: 200m 200m on the spot.
Remarks: Lac Verte Vallée.

Camaret-sur-Mer 14B1

Rue Georges Ancey. **GPS**: n48,27513 w4,60793.

75 free, 01/04-31/10 € 6, only exact change €2/100liter Ch €2/55minutes. **Location:** Rural, comfortable, quiet.
Surface: gravel. 01/01-31/12.
Distance: 1km 500m 500m 500m on the spot on the spot.
Remarks: Max. 72h.

Campénéac 18A1

Rue de l'Étang. **GPS**: n47,95736 w2,29039.

FR

30 free €2 WC. **Location:** Rural. **Surface:** grassy.
01/01-31/12.
Distance: 250m 250m 250m.
Remarks: Coins at Fauchoux, rue nationale 32.

S **Campénéac** 18A1

Rue de la Fontaine. **GPS**: n47,95674 w2,29364.
€2 Ch WC.
Distance: on the spot on the spot on the spot.
Remarks: Coins at town hall and supermarket.

S **Cancale** 15B3

Aire camping-car Ville Ballet, Rue des Français Libres.
GPS: n48,67004 w1,86583.

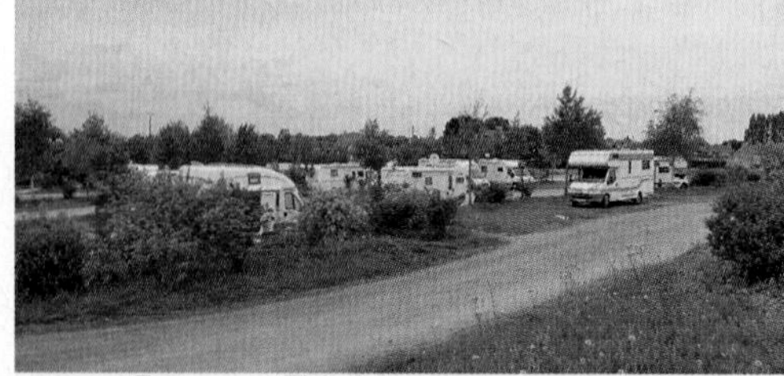

30 € 10 10minutes Ch 55minutes,€3,40.
Location: Simple. **Surface:** grassy. 01/01-31/12.
Distance: 300m 1km 800m 100m.
Remarks: Bread-service.

Tourist information Cancale:
La Ferme Marine. Guided tour oyster farm. summer 11h,15h,17h Français, 14h English, 16h Deutsch.

S **Carantec** 14C1

Aire du Meneyer, Rue Castel an Dour. **GPS**: n48,65967 w3,9138.

20 free €2/100liter Ch €2/55minutes.
Surface: gravel/metalled. 01/01-31/12.
Distance: 500m.
Remarks: Max. 48h.

Carantec 14C1

Chemin du Roch Glaz. **GPS**: n48,65235 w3,90308.

10 free. **Surface:** asphalted. 01/01-31/12.
Distance: beach 300m on the spot.
Remarks: Max. 24h, seaview.

Carantec 14C1

Rue Pen Al Lann. **GPS**: n48,66861 w3,895.

15 free. **Surface:** asphalted. 01/01-31/12.
Distance: 500m 150m 150m 1km 1km.
Remarks: At tennis-courts, max. 48h.

Carantec 14C1

Square du Grand Sacconex, Rue du Kélenn. **GPS**: n48,66892 w3,91085.

10 free. **Surface:** unpaved.
Distance: 300m on the spot on the spot on the spot 300m on the spot.
Remarks: At gymnasium.

Tourist information Carantec:
M Musée Maritime. Navigation museum. 15/05-15-09 Thu.

S **Carhaix-Plouguer** 14C2

Rue de Bazeilles/Rue des Augustins. **GPS**: n48,27829 w3,57257.

10 free Ch free. **Location:** Urban, simple, central.
Surface: asphalted. 01/01-31/12.
Distance: 200m 200m 200m.

S **Carnac** 14D3

Square d'Illertissen. **GPS**: n47,58505 w3,08242.

40 free €2/10minutes Ch €2/2h.
Location: Simple. **Surface:** asphalted. 01/01-31/12.
Distance: 50m 1,5km 50m 50m.
Remarks: Max. 1 night.

Tourist information Carnac:
Office de Tourisme, 74, avenue des Druides, http://www.ot-carnac.fr/. Seaside resort and important place of finding of 30.000 prehistoric menhirs.
M Musée de Préhistoire. Prehistoric museum. 10-12.30h and 14-18h 01/12-01/04.

S **Caulnes** 15A3

Lavoir Fontaine, Rue de Dinan. **GPS**: n48,28655 w2,15517.

10 free €2/10minutes Ch €2/1h WC.
Location: Urban, simple, quiet. **Surface:** gravel.
15/03-15/11.
Distance: 500m 100m 100m 200m.
Remarks: Max. 24h.

S **Cesson-Sévigné** 18B1

Route de La Valette. **GPS**: n48,11802 w1,59121.

8 free €2,30/10minutes Ch €2,30/55minutes.
Location: Rural, simple, central, quiet. **Surface:** metalled.
01/01-31/12.
Distance: 500m on the spot on the spot 100m 100m 500m on the spot.

Châteauneuf-du-Faou 14C2

Penn ar Pont. **GPS**: n48,18286 w3,81576.

15 free.
Location: Simple, quiet. **Surface:** gravel. 01/01-31/12.
Distance: 1,3km on the spot on the spot.

S **Châtillon-en-Vendelais** 18B1

D108. **GPS**: n48,23112 w1,17959.

10 free Ch free. **Location:** Rural, simple, quiet.
Surface: asphalted.
Distance: 2km lake on the spot on the spot.
Remarks: At the lake, next to campsite.

S **Cléden-Cap-Sizun** 14B2

Place du 19 mars 1962, Rue de la ville d'ys.
GPS: n48,04803 w4,65008.

20 free €2/10minutes Ch. **Location:** Rural, simple, quiet.
Surface: asphalted/metalled. 01/01-31/12.
Distance: on the spot on the spot.

FR

S Cléden-Cap-Sizun 14B2

Pointe du Van, D7. **GPS**: n48,05936 w4,70727.

20 free.
Location: Simple, quiet. **Surface:** gravel. 01/01-31/12.
Distance: Cléden-Cap-Sizun ± 5km on the spot on the spot on the spot.

Cléden-Cap-Sizun 14B2

Route de Kastel Koz, Beuzec-Cap-Sizun. **GPS**: n48,08473 w4,51844.

20 free. **Location:** Rural, simple, isolated, quiet.
Surface: asphalted/gravel. 01/01-31/12.
Distance: on the spot on the spot.

S Cléden-Poher 14C2

Route du Stade. **GPS**: n48,23686 w3,67165.

4 free Ch (4x)free. **Location:** Simple, quiet.
Surface: asphalted. 01/01-31/12.
Distance: 300m 50m bakery 200m 400m.
Remarks: Voluntary contribution.

S Clohars-Carnoët 14C2

Place de NAVA, Route de Quimperlé. **GPS**: n47,79790 w3,585.

4 free €2/70liter Ch €2/50minutes. **Location:** Simple.
Surface: asphalted. 01/01-31/12.
Distance: 200m 10km 4,5km bakery 200m.

S Combrit 14B2

Place du 19 mars 1962, Hent Ty Plouz. **GPS**: n47,88755 w4,1546.

10 free €2/10minutes Ch €2/60minutes. **Location:** Urban, simple, quiet. **Surface:** metalled. 01/01-31/12.
Distance: on the spot 5km 200m 1,3km on the spot.
Remarks: Coins at the shops in the village.

S Commana 14C1

Place du salles de Sports, D11. **GPS**: n48,41611 w3,96139.

5 free free. **Location:** Rural, simple, isolated, quiet.
Surface: grassy. 01/01-31/12.
Distance: 200m 300m bakery 300m on the spot on the spot.

S Concarneau 14C2

Le Porzou, Allée Jean Bouin. **GPS**: n47,86320 w3,9051.

40 free €4/10minutes Ch €4/55minutes WC.
Location: Urban, simple. **Surface:** asphalted. 01/01-31/12.
Distance: city centre 2km on the spot.
Remarks: Foot ferry to centre.

S Concarneau 14C2

Parking de la Gare, Avenue de la Gare. **GPS**: n47,87864 w3,9202.

47 € 2/20-08h €4 Ch €4/55minutes.
Location: Simple. **Surface:** asphalted. 01/01-31/12.
Distance: 500m beach 1,4km on the spot on the spot.
Remarks: Parking station.

Tourist information Concarneau:
Mo, Fri.

S Crac'h 14D3

Intermarché, AC Les Alizés. **GPS**: n47,60421 w2,99669.

8 free €2/10minutes Ch. **Surface:** asphalted.
01/01-31/12.
Distance: on the spot on the spot.

S Crozon 14B1

Parking du Loc'h, Rue de l'Atlantique, Morgat.
GPS: n48,22523 w4,50851.

30 € 4,50/24h €2,30/10minutes Ch €2,30/55minutes WC.
Location: Urban, simple. **Surface:** asphalted.
01/01-31/12.
Distance: 300m on the spot on the spot 100m on the spot.
Remarks: Max. 48h, market Wednesday.

S Crozon 14B1

Le Fret, Le Sillon, D55. **GPS**: n48,28457 w4,50934.

15 free €2,20/10minutes Ch. **Location:** Rural, simple, quiet.
Surface: unpaved. 01/01-31/12.
Distance: 5,5km 50m 250m 5,5km on the spot.

S Crozon 14B1

Parking Office de Tourisme, Boulevard de Pralognan, D887.
GPS: n48,24770 w4,4934.

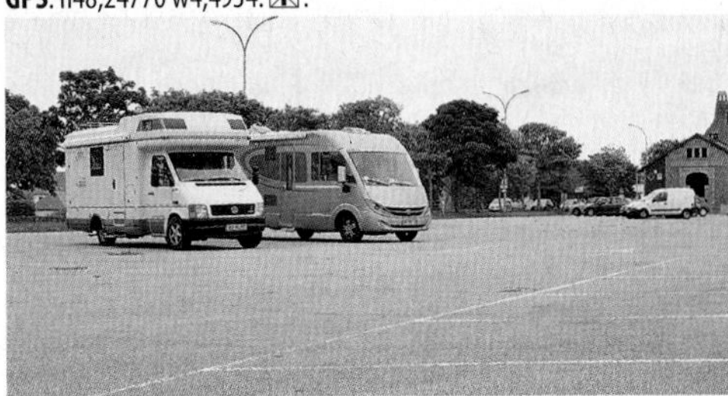

20 free €2,30/100liter. **Location:** Urban, simple.
Surface: asphalted. 01/01-31/12.
Distance: 50m on the spot on the spot.
Remarks: Nearby Office de Tourisme, max. 48h.

S Damgan 14D3

Parking de Kervoyal. **GPS**: n47,51465 w2,56038.

76 € 7,50 Chincluded. **Location:** Rural, comfortable, quiet.
Surface: metalled/sand. 01/01-31/12.
Distance: 600m Sandy beach.
Remarks: Parking at the beach, max. 48h.

Dinan 15A3

Rue du Port, D12. **GPS**: n48,45450 w2,0389.

30 € 0,30/30min 9-19h, overnight stay free. **Location:** Urban, simple, central. **Surface:** asphalted. 01/01-31/12.
Distance: 800m 800m on the spot 500m.

S Dol-de-Bretagne 15B3

Place Jean Hamelin. **GPS**: n48,54736 w1,75442.

FR

16 free €2 Ch €2. **Location:** Urban, simple, noisy.
Surface: asphalted. 01/01-31/12.
Distance: on the spot 100m 100m 150m.

Douarnenez 14B2

Rue Jean Barre. **GPS**: n48,09192 w4,3328.

4 free.
Location: Urban, simple, noisy. **Surface:** asphalted.
01/01-31/12.
Distance: on the spot 200m 200m.
Remarks: Max. 24h, narrow road, not suitable for motorhomes +7m.

Elven 14D3

Avenue des Martyrs de la Résistance, Le Guého.
GPS: n47,73879 w2,58134.

26 free €2 Ch (12x)€2/4h.
Location: Rural, simple, quiet. **Surface:** grassy/gravel.
parking 01/01-31/12 service 01/07-31/08.
Distance: 1,5km 800m 800m.

Erdeven 14D3

Chemin De Kerouriec. **GPS**: n47,62717 w3,17988.

10 € 7 €2 Ch (10x)€2/night WC. **Location:** Rural, simple, isolated, quiet. **Surface:** grassy. 01/01-31/12.
Distance: 1,1km.

Erdeven 14D3

Parc Kerhillio, Boulevard d'Atlantique. **GPS**: n47,61429 w3,15958.

70 € 6,50/24h Ch included.
Location: Rural, simple. **Surface:** grassy. 01/01-31/12.
Distance: 500m 200m 200m on the spot on the spot.

Erquy 15A3

Caroual Plage, Rue des Hirondelles. **GPS**: n48,62120 w2,4724.

44 € 6/24h €2/100liter Ch €2. **Location:** Urban, comfortable, central. **Surface:** asphalted/metalled.
Distance: 2,5km on the spot.
Remarks: Beach parking, max. 48h, baker at 8am.

Étel 14D3

Camping municipal, Rue de la Barre. **GPS**: n47,65100 w3,202.

25 € 7/night €2/100liter Ch (16x)against payment.
Location: Rural, simple. **Surface:** grassy. 01/04-30/09.
Distance: 500m 200m on the spot on the spot.
Remarks: Baker every morning (Jul/Aug).

Fouesnant 14C2

Plage Mousterlin, Chemin de Kerneuc. **GPS**: n47,85144 w4,04662.

15 free. **Location:** Rural, simple, quiet. **Surface:** grassy/sand.
01/01-30/12 31/12.
Distance: beach 50m 400m 500m on the spot.
Remarks: Beach parking, max. 48h.

Fouesnant 14C2

Leclerc, D45, Route de Quimper. **GPS**: n47,90234 w4,02938.

12 free €2/10minutes Ch €2/55minutes.
Surface: asphalted. 01/01-31/12.
Distance: on the spot.

Fougères 15B3

Allée des Fêtes. **GPS**: n48,35660 w1,20242.

25 free Ch WC free. **Location:** Urban, simple.
Surface: asphalted. 01/01-31/12.
Distance: 500m 200m 200m.

Fougères 15B3

Parking de la Poterne, Boulevard de Rennes.
GPS: n48,35524 w1,2113.

16 free Ch free. **Location:** Urban, simple, central.
Surface: metalled. 01/01-31/12.
Distance: on the spot 250m 300m on the spot.
Remarks: Castle of Fougères 500m.

Fréhel 15A3

La Ville Oie, Rue des Sports, D117, Pléhérel-plage.
GPS: n48,65032 w2,35241.

40 € 6 80liter Ch 1h, Service € 4.
Location: Rural, simple, isolated. **Surface:** gravel/metalled.
01/01-31/12.
Distance: 1,1km beach 1,2km on the spot.

Gâvres 14C3

Les Joncs, Rue des Filets Bleus. **GPS**: n47,69515 w3,35097.
40 € 5-7,60, 16/06-31/08 tariff camp site €2 Ch included.
Surface: grassy. 01/01-31/12.
Distance: 100m 100m.

Glomel 14C2

Etang du Coronc, Rue du Lac. **GPS**: n48,22052 w3,38972.

12 free €2/100liter Ch €2/1h. **Location:** Rural, simple, quiet. **Surface:** asphalted/gravel. 01/01-31/12.
Distance: 150m 400m.
Remarks: At lake.

Goulven 14B1

Aire Naturelle Ty Poas. **GPS**: n48,63109 w4,30833.

15 € 5,50 + tourist tax €2 Ch €2 WC.
Location: Comfortable, quiet. **Surface:** grassy/metalled.
15/06-30/09.
Distance: 500m beach 200m 500m.

Grand-Fougeray 18B2

Rue Camille de Jourdan. **GPS**: n47,72233 w1,7298.
5 free Ch. **Surface:** asphalted. 01/01-31/12.
Distance: 300m 300m.

Gueltas 14D2

Boju, Keriffe. **GPS**: n48,10406 w2,79064.

16 free ChWCfree. **Location:** Rural, simple, quiet. **Surface:** gravel. 01/01-31/12.
Distance: 1km on the spot.
Remarks: At the Nantes-Brest Canal.

S Gueltas 14D2

Cité des Écureuils, D125. **GPS:** n48,09667 w2,80111.

10 free Chfree.
Location: Rural, simple, isolated, quiet. **Surface:** gravel.
Distance: 200m.
Remarks: Nearby sports park.

S Guern 14D2

Kervazo, Rue de la Vallée, D1. **GPS:** n48,02815 w3,09215.

8 free Chfree. **Location:** Rural, simple, quiet. **Surface:** asphalted. 01/01-31/12.
Distance: 250m bakery 300m.

Guern 14D2

Etang du Ponterre, D1. **GPS:** n48,03472 w3,0975.

6 free.
Location: Rural, simple. **Surface:** gravel. 01/01-31/12.
Distance: 700m on the spot 700m bakery.

S Guichen 18B1

Le Boel, Pont Réan. **GPS:** n48,00221 w1,77336.

5 €5 ChWCfree. **Location:** Simple, quiet. **Surface:** metalled. 01/01-31/12.
Distance: 500m on the spot on the spot on the spot bakery 150m.
Remarks: Max. 48h.

Guidel 14C2

D152, Guidel-Plage > Fort-Bloqué. **GPS:** n47,75035 w3,50574.

15 free. **Location:** Rural, simple. **Surface:** gravel/sand. 01/01-31/12.
Distance: 1,5km 100m 1,5km on the spot on the spot.
Remarks: Behind Résidence Maéva, beach parking, max. 24h.

Guidel 14C2

La Falaise, Guidel plage. **GPS:** n47,76640 w3,5258.

7 free.
Location: Simple. **Surface:** metalled. 01/01-31/12.
Distance: on the spot.
Remarks: Behind yachting school, max. 24h.

Guidel 14C2

Plage du Loc'h, D152. **GPS:** n47,75650 w3,5159.

8 free. **Location:** Quiet. **Surface:** sand. 01/01-31/12.
Distance: 250m.

S Guidel 14C2

Arc-en-Ciel, ZA de Pen Mané. **GPS:** n47,80980 w3,4633.
service €2, during opening hours Ch WC. 01/01-31/12.

S Guimiliau 14C1

Parking Salle Polyvalente, Rue des Bruyeres.
GPS: n48,48676 w3,99665.

15 free free. **Location:** Simple, central, noisy. **Surface:** metalled. 01/01-31/12.
Distance: on the spot 400m 400m on the spot on the spot.
Remarks: Max. 2 nights.

S Guingamp 14D1

Place du Vally. **GPS:** n48,56024 w3,1489.

free Chfree WC. **Location:** Simple, central. **Surface:** asphalted. 01/01-31/12 Fri market.

Distance: on the spot.
Remarks: Max. 24h.

S Guiscriff 14C2

La Gare de Guiscriff, Rue de la Gare. **GPS:** n48,05722 w3,65401.

4 free Ch (4x)€5. **Location:** Rural. **Surface:** metalled. 01/01-31/12.
Distance: 1km bakery 1km on the spot on the spot.

S Guissény 14B1

Rue de Plouguerneau. **GPS:** n48,63299 w4,41127.

free €2 Ch. **Location:** Comfortable. **Surface:** gravel. 01/01-31/12.
Distance: on the spot beach 550m 250m bakery.
Remarks: Coins at the shops and town hall.

Hédé-Bazouges 15B3

La Magdelaine. **GPS:** n48,30592 w1,79218.

50 free. **Location:** Rural, simple. **Surface:** grassy/gravel. 01/01-31/12.
Distance: 1km on the spot on the spot 50m on the spot on the spot.

S Hillion 14D1

Le Tertre Piquet, Lermot-plage. **GPS:** n48,53098 w2,66387.

20 free ChWCfree. **Location:** Simple, isolated. **Surface:** grassy. 01/01-31/12.
Distance: sandy beach 100m.
Remarks: Beach parking, no camping activities.

S Hillion 14D1

Rue Olivier Provost. **GPS:** n48,51743 w2,66772.

7 free Chfree. **Location:** Simple, central, quiet. **Surface:** gravel. 01/01-31/12.

FR

Distance: 500m 100m on the spot.

S Hirel 15B3

D155. **GPS**: n48,60841 w1,82032.

100 free, night € 6 €2/100liter Ch €2/55minutes.
Location: Rural, simple. **Surface:** grassy/gravel.
01/01-31/12.
Distance: 700m 200m 200m.

S Huelgoat 14C1

Place du Camping-cars, Route du Fao, D769a.
GPS: n48,36115 w3,75612.

30 free €5/10minutes Ch 1h. **Location:** Rural, simple, quiet. **Surface:** metalled. 01/01-31/12.
Distance: 500m on the spot on the spot 500m 500m 500m 500m 500m.
Remarks: In front of campsite municipal, service 100m.

S Janzé 18B1

Aire du Hardier, D41. **GPS**: n47,97258 w1,53825.

5 € 10 €2 Ch WC free. **Location:** Motorway, simple, simple.
Surface: asphalted.
Distance: on the spot.
Remarks: At petrol station.

S Josselin 14D2

Place St.Martin. **GPS**: n47,95639 w2,55056.

50 free €2,50 Ch €2,50/h WC.
Location: Urban, central. **Surface:** metalled.
01/01-31/12 Sa 9-14h.
Distance: 300m N24 900m 300m bakery 300m 1km on the spot.
Remarks: Castle of Josselin 400m.

Tourist information Josselin:
Office de Tourisme, Place de la Congregation, www.paysdejosselin.com. City is dominated by the castle of Rohan.

S Kerlouan 14B1

Lestonquet. **GPS**: n48,66952 w4,36161.

free €2 Ch. **Surface:** grassy. 01/01-31/12.
Remarks: Former campsite.

Kerlouan 14B1

La Digue. **GPS**: n48,66195 w4,37879.

4 free. **Location:** Isolated. **Surface:** gravel. 01/01-31/12.
Distance: 100m on the spot on the spot.

S Kernascléden 14C2

Domaine du Scroff, Canquisquelen. **GPS**: n47,99785 w3,31845.
2 € 10 Ch WC included. **Location:** Comfortable.
01/01-31/12.
Distance: 1km on the spot on the spot.
Remarks: Heated pool.

S La Chèze 14D2

Chemin d'Alénor, Allée du 19 mars 1962.
GPS: n48,13419 w2,65787.

10 € 4, weekend/holidays free Ch (6x) WC free.
Location: Simple, quiet. **Surface:** asphalted.
01/01-31/12.
Distance: 200m 200m mountainbike trail.
Remarks: Parking at small lake.

S La Fontenelle 15B3

Rue de Chevrigné. **GPS**: n48,46575 w1,50495.

6 free €2/10minutes Ch €2/55minutes.
Location: Rural, simple, quiet. **Surface:** asphalted.
01/01-31/12.
Distance: on the spot 350m on the spot on the spot.
Remarks: Next to cemetery, adjacent walking and bicycle area.

S La Martyre 14C1

Route de Ploudiry, D35. **GPS**: n48,44861 w4,15694.

10 free Ch WC free.
Surface: gravel. 01/01-31/12.
Distance: 100m 100m 100m.
Remarks: Nearby Maison du Plateau.

La Roche-Bernard 18A2

Place du Dôme. **GPS**: n47,51753 w2,29733.

>20 free. **Location:** Urban, simple, central. **Surface:** asphalted.
01/01-31/12.
Distance: 50m 100m 50m.

S La Roche-Bernard 18A2

Halte Camping-car, Rue du Patis. **GPS**: n47,52012 w2,30466.

15 € 9,60, 01/07-25/08 € 11,10 Ch €4,60 WC.
Location: Urban, comfortable, quiet. **Surface:** grassy.
02/04-16/09.
Distance: 100m 50m 50m 100m 100m.
Remarks: Next to campsite du Patis.

Tourist information La Roche-Bernard:
Small town especially known for the beautiful hanging bridge over the Vilaine river, 50m high and over 400m long.

S La Roche-Derrien 14D1

Rue du Jouet. **GPS**: n48,74696 w3,25976.

12 € 2 €2 Ch (6x)€2.
Location: Rural, simple, central, quiet. **Surface:** gravel.
01/01-31/12.
Distance: 100m 100m 100m.
Remarks: Coins at the shops and town hall.

S Lampaul-Plouarzel 14B1

Aire de Porspaul, Rue de Beg ar Vir. **GPS**: n48,44667 w4,77722.

50 free, 15/04-15/10 € 3,50, Jul/Aug + € 0,30/pp €2/20minutes Ch €2/55minutes WC €1,60 €3/3,50.
Location: Comfortable. **Surface:** grassy. 01/01-31/12.
Distance: 150m 100m 200m 500m on the spot on the spot.
Remarks: Shower and washing machine Jul/Aug.

S Landerneau 14B1

Rue du Calvaire. **GPS**: n48,44694 w4,25667.

FR

25 €5, incl. electricity €2 Ch included .
Location: Comfortable. **Surface:** grassy/gravel. 01/01-31/12.
Distance: 500m river 500m 500m on the spot.

Landivisiau 14C1

P de Keravel, Rue du Manoir. **GPS**: n48,51015 w4,0758.

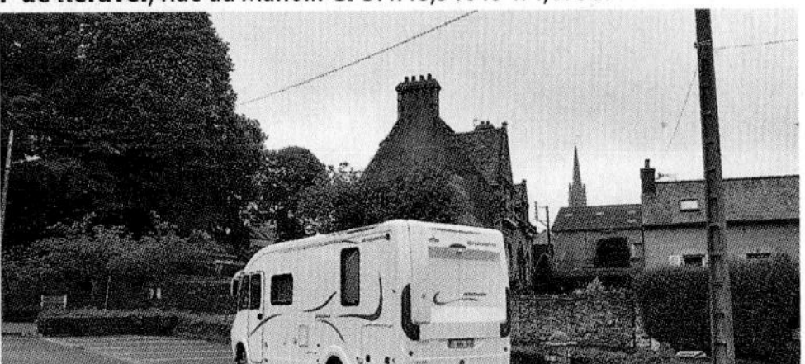

3 free Chfree. **Surface:** asphalted. 01/01-31/12.
Distance: on the spot on the spot 100m centre.

Landudec 14B2

Super U, Rue des Écoles. **GPS**: n48,00143 w4,34088.

5 free €2/10minutes Ch €2/55minutes. **Location:** Rural, simple. **Surface:** asphalted. 01/01-31/12.
Distance: 1km on the spot on the spot.
Remarks: Motorhome washing place.

Lanfains 14D1

Étang du Pas, Le Pas, D7. **GPS**: n48,36466 w2,87938.

6 free ChWCfree. **Location:** Simple, quiet.
Surface: asphalted/grassy. 01/01-31/12.
Distance: on the spot on the spot.
Remarks: Parking at small lake.

Languidic 14D2

Zone Lanveur, Place du Bouilleur de Cru.
GPS: n47,83722 w3,16188.

20 free Chfree. **Location:** Motorway, simple, noisy.
Surface: metalled. 01/01-31/12.
Distance: 700m N24 300m.

Lanloup 14D1

Rue de Saint-Roch. **GPS**: n48,71359 w2,96389.

2 free WCfree. **Location:** Rural, simple, quiet. **Surface:** gravel.
01/01-31/12.
Distance: on the spot.

Lannilis 14B1

Aire Fontaine Rouge. **GPS**: n48,55667 w4,50528.

12 free ChWC. **Surface:** metalled. 01/01-31/12.
Distance: 1km 1,5km 1,5km.

Lannilis 14B1

Rue Haie Blanche. **GPS**: n48,57125 w4,52151.

free Chfree. **Surface:** asphalted. 01/01-31/12.
Distance: 100m bakery 150m.
Remarks: In front of cemetery.

Lanvallay 15A3

Rue du terrain des sports. **GPS**: n48,45420 w2,03028.

5 free €2/100liter Ch €2. **Location:** Urban, simple.
Surface: asphalted. 01/01-31/12.
Distance: 50m 50m 50m.

Larmor-Baden 14D3

Route d'Auray. **GPS**: n47,58816 w2,89868.

3 free. **Location:** Simple. **Surface:** asphalted. 01/01-31/12.
Distance: 50m 100m 100m.
Remarks: Max. 6,5m.

Larmor-Plage 14C3

Parking les Pins, Rue des Pins. **GPS**: n47,70970 w3,3791.

4 free ChWCfree. **Location:** Central. **Surface:** asphalted.
01/01-31/12.
Distance: on the spot 50m 100m 100m.
Remarks: Nearby plage de Toulhars, max. 72h.

Le Conquet 14B1

Parking Parklec'H, Rue Général Leclerc. **GPS**: n48,36055 w4,7701.

+10 free €2/100liter Ch €2/1h. **Surface:** gravel.
01/01-31/12.
Distance: 200m beach 800m 400m bakery 300m on the spot.
Remarks: Coins at tourist info and town hall.

Le Croisty 14C2

Aire de pique-nique, D132, Kergoff. **GPS**: n48,06510 w3,38144.

8 free €2 Ch €2/55minutes WC. **Location:** Comfortable, isolated, quiet. **Surface:** asphalted. 01/01-31/12.
Distance: 1,5km on the spot.

Le Faou 14C1

Rue de la Grève. **GPS**: n48,29529 w4,18501.

8 15/06-15/09 € 3,50 €2/100liter Ch. **Location:** Urban, simple.
Surface: metalled. 01/01-31/12.
Distance: 500m 600m 1,5km.

Le Faouët 14C2

Restaurant Ty Blomen, Le Grand Pont. **GPS**: n48,03575 w3,48125.

15 free €2 Ch. **Location:** Rural, simple. **Surface:** asphalted.
01/01-31/12.
Distance: on the spot.

Le Folgoët 14B1

Parking Frepel, Route de Gorrékear. **GPS**: n48,56002 w4,33507.

FR

30 free Ch free. **Surface:** gravel/metalled.
01/01-31/12.
Distance: on the spot 100m 100m.
Remarks: Nearby basilica.

Le Guilvinec 14B2

Parking de la Petite Sole, Rue Jean Baudry.
GPS: n47,79588 w4,27997.

16 €4 €2/100liter Ch €2/10minutes.
Location: Urban, simple, noisy. **Surface:** asphalted.
01/01-31/12 Su market.
Distance: on the spot on the spot 100m 100m on the spot.
Remarks: Coins at tourist info.

Le Trévoux 14C2

Rue des Sports. **GPS**: n47,89683 w3,64228.

4 free Chfree. **Location:** Simple. **Surface:** gravel.
01/01-31/12.
Distance: on the spot.
Remarks: Nearby tennis-courts, max. 48h.

Le Trévoux 14C2

Plan d'Eau, Rue de Quimperlé. **GPS**: n47,89356 w3,6386.

10 free. **Location:** Simple. **Surface:** gravel. 01/01-31/12.
Distance: on the spot bakery.
Remarks: At lake.

Le Vivier-sur-Mer 15B3

Camping-Car Park, Rue de l'Abri des Flots.
GPS: n48,60291 w1,77255.

49 € 8,40, 01/06-30/09 € 9,60 Ch (49x) included.
Location: Rural, comfortable, quiet. **Surface:** asphalted.
01/01-31/12.
Distance: on the spot 100m 100m 150m 150m on the spot.

Léhon 15A3

Parking Club de Tennis. GPS: n48,44177 w2,04233.

6 free Chfree. **Location:** Urban, simple. **Surface:** asphalted.
01/01-31/12.
Distance: on the spot bakery 100m.

Les Forges 14D2

Place de l'Église, D117. **GPS**: n48,01820 w2,6482.

5 free WCfree.
Surface: metalled. 01/01-31/12.
Distance: 100m 100m.

Lézardrieux 14D1

Rue de l'Île à Bois. **GPS**: n48,83002 w3,08165.

5 free. **Location:** Simple, isolated, quiet. **Surface:** gravel/sand.
01/01-31/12.
Distance: Lézardrieux 6km 50m on the spot.
Remarks: Max. 24h.

Lézardrieux 14D1

Camping Municipal, Cité des Gardiens de Phare.
GPS: n48,78021 w3,1147.
Chfree. 01/01-31/12.
Distance: on the spot.

Liffré 18B1

Intermarché. GPS: n48,22459 w1,50165.

free Ch free. **Location:** Urban, simple.
Surface: asphalted. 01/01-31/12.
Distance: 300m on the spot.

Locmaria-Plouzané 14B1

Zône détente Ty Izella, Rue de la Fontaine.
GPS: n48,37306 w4,64306.

12 free €2 Ch €2. **Location:** Quiet. **Surface:** gravel.
01/01-31/12.
Distance: 100m 250m 250m.
Remarks: Coins at town hall.

Locmaria-Plouzané 14B1

Plage de Portez, Rue de Portez, Porsmilin.
GPS: n48,35501 w4,67269.

8 € 5 + tourist tax Chincluded €3.
Surface: gravel. 18/04-18/09.
Distance: 3,5km beach 50m on the spot on the spot.
Remarks: To be paid at campsite.

Locmariaquer 14D3

Aire de Pierres Plates, > Route des Plages.
GPS: n47,55720 w2,9486.

18 free.
Location: Simple. **Surface:** metalled. 01/01-31/12.
Distance: beach 50m on the spot.
Remarks: Max. 24h, 500m from 'Les Pierres Plates'.

Locmariaquer 14D3

Résidence de Cresidui. **GPS**: n47,57204 w2,95328.
€2/100liter Ch.

Tourist information Locmariaquer:
Office de Tourisme, Rue de la Victoire, www.ot-locmariaquer.com. Port city with many megalithics, signed dolmen.

Locminé 14D2

Rue Laennec / rue du Pont Person. **GPS**: n47,88788 w2,83174.

6 free Chfree. **Location:** Simple. **Surface:** gravel.
01/01-31/12.
Distance: 1km N24 1,4km 600m.
Remarks: Max. 48h.

Locmiquelic 14C3

Port de Ste. Catherine, Quai Rallier du Baty.
GPS: n47,72364 w3,34958.

FR

free. **Location:** Simple. **Surface:** asphalted.
Distance: on the spot on the spot on the spot.
Remarks: Parking at marina, max. 1 night.

Locqueltas 14D3

Rue de la Fontaine. **GPS**: n47,75841 w2,76901.

6 free Ch (4x)€3,50 WC free.
Location: Rural, simple, quiet. **Surface:** gravel.
01/01-31/12.
Distance: 100m 600m 100m 100m.
Remarks: Max. 24h, coins at Bar-Tabac, 18 Place de la Mairie, town hall.

Locronan 14B2

Parking de la Croix de Mission, Rue du Prieuré.
GPS: n48,09811 w4,21245.

10 free, 01/06-15/10 € 6/24h €2/10minutes Ch €2/2h.
Location: Urban, simple, quiet. **Surface:** grassy/sand.
01/01-31/12.
Distance: 100m 50m on the spot on the spot.

Loctudy 14B2

Plage des Sables Blancs, Chemin de Toul Pesked.
GPS: n47,80110 w4,20044.

6 free. **Location:** Rural, simple. **Surface:** grassy/sand.
01/01-31/12.
Distance: 4km beach 80m on the spot on the spot.
Remarks: Beach parking.

Loudéac 14D2

Parking de la Gare, Boulevard de la Gare.
GPS: n48,18058 w2,76277.

3 free Ch free. **Location:** Urban, simple. **Surface:** asphalted.
01/01-31/12.
Distance: 600m 50m 200m 200m on the spot.

Maël-Carhaix 14C2

Place de l'école, Route de Rostrenen. **GPS**: n48,28344 w3,42148.

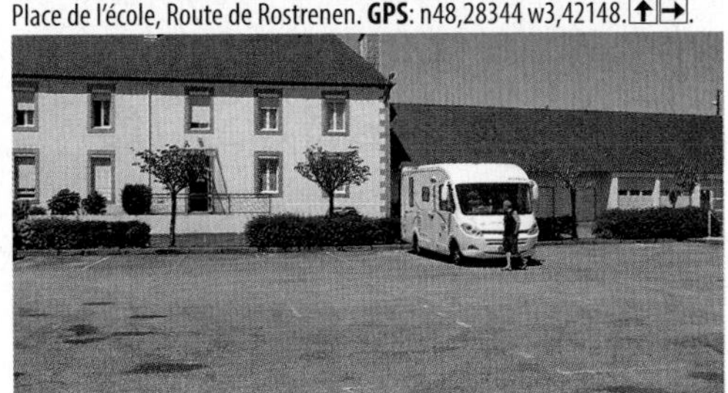

5 free €2 Ch WC. **Location:** Urban, simple.
Surface: asphalted. 01/01-31/12.
Distance: 100m 100m 100m.
Remarks: At fire-station, coins at town hall.

Malansac 18A2

Rue Saint Fiacre. **GPS**: n47,67820 w2,29942.

5 free Ch free. **Location:** Rural, comfortable, quiet.
Surface: grassy.
Distance: 100m 100m 100m.

Malestroit 18A1

Chemin des Tanneurs. **GPS**: n47,80772 w2,37885.

12 free. **Location:** Comfortable, quiet. **Surface:** gravel/metalled.
01/01-31/12.
Distance: 500m on the spot 350m.
Remarks: Max. 48h.

Malestroit 18A1

Chemin de l'Écluse. **GPS**: n47,81250 w2,38197.

12 free. **Location:** Rural, comfortable, quiet.
Surface: gravel/metalled. 01/01-31/12.
Distance: 100m on the spot on the spot 100m 100m 200m.
Remarks: Max. 48h.

Malestroit 18A1

Rue de Narvik. **GPS**: n47,80896 w2,37591.
Ch free. **Surface:** asphalted.
Distance: 1,5km 600m 600m 2km 1km.

Marzan 18A2

Rue de la Source. **GPS**: n47,54023 w2,32383.

+20 free Ch WC free. **Location:** Urban, simple, quiet.
Surface: asphalted.
Distance: 50m 20m.

Maure-de-Bretagne 18A1

Rue de Campel, D65. **GPS**: n47,89230 w1,99031.

3 free Ch free. **Location:** Urban, simple, central, quiet.
Surface: gravel. 01/01-31/12.
Distance: 200m on the spot 200m 200m on the spot on the spot on the spot.

Mauron 18A1

Rue de la Libération. **GPS**: n48,08024 w2,27677.

12 free €2,50/100liter Ch WC. **Location:** Rural, simple, comfortable, quiet. **Surface:** asphalted.
Distance: 150m on the spot on the spot 150m 150m on the spot on the spot.

Mégrit 15A3

Rue des Granitiers. **GPS**: n48,37817 w2,24722.
free Ch free. **Surface:** asphalted/gravel. 01/01-31/12.
Distance: on the spot.

Mellé 15B3

Rue Rouviel. **GPS**: n48,48919 w1,18814.

6 free Ch WC free. **Surface:** metalled.
Distance: 200m 200m.
Remarks: Nearby football ground, max. 48h.

Meslin 14D1

Allée des Loisirs, D28. **GPS**: n48,44363 w2,56994.

10 free Ch free. **Location:** Urban, simple, central.
Surface: metalled. 01/01-31/12.
Distance: 300m bar/crêperie 50m 50m.

FR

Moëlan-sur-Mer 14C2

Kerdoualen, Route de l'Île Percée. **GPS**: n47,79045 w3,70314.

4 free. **Location:** Rural. **Surface:** gravel. 01/01-31/12.
Distance: 200m.

Moëlan-sur-Mer 14C2

Rue de Beg Tal Gward. **GPS**: n47,77749 w3,64404.

4 free. **Location:** Rural, isolated, quiet. **Surface:** asphalted.
01/01-31/12.
Distance: Moëlan 5km sea 50m.

Moncontour 14D2

Camping la Tourelle, Rue François Lorant.
GPS: n48,35271 w2,63719.

4 €2 €2 Ch €2/55minutes. **Location:** Rural, simple, quiet. **Surface:** gravel. 01/01-31/12.
Distance: 1,5km 1,5km 1,5km.
Remarks: Max. 48h.

Morlaix 14C1

Rue de Brest. **GPS**: n48,57422 w3,8316.
5 free Ch free. **Location:** Urban, simple, central, noisy.
Surface: asphalted. 01/01-31/12.
Distance: on the spot on the spot 200m 100m 200m on the spot on the spot.

Mûr-de-Bretagne 14D2

L'ancienne Gare, Place de la Gare. **GPS**: n48,19814 w2,98961.
4 free Ch. **Location:** Urban, simple. **Surface:** metalled.
01/01-31/12.
Distance: 700m 500m.

Mûr-de-Bretagne 14D2

Anse de Leandroanec, Plage de Leandroanec.
GPS: n48,20969 w3,01309.
10 free. **Location:** Rural, simple, quiet. **Surface:** metalled.
01/01-31/12.
Distance: 2,5km on the spot.

Mûr-de-Bretagne 14D2

Place Ste Suzanne. **GPS**: n48,20260 w2,98835.
4 free. **Location:** Urban, simple. **Surface:** metalled.
01/01-31/12.
Distance: 300m 100m.

Neulliac 14D2

Rue des Deux Croix, D767. **GPS**: n48,12812 w2,98552.

4 free €2 Ch €2. **Location:** Simple, isolated, quiet.
Surface: asphalted.
Distance: 300m 300m.

Névez 14C2

Rue de Port Manech, Impasse du Stade. **GPS**: n47,81560 w3,7894.

20 free €2/10minutes Ch €2/55minutes WC.
Location: Simple. **Surface:** asphalted. 01/01-31/12.
Remarks: Parking next to stadium, max. 24h, service only with 2-euro coins.

Névez 14C2

Plage de Dourveil, Rue de Dourveil, D1. **GPS**: n47,79407 w3,8101.

5 free. **Surface:** sand.
Distance: on the spot.
Remarks: Max. 24h, no camping activities.

Névez 14C2

Plage de Tahiti, Kerstalen. **GPS**: n47,79287 w3,79011.

± 11 free.
Location: Simple. **Surface:** grassy/sand. 01/01-31/12.
Distance: beach 150m.
Remarks: Beach parking, max. 24h.

Névez 14C2

Rue de la Plage. **GPS**: n47,80499 w3,74261.

5 free.
Location: Rural, simple. **Surface:** sand. 01/01-31/12.
Distance: 50m.
Remarks: Max. 24h.

Névez 14C2

Rue des Iles, Raguénez. **GPS**: n47,78908 w3,80174.

10 free. **Location:** Simple. **Surface:** asphalted. 01/01-31/12.
Distance: sea 10m, beach 150m 100m.
Remarks: Max. 24h.

Noyal-Pontivy 14D2

Le Valvert, Caudan. **GPS**: n48,07833 w2,91583.

20 free WC free. **Location:** Rural, comfortable, isolated, quiet.
Surface: asphalted. 01/01-31/12.
Distance: Noyal-Pontivy 4,5km on the spot on the spot 50m.
Remarks: At small lake.

Paimpol 14D1

Parking Pierre Loti, Rue Pierre Loti. **GPS**: n48,78404 w3,0463.

15 free €3,30/100liter Ch €3,30/55minutes.
Surface: gravel/sand. 01/01-31/12.
Distance: on the spot 1km 400m 100m on the spot on the spot.
Remarks: Service 100m.

Paimpol 14D1

Parking de Goas Plat, Rue de Goas Plat. **GPS**: n48,77535 w3,04009.

37 € 8. **Location:** Urban, simple, central, quiet.
Surface: asphalted.
Distance: centre 500m 2km 500m 500m.
Remarks: Max. 24h.

Paimpont 18A1

Rue de l'Enchanteur Merlin. **GPS**: n48,02286 w2,17128.

70 € 3, 01/05-27/09 € 4 €3,70/10minutes Ch WC.
Location: Simple. **Surface:** gravel.
Distance: 200m 200m 200m 200m 200m on the spot 100m.

FR

Remarks: Coins at tourist info and supermarket.

Pénestin 14D3

Allée du Grand Pré. **GPS**: n47,48111 w2,47361.

7 free, € 6/night + € 0,20/pp €2,50/100liter Ch €2,50/1h.
Location: Urban. **Surface:** asphalted.
Distance: 500m 1,5km 500m.
Remarks: Check in all aires in Pénestin: Office de tourisme; Bar-PMU Le Narval, Rue Calvaire; Café 0 20 100 0, Port de Tréhiguier, max. 48h, coins at tourist info.

Pénestin 14D3

Aire camping-car de la Pointe du Bile, Route de l'Espernel.
GPS: n47,44524 w2,48029.

free, € 6/night + € 0,20/pp. **Location:** Rural, simple, quiet.
Surface: grassy/sand. 01/01-31/12.
Distance: 100m.
Remarks: Max. 48h.

Pénestin 14D3

Allée de Poudrantais. **GPS**: n47,46681 w2,48716.

4 free, € 6/night + € 0,20/pp. **Location:** Urban, simple, quiet.
Surface: gravel/metalled.
Distance: 50m.
Remarks: Max. 48h.

Pénestin 14D3

Chemin de Camaret. **GPS**: n47,49386 w2,49075.

4 free, € 6/night + € 0,20/pp. **Location:** Urban, simple, quiet.
Surface: gravel.
Distance: 100m.
Remarks: Max. 48h.

Pénestin 14D3

Plage de la Source, Allée du Maro. **GPS**: n47,48158 w2,49005.

10 free, € 6/night + € 0,20/pp. **Location:** Rural, simple, quiet.
Surface: grassy/metalled.
Distance: 300m.
Remarks: Max. 48h.

Pénestin 14D3

Plage du Palandrin, L'Isle du Clos Parc, Kerséguin.
GPS: n47,45000 w2,46417.

6 free, € 6/night + € 0,20/pp tourist tax.
Location: Rural, simple, isolated. **Surface:** grassy/sand.
01/01-31/12.
Distance: Sandy beach 1km.
Remarks: Pay at tourist office.

Pénestin 14D3

Route du Loguy. **GPS**: n47,49050 w2,49667.

20 free, € 6/night + € 0,20/pp. **Location:** Rural, simple, quiet.
Surface: grassy/metalled.
Distance: 150m.
Remarks: Max. 48h.

Penmarch 14B2

Aire de Kérity, Rue Victor Hugo. **GPS**: n47,79981 w4,34794.

10 free, 01/04-31/10 € 4/19-9h. **Location:** Rural, simple, quiet.
Surface: grassy/gravel. 01/01-31/12.
Distance: 1,5km 50m 1km 5km on the spot on the spot.

Penmarch 14B2

Aire du Ster, Rue de la Grande Grève. **GPS**: n47,80042 w4,31807.

15 free, 01/04-31/10 € 4/19-9h.
Surface: sand. 01/01-31/12.
Distance: Sandy beach 2km on the spot on the spot.

Remarks: Beach parking.

Penmarch 14B2

Aire du Viben, Rue de la Plage. **GPS**: n47,82390 w4,3708.

30 free, 01/04-31/10 € 4/19-9h. **Location:** Rural, simple, quiet.
Surface: metalled. 01/01-31/12.
Distance: bakery 1km 50m 900m on the spot on the spot.
Remarks: Sandy beach.

Penmarch 14B2

Aire de Kerameil, Rue du Pont Nevez. **GPS**: n47,81369 w4,36077.
€2/10minutes Ch WC. 01/01-31/12.
Remarks: Only overnight stays 19-9h.

Penvins 14D3

Camping La Gree Penvins, Chemin du Marais 20.
GPS: n47,49746 w2,68606.

22 € 5. **Location:** Urban, comfortable, quiet. **Surface:** grassy.
01/01-31/12.
Distance: on the spot 350m.
Remarks: Max. 48h.

Penzé 14C1

Rue du Dossen. **GPS**: n48,59811 w3,93439.

5 free €2 Ch €2 WC. **Location:** Simple, quiet.
Surface: asphalted. 01/01-31/12.
Distance: 100m on the spot on the spot 50m 250m on the spot on the spot.
Remarks: Nearby port.

Piré-sur-Seiche 18B1

Rue de Boistrudan. **GPS**: n48,00719 w1,42871.

15 free Ch free.
Location: Rural, simple. **Surface:** metalled.
Distance: 300m on the spot 300m 500m.
Remarks: At fish lake.

Plabennec 14B1

Rue de l'Aber. **GPS**: n48,50155 w4,43374.

FR

5 free Chfree. **Location:** Simple. **Surface:** metalled.
01/01-31/12.
Distance: on the spot.
Remarks: Parking at small lake.

S **Planguenoual** 15A3

Bien y Vient. GPS: n48,53447 w2,54506.

6 €5 €2/24h. **Location:** Rural, comfortable, isolated, quiet. **Surface:** grassy. 01/01-31/12.
Distance: on the spot.

S **Planguenoual** 15A3

Ferme Gesbert, D786. **GPS:** n48,54883 w2,5556.

6 free €2 Ch €2 . **Location:** Rural.
Surface: grassy/gravel. 01/01-31/12.
Distance: 1km 1km 1km.
Remarks: Regional products.

S **Plémet** 14D2

Rue de l'Étang, D16. **GPS:** n48,17897 w2,58918.

15 free €2/100liter Ch €2/55minutes.
Surface: gravel. 01/01-31/12.
Remarks: Parking at small lake.

S **Pléneuf-Val-André** 15A3

Avenue du Général Leclerc. **GPS:** n48,58355 w2,55669.

30 €6 €2 Ch. **Location:** Urban, simple, central, quiet.
Surface: grassy/gravel. 01/01-31/12.
Distance: 1km 450m.
Remarks: Max. 72h.

S **Plerguer** 15B3

Route de Saint Mâlo. **GPS:** n48,52975 w1,85237.
6 Ch. 01/01-31/12.

Distance: 500m 500m on the spot 500m.
Remarks: At supermarket.

S **Plérin** 14D1

Sous la Tour, Rue de la Tour, D24. **GPS:** n48,53146 w2,72483.

16 free Chfree. **Location:** Simple, quiet. **Surface:** gravel.
01/01-31/12.
Distance: on the spot 300m 1km.

S **Pleslin-Trigavou** 15A3

D28. **GPS:** n48,53631 w2,05009.

20 free Chfree.
Location: Urban, simple. **Surface:** asphalted.
Distance: on the spot 400m on the spot on the spot.
Remarks: Cycle and hiking routes: voie verte, Circuit des Mégalithes.

S **Plessala** 14D2

Rue de l'Étang. **GPS:** n48,27394 w2,62427.

12 free Chfree. **Location:** Urban, simple, quiet.
Surface: gravel. 01/01-31/12.
Distance: 200m on the spot.
Remarks: At fish lake, max. 48h, fishing permit available.

Plestin-les-Grèves 14C1

Voie Communale de l'Armorique. **GPS:** n48,68157 w3,63411.

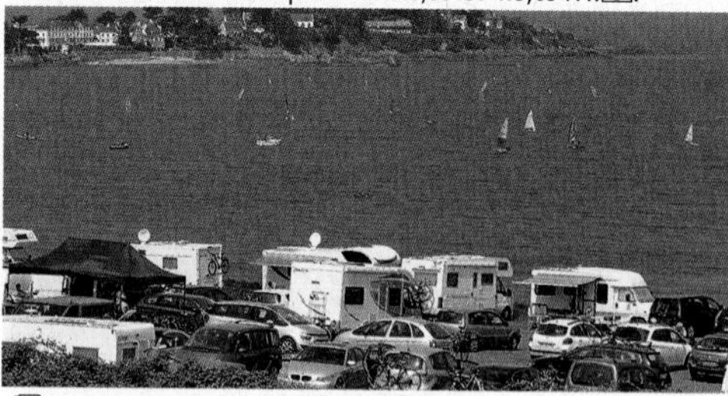

6 free. **Surface:** unpaved. 01/01-31/12.
Distance: 3km 50m 2km on the spot.
Remarks: Beach parking, max. 24h.

Plestin-les-Grèves 14C1

Du Grand Rocher, Avenue de la Lieue de Grève.
GPS: n48,66968 w3,5858.

free. **Location:** Simple, isolated, quiet.
Distance: 1,3km 100m 1,3km.

Plestin-les-Grèves 14C1

Route de la Corniche. **GPS:** n48,67235 w3,63602.

6 free. **Location:** Rural, simple, quiet. **Surface:** grassy/sand.
01/01-31/12.
Distance: 1km on the spot 300m Lidl 2km.
Remarks: Max. 24h.

S **Plestin-les-Grèves** 14C1

Rue de Guergay. **GPS:** n48,66232 w3,62562.
€2/10minutes Ch €2/1h.
Remarks: Motorhome washing place.

Pleubian 14D1

Port Béni. **GPS:** n48,84834 w3,17053.

4 free. **Location:** Rural, simple, isolated, quiet.
Surface: asphalted. 01/01-31/12.
Distance: Pleubian 2,5km on the spot 2,5km on the spot.
Remarks: Max. 24h.

Pleubian 14D1

Rue de Kermagen, Kermagen. **GPS:** n48,85667 w3,14194.

4 free. **Surface:** grassy. 01/01-31/12.
Distance: Pleubian 1,6km beach 100m on the spot.
Remarks: Max. 24h.

Pleubian 14D1

Rue de Pen Lan, Lanéros. **GPS:** n48,85760 w3,07883.

4 free. **Surface:** asphalted. 01/01-31/12.
Distance: Pleubian 5,5km on the spot on the spot.
Remarks: Max. 24h.

S **Pleumeur-Bodou** 14C1

Parking de Toul ar Stang, Rue de Toul ar Stang, Ile Grande.
GPS: n48,79868 w3,58342.

6 € 6/night €2/10minutes Ch €2/1h.
Location: Rural, simple, quiet. **Surface:** grassy.
01/01-31/12.
Distance: Plemeur-Bodu 6km sandy beach 150m 150m on the spot.

Pleumeur-Bodou 14C1

Cosmopolis-Parc Scientifique, Route du Radome.
GPS: n48,78297 w3,52587.

20 parking free, € 5/night Ch WC.
Surface: gravel/sand. 01/01-31/12.
Distance: 1km 1km on the spot on the spot.

Plévenon 15A3

Parking Cap Fréhel. **GPS**: n48,68174 w2,31811.

40 free, 01/06-30/09 € 4. **Surface:** metalled.
Distance: 50m.
Remarks: Max. 1 night.

Pleyben 14C2

Pont Coblant. **GPS**: n48,19337 w3,98182.

80 free WC. **Location:** Rural, simple, quiet. **Surface:** grassy.
15/06-15/09.
Distance: 300m on the spot 300m 300m on the spot.
Remarks: On the canal, former campsite.

Ploemeur 14C2

Aire de la Vraie Croix, Route de Larmor. **GPS**: n47,72784 w3,41423.
free Chfree.
Remarks: Industrial area, max. 48h.

Ploemeur 14C2

Rue Louis Lessart. **GPS**: n47,73681 w3,43051.

7 free. **Surface:** asphalted. 01/01-31/12.
Distance: on the spot.
Remarks: Parking centre, max. 24h.

Ploemeur 14C2

Golf Ploemeur, D152, Boulevard de l'Atlantique.
GPS: n47,72316 w3,48156.

9 free.
Location: Rural, quiet. **Surface:** gravel.
01/01-31/12.
Distance: Ploemeur 5km N165 10km beach 300m 1,8km.

Plogoff 14B2

Aire Naturelle Kerguidy Izella, Rue Guillaume Pennamen.
GPS: n48,03694 w4,68139.

30 € 12 Ch WC included. **Location:** Rural, comfortable, luxurious, quiet. **Surface:** grassy. 01/01-31/12.
Distance: 2km 4km 1km 2km on the spot.
Remarks: 9><20h.

Plogoff 14B2

Parking de l'Eglise, Rue Cleder cap Sizum.
GPS: n48,03727 w4,6652.

3 free €2/10minutes Ch. **Location:** Rural, simple.
Surface: asphalted. 01/01-31/12.
Distance: centre.

Plogoff 14B2

Aire de la Pointe du Raz, Route des Langoustiers.
GPS: n48,03651 w4,7173.

40 € 15.
Location: Rural, simple, quiet. **Surface:** unpaved. 01/01-31/12.
Distance: 3km 50m on the spot on the spot.

Plogoff 14B2

Parking du Stade, Rue du 19 Mars 1962. **GPS**: n48,03245 w4,66316.

50 free. **Location:** Rural, simple, quiet. **Surface:** grassy/metalled.
01/01-31/12.
Distance: on the spot 450m 450m bakery.

Plomelin 14B2

Rue Hent Keramer. **GPS**: n47,93410 w4,1515.

4 free €2/10minutes Ch €2/h. **Location:** Rural, simple, quiet. **Surface:** asphalted. 01/01-31/12.
Distance: on the spot 400m 200m.
Remarks: Parking sports park, max. 24h.

Plonévez-Porzay 14B2

Plonévez-Porzay, Rue des Eglantines. **GPS**: n48,12469 w4,22414.

15 free €2/10minutes Ch €2/55minutes.
Location: Rural, comfortable, quiet. **Surface:** grassy.
01/01-31/12.
Distance: 600m 450m bakery + Spar on the spot.

Plonévez-Porzay 14B2

Kervel Izella. **GPS**: n48,11570 w4,28065.

10 free. **Location:** Rural, simple, simple. **Surface:** grassy/sand.
01/01-31/12.
Distance: 8km 50m on the spot on the spot.
Remarks: Beach parking, max. 48h.

Plouarzel 14B1

Aire de camping-car de Ruscumunoc, Route de Ruscumunoc.
GPS: n48,42232 w4,78486.

free, 15/05-15/09 € 4,60 €2,50/10minutes Ch €2,60/50minutes €1. **Location:** Comfortable, quiet.
Surface: grassy. 01/01-31/12.
Distance: 3km 100m.

FR

Ploubalay 15A3

Rue des Ormelets. **GPS**: n48,58057 w2,14524.

3 free Ch free. **Location:** Simple. **Surface:** asphalted. 01/01-31/12.
Distance: 250m 100m 500m on the spot.

Ploubazlanec 14D1

Park Nevez, Cité de Lan ar Mendy. **GPS**: n48,80090 w3,0305.
3 free. **Location:** Simple. 01/01-31/12.
Distance: bakery.
Remarks: Max. 24h.

Ploubazlanec 14D1

Pointe de l'Arcouest, Route de l'Embarcadère.
GPS: n48,82102 w3,01948.

20 free, 30/06-30/09 € 6/24h. **Location:** Simple, isolated, quiet.
Surface: grassy. 01/01-31/12.
Distance: 2km 50m on the spot.

Ploubazlanec 14D1

Rue du Port Loguivy. **GPS**: n48,82011 w3,06279.

6 free. **Surface:** asphalted. 01/01-31/12.
Distance: 100m on the spot 100m 100m.

Plouescat 14C1

Rue de Pen an Théven. **GPS**: n48,65902 w4,21863.

6 free. **Surface:** metalled. 01/01-31/12.
Distance: 3,5km 100m.

Plouescat 14C1

Intermarché, La Rocade-Kerchapalain.
GPS: n48,65083 w4,18444.

4 free €2 Ch €2 €5/1. **Location:** Comfortable.
Surface: asphalted. 01/01-31/12.
Distance: 500m 600m on the spot on the spot.
Remarks: Parking supermarket.

Plouézec 14D1

Parking A. Le Calvez, Route de Paimpol. **GPS**: n48,75041 w2,98651.

3 free. **Surface:** asphalted. 01/01-31/12.
Distance: 100m 200m 100m.

Plouézec 14D1

Parking de la Corniche, Bréhec. **GPS**: n48,72875 w2,9455.

5 free. **Surface:** asphalted. 01/01-31/12.
Distance: on the spot.
Remarks: Beautiful view.

Plouézec 14D1

Place du 19 mars 1962. **GPS**: n48,74788 w2,9853.

3 free. **Surface:** asphalted. 01/01-31/12.
Distance: on the spot.
Remarks: Service at camping municipal.

Plouézec 14D1

Route de Paimpel. **GPS**: n48,75049 w2,98643.

3 free. **Location:** Urban, simple. **Surface:** asphalted.
01/01-31/12.
Distance: 100m 100m.

Plougasnou 14C1

Parking de la Métairie, Rue Charles de Gaulle.
GPS: n48,69404 w3,79209.

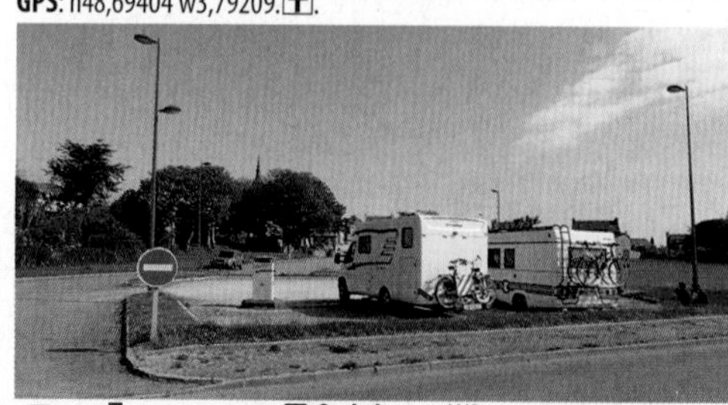

7 free €2/10minutes Ch €2/1h WC. **Location:** Rural.
Surface: gravel. 01/01-31/12.
Distance: on the spot sandy beach 1,4km 200m 250m bakery on the spot on the spot.
Remarks: Tuesday morning market.

Plougasnou 14C1

Rue des Grands Viviers, Le Diben. **GPS**: n48,70811 w3,82731.

7 free €2 Ch. **Location:** Rural, simple, isolated, quiet.
Surface: asphalted. 01/01-31/12.
Distance: 300m on the spot on the spot 300m on the spot.
Remarks: Max. 48h, coins at town hall.

Plougastel-Daoulas 14B1

Rue de la Fontaine Blanche. **GPS**: n48,37111 w4,36428.

15 free Ch free.
Surface: asphalted. 15/05-15/10.
Distance: 450m 450m 450m.
Remarks: Parking at sports grounds.

Plougonvelin 14B1

Rue de Bertheaume. **GPS**: n48,33792 w4,70742.

50 € 6 Ch WC included. **Location:** Comfortable, quiet. **Surface:** grassy/sand. 01/01-31/12.
Distance: 1km beach 650m.

Plougonvelin 14B1

Intermarché, Rue du Stade. **GPS**: n48,34245 w4,72248.

€7 €2/100liter Ch €1/1h €5.
Surface: asphalted.
Distance: on the spot.

Plouguerneau 14B1

Lilia. **GPS**: n48,61891 w4,55341.

10 free €4/10minutes Ch €4/55minutes.
Location: Comfortable. **Surface:** asphalted. 01/01-31/12.
Distance: 400m 850m 450m.

FR

Plouha 14D1

Plage de Palus, Route du Palus. **GPS**: n48,67667 w2,88556.

10 free. **Location:** Rural, simple, isolated, quiet. **Surface:** grassy.
01/03-31/10.
Distance: 3km sandy/pebbled beach 100m 50m on the spot.
Remarks: Max. 3 days.

Ploumoguer 14B1

Rue Huon de Kermadec, D28. **GPS**: n48,40507 w4,72492.

30 free, July-Aug € 3 €2/80liter Ch €2/45minutes WC €2 €4/2,30. **Surface:** metalled. 01/04-30/11.
Distance: 200m 200m 200m.
Remarks: Next to stadium, max. 48h, coins at town hall, supermarket, bakery and Tabac.

Plouneour 14B1

Parking des Menhirs. **GPS**: n48,65090 w4,30573.
10 free. **Surface:** metalled. 01/01-31/12.
Distance: 1km 50m.
Remarks: At sea.

Plouvorn 14C1

Plan d'Eau de Lanorgant. **GPS**: n48,57722 w4,03056.

15 free €2 Ch €2 WC.
Location: Simple, quiet. **Surface:** metalled. 01/01-31/12.
Distance: 500m 100m 100m 500m 500m.
Remarks: Parking at small lake.

Pluméliau 14D2

Allée du vieux Blavet. **GPS**: n47,98229 w3,04209.

15 free Chfree. **Location:** Rural, comfortable.
Surface: gravel. 01/01-31/12.
Distance: 500m on the spot 250m on the spot on the spot.
Remarks: Along the Blavet river, attention: max. ^3.1m.

Pont-Aven 14C2

Rue Louis Lomenech. **GPS**: n47,85401 w3,74333.

30 free €2,45/10minutes Ch €2,45/55minutes.
Location: Simple. **Surface:** asphalted.
01/01-31/12.
Distance: 450m 450m.
Remarks: Parking near stadium Sinquin, coins at tourist info (D783).

Pont-Aven 14C2

Rue des Abbès Tanguy. **GPS**: n47,85646 w3,75203.

free. **Location:** Simple. **Surface:** asphalted. 01/01-31/12.
Distance: 400m.

Pont-l'Abbé 14B2

Parking de la Gare, Rue de la Gare. **GPS**: n47,86754 w4,22591.

30 free. **Location:** Urban, simple. **Surface:** unpaved.
01/01-31/12.
Distance: on the spot 50m 400m 1km.

Pont-l'Abbé 14B2

Leclerc, Route de Saint Jean Trolimont. **GPS**: n47,86414 w4,23646.

13 free €2/100liter Ch €2/2h.
Location: Urban, simple. **Surface:** asphalted. 01/01-31/12.
Distance: 1,5km on the spot on the spot on the spot.
Remarks: At supermarket.

Pontivy 14D2

Rue de la Fontaine. **GPS**: n48,06758 w2,96941.

6 free free. **Location:** Urban, simple. **Surface:** asphalted.
01/01-31/12.
Distance: 800m on the spot bakery 300m on the spot.

Port-Louis 14C3

Aire de la Côte Rouge, D781 Port-Louis > Riantec.
GPS: n47,70873 w3,34295.

14 € 5/24h, 01/06-15/09 € 10/24h Ch (4x)included . **Surface:** asphalted. 01/01-31/12.
Distance: on the spot on the spot.

Port-Louis 14C3

Aire des Remparts, Promenade Henri François Buffet.
GPS: n47,70496 w3,35602.

30 € 5/24h, 01/06-15/09 € 10/24h Ch included .
Location: Urban. 01/01-31/12.
Distance: 100m 100m on the spot.
Remarks: In front of campsite.

Portsall 14B1

Aire camping-cars Kerros, Rue de Porsguen.
GPS: n48,56583 w4,69944.

37 € 5,20/24h Ch included .
Location: Comfortable, quiet. **Surface:** grassy. 01/01-31/12.
Distance: on the spot 350m 200m 200m.
Remarks: Max. 3 days.

Poullaouen 14C1

D236, Rue de Ty Meur. **GPS**: n48,33672 w3,64218.

5 free Chfree.
Location: Rural, comfortable, quiet. **Surface:** gravel.
01/01-31/12.
Distance: 200m 150m Véloroute Roscoff-Nantes on the spot.

Primelin 14B2

Camping Municipal de Kermaléro, Route de l'Océan.
GPS: n48,02550 w4,61821.

15 free, 13/06-13/09 € 3 €2/100liter Ch €3/h.
Location: Rural, simple, quiet. **Surface:** metalled.
01/01-31/12.

FR

Distance: 1km 1km.

Priziac 14C2

Base de Loisirs du Lac du Bel Air, Etang du Bel Air.
GPS: n48,06183 w3,41132.

€ 5,50 Ch included.
Distance: 300m.

Quiberon 14D3

Rue de Port Kerné. **GPS**: n47,49165 w3,13941.

140 € 6,40/24h €1/2minutes Ch.
Location: Rural, simple. **Surface:** gravel.
01/01-31/12 service: 15/10-01/04.
Distance: 2km sea 250m 2km 2km on the spot on the spot on the spot.
Remarks: Next to camping municipal, max. 3 days, bread-service only in summer, seaview.

Quimper 14C2

Route de l'Innovation. **GPS**: n47,97399 w4,09319.

2 free €2/100liter Ch €2/10minutes.
Location: Urban, simple, noisy. **Surface:** asphalted.
01/01-31/12.
Distance: 1km on the spot on the spot on the spot on the spot.
Remarks: Parking at centre commercial, special part for motor homes.

Quimperlé 14C2

Aire Saint Nicolas, Rue du Viaduc. **GPS**: n47,86640 w3,54334.

3 free Chfree. **Location:** Simple. **Surface:** metalled.
01/01-31/12.

Quintin 14D1

Place du Champ de Foire. **GPS**: n48,40056 w2,90222.

7 free Chfree. **Location:** Urban, simple, quiet.
Surface: asphalted. 01/01-31/12 Service: winter.
Distance: on the spot on the spot.
Remarks: Next to swimming pool, near the lake, tuesday market.

Tourist information Quintin:
Tue-morning.

Radenac 14D2

Sente Verte, Les Gambris. **GPS**: n47,95778 w2,71333.

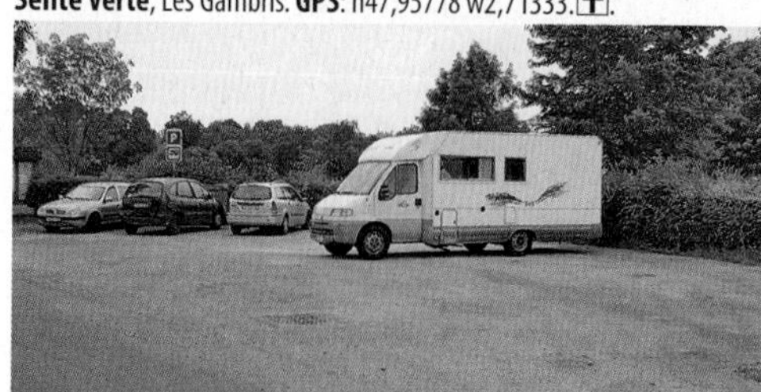

5 free. **Location:** Rural, simple, quiet. **Surface:** gravel.
01/01-31/12.
Distance: 700m on the spot on the spot on the spot.
Remarks: At small lake.

Redon 18A2

Quai Surcouf. **GPS**: n47,64510 w2,0897.

10 free Chfree. **Location:** Simple. **Surface:** asphalted.
01/01-31/12.
Distance: 500m on the spot 100m 200m 200m.
Remarks: In front of Bureau du Port de Plaisance.

Tourist information Redon:
Manoir de l'Automobile de Loheac. Car collection: Ferrari, Lamborghini, Porsche, Maserati.

Réguiny 14D2

Base de Loisirs, Rue de la Piscine. **GPS**: n47,96843 w2,73828.

10 free Chfree. **Location:** Rural, simple, quiet.
Surface: unpaved. 01/01-31/12.
Distance: 1,3km bakery 1,3km on the spot on the spot.

Rennes 18B1

Rue du Professeur Maurice Audin. **GPS**: n48,13531 w1,64542.

5 free €2/100liter Ch €2/1h €1/30minutes.
Location: Rural, simple. **Surface:** asphalted. 01/01-31/12.
Distance: 3km 100m 100m 3km on the spot.
Remarks: In park, max. 48h.

Tourist information Rennes:
Musée de Britanny. Regional museum.
Tue-Sa.

Riantec 14C3

Camping-car Park de Kerdurand. **GPS**: n47,71735 w3,31778.
49 Ch (40x)included.
Location: Rural. 01/01/-31/12.
Distance: 800m 1,5km.
Remarks: Video surveillance.

Riantec 14C3

Leclerc, Rond-point de Kersabiec. **GPS**: n47,72611 w3,32137.

10 free €2 Ch €2/55minutes.
Location: Simple. **Surface:** asphalted. 01/01-31/12.
Distance: on the spot.

Riantec 14C3

Route de Plouhinec. **GPS**: n47,71163 w3,29858.

4 free €2/10minutes Ch €2/55minutes.
Location: Rural, simple. **Surface:** metalled. 01/01-31/12.
Distance: 1,5km.
Remarks: Near old laundry place (still operational!), max. 24h.

Rochefort-en-Terre 18A2

Parking des Grées, Rue du Souvenir. **GPS**: n47,69975 w2,33384.

>100 € 2/24h. **Location:** Rural, simple, quiet. **Surface:** gravel.
01/01-31/12.
Distance: 200m.

Rohan 14D2

Port de Plaisance, Rue Saint-Gouvry. **GPS**: n48,07187 w2,75559.

14 free ChWCfree. **Location:** Rural, comfortable, quiet.
Surface: asphalted. 01/01-31/12.
Distance: 500m on the spot on the spot 500m on the spot.
Remarks: At the Nantes-Brest Canal.

Romagné 15B3

Allée des Prunus, D812. **GPS**: n48,34409 w1,27415.

5 free ChWCfree. **Location:** Urban, simple.
Surface: metalled. 01/01-31/12.

FR

Distance: 100m 1,7km 200m 50m.

Roscoff — 14C1

Route du Laber. **GPS:** n48,71215 w3,99918.

30 free Chfree. **Location:** Isolated. **Surface:** asphalted.
01/01-31/12.
Distance: 2km.
Remarks: Service 200m.

Tourist information Roscoff:
Office de Tourisme, 46, rue Gambetta, www.roscoff-tourisme.com.
Seaside resort and former pirates town.
Wed.

Rostrenen — 14D2

Rue Rosa l'Hénaff, D23. **GPS:** n48,23318 w3,32019.

6 free €2/100liter Ch €2/1h.
Location: Urban, simple. **Surface:** gravel.
01/01-31/12.
Distance: 400m 100m.
Remarks: Coins at tourist info, town hall, maison de presse, tabac.

Sains — 15B3

Rue du Puits Rimoult. **GPS:** n48,55305 w1,58603.

10 € 5, tourist tax € 0,20/pp Chfree.
Location: Rural, simple, quiet. **Surface:** grassy/metalled.
01/01-31/12.
Distance: 100m 2km 150m 150m on the spot 100m on the spot.

Saint Aignan — 14D2

Place de l'Église. **GPS:** n48,18306 w3,01361.

20 free ChWCfree. **Location:** Comfortable, quiet.
Surface: asphalted. 01/01-31/12.
Distance: 100m on the spot on the spot.
Remarks: Square behind the church.

Saint Gérand — 14D2

Keroret, D322. **GPS:** n48,11333 w2,89028.

12 free ChWCfree. **Location:** Rural, comfortable, quiet.
Surface: gravel. 01/01-31/12.
Distance: 800m on the spot 150m on the spot on the spot.
Remarks: At the Nantes-Brest Canal.

Saint-Aubin-d'Aubigné — 18B1

Rue de Rennes. **GPS:** n48,26147 w1,60621.

5 free ChWCfree. **Location:** Urban, simple.
Surface: asphalted. 01/01-31/12.
Distance: on the spot 100m on the spot on the spot.

Saint-Barnabé — 14D2

Place du Vieux Chêne, Rue Pierre Loti. **GPS:** n48,13672 w2,70146.

10 free Chfree. **Location:** Urban, simple, central.
Surface: gravel. 01/01-31/12.
Distance: 200m bakery 50m.

Saint-Benoît-des-Ondes — 15B3

Rue Bord de Mer. **GPS:** n48,61681 w1,84714.

10 free €3/50liter Ch €3/15minutes.
Location: Rural, simple. **Surface:** asphalted.
Distance: 100m on the spot on the spot 100m 200m on the spot on the spot.

Saint-Brice-en-Coglès — 15B3

Espace Jules Verne, Rue de Normandie, D102.
GPS: n48,41126 w1,36252.

8 free €2/100liter Ch €2/55minutes WC.
Location: Urban, simple, central. **Surface:** asphalted/metalled.
01/01-31/12.
Distance: 300m 500m 400m 300m on the spot.

Saint-Carreuc — 14D1

Rue de la Lande, D27. **GPS:** n48,40300 w2,73923.

12 free €2/10minutes Ch €2/55minutes.
Location: Rural, simple, isolated, noisy. **Surface:** metalled.
01/01-31/12.
Distance: 300m on the spot on the spot.
Remarks: At Etang-du-Plessis, max. 24h.

Saint-Derrien — 14C1

GPS: n48,54820 w4,1817.

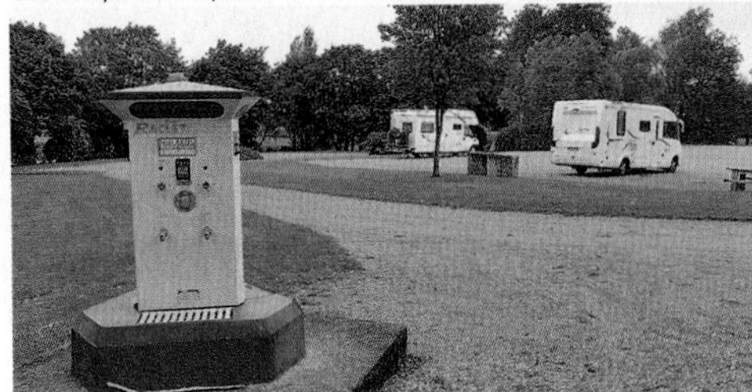

20 free €3 Ch €3 WC. **Location:** Quiet.
Surface: gravel/metalled. 01/05-31/10.
Distance: 100m on the spot on the spot 300m 300m.
Remarks: Nearby recreation area.

Saint-Gelven — 14D2

Rue de l'Ecole, D95. **GPS:** n48,22442 w3,09589.

10 free Chfree. **Location:** Urban, simple. **Surface:** gravel.
01/01-31/12.
Remarks: Service 100m.

Saint-Gelven — 14D2

Tregnanton, D117. **GPS:** n48,21153 w3,08457.

free.
Location: Rural, isolated, quiet. **Surface:** grassy/metalled.
Distance: 2,5km on the spot on the spot on the spot.

Saint-Gildas-de-Rhuys — 14D3

Camping municipal de Kerver, Route du Rohu.
GPS: n47,52238 w2,85803.

35 € 6/24h €2 Ch **Location:** Rural, simple, quiet.
Surface: asphalted. 15/03-04/11.
Distance: 4km 50m 400m 4km.

FR

Saint-Guyomard 14D3

Route de Malestroit, D112. **GPS**: n47,78166 w2,51188.

20 € 5/night €3 Ch €3.
Location: Rural, simple, quiet. **Surface:** asphalted.
Distance: 300m 100m.
Remarks: Behind church, check in at town hall.

Saint-Jacut-de-la-Mer 15A3

Rue de la Manchette. **GPS**: n48,58969 w2,18947.

26 € 6 Ch included. **Location:** Comfortable.
Surface: grassy/gravel. 01/01-31/12.
Distance: 1km 500m.
Remarks: Baker at 8am.

Saint-Malo 15A3

Les Iltots, Avenue de la Guimorais, Rothéneuf.
GPS: n48,68109 w1,96348.

150 € 7, 25/06-04/09 € 12, 2 pers. incl €3 Ch (40x) included. **Location:** Rural, comfortable. **Surface:** grassy.
08/03-14/11 and 16/12-03/01.
Distance: sandy beach 100m 100m 200m.

Saint-Malo 15A3

Parking Paul Féval, Rue Paul Féval. **GPS**: n48,64341 w1,99385.

200 € 7,50, overnight stay 19-9h free €2,50 Ch.
Location: Urban, simple. **Surface:** gravel. holidays + 01/07-07/09.
Distance: 800m 800m on the spot.
Remarks: Free bus to centre.

Saint-Malo 15A3

Avenue Louis Martin. **GPS**: n48,64876 w2,01776.

free 19.00-09.00h. 01/01-31/12.
Distance: 5 min 100m 1km.
Remarks: Max. 24h.

Saint-Malo 15A3

Parking du Grand Domaine. **GPS**: n48,61568 w2.
01/01-31/12.

Saint-Malo 15A3

Parking Le Davier, Avenue J. Kennedy. **GPS**: n48,67356 w1,98098.
free 19.00-09.00h. 01/01-31/12.
Distance: 100m 400m.
Remarks: Max. 24h.

Saint-Malo 15A3

Parking Le Naye, Port des Bas-Sablons, Terre-Plein du Naye.
GPS: n48,64111 w2,02322.

free 19.00-09.00h. 01/01-31/12.
Distance: on the spot 650m.
Remarks: Behind swimming pool, max. 24h.

Saint-Malo 15A3

Parking Marville, Avenue de Marville. **GPS**: n48,64142 w2,00226.

free 19.00-09.00h. **Surface:** asphalted. 01/01-31/12.
Distance: 300m 300m 100m.
Remarks: Max. 24h.

Saint-Malo 15A3

Rue Henri Lemairié. **GPS**: n48,65467 w1,97374.

free 19.00-09.00h.
01/01-31/12.
Distance: on the spot 1km 1km.
Remarks: Max. 24h.

Tourist information Saint-Malo:
Château. Castle, 14/15th century, historical museum. 10-12h, 14-18h.
Fort National. Fort designed by Vauban. At ebb accessible by foot.

Saint-Pierre-Quiberon 14D3

Rue du Stade. **GPS**: n47,51160 w3,13903.

40 € 5/24h €2/10minutes Ch €2/45minutes.
Location: Simple. **Surface:** asphalted. 01/01-31/12.
Distance: 1km 1,5km on the spot on the spot.
Remarks: Max. 48h.

Saint-Pol-de-Léon 14C1

Quai de Pempoul. **GPS**: n48,68361 w3,97083.

30 € 6 €2 Ch €2 WC.
Surface: metalled. 01/01-31/12.
Distance: 800m on the spot on the spot 800m 800m.
Remarks: At sea.

Saint-Pol-de-Léon 14C1

Rue Hervé Mesguen. **GPS**: n48,67919 w3,99749.

8 free €2/10minutes Ch €2/55minutes.
Location: Comfortable. **Surface:** asphalted. 01/01-31/12.
Distance: on the spot.
Remarks: In front of supermarket Leclerc.

Saint-Renan 14B1

Route de l'Aber. **GPS**: n48,43878 w4,63063.

10 free €2 Ch €2.
Surface: gravel. 01/01-31/12.
Remarks: Jul/Aug max. 48h.

Saint-Rivoal 14C1

Saint-Rivoal, D42. **GPS**: n48,34930 w3,99782.

6 free Ch free. **Location:** Rural, simple, isolated, quiet.
Surface: grassy/metalled. 01/01-31/12.
Distance: 300m 500m on the spot on the spot.

Saint-Servais 14C1

Cité Yan d'Argent. **GPS**: n48,50984 w4,15434.

10 free Ch free WC. **Location:** Simple, quiet.
Surface: gravel/metalled. 01/01-31/12.
Distance: 200m 200m 200m.

Saint-Thégonnec 14C1

Park an Iliz, D118. **GPS**: n48,52215 w3,94637.

FR

25 free Ch free. **Location:** Urban, comfortable, central, quiet. **Surface:** gravel. 01/01-31/12.
Distance: on the spot 150m 150m on the spot on the spot.
Remarks: Free coins available at shops.

Tourist information Saint-Thégonnec:
Fri.
Crêperie Steredenn, Rue de la Gare 6.

Santec 14C1

Le bistrot à Crèpes, Rue de Méchouroux. **GPS**: n48,70102 w4,03868.

15 free €2 Ch WC free. **Location:** Quiet.
Surface: grassy. 01/01-31/12 Wed.
Distance: La plage du Staol 100m on the spot 800m.
Remarks: Max. 24h, bread-service.

Sarzeau 14D3

Aire du Rohaliguen, Rue du Raker/Rue du Pont Neui.
GPS: n47,49769 w2,76748.

10 € 5,50/18-10h Ch WC free. **Location:** Rural, simple, quiet.
Surface: metalled. 01/01-31/12.
Distance: on the spot 200m.

Sarzeau 14D3

Rue de Brénudel. **GPS**: n47,52969 w2,7598.

20 € 5,50/24h €2 Ch €2. **Location:** Urban, simple, quiet.
Surface: asphalted. 01/01-31/12 school hours (8-16h).
Distance: on the spot 750m.

Sarzeau 14D3

Rue du Port St.Jacques, Kerbodo. **GPS**: n47,48906 w2,79297.

15 € 5,50/18-8h Ch WC free €2. **Location:** Urban, comfortable, quiet. **Surface:** asphalted. 01/01-31/12.
Distance: 200m 500m 100m 200m.
Remarks: Nearby port, max. 48h.

Sarzeau 14D3

Rue du Stang, St.Colombier. **GPS**: n47,54665 w2,72151.

5 € 5,50/18-10h Ch free.
Location: Urban, simple, quiet. **Surface:** asphalted.
Distance: St.Colombier 100m 50m 50m 50m.
Remarks: Max. 48h.

Scaër 14C2

Rue Louis Pasteur. **GPS**: n48,02774 w3,6951.

free €2/10minutes Ch €2/55minutes WC.
Location: Rural, simple, quiet. **Surface:** asphalted.
01/01-31/12.
Distance: 500m bakery 200m on the spot on the spot.
Remarks: Max. 72h, coins at camping municipal.

Sérent 14D2

Du Pont Salmon, Rue du Général De Gaule,.
GPS: n47,82445 w2,50194.

10 free. **Location:** Urban, simple, quiet. **Surface:** asphalted.
01/01-31/12.
Distance: 400m 400m 400m on the spot.

Silfiac 14D2

P Salle Polyvalente, Rue du Résistant P. le Bourlay.
GPS: n48,14816 w3,15668.
free Ch free. **Location:** Simple. **Surface:** asphalted.
01/01-31/12.
Distance: 150m 150m on the spot on the spot.

Silfiac 14D2

Etang de pont Samuel, Pont Samuel. **GPS**: n48,12847 w3,17109.

5 . **Location:** Rural, simple, isolated. **Surface:** unpaved.
01/01-31/12.
Distance: 300m 200m 200m.

Sougéal 15B3

Le Placis, D15. **GPS**: n48,50651 w1,52562.

30 free Ch WC free. **Location:** Rural, simple, quiet.
Surface: gravel/metalled. 01/01-31/12.
Distance: on the spot 300m bakery 300m.
Remarks: Bakery 500m.

Sulniac 14D3

Salle des Fêtes, Rue des Écoles. **GPS**: n47,67756 w2,56642.

15 free Ch free. **Location:** Rural, simple, quiet.
Surface: asphalted. 01/01-31/12.
Distance: 400m bakery 500m.

Theix 14D3

Allée de Noyalo. **GPS**: n47,62726 w2,66183.

4 free Ch free. **Location:** Urban, simple, quiet.
Surface: asphalted. Service: winter.
Distance: 500m 500m 500m 50m 50m.

Tinténiac 15B3

Quai de la Donac. **GPS**: n48,33168 w1,83202.

10 € 3 Ch free. **Location:** Rural, simple.
Surface: grassy/gravel. 01/04-31/10.
Distance: 500m Along river on the spot 100m 550m.

Trébeurden 14C1

Route de Lannion, D65. **GPS**: n48,76711 w3,5514.

5 parking free, € 7/night €4,30 Ch €4,30.
Location: Rural, comfortable, central, quiet.
Surface: asphalted.
Distance: on the spot 1,4km 1,5km 1km bakery, Intermarché 1,5km.

Trébeurden 14C1

Corniche de Pors Mabo. **GPS**: n48,76886 w3,57794.
parking free, € 7/night. **Surface:** unpaved.

FR

Distance: on the spot 800m 800m 300m 300m.

Trébeurden 14C1

Impasse du Vieux Puits. **GPS:** n48,76999 w3,56849.
parking free, € 7/night. **Surface:** asphalted.
Distance: on the spot 1,5km on the spot on the spot.

Trébeurden 14C1

Route de Pors Mabo. **GPS:** n48,76194 w3,56537.
parking free, € 7/night. **Surface:** metalled.
Distance: 1,5km 200m 200m.

Trébeurden 14C1

Rue Pierre Marzin. **GPS:** n48,76842 w3.
parking free, € 7/night.
Surface: metalled. 01/01-31/12.
Distance: on the spot 1km 300m 600m.

Trégastel 14C1

Rue de Poul-Palud. **GPS:** n48,82437 w3,49874.

56 € 8 Ch included. **Location:** Rural, comfortable, isolated, quiet. **Surface:** asphalted. 01/01-31/12.
Distance: 1km 1km Super U on the spot.
Remarks: Aug max. 3 nights, max. 5 nights.

Tréguier 14D1

Bois du Poète, Boulevard Anatole le Braz. **GPS:** n48,78932 w3,23144.

20 free Ch free. **Surface:** asphalted. 01/01-31/12.
Distance: 100m 20m 20m 100m 100m.

Tréguier 14D1

Super U, Boulevard Jean Guehenno. **GPS:** n48,77892 w3,23346.
€1/10minutes Ch €1/55minutes. 01/01-31/12.
Distance: 200m on the spot.

Trégunc 14C2

Parking Quentel, Place de la Mairie, Rue de Pont-Aven.
GPS: n47,85472 w3,85139.

6 free €3 Ch €3.
Surface: metalled. 01/01-31/12.
Remarks: Behind town hall, max. 24h.

Trégunc 14C2

Parking de Pouldohan, Route de Pouldohan.
GPS: n47,84435 w3,88832.

5 free. **Location:** Rural, simple, isolated. **Surface:** grassy.
01/01-31/12.
Distance: 400m 400m.

Trégunc 14C2

Plage Ster Greich. GPS: n47,84918 w3,88656.
6 free. **Surface:** sand. 01/01-31/12.
Distance: on the spot.
Remarks: Max. 24h.

Trégunc 14C2

Route de Kerlaëron. **GPS:** n47,82964 w3,8872.

6 free.
Location: Rural, simple. **Surface:** grassy. 01/01-31/12.
Distance: 200m.
Remarks: Max. 24h.

Trégunc 14C2

Rue de Porzh Breign. **GPS:** n47,84079 w3,89736.

5 free. **Location:** Rural, simple, quiet. **Surface:** grassy.
01/01-31/12.
Distance: 200m.
Remarks: Max. 24h.

Trégunc 14C2

Supermarché Casino, Route de Concarneau, D783.
GPS: n47,85633 w3,86343.

4 free €2 Ch €2/55minutes.
Location: Simple. **Surface:** asphalted.
Distance: on the spot.

Tremblay 15B3

Route de Fougères. **GPS:** n48,42328 w1,47095.

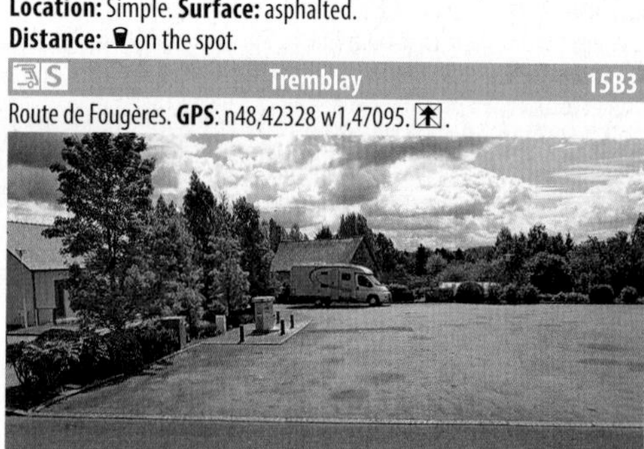

15 free €2/10minutes Ch €2/55minutes.
Location: Urban, simple. **Surface:** asphalted. 01/01-31/12.
Distance: 400m 200m on the spot.

Trémuson 14D1

Aire du Buchon, Rue de Brest, D712. **GPS:** n48,52250 w2,85278.

5 free Ch free. **Location:** Urban, simple. **Surface:** asphalted.
01/01-31/12.
Distance: 500m 50m 200m.
Remarks: Max. 48h.

Val-d'Izé 18B1

Rue du Château. **GPS:** n48,17904 w1,30133.

3 free Ch WC free. **Location:** Urban, simple, quiet.
Surface: asphalted. 01/01-31/12.
Distance: 100m on the spot 100m 100m on the spot.
Remarks: Next to sports fields.

Vannes 14D3

Camping-car Parc, Avenue du Maréchal Juin.
GPS: n47,63283 w2,77996.

34 € 9,60, Jul/Aug € 12 Ch €4 WC included.
Location: Urban, comfortable, quiet. **Surface:** asphalted.
01/01-31/12.
Distance: Vannes 4km 200m 200m 1km on the spot on the spot on the spot.
Remarks: Note: access only after buying entrance (3 formulas) via www.campingcarpark.com (wifi available), free shuttle (summer).

Tourist information Vannes:

Office de Tourisme, 1, rue Thiers, www.tourisme-vannes.com. The old district is surrounded by ramparts with gates and parks with historical wash places.

Cathédrale St Pierre.

Pays de la Loire

Angers 18C2

Boulevard Olivier-Couffon. **GPS:** n47,46616 w0,56549.

30 € 14/24h Ch free.
Location: Urban, noisy. **Surface:** asphalted. 01/01-31/12.
Distance: centre 950m 3km.
Remarks: Max. 72h, monitored parking, Château d'Angers 600m.

Tourist information Angers:

Haras National du Lion d'Angers. National stud-farm. 10-18h. free.

Château d' Angers. Fortified castle, museum for contemporary art. 10-17.30h. € 8,50.

Angrie 18C2

Route du Vieux Bourg. **GPS**: n47,57176 w0,97312.

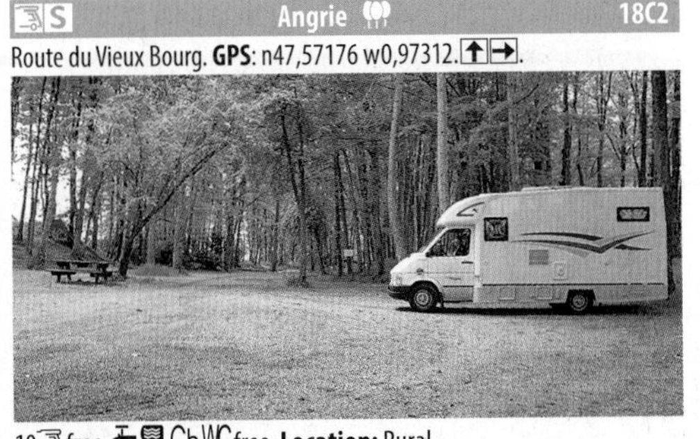

10 free Ch WC free. **Location:** Rural. **Surface:** gravel/metalled. 01/01-31/12 1st weekend Aug.
Distance: 400m on the spot.
Remarks: Max. 48h.

Arnage 18D1

Rue du Port. **GPS**: n47,93035 e0,18418.

2 free €2 Ch €2/15minutes. **Location:** Urban, simple, quiet. **Surface:** asphalted. 01/01-31/12.
Distance: 250m on the spot 500m on the spot.

Asnières-sur-Vègre 18D2

D190. **GPS**: n47,88950 w0,23716.
WC. **Surface:** gravel.
Distance: 200m.

Assérac 14D3

Pen-Bé. **GPS**: n47,42556 w2,45528.

5 free WC.
Location: Simple. **Surface:** grassy. 01/01-31/12.
Distance: 50m 100m 100m 200m 200m.

Assérac 14D3

Chemin de la Marché aux Bœufs. **GPS**: n47,43111 w2,45194.

free WC. **Surface:** metalled.
Distance: 1km 300m 300m 2km 2km.

Aubigné-sur-Layon 18C3

Rue de 17 mars 1962. **GPS**: n47,21167 w0,46383.

5 free Ch free. **Location:** Simple, quiet. **Surface:** metalled. 01/01-31/12.
Distance: 100m on the spot on the spot.

Auvers-le-Hamon 18D1

Chemin du tour. **GPS**: n47,90115 w0,34654.
Distance: 500m on the spot 500m.
Remarks: At small lake.

Averton 18D1

Étang des Perles. **GPS**: n48,34744 w0,24468.

10 free €2,50 Ch €2,50 WC. **Location:** Rural. **Surface:** gravel. 01/01-31/12.
Distance: lake on the spot on the spot on the spot.

Batz-sur-Mer 14D3

Route de la Govelle. **GPS**: n47,26747 w2,4537.

7 € 8 €2 Ch €2 WC. **Location:** Simple. **Surface:** metalled. 01/01-31/12.
Distance: 1,5km 100m 100m 1,5km 50m.
Remarks: Max. 48h, coins at tourist info and town hall, no camping activities.

Baugé-en-Anjou 18D2

Parking du plan d'eau, Rue de la Croix de Mission, Le Vieil Baugé. **GPS**: n47,53066 w0,11899.

15 free Ch free.
Location: Rural. **Surface:** gravel. 01/01-31/12.
Distance: on the spot bakery 100m.
Remarks: Service 50m.

Baugé-en-Anjou 18D2

Rue du Pont des Fées. **GPS**: n47,53886 w0,09637.

10 free €3/15minutes Ch €3/15minutes.
Location: Rural. **Surface:** gravel. 01/01-31/12.
Distance: 2km 400m.

Baugé-en-Anjou 18D2

Super U, Avenue d'Angers. **GPS**: n47,53886 w0,09637.
15 free Ch. 01/01-31/12.
Distance: 300m on the spot.

Bazouges-sur-le-Loir 18D2

Voie de la Liberté. **GPS**: n47,68994 w0,16952.

free.
Location: Rural, quiet. **Surface:** gravel. 01/01-31/12.
Distance: 200m 200m.

Beauvoir-sur-Mer 18A3

Place des Paludier, Rue de Nantes. **GPS**: n46,91685 w2,0465.

24 free, night € 5 €2,50/3minutes Ch €2,50/15minutes WC. **Location:** Urban, simple. **Surface:** asphalted. 01/01-31/12.
Distance: 400m 800m 800m.
Remarks: Max. 48h.

Belleville-sur-Vie 21B1

Rue des Écoliers. **GPS**: n46,78160 w1,42875.

15 free. **Surface:** grassy/gravel. 01/01-31/12.
Distance: 500m 500m 200m.
Remarks: Near Salle des Fêtes.

Benet 21C2

Rue de la Gare. **GPS**: n46,36896 w0,59482.

10 free Ch WC free. **Location:** Rural, simple. **Surface:** asphalted.
Distance: 300m 300m on the spot 50m.

Blain 18A2

Place Jollan de Clerville, Rue Victor Schoelcher. **GPS**: n47,47444 w1,76139.

30 free Ch free. **Surface:** gravel. 01/01-31/12.
Distance: 100m 100m.

Blaison-Gohier 18C3

Aire de Bajun, Rue Thibaut de Blaison. **GPS**: n47,39897 w0,37513.

FR

4 free Ch WC free. **Location:** Urban, simple, quiet.
Surface: asphalted. 01/01-31/12.
Distance: 400m on the spot 300m 1,5km on the spot on the spot.
Remarks: Automatic bread distributor.

S Blaison-Gohier 18C3

Rue de Thibaut de Blaison. **GPS**: n47,39923 w0,37515.

5 free Ch free. **Surface:** asphalted. 01/01-31/12.
Distance: on the spot 200m 200m.

S Bouchemaine 18C2

25 rue Chevrière. **GPS**: n47,41913 w0,61117.

45 € 13,50 €0,50/50liter Ch WC €1 included.
Surface: grassy/gravel. 01/01-31/12 service: 01/12-28/02.
Distance: 50m.
Remarks: Along the river Maine, former campsite, baker every morning (Jul/Aug).

S Bouère 18C2

Rue des Sencies. **GPS**: n47,86320 w0,47661.

16 free €2/80liter Ch €2.
Location: Quiet. **Surface:** grassy. 01/01-31/12.
Distance: on the spot 50m bakery 100m.

S Bouin 18A3

Port du Bec, Rue du Port du Bec. **GPS**: n46,93871 w2,07318.

33 free €2,50/10minutes Ch €2,50/4h.
Surface: gravel. 01/01-31/12.
Distance: on the spot on the spot.

Bouin 18A3

GPS: n47,00918 w2,02782.

10 free. **Location:** Rural, simple. **Surface:** grassy/gravel.
01/01-31/12.
Distance: on the spot.

Bouin 18A3

GPS: n46,99821 w2,03314.

10 free.
Location: Simple. **Surface:** metalled. 01/01-31/12.
Distance: on the spot on the spot.

S Bourgneuf-en-Retz 18A3

D758. **GPS**: n47,04028 w1,95704.

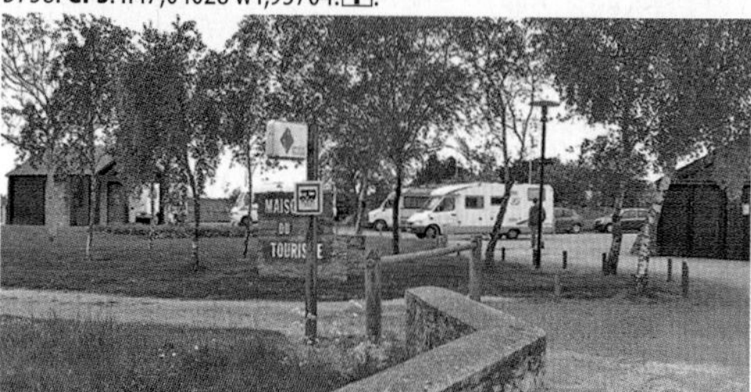

12 free Ch WC free. **Location:** Simple. **Surface:** asphalted.
01/01-31/12 Service: winter.
Distance: 300m 200m 300m 300m.
Remarks: Parking tourist info, max. 48h.

S Boussay 18B3

Place des Marronniers. **GPS**: n47,04240 w1,18648.

4 free €2/100liter Ch €2/60minutes.
Location: Simple. **Surface:** asphalted. 01/01-31/12.
Distance: 200m 200m 200m on the spot.
Remarks: Max. 48h, coins at town hall, poste.

Brétignolles-sur-Mer 21A1

Parking de la Normandelière, Rue de la Source.
GPS: n46,61664 w1,85974.

25 free.
Location: Simple. **Surface:** metalled. 01/01-31/12.
Distance: 1,5km sandy beach 500m 1,5km on the spot on the spot.
Remarks: Service: Super U D38, GPS 46,62537 -1,85787.

Tourist information Brétignolles-sur-Mer:

Thu, Su.

S Briollay 18C2

Plage de Briollay. **GPS**: n47,56766 w0,50733.
10 free €2 Ch. **Surface:** grassy/gravel. 01/01-31/12.
Remarks: Along Sarthe River, closed when frosty and high water.

S Brissac-Quincé 18C3

Aire Communale, Rue de l'Aubance. **GPS**: n47,35465 w0,4463.

10 € 4 Ch included. **Location:** Urban, simple, quiet.
Surface: asphalted. 01/01-31/12.
Distance: 300m 300m 300m on the spot on the spot.
Remarks: Max. 2 days.

S Brissac-Quincé 18C3

Domaine de la Belle Etoile, La Belle Étoile.
GPS: n47,33404 w0,43597.

8 € 12 Ch WC €3 included. **Location:** Rural, comfortable, quiet. **Surface:** grassy. 31/10-01/04.

S Brissac-Quincé 18C3

Domaine de L'Etang, Route de Saint-Mathurin.
GPS: n47,36103 w0,43529.

6 € 12-15 Ch WC €5 included.
Location: Rural, comfortable, quiet. **Surface:** grassy.
01/01-31/12.
Distance: 1,5km 500m 2km on the spot on the spot.
Remarks: To be paid at campsite.

S Chailland 18C1

Coccimarket. **GPS**: n48,22139 w0,86583.

4 free Ch free. **Location:** Rural, simple. **Surface:** asphalted.
01/01-31/12.
Distance: 300m 300m on the spot.
Remarks: Max. 24h.

S Chaille-les-Marais 21B2

Rue du 8 Mai 1945. **GPS**: n46,39228 w1,02127.

FR

20 free €3 WC free. **Location:** Simple, quiet. **Surface:** grassy.
01/01-31/12 Thu-morning.
Distance: 100m 100m 300m 50m.
Remarks: At fire-station and sports park.

S Challans 18A3

Parking du Viaud Marais. GPS: n46,85027 w1,8742.

15 free Ch free. **Location:** Urban. **Surface:** asphalted.
01/01-31/12.
Distance: 1km 500m 500m 100m.
Remarks: Max. 3 days.

S Chalonnes-sur-Loire 18C3

Le Champ du Bois, D751. **GPS:** n47,35105 w0,74466.

20 €9 €2 Ch included. **Location:** Rural, comfortable.
Surface: grassy. 01/01-31/12.
Distance: 1km on the spot 1km on the spot.
Remarks: Nearby camp site.

S Chambretaud 18C3

Aire des Diamants, Rue Notre Dame. **GPS:** n46,92300 w0,9717.

5 free €2/150liter Ch WC. **Location:** Rural, simple.
Surface: asphalted. 01/01-31/12.
Distance: 1km 5km on the spot 1km.

S Champ-Sur-Layon 18C3

Rue du Soleil Levant. **GPS:** n47,26369 w0,57289.

2 free Ch (1x) WC free. **Location:** Rural, simple, quiet.
Surface: asphalted/metalled. 01/01-31/12.
Distance: 150m 6km 6km on the spot on the spot.

S Champtocé-sur-Loire 18C2

Rue de la Hutte. **GPS:** n47,41143 w0,86958.

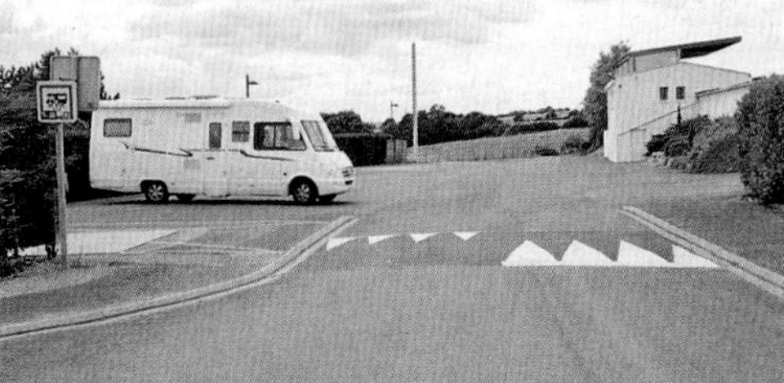

8 free Ch free. **Location:** Rural, simple. **Surface:** asphalted.
01/01-31/12.
Distance: 300m 5,7km 400m 400m.
Remarks: At stadium.

S Champtoceaux 18B3

Parking Champalud, Place de Niederheimbach.
GPS: n47,33816 w1,2649.

8 €4 Ch h WC included. **Location:** Urban, simple, quiet. **Surface:** asphalted. 01/01-31/12.
Distance: 150m 100m 150m on the spot on the spot on the spot.
Remarks: Square behind the church, max. 48h, payment and wifi code at tourist office.

S Champtoceaux 18B3

Le Port du Moulin, Le Cul du Moulin, D751.
GPS: n47,33913 w1,27445.

5 free WC free. **Location:** Rural, simple, quiet.
Surface: gravel/metalled. 01/01-31/12.
Distance: 1,5km on the spot on the spot on the spot 1,5km.
Remarks: Along Loire river, max. 48h.

S Changé 18C1

Parking du plan d'eau du Port, Rue du Bac.
GPS: n48,10047 w0,78584.

10 free Ch free. **Location:** Urban, simple.
Surface: gravel/sand. 01/01-31/12.
Distance: 5km 800m.
Remarks: Along the Mayenne river.

S Chantenay-Villedieu 18D1

Plan d'eau. GPS: n47,91668 w0,16849.
free Ch WC free. 01/04-31/10.

S Chantonnay 21B1

Rue de l'Arc en Ciel. **GPS:** n46,68754 w1,04104.

5 free €2/100liter Ch €2/60minutes. **Location:** Rural, simple, noisy. **Surface:** asphalted. 01/01-31/12.
Distance: 1km 500m 1km.
Remarks: Next to sports fields, coins at tourist info.

S Chanzeaux 18C3

Aire de Ploizeau, Rue de Bel Air a Chanzeaux D121.
GPS: n47,25548 w0,63848.

6 free €2/100liter Ch WC. **Location:** Rural, simple, quiet.
Surface: metalled. 01/01-31/12.
Distance: 1km on the spot 1km 1km on the spot on the spot.

S Charcé-Saint-Ellier-sur-Aubance 18C3

Rue Saint Ellier. **GPS:** n47,35647 w0,41146.

free Ch WC free. **Location:** Urban, simple, quiet.
Surface: metalled/sand. 01/01-31/12.
Distance: 100m 3km 3km.

Charcé-Saint-Ellier-sur-Aubance 18C3

Rue Saint Ellier. **GPS:** n47,35647 w0,41146.
free Ch free. **Location:** Urban, simple, quiet.
Surface: metalled/sand. 01/01-31/12.
Distance: 100m 3km 3km.

Château-d'Olonne 21A1

Les Plesses, Rue des Plesses. **GPS:** n46,49132 w1,74293.

20 € 7,30/night, € 12,30/2 nights €2,07/6minutes Ch.
Location: Simple. **Surface:** asphalted. 01/01-31/12.
Distance: 2km 500m.

Château-Gontier 18C2

Quai-du-Docteur Lefevre. **GPS:** n47,82450 w0,70206.

30 free. **Location:** Urban, simple, central. **Surface:** asphalted.

FR

01/01-31/12.
Distance: 200m on the spot 50m.
Remarks: Along the Mayenne river.

Châteauneuf-sur-Sarthe 18C2

L'aire de repos, Rue de la Gare. **GPS**: n47,67774 w0,4866.
€ 5,16 Ch. 01/01-31/12 service: 01/10-01/05.
Distance: 400m 400m 500m.
Remarks: Along Sarthe River.

Chavagne-en-Paillers 18B3

Place des Arcades. **GPS**: n46,89083 w1,24917.

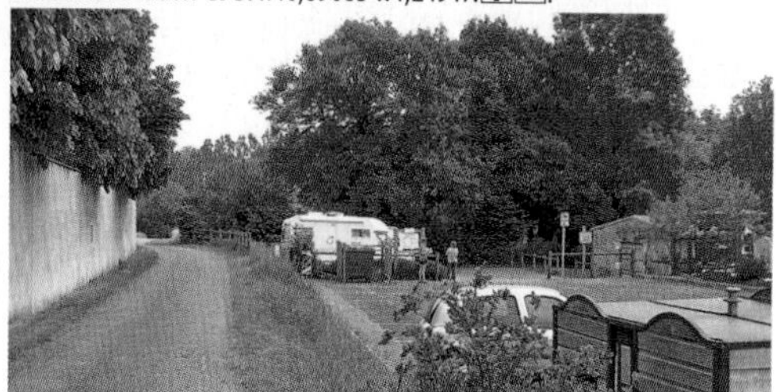

3 free €2/10minutes Ch €2/55minutes.
Location: Simple, central, quiet.
Surface: asphalted.
01/01-31/12.
Distance: 300m 50m 100m 300m.
Remarks: Coins at tourist office/Rest. Le petit Marmiton/Boulanger de Quartier, 8 rue G de Gaulle/ Carrefour Express, 197 rue G de Gaulle.

Chavagnes les Eaux 18C3

Rue de l'Église. **GPS**: n47,27024 w0,45437.

4 free Chfree. **Location:** Simple, quiet. **Surface:** metalled.
01/01-31/12.
Distance: on the spot 150m.
Remarks: Behind church.

Chemillé-Melay 18C3

La ferme Cabri d'Anjou, La Chaperonnière.
GPS: n47,22275 w0,7524.

2 free. **Location:** Rural, simple, simple, isolated, quiet.
Surface: grassy. 01/01-31/12.
Distance: 2km 3km 3km on the spot on the spot.
Remarks: Cheese farm.

Chênehutte-Trèves-Cunault 18D3

Rue Beauregard, D751, Cunault. **GPS**: n47,32685 w0,19459.

40 free €3/100liter Ch €3/6h . **Location:** Rural, simple, quiet. **Surface:** grassy. 01/01-31/12.
Distance: 500m 500m 500m on the spot on the spot.
Remarks: Max. 72h.

Chenillé-Changé 18C2

Le Pin, D78. **GPS**: n47,69919 w0,66693.

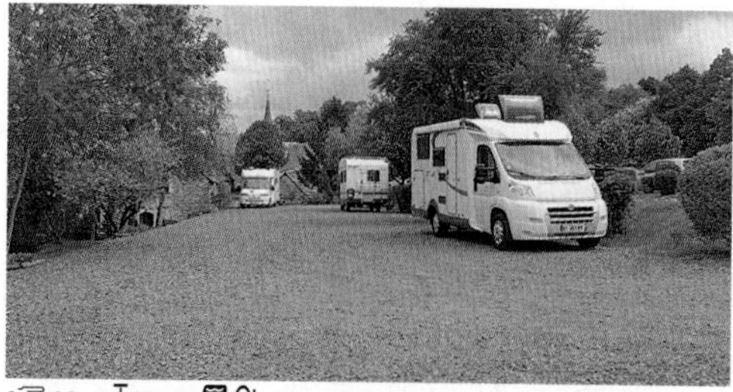

8 € 3-4 €2,80 Ch. **Location:** Simple. **Surface:** gravel.
01/01-31/12.
Distance: on the spot 100m.
Remarks: Along the Mayenne river, coins at cafe.

Clefs-Val d'Anjou 18D2

D938. **GPS**: n47,62442 w0,07698.
10 free. **Surface:** metalled. 01/01-31/12.
Distance: 500m 500m 500m.

Coëx 21A1

Rue des Goélettes. **GPS**: n46,69668 w1,76397.

4 free €2/10minutes Ch €2/55minutes.
Location: Rural. **Surface:** asphalted. 01/01-31/12.
Distance: 200m 500m 500m.
Remarks: Max. 48h, coins at town hall.

Combrée 18C2

Rue de Britanny, Bel-Air. **GPS**: n47,71281 w0,9989.

3 free ChWCfree. **Location:** Rural. **Surface:** unpaved.
01/01-31/12.
Distance: 100m.

Combrée 18C2

Aire du Plan d'Eau, D203. **GPS**: n47,70321 w1,02755.

3 free.
Location: Rural, quiet. **Surface:** asphalted. 01/01-31/12.
Distance: 200m on the spot on the spot 50m.
Remarks: Behind tennis-court.

Concourson-sur-Layon 18C3

Place du Prieuré. **GPS**: n47,17372 w0,34199.

10 free €3/100liter ChWC. **Location:** Urban, simple, quiet.
Surface: asphalted. 01/01-31/12.
Distance: 400m 400m 400m on the spot on the spot on the spot.
Remarks: Coins at the bakery and auberge du Haut Layon, service 200m.

Dampierre-sur-Loire 18D3

L'aire d'accueil de Dampierre-sur-Loire, Route de Montsoreau.
GPS: n47,24157 w0,0232.

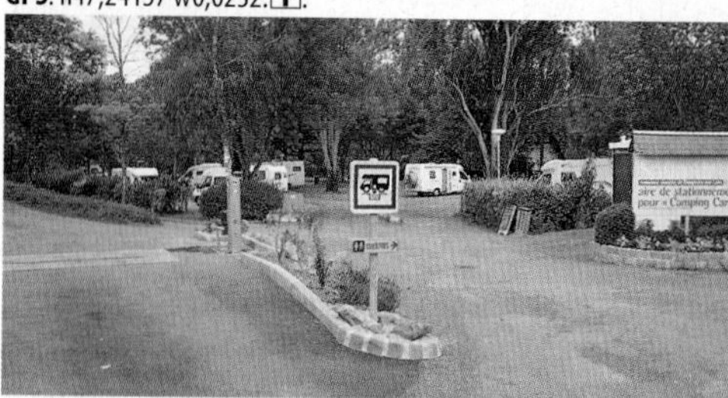

80 € 6 + € 0,50/pp tourist tax Chincluded WCfree.
Location: Urban, simple, central, quiet. **Surface:** forest soil.
01/04-31/10.
Distance: on the spot 100m on the spot 4,5km on the spot on the spot.
Remarks: On the river Loire, behind town hall.

Deux-Evailles 18C1

Site de la Fenderie, Champ de Vigne, D129.
GPS: n48,20203 w0,52018.

20 free €2 Ch €2 WC. **Location:** Rural, comfortable, quiet.
Surface: grassy/gravel. 01/01-31/12.
Distance: 1km 20m 20m 20m 5km Montsurs on the spot.
Remarks: Coins at Auberge.

Doué-la-Fontaine 18D3

Domaine des Sablonniéres, Rue Jean Gaschet.
GPS: n47,18280 w0,25742.

3 free Chfree. **Location:** Urban, simple, quiet.
Surface: gravel/metalled.
Distance: 500m 300m 500m on the spot on the spot.

Doué-la-Fontaine 18D3

Roseraie les Chemins, Route de Cholet. **GPS**: n47,18554 w0,31436.

8 free. **Location:** Rural, simple, quiet. **Surface:** gravel.
01/01-31/12.
Distance: 2km 2km 3km on the spot on the spot.
Remarks: Rose grower.

Durtal 18D2

Rue du Petit Port. **GPS**: n47,66842 w0,24172.

5 free. **Location:** Rural, quiet. **Surface:** asphalted.
Distance: 300m 2,4km.

Durtal 18D2

Rue Beausite. **GPS:** n47,67139 w0,2406.

2 free €2/10minutes Ch €2/60minutes.
Location: Simple. **Surface:** asphalted. 01/01-31/12.
Distance: 300m 2,4km.
Remarks: Inclining pitches.

Ernée 18C1

Plan d'eau d'Ernée, Plan d'eau d'Ernée. **GPS:** n48,29670 w0,93997.

2 free WC free. **Location:** Urban, simple, quiet.
Surface: asphalted. 01/01-31/12.
Distance: 500m on the spot 500m 500m.
Remarks: Parking at small lake.

Faye d'Anjou 18C3

Chateau du Fresne, D55, Rue des Monts.
GPS: n47,29923 w0,53806.

10 free ChWC free. **Location:** Rural, simple, quiet.
Surface: gravel. 01/01-31/12.
Distance: 2km 3km.

Feneu 18C2

Port Albert. **GPS:** n47,56560 w0,60994.

6 free €2 Ch. **Location:** Rural, quiet. **Surface:** gravel.
01/01-31/12.
Distance: 1,5km.
Remarks: Along the Mayenne river.

Fontaines 21C2

Place du Champ de Foire. **GPS:** n46,42291 w0,81952.

20 free ChWC free.
Location: Rural, simple. **Surface:** gravel.
Distance: 2km.

Fontenay-le-Comte 21C1

Avenue du Général de Gaulle. **GPS:** n46,46203 w0,80544.

10 € 5 €2/4minutes Ch included. **Location:** Simple, isolated, noisy. **Surface:** asphalted. 01/01-31/12.
Distance: 500m 500m 500m.
Remarks: In front of police station, max. 24h, centre.

Fontevraud l'Abbaye 18D3

Allée des Jardins. **GPS:** n47,18444 e0,04917.

8 free ChWC free. **Location:** Urban, simple, central.
Surface: asphalted. 01/01-31/12.
Distance: 400m 400m 400m 300m.

Foussais-Payré 21C1

Place du Prieuré. **GPS:** n46,53000 w0,68275.

20 free Ch free. **Location:** Rural, simple. **Surface:** gravel.
01/01-31/12.
Distance: 500m 500m 200m.

Freigné 18B2

Aire du Plan d'Eau, D185. **GPS:** n47,55071 w1,12686.
free. **Surface:** grassy. 01/01-31/12.
Distance: on the spot 400m 400m.

Fresnay-sur-Sarthe 18D1

Rue de la Gare. **GPS:** n48,28171 e0,02978.

8 free Ch free. **Location:** Simple. **Surface:** gravel.
01/01-31/12.
Distance: 600m 600m 50m.

Gené 18C2

Escale du Haut Anjou, La Petite Fenouillère.
GPS: n47,63770 w0,79641.

7 € 14 Ch included. **Location:** Rural, simple.
Surface: gravel. 01/01-31/12.
Distance: 1,2km fish pond.
Remarks: Cheese farm.

Gorron 15C3

Route de Brecé, Rue du Maine. **GPS:** n48,40735 w0,80993.
6 free Ch free. **Surface:** gravel. 01/01-31/12.
Remarks: Max. 2 nights.

Grez-en-Bouère 18C2

Place A. Peigné. **GPS:** n47,87306 w0,52306.

6 free Ch free WC. **Location:** Rural, simple.
Surface: asphalted. 01/01-31/12, service: 01/04-30/11.
Distance: 50m 50m 100m.
Remarks: Max. 48h.

Grez-Neuville 18C2

Rue du Port, D291. **GPS:** n47,60119 w0,68504.

8 free Ch free. **Location:** Rural, simple. **Surface:** grassy.
01/01-31/12.
Remarks: Former campsite.

Guenrouet 18A2

Rue des Hauts du Port. **GPS:** n47,52198 w1,94978.

2 free €2 Ch €2. **Surface:** asphalted. 01/04-31/10.
Distance: 200m 50m 200m 200m.
Remarks: Along canal of Nantes/Brest, next to campsite Saint Clair, max. 24h.

Guérande 14D3

Avenue de la Brière, D99E. **GPS:** n47,33389 w2,42083.

FR

20 free €5/100liter Ch €5/1h. **Location:** Simple, noisy. **Surface:** asphalted/grassy. 01/01-31/12.
Distance: 1km.

Jans 18B2

Place de l'Église. **GPS:** n47,62222 w1,61222.

6 free Ch WC free. **Surface:** gravel. 01/01-31/12.
Remarks: Behind town hall.

Jard-sur-Mer 21A1

Route des Goffineaux. **GPS:** n46,41074 w1,59358.

16 € 6,10/24h, € 10,20/48h €2/10minutes Ch.
Location: Rural, simple. **Surface:** asphalted. 01/01-31/12.
Distance: 1km 50m 1,5km 1,5km.

Juigne-sur-Loire 18C3

Domaine des 2 moulins, Route de Martigneau.
GPS: n47,40374 w0,47702.

5 € 5 Ch WC included.
Location: Rural, comfortable, quiet. **Surface:** gravel. 01/01-31/12.
Distance: 1km 4km 2km 1km 500m on the spot on the spot.
Remarks: When buying wine 1 night free.

Juvigné 18C1

Plan d'Eau de Saint Martin, Rue de la Croixille, D29.
GPS: n48,22806 w1,03806.

20 free Ch WC free. **Location:** Urban, simple. **Surface:** gravel. 01/01-31/12.
Distance: 200m 20m 200m 100m on the spot.
Remarks: Max. 72h.

La Baconnière 18C1

Place de l'Eglise. **GPS:** n48,18361 w0,89139.

5 free Ch free.
Location: Urban, simple. **Surface:** asphalted.
01/01-31/12.
Distance: on the spot 100m.
Remarks: Behind church, service (winter) on demand (town hall).

La Barre-de-Monts 18A3

La Grande Côte. **GPS:** n46,88528 w2,15196.
39 € 8,40-10,60 Ch included.
Surface: metalled/sand. 01/01/-31/12.
Distance: 800m 200m 800m.

La Baule 14D3

Boulevard Guy de Champsavin, La Baule-Escoublac.
GPS: n47,28196 w2,42509.

20 free €3 Ch (20x)€3/55minutes.
Location: Comfortable, quiet. **Surface:** metalled.
Distance: beach 700m.

La Bernerie-en-Retz 18A3

Parking Wilson, Avenue de Jean d Arc. **GPS:** n47,07871 w2,03399.

30 € 7, 15/06-15/09 € 8 €3,50/100liter Ch €3,50/55minutes WC. **Surface:** asphalted. 01/01-31/12.
Distance: 300m 100m 300m 300m on the spot.
Remarks: Max. 48h, coins at tourist info.

La Chapelle-Saint-Florent 18B3

Aire du Stade, Rue de l'Evre. **GPS:** n47,33411 w1,05178.

6 free Ch free. **Location:** Rural, simple, quiet.
Surface: gravel/metalled. 01/01-31/12.
Distance: 300m 300m 50m.

La Daguenière 18C2

Chemin de Beausse, Rue de Stade. **GPS:** n47,42222 w0,43936.

12 free Ch free. **Location:** Rural. **Surface:** asphalted.
01/01-31/12.
Distance: 200m 300m 300m.
Remarks: Next to sports fields.

La Daguenière 18C2

Port Maillard. **GPS:** n47,41743 w0,43781.

6 free WC.
Location: Rural. **Surface:** unpaved. 01/01-31/12.
Remarks: Along Loire river.

La Faute-sur-Mer 21B2

Camping-Car Park, Rond Point Fleuri. **GPS:** n46,33297 w1,32231.

31 € 8,41, tourist tax incl Ch included.
Surface: asphalted. 01/01-31/12.
Distance: on the spot 850m 100m.
Remarks: At tourist office.

La Flèche 18D2

Promenade du Maréchal Foch. **GPS:** n47,69767 w0,07875.

10 free Ch free. **Location:** Urban. **Surface:** asphalted.
01/01-31/12 tue-evening (market).
Distance: 100m 100m 100m.

La Fresnaye-sur-Chédouet 15E3

La forêt de Perseigne, Les Ventes du Four, D236.
GPS: n48,43469 e0,25972.

20 free Ch free. **Location:** Rural, quiet. **Surface:** gravel.
01/01-31/12.
Distance: La Fresnaye 1,5km on the spot.

La Meilleraie-Tillay 21C1

Rue des Ombrages. **GPS:** n46,73923 w0,84578.

6 free €2/5minutes Ch WC €1. **Location:** Simple, isolated,

quiet. **Surface:** asphalted. 01/04-31/10.
Distance: 700m 700m 700m.

La Plaine-sur-Mer 18A3

Boulevard des Nations Unies. **GPS:** n47,13994 w2,19057.

8 free Chfree. **Location:** Simple, isolated.
Surface: asphalted. 01/01-31/12.
Distance: 300m 800m 500m.
Remarks: Max. 24h.

La Poitevinière 18C3

Aire de la Fontaine, Place de la Fontaine, D15.
GPS: n47,22750 w0,897.

5 free Ch WCfree. **Location:** Urban, comfortable, quiet.
Surface: asphalted. 01/01-31/12.
Distance: 50m on the spot 50m on the spot on the spot.
Remarks: Coins available at bar.

La Roche-sur-Yon 21B1

Boulevard Italie. **GPS:** n46,66833 w1,41861.

20 free Chfree.
Location: Urban. **Surface:** metalled. 01/01-31/12.
Distance: 500m 500m 500m.
Remarks: Max. 36h.

La Séguinière 18C3

Avenue de Nantes. **GPS:** n47,06005 w0,93668.

10 free €2/100liter Ch €2/1h WC.
Location: Simple. **Surface:** asphalted.
Distance: 100m on the spot 50m.

La Selle-Craonnaise 18C1

La Rincerie. **GPS:** n47,86330 w1,06843.
free Ch.
Distance: on the spot on the spot on the spot.
Remarks: At lake.

La Suze-sur-Sarthe 18D2

Rue du Camping. **GPS:** n47,88917 e0,03040.

10 €5 Ch free WC. **Location:** Urban, simple.
Surface: grassy/gravel. 01/01-31/12.
Distance: 300m 300m on the spot on the spot.
Remarks: Along Sarthe River, in harbour.

La Tranche-sur-Mer 21B2

Boulevard de la Petite Hollande. **GPS:** n46,34965 w1,44769.

20 free, 14/06-14/09 € 10 €3,50/10minutes Ch .
Location: Simple, quiet. 01/01-31/12.
Remarks: Max. 7 days.

La Tranche-sur-Mer 21B2

Parking de la Baleine, Place des Baleines.
GPS: n46,34340 w1,46222.

10 free, 14/06-14/09 € 10 .
Location: Rural, quiet. **Surface:** gravel. 01/01-31/12.
Distance: 200m on the spot on the spot.
Remarks: Max. 7 days.

La Tranche-sur-Mer 21B2

Parking du Stade, Avenue du Général de Gaulle.
GPS: n46,35028 w1,43688.

30 free, 14/06-14/09 € 10 €3,50 Chfree.
Location: Rural. **Surface:** asphalted.
Distance: 1km.
Remarks: Max. 7 days.

La Turballe 14D3

GPS: n47,35150 w2,50558.
24 € 9 Ch included. **Surface:** metalled.
01/01/-31/12.
Distance: 800m 800m 600m 400m on the spot.

La Turballe 14D3

Boulevard de la Grande Falaise. **GPS:** n47,33106 w2,49919.

23 € 7,40/24h, tourist tax incl Chincluded.
Location: Comfortable. **Surface:** gravel. 01/01-31/12.
Distance: 2km 300m.
Remarks: Max. 72h.

La Turballe 14D3

Rue Alphonse Daudet. **GPS:** n47,34870 w2,50804.

15 free, June-Sep € 3 Chfree.
Location: Simple, quiet. **Surface:** gravel. 01/01-31/12.
Distance: 800m 500m 100m 100m.
Remarks: Max. 5 days.

Lassay-les-Châteaux 15C3

Allée du Haut Perrin. **GPS:** n48,43777 w0,49822.

free €2 Ch. **Location:** Urban, simple, central.
Surface: asphalted. 01/01-31/12.
Distance: 100m.
Remarks: Coins at Tourist Info and bakery.

Laval 18C1

Parking de la Halte Fluviale, Rue du Vieux Saint-Louis.
GPS: n48,07589 w0,77142.

10 free Chfree.
Location: Urban, simple. **Surface:** asphalted. 01/01-31/12.
Distance: 300m on the spot on the spot on the spot.
Remarks: Parking nearby viaduct.

Tourist information Laval:
Vieux Château. Medieval castle, museum with collection of naive art. 9.30-12h and 13.30-18.30h.

Le Coudray Macouard 18D3

Route de Bron. **GPS:** n47,18806 w0,11722.

5 free Chfree. **Location:** Rural, simple, isolated, quiet.

FR

Surface: grassy/sand. 01/01-31/12.
Distance: 800m 800m.
Remarks: Near sports fields.

S Le Croisic 14D3

Le Lin Gorzé, Rue du Lin Gorzé. **GPS**: n47,29917 w2,52194.

9 € 6,30, € 0,75/pp tourist tax €2 Ch.
Location: Simple, quiet. **Surface:** asphalted. 01/01-31/12.
Distance: 500m 500m 500m 800m.
Remarks: Max. 48h, no camping activities.

S Le Croisic 14D3

Les Courlis, Rue des Courlis. **GPS**: n47,29000 w2,505.

15 € 6,30, € 0,75/pp tourist tax €2 Ch.
Location: Simple. **Surface:** gravel. 01/04-31/10.
Distance: 500m 500m 500m 500m.
Remarks: Max. 48h, no camping activities.

Le Croisic 14D3

La Vigie, Avenue de Pierre Longue, D45. **GPS**: n47,28917 w2,53667.

9 € 6,30, € 0,75/pp tourist tax.
Location: Simple. **Surface:** asphalted. 01/01-31/12.
Distance: 3km 50m 3km 3km.
Remarks: Max. 48h, no camping activities.

Le Croisic 14D3

P1 Kerdavid, Rue Kerclavid 1. **GPS**: n47,29835 w2,51995.

8 € 6,30, € 0,75/pp tourist tax. **Location:** Urban, simple, quiet. **Surface:** asphalted. 01/01-31/12.
Distance: 500m 500m 500m 800m.
Remarks: Max. 48h, no camping activities.

Tourist information Le Croisic:

Océarium du Croisic. Sea aquarium. 01/06-31/08 10-20h, 01/05-31/05, 01/09-30/09 10-13h, 14-19h, 01/10-30/04 14-19h.

S Le Guédéniau 18D2

Plan d'eau, Rue du Lavoir. **GPS**: n47,49405 w0,04488.

25 free ChWCfree.
Location: Rural. **Surface:** metalled. 01/01-31/12.
Distance: on the spot.
Remarks: Recreation area at lake.

S Le Mans 18D1

Quai de l'Amiral Lalande. **GPS**: n48,00233 e0,18915.

7 free Chfree. **Location:** Urban, simple. **Surface:** asphalted. 01/01-31/12.
Distance: centre 1km 8km.
Remarks: Along Sarthe River.

Le Mans 18D1

Rue Denfert Rochereau. **GPS**: n48,01111 e0,19750.

free. **Location:** Urban, simple, noisy. **Surface:** asphalted. 01/01-31/12.
Distance: 500m 500m 500m.
Remarks: Max. 24h, sunday morning market.

Tourist information Le Mans:

M Le Musée des 24 Heures - Circuit de la Sarthe, 9 Place Luigi Chinetti. Motorcar museum.

Place des Jacobins. Wed + Su-morning, Fri.

S Le Pallet 18B3

Rue Pierre Abelard. **GPS**: n47,13494 w1,3305.

20 free €1 Ch. **Location:** Rural, simple. **Surface:** asphalted. 01/01-31/12.
Distance: 500m 500m 500m on the spot on the spot.
Remarks: Wine museum, coins at the shops in the village.

S Le Poiré-sur-Vie 21B1

Rue de Roc. **GPS**: n46,76773 w1,51162.

5 free Ch free. **Location:** Central, quiet. **Surface:** gravel.
01/01-31/12.
Distance: 500m 500m 500m.

S Le Puy-Notre-Dame 18D3

Place du Gâte Argent, Rue du Parc. **GPS**: n47,12390 w0,23155.

15 free Chfree. **Location:** Urban, simple, quiet.
Surface: metalled. 01/01-31/12.
Distance: 100m 200m 200m.
Remarks: Next to cemetery.

S Le Puy-Notre-Dame 18D3

Cave-Champignonnière St.Maur, 1 Rue du Chateau, Sanziers. **GPS**: n47,11755 w0,20526.

8 free (1x)on demand WCfree.
Location: Simple, quiet. **Surface:** metalled. 01/03-30/10.
Distance: 2km.
Remarks: At mushroom grower.

S Le Puy-Notre-Dame 18D3

Domaine de la Renière, Les Caves. **GPS**: n47,13429 w0,24256.

5 € 6 included €5/24h.
Location: Simple, quiet. **Surface:** metalled. 01/03-01/11.
Distance: 700m.
Remarks: When buying wine 1 night free.

S Le Puy-Notre-Dame 18D3

Domaine du Vieux Tuffeau, Les Caves. **GPS**: n47,13498 w0,24704.

6 free free €5/night. **Location:** Rural, simple, quiet.
Surface: metalled. 01/01-31/12.
Distance: 1km.

Le Puy-Notre-Dame 18D3

Domaine de la Girardrie, Rue Fontaine de Cix. **GPS**: n47,11616 w0,24127.

FR

5 free free. **Location:** Rural, simple, quiet. **Surface:** gravel.
01/01-31/12.
Distance: 1km 1km 1km.

Le Puy-Notre-Dame 18D3

Domaine des Hauts Buards, 17 Rue des Troglodytes.
GPS: n47,11149 w0,22544.

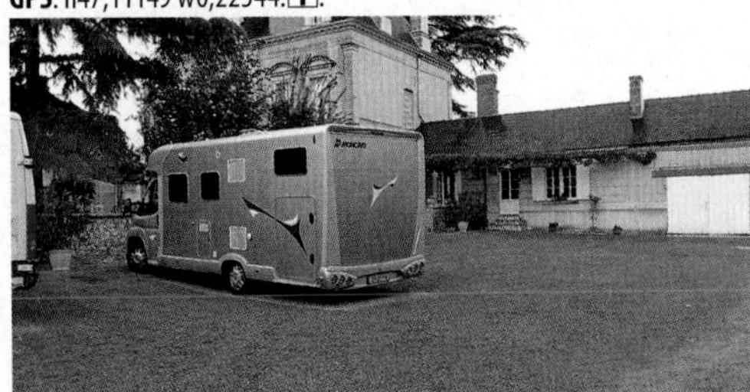

5 free. **Location:** Rural, simple, isolated, quiet. **Surface:** gravel.
01/01-31/12.
Distance: 7km 7km 7km on the spot on the spot.

Le Vaudelnay 18D3

Domaine du Vieux Pressoir, 235, Rue Château d'Oiré.
GPS: n47,14669 w0,25239.

4 free. **Location:** Rural, simple, quiet. **Surface:** metalled.
01/01-31/12.
Distance: 3km 3km 3km on the spot on the spot.
Remarks: No arrival on Sunday.

Les Epesses 21C1

Le Puy du Fou, D27. **GPS**: n46,89425 w0,92506.
100 € 5 €2/100liter Ch (36x)€2/12h.
Location: Simple, isolated, noisy.
Surface: grassy.
Remarks: Baker at 8am, free shuttle to Puy du Fou.

Les Essarts 21B1

Rue de la piscine. **GPS**: n46,77380 w1,23499.

10 free €2/10minutes Ch (2x)€2/55minutes.
Location: Rural, simple. **Surface:** asphalted. 01/01-31/12.
Distance: 600m 5,6km 600m 600m.
Remarks: At swimmingpool and campsite.

Les Herbiers 21B1

Rue Saint Exupéry. **GPS**: n46,87410 w1,01765.

8 free Chfree.
Location: Simple. **Surface:** asphalted. 01/01-31/12.
Distance: 600m 600m 600m.
Remarks: Max. 24h.

Les Sables-d'Olonne 21A1

Aire camping-cars Port Olona, Rue des Bossis.
GPS: n46,50765 w1,78898.

38 € 8, tourist tax incl Ch.
Surface: asphalted. 01/01-31/12.
Distance: city centre 1,5km 1,6km 100m 2,6km 150m.
Remarks: Jul/Aug max. 48h, max. 72h.

Les Sables-d'Olonne 21A1

Indigo Parking Plage, Rue Printanière. **GPS**: n46,49646 w1,77493.

150 € 15,10/24h, winter free Ch WCincluded.
Location: Urban, simple. **Surface:** gravel.
01/01-31/12 service 06/11-31/03.
Distance: on the spot beach 600m 600m 400m.

Les Sables-d'Olonne 21A1

Les Salines, 120 route de l'Aubraie. **GPS**: n46,51635 w1,80533.

20 € 5 Chincluded €4 free.
Location: Rural. **Surface:** sand.
01/04-30/09.
Distance: 600m on the spot.
Remarks: Baker every morning, july/Aug only overnight stays (18-11h).

Tourist information Les Sables-d'Olonne:
Cours Dupont. Wed + Sa morning.
Zoo d'Olonne. Zoo.

Longué-Jumelles 18D3

Boulevard Victor Hugo. **GPS**: n47,38119 w0,11254.

10 free ChWCfree. **Location:** Simple, quiet. **Surface:** gravel.
01/01-31/12.
Distance: 100m 3,3km on the spot on the spot.
Remarks: Service 300m: N 47,38046 W -0,11488, attention: follow the signs.

Luçon 21B1

Domaine des Guifettes. **GPS**: n46,43339 w1,18189.

€ 10,50, dog € 2,60 Ch included.
Location: Rural, comfortable, isolated, quiet.
Surface: gravel/metalled.
Distance: on the spot on the spot on the spot on the spot on the spot on the spot.
Remarks: Free entrance swimming pool, jacuzzi, sauna, midget golf.

Tourist information Luçon:
Centre Ville. Wed + Sa morning.

L'Aiguillon-sur-Mer 21B2

Centre de Voile, Avenue Amiral Coubert.
GPS: n46,33238 w1,30726.

50 € 5 €2/100liter ChWC. **Location:** Rural, simple.
Surface: asphalted. 01/01-31/12.
Distance: 300m 300m on the spot 300m 300m.
Remarks: At lake, yachting school.

Maillé 21C2

La Petite Cabane. **GPS**: n46,34082 w0,79349.

€ 8 Chincluded.
Location: Rural, simple, quiet. **Surface:** grassy.
Distance: 500m 200m.
Remarks: Check in at harbourmaster, service passerby € 3, bicycle rental 500m.

Maillezais 21C2

Rue de l'Ecole. **GPS**: n46,37081 w0,74123.

20 free €2/100liter Ch. **Location:** Simple.
Surface: asphalted. 01/01-31/12.
Distance: 500m 500m 200m.

Maisdon-sur-Sèvre 18B3

Domaine des Croix, Les Croix. **GPS**: n47,10710 w1,38757.

12 free Ch €4/24h WC €1.
Location: Rural. **Surface:** gravel. 01/01-31/12.
Distance: 1km.
Remarks: Max. 72h, wine tasting.

Mamers 18E1

Rue de la Piscine. **GPS**: n48,35523 e0,37187.

FR

8 € 7/night, € 18/3 nights Ch included.
Location: Rural, comfortable. **Surface:** grassy/gravel.
01/01-31/12.
Distance: 1km 500m 500m 1km 1km.
Remarks: Entrance code available at campsite.

S Mansigné 18D2

Camping de la Plage, Route du Plessis. **GPS:** n47,75130 e0,13233.
€ 10 €2 Ch €2/h.

S Martigné-Briand 18C3

Jardin des Vieux Pressoirs, Rue d'Anjou.
GPS: n47,23584 w0,42851.

4 free Chfree. **Surface:** metalled. 01/01-31/12.
Distance: 200m 200m 100m.
Remarks: Closed when frosty.

S Martigné-Briand 18C3

Domaine de la Touche Blanche, La Touche Blanche.
GPS: n47,26977 w0,45274.

6 free €3/day. **Location:** Rural, simple, quiet.
Surface: gravel. 01/01-31/12.
Distance: 3km 3km 3km on the spot on the spot.

S Mayenne 18C1

Quai Carnot. **GPS:** n48,30000 w0,62.

4 free €1,50 Ch. **Location:** Urban, simple, noisy.
Surface: asphalted. 01/01-31/12.
Distance: 1km 10m.
Remarks: Max. 24h, coins at tourist info.

S Mervent 21C1

Chemin du Chêne Tord. **GPS:** n46,52385 w0,76432.

free €2/100liter Ch. **Location:** Rural, simple, isolated, quiet.
Surface: gravel.
Distance: 1km.
Remarks: At cemetery, coins at tourist info.

S Mesnard-la-Barotière 21B1

Base de Loisirs de la Tricherie. **GPS:** n46,85280 w1,11764.

free €3 Ch .
Location: Rural, simple. **Surface:** grassy.
Distance: 2km beach on the spot on the spot on the spot.
Remarks: At lake of Tricherie.

Mesquer 14D3

Aire du Parc de la Lande, Route de Campzillon.
GPS: n47,39309 w2,46549.
€ 5,50/night. 01/04-31/10.
Distance: 1,2km.
Remarks: Max. 72h.

Mesquer 14D3

Avenue de Praderoi, Quimiac. **GPS:** n47,40564 w2,48739.

10 free. **Surface:** forest soil. 01/01-31/12.
Distance: 400m sandy beach 300m.
Remarks: Tuesday morning market.

Mesquer 14D3

Route de la Bôle de Merquel. **GPS:** n47,41474 w2,46826.

15 free. **Surface:** gravel/metalled. 01/01-31/12.
Distance: 300m.
Remarks: Max. 48h.

S Mesquer 14D3

Route de Kerlagadec. **GPS:** n47,39567 w2,46752.
Chfree. 01/01-31/12.

S Mezeray 18D2

Rue de la Vezanne. **GPS:** n47,82300 w0,01485.

8 free €2 Ch €2. **Location:** Rural, simple. **Surface:** gravel.
01/01-31/12.
Distance: 300m.

S Montfort-le-Gesnois 18E1

Parc des Sittelles. GPS: n48,03763 e0,41375.

16 € 10 Ch included. **Location:** Rural, simple, quiet.
Surface: forest soil. 01/01-31/12.
Distance: 50m.

S Montreuil-Bellay 18D3

Place Dom Deschamps, Rue Georges Girouy.
GPS: n47,13272 w0,15835.

30 free €2,20/10minutes ChWC.
Location: Urban, simple. **Surface:** gravel/metalled.
01/01-31/12 15/06-15/09 10-19h.
Distance: 150m on the spot 150m 150m on the spot on the spot on the spot.
Remarks: Along river, nearby campisite Les Nobis, coins at the shops and town hall.

S Montreuil-Bellay 18D3

Caveau de la Prévoté, Rue du Cohu 55, Méron.
GPS: n47,13522 w0,11121.

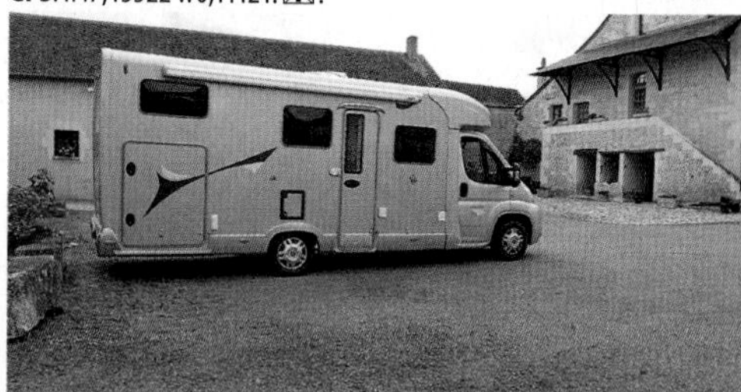

3 free Ch free. **Location:** Simple, quiet.
Surface: metalled. 01/01-31/12.
Distance: 50m 3km 3km.

Tourist information Montreuil-Bellay:

Office de Tourisme, Place du Concorde, www.ville-montreuil-bellay.fr. City with a fortress from 1025.

S Montreuil-Juigné 18C2

Rue Saint Jean Baptiste. **GPS:** n47,54132 w0,61526.

8 free €2/100liter Ch. **Location:** Rural, simple.
Surface: gravel/metalled. 01/01-31/12.
Distance: 1km 50m 800m.
Remarks: Along the Mayenne river, max. 72h, coins at camping municipal.

Montsoreau 18D3

Domaine de la Perruche, 29, Rue de la Maumenière.
GPS: n47,21828 e0,05079.
. **Location:** Simple, central.
Distance: 500m 500m.
Remarks: 10.30><18.30h.

S Moutiers-sur-le-Lay 21B1

Palias. **GPS:** n46,55375 w1,15483.

FR

6 free Ch WC free. **Location:** Simple. **Surface:** grassy.
01/01-31/12.
Distance: 400m 400m 400m 200m.
Remarks: At gymnasium.

S Mouzillon 18B3

Route de la Vendée. **GPS:** n47,13944 w1,28194.

12 free €2 Ch. **Location:** Simple. **Surface:** asphalted.
Distance: 200m 200m 200m on the spot.

S Nantes 18B3

Camping-car park du Petit Port, Boulevard du Petit Port.
GPS: n47,24252 w1,5568.

15 € 12/24h Ch included. **Location:** Urban, simple, central.
Surface: grassy/metalled. 01/01-31/12.
Distance: on the spot 3,5km on the spot 300m tram 150m.
Remarks: Wifi code: 44-2207, entrance code: 2207A.

Tourist information Nantes:
Musée Jules Verne.

S Noirmoutier-en-l'Ile 18A3

Aire de La Guérinière, Rue de la Tresson. **GPS:** n46,96591 w2,21482.

49 € 8-10, 02/07-27/08 € 13 Ch included.
Surface: gravel. 01/01-31/12.
Distance: sandy beach 450m 200m 100m.
Remarks: Max. 48h, video surveillance.

S Noirmoutier-en-l'Ile 18A3

La Place de l'ancien moulin à eau, Noirmoutier-en-l'Ile.
GPS: n47,00139 w2,25167.

220 € 5, 01/04-30/10 € 8, parking free €2/100liter Ch €2/1h free. **Surface:** asphalted. 01/01-31/12.
Distance: 750m sandy beach 2,5km 750m.
Remarks: Max. 72h.

S Noirmoutier-en-l'Ile 18A3

Place des Ormeaux, L'Epine. **GPS:** n46,98060 w2,26404.

51 € 8/24h, € 14/48h, € 20/72h 100liter Ch included50minutes WC.
Surface: metalled. 01/01-31/12.
Distance: 100m 1,3km on the spot 200m 3km on the spot.
Remarks: Max. 72h.

S Noirmoutier-en-l'Ile 18A3

Place R. Ganachaud, l'Herbaudière. **GPS:** n47,02016 w2,30061.

18 € 5, 01/04-30/10 € 8, parking free €2/100liter Ch €2/1h.
Surface: asphalted. 01/01-31/12.
Distance: on the spot 350m.
Remarks: Parking behind town hall, max. 72h.

Tourist information Noirmoutier-en-l'Ile:
Place de la République. Fri.
Sealand Aquarium, Le Vieux Port.

S Nort-sur-Erdre 18B2

13 Place du Bassin. **GPS:** n47,43746 w1,49546.

6 free €2 Ch WC free . **Location:** Simple, quiet.
Surface: asphalted. 01/01-31/12.
Distance: 300m 100m 300m 300m.
Remarks: Max. 24h.

S Notre-Dame-de-Monts 18A3

Aire de la Clairière, Rue de la Clairière.
GPS: n46,83460 w2,14282.

35 € 7/20-8h, 01/10-31/03 € 5/20-8h Ch free.
Location: Rural, simple. **Surface:** gravel. 01/01-31/12 service: 01/12-01/04.
Distance: 800m 200m 200m 800m 800m.
Remarks: Motorhome parking at the beach.

S Notre-Dame-de-Monts 18A3

Parking De Gaulle, Rue de La Barre. **GPS:** n46,83118 w2,13006.

20 € 7/20-8h, 01/10-31/03 € 5/20-8h Ch WC free.
Surface: asphalted. 01/01-31/12 service: 01/12-01/04.
Distance: 300m 500m 300m.

S Nozay 18B2

Étang de Nozay. **GPS:** n47,57500 w1,62528.

16 € 8 Ch (16x) WC included.
Surface: gravel. 01/01-31/12 service: frost.
Distance: 1,5km 2km 10m 200m 400m.

S Olonne-sur-Mer 21A1

Aire camping-cars OlonnEscale, Rue des Anciens Combattants d'Afrique du Nord. **GPS:** n46,53814 w1,77517.

21 € 8/24h Ch included.
Location: Simple. 01/01-31/12.
Distance: 300m 6km 600m 300m.
Remarks: Jul/Aug max. 48h, max. 72h.

S Oudon 18B3

Aire de Camping-Car Oudon, Rue de la Vieille Cour.
GPS: n47,34567 w1,28415.

8 free Ch. **Location:** Rural, simple, quiet. **Surface:** gravel.
01/01-31/12.
Distance: 300m 500m 400m on the spot on the spot.
Remarks: Servicepoint at campsite 1km.

S Pellouailles-les-Vignes 18C2

Impasse de la Chapelle, D323. **GPS:** n47,52141 w0,43698.

3 free Ch free. **Location:** Rural. **Surface:** asphalted.
01/01-31/12.
Distance: on the spot 1,4km 100m bakery 50m.

FR

Piriac-sur-Mer 14D3

Parking de Brambel, Avenue du Général de Gaulle, D452.
GPS: n47,39647 w2,51292.

12 € 6,50 €2/100liter Ch WC
Location: Comfortable. **Surface:** metalled. 01/01-31/12.
Distance: 2km sandy beach 50m 2km 2km.
Remarks: Parking to sea.

Piriac-sur-Mer 14D3

Parking de Lérat, Route de Mesquêne, D99, Lieu-dit Lérat.
GPS: n47,36807 w2,53273.

25 € 6,50 €2/100liter Ch **Location:** Simple.
Surface: metalled. 01/01-31/12.
Distance: 2,5km 600m 600m 500m 500m.

Piriac-sur-Mer 14D3

Port de Piriac, Rue de la Tranchée. **GPS**: n47,37861 w2,5422.

15 € 6,50 €2/100liter Ch
Surface: gravel. 01/01-31/12.
Distance: 500m 500m 500m.

Tourist information Piriac-sur-Mer:
01/06-30/09 Mo + Wed + Sa-morning, 01/10-30/05 Tue.
Arts market. 01/07-31/08 Thu-evening.

Pontmain 15C3

Parking de la Mairie, Le Bourg. **GPS**: n48,43796 w1,06042.
50 free Ch free. 01/01-31/12.
Distance: on the spot.
Remarks: Max. 1 night.

Pornic 18A3

Le Val Saint-Martin. **GPS**: n47,12053 w2,09162.

7 free €2/100liter Ch **Location:** Comfortable, isolated.
Surface: asphalted. 01/01-31/12.
Distance: city centre 1,5km.
Remarks: Next to swimming pool.

Pouancé 18B2

Rue de l'Hippodrome, Aubin. **GPS**: n47,75223 w1,18007.

5 € 4,40 Ch (4x) WC free. **Location:** Rural, simple, quiet.
Surface: grassy. 01/01-31/12.
Distance: 500m small beach 20m 20m 1km 1km.
Remarks: Along étang de Saint-Aubin.

Pouzauges 21C1

Parking de la Vallée, D49/D203. **GPS**: n46,77639 w0,82861.

10 free Ch free. **Location:** Simple. **Surface:** asphalted.
01/01-31/12.
Distance: 1km 1km 1km.

Préfailles 18A3

Camping-Car Park de La Pointe, Chemin du Port aux Anes.
GPS: n47,13872 w2,22213.

49 € 12/24h Ch included **Location:** Comfortable. **Surface:** grassy/gravel. 01/01-31/12.

Préfailles 18A3

Aire de Biochon, Chemin de Levertrie. **GPS**: n47,12973 w2,19028.

75 € 3. **Location:** Rural, simple, quiet. **Surface:** gravel/sand.
01/01-31/12.
Distance: 3km 500m 500m 3km 3km.
Remarks: Max. 48h, baker every morning.

Préfailles 18A3

Aire de la Pointe St-Gildas, D313, chemin des Pinettes.
GPS: n47,13663 w2,23843.

45 € 5. **Location:** Rural, simple, quiet. **Surface:** grassy/gravel.
01/01-31/12.
Distance: 3km 50m 200m 3km.
Remarks: Max. 48h, baker every morning.

Préfailles 18A3

Rue de la Prée. **GPS**: n47,13439 w2,2117.
€2,50/100liter Ch. **Location:** Simple. 01/01-31/12.
Remarks: Coins at tourist info.

Pruillé-l'Éguillé 18E2

Berce Loisirs, La Quellerie. **GPS**: n47,82714 e0,42822.
23 € 7 €2 Ch €2 €1. **Surface:** grassy. 01/01-31/12.
Distance: 1,2km on the spot 1,2km on the spot on the spot.
Remarks: At fish pond.

Rablay sur Layon 18C3

Parking les Lavandières, D54. **GPS**: n47,29772 w0,57767.

5 free Ch WC free. **Location:** Rural, simple, quiet.
Surface: gravel/sand. 01/01-31/12.
Distance: 300m.

Riaille 18B2

Rue de la Benate. **GPS**: n47,51412 w1,28803.

5 free Ch WC free. **Location:** Rural, simple, quiet.
Surface: gravel. 01/01-31/12.
Distance: 700m 700m 700m.
Remarks: Max. 48h.

Rouans 18A3

Aire naturelle de Messan, Route des Marais.
GPS: n47,19272 w1,85419.

8 € 3 Ch WC free. **Location:** Rural, simple.
Surface: grassy/metalled. 01/01-31/12.
Distance: 1km on the spot on the spot 1km.
Remarks: To be paid at town hall.

Saint-Aubin-de-Luigné 18C3

Domaine La Biquerie, Domaine viticole de la Biquerie D17.
GPS: n47,30843 w0,70211.

30 free Ch free.
Location: Rural, simple, quiet. **Surface:** grassy.
01/01-31/12.
Distance: 5km 5km 5km 5km on the spot on the spot.

Saint-Aubin-de-Luigné 18C3

Camping du Layon, Rue Jean de Pontoise.
GPS: n47,32796 w0,67112.

10 € 4 Ch included. **Location:** Urban, central, quiet. **Surface:** asphalted. 01/05-30/09.
Distance: 50m 100m 250m 250m 250m on the spot on the spot.
Remarks: Pay at campsite or town hall.

Saint-Calais 18E2

Boulevard du Docteur Gigon. **GPS:** n47,92416 e0,74459.

4 free ChWC free. **Location:** Rural, simple.
Surface: asphalted. 01/01-31/12.
Distance: 400m on the spot.

Saint-Calais 18E2

Le Champ Long, D249. **GPS:** n47,93375 e0,74568.

15 free WC.
Location: Rural. **Surface:** asphalted. 01/01-31/12.
Distance: 1,6km lake on the spot on the spot.

Saint-Clément-des-Levées 18D3

Rue de la Laiterie. **GPS:** n47,33064 w0,18042.

10 free €2 Ch. **Surface:** metalled. 01/01-31/12.
Distance: 300m.
Remarks: Coins at the shops and town hall.

Saint-Cyr-en-Bourg 18D3

Cave de Saumur, Route de Saumoussay.
GPS: n47,19642 w0,07266.

15 free ChWC free. **Location:** Rural, simple, quiet.
Surface: asphalted. 15/03-15/09.
Distance: 3km.
Remarks: Max. 48h, wine tasting 300m.

Saint-Georges-sur-Loire 18C2

Rue de la Villette. **GPS:** n47,40610 w0,76301.

12 free Ch free. **Location:** Rural, simple, quiet.
Surface: asphalted. 01/01-31/12.
Distance: 300m 100m 300m 300m.
Remarks: Next to the old abbey, max. 24h.

Saint-Gervais 18A3

Route de St Urbain. **GPS:** n46,89999 w2,00134.
10 €3/10minutes Ch €3/55minutes. 01/01-31/12.
Distance: 300m 300m.

Saint-Gilles-Croix-de-Vie 21A1

La Rabalette, Rue de la Rabalette. **GPS:** n46,70302 w1,94728.

35 15/03-15/11 € 6/night €2,60/10minutes Ch.
Location: Urban, simple. **Surface:** asphalted. 01/01-31/12.
Distance: 500m 1km 500m 500m.
Remarks: Nearby lake Soudinière, coins at tourist info.

Saint-Gilles-Croix-de-Vie 21A1

Stade de la Chapelle, Rue du Bois. **GPS:** n46,69449 w1,92716.

€ 6 €2,60 Ch. **Location:** Urban. **Surface:** unpaved.
01/04-30/09 weekend and school holidays.
Distance: centre 500m.
Remarks: Coins at tourist info.

Tourist information Saint-Gilles-Croix-de-Vie:
St.Gilles: Tue, Thu, Su; Croix de Vie; Wed, Sa.

Saint-Hilaire-de-Chaléons 18A3

Rue Eloi Guitteny, D61. **GPS:** n47,10389 w1,86639.

2 free ChWC free. **Surface:** asphalted. 01/01-31/12.
Distance: 100m 500m 100m.
Remarks: Next to campsite de l'Etoile, max. 24h.

Saint-Hilaire-de-Riez 21A1

Base des vallées, Chemin des Vallées. **GPS:** n46,73154 w1,91132.

10 free €2,60/10minutes Ch.
Location: Rural, simple. **Surface:** asphalted. 01/01-31/12.
Distance: St.Hilaire 3,7km 7km.

Saint-Hilaire-de-Riez 21A1

Parking des Becs, Avenue des Becs. **GPS:** n46,76040 w2,02656.

25 € 6/24h €2,60/10minutes Ch.
Surface: asphalted. 01/01-31/12.
Distance: 100m sandy beach 750m 200m.
Remarks: Max. 3 nights.

Saint-Hilaire-de-Riez 21A1

Allée de la Plage de la Parée Préneau. **GPS:** n46,72865 w1,99167.

48 free, night € 5. **Location:** Rural. **Surface:** metalled.
01/01-31/12.
Distance: on the spot.
Remarks: Beach parking.

Saint-Hilaire-de-Riez 21A1

Champ Gaillard, Avenue de Baisse. **GPS:** n46,76903 w2,03337.

28 free.
Location: Rural, isolated. **Surface:** gravel. 01/01-31/12.
Distance: sandy beach 1km.

Saint-Jean-de-Monts 21A1

Le Repos des Tortues, Route de Notre Dame de Monts 38.
GPS: n46,79879 w2,07344.

98 € 8, 01/07-31/08 € 12 Ch (49x),4Amp WC €5/stay €4 included. **Location:** Rural, luxurious.
Surface: grassy/gravel. 01/01-31/12.
Distance: 800m 1,5km 50m 2km.
Remarks: Video surveillance.

FR

S Saint-Jean-de-Monts 21A1

Aire de stationnement des Pimprenelles, Rue des Pimprenelles. **GPS**: n46,78837 w2,07986.

20 € 8,50-12, tourist tax incl Ch included.
Location: Comfortable. **Surface:** asphalted. 01/04-01/11.
Distance: sandy beach 200m.

Tourist information Saint-Jean-de-Monts:
Wed, Sa.

S Saint-Jean-sur-Mayenne 18C1

Les Marchanderies. **GPS**: n48,12793 w0,75244.

25 € 7,60 Ch WC included. **Location:** Rural, luxurious, quiet. **Surface:** grassy/gravel. 01/01-31/12.
Distance: 500m on the spot 300m 400m bakery on the spot.
Remarks: Along the Mayenne river.

S Saint-Léonard-des-Bois 18D1

Aire Municipale, Le Gué Plard. **GPS**: n48,35318 w0,08127.

10 free Ch WC free.
Location: Simple, quiet. 01/01-31/12.
Distance: 500m on the spot on the spot 500m on the spot on the spot on the spot.

S Saint-Loup-du-Gast 15C3

Zone d'Activité du Creusot. **GPS**: n48,38750 w0,58548.

6 free Ch free.
Location: Rural, simple. **Surface:** asphalted/grassy.
01/01-31/12.
Distance: 350m.
Remarks: Max. 1 night, departure Vélorail, € 15 per bike for 4 pers.

S Saint-Mars-la-Jaille 18B2

Rue Neuve. **GPS**: n47,52327 w1,18357.

12 free Ch WC free. **Location:** Rural. **Surface:** asphalted.
01/01-31/12.
Distance: 200m on the spot.
Remarks: Parking at small lake.

S Saint-Michel-Chef-Chef 18A3

Camping-Car Park Le Thar-Cor La Plaine sur Mer, Avenue Cormier. **GPS**: n47,16017 w2,16881.

24 € 12/24h Ch included.
Location: Simple, isolated, quiet. 01/01-31/12.
Distance: sandy beach 400m 400m 400m.

S Saint-Michel-Chef-Chef 18A3

Rue du Chevecier. **GPS**: n47,18209 w2,14664.

30 free, 20-8h € 6 €2,95/100liter Ch.
Location: Simple. **Surface:** asphalted.
01/01-31/12.
Distance: 300m 300m 300m.
Remarks: Parking townhall, coins at tourist info and town hall.

S Saint-Michel-Chef-Chef 18A3

Camping Clos Mer et Nature, Route de Tharon. **GPS**: n47,17309 w2,15779.

€ 6 €2/100liter Ch €2. **Location:** Simple, quiet.
Surface: grassy. 01/01-31/12.
Distance: 500m sandy beach 400m 300m.
Remarks: Check in at reception campsite.

S Saint-Michel-en-l'Herm 21B2

Route de la Mer. **GPS**: n46,35161 w1,24821.

4 free €2 Ch.
Location: Simple. **Surface:** asphalted/gravel.
Distance: 200m 200m 200m.

Remarks: Coins at the shops.

S Saint-Michel-et-Chanveaux 18B2

Aire de la Coulée Verte, Rue de Britanny. **GPS**: n47,68034 w1,13252.
4 free WC. **Surface:** unpaved. 01/01-31/12.
Distance: 100m.

S Saint-Michel-Mont-Mercure 21C1

Place du Sommet. **GPS**: n46,83222 w0,88222.

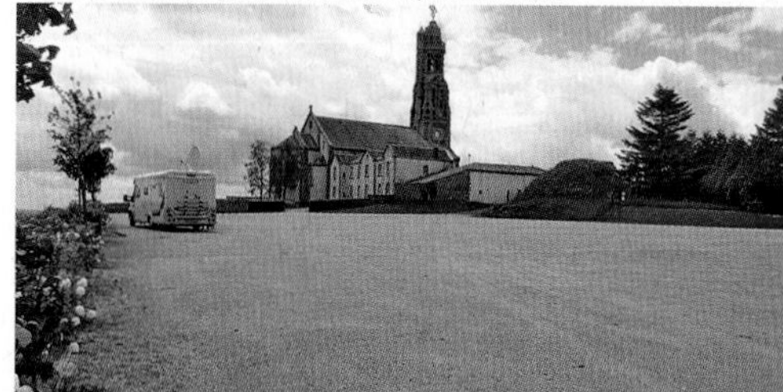

50 free €2/150liter Ch. **Location:** Simple, isolated.
Surface: gravel/sand. 01/01-31/12.
Distance: 500m on the spot 500m.

S Saint-Nazaire 18A3

Parking du Théâtre, Boulevard Paul Leferme. **GPS**: n47,27895 w2.

28 € 7, tourist tax € 0,65/pp €4/10minutes Ch included.
Location: Urban, simple, isolated. **Surface:** metalled.
01/01-31/12.
Distance: on the spot 500m 50m.
Remarks: Free bus to centre.

S Saint-Nazaire 18A3

Route de l'Océan, D292, Saint-Marc-sur-Mer.
GPS: n47,23700 w2,30033.

15 free €4/100liter Ch €4/1h.
Location: Rural, simple, quiet. **Surface:** gravel. 01/01-31/12.
Distance: 2km 100m 100m.

Saint-Nazaire 18A3

Quai du Port de Méan. **GPS**: n47,29937 w2,18333.
6 free. **Surface:** metalled.
Distance: 4km 1km 150m.

Saint-Nazaire 18A3

Route du Bois Joalland. **GPS**: n47,27954 w2,26229.

5 free.
Location: Simple, central. **Surface:** gravel. 01/01-31/12.
Distance: 500m 10m 10m on the spot on the spot.

S Saint-Philbert-de-Grand-Lieu 18B3

Chemin de la Plage. **GPS**: n47,04500 w1,64172.

FR

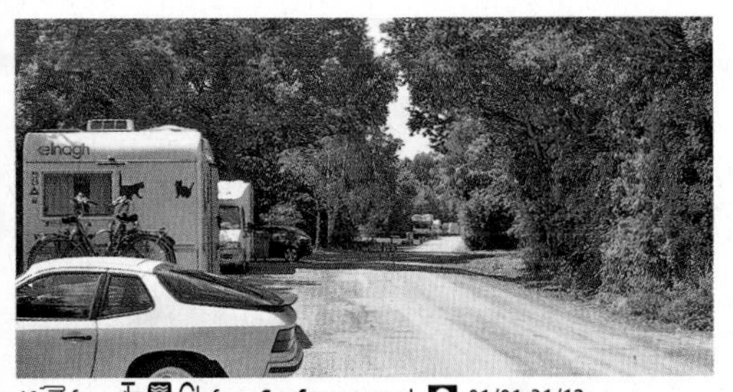

10 free Ch free. **Surface:** gravel. 01/01-31/12.
Distance: 1km on the spot on the spot 550m 1km.

Saint-Rémy-la-Varenne 18D3

Rue St Aubin-D132. **GPS:** n47,39805 w0,31612.

3 free ChWC free. **Location:** Urban, simple, quiet.
Surface: asphalted. 01/01-31/12.
Distance: on the spot 100m 100m 150m on the spot on the spot.

Saint-Saturnin-sur-Loire 18C3

Route de Saumur, D751. **GPS:** n47,39267 w0,43285.

3 free Ch free. **Location:** Urban, simple, quiet.
Surface: metalled. 01/01-31/12.
Distance: on the spot 100m 100m 100m on the spot on the spot.

Saint-Viaud 18A3

Rue du Parc des Sports. **GPS:** n47,25917 w2,015.

10 free Ch (2x). **Location:** Rural, comfortable, quiet.
Surface: metalled. 01/01-31/12.
Distance: 500m 100m 500m 500m.
Remarks: At recreational lake, max. 8 days.

Saint-Vincent-sur-Jard 21B1

Chemin des Roulettes, Le Goulet. **GPS:** n46,41038 w1,5413.

43 € 0,35/h €2/10minutes Ch €2/55minutes.
Location: Rural, simple. **Surface:** metalled.
01/01-31/12 Service: winter.
Distance: 1km 100m 400m.

Sainte-Foy 21A1

Rue Maurice Raimbaud. **GPS:** n46,54568 w1,67306.
3 free Ch free. **Surface:** asphalted. 01/04-31/10.

Distance: on the spot on the spot.

Saulgé l'Hôpital 18C3

Terrain de Loisirs, Chemin de la Planche.
GPS: n47,29853 w0,38344.

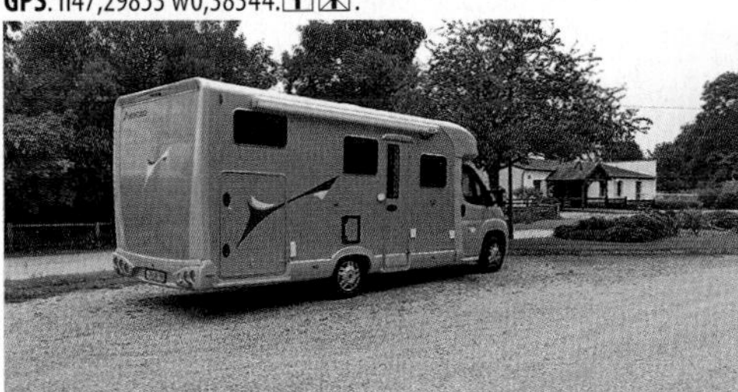

15 free Ch free. **Location:** Rural, simple, quiet.
Surface: gravel. 01/01-31/12.
Distance: 100m 100m 100m.
Remarks: Service 100m.

Segré 18C2

Aire de l'Europe, D775. **GPS:** n47,68497 w0,85719.

free ChWC free. **Location:** Rural. **Surface:** asphalted.
01/01-31/12.
Distance: 1km.

Segré 18C2

Place du Moulin sous la Tour, Rue Emile Zola.
GPS: n47,68409 w0,87436.

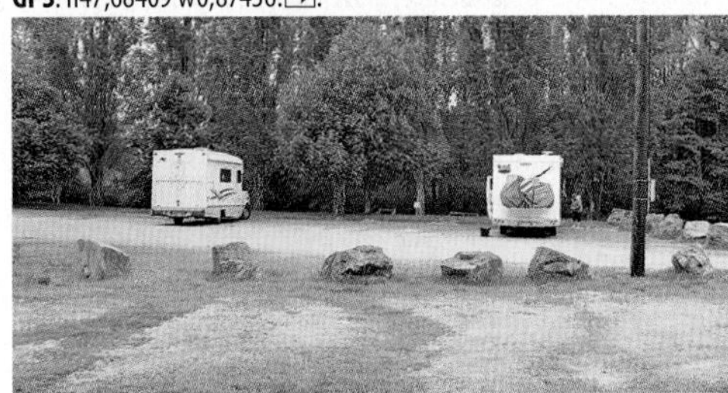

10 free Ch free. **Location:** Rural, simple. **Surface:** gravel.
01/01-31/12 Service: winter.
Distance: 300m on the spot 100m on the spot.

Sillé-le-Guillaume 18D1

2, Place de la Gare. **GPS:** n48,18167 w0,13111.

8 free €3 Ch €3. **Location:** Urban, simple.
Surface: asphalted. 01/01-31/12.
Distance: 300m 300m 400m train 50m.
Remarks: Coins at tourist info.

Souvigné-sur-Sarthe 18D2

Le Val de Taude, Rue de la Vallée. **GPS:** n47,82782 w0,38896.
free.

Talmont-Saint-Hilaire 21A1

Parking des Gâtines, Rue des Gâtines. **GPS:** n46,46761 w1,61718.

16 € 7,40/24h €3/10minutes Ch €3/50minutes.
Location: Rural, simple. **Surface:** asphalted. 01/01-31/12.
Distance: 500m Small lake (100m) 100m.

Talmont-Saint-Hilaire 21A1

Parking du Château Guibert, Avenue de la Plage.
GPS: n46,44098 w1,66351.

16 € 7,40/24h €3 Ch €3 WC.
Location: Rural, simple. **Surface:** metalled. 01/01-31/12.
Distance: 1km.
Remarks: Max. 48h.

Tennie 18D1

Rue du Camping. **GPS:** n48,10636 w0,0786.
free. 01/01-31/12.
Distance: 250m.
Remarks: At lake.

Thoiré-sur-Dinan 18E2

19 rue Gabriel Guyon. **GPS:** n47,75343 e0,44621.
4 € 5 Ch included. 01/01-31/12.
Remarks: Picnic and barbecue place.

Turquant 18D3

Aire Municipal, Rue des Ducs d'Anjou. **GPS:** n47,22393 e0,02858.

20 free €2,50 ChWC free.
Location: Simple, central. **Surface:** metalled. 01/01-31/12.
Distance: 100m 50m 50m on the spot on the spot on the spot.
Remarks: Behind church, coins at the shops in the village.

Vaiges 18C1

Rue Robert Gletron, D57. **GPS:** n48,04189 w0,48285.

5 free €2 Ch. **Location:** Urban, simple, noisy. **Surface:** gravel.
01/01-31/12.
Distance: 500m 1,7km 20m 700m bakery.

Valanjou 18C3

Aire de Plaisance, Rue de la Mairie. **GPS:** n47,21658 w0,60326.

FR

6 free free. **Location:** Rural, simple, quiet.
Surface: metalled. 01/01-31/12.
Distance: 200m on the spot 300m 300m on the spot on the spot.
Remarks: Nearby town hall.

S Vauchrétien 18C3

Domaine Dittiére, Chemin de la Grouas Vauchrétien.
GPS: n47,33273 w0,47231.

5 free free. **Location:** Rural, simple, quiet. **Surface:** gravel.
01/01-31/12.
Distance: 500m 500m.

Venansault 21B1

Rue Pierre Nicolas Loué. **GPS**: n46,68250 w1,51472.

5 free. **Surface:** sand. 01/01-31/12.
Distance: 500m 100m 300m 500m.

S Vendrennes 21B1

Route de l'Océan. **GPS**: n46,82690 w1,1217.

5 free €3/150liter Ch free. **Location:** Rural, simple, quiet.
Surface: metalled/sand. 01/01-31/12.
Distance: 200m.
Remarks: Coins at the bakery.

S Vihiers 18C3

Rue Champ de Foire des Champs. **GPS**: n47,14355 w0,5358.

5 free ChWC free. **Location:** Urban, simple, quiet.
Surface: asphalted. 01/01-31/12.
Distance: 50m 100m 100m.

S Villebernier 18D3

Le Port Roux. **GPS**: n47,25395 w0,03454.
40 Ch.

Remarks: Along Loire river.

S Villeveque 18C2

Rue du Port. **GPS**: n47,56222 w0,42257.
6 free €1 ChWC. 01/01-31/12.
Distance: 100m 50m bakery 200m.

S Villiers-Charlemagne 18C1

Village Vacances et Pêche, Rue des Haies.
GPS: n47,92083 w0,68167.

25 € 8,40, first night free €2 Ch .
Location: Rural, comfortable, quiet.
Surface: grassy.
01/01-31/12.
Distance: on the spot day pass available 500m on the spot.

S Vouvant 21C1

Rue de Château Neuf. **GPS**: n46,57462 w0,77462.

20 free Ch free. **Surface:** gravel. 01/01-31/12.
Distance: 500m 500m 500m.

Centre-Val de Loire

S Ainay-le-Vieil 21H1

La Tuilerie. **GPS**: n46,66159 e2,55582.

6 free ChWC free. **Location:** Rural, simple, quiet.
Surface: grassy. 01/01-31/12.
Distance: 850m 800m.

S Allogny 18G3

D944. **GPS**: n47,21913 e2,32329.

3 free WC free. **Location:** Rural, simple, isolated, noisy.
Surface: asphalted. 01/01-31/12.
Distance: 800m 50m 50m.

S Amboise 18E3

Vinci Park, Allée de la Chapelle Saint-Jean.
GPS: n47,41761 e0,98742.

20 € 12/24h Ch included (20x)€2
Location: Rural, comfortable, central, quiet.
Surface: asphalted/grassy. 01/01-31/12.
Distance: 200m 200m 200m 200m on the spot on the spot.
Remarks: Next to campsite, castle 500m.

Amboise 18E3

Parking St. Jean, Avenue Leonardo da Vinci 43, D61.
GPS: n47,40814 e0,98986.

11 free. **Location:** Urban, simple, isolated, quiet.
Surface: asphalted. 01/01-31/12.
Distance: on the spot 1,5km 1,5km on the spot.

S Angé 18F3

Place de la Mairie. **GPS**: n47,33239 e1,24450.

20 free €3/100liter Ch . **Location:** Simple, isolated, quiet.
Surface: sand. 01/01-31/12.
Remarks: Coins at town hall and supermarket.

S Ardentes 21G1

Avenue de Verdun. **GPS**: n46,74682 e1,82826.

5 free €2,50/10minutes Ch (4x) WC .
Location: Rural, noisy. **Surface:** gravel.
Distance: on the spot on the spot.

Argenton-sur-Creuse 21F1

Rue de la Grenouille. **GPS**: n46,58715 e1,52497.

50 free. **Location:** Simple. **Surface:** gravel. 01/01-31/12.
Distance: 50m 3,4km 50m 50m.

S Argenton-sur-Creuse 21F1

Alleé du Champ de Foire. **GPS**: n46,58501 e1,52283.
ChWC free. **Location:** Rural, simple. 01/01-31/12.

FR

Distance: on the spot.

Athée-sur-Cher 18E3

Aire d'Athée-sur-Cher, D83, Rue de Cigogné.
GPS: n47,31439 e0,91756.

3 free Chfree. **Location:** Rural, simple, isolated, quiet.
Surface: metalled. 01/01-31/12.
Distance: 800m 11km 1,5km 1km on the spot.
Remarks: Max. 24h.

Aubigny-sur-Nère 18H3

Parc des Sports, D7. **GPS**: n47,48201 e2,44995.

9 free Chfree. **Location:** Rural, simple, isolated, quiet.
Surface: asphalted. 01/01-31/12.
Distance: 1km 1km 2km on the spot on the spot.
Remarks: Playground.

Aubigny-sur-Nère 18H3

Parking du Pré qui Danse, Mail Guichard.
GPS: n47,49140 e2,43830.

17 free ChWCfree. **Location:** Urban, simple.
Surface: asphalted. 01/01-31/12.
Distance: 200m 200m 200m 100m.

Avoine 18D3

Avenue de la République. **GPS**: n47,21287 e0,17706.

11 € 4 €2/10minutes Ch (11x)€2/24h .
Location: Rural, comfortable, luxurious, central, quiet.
Surface: asphalted/metalled. 01/01-31/12.
Distance: 1km Lac Mousseau 300m 300m 300m.
Remarks: Max. 3 nights.

Azay-le-Rideau 18E3

Camping municipal Le Sabot, Rue du Stade.
GPS: n47,25925 e0,46992.

8 free €3/100liter Ch €1,70,on camp site.
Location: Urban, comfortable, central, quiet. **Surface:** asphalted.
01/04-01/10.
Distance: 200m 300m on the spot on the spot.
Remarks: Max. 24h, coins at camping (9/16h), castle 300m.

Azé 18F2

M et Mme Hersant, Les Places, D957 Épuisay-Galette.
GPS: n47,86451 e0,97659.

6 € 10 Ch included. **Location:** Rural, comfortable, isolated, quiet. **Surface:** grassy/gravel. 01/01-31/12.
Distance: 7km on the spot.

Barlieu 18H3

Base de loisirs de Badineau. **GPS**: n47,47918 e2,63168.

15 € 2, first night € 3,50 €2/100liter Ch €2/h WC.
Location: Rural, simple, quiet. **Surface:** grassy/gravel.
19/04-31/10.
Distance: 1km on the spot on the spot.
Remarks: At small lake.

Benais 18D3

Rue Saint-Vincent. **GPS**: n47,29875 e0,21598.

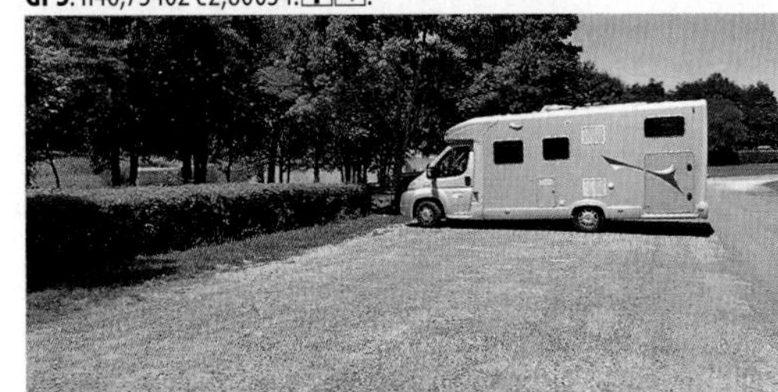

6 free. **Location:** Rural, simple, quiet. **Surface:** grassy.
01/01-31/12.
Distance: 350m 350m on the spot on the spot.

Bessais-le-Fromental 21H1

Base de loisirs de l'Étang de Goule, Champ de la Croix.
GPS: n46,73402 e2,80034.

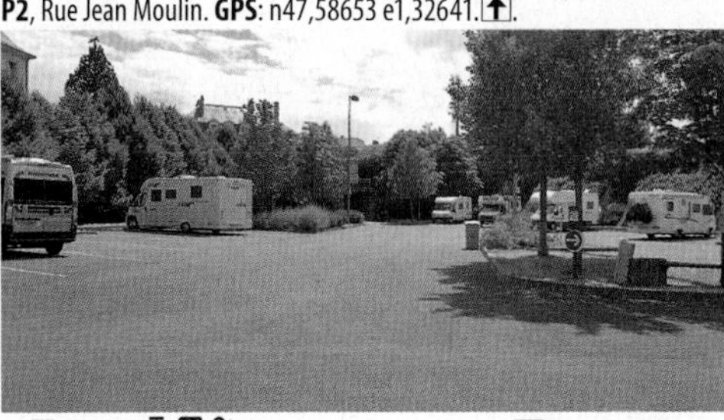

50 free €2 Ch. **Location:** Simple, isolated, quiet.
Surface: asphalted/grassy. service: frost.
Distance: 4km on the spot on the spot on camp site on camp site.

Blois 18F2

P2, Rue Jean Moulin. **GPS**: n47,58653 e1,32641.

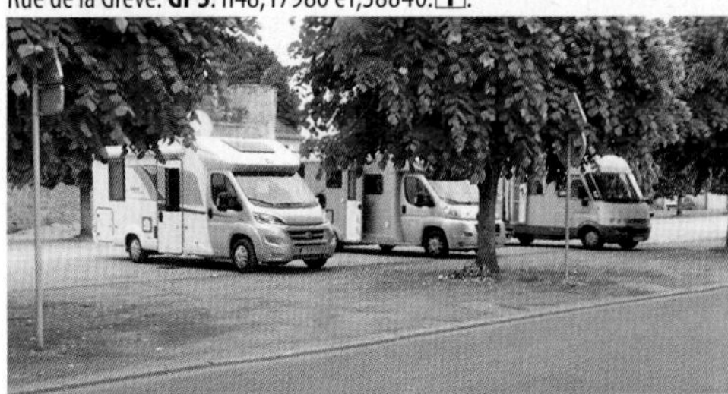

20 € 5/24h Chfree. **Surface:** asphalted. 01/05-30/09.
Distance: on the spot 6,9km 100m 100m on the spot.

Tourist information Blois:
Château de Blois.
Cathédrale St Louis.
Quatier Coty. Wed 7-13h.

Bonneval 18F1

Rue de la Grève. **GPS**: n48,17980 e1,38840.

8 free ChWCfree. **Surface:** asphalted. 01/01-31/12.
Distance: 200m 200m 350m.

Bonny-sur-Loire 18H2

Chemin de la Cheuille. **GPS**: n47,55925 e2,83967.

6 free €2/liter Ch €2/30minutes WC. **Location:** Rural, simple, central. **Surface:** gravel. 01/05-30/09.
Distance: 150m 50m 300m on the spot on the spot.
Remarks: Along La Cheuille river.

Boulleret 18H3

Place des Charmes. **GPS**: n47,42304 e2,87244.

4 free €2/100liter Ch (1x)€2/6h WC free.
Location: Urban, simple, central. **Surface:** asphalted. 01/01-31/12.
Distance: on the spot on the spot on the spot on the spot on the spot.
Remarks: Coins at the shops and restaurant, sanitary building: 01/05-30/09.

Bourges 18H3

Rue Jean Bouin. **GPS**: n47,07597 e2,39897.

FR

50 free Ch free. **Location:** Urban, simple, central.
Surface: asphalted. 01/01-31/12.
Distance: 50m 500m 500m.
Remarks: Max. 48h.

Tourist information Bourges:
Ballades de Bourges. Festivities and market in the city centre.
01/07-31/08.

Bourgueil 18D3

Jardin de Tanneries, Rue des Tanneries. **GPS**: n47,28014 e0,17058.

6 free. **Location:** Simple, central, quiet. **Surface:** gravel/sand.
01/01-31/12.
Distance: 300m 150m.
Remarks: Max. 1 night.

Bourré 18F3

Domaine Deniau, Route des Vaublins 18.
GPS: n47,35101 e1,24603.

6.
Location: Rural, simple. **Surface:** gravel. 01/01-31/12.

Brézolles 15F3

Rue de Verneuil, D939. **GPS**: n48,69083 e1,06972.

10 free Ch free. **Surface:** gravel. 01/01-31/12.
Distance: 200m 200m.

Briare-le-Canal 18H2

Flot Bleu Park, Boulevard Lereou. **GPS**: n47,64304 e2,72270.

12 € 7/24h Ch included. **Location:** Urban, comfortable, quiet. **Surface:** grassy. 01/01-31/12.
Distance: on the spot 4,5km on the spot on the spot 800m 800m 100m 500m.
Remarks: Max. 72h.

Briare-le-Canal 18H2

Rue des Vignes. **GPS**: n47,63215 e2,73981.

40 free €2/100liter Ch . **Location:** Urban, simple.
Surface: gravel. 01/01-31/12.
Distance: 300m 4,5km 50m 500m 800m on the spot on the spot.

Briare-le-Canal 18H2

Port du Commerce, Quai de Mazoyer. **GPS**: n47,63470 e2,74030.

10 free WC free. **Location:** Simple. **Surface:** asphalted.
01/01-31/12.
Distance: 200m 4,5km on the spot on the spot 800m on the spot on the spot.

Céré-la-Ronde 18F3

Rue du Stade. **GPS**: n47,25788 e1,18232.
10 € 8,40-10,80 Ch included. 01/01/-31/12.
Distance: 500m.

Chabris 18F3

Place du Champ de Foire. **GPS**: n47,25317 e1,65211.

5 free €2 Ch €2.
Location: Rural, central, quiet. **Surface:** gravel/metalled.
01/01-31/12.
Distance: on the spot 250m 250m.
Remarks: Coins at Tourist Info and Maison de la Presse (250m).

Chambord 18F2

Château de Chambord, Place St.Louis. **GPS**: n47,61608 e1,51057.

100 <7.90m € 7/day + € 10/night, >7.90m € 45/day + € 45/night.
Surface: asphalted.
Distance: 100m 100m.
Remarks: Parking castle, max. 1 night.

Champigny-sur-Veude 18D3

Place du Chapeau Rouge, Rue de la Bonne Dame.
GPS: n47,06499 e0,31773.
8 free Ch. **Surface:** asphalted. 01/01-31/12.
Remarks: At small lake.

Chaon 18G2

La Maison du Braconnage, Rue des Genêts, D129.
GPS: n47,60942 e2,16611.

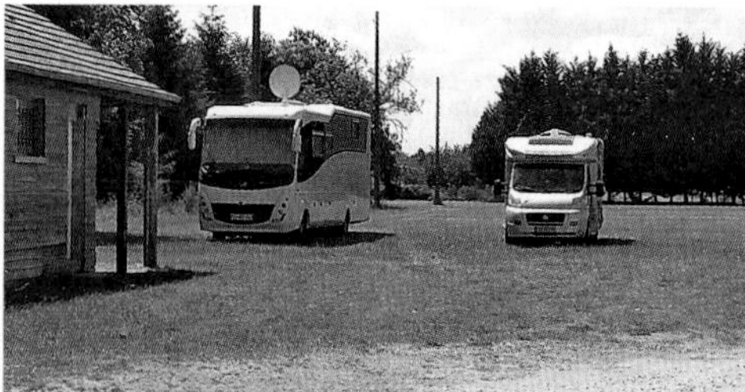

10 free Ch free. **Location:** Rural, isolated, quiet.
Surface: grassy/metalled. 01/01-31/12.
Distance: 200m 200m bakery 50m.
Remarks: Video surveillance.

Châteaudun 18F1

Aire de Châteaudun, Rue des Fouleries.
GPS: n48,07172 e1,32421.

15 free €2/100liter Ch €2/20minutes WC.
Location: Urban, comfortable, central, quiet. **Surface:** asphalted.
01/01-31/12.
Distance: 400m Canoe rental on the spot on the spot.
Remarks: Along Loir river, castel of Châteaudun 300m.

Châteauroux 21F1

17, Avenue de Parc des Loisirs. **GPS**: n46,82278 e1,69507.

5 free €2,50/100liter Ch €2,50/h.
Location: Simple. **Surface:** asphalted. 01/05-31/10.
Distance: 3,6km 2km 2km.
Remarks: Coins at campsite.

Châtillon-sur-Loire 18H2

Rue du Port. **GPS**: n47,59128 e2,76044.

±6 € 9 Ch WC included.
Location: Rural, comfortable, quiet. **Surface:** asphalted/gravel.
Distance: 800m 9km A77 400m bakery 500m.
Remarks: At the canal.

Chenonceaux 18F3

Aire de Chenonceaux, Chemin de la Varenne.
GPS: n47,33053 e1,06824.

10 free. **Location:** Rural, simple, isolated, noisy. **Surface:** grassy.
01/01-31/12.

Distance: 500m ⊗500m on the spot on the spot.
Remarks: Along railwayline.

Chenonceaux 18F3
Rue du Château. **GPS**: n47,33020 e1,06648.

20 free. **Location:** Rural, simple, isolated. **Surface:** metalled.
01/01-31/12.
Distance: 500m ⊗500m on the spot.
Remarks: Parking at castle of Chenonceaux.

Tourist information Chenonceaux:
Castle.

Cheverny 18F2
Château Cheverny P3, D102. **GPS**: n47,49762 e1,46097.

20 free. **Surface:** metalled.
9.30-12h, 14.15-17h, Apr-Sep 9.30-18.15h.
Distance: 100m ⊗100m.

Tourist information Cheverny:
Château Cheverny. Castle. 9.30-12h, 14.15-17h, Apr-Sep 9.30-18.15h.

Chouzé-sur-Loire 18D3
Aire de Chouzé-sur-Loire, Rue de l'Eglise.
GPS: n47,23809 e0,12649.

6 free €2 Ch. **Location:** Rural, comfortable, central, quiet.
Surface: gravel. 01/01-31/12.
Distance: on the spot ⊗250m on the spot on the spot on the spot.
Remarks: Coins at the shops and town hall.

Civray-de-Touraine 18F3
Caves du Père Auguste, 14 rue des Caves. **GPS**: n47,33497 e1,04718.

5 free €2/120liter (4x)€4/24h WC €3.
Surface: asphalted/grassy. 02/01-31/12.
Distance: 500m ⊗1,5km 4km on the spot.

Cloyes-sur-le-Loir 18F1
Rue du Colonel Boussa. **GPS**: n47,99172 e1,23218.
5 free. **Surface:** asphalted. 01/01-31/12.
Distance: ⊗450m 800m.

Coullons 18H2
Place du Monument. **GPS**: n47,62012 e2,49319.

3 free ChWCfree. **Location:** Urban, simple, quiet.
Surface: gravel. 01/01-31/12.
Distance: on the spot ⊗500m 50m 50m on the spot.

Courville-sur-Eure 15F3
Avenue Thiers. **GPS**: n48,44600 e1,24166.
6 free €2,50/100liter Ch €2,50/55minutes.
Surface: asphalted. 01/01-31/12.
Remarks: Coins at campsite and shops.

Culan 21G2
Place du Champ de Foire. **GPS**: n46,54727 e2,34630.

20 free €1,50/10minutes Ch €1,50/h WC.
Surface: asphalted. 01/01-31/12.
Distance: 50m ⊗50m 50m.
Remarks: Near office de tourisme, coins available at the shops.

Cuzion 21F2
Base de Loisirs Pont des Piles, Rue des Petites Côtes.
GPS: n46,45639 e1,61167.

6 free. **Location:** Isolated, quiet. **Surface:** grassy/metalled.
01/01-31/12.
Remarks: At castle, max. 1 night.

Dampierre-en-Burly 18H2
Etang du Bourg, Rue nationale. **GPS**: n47,76250 e2,51413.

6 free Ch WCfree. **Location:** Rural, simple, quiet.
Surface: gravel. 01/01-31/12.
Distance: 1km on the spot on the spot ⊗1km 1,5km 500m on the spot.

Dreux 15F3
Camping-Car Park, Rue Jean-Louis Chanoine. **GPS**: n48,74029 e1,33227.
9 €9,60 Ch (8x) included. 01/01-31/12.
Distance: 2,5km ⊗on the spot 2km.

Dry 18G2
Rue de Meung. **GPS**: n47,79824 e1,71419.

10 free €2/10minutes Ch €2/55minutes.
Location: Simple. **Surface:** metalled. 01/01-31/12.
Distance: on the spot 1km ⊗50m.
Remarks: Coins at town hall.

Épineuil-le-Fleuriel 21H1
Le Bourg. **GPS**: n46,55690 e2,58265.

5 free Chfree. **Location:** Rural, simple. **Surface:** gravel.
01/01-31/12.
Distance: 500m.

Esvres-sur-Indre 18E3
Salle des Fêtes, Impasse Auguste Noyant. **GPS**: n47,28291 e0,78418.

7 free free.
Location: Urban, simple, central, quiet. **Surface:** gravel.
01/01-31/12 water disconnected in winter.
Distance: on the spot ⊗100m 250m on the spot on the spot on the spot.

Genillé 18F3
Rue de la Varenne. **GPS**: n47,18442 e1,09201.
6 €5 €2/100liter Ch included. 01/01-31/12.
Distance: 150m ⊗200m on the spot.

Genillé 18F3
Ferme Jouvin, La Galerie, D 764 Loches> Montrichard.
GPS: n47,21409 e1,10871.

€2 service€3 Ch included. **Location:** Rural, simple, isolated, quiet. **Surface:** grassy. 01/01-31/12.
Distance: 2,7km on the spot.

Germigny-des-Prés 18G2
21 Route de Saint-Benoît. **GPS**: n47,84430 e2,26798.

5 free Chfree. **Location:** Rural, simple, quiet.

FR

Surface: gravel/metalled. 01/01-31/12.
Distance: 100m 1,5km, bakery 600m.

Gien 18H2

Quai de Nice. **GPS**: n47,67985 e2,64308.

8 free €2,10 Ch €2,10. **Location:** Urban, noisy.
Surface: asphalted. 01/01-31/12.
Distance: 2km on the spot.
Remarks: Max. 48h, coins at swimming pool.

Gizeux 18D3

Aire de Gizeux, Route du Lavoir. **GPS**: n47,39275 e0,19689.

10 free €3/100liter Ch stay.
Location: Rural, comfortable, central, quiet.
Surface: gravel.
01/01-31/12.
Distance: 200m 500m 200m on the spot on the spot on the spot.
Remarks: Coins at the shops and town hall, Château de Gizeux 400m.

Guilly 18G3

Le Prieuré Chambres d'Hôtes, Rue du Prieuré.
GPS: n47,07920 e1,72100.

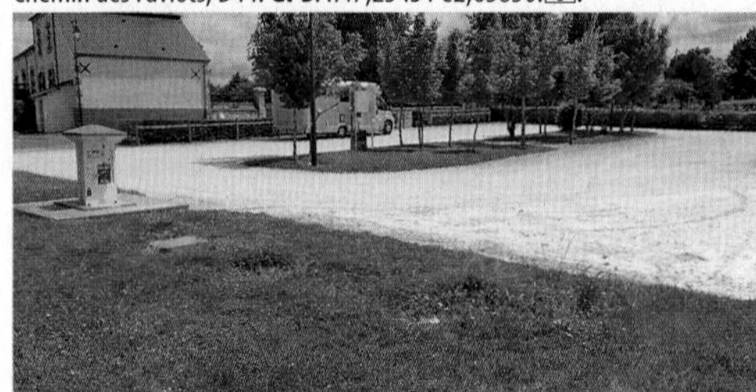

10 €5 €3 Ch . **Location:** Rural, quiet.
Surface: grassy/metalled. 01/01-31/12.
Distance: 150m on the spot 150m.

Humbligny 18H3

Chemin des Faviots, D44. **GPS**: n47,25451 e2,65850.

8 free €2/100liter Ch €2/60minutes. **Location:** Rural, simple. **Surface:** gravel. 01/01-31/12.
Distance: on the spot 1km 3km 50m.
Remarks: Coins at town hall.

La Chapelle-Saint-Mesmin 18G2

Aire camping-cars, Chemin de Fourneaux.
GPS: n47,88550 e1,83990.

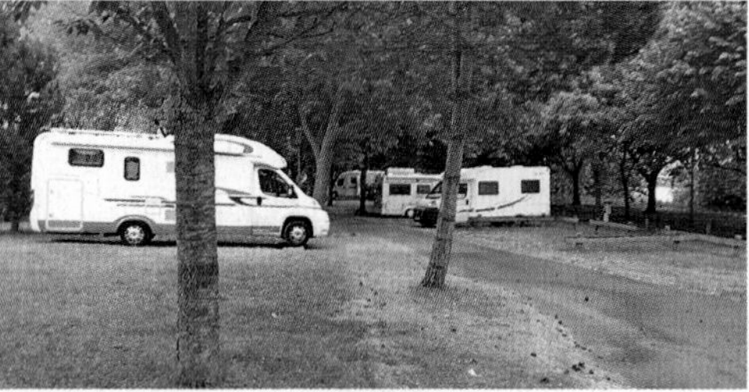

23 € 5/24h, € 9/48h, € 12/72h Ch included.
Location: Urban, comfortable, quiet. **Surface:** grassy.
01/04-31/12.
Distance: 500m, Orléans 5km 2,7km 50m 50m 500m 500m on the spot on the spot.
Remarks: Along Loire river, market Saturday.

La Châtre 21G1

Rue du Champ de Foire. **GPS**: n46,58250 e1,98250.

10 € 2. **Location:** Urban, simple. **Surface:** asphalted.
Distance: 50m 50m 50m.

La Châtre 21G1

Supermarché Super U, Avenue d'Auvergne, D943.
GPS: n46,58278 e2,00139.
10 free €2/10minutes Ch €2/1h. **Location:** Simple.
Surface: asphalted. 01/01-31/12.
Distance: 800m 50m.

La Ferte-Beauharnais 18G2

D922. **GPS**: n47,54455 e1,84882.

12 free €2/10minutes Ch €2/55minutes WC.
Location: Simple, noisy. **Surface:** grassy/metalled.
01/01-31/12.
Distance: 300m on the spot on the spot 250m 100m.
Remarks: At small lake.

La Ferté-Saint-Cyr 18G2

D925, Rue Faubourg de Britanny. **GPS**: n47,65623 e1,67249.
4. **Surface:** metalled.

La Loupe 15F3

Place du 8 mai, Docteur Moenner St. **GPS**: n48,47262 e1,01768.
3 €2,20 Ch €2,20. **Surface:** asphalted. 01/01-31/12.
Distance: 300m 100m 800m.
Remarks: Coins at tourist info.

La Pérouille 21F1

Étang de la Roche, Le Champ Perrot. **GPS**: n46,70507 e1,52259.

free €2/10minutes Ch WC.
Location: Rural, isolated, quiet. **Surface:** grassy/gravel.
01/01-31/12.
Distance: 750m 5km A20 750m.
Remarks: At small lake, coins at town hall and restaurant (750m).

Lailly-en-Val 18G2

Place de l'Église. **GPS**: n47,77023 e1,68544.

30 free Ch WC free. **Surface:** gravel. 01/01-31/12.
Distance: 100m 50m 300m 200m.

Lamotte-Beuvron 18G2

Aire municipale, Chemin de Maisonfort. **GPS**: n47,59795 e2,02524.

10 free Ch WC free.
Location: Urban, central. **Surface:** metalled.
01/01-31/12 Fri-morning, water disconnected in winter.
Distance: 200m 4,5km on the spot on the spot 200m 300m 100m.
Remarks: At the canal.

Tourist information Lamotte-Beuvron:
Avenue de la Republique. Market. Fri-morning.

Langon (Loir-et-Cher) 18G3

Parking Canal du Berry, D976. **GPS**: n47,28253 e1,82862.

7 free €2/10minutes Ch €2/1h. **Location:** Rural, quiet.
Surface: asphalted. 01/01-31/12 Service: winter.
Distance: 50m on the spot 100m 100m.
Remarks: Coins at the shops and town hall.

Le Blanc 21E1

Place du Général de Gaulle. **GPS**: n46,63154 e1,06164.

free €2/100liter Ch €2/h.
Location: Central, noisy. **Surface:** asphalted.
01/01-31/12 service: 01/11-01/04.
Distance: on the spot 250m.
Remarks: Coins at tourist info.

Le Châtelet 21G1

Le Tivoli, Avenue de la Gare. **GPS**: n46,64502 e2,27863.

FR

5 free €2 Ch €2/h. **Location:** Simple. **Surface:** asphalted.
01/01-31/12.
Distance: 50m 50m 300m.

Léré 18H3

Le Port, Rue du Champ des Noyers. **GPS**: n47,47485 e2,87477.

4 free Ch free. **Location:** Rural, simple, quiet.
Surface: asphalted. 01/01-31/12.
Distance: 400m on the spot on the spot.
Remarks: At the canal.

Les Bordes 18H2

Etang du Petit Moulin, Route de Gien.
GPS: n47,81041 e2,40729.

6 free Chfree.
Location: Rural, simple, quiet. 01/01-31/12.
Distance: 400m 100m 150m 2km 500m on the spot on the spot.

Les Montils 18F2

Camping-Car Park des Montils, Route de Seur.
GPS: n47,49308 e1,30571.
45 € 12 Ch (36x) included. **Location:** Rural.
Surface: grassy.
Distance: 500m.
Remarks: Along river, former campsite.

Levet 21H1

Chemin du Crot A Thibault. **GPS**: n46,92306 e2,40639.

3 free (3x). **Location:** Rural, simple, isolated, quiet.
Surface: gravel. 01/03-31/10.
Distance: 250m 250m 250m.
Remarks: Max. 24h.

Loches 18E3

Allée du Maquis César io. **GPS**: n47,12656 e1,00221.
4 free. 01/01-31/12.
Distance: 700m 700m.

Loches 18E3

Avenue Louis XI. **GPS**: n47,13315 e1,00023.
5 free. **Surface:** gravel. 01/01-31/12.
Distance: centre 250m.
Remarks: Max. 24h.

Loches 18E3

Rue de l'Amiral de Pointis. **GPS**: n47,13744 e1,00115.
4 free. **Location:** Simple, noisy. **Surface:** asphalted.
01/01-31/12.
Distance: 1,4km 1,4km.

Loches 18E3

Avenue Aristide Briand. **GPS**: n47,12240 e1,00164.
Ch free. 01/01-31/12.

Louzouer 18H1

Cidre Chivet, 323 Les Mussereaux. **GPS**: n48,02833 e2,87062.

5 € 5 €3 Ch. **Location:** Comfortable.
Surface: asphalted/metalled. 15/03-31/12.
Distance: 1,5km.
Remarks: Max. 24h.

Luant 21F1

L'Étang Duris. **GPS**: n46,72222 e1,57338.

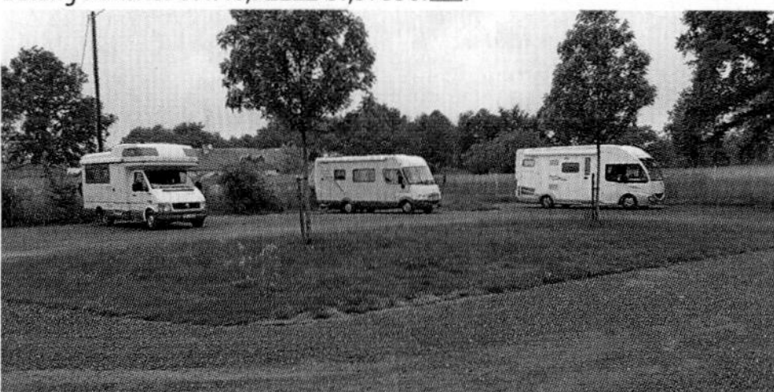

10 free €2 Ch €2.
Location: Rural, isolated, quiet. **Surface:** gravel.
01/01-31/12.
Distance: 3km 3,3km A20 lake bar/brasserie on the spot.
Remarks: Coins at town hall and restaurant.

Marboué 18F1

L'Espace Loisirs des Fontaines, Rue du Croc Marbot.
GPS: n48,11240 e1,32870.

13+5 free €2/10minutes Ch €2/50minutes.
Location: Rural, comfortable, central, quiet. **Surface:** grassy/metalled.
01/01-31/12.
Distance: on the spot 500m 150m on the spot on the spot.

Marcilly-en-Villette 18G2

Rue du Lavoir. **GPS**: n47,76197 e2,02448.

6 free Chfree. **Location:** Rural, simple, quiet.
Surface: gravel. 01/01-31/12.
Distance: 200m 400m 500m on the spot.
Remarks: At tennis-court.

Martizay 21E1

Aire de Loisirs, Rue des Afrique du Nord.
GPS: n46,80528 e1,03806.

9 free Ch (4x)WCfree. **Location:** Rural, quiet.
Surface: metalled/sand. 01/01-31/12.
Distance: on the spot bakery 500m.

Mehun-sur-Yèvre 18G3

Quai du Canal. **GPS**: n47,14409 e2,21010.

6 € 2,50 Ch.
Location: Rural, quiet. **Surface:** asphalted. 01/01-31/12.
Distance: 500m 400m.
Remarks: At the canal.

Menetou-Salon 18H3

Rue de la Liberté. **GPS**: n47,23162 e2,49002.

6 free Ch (6x)free.
Surface: gravel/metalled. 01/04-31/10.
Distance: on the spot 50m 100m 100m.

Mennetou-sur-Cher 18G3

Place du 11 Novembre, N76. **GPS**: n47,26861 e1,86472.

8 free €2/10minutes Ch €2/h.
Location: Rural, quiet. **Surface:** sand. 01/01-31/12.
Distance: 150m 100m 150m 150m.
Remarks: Coins at shops and tourist office, small fortified town.

Méry-sur-Cher 18G3

Chemin Lucien Bonneau/N76. **GPS**: n47,24586 e1,98989.

6 € 7,55/24h €1/12minutes Ch (7x)WCincluded.
Location: Rural, quiet. **Surface:** metalled. 01/01-31/12.
Distance: 150m 100m.
Remarks: Nights closed with barrier.

Meung-sur-Loire 18G2

Chemin des Grèves. **GPS**: n47,82327 e1,69814.
8 free €2 Ch. **Location:** Rural. **Surface:** gravel.
01/01-31/12.
Distance: 250m 300m 250m bakery.
Remarks: At swimming pool.

Montigny 18H3

Le Vieux Château. **GPS**: n47,24283 e2,68627.

FR

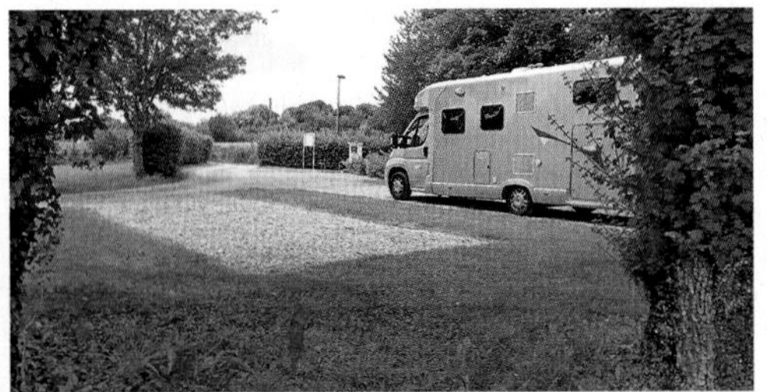

2 free €2/100liter €2/60minutes. **Location:** Rural, simple, isolated, quiet. **Surface:** gravel. 01/01-31/12.
Distance: 800m 850m.
Remarks: Coins at town hall, poste.

S Montoire-sur-le-Loir 18E2

Avenue de la République. **GPS:** n47,75750 e0,86928.

15 free Chfree €1. **Location:** Urban, comfortable, quiet. **Surface:** asphalted. 01/01-31/12.
Distance: on the spot 500m 500m on the spot.
Remarks: At former station.

Montoire-sur-le-Loir 18E2

Aire de Montoire-sur-le-Loir, Boulevard des Alliés, Quartier Marescot. **GPS:** n47,74990 e0,86317.

8 free. **Location:** Urban, simple, central, quiet. **Surface:** asphalted. 01/01-31/12.
Distance: 50m on the spot on the spot 500m 500m on the spot on the spot.

S Montrésor 18F3

Rue du 8 Mai. **GPS:** n47,15750 e1,20169.
10 free Chfree. **Surface:** asphalted. 01/01-31/12.
Distance: 200m.

S Montrichard 18F3

Rue Frideloux. **GPS:** n47,34016 e1,17045.
40 € 9,60 Ch included. 01/01/-31/12.
Distance: 500m 500m 500m 400m.

S Morogues 18H3

Route des Aix, D46. **GPS:** n47,23990 e2,59857.

4 free €2/100liter Ch €2/60minutes. **Location:** Rural, simple, quiet. **Surface:** gravel. 01/01-31/12.
Distance: on the spot 200m 1km 800m.
Remarks: Coins at tourist info Henrichemont (12km).

S Neuillay-les-Bois 21F1

Route de Buzançais, D1. **GPS:** n46,76917 e1,47333.

5 free Ch (2x)WCfree. **Location:** Simple, quiet. **Surface:** metalled. 01/05-31/10.
Distance: 50m 50m 50m 50m.
Remarks: Max. 24h.

S Neuvy-Le-Barrois 21H1

La Prairie, Le Pénisson, D45. **GPS:** n46,86159 e3,03930.

6 € 6 €2/100liter Ch €4/24h €2.
Location: Rural, comfortable, isolated, quiet.
Surface: gravel/metalled. 01/01-31/12.
Distance: 200m 200m.

S Neuvy-Pailloux 21G1

Les Gloux, RN151. **GPS:** n46,88278 e1,83682.

15 free ChWCfree. **Location:** Rural, simple, isolated. **Surface:** asphalted. 01/01-31/12.

S Nogent-le-Roi 15F3

Rue du Pont des Demoiselles. **GPS:** n48,65059 e1,52894.
4 free Ch free. **Surface:** asphalted.
Distance: 400m 400m 400m.
Remarks: Next to sports fields.

Nogent-sur-Vernisson 18H2

Rue du Gué Mulet. **GPS:** n47,84055 e2,73996.

6 free.
Location: Simple, quiet. **Surface:** gravel. 01/01-31/12.
Distance: 1km on the spot on the spot 1km.

S Nogent-sur-Vernisson 18H2

Rue Georges Bannery. **GPS:** n47,85363 e2,74014.
€2 Ch €2.
Remarks: Coins at tourist info, PMU Rue Bannery or bar in Rue A. Briand.

Nouan-le-Fuzelier 18G2

Rue des Peupliers. **GPS:** n47,53324 e2,03437.

6 free. **Location:** Urban, simple. **Surface:** asphalted/metalled. 01/01-31/12.
Distance: 300m 300m 300m.

S Orléans 18G2

Parc des expositions, Rue du Président Robert Schumann. **GPS:** n47,87408 e1,91351.
free .

Tourist information Orléans:

- Office de Tourisme, 6, rue Albert 1er, www.ville-orleans.fr. City with many old bldg. And monuments.
- Maison Jeanne d'Arc. Museum about the life of Jeanne d'Arc. 01/04-31/10 Mo.
- Cathédrale Ste Croix. Gothic cathedral.
- Église Nôtre Dame de recouvrance. Church 16th century.
- Tour Saint Paul. Church 17th century.
- Allée Pierre Chevallier. Su morning.
- Quai du Roi. Sa-morning.
- Fête de Jeanne d'Arc. Historical celebration. 08/05.
- Parc Floral. Flowers and zoo. daily.

S Oulches 21F1

Impasse de l'Étang. **GPS:** n46,61339 e1,29547.

5 free €2 Ch €2.
Location: Rural, simple. **Surface:** gravel. 01/01-31/12.
Distance: on the spot 100m.
Remarks: Coins at town hall.

S Ouzouer-sur-Trézée 18H2

Parking halte nautique, Rue Saint-Roche. **GPS:** n47,67000 e2,80888.

5 free ChWC free. **Location:** Urban, comfortable, quiet. **Surface:** asphalted. 01/04-31/10.
Distance: 500m on the spot 500m 700m 50m.
Remarks: At canal 'de Briare', max. 48h.

S Ouzouer-sur-Trézée 18H2

Camping municipal, Chemin du Rochoir. **GPS:** n47,66819 e2,80611.

6 € 4,50 Ch €2,60 WC included .
Surface: grassy/gravel. 01/04-31/10.

S Paucourt 18H1

Rue de l'Église. **GPS:** n48,03441 e2,79179.

FR

free Chfree. **Location:** Rural. **Surface:** asphalted.
01/01-31/12.
Distance: on the spot 4,5km.

S Pont-de-Ruan 18E3

D17. **GPS:** n47,26373 e0,57632.
free €2 Ch €2. **Location:** Simple, isolated.
Surface: gravel/sand.
Distance: 300m.

S Pontlevoy 18F3

4 rue de Coutant. **GPS:** n47,38619 e1,25905.
free Ch . 01/01-31/12.
Distance: 500m.

S Pouligny-Saint-Pierre 21E1

Route du Blanc, D950, Bénavent. **GPS:** n46,65591 e1,02054.

10 free €2 €2 Ch€2 €2. **Location:** Rural, simple, quiet.
Surface: gravel.
Distance: bakery 50m.
Remarks: Coins at the bakery.

S Reignac-sur-Indre 18E3

Rue Louis de Barberin, D58. **GPS:** n47,22922 e0,91585.

5 free €2/100liter Ch. **Location:** Rural, simple, central, noisy.
Surface: asphalted. 01/01-31/12.
Distance: 300m 20km on the spot on the spot on the spot.
Remarks: Max. 24h, coins at the shops in the village.

S Restigné 18D3

Rue Basse. **GPS:** n47,28041 e0,22614.
4 free €2/100liter Ch. **Location:** Urban, simple, central, quiet.
Surface: gravel. 01/01-31/12.
Distance: on the spot on the spot on the spot on the spot.
Remarks: Coins at town hall.

S Richelieu 18D3

Avenue Pasteur. **GPS:** n47,01098 e0,32265.
10 free €4 . **Surface:** metalled. 01/01-31/12.
Distance: 300m 300m bakery 300m on the spot on the spot.
Remarks: Servicepoint at campsite 1km.

S Saint-Amand-Montrond 21H1

Base de Loisirs Virlay, Etangs de Goule.
GPS: n46,73362 e2,48851.

21 free Chfree. **Location:** Rural, simple, quiet.
Surface: asphalted/grassy. 01/01-31/12.
Distance: 1km 5km 500m 500m on the spot on the spot.

S Saint-Amand-Montrond 21H1

Quai Lutin, via Avenue Maréchal Foch. **GPS:** n46,71818 e2,50480.

4 free Chfree. **Location:** Urban, simple.
Surface: asphalted/gravel. 01/01-31/12.
Distance: 200m on the spot on the spot 200m 200m.
Remarks: On the canal.

S Saint-Benoît-du-Sault 21F2

Place du Champ de Foire. **GPS:** n46,44117 e1,39249.

3 free €2/120liter Ch €2/4h .
Location: Rural. **Surface:** asphalted. 01/01-31/12.
Distance: 300m 300m.
Remarks: At tourist office.

S Saint-Brisson-sur-Loire 18H2

Rue des Ruets, route d'Autry, D52. **GPS:** n47,64680 e2,68028.

6 free Chfree . **Location:** Urban, simple, quiet.
Surface: asphalted. 01/01-31/12.
Distance: 100m 100m 100m 50m.
Remarks: Parking nearby town hall.

S Saint-Claude-de-Diray 18F2

Rue du Moulin D98. **GPS:** n47,61356 e1,41402.
4 free Chfree.
Location: Simple, quiet. **Surface:** gravel.
Distance: 500m.
Remarks: Next to cemetery.

S Saint-Denis-les-Ponts 18F1

Aire de Saint Denis-les-Ponts, Rue Jean Moulin.
GPS: n48,06643 e1,28950.

+10 free €2/100liter Ch.
Location: Urban, comfortable, central, quiet. **Surface:** gravel.
01/01-31/12 Service: winter.
Distance: Châteaudun 3km on the spot on the spot 100m on the spot on the spot.
Remarks: Coins at the shops in the village, Châteaudun (city and castle) 4km.

Saint-Dyé-sur-Loire 18F2

Parking de la base nautique. **GPS:** n47,65454 e1,47852.
4 free. **Surface:** grassy. 01/01-31/12.
Distance: 800m on the spot.
Remarks: Along Loire river, max. 48h.

S Saint-Épain 18E3

Plan d'eau. **GPS:** n47,14444 e0,53960.
€ 5,10 Ch €1,70.
Distance: 300m on the spot.
Remarks: Pay at town hall, fishing permit available at Tabac and supermarket.

S Saint-Genouph 18E3

Rue de l'Auberdière. **GPS:** n47,37702 e0,60200.
free Ch. **Surface:** metalled. 01/01-31/12.
Distance: 350m 350m.

S Saint-Georges-sur-Arnon 21G1

Allée de la Presle. **GPS:** n46,99999 e2,09884.

10 free Chfree. **Location:** Rural, isolated, quiet.
Surface: gravel. 01/01-31/12.
Distance: on the spot on the spot.
Remarks: At small lake, former campsite, max 3,5t.

S Saint-Georges-sur-Arnon 21G1

N151. **GPS:** n46,97740 e2,06908.

10 free ChWCfree. **Location:** Simple, isolated.
Surface: asphalted.
Remarks: May 2016 during inspection service out of order.

S Saint-Georges-sur-Moulon 18H3

Route de Ville. **GPS:** n47,18596 e2,41786.

2 free Chfree. **Location:** Simple, isolated, quiet.
Surface: gravel. 01/01-31/12.
Distance: 1,5km 1km 1,5km.

S Saint-Gondon 18H2

Rue de Sully. **GPS:** n47,69808 e2,53876.

FR

3 free Chfree. **Location:** Rural, simple, quiet.
Surface: asphalted. 01/01-31/12.
Distance: 300m 300m 200m.
Remarks: Max. 48h.

Saint-Gondon 18H2

Rue du Petit Clou. **GPS**: n47,69995 e2,54356.

10 free Chfree. **Location:** Rural, simple. **Surface:** metalled. 01/01-31/12.
Distance: 100m.
Remarks: In front of cemetery.

Saint-Jean-le-Blanc 18G2

Base de loisirs de l'Ile Charlemagne, Levée de la Chevauchée.
GPS: n47,89437 e1,93870.

free €2/100liter Ch. **Location:** Simple, isolated.
Surface: sand. 01/01-31/12.
Distance: Orléans 3km on the spot on the spot.

Saint-Lubin-en-Vergonnois 18F2

Place Jacques Michaux. **GPS**: n47,61241 e1,23927.
free Ch. **Surface:** gravel.
Distance: on the spot.

Saint-Nicolas-de-Bourgueil 18D3

Rue de la Treille. **GPS**: n47,28496 e0,12528.

5 free. **Location:** Rural, simple, quiet. **Surface:** gravel/sand. 01/01-31/12.
Distance: 150m 150m 250m.

Saint-Saturnin 21G2

Route de Perassay. **GPS**: n46,50565 e2,23585.

free €2 Ch. **Location:** Rural, simple, quiet.
Surface: gravel. 01/01-31/12.

Distance: 300m.

Sainte-Maure-de-Touraine 18E3

Aire du Bois Chaudron, D910, Le Bois Caudron.
GPS: n47,09315 e0,61275.

40 € 2,50, 2 pers.incl €2 €1 Ch€3 (4x)€2/12h WC €2 €4/3. **Location:** Rural, comfortable, isolated, quiet.
Surface: grassy. 01/01-31/12.
Distance: 1,5km 4,4km 1,5km 1,5km on the spot.
Remarks: Bread-service.

Sainte-Maure-de-Touraine 18E3

Parking Ronsard, Rue de la Métairie. **GPS**: n47,11096 e0,61640.

15 free Chfree WC. **Location:** Urban, simple, central, quiet.
Surface: asphalted. 01/01-31/12.
Distance: 200m 3km 200m 200m on the spot.

Sainte-Sévère-sur-Indre 21G2

Place du Champ de Foire, rue de Verdun. **GPS**: n46,48724 e2,07167.

free €2 Ch.
Location: Rural, simple. **Surface:** gravel/sand.
Distance: 100m 200m.

Sancoins 21H1

Quai du Canal. **GPS**: n46,83356 e2,91568.

20 free €2,50/100liter ChWC. **Location:** Simple, quiet.
Surface: gravel/metalled. 01/01-31/12.
Distance: 200m on the spot on the spot 200m 150m on the spot on the spot.

Saran 18G2

Allée Claude Bernard. **GPS**: n47,95106 e1,87315.

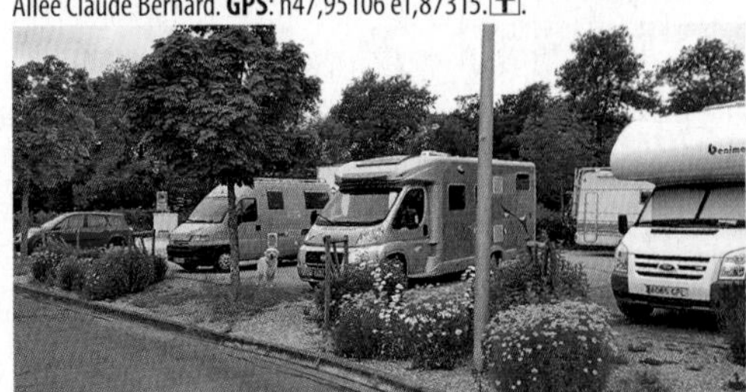

10 free Chfree. **Location:** Simple, central. **Surface:** gravel. 01/01-31/12.

Distance: on the spot on the spot 1,5km 1km 800m on the spot on the spot.

Selles-sur-Cher 18F3

Avenue Kleber-Loustau, D856. **GPS**: n47,27639 e1,55889.

15 €5 Ch. **Location:** Rural, comfortable, quiet.
Surface: asphalted. 01/04-30/09.
Distance: 500m 200m 500m 500m.
Remarks: To be paid at campsite, service on campsite.

Sully-sur-Loire 18H2

Espace Loisirs Georges Blareau, Chemin de la Salle Verte.
GPS: n47,77139 e2,38451.

16 free Chfree. **Location:** Comfortable, quiet.
Surface: gravel/metalled. 01/01-31/12.
Distance: 800m on the spot on the spot 800m 800m.
Remarks: Nearby castle of Sully, narrow entrance.

Sury-près-Léré 18H3

Route de Savigny. **GPS**: n47,48301 e2,86527.

6 free €2/100liter Ch €2/60minutes.
Location: Rural, simple, quiet. **Surface:** asphalted. 01/01-31/12.
Distance: 1,5km 50m 1,5km.
Remarks: Coins at town hall and restaurant.

Theillay 18G3

Chemin du Ronaire. **GPS**: n47,31849 e2,03775.

10 free Chfree. **Location:** Rural, quiet.
Surface: gravel/metalled. 01/04-30/10.
Distance: 250m 250m.
Remarks: At cemetery.

Thenay 21F1

Rue de la Paix, D48. **GPS**: n46,63199 e1,43096.

FR

5 free €2 Ch €2. **Location:** Rural, simple, quiet.
Surface: metalled. 01/01-31/12.
Distance: 200m.
Remarks: Coins at the shops and town hall.

S Thiron-Gardais 18F1

Aire de Thiron-Gardais, Avenue de la Gare.
GPS: n48,31194 e0,99583.

10 free Chfree.
Location: Urban, simple.
Surface: asphalted.
Distance: 100m 300m 300m 300m on the spot 100m.

S Tour-en-Sologne 18F2

Rue de la Mairie. **GPS**: n47,53786 e1,49973.

10 free €2,50/100liter Ch €2,50/h WC.
Surface: gravel.
Distance: 50m 200m bakery 100m.
Remarks: Coins at townhall and bakery.

S Tours 18E3

Parking relais du Lac, Avenue du Général Niessel.
GPS: n47,36700 e0,70007.
6 € 2,60 €2/100liter Ch **Surface:** asphalted.
Distance: 2,5km.

S Vailly-sur-Sauldre 18H3

Rue du Pont. **GPS**: n47,45727 e2,64665.

20 € 3,50 Chfree €2,50 WC €0,80.
Location: Comfortable, central. **Surface:** gravel/metalled.
01/04-31/10.
Distance: 300m on the spot nearby nearby.
Remarks: Along the Sauldre river.

Tourist information Vailly-sur-Sauldre:
Fri.

S Valençay 18F3

Avenue de la Résistance. **GPS**: n47,16080 e1,56163.

10 free €2 Ch €4 . **Location:** Rural, quiet.
Surface: metalled. 01/01-31/12.
Distance: 100m 100m 100m.
Remarks: Nearby entrance castle.

Tourist information Valençay:
Château. Castle, 15th-18th century. 01/03-30/11.

S Vendôme 18F2

Aire de Vendôme, Rue Geoffroy Martel. **GPS**: n47,79111 e1,07528.

5 free. **Location:** Urban, simple, central. **Surface:** asphalted.
01/01-31/12.
Distance: 500m.

S Véretz 18E3

Camping-car Park Véretz, Rue des Isles. **GPS**: n47,35810 e0,81466.
63 € 9,60 Ch (35x) . 01/01-31/12.
Distance: 800m 800m 750m.
Remarks: Along river.

S Villaines les Rochers 18E3

Aire de Villaines-les-Rochers, Place de la Mairie/ Rue des Ecoles.
GPS: n47,22083 e0,49583.

6 free ChWCfree. **Location:** Urban, comfortable, central, quiet. **Surface:** asphalted. 01/01-31/12.
Distance: on the spot 100m 100m on the spot on the spot.
Remarks: Max. 24h.

S Villandry 18E3

Aire de Villandry, Rue Principale. **GPS**: n47,34100 e0,51127.

25 free €2/100liter ChWC .
Location: Rural, comfortable, central, quiet.
Surface: grasstiles.
01/01-31/12.
Distance: 50m 3,1km 300m 100m 100m on the spot on the spot on the spot.
Remarks: Coins at tourist info(100m), Château de Villandry 200m.

S Villedômer 18E2

Aire de Loisirs de Lavoir, Rue du Lavoir.
GPS: n47,54465 e0,88727.

5 free, 15/06-15/09 € 5 €2/100liter Ch €4/1h.
Location: Rural, simple, central, quiet. **Surface:** metalled.
01/01-31/12.
Distance: 100m 8,1km 100m 200m 200m on the spot on the spot.
Remarks: Max. 24h, coins at town hall (200m), bakery (200m) and supermarket (50m).

S Villequiers 18H3

L'Étappe Berrichonne, Le Petit Azillon.
GPS: n47,08828 e2,77429.

6 € 7 Ch included. **Location:** Isolated, quiet.
Surface: gravel/metalled. 01/01-31/12.
Distance: 3km.

S Vitry-aux-Loges 18G2

Rue des Érables. **GPS**: n47,93915 e2,27078.
free Chfree. **Location:** Rural. **Surface:** asphalted.
01/01-31/12.
Distance: 100m 100m on the spot on the spot.
Remarks: At canal of Orléans.

S Vouvray 18E3

Parking Bec de Cisse, Rue Bec de Cisse.
GPS: n47,40929 e0,79735.

3 free €2/100liter Ch €2/1h WC.
Location: Rural, comfortable, central, quiet. **Surface:** asphalted.
01/01-31/12 Service: winter.
Distance: on the spot 8,5km 500m 150m 150m on the spot on the spot.
Remarks: Max. 48h, coins at campsite and tourist info.

FR

Bourgogne-Franche-Comté

S Anost 19B3

Place Centrale. **GPS**: n47,07738 e4,09869.

10 free Chfree. **Location:** Rural, simple, quiet.
Surface: metalled. 01/01-31/12.
Distance: on the spot.

S Arc-et-Senans 22E1

Grande rue. **GPS**: n47,03343 e5,78120.

10 free €2 Ch. **Location:** Simple. **Surface:** gravel.
01/01-31/12.
Distance: 500m 500m.
Remarks: Coints at mairie, supermarket and campsite.

S Arinthod 22D2

Rue de la Prélette. **GPS**: n46,39654 e5,57013.

5 €6 Ch included.
Location: Rural. **Surface:** gravel. 01/01-31/12.
Distance: 100m.
Remarks: Near sports fields.

Arsure-Arsurette 22E1

Châlet des Arches, Route de l'Aliance de vie blanc.
GPS: n46,72168 e6,08402.

10 free €2 WC . **Location:** Isolated. **Surface:** asphalted.
01/01-31/12.

Autun 22B1

Route de Chalon. **GPS**: n46,95548 e4,31667.

17 free €3,50 ChWC.
Location: Urban, simple. **Surface:** asphalted.
01/01-31/12.
Distance: city centre 2km 100m 100m supermarket 900m on the spot on the spot.
Remarks: Parking at small lake Le Vallon at N80, in front of McDonalds.

Tourist information Autun:
Musée Rolin. Roman and Medieval excavations.
Wed, Fri, Su.

Auxerre 19A2

Quai de l'Ancienne Abbaye. **GPS**: n47,79742 e3,57738.

10 free. **Surface:** asphalted. 01/01-31/12.
Distance: 300m 300m 300m.
Remarks: Along the Yonne river.

Tourist information Auxerre:
Tue, Fri.

Baume-les-Dames 19E3

Quai du Canal. **GPS**: n47,34023 e6,35778.

30 € 9,30 + € 0,20/pp tourist tax €2 Ch WCincluded €1,70. **Location:** Rural, comfortable. **Surface:** asphalted/grassy.
01/01-31/12.
Distance: on the spot 5,3km on the spot on the spot on the spot.
Remarks: Bread-service.

Tourist information Baume-les-Dames:
Abbaye Nôtre Dame. Historical monument, 18th century.

Baume-les-Messieurs 22D1

Cascade des Tufs, Rue des Moulins. **GPS**: n46,69124 e5,63946.

10 free. **Location:** Simple.

Beaune 22C1

Avenue Charles de Gaulle. **GPS**: n47,01731 e4,83628.

5 free €3 Ch €3/2h .
Location: Urban, simple, central.
Surface: asphalted.
Distance: 500m 2,6km 200m centre commercial 300m.
Remarks: 5 special pitches, all parking places permitted.

Tourist information Beaune:
Hôtel Dieu et Musée. Former hospital, 15th century, museum.
Château de Meursault, Meursault. Castle with vineyard and wine tastery.

Belvoir 19F3

Chateaux Belvoir. **GPS**: n47,32139 e6,61097.

3 free. **Location:** Rural, simple. **Surface:** asphalted/gravel.
01/01-31/12.

Besançon 19E3

Parking du Crous, Cité Carnot, Quai Veil Picard.
GPS: n47,23702 e6,01644.

12 € 5/24h Chfree. **Location:** Urban, simple.
Surface: asphalted. 01/01-31/12.
Distance: on the spot 500m 500m on the spot.

Tourist information Besançon:
Jardin Botanique, Avenue de la Paix. Botanical gardens. 7-19
Sa after11. free.
Château, Vaire-le-Grand. 15/08-18/09, 19/09-14/08 by agreement.
Tue, Fri, Su.
Parc Zoologique de la Citadelle, Citadelle. Zoo. 10-17/19h.

Bois-d'Amont 22E2

Impasse de l'Eglantine. **GPS**: n46,53771 e6,13934.

10 free €2 Ch €2. **Location:** Rural, comfortable, quiet.
Surface: asphalted. 01/01-31/12.
Distance: on the spot on the spot on the spot on the spot.

Brognard 19F2

Base de Loisirs de la Savoureuse, Rue de Paquis.
GPS: n47,52834 e6,85652.

3 free Chfree. **Location:** Rural, noisy. **Surface:** asphalted.
01/01-31/12.
Distance: 50m 1,3km.
Remarks: Max. 48h.

Broindon 19C3

Aire Du Cerisier Chambertin, Rue du cerisier.
GPS: n47,19834 e5,04522.
free . 01/04-30/11.

Bucey-les-Gy 19E3

Chemin de Tranot 1. **GPS**: n47,42456 e5,83974.

5 free €2/20minutes Chfree (5x)€2/4h.
01/01-31/12.
Remarks: Coins available at the shop.

Bussy-le-Grand 19C2

Château de Bussy, Rue du Château. **GPS**: n47,56069 e4,52544.
5 free. **Surface:** metalled. 01/01-31/12.
Distance: 200m.
Remarks: At castle.

Chablis 19B2

Route d'Auxerre, D235. **GPS**: n47,81711 e3,78425.

5 free free.
Location: Simple, quiet. **Surface:** asphalted.
Distance: centre 500m on the spot.

Chalon-sur-Saône 22C1

P Ville Historique, Promenade Sainte Marie.
GPS: n46,78365 e4,86046.

FR

2 free Chfree. **Location:** Simple. **Surface:** asphalted.
01/01-31/12.
Distance: 500m 50m.
Remarks: Free shuttle to centre.

Champagnole 22E1

20, Rue Georges Vallerey. **GPS:** n46,74633 e5,89918.

5 €6 €4 Ch €4 WC €3.
Location: Simple. **Surface:** gravel/sand. 25/03-30/09.
Distance: 500m 250m.
Remarks: Max. 1 night, coins at campsite.

Charolles 22B2

Route de Viry. **GPS:** n46,43956 e4,28203.

8 €3 Ch €3. **Location:** Simple. **Surface:** gravel.
01/04-01/10.
Distance: 300m.
Remarks: Max. 48h.

Château-Chinon 19B3

Rue Jean Sallonnyer. **GPS:** n47,06304 e3,93627.

4 free Chfree WC.
Location: Simple. **Surface:** metalled. 01/05-30/10.
Distance: 200m 250m 250m.
Remarks: Max. 24h.

Châtillon-en-Bazois 22A1

Place Pierre Saury. **GPS:** n47,05310 e3,65511.

5 free Ch. **Surface:** metalled. 01/04-31/10.
Distance: 50m.

Chiddes 22B1

Le Bourg. **GPS:** n46,86108 e3,94091.

4 free Chfree WC. **Location:** Simple. **Surface:** gravel.
01/01-31/12.
Distance: on the spot on the spot.
Remarks: Max. 48h, free coins available at restaurant.

Chiddes 22B1

Augendre. GPS: n46,86781 e3,94364.
€3 + €2,20/pp €2 €2,50. **Surface:** gravel.

Clairvaux-les-Lacs 22E1

Route de Lons-le-Saunier, D678. **GPS:** n46,58246 e5,74660.

6 free Chfree.
Location: Urban, simple. 01/01-31/12.
Distance: nearby.
Remarks: On entering village, nearby police station.

Clamecy 19A3

Rue de l'Abattoir. **GPS:** n47,46222 e3,52250.

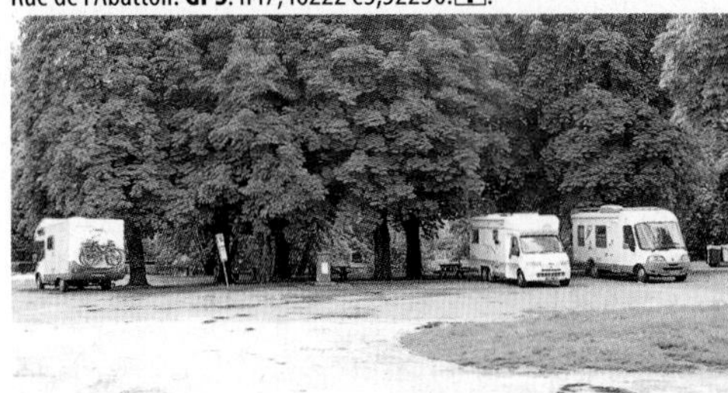

6 free. **Location:** Simple. **Surface:** gravel. 01/01-31/12.
Distance: 350m 150m.

Conliège 22D1

Rue du Saugeois. **GPS:** n46,65270 e5,59981.

2 free ChWCfree. **Location:** Urban, simple.
Surface: asphalted.
Distance: 100m.

Consolation-Maisonnettes 19F3

Parc du Seminaire du Cirque de Consolation., D377.
GPS: n47,15848 e6,60600.

10 € 10/24h Ch WCincluded. **Location:** Rural, simple.
Surface: asphalted.
Distance: on the spot.
Remarks: Check in at shop.

Corravillers 19F2

Rue de la Mairie. **GPS:** n47,89431 e6,62162.

2 free €2/23minutes Chfree €2/23minutes.
Location: Rural, simple. **Surface:** grassy/gravel.
01/01-31/12.
Distance: 500m 500m.

Corre 19E2

Fluvial Loisirs, Pré le Saônier. **GPS:** n47,91402 e5,99308.

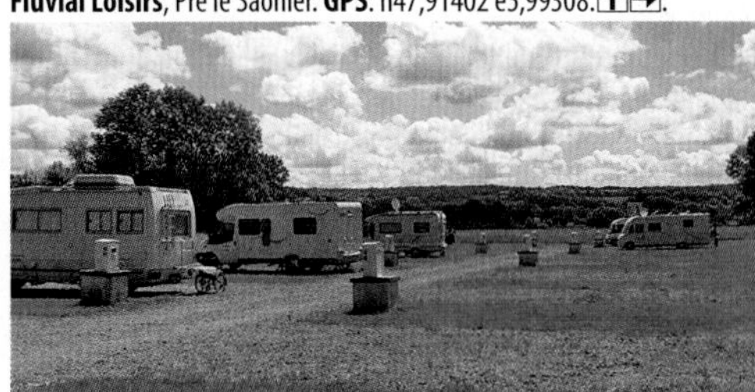

32 € 10 Ch included €4/3 €3/day.
Location: Rural, comfortable, quiet. **Surface:** grassy.
01/01-31/12.
Distance: 200m 50m 50m bakery 300m, supermarket 500m 100m.

Cousance 22D2

Grande rue, Champs de foire. **GPS:** n46,52929 e5,39154.

4 free ChWCfree. **Surface:** asphalted. 01/01-31/12.
Distance: 100m 6,6km 100m.

Crosey-le-Petit 19F3

Rue de begin. **GPS:** n47,35039 e6,48913.

1 free. **Location:** Rural, simple. **Surface:** asphalted/gravel.
01/01-31/12.
Distance: on the spot on the spot.

Digoin 22B2

Place de la Grève, Route de Vichy. **GPS:** n46,48102 e3,97288.

± 15 free (4x) WC. **Location:** Simple, central.
Surface: asphalted. 01/01-31/12.
Distance: on the spot on the spot on the spot on the spot.
Remarks: Next to office de tourisme.

FR

Dijon 19C3

Aire de Dijon, 3, Boulevard Chainoine Kir. **GPS**: n47,32125 e5,01090.

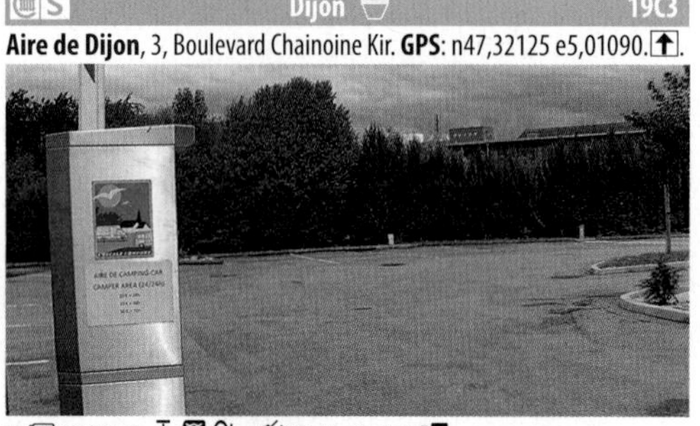

16 € 10/24h Ch (17x)included.
Location: Urban, comfortable, noisy. **Surface:** asphalted.
01/01-31/12 water: frost.
Distance: centre Dijon 1,5km 10km 300m 300m 500m 500m >Dijon 150m 10m.
Remarks: Attention: motorhomes ^3m take access road from southerly direction.

Tourist information Dijon:
Office de Tourisme, 11 Rue des Forges, Place Darcy, www.destinationdijon.com. City worth a visit with a number of large mansions and streets with half-timbered houses.

Dôle 19D3

Parking de Lahr, Avenue de Lahr. **GPS**: n47,08983 e5,49641.

20 free. **Location:** Simple, central, noisy. **Surface:** asphalted.
Village fair: mid-May.
Distance: on the spot on the spot.

Tourist information Dôle:
Maison natale de Louis Pasteur, 43 Rue Pasteur. Birth house Pasteur, museum. 1/4-31/10 10-12h, 14-18h, 01/11-31/03 Sa-Su 14-18h Su-morning.

Ecuisses 22C1

Place Marcel Pagnol, Route du Bourg. **GPS**: n46,76019 e4,52283.

20 free €2 Ch €2.
Location: Simple. **Surface:** metalled.
01/01-31/12.
Remarks: At lake, max. 48h, coins at townhall and bakery.

Esmoulières 19F2

D236. **GPS**: n47,85243 e6,61502.

2 free. **Location:** Rural, simple. **Surface:** asphalted.
01/01-31/12.

Étang-sur-Arroux 22B1

Place du Mousseau. **GPS**: n46,86631 e4,18946.

free Chfree.
Location: Simple. **Surface:** asphalted. 01/01-31/12.
Distance: 100m 100m.

Faucogney-et-la-Mer 19F2

Rue des Chars. **GPS**: n47,83735 e6,56003.

6 free €2/23minutes Chfree €2/20minutes.
Location: Rural, simple. **Surface:** grassy/gravel.
01/01-31/12.
Distance: 800m.

Fontaine-Française 19D3

Rue Berthault. **GPS**: n47,52487 e5,36768.

5 free €3 Ch. **Location:** Rural, simple.
Surface: asphalted/grassy. 01/01-31/12.
Distance: 100m 16km on the spot 250m bakery.
Remarks: Along river and betwee 2 lakes, coins at shops in the village 08-21h.

Fours 22A1

Rue des Saules, D981. **GPS**: n46,81720 e3,71806.

10 free Ch free.
Location: Simple. **Surface:** gravel. 01/01-31/12.
Distance: 200m 200m 200m.

Génelard 22B2

Place du Bassin, D974. **GPS**: n46,57750 e4,23500.

2 free Ch free. **Location:** Simple. **Surface:** asphalted.
01/01-31/12.
Distance: on the spot.

Gilly-sur-Loire 22B2

Le Gatefer. **GPS**: n46,53768 e3,78218.
10 free Chfree. **Surface:** metalled. 01/01-31/12.

Givry 22C1

Relais camping-car, Rue de la Gare. **GPS**: n46,78000 e4,74830.

15 free €2/100liter Ch €2/1h.
Location: Comfortable. **Surface:** asphalted. 01/01-31/12.
Distance: on the spot 300m bakery 300m on the spot on the spot.
Remarks: Coins at restaurant.

Tourist information Givry:
Marché. Market. Thu.
La Voie Verte de Givry à Cluny. Cycle route on former railway,.

Gray 19D3

Rue de la Plage. **GPS**: n47,46045 e5,61874.

12 free Chfree. **Location:** Comfortable.
Surface: grassy/gravel. 01/01-31/12.
Remarks: Near camping municipal.

Gron 19A1

Rue des Petits Prés. **GPS**: n48,16011 e3,25636.
5 free ChWC. **Location:** Simple, quiet. **Surface:** asphalted.
01/01-31/12.

Gurgy 19A2

Quai des Fontaines. **GPS**: n47,86348 e3,55376.

20 €7 Chincluded .
Surface: grassy/gravel. 01/04-31/10.
Distance: 50m 7km on the spot 500m 300m.
Remarks: Along the Yonne river, coins at supermarket.

Heuilley-sur-Saône 19D3

Rue Condé. **GPS**: n47,32800 e5,45471.

20 free €3 ChWC. **Location:** Rural, quiet.
Surface: gravel/sand. 01/01-31/12.
Distance: on the spot 100m 100m.
Remarks: Coins at town hall.

Jeurre 22D2

35, Rue Principale. **GPS**: n46,36662 e5,70769.

FR

40 €5 €2 Ch €2 €3/day. **Location:** Rural, simple. **Surface:** grassy. 01/05-31/10.

La Chapelle des Bois 22E1

Station de ski, Chemin du Marais Blanc. **GPS**: n46,60307 e6,11317.

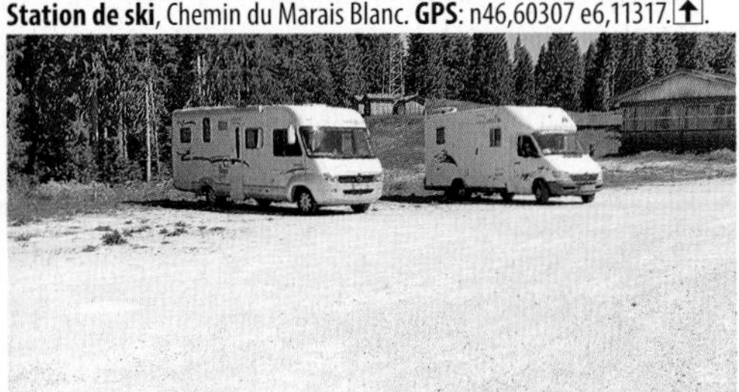

free. **Surface:** unpaved.
Distance: on the spot.

La Chapelle-de-Guinchay 22C2

Le Clos Meziat. **GPS**: n46,21017 e4,76720.

± 10 free ChWCfree. **Location:** Rural, comfortable, quiet. **Surface:** gravel/metalled. 01/01-31/12.
Distance: centre 1,2km A6 10km 1,2km 1,2km.

La Charité-sur-Loire 18H3

Quai de la Tête de l'Ourth. **GPS**: n47,17577 e3,01254.
3 free. **Surface:** asphalted. 01/01-31/12.
Remarks: Parking at river.

La Charité-sur-Loire 18H3

Quai Romain Mollot. **GPS**: n47,17483 e3,01123.

5 free. **Surface:** asphalted. 01/01-31/12.
Distance: 250m on the spot on the spot on the spot on the spot on the spot.
Remarks: Parking at the river, max. 24h.

La Montagne 19F2

D136. **GPS**: n47,92581 e6,58710.

2 free. **Location:** Rural, simple. **Surface:** asphalted. 01/01-31/12.
Remarks: Parking at skipistes.

La Pesse 22E2

Rue de l'Epicéa, D25. **GPS**: n46,28400 e5,84764.

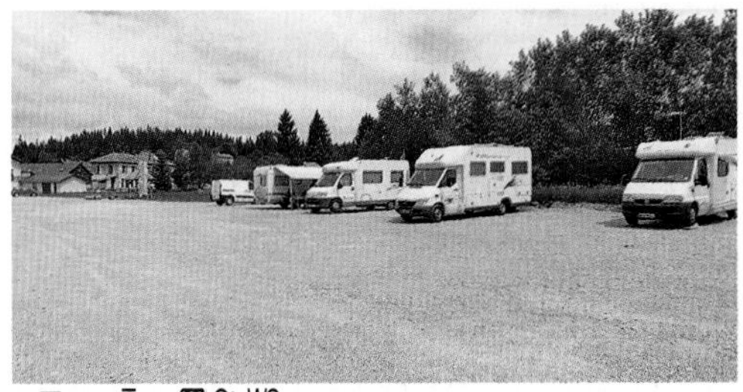

15 free €2 ChWC. **Location:** Rural, simple. **Surface:** unpaved. 01/01-31/12.
Distance: on the spot on the spot.
Remarks: At start of langlauf circuit.

La Pesse 22E2

Ferme Auberge de La Combe aux Bisons, Lieu-dit Pré Reverchon. **GPS**: n46,29278 e5,86011.

3 guests free .
Location: Simple, isolated. 01/01-31/12 Mon, Tue.
Distance: on the spot.

Laignes 19B2

Chemin du Moulin Neuf, D965. **GPS**: n47,84850 e4,36132.

7 free . **Location:** Simple, quiet. **Surface:** grassy. 01/01-31/12.
Distance: 1km on the spot.
Remarks: Parking at river, max. 24h.

Lamoura 22E2

Route de Prémanon, D25. **GPS**: n46,41107 e5,99458.

20 free Chfree WC. **Location:** Rural, simple. **Surface:** asphalted.
Distance: winter on the spot on the spot.
Remarks: Service sportcentre La Serra, only in winter time.

Lamoura 22E2

Route de Prémanon, D25. **GPS**: n46,40139 e5,98561.

6 free .
Distance: on the spot on the spot.

Larochemillay 22B1

Centre Bourg. **GPS**: n46,87793 e4,00155.
4 free Chfree. 01/01-31/12.

Distance: on the spot on the spot.
Remarks: Coins at town hall and restaurant, max. 48h.

Le Vernois 22D1

Caveau des Byards. **GPS**: n46,73342 e5,59405.

2 free.
Location: Urban, simple. **Surface:** grassy/gravel.

Les Rousses 22E2

Parking l'Aube, Route du Lac. **GPS**: n46,48779 e6,06690.

30 free, € 4/Winter €3,60/100liter Ch €3,60/1h .
Location: Simple. **Surface:** asphalted. 01/01-31/12.
Distance: 500m 500m 200m.

Les Rousses 22E2

Porte du Balanciers, Route Blanche, N5. **GPS**: n46,44852 e6,07591.

30 free, € 4/Winter €3,50 Ch WC.
Surface: asphalted.
01/01-31/12.
Distance: Restaurant 5km.
Remarks: Coins at tourist info, ski station, ski rental, ski school.

Louhans 22D1

Halte nautique, Rue du Port. **GPS**: n46,62952 e5,21302.

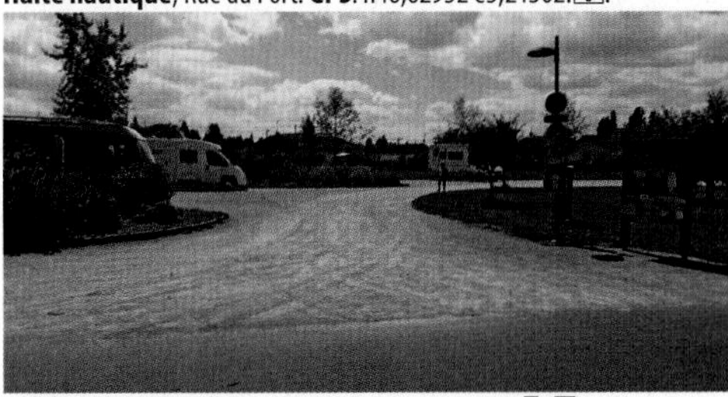

22 free, 01/04-30/09 € 6 + € 0,20/pp tourist tax ChWCincluded. **Location:** Comfortable, quiet. **Surface:** gravel.
Distance: 400m on the spot.
Remarks: To be paid at Halte Nautique, sanitary building: 01/05-30/09.

Luxeuil-les-Bains 19E2

Place de l'Etang de la Poche, Rue Gambetta. **GPS**: n47,81679 e6,38659.

20 free €2/100liter Ch €2/1h. **Location:** Simple, quiet. **Surface:** gravel. 01/01-31/12 Service: winter.

FR

Distance: 1km 100m 1km Auchan/Aldi 500m 1km.
Remarks: Max. 72h, coins at tourist info.

Tourist information Luxeuil-les-Bains:
Fougerolles. Since the 16th century the small town is the centre of distilleries (Kirsch and cherry brandy).

S Luzy 22B1
Place du champ De Foire. **GPS**: n46,79028 e3,96840.

4 free Ch WC free. **Location:** Simple. **Surface:** metalled.
01/01-31/12.
Distance: centre 300m 100m 200m 500m.
Remarks: Max. 48h, coins at the shops and restaurant.

S Mailly-le-Château 19A2
L'espace naturel du Beauvais, Rue du Beauvais.
GPS: n47,59308 e3,63059.
free €3 Ch €3. **Location:** Isolated, quiet.
Surface: grassy. 01/01-31/12.
Distance: 650m.
Remarks: Coins at the shops.

S Maisod 22D2
La Mercantine. **GPS**: n46,46500 e5,68864.

40 €6 €2 Ch.
Location: Rural, simple. **Surface:** gravel.
Distance: 100m 200m.
Remarks: At lake Vouglans, max. 24h.

Marigny-le-Cahouët 19C3
Chemin des Écluses. **GPS**: n47,46370 e4,45598.
free. **Surface:** gravel/metalled. 01/01-31/12.
Distance: 200m bakery 200m on the spot on the spot.
Remarks: At the canal, picnic area.

S Marsannay-la-Côte 19C3
Espace du Rocher, Rue du Rocher. **GPS**: n47,27099 e4,99224.

5 free Ch free. **Location:** Urban, simple, quiet.
Surface: asphalted. 01/01-31/12.
Distance: 500m 3,5km 750m.

Marsannay-la-Côte 19C3
Rue de Mazy, D122. **GPS**: n47,27027 e4,98761.
free. **Surface:** asphalted. 01/01-31/12.
Distance: on the spot 5km.
Remarks: Parking next to Office du Tourisme.

S Marzy 22A1
Aire de camping-cars, Allée des Vignes du Clos.
GPS: n46,97982 e3,09357.
3 free €2 Ch. **Location:** Simple, quiet. **Surface:** asphalted.
01/01-31/12.
Distance: 100m.
Remarks: Max. 72h.

S Mesnay 22E1
Rue Vermot. **GPS**: n46,89834 e5,80036.

5 free €2/10minutes Ch free €2/55minutes.
Location: Simple. 01/01-31/12.
Distance: 500m, 2,5km Arbois.

S Montbéliard 19F3
Parking du Champ de Foire. **GPS**: n47,50663 e6,79128.

4 free €1,60 Ch €1,60. **Location:** Urban.
Surface: asphalted.
Remarks: Max. 48h.

S Montreux-Château 19F2
D11. **GPS**: n47,60283 e7,00252.

8 € 5/24h €5/10minutes Ch (8x) WC included. **Location:** Simple. **Surface:** gravel.

S Moussières 22E2
GPS: n46,32111 e5,89778.

6 free €2 Ch €2. **Location:** Rural, simple. **Surface:** gravel.
01/01-31/12.
Distance: on the spot.
Remarks: In front of cheese farm.

S Mouthe 22E1
Place de l'Eglise. **GPS**: n46,71042 e6,19570.

20 free €3 Ch . **Location:** Rural, simple.
Surface: asphalted.
Remarks: Coins at the bakery, supermarket, tourist office.

S Nolay 22C1
Avenue de la Liberté. **GPS**: n46,95016 e4,62828.

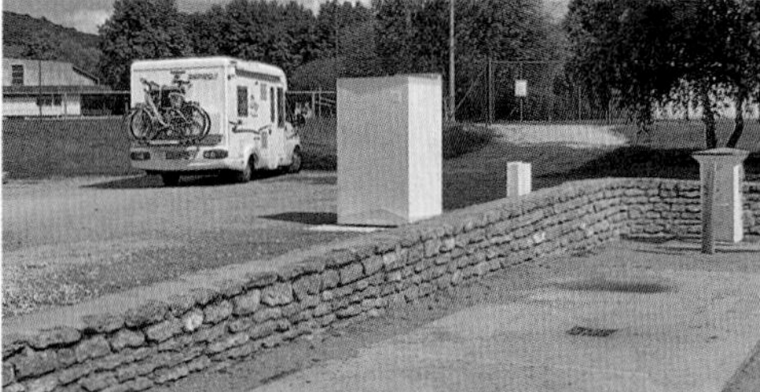

± 10 free €3 Ch €3. **Location:** Urban, simple.
Surface: gravel. 01/01-31/12.
Distance: 100m 300m 300m.
Remarks: Coins at tourist info and town hall.

Tourist information Nolay:
Site Champetre du Bout du Monde, Vauchignon. Water falls.

S Nozeroy 22E1
Rue des Remparts. **GPS**: n46,77249 e6,03516.

10 € 6 Ch included,2Amp. **Location:** Rural, isolated, quiet.
Surface: grassy/gravel. 01/01-31/12.
Distance: 200m.

S Nuits-Saint-Georges 19C3
Rue de Cussigny. **GPS**: n47,13178 e4,95189.

10 free Ch free. **Location:** Urban, simple. **Surface:** asphalted.
01/01-31/12.
Distance: 400m 2,1km 500m Intermarché 300m.

Tourist information Nuits-Saint-Georges:
Fri.

S Orgelet 22D2
Place Ancien Champ de Foire, Rue du Faubourg de l'Orme.
GPS: n46,52232 e5,60860.

20 free Ch WC free. **Location:** Simple.
Surface: grassy/metalled. 01/01-31/12.
Distance: 300m.
Remarks: Closed when frosty.

S Pougues-les-Eaux 19A3
D907. **GPS**: n47,08315 e3,09382.

5 free €2/10minutes Ch €2/10minutes.
Surface: asphalted. 01/01-31/12.

FR

Distance: 250m 1,4km 100m.
Remarks: Coins at campsite and tourist info.

S Prissé 22C2

Vignerons des Terres Secrètes, Les Grandes Vignes.
GPS: n46,32226 e4,75257.

5 free €2 ChWC. **Location:** Rural, simple. **Surface:** gravel.
01/01-31/12.
Distance: 500m 3km.
Remarks: Max. 24h.

S Pruzilly 22C2

La Croix Blanche, salle des Fêtes. GPS: n46,25708 e4,69792.

6 free ChWCfree. **Location:** Rural, simple.
Surface: asphalted. 01/01-31/12.
Distance: on the spot on the spot.
Remarks: Max. 48h, vins de Côte de Beaujolais.

S Quarre-les-Tombes 19B3

Rue des Ecoles. **GPS**: n47,36853 e3,99936.
6 free free. **Surface:** metalled. 01/04-31/10.
Distance: 100m 100m 100m.

S Raddon-et-Chapendu 19F2

GPS: n47,84899 e6,47427.

6 free €2/23minutes €2/23minutes. **Location:** Rural, simple.
Surface: gravel.
Remarks: Near sports fields.

Randevillers 19F3

Rue de la Cote. **GPS**: n47,30944 e6,52707.

3 free. **Location:** Rural. **Surface:** asphalted/gravel.

S Rémilly 22B1

Le Bourg. **GPS**: n46,81995 e3,81171.
4 free Chfree. **Surface:** grassy. 01/01-31/12.
Distance: 200m 200m.
Remarks: Coins at town hall and restaurant, max. 48h.

S Rogny-les-Sept-Écluses 18H2

Quai Sully. **GPS**: n47,74673 e2,88104.
4 free Chfree. **Location:** Simple, quiet. **Surface:** grassy.
01/01-31/12.
Distance: on the spot 350m.
Remarks: At the canal.

S Rouvray 19B3

Place du Champs de foire, D906. **GPS**: n47,42271 e4,10412.

4 free Chfree. **Surface:** metalled.
Distance: on the spot.
Remarks: Max. 48h.

S Saint-Benin-d'Azy 22A1

1 rue François Mitterrand. **GPS**: n47,00381 e3,40113.
3 free Ch free. 01/01-31/12.

Saint-Bresson 19F2

La Rue Saint Bresson. **GPS**: n47,86999 e6,50226.

2. **Location:** Rural, simple. **Surface:** asphalted.

S Saint-Claude 22E2

Avenue de la Libération, D436. **GPS**: n46,38049 e5,85209.

3 free Ch free. **Location:** Urban, simple, noisy.
Surface: asphalted. 01/01-31/12.
Distance: 1km.

Tourist information Saint-Claude:
Tourist town, production of pipes.
Musée du Pipe et Diamant. Pipes and diamond exhibition.
01/06-30/09 9.30-12h, 14-18.30h, 01/10-31/05 14-18h Su.

S Saint-Fargeau 19A2

Rue de Laveau, D18. **GPS**: n47,63968 e3,06999.

10 free ChWCfree. 01/01-31/12.
Distance: 50m 50m.

S Saint-Gengoux-le-National 22C1

GPS: n46,60624 e4,66844.

16 free €3/15minutes Ch €3/50minutes WC .
Location: Simple, quiet. **Surface:** gravel. 01/01-31/12.
Distance: 500m.
Remarks: At former station.

Tourist information Saint-Gengoux-le-National:
La Voie Verte. Cycle route on former railway,.

S Saint-Honoré-les-Bains 22B1

Allée de la Cressonnière. **GPS**: n46,90471 e3,84059.

4 free €2 Ch €2. **Location:** Simple. **Surface:** gravel.
01/01-31/12.
Distance: 300m 300m 50m.
Remarks: Max. 48h, coins at town hall and supermarket.

S Saint-Julien-du-Sault 19A1

Stade Jean Sax, Rue du Stade. **GPS**: n48,02906 e3,30116.
13 free Chfree. 01/01-31/12.

S Saint-Léger-sur-Dheune 22C1

Route de Saint-Bérain. **GPS**: n46,84648 e4,63248.

12 € 7/24h Ch included. 01/01-31/12.
Distance: on the spot.

S Saint-Loup-sur-Semouse 19E2

Rue de Champ de Tir. **GPS**: n47,88643 e6,27051.

4 free €3 Ch. **Surface:** asphalted. 01/03-30/11.
Distance: on the spot 500m on the spot on the spot
on the spot.
Remarks: Behind church, max. 24h.

S Saint-Point-Lac 22E1

Aire d'acceuil pour camping-cars, Rue du lac.
GPS: n46,81268 e6,30375.

40 € 6 10minutes Ch 55minutes WCfree.
Surface: gravel/sand. 01/03-30/11.
Distance: on the spot.
Remarks: Max. 3 nights, no camping activities.

Sainte-Marie-en-Chanois 19F2

Rue de la Lolonge. **GPS**: n47,83663 e6,51216.

FR

5 free. **Location:** Rural, simple. **Surface:** asphalted.

Salins-les-Bains 22E1

Rue de la République, D472. **GPS**: n46,93254 e5,87899.

8 free Ch free. **Location:** Simple. **Surface:** asphalted.
01/01-31/12.
Distance: 50m.
Remarks: Permitted to park/stay overnight on all parkings.

Sancey-le-Grand 19F3

D-31. **GPS**: n47,29040 e6,57742.

2 free.
Location: Rural, simple. **Surface:** gravel. 01/01-31/12.
Distance: 500m.

Sancey-le-Long 19F3

D31/D464. **GPS**: n47,30513 e6,59477.

2 free €2 Ch €2.
Location: Rural, simple. **Surface:** gravel.
Remarks: Coins at supermarket, cafe, centre commercial.

Saulx 19E2

Place de l'Eglise. **GPS**: n47,69620 e6,28030.
€2/100liter €2/2h WC free. **Location:** Simple, quiet.

Savigny-le-Sec 19C3

Rue de la Mare. **GPS**: n47,43365 e5,04607.

10 € 3,50 Ch included WC. **Location:** Rural, simple, isolated, quiet. **Surface:** asphalted/gravel. 01/01-31/12.
Distance: 1,3km bakery 1,3km.

Savoyeux 19D2

Port de plaisance, Rue des Chênes. **GPS**: n47,56270 e5,73971.
4 € 5 Ch €2 WC €2 €1/12h. 01/01-31/12.
Distance: 1km.
Remarks: Pay at harbourmaster.

Semur-en-Auxois 19B3

Avenue Pasteur. **GPS**: n47,49506 e4,34945.

30 free Ch free.
Location: Simple, quiet. **Surface:** asphalted.
01/01-31/12 water: Nov-March.
Distance: historical centre 1,3km 10km 800m 800m.
Remarks: At football ground.

Tourist information Semur-en-Auxois:
Alise-Ste-Reine. Findings of Gallo-Roman city. 01/04-31/10 daily.

Sermamagny 19F2

Rue Alfred Lallemand. **GPS**: n47,68351 e6,81416.

30 free. **Surface:** grassy.

Seurre 22D1

Rue de la Perche à l'Oiseau. **GPS**: n47,00405 e5,14318.

15 free €4,70/20minutes Ch Service €4/20min.
Location: Rural, simple, quiet. **Surface:** asphalted.
01/01-31/12.
Distance: 800m 100m 100m 700m 700m.
Remarks: Camper service 8-20h.

Thoirette 22D2

Grande Rue. **GPS**: n46,26924 e5,53529.

5 € 6 Ch included.
Location: Simple. **Surface:** gravel.
Distance: 25m 50m 25m.

Tournus 22C2

Quai de la Marine. **GPS**: n46,56757 e4,91118.
8 free Ch. **Location:** Urban. **Surface:** metalled.
01/01-31/12.
Distance: 300m 300m 500m 300m.
Remarks: Market Saturday.

Treigny 19A2

Rue du Champ de Foire. **GPS**: n47,54982 e3,18159.
2 free Ch. **Location:** Simple, quiet. **Surface:** asphalted.
01/01-31/12.
Distance: 200m 200m 200m.

Vaivre-et-Montoille 19E2

Avenue des Rives du Lac. **GPS**: n47,62938 e6,12701.

7 free €2,50 Ch. **Location:** Rural, simple, quiet.
Surface: sand. 01/01-31/12.
Distance: 1,5km beach 100m 100m 25m on the spot on the spot.
Remarks: Swimming pool complex, lake.

Vaivre-et-Montoille 19E2

Avenue du Lac. **GPS**: n47,63718 e6,10752.

5 free. **Location:** Rural. **Surface:** asphalted. 01/01-31/12.
Distance: on the spot on the spot on the spot.
Remarks: Directly at lake.

Vellevans 19F3

D464. **GPS**: n47,31042 e6,49139.

2 free. **Location:** Rural. **Surface:** grassy/gravel.

Villers-le-Lac 19F3

Vedettes Panoramiques, Rue du Clos Rondot.
GPS: n47,05948 e6,67195.

8 free €2 Ch free. **Location:** Simple.
Surface: concrete. 01/01-31/12.
Distance: 50m.
Remarks: Small pitches.

Villers-le-Lac 19F3

Bateaux du Saut du Doubs. **GPS**: n47,05500 e6,67000.

50 € 8, free with boat trip €3,50 Ch at ofÔce/shop.
Location: Simple, central. **Surface:** grassy/gravel. 01/04-31/10.
Distance: 100m.
Remarks: Check in at Bateaux.

FR

Vinzelles 22C2

Clos Bonin. **GPS**: n46,27145 e4,77008.

10 free Chfree. **Location:** Rural, simple. **Surface:** asphalted.
01/01-31/12.
Distance: 200m A6 2,8km on the spot on the spot on the spot.

Auvergne-Rhône-Alpes

Aiguebelle 25E1

Pré de foire. **GPS**: n45,54289 e6,30635.

18 free €2/100liter Ch. **Surface:** asphalted/grassy.
01/01-31/12 Thu-morning closed because of market.
Distance: on the spot 6,1km.

Tourist information Aiguebelle:
Tue-morning.

Aigueperse 22A3

Place du Foirail, Rue de la Porte aux Boeufs. **GPS**: n46,02634 e3,20313.

15 free €2/10minutes Ch €2/1h.
Location: Urban, simple, central, quiet. **Surface:** asphalted.
01/01-31/12 17/08-28/08.
Distance: on the spot nearby nearby.
Remarks: Market square.

Aiguilhe 25B2

Avenue de Bonneville. **GPS**: n45,05063 e3,88356.

6 free. **Location:** Urban, simple, central. **Surface:** asphalted.
01/01-31/12.
Distance: on the spot 350m.
Remarks: Max. 24h.

Aix-les-Bains 22E3

Avenue du Grand Port. **GPS**: n45,70504 e5,88810.

16 free free WC. **Location:** Urban, simple, noisy. **Surface:** gravel.
01/01-31/12.
Distance: city centre 2km 2km Lake 100m 150m bread service 500m on the spot.
Remarks: Max. 48h, market Wednesday and Saturday.

Aix-les-Bains 22E3

Camping-Car Park, Rue des Goélands. **GPS**: n45,69627 e5,88926.
77 € 13 Ch (52x) €5/3 included.
Surface: grassy. 01/01-31/12.
Distance: 500m on the spot 200m 500m 200m.
Remarks: At lake.

Alba-la-Romaine 25C3

Bragigous. **GPS**: n44,55329 e4,59741.

35 € 4 €2 Ch. **Location:** Rural, quiet. **Surface:** grassy/gravel.
01/01-31/12.
Distance: on the spot 200m 200m.
Remarks: Service to be paid at retirement home.

Albertville 22F3

Parking Conflans, Montée Adolphe Hugues, Conflans.
GPS: n45,67389 e6,39694.
6 free €3,50 Ch. **Surface:** asphalted.
Distance: 10 min walking.

Tourist information Albertville:
Quai des Allobroges. Thu 6-18h.

Allanche 24H1

Aire de la Gare, Chemin de la Roche Marchal.
GPS: n45,23000 e2,93139.

25 free €2 Ch. **Location:** Rural, simple, quiet.
Surface: gravel/sand. 01/05-30/09, parking 01/01-31/12.
Distance: 300m 300m 300m.
Remarks: Altitude 1000m, coins at camping, tourist info and town hall, accessed via Allanche centre.

Allevard 25E1

Place du David. **GPS**: n45,38838 e6,07110.
+10 € 4 ChWCfree. **Location:** Rural. **Surface:** unpaved.
01/01-31/12.
Distance: 500m 300m.
Remarks: Max. 48h.

Alpe d'Huez 25E2

Parking de Brandes. **GPS**: n45,08654 e6,07916.

75 € 10/day + € 0,40/pp tourist tax Ch WC.
Surface: asphalted.
Distance: 1km on the spot.
Remarks: First buy a parking ticket at Palais des Sports et des Congrès.

Alpe d'Huez 25E2

Parking l'Eclose, Rue du 93me Ram. **GPS**: n45,08796 e6,07019.
25 € 10/day + € 0,20/pp tourist tax Ch WCincluded.
Surface: asphalted.
01/12-01/04, 11/07-31/08.
Distance: 200m 200m 200m on the spot.
Remarks: First buy a parking ticket at Palais des Sports et des Congrès.

Ambierle 22B2

Complexe sportif, Rue Sainte Claude. **GPS**: n46,10663 e3,89384.

3 free Chfree. **Location:** Rural, simple, quiet.
Surface: asphalted. 01/01-31/12.
Distance: on the spot 200m 300m.
Remarks: At sports park.

Amplepuis 22B3

Rue Paul de la Goutte. **GPS**: n45,97027 e4,33085.
free Chfree. **Surface:** asphalted.
Distance: on the spot 50m 100m on the spot.
Remarks: Behind gymnasium.

Annecy 22E3

Parking de Colmyr, Rue des Marquisats, N1508.
GPS: n45,89070 e6,13915.

14 free Chfree.
Location: Urban, simple, central, quiet. **Surface:** asphalted.
01/01-31/12.
Distance: 700m 100m on the spot 700m 700m.
Remarks: Max. 24h, market days Tuesday, Friday, Sunday.

Tourist information Annecy:
Office de Tourisme, Bonlieu, 1 rue Jean Jaurès, www.lac-annecy.com. Located on lake of the same name and surrounded by mountain peaks. The old city centre exists of covered lanes, canals and bridges.
Place de Romains. Tue 7-19h.

Anse 22C3

Cave Saint Cyr, 31 chemin de Trechen. **GPS**: n45,93169 e4,68623.
4 free Ch . **Location:** Rural. **Surface:** gravel/metalled.
01/01-31/12.

Anthy-sur-Léman 22F2

Rue du Lac. **GPS**: n46,35889 e6,42192.

FR

5 free. **Surface:** gravel.
Distance: 700m 50m on the spot.
Remarks: Max. 48h, max. 7m.

S Archignat 21H2

Rue des Chalets. **GPS**: n46,37336 e2,42408.
5 €5 + €0,20/pp tourist tax €2 Ch €3 WC.
Location: Quiet. **Surface:** grassy/gravel.
Distance: on the spot.

S Arçon 22B3

Le Bourg. **GPS**: n46,00977 e3,88793.

3 free Chfree. **Location:** Rural, simple, quiet.
01/01-31/12.
Distance: on the spot 50m.

S Arlanc 25A1

Loumans. **GPS**: n45,41233 e3,71782.

+10 free €2 Ch. **Location:** Rural, simple, quiet.
Surface: asphalted/grassy. 01/04-31/10.
Distance: 500m on the spot 100m 1km on the spot.
Remarks: At swimming pool and small lake, coins at tourist info.

S Arlebosc 25C2

Place du Marché aux Fruits. **GPS**: n45,03683 e4,65238.

10 free Chfree. **Location:** Rural, simple. **Surface:** gravel.
01/01-31/12.
Distance: on the spot bakery 150m on the spot.

S Arnac (Cantal) 24G2

Aire camping-cars, RD61. **GPS**: n45,06056 e2,23389.

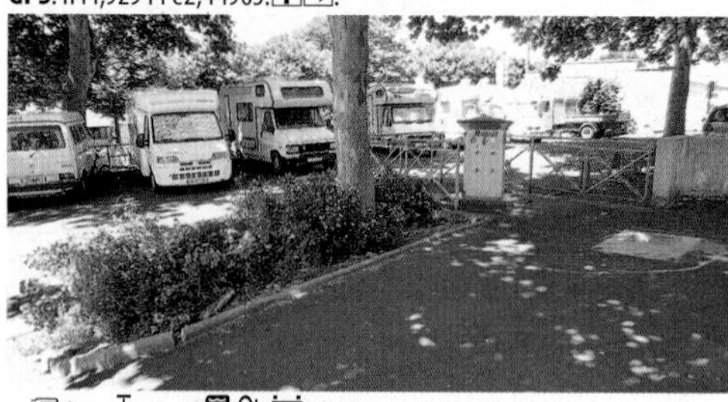

2 free €2/100liter Ch €2/1h. **Location:** Rural, simple, quiet. **Surface:** grassy/gravel. 01/01-31/12.
Distance: 50m 150m 150m.

S Aubignas 25C3

Aire camping-cars. GPS: n44,58732 e4,63177.

10 voluntary contribution €2 €2/100liter ChWC.
Surface: gravel.
Distance: 300m.
Remarks: Beautiful view.

S Aubusson-d'Auvergne 22A3

Base de Loisirs-lac d'Aubusson. GPS: n45,75377 e3,61079.

50 €6 ChWC free.
Location: Rural, simple, isolated, quiet. **Surface:** metalled.
01/01-31/12.
Distance: on the spot on the spot 200m 8km on the spot.

S Aurec-sur-Loire 25B1

Place de la Gare. **GPS**: n45,37164 e4,19919.

3 free Chfree. **Location:** Urban, simple, central, quiet.
Surface: gravel/sand. 01/01-31/12.
Distance: 450m 450m 500m 50m.
Remarks: At station, max. 48h.

S Aurillac 24G2

Place du Champ de Foire, Cours d'Angoulême.
GPS: n44,92944 e2,44963.

10 free €3,50 Ch €3,50.
Location: Urban, simple, noisy. **Surface:** asphalted.
01/01-31/12 service: 31/10-01/05.
Distance: on the spot 100m 100m.
Remarks: Max. 24h, coins at tourist info.

Tourist information Aurillac:
European street theatre and festival. 3rd week Aug.

S Avermes 22A1

Avenue des Isles. **GPS**: n46,58611 e3,30667.
3 free €2 ChWC. **Surface:** metalled. 01/01-31/12.
Remarks: At sports centre.

S Aydat 21H3

Aire camping-cars. GPS: n45,66025 e2,97778.

41 €9,50/24h Ch (28x)WC included.
Location: Rural, comfortable, quiet. **Surface:** grassy.
01/01-31/12.
Distance: 200m on the spot on the spot on the spot 250m.
Remarks: Former campsite, max. 8,20m.

Balazuc 25B3

Parking Champsgelly, La Croisette. **GPS**: n44,50601 e4,37366.

free. **Location:** Rural. **Surface:** gravel. 01/01-31/12.
Distance: 1km.

S Banne 25B3

Quartier l'Eglise, D251. **GPS**: n44,36539 e4,15691.

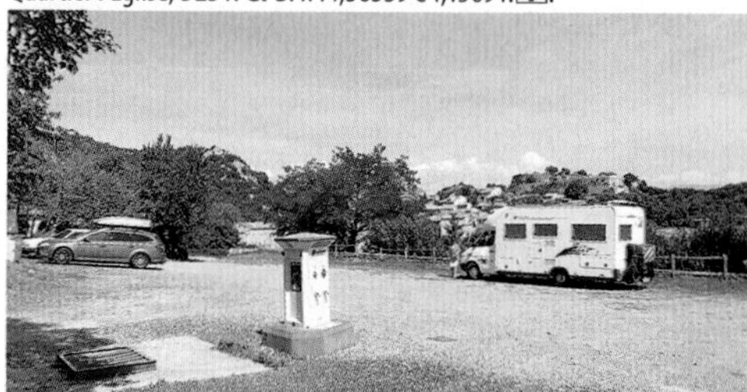

25 free €3/60liter Ch €3/1h. **Surface:** gravel/metalled.
01/01-31/12.
Distance: 500m.
Remarks: Behind church, beautiful view.

S Barjac 25B3

Rue Pierre Andre Benoit. **GPS**: n44,30589 e4,34343.

20 free Ch €3,water 10min+electricity 55min.
Location: Simple.
01/01-31/12.
Distance: 100m 100m on the spot.
Remarks: Coins at tourist info and town hall, friday market.

S Beaulieu 25B2

Lous Saux. **GPS**: n45,12662 e3,94799.

5 free Ch (2x)free. **Location:** Rural, simple, quiet.
Surface: gravel. 01/04-31/10 service 01/11-31/03.
Distance: 800m 300m on the spot on the spot.
Remarks: Max. 48h.

Beaulon 22A1

Écluse de Beaulon, La Curesse. **GPS**: n46,60443 e3,65840.

+10 free Ch (10x)free. **Location:** Rural, simple, isolated, quiet. **Surface:** gravel. 01/01-31/12.
Distance: 1,2km Canal on the spot 1,2km 1,2km on the spot on the spot.

Beausemblant 25C1

Drôme des Collines, Rue des Glycines, D122.
GPS: n45,21826 e4,83282.

4 free Chfree. **Location:** Simple. **Surface:** gravel.
01/01-31/12.
Distance: 100m 100m on the spot.
Remarks: Max. 48h.

Beauzac 25B1

Espace La Dorlière, D42. **GPS**: n45,26161 e4,10170.

8 free Chfree. **Location:** Rural, simple, quiet.
Surface: gravel/sand. 15/04-31/10.
Distance: 250m 300m.

Bellerive-sur-Allier 22A2

Riv'Air Camp, Rue Claude Decloitre. **GPS**: n46,11514 e3,43114.

39 € 10 Ch (50x)WC included. **Location:** Urban, comfortable, isolated, quiet. **Surface:** metalled. 01/01-31/12.
Distance: 2,5km 17km on the spot on the spot on the spot 800m.
Remarks: Along the Allier river.

Belleville 22C2

Ancienne Avenue du Port. **GPS**: n46,10626 e4,75470.

8 free Chfree. **Surface:** asphalted. 01/01-31/12.
Distance: centre 500m A6 900m 500m 500m.

Belley 22D3

Route de Saint-Germain, D41. **GPS**: n45,75535 e5,67790.

20 free €2 Ch €2. **Location:** Urban, simple, central, quiet.
Surface: asphalted. 01/01-31/12.
Distance: city centre 1km 1km 1km 1km.
Remarks: Near sports park, service only with 1-euro coins.

Belleydoux 22E2

Relais Flot Bleu, Route Principale. **GPS**: n46,25556 e5,77994.
free €2 Ch €2/20minutes. 01/01-31/12.

Belmont-de-la-Loire 22B2

Place de l'Église. **GPS**: n46,16543 e4,34634.

2 free Ch WC. **Location:** Rural, simple, quiet.
Surface: metalled. 03/03-19/07, 01/08-31/10.
Distance: 50m 100m 100m on the spot.

Bibost 22C3

D91. **GPS**: n45,79500 e4,55144.
free Ch free. **Location:** Rural, quiet. **Surface:** gravel.
01/01-31/12.
Remarks: Beautiful view.

Billy 22A2

Rue de la Fontaine. **GPS**: n46,23586 e3,43044.

free Chfree. **Surface:** asphalted. 01/01-31/12.
Distance: on the spot.
Remarks: Max. 48h.

Blesle 25A1

Route du Babory, D8. **GPS**: n45,31733 e3,17424.

6 free. **Location:** Rural, simple, quiet. **Surface:** gravel/sand.
01/01-31/12.
Distance: 300m 300m 300m on the spot.
Remarks: Max. 2 nights, service at camping municipal.

Blesle 25A1

Hôtel-Restaurant Le Scorpion, Le Basbory, D909.
GPS: n45,31219 e3,18677.

25 € 12,50 Ch (8x)WC included. **Location:** Rural, comfortable, quiet. **Surface:** grassy. 01/01-31/12.
Distance: 5,8km on the spot on the spot.

Boën 22B3

Boulevard Moizieux. **GPS**: n45,74401 e4,00263.

free Chfree. **Surface:** gravel. 01/01-31/12.
Distance: 200m 200m 300m.

Boulieu-lès-Annonay 25C1

Chemin du Lavoir. **GPS**: n45,26928 e4,66963.

6 free ChWCfree. **Location:** Rural, comfortable, quiet.
Surface: gravel.
Distance: 400m 400m 400m.
Remarks: Voluntary contribution, market on Sunday.

Bourg-en-Bresse 22D2

Parking V.L./Bus, Boulevard de Brou. **GPS**: n46,19854 e5,23766.

10 free WC100m. **Location:** Urban, simple, central, noisy.
Surface: asphalted. Wed, Sa.
Distance: on the spot 6km 100m 200m on the spot on the spot.

Bourg-Saint-Andéol 25C3

Chemin de la Barrière. **GPS**: n44,37520 e4,64327.

30 free Ch free. **Surface:** asphalted. 01/01-31/12.
Distance: 750m 50m Lidl.
Remarks: Along railwayline, max. 48h.

Bourg-Saint-Maurice 25F1

Arc1600. **GPS**: n45,59523 e6,78951.
20 €2 Ch €2. 01/01-31/12.
Distance: Bourg St.Maurice 15km.

FR

Bourget-du-Lac 22E3

International au l'Lle de Cygnes. **GPS**: n45,65250 e5,86378.

32 € 6,20-12,50 Ch WC included.
Location: Rural, comfortable, quiet. **Surface:** metalled.
01/01-31/12 service: 01/12-01/03.
Distance: 500m 500m beach 300m 100m on the spot on the spot 100m on the spot on the spot.

Bourgneuf 25E1

Aire camping-cars, D925. **GPS**: n45,55257 e6,21091.

30 free €2 Ch. 01/01-31/12.
Distance: 5km Brasserie/Pizzeria bakery.
Remarks: Coins available at Pizzeria/Tabac.

Bouvante 25D2

Village de Font d'Urle, Font d'Urle. **GPS**: n44,89789 e5,32195.

10 free €2/100liter Ch (5x)€7/24h WC €2.
Location: Simple, quiet. **Surface:** gravel. 15/05-30/09.
Distance: on the spot nordic walking on the spot.
Remarks: Altitude 1550m, coins at riding school.

Brioude 25A1

Parking Centre Historique, Avenue de Lamothe, D588.
GPS: n45,29444 e3,38778.

30 free €2 Ch €2. **Location:** Urban, simple, central, quiet.
Surface: asphalted/gravel. 01/01-31/12.
Distance: 100m 100m 100m on the spot.
Remarks: Coins at tourist info(100m).

Tourist information Brioude:
L'aquarium-la Maison du Saumon et de la Rivière, Place de la Résistance. Museum about the salmon. 01/04-30/11.

Calvinet 24G2

Aire de Calvinet, Terrain de sport. **GPS**: n44,71023 e2,35914.

6 free €2 Ch €2. **Location:** Rural, simple, quiet.
Surface: gravel. 01/01-31/12 service 01/11-31/03.
Distance: 1,5km 1,5km 1,5km.
Remarks: Nearby sports ground.

Cassaniouze 24G2

Aire camping-cars, Le Bourg. **GPS**: n44,69347 e2,38233.

6 free €2/80liter Ch €2/1h €1.
Location: Rural, simple, quiet. **Surface:** gravel.
01/01-31/12 service 01/11-31/03.
Distance: 600m 600m 600m.

Cayrols 24G2

Aire camping-cars, La Devèze, D51. **GPS**: n44,83000 e2,23278.

10 free €3,80 Ch €3,80 WC.
Location: Rural, comfortable, quiet. **Surface:** metalled.
01/01-31/12 service 01/11-31/03.
Distance: 100m 200m.
Remarks: Max. 1 week, coins at the shops in the village and petrol station.

Chalmazel 22B3

Le Bourg Le Pont d'Ouest. **GPS**: n45,70149 e3,85459.

8 free €2 Ch €2/4h. **Location:** Comfortable.
Surface: metalled. 01/01-31/12.
Distance: 50m on the spot 50m 50m on the spot on the spot 2km.
Remarks: Along river.

Chambéry 25E1

Rue Costa de Beauregard. **GPS**: n45,56289 e5,93302.
6 free Ch free.
Location: Urban. **Surface:** asphalted.
Distance: 500m 1,2km 500m 500m.
Remarks: Water closed during wintertime.

Tourist information Chambéry:
Vieux Cité. Historical centre with old mansions.
Château des Ducs de Savoie. Complex of buildings, 13-14th century.

Chambon-sur-Lac 24H1

Camping Les Bombes, La Vergne. **GPS**: n45,56991 e2,90176.

30 €7 €3 Ch. **Location:** Rural, simple, quiet.
Surface: grassy/gravel. 01/01-31/12 service: 15/09-01/05.
Distance: 500m 200m 1km 500m 500m bakery on the spot on the spot.
Remarks: Pay and coins at campsite.

Chamonix-Mont-Blanc 22F3

Parking Grépon, Aiguille du Midi, D1506. **GPS**: n45,91578 e6,86970.

50 € 12,50/24h Ch WC free. **Surface:** asphalted.
01/01-31/12, service only during summer period.
Distance: 1km 350m 600m.

Tourist information Chamonix-Mont-Blanc:
Aiguille du Midi. Telpher carrier from Chamonix (1036 m.) To Aiguille de Midi (3842m).
Montenvers et mer de Glace. Tramline from Montenvers to the ice lake, a glacier of 7 km long and 1.2 km broad.

Champagnac 24G1

D12. **GPS**: n45,35806 e2,39929.

4 free Ch WC free. **Location:** Simple, quiet.
Surface: asphalted.
Distance: on the spot on the spot.

Champeix 25A1

Champeix, Route de Montaigut, D996. **GPS**: n45,58845 e3,11568.

20 free €2 Ch. **Location:** Rural, simple, isolated, quiet.
Surface: grassy/gravel. 01/04-31/10.
Distance: 1,3km 1,3km 500m.

Champoly 22B3

La Péniche, Chemin de la salle des fêtes. **GPS**: n45,85583 e3,83227.
2 free €2 Ch €2 WC . 01/01-31/12.

Chamrousse 25E2

Place des Niverolles, Rue de la Cembraie. **GPS**: n45,12666 e5,87356.

FR

12 €8 Ch included. **Surface:** asphalted. 01/01-31/12.
Distance: 400m 400m 400m.
Remarks: Max. 24h.

S Chanaleilles 25A2

Le Bourg. **GPS**: n44,85971 e3,49052.

5 free Ch WC free. **Location:** Rural, simple, isolated, quiet.
Surface: asphalted. 01/01-31/12.
Distance: 500m 400m on the spot.

S Chanteuges 25A2

Ancienne Gare. **GPS**: n45,07234 e3,53005.

6 free Ch free. **Location:** Rural, simple, isolated, quiet.
Surface: gravel. 01/01-31/12.
Distance: 200m.
Remarks: Max. 8M.

S Charbonnières-les-Varennes 21H3

Route de Saint-Georges, Paugnat. **GPS**: n45,88457 e2,97993.

10 free €2/10minutes Ch €2/55minutes.
Location: Rural, comfortable, quiet.
Surface: grassy.
01/01-31/12.
Distance: 500m bakery 500m on the spot.
Remarks: Coins at the shops in the village, trail to volcano crater.

S Charix 22D2

Auberge du Lac Genin. **GPS**: n46,21981 e5,69556.

20 € 5 + € 0,20/pp tourist taks, guests free Ch free.
Location: Rural, simple, isolated, quiet. **Surface:** gravel.
01/05-30/09.
Distance: 4,7km lake on the spot on the spot on the spot on the spot.

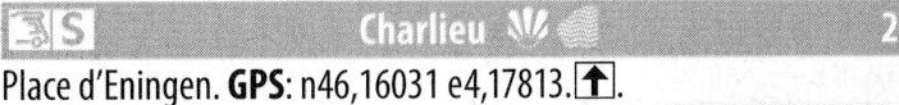

S Charlieu 22B2

Place d'Eningen. **GPS**: n46,16031 e4,17813.

5 free Ch WC free. **Location:** Rural. **Surface:** gravel/metalled.
01/01-31/12.
Distance: historical centre 500m 500m 500m.
Remarks: In front of police station.

S Charols 25C3

Aire municipale, D9. **GPS**: n44,59160 e4,95441.

10 free free. **Surface:** asphalted. 01/01-31/12.
Distance: 200m 200m 50m.

S Chaspuzac 25A2

Aérodrome du Puy-en-Velay, Rue du Vol à Voile.
GPS: n45,07491 e3,76131.

4 free €2 Ch. **Location:** Rural, simple, quiet.
Surface: asphalted. 01/01-31/12 service 01/11-28/02.
Distance: 50m on the spot.
Remarks: View on airport.

S Chastreix 24H1

Parking Station de Ski, Chastreix Sancy. **GPS**: n45,53507 e2,77695.

14 free Ch €9,(winter) WC €2,(winter).
Location: Rural, simple, quiet. **Surface:** metalled.
01/01-31/12.
Distance: Chastreix 6km on the spot.
Remarks: Check in between 9-17h.

S Château-sur-Allier 21H1

Domaine Fessebois. **GPS**: n46,76379 e3,02714.
4 free €3 Ch. **Location:** Rural, simple, isolated, quiet.
Surface: gravel. 01/01-31/12.
Remarks: Picnic area.

S Châtel-Guyon 21H3

Place de la Musique Nationale. **GPS**: n45,92324 e3,06590.

7 € 5/day €2 Ch WC. **Location:** Urban, comfortable, central, quiet. **Surface:** asphalted. 01/01-31/12.
Distance: nearby 400m 400m on the spot.
Remarks: Check in at police station, coins at tourist info.

Châtel-Guyon 21H3

Parking des Roches, Chemin de Bussane.
GPS: n45,91789 e3,06545.

10 free. **Location:** Urban, simple, quiet. **Surface:** asphalted.
01/01-31/12.
Distance: 500m 600m 600m.

Châtel-Guyon 21H3

Pré Morand, Avenue de Russie. **GPS**: n45,91713 e3,05724.
free. **Surface:** gravel. 01/01-31/12.
Remarks: Next to spa resort.

S Chaudes-Aigues 24H2

Parking Beauredon, Avenue Georges Pompidou, D921.
GPS: n44,84972 e3,00306.

10 free €2 Ch €2/55minutes. **Location:** Urban, simple, quiet. **Surface:** gravel. 15/04-15/10.
Distance: 400m 400m 400m on the spot.

Tourist information Chaudes-Aigues:
Office de Tourisme, 1, avenue Georges Pompidou, www.chaude-saigues.com. Small town with warm thermal sources (82°C).

S Chevagnes 22A1

Route Nationale. **GPS**: n46,61028 e3,55219.
4 free €2 Ch €2. **Location:** Comfortable, isolated, quiet.
Surface: gravel. 01/01-31/12.
Distance: on the spot 200m.

S Chichilianne 25D2

Passière. **GPS**: n44,81226 e5,57532.

free €3 Ch. **Surface:** grassy.
01/01-31/12 water disconnected in winter.
Distance: on the spot on the spot.
Remarks: Coins at town hall or Maison du Parc.

S Chomelix 25B1

Centre Multi Activités Chomelix, Route d'Estables, D135.
GPS: n45,26219 e3,82573.

5 free €4 Ch. **Location:** Rural, simple, quiet. **Surface:** gravel.
01/01-31/12.
Distance: on the spot on the spot on the spot on the spot.

S Clansayes 25C3

Aire de Toronne, Quartier Toronne RD133.
GPS: n44,36975 e4,79901.

25 € 10, 2 pers. incl., dog € 1,50 Ch €4/day WC €4.
Location: Rural, comfortable, luxurious, isolated, quiet.
Surface: grassy/gravel. 01/01-31/12.
Distance: 2km 10km buvette-menu rapide-restauration 3km.
Remarks: Bread-service, regional products, swimming pool (summer).

S Clermont Ferrand 22A3

P&R Les Pistes, Rue de la Fontaine de la Ratte.
GPS: n45,79810 e3,11222.

6 € 5 Chfree. **Location:** Urban. **Surface:** asphalted.
01/01-31/12.
Distance: historical centre 3km 50m.
Remarks: Nearby Michelin museum, check in at parking attendant.

S Colombier-le-Jeune 25C2

Place de la Marie, Le Bourg. **GPS**: n45,01106 e4,70132.

free Chfree. **Location:** Rural. **Surface:** metalled.
01/01-31/12 water disconnected in winter.
Distance: on the spot on the spot on the spot on the spot.

S Coltines 24H2

D40. **GPS**: n45,09612 e2,98555.

5 free €2/100liter Ch €2/60minutes.
Location: Rural, simple, quiet. **Surface:** gravel.
15/04-15/10.
Distance: 400m 400m 400m.
Remarks: Coins at Epicerie-Presse, Centre Chantarisa and town hall.

S Condat 24H1

Parking au Pont, D678. **GPS**: n45,33889 e2,76250.

4 free Service€2,50 Ch. **Location:** Simple.
Surface: asphalted. 01/01-31/12 service: 01/10-01/05.
Distance: 50m 10m 50m.
Remarks: Coins at campsite La Borie Basse (500m).

S Cornas 25C2

Impasse de Iris, Grande Rue, D86. **GPS**: n44,96024 e4,84722.

5 free Chfree. **Location:** Simple. **Surface:** gravel.
01/01-31/12.
Distance: 200m 200m bakery 200m.
Remarks: Max. 48h, several 'Caves' with wine tasting.

S Coubon 25B2

Route du Plan d'Eau. **GPS**: n44,99735 e3,91742.

5 free €3 ChWC. **Surface:** asphalted.
01/01-31/12 water disconnected in winter.
Remarks: Along Loire river, key service at supermarket Vival and bar/tabac 75m.

S Coucouron 25B2

Les Eygades. **GPS**: n44,80168 e3,96148.

33 01/05-30/09 € 8/day Ch included. **Location:** Rural, simple. **Surface:** gravel. 01/01-31/12.
Distance: 1km on the spot on the spot 1km on the spot.
Remarks: At Lac de Coucouron, max. 7 days, outside season free stay on campsite municipal (no facilities).

S Cournon d'Auvergne 22A3

Les Pres des Laveuses, Rue de Laveuses. **GPS**: n45,73994 e3,22225.
10 € 5 €2,30 Chfree. **Location:** Rural, simple. **Surface:** gravel.
01/01-31/12.
Distance: on the spot on the spot on the spot.

S Cours-la-Ville 22B2

La Rivière. **GPS**: n46,10399 e4,32315.

10 free Chfree. **Location:** Rural, simple.
Surface: grassy/gravel. 01/01-31/12.
Distance: 300m on the spot on the spot on the spot.
Remarks: Along the river Trambouze, to be reached from northern direction, Boulevard Pierre de Coubertin.

Courtenay 22D3

Etang de Salette. **GPS**: n45,72417 e5,37124.

7 free. **Location:** Rural, isolated, quiet. **Surface:** gravel.
Distance: 1km Pizzeria bread service 1,2km on the spot.

S Crandelles 24G2

Aire camping-cars, Lac des Genevrières. **GPS**: n44,95877 e2,34289.

10 free €3,50 Ch. **Location:** Comfortable, central, quiet.
Surface: gravel. 01/01-31/12 service: 01/11-01/04.
Distance: 300m 50m 50m 50m 300m.

S Craponne-sur-Arzon 25B1

Place de la Gare. **GPS**: n45,33381 e3,84996.

+20 free €2 Ch €2/h.
Location: Urban, simple, quiet. **Surface:** asphalted/gravel.
01/01-31/12 service 01/11-31/03.
Distance: 150m 150m on the spot.

S Crémieu 22D3

Rue du 19 mars 1962. **GPS**: n45,72549 e5,24670.

12 free Chfree. **Location:** Urban, simple, central.
Surface: asphalted. 01/01-31/12.
Distance: 300m 250m 300m 100m.

S Crest 25C2

Place du Champ de Mars, Avenue Agirond. **GPS**: n44,72600 e5,02100.

FR

17 €5 €3 Ch €3 free. **Location:** Urban, simple.
Surface: asphalted. 01/01-31/12.
Distance: 200m pizzeria bakery 50m.

Cros-de-Géorand 25B2

Lac de la Palisse. GPS: n44,78041 e4,10356.
6 €8,40 Ch (4x) included. 01/01-31/12.

Die 25D2

Aire de Meyrosse, Avenue du Maréchal Leclerc, D238.
GPS: n44,75103 e5,37385.

30 €5/24h ChWCfree.
Surface: grassy/gravel. 01/01-31/12.
Distance: 300m 300m 1km.
Remarks: Max. 1 night, pay at Police Municipale.

Diou 22B2

Camping du Gué de Loire, Chemin de la Procession.
GPS: n46,53523 e3,74401.
6 free, 15/06-30/09 €5 Ch. **Surface:** grassy.
01/01-31/12.

Dompierre-sur-Besbre 22A2

Les Gauffroux. GPS: n46,51967 e3,67907.
7 free Ch free. 01/01-31/12.
Distance: on the spot 300m 200m.

Donzère 25C3

Aire de respos de Combelonge, RN 7.
GPS: n44,44060 e4,71899.

15 free ChWCfree. **Surface:** asphalted. 01/01-31/12.
Distance: 500m 7km.
Remarks: Near RN7.

Drugeac 24G1

Aire de camping-cars, La Gare SNCF. **GPS:** n45,16694 e2,38667.

4 free €2/100liter Ch €2/1h.
Location: Rural, simple, quiet. **Surface:** asphalted.
01/01-31/12 service: 01/11-01/05.
Distance: 100m 100m 100m.
Remarks: At former station, now start Vélorail.

Ebreuil 21H2

Parking du Stade, D915. **GPS:** n46,10954 e3,07606.

10 free. **Location:** Simple. **Surface:** gravel. 01/01-31/12.
Distance: 6,5km.
Remarks: In front of campsite municipal, service 500m.

Ebreuil 21H2

Chemin des Nières. **GPS:** n46,11083 e3,08111.
Chfree. 01/01-31/12.
Remarks: Overnight stay on Parking du Stade.

Estivareilles 21H2

Salle Polyvalente, Rue de la République.
GPS: n46,42471 e2,61529.

20 free Chfree. **Location:** Urban, simple. **Surface:** gravel.
01/01-31/12.
Distance: on the spot 9km 200m bakery 200m.

Eyzin-Pinet 25C1

Rue du Stade. **GPS:** n45,47463 e4,99965.

6 free Chfree. **Location:** Rural, simple, central, quiet.
Surface: gravel. 01/01-31/12.
Distance: 50m 50m 20m on the spot on the spot.

Faverges 22E3

Route d'Annecy, D2508. **GPS:** n45,74943 e6,28626.

20 free Chfree. **Location:** Rural, simple, noisy.
Surface: gravel. 01/01-31/12 Service: winter.
Distance: 800m 800m on the spot 100m 100m.
Remarks: Max. 48h, market Wednesday.

Faverolles 25A2

Place de la mairie, Le Bourg, D248. **GPS:** n44,93906 e3,14756.

4 free €2/10minutes Ch €2/55minutes.
Location: Urban, simple. **Surface:** gravel/metalled.
01/01-31/12.

Distance: 200m 200m on the spot.

Flaine 22F3

Parking P1. GPS: n46,00377 e6,69083.

25 €5. **Surface:** gravel. 01/01-31/12.
Distance: on the spot.
Remarks: Parking at skipistes.

Fontanes 25C1

Hameau Chantemerle. **GPS:** n45,54681 e4,44027.

3 free Chfree. **Location:** Rural, simple, quiet.
Surface: asphalted. 01/01-31/12.
Distance: 500m 13km 400m.
Remarks: At tennis-courts, inclining pitches.

Gervans 25C2

Place des Amandiers, Rue de l'école. **GPS:** n45,10932 e4,83031.

4 free Chfree. **Location:** Simple. **Surface:** gravel.
Distance: on the spot on the spot on the spot.
Remarks: Max. 24h, no camping activities.

Grane 25C2

Domaine Distaise, D104. **GPS:** n44,75564 e4,86768.

15 €2/pp . **Surface:** grassy. 01/01-31/12.

Gresse-en-Vercors 25D2

D8D, La Ville. **GPS:** n44,89184 e5,54766.

free Ch. **Surface:** gravel.
Distance: on the spot.
Remarks: Max. 24h, service on campsite.

Hauteluce 22F3

Parking de la Fôret, Tetras, D123. **GPS:** n45,74633 e6,53441.

FR

5 free €2 Ch €2. **Surface:** gravel. 01/01-31/12.
Distance: 3km 3km 3km.

S Hauteluce 22F3

Parking Du Col des Saisies, D218b. **GPS**: n45,76297 e6,53382.

40 € 8 €2 Ch €2 WC. **Surface:** asphalted. 01/01-31/12.
Distance: 500m on the spot 500m 200m 200m.

S Hauterives 25C1

D538. **GPS**: n45,25497 e5,03022.

free, 01/04-31/10 € 5/24h €3/50liter Ch WC.
Location: Rural, simple. **Surface:** gravel.
Distance: 250m 250m.
Tourist information Hauterives:
Palais Idéal du Facteur Cheval.

S Illiat 22C2

GPS: n46,18495 e4,88802.

4 free Ch WC free. **Location:** Rural, simple, quiet.
Surface: gravel. 01/01-31/12.
Distance: 650m on the spot on the spot 650m on the spot on the spot.
Remarks: At small lake.

Issoire 25A1

Boulevard André Malraux. **GPS**: n45,54521 e3,24107.
8 free. **Surface:** gravel/metalled. 01/01-31/12.
Distance: 300m 300m 100m on the spot.

S Izernore 22D2

Rue de l'Oignin. **GPS**: n46,21847 e5,55041.

15 free Ch free.
Location: Rural, simple, central, quiet.
01/01-31/12.
Distance: on the spot 6km 500m 500m 500m 500m.
Remarks: On the foot of the Monts Berthiand.

S Jaligny-sur-Besbre 22A2

Rue de la Chaume. **GPS**: n46,38155 e3,59147.

5 free Ch (5x)free. **Location:** Rural, simple, quiet.
Surface: gravel. 01/01-31/12.
Distance: 200m on the spot on the spot 250m 250m.
Remarks: Along the Besbre river.

S Job 22A3

25 Route de Chansert, D255. **GPS**: n45,62019 e3,74502.
free Ch . **Surface:** gravel.
Distance: 500m 500m.

S Joux 22B3

Salle des Fêtes, La Noirie, D79. **GPS**: n45,88869 e4,37587.

10 free Ch free. **Location:** Rural. **Surface:** asphalted.
01/01-31/12 water disconnected in winter.
Distance: 200m 3,2km 200m 200m.
Remarks: Nearby castle garden.

S La Balme de Sillingy 22E3

Aire de Camping-cars Domaine du Tornet, D508.
GPS: n45,97124 e6,03135.

30 € 5 Ch free. **Location:** Rural, simple, central, quiet.
Surface: gravel. 01/04-31/10.
Distance: 100m (fishing permit available) 100m on the spot.
Remarks: Recreation park, max. 48h.

La Bénisson-Dieu 22B2

Parking de l'école, Rue des Comtes du Forez.
GPS: n46,15094 e4,00000.
2 free. 01/01-31/12.

S La Bourboule 24H1

Chemin de la Suchére. **GPS**: n45,58572 e2,73489.
10 free €5 Ch. **Surface:** metalled.
Distance: 500m 500m.
Remarks: Max. 48h.

La Bourboule 24H1

Plateau de Charlannes. **GPS**: n45,57811 e2,73513.

10 free. **Location:** Rural, simple, quiet. **Surface:** asphalted.
01/01-31/12.
Distance: 6,5km Snackbar on the spot on the spot.
Remarks: Parking at funicular railway.

S La Chaise-Dieu 25A1

Esplanade de la Gare. **GPS**: n45,31682 e3,69694.

8 free €2 Ch. **Location:** Urban, simple, quiet.
Surface: gravel/sand. 01/04-31/10.
Distance: 500m on the spot.
Remarks: Coins at shops and tourist office.

S La Chapelle-Laurent 25A1

Aire camping-cars, D10. **GPS**: n45,18028 e3,24389.

20 free voluntary contribution Ch free.
Location: Rural, simple, quiet. **Surface:** grassy.
01/01-31/12 service 15/11-30/04.
Distance: 50m nearby 100m 100m on the spot on the spot.

La Clusaz 22F3

Route des Confins. **GPS**: n45,92298 e6,48380.
free. **Surface:** asphalted. 01/01-31/12.
Remarks: Parking at pistes.

S La Féclaz 22E3

Aire Camping-cars de la Féclaz, D206a. **GPS**: n45,64210 e5,98411.

40 € 4 €1,50 Ch €1,50.
Surface: asphalted. 01/01-31/12.
Distance: on the spot on the spot on the spot 300m.

S La Roche-Blanche 22A3

Les Trolières, La Pigné Sud, Route des Fours à Chaux.
GPS: n45,71567 e3,14790.

100 € 6 €2/100liter Ch (4x)€6/6h.
Location: Rural, simple, isolated, quiet. **Surface:** grassy.
01/03-30/11.
Distance: 1,1km.
Remarks: Max. 48h.

S La Tour-d'Auvergne 24H1

Route de Bagnols. **GPS**: n45,53290 e2,68213.

FR

25 free €2/100liter Ch €2. **Location:** Simple, quiet. **Surface:** metalled. 01/01-31/12.
Distance: on the spot 650m 650m bakery.

S Lablachère 25B3

La Ferme Théâtre, D104, Notre Dame. **GPS**: n44,45481 e4,22004.

20 € 5/24h €2 €3/12h.
Location: Rural. **Surface:** gravel.
01/01-31/12.
Distance: 1km 150m.
Remarks: Max. 24h, theater, regional products.

S Lacapelle-Viescamp 24G2

Aire camping-cars, D18. **GPS**: n44,92167 e2,26361.

5 free €3/100liter Ch €3/1h.
Location: Rural, simple. **Surface:** metalled. 01/01-31/12.
Distance: 100m 100m on the spot.
Remarks: Coins available at the shop.

S Lachamp-Raphaël 25B2

D122, Le Village. **GPS**: n44,81133 e4,28860.

5 free €2 Ch.
Location: Rural, simple, quiet. **Surface:** gravel.
01/01-31/12.
Distance: 300m 300m Bread 300m departure Nordic.
Remarks: Altitude 1330m, coins at bar/hotel, beautiful view.

Lagorce 25B3

Le Sainte Anne, Leyris. **GPS**: n44,49581 e4,42190.
free. 01/01-31/12.

S Lalouvesc 25C2

Vallon d'Or, Sainte Agathe. **GPS**: n45,11947 e4,53384.

3 free WC. **Location:** Simple, central. **Surface:** asphalted.
01/01-31/12.
Distance: on the spot 100m 100m.

S Lalouvesc 25C2

La Fontaine. **GPS**: n45,12149 e4,53393.
€2/15minutes Ch €2.
15/05-15/10.
Remarks: Coins at petrol station and camping municipal.

S Lamastre 25C2

Parking Pont de Tain, Place Pradon. **GPS**: n44,98672 e4,58001.

20 free €4,40/100liter Ch €2,50/1h . **Location:** Simple.
Surface: asphalted. 01/01-31/12.
Distance: on the spot on the spot on the spot.
Remarks: Coins at tourist info.

S Lamure-sur-Azergues 22C3

Place de la gare. **GPS**: n46,06120 e4,49185.

10 free €2 Ch €2 WC.
Location: Rural, simple. **Surface:** asphalted.
01/01-31/12.
Distance: on the spot 100m 100m train/bus on the spot.
Remarks: Near train station.

S Lanarce 25B2

Camping Municipal. **GPS**: n44,72578 e4,00403.
free, 15/06-15/09 € 10 Ch €3 WC included.
Surface: grassy. 01/01-31/12 Service: winter.
Distance: 700m on the spot on the spot 700m.
Remarks: Beside river.

S Lans-en-Vercors 25D2

Route de l'Aigle. **GPS**: n45,12418 e5,59125.

30 free Ch WC free. **Location:** Rural, simple. **Surface:** gravel.
01/01-31/12.
Distance: 500m on the spot.
Remarks: Large parking, tuesday and Saturday market.

S Lapalisse 22A2

Place Jean Moulin, RN7 dir Roanne. **GPS**: n46,25000 e3,63500.

50 free Ch WC. **Location:** Urban, simple, central, quiet.
Surface: asphalted. 01/01-31/12.
Distance: 300m on the spot on the spot on the spot.
Remarks: Coins at tourist info.

S Laprugne 22A3

Domaine La Bourbonnaise, D477. **GPS**: n45,98661 e3,74569.
€ 8 Ch . **Surface:** asphalted. 01/01-31/12.
Distance: on the spot.

S Laqueuille 21H3

Place de Foirail, Le Bourg. **GPS**: n45,65008 e2,73289.
2 free €2/10minutes Ch €4/8h WC .
01/01-31/12.
Distance: 100m.

S Lathuile 22E3

Les Jardin du Tailleter, 190 route de la Porte, Bout du lac, N 508.
GPS: n45,79480 e6,20796.

24 € 8 Ch included (24x)€2 .
Location: Rural, simple. **Surface:** grassy. 01/06-31/08.
Distance: Lake of Annecy 750m.
Remarks: Max. 24h.

Lavaudieu 25A1

Le Bourg. **GPS**: n45,26297 e3,45606.

+10 free. **Location:** Simple, isolated, quiet. **Surface:** grassy/gravel.
01/01-31/12.
Distance: 200m on the spot on the spot on the spot.

S Le Bessat 25C1

Croix de Chaubouret. **GPS**: n45,36812 e4,52768.

4 free €2,50/20minutes Ch (4x)€2,50/6h.
Location: Rural. **Surface:** asphalted.
01/01-31/12.
Distance: 1km 100m mountainbike trail on the spot on the spot.
Remarks: Altitude 1200m, coins at Chalet des Alpes and the shops.

S Le Breuil-sur-Couze 25A1

Allée de Treize Vents. **GPS**: n45,46867 e3,26121.

8 free Ch free. **Location:** Urban, simple. **Surface:** gravel.
01/01-31/12.
Distance: 900m 700m bakery, supermarket.
Remarks: Along railwayline.

S Le Cheix-sur-Morge 22A3

D425. **GPS**: n45,95138 e3,17812.

FR

6 free Chfree. **Location:** Rural, simple, isolated, quiet.
Surface: gravel. 01/01-31/12.
Distance: 500m.
Remarks: Max. 48h.

Le Cheylard 25C2

Super U, Chemin du pre-jalla, ZI la Palisse.
GPS: n44,91143 e4,44162.

20 free €2 Ch €2. **Location:** Simple, noisy.
Surface: asphalted. 01/01-31/12.
Distance: on the spot on the spot.
Remarks: Max. 24h.

Le Cheylas 25E1

Avenue de la Libération. **GPS**: n45,37170 e5,99014.
free ChWCfree. **Surface:** asphalted/metalled.
Distance: on the spot nearby.

Le Crozet 22B2

Les Minières, Le Bourg. **GPS**: n46,16934 e3,85727.
2 free €2/30minutes Ch €2/4h. **Surface:** metalled.
01/01-31/12.
Distance: 150m.

Le Grand Bornand 22F3

Route de La Broderie. **GPS**: n45,94144 e6,43636.

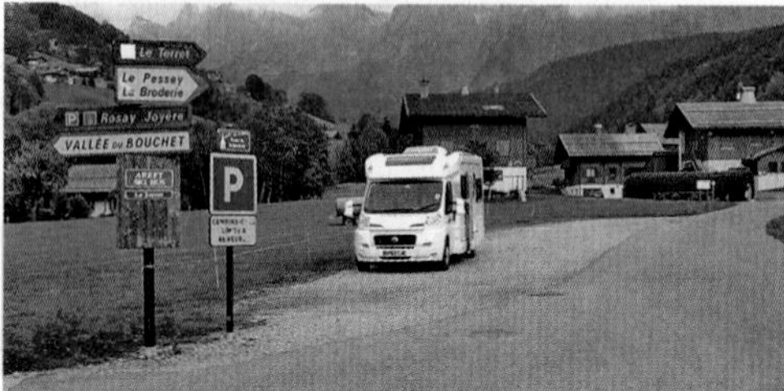

10 free. **Surface:** metalled. 01/01-31/12.
Distance: 600m on the spot.
Remarks: Max. 48h.

Le Lac d'Issarlès 25B2

D16. **GPS**: n44,81948 e4,06156.

24 € 11 + € 0,25/pp tourist tax Ch WC included.
Location: Central. **Surface:** metalled.
15/04-01/11.
Distance: 100m 100m 100m.
Remarks: Attention: this town is not Issarlès!.

Le Monastier-sur-Gazeille 25B2

Rue Augustin Ollier. **GPS**: n44,93720 e3,99250.

10 free €2/5minutes Ch. **Location:** Rural, simple, quiet.
Surface: gravel. 01/03-31/10.
Distance: 300m 300m 500m on the spot.

Le Monestier 25A1

D39. **GPS**: n45,56364 e3,66088.
free Ch. **Surface:** grassy/gravel.

Le Puy-en-Velay 25B2

Place Maréchal Leclerc. **GPS**: n45,04489 e3,89498.

26 € 12 Ch (26x) included.
Location: Urban, comfortable, central, quiet. **Surface:** asphalted.
01/01-31/12.
Distance: 1km 1km 2km 300m.

Le Puy-en-Velay 25B2

Boulevard de Cluny. GPS: n45,04963 e3,88976.
€2 Ch.

Le Reposoir 22F3

Route Departementale D204. **GPS**: n46,01010 e6,53648.

10 free Chfree WC. **Surface:** metalled.
Distance: 150m on the spot.

Le Teil 25C3

Alleé Paul Avon. **GPS**: n44,55138 e4,68972.

6 free Chfree.
Location: Noisy. **Surface:** grassy/metalled.
Distance: on the spot on the spot 500m.
Remarks: Nearby D86.

Tourist information Le Teil:
Thu morning.

Le Vernet 25A2

Place de l'étang, D48. **GPS**: n45,03560 e3,66952.

14 € 3 Chincluded (14x)€3/night.
Location: Rural, simple, isolated, quiet. **Surface:** grassy/sand.
01/01-31/12 service 01/11-30/04.
Distance: 50m on the spot on the spot.
Remarks: Max. 72h.

Les Ancizes-Comps 21H3

Camping de Comps les Fads, Le Moulin. **GPS**: n45,93986 e2,79985.
€ 8,40, 2 pers.incl Ch €2. **Surface:** grassy.
01/01-31/12.

Les Carroz-Arâches 22F3

Télécabine Les Cluses. GPS: n46,02500 e6,64361.

free Ch free. 01/06-30/11.
Distance: 500m 500m.
Remarks: Parking funicular railway.

Les Deux-Alpes 25E2

Avenue de la Muzelle, D213. **GPS**: n45,02394 e6,12120.
€ 7 Ch included. **Surface:** asphalted. winter.
Remarks: Beautiful view.

Les Estables 25B2

Foirail de la Mézine, Le Bourg. **GPS**: n44,90231 e4,15679.

8 free ChWC free.
Location: Rural, simple. **Surface:** asphalted.
01/01-31/12.
Distance: 50m 50m on the spot 500m on the spot.
Remarks: Service at petrol station, free wifi, code at tourist info.

Les Gets 22F2

Route du Front de Neige. **GPS**: n46,14992 e6,65673.

25 € 0,90/pp tourist tax, winter € 17 Ch .
Surface: gravel. 01/01-31/12.
Distance: 1km on the spot.
Remarks: Max. 7 days, bus to centre every 30 minutes.

Tourist information Les Gets:
Week market. Thu-morning.

Les Granges-Gontardes 25C3

Domaine de la Tour d'Elyssas, Quartier Combe d'Elissas.
GPS: n44,41811 e4,75465.

FR

8 free Ch free. **Surface:** gravel. 01/01-31/12.
Distance: 9km.
Remarks: At wine-grower, max. 48h.

Les Houches 22F3

Aire d'accueil camping-car Mont Blanc, 500 route du Pont.
GPS: n45,89257 e6,81706.
22 € 15 Ch included. **Location:** Comfortable, isolated, quiet. **Surface:** gravel. 01/04-30/11.
Distance: 2,5km 1km 1km 500m.

Les Karellis 25F1

GPS: n45,22778 e6,40639.
free. 01/01-31/12.
Remarks: Mountain station nearby St.Jean-de-Maurienne.

Les Menuires 25F1

Les Bruyères, Dir Val Thorens. **GPS:** n45,32557 e6,53414.
70 € 10/24h + € 0,20/pp tourist tax Ch (7x)€2/4h WC.
Surface: asphalted. 01/01-31/12.
Distance: on the spot on the spot on the spot.
Remarks: Near the pistes.

Les Noës 22B3

Le Bourg, D47. **GPS:** n46,04083 e3,85206.

5 free ChWCfree. **Location:** Rural, simple, quiet.
Surface: gravel. 01/01-31/12.
Distance: on the spot 50m on the spot.

Les Sauvages 22B3

D121. **GPS:** n45,92083 e4,37711.

free Chfree. **Location:** Rural, simple, quiet. **Surface:** gravel. 01/01-31/12.
Distance: on the spot 100m 100m on the spot.

Lezoux 22A3

Parking Musée départemental de la Céramique, Rue de la République. **GPS:** n45,82686 e3,38459.

30 free ChWCfree.
Location: Comfortable, central, quiet. **Surface:** gravel.
01/01-31/12 water: 01/11-31/03.
Distance: 500m 3,5km 500m 500m.

Lurcy-Lévis 21H1

Plan d'eau des Sézeaux, Rue de Fontgroix.
GPS: n46,73797 e2,93863.

6 free €3/100liter Ch €3/55minutes WC.
Location: Rural, comfortable, quiet. **Surface:** grassy/gravel.
01/01-31/12.
Distance: 800m Small lake on the spot 800m 800m.
Remarks: Coins at cafe, in front of the church.

Lus-la-Croix-Haute 25D2

D 505. **GPS:** n44,66712 e5,70800.
6 free ChWCfree. **Surface:** metalled. 01/01-31/12.
Distance: 500m on the spot on the spot.
Remarks: At fire-station, tenniscourt.

Mâcot-la-Plagne 25F1

GPS: n45,50677 e6,68652.
46 free, Winter € 10 €2 Ch €4/8h. **Surface:** asphalted.
01/01-31/12.
Distance: on the spot.

Mandailles-Saint-Julien 24H2

Le Mas, D17. **GPS:** n45,06916 e2,65611.

5 free €3,50 Ch. **Location:** Rural, simple, quiet.
Surface: metalled. 01/01-31/12 service: 30/09-01/05.
Distance: 200m 200m 200m on the spot.
Remarks: Max. 24h, coins at restaurants.

Manzat 21H3

Place du 14 Juillet. **GPS:** n45,96180 e2,93883.

20 free Chfree. **Location:** Rural, simple, quiet.
Surface: unpaved. 01/01-31/12.
Distance: on the spot 5,6km 250m 200m.
Remarks: In front of police station.

Marcolès 24G2

Aire camping-cars, Terrain de sport. **GPS:** n44,78028 e2,35389.

5 €2 Chfree. **Location:** Rural, simple, quiet.
Surface: gravel. 01/01-31/12 service 01/11-31/03.
Distance: 100m 100m 100m.
Remarks: Artists village.

Marsanne 25C3

Avenue de Bailliencourt, D57. **GPS:** n44,64568 e4,87175.

5 free Chfree.
Location: Rural, quiet. **Surface:** grassy. 01/01-31/12.
Distance: 300m 300m nearby.
Remarks: Max. 48h, medieval village.

Massiac 25A1

Aire du Bouclier Arverne, Rue Jacques Chaban Delmas.
GPS: n45,25364 e3,19376.

8 free Chfree. **Location:** Urban, simple, quiet.
Surface: asphalted. 01/01-31/12.
Distance: 350m 400m 400m on the spot.

Massiac 25A1

Aire de Massiac, Rue Jacques Chaban Delmas.
GPS: n45,25267 e3,19433.

8 free. **Location:** Rural, simple, quiet. **Surface:** grassy.
01/01-31/12.
Distance: 400m 1,4km on the spot on the spot 400m 400m 200m on the spot.

Mauriac 24G1

Aire camping-cars, Rue du Val Saint Jean.
GPS: n45,21863 e2,32183.

10 free €2/100liter Ch €2/1h. **Location:** Rural, simple, quiet. **Surface:** metalled. 01/01-31/12.
Distance: 1km beach 300m 1,2km 1,2km.

Maurs 24G2

Maurs La Jolie, Route de Quezac. **GPS:** n44,71442 e2,19615.

5 free €2/100liter Ch €2/1h.
Location: Urban, simple, central, quiet. **Surface:** asphalted.
01/01-31/12.
Distance: 300m 300m 300m 300m.

FR

Remarks: Coins at Papetterie and tourist office.

Megève 22F3

Chemin des Ânes. **GPS**: n45,86401 e6,62010.
free. 01/01-31/12.
Remarks: In front of parking Télécabine du Jaillet.

Messeix 21H3

Place des Pins. **GPS**: n45,61576 e2,55621.

6 free €2/10minutes Ch €2/55minutes.
Location: Urban, simple, quiet. **Surface:** asphalted.
01/01-31/12.
Distance: 500m 18km 1,7km on the spot.
Remarks: Coins at the shops.

Meyras 25B2

Grande rue, D26. **GPS**: n44,67939 e4,26847.

15 €4/48h €4/100liter Ch €4/5kWh.
Surface: asphalted. 01/04-31/10.
Distance: 500m 200m 200m.
Remarks: Max. 48h, coins at the shops in the village.

Mijoux 22E2

D50, Route de la Combe-en-Haut. **GPS**: n46,36963 e6,00247.

20 free €3,50 Ch €3,50. **Surface:** gravel. Service: winter.
Distance: 500m 500m 500m on the spot on the spot.
Remarks: Coins at town hall and supermarket.

Mirabel-aux-Baronnies 25D3

Aire camping-cars, Chemin des Grottes. **GPS**: n44,31260 e5,09968.

6+10 voluntary contribution Chfree. **Location:** Rural.
Surface: grassy/metalled. 01/01-31/12.
Distance: 200m.

Montalieu-Vercieu 22D3

Chamboud. **GPS**: n45,82776 e5,42100.

6 free ChWCcampsite. **Location:** Rural, simple, isolated, quiet. **Surface:** asphalted.
Distance: 2km 2km 2km 1,5km.
Remarks: Next to campsite/Base de Loisirs de la Vallée Bleue, max. 2 nights.

Montbrison-sur-Lez 25C3

Place Publique. **GPS**: n44,43663 e5,01779.

4 free free. **Surface:** metalled. 01/01-31/12.
Distance: 100m 100m 100m.

Montbrison-sur-Lez 25C3

Quartier le Chatelard. **GPS**: n44,42751 e5,02438.

6 €5 €2/60liter Ch €2. **Location:** Isolated.
Surface: gravel/metalled. 01/01-31/12.
Remarks: Coins at bar and garage.

Montbrun-les-Bains 28D1

Toscan. **GPS**: n44,17247 e5,43881.

10 free. **Location:** Rural, quiet. **Surface:** grassy.
01/01-31/12.
Distance: 500m 300m 400m on the spot 400m Tour de la Citadelle.

Montbrun-les-Bains 28D1

Condamine. **GPS**: n44,17413 e5,44071.
€2 Ch €2.

Montélimar 25C3

Domaine du Bois de Laud, Chemin du Bois de Laud.
GPS: n44,56522 e4,75691.

17 €4,30 Chincluded. **Location:** Urban.
Surface: grassy/metalled. 01/01-31/12.
Distance: 500m 100m.

Remarks: Near centre commercial Leclerc, max. 48h.

Montluçon 21H2

Route de l'Etang de Sault, Prémilhat. **GPS**: n46,33469 e2,55855.

8 free €6/150liter Ch (6x)€2,50/10h.
Location: Rural, comfortable. **Surface:** gravel. 01/01-31/12.
Distance: 5km Montluçon 2,6km 150m 150m 500m.
Remarks: Max. 72h.

Montluçon 21H2

Place de la Fraternité, Rue des Marais. **GPS**: n46,35535 e2,58686.

15 free €5/150liter Ch €2,50/10minutes WC.
Location: Urban, simple, noisy.
Surface: asphalted.
01/01-31/12 water: Nov-March.
Distance: on the spot A71 16km on the spot on the spot on the spot.
Remarks: Thu-morning closed because of market (6-15h).

Montmurat 24G2

Aire camping-cars, Le Bourg, D345. **GPS**: n44,62811 e2,19804.

10 free €1 Ch. **Location:** Rural, simple, isolated, quiet.
Surface: gravel. 01/01-31/12.
Distance: on the spot.

Montoldre 22A2

D21. **GPS**: n46,33272 e3,44727.

+10 free €2/100liter Ch. **Location:** Rural, simple, quiet.
Surface: asphalted. 01/01-31/12.
Distance: centre on the spot.
Remarks: In front of town hall.

Montpeyroux 22A3

D797C, Rue De l'Hume. **GPS**: n45,62373 e3,19911.

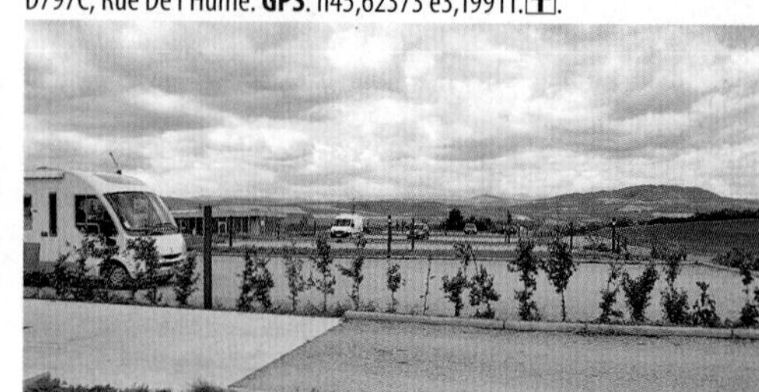

FR

+10 free €2,50 Ch €2,50/1h. **Location:** Rural, simple, quiet. **Surface:** gravel. 01/01-31/12.
Distance: 100m 200m 200m.
Remarks: Coins at the shops in the village.

Tourist information Montpeyroux:
Small town with wine-cellar Cave de Montpeyroux. Mo/Sa 8.30-12.30h, 14-18/19h, Su 10.30-12h, 16-19h.

Montsalvy 24G2

Route de Junhac. **GPS**: n44,70778 e2,49667.

11 free €2 Ch €2 WC €1. **Location:** Rural, comfortable, quiet. **Surface:** asphalted. 01/01-31/12.
Distance: 400m 400m 400m.

Morillon 22F3

GPS: n46,08289 e6,67968.
10 free ChWCfree. **Surface:** asphalted.
Distance: 200m 100m 300m 100m.

Moulins 22A2

Flot Bleu Park, Chemin de Halage. **GPS**: n46,55852 e3,32491.

92 € 0,10/h €2 Ch€2 (12x)€2/4h
Location: Urban, comfortable, central, quiet.
Surface: grassy/metalled. 01/01-31/12.
Distance: city centre 1km 100m 300m on the spot.

Murat 24H2

Place du 19 mars. **GPS**: n45,10912 e2,86728.

8 free €2/10minutes Ch €2/1h WCfree.
Location: Urban, simple, central, noisy. **Surface:** asphalted.
01/01-31/12.
Distance: 300m 100m 1,5km 100m on the spot.
Remarks: Coins at tourist info, marked pitches in the back of de parking.

Tourist information Murat:
Fri-morning.

Murat-le-Quaire 21H3

Les Rives du Lac, Route de la Banne d'Ordanche.
GPS: n45,60274 e2,73797.

37 € 9,60/24h Ch (8x)WC €1 included.
Location: Rural, comfortable, quiet. **Surface:** grassy/metalled.
01/01-31/12.
Distance: 1,2km 12km 100m 100m day pass available
on the spot on the spot 100m 5km.
Remarks: Bread-service.

Murol 24H1

Domaine du lac Chambon, Plage Est. **GPS**: n45,57158 e2,92959.
15 € 10 Ch (15x)included. **Surface:** grassy.
20/04-01/09.
Distance: 100m.
Remarks: Entrance code available at campsite.

Nantua 22D2

D74. **GPS**: n46,15497 e5,59656.

13 € 7,50 + € 0,20/pp tourist tax Ch WCincluded.
Location: Urban, comfortable, central. **Surface:** gravel.
01/04-30/10.
Distance: 700m 7km on the spot on the spot 150m 150m on the spot on the spot.
Remarks: At Nantua lake.

Naucelles 24G2

Aire camping-cars, Rue du Terrou. **GPS**: n44,95694 e2,41757.

5 free €3,50/100liter Ch €3,50/1h. **Location:** Urban, simple, quiet. **Surface:** asphalted. 01/01-31/12.
Distance: Spar 300m.
Remarks: Coins at supermarket in the village.

Néris-les-Bains 21H2

Camping du Lac, Avenue Marrx Dormoy, D155.
GPS: n46,28673 e2,65235.

6 € 7 Ch (6x)WCincluded €1,50/h.
Location: Urban, comfortable. **Surface:** gravel. 01/03-31/10.
Distance: 500m 12km bakery 500m.
Remarks: Max. 3 nights, to be paid at campsite.

Neussargues-Moissac 24H1

Allée des Peupliers. **GPS**: n45,13438 e2,98130.

5 free €2/100liter Ch €2/2h WC . **Location:** Rural, comfortable, quiet. **Surface:** gravel. 01/01-31/12 water disconnected in winter.
Distance: 300m 50m 300m on the spot on the spot.
Remarks: Coins at town hall and restaurant.

Neuvéglise 24H2

Le Bourg. **GPS**: n44,92924 e2,98344.
3 free ChFree. **Location:** Urban, simple, central.
Surface: asphalted. 01/01-31/12.
Distance: on the spot 100m 200m.

Noailly 22B2

Parking Maison du Temps Libre. **GPS**: n46,13649 e4,00000.
3 free. **Surface:** asphalted. 01/01-31/12.
Distance: 200m.

Noirétable 21H3

Aire d'accueil de camping-cars, Lieu-dit La Roche.
GPS: n45,80739 e3,00000.

7 free €3 Ch €1/2h . **Location:** Simple, quiet.
Surface: metalled. 01/01-31/12.
Distance: 800m 100m 100m 100m 800m on the spot on the spot on the spot.
Remarks: Next to campsite (50m), coins at campsite.

Nyons 25D3

Promenade de la Digue. **GPS**: n44,35778 e5,13861.

20 € 10/24h ChWC included.
Surface: gravel. 01/01-31/12.
Distance: 250m 250m 250m 250m.
Remarks: Next to Parc loisirs aquatique, max. 48h.

Nyons 25D3

Domaine Rocheville, Route de Montélimar, RD 538.
GPS: n44,36850 e5,11775.

6 € 7, tourist tax € 0,20/pp €4/100liter Ch €4 WC included,summer free. **Surface:** grassy. 01/01-31/12.

Tourist information Nyons:
Pavillon du Tourisme, Place de la Libération. Important Olive-city in the Provence.
Musée de l'Olivier, Espace Vignolis. Museum about the olive-tree and production of olive oil. daily 01/11-28/02 Su.
Centre-ville. Regional market. Thu-morning.

Orcines 21H3

Route du Puy de Dôme, D68. **GPS**: n45,76958 e2,98624.
free Chfree. **Location:** Rural, isolated. **Surface:** asphalted.
01/01-31/12 Service: winter.

Orcines 21H3

D941. **GPS**: n45,80394 e2,98726.

10 free. **Location:** Simple, noisy. **Surface:** metalled.
01/01-31/12.

FR

Distance: on the spot.

S Orcines 21H3

D941B dir Orcines Vulcania. **GPS**: n45,78765 e3,00947.
€2/100liter Ch €2/1h. **Location:** Simple, noisy.
01/01-31/12.

S Orgnac l'Aven 25B3

Le Fez, D217. **GPS**: n44,30419 e4,43240.

5 free Chfree. **Location:** Rural. **Surface:** gravel.
01/01-31/12.
Distance: 200m 10m 300m.
Remarks: Caves of Aven d'Orgnac 2km.

S Panissières 22B3

Aire camping-cars, Allée des Acacias. **GPS**: n45,78835 e4,34355.

4 €6,50 Ch included4 WC use sanitary €3,30/pp.
Location: Rural, simple, quiet. **Surface:** metalled.
01/01-31/12 Service: winter.
Distance: 300m 300m 300m.
Remarks: Use sanitary € 2,40/pp per day.

S Paray-le-Frésil 22A1

Le Bourg. **GPS**: n46,65472 e3,61294.
3 free €2 Ch €2/55minutes. **Location:** Quiet.
Surface: sand. 01/01-31/12.
Distance: on the spot on the spot.
Remarks: Service only by credit card.

S Paulhac 24H2

Place des Chausseurs. **GPS**: n45,00669 e2,90394.

3 free Chfree At townhall. **Location:** Rural, simple, isolated, quiet. **Surface:** grassy. 01/01-31/12.
Distance: on the spot on the spot.

S Périgny 22A2

Rue de l'Église. **GPS**: n46,25306 e3,55307.
8 free ChWC. **Location:** Rural, simple, isolated, quiet.
Surface: gravel. 01/01-31/12.

S Pierrefort 24H2

Côte de Chabridet. **GPS**: n44,92172 e2,84199.

20 free €2/100liter Ch €2. **Location:** Rural, simple.
Surface: gravel. 01/01-31/12.
Distance: 200m 300m 300m on the spot.
Remarks: Coins at tourist info, service 100m.

S Planfoy 25C1

Chemin du Vignolet. **GPS**: n45,37445 e4,44910.

10 free €2,50/15minutes Ch (8x)€2,50/6h.
Location: Rural, comfortable, quiet. **Surface:** asphalted.
01/01-31/12.
Distance: 1,3km 7km 1,3km on the spot.
Remarks: Coins at the shops in the village.

S Pleaux 24G1

Parc des Auzerals, Place d'Empeyssine.
GPS: n45,13556 e2,22833.

30 free Ch WCfree. **Location:** Urban, simple, central, quiet. **Surface:** asphalted/gravel. 01/01-31/12.
Distance: on the spot 100m 100m.

S Pont-de-Veyle 22C2

D933, Rue de la Poste. **GPS**: n46,26437 e4,88697.

20 free . **Location:** Urban, simple, central, noisy.
Surface: gravel.
Distance: on the spot 3,5km on the spot on the spot 50m 150m.

S Pontcharra-sur-Turdine 22C3

Place A. Schweitzer. **GPS**: n45,87405 e4,49133.

4 free ChWCfree. **Location:** Urban. 01/01-31/12.
Distance: 50m on the spot 50m 50m on the spot.

S Pouilly-sous-Charlieu 22B2

Place du Marché, Rue de la République. **GPS**: n46,14335 e4,10832.
free ChWCfree. **Surface:** asphalted. Su-morning (market).
Distance: on the spot.

S Pouilly-sous-Charlieu 22B2

Rue de la Berge. **GPS**: n46,14699 e4,10075.
4 free. **Surface:** gravel. 01/01-31/12.
Distance: on the spot.
Remarks: Parking at the Loire river.

S Pradelles 25B2

Aire de la Salaison, N88. **GPS**: n44,77540 e3,88752.

40 free Ch (8x)€2 free. **Location:** Rural, comfortable.
Surface: grassy/gravel. 01/01-31/12.
Distance: 1km on the spot on the spot on the spot.
Remarks: Max. 24h, regional products and bread.

S Prapoutel-les-Sept-Laux 25E1

D281. **GPS**: n45,25769 e5,99785.

free WC. **Surface:** metalled. 01/01-31/12.
Distance: 50m.
Remarks: Parking at pistes.

S Privas 25C2

Avenue de la gare. **GPS**: n44,73134 e4,59309.

10 free Ch. **Location:** Urban. **Surface:** gravel/metalled.
01/01-31/12.
Distance: centre 750m.

S Prunet 24G2

Aire camping-cars, Le Bourg. **GPS**: n44,82049 e2,46398.

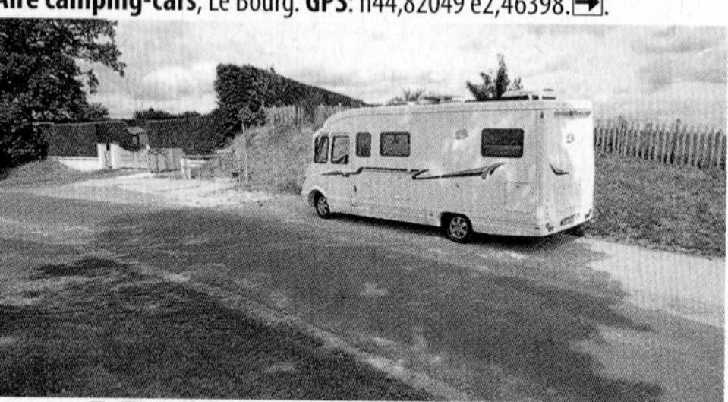

3 free Ch free. **Location:** Rural, simple, quiet.
Surface: gravel. 01/01-31/12 service 01/11-31/03.
Distance: 300m 300m.

S Puy-Saint-Martin 25C3

Aire de camping-car. **GPS**: n44,62753 e4,97492.

13 free Ch.
Location: Rural, comfortable. **Surface:** grassy.
Distance: on the spot 50m bakery 300m.
Remarks: Former campsite, max. 48h, voluntary contribution.

S Randan 22A3

Rue du Puy de Dôme. **GPS**: n46,01630 e3,35075.

FR

5 free €2/15minutes Ch €2/15minutes.
Location: Urban, simple, quiet. **Surface:** gravel.
01/01-31/12.
Distance: 500m 500m 200m.
Remarks: Coins at Maison de la Presse, Rue de Commerce.

S Raucoules 25B1

Le Bourg. **GPS**: n45,18640 e4,29750.

4 free €2/20minutes Ch (4x)€2/4h.
Location: Rural, simple, central, quiet. **Surface:** asphalted.
01/01-31/12.
Distance: 200m 300m on the spot on the spot.
Remarks: Coins available at the shops.

S Renaison 22B3

La Rivière. **GPS**: n46,04757 e3,92124.

10 free Chfree. **Location:** Rural, simple, quiet.
Surface: grassy/gravel. 01/01-31/12.
Distance: 400m on the spot 700m.
Remarks: Along river.

S Retournac 25B1

Aire de la Chaud, Rue de la Loire. **GPS**: n45,20328 e4,04501.

20 free Chfree. **Location:** Rural, simple, isolated, quiet.
Surface: gravel. 01/01-31/12 Service: winter.
Distance: city centre 1km on the spot on the spot 650m on the spot on the spot.
Remarks: Along Loire river.

S Reventin-Vaugris 25C1

Rue Mouret. **GPS**: n45,46821 e4,84239.

10 free WC. **Location:** Rural, simple, central, quiet.
Surface: gravel/metalled. 01/01-31/12.

Distance: on the spot 6km 100m bakery 100m.

S Riom 22A3

Route d'Ennezat, D224. **GPS**: n45,89455 e3,12477.

4 free €2/15minutes Ch €2/15minutes.
Location: Urban, simple, central, noisy. **Surface:** gravel.
01/01-31/12.
Distance: 700m 2,5km nearby nearby.

S Riom-es-Montagnes 24H1

Rue du Champ de Foire. **GPS**: n45,28444 e2,65389.
€2/100liter Ch €2/1h.
Location: Simple. 01/01-31/12.
Distance: on the spot 100m 100m.
Remarks: Overnight stay on Parking de la Piscine, GPS N 45,27902 E 2,66403.

S Roanne 22B3

Port de Plaisance, Quai Commandant de Fourcauld.
GPS: n46,03750 e4,08306.

10 €6 €2,50/15minutes €2,50 Ch€2,50 €2,50/4h WC .
Location: Urban, comfortable, quiet. **Surface:** gravel.
01/01-31/12.
Distance: 500m 500m 2km 2km on the spot on the spot on the spot.
Remarks: Max. 6 days.

Romans-sur-Isère 25C2

Avenue Gambetta. **GPS**: n45,04521 e5,05879.

4 free. **Location:** Urban, simple. **Surface:** metalled.
01/01-31/12.
Distance: centre 700m.
Remarks: Parking in front of Marques Avenue, max. 48h.

S Ruoms 25B3

La Grand Terre. GPS: n44,42381 e4,33253.
15 € 10,80-12 Ch (12x) included.
Location: Rural. **Surface:** grassy/metalled. 01/01/-31/12.
Distance: 3km 200m on the spot on the spot.
Remarks: In front of campsite.

S Ruynes-en-Margeride 25A2

Le Bourg. **GPS**: n45,00111 e3,22389.

8 free €2/10minutes Ch €2/55minutes.
Location: Urban, simple, quiet. **Surface:** gravel/sand.

01/01-31/12.
Distance: 50m 6km 50m 50m.

S Saillans 25D2

La Roche, Quartier Tourtoiron, Montmartel.
GPS: n44,69549 e5,19350.

20 €3 €2 Ch.
Location: Rural, simple. **Surface:** gravel.
01/01-31/12.
Distance: 300m.
Remarks: Along the Drôme river, max. 24h, closed when high water.

S Saint-Agrève 25B2

Coussac. **GPS**: n45,01042 e4,39339.

free €3 Ch €3,water 10min + electricity 50min WC.
Location: Simple. **Surface:** asphalted. 01/01-31/12.
Distance: 500m 500m 500m.
Remarks: Coins at tourist info.

S Saint-Agrève 25B2

Le Lac de Véron, Pré de Gardy, D120. **GPS**: n44,99981 e4,40164.

5 € 5/24h on demand free. **Location:** Rural, comfortable, quiet. **Surface:** unpaved. 01/04-31/10.
Distance: village 1km on the spot on the spot on the spot on the spot.
Remarks: At fish lake.

S Saint-Alban-Auriolles 25B3

Rue Marius Perbost. **GPS**: n44,42693 e4,30096.

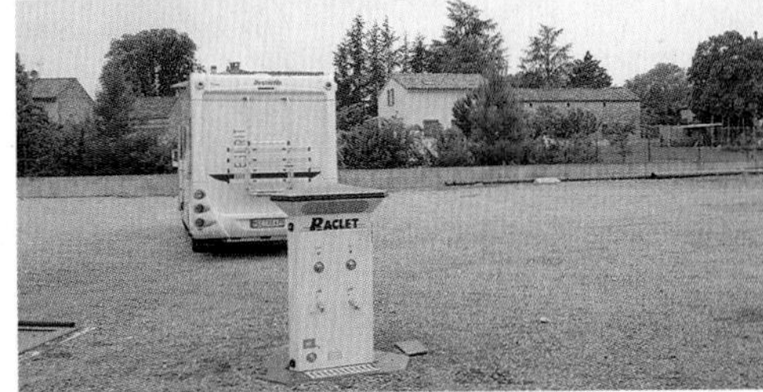

free €3 Ch €3. **Surface:** gravel.
Distance: 300m 200m.

S Saint-André-d'Apchon 22B3

La Prébande. GPS: n46,03385 e3,92705.

FR

3 free Ch free. **Location:** Rural, simple, quiet.
Surface: gravel. 01/01-31/12.
Distance: 300m 100m.

Saint-Bonnet-le-Château 25B1

Esplanade de la Boule. **GPS:** n45,42514 e4,06436.

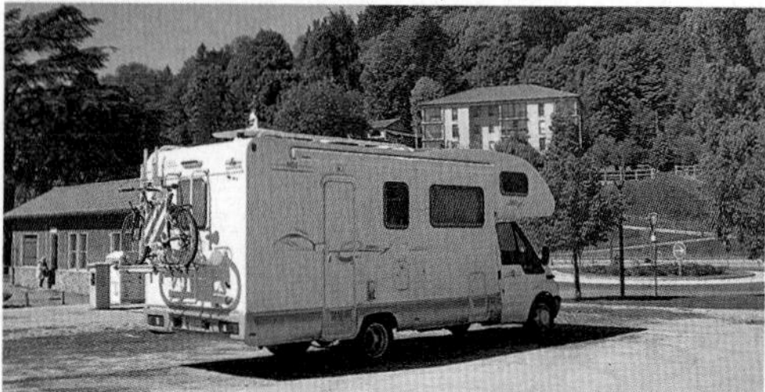

50 free Ch WC free.
Location: Simple. **Surface:** metalled. Fri.
Distance: 200m 1km 200m 200m.

Tourist information Saint-Bonnet-le-Château:
Musée de la Pétanque et des Boules, Esplanade de la Boule. All about the beloved French national sport. 01/04-31/10.
Musée International Pétanque et Boules, Boulevard des Chauchères. Fri.

Saint-Bonnet-le-Froid 25C1

Chemin de Brard. **GPS:** n45,14136 e4,43454.

6 €5 Ch included. **Location:** Urban, simple, central, quiet. **Surface:** gravel. 01/03-15/11.
Distance: 150m 150m 150m on the spot.
Remarks: Access via D105.

Saint-Bonnet-Tronçais 21H1

Parking du Stade, Route de Tronçais, D39.
GPS: n46,66001 e2,69717.
10 free €5 Ch. **Surface:** gravel. 01/01-31/12 water disconnected in winter.
Distance: 300m.
Remarks: Coins at the bakery and campsite.

Saint-Bonnet-Tronçais 21H1

Rue de l'Étang. **GPS:** n46,65896 e2,69228.
10 free. **Location:** Simple, central. **Surface:** gravel.
01/01-31/12.
Distance: on the spot 27km Lake 450m bakery 200m.

Saint-Christophe-sur-Dolaison 25B2

Place des Jardins, Le Bourg. **GPS:** n44,99802 e3,82158.

6 free €2 Ch €2. **Location:** Rural, simple, quiet.
Surface: asphalted. 01/01-31/12.
Distance: 100m 150m on the spot on the spot.
Remarks: Coins at town hall.

Saint-Désirat 25C1

Musée de l'Alambic,Distillerie Jean Gauthier, D291.
GPS: n45,25856 e4,79261.

free WC free. **Location:** Simple. **Surface:** asphalted.
Distance: 300m 300m.
Remarks: Max. 1 night.

Saint-Donat-sur-l'Herbasse 25C2

Route de St.Bardoux. **GPS:** n45,11902 e4,98284.

free Ch free. **Location:** Simple. 01/01-31/12.
Distance: 400m 400m 1km.
Remarks: In front of gymnasium, max. 1 night.

Saint-Éloy-les-Mines 21H2

Rue du Puy-de-Dôme, RN144. **GPS:** n46,15559 e2,83615.

30 free €2 Ch €2. **Location:** Rural, simple.
Surface: metalled. 01/01-31/12.
Distance: on the spot 700m 400m Carrefour Market.
Remarks: Max. 48h.

Saint-Étienne-la-Varenne 22C3

Le Bourg. **GPS:** n46,07731 e4,63024.

4 free Ch free. **Location:** Rural, simple, quiet.
Surface: gravel/metalled. 01/01-31/12.
Distance: on the spot 50m on the spot on the spot.
Remarks: Next to church.

Saint-Félicien 25C2

Place du Pré Lacour. **GPS:** n45,08453 e4,62848.

6 free €2 Ch. **Location:** Urban, simple.
Surface: asphalted/gravel. 01/01-31/12.
Distance: on the spot on the spot on the spot.
Remarks: Behind police station, max. 2 nights.

Saint-Flour 24H2

Cours Chazerat. **GPS:** n45,03389 e3,08750.

20 free €2 Ch €2/55minutes. **Location:** Urban, simple.
Surface: metalled. 01/01-31/12.
Distance: on the spot 4,6km 50m 50m on the spot on the spot.
Remarks: Higher part of the city.

Saint-Flour 24H2

Place de l'Ander, ville basse. **GPS:** n45,03556 e3,09750.

8 free €2/100liter Ch €2/55minutes. **Location:** Urban, simple. **Surface:** asphalted. 01/01-31/12.
Distance: 300m 4km 300m 300m on the spot.
Remarks: Near campsite, lower part of the city.

Tourist information Saint-Flour:
Office de Tourisme, 17bis, place d'Armes, www.saint-flour.com. City with car-free historical centre, Vieux Saint Flour.

Saint-Forgeux 22C3

Le Tram. **GPS:** n45,85733 e4,47566.

free Ch free WC. **Location:** Rural, simple, quiet.
Surface: metalled. 01/01-31/12.
Distance: 300m 300m 300m on the spot.

Saint-Genest-de-Beauzon 25B3

Domaine la Pize, La Pize. **GPS:** n44,43759 e4,19431.

€ 10 Ch WC included. **Location:** Rural, isolated, quiet.
Surface: unpaved. 01/01-31/12.
Distance: 1,6km.

Saint-Georges 25A2

Aire du Cantal. GPS: n45,03167 e3,13500.

20 free €2 Ch €2 WC. **Location:** Motorway, simple, noisy.
Surface: asphalted. 01/01-31/12.
Distance: 3km 500m 200m 500m.

Remarks: At petrol station Esso.

S Saint-Georges-d'Espéranche 25C1

Chemin des Platières. **GPS**: n45,55560 e5,07478.

14 free Chfree. **Location:** Rural, simple, central, quiet.
Surface: metalled. 01/01-31/12.
Distance: on the spot 100m 500m.
Remarks: Max. 48h.

S Saint-Gérand-de-Vaux 22A2

Etang du Moulin, Les Gaillards. **GPS**: n46,38416 e3,39972.

30 free €2/100liter Ch €2/1h. **Location:** Quiet.
Surface: grassy. 01/01-31/12.
Distance: on the spot.

S Saint-Germain-Lespinasse 22B2

Place du 8 mai 1945. **GPS**: n46,10510 e3,96229.

3 free Chfree. **Location:** Rural, simple, quiet.
Surface: gravel. 01/01-31/12.
Distance: 200m 50m 50m.

S Saint-Gérons 24G2

Plage d'Espinet. **GPS**: n44,93257 e2,23190.
26 € 8,40-10,80 Ch included. 01/01-31/12.
Distance: 2km Snackbar.
Remarks: Video surveillance.

S Saint-Gervais-les-Bains 22F3

77, impasse Cascade. **GPS**: n45,88864 e6,71287.

20 free €2 Ch €2. **Surface:** asphalted.
Distance: 200m 200m 200m 300m.
Remarks: Parking skating rink.

S Saint-Haon-le-Châtel 22B3

Fondanges, Route de la Croix du Sud, D39.
GPS: n46,06362 e3,91313.

3 free Chfree. **Location:** Rural, quiet. **Surface:** metalled.
01/01-31/12.
Distance: 400m 400m 400m 400m.

S Saint-Hilaire-sous-Charlieu 22B2

Le Grand Couvert, Les Perches. **GPS**: n46,11247 e4,18602.
2 free. 01/01-31/12.

S Saint-Jean-d'Ardières 22C2

Domaine de Grande Ferrière, 831 route des Rochons.
GPS: n46,12954 e4,71581.

5 free Chfree €5/4night WC. **Location:** Rural, simple.
Surface: gravel.
Distance: 3km 6km 5km 500m 3km 3km.

S Saint-Jean-de-Bournay 25D1

Place du Marche. **GPS**: n45,50130 e5,13845.

10 free free Ch. **Location:** Rural, simple, central, quiet.
Surface: asphalted. 01/01-31/12.
Distance: on the spot 100m 100m.

S Saint-Jean-de-Maurienne 25E1

Rue Louis Sibue. **GPS**: n45,27995 e6,34776.
10 free €2 Ch €2 WC.
Surface: asphalted. 01/01-31/12.
Distance: 2,5km 100m.

S Saint-Jean-en-Royans 25D2

Rue de la Gare. **GPS**: n45,02028 e5,29032.

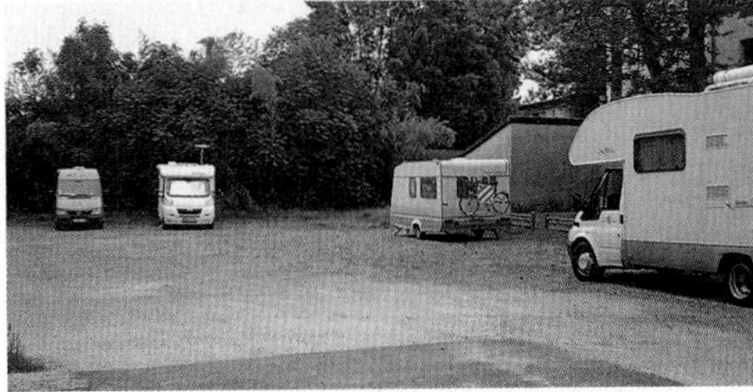

3 free Chfree. **Location:** Simple. **Surface:** gravel.
01/01-31/12.
Distance: 200m 200m 200m.

S Saint-Julien-Chapteuil 25B2

L'Holme, La Croix Blanche. **GPS**: n45,03917 e4,06305.
€3 Ch. 01/01-31/12.
Remarks: Service in front of campsite.

S Saint-Julien-la-Geneste 21H3

Les Marceaux. **GPS**: n46,03221 e2,75787.
12 € 8 Ch (10x). **Location:** Isolated, quiet.

S Saint-Just 25A2

Camping Municipal, Le Bourg. **GPS**: n44,88972 e3,20889.

10 € 8 €2/100liter Ch €2/55minutes (4x)€3,50/night WC included. **Location:** Rural, comfortable, quiet.
Surface: grassy. 01/01-31/12.
Distance: 50m 6,2km 100m 100m on the spot.
Remarks: Incl. use camp-site facilities.

S Saint-Just-d'Ardèche 25C3

Domaine La Favette, D86, route des Gorges d'Ardèche.
GPS: n44,30134 e4,60649.

6 € 5 €2 Ch €2. 01/01-31/12.
Remarks: At wine-grower, max. 24h.

Tourist information Saint-Just-d'Ardèche:
Good starting point to discover the Ardèche gorges.
Thu.

S Saint-Just-en-Chevalet 22B3

Boulevard de l'Astrée. **GPS**: n45,91411 e3,84727.

5 free ChWCfree. **Location:** Rural, simple.
01/01-31/12 Thu-morning.
Distance: on the spot on the spot on the spot on the spot.

S Saint-Mamet-la-Salvetat 24G2

Aire camping-cars, D20. **GPS**: n44,85714 e2,30981.

3 free €2/100liter Ch €2/1h WC. **Location:** Rural, simple, quiet. **Surface:** asphalted. 01/01-31/12.
Distance: 500m 350m.
Remarks: Coins at the shops and town hall.

S Saint-Marcel-d'Urfé 22B3

Le Bourg. **GPS**: n45,87361 e3,88391.
3 free Chfree. **Surface:** gravel.
Distance: on the spot on the spot.
Remarks: At tennis-court.

S Saint-Marcel-en-Murat 21H2

D243. **GPS**: n46,32184 e3,00837.

FR

10 free €2/100liter Ch €2/1h. **Location:** Rural, simple. **Surface:** gravel. 01/01-31/12.
Distance: 3,5km exit 11 A71 nearby.
Remarks: Coins at town hall and restaurant.

Saint-Martin-d'Estréaux 21H2

Place des Gouttes. GPS: n46,20713 e3,00000.
3 free. **Surface:** metalled. 01/01-31/12.
Distance: 200m 200m 200m.

Saint-Martin-en-Haut 22C3

Etang du Kaiser, Lieu-dit-Jeangouttière. **GPS:** n45,64206 e4,53511.

4 free Ch WC.
Location: Rural, comfortable, quiet. **Surface:** gravel. 01/01-31/12.
Distance: St.Martin 4km on the spot on the spot on the spot.
Remarks: At small lake, max. 72h.

Saint-Ours-les Roches 21H3

Vulcania, 2 route de Mazayes. **GPS:** n45,81467 e2,94309.
65 € 10 €2/100liter Ch (20x)€2/6h. 15/03-13/11.
Remarks: Max. 2 nights.

Saint-Paul-des-Landes 24G2

Aire camping-cars, Rue du Moinac. **GPS:** n44,94250 e2,31694.

3 free €3,50 Ch €3,50. **Location:** Rural, simple, central, quiet. **Surface:** asphalted. 01/01-31/12.
Distance: 50m 200m 50m.
Remarks: Coins at petrol station.

Saint-Paul-le-Jeune 25B3

Rue Louis Roux, D901. **GPS:** n44,33999 e4,15322.

free €2 Ch €2. **Location:** Rural. **Surface:** grassy. 01/01-31/12.
Distance: on the spot 100m.
Remarks: Coins at the shops in the village.

Saint-Paul-Trois-Châteaux 25C3

Parking Office de Tourisme, Le Courreau, Place Chausy.
GPS: n44,34786 e4,76995.

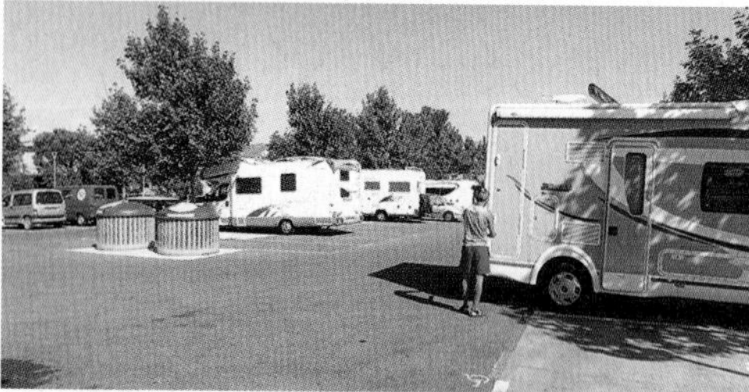

free Chfree WC. **Location:** Urban. **Surface:** asphalted.
Distance: 50m 50m.
Remarks: Max. 24h.

Tourist information Saint-Paul-Trois-Châteaux:
Marché. Tue-morning.
Marché aux truffes du Tricastin. Dec-Mar Su-morning.

Saint-Pierre-en-Faucigny 22E3

Avenue de la Gare. **GPS:** n46,05884 e6,37450.

4 free Ch free. **Surface:** asphalted. 01/04-30/11.
Distance: on the spot 60m on the spot on the spot.
Remarks: Nearby railway station.

Saint-Pourçain-sur-Sioule 22A2

Aire Camping-car de la Moutte, Rue de la Moutte.
GPS: n46,31262 e3,29656.

73 free €4 Ch (8x)€4/4h.
Location: Urban, comfortable, central, quiet. **Surface:** grassy. 01/01-31/12.
Distance: 800m on the spot on the spot on the spot.
Remarks: Along the Sioule river.

Saint-Rémèze 25C3

Les Chais du Vivarais, D362. **GPS:** n44,39536 e4,50576.

free Chfree. **Surface:** asphalted. 01/03-15/11.
Distance: 500m 200m.
Remarks: Max. 48h.

Tourist information Saint-Rémèze:
Grotte Aven Marzal. Caves. Sa/Su/Holidays, 01/04-30/09 10.30-18h.
Grotte de la Madelaine. Caves. Apr-Oct 10-18h.
Musée de la lavande. Museum and distillery with lavender fields. 01/05-30/09 10-17h, Apr + Oct Sa-Su-holiday 10-17h.
Zoo préhistorique, Route des Gorges. Prehistoric park. 10.30-17.30h.

Saint-Rémy-de-Blot 21H3

Place du Bourg. **GPS:** n46,07722 e2,93139.

7 free WC. **Location:** Rural, simple, isolated, quiet. **Surface:** grasstiles. 01/01-31/12.
Distance: on the spot.

Saint-Restitut 25C3

Le Village. **GPS:** n44,33144 e4,79093.

free Chfree. **Surface:** asphalted. 01/01-31/12.
Distance: on the spot.

Saint-Rirand 22B3

Le Bourg. **GPS:** n46,07589 e3,84965.
3 free Chfree. **Surface:** gravel. 01/01-31/12.

Saint-Romain-d'Ay 25C1

Praperier, D6. **GPS:** n45,16430 e4,66339.

4 free €2/20minutes Ch (4x)€2/4h WC.
Location: Simple. **Surface:** asphalted. 01/01-31/12.
Distance: 550m 100m.
Remarks: Coins at town hall and superette.

Saint-Romain-de-Lerps 25C2

Le Village, D287. **GPS:** n44,98029 e4,79596.

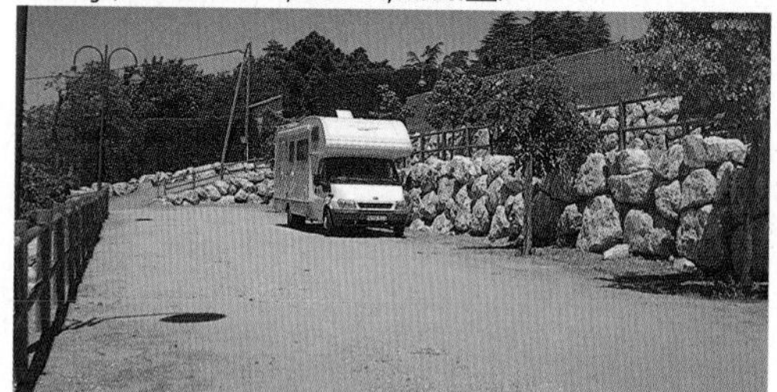

10 free Ch €4,100liter water + 1h electricity WC.
Location: Rural, simple, quiet. **Surface:** gravel. 01/01-31/12 01/10 and 01/04.
Distance: 100m 100m bakery 100m.
Remarks: Less suitable for motorhomes >6,5m, coins at bakery, bar/resto 3duPic and town hall, panoramic view over the Rhône-valley 200m.

Saint-Romain-Lachalm 25B1

Rulière. **GPS:** n45,26399 e4,33576.

4 free €2/10minutes Ch (4x)€2/4h.
Location: Rural, simple, isolated. **Surface:** asphalted.

FR

01/01-31/12.
Distance: 100m bakery 200m.
Remarks: Coins at the shops and town hall.

Saint-Sauves-d'Auvergne 21H3

Domaine de Lavaux, D82. **GPS**: n45,61688 e2,68975.

50 € 8 Ch (10x)€4/day WC included €1,25 €5.
Location: Rural, comfortable, isolated, quiet. **Surface:** grassy.
15/05-30/09.
Distance: 1km on the spot.

Saint-Symphorien-sur-Coise 22C3

Bois des Pinasses. **GPS**: n45,62578 e4,45837.

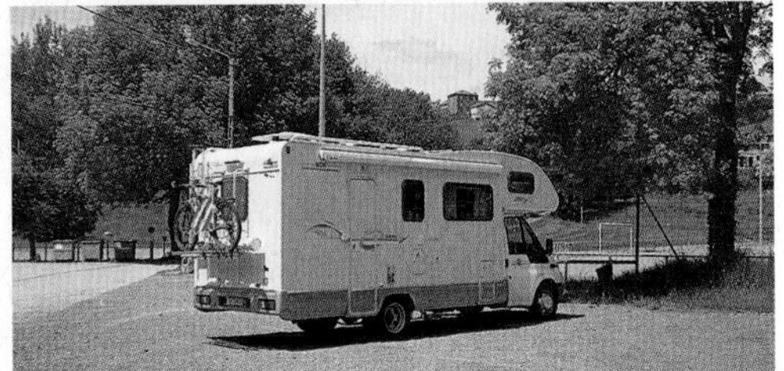

free.
Location: Rural, simple. **Surface:** gravel. 01/01-31/12.
Distance: 1km 50m.
Remarks: Next to sports fields.

Saint-Symphorien-sur-Coise 22C3

Rue des Rameaux. **GPS**: n45,63378 e4,45883.
Chfree. **Location:** Simple. 01/01-31/12.
Remarks: Free coins at Bar-Tabac and town hall.

Saint-Théoffrey 25E2

Camping Ser-Sirant, Chemin du Lavoir. **GPS**: n45,00034 e5,77819.
4 € 8-9,50 €1,50 Ch. **Location:** Rural. **Surface:** grassy.
Distance: beach Saint Théoffrey.
Remarks: At lake Laffrey, pay at reception campsite.

Saint-Thomé 25C3

N107, Les Crottes. **GPS**: n44,50059 e4,63445.

1 free Chfree. **Surface:** asphalted.

Saint-Victor-sur-Loire 25B1

Base Nautique du lac de Grangent. **GPS**: n45,44787 e4,25626.

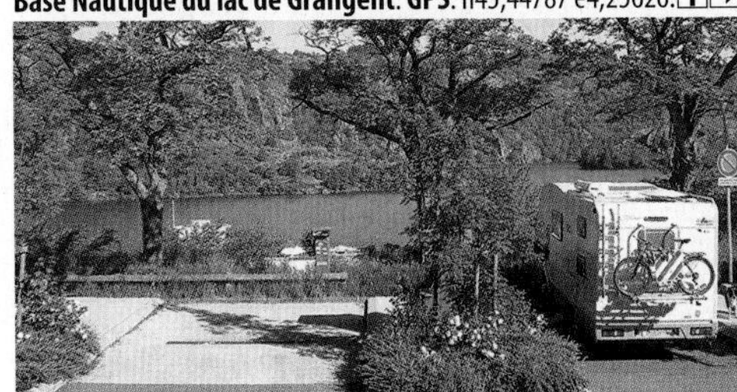

12 free Chfree (4x)€2,60/4h WC. **Location:** Rural, comfortable. **Surface:** asphalted. 01/01-31/12.
Distance: on the spot on the spot on the spot.
Remarks: Max. 72h, coins at the shops in the village.

Saintt-André-de-Chalencon 25B1

Place des Droits de l'Homme. **GPS**: n45,27254 e3,97010.
2 free €2/10minutes Ch €2/1h. **Location:** Urban, simple, central. **Surface:** gravel/sand. 01/01-31/12.
Distance: on the spot.

Salers 24H1

Le Mouriol, Route du Puy Mary. **GPS**: n45,14718 e2,49900.

15 € 3,70 + € 0,50 tourist tax €2,10 Ch €1,50,on campsite.
Location: Rural. **Surface:** gravel.
Distance: 1,2km 50m.
Remarks: Next to camping municipal, coins at campsite and tourist info.

Salers 24H1

D680. **GPS**: n45,14010 e2,49478.
12 € 3. **Location:** Rural. **Surface:** asphalted/metalled.
Distance: 500m.
Remarks: Max. 24h, no camping activities.

Salers 24H1

Rue Notre-Dame. **GPS**: n45,13898 e2,49583.
6 € 3. **Surface:** asphalted. 01/01-31/12.
Distance: 250m.
Remarks: Max. 24h, no camping activities.

Samoëns 22F3

Aire d'accueil camping-car de Vercland, Hameau de Vercland. **GPS**: n46,07283 e6,69957.

10 free Ch €5.
Surface: metalled. 01/01-31/12 Service: winter.
Distance: 2km 100m 2km.

Samoëns 22F3

Parking du Giffre. **GPS**: n46,07666 e6,71899.

5 € 10 Ch .
Surface: asphalted. 01/01-31/12 Service: winter.
Distance: 100m 100m 100m Skibus to Samoëns 1600 100m on the spot.
Remarks: Near campsite du Giffre, parking 150m.

Sansac-de-Marmiesse 24G2

Aire camping-cars, Rue de la Vidalie. **GPS**: n44,88389 e2,34639.

3 free €3,50 Ch €3,50.
Location: Urban, simple, central. **Surface:** asphalted.
01/01-31/12 service: 01/10-30/04.
Distance: on the spot 200m on the spot.
Remarks: Coins at the bakery.

Sassenage 25D1

Rue Pierre de Coubertin. **GPS**: n45,21346 e5,66858.

9 free Chfree. **Surface:** asphalted. 01/01-31/12.
Distance: on the spot on the spot.
Remarks: At sports grounds, max. 48h.

Saugues 25A2

Place du Brieul. **GPS**: n44,95940 e3,54395.

10 free Chfree. **Location:** Simple. **Surface:** asphalted.
01/01-31/12.
Distance: on the spot bakery 200m.

Sauret-Besserve 21H3

D523. **GPS**: n45,99245 e2,80746.

4 free €2 Ch. **Location:** Rural, simple, isolated.
01/01-31/12.
Remarks: Near church.

Ségur-les-Villas 24H1

Aire de camping-cars, Le Bourg. **GPS**: n45,22311 e2,81818.

10 free €3/100liter Ch €3/1h. **Location:** Rural, simple, quiet. **Surface:** grassy. 01/05-31/10.
Distance: 200m 300m 200m.
Remarks: Nearby football ground, coins at the shops in the village.

Serrières-en-Chautagne 22E3

GPS: n45,87964 e5,84230.

15 free ChWCfree. **Location:** Rural, central, quiet.
Surface: metalled. 01/01-31/12 Service: winter.
Distance: on the spot 1km beach 50m on the spot 200m 100m 100m.
Remarks: At little mountain stream.

Seyssel 22E3

Parking Base de Loisirs, Quai du Rhône. **GPS**: n45,95146 e5,83343.

4 free Chfree. **Location:** Rural, simple, central, quiet.

FR

Surface: gravel. 01/01-31/12.
Distance: 800m on the spot on the spot 500m 800m on the spot.
Remarks: At recreational lake and Rhone river.

Seyssel 22E3

Quai du Rhône. **GPS**: n45,95001 e5,83406.

12 free. **Location:** Rural, simple, central, quiet. **Surface:** gravel. 01/10-01/06.
Distance: 400m on the spot on the spot 400m 400m 400m on the spot.

Siaugues-Sainte-Marie 25A2

D590. **GPS**: n45,09303 e3,62784.

4 free €2/10minutes Ch €2/h. **Location:** Rural, simple.
Surface: grassy. 01/01-31/12.
Distance: 300m.

Sixt-Fer-à-Cheval 22F3

Route du Cirque du Fer à Cheval. **GPS**: n46,05698 e6,78048.

20 free Ch €4/12h.
Surface: asphalted. 01/01-31/12.
Distance: 500m on the spot 500m.

Solignac-sur-Loire 25B2

Le Vis. **GPS**: n44,96471 e3,88001.

20 € 12 Ch WCincluded. **Location:** Rural, comfortable, isolated, quiet. **Surface:** grassy. 01/05-01/11.
Distance: 800m.

Solignat 25A1

Route des Dauphins d'Auvergne, D32. **GPS**: n45,51701 e3,17074.

+50 free €2/100liter Ch €2/1h. **Location:** Rural, simple, quiet. **Surface:** grassy. 01/01-31/12.
Distance: 100m.

St Anthème 25B1

Rambaud. **GPS**: n45,52354 e3,91464.

30 € 3 Chincluded.
Location: Rural, simple, central, quiet. **Surface:** grassy/gravel.
01/01-31/12 Water when frosty.
Distance: 200m beach 250m 200m on the spot.
Remarks: Next to campsite Rambaud, water disconnected.

Super Besse 24H1

La Binche, Ronde de Vassivière. **GPS**: n45,50644 e2,85342.

172 € 5,60/24h, € 37,80/8 days €1/20minutes Ch (100x) €2,50/4h . **Location:** Comfortable, quiet.
Surface: asphalted. 01/01-31/12.
Distance: 300m 300m on the spot 300m.
Remarks: On ring-road around the lake, P5, P7 and P10, no camping activities.

Super Lioran 24H2

Aire de Laveissière, Parking Font d'Alagnon.
GPS: n45,08856 e2,73819.

25 free. **Location:** Rural, simple, quiet. **Surface:** asphalted. 01/01-31/12.
Distance: 200m 200m 50m 30m 30m.

Suze-la-Rousse 25C3

Route de Bollène, D94. **GPS**: n44,28598 e4,83185.

free free. **Surface:** grassy/gravel. 01/01-31/12.
Distance: 850m on the spot on the spot.
Remarks: At sports grounds.

Suze-la-Rousse 25C3

50 Impasse de la Zone Artisanale. **GPS**: n44,28965 e4,84783.
Chfree. 01/01-31/12.
Distance: 1,5km.

Talizat 24H2

Place du 19 mars 1962. **GPS**: n45,11417 e3,04583.

3 free €2 Ch €2.
Location: Rural, simple, quiet. **Surface:** asphalted.
01/01-31/12.
Distance: on the spot 100m 100m on the spot.
Remarks: Coins at town hall and restaurant, behind town hall.

Tence 25B2

Place du Fieu. **GPS**: n45,11580 e4,29220.

6 free €2/10minutes Ch. **Location:** Urban, simple, quiet.
Surface: gravel/metalled. 01/01-31/12.
Distance: 200m 200m on the spot.

Thiel-sur-Acolin 22A2

Rue de la Motte. **GPS**: n46,52269 e3,58776.
11 free €2 Ch €2. **Location:** Rural, isolated, quiet.
Surface: gravel. 01/01-31/12.
Distance: 650m.
Remarks: Service only by credit card.

Thiel-sur-Acolin 22A2

Route Départementale 914. **GPS**: n42,63763 e2,93675.
6 € 12 Ch included.

Thiers 22A3

Base de loisirs Iloa, D44 > Dorat. **GPS**: n45,87070 e3,48311.

10 free free. **Location:** Rural, simple, isolated, quiet.
Surface: metalled. 01/01-31/12.
Distance: 2,6km.

Thiézac 24H2

Aire de camping-car La Sapinière, D59.
GPS: n45,01583 e2,66278.

8 free €2 Ch €2. **Location:** Rural, simple, quiet.
Surface: asphalted. 01/01-31/12.
Distance: 50m 100m 100m.
Remarks: Max. 24h, coins at petrol station.

Thueyts 25B2

Chemin d'Echelle du Roi, via N102. **GPS**: n44,67274 e4,21917.

10 free 5minutes Ch 10minutes,service €2.
Location: Rural, simple, quiet. **Surface:** grassy/gravel.
15/03-15/11.
Distance: 200m 200m on the spot.
Remarks: Near the Ardèche river and Pont du Diable, next to sports fields, max. 24h.

Tiranges 25B1

Accueil Camping Car, La Nerceyre. **GPS**: n45,30702 e3,99107.

10 free €2 Ch. **Location:** Rural, simple, quiet.
Surface: asphalted. 01/01-31/12.
Distance: 400m 400m 400m.

Tournon-sur-Rhône 25C2

Chemin de la Beaume/D86. **GPS**: n45,07337 e4,82150.

25 €5 Ch free. **Location:** Urban, simple. **Surface:** asphalted.
01/01-31/12.
Distance: 1km 5km 1km 1km.
Remarks: Max. 24h.

Tourist information Tournon-sur-Rhône:
Wed, Sa.
Route Panoramique, place Jean Jaurès. Starting point touristic route.

Tourzel-Ronzières 25A1

Aire camping-car, Chemin du Clos, D23. **GPS**: n45,52989 e3,13504.

15 free Ch WC free. **Location:** Rural, simple, isolated, quiet. **Surface:** grassy/gravel. 01/01-31/12.
Distance: 500m 500m.

Treffort 25D2

Plage de la Salette, D110b. **GPS**: n44,90732 e5,67208.

12 € 10/24h €2 Ch €2 WC. **Surface:** gravel.
01/05-31/10.
Distance: 3km lake lake on the spot on the spot on the spot.
Remarks: At lake Monteynard.

Treteau 22A2

Rue du Rosier, D21. **GPS**: n46,36800 e3,51758.

+10 € 3,50/night €2 Ch €2 WC. **Location:** Rural, simple, quiet. **Surface:** grassy/metalled. 01/03-31/10.
Distance: 500m on the spot day pass available 100m on the spot.
Remarks: At small lake.

Trévoux 22C3

Chemin du Camping. **GPS**: n45,94017 e4,76694.

4 €5 €3 Ch €3 WC €2.
Location: Urban, simple, central, quiet. **Surface:** grassy/gravel.
01/01-31/12.
Distance: on the spot 7km 100m 1km 1km 1km.
Remarks: Along river, at entrance campsite, pay at campsite or town hall.

Ugine 22F3

Place du 8 Mai 1945. **GPS**: n45,74634 e6,41774.
free €2 €2 WC. **Surface:** asphalted. 01/01-31/12.
Distance: 50m 50m 50m.

Tourist information Ugine:
Wed, Sa-morning.

Val d'Isère 25F1

Le Pont Saint-Charles, Route du Col de l'Iseran, D902.
GPS: n45,45432 e6,97005.

50 free free. **Surface:** gravel. 01/01-31/12.
Distance: on the spot.
Remarks: Parking at skipistes.

Valette 24H1

Aire camping-cars, D678. **GPS**: n45,27000 e2,60222.

5 free €2 Ch €2. **Location:** Rural, comfortable, quiet.
Surface: gravel. 01/01-31/12 service: 01/11-01/05.
Distance: 50m 100m 150m.

Valloire 25F1

Camping-Car Park Les Verneys, Route du Galibier.
GPS: n45,14591 e6,42011.
30 € 12 Ch WC included. **Surface:** asphalted.
01/01-31/12.
Distance: on the spot 250m.
Remarks: Free shuttle.

Vallon-Pont-d'Arc 25B3

Chemin du Chastelas. **GPS**: n44,40537 e4,39683.

20 € 6/24h €2 Ch €2 WC. 01/01-31/12.
Distance: 100m 100m 100m.
Remarks: Free shuttle to the Pont d'Arc, 2x per hour.

Vallon-Pont-d'Arc 25B3

Domaine de l'Esquiras, Chemin du Fez. **GPS**: n44,41583 e4,37738.

5 € 8, peak season € 10 + € 0,60/pp tourist tax Ch €3 WC free. **Surface:** gravel. 12/04-21/09.
Distance: 800m.
Remarks: Use sanitary facilities + swimming pool € 4/pp.

Tourist information Vallon-Pont-d'Arc:
Office de Tourisme, 1 Place de l'Ancienne Gare, http://pontdarc-ardeche.fr. Small tourist town with the well-known Pont d'Arc, a natural arc over the Ardèche river.
Grotte des Huguenots. Former shelter of the Huguenots. 15/06-31/08.
Thu-morning.

Valuéjols 24H2

Place de 19 Mars 1962. **GPS**: n45,05349 e2,92927.

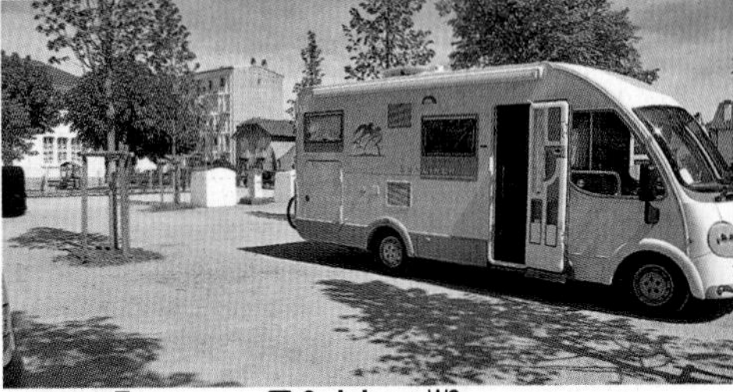

15 €3 Ch included. **Location:** Rural, simple.
Surface: asphalted. 01/01-31/12.
Distance: 400m 400m 400m on the spot on the spot on the spot.

Varennes-sur-Allier 22A2

Place Hôtel de Ville, Rue de Beaupuy. **GPS**: n46,31288 e3,40476.

30 free €2/100liter Ch €2/h WC.
Location: Urban, simple, central, noisy. **Surface:** metalled.
01/01-31/12.
Distance: on the spot on the spot on the spot.
Remarks: Coins at town hall.

Vassieux-en-Vercors 25D2

Avenue du Mémorial, D76. **GPS**: n44,89703 e5,36927.

FR

30 free Chfree.
Location: Rural, simple. **Surface:** metalled. service in winter.
Distance: 200m 200m 200m on the spot 7km Font D'Urle on the spot.
Remarks: Next to football ground.

Vaujany 25E1

Télécabine. GPS: n45,15694 e6,08011.

15 free Chfree €5.
Surface: gravel. 01/01-31/12.
Distance: 300m 300m 300m 300m.
Remarks: Max. 24h, coins at tourist info (electricity).

Védrines-Saint-Loup 25A2

Route du Plan d'Eau. **GPS**: n45,06758 e3,27565.

5 free €2/10minutes Ch €2/55minutes.
Location: Rural, simple, isolated, quiet. **Surface:** gravel/metalled.
01/01-31/12.
Distance: 400m on the spot on the spot on the spot.

Velzic 24H2

Lavernière, Rue de Fracort. **GPS**: n45,00166 e2,54638.

5 free €3,50 Ch. **Location:** Rural, simple, isolated.
Surface: asphalted. 01/01-31/12 service: 31/10-01/04.
Distance: 1km 1km 1km on the spot.
Remarks: Coins at épicerie Pas de Peyrols.

Vernosc-lès-Annonay 25C1

257 rue du Centre. **GPS**: n45,21914 e4,71409.
6 free Ch . 01/01-31/12.
Distance: 200m 200m.
Remarks: Next to town hall.

Vézac 24H2

Aire de camping-cars, Route de Cavanière.
GPS: n44,89059 e2,51779.

8 free €3,50 Ch.
Location: Rural, simple. **Surface:** asphalted. 01/01-31/12.
Distance: 100m 50m 700m.
Remarks: At golf court, coins at bar/tabac, 50m.

Vic-sur-Cère 24H2

Aire de camping-cars, Avenue des Tilleuls.
GPS: n44,98194 e2,63111.

10 free €2 Ch €2. **Location:** Rural, comfortable, quiet.
Surface: asphalted. 01/01-31/12.
Distance: 200m 200m 150m.
Remarks: Coins at tourist info, Avenue Mercier.

Vieille-Brioude 25A1

Rue de Combevignouse. **GPS**: n45,26540 e3,40557.

6 free €2/10minutes Ch €2/55minutes .
Location: Urban, simple, central, quiet. **Surface:** asphalted.
01/01-31/12.
Distance: 150m 200m.
Remarks: Service 200m.

Vieillevie 24G2

Aire de Vieillevie, Le Bourg. **GPS**: n44,64432 e2,41773.

5 free €2 Ch €2. **Location:** Rural, comfortable, quiet.
Surface: gravel. 01/01-31/12.
Distance: 50m 100m 50m 50m.

Vienne 25C1

Place Joseph Muray et Jean Tardy, N7. **GPS**: n45,53860 e4,87271.

10 free Chfree. **Location:** Urban, simple, central, noisy.
Surface: asphalted. Wed-afternoon (market).
Distance: 50m 2km 50m 50m 50m.

Villards-de-Lans 25D2

Chemin des Bartavelles. **GPS**: n45,06619 e5,55609.

15 free. **Surface:** asphalted.
Distance: 600m 600m 600m.
Remarks: Max. 48h.

Villars-les-Dombes 22C3

Parc des Oiseaux, RN83. **GPS**: n45,99126 e5,02582.

100 guests free. **Location:** Simple, quiet. **Surface:** asphalted/grassy.
01/01-31/12 sundays, holidays, winter.
Distance: 2km 1km 1km 2km 2km on the spot.
Remarks: Parking bird park, max. 1 night, gate closed from 21-8h.

Tourist information Villars-les-Dombes:
Parc des Oiseaux. Bird park, 23ha. 9.30-18.30h, winter 10-17.30h.

Villefranche-d'Allier 21H2

Avenue du 8 Mai 1945. **GPS**: n46,39565 e2,85672.

4 free €2/10minutes Ch (4x)€2/2h.
Surface: asphalted. 01/01-31/12.
Distance: 150m 12km 150m 150m.
Remarks: Coins available at the shops.

Villerest 22B3

Aire camping-car du Grezelon, D18, Route de Seigne.
GPS: n45,98610 e4,04300.

15 € 6, tourist tax € 0,25/pp €4 Ch.
Surface: gravel. 01/01-31/12 service: 01/10-30/04.
Distance: on the spot 1km on the spot.
Remarks: At Lac du Villerest and barrage, max. 48h.

Violay 22B3

Place Giroud. **GPS**: n45,85268 e4,35564.

FR

3 free €2 Ch€2. **Location:** Rural, simple, quiet.
Surface: metalled. 01/01-31/12.
Distance: 100m A89 9km 200m 150m.
Remarks: Beautiful view.

S Virieu 25D1

Rue du May, D17. **GPS**: n45,48166 e5,47746.

4 free ChWCfree. **Location:** Rural, simple, central, quiet.
Surface: gravel.
Distance: on the spot 200m 200m on the spot.
Remarks: Picnic area at edge of the village.

S Viverols 25B1

Camping Le Pradoux, Le Ruisseau. **GPS**: n45,43123 e3,88279.

6 free €2 Ch €2. **Surface:** gravel. 01/04-31/10.

Vogüé 25B3

Chemin de Setras. **GPS**: n44,55163 e4,41308.

20 free. **Surface:** asphalted. 01/01-31/12.
Distance: 50m Ardèche 200m.
Remarks: At cemetery.

S Vorey-sur-Arzon 25B1

Aire Les Moulettes, Chemin de Félines. **GPS**: n45,18667 e3,90489.

5 €2 €3 Ch €4. **Location:** Rural, simple.
Surface: gravel. 01/01-31/12 service 15/09-30/04.
Distance: 200m on the spot 200m 200m on the spot on the spot.
Remarks: Along river Arzon, coins and code wifi available at campsite.

S Ytrac 24G2

Aire camping-cars, Impasse Jean de la Fontaine.
GPS: n44,91510 e2,36368.

3 free €3,50 Ch €3,50. **Location:** Rural, simple, central.

Surface: asphalted. 01/01-31/12.
Distance: 150m 100m 150m.
Remarks: Coins at shops and tourist office.

Nouvelle-Aquitaine

S Accous 27B3

La Nabe, D339. **GPS**: n42,91028 w0,61939.

20 € 12 Ch WC included. **Location:** Rural, comfortable, isolated, quiet. **Surface:** grassy/gravel.
Distance: 7km 100m on the spot.

S Agris 21D3

Le Pont d'Agris, D6. **GPS**: n45,78619 e0,33944.

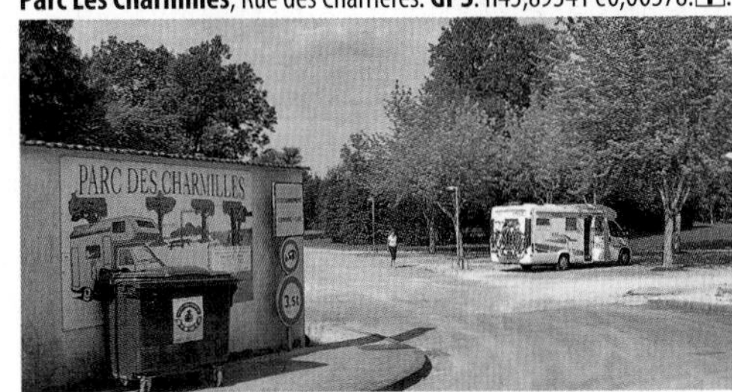

6 free €2 Ch €2. **Surface:** asphalted. 01/01-31/12.
Distance: on the spot on the spot on the spot.

S Aigre 21D3

Parc Les Charmilles, Rue des Charrières. **GPS**: n45,89341 e0,00578.

10 € 5,50 Ch (4x)WCincluded . **Surface:** metalled.
01/04-31/10.
Distance: on the spot on the spot on the spot.
Remarks: 4th night free.

S Aillas 24C3

À Bourg. **GPS**: n44,47514 w0,07318.

5 free Chfree. **Location:** Urban, simple, quiet.
Surface: gravel. 01/01-31/12.
Distance: 200m 100m.
Remarks: Next to sports fields.

S Aire-sur-l'Adour 27C1

Rue des Graviers. **GPS**: n43,70333 w0,25535.

50 € 3, 01/07-31/08 € 4 €1 Ch. **Location:** Rural, simple, quiet. **Surface:** gravel.
01/01-31/12 3rd week Jun.
Distance: 200m on the spot on the spot 200m.
Remarks: Near campsite, max. 72h.

S Airvault 21D1

Rue Faubourg des Cyprès. **GPS**: n46,82516 w0,14219.

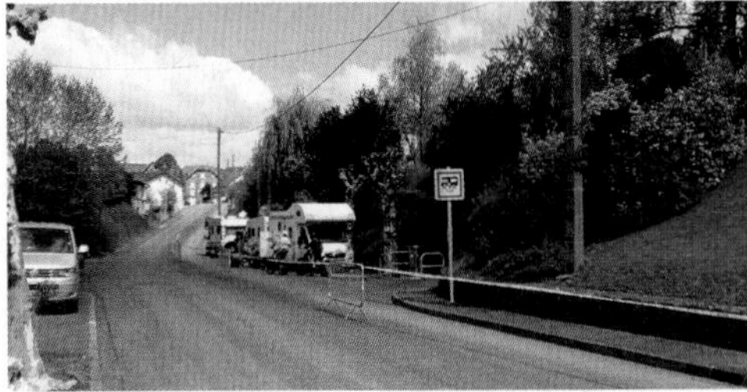

10 free ChWCfree. **Location:** Urban, simple, central.
Surface: asphalted. 01/01-31/12.
Distance: 250m 250m 250m.

S Allassac 24F1

Avenue du Saillant. **GPS**: n45,25897 e1,47358.

4 free Ch (2x)free. **Location:** Urban, simple, noisy.
Surface: gravel/sand. 01/01-31/12.
Distance: 500m 5km 500m 500m.
Remarks: Parking station.

S Andernos-les-Bains 24B2

Port Ostréicole, Avenue du Commandant Allègre.
GPS: n44,74477 w1,10969.

60 € 9,20 €2,50/100liter Ch €2,10 .
Location: Urban, comfortable, quiet. **Surface:** grassy/metalled.
01/01-31/12.
Distance: 500m on the spot on the spot 50m.
Remarks: In harbour, max. 48h.

S Anglet 27A1

Aire de camping-car de La Barre, Avenue de l'Adour, D405.
GPS: n43,52608 w1,51488.

50 free, Apr/June € 6, July/Aug € 10 €3 Ch.
Surface: grassy/metalled. 13/04-11/11.
Distance: 1km 300m 50m 500m 500m 100m.
Remarks: Private property.

S Anglet 27A1

Parking "Haut" - Plage des Corsaires, Boulevard des Plages.
GPS: n43,50696 w1,53373.

FR

80 free, Apr/June € 6, July/Aug € 10 Chincluded.
Surface: asphalted. 01/01-31/12.
Distance: 500m, Biarritz 2km 500m 500m 500m.
Remarks: Max. 24h, baker every morning.

S Angliers 18D3

Aire de repos de la Briande, D347. **GPS**: n46,95861 e0,10472.

8 free Ch WCfree. **Location:** Rural, comfortable, quiet.
Surface: asphalted. 01/01-31/12.
Distance: Angliers 1km 50m.

S Angoisse 24E1

Le Pont du Jour, L'Hépital, D704. **GPS**: n45,43296 e1,14413.

8 € 5 Chincluded €3 €3. **Location:** Rural, simple.
Surface: grassy.
Distance: 500m 1km 4,5km.

S Angoulins 21B2

Rue du Chay. **GPS**: n46,10623 w1,13565.

17 free. **Location:** Rural, simple. **Surface:** asphalted.
Distance: 1km 20m.

S Arcachon 24B2

Boulevard Mestrézat, D650. **GPS**: n44,65142 w1,14864.

20 free Chfree. **Location:** Urban, simple, noisy.
Surface: asphalted/gravel. 01/01-31/12.
Distance: 1km 50m.
Remarks: Max. 24h.

Arcachon 24B2

Avenue du Parc. **GPS**: n44,64868 w1,19672.

free.
Location: Simple. **Surface:** gravel. 01/01-31/12.
Distance: on the spot on the spot.

Tourist information Arcachon:
place du XI Novembre. Covered market. 01/06-31/08 daily 7-13h.

S Arçais 21C2

Aire camping-cars du Coursault, Rue de Coursault.
GPS: n46,29583 w0,69.

20 € 8 ChWCfree. **Location:** Simple, quiet.
Surface: grassy. 01/01-31/12.
Distance: 400m on the spot nearby nearby.

S Arette 27B2

Aire de camping car d'Arette, Place de la Mairie.
GPS: n43,09477 w0,71511.

10 free ChWC. **Location:** Simple. **Surface:** asphalted.
01/01-31/12.

S Arzacq-Arraziguet 27C2

Aire de camping cars, Place du Marcadieu.
GPS: n43,53481 w0,41035.

10 free ChWCfree. **Location:** Urban. **Surface:** asphalted.
01/01-31/12.
Distance: on the spot 500m 500m 100m 100m.

S Aubeterre-sur-Dronne 24D1

Base de Loisirs, D2, Route de Ribérac. **GPS**: n45,26934 e0,17586.

7 free Chfree. **Location:** Rural, simple, isolated, quiet.
Surface: gravel/metalled. 01/01-31/12.
Distance: 500m on the spot 300m 500m.
Remarks: At tennis-courts.

Tourist information Aubeterre-sur-Dronne:
Place de Village. Thu, Su.

S Aubusson 21G3

Parking Champ de Foire, Rue des Fusilles, D988.
GPS: n45,95694 e2,17528.

70 free Ch WCfree. **Location:** Urban. **Surface:** asphalted.
01/01-31/12.
Distance: 500m 500m 500m.

S Aulnay 21C2

Rue de Salles. **GPS**: n46,02239 w0,34528.

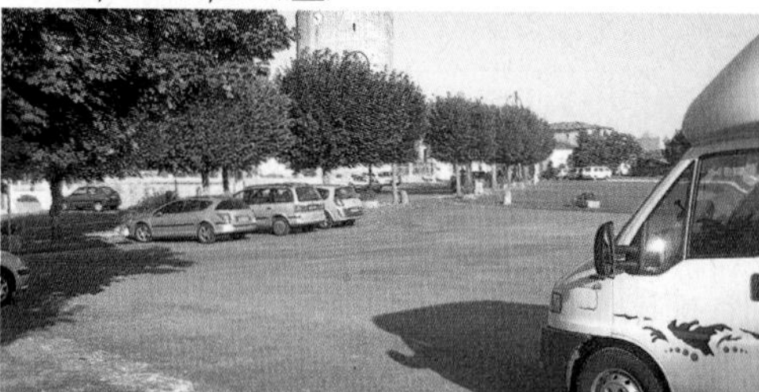

10 free Chfree. **Surface:** gravel.
Distance: 200m 200m 200m.
Remarks: Max. 24h.

Aulnay 21C2

Place Charles de Gaulle, Rue Haute de l'Eglise.
GPS: n46,02306 w0,35444.

10 free. **Surface:** metalled. 01/01-31/12.
Distance: 200m 200m 200m.

S Auriat 21F3

Etang d'Auriat. **GPS**: n45,87790 e1,64277.

3 free Chfree. **Location:** Rural, isolated, quiet.
Surface: metalled. 01/01-31/12.
Distance: on the spot on the spot.
Remarks: At small lake.

S Ayen 24F1

Route de la Noix, Ayen Bas. **GPS**: n45,24964 e1,32343.

20 free Chfree. **Location:** Rural, simple, quiet.
Surface: grassy/gravel. 01/01-31/12.
Distance: 300m.
Remarks: Nearby D39, campsite and sports grounds.

Azerat 24E1

Le Bourg. **GPS**: n45,14954 e1,12496.

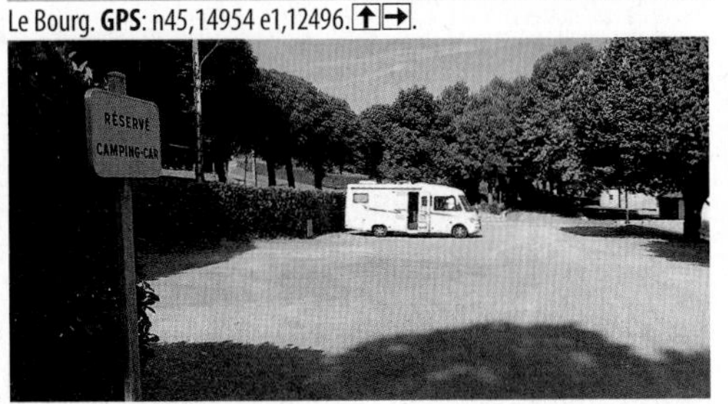

6 €2 €3 Ch. **Location:** Urban, simple, quiet. **Surface:** gravel. 01/01-31/12.
Distance: 50m 150m.
Remarks: Pay at town hall.

Azur 27A1

Camping-Car Park, Route du Lac. **GPS**: n43,78842 w1,3119.

31 € 9,60 + one-time Pass'Etapes € 4 Ch included. **Location:** Rural, quiet. **Surface:** gravel. 01/01-31/12.
Distance: 1,5km 150m 150m 200m on the spot on the spot.

Badefols-sur-Dordogne 24E2

Le Bourg. **GPS**: n44,84254 e0,79160.

10 free €2/100liter Ch WC free. **Location:** Rural, simple.
Surface: asphalted. 01/01-31/12 Sa market.
Distance: on the spot bakery 50m.
Remarks: Coins at town hall.

Barbezieux-Saint-Hilaire 24C1

E.Leclerc, Rue du Commandant Foucaud. **GPS**: n45,47047 w0,16032.

8 free €2/100liter Ch. **Location:** Urban, simple, central, noisy.
Surface: asphalted. 01/01-31/12.
Distance: 500m on the spot on the spot.

Bazas 24C3

Rue de l'Eyrevieille. **GPS**: n44,43389 w0,21509.

5 Ch WC free. Service: winter.

Beaumont du Périgord 24E2

Avenue Rhinau, D660. **GPS**: n44,77469 e0,76559.

20 free Ch free. **Surface:** asphalted. 01/01-31/12.
Distance: 800m.

Tourist information Beaumont du Périgord:
Bastide de Beaumont.

Bellac 21E2

Aire d'accueil camping-car rives du Vincou, Rue des Tanneries.
GPS: n46,11513 e1,05242.

4 free Ch free. **Location:** Rural, isolated, quiet.
Surface: asphalted. 01/01-31/12.
Distance: 1km.
Remarks: Service 100m.

Bellac 21E2

Le Champ de foire, Rue des Doctrinaires.
GPS: n46,12085 e1,05018.

4 free. **Location:** Urban, simple. **Surface:** asphalted.
Distance: on the spot on the spot on the spot.
Remarks: >3,5t not allowed.

Bellac 21E2

Parking de la Mairie, Place de la République.
GPS: n46,12155 e1,04604.

2 free. **Location:** Urban, simple. **Surface:** asphalted. 01/01-31/12.
Distance: 300m.

Bénéjacq 27C2

L'Esplanade du Lagoin, Place de la Fontaine.
GPS: n43,19009 w0,20914.

6 free €2/100liter Ch €2/h. **Location:** Urban, comfortable, quiet. **Surface:** asphalted. 01/01-31/12.
Distance: 500m 50m 500m.

Remarks: Max. 48h, coins at the bakery, restaurant and pharmacy.

Bergerac 24D2

Parc Public de Pombonne, Avenue Marceau Feyry.
GPS: n44,87104 e0,50408.

6 free €2/100liter Ch. **Location:** Simple.
Surface: metalled.
Distance: city centre 3km 1km.
Remarks: Max. 24h.

Tourist information Bergerac:
Musée du Tabac, Maison Peyrarède, Place du Feu. History of tobacco. Mo-Fri 10-12h, 14-18, Sa 10-12h, 14-17h, Su 14.30-17.30h, Nov-Mar Mo-Fr.
Église Notre Dame, Rue Saint Esprit. Wed, Sa 7-13h.

Bernos-Beaulac 24C3

La Grande Route, N524. **GPS**: n44,36949 w0,24257.

10 € 4 €2/10minutes Ch.
Location: Rural, simple, quiet. **Surface:** metalled.
01/01-31/12 water: frost.
Distance: river on the spot bakery 100m.
Remarks: Coins at petrol station.

Bessines-sur-Gartempe 21F2

Place du Champ de Foire, Rue d'Ingolsheim.
GPS: n46,10979 e1,37008.

4 free €2 Ch €2. **Location:** Urban, simple.
Surface: asphalted. 01/01-31/12.
Distance: on the spot 900m 100m 50m.

Beynac-et-Cazenac 24E2

Le Parc, D703. **GPS**: n44,84466 e1,14560.

20 free.
Location: Rural, simple. **Surface:** gravel. 01/01-31/12.
Distance: historical centre 500m 500m.

Biarritz 27A2

Aire de camping-cars Gabrielle Dorziat, Allée Gabrielle Dorziat.
GPS: n43,45974 w1,56893.

FR

19 € 12/24h Ch included. 01/01-31/12.
Remarks: Max. 48h.

Biarritz 27A2

Parking Milady, Avenue de la Milady. **GPS**: n43,46536 w1,57162.

50 € 12 Ch included.
Location: Urban, simple. **Surface:** asphalted. 01/01-31/12.
Distance: 500m 300m 500m 500m.
Remarks: Baker every morning.

Tourist information Biarritz:
Rue des Halles. daily.

Biron 24E2

Route de Vergt de Biron. **GPS**: n44,63080 e0,87055.

10 free €2/100liter Ch €2/1h. **Location:** Simple.
Surface: grassy/metalled. 01/01-31/12 service 01/11-31/03.
Distance: 250m 250m.
Remarks: Coins at grocery.

Biscarrosse 24B3

Biscarrosse Plage Sud, Chemin de Navarosse.
GPS: n44,43223 w1,16566.

30 € 8, Jul/Aug € 15 Chfree WC. **Location:** Simple.
Surface: metalled. 01/01-31/12.
Distance: 4km 50m 100m 50m on the spot.
Remarks: Video surveillance.

Biscarrosse 24B3

Rue des Viviers, Biscarrosse-plage. **GPS**: n44,46027 w1,24627.

80 € 12,50, 15/09-14/06 € 8, 15/07-31/08 € 16
Ch included. **Location:** Simple, quiet. **Surface:** forest soil.
01/05-31/10.
Distance: 2,5km 400m 100m 50m on the spot.

Remarks: Video surveillance.

Blanquefort 24C2

Château Saint Ahon, Rue de Saint-Ahon.
GPS: n44,92663 w0,63217.

4 € 3 free.
Location: Urban, simple, central, quiet. **Surface:** gravel/metalled.
01/01-31/12 Su/holidays.
Distance: 300m 12km 300m on the spot.
Remarks: Arrival < 19h, max. 48h.

Blasimon 24C2

Rue Abbé Greciet. **GPS**: n44,74836 w0,07537.

4 free Chfree. **Location:** Urban, simple, quiet.
Surface: gravel. 01/01-31/12.
Distance: 100m 100m 100m.

Blasimon 24C2

Château la Peyraude, Bleurette. **GPS**: n44,73463 w0,09942.

15 free Ch WC free.
Location: Rural, simple. **Surface:** grassy. 01/01-31/12.
Distance: 3km.
Remarks: Arrival <22h, regional products.

Blaye 24C1

Parking de la Citadelle, Rue Pierre Semard.
GPS: n45,12549 w0,66535.

30 free. **Location:** Urban, simple, central, quiet.
Surface: gravel/metalled. 01/01-31/12.
Distance: 250m on the spot on the spot 300m 2km
300m.

Blaye 24C1

Château le Cône, Route des Cônes. **GPS**: n45,13742 w0,66507.

12 free Ch (4x). **Location:** Rural, comfortable, quiet.
Surface: asphalted/gravel. 01/01-31/12.
Distance: 2km on the spot on the spot.

Boismé 21C1

Rue des Essarts. **GPS**: n46,77765 w0,43347.

4 free ChWCfree. **Location:** Rural, isolated, quiet.
Surface: metalled. 01/01-31/12.
Distance: on the spot 500m 500m on the spot
on the spot.
Remarks: At small lake, playground.

Bort-les-Orgues 24H1

Rue de la Fontaine Grande. **GPS**: n45,39913 e2,49710.

6 free Chfree. **Location:** Urban, simple, central, quiet.
Surface: asphalted. 01/01-31/12.
Distance: 200m river 200m 200m.

Bosmoreau-les-Mines 21F3

Le Bourg. **GPS**: n45,99936 e1,75194.

5 free Chfree. **Location:** Rural, simple, quiet.
Surface: gravel. 01/01-31/12.
Distance: 500m.

Bouglon 24D3

Aire de Repos, Le Clavier. **GPS**: n44,38599 e0,10271.

4 free WCfree. **Location:** Rural, simple, quiet.
Surface: asphalted. 01/01-31/12.
Distance: 500m 500m 500m.
Remarks: Picnic area.

Bougon 21D2

Musée des Tumulus, La Chapelle. **GPS**: n46,37845 w0,06825.

10 free free. **Location:** Rural, simple, isolated.

Surface: asphalted. 01/01-31/12.
Distance: 3km.
Remarks: Parking museum.

Bourcefranc-le-Chapus 21B3

Bois de Pin, Prise du Portail Rouge. **GPS:** n45,82611 w1,14278.

20 € 6. **Location:** Isolated, quiet. **Surface:** gravel.
01/01-31/12.
Distance: 4km on the spot on the spot 3km.

Bourcefranc-le-Chapus 21B3

Rue du Président Kennedy. **GPS:** n45,84546 w1,14929.

10 free. **Location:** Urban, simple, central. **Surface:** asphalted.
01/01-31/12.
Distance: 250m 750m 250m 250m.
Remarks: Max. 24h.

Bourcefranc-le-Chapus 21B3

Camping de la Giroflée, Fief de Bonnemort.
GPS: n45,83112 w1,15073.
€2,60/100liter Ch. 01/05-31/10.
Distance: 2,5km on the spot.
Remarks: Coins at tourist info and town hall.

Bourdeilles 24E1

Plaine des Loisirs, Le Bourg. **GPS:** n45,32270 e0,58260.

40+ € 4,50 €2/100liter Ch. **Location:** Comfortable, quiet.
Surface: grassy. 01/01-31/12.
Distance: 500m on the spot on the spot 200m 200m.
Remarks: Coins at the shops.

Bourg-sur-Gironde 24C1

Quai Jean Bart. **GPS:** n45,03794 w0,55699.

10 € 5 €3. **Location:** Urban, simple, central. **Surface:** asphalted.
01/01-31/12.
Distance: on the spot On the river Gironde on the spot on the spot.

Bourganeuf 21F3

Place de l'Etang, Avenue du Dr Butaud. **GPS:** n45,95444 e1,75750.

10 free Chfree. **Location:** Urban. **Surface:** gravel.
01/01-31/12 tue-evening, wed-morning (market).
Distance: on the spot 300m on the spot.
Remarks: Max. 48h.

Branne 24C2

Route de Cabara. **GPS:** n44,83191 w0,18448.

3 free €2/100liter Ch €2/1h. **Location:** Urban, simple, noisy.
Distance: on the spot on the spot 500m 500m.

Brantôme 24E1

Chemin de Vert Galant. **GPS:** n45,36134 e0,64842.

50 € 5,50 €2/12minutes Ch. **Location:** Simple, quiet.
Surface: grassy. 01/01-31/12.
Distance: 200m 100m 300m.

Brantôme 24E1

Aire Camping-cars Font Vendôme, Route de Nontron.
GPS: n45,37924 e0,64588.

4 € 2 €2 Ch €1/night WC. **Location:** Simple.
Surface: asphalted. 01/01-31/12.
Distance: 3,5km 1km 1km.
Remarks: Money in envelope in mail box.

Tourist information Brantôme:
Fri-morning.

Bressuire 21C1

Place Labâte. **GPS:** n46,84417 w0,49086.

5 free Chfree. **Location:** Urban, simple, noisy. **Surface:** sand.
01/01-31/12.
Distance: 400m 400m 400m.

Brive-la-Gaillarde 24F1

Rue des 3 Provinces. **GPS:** n45,16486 e1,54170.

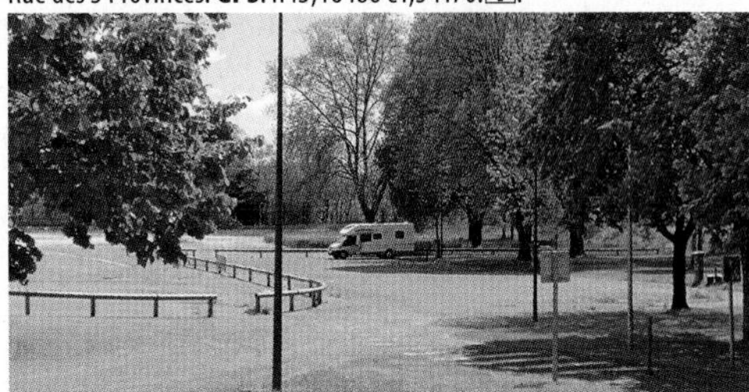

12 first night € 9, € 7 each additional night + tourist tax € 0,60/pp Ch (12x)€3/6h. **Location:** Urban, simple.
Surface: asphalted.
Distance: 1km 150m 500m.
Remarks: Free bus to centre.

Bujaleuf 21F3

Route du Champ de Foire. **GPS:** n45,80418 e1,63696.

5 free Chfree. **Location:** Rural, simple, quiet.
Surface: gravel. 01/01-31/12.
Distance: 1,5km on the spot 1,5km.
Remarks: Max. 24h, service 1,5km GPS N45,79747 E1,63141.

Bussière-Poitevine 21E2

Croix de l'Hosanne, Rue du Quatriéme Zouave.
GPS: n46,23670 e0,90173.

10 €2/100liter Ch WC. **Location:** Rural.
Surface: asphalted. 15/03-14/11.
Distance: 450m.
Remarks: Coins at the shops.

Buzet-sur-Baïse 24D3

Port de Buzet-Val d'Albret. **GPS:** n44,25799 e0,30569.

20 € 7 €2 Ch €2 WC €2 €2 €2/24h.
Location: Rural, comfortable. **Surface:** grassy. 01/01-31/12.
Distance: 6,5km on the spot 350m 350m on the spot on the spot.

Cadillac 24C2

Avenue du Parc. **GPS:** n44,63871 w0,31721.

10 free Chfree €2/3h. **Location:** Urban, simple.

FR

FR

Surface: asphalted. 01/01-31/12.
Distance: on the spot 100m 100m 100m.
Remarks: Max. 3 nights, closed when frosty.

S Cambo-les-Bains 27A2

Chemin Arroka. **GPS:** n43,35537 w1,41173.
8 € 10 Ch included. **Surface:** metalled.
01/01-31/12.
Distance: 500m 100m 500m 200m.

S Cancon 24E3

Rue des Écoles. **GPS:** n44,53638 e0,62562.

10 free Ch WC free. **Location:** Simple. **Surface:** metalled.
01/01-31/12.
Distance: 100m 100m 100m.

S Capbreton 27A1

Plage l'Océanide, Parking des Ortolans, Allée des Ortolans.
GPS: n43,63578 w1,44681.

133 € 8,80-13,50 Ch (120x) WC included.
Surface: asphalted. 15/11-31/03.
Distance: 1,5km on the spot on the spot 1,5km 1,5km.
Remarks: Beach parking, 14/07-20/08: max. 2 nights.

S Capian 24C2

D13/Chemin de Lavergne. **GPS:** n44,71177 w0,33093.

25 free €2/10minutes Ch €2/55minutes.
Location: Rural, simple, quiet. **Surface:** gravel.
01/01-31/12.
Distance: 500m.

S Carcans 24B1

Route de Bombannes, Maubuisson. **GPS:** n45,08545 w1,14866.

20 € 6,10 Ch free €2. **Location:** Rural, simple, isolated, quiet. **Surface:** asphalted/gravel. 01/07-31/08.
Distance: 2km 400m 2km 2km on the spot on the spot.

Tourist information Carcans:
Office de Tourisme, Maison de la Station, www.carcans-maubuisson.com. Touristic town between the ocean and a wine region, 120km signposted cycle routes.

S Casseneuil 24E3

Rue Grande, D225. **GPS:** n44,44667 e0,61861.

20 free Ch free. **Location:** Rural, simple. **Surface:** asphalted.
01/01-31/12.
Distance: 100m on the spot on the spot 100m 800m.

S Castelculier 24E3

GPS: n44,17475 e0,69452.

5 free €2 Ch. **Location:** Urban, simple, quiet.
Surface: metalled. 01/01-31/12.
Distance: 200m.

S Casteljaloux 24D3

Ste Castel Chalets, D933. **GPS:** n44,29230 e0,07361.

11 € 10, Jul/Aug € 15, dog € 3 Ch WC included.
Location: Rural, comfortable, quiet. **Surface:** gravel/sand.
01/04-31/10.
Distance: 2km Lac de Clarens.

S Casteljaloux 24D3

Impasse de la Fôret. **GPS:** n44,31068 e0,07933.

4 free Ch free. **Location:** Rural, simple, quiet.
Surface: asphalted. 01/01-31/12.
Distance: 250m 250m.
Remarks: Parking at swimming pool, max. 48h.

S Casteljaloux 24D3

La Taillade, Route de la Forge, La Réunion.
GPS: n44,26998 e0,08004.

4 € 8 Ch included. **Location:** Rural, isolated, quiet.
Surface: forest soil. 01/04-31/10.

S Caumont-sur-Garonne 24D3

Bourg de Caumont. **GPS:** n44,44202 e0,17887.

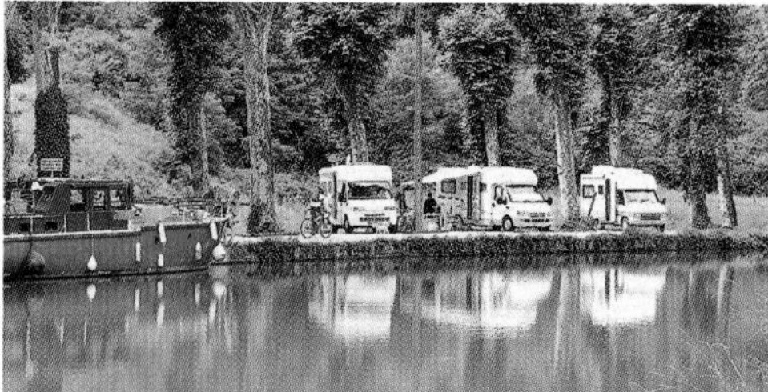

14 free €1 Ch €1/2h. **Location:** Rural, simple, quiet.
Surface: gravel. 01/01-31/12.
Distance: 8km on the spot.

S Cellefrouin 21D3

D739. **GPS:** n45,89361 e0,38639.

50 free Ch WC free. **Location:** Simple, isolated, quiet.
Surface: gravel. 01/01-31/12.
Distance: 300m.

S Celles-sur-Belle 21D2

Place de l'Aumônerie, Rue des Halles.
GPS: n46,26278 w0,20806.

10 free Ch free. **Location:** Urban, simple, quiet.
Surface: gravel. 01/01-31/12.
Distance: 100m 100m 100m.

Chabanais 21E3

Chemin des Tanneries, N141. **GPS:** n45,87447 e0,72008.

4 free. **Location:** Rural, simple. **Surface:** asphalted.
01/01-31/12 Thu.
Distance: on the spot 100m 100m.
Remarks: Along the river Vienne.

S Chalus 21E3

Aire des Energies, Avenue Jean Jaurès. **GPS:** n45,66095 e0,98798.

10 free €2 Ch €2.
Location: Simple. **Surface:** gravel.
Distance: 1,2km on the spot.
Remarks: Behind petrol station.

S Chamberet 21F3

Ris Combeix. **GPS:** n45,57926 e1,70843.

7 free (1x). **Location:** Rural, comfortable, isolated, quiet. **Surface:** grassy.
Distance: 1,3km 1,3km.

Chamberet 21F3

Route de St Dulcet. **GPS**: n45,57961 e1,72051.

4 free Ch. **Location:** Urban, simple, quiet.
Surface: gravel. 01/01-31/12.
Distance: 900m.
Remarks: Next to football ground.

Chambon-sur-Voueize 21H2

Rue du Stade. **GPS**: n46,18579 e2,43426.

4 free €2/10minutes Ch €2/1h. **Location:** Rural, quiet.
Surface: asphalted. 01/01-31/12 service 01/11-31/03.
Distance: 500m 500m 200m.
Remarks: Near camping municipal.

Chamboulive 24F1

GPS: n45,42255 e1,71639.
10 free €2 Ch €2/h. 01/01-31/12.
Distance: 1,2km 1,2km 1,2km.

Château-Larcher 21D2

Val de Clouère. **GPS**: n46,41444 e0,31556.

10 €5 Ch WC included.
Location: Rural, comfortable, isolated, quiet. **Surface:** grassy/gravel.
01/03-31/11.
Distance: 300m 100m 300m 300m.
Remarks: At small lake, former campsite, baker every morning.

Château-l'Evêque 24E1

Place de la Fontaine. **GPS**: n45,24472 e0,68743.

8 free €2 Ch €2. **Location:** Urban. **Surface:** gravel.
01/03-31/10 summer: Su (flea market).
Distance: 50m 100m on the spot.
Remarks: Max. 48h, coins at shops in the village 08-21h.

Châtelaillon-Plage 21B2

GPS: n46,07253 w1,07886.

51 €8,40-10,80 Ch (48x) included.
Location: Rural, simple. **Surface:** asphalted/grassy.
01/01-31/12.
Distance: 700m 800m 700m.

Châtelaillon-Plage 21B2

Parking de l'Office du Tourisme, Avenue de Strasbourg.
GPS: n46,07679 w1,08859.

5 free. **Location:** Urban, simple. **Surface:** metalled.
01/01-31/12.
Distance: on the spot 500m on the spot on the spot.

Châtelaillon-Plage 21B2

Les Boucholeurs, Avenue de l'Abbé Guichard.
GPS: n46,05538 w1,08738.

7 free. **Surface:** asphalted. 01/01-31/12.
Distance: 150m 150m 150m.
Remarks: Max. 48h.

Châtelus-le-Marcheix 21F3

Rue du Tursaud. **GPS**: n45,99894 e1,60339.

8 free €2 Ch €2. **Location:** Rural.
Surface: gravel/metalled. 01/01-31/12.
Distance: 300m 300m 300m.
Remarks: Next to camping municipal.

Chef-Boutonne 21D2

Aire camping-cars, Chemin du Parc. **GPS**: n46,10982 w0,07869.

20 free Ch WC free.
Surface: grassy/gravel. 01/04-31/10.
Distance: 800m 300m 800m on the spot.

Chénérailles 21G2

Route d'Aubusson, lotissement Marlaud, D990.
GPS: n46,11058 e2,17753.

5 free €4 Ch €4. **Location:** Simple. **Surface:** asphalted.
01/01-31/12.
Distance: 200m 50m 100m.
Remarks: Coins available at restaurant le Coq d'Or (50m).

Cherves-Richemont 21C3

Allee des Coquelicots. **GPS**: n45,74030 w0,35607.

6 free Ch free. **Surface:** asphalted.
01/01-31/12 service 01/11-15/04.
Distance: 500m 100m 500m.

Chey 21D2

Place de la Liberté. **GPS**: n46,30412 w0,05002.

4 free Ch WC free. **Location:** Rural, comfortable, quiet.
Surface: asphalted. 01/01-31/12.
Distance: on the spot.

Cieux 21E3

Avenue du Lac. **GPS**: n45,99173 e1,04939.

25 €8 €2 Ch €1,50.
Location: Simple. **Surface:** grassy. 15/04-15/10.
Distance: 100m.

Civrac-en-Médoc 24B1

Route de Montignac, Montignac. **GPS**: n45,33619 w0,922.

5 free. **Location:** Rural, simple, isolated, quiet. **Surface:** gravel.
01/01-31/12.

FR

Distance: 2km.

Clérac 24C1

Étang des Prés de Réaux, Route des Vignes.
GPS: n45,17906 w0,228.

8 free Ch free. **Location:** Rural, simple, isolated, quiet.
Surface: gravel. 01/01-31/12.
Distance: 200m on the spot 100m 100m on the spot on the spot.
Remarks: At small lake, max. 1 night.

Cognac 21C3

Place de la Levade, Quartier Saint-Jacques. **GPS**: n45,69847 w0,33265.

4 free €2 Ch. **Location:** Urban, simple, central.
Surface: asphalted. 01/01-31/12.
Distance: 100m on the spot 100m 500m on the spot.

Tourist information Cognac:
Otard. Cognac distillery in 16th century castle. Guided tour and tasting. daily 01/10-31/03 weekend.
Cognac-musée. Culture around the Cognac. 01/10-31/05 14-17.30h, 01/06-30/09 10-12h, 14-18h.

Collonges-la-Rouge 24F2

Parking le Marchadial. **GPS**: n45,05833 e1,65889.

20 free, 01/03-31/10 € 8/24h Ch WC included.
Location: Rural, simple, quiet. **Surface:** gravel.
01/01-31/12.
Distance: 500m 500m 500m 1km.

Concèze 24F1

D56E. **GPS**: n45,35472 e1,34583.

3 free Ch free. **Location:** Rural, simple, quiet.
Surface: gravel. 01/01-31/12.
Distance: on the spot.

Confolens 21E2

Camping les Ribières, Avenue de Sainte-Germain.
GPS: n46,01894 e0,67570.

free, May-Sep € 5 Ch WC included.
Surface: metalled. 01/01-31/12 service: 16/09-14/05.
Distance: 750m.

Tourist information Confolens:
Wed, Sa.

Contis-Plage 24A3

Avenue du Phare. **GPS**: n44,09333 w1,31861.

70 € 9, 01/06-01/09 € 13/24h, 01/12-28/02 free €2 Ch WC.
Location: Simple. **Surface:** gravel.
01/01-31/12.
Distance: 200m on the spot.
Remarks: Max. 72h.

Couhé 21D2

Place du Marché. **GPS**: n46,29906 e0,17882.

25 free Ch WC free. **Location:** Urban, simple, central, quiet.
Surface: asphalted. 01/01-31/12.
Distance: 200m 200m 200m.

Coulon 21C2

Parking d'Autremont, Rue André Cramois.
GPS: n46,32102 w0,59063.

80 € 8,50 Ch WC included. **Location:** Urban, comfortable. **Surface:** grassy/gravel. 01/04-30/11.
Distance: 350m 350m 350m on the spot on the spot.

Coulonges-sur-l'Autize 21C1

Avenue de la Gare. **GPS**: n46,48011 w0,59393.

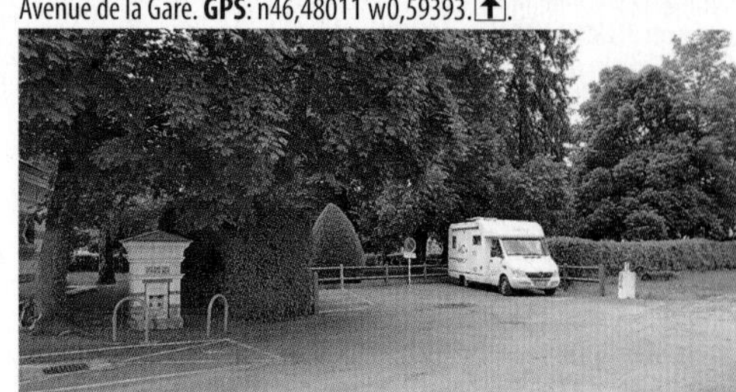

2 free Ch WC free. **Location:** Urban, simple, noisy.
Surface: asphalted. 01/01-31/12.
Distance: 450m 350m 350m.
Remarks: Max. 24h, picnic area.

Créon 24C2

Vélo-centre, Boulevard Victor Hugo, D20.
GPS: n44,77663 w0,34806.

5 free €3 Ch €3/4h.
Location: Urban, simple. **Surface:** asphalted.
01/01-31/12 tue-evening, wed-morning (market).
Distance: 500m 500m on the spot.

Cressat 21G2

D990, Rue de la Prade. **GPS**: n46,13956 e2,11015.

5 free €3/100liter Ch €3/h. **Location:** Rural.
Surface: asphalted. 01/01-31/12.
Distance: 100m 500m.
Remarks: At fish lake, coins at superette 'la Montagne' (500m) and town hall.

Criteuil la Magdeleine 21C3

Le Bourg. **GPS**: n45,53788 w0,21597.

3 free Ch WC free. **Location:** Rural, simple, quiet.
Surface: asphalted. 01/01-31/12.
Distance: on the spot.

Cussac 21E3

Jardin de la Palène, Rue du 8 Mai 1945.
GPS: n45,70519 e0,84936.

4 €2 Ch (2x)€2. **Location:** Rural, comfortable, quiet.
Surface: grassy/gravel. 01/04-31/10.
Distance: 200m 200m 100m.
Remarks: Coins at town hall, bar and restaurant.

Damazan 24D3

Gites La Vignerai, Route Cap de Bosc. **GPS**: n44,28130 e0,26285.

6 € 9 €1 Ch €1 €1/day WC €5 . **Location:** Simple.

01/01-31/12.
Distance: 500m ⊗1km.

Dampniat 24F1

Stade, Le Mas. **GPS**: n45,16262 e1,63728.

4 free €2/10minutes Ch (2x)€2/55minutes.
Location: Rural, simple, quiet. **Surface:** gravel.
Distance: 850m.
Remarks: At sports centre.

Dax 27B1

Parking du Pont des Arènes, Boulevard des Sports.
GPS: n43,71427 w1,04931.

8 free free. **Location:** Urban, simple, noisy.
Surface: asphalted. 01/01-31/12.
Distance: on the spot ⊗on the spot 1km.
Remarks: Max. 72h, saturday market in the halls.

Tourist information Dax:
Office de Tourisme, 11, cours Foch, www.dax.fr. Health resort with warm water sources and medicinal mud.

Dolus-d'Oléron 21B3

Route du Stade. **GPS**: n45,91137 w1,25255.

40 € 6 €4/100liter €4/1h. **Location:** Rural, simple.
Surface: grassy. 01/01-31/12.
Distance: 500m 1,2km Hypermarché.
Remarks: Coins at tourist info.

Domme 24F2

Le Pradal. **GPS**: n44,80053 e1,22156.

20 free, night € 5 €2/100liter Ch €2/1h.
Location: Simple, quiet. **Surface:** asphalted. 01/01-31/12
Service: winter.
Distance: 500m ⊗500m.

Tourist information Domme:
Office de Tourisme, Place de la Halle, www.ot-domme.com. Fortified city worth seeing, parking for motorhomes outside of the town, being indicated.

Dompierre-sur-Charente 21C3

Camping Municipal du Pré St Jean, Rue de Saintonge.
GPS: n45,70099 w0,49438.

5 free €4 Ch. **Location:** Rural, simple, isolated.
Surface: gravel/metalled. 15/06-15/09.
Distance: on the spot 300m ⊗100m 100m.
Remarks: Coins at the bakery and campsite.

Donzenac 24F1

Village de Vacance La Rivière, Rue de la Riviere.
GPS: n45,21897 e1,51829.

10 free Ch €4,20/night WC free. **Location:** Rural, simple, quiet. **Surface:** gravel. 01/01-31/12.
Distance: 4km 1,3km ⊗4km 400m.
Remarks: Max. 48h.

Douchapt 24D1

Beauclair. **GPS**: n45,25145 e0,44335.

€ 5 €2/100liter Ch €2/1h. **Location:** Rural, simple, isolated. **Surface:** metalled. 01/01-31/12.
Distance: 1,5km Dronne river ⊗1,5km.
Remarks: Pay and coins at Village Vacances Beauclair.

Duras 24D2

Municipal du Château de Duras, Le Bourg.
GPS: n44,67755 e0,17854.

5 free, July-Aug € 2,60 + € 3,15/pp Ch free €2,10.
Location: Rural, simple, quiet. **Surface:** grassy.
01/01-31/12.
Distance: 350m ⊗350m 350m.

Eaux-Bonnes 27C3

Parking du Ley, D918, Gourette. **GPS**: n42,96304 w0,33933.

60 € 10 Ch €5 WC included. **Location:** Rural, simple.
Surface: asphalted. 01/01-31/12.
Distance: 1,4km 1,4km ⊗1,4km 1,4km.

Echillais 21B3

Place de la Carrière. **GPS**: n45,89753 w0,95545.

15 € 5,10 €3 Ch. **Location:** Rural, simple.
Surface: asphalted.
Remarks: Access via rue de l'église.

Egletons 24G1

Parking Espace Ventadour, Rue Henri Dignac.
GPS: n45,40406 e2,04791.

20 free €2/100liter Ch.
Location: Urban, simple, quiet. **Surface:** gravel.
01/01-31/12 Service: winter.
Distance: 300m 3,5km ⊗300m 300m.

Espés Undurein 27B2

Etche Gochoki, D11. **GPS**: n43,26388 w0,88083.

6 € 8 €2 Ch €2. **Surface:** grassy/metalled.
01/01-31/12.
Distance: 500m ⊗500m 400m.

Excideuil 24E1

Rue Léon Barreau. **GPS**: n45,33614 e1,05269.

4 free Ch €3. **Location:** Urban, simple, noisy.
Surface: asphalted. 01/01-31/12.
Distance: on the spot ⊗100m 100m.

Felletin 21G3

Parking Lagrange, Avenue Joffre. **GPS**: n45,88308 e2,17667.

10 free Ch WC free. **Location:** Urban, quiet. **Surface:** gravel.
01/01-31/12.
Distance: on the spot.

FR

Fontet 24D2

Base de Loisirs Fontet. **GPS**: n44,56118 w0,02282.

20 € 9 Ch WC included €1. **Location:** Rural, comfortable, quiet. **Surface:** grassy/gravel. 01/01-31/12.
Distance: on the spot bakery 500m, supermarket 4km.
Remarks: At lake, near marina.

Forgès 24G1

Camping-Car Park, Rue Pierre et Marie Curie.
GPS: n45,15403 e1,87089.

33 € 8,40, tourist tax € 0,75/pp Ch (12x)included.
Location: Rural, comfortable, quiet. **Surface:** grassy.
01/01-31/12.
Distance: on the spot on the spot.

Fouras 21B2

Plage Nord, Avenue du Cadoret. **GPS**: n45,99194 w1,08694.

15 € 7 €1/50liter. **Location:** Urban, simple.
Surface: metalled. 01/01-31/12.
Distance: on the spot on the spot on the spot.
Remarks: In front of campsite Cadoret, Fun golf, max. 48h, coins at campsite and tourist info.

Fouras 21B2

Prairie du Casino, Dir pointe de la Fumée. **GPS**: n45,99583 w1,10611.

30 € 6 liter. **Location:** Rural, simple. **Surface:** metalled.
01/01-31/12.
Distance: on the spot on the spot on the spot.
Remarks: Max. 48h.

Fourques-sur-Garonne 24D3

Halte Nautique d Pont des Sables, Pont des Sables, D933.
GPS: n44,46081 e0,13932.

4 free Ch free. **Location:** Urban, simple. **Surface:** metalled.
01/03-31/10.
Distance: Fourques 2,5km 3km on the spot.

Fromental 21F2

Place Jean Theillaud. **GPS**: n46,15950 e1,39643.

4 free Ch (4x) WC free. **Location:** Rural, quiet.
Surface: gravel. 01/01-31/12.
Distance: on the spot on the spot.
Remarks: Near church.

Frontenac 24C2

D236. **GPS**: n44,73781 w0,16308.

10 free WC free. **Location:** Rural, simple.
Surface: grassy/gravel. 01/01-31/12.
Distance: 200m 200m bakery 200m on the spot.
Remarks: Behind town hall, max. 48h.

Fumel 24E3

Place Du Saulou, rue Massenet, D911. **GPS**: n44,49809 e0,97165.

10 free Ch WC free. **Location:** Urban, simple.
Surface: asphalted. 01/01-31/12.
Distance: 200m 200m.
Remarks: Château de Bonaguil 7km.

Gan 27C2

Cave de Gan Jurançon, Avenue Henri IV. **GPS**: n43,23670 w0,38979.

free €2 Ch WC.
Location: Simple.
Surface: asphalted.
Distance: 900m on the spot bakery.
Remarks: Coins at Cave de Gan Jurançon, service accross the street.

Gan 27C2

Le Clos Husté, Chemin de Cours-Husté. **GPS**: n43,19703 w0,41247.
5 free. **Location:** Simple.
Distance: 5km.

Gastes 24B3

Port de Gastes, Avenue du lac. **GPS**: n44,32880 w1,15068.

100 € 2-4,50, 01/06-30/09 € 8 Ch WC included.
Location: Comfortable. **Surface:** grassy.
01/01-31/12 service in winter.
Distance: Parentis-en-Born 7km on the spot on the spot 800m 800m.
Remarks: Along lake, baker every morning.

Gastes 24B3

Camping Les Echasses, 193 rue de Bernadon.
GPS: n44,31871 w1,13879.

6 € 6,50-8,50 €3 Ch included. **Location:** Simple.
Surface: grassy. 01/01-31/12.
Distance: Gastes Lac 2km on the spot.
Remarks: Max. 1 night, no camping activities.

Gencay 21D2

Place du Champs de Foire. **GPS**: n46,37315 e0,40638.

10 free €2 Ch €2 WC. **Location:** Urban, simple, noisy.
Surface: grassy/metalled. 01/01-31/12.
Distance: 200m 200m 200m.
Remarks: Coins at the shops.

Genté 21C3

Rue de l'Eglise. **GPS**: n45,62861 w0,315.

6 free Ch (6x) WC free. **Surface:** asphalted.
01/01-31/12.
Distance: on the spot 350m on the spot.

Gornac 24C2

Aire Municipale, Esplanade Fongave. **GPS**: n44,66020 w0,18129.

30 free Ch free. **Location:** Rural, simple, quiet.
Surface: asphalted. 01/01-31/12.
Distance: 200m 200m.

FR

Gouzon 21G2

Place du Champ de Foire, Rue d'Alcantera.
GPS: n46,19139 e2,24028.

6 free Chfree. **Location:** Rural, simple, quiet.
Surface: metalled/sand. 01/01-31/12.
Distance: 300m 300m 300m.

Grayan-et-l'Hôpital 24B1

Route de l'Océan. **GPS**: n45,43332 w1,1437.

10 free €2/100liter Ch €2. **Location:** Rural, simple, isolated, quiet. **Surface:** forest soil.
Distance: 5km 200m 100m on the spot on the spot on the spot.
Remarks: Near campsite.

Grenade-sur-l'Adour 27C1

Place du 19 mars 1962. **GPS**: n43,77500 w0,43472.

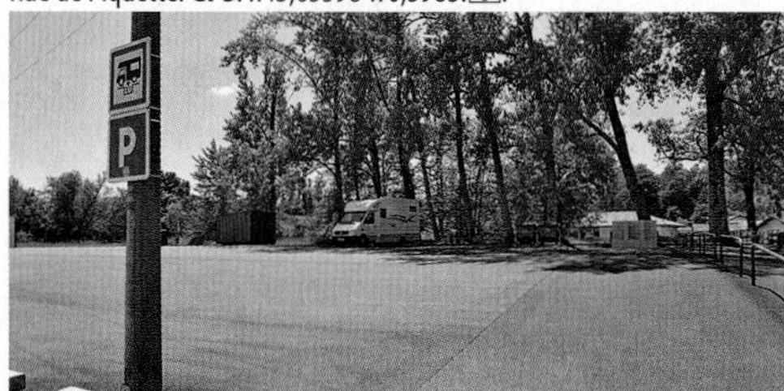

10 free ChWCfree. **Location:** Rural, simple.
Surface: asphalted/gravel.
Distance: 100m 100m 100m.
Remarks: Next to cemetery, max. 24h.

Grézillac 24C2

Le Bourg. **GPS**: n44,81727 w0,21692.
2 free. **Surface:** gravel. 01/01-31/12.

Guéret 21G2

Aire des Monts de Guéret, RN145. **GPS**: n46,18189 e1,85837.
16 free €2/100liter Ch free. **Surface:** asphalted.
01/01-31/12.
Distance: centre 4km 500m.

Hagetmau 27C1

Rue de Piquette. **GPS**: n43,65398 w0,5983.

5 free Chfree.
Location: Rural, quiet. **Surface:** asphalted.
Distance: 500m 500m 1,5km.

Hautefort 24E1

Route de Boisseuil. **GPS**: n45,26017 e1,14907.

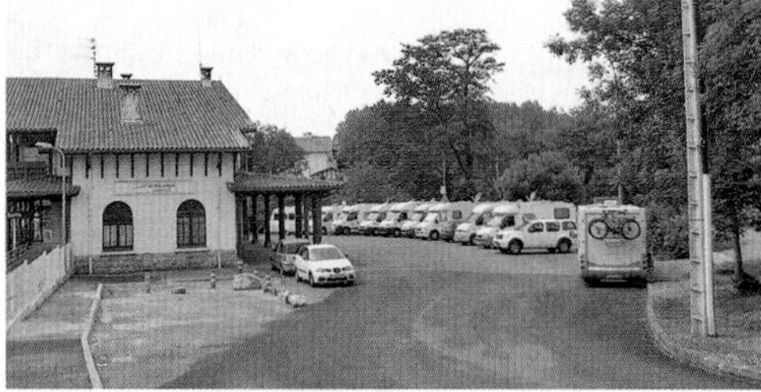

3 free Ch €2 WCfree. **Location:** Simple.
Surface: asphalted. 01/01-31/12.
Distance: 50m 100m Intermarché 1km.

Tourist information Hautefort:
Château Hautefort. Classified castle. 01/04-30/09 daily, 01/10-31/03 afternoons 12/11-29/02.
Wed-morning.

Hendaye 27A2

Gare des deux Jumeaux, Rue d'Ansoenia.
GPS: n43,37019 w1,7648.

25 € 10 €2/100liter Ch €2/1h. **Location:** Urban, simple.
Surface: asphalted. 01/01-31/12.
Distance: on the spot 800m 450m 450m on the spot.
Remarks: Railway-station Hendaye-plage, max. 72h, nights closed with barrier.

Hiers-Brouage 21B3

D3. **GPS**: n45,86250 w1,07667.

20 free.
Location: Rural. **Surface:** grassy/gravel. 01/01-31/12.
Distance: 250m 250m 250m.
Remarks: Arrival >20h, departure <9h.

Hiers-Brouage 21B3

Rue Palissy, D3. **GPS**: n45,85284 w1,07745.
€4 Ch. **Surface:** metalled. 01/01-31/12.

Hostens 24C3

Parking, La Hourcade. **GPS**: n44,49718 w0,64867.
5 free WC. **Surface:** metalled/sand.
Distance: 1,2km 1.2km on the spot on the spot.
Remarks: At lake, picnic area.

Houeillès 24D3

Aire de Repos, Rue du 19 Mars 1962. **GPS**: n44,19611 e0,03250.

15 free WCfree. **Location:** Rural, simple, quiet.
Surface: grassy/gravel. 01/01-31/12.
Distance: 100m 250m.
Remarks: Max. 24h.

Hourtin 24B1

Aire de camping Car Hourtin, 108, Avenue du Lac.
GPS: n45,18083 w1,08056.

90 € 7,90, 01/04-30/09 € 10,50 Ch (40x)€2 WCincluded.
Location: Urban, comfortable, central, quiet.
Surface: gravel/metalled. 01/01-31/12.
Distance: 50m 50m 50m.

Jarnages 21G2

Route des Promenctes, D65. **GPS**: n46,18417 e2,08098.

6 free €2 Ch €2. **Location:** Rural, simple, quiet.
Surface: asphalted. 01/01-31/12.
Distance: 500m on the spot 500m 500m.
Remarks: At tennis-courts.

Javerdat 21E3

Le Bourg. **GPS**: n45,95249 e0,98582.

4 free €2/100liter Ch €2/55minutes WC.
Location: Rural, quiet. **Surface:** gravel. 01/01-31/12.
Distance: 100m.
Remarks: Coins at Auberge Limousine (100m).

Jonzac 24C1

Place du 8 Mai 1945. **GPS**: n45,44800 w0,433.

18 free €4,20/100liter Ch €4,20/h. **Location:** Urban, simple, central. **Surface:** asphalted. 01/01-31/12.
Distance: 500m 200m 200m on the spot.
Remarks: Max. 24h, coins at tourist info.

Jonzac 24C1

Chez M. Alex Beurg, Chez Marchand. **GPS**: n45,44121 w0,40427.
3 free. **Location:** Rural, simple, isolated, quiet. **Surface:** grassy.
01/01-31/12.
Remarks: Max. 24h.

Jumilhac-le-Grand 24E1

Boulevard du Pigeonnier, D78. **GPS**: n45,49219 e1,06092.

FR

2 free Chfree. **Location:** Urban, simple. **Surface:** asphalted. 01/01-31/12.
Distance: on the spot 200m bakery 200m.
Remarks: Near Château de Jumilhac.

L'Hôpital-Saint-Blaise 27B2

Parking l'Église, D25. **GPS:** n43,25088 w0,76925.

5 free WCfree. **Location:** Rural, simple. **Surface:** asphalted. 01/01-31/12.
Distance: on the spot on the spot on the spot on the spot.

La Brée-les-Bains 21B2

Rue de la Baudette. **GPS:** n46,00810 w1,35764.

50 free Ch. **Location:** Rural, simple, quiet.
Surface: asphalted. 01/01-31/12.
Remarks: Coins at tourist info.

La Coquille 24E1

N21, Place de l'église. **GPS:** n45,54245 e0,97702.

5 free ChWCfree. **Location:** Urban, simple, central.
Surface: asphalted. 01/01-31/12.
Distance: 100m 200m 200m.

La Couronne 21D3

Rue du Champs de Foire. **GPS:** n45,60619 e0,10015.

free ChWCfree.
Location: Simple, central. **Surface:** asphalted.
01/01-31/12 Wed-morning, Sa-morning market.
Distance: on the spot on the spot on the spot on the spot.

La Courtine 21G3

Rue Impasse J Bayle. **GPS:** n45,70591 e2,25890.

5 free €2/100liter Ch €2/1h. **Location:** Simple, quiet.
Surface: asphalted. 01/01-31/12.

Distance: 1km 100m.

La Mothe-Saint-Héray 21D2

Rue du Pont l'Abbé. **GPS:** n46,35971 w0,11775.

4 free €1/50liter ChWC. **Location:** Rural, comfortable.
Surface: gravel. 01/01-31/12.
Distance: 500m 200m 200m.

La Pierre-Saint-Martin 27B3

Aire de campingcar de la Pierre-Saint-Martin, Braça de Guilhers.
GPS: n42,97918 w0,7487.

40 € 10 Ch (winter). **Location:** Simple.
Surface: asphalted. 01/01-31/12.
Distance: 300m 300m 150m.

La Réole 24D2

Les Justices, Avenue Gabriel-Chaigne. **GPS:** n44,58059 w0,03036.

10 € 4 Chfree. **Location:** Urban, simple, noisy.
Surface: grassy. 15/04-01/10.
Distance: 800m 700m.
Remarks: Nearby Musée Automobile et Militaire.

La Roche-Chalais 24D1

Halte Nautique, D730. **GPS:** n45,15701 e0,00419.

4 free ChWCfree.
Location: Rural, simple. **Surface:** metalled.
01/01-31/12.
Distance: 400m 100m 100m.
Remarks: Service at Intermarché, Av.d'Aquitaine, n45,14633 o0,00569.

La Roche-Posay 21E1

Super U, ZA Les Chaumettes. **GPS:** n46,79361 e0,79750.

free Chfree. **Location:** Simple, noisy. **Surface:** asphalted.
01/01-31/12.

Distance: 1,5km on the spot.

La Rochefoucauld 21D3

Aire camping-car, Rue des Flots, Rivières. **GPS:** n45,74505 e0,38085.

+20 Ch WC. 01/01-31/12.
Distance: 1km.
Remarks: Beside river Tardoire, next to campsite, Château de La Rochefoucauld 1,3km.

La Rochelle 21B2

Esplanade des Parc, Chemin des Remparts.
GPS: n46,16620 w1,1544.

24 free. **Location:** Urban. **Surface:** asphalted. 01/01-31/12.
Distance: 250m 100m 250m 50m.

La Rochelle 21B2

Port Neuf, 6 boulevard Aristide Rondeau.
GPS: n46,16046 w1,18453.

171 € 8, tourist tax incl Chincluded free.
Location: Urban. **Surface:** gravel. 01/01-31/12.
Distance: centre 2,5km 1km on the spot.

La Rochelle 21B2

Vieux Port, Avenue Jean Moulin. **GPS:** n46,15250 w1,13944.

50 € 10,50/24h Ch. **Surface:** asphalted. 01/01-31/12.
Distance: 1,5km free.
Remarks: Pay at reception, shuttle bus to city centre.

La Rochelle 21B2

Quai du Lazaret. **GPS:** n46,14213 w1,16773.

40 free. **Location:** Urban, simple. **Surface:** asphalted.
01/10-30/06.

Tourist information La Rochelle:

FR

La Maison Henri II, Rue de Augustins. Archeological museum. 15/5-30/9 Sa-Fr 10-19h Sa-Su 14-19h.
Musée Maritime de la Rochelle, Bassin des Chautiers. Shipping museum. daily 10-18.30h.
Aquarium, Quai Louis Prunier. Sea aquarium. 01/07-31/08 9-23h, 01/09-30/06 10-20h.

S La Roque-Gageac 24E2
D703. **GPS**: n44,82428 e1,18376.

20 € 7 €2/10minutes Ch €2/1h.
Location: Simple. **Surface:** metalled. 01/01-31/12.
Distance: 200m 100m 100m 200m 200m.
Remarks: Along the Dordogne river, canoe rental.

Tourist information La Roque-Gageac:
www.cc-perigord-noir.fr. Small town worth seeing, in the Dordogne valley.

S La Teste-de-Buch 24B2
Aire de Camping Car du Lac de Cazaux, Rue Guynemer.
GPS: n44,53158 w1,16025.

30 € 12/24h Ch included. **Location:** Comfortable, quiet. **Surface:** gravel/metalled. 01/01-31/12.
Distance: 450m 450m on the spot.

S La Teste-de-Buch 24B2
Centre LeClerc, Rue Pierre et Marie Curie. **GPS**: n44,61628 w1,11403.

15 free €2/10minutes Ch €2/30minutes.
Surface: asphalted.
Distance: on the spot on the spot.

S La Tremblade 21B3
85 Rue Marcel Gaillardon. **GPS**: n45,78268 w1,15228.

49 € 10/24h Ch ,16Amp included.
Location: Rural, comfortable, central, quiet. **Surface:** gravel/metalled.
01/01-31/12.
Distance: 2,2km on the spot 500m on the spot.
Remarks: Max. 72h, baker every morning.

S Labastide-d'Armagnac 27C1
Les Embarrats. **GPS**: n43,97205 w0,18602.

20 free Ch free. **Location:** Rural, simple, quiet.
Surface: grassy.
Distance: 300m.

S Labenne 27A1
Route Océane. **GPS**: n43,59616 w1,45492.

50 € 10 Ch included.
Surface: metalled. 10/04-01/10.
Distance: 1km 2km 2km 1km 1km.
Remarks: Max. 48h, no camping activities.

S Lacanau 24B1
Le Huga, Alleé des Sauviels. **GPS**: n45,00583 w1,16528.

125 € 13,80/24h Ch included.
Location: Rural, comfortable, quiet. **Surface:** unpaved.
01/01-31/12.
Distance: 2km 2km 100m 2km on the spot on the spot.
Remarks: In front of heliport, max. 48h.

S Ladaux 24C2
Vignobles Lobre & Fils, Le Bos. **GPS**: n44,69677 w0,24393.

5 free Ch WC. **Location:** Rural, simple.
Surface: grassy/metalled. 01/01-31/12.
Distance: 300m.

S Lalinde 24E2
Avenue Général Leclerc. **GPS**: n44,83938 e0,74302.

2 free Ch free. **Location:** Simple. **Surface:** unpaved.
01/01-31/12.
Distance: 500m 500m 500m on the spot.
Remarks: Near train station.

S Lanouaille 24E1
Rue du Chemin Neuf. **GPS**: n45,39248 e1,14002.

6 free Ch WC free. **Location:** Simple, central, quiet.
Surface: asphalted. 01/01-31/12.
Distance: 50m 100m 100m on the spot.
Remarks: Max. 48h.

S Lanton 24B2
Allée Albert Pitres, Taussat. **GPS**: n44,71710 w1,06991.

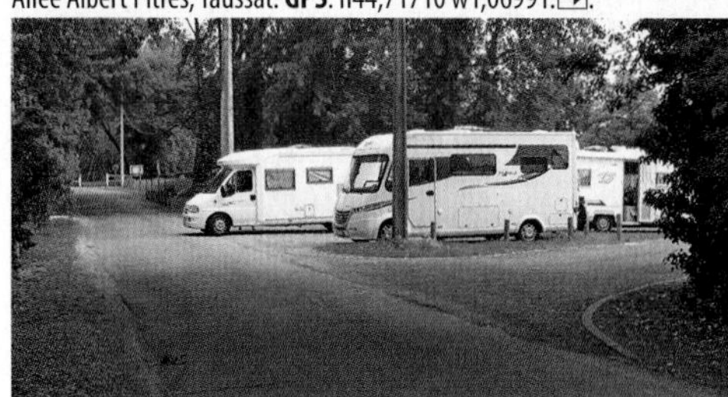

8 free Ch free. **Location:** Urban, simple, isolated.
Surface: asphalted. 01/01-31/12.
Distance: 2km sandy beach 100m 100m 4km.

S Lantueil 24F1
Route du Doux. **GPS**: n45,12900 e1,66138.

5 free Ch free. **Location:** Urban, simple, quiet.
Surface: gravel.
Distance: 100m 100m.

S Laruns 27C3
Artouste Fabrèges. **GPS**: n42,87914 w0,39693.

80 free €5/100liter Ch €5/1h WC. **Location:** Rural, simple.
Surface: asphalted/grassy. 01/01-31/12.
Distance: 200m on the spot on the spot on the spot on the spot 1km.
Remarks: Coins at tourist info.

S Laruns 27C3
Parking du Cinéma, Avenue de la Gare. **GPS**: n42,98919 w0,42481.

30 € 6 Ch WC. **Location:** Urban, simple.
Surface: asphalted. 01/01-31/12.
Distance: 100m 100m 100m 400m.
Remarks: Max. 24h, coins at tourist info.

FR

S Lauzun 24D2

Rue Saint-Colomb. **GPS**: n44,62762 e0,45979.

2 free WC free. **Surface:** gravel. 01/01-31/12.
Distance: 350m on the spot 350m 350m on the spot.
Remarks: At small lake, max. 48h.

S Lavardac 24D3

Rue de la Victoire - Place du Foirail. **GPS**: n44,17883 e0,29928.

3 free Ch free. **Location:** Rural, simple. **Surface:** asphalted. 01/01-31/12.
Distance: on the spot bakery 150m.

S Layrac 24E3

Aire de Layrac, Rue du 19 Mars 1962. **GPS**: n44,13233 e0,65946.

4 free Ch WC free. **Location:** Urban, simple.
Surface: asphalted. 01/01-31/12.
Distance: on the spot 150m 150m.

S Layrac 24E3

Le Moulin, D129. **GPS**: n44,13640 e0,66441.

max. 4 € 10/24h Ch WC included. **Location:** Simple, noisy. **Surface:** gravel. 01/01-31/12.
Distance: on the spot.
Remarks: Call if no one is present, video surveillance.

Le Bois-Plage-en-Ré 21B2

Parking Municipal, Avenue du Pas des Boeufs.
GPS: n46,17708 w1,38613.
15 free. **Location:** Simple. **Surface:** gravel/sand.
Distance: 150m.

S Le Bois-Plage-en-Ré 21B2

Aire Camping-Car Campéole, Avenue du Pas des Boeufs.
GPS: n46,17741 w1,38674.

35 € 8,60-12,80 €3 Ch €2/12h. **Location:** Rural, simple. **Surface:** gravel/metalled. 01/01-31/12.
Distance: 150m.
Remarks: Payment also possible at campsite.

S Le Bugue 24E2

Place Léopold Salme. **GPS**: n44,91679 e0,92775.

50 € 7 Ch WC free. **Location:** Simple. **Surface:** grassy. 01/01-31/12 Service: winter.
Distance: 200m 20m 100m Intermarché 100m.
Remarks: Along the river Vézère, tuesday and Saturday market.

S Le Château d'Oléron 21B3

Boulevard Philippe Daste. **GPS**: n45,89641 w1,20236.

90 € 10 Ch WC included. **Location:** Rural, comfortable. **Surface:** grassy.
Distance: on the spot.
Remarks: Former campsite.

S Le Grand Village Plage 21B3

Allée des Pins. **GPS**: n45,86222 w1,24111.

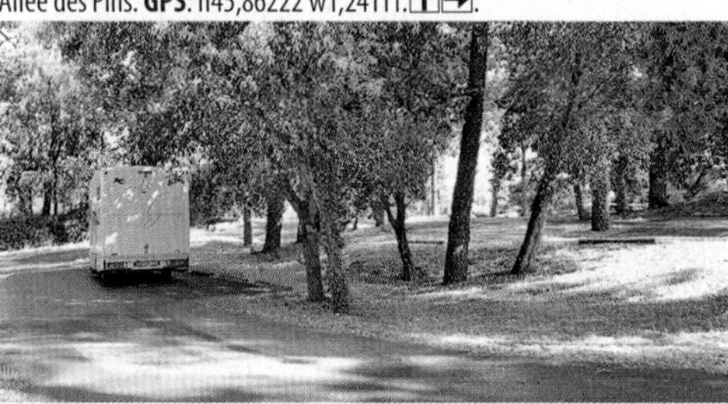

8 € 6 €4/100liter Ch €4. **Location:** Rural, simple.
Surface: asphalted. 01/01-31/12.
Remarks: 01/04-30/09 max. 24h.

S Le Mas-d'Agenais 24D3

Grande Garesse. **GPS**: n44,40656 e0,22030.

8 free Ch (8x)free. **Location:** Urban, comfortable.
Surface: gravel. 01/01-31/12.
Distance: 600m 600m.

Le Porge 24B2

Avenue de l'Océan. **GPS**: n44,89437 w1,2131.

10 free. **Location:** Rural, simple, isolated. **Surface:** forest soil. 01/01-31/12.
Distance: Le Porge 10km on the spot on the spot on the spot on the spot.
Remarks: Max. 24h.

S Le Porge 24B2

Intermarché, D107. **GPS**: n44,87574 w1,07883.
€2/20minutes Ch. **Location:** Simple. 01/01-31/12.
Distance: on the spot on the spot.

S Le Teich 24B2

Parking de la Gare, Rue de l'Industrie. **GPS**: n44,63303 w1,02643.
free €5/100liter Ch €5/h. 01/01-31/12.
Distance: 700m 1km on the spot.

S Le Temple-sur-Lot 24D3

Avenue de Verdun. **GPS**: n44,38000 e0,52639.

4 free Ch WC free. **Location:** Urban, simple, quiet.
Surface: asphalted. 01/01-31/12.
Distance: 100m 100m.

S Le Temple-sur-Lot 24D3

Le Bosc, D911. **GPS**: n44,38144 e0,53649.
10 € 5 Ch according consumption included.
Location: Rural. **Surface:** grassy. 01/01-31/12.
Distance: 800m 800m 800m on the spot.
Remarks: Picnic and barbecue place.

S Le Verdon-sur-Mer 21B3

Plage fluviale, Allée des Baïnes. **GPS**: n45,54633 w1,0541.

31+19 € 5/24h, 01/06-30/09 € 8/24h €2/100liter Ch. **Location:** Urban, comfortable, isolated, quiet.
Surface: gravel/metalled.
01/01-31/12.
Distance: 50m 500m 2km on the spot.
Remarks: Coins at town hall, tourist info and the shops at the beach.

S Lège-Cap-Ferret 24B2

Route des Pastourelles, Avenue Charles de Gaulle, D106, Claouey.
GPS: n44,75127 w1,18033.

10 free Ch (2x)free. **Location:** Urban, simple, noisy.
Surface: forest soil. 01/01-31/12.
Distance: on the spot 1km 600m 600m on the spot.
Remarks: Coins at camping municipal, day parking also allowed,

FR

overnight stay on motorhome stopovers.

Lège-Cap-Ferret 24B2

Avenue Edouard Branly. **GPS**: n44,75203 w1,18809.

15 free.
Location: Rural, simple. **Surface:** forest soil.
01/01-31/12.
Distance: 2km 600m 600m 600m 600m on the spot.
Remarks: Near campsite Les Embruns.

Lège-Cap-Ferret 24B2

D106, Avenue de Bordeaux, L'Herbe. **GPS**: n44,68655 w1,2451.

15 free. **Location:** Rural, simple, quiet. **Surface:** asphalted/metalled.
01/01-31/12.
Distance: 2km 1km 2km 2km.

Léguillac-de-l'Auche 24E1

Glenon. **GPS**: n45,20319 e0,55876.
6 free €2 €3/24h. **Location:** Rural, isolated, quiet.
Surface: grassy.
Distance: 2km 2km 2km.

Lembras 24D2

Aire de Caudeau, Impasse de l'Anguillère.
GPS: n44,88300 e0,52522.

free Chfree (10x)€4/12h. **Location:** Rural, comfortable, central. **Surface:** gravel. 01/01-31/12.
Distance: 200m 200m 200m 2,5km.

Léon 27A1

Route de Puntaou. **GPS**: n43,88444 w1,31861.

80 € 11 Chincluded. **Location:** Simple.
Surface: grassy/gravel. 01/01-31/12.
Distance: 1km 250m 50m 50m 50m.
Remarks: Nearby lake.

Les Eyzies 24E2

Parking de la Vézère, Promenade de la Vézère.
GPS: n44,93863 e1,00907.

25 € 5/night €2/100liter Ch.
Location: Urban, comfortable, quiet. **Surface:** grassy/sand.
01/01-31/12.
Distance: 200m 200m 200m.
Remarks: Along the river Vézère, summer max. 48h, parking fee being collected at 9AM.

Tourist information Les Eyzies:

Village Troglodytique de la Madeleine, Tursac. Troglodyte-village.
Le Village du Bournat, Le Bugue. Open air museum. 01/03-31/10 10-18/19h.

Les Mathes/La Palmyre 21B3

Aire de la Garenne, Rue de la Garenne, Les Mathes.
GPS: n45,71433 w1,14752.

20 € 8/24h €4/100liter ChWC.
Location: Rural, simple, isolated. **Surface:** metalled. 01/01-31/12.
Distance: 400m.
Remarks: Coins at town hall Mo-Fri 9-18h and tourist info La Palmyre daily 9-19h in July/Aug.

Les Mathes/La Palmyre 21B3

Aire du Corsaire, Avenue de lAtlantique. **GPS**: n45,69193 w1,18896.

90 € 8/24h €4/100liter Ch €2/1h .
Location: Simple, central, quiet. **Surface:** asphalted.
01/01-31/12.
Distance: 1km 200m 200m on the spot.
Remarks: Max. 7 days.

Les Mathes/La Palmyre 21B3

Boulevard de la Plage, La Palmyre. **GPS**: n45,68287 w1,17942.

50 € 8/24h. **Location:** Urban, simple, central, quiet.
Surface: asphalted. 01/01-31/12 01/07-31/08.
Distance: 1,2km 100m 200m on the spot.

Tourist information Les Mathes/La Palmyre:

Zoo de la Palmyre. Zoo, 1600 animals, 14Ha. 01/04-30/09 9-20.30h, 01/10-31/03 9-12h, 14-18h.

Les Portes-en-Ré 21B2

Parking de la Patache, Route du Fier. **GPS**: n46,22925 w1,48315.

10 € 10/24h ChWCfree. **Location:** Rural, simple.
Surface: metalled. 01/01-31/12.
Distance: on the spot on the spot 3,5km.
Remarks: Max. 24h, payment only with coins.

Les Salles-Lavaugyon 21E3

Le Tilleul, Route de St Mathieu. **GPS**: n45,73998 e0,70100.

6 € 5 (3x)included. **Location:** Rural, simple, isolated.
Surface: gravel. 01/01-31/12.

Lescar 27C2

Parking Jacques Monod, Chemin de Beneharnum.
GPS: n43,33062 w0,43458.
5 free. **Surface:** asphalted. 01/01-31/12.
Distance: on the spot on the spot on the spot on the spot.
Remarks: Max. 48h.

Lescar 27C2

Place de l'Evêché. **GPS**: n43,33348 w0,43401.
3 free. **Surface:** metalled. 01/01-31/12.
Distance: on the spot 150m on the spot.
Remarks: Near office de tourisme, max. 48h.

Lescar 27C2

Impasse du Vert Galant. **GPS**: n43,32669 w0,44373.
Chfree.

Lestelle-Bétharram 27C2

D937. **GPS**: n43,12522 w0,2074.
10 free. **Location:** Urban, simple, noisy. **Surface:** asphalted.
01/01-31/12.
Distance: 500m 250m.

Lezay 21D2

Rue de Gâte Bourse. **GPS**: n46,26500 w0,01139.

15 free Chfree. **Location:** Urban, simple. **Surface:** asphalted.
01/01-31/12.
Distance: 200m 200m.

Liginiac 24G1

Le Maury-Liginiac. **GPS**: n45,39158 e2,30387.

2 free Ch (1x)free. **Location:** Rural, simple, isolated, quiet. **Surface:** gravel. 01/01-31/12.
Distance: 4,5km Sandy beach on the spot.
Remarks: At lake Neuvic. Follow restaurant Le Maury.

FR

Limeuil 24E2

D31. **GPS**: n44,88564 e0,89151.

10 free. **Location:** Rural, simple, isolated. **Surface:** grassy/gravel. 01/01-31/12.
Distance: 400m 400m 750m.

Lissac-sur-Couze 24F1

Parking du poste de secours. GPS: n45,09914 e1,46277.

15 € 4/stay €4/100liter Ch (12x)€4/6h.
Location: Rural, comfortable. **Surface:** gravel. 01/01-31/12.
Distance: on the spot on the spot.

Lit-et-Mixe 24A3

Cap de l'Homy, 600, avenue Océan. **GPS**: n44,03730 w1,33419.

36 € 11,30-21,30 + € 0,61/pp tourist taks Ch WC.
Location: Simple, quiet. **Surface:** forest soil. 01/05-30/09.
Distance: 400m 200m 200m on the spot.
Remarks: Next to camping municipal.

Lizant 21D2

D107. **GPS**: n46,08614 e0,27834.
8 free Ch WC. **Surface:** gravel.
Distance: 100m on the spot.
Remarks: Playground.

Londigny 21D2

Place de l'Eglise. **GPS**: n46,08333 e0,13472.

5 free Ch WCfree. **Location:** Isolated, quiet.
Surface: gravel. 01/01-31/12.
Remarks: Max. 48h.

Loudun 18D3

Place de la Porte Saint Nicolas. **GPS**: n47,01357 e0,07833.

3 free €2/10minutes Ch €2/55minutes.
Location: Urban, simple, noisy. **Surface:** asphalted.
01/01-31/12.
Distance: 500m 500m 100m, bakery 10m.
Remarks: Max 3,5t.

Lussac-les-Châteaux 21E2

GPS: n46,40250 e0,72583.

20 free Ch WCfree. **Location:** Urban, simple, central.
Surface: metalled. 01/01-31/12 Wed, market.
Distance: 200m 200m 200m.

Marennes 21B3

1 Avenue William Bertrand. **GPS**: n45,82140 w1,13828.

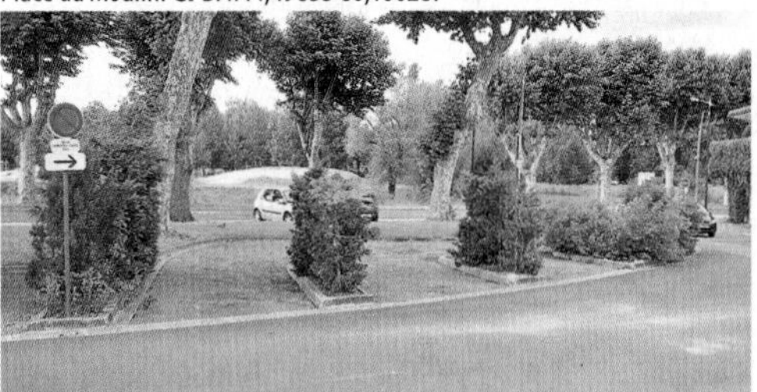

5 free.
Location: Rural, simple. **Surface:** metalled. 01/01-31/12.
Distance: on the spot.
Remarks: Max. 6,5m.

Marmande 24D3

La Filhole, Rue de la Filhole. **GPS**: n44,49667 e0,16412.

30 € 8 Ch included. **Location:** Rural, simple, quiet.
Surface: grassy. 01/04-01/11.
Distance: 500m 500m 1km.

Marmande 24D3

Place du Moulin. **GPS**: n44,49833 e0,16028.

2 free Chfree. **Location:** Urban. **Surface:** asphalted.
01/11-01/04.
Distance: 150m on the spot.
Remarks: Max. 48h.

Marquay 24E2

D6. **GPS**: n44,94401 e1,13529.
free Ch. **Surface:** gravel.
Distance: 100m.

Mauléon 18C3

Rue de la Bachelette. **GPS**: n46,91904 w0,75267.

4 free Chfree. **Location:** Rural, simple, quiet.
Surface: asphalted. 01/01-31/12.
Distance: 500m 500m 500m.
Remarks: Next to swimming pool.

Mauzé-sur-le-Mignon 21C2

Le Port, Rue du Port. **GPS**: n46,19989 w0,67952.

10 free €4 Ch WC.
Location: Rural. **Surface:** gravel. 01/01-31/12.
Distance: 1km on the spot.
Remarks: Coins at campsite and shops.

Ménigoute 21D1

Rue des Vignes. **GPS**: n46,49790 w0,05795.

4 free Chfree. **Location:** Urban, simple, quiet.
Surface: gravel.
Distance: on the spot.

Mensignac 24E1

Combecouyere-Sud. **GPS**: n45,22309 e0,56553.
3 free €2 Ch. **Location:** Rural. **Surface:** metalled.
01/03-31/10.

Meschers-sur-Gironde 21B3

Port de Plaisance, Route des Salines. **GPS**: n45,55614 w0,9451.

10 € 7/24h €2/100liter Ch (8x) €1,50 €2/2 .
Location: Rural, comfortable, isolated, quiet. **Surface:** asphalted.
01/01-31/12.
Distance: 1km 100m 100m 1km.

Messanges 27A1

Plage principale, Avenue de la Plage. **GPS**: n43,81549 w1,40088.

10 free WC. **Location:** Simple. **Surface:** metalled/sand.
Distance: 1,5km 200m.

FR

Remarks: Max. 48h.

Messé 21D2

D114. **GPS**: n46,26306 e0,11203.

20 free Ch WC free. **Location:** Rural, isolated, quiet.
Surface: gravel. 01/01-31/12.
Distance: on the spot 10km.

Meuzac 24F1

Étang de la Roche, D243. **GPS**: n45,54805 e1,44017.

15 free Ch free. **Location:** Rural, simple, quiet.
Surface: gravel. 01/01-31/12.
Distance: 100m 5km on the spot on the spot 100m 100m on the spot.
Remarks: Service 200m.

Meymac 24G1

Parking Lac de Sechemailles, Le Montbazet.
GPS: n45,52500 e2,12761.

20 free €2,60 Ch €2,60. **Location:** Rural, comfortable, quiet. **Surface:** gravel. 01/01-31/12.
Distance: 2km 500m 500m.
Remarks: Coins available at Office du Tourisme and bar.

Meymac 24G1

Boulevard de la Garenne. **GPS**: n45,53973 e2,15381.
30 free €2 Ch (1x)€2. **Location:** Rural, simple.
Surface: gravel. 20/04-02/11.
Remarks: Coins at campsite and tourist info.

Mézières-sur-Issoire 21E2

Place de la République. **GPS**: n46,10726 e0,91014.

4 free Ch free. **Location:** Rural. **Surface:** asphalted.
01/01-31/12.
Distance: on the spot.

Mimizan 24B3

Hélistation Plage Sud, Rue des Lacs, Mimizan-Plage.
GPS: n44,20517 w1,29675.

85 € 14,50 Ch included.
Location: Comfortable. **Surface:** asphalted.
01/01-31/12.
Distance: 500m on the spot 500m 200m.
Remarks: Parking at dune, no trailers allowed.

Mimizan 24B3

Route du C.E.L.. **GPS**: n44,21375 w1,28239.

150 € 7,50 €3/20minutes Ch. **Location:** Simple.
Surface: gravel/sand. 01/06-31/09.
Distance: 1,5km on the spot.

Mimizan 24B3

Camping du Lac, Avenue de Woolsack, Mimizan-lac.
GPS: n44,21956 w1,22972.

21 € 11-18 + € 0,22/pp tourist tax, dog € 1,10-1,90 €2/15minutes Ch WC €3 . **Location:** Comfortable. **Surface:** gravel.
30/04-30/09.
Distance: 6km on the spot on the spot.

Mirambeau 24C1

92, avenue de la République. **GPS**: n45,37816 w0,56872.
20 € 8 Ch included. **Surface:** grassy.
01/01-31/12.
Distance: 500m 3km 50m Super U 150m.
Remarks: Former campsite.

Mirebeau 21D1

14 rue du Pas Martin. **GPS**: n46,78064 e0,19430.
€ 7 €2 €2 Ch €5. 01/01-31/12.
Remarks: Barbecue place.

Moliets-et-Maa 27A1

Avenue de l'Océan, Moliets-Plage. **GPS**: n43,85091 w1,38188.

120 € 7, 01/04-31/08 € 13 Ch WC.
Location: Comfortable, noisy. **Surface:** forest soil.
Distance: 200m 750m 200m 200m.
Remarks: Shady.

Monbahus 24D3

Rue du Moulin, Le Bourg. **GPS**: n44,54738 e0,53517.

3 free Ch (2x)free. **Location:** Rural, simple.
Surface: asphalted. 01/01-31/12 Service: winter.
Distance: 300m 200m 300m.
Remarks: Beautiful view, steep entrance road.

Monbazillac 24D2

Château du Haut Pezaud, Les Pezauds. **GPS**: n44,78471 e0,48687.

10 € 5, first night free €1,50 €21/day WC free €1/pppd €1,50/day. **Location:** Rural, simple. **Surface:** grassy.
01/01-31/12.
Distance: table d'hôtes through the vineyards.
Remarks: Max. 7 nights, baker every morning, tasting of regional products.

Monbazillac 24D2

Domaine La Lande, Route de Ribagnac, D13.
GPS: n44,78822 e0,49587.

10 free Ch WC free. **Location:** Rural, simple. **Surface:** grassy.
01/01-31/12.
Distance: 800m 200m on the spot.
Remarks: Baker every morning, sale of wines.

Monflanquin 24E3

Chemin de la Source, 3, Allée des Érables.
GPS: n44,52812 e0,75537.

free Ch free.
Location: Simple. **Surface:** gravel.
01/01-31/12.
Distance: 1,5km Lac de Coulon 150m 1,3km 250m.
Remarks: Service 500m n44,52477 o0,75642.

Tourist information Monflanquin:
Office de Tourisme, Place des Arcades, www.monflanquin-tourisme.com. Medieval town.

Monpazier 24E2

La Duelle-nord. **GPS**: n44,68499 e0,89362.

FR

10 free Chfree. **Surface:** gravel. 01/01-31/12.
Distance: 300m 400m 500m.

Monségur 24D2

Place du 8 mai. **GPS**: n44,65060 e0,08363.

4 free WCfree. **Location:** Simple, noisy. **Surface:** gravel. 01/01-31/12.
Distance: on the spot.
Remarks: Max. 48h. No access via La Bastide.

Mont-de-Marsan 27C1

Aire du Camping-Cars du Marsan, 541 Avenue de Villeneuve. **GPS**: n43,88992 w0,47559.

45 € 5,10-8,40, tourist tax € 0,33/pp €1/5minutes Ch (3x)€1/4h. **Location:** Rural, central. **Surface:** asphalted/grassy. 01/01-31/12.
Distance: 2,3km 500m.

Montalivet-les-Bains 24B1

Boulevard de Lattre de Tassigny, Montalivet-sud. **GPS**: n45,37611 w1,15667.

30 €5 €1 Ch. **Location:** Urban, simple, quiet. **Surface:** grassy/metalled. 01/05-30/09.
Distance: on the spot 100m 400m 400m.
Remarks: At sea, max. 48h, service at Aldi 1km.

Tourist information Montalivet-les-Bains:
Fri.

Montboucher 21F3

GPS: n45,95152 e1,68069.

10 free ChWCfree. **Location:** Rural, quiet. **Surface:** grassy/gravel. 01/01-31/12.
Distance: 8km 8km 8km.

Montcaret 24D2

Le Chalet du Gourmet, D936. **GPS**: n44,85337 e0,03988.

16 € 6,50 Ch included WC €2 €3.
Location: Rural, simple. **Surface:** gravel. 01/01-31/12.
Distance: 1,2km on the spot.
Remarks: Bread-service, fruit-vegetables-wine-regional products for sale.

Montendre 24C1

Place de la Paix. **GPS**: n45,28627 w0,41116.

15 free ChWCfree. **Location:** Urban, simple, central, quiet. **Surface:** asphalted. 01/01-31/12 Thu 6-14h.
Distance: 100m 100m 500m.

Monteton 24D2

D423. **GPS**: n44,62249 e0,25745.

25 free Chfree. **Location:** Rural, simple. **Surface:** grassy. 01/01-31/12.
Distance: on the spot 150m.
Remarks: Beautiful view.

Montguyon 24C1

Plaine des Sports, Rue de Vassiac. **GPS**: n45,21796 w0,18368.

15 free ChWCfree. **Location:** Urban, simple, central, quiet. **Surface:** gravel. 01/01-31/12.
Distance: 500m 500m 500m on the spot.
Remarks: Max. 72h.

Montignac 24E1

P Vieux Quartiers, Rue des Sagnes. **GPS**: n45,06800 e1,16547.

35 € 5/night Ch included. **Location:** Comfortable, central. **Surface:** gravel. 01/01-31/12.
Distance: 200m 200m 200m.

Montignac 24E1

Ferme du Bois Bareirou, Les Baraques, Montignac-Lascaux. **GPS**: n45,09053 e1,11143.

20 free €3 Ch €3. **Location:** Rural, isolated, quiet. **Surface:** grassy. 01/01-31/12.
Distance: 5km.
Remarks: Max. 3 days.

Montils 21C3

Le Vignolet, D233. **GPS**: n45,65285 w0,50576.

20 free Ch free. **Location:** Rural, simple, isolated. **Surface:** gravel/metalled. 01/01-31/12.
Distance: 300m.

Montmorillon 21E2

Rue Léon Dardant. **GPS**: n46,42326 e0,86788.

10 free €2/10minutes Ch €2.
Location: Urban, simple, central, quiet. **Surface:** asphalted. 01/01-31/12.
Distance: 500m 500m 2km.
Remarks: Along theGartempe river, max. 24h.

Montpon-Ménestérol 24D2

Chez Lou Cantou, 46 rue Gustave Eiffel, D730. **GPS**: n45,02101 e0,15997.
4 € 10/24h €3/100liter Ch €3.
01/04-31/10 frost.

Morcenx 24B3

Chemin des Abattoirs. **GPS**: n44,03811 w0,90914.

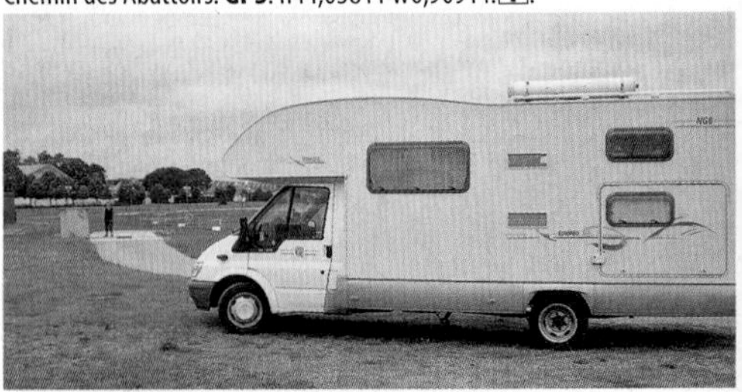

free Chfree. **Location:** Simple.
Distance: 500m 8,8km.
Remarks: Along railwayline.

Mortagne-sur-Gironde 21C3

Le Port de Mortagne, Quai des Pêcheurs. **GPS**: n45,47472 w0,79778.

FR

50 € 8 Ch WC against payment included.
Location: Rural, simple, isolated, quiet. **Surface:** grassy.
01/01-31/12.
Distance: 750m 200m 750m on the spot.
Remarks: In front of Capitainerie.

S Moulismes 21E2

RN147. **GPS**: n46,33306 e0,81000.

50 free €3 Ch WC. **Location:** Rural, simple, quiet.
Surface: grassy/metalled. 01/01-31/12.
Distance: 400m on the spot on the spot 400m.
Remarks: At small lake (plan d'eau).

S Mugron 27B1

Avenue des Martyrs de la Résistance, D32e.
GPS: n43,74846 w0,75063.

4 free Ch (4x)free. **Location:** Rural, simple.
Surface: gravel. 01/01-31/12.
Distance: 300m on the spot.
Remarks: Max. 24h.

S Nailhac 24E1

Lorserie, D62E3. **GPS**: n45,23276 e1,14214.

6 free Chfree €3,50/24h. **Location:** Rural, simple.
Surface: metalled.
Distance: 1,5km 1,5km.

S Nantiat 21F3

L'Étang des Haches, Route de Chamboret. **GPS**: n46,00484 e1,15332.
free €2/100liter Ch €2/4h. 01/01-31/12.

Naujan-et-Postiac 24C2

Lafuge. **GPS**: n44,78715 w0,17928.

free. **Location:** Rural, simple. **Surface:** gravel.

01/01-31/12.
Distance: 200m.

S Nérac 24D3

Place du Foirail. **GPS**: n44,13435 e0,33655.

2 free ChWC. **Location:** Urban, simple. **Surface:** asphalted.
01/01-31/12.
Distance: 50m on the spot on the spot.

S Nersac 21D3

Rue d'Epagnac. **GPS**: n45,62599 e0,05015.

7 free Ch (4x)free.
Surface: asphalted. 01/01-31/12.
Distance: on the spot 100m 100m 100m.
Remarks: Max. 48h.

S Nespouls 24F2

GPS: n45,05244 e1,49568.

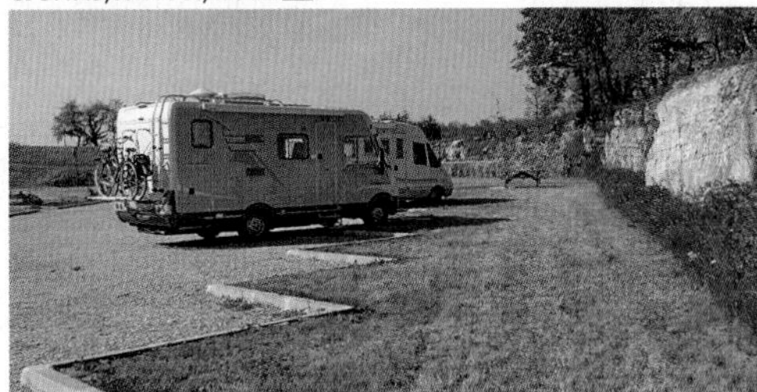

10 Chfree.
Location: Rural, comfortable. **Surface:** gravel.
Distance: 1km 500m on the spot on the spot.

S Nieuil-l'Espoir 21E2

Allée du champ de foire. **GPS**: n46,48505 e0,45417.

10 free €2 Ch €2. **Location:** Rural, comfortable, quiet.
Surface: grassy/metalled. 01/01-31/12.
Distance: 200m 150m on the spot on the spot.
Remarks: At Base de Loisirs, coins at the shops.

S Nieul 21F3

19 Mars 1962, D28. **GPS**: n45,92564 e1,17236.

15 free ChWCfree. **Location:** Rural, central, quiet.
Surface: grassy/gravel. 01/04-31/10.
Distance: 400m 400m 400m.

Remarks: Max. 72h.

S Nieulle-sur-Seudre 21B3

Place de la Mairie. **GPS**: n45,75275 w1,00209.

4 free €4/100liter Ch against payment.
Location: Urban, simple, central, quiet. **Surface:** asphalted.
01/01-31/12.
Distance: on the spot.
Remarks: Coins at town hall.

S Niort 21C2

Aire des camping-cars du Pré Leroy, Rue de Bessac.
GPS: n46,32917 w0,46444.

14 € 7,70 Ch included.
Location: Urban, comfortable, quiet. **Surface:** metalled.
01/01-31/12.
Distance: 1,2km 150m 300m.

Tourist information Niort:
Tue, Sa.
Marais Poitevin. Swamp area, possibility of making boat trips.

S Objat 24F1

Parc Aquatique Espace Loisirs, Avenue Jules Ferry.
GPS: n45,27110 e1,41147.

20 € 6,60, 01/04-31/10 € 8,60 €2/100liter Ch WC €2 .
Location: Rural, comfortable, quiet.
Surface: grassy/metalled.
01/01-31/12.
Distance: 500m 500m.
Remarks: Max. 7 days, baker on site: Tue-Sa, free electricity 72h, swimming pool 200m, entrance code available at tourist info.

S Ogeu-les-Bains 27C2

Avenue de Pau. **GPS**: n43,15349 w0,5022.

4 free Chfree. **Location:** Urban, simple, simple.
Surface: asphalted/gravel. 01/01-31/12.
Distance: 100m 500m.
Remarks: Max. 48h.

S Oloron-Sainte-Marie 27B2

Parking Tivoli, Rue Adoue. **GPS**: n43,18399 w0,60854.

FR

7 free €4/55minutes Ch €4/55minutes.
Surface: asphalted. 01/01-31/12.
Distance: 100m on the spot on the spot 400m 400m.
Remarks: Max. 48h, coins at tourist info.

S Ondres 27A1

P3, Avenue de la Plage, Ondres-Plage. **GPS**: n43,57611 w1,48611.

41 €8, Jul/Aug €10 Ch WCfree.
Surface: asphalted. 15/04-01/11.
Distance: 3km on the spot on the spot on the spot on the spot on the spot.
Remarks: Max. 48h.

S Oradour-sur-Glane 21E3

Aire de camping-cars, Rue du Stade. **GPS**: n45,93570 e1,02471.

30 free €2/100liter Ch €2 WC.
Location: Rural. **Surface:** asphalted.
01/01-31/12 Service: winter.
Distance: 800m 800m 800m.
Remarks: Coins at tourist info, playground.

Tourist information Oradour-sur-Glane:
Office de Tourisme, Place du Champ de Foire. Martyre town, was attacked by 200 SS-soldiers on 10 June 1944. They assassinated the population. Afterwards the village was burned down. In commemoration a wall was built round the the city after the war. free.

S Oradour-sur-Vayres 21E3

Rue Jean Giraudoux. **GPS**: n45,73269 e0,86592.

10 Chfree.
Location: Urban, simple. **Surface:** gravel.
Distance: 200m 200m.

S Pageas 21E3

RN21. **GPS**: n45,67758 e1,00224.

20 free €3 Ch €3 WC. **Location:** Rural, comfortable.
Surface: grassy/gravel. 01/01-31/12.
Distance: 100m on the spot on the spot on the spot.
Remarks: Near N21, coins at town hall.

S Pamproux 21D2

Rue de la Cueille. **GPS**: n46,39625 w0,05874.

3 free €2/20minutes Ch €2/20minutes.
Location: Rural, simple, quiet. **Surface:** asphalted.
01/01-31/12.
Distance: 100m 5,2km 100m.

S Parentis-en-Born 24B3

Site du Lac, Route des Campings. **GPS**: n44,34432 w1,09879.

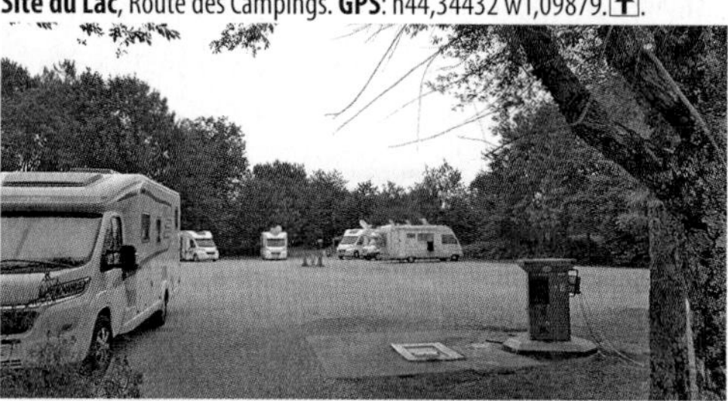

25 €7 Ch (4x)included. **Location:** Comfortable.
Surface: gravel. 01/01-31/12 service in winter.
Distance: 3km 50m 50m.

S Parthenay 21D1

Aire base de loisirs Bois Vert, Rue de Boisseau 14.
GPS: n46,64088 w0,26689.

8 €9-10 Ch included €3 €2 €4/day.
Location: Urban. **Surface:** gravel.
05/04-31/10.
Distance: 2,5km on the spot nearby 2km 100m.
Remarks: Along the Thouet river, check in at campsite.

Tourist information Parthenay:
Les Halles. Weekly market in the halls and streets. Wed.

Pau 27C2

Place de Verdun, Rue Ambroise Bordelongue.
GPS: n43,29848 w0,37811.

20 free. **Location:** Urban. **Surface:** asphalted. 01/01-31/12.
Distance: on the spot on the spot 200m.
Remarks: Max. 48h, free shuttle.

S Payzac 24F1

Le Bourg. **GPS**: n45,40008 e1,21950.

2 free Ch free. **Location:** Simple. **Surface:** asphalted.
01/01-31/12.
Distance: on the spot on the spot on the spot on the spot.

S Pellegrue 24D2

Le Touran, Rue du Lavoir. **GPS**: n44,74514 e0,07416.

3 free Ch free. **Location:** Urban, simple.
Surface: metalled. 01/01-31/12.
Distance: 100m 200m 700m.

S Pérignac 21C3

Pla de l'Église. **GPS**: n45,62532 w0,46309.
10 free Ch. **Surface:** asphalted. 01/01-31/12.
Distance: on the spot on the spot.
Remarks: Behind church.

S Périgueux 24E1

Espace des Prés, Rue des Prés. **GPS**: n45,18770 e0,73081.

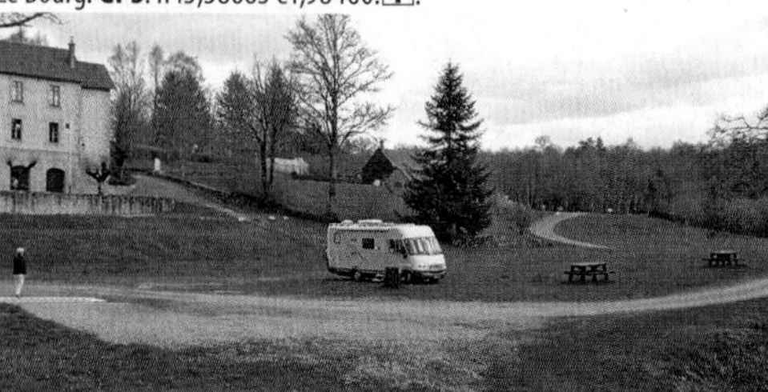

40 €6 Chincluded. **Location:** Urban, comfortable, central. **Surface:** asphalted. 01/01-31/12 water disconnected in winter.
Distance: 800m on the spot.
Remarks: Max. 48h.

S Pérols-sur-Vézère 21G3

Le Bourg. **GPS**: n45,58665 e1,98460.

10 free €2 Ch. **Location:** Rural, comfortable, quiet.
Surface: grassy.
Distance: 50m on the spot on the spot on the spot.
Remarks: Coins at tourist info.

S Peyrat-le-Château 21F3

Auphelle. **GPS**: n45,80750 e1,84111.

FR

100 € 4,20, Jul/Aug € 6 €2,50/100liter €6/4h. **Location:** Rural, quiet. **Surface:** grassy. 12/04-07/11.
Distance: Lac de Vassivière 300m.
Remarks: In front of campsite, bread-service in summer period.

S Peyrat-le-Château 21F3

Parking Pré de l'Age. GPS: n45,81468 e1,77085.
€2 Ch.
Remarks: Coins at tourist info and town hall.

Tourist information Peyrat-le-Château:
Office de Tourisme, 1, Rue du Lac, www.peyrat-tourisme.com. Tourist town close water sports lake, Lac de Vassivière, marked cycle and hiking routes. Sa-Su 15-17h.

S Peyrehorade 27B1

Des Gaves, Route de la Pêcherie. **GPS:** n43,54300 w1,1071.
16 € 9 Ch €2,50 WC . **Surface:** grassy.
01/06-30/09.
Distance: 150m on the spot on the spot 150m 150m 200m.

S Peyrehorade 27B1

Place Jean Bridart, Rue du Sablot, D817.
GPS: n43,54300 w1,09994.

10 free Chfree. **Location:** Urban, simple. **Surface:** metalled.
01/01-31/12.
Distance: 50m on the spot on the spot 100m on the spot.

S Pomarez 27B1

Rue de la Mairie. **GPS:** n43,62853 w0,82895.
5 free Ch WC. **Location:** Urban, noisy.
Surface: asphalted. 01/01-31/12.
Distance: on the spot 200m 400m.
Remarks: At townhall, max. 72h.

S Pomarez 27B1

Ferme du Grand Castagnet, Chemin du Lucq.
GPS: n43,62040 w0,86525.
3 free Ch WC.
Surface: gravel/metalled. 01/01-31/12.
Distance: 2km.

S Pons 21C3

Place de l'Europe. **GPS:** n45,58086 w0,5528.
10 free WC . 01/01-31/12.
Distance: 400m 400m 400m.
Remarks: Max. 24h.

Pons 21C3

Chateau Renaud, D234E5, Bougneau. **GPS:** n45,60102 w0,5367.
10 free. **Location:** Isolated. 01/01-31/12.
Distance: on the spot 1,2km.
Remarks: Along river.

S Pons 21C3

Camping municipal Le Paradis, Avenue du Poitou.
GPS: n45,57765 w0,55536.

5 free €6 Ch €6/h.
Location: Urban, simple. **Surface:** asphalted.
Distance: 300m.

S Port-des-Barques 21B2

Pré des Mays, Avenue des Sports. **GPS:** n45,94722 w1,09.

30 € 6,20/24h €2/10minutes Chfree €2/55minutes
Location: Rural, simple. **Surface:** metalled.
15/03-15/11.
Remarks: In front of stadium.

S Port-Sainte-Foy-et-Ponchapt 24D2

Rue Jacques Jasmin. **GPS:** n44,84210 e0,20915.

4 free Chfree. **Location:** Urban, simple, central, quiet.
Surface: asphalted. 01/01-31/12.
Distance: on the spot 600m 600m.
Remarks: Along the Dordogne river, service 200m.

Prats-de-Carlux 24F2

Les Oies du Périgord Noir, D47B. **GPS:** n44,89936 e1,31503.

4 free. **Location:** Rural, simple, quiet. 01/01-31/12.
Distance: 3km 3km 3km.
Remarks: Max. 24h.

S Rébénacq 27C2

Chemin de Montés. **GPS:** n43,15690 w0,39733.

4 free Ch free. **Location:** Rural, simple, quiet.
Surface: asphalted.
Distance: 400m on the spot on the spot.
Remarks: At football ground, max. 48h.

S Ribérac 24D1

Camping de la Dronne, 91 Rue des Etats Unis.
GPS: n45,25704 e0,34255.

10 free, 01/06-15/09 € 5,60 Chfree. **Location:** Urban, simple. **Surface:** metalled. 01/01-31/12 Water when frosty.
Distance: 1,3km 50m Leclerc 900m.

S Rivedoux-Plage 21B2

Campéole Le Platin, 125, Av Gustave Perreau.
GPS: n46,15889 w1,27139.

17 € 14-17 €3 Ch . **Location:** Urban, simple.
Surface: asphalted. 01/01-31/12.
Distance: 100m Plage Nord.
Remarks: Next to campsite Le Platin, to be paid at campsite.

S Rochefort 21B2

Rue de la Fosse aux Mâts. **GPS:** n45,92735 w0,95467.

25 € 6/24h Chincluded. **Location:** Urban, simple.
Surface: asphalted. 01/01-31/112.

Rochefort 21B2

Avenue Marcel Dassault. **GPS:** n45,94661 w0,96002.

15 € 6. **Location:** Urban, simple. **Surface:** asphalted.
01/01-31/12.
Distance: 1km.

Rochefort 21B2

Pont Transbordeur, Chemin de Charente.
GPS: n45,91792 w0,96388.

5 free. **Location:** Urban, simple. **Surface:** grassy/gravel.
01/01-31/12.

Rochefort 21B2

Rue de la Vieille Forme. **GPS:** n45,94448 w0,95554.
10 € 6. **Location:** Simple. **Surface:** gravel.
Remarks: Near marina.

FR

S Rochefort 21B2
Port de Plaisance, Quai Lemoigne de Sérigny.
GPS: n45,94444 w0,95556.
Ch free.
01/01-31/12.
Tourist information Rochefort:
Corderie Royale. Old royal rope-walk.
Tue, Thu, Sa.

S Romagne 21D2
Rue du Vigneau. **GPS**: n46,26884 e0,30373.

6 free Ch WC free. **Location:** Rural, comfortable, quiet.
Surface: gravel. 15/03-31/10.
Distance: 250m 250m.

S Roquefort 24C3
Allée de Nauton. **GPS**: n44,04754 w0,32255.

6 free Ch. **Location:** Rural. **Surface:** grassy/gravel.
01/01-31/12.
Distance: 1,7km 5km.
Remarks: Next to camping municipal.

S Rouillac 21D3
Super U, Rue de Genac. **GPS**: n45,77650 w0,06133.

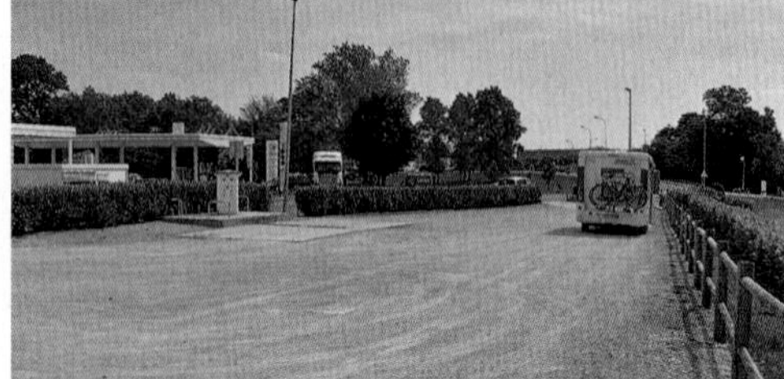

8 free €3 Ch. **Surface:** gravel. 01/01-31/12.
Distance: 500m 500m 50m.
Remarks: Coins available at supermarket.

S Roullet-Saint-Estèphe 21D3
Aire de camping-car Roullet, D210. **GPS**: n45,58086 e0,04461.
20 free Ch free. **Location:** Rural. **Surface:** gravel.
01/01-31/12.
Distance: 300m 150m 350m.

S Roumazières-Loubert 21E3
Aire de Détente de Ronmatières, RN141.
GPS: n45,88275 e0,57287.

3 free Ch WC free.
Surface: asphalted. 01/01-31/12.
Distance: 500m 100m 300m.

S Royan 21B3
Camping-Car Park Royan, Rue Bel-air. **GPS**: n45,62834 w1,01204.

28 € 9,60 Ch included.
Location: Urban, comfortable, central, quiet.
Surface: gravel/metalled. 01/01-31/12.
Distance: 500m 500m 500m.

S Royère-de-Vassivière 21G3
Le Bourg. **GPS**: n45,84012 e1,91122.

6 free Ch WC free. **Location:** Rural, simple.
Surface: asphalted. 01/01-31/12 Thu>14h (market).
Distance: on the spot 200m on the spot.
Remarks: Max. 48h.

S Ruffec 21D2
SARL Remy Frères Camping-Cars, D26. **GPS**: n46,03316 e0,18366.

10 free Ch free. **Surface:** asphalted.
Distance: 1km.
Remarks: At motorhome dealer.

S Sadroc 24F1
Place du Château. **GPS**: n45,28325 e1,54854.

6 free Ch free. **Location:** Urban, simple, quiet.
Surface: asphalted. 01/01-31/12.
Distance: on the spot 5,2km 50m.
Remarks: Max. 24h.

S Saint Césaire 21C3
Parking Paléosite, Rue de Groies. **GPS**: n45,75406 w0,50751.

20 free Ch free. **Location:** Rural, simple, isolated, quiet.
Surface: asphalted/metalled. 01/01-31/12.
Distance: on the spot 500m 100m on the spot.
Tourist information Saint Césaire:
Paléosite, Route de la Montée Verte. Interactive park, in the footsteps of the Neanderthals. 10.30-18.30, Jul-Aug 10-20 January.

S Saint Estèphe 21E3
Etang de Saint Estèphe, Route du Grand Etang.
GPS: n45,59458 e0,67437.

10 € 5 Ch included. **Location:** Rural, comfortable.
Surface: forest soil. 01/01-31/12.
Distance: 700m lake on the spot on the spot 3km, bakery 800m.
Remarks: Max. 48h, summer: beach, bar, restaurant.

S Saint Laurant de la Prée 21B2
La Cabane, Route de l'Océan. **GPS**: n45,99043 w1,04942.

10 € 7 Ch included. **Location:** Rural, simple.
Surface: gravel. 01/01-31/12.

S Saint-Agnant 21B3
Place de Verdun. **GPS**: n45,86635 w0,9641.

10 free Ch free. **Location:** Rural, simple. **Surface:** asphalted.
01/01-31/12.
Remarks: Next to town hall.

S Saint-Amand-sur-Sèvre 21C1
Boulevard de Maumusson. **GPS**: n46,86903 w0,8.

5 free Ch free. **Location:** Rural, simple, quiet.
Surface: grasstiles. 01/01-31/12.
Distance: 500m 500m 500m.

S Saint-Amand-sur-Sèvre 21C1
Le Moulin Chaligny. **GPS**: n46,88493 w0,82342.

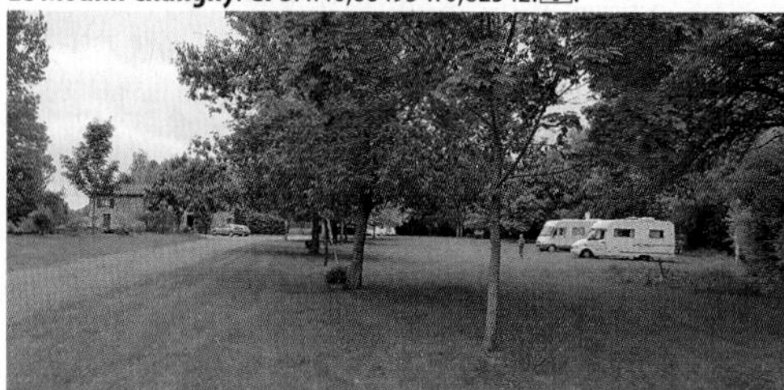

10 € 10 Ch WC included. **Location:** Rural, isolated, quiet.
Surface: grassy. 01/01-31/12.
Distance: 3km 3km 3km on the spot on the spot.

Saint-Antoine-Cumond 24D1

Le Bourg, D43. **GPS**: n45,25553 e0,19963.

10 free Ch WC free. **Location:** Rural, simple.
Surface: asphalted/gravel. 01/01-31/12.
Distance: on the spot.

Saint-Antoine-de-Breuilh 24D2

Camping-Car Park, 86 bis avenue du Périgord.
GPS: n44,84516 e0,15847.
26 € 9,60-10,80 Ch (24x) included.
Location: Comfortable, quiet. 01/01-31/12.
Distance: 200m 200m 300m 500m on the spot on the spot.

Saint-Caprais-de-Blaye 24C1

Route de Saintes, RN137, Ferchaud. **GPS**: n45,29120 w0,5692.

8 free service €2 Ch WC free, cold shower.
Surface: asphalted. 01/01-31/12.
Distance: 6,4km on the spot on the spot.
Remarks: Tourist information and picnic tables available.

Saint-Clément-des-Baleines 21B2

Rue de la Forêt. **GPS**: n46,22756 w1,54644.

30 € 11/night, € 18/2 nights Ch €4/1h free.
Location: Rural, simple. **Surface:** metalled.
01/01-31/12.
Distance: 250m 500m.
Remarks: Next to campsite, payment only with coins.

Saint-Cyprien 24E2

Place Mackenheim, Rue du Priolat. **GPS**: n44,86828 e1,04435.

8 € 3,50 Ch.
Location: Simple. **Surface:** asphalted.
01/01-31/12.
Distance: 50m bakery 50m, supermarket 100m.
Remarks: Max. 24h, coins at tourist info and restaurant La Sivade.

Tourist information Saint-Cyprien:
Marché repas gourmand. summer Thu-evening.

Saint-Denis-d'Oléron 21B2

Aire du Moulin, Route des Huttes. **GPS**: n46,02750 w1,38306.

170 € 10/24h Ch WC included. **Location:** Rural, simple. **Surface:** grassy. 01/01-31/12.
Distance: 1km.
Remarks: Max. 4 nights.

Saint-Dizant-du-Gua 24C1

Les berges du Taillon, 6 Rue du Pérat. **GPS**: n45,43062 w0,707.
25 free €2 Ch €2. **Surface:** grassy/metalled.
01/01-31/12.
Distance: 200m on the spot on the spot on the spot on the spot.

Saint-Estèphe 24C1

Rue du Littoral. **GPS**: n45,26544 w0,7582.

5 free Ch Service €5. **Location:** Rural, simple, quiet.
Surface: gravel/metalled. 01/01-31/12.
Distance: 2km on the spot on the spot on the spot on the spot.
Remarks: Free, coins available at restaurant.

Saint-Front-la-Rivière 24E1

Chez Boutau, D83. **GPS**: n45,46645 e0,72419.

10 free Ch (2x) free. **Location:** Rural, comfortable, isolated, quiet. **Surface:** metalled. 01/01-31/12.
Remarks: Max. 72h, picnic area.

Saint-Genis-de-Saintonge 21C3

Rue Fanny. **GPS**: n45,48330 w0,56569.

20 € 6/24h 10minutes Ch (20x) included 4h.
Location: Urban, comfortable, central, quiet. **Surface:** asphalted.
01/01-31/12.
Distance: 400m.
Remarks: Behind cinema, max. 72h.

Saint-Georges-de-Didonne 21B3

Parking Maudet, Rue du Docteur Maudet.
GPS: n45,60408 w0,99964.

19 € 6/24h Ch included.
Location: Urban, simple, central, quiet. **Surface:** asphalted.
01/01-31/12.
Distance: 400m 500m.
Remarks: Max. 72h.

Saint-Georges-de-Didonne 21B3

Front de Mer, Boulevard de la Côte de Beauté.
GPS: n45,59557 w0,99163.

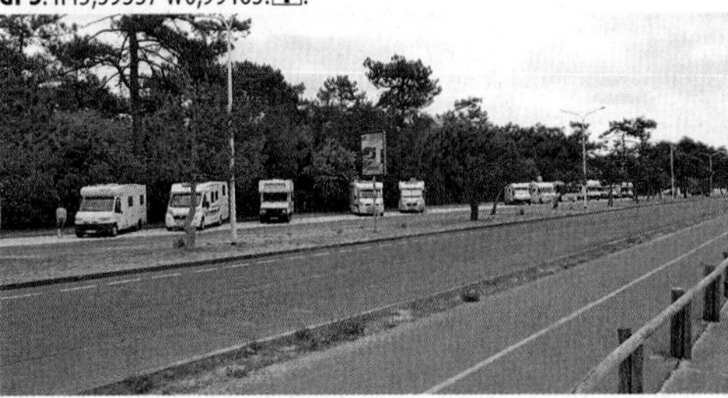

20 € 6/24h. **Location:** Urban, simple, quiet.
Surface: gravel/metalled. 01/01-31/12.
Distance: 500m on the spot 350m on the spot.
Remarks: Beach parking, max. 72h.

Saint-Georges-de-Didonne 21B3

Parking Gillet, Rue du Professeur Langevin.
GPS: n45,60324 w0,9921.

13 € 6/24h. **Location:** Urban, simple, central, quiet.
Surface: asphalted. 01/01-31/12.
Distance: on the spot 800m on the spot on the spot.
Remarks: Max. 72h.

Saint-Georges-de-Didonne 21B3

Parking Miramar, Rue du Port. **GPS**: n45,60031 w1,007.

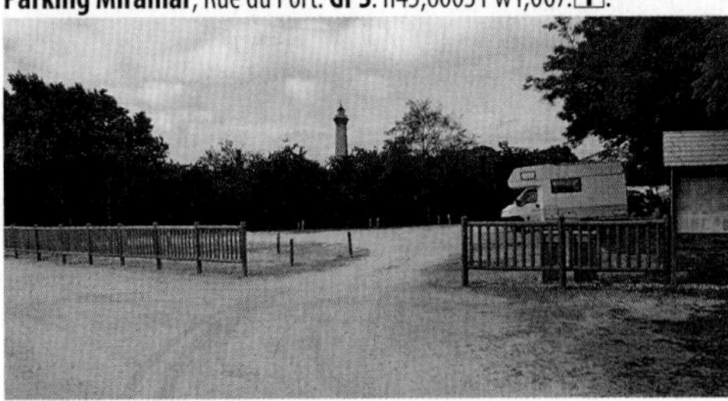

15 € 6/24h. **Location:** Urban. **Surface:** gravel/metalled.
01/01-31/12.
Distance: 1km 100m on the spot 200m 1km.
Remarks: Max. 72h.

Saint-Germain-de-Marencennes 21C2

Rue du Moulin Neuf. **GPS**: n46,07882 w0,78283.
10 € 6 Ch WC included. **Location:** Simple, quiet.
Surface: asphalted. 15/03-15/11.
Distance: 500m.

Saint-Hilaire-de-Lusignan 24D3

D813. **GPS**: n44,22491 e0,51364.

FR

3 free €3/10minutes Ch. **Location:** Urban, simple, noisy. **Surface:** gravel. 01/01-31/12.
Distance: on the spot 1km 5km, bakery 500m.

Saint-Hilaire-la-Palud 21C2

Place de la Marie. **GPS:** n46,26444 w0,71306.

10 free. **Surface:** asphalted. 01/01-31/12.
Distance: on the spot on the spot on the spot.
Remarks: Parking in front of town hall, max. 2 nights.

Saint-Jean-d'Angély 21C3

Base de Plein Air, Avenue de Marennes, D18.
GPS: n45,94537 w0,53735.

10 free Chfree. **Surface:** gravel. 01/01-31/12.
Distance: 1km 100m 100m 200m 1km.
Remarks: Max. 2 nights.

Saint-Jean-de-Côle 24E1

Le Bourg. **GPS:** n45,41984 e0,84048.

3 free €2 Ch €2. **Location:** Urban, simple, quiet. **Surface:** metalled. 01/01-31/12.
Distance: on the spot 200m 300m 200m.
Remarks: At tennis-court, coins at tourist info.

Saint-Jean-de-Luz 27A2

Avenue Geneviève Antonios de Gaulle, D810.
GPS: n43,38527 w1,6629.

18 free Ch free. **Surface:** asphalted.
Distance: 200m 2,2km 300m 300m 100m 100m.
Remarks: Max. 48h.

Tourist information Saint-Jean-de-Luz:
Office de Tourisme, Place du Maréchal Foch, www.saint-jean-de-luz.com. Tourist town with beautiful shops. The local speciality is chipirones, octopus cooked in its own ink.
Halles, Bd Victor Hugo. morning.

Saint-Jean-Pied-de-Port 27A2

Parking du Lai Alai. GPS: n43,16519 w1,23208.

50 € 5,50 Ch WC .
Surface: metalled.
01/01-31/12.
Distance: 350m 350m 350m 350m 350m on the spot.
Remarks: Nearby stadium, max. 48h.

Tourist information Saint-Jean-Pied-de-Port:
Office de Tourisme, 14, Place Charles de Gaulle, www.pyrenees-basques.com. Fortified city on the foot of the Roncesvallespass on the road to Santiago de Compostela.
Forêt d'Iraty. Nature reserve, hiking trails available at OT.

Saint-Julien-le-Petit 21F3

Route de la Plage. **GPS:** n45,82142 e1,70531.

12 € 5, 2 pers.incl Ch WC . **Location:** Rural, quiet. **Surface:** grassy. 01/01-31/12.

Saint-Junien-la-Bregère 21F3

Rue du Chevalier de Châteauneuf. **GPS:** n45,88236 e1,75282.

3 free Chfree. **Location:** Rural, quiet. **Surface:** asphalted. 01/01-31/12.

Saint-Laurent 21G2

Rue des Cerisiers. **GPS:** n46,16639 e1,96167.

4 free Ch free. **Location:** Rural. **Surface:** metalled. 01/01-31/12.
Distance: on the spot on the spot.

Saint-Laurent-Médoc 24B1

Place du 8 mai 1945. **GPS:** n45,14903 w0,8215.

6 free Ch . **Location:** Urban, simple, comfortable. **Surface:** gravel/metalled. 01/01-31/12.
Distance: on the spot 300m 300m.

Saint-Laurent-sur-Gorre 21E3

Les Chênes, Allée des Primevères. **GPS:** n45,76528 e0,95639.

20 € 6 €2/100liter Ch (7x)€2/4h WC included.
Location: Rural, comfortable, quiet. **Surface:** grassy. 01/01-31/12.
Distance: 300m on the spot on the spot 300m 300m.

Saint-Leon-sur-l'Isle 24D1

Skate Park Bord de l'Isle, D41E2. **GPS:** n45,12002 e0,49628.

6 free Chfree. **Location:** Rural, simple.
Surface: metalled/sand. 01/01-31/12.
Distance: 2km 5,3km on the spot 2km 2km.
Remarks: Service in village 750m, n45.11515 o0.5003400.

Saint-Léon-sur-Vézère 24E2

Le Bourg, C201. **GPS:** n45,01230 e1,08978.

15 free, 01/04-15/11 € 6 €2 WC. **Location:** Rural, simple, quiet. **Surface:** grassy/gravel. 01/01-31/12.
Distance: 100m 200m 150m.
Remarks: Coins at tourist info.

Saint-Martial-d'Artenset 24D2

Le Gaec du Petit Clos, Ferrachat. **GPS:** n44,99877 e0,22052.
€ 5, € 10 service incl Ch . **Location:** Comfortable, isolated, quiet.
Distance: 2,5km 9km 2,5km.

Saint-Martin-de-Ré 21B2

Rue de Rempart. **GPS:** n46,19925 w1,36514.

17 € 11 Chincluded. **Location:** Rural. **Surface:** gravel.

01/01-31/12.
Distance: 500m 700m 500m 500m.
Remarks: 01/04-30/09 max. 72h.

S Saint-Mathieu 21E3

Les Champs. **GPS**: n45,71465 e0,78720.

15 free €2/100liter Ch. **Location:** Rural, simple, quiet.
Surface: asphalted. 01/01-31/12.
Distance: 2km on the spot on the spot.

S Saint-Médard-de-Guizières 24D2

Place du 14 Juillet. **GPS**: n45,01526 w0,05813.
3 free ChWCfree. **Surface:** asphalted. 01/01-31/12.
Distance: on the spot on the spot 300m.

S Saint-Merd-les-Oussines 21G3

D109 > Tarnac. **GPS**: n45,63500 e2,03719.

6 free €2 Ch. **Location:** Rural, simple, isolated, quiet.
Surface: grassy/gravel. 01/01-31/12.
Distance: 400m.
Remarks: Coins at Auberge du Mont-Chauvet.

S Saint-Palais-sur-Mer 27B2

Parking Place Ste. Elisabeth, Rue Gaztelu Zena.
GPS: n43,32944 w1,0325.

10 free ChWCfree. **Location:** Simple. **Surface:** asphalted.
01/01-31/12.
Distance: 200m 250m 250m.

S Saint-Paul-lès-Dax 27B1

Allée Salvador Allende. **GPS**: n43,73460 w1,07865.

8 free Chfree. **Location:** Simple. **Surface:** gravel/sand.
01/01-31/12.
Distance: 500m 500m.
Remarks: Max. 72h, shady.

S Saint-Pée-sur-Nivelle 27A2

Flot bleu park St. Pée sur Nivelle, Promenade du Parlement de Navarre. **GPS**: n43,34945 w1,5215.

50 € 9,50/24h €2,50/120liter Ch €2,50/4h.
Surface: asphalted. 01/01-31/12.
Distance: 3km on the spot 500m Restaurant Aintzira Le Lac.
Remarks: Parking at lake, max. 48h, bread-service.

S Saint-Pey-d'Armens 24C2

Château Gerbaud, Gerbaud. **GPS**: n44,85310 w0,10699.

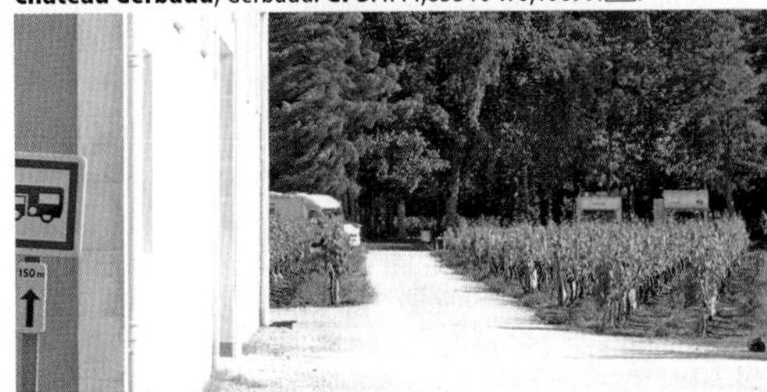

40 € 5 Chincluded (8x)€3. **Location:** Rural, simple.
Surface: grassy. 01/01-31/12.
Distance: 1km bakery 1km, supermarket 2km.
Remarks: Max. 48h.

S Saint-Pierre-d'Oléron 21B2

Avenue des Pins, La Cotinière. **GPS**: n45,92393 w1,3427.

10 € 9 €4/stay Ch. **Location:** Rural, simple.
Surface: grassy/gravel.
Remarks: In front of campsite municipal, pay at reception.

S Saint-Porchaire 21C3

Place du Champ de Foire. **GPS**: n45,82063 w0,78215.

10 free ChWCfree. **Location:** Urban, simple, central, quiet.
Surface: gravel. 01/01-31/12.
Distance: 400m 200m 1km.
Remarks: Max. 48h.

S Saint-Privat 24G1

Rue des Chanaux. **GPS**: n45,14037 e2,09765.

10 free €2 Ch €2. **Location:** Urban, simple, central, quiet.
Surface: grassy/metalled. 01/01-31/12.
Distance: 200m 200m 200m.

S Saint-Romain-la-Virvée 24C2

Rue des Milonis. **GPS**: n44,96449 w0,40139.

5 free Chfree. **Location:** Rural, comfortable, quiet.
Surface: asphalted. 01/01-31/12.
Distance: on the spot 10km 250m.
Remarks: Next to sports fields.

S Saint-Saud-Lacoussière 21E3

Étang de la Gourgousse, Route du Grand Etang.
GPS: n45,55780 e0,82237.

free.
Location: Rural, isolated, quiet. **Surface:** forest soil.
Distance: Sandy beach on the spot on the spot.
Remarks: Max. 72h.

S Saint-Saud-Lacoussière 21E3

Domaine Sous Chardonnièras, 4, Impasse Sous Chardonnièras.
GPS: n45,54053 e0,81909.

4 € 12,50 WC included.
Location: Simple, quiet. **Surface:** grassy. 01/01-31/12.
Distance: 500m 2km 2km 500m 500m.

S Saint-Sauveur 24E2

Le Bourg, D21. **GPS**: n44,86850 e0,58834.

3 free ChWCfree. **Location:** Simple. **Surface:** asphalted.
01/01-31/12.
Distance: 100m 100m 100m.

S Saint-Savin 24C1

Aire de Civrac-de-Blaye, Parc de la Mairie, D36, Civrac-de-Blaye.
GPS: n45,11222 w0,44444.

1 free WCfree. **Surface:** grassy. 01/01-31/12.
Distance: 50m 100m.

FR

Saint-Savin 24C1

Aire de St.Girons d'Aiguevives, St.Girons d'Aiguevives. **GPS**: n45,13972 w0,5425.

2 free. **Surface:** grassy/gravel. 01/01-31/12.
Distance: on the spot 4km 10km.
Remarks: Parking in front of church.

Saint-Savin 24C1

Aire des Lacs du Moulin Blanc, St.Christoly-de-Blaye. **GPS**: n45,15167 w0,47583.

2 free WC free. **Surface:** gravel. 01/01-31/12.
Distance: 800m 50m on the spot on the spot 3km.
Remarks: Parking at lake.

Saint-Savin 24C1

Aire des Lagunes, St.Mariens. **GPS**: n45,11790 w0,40243.

2 free WC free. **Surface:** asphalted. 01/01-31/12.
Distance: on the spot 6km 6km 2km 3km.

Saint-Savin 24C1

Parking Centre Culturel. **GPS**: n45,13800 w0,4465.

2 free WC. **Surface:** gravel. 01/01-31/12.
Distance: on the spot 3km 3km 150m 800m, bakery 50m.
Remarks: Max. 48h.

Saint-Savin 24C1

Aire de l'Église, Générac. **GPS**: n45,18000 w0,54.
2 free. 01/01-31/12.
Distance: on the spot 6km 10km.

Saint-Savin 24C1

Aire de Marcenais, Marcenais. **GPS**: n45,05808 w0,33889.

2 free. 01/01-31/12.
Distance: on the spot 6km 6km.
Remarks: Next to community centre.

Saint-Savin 24C1

Aire de Saugon, Saugon. **GPS**: n45,17795 w0,50243.
2 free. 01/01-31/12.
Distance: on the spot 6km 6km 3km 6km.
Remarks: Behind town hall.

Saint-Savin 24C1

Aire de St. Vivien, RN137, St.Vivien-de-Blay. **GPS**: n45,09917 w0,51666.

2 free. 01/01-31/12.
Distance: on the spot 3km 3km 3km 3km.
Remarks: Parking at church.

Saint-Savin 24C1

Aire du Dojo, Cézac. **GPS**: n45,09000 w0,41.

1 free. 01/01-31/12.
Distance: on the spot 6km 6km 3km 3km.
Remarks: Nearby town hall.

Saint-Savin 24C1

Aire du Lac des Vergnes, Laruscade. **GPS**: n45,10000 w0,34.
2 free. 01/01-31/12.
Distance: 200m on the spot 500m 2km.
Remarks: Parking at lake.

Saint-Savin 24C1

Aire Maison de la Forêt, Donnezac. **GPS**: n45,24000 w0,44.

2 free. 01/01-31/12.
Distance: on the spot 6km 6km.
Remarks: Next to community centre.

Saint-Savin 24C1

Parking communal Aire de Cavignac, Rue de Paix, Cavignac. **GPS**: n45,10019 w0,39192.

2 free. 01/01-31/12.
Distance: on the spot 8km 50m 300m.

Saint-Savin 24C1

Parking communal Aire de Saint Yzan, Parking de la Gare, St.Yzan-de-Soudiac. **GPS**: n45,14006 w0,40996.
2 free. 01/01-31/12.
Distance: on the spot 12km 800m 3km 3km on the spot.

Saint-Savin 24C1

Parking de Marsas, Rue Chaignaud, Marsas. **GPS**: n45,06770 w0,3849.
2 free. 01/01-31/12.
Distance: on the spot 4km 4km.

Saint-Savin 24C1

Parking Maison des Jeunes, Cubnezais. **GPS**: n45,07500 w0,40861.

free. **Surface:** asphalted. 01/01-31/12.
Distance: 50m 3km 3km.

Saint-Séverin 24D1

Rue de la Pavancelle. **GPS**: n45,31269 e0,25527.

2 free Ch WC free. **Location:** Rural. **Surface:** asphalted. 01/01-31/12.
Distance: 200m 200m Spar 100m.

Saint-Sorlin-de-Conac 24C1

Pôle Nature de Vitrezay. **GPS**: n45,32780 w0,71053.
20 free Ch free. 01/01-31/12.
Distance: 400m.
Remarks: Nature reserve.

Saint-Sulpice-le-Guérétois 21G2

Le Masgerot. **GPS**: n46,18265 e1,84714.

16 €2/100liter Ch.
Location: Noisy. **Surface:** asphalted.
Distance: on the spot on the spot.
Remarks: Next to petrol station.

Saint-Sylvestre-sur-Lot 24E3

Place du Lot, Avenue Jean Moulin. **GPS**: n44,39621 e0,80499.

12 free Ch free.
Location: Urban, simple. **Surface:** asphalted. 01/01-31/12.
Distance: 150m, Penne d'Agenais centre 1,8km 100m 50m.
Remarks: Service 100m.

Saint-Trojan-les-Bains 21B3

Parking de la Liberté, Rue Marie Curie. **GPS**: n45,84371 w1,20899.

9 free €4. **Location:** Urban, simple. **Surface:** asphalted.
01/01-31/12.
Distance: 200m on the spot.
Remarks: Max. 72h.

Saint-Trojan-les-Bains 21B3

Parking Patoizeau, Boulevard de la plage. **GPS**: n45,84100 w1,20491.

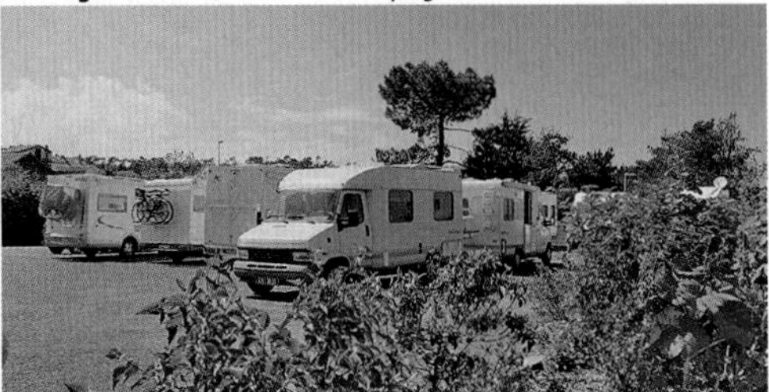

10 free. **Location:** Rural, simple. **Surface:** asphalted.
01/01-31/12.
Distance: 600m 100m.
Remarks: In front of fire-station, max. 72h.

Tourist information Saint-Trojan-les-Bains:
Bureau Municipal de Tourisme, Carrefour du Port, www.st-trojan-les-bains.fr. Seaside resort on the island of Oléron, well-known for the mimosa and oyster culture.
place de Filles de la Sagesse. Food and drugs market. Thu + Sa-morning, summer daily.
Marche Nocturne, rue de la République. Evening market. Thu from 17h.

Saint-Vincent-de-Cosse 24E2

Ferme d'Enveaux. **GPS**: n44,82669 e1,09822.

50 guests free Chfree.
Surface: unpaved. 01/01-31/12.
Distance: pebbled beach 50m on the spot on the spot.
Remarks: Along the Dordogne river, max. 48h, key service at canoe rental.

Saint-Vincent-Jalmoutiers 24D1

Le Bourg. **GPS**: n45,20055 e0,19091.

25 free ChWCfree. **Location:** Rural, simple.
Surface: grassy/sand. 01/01-31/12.
Distance: 350m 350m.

Saint-Ybard 24F1

Foyer Rural, Rue des Fontaines. **GPS**: n45,44886 e1,52271.

2 free free.
Location: Urban, simple, central, quiet.
Distance: on the spot 200m on the spot on the spot.

Saint-Yrieix-la-Perche 24F1

Parking J.P Fabrègue, Avenue de Lattre de Tassigny, D901.
GPS: n45,51271 e1,20646.

5 free €3,50 Ch. **Location:** Urban, simple.
Surface: asphalted. 01/01-31/12.
Distance: 300m 300m 300m.
Remarks: Coins at Tourist Info and Maison de la Presse.

Saint-Yrieix-la-Perche 24F1

Ferme du Poumier, Lieu-dit Poumier, Marcognac.
GPS: n45,52065 e1,26853.

4 €6 Ch included. **Location:** Rural, isolated, quiet.
Surface: gravel. 01/01-31/12.
Distance: St.Yrieix 5km.

Saint-Yrieix-sur-Charente 21D3

Camping du Plan d'eau, Rue du Plan d'Eau, Impasse des Ooyères.
GPS: n45,69176 e0,14517.

14 €7,20, Jul/Aug €9,25 Chfree €3,65.
Location: Comfortable, luxurious. **Surface:** asphalted.
01/04-31/10. **Distance:** 2km 1km 1km 1km 3km.

Sainte-Alvère 24E2

Rue de la Fontaine Saint Jean. **GPS**: n44,94500 e0,80499.

10 free €2,50/100liter Ch €2,50/h.
Location: Rural, simple. **Surface:** gravel. 01/01-31/12.
Distance: 500m 500m 500m.
Remarks: At sports centre, coins at town hall.

Sainte-Colombe-en-Bruilhois 24D3

Lieu-dit Bécade. **GPS**: n44,17889 e0,51692.

4 free ChWCfree. **Location:** Rural, simple, quiet.
Surface: gravel. 01/01-31/12.
Distance: on the spot 200m 200m.

Sainte-Eulalie-en-Born 24B3

Route du Port, D652. **GPS**: n44,30634 w1,18206.

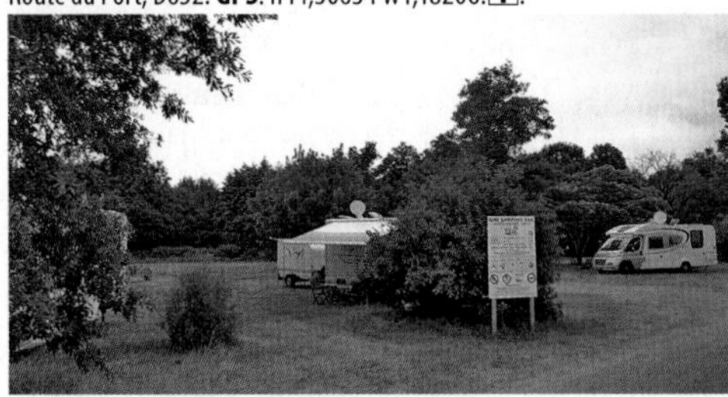

40 €4,50-7 Ch WC included €3.
Location: Comfortable, quiet. **Surface:** grassy.
01/04-31/10 service 01/11-01/03.
Distance: 50m 50m on the spot on the spot.
Remarks: At marina, to be paid at campsite.

Sainte-Livrade-sur-Lot 24E3

Avenue René Bouchon. **GPS**: n44,39588 e0,59179.

8 free Chfree. **Location:** Urban, simple. **Surface:** asphalted.
01/01-31/12.
Distance: on the spot 850m.
Remarks: At fire-station.

Sainte-Nathalène 24F2

Les Ch'tis, Le Bourg, D47. **GPS**: n44,90409 e1,28765.

6 €10 Ch included. **Location:** Rural, simple.
Surface: gravel. 01/01-31/12.
Distance: Sarlat 7km 50m bread service 50m.
Remarks: Market Wednesday (July-August).

Saintes 21C3

Aire camping-cars Avenue de Saintonge, Chemin de la Prairie.
GPS: n45,74047 w0,62696.

12 €5/24h Ch Service €5 .
Location: Urban, simple, central. **Surface:** asphalted.

FR

01/01-31/12.
Distance: 1km 200m Leclerc 100m.
Remarks: Max. 7 days.

Tourist information Saintes:
Les Arènes. Roman anfiteatro.
Place 11 November. Tue + Fri morning.
Grande Foire. Large regional market. 1st Mon of the month.

S **Salies-de-Béarn** 27B2

Aire Camping-car du Herre, Chemin du Herré.
GPS: n43,47270 w0,9339.

24 € 6,70 €2,50 Ch. **Location:** Rural, simple, quiet. **Surface:** gravel. 01/01-31/12.
Distance: 300m on the spot on the spot 300m 300m 300m.

S **Salignac-Eyvigues** 24F2

Rue des Ecoles. **GPS**: n44,97257 e1,32061.

10 free Chfree. **Location:** Simple, quiet. **Surface:** grassy.
01/01-31/12.
Distance: 300m 300m 250m.

Salignac-Eyvigues 24F2

Les Jardins du Manoir d'Eyrignac, Rte des Jardins du Manoir.
GPS: n44,93875 e1,31609.

40 free. **Location:** Rural. **Surface:** grassy/gravel.
Distance: Sarlat 13km on the spot.

S **Sanguinet** 24B2

Aire Des Bardets, 1131, Avenue de Losa. **GPS**: n44,48399 w1,09154.

15 free, 01/05-18/10 € 8 Chfree. **Location:** Simple, quiet. **Surface:** metalled. 01/01-31/12.
Distance: 800m on the spot on the spot 50m on the spot.
Remarks: At lake, max. 48h.

S **Sanguinet** 24B2

Parking du Pavillon, 459, Avenue de Losa.
GPS: n44,48579 w1,08479.

30 free, 01/06-15/09 € 9 ChWC. **Location:** Simple, quiet.
Surface: forest soil. 01/01-31/12.
Distance: on the spot Le Pavillon.
Remarks: Max. 48h.

S **Sare** 27A2

Route des Platane. **GPS**: n43,31179 w1,5839.

23 € 6 Ch. **Location:** Simple. **Surface:** asphalted.
01/01-31/12.
Distance: 400m 400m on the spot.
Remarks: Nearby swimming pool.

Tourist information Sare:
Office de Tourisme, Bourg, www.sare.fr. Typical Basque village in Labourd-region.
Le petit train de la Rhune, Col de Saint Ignace. The little train runs through the mountains in the Basque Country on the Franco-Spanish border. 15/03-15/11 from 9h.
Les Grottes de Sare. Caves, prehistoric park and museum. 01/02-31/12.

S **Sarlat-la-Canéda** 24F2

Place Flandres Dunkerque. **GPS**: n44,89530 e1,21266.

50 € 7/24h, € 15/48h €2 Ch €2
Location: Urban, simple, noisy. **Surface:** asphalted.
01/01-31/12.
Distance: 1km 100m bakery 50m.

Tourist information Sarlat-la-Canéda:
Centre ville. Centre of the French trade in foie grass. Sa-morning.

S **Saujon** 21B3

Route des Ecluses. **GPS**: n45,67503 w0,932.

14 € 4/24h €2/100liter Ch €2/1h.
Location: Urban, simple, central, quiet. **Surface:** asphalted.
01/01-31/12.
Distance: 900m.
Remarks: Max. 6 days, coins at town hall.

S **Sauvagnon** 27C2

Champ de Foire, Rue du Béarn. **GPS**: n43,40361 w0,38635.

7 free ChWCfree. **Location:** Rural. **Surface:** asphalted.
01/01-31/12.
Distance: on the spot on the spot on the spot on the spot.
Remarks: Max. 48h.

Sauvagnon 27C2

Rue du Béarn. **GPS**: n43,40310 w0,3876.

5 free. **Location:** Rural, simple, quiet. **Surface:** grasstiles.
01/01-31/12.
Distance: on the spot.

S **Sauveterre de Guyenne** 24C2

Boulevard de 11 Novembre. **GPS**: n44,69022 w0,08624.

4 free €1,50/90minutes Ch €1,50/90minutes.
Location: Urban, simple, noisy. **Surface:** metalled.
01/01-31/12.
Distance: 350m 1000m, bakery 100m.
Remarks: Coins at tourist info, supermarket.

S **Sauzé-Vaussais** 21D2

Place des Halles. **GPS**: n46,13540 e0,10660.

free Ch WCfree. **Surface:** asphalted.
01/01-31/12 water: Nov-March.
Distance: on the spot on the spot on the spot.

S **Savignac-Lédrier** 24F1

Route de Juillac. **GPS**: n45,36401 e1,22066.

15 free Ch free. **Location:** Rural. **Surface:** gravel.
01/01-31/12.
Distance: on the spot 100m.
Remarks: Coins at restaurant des Forges.

S **Segonzac** 21C3

Place Blanche. **GPS**: n45,61456 w0,22113.

4 free Ch (4x) WC free.
Surface: gravel. 01/01-31/12.
Distance: 500m, Cognac 8km 500m 500m.

Segonzac 21C3

Cognac Forgeron, Chez Richon. **GPS:** n45,62545 w0,17514.

6 free.
Location: Rural, quiet. **Surface:** grassy. 01/01-31/12.
Distance: 500m.
Remarks: Check in on arrival, wine tasting.

Seignosse 27A1

Camping-car Park, D79. **GPS:** n43,69089 w1,42539.

110 € 11 Ch WC included.
Surface: grassy/gravel. 01/01-31/12.
Distance: 500m 500m 500m 500m 500m.
Remarks: Next to campsite municipal Hourn-Nao, video surveillance.

Séreilhac 21E3

Allée Catherine Tabaraud. **GPS:** n45,76751 e1,07903.

10 free €2/10minutes Ch (2x)€2/1h.
Location: Rural, comfortable, quiet. **Surface:** gravel.
01/01-31/12.
Distance: 200m on the spot 400m on the spot.

Servières-le-Château 24G1

Centre touristique du lac de Feyt. GPS: n45,14415 e2,03665.

15 free, 29/03-27/09 € 5 €2/100liter Ch €2/1h.
Location: Rural, comfortable, isolated, quiet.
Surface: grassy/metalled. 01/01-31/12.
Distance: Sandy beach on the spot.

Sévignacq Méracq 27C2

Aire du gave d'Ossau, Quartier Raguette.
GPS: n43,10681 w0,42082.

20 € 10 €3 Ch €2 WC . **Location:** Simple, quiet.
Surface: grassy/gravel. 15/02-10/11.
Distance: 1km on the spot on the spot 1km 1km.

Soorts-Hossegor 27A1

Route des Lacs. **GPS:** n43,67279 w1,42087.

85 € 6/24h, 01/06-30/09 € 12 €2/30weekend Ch WC .
Location: Rural, quiet. **Surface:** gravel. 01/01-31/12.
Distance: 550m.
Remarks: Max. 5 days.

Sorges 24E1

Aire de repos Grangearias, Le Bourg, N21.
GPS: n45,30570 e0,87238.

4 free Ch free. **Location:** Urban, simple. **Surface:** metalled.
01/01-31/12.
Distance: 100m 200m 250m.
Remarks: Service 100m.

Soubise 21B3

Aire camping-car, Le Port/rue Colbert. **GPS:** n45,92833 w1,00666.

17 € 7 Ch WC included.
Location: Rural, simple. **Surface:** grassy/metalled.
01/01-31/12.
Distance: on the spot 50m.
Remarks: Along river, max. 24h, incl. showers and warm water.

Soubrebost 21G3

La Martinèche Maison Martin Nadaud Parking, D13.
GPS: n45,98489 e1,85317.

10 free Ch free. **Location:** Rural, isolated, quiet.
Surface: asphalted. 01/01-31/12.
Distance: 9km.

Soulac-sur-Mer 21B3

Boulevard de L'Amélie. **GPS:** n45,49938 w1,1373.

45 € 4, 15/06-15/09 € 8 €3,70/10minutes Ch €3,70/h . **Location:** Urban, comfortable. **Surface:** gravel/metalled.
01/01-31/12.
Distance: 2km 50m 2,5km 2,5km on the spot on the spot.

Sourzac 24D1

D6089. **GPS:** n45,05147 e0,39518.

8 free €2/100liter Ch WC.
Location: Rural, central. **Surface:** gravel/metalled.
01/01-31/12 water disconnected in winter.
Distance: 600m 100m.
Remarks: Coins at petrol station.

Soustons 27A1

Parking du Lac Marin, Avenue de la Pêtre, Soustons Plage.
GPS: n43,77525 w1,41076.

82 01/10-31/04 € 7,00, 01/05-30/09 € 13,00 Ch WC included.
Location: Simple. **Surface:** gravel/metalled. 01/01-31/12.
Distance: city centre 3km lake 50m, ocean 300m 50m 50m on the spot.
Remarks: Max. 72h.

Terrasson-Lavilledieu 24F1

MCD Camping-cars, Rue Alphonse Daudet.
GPS: n45,13389 e1,30832.

25 € 6 €2 Ch €3. **Location:** Rural, comfortable, quiet.
Surface: grassy. 01/03-31/11.
Distance: 1km 600m 600m.

Thouars 18D3

Rue Felix Gellusseau. **GPS:** n46,97614 w0,21151.

FR

10 free free. **Location:** Urban, simple, quiet.
Surface: sand. 01/01-31/12.
Distance: 200m 200m 200m.

Tourist information Thouars:
Tue, Fri.

Thurageau 21D1

Fam. Turpeau, Agressais. **GPS:** n46,78388 e0,25644.

5 free free. **Location:** Rural, simple, quiet.
Surface: gravel. 01/01-31/12.
Distance: 2,5km.
Remarks: Goat farm, farm products.

Tocane-Saint-Apre 24D1

Pré Sec, D103. **GPS:** n45,25712 e0,49471.

8 free €2/100liter Ch €2/1h. **Location:** Rural, simple.
Surface: metalled. 01/01-31/12.
Distance: 300m 100m 300m 300m.
Remarks: Coins at the shops in the village.

Tonnay-Charente 21B3

Quai des Capucins. **GPS:** n45,93921 w0,88171.

15 free free. **Location:** Urban, simple. **Surface:** gravel.
01/01-31/12.
Distance: 1km 500m.

Tournon-d'Agenais 24E3

Base de Loisirs Camp Beau, Pont Roumio, Route de Libos, D102.
GPS: n44,40444 e0,99833.
15 free free. **Location:** Rural, simple. **Surface:** metalled.
01/01-31/12.
Distance: 500m.

Touvre 21D3

Route de Pontil. **GPS:** n45,66085 e0,25834.
7 free Ch. **Surface:** gravel. 01/01-31/12.

Treignac 24F1

Les rivières, Route du lac, D940. **GPS:** n45,54341 e1,79950.

25 free free. **Location:** Rural, simple, quiet.
Surface: grassy/gravel. 01/04-01/10 service: frost.
Distance: 2km on the spot.
Remarks: Along river.

Tourist information Treignac:
Office de Tourisme, 1, Place de la République. Free itinerary city tour along all curiosities, available at OT.

Trémolat 24E2

D30. **GPS:** n44,87378 e0,83065.

5 free €2/25minutes Ch. **Location:** Rural, simple.
Surface: asphalted. 01/01-31/12.
Distance: 300m 300m 300m on the spot.
Remarks: Coins at town hall.

Turenne 24F2

Aire camping-cars, Avenue du Sénateur Labrousse, D8.
GPS: n45,05391 e1,57988.

10 free €2 Ch €2 WC. **Location:** Rural, comfortable, central. **Surface:** gravel. 01/01-31/12.
Distance: on the spot 100m 100m.
Remarks: Behind tourist info, coins at tourist info and supermarket, narrow road, not suitable for motorhomes +7m.

Tourist information Turenne:
Tour de Cesar. Easter-Oct daily, winter Su.

Uhart-Mixe 27B2

Parking de la salle polyvalente d'Airetik, Route départementale 933.
GPS: n43,27780 w1,02245.

4 €5 €2 .
Location: Rural, simple, quiet. **Surface:** asphalted.
Distance: 1km.
Remarks: Max. 24h.

Ussel 24G1

Aire du lac de Ponty. GPS: n45,54762 e2,28330.

15 free €2 Ch €2 WC. **Location:** Rural, simple, quiet.
Surface: grassy/gravel. 01/01-31/12.
Distance: Ussel 3km 8,5km on the spot on the spot.
Remarks: At lake, in front of campsite.

Uzerche 24F1

Place de la Petite Gare, Rue Paul Langevin.
GPS: n45,42477 e1,56696.

20 free free.
Location: Urban, simple, central, quiet. **Surface:** asphalted.
01/01-31/12 every twentieth day of the month.
Distance: 300m 4,4km little stream.

Valeyrac 24B1

Port de Goulée, Route Castillonaise. **GPS:** n45,40500 w0,91028.

5 free. **Location:** Rural, simple, isolated, quiet.
Surface: gravel/metalled. 01/01-31/12.
Distance: 50m on the spot on the spot 20m on the spot on the spot.
Remarks: At harbour.

Vanxains 24D1

Le Petit Verteillac, D708. **GPS:** n45,21204 e0,28399.

2 free Ch WC free. **Location:** Rural, simple.
Surface: asphalted. 01/01-31/12.
Distance: 400m 700m.

Vasles 21D1

Mouton Village, Rue de la Cité. **GPS:** n46,57329 w0,02309.

10 free free. **Location:** Rural, simple, quiet.
Surface: gravel. 01/01-31/12.
Distance: 400m 400m.

FR

S Vertheuil 24B1

Château Ferré, 3 rue des Aubépines. **GPS**: n45,26225 w0,82798.

4 free ChWC. **Location:** Rural, comfortable.
Surface: grassy/gravel. 01/01-31/12.
Distance: 2km 8km 2,5km.

S Veyrines-de-Domme 24E2

Boutique des Bois d'Envaux, Route des Milandes, 6-102 Le Falgueyrat.
GPS: n44,82090 e1,10394.

30 free. **Location:** Simple, isolated. **Surface:** grassy.
Distance: on the spot.
Remarks: Sale of foie gras and wine, monday evening marché gourmand.

S Vézac 24E2

Camping-Car Park, La Malartrie. **GPS**: n44,82440 e1,16950.

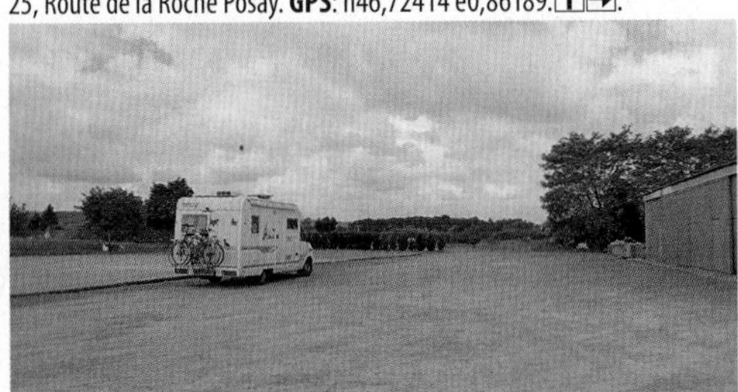

15 € 9,60, 01/07-31/08 € 12 + tourist tax € 1,22/pp Ch included. **Surface:** grassy/gravel. 01/01-31/12.

S Vicq-sur-Gartempe 21E1

25, Route de la Roche Posay. **GPS**: n46,72414 e0,86189.

10 free ChWCfree. **Location:** Rural, simple, quiet.
Surface: gravel. 01/01-31/12.
Distance: 500m.

S Vielle-Saint-Girons 27A1

Lac de Léon, plage de Vielle. **GPS**: n43,90279 w1,30944.

30 € 8-14 + tourist tax € 0,61/pp, dog € 5,10 Ch (30x)€5/night WC. **Location:** Simple. **Surface:** gravel/metalled.
01/04-30/09.
Distance: 100m 300m 50m 100m.
Remarks: Max. 48h.

S Vielle-Saint-Girons 27A1

Les Tourterelles, Saint Girons-Plage. **GPS**: n43,95278 w1,35778.

40 € 9,90 02/07-27/08 € 15,50 16/07-20/08 € 15,95 Ch €4/24h WC. **Location:** Comfortable.
Surface: gravel/metalled. 01/04-30/09.
Distance: 300m 500m 500m.
Remarks: Sanitary at campsite.

S Vieux-Boucau-les-Bains 27A1

Aire camping-cars Village, Avenue des Pêcheurs.
GPS: n43,77971 w1,40041.

150 € 6, 01/05-30/09 € 12 Ch included .
Location: Comfortable. **Surface:** gravel/sand. 01/01-31/12.
Distance: 500m 200m 500m 500m on the spot.
Remarks: >3,5t not allowed.

S Vigeois 24F1

D7, route de Brive. **GPS**: n45,36717 e1,53392.

12 free €3/150liter Ch €3. **Location:** Rural, simple, isolated, quiet. **Surface:** grassy/gravel. 01/04-31/10.
Distance: 2km 7,2km beach 150m.
Remarks: Coins at town hall and bars in the village.

S Villefranche-du-Périgord 24E2

Plan d'eau, Le Bourg. **GPS**: n44,63104 e1,07728.

15 free €2,50 Ch €2,50 . **Location:** Rural, quiet.
Surface: metalled. 01/01-31/12.
Distance: 300m.

S Villeneuve-de-Marsan 27C1

Avenue du Stade 40. **GPS**: n43,88737 w0,30595.

7 free Ch (2x)free,16Amp. **Location:** Rural, simple, quiet.
Surface: asphalted. 01/01-31/12.

Distance: 1km 1km 1km.
Remarks: Max. 48h.

S Villeréal 24E2

Aire de Jeux, Boulevard Alphonse de Poitiers, D104.
GPS: n44,63798 e0,74065.
free Ch. **Surface:** asphalted. 01/01-31/12.
Distance: 300m 300m 300m.

S Villeton 24D3

D120. **GPS**: n44,36386 e0,27279.

4 € 4,60, 01/04-31/10 € 5,60 €4 Ch €2/4h WC.
Location: Rural, comfortable. **Surface:** gravel.
01/01-31/12 water disconnected in winter.
Distance: 10,5km on the spot on the spot on the spot 500m.

S Vitrac 24F2

Montfort, D703. **GPS**: n44,83558 e1,24852.

10 free €3/100liter Ch €3/h WC. **Location:** Rural, simple.
Surface: grassy/gravel. 01/01-31/12.
Distance: 50m 2km beach at Dordogne river 200m.
Remarks: Coins available at restaurant Le Point Vue (200m).

Occitanie

S Adé 27C2

Feerie-des-Eaux, 70 Avenue des Pyrénées, N21.
GPS: n43,12834 w0,0277.

27 € 10 Ch included. **Location:** Comfortable, noisy.
Surface: asphalted/grassy. Easter-31/10.
Distance: Lourdes 2km 1km 500m 200m.

S Agde 28A2

Les Canoës, Route de la Tamarissière. **GPS**: n43,29871 e3,45391.
€ 12-15 + € 0,83/pp tourist tax, dog € 3 Ch .
01/04-31/10.
Remarks: Former campsite.

Tourist information Agde:
Cathédrale Ste Étienne. Romanesque fortified cathedral, 12th century.

S Agos-Vidalos 27C3

Le Pibeste, Avenue du Lavedan. **GPS**: n43,03552 w0,07069.

30 € 9,60, 01/07-31/08 €10,80 Ch included.
Location: Rural, comfortable. **Surface:** grassy/gravel.

FR

01/01-31/12.
Distance: on the spot 10km on the spot 3km on the spot on the spot.

S Aigues-Mortes 28B2

Les Poissons d'Argent, CD62. **GPS**: n43,56476 e4,16289.

120 € 10 Chincluded (32x)€3/24h,5Amp.
Location: Simple. **Surface:** gravel.
01/03-31/10.
Distance: 3km 3km on the spot on the spot 1,5km Lidl 500m 500m.
Remarks: At fish lake, fishing permit incl, bread-service.

S Aigues-Mortes 28B2

Rue du Port. **GPS**: n43,56631 e4,18575.

50 € 16 Chfree.
Location: Simple. **Surface:** metalled. 01/01-31/12.
Distance: 600m.
Remarks: Max. 24h.

Tourist information Aigues-Mortes:
Office de Tourisme, Place Saint Louis, ot-aiguesmortes.com. Medieval fortress, 13th century, in the swamp of the Camargue, tourist attraction.
La Tour Carbonnière, Place Saint Louis. Tower, guard-post for the defence of the city.

Aiguèze 25C3

GPS: n44,30530 e4,55250.

+20 free. **Location:** Rural, simple, quiet. **Surface:** grassy/gravel.
01/01-31/12.
Distance: 300m 300m.

S Albas 24F3

Pech del Gal. **GPS**: n44,47480 e1,23275.

10 free Chfree. **Location:** Simple, isolated, noisy.
Surface: gravel. 01/01-31/12 water disconnected in winter.
Remarks: At weir.

S Albi 27G1

Base de Loisirs Pratgraussals, Rue de Lamothe.
GPS: n43,92951 e2,13480.

20 free Chfree. **Location:** Rural, simple, isolated, quiet.
Surface: asphalted. 01/01-31/12.
Distance: 1,5km.
Remarks: At cemetery, service 200m.

Albi 27G1

Parking Cathédrale. GPS: n43,92750 e2,14111.

10 free. **Location:** Urban, simple, noisy. **Surface:** asphalted.
01/01-31/12.
Distance: 50m 50m 100m.
Remarks: Parking nearby cathedral Sainte Cécile, max. 48h.

S Albi 27G1

Supermarkt Leclerc, Les portes d'Albi. **GPS**: n43,91846 e2,10968.

free €2/10minutes Ch €2/55minutes.
Location: Urban, simple, noisy. **Surface:** asphalted.
01/01-31/12.
Distance: 3km on the spot on the spot on the spot.
Remarks: Parking supermarket.

S Albi 27G1

Rue Michelet. **GPS**: n43,94583 e2,15111.
Ch free. 01/01-31/12.

S Alès 28B1

Place du camping-car, Avenue Jules Guesde.
GPS: n44,12013 e4,08207.

6 free Chfree. **Location:** Urban, comfortable, central, noisy.
Surface: asphalted. 01/01-31/12.
Distance: on the spot on the spot on the spot 400m 600m on the spot routes available at tourist office.

S Alvignac 24F2

Parc du Samayou, Route de Padirac. **GPS**: n44,82504 e1,69711.

10 free ChWC. **Surface:** asphalted.
Distance: 100m 200m 200m.

S Alzon 28A1

D999. **GPS**: n43,96567 e3,43902.
20 free €2/100liter Ch. **Surface:** gravel/metalled.
01/01-31/12.
Distance: 100m.
Remarks: Coins at restaurant.

S Amélie-les-Bains-Palalda 32G1

Carrer de l'Oreneta. **GPS**: n42,48063 e2,67951.

40 € 7 Chincluded. **Surface:** gravel. 01/01-31/12.
Distance: 2km 500m.
Remarks: Behind hotel du Lion D'Or, max. 7 days.

S Amélie-les-Bains-Palalda 32G1

Camping Amélie, Avenue Beau Soleil, D115.
GPS: n42,47894 e2,67414.

8 € 6 €4. **Location:** Simple, noisy. **Surface:** grassy/gravel.
01/01-31/12.
Distance: on the spot 1km 1km.
Remarks: Max. 48h, coins at campsite.

S Anduze 28B1

Place de la Gare. **GPS**: n44,05000 e3,98444.

20 free €2 Ch €2/55minutes.
Location: Urban, simple, central, quiet. **Surface:** asphalted.
01/01-31/12.
Distance: on the spot 300m 400m on the spot on the spot.
Remarks: Max. 48h.

Tourist information Anduze:
Bambousserie de Prafrance, 552 rue de Montsauve. Bamboo garden laid out in 1835, with a large variety of bamboo species. 01/02-15/11.
Train Touristique, 38 Place de la Gare. Tourist train from Anduze to St. Jean-du-Gard. 26/03-31/10.

S Anglès 27H2

Route de Saint-Pons. **GPS**: n43,56553 e2,56544.
4 free Ch. **Surface:** metalled.
Distance: 500m.

S Aniane 28A2

Le Pont du Diable. GPS: n43,70270 e3,55988.

FR

€ 5/day, € 18/24h €3 Ch.
Location: Rural, isolated. **Surface:** gravel.
01/01-31/12.
Distance: 9km.
Remarks: Max. 48h, Pont du Diable 600m, St.Guilhem-le-Désert 4km, free shuttlebus Mai-Sept: weekend (11-19h), July-Aug daily (10-23h).

Aniane 28A2

Lotissement du Camp de Sauve. **GPS**: n43,68652 e3,58254.

15 free. **Surface:** gravel. 01/01-31/12.
Distance: 300m nearby 300m 300m.

Aragnouet 27D3

Piau Engaly. **GPS**: n42,78599 e0,15800.

120 free, Winter € 15 Ch (120x) WC.
Location: Comfortable, isolated, quiet. **Surface:** asphalted.
01/12-31/08.
Distance: 300m 300m 300m.
Remarks: Service only during winter period.

Arfons 27G2

Pierron-Les Escudiés. **GPS**: n43,43972 e2,19472.

4 € 5. **Surface:** grassy. 01/01-31/12.
Distance: 4km 1km 4km 4km.

Argelès-Gazost 27C3

Carrefour Market, Route du Stade. **GPS**: n43,00455 w0,08636.

26 free Ch. **Location:** Rural, comfortable, quiet.
Surface: asphalted. 01/01-31/12.
Distance: 4km 350m on the spot on the spot.

Arre 28A1

D999. **GPS**: n43,96771 e3,52139.

6 free €2/100liter Ch €2/1h WC.
Location: Rural, simple, central, quiet. **Surface:** metalled.
01/01-31/12.
Distance: on the spot on the spot on the spot on the spot bakery 200m on the spot.

Arreau 27D3

Chemin de Fregel. **GPS**: n42,90708 e0,35912.

25 free, July-Aug € 2 Chfree. **Location:** Urban, simple, central. **Surface:** metalled. 01/01-31/12.
Distance: 100m 100m 150m 300m 200m on the spot on the spot.

Arrens-Marsous 27C3

D918. **GPS**: n42,95806 w0,20722.

10 free €2/100liter Ch €2. **Location:** Rural, simple, isolated, quiet. **Surface:** asphalted. 01/01-31/12.
Distance: 650m 550m 500m on the spot on the spot.

Arvieu 24H3

GPS: n44,19246 e2,65916.

6 free €2/80liter Chfree.
Location: Simple, quiet. **Surface:** gravel.
01/01-31/12.
Distance: 100m on the spot 100m 100m on the spot.
Remarks: At sports centre, max. 72h, coins at the shops and town hall.

Aubrac 24H3

D533. **GPS**: n44,62026 e2,98705.
10 free ChWCfree. **Location:** Simple, quiet. **Surface:** gravel.
01/01-31/12.
Distance: 50m on the spot on the spot on the spot on the spot.

Auch 27D1

Camping municipal, Rue des Cormorans.
GPS: n43,63654 e0,58854.

3 € 4 Chfree €1,50. **Surface:** asphalted. 01/01-31/12.
Distance: 15min 15min 15min.

Auterive 27F2

Grande Allée du Ramier. **GPS**: n43,35025 e1,47730.

6 free Chfree. **Surface:** asphalted. 01/01-31/12.
Remarks: At fire-station.

Auterive 27F2

Rue des Docteurs Basset. **GPS**: n43,35182 e1,47641.
10 free. **Surface:** asphalted.
Distance: 200m 200m.
Remarks: Along river.

Auzas 27E2

La Grangère. **GPS**: n43,17016 e0,88690.

10 € 4 Ch (4x)included. **Surface:** asphalted.
Distance: on the spot.
Remarks: At lake.

Avèze 28A1

Aire de Loisirs du Pont Vieux, D999. **GPS**: n43,97517 e3,59899.

6 free €2 Ch €2/1h.
Surface: metalled. 01/01-31/12.
Distance: 500m on the spot on the spot 500m 1,3km on the spot.
Remarks: Next to campsite municipal, max. 48h.

Ax-les-Thermes 27F3

A Bonascre, Rue des Chalets. **GPS**: n42,70340 e1,81657.
40 free €2/100liter Ch €6/24h. **Location:** Isolated, quiet. **Surface:** gravel. 01/01-31/12.

Ax-les-Thermes 27F3

N20. **GPS**: n42,72565 e1,83154.
30 € 8 100liter included1h. **Location:** Simple, noisy.
Surface: asphalted.
Distance: 1km.

Ax-les-Thermes 27F3

Parc d'Espagne. **GPS**: n42,71504 e1,84142.

FR

35 € 5. **Surface:** asphalted. 01/01-31/12.
Distance: 500m 500m 500m.

S Bagnères-de-Bigorre 27D3

Rue René Cassin. **GPS:** n43,07319 e0,15256.

30 free Ch WC free. **Location:** Rural, simple, noisy.
Surface: gravel. 01/01-31/12.
Distance: 500m 15km 500m 650m.

Bagnères-de-Bigorre 27D3

Avenue de Belgique. **GPS:** n43,06917 e0,14889.

10 free. **Location:** Urban, simple, central, noisy. **Surface:** asphalted.
01/01-31/12.
Distance: 200m 15km 200m 200m on the spot on the spot on the spot.
Remarks: At station.

S Bagnères-de-Luchon 27D3

Lac de Badech, Rue Jean Mermoz. **GPS:** n42,79540 e0,59875.

50 € 4/24h Service € 4 Ch .
Location: Rural, simple, quiet. **Surface:** asphalted.
01/01-31/12 service: 01/12-01/04.
Distance: 1km 1km 500m on the spot on the spot.
Remarks: Coins at tourist info.

S Bagnols-sur-Cèze 28C1

Av. de l Europe, D8086. **GPS:** n44,16820 e4,61958.

20 free Ch free. **Surface:** gravel.
Distance: 200m 200m 200m.
Remarks: Max. 24h.

S Balaruc-les-Bains 28A2

Avenue des Hespérides 335. **GPS:** n43,44499 e3,67564.

6 € 8,50 Ch. **Location:** Rural, quiet. **Surface:** unpaved.
01/01-31/12.
Distance: on the spot.

S Balaruc-les-Bains 28A2

Thermes Hespérides, Allée des Sources.
GPS: n43,44574 e3,67770.

6 € 7 Ch 55minutes WC included . **Location:** Simple, quiet. **Surface:** asphalted. 01/01-31/12.
Distance: 1km.
Remarks: Free bus to centre.

S Baraqueville 24G3

Rue du Val de Lenne. **GPS:** n44,27850 e2,43407.

10 free € 3 Ch . **Location:** Simple, quiet.
Surface: asphalted. 01/01-31/12 service 01/11-31/03.
Distance: on the spot 50m on the spot on the spot.
Remarks: Coins at the shops in the village, inclining pitches.

Barbotan-les-Thermes 27C1

Avenue des Thermes. **GPS:** n43,94884 w0,04344.

6 free, night € 4,50. **Surface:** asphalted. 01/01-31/12.
Distance: 500m 50m 500m.

S Bardigues 27E1

GPS: n44,03869 e0,89271.

4 free € 2/100liter Ch. **Surface:** gravel. 01/01-31/12.
Distance: 150m 8,6km 150m 150m.

Barèges 27D3

Le Tournabou, Route de Tourmalet, D918. **GPS:** n42,90329 e0,10151.

15 free. **Location:** Rural, isolated, quiet. **Surface:** asphalted.
01/01-31/12.
Distance: 2,5km on the spot 3km on the spot on the spot on the spot on the spot.

S Beaucaire 28C1

Les Marguilliers, Chemin des Marguilliers.
GPS: n43,81667 e4,64107.

9 € 15/24h Ch included.
Surface: gravel. 01/01-31/12.
Distance: 500m 500m 500m 500m.

S Beaucaire 28C1

Quai de la Paix. **GPS:** n43,80615 e4,63739.

10 free € 2/100liter Ch € 2/1h. **Location:** Urban, simple.
Surface: asphalted. 01/01-31/12 water disconnected in winter.
Distance: 300m 300m bakery 300m.
Remarks: Coins at tourist info.

S Bédarieux 27H2

Avenue Jean Moulin. **GPS:** n43,61071 e3,15329.

10 free Ch free. **Location:** Urban, simple, central, quiet.
Surface: grassy. 01/01-31/12.
Distance: on the spot on the spot on the spot 800m.
Remarks: Along the Orb river.

S Bélesta 27H3

Rue des Loisirs. **GPS:** n42,71560 e2,60786.

10 € 5 € 2/20minutes (8x) € 2/4h. **Location:** Rural, simple, quiet. **Surface:** grassy/gravel. 01/04-31/10.
Distance: 100m on the spot.

S Bellas 24H3

D995. **GPS:** n44,31256 e3,12689.

10 €5 free €3. **Location:** Rural, quiet. **Surface:** grassy/metalled. 01/01-31/12. **Distance:** on the spot on the spot.

Bellegarde 28C1

Port de plaisance, Las Courrejos Est. **GPS**: n43,74422 e4,51890.

free €2 Ch €2/1h. **Location:** Rural, simple. **Surface:** gravel/sand. 01/01-31/12. **Distance:** city centre 1,5km. **Remarks:** Max. 48h, coins at harbourmaster.

Belmont sur Rance 27H1

Parking de la Mairie, Route de Lacaune. **GPS**: n43,81630 e2,75269.

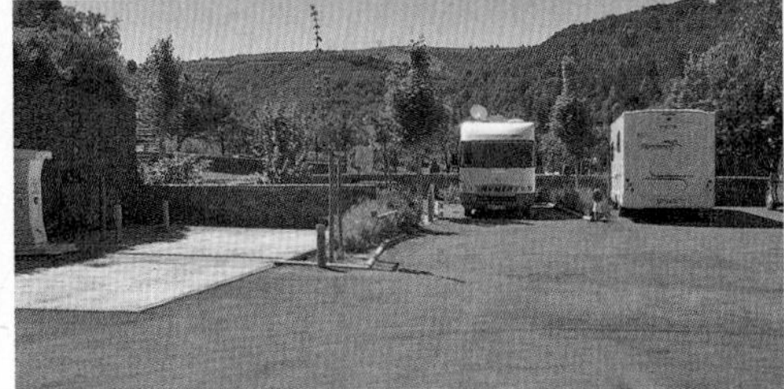

3 free Ch free. **Surface:** asphalted. 01/01-31/12. **Distance:** on the spot.

Belpech 27F2

Stade municipal, Rue du Stade. **GPS**: n43,19864 e1,74472.

15 free Ch free WC. **Surface:** grassy. 01/01-31/12. **Distance:** 1km 1km 1km. **Remarks:** At football ground.

Boisse Penchot 24G3

Rue du Chateau Bas. **GPS**: n44,59201 e2,20567.

8 free €3/100liter Ch €3/1h. **Surface:** asphalted. 01/01-31/12. **Distance:** 100m on the spot on the spot on the spot on the spot.

Bonac Irazein 27E3

Lac Bonac. GPS: n42,87541 e0,97565.

10 €6 Ch included. **Surface:** grassy/gravel. 01/03-30/11. **Distance:** on the spot. **Remarks:** At artificial lake of Bonac.

Bouillac 24G3

Aire de Bouillac, D840. **GPS**: n44,57333 e2,15750.

6 free €3 Ch. **Surface:** metalled. 01/03-30/11. **Distance:** on the spot on the spot on the spot 600m. **Remarks:** Max. 24h, coins at the shops.

Branoux-les-Taillades 25B3

Aire de la Placette, La placette. **GPS**: n44,22607 e4,01036. 4 free €4/10minutes Ch. **Surface:** metalled. 01/01-31/12. **Distance:** 100m. **Remarks:** Picnic area.

Bréau-et-Salagosse 28A1

Le Rieumage, D272. **GPS**: n43,99338 e3,56716. 6 €2 €2 Ch. **Location:** Rural, isolated, quiet. **Surface:** gravel. 01/01-31/12.

Broquies 27H1

Route de Mazies. **GPS**: n44,00498 e2,69371.

30 free Ch WC. **Surface:** gravel. 01/04-30/11. **Distance:** 50m on the spot on the spot. **Remarks:** Coins at supermarket.

Cadours 27E1

Rue Malakoff. **GPS**: n43,72320 e1,04861.

5 free Ch free. **Location:** Rural. **Surface:** grassy. 01/01-31/12 tue-evening, wed-morning. **Distance:** 1km 1km. **Remarks:** At football ground.

Cahors 24F3

Parking Chartreux, Rue de la Chartreuse. **GPS**: n44,44016 e1,44119.

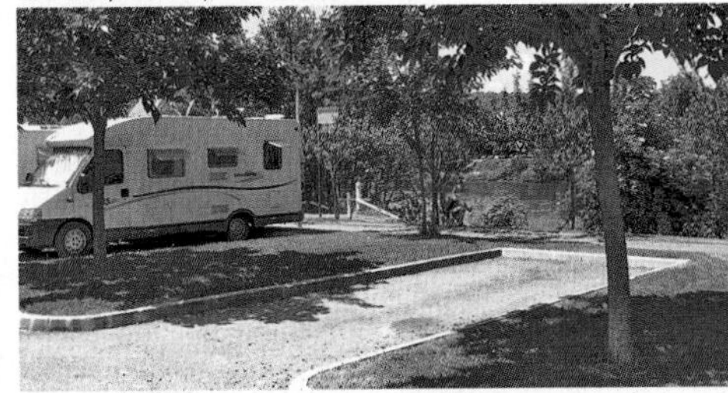

3 free Ch free. **Surface:** gravel. 01/01-31/12. **Distance:** 500m on the spot 250m 50m on the spot. **Remarks:** Along river.

Cahors 24F3

Parking Saint George, Rue Saint George. **GPS**: n44,43875 e1,44111. 20 free. **Surface:** asphalted. 01/01-31/12. **Distance:** 1,2km 15km 100m on the spot. **Remarks:** Shuttle bus to city centre.

Tourist information Cahors:
Wed, Sa.

Cahuzac-sur-Vère 27G1

Place du Mercadial. **GPS**: n43,98194 e1,91111.

5 free Ch WC free. **Location:** Rural, simple. **Surface:** gravel. **Distance:** 200m 200m 200m on the spot. **Remarks:** At cemetery.

Cajarc 24F3

Place de la Gare. **GPS**: n44,48458 e1,84573.

8 free €1 Ch. **Surface:** grassy. 01/01-31/12. **Distance:** 100m 200m 200m.

Camares 27H1

Base de loisirs des Zizines. **GPS**: n43,81654 e2,87988.

16 free, night €3 Ch WC free. **Surface:** gravel. 15/04-31/10. **Distance:** 100m on the spot on the spot.

Campagnac 24H3

La Sagne. **GPS**: n44,41885 e3,08875.

5 free, 13/06-13/09 €3 Ch. **Surface:** metalled. 01/01-31/12. **Distance:** 400m 400m 400m. **Remarks:** Coins at campsite and town hall.

Campan 27D3

Le Bourg. **GPS**: n43,01817 e0,17828.

5 free Ch WC. **Location:** Rural, simple, quiet. **Surface:** gravel. 01/01-31/12.

FR

Distance: 100m on the spot 300m 200m.
Remarks: Max. 48h.

Campan 27D3

Serre Crampe, Payolle. **GPS**: n42,93711 e0,30259.

15 free Ch WC free. **Location:** Rural, isolated, quiet.
Surface: gravel. 01/01-31/12.
Distance: 5km 150m 150m 600m 6km on the spot on the spot on the spot on the spot.
Remarks: Max. 48h, service 100m.

Campuac 24H3

GPS: n44,57027 e2,59162.
10 free Ch WC free. **Surface:** gravel. 01/01-31/12.
Distance: 100m on the spot.

Canet-de-Salars 24H3

Les Fontanelles. **GPS**: n44,23260 e2,74716.

6 € 6, tourist tax € 0,60/pp €2/20minutes Ch WC included.
Location: Rural, simple, quiet. **Surface:** grassy/gravel.
01/04-30/10.
Distance: 750m 5km 750m on the spot.
Remarks: Coins at bar and garage.

Capdenac-Gare 24G3

Camping-Car Park, Boulevard Paul Ramadier.
GPS: n44,57302 e2,07292.
50 € 8,40, 01/07-31/08 € 9,60 Ch WC .
01/01-31/12.
Distance: on the spot.
Remarks: Former campsite.

Carcassonne 27G2

Camping de la Cité, Route de Saint-Hilaire.
GPS: n43,19980 e2,35317.
38 € 12/24h + € 0,20/pp tourist tax €2 Ch.
Surface: gravel. 01/01-31/12.
Distance: 3,5km.

Tourist information Carcassonne:
Office de Tourisme, 15, Boulevard Camille Pelletan, www.carcassonne-tourisme.com. Medieval fortified city, museum city with many curiosities.
The new city has a modern shopping centre.

Cardaillac 24G2

Le Pré del Prie. GPS: n44,67868 e1,99805.

12 free €2/100liter Ch €2/h. **Location:** Isolated, quiet.
Surface: gravel. 01/01-31/12.
Distance: 100m on the spot 100m.
Remarks: Behind church.

Carnon 28B2

Les Saladelles, Avenue Grassion Cibrand, Carnon-plage.
GPS: n43,55097 e3,99417.

18 € 11,50, 01/07-31/08 € 13 Ch WC included,on campsite €5.
Location: Rural. **Surface:** asphalted.
01/04-15/10.
Distance: 1km 80m 50m.
Remarks: Next to campsite Les Saladelles.

Castanet 24G3

GPS: n44,27889 e2,28944.

4 € 8 Ch included. **Location:** Rural, comfortable, quiet.
Surface: gravel. 01/01-31/12.
Distance: on the spot on the spot.
Remarks: Money in envelope in mail box.

Casteil 32G1

D116. **GPS**: n42,53324 e2,39230.

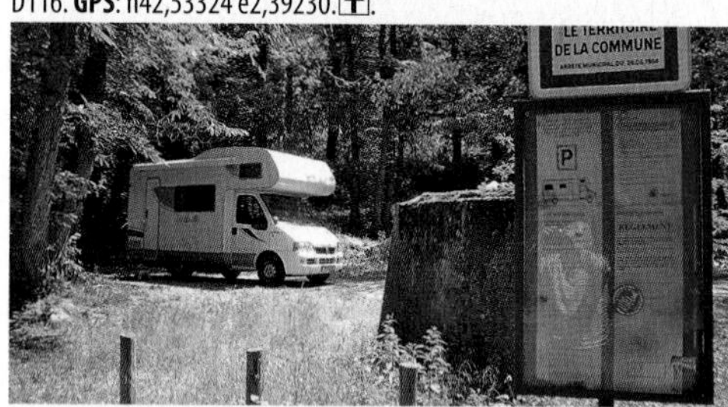

5 free. **Location:** Rural, simple, isolated, quiet. **Surface:** forest soil.
01/04-31/10.
Distance: 1km on the spot on the spot.

Castelnau-de-Montmiral 27F1

Domaine Les Miquels. GPS: n43,96667 e1,80278.

6 € 10 Ch included. **Location:** Rural, comfortable, isolated, quiet. **Surface:** grassy. 01/01-31/12.
Distance: 2,5km on the spot 2,5km.

Castelnau-Durban 27F3

D117. **GPS**: n42,99994 e1,33976.

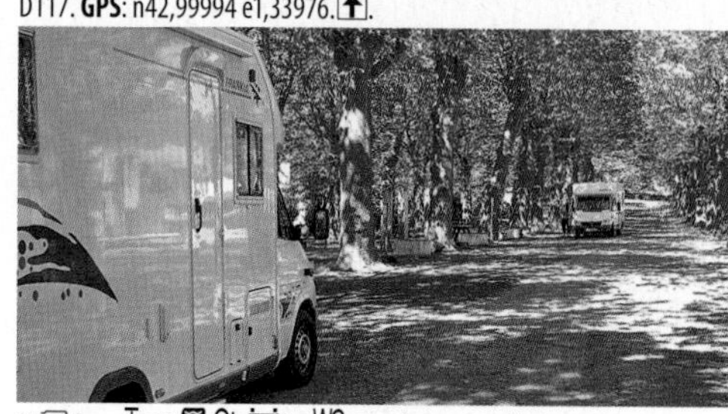

10 free €2 Ch €2 WC. **Surface:** metalled.
Remarks: Parking in front of church, max. 48h.

Castelnaudary 27G2

Camping-Car Park Castelnaudary, Passage des Lavandières.
GPS: n43,31427 e1,94899.

14 € 8,40, 01/07-31/08 € 9,60 Ch (8x) included.
Location: Urban, comfortable. **Surface:** grassy/gravel.
01/01-31/12.
Distance: on the spot on the spot on the spot.
Remarks: At Canal du Midi.

Castelsarrasin 27E1

Allée de la Source. **GPS**: n44,03861 e1,10221.

40 € 3/24h €2,50/100liter Ch €2,50/24h.
Surface: gravel. 01/01-31/12.
Distance: 500m 500m 500m.

Castres 27G2

Place Gerard Philipe, Chemin des Porches. **GPS**: n43,60168 e2,24939.

free. **Location:** Urban. **Surface:** asphalted. 01/01-31/12.
Distance: 2km 2km 2km.
Remarks: Max 3,5t, free bus to centre.

Castres 27G2

Route de l'Industrie Z.I. de Melou. **GPS**: n43,59069 e2,20648.
Ch free. 01/01-31/12.

Tourist information Castres:
Palais Episcopal. Episcopal palace.
Tue, Thu-Su.

Cauterets 27C3

Ancien Boulodrome, Avenue Charles Thierry.
GPS: n42,88628 w0,11522.

24 € 10 Ch included. **Location:** Rural, simple, quiet.
Surface: asphalted. 01/01-31/12.
Distance: 300m 20km 300m 350m on the spot on the spot on the spot.

Cauterets 27C3

Place de la Patinoire, D920. **GPS**: n42,89361 w0,11256.

50 € 10/24h Ch included. Location: Rural, comfortable, quiet. Surface: asphalted. 01/01-31/12.
Distance: 300m 20km 300m 300m on the spot on the spot.
Remarks: Max. 21 nights.

Caylus 24F3

Base de loisirs Labarthe, D19. **GPS:** n44,23363 e1,77225.

6 free Chfree. **Location:** Rural, simple.
Surface: grassy/gravel. 01/01-31/12.
Distance: 200m 200m 200m.

Tourist information Caylus:
St.Antonin. Small town with the oldest town hall of France.

Chusclan 28C1

Cave Chusclan, Route d'Orsan, D138. **GPS:** n44,14552 e4,67762.

40 free Chfree. **Surface:** gravel. 01/01-31/12.
Distance: 500m 500m.

Clermont-l'Hérault 28A2

Aire de stationnement camping-car, Lac du Salagou.
GPS: n43,64677 e3,38915.

8 € 5-7 €2/100liter Ch (6x). **Location:** Rural, simple, isolated, quiet. **Surface:** gravel. 01/01-31/12.
Distance: 7km on the spot on the spot on the spot 7km on the spot on the spot.
Remarks: Coins at campsite.

Collioure 32H1

Route de Madeloc. **GPS:** n42,52566 e3,06861.

15 € 10/24h Ch (12x) WC included.
Location: Comfortable, quiet. **Surface:** asphalted. 01/01-31/12.
Distance: 2km 2,3km 2km 2km.
Remarks: Monitored parking, may-Sep free shuttle to Collioure.

Comps 28C1

Place des Arènes. **GPS:** n43,85402 e4,60724.

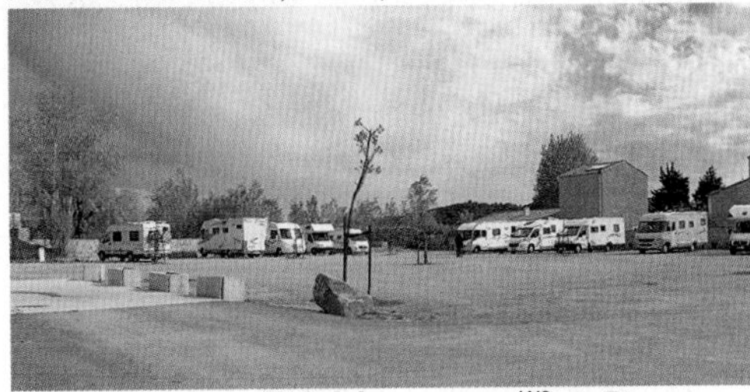

50 € 5 €2/110liter Ch €2/50minutes WC.
Location: Rural. **Surface:** grassy/gravel. 01/01-31/12.
Distance: 50m on the spot on the spot 50m on the spot on the spot.

Comps 28C1

GPS: n43,85390 e4,60912.

30 € 5.
Location: Rural. **Surface:** unpaved. 01/01-31/12.
Remarks: Along river.

Condom 27D1

Avenue des Mousquetaires. **GPS:** n43,94836 .
12 free Ch. **Location:** Comfortable, isolated, quiet.
Surface: metalled. 01/01-31/12.
Distance: 500m.
Remarks: Max. 5 days.

Condom 27D1

Ferme de Parette, Route de Nérac, RN930.
GPS: n43,98802 e0,35046.

8 € 8, 2 pers.incl Ch included €4.
Location: Comfortable, isolated, quiet. **Surface:** grassy.
01/01-31/12.
Distance: 2km 2km 2km.

Tourist information Condom:
Musée de l'Armagnac. All about Armagnac.

Cordes-sur-Ciel 27G1

Parking les Tuileries. GPS: n44,06453 e1,95802.

40 € 6 60liter Ch included3h.
Location: Rural, simple, isolated, quiet. **Surface:** grassy/gravel.
01/01-31/12.
Distance: 500m 500m.

Coupiac 27H1

Route de Martin. **GPS:** n43,95174 e2,58464.
10 free Chfree. **Surface:** grassy. 01/01-31/12.
Distance: 500m 450m.
Remarks: Max. 72h.

Cransac 24G3

Aire de Camping-car Cransac, Route de la Gare.
GPS: n44,52278 e2,27444.

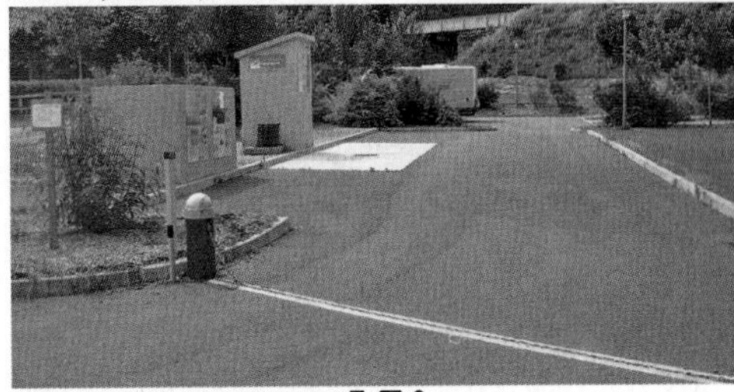

6 € 6,30, tourist tax € 0,40/pp Chincluded.
Surface: gravel. 01/03-23/11.
Distance: 500m 500m 500m.
Remarks: Max. 48h.

Cuxac-Cabardès 27G2

La Cabasse. **GPS:** n43,36126 e2,30185.
8 € 5 €2 Ch €3. **Location:** Isolated, quiet.
Surface: metalled.

Donzac 24E3

Lac de Sources, D30. **GPS:** n44,11308 e0,82044.

10 free Chfree. **Location:** Rural. **Surface:** gravel.
01/01-31/12.
Distance: on the spot.
Remarks: Max. 48h.

Douelle 24F3

Domaine Marcilhac, D8. **GPS:** n44,47927 e1,34947.

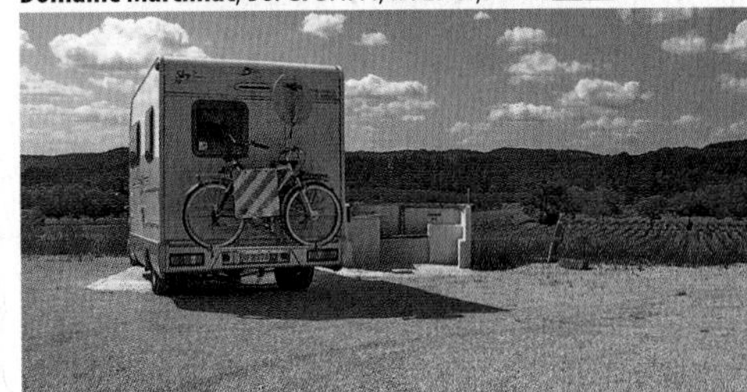

10 free €2 Ch. **Location:** Rural. **Surface:** gravel.
01/01-31/12.
Distance: 1km 1km 1km 1km.

Duilhac-sous-Peyrepertuse 27G3

Route du château. **GPS:** n42,86160 e2,56527.

25 free ChWCfree. **Location:** Rural, simple, quiet.
Surface: asphalted. 01/04-31/10.
Distance: 200m 200m.

Entraygues-sur-Truyère 24H2

Route de Villecomtal, D904. **GPS:** n44,64020 e2,56925.

FR

free. **Surface:** grassy. 01/04-31/12.
Distance: 50m on the spot on the spot 50m 50m.

Entraygues-sur-Truyère 24H2

Rue de la Grave. **GPS:** n44,64417 e2,56278.

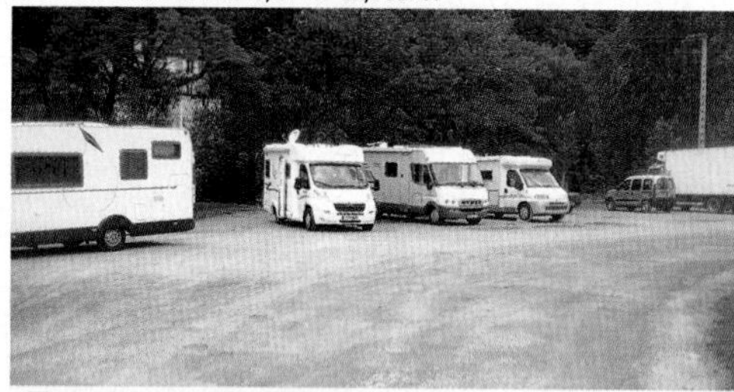

5 free. **Surface:** gravel. 01/01-31/12.
Distance: 50m 150m 150m.

S Entraygues-sur-Truyère 24H2

Rue du 16 Août 1944. **GPS:** n44,64269 e2,56577.
€3 Ch.
Remarks: Coins at tourist info.

S Espalion 24H3

Avenue Pierre Monteil. **GPS:** n44,52156 e2,76921.
25 € 9,60-10,80 Ch (8x) included.
Surface: gravel/metalled. 01/01/-31/12.
Distance: 1km 1km 1km.
Remarks: At swimming pool.

S Espéraza 27G3

Promenade François Mitterand. **GPS:** n42,93370 e2,21589.

20 free Chfree. **Location:** Rural, simple, quiet.
Surface: grassy.
Distance: 500m on the spot on the spot 500m.

S Fanjeaux 27G2

Chemin des Fontanelles. **GPS:** n43,18611 e2,03222.

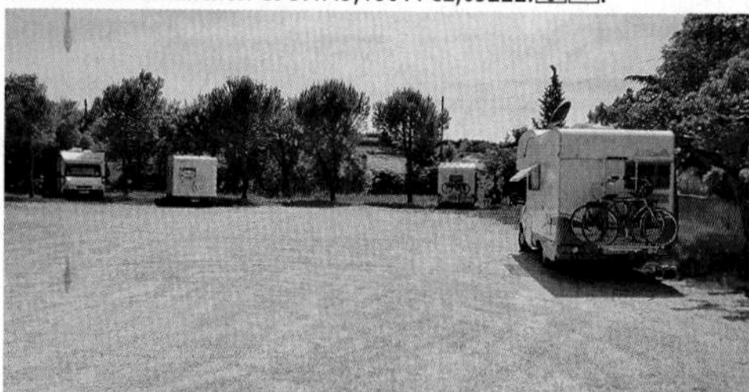

15 free Chfree. **Location:** Rural, simple.
Surface: grassy/gravel. 01/01-31/12.
Distance: 100m 100m 100m.
Remarks: Next to maison de retraite (home for the elderly), max. 48h.

S Félines-Termenès 27H3

Av. de Termenes, dir Mouthoumet. **GPS:** n42,98691 e2,61285.

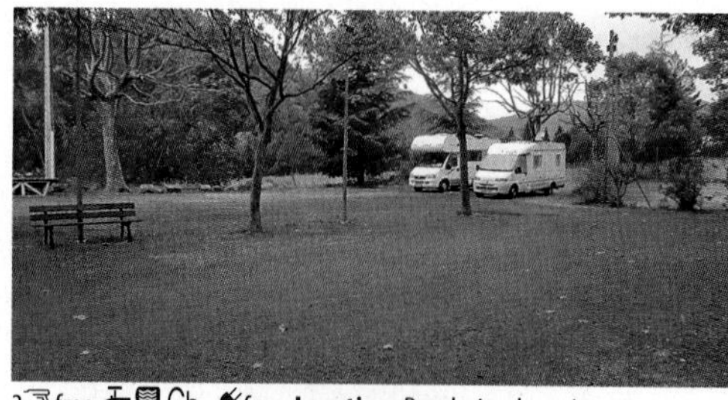

3 free Ch free. **Location:** Rural, simple, quiet.
Surface: gravel. 01/01-31/12.
Distance: 50m.
Remarks: Closed when frosty.

Tourist information Félines-Termenès:
Cité Médiéval, Villerouge Termenes. Medieval village and castle from 12-14th century. 01/07-30/09.

S Figeac 24G3

Parking le Foiral, Boulevard Colonel Teulié.
GPS: n44,61089 e2,03674.

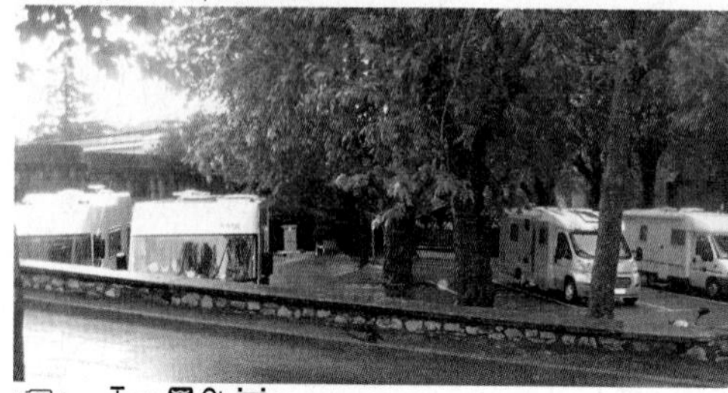

5 free €2 Ch €2. **Location:** Central, noisy.
Surface: asphalted. 01/01-31/12.
Distance: 100m 400m 100m 100m.

Tourist information Figeac:
Marché régional. Regional market. Sa-morning.

S Fitou 27H3

Aragon, Route Nationale 9, Les Cabanes de Fitou.
GPS: n42,89275 e2,99672.

15 € 5/12h, € 7/24h Ch €2,50 included.
Location: Rural. **Surface:** gravel. 01/01-31/12.
Distance: A9 6,5km on the spot 500m.
Remarks: Video surveillance.

S Fleurance 27E1

Boulevard de Metz. **GPS:** n43,85164 e0,66184.

20 free €2 Ch €2. **Surface:** gravel.
Distance: 200m on the spot on the spot.

S Fleury-d'Aude 28A2

Base de Loisirs Étang de Pissevache, Saint-Pierre-la-Mer.
GPS: n43,18972 e3,19694.

100 € 5/24h, 01/04-31/10 € 8,75/24h Chincluded €2/4h **Surface:** unpaved. 01/01-31/12.
Distance: sandy beach 300m.
Remarks: Parking directly behind the beach, next to tennis park and small surf lake, follow Base de Loisirs.

S Fleury-d'Aude 28A2

Les-Cabanes-de-Fleury. **GPS:** n43,21529 e3,23315.

100 € 7 €2 Ch.
Surface: metalled/sand. 01/01-31/12.
Distance: on the spot on the spot 200m.
Remarks: Next to campsite municipal Rive d'Aude, coins at capitainerie (1km).

S Florac 25A3

D16. **GPS:** n44,32582 e3,59032.

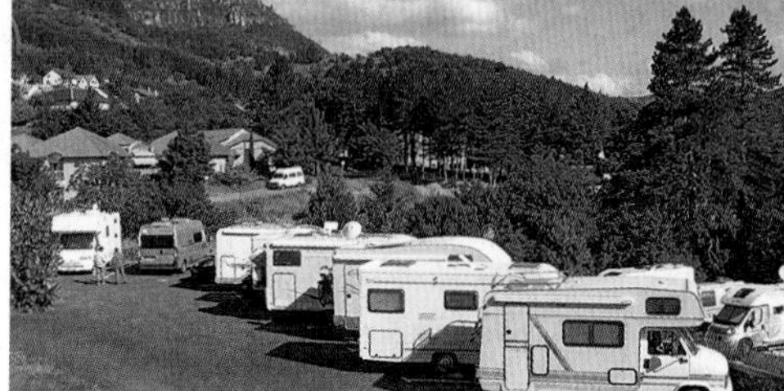

23 free €2/100liter Ch €2/1h WCfree.
Location: Rural, comfortable, central, quiet. **Surface:** asphalted.
01/01-31/12.
Distance: 150m 300m 300m 150m 150m mountain-bike trail on the spot.
Remarks: Nearby cemetery.

S Florensac 28A2

Domaine de Veyrac, Route de Bessan, D28.
GPS: n43,36221 e3,47671.

10 € 7 .
Location: Simple, isolated, quiet. **Surface:** gravel.
Distance: 5km 3,6km.

S Fraïsse-sur-Agout 27H2

Allée des Tilleuls. **GPS:** n43,60583 e2,79778.

15 € 7 Ch (1x)included. **Surface:** asphalted/grassy.
01/01-31/12.
Distance: 400m 20m 20m 400m.
Remarks: At the edge of village, on the Agout river.

S Frejairolles 27G1

Domaine du Grand Chêne, D81. **GPS:** n43,86043 e2,24799.
10 € 10 Ch WC €5/3 included.
Surface: grassy/gravel.

S Gaillac 27F1

Parking des Rives Thomas, Rue Claude Nougaro.
GPS: n43,89951 e1,89494.

4 free Chfree. **Location:** Urban, simple, noisy. **Surface:** asphalted. 01/01-31/12. **Distance:** 200m 200m 200m.

Gavarnie 27C3

Parking Holle, Route de la station des Espécières, D923. **GPS**: n42,73857 w0,01959.

20 free, July-Aug € 7 Chincluded. **Location:** Rural, simple, isolated, quiet. **Surface:** metalled. 01/01-31/12. **Distance:** 1,5km 100m 800m 800m 800m on the spot 100m 1,5km.

Gavarnie 27C3

Parking du Cirque, Baretge. **GPS**: n42,73549 w0,0116.

20 € 7. **Location:** Rural, simple. **Surface:** asphalted. 01/07-31/08. **Distance:** 200m 200m 200m 200m on the spot on the spot on the spot.

Tourist information Gavarnie:

Cirque de Gavarnie. Can be reached with a donkey, a horse or by foot. A giant waterfalll, snow pillars and mountain slopes.

Gèdre 27C3

Aire de stationnement de Héas, D922. **GPS**: n42,74916 e0,08935. free. **Location:** Rural, simple, isolated, quiet. **Surface:** grassy. winter. **Distance:** 9km 600m. **Remarks:** At Chapelle de Héas.

Gèdre 27C3

Place de la Bergère, Gedre Débat. **GPS**: n42,78860 e0,01967.

12 free. **Location:** Rural, simple. **Surface:** asphalted. 01/01-31/12. **Distance:** on the spot 250m 50m.

Gèdre 27C3

Auberge de la Munia, Héas, D922. **GPS**: n42,73643 e0,08631. 5 € 6. **Distance:** on the spot.

Génolhac 25B3

Les Taillades, Place du 19 Mars 1962, D906. **GPS**: n44,35388 e3,94844.

10 free Chfree. **Location:** Rural, simple, isolated, quiet. **Surface:** metalled. 01/01-31/12. **Distance:** 200m 800m on the spot.

Gignac 24F2

Le Moulin, Place des Troubadours. **GPS**: n45,00624 e1,45687.

10 free Ch. **Surface:** metalled. 01/01-31/12. **Distance:** 50m 150m 150m.

Gimont 27E1

Avenue de Cahuzac, RN124. **GPS**: n43,62987 e0,87009.

12 free Ch free. **Location:** Simple, noisy. **Surface:** gravel. 01/01-31/12. **Distance:** 100m on the spot on the spot 300m 300m 300m. **Remarks:** At lake, max. 48h, market Wednesday and Sunday.

Gourdon 24F2

Esplanade du foirail. **GPS**: n44,73423 e1,38523.

8 € 1/6h Ch (8x)included. **Location:** Comfortable, quiet. **Surface:** gravel. 01/01-31/12. **Distance:** 200m 100m 200m on the spot.

Gramat 24F2

La Garenne, Avenue Paul Mezet. **GPS**: n44,77966 e1,72904.

10 free Ch. **Surface:** gravel. 01/01-31/12. **Distance:** 400m 400m 400m. **Remarks:** Max. 48h.

Grenade-sur-Garonne 27F1

Quai de Garonne. **GPS**: n43,77201 e1,29673.

4 free Ch. **Surface:** gravel. **Distance:** 100m 100m 100m 100m. **Remarks:** Service: Allées Alsace Lorraine (100m).

Gruissan 27H3

Aire des 4 Vents, Avenue des quatre vents. **GPS**: n43,10444 e3,09944.

120 free, 12/02-30/11 € 9 ChWC included. **Surface:** gravel. 01/01-31/12. **Distance:** on the spot on the spot on the spot on the spot on the spot.

Gruissan 27H3

Aire des Châlets, Avenue de la Jetée, Gruissan-plage. **GPS**: n43,09583 e3,11111.

80 € 9 Chincluded. **Surface:** gravel. 01/04-30/09. **Distance:** 2km on the spot on the spot 2km 2km.

Gruissan 27H3

Étang de Mateille, Gruissan dir Narbonne-Plage, base de voile, D332. **GPS**: n43,12083 e3,11417.

150 € 9 Ch (24x)€ 1,50 WC. **Surface:** grassy/metalled. 01/07-31/08. **Distance:** 4km on the spot on the spot 800m Lidl 2km.

Tourist information Gruissan:

L'Hospitalet. Probably the largest wine-cellar of the world.

Vieux Port. Old fishing-port.

Guzet-Neige 27E3

Station de ski de Guzet. **GPS**: n42,78007 e1,29979. free WC. 01/01-31/12. **Distance:** on the spot on the spot.

La Bastide-de-Sérou 27F3

Bargnac, D15. **GPS**: n43,00194 e1,44556.

FR

15 € 14,60, Jul/Aug € 18,60 Ch WC included.
Location: Rural, isolated, quiet. **Surface:** asphalted/gravel.
11/04-03/11.

La Canourgue 25A3

Avenue du Lot, D998. **GPS:** n44,43325 e3,20775.

10 free Chfree. **Location:** Rural, simple, isolated, quiet.
Surface: metalled. 01/01-31/12 Jul/Aug: tue.
Distance: 500m 1,3km 600m 600m 600m.
Remarks: Max. 24h.

La Cavalerie 27H1

Camping-Car Park. GPS: n44,00876 e3,15228.
32 € 9,60 Ch . **Surface:** gravel.
Distance: 200m 200m.

La Couvertoirade 28A1

GPS: n43,91012 e3,31276.

10 € 3 €3/100liter WC. **Location:** Rural, isolated, quiet.
Surface: gravel. 01/01-31/12.
Distance: 50m 50m.
Remarks: Large parking on edge from village.

Tourist information La Couvertoirade:
Citadelle de l'Ordre de Tempeliers. Fortified city in original state. Now many old craft industries are exercised. There is a toll-house at the entrance of the village, entrance fee is charged.

La Grande Motte 28B2

Aire camping-car Les Cigales, Avenue de la Petite Motte.
GPS: n43,56789 e4,07404.

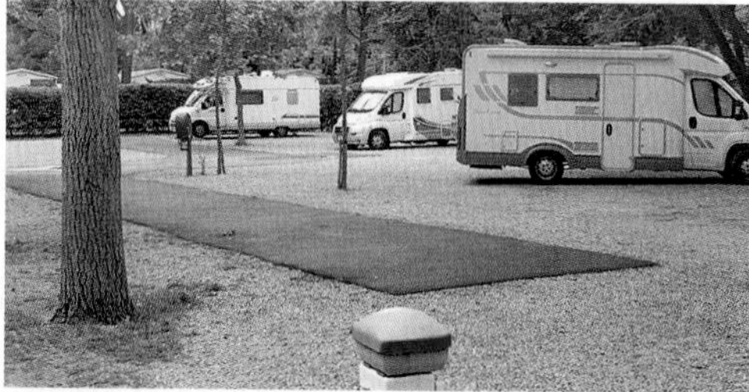

50 € 11-13, Jul-Aug € 16 + € 1/pp tourist tax ChWC .
Location: Rural. **Surface:** gravel. 01/01-31/12.
Distance: 2km 1,2km 2km 2km.

La Palme 27H3

Les Salins de La Palme, Route de Port la Nouvelle.
GPS: n42,98033 e3,01858.
49 € 12 Ch (49x) . **Location:** Rural, comfortable, isolated, quiet. **Surface:** grassy. 01/01-31/12.
Distance: 2,5km 2km on the spot.

Labastide-Murat 24F2

Route de Gramat. **GPS:** n44,64944 e1,57061.
free Ch.
Location: Rural, simple. **Surface:** asphalted.

Distance: 300m on the spot.
Remarks: At supermarket Carrefour.

Labruguiere 27G2

Domaine d'en Laure, Avenue Arthur Batut.
GPS: n43,53139 e2,25528.

10 free €2/10minutes Ch €2/minutes.
Location: Rural, simple, isolated, quiet. **Surface:** grassy.
01/01-31/12.
Distance: 2km on the spot on the spot 1,3km 1,3km.

Lacapelle Marival 24G2

Place de Larroque. **GPS:** n44,72806 e1,92944.

50 free €2/100liter Ch €2/h.
Surface: asphalted. service 15/05-30/09.
Distance: on the spot 100m 50m.

Lacaune 27H1

Rue de la Balme. **GPS:** n43,70795 e2,69010.

20 free. **Surface:** gravel. 01/01-31/12.
Distance: on the spot on the spot.

Lacroix-Barrez 24H2

Le Ventoux. **GPS:** n44,77793 e2,63086.
10 € 2,50 + € 0,30 tourist tax Chfree. **Surface:** grassy.
01/01-31/12 service: 01/11-17/04.
Distance: 400m.

Lagrasse 27H3

Parking de la Promenade, P2, Les Condamines.
GPS: n43,09273 e2,62004.

40 € 3, 01/06-30/09 € 5 ChWCfree. **Location:** Rural, simple, quiet. **Surface:** grassy/gravel. 01/01-31/12.
Distance: on the spot on the spot on the spot on the spot on the spot.

Laguepie 24G3

Chemin de Saint Cambraire. **GPS:** n44,14578 e1,97298.

6 free Chfree. **Location:** Rural, simple, quiet.
Surface: grassy/gravel. 01/01-31/12.
Distance: 600m 600m 500m.

Laguiole 24H2

Du Bouyssou, La Serre. **GPS:** n44,67199 e2,92451.
€ 8 €3. **Surface:** asphalted.
Distance: 7km on the spot.

Laguiole 24H2

Rue de Lavernhe. **GPS:** n44,68408 e2,85048.

10 free Chfree. **Surface:** gravel.
01/01-31/12, service: 17/04-15/10.
Distance: on the spot.

Laguiole 24H2

La Montagnettte, Les Clauzades. **GPS:** n44,70457 e2,84037.
5 free €3. **Location:** Simple, isolated, quiet. **Surface:** gravel.
01/01-31/12.
Distance: 4km.

Laissac 24H3

Place du Foirail des Ovins, RN88. **GPS:** n44,38590 e2,82160.

6 free Chfree. **Surface:** asphalted. 01/03-30/11.
Distance: 500m 500m 500m.
Remarks: Max. 24h.

Langogne 25B2

Camping-Car Park, Route du lac. **GPS:** n44,73700 e3,83448.

40 € 9,10-10,30 Ch (16x) included.
Location: Rural, comfortable, quiet. **Surface:** unpaved.
01/01-31/12.
Distance: 2km beach 1km on the spot 2km 2km.
Remarks: At lake Naussac.

Langogne 25B2

Centre Polyvalente. GPS: n44,72281 e3,85419.

10 free, €2/100liter Ch. **Location:** Central, quiet.
Surface: asphalted. 01/01-31/12.
Distance: on the spot 300m 300m on the spot.
Remarks: Coins at tourist info.

S Lannemezan 27D2

L'Espace du Nébouzan, Chemin du Carrérot de Blazy.
GPS: n43,12779 e0,38085.

20 free Ch free. **Location:** Rural, comfortable.
Surface: gravel. 01/01-31/12.
Distance: 450m 200m 250m.

S Lanuéjouls 24G3

Aire Campingcar Lanuéjouls, Avenue du Rouergue, D1.
GPS: n44,42528 e2,16139.

14 €5 Ch WC included. **Location:** Rural, comfortable.
Surface: gravel. 01/01-31/12.
Distance: 100m 100m 100m.
Remarks: Ticket for access at shops in the village.

S Lapradelle Puilaurens 27G3

D117. **GPS**: n42,81003 e2,30854.

6 free Ch free. **Location:** Rural, simple, quiet.
Surface: metalled. 01/01-31/12.
Distance: on the spot on the spot on the spot.
Remarks: At fire-station.

S Latour-Bas-Elne 32H1

Aire de Latour Bas Elne, Route de la Mer.
GPS: n42,60017 e3,00667.

40 € 10, € 14 Jun-Aug, trailer € 4 Ch included €3/48h.
Location: Comfortable. **Surface:** grassy.
01/01-31/12.
Distance: 3km.
Remarks: Baker at 9am, monitored parking.

S Latour-de-Carol 32F1

Village Club Yravals, 2 Rue de Saneja. **GPS**: n42,45829 e1,89460.

5 € 10, 2 pers.incl, extra pers € 1 Ch WC included €2/day. **Surface:** grassy. 01/04-31/10.
Distance: 2km.

S Latronquière 24G2

Place du Foirail. **GPS**: n44,79917 e2,07917.

4 free Ch WC free.
Surface: asphalted. 01/01-31/12.
Distance: 300m 3km 3km 300m 300m.

S Laudun-l'Ardoise 28C1

Place des Arènes. **GPS**: n44,10791 e4,65556.

3 free €4 Ch. **Location:** Simple, central, noisy.
Surface: asphalted. 01/01-31/12.
Distance: 300m 300m 300m.

S Laudun-l'Ardoise 28C1

Route d'Avignon, N580. **GPS**: n44,09527 e4,70164.

free Ch free.
Location: Simple, central. **Surface:** asphalted. 01/01-31/12.
Distance: 5,5km.
Remarks: Behind police station, at tennis-court.

S Laudun-l'Ardoise 28C1

Vignerons de Laudun, Avenue du Général de Gaulle.
GPS: n44,10388 e4,66362.

10 free Ch. **Surface:** grassy/gravel.
Distance: 750m 300m 750m.
Remarks: Max. 3 days.

S Lauzerte 24E3

1, Place du Foirail. **GPS**: n44,25432 e1,13666.

10 free Ch WC free.
Surface: asphalted. 01/01-31/12 tue-evening, wed-morning.
Distance: 500m on the spot on the spot.

S Lauzerte 24E3

D2, Vignals. **GPS**: n44,26750 e1,14083.

20 free Ch WC free.
Surface: grassy/gravel. 01/01-31/12.
Distance: Lauzerte 1km on the spot 2km.

Tourist information Lauzerte:
Wed-morning.

S Le Barcarès 27H3

Barcares le Port, Quai des Tourettes. **GPS**: n42,80165 e3,03277.
49 € 9,60, Jul/Aug € 12 Ch (16x) included.
01/01-31/12.
Distance: 1,5km 2km on the spot on the spot 1,5km.

S Le Bosc 28A1

Parc Activités Méridienne. **GPS**: n43,68932 e3,35328.

10 free €2/100liter Ch €2/1h. **Location:** Motorway, simple, isolated. **Surface:** asphalted. 01/01-31/12.
Distance: 400m on the spot Intermarché 50m.

S Le Boulou 32H1

Chemin du Moulin Nou. **GPS**: n42,52719 e2,83704.

21 free €2 Ch WC. **Location:** Rural, simple, comfortable.
Surface: asphalted. 01/01-31/12.
Distance: 300m 1km 300m 300m.
Remarks: In front of cemetery, max. 24h.

S Le Cap d'Agde 28A2

Rue du Gouverneur. **GPS**: n43,28600 e3,51739.

FR

30 € 5, 27/03-02/11 € 10 €2 Ch included.
Location: Rural, comfortable, central. **Surface:** asphalted/metalled.
01/01-31/12.
Distance: on the spot 500m 500m 500m.
Remarks: Nearby Camping La Clape, video surveillance.

Le Caylar 28A1

Domaine des Templiers, Route de la Couvertoirade, D609.
GPS: n43,86944 e3,31466.

30 € 10 Ch (9x)included12h WC €4/pp.
Location: Comfortable, isolated, quiet. **Surface:** gravel.
01/04-31/10.
Distance: 600m 500m on the spot.

Le Fossat 27F2

Aire des Lallières, Place de la Mairie. **GPS:** n43,17201 e1,41170.

21 € 12 Ch WC included. **Location:** Luxurious.
Surface: gravel. 01/03-30/11.

Le Grau du Roi 28B2

Parking de la plage, Rue du Commandant Marceau.
GPS: n43,54061 e4,13349.

40 € 8,80, June-Aug € 12,50 €2/100liter Ch €2/55minutes.
Surface: asphalted. 01/01-31/12.
Distance: centre 550m sandy beach 20m on the spot on the spot.
Remarks: Beach parking, video surveillance.

Le Houga 27D1

Ferme aux Cerfs, Route de Mont de Marsan, D6.
GPS: n43,78430 e0,20997.

15 € 3 Chfree. **Surface:** grassy. 01/01-31/12.
Distance: 2,5km on the spot.

Le Malzieu-Ville 25A2

Place Foirail. **GPS:** n44,85506 e3,33385.

6 free ChWCfree.
Location: Rural, simple, comfortable, central, quiet.
Surface: asphalted. 01/01-31/12.
Distance: on the spot 10km on the spot 200m 200m on the spot.

Le Monastier-Pin-Moriès 25A3

Place de la Gare. **GPS:** n44,50896 e3,25162.

4 free ChWCfree. **Location:** Rural, simple, isolated, quiet.
Surface: asphalted. 01/01-31/12.
Distance: 1km 1,5km 1km.
Remarks: Coins at petrol station (200m), picnic area.

Le Ségala 27F2

Esplanade du Canal. **GPS:** n43,34089 e1,83544.

10 free WC. **Location:** Rural, simple, quiet. **Surface:** gravel.
01/01-31/12.
Distance: on the spot 1km on the spot on the spot on the spot on the spot.
Remarks: No camping activities.

Le Ségur 27G1

Place de Marie. **GPS:** n44,10889 e2,05861.

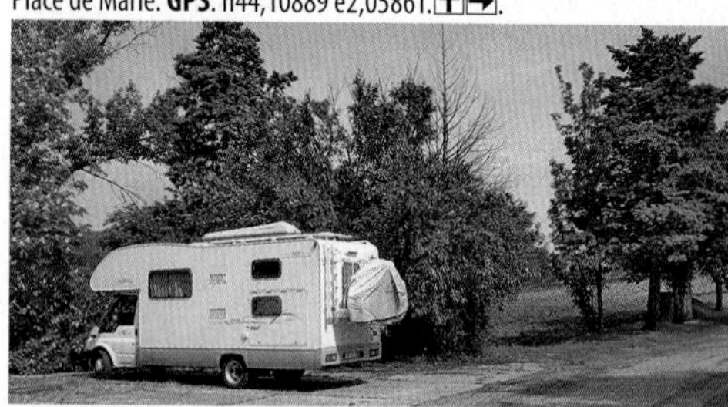

3 free ChWCfree. **Location:** Rural, simple, quiet.
Surface: metalled. 01/01-31/12.
Distance: 50m 100m 100m.
Remarks: At townhall.

Les Angles 32G1

Pla del Mir. GPS: n42,56321 e2,06780.

100 free €3,50 ChWC. **Location:** Rural, simple, quiet.
Surface: asphalted. 01/01-31/12.
Distance: 2,6km on the spot.

Les Cabannes 27F3

Quartier la Bexane. **GPS:** n42,78493 e1,68301.

30 € 4/24h €2/100liter ChWC. **Surface:** asphalted.
Distance: 300m 300m.

Les Mages 25B3

Serre Marine, D904, St. Ambroix/Alés. **GPS:** n44,23442 e4,16967.

7 free Chfree. **Location:** Rural, simple, isolated, noisy.
Surface: metalled. 01/01-31/12.
Distance: 700m 700m 800m.
Remarks: Picnic area.

Leucate 27H3

Chemin des Coussoules, La Franqui. **GPS:** n42,94329 e3,02917.

70 € 6 Chon campsite €5.
Surface: unpaved.
01/02-30/11.
Distance: 2km on the spot on the spot 2km 2km.
Remarks: Next to campsite Coussoules, check in at reception campsite.

Leucate 27H3

Le Goulet, D627. **GPS:** n42,91145 e3,01946.

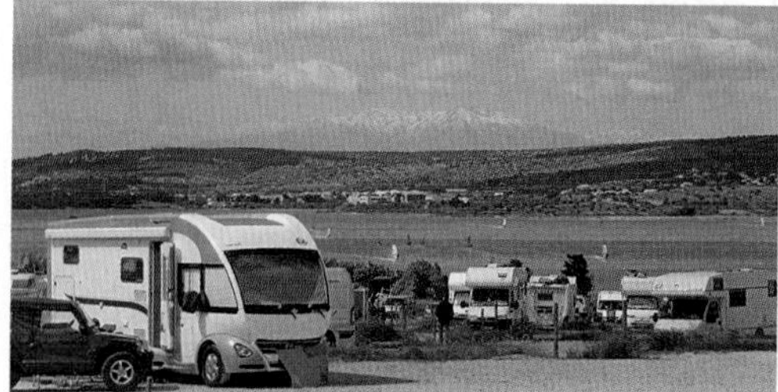

150 € 10,20-13,80 €2 Ch €2.
Location: Rural, simple. **Surface:** unpaved.
01/01-31/12.
Distance: centre Leucate 850m on the spot on the spot.
Remarks: Terraces, at lake of Leucate, baker on site (20/03-31/10).

Leucate 27H3

Mouret, Chemin du Mouret, Leucate Plage.
GPS: n42,90022 e3,05272.

FR

236 € 10,20-13,80/24h Ch included
Location: Rural, simple. **Surface:** asphalted/gravel.
01/01-31/12.
Distance: 300m on the spot on the spot.
Remarks: Beach parking, baker on site (20/03-31/10).

S Limoux 27G3

Parking, Rue Louis Braille. **GPS**: n43,05741 e2,21490.

30 free Ch free. **Location:** Urban, simple, quiet.
Surface: metalled. 01/01-31/12.
Distance: 200m on the spot 200m.

S Lisle sur Tarn 27F1

Aire de Bellevue, Rue des Aulnes. **GPS**: n43,86167 e1,81833.

12 free €2/100liter Ch. **Location:** Rural, simple, isolated, quiet. **Surface:** sand. 01/01-31/12.
Distance: 1,5km on the spot on the spot 1,5km 1,5km.
Remarks: Coins at Tourist Info and Maison de la Presse.

Lodève 28A2

Baie des Vailhés, Celles. **GPS**: n43,67087 e3,35565.
€ 5, 01/07-31/08 € 8 + tourist tax € 0,20/pp.

Tourist information Lodève:
Maison de Tourisme, 7, Place de la République, www.lodeve.com. Old city to the gate of the Mediterranean.

S Lombez 27E2

Route de Toulouse, D632. **GPS**: n43,47417 e0,91592.

20 free WC free. **Surface:** gravel.
Distance: 200m 150m 200m.

S Loudenvielle 27D3

Aire de campingcar Les Seguettes, Chemin du Hourgade.
GPS: n42,80163 e0,41088.

30 free, 01/07-15/09 € 3 €2/100liter Ch €2/h.
Location: Rural, quiet. **Surface:** gravel.
01/01-31/12.
Distance: 700m 700m 800m.
Remarks: At lake, coins at Tourist Info and Maison de la Presse.

Loudenvielle 27D3

La Ribère, D25 Génos. **GPS**: n42,79963 e0,40813.
6 free, 01/07-15/09 € 3. **Location:** Rural, simple, quiet.
Surface: gravel. 01/01-31/12.
Distance: 500m on the spot on the spot 500m on the spot on the spot.

S Lourdes 27C2

Le Vieux Berger, Route de Julos. **GPS**: n43,10451 w0,0332.

27 € 11, May-Jun € 13, Jul-Sep € 14 Ch WC €3/3 included. **Location:** Rural, luxurious, noisy.
Surface: grassy/gravel. 01/01-31/12.
Distance: 1km 2km 700m 700m 100m on the spot.
Remarks: Next to campsite.

Tourist information Lourdes:
Office de Tourisme, Place Peyramale, www.lourdes-infotourisme.com. Lively place of pilgrimage.
Basilique St.Pius X. Underground basilica, of the largest sanctuaries in the world, there is place for 25,000 people.

S Lunas 28A1

Base de Loisirs Prade, D35. **GPS**: n43,70555 e3,18555.

75 free Ch free. **Location:** Simple, isolated, quiet.
Surface: grassy/metalled. 01/01-31/12.
Distance: 900m on the spot on the spot 200m 700m 200m.

S Luzech 24F3

Les Berges de Caïx, D9. **GPS**: n44,49068 e1,29506.

15 € 8,50 + € 0,22/pp tourist tax Ch WC included €2.
Surface: gravel. 01/01-31/12.
Distance: 2km.
Remarks: Along Lot river.

S L'Hospitalet-près-l'Andorre 32F1

N22. **GPS**: n42,58823 e1,79833.

5 free €2 Ch €6. **Surface:** asphalted.
Distance: 100m.

Marbre 27D3

Lac de Payolle, D918, Campan > Col de Aspin.
GPS: n42,93528 e0,29222.

free.
Location: Rural, simple, isolated. **Surface:** grassy/gravel.
Distance: 5km 50m 50m 700m 5km on the spot on the spot.

S Marseillan-Plage 28A2

Rue des Goélands. **GPS**: n43,31902 e3,54864.

122 € 4-6-12/24h €2/10minutes Ch
Location: Comfortable, quiet. **Surface:** gravel. 01/01-31/12.
Distance: on the spot sandy beach 600m on the spot on the spot.
Remarks: Max. 48h.

S Martel 24F2

La Fontanelle, Avenue de Nassogne. **GPS**: n44,93505 e1,60656.

12 free Ch. **Surface:** gravel. 01/01-31/12.
Distance: 250m 250m 250m.

Martel 24F2

Parking Monti. GPS: n44,93957 e1,60827.
12 free. **Surface:** asphalted. 01/01-31/12.
Distance: 400m 400m 400m.

S Marvéjols 25A3

Boulevard Aurelle de Paladines, Le Pré de Suzon.
GPS: n44,55406 e3,28753.

10 free Ch WC free.
Location: Central. **Surface:** asphalted.
Distance: on the spot 7,5km on the spot on the spot.

Tourist information Marvéjols:
Maison de Tourisme, Porte du Soubeyran, www.ville-marvejols.fr. Old fortress city, gates with battlements and towers.

S Matemale 32G1

GPS: n42,57964 e2,10227.

FR

10 free €1 ChWC. **Location:** Rural, simple, isolated, quiet.
Surface: asphalted. 01/01-31/12.
Distance: 3km on the spot on the spot 300m.
Remarks: Parking at lake.

Matemale 32G1

Rue de la Truite. **GPS:** n42,56559 e2,10433.

10 free. **Location:** Rural, simple, isolated, quiet. **Surface:** gravel.
01/01-31/12.
Distance: 1,5km 20m 1,5km 1,5km.
Remarks: Parking at lake.

Maureillas-Las-Illas 32H1

GPS: n42,48711 e2,80748.
20 € 8-12,50 Ch €4.
Surface: metalled. 01/01-31/12.
Distance: 500m 500m 500m.

Mazamet 27G2

D118. **GPS:** n43,46278 e2,34609.
free Chfree. **Location:** Rural, isolated, quiet.
Surface: grassy/gravel. 01/01-31/12.
Distance: 8km on the spot on the spot on the spot.

Mazamet 27G2

Rue Galibert-Ferret, Champ de la Ville. **GPS:** n43,49089 e2,37918.

10 free Chfree. **Location:** Urban. **Surface:** asphalted.
01/01-31/12 Fri-Sa market.
Distance: on the spot on the spot.
Remarks: At townhall, max. 24h.

Mazères-sur-Salat 27E3

Rue de Vieux Ruisseau. **GPS:** n43,13457 e0,97633.

15 free Chfree. **Surface:** metalled. 01/01-31/12.
Distance: 4,5km river.

Mende 25A3

Rue du Faubourg Montbel. **GPS:** n44,52063 e3,49660.

20 free €2/10minutes Chfree €2/55minutes.
Location: Urban, comfortable, central, quiet. **Surface:** asphalted.
01/01-31/12.
Distance: on the spot on the spot 200m 400m on the spot on the spot.
Remarks: Along Lot river, max. 96h.

Mende 25A3

Camping-car Park, Aérodrome Mende-Brenoux.
GPS: n44,52063 e3,49660.
38 € 9,60/24h. **Surface:** grassy. 01/01-31/12.
Remarks: At airfield.

Mèze 28A2

Complexe sportif des Sesquiers, Route de Villeveyrac.
GPS: n43,44135 e3,59436.

6 free Chfree.
Location: Simple, noisy. **Surface:** gravel.
Distance: 2,5km 10km.

Miélan 27D2

Rue du Cubet. **GPS:** n43,43319 e0,30900.

6 free Chfree. **Location:** Rural, simple. **Surface:** gravel.
01/01-31/12.
Distance: 350m 350m 350m.

Millau 27H1

Camping-car Park, Rue de la Saunerie 19.
GPS: n44,09610 e3,08577.

41 € 9,60/24h Ch included. **Location:** Comfortable.
Surface: gravel. 01/01-31/12.
Distance: 500m.
Remarks: Motorhomes <7.5m, entrance code night: parknight, video surveillance.

Tourist information Millau:

Office de Tourisme, 1, Place du Beffroi, www.ot-millau.fr. City tourist in the Valley of the Tarn and the Dourbie. Important for the leather trade.

Vieux Millau. Historical hiking route, info at Office de Tourisme.

Mirandol-Bourgnounce 24G3

Place de Foirail. GPS: n44,14167 e2,16667.

8 free ChWCfree. **Location:** Rural, simple, quiet.
Surface: asphalted. 01/01-31/12.
Distance: on the spot on the spot 50m on the spot.

Mirepoix 27F3

Parking des Capitouls, Alée des Soupirs. **GPS:** n43,08491 e1,87399.

20 free ChWCfree. **Surface:** asphalted. 01/01-31/12.
Distance: centre 500m 200m 400m.
Remarks: Next to community centre.

Tourist information Mirepoix:

Cattle market. winter 2nd, 4th Mo of the month.

Thu, Sa.

Moissac 27E1

Promenade Sancert. **GPS:** n44,10011 e1,08540.

4 free €2/4h. **Location:** Urban, simple. **Surface:** metalled.
01/01-31/12.
Distance: 100m 100m.
Remarks: Coins at tourist info.

Mont Roc 27G1

Salle de Fêtes. **GPS:** n43,80330 e2,37192.

8 free €2 Ch €2 WC.
Surface: metalled. 01/01-31/12.
Distance: 50m on the spot on the spot.

Mont-Louis 32G1

Parking des Remparts. GPS: n42,50765 e2,12273.

20 € 5 included. **Location:** Urban, simple, quiet.
Surface: asphalted.
Distance: 200m 200m 200m.
Remarks: Parking at city wall.

FR

Montagnac 28A2

D613. **GPS**: n43,47520 e3,49129.

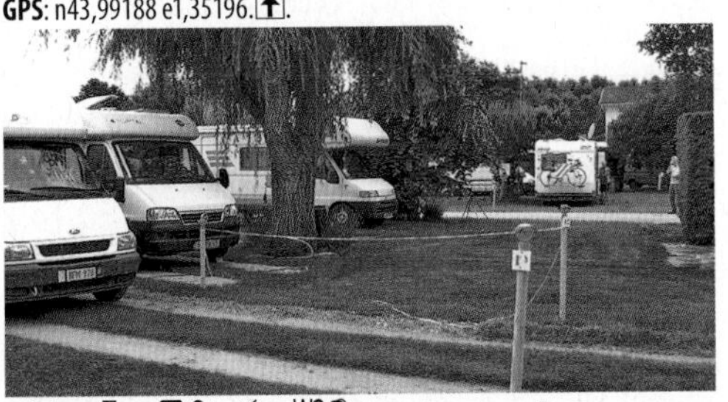

3 free Ch free. **Surface:** gravel.
Distance: 1km 1km 1km.

Montauban 27F1

Mr. Lacaze, aire camping-car, 225, route de Corbarieu, D21.
GPS: n43,99188 e1,35196.

15 € 6 €1 Ch €2 WC €1. **Surface:** gravel.
01/01-31/12.
Distance: Montauban 3km 1km.
Remarks: Max 3,5t.

Montauban 27F1

Port Canal, Rue des Oules. **GPS**: n44,00744 e1,34105.
10 € 6 Ch . **Location:** Comfortable, quiet.
Surface: grassy/gravel. 01/01-31/12.
Distance: 2,5km.
Remarks: At the canal.

Montauban 27F1

La Ferme des Pibouls, Route de Saint-Antonin.
GPS: n44,03658 e1,40499.
12 free Ch.
Surface: grassy.
Distance: 5km.

Tourist information Montauban:
Office de Tourisme, 2, rue du Collège, officetourisme.montauban.com. City of roses.
Sa.

Montcalm 28B2

Le Caveau du Chêne, Route d'Aigues Mortes, D58.
GPS: n43,57322 e4,30505.

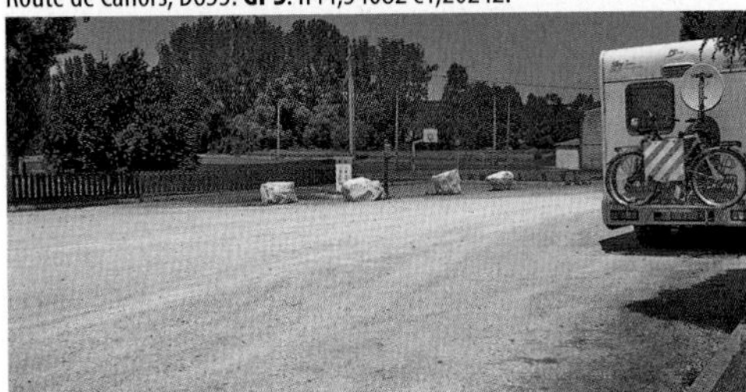

40 free for clients. **Location:** Rural, isolated, quiet. **Surface:** grassy.
01/01-31/12.

Montcuq 24E3

Route de Cahors, D653. **GPS**: n44,34082 e1,20242.

15 free €2 Ch €2.
Surface: gravel. 01/01-31/12.
Distance: 250m 250m 250m.
Remarks: Coins at Tourist Info and petrol station.

Montdardier 28A1

Rue de l'église. **GPS**: n43,92885 e3,59073.
5 free.
Distance: 350m.
Remarks: Max. 72h.

Monteils 24G3

D47. **GPS**: n44,26694 e1,99667.

4 free Ch free. **Location:** Rural, simple, quiet.
Surface: grassy/gravel. 01/01-31/12.
Distance: 100m 100m 50m.

Montézic 24H2

Les Prades Sud. **GPS**: n44,71054 e2,64413.

4 free Ch. **Surface:** asphalted. 01/03-31/10.
Distance: 500m on the spot on the spot.

Montferrand 27F2

Col de Naurouze, Route du Ségala, N113> D218.
GPS: n43,35238 e1,82390.

20 free. **Location:** Rural, simple, quiet. **Surface:** gravel.
01/01-31/12.
Distance: 2km on the spot 2km on the spot on the spot.

Montpellier 28B2

Parking Joffre, Rue d'Argencour. **GPS**: n43,61316 e3,88608.
€ 1/h. **Surface:** asphalted. 01/01-31/12.
Distance: 4km.
Remarks: Overnight stay possible. Via avenue Jean Mermoz.

Tourist information Montpellier:
Corum. Opera-complex.
Place de la Comédie. Square with many cafés.

Montréal (Gers) 27D1

Stade André Daubin, D29. **GPS**: n43,95375 e0,19730.

free Ch free. **Surface:** gravel. 01/01-31/12.
Distance: 200m 500m 500m.
Remarks: Parking at rugby ground.

Tourist information Montréal (Gers):
Office de Tourisme, place de l'Hôtel de Ville, www.montrealdugers.com/. Fortified city with ramparts, square with arcades and picturesque alleys.

Montréjeau 27D3

Grande Halle, Place de Verdun. **GPS**: n43,08448 e0,57112.

4 free. **Location:** Urban, simple, central, noisy. **Surface:** asphalted.
01/01-31/12.
Distance: 100m 400m on the spot.

Monze 27G3

La Bretonne. **GPS**: n43,15475 e2,45867.

2 free. **Location:** Rural, simple, isolated, quiet. **Surface:** asphalted.
01/01-31/12.
Distance: 50m 500m.
Remarks: Max. 48h.

Mourèze 28A2

D8. **GPS**: n43,61728 e3,36111.

6 € 6 Ch WC included. **Location:** Simple, isolated, quiet.
Surface: gravel. 01/01-31/12.
Distance: on the spot 300m on the spot.

Mur de Barrez 24H2

Parc de la Corette, Place du Foirail. **GPS**: n44,84842 e2,65980.

6 free Ch. **Surface:** asphalted. 01/04-15/11.
Distance: 100m on the spot 50m.
Remarks: Max. 72h.

Murviel-lès-Béziers 27H2

Camping-Car Park, Route de Réals, D36. **GPS**: n43,43953 e3,13420.

25 € 9,60-10,80 Ch (20x) WC included.
Location: Rural, comfortable, isolated, quiet. **Surface:** unpaved.
01/01-31/12.
Distance: 700m 10km 700m 1,7km on the spot.
Remarks: Historical centre.

Nages 27H2

Aire de camping car du Lac, Lac du Laouzas, D162.
GPS: n43,64694 e2,78194.

FR

22 € 7 Ch included. **Location:** Isolated, quiet.
Surface: grassy/gravel. 31/03-01/11.
Distance: on the spot.
Remarks: Nearby base nautique.

S Najac 24G3

Le Pontet. **GPS**: n44,22167 e1,96778.

10 € 6, 01/04-30/09 € 8 Ch (12x)included.
Location: Comfortable, quiet. **Surface:** asphalted. 01/01-31/12.
Distance: 1,8km on the spot on the spot 1,8km on the spot on the spot.
Remarks: Historical centre.

S Narbonne 27H3

Parking du Parc des Sports, Avenue Maître Hubert Mouly.
GPS: n43,18017 e3,02294.

36 € 9/24h €2/20minutes Ch €2
Surface: asphalted.
01/01-31/12.
Distance: on the spot 2,3km Carrefour.
Remarks: Free bus to centre every 30 minutes.

Tourist information Narbonne:

Autorail Touristique du Minervois. Train tourist from Narbonne to Bize. 01/07-17/09.

Palais des Archevêques. Palace, 11th century, with cathedral. Thu, Su.

S Narbonne-Plage 27H3

Créneau Naturel, Route de Gruissan. **GPS**: n43,14725 e3,15408.
100 € 10 Ch WC included. 01/01-31/12.
Distance: Narbonne 16km on the spot on the spot 1km.

S Naucelle 24G3

Place du Ségala. **GPS**: n44,19723 e2,34175.

4 free Ch free. **Location:** Simple, noisy. **Surface:** asphalted.
01/01-31/12.
Distance: on the spot 500m 500m on the spot on the spot.

S Nègrepelisse 27E1

Avenue Jean Fleury. **GPS**: n44,07408 e1,52664.
15 free Ch free. **Surface:** grassy/gravel.
01/01-31/12 service: 01/12-01/04.
Distance: 500m 500m on the spot.

Remarks: Near sports fields.

S Nîmes 28B1

Domaine de Fontbespierre, 3359, route d'Anduze.
GPS: n43,87142 e4,27746.

50 € 10 €2 Ch €2/day WC. **Location:** Rural.
Surface: grassy. 01/01-31/12.
Distance: 6km 6km 6km.
Remarks: Terrain with video surveillance.

Octon 28A2

Avenue de la Molière. **GPS**: n43,65390 e3,30378.

8 free.
Location: Simple, quiet. **Surface:** asphalted.
Distance: 50m 50m 50m Lac du Salagou Lac du Salagou.
Remarks: Parking behind 'Clamery', Lac du Salagou.

S Oust 27E3

Aire camping-car, Foute d'Aulus les Bains.
GPS: n42,87167 e1,21833.

10 € 14,50, 2 pers.incl. Ch WC.
Surface: gravel.
01/01-31/12.
Remarks: Next to campsite Les 4 Saisons, arrival >14h departure <12h.

S Ouveillan 27H2

Place Cave Coopératieve. **GPS**: n43,29204 e2,97080.

7 free Ch free.
Surface: gravel/metalled. 01/01-31/12.
Distance: 2km 2km 2km.

S Palavas-les-Flots 28B2

D62E2. **GPS**: n43,53281 e3,92654.

23 € 11-19 Ch included. **Surface:** asphalted.
01/01-31/12.
Distance: centre 600m sandy beach 800m.

S Palavas-les-Flots 28B2

Port Fluvial, Base Paul Riquet, Avenue de Lattre Tassigny.
GPS: n43,53091 e3,92316.

135 € 14, 01/06-30/09 € 17 + € 0,83/pp tourist tax, extra charge >8m and trailer €3 Ch €3 WC included. **Surface:** asphalted.
01/01-31/12.
Distance: 1km 1km 1km.
Remarks: Bicycle rental.

S Peyragudes 27D3

Parking de Balestas, Culas. **GPS**: n42,79629 e0,44015.

25 free €2/100liter €2/1h. **Location:** Rural, simple, isolated, quiet. **Surface:** gravel. 01/01-31/12.
Distance: 10km 150m 850m on the spot on the spot on the spot.
Remarks: Coins at Maison de Peyragudes.

S Peyriac-de-Mer 27H3

Route des Bages. **GPS**: n43,09372 e2,96205.

20 € 5/24h Ch. **Location:** Rural, simple, simple.
Surface: grassy/metalled. 01/01-31/12.
Distance: 1km on the spot 1km 1km on the spot on the spot.
Remarks: Next to rugby ground.

S Peyrusse le Roc 24G3

D87. **GPS**: n44,49500 e2,13972.

12 free Ch free. **Surface:** grassy/sand. 01/01-31/12.
Distance: 500m 500m 500m.

S Pezens 27G2

Place de la Liberté, D6113. **GPS**: n43,25528 e2,26361.

5 free free. **Location:** Urban, simple, noisy. **Surface:** gravel. 01/01-31/12.
Distance: 50m 50m 50m.

S Pierrefitte-Nestalas 27C3

Chemin de la Portere. **GPS**: n42,96048 w0,07638.

15 free €1/50liter ChWC. **Location:** Rural, isolated, quiet. **Surface:** asphalted. 01/01-31/12.
Distance: 200m 10km 200m 200m on the spot on the spot.
Remarks: Max. 8 days.

S Pinsac 24F2

Parking Salle des Fêtes, D43. **GPS**: n44,85500 e1,51222.

5 free €2 Ch. **Surface:** gravel. 01/01-31/12.
Distance: on the spot 9,5km 700m.

S Pont-de-Salars 24H3

Place de la Rivière. **GPS**: n44,27822 e2,72853.

5 free €5/80liter Ch. **Location:** Simple. **Surface:** asphalted. 01/05-31/10.
Distance: 100m 2km 2km on the spot 100m on the spot.
Remarks: Along river, max. 3 days, coins at the shops.

S Port Vendres 32H1

L'Anse des Tamarins, Route de la Jetée. **GPS**: n42,51778 e3,11375.

40 € 6, May/Okt € 10 €2/100liter ChWC. **Location:** Rural, simple. **Surface:** gravel. 01/01-31/12.
Distance: 1,3km 100m on the spot.

S Port-la-Nouvelle 27H3

Chemin des Vignes. **GPS**: n43,01366 e3,04077.

30 free, Apr/June-Sep/Nov € 4, July/Aug € 9 €2/15minutes Ch €2/15minutes included,on campsite .
Location: Rural, simple. **Surface:** grassy/gravel.
Distance: 2km 8,6km 2km 2km 1km Huit-à-huit, Passage de l'Abbé Gavanon.

S Port-la-Nouvelle 27H3

Parking Super U, Avenue du Général de Gaulle.
GPS: n43,01609 e3,04933.
free €2/10minutes Chfree €2/55minutes against payment. **Surface:** asphalted. 01/01-31/12, 19.30-08.30h.
Distance: 1km 1km 1km on the spot.

Portiragnes 28A2

Avenue de la Grande Maïre. **GPS**: n43,27558 e3,35156.

± 15 free. **Location:** Rural, simple, quiet. **Surface:** unpaved. 01/01-31/12.
Distance: sandy beach 200m.
Remarks: Max. 2 days.

Pradinas 24G3

Place de l'Eglise. **GPS**: n44,23855 e2,26583.

5 Chfree. **Location:** Rural, simple, quiet.
Surface: grassy/sand.
Distance: on the spot.

S Prayssac 24E3

Avenue Maréchal Bessières. **GPS**: n44,50352 e1,19197.

15 free ChWC. **Surface:** grassy/gravel. 01/01-31/12.

S Preignan 27D1

Rue Emile Zola. **GPS**: n43,71243 e0,63378.

20 free Chfree. **Surface:** gravel.
Distance: 1km.

Remarks: At sports park.

S Puy l'Eveque 24E3

Place de la Gendarmerie. **GPS**: n44,50699 e1,13560.

4 free ChWCfree.
Surface: gravel. 01/01-31/12 05/08-14/08.
Distance: 250m 300m 300m.
Remarks: In front of town hall, max. 24h, upper city.

S Puylaurens 27G2

Rue Albert Thorel. **GPS**: n43,56861 e2,01194.

17 free Chfree . **Surface:** gravel. 01/01-31/12.
Distance: 700m 700m 400m.
Remarks: Max. 48h, wifi at supermarket.

S Quillan 27G3

Parking Joseph Courjétaire, D117. **GPS**: n42,87366 e2,18266.

10 free €3,10 ChWC. **Location:** Urban, simple, quiet.
Surface: asphalted. 01/01-31/12.
Distance: on the spot on the spot on the spot on the spot on the spot.
Remarks: Nearby railwayline, coins available at Office du Tourisme and bar.

S Remoulins 28C1

N86. **GPS**: n43,93789 e4,55851.

10 free €5/20minutes Ch. **Location:** Urban.
Surface: asphalted.
Distance: 100m 100m 100m.
Remarks: Parking nearby river, service on the other side of the bridge: Route du Pont du Gare.

Tourist information Remoulins:
Pont du Gard. Roman aqueduct.

S Rennes-les-Bains 27G3

Plateau Sport Nature, Route des Corbières.
GPS: n42,91479 e2,31814.

FR

7 € 5/24h Chfree. **Location:** Rural, simple, quiet.
Surface: asphalted. 01/01-31/12.
Distance: 500m 100m.

Requista 27H1

Place François Fablé. **GPS:** n44,03465 e2,53599.

6 free free. **Surface:** gravel. 01/01-31/12.
Distance: 200m.

Revel 27G2

Roy des Eaux, Chemin de la Pergue. **GPS:** n43,45286 e2,01233.
28 € 7, 01/06-31/08 € 9, tourist tax excl Ch included.
Surface: gravel. 01/01-31/12.
Distance: 1km 1km 1km.
Remarks: Max. 7 nights.

Rieupeyroux 24G3

15 Rue de la Calquière. **GPS:** n44,30861 e2,23194.

3 free Ch free. **Location:** Simple. **Surface:** asphalted.
01/04-01/11.
Distance: 500m 500m 1,5km.
Remarks: Next to school.

Rieutort-de-Randon 25A3

Lac de Charpal. **GPS:** n44,62491 e3,56046.

10 free. **Location:** Rural, isolated, quiet. **Surface:** unpaved.
01/01-31/12.
Distance: 8km 18km on the spot on the spot on the spot on the spot.
Remarks: At lake Charpal.

Rignac 24G3

Hameau du Lac, La Peyrade. **GPS:** n44,40456 e2,28958.

12 free, June-Aug € 5 Chfree. **Location:** Rural, simple, quiet. **Surface:** grassy. 01/01-31/12.
Distance: 1km on the spot 1km 1km on the spot.

Rivières 27G1

Aire de Salta, La Courtade Haute. **GPS:** n43,91072 e1,98889.

6 € 12 Ch (6x)included. **Location:** Rural, comfortable, quiet. **Surface:** gravel. 01/06-30/09.
Distance: 2km on the spot on the spot 2km.
Remarks: Along the Tarn river.

Rocamadour 24F2

Le Château, D673. **GPS:** n44,80000 e1,61528.

30 free. **Surface:** gravel. 15/06-15/09.
Distance: 100m.

Rodez 24H3

Route du Gué de Salelles. **GPS:** n44,35731 e2,59374.

6 free Chfree. **Location:** Urban, simple, noisy.
Surface: gravel. 01/01-31/12.
Distance: 1km 1km.
Remarks: Max. 72h.

Roquecor 24E3

Place du Foirail. **GPS:** n44,32346 e0,94496.

6 free Chfree. **Surface:** asphalted. 01/01-31/12.
Distance: 250m 300m 250m.
Remarks: Max. 48h.

Roquefort-sur-Soulzon 27H1

D23. **GPS:** n43,98120 e2,98163.

free ChWCfree. **Surface:** asphalted. 01/01-31/12.
Distance: 100m.
Remarks: Parking behind tourist info, water closed during wintertime.

Routier 27G3

Sous la Serre. **GPS:** n43,10813 e2,12362.

7 free Chfree.
Location: Rural, simple, quiet. **Surface:** grassy/gravel.
01/01-31/12 water disconnected in winter.
Distance: on the spot.

Tourist information Routier:
Corbières. Region is known for its wines and the Cathar citadels, the castle of Queribus in Cucugan is one of the last bastions of the Cathars.

Saillagousse 32F1

Rue des Sports. **GPS:** n42,45764 e2,03766.

7 free € 4 Ch WC. **Location:** Urban, simple, quiet.
Surface: asphalted. 01/01-31/12.
Distance: on the spot on the spot on the spot.
Remarks: Coins at tourist info and town hall.

Saint-André 32H1

Parking de Taxo. **GPS:** n42,55248 e2,97303.

6 € 2,30 € 2 Ch € 2. **Surface:** asphalted. 01/01-31/12.
Distance: on the spot.
Remarks: Max. 3 nights, coins at tourist info.

Saint-Antoine 27E1

GPS: n44,03587 e0,84209.

10 free Chfree. **Location:** Rural, simple, quiet.
Surface: asphalted.
Distance: 200m 4,3km 200m.

Saint-Antonin-Noble-Val 24F3

Chemin de Roumégous. **GPS:** n44,15222 e1,75139.

15 free Chfree. **Location:** Rural, simple, quiet.
Surface: asphalted/gravel. 01/01-31/12.

FR

Distance: 200m 300m 100m on the spot.

Saint-Bertrand-de-Comminges 27D3

Parking Cathédrale, D26a. **GPS**: n43,02944 e0,57221.

25 free WC. **Location:** Rural, quiet. **Surface:** asphalted/grassy.
01/01-31/12.
Distance: 200m 200m 3km on the spot on the spot.

Saint-Céré 24G2

Rue du Stade. **GPS**: n44,86139 e1,88583.

3 free Ch free. **Location:** Simple, central. **Surface:** asphalted.
01/01-31/12.
Distance: 200m 200m 150m.
Remarks: Behind stadium, nearby cemetery.

Saint-Chély-d'Apcher 25A2

Parking du Péchaud, Boulevard G. d'Apcher, N9.
GPS: n44,80084 e3,27296.

2 free €2/100liter Ch €2/10minutes.
Location: Simple, central, quiet. **Surface:** asphalted.
01/01-31/12.
Distance: 200m 2,5km 200m 200m on the spot.
Remarks: Coins at tourist info.

Saint-Cirq-Lapopie 24F3

Porte Roques, D662. **GPS**: n44,47055 e1,68050.

40 € 7,50 €2/100liter Ch €2 WC €2.
Location: Isolated, quiet. **Surface:** grassy/gravel. 01/01-31/12.
Distance: 1,5km on the spot 50m.
Remarks: Along Lot river, near campsite, max. 48h.

Tourist information Saint-Cirq-Lapopie:

Village, entirely under preservation order, has been built on a rock above the river Lot.

Grotte de Pech-Merle, Cabrerets. Temple cave, monument from the Paleolithicum with images of mammoth, horses and bizons.

Saint-Clar 27E1

Aire de repos, Avenue de la Garlepe. **GPS**: n43,89111 e0,77250.

10 free Ch WC free. **Location:** Comfortable, isolated, quiet.
Surface: grassy/gravel. 01/01-31/12.
Distance: 500m 250m.

Saint-Côme-d'Olt 24H3

Rue des Ginestes. **GPS**: n44,51647 e2,82072.
9 Ch . 01/01/-31/12.
Distance: 500m 500m 500m.
Remarks: Coins at tourist info and supermarket.

Saint-Couat-d'Aude 27H2

La Bellevue. **GPS**: n43,21429 e2,63052.
€ 5 €3 Ch €3 WC . **Location:** Comfortable, isolated, quiet.

Saint-Cyprien 32H1

Aire du Théâtre de la Mer, Quai Arthur Rimbaud.
GPS: n42,61776 e3,03512.

49 € 12,50/24h15/10-31/03 € 10,15/24h Ch included.
Location: Comfortable. **Surface:** asphalted.
01/01-31/12 service 15/10-31/03.
Distance: 450m marina 300m.

Saint-Cyprien-sur-Dourdou 24G3

La Citarelle. **GPS**: n44,54782 e2,40844.
13 € 5 Ch. **Surface:** grassy/gravel. 01/01-31/12.
Distance: on the spot 350m.

Saint-Félix-Lauragais 27F2

Lac de Lenclas, D622. **GPS**: n43,42667 e1,89806.

10 free Ch WC. **Location:** Simple, isolated, quiet.
Surface: gravel. 01/01-31/12.
Distance: 100m 100m.
Remarks: Max. 24h.

Saint-Geniez-d'Olt 24H3

Avenue de la gare. **GPS**: n44,46305 e2,97563.

10 free WC free. **Surface:** gravel. 01/01-31/12.
Distance: on the spot on the spot on the spot on the spot on the spot.
Remarks: Max. 24h.

Saint-Géry 24F3

Domaine du Porche, D662. **GPS**: n44,47818 e1,58091.
15 € 5,50 €2/100liter Ch €2/1h. **Surface:** gravel.
01/01-31/12.

Distance: 100m 100m.
Remarks: Market on Sunday.

Saint-Gilles 28B2

Quai du Canal. **GPS**: n43,67154 e4,43281.

free. **Location:** Rural. **Surface:** asphalted. 01/01-31/12.
Distance: 500m 200m 500m.

Tourist information Saint-Gilles:

Abbay St.Gilles. Abbey with underground church.

Saint-Girons 27E3

Rue Aristide Berges. **GPS**: n42,98865 e1,13852.

7 free €2/150liter Ch €2/15minutes. **Surface:** asphalted.
Distance: 100m.
Remarks: Max. 48h.

Saint-Jean-du-Gard 28B1

Av. de la Résistance. **GPS**: n44,10210 e3,88347.

20 free Ch WC free. **Location:** Urban, simple.
Surface: metalled. 01/01-31/12.
Distance: on the spot 100m 100m 50m 300m on the spot.
Remarks: Tourist train.

Saint-Jean-et-Saint-Paul 27H1

Saint Jean d'Alcas. **GPS**: n43,92646 e3,00887.
10 free Ch WC free. **Surface:** gravel. 01/01-31/12.
Distance: on the spot.

Saint-Just-sur-Viaur 27G1

Parking La Fabrie, D532. **GPS**: n44,12402 e2,37588.

4 free Ch WC free. **Location:** Rural, isolated, quiet.
Surface: gravel. 01/01-31/12 service 01/11-31/03.
Distance: 10km on the spot on the spot.

Saint-Lary-Soulan 27D3

Parking du Stade, Route de Vieille Aure. **GPS**: n42,82248 e0,32329.

FR

44 € 6/night € 2/100liter Ch €2/h.
Location: Rural, simple, noisy. **Surface:** asphalted.
01/01-31/12.
Distance: 500m 500m 500m on the spot on the spot.
Remarks: Parking behind stadium.

S Saint-Laurent-de-Carnols 25C3

Cave Coopérative Vinicole, Route de Bagnols D166.
GPS: n44,21002 e4,53132.
5 free Ch. 01/01-31/12.
Distance: 200m.

S Saint-Laurent-de-Cerdans 32G1

Parking Halle Polyvalente, Place du Syndicat.
GPS: n42,38336 e2,61572.

15 free ChWCfree. **Location:** Urban, simple, quiet.
Surface: gravel. 01/01-31/12.
Distance: 500m 100m 500m on the spot.
Remarks: Max. 48h.

Saint-Mamert-du-Gard 28B1

Rue des Fraisses. **GPS**: n43,88965 e4,19039.

6 free. **Location:** Simple. **Surface:** asphalted. 01/01-31/12.
Distance: 400m.

S Saint-Mamert-du-Gard 28B1

Route du Stade. **GPS**: n43,88491 e4,19054.
Chfree. 01/01-31/12.

S Saint-Mamet 27D3

Rue Pierre Baysse, D27. **GPS**: n42,78399 e0,60393.

7 € 5 Chfree. **Location:** Rural, quiet. **Surface:** asphalted.
01/01-31/12.
Distance: 200m 850m 150m.
Remarks: Next to cemetery, max. 3 nights, to be paid at town hall.

S Saint-Marsal 32G1

GPS: n42,53755 e2,62242.

25 € 3 free. **Location:** Rural, simple. **Surface:** asphalted.
01/01-31/12.
Distance: on the spot.

S Saint-Martin-de-Londres 28A1

Rue des Sapeurs. **GPS**: n43,79046 e3,73470.

6 € 4 included. **Location:** Simple. 01/01-31/12.
Distance: 150m on the spot.

S Saint-Martory 27E2

Place Nationale, D52E, D117. **GPS**: n43,14141 e0,93033.

7 free ChWCfree. **Surface:** asphalted. Thu (market).
Distance: 3km.
Remarks: Along river, max. 1 night.

S Saint-Mathieu-de-Tréviers 28B1

D17. **GPS**: n43,76206 e3,86016.

8 € 5 Ch included. **Surface:** gravel. 01/01-31/12.
Distance: 1km.
Remarks: Check in at gymnasium.

Saint-Maurice-en-Quercy 24G2

Place de l'église. **GPS**: n44,74306 e1,94722.

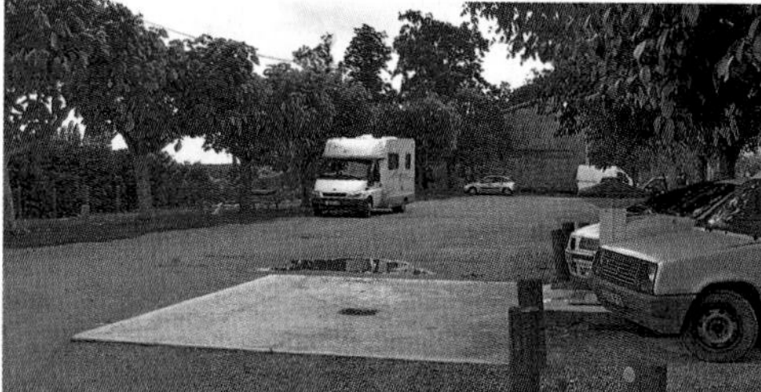

10 free.
Location: Simple, quiet. **Surface:** gravel. 01/01-31/12.

S Saint-Nicolas-de-la-Grave 27E1

Rue de la Calle. **GPS**: n44,06379 e1,02471.

free Chfree. **Surface:** asphalted/gravel. 01/01-31/12.
Distance: 100m 50m 100m.

S Saint-Puy 27D1

Grande Rue, D654. **GPS**: n43,87611 e0,46250.

3 free ChWCfree. **Surface:** gravel. 01/01-31/12.
Distance: 20m 50m 20m.

S Saint-Sauveur-Camprieu 28A1

D710 Maison du Bois. **GPS**: n44,10843 e3,48304.
6 free € 2/100liter Ch. **Location:** Rural, isolated.
01/01-31/12.
Distance: on the spot.
Remarks: Altitude 1000m.

S Saint-Thibéry 28A2

Domaine de la Vière, Chemin de la Vière.
GPS: n43,38301 e3,40137.

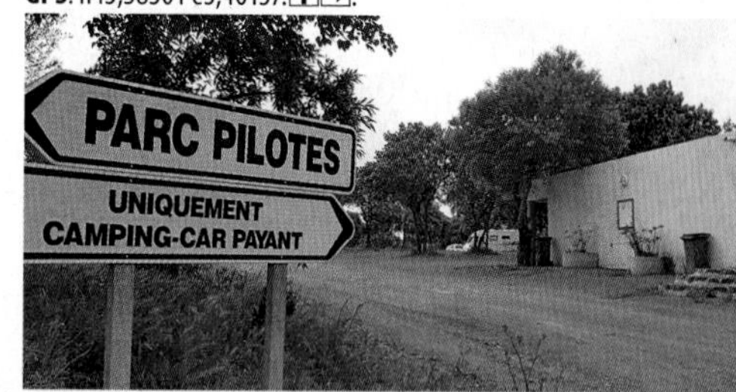

26 € 10 Ch WC included. **Location:** Rural, comfortable, isolated. **Surface:** unpaved. 01/01-31/12.
Distance: 2km A9 3km 14km 3km 4km.
Remarks: During the weekend possible inconvenience of motocross.

S Saint-Thomas 27E2

Ferme Le Gros, D58. **GPS**: n43,50190 e1,07451.
10 € 3 Ch included. **Location:** Rural.
Surface: grassy/gravel.
Distance: 2km.

S Sainte-Croix-Volvestre 27E3

Lenclos. **GPS**: n43,12673 e1,17094.

free Chfree. **Location:** Simple, isolated, quiet.
Surface: grassy/gravel. 01/01-31/12.
Remarks: At football ground.

S Sainte-Eulalie-d'Olt 24H3

La Grave. **GPS**: n44,46466 e2,94974.

10 € 7, 15/05-15/09 € 8 Ch WC included.
Location: Rural, quiet. **Surface:** gravel. 01/01-31/12.
Distance: 300m on the spot 250m 350m.
Remarks: Along Lot river, next to campsite.

S Sainte-Geneviève-sur-Argence 24H2

Rue de l'Argence. **GPS:** n44,80194 e2,76222.

30 free €2 Ch . **Surface:** gravel. 01/01-31/12.
Distance: 300m 500m 500m 300m 300m.

S Sainte-Marie-de-Campan 27D3

Place du 19 Mars 1962, D918. **GPS:** n42,98234 e0,22821.

5 free Chfree. **Location:** Rural, simple, quiet.
Surface: asphalted. 01/01-31/12.
Distance: 100m 250m 200m on the spot on the spot.
Remarks: Max. 48h.

Salasc 28A2

Route de la Gloriette, D148. **GPS:** n43,61746 e3,31709.
2 free. 01/01-31/12.
Distance: 300m 300m.

S Salles-Curan 24H3

Aire de camping-car des Vernhes, Lac de Pareloup.
GPS: n44,20002 e2,77573.

80 € 11/24h €4 Ch (80x) WC included.
Location: Rural, comfortable, quiet. **Surface:** grassy/gravel.
01/04-31/10.
Distance: 4km on the spot on the spot 4km 4km on the spot.
Remarks: At lake, former campsite.

S Salles-sur-l'Hers 27F2

Allée des Platanes. **GPS:** n43,29194 e1,78844.

10 free Ch free. **Location:** Rural, simple, isolated, quiet.
Surface: gravel. 01/01-31/12.
Distance: on the spot 100m 100m.
Remarks: At football ground.

S Samatan 27E2

Les Rivages Base de Loisirs, Avenue de Lombez, D39.
GPS: n43,48791 e0,92616.

10 € 3 + € 0,20/pp tourist tax Ch WC included.
Surface: asphalted. 01/01-31/12.
Distance: 500m on the spot on the spot 250m 250m 250m.

S Sarrant 27E1

Route de Solomiac. **GPS:** n43,77532 e0,92822.

20 free Chfree. **Surface:** grassy/gravel. 01/01-31/12.
Distance: 150m 150m.
Remarks: In front of football stadium.

S Sauve 28B1

D999. **GPS:** n43,94017 e3,95218.

5 free Chfree. **Location:** Urban, simple, central, noisy.
Surface: metalled. 01/01-31/12.
Distance: 50m 50m on the spot.

S Sauveterre-de-Comminges 27D3

Hameau de Bruncan, D9. **GPS:** n43,03391 e0,66711.

5 € 6 Ch WC included. **Location:** Rural, simple, quiet.
Surface: grassy/gravel. 01/01-31/12.
Distance: on the spot on the spot 10km on the spot on the spot.
Remarks: Check in at bar, service passerby € 3.

S Sauveterre-de-Rouergue 24G3

Le Sardou, D997. **GPS:** n44,21613 e2,31700.

15 free Chfree €2/day WC €1,50/12minutes.
Location: Rural, comfortable, quiet. **Surface:** gravel.
01/05-31/10.
Distance: 500m 500m 500m.
Remarks: Coins at tourist info.

S Ségur 24H3

Impasse du Pré Amat. **GPS:** n44,29087 e2,83503.

3 free ChWCfree €2/6minutes. **Location:** Rural, simple.
Surface: asphalted. 01/05-31/10.
Distance: 500m 500m.
Remarks: Coins at town hall and supermarket, small pitches, covered picnic area with electricity.

S Senergues 24G3

La Ferme des Autruches, La Besse. **GPS:** n44,58861 e2,48361.
5 free, voluntary contribution Chfree. **Surface:** grassy/gravel.
01/03-30/11.
Distance: 2km.

S Sérignan-Plage 28A2

Camping-Car Park Serignan Plage. GPS: n43,26909 e3,33149.
€ 9,60, 01/07-31/08 € 12 Ch . **Surface:** grassy.
15/03-14/10.
Distance: 200m 200m.
Remarks: In front of campsite.

S Sérignan-Plage 28A2

Mini Golf du Lion, Avenue de la Plage. **GPS:** n43,26892 e3,33629.

20 € 8, 01/05-30/09 € 13 + tourist tax € 2/pp Ch WC included €4. **Location:** Rural, comfortable, quiet.
Surface: unpaved. 01/01-31/12.
Distance: 150m on the spot 150m.
Remarks: Behind restaurant, bread-service, swimming pool.

S Serres-sur-Arget 27F3

GPS: n42,96990 e1,51972.

€ 5 Ch included. **Location:** Isolated, quiet.
Surface: metalled. 01/01-31/12.
Remarks: Next to community centre.

S Sète 28A2

Parking Les 3 Digues. GPS: n43,36663 e3,61523.

FR

70 € 6,66-9,66, Jul/Aug € 11,66 €1/10minutes Ch.
Location: Rural, simple. **Surface:** gravel. 01/01-31/12.
Distance: 50m on the spot on the spot.
Remarks: Beach parking, max. 72h, 01/06-30/09 no dogs allowed on the beach.

S Sommières 28B1

Chemin de la Princesse. **GPS**: n43,78701 e4,08717.

25 free €3 Ch. **Location:** Simple. **Surface:** gravel.
Distance: 500m 100m 300m.
Remarks: In front of campsite municipal.

S Souillac 24F2

Parking de Baillot, Chemin de Baillot. **GPS**: n44,89139 e1,47667.

20 free €3 Ch €3.
Surface: asphalted. 01/01-31/12.
Distance: 400m 4,5km 400m 500m.

Tourist information Souillac:
Bd Louis-Jean Malvy. Monastery-city, 12th century, between the regions Périgord and Quercy.

S Soulom 27C3

Place des Fêtes, D921. **GPS**: n42,95611 w0,0725.

15 free free. **Location:** Rural, simple, noisy. **Surface:** asphalted. 01/01-31/12.
Distance: 200m 500m 200m 200m.

S Sousceyrac 24G2

Place des Condamines. **GPS**: n44,87255 e2,03649.

10 free Ch WCfree. **Location:** Simple, central, noisy.
Surface: asphalted. 01/04-30/10.
Distance: on the spot on the spot on the spot 100m.
Remarks: In front of town hall, max. 1 night.

S Tarbes 27D2

Aire de Service Camping-car Ambulance Didier, Avenue de la Libération. **GPS**: n43,24284 e0,06790.

30 € 10 Chincluded €2/night.
Location: Quiet. **Surface:** asphalted. 01/01-31/12.
Distance: 1km 1km 800m 1km.
Remarks: Service only: water € 2, water + electricity € 5, video surveillance.

S Thémines 24F2

Place de L'église. **GPS**: n44,74083 e1,82972.

3 Ch free. **Surface:** asphalted. 01/01-31/12.
Distance: on the spot 100m 100m.
Remarks: Near church.

S Therondels 24H2

La Cazournie. **GPS**: n44,89833 e2,75937.
10 free Chfree. **Surface:** grassy. 01/04-15/11.
Distance: on the spot 100m 100m.

S Theza 32H1

Route Départementale 914. **GPS**: n42,63763 e2,93675.
6 € 12 Ch WCincluded. 01/01-31/12.
Remarks: Service passerby € 6.

S Thues-entre-Valls 32G1

Gorges de la Carança. **GPS**: n42,52346 e2,22517.

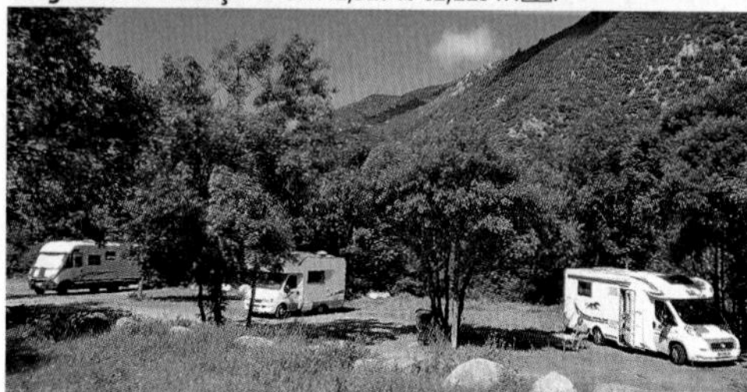

25 € 9/24h Ch included.
Location: Simple, isolated, quiet. **Surface:** grassy/gravel.
01/01-31/12 frost.
Distance: 2km on the spot on the spot on the spot.

S Trouillas 32H1

Les Oliviers de la Canterrane, Solt de las Moles, D612.
GPS: n42,61399 e2,81599.

20 free Chfree. **Location:** Rural, isolated, quiet.
Surface: gravel. 01/01-31/12.
Distance: 500m 4km on the spot.

S Vabre 27G1

Route de Castres. **GPS**: n43,69401 e2,42595.

free Chfree. **Surface:** asphalted.
Distance: 500m 500m on the spot on the spot.
Remarks: Tenniscourt, swimming pool (summer).

S Vabres-l'Abbaye 27H1

Le Coustel, Rue de la Vigne. **GPS**: n43,94575 e2,83957.
15 free Chfree. **Surface:** gravel. 01/04-30/10.
Distance: 50m on the spot on the spot.

S Vailhan 28A2

Parking de l'Eglise. **GPS**: n43,55527 e3,29882.

6 € 5 Chincluded. **Surface:** gravel. 01/01-31/12.
Distance: 1km 200m 50m.

S Valderiés 27G1

Place de Mairie, D91. **GPS**: n44,01167 e2,23333.

5 free ChWCfree. **Location:** Simple. **Surface:** asphalted.
01/01-31/12.
Distance: on the spot on the spot on the spot on the spot.
Remarks: Service 100m, weighbridge.

S Valence (Tarn-et-Garonne) 24E3

Aire de camping-car à Valence d'Agen, D953EC.
GPS: n44,10547 e0,88608.
€ 4 Ch. **Surface:** asphalted.
Distance: 600m.

S Valence (Tarn-et-Garonne) 24E3

M. Cadot, aire privée, 341, Route des Charretiers, Valence-sud.
GPS: n44,09803 e0,89043.
8 € 8 Ch included. **Location:** Rural, comfortable, isolated, quiet. **Surface:** gravel. 01/01-31/12.
Distance: 1,2km 1,2km 1,2km.

S Valence-sur-Baïse 27D1

Route d'Auch, D930. **GPS**: n43,87272 e0,38787.

7 free ChWCfree. **Location:** Simple, noisy. **Surface:** gravel.
01/01-31/12.
Distance: 500m 500m 500m on the spot.

S Vallabrègues 28C1

Route d'Aramon, D183A. **GPS**: n43,85763 e4,62639.

FR

5 free €2 Ch €2/h. **Location:** Rural. **Surface:** gravel.
01/01-31/12 high water.
Distance: 500m.
Remarks: At lake and along the Rhone river.

S Valleraugue 28A1

Avenue de l'Aigoual, D986. **GPS**: n44,08054 e3,63613.
6 free €2 Ch. **Surface:** asphalted. 01/01-31/12.
Distance: 450m.

S Valras-Plage 28A2

Avenue du Casino. **GPS**: n43,24230 e3,28162.

30 free €2 Ch. **Surface:** asphalted/metalled.
01/10-30/06 summer.
Distance: on the spot 200m on the spot on the spot on the spot.
Remarks: Behind casino/disco, service: Boulevard Pierre Giraud 200m, no camping activities.

S Valras-Plage 28A2

Boulevard de la Recanette. **GPS**: n43,25310 e3,29623.
20 € 12 Ch (9x)included. **Surface:** gravel.
Distance: 800m 800m 800m.

S Vénerque 27F2

Allée du Duc de Ventadour. **GPS**: n43,43356 e1,44021.

10 free Ch free. **Surface:** gravel/metalled.
Distance: on the spot.

S Vernet-les-Bains 32G1

Chemin de la Laiterie. **GPS**: n42,54268 e2,39092.

7 free €2,50/20minutes Ch €2,50/20minutes.
Location: Rural, simple, quiet. **Surface:** gravel.
01/03-31/10.
Distance: 600m on the spot 600m.
Remarks: Coins at tourist info and town hall.

S Vers 24F3

Halte Nautique. **GPS**: n44,48551 e1,55503.

20 € 5 Ch WC free.
Surface: grassy. 01/05-30/09.
Distance: 100m 100m 200m 100m on the spot on the spot.

S Vézénobres 28B1

Parc Audibal. **GPS**: n44,03851 e4,14118.
3 € 7 Ch included. 01/01-31/12.

Vézins-de-Lévézou 24H3

La Ferme du Lévézou, Les Vialettes du Ram.
GPS: n44,26275 e2,92293.

6 free. **Location:** Rural, isolated, quiet. **Surface:** gravel.
Distance: 6km 25km.
Remarks: Max. 24h, regional products.

S Vias 28A2

Aire de l'Espagnac, 2080 chemin de Portiragnes.
GPS: n43,31013 e3,36226.
27 Ch €3 included. **Surface:** grassy/gravel.
01/01-31/12.
Distance: 9km.

S Vic-en-Bigorre 27D2

Rue du Stade, Avenue de Pau D6. **GPS**: n43,38472 e0,04917.

4 free Ch free. **Location:** Rural, noisy. **Surface:** gravel.
01/01-31/12.
Distance: 500m 300m 50m 50m.

S Vicdessos 27F3

GPS: n42,76891 e1,50257.

20 € 6 Ch included.
Surface: metalled. 01/01-31/12.
Distance: on the spot.

S Villasavary 27G2

Camping-Car Park des Collines, Zone du Pradel.
GPS: n43,21881 e2,03242.

11 € 8,40, 01/07-31/08 € 9,60 Ch included.
Location: Rural, comfortable, isolated, quiet. **Surface:** asphalted.
01/01-31/12.
Distance: 650m 10km on the spot.
Remarks: Video surveillance.

S Villecomtal-sur-Arros 27D2

Rue de la Fontaine. **GPS**: n43,40286 e0,19852.

15 free €1,50/100liter Ch €1,50/h. **Location:** Rural, simple, quiet. **Surface:** gravel. 01/01-31/12.
Distance: on the spot 100m 200m 50m.
Remarks: Coins at townhall and bakery.

Villefranche-de-Rouergue 24G3

Parking des Ruelles, Traverse des Ruelles.
GPS: n44,35111 e2,03333.

3 free. **Location:** Urban, simple, noisy. **Surface:** asphalted.
01/01-31/12.
Distance: 100m 100m 100m.

Tourist information Villefranche-de-Rouergue:
place Notre Dame. Thu.

S Villeneuve (Aveyron) 24G3

La Coustone. **GPS**: n44,44104 e2,03737.

10 € 7 Ch (4x) WC included. **Location:** Rural, simple, quiet. **Surface:** gravel. 12/04-01/11.
Distance: 200m 200m 200m.

S Villeneuve-lès-Maguelone 28B2

Avenue René Poitevin. **GPS**: n43,52980 e3,86584.

26 € 9, 01/05-14/09 € 15/24h Ch included.
Location: Rural. **Surface:** asphalted. 01/01-31/12.
Distance: 500m 8km 2,5km 500m 250m 50m on

FR

the spot.
Remarks: 26/04-30/09: also cash payment at office de tourisme (200m).

S Villeneuve-Minervois 27G2

Avenue du Jeu de Mail. **GPS**: n43,31516 e2,46432.

20 free Ch WC. **Surface:** asphalted/metalled.
01/01-31/12.
Distance: on the spot on the spot on the spot.
Remarks: In front of town hall, max. 48h.

S Vinça 32G1

Portes du Canigou. GPS: n42,64939 e2,53184.
35 € 10,80-12 Ch (32x) included.
Surface: metalled. 01/01-31/12.
Distance: 650m on the spot on the spot 100m 650m 500m on the spot on the spot.
Remarks: Video surveillance.

Tourist information Vinça:
Office de Tourisme, Place Bernard Alart, www.ville-vinca.fr. Catalan city on a lake of 10ha.

Andorra

S Pas de la Casa 32F1

Avinguda del Consell General. **GPS**: n42,54468 e1,73525.
20-8h € 2,10 . **Surface:** metalled.

S Sant-Julia-de-Lòria 32F1

Carretera de la Rabassa. **GPS**: n42,46573 e1,49462.

4 € 0,50/h, 20.00-08.00 free Ch (4x) included.
Surface: asphalted. 01/01-31/12.
Distance: 1km.

Provence-Alpes-Côte d'Azur

S Allos 25F3

Les Prés. **GPS**: n44,24289 e6,62220.

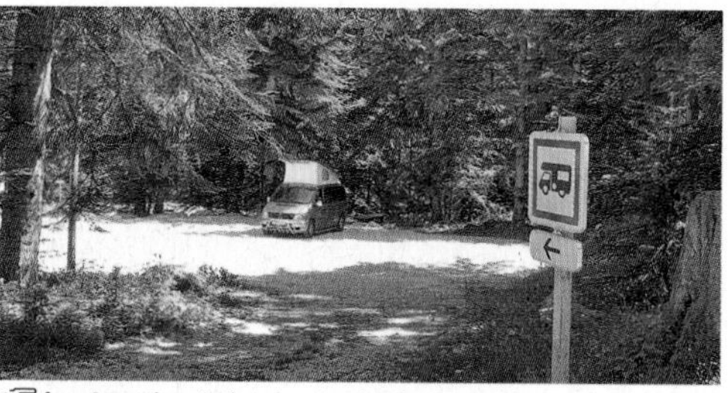

30 € 6 Ch (9x) included WC. **Surface:** asphalted.
01/01-31/12.
Distance: 500m 200m 500m 500m 200m 200m.
Remarks: Max. 72h.

Allos 25F3

Parking de la Cluite. GPS: n44,24677 e6,66918.

6 free. **Location:** Isolated, quiet. **Surface:** gravel.
Distance: Allos 6,5km.
Remarks: Isolated parking, jul/Aug shuttle bus to Lac d'Allos.

S Allos 25F3

La Foux d'Allos. **GPS**: n44,29583 e6,56944.

5 free Ch WC free. **Surface:** asphalted.
Distance: 1km 100m 100m Skibus 50m 50m.

S Annot 28F1

Chemin de la Colle Basse. **GPS**: n43,96351 e6,66386.

20 free Ch free. **Surface:** grassy/gravel. 01/01-31/12.
Distance: 400m 400m 400m.

S Arles 28C2

Quai Kalymnos, Avenue de la Camargue. **GPS**: n43,67796 e4,61802.
€ 5, overnight stay free Ch. 01/01-31/12.
Distance: city centre ± 1km 300m.
Remarks: Along the Rhone river.

Tourist information Arles:
Office de Tourisme, Boulevard des Lices, www.tourisme.ville-arles.fr. City on the border of the nature reserve Camargue with Roman ruin. The painter Van Gogh lived in Arles, 1888-89.
Église St.Trophine. Romanesque and Gothic construction.
Palais Constantin. Large Roman imperial palace of which only the baths are left.

S Avignon 28C1

Aire de camping-car Pont dÁvignon, 10 chemin de la Barthelasse.
GPS: n43,95691 e4,80184.
35 € 11,50-18,50, tourist tax incl €2,50 Ch €2,50.
Surface: grassy. 05/03-01/11.
Distance: city centre 1,5km 200m 200m on the spot on the spot.

P Avignon 28C1

Chemin de l'Ile Piot. **GPS**: n43,95167 e4,79361.

20 free. **Surface:** asphalted. 01/01-31/12.
Distance: 800m 800m 800m on the spot.
Remarks: Max. 24h, free bus to centre every ten minutes.

Tourist information Avignon:
Office de Tourisme, 41, cours Jean Jaurès, www.ot-avignon.fr. Roman city dominated by the Palais du Papes. 01/04-31/08, 01/10-31/10 9-17h, 01/09-30/09 9-20h, 01/11-31/03 9-12.45h, 14-18h.
Place d'Horloge. Cosy square in the old centre of the city.
Pont Saint Bénézet. Known as the Pont d'Avignon, bridge over the river Rhône.
Petit Palais. Former residence of the archbishop.

S Bagnols-en-Fôret 28F2

Parc de Notre-Dame Les Merles, 1 chemin des Meules, D47.
GPS: n43,53590 e6,68893.

15 € 5 €4 . **Location:** Rural, comfortable, isolated, quiet.
Surface: grassy. 01/01-31/12.
Distance: 1km 1km 1km on the spot.

S Banon 28D1

Espace de la Grand Fontaine, Rue de la Grande Fontaine.
GPS: n44,03982 e5,63006.

± 15 € 3/24h Ch free WC. **Location:** Rural, simple.
Surface: gravel/metalled.
Distance: 250m 250m 100m on the spot on the spot.
Remarks: Max. 7 days, tuesday morning market.

S Banon 28D1

Fontaine de Crême, Route de La Rochegiron D112.
GPS: n44,05960 e5,66880.
€ 10 included €3 . 01/01-31/12.
Distance: 3km on the spot on the spot.
Remarks: Regional products.

S Barcelonnette 25F3

Parking du Bouguet, Chemin des Alpages.
GPS: n44,38222 e6,65778.

15 € 6 €2/100liter Ch €2/1h . **Location:** Isolated, quiet.
Surface: grassy. 01/01-31/12.
Distance: 500m 200m 500m 500m.

Barcelonnette 25F3

GPS: n44,38717 e6,64626.
3 free. **Location:** Simple. **Surface:** asphalted. 01/01-31/12.
Distance: 500m 500m 600m.
Remarks: Max. 48h.

S Bédoin 28D1

Chemin des Sablières. **GPS**: n44,12472 e5,17167.

€ 3 €2/10minutes,only 2-euro coins Ch free €2/55minutes,only 2-euro coins.
Location: Rural, simple, quiet. **Surface:** grassy/metalled.

FR

01/01-31/12.
Distance: 600m 600m 600m Mont-Ventoux on the spot.
Remarks: Next to campsite La Pinède, max. 3 nights.

Bollène 25C3

Centre Leclerc, Route de Saint Paul Trois Châteaux, D26.
GPS: n44,32222 e4,74306.

free Chfree. 01/01-31/12.
Distance: 4,3km.
Remarks: Service only during opening hours shop.

Tourist information Bollène:
Village Troglodyte. Cave dwelling village. 01/04-31/10 9.30-19h, 01/11-31/03 Sa-Su, holidays, vacation 14-18h 01/12-31/01.

Briançon 25F2

Parc des Sports, Rue Jean Moulin. **GPS**: n44,89028 e6,62883.
4 free €2/100liter Ch €2.
Surface: asphalted.
Distance: 1km.
Remarks: At sports park, max. 24h.

Tourist information Briançon:
Office de Tourisme, 1, place du Temple, www.ot-briancon.fr. Highest city of Europe, fortress is now a tourist centre, in winter as winter sports resort and in summer parapente, rafting and biking.
Parc des Écrins. Nature reserve.

Caille 28F1

Aire de Caille, Chemin de la Plaine. **GPS**: n43,77893 e6,73331.

3 free €4/15minutes Ch €2/15minutes.
Location: Simple, quiet. **Surface:** asphalted.
01/01-31/12.
Distance: 50m 50m 100m on the spot 10km 150m.

Carpentras 28C1

Parking de Coubertin, Avenue de Coubertin.
GPS: n44,04398 e5,05372.

8 free Chfree.
Location: Urban, simple. **Surface:** asphalted.
Distance: 1,5km.
Remarks: At sports centre P.de Coubertin, max. 24h.

Tourist information Carpentras:
Hôtel Dieu. Former hospital, 18th century.
Centre-ville. Fri-morning.

Carro 28C2

Quai Jean Verandy. **GPS**: n43,32931 e5,04076.

70 € 6,30, 01/04-30/06 € 8,40, 01/07-31/08 € 10,50 Ch included. **Location:** Comfortable, central, quiet. **Surface:** gravel.
01/01-31/12.
Distance: on the spot on the spot on the spot 200m 200m.
Remarks: Max. 72h, fish sales from 08h.

Carry-le-Rouet 28D2

Avenue Pierre Sémard. **GPS**: n43,33829 e5,15921.

4 free. **Location:** Simple, noisy. **Surface:** asphalted.
01/01-31/12.
Distance: 1km 1km 500m.
Remarks: Nearby police station, max. 48h.

Castellane 28F1

Ancienne Route de Grasse. **GPS**: n43,84600 e6,51471.

28 € 6,50 Chincluded WC. **Surface:** asphalted.
01/01-31/12.
Distance: 100m.
Remarks: Directly at the river, near Pont du Roc.

Castellane 28F1

Route de Digne. **GPS**: n43,85468 e6,50159.
25 € 5,50 Chincluded €3. **Surface:** grassy/metalled.
01/01-01/11.
Distance: 800m 800m 500m on the spot.
Remarks: At museum.

Castellane 28F1

Supermarché Casino. **GPS**: n43,85222 e6,50791.
6 free €2 Ch. **Surface:** metalled. 01/01-31/12.
Distance: 400m 300m on the spot 400m.

Tourist information Castellane:
Sa-morning.

Cavalière 28F3

Avenue du Cap Nègre, D559. **GPS**: n43,15228 e6,43078.

50 € 16-18 Ch included. **Surface:** sand.
Distance: 50m 50m 50m 200m.

Château-Arnoux-Saint-Auban 28E1

Avenue Gén. de Gaulle, N85. **GPS**: n44,09543 e6,01022.

+10 free Chfree. **Location:** Urban, central, noisy.
Surface: asphalted.
Distance: on the spot 2,3km.
Remarks: Max. 48h, service 50m.

Chorges 25E3

Place du champ de foire. **GPS**: n44,54600 e6,28008.

10 free free. **Surface:** gravel. 01/01-31/12.
Distance: 400m 400m 1km.
Remarks: Max. 12h.

Tourist information Chorges:
Lac de Serre Ponçon, Serre Ponçon. Clear blue artificial lake, many water sports.

Colmars-les-Alpes 25F3

Parking de la Lance, La Bourgade. **GPS**: n44,17943 e6,62695.

10 free €2 Ch. **Surface:** asphalted. 01/01-31/12.
Distance: 300m 50m 50m 300m 300m.
Remarks: Max. 24h, tuesday market.

Comps-sur-Artuby 28F1

La Grange du Roux, D955. **GPS**: n43,70652 e6,50678.

10 free €3 ChWC. **Location:** Rural, comfortable, isolated, quiet. **Surface:** gravel. 01/01-31/12.
Distance: 350m pizzeria/crêperie 50m 350m.
Remarks: Coins at the shops.

Crots 25F3

Park de Crots, Plage de Canterenne. **GPS**: n44,53830 e6,45489.
40 € 10,80-9,60 Ch (16x) included.
Surface: metalled. 01/01-31/12.
Distance: 1km 100m 500m on the spot on the spot.
Remarks: Historical centre.

Cuges-les-Pins 28E2

Le Jardin de la Ville. **GPS**: n43,28150 e5,70558.

FR

10 €3 €1,50 Ch. **Location:** Rural, comfortable, isolated, quiet. **Surface:** grassy/gravel. 01/01-31/12.
Distance: 500m 500m 500m.
Remarks: Monitored parking.

Tourist information Cuges-les-Pins:
Musée Légion Etrangères, Aubagne. Museum about the French Foreign Legion.

Dauphin 28E1

Route de la Rencontre. **GPS**: n43,90028 e5,78417.

4 free.
Location: Rural, simple, quiet. **Surface:** metalled.
Distance: 300m 300m on the spot on the spot.
Remarks: Near Salle des Fêtes.

Digne-les-Bains 28E1

La Halle des Sports, Avenue René Cassin. **GPS**: n44,08280 e6,22170.

20 free €2,50/10minutes Ch. **Surface:** gravel. 01/01-31/12 during fair.
Distance: city centre 1,4km.

Digne-les-Bains 28E1

Le Vallon des Sources, Avenue des Thermes.
GPS: n44,07998 e6,26091.

25 free €2 Ch. 01/01-31/12.
Distance: 2,5km 750m 2km 100m.
Remarks: Coins available at pay-desk of theTherme.

Ensuès-la-Redonne 28D2

Avenue de la Côte Bleue. **GPS**: n43,35530 e5,18915.

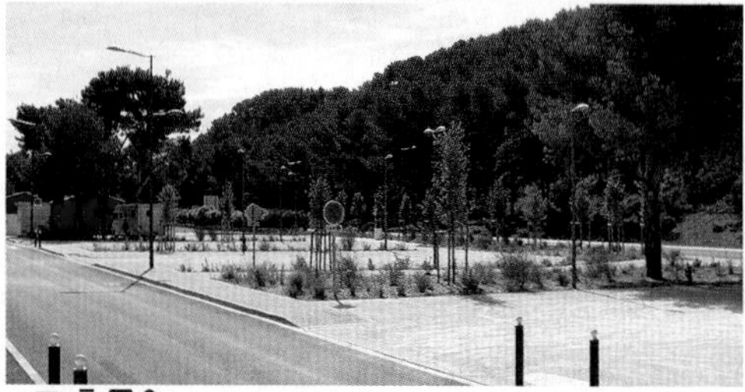

20 Chfree. **Location:** Isolated, noisy. **Surface:** gravel. 01/01-31/12.
Distance: 1,2km 3km 1km 1km 100m.

Esparron de Verdon 28E1

D82. **GPS**: n43,74233 e5,97366.

7 free . **Location:** Rural, simple.
Distance: 500m 500m 500m 500m on the spot.

Fayence 28F2

Allée des Jardins. **GPS**: n43,62308 e6,68982.

2 free €4 Ch. **Location:** Simple, central, noisy.
Surface: asphalted.
Distance: 750m 750m 300m.
Remarks: At tennis-court and swimming pool, max. 48h.

Fontaine-de-Vaucluse 28D1

Camping-Car Park, Route de Cavaillon. **GPS**: n43,92024 e5,12452.

€12 Ch (2x) included. **Location:** Rural, comfortable, quiet. **Surface:** gravel/metalled. 01/01-31/12.
Distance: 500m 500m on the spot on the spot.

Fontvieille 28C1

Parking du Moulin de Daudet, Allée des Pins.
GPS: n43,72000 e4,71200.

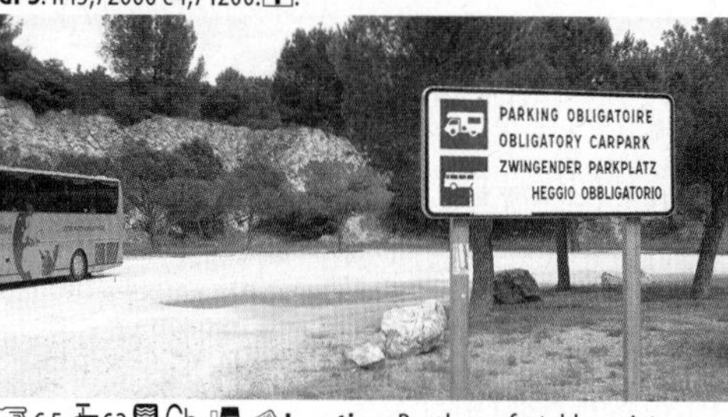

€5 €2 Ch. **Location:** Rural, comfortable, quiet.
Surface: gravel.
Distance: 800m 800m.

Gap 25E3

Parking Dumont, Avenue Commandant Dumont, N85.
GPS: n44,56544 e6,08447.

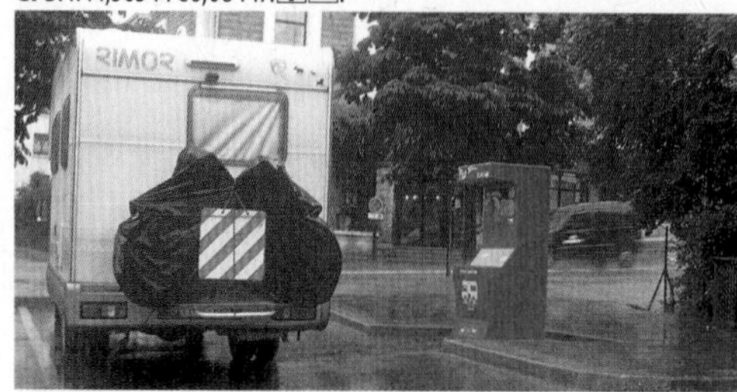

3 free €3 Ch €3 . **Surface:** asphalted.
Distance: 500m on the spot on the spot.
Remarks: Stay overnight allowed at other pitches.

Gap 25E3

Avenue d'Embrun 93. **GPS**: n44,56958 e6,10249.
6 free Chfree. **Surface:** metalled. 01/01-01/11.
Distance: 800m 100m 100m 50m.
Remarks: Free bus to centre.

Gémenos 28D2

Cours Sudre. **GPS**: n43,29772 e5,62953.

3 free ChWCfree. **Location:** Central, quiet.
Surface: metalled. 01/01-31/12.
Distance: 100m 100m 100m 50m.
Remarks: Near office de tourisme, max. 24h.

Gigondas 28C1

Domaine des Florets, Route des Dentelles, D80.
GPS: n44,16220 e5,01725.

3 free free. **Location:** Rural, simple, quiet. **Surface:** gravel. 01/01-31/12.
Distance: 1,7km 500m on the spot Des Dentelles.
Remarks: Check in at tasting room.

Gordes 28D1

D2. **GPS**: n43,90056 e5,19306.

20 free.
Location: Rural, simple. **Surface:** gravel. 01/01-31/12.
Distance: 2km 2km 2km.

Greasque 28D2

Musée de la Mine, Route de Puits Hely d'Oissel.
GPS: n43,43281 e5,53439.

15 free Chfree. **Surface:** gravel. 16/01-20/12.
Distance: 600m.

Gréoux-les-Bains 28E1

Aire Camping-car, Chemin de la Barque.
GPS: n43,75562 e5,88862.

FR

80 € 10/24h Ch WC included. Location: Urban, simple, noisy. Surface: gravel. 01/01-31/12.
Distance: 150m 150m 150m on the spot.
Remarks: Max 3,5t, max. 30 days.

S Grimaud 28F2

Saint Pons Les Mûres, D98. GPS: n43,28000 e6,57806.

12 € 15 Ch included €2,50. Location: Simple, noisy.
Surface: asphalted. 01/01-31/12.
Distance: 800m 800m 200m 500m.
Remarks: Max. 72h.

S Guillaumes 28F1

D2202. GPS: n44,08861 e6,85285.

10 free €2/100liter Ch €2/1h.
01/01-31/12.
Distance: 50m on the spot on the spot 50m 50m.
Remarks: Coins at Bar-Tabac, tourist info, town hall.

S Hyères 28E3

Les Etangs de Sauvebonne, 566 Route de Pierrefeu.
GPS: n43,16220 e6,12291.

20 € 10 Ch included €3/day. Location: Rural, comfortable, quiet. Surface: grassy. 01/01-31/12.
Distance: on the spot on the spot.

Hyères 28E3

Parking des îles, Avenue des Arbannais. GPS: n43,02864 e6,15438.
4 . Location: Urban. 01/01-31/12.
Distance: 100m bakery 100m.
Remarks: At harbour.

S Jausiers 25F3

Route de Jausiers-Barcelonette, D900. GPS: n44,41266 e6,72936.

3 free €3 Ch . Surface: metalled. 01/01-31/12.
Distance: 600m 50m 100m 400m.

Jausiers 25F3

Pont de Barnuquel, Lotissement des Neiges. GPS: n44,41278 e6,72472.

20 free. Surface: unpaved. 01/01-31/12.
Distance: 600m on the spot 100m 400m.
Remarks: Service 200m.

S Jouques 28D2

Parking Saint Honorat, D11. GPS: n43,63176 e5,64414.
5 free Ch . Surface: asphalted.
Distance: 750m 750m 750m.

L'Isle-sur-la-Sorgue 28C1

Parking de la Gare, Avenue Julien Guigue.
GPS: n43,91768 e5,04686.
free. Location: Simple, noisy. Surface: gravel.
Distance: 500m 150m 700m on the spot.
Remarks: At station.

S La Bréole 25E3

Bourg La Bréole. GPS: n44,45777 e6,29194.

6 free Ch WC free. Location: Simple, quiet.
Surface: asphalted. 01/01-31/12.
Distance: on the spot 2km 2km Lac de Serre Ponçon 100m 100m.

S La Crau 28E3

Espace Lavage Auto Grand Bleu, La Moutonne.
GPS: n43,12417 e6,07444.

3 free €4 Ch. Location: Simple, noisy. Surface: concrete.
01/01-31/12.

S La Londe-les-Maures 28E3

Rond-point Ducourneau, chemin du Pansard.
GPS: n43,13185 e6,23053.

4 free €3 Ch .
Location: Simple, isolated, quiet. Surface: asphalted.
01/01-31/12.
Distance: 800m 3km 800m 800m.
Remarks: 03/07/2015 during inspection service out of order, max. 24h.

S La Martre 28F1

Chemin de Fontvieillle. GPS: n43,77233 e6,60255.

3 € 5 Ch included. Location: Comfortable, isolated, quiet.
Surface: grassy/gravel. 01/01-31/12.
Distance: 300m 300m 300m.

S La Motte 28F2

Chemin des Correns. GPS: n43,48860 e6,54212.

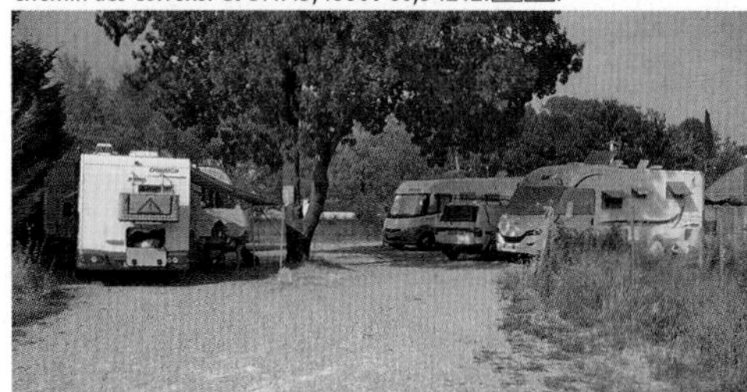

10 free €2 Ch. Location: Rural, simple, isolated, quiet.
Surface: gravel. 01/01-31/12.
Distance: 800m 300m.
Remarks: At tennis-courts, max. 24h, coins at the shops.

S La Motte 28F2

Moulin de Vallongues, Avenue Fréderique Mistral, D47.
GPS: n43,49630 e6,53134.

10 free €2/100liter Ch €2/h . Location: Isolated, quiet.
Surface: gravel. 01/01-31/12.
Distance: 600m 600m 4km.
Remarks: Max. 24h.

La Roche-des-Arnauds 25E3

D994, Chemin des Digues. GPS: n44,56134 e5,95637.

5 free. Surface: asphalted. 01/01-31/12.
Distance: 100m on the spot on the spot 100m.
Remarks: Max. 24h.

S La Salle-les-Alpes 25F2

Aire camping car Pontillas, Hameau de Bez.
GPS: n44,94805 e6,55564.
20 € 8 Ch included. Surface: metalled.
Distance: 400m 400m 400m 20m.
Remarks: Pay at tourist office.

S La Salle-les-Alpes 25F2

Chemin de l'Oratoire, Villeneuve. GPS: n44,94417 e6,55583.

FR

15 € 8, winter € 18 Ch included. **Surface:** gravel.
01/01-31/12.
Distance: 200m 50m.
Remarks: Parking at skipistes.

S Laragne-Montéglin 25E3

Avenue de Provence, D1075. **GPS**: n44,31212 e5,82543.

15 free Ch free. **Surface:** asphalted. 01/01-31/12.
Distance: 300m 300m 300m.

S Laragne-Montéglin 25E3

Intermarché, D1075. **GPS**: n44,30300 e5,83700.

30 free €2 Ch. 01/01-31/12.
Distance: 2km.

Le Lauzet-Ubay 25F3

D900. **GPS**: n44,42833 e6,43389.

10 free.
Location: Isolated, quiet. **Surface:** gravel. 01/01-31/12.
Distance: 50m 50m 50m 100m.
Remarks: At small lake.

S Le Monêtier-les-Bains 25F2

Aire camping car les Charmettes, Route des Bains.
GPS: n44,97602 e6,50933.
40 € 4,80/day + tourist tax Ch free. **Surface:** metalled.
01/01-31/12.
Distance: on the spot.
Remarks: Parking at skipistes.

S Le Thoronet 28E2

D17, boulevard du 17 aout 1944. **GPS**: n43,45097 e6,30411.

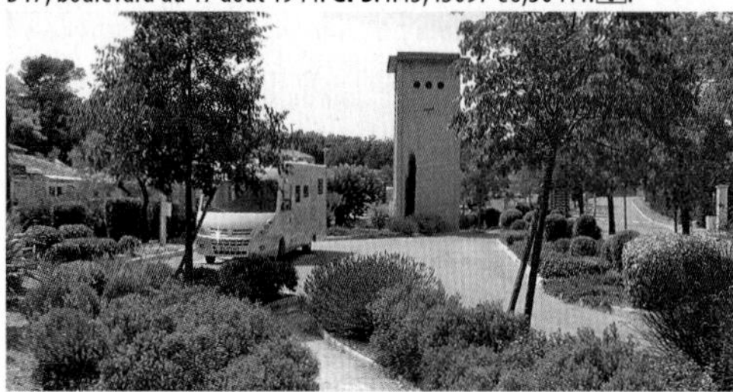

2 free €2 Ch. **Location:** Rural, simple, central, noisy.
Surface: asphalted. 01/01-31/12.
Distance: on the spot 50m.
Remarks: Max. 48h, coins at tourist info.

S Les Issambres 28F2

Chez Marcel, Plage La Gaillarde, N98. **GPS**: n43,36559 e6,71202.

40 € 11, peak season € 16 Ch included €3/day €0,50
€5/5 . **Location:** Comfortable, isolated, quiet.
Surface: gravel/sand. 01/01-31/12.
Distance: 3km 50m 200m 200m 50m.

S Les Salles-sur-Verdon 28E1

L'Ermitage, D957. **GPS**: n43,77434 e6,21773.

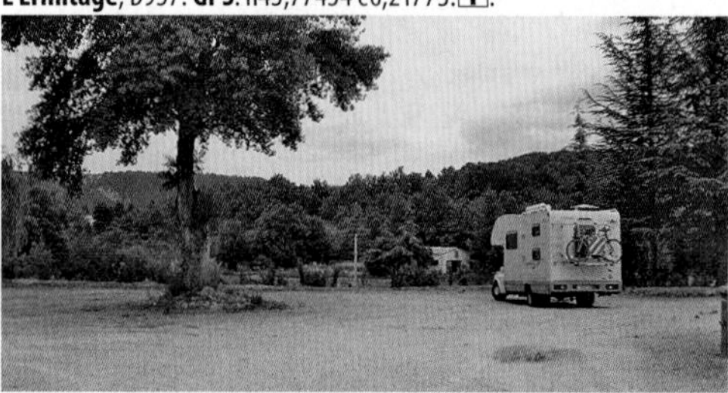

5 € 6, Jul/Aug € 8 Ch €5 included.
Location: Rural, simple. **Surface:** gravel/sand.
Distance: 700m Lac de Ste Croix 1km on the spot on the spot on the spot.
Remarks: Service passerby € 5, swimming pool incl.

S Malaucène 25D3

Avenue Charles de Gaulle. **GPS**: n44,17792 e5,12970.

40 € 3,50 excl. tourist tax Ch free.
Location: Rural, simple, noisy.
Surface: unpaved.
01/01-31/12.
Distance: 150m 150m 150m Mont-Ventoux on the spot.
Remarks: Between sports fields and gendarmerie.

Tourist information Malaucène:
Marché Provencal. Wed-morning.

S Malemort-du-Comtat 28D1

Avenue Docteur Tondut, D5. **GPS**: n44,02175 e5,15714.

free Ch free.
Location: Rural, simple. **Surface:** gravel.
Distance: 200m on the spot.
Remarks: Near Salle des Fêtes.

S Marseille 28D2

Marlyparc, Chemin de Morgiou 120. **GPS**: n43,24085 e5,40693.

40 € 12 Ch included €5 . **Location:** Urban, simple, central, quiet. **Surface:** metalled. 01/01-31/12.
Distance: 7km Marseille 3km 1km on the spot.

Ménerbes 28D1

Parking Longue Durée. GPS: n43,83193 e5,20828.

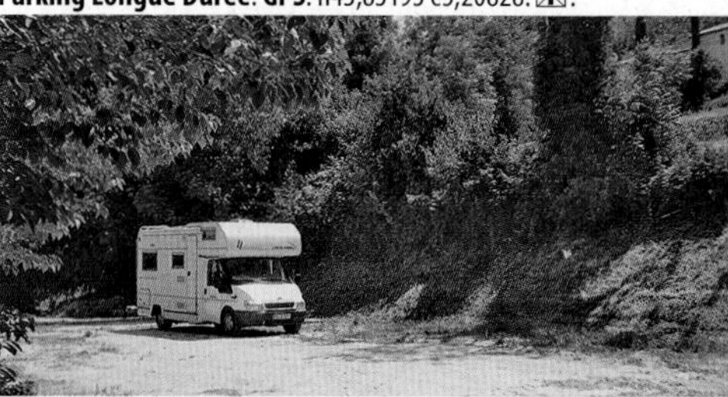

free. **Location:** Rural, simple. **Surface:** gravel.
Distance: 250m 100m on the spot.

S Montgenèvre 25F2

Aire des Marmottes. GPS: n44,93417 e6,73317.

250 € 10 Ch (80x)included. **Location:** Comfortable, isolated, quiet. **Surface:** metalled. 01/01-31/12.
Distance: 500m 500m on the spot.

S Moustiers-Sainte-Marie 28E1

P5, D952. **GPS**: n43,84361 e6,21874.

€ 8,50/night €2/10minutes Ch €2/10minutes.
Location: Rural, simple. **Surface:** gravel.
Distance: 10 min walking on the spot on the spot.
Remarks: Max. 2 nights.

S Névache 25F2

D994G. **GPS**: n45,01666 e6,64261.

free, 01/07-31/08 € 5 free. **Location:** Isolated.
Surface: grassy. 01/01-31/12.

Ollioules 28E3

Route des Gorges, DN8. **GPS**: n43,13868 e5,85002.
8 € 3. 01/04-30/09.
Distance: 600m 600m 450m.
Remarks: Max. 48h.

S Oppède-le-Vieux 28D1

Parking Oppède-le-Vieux. GPS: n43,83094 e5,15897.

2 € 5/day free WC.
Location: Rural, simple. **Surface:** gravel.
Distance: 500m 500m.

Tourist information Oppède-le-Vieux:
Hiking route through medieval top-hill village.

S Orcières-Merlette 25E2

Camping-car Casse Blanche, Pra Palier, P2.
GPS: n44,69517 e6,32567.
24 € 10/24h Ch included. **Surface:** asphalted.
01/01-31/12.
Distance: on the spot on the spot.
Remarks: Summer: pay at tourist office.

S Pélissanne 28D2

Prouvenque, Chemin de la Prouvenque.
GPS: n43,62805 e5,15307.

6 free Ch free. **Location:** Urban, simple, quiet.
Surface: asphalted.
Distance: 500m 8km.
Remarks: Parking stadium.

Plan-de-la-Tour 28F2

Parking Foch. **GPS**: n43,33787 e6,54532.

free.
Location: Simple, central, quiet. **Surface:** gravel.
Distance: on the spot 100m 150m.
Remarks: Max. 48h.

Tourist information Plan-de-la-Tour:
Thu morning 6-12h.

S Port Saint-Louis-du-Rhône 28C2

Av. de la 1 Dfl. **GPS**: n43,38424 e4,81909.

50 € 6,25 Ch included. **Location:** Simple, isolated, quiet.
Surface: asphalted/gravel. 01/01-31/12.
Distance: 1,5km 2km on the spot 1km 1,5km.
Remarks: Max. 48h.

S Pra-Loup 25F3

Parking des Choupettes. **GPS**: n44,36806 e6,60611.

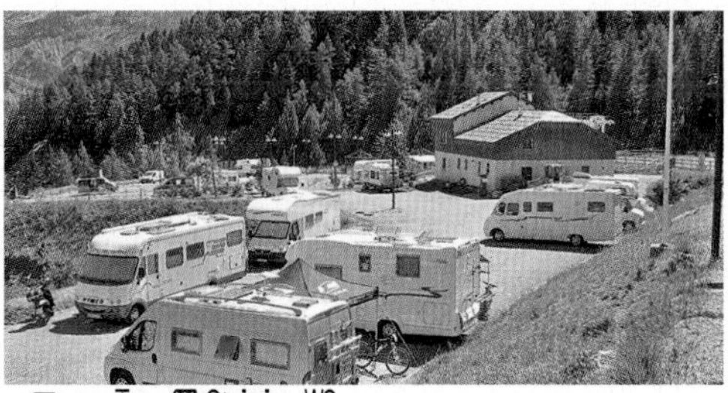

50 free €3 Ch €3 WC.
Surface: asphalted. 01/01-31/12.
Distance: 400m 400m 400m 50m.
Remarks: Parking at skipistes.

S Puget Theniers 28F1

Aire de la Condamine, Route des Grandes Alpes.
GPS: n43,95306 e6,89944.

10 € 3,50 Ch included. **Surface:** asphalted.
01/01-31/12.
Distance: 300m 20m 300m 300m.

S Puimoisson 28E1

Les Lavandins, Basses Touires. **GPS**: n43,87006 e6,12979.

40 € 5/24h €0,50/100liter.
Surface: gravel. 01/04-31/10.
Distance: 650m 650m.

S Puy-Saint-Vincent 25F2

Clôt de Saint-Romain, D4. **GPS**: n44,83245 e6,48331.
20 € 6 Ch included. 18/12-25/04.
Remarks: Altitude 1600m, max. 15 days, information at cableway.

S Puyvert 28D1

Super U, D118. **GPS**: n43,74763 e5,33727.

5 free Ch (2x)free €4. **Location:** Rural.
Surface: asphalted. 01/01-31/12.
Distance: 1,5km on the spot.
Remarks: Parking near Super-U.

S Quinson 28E1

Les Prés du Verdon, Allée des Prés du Verdon.
GPS: n43,69801 e6,03911.

5 free Ch free. **Location:** Rural, simple, quiet.
Surface: gravel/sand. 01/01-31/12.
Distance: 100m 100m 300m 500m on the spot.
Remarks: Near the prehistoric museum of the gorges du Verdon.

S Ramatuelle 28F2

Parking de Tamaris, Plage de Pamplonne, Route des Tamaris.
GPS: n43,23893 e6,66149.

60 € 5/day, € 5/night, 1/7-31/8 € 9day, € 9/night, dog € 1 Ch (20x)€7/day. **Location:** Rural. **Surface:** gravel.
Distance: on the spot on the spot on the spot.
Remarks: Beach parking.

S Ramatuelle 28F2

Parking Municipal, Plage de Pamplonne, Route de Bonne-Terrasse.
GPS: n43,21126 e6,66217.

130 € 8,20, 02/11-10/03 € 5,10 Ch WC.
Location: Rural. **Surface:** gravel. 01/04-31/10.
Distance: 200m 200m 2km.
Remarks: Beach parking, max. 48h, bread-service.

Tourist information Ramatuelle:
La place de l'Ormeau. Provencal Market. Thu, Su.

S Riez 28E1

P de l'Auvestre, Chemin du Relais. **GPS**: n43,82180 e6,09197.

30 € 5/24h Ch free. **Location:** Rural, comfortable, quiet.
Surface: gravel.
Distance: 500m 500m 100m on the spot on the spot.

Roussillon 28D1

Parking Saint Joseph, D149. **GPS**: n43,89660 e5,29593.

20 € 2/day, € 7/night. **Location:** Rural, comfortable.
Surface: gravel.
Distance: 800m 800m on the spot on the spot.
Remarks: Max. 48h, no camping activities.

Tourist information Roussillon:
Sentier des Ocres. Hiking trail, 45 min.

S Sablet 25C3

Domaine du Parandou, D977. **GPS**: n44,19325 e4,99522.

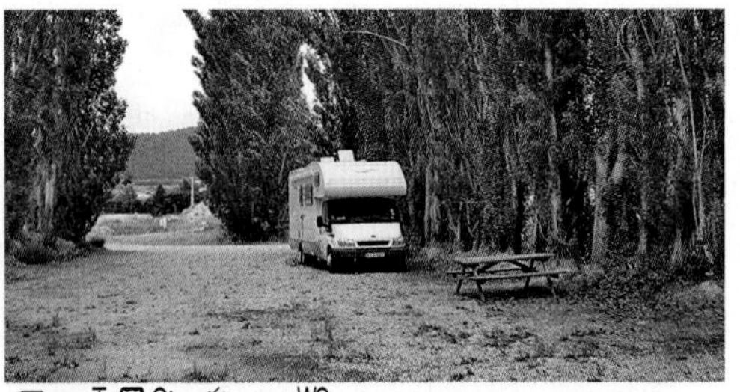

5 € 2 Ch (2x)€3 WCincluded. **Location:** Rural, simple. **Surface:** gravel. 01/01-31/12.
Distance: 2km.

Saint-André-les-Alpes 28F1

Grand Rue. **GPS**: n43,96525 e6,50735.

30 free €3/10minutes Ch. **Location:** Comfortable, quiet. **Surface:** asphalted. 01/01-31/12.
Distance: 250m 100m 250m.

Saint-Chamas 28C2

Avenue Marx Dormoy. **GPS**: n43,54636 e5,03246.
10 free Ch. **Location:** Urban, simple. **Surface:** gravel. 01/01-31/12.
Distance: on the spot on the spot.
Remarks: Near marina.

Saint-Crépin 25F2

D138. **GPS**: n44,70562 e6,60196.

€ 6 + € 0,40/pp tourist tax Ch WC included.
Location: Quiet. **Surface:** grassy. 01/01-31/12.
Distance: 500m on the spot.
Remarks: Service on the other side of the bridge.

Saint-Étienne-de-Tinée 25F3

Camping du Plan d'Eau, Boulevard de la Digue.
GPS: n44,25847 e6,92307.
6 € 10 €3 Ch. **Location:** Comfortable, quiet.
Surface: gravel. 01/06-30/09.
Remarks: At lake, in the village.

Saint-Jean-Saint-Nicolas 25E2

GPS: n44,66782 e6,23484.

Saint-Laurent-du-Var 28G1

Route des Pugets. **GPS**: n43,68584 e7,18459.

7 free Chfree. **Location:** Isolated, noisy. **Surface:** asphalted. 01/01-31/12.
Distance: 1,2km 4,5km 1,2km 1,2km.
Remarks: Max. 7 days.

Saint-Laurent-du-Var 28G1

Avenue Francis Teisseire. **GPS**: n43,66628 e7,19595.

5 free. **Location:** Simple, central, noisy. **Surface:** asphalted. 01/01-31/12.
Distance: city centre 2km 200m 600m 500m 500m 500m.
Remarks: Max. 8M.

Saint-Mandrier-sur-Mer 28E3

Pin Roland, Impasse de la Mer. **GPS**: n43,07771 e5,90444.

6 free Chfree. **Surface:** asphalted. 01/01-31/12.
Distance: 500m 500m.
Remarks: Max. 48h.

Saint-Martin-de-Crau 28C2

Place François Miterrand. **GPS**: n43,63859 e4,81454.
3 free ChWCfree. **Location:** Urban. **Surface:** metalled. 01/01-31/12.
Distance: 400m 400m 1,5km.
Remarks: In front of town hall, max. 48h.

Saint-Michel-l'Observatoire 28E1

Place du Serre. **GPS**: n43,90908 e5,71750.

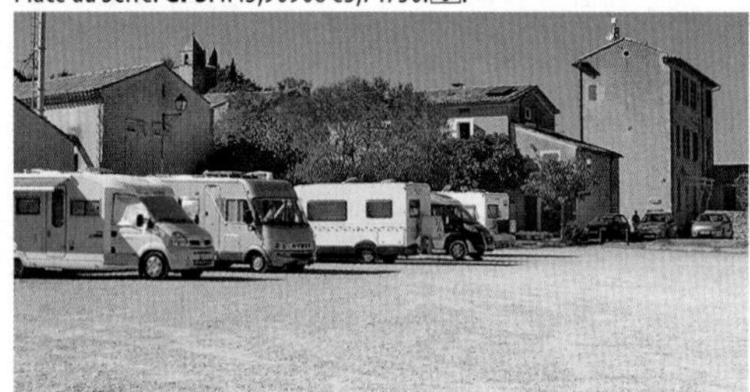

10 free.
Location: Simple. **Surface:** gravel. 01/03-15/11.
Distance: 200m 200m on the spot.
Remarks: Beautiful panorama.

Saint-Paul-lès-Durance 28E2

Rue du Camping le Retour. **GPS**: n43,68700 e5,70588.

6 free Chfree. **Location:** Rural, simple, quiet.
Surface: gravel. 01/01-31/12.
Distance: 500m 4km 500m 700m.
Remarks: Max. 48h.

Saint-Tropez 28F2

Aire camping-car, Chemin Fontaine du pin, Chemin de la Moutte.
GPS: n43,26468 e6,67227.

15 € 16 €2 Ch €2,50 WC €1. **Location:** Isolated.
Surface: grassy/sand. 01/01-31/12.
Distance: 3km 800m.

Tourist information Saint-Tropez:
La Citadelle, musée de la Marine. Navy museum.
Place des Lices. Week market. Wed + Sa morning.

Saint-Véran 25F2

D5. **GPS**: n44,70447 e6,86091.
20 € 2/day, € 5/night ChWCfree. **Location:** Isolated, quiet.
Surface: metalled. 01/01-31/12.
Distance: 100m 100m 200m on the spot 200m.

Sainte-Croix-du-Verdon 28E1

Route du Lac. **GPS**: n43,76077 e6,15102.

20 € 6,50/24h €2/10minutes ChWCincluded.
Location: Rural, simple. **Surface:** asphalted.
Distance: 100m 100m on the spot on the spot.
Remarks: Max. 3 nights, water closed during wintertime.

Sainte-Maxime 28F2

D25, le Muy dir Ste.Maxime. **GPS**: n43,31730 e6,62999.

50 € 10/24h, 01/10-31/03 € 5 Chfree. **Location:** Comfortable, quiet. **Surface:** metalled. 01/01-31/12.
Distance: city centre 1km 1,2km McDonalds 50m Lidl 200m.
Remarks: Max. 48h.

Tourist information Sainte-Maxime:
Thu-morning.
Les Greniers du Golfe, Aire des Magnoti. Bric-a-brac. Wed 08-18h.

Saintes-Maries-de-la-Mer 28B2

Avenue d'Arles, D570. **GPS**: n43,45535 e4,42750.

60 € 13 ChWCincluded. **Location:** Simple, central, quiet.
Surface: asphalted. 01/01-31/12.
Distance: 200m beach 400m 100m 50m 100m.
Remarks: Max. 48h, service: 8.30-11.30h, 16-19.30h.

Saintes-Maries-de-la-Mer 28B2

Plage Ouest, Route d'Aigues-Mortes, D38. **GPS**: n43,44991 e4,40407.

FR

50 € 12, >7.50m € 24 Ch included. **Location:** Isolated, quiet. **Surface:** asphalted/gravel. 01/01-31/12.
Distance: 1,5km 50m.
Remarks: Beach parking.

S Saintes-Maries-de-la-Mer 28B2

Valée des Lys, Parking Plage Est, Avenue Cousteau. **GPS**: n43,45364 e4,43695.

150 € 12 Ch free. **Surface:** metalled. 01/01-31/12.
Distance: 250m beach 50m 100m 250m.

CS Saintes-Maries-de-la-Mer 28B2

Camping de la Brise. **GPS**: n43,45572 e4,43620.

50 € 16 + tourist tax Ch WC included.
Location: Comfortable, central, quiet. **Surface:** grassy/gravel. 16/12-11/11.
Distance: 850m direct access to sandy beach 800m 800m on the spot on the spot.
Remarks: Max. 48h.

P Saintes-Maries-de-la-Mer 28B2

Parking du Large, Avenue du Docteur Cambon. **GPS**: n43,45430 e4,43326.

20 free.
Location: Simple, central. **Surface:** gravel.
Distance: 250m 700m 250m 250m.

P Saintes-Maries-de-la-Mer 28B2

Route de Cacharel. **GPS**: n43,45684 e4,43305.

10 free. **Location:** Simple, isolated, quiet.
Distance: 700m 750m.

S Salernes 28E2

Aire Municipal, Route des Quatre Chemins. **GPS**: n43,55923 e6,23381.

35 free Ch free. **Surface:** grassy/gravel. 01/01-31/12.
Distance: 300m.
Remarks: Max. 24h.

S Salin-de-Giraud 28C2

Rue de la Bouvine. **GPS**: n43,41222 e4,73056.

20 free € 2 Ch € 0,80.
Location: Simple, quiet. **Surface:** gravel. 01/04-31/10.
Distance: 500m 500m 500m.
Remarks: At fire-station, coins at town hall, showers only in july/aug.

S Sarrians 28C1

Avenue de la Camargue. **GPS**: n44,07943 e4,97788.

10 € 3/day Ch free . **Location:** Rural, simple. **Surface:** gravel. 01/01-31/12.
Distance: 800m 500m.

S Sault 28D1

P3, Route de Saint-Trinit. **GPS**: n44,09434 e5,41308.

15 free € 2/10minutes Ch stay. **Location:** Rural, simple. **Surface:** gravel. 01/01-31/12.
Distance: 500m 500m on the spot 4km chemin des Lavandes.

S Sausset-les-Pins 28D2

Avenue Pierre Matraja. **GPS**: n43,33890 e5,10916.

15 free € 4/100liter Ch € 4/1h. **Location:** Simple, isolated, quiet. **Surface:** asphalted. 01/01-31/12.
Distance: 1,2km 1,2km 1,2km 5m.
Remarks: At stadium, max. 72h.

S Savines-le-Lac 25F3

Parking du Barnafret, Av. du Faubourg, D954. **GPS**: n44,52495 e6,40090.

17 € 8 € 2/120liter Ch (20x). **Location:** Comfortable, central. **Surface:** asphalted.
Distance: 300m 500m 100m.

S Selonnet 25E3

Quartier de Boulangère. **GPS**: n44,36862 e6,31525.

7 free € 2/10minutes Ch € 2/55minutes .
Location: Rural. **Surface:** gravel. 01/01-31/12.
Distance: 300m 300m 300m.
Remarks: Coins at town hall, supermarket, bakery and Tabac, free wifi at town hall.

S Sénas 28D1

Avenue des Jardins. **GPS**: n43,74403 e5,08020.

6 free € 3/10minutes Ch. **Location:** Urban, simple. **Surface:** asphalted. 01/01-31/12.
Distance: 200m 1,5km 200m 200m.
Remarks: Coins at tourist info and maison de presse.

S Sillans-la-Cascade 28E2

Route de Salernes. **GPS**: n43,56692 e6,18277.
free, July-Aug € 2 € 3 Ch. 01/01-31/12.
Distance: 500m 500m.
Remarks: Free entrance swimming pool.

S Sisteron 25E3

Aire camping-cars, Avenue de la Libération. **GPS**: n44,19105 e5,94542.
12 € 2/12h € 2/20minutes Ch € 2/4h .
Surface: asphalted. 01/01-31/12.
Distance: 800m.
Remarks: Along railwayline.

S Sisteron 25E3

Parking Melchior Donnet, D4085. **GPS**: n44,20028 e5,94389.

10 free € 2 Ch € 2/12h. **Surface:** asphalted. 01/01-31/12.
Distance: 4,5km.

S Six-Fours-les-Plages 28E3

Port de la Coudoulière. **GPS**: n43,09750 e5,81194.

FR

5 € 10 WC included €2. **Location:** Central.
Surface: asphalted. 01/10-30/04.
Distance: 100m 100m 100m.

Six-Fours-les-Plages 28E3

Promenade Gén. Charles de Gaulle. **GPS**: n43,11252 e5,81172.
€3 Ch. 01/01-31/12.
Remarks: Behind tourist info, 8-12, 14-19h.

Sospel 28G1

Stade E. Donato, D2566. **GPS**: n43,87876 e7,44213.

4 free Ch free. **Surface:** asphalted. 01/01-31/12.
Distance: 300m 300m 300m.

Thorenc 28F1

Lac de Thorenc, D2. **GPS**: n43,79921 e6,80802.

10 free €5 Ch WC. **Location:** Rural, simple, isolated, quiet.
Surface: metalled. 01/01-31/12.
Distance: 750m on the spot on the spot on the spot épicerie 750m on the spot.
Remarks: Along Lake Thorenc.

Trigance 28F1

Quartier Saint Roch. **GPS**: n43,76060 e6,44255.

5 €5 Ch included. **Location:** Isolated, quiet.
Surface: asphalted/gravel. 01/01-31/12.
Remarks: Max. 2 days.

Uvernet-Fours 25F3

Losissement Le Bachelard, D902. **GPS**: n44,36816 e6,62783.

6 free €2 Ch €2. **Location:** Isolated, quiet.
Surface: gravel/sand. 01/01-31/12.
Distance: 900m.

Vaison-la-Romaine 25D3

Aire camping-car, Avenue André Coudray.
GPS: n44,24650 e5,07392.

30 € 8/24h, tourist tax € 0,55/pp Ch free.
Location: Urban, comfortable. **Surface:** gravel.
01/01-31/12 Tue-morning.
Distance: 800m.

Tourist information Vaison-la-Romaine:
Le Pont Romain. Bridge from the Roman Empire.
Le Château. Ruins of the castle of the Counts of Toulouse.
Tue.

Valberg 28F1

Le Lagopède, Route de Rouya. **GPS**: n44,09615 e6,93675.

21 € 10 + € 0,20/pp tourist tax Ch (21x) WC included.
Location: Comfortable, isolated, quiet. **Surface:** asphalted.
01/01-31/12.
Distance: 500m on the spot 500m 500m 600m.

Valréas 25C3

Aire camping-car. **GPS**: n44,38713 e4,99245.

5 free. **Location:** Simple. **Surface:** asphalted. 01/01-31/12.
Distance: 400m 250m.
Remarks: Behind tourist info, max 3,5t.

Valréas 25C3

Domaine du Lumian, Route de Montélimar, D941.
GPS: n44,39384 e4,96325.

6 free Ch free. **Surface:** gravel. 01/01-31/12.
Distance: 2,5km.

Vauvenargues 28D2

Boulevard Moraliste. **GPS**: n43,55485 e5,59764.
3 free. **Surface:** asphalted. 01/01-31/12.
Distance: 300m on the spot 300m.
Remarks: At cemetery.

Veynes 25E3

Base de Loisirs Les Iscles, Les Graviers, D994.
GPS: n44,51830 e5,79860.
€ 5,50 . **Location:** Rural, simple, quiet. **Surface:** gravel.
Distance: on the spot on the spot.
Remarks: Wifi at restaurant.

Villeneuve 28E1

GPS: n43,89611 e5,86167.

12 free Ch free. **Location:** Rural, simple, quiet.
Surface: gravel. 01/01-31/12 service: 30/11-01/03.
Distance: 200m 5,5km on the spot on the spot.
Remarks: Max. 48h.

Vinon sur Verdon 28E1

Chemin du Plan. **GPS**: n43,72952 e5,80141.

20 free €2/20minutes Ch included. **Location:** Rural, simple.
Surface: asphalted.
Distance: 3km on the spot on the spot.
Remarks: Parking Carrefour Market, coins at petrol station.

Visan 25C3

Domaine de Lucena, 1600 chemin du Rastelet.
GPS: n44,31576 e4,98406.
5 Ch . **Location:** Isolated, quiet. **Surface:** gravel.
01/01-31/12.
Distance: 4km.

Visan 25C3

Domaine des Lauribert, D976. **GPS**: n44,34833 e4,97276.

20 free Ch (8x)€2 WC. **Surface:** unpaved.
01/01-31/12.
Remarks: At wine-grower, max. 72h.

Corsica

Aléria 33G1

Le Banana's, Casaperta. **GPS**: n42,17353 e9,42103.

16 € 15 Ch €5 included. **Location:** Rural, comfortable. **Surface:** asphalted/grassy. 01/01-31/12.
Distance: river 200m 800m on the spot.
Remarks: Swimming pool available.

Barretalli 33G1

Marine de Giottani. **GPS**: n42,86593 e9,34370.

FR

10 € 10 Ch included. **Location:** Rural, simple, isolated.
Surface: gravel/sand. 01/01-31/12.
Distance: 300m 300m.
Remarks: Narrow entrance.

P Col de Bavella 33G1

Parking du Col, D268. **GPS**: n41,79567 e9,22470.

15 € 4. **Location:** Simple, isolated. **Surface:** gravel/sand.
01/01-31/12.
Distance: 250m.
Remarks: Overnight stay allowed.

S Col de Vergio 33G1

D84. **GPS**: n42,28647 e8,89441.

20 € 12 Ch included. **Location:** Rural, simple, isolated.
Surface: gravel/sand. 01/01-31/12.
Distance: 100m on the spot 1km.

Galéria 33G1

D351. **GPS**: n42,41661 e8,65660.

20 free, night € 20. **Location:** Rural, simple, isolated.
Surface: gravel.
Distance: 600m 400m on the spot.
Remarks: Canoe safari ± 1 hour, € 6/pp.

S Ogliastro 33G1

Parking de la Plage, Marine d'Albo D80. **GPS**: n42,81041 e9,33592.

10 free, July-Aug € 6 service € 2 Ch. **Location:** Simple.
Surface: unpaved. 01/01-31/12.
Distance: 100m 100m.
Remarks: Coins at the shops and restaurant.

S Porto Vecchio 33G2

Camperpark Guiseppe, Route de Palombaggia.
GPS: n41,55015 e9,30636.

25 € 25 Ch WC included € 0,50 at restaurant.
Location: Comfortable. **Surface:** unpaved.
Distance: Porto Vecchio 9km white sandy beach 150m 150m.

S Porto Vecchio 33G2

Parking de la Plage, Route de Palombaggia.
GPS: n41,56389 e9,33601.

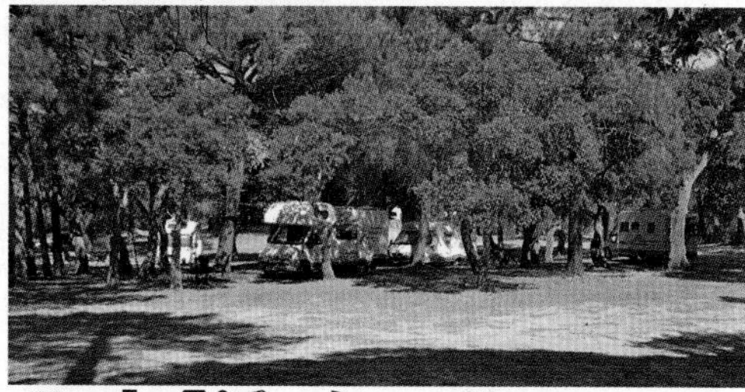

50 € 14 € 2 Ch ,cold included. **Location:** Comfortable.
Surface: sand. 15/05-15/09.
Distance: Porto Vecchio 10km 500m 500m.
Remarks: Bread-service.

Rogliano 33G1

Parking de Tollare, D153, Ersa. **GPS**: n43,00733 e9,38831.

+10 free, July-Aug € 10. **Location:** Simple, isolated.
Surface: grassy/sand. 01/01-31/12.
Distance: on the spot on the spot on the spot.
Remarks: Attention: narrow road, 5,5km.

FR

United Kingdom

Capital: London
Government: Constitutional monarchy
Official Language: English
Population: 64,088,222 (2015)
Area: 243,610 km²

General information
Dialing code: 0044
General emergency: 112
Currency: Pound sterling (GBP),
£1 = € 1,11, € 1 = £0.89 (October 2016)

Regulations for overnight stays
Wild camping is forbidden in the UK. Motorway service stations allow overnight parking.

Additional public holidays 2017
March 17 St. Patricksday (Northern Ireland)
April 14 Good Friday
April 17 Easter monday
May 1 Labour Day
May 1 Early May Bank Holiday
May 29 Spring Bank Holiday
July 12 Orangemens' Day (Northern Ireland)
August 28 Summer Bank Holiday
October 31 Halloween
November 5 Guy Fawkes Day
December 26 Boxing Day

Time Zone
Winter (Standard Time) GMT+0
Summer (DST) GMT+1

GB

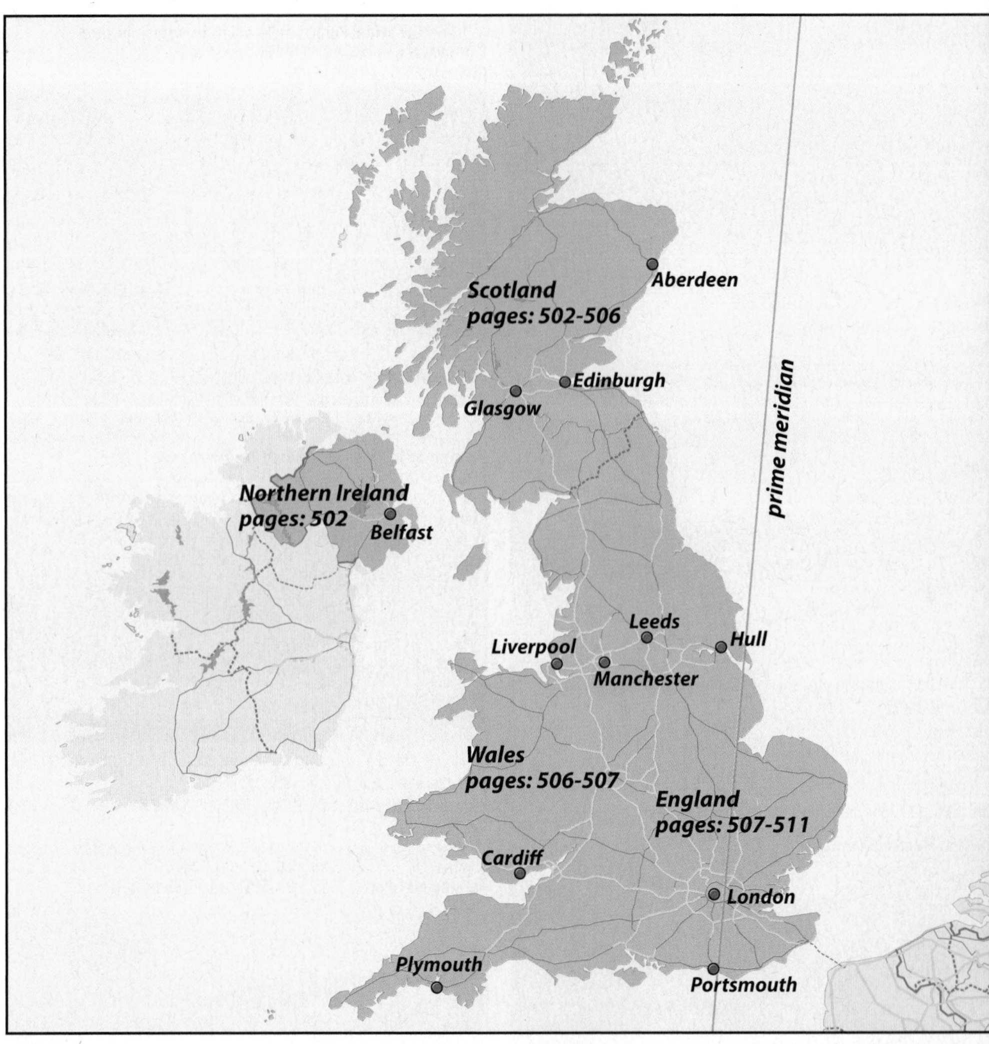

Northern Ireland

Aghadowey 1C1
Golf Car Park, Brown Trout Golf and Country Inn, 209 Agivey Road, A54. **GPS**: n55,02413 w6,59985.
free.
Remarks: Max. 48h.

Antrim 1D1
The Ramble Inn, 236 Lisnevenagh Road. **GPS**: n54,76198 w6,24265.
free.
Distance: Antrim 7km.

Ballinamallard 1C1
Ballinamallard Football Club, Ferney Park. **GPS**: n54,41474 w7,60092.

free. **Surface:** gravel.
Distance: 1,5km.
Tourist information Ballinamallard:
Ballinamallard River, Kilgortnaleague Bridge, A35 Enniskillen > Irvinestown. Wild Salmon and Trout River.

Ballymoney 1C1
Anglers' Rest, 139 Vow Road. **GPS**: n54,99087 w6,56672.
free.
Distance: on the spot.
Tourist information Ballymoney:
Leslie Hill Open Farm, 9, Macfin Road. Living history on the farm, picnic area, playground, Tea-room etc. Easter-31/05: Su-Bank Holidays 14-18h, 01/06-30/06: Sa-Su 14-18h, 01/07-31/08: Mo-Sa 11-18h, Su 14-18h.
Old Bushmills Distillery, Main Street, Bushmills. World's oldest licensed whiskey distillery.
Mo-Sa 09.15-16.45h, Su 12-16.45h.

Broughshane 1D1
Houston Mills, Buckna road. **GPS**: n54,89352 w6,20076.

free £1 Ch (4x)£1. **Location:** Central, noisy.
Surface: asphalted.
Distance: on the spot on the spot.
Remarks: Coins at supermarket.

Carrickfergus 1D1
Carrickfergus Harbour Car Park, Rodgers Quay.
GPS: n54,71177 w5,8119.
free £1 Ch £1.
Remarks: Coins at harbourmaster and tourist office.

Donaghadee 1D1
The Commons Parks, Millisle Road. **GPS**: n54,63475 w5,5312.
free £2/100liter £2/h. **Surface:** asphalted.
Distance: on the spot on the spot on the spot on the spot on the spot.
Remarks: Coins at petrol station.

Newtownards 1D1
Daft Eddys, Sketrick Island. **GPS**: n54,48812 w5,64807.

free.
Distance: Newtownards 17km.
Tourist information Newtownards:
Somme Heritage Centre, 233 Bangor Road, Conlig, A21. The centre examines Ireland's role in the 1st World War.
Castle Espie Wildfowl And Wetlands Centre, 78 Ballydrain Road, Comber. 01/01-31/12 10-17 23-25/12.

Portrush 1C1
Sandhill Drive. **GPS**: n55,20107 w6,65253.
10 £1,25/100liter Ch £1,25/kWh.
Location: Simple, central. **Surface:** asphalted.
Distance: on the spot 600m.

Whitehead 1D1
Bentra Golf Club, Slaughterford Road. **GPS**: n54,75908 w5,72012.
free £1 Ch. **Surface:** asphalted.
Distance: 1km 1,5km 150m.

Scotland

Aberdeen 2C2
Aberdeen Lighthouse parking, Greyhope Rd, Aberdeen.
GPS: n57,14219 w2,05728.

8 free. **Location:** Rural, simple, quiet. **Surface:** asphalted.
01/01-31/12.
Distance: 3km on the spot 2,5km 1,5km on the spot.
Remarks: Whale and dolphin spotting.

S Aberlour 2B1

Aberlour Parking, Aberlour, Elchies road.
GPS: n57,47020 w3,22929.

20 free WC free.
Location: Rural, simple, quiet. **Surface:** asphalted. 01/01-31/12.
Distance: 500m 100m 100m 500m 500m 250m on the spot.

S Ardfern 2A2

Ardfern Motorhome Park, Lochgilphead PA31 8US.
GPS: n56,17402 w5,54799.

10 £15, 01/06-15/08 £20 Ch WC included.
Location: Rural, comfortable, isolated, quiet. **Surface:** gravel.
01/01-31/12.
Distance: 1km on the spot on the spot 1km 1km.

S Ardmair 2B1

Ardmair Point Campsite, Ullapool IV26 2TN.
GPS: n58,03430 w5,07101.

50 £21 Ch WC included £4.
Location: Rural, comfortable, isolated, quiet.
Surface: grassy/metalled. 01/04-01/10.
Distance: 6km on the spot on the spot on the spot on the spot.

Auchtertyre 2A1

Auchtertyre Parking, A890 Auchtertyre.
GPS: n57,28867 w5,57118.

8 free. **Location:** Rural, simple, quiet. **Surface:** asphalted.
01/01-31/12.
Distance: 2km.

Balchrick 2B1

Droman Pier parking, Balchrick. **GPS**: n58,48394 w5,11249.

5 free. **Location:** Rural, simple, quiet. **Surface:** asphalted.
01/01-31/12.
Distance: on the spot 1km.

S Ballachulish 2B2

Glencoe Mountain Resort Campsite, Glencoe, A82 Ballachulish > Achallader. **GPS**: n56,63295 w4,82744.

9 £15 Ch WC included.
Location: Rural, comfortable, isolated, quiet.
Surface: asphalted/gravel. 01/01-31/12.
Distance: 15km on the spot on the spot on the spot.
Remarks: Parking ski-lifts.

S Balmacara 2A1

Reraig, Kyle Of Lochalsh. **GPS**: n57,28290 w5,62608.

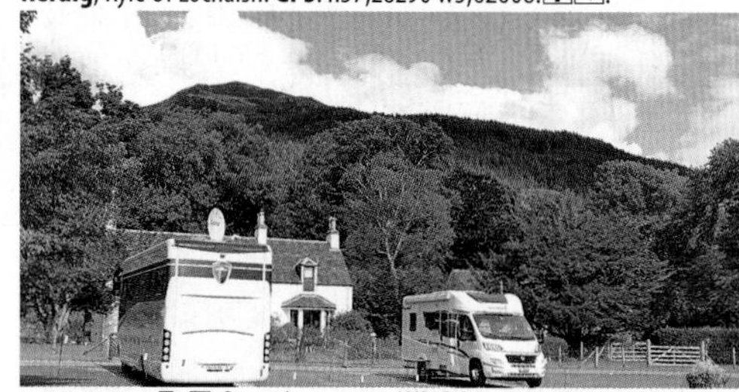

40 £15.90 Ch £1,50/day WC £3/h.
Location: Rural, comfortable, quiet.
Surface: grassy/gravel.
01/05-30/09. **Distance:** 8km on the spot on the spot 8km on the spot.

S Banff 2C1

Gamrie Bay, Easter Cushnie, Gardenstown.
GPS: n57,65139 w2,33382.

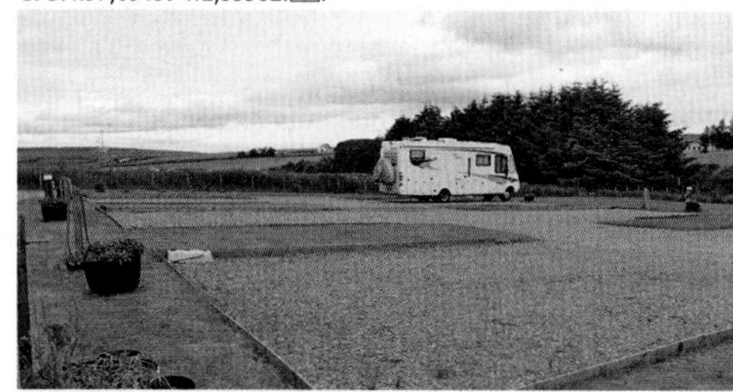

6 £12, 01/04-30/09 £14 Ch included.
Location: Rural, luxurious, isolated, quiet. **Surface:** gravel.
01/01-31/12.
Distance: 2,5km 2,5km 2,5km 1km.

S Banff 2C1

Quayside parking, 11 Quayside Banff. **GPS**: n57,67092 w2,52462.

10 free WC free.
Location: Urban, simple, quiet. **Surface:** concrete. 01/01-31/12.
Distance: 300m on the spot on the spot 700m 700m 400m.

Banff 2C1

Banff parking, Temple View, Banff. **GPS**: n57,66366 w2,51905.

25 free.
Location: Urban, simple, quiet. **Surface:** concrete. 01/01-31/12.
Distance: 1km 300m 300m 200m 200m 400m.

S Callander 2B2

The Cabin at Loch Lubnaig, A84. **GPS**: n56,27765 w4,2834.

2 £10 Ch £2 £1. **Location:** Rural, simple, isolated, noisy.
Surface: asphalted. 01/01-31/12.
Distance: 7,5km on the spot on the spot 7,5km 7,5km on the spot 1km.
Remarks: Max. 3 nights, gate closes at 20h.

S Cruden Bay 2C1

Port Errol, Harbour Street. **GPS**: n57,41130 w1,84546.

voluntary contribution (£10) free. **Location:** Rural, simple, quiet.
Surface: metalled. 01/01-31/12.
Distance: on the spot on the spot on the spot 850m on the spot.
Remarks: Max. 3 days.

S Cullen 2B1

Cullen Harbour parking, Port Long Rd, Cullen, Moray.
GPS: n57,69408 w2,81992.

6 free WC free. **Location:** Rural, simple, simple, quiet.
Surface: gravel. 01/01-31/12.
Distance: 400m on the spot on the spot 400m 400m

GB

on the spot.

Dumfries 2B3

P Long Stay, White Sands. **GPS**: n55,06722 w3,6125.

10 free. **Location:** Simple, noisy. **Surface:** asphalted.
01/01-31/12.
Distance: 100m on the spot on the spot on the spot on the spot on the spot.

Dundonnell 2B1

Corrieshalloch Parkiing, A832 Garve. **GPS**: n57,75898 w5,03397.

8 free. **Location:** Rural, simple, quiet. **Surface:** asphalted.
01/01-31/12.
Distance: 5km 300m.

Dunthulm 2A1

Camus More Campsite, Isle of Skye. **GPS**: n57,65020 w6,40459.

7 £8 WC included. **Location:** Rural, simple, isolated, quiet.
Surface: grassy. 15/05-07/09.
Distance: 10km on the spot 10km 10km.
Remarks: Nearby Dunthulm Castle.

Durness 2B1

Sango Sands Oasis campsite, Durness IV27 4PZ, UK.
GPS: n58,57013 w4,74269.

60 £20 Ch WC included £2/2 £5/day.
Location: Rural, comfortable, quiet. **Surface:** grassy/metalled.
01/04-31/10.
Distance: on the spot 100m 200m on the spot on the spot.

Easdale 2A2

Souvenir shop, Ellenabeich, Isle of Seil. **GPS**: n56,29521 w5,64926.

10 £10 WC. **Location:** Rural, simple, quiet.
Surface: metalled. 01/01-31/12.
Distance: on the spot on the spot on the spot on the spot 4,5km on the spot on the spot.

Falkirk 2B2

The Falkirk Wheel, Lime Road. **GPS**: n56,00031 w3,83982.

30 £15 WC .
Location: Rural, simple, quiet. **Surface:** asphalted. 01/01-31/12.
Distance: 4km on the spot on the spot 4km on the spot on the spot on the spot on the spot.
Remarks: Check in during opening hours or call: 01324676912, caution key sanitary £20.

Fettercairn 2B2

Car Park Bowling Club, Fettercairn, Laurencekirk.
GPS: n56,84971 w2,57306.

. **Location:** Rural, simple, noisy. **Surface:** asphalted.
01/01-31/12.
Distance: 100m 100m 250m 100m.

Tourist information Fettercairn:

Fettercairn Distillery Visitor Centre Information, Distillery Road. One of Scotland's oldest malt whiskey distilleries. 01/05-30/09, Mon-Sa 10-14.30h. £5.

Fort William 2A2

Fort William parking long stay, West End Roundabout, Fort William.
GPS: n56,81522 w5,11686.

10 £2. **Location:** Urban, simple, noisy. **Surface:** asphalted.
01/01-31/12.
Distance: 200m 200m 200m 200m 200m 10km.

Girvan 1D1

Harbour street- Henriettastreet. **GPS**: n55,24324 w4,85869.

50 free WC. **Location:** Rural, simple, quiet. **Surface:** asphalted.
01/01-31/12.
Distance: 100m sandy beach 50m 50m 500m 600m 50m on the spot.

Glenbrittle 2A1

Glenbrittle Campsite, Carbost. **GPS**: n57,20251 w6,29021.

33 £9 Ch £2 £6 WC included.
Location: Rural, comfortable, isolated, quiet.
Surface: grassy/metalled. 01/04-01/10.
Distance: 10km on the spot on the spot on the spot on the spot.

Hawick 2B3

Common Haugh, Victoria Rd, Hawick. **GPS**: n55,42310 w2,79114.

50 free WC. **Location:** Urban, simple, central. **Surface:** asphalted.
01/01-31/12.
Distance: 800m 800m on the spot on the spot on the spot.
Remarks: Max. 24h, special part for motor homes.

Helensburgh 2B2

Helensburgh Pier Car Parking, Sinclair St. Helensburgh.
GPS: n56,00198 w4,73503.

20 £1.20/h 9-18h WC free. **Location:** Urban, simple, central, noisy. **Surface:** asphalted. 01/01-31/12.
Distance: 200m on the spot on the spot 200m 250m 300m on the spot on the spot.

Irvine 1D1

Irvine Beach Drive Parking, Irvine Beach Drive.
GPS: n55,60628 w4,69263.

100 free WC free. **Location:** Rural, simple, quiet. **Surface:** asphalted.
01/01-31/12.
Distance: 1,5km 4km on the spot 1,2km 850m 400m on the spot.
Remarks: At sea, historical centre.

Jedburgh 2B3

Canongate Parking, 7 Queen Street, Jedburgh.
GPS: n55,47761 w2,55313.

GB

15 free WC free. **Location:** Urban, simple, central, noisy.
Surface: concrete. 01/01-31/12.
Distance: on the spot on the spot 100m on the spot on the spot on the spot.
Remarks: At tourist office.

Kalnakill 2A1

Kalnakill parking, IV54 Kalnakill. **GPS:** n57,54182 w5,84807.

4 free. **Location:** Rural, simple, isolated, quiet. **Surface:** asphalted.
01/01-31/12.
Distance: 2,2km.

Kilchoan 2A2

Far View Campsite, Pier Road. **GPS:** n56,69409 w6,09621.

2 £15 Ch included. **Location:** Rural, comfortable, isolated, quiet. **Surface:** grassy/gravel. 01/01-31/12.
Distance: 1,5km 500m 500m 500m on the spot on the spot.
Remarks: Ferry boat to Isle of Mull 400m.

Kilchoan 2A2

Kilchoan Ferry Port Parking, Pier Road.
GPS: n56,69008 w6,09603.

15 free. **Location:** Rural, simple, isolated, quiet. **Surface:** asphalted.
01/01-31/12.
Distance: 2km on the spot on the spot 1km.

Kirkcudbright 1D1

Kirkcudbright Parking, Beaconsfield Place, Kirkcudbright.
GPS: n54,83707 w4,05045.

5 free WC free. **Location:** Simple, central, noisy. **Surface:** asphalted.
01/01-31/12.
Distance: on the spot on the spot on the spot on the spot on the spot on the spot on the spot.

Kylesku 2B1

Kylesku Parking, A894 Kylesku. **GPS:** n58,25756 w5,02726.

10 free. **Location:** Rural, simple, isolated, quiet. **Surface:** asphalted.
01/01-31/12.
Distance: 1Km on the spot on the spot 1km.

Lendalfoot 1D1

Lendalfoot Parking, 8 A77 Girvan. **GPS:** n55,16301 w4,94904.

4 free. **Location:** Rural, simple, noisy. **Surface:** concrete.
01/01-31/12.
Distance: 500m on the spot.

Lochwinnoch 1D1

Clyde Muirshiel parking, 22 Saint Winnoc Road, Lochwinnoch.
GPS: n55,79569 w4,62302.

10 free WC free. **Location:** Rural, simple, quiet. **Surface:** asphalted.
01/01-31/12.
Distance: 500m on the spot on the spot on the spot 300m on the spot on the spot.

Luskentyre 2A1

Luskentyre Parking, Luskentyre, Isle of Harris HS3.
GPS: n57,86673 w6,91537.

3 £5. **Location:** Rural, simple, isolated, noisy.
Surface: asphalted/metalled. 01/01-31/12.
Distance: on the spot on the spot.
Remarks: Online payment with PayPal.

Moffat 2B3

Grey Mare's Tail Nature reserve, Moffat Water Valley, Dumfries and Galloway. **GPS:** n55,41779 w3,28646.

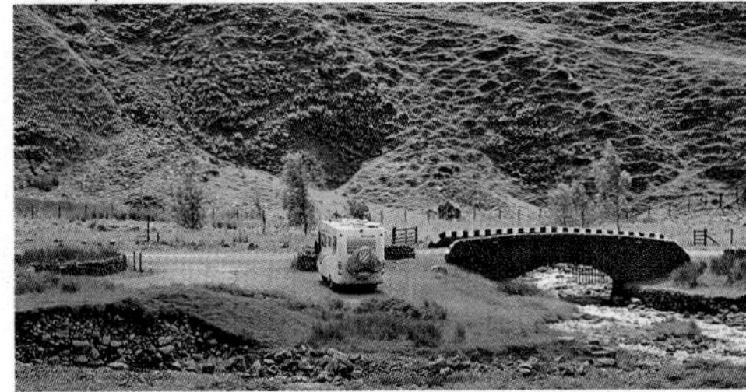

10 £2. **Location:** Rural, simple, isolated, quiet. **Surface:** gravel.
01/01-31/12.
Distance: on the spot on the spot.

New Abbey 2B3

Parking Sweetheart Abbey, A710, Main Street.
GPS: n54,98070 w3,61966.

6 free WC. **Location:** Simple, quiet. **Surface:** asphalted/metalled.
01/01-31/12.
Distance: 200m on the spot 200m 200m on the spot.

Newton Steward 1D1

Newton Steward parking, Galloway Forrest Park.
GPS: n54,97358 w4,43804.

3 free. **Location:** Rural, simple, isolated, quiet.
Surface: asphalted/gravel. 01/01-31/12.
Distance: 6km 500m on the spot.

Oban 2A2

Oban, Lochavuling Parking, Lochavullin road,Oban.
GPS: n56,40948 w5,47142.

4 £10. **Location:** Urban, simple, noisy. **Surface:** asphalted.
01/01-31/12.
Distance: 400m 400m on the spot 400m.
Remarks: At tourist office.

Oban 2A2

The Wide Mouthed Frog, A85 Oban, Dunbeg.
GPS: n56,44856 w5,4319.

5 free. **Location:** Urban, simple, noisy.
Surface: gravel.
01/01-31/12.
Distance: 6km on the spot on the spot on the spot 5km.

Scourie 2B1

Scourie campsite, Scourie Lairg IV27 4SE, UK.
GPS: n58,35157 w5,15523.

GB

50 £20 Ch WC included £2/1.
Location: Rural, comfortable, isolated, quiet.
Surface: grassy/metalled. 01/04-30/09.
Distance: 200m on the spot on the spot on the spot 200m on the spot.

Seilebost 2A1

Seilebost Parking, A859 Seilebost, Isle of Harris.
GPS: n57,86615 w6,88152.

10 £5. **Location:** Rural, simple, quiet. **Surface:** gravel/metalled.
01/01-31/12.
Distance: 6km 2km.
Remarks: Online payment with PayPal.

S Shawbost 2A1

Eilean Fraoich campsite, 77 N Shawbost, Isle of Lewis.
GPS: n58,31989 w6,68753.

25 £18 Ch WC included £4/3 £5/day. **Location:** Rural, comfortable, isolated, quiet.
Surface: gravel/metalled. Easter-01/10.
Distance: 500m 1km 500m on the spot.

S Sligachan 2A1

Sligachan campsite, A87 Sligachan, Isle of skye, UK.
GPS: n57,29146 w6,17696.

100 £7.50/pp Ch £5 WC £3 included.
Location: Rural, simple, isolated, quiet. **Surface:** grassy/gravel.
01/04-16/10.
Distance: 10km on the spot 100m 10km on the spot 100m.

S Tomintoul 2B2

Tomintoul Bowlingclub Campsite, Lecht Drive, Tomintoul.
GPS: n57,25073 w3,37636.

£7 WCincluded. **Location:** Urban, simple, central, quiet.
Surface: gravel. 01/01-31/12.
Distance: 300m 300m 300m 300m 300m 300m 12km.
Remarks: Money in envelope in mail box.

Tourist information Tomintoul:
Tourist Information Centre, The Square.
Tomintoul Museum, Tomnabat Lane. Historical regional museum.
Easter-31/10, mon-sa 9.30-12h, 14-16h.

S Uig 2A1

Uigbay Campsite, A87 Uig, Portree, isle of skye, UK.
GPS: n57,58559 w6,37971.

15 £7 Ch £3 WC £3 included. **Location:** Rural, simple, isolated, quiet. **Surface:** gravel/metalled.
01/01-31/12.
Distance: 200m on the spot 100m 200m on the spot.

Wales

S Abergynolwyn 1D3

Riverside Guest House, Llanegryn Street.
GPS: n52,64584 w3,95856.

5 £10/night Chincluded £6/night. **Location:** Rural, comfortable, central, quiet. **Surface:** grassy/metalled.
01/01-31/12.
Remarks: Arrival <18h, narrow entrance (2.6m), Snowdonia National Park.

S Brecon 1D3

The Watton Car Park, Heol Gouesnou. **GPS**: n51,94609 w3,38531.

25 £0.70/h, max. £3.20 8-18h, overnight stay free WCfree,150m.
Location: Urban, simple, quiet. **Surface:** asphalted.
01/01-31/12.
Distance: on the spot on the spot.
Remarks: 1 night per 7 nights.

Brecon 1D3

Canal Road Car/Coach-Lorry Park, Canal Road.
GPS: n51,94486 w3,38993.

10 £0.70/h, max. £3.20 8-18h, overnight stay free.
Location: Urban, simple, central, quiet. **Surface:** asphalted.
01/01-31/12.
Distance: 100m 100m.
Remarks: 1 night per 7 nights.

Brecon 1D3

The Promenade Car Park, Fenni-Fach Rd. **GPS**: n51,95089 w3,4036.

25 £0.70/h, max. £3.20 8-18h, overnight stay free.
Location: Urban, simple, isolated, quiet. **Surface:** asphalted.
01/01-31/12.
Distance: 600m on the spot 700m.
Remarks: 1 night per 7 nights.

S Builth Wells 1F2

The Groe Car Park, The Strand. **GPS**: n52,14969 w3,40252.

20 £0.70/h, max. £3.20 8-18h, overnight stay free WC.
Location: Urban, simple, quiet. **Surface:** asphalted.
01/01-31/12.
Distance: on the spot on the spot on the spot.
Remarks: 1 night per 7 nights.

Builth Wells 1F2

Smithfield Car Park, Brecon Rd. **GPS**: n52,14714 w3,40261.

50 £0.70/h, max. £3.20 8-18h, overnight stay free.
Location: Urban, simple, central. **Surface:** asphalted.
01/01-31/12.
Distance: 200m.
Remarks: 1 night per 7 nights.

Crickhowell 1F2

Beaufort Street Car Park, Greenhill Way. **GPS**: n51,85838 w3,13557.

8 £0.70/h, max. £3.20 8-18h, overnight stay free.

GB

simple, quiet. **Surface:** grassy/gravel. 01/01-31/12.
Distance: on the spot on the spot 600m.
Remarks: Max. 72h, key service at Touristinformation (900m).

Holsworthy 1E3

The Manor Car Park, Western Road. **GPS**: n50,81133 w4,35282.

6 £5 18-10h, £3 day. **Location:** Urban, simple, quiet.
Surface: asphalted. 01/01-31/12.
Distance: on the spot 150m 150m.
Remarks: Max. 2 nights, min. 6m space between motorhomes.

Huntingdon 1G2

Wellsbridge Motorhomes Sales, Ramsey Forty Foot, Ramsey.
GPS: n52,47540 w0,08834.

5 £5 WC. **Location:** Rural, simple, isolated, quiet.
Surface: asphalted. 02/01-23/12.
Distance: on the spot.

Ipswich 1H2

Burnt House Farm, Wash Lane, Witnesham.
GPS: n52,11418 e1,20094.

5 £8 Ch WC included. **Location:** Rural, comfortable, isolated, quiet. **Surface:** grassy/metalled. 01/01-31/12.
Distance: 2km 2km.

Ipswich 1H2

Orwell Crossing Lorry Park, A14 Eastbound, Nacton.
GPS: n52,02473 e1,22678.

20 £12. **Location:** Motorway, simple, noisy.
Surface: asphalted. 01/01-31/12.
Distance: on the spot.

Ivybridge 1E3

Lee Mill Services, A38. **GPS**: n50,38493 w3,97041.

10 £17.50/night WC included. **Location:** Simple, noisy.
Surface: asphalted. 01/01-31/12.
Distance: on the spot 500m.
Remarks: Behind petrol station, discount at restaurant £5.

Maidstone 1H3

Maidstone Services, M20. **GPS**: n51,26687 e0,61502.

8 £20/24h, first 2 hours free WC against payment.
Location: Motorway, simple, noisy. **Surface:** asphalted.
01/01-31/12.
Distance: 200m on the spot 150m.
Remarks: Payment with mobile phone.

Tourist information Maidstone:
M Museum of Kent Life, Lock Lane, Sandling. History and traditions of Kent. 10-17h.

Mevagissey 1E3

Willow Car & Coach Park, Valley Road. **GPS**: n50,27155 w4,79044.

10 10-18h parking rate, overnight stay £7.50 on demand.
Location: Simple, central. **Surface:** metalled.
01/01-31/12.
Distance: 150m 1km 300m.

New Milton 1F3

Orchard Lakes, New Lane, Bashley. **GPS**: n50,77182 w1,6645.

5 £15 Ch included. **Location:** Rural, comfortable, isolated, quiet. **Surface:** grassy/metalled. 01/01-31/12.
Distance: 400m 6,5km on the spot New Forest.
Remarks: Arrival >18h.

Newhaven 1G3

West Side Promenade. **GPS**: n50,78189 e0,05530.

30 £3. **Surface:** concrete. Easter-30/09.
Distance: 2km on the spot on the spot 400m 850m 2km.
Remarks: Arrival 8><17h.

Newnham on Severn 1F2

Elton Farm, Littledean Road, A4151. **GPS**: n51,82355 w2,44753.
5 £5 Ch. **Location:** Rural, simple, isolated.
Surface: grassy. 01/01-31/12.
Distance: on the spot on the spot.

Newton Abbot 1F3

Sunnyside, Yvonne Bassett, Totnes Road, A381, Ipplepen.
GPS: n50,48591 w3,63376.

5 £8.50/night Ch £1,50/day WC included.
Location: Rural, simple, quiet. **Surface:** grassy/metalled.
01/03-31/10.
Distance: 100m.
Remarks: Arrival <18h.

Northcumberland 2C2

Hazlehead Park, Hazledene Road. **GPS**: n57,13987 w2,17956.

20 free. **Location:** Simple, noisy. **Surface:** asphalted.
01/01-31/12.
Distance: 6km 2km 2km on the spot.

Northcumberland 2C2

The Barn at Beal, TD15 2PB, Northcumberland.
GPS: n55,67754 w1,89434.

9 £15 Ch WC included. **Location:** Rural, comfortable, quiet. **Surface:** gravel/metalled. 01/01-31/12.
Distance: 2km on the spot on the spot on the spot.
Remarks: Possibility for reservation.

Oldham 1F1

The Hawthorn, Roundthorn Road. **GPS**: n53,53352 w2,08637.
5 £9 £2,50/night WC.
Distance: 3km.

Pickering 1G1

Antiques Centre, Southgate. **GPS**: n54,24413 w0,78026.

5 £10 Ch. **Location:** Simple. **Surface:** asphalted.
01/01-31/12.
Distance: 500m.

Praa Sands 1E3

Sydney Cove Car Park, Castle Drive. **GPS**: n50,10440 w5,3919.

GB

10 £8/24h. Location: Simple.
Distance: 100m 100m.

Rake 1G3

The Flying Bull, London Road. **GPS**: n51,04419 w0,85418.

5 £5 included WC at restaurant. **Location:** Rural, isolated, quiet. **Surface:** grassy. 01/01-31/12.
Distance: 3km on the spot.
Remarks: Max. 1 night, check in at restaurant.

Rye 13B2

The River Haven Hotel, Winchelsea Rd. **GPS**: n50,94880 e0,72990.

5 £5. **Surface:** gravel. 01/01-31/12.
Distance: 400m on the spot 100m.
Remarks: Pay at hotel.

Scarborough 1G1

South Moor Farm, Dalby Forest Drive. **GPS**: n54,30049 w0,61169.
5 £10 Ch. **Location:** Rural, simple. **Surface:** grassy.
01/01-31/12.

Sewerby 1G1

The Ship Inn, Cliff Road. **GPS**: n54,10167 w0,16411.
5 £15 Ch. **Surface:** unpaved.
Distance: on the spot.

Southampton 1G3

Long Stay Car Park, West Quay Road. **GPS**: n50,90090 w1,4083.

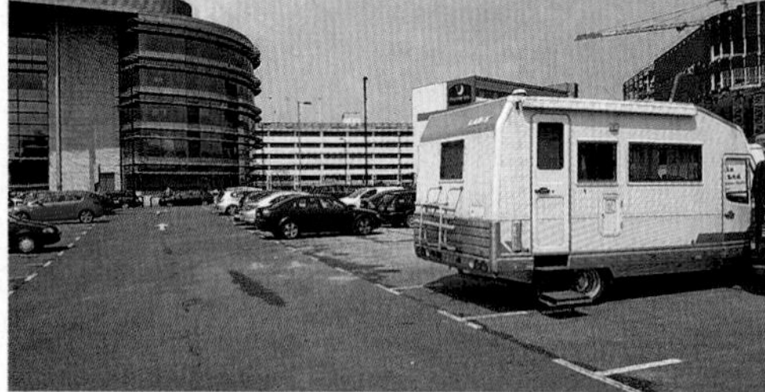

day max. £7.50, night £2. 01/01-31/12.
Distance: 800m 800m 800m.
Remarks: Max 3,5t.

St Austell 1E3

Edgemoor, Enniscaven, St.Dennis. **GPS**: n50,39636 w4,8676.

5 £5/night WC included. **Location:** Comfortable, quiet.
Surface: grassy/metalled. 01/01-31/12.
Distance: St.Austell 14,5km on the spot on the spot.

St Ives 1G2

The Seven Wives, Ramsey road. **GPS**: n52,33193 w0,07634.

5 £5 Ch £6/night WC. **Location:** Urban, simple, central. **Surface:** metalled. 01/01-31/12.
Distance: 1,4km on the spot.

St Jidgey 1E3

Halfway House Inn. **GPS**: n50,48949 w4,89943.
4 £10, guests free. **Location:** Rural, isolated, quiet.
Surface: grassy.
Distance: on the spot.

Staple Fitzpaine 1F3

Home Mead, New Rd. **GPS**: n50,95970 w3,0489.

5 £5 included. **Location:** Rural, isolated, quiet.
Surface: grassy. 01/01-31/12.
Distance: on the spot.

Stoke St Gregory 1F3

The Royal Oak, The Square. **GPS**: n51,04050 w2,9318.

5 guests free Ch free £4.
Surface: asphalted. 01/01-31/12.
Distance: on the spot 50m 50m.
Remarks: Parking in front of church.

Stratford-upon-Avon 1G2

Stratford Marina Car Park, Bridgeway. **GPS**: n52,19280 w1,70154.

10 9-18h £8, overnight stay £15. **Location:** Urban, simple, central. **Surface:** asphalted. 01/01-31/12.
Distance: 200m 200m 200m.

Stratford-upon-Avon 1G2

The New Inn Hotel, Clifford Chambers. **GPS**: n52,16929 w1,7168.

5 £8 £4,80.
Location: Rural, simple. **Surface:** grassy. 01/01-31/12.
Distance: on the spot on the spot.

Tourist information Stratford-upon-Avon:
Birthplace of William Shakespeare.

Tarrington 1F2

The Tarrington Arms, Ledbury road. **GPS**: n52,06473 w2,5604.

5 free WC free.
Location: Rural, simple. **Surface:** metalled.
Distance: 200m on the spot.

Tenby 1D3

Carew Airfield & Pavilion, Sageston. **GPS**: n51,69362 w4,80973.

5 £15-20/night Ch WC included.
Location: Comfortable, quiet. **Surface:** concrete. 01/01-31/12.
Distance: 150m 8km 500m 1,5km 1,5km.

Thaxted 1G2

Margaret Street Car Park, Margaret Street.
GPS: n51,95530 e0,34328.

2 free WC free. **Location:** Urban, simple, central, quiet.
Surface: concrete. 01/01-31/12.
Distance: 150m 150m.
Remarks: Max. 48h in fortnight.

Tintagel 1E3

King Arthur's Car Park, Fore Street. **GPS**: n50,66441 w4,75119.

50 £3.90 10-16h, £3 16-10h WC. **Location:** Simple.
Surface: asphalted.
Distance: on the spot on the spot 100m.
Remarks: Opposite Tintagel Old Post Office.

GB

Tintagel 1E3

Mayfair Car Park, Fore Street. **GPS**: n50,66386 w4,75061.

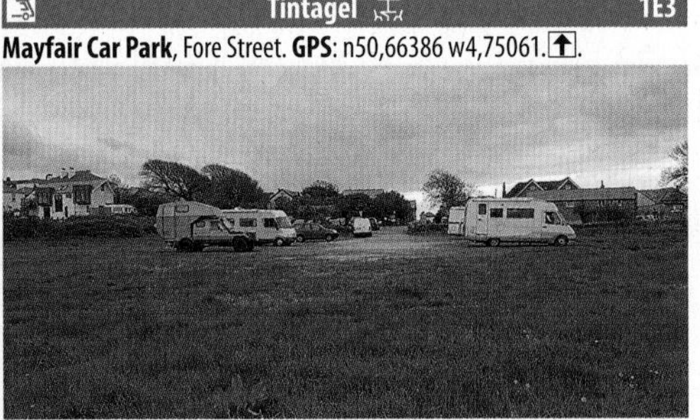

30 £2 8.00-20h, £3.50 20-08h. **Location:** Urban, simple, central.
Surface: grassy. 01/01-31/12.
Distance: on the spot 100m on the spot.
Remarks: Next to King Arthur's Car Park.

Tintagel 1E3

Sword in Stone Car Park, Bossiney Road. **GPS**: n50,66257 w4,74763.

20 £5/24h. **Location:** Urban, simple. **Surface:** asphalted.
01/01-31/12.
Distance: 150m 250m.

Tourist information Tintagel:

Tintagel Old Post Office, Fore Street. 600 year-old traditional Cornish Longhouse.

King Arthur's Castle, Castle Road. 25/03-30/10.

Torrington 1E3

Sydney House Car Park, South Street. **GPS**: n50,95121 w4,14438.

20 £5 18-10h, £3 day. **Location:** Urban, simple, quiet.
Surface: asphalted. 01/01-31/12.
Distance: 300m 250m 250m.
Remarks: Max. 2 nights, min. 6m space between motorhomes.

Westward Ho! 1E3

Main Car Park, Golf Links Rd. **GPS**: n51,04069 w4,23728.

8 £7, 01/11-14/03 £3, night £5. **Location:** Urban, simple, central, quiet. **Surface:** asphalted.
01/01-31/12.
Distance: on the spot 200m 200m.
Remarks: Max. 5000kg, min. 6m space between motorhomes.

Whaplode St Catherines 1G2

The Bleu Bell Inn, Cranesgate S. **GPS**: n52,75956 w0,0155.
5 £5, free with a meal Ch (2x)£2,50/night.
Location: Simple. 01/01-31/12 Mo.
Distance: on the spot.

Winchester 1G3

Coach Park, Worthy Lane, B3044. **GPS**: n51,06931 w1,31628.

10 £7, overnight stay free. **Location:** Urban, simple.
Surface: asphalted.
Distance: 850m 500m 50m.
Remarks: Max. 24h.

Yeovil 1F3

Cartgate and Picnic Area, A303/A3088 roundabout.
GPS: n50,96926 w2,74087.

20 free WC Password at the restaurant. **Location:** Motorway, simple, noisy. **Surface:** asphalted. 01/01-31/12.
Distance: 15km on the spot.

GB

Greece

Capital: Athens
Government: Parliamentary democracy
Official Language: Greek
Population: 10,775,600 (2015)
Area: 131,990 km²

General information
Dialling code: 0030
General emergency: 112
Currency: Euro

Regulations for overnight stays
Wild camping and overnight parking is not officially allowed. Overnight parking places mentioned here are not official motorhome stopovers but tolerated areas.

Additional public holidays 2017
January 6 Epiphany
February 27 Ash Monday, 41 days before Easter
March 25 Independence Day
April 16-17 Orthodox Easter
May 1 Labor Day
August 15 Assumption of the Virgin Mary
October 28 National Holiday, Ochi day

Time Zone
Winter (Standard Time) GMT+2
Summer (DST) GMT+3

Greece North
pages: 517

Central Greece
pages: 512-513

Igoumentisa

Athens

Patras

Peloponnisos/Attica
pages: 513-517

GR

Central Greece

Achillio 35G1

Epar. Od. Archilliou-Glifas. **GPS**: n39,00943 e22,95758.

Distance: on the spot on the spot on the spot.

Agios Nikolaos 35F2

GPS: n38,34959 e22,15661.

01/10-30/04.

Remarks: Parking at harbour.

Ammoudia 35E1

GPS: n39,23636 e20,48073.

Surface: gravel/sand.

Distance: on the spot 50m on the spot 100m 250m.

Remarks: At harbour.

Ammoudia 35E1

GPS: n39,23989 e20,48116.

Surface: sand.

Distance: on the spot on the spot on the spot 200m 50m.

Remarks: Beach parking.

Arahova 35G2

GPS: n38,47948 e22,58164.

01/01-31/12.

Arillas 35E1

Restaurant Soukas, Aglias-Platarias. **GPS**: n39,35278 e20,28861.

free for clients WC . **Location:** Rural.

Surface: grassy/sand. 01/05-01/10.

Distance: on the spot on the spot.

Boukka 35F1

GPS: n38,93125 e21,14200.

Surface: sand.

Distance: on the spot 100m.

Remarks: Next to sports fields, beach parking.

Corfu 35E1

Dionysus, Dassia. **GPS**: n39,66472 e19,84440.

€ 18,20-21 Ch WC. 01/04-20/10.

Corfu 35E1

Dolphin Camping, Sidari. **GPS**: n39,78890 e19,72354.

€ 12-14,10 Ch WC. 01/07-10/09.

Corfu 35E1

Karda Beach, Dassia. **GPS**: n39,68611 e19,83861.

€ 22,30-23,60 Ch WC. 26/04-01/09.

Distance: on the spot.

Tourist information Corfu:

Esplanada, Kerkyra (Corfu). Meeting point for inhabitants and tourists.

Kerkyra (Corfu).

Frurion, Kerkyra (Corfu). Citadel, 1550.

Aqualand, Corfu Water Park, Ag.Ioannis. Leisure pool park.

Delphi 35F2

Apollon. **GPS**: n38,48388 e22,47550.

Ch. 01/01-31/12.

Delphi 35F2

Chrissa. **GPS**: n38,47267 e22,46206.

55 € 18,50-22,50 Ch WC. 01/01-31/12.

Delphi 35F2

Delphi Camping. **GPS**: n38,47833 e22,47450.

€ 19,60-21,80 Ch WC. 01/04-31/10.

Tourist information Delphi:

Site of Delphi. Archeological site. 7.30-17.30h holiday. € 9.

Eratini 35F2

N48/E65 km 47. **GPS**: n38,33769 e22,19198.

Surface: grassy/sand.

Distance: on the spot on the spot.

Remarks: Beach parking, max 3,5t.

Erétria 35G2

Milos Camping. **GPS**: n38,39139 e23,77556.

€ 25-32 ChWC. 15/04-30/09.

Tourist information Erétria:

Seaside resort and archological site Antique Eretria.

Gliki 35E1

Taverne Panorama. **GPS**: n39,32726 e20,61568.

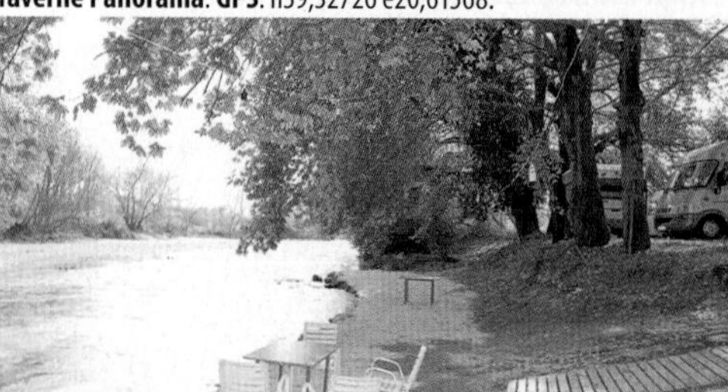

guests free WC. **Surface:** grassy.

Distance: 500m 500m.

Remarks: Along the Acheron river.

Hiliadou 35F2

GPS: n38,39408 e21,92096.

Surface: gravel.

Distance: Nafpaktos 7km on the spot.
Remarks: Beach parking.

Igoumenítsa — 35E1
GPS: n39,51540 e20,21087.

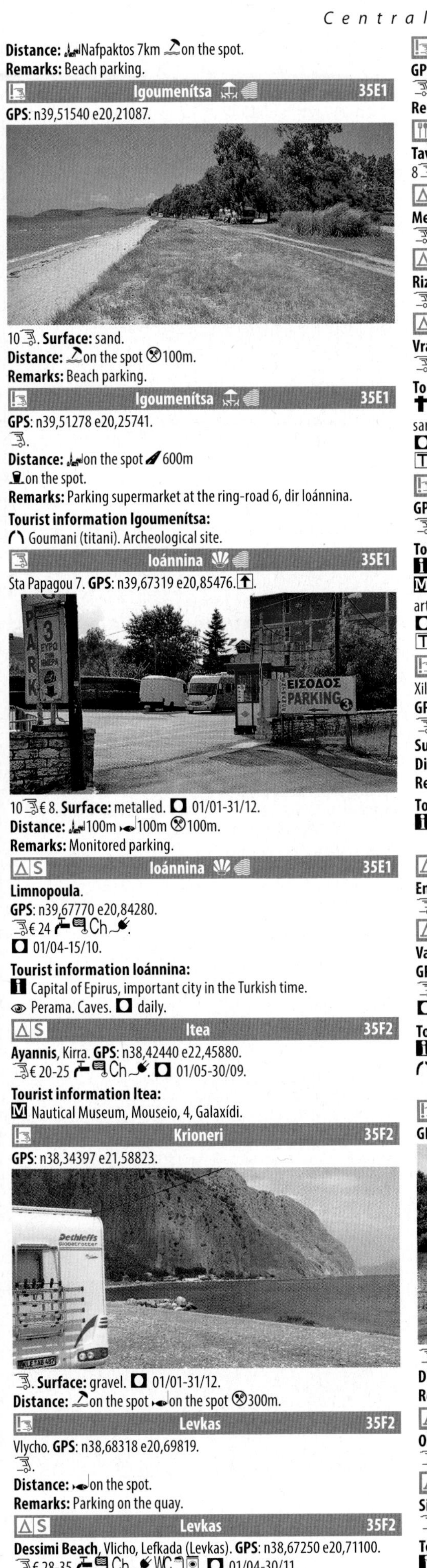

10. **Surface:** sand.
Distance: on the spot 100m.
Remarks: Beach parking.

Igoumenítsa — 35E1
GPS: n39,51278 e20,25741.
Distance: on the spot 600m on the spot.
Remarks: Parking supermarket at the ring-road 6, dir Ioánnina.

Tourist information Igoumenítsa:
Goumani (titani). Archeological site.

Ioánnina — 35E1
Sta Papagou 7. **GPS:** n39,67319 e20,85476.

10 € 8. **Surface:** metalled. 01/01-31/12.
Distance: 100m 100m 100m.
Remarks: Monitored parking.

Ioánnina — 35E1
Limnopoula.
GPS: n39,67770 e20,84280.
€ 24 Ch.
01/04-15/10.

Tourist information Ioánnina:
Capital of Epirus, important city in the Turkish time.
Perama. Caves. daily.

Itea — 35F2
Ayannis, Kirra. **GPS:** n38,42440 e22,45880.
€ 20-25 Ch. 01/05-30/09.

Tourist information Itea:
Nautical Museum, Mouseio, 4, Galaxídi.

Krioneri — 35F2
GPS: n38,34397 e21,58823.

. **Surface:** gravel. 01/01-31/12.
Distance: on the spot on the spot 300m.

Levkas — 35F2
Vlycho. **GPS:** n38,68318 e20,69819.
Distance: on the spot.
Remarks: Parking on the quay.

Levkas — 35F2
Dessimi Beach, Vlicho, Lefkada (Levkas). **GPS:** n38,67250 e20,71100.
€ 28-35 Ch WC. 01/04-30/11.

Levkas — 35F2
Poros Beach, Poros, Lefkada (Levkas). **GPS:** n38,64094 e20,69698.
Ch WC. 01/05-30/09.

Mesolóngi — 35F2
GPS: n38,36358 e21,42016.
01/01-31/12.
Remarks: Parking in harbour.

Metéora — 35F1
Taverna Arsenis, East Street, Kalambaka. **GPS:** n39,69923 e21,64109.
8 guests free WC. 01/01-31/12.

Metéora — 35F1
Meteora Garden, Kalambaka. **GPS:** n39,70869 e21,60915.
Ch WC. 01/01-31/12.

Metéora — 35F1
Rizos International, Kalambaka. **GPS:** n39,69010 e21,64564.
Ch. 01/01-31/12.

Metéora — 35F1
Vrachos Kastraki, Kastraki. **GPS:** n39,71338 e21,61588.
€ 18 Ch. 01/01-31/12.

Tourist information Metéora:
Important cultural inheritance, 24 monasteries built on enormous sandstone peaks, of which 6 can be visited.
9-13h, 15-17h.
against payment.

Métsovo — 35F1
GPS: n39,76898 e21,17749.

Tourist information Métsovo:
Traditional mountain village.
Archotiko Tositsa. Restored 18th century mansion, museum or folk art.
8.30-13h, 16-18h.
€ 3.

Nafpaktos — 35F2
Xiliadou, N48/E65 km 80,5.
GPS: n38,38139 e21,81661.
Surface: gravel/sand.
Distance: on the spot on the spot nearby.
Remarks: Parking at the beach.

Tourist information Nafpaktos:
Old city with Venetian Castle and circular walled harbor.

Parga — 35E1
Enjoy Lichnos. GPS: n39,28358 e20,43340.
€ 28-36 Ch WC. 01/05-15/10.

Parga — 35E1
Valtos Camping.
GPS: n39,28556 e20,38972.
€ 20-21,50 Ch.
01/05-30/09.

Tourist information Parga:
Lively bathing resort.
Necromanteion of Ephyra. Oracle of death.

Perdika — 35E1
GPS: n39,38607 e20,27473.

free.
Distance: Perdika 7km on the spot.
Remarks: Beach parking.

Pilion — 35G1
Olizon, Milina. **GPS:** n39,16472 e23,21666.
€ 24-32 Ch WC. 01/05-15/10.

Pilion — 35G1
Sikia Fig Tree, Kato Gatzea. **GPS:** n39,31025 e23,10977.
€ 19-24,50 Ch WC. 01/04-31/10.

Tourist information Pilion:
Mythological peninsula, beautiful nature, authentic mountain villages and fishing towns.
Makrinitsa. Village worth seeing, car-free.
Miliés. Folk museum. 01/04-31/10 Tue-Su, 01/11-31/03 Wed-Su.
Archeological Museum, Athanasáki 1, Vólos. Tue-Su holiday.

Plataria — 35E1
Nautilos. GPS: n39,44389 e20,25806.
€ 21-23,50 Ch. 01/04-20/10.

Préveza — 35F1
Mitikas. GPS: n39,01719 e20,71555.

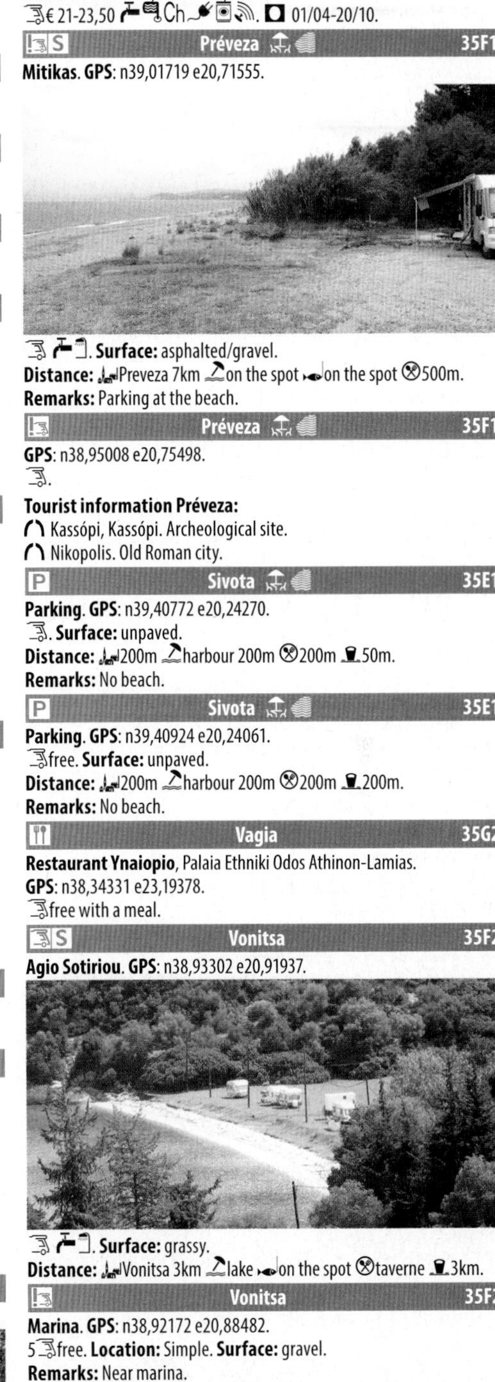

. **Surface:** asphalted/gravel.
Distance: Preveza 7km on the spot on the spot 500m.
Remarks: Parking at the beach.

Préveza — 35F1
GPS: n38,95008 e20,75498.

Tourist information Préveza:
Kassópi, Kassópi. Archeological site.
Nikopolis. Old Roman city.

Sivota — 35E1
Parking. GPS: n39,40772 e20,24270.
. **Surface:** unpaved.
Distance: 200m harbour 200m 200m 50m.
Remarks: No beach.

Sivota — 35E1
Parking. GPS: n39,40924 e20,24061.
free. **Surface:** unpaved.
Distance: 200m harbour 200m 200m 200m.
Remarks: No beach.

Vagia — 35G2
Restaurant Ynaiopio, Palaia Ethniki Odos Athinon-Lamias.
GPS: n38,34331 e23,19378.
free with a meal.

Vonitsa — 35F2
Agio Sotiriou. GPS: n38,93302 e20,91937.

. **Surface:** grassy.
Distance: Vonitsa 3km lake on the spot taverne 3km.

Vonitsa — 35F2
Marina. GPS: n38,92172 e20,88482.
5 free. **Location:** Simple. **Surface:** gravel.
Remarks: Near marina.

Peloponnisos/Attica

Agia Kyriaki — 35G3
GPS: n36,71883 e23,02305.
Remarks: At the beach.

Agios Andreas — 35G2
GPS: n37,37120 e22,78262.

WC free. **Surface:** gravel.
Distance: 3km on the spot on the spot on the spot.
Remarks: At harbour.

GR

Agios Andreas 35G2

Camping Agios Andreas. **GPS**: n36,86664 e21,92087.
. 20/04-30/09.
Distance: on the spot.

Agios Fokas 35G3

GPS: n36,59565 e23,06108.

5 . **Surface:** sand.
Distance: Monemvasia 13km.
Remarks: Parking at pier.

Agios Kiriaki 35F3

Filiatra, Epar.Od.Filiatron. **GPS**: n37,11963 e21,57611.
. 01/01-31/12.

Assini 35G2

Kastraki. **GPS**: n37,52861 e22,87556.
€ 24,50-26,50 Ch WC . 01/04-01/10.

Athens 35G2

GPS: n37,96987 e23,72263.
. 01/01-31/12.
Remarks: Parking of the Acropolis, guarding after authorization Probably only outside the main season.

Athens 35G2

Athens camping, Leoforis Athinon.
GPS: n38,00889 e23,67222.
€ 29 Ch WC .
01/01-31/12.

Tourist information Athens:
Monasteraki. Old district with Athenian flea market.
Su 8-14h.
Panathenaic Stadium. Stadium of the first Olympic Games in 1896.
Plaka. Old district around the Acropolis.
Tomb of the Unknown Soldier, Plateía Syntágmatos. Sunday 11h changing of the guard.
Acropolis. Archeological site.
01/05-31/10 Mo-Fri 8-18.30h, Sa-Su 8.30-14.30h, 01/11-30/04 8.30-16.30h
01/05, 28/10, holiday.

Bozas 35G3

GPS: n36,70437 e22,82144.

20 free for clients Ch.
Location: Isolated. **Surface:** sand. 01/01-31/12.
Distance: on the spot on the spot.

Diakofto 35F2

GPS: n38,19747 e22,20167.

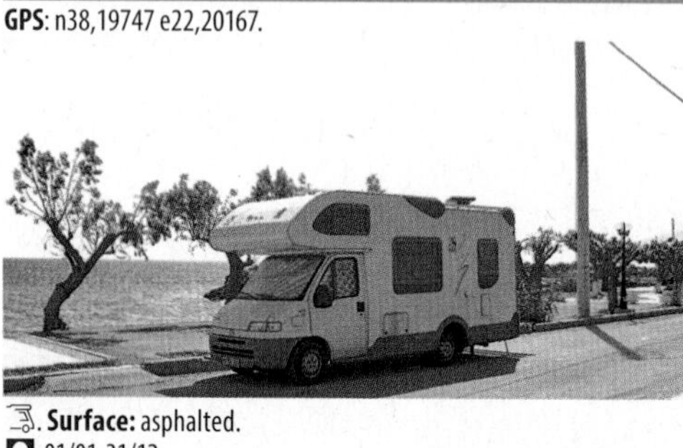

. **Surface:** asphalted.
01/01-31/12.
Distance: on the spot on the spot on the spot 500m.
Remarks: Parking at harbour.

Tourist information Diakofto:
Rack railway, Kalavryta. Train journey with rack-railway.

Dimitsána 35F2

Kefalari tou Ai-Yanni. **GPS**: n37,59058 e22,04286.
4 .
Remarks: Parking water museum.

Dimitsána 35F2

Taverna Koustenis, Eparchiaki Odos Kato Davias.
GPS: n37,58650 e22,04459.
5 free. **Location:** Rural, simple.
Surface: gravel.
Distance: 9km on the spot.

Tourist information Dimitsána:
Loúsios-kloof. 5km long and 300m deep, marked trails.

Elefsina 35G2

GPS: n38,04235 e23,53942.
. 01/01-31/12.
Remarks: Parking in front of the ruins in the city center.

Epidaurus 35G2

GPS: n37,59675 e23,07444.

WC free.
Surface: gravel.
Remarks: Overnight stay on parking at the Ancient theater is generally tolerated.

Tourist information Epidaurus:
Ancient Epidaurus. Archeological site. 8-19h.

Ermioni 35G2

Hydras Wave. **GPS**: n37,40583 e23,31556.
€ 18 Ch WC . 15/04-15/10.

Galatas 35G2

Epar.Odos Ermionis. **GPS**: n37,49491 e23,45546.
20 .
Distance: on the spot on the spot.
Remarks: At the quay.

Gerolimenas 35G3

GPS: n36,48230 e22,39969.

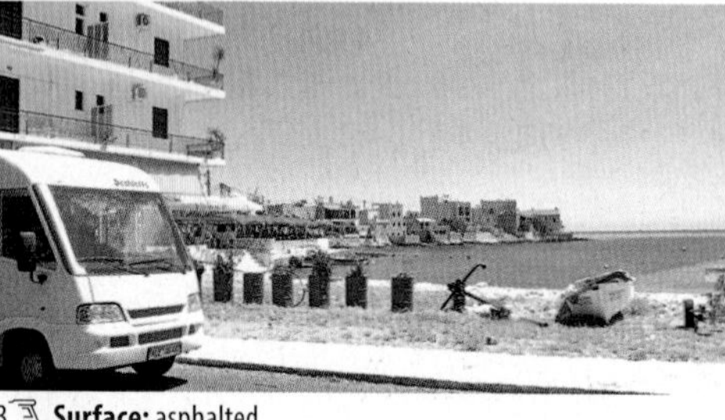

3 . **Surface:** asphalted.
Distance: on the spot on the spot 50m on the spot.
Remarks: Parking at the beach.

Gialova Pylou 35F3

Navarino Beach. **GPS**: n36,94770 e21,70620.
€ 20-23 Ch WC . 01/04-31/10.

Glifa Kyllini 35F2

Ionion. **GPS**: n37,83640 e21,13340.
€ 21-24,50 Ch . 01/01-31/12.

Gythion 35G3

Valtaki beach, Valtaki. **GPS**: n36,78883 e22,58225.

. **Surface:** sand.
Distance: on the spot on the spot.
Remarks: At the beach, ± 5km from Gythion dir Skala.

Gythion 35G3

Gythion Bay. **GPS**: n36,72942 e22,54535.
€ 20,50-22 Ch . 01/04-31/10.

Kakovatos 35F2

GPS: n37,45721 e21,63869.
. **Surface:** metalled.
Remarks: Parking at the beach.

Kalo Nero 35F2

GPS: n37,29786 e21,69525.

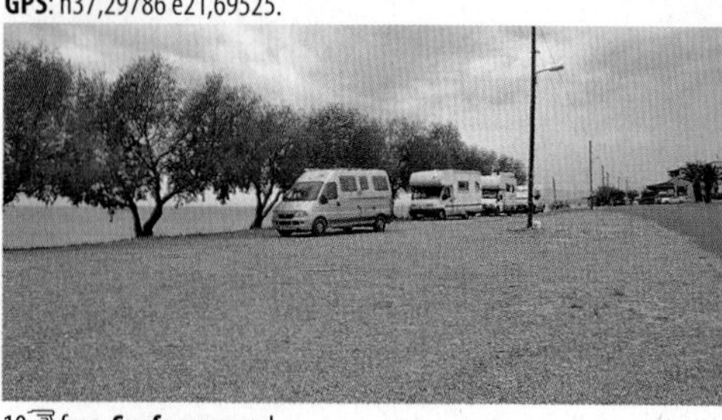

10 free. **Surface:** gravel.
Distance: 100m Sandy beach 100m.

Kalogria 35F2

Camper Stop Kalogria, Kalogria. **GPS**: n38,15986 e21,37162.

40 € 10, 16/07-31/08 € 12 Ch (20x)€3/day WC included.
Surface: unpaved. 01/05-31/10.
Distance: 5km 11km 500m 300m 50m on the spot on the spot on the spot on the spot.

Tourist information Kalogria:
Kotychi, Lapas. Visitors centre, swamp area.

Kamares 35G3

GPS: n36,68203 e22,52090.

. **Surface:** sand.
Distance: on the spot on the spot 350m.

Kameras Irion 35F1

Poseidon. **GPS**: n40,01305 e22,59039.
€ 30-38 Ch WC . 01/04-31/10.

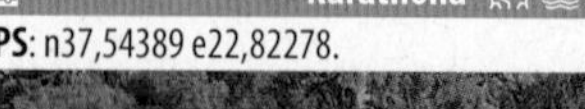

Karathona 35G2

GPS: n37,54389 e22,82278.

50 free.
Distance: Sandy beach.

GR

Karavostasi 35G3

Taverna Faros
Karavostasi
Located directly at see
Restaurant with regional specialties
Paved and flat motorhome pitches
www.taverna-faros.eu
faroskaravostasimani@gmail.com

Taverna O Faros, Karavostasi. **GPS**: n36,69733 e22,38073.
15 free. **Location:** Rural, simple. **Surface:** gravel.
Distance: on the spot on the spot.
Remarks: No beach.

Kastro 35F2

Killinis Beach. **GPS**: n37,87413 e21,10748.

free. **Surface:** grassy/sand.
Distance: 2km on the spot on the spot Beach taverne.
Remarks: Beach parking.

Tourist information Kastro:
Chlemoutsi. Medieval castle.

Kato Alissos 35F2

Kato Allissos. GPS: n38,14986 e21,57740.
€ 18,30-19 Ch WC. 30/06-01/09.

Kifisiá 35G2

Dionissiotis. GPS: n38,10535 e23,81355.
€ 19 Ch WC. 01/01-31/12.
Remarks: 18km north of Athens, route Athens dir Lamia.

Tourist information Kifisiá:
Holiday resort of the Athenian since the Roman time.
Gouländris, Levidou 13. History of nature.

Killini 35F2

Epar Od. Andravidas-Killinis. **GPS**: n37,92598 e21,16699.
Distance: 2km.
Remarks: Parking at the beach.

Kiveri 35G2

GPS: n37,52761 e22,73120.

10 free. **Surface:** gravel.
Distance: 200m pebbled beach 50m 100m.
Remarks: At harbour.

Kokkinia 35G3

GPS: n36,79762 e22,78485.

20 free. **Surface:** metalled.
Distance: Sandy beach 400m.
Remarks: Beach parking.

Korfos 35G2

GPS: n37,76361 e23,13302.

Surface: gravel.
Remarks: At fishing port.

Korinthos 35G2

Afrodites Waters, Ancient Corinth. **GPS**: n37,91139 e22,87861.

20 € 10 Ch WC included. 01/01-31/12.
Distance: 350m 350m 350m.

Korinthos 35G2

Ancient Corinth. **GPS**: n37,90750 e22,87806.

Tourist information Korinthos:
Important trade centre.
Korinth Canal. Canal, 23m wide.
Acrocorinth. Fortress.
8-19h, winter 8-17h. free.
Ancient Korinthos. Archeological site.
01/04-31/10 8-19h, 01/11-31/03 8-17h
25/12-26/12, 01/01, 25/03, Easter, 01/05.

Koroni 35F3

GPS: n36,79729 e21,96002.

Remarks: Parking at harbour.

Koroni 35F3

Camping Koroni. GPS: n36,79942 e21,95068.
€ 25 Ch WC. 01/01-31/12.
Distance: 600m on the spot on the spot.

Tourist information Koroni:
Port city with Venetian castle, 1206.

Kosmas 35G2

Epar.Od.Leonidiou-Kosma. **GPS**: n37,09180 e22,74043.

Surface: metalled.
Distance: on the spot on the spot on the spot.
Remarks: Behind church.

Kotronas 35G3

GPS: n36,61899 e22,49367.

free. **Surface:** concrete.
Distance: on the spot on the spot 50m.
Remarks: Parking at pier.

Lambiri 35F2

Tsolis, Old National Road. **GPS**: n38,32083 e21,97194.
€ 17-20 Ch WC. 01/01-31/12.

Legrena 35G2

GPS: n37,66206 e23,99772.
01/01-31/12.

Marathon 35G2

Ramnous.
GPS: n38,13139 e24,00722.
€ 27-35 Ch WC.
01/04-31/10.

Tourist information Marathon:
www.marathon.gr. The name marathon, course of 41 km, comes from this town.

Mayroyouni/Gythion 35G3

Meltemi.
GPS: n36,72986 e22,55360.
€ 19 Ch WC.

Tourist information Mayroyouni/Gythion:
Tourist Information Areópoli, Vasiléos Pávlou 21, Máni. Peninsula.
Pýrgos Diroú, Máni. Caves.

Monemvasía 35G3

GPS: n36,68240 e23,03821.
Remarks: Parking harbour.

Monemvasía 35G3

GPS: n36,68875 e23,05076.
Surface: asphalted.
Distance: on the spot on the spot shuttle to old town.

Tourist information Monemvasía:
Fortified city, lower town have been restored.
Agía Sofia. Church 13th century.

Mycenae 35G2

Atreus. GPS: n37,71911 e22,74114.
€ 24-32 Ch WC. 01/01-31/12.

Tourist information Mycenae:
Archeological Museum, Argos. € 12.
Archeological site. 1/4-31/10 8-19h, 1/11-31/3 8-17h holi-

GR

day.
Agora Argos, Argos. Archeological site.
summer 8.30-15h.

Nafplio 35G2
GPS: n37,56823 e22,80170.

free.
Surface: asphalted.
Distance: 500m 300m.
Remarks: Parking marina.

Tourist information Nafplio:
Tourist information, Ikostispémtis Martiou 2. First Greek capital.
Archeological Museum. Tue-Su 8.30-15h Mo.
Palamídi. Citadel 18th century.

Neo Itylo 35G3
Black Pirate. **GPS**: n36,69154 e22,38986.

10 free. **Surface:** grassy/gravel.
Distance: on the spot pebbled beach on the spot 50m.

Olympia 35F2
Alphios. **GPS**: n37,64360 e21,61930.
€ 24-33 Ch WC. 01/04-31/10.

Tourist information Olympia:
Archeological Museum. Important Greek archeological museum.
Mo 11-19h, Tue-Su 8-19h.

Paralia Astros 35G2
GPS: n37,44475 e22,74800.

. **Surface:** gravel.
Distance: on the spot on the spot 200m.
Remarks: At the beach.

Paralia Platanou 35F2
GPS: n38,17104 e22,26828.

. **Surface:** gravel.
Distance: on the spot.
Remarks: At the beach.

Paralia Rizomilos 35F2
GPS: n38,21898 e22,14745.

free. **Surface:** gravel.
Distance: on the spot on the spot on the spot mini market (summer).
Remarks: Not in front of hotel.

Pátra 35F2
Golden Sunset, Old national Road km 19. **GPS**: n38,14389 e21,58778.
€ 32-39 Ch WC. 01/04-15/10.

Tourist information Pátra:
Archaïa Klauss. First commercial producer of wine of Greece.

Perahóra 35G2
Limni Vouliagmenis. **GPS**: n38,03188 e22,87293.

.
Distance: on the spot on the spot.
Remarks: At the lake.

Petalidi 35F3
GPS: n36,95871 e21,93418.
. **Surface:** asphalted.
Remarks: Nearby port.

Petalidi 35F3
GPS: n36,95915 e21,92870.

. **Surface:** asphalted.
Distance: on the spot.
Remarks: Parking in village, near the sea.

Pírgos Dhiroú 35G3
Diros. **GPS**: n36,64206 e22,38357.

20. **Location:** Isolated. **Surface:** unpaved.
Distance: on the spot.

Porto Kagio 35G3
Taverna Porto. **GPS**: n36,42811 e22,48697.
max. 3 guests free. **Surface:** grassy.
Distance: on the spot on the spot on the spot mini market.

Rafina 35G2
GPS: n38,01835 e24,01227.
. 01/01-31/12.

Salandi 35G2
GPS: n37,44748 e23,12474.

. **Location:** Isolated. **Surface:** gravel.
Distance: Didyma 5km on the spot on the spot.
Remarks: At the beach.

Savalia 35F2
Savalia Beach. **GPS**: n37,79685 e21,25578.

. **Surface:** asphalted.
Distance: on the spot on the spot.

Skoutari 35G3
GPS: n36,65921 e22,49962.

max. 3. **Surface:** concrete.
Distance: on the spot on the spot within walking distance.
Remarks: Near fishing-port.

Sounion 35G2
Camping Bacchus.
GPS: n37,67694 e24,04750.
€ 23 Ch WC.
01/01-31/12.

Tourist information Sounion:
Mineralogical Museum, Lavrió. Old mine shaft of the silvermines.
Wed, Sa-Su.
Archeological site.

Tolo 35G2
GPS: n37,51469 e22,85662.

WC. **Surface:** asphalted.
Distance: 500m 100m on the spot 200m.
Remarks: Near fishing-port.

Tyrchu 35G2
Taverne Ostria. **GPS**: n37,31414 e22,82054.

GR

3 guests free. **Surface:** gravel.
15/05-30/09.
Distance: Tyros 10km on the spot on the spot on the spot.
Remarks: At the beach, attention: via steep path.

Zacharo 35F2

GPS: n37,51917 e21,60248.

Distance: on the spot.

Zacharo 35F2

Tholo Beach. GPS: n37,41160 e21,66830.
€ 18,50 Ch WC . 01/04-31/10.

Greece North

Ag.Mamas Moudania 35H1

Ouzoni Beach. GPS: n40,21611 e23,31833.
€ 17,60-23 Ch WC . 01/05-30/09.

Akt Armenistis Sithonia 35H1

Armenistis. GPS: n40,15222 e23,91361.
€ 31-40 Ch WC . 01/05-15/09.

Alexandroúpoli 35H1

GPS: n40,84364 e25,87693.

Remarks: Parking harbour.

Alexandroúpoli 35H1

Apollonias.
GPS: n40,84342 e25,86477.
Surface: asphalted.
Remarks: Parking near stadium.

Tourist information Alexandroúpoli:
Tourist Information, Mákris. Large holiday resort, beautiful beach.

Gerakani 35H1

Kouyoni. GPS: n40,26464 e23,46347.
€ 22,25-24,50 Ch . 01/05-30/09.

Kalamaria 35G1

Zampetaz, Tessaloniki-Perea. **GPS:** n40,50289 e22,97053.
10 free Ch free. **Location:** Simple.
Surface: asphalted.
Distance: 10km 3km on the spot.

Kastoriá 35F1

GPS: n40,50461 e21,27977.
against payment .
Remarks: Voluntary contribution.

Metamorphosi 35H1

Sunny Bay. GPS: n40,22694 e23,58944.
€ 18,90-21,70 Ch WC . 01/05-31/10.

Moustheni 35H1

Moysthenі Station. GPS: n40,84413 e24,11506.
10 free Ch . **Surface:** asphalted.
Distance: 100m on the spot mini market.
Remarks: Special part for motor homes, shop, restaurant, station 24/24.

Ouranoupoli 35H1

Ouranoupoli. GPS: n40,33944 e23,97056.
€ 28-31 Ch . 01/04-31/10.

Paralia Epanomi 35G1

Golden Beach. GPS: n40,40469 e22,89925.
10 € 10 €5. **Location:** Rural, simple.
Surface: grassy/sand.
Distance: on the spot on the spot.

Porto Lagos 35H1

GPS: n41,00633 e25,12028.

5 free . **Surface:** asphalted.
Distance: on the spot.
Remarks: Parking at pier.

Vergina 35G1

Parking, Aristotelos 25. **GPS:** n40,48506 e22,31978.
25 € 4 €2. **Location:** Urban, simple. **Surface:** asphalted.
Distance: on the spot 200m 450m.

GR

Croatia

Capital: Zagreb
Government: parliamentarian democracy
Official Language: Croatian
Population: 4,491,000 (2014)
Area: 56,594 km²

General information
Dialling code: 00385
General emergency: 112
Currency: Kuna, kn, 1 kuna = 100 lipa
1kn = € 0,13, € 1 = 7,52 kn
10kn = £1.15, £1 = 8,73 kn (November 2016)
Credit card are accepted almost everywhere.

Regulations for overnight stays
Wild camping is forbidden.

Additional public holidays 2017
January 6 Epiphany
May 1 Labor Day
June 15 Corpus Christi
June 22 Dan antifasisticke borbe, Anti-Fascist Resistance Day
June 25 Dan drzavnosti, National Holiday
August 5 Victorie Day and National Thanksgiving
August 15 Assumption of the Virgin Mary
October 8 Independence Day

Time Zone
Winter (Standard Time) GMT+1
Summer (DST) GMT+2

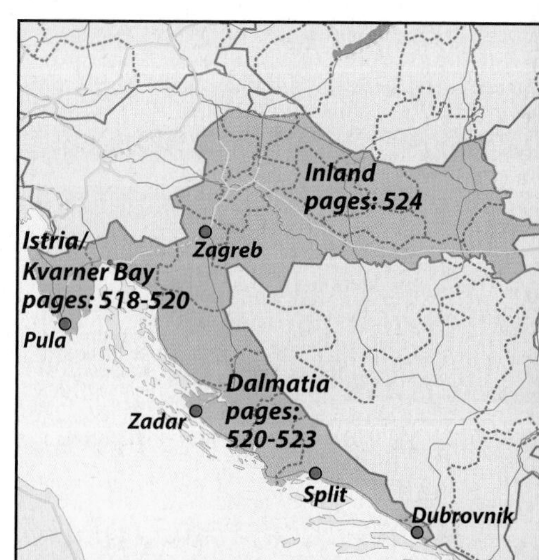

HR

Istria/Kvarner Bay

S Baderna 38A2
Farm Pino, Katun 1. **GPS**: n45,22020 e13,72908.

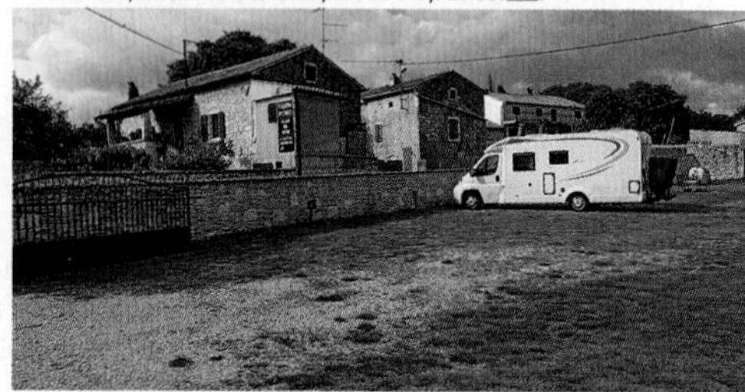

14 € 10 + € 3/pp Ch (23x) WC Service €4 €2
Location: Rural, isolated, quiet. **Surface:** grassy.
01/01-31/12.
Distance: 2km 6km 2km 400m on the spot on the spot.

S Cres/Cres 38A2
Kovačine, Melin I, 20. **GPS**: n44,96278 e14,39694.
€ 19,20-41,10 Ch WC. 19/03-16/10.
Distance: on the spot.

Tourist information Cres/Cres:
Turisticka zajednica, Riva Creskih Kapetana, www.tzg-cres.hr. Island can be reached with ferry service from Brestova, south of Rijeka and Valbiska, west Krk.

S Cres/Martinšćica 38A3
Slatina. **GPS**: n44,82091 e14,34238.
€ 16-28,20 Ch WC. 19/03-31/10.

S Cres/Nerezine 38A3
Lopari, Nerezine. **GPS**: n44,68253 e14,39846.
€ 13-24,50 Ch WC. 25/03-10/10.

S Cres/Nerezine 38A3
Preko Mosta, Osor 76, Nerezine. **GPS**: n44,69250 e14,39167.
KN 129-179 Ch WC. 01/04-30/09.

S Cres/Nerezine 38A3
Rapoća, Rapoća, Nerezine. **GPS**: n44,66357 e14,39756.
€ 20-28 Ch WC. 22/04-10/10.

S Crikvenica 38A2
Kacjak, Kacjak BB. **GPS**: n45,16703 e14,70511.
Ch WC. 15/05-15/09.

S Dobrinj 38A2
Slamni Camping, Klimno 8a. **GPS**: n45,15360 e14,61758.
€ 20,27 Ch WC. 22/04-10/10.

S Fažana 38A3
Ul.1.Maja. **GPS**: n44,92880 e13,80255.

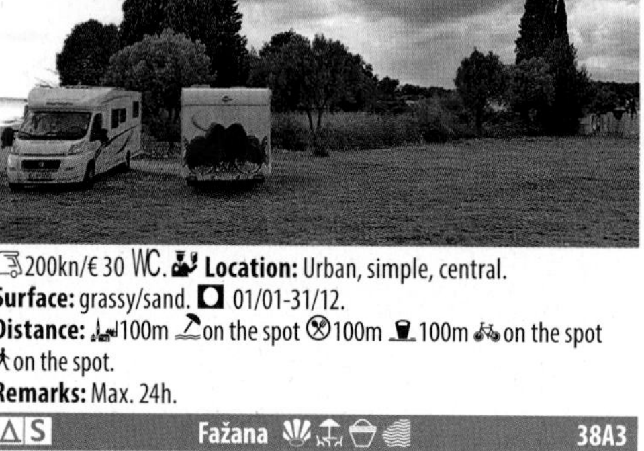

200kn/€ 30 WC. **Location:** Urban, simple, central.
Surface: grassy/sand. 01/01-31/12.
Distance: 100m on the spot 100m 100m on the spot on the spot.
Remarks: Max. 24h.

S Fažana 38A3
Bi Village, Dragonja 115. **GPS**: n44,91750 e13,81111.
€ 21-46 Ch WC. 21/04-30/09.

S Fažana 38A3
Pineta Fažana, Perojska cesta bb.
GPS: n44,93835 e13,79554.
€ 11,10-24,10 Ch WC.
27/04-30/09.

Tourist information Fažana:
Nationaal Park Brijuni, Brijuni. Nature reserve, boat connection from Fažana. daily.

Grožnjan 38A2
Parking bus. **GPS**: n45,38163 e13,72375.

20 free. **Location:** Rural, simple, isolated, quiet.
Surface: gravel. 01/01-31/12.
Distance: 200m 200m on the spot on the spot on the spot.
Remarks: Next to cemetery.

S Ičići 38A2
Opatija. **GPS**: n45,31083 e14,28472.
Ch WC. 27/04-13/10.

S Klenovica 38A2
Klenovica, Zidinice BB. **GPS**: n45,09788 e14,84393.
€ 19-26,60 Ch. 01/05-30/09.
Distance: on the spot on the spot.

S Koromačno 38A2
Tunarica. **GPS**: n44,96917 e14,09889.
€ 20,50-24,10 Ch WC. 29/04-30/09.

S Kraljevica 38A2
Ostro. **GPS**: n45,27109 e14,56402.
Ch. 01/05-30/09.

S Krk/Baška 38A2
Kamp Mali, Put Zablace 100. **GPS**: n44,96609 e14,74710.

33 € 10-20 Ch (30x),10Amp WC €5 included.
Location: Urban, comfortable, central, quiet. **Surface:** grasstiles.
01/03-30/10.
Distance: 300m 150m on the spot on the spot 50m on the spot on the spot.

S Krk/Baška 38A2
Zablace, Emila Geitslicha 34, Baška. **GPS**: n44,96694 e14,74528.
€ 38,50-47,30 Ch WC. 01/05-01/10.

S Krk/Klimno 38A2
Slamni, Klimno 8a. **GPS**: n45,15351 e14,61770.
€ 18-38 Ch. 22/04-10/10.
Remarks: Mini-camp.

S Krk/Krk 38A2
Camper Stop Felix, Ulica Narodnog preporoda 51.
GPS: n45,02928 e14,58149.

12 € 25 Ch (12x),16Amp WC €5 included.
Location: Urban, comfortable, central, quiet. **Surface:** grassy/gravel.
01/01-31/12.
Distance: 300m 300m 300m 50m 50m on the spot on the spot on the spot.

S Krk/Krk 38A2
Bor. **GPS**: n45,02250 e14,56194.
€ 20,40-29 Ch WC. 01/01-31/12.

S Krk/Krk 38A2
Jezevac, Plavnička bb. **GPS**: n45,01963 e14,57000.
€ 26-38 Ch WC. 25/03-01/10.

S Krk/Krk 38A2
Marta, Škrbcici 29. **GPS**: n45,04930 e14,48940.
€ 12,30-17,10 Ch WC. 01/05-30/09.
Remarks: Mini-camp.

Tourist information Krk/Krk:
Tourist Information, Vela placa 1/1, www.krk.hr. Krk accessible via toll-bridge south-east from Rijeka.
Jazz-festival, Kamplin. Aug.

Krk/Malinska 38A2

Draga, Palih Boraca 4. **GPS**: n45,12052 e14,52494.
€ 12,90-17 Ch WC. 01/04-15/10.
Remarks: Mini-camp.

Krk/Malinska 38A2

Glavotok, Glavokok 4. **GPS**: n45,09472 e14,44111.
€ 17,95-43,15 Ch WC. 22/04-02/10.
Distance: on the spot.

Krk/Njivice 38A2

Njivice, Primorska bb. **GPS**: n45,16963 e14,54740.
€ 20,80-40,20 Ch WC. 09/04-30/10.

Krk/Omišalj 38A2

Pusca, Pušča bb. **GPS**: n45,23613 e14,55108.
Ch WC. 01/06-30/09.

Krk/Pinezici 38A2

Amar, Njivine 8. **GPS**: n45,04351 e14,47985.
Remarks: Mini-camp.

Krk/Punat 38A2

Maslinik, Nikole Tesle 1. **GPS**: n45,01809 e14,63478.
€ 13,33-21,99 Ch WC. 01/04-04/10.
Remarks: Mini-camp.

Krk/Punat 38A2

Pila, Setalište Ivana Brusića. **GPS**: n45,01581 e14,62860.
250 € 15-20 Ch. 22/04-09/10.

Krk/Punat 38A2

Škrila, Stara Baška. **GPS**: n44,96611 e14,67389.
350 € 20,60-33,20 Ch.
01/04-01/10.

Tourist information Krk/Punat:
Otočić Košljun. Monastery.

Krk/Šilo 38A2

Tiha Šilo, Konjska bb. **GPS**: n45,14876 e14,67150.
€ 16,50-26 Ch WC. 01/04-15/10.
Remarks: Mini-camp.

Labin 38A2

Kamp Tunarica, Koromačno. **GPS**: n44,96933 e14,09979.

50 € 15, 01/07-31/08 € 19 Ch (50x)€4/night,16Amp WC €5 included. **Location:** Rural, simple, isolated, quiet.
Surface: forest soil. 01/05-30/09.
Distance: 15km on the spot on the spot on the spot on the spot 2km on the spot.

Labin 38A2

Camping Romantik, Kapelica 47b. **GPS**: n45,08167 e14,10188.
20 € 17-24 Ch WC €5,30 included.
Distance: 2km on the spot on the spot.
Remarks: Mini-camp.

Labin 38A2

Marina. **GPS**: n45,03333 e14,15806.
€ 27,80-42,10 Ch WC. 25/03-30/10.

Labin 38A2

Marina, Sveta Marina.
GPS: n45,03387 e14,15723.
€ 37-47 Ch WC. 25/03-30/10.
Remarks: Mini-camp.

Tourist information Labin:
Narodni muzej, N. Katunara 6. Ethnological museum.
daily 10-13h, 17-19h.

Lošinj/Mali Lošinj 38A3

Čikat. **GPS**: n44,53750 e14,45056.
940 € 22,50-36,60 Ch WC. 01/01-31/12.

Lošinj/Mali Lošinj 38A3

Poljana. **GPS**: n44,55556 e14,44167.
€ 16,50-21 Ch WC. 17/03-17/10.

Tourist information Lošinj/Mali Lošinj:
Dolphins day, action day with possibility for adoption of a dolphin.
1st Sa Aug.

Medulin 38A3

Indije, Banjole. **GPS**: n44,82398 e13,85090.
Ch WC. 01/05-01/10.

Medulin 38A3

Kazela. **GPS**: n44,80695 e13,95015.
Ch WC. 01/04-15/10.

Medulin 38A3

Kranjski Kamp, Runke 52, Premantura. **GPS**: n44,80694 e13,91616.
€ 19,80-27,10 Ch WC. 01/06-18/09.
Remarks: Mini-camp.

Medulin 38A3

Medulin. **GPS**: n44,81417 e13,93194.
1500 Ch WC. 03/04-09/10.

Medulin 38A3

Piškera, Indie 49, Banjole. **GPS**: n44,82332 e13,84855.
KN 170-200 Ch WC.
Remarks: Mini-camp.

Medulin 38A3

Pomer, Pomer. **GPS**: n44,82064 e13,90205.
Ch WC.
Remarks: Mini-camp.

Medulin 38A3

Postolovic, Bumbište 10. **GPS**: n44,82037 e13,85749.
Ch.
Remarks: Mini-camp.

Medulin 38A3

Runke, Premantura. **GPS**: n44,80742 e13,91632.
€ 28-37 Ch WC. 01/05-30/09.

Medulin 38A3

Širola, Rupice Bd. **GPS**: n44,82113 e13,85872.
10 Ch.
Remarks: Mini-camp.

Medulin 38A3

Stupice, Premantura. **GPS**: n44,79779 e13,91354.
Ch. 01/05-25/09.

Medulin 38A3

Tasalera, Premantura.
GPS: n44,81425 e13,91275.
€ 27-35 Ch WC. 01/04-30/09.

Tourist information Medulin:
Premantura. Most Southern place of Istria.
Banjole. Fisherman's village with natural harbour.

Moščenička Draga 38A2

Draga. **GPS**: n45,24023 e14,25021.
131-186kn Ch. 15/04-01/10.
Remarks: Mini-camp.

Moščenička Draga 38A2

Draga. **GPS**: n45,24000 e14,25028.
165. 15/04-15/10.

Motovun 38A2

Motovun Camping, Rizanske skupstine 1a.
GPS: n45,33446 e13,82523.

12 € 15-25 + tourist tax € 1/pp Ch WC included.
Location: Rural, comfortable.
Surface: gravel. 01/01-31/12.
Distance: 50m on the spot 50m 50m 100m on the spot on the spot.
Remarks: Free entrance swimming pool, discount longer stays.

Novi Vinodolski 38A2

Autocamp Sibinje, Sibinj. **GPS**: n45,04405 e14,87751.
80 € 24 Ch WC. 01/04-30/09.
Distance: on the spot 50m 50m.
Remarks: Mini-camp.

Novigrad (Istria) 23H3

Mareda. **GPS**: n45,34149 e13,54610.
800 from € 17 Ch WC included. 15/04-30/09.

Novigrad (Istria) 23H3

Sirena. **GPS**: n45,31528 e13,57556.
€ 32-52 Ch WC. 01/04-30/09.

Tourist information Novigrad (Istria):
Hoofdstraat van de oude stad. Farmers market. daily.
Feest van de beschermheilige Pelegrinus, Umag. 23/05.

Poreč 38A2

30. Travinja/Karla Huguesa. **GPS**: n45,22104 e13,60742.

28 200kn, winter free. **Location:** Simple, central, noisy.
Surface: asphalted. 01/01-31/12.
Distance: 800m 2km 2km 400m 2km 500m on the spot on the spot.

Poreč 38A2

Bijela Uvala. **GPS**: n45,19139 e13,59667.
2000 € 35-52 Ch WC. 01/04-15/10.

Poreč 38A2

Laternacamp. **GPS**: n45,29639 e13,59444.
3000 from € 22,65 Ch WC. 01/04-15/10.

Poreč 38A2

Puntica, Funtana. **GPS**: n45,17749 e13,60406.
250 Ch WC. 11/04-13/10.

Poreč 38A2

Zelena Laguna. **GPS**: n45,19611 e13,58917.
1000 € 32,50-55 Ch WC. 01/04-15/10.

Poreč 38A2

Materada, Materada. **GPS**: n45,24628 e13,59600.
Remarks: Mini-camp.

Tourist information Poreč:
Turisticka zajednica, Zagrebacka 9, www.istra.com/porec. Old city, centre tourist and cultural.
Decumanus. Roman main street with palazzi from the Venetian time.
Zavicajnog muzeja poreštine. Native museum of Porec. daily 10-13h, 18-22h.
Eufrazijeva bazilika. Basilica, 6th century, in the centre. daily 7-19h.

Pula 38A3

Puntižela. **GPS**: n44,89806 e13,80722.
Ch WC included. 01/05-31/10.

Pula 38A3

Stoja. **GPS**: n44,86000 e13,81472.
750 € 32,50-40,90 Ch WC.
03/04-02/11.

Tourist information Pula:
Arheoloski Muzej Istre, Carrarina 3. Archeological museum. winter Mo-Fri 9-14h, summer Mo-Sa 9-19h.
Amfiteatar. Large anfiteatro from Roman time. daily 8-21h.
Ljetni klasicni Festival, Amfitheatar. Opera festival. Aug.

Rab 38A3

Camperpark Lando Resort, Kampor 321. **GPS**: n44,78404 e14,70682.
Ch WC €7 included. **Location:** Comfortable.
Surface: grassy/metalled. 01/01-31/12.
Distance: city centre 1,5km 50m 50m 1,5km on the spot on the spot.
Remarks: Heated pool.

Rab 38A3

Mel, Kampor 319. **GPS**: n44,79390 e14,70302.
Remarks: Mini-camp.

Rab 38A3

Planka, Kampor 326. **GPS**: n44,78049 e14,72048.
Remarks: Mini-camp.

Rabac 38A2

Oliva. **GPS**: n45,07960 e14,14777.
300 Ch WC. 15/03-30/09.
Distance: on the spot.

HR

Ribnik 38B2
Srce Prirode/Heart of Nature Camp, Gorica Lipnička 8.
GPS: n45,56389 e15,39278.
30 € 29,40-35 Ch WC. 01/04-31/10.
Remarks: Mini-camp.

Rijeka 38A2
Preluk Katalinic, Preluk 1.
GPS: n45,35340 e14,33235.
90 Ch WC.
Remarks: Mini-camp.

Tourist information Rijeka:
Tourist Information, Kastav 47, Kastav. Walled city with rich history.
Pomorski i povijesni muzej, Muzejski trg 1. Navy museum. Mo-Fri 10-13h, 18-21h.
Velika trznica. Market opposite to Modello palace.
Carnaval van Rijeka. Feb.

Rovinj 38A2
Aleja Ruera Boskovica. **GPS**: n45,08898 e13,64537.
30 25kn/h 6-23h (± € 55), overnight stay free ChWCincluded.
Location: Urban, simple, central, noisy. **Surface:** asphalted.
01/01-31/12.
Distance: 1km 300m 300m 300m 1km 300m on the spot on the spot.

Rovinj 38A2
Camping Polari. **GPS**: n45,06300 e13,67480.
40 € 12-32 Ch WC included 25kn 100kn.
Location: Rural, simple, quiet. **Surface:** grassy/metalled.
22/04-04/10.
Distance: 3km on the spot on the spot on the spot on the spot on the spot June/July/Aug on the spot on the spot.
Remarks: Camperstop max. 48h.

Rovinj 38A2
Mon Paradiso, Uvala Veštar. **GPS**: n45,04947 e13,69000.
40 € 36-50 Ch WC. 01/06-30/09.
Remarks: Mini-camp.

Rovinj 38A2
Polari. **GPS**: n45,06258 e13,67477.
2150 € 18-44,80 Ch WC. 22/04-02/10.

Rovinj 38A2
Porton Biondi. **GPS**: n45,09410 e13,64232.
396 KN 114-226 Ch WC. 15/03-30/10.

Rovinj 38A2
Valdaliso. **GPS**: n45,10389 e13,62500.
400 Ch WC included. 20/04-15/10.

Rovinj 38A2
Vestar. **GPS**: n45,05389 e13,68639.
800 € 15-52,40 Ch WC. 22/04-25/09.

Rovinj 38A2
Ulika, Polari Bd. **GPS**: n45,06528 e13,67583.
01/04-01/10.
Remarks: Mini-camp.

Tourist information Rovinj:
Turisticka zajednica, Budicin 12, www.istra.com/rovinj. City has been a cultural monument since 1963.
Aquarium, Obala G. Paliage 5. daily 9-21h.
Palazzo Califfi, Trg Marsala Tita 11. Tue-Su 10.30-14h, summer 18-20h.
Market.
Grisia, Grisia. Art festival. 2nd week Aug.

Savudrija 23H3
Pineta. **GPS**: n45,48667 e13,49250.
460 € 15,70-36,70 Ch WC. 22/04-25/09.

Savudrija 23H3
Veli Jože, Borozija. **GPS**: n45,49556 e13,50444.
Ch WC. 01/04-30/09.

Savudrija 23H3
Ravna Dolina. **GPS**: n45,49246 e13,50490.
01/05-30/09.

Selce 38A2
Selce. **GPS**: n45,15408 e14,72533.
€ 17,50-31,10 Ch. 01/04-15/10.

Selina 38A2
Camp Terre, 79. **GPS**: n45,15770 e13,76765.
10 100-125kn Ch (14x),16Amp WC €5 included.
Location: Rural, luxurious, isolated, quiet.
Surface: gravel.
01/01-31/12.
Distance: 3km 5km 3km 3km on the spot on the spot.

Umag 23H3
Finida. **GPS**: n45,39278 e13,54194.
204 € 15,70-36,30 Ch WC. 22/04-25/09.

Umag 23H3
Stella Maris. **GPS**: n45,45056 e13,52278.
400 € 15,50-24,40 Ch WC. 24/04-25/09.

Vižinada 38A2
Agroturizam Jadruhi, Jadruhi 11. **GPS**: n45,29978 e13,74819.
10 50kn Ch (6x)included,16Amp WC free.
Location: Rural, simple, isolated, quiet. **Surface:** gravel/metalled.
01/01-31/12.
Distance: 4km 6km on the spot 4km on the spot on the spot on the spot.
Remarks: Check in at restaurant.

Vrsar 38A2
Camperstop Valkanela, Fontana. **GPS**: n45,16501 e13,60804.
20 € 12-32 Ch WC included 100kn/24h.
Location: Urban, simple, central, quiet.
Surface: grassy.
22/04-03/10.
Distance: 500m on the spot on the spot on the spot 1km on the spot on the spot.
Remarks: Camperstop, max. 48h, use camp-site facilities incl.

Vrsar 38A2
Dalmatinska ulica. **GPS**: n45,14706 e13,60422.
30 50kn/day. **Location:** Urban, simple, central, noisy.
Surface: asphalted. 01/01-31/12.
Distance: 350m 350m 350m 350m 350m 350m on the spot on the spot.

Vrsar 38A2
Porto Sole. **GPS**: n45,14139 e13,60222.
800 € 15,40-38,60 Ch WC. 01/03-01/11.

Dalmatia

Babino Polje 39B2
Mungos. **GPS**: n42,73885 e17,53441.
€ 25-35 Ch. 15/05-30/09.
Remarks: Mini-camp.

Baška Voda 39A2
Basko Polje. **GPS**: n43,34561 e16,96272.
€ 29-37 Ch WC. 15/05-30/09.

Bibinje 38B3
Andela. **GPS**: n44,05557 e15,29263.
Ch.
Remarks: Mini-camp.

Bibinje 38B3
Dido, Težački put. **GPS**: n44,05708 e15,29116.
Ch WC.
Remarks: Mini-camp.

Bibinje 38B3
Kero, Punta Bibinje. **GPS**: n44,05730 e15,28918.
€ 20 Ch WC.
Remarks: Mini-camp.

Bibinje 38B3
Punta, Težački put. **GPS**: n44,05680 e15,29162.
Remarks: Mini-camp.

Biograd na Moru 38B3
Dijana & Josip, Put Solina 26. **GPS**: n43,93229 e15,45252.
€ 42-50 Ch WC. 01/05-30/09.
Remarks: Mini-camp.

Biograd na Moru 38B3
Ljutic, Put Solina. **GPS**: n43,92654 e15,45353.
€ 26-36 Ch WC. 01/05-01/10.
Remarks: Mini-camp.

Biograd na Moru 38B3
Mia, Put Solina 47. **GPS**: n43,93441 e15,44803.
€ 18-40 Ch. 01/01-31/12.
Remarks: Mini-camp.

Biograd na Moru 38B3
Soline, Put Kumenta. **GPS**: n43,92756 e15,45595.
€ 21,90-39,20 Ch WC. 22/04-30/09.

Bol 39A2
Kito, Ante Radića 1. **GPS**: n43,26407 e16,64820.
KN 110-180 Ch WC. 01/01-31/12.

Drace-Pelješac 39B2
Plaža, Janjina. **GPS**: n42,92477 e17,43079.
Remarks: Mini-camp.

Dubrovnik 39B2
Solitudo, Vatroslava Lisinskog 17. **GPS**: n42,66178 e18,07052.
€ 24,20-51,60 Ch WC.
01/04-31/10.

Tourist information Dubrovnik:
Akvarij Dubrovnik, D. Jude 2. Sea aquarium. Mo-Sa 9-13h.
City Walls, Gundulićeva poljana 2. City wall surround the entire Old City. 10-12h, 01/04-31/10 10-18.30h. 90kn.
Place Stradun. Main street with Onofrio-fountain and Sveti Frane monastery.
Dubrovacki Muzej, Pred Dvorom 3. History of the city. Mo-Sa 9-14h.
Pomorski Muzej, Sveti Ivan. Shipping museum. Tue-Sa 9-16h.
Zomerfestival. 10/07-25/08.

HR

Dugi Rat 39A1

Ivo, Duce Rogac. **GPS**: n43,44111 e16,65778.
€ 11-20 Ch WC. 15/04-15/11.
Remarks: Mini-camp.

Dugi Rat 39A1

Luka, Duce Rogac. **GPS**: n43,44164 e16,65347.
€ 12,50-21 Ch WC. 30/06-01/09.
Remarks: Mini-camp.

Dugi Rat 39A1

Orij, Orij, Duce Rogac. **GPS**: n43,44631 e16,63429.
Remarks: Mini-camp.

Grebaštica 39A1

Ante&Toni, Brodarica. **GPS**: n43,63833 e15,95833.
25 Ch WC. 01/05-01/10.
Distance: 100m on the spot.
Remarks: Mini-camp.

Grebaštica 39A1

Tomas, D8. **GPS**: n43,63003 e15,93764.
30 € 10,70 Ch WC. 01/05-01/11.
Distance: on the spot.
Remarks: Mini-camp.

Kaštel Kambelovac 39A1

U Dragama, A. Starcevica 39. **GPS**: n43,54951 e16,37778.
Remarks: Mini-camp.

Kaštel Štafilic 39A1

Koludrovac, Resnik Bb. **GPS**: n43,54373 e16,31753.
Remarks: Mini-camp.

Kaštel Stari 39A1

Kamp- Biluš Josip. **GPS**: n43,55162 e16,34978.
KN 95-138 Ch WC. 01/04-30/09.
Remarks: Mini-camp.

Kaštel Stari 39A1

Adria. **GPS**: n43,55143 e16,35349.
Remarks: Mini-camp.

Kolan 38B3

Sveti Duh. **GPS**: n44,51518 e14,95525.
KN 120-150 Ch. 01/06-30/09.
Remarks: Mini-camp.

Korčula 39A2

Kalac. **GPS**: n42,95056 e17,14500.
€ 40-50 Ch WC. 01/06-01/10.

Korčula 39A2

Oskorušica, Oskorušica 27/ VI, Racišce. **GPS**: n42,96795 e17,07335.
Ch WC.
Remarks: Mini-camp.

Korčula 39A2

Vela Postrana, Lumbardra 142.
GPS: n42,92230 e17,17266.
Ch WC.
Remarks: Mini-camp.

Tourist information Korčula:
Turisticka zajednica, Obala Tudmana, www.korcula.net. City with historical centre, birth-place Marco Polo.
Marco Polo fest. 09/07-11/07.
Zwaarddansfestival. daily 04/07-23/08.

Korenica 38B2

Bistro Marina, Zagrebaćka 6. **GPS**: n44,74702 e15,70464.

12 guests free €2/100liter €2/night,10Amp WC.
Location: Urban, simple, central, quiet.
Surface: asphalted.
06/01-30/01.
Distance: 100m on the spot 10m 100m on the spot on the spot.
Remarks: Guests free.

Kornati/Murter 38B3

Jazina, Tisno. **GPS**: n43,80940 e15,62760.
KN 93,20-155 Ch WC. 01/04-15/10.

Kornati/Murter 38B3

Jezera-Lovišća, Jezera. **GPS**: n43,79370 e15,62867.
€ 16,55-36 Ch WC. 28/04-10/10.

Kornati/Murter 38B3

Kosirina, Betina. **GPS**: n43,79727 e15,61004.
Ch WC. 01/05-30/09.

Kornati/Murter 38B3

Plitka Vala, Betina. **GPS**: n43,80515 e15,61284.
€ 14,50-23,60 Ch WC. 01/04-31/10.

Kornati/Murter 38B3

Slanica, Jurija Dalmatinca 17. **GPS**: n43,81682 e15,57733.
KN 109,40-173,40 Ch WC. 15/04-15/10.

Krvavica 39A2

Autocamp Krvavica. **GPS**: n43,32375 e16,98559.
Distance: 100m.

Kucište 39A2

Palme. **GPS**: n42,97639 e17,12917.
€ 16,50-26 Ch WC. 01/06-01/10.

Kucište 39A2

Plaža, Viganj 4, Od Gaja. **GPS**: n42,97935 e17,10400.
Remarks: Mini-camp.

Lokva Rogoznica 39A2

Danijel, Ruskamen bb. **GPS**: n43,40973 e16,74529.
Ch WC.
Remarks: Mini-camp.

Lokva Rogoznica 39A2

Linda. **GPS**: n43,40834 e16,75683.
Ch WC.
Remarks: Mini-camp.

Lovište 39A2

Lupiš. **GPS**: n43,02790 e17,03012.
€ 20-30 Ch WC. 01/03-01/11.
Remarks: Mini-camp.

Lukoran 38B3

Novi Kamp, Punta 28. **GPS**: n44,10538 e15,15518.
Remarks: Mini-camp.

Mlini 39B2

Kate, Tupina 1. **GPS**: n42,62472 e18,20806.
KN 158-214 Ch. 04/04-28/10.
Remarks: Mini-camp.

Mlini 39B2

Kupari, Kupari bb. **GPS**: n42,62462 e18,18833.
€ 11,50-15,20 Ch WC. 01/04-30/09.
Remarks: Mini-camp.

Mlini 39B2

Matkovica, Srebreno 8. **GPS**: n42,62450 e18,19295.
€ 20-24 Ch WC.
Remarks: Mini-camp.

Mlini 39B2

Paradiso Laguna, Za Gospom, Plat. **GPS**: n42,60759 e18,22838.
KN 109-130 Ch.
Remarks: Mini-camp.

Mlini 39B2

Porto, Srebreno. **GPS**: n42,62433 e18,19107.
Ch.
Remarks: Mini-camp.

Mljet 39B2

Marina, Marina Matana,Ropa 11. **GPS**: n42,75260 e17,46000.
€ 27,80-42,10 Ch WC. 25/03-30/10.
Remarks: Mini-camp.

Mokalo 39B2

Adriatic. **GPS**: n42,97694 e17,22500.
01/04-31/10.

Molunat 39B2

Adriatic I, Višnjici 4, Đurinici. **GPS**: n42,45341 e18,43554.
Ch.
Remarks: Mini-camp.

Molunat 39B2

Monika, Molunat 10. **GPS**: n42,45284 e18,42871.
KN 80-180 Ch. 01/01-31/12.
Remarks: Mini-camp.

Molunat 39B2

Adriatic II. **GPS**: n42,45327 e18,43582.
Remarks: Mini-camp.

Nin 38B3

Dišpet, Put Ždrijaca 13. **GPS**: n44,24618 e15,18971.
€ 26-35 Ch WC. 01/04-15/10.
Remarks: Mini-camp.

Nin 38B3

Nin, Put Venere Anzotike 41. **GPS**: n44,24541 e15,17401.
KN 100-132 Ch. 01/05-15/10.
Remarks: Mini-camp.

Nin 38B3

Ninska Laguna, Put blata 10. **GPS**: n44,24639 e15,17389.
€ 10-20 Ch WC. 15/04-15/10.
Remarks: Mini-camp.

Tourist information Nin:
Arheološka zbirka Nin, Trg Kraljevac 8. Archeological museum.
01/10-31/5 8-14h, 01/06-30/09 8-22h.

Novigrad (Dalmatia) 38B3

Adria-Sol Mulic. **GPS**: n44,19019 e15,54703.
€ 17,70-19,70 Ch WC. 01/05-30/09.
Remarks: Mini-camp.

Obrovac 38B3

Zrmanja Camping Village, Kruševo, Župani - Drage bb.
GPS: n44,18506 e15,69279.
Remarks: Mini-camp.

Omiš 39A1

Galeb. **GPS**: n43,44061 e16,68128.
KN 126,80-248,60 Ch WC. 13/05-01/11.

Omiš 39A1

Lisičina, Lisičina 2. **GPS**: n43,44737 e16,69038.
KN 76-131 Ch WC. 01/01-31/12.
Remarks: Mini-camp.

Opuzen 39B2

Rio, Put Zlatinovca 23. **GPS**: n43,01147 e17,47035.
€ 18-25 Ch WC. 01/04-30/10.

Orašac 39B2

Pod Maslinom, Put prema moru b.b.. **GPS**: n42,69907 e18,00592.
KN 96-138 Ch. 01/04-01/11.
Remarks: Mini-camp.

Pag 38B3

Košljun, Košljun B.B.. **GPS**: n44,39849 e15,07936.
KN 131-156 Ch WC. 01/06-01/10.
Remarks: Mini-camp.

Pag 38B3

Pere, Dinjiška. **GPS**: n44,35939 e15,18641.
€ 15 WC. 01/05-15/10.
Remarks: Mini-camp.

Pag 38B3

Porat, Stjepana Radića bb., Povljana. **GPS**: n44,34914 e15,10547.
60 € 12,66-20,94 Ch WC. 23/04-30/09.
Remarks: Mini-camp.

Pag 38B3

Simuni, V. Nazora b.b, Simuni. **GPS**: n44,45979 e14,97670.
94-379kn Ch WC. 01/01-31/12.

Pakoštane 38B3

Blaž. **GPS**: n43,90763 e15,50089.
Ch.
Remarks: Mini-camp.

Pakoštane 38B3

Kozarica. **GPS**: n43,90970 e15,49881.
€ 16,90-48,90 Ch WC. 15/04-15/10.

Pakoštane 38B3

Marin. **GPS**: n43,90442 e15,51866.
€ 13,50-32,50 Ch WC. 01/07-31/10.
Remarks: Mini-camp.

Pakoštane 38B3

Nordsee. **GPS**: n43,90525 e15,51617.
€ 14,40-27,50 Ch WC. 01/03-05/11.

Pakoštane 38B3

Oaza Mira, Dr. Franje Tuđmana bb, Drage. **GPS**: n43,88607 e15,53290.
150 € 23-56 Ch WC. 01/04-15/10.
Remarks: Mini-camp.

Pakoštane 38B3

Oaza, Drage. **GPS**: n43,87035 e15,55917.

HR

€ 14-24 Ch WC. 01/04-15/10.
Remarks: Mini-camp.

Pakoštane — 38B3

Pakoštane. **GPS**: n43,91258 e15,49772.
Remarks: Mini-camp.

Pašman — 38B3

Camp Arboretum, Barotul 8. **GPS**: n43,96283 e15,36082.
€ 20-22 Ch WC. 01/06-30/09.
Remarks: Mini-camp.

Pelješac/Orebić — 39B2

Camping Ponta, Kvaternikova 3. **GPS**: n42,97722 e17,22444.
30 65-80kn WC.
Distance: on the spot on the spot.

Pelješac/Orebić — 39B2

Ulica Bana Josipa Jelačića. **GPS**: n42,97499 e17,16929.
±10 70kn. **Surface:** grassy/gravel. 01/01-31/12.
Distance: pebbled beach 500m.

Pelješac/Orebić — 39B2

Camping Adriatic, Mokalo 6. **GPS**: n42,97672 e17,22489.
€ 14-35,50 Ch WC. 01/04-31/10.
Remarks: Mini-camp.

Pelješac/Orebić — 39B2

Glavna Plaža. **GPS**: n42,97583 e17,18917.
€ 12-20,20 Ch WC. 15/05-15/10.

Pelješac/Orebić — 39B2

Paradiso. **GPS**: n42,96750 e17,24293.
Ch.
Remarks: Mini-camp.

Pelješac/Orebić — 39B2

Perna. **GPS**: n42,97638 e17,13272.
€ 13,50- 18,80 Ch. 16/04-14/10.

Pelješac/Orebić — 39B2

Trstenica, Šetalište Kneza Domagoja 50. **GPS**: n42,97725 e17,18995.
25 Ch WC.
Remarks: Mini-camp.

Pelješac/Orebić — 39B2

Paradiso, Obala Pomoraca 70 A. **GPS**: n42,96693 e17,24230.
Remarks: Mini-camp.

HR

Pelješac/Trpanj — 39B2

Divna. **GPS**: n43,00944 e17,26806.
100 Ch. 01/06-30/09.
Remarks: Mini-camp.

Pelješac/Trpanj — 39B2

Vrila. **GPS**: n43,00360 e17,28467.
Ch WC. 20/05-10/10.

Petrcane — 38B3

Pineta, Punta Radman 21. **GPS**: n44,17805 e15,16161.
KN 110-138 Ch WC. 01/05-01/09.
Remarks: Mini-camp.

Podgora — 39A2

Sutikla. **GPS**: n43,23455 e17,07759.
KN 99-198 Ch WC. 22/06-15/09.

Podstrana — 39A1

Tamaris, Sv.Martin 114. **GPS**: n43,47551 e16,56383.
50 € 18,70-21,37 Ch WC. 15/06-15/09.
Distance: on the spot.
Remarks: Mini-camp.

Podstrana — 39A1

Car, Sv. Martin 180. **GPS**: n43,47479 e16,56624.
Remarks: Mini-camp.

Tourist information Podstrana:
Sinjska alka, Sinj. Knight celebration. 5th August.

Posedarje — 38B3

Kristina. **GPS**: n44,21288 e15,49820.
€ 12,80-15,80 Ch. 01/05-30/09.
Remarks: Mini-camp.

Posedarje — 38B3

Bristi. **GPS**: n44,21231 e15,48038.
Remarks: Mini-camp.

Povijana — 38B3

Mali Dubrovnik, Kralja P. Svacica 1. **GPS**: n44,34931 e15,10060.
Ch WC.
Remarks: Mini-camp.

Povijana — 38B3

Porat, Ante Starcevica Bb. **GPS**: n44,14466 e15,08569.
30 KN 120-136 Ch WC. 01/05-01/10.
Remarks: Mini-camp.

Primošten — 39A1

Zagrebacka ul.. **GPS**: n43,58854 e15,92632.
10 € 7/24h.
Distance: 200m 200m 200m 200m.

Primošten — 39A1

Adriatic, Huljerat b.b.. **GPS**: n43,60645 e15,92193.
€ 16,80-30,90 Ch WC. 07/04-31/10.

Privlaka — 38B3

Dalmacija, Ivana Pavla II 40. **GPS**: n44,25613 e15,12557.
€ 15,70-40,40 Ch WC. 01/05-15/10.

Privlaka — 38B3

Medanić, Put Brtalica 47. **GPS**: n44,24887 e15,13379.
Ch WC.
Remarks: Mini-camp.

Ražanac — 38B3

Kamp Miočić, Rtina I 139, Rtina. **GPS**: n44,29219 e15,30179.
Ch WC.

Ražanac — 38B3

Kamp Odmoree, Rtina Stošići bb. **GPS**: n44,30040 e15,28881.
13 KN 345 Ch.

Ražanac — 38B3

Planik. **GPS**: n44,27778 e15,34472.
€ 14,94-19,33 Ch WC. 01/01-31/12.
Remarks: Mini-camp.

Ražanac — 38B3

Puntica, Puntica 1. **GPS**: n44,28389 e15,34306.
€ 12-18,80 Ch WC. 01/05-15/10.
Remarks: Mini-camp.

Rovanjska — 38B3

Tamaris. **GPS**: n44,25037 e15,53735.
30 KN 112-142 Ch WC. 01/05-01/10.
Remarks: Mini-camp.

Senj — 38A2

Kamp Škver, Filipa Vukasovica 5. **GPS**: n44,99385 e14,90012.

50 69kn, Jun/Sep 89kn, Jul/Aug 106kn Ch night,20kn, 16Amp WC 35kn included **Location:** Urban, comfortable. **Surface:** gravel/metalled. 01/04-01/10.
Distance: 500m on the spot on the spot on the spot 150m 500m on the spot on the spot.
Remarks: Fishing permit available.

Senj — 38A2

Bunica, Bunica 33. **GPS**: n45,02607 e14,88630.
Ch.
Remarks: Mini-camp.

Senj — 38A2

Ujca, M. Cihlar Nehajeva, 4. **GPS**: n44,96833 e14,92167.
KN 100-150 Ch WC. 01/05-01/10.
Distance: on the spot.
Remarks: Mini-camp.

Šibenik — 38B3

Cikada, Konjevodci 63. **GPS**: n43,78200 e15,99116.
10 € 9-12 + € 0,50-1/pp tourist tax Ch €2,50 WC. **Location:** Rural. **Surface:** gravel. 01/05-31/10.

Šibenik — 38B3

Camperstop, Lozovac-Gradina. **GPS**: n43,79207 e15,97042.

kn 40. **Surface:** unpaved. 01/01-31/12.
Remarks: 1km from Krka waterfalls.

Šibenik — 38B3

Solaris. **GPS**: n43,69917 e15,87795.
€ 15-62 Ch WC. 24/03-20/10.

Šibenik — 38B3

Solaris-Zablaće, Obala palih boraca 2a. **GPS**: n43,70524 e15,86850.
€ 30-32,50 Ch WC. 01/05-30/09.

Tourist information Šibenik:
Internationaal kinderfestival. 22/06-06/07.
Nacionalni Park Krka, Krka. Nature reserve.

Skradin — 38B3

Robeko Camping, Piramatovci. Bilostanovi 12.
GPS: n43,89193 e15,82320.
Ch WC.
Remarks: Mini-camp.

Slano — 39B2

Baldo. **GPS**: n42,79683 e17,84989.
€ 26-32 Ch. 19/04-09/10.
Remarks: Mini-camp.

Slano — 39B2

Bambo. **GPS**: n42,77513 e17,88500.
Ch.
Remarks: Mini-camp.

Slano — 39B2

Banja, Put Od Banje. **GPS**: n42,77414 e17,88405.
Ch.
Remarks: Mini-camp.

Slano — 39B2

Rogac, Grgurici. **GPS**: n42,78229 e17,87536.
KN 64-76 Ch WC. 01/04-01/10.
Remarks: Mini-camp.

Slano — 39B2

Sladenovici, Sladenovici 9. **GPS**: n42,78451 e17,85984.
€ 11 Ch.
Remarks: Mini-camp.

Slatine — 39A1

Domic, Put Porta 71, Ciove. **GPS**: n43,49784 e16,34060.
Remarks: Mini-camp.

Soline — 38B3

Camping Mandarino. **GPS**: n44,14148 e14,86495.
€ 20-48 Ch WC. 14/05-30/09.
Remarks: Mini-camp.

Split — 39A1

Stobreč. **GPS**: n43,50401 e16,52644.

€ 16,70-30,30 Ch WC.
01/01-31/12.
Distance: centre 7km on the spot.

Tourist information Split:
Arheoloski Muzej, Zrinjsko-Frankopanska 25. Findings from Roman time and Middle Ages. Tue-Fri 9-14h, Sa-Su 9-13h, 01/06-30/09 Tue-Fri 9-12, 13-20h, Sa-Su 9-13h.
Galerija Ivana Mestrovica, Setaliste I. Mestrovica 46. Gallery. Mo-Sa 10-18h, Su 10-14h.
Muzej Hrvatskih Arheoloskih Spomenika, S. Gunjace bb. Archeological findings. Mo-Sa 9-20h.
Dioklecijanova palača. Roman palace.

Starigrad/Paklenica 38B3

Camp National Park, Paklenica. **GPS**: n44,28832 e15,44573.
€ 35-50 Ch WC. 15/03-15/10.
Remarks: Mini-camp.

Starigrad/Paklenica 38B3

Marko, Paklenicka 7, Paklenica. **GPS**: n44,28643 e15,45247.
€ 16-19 Ch WC. 01/01-31/12.
Remarks: Mini-camp.

Starigrad/Paklenica 38B3

Pinus, Ive Senjanina 5, Paklenica. **GPS**: n44,32242 e15,39288.
€ 12,70-16,80 Ch WC. 01/05-01/09.
Remarks: Mini-camp.

Starigrad/Paklenica 38B3

Pisak, Paklenica. **GPS**: n44,27285 e15,47806.
KN 124-146 Ch WC. 01/05-01/10.
Remarks: Mini-camp.

Starigrad/Paklenica 38B3

Plantaža, Put Plantaže 2, Paklenica. **GPS**: n44,30056 e15,43211.
€ 27-33 Ch WC. 01/01-31/12.
Remarks: Mini-camp.

Starigrad/Paklenica 38B3

Vesna, Paklenicka 103, Paklenica. **GPS**: n44,28610 e15,45243.
Ch WC. 01/01-31/12.
Remarks: Mini-camp.

Starigrad/Paklenica 38B3

Jaz, Seline, Paklenica. **GPS**: n44,28323 e15,46028.
01/05-30/09.
Remarks: Mini-camp.

Tourist information Starigrad/Paklenica:
Nacionalni park "Paklenica". Nature reserve, 150 km biking ad hiking trails, bird observation, tunnels and caves.

Ston 39B2

Prapratno. **GPS**: n42,81778 e17,67611.
€ 35-50 Ch WC. 01/05-30/09.

Ston 39B2

Vrela, Brijesta 10. **GPS**: n42,90397 e17,53266.
€ 22-30 Ch WC. 01/04-30/10.
Remarks: Mini-camp.

Sukošan 38B3

Brajde. **GPS**: n44,04256 e15,30755.
Ch WC.
Remarks: Mini-camp.

Sukošan 38B3

Malenica, Vl. Milan Gašparović. **GPS**: n44,03658 e15,32790.
50 WC. 01/05-01/10.
Remarks: Mini-camp.

Sukošan 38B3

Oliva. **GPS**: n44,04247 e15,30805.
Ch WC. 01/01-31/12.
Remarks: Mini-camp.

Sukošan 38B3

Kaj. **GPS**: n44,04278 e15,30655.
Remarks: Mini-camp.

Supetar 39A2

Waterman Beach. **GPS**: n43,38076 e16,56439.
Ch WC. 01/05-30/09.

Sutivan 39A2

Mlin, Brac. **GPS**: n43,38316 e16,47795.
Remarks: Mini-camp.

Sutivan 39A2

Sutivan, Gorana Pavlova 12. **GPS**: n43,38523 e16,48460.
01/01-31/12.

Sv. Filip I Jakov 38B3

Antonio, Turanj. **GPS**: n43,97488 e15,39990.
Ch WC.
Remarks: Mini-camp.

Sv. Filip I Jakov 38B3

Djardin, Sveti Filip i Jakov bb. **GPS**: n43,96139 e15,42750.
€ 14,60-26,20 Ch WC. 23/04-01/10.

Sv. Filip I Jakov 38B3

Filip, Put Primorja 10a. **GPS**: n43,96055 e15,42910.
€ 9,73-26,66 Ch WC. 01/04-01/10.
Remarks: Mini-camp.

Sv. Filip I Jakov 38B3

Maestral, Turanj 90. **GPS**: n43,96611 e15,41162.
KN 122-152 Ch WC. 01/05-31/10.
Remarks: Mini-camp.

Sv. Filip I Jakov 38B3

Moce, Put Primorja 8. **GPS**: n43,95968 e15,42915.
€ 13,32-26,66 Ch WC. 01/04-01/10.
Remarks: Mini-camp.

Sv. Filip I Jakov 38B3

Rio, Put Primorja. **GPS**: n43,95583 e15,43500.
€ 33-44 Ch WC.
Remarks: Mini-camp.

Sv. Filip I Jakov 38B3

Ante, Turanj. **GPS**: n43,99637 e15,37915.
Remarks: Mini-camp.

Sv. Filip I Jakov 38B3

Bepo, Turanj. **GPS**: n43,96562 e15,41254.
Remarks: Mini-camp.

Sv. Filip I Jakov 38B3

Bozo, Sv. Petar. **GPS**: n43,99688 e15,37838.
Remarks: Mini-camp.

Sv. Filip I Jakov 38B3

Jugo, Turanj. **GPS**: n43,96605 e15,41173.
Remarks: Mini-camp.

Sv. Filip I Jakov 38B3

Livada. **GPS**: n43,95976 e15,43108.
Remarks: Mini-camp.

Sv. Filip I Jakov 38B3

Milan, Sv. Petar. **GPS**: n44,00205 e15,36859.
Remarks: Mini-camp.

Sv. Filip I Jakov 38B3

R & B, Turanj. **GPS**: n43,96592 e15,41196.
Remarks: Mini-camp.

Sveti Juraj 38A2

Camping Ujča, Ujča 146/A. **GPS**: n44,96853 e14,92223.
100-110kn Ch WC. 01/05-01/10.
Remarks: Mini-camp.

Sveti Petar na Moru 38B3

Autocamp Martin. **GPS**: n44,00003 e15,36880.
15 € 14 Ch €3 WC. **Surface:** grassy/gravel.
01/01-31/12.
Distance: on the spot on the spot.

Tkon 38B3

Brist. **GPS**: n43,92312 e15,41493.
Ch.
Remarks: Mini-camp.

Tkon 38B3

Adriana. **GPS**: n43,91734 e15,42596.
Remarks: Mini-camp.

Tribanj 38B3

Camp CTT, D8. **GPS**: n44,34673 e15,32444.
7. **Surface:** grassy/gravel. 01/01-31/12.
Distance: 900m on the spot.
Remarks: Not suitable for motorhomes +7m.

Tribanj 38B3

Punta Šibuljina, Šibuljina. **GPS**: n44,33631 e15,34627.
150 € 13,95-22 Ch WC. 23/04-08/10.
Remarks: Mini-camp.

Tribanj 38B3

Ante, Krušcica. **GPS**: n44,34469 e15,32842.
Remarks: Mini-camp.

Trogir 39A1

Seget, Seget Donji. **GPS**: n43,51904 e16,22430.
50 from € 21 Ch WC. 01/03-31/10.
Distance: 800m on the spot.
Remarks: Mini-camp.

Trogir 39A1

Vranjica Belvedere, Seget Vranjica. **GPS**: n43,51196 e16,19159.
451 Ch WC. 15/04-15/10.

Tourist information Trogir:
Tourist Information, Ivana Pavla II Square, www.trogir-online.com.
City with rich culture from Greek, Roman and Venetian time.
Town Museum, Fanfogna palace, Garagnin. History of the city.
16/09-14/06 by request 8-14h, 15/06-15/09 9-21h.
Zbirka Kairos. Ecclesiastical art collection. 15/6-15/9 8-13, 15-19h.
Fortress Kamerlengo. Fortress. 15/6-15/9 9-20h.
Katedrala St. Lawrence. Bell-tower of Cathedral of St. Lawrence, 47m. 15/6-15/9 9-12, 16-19h. 5kn.

Vela Luka 39A2

Mindel, Stani 193. **GPS**: n42,98369 e16,67060.
€ 14 Ch WC. 01/01-31/12.

Veli Rat 38A3

Camping Kargita, Veli Rat 67. **GPS**: n44,15402 e14,82221.
30 € 17,10-31 Ch WC. 23/04-01/10.
Remarks: Mini-camp.

Viganj 39A2

Antony Boy. **GPS**: n42,97889 e17,10752.
KN 134-170 Ch WC. 01/01-31/12.

Vir 38B3

Luka. **GPS**: n44,29610 e15,10605.
Remarks: Mini-camp.

Vir 38B3

Sapavac, Put Bunara 101. **GPS**: n44,29432 e15,07640.
Remarks: Mini-camp.

Vodice 38B3

Imperial, Vatroslava Lisinskog 2/I. **GPS**: n43,75287 e15,78992.
145 € 23-41 Ch WC. 21/03-11/11.

Vransko Jezero 38B3

Crkvine. **GPS**: n43,93035 e15,51012.
€ 23-29 Ch WC. 15/04-15/10.

Vrsi 38B3

Mulic, Mulo. **GPS**: n44,26174 e15,21246.
Remarks: Mini-camp.

Zaboric 39A1

Jasenovo. **GPS**: n43,65116 e15,95025.
50 € 13-29 Ch WC. 01/05-01/10.
Distance: on the spot.
Remarks: Mini-camp.

Zadar 38B3

Borik, Radovana 7. **GPS**: n44,13528 e15,21528.
500 € 19,20-30,10 Ch WC. 01/05-01/10.

Tourist information Zadar:
Trg Pet Bunara. Square of the five fountains.
Arheoloski Muzej, Simuna Kozicica Benje bb. Archeological findings.
Mo-Sa 9-13h, 18-20h.
Muziekavonden in de St. Donatius van Zadar. 01/07-15/08.

Zaostrog 39B2

Uvala Borova, Mkarska. **GPS**: n43,13123 e17,28750.
90 € 21,80-32,60 Ch WC. 01/05-30/09.

Zaton 38B3

Zaton. **GPS**: n44,23385 e15,16671.
€ 22,60-57,70 Ch WC. 30/04-30/09.

Ždrelac 38B3

Ruža. **GPS**: n44,00987 e15,27653.
40 WC.
Remarks: Mini-camp.

Živogošće 39A2

Dole. **GPS**: n43,17118 e17,19669.
€ 36-45 Ch WC. 01/05-30/09.

Žrnovo 39A2

Vrbovica, Vrbovica bb. **GPS**: n42,95882 e17,11394.
KN 120-160 Ch WC. 01/06-01/09.
Remarks: Mini-camp.

Žrnovo 39A2

Tri Žala, Uvala Tri Žala 808. **GPS**: n42,96407 e17,09104.
Remarks: Mini-camp.

Žuljana 39B2

Vucine. **GPS**: n42,88257 e17,45135.
Ch WC.
Remarks: Mini-camp.

HR

Inland

Kopačevo 38D1

Family-Camperstop, Ferenca Kiša 7. **GPS**: n45,59832 e18,78467.
20. 01/04-30/09.

Koprivnica 38C1

Cerine, Miroslava Krleze 81. **GPS**: n46,15361 e16,84250.

11 first night 110kn, 75kn each additional night, 2 pers incl. + 7kn tourist tax Ch WC included. **Location:** Comfortable. **Surface:** grasstiles. 01/01-31/12.
Distance: 1,5km 300m 1km.
Remarks: Parking spa resort, wifi code at swimming pool.

Lipovac 38D2

Spacva. **GPS**: n45,04593 e18,99682.
. 01/05-01/10.

Plitviča 38B2

Bear, Selište Drežničko 52. **GPS**: n44,94804 e15,63639.

30 130kn, 01/06-30/09 150kn, 01/07-31/08 170kn Ch (30x),16Amp WC included. **Location:** Rural, comfortable, central, quiet. **Surface:** asphalted/gravel. 01/04-15/10.
Distance: 300m 700m 20km 150m 400m on the spot on the spot on the spot.
Remarks: Baker every morning, water falls Plitvica 5km.

Plitviča 38B2

Cvetkovic, Jezerce 28. **GPS**: n44,86338 e15,63967.

20 € 10/pp Ch WC included.
Location: Rural, comfortable, central, quiet. **Surface:** grassy/gravel. 01/01-31/12.
Distance: 800m 10km 800m 800m on the spot on the spot 800m 800m.
Remarks: Water falls Plitvica 2km.

Plitviča 38B2

Korana. **GPS**: n44,99260 e15,64916.
€ 20-24 Ch. 25/03-31/10.

Tourist information Plitviča:
Nacionalni Park Plitviča Jezera, www.np-plitvicka-jezera.hr. National park Plitvice lakes. 9-17h.

Racovica 38B2

Turist, Grabovac 102. **GPS**: n44,97222 e15,64750.
€ 20-26,40 Ch WC. 30/04-01/10.

Zagreb 38B2

Camp-Zagreb, Jezerska 6. **GPS**: n45,80253 e15,82622.

50 € 23-31 Ch WC included.
Location: Urban, luxurious. **Surface:** metalled.
Distance: on the spot on the spot on the spot on the spot on the spot.
Remarks: Bus to Zagreb € 8/round trip.

Tourist information Zagreb:
http://www.infozagreb.hr/. Capital, surface 64133 km², inhabitants 885,000, 11 theaters and 22 museums.
M Archeological Museum, 19 Nikola Subic Zrinski Square. Tue-Fri 10-17h, Sa-Su 10-13h.
M Atelje Mestrovic, Mletacka 8. Former dwellinghouse of sculptor Ivan Mestrovic. Tue-Fri 10-18h, Sa-Su 10-13h.
M Ethnographic Museum, Mazuranicev trg 14. Tue-Thu 10-18h, Fri-Su 10-13h.
M Muzej Grada Zagreb, Opaticka 20. City museum. Tue-Fri 10-18h, Sa 11-19h, Su 10-14h.
M Tehnicki Muzej, Savska cesta 18. Technical museum. Tue-Fri 9-17h, Sa-Su 9-13h.
Medjunarodna Smotra Folklora. International folk festival. 20/07/05-24/07/05.
Zomerfestival van Zagreb. 01/07-15/08.
Park Prirode Kopacki Rit. Nature reserve, boat rental. daily 8-16h.

HR

Hungary

Capital: Budapest
Government: parliamentary constitutional republic
Official Language: Hungarian
Population: 9,897,000 (2015)
Area: 93,024 Km²

General information
Dialling code: 0036
General emergency: 112
Currency: Forint (HUF)
€ 1 = 310 HUF, 100 HUF = € 0,32
£1 = 360 HUF, 100 HUF = £0.28 (November2016)
Credit cards are accepted almost everywhere.

Regulations for overnight stays
Free overnight stay is not allowed.

Additional public holidays 2017
March 15 Revolution Memorial Day 1848
March 28 Easter Monday
August 20 Hungarian National Day
October 23 Revolution Memorial Day 1956
November 1 All Saints' Day

Time Zone
Winter (Standard Time) GMT+1
Summer (DST) GMT+2

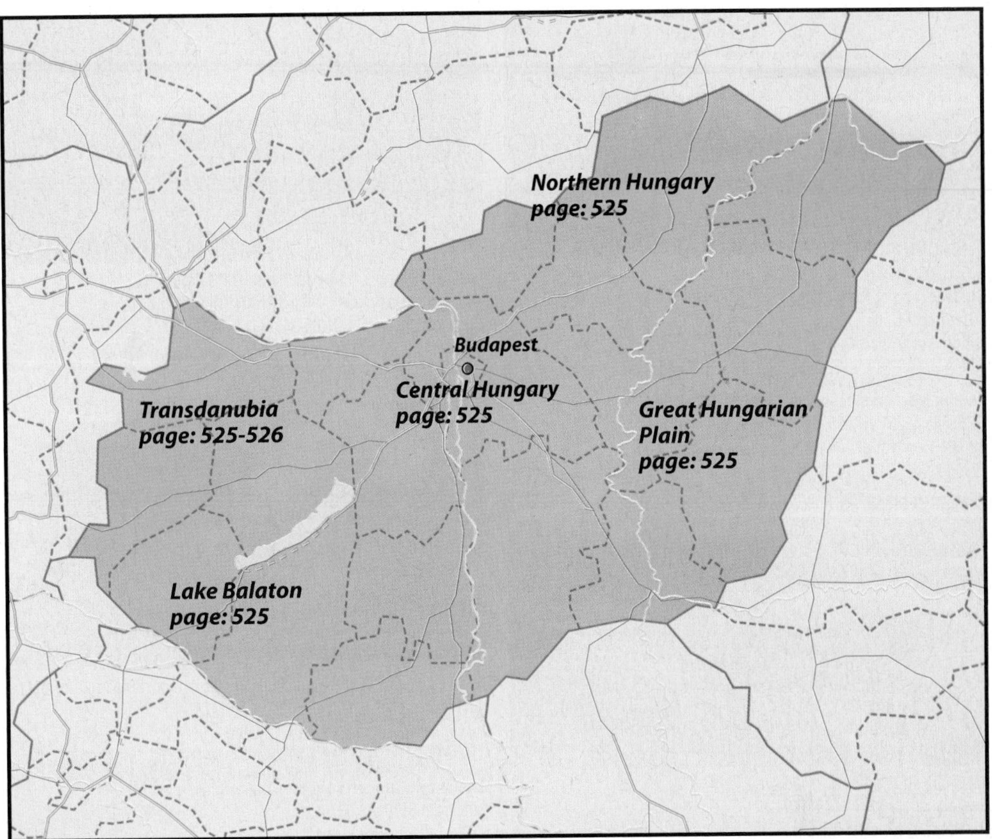

Northern Hungary

Bekölce 37C3
Camping Bekölce, Béke út 252. **GPS**: n48,08260 e20,24904.
10 € 15 Ch included. 01/01-31/12.

Borsodbóta 37C2
Camping Amedi, Rákóczi út 181. **GPS**: n48,21329 e20,40569.
40 € 12,50, 01/07-31/08 € 16,50 Chincluded €4.
Surface: grassy. 01/05-30/09.

Budapest 37C3
Ave Natura, Csermely u 3.
GPS: n47,51416 e18,97300.

12 € 18,50 Ch (12x)€3,80 WC included.
Surface: grassy/sand. 01/04-10/11.
Distance: 5km 100m 2km on the spot on the spot on the spot.

Hernádvécse 37C2
Zonnebloempaleis, Rákóczi út 96. **GPS**: n48,43360 e21,17230.
1 € 10, 15/06-28/08 € 12 Ch included. **Location:** Rural.
Surface: grassy. 14/04-01/10.
Distance: 2km.

Pécs 38C1
Família Camping, Gyöngyösi utca 6. **GPS**: n46,08559 e18,26206.
15 € 15 Ch included.
Location: Rural. **Surface:** metalled. 01/05-30/09.
Distance: 2,5km 200m 100m.

Great Hungarian Plain

Püspökladány 37C3
Árnyas Thermal Camping és Üdülőpark, Petőfi Sándor Ut 62.
GPS: n47,32192 e21,10273.
50 € 15 Ch included. **Location:** Rural.
Surface: grassy/metalled. 01/05-30/09.
Distance: on the spot.

Szentkirály 37C3
Fantazia Tanya, Felsö Tanya 165. **GPS**: n46,94087 e19,93109.
20 € 13 Chincluded €4. **Location:** Rural. **Surface:** grassy.
01/04-01/11.
Distance: on the spot.

Zsana 38D1
Camping Oázis Tanya, L Körzet 15. **GPS**: n46,41438 e19,61111.
20 € 16,20, 01/07-31/08 €18 Ch €2,50 included.
Location: Rural. **Surface:** grassy. 15/04-30/09.
Distance: 10km.

Central Hungary

Csemő 37C3
Békés Föld, Bezzeg dülö. **GPS**: n47,13217 e19,73983.
4 € 12,50 Ch included. **Surface:** grassy/sand.
01/01-31/12.

Lake Balaton

Balatonkeresztúr 38C1
Bertalan, Ady Endre utca 51. **GPS**: n46,70333 e17,37047.

6 € 12 Ch WC included. **Location:** Urban, simple.
Surface: grassy. 01/01-31/12 service: Jul/Aug.
Distance: on the spot lake Balaton 300m 200m 150m 500m.

Cserszegtomaj 38C1
Camping Panorama, Panoráma köz 1. **GPS**: n46,80667 e17,21306.
15 € 16 Ch included. **Surface:** grassy. 01/04-31/10.
Distance: 5km 5km 2km 2km.

Gyenesdiás 38C1
Wellnes-Park, Napfény utca 6. **GPS**: n46,76417 e17,30250.
€ 15,80-18,80 Ch included. **Surface:** grassy.
01/04-15/10.
Distance: 2km lake Balaton 2km 200m 500m 2km.

Kisbárapáti 38C1
Camping Jó Napot, Ady Endre utca 46. **GPS**: n46,59827 e17,86750.
15 € 15,50 Chincluded €3,50. **Location:** Rural.
Surface: grassy. 15/04-15/09.

Koppányszántó 38C1
Tranquil Pines, Dózsa György utca 334. **GPS**: n46,59027 e18,10344.

10 € 11,50 Ch included €5,50. **Location:** Rural.
Surface: metalled. 01/01-31/12.
Distance: 1,5km.

Somogyvár 38C1
Kimis Camp, Bartók Béla utca 58. **GPS**: n46,58275 e17,62398.

36 € 9 Ch (24x)WC included €1.
Location: Rural, comfortable. **Surface:** grassy. 01/05-30/09.
Distance: 500m on the spot.

Transdanubia

Bozsok 37B3
Nagy Vendégház, Rákoczi út 105. **GPS**: n47,32059 e16,48590.

HU

5 € 5 Ch WC. **Location:** Rural, simple, comfortable.
Surface: grassy. 01/01-31/12.
Distance: 30m 400m.
Remarks: Arrival >14h departure <12h.

S Felsőszentmárton 38C1

Camping de-ommekeer, Szent Lhászló Utca 38.
GPS: n45,85261 e17,69925.
10 € 15 Ch included. **Surface:** grassy. 01/04-30/09.

S Győr 37B3

Camping Pihenö, Mártírok útja. **GPS**: n47,72515 e17,71406.

35 € 15,50 Ch included.
Surface: grassy. 01/01-31/12.
Distance: 7km 9km.

S Halászi 37B3

Party Csárda, Duna sétány. **GPS**: n47,88586 e17,32201.

5 € 15 + € 1,75/pp tourist tax Ch €2 WC ,cold included.
Location: Rural, simple. **Surface:** grasstiles. 01/01-31/12.
Distance: 300m on the spot on the spot on the spot 200m.
Remarks: Wifi at restaurant.

S Lenti 38B1

Rudas, Béke utca 32. **GPS**: n46,62582 e16,53266.

6 € 10 Ch on demand WC included.
Location: Rural, simple. **Surface:** grassy. 01/01-31/12.
Distance: 200m 800m 800m 30m 300m 600m.

S Magyaregregy 38C1

Camping Máré Vára, Várvölgyi utca 2. **GPS**: n46,23407 e18,30913.
36 € 17,50 Ch (36x) WC included. **Location:** Rural.
Surface: grassy. 15/04-30/09.
Distance: 500m on the spot 1km 1km on the spot on the spot.
Remarks: Bread-service, swimming pool 200m.

S Mosonmagyaróvár 37B3

AquaThermalcamp, Kigyo utca 1. **GPS**: n47,87715 e17,27948.

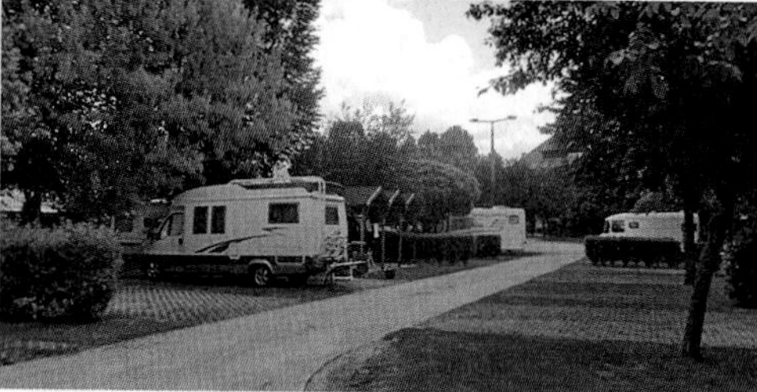

40 € 9 + 9/pp + € 1/pp tourist tax Ch €3/24h WC included. **Location:** Urban, comfortable.
Surface: grassy. 01/01-31/12.
Distance: 100m on the spot on the spot 100m.

S Mosonmagyaróvár 37B3

Kocisi Joseph, Vízpart utca 59. **GPS**: n47,87335 e17,27851.

8 € 15 Ch included. **Location:** Rural, comfortable.
Surface: grassy/metalled. 01/01-31/12.
Distance: 300m 200m 200m.

S Nagysáp 37B3

Granárium Camper-port, Granárium domb 3.
GPS: n47,68573 e18,60741.

7 € 10 Ch (4x),16Amp WC €10 included.
Surface: gravel. 01/01-31/12.
Distance: 500m on the spot 500m 50m on the spot on the spot.

S Pápa 37B3

Thermalcamping Pápa, Varkert Utca 7. **GPS**: n47,33781 e17,47359.

6 € 12 + € 1,60/pp tourist tax Ch WC included. **Location:** Urban, simple.
Surface: gravel. 01/01-31/12.
Distance: 500m on the spot 500m.
Remarks: Use sanitary facilities at campsite.

S Patosfa 38C1

Camping Farkas, Petőfi utca 52-56. **GPS**: n46,12545 e17,65788.
9 € 19 Ch WC included. **Location:** Rural.
Surface: sand. 01/05-30/09.
Remarks: Natural swimming pool, bread-service, regional products.

S Sormás 38C1

István Parkhotel & Restaurant, Külterület 28.
GPS: n46,46071 e16,90783.
16 € 7 Ch (16x)€3,50,10Amp WC €3 included.
Location: Rural, comfortable, luxurious. **Surface:** grassy/metalled.
01/01-31/12.
Distance: 2km 1km on the spot on the spot on the spot 200m on the spot on the spot.

HU

Ireland

Capital: Dublin
Government: parliamentary constitutional republic
Official Language: Irish and English
Population: 4,892,000 (2015)
Area: 69,825 Km²

General information
Dialling code: 00353
General emergency: 112
Currency: Euro
Credit cards are accepted almost everywhere.

Regulations for overnight stays
Free overnight stay is allowed with consent of the landowner, and up to 24 hours on regular parking spaces.

Additional public holidays 2017
March 17 Saint Patrick's Day
April 14 Good Friday
April 17 Easter Monday
May 1 Early Bank Holiday
June 5 June Bank Holiday
August 7 First Moday in August
October 30 October Bank Holiday
November 1 All Saints'Day

Time Zone
Winter (Standard Time) GMT+0
Summer (DST) GMT+1

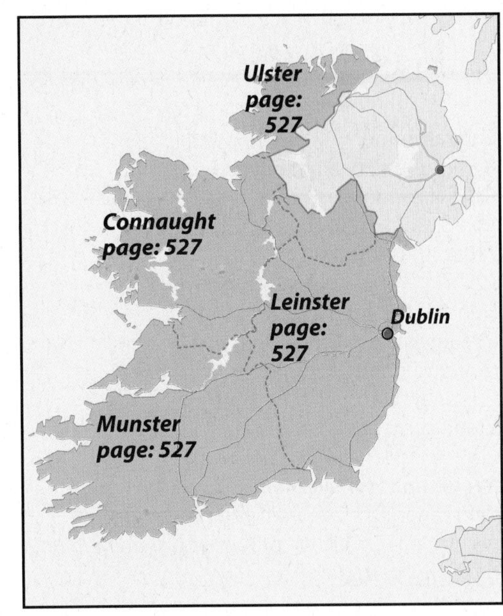

Ulster

S — Buncrana — 1C1
R238. **GPS**: n55,12828 w7,45782.
3 free free €5. **Surface:** metalled. 01/01-31/12.

Donegal — 1C1
Parking 4 Port, Quaystreet. **GPS**: n54,65183 w8,1123.
4 € 2,70. **Location:** Urban. **Surface:** asphalted. 01/01-31/12.

S — Dunfanaghy — 1C1
N56. **GPS**: n55,18392 w7,97303.
10 Ch. 01/01-31/12.

Connaught

Corraguan — 1B2
White Strand. **GPS**: n53,66904 w9,90211.
10 free. **Location:** Rural. 01/01-31/12.

S — Galway — 1B2
Galway Harbour, Dockstreet. **GPS**: n53,27004 w9,04885.
15 8-19h € 2/h, 19-8h € 4 €3/10kWh. **Location:** Urban.
Surface: asphalted. 01/01-31/12.

S — Portumna — 1B2
Castle Avenue. **GPS**: n53,08388 w8,22038.
8 free WC free. **Location:** Rural. **Surface:** asphalted.
01/01-31/12.

S — Templeboy — 1B1
Beach Bar, Aughris head. **GPS**: n54,26908 w8,75696.
10 € 20 Ch included. **Location:** Rural. **Surface:** grassy.
01/01-31/12.

Leinster

Glenmalure — 1C2
Glenmalure lodge, Wicklow Way. **GPS**: n52,95743 w6,35405.
4. **Location:** Rural. **Surface:** metalled. 01/01-31/12.

Munster

Askeaton — 1B2
Askeaton Leisurecenter, The Quay. **GPS**: n52,60273 w8,97511.
4. **Location:** Urban. **Surface:** asphalted. 01/01-31/12.

Ballinskellig — 1A3
Cois Tra Lower. **GPS**: n51,82093 w10,27323.
10 free. **Location:** Rural. **Surface:** asphalted. 01/01-31/12.

S — Castletownbere — 1B3
Berehaven Golf Club, Filane West. **GPS**: n51,65417 w9,86125.
10 € 18 included Ch €2 WC free. **Location:** Rural.
Surface: metalled. 01/01-31/12.

Cobh — 1B3
Whitepoint Moorings. **GPS**: n51,84716 w8,30735.
10 free. **Location:** Urban. **Surface:** asphalted. 01/01-31/12.

Liscanor — 1B2
Cliffs of Moher. **GPS**: n52,97145 w9,42475.
€ 6/pp. **Location:** Rural. **Surface:** metalled. 01/01-31/12.

S — Midleton — 1B3
Distillery Road Car Park. **GPS**: n51,91344 w8,16981.
6 €0,25 €0,25 Ch €0,25. **Location:** Urban.
Surface: asphalted. 01/01-31/12.

IE

Italy

Capital: Rome
Government: parliamentarian republic
Official Language: Italian
Population: 61,680,000 (2014)
Area: 301,318 km²

General information
Dialling code: 0039
General emergency: 112
Currency: Euro
Credit cards are accepted almost everywhere.

Regulations for overnight stays
Wild camping is allowed with permission of municipality, police or property owner when no problems occur.

Additional public holidays 2017
January 6 Epiphany
April 25 Liberation Day
May 1 Labor Day
June 2 Festa della Republica, National Holiday
August 15 Assumption of the Virgin Mary
November 1 All Saints' Day
November 4 Armistice Day
December 8 Immaculate Conception

Time Zone
Winter (Standard Time) GMT+1
Summer (DST) GMT+2

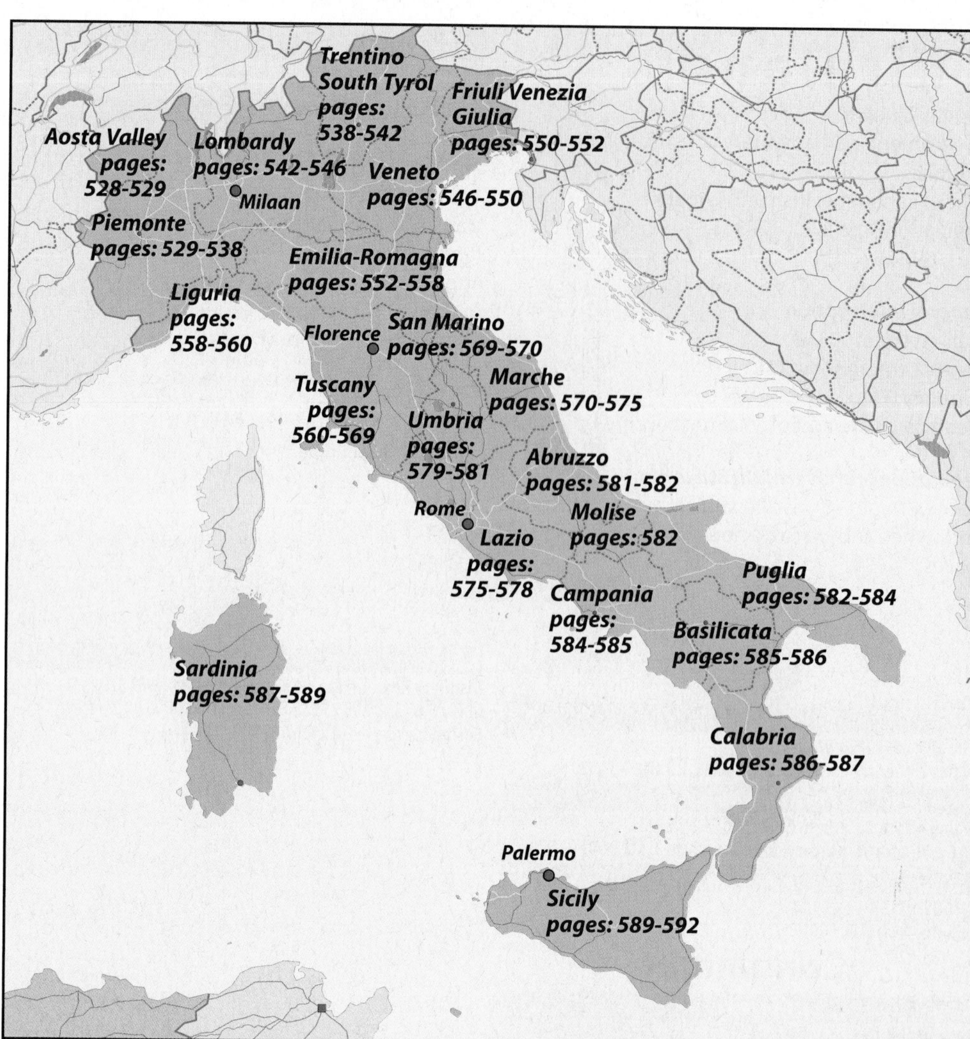

IT

Aosta Valley

Antey-Saint-André 22G3
Località Filey, SR46. **GPS**: n45,81246 e7,58898.
15 € 8, tourist tax € 0,20/pp Ch included.
Surface: metalled. 01/01-31/12.
Distance: 850m.
Remarks: To be paid at bar, service passerby € 5.

Aosta 22G3
Via Cadutti del Lavoro. **GPS**: n45,73600 e7,33035.

30 € 12/24h Ch included € 1/kWh.
Location: Urban, noisy. **Surface:** asphalted.
01/01-31/12 Thu-morning closed because of market.
Distance: on the spot 4,5km 200m on the spot.
Remarks: Parking closes at 22h, video surveillance.

Aymavilles 22G3
Strada Comunale del Moulins. **GPS**: n45,70125 e7,23960.

20 € 8/24h . **Surface:** metalled. 01/05-31/10.
Distance: on the spot 2km.

Bard 22H3
SS 26 della Valle d'Aost. **GPS**: n45,61564 e7,74204.
free. **Surface:** metalled. 01/01-31/12.
Distance: on the spot.

Bionaz 22G3
Area Attrezzata Bosco di Lexert. GPS: n45,87458 e7,42381.
€ 10/night Ch. **Surface:** grassy/gravel.
Remarks: Picnic area at small lake.

Brusson 22H3
Foyer du Ski, Rue Vollon. **GPS**: n45,76617 e7,71117.

50 € 10,80/24h Ch included. **Surface:** grassy/metalled.
01/01-31/12.
Distance: on the spot.
Remarks: At lake.

Cervinia/Breuil 22G3
Area Camper del Breuil. GPS: n45,92614 e7,62026.
50 € 7/24h Ch. **Surface:** asphalted. 01/01-31/12.
Distance: 1km Lago Blu 400m on the spot.
Remarks: Altitude 2000m, shuttle bus to city centre.

Champorcher 22G3
Area pic-nic, Loc. Chardonney. **GPS**: n45,62141 e7,60992.
35 € 6 free. **Surface:** grassy.
Distance: 300m 300m.
Remarks: Nearby parking funicular railway.

Chatillon 22G3
Area Camper attrezzata Chatillon, Frazione Perolle.
GPS: n45,74889 e7,62388.

16 € 6/12h Ch . **Surface:** metalled. 01/01-31/12.
Distance: historical centre 500m.

Cogne 22G3
Fraz. Lillaz. **GPS**: n45,59602 e7,38815.

37 € 8,70, Jul-Aug and 24/12-6/1 € 10,70, tourist tax excl Ch € 2,50. **Surface:** asphalted. 01/01-31/12.
Distance: 100m on the spot 100m 100m on the spot 1km.
Remarks: Altitude 1650m.

Cogne 22G3
Fraz. Revettaz. **GPS**: n45,60840 e7,35830.

130 € 8,70, Jul/Aug and 24/12-06/01 € 10,70 Ch €2,50.
Surface: asphalted. 01/01-31/12 water disconnected in winter.

Tourist information Cogne:
Parco Nazionale Gran Paradiso, Vall d'Aosta. Nature reserve, information centres: Dégioz, Rhêmes-Notre-Dame and Cogne.

Courmayeur 22F3

Funivia Val Veny. **GPS:** n45,81428 e6,95612.
free . **Surface:** metalled. 01/01-31/12.
Distance: 3km on the spot.

Étroubles 22G3

Camping Tunnel, Rue des Chevrières, 4. **GPS:** n45,81874 e7,22922.
9 € 13, 22/07-27/08 € 18 Ch included.
Surface: grassy/metalled.
Remarks: Max. 48h.

Fénis 22G3

Località Chez Sapin. **GPS:** n45,73939 e7,48553.
free. **Surface:** asphalted.
Distance: 500m.
Remarks: At cemetery.

Fontainemore 22H3

SR44. **GPS:** n45,64598 e7,85916.
2 € 6 Ch €3 WC €1,summer. 01/01-31/12.
Distance: 350m 350m.
Remarks: To be paid at bar.

Gaby 22H3

Piazzale Vourry. **GPS:** n45,70157 e7,87295.
9 free . 01/01-31/12 Service: winter.
Distance: 1,5km.
Remarks: Altitude 1000m.

Gressoney-Saint-Jean 22H3

P Weissmatten, Via Bildschocke, Saint Jean.
GPS: n45,76028 e7,83556.

€ 6/12h then € 0,50/h, 01/05-30/06 gratis Ch included.
Surface: asphalted. 01/01-31/12.
Remarks: Parking funicular railway.

Gressoney-Saint-Jean 22H3

Tschaval, La Trinité. **GPS:** n45,85657 e7,81362.

36 € 12/24h + € 0,80/pp tourist tax Ch €3 WC .
Surface: metalled. 01/01-31/12, 24/24h.
Distance: 2 restaurants 300m on the spot on the spot on the spot 200m.

Hône 22H3

Via Raffort. **GPS:** n45,61169 e7,73262.
18 € 8 Chincluded €1/4h. **Surface:** metalled.
01/01-31/12.
Distance: 350m 7km.
Remarks: Max. 48h.

La Thuile 22F3

Azzurra Camper. **GPS:** n45,70823 e6,95335.

80 € 13-18 + € 0,80/pp tourist tax Ch (45x)€3 €3 €5.
Surface: metalled. 01/01-31/12.
Distance: 500m 500m 100m.
Remarks: Bread-service, video surveillance.

Pont-Saint-Martin 22H3

Piazzale Palazzetto dello Sport. **GPS:** n45,60025 e7,79338.
free. **Surface:** asphalted.
Distance: 1km.

Rhemes Notre Dame 25G1

Gipeto, Loc. Chanavey. **GPS:** n45,57960 e7,12392.
30 € 6/12h, >1 hour € 0,50/h included. **Surface:** metalled.
01/01-31/12.
Distance: on the spot.

Rhemes Notre Dame 25G1

Frazione Bruil. **GPS:** n45,57148 e7,11848.
20 free. **Surface:** asphalted.

Saint-Denis 22G3

Strada Regionale del Col Saint Pantaléon, Loc. Plaù.
GPS: n45,77129 e7,56092.

4 € 7/24h Ch WC. **Location:** Quiet.
Surface: grasstiles/grassy. 15/04-31/10.
Distance: 16km.

Saint-Oyen 22G3

Rue de Flassin. **GPS:** n45,82133 e7,20822.
€ 15/24h Ch WCincluded €1. 01/01-31/12.
Distance: 22km on the spot on the spot.

Saint-Pierre 22G3

Place des Valdôtains à l'étranger, Località Pommier.
GPS: n45,70831 e7,22402.
8 free . 01/01-31/12.
Distance: 300m 300m on the spot.

Torgnon 22G3

Plan Proriond. **GPS:** n45,80397 e7,55490.
25 € 8/24h Ch . **Surface:** grasstiles/metalled.
01/01-31/12.
Distance: 50m.

Valgrisenche 22G3

Frazione Bonne. **GPS:** n45,61931 e7,05930.

20 € 10/24h Ch €3. **Surface:** grassy/sand.
Remarks: At weir.

Valgrisenche 22G3

Localita' Mondanges. **GPS:** n45,62638 e7,06252.
20 . **Location:** Rural.
Surface: asphalted. 01/01-31/12.
Distance: on the spot.

Valsavarenche 25G1

Località Dégioz. **GPS:** n45,59404 e7,20721.
11 € 5/12h Ch. **Surface:** grasstiles/metalled.
01/04-31/10.
Distance: 100m.
Remarks: Check in at town hall Tabaccheria or Bar Lo Fourquin, with registration number motorhome.

Verrès 22G3

Piazzale Grand Ronc, Via Stazione. **GPS:** n45,66226 e7,69392.

6 € 5 free. **Surface:** asphalted. 01/01-31/12.
Distance: 200m 1,5km.

Piedmont

Acceglio 25F3

SP422. **GPS:** n44,47526 e6,98530.
free. **Location:** Rural, isolated, quiet. **Surface:** grassy/gravel.
01/01-31/12.
Remarks: Max. 24h.

Acqui Terme 26A2

Area comunale, SS456, Viale Einaudi. **GPS:** n44,66533 e8,47228.

150 € 8 Ch (16x)included WC.
Location: Urban, comfortable, central, noisy.
Surface: grasstiles/metalled. 01/01-31/12.
Distance: 1,5km 25km 50m 250m.

Agliè 25H1

Via della Gula. **GPS:** n45,36662 e7,76381.

40 free.
Location: Urban, simple. **Surface:** metalled. 01/01-31/12.
Distance: on the spot.

Alba 25H2

Alba Village, Corso Piave 219, loc. San Cassiano.
GPS: n44,68553 e8,01095.

20 € 8 + € 0,50/pp tourist tax €0,50/30liter Ch free .
Location: Urban, comfortable, central. **Surface:** grassy.
01/01-31/12.
Distance: 2,5km 1km on the spot 100m on the spot.
Remarks: Nearby Hotel&Camping Alba Village, max. 48h, check in at reception, monitored parking.

Alessandria 26A2

Area comunale, Viale Teresa Michel. **GPS:** n44,92075 e8,62722.

IT

25 free Ch.
Location: Urban, simple. **Surface:** asphalted. 01/01-31/12.
Distance: 2km 2km on the spot 500m on the spot.

Arona 23A3

Via Michelangelo Buonarotti. **GPS:** n45,76879 e8,54495.
20 free. **Surface:** metalled. 01/01-31/12.
Distance: 2km 200m 2km.

Asti 25H2

Piazza Campo del Palio. **GPS:** n44,89712 e8,21057.
>50 free . **Location:** Urban, simple, central, noisy.
Surface: asphalted. 01/01-31/12 Wed-Sa.
Distance: on the spot on the spot on the spot.

Avigliana 25G2

Via Giovanni Suppo. **GPS:** n45,07304 e7,39004.

8 free Chfree. **Location:** Urban, simple, quiet.
Surface: asphalted.
Distance: 1km 4,6km.
Remarks: Nearby sports complex.

Tourist information Avigliana:
Thu.

Barge 25G2

Via Carlo Alberto. **GPS:** n44,73108 e7,32000.

4 free Chfree. **Location:** Simple. **Surface:** asphalted.
Distance: 800m on the spot.

Battifollo 25H3

Cian del Mondo, Loc. Piano del Mondo.
GPS: n44,31994 e8,01858.

20 € 15 Ch (20x)€2,50/day WC included.
Location: Rural, comfortable. **Surface:** gravel. 01/03-08/12.
Distance: 700m 500m on the spot on the spot.

Baveno 23A3

Area Comunale, Piazza Umberto Giordano.
GPS: n45,91139 e8,50056.

40 € 12/24h ChWCincluded.
Location: Noisy. **Surface:** metalled. 01/01-31/12.
Distance: 500m 2,8km Lago Maggiore 300m 300m.
Remarks: Behind railway station, max. 72h, no camping activities, weekend: noisy.

Bibiana 25G2

Piazza 3° Alpini. **GPS:** n44,79581 e7,29366.

8 free Ch. **Location:** Urban, simple.
Surface: metalled.
Distance: 500m 500m.

Biella 25H1

Area Comunale, Piazzale Sandro Pertini. **GPS:** n45,55559 e8,06760.

30 free free.
Location: Urban. **Surface:** asphalted. 01/01-31/12.
Distance: on the spot 100m station 100m.
Remarks: Square next to station F.S San Paolo.

Bielmonte 22H3

Piazzale 2, SS232. **GPS:** n45,66250 e8,08472.
8 € 3,50 Chincluded €3,50.

Borgo San Dalmazzo 25G3

P Area Camper, Strada Communale Del Cimitero.
GPS: n44,32889 e7,49167.

15 free Chfree.
Location: Urban, simple, quiet. **Surface:** asphalted. 01/01-31/12.
Distance: 100m.
Remarks: At sports park.

Borgosesia 22H3

Piazza Milanaccio, Via Varallo. **GPS:** n45,72005 e8,27408.

8 free Chfree. **Location:** Urban. **Surface:** asphalted.
01/01-31/12 Jun.
Distance: 300m.
Remarks: Market Saturday.

Candelo 25H1

Area Comunale, Via Cesare Pavese. **GPS:** n45,54163 e8,11595.

2 free Chfree. **Location:** Urban, quiet. **Surface:** gravel.
01/01-31/12.
Distance: 400m 400m 100m.
Remarks: Nearby sports center.

Candelo 25H1

Area Ricetto, Via Mulino. **GPS:** n45,54624 e8,11573.

25 free Ch free. **Location:** Comfortable.
Surface: metalled. 01/01-31/12.
Distance: 400m 400m.

Canelli 25H2

Piazza Unione Europea. **GPS:** n44,72039 e8,29369.

15 free Chfree. **Location:** Urban, simple, noisy.
Surface: asphalted. 01/01-31/12.
Distance: 500m on the spot on the spot on the spot.

Cannobio 23A2

Area Comunale, Via Al Fiume / Via San Rocco.
GPS: n46,06179 e8,69242.

55 € 15/24h ChWCincluded.
Location: Rural. **Surface:** grasstiles. 01/01-31/12.
Distance: 500m on the spot 500m 300m.
Remarks: Along river, max. 3 days.

Tourist information Cannobio:
Su.

Carcoforo 22H3

Le Giare, SP11, Loc. Tetto Minocco. **GPS:** n45,90769 e8,05130.

100 € 10/day, € 15/weekend, € 40/week Chfree (16x)€1,50 WC €1. **Surface:** grassy. 01/01-31/12.
Distance: on the spot 50m 300m on the spot.
Remarks: Along the Egua river.

S Casale Monferrato 26A1

Palazzetto dello Sport Paolo Ferraris, Via Visconti.
GPS: n45,12556 e8,46194.

15 free in shopping centre. **Location:** Rural.
Surface: asphalted. 01/01-31/12.
Distance: 1,5km 3,6km 200m 200m.
Remarks: At sports centre.

Casale Monferrato 26A1

Parcheggio Castello, Piazza Castello. **GPS:** n45,13722 e8,44806.

>10 free. **Location:** Urban, simple, central, noisy.
Surface: asphalted. Tue, Fri 6-16h (market).
Distance: 200m 4km 100m 250m on the spot on the spot.

S Casaleggio Boiro 26A2

Via Castello. **GPS:** n44,63354 e8,73254.

8 free Chfree (6x)included. **Location:** Rural, comfortable, quiet. **Surface:** gravel. 01/01-31/12.
Distance: 250m 10km 150m 250m.

S Castelletto Stura 25G3

Via Cuneo. **GPS:** n44,44194 e7,63444.

20 free free.
Location: Rural, simple. **Surface:** gravel.
Remarks: Nearby sports park.

S Castiglione Falletto 25H2

Area comunale, Piazzale Muntelier. **GPS:** n44,62379 e7,97486.

10 free Chfree . **Location:** Rural, comfortable, quiet.
Surface: metalled. 01/01-31/12.
Distance: 100m 100m 100m.

S Castiglione Tinella 25H2

Camperstop Ai Ciuvin, Agriturismo, Strada Manzotti 3.
GPS: n44,73357 e8,18140.

12 € 20 Ch WC included. **Location:** Rural, comfortable, isolated, quiet. **Surface:** grassy. 01/01-31/12.
Distance: 15km 20km on the spot 15km.
Remarks: Max. 48h.

S Cavour 25G2

Via Vigone. **GPS:** n44,78766 e7,37660.

18 € 5/24h Chfree. **Surface:** metalled.
Distance: 400m 100m.

S Ceresole Reale 25G1

Area sosta Camper Lungolago, Strada Provinciale 50.
GPS: n45,43407 e7,22783.
€ 8 free Ch €3 WC €0,50/15minutes. 01/01-31/12.
Distance: 300m 300m 300m on the spot on the spot.

S Ceresole Reale 25G1

Borgata Chiapili Inferiore, SP50. **GPS:** n45,45049 e7,18765.
€ 8 €4 Ch €3. **Surface:** unpaved.
Distance: 4km Ristorante Lo Sciatore 2km.
Remarks: Along the Orco river, national Park 'Gran Paradiso'.

S Cesana Torinese 25F2

Area Sosta Camper Casa Cesana, Viale Sen. Bouvier.
GPS: n44,94782 e6,79516.

12 € 10/24h Chincluded (12x)€3/day,6Amp.
Location: Simple. **Surface:** asphalted. 01/06-01/11.
Distance: 300m 50m 100m.
Remarks: Check in at hotel.

S Cherasco 25H2

Parking Area Camper, Piazza Giovanni Paolo II.
GPS: n44,64946 e7,85529.

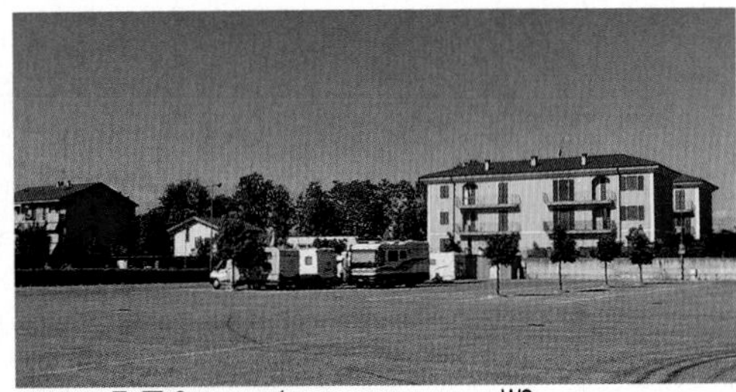

9 free Chfree (8x)against payment WC.
Location: Rural, simple, quiet.
Surface: asphalted. 01/01-31/12.
Distance: 400m 3,7km 200m 300m.
Remarks: Max. 48h.

S Chianocco 25G1

Area Camper Giraude. GPS: n45,14110 e7,16592.

20 € 3-10 ChWCincluded. **Location:** Rural, simple.
Surface: grassy/gravel. 01/04-31/10.
Distance: 1km.
Remarks: Max. 48h.

S Chiaverano 25H1

Area Camper Lago Sirio, Strada Provinciale 75.
GPS: n45,48585 e7,88815.

€ 10 Ch €2 WC . **Surface:** grassy. 01/01-31/12.
Distance: on the spot on the spot on the spot on the spot.

S Chieri 25H2

Piazza Quarini, via Bernardo Vittone. **GPS:** n45,00391 e7,82744.

12 free Chfree. **Surface:** asphalted. 01/01-31/12.
Distance: on the spot 200m > Turin.
Remarks: Behind Barracks, tuesday market.

S Chieri 25H2

Strada San Silvestro. **GPS:** n45,01460 e7,83214.

10 free Chfree.
Location: Urban, simple. **Surface:** asphalted.
Distance: on the spot 50m 50m.

S Chiusa di Pesio 25H3

Via Provinciale (SP42). **GPS:** n44,27233 e7,66361.

IT

8 €4 Ch.
Distance: on the spot 300m 700m on the spot on the spot.

S Chiusa di San Michele 25G2

Via Pragallo. **GPS**: n45,10294 e7,33034.

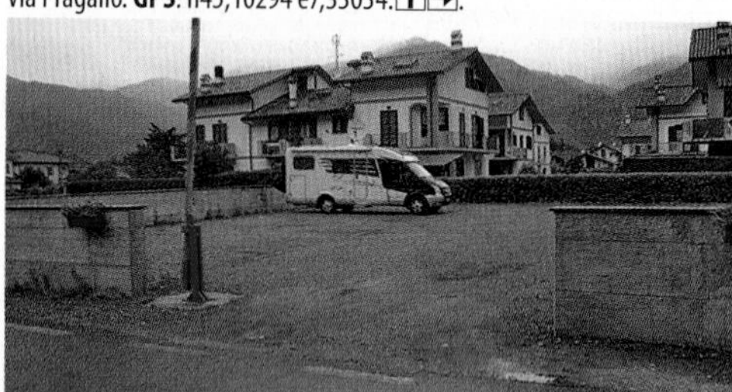

5 €8 included.
Location: Simple, comfortable.
Surface: gravel. 01/04-31/10.
Distance: 8km 600m.
Remarks: Max. 48h, to be paid at Uffici Comunali, Piazza Bauchiero 2.

S Chivasso 25H1

Piazza Libertini, Via Gerbido. **GPS**: n45,18514 e7,89296.

20 free €2 . **Location:** Urban, simple.
Surface: asphalted.
Distance: 300m Carrefour 100m.
Remarks: Parking swimming pool.

S Collegno 25G2

Collegno Area Sosta Camper, Corso Pastrengo.
GPS: n45,08070 e7,58313.

30 free €0,50 €0,50 Ch€1 €1/4h. **Location:** Quiet.
Surface: asphalted.
Distance: 4km on the spot.
Remarks: Coins at Autolavaggio Il Draghetto, video surveillance.

S Cortemilia 25H3

Strada San Roco. **GPS**: n44,57848 e8,18567.
10 free Chfree. **Location:** Simple. **Surface:** gravel.
Distance: 500m 500m.
Remarks: Max. 48h.

S Cravagliana 22H3

Pian delle Fate, Loc. Brugarolo, SP di Valle Mastallone.
GPS: n45,85223 e8,22473.

30 € 14 + € 1/pp Ch (4x)WC included.
Surface: grassy. 15/03-15/10.
Distance: on the spot on the spot.

S Crissolo 25G2

Via Ruata. **GPS**: n44,69771 e7,15931.

20 €5 ChWCincluded. **Location:** Urban, simple, quiet.
Surface: asphalted.
Distance: on the spot on the spot.

S Cuceglio 25H1

Area Camper Erbaluce, Via Porta Pia 69/71. **GPS**: n45,34724 e7,81168.

10 € 12 (10x) included.
Location: Rural, comfortable. **Surface:** gravel.

S Donato 25H1

Area Camper Fabrizio de André, Via S. Pertini, SP405.
GPS: n45,52774 e7,90944.

6 €5 WCfree.
Location: Rural. **Surface:** grasstiles. 01/01-31/12.
Distance: 300m 300m.
Remarks: Pay at Tabaccheria in the village.

S Entracque 25G3

Area C'era una Volta, SS22. **GPS**: n44,25151 e7,38975.

18 € 15 Ch (16x)WC €5/day €1 included.
Location: Rural. **Surface:** unpaved. 01/01-31/12.
Distance: 1km river-beach 500m 500m on the spot 1km
> Cuneo on the spot on the spot 1km.

S Entracque 25G3

Parcheggio Camper Real Park, Ponterosso.
GPS: n44,26111 e7,37750.

66 €6 Ch included. **Location:** Rural.
Surface: grassy/gravel.
Distance: 3km on the spot on the spot 6km.
Remarks: Recreation park, max. 2 days.

S Entracque 25G3

Via del Mulino. **GPS**: n44,23389 e7,39723.

60 € 12/24h, € 20/48h (50x)included €2.
Location: Rural, simple. **Surface:** gravel.
Distance: 300m.

S Fenestrelle 25G2

GPS: n45,03889 e7,04583.

9 free free. **Surface:** asphalted.
Remarks: Next to cemetery.

S Fenestrelle 25G2

Le Casermette. **GPS**: n45,03671 e7,05090.

20 free, fri-su € 5-10, Jun-Aug € 10 Ch included.
Surface: unpaved. 01/01-31/12.

S Frabosa Soprana 25H3

Fontane. **GPS**: n44,23554 e7,83561.
free Chfree. **Location:** Rural, isolated, quiet.
01/01-31/12.

S Frabosa Soprana 25H3

Grotta di Bossea, Loc.Bossea 10. **GPS**: n44,24077 e7,83939.
5 free Chfree WC. **Location:** Rural, simple, isolated.
Surface: asphalted. 01/01-31/12.
Distance: 12km on the spot on the spot 12km on the spot.
Remarks: Parking at the caves.

S Garessio 25H3

Area Comunale, Str.Provinciale del Colle di San Bernardo (P582).
GPS: n44,19927 e8,02587.

IT

30 free Chfree.
Location: Rural, simple. **Surface:** asphalted. 01/01-31/12.
Distance: 1km 22km 1km 1km.

Genola 25H3

Grosso Vacanze, Via Divisione Alpina Cuneense 2, SS20.
GPS: n44,59751 e7,65982.

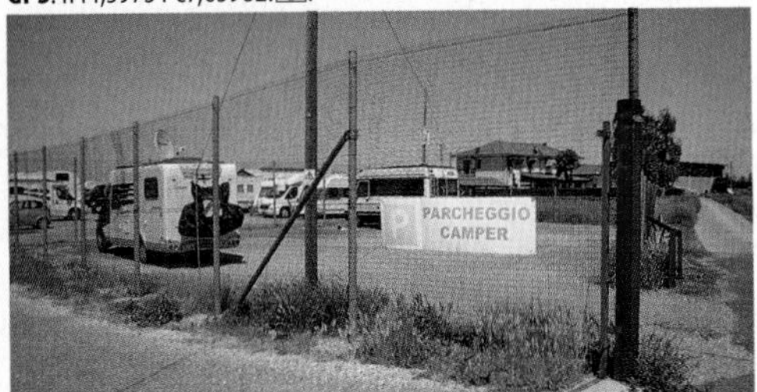

free Ch . **Surface:** metalled. 01/01-31/12.
Remarks: Motorhome dealer, accessory shop.

Giaveno 25G2

SP187, via Torino. **GPS:** n45,04154 e7,36096.

free free. **Surface:** asphalted.
Distance: 100m.

Grinzane Cavour 25H2

Piazza Ugo Genta, Via Bricco. **GPS:** n44,65515 e7,98936.

3 free Chfree. **Location:** Rural, simple, isolated, noisy.
Surface: asphalted. 01/01-31/12.
Distance: 500m 500m 2km on the spot.

Ivrea 25H1

La Dora d'Ivrea, Via Dora Baltea. **GPS:** n45,46334 e7,87621.

10 € 5 Chincluded. **Location:** Comfortable.
Surface: asphalted. 01/01-31/12.
Distance: 500m 4,5km Ipermercato 800m 350m.
Remarks: Beside river.

Locana 25G1

Via Nusiglie. **GPS:** n45,41361 e7,46278.
€ 8/24h €4/24h WC.

Macugnaga 22H3

Pecetto, Di Iacchine Pierluigi Loc. Pecetto. **GPS:** n45,97015 e7,95352.

28 € 10, 2 nights € 15 ChWCfree.
Location: Rural, simple, quiet.
Surface: concrete. 01/05-30/11.
Distance: 1km 100m 500m 100m on the spot.
Remarks: At ski-lift.

Madonna del Sasso 23A3

Area Comunale, Via Santuario, Fraz. Boleto.
GPS: n45,78974 e8,37222.

8 free Chfree. **Surface:** grasstiles. 01/01-31/12.
Distance: 200m Lago d'Orta 700m 100m 50m.
Remarks: Narrow entrance, view at Lago d'Orta.

Maglione 25H1

SP78, Via Cigliano. **GPS:** n45,34338 e8,01456.

20 free. **Location:** Rural, simple, quiet. **Surface:** grassy.
Distance: on the spot 50m.
Remarks: Art city.

Marsaglia 25H3

Via della Stazione, SP115. **GPS:** n44,45228 e7,97929.
18 € 13 Ch WC . **Surface:** asphalted/grassy.
01/01-31/12.
Distance: on the spot.
Remarks: Inspection june 2013: closed because of renovation.

Marsaglia 25H3

Agriturismo Cascina Zanot, Strada S. Rocco, 17.
GPS: n44,46506 e7,95838.
€ 15-25 ChWC included.
Remarks: Beautiful view.

Melle 25G3

SP8. **GPS:** n44,56245 e7,31739.

22 € 3, 01/06-01/10 € 5 ChWCincluded.
Location: Comfortable. **Surface:** metalled. 01/01-31/12.
Distance: 250m.

Mergozzo 23A3

Parcheggio Area Camper, Via Sempione 49.
GPS: n45,96204 e8,44320.
6 € 10/24h Chincluded €5. **Surface:** asphalted.
01/01-31/12.
Distance: 300m Lake Mergozzo 500m 300m.

Mirabello Monferrato 26A2

SS31. **GPS:** n45,02976 e8,52939.

8 free €2 Ch€1. **Location:** Simple, isolated, quiet.
Surface: asphalted. 01/01-31/12.
Distance: 900m 10km 800m 50m 50m.

Mombarcaro 25H3

SP103. **GPS:** n44,46900 e8,08352.
8 € 5 Ch included. **Location:** Rural, comfortable.
Surface: metalled. 01/01-31/12.
Distance: 500m.

Mondovì 25H3

Piazza le Giardini. **GPS:** n44,39430 e7,82370.
free Chfree. **Location:** Simple, noisy. **Surface:** asphalted.
01/01-31/12.
Distance: 500m.
Remarks: Nearby bus station, parking under railway bridge.

Mondovì 25H3

Piazza Republica. **GPS:** n44,38964 e7,81930.
free. **Location:** Urban, simple, central. **Surface:** asphalted.
01/01-31/12.
Distance: 400m 5km 50m 100m on the spot.
Remarks: Nearby the old station.

Mondovì 25H3

Mondovicino Outlet Center. GPS: n44,41889 e7,84966.
free Ch. **Location:** Simple. **Surface:** asphalted. 25/12, 01/01.
Distance: 4km 1,2km on the spot.
Remarks: Parking at Outlet Center and Centro Commercial.

Mongrando 25H1

Area Comunale, Via dei Giovanni. **GPS:** n45,52543 e8,00595.

15 free Chfree . **Location:** Urban, quiet.
Surface: grasstiles. 01/01-31/12.
Distance: 900m.
Remarks: At sports centre.

Montiglio Monferrato 25H2

Via Padre Carpignano. **GPS:** n45,06261 e8,10045.
25 free . 01/01-31/12.
Distance: 200m.

Neive 25H2

Via Crocetta. **GPS:** n44,72753 e8,11332.

6 € 10 Ch (6x)WC included. **Surface:** grassy/gravel.
Distance: 100m 100m.
Remarks: Check in at sport centre.

Niella Belbo 25H3

Agriturismo Ca'd Tistu, Via Pian Lea, 2.
GPS: n44,49941 e8,07991.
6 € 6. **Location:** Rural, isolated, quiet. 01/01-31/12.
Distance: 1,8km on the spot.

IT

Niella Tanaro 25H3

Agriturismo I Fornelli, Via Fornello 1. **GPS**: n44,41418 e7,90988.

3 € 5 €3,50 Ch €2,50/24h WC.
Location: Rural, simple, isolated, quiet. **Surface:** grassy/gravel.
01/01-31/12.
Distance: 4km 2km 1km 10km.
Remarks: Farm products.

Nizza Monferrato 26A2

Parking Camper Piazzale S.Pertini, Piazzale Sandro Pertini.
GPS: n44,77140 e8,35346.

13 € 5 Ch Service, electricity incl. €3.
Location: Urban, comfortable, central, quiet. **Surface:** grassy.
01/01-31/12.
Distance: 200m 500m 500m.
Remarks: Gate closed, first call Motorhome Club Nicese between 9-20h.

Novi Ligure 26A2

Viale Pinan Cichero, zona stadio comunale. **GPS**: n44,77041 e8,78181.

25 free free. **Location:** Urban, simple, noisy.
Surface: asphalted. 01/01-31/12.
Distance: 1,5km 2km on the spot 600m.
Remarks: Parking gymnasium.

Occimiano 26A2

Via Circonvallazione. **GPS**: n45,05834 e8,50940.

5 € 5 Ch included.
Location: Rural, comfortable. **Surface:** asphalted. 01/01-31/12.
Distance: 250m 15km 250m 400m.
Remarks: To be paid at bar Concordia.

Oggebbio 23A3

Area Camper Oggebbio, Via Martiri Oggebbiesi 6.
GPS: n45,99680 e8,65304.

22 € 18/24h Ch WC included €1 €5/24h.
Location: Luxurious. **Surface:** gravel.
01/03-01/12.
Distance: on the spot 700m.
Remarks: Attention: narrow road, view on Lago Maggiore, video surveillance.

Omegna 23A3

Area Camper Lago d'Orta, Via Caduti di Bologna 1.
GPS: n45,86340 e8,39840.

25 € 8/12h, 01/06-30/09 € 10/12h Ch WC included.
Surface: metalled. 01/01-31/12.
Distance: 1,8km beach on the spot on the spot.
Remarks: Caution key electricity € 30, cash payment, video surveillance.

Ormea 25H3

Via Orti della Rana. **GPS**: n44,14532 e7,90751.

10 € 10 Ch. **Location:** Rural, comfortable, quiet.
Surface: grasstiles. 01/01-31/12.
Distance: 1km 500m 1km.
Remarks: Pay at tourist office.

Ormea 25H3

Riserva la Regina, Via Martinetto. **GPS**: n44,15162 e7,90929.
€ 10/24h WC €1,50.
Surface: gravel. Easter-30/10.
Distance: 500m fishing permit obligatory on the spot 500m on the spot.
Remarks: Regional products.

Oropa 22H3

Area di Santuari, Via Santuario di Oropa.
GPS: n45,62864 e7,97530.

31 € 10 Ch WC.
Location: Rural. **Surface:** metalled. 01/05-31/10.
Distance: 200m.

Orta San Giulio 23A3

Parco del Sacro Monte, Via Sacro Monte. **GPS**: n45,79732 e8,41204.

8 free. **Surface:** gravel. 01/01-31/12.
Distance: 900m 400m.
Remarks: Max. 48h.

Orta San Giulio 23A3

Via Panoramica. **GPS**: n45,79729 e8,41527.

20 € 10/24h. **Surface:** asphalted. 01/01-31/12.
Distance: 500m Lago d'Orta 500m 100m.

Ovada 26A2

Via Gramsci. **GPS**: n44,64084 e8,64920.

25 free free. **Location:** Simple, central. **Surface:** grasstiles.
01/01-31/12.
Distance: 300m 3km 100m 500m.

Piatto 22H3

Area Comunale, Fraz. Malina. **GPS**: n45,58908 e8,13630.

10 free Ch.
Location: Urban. **Surface:** asphalted. 01/01-31/12.
Remarks: At sports park.

Pietraporzio 25G3

Area Camper Pontebernardo, Via Nazionale, SS21.
GPS: n44,34868 e7,01831.

21 € 5/24h Ch.
Location: Rural, comfortable. **Surface:** gravel. 01/01-31/12.
Distance: 100m.
Remarks: 3rd night free.

Pinerolo 25G2

Olimpico, Via Alpi Cozie. **GPS**: n44,88917 e7,35111.

IT

10 free Ch (10x)against payment. **Location:** Urban, simple. **Surface:** metalled. 01/03-01/11.
Distance: 2km 1,5km 300m 300m 200m.
Remarks: Nearby sports park.

Pollone 22H3

Burcina di Pollone, Via Felice Piacenza.
GPS: n45,58548 e8,00521.

21 € 16/24h Ch WC included €2 .
Location: Rural, comfortable. **Surface:** grasstiles.
01/01-31/12.
Distance: 600m on the spot.
Remarks: At parco Naturale Burcina, max. 48h.

Pombia 23A3

Safari Park, SS 32 km 23,4. **GPS:** n45,64167 e8,61740.
free WC. **Surface:** asphalted.

Ponderano 25H1

Area Comunale, Strada Vicinale al Cimitero.
GPS: n45,53683 e8,04949.

10 free free. **Location:** Urban, simple. **Surface:** gravel.
01/01-31/12.
Distance: 400m.
Remarks: Nearby sports park.

Pont Canavese 25G1

Feiteria, Via Soana. **GPS:** n45,42153 e7,60020.
12 € 7,50 €2,50 Ch €2,50. **Surface:** grassy.
01/01-31/12.
Distance: on the spot.
Remarks: Max. 48h, video surveillance.

Pontechianale 25G3

Area Camper, Fraz Maddalena. **GPS:** n44,62158 e7,02776.
€ 7/24h Ch. **Surface:** grassy. 01/05-30/09.
Distance: 200m 200m 200m 200m.
Remarks: Next to campsite.

Pontechianale 25G3

Chianle, SP 251. **GPS:** n44,65055 e6,99280.
15 free. **Location:** Simple, isolated. **Surface:** grassy/gravel.
Distance: 4km on the spot.

Pragelato 25F2

Villagio GoFree, SS23. **GPS:** n45,02187 e6,94914.

€ 16-21, 4 pers.incl Ch €1,50 WC . 12/06-13/09.
Distance: on the spot on the spot on the spot on the spot.
Remarks: Spa, ski, tennis, golf.

Prali 25G2

Fraz.Ghigo. **GPS:** n44,89176 e7,04956.

free Chfree. **Surface:** grassy.
Distance: 300m on the spot.
Remarks: Altitude 1450m, along river.

Prarostino 25G2

Porto di Montagne, Via Piani. **GPS:** n44,86488 e7,26970.

15 € 7 Ch WC included. **Location:** Comfortable.
Surface: grassy/gravel. 01/01-31/12 With snow.
Distance: 300m 200m on the spot.
Remarks: To be paid at bar.

Prato Nevoso 25H3

Area Stalle Lunghe, Via Corona Boreale. **GPS:** n44,25200 e7,78192.

€ 15-20 Ch included.
Surface: asphalted. 01/01-31/12.
Distance: on the spot A6 33km on the spot 50m on the spot.

Prato Nevoso 25H3

Piazza G. Dodero. **GPS:** n44,25200 e7,78192.

10 free. **Location:** Rural, simple, central. **Surface:** asphalted.
01/01-31/12.
Distance: on the spot on the spot on the spot on the spot.

Rimasco 22H3

Il Laghetto, Strada del Lago. **GPS:** n45,86109 e8,06450.

20 € 10/24h Ch €3/day WC included.
Surface: grassy. 01/05-30/09 Restaurant: Tue.
Distance: on the spot on the spot.
Remarks: At lake.

Riva Valdobbia 22H3

Area Lo Chalet, Via Circonvallazione. **GPS:** n45,83476 e7,95486.

48 € 13/24h Ch €2 WC included .
Surface: grassy/metalled. 01/04-31/10.
Distance: on the spot on the spot on the spot.
Remarks: Along river.

Roaschia 25G3

Area camper I Funtanil, Via Circonvallazione, SP 108.
GPS: n44,26758 e7,45860.

15 € 9 Ch WC included.
Location: Rural, comfortable, quiet. **Surface:** gravel.
Distance: on the spot.

Romano Canavese 25H1

Strada provinciale 56. **GPS:** n45,38644 e7,86177.

10 . **Location:** Rural, simple.
Surface: grasstiles/metalled.
Distance: 2,2km.

Rosta 25G2

Via Buttigliera Alta 2, Via Piave. **GPS:** n45,07106 e7,46333.

5 free €2 Ch€2. **Location:** Urban. **Surface:** asphalted.
01/01-31/12.
Distance: on the spot train > Turin 19min.

Saluzzo 25G2

Area Bodoni, Via Olivero Matteo. **GPS:** n44,63886 e7,49192.

17 free free.
Location: Urban, simple. **Surface:** grasstiles. 01/01-31/12.
Distance: 700m 200m.

Remarks: Small pitches.

Saluzzo 25G2

Via Cuneo 16. **GPS**: n44,63739 e7,49740.

±10 free free.
Location: Urban. **Surface:** asphalted. 01/01-31/12.
Distance: 1km.

San Damiano d'Asti 25H2

Via Monsignor Franco. **GPS**: n44,82659 e8,05921.

50 free Ch. **Location:** Rural, simple. **Surface:** gravel.
01/01-31/12.
Distance: 1km 1km 1km.
Remarks: At cemetery.

San Damiano d'Asti 25H2

Agriturismo Gran Collina, Frazione Stizza 38.
GPS: n44,00000 e8,04979.
€ 10 included according consumption.
Distance: km.
Remarks: Bicycle rental, regional products.

San Damiano d'Asti 25H2

Azienda Agricola Cascina Piana, Fraz S.Grato.
GPS: n44,85136 e8,07417.

25 € 8-10 Ch (8x) WC included.
Location: Rural, comfortable, isolated, quiet. **Surface:** grassy.
01/02-30/06 and 01/09-30/11.
Distance: 1,5km 1,5km 500m.
Remarks: Farm products.

Sanfront 25G2

Via Montebracco, SP26. **GPS**: n44,64944 e7,32056.

15 free Chfree. **Location:** Urban, simple.
Surface: unpaved.
Remarks: At sports park, max. 24h.

Santa Maria Maggiore 23A2

Area Verde Attrezzata, Via Alfredo Belcastro/via Pineta.
GPS: n46,13219 e8,45500.

32 € 20/24h Ch .
Location: Rural. **Surface:** grassy/gravel. 01/01-31/12.
Distance: 200m on the spot.
Remarks: Max. 48h.

Santa Maria Maggiore 23A2

Agriturismo Al Piano delle Lutte, Via Domodossola 57.
GPS: n46,13569 e8,44753.

6 € 10/24h Ch according consumption WC .
Location: Rural, simple. **Surface:** grassy/gravel.
01/01-31/12.
Distance: on the spot.
Remarks: Regional products.

Sant'Antonino di Susa 25G2

Area Sosta Il Sentiero Dei Franchi, Borgo Cresto 16/1.
GPS: n45,09973 e7,27754.

20 € 10 Ch €2. **Location:** Simple, comfortable, quiet.
Surface: grassy/gravel. 01/01-31/12.
Distance: on the spot on the spot.
Remarks: Check in at restaurant.

Sestriere 25F2

Lago Losetta, Strada Azzurri d'Italia. **GPS**: n44,96465 e6,88141.

60 € 15/24h Ch included.
Surface: unpaved. 01/01-31/12.
Distance: 800m Shuttle bus to ski-piste.

Sommariva Perno 25H2

Area comunale, Loc.Piano, SP0. **GPS**: n44,75126 e7,89667.

10 free Chfree. **Location:** Rural, simple, noisy.
Surface: gravel. 01/01-31/12.
Distance: 500m 13km 250m 250m.

Susa 25G1

Piazza Repubblica. **GPS**: n45,13861 e7,05389.

12 free Chfree €1. **Location:** Urban, simple, central.
Surface: asphalted. 01/01-31/12.
Distance: 300m 500m 800m.

Tagliolo Monferrato 26A2

Str. del Varo. **GPS**: n44,63960 e8,67126.
21 € 5/24h Ch.
Location: Rural, simple, quiet. **Surface:** grassy/gravel.
01/01-31/12.
Distance: 250m 2km 200m 400m.
Remarks: Max. 72h, keycard barrier at Bar/Tabac, caution € 10.

Torino 25H2

Corso Casale 327. **GPS**: n45,08084 e7,72993.

free free. **Location:** Urban, noisy.
Surface: asphalted.
Distance: 800m 100m 150m.

Torino 25H2

Corso Giovanni Agnelli. **GPS**: n45,02888 e7,63924.

57 € 10 Chincluded €0,50 WC €1 .
Location: Urban, comfortable.
Surface: grasstiles. 01/01-31/12.
Distance: 4km 4km 100m 100m on the spot.
Remarks: Max. 5 days, monitored parking 24/24.

Torino 25H2

Parco Ruffini, Corso Lione/Corso Carlo Piaggia, Turin (Torino).
GPS: n45,05686 e7,63166.

20 free Chfree.
Location: Urban, simple, noisy. **Surface:** asphalted.
Distance: city centre 5km on the spot.

Tourist information Turin (Torino):

- Mole Antonelliana. National Film museum.
- Museo Nazionale dell'Automobile, Corso Unità d'Italia 40. Museum of motor-cars. Tue-Sa, 10-18.30h, Su 10-20.30h Mo.
- Palazzo Madame. Historical art.
- Palazzo Reale. Royal palace.
- Cathedral, 1498.
- Basilica di Superga. Baroque basilica.

S Usseaux 25G2

Magic Forest, Strada Comunale dell'inverso 1.
GPS: n45,04170 e6,98518.

100 € 15 Ch WC €1 €5 included. **Location:** Rural, comfortable. **Surface:** grassy. 01/06-01/09.

S Usseaux 25G2

Area sosta Usseaux, Fraz. Fraisse-Pourrières. **GPS**: n45,04146 e6,98500. € 15 ChWC. **Surface:** grassy.

S Usseaux 25G2

Lago di Laux, Via Lago 7. **GPS**: n45,04166 e7,02222.

100 € 15/24h €3 €3 Ch (54x)€2,50/24h. **Location:** Rural, simple, isolated, quiet.
Surface: grassy. 01/06-31/09.
Distance: 500m 200m on the spot 5km.
Remarks: Pay at restaurant.

S Valdieri 25G3

Centro Alpino S.Anna, Loc. S. Anna. **GPS**: n44,24513 e7,32548.

40 € 12 Ch included.
Location: Rural. **Surface:** grassy/gravel.
Distance: 100m on the spot 100m.
Remarks: Narrow entrance (bridge).

S Valdieri 25G3

Parco Alpi Marittime, Terme di Valdieri. **GPS**: n44,20546 e7,26840.

€ 10 Ch. **Surface:** gravel. 01/01-31/12.

S Valle Mosso 22H3

Piazza Alpini d'Italia. **GPS**: n45,63316 e8,14629.

3 free Chfree.
Location: Urban. **Surface:** asphalted. 01/01-31/12.

Distance: on the spot Conad 20m 50m.

S Varallo 22H3

Area Comunale, Via Sant'Antonio. **GPS**: n45,81797 e8,24857.

8 € 10/24h Ch (4x)included. **Location:** Urban, quiet.
Surface: gravel/sand. 01/01-31/12.
Distance: 500m 500m.
Remarks: To be paid at town hall.

S Venaria Reale 25G1

Relax and Go, Via Scodeggio 15. **GPS**: n45,14108 e7,62404.

15 € 18-20 Chincluded €2/day. **Location:** Simple.
Surface: grassy.
Distance: 2km 500m 500m bus GTT, tram 72>Turin.

S Venasca 25G3

SP8, Via Provinciale. **GPS**: n44,56620 e7,39328.

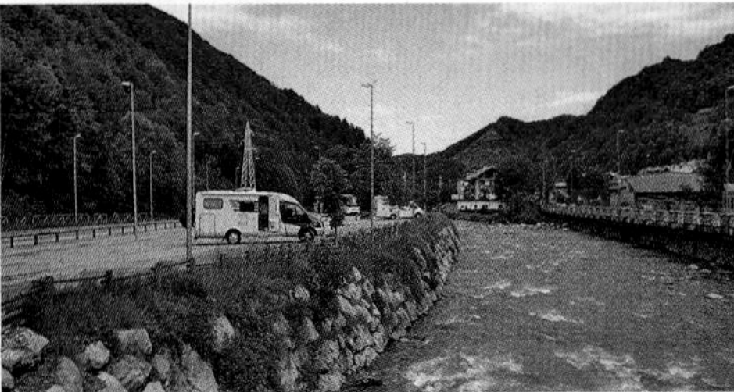

20 free Chfree.
Location: Rural, simple, noisy. **Surface:** asphalted.
Distance: 600m.

S Verbania 22H3

Punto Sosta Camper, Viale Azari 97. **GPS**: n45,93122 e8,00000.
34 € 6/12h, € 12/24h (18x). **Surface:** asphalted.
Distance: 900m 1,2km 200m.

Verbania 22H3

Via Brigata Cesare Battisti. **GPS**: n45,94027 e8,57676.
10.
Distance: 350m on the spot 350m.
Remarks: Along river.

S Verbania 22H3

Corso Europa. **GPS**: n45,92732 e8,56266.
Ch.

S Vercelli 26A1

Via Trento, c/o piazzale Pala-hockey. **GPS**: n45,33417 e8,41861.

10 free free.
Location: Urban, simple. **Surface:** asphalted. 01/01-31/12.
Distance: 1,5km 6km 50m 1,5km on the spot.

Tourist information Vercelli:

Basilica di Sant'Andrea. Basilica, part of abbey.

S Vergne 25H3

Piazza della Vite e del dell Vina. **GPS**: n44,61298 e7,92064.

6 free Chfree. **Location:** Simple. **Surface:** metalled.
Distance: on the spot on the spot.

S Vernante 25G3

E74. **GPS**: n44,24489 e7,53219.

20 € 5 free. **Location:** Urban, simple. **Surface:** asphalted.
Distance: 200m 200m 300m on the spot.

S Vialfrè 25H1

Via Luigi Emanuel, SP55. **GPS**: n45,38298 e7,81754.

7 free Chfree. **Location:** Rural, simple.
Surface: grasstiles.
Distance: on the spot 6km 300m 300m.

S Vidracco 25H1

Damanhur Crea, Via Baldissero 21. **GPS**: n45,42884 e7,75327.

30 € 8/24h Ch (24x)WC included.
Location: Simple, quiet. **Surface:** asphalted.
Distance: cafetaria on the spot.

Tourist information Vidracco:

Damanhur Crea, Via Baldissero 21. Extraordinary Italian artistic and spritual community.

S Villar Focchiardo 25G2

Area Camper Villar Focchiardo, Via Fratta, SS24.
GPS: n45,11336 e7,22408.

54 € 5-10, weekend € 15 Chfree. **Location:** Rural, simple, comfortable, quiet. **Surface:** grassy. 01/01-31/12 camper service: 01/11-31/03.
Distance: 4,5km.

S Villar Pellice 25G2

Parco Flissia, Via Cave del Fin. **GPS**: n44,80472 e7,15083.

IT

20 € 6 ChWCfree. **Location:** Rural, simple, isolated.
Surface: grassy. 01/04-01/10.
Distance: 500m on the spot fishing permit obligatory agriturismo.
Remarks: Service passerby € 3.

S **Vinadio** 25G3
Area di Sosta Communale, Bagni di Vinadio, Fraz. Strapesi.
GPS: n44,28747 e7,07534.

30 € 11/24h Ch free. **Location:** Rural, simple.
Surface: grassy/gravel.
Distance: 300m, Vinadio 10km on the spot on the spot.
Remarks: Altitude 1350m, parking at the spa resort of Strapeis.

S **Vinadio** 25G3
Piazza d'Armi, SS21. **GPS:** n44,30667 e7,17083.

01/06-31/08 € 5 Chfree. **Surface:** asphalted.
Distance: 400m.

S **Volpedo** 26B2
Lungo Curone Matteotti. **GPS:** n44,88512 e8,98707.

6 free Chfree. **Surface:** grassy/gravel.
Distance: 600m.
Remarks: At sports park.

Trentino South Tyrol

S **Andalo** 23D2
Via Rindole, 6, Loc. Rindole. **GPS:** n46,16113 e11,00647.

80 € 15-20 Ch (20x)€5. **Location:** Rural, simple, quiet.
Surface: asphalted. summer.
Distance: 200m on the spot on the spot.
Remarks: Service passerby € 10, beautiful view.

Arco 23D3
Piazzale Carmellini, Viale Paolina Caproni.
GPS: n45,92232 e10,89032.

14 € 1/4h, max. € 10/24h.
Location: Urban, simple. **Surface:** asphalted. 01/01-31/12.
Distance: 200m 200m on the spot.
Remarks: Max. 72h.

S **Arco** 23D3
Viale Rovereto. **GPS:** n45,91820 e10,89225.
Chfree. water disconnected in winter.

S **Avio** 23D3
Agriturismo Erta, Via Pozza, Località Erta 2.
GPS: n45,74292 e10,96807.

25 € 15 Ch (16x) included. **Location:** Rural.
Surface: grassy. 01/01-31/12.
Distance: 800m 200m 300m on the spot 800m on the spot on the spot on the spot 20km.

S **Barbiano** 23E1
Kollmann Stop, Frazione Colma, SS12. **GPS:** n46,58728 e11,52401.

15 € 12, in envelope in mail box €5 Ch included.
Location: Simple, noisy. **Surface:** gravel. 01/01-31/12.
Distance: 300m 9km 300m 300m on the spot on the spot.
Remarks: Along through road, max. 48h.

Baselga di Pine 23E2
Ice Rink Piné, Via Dello Stadio. **GPS:** n46,12617 e11,25382.

10 free. **Location:** Rural, simple, quiet.
Surface: metalled.
Distance: 1km.
Remarks: >18.00h free.

S **Bezzecca** 23D3
Via Peluca. **GPS:** n45,89861 e10,71833.

22 € 10/24h Chfree. **Location:** Rural, simple, isolated, quiet. **Surface:** grasstiles. 01/04-01/11.
Distance: 450m 2km 300m.

S **Bolzano/Bozen** 23E1
Parking Fiera Messe, Via Bruno Buozzi. **GPS:** n46,47417 e11,32617.

30 free Chfree.
Location: Urban, simple, noisy. **Surface:** asphalted. 01/01-31/12.
Distance: centre 4km 1,1km on the spot 4km on the spot.
Remarks: Along railwayline.

S **Bolzano/Bozen** 23E1
Via Maso della Pieve. **GPS:** n46,47327 e11,33693.

8 € 1/h 8-19h, Sa 8-13h, overnight stay free Ch.
Location: Urban, simple, noisy.
Surface: asphalted. 01/01-31/12.
Distance: city centre 3km 100m on the spot.

S **Borgo Valsugana** 23E2
Via Tommaso Temanza. **GPS:** n46,05444 e11,46361.

18 € 10/24h Ch included.
Location: Urban, simple.
Surface: grasstiles.
Distance: 100m 20m 20m 100m 100m on the spot.
Remarks: Max. 48h, service passerby € 5.

S **Braies** 23F1
P2, Lago di Braies, Fraz. San Vito. **GPS:** n46,70265 e12,08520.

25 € 12 €0,50.
Location: Rural, simple, quiet. **Surface:** gravel. 30/05-31/10.
Distance: Braies 5km Lago di Braies 250m 250m 5km on the spot on the spot.

Braies 23F1
P1, Lago di Braies, Fraz. San Vito. **GPS:** n46,70577 e12,08698.
€ 9/day, € 7/night. **Surface:** gravel. 01/01-31/12.
Distance: Lake Prags 850m.

S **Brentonico** 23D3
Via al Dosset. **GPS:** n45,81540 e10,95581.

11 € 7 €2/100liter Chincluded €3/24h.
Location: Rural, comfortable, quiet. **Surface:** grasstiles.
01/01-31/12.
Distance: 400m 10km 250m 300m.

Brunico/Bruneck 23F1

P2, Piazza Mercato di Stegona. **GPS:** n46,79558 e11,93006.

>25 € 7. **Location:** Urban, simple, noisy. **Surface:** gravel.
01/01-31/12.
Distance: 800m 500m 500m on the spot on the spot on the spot.

Tourist information Brunico/Bruneck:
Associazione Turistica, Via Europa,24. Fortified city, 14th century.
Regional museum.
Annual fair. last week Oct.

Caldes 23D2

Rafting Val di Sole, Loc. Contrè. **GPS:** n46,36139 e10,94528.

30 € 10, Jul € 13, Aug € 15 €6. **Surface:** asphalted.
01/04-30/09.
Distance: 2km 200m 2km.

Caldonazzo 23E2

Via al Lago. **GPS:** n46,00501 e11,26307.

30 € 8/6-22h (01/04-30/9), € 10/night.
Location: Simple. **Surface:** grassy/sand. 01/01-31/12.
Distance: 2km 50m 300m.
Remarks: Payment only with coins.

Castelfondo 23E1

Belverde, Via Alfonso Lamarmora. **GPS:** n46,45831 e11,13163.

16 € 12/24h (16x) WC. **Surface:** gravel.
Distance: 800m 800m 300m on the spot.

Remarks: Max. 72h.

Cavalese 23E2

P Fondovalle, SP232. **GPS:** n46,28438 e11,47256.

50 € 12. **Location:** Simple. **Surface:** grasstiles/metalled.
01/01-31/12.

Chiusa 23E1

Gamp, Via Gries 10. **GPS:** n46,64128 e11,57244.

20 € 14,50-16/24h 2 pers. + 2 children incl, dog € 2 Ch included. **Location:** Rural, simple.
Surface: grassy. 01/01-31/12.
Distance: 300m 800m on the spot mini market 100m on the spot on the spot.

Corvara in Badia 23F1

P Corvara, Strada Planac SS244. **GPS:** n46,54105 e11,88388.

10 free. **Location:** Rural, simple, isolated. **Surface:** gravel.
01/01-31/12.
Distance: 3,5km on the spot 3,5km on the spot on the spot.

Dimaro 23D2

Camper Solander, Loc. Rovina. **GPS:** n46,32488 e10,86215.

10 € 20/24h, € 10/night Ch WC included.
Surface: gravel. 01/01-31/12.
Distance: 500m on the spot.
Remarks: Near campsite Dolomiti.

Dimaro 23D2

Dolomiti, Via Gole. **GPS:** n46,32507 e10,86267.
€ 20-31 Ch included. **Location:** Rural.
Surface: asphalted. 01/01-31/12.
Distance: on the spot on the spot.

Eppan 23E1

Camper Stop Eppan, Sillnegg 2. **GPS:** n46,44871 e11,26418.
27 € 18/24h Ch WC included. **Location:** Comfortable, luxurious, quiet. **Surface:** gravel.
Distance: 800m pizzeria 200m 800m 100m on the spot on the spot.

Folgaria 23E3

Area Sosta Bucaneve, Via Negheli 87. **GPS:** n45,91849 e11,19255.

25 € 8. **Location:** Simple.
Surface: grasstiles.
01/01-31/12.
Distance: 300m 100m.
Remarks: Check in and pay at reception, golf court, shuttle bus.

Folgaria 23E3

SS3501. **GPS:** n45,91397 e11,17081.
€1 Ch.

Folgarida 23D2

Hotel Belvedere, Piazzale Belvedere. **GPS:** n46,29716 e10,86741.
€ 15 €5.
Distance: on the spot 200m 150m.

Gargazzone 23E1

Weißhof-Keller, Landstrasse 65 SS38. **GPS:** n46,58500 e11,20528.

10 € 10 Ch €2/24h WC €1. **Location:** Rural, simple, quiet. **Surface:** grassy/gravel. 01/01-31/12.
Distance: 2km 1,5km 500m 2km on the spot on the spot on the spot.
Remarks: Reservation for Christmas holidays, tel.: +39 (0)473 292448.

Tourist information Gargazzone:
Consorzio Turistico, Via Maria Trost, 5, Merano, www.meranerland.com. Place with medicinal sources.
Castel Tirolo, 4km N. de Merano. Regional museum. 01/03-31/12.
Merano. Tue, Fri.
Festa della Città, Merano. 1st weekend Aug.

Glorenza 23D1

Glurms Camping im Park, > SS41. **GPS:** n46,67067 e10,54520.

40 € 12 Ch €2 WC. **Surface:** grassy.
Distance: 500m on the spot.
Remarks: Along the Adige river.

La Villa in Badia 23F1

Odlina, Strada Ninz, 49. **GPS:** n46,58889 e11,90028.

45 summer € 25, winter € 30 Ch WC included €5 €3. **Location:** Rural, luxurious, quiet. **Surface:** metalled.
01/01-31/12.
Distance: 400m 150m 150m on the spot on the spot on the spot 300m.
Remarks: Reservation for Christmas holidays: info@odina.it, use of

IT

sauna against payment.

Lago 23E2

Via Tresselume. **GPS**: n46,28291 e11,52557.

30 free €1 €2 Ch€1 (12x)€2/8h.
Location: Rural, simple. **Surface:** metalled. 01/01-31/12.
Distance: 200m 200m.

Lavarone 23E2

Prà Grando, Via Padova. **GPS**: n45,93602 e11,27099.

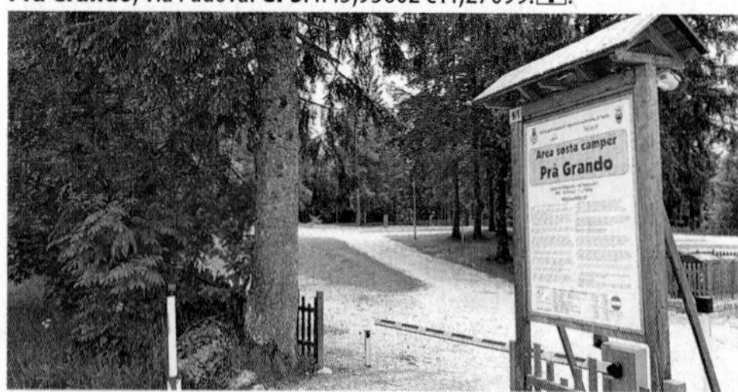

40 € 16,50 May/June/July, € 19 Aug, € 18 Dec-April Ch (3x) €1/3minutes included. **Location:** Rural, simple, quiet.
Surface: grassy/gravel. 01/05-30/09, 01/12-31/03.
Distance: 300m 32km Lago di Lavarone 1km 1km 300m 300m 300m 1km 1km.

Lavarone 23E2

SS 349, Loc Moar. **GPS**: n45,94575 e11,26397.

18 € 13/24h €0,50 Chfree. **Location:** Rural, simple, quiet.
Surface: metalled. 01/01-31/12.
Distance: 800m Lago di Lavarone 1,9km 500m.
Remarks: Next to sports fields, max. 72h.

Levico Terme 23E2

Area Sosta Camper Valsugana, Loc Pleina.
GPS: n46,00691 e11,28706.

50 € 19/24h Ch WC €4 included.
Location: Rural, comfortable. **Surface:** grassy. 01/01-31/12.
Distance: 1,3km 200m, Lido di Levico 1,1km 50m 50m on the spot on the spot on the spot.
Remarks: Max. 3 nights, check in at reception campsite.

Levico Terme 23E2

Area 47, SP1. **GPS**: n46,00415 e11,28880.

18 € 18, 01/06-30/09 € 25 ChWC included.
Location: Rural, comfortable. **Surface:** asphalted.
Distance: 1,3km on the spot.
Remarks: Including access to swimming pool and private beach.

Moena 23E2

Bar Il Giardino, SS 48 Forno di Moena. **GPS**: n46,35238 e11,63149.

40 € 12, 01/07-31/08 and 25/12-08/01 € 14 €4 Ch €4/24h WC. **Location:** Rural, comfortable, central. **Surface:** grassy/metalled. 01/01-31/12.
Distance: 3,5km 500m 2km 300m on the spot on the spot on the spot.
Remarks: Max. 48h, skibus comes at parking.

Molveno 23D2

Area attrezzata per camper Lago di Molveno, Via Lungolago, 25, Loc. Ischia. **GPS**: n46,14122 e10,95819.

50 € 15-30 Ch included. **Location:** Rural, simple, quiet. **Surface:** metalled. 01/01-31/12.
Distance: 800m 200m 200m 100m.

Pergine Valsugana 23E2

Soleando Camperparking, Via al lago 23/A.
GPS: n46,05121 e11,23593.

10 € 12 Ch included. **Location:** Urban, simple, noisy.
Surface: gravel. 01/01-31/12.
Distance: 600m Lago di Caldonazzo 1km 300m 300m 100m on the spot.

Tourist information Pergine Valsugana:
www.apt.trento.it. City at the foot of the Dolomites with historical centre.
Palazzo Pretorio, Trento. Ecclesiastical museum.

Predazzo 23E2

Latemar 2200, SS48, dir Moena. **GPS**: n46,32582 e11,59970.

50 free, peak season € 7-10/24h Chincluded.
Location: Rural, simple, noisy. **Surface:** asphalted/gravel. 01/01-31/12.
Distance: 2,5km 2,5km on the spot on the spot on the spot on the spot on the spot.
Remarks: Parking ski-lifts.

Rabbi 23D2

Al Plan, Loc. Plan, Bagni di Rabbi. **GPS**: n46,40768 e10,79559.

105 € 18-23, 2 pers. incl., dog € 1 Ch WCincluded against payment.
Location: Rural. **Surface:** metalled. 01/05-30/09.
Distance: 600m 600m on the spot on the spot on the spot.
Remarks: Max. 48h.

Racines 20E3

Sportzone Ratschings, Belprato, Stanghe.
GPS: n46,88254 e11,38383.

20 free. **Location:** Rural, simple.
Surface: gravel. 01/01-31/12.
Distance: 400m 5km 400m 400m 400m Gilfenklammroute.

Riva del Garda 23D3

Via Monte Brione. **GPS**: n45,87986 e10,85872.

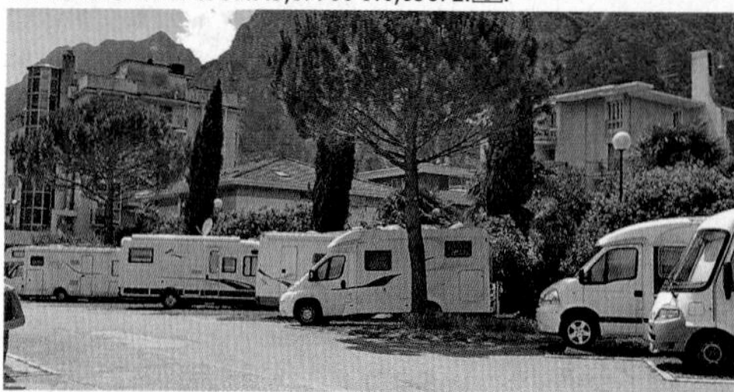

41 € 0,50/h, max. € 24/48h Chincluded.
Location: Urban, simple.
Surface: grasstiles. 01/11-07/12.
Distance: 1,5km 200m.
Remarks: Max. 48h.

Tourist information Riva del Garda:
Museo Civico, Piazza Battisti.

Rovereto 23E3

Area Camper Quercia, Via Palestrina. **GPS**: n45,90232 e11,03704.

15 € 8/12h, € 16/24h Ch WC included.
Location: Simple. **Surface:** grasstiles. 01/01-31/12.
Distance: 1,5km 2km.
Remarks: Caution € 5, bicycle rental, picnic tables available.

Tourist information Rovereto:
Museo Storico Italiano della Guerra, Via Castelbarco, 7. War museum.
Mo-Fri 8.30-12.30h, 14-18h 01/01-28/02.
Castel Beseno, Besenello. Tue-Su.

San Candido 23F1

Area di Sosta Camper, Via Prato alla Drava, 1/A.
GPS: n46,73924 e12,36559.

IT

90 € 20 Ch WCincluded €2. Location: Rural, comfortable, quiet. Surface: gravel. 01/01-31/12.
Distance: 6km on the spot 500m on the spot on the spot on the spot 2km 500m.
Remarks: Bicycle rental, shuttle bus San Candido and skipistes € 1/pp.

S San Guiseppe al Lago 23E2

Posteggio Camper Lago di Caldero, San Guiseppe 18.
GPS: n46,39038 e11,25663.

35 € 20/night Ch WC. **Location:** Rural, comfortable, quiet. **Surface:** gravel. 13/03-15/11.
Distance: 5km Caldero Private beach 50m Nearby campsite on the spot on the spot on the spot.
Remarks: Next to campsite, max. 4 days.

S San Martino di Castrozza 23F2

Area Sosta Tognola, Loc.Tognola. **GPS**: n46,25373 e11,80158.

90 € 15 included Ch €1/80minutes.
Location: Rural, comfortable, quiet. **Surface:** gravel. 01/01-31/12.
Distance: 1,5km 500m on the spot on the spot on the spot.
Remarks: Next to ski-lift, free shuttle.

S San Vigilio di Marebbe 23F1

Restaurant Pizzeria Rittenkeller, Str. Ras Costa, 2.
GPS: n46,70630 e11,92920.

120 01/04-30/11 € 25, 01/12-31/03 € 30 Ch included.
Location: Rural, simple, quiet.
Surface: gravel. 01/01-31/12.
Distance: 600m 500m on the spot 600m 600m on the spot 600m.
Remarks: Next to ski-lift, breakfast-service, reservation for Christmas holidays: info@ritterkeller.it.

Santa Cristina Valgardena 23E1

P1 Monte Pana, Strada Pana. **GPS**: n46,55174 e11,71624.

50 € 15/24h.
Location: Simple, isolated, quiet. **Surface:** gravel. 01/01-31/12.
Distance: 2,5km on the spot 2,5km on the spot on the spot on the spot.
Remarks: Altitude 1650m, max. 7 days, narrow entrance.

Selva di Val Gardena 23F1

Piz Sella, Strada Plan de Gralba. **GPS**: n46,53204 e11,77230.

50 € 12/24h. **Location:** Rural, simple. **Surface:** gravel. 01/01-31/12.
Distance: 4km 150m on the spot on the spot.
Remarks: Inclining pitches.

S Sesto/Sexten 23F1

Caravanpark Sexten, SS52 St Josefstrasse 54.
GPS: n46,66741 e12,39996.

35 € 23-27 Ch ,4Amp WC included €4 €2.
Location: Rural, luxurious, quiet.
Surface: grasstiles. 01/01-31/12.
Distance: 3km on the spot on the spot on the spot on the spot on the spot 900m on the spot.
Remarks: Max. 48h, sauna and spa.

Silandro 23D1

Via Ospedale, Silandro/Schlanders. **GPS**: n46,62721 e10,78185.

€ 3. **Surface:** grasstiles.
Distance: 500m 500m.

S Smarano 23E2

Area Sosta Ostaria del Filò, Viale Merlonga 48/a.
GPS: n46,34962 e11,10956.

43 € 10-13 Ch WC €1. **Surface:** grassy. 01/01-31/12.
Distance: 1km on the spot.
Remarks: Check in at restaurant.

Solda 23D1

GPS: n46,51448 e10,59578.
25 free. **Location:** Simple. **Surface:** gravel. 01/01-31/12.
Distance: 1km 100m on the spot on the spot.

S Tirolo 23E1

Schneeburghof, Monte Benedetto 26. **GPS**: n46,67789 e11,16495.

20 € 23 Ch included.
Location: Comfortable. **Surface:** gravel.
Distance: on the spot.
Remarks: Bread-service, swimming pool (summer).

S Tonadico 23F2

Lanterna Verde, Via Zocchet 10. **GPS**: n46,18216 e11,84318.

46 € 16 Ch WCincluded. **Location:** Rural, comfortable, quiet. **Surface:** grasstiles. 01/01-31/12.
Distance: 1km 100m 1km on the spot on the spot on the spot 15km 15km.
Remarks: Max. 48h, check in at restaurant.

S Trento 23E2

P Zuffo, Loc. Vela. **GPS**: n46,07650 e11,11050.

20 € 5 €1 Ch.
Location: Simple, noisy. **Surface:** asphalted. 01/01-31/12.
Distance: 1,8km 150m 200m.
Remarks: Max. 48h.

S Trento 23E2

Camper Trento Park, Via Brennero, 181. **GPS**: n46,09438 e11,11335.
200 € 12/24h Ch included €1 . **Surface:** asphalted. 01/01-31/12.
Distance: city centre 3km 2km 400m 400m bus 3-11-17 > centre.
Remarks: Inspection 2015: closed because of renovation.

S Trento 23E2

Parking Trentino, Via Santi Cosma e Damiano 64.
GPS: n46,07674 e11,10411.

20 € 15 Ch included. **Location:** Urban, simple, noisy.
Surface: grasstiles. 01/01-31/12.
Distance: 1,8km 300m 300m bus > centre 15 min.
Remarks: Call for entrance code: 3389004343 Mr. Pisetta.

IT

Trento 23E2

P3 Giardino Botanico Fondo Viote, SP85.
GPS: n46,02445 e11,03973.

100 € 4-10/10h, overnight stay free. **Location:** Rural, simple, isolated, quiet. **Surface:** asphalted. 01/01-31/12.
Distance: 18km Trento 150m on the spot on the spot on the spot on the spot.
Remarks: Altitude 1450m, max. 48h.

Tres 23E2

Batuda, SP della Predaia. **GPS**: n46,32040 e11,10202.

15 € 12/24h Ch WC included. **Location:** Rural.
Surface: grasstiles/metalled. 01/01-31/12.
Distance: 800m.

Vezzano 23D2

Vecchio Mulino, SS45bis. **GPS**: n46,07684 e11,01980.
10. **Location:** Rural, simple.
Surface: grassy. 25/04-10/11.
Distance: on the spot.

Lombardy

Alzano Lombardo 23C3

Via Europa. **GPS**: n45,73690 e9,72007.

3 . **Surface:** asphalted. Sa 6-15h market.
Remarks: At sports park.

Biassono 23B3

Via al Parco/Via della Sciavatera. **GPS**: n45,63102 e9,28865.

10 free Ch free. **Location:** Rural, simple, isolated.
Surface: asphalted. 01/01-31/12.
Distance: 500m Centro Commerciale Vilasanta 4km train > Milan 500m.

Borgofranco sul Po 26E1

Via Filipo Turati. **GPS**: n45,04775 e11,20524.

4 free Ch free. **Location:** Simple, quiet. **Surface:** grassy.
01/01-31/12 water: frost.
Distance: 600m 1km 200m 300m 200m 200m.

Bormio 23C1

Bormio 2000, Via Battaglion Morbegno. **GPS**: n46,46260 e10,37190.

€ 8/24h Ch included. **Surface:** sand. 01/01-31/12.
Distance: 500m 500m on the spot.
Remarks: Parking funicular railway, service passerby € 5.

Tourist information Bormio:
Ufficio Informazioni e di Accoglienza Turistica, Via Roma, 131/b. Alps city, large winter sport area, also summer skiing.
Parco Nazionale dello Stelvio. Region with 50 glacier lakes and high mountain peaks. Access around Bormio.

Brescia 23C3

Agriturismo Cascina Maggi, Via della Maggia 3.
GPS: n45,51232 e10,23634.

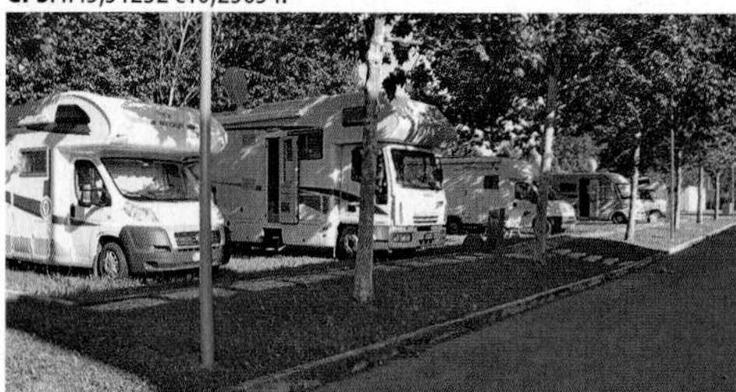

16 € 15 Ch included.
Surface: metalled. 01/01-31/12.
Distance: 2,5km on the spot 500m on the spot.
Remarks: Check in at hotel, market Saturday.

Campione 23D3

Area Camper Campione del Garda, Via Verdi.
GPS: n45,75651 e10,74985.

30 € 15/24h . **Surface:** unpaved. 01/04-31/10.
Distance: 500m on the spot 200m.

Capo di Ponte 23C2

Concarena, Via Santo Stefano. **GPS**: n46,02447 e10,34325.

12 € 8/24h, 1/10-28/2 free Ch WC included.
Surface: asphalted. 01/01-31/12.
Distance: 300m 300m 300m.

Carenno 23B3

Via per il Colle. **GPS**: n45,79952 e9,46606.
8 € 5 Ch included. **Surface:** asphalted. 01/01-31/12.
Distance: 250m.
Remarks: Next to sports fields, max. 72h.

Certosa di Pavia 26B1

Parking Certosa, Via di Vittorio, SP27. **GPS**: n45,25735 e9,14161.

20 € 15/24h Ch WC free. **Location:** Simple.
Surface: grassy/gravel. 01/01-31/12 water disconnected in winter. **Distance:** 1km 200m on the spot on the spot.
Remarks: Monastery Certosa di Pavia 450m.

Chiavenna 23B2

Piazzale Leonardo da Vinci, Via A. Moro, SS36.
GPS: n46,31424 e9,39631.

free Ch free. **Surface:** asphalted.
Distance: 800m 200m.

Chiesa in Valmalenco 23C2

Loc. Vassalini. **GPS**: n46,27020 e9,85670.

free € 3 . **Surface:** gravel.
Distance: 1km 200m.

Clusone 23C3

Busgarina, Via Vago 6, loc Fiorine. **GPS**: n45,87312 e9,91642.

80 € 13 Ch (33x)€2 €1/7minutes. 01/01-31/12.
Distance: on the spot.

Clusone 23C3

Viale Vittorio Emanuele. **GPS**: n45,88926 e9,95812.

5 free Ch free. **Surface:** asphalted. 01/01-31/12.

Distance: 600m on the spot.
Remarks: Max. 48h.

Colico 23B2

L'Ontano, Via Montecchio Nord. **GPS**: n46,14213 e9,37452.

25 € 20/24h Ch WC €1/3minutes. **Surface:** metalled.
01/02-31/12.
Distance: 500m on the spot on the spot.
Remarks: View on Lake Como.

Como 23B3

Area Camper Como, Via Brennero 7, Tavernola.
GPS: n45,83518 e9,06140.

10 € 0,50/h, € 12/24h €1,50 Ch€2,50 €1/kWh.
Location: Comfortable. **Surface:** grasstiles. 01/01-31/12.
Distance: city centre Como 4,5km 800m 400m 200m on the spot on the spot.

Como 23B3

Via Aldo Moro. **GPS**: n45,80286 e9,09155.

3 € 0,50/h €1,50 Ch€2,50 €0,50/kWh.
Location: Urban, central, noisy.
Surface: asphalted. 01/01-31/12.
Distance: city centre 1km 150m 100m.

Costa Volpino 23C3

Via Nazionale 24. **GPS**: n45,82298 e10,08680.
25 € 12/24h Ch WC €1. 01/01-31/12.
Distance: 900m on the spot 100m on the spot on the spot.
Remarks: At lake.

Cremona 26C1

Piazzale della Croce Rossa, Via Mantova.
GPS: n45,13744 e10,03464.

free Chfree.
Location: Simple. **Surface:** asphalted. 01/01-31/12.
Distance: on the spot 3km on the spot 200m on the spot.
Remarks: Nearby stadium.

Desenzano del Garda 23D3

Area Sosta Camper La Spiaggia, Via Vò, 19.
GPS: n45,48747 e10,52180.

100 € 12/24h Chincluded WC.
Surface: gravel.
01/01-31/12.
Distance: 200m Pizzeria Stella Del Garda 10m on the spot.
Remarks: Video surveillance, barbecue place.

Esine 23C3

Fontanelle on the Road, Via Toroselle 12, SS42.
GPS: n45,90302 e10,21820.

15 Ch. **Surface:** grassy. 01/01-31/12.
Distance: 4km on the spot.

Gandino 23C3

Via Giovanni Pascoli. **GPS**: n45,81286 e9,90538.

2 free Chfree. **Surface:** grasstiles. 01/01-31/12.
Distance: historical centre 250m.
Remarks: Max. 48h.

Gavirate 23A3

Via Cavour. **GPS**: n45,83913 e8,72105.

30 € 8/day €2 Ch€1 €1/12h.
Location: Rural, simple, quiet. **Surface:** grasstiles.
01/01-31/12.
Distance: 200m 10m on the spot on the spot on the spot.
Remarks: At lake of Varese, friday market.

Germignaga 23A3

Via A. Bodmer. **GPS**: n45,99630 e8,72421.

6 € 1,50/h, € 15/24h €1 Ch €3 WC.
Location: Simple, central, quiet. **Surface:** asphalted.
01/01-31/12.
Distance: 500m on the spot on the spot 500m 500m.
Remarks: Max. 48h, key electricity at pay-desk.

Iseo 23C3

Viale Europa. **GPS**: n45,65396 e10,04449.

free. **Surface:** unpaved. 01/01-31/12.
Distance: 1km 250m 600m.

Tourist information Iseo:
I.A.T. (Ufficio Informazioni e di Accoglienza Turistica), Lungolago Marconi, 2. Old fishermen's village.
Week market. Fri.

Lecco 23B3

Via Arturo Toscanini, Loc. Bione di Lecco. **GPS**: n45,83136 e9,40779.

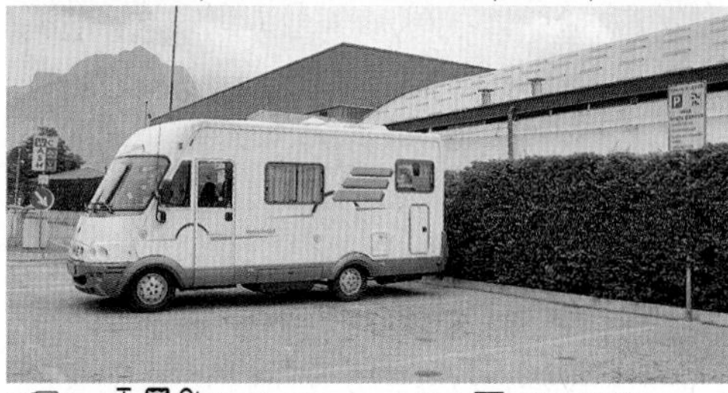

12 free Chfree. **Surface:** asphalted. 01/01-31/12.
Distance: 2,8km.
Remarks: At lake Garlate, cycle routes.

Livigno 23C1

Aquafresca, Via Palipert 374. **GPS**: n46,50713 e10,11952.
Ch WC. 01/01-31/12.
Distance: on the spot on the spot.
Remarks: Free shuttle.

Livigno 23C1

Stella Alpina, Via Palipert 570. **GPS**: n46,50515 e10,11958.

28 € 15 Ch €3 WC.
Surface: gravel. 01/01-31/12.
Distance: 400m Free bus on the spot.
Remarks: Free shuttle to ski-lifts.

Livigno 23C1

Trepalle, SS301. **GPS**: n46,52655 e10,17578.

50 € 10 Chfree. **Surface:** asphalted.
Distance: Livigno 6,6km 200m bus to Livigno every 40 minutes on the spot.
Remarks: Altitude 2000m.

Tourist information Livigno:
Latteria di Livigno, Via Pemonte 911. Discover the secrets of dairy products from Livigno. On Wednesday the possibility of preparing meals, costs € 7, from 14h. summer Mo-Fr 8-20h.

Lodrino 23C3

Via Kennedy, Localité Dade. **GPS**: n45,71450 e10,28107.

IT

3 free free. **Surface:** asphalted. 01/01-31/12.
Distance: 500m.

Luino 23A3

Via Gorizia. **GPS:** n45,97255 e8,75275.

16 € 9 Ch. **Location:** Rural, isolated, quiet.
Surface: asphalted/grassy. 01/01-31/12.
Distance: 3km on the spot 3km.
Remarks: At sports grounds.

Maccagno 23A2

Via Virgilio Parisi. **GPS:** n46,04010 e8,73545.

18 free free. **Location:** Rural, simple, central, quiet.
Surface: gravel.
Distance: 300m 200m 200m 300m 300m 300m on the spot on the spot.
Remarks: At sports centre, max. 72h, friday market.

Magnacavallo 26E1

Via Salvador Allende. **GPS:** n45,00587 e11,17906.

4 free Chfree. **Location:** Simple. **Surface:** asphalted.
01/01-31/12.
Distance: 200m 200m 200m 50m.
Remarks: At sports park.

Mandello del Lario 23B3

Area Cima, Via Giulio Cesare. **GPS:** n45,91830 e9,31589.

12 € 10 Ch. **Surface:** asphalted. 01/01-31/12.
Distance: 800m Lago di Lecco 400m.

Mantova 26D1

Parco Paganini, Via Fiera 11, Grazie di Curtatone.
GPS: n45,15333 e10,69111.

108 € 12 Ch WC included. **Location:** Simple, central.
Surface: asphalted/grassy. 01/03-13/11.
Distance: 300m, Mantova 6km 300m 4km, bakery 300m.

Mantova 26D1

Sparafucile, Via Legnago 1/a. **GPS:** n45,16336 e10,81244.

54 € 10/12-12h, € 15/24h Ch WC included.
Location: Comfortable, luxurious, quiet. **Surface:** grassy/metalled.
01/01-31/12.
Distance: 1km 4km 500m 500m on the spot on the spot.
Remarks: Thursday market.

Mantova 26D1

Anconetta. **GPS:** n45,15322 e10,79864.

free. **Location:** Urban, simple. **Surface:** asphalted.
01/01-31/12.
Distance: centre 800m on the spot.
Remarks: Marina.

Menaggio 23B2

Via Armando Diaz 12. **GPS:** n46,02454 e9,23900.
20 free. 01/01-31/12.
Distance: 550m on the spot on the spot.

Merate 23B3

Via Papa Giovanni Paolo I, loc. Sartirana. **GPS:** n45,71326 e9,41865.

10 € 5,50 Ch. **Surface:** grasstiles.
Remarks: Max. 72h.

Milano 26B1

Ripamonti SNC, Via Ripamonti 481, Milan (Milano).
GPS: n45,40914 e9,20937.

30 € 20/24h Ch €5 WC included. **Surface:** asphalted.
Distance: on the spot Milan 40min.
Remarks: Monitored parking.

Milano 26B1

Camper Village Linate Parking, Viale Enrico Forlanini, 123, Milan (Milano). **GPS:** n45,46245 e9,27024.
€ 20/24h. **Location:** Urban.
Surface: metalled. 01/01-31/12.
Distance: centre 7km N 74 > centre.

Milano 26B1

Agriturismo Cascina Gaggioli, Via Selvanesco 25, Milan (Milano).
GPS: n45,41785 e9,19578.
8 € 20 WC . **Surface:** metalled.
Distance: 6km 500m 250m.

Tourist information Milan (Milano):
Castello Sforzesco.
Duomo. History of Gothic architecture. Tue-Su.
Via Fauché. Tue, Sa.
Mercatone del Naviglio Grande, Naviglio Grande. Antiques market, 400 stalls. last Su of the month.
Galleria.

Moglia 26E2

Via Tazio Nuvolari. **GPS:** n44,93639 e10,91582.

14 free Chfree. **Surface:** asphalted. 01/01-31/12.
Distance: 300m A22 7km 300m.
Remarks: At swimming pool.

Monte Marenzo 23B3

Via Papa Gionvanni. **GPS:** n45,77639 e9,45222.

6 free free. **Surface:** gravel. 01/01-31/12.
Distance: 300m.

Monzambano 26D1

Area attrezzata camper Comunale di Monzambano, Via Degli Alpini n. 9. **GPS:** n45,38916 e10,69277.

130 € 13/24h (24x) €0,50 included.
Surface: gravel. 01/01-31/12.
Distance: 200m 100m 300m, bakery 100m on the spot on the spot.
Remarks: Max. 48h, market on Sunday.

Morbegno 23B2

Area Sosta Camper Morbegno, Via del Foss.
GPS: n46,14419 e9,57500.
22 € 10 Ch included. **Location:** Rural.
Surface: grasstiles.
01/01-31/12.
Distance: historical centre 500m 100m Skibus on the spot.

Niardo 23C2

Area di sosta Mr. Sanders, Località Crist.
GPS: n45,97690 e10,31959.

20 € 10 Ch €2 WC.
Surface: metalled. 01/01-31/12.
Distance: Niardo 1,3km on the spot on the spot.
Remarks: Bread-service.

S Nova Milanese 23B3

Via G. Brodolini. **GPS**: n45,58298 e9,19668.

4 free free.
Location: Urban, simple. **Surface:** asphalted. 01/01-31/12.
Distance: 500m 1,6km 200m.
Remarks: Video surveillance.

Novate Mezzola 23B2

Via al Lido. **GPS**: n46,21083 e9,45000.

25 free. **Surface:** grassy/gravel. 01/01-31/12.
Distance: 800m 40m 800m on the spot.
Remarks: At lake Mezzola, signposted cycle routes.

S Olginate 23B3

Via Cesare Cantù. **GPS**: n45,79523 e9,41610.

46 € 14/24h Ch included. **Surface:** metalled.
01/01-31/12 Thu>16h-Fri<16h (market).
Distance: 200m on the spot.
Remarks: At Olginate lake.

S Pizzighettone 26C1

Via De Gasperi. **GPS**: n45,18538 e9,79402.

4 free Chfree. **Location:** Simple. **Surface:** gravel.
01/01-31/12.
Distance: 400m 300m Lidl 100m.

S Rovetta 23C3

Campo sportivo, Via Papa Giovanni XIII. **GPS**: n45,88892 e9,98224.

free Ch. **Surface:** asphalted.
Distance: 400m.
Remarks: Parking at gymnasium.

S Ruino 26B2

Agriturismo Adriana Tarantani, Loc. Tre Venti.
GPS: n44,92833 e9,26311.

6 free with a meal Ch. **Location:** Rural, simple.
Surface: grassy/gravel. 01/01-31/12.
Distance: 1km on the spot 1km 100m.

S Sabbioneta 26D2

Via Piccola Atene. **GPS**: n44,99459 e10,48849.

15 free Chfree. **Location:** Simple, quiet. **Surface:** metalled.
01/01-31/12.
Distance: 200m 400m 500m.

S San Benedetto Po 26E1

Via Cardinal Ruffini. **GPS**: n45,04292 e10,93432.
4 free Chfree. **Surface:** asphalted. 01/01-31/12.
Distance: 500m on the spot.

S Santa Caterina Valfurva 23D2

Agriturismo Zia Edda, Via Forni, loc. Nassegno.
GPS: n46,40917 e10,50833.

€ 12 Ch €3. **Surface:** grassy.
Distance: 500m on the spot on the spot.

S Saronno 23B3

Via E.H.Griegh. **GPS**: n45,61265 e9,04274.

2 free €1/100liter Ch. **Location:** Simple, simple.
Surface: asphalted. 01/01-31/12.
Distance: 1,5km 3,5km 500m 200m.

Saronno 23B3

Via Dalmazia 11. **GPS**: n45,62446 e9,02469.

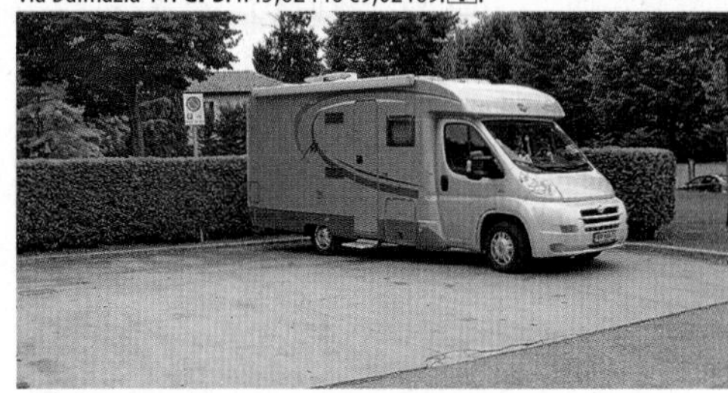

2 free. **Location:** Urban, central. **Surface:** concrete.
01/01-31/12.
Distance: on the spot 2km 1km 1km.
Remarks: Max. 24h.

S Sartirana Lomellina 26A1

Via Cavour. **GPS**: n45,11337 e8,66936.

3 free €2/100liter Ch. **Location:** Simple. **Surface:** asphalted.
01/01-31/12 Sa-morning market.
Distance: 100m 200m 100m on the spot.

S Sirmione 23D3

Camper Park Sirmione, Via Cantarane. **GPS**: n45,46083 e10,63333.

150 € 20/24h, € 11/20.30-9.30h Ch €3 included.
Surface: gravel. 15/03-31/10.
Distance: 1,5km Lake Garda 100m 1km 100m.

S Sirmione 23D3

Piazzale Montebaldo. **GPS**: n45,48694 e10,61028.

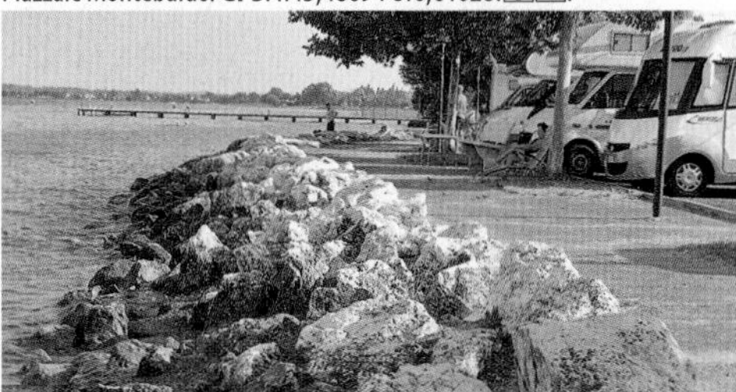

21 from € 2,50 1/2h till-€ 21/24h ChWC.
Surface: asphalted. 01/01-31/12.
Distance: 200m on the spot 50m 200m.

S Sondrio 23C2

Area Sportiva, Via Vanoni. **GPS**: n46,16064 e9,86957.

6 free Chfree. **Surface:** asphalted.
Distance: 600m.
Remarks: Parking sports park.

S Stezzano 23B3

Via Pietro Mascagni. **GPS**: n45,65594 e9,65301.

IT

free Chfree. **Surface:** asphalted.

S **Sulzano** 23C3

Parking Gerolo, Via Tassano 14. **GPS**: n45,68830 e10,10341.

25 € 15/24h, € 10/night ChWC.
Surface: grassy. 01/01-31/12.
Distance: 300m Lago Iseo 400m 300m.

S **Ternate** 23A3

Via Roma. **GPS**: n45,78006 e8,69780.

8 € 10 Ch (4x)free. **Location:** Simple, central, quiet.
Surface: unpaved. 01/01-31/12.
Distance: 200m on the spot on the spot 100m 200m on the spot on the spot.
Remarks: At Comabbio lake.

S **Tirano** 23C2

Area Camper Tirano, Via Polveriera/Via Sala Piero.
GPS: n46,21361 e10,15722.

20 € 15/24h Ch included.
Location: Comfortable. **Surface:** grasstiles. 01/01-31/12.
Distance: 1km station 800m.

Tourist information Tirano:
Bernina Express. The highest-altitude trans-Alpine line in Europe, with one of the steepest gradients in the world between Tirano (It) and Chur (Ch). UNESCO's List of World Heritage. ± € 100/pp return ticket (Tirano-Chur), ± € 45/pp return ticket (Tirano-Pontresina).

S **Torbole** 23D3

Camperstop Torbole, Via Al Cor. **GPS**: n45,87264 e10,87260.

120 € 20-34 Ch WC included. **Surface:** grassy.
01/01-31/12.
Distance: on the spot on the spot on the spot on the spot.

Remarks: Along Lake Garda.

S **Treviglio** 23B3

Via al Malgari. **GPS**: n45,53142 e9,59710.

4 free Chfree. **Surface:** metalled. 01/01-31/12.
Distance: 700m 400m.
Remarks: At sports park.

S **Varzi** 26B2

Strada Circonvallazione. **GPS**: n44,82172 e9,19727.

30 free, summer € 5 ChWCfree. **Location:** Simple, central.
Surface: asphalted/metalled. 01/01-31/12.
Distance: 200m 50m 50m.
Remarks: Along the Staffora river, friday market.

Veneto

S **Arquà Polesine** 26F1

Ostello Canalbianco, SS 16, n15. **GPS**: n44,99665 e11,76243.
12 € 10 Ch WC.
Distance: on the spot.

Asiago 23E3

P Verdi Mosele, SS349, Via Giuseppe Verdi.
GPS: n45,87129 e11,50026.

20 € 1/h, € 4/day. **Surface:** asphalted. 01/01-31/12.
Distance: 300m 500m.

S **Asolo** 23F3

Area Camper Communale, Via Forestuzzo.
GPS: n45,79637 e11,91283.

20 € 7/24h Ch (14x)included.
Location: Rural, comfortable.
Surface: grassy/sand. 01/01-31/12.
Distance: 400m 400m 400m.
Remarks: Access 8-19.30h, barbecue place, picnic area.

S **Auronzo di Cadore** 23F1

Taiarezze, SR48, Via Reaneloc. **GPS**: n46,56217 e12,41640.

30 € 12, 01/07-31/08 and 24/12-06/01 € 18 Chincluded.
Location: Rural, simple, quiet. **Surface:** asphalted.
01/01-31/12.
Distance: 1,5km on the spot on the spot on the spot on the spot on the spot on the spot 1,6km 1,6km.
Remarks: Max. 48h, payment only with coins.

S **Barbarano Vicentino** 26E1

Viale Vittorio Veneto 66. **GPS**: n45,40725 e11,54654.

3 free free. **Surface:** asphalted. 01/01-31/12.
Distance: 200m 200m 200m.

S **Bardolino** 23D3

Parking Serenella, Via Gardesana dell'Acqua.
GPS: n45,56115 e10,71412.

10 € 17/24h Chincluded. **Location:** Rural, simple, quiet.
Surface: grasstiles. 01/01-31/12.
Distance: 2km on the spot on the spot on the spot Lidl 2km on the spot on the spot on the spot.

Tourist information Bardolino:
I.A.T. (Ufficio Informazioni e di Accoglienza Turistica), Piazzale Aldo Moro.

S **Bassano del Grappa** 23F3

Parcheggio Gerosa, Via Alcide de Gasperi.
GPS: n45,75831 e11,73091.

20 € 12/24h Ch included.
Surface: asphalted. 01/01-31/12.
Distance: 300m 300m 300m on the spot.
Remarks: Max. 48h.

Bassano del Grappa 23F3

Prato Santo Caterina, Via Chini 6. **GPS**: n45,76009 e11,73413.
free.
Distance: on the spot.

S **Belluno** 23F2

Rio Cavalli, Via Sagrogna 74. **GPS**: n46,15646 e12,26136.

IT

20 € 15 . €5 WC. **Location:** Comfortable, central, quiet. **Surface:** grassy/sand. 01/01-31/12.
Distance: 3km 6km on the spot on the spot 3km on the spot.

Belluno 23F2

Viale dei Dendrofori, loc. Lambioi. **GPS**: n46,13712 e12,21371.

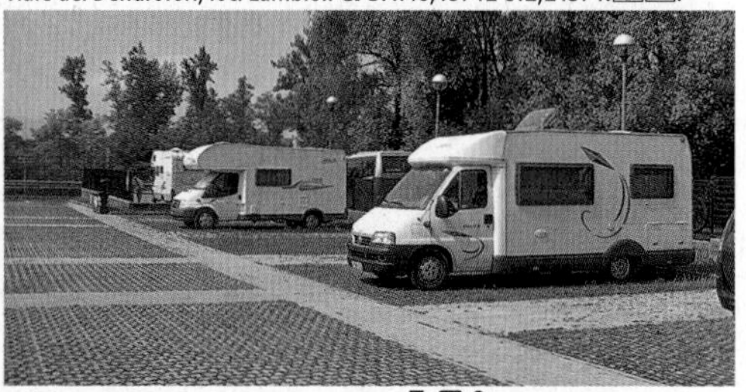

12 8-18 € 0,80/h, overnight stay free Chfree.
Location: Simple, central, noisy. **Surface:** grasstiles/metalled.
01/01-31/12.
Distance: 100m 100m 100m.
Remarks: Nearby swimming pool and skating rink.

Bibione 23H3

Valle Vecchia, Strada Brussa. **GPS**: n45,62458 e12,95866.

100 € 10/08-18h, overnight stay free free WC.
Location: Rural, simple, isolated, quiet. **Surface:** grassy.
01/01-31/12.
Distance: 12km sandy beach 250m 12km 12km on the spot on the spot.
Remarks: Guarded during the day, shower during opening hours, dog permitted on the beach.

Borghetto di Valeggio sul Mincio 26D1

Camper Parking Visconteo, Strada provinciale 55.
GPS: n45,35537 e10,72017.
60 € 10/24h €3 Ch €2/24h. **Location:** Rural, comfortable. **Surface:** gravel. 01/01-31/12.
Distance: on the spot Lake Garda 13km 250m on the spot on the spot.
Remarks: Borghetto 200m.

Castelguglielmo 26E1

Via Alessandro Volta. **GPS**: n45,02246 e11,53518.

10 free Ch free. **Surface:** metalled.
Distance: 500m 500m.

Cavallino-Treporti 23G3

Spiaggia di Cà Ballarin, Via Gabrielle Berton.
GPS: n45,45998 e12,51659.

4 free. **Location:** Rural, simple, quiet.
Surface: sand. 01/05-31/10.
Distance: 1km on the spot on the spot on the spot 1km 300m.
Remarks: Beach parking.

Tourist information Cavallino-Treporti:
Week market. Tue-Thu morning.

Chioggia 26G1

2 Palme, Lungomare Adriatica. **GPS**: n45,22122 e12,29624.

100 € 12, peak season € 20, Su/holidays € 15 Ch (100x)WCincluded €0,50. **Location:** Urban, simple, central.
Surface: grassy/gravel. 01/01-31/12.
Distance: centre 1,8km 200m.
Remarks: Chioggia: little Venice.

Colà di Lazise 23D3

Villa dei Cedri, Via Possoi. **GPS**: n45,46777 e10,74972.

200 € 1/h, 5 hours min Ch included. **Location:** Rural, comfortable, quiet. **Surface:** grasstiles. 01/01-31/12.
Remarks: Parco Termale 300m.

Conegliano 23F2

Area de Sosta Campeggio Club Conegliano, Via San Giovanni Bosco, SS13. **GPS**: n45,87799 e12,30111.

30 € 12/24h Ch (16x)included WC.
Location: Simple, central, quiet.
Surface: grassy. 01/01-31/12.
Distance: 2km nearby on the spot.

Domegge di Cadore Belluno 23F1

Camping Cologna, Vallesella di Cadore. **GPS**: n46,44605 e12,40658.

30 € 10 Ch. **Location:** Rural, simple, quiet. **Surface:** grassy.
01/05-20/10.
Distance: 1km At the lake on the spot on the spot 1km 1km on the spot on the spot.
Remarks: Max. 24h, narrow entrance.

Feltre 23F2

Area Camper Vincheto, Via Casonetto 158C.
GPS: n46,03124 e11,95911.
12 € 15 Chincluded €3. **Surface:** grassy/metalled.
01/01-31/12.

Feltre 23F2

Piazale Pra del Vescovo, Viale A. Gaggia.
GPS: n46,02013 e11,90792.

15 free Chfree. **Surface:** metalled. 01/01-31/12.
Distance: 500m 500m 500m 500m.
Remarks: Max. 48h.

Ferrara di Monte Baldo 23D3

Via Chiesa. **GPS**: n45,67794 e10,85491.

16 free Chfree (16x)€5/day. **Location:** Rural, simple, isolated, quiet. **Surface:** gravel. 01/01-31/12.
Distance: 300m 300m 300m 300m on the spot on the spot on the spot.
Remarks: To be paid at bar.

Garda 23D3

P Centro, SS249. **GPS**: n45,57501 e10,71019.

20 € 17/24h ChWCincluded.
Location: Simple. **Surface:** metalled. 01/01-31/12.
Distance: 200m on the spot on the spot.

Garda 23D3

Via Preite. **GPS**: n45,57620 e10,71404.

30 € 17/24h Chincluded.
Location: Quiet. **Surface:** grasstiles. Easter-31/10.
Distance: 300m Lake Garda 300m.

Lazise 23D3

Parking Lazise Dardo, Via San Martino, SP31.
GPS: n45,50623 e10,73584.

IT

15 € 17/24h. **Surface:** asphalted. 01/01-31/12.
Distance: 200m 5,8km 200m 200m 200m.

S Lido di Jesolo 23G3

Area camping Albatros, Via Correr 102/A.
GPS: n45,52477 e12,68995.

131 € 12-32 Ch WC included. **Location:** Rural, comfortable, isolated, quiet. **Surface:** grassy. 01/03-31/10.
Distance: 500m 700m 100m 100m 100m 100m.

S Lido di Jesolo 23G3

Boscopineta, Via Vettor Pisani. **GPS:** n45,52278 e12,69178.

250 € 11-20 Ch WC €1 €5 included.
Location: Rural, comfortable, central. **Surface:** grassy.
Easter-31/10.
Distance: 100m 400m 250m on the spot.

S Lido di Jesolo 23G3

Camping Park dei Dogi, Viale Oriente. **GPS:** n45,52146 e12,68828.

200 € 14-26, 4 pers.incl. Ch WCincluded €0,50 €5 €1/week. **Location:** Rural, comfortable, central, quiet.
Surface: grassy. 01/01-31/12.
Distance: 200m sandy beach 200m 40m 150m 20m.

S Lido di Jesolo 23G3

Jesolo Camper Don Bosco, Via Oriente/via G.Don Bosco.
GPS: n45,52188 e12,68943.

250 € 11-20 Ch €3 WC €1 €5 included.
Location: Rural, comfortable. **Surface:** grassy/gravel.
01/01-31/12.
Distance: 100m 100m on the spot 100m on the spot.
Remarks: Bus to Venice stops in front of motorhome parking.

S Livinallongo del Col di Lana 23F1

Sportbar del Ghiaccio, Via Piagn,6 Arabba.
GPS: n46,49678 e11,87692.

50 € 17 Ch (17x)€3/24h WC €3. **Location:** Rural, comfortable, quiet. **Surface:** grassy/gravel. 01/01-31/12.
Distance: on the spot on the spot 200m 200m on the spot on the spot 200m.
Remarks: At the skating rink, check in at bar, service passerby € 6.

S Malcesine 23D3

Camping Lombardi, Via Navene 141, loc. Campagnola.
GPS: n45,78429 e10,82187.

20 € 18/24h, 28/06-01/09 € 21/24h Ch €1/24h WCincluded €1,50 according consumption. **Location:** Rural, simple, quiet. **Surface:** grasstiles. 01/04-31/10.
Distance: 3km Lake Garda 500m 50m on the spot on the spot on the spot.
Remarks: Max. 48h.

P Marghera 23F3

Parcheggio Terminal Service, Via dei Petroli 1/3 angolo via della Libertà. **GPS:** n45,46806 e12,26589.

€ 20/24h.
Location: Simple, central, quiet. 01/01-31/12.
Distance: > Venice.
Remarks: Monitored parking.

S Mirano 23F3

Camper Club Mirano, Via viasana, 4. **GPS:** n45,49322 e12,08968.

€ 15 Ch included.
Location: Rural, comfortable. **Surface:** grasstiles. 01/01-31/12.
Distance: historical centre 1,5km 8km 500m 600m 300m Padua-Venice.
Remarks: For entrance email: camperclubmirano@libero.it of phone 3479831010.

S Misurina 23F1

Piazzale Loita, Via Monte Piana. **GPS:** n46,58839 e12,25737.

50 € 2/h, € 18/day Ch included.
Location: Rural, simple, simple, central, noisy. **Surface:** gravel.
01/01-31/12.
Distance: 300m 500m 50m 300m on the spot on the spot on the spot 3km.
Remarks: Max. 48h, cash payment.

Misurina 23F1

P camper Rifugio Auronzo, Rifugio Auronzo.
GPS: n46,61267 e12,29342.

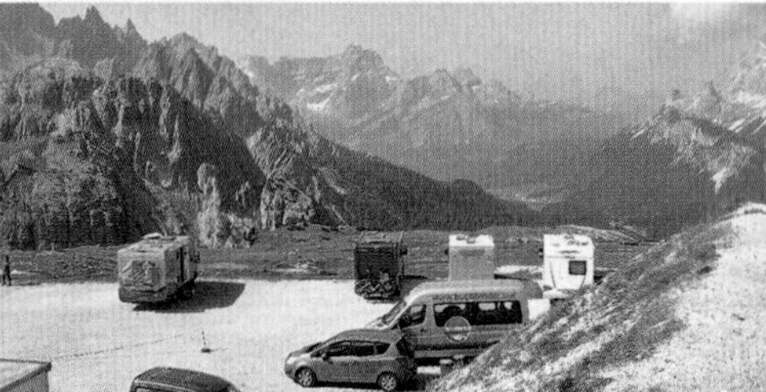

40 € 40 toll road incl., extra night € 15. **Location:** Rural, simple, isolated. **Surface:** gravel. 01/05-30/10.
Distance: Misurina 12km on the spot 12km on the spot Tre Cime di Lavadero 15km.
Remarks: Beautiful view.

S Molina 23D3

Camper el Crear, Via Bartolomeo Bacilieri 145.
GPS: n45,61229 e10,90855.

20 € 5 free. **Location:** Rural, simple, quiet.
Surface: grassy/gravel. 01/01-31/12.
Distance: on the spot on the spot.
Remarks: Max. 48h, pay at restaurant.

S Montagnana 26E1

Via Circonvallazione. **GPS:** n45,23528 e11,46639.

20 free Ch WC free. **Surface:** asphalted. 01/01-31/12.
Distance: 200m 200m 200m.
Remarks: At sports centre.

Padova 26F1

P1, Piazza della Pace Ytzhak Rabbin, Via cinquantottesimo Fanteria, Padua (Padova).
GPS: n45,39686 e11,87673.
8-20h € 10, 20-8h € 10, 18-10h € 20. **Surface:** asphalted.
01/01-31/12.
Distance: on the spot 6km on the spot on the spot on the spot.

Tourist information Padua (Padova):
- Caffe Pedrocchi, Via Oberdan. Café, meeting point for students.
- Capella degli Scrovegni. Chapel.

S Peschiera del Garda 26D1

Area camper Peschiera, Via Milano. **GPS:** n45,43995 e10,68474.

IT

100 € 15/24h Ch WC €1 included.
Location: Simple, quiet. **Surface:** gravel. 01/01-31/12.
Distance: 200m 1km 400m 400m on the spot on the spot on the spot.
Remarks: Monday-morning market.

S Peschiera del Garda 26D1

Nuova Area Camper, Via Frassino 11. **GPS**: n45,43115 e10,67500.

80 € 15 Ch WC included.
Location: Rural, simple. **Surface:** gravel. 01/01-31/12.
Distance: 1,5km 300m.

Tourist information Peschiera del Garda:
Tourist town at Lake Garda.
Mo-morning.

Porto Tolle 26G2

Via strada del Mare, loc. Barricata, SP38. **GPS**: n44,84997 e12,46342.

50 € 3,50. **Location:** Rural, quiet. **Surface:** grassy/sand.
Distance: 50m.
Remarks: Beach parking.

S Porto Tolle 26G2

Agriturismo La Ca' del Delta, Via Mazzini, 1.
GPS: n44,97798 e12,39785.
8 € 15 €2/day. **Location:** Isolated, quiet.
Distance: on the spot.

S Punta Sabbioni 23G3

Parking Dante Alighieri, Dante Alighieri 26.
GPS: n45,44132 e12,42131.

36 € 17-20 + € 3/pp Ch €3/24h WC included €3 free. **Location:** Urban, simple, central, quiet.
Surface: grassy.
01/03-01/11.
Distance: 1,5km 1,5km 1,5km 500m.
Remarks: Arrival <22h, monitored parking, ferry boat to Venice 500m.

S Punta Sabbioni 23G3

Agricamping da Scarpa, Via Pealto 15.
GPS: n45,44279 e12,44055.

15 € 16-20 + € 6-7/pp Ch WC €3 included.
Location: Rural, comfortable, quiet.
Surface: grassy.
01/01-31/12.
Distance: 500m on the spot 500m ferry Venice 1,5km.
Remarks: Breakfast-service.

S Recoaro Terme 23E3

Area Communale, Via Della Restistenza.
GPS: n45,70430 e11,22902.

16 € 5/24h €0,10/10liter Ch (16x)€0,50/2h,6Amp.
01/01-31/12.
Distance: on the spot on the spot on the spot on the spot on the spot.

S Santo Stefano di Cadore 23G1

Albergo Gasperina, Loc. Cima Canale, Val Visdende.
GPS: n46,60835 e12,63053.

49 € 12/24h, Aug € 14 Ch (49x)€2,50/day WC included €2. **Surface:** gravel. 01/06-01/10.
Distance: 12km 300m on the spot 6km on the spot on the spot.
Remarks: Check in at restaurant, bread-service, 10% discount at restaurant.

S Sappada 23G1

Borgata Palù. **GPS**: n46,56254 e12,67991.

40 € 12/24h Ch (24x)included. **Location:** Rural, simple, quiet. **Surface:** gravel. 01/01-31/12.
Distance: 1,1km 500m 1km on the spot on the spot 100m.
Remarks: Keycard at townhall, caution € 10.

S Schio 23E3

Parking Palasport, Viale dell'Industria. **GPS**: n45,71389 e11,37599.

4 free Ch free. **Surface:** asphalted. 01/01-31/12.
Distance: 1km 1km 1km on the spot on the spot.

S Sernaglia della Battaglia 23F3

Area attrezzata Le Grave, Via Passo Barca, Falzè di Piave.
GPS: n45,85676 e12,16566.

24 € 5/12h Ch included €2/24h. **Location:** Rural, simple. **Surface:** grassy. 01/01-31/12.
Distance: 500m on the spot 100m 500m 300m.

S Soave 26E1

Via Invalidi del Lavoro. **GPS**: n45,42340 e11,24541.

8 € 5 Ch (8x)free,16Amp.
Surface: grasstiles.
01/01-31/12.
Distance: 200m 3km on the spot 200m 200m 300m.

S Torre di Mosto 23G3

Agriturismo La Via Antiga, Via S. Martino 13.
GPS: n45,64389 e12,67056.

8 € 15 Ch (5x)included. **Location:** Rural, simple, isolated, quiet. **Surface:** grassy/gravel. 01/03-30/09.
Distance: 7km on the spot.

S Treviso 23F3

Parking ex Foro Boario, Via Castello d'Amore.
GPS: n45,67014 e12,25733.

13 free Ch free.
Location: Rural, simple. **Surface:** metalled. 01/01-31/12.
Distance: 500m 11,5km 500m 500m 200m.
Remarks: Max. 48h.

S Treviso 23F3

Via Giovanni Boccaccio. **GPS**: n45,66769 e12,26361.

IT

24 free Chfree. **Location:** Urban, simple, central, noisy.
Surface: asphalted. 01/01-31/12.
Distance: 1km 500m 500m 300m.
Remarks: Along railwayline.

Tourist information Treviso:
Sile. Fish-market on island.

S **Venezia** 23G3
Parcheggio Al Tronchetto, Venice (Venezia).
GPS: n45,44146 e12,30514.

40 € 21/0-12h, 12-24h € 16 included.
Location: Urban, simple, central, quiet. **Surface:** asphalted.
01/01-31/12.
Distance: 2km on the spot 2km 2km ferry, train.

S **Venezia** 23G3
Parco di San Giuliano, Via San Giuliano, Venice (Venezia).
GPS: n45,46742 e12,27916.

100 € 18/24h €3 Ch (30x)€4/24h WC included.
Location: Urban, comfortable, central, quiet.
Surface: grassy.
01/01-31/12.
Distance: 4km 200m 1,5km ferry Venice 100m, bus.

Tourist information Venice (Venezia):
A.P.T. (Azienda di Promozione Turistica), www.turismovenezia.it. Historical city consits of 117 islands, 150 canals and 400 bridges.

S **Verona** 26E1
Area sosta camper Porta Palio, Via dalla Bona.
GPS: n45,43354 e10,97879.

37 € 5/4h, € 10/24h Chincluded. **Location:** Urban, simple, central. **Surface:** asphalted.
01/01-31/12.
Distance: 500m Pizza (ordering service) bus 62 > centre.

S **Verona** 26E1
Agricamping Corte Finiletto, Strada Bresciana, 41.
GPS: n45,44651 e10,91917.

15 € 21, 2 pers.incl Ch €2 WC included.
Location: Rural. **Surface:** grassy.
Distance: 6km 3km 3km on the spot 1,5km 1,5km.
Remarks: 10% discount on presentation of the most recent guide.

Tourist information Verona:
Arena. Large anfiteatro, in July/August opera performances.
Via Capella. Known for the love drama of Romeo and Juliet.
Piazza dellen Erbe. daily.

S **Vicenza** 23E3
Park Interscambio CentroBus, Via Bassano, Zona sud-est.
GPS: n45,54321 e11,55886.

40 € 10/24h WCincluded. **Surface:** asphalted.
01/01-31/12 during event.
Distance: 2km on the spot Free bus to centre, every 15 min.
Remarks: At stadium.

S **Vicenza** 23E3
Park Interscambio CentroBus, Viale Cricoli, Zona nord.
GPS: n45,56418 e11,54903.

18 € 8,40/24h Ch WCincluded.
Surface: asphalted.
01/01-31/12.
Distance: 1,6km on the spot on the spot Free bus to centre.

Tourist information Vicenza:
Quartiere delle Barche. District with palaces in Venetian style.

Friuli Venezia Giulia

S **Ampezzo** 23G1
Via Laucjit. **GPS:** n46,41170 e12,80073.
6 € 7/24h Ch WC. **Surface:** grassy/metalled.
01/01-31/12.
Distance: 500m 650m on the spot.
Remarks: Next to sports fields.

S **Andreis** 23G2
SP20. **GPS:** n46,19880 e12,61157.

€ 5/day. **Location:** Simple. **Surface:** grassy/gravel.
Distance: little stream.

S **Aquileia** 23H3
Via Achille Grandi. **GPS:** n45,76549 e13,36898.
20 € 10/24h Ch. **Surface:** grasstiles. 01/01-31/12.
Distance: 500m 200m on the spot.
Remarks: Max. 48h.

S **Arta Terme** 23G1
Terme di Arta. **GPS:** n46,47554 e13,01677.
7 free Ch. **Surface:** grasstiles. 01/01-31/12.
Distance: 1km.
Remarks: Nearby football ground.

Artegna 23H2
Via Vicenza. **GPS:** n46,23465 e13,14919.
3 free. 01/01-31/12.
Distance: 800m 800m.

S **Barcis** 23G2
Loc. Portuz, SS251. **GPS:** n46,19055 e12,56507.

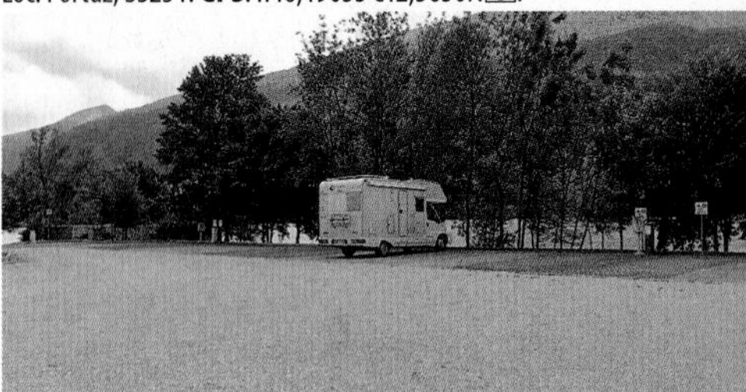

20 € 12/24h Ch. **Location:** Comfortable, isolated, quiet.
Surface: grasstiles/metalled. 01/01-31/12.
Distance: 400m on the spot 500m 500m.
Remarks: At the lake of Barcis, max. 48h.

S **Brugnera** 23G2
Parco Di Villa Varda, Via Villa Varda di S. Cassiano.
GPS: n45,88861 e12,52980.
40 free Ch. **Surface:** gravel. 01/01-31/12.

S **Capriva del Friuli** 23G2
Via degli Alpini. **GPS:** n45,94657 e13,00000.
6 free Ch WC. **Surface:** metalled. 01/01-31/12.
Distance: 600m.

S **Cavasso Nuovo** 23G2
Via Dante Alighieri. **GPS:** n46,19514 e12,77467.
4 free Ch. **Surface:** asphalted. 01/01-31/12.
Distance: 400m.

S **Cividale del Friuli** 23H2
Via delle Mura. **GPS:** n46,09446 e13,43618.
4 free Chfree. **Surface:** asphalted.
Distance: 500m 500m on the spot.
Remarks: Max. 72h.

S **Clauzetto** 23G2
Ambito delle Grotte di Pradis, Via Pradis di sotto,76.
GPS: n46,24538 e12,88974.
8 free Chfree. **Location:** Rural, isolated. **Surface:** forest soil.
01/01-31/12.
Distance: Clauzetto 3km 150m on the spot.
Remarks: Parking at the caves.

S **Codroipo** 23H2
Strada vicinale molino della sega, Passariano.
GPS: n45,94649 e13,00836.
30 € 3/6h Ch. 01/01-31/12.
Distance: centre 3,5km 300m.
Remarks: Coins at tourist info.

Colloredo di Monte Albano 23H2
Strada Provinciale 49. **GPS:** n46,16556 e13,13932.
10 free. **Surface:** metalled. 01/01-31/12.
Distance: 100m 100m.

S **Cormons** 23H2
P.le Luciano Zani, Salita del Monte Quarin.
GPS: n45,96672 e13,47341.
4 free free. **Location:** Rural. **Surface:** metalled.
01/01-31/12.
Distance: 3,5km 2km 2,5km on the spot.

S **Corno di Rosazzo** 23H2
Via dei Pini. **GPS:** n45,98955 e13,43917.

8 free Ch free. **Location:** Rural, simple, quiet. **Surface:** asphalted. 01/01-31/12.
Distance: 300m 1,5km 1km.
Remarks: Max. 48h.

S Forni di Sopra 23G1

Santa Viela, SS52. **GPS:** n46,42500 e12,57036.

20 € 7-9 Ch free. **Location:** Rural, simple, noisy. **Surface:** asphalted. 01/01-31/12.
Distance: 800m on the spot 800m 400m on the spot on the spot on the spot on the spot.
Remarks: No camping activities.

S Gemona del Friuli 23H2

Piazzale Mons. Battista Monai. **GPS:** n46,27585 e13,13728.

15 free Ch free. **Location:** Rural, simple, central, noisy. **Surface:** asphalted. 01/01-31/12.
Distance: on the spot 3,3km 300m 500m on the spot.

S Gorizia 23H2

Viale Oriani. **GPS:** n45,94554 e13,61603.

30 free Ch free. **Location:** Simple, quiet. **Surface:** asphalted. 01/01-31/12.
Distance: centre 500m on the spot.

S Gradisca d'Isonzo 23H2

Viale Trieste. **GPS:** n45,88577 e13,49582.

3 free Ch free. **Location:** Central. **Surface:** asphalted. 01/01-31/12.
Distance: on the spot 2,3km on the spot on the spot.
Remarks: Max. 48h.

Gradisca d'Isonzo 23H2

Agriturismo Ai Feudi di Marizza Monica e Villi, Via Venuti, 11.
GPS: n45,89214 e13,46782.
guests free.
Distance: on the spot.

S Grado 23H3

Viala Italia. **GPS:** n45,68218 e13,41230.

41 € 16/24h Ch included. **Location:** Simple. **Surface:** asphalted. 01/01-31/12.
Distance: 2km 24km 600m on the spot.
Remarks: Video surveillance.

S Latisana 23H3

Via Gasperi. **GPS:** n45,77943 e12,99523.
10 free Ch. 01/01-31/12.
Distance: 500m.
Remarks: At supermarket.

Malborghetto Valbruna 23H1

Malga Saisera. **GPS:** n46,45624 e13,46955.
€ 8. **Location:** Rural, isolated, quiet. **Surface:** gravel.
Distance: 5,5km 5,5km on the spot.

S Maniago 23G2

Via Colvera. **GPS:** n46,17632 e12,71149.
5 free Ch free.
Surface: grasstiles. 01/01-31/12.
Distance: 500m 500m.

S Monfalcone 23H2

Areacamper F.V.G, Via Consiglio d'Europa, 13.
GPS: n45,79754 e13,55867.
36 € 15/24h Ch WC . **Surface:** metalled. 01/01-31/12.
Distance: city centre 3km on the spot.
Remarks: Nearby port, video surveillance.

S Montereale Valcellina 23G2

Via dell'Omo. **GPS:** n46,15168 e12,66122.

15 € 5 Ch included. **Location:** Urban, simple. **Surface:** asphalted. 01/01-31/12.
Distance: 500m 300m.
Remarks: Service passerby € 2, key at petrol station/bar.

Mossa 23H2

Via delle Fornaci. **GPS:** n45,94563 e13,54536.
5 free. **Surface:** metalled. 01/01-31/12.
Distance: 1km on the spot.

S Oleis 23H2

Via Rosazzo. **GPS:** n46,01634 e13,39311.
10 free Ch free. **Location:** Isolated, quiet. **Surface:** metalled. 01/01-31/12.
Distance: 100m.

S Paluzza 23G1

Ponte di Sutrio, Via Nazionale. **GPS:** n46,51148 e13,00203.
10 free Ch free. **Surface:** gravel. 01/01-31/12.
Distance: 150m 150M.

S Piancavallo 23G2

Via Barcis. **GPS:** n46,11141 e12,51411.
70 € 13/24h Ch .
Surface: metalled. 01/01-31/12.
Distance: 600m.
Remarks: Max. 7 days, check in at hotel.

S Pordenone 23G2

SS13, Pordenone. **GPS:** n45,97236 e12,64332.

8 € 3 Ch. **Location:** Urban, simple, noisy. **Surface:** asphalted. 01/01-31/12.
Distance: 1km 3km 200m on the spot.
Remarks: Max. 48h, to be paid at petrol station.

S Preone 23G1

Strada Provinciale 12. **GPS:** n46,39736 e12,86561.
12 € 13/24h Ch . **Surface:** grasstiles. 01/01-31/12.
Distance: 500m 350m 350m.

S Quinto di Trevisio 23F3

Camper Resort Quinto, Via Costamala 26.
GPS: n45,63901 e12,15728.

28 € 15 Ch WC included. **Location:** Luxurious. **Surface:** gravel. 01/01-31/12.
Distance: 800m on the spot 500m 650m on the spot on the spot.
Remarks: Max. 5 days.

S Ravascletto 23G1

Via Valcalda. **GPS:** n46,52348 e12,92790.
20 € 6 Ch. **Surface:** grasstiles. 01/01-31/12.
Distance: 500m 200m.
Remarks: To be paid at town hall.

S Sacile 23G2

Viale Repubblica. **GPS:** n45,95672 e12,49667.
7 € 9/24h Ch. **Surface:** metalled. 01/01-31/12.
Distance: 600m 300m on the spot.
Remarks: Max. 48h, video surveillance.

S San Daniele del Friuli 23G2

Via Udine, SP16. **GPS:** n46,15610 e13,01368.

20 free Ch free. **Location:** Rural, central, quiet. **Surface:** grasstiles. 01/01-31/12.
Distance: 300m 300m 300m 200m.
Remarks: Parking sports park.

S San Vito al Tagliamento 23G2

Area di sosta San Vito al Tagliamento, Via Pulet.
GPS: n45,91224 e12,86590.

12 € 5/12h, € 8/24h, € 15/48h € 1 Ch included. **Location:** Rural, simple, isolated, quiet. **Surface:** asphalted. 01/01-31/12.

IT

Distance: 500m 15km 500m 500m 500m.
Remarks: Max. 48h, gate can be opened manually.

S **Sauris** 23G1

Prosciuttificio Wolf Sauris, Sauris di Sotto 88.
GPS: n46,46756 e12,70833.
10 free WC free. **Location:** Rural, simple, quiet.
Surface: asphalted. 01/01-31/12.
Distance: on the spot 150m on the spot.
Remarks: Regional products.

S **Sesto al Reghena** 23G2

Viale degli Olmi. **GPS**: n45,84615 e12,81273.
6 €5 €0,10/10liter €3 Ch€2 €1/12h.
Surface: asphalted. 01/01-31/12.
Distance: 500m 500m.

S **Spilimbergo** 23G2

Via Udine. **GPS**: n46,10814 e12,90411.

10 free Ch free. **Location:** Urban, simple, central.
Surface: grasstiles. 01/01-31/12.
Distance: 300m 300m 400m.
Remarks: Max. 48h.

S **Tarcento** 23H2

Plein-air Torre, Via Sottocolleverzan. **GPS**: n46,21446 e13,22504.

10 free Ch free .
Location: Urban, simple, quiet.
Surface: grasstiles. 01/01-31/12.
Distance: 200m 200m 200m.
Remarks: Nearby sports center, max. 72h, no camping activities.

S **Tarvisio** 23H1

Parcheggio P3, Via Armando Diaz. **GPS**: n46,50426 e13,57157.

32 € 15/24h Ch .
Location: Urban, simple, central. **Surface:** metalled.
10/06-18/09 and 19/12-06/01.
Distance: 900m 100m 100m.
Remarks: Max. 2 days.

S **Timau** 23G1

Strada Statale 52bis. **GPS**: n46,58974 e12,97102.
5 € 10/24h Ch . **Location:** Rural, isolated.
Surface: grasstiles/grassy. 01/06-30/09.
Distance: 2,5km.
Remarks: At small lake, to be paid at bar.

S **Tramonti di Sopra** 23G2

Area picnic Sot Trivea, Strada Da Lis Fornas. **GPS**: n46,30133 e12,77974.
4 € 10/24h Ch . **Location:** Rural, isolated, quiet.
Surface: grassy/gravel. 01/01-31/12.
Distance: 1,5km 1,5km.
Remarks: Beside river.

S **Trieste** 38A2

Mamaca park, Via del Pane Bianco. **GPS**: n45,62539 e13,78707.
49 € 18 Ch €4 WC . 01/01-31/12.
Distance: 200m 100m.
Remarks: Narrow entrance.

S **Trieste** 38A2

Via Karl Ludwig Von Bruck. **GPS**: n45,63710 e13,76990.

50 € 4 Ch free. **Location:** Motorway, simple, noisy.
Surface: asphalted. 01/01-31/12.
Distance: 3km shuttle to centre.
Remarks: Max. 72h, pitches under motorway.

Trieste 38A2

Via Ottaviano Augusto. **GPS**: n45,64599 e13,75654.

free. **Location:** Urban, noisy.
Surface: asphalted. 01/01-31/12.
Distance: centre 500m 100m on the spot.
Remarks: In opposite of Piazza Unitá d'Italia.

Trieste 38A2

Piazzale 11 settembre 2001, Viale Miramare.
GPS: n45,68250 e13,75138.

20 free. **Location:** Urban, simple, quiet.
Surface: metalled.
Distance: on the spot.
Remarks: In front of porticciolo di Barcola, quiet at night, crowdy during the day.

Tourist information Trieste:
Grotta del Giganta. Caves. Tue-Su, 01/07-31/08 Mo-Su.

S **Udine** 23H2

Via Chiusaforte. **GPS**: n46,08115 e13,22317.

50 free Ch free. **Location:** Urban, simple, noisy.
Surface: grasstiles. 01/01-31/12.
Distance: city centre 2km 3,5km 160m 400m line 1 > centre.

S **Valvasone** 23G2

Via Pier Pasolini. **GPS**: n45,99819 e12,86031.

8 free Ch free. **Location:** Rural, simple, quiet.
Surface: asphalted. 01/01-31/12.
Distance: 350m 350m 400m.
Remarks: Max. 48h.

S **Villa Vicentina** 23H2

Via Duca d'Aosta. **GPS**: n45,81738 e13,39369.
10 free Ch . **Surface:** asphalted. 01/01-31/12.
Distance: 200m on the spot.

S **Vito d'Asio** 23G1

Via Gialinars, San Francesco. **GPS**: n46,31244 e12,93427.
5 free Ch . **Location:** Rural, isolated, quiet.
Surface: metalled. 01/01-31/12.
Distance: Vito d'Asio 15km 350m.

S **Zoppola** 23G2

Via Manteghe. **GPS**: n45,96502 e12,78019.

20 free Ch free. **Location:** Rural, isolated, quiet.
Surface: metalled. 01/01-31/12.
Distance: centre 500m 850m 1,5km.
Remarks: At gymnasium, max. 48h.

Emilia-Romagna

S **Anita** 26F2

Agriturismo Prato Pozzo, Via Rotta Martinella 34/a.
GPS: n44,54892 e12,13322.

20 € 6 + € 6/pp, guests free Ch (12x)€2,60/day WC included . **Location:** Rural, comfortable, isolated, quiet.
Surface: grassy/metalled. 01/01-31/12.
Distance: 1km 500m 500m on the spot 1km 1km.

S **Argenta** 26F2

Area Golf Club, Via Poderi. **GPS**: n44,63027 e11,81112.
5 € 5 Ch included. **Surface:** gravel/metalled.
01/01-31/12.
Distance: 3km.
Remarks: Key at Golf Club.

S **Argenta** 26F2

Via Galassi. **GPS**: n44,61265 e11,83972.

10 free free. **Surface:** metalled. 01/01-31/12.
Distance: 200m 200m 200m 200m.
Remarks: At tennis-courts.

Bagno di Romagna 34C1

Area camper Diga di Ridracoli, SP112, Santa Sofia.
GPS: n43,88477 e11,83343.
13 € 21 Ch WC included. **Location:** Isolated.
Surface: grassy. 01/03-31/10.
Remarks: In nature reserve.

Bagno di Romagna 34C1

Via Lungo Savio 1. **GPS**: n43,84108 e11,96532.

10 free. **Surface:** metalled. 01/01-31/12.
Distance: 500m 1km 500m 500m.
Remarks: Parking swimming pool.

Tourist information Bagno di Romagna:
Week market. Fri 7.30-12.30h.

Bellaria-Igea Marina 26G3

Parking delle Robinie, Via Pinzon 260, Igea Marina, Zona sud.
GPS: n44,12783 e12,48873.

106 € 10-19 Ch €2,50/day €1.
Location: Rural, comfortable, central, quiet. **Surface:** grassy/gravel.
12/03-15/10, 8-23h.
Distance: 10m 200m 100m 50m.

Bellaria-Igea Marina 26G3

Mare d'Inverno, Via Murri, 13. **GPS**: n44,11639 e12,49972.

45 € 11, 21/06-31/08 € 17,50, holidays + € 2 Ch €2,50/day €1. **Location:** Rural, comfortable, quiet. **Surface:** grassy.
15/03-30/09.
Distance: 800m 200m 800m 1,5km, bakery 800m 100m.

Bellaria-Igea Marina 26G3

Area Sosta Rio Pircio, Via Benivieni 4, Igea Marina.
GPS: n44,12688 e12,48849.

68 € 14, 21/06-31/08 € 19 Ch €2/day WC €1 hot shower €1. **Location:** Rural, comfortable, central, quiet. **Surface:** grassy.
01/03-31/10.
Distance: 100m 200m 250m.

Bellaria-Igea Marina 26G3

L'Adriatico Parking, Via Benivieni, 12. **GPS**: n44,12644 e12,48740.

60 € 10, 21/06-31/08 € 19 Ch €2,50/day €1 against payment €1/24h,€5/week.
Location: Rural, comfortable, quiet. **Surface:** grassy. 15/03-31/12.
Distance: 250m.

Berceto 26C3

Via P. Salas. **GPS**: n44,51123 e9,98589.

20 € 7 Ch WC included.
Surface: asphalted.
01/01-31/12.
Distance: 200m 4km 200m 200m on the spot on the spot.
Remarks: Caution € 20, key at kiosk in front of restaurant Rina.

Bertinoro 26G3

Via Superga, SP 83, Loc. Fratta Terme. **GPS**: n44,13749 e12,10313.

free Ch free. **Surface:** asphalted. 01/01-31/12.
Distance: 1km 1km 1km 300m.
Remarks: Near spa resort and sports centre.

Bomporto 26E2

Piazza dello Sport, Via Verdi. **GPS**: n44,72886 e11,03585.

10 free free. **Location:** Urban, simple.
Surface: metalled.
Distance: 500m 500m.
Remarks: Parking at sports park.

Brisighella 26F3

Piazzale Donatori di Sangue. **GPS**: n44,22168 e11,77883.

18 € 8 Ch free €2/12h.
Surface: asphalted. 01/01-31/12.
Distance: 1km 1km 1km 500m.
Remarks: Near spa resort.

Carpi 26D2

Bruno Losi, Piazzale delle Piscine. **GPS**: n44,78444 e10,86817.

free Ch free. **Surface:** metalled. 01/01-31/12.
Distance: 300m 50m on the spot.
Remarks: Parking swimming pool, max. 72h.

Casal Borsetti 26G2

Area Sosta Camper Mare e Parco, Via Ortolani.
GPS: n44,55000 e12,27997.

238 € 10, 01/06-01/09 € 12/24h, 01/11-28/02 free Ch included €3/24h WC . **Location:** Rural, comfortable, central, quiet.
Surface: grassy/metalled. 01/01-31/12.
Distance: 150m 150m.
Remarks: Dogs beach.

Casola Valsenio 26F3

Via don Milani/Via Antonio Gramsci. **GPS**: n44,22597 e11,62953.

3 free free. **Surface:** asphalted. 01/01-31/12.
Distance: 300m 500m 500m.
Remarks: At swimming pool.

Casola Valsenio 26F3

Viale Domenico Neri. **GPS**: n44,22483 e11,62392.
4 free free. **Surface:** asphalted. 01/01-31/12.
Distance: 100m 500m 100m.

Castel San Pietro Terme 26F3

Via Oriani. **GPS**: n44,39725 e11,59197.

8 free €1 Ch WC €0,20.
Surface: asphalted. 01/01-31/12.
Distance: 300m 4,2km 200m 250m 250m 250m.
Remarks: Nearby hospital.

Castellarano 26D2

Parco Don Reverberi, Via Don Reverberi.
GPS: n44,50777 e10,73419.

IT

5 free Chfree. **Location:** Rural, simple. **Surface:** asphalted.
01/01-31/12.
Distance: 500m 500m 500m 500m 500m.

Castelnovo ne' Monti 26D3

Impianti Sportivi, Zona PEP, Via Fratelli Cervi, SS63.
GPS: n44,43277 e10,41133.

4 free Chfree.
Location: Simple, quiet. **Surface:** asphalted. 01/01-31/12.
Distance: 500m on the spot.

Cervia 26G3

Via Aldo Ascione, Cervia-nord. **GPS:** n44,28151 e12,32459.

50 free Chfree. **Location:** Simple, isolated, noisy.
Surface: asphalted. 01/01-31/12.
Distance: 3km 3km 1,3km.
Remarks: No camping activities.

Cervia 26G3

Viale Tritone, Fraz. Pinarella. **GPS:** n44,23984 e12,35883.

40 free Chfree. **Location:** Urban, simple, noisy.
Surface: asphalted/metalled. 01/01-31/12.
Distance: 750m 900m on the spot.
Remarks: No camping activities.

Cervia 26G3

Via Ravenna. **GPS:** n44,27597 e12,34107.
against payment. 01/01-31/12.
Distance: 500m 1km 500m 500m.
Remarks: No camping activities.

Cervia 26G3

Terme di Cervia, Viale C. Forlanini, Cervia-nord.
GPS: n44,27335 e12,32964.

50 € 10/24h (6x)€2. **Location:** Rural, quiet.
Surface: grassy/gravel. 01/04-30/11.
Distance: 3km 3km 50m.
Remarks: Parking spa resort.

Tourist information Cervia:
Week market. Thu.

Cesena 26G3

Zona Ippodromo, Via G. Ambrosini. **GPS:** n44,14549 e12,22865.
free €1 €2 Ch. **Location:** Urban. **Surface:** grasstiles.
Distance: 500m.

Cesena 26G3

Agriturismo Macin, Via San Mauro 5280. **GPS:** n44,13592 e12,16953.

4 € 5, free for clients Ch WC included.
Surface: grassy/metalled. 01/01-31/12.
Distance: 5km 8,4km 5km 5km.

Cesenatico 26G3

Area Camper Cesenatico, Viale Camillo Benso Cavour 1/b.
GPS: n44,20620 e12,38875.
160 € 10, Apr/May € 14, Jun/Sep € 18, Jul/Aug € 23 Ch €3 WC included. **Surface:** grassy. 01/01-31/12.
Distance: 500m on the spot.
Remarks: Check in on arrival, monitored parking 24/24.

Cesenatico 26G3

Piazzale della Rocca. **GPS:** n44,19855 e12,39086.

35 free €0,50/25liter Ch. **Location:** Simple.
Surface: metalled. 01/01-31/12.
Distance: 500m 2km 200m 500m 200m.

Cesenatico 26G3

Via Mazzini, zona Ponente. **GPS:** n44,21408 e12,38008.

21 € 12/24h Ch included.
Location: Rural, simple. **Surface:** grassy/gravel. 01/01-31/12.
Distance: centre 3,5km 800m.
Remarks: At entrance campsite Cesenatico, max. 48h.

Civitella di Romagna 26F3

Agriturismo Acero Rosseo, Via Seggio.
GPS: n44,00200 e11,97539.

20 guests free free.
Surface: grassy. 01/01-31/12.
Distance: 5km on the spot 5km.

Collecchio 26C2

Via Spezia. **GPS:** n44,75178 e10,22265.

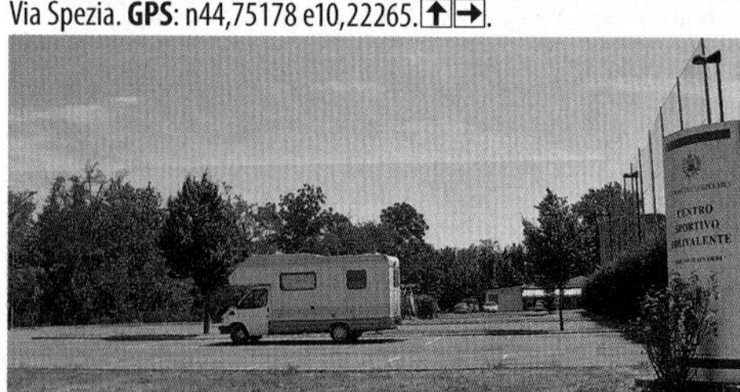

8 free Ch. **Location:** Simple. **Surface:** asphalted.
01/01-31/12.
Distance: 500m.

Comacchio 26F2

Area di sosta Cavallari, Via Villaggio San Carlo 9.
GPS: n44,70297 e12,16862.

80 € 18 Ch included WC €2. **Location:** Rural, luxurious, quiet. **Surface:** grassy. 16/02-30/11.
Distance: 1km on the spot.
Remarks: Bicycle rental.

Comacchio 26F2

Via Fattibello. **GPS:** n44,69095 e12,18447.

13 free. **Location:** Rural, central, quiet. **Surface:** metalled.
01/01-31/12.
Distance: 300m 100m.

Conselice 26F2

Agriturismo Massari, Via Coronella 110, Chiesanuova di Conselice.
GPS: n44,53167 e11,81856.

10 € 9/pp, guests free Ch WC included.
Surface: metalled.
01/01-31/12.
Distance: 1,5km 200m on the spot 1,5km.

Faenza 26F3

Via Proventa. **GPS:** n44,31272 e11,89289.

2 free Chfree. **Surface:** asphalted. 01/01-31/12.
Distance: 4km 2km.

IT

S Faenza 26F3

Agriturismo Trerè, Via Casale 19. **GPS**: n44,29968 e11,80368.

5 € 8 + € 5/pp, guests free Ch €2 WC.
Surface: metalled. 01/01-31/12.
Distance: 7km on the spot 200m on the spot.
Remarks: Dog € 3, swimming pool € 5.

S Farini 26B2

Viale dei Sassi Neri. **GPS**: n44,70994 e9,56611.

50 free Chfree. **Surface:** grassy/gravel. 01/01-31/12.
Distance: 400m on the spot.

S Ferrara 26F2

Via Rampari di San Paolo. **GPS**: n44,83544 e11,61090.
30 € 6/24h €1/100liter €2 Ch€1 €5/2h.
Location: Central, noisy.
Surface: metalled. 01/01-31/12.
Distance: 800m 6,5km 250m 500m 50m.

Tourist information Ferrara:
M Museo della Cattedrale. T € 6.
Castello Estence.
Palazzo Scifanoia.
Mo, Fri.

S Fontanellato 26C2

Via XXIV Maggio. **GPS**: n44,87797 e10,16987.

20 € 10/24h Ch (16x)WCfree. **Surface:** asphalted.
01/01-31/12.
Distance: 300m 6km 200m 500m.
Remarks: Motorhome washing place.

Forlimpopoli 26G3

Via De Gasperi. **GPS**: n44,19044 e12,12608.

free. **Surface:** asphalted. 01/01-31/12.
Distance: 100m 100m 100m 100m.
Remarks: Nearby railway station.

S Forlimpopoli 26G3

Palazzetto dello Sport, Via del Tulipano. **GPS**: n44,18534 e12,11960.
Chfree.

S Gropparello 26C2

Via D. Aligieri. **GPS**: n44,83521 e9,73051.

€ 10 free. **Location:** Rural, simple, quiet.
Surface: asphalted. 01/01-31/12.
Distance: 100m 500m.
Remarks: Castello di Gropparello 300m.

S Guastalla 26D2

Piazzale Ugo Foscolo. **GPS**: n44,92364 e10,65148.

6 free free (6x)€3.
Surface: asphalted. 01/01-31/12.
Distance: historical centre 300m 1,5km 600m 100m on the spot.
Remarks: Cycle route along the Po river.

S Imola 26F3

Via Pirandello. **GPS**: n44,34628 e11,70922.

30 free free. **Surface:** grassy/sand. 01/01-31/12.
Distance: 700m 50m 80m 50m supermercato Famila.
Remarks: In front of the Ferrari Circuit.

Tourist information Imola:
Piazza Gramsci. Mo-Thu, Sa 8-12.30h.

S Lagosanto 26F2

Locanda Il Varano, Via Valle Oppio 6, Marozzo di Lagosanto.
GPS: n44,78167 e12,12533.

36 € 15, guests free Ch (36x) WC.
Location: Rural, comfortable, quiet.
Surface: gravel. 01/01-31/12.
Distance: 3km 12km on the spot 500m.

S Langhirano 26D2

Salumificio La Perla, Quinzano. **GPS**: n44,58748 e10,23783.

10 free . **Location:** Rural, simple, quiet.
Surface: gravel.
01/01-31/12.
Distance: 3km on the spot 3km on the spot.
Remarks: Producer Parma ham.

S Langhirano 26D2

La Fazenda, Cascinapiano di Langhirano. **GPS**: n44,63322 e10,27410.

50 € 10, guests € 5 WCincluded. **Location:** Simple, quiet.
Surface: grassy/gravel. 01/01-31/12.
Distance: 1km on the spot on the spot 500m.

S Lido di Dante 26G3

Via Marabina 208. **GPS**: n44,38867 e12,31364.

30 € 6 Chincluded. **Surface:** grassy. 01/04-30/09.
Distance: 100m 100m 50m 200m 50m.

S Maranello 26E2

Area Camper Maranello, Via Fondo Val Tiepido 77, Torre Maina.
GPS: n44,50008 e10,87384.

10 € 7 €2 Ch WC.
Location: Rural, comfortable, quiet. **Surface:** unpaved.
01/01-31/12.
Distance: on the spot shuttle Bologna-Modena on the spot.
Remarks: Entrance code available at bar.

S Marzaglia 26D2

Area di sosta Marzaglia, Strada Pomposiana 305.
GPS: n44,63514 e10,80733.

30 € 15, 2 pers.incl Ch €1,50/day WC.
Location: Rural, comfortable, quiet.
Surface: gravel. 01/01-31/12.
Distance: Modena 10km 7km.

S Mesola 26G2

Oasi Park II, Via Cristina 84, SP27, Bosco Mesola.
GPS: n44,86822 e12,24898.

IT

130 € 8-15 Ch (100x)€2/day WC against payment included. **Location:** Rural, comfortable, quiet. **Surface:** grassy. 01/03-01/11.
Distance: 400m 1km.
Remarks: Free bicycles available.

S Mesola 26G2
Via Beatrice d'Este. **GPS:** n44,92331 e12,23469.

6 free Ch.
Location: Rural, simple. **Surface:** asphalted. 01/01-31/12.
Distance: 400m 400m 150m.
Remarks: Parking sports park.

S Mesola 26G2
Agriturismo Ca'Laura, SP 27, Bosco Mesola.
GPS: n44,87122 e12,24444.

6 € 15 Ch WC. **Location:** Luxurious, quiet.
Surface: metalled. 01/01-31/12.
Distance: 10km on the spot 1km 1km.
Remarks: Swimming pool, training golf course.

S Mirandola 26E2
Via Luigi Galvani. **GPS:** n44,89812 e11,06199.
10 free Ch free.
Location: Simple, quiet. **Surface:** gravel.
Distance: 500m 1km 1km 500m.
Remarks: At cemetery.

S Misano Adriatico 26G3
Centro Caravan Misano, Via Taveleto 53. **GPS:** n43,96694 e12,67306.

12 € 20 Ch (12x)€1,50,6Amp WC €0,50 €1 included. **Location:** Luxurious, quiet. **Surface:** grassy. 01/01-31/12. **Distance:** 500m 5km 2km 500m 500m. **Remarks:** Arrival < 19h, caution key € 10, video surveillance.

S Modena 26E2
Camper Club Mutina, Strada Collegarola 76/A, zona Vaciglio.
GPS: n44,61361 e10,94444.

32 € 16/24h Ch WC included. **Location:** Rural, comfortable, luxurious, quiet. **Surface:** asphalted. 01/01-31/12.
Distance: 600m 3km 600m on the spot.

S Modena 26E2
Taverna Napoleone, Via San Lorenzo 44, Castelnuovo Rangone.
GPS: n44,57766 e10,96552.

10 free free.
Location: Rural. **Surface:** metalled. 01/01-31/12.
Distance: 5km 2,8km pizzeria 5km.
Remarks: 10% discount at restaurant.

Tourist information Modena:
M Galleria Ferrari, Via Dino Ferrari 43, Maranello. Museum of motor-cars.

S Monticelli d'Ongina 26C1
Piazza Resistenza. **GPS:** n45,09050 e9,93537.

10 free Ch free. **Location:** Simple, quiet. **Surface:** asphalted. 01/01-31/12.
Distance: centre 300m 6,2km 300m 300m.

S Parma 26D2
Area Camper Parma, Largo XXIV Agosto 1942, n° 21/a.
GPS: n44,80931 e10,28495.

26 € 20 Ch included WC €1.
Location: Comfortable. **Surface:** grasstiles. 01/01-31/12.
Distance: centre 3,5km 7km Lidl 100m 100m.
Remarks: Monitored parking, arrival <22h, service passerby € 4, motorhome washing place 50m.

Tourist information Parma:
Palazzo Pilotta. morning.
Via Verdi. Week market. Wed-Sa 7-14h.

S Pavullo nel Frignano 26D3
Via Marchiani. **GPS:** n44,34294 e10,83309.

12 free Ch free. **Location:** Comfortable, quiet.
Surface: gravel/sand. 01/01-31/12.
Distance: 700m 600m 600m 600m.
Remarks: Picnic area.

S Porto Corsini 26G2
Ancora Blu, Via G. Guizzetti. **GPS:** n44,49620 e12,27950.

163 € 9, 01/06-31/08 € 11 Ch (20x)€3/day WC.
Location: Rural, comfortable, quiet.
Surface: grassy. 01/03-31/10.
Distance: 500m 200m 300m 300m 300m.
Remarks: Video surveillance.

S Portomaggiore 26F2
Via Giuseppe Mazzini. **GPS:** n44,69584 e11,81389.

10 free free. **Surface:** asphalted. 01/01-31/12.
Distance: 500m 500m 500m.
Remarks: Nearby cemetery.

Tourist information Portomaggiore:
Valli di Comacchio. Nature reserve, in winter whereabouts birds.

Premilcuore 26F3
Parcheggio Fluviale, Loc. Fontanalba. **GPS:** n43,97618 e11,77615.

€ 1. **Surface:** metalled. 01/01-31/12.
Distance: 500m 20m 500m 50m.
Remarks: Along river.

S Ravenna 26G3
Parking Bus-Camper, Via E.Ferrari. Loc.Classe.
GPS: n44,37849 e12,23461.

30 € 2,25/24h free. **Location:** Urban, simple.
Surface: grasstiles. 01/01-31/12.
Distance: Ravenna centre 6km.

emarks: Nearby basilica.

S Ravenna 26G3

iazza della Resistenza. **GPS**: n44,41433 e12,18852.

0 € 0,50/h, € 2,50/24h Chfree.
ocation: Urban, simple, central.
urface: grasstiles.
01/01-31/12.
istance: historical centre 500m 5km 150m 500m 50m.
emarks: Max. 24h.

S Ravenna 26G3

ia Pomposa. **GPS**: n44,43002 e12,20827.

0 free Chfree. **Surface:** asphalted. 01/01-31/12.
istance: city centre 2km 100m on the spot.

S Ravenna 26G3

ia Teodorico. **GPS**: n44,42317 e12,20981.

0 free Chfree. **Location:** Urban, simple, quiet.
Surface: asphalted. 01/01-31/12.
Distance: 500m on the spot.
Remarks: In front of the Mausoleum.

Ravenna 26G3

Via Brancaleone/circonvallazione S. Gaetanino.
GPS: n44,42339 e12,20478.

25 free. **Location:** Urban, simple, noisy. **Surface:** metalled.
01/01-31/12.
Distance: 200m 5km 100m 200m 200m 10m.
Remarks: Next to Rocca Brancaleone.

S Ravenna 26G3

Area Camper Atrezzata, Eurolandia, SS16.
GPS: n44,33533 e12,26949.

72 € 10/day, € 15/2 days Chincluded €0,50/30minutes.
Location: Rural, simple. **Surface:** gravel.
01/04-31/10.
Remarks: Video surveillance.

S Ravenna 26G3

Parco Divertimenti Mirabilandia, SS16, via Romea Sud 463.
GPS: n44,33290 e12,26966.

400 € 15 included. **Location:** Rural, simple, noisy.
Surface: gravel.
Distance: Ravenna centre 10km McDonalds.
Remarks: Max. 48h.

Tourist information Ravenna:

U.I.A.T. (Ufficio Informazioni e di Accoglienza Turistica), Piazza S. Francesco, 7, http://www.turismo.ra.it/. City of the mosaics, historical city with many curiosities.
Piazza Garibaldi. Antiques market. 3rd weekend of the month.
Parco Divertimenti Mirabilandia, SS16, via Romea Sud 463. Amusement park. 01/04-15/09.

S Reggio nell'Emilia 26D2

Parking Ex Foro Boario, Via XX Settembre.
GPS: n44,70941 e10,62463.

50 free Chfree.
Location: Urban, simple.
Surface: grasstiles. 01/01-31/12.
Distance: 1km 3,7km 100m 500m Free bus to centre.

S Riccione 26G3

Piazza 1° Maggio. **GPS**: n44,00392 e12,65115.

10 free €4 Ch.
Location: Urban, simple, central, quiet. **Surface:** asphalted.
01/01-31/12 Service: winter.
Distance: 100m 500m 500m 100m 50m.

S Rimini 26G3

La Valletta Sosta Verde, Via Della Lama 47, SS 16.
GPS: n44,09889 e12,49867.

200 € 11, >7,3m € 18, dog € 1 Chincluded €3 WC €1.
Location: Rural, noisy.
Surface: grassy/gravel. 01/04-30/09.
Distance: Rimini 11km 3,8km 2km 800m 800m.
Remarks: Shuttle bus to beach.

S Rimini 26G3

Parking Settebello, Via Roma 86. **GPS**: n44,05982 e12,57669.

300 € 10/24h €2 Ch€2 (80x)€3/day.
Location: Urban, simple, central, noisy.
Surface: metalled. 01/01-31/12.
Distance: 200m 500m.
Remarks: Next to cinema Settebello.

Rimini 26G3

P30 Chiabrera, Via Chiabrera. **GPS**: n44,04803 e12,59548.
01/05-30/09 € 12,10. **Location:** Urban, simple, central, noisy.
Surface: asphalted.

S Rimini 26G3

Camper Nautica, Via Ortigara 78/80. **GPS**: n44,07461 e12,57005.
20 € 20-30/24h €1,50 . 01/01-31/12.
Distance: on the spot on the spot on the spot.
Remarks: Monitored parking 24/24.

Tourist information Rimini:

Casa Zanni, Via Casale, 205, Villa Verucchio. Restaurant with authentic Italian cuisine.

S Ro 26F1

Mulino sul Po. GPS: n44,95498 e11,75668.

4 free (4x)free WC . **Location:** Rural, simple, noisy.
Surface: metalled.
Distance: 1km on the spot on the spot.
Remarks: Along the Po river.

S Rocca San Casciano 26F3

GPS: n44,06173 e11,84604.
4 free €1/100liter Ch €1/4h. **Location:** Rural.
Surface: metalled. 01/01-31/12.
Distance: 300m 100m.

S Sala Baganza 26C2

Via Vittorio Emanuele, 42. **GPS**: n44,70856 e10,23070.

4 free Ch (4x)free. **Location:** Rural, simple, quiet.
Surface: asphalted. 01/01-31/12.
Distance: 500m 15km 500m.

S Salsomaggiore Terme 26C2

Via Antonio Gramsci. **GPS**: n44,82005 e9,98981.

20 free free. **Location:** Urban, simple, quiet. **Surface:** gravel.
01/01-31/12.

IT

Distance: 800m.
Remarks: Parking next to station.

S San Giuseppe 26G2

Ariaperta Sosta Camper, Via Delle Nazioni 39.
GPS: n44,72578 e12,22528.
99 € 15 Ch (32x)included WC. **Surface:** grassy.
Distance: 500m 1,5km 500m 500m.

San Piero in Bagno 34C1

Via G.Mazzini. **GPS**: n43,86353 e11,97692.

5 free. **Surface:** asphalted. 01/01-31/12.
Distance: 500m 1km 500m 500m 200m.

S Santa Sofia 34C1

Piazzale K. Marx. **GPS**: n43,94165 e11,90930.

free Chfree. **Surface:** asphalted. 01/01-31/12.
Distance: 200m.

Tourist information Santa Sofia:
Foreste Casentinesi. National nature reserve.

S Serramazzoni 26D3

Piazzale Largo Olimpico. **GPS**: n44,42223 e10,79402.

20 free Chfree. **Location:** Urban. **Surface:** asphalted.
01/01-31/12.
Distance: 300m 100m 300m 300m 300m 800m.

S Serramazzoni 26D3

Ristorante La Roccia, Via Giardini Nord, Montagnana di Serramazzoni.
GPS: n44,47157 e10,82050.

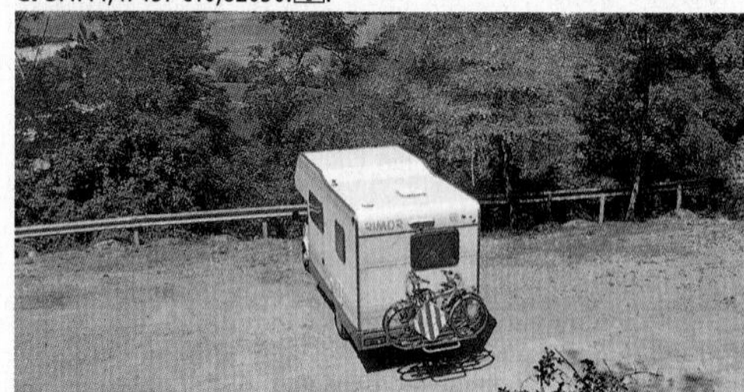

15 free.
Location: Rural, simple, quiet. **Surface:** gravel. 01/01-31/12.
Distance: 8km Maranello on the spot 8km.
Remarks: Maranello: Ferrari factory and museum.

Sestola 26D3

Via Guidellina. **GPS**: n44,22591 e10,77374.
10 free. **Surface:** asphalted. 01/01-31/12.
Distance: 300m 800m 500m on the spot.

S Soragna 26C2

Via Matteotti / via Gramsci. **GPS**: n44,92988 e10,12566.

10 free Chfree. **Location:** Urban, simple, quiet.
Surface: asphalted. 01/01-31/12.
Distance: 120m 200m 200m.

Suviana 26E3

Via Lungo Lago. **GPS**: n44,12039 e11,04592.

60 Free, hollidays € 9. **Location:** Rural, simple, quiet.
Surface: asphalted. 01/01-31/12.
Distance: on the spot on the spot on the spot.
Remarks: At lake Suviana, canoe rental.

S Terenzo 26C2

Loc. Bardone. **GPS**: n44,62528 e10,10083.

8 € 13 Ch WC included. **Location:** Rural, comfortable, quiet. **Surface:** metalled. 01/01-31/12.
Distance: 200m 12km 12km on the spot.
Remarks: Max. 2 nights.

S Tredozio 26F3

Area Le Volte, Via Salvo D'Acquisto. **GPS**: n44,07431 e11,73228.

40 € 5 Ch €2,50. **Surface:** metalled. 01/01-31/12.
Distance: 1,5km 200m camping 1,5km.
Remarks: Next to campsite Le Volte, max. 48h, discount at restaurant/swimming-pool.

S Tresigallo 26F2

Fraz. Finale di Rero. **GPS**: n44,81643 e11,90050.
free.
Remarks: Nearby sports park.

S Vergato 26E3

SS 64, Bologna-Pistoia. **GPS**: n44,28952 e11,11270.

25 free Chfree. **Location:** Rural, simple. **Surface:** asphalted.
01/01-31/12.

Distance: 400m 400m 500m 500m.

S Vezzano Sul Crostolo 26D2

Area Sosta Camper Matildica, SS63. **GPS**: n44,58960 e10,53608.
10 Ch. **Surface:** asphalted. 01/01-31/12.
Distance: 1,5km on the spot on the spot on the spot.
Remarks: Eco Parco di Vezzano, keycard at Bar Sport, Via Roma, SS63, n44,59963, o10,54542.

Liguria

S Borghetto Santo Spirito 28H1

Val Varatella, Via Tiziano. **GPS**: n44,11565 e8,23507.
24 € 18-27 WC.
Distance: 500m 1km.

S Borghetto Santo Spirito 28H1

Via Tevere. **GPS**: n44,11548 e8,23758.

150 € 10/24h, Jul-Aug-Dec € 13 Ch (50x)€3/day,16Amp.
Surface: gravel.
Distance: 1,1km 2,5km 400m.
Remarks: Along the river Varatella.

S Castelnuovo Magra 26C3

Agriturismo Cascina dei Peri, Via Montefrancio 71.
GPS: n44,10355 e10,00734.

3 € 10/pp, child € 3 Ch €3 WC included €5.
Surface: grassy/gravel. 01/01-31/12.
Distance: 2,4km.
Remarks: Dinner € 20/pp wine incl. (to order <16h), selling of wine and olive oil, swimming pool from june.

S Celle Ligure 26A3

Via Natta. **GPS**: n44,34888 e8,55674.

25 Ch. **Surface:** asphalted. 01/01-31/12.
Distance: 300m 200m 500m 200m 300m 100m.

S Cengio 25H3

Area Attrezzata Cengio Isole, Via Isole.
GPS: n44,39083 e8,20194.

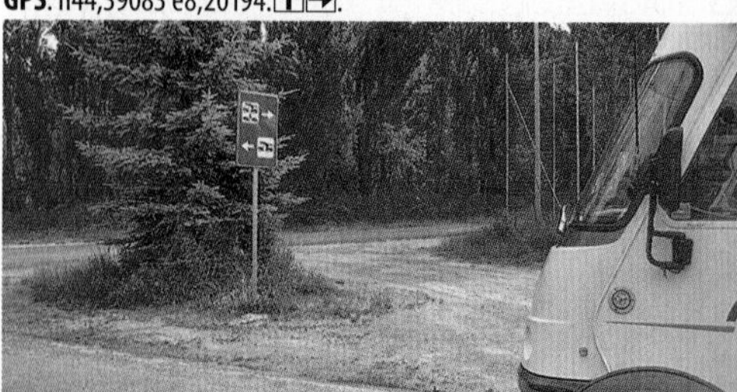

free Chfree. **Surface:** asphalted.
Distance: 600m on the spot on the spot.
Remarks: Nearby sports park.

S Cervo 28H1

Camper Cervo, Via Steria. **GPS**: n43,92833 e8,10527.

IT

130 € 12-15/day Ch included €3/24h. **Surface:** gravel.
01/01-31/12.
Distance: 2,5km.

S Diano Marina 28H1

Oasi Park, Via Sori 5. **GPS**: n43,90667 e8,07083.

300 € 8-15/day Ch €3 WC €1 .
Surface: grassy/gravel. 01/01-31/12.
Distance: 600m 6,8km 800m 600m 600m 600m mountainbike trail.
Remarks: Beachshuttle with bar/restaurant.

S Diano Marina 28H1

Il bowling di Diano, Via Diano S. Pietro, 71 - Diano Castello.
GPS: n43,91683 e8,07576.

€ 18/day Ch €4.
Surface: unpaved. 01/01-31/12.
Distance: 1km 5,5km 1,2km on the spot 50m.
Remarks: Narrow entrance, swimming pool, bar, bowling.

S Diano Marina 28H1

Al Roseto, Via Case Parse, San siro, Diano Castello.
GPS: n43,91983 e8,07733.

€ 12-15 Ch WC €2 . 01/01-31/12.
Distance: 5,5km.
Remarks: At Floriculturist, shuttle bus to beach.

S Finale Ligure 26A3

Area Caprazoppa, Via Aurelia, SS1. **GPS**: n44,16549 e8,33750.

40 € 18/24h Ch included.
Surface: gravel/sand. 01/01-31/12.
Distance: 500m 4km 700m.

Imperia 28H1

Francy Park, Via dei Giardini. **GPS**: n43,86917 e8,00010.

32 € 10, 01/06-30/09 € 13.
Surface: metalled. 01/01-31/12.
Distance: centre 4km sea 150m 150m.

S La Spezia 26C3

Viale San Bartolomeo. **GPS**: n44,10417 e9,85917.

100 € 5 free.
Surface: grassy. 8-20h 12.30-13.30h.
Distance: 4km.
Remarks: Monitored parking.

Tourist information La Spezia:
- Lerici. Former fishing village, nowadays holiday resort.
- Cinque Terre. Protected coast area.
- Castello di Lerici, Lerici. 01/04-31/10.
- Lerici. Sa-morning.

S Levanto 26C3

SP556, Loc. Moltedi. **GPS**: n44,17476 e9,61836.

16 € 18/24h Ch included. 01/01-31/12.
Distance: 500m 1km train 100m.
Remarks: Behind railway station, well situated for visiting the Cinque Terre by train.

S Loano 25H3

La Sosta, Via delle Fornaci, 31. **GPS**: n44,13115 e8,24111.
41 € 15 Ch WC included. **Surface:** gravel.
01/01-31/12.
Distance: 2km 400m.
Remarks: Shuttle bus.

Tourist information Loano:
- Grotta di Santa Lucia, Toirano. Stalactites and stalagmites.
- Grotta della Basura, Toirano. Man and beast from the stone age.

S Pietra Ligure 26A3

Area Camper, Via Crispi 43. **GPS**: n44,15484 e8,28397.

53 € 13/24h, 01/06-30/09 € 16/24h Ch (53x)included WC €0,70. **Surface:** gravel. 01/01-31/12.
Distance: 200m.

S Portovenere 34A1

Via Olivo, Loc. Cavo. **GPS**: n44,05961 e9,84843.

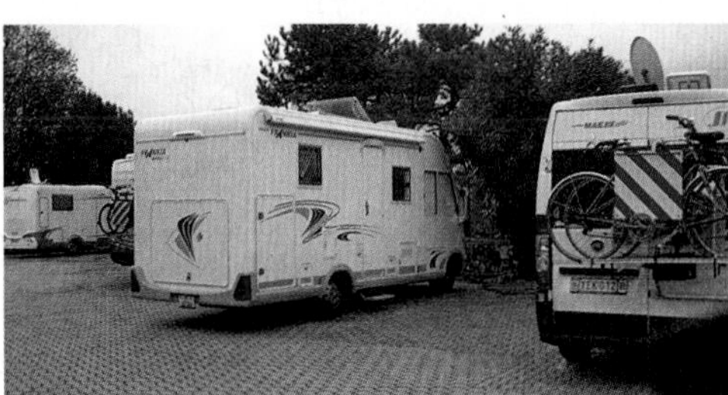

20 € 1,85/h 8-20h, overnight stay free Ch.
Surface: metalled. 01/01-31/12.
Distance: 2km 750m 600m 50m.

S San Lorenzo al Mare 28H1

Area Camper Il Pozzo, Via Gaetano Salvemini.
GPS: n43,85512 e7,96083.

30 € 15-23 Ch WC €4 included.
Location: Luxurious. **Surface:** gravel.
Distance: 400m 600m 400m.
Remarks: Max. 7m.

San Rocco 26B3

Viale Franco Molfino, Camogli. **GPS**: n44,33472 e9,16084.

9 € 9/8-20h. **Surface:** asphalted.
Distance: 150m on the spot.
Remarks: Marked hiking trails in Parco di Portofino (45min-2h).

S Santo Stefano al Mare 28H1

Camper Village, Strada Porsani. **GPS**: n43,84378 e7,90824.

60 € 12-30/24h Ch €3 WC €1. **Surface:** gravel.
Distance: 10km 800m on the spot.
Remarks: Free shuttle, swimming pool.

Santo Stefano al Mare 28H1

Marina degli Aregai, Via Gianni Cozzi. **GPS**: n43,83723 e7,90581.

± 30 € 1,50/h, € 5-10/day. **Surface:** asphalted.
Distance: on the spot Sandy beach on the spot on the spot.

S Torriglia 26B3

Area Comunale Piscina, Via degli Alpini. **GPS**: n44,51667 e9,16000.

IT

10 free Chfree. **Surface:** grasstiles.
Distance: 200m.
Remarks: Next to swimming pool, market Saturday.

S Vado Ligure 26A3

Area Sosta Camper, Via Aurelia 16, SS1. **GPS:** n44,27797 e8,44171.

68 € 8/12h, € 16/24h Ch included.
Surface: metalled. 01/01-31/12.
Distance: 600m 50m 50m.
Remarks: Ferry > Corsica 2km.

Tuscany

S Alberese 34B2

Parco Naturale della Maremma, Via del Bersagliere.
GPS: n42,66944 e11,10416.

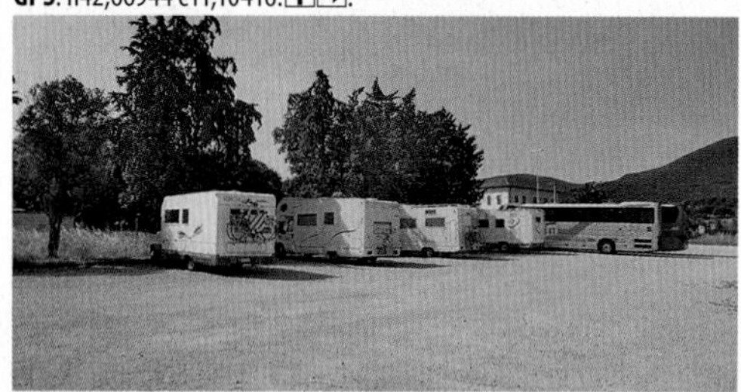

50 free. **Location:** Rural.
Surface: gravel/sand.
01/04-30/09.
Distance: 100m 7km on the spot on the spot on the spot.

S Albinia 34B2

Ai Delfini, Via Aurelia km 153. **GPS:** n42,50882 e11,19552.

24 € 1/h, Aug € 1,50/h 4 pers incl. + tourist tax Ch WCincluded € 1 € 5 1h incl., € 10/15 days.
Location: Comfortable, quiet.
Surface: grassy/sand. 24/04-31/10.
Distance: 2km 50m on the spot 2km.

S Anghiari 34C1

Via Campo della Fiera. **GPS:** n43,53904 e12,05291.

8 free Chfree. **Location:** Simple, quiet. **Surface:** asphalted.
01/01-31/12.
Distance: on the spot on the spot on the spot.

S Anghiari 34C1

Agriturismo Val della Pieve, Via della Fossa 8.
GPS: n43,53657 e12,05131.

10 € 15/24h, Jul/Aug € 20 Ch WC €3 included.
Location: Comfortable, isolated, quiet. **Surface:** gravel.
01/01-31/12.
Distance: 300m 300m 300m 300m.
Remarks: Swimming pool € 3/pppd.

S Anghiari 34C1

Agriturismo La Taverna dei Sorci, San Lorenzo.
GPS: n43,51467 e12,07799.

20 free free. **Location:** Simple, quiet. **Surface:** metalled.
01/01-31/12.
Distance: 3km on the spot.

S Arcidosso 34B2

Parco Faunistico Monte Amiata, Località Poderi.
GPS: n42,83740 e11,52922.

15 free Ch.
Location: Rural, isolated, quiet. **Surface:** grassy. 01/01-31/12.
Distance: 10km.
Remarks: Nature reserve.

S Arezzo 34C1

Via Da Palestrina/via Tarlati (centro-nord). **GPS:** n43,47213 e11,88773.

30 € 0,80/h, € 8/24h Ch free.
Location: Simple, quiet. **Surface:** asphalted. 01/01-31/12.
Distance: historical centre 1km.
Remarks: Escalator to city centre.

Arezzo 34C1

P Tarlati, Via Guido Tarlati. **GPS:** n43,47237 e11,88362.

50 free. **Location:** Urban, simple, central. **Surface:** grasstiles.
01/01-31/12.
Distance: city centre 1km 500m 300m.

Tourist information Arezzo:
Week market.

S Barberino di Mugello 26E3

SS65, Fraz. Monte di Fó. **GPS:** n44,07613 e11,28062.

30 free Chfree. **Location:** Simple, quiet. **Surface:** metalled.
01/01-31/12.
Distance: 4km 150m (camping) 150m (camping).
Remarks: In front of campsite Il Sergente.

S Barga 26D3

Area San Cristoforo, Via Hayange. **GPS:** n44,07234 e10,48131.

€ 10/24h Ch (10x) WC 200m. **Surface:** gravel.
Distance: centro storico within walking distance.

S Bibbiena 34C1

La Collina delle Stelle, Loc. Casanova 63.
GPS: n43,71669 e11,85173.

8 € 15, 01/05-30/09 € 20 2 pers. incl., extra pers. € 4 Ch €2/day WC €5, ironing services €5 included. **Location:** Comfortable, quiet. **Surface:** gravel. 15/03-01/11, Christmas.
Distance: 7km on the spot on the spot.
Remarks: Swimming pool € 5/pp (free with a meal).

S Borgo a Mozzano 34A1

Via I° Maggio, SP2. **GPS:** n43,97612 e10,54113.

4 free Ch (4x)free. **Surface:** gravel.
Distance: 200m Serchio river.
Remarks: At tourist office.

IT

Borgo San Lorenzo 34B1

Via Caduti di Montelungo. **GPS**: n43,95112 e11,38518.

10 Chfree. **Location:** Simple. **Surface:** asphalted.
01/01-31/12 Fri.
Distance: 500m 500m 300m.
Remarks: Friday market.

Buonconvento 34B2

Viale della Liberta. **GPS**: n43,13854 e11,48109.

free. **Location:** Simple. **Surface:** unpaved.
Distance: 50m 50m.
Remarks: At the city walls.

Buonconvento 34B2

Viale Ferruccio Parri. **GPS**: n43,13065 e11,48349.
€1 Ch. 01/01-31/12.

Calci 34A1

Via Brogiotti. **GPS**: n43,72769 e10,51722.

6 € 8/24h Ch included.
Surface: asphalted. 01/01-31/12.
Distance: 100m 200m.
Remarks: At sports park, payment only with coins.

Campiglia Marittima 34B2

Parcheggio La Pieve, Via di Venturina. **GPS**: n43,05672 e10,61439.

4 free Chfree. **Location:** Rural. **Surface:** asphalted.
01/01-31/12.
Distance: 350m 450m 500m.
Remarks: In front of cemetery, near gymnasium.

Campiglia Marittima 34B2

Via di Caldana. **GPS**: n43,03662 e10,59969.
free €1/100liter Ch. 01/01-31/12.
Distance: 800m 250m.

Capalbio 34B3

Via della Torba. **GPS**: n42,40753 e11,31566.
€ 6. **Surface:** sand.
Distance: 150m on the spot.
Remarks: Beach parking.

Capraia e Limite 34B1

Via delle Ginestre, zona industriale, loc. Capraia Fiorentina.
GPS: n43,73660 e11,00442.

free Chfree. **Surface:** metalled.

Casola in Lunigiana 26C3

Area La Linea del Drago. **GPS**: n44,19916 e10,17333.

20 € 7 + € 5/pp Ch WC included. **Surface:** grassy.
01/01-31/12.
Distance: on the spot.
Remarks: At little stream with swimming area.

Castagneto Carducci 34A2

Camperesort, Via Aurelia 373/B. **GPS**: n43,15630 e10,56097.

50 € 10 + € 5/pp, 15/06-15/09 € 10/Pp Ch WC €1
€3 included. **Location:** Luxurious. **Surface:** grassy/gravel.
01/01-31/12. **Distance:** 1,2km on the spot.
Remarks: Video surveillance, swimming pool incl.

Castagneto Carducci 34A2

Via del Seggio, Marina di Castagneto. **GPS**: n43,18401 e10,54841.

30 € 10/24h Chfree. **Surface:** unpaved.
01/01-31/12.
Distance: 2km 500m 2,5km 2,5km.

Castagneto Carducci 34A2

Viale delle Palme, Marina di Castagneto. **GPS**: n43,19323 e10,54152.

20 € 20-30/24h Ch. **Surface:** unpaved.
Distance: 100m.
Remarks: Max. 48h, dogs beach.

Castel del Piano 34B2

Via Po. **GPS**: n42,88872 e11,53733.

30 free Chfree. **Location:** Rural, simple. **Surface:** asphalted.
01/01-31/12.
Distance: 500m.

Castelfiorentino 34B1

Via Che Guevara, circonvallazione Ovest. **GPS**: n43,60885 e10,96365.

5 free free.
Location: Simple, isolated. **Surface:** asphalted.
Distance: 1,5km 1,5km 1,5km.

Castellina in Chianti 34B1

La Strada del Chianti, SR222. **GPS**: n43,47330 e11,28760.

15 € 12/24h €0,20/10liter Ch (8x)included WC €0,50.
Location: Rural, comfortable. **Surface:** asphalted. 01/01-31/12.
Distance: 200m.

Tourist information Castellina in Chianti:
Via IV Novembre. Week market. Sa-morning.

Castelnuovo di Garfagnana 26D3

Via Valmaira. **GPS**: n44,11447 e10,40304.

free Chfree. **Surface:** metalled. 01/01-31/12.
Distance: 1km.
Remarks: At sports park.

Castiglion Fiorentino 34C1

Piazza Garibaldi, viale Marconi. **GPS**: n43,34465 e11,92278.

20 free Chfree WC. **Location:** Rural, simple.
Surface: asphalted. 01/01-31/12 Fri-morning market.
Distance: on the spot on the spot.

Castiglione della Pescaia 34B2

Paduline, Via Andromeda. **GPS**: n42,76888 e10,89079.

120 € 12-15 €2 €3.
Location: Rural, simple. **Surface:** gravel. 01/05-30/09.
Distance: 1km.
Remarks: Market Saturday.

IT

Castiglione della Pescaia 34B2

Rocchette Serignano, Via Rio Palma, Rocchette.
GPS: n42,77970 e10,79955.

120 € 20/day € 3 Ch (18x) €1. **Location:** Rural, comfortable. **Surface:** gravel. 01/04-15/09.
Distance: Castiglione della Pescaia 7km 200m 200m.
Remarks: Beach parking, unguarded.

Castiglione della Pescaia 34B2

Via Ponte Giorgini. **GPS**: n42,76515 e10,88545.

5 € 1,50h, € 10/24h. **Location:** Urban, simple.
Surface: asphalted. 01/01-31/12.
Distance: on the spot.
Remarks: Market Saturday.

Castiglione d'Orcia 34C2

Area Pro Loco, Viale Marconi. **GPS**: n43,00292 e11,61552.

5 free free. **Location:** Rural, simple. **Surface:** gravel/sand.
01/01-31/12.
Distance: 200m on the spot.

Tourist information Castiglione d'Orcia:
Rocco d'Orcia. Medieval citadel.

Cecina 34A2

Agricamper Impalancati, Via Aurelia Nord, 108.
GPS: n43,33682 e10,49946.
20 € 10, Jun/Sep € 15, Jul € 20, Aug € 25 Ch included WC . **Location:** Comfortable, isolated, quiet.
Surface: grassy/gravel.

Cecina 34A2

Agricamper Gioia Selvaggia e Fabio, Via Paratino Alto, 53.
GPS: n43,28780 e10,55314.
18 € 10, Jul/Aug € 15 Ch included.
Surface: grassy/gravel.
Distance: city centre 5km 6km.
Remarks: Swimming pool (summer).

Certaldo 34B1

Area Comunale, Piazza dei Macelli. **GPS**: n43,54629 e11,04611.

10 free Chfree. **Location:** Rural. **Surface:** metalled.
01/01-31/12.
Distance: medieval centre 150m (elevator) 150m 250m.

Chifenti 34A1

Area sosta Chifenti, SS12. **GPS**: n44,00492 e10,56337.
10 free Chfree. **Surface:** asphalted/gravel.
01/01-31/12.
Distance: 500M.

Chiusdino 34B2

Abbazia San Galgano, SS441. **GPS**: n43,15283 e11,15137.

15 € 1,50/h, € 10/8-20h, overnight stay free (9x)free.
Location: Rural, isolated, quiet.
Surface: grasstiles. 01/01-31/12.
Distance: 12km 300m.
Remarks: Abbey of San Galgano 300m.

Chiusi 34C2

Via Torri del Fornello. **GPS**: n43,01461 e11,94972.

5 free free. **Surface:** asphalted.
Distance: 100m 4,5km.
Remarks: Next to school.

Chiusi 34C2

Loc. Sbarchino. **GPS**: n43,05049 e11,95756.
10 free. 01/01-31/12.
Distance: Pesce d'Oro on the spot on the spot.

Cutigliano 26D3

Via di Risorgimento/Sp37. **GPS**: n44,09877 e10,75450.
14 € 1,50/h, € 15/24h Ch included.
Surface: metalled.
Remarks: Max. 48h.

Dicomano 34B1

SS67, Tosco Romagnola. **GPS**: n43,89407 e11,53715.

4 free Chfree. **Location:** Simple. **Surface:** asphalted.
01/01-31/12.
Distance: 1km 200m.

Equi Terme 26C3

Via della Stazione. **GPS**: n44,17009 e10,15513.

40 € 10/night Ch included. **Surface:** gravel.
Distance: 100m.
Remarks: Near spa resort (100m), caves (500m) and marble quarry.

Firenze 34B1

FiPark, Viale Europa, Fraz. Bagno a Ripoli, Florence (Firenze).
GPS: n43,75554 e11,30609.

40 7-19h € 2/h, 19-7h € 1/h, € 15/24h Ch.
Location: Simple. **Surface:** metalled. 01/01-31/12.
Distance: bus 23/33 > centre.

Firenze 34B1

Area sociale 'Flog', Via M Mercati 24/b, zona Careggi, Florence (Firenze).
GPS: n43,79491 e11,24835.

25 € 15/24h € 3 Ch. **Location:** Simple. **Surface:** gravel.
01/01-31/12.
Distance: city centre 2km Pizzeria centre : bus 4, 6-24h.

Firenze 34B1

Florence Park Scandicci, Via di Scandicci 241, Florence (Firenze).
GPS: n43,76267 e11,20875.

25 € 15 included. **Location:** Urban, comfortable, central, quiet.
Surface: metalled. 01/01-31/12.
Distance: 4km 5km 150m.
Remarks: Video surveillance.

Firenze 34B1

Gelsomino SCAF, Via del Gelsomino 11, Florence (Firenze).
GPS: n43,75173 e11,24388.

150 € 15/24h Ch included.
Surface: grasstiles.
01/01-31/12.
Distance: 2km bus 37 > centre.
Remarks: Max. 7m.

Tourist information Florence (Firenze):
U.I.A.T. (Ufficio Informazioni e di Accoglienza Turistica), Piazza Stazione, 4, www.firenze.turismo.toscana.it. Renaissance city with many curiosities.
Ponte Vechio. Famous bridge with jeweller's shops.
Cappella Brancacci, Santa Maria del Carmine. Renovated frescoes.
The Mall, le griffe, Via Europa 8, Leccio Reggello. Factory outlet.

Firenzuola 26E3

Loc. Pieve di Camaggiore. **GPS**: n44,14594 e11,45361.

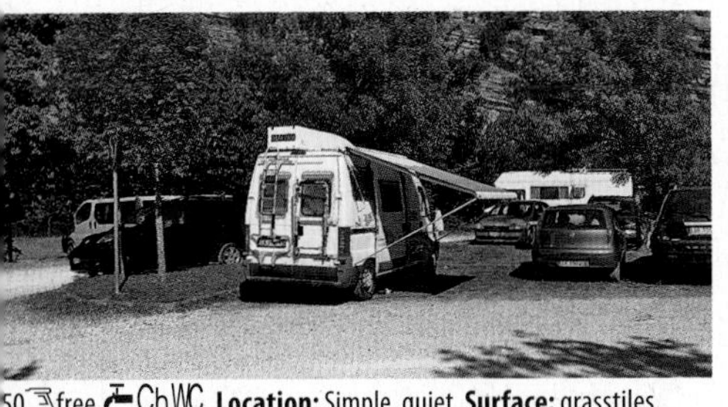

50 free ChWC. **Location:** Simple, quiet. **Surface:** grasstiles.
01/01-31/12.
Distance: Firenzuola 10km river 100m 1km.
Remarks: Playground.

Firenzuola 26E3

Area Picnic, Loc. Badia a Moscheta. **GPS**: n44,07586 e11,42030.

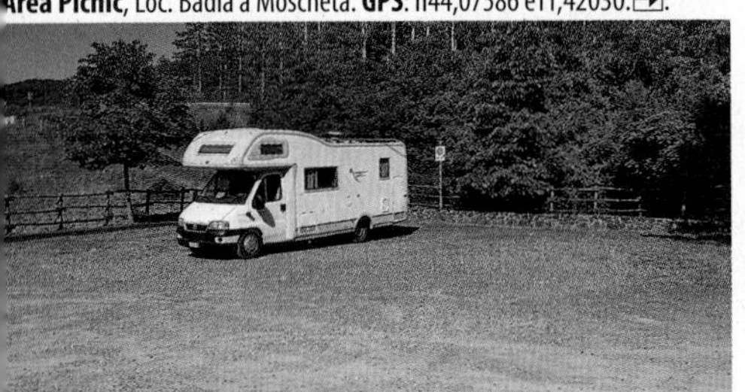

10 free. **Location:** Simple, isolated, quiet.
Surface: gravel.
01/01-31/12.
Distance: Firenzuola 8km 500m agriturismo Badia di Moscheta.

Fivizzano 26C3

Agriturismo Ristorante Al Vecchio Tino, Loc. Germalla 1, Monte dei Bianchi. **GPS**: n44,17155 e10,13325.
6 € 12 Ch included. **Surface:** gravel. 01/01-31/12.

Foiano della Chiana 34C1

Outlet Village Valdichiana, Via Enzo Ferrari 5, loc. Farniole.
GPS: n43,22398 e11,80301.

10 free. **Location:** Simple. **Surface:** asphalted. 01/01-31/12.
Distance: on the spot on the spot.
Remarks: Motorhome parking at Outlet.

Follonica 34B2

Eucalyptus Camper Park, Via Sanzio. **GPS**: n42,92804 e10,77569.

40 € 10 €4 Ch included €1. 01/06-30/09.
Distance: beach 1,8km 1km 1km.
Remarks: At paradise pool.

Follonica 34B2

Agriturismo dal Pastore, Via Cassarello, 342.
GPS: n42,92835 e10,78912.
10 € 10 + € 1/pp tourist tax Ch. **Location:** Rural.
Surface: grassy.
Distance: city centre 3km 2,5km.
Remarks: Regional products.

Fonteblanda 34B2

Talamone Wind Beach Parking, Strada Provinciale Talamone.
GPS: n42,56334 e11,15659.

150 free, June-Sep € 15. **Location:** Rural, simple, isolated.
Surface: gravel. 01/01-31/12.
Distance: 1,5km on the spot on the spot 1,5km 1,5km.
Remarks: Beach parking, shuttle bus to village.

Gaiole in Chianti 34B1

Via Michelangelo Buonarroti. **GPS**: n43,46470 e11,43428.

free Chfree. **Location:** Rural, simple. **Surface:** metalled.
01/01-31/12.
Distance: 400m on the spot.
Remarks: At footballstadium.

Gallicano 26D3

Via dei Cipressi. **GPS**: n44,05827 e10,44565.

4 free Ch (2x)free.
Surface: metalled. 01/01-31/12.
Distance: 500m.
Remarks: Grotta del Vento.

Greve in Chianti 34B1

Monte S. Michele, Via Montebeni. **GPS**: n43,59066 e11,31355.

17 free free. **Location:** Rural, comfortable, quiet.
Surface: metalled. 01/01-31/12.
Distance: 500m 500m.

Tourist information Greve in Chianti:
Sa-morning.

Isola dElba 34A2

Area Camper Cavo, San Bennato, Cavo, Elba (Isle) (Isola dElba).
GPS: n42,85459 e10,42267.
50 € 18/24h Ch €2 €1. **Surface:** gravel.
01/04-30/10.
Distance: 600m 400m.

Isola dElba 34A2

Area Camper La Perla, Loc. Campo All'Aia, Procchio, Elba (Isle) (Isola dElba). **GPS**: n42,78893 e10,24877.
20 € 18, Jun/Sep € 24, Jul € 30, Aug € 39 €3,50 .
Surface: gravel. 01/01-31/12.
Distance: on the spot.

Isola dElba 34A2

Loc. Bocchetto, Porto Azzurro. **GPS**: n42,77114 e10,39985.
60 free, peak season € 10/24h Chfree.
Surface: asphalted.

Distance: city centre 1km.
Remarks: Nearby cemetery.

Isola dElba 34A2

Sighello, area La Pila, Marina di Campo. **GPS**: n42,75357 e10,24228.
30 € 15 Ch €3. **Surface:** unpaved. 01/05-30/09.
Distance: 400m 200m.
Remarks: At sports park.

Larciano 34B1

Agriturismo Poggetto, Via Stradella 1489.
GPS: n43,83319 e10,88042.

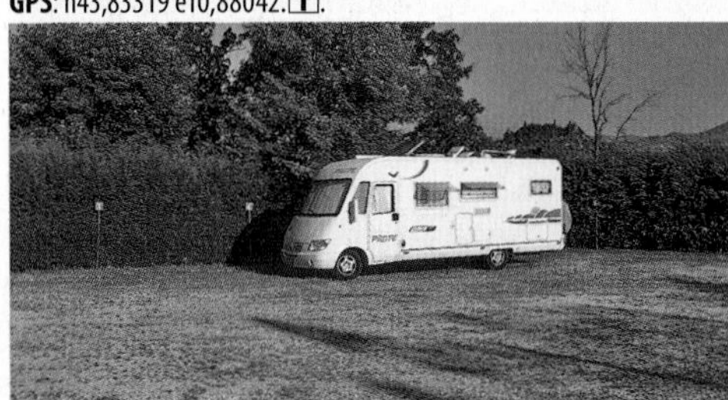

25 € 15/24h, free with a meal Ch. **Surface:** grassy/gravel.
01/01-31/12.
Distance: 1km 1km.

Livorno 34A1

Parco del Mulino, Via Voltolino Fontani. **GPS**: n43,51394 e10,32503.
25 € 10, May/Sep € 12 Ch included. **Surface:** grassy.
01/01-31/12.
Distance: city centre 3km 1km 350m.

Livorno 34A1

Parco Marina del Boccale, Via del Littorale,238.
GPS: n43,47861 e10,33138.
€ 20 ChWC. **Surface:** grassy. 01/04-31/09.
Distance: Livorno 8km on the spot on the spot.

Livorno 34A1

Piazza Ordoardo Borrani, Viale d'Antignano.
GPS: n43,50465 e10,32144.

50 free. **Location:** Rural.
Surface: asphalted.
Distance: 400m Antignano 100m 300m.

Tourist information Livorno:
Ufficio Informazioni, Piazza del Municipio. Medieval port city.

Lucca 34A1

Il Serchio, Via del Tiro a Segno 704, loc. Sant'Anna.
GPS: n43,85000 e10,48583.

66 € 25/24h, dog € 1 Ch (66x)WC €4,50 included.
Surface: grasstiles. 01/03-31/01.
Distance: 1km 2km 500m on the spot 2km on the spot.
Remarks: Waste dump € 2/day, shuttle € 1/pp, swimming pool € 5/pp.

Lucca 34A1

Area Sosta Lucca, Viale Gaetano Luporini.
GPS: n43,84028 e10,48878.

IT

65 € 10/24h, peak season € 14/24h, € 3/h Ch included.
Surface: asphalted.
Distance: 5 min walking 2km.

Tourist information Lucca:
Casa di Puccini, Via di Poggio. Birth place of the composer. Tue-Su.
Wed, Sa, 3rd Su of the month antiques market.

S Lucignano 34C1
SP19. **GPS**: n43,27664 e11,74512.

20 free Ch (9x)free. **Location:** Rural, simple.
Surface: grassy. 01/01-31/12.
Distance: 500m.
Remarks: At the edge of village.

S Marina di Bibbona 34A2
Via dei Cipressi. **GPS**: n43,24825 e10,53389.
€ 10/24h Ch €2 WC free €1. 01/04-31/10.
Distance: 1km 500m 500m.

S Marina di Cecina 34A1
Parcheggio Aqua Park, Via Tevere. **GPS**: n43,30070 e10,49948.

100 € 8 Ch. **Location:** Rural. **Surface:** metalled.
01/03-15/11.
Distance: 2km 1km 200m 200m.

S Marina di Cecina 34A1
Via della Cecinella. **GPS**: n43,29278 e10,50785.

30 € 8/24h Ch. **Location:** Rural, simple, quiet.
Surface: asphalted. 01/03-15/11.
Distance: 2km 300m 2km 2km.

S Marina di Cecina 34A1
New Camping Le Tamerici, Via della Cecinella, 5.
GPS: n43,29192 e10,51053.
€ 25-44 Ch WC included. 11/05-03/10.
Distance: 1,5km 1km on the spot on the spot.
Remarks: Swimming pool.

S Marina di Grosseto 34B2
Oasi di Maremma, SP158 delle Collacchie Km 34,4.
GPS: n42,72611 e10,99055.

50 € 16, peak season € 20, 4 pers.incl Ch (100x)€2 WC €1 €4. **Location:** Comfortable, quiet.
Surface: grassy. 01/04-30/09.
Distance: 1km 1km 1km 1km on the spot.
Remarks: Water at each pitch, shuttle € 1/pp.

S Marina di Grosseto 34B2
Area di sosta l'Oasi, S332 > dir San Vincenzo d'Elba.
GPS: n42,73466 e10,97483.

50 € 12, Jun € 15, Jul/Aug € 20 Ch €2 WC €2
Location: Rural, comfortable. **Surface:** grassy. Easter-30/09.
Distance: Marina 1,5km 1,1km 400m nearby.

Marina di Grosseto 34B2
Via Costiera, SP158. **GPS**: n42,73722 e10,96388.

50 free. **Location:** Rural, simple.
Surface: gravel. 01/01-31/12.
Distance: 2km 400m.

P Marina di Grosseto 34B2
Via Grossetana. **GPS**: n42,71552 e10,98646.

8 free. **Location:** Urban. **Surface:** sand.
Distance: 400m 400m on the spot.
Remarks: At harbour.

Tourist information Marina di Grosseto:
Parco Naturale della Maremma. Nature reserve. Wed, Sa, Su, holidays 9h 01/06-30/09 guided walk 7h, 16h.

S Marina di Pisa 34A1
Parcheggio Camper Pisamo, Viale Gabriela d'Annunzio.
GPS: n43,67909 e10,27887.
130 € 15/24h Ch. **Surface:** sand. 01/01-31/12.
Distance: sea 1km on the spot.

S Marradi 26F3
Area sosta Marradi, Via San Benedetto. **GPS**: n44,07347 e11,61166.

30 free 100liter Ch 8kWh,Service€5. **Location:** Simple, quiet. **Surface:** asphalted. 01/01-31/12.
Distance: 50m on the spot 100m 200m.
Remarks: Caution key service € 7.

S Massa Marittima 34B2
Viale del Risorgimento. **GPS**: n43,04530 e10,89050.

7 free Ch free.
Surface: asphalted. 01/01-31/12.
Distance: historical centre 650m 600m 500m on the spot.

S Montalcino 34B2
Via Osticcio. **GPS**: n43,04913 e11,48749.

30 € 5/24h Ch free. **Location:** Rural, comfortable, quiet.
Surface: asphalted/metalled. 01/01-31/12.
Distance: 700m 700m 700m.

Montalcino 34B2
Agriturismo la Croce, La Croce 9. **GPS**: n43,03931 e11,50373.
15 € 20, guests free. **Location:** Rural, isolated, quiet.
Surface: grassy. 01/04-31/10.
Distance: 3,5km on the spot.
Remarks: Regional products and wine.

S Monte San Savino 34C1
Via del Casalino. **GPS**: n43,33177 e11,72204.

20 free Ch free. **Location:** Rural, simple. **Surface:** gravel.
01/01-31/12.
Distance: on the spot 4,2km 200m.
Remarks: Steep ramp.

Montecatini Terme 34B1
Piazza Pietro Leopoldo, SS 436. **GPS**: n43,88286 e10,76386.
40 free. **Surface:** asphalted. 01/01-31/12 Thu (market).
Distance: 3km 500m 500m.
Remarks: In front of stadium, tuesday market.

S Montepulciano 34C2
P5, Piazza Pietro Nenni. **GPS**: n43,09577 e11,78684.

IT

32 € 10/24h free. **Location:** Rural, simple. **Surface:** asphalted. 01/01-31/12 Wed morning, market.
Distance: 200m 100m 400m.
Remarks: Cash payment.

Montepulciano 34C2

La Buca Vecchia, Strada per Pienza, 38. **GPS**: n43,09903 e11,73939.
7 € 20 + € 1/pp tourist tax Ch included.
Location: Comfortable, isolated, quiet. **Surface:** metalled.
01/01-31/12.
Distance: 5km.
Remarks: Check in on arrival, barbecue place.

Monteriggioni 34B1

Via Cassia Nord 142. **GPS**: n43,38560 e11,22784.
30 € 16/24h Ch included WC. **Surface:** metalled.
Distance: 400m 400m.
Remarks: Service passerby € 4.

Monteriggioni 34B1

Strada di Monteriggioni. **GPS**: n43,38801 e11,22511.

12 € 2/h 8-20h, max. € 6, overnight stay free. **Location:** Rural, comfortable. **Surface:** gravel. 01/01-31/12.
Distance: 300m 1,4km 300m on the spot.

Monteriggioni 34B1

Agriturismo "Il Sambuco", Via Maestri del Lavoro 12, Uopini.
GPS: n43,35266 e11,29415.
8 € 15/24h free Ch included WC. **Surface:** gravel.
01/01-31/12.
Distance: 1km 350m 300m.
Remarks: Regional products, swimming pool € 5.

Monteroni d'Arbia 34B1

Via San Giusto. **GPS**: n43,23048 e11,42371.

free Ch free. **Location:** Rural, simple. **Surface:** sand.
01/01-31/12.
Distance: 50m.
Remarks: P centre.

Montespertoli 34B1

Molino del Ponte, Via Volterrana Nord. **GPS**: n43,65606 e11,08445.

5 free € 1/100liter € 2 Ch. **Location:** Rural. **Surface:** metalled.
01/01-31/12.
Distance: Montespertoli 2,3km on the spot 400m.

Montevarchi 34B1

Via B. Latini. **GPS**: n43,53052 e11,56784.

free free. **Location:** Urban, simple. **Surface:** asphalted.
01/01-31/12.
Distance: 7km Coop.
Remarks: Nearby stadium.

Montopoli in Val d'Arno 34B1

Piazza Amerigo Vespucci, Via di Masoria. **GPS**: n43,67333 e10,75222.

31 free Ch free. **Surface:** metalled. 01/01-31/12.
Distance: within walking distance.

Orbetello 34B3

Lanino Parco Sosta, Loc. Santa Liberata.
GPS: n42,43346 e11,15959.

50 € 10/motorhome, € 8/pp, € 5/child Ch (40x)included WC. **Location:** Rural.
Surface: grassy/gravel. 01/01-31/12.
Distance: Orbetello 5km 50m 200m alimentari.
Remarks: Max. 72h.

Palazzuolo sul Senio 26F3

Parcheggio Casone, Via Casone. **GPS**: n44,11073 e11,54968.

100 free Ch free. **Location:** Simple. **Surface:** asphalted.
01/01-31/12.
Distance: 100m 100m 100m.
Remarks: Narrow entrance.

Palazzuolo sul Senio 26F3

Via Francesco Pagliazzi. **GPS**: n44,11551 e11,55000.

6 free. **Location:** Isolated. **Surface:** metalled.
01/01-31/12.
Distance: on the spot.

Remarks: Next to cemetery, upper part of the parking.

Pienza 34C2

Via Mencattelli e Foro Boario. **GPS**: n43,07799 e11,68087.

8-22h: € 1,50/1h, € 5/4h, € 10/8h, overnight stay free Ch included WC. **Location:** Rural, simple. **Surface:** asphalted.
01/01-31/12 Fri-morning market.
Distance: 100m.

Pienza 34C2

Podere il Casale, Via Podere Il Casale 64. **GPS**: n43,08090 e11,71161.
8 € 26, 2 pers. incl € 3 WC. **Location:** Quiet.
Surface: gravel. 01/01-31/12.
Distance: on the spot.
Remarks: Regional products.

Pieve Santo Stefano 34C1

Grey camper, Via della Verna. **GPS**: n43,67058 e12,03729.

20 € 10 Ch WC included € 1. **Location:** Simple, noisy.
Surface: metalled. 01/01-31/12.
Distance: on the spot 1,7km.
Remarks: Nearby viaduct E45.

Piombino 34A2

Camperoasi, Loc. Mortelliccio, Riotorto.
GPS: n42,95416 e10,66638.

93 € 20, Apr-Jun, Sep € 30, Jul/Aug € 40 Ch WC € 0,50 included.
Location: Comfortable. **Surface:** grasstiles/grassy. 01/01-31/12
01/10-31/03 Mo-Thu.
Distance: 200m 50m 50m.
Remarks: Water/drainage at each pitch, 10% discount on presentation of the most recent guide, reception open: 9.30-12.30 14-19.30.

Piombino 34A2

Area Sosta Camper Isolotto, Loc. Mortelliccio, 7, Riotorto.
GPS: n42,95765 e10,67374.
23 € 20, Jul/Aug € 27 Ch included. **Surface:** gravel.
Distance: 200m.
Remarks: Fruit-vegetables-wine-regional products for sale, swimming pool available.

Piombino 34A2

Area Sosta l'OrtiCillo, Loc. Le Pinete, 3 Riotorto.
GPS: n42,98414 e10,68011.
12 € 8-10, 01/07-31/08 € 14 + tourist tax € 0,50/pp Ch included.
Surface: gravel. 01/01-31/12.
Distance: 300m.
Remarks: Barbecue place, borrow cycles for free, regional products.

Piombino 34A2

Carbonifera 1, Loc. Torre Mozza. **GPS**: n42,94750 e10,69277.

IT

± 75 € 2,20/h, € 18,70/24h Ch included.
Surface: gravel. 01/01-31/12.
Distance: 50m.
Remarks: Beach parking, no camping activities.

S **Piombino** 34A2

Parcheggio Caldanelle, Loc. Caldanelle. **GPS**: n43,00216 e10,52816.

150 € 2/h, € 17/8-20h, overnight stay free Ch.
Location: Isolated, quiet. **Surface:** grassy. 01/01-31/12.
Distance: Piombino 9km 1,5km.
Remarks: Beach parking, camper service 8-20h, no camping activities, shuttle bus.

S **Piombino** 34A2

Perelli 1-3, Loc. Perelli. **GPS**: n42,95527 e10,61944.

50 € 2,20/h, € 18,70/8-20h, overnight stay free Ch free.
Location: Quiet. **Surface:** grassy/sand. 01/06-30/09.
Distance: Sandy beach Perelli 1.
Remarks: Beach parking, service: Perelli 3, no camping activities, dogs beach.

S **Piombino** 34A2

Podere Mortelliccio, Loc. Mortelliccio 8, Riotorto.
GPS: n42,95700 e10,67884.
8 € 20-25, Jul/Aug € 32 Ch included €3,50.
Surface: gravel. 01/01-31/12.
Distance: 400m on the spot.
Remarks: Regional products and wine, barbecue place.

S **Piombino** 34A2

Via della Pace. **GPS**: n42,93777 e10,52194.

15 free €0,10/10liter Ch. **Location:** Urban, noisy.
Surface: metalled. 01/01-31/12.
Distance: 500m 1km 700m 800m.

S **Piombino** 34A2

Parcheggio di Alvin, Piazzale Salvatore Allende.
GPS: n42,92578 e10,54219.
€ 15/24h Ch. 01/04-31/10.
Distance: 200m.

S **Pisa** 34A1

Parcheggio camper, Via di Pratale 78. **GPS**: n43,72106 e10,42066.

100 € 12/night, € 1/h, € 5/6h €3 Ch.
Location: Quiet. **Surface:** asphalted.
Distance: 800m 7km on the spot.
Remarks: Monitored parking.

S **Pistoia** 34B1

Via Marino Marini/via della Quiete. **GPS**: n43,94389 e10,91556.
50 free . **Surface:** asphalted.
Distance: city centre 1km 6km on the spot.
Remarks: At sports park.

S **Pistoia** 34B1

Agricamper Podere Campofossato. **GPS**: n43,99503 e10,89520.
8 € 20 Ch included.
Distance: 50m.
Remarks: Regional products.

S **Poggibonsi** 34B1

Via Fortezza Medicea, loc. Vallone. **GPS**: n43,46203 e11,14593.

± 15 free €0,10/10liter Ch (6x)€1/12h.
Location: Rural. **Surface:** gravel. 01/01-31/12.
Distance: centre 500m 400m 500m.

Tourist information Poggibonsi:
Monteriggioni. Walled small town.

S **Pontassieve** 34B1

Viale Hanoi/viale Lisbona. **GPS**: n43,77355 e11,42764.

free Ch free. **Location:** Simple. **Surface:** asphalted.
01/01-31/12.
Distance: 500m.

S **Poppi** 34C1

La Crocina, Viale dei Pini. **GPS**: n43,71982 e11,76529.

12 free Ch free €3/5h. **Location:** Simple, quiet.
Surface: asphalted. 01/01-31/12.
Distance: historical centre 500m 300m.

S **Porto Ercole** 34B3

Le Miniere, SP di Porto Ercole. **GPS**: n42,41749 e11,20386.

130 € 20-25, Aug € 30 Ch WC €0,50 €5 included.
Location: Comfortable, noisy.
Surface: grassy. Easter-30/09.
Distance: Porto Ercole 2km 800m 800m 2km.
Remarks: Bread-service, borrow cycles for free, free shuttle to beach every 30 minutes.

S **Porto Ercole** 34B3

Parking Da Renzo, SC della Feniglia. **GPS**: n42,41527 e11,20777.

150 € 18 Ch €3 WC included. **Location:** Rural, comfortable, quiet.
Surface: grassy.
Easter-01/10.
Distance: Porto Ercole 3km beach 1km 800m on the spot.
Remarks: No camping activities, bike/car rental, beach shuttle (August).

S **Pratovecchio** 34C1

Via Uffenheim. **GPS**: n43,78666 e11,71952.

12 free Ch free. **Location:** Simple, quiet.
Surface: asphalted. 01/01-31/12.
Distance: 50m 100m 100m.
Remarks: Along river, follow signs instead of GPS.

S **Radda in Chianti** 34B1

Via Degli Ulivi. **GPS**: n43,48643 e11,37543.

6 € 12/24h WC free. **Location:** Rural, simple.
Surface: metalled. 01/01-31/12.
Distance: 200m (stairs).

S **Radicofani** 34C2

Via A. de Gasperi. **GPS**: n42,89471 e11,77506.

5 free Ch free. **Location:** Rural, simple.

IT

Surface: grassy/gravel. 01/01-31/12.
Distance: 400m ⊗800m.

S Radicondoli 34B1

Il Pianetto. GPS: n43,25888 e11,04250.

free Ch €1/h.
Surface: grassy/gravel. 01/01-31/12.
Distance: medieval centre 300m ⊗300m 2km.

S Rapolano Terme 34C1

Area di sosta camper Il Pini, Via Vittorio Veneto.
GPS: n43,29601 e11,60312.
50 € 10/24h, € 8/12h, € 6/6h €3 included.
Surface: gravel. 01/01-31/12.
Distance: on the spot 1km ⊗300m.
Remarks: Terme Antica Querciolaia 200m.

S Rapolano Terme 34C1

Villa dei Boschi, Loc. Villa dei Boschi 50, Fraz San Gimignanello, SP10.
GPS: n43,22829 e11,65429.

20 € 20/24h, free with a meal WC included.
Location: Rural, simple, isolated. **Surface:** grassy. 01/01-31/12.
Distance: ⊗on the spot.

S Rapolano Terme 34C1

Area di sosta Le Terme, Via Trieste. **GPS:** n43,29268 e11,60781.

64 € 5/6h, € 8/12h, € 12/24h Ch WC included €2.
Location: Rural, comfortable. **Surface:** gravel/metalled.
01/01-31/12.
Distance: 500m ⊗50m 200m.
Remarks: Terme Antica Querciolaia 50m.

S Rosignano Marittimo 34A1

Molino a Fuoco, Via dei Cavalleggeri Antica, Vada.
GPS: n43,32816 e10,46005.

70 01/04-15/09 € 15 Ch included. **Surface:** grassy/gravel.
Distance: 400m 500m ⊗400m 400m.
Remarks: Max. 72h.

S Rosignano Marittimo 34A1

Il Fortullino, Località il Fortullino. **GPS:** n43,43005 e10,39632.

150 € 18/night, Jul-Aug € 23 Ch included.
Surface: unpaved. 01/04-30/09.
Distance: Castiglioncello 4km, Livorno 20km, Pisa 40km 150m ⊗Pizzeria 100m 5km.

S Rosignano Marittimo 34A1

SP39, Via Aurelia, Loc Caletta. **GPS:** n43,39900 e10,42807.

18 € 10 free. **Surface:** metalled.
Distance: on the spot 300m 100m.
Remarks: Along busy road, max. 48h.

Rosignano Marittimo 34A1

Parcheggio del Lillatro, Via Fratelli Gigli, loc Lillatro.
GPS: n43,38380 e10,43206.

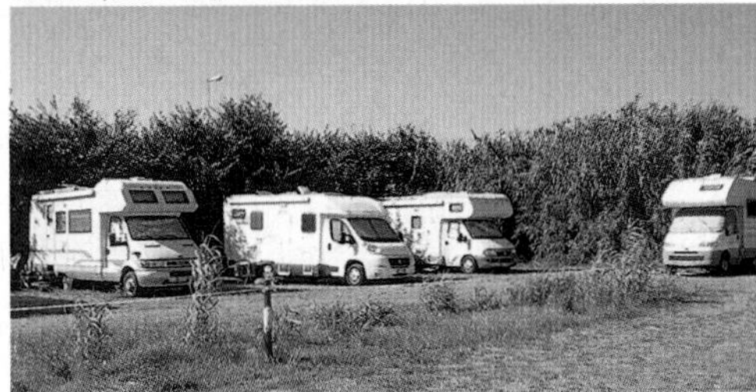

40 € 9. **Location:** Simple, isolated, quiet. **Surface:** sand.
Easter-31/10.
Distance: 50m ⊗50m.

Rosignano Marittimo 34A1

Sportiva Vada, Via Mare Mediterraneo, Vada.
GPS: n43,35208 e10,45183.

75 € 10/day. **Location:** Rural, quiet. **Surface:** unpaved.
01/04-01/10.
Distance: 400m 200m ⊗200m 400m.

San Casciano dei Bagni 34C2

Via Della Pineta. **GPS:** n42,86530 e11,87383.

15 free. **Location:** Rural, simple. **Surface:** gravel/sand.
01/01-31/12.
Distance: 500m.

S San Casciano dei Bagni 34C2

Piazzale del Ponte. **GPS:** n42,87024 e11,87742.

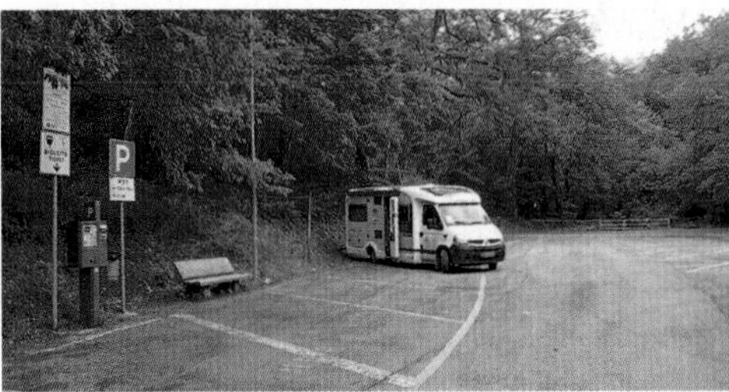

15 € 6/12h, € 12/24h Ch. **Surface:** asphalted.
01/01-31/12.
Distance: 100m.
Remarks: Near spa resort.

S San Casciano in Val di Pesa 34B1

Parco Il Poggione. GPS: n43,65395 e11,18768.

5 € 8 free.

S San Gimignano 34B1

Sosta Camper Santa Chiara, Via di Castel San Gimignano, Loc. Fornace.
GPS: n43,45572 e11,03476.

30 € 22/24h €2 Ch WC included. **Location:** Rural, luxurious. **Surface:** gravel. 01/01-31/12.
Distance: 3km ⊗Osteria/bar 1,5km shuttle.
Remarks: Barbecue place, free shuttle bus to San Gimignano, tenniscourt.

S San Gimignano 34B1

Park Santa Lucia, Loc. Santa Lucia. **GPS:** n43,45205 e11,05586.

50 € 1/h, € 15/24h Ch (14x)included.
Location: Rural, simple. **Surface:** gravel. 01/01-31/12.
Distance: 3km Citybus Linea 1.
Remarks: Next to swimming pool, 24/24 video surveillance, shuttle bus to city centre.

S San Miniato Basso 34B1

Piazza G. Impastato, Via Pestalozzi/Via G. Pizzigoni, zona industriale.
GPS: n43,69417 e10,83638.

€ 0,50/h free. **Surface:** asphalted. 01/01-31/12.
Distance: 800m ⊗50m Superal.

IT

San Miniato Basso 34B1

Area Camper Il Salice, Via Pier delle Vigne 28/A, loc. La Catena.
GPS: n43,68434 e10,82224.

20 € 15/24h Ch WC.
Surface: gravel. 01/01-31/12.
Distance: 1km on the spot.
Remarks: Max. 3 days, shuttle bus to city centre.

San Piero a Sieve 34B1

GPS: n43,96260 e11,32732.

20 free Chfree. **Location:** Simple, quiet. **Surface:** metalled.
01/01-31/12.
Distance: 500m 250m.

San Quirico d'Orcia 34C2

Via delle Scuole. **GPS**: n43,05607 e11,60682.

30 € 10/24h free. **Location:** Rural, simple.
Surface: asphalted. 01/01-31/12.
Distance: 200m.
Remarks: Picnic area, playground.

San Quirico d'Orcia 34C2

Strada di Bagno Vignoni, Bagno Vignoni.
GPS: n43,02904 e11,62450.

± 20 free. **Location:** Rural, simple, quiet.
Surface: unpaved.
01/01-31/12.
Distance: 500m 350m.
Remarks: Parco dei Mulini: natural hot springs, free entrance, 400m.

San Romano in Garfagnana 26D3

Via Campo Sportivo/via Prà di Lago. **GPS**: n44,17243 e10,34199.

15 free Chfree. **Surface:** grassy.

01/01-31/12.
Remarks: At sports park, Parco Avventura Selva del Buffardello 100m.

San Vincenzo 34A2

Via Biserno. **GPS**: n43,08790 e10,54134.

50 01/04-30/09 € 10/24h free.
Surface: grassy/gravel.
01/01-31/12.
Distance: 1km beach 200m 50m 50m.
Remarks: Beach parking, no camping activities, bicycle rental.

San Vincenzo 34A2

SS. Annunziata, Via del Castelluccio, 142. **GPS**: n43,10086 e10,56001.
€ 16, Jul/Aug € 25-35 Ch included €0,50 €3.
Distance: 1km 1km on the spot 50m.
Remarks: Playground, swimming pool.

Sansepolcro 34C1

Viale Alessandro Volta. **GPS**: n43,56976 e12,13727.

20 free Chfree. **Location:** Urban, simple. **Surface:** asphalted.
01/01-31/12.
Distance: 200m.

Sansepolcro 34C1

Podere Violino, Via del Tevere 1150, Gricignano.
GPS: n43,55539 e12,12312.

8 € 6 + € 5/pp Ch WC included.
Location: Comfortable, isolated, quiet. **Surface:** grassy.
01/03-31/12.
Distance: 2km river on the spot 500m.
Remarks: Restaurant closed on Sunday, swimming pool available.

Santa Fiora 34C2

Via Martiri della Niccioleta. **GPS**: n42,83531 e11,58397.

20 free Chfree (6x)€1/2h. **Location:** Rural, simple.
Surface: gravel/sand. 01/01-31/12.
Distance: 450m.

Sasso Pisano 34B2

Buca San Rocco. **GPS**: n43,16748 e10,86586.

10 free €2 Ch €3/12h. **Location:** Rural.
Surface: metalled. 01/01-31/12.
Distance: 100m 200m.

Saturnia 34B2

L'Alveare dei Pinzi, Strada della Peschiera, Saturnia.
GPS: n42,65597 e11,50368.

400 € 14/24h Ch (120x)€2 WC €0,50 €6 included
. **Location:** Rural, comfortable, quiet. **Surface:** gravel.
01/01-31/12.
Distance: Saturnia 3km 1,5km.
Remarks: Panoramic view, free shuttle to spa resort and Saturnia, bar/snack/fruit, terme di Saturnia (sulfur baths) 1,7km, Cascate del Mulino (water fall, free entry) 2,5km, friday market.

Saturnia 34B2

La Quercia, Via Aurina 15. **GPS**: n42,66667 e11,50457.

30 € 16/24h Ch WC €1 included.
Location: Rural, comfortable, central.
Surface: gravel. 01/01-31/12.
Distance: 200m 100m 100m.
Remarks: Shuttle bus, terme di Saturnia (sulfur baths) 1,7km, Cascate del Mulino (water fall, free entry) 2,5km.

Scarperia 26E3

Ranch Ricavo, Via di Galliano 21. **GPS**: n44,01189 e11,30681.

20 € 10 Ch WCincluded. **Location:** Simple, quiet.
Surface: grassy. 01/01-31/12.
Distance: 5km on the spot 5km.

Sestino 34C1

Via Travicello. **GPS**: n43,71223 e12,30356.

12 free free. **Surface:** grasstiles.

Distance: 2km.
Remarks: Nearby sports park.

S Sesto Fiorentino 34B1

Area Antica Etruria, Via Ferruccio Parri. **GPS**: n43,84150 e11,17667.

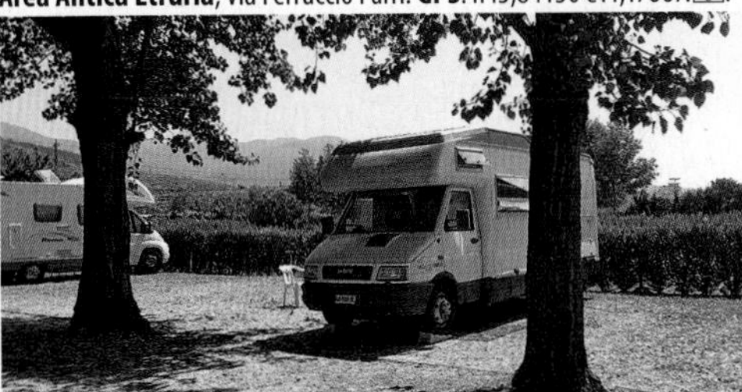

50 € 18/24h Ch WC included €1,50/day.
Location: Comfortable. **Surface:** asphalted. 01/01-31/12.
Distance: 1,5km 400m 400m 30m > Florence.
Remarks: Monitored parking.

S Sesto Fiorentino 34B1

Viale Ariosto. **GPS**: n43,83238 e11,18997.

15 free. **Location:** Simple, quiet. **Surface:** asphalted.
01/01-31/12.
Distance: 500m 3km 200m 500m train 100m.
Remarks: In front of Lidl supermarket, 20 mins to Florence by train.

S Siena 34B1

P1, Palasport, Via Achille Sclavo. **GPS**: n43,33323 e11,31739.

35 € 20/motorhome (8.00-20.00h) Ch WC free.
Location: Urban, simple. **Surface:** metalled. 01/01-31/12.
Distance: on the spot.

S Siena 34B1

P2, Il Fagiolone, Via di Pescaia. **GPS**: n43,31456 e11,31760.

60 € 20/motorhome (8-20h), overnight stay free WC free.
Location: Urban, simple, noisy.
Surface: metalled. 01/01-31/12.
Distance: on the spot.
Remarks: Along busy road.

Siena 34B1

Acqua Calda, Via Fausto Coppi. **GPS**: n43,33627 e11,29695.

free. **Location:** Urban, simple. **Surface:** grasstiles.
01/01-31/12.
Distance: 650m bus 10 centre Siena.

Siena 34B1

Via delle Province/via Napoli. **GPS**: n43,34168 e11,30512.

free. **Location:** Urban, simple, noisy. **Surface:** asphalted.
01/01-31/12.
Distance: 200m McDonalds 200m on the spot.

Tourist information Siena:

- Palazzo Publico. Gothic town hall from 1342.
- Torre del Mangia. Bell tower. daily.
- Duomo. Romanesque Gothic cathedral.
- La Lizza. Week market. Wed morning.
- Palio, Piazza del Campo. Famous historical horse race. 02/07, 16/08.

S Stia 34C1

Parco comunale del Canto della Rana, Via Londa, SP556.
GPS: n43,80417 e11,70326.

6 free Ch free. **Location:** Simple, quiet. **Surface:** gravel.
01/01-31/12.
Distance: 500m.

S Suvereto 34B2

Via dei Forni. **GPS**: n43,07572 e10,67802.

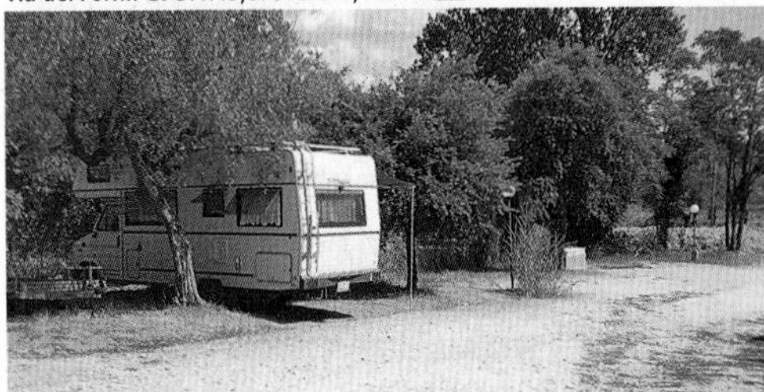

12 free free. **Location:** Rural, simple, quiet. **Surface:** grassy.
01/01-31/12.
Distance: medieval centre 200m 300m 300m.

S Torrita di Siena 34C2

Via di Ciliano. **GPS**: n43,16475 e11,77173.

6 free Ch free. **Location:** Rural, comfortable, quiet.
Surface: metalled. 01/01-31/12.
Distance: 400m 200m on the spot on the spot.

S Venturina 34B2

Parco Termale Calidario, Via del Bottaccio.
GPS: n43,03666 e10,60000.

20 free €0,10/10liter Ch. **Location:** Quiet. **Surface:** metalled.
01/01-31/12.
Distance: 800m 50m 800m.
Remarks: Thermal centre 50m.

S Viareggio 34A1

Via Martiri di Belfiore. **GPS**: n43,88120 e10,25080.

44 € 15/24h Ch included.
Surface: asphalted.
01/01-31/12.
Distance: 1km 2,5km.
Remarks: Check in at All Events Festival Puccini Viareggio, Viale Regina Margherita 1, 43,8673339 10,2431529, terrain with video surveillance.

S Vinci 34B1

Via Girolamo Calvi. **GPS**: n43,78080 e10,92830.
12 free Ch free. **Surface:** metalled. 01/01-31/12.
Distance: 300m.
Remarks: At sports park.

S Volterra 34B1

Parking P3, Fonti Docciola, Viale Dei Filosofi.
GPS: n43,40306 e10,86417.

15 € 10 8-20h, overnight stay free Ch free.
Location: Urban. **Surface:** gravel. 01/01-31/12.
Distance: historical center 100m 200m 300m.

San Marino

S San Marino 26G3

Camper Stop, Via del Serrone 94. **GPS**: n43,92057 e12,45056.
free. **Surface:** grassy.
Distance: city centre 3km on the spot.

S San Marino 26G3

P13, Baldasserona, Borgo Maggiore. **GPS**: n43,94054 e12,44289.

50 free Ch. **Surface:** asphalted. 01/01-31/12.
Remarks: Service 300m.

S San Marino 26G3

Strada Genghe di Atto, Acquaviva. **GPS**: n43,94491 e12,42963.

IT

5 free Ch WC free. **Surface:** asphalted.

San Marino 26G3

P10, Via Napoleone Boneparte. **GPS:** n43,93567 e12,44362.

20 € 8/24h. **Surface:** asphalted. 01/11-31/03.
Remarks: Elevator to centre 50m.

Tourist information San Marino:
Borgo Maggiore. Week market. Thu.

Marche

Amandola 34D2

Area Sosta Sibillini, Piazzale Sandro Pertini. **GPS:** n42,97085 e13,35488.
42 € 10 Ch €2 WC included. **Surface:** asphalted.
01/01-31/12.
Distance: 850m.

Ancona 34D1

Area di sosta Posatora, Via Sanzio Blasi, Loc. Posatore.
GPS: n43,59964 e13,48530.

30 € 12 Ch (24x)included.
Location: Simple.
Surface: metalled. 01/01-31/12.
Distance: 4,5km 10m.
Remarks: Max. 72h, only exact change, entrance between 8-22h.

Ancona 34D1

Centro Commerciale Auchan, Via Scataglini, Zona Industriale Baraccola, SS16, Ancona-sud. **GPS:** n43,55133 e13,51506.

25 free free. **Location:** Simple. **Surface:** grasstiles.
01/01-31/12.
Distance: 8km 3,6km.

Tourist information Ancona:
Riviera del Conera. Touristic peninsula with beaches and several bathing resorts.

Apecchio 34C1

Via Isidoro Pazzaglia. **GPS:** n43,55938 e12,41969.
30 free Ch (6x)free. **Surface:** metalled. 01/01-31/12.
Distance: 100m 50m.

Tourist information Apecchio:
Week market. Fri-morning.

Ascoli Piceno 34E2

Ex Seminario, Viale Alcide Gasperi. **GPS:** n42,85222 e13,58222.

20 € 3/night,20/h, night € 3 . **Location:** Urban.
Surface: asphalted.
Distance: centre 500m 200m 200m.
Remarks: Guarded parking.

Ascoli Piceno 34E2

Bed & Breakfast Chartaria, Via Adriatico.
GPS: n42,84792 e13,57306.
7 € 15 €3. **Surface:** grassy.

Tourist information Ascoli Piceno:
City with many monumental bldg.
Wed, Sa.

Camerino 34D1

Via Macario Muzio. **GPS:** n43,13677 e13,06718.

8 free Ch free €1/4h WC . **Location:** Rural.
Surface: asphalted. 01/01-31/12.
Distance: centre 500m 350m.
Remarks: Beautiful view, escalator to city centre.

Carpegna 34C1

Via Aldo Moro. **GPS:** n43,78083 e12,34040.

10 free €1 Ch €0,60/h. **Surface:** concrete.
01/01-31/12.
Distance: 300m 300m.

Castelfidardo 34D1

Croce Verde, Via Lumumba/via Donato Bramonte.
GPS: n43,46603 e13,55563.

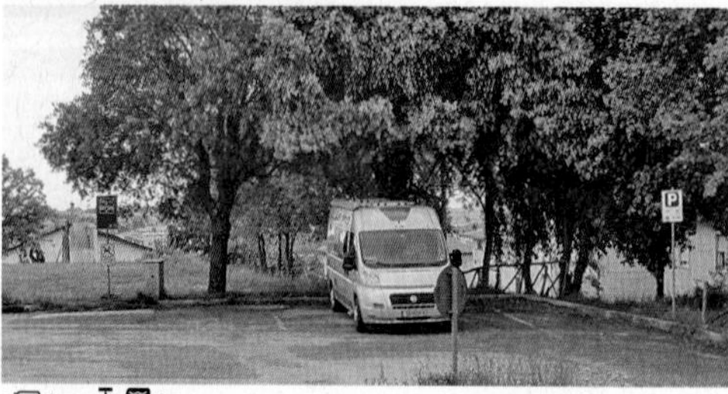

3 free free.
Location: Simple. **Surface:** asphalted. 01/01-31/12.
Distance: 200m.
Remarks: Max. 48h.

Castelsantangelo sul Nera 34D2

Strada Provinciale 136. **GPS:** n42,89117 e13,15355.
8 free Ch free. **Location:** Isolated, quiet. **Surface:** asphalted.
01/01-31/12.
Distance: 200m.

Cerreto D'Esi 34D1

Via Dante Alighieri. **GPS:** n43,32714 e12,99114.

10 free . **Location:** Simple. **Surface:** metalled.
01/01-31/12.
Distance: 500m.

Cingoli 34D1

Area Balcone delle Marche, Via San Esuperanzio.
GPS: n43,37643 e13,20943.
€ 10 Ch included. **Location:** Rural.
Surface: asphalted/gravel. 01/01-31/12.
Distance: 200m 200m 100m on the spot.

Colmurano 34D1

Via Piero della Francesca, Contrada Peschiera.
GPS: n43,16260 e13,35828.

8 free Ch WC free. **Surface:** asphalted. 01/01-31/12.
Distance: 400m.
Remarks: Near sports park and historical centre.

Corinaldo 34D1

CoriCamper, Via Pecciameglio. **GPS:** n43,64688 e13,04850.
14 free Ch free.
Surface: metalled. 01/01-31/12.
Distance: 200m 300m 200m.
Remarks: Max. 48h.

Corinaldo 34D1

Via Lepri 3. **GPS:** n43,64703 e13,04910.

8 free Ch free. **Location:** Simple. **Surface:** asphalted.
01/01-31/12.
Distance: 400m 50m.

Corinaldo 34D1

Ristorante Camping Colverde, Via per Montalboddo 52.
GPS: n43,63504 e13,09743.

10 € 15, guests € 10 Ch WC,on campsite included,on campsite. **Location:** Rural, simple. **Surface:** grassy.
01/01-31/12.
Distance: 5km on the spot.
Remarks: Max. 48h.

Cossignano 34E2

Via Gallo. **GPS:** n42,98050 e13,69213.
6 € 6 €3 Ch included. **Location:** Simple.
Surface: metalled. 01/01-31/12.
Distance: 500m.

IT

S Cupramontana 34D1

Verdicchio, SP 11. **GPS**: n43,43934 e13,11837.

10 free free Ch (10x). **Location:** Simple, noisy.
Surface: metalled. 01/01-31/12.
Distance: 100m 500m.
Remarks: Beautiful view of Monte San Vicino.

S Fabriano 34D1

Fraz. Poggio San Romualdo. **GPS**: n43,36473 e13,02534.

35 free free. **Location:** Rural, simple, quiet. **Surface:** grassy.
01/01-31/12.
Distance: 3,5km on the spot.

S Fabriano 34D1

Via Bruno Buozzi. **GPS**: n43,34650 e12,91645.

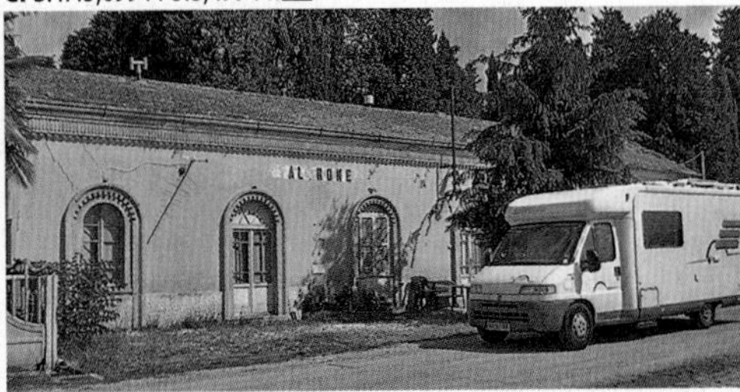

16 free €2/100liter Ch (6x)€3/12h. **Location:** Simple.
Surface: grassy. 01/01-31/12.
Distance: 3km.
Remarks: Next to sports centre.

S Falerone 34D1

Ex-stazione FS di Piane di Falerone, Via Togliatti.
GPS: n43,09944 e13,49944.

15 free Ch free.
Surface: metalled. 1st Su of the month.
Distance: 100m 200m.
Remarks: Nearby the old station and theatre Romano.

S Fano 34D1

Lungomare Sassonia, Via Ruggeri. **GPS**: n43,84238 e13,03197.

60 € 7-8,50 (20x)€2 . **Surface:** grassy/gravel.
01/01-31/12.
Distance: 1km 2km 50m 50m 600m.

S Fano 34D1

Area di Sosta Adriatico, SS16, Torrette di Fano.
GPS: n43,80789 e13,08198.

30 € 10-23, camperstop 18-9h € 8-10 Ch (12x)WC included €0,50 €3. **Location:** Comfortable. **Surface:** grassy/gravel.
22/04-11/09.
Distance: 4km 9km 200m 50m 500m.
Remarks: Service passerby € 5.

S Fano 34D1

Viale Kennedy. **GPS**: n43,84557 e13,01133.

16-20 free Ch free. **Location:** Simple. **Surface:** asphalted.
01/01-31/12.
Distance: 200m 2,7km 800m.
Remarks: Nearby cemetery.

S Fano 34D1

Campo Nunzia, SS Adriactica Sud-Loc. Torrette di Fano.
GPS: n43,80474 e13,08488.

28 € 10-15 Ch €2,50/24h WC €1. **Location:** Comfortable.
Surface: grassy/gravel. 24/04-01/09.
Distance: 7km 10km 150m.

Fano 34D1

Ristorante La Tratta Maria Angela, Via Fratelli Zuccari 37.
GPS: n43,83589 e13,04182.

14 € 7. **Location:** Simple, quiet. **Surface:** grassy.
01/04-01/10.
Distance: 2,5km 50m on the spot on the spot.
Remarks: P camper.

Tourist information Fano:
Wed, Sa.

S Fermo 34E1

Area Camper 2004, Lungomare Marina Palminese.
GPS: n43,15085 e13,81382.

64 € 10, electricity included € 12 Ch (32x)included hot shower against payment. **Surface:** grassy. 01/04-30/09.
Distance: 2,5km on the spot.

S Fermo 34E1

Baia dei Gabbiani, Viale A. de Gasperi, Lido S. Tomasso.
GPS: n43,22158 e13,78113.

50 € 13-20, Aug € 25 Ch included €0,50 .
Surface: grassy/gravel. 01/04-30/09.
Distance: 6,6km Private beach.

S Fermo 34E1

Onda Verde, Via Usodimare, Lido di Fermo.
GPS: n43,20289 e13,78825.

100 € 10 to € 20 (Aug) Ch 2Amp WC included.
Surface: grassy. 01/04-30/09.
Distance: Fermo 10km 5,4km 10m 10-500m 200m.

S Fossombrone 34D1

Via Oberdan. **GPS**: n43,69301 e12,81835.

8 free Ch free. **Surface:** asphalted. 01/01-31/12.
Distance: 500m 1,4km.

Tourist information Fossombrone:
Week market. Mo.

S Genga 34D1

Frasassi, Fraz San Vittore. **GPS**: n43,40321 e12,97597.

50 free WC free. **Location:** Simple, quiet.
Surface: gravel.
01/01-31/12.
Distance: 7km on the spot.
Remarks: Nearby pay-desk Gole di Frasassi, free shuttle to the caves.

IT

Gradara 26H3

Parcheggio dei Cipressi, Via Mancini.
GPS: n43,94163 e12,77461.
€ 5/6h, € 10/24h €3/6h. **Surface:** grassy. 01/01-31/12.
Distance: on the spot on the spot.

Gradara 26H3

Parking P1, Piazza Paolo e Francesca. **GPS**: n43,94083 e12,77083.

14 € 10/24h ChWCfree.
Location: Simple, central.
Surface: asphalted. 01/01-31/12.
Distance: historical center 100m 7,3km on the spot 400m.
Remarks: Parking centre, castle 500m.

Grottammare 34E2

Sosta Camper 43° Parallelo, Via Carlo Alberto dalla Chiesa.
GPS: n42,96673 e13,87694.
40 € 15 Ch WC. **Surface:** asphalted.
Distance: 2,7km 500m 500m 100m on the spot.
Remarks: Behind centro commerciale Cityper, along railwayline.

Grottammare 34E2

Briciola di Sole, Contr. Granaro 19. **GPS**: n42,98278 e13,84000.

14 € 15, guests free Ch included.
Surface: gravel/metalled.
01/04-31/10.
Distance: 2,5km sea 5km on the spot 2km.
Remarks: Restaurant with traditional kitchen, located on estate.

Jesi 34D1

Via Alfredo Zannoni. **GPS**: n43,51882 e13,24180.

10 free free.
Location: Simple, quiet. **Surface:** asphalted. 01/01-31/12.
Distance: 500m centro storico.

Tourist information Jesi:
Area with many vineyards.
Grotte di Frasassi. Caves.

Loreto 34D1

Area Camper Pro Loco, Via Maccari. **GPS**: n43,44125 e13,61491.

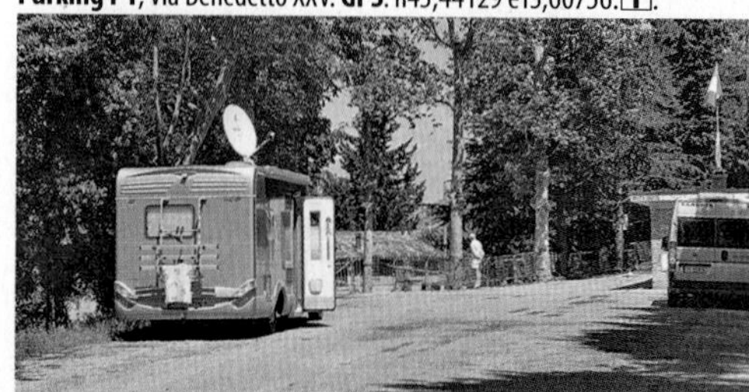

65 € 12/24h Chincluded (20x)€3/day WC €1 €2/8h.
Location: Comfortable. **Surface:** grasstiles.
01/01-31/12.
Distance: 150m 15km.
Remarks: Max. 48h.

Loreto 34D1

Parking P1, Via Benedetto XXV. **GPS**: n43,44129 e13,60756.

6 € 6/day, overnight stay free WC. **Surface:** asphalted.
Distance: 300m 50m.
Remarks: Parking at city wall.

Macerata 34D1

Sferisterio, Via Paladini. **GPS**: n43,29806 e13,45694.
8 € 5 Ch . **Surface:** asphalted. 01/01-31/12.
Distance: 200m 200m.

Macerata Feltria 34C1

Loc. San Gasparre. **GPS**: n43,80098 e12,42886.

4 free ChWC free.
Surface: metalled. 01/01-31/12.
Distance: 1km on the spot Pizzeria.
Remarks: Along Aspa river.

Tourist information Macerata Feltria:
Week market. Tue.

Marina di Montemarciano 34D1

Lungomare Alfredo Cappellini. **GPS**: n43,65936 e13,32780.

40 € 0,70/h Ch (32x)€2.
Location: Simple, noisy. **Surface:** grassy. 15/05-15/09.
Distance: 4km 9km 50m pebbled beach 100m.
Remarks: To coast road and railwayline.

Marotta 34D1

Area di Sosta Marotta, Lungomare Colombo 157, Mondolfo.
GPS: n43,76067 e13,15312.

80 € 6,50-14 Ch (80x)€2/24h WC included, cold.
Location: Simple. **Surface:** grassy. 01/04-30/09.
Distance: 500m 1,5km 50m on the spot.
Remarks: Between coast road and railwayline.

Matelica 34D1

Porte Capamante, Via Circonvallazione. **GPS**: n43,25917 e13,01083.

6-8 free free. **Location:** Simple. **Surface:** asphalted.
01/01-31/12.
Distance: 200m 200m 200m.

Matelica 34D1

Country House Salomone, Località Salomone 437.
GPS: n43,29635 e13,00031.

40 € 7, free with a meal (16x)included WCatrestaurant.
Location: Rural, simple.
Surface: grassy/gravel. 01/01-31/12.
Distance: on the spot.
Remarks: Beautiful view.

Mergo 34D1

Area Sosta Comunale, Via Colli. **GPS**: n43,47394 e13,03598.

10 free Chfree (8x).
Location: Simple. **Surface:** concrete. 01/01-31/12.
Distance: 300m.
Remarks: Nearby sports park.

Mondavio 34D1

Via Cappuccini. **GPS**: n43,67744 e12,96165.
10 free Ch free. **Surface:** asphalted. 01/01-31/12.
Distance: 500m 700m.
Remarks: Nearby police station.

Tourist information Mondavio:
Week market. Mo.

Montalto delle Marche 34E2

Via Cuprense. **GPS**: n42,98726 e13,60870.

6 free free. **Surface:** metalled. 01/01-31/12.
Distance: 100m.

Monte San Giusto 34D1

Campo Sportivo, Via Magellano, Villa San Filippo.
GPS: n43,26343 e13,60070.

IT

20 free Chfree. **Surface:** asphalted. 01/01-31/12.
Distance: 1km.
Remarks: Outlet center leather and shoes.

Monte Vidon Corrado 34D1

Viale Trento e Trieste. **GPS:** n43,12205 e13,48381.

4 free Chfree. **Surface:** metalled. 01/01-31/12.
Distance: 200m 200m.

Montecosaro 34E1

Via Martiri della Libertà Ungherese. **GPS:** n43,31779 e13,63653.

30 free Chfree. **Surface:** concrete. 01/01-31/12.
Distance: 100m 100m 100m 50m.

Montefiore dell'Aso 34E1

Piazza Pietro Nenni. **GPS:** n43,04992 e13,75021.

10 free Chfree. **Surface:** sand. 01/01-31/12.
Distance: 200m.

Montefiore dell'Aso 34E1

Agricamper Il Poggio del Belvedere, Contrada Aso no. 11.
GPS: n43,04611 e13,72500.

6 € 8/pp Ch WC included. **Surface:** metalled.
01/01-31/12.

Montelupone 34D1

Loc. San Firmano. **GPS:** n43,36383 e13,54950.

20 free free. **Location:** Simple. **Surface:** asphalted.
Distance: 500m.
Remarks: Parking sports park.

Montelupone 34D1

Via Allesandro Manzoni. **GPS:** n43,34300 e13,57080.

10 free free. **Location:** Simple. **Surface:** asphalted.
01/01-31/12.
Remarks: Parking city park.

Morro d'Alba 34D1

Area Comunale, Via degli Orti. **GPS:** n43,60198 e13,21263.

30 free free.
Location: Simple, quiet.
Surface: asphalted. 01/01-31/12.
Distance: 500m.
Remarks: Access with electronic card, Bar Pro Loco or town hall.

Offida 34E2

Via Tommaso Castelli. **GPS:** n42,93689 e13,69180.

3 free free. **Surface:** unpaved. 01/01-31/12.
Remarks: At the city walls.

Pedaso 34E1

Via Martiri della Libertà. **GPS:** n43,09985 e13,84272.
free. **Surface:** asphalted. 01/01-31/12.
Distance: on the spot on the spot 150m.
Remarks: Parking at the beach.

Pesaro 26H3

Via dell Aquedotto. **GPS:** n43,90842 e12,90097.

12 free Chfree (12x)€1. **Surface:** asphalted.
Distance: 1km 7,5km.

Pesaro 26H3

Waterfront Parking, Via Calata Caio Duilio.
GPS: n43,92244 e12,90657.
20 € 12. 01/01-31/12.
Distance: on the spot.
Tourist information Pesaro:
Week market. Tue.

Petritoli 34E1

Impianti Sportivi. GPS: n43,07306 e13,65139.

10 free Chfree. **Surface:** sand. 01/01-31/12.
Distance: 1km.
Remarks: At sports park.

Piandimeleto 34C1

Via Giacomo Leopardi. **GPS:** n43,72541 e12,41328.

9 free Chfree. **Surface:** grassy. 01/01-31/12.
Distance: 100m.

Pietrarubbia 34C1

Vulcangas, Via Montefeltresca 107, Ponte Cappuccini.
GPS: n43,80278 e12,36667.

2 free WCfree. **Surface:** metalled. 01/01-31/12.
Distance: 200m.

Pievebovigliana 34D2

Via Rancia. **GPS:** n43,06583 e13,08526.

10 free Ch . **Surface:** asphalted. 01/01-31/12.
Distance: 300m.

Pioraco 34D1

Loc. Buchetto, SS361 km77. **GPS:** n43,18010 e12,97422.

18 (+20) € 13 (16x)WC included. **Location:** Rural,

comfortable, quiet. **Surface:** gravel. 01/01-31/12.
Distance: 700m on the spot summer on the spot.

Pollenza — 34D1

Contrada Morazzano. **GPS:** n43,26482 e13,34614.

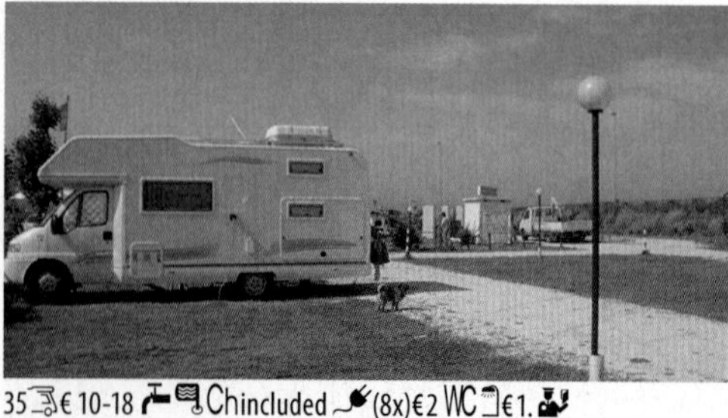

8 free free. **Location:** Simple. **Surface:** asphalted. 01/01-31/12.
Distance: 500m.
Remarks: Nearby elevator to centre, max. 48h.

Porto Recanati — 34E1

Area sosta camper Porto Recanati, Viale Scarfiotti, loc. Scossicci.
GPS: n43,44605 e13,65639.

35 € 10-18 Ch included (8x)€2 WC €1.
Location: Simple. **Surface:** grassy. 01/01-31/12.
Distance: 500m 3km 50m 200m 1km.
Remarks: Max. 72h, video surveillance, dogs beach.

Porto Recanati — 34E1

Karting Club Pista del Conero, Viale Scarfiotti, loc. Scossicci.
GPS: n43,47067 e13,64246.

80 € 25/24h Ch (80x)WC included €1 free.
Location: Simple, noisy. **Surface:** gravel. 01/04-30/09.
Distance: 100m 200m.

Porto Recanati — 34E1

Campeggio Club Adriatico, Via Scossicci, Scossicci.
GPS: n43,46393 e13,64642.
€ 17-30 Ch WC included. **Surface:** grassy.
09/04-29/09.
Distance: on the spot on the spot on the spot on the spot.

Porto San Giorgio — 34E1

La Perla Adriatico, Via San Martino 13. **GPS:** n43,16400 e13,80836.
75 € 15/20 Ch WC included, cold .
Surface: unpaved. 01/04-30/09.
Distance: beach 200m 300m.
Remarks: Shuttle bus.

Potenza Picena — 34E1

Via Togliatti, Porto Potenza Picena. **GPS:** n43,36167 e13,69306.

45 € 7/24h, € 10/48h, € 15/72h Ch included (12x)€2.
Surface: asphalted. 01/01-31/12.
Distance: 200m 600m 200m 200m.
Remarks: Thursday market.

Recanati — 34D1

Camperclub Recanati, Viale Giovanni XXIII.
GPS: n43,40245 e13,55777.

25 free (22x)free. **Location:** Urban, simple.
Surface: asphalted. 01/01-31/12.
Distance: 500m.

San Benedetto del Tronto — 34E2

Sosta Camper 43° Parallelo, Via Domenico Bruni.
GPS: n42,96677 e13,87670.
40 € 15 Ch €3 . **Surface:** asphalted.
Distance: on the spot sandy beach 100m 80m.

San Benedetto del Tronto — 34E2

Viale dello Sport. **GPS:** n42,92312 e13,89527.

70 € 7, Jul/Aug € 10 Ch included €2. **Surface:** asphalted.
Distance: 4,3km 500m on the spot.
Remarks: Along railwayline, under viaduct.

San Ginesio — 34D1

Via Ciarlatini. **GPS:** n43,10945 e13,31801.

8 free. **Surface:** gravel. 01/01-31/12.
Distance: 200m 200m 200m 1km.

San Leo — 34C1

Via Michele Rosa. **GPS:** n43,89871 e12,34950.

20 free Ch free.
Surface: asphalted. 01/01-31/12 festivities.
Distance: 500m on the spot.

San Severino Marche — 34D1

P7, Viale Mazzini. **GPS:** n43,22757 e13,18836.

12 free free (12x)€0,50/4h. **Location:** Simple, quiet.
Surface: asphalted. 01/01-31/12.
Distance: 800m.
Remarks: Parking sports park.

Sant'Agata Feltria — 34C1

Piazzale Europa. **GPS:** n43,86386 e12,20549.

40 € 8/24h (6x)free. **Surface:** asphalted.
Distance: 100m.

Sarnano — 34D2

Via Corridoni. **GPS:** n43,03444 e13,29972.

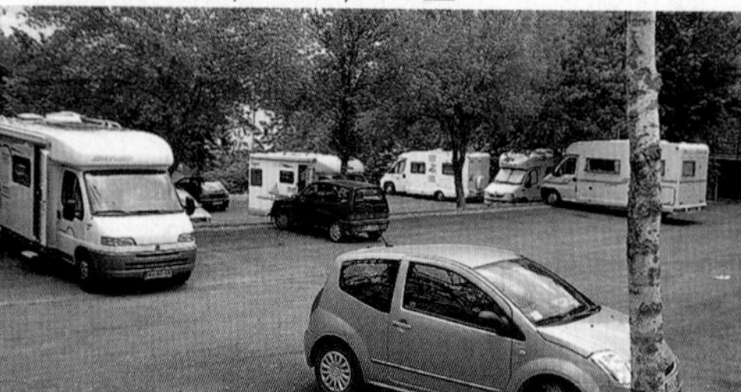

15 free ChWC free. **Surface:** asphalted. 01/01-31/12.
Distance: 100m 100m 100m.

Sassoferrato — 34D1

Via Raffaello Sanzio. **GPS:** n43,43122 e12,85471.

7 free free (6x)€1/day. **Location:** Simple.
Surface: asphalted. 01/01-31/12.
Distance: 500m.

Senigallia — 34D1

Via F. Podesti 234, SS16, Senigallia-sud. **GPS:** n43,70483 e13,23764.

14 € 10 free.
Location: Simple, noisy. **Surface:** asphalted. 01/01-31/12.
Distance: 3km 3,3km 150m.
Remarks: Along busy road, next to petrol station, max. 48h.

Tolentino — 34D1

Viale Foro Boario. **GPS:** n43,20773 e13,28784.

15 free free. **Surface:** asphalted.
01/01-31/12.
Distance: 200m 200m.

IT

S Urbania 34C1

Area camper Barco, Loc. Barco Ducale Colonia.
GPS: n43,67916 e12,51277.
65 free Ch free.
Location: Rural. **Surface:** gravel/sand.
Distance: 1km.
Remarks: Biking trail, behind former summer residence of dukes of Urbania.

S Urbania 34C1

Piazzale Fosso del Maltempo, Viale Michelangelo.
GPS: n43,66482 e12,52191.

50 free Ch free. **Surface:** asphalted. 01/01-31/12.
Distance: 500m.

Tourist information Urbania:
Week market. Thu.

S Urbino 34C1

Via Pablo Neruda. **GPS**: n43,73333 e12,62722.

10 free Ch free. **Surface:** asphalted. 01/01-31/12.
Distance: historical centre 2,5km.
Remarks: Shuttle bus to city centre.

S Urbino 34C1

Corte della Miniera, Via Miniera, 10. **GPS**: n43,78336 e12,59091.
5 guests free Ch.
Distance: Urbino 11km on the spot.

Tourist information Urbino:
Week market. Sa.

S Urbisaglia 34D1

Abbadia di Fiastra, P4. **GPS**: n43,22111 e13,40722.

20 free Ch free. **Surface:** metalled.
01/01-31/12.
Distance: 4km 50m.
Remarks: Parking monastery, archaeological park Urbs Salvia 3km, hiking area.

S Visso 34D2

Largo Gregorio XIII. **GPS**: n42,93139 e13,09141.

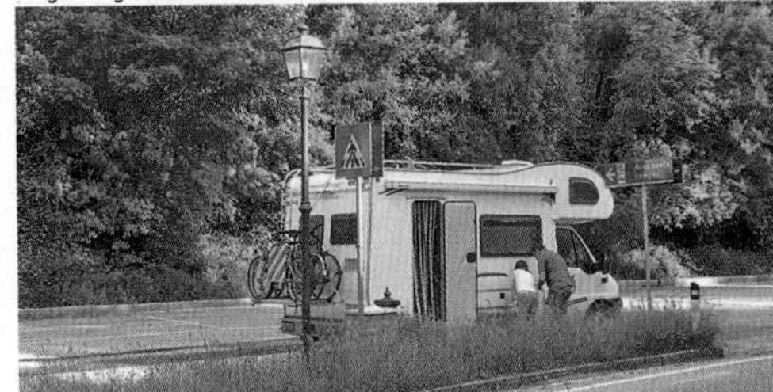

15 free Ch free €0,80/h. **Surface:** asphalted.
Distance: 800m.

Lazio

S Acquapendente 34C2

Agriturismo Buonomore, SS Cassia Km 130.
GPS: n42,73367 e11,88361.

8 € 15-20, Aug € 25 Ch WC included. **Location:** Rural, simple, quiet. **Surface:** grassy/gravel.
01/01-31/12.
Distance: 3km on the spot.
Remarks: Swimming pool incl.

S Acquapendente 34C2

Via Campo Boario. **GPS**: n42,74203 e11,86240.

20 free Ch free. **Location:** Urban.
Surface: asphalted/metalled. 01/01-31/12.
Distance: 250m 250m.
Remarks: At sports park.

S Albano Laziale 34D3

Piazza Guerucci, Via Riccardo Lombardi. **GPS**: n41,73206 e12,65213.

8 free Ch free. **Location:** Simple, noisy.
Surface: asphalted.
Distance: 1km train > Rome 55min.
Remarks: Next to post office and sports park.

S Amatrice 34D2

AgriCamper Amatrice, Località Retrosi. **GPS**: n42,62349 e13,31788.
20 € 10 Ch included. **Location:** Isolated. **Surface:** gravel.
01/01-31/12.
Remarks: Located in national nature reserve Gran Sasso.

S Bolsena 34C2

Guadetto, Via della Chiusa. **GPS**: n42,63604 e11,98695.

60 € 15/24h Ch included WC. **Location:** Rural.
Surface: grassy/sand. 01/01-31/12.
Distance: 1km 10m 300m 1,5km on the spot on the spot.
Remarks: Bread-service, tuesday market.

Bolsena 34C2

Via Santa Maria. **GPS**: n42,63898 e11,98562.

50 € 5/12h, € 10/24h. **Location:** Urban, simple.
Surface: asphalted. 01/01-31/12.
Distance: 800m 100m on the spot 400m 400m 100m on the spot on the spot.

S Bolsena 34C2

Agricampeggio Le Calle, Via Cassia km 111,200.
GPS: n42,63029 e11,99716.
€ 15-19, 2 pers.incl Ch WC included. 01/04-01/11.
Distance: 1km on the spot.

Tourist information Bolsena:
Citadel and ramparts.

S Bracciano 34C3

Le Mimose, Via del Lago 25. **GPS**: n42,10856 e12,17893.

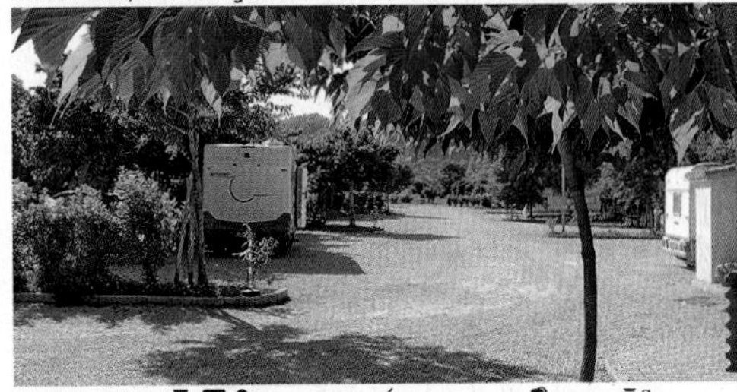

50 € 14/24h Ch included (40x)€3/24h €0,50.
Location: Rural, comfortable, quiet.
Surface: gravel. 01/01-31/12.
Distance: 800m Lago di Bracciano 250m 150m 800m 200m.

S Capodimonte 34C2

Temporanea. **GPS**: n42,55979 e11,88714.

50 € 10/24h €3 Ch. **Location:** Urban, simple, quiet.
Surface: grassy. 01/01-31/12.
Distance: 2km on the spot.
Remarks: At lake Bolsena, check in at bar.

S Cassino 35B1

Parking Europa, Via Agnone 5. **GPS**: n41,48289 e13,83750.

20 € 13,50-16,50, 2 pers.incl Service €2,50 Ch €3 WC €1 €4/day. **Location:** Rural, luxurious, quiet.
Surface: grassy/gravel. 01/01-31/12.
Distance: 800m 4km 1km 1km 1,5km.
Remarks: Service passerby € 7.

S Castel di Tora 34D3

Via Turano, SP34. **GPS**: n42,21362 e12,96888.
15 € 15/24h Ch WC included. **Surface:** gravel.
01/01-31/12.
Distance: 1km on the spot 250m.
Remarks: At Turano lake.

IT

Castel Gandolfo 34D3

Parcheggio Bus Lago Albano, Via Spiaggia del Lago.
GPS: n41,75797 e12,65359.

17 € 10/24h.
Location: Rural, simple, noisy. **Surface:** metalled. 01/01-31/12.
Distance: on the spot on the spot 800m > Rome.
Remarks: At lake Albano.

Ciampino 34D3

Il Sassone, Via Doganale 1. **GPS**: n41,78507 e12,62640.

70 € 12/24h Ch €2/24h included.
Location: Rural, comfortable, quiet.
Surface: grassy. 01/01-31/12.
Distance: 3km 1,5km 1,5km 50m.

Civita Castellana 34C3

Via Terni. **GPS**: n42,29905 e12,41520.

+50 free. **Location:** Simple.
Surface: asphalted. 01/01-31/12.
Distance: 500m 50m.
Remarks: At cemetery.

Tourist information Civita Castellana:
Palazzo Farnese, Caprarola. Pentagonal country house, accessed by winding staircase.

Colle di Tora 34D3

Via Maria Letizia Giuliani. **GPS**: n42,20898 e12,94915.

25 € 10/24h Ch WCincluded.
Location: Rural, simple, quiet. **Surface:** gravel. 01/01-31/12.
Distance: on the spot on the spot on the spot.
Remarks: At Turano lake, pay at restaurant.

Colleferro 34D3

Viale Europa. **GPS**: n41,72540 e13,00989.
free Chfree.
Distance: 5km train > Rome.
Remarks: Next to swimming pool.

Tourist information Colleferro:
Anagni. Region with number of old settlements.

Farfa in Sabina 34D3

Abbazia di Santa Maria, SP41A. **GPS**: n42,22166 e12,71603.

20 free Chfree.
Location: Rural, simple, isolated. **Surface:** gravel. 01/01-31/12.
Distance: 4,7km.

Gaeta 35B1

Playa Colorada, Località S.Agostino, SS 213, Sperlonga>Gaeta.
GPS: n41,22812 e13,50281.

60 € 25-30, 2 pers.incl Ch WCincluded €1 €0,50/h.
Location: Rural, comfortable, central. **Surface:** gravel.
01/04-30/09.
Distance: 50m bar/restaurant 200m.
Remarks: Shuttle to Gaeta, market Wednesday.

Gaeta 35B1

Sosta Camper Internationale, Via Flacca km 20.500.
GPS: n41,23598 e13,49045.

30 € 20-25 Ch WCincluded €1. **Surface:** gravel.
Distance: on the spot on the spot.
Remarks: Monitored parking.

Gaeta 35B1

Copacabana Beach, Via flacca Km 20.350, S.agostino Gaeta.
GPS: n41,23743 e13,48781.

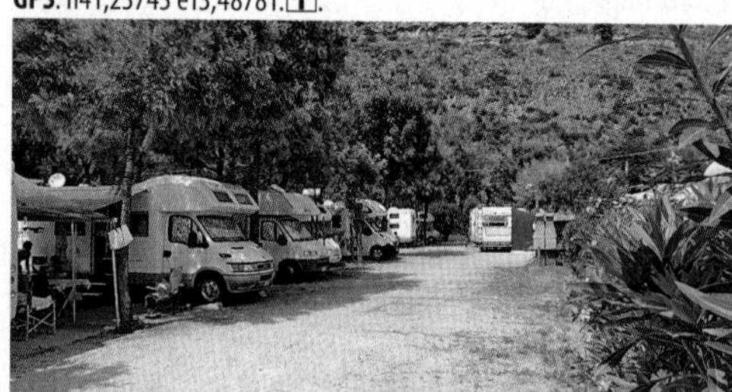

18 € 25-30, 4 pers.incl €0,50 Ch WC €0,50 €1.
Location: Rural, simple.
Surface: gravel/sand. 01/04-30/09.
Distance: 6km on the spot on the spot.
Remarks: Shuttle to Gaeta.

Gradoli 34C2

Parcheggio camper San Magno, Strada di Gradoli, SP114 km 6+137.
GPS: n42,59925 e11,86547.

50 € 15 Ch included. **Location:** Comfortable, isolated, quiet. **Surface:** grassy. 01/01-31/12.
Distance: 7km on the spot 500m.
Remarks: At lake Bolsena, discount longer stays.

Latina 35A1

Area Camper Alta Marea, Strada Lungomare 3253, SP39, Loc. Foce Verde. **GPS**: n41,41043 e12,86008.

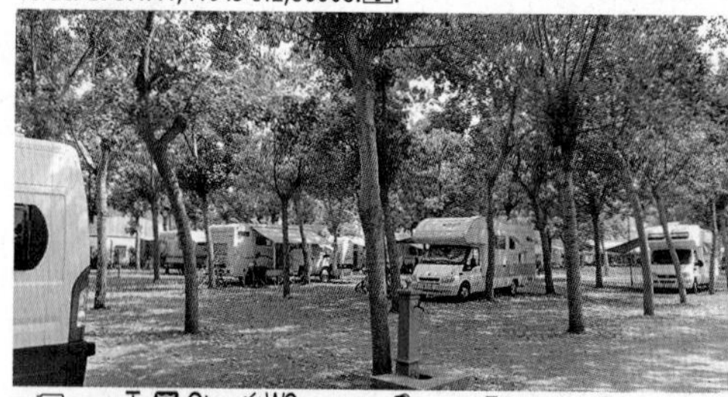

91 € 15 Ch WCincluded €0,50.
Location: Rural, comfortable, quiet.
Surface: grassy. 01/04-30/09.
Distance: on the spot 50m on the spot 200m.

Latina 35A1

Museo di Piana delle Orme, Strada Migliara 43 Mezza.
GPS: n41,44452 e12,98479.

25 free Ch. **Location:** Rural, simple, quiet. **Surface:** gravel.
01/01-31/12.
Distance: Latina 10km 2km.
Remarks: At museum.

Leonessa 34D2

GPS: n42,56436 e12,96172.

50 free Ch. **Surface:** asphalted. Market day.
Distance: 500m 500m 500m 300m.

Lubriano 34C2

Parco Paime, Piazza Palme. **GPS**: n42,63500 e12,10512.

17 € 5/24h Ch (36x)WC included.
Location: Comfortable, quiet.
Surface: grasstiles. 01/01-31/12.
Distance: 1km on the spot.
Remarks: Nights closed with barrier.

Lunghezza 34D3

Camper Club Antichi Casali, Via Lunghezzina 302/a.
GPS: n41,93039 e12,70454.

40 € 15/24h Ch WC included.
Location: Rural, comfortable, isolated, quiet. **Surface:** gravel.
01/01-31/12.
Distance: 3km 5km Rome 20min.
Remarks: Monitored parking 24/24, shuttle bus.

S Lunghezza 34D3

Camper Club Mira Lago Roma, Via Lunghezzina 75.
GPS: n41,93159 e12,67642.

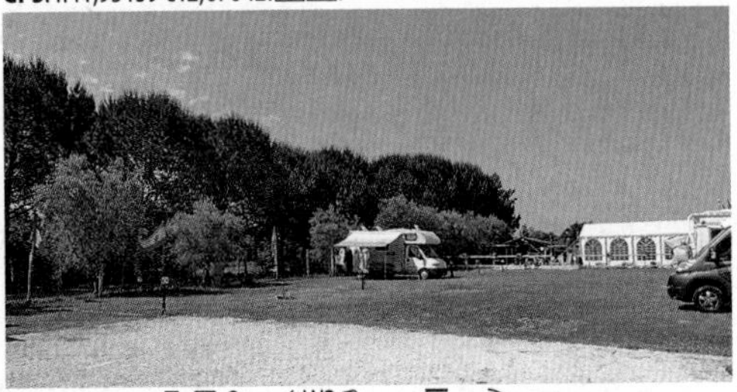

60 € 18/24h Ch WC €0,50 €4 included.
Location: Rural, comfortable, isolated, quiet. **Surface:** grassy.
01/01-31/12.
Distance: 700m on the spot on the spot on the spot on the spot on the spot.
Remarks: At 2 small lakes, service passerby € 5.

S Montalto di Castro 34C3

Via Arbea, Marina di Montalto di Castro.
GPS: n42,32981 e11,57699.

50 € 7,50/day, overnight stay free Chfree. **Location:** Rural, simple, quiet. **Surface:** grassy/gravel. 01/01-31/12.
Distance: 250m 200m 200m 200m.
Remarks: Shady, thursday market.

S Montalto di Castro 34C3

Via Torre Marina, Marina di Montalto di Castro.
GPS: n42,32137 e11,59015.

64 free, 01/06-15/09 8-20h € 7,50 Chincluded.
Location: Rural, simple. **Surface:** gravel. 01/01-31/12.
Distance: 500m 200m 400m 300m.

S Montefiascone 34C2

Cantina di Montefiascone, Via Grilli 2. **GPS:** n42,53346 e12,04293.

30 free Ch free. **Location:** Urban, comfortable, noisy.
Surface: metalled. 01/01-31/12.
Distance: 1km.

S Montefiascone 34C2

Agricamper Bella Cima, Strada Limitone.
GPS: n42,52241 e12,00767.

18 € 15/24h Ch included. **Surface:** gravel.
01/01-31/12.
Distance: 4km 4km 4km.
Remarks: Swimming pool.

S Nettuno 35A1

Area Sosta L'Ippocampo, Via Palestrina 9.
GPS: n41,47354 e12,68916.

50 € 15 Ch WC included.
Location: Rural, simple, quiet. **Surface:** gravel. 01/01-31/12.
Distance: 3km 3km.

S Oriolo Romano 34C3

Viale degli Artigiani. **GPS:** n42,16699 e12,13902.

3 free free. **Location:** Simple. **Surface:** asphalted.
01/01-31/12.
Distance: 850m on the spot station 600m Roma-Viterbo.

S Pescia Romana 34B3

Area La Pineta, Loc. Marina di Pescia Romana.
GPS: n42,36552 e11,49389.

50 € 10-22 Chincluded €3 €1. **Location:** Rural, comfortable, quiet. **Surface:** grassy. Easter-30/09.
Distance: Pescia Romana 5km 100m 100m.
Remarks: Bread-service, monday market.

S Rieti 34D2

Via Fonte Cottorella. **GPS:** n42,39548 e12,86463.

10 free . **Surface:** asphalted. 01/01-31/12.
Distance: historical center 100m.

S Roma 34D3

Area Attrezzata per Camper LGP Roma, Via Casilina 700, Rome (Roma). **GPS:** n41,87595 e12,55515.

200 € 15/<8m, € 22/8><10m, € 30/10><15m + tourist tax € 2/pp Ch included against payment € 1/h
Location: Urban, luxurious, central, quiet.
Surface: grassy.
01/01-31/12.
Distance: 100m 100m bus service to city centre day and night.
Remarks: Accessory shop, trailer/additonal car € 15 on separate parking € 7, repairs. Exit 18 ring road (G.R.A.), follow Roma centro, ± 4km dir centre, company is on the left side of the road, turning after 2nd lights.

S Roma 34D3

Prato Smeraldo, Via Ardeatina/Via di Tor Pagnotta 424, Rome (Roma).
GPS: n41,80970 e12,52857.

16 € 14 Ch €2/24h included.
Location: Motorway, simple, noisy. **Surface:** grassy/metalled.
01/01-31/12, 24/24h.
Distance: on the spot on the spot on the spot.
Remarks: Service passerby € 5. Exit 25 ring road (G.R.A.), second light to the right, Via di Tor Pagnotta.

S Roma 34D3

Le Terrazze, Via di Fioranello 170, Rome (Roma).
GPS: n41,79250 e12,54083.

40 € 20, max. 4 pers.incl Ch (40x)included.
Location: Simple, quiet. **Surface:** metalled. 01/01-31/12.
Distance: 750m 1km on the spot on the spot.
Remarks: Video surveillance, car rental, excursions. Exit 25 ring road (G.R.A.), dir Santuario Divino Amore.

S Roma 34D3

Parcheggio IAT, Air terminal Ostiense, Piazza G. da Verrazzano 9, Zone Mercati Generali, Rome (Roma). **GPS:** n41,86931 e12,48944.

IT

€ 1,50, at least € 6, € 27/24h Ch included €3,65/24h.
Location: Urban, simple, central, noisy. **Surface:** asphalted.
01/01-31/12.
Distance: metro 1km.
Remarks: Motorhome and Coach Parking.

Roma 34D3

Area Sosta Camper Park Colombo, Via C. Colombo 170, Rome (Roma).
GPS: n41,86236 e12,49713.
€ 20 Ch Service € 5. 01/01-31/12.
Distance: 100m.
Remarks: Monitored parking 24/24.

Tourist information Rome (Roma):

Città del Vaticano. Domicile of the pope. Independent state since 1929.

A.P.T. (Azienda di Promozione Turistica), Via Parigi, 11. Capital of the country, a lot of curiosities in the old town centre. Roma Archeologica Card: 7-days ticket € 27,50, free entrance to Roman National Museum, Colosseum, Palatine, Baths of Caracalla, Tomb of Cecilia Metella and Villa of the Quintili.

Piazza del Campidoglio.

Palatino, Via di S. Gregorio, 30. Archeological site. 9h-sunset. € 16, incl. Colosseum.

Subiaco.

Musei Vaticani, Città del Vaticano. Paintings and art objects.

Basilica di San Pietro. Basilica with Sistine Chapel.

Colosseo, Piazza del Colosseo. Colosseum, anfiteatro, the most important monument of ancient Rome. 9h-sunset. € 12, entrance Palatine Hill incl.

Forum Romanum, Via dei Fori Imperiali. Novel Forum, the political, economic, and religious centre of ancient Rome. 9h-sunset.

Pantheon, Piazza della Rotonda. Church of Santa Maria ad Martyres. 9-19.30h, Su 9-18h, holidays 9-13h, Mass Sa 17, Su 10.30h, 16.30h. free.

Città del Vaticano. Pope blesses the mob for the window of the library. Su 12h.

Piazza di Spagna.

San Felice Circeo 35B1

Circeo Camper, Viale Europa 1. **GPS**: n41,24095 e13,10426.

50 € 23-33, 4 pers. incl Ch €3/24h WC €1 €7 included.
Location: Rural, luxurious, central. **Surface:** grassy. 01/04-20/09.
Distance: 100m 10m 10m 100m 100m.

San Felice Circeo 35B1

CirceMed, Via Molella 2/A. **GPS**: n41,25684 e13,12089.

60 € 18-27 Ch (50x) WC €1 €1 €3 included.
Location: Rural, comfortable, quiet. **Surface:** grassy. 01/04-30/09.
Distance: 500m 200m 200m on the spot.

Tourist information San Felice Circeo:

Tue-morning.

Terracina 35B1

Via Amerigo Vespucci. **GPS**: n41,28528 e13,25450.

20 € 12. **Location:** Urban, simple. **Surface:** asphalted.
Distance: on the spot 100m on the spot 200m 300m.

Tivoli 34D3

Via Aquaregna. **GPS**: n41,95841 e12,80465.

30 free Ch. **Location:** Urban, simple, central, quiet.
Surface: asphalted. 01/01-31/12 Wed, market.
Distance: 400m.
Remarks: Along the Aniene river.

Tourist information Tivoli:

Villa d'Este. Country house with gardens and fountains, 16th century. Villa Adriana. Roman villa.

Trevignano Romano 34C3

Blue Lake Camper, Via della Rena. **GPS**: n42,15877 e12,22411.
Ch. **Surface:** gravel.
Distance: on the spot on the spot.
Remarks: At the lake.

Tuscania 34C2

Via Nazario Sauro. **GPS**: n42,42217 e11,87520.

12 free free. **Location:** Urban, simple.
Surface: grasstiles/metalled. 01/01-31/12.
Distance: 250m 250m 250m.

Villa San Giovanni in Tuscia 34C3

Viale Europa. **GPS**: n42,28160 e12,05282.

free. **Location:** Rural, simple, quiet. **Surface:** asphalted.
01/01-31/12.
Distance: 200m.

Viterbo 34C2

Agricampeggio Paliano, Strada Pian di Tortora.
GPS: n42,39301 e12,08601.
100 € 15, 2 pers.incl, extra pers € 5 Ch WC.
Surface: grassy.
Distance: city centre 2km.
Remarks: Video surveillance.

Viterbo 34C2

Piazza Mariano Romiti, loc. Belcolle. **GPS**: n42,40897 e12,11049.

50 free free. **Location:** Urban, simple. **Surface:** asphalted.
01/01-31/12.
Distance: Lazise centre 300m on the spot.
Remarks: At station.

Viterbo 34C2

Bed&breakfast Axia, Strada Procoio 2/C.
GPS: n42,41157 e12,05061.

5 € 18 Ch €3 included. **Location:** Rural.
Surface: grassy. 01/01-31/12.
Distance: Viterbo 4km.
Remarks: 10% discount at entrance Terme dei Papi (900m), bus to Viterbo € 5.

Viterbo 34C2

Agriturismo Monteparadiso, Loc. Monterazzano.
GPS: n42,44161 e12,03062.

5 guests free. **Location:** Simple, isolated. **Surface:** gravel.
01/01-31/12.
Distance: 7km.
Remarks: Near Termale Bullicame and Terme dei Papi.

Viterbo 34C2

Terme dei Papi, Strada Montarone. **GPS**: n42,41487 e12,06351.

100 guests free. **Surface:** grassy/gravel. 01/01-31/12.
Distance: 3km.
Remarks: At Terme dei Papi.

Vitorchiano 34C2

SP23 Via della Teverina. **GPS**: n42,47152 e12,17212.

10 free Ch. **Surface:** asphalted. 01/01-31/12.
Distance: 500m.

Umbria

Amelia 34C2

Piazzale del Mercato, Via Rimembranze.
GPS: n42,55200 e12,41880.
10 free Ch free. **Surface:** asphalted. 01/01-31/12 Mo-morning (market).
Distance: 50m 50m 50m.

Assisi 34C2

Via Giosuè Borsi, loc. Santa Maria degli Angeli.
GPS: n43,05972 e12,58747.

€ 18/24h, € 1,80/h Ch. **Surface:** asphalted.
01/01-31/12.
Distance: 2km bus >Assisi 20min (retour € 1,80).

Assisi 34C2

Area San Vittorino, Via San vittorino. **GPS**: n43,07848 e12,60229.

30 € 14/24h, € 2/h. **Surface:** asphalted. 01/01-31/12.
Distance: 500m.
Remarks: Convento di San Francesco 1km.

Assisi 34C2

Viale Vittorio Emanuele II/SS147. **GPS**: n43,06864 e12,61420.

10 € 20/24h. **Surface:** gravel. 01/01-31/12.
Distance: city centre 100m.

Bevagna 34D2

Piazza dell'Accoglienza, Via Raggiolo. **GPS**: n42,93417 e12,60639.

50 free Ch WC free. **Surface:** gravel.
Distance: 100m 100m 100m.

Borghetto 34C1

Via Pontile. **GPS**: n43,18415 e12,02372.

4 free free. **Surface:** asphalted. 01/01-31/12.
Distance: 150m 100m.
Remarks: At lake Trasimeno.

Cannara 34C2

Via Giaime Pintor, Loc. Casone. **GPS**: n42,99272 e12,57840.

20 free Ch free. **Surface:** asphalted.
Distance: 300m 300m on the spot.
Remarks: At sports park XXV Aprile, cycle routes.

Tourist information Cannara:
Assisi. Historical city.

Cascia 34D2

Piazzale Papa Leone XIII, Via della Molinella.
GPS: n42,71968 e13,01605.

14 € 8/24h Ch included (8x)€0,50/2h.
Surface: asphalted. 01/01-31/12 Service: winter.
Distance: 300m 300m 300m 100m 100m.
Remarks: Escalator to city centre.

Cascia 34D2

SS Discascia. **GPS**: n42,72139 e13,01778.
20 free . **Surface:** gravel. 01/01-31/12.
Distance: 1km.
Remarks: Next to petrol station.

Castelluccio di Norcia 34D2

Pian Grande. **GPS**: n42,80045 e13,18947.

free. **Surface:** grassy. 01/01-31/12.
Distance: Castelluccio 5km.
Remarks: Parco Nazionale dei Monti Sibilini.

Castiglione del Lago 34C2

Viale Divisione Partigiani Garibaldi. **GPS**: n43,12389 e12,05054.

free, summer € 12 Ch included. **Surface:** asphalted/sand.
01/01-31/12.
Distance: 800m on the spot.
Remarks: At lake Trasimeno.

Città di Castello 34C1

Piazzale E. Ferri, Viale Nazario Sauro. **GPS**: n43,45892 e12,23465.
free €0,10/10liter Ch. **Location:** Urban. **Surface:** asphalted.
01/01-31/12.
Distance: 300m 1,5km.
Remarks: Escalator to city centre.

Città di Castello 34C1

La Fontana del Boschetto, Via Aretina 38. **GPS**: n43,45737 e12,22882.
20 € 12 Ch .
Distance: 2km on the spot.
Remarks: Free shuttle.

Ferentillo 34D2

Loc. Precetto. **GPS**: n42,61802 e12,79347.
5 free .
Surface: asphalted.
Distance: 200m.

Ficulle 34C2

Parco Cittadino, Via Orvieto SR 71. **GPS**: n42,83044 e12,06828.

25 free Ch free. **Surface:** gravel.
Distance: 500m 10km 1km 500m.

Gualdo Cattaneo 34C2

Parco Acquarossa, Via Bonifacio 6. **GPS**: n42,89168 e12,53591.
€ 5 Ch WC included. **Location:** Rural.
Surface: gravel.
Distance: on the spot on the spot.
Remarks: Excursions, regional products.

Gualdo Tadino 34D1

Piazza Federico II di Svevia. **GPS**: n43,23143 e12,78062.
free Ch free. **Surface:** asphalted. Thu (market).

Gualdo Tadino 34D1

Via Perugia. **GPS**: n43,23756 e12,77235.
100 free free.
Distance: 400m 20m.
Remarks: Nearby stadium.

Gubbio 34C1

Camperclub Gubbio, Via del Bottagnone.
GPS: n43,35000 e12,56389.

80 free, 20-8h € 5 Ch free (8x)€1/h.
Surface: asphalted. 01/01-31/12.
Distance: historical centre 1,5km 100m 200m.
Remarks: Teatro Romano 500m.

Monte Castello di Vibio 34C2

Via Bartolomeo Jacopo della Rovere. **GPS**: n42,84168 e12,35055.

IT

10 free Chfree. **Surface:** gravel. 01/01-31/12.
Distance: 350m 50m.

S Montefalco 34D2
Viale delle Vittoria. **GPS:** n42,89230 e12,64791.

15 free Ch €1/h WC. **Surface:** grasstiles.
Distance: 100m.

S Montone 34C1
Via Aldo Bologni. **GPS:** n43,36346 e12,32499.
€ 10/24h Ch. **Surface:** asphalted. 01/01-31/12.
Distance: 200m 250m.
Remarks: At sports park.

S Orvieto 34C2
Area Sosta Camper Orvieto, Strada della Direttissima, Piazza delle Pace. **GPS:** n42,72562 e12,12736.

50 € 18/day Ch WC included.
Surface: metalled. 01/01-31/12.
Distance: funicular (retour € 1,60) 5 min 2,4km 50m pizzeria 50m.

Tourist information Orvieto:
U.I.A.T. (Ufficio Informazioni e di Accoglienza Turistica), Piazza Duomo, 24. City on volcanic plateau.
Del Crocifisso del Tufo. Ruins of Etruscan city.

S Panicale 34C2
Area Camper, Viale della Repubblica. **GPS:** n43,02806 e12,10222.

8 € 8/24h €0,50/180liter Ch €0,50/kWh.
Surface: grasstiles. 01/01-31/12.
Distance: 100m 100m 50m.
Remarks: Max. 72h.

S Passignano sul Trasimeno 34C1
Airone Area Camper, Lungolago Giappesi.
GPS: n43,18445 e12,14526.
€ 15 Ch WC €0,50 included. **Surface:** grassy.
01/01-31/12.
Distance: 500m beach 200m 50m.
Remarks: At lake Trasimeno.

S Passignano sul Trasimeno 34C1
Via Europa, SS75bis, km 35,8. **GPS:** n43,18509 e12,14348.

4 free €0,30/100liter Ch €0,30/h WC.
Surface: asphalted. 01/01-31/12.
Distance: 400m 100m.
Remarks: At lake Trasimeno.

S Perugia 34C2
Il Bove, Via Giovanni Ruggia. **GPS:** n43,09810 e12,38386.

50 € 5/12h, € 18/24h Ch WC.
Location: Urban. **Surface:** asphalted. 01/01-31/12.
Distance: 1,5km 500m 100m 200m on the spot.
Remarks: Parking police station.

Tourist information Perugia:
Palazzo dei Priori.
Tue.

S San Gemini 34D2
Via della Libertà. **GPS:** n42,61200 e12,54372.

16 Ch WC. **Surface:** metalled. 01/01-31/12.
Distance: 300m 100m.

S Sant'Anatolia di Narco 34D2
Purchetta, SP209. **GPS:** n42,73599 e12,83598.
8 free. 01/01-31/12.
Distance: on the spot on the spot on the spot.

S Scheggia e Pascelupo 34D1
Camper Scheggia, Via Campo Sportivo. **GPS:** n43,40007 e12,66674.
€ 12/24h Chincluded €2. **Surface:** gravel.
01/01-31/12.
Distance: 450m 500m.

S Spello 34D2
Via Centrale Umbra. **GPS:** n42,99371 e12,66730.

70 € 6/24h Ch. **Surface:** asphalted.
Distance: 500m 1,1km 500m 500m.
Remarks: Parking sports park.

S Spello 34D2
Terme Francescane Village, Via Fonte Citerna.
GPS: n43,00619 e12,62116.
30 € 13 Ch €3 WC. **Surface:** gravel. 01/01-31/12.
Distance: Spello 6km.

Spoleto 34D2
Parcheggio Ponciano, Via del Tiro a Segno.
GPS: n42,73687 e12,74212.

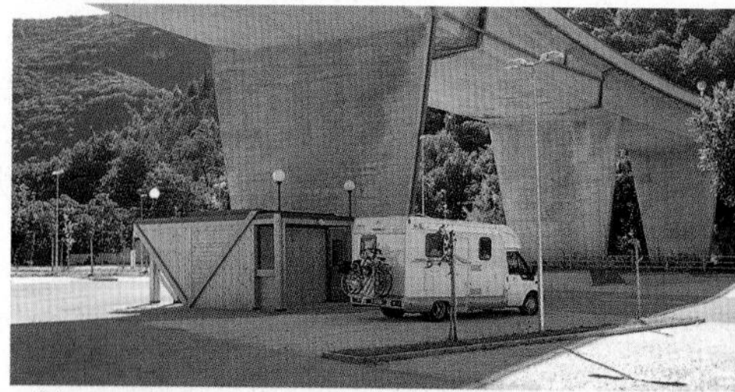

20 € 1/h, € 5/24h. **Surface:** gravel. 01/01-31/12.
Distance: 500m 500m 500m.
Remarks: Escalator to city centre.

S Spoleto 34D2
Via dei Filosofi. **GPS:** n42,74619 e12,73214.

free free. **Surface:** gravel.
Distance: 800m.

Tourist information Spoleto:
Montefalco. Village worth seeing, parking outside village, narrow streets.
Ponte delle Torri. Aqueduct, 14th century.
Tue, Fri.
Art festival. 01/06-31/07.

S Terni 34D2
Via Lombardo Radice. **GPS:** n42,56634 e12,63577.

€ 4/48h €0,50 Ch included. **Surface:** asphalted.
Distance: 50m 50m.

Terni 34D2
Piazzale Felice Fatati, SR209. **GPS:** n42,55690 e12,72006.

free. **Surface:** unpaved.
Distance: Terni 7km on the spot.
Remarks: Along river, nearby waterfalls.

S Todi 34C2
Area Porta Orvietana, Viale di Montesanto.
GPS: n42,78120 e12,40168.

16 € 15,40/24h, € 3/h Ch. **Surface:** asphalted. Sa-

IT

morning market.
Remarks: Elevator (free) to centre.

S Torgiano 34C2

Via Perugia. **GPS:** n43,02917 e12,43833.

10 free Chfree. **Surface:** asphalted. 01/01-31/12.
Distance: 200m 3,5km 200m 300m.

S Trevi 34D2

Via Costa San Paolo. **GPS:** n42,87829 e12,75221.

20 free Chfree. **Surface:** grasstiles. 01/01-31/12.
Distance: 500m 5,1km.
Remarks: At swimming pool.

Abruzzo

S Anversa degli Abruzzi 34E3

Il Sagittario, Loc. Ponte delle Fornaci. **GPS:** n41,99995 e13,80960.
10 € 12 Ch WC. **Surface:** gravel. 01/01-31/12.
Distance: 1km 1km 1km.

S Anversa degli Abruzzi 34E3

Bioagriturismo La Porta dei Parchi, Piazza Roma 3.
GPS: n42,00014 e13,79899.

4 € 10, free with a meal Ch WC included.
Surface: metalled. 01/01-31/12.
Distance: on the spot.

S Campotosto 34D2

Via Lago, SR557. **GPS:** n42,56208 e13,34805.
€ 5. **Surface:** grassy. 01/01-31/12.
Distance: Campotosto 3km on the spot.
Remarks: At lake Campotosto.

Casalbordino 34F3

Via Alessandrini. **GPS:** n42,19952 e14,61800.
20 € 5. **Surface:** grassy/sand. 01/01-31/12.
Distance: on the spot on the spot on the spot.

S Casalbordino 34F3

Area di sosta Ass Villa Sarda, Contr. Piana Sabelli.
GPS: n42,17773 e14,59994.
20 Ch WC. **Surface:** grassy. 01/01-31/12.
Distance: 1km on the spot.

S Fossacesia 34F2

Area Camper, Via Lungomare 16b. **GPS:** n42,24067 e14,52988.

24 € 10 Ch included. **Surface:** gravel/sand.
01/03-30/11.
Distance: 6,5km on the spot.
Remarks: Pebbled beach.

S Isola del Gran Sasso 34E2

S.Gabriele dell Addolorata. **GPS:** n42,51712 e13,65634.

free Ch. **Surface:** gravel/sand.
Distance: on the spot 4km on the spot on the spot.
Remarks: Nearby basilica.

S Lanciano 34E2

Area Attrezzata, Strada provinciale Lanciano-Frisa, Lancianovecchia.
GPS: n42,23385 e14,39106.

50 free ChWCfree.
Surface: asphalted. Sa-morning market.
Distance: 300m (stairs and elevator).
Remarks: At city walls, upper part of the parking, escalator to city centre.

Tourist information Lanciano:
Historical city with medieval Jewish district, Ripa Sacca.

S L'Aquila 34D2

Via porta Napoli. **GPS:** n42,34175 e13,39510.
10 free Ch. 01/01-31/12.
Distance: 700m 500m.

S L'Aquila 34D2

Via Strinella. **GPS:** n42,35323 e13,40708.

10 free Chfree. **Surface:** asphalted. 01/01-31/12.
Distance: 500m.
Remarks: In front of Hotel Federico II, adjacent Parco del Castello.

S Notaresco 34E2

Via Martiri della Libertà. **GPS:** n42,65527 e13,89578.
10 free Chfree against payment. **Surface:** asphalted.
Distance: on the spot.
Remarks: At tennis-courts.

S Ovindoli 34E3

Via Statale. **GPS:** n42,14143 e13,51740.

50 free Chfree. **Location:** Simple.
Distance: 500m 600m 2km.

S Penne 34E2

Agriturismo Il Portico, Contrada Colle Serangelo 26.
GPS: n42,45592 e13,95165.

15 € 10, free with a meal Ch (7x)€3 WC included.
Surface: grassy.

S Pescasseroli 34E3

Area Camper S.Andrea, Loc. Sant'Andrea.
GPS: n41,79888 e13,79222.

€ 15, 2 pers.incl Ch WC included.
8-13h, 14.30-20h.
Remarks: Free shuttle to centre.

Tourist information Pescasseroli:
Parco Nazionale d'Abruzzo. Nature reserve.

S Pineto 34E2

Sand stone beach, Via Tremiti, fraz. Scerne.
GPS: n42,64270 e14,04505.
ChWC. **Surface:** grassy. 01/05-31/10.
Distance: on the spot on the spot.

S Roccaraso 34E3

Park Hotel Il Poggio, SS17, C.da Poggio, 1, Loc Il Poggio.
GPS: n41,82638 e14,10111.

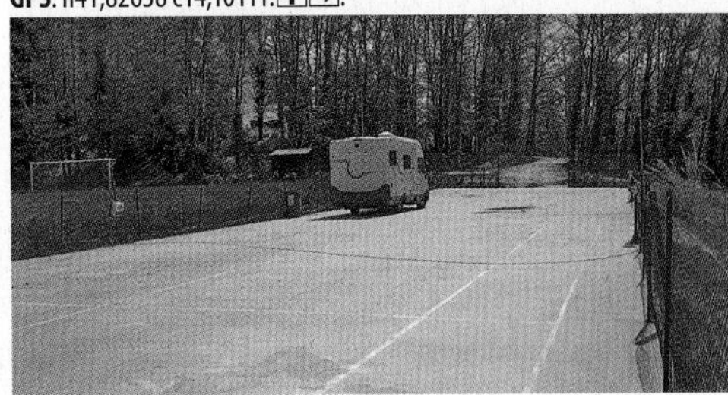

18 € 20 Ch (18x)included. 01/01-31/12.
Distance: on the spot.
Remarks: Discount longer stays, shuttle bus to ski-piste.

S Roseto degli Abruzzi 34E2

Area di Sosta Camper Romeo, Via degli Orti 13, loc. Cologna Spiaggia.
GPS: n42,72287 e13,98076.

IT

40 € 20/24h Ch (40x)WC included €1.
Surface: grassy. 01/01-31/12.
Distance: 200m 750m on the spot 100m.

Roseto degli Abruzzi 34E2

Area di sosta Isola del Sole, Piana degli Ulivi.
GPS: n42,66902 e14,01189.

11 € 20 Ch (11x)€2 WC included.
Surface: metalled. 01/01-31/12.
Distance: 3km 3km.
Remarks: Swimming pool (summer).

Roseto degli Abruzzi 34E2

Palazzo dello Sport. GPS: n42,66012 e14,02382.

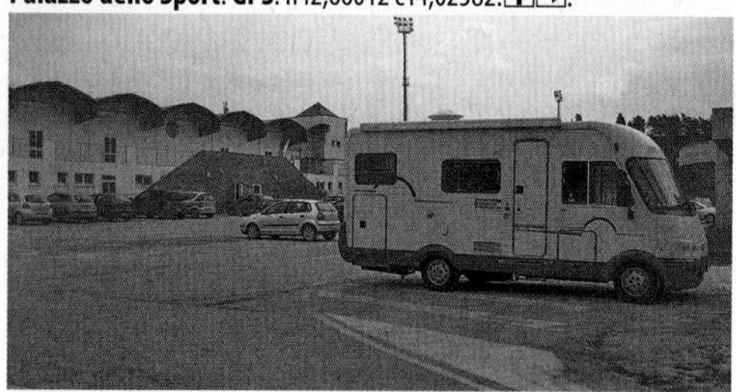

free Chfree. **Surface:** asphalted. Tue.
Distance: 200m.
Remarks: Tuesday market.

San Demetrio nei Vestini 34E3

La Grotta di Stiffe, Via del Mulino, Fraz. Stiffe.
GPS: n42,25567 e13,54811.

free €2,50 €2,50.
Surface: metalled/sand. 01/01-31/12.
Distance: l'Aquila 18km.

San Salvo Marina 34F3

Area Sosta Communale per Autocaravan.
GPS: n42,07195 e14,76289.
30 € 16/24h, € 20/48h, € 30/72h ChWC included cold shower.
Surface: grassy. 01/05-15/09.
Distance: 300m 2,2km 300m.

Santo Stefano di Sessanio 34E2

Ostello del Cavaliere, Piazza Della Giudea.
GPS: n42,34429 e13,64314.
5 guests free . **Surface:** metalled.
Distance: 300m.

Sant'Egidio alla Vibrata 34E2

Zona industriale. **GPS:** n42,81937 e13,69915.

free Chfree. **Surface:** asphalted.

Torino di Sangro 34F2

Area camper Vitale, Lido le Morgie. **GPS:** n42,20403 e14,60349.
100 € 15/24h Chincluded €2 WC €0,50.
Surface: grassy/sand.
Distance: 8km beach 70m on the spot.

Tortoreto Lido 34E2

Frontemare Easy Park, Via Napoli. **GPS:** n42,78425 e13,94966.
30 € 15 Ch included WC . **Surface:** asphalted.
01/04-01/10.
Distance: beach 200m.

Tortoreto Lido 34E2

Lungomare Sirena. **GPS:** n42,78863 e13,94989.
6 free. 01/01-31/12.
Distance: beach 100m.
Remarks: Max. 48h.

Villalago 34E3

SP82b. **GPS:** n41,92255 e13,85621.

13 free Chfree. **Surface:** asphalted.
Distance: on the spot.
Remarks: At lake Scanno, nearby beach and kosk.

Molise

Campobasso 34F3

Area di sosta Dominick Ferrante, Contrada Macchie 1.
GPS: n41,56886 e14,65118.

20 € 10/24h, € 15/48h Ch included.
Surface: gravel.
Distance: 800m.

Monteroduni 34E3

Oasi San Nazzaro. GPS: n41,53448 e14,15924.

40 € 10, free with a meal Ch (6x)included.
Surface: grassy. 01/01-31/12.
Distance: Fish lake on the spot.

Petacciato Marina 34F3

Villagio la Torre, SS16 Adriatica km535,5, Termoli ri Vasto.
GPS: n42,02432 e14,88739.

60 € 10-20 Ch (50x)included WC . **Surface:** gravel/sand.
01/01-31/12.
Distance: on the spot on the spot on the spot.
Remarks: Access via gate next to tower ruins.

Petacciato Marina 34F3

Parking spiaggia, Via del Mare, SS16. **GPS:** n42,03543 e14,85337.

40 € 6, 8-20h against payment. **Surface:** asphalted.
Distance: 9,5km 50m.
Remarks: Reserved place for motorhomes.

Petacciato Marina 34F3

Parking Tolomei, Via Marinelle, SS 16. **GPS:** n42,03219 e14,85844.
50 € 15 Ch WC .
Surface: gravel. 01/01-31/12.
Distance: Direct access.
Remarks: Shuttle bus.

Puglia

Alberobello 35D1

Parcheggio Nel Verde, Via Cadore. **GPS:** n40,78266 e17,23418.

60 € 15-18/24h, € 10/12h, € 8/6h Ch €3 included.
Surface: grassy/gravel. 01/01-31/12.
Distance: Trulli-centre 50m 50m 100m.
Remarks: No camping activities.

Tourist information Alberobello:
Centre of the Trulli-region. Trulli houses are curious houses built without motar.
Thu-morning.

Bari 35C1

Area Hobby Park Wash, Via Giovanni del Conte.
GPS: n41,11581 e16,88501.
€ 15/24h Ch . **Surface:** metalled. 01/01-31/12.
Distance: centre 500m 700m.
Remarks: Monitored parking.

Bari 35C1

Gran Parcheggio Alberotanza, Via Alberotaza, 43A.
GPS: n41,09520 e16,87868.

250 € 15 €0,50/30liter €2,50 Ch €0,50/kWh .
Surface: asphalted. 01/01-31/12.
Distance: 7,8km 500m 500m.

IT

Remarks: Monitored parking.

Brindisi — 35D1

Area Attrezzata, Strada Minnuta 6. **GPS**: n40,63517 e17,91824.

€ 10 Ch €3 WC included. **Surface:** asphalted.
01/01-31/12.
Remarks: 24/24 surveillance.

Castellana Grotte — 35D1

Area Sapori & Sapori, Via Turi. **GPS**: n40,88560 e17,15722.
10 free Ch free. **Surface:** asphalted.
Distance: 1km.
Remarks: Caves 1,8km.

Castellana Grotte — 35D1

Le Grotte di Castellana, SS32. **GPS**: n40,87543 e17,14900.

€ 5. **Surface:** grassy/gravel.
01/01-31/12.
Remarks: Parking at the caves of Castellana, overnight stay allowed.

Foggia — 34G3

Parking 92. GPS: n41,43430 e15,48063.
€ 10 Ch included.
Distance: 6km.

Gallipoli — 35D1

Area Sosta Camper Nuovi Orizzonti, Sp 221 Contrada L'Ariò.
GPS: n40,00286 e18,03374.
40 € 21, Aug € 26 Ch WC included.
Location: Comfortable, quiet. **Surface:** forest soil.
01/01-31/12.
Distance: Gallipoli 5km 1,5km.
Remarks: Free shuttle to beach.

Gallipoli — 35D1

Autopark Spiaggia D'oro San Mauro, Loc. Padula Bianca.
GPS: n40,09568 e18,01625.
50 € 20 Ch. **Location:** Quiet. 01/06-31/09.
Distance: Gallipoli 4km 100m.

Gallipoli — 35D1

CamperPark Baia Verde, Via Rosa dei Venti, Loc. Baia Verde.
GPS: n40,03375 e18,02088.
70 € 20 Ch included.
Surface: grassy. 01/06-31/09.
Distance: Gallipoli 4km 200m 200m.

Gallipoli — 35D1

Campo delle Bandiere, Loc. Padula Bianca. **GPS**: n40,09681 e18,01297.
€ 15-25 ChWC. **Surface:** sand. 01/06-01/09.
Distance: Sandy beach.

Gallipoli — 35D1

La Sosta, Via Beneficati Rossi, Loc. Padula Bianca.
GPS: n40,09454 e18,01572.
ChWC. **Surface:** sand. 01/01-31/12.
Distance: 50m on the spot.
Remarks: Video surveillance.

Gallipoli — 35D1

Via Cimitero. **GPS**: n40,05479 e17,99689.
20 € 10/24h. **Surface:** asphalted. 01/01-31/12.
Distance: centre 400m 650m 400m 200m.

Lequile — 35D1

Salento Sosta Camper, Via Preti di Campi 6. **GPS**: n40,28266 e18,13179.

18 € 15/24h Ch.
Location: Comfortable, quiet. **Surface:** gravel. 01/01-31/12.
Distance: city centre Lecce 8km.
Remarks: Bike/car rental, swimming pool, bar.

Lesina — 34F3

Oasi, Via Ludovica Ariosto. **GPS**: n41,86472 e15,35806.

15 € 12, Sept-Mar-Apr € 15, May/Aug € 18 Ch WC included. **Surface:** asphalted. 01/01-31/12.
Distance: 300m on the spot 500m.

Lucera — 34G3

Via Montello. **GPS**: n41,49987 e15,33223.

100 free. **Surface:** asphalted. 01/01-31/12.
Remarks: At station.

Lucera — 34G3

Centro sportivo Casanova, Strada Contrada Casanova.
GPS: n41,48849 e15,26008.
€ 10 Ch. **Location:** Isolated. 01/01-31/12.
Distance: Lucera 9km.

Margherita di Savoia — 39A3

Lido Baywatch, Via Barletta. **GPS**: n41,36222 e16,17361.

12 € 20, 01/06-30/09 € 25 Ch WC included.
Surface: gravel. 01/01-31/12.
Distance: 2km on the spot on the spot.

Massafra — 35D1

Area di Sosta La Stella, SS7, SS Appia km 633, Le Forche.
GPS: n40,59201 e17,09904.

20 € 10/16-12h, € 20/24h Ch (18x) WC included €1.
Surface: grassy. 01/01-31/12.
Distance: 1km 500-700m 1km.

Remarks: Beachshuttle € 2.

Mattinata — 34G3

Eden Park, Porto di Mattinata, SP53. **GPS**: n41,70667 e16,06556.

25 € 13-26,60 ChWC included €0,50.
Surface: grassy/sand. 01/06-31/08.
Distance: 1km pebbled beach on the spot 1km 1km.

Melendugno — 35D1

Area Camper Salento I Faraglioni, SP366 km 20.5, Sant'Andrea.
GPS: n40,25550 e18,43748.
15 € 12-27/24h Ch WC. 01/01-31/12.
Distance: 700m on the spot.
Remarks: Shuttle bus to beach.

Melendugno — 35D1

Gran Pasha, Strada provinciale Lecce-Melendugno-San Foca, km.18.
GPS: n40,27724 e18,40510.
50 € 10-15, 20/07-31/08 € 25 + tourist tax Ch €3 WC.
Surface: unpaved. 01/01-31/12.
Distance: 1,5km.
Remarks: Free shuttle.

Monopoli — 35D1

Area du Sosta Camper Lido Millennium, SP90, Loc. Capitolo, SS16 km850 Uscita Capitolo. **GPS**: n40,90374 e17,35261.

100 € 15-18-23 Ch 6Amp WC included €1.
Surface: gravel. Easter-30/09.
Distance: 500m 50m 50m 50m.
Remarks: Private beach.

Otranto — 35D1

Oasy Park, Via Renis. **GPS**: n40,13795 e18,48922.

50 € 18, Aug € 20, 2 pers. Incl Ch (70x),16Amp WC included €1 €4. **Surface:** grassy/gravel. 01/01-31/12.
Distance: 400m 700m 400m 400m.

Otranto — 35D1

Area Camper Fontanelle, Sp366, km28. **GPS**: n40,19159 e18,45494.

€ 15/24h, Jul-Aug € 25, 4 pers incl. + tourist tax Ch €3 WC included €0,50.
Distance: Otranto 5km beach 200m.
Remarks: Shuttle bus to Otranto.

IT

S Peschici 34G3

Camper Marina Picola, Loc. Pantanello, Baia di Peschici.
GPS: n41,94528 e16,00528.

45 Apr € 12, May € 13, Jun/Sep € 15, Jul € 20, Aug € 25 Ch WC included €0,50.
Surface: grassy/sand. 01/04-30/09.
Distance: 2,5km, walking 800m (stairs) sandy beach 50m.

S Peschici 34G3

AgriCamper Pane e Vino, SS89 km 2,6. **GPS**: n41,92372 e16,01534.
20 € 10 Ch WC. **Surface:** sand.
Distance: 3,5km on the spot.

S Peschici 34G3

Area attrezzata per camper Dattoli, Via Spiaggia, SS89.
GPS: n41,94522 e16,01138.
14 € 15-20 Ch WC included €0,50.
Surface: unpaved.
Distance: Old city 300m (stairs) 100m 100m.

Putignano 35D1

Grotte di Putignano, SS172. **GPS**: n40,85706 e17,10944.
free. 01/01-31/12.

S Rodi Garganico 34G3

Area sosta camper Isola Bella, Via delle More.
GPS: n41,92444 e15,84166.

30 € 15-20, Aug € 25 Ch WC included.
Surface: grassy/sand. 01/06-15/09.
Distance: Lido del Sole 1,5km, Rodi Garganico 3,8km sandy beach 10m on the spot 100m 1,5km.

S San Giovanni Rotondo 34G3

Coppa Cicuta, Strada Comunale Pozzocavo-Tre Carrini.
GPS: n41,69599 e15,70423.

30 € 12 Ch (30x)€1,50/night WC included €10.
Surface: gravel. 01/01-31/12.
Distance: 3km on the spot.
Remarks: Shuttle € 2/pp.

S San Giovanni Rotondo 34G3

Lo Chalet, Viale Padre Pio. **GPS**: n41,70658 e15,69799.
€ 15/24h Ch WC. **Surface:** metalled.
01/01-31/12.
Distance: on the spot.
Remarks: Free shuttle, santuario 300m.

S San Giovanni Rotondo 34G3

Di Cerbo, Circonvallazione Sud, SP45bis. **GPS**: n41,69725 e15,73097.

20 € 5,20/day, € 7,80/night Ch WC €0,50 €1.
Surface: asphalted. 01/01-31/12.
Distance: 1km on the spot on the spot on the spot.
Remarks: Shuttle bus.

P San Giovanni Rotondo 34G3

Viale Padre Pio. **GPS**: n41,70679 e15,69927.
150 € 2,50, overnight stay free. **Surface:** asphalted.
Remarks: Shrine Padre Pio 200m.

S San Pietro in Bevagna 35D1

La Salina, SP122, Manduria. **GPS**: n40,30121 e17,72630.
€ 14-20, 4 pers.incl Ch €2,50 WC included.
Surface: gravel. 01/06-30/09.
Distance: on the spot.

San Pietro in Bevagna 35D1

La Marina, Via Favignana, Manduria. **GPS**: n40,30888 e17,67750.

80 € 20/24h. **Surface:** unpaved.
Distance: 300m.

S Santa Maria al Bagno 35D1

Area Camper Mondonuovo, Via Torremozza.
GPS: n40,13494 e18,00166.
20 € 15, Aug € 17 Ch.
Surface: gravel. 01/01-31/12.
Distance: beach 500m 900m.

S Torre Canne di Fasano 35D1

Lido Tavernese, SS379, uscita Torre Canne Sud.
GPS: n40,82023 e17,49875.

100 € 15-22 Ch (80x)€2 WC included €1.
Surface: grassy.
Distance: 3,5km on the spot 01/07-31/08.

S Torre Canne di Fasano 35D1

Il Privilegio Camper Service, Via Appia, SP90 > Savelletri.
GPS: n40,84363 e17,46359.
€ 15-20 Ch WC. **Surface:** gravel.
Distance: on the spot.
Remarks: Beach club.

S Torre dell'Orso 35D1

Camper Park Area La Torre. **GPS**: n40,27824 e18,41413.
20 € 10-35 Ch. 01/06-30/09.
Distance: 700m.
Remarks: Regional products.

S Troia 34G3

Campo della Fiera, Via Sant'Antonio. **GPS**: n41,36158 e15,30616.

12 free Ch. **Surface:** asphalted. 01/01-31/12.
Distance: 200m.
Remarks: Near the cathedral.

S Vico del Gargano 34G3

Lido Azzurro. **GPS**: n41,94208 e15,98303.

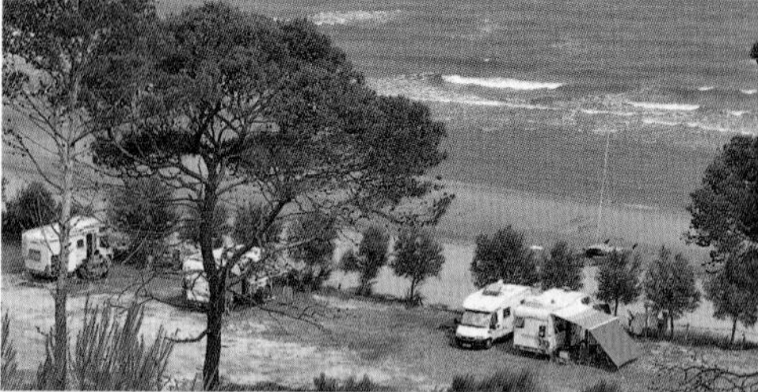

80 € 15, July € 20, Aug € 25 Ch €3,(Aug) WC included.
Surface: sand. 01/01-31/12.
Distance: Valazzo 4km Sandy beach 1km (camping).

S Vieste 34G3

Fusilo Rosina, Contrada S.Lucia. **GPS**: n41,91028 e16,12944.

70 Jun-Sep € 15, Jul € 20, Aug € 27,50 Ch (70x)included WC €0,50. **Surface:** grassy. 01/06-15/09.
Distance: 4km 300m 50m 100m 50m.

S Vieste 34G3

Area Eden Blu, Lungomare Enrico Mattei.
GPS: n41,85985 e16,17396.
40 € 22 Ch WC.
Surface: unpaved. 01/04-31/10.
Distance: on the spot.

Tourist information Vieste:
Mo.

S Zapponeta 39A3

Zapponeta Beach, Via del Mare. **GPS**: n41,45694 e15,96083.

30 € 13, 13/06-10/07, 22/08-11/09 € 14, 11/07-21/08 € 16, 2 pers incl Ch €3 WC included €1. **Surface:** grassy/metalled.
01/04-30/09.
Distance: 250m on the spot on the spot 500m 500m.
Remarks: Narrow entrance.

Campania

S Bacoli 35B1

Sea Oasi Village, Via Strada Romana, loc. Fusaro.
GPS: n40,82194 e14,04791.
± 100 € 15/20/24h, 4 pers.incl Ch €5 WC €1.
Surface: grassy/sand.
Distance: on the spot.
Remarks: At the beach.

Bacoli 35B1

Sea Oasi Village, Via Strada Romana. **GPS**: n40,82194 e14,04791.

100 € 18-20, 4 pers.incl. **Surface:** grassy.
Distance: on the spot on the spot.

S Bacoli 35B1

Parco Naturale Agriturismo Fondi di Baia, Via Fondi di Baia.
GPS: n40,81157 e14,07412.

20 € 10 Ch included. **Surface:** asphalted.
01/01-31/12.
Distance: 3km Baia 700m 100m.

S Baia e Latina 35B1

Il Baglio Country Village, Via Sturzo 13. **GPS:** n41,30386 e14,24754.
guests free Ch WC . 01/01-31/12.
Distance: village 2km on the spot.
Remarks: Use of sauna against payment.

S Battipaglia 35B1

Camperstop Lagomare, Via Andrea Doria 1, Fraz. Lago.
GPS: n40,55296 e14,90615.
40 € 20/24h, max. 4 pers Ch ,3kWh WC included.
Surface: grasstiles. 01/01-31/12.
Distance: 100m 50m.

S Benevento 35B1

Sannio Camper Club, Via Domenico Mustilli.
GPS: n41,13141 e14,78960.

50 € 10/24h Ch included. 01/01-31/12.
Distance: 500m 1,8km 300m.

Tourist information Benevento:
Piazza Risorgimento en Piazza Santa Maria. Wed, Sa 8-13h.

Casalbore 35B1

Agriturismo Le Mainarde. **GPS:** n41,24516 e15,00242.
30 € 15. 01/01-31/12.
Distance: on the spot.

S Cava de' Tirreni 35B1

Via Ido Longo, loc. Sant'Arcangelo. **GPS:** n40,69984 e14,69553.
free Chfree. **Surface:** grasstiles. 01/01-31/12.
Distance: 2,3km.

Tourist information Cava de' Tirreni:
Salerno. City with medieval centre.
Museo Civico, Amalfi. Museum with Tavole Amalfitane, the old Law of the Sea. 8-14h, Sa 8-12h holiday.

S Contursi Terme 35C1

Agriturismo Il Giardino, Loc. Prato. **GPS:** n40,64891 e15,23002.
€ 10 Ch . **Surface:** metalled.
Distance: 4,4km on the spot.
Remarks: Le Terme Vulpacchio 50m.

S Marina di Camerota 35C1

Parcheggio Europa, Via Sirene. **GPS:** n40,00302 e15,36493.
€ 18 . **Surface:** unpaved. Easter-30/09.
Distance: 300m.

S Mondragone 35B1

Dun Area Camper, Via Domiziana, km 15.250.
GPS: n41,13159 e13,86150.
50 Ch . **Surface:** grassy/sand.
Distance: Mondragone 4km on the spot on the spot 3km on the spot.
Remarks: Monitored parking 24/24.

S Napoli 35B1

Parking IPM, Via Colli Aminei 27, Naples (Napoli).
GPS: n40,87038 e14,24616.

7-21h € 10 21-8h €10 Chincluded €2. **Surface:** asphalted.
01/01-31/12.
Distance: 1,2km bus R4 centre Napoli 30m.
Remarks: Monitored parking.

S Napoli 35B1

Parking Patry, Via Nuova Poggioreale 120, Naples (Napoli).
GPS: n40,86788 e14,29436.
€ 24/24h Ch included. **Location:** Urban.
Surface: metalled. 01/01-31/12.
Distance: metro 300m.
Remarks: Monitored parking.

Tourist information Naples (Napoli):
A.A.C.S.T.(Azienda Autonoma di Cura Soggiorno e Turismo), Palazzo Reale, www.regione.campania.it. Capital of the province with many monuments and cultural treasures.
Vesuvio. Volcano, observatorium on western edge of the crater. Visit with guide possible.
Mergellina. Small peninsula with fishing-port and marina.
Teatro San Carlo. Opera building.
Museo Nazionale Archeologico di Napoli, Piazza Museo Nazionale 19. Antique hellenic-roman civilisation. Tue-Su 9-14h.
Palazzo Reale. Royal palace. 9-13.30h Mo.
Duomo San Gennaro. Cathedral with original interior.
Ercolano/Herculaneum. Ancient city buried together with Pompeii. 9-14.45h, holidays 9-18.15h.
Mercato Corso Malta. Mo, Fri.

S Paestum 35C1

Camper Village Maremirtilli, Via Linora di Paestum, SP278.
GPS: n40,37607 e15,00119.
70 € 15-25 Ch WC . **Surface:** grassy. 01/01-31/12.
Distance: on the spot.

S Paestum 35C1

Camper Park Zone Archeologica, Via Magna Grecia, Capaccio Paestum.
GPS: n40,41851 e15,00697.
30 € 10 Chincluded.
Surface: unpaved. 01/01-31/12.
Distance: 300m 1,6km 50m.
Remarks: Paestum Excavations 200m.

S Paestum 35C1

Gli Eucalipti Area di Sosta, Via Linora, 76, Capaccio.
GPS: n40,38565 e15,00308.
25 € 14/17 Ch included. **Surface:** grassy.
01/05-01/10.
Distance: 4km 50m.

S Paestum 35C1

Fattoria del Casaro, Via Licinella 5, Capaccio Paestum.
GPS: n40,41504 e15,00505.
100 € 12/24h Ch included.
Distance: 600m beach 1,8km on the spot.
Remarks: Paestum Excavations 300m, regional products and bread.

Tourist information Paestum:
A.A.C.S.T.(Azienda Autonoma di Cura Soggiorno e Turismo), Via Magna Grecia, 151. Old city, founded by the Greeks. In the surroundings many vestiges from that time.
9h-sunset.

S Palinuro 35C1

Sosta Camper Palorcio, Via San Sebastiano, 39.
GPS: n40,03831 e15,31236.
35 € 12-22, 08/08-24/08 € 30 Ch WC included.
Surface: grassy. 01/06-30/09.
Distance: 1km.

S Palinuro 35C1

Via Palorcio. **GPS:** n40,03722 e15,30944.
€ 20/24h ChWC included.
Distance: 700m.

S Pompei 35B1

Camping Pompei, Via Plinio 113.
GPS: n40,74675 e14,48496.
€ 15,50-20, 2 pers.incl Ch WC included. **Location:** Urban. **Surface:** grassy. 01/01-31/12.
Remarks: Entrance acient city 150m.

Tourist information Pompei:
Ancient city at the foot of Vesuvius.
9h-sunset holiday.

S Pozzuoli 35B1

Castagnaro Park, Via del Castagnaro 1. **GPS:** n40,86939 e14,12150.
85 € 15 Ch (80x)€3/24h WC €1,50 included.
Surface: grassy/gravel.
01/01-31/12.
Distance: 300m 4km 300m 300m 200m.
Remarks: Monitored parking, reservation during Christmas period.

Tourist information Pozzuoli:
Cuma. Archeological site. 9-14.45h, summer 18h.

S Sala Consilina 35C1

Via Santa Maria della Misericordia. **GPS:** n40,41376 e15,56397.
20 € 5/night Ch included. **Surface:** metalled.
01/01-31/12.
Distance: 1,5km 300m 500m 2,5km 1,5km 15km 15km.
Remarks: Behind hotel Vallis Dea.

S Tramonti 35B1

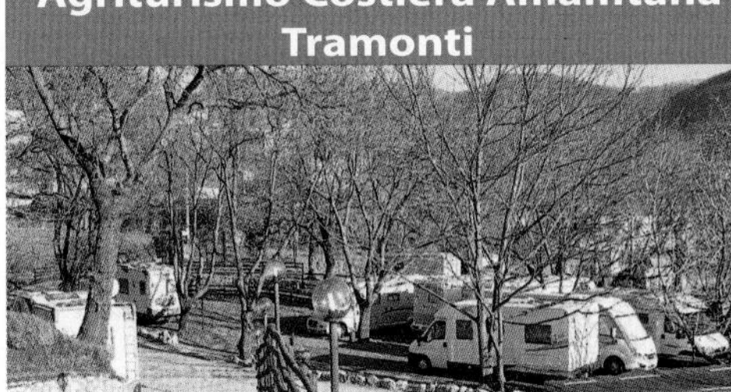

Agriturismo Costiera Amalfitana, Via Falcone, 12 - Frazione Pietre.
GPS: n40,69929 e14,61811.
22 01/09-14/06 € 22, 15/06-31/08 - 23/12-06/01 € 30 Ch WC included.
Location: Rural, comfortable. **Surface:** grassy/gravel. 01/01-31/12.
Distance: 50m 15km 6km on the spot 30m 500m on the spot.
Remarks: Amalfi Coast, regional products.

Basilicata

S Grumento Nova 35C1

Agriturismo Al Parco Verde, Contrada Spineto, Moliterno-Grumento.
GPS: n40,28110 e15,90563.
20 € 20 Ch WC included . **Surface:** grassy.
01/06-01/10.
Distance: 8km 2km 5km on the spot 2km 1km.
Remarks: Archeological site 200m.

S Matera 35C1

Area Camper Matera, SS7, Via Appia. **GPS:** n40,67981 e16,62126.
25 € 14/24h Ch WC included. **Surface:** metalled.
01/01-31/12.

IT

Distance: centre 3,5km.

Matera 35C1

Parco Serra Venerdì, Via dei Normanni. **GPS:** n40,66814 e16,58960.

12 € 18/24h Ch WC.
Surface: metalled. 01/01-31/12.
Distance: 1,8km 200m on the spot.

Metaponto 35C1

Camper parking Nettuno, Viale Magna Grecia, Metaponto Lido.
GPS: n40,35693 e16,83221.

50 € 13/24h, Jul/Aug € 18 Ch WCincluded €1.
Surface: grassy/gravel. 01/01-31/12.
Distance: 50m on the spot 300m.

Tourist information Metaponto:
Archeological site. 9h-sunset.

Calabria

Amantea 35C2

Garden Park Caterina, SS. 18, loc Coreca.
GPS: n39,09383 e16,08508.
10 € 20-25, 4 pers.incl Ch €2,50 WCincluded €1 €5.
Surface: grassy. 15/06-15/09.
Distance: on the spot on the spot on the spot nearby.

Bova Marina 35C3

Mafalda's Camper Park, Via Sotto Ferrovia, loc. San Pasquale.
GPS: n37,92422 e15,94800.
20 € 10-20 Ch included. **Surface:** gravel/sand.
Distance: 3km on the spot on the spot 200m 500m.
Remarks: Accessible via unpaved road, video surveillance.

Catanzaro Marina 35C2

Il Chioschetto, Via Carlo Pisacane 24. **GPS:** n38,83321 e16,64862.

10 free. **Location:** Simple. **Surface:** sand.
Distance: Sandy beach.

Cirella 35C1

Area Camper Ulisse, SS 18 km 270, Diamante.
GPS: n39,72500 e15,80930.

130 € 8-25, 4 pers.incl Ch WC included.
Surface: grassy/sand. 01/04-31/10.
Distance: 800m on the spot on the spot on the spot on the spot on the spot.

Cirella 35C1

Lido Alexander, SS 18, Diamante. **GPS:** n39,72168 e15,81097.

50 € 8-17 Ch €3 WCincluded €1 €3.
Surface: grassy/gravel. 01/01-31/12.
Distance: 1,5km on the spot on the spot on the spot on the spot.

Cirella 35C1

Lido delle Sirene, SS 18, Contr. Riviere. **GPS:** n39,71822 e15,81137.

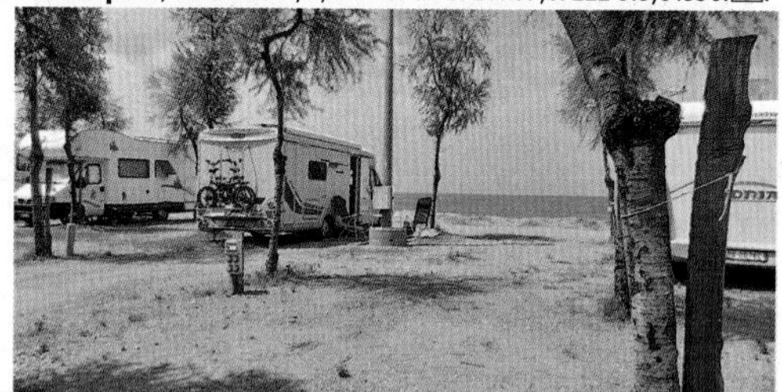

100 Ch WC. **Surface:** grassy.
01/06-20/09.
Distance: 1km on the spot on the spot on the spot 1km.

Cirella 35C1

Lido Tropical, Viale Glauco, 9, Diamante. **GPS:** n39,69222 e15,81556.

200 € 8-30, 4 pers.incl Ch WC.
Surface: grassy/sand. 01/01-31/12.
Distance: 1,5km on the spot on the spot 200m 200m shuttle to town.

Cirò Marina 35D2

Via Maddalena. **GPS:** n39,35998 e17,12910.
25 € 6, 01/06-31/08 € 12.
Surface: unpaved. 01/01-31/12.
Distance: 1,2km 50m.

Cittadella del Capo 35C2

Torre Parise, Via Parise. **GPS:** n39,56580 e15,87399.
16 € 15, Jul/Aug € 18 Ch WCincluded. **Surface:** grassy.
01/01-31/12.
Distance: 1,5km 200m 500m.
Remarks: Swimming pool.

Condofuri Marina 35C3

Agriturismo Antonino Gemelli, Via Salinella 37.
GPS: n37,92372 e15,85150.
20 € 15-20 Ch WC. **Surface:** gravel/sand.
01/01-31/12.
Distance: 500m 100m.

Corigliano Calabro 35C1

B&B Club Tepee, Contrada Sant'Agata 42, SS106bis > Cantinella.
GPS: n39,64140 e16,38617.
€ 10 Ch.
Distance: Corigliano 14km.

Cropani Marina 35D2

Sena Park, Viale Venezia 34. **GPS:** n38,91143 e16,80963.
25 € 12-28, 2 pers.incl Ch WC €0,50 included.
Surface: grassy/sand.
01/01-31/12.
Distance: 500m 400m 400m ristorante/pizzeria 500m.
Remarks: Washing motorhome € 20.

Crotone 35D2

Hera Lacinia Mare, Via Filippo, 47, Campione III.
GPS: n39,00311 e17,16984.

10 € 25 Ch. **Surface:** gravel/metalled.
Distance: on the spot on the spot on the spot 100m 200m.

Morano Calabro 35C1

Via Gaetano Scorza. **GPS:** n39,84098 e16,13731.

10 free. **Surface:** asphalted. 01/01-31/12.
Distance: 200m 7km 200m 200m.
Remarks: Next to church of San Bernardino, panoramic view.

Palmi 35C2

Sosta Camper Prajola, Lungomare Donna Canfora.
GPS: n38,39333 e15,86277.

25 € 15/24h Ch WCincluded. **Location:** Simple.
Surface: gravel. 01/01-31/12.
Distance: on the spot.

Praia a Mare 35C1

Nuova Playa, Contr. Fiucci. **GPS:** n39,86885 e15,78943.

15 € 15, peak season € 30 Ch included. **Surface:** grassy.
01/01-31/12.
Distance: 2km on the spot on the spot 100m 2km.
Remarks: Black sandy beach, in front of Dino island.

Praia a Mare 35C1

Punto Mare, Loc. Fiuzzi. **GPS:** n39,87633 e15,78727.

30 € 6 €2,50 €2,50 Ch €2. **Surface:** grassy.
01/06-30/09.
Distance: 800m 600m 600m 500m 500m on the spot.

Rossano 35C1

Sosta Camper Il Faro, C. da Foresta Faro Campo Trionto.
GPS: n39,62148 e16,75146.

12 € 13-25 Ch WC included. **Location:** Comfortable, isolated. **Surface:** grassy. 01/01-31/12.
Distance: 2km, Rossano 12km Sandy beach on the spot.

S Scalea 35C1

Dolce Vita, Via Fiume Lao 7. **GPS:** n39,79667 e15,79265.

100 € 16-21 Ch €5 WC €0,50 . **Surface:** grassy. 01/05-30/09.
Distance: on the spot on the spot on the spot on the spot 800m.

S Scalea 35C1

Lido Zio Tom, Corso Mediterraneo km 261,7.
GPS: n39,81306 e15,78917.

140 € 10-18 Ch included,4Amp WC hot shower against payment. **Surface:** grassy/gravel. 15/04-15/10.
Distance: on the spot 300m 1km 1,5km.

S Scalea 35C1

Lido Aqua Mar Sosta Camper Martina, Corso Mediterraneo.
GPS: n39,80092 e15,79087.
€ 20/24h Ch WC €0,50.
Distance: on the spot.

Sardinia

S Aglientu 33G2

Oasi Gallura, Localita'Vignola Mare 19, SP 90 km 53.
GPS: n41,12556 e9,06167.

95 € 16-22,50, 2 pers. incl Ch €3 WC €5 included. **Location:** Comfortable, quiet. **Surface:** grassy/sand.
Distance: 25m sandy beach 50m 100m 100m.

S Alghero 33G2

Camperpark I Platani, Ss 291 Km 32,5 S.Maria la Palma - Fertilia.
GPS: n40,60699 e8,27463.

€ 16, 01/06-160/09 € 20-25 Ch , hot shower €0,50 €5 included. **Location:** Comfortable.
Surface: grassy. 01/01-31/12.
Distance: Alghero 7km 1,5km.
Remarks: Monitored parking 24/24, free shuttle to beach and supermarket, dogs beach.

S Alghero 33G2

Paradise Park, Loc. Le Bombarde. **GPS:** n40,59180 e8,25610.

150 € 16-23 Ch WC €0,50 €5 included.
Location: Comfortable, quiet. 01/01-31/12.
Distance: 350m 350m on the spot on the spot 50m.

Arborea 33G3

Corsaro Beach, Str. 26 Ovest. **GPS:** n39,80187 e8,54956.

10 € 5-10. **Surface:** forest soil. 15/06-15/09.
Distance: sandy beach 100m 400m.

S Arbus 33G3

Spiaggia Scivu, SC Scivu. **GPS:** n39,49426 e8,41444.

+50 free, summer € 12/day, overnight stay free €1.
Location: Isolated. **Surface:** gravel/sand. 01/01-31/12.
Distance: sandy beach 100m, stairs.
Remarks: Bar.

S Bosa 33G2

S'Abba Drucche Spiagge, SP49 Alghero-Bosa km 38+800.
GPS: n40,31641 e8,47352.

100 € 20 Ch (96x),6Amp WC included €1 €5 €2.
Surface: unpaved. 15/03-30/10.
Distance: on the spot on the spot.
Remarks: Discount longer stays.

Bosa 33G2

Parcheggio Nassiriya, Via Sas Conzas. **GPS:** n40,29472 e8,49922.

±10 free. **Location:** Urban. **Surface:** asphalted. 01/01-31/12.
Distance: 300m 150m.
Remarks: Along river.

S Bosa 33G2

Casa del Vento, SP49. **GPS:** n40,32886 e8,43628.

±5 € 10 Ch included.
Location: Rural. **Surface:** gravel/sand.
Distance: Bosa 8km At the sea, no beach on the spot.
Remarks: Beautiful view, narrow entrance.

S Buggerru 33G3

Area Camper Il Porto, Via Roma. **GPS:** n39,40317 e8,40250.

50 € 5-15, Jul/Aug € 20 Ch €5. **Surface:** sand. 01/04-31/10.
Distance: 800m on the spot 400m 800m.
Remarks: Beach parking.

S Buggerru 33G3

Punta Sosta San Nicolao, Loc. Cala Domestica.
GPS: n39,41757 e8,41147.

20 € 10 Ch included cold shower.
Surface: grassy/sand. 01/05-30/10.
Distance: 4km sandy beach 50m 50m.
Remarks: Beach parking.

S Cabras 33G3

Tanca Is Muras, Località Mari Ermi. **GPS:** n39,96226 e8,40324.

€ 12 €5 Ch €4 €0,50. **Location:** Isolated. 01/05-01/10.
Distance: Sandy beach.

S Cagliari 33G3

Campernow, Via Gerolamo Cardano. **GPS:** n39,23580 e9,13832.

10 € 17 Ch WC included. **Location:** Urban, central, noisy. **Surface:** metalled. 20/04-15/10.
Distance: city centre 3km 150m Lidl 100m 100m.

S Cagliari 33G3

Camper Cagliari Park, Via Stanislao Caboni. **GPS:** n39,21024 e9,12772.

IT

150 € 20 Ch €5 WC included. **Location:** Urban. **Surface:** asphalted. 01/01-31/12. **Distance:** city centre 1,5km 300m. **Remarks:** Monitored parking.

Cala Gonone 33G2

Palmasera, Viale Bue Marino. **GPS**: n40,27954 e9,62993.

€ 20, Jul/Aug € 25-30 Ch WC €0,50 €5 included. **Surface:** unpaved. 01/04-31/10. **Distance:** 800m 500m ristoro 200m on the spot. **Remarks:** Shuttle bus to beach.

Cala Sinzias 33G3

SP18. **GPS**: n39,18912 e9,56273.

10 free, summer € 10. **Surface:** sand. 01/01-31/12. **Distance:** sandy beach 50m on the spot. **Remarks:** Beach parking, pay in at kiosk.

Cardedu 33G3

Cucamonga, Marina di Gairo. **GPS**: n39,75397 e9,67130.

±20 € 10 Ch included. **Location:** Rural, isolated, quiet. **Surface:** sand. 01/01-31/12. **Distance:** pebbled beach 7km.

Domus de Maria 33G3

Area Camper Chia, Su Giudeu, Capo Spartivento, Chia. **GPS**: n38,89128 e8,86264.

100 € 16-20 Ch WC included €0,50. **Location:** Comfortable. **Surface:** sand. Easter-01/11. **Distance:** on the spot 400m 900m.

Golfo Aranci 33G2

Playa Vistas Chulas, Via Cala Moresca. **GPS**: n40,98826 e9,63589.

±20 free. **Location:** Isolated. **Surface:** gravel/sand. 01/01-31/12. **Distance:** 2km on the spot on the spot. **Remarks:** 1km unpaved road, max. ^3.2m, beach parking, no camping activities.

Masua 33G3

La Nuova Colonia, Masua Porto Flavia. **GPS**: n39,33409 e8,42052.

50 € 14-17 Ch included free,at restaurant. **Location:** Rural, isolated, quiet. **Surface:** unpaved. 01/04-31/10. **Distance:** sandy beach 50m, stairs on the spot. **Remarks:** Former mineral mines, tour Porto Flavia.

Nuoro 33G2

P.le Anfiteatro cittadino, Piazza Veneto. **GPS**: n40,31447 e9,32807.

5 free Ch free. **Surface:** asphalted. 01/01-31/12. **Distance:** 1,2km.

Olbia 33G2

Camper service Marina di Cugnana, Località Marina di Cugnana, SP73. **GPS**: n41,02042 e9,51441.

30 € 1,50/h, € 25/24h Ch WC included. **Location:** Noisy. 01/05-30/09. **Distance:** Olbia 12km on the spot on the spot. **Remarks:** Shuttle bus to beach, swimming pool.

Oristano 33G3

Stadio Tharros, Via Dorando Petri. **GPS**: n39,89710 e8,58927. Ch free. 01/01-31/12.

Orosei 33G2

Osalla Beach Garden, Osalla di Orosei. **GPS**: n40,34474 e9,68619.

34 € 15-20 Ch WC included,cold shower. **Surface:** gravel/sand. Easter-31/10. **Distance:** 3,5km.

Quartu Sant'Elena 33G3

Is Canaleddus, Viale L. da vinci, SP17. **GPS**: n39,17957 e9,36489.

€ 10 . **Surface:** unpaved. 01/05-01/10. **Distance:** pebbeled beach 150m on the spot. **Remarks:** Beach parking.

San Nicolò d'Arcidano 33G3

Viale Dei Giardini. **GPS**: n39,68530 e8,64570.

4 free €4 €4 Ch€4 €4. **Surface:** asphalted. 01/01-31/12. **Distance:** on the spot.

San Teodoro 33G2

Via Donat Cattin. **GPS**: n40,76658 e9,66884.

30 € 1/h, € 4/6h. **Location:** Noisy. **Surface:** asphalted. **Distance:** 800m 1,8km 100m.

Sant'Anna Arresi 33G3

Sosta camper Il Ruscello, Via del Cormorano, loc. Is Pillonis. **GPS**: n38,97772 e8,62317.

80 € 16-20 Ch WC €4 included. **Location:** Rural, comfortable, isolated. **Surface:** grassy/gravel. 01/01-31/12. **Distance:** 3,5km on the spot. **Remarks:** Shuttle bus to beach.

Siniscola 33G2

Spiaggia di Berchida. **GPS**: n40,48064 e9,80680.

+50 € 10/day. **Location:** Rural, isolated. **Surface:** unpaved. 01/01-31/12. **Distance:** on the spot.

IT

Solanas 33G3

Via al Mare. **GPS**: n39,13333 e9,43254.

10 free. **Surface:** sand.
Distance: 300m Sandy beach 300m.
Remarks: Beach parking.

Sorso 33G2

Camp Site International, Via degli Oleandri, SP 81 km 13, Platamona Lido. **GPS**: n40,81566 e8,46563.

120 € 14-20 Ch WC €3 included.
Location: Simple. **Surface:** unpaved. 01/04-30/09.
Distance: 350m 2km on the spot.

Stintino 33G2

La Pineta, Loc. Pozzo S.Nicola, SP34. **GPS**: n40,86843 e8,23610.

40 € 17-19-21 Ch WC included hot shower €1 €5.
Location: Rural. **Surface:** grassy/sand. 01/01-31/12.
Distance: 3,5km on the spot.

Tancau sul Mare 33G3

Area attrezzata Costa Orientale, Viale Mare.
GPS: n39,98321 e9,68608.

55 € 10-20, Jul/Aug electricity € 3 Ch WC included €4.
Location: Comfortable. **Surface:** asphalted/sand.
Easter-31/10.
Distance: Santa Maria Navarese 900m sandy beach 50m 50m 250m. **Remarks:** Shady.

Tonara 33G3

Ostello delle Gioventù, Via Muggianeddu, 2. **GPS**: n40,02855 e9,17542.
€ 10 Ch. 01/01-31/12.
Distance: 500m on the spot.

Tortolì 33G3

Tanca Orrì, Lido Orrì. **GPS**: n39,90364 e9,68204.

80 € 16-20 Ch €2,2Amp WC included, cold shower.
Location: Comfortable. **Surface:** unpaved. 01/01-31/12.
Distance: Tortolì 5km sandy beach 50m 100m.

Tortolì 33G3

Area Camper Rocce Rosse, Via del Muflone. **GPS**: n39,86865 e9,67924.

70 € 15-25, Aug € 35 €4. **Location:** Rural. **Surface:** sand.
01/06-30/09.
Distance: Tortolì 9km sandy beach 250m on the spot mini market.
Remarks: Shady.

Tortolì 33G3

Baia Cea, Via del Muflone. **GPS**: n39,86874 e9,68034.

60 € 15-30 Ch WC included.
Location: Rural. **Surface:** sand. 01/05-30/09.
Distance: Tortolì 9km on the spot on the spot.

Valledoria 33G2

Punto Maragnani, Via La Ciaccia, Loc. Maragnani.
GPS: n40,92021 e8,79240.

90 € 15/24h Ch WC included. **Surface:** unpaved.
01/01-31/12.
Distance: 50m 200m.
Remarks: Motorhome washing place.

Villaputzu 33G3

Bella Vista Camper Service, Località Prumari, Porto corallo.
GPS: n39,43820 e9,63243.

50 € 10-25 Ch WC €1 €5 included.
Location: Rural. **Surface:** gravel.
Distance: Villaputzu 6km 50m 500m 7km.

Villasimius 33G3

Gli Aranci, Viale dei Carrubi, loc. Pranu Zinnigas.
GPS: n39,15977 e9,50865.

100 € 23 Ch WC included. **Location:** Comfortable, quiet. **Surface:** unpaved. 01/01-31/12.
Distance: 2km 4km 100m Eurospin 1km.
Remarks: Shuttle bus to beach.

Sicily

Agrigento 35B3

Sosta Camper Quality, Via delle Dune, San Leone.
GPS: n37,24566 e13,61114.
50 € 20 Ch WC included. **Location:** Comfortable, quiet. **Surface:** sand. 01/06-31/10.
Distance: Dune sandy beach 10m 50m.

Agrigento 35B3

Valle dei Templi, Viale Caduti di Marzabotto. **GPS**: n37,28881 e13,58181.
50 € 5. **Location:** Simple. **Surface:** sand. 01/01-31/12.
Remarks: Near entrance and pay-desk of Valle dei Templi.

Augusta 35C3

Area Attrezzata Camper Nelly, SS114 - Km 118,5, Contrada Agnone Bagni. **GPS**: n37,31148 e15,09260.
€ 18-22 Ch WC included €1 €3. 15/05-15/09.
Distance: 6km 1,5km 180m.

Caccamo 35B3

SS 285. **GPS**: n37,93410 e13,66115.
10 free Ch free. **Location:** Simple.
Surface: gravel/metalled.
Distance: 900m 300m.

Caltagirone 35C3

Piazzale San Giovanni, Loc. San Giovanni.
GPS: n37,23949 e14,50717.
free. **Surface:** asphalted. 01/01-31/12.
Distance: historical centre 700m.

Caltanissetta 35B3

Via Guastaferro. **GPS**: n37,48959 e14,04515.
25 free Ch free. **Location:** Urban, simple, noisy.
Surface: asphalted.
Distance: 2km on the spot on the spot.

Castelbuono 35B3

Via Guiseppe Mazzini. **GPS**: n37,93694 e14,09296.
10 free Ch. **Location:** Simple, quiet.
Distance: 700m 700m.

Castellammare del Golfo 35B3

Playtime, Viale Leonardo da Vinci, SS187.
GPS: n38,02494 e12,89086.
€ 15/24h Ch WC . **Surface:** grassy.
Distance: 200m 1km.

Castelluzzo 35B3

SP16. **GPS**: n38,12220 e12,72524.

free. **Surface:** gravel.
Distance: on the spot.
Remarks: Beach parking, beach train.

Castelluzzo 35B3

Parking Macari, SP16. **GPS**: n38,13564 e12,73638.

IT

free. **Surface:** sand.

S Enna 35B3

Ennacamper, C/da S.Giuseppe, Pergusa. **GPS:** n37,52277 e14,29000.
30 € 20/24h Ch Service € 5 € 4. **Location:** Simple.
Surface: sand.
Remarks: Free shuttle, cleaning motorhome € 5.

S Francavilla di Sicilia 35C3

Maremonti, Via Cappuccini. **GPS:** n37,90855 e15,14347.

±50 gift. **Surface:** unpaved. 01/01-31/12.
Distance: 400m Riverbed.
Remarks: Gole dell'Alcantara 6km.

S Furnari 35C2

Tonnarella, Corso Palermo 6. **GPS:** n38,13218 e15,12469.

44 € 13-24 Ch WC included € 0,50 € 4.
Location: Simple. **Surface:** gravel. 01/01-31/12.
Distance: on the spot on the spot 150m 250m.
Remarks: Monitored parking, excursion to the Eolie-islands.

S Gangi 35B3

SS14. **GPS:** n37,79203 e14,21079.
15 free Ch free.
Surface: gravel/sand. 01/01-31/12.
Distance: 750m 750m.

S Giardini Naxos 35C3

Parking Lagani, Via Stralcina 22, zona Recanati.
GPS: n37,82092 e15,26753.

30 € 15-30 Ch WC included € 1,(summer) € 5.
Surface: metalled. 01/01-31/12.
Distance: on the spot 200m 50m 200m Bus to Taormina 300m.
Remarks: Special tariff for long stay during the winter, bar, view on Etna and Taormina.

S Giardini Naxos 35C3

Eden Parking, Via Stracina. **GPS:** n37,82188 e15,26701.

30 € 7-25 Ch € 0,35/kWh WC € 1. **Surface:** grassy.
01/01-31/12.
Distance: 500m > Taormina.

S Giardini Naxos 35C3

Holiday Sun, Viale Stracina 20. **GPS:** n37,82109 e15,26784.
30 € 7-25 Ch WC. **Surface:** grassy/gravel.
Distance: beach 500m on the spot > Taormina.

Tourist information Giardini Naxos:
Sa-morning.

S Ispica 35C3

Associazione Camper Club Porto Ulisse.
GPS: n36,69761 e14,98647.
30 € 16/24h Ch.
Surface: grassy. Easter-30/09.
Distance: 100m.

S Licata 35B3

Ristorante La Sorgente, Loc. Pisciotto.
GPS: n37,12666 e13,85194.

80 Jun € 15, Jul € 20, Aug € 25 Ch WC included.
Surface: gravel.
Distance: Licata 9km on the spot on the spot.
Remarks: Stairs to sandy beach.

S Marina di Ragusa 35C3

Marina Caravan, Via Portovenere 57. **GPS:** n36,78472 e14,56486.

60 € 15-20 Ch WC € 4 included. **Surface:** grassy.
01/01-31/12.
Distance: 500m 300m 100m 100m 200m.
Remarks: Water/drainage at each pitch, bicycle rental.

S Marina di Ragusa 35C3

Via Falconara. **GPS:** n36,78821 e14,54697.
40 free Ch free WC. **Surface:** asphalted. 01/01-31/12.
Distance: 1km 1km.

S Marsala 35A3

Sibiliana Beach Village, Contrada Fossarunza 205/z 14.
GPS: n37,73520 e12,47497.
100 € 20 Ch WC included. **Surface:** unpaved.
Distance: 50m.

S Marsala 35A3

Nautisub Club S. Teodoro, Contrada Birgi.
GPS: n37,91046 e12,46178.

± 50 € 15/20 Ch. **Surface:** grassy. 01/05-30/09.
Distance: 5km Sandy beach on the spot.

S Marsala 35A3

Via Colonnello Maltese. **GPS:** n37,79497 e12,43270.
free Ch. **Surface:** asphalted. 01/01-31/12.
Distance: 500m on the spot.

S Mineo 35C3

Le Bave di Bacco, Strada Provinciale 86. **GPS:** n37,24137 e14,72239.
customers free. **Location:** Rural, simple, isolated.
Surface: grassy. 01/01-31/12.

S Montallegro 35B3

Vizzi Parking, Via Lungomare, SP87. **GPS:** n37,38206 e13,30932.
€ 15 € 3 Ch € 2. **Surface:** gravel. 01/06-01/10.
Distance: 100m.

S Montallegro 35B3

Agriturismo Torre Salsa, Bove Marina.
GPS: n37,37583 e13,32222.

20 € 17-24 € 4 Ch according consumption WC € 1 € 6 € 1,50/h. **Surface:** grassy. 01/01-31/12.
Distance: 700m.
Remarks: Also pitches on the beach without service, estate 300 acres, hiking and mountain bike trails.

S Montevago 35B3

Agricamper Villa dei Pini, Via Piersanti Mattarella.
GPS: n37,70083 e12,98000.
€ 15 Ch included. 01/01-31/12.
Distance: 200m.

S Montevago 35B3

Centro Terme Acqua Pia, Loc. Acque Calde. **GPS:** n37,70602 e12,98092.
20 2 days-1night € 15 + € 15/pp € 3. 01/04-31/10.
Remarks: Including access spa resort.

S Motta Camastra 35C3

S185, fraz. Ficarazzi. **GPS:** n37,88870 e15,17633.

10 € 15 Ch WC included. **Location:** Rural.
Surface: grassy/gravel. 01/01-31/12.
Distance: 300m 1km.
Remarks: In front of entrance of Gole dell'Alcantara.

S Mussomeli 35B3

Piazzale Mongibello. GPS: n37,58343 e13,74956.
free Ch.
Distance: historical centre.

S Noto 35C3

Airone, Via San Corrado, Lido di Noto. **GPS:** n36,85916 e15,11555.

IT

50 Jun/Sep € 14-16, Aug € 20 Ch €2 WC hot shower €0,50. **Surface:** grassy/sand. 01/04-30/09.
Distance: 100m 100m 750m Bus to Noto 100m.

S Noto 35C3

Il Canneto, Viale Lido di Noto, Lido di Noto.
GPS: n36,86083 e15,11944.

55 € 10-18 Ch €2 WC.
Surface: grassy/sand.
Distance: on the spot 1,2km.
Remarks: Bread-service and meals, direct access to the sandy beach.

S Noto 35C3

NotoParking, Contrada Faldino, Noto. **GPS:** n36,88353 e15,08595.

40 € 18 Ch €3 WC €1. **Surface:** grassy/gravel.
01/01-31/12.
Distance: 1km 3km 200m 200m.
Remarks: Organised excursions in the surroundings, free shuttle bus to Noto.

S Noto 35C3

Oasi Park Falconara, Viale Ionio, Lido di Noto.
GPS: n36,87001 e15,12872.
50 € 15, 01/06-31/10 € 17-24 Ch WC included.
Surface: gravel. 01/01-31/12.
Distance: Noto 4km beach 700m pizzeria 50m.
Remarks: Shuttle bus to Noto and beach.

S Noto 35C3

Parcheggio Calamosche, Oasi di Vendicari.
GPS: n36,81611 e15,09888.

40-50 € 15 WC included. **Surface:** grassy.
01/06-30/09.
Distance: Noto 10km 20 min walking bar/restaurant.

S Oliveri 35C2

Azimut Sosta Camper, Corso Cristoforo Colombo.
GPS: n38,12840 e15,05833.
100 € 12-15-20-22 Ch (100x),6Amp WC included.
Location: Comfortable. **Surface:** grassy/gravel. 01/03-31/10.
Distance: 500m, Tindari 1,2km 2,5km beach 50m 50m 50m 200m 10m 100m 100m 200m.

S Pachino 35C3

Area camper Venere, Contrada Granelli. **GPS:** n36,70100 e15,02790.
€ 20-26, 5 pers. incl Ch WC included.
Surface: unpaved. 01/06-30/09.
Distance: Sandy beach.

S Pachino 35C3

Dragomar, Strada Marzamemi Portopalo di Capo Passero, Marzamemi.
GPS: n36,72732 e15,12083.

30 € 12-21 Ch €3 WC included. **Surface:** gravel.
01/01-31/12.
Distance: on the spot 400m 600m.
Remarks: Seaview, no beach.

S Palermo 35B3

Green Car Palermo, Via Quarto dei Mille 11b.
GPS: n38,11016 e13,34307.
€ 20/24h Ch included. **Location:** Simple.
Surface: asphalted.
Distance: piazza Indipendenza 300m.

S Palermo 35B3

Parking Giotto, Piazzale John Lennon. **GPS:** n38,13240 e13,33148.
36 € 20/24h Ch free. **Location:** Central.
Surface: asphalted. 01/01-31/12.
Remarks: 3 nights stay 10% discount.

S Palermo 35B3

Parking Ospedale Cervello, Via Trabucco. **GPS:** n38,15619 e13,31354.
. **Location:** Simple, isolated.
Remarks: Nearby hospital.

S Palermo 35B3

Via Uditore 17. **GPS:** n38,13140 e13,32515.
Ch WC. **Surface:** gravel.
Remarks: Monitored parking, shuttle bus to city centre.

Palermo 35B3

Piazza Alcide De Gasperi. **GPS:** n38,15170 e13,33944.
free. **Surface:** asphalted.
Distance: on the spot.
Remarks: Nearby stadium.

S Palermo 35B3

Freesbee Parking, Via Imperatore Federico 116.
GPS: n38,14722 e13,35277.
100 € 15-18 Ch WC €1. **Surface:** asphalted.
Distance: Cathedral Palermo 400m 2km 150m.
Remarks: At motorhome dealer, 24/24 surveillance.

Tourist information Palermo:

U.I.A.T. (Ufficio Informazioni e di Accoglienza Turistica), Piazza Castelnuovo, 34, www.regione.sicilia.it/turismo. Capital of Sicilly, port and economical heart of the Island.
San Giovanni degli Eremiti.
Santa Catarina.
Vucciria, Via Cassari-Argenteria. Palermo's most famous, picturesque and historic market.

Piazza Armerina 35B3

Via G. Lo Giudice. **GPS:** n37,38711 e14,37041.
free. **Location:** Simple. **Surface:** asphalted. 01/01-31/12.
Distance: 200m.

S Piazza Armerina 35B3

Agricamper Valle Dell'Elsa, SS65. **GPS:** n37,30173 e14,39605.
12 € 15/24h Ch WC included. **Location:** Rural, comfortable, isolated, quiet. **Surface:** metalled. 01/01-31/12.
Distance: Piazza Armerina 20km on the spot.

S Piazza Armerina 35B3

Agriturismo Agricasale, Contrada Ciavarina.
GPS: n37,34032 e14,38840.
40 € 15 Ch included. **Location:** Rural, comfortable, isolated, quiet.
Distance: Piazza Armerina 13km bar/restaurant.
Remarks: Swimming pool € 3/pppd.

S Piazza Armerina 35B3

Agriturismo Gigliotto, SS 117bis km60. **GPS:** n37,29051 e14,38721.
20 € 20, 01/04-31/10 € 30 Ch WC included.
Location: Comfortable, quiet. **Surface:** gravel. 01/01-31/12.
Distance: Piazza Armerina 13km.
Remarks: Swimming pool incl.

S Piazza Armerina 35B3

SP90. **GPS:** n37,36805 e14,33421.
20 € 15/24h Ch included. **Location:** Simple.
01/01-31/12.
Distance: Piazza Armerina 4,5km on the spot.
Remarks: Villa Romana del Casale 400m.

S Porto Empedocle 35B3

Punta Piccola Park, Scala dei Turchi, SP68.
GPS: n37,28916 e13,49250.

99 € 15-20, 01/07-31/08 € 23 Ch (65x) WC €1 included. **Surface:** gravel. 01/01-31/12.
Distance: 2,5km on the spot 200m 1km.
Remarks: Shopping service, direct access to the sandy beach.

Tourist information Porto Empedocle:

Valle dei Templi, Agrigento. The Valley of The Temples, archeology.

S Portopalo di Capo Passero 35C3

Cicogna, Via Carlo Alberto, 2. **GPS:** n36,68333 e15,13638.
20 Jun/Sep € 12, Jul/Aug € 16 Ch (20x)included.
Surface: gravel.
Distance: 50m sandy beach 300m.

S Pozzallo 35C3

Il Giardino di Epicuro, SP67. **GPS:** n36,73128 e14,86240.

50 € 20 Ch (22x)€3 cold shower. **Surface:** grassy/sand.
01/05-30/09.
Distance: 500m on the spot 50m 300m.
Remarks: Sandy beach.

S Pozzallo 35C3

Salvamar, Zona Porto di Pozzallo. **GPS:** n36,71541 e14,82240.

30 11/09-31/05 € 15, 01/06-10/09 € 20 2 pers. incl Ch included. **Surface:** grassy. 01/01-31/12.
Distance: 200m 500m 1km.

S Realmonte 35B3

Sosta camper Zanzibar, C/o Capo Rossello.
GPS: n37,29495 e13,45438.

100 € 12-22, 01/10-30/03 € 10 Ch WC included hot shower €1. **Surface:** gravel. 01/01-31/12.
Distance: sandy beach on the spot 150m.
Remarks: Bus to Valle dei Templi (€ 7/pp, min. 4 pers).

IT

Reitano 35B3

Via Lungomare Colonna. **GPS**: n38,01407 e14,33081.
70 € 10 Ch €0,50. **Location:** Simple. 15/07-18/09.
Distance: 500m on the spot.

Ribera 35B3

Kamemi, SS115, Secca Grande. **GPS**: n37,43840 e13,24469.
Camperstop € 10 Ch. 01/01-31/12 01/08-24/08 No Camperstop.

Roccalumera 35C3

Park Jonio, Via Collegio, SS114 Roccalumera > Nizza di Sicilia.
GPS: n37,97943 e15,39752.

60 € 11-17, Jul/Aug € 15-20, 3 pers. incl Ch (60x) .
Surface: gravel.
Distance: within walking distance 250m Bar/snack on the spot. **Remarks:** In front of Centro Sportivo.

San Giovanni La Punta 35C3

Entertainmentcity Isivillage, Via Fisichelli 63.
GPS: n37,58929 e15,08612.
guests free. **Surface:** asphalted.

San Vito Lo Capo 35B3

Al Faro, Via Faro 36. **GPS**: n38,18472 e12,73277.

30 € 18-30 Ch included hotshower € 1.
Surface: asphalted/grassy. 01/05-31/10.
Distance: 1km on the spot 300m 1km.
Remarks: Terrace on the sea, no beach, sandy beach 400m.

San Vito Lo Capo 35B3

Parking camper Giovanni, Via Savoia 13.
GPS: n38,16222 e12,73666.

90 € 12-18 Ch (90x) WC €0,50 €5 included.
Surface: gravel. 01/01-31/12.
Distance: 300m 1,4km 1km 1km.
Remarks: Free shuttle to beach.

San Vito Lo Capo 35B3

Monte Monaco, Via del Secco, 80. **GPS**: n38,17438 e12,74552.
€ 12, Jun € 15, Jul € 20, Aug € 25 Ch WC €1.
Surface: gravel. 01/04-31/10.
Distance: 850m 300m 300m 850m.

San Vito Lo Capo 35B3

Via la Piana. **GPS**: n38,16886 e12,74307.

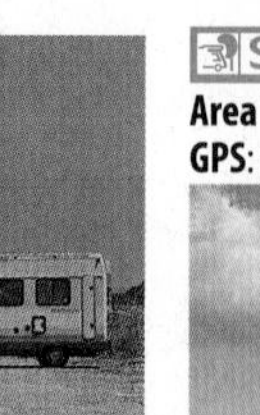

free. **Surface:** unpaved.
Distance: 800m 800m.
Remarks: Free shuttle to centre.

Scicli 35C3

Club Piccadilly, Via Mare Adriatico, Donnalucata.
GPS: n36,74750 e14,66306.
€ 12-35 Ch WC . 01/01-31/12.
Distance: 3km sandy beach 100m.

Scopello 35B3

Fontana Andrea, Contrada Ciauli, SS 187.
GPS: n38,05492 e12,84290.
€ 12/24h Ch included.
Surface: grassy. 01/04-01/10.
Distance: beach 300m.

Scopello 35B3

Agricampeggio Scopello, Via Finanzierè Vincenzo Mazzarell.
GPS: n38,06777 e12,81777.

50 € 22/24h Ch included €1. **Surface:** gravel.
01/05-30/09.
Distance: historical centre 200m 1,5km 100m 400m.
Remarks: Farm products, shuttle to beach and Riserva dello Zingaro € 2,50/pp.

Siracusa 35C3

Parcheggio Von Platen, Via Augusto Von Platen 38.
GPS: n37,07692 e15,28738.
€ 0,90/h.
Remarks: Near archeological site and museum.

Siracusa 35C3

Via Procione 6, zona Golfetto, Fontane Bianche.
GPS: n36,96361 e15,22027.
€ 20 Ch WC . **Surface:** unpaved.
Distance: Siracusa 15km on the spot on the spot.
Remarks: Bus to Siracusa, natural swimming pool in sea.

Siracusa 35C3

Area sosta Siracusa, Via Rodi 15. **GPS**: n37,06436 e15,28710.
€ 0,60/h, night € 1. **Surface:** asphalted. 01/01-31/12.
Distance: Ortigia 500m 50m.

Sutera 35B3

Piazza Rettore Carruba. **GPS**: n37,52450 e13,72960.
free Ch. **Surface:** asphalted.
Distance: on the spot on the spot.

Taormina 35C3

Sosta Camper Pier Giovanni, Trappitello, Via Spagnuolo.
GPS: n37,82196 e15,24502.

15 € 10-20 Ch WC included. **Surface:** grassy/metalled.
01/01-31/12.
Distance: 500m 4km 300m 300m.
Remarks: Shuttle bus to city centre.

Terme Vigliatore 35C2

Area Trinacria, Via Lungomare Marchesana.
GPS: n38,14018 e15,14596.

120 € 15, Aug € 18 Ch included.
Surface: grassy. 01/01-31/12.
Distance: 50m pizzeria 200m 200m.
Remarks: Excursion to the Eolie-islands.

Trapani 35A3

Hotel Le Saline, SP21 km4, contrada Nubia-Paceco.
GPS: n37,98304 e12,53106.
20 € 15-20 Ch . **Surface:** metalled.
01/01-31/12.

IT

Luxembourg

Capital: Luxembourg
Government: Grand duchy
Official Language: French, German, Luxembourgish
Population: 570.250 (2015)
Area: 2,586 km²

General information
Calling code: 00352
General emergency: 112
Currency: Euro

Regulations for overnight stays
Parking overnight and camping by public road is forbidden. Motorhome-service only on campsites.

Additional public holidays 2017
May 1 Labor day
June 23 National Holiday
August 15 Assumption of the Virgin Mary
November 1 All Saints' Day

Time Zone
Winter (Standard Time) GMT+1
Summer (DST) GMT+2

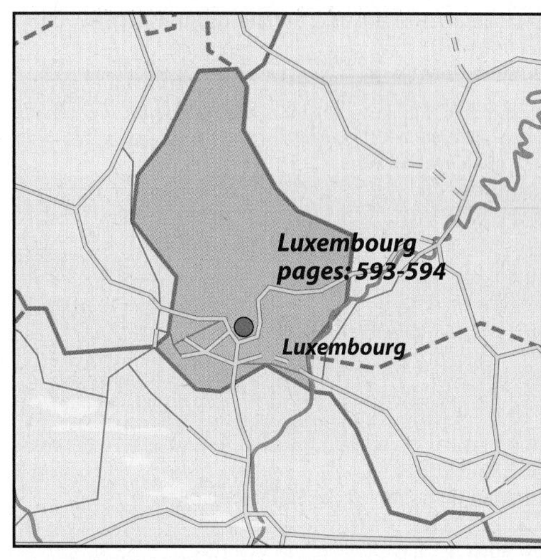

S Berdorf 16E1

Camperhafen Martbusch, 3, Beim Martbusch.
GPS: n49,82660 e6,34599.

9 € 8-10 €1/100liter Ch €0,50/kWh €3 included. **Location:** Rural, comfortable, quiet. **Surface:** asphalted.
01/01-31/12.
Distance: 500m on the spot 7km 500m on the spot on the spot.
Remarks: Max. 2 nights, check in at reception campsite.

S Bleesbrück 16E1

Camping Bleesbrück, 1, Bleesbreck. **GPS**: n49,87270 e6,18940.

3 € 15 Ch WC included. **Location:** Rural, simple, noisy. **Surface:** grassy.
01/04-15/10.
Distance: 2,5km on the spot 2,5km.
Remarks: Arrival >18h departure <9h, if not camping tariff.

S Diekirch 16E1

Camping de la Sûre, Route de Gilsdorf.
GPS: n49,86597 e6,16489.

8 € 12-15 Ch WC included, sanitary only summer €3 free.
Location: Comfortable, central. **Surface:** grasstiles. 01/01-31/12.
Distance: 100m 100m 100m (permit € 4/month) 100m 100m.
Remarks: Max. 2 days.

Tourist information Diekirch:
Conservatoire National de véhicules historique, 20-22, rue de Stavelot. Exhibition of historical vehicles. 10-18h Mo.
Musée National de l'histoire militaire, 10, Bamertal. War museum.
Tue-Su 10-18h Mo.
Rue de Marché. Tue 8-12h.
Al Dikkirch. Folk festival. 2nd week Jul.

S Dudelange 16E1

Parking Gare-Usines. GPS: n49,47176 e6,07772.

8 free Ch free. **Location:** Simple, noisy. **Surface:** grasstiles/grassy. 01/01-31/12.
Distance: 1km 4,1km near train station.
Remarks: Well situated for visiting Luxembourg city, 20min by train, max. 48h.

Tourist information Dudelange:
Musée National des Mines de Fer, Carreau de la Mine, Rumelange. History of the mines.

S Ermsdorf 16E1

Neumühle. GPS: n49,83917 e6,22503.
€ 16-20,50 Ch WC €4 included. L ocation: Rural, comfortable, isolated, quiet. **Surface:** grassy.
15/03-31/10.
Distance: 1km on the spot 6km.

S Heiderscheid 16E1

Camperhafen Fuussekaul, Fuussekaul 4.
GPS: n49,87806 e5,99278.
35 € 10, Jul/Aug € 15 Ch (35x),16Amp WC included €1/5minutes €4/2,50 €4,90/day.
Location: Luxurious, isolated, quiet. **Surface:** grasstiles/metalled.
01/01-31/12.
Distance: 1km 8km 8km 5km on the spot on the spot on the spot on the spot.

Tourist information Heiderscheid:
Heischter Mart. Traditional market. end Jul.

S Heiderscheidergrund 16E1

Camping Bissen, 11, Millewee. **GPS**: n49,90495 e5,95595.
3 € 10, 10/07-15/08 € 15 Ch included. **Surface:** gravel.
01/01-31/12.
Distance: on the spot on the spot.
Remarks: Quick-Stop: >17h - <10h, along river.

S Hoscheid 11E3

Hotel-Restaurant Des Ardennes, Haaptstrooss.
GPS: n49,94675 e6,08084.

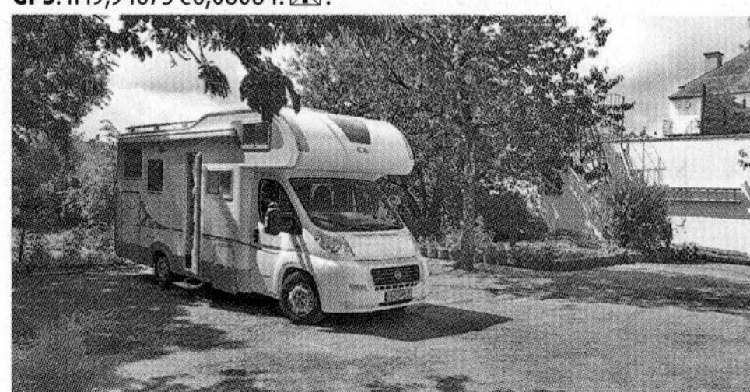

4 free with a meal WC included. **Location:** Simple, quiet. **Surface:** asphalted. 01/02-15/12.
Distance: on the spot on the spot on the spot.
Remarks: Parking behind hotel.

S Junglinster 16E1

Rue Emile Nilles. **GPS**: n49,70421 e6,25123.

3 free €0,10/10liter Ch (4x)€0,50/kWh. **Location:** Simple. **Surface:** asphalted. 01/01-31/12.
Distance: 200m.

S Larochette 16E1

Camping Auf Kengert. GPS: n49,80021 e6,19788.
2 € 17-26 Ch included. 01/03-08/11.
Remarks: Quick-Stop: >19h - <9h.

Tourist information Larochette:
Schiessentümpel. Waterfall with three cascades.
Château. Easter-Oct, 10-18h, daily.

S Liefrange 16E1

Camperhafen Leifreg, 14, Haaptstrooss. **GPS**: n49,91136 e5,87438.

23 € 10, Jul/Aug € 15 Ch WC included €1.

LU

Location: Rural, isolated, quiet. **Surface:** grasstiles/metalled.
01/04-01/11.
Distance: on the spot Obersauer Stausee 500m on the spot.

P Luxemburg 16E1

Glacis, Boulevard de la Foire /Av. de la Faiencerie.
GPS: n49,61602 e6,12246.

20 Mo-Fr € 0,80/h.
Location: Urban, simple, noisy. **Surface:** asphalted.
01/01-31/12.
Distance: centre 650m on the spot.
Remarks: Overnight stay allowed.

Tourist information Luxemburg:
Luxembourg City Tourist Office, Place d'Armes, www.lcto.lu. Citadel and fortifications have been changed in parks and walks, especially in the lower city.
01/04-31/10 Mo-Sa 9-19h, Su 10-18h, 01/11-31/03 Mo-Sa 9-18h.
Casemates du Bock, Montée de Clausen. Casemates, 21km.
01/03-31/10 10-20.30h.
Musée National d'histoire et d'art, Marché-aux-Poissons. Archeological findings.
Tue-Su 10-18h.
Palais Grand Ducal, 17, rue du Marché-aux-Herbes. Ducal palace.
01/07-31/08.
Cathédrale Notre-Dame, Rue Notre Dame.
daily 10-12h, 14-17.30h.
Crypte Archéologique, Montée de Clausen.
01/03-31/10 10-17h. T free.
Marché-aux-puces, place d'Armes. Bric-a-brac.
2nd + 4th Sa of the month.
Markt, place Guillaume.
Wed + Sa morning.
Schueberfouer. Folk festival. 30/08-15/09.

LU

S Nommern 16E1

Europacamping Nommerlayen, Rue Nommerlayen.
GPS: n49,78450 e6,16414.

13 € 10-20 Ch €2/2kWh WC €5,25/4,75 included.
Location: Rural, comfortable, isolated, quiet.
Surface: grasstiles.
01/03-06/11.
Distance: 1km on the spot on the spot 1,5km on the spot.
Remarks: Quick-Stop: >17h - <10h.

S Obereisenbach 11E3

Kohnenhof. **GPS**: n50,01630 e6,13682.

12 € 14 Ch WC included €10.
Location: Rural, comfortable, isolated, quiet.
Surface: grasstiles/metalled. 01/04-01/11.
Distance: 4km on the spot on the spot on the spot 9km on the spot on the spot.

S Redange/Attert 16E1

Rue de la Piscine 24. **GPS**: n49,76918 e5,89459.

12 free Ch (5x)free.
Location: Rural, simple, quiet. **Surface:** asphalted. 01/01-31/12.
Distance: 800m on the spot.
Remarks: Max. 48h.

S Schwebsange 16E1

Camport, Rue du Port. **GPS**: n49,51163 e6,36249.

18 € 10, 2 pers.incl Ch €2,50 WC €2 included,at restaurant. **Location:** Rural, comfortable, quiet. **Surface:** grasstiles.
01/04-31/10.
Distance: 500m fishing permit obligatory on the spot on the spot 500m.

Tourist information Schwebsange:
A Possen, 1 rue Aloyse Sandt, Bech-Kleinmacher. Folkore and wine museum. 01/05-31/10 14-19h, 01/03-30/04, 01/11-31/12 Fri-Su 14-19h Mo.

Vianden 16E1

39, rue du Sanatorium. **GPS**: n49,93717 e6,20556.

free. **Location:** Simple, central, quiet. **Surface:** asphalted.
01/01-31/12.
Distance: 500m 100m 500m 500m on the spot on the spot on the spot.
Remarks: At the chair-lifts (télesiege).

Tourist information Vianden:
SEO. Large hydro-electric power-station. Easter-Sep 10-20h.
T free.
Bakkerij museum, 96-98, Grand-Rue. Easter-Oct 11-17h Mo.
Château de Vianden. 10-16 02/11, 25/12, 01/01.
Nessmoort. Nuts market. 2nd Su Oct.
Télesiège. Chair-lift. Easter-Oct.

S Wiltz 11E3

Kaul, Rue Joseph Simon. **GPS**: n49,97173 e5,93433.

3 free €1 Ch. **Location:** Rural, simple, isolated, quiet.
Surface: gravel. 01/01-31/12.
Distance: 500m 500m.
Remarks: Recreation park, near campsite.

Montenegro

Capital: Podgorica
Government: parliamentary republic
Official Language: Montenegrin
Population: 647,000 (2015)
Area: 13,812 Km²

General information
Dialling code: 0382
General emergency: 112
Currency: Euro
Credit cards are accepted almost everywhere.

Regulations for overnight stays
Free overnight stay is not allowed.

Additional public holidays 2017
January 7-8 Christmas (Orthodox)
May 1 Labour Day
May 21 Independence Day
July 13 Statehood Day

Time Zone
Winter (Standard Time) GMT+1
Summer (DST) GMT+2

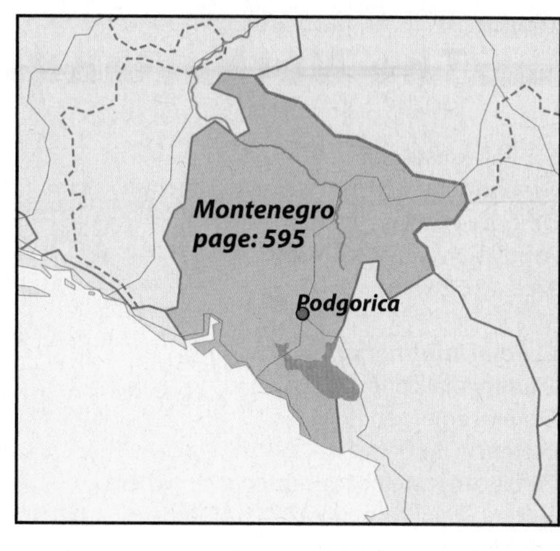

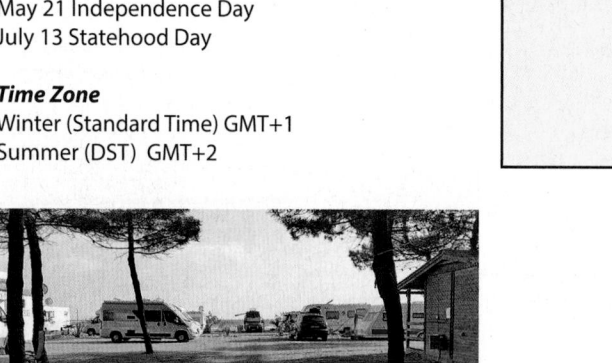

Bijela 39C2
Zlokovic. GPS: n42,45768 e18,66873.
50 € 21 Ch included.
Surface: grassy/sand. 01/03-01/11.
Distance: 2km on the spot on the spot on the spot.

Dobrilovina 39C2
Kamp Eco Oaza. GPS: n43,01780 e19,40936.
25 € 15 Ch included.
Location: Rural. **Surface:** grassy. 01/01-31/12.
Distance: 200m on the spot.

Gusinje 39C2
Krojet. GPS: n42,55053 e19,82502.
15 € 10. **Location:** Rural. **Surface:** grassy. 01/04-30/10.
Distance: on the spot.

Kotor 39C2
E65. **GPS**: n42,42761 e18,76881.
20 € 1/h Ch free.
Location: Urban. **Surface:** gravel. 01/01-31/12.
Distance: 500m on the spot on the spot 200m 200m.

Morinj 39C2
Naluka. GPS: n42,48694 e18,65214.
40 € 20 Ch included. **Surface:** grassy/sand.
01/05-01/10.
Distance: on the spot on the spot 600m.

Petnjica 39C2
Jatak. GPS: n42,97815 e19,07510.
10 € 10 Ch included €2 €2.
Surface: grassy. 01/06-01/09.
Distance: on the spot.

Petrovac 39C2
Maslina, Buljarica bb 300. **GPS**: n42,19833 e18,96583.
100 € 15,60 Ch included €3 .
Surface: grassy. 01/01-31/12.
Distance: 2km 200m 300m.

Podgorica 39C2
Hostel Izvor. GPS: n42,48363 e19,30621.
10 € 15 Ch included.
Surface: concrete. 01/01-31/12.
Distance: on the spot.

Rasova 39C1
Miro Tara-Regata, Djrdjevica Tara. **GPS**: n43,14862 e19,29217.
20 € 15 Ch included.
Surface: grassy/gravel. 01/04-30/10.

Ulcinj 39C3
Miami beach. GPS: n41,90870 e19,24978.
30 € 20 Ch included.
Surface: grassy/sand. 01/05-01/10.
Distance: on the spot on the spot on the spot.

Ulcinj 39C3
Safari beach. GPS: n41,90466 e19,26533.

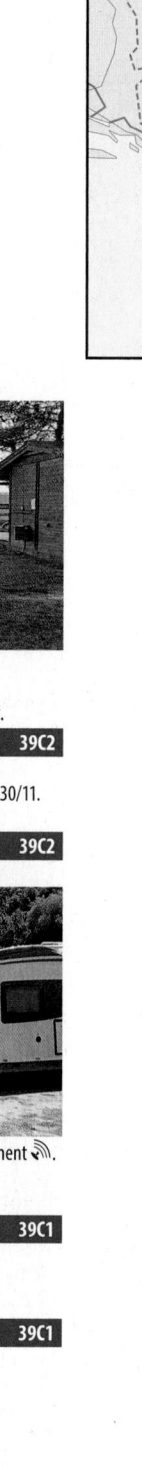

130 € 15, 15/6-15/9 € 30 Ch included €3 .
Surface: grassy. 01/01-31/12.
Distance: 7km on the spot on the spot on the spot.

Utjeha-Bušat 39C2
Oliva, Uvala Maslina-Utjeha. **GPS**: n42,01028 e19,15111.
25 € 15 Ch included. **Surface:** grassy. 01/04-30/11.
Distance: on the spot on the spot on the spot.

Utjeha-Bušat 39C2
Utjeha, Uvala Maslina-Utjeha. **GPS**: n42,01012 e19,15095.

20 € 14, 20/6-1/9€ 16 Ch included against payment .
Surface: grassy. 15/04-01/11.
Distance: on the spot on the spot on the spot.

Žabljak 39C1
Kod Boce. GPS: n43,14352 e19,11580.
30 € 6 Ch included €2.
Surface: grassy/gravel. 15/04-30/10.

Žabljak 39C1
Razvrsje. GPS: n43,14443 e19,11510.
20 € 10 Ch included.
Surface: grassy/gravel. 01/01-31/12.
Distance: 900m on the spot.

ME

The Netherlands

Capital: Amsterdam
Government: Constitutional monarchy
Official Language: Dutch
Population: 16,947,904 (2015)
Area: 41,526 km²

General information
Country dial code: 0031
General emergency: 112
Currency: Euro
Credit cards are not accepted everywhere.

Regulations for overnight stays
Wild camping is forbidden in the Netherlands. Several motorhome-friendly municipalities have regulated facilities where overnight parking is allowed.

Additional public holidays 2017
April 17 Easter Monday
April 27 King's day
May 5 Liberation day
June 5 Pentecost Monday
December 26 Boxing day

Time Zone
Winter (Standard Time) GMT+1
Summer (DST) GMT+2

NL

North Holland

Abbenes 9C2

Camperplaats 't Groene Hart, Kaagweg 50.
GPS: n52,22630 e4,61911.

25 € 10, Apr-May € 12, 2 pers. incl Chincluded (6x)€ 2/24h, 10Amp WC € 0,20 € 1 free. **Location:** Rural, comfortable, quiet. **Surface:** grassy/gravel. 15/03-01/11.
Distance: 4km 900m 1,5km 1,5km 1,5km 4km Leiden <> Amsterdam on the spot on the spot.
Remarks: Bicycle rental.

Amsterdam 9C1

Amsterdam City Camp, Papaverweg 55. **GPS**: n52,39847 e4,90010.

60 € 18, 01/08-31/08 € 21 + tourist tax € 1,50/pp Ch (30x)€ 4,10Amp included .
Location: Urban, comfortable. **Surface:** metalled. 01/01-31/12.
Distance: 2km 20m 100m 1km 1,5km 500m.

Remarks: Video surveillance, free ferry to city centre.

Amsterdam 9C1

Fam. Ackermann, Lutkemeerweg 149, Amsterdam-Osdorp.
GPS: n52,36358 e4,77240.

16 € 17,50, 2 pers. incl € 4 Ch € 4,50/day.
Surface: metalled.
01/01-31/12.
Distance: 10km city centre 2km Tram > Amsterdam 1,2km.
Remarks: Via Osdorperweg, special license.

Amsterdam 9C1

Het Amsterdamse Bos, Kleine Noorddijk 1, Amsterdam-zuid.
GPS: n52,29271 e4,82171.
100 € 21,60-25 Ch WC .
15/03-01/12.
Distance: 1km on the spot on the spot on the spot 100m.

Tourist information Amsterdam:
VVV, Stationsplein 10 en Leidseplein 1, www.iamsterdam.com. City Card gives entrance to museums, public transport, boattrip on the canals etc., 24h/€ 55, 48h/€65, 72h/€ 75, available at VVV.
Canalbus. Boat trip on the canals.
€ 21.
Stelling van Amsterdam. Forts built to protect Amsterdam.
Albert Cuyp, Albert Cuyp. Market with over 260 stalls.
daily 9-17h Su.
Antiek, Noordermarkt.
Sa 9-17h.
Artis, Plantage Kerklaan 38-40. City-zoo.
9-17/18h.
Villa Arena, Arena boulevard. Furniture mall, 50 shops. Tue-Sa 10-18h, Mo 13-18h.

De Rijp 9C1

Bloembolbedrijf Stoop, Zuiddijk 34. **GPS**: n52,54813 e4,83416.

4 € 7 € 1/100liter (4x)€ 2/day.
Location: Rural, simple, quiet. **Surface:** concrete. 01/01-31/12.
Distance: 3km 200m 200m 3km 3km.

Den Helder 7C3

Willemsoord, Willemsoord 47. **GPS**: n52,96134 e4,76856.

40 € 12,50, tourist tax incl Ch (3x)€ 1/2kWh included.
Location: Simple, central, quiet. **Surface:** metalled.
01/01-31/12.
Distance: 400m 300m 300m 400m 1km 600m.
Remarks: Max. 48h, ferry boat to Texel 500m.

Den Oever 7C3

Haventerrein Oostkade, Oostkade 3. **GPS**: n52,93395 e5,03974.

10 € 10 € 0,50/100liter € 0,50 Ch (8x) WC included.
Location: Motorway, simple, isolated, noisy. **Surface:** metalled.
01/01-31/12.
Distance: 500m 1,4km 200m offshore fishing 500m 500m on the spot.
Remarks: At old harbour, max. 3 days, saturday-morning fishmarket.

S Enkhuizen 9D1

Gependam, Dirck Chinaplein. **GPS**: n52,69806 e5,29005.

6 € 10,85 WC € 0,20 € 1.
Location: Urban, simple, central.
Surface: asphalted. 01/01-31/12.
Distance: 1km on the spot on the spot 100m 1km 100m.
Remarks: Max. 48h.

Tourist information Enkhuizen:
M Zuiderzeemuseum. Historical little town.
01/04-31/10 10-17h.

S Het Zand 7C3

Camperplaats de Hoop, Parallelweg 33.
GPS: n52,83628 e4,74931.
14 € 15 Ch included . **Location:** Rural.
Surface: grassy/metalled. 01/02-21/12.
Distance: centre 500m 5km 300m 350m 550m 150m on the spot on the spot.
Remarks: Near mill, money in envelope in mail box, call for entrance code.

S Hoorn 9C1

Jachthaven Hoorn, Visserseiland 221. **GPS**: n52,63467 e5,05676.

27 € 14,60 Ch WC € 0,50 included.
Location: Quiet. **Surface:** metalled. 01/04-31/10.
Distance: 500m 2,8km on the spot on the spot 100m on the spot.
Remarks: Check in at harbourmaster.

S Huizen 9D2

Recreatieterrein Wolskamer, IJsselmeerstraat.
GPS: n52,30860 e5,24046.

8 free Ch. **Location:** Simple, quiet. **Surface:** grassy.
01/01-31/12.
Distance: 1km 200m 200m 1km Lidl 300m on the spot on the spot.
Remarks: Max. 48h, service at harbourmaster.

Tourist information Huizen:
Sa.

Katwoude 9C1

De Simonehoeve, Wagenweg 2. **GPS**: n52,48620 e5,03196.

10 free. **Location:** Simple. **Surface:** asphalted. 01/01-31/12.
Distance: 2km 2km 2km on the spot 2km 100m.
Remarks: Cheese farm, nearby Hotel Volendam, free guided tour.

S Laren 9D2

Sportcomplex De Biezem, Schapendrift 64. **GPS**: n52,25717 e5,23884.

2 free Ch WC . **Surface:** metalled. 01/01-31/12.
Distance: 1km 1km.
Remarks: Max. 1 night.

S Medemblik 9D1

Haven Medemblik, Pekelharinghaven 50. **GPS**: n52,77139 e5,11361.

5 € 12,50, 2 pers.incl Ch WC included.
Location: Simple, quiet. **Surface:** metalled. 01/01-31/12.
Distance: 1km 200m on the spot 50m 1km 50m on the spot.
Remarks: Max. 48h, check in at harbourmaster.

Tourist information Medemblik:
M Museum Stoomtram. Steam tram museum: Hoorn-Medemblik.

S Middenmeer 9C1

Jachthaven Middenmeer, Havenstraat. **GPS**: n52,81236 e4,99112.

12 € 10 Ch WC included € 5/2 € 2.
Location: Comfortable. **Surface:** metalled. 01/01-31/12.
Distance: 500m 1,7km 50m 50m 500m 150m on the spot.
Remarks: Max. 48h, check in at harbourmaster.

S Monnickendam 9C1

Jachthaven Waterland, Galgeriet 5a. **GPS**: n52,45920 e5,04059.

6 € 18,50 Ch € 0,50/2kWh WC € 4,50 included.
Location: Urban, simple, quiet.
Surface: metalled. 30/04-15/10.
Distance: 500-800m on the spot on the spot.
Remarks: Check in at harbourmaster, caution sepkey € 20, bookings in peak season.

S Naarden 9D2

Jachthaven Naarden, Onderwal 4. **GPS**: n52,30874 e5,14703.

10 € 17,50 + € 2/pp tourist tax Ch WC € 5/3 included. **Location:** Rural, comfortable, quiet.
Surface: grassy/metalled. 01/01-31/12.
Distance: Naarden-vesting (fortress) 2,3km 600m 500m lake Gooi on the spot on the spot on the spot.

Tourist information Naarden:
M Vestingmuseum. Fortress museum. Tue-Fri 10.30-17h, Sa/Su/holidays 12-17h.

S Nieuw Vennep 9C2

Allesonda Hoeve, IJweg 1281. **GPS**: n52,28705 e4,62614.
15 € 12 Ch included. **Location:** Rural. **Surface:** metalled.
01/04-01/10.
Distance: 1,5km 1,5km 1,5km.
Remarks: Only cash payment.

Oosthuizen 9C1

Recreatieknooppunt Oosthuizen, Hoornse Jaagweg.
GPS: n52,57609 e4,99719.

2 free. **Location:** Rural, isolated, noisy. **Surface:** asphalted.
01/01-31/12.
Distance: 250m on the spot on the spot 200m 500m 100m > Volendam on the spot on the spot.
Remarks: Max. 48h.

S Opperdoes 9C1

Imkerij de Bijenstal, Zwarte pad. **GPS**: n52,76255 e5,08027.

3 € 11,10, 2 pers.incl (2x) € 3,50 .
Location: Rural, simple, isolated, quiet. **Surface:** gravel.
Distance: 500m 2km 300m 500m.
Remarks: Boat rental.

Tourist information Opperdoes:
M Museum stoomtram, Van Dedemstraat 8, Medemblik. Steam tram museum: Hoorn-Medemblik.

NL

Oudendijk 9C1

Bruin Eetcafé Les Deux Ponts, Slimdijk 2.
GPS: n52,60462 e4,95983.

10 free, use of a meal obligated. **Location:** Rural, simple, quiet.
Surface: gravel. 01/01-31/12 Tue.
Distance: 2km on the spot on the spot on the spot.

Purmerend 9C1

Het Bolwerk, Nieuwstraat. **GPS**: n52,50681 e4,95049.

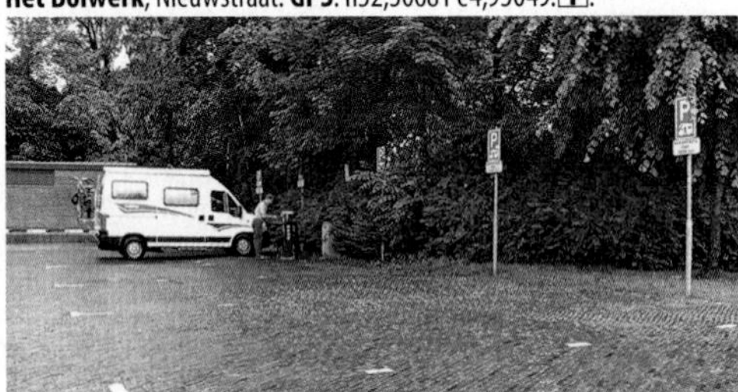

5 € 6,90 € 1 € 0,15/h free.
Location: Urban, simple, quiet. **Surface:** metalled.
01/01-31/12 water: 01/11-01/04.
Distance: 200m 200m.
Remarks: Max. 72h, tuesday morning market.

Tourist information Purmerend:
Centrum. Tue.

Schagen 9C1

Jachthaven Schagen, Lagedijkerweg 2B. **GPS**: n52,79088 e4,78746.

15 € 7,50 + € 0,97/pp tourist tax € 0,50/100liter Ch included WC € 0,50 € 4/4 € 1.
Surface: metalled. 01/01-31/12.
Distance: 500m on the spot 400m 500m.
Remarks: Check in at harbourmaster, caution key sanitary building € 15.

Tourist information Schagen:
West Friese Folkloremarkt. Folkore market. Jun-Jul-Aug: Thu.

Slootdorp 7C3

De Tulpentuin, Wierweg 7. **GPS**: n52,85627 e5,01010.

8 € 11,50 Ch (8x)WC included.
Location: Rural, isolated, quiet. **Surface:** metalled. 01/01-31/12.
Distance: Wieringerwerf 2km 2km 500m 2km 2km on the spot on the spot.
Remarks: At tulip grower, regional products.

Stompetoren 9C1

Het Schermer Wapen, Oterlekerweg 3. **GPS**: n52,61285 e4,82096.

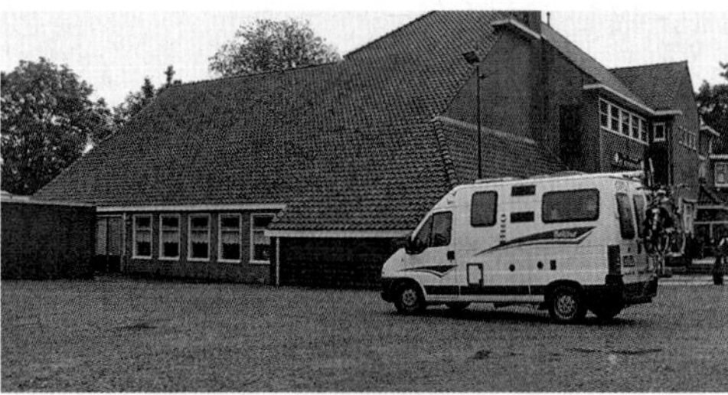

4 free, use of a meal obligated. **Location:** Urban, simple.
Surface: gravel. 01/01-31/12 Wed.
Distance: 500m on the spot 500m.

Texel/De Cocksdorp 7C3

De Krim, Roggeslootweg 6. **GPS**: n53,15110 e4,85996.
10 € 16-26 Ch included. **Surface:** grassy/metalled.
01/01-31/12.

Volendam 9C1

Marinapark Volendam, De Pieterman 1.
GPS: n52,48944 e5,05972.

36 € 14 10-17h, € 20/24h Ch included € 5 .
Location: Comfortable, quiet.
Surface: grasstiles/metalled.
01/01-31/12.
Distance: 1,5km 50m 50m 300m 300m 300m.

Tourist information Volendam:
VVV, Zeestraat 37, www.vvv-volendam.nl. Old fishermen's village.
Volendams Museum, Zeestraat 41. Life and Work in Volendam, 1800-1900.
01/03-30/11 10-17h.

Weesp 9C2

Vecht & Weide, Dammerweg 5c. **GPS**: n52,28729 e5,07152.
8 € 12, tourist tax incl Ch (8x)WC included.
Location: Rural. **Surface:** metalled. 01/01-31/12.
Distance: 4km 400m 400m 3.5km Bus 300m on the spot on the spot.
Remarks: Max. 8M.

Friesland

Akkrum 7D3

Tusken de Marren, Ulbe Twijnstrawei 31. **GPS**: n53,04853 e5,82577.

20 € 15 € 0,50/100liter Ch € 2/night WC € 4/2 included. **Surface:** grassy/metalled. 15/03-01/11.
Distance: 200m on the spot on the spot 700m 500m on the spot.
Remarks: Information at harbourmaster, boat rental.

Anjum 7E2

It Tún-Hûs, Bantswei 1a. **GPS**: n53,37751 e6,12999.

20 € 10 Ch WC . **Surface:** metalled.
15/03-31/10.
Distance: 400m 2km 350m 550m.

Appelscha 7E3

De Compagnonshoeve, Vaart Noordzijde 104.
GPS: n52,95222 e6,36278.

10 € 8 Ch € 1,50 included.
Location: Rural, simple, quiet. **Surface:** grassy. 01/01-31/12.
Distance: on the spot 3km on the spot 200m 400m 400m 50m.

Appelscha 7E3

Camperplaats Appelscha, Noorder Es. **GPS**: n52,95459 e6,33619.

10 € 10 € 0,10/20liter Ch (10x) € 0,50/kWh WC € 0,50 included. **Surface:** grassy/metalled. 01/01-31/12.
Distance: on the spot 5km 900m on the spot 1km 500m on the spot on the spot.

Balk 7D3

Jachthaven Lutsmond, Sleatemar 1a. **GPS**: n52,90389 e5,59694.

10 € 10 + € 1/pp tourist tax Ch € 3 WC .
Surface: grassy. 01/01-31/12.
Distance: 1km on the spot on the spot nearby 1km on the spot on the spot.

Bergum 7E3

Camperterrein Prinses Margriet Kanaal, Opperdijk van Veenweg 22.
GPS: n53,18643 e6,00176.

25 € 10/night Ch included € 2/night 1h free, 1 day € 7,50.
Location: Urban, comfortable, quiet. **Surface:** grassy/metalled.
01/01-31/12.
Distance: 2km 2km on the spot 2km 200m on the spot on the spot on the spot.

Bergum 7E3

Jachthaven Burgumerdaam, Bergumerdaam 51.
GPS: n53,18705 e5,99299.

NL

10 € 9 + € 1/pp tourist tax € 0,50/100liter Ch € 0,50/kWh WC € 0,50/5minutes € 3,50/3,50 included.
Location: Urban, comfortable, central, quiet. **Surface:** metalled.
15/03-01/11.
Distance: 500m 500m 5km on the spot 500m 500m 500m on the spot on the spot.
Remarks: Max. 72h.

Blesdijke 7E3

Stoutenburght, Markeweg 35a. **GPS**: n52,83850 e6,03339.

12 € 10 Ch (12x),6Amp WC included.
Location: Rural. **Surface:** grassy. 15/03-01/10.
Distance: 5km 2km 2km on the spot on the spot.

Bolsward 7D3

Camperplaats Half-Hichtum, Hichtumerweg 14.
GPS: n53,07365 e5,52253.

6 € 13,50 Ch WC included € 3,50 .
Location: Rural, comfortable, quiet. **Surface:** grassy/metalled.
01/04-01/11.
Distance: 1km 1,3km 6km 500m 1km 1km 200m on the spot on the spot.

Brantgum 7E2

Camperplaats Veldzicht, Veldbuurtsterweg 9.
GPS: n53,35556 e5,93632.

20 € 11 Ch included.
Location: Rural, comfortable, isolated, quiet.
Surface: grassy/metalled. 01/01-31/12.
Distance: Dokkum 7km 2km 3km 3km on the spot on the spot.
Remarks: Ferry boat to Ameland 3km.

Burdaard 7E3

Jachthaven Mouneheim, Mounewei 17. **GPS**: n53,29711 e5,88261.

12 € 10 Ch € 1/night,10Amp WC € 0,50/5minutes € 4,50/2,50 included. **Location:** Rural, comfortable, quiet.
Surface: grassy/gravel. 01/01-31/12.
Distance: on the spot 2km on the spot on the spot 100m 500m 2km on the spot on the spot.
Remarks: Passerby € 1/100l.

Dokkum 7E2

Van Kleffenstraat 8. **GPS**: n53,32496 e5,99254.
5 € 12, 2 pers.incl Ch WC free.
Location: Central.
Surface: grassy/metalled. 01/01-31/12.
Distance: on the spot on the spot 400m 200m 400m on the spot on the spot.
Remarks: Max. 72h.

Dokkum 7E2

Kalkhuisplein, Kalkhuisplein. **GPS**: n53,32650 e6,00936.

3 € 5.
Location: Urban, simple, quiet. **Surface:** metalled. 15/03-31/12.
Distance: 500m 1km 20m 20m 1km 1km 1km on the spot on the spot.
Remarks: Max. 1 night, only overnight stays 18-9h.

Drachten 7E3

VV Drachten, Gauke Boelensstraat. **GPS**: n53,10289 e6,08832.

5 free. **Surface:** asphalted. 01/01-31/12.
Distance: 500m on the spot 500m on the spot on the spot.

Earnewâld 7E3

Eilansgrien. **GPS**: n53,12958 e5,93630.

5 € 5,40 + € 1/pp tourist tax Ch included WC € 0,50 € 3,50,€ 3,50/3,50 .
Surface: asphalted. 01/01-31/12.
Distance: 200m 500m 200m.
Remarks: Max. 72h, sanitary/washing machine at tourist office (Summer season).

Harlingen 7D3

Tsjerk Hiddesluizen, Nieuwe Vissershaven 17.
GPS: n53,17938 e5,41731.

10 € 7,50 € 1 Ch (16x)€ 1/2kWh WC .
Surface: asphalted. 01/01-31/12.
Distance: 500m 500m 500m 100m.
Remarks: Max. 72h, laundromat/toilets/shower 500m.

Heerenveen 7E3

Thialf, Pim Mulierlaan 1. **GPS**: n52,93843 e5,94495.

4 free. **Surface:** metalled.
01/01-31/12 during event.
Distance: 2km 2km 2km.
Remarks: On parking ground of skating rink, max. 72h.

Heerenveen 7E3

De Koningshof, Prinsenweg 1. **GPS**: n52,94759 e5,94438.

4 free. **Surface:** asphalted. 01/01-31/12.
Distance: 1km on the spot 4km 500m.
Remarks: Large parking near A32, max. 72h.

Heerenveen 7E3

Gemeentewerf, Venus 4. **GPS**: n52,96663 e5,93502.
free. Mon-Fri 9-15u.

Hogebeintum 7D2

Bezoekerscentrum Terp Hegebeintum, Pijpkedijk 4.
GPS: n53,33612 e5,85266.

4 free. **Location:** Simple, isolated. **Surface:** asphalted.
Distance: 4km.
Remarks: Parking information centre/VVV, highest mound in the Netherlands, max. 2 days, ferry boat to Ameland 3km.

IJlst 7D3

De Tsjalk, De Tsjalk. **GPS**: n53,00846 e5,62741.

4 € 7,50 WC free € 0,50/5minutes.
Location: Urban, simple, central, quiet. **Surface:** metalled.

NL

01/01-31/12.
Distance: 200m on the spot 200m 200m 200m on the spot on the spot.

Joure 7D3

Jachthaven, Grienedyk. **GPS**: n52,97210 e5,78836.

4 € 10 + € 1/pp tourist tax € 0,50/70liter € 3 € 1 € 7,50.
Surface: metalled. 01/03-01/11.
Distance: 500m 50m.
Remarks: Max. 72h.

Kollum 7E3

Jachthaven de Rijd, Cantecleer 2. **GPS**: n53,28727 e6,15139.

12 € 10 Ch ,10Amp WC included.
Location: Urban, simple, central, quiet. **Surface:** metalled.
01/05-01/10.
Distance: on the spot on the spot 500m 500m 500m on the spot on the spot.
Remarks: Max. 72h.

Koudum 7D3

De Kuilart, De Kuilart 1. **GPS**: n52,90305 e5,46706.

10 + 2 € 17,50-25 + € 1/pp tourist tax, Quick-Stop € 8 Chincluded € 1/night,6Amp WC € 0,35/5minutes € 4,40/2,35 .
Location: Rural, luxurious, noisy. **Surface:** grassy/metalled.
01/01-07/05, 22/05-05/07, 25/08-31/12 holidays.
Distance: 1,5km on the spot on the spot on the spot 1km 1km on the spot on the spot.

Langweer 7D3

Brandweerkazerne, Pontdyk. **GPS**: n52,96000 e5,71972.

4 free free. **Location:** Simple. **Surface:** metalled.
01/01-31/12.
Distance: 500m 500m 500m 500m.
Remarks: Max. 72h.

Langweer 7D3

Passantenhaven Langweer, Pontdyk. **GPS**: n52,96091 e5,72240.

3 € 7, tourist tax € 0,20/pp € 0,20 Ch € 2 WC € 0,50 € 3,50/3,50 . **Surface:** grassy. 01/04-31/10.
Distance: 500m on the spot on the spot 500m 500m 500m.

Leeuwarden 7D3

Prinsentuin, Wissesdwinger 1. **GPS**: n53,20528 e5,79659.

4 € 9,08 Ch € 0,34/kWh,6Amp WC € 4,31/3 included.
Location: Urban, comfortable, central, quiet. **Surface:** metalled.
01/01-31/12 sanitary building: 01/11-01/04.
Distance: on the spot 2km on the spot on the spot on the spot on the spot on the spot on the spot on the spot.

Leeuwarden 7D3

Harlingertrekweg. **GPS**: n53,19839 e5,77098.

5 free. **Location:** Noisy.
Surface: metalled. 01/01-31/12.
Distance: 1km 1km 1km 500m.

Leeuwarden 7D3

Leeuwarder Jachthaven, Jachthavenlaan 3.
GPS: n53,19886 e5,83019.

6 € 12,50 Ch WC € 1/5minutes included.
Location: Urban, comfortable, isolated, quiet. **Surface:** grassy/gravel.
01/01-31/12.
Distance: 2,5km 1km on the spot on the spot 500m 500m 300m on the spot on the spot.
Remarks: Check in at harbourmaster.

Leeuwarden 7D3

Taniaburg, Vierhuisterweg 72. **GPS**: n53,21955 e5,79286.

8 € 12,50 Ch € 2/night,6Amp WC € 2,50,€ 2,50/3 included. **Location:** Rural, comfortable, quiet.
Surface: grassy/gravel. 01/04-01/11.
Distance: 3km 1km on the spot on the spot 500m 500m on the spot on the spot.
Remarks: Canoe and bicycle rental.

Lemmer 7D3

Jachthaven Lemmer, Plattedijk 4-12. **GPS**: n52,84708 e5,69696.

25 € 13 + tourist tax € 1/pp € 0,50 Ch € 0,50 WC € 0,50 . **Surface:** metalled. 01/01-31/12.
Distance: 1km 2,7km on the spot 1km.

Lemmer 7D3

Watersportcentrum Tacozijl, Plattedijk 20. **GPS**: n52,85104 e5,68189.

20 € 12,50-21 Ch € 0,50/kWh WC included .
Surface: grassy/metalled. 01/01-31/12.
Distance: centre 2,2km 3km 1,5km on the spot on the spot on the spot.

Tourist information Lemmer:
Ir. D.F. Woudagemaal. The biggest steam pumpingstation of Europe.
Tue-Sa 10-17h, Su 13-17h.

Lollum 7D3

Camperplaats Landgoed Hizzard, Hizzaarderlaan 16.
GPS: n53,11913 e5,51428.
2 € 12, tourist tax incl Chincluded (2x)€ 2,50/24h WC € 2,50 . **Location:** Rural. **Surface:** metalled.
01/01-31/12.
Distance: city centre Winsum 3,8km on the spot 3,8km 1,4km on the spot on the spot.

Makkum 7D3

Gemeentehaven Makkum, Workumerdijk 2.
GPS: n53,05329 e5,40317.

2 € 10 ChWC included € 2/2.
Location: Urban, simple, central, noisy. **Surface:** metalled.
01/04-31/10 service: 01/11-01/04.
Distance: 100m on the spot 400m 950m 950m on the spot on the spot.
Remarks: Max. 72h.

Mirns 7D3

De Braamberg, Murnserdyk. **GPS**: n52,85249 e5,48190.

10 € 10 + € 1/pp tourist tax Chincluded € 2 WC .

NL

Location: Rural. **Surface:** gravel. 01/01-31/12.
Distance: beach 250m.

Molkwerum 7D3

Camperplaats 't Seleantsje, 't Seleantsje 2.
GPS: n52,90419 e5,39493.

18 € 12 Ch WC included € 0,50/6minutes € 4/2,50 € 5/day. **Location:** Rural, comfortable, quiet. **Surface:** grasstiles. 15/03-01/11.
Distance: 300m on the spot on the spot on the spot 4km 1km on the spot on the spot.

Nes 7E3

Manege Nes, Burdineweg 2. **GPS**: n53,05468 e5,85558.

10 € 5 Ch € 2/night,16Amp WC included.
Location: Rural, simple, quiet. **Surface:** grassy/metalled. 01/01-31/12.
Distance: 700m 1km 10km 50m 700m 700m 700m on the spot on the spot.
Remarks: At manege.

Nijetrijne 7E3

Paviljoen Driewegsluis, Lindedijk 2a. **GPS**: n52,83261 e5,92467.

customers free. **Surface:** metalled.
Distance: on the spot on the spot on the spot on the spot.

Oudega 7E3

Jachthaven Oudega, Roundeel. **GPS**: n53,12315 e5,99961.

2 € 7 € 1/100liter € 1 € 1. **Location:** Simple. **Surface:** grassy. 01/04-01/11.
Distance: 200m 200m 200m.
Remarks: Max. 48h.

Oudemirdum 7D3

Landgoed de Syme, Jan Schotanuswei 106a, via Oude Balksterweg.
GPS: n52,85746 e5,51115.

2 € 7,50 included € 2,50/night.
Location: Rural, simple, isolated, quiet. **Surface:** grassy/metalled. 01/01-31/12.
Distance: 4km 6km 6km 4km 4km on the spot on the spot.

Oudeschoot 7E3

Minicamping 't Woutersbergje, Van Bienemalaan 15-17.
GPS: n52,93544 e5,96009.

7 € 10,40 Ch € 2,50/night,6Amp WC € 3/2 included. **Location:** Rural, comfortable, central, quiet. **Surface:** metalled. 01/01-31/12.
Distance: 3,5km 300m on the spot on the spot.

Ried 7D3

Jachthaven it Kattegat, Berlikumerweg 13. **GPS**: n53,22416 e5,59330.

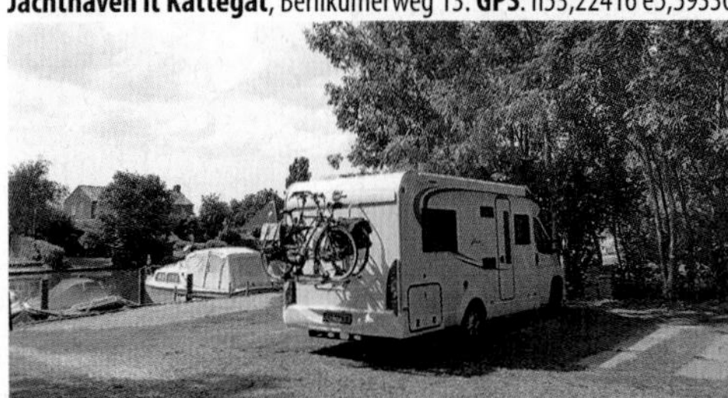

3 + 4 € 9,50 . **Location:** Rural, simple, quiet. **Surface:** grassy/metalled. 01/04-01/10.
Distance: on the spot 500m on the spot on the spot 500m on the spot on the spot.

Rohel 7D3

Aktiviteitenboerderij, Vierhuisterweg 29. **GPS**: n52,90337 e5,84540.

5 € 15 Ch WC included. **Location:** Quiet. **Surface:** metalled. 01/01-31/12.
Distance: on the spot on the spot on the spot on the spot.

Sexbierum 7D3

Restaurant Liauckama State, Liauckamaleane 2.
GPS: n53,22028 e5,47656.

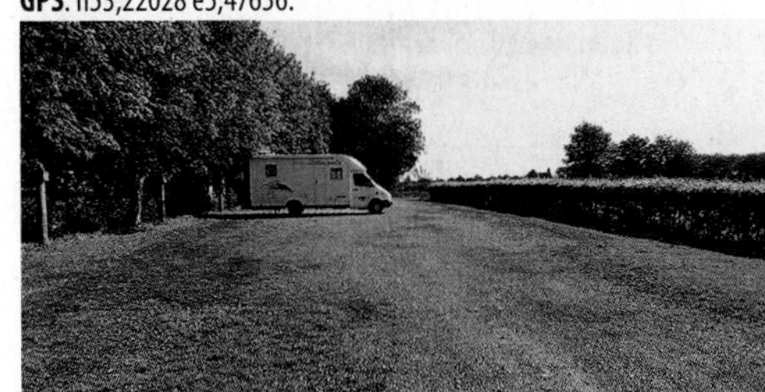

5 € 10, free for clients. **Surface:** grassy/gravel. 01/01-31/12.
Distance: 1km 1km 1km.

Sint Jacobiparochie 7D3

Zeedijk, Zwarte Haan. **GPS**: n53,30915 e5,63051.

25 free. **Surface:** grassy. 01/01-31/12.
Distance: Sint Jacobiparochie 8km Wadden Sea 100m on the spot on the spot.

Sloten 7D3

Jachthaven Lemsterpoort, Jachthaven 7.
GPS: n52,89265 e5,64486.

10 € 12 € 0,50/100liter Ch € 2,50/24h,6Amp WC € 1/5minutes included. **Location:** Urban, comfortable, quiet. **Surface:** grassy/metalled. 01/01-31/12.
Distance: 100m 2km on the spot on the spot 100m 100m 500m on the spot on the spot.

Sneek 7D3

Jachthaven Holiday Boatin, Eeltjebaasweg 3.
GPS: n53,01996 e5,69562.

4 € 12 Ch € 1/night,10Amp WC included.
Location: Urban, comfortable, quiet. **Surface:** concrete. 01/01-31/12.
Distance: 3,6km 2km on the spot on the spot 4km 2km, bakery 300m 300m on the spot on the spot.

Sneek 7D3

Amicitia Hotel Sneek, Alexanderstraat.
GPS: n53,02378 e5,67595.

10 € 9,50, free with a meal Ch included.
Surface: metalled. 01/01-31/12.
Distance: 1,5km 400m 8km on the spot.
Remarks: Reservation during Sneek sailing week: info@amicitiahotel.nl, 1st week of August.

NL

Stavoren 7D3

Marina Stavoren Buitenhaven Stavoren

- Paved motorhome pitches
- Located directly at lake
- Located directly on the beach

Marina Stavoren Buitenhaven, Suderstrand 2.
GPS: n52,87360 e5,36715.
25 € 12,50 Ch € 2,16Amp WC € 4,50/2,50 included. **Surface:** asphalted. 01/04-31/10.
Distance: Stavoren 500m on the spot on the spot on the spot 500m 500m on the spot on the spot.
Remarks: Max. 3 nights, check in at harbourmaster.

Sumar 7E3

Recreatiecentrum Bergumermeer, Solcamastraat 30.
GPS: n53,19044 e6,02316.

10 € 19,50 Ch WC included. **Location:** Rural, luxurious, quiet. **Surface:** grassy/metalled. 01/04-31/10.
Distance: 5km.

Sumar 7E3

Recreatiecentrum Bergumermeer, Solcamastraat-30.
GPS: n53,19044 e6,02316.

1 € 8 17-10h. 01/04-31/10.

Surhuisterveen 7E3

Zwembad Wettervlecke, Badlaan 3. **GPS**: n53,17987 e6,16124.

5 € 5 € 1 € 1 WC included. **Surface:** grassy.
Distance: 500m 500m.

Tersoal 7D3

Watersportbedrijf Lege Geaen, Buorren 2.
GPS: n53,07729 e5,74360.

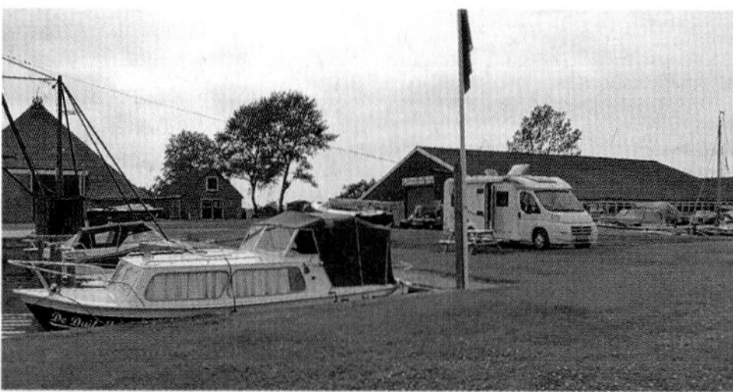

6 € 12 Ch € 2,50/night WC included.
Location: Rural, comfortable, quiet. **Surface:** grassy/gravel.
01/01-31/12.
Distance: 8km 1,5km on the spot on the spot 1,5km 8km on the spot on the spot.

Wartena 7E3

Jachthaven Wartena, Stukenwei. **GPS**: n53,15145 e5,90532.

10 € 10 € 0,50/100 Ch WC € 1 € 6 .
Location: Central.
Surface: grassy/metalled. 01/01-31/11.
Distance: 200m on the spot on the spot 500m 500m on the spot on the spot.
Remarks: Bicycle rental.

Winsum 7D3

Camperplaats Winsum, Skans 12. **GPS**: n53,15177 e5,63111.

4 € 12 Ch included WC . **Location:** Simple.
01/01-31/12.

Wommels 7D3

Jachthaven Wommels, Terp 14. **GPS**: n53,10957 e5,58765.

8 € 11 Ch WCincluded € 0,50.
Location: Simple. **Surface:** grassy/metalled. 01/04-01/10.
Distance: 300m on the spot 100m.
Remarks: Market 100m, museum 200m.

Tourist information Wommels:
Tue-morning.

Workum 7D3

Jachthaven Bouwsma, Moleburren 11. **GPS**: n52,98230 e5,45518.

10 € 10-14 excl. tourist tax Ch € 2,50/night,6Amp WC € 2 € 1/7minutes € 8/0 included. **Location:** Urban, central, quiet. **Surface:** grassy/metalled.
01/04-31/10.
Distance: 750m 1,5km on the spot 500m 500m 200m on the spot on the spot.

Tourist information Workum:
M Jopie Huisman Museum, Noard 6. Autodidact, paintings and drawings. T € 8,50.

Woudsend 7D3

Recreatiecentrum De Rakken, Lynbaen 10.
GPS: n52,94649 e5,62732.

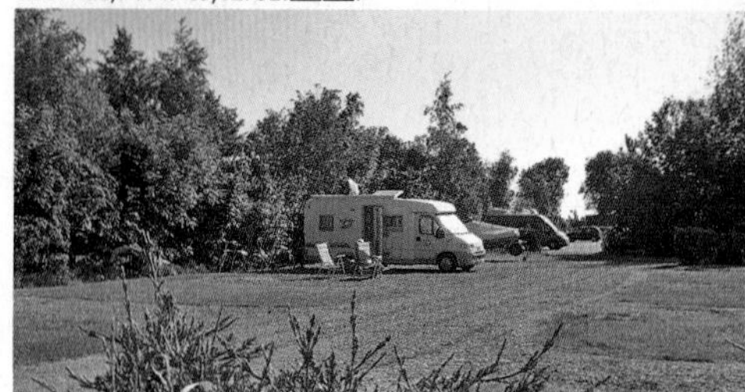

15 € 17,50 + € 1/pp tourist tax Ch WC included € 4,50/2,50 . **Surface:** grassy/metalled. 15/03-15/10.
Distance: 200m 2,5km 200m 200m 200m.

Ypecolsga 7D3

Camperplaats Waterloo, Nr. 19. **GPS**: n52,92758 e5,59549.

13 € 10, 2 pers.incl Ch WC use sanitary € 1,50/pp € 4,50/2 included. **Surface:** grasstiles. 01/01-31/12.
Distance: 3km 1km 1km 3,5km 3,5km nearby on the spot.

Zurich 7D3

Camperplaats Zurich, Caspar di Roblesdijk 3.
GPS: n53,11235 e5,39335.

3 € 3. **Location:** Urban, simple, central, noisy. **Surface:** metalled.
01/01-31/12.
Distance: on the spot 1,5km on the spot on the spot on the spot on the spot.
Remarks: Max. 72h.

Zwaagwesteinde 7E3

Camperpark Kuikhorne, Kuikhornsterweg 31.
GPS: n53,24124 e6,01875.

25 € 10, 2 pers.incl € 1/100liter Ch € 1 WC € 0,50 € 4/3 . **Surface:** asphalted/grassy. 15/03-01/11.
Distance: 2km on the spot 2km, pizzeria within walking distance 2km.
Remarks: Max. 72h, boat rental.

NL

Groningen

Appingedam 7F2

Camperplaats Appingedam, Farmsumerweg 21.
GPS: n53,32062 e6,86689.

10 free free € 1/kWh,10Amp.
Location: Urban, simple, central, noisy. **Surface:** metalled.
01/01-31/12.
Distance: 750m Damsterdiep 500m 500m on the spot on the spot on the spot.
Remarks: Max. 72h.

Tourist information Appingedam:
Solwerderstraat. Sa 09-16h.

Blijham 7F3

Camperpark Turfstee, Turfweg 28. **GPS**: n53,11118 e7,02912.

55 € 10 + € 0,75 tourist tax Ch WC € 0,50/5minutes € 7,50/0 included. **Location:** Rural, comfortable, isolated.
Surface: grassy/gravel.
Distance: 3km 3km 3km on the spot on the spot.

Delfzijl 7F2

Zeebadweg, Zeebadweg. **GPS**: n53,33582 e6,92650.

8 free Chfree € 1.
Distance: 500m on the spot on the spot 100m 300m.
Remarks: Max. 48h.

Doezum 7E3

Landgoed Jonker, Provincialeweg 133a.
GPS: n53,20411 e6,26018.

60 € 10, 2 pers.incl Ch (20x)€ 0,50/kWh,16Amp WC included.
Location: Luxurious.
Surface: grassy/metalled.
25/03-01/10.
Distance: 1,5km on the spot on the spot on the spot.

Tourist information Doezum:
Abel Tasman Kabinet, Kompasstraat 1, Grootegast. Local archaeological museum seafarer Abel Tasman. Thu-Sa 13.30-16.30h.

Eenrum 7E2

Jachthaven De Dobbe, Dobbepad. **GPS**: n53,36311 e6,45151.

4 € 3 + € 3/pp + € 1,15/pp tourist tax Ch € 2 WCincluded € 0,50. **Location:** Rural, simple, quiet.
Surface: grassy/metalled.
Distance: 500m on the spot 500m 500m.
Remarks: Check in at harbourmaster.

Groningen 7E3

Sportcentrum Kardinge, Bieskemaar. **GPS**: n53,23946 e6,59680.

15 tourist tax. **Location:** Rural, simple, quiet. **Surface:** metalled.
01/01-31/12.
Distance: 3km 1km on the spot.
Remarks: Max. 72h.

Tourist information Groningen:
Prinsenhof en prinsenhoftuin. 15/03-15/10.

Haren 7E3

De Lijste, Meerweg. **GPS**: n53,16298 e6,57878.
10 free. **Surface:** grassy.
Distance: 1,3km no bathing 250m.

Lauwersoog 7E2

Lauwersmeerplezier, Kustweg 30. **GPS**: n53,40625 e6,20044.

23 € 17, 2 pers. incl WC € 3 included.
Surface: grassy/metalled. 01/01-31/12.
Distance: 500m on the spot on the spot 500m 500m.

Lauwersoog 7E2

Havenkantoor Lauwersoog, Haven 2.
GPS: n53,40819 e6,19768.

2 € 1,50/m Ch WC included.
Location: Urban, simple, quiet. **Surface:** metalled. 01/01-31/12.
Distance: on the spot on the spot on the spot on the spot on the spot.

Lauwersoog 7E2

Jachthaven Noordergat, Noordergat 1.
GPS: n53,40493 e6,20311.

30 € 15 + € 1,15/pp tourist tax Ch included WC € 0,50/5minutes € 3/2,50 . **Location:** Rural, simple, quiet.
Surface: concrete. 01/01-31/12.
Distance: on the spot on the spot on the spot on the spot.

Tourist information Lauwersoog:
Lauwersmeergebied. Breeding area for birds and recreation area.
01/04-31/10 Tue-Su 11-17h.

Leens 7E2

Leenstertillen, Leenstertillen 2. **GPS**: n53,35066 e6,37002.

15 € 12,50 Chservice € 3 included WC € 1.
Location: Rural, simple, quiet.
Surface: metalled. 01/01-31/12.
Distance: 1,5km 50m 50m 1,5km 1,6km.
Remarks: Dog € 1,50/night, barbecue place.

Losdorp 7F2

Restaurant Eemshaven, Schafferweg 29.
GPS: n53,37214 e6,84411.

4 consuming is appreciated Ch € 5,customers WC free . **Location:** Rural, simple, quiet. **Surface:** metalled.
01/01-31/12 Mo.
Distance: 2km 2km 1km on the spot on the spot.
Remarks: Code wifi in restaurant.

Lutjegast 7E3

't Kompas, Kompasstraat 1. **GPS**: n53,23498 e6,25972.

5 free. **Surface:** metalled. 01/01-31/12.
Distance: 200m on the spot 200m on the spot.
Remarks: Behind the club-building.

Midwolda 7F3

Blauwestadhoeve, Hoofdweg 156. **GPS**: n53,19424 e7,00751.
6 € 10 € 2,25 € 1,50 Ch€ 1,50 (6x)€ 1,45 WC € 1 € 1 € 1,45 . **Location:** Rural. **Surface:** grassy/metalled.
01/01-31/12.
Distance: 250m 2km 900m 500m 100m 250m 100m on the spot on the spot.

NL

Midwolda 7F3

Jachthaven Midwolda, Strandweg 1. **GPS**: n53,19634 e7,03068.
5 € 11,90 € 0,50/100liter Ch € 1/day WC included.
Location: Rural, comfortable, quiet.
Surface: grassy. 01/04-31/10.
Distance: city centre 1km on the spot on the spot 1km 500m on the spot.
Remarks: View at Lake Oldambt.

Musselkanaal 7F3

Jachthaven Spoordok, Havenkade 1. **GPS**: n52,92694 e7,01389.

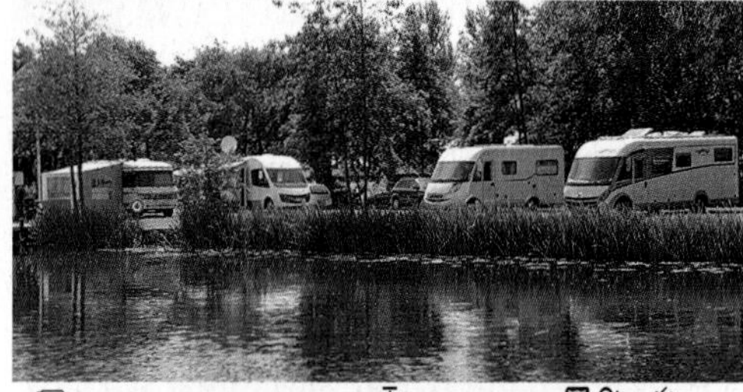

35 € 9,50 + € 0,75/pp tourist tax € 0,50/100liter Ch (35x)WC included.
Location: Rural, comfortable, quiet. **Surface:** grassy/metalled.
01/04-01/11.
Distance: 200m on the spot on the spot on the spot nearby on the spot on the spot. **Remarks:** Max. 72h.

Nuis 7E3

Het Knooppunt, Oudeweg 47. **GPS**: n53,15061 e6,31021.

12 € 10 Ch WC included.
Location: Rural. **Surface:** grassy/metalled. 01/04-01/10.
Distance: on the spot 3km 5km 2km 3,5km on the spot on the spot on the spot. **Remarks:** Breakfast-service, charging point for electric bicycles.

Onderdendam 7E2

Watersportvereniging Onderdendam, Warffumerweg 12.
GPS: n53,33652 e6,58600.

6 € 6 + € 1/pp Ch (6x)€ 2,50 WCincluded € 0,50.
Location: Simple, quiet. **Surface:** grassy/metalled.
Distance: 500m on the spot on the spot 500m 500m.

Onstwedde 7F3

Holte 9. **GPS**: n53,05021 e7,04459.

5 € 3 Chincluded € 2.
Location: Rural, simple. **Surface:** grassy. 01/01-31/12.
Distance: 1km 1km 1km 1km bike junction.

Sellingen 7F3

Camperpark Westerwolde, Zevenmeersveenweg 1a.
GPS: n52,95412 e7,13174.

10 € 8 + € 1/pp tourist tax € 1 ChWC included € 4.
Location: Rural, simple, quiet.
Surface: grassy. 01/01-31/12.
Distance: 1km on the spot 1km 1km on the spot on the spot.
Remarks: Arrival after 7pm.

Sellingen 7F3

De Barkhoorn, Beetserweg 6. **GPS**: n52,94617 e7,13421.

5 € 9 + tourist tax, dog € 3 € 3,50.
Location: Rural, simple, quiet. **Surface:** grasstiles.
01/04-31/10 01/07-22/08.

Slochteren 7F3

Duurswoldje, Edserweg. **GPS**: n53,20051 e6,79020.

7 € 7 Ch included € 1/24h.
Location: Rural, simple, quiet. **Surface:** grassy. 01/01-31/12.
Distance: 500m on the spot on the spot 1km on the spot.
Remarks: Covered picnic area, small stock accommodation.

Stadskanaal 7F3

De Roo Campers, Unikenkade 1. **GPS**: n53,03556 e6,87617.

10 € 5 ChWCincluded.

Location: Rural, simple, quiet.
Surface: grassy. 01/01-31/12.
Distance: 8km 4km on the spot on the spot 8km 8km.

Tourist information Stadskanaal:
Pagedal, www.stadskanaal.nl. Daytime recreation.

Ter Apel 7F3

Jachthaven De Runde, Oosterkade 5. **GPS**: n52,87179 e7,07329.

10 € 7,50 + € 0,75/pp tourist tax € 0,50 Ch € 1 WC € 0,50 € 4,€ 4/2 free,5h. **Location:** Rural, comfortable, quiet.
Surface: grassy. 01/01-31/12.
Distance: 1km on the spot on the spot on the spot 1km 500m on the spot.
Remarks: Wifi 5h free.

Termunterzijl 7F2

Zeestrand, Schepperbuurt 4a. **GPS**: n53,30173 e7,03085.

15 € 10 ChWCincluded € 1 € 4/2 € 2,50.
Surface: metalled. 01/01-31/12.
Distance: 100m 100m 100m 200m 200m.
Remarks: Registration via intercom or phone.

Usquert 7E2

't Zielhuis, Zijlweg. **GPS**: n53,43203 e6,58396.

+10 free. **Location:** Rural, simple, isolated, quiet. **Surface:** gravel.
01/01-31/12.
Distance: Usquert 4,5km Wadden Sea on the spot on the spot.

Veendam 7F3

Borgerswold, Flora 2. **GPS**: n53,10637 e6,84826.

60 € 5 + € 2,50/pp Ch WC included.
Location: Rural, simple, quiet.
Surface: grassy.
01/01-31/12.
Distance: 2km beach 50m on the spot 2km 1km 1,5km on the spot.

Tourist information Veendam:
Museumspoorlijn STAR, Parallelweg 4, Veendam. Museum railway line, tickets available at railwaystation. round trip € 15.
Veenkoloniaalmuseum, Museumplein 5. History of the peat, shipping and industry. Tue-Thu 11-17h, Fri-Mo 13-17h 01/09-30/06 Mo. € 7,50.

NL

Winschoten 7F3

achthaven de Rensel, Hellingbaan 4. **GPS**: n53,14405 e7,04760.

0 € 11, 2 pers.incl € 0,50 Ch WCincluded.
ocation: Simple, quiet. **Surface:** concrete. 01/01-31/12.
istance: 800m 200m McDonalds 200m AH.

Winschoten 7F3

otel Café Restaurant Bowling In den Stallen, Oostereinde 10.
PS: n53,15371 e7,06528.

0 consuming is appreciated on demand .
Location: Rural, simple, quiet.
urface: asphalted/metalled.
Distance: 1km 600m 600m on the spot 1km 600m.
ourist information Winschoten:
Stoomgemaal, Winschoter Oostereinde. Steam-engine 1895.

Winsum 7E2

achthaven/Camping Marenland, Winsumerstraatweg.
GPS: n53,33177 e6,51015.

10 € 14,50 Ch ,4Amp WC € 6,50,€ 6,50/0 included, at restaurant. **Location:** Urban, comfortable, quiet.
Surface: grassy/metalled. 01/04-01/11.
Distance: 300m 200m on the spot on the spot 500m 200m on the spot Pieterpad.

Zoutkamp 7E2

Jachthaven Hunzegat, Strandweg 17. **GPS**: n53,34114 e6,29406.

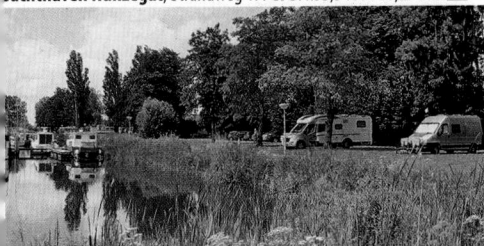

10 € 12,50 + tourist tax Ch,dump chem.toilet only with biodegradable liquid (10x),4A WCincluded € 0,50 € 7,40/0 .
Location: Rural, comfortable, quiet. **Surface:** grassy/metalled.
01/01-31/12.
Distance: 1km on the spot on the spot 500m 500m 300m on the spot.
Remarks: Bread-service.
Tourist information Zoutkamp:
Zeehondencrèche, Hoofdstraat 94a, Pieterburen. Sanctory to cure sick seals. Mo-Fr 9-17h, Sa-Su 10-17h. € 10,50.

Zuidbroek 7F3

De Broeckhof, W.A. Scholtenweg 18. **GPS**: n53,16118 e6,86054.

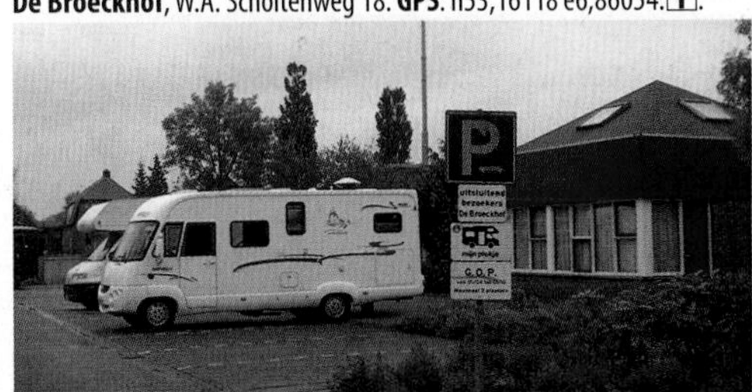

3 free ChWC free.
Location: Rural, simple, central, quiet. **Surface:** metalled.
01/01-31/12 3rd week Jun.
Distance: 500m on the spot on the spot 1km on the spot on the spot on the spot.
Remarks: Max. 72h.

Drenthe

Barger Compascuum 9F1

Nationale Veenpark, Berkenrode 4. **GPS**: n52,75504 e7,02546.

20 € 6 + € 1,20/pp tourist tax included.
Location: Rural, simple, quiet.
Surface: grassy.
01/05-31/10.
Distance: 100m on the spot on the spot.
Remarks: Max. 3x24h, after visiting Veenpark 2nd night free.
Tourist information Barger Compascuum:
Veenpark-Wereld van Veen, Berkenrode 4. Life and Work in peat area, 160 acres of nature, peat and villages. 01/04-31/10 10-17h, 01/07-31/08 10-18h.

Borger 7F3

Nuuverstee, Rolderstraat 4. **GPS**: n52,92633 e6,77447.

9 € 15 Ch (9x),10Amp WC included.
Location: Rural, comfortable, luxurious.
Surface: grassy/metalled. 01/01-31/12.
Distance: 800m 600m 2km 500m 600m 1km 500m on the spot on the spot.
Remarks: Bread-service, charging point for electric bicycles, use of sauna against payment.

Dwingeloo 9E1

Torentjeshoek, Leeuweriksveldweg 1. **GPS**: n52,81927 e6,36077.

6 € 10-17 + € 1,10 tourist tax Ch 10Amp WC included, on campsite.
Location: Rural, luxurious, quiet. **Surface:** grassy/metalled.
01/01-31/12.
Distance: 2km 2km 200m 200m 2km 2km 1km on the spot on the spot.
Remarks: Arrival >16h, departure <11h.

Eelderwolde 7E3

Scandinavisch Dorp, Oude Badweg 1. **GPS**: n53,16984 e6,55391.

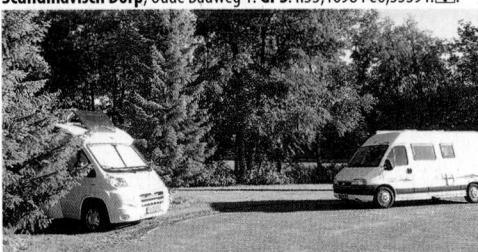

5 free.
Location: Rural, simple, quiet. **Surface:** asphalted/grassy.
01/01-31/12 Restaurant: Tue, 01/10-01/04 Mo-Tue.
Distance: 2km 5km 500m on the spot on the spot 2km 200m on the spot on the spot.
Remarks: Guests free.

Eext 7F3

Schaopvolte, Stationsstraat 60a. **GPS**: n53,00007 e6,72862.

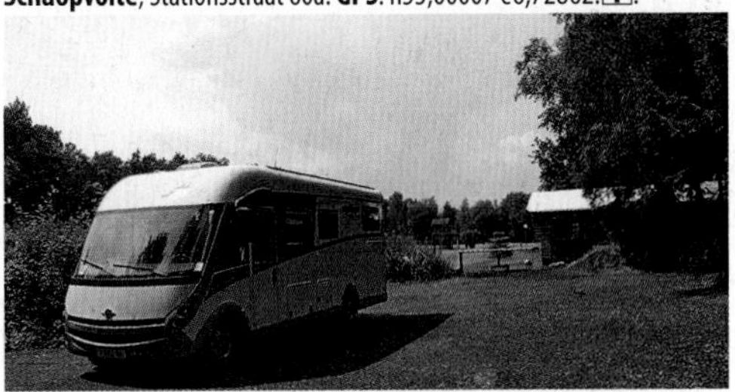

10 € 8,50, tourist tax excl € 1 Ch (6x)€ 1/4kWh WC € 0,50 € 4,50 € 2/day. **Location:** Rural, simple, quiet.
Surface: grassy/gravel. 01/04-01/11.
Distance: 2km.

Elim 9E1

De Barswieke, Barsweg 9. **GPS**: n52,67144 e6,57821.

10 € 6 + tourist tax Chincluded € 1,50 WC € 0,50 .
Surface: grassy/metalled. 01/01-31/12.
Distance: 1km 1km.

Emmen 9F1

Kerkhoflaan/Emmalaan. **GPS**: n52,78091 e6,90330.

10 free. **Location:** Urban, simple.
Surface: grassy.
01/01-31/12.
Distance: 1km Albert Heijn 600m.
Remarks: Behind hotel Eden, max. 72h, zoo Emmen 900m.
Tourist information Emmen:
Wildlands Adventure Zoo, Raadhuisplein 99. Zoo.
10-17h.

Erica 9F1

Achter op Erica, Verlengde Herendijk. **GPS**: n52,73006 e6,92256.

NL

15 € 8 Ch included € 3 € 1.
Location: Rural. **Surface:** grassy. 01/01-31/12.
Distance: 3,5km on the spot on the spot.
Remarks: Closed when frosty, possibility for reservation.

Hoogeveen 9E1

Terpweg 3. **GPS**: n52,72639 e6,50040.

3 free. **Location:** Rural, simple, isolated.
Surface: metalled. 01/01-31/12.
Distance: 2km 2,2km 100m 1km 1km.
Remarks: At sports park, max. 72h.

Matsloot 7E3

Camping Pool, Matsloot 1a. **GPS**: n53,19354 e6,44980.

10 € 10 Ch WC included. **Location:** Rural, simple, isolated, quiet. **Surface:** metalled. 01/01-31/12.
Distance: 5km on the spot on the spot on the spot.
Remarks: On Leekster lake.

Meppel 9E1

Jachthaven, Westeinde 32. **GPS**: n52,69615 e6,18096.

15 € 7,70, 2 pers.incl. € 0,50 Ch € 0,50/kWh WC € 3/3. **Location:** Urban, comfortable, central, quiet. **Surface:** grassy. 01/01-31/12.
Distance: 500m on the spot on the spot on the spot 400m.

Nieuwlande 9F1

Bonenstee, Brugstraat 87. **GPS**: n52,67889 e6,61194.

20 € 7,50, 01/11-31/03 € 6 Ch (6x)€ 1,50 WC € 1 included. **Location:** Rural. **Surface:** grassy/metalled. 01/01-31/12 service 01/11-31/03.
Distance: 2km 4km 4km 2km 2km 100m bike junction on the spot.
Remarks: Max. 72h.

Noord-Sleen 9F1

De Kalverweide, Zweeloërstraat 1. **GPS**: n52,79330 e6,79475.

10 € 12 Ch WC included.
Location: Rural, comfortable, quiet. **Surface:** grassy. 01/01-31/12.
Distance: 500m on the spot on the spot.
Remarks: Use of sauna against payment.

Oosterhesselen 9F1

Sauna Hesselerbrug, Verlengde Hoogeveensevaart 32.
GPS: n52,73535 e6,72029.

use of sauna obligatory. **Surface:** metalled.
Distance: 4km 4km.

Ruinen 9E1

De Wiltzangh, Witteveen 2. **GPS**: n52,78140 e6,36581.

10 € 12,50, tourist tax incl Ch € 0,50/kWh WC € 4,50 included. **Surface:** grassy/sand. 01/01-31/12.
Distance: 2km 2km on the spot 2km on the spot on the spot.

Schoonloo 7F3

Camping BuitenGewoon, Elperstraat 16. **GPS**: n52,90114 e6,67965.
€ 10 Ch WC .
Distance: 1,5km.

Ufelte 9E1

De Blauwe Haan, Weg achter de es 11.
GPS: n52,80220 e6,27264.

6 € 10 excl. tourist tax Ch € 2,50/night,10Amp WC included . **Location:** Rural, luxurious, quiet.
Surface: grassy/metalled. 01/04-31/10.
Distance: 5km 2km 3km 3km 2,5km 5km 2km on the spot on the spot.

Westerbork 7F3

Landgoed het Timmerholt, Gagelmaat 4.
GPS: n52,86850 e6,61748.

4 € 10, 19/07-02/08 € 12,50 Ch included WC € 1,50/pppd € 1,50/pppd € 3,90/2,75 h. **Location:** Rural, luxurious, quiet. **Surface:** grassy/metalled. 01/01-31/12.
Distance: 2km 4km on the spot on the spot on the spot 2km 2km on the spot on the spot.

Tourist information Westerbork:
Herinneringscentrum Kamp Westerbork, Oosthalen 8, Hooghalen. Mo-Fri 10-17h, Sa-Su 11-17h, 01/07-31/08 and holidays 11-17h.

Wijster 9E1

Grondsels, Grondselweg 7. **GPS**: n52,80143 e6,49025.

10 € 5 Ch € 2 WC included.
Location: Rural, simple, isolated, quiet.
Surface: grassy/metalled. 15/03-31/10.
Distance: 3km on the spot 3km 5km on the spot.

Overijssel

Almelo 9F1

Stationsstraat. **GPS**: n52,35827 e6,65589.
3 free. **Location:** Urban. **Surface:** metalled. 01/01-31/12.
Distance: 600m.

Tourist information Almelo:
Markt- en Centrumplein. Thu 8.30-14h, Sa 8.30-17h.

Bathmen 9E2

Prinses Margrietlaan. **GPS**: n52,25025 e6,29927.

2 free. **Location:** Urban, simple, central, quiet. **Surface:** metalled. 01/01-31/12.
Distance: 1km 2,5km 1km 1km on the spot on the spot.
Remarks: Parking gymnasium.

Belt Schutsloot 9E1

Café-Restaurant de Belt, Havezatheweg 4. **GPS**: n52,66774 e6,05189.

10 free for clients WC .
Surface: asphalted. 01/01-31/12.
Distance: 3km 1km 1km on the spot 3km.
Remarks: North of Zwartsluis, at Belter- and Beulakerwijde.

Bentelo 9F2

Camperplaats de Bentelose Esch, Eschweg 2.
GPS: n52,21250 e6,67010.

NL

25 € 15 Ch (25x)WC included.
Location: Rural, luxurious, quiet. **Surface:** grassy/gravel.
15/03-01/11.
Distance: 2km 5km 2km 2km 400m on the spot on the spot.

Beuningen 9F1

De Nijenhaer, Nijenhaerweg 25. **GPS:** n52,34471 e6,99325.

15 € 10 Ch included.
Location: Rural. **Surface:** grassy. 01/01-31/12.
Distance: 3km on the spot on the spot.

Borne 9E2

De Aak. GPS: n52,30204 e6,00000.
1 free. **Location:** Urban. **Surface:** metalled. 01/01-31/12.
Distance: 200m 200m 500m.

Dalfsen 9E1

Stationsweg 4. **GPS:** n52,49944 e6,25949.

5 free. **Location:** Rural, simple, central, quiet.
Surface: grasstiles. 01/01-31/12.
Distance: 500m 500m 800m on the spot on the spot on the spot.
Remarks: Max. 48h, service on campsite.

Dalfsen 9E1

Starnbosch, Sterrebosweg 4. **GPS:** n52,47538 e6,26336.

7 € 10 + € 0,85/pp tourist tax Ch (8x)WC included € 0,40/5minutes € 5/0,50 € 1/1h. **Location:** Rural, comfortable, quiet. **Surface:** grassy/sand. 01/01-31/12.
Distance: 4km on the spot 4km 3,3km on the spot on the spot.
Remarks: Max. 48h.

De Lutte 9F2

Erve Velpen, Beuningerstraat 25. **GPS:** n52,33224 e7,01197.

20 € 7, tourist tax € 1/pp Ch € 2/day € 1/8minutes included. **Location:** Rural, comfortable, isolated, quiet.
Surface: grassy. 01/01-31/12.
Distance: 4km 300m bike junction on the spot.

Dedemsvaart 9E1

Camperplaats Dedemsvaart, Langewijk 112.
GPS: n52,60435 e6,45108.

10 € 6,50 € 1,50 € 2,50 .
Surface: metalled. 01/01-31/12.
Distance: 700m 300m 200m.
Remarks: Max. 48h.

Den Ham 9E1

De Linderbeek, Zomerweg 56. **GPS:** n52,44526 e6,49870.

4 € 12,50 Ch WC € 5 included. 01/04-01/10.
Distance: on the spot on the spot.
Remarks: Max. 7 nights, € 2,50 discount on presentation of the guide 2012.

Diepenheim 9E2

Camperpark Ravenhorst/Diepenheim, Esweg 6.
GPS: n52,18307 e6,57872.

30 € 12,50 2p incl. + tourist tax Ch (30x),6Amp WC € 1 included . **Location:** Rural, luxurious, quiet.
Surface: grassy/metalled. 15/03-01/11.
Distance: 2km 2km 2km on the spot on the spot.
Remarks: Money in envelope in mail box.

Diepenheim 9E2

't Holt, Hengevelderweg 1A. **GPS:** n52,19500 e6,59186.

3 € 5, free for clients Ch free.
Surface: metalled.

01/01-31/12.
Distance: 3km on the spot on the spot 3km on the spot.
Remarks: Golf court (pitch+putt).

Diepenheim 9E2

In de Kokkerieje, Grotestraat 94. **GPS:** n52,19923 e6,55452.

free with a meal. Mo-Tue.
Distance: on the spot 1km 500m.
Remarks: Parking behind restaurant.

Enschede 9F2

De Loeks, Moorvenweg 2a. **GPS:** n52,17757 e6,86599.

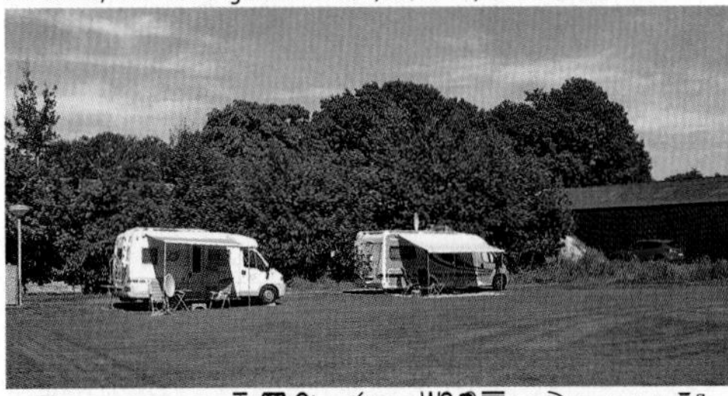

15 € 18,50, dog € 1 Ch (15x)WC € 2 included.
Location: Rural, luxurious, isolated, quiet. **Surface:** grassy/metalled.
01/01-31/12 sanitary 01/11-31/03.
Distance: 3km 2km 2km on the spot on the spot.

Enschede 9F2

Diekmanterrein, Weggelhorstweg. **GPS:** n52,20543 e6,90096.

5 free. **Location:** Urban, simple, isolated, quiet. **Surface:** asphalted.
01/01-31/12.
Distance: 2km 1,4km on the spot.

Enter 9E2

Werfstraat. **GPS:** n52,29808 e6,58271.

3 free. **Location:** Urban, simple. **Surface:** grassy/gravel.
01/01-31/12.
Distance: 600m on the spot on the spot 600m 700m on the spot on the spot.
Remarks: Max. 72h.

Geesteren 9F1

Zalencentrum Spalink, Koelenbeekweg 10. **GPS:** n52,44060 e6,69555.

15 € 8,50 Ch WC. **Surface:** grassy/gravel.

NL

01/01-31/12.
Distance: 3,5km ⊗on the spot 3,5km on the spot on the spot.
Remarks: Guests free.

S **Giethoorn** 9E1

Passantenhaven Zuidercluft, Vosjacht 1G. **GPS**: n52,72134 e6,07449.

30 € 12, 2 pers.incl., 1/11-1/4 € 6 € 0,50/100liter Ch € 1/2kWh WC € 0,50. **Surface:** grassy. 01/01-31/12.
Distance: 1km on the spot on the spot.
Remarks: Check in at harbourmaster, water closed during wintertime.

S **Giethoorn** 9E1

Camperplaats Haamstede, Kanaaldijk 17.
GPS: n52,72828 e6,07570.

35 € 10, 2 pers.incl € 0,50 Ch € 3 WC € 0,50.
Location: Rural, comfortable, central, quiet. **Surface:** grassy.
01/04-31/10.
Distance: 2km 1km 20m ⊗1km 1km on the spot on the spot.

S **Giethoorn** 9E1

Camperresort Bodelaeke, Vosjacht 10A.
GPS: n52,71703 e6,07668.
99 € 10, 2 pers. incl., dog € 1,50 € 0,50/100liter Ch € 3,16Amp WC € 6/4 included.
Location: Rural, comfortable. **Surface:** grasstiles/grassy.
02/03-31/10.
Distance: 1km on the spot on the spot.

Tourist information Giethoorn:
VVV, Eendrachtsplein 1, www.kopvanoverijssel.nl. Village in nature reserve De Weerribben, Dutch Venice, boat trips possible.

S **Haaksbergen** 9F2

Henk Pen Caravans en Kampeerauto's, Westsingel 2.
GPS: n52,14917 e6,71167.

2 free free. **Location:** Simple, noisy. **Surface:** asphalted.
01/01-31/12.
Distance: 1km on the spot ⊗on the spot 1km.
Remarks: Motorhome dealer.

S **Haaksbergen** 9F2

Camping Scholtenhagen, Scholtenhagenweg 30.
GPS: n52,14820 e6,72467.

24 € 10 Ch (24x) WC € 0,90 € 5,25 included.
Location: Rural, luxurious, quiet. **Surface:** grassy. 01/01-31/12.
Distance: 2km 7km 3km 2,5km 1km on the spot on the spot.
Remarks: Max. 72h, bread-service, excl use swimming pool.

S **Hardenberg** 9E1

De Kuserbrink, Parkweg. **GPS**: n52,57746 e6,62927.

4 € 10 € 0,50/100liter Chfree (4x) € 1/kWh.
Location: Rural, comfortable, central, quiet. **Surface:** grasstiles.
01/01-31/12.
Distance: centre 500m on the spot on the spot.
Remarks: Max. 72h.

S **Hardenberg** 9E1

Fam. Pullen, Allemansweg 1a, Collendoorn.
GPS: n52,58845 e6,59146.

20 € 10 Ch included. **Location:** Rural, comfortable, isolated, quiet. **Surface:** grassy. 01/01-31/12.
Distance: 3km ⊗3km bike junction on the spot.
Remarks: Dog on leads.

S **Hasselt** 9E1

Jachthaven de Molenwaard, Van Nahuysweg 151.
GPS: n52,59367 e6,08741.

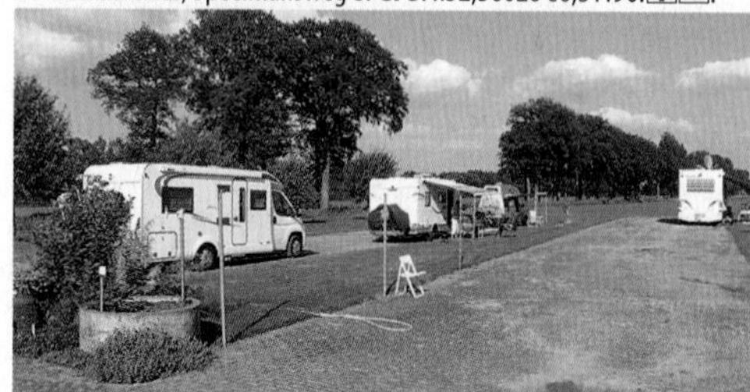

10 € 8,50, tourist tax € 0,70/pp Ch (10x) € 2/night WC € 0,50/6minutes € 3,75/3,75 included.
Location: Luxurious, quiet. **Surface:** metalled. 01/01-31/12.
Distance: 500m on the spot on the spot ⊗500m 500m 500m on the spot on the spot.
Remarks: Check in at harbourmaster.

S **Heeten** 9E1

De Baanbreker, Speelmansweg 8. **GPS**: n52,36026 e6,31190.

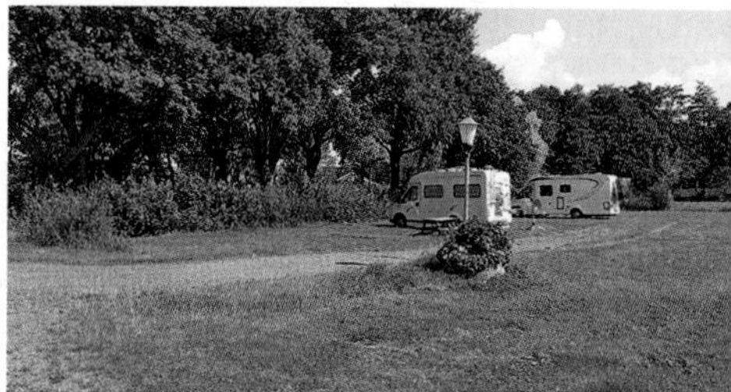

10 € 4,50 Ch. **Surface:** metalled. 01/01-31/12.
Distance: 2km ⊗2km 2km on the spot on the spot.
Remarks: Max. 48h.

S **Hellendoorn** 9E1

Camperplaats Hancate, Zuidelijke Kanaaldijk.
GPS: n52,43418 e6,44060.

10 € 10 Ch (4x) included.
Location: Rural, simple, quiet. **Surface:** grassy. 01/01-31/12.
Distance: 5km on the spot ⊗100m 200m on the spot on the spot.

S **Hengelo** 9F2

Jachthaven Hengelo, Kanaalweg 8. **GPS**: n52,25123 e6,76216.
6 € 10 + € 1/pp tourist tax Ch included.
Location: Rural. **Surface:** grassy/metalled. 01/05-01/10.
Distance: 3km on the spot ⊗on the spot 3km on the spot on the spot.
Remarks: Max. 72h, max. 7m.

S **Hengelo** 9F2

Camperplaats Eulerhook, Vöckersweg 19.
GPS: n52,24652 e6,75365.

15 € 10 Ch (15x) WC included. **Location:** Rural, comfortable, noisy. **Surface:** metalled. 01/01-31/12.
Distance: 4km 2km 500m ⊗4km 3km 1km on the spot on the spot.
Remarks: Nearby motorway.

S **Hertme** 9F2

Camperpark Rabo Scheele, Hertmerweg 37.
GPS: n52,32663 e6,74691.

25 € 12, 2 pers.incl Ch WC included.
Location: Rural, comfortable, quiet. **Surface:** grassy/metalled.
01/01-31/12.
Distance: Hertme 500m, Borne 2km 100m ⊗500m 2km 2km on the spot on the spot.

S **Holten** 9E2

Camperplaats Holten, Schreursweg 5. **GPS**: n52,27862 e6,44847.
25 € 11 Ch included. **Location:** Rural.
01/04-31/10.
Distance: 2km 2km ⊗500m on the spot on the spot.

S **Holten** 9E2

Camperplaats Lookerland, Rijssenseweg 34A.
GPS: n52,28515 e6,43866.

20 € 10 Ch (10x)included WC free.
Location: Rural, quiet.
Surface: grassy/metalled.
01/04-31/09.

NL

Distance: 1,3km 3km 1,3km 1,3km 100m on the spot Pieterpad. **Remarks:** Money in envelope in mail box.

Tourist information Holten:
VVV, Dorpsstraat 27, www.vvvholten.nl.

Kampen 9E1

Burgemeester Berghuisplein 1. **GPS:** n52,55268 e5,91356.

25 € 7,50 Ch WC included € 0,50/6minutes.
Location: Urban, comfortable, central, quiet.
Surface: metalled.
01/01-31/12.
Distance: historical centre 500m 1,5km 1,5km 900m 1km on the spot on the spot.
Remarks: Max. 72h, entrance code sanitary building at town hall.

Tourist information Kampen:
VVV, Oudestraat 151, www.vvvkampen.nl. Former Hanseatic town on the Ijssel.

Losser 9F2

Brilmansdennen, Bookholtlaan. **GPS:** n52,26927 e7,01378.

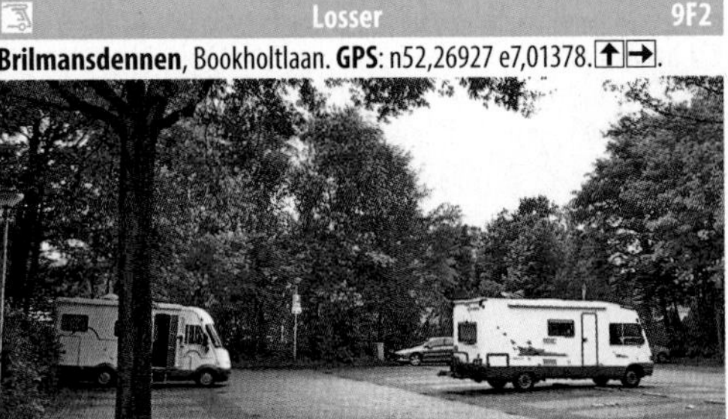

3 free. **Surface:** metalled. 01/01-31/12.
Distance: 1km.
Remarks: At sports park, max. 72h.

Nieuwleusen 9E1

Koninging Julianalaan. **GPS:** n52,58213 e6,28076.

3 free. **Location:** Urban, simple. **Surface:** metalled.
01/01-31/12.
Distance: 300m on the spot on the spot.
Remarks: Max. 48h.

Nijverdal 9E1

De Wilgenweerd, Sportlaan 6. **GPS:** n52,37118 e6,46538.

3 € 5 + € 0,50/pp tourist tax.
Surface: grasstiles/metalled. 01/01-31/12.
Distance: 500m on the spot on the spot on the spot 500m 200m on the spot on the spot.

Oldemarkt 9E1

Vaartjes partycentrum, Kruisstraat 86-88.
GPS: n52,82095 e5,96698.

10 free for clients. **Surface:** asphalted. 01/01-31/12.
Distance: 200m on the spot on the spot on the spot 200m.

Ommen 9E1

Landgoed De Stekkenkamp, Beerzerweg 3.
GPS: n52,51128 e6,43933.

8 € 7,50 + € 0,80/pp tourist tax € 0,50/4minutes Ch (8x) included. **Location:** Rural, simple, quiet. **Surface:** grasstiles/grassy.
01/01-31/12.
Distance: 1,2km 1,2km 1,2km 1,2km 1,2km 1,2km on the spot on the spot.
Remarks: At historical farmhouse, max. 72h.

Overdinkel 9F2

Camperplaats Skop'nboer, Schaapskooiweg 2.
GPS: n52,24692 e7,03581.

25 € 15 Ch WC included. **Location:** Rural, luxurious, quiet. **Surface:** grasstiles/grassy. 01/01-31/12.
Distance: 3km 3km on the spot on the spot.

Steenwijk 9E1

Jachthaven, Houthaven. **GPS:** n52,78627 e6,10006.

20 € 10 € 1. **Surface:** grassy. 01/01-31/12.
Distance: 1km on the spot on the spot 300m.
Remarks: Check in at harbourmaster.

Tubbergen 9F1

De Vlaskoel, Sportlaan 3. **GPS:** n52,41043 e6,78316.

2 free free. **Location:** Simple, simple. **Surface:** metalled.
01/01-31/12.
Distance: 500m 600m 600m on the spot on the spot.
Remarks: At swimming pool.

Vollenhove 9E1

De Haven. **GPS:** n52,68277 e5,94862.

6 € 12 Ch € 1 WC € 0,50. **Surface:** metalled.
01/01-31/12.
Distance: 100m 100m 1km.
Remarks: Check in at harbourmaster.

Vollenhove 9E1

Recreatiecentrum 't Akkertien, Op de Voorst, Noordwal 3.
GPS: n52,67609 e5,93914.

20 € 8 Ch included. 01/01-31/12.
Distance: 900m on the spot on the spot 400m peak season.

Wierden 9E1

De Huurne, Zandinksweg 22. **GPS:** n52,35003 e6,57474.

10 € 10 Ch included. 01/01-31/12.
Distance: 2km 3km 2km 700m.
Remarks: Max. 3 nights, max 3,5t.

Wierden 9E1

Wijngaard Baan, Kloosterhoeksweg 15. **GPS:** n52,32172 e6,56709.

24 € 12 Ch WC included.
Surface: metalled. 01/01-31/12.
Distance: 3km on the spot on the spot 3km on the spot on the spot.
Remarks: Vineyard.

Wijhe 9E1

Passantenhaven, Veerweg. **GPS:** n52,38639 e6,12830.

10 € 6, tourist tax € 0,50/pp Ch WC included .
Location: Simple, central. **Surface:** asphalted/metalled.
24/04-02/11.

NL

Distance: 500m on the spot on the spot 500m 500m on the spot on the spot.
Remarks: Max. 3 nights.

Tourist information Wijhe:
Marktplein. Tue-morning.

Zwartsluis 9E1

Voetbalvereniging DESZ, Clingellanden. **GPS:** n52,63850 e6,07536.

15 € 10, 2 pers.incl Ch. **Surface:** gravel.
Distance: 400m.
Remarks: Service at marina.

Tourist information Zwartsluis:
Stoomgemaal Mastenbroek, Kamperzeedijk 5, Genemuiden. Pumping-engine, 1856.

Zwolle 9E1

Turfmarkt. **GPS:** n52,51326 e6,10380.

7 mo-sa 8-18h € 5/day, free overnight stay.
Location: Urban, simple, central. **Surface:** metalled. 01/01-31/12.
Distance: 800m 1km 650m on the spot on the spot.
Remarks: Max. 72h.

Zwolle 9E1

Jachthaven de Hanze, Holtenbroekerdijk 44.
GPS: n52,53122 e6,07345.

15 € 10, tourist tax incl Ch (15x)€ 0,50/kWh WC € 1/7minutes included. **Location:** Rural, comfortable, central, quiet. **Surface:** grassy/metalled. 01/01-31/12.
Distance: 2,5km 2km on the spot on the spot 1km 1km 500m on the spot on the spot.
Remarks: Max. 72h.

Tourist information Zwolle:
Sassenpoort, Koestraat 46. Medieval gate building. Wed-Fri 14-17h, Sa/Su/holidays 12-17h.

Flevoland

Almere 9D2

Marina Muiderzand, IJmeerdijk 4. **GPS:** n52,34155 e5,13493.

10 (01/10-30/04 2 pl € 14,50 Ch WC € 5/3 included. **Surface:** asphalted. 01/01-31/12.
Distance: 8km on the spot on the spot on the spot on the spot 1km.
Remarks: Check in at harbourmaster.

Tourist information Almere:
VVV, De Diagonaal 199, www.vvvalmere.nl.
Stadhuisplein. Wed, Sa 9-16h.
Biologische Boerenmarkt, Kempenhaanpad 14, www.stadsboerderijalmere.nl. Sa 9.30-13h.

Almere-Haven 9D2

WSV Almere, Sluiskade 11. **GPS:** n52,33257 e5,21715.

40 € 15,50, 2 pers. incl Ch (12x)€ 0,50/2kWh WC € 5 included.
Location: Urban, simple. **Surface:** grassy. 01/01-31/12.
Distance: on the spot on the spot 200m on the spot.

Almere-Haven 9D2

Haven, Sluis. **GPS:** n52,33366 e5,22170.

2 € 7 Ch WC € 0,50.
Surface: metalled. 02/05-04/09.
Distance: on the spot 1km on the spot on the spot 1km.
Remarks: Max. 72h, check in at harbourmaster.

Tourist information Almere-Haven:
De Brink. Fri 9-16h.

Emmeloord 9D1

Camperplaats Emmeloord, Casteleynsweg 1.
GPS: n52,73981 e5,77235.
12 € 9, 2 pers. incl Ch € 2/day included.
Surface: grassy. 11/04-31/10.
Distance: 4,9km 150m.
Remarks: 2 bicycles available.

Lelystad 9D1

P Houtribhoek, Houtribslag. **GPS:** n52,54762 e5,45666.

4 free.
Surface: metalled.
01/01-31/12.
Distance: 2km on the spot on the spot on the spot 2km.
Remarks: Max. 48h.

Tourist information Lelystad:
Oostvaardersplassen. 6000 acres of lakes, mud fields, reed swamps, hiking route 5km and cycle route 35km.
Batavia Stad, Bataviaplein 60. Outlet-shopping.
daily 10-18h.
free, parking € 3.

Luttelgeest 9D1

Recreatie en Horeca bedrijf Craneburcht, Kuinderweg 52.
GPS: n52,78304 e5,84331.

10 € 13,50 + € 0,75/pp tourist tax € 2 WC.
Surface: metalled. 01/03-30/11 winter: Mo-Tue.
Distance: 200m on the spot 7km.
Remarks: Arrival >17h, departure <10h.

Nagele 9D1

Afslag Nagele, Han Stijkelweg 11. **GPS:** n52,65034 e5,68610.

20 € 12 Ch € 2/night WC included free.
Location: Comfortable, isolated, quiet. **Surface:** grassy/metalled.
01/01-31/12.
Distance: 3km.
Remarks: Max. 5 days.

Urk 9D1

Haven, Burgemeester Schipperkade. **GPS:** n52,66040 e5,59975.

20 € 15 Ch (18x) WC included.
Surface: metalled.
01/01-31/12.
Distance: 200m 100m 100m, bakery 300m.

Tourist information Urk:
VVV, Wijk 2 2, www.vvvflevoland.nl. Old fishermen's village, former island.
Het Oude Raadhuis, Wijk 2 2. Regional museum.
01/04-31/10 Mo-Fr 10-17h, Sa 10-16h, 01/03-30/11 Mo-Sa 10-16h.
Urkerhard. Sa 8.30-13h.
Stegentocht/Ginkiestocht. Guided walk, reservation at Touristinfo Urk.

Zeewolde 9D2

Camperpark De Wielewaal, Wielseweg 9. **GPS:** n52,25981 e5,43727.

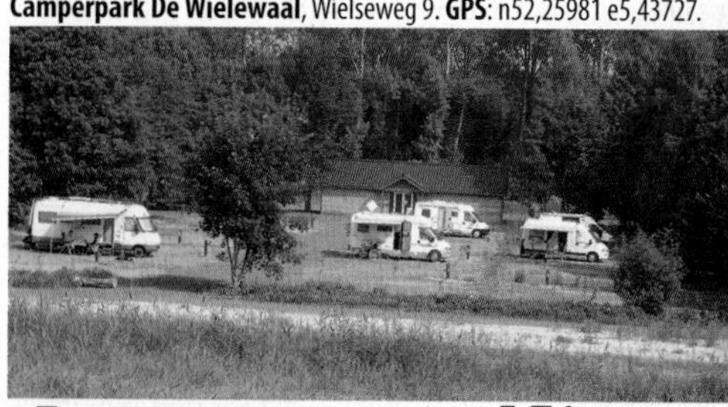

50 € 12, 2 pers.incl, tourist tax € 1/pp, dog € 1 Ch included € 2 WC against payment.
Surface: metalled. 01/01-31/12.
Distance: 7km on the spot on the spot 7km.

Gelderland

Aalten 9F2

t Noorden, Lichtenvoordsestraatweg 44.
PS: n51,93402 e6,58206.

€ 10 € 1/80liter Chfree (4x)included.
Location: Rural, simple, noisy.
Surface: gravel.
01/01-31/12.
Distance: 700m on the spot on the spot.
Tourist information Aalten:
Wijngoed De Hennepe, Romienendiek 3, www.wijngoeddehennepe.nl. Guided tour and tastery. shop Tue-Fr 13.30h-sunset, Sa 10h, guided tour/tasting Jul/Aug We 15h.
Hoge Blik. Thu 8-12h.

Aerdt 9E2

De Aerdtse Wacht, Heuvelakkersestraat 18.
GPS: n51,88634 e6,08861.

4 € 10 € 1/80liter Ch included. Location: Rural, comfortable, isolated, quiet. Surface: metalled. 01/01-31/12.
Distance: 1km 1,5km 1,5km on the spot on the spot on the spot on the spot on the spot on the spot.

Almen 9E2

De Nieuwe Aanleg, Scheggertdijk 10. GPS: n52,16711 e6,29744.

12 € 10 € 0,75/100liter Ch (12x)included WC € 0,75/5minutes . Location: Rural, comfortable, quiet.
Surface: metalled. 01/01-31/12.
Distance: 2km on the spot on the spot on the spot 2km on the spot on the spot on the spot.
Remarks: At the Twentekanaal.
Tourist information Almen:
Dorpsstraat. Small week market. Tue 11-13h.

Apeldoorn 9E2

Malkander, Dubbelbeek 38. GPS: n52,18305 e5,96673.

4 free. Location: Simple, isolated. Surface: metalled.
01/01-31/12, 15-09h.
Distance: 2km 150m 1km.
Remarks: At swimming pool.
Tourist information Apeldoorn:
Marktplein. Wed 8-13h, Sa 8-17h.

Appeltern 9D3

Strand Maaslanden, Hamsestraat 2. GPS: n51,83107 e5,56193.

10 € 10 Ch included WC € 1.
Location: Rural. Surface: grassy/metalled.
Distance: 2km on the spot on the spot on the spot on the spot.
Remarks: Boat rental, bicycle rental, show-garden Appeltern 3km.

Appeltern 9D3

Herberg 't Mun, Molenstraat 10, Blauwe Sluis.
GPS: n51,84048 e5,56360.

50 € 5 Ch (12x)€ 2,6Amp WC included.
Location: Rural, simple, isolated, quiet. Surface: grassy/metalled.
01/01-31/12.
Distance: 2km 300m Trout farm on the spot 2km on the spot on the spot on the spot.
Remarks: Show-garden Appeltern 3km.

Arnhem 9E2

Nieuwe Kade. GPS: n51,97327 e5,91593.

4 € 9 € 2,50 Ch (4x)€ 0,50/kWh WC .
Location: Urban, simple, central, quiet. Surface: metalled.
01/01-31/12.
Distance: 1km 4,7km 200m 1km 1km on the spot on the spot.
Remarks: Along the Rhine river, max. 48h, service at petrol station n51,970749 e5,94796.
Tourist information Arnhem:
Jansplaats. Small week market. Tue 7.30-15h.

Bemmel 9E2

Dijkstraat/Wardstraat. GPS: n51,88972 e5,90972.

3 free. Location: Urban, simple, central, quiet. Surface: metalled.
01/01-31/12.
Distance: 400m 400m 400m 400m on the spot on the spot.
Remarks: Max. 72h.

Borculo 9E2

Hambroekplas/Berkelpalace, Hambroekweg 10.
GPS: n52,11573 e6,53758.

4 € 10 € 1/80liter Ch (4x)included. Location: Rural, simple, noisy. Surface: grassy/gravel. 01/03-31/10.
Distance: 500m 150m 50m 500m on the spot on the spot.

Borculo 9E2

Bruggink Campers, Kamerlingh Onnestraat 19.
GPS: n52,12281 e6,52682.

3 free on demand. Location: Urban, simple, noisy.
Surface: metalled. 01/01-31/12, 18-9h.
Distance: 1,5km 2km 500m 1,5km 1,5km on the spot.

Bredevoort 9F2

P2, recreatieplas Slingeplas, Kruittorenstraat 10b.
GPS: n51,94722 e6,62318.

8 € 10 € 1/80liter Ch (8x)included.
Location: Rural, simple, quiet.
Surface: metalled.
01/04-01/10.
Distance: 500m 100m 400m 500m on the spot.
Remarks: Max. 72h.
Tourist information Bredevoort:
VVV, Markt 8. City with half-timbered houses.
Book market. 3rd Sa of the month 10-17.

Culemborg 9D2

Jachthaven de Helling, Beusichemsedijk.
GPS: n51,96117 e5,22148.

20 € 16,50 + tourist tax Ch WC € 0,50 € 4/4 included. Surface: grassy/sand. 01/04-01/11.
Distance: 500m on the spot on the spot 100m 500m 1,5km.
Remarks: Check in at harbourmaster.

De Heurne 9E2

De Haar, Caspersstraat 14. GPS: n51,89802 e6,50035.

NL

18 € 10 € 1/80liter Ch (15x) included.
Location: Rural, comfortable, quiet.
Surface: grassy. 01/01-31/12.
Distance: 1km 8km 1km on the spot on the spot.
Remarks: Filling station gas bottles 300m.

S **Doesburg** 9E2

Jachthaven Doesburg, Turfhaven. **GPS**: n52,01109 e6,13368.

6 € 7,50 Ch (6x)€ 0,50/kWh WC included € 0,50/4minutes. **Location:** Urban, comfortable, central, quiet.
Surface: concrete. 01/01-31/12.
Distance: 500m 4km on the spot 500m 1km 500m on the spot on the spot.
Remarks: Check in at harbourmaster.

Doornenburg 9E2

Kerkstraat. **GPS**: n51,89416 e6,00129.

3 free. **Location:** Rural, quiet.
Surface: metalled. 01/01-31/12.
Distance: 400m 200m cafetaria 200m 400m on the spot.
Remarks: Max. 3 days, view on castle Doornenburg.

S **Elburg** 9D1

Gemeentehaven Elburg, Havenkade 1. **GPS**: n52,45110 e5,82933.

18 € 7,50 + € 1,05/pp tourist tax Ch € 0,50/24h WC € 0,50 included. **Location:** Comfortable, central, quiet.
Surface: grasstiles/metalled. 01/01-31/12.
Distance: 250m on the spot on the spot 300m 300m on the spot on the spot on the spot.
Remarks: Max. 3 days, water closed during wintertime.

S **Emst** 9E2

Recreatiepark 't Smallert, Smallertsweg 8.
GPS: n52,30910 e5,98126.

20 € 5 free. **Surface:** metalled. 01/01-31/12.
Distance: 2km 200m 200m on the spot on the spot on the spot.
Remarks: Check in on arrival.

S **Ermelo** 9D2

Camperpark Strand Horst, Buitenbrinkweg 82.
GPS: n52,31181 e5,56643.

40 € 14-16, 2 pers. incl € 1 Ch (50x) WC € 0,50/6minutes included. **Location:** Rural, comfortable, noisy.
Surface: grassy/metalled. 01/03-01/11.
Distance: 4km 50m 200m 200m 500m 4km.

S **Garderen** 9D2

Hotel Restaurant Overbosch, Hooiweg 23.
GPS: n52,22577 e5,70504.

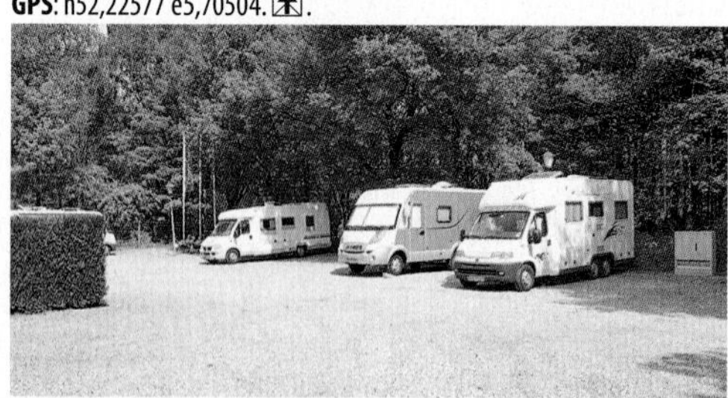

10 € 7,50 € 2,50/24h . **Location:** Rural, simple, quiet.
Surface: gravel. 01/01-31/12.
Distance: 1km on the spot 1km on the spot on the spot on the spot.
Remarks: Use of a meal desired.

Garderen 9D2

Gasterij Zondag, Apeldoornsestraat 163-165.
GPS: n52,21443 e5,70696.

10 free .
Location: Rural.
Surface: gravel. 01/01-31/12 Restaurant: Tue.
Distance: 2km 3,5km on the spot on the spot on the spot.
Remarks: Max. 1 night, entrance next to restaurant, restaurant visit appreciated.

Geldermalsen 9D2

Kostverlorenkade. **GPS**: n51,88507 e5,29030.

1 free. **Surface:** metalled.
Distance: 100m 3,6km on the spot on the spot on the spot.
Remarks: Parking at departure excursion boat.

Gendringen 9E2

Willem Alexanderplein. **GPS**: n51,86999 e6,37948.

2 free. **Location:** Urban, simple, central. **Surface:** asphalted. 01/01-31/12.
Distance: 200m 100m 500m.
Remarks: Max. 72h.

S **Gendringen** 9E2

Diekshuus, Ulftseweg 4a. **GPS**: n51,87412 e6,38586.

8 € 10 € 1/80liter Ch (4x)included.
Location: Rural, simple, quiet. **Surface:** gravel. 01/01-31/12.
Distance: 600m 600m on the spot on the spot.
Remarks: At manege.

S **Gorssel** 9E2

De Vlinderhoeve, Bathmenseweg 7. **GPS**: n52,21825 e6,26255.

5 € 14 Ch WC € 6/2 included.
Location: Rural, comfortable, luxurious, isolated, quiet.
Surface: forest soil.
01/04-31/10.
Distance: 4,5km 5km on the spot on the spot on the spot.
Remarks: To be paid at campsite.

S **Groenlo** 9F2

Camping Marveld, Elshofweg 6. **GPS**: n52,03604 e6,63134.
6 € 10 € 1/80liter Ch (4x)included. **Location:** Urban, simple. **Surface:** metalled. 01/01-31/12.
Distance: 1km 500m.

Harderwijk 9D2

P Parkweg, Parkweg. **GPS**: n52,34088 e5,62977.

NL

3 free. **Location:** Urban, simple. **Surface:** metalled.
01/01-31/12.
Distance: 1,2km 3km 1,3km 800m.

Hattem 9E1

Jachthaven Hattem, Geldersedijk 20. **GPS:** n52,47699 e6,06945.

22 € 10 + € 1,25/pp tourist tax Ch (4x)€ 2/24h WC € 0,50 € 4,00/4,00 included.
Location: Urban, comfortable, central, quiet.
Surface: grasstiles/grassy. 01/01-31/12.
Distance: 200m on the spot on the spot 200m 200m 50m on the spot on the spot.
Remarks: Max. 72h, check in at harbourmaster, bread-service.

Heerde 9E1

Brasserie Meet & Eat, Eperweg 55. **GPS:** n52,37084 e6,02079.

10 free, use of a meal desired (2x)included WC .
Surface: grassy/gravel.
Su (01/10-30/04).
Distance: 3km 1,5km 1,5km on the spot 2km 100m.

Hengelo 9E2

Elderinkweg 1-9. **GPS:** n52,04457 e6,30377.

2 free. **Location:** Rural, simple.
Surface: asphalted. 01/01-31/12.
Distance: 500m 100m.
Remarks: Next to sports fields, max. 24h.

Heteren 9D2

Steenkuil, N837. **GPS:** n51,95456 e5,73094.

3 free. **Location:** Rural, simple, isolated, quiet.
Surface: gravel/metalled.
01/01-31/12.
Distance: 2km 2km 2km 2km on the spot on the spot.
Remarks: Max. 72h.

Heteren 9D2

Landgoed Overbetuwe, Uilenburgsestraat 3.
GPS: n51,94853 e5,77266.
10 € 12 € 2 Ch€ 2 € 2 WC€ 2 . **Surface:** grassy.
01/01-31/12.
Distance: 2km.

Huissen 9E2

Looveer. **GPS:** n51,93578 e5,94467.

3 free. **Location:** Simple, central.
Surface: grasstiles/metalled. 01/01-31/12.
Distance: 200m 200m 200m 200m on the spot 500m on the spot on the spot.
Remarks: Max. 72h.

Hurwenen 9D3

Het Uilennest, Groenestraat 2a. **GPS:** n51,81367 e5,31880.
10 € 12,50 Ch included. **Surface:** grassy.
01/01-31/12.
Distance: 600m 600m.

Kerkwijk 9D3

Hippisch Centrum Bommelerwaard, Jan Stuversdreef 1-3.
GPS: n51,78876 e5,19929.

5 € 10 WC included.
Surface: metalled. 01/01-31/12.
Distance: 2km 1,5km 1,5km 1,5km.

Lathum 9E2

Jachthaven 't Eiland, De Muggenwaard 16.
GPS: n51,98819 e6,04462.

20 € 8,50 Ch (20x)€ 1,50/day WC included € 0,50/4minutes € 3/day. **Location:** Rural, comfortable, quiet.
Surface: grassy/metalled. 01/01-31/12.
Distance: 1km 5km on the spot on the spot on the spot 1km 500m on the spot.
Remarks: Max. 48h.

Lichtenvoorde 9E2

Zieuwentseweg. **GPS:** n51,99067 e6,55990.

4 € 10 € 1/80liter Ch (4x)included.
Location: Urban, simple, central. **Surface:** gravel/sand.
01/01-31/12.
Distance: 500m on the spot 500m 100m.
Remarks: Next to sports centre.

Maasbommel 9D3

Eeterij 't Pont, Veerweg 1. **GPS:** n51,81963 e5,54507.

10 € 10 . **Location:** Rural.
Surface: gravel. 01/01-31/12.
Distance: 750m on the spot on the spot.
Remarks: Along the Meuse river, beautiful view.

Maasbommel 9D3

Saletmeubelen, Kapelstraat 30. **GPS:** n51,82459 e5,53193.

5 € 10 Ch included. 01/01-31/12.
Distance: 300m 1km 1km 1km 300m.

Megchelen 9E3

Theetuin, B&B Vita Verde, Nieuweweg 10. **GPS:** n51,83895 e6,38022.

3 € 10 included. **Surface:** grassy/gravel. 01/01-31/12.
Distance: 500m 5km 500m 4km on the spot on the spot.
Remarks: Bread-service.

Meteren 9D3

Restaurant 3 Zussen, Rijksstraatweg 80. **GPS:** n51,85722 e5,28033.

5 free.
Distance: on the spot.
Remarks: Use of a meal desired.

Millingen a/d Rijn 9E3

't Crumpse Hoekje, Crumpsestraat 28.
GPS: n51,85624 e6,03145.

12 € 8, 2 pers.incl € 1/90liter Ch (12x)€ 2/day WC € 1/6minutes included. **Location:** Rural, luxurious,

NL

isolated, quiet. **Surface:** gravel. 01/01-31/12.
Distance: 1,4km 2km 1,4km 1,4km 1,5km on the spot.

Neede 9F2

Café restaurant De Olde Mölle, Diepenheimseweg 21.
GPS: n52,14153 e6,61035.

8 € 10 € 1/80liter Chfree .
Surface: metalled. 01/01-31/12.
Distance: 1km on the spot.
Remarks: Max. 72h.

Neede 9F2

Camperpark Achterhoek, Diepenheimseweg 44.
GPS: n52,18023 e6,58588.

24 € 14,50, 04/07-23/08 € 16, 2 pers.incl Ch (24x)WC € 0,12/minutes € 5,50/3,50 included.
Location: Rural, comfortable, noisy. **Surface:** grassy.
25/03-25/09.
Distance: 4.5 km on the spot on the spot 4,5km on the spot on the spot.
Remarks: To be paid at campsite, bread-service, bicycle rental.

Nijkerk 9D2

Camperplaats Nijkerk, Watergoorweg 31.
GPS: n52,22641 e5,47711.

4 free Chfree. **Location:** Urban, simple, noisy. **Surface:** metalled.
01/01-31/12.
Distance: 500m 2km 2km 500m 500m 500m 200m on the spot on the spot.

Nunspeet 9D1

Camperplaats De Zwaan, Hardenbrinkweg 46.
GPS: n52,37901 e5,75363.

35 € 13 Ch (45x)WC € 3/3 included.
Location: Rural, comfortable, luxurious, quiet.
Surface: grasstiles/grassy. 01/01-31/12.
Distance: 2,5km 3,5km 2,5km 2,5km 1km 2km 900m Zwanenroute on the spot.
Remarks: No arrival on Sunday.

Nunspeet 9D1

Routiers Nunspeet, Rijksweg A28. **GPS:** n52,36199 e5,77061.

3 free WC . **Surface:** asphalted. 01/01-31/12.
Remarks: Use of sanitary free with a meal.

Tourist information Nunspeet:
Thu-morning.

Otterlo 9D2

De Wije Werelt, Arnhemseweg 100-102. **GPS:** n52,08592 e5,77319.

50 € 18-25 Ch (10x)WC included € 5/2 € 3,50/day.
Location: Rural, simple.
Surface: grassy.
01/01-31/12.
Distance: 500m 500m on the spot campsite supermarket on the spot on the spot on the spot.

Tourist information Otterlo:
Kröller Müller Museum. Collection.

Poederoijen 9C3

Slot Loevestein, Loevestein 1. **GPS:** n51,81722 e5,02086.
4 free. 01/01-31/12.
Distance: 6km 6km 6km on the spot on the spot.

Putten 9D2

Camperplaats De Driest, Driestweg 10. **GPS:** n52,23386 e5,61533.
15 voluntary contribution . 01/01-31/12.
Distance: 2,5km on the spot on the spot.
Remarks: Max. 72h.

Putten 9D2

Brinkstraat. **GPS:** n52,26244 e5,60756.

2 free. **Location:** Urban, simple, central. **Surface:** metalled.
01/01-31/12.
Distance: 200m 300m 300m 250m on the spot on the spot.
Remarks: Max. 48h.

Tourist information Putten:
Wed.

Rekken 9F2

Grensovergang, Oldenkotseweg. **GPS:** n52,09783 e6,75568.

5 € 5. **Surface:** metalled. 01/01-31/12.
Distance: on the spot on the spot on the spot.
Remarks: Max. 72h, cycle and hiking routes.

Ressen 9E2

De Woerdt, Woerdsestraat 4. **GPS:** n51,88867 e5,87215.

15 € 7,50 + € 1/pp tourist tax (10x)€ 1.
Location: Rural.
Surface: grassy/metalled. 01/01-31/12.
Distance: 2km 3,6km 2km.
Remarks: Regional products, pitches in the orchard.

Ruurlo 9E2

Camping Tamaring, Wildpad 3. **GPS:** n52,10239 e6,44257.

2 € 10 € 1/80liter Ch (4x)included. **Location:** Rural, simple, quiet. **Surface:** gravel/metalled. 01/01-31/12.
Distance: 2km on the spot on the spot.
Remarks: Max. 8M.

Silvolde 9E2

Parking de Paasberg, Terborgseveld. **GPS:** n51,91633 e6,37194.

4 free. **Location:** Urban, simple, quiet. **Surface:** metalled.
01/01-31/12.
Distance: city centre 1km 300m.
Remarks: Parking at swimming pool, max. 72h.

Sinderen 9E2

NatuurlijkBUITEN, Toldijk 11. **GPS:** n51,91297 e6,42384.

2 € 12 € 1/80liter (2x) included.
Location: Rural, comfortable, isolated, quiet. **Surface:** grassy/gravel.
01/01-31/12.
Distance: 3km 3km on the spot 3km 3km 2km on the spot on the spot.
Remarks: Bread-service + breakfast-service, bicycle rental.

Sinderen 9E2

Biezenhof, Kapelweg 42a. **GPS:** n51,90424 e6,45180.

4 € 10 € 1/80liter Ch included.
Location: Rural, simple, quiet. **Surface:** gravel. 01/01-31/12.

NL

Distance: 4km 4km 4km on the spot.

Steenderen 9E2

Camperplaats Landlust, Landlustweg 2.
GPS: n52,06086 e6,18866.

12 € 12,50 Ch (12x) WC included.
Location: Rural, luxurious, central, quiet.
Surface: grassy/metalled. 01/01-31/12.
Distance: on the spot 1,5km 300m 150m 150m on the spot on the spot.

Stokkum 9E2

Camping Brockhausen, Eltenseweg 20. **GPS**: n51,87778 e6,21167.

4 € 10 € 1/80liter Ch (4x)included € 2,50/day.
Location: Rural, simple. **Surface:** gravel. 01/01-31/12.
Distance: 800m 500m 2,5km 2km on the spot on the spot.
Remarks: Bread-service.

Terschuur 9D2

Camperplaats Groot Westerveld, Leemweg 2.
GPS: n52,16819 e5,53239.

4 €7,50 Ch € 2,50/night,10Amp WC included.
Location: Rural, simple, quiet. **Surface:** grassy/metalled.
01/03-30/09.
Distance: 1,5km 4km 2km 3km 2km 1km on the spot on the spot.

Terwolde 9E2

Dorpsstraat 53, N792. **GPS**: n52,28173 e6,09962.

2 free. **Location:** Simple, central, quiet. **Surface:** metalled.
01/01-31/12.
Distance: 100m on the spot on the spot on the spot on the spot.

Tiel 9D2

Parking Waalkade, Waalkade. **GPS**: n51,88518 e5,44079.

4 € 5,10. **Surface:** asphalted. 01/01-31/12.
Distance: 500m on the spot on the spot on the spot 500m on the spot.
Remarks: Max. 2 nights, cash payment.

Tiel 9D2

Restaurant de Betuwe, Hoog Kellenseweg 7.
GPS: n51,90391 e5,44286.
10 € 8 . **Surface:** asphalted. 01/01-31/12.
Distance: 2km on the spot.

Toldijk 9E2

Prinsen, Hardsteestraat 4. **GPS**: n52,04489 e6,21737.

2 €6 Chincluded (1x)€ 2,50.
Location: Rural, simple, quiet. **Surface:** grassy. 01/01-31/12.
Distance: 1,5km 5km 5km 1,5km 2km 300m on the spot.
Remarks: Max. 3 nights.

Tolkamer 9E3

Europakade, Europakade. **GPS**: n51,85122 e6,09938.

15 €7,50 + € 0,90/pp tourist tax (6x)€ 1/kWh.
Location: Simple, central, quiet. **Surface:** metalled.
01/01-31/12 high water.
Distance: 200m 150m 200m 500m on the spot on the spot.
Remarks: Max. 48h.

Tolkamer 9E3

Jachthaven de Bijland, Zwarteweg 2. **GPS**: n51,85923 e6,09775.

20 € 8/day, € 10/night Ch WC € 1/4minutes included.
Location: Rural, comfortable, central. **Surface:** grassy.
15/04-15/10.
Distance: 200m 200m on the spot on the spot.

Tolkamer 9E3

De Swaenebloem, Bijland 3. **GPS**: n51,86235 e6,07937.

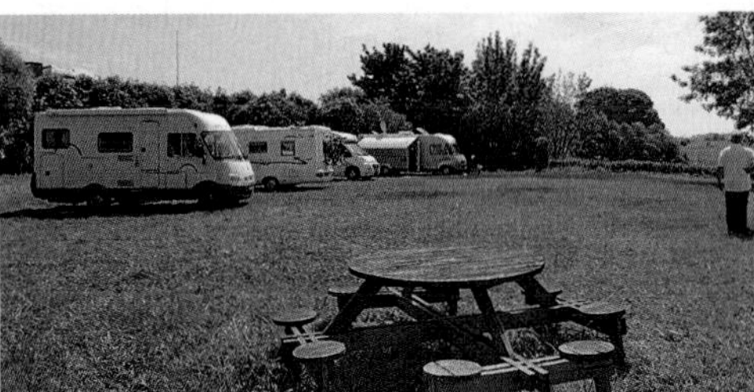

15 € 11,20 Ch (12x)€ 1,50/day WC included.
Location: Rural, comfortable, quiet.
Surface: grassy. 01/01-31/12.
Distance: 3,5km 100m on the spot on the spot 3,5km 3km on the spot on the spot.
Remarks: Charging point for electric bicycles.

Twello 9E2

Jachtlustplein 7. **GPS**: n52,23439 e6,09847.

1 free. **Location:** Urban, simple, central, quiet. **Surface:** metalled.
01/01-31/12.
Distance: 100m 100m 100m on the spot on the spot on the spot.

Varik 9D3

Pleisterplaats Bol Varik, Waalbandijk 8. **GPS**: n51,82589 e5,37829.
5 € 8, tourist tax incl free. 01/01-31/12.
Distance: 50m 500m 100m.
Remarks: Max. 48h, check in at restaurant.

Varsseveld 9E2

Pallandtbad, Grutterinkpad. **GPS**: n51,94345 e6,46691.

3 free. **Location:** Urban, simple, central. **Surface:** metalled.
01/01-31/12.
Distance: 200m 200m 200m 200m.
Remarks: Behind swimming pool, max. 24h.

Vierakker 9E2

Hanzestadcampers, Vierakkersestraatweg 19.
GPS: n52,10659 e6,24122.

3 € 7,50 Ch (3x) included.
Location: Rural, simple, quiet. **Surface:** gravel. 01/01-31/12.
Distance: 500m 1km 500m 500m on the spot on the spot.

Voorst 9E2

De Adelaar, Rijksstraatweg 49. **GPS**: n52,17760 e6,14150.

NL

12 € 13 free Ch (12x)€ 2,50 WC € 0,50/time € 4/time,€ 4/4 included. **Location:** Rural, luxurious, quiet.
Surface: grassy/metalled. 01/01-31/12.
Distance: 500m 7km on the spot on the spot 150m 1km on the spot.
Remarks: Incl. use camp-site facilities, playground.

Voorst 9E2

Boerderij de Kolke, Klarenbeekseweg 30. **GPS**: n52,17355 e6,13318.

16 € 7,90 Ch (16x)€ 1/kWh included.
Location: Rural, comfortable, central, quiet. **Surface:** grassy/metalled.
01/01-31/12.
Distance: 1km 500m.
Remarks: Regional products.

Voorthuizen 9D2

Ackersate, Harremaatweg 26. **GPS**: n52,18683 e5,62547.

5 € 23 Ch WC included € 1 € 5,50,on campsite
Location: Rural, simple.
Surface: metalled. 01/04-27/10.
Distance: 1,3km 4,2km on the spot on the spot on the spot on the spot.

Wageningen 9D2

Pabstendam. **GPS**: n51,96107 e5,65923.
3 free. **Surface:** grasstiles. 01/01-31/12.
Distance: 650m 650m.
Remarks: Nearby port.

Westendorp 9E2

Recreatieoord Hippique, Doetinchemseweg 141.
GPS: n51,94964 e6,42084.

8 € 10 € 1/80liter Ch (8x) WC € 1,75/24h € 1,75/24h € 5/time included.
Location: Rural, luxurious. **Surface:** grasstiles. 01/01-31/12.
Distance: 500m 2km 3km 1,5km 3km 1,5km on the spot on the spot.
Remarks: Arrival 9><20h.

Wijchen 9D3

Oude Klapstraat 80. **GPS**: n51,80840 e5,72140.
2 free. **Surface:** metalled. 01/01-31/12.
Distance: 500m.

Wilp 9E2

Kampeerhoeve Bussloo, Grotenhuisweg 50. **GPS**: n52,20883 e6,10961.

10 € 11-13,50, tourist tax incl Ch (10x) € 3,50/day € 5/4 included. **Location:** Rural, luxurious, isolated, quiet.
Surface: grassy/metalled. 01/01-31/12.
Distance: 4,5km 2km 400m 400m 1km 4,5km on the spot on the spot.
Remarks: Use sanitary facilities at campsite.

Winterswijk 9F2

Landgoed Kreil, Heenkamppieperweg 1.
GPS: n51,93734 e6,67493.

2 € 10 € 1/80liter Ch included against payment.
Location: Rural, simple, isolated, quiet. **Surface:** metalled.
01/03-31/10.
Distance: Breedevoort 4,5km Located on estate.

Winterswijk 9F2

Camping Ten Hagen, Waliënsestraat 139A.
GPS: n51,99131 e6,71898.

4 € 10 € 1/80liter Ch (4x)included € 3/24h
Location: Rural, simple, isolated, quiet. **Surface:** grassy.
01/01-31/12.
Distance: city centre 3km 3km 2km on the spot on the spot.
Remarks: Max. 24h, manufacturer of wooden clogs.

Winterswijk 9F2

Het Winkel, De Slingeweg 20. **GPS**: n51,95176 e6,73621.

4 € 10 € 1/80liter Ch (4x)included.
Location: Rural, simple, quiet. **Surface:** gravel/sand. 01/01-31/12.
Distance: 4,5km on the spot on the spot on the spot.

Winterswijk 9F2

Vreehorst, Vreehorstweg 43. **GPS**: n51,95028 e6,69251.

4 € 10 € 1/80liter Ch (4x)included. **Location:** Rural, simple, comfortable, quiet. **Surface:** sand. 01/01-31/12.
Distance: 3,6km on the spot on the spot.

Zaltbommel 9D3

De Beersteeg, Beersteeg. **GPS**: n51,81040 e5,24083.
6 . 01/01-31/12.

Zelhem 9E2

Carpoolplaats, Stikkenweg/N330. **GPS**: n51,99893 e6,34541.

2 free. **Location:** Rural, simple, noisy. **Surface:** asphalted.
01/01-31/12.
Distance: 1km.
Remarks: Max. 24h.

Zutphen 9E2

Houtwal. **GPS**: n52,13609 e6,19747.

8 € 2, overnight stay free € 1/80liter (8x)€ 1/kWh.
Location: Urban, simple, quiet.
Surface: metalled. 01/01-31/12.
Distance: 1km.
Remarks: Nearby police station, max. 48h, beautiful view.

Zutphen 9E2

IJsselkade. **GPS**: n52,13953 e6,19154.

2 € 1,30/h, >18.00h free. **Location:** Urban, simple, central, noisy. **Surface:** metalled. 01/01-31/12.
Distance: 1km.
Remarks: Motorhome max. 6m, max. 48h.

Tourist information Zutphen:
Groenmarkt-Houtmarkt-Zaadmarkt. Thu 8-12h, Sa 8-17h.
Lange Hofstraat. Farmers market. Thu 8-13h.

Utrecht

Amersfoort 9D2

Aan de Eem, Grote Koppel. **GPS**: n52,16083 e5,38286.

NL

3 € 1,10/meter WC included.
Location: Urban, noisy. **Surface:** metalled. 01/01-31/12.
Distance: 600m 500m 500m on the spot.
Remarks: At fire-station, max. 24h.

Tourist information Amersfoort:
VVV, Breestraat 1, www.vvvamersfoort.nl.

Baarn 9D2

De Zeven Linden, Zevenlindenweg 4. **GPS**: n52,19721 e5,24838.

3 € 19 € 2,50 Ch. **Location:** Simple.
Surface: metalled. 01/04-01/11.
Distance: 2km 1km 2km 300m on the spot on the spot.

Tourist information Baarn:
Brink. Tue 8.30-14h.

Bunnik 9D2

Camping de Boomgaard, Parallelweg 9. **GPS**: n52,06065 e5,19943.

16 € 17-19 Ch WC € 2.
Surface: metalled.
26/03-15/10.
Distance: 3km 800m.
Remarks: Arrival >17h departure <10h check in at reception next morning, use camp-site facilities allowed.

Bunschoten-Spakenburg 9D2

Jachthaven Nieuwboer, Westdijk 36. **GPS**: n52,26070 e5,37238.

8 € 18, 2 pers. incl Ch WC € 3,50 included.
Location: Rural, simple, comfortable, quiet. **Surface:** grassy.
01/01-31/12.
Distance: 800m 6km 100m 700m 700m 700m on the spot on the spot.

IJsselstein 9C2

Jachthaven Marnemoende, Noord IJsseldijk 107b.
GPS: n52,04583 e5,01861.

3 € 15 Ch WC € 4/2 included.
Location: Rural, comfortable, luxurious, quiet.
Surface: gravel. 01/01-31/12.
Distance: 2km on the spot on the spot on the spot 2km 2km on the spot.

Leersum 9D2

Touché, Rijksstraatweg 54. **GPS**: n52,00974 e5,43507.

5 free. **Location:** Urban, simple.
Surface: gravel. 01/01-31/12 Mo-Tue.
Distance: 200m on the spot 200m on the spot on the spot.

Leusden 9D2

De Mof, Arnhemseweg 95. **GPS**: n52,10654 e5,41445.

5 free, use of a meal desired.
Location: Rural, simple. **Surface:** gravel.
01/01-31/12 Mon, Tue.
Distance: 4km 4km on the spot on the spot on the spot.
Remarks: First check in at restaurant.

Mijdrecht 9C2

Rondweg. **GPS**: n52,20804 e4,86879.

4 free. **Location:** Urban, simple, noisy. **Surface:** metalled.
01/01-31/12.
Distance: 500m 500m 500m 500m.
Remarks: Max. 48h.

Rhenen 9D2

Restaurant 3 Zussen, Kerkewijk-zuid 115. **GPS**: n52,00682 e5,54006.

5 free. **Location:** Rural, simple. **Surface:** asphalted.
01/01-31/12.
Distance: 1km Veenendaal on the spot 1km on the spot on the spot on the spot.
Remarks: Use of a meal desired.

Vianen 9D2

Kanaalweg, P1. **GPS**: n51,99549 e5,09620.

4 free. **Surface:** metalled. 01/01-31/12.
Distance: 500m.
Remarks: During events: Hazelaarplein, max. 48h.

Vianen 9D2

Ponthoeve, Buitenstad 58.
GPS: n51,99829 e5,09035.
4 free. **Surface:** metalled. 01/01-31/12.
Distance: centre 400m 300m 800m 900m on the spot on the spot.
Remarks: Max. 72h.

Tourist information Vianen:
VVV, Voorstraat 97, www.vvv-vianen.nl. Historical centre.
Voorstraat (zuid). Wed 10-16h.

South Holland

Alblasserdam 9C3

Camperpark Kinderdijk, Marineweg 3a.
GPS: n51,85971 e4,65816.

44 € 15, tourist tax incl Ch WC included.
Location: Central.
Surface: metalled. 01/02-27/12.
Distance: on the spot 2km on the spot on the spot 300m 200m on the spot on the spot.
Remarks: World Heritage site Kinderdijk, 19 mills, 5km, waterbus ferry 300m.

Tourist information Alblasserdam:
Werelderfgoed Kinderdijk, Nederwaard 1, Kinderdijk. World famous mill-area. 12/03-30/10 9-17.30, 31/10-30/12 11-16.
Wilgenplein. Mo-afternoon.

Bleiswijk 9C2

Jan van de Heidenstraat. **GPS**: n52,01415 e4,53411.

2 free. **Location:** Urban. **Surface:** metalled. 01/01-31/12.
Distance: 300m 5km 500m Jumbo 400m.
Remarks: Next to fire-station.

Bleskensgraaf 9C3

Farm Nescio, Elzenweg 19. **GPS**: n51,85674 e4,75266.

NL

8 € 14 Ch WC included. **Location:** Rural, comfortable, isolated, quiet. **Surface:** metalled. 01/01-31/12.
Distance: 2,5km 1,5km 1,5km 1km 2,5km.
Remarks: Possibility of guided tour.

S Delft 9C2

Delftse Hout, Korftlaan 5. **GPS:** n52,01772 e4,37945.

20 € 20-28 Ch (20x) € 6,50 included.
Location: Urban, comfortable, central.
Surface: grasstiles. 01/04-01/11.
Distance: 1,5km 1,2km 500m on the spot on the spot on the spot summer > centre on the spot on the spot.
Remarks: Check in at reception campsite.

Tourist information Delft:
VVV, Hippolytusbuurt 4, www.delft.nl. Historical centre with canals and merchant houses. church 01/03-31/10 Mo-Sa 9-18h, 01/11-28/02 Mo-Sa 11-16h.

S Den Haag 9C2

Camperpark Den Haag, Valutapad, The Hague. **GPS:** n52,05282 e4,38013.

100 € 19,95, 2 pers. incl Ch (30x)€ 3,75/24h,10Amp WC included.
Location: Urban, comfortable. **Surface:** grassy/metalled. 01/01-31/12.
Distance: 7km 1,7km 12km 1km 1km 500m.
Remarks: Bread-service.

Tourist information The Hague (Den Haag):
VVV, Spui 68, www.denhaag.com. Government city and royal residence.
Bezoekerscentrum Binnenhof, Binnenhof 8a. Guided tours in government buildings. Mo-Sa 10-16h. € 5-10.
Madurodam, George Maduroplein 1. Miniature Holland.

S Dordrecht 9C3

Camperplaats Stadswerven, Maasstraat. **GPS:** n51,81793 e4,68750.

12 Mo-Sa € 6,50/24h, Su free € 1/60liter Ch.
Location: Simple, quiet. **Surface:** metalled. 01/01-31/12.
Distance: city centre 3km 5km on the spot on the spot 3km 1km waterbus.
Remarks: Max. 72h, near Noah's Ark.

Dordrecht 9C3

Weeskinderendijk 5. **GPS:** n51,80861 e4,65611.

2 € 1/4h, first 24h free. **Location:** Urban, simple, noisy. **Surface:** metalled. 01/01-31/12.
Distance: 500m 500m 500m 100m.
Remarks: Max. 72h.

S Dordrecht 9C3

Jachthaven Westergoot, Baanhoekweg 1. **GPS:** n51,81518 e4,72467.
€ 10 Ch € 2 WC € 0,50/7minutes € 5.
Distance: on the spot.

S Giessenburg 9C3

Boerenterras De Groot, A.M.A. Langeraadweg 9. **GPS:** n51,85327 e4,92205.

6 € 10 Ch WC included. **Location:** Rural, simple, isolated, quiet. **Surface:** concrete. 01/01-31/12.
Distance: 1,5km 3km on the spot 1,5km 3,5km on the spot.

S Giessenburg 9C3

Halfomhoeve, Bovenkerkseweg 76/78. **GPS:** n51,84628 e4,87548.

5 € 10 Ch WC included. **Location:** Rural, simple, isolated, quiet. **Surface:** concrete. 01/05-15/10.
Distance: 2km 3km on the spot 1,5km 1,5km on the spot on the spot.

S Giessenburg 9C3

Landscheiding Giessenburg, Landscheiding 1. **GPS:** n51,84753 e4,92294.

10 € 10 Ch WC included.
Location: Rural, comfortable, isolated, quiet.
Surface: grassy/metalled. 01/01-31/12.
Distance: 2km 2km 2km on the spot on the spot.

S Gorinchem 9C3

WSV Merwede, Buiten de Waterpoort 8. **GPS:** n51,82697 e4,96477.

16 € 10 Chincluded € 0,75 € 5/4.
Location: Comfortable, isolated, quiet.
Surface: gravel/metalled.
01/01-31/12.
Distance: 500m on the spot on the spot 300m 1km on the spot.
Remarks: Max. 72h, check in at harbourmaster.

Tourist information Gorinchem:
VVV, Grote Markt 17, www.gorinchem.nl. Historical centre with city walls.
Slot Loevestein, Loevestein 1, Poederoijen. Castle, 14th century.
Grote Markt. Mo 8.30-12.30h.

S Gouda 9C2

Parking Klein Amerika, Fluwelensingel. **GPS:** n52,01185 e4,71576.

30 € 8 Ch (12x)WCincluded.
Location: Urban, simple, quiet.
Surface: metalled. 01/01-31/12.
Distance: 300m.
Remarks: Max. 3 days.

Tourist information Gouda:
VVV, Markt 35, www.vvvgouda.nl. Historical centre with 300 monuments, famous for its Gouda-cheese.
Kaaswaag, Markt. History of the Gouda cheese, cheesetasting. 01/04-30/09 13-17h, Thu 10-17h. € 7,50.
Markt. Thu 8.30-13h, Sa 8.30-17h.
Montmartre, Markt. Antiques and flea market. 01/05-30/09 We 9-17h.

S Goudriaan 9C2

Boerderij de Verwondering, De Hoogt 14. **GPS:** n51,89150 e4,90741.

2 € 10 Ch included. **Location:** Rural, simple, isolated. **Surface:** concrete.
Distance: 2,5km 7km.

S Hoogblokland 9C2

Landwinkel De Bikkerhoeve, Bazeldijk 66. **GPS:** n51,89716 e4,99563.

6 € 10 Ch WCincluded. **Location:** Rural, simple, isolated, quiet. **Surface:** concrete. 01/03-31/10.
Distance: 2km 1,4km 2km 2km on the spot on the spot.

NL

S Langerak 9C2

Camperplaats Langerak, Melkweg 3.
GPS: n51,92069 e4,89975.
3 € 15 WC . **Location:** Rural. **Surface:** metalled.
Distance: on the spot on the spot.
Remarks: Max. 8M, bicycle rental.

S Leerdam 9C2

De Galgenwaard, Lingedijk 8a, Oosterwijk.
GPS: n51,87451 e5,07311.

3 € 8 included € 2 WC. **Location:** Rural, simple, quiet.
Surface: metalled. 01/04-01/10.
Distance: Leerdam 2km on the spot on the spot 300m
Along the river Linge.
Remarks: Opening hours 7-22h, passenger ferry across the Linge.

Leerdam 9C2

Groenzoom, Lingedijk. **GPS**: n51,88288 e5,08670.

3 free. **Location:** Urban, simple. **Surface:** metalled.
01/01-31/12.
Distance: 2,5km 2,5km 2,5km on the spot.
Remarks: In front of Lingedijk 27, small pitches.

Leerdam 9C2

Parking Glasmuseum, Lingedijk. **GPS**: n51,88676 e5,08699.

2 free. **Location:** Rural, simple. **Surface:** asphalted.
01/01-31/12.
Distance: 1km on the spot 1km on the spot.

Leerdam 9C2

Jachthaven Oude Horn, Sundsvall 1. **GPS**: n51,88984 e5,09532.

3 free. **Location:** Urban, simple.
Surface: gravel. 01/01-31/12.
Distance: 300m 300m 300m.
Remarks: Max. 72h.

Leiden 9C2

P Haagweg, Haagweg 6. **GPS**: n52,15963 e4,47852.

15 € 12/24h. **Location:** Urban.
Surface: metalled.
01/01-31/12.
Distance: 800m 800m 800m Free bus to centre.
Remarks: Along railwayline, video surveillance, free shuttle (till 2am).

S Lexmond 9C2

De Fruithof, Achthoven 39. **GPS**: n51,97414 e5,00254.
2 € 12 included. **Location:** Rural. **Surface:** metalled.
Distance: 150m on the spot on the spot on the spot.
Remarks: Max. 7m.

S Maassluis 9B2

Camperplaats Maassluis, Govert van Wijnkade 50.
GPS: n51,91628 e4,24535.

3 free free. **Surface:** asphalted. 01/01-31/12.
Distance: city centre 1km 500m 1,2km 450m on the spot on the spot.
Remarks: Max. 48h.

S Nieuwland 9C2

De Grienduil, Geer 25. **GPS**: n51,90106 e5,02622.

4 € 7-13 + € 1/pp tourist tax Ch WC included.
Location: Simple, quiet. **Surface:** gravel. 01/01-31/12.
Distance: on the spot 2km 4km on the spot on the spot.
Remarks: In winter limited services.

S Noordeloos 9C2

Huis den Dool, Botersloot 67. **GPS**: n51,91170 e4,95995.
3 € 12,50 Ch included . **Location:** Rural.
Distance: on the spot on the spot.
Remarks: Charging point for electric bicycles.

S Numansdorp 9C3

Fort Buitensluis, Fortlaan 10. **GPS**: n51,71727 e4,43866.
5 € 15 Ch included. **Surface:** unpaved.
01/04-01/10.
Distance: 1,5km 5km on the spot on the spot 1,5km on the spot on the spot.
Remarks: At Hollands Diep, golf court 3km.

Oud Beijerland 9C3

De Oude Tol, Randweg 31a. **GPS**: n51,82933 e4,39585.

4 free. **Location:** Rural, simple, isolated, quiet.
Surface: asphalted.
01/01-31/12.
Distance: 2km on the spot 100m on the spot on the spot.
Remarks: Arrival >16h, max. 24h.

S Ouddorp 9B3

Drive-in Camperpark Klepperduinen, Vrijheidsweg 1.
GPS: n51,81724 e3,89850.

51 € 8,50-10,50/12h, € 15-18,50/24h + tourist tax € 0,95/pp, dog € 2,50/day Ch (51x)€ 4/24h WC included .
Location: Rural, luxurious, isolated, quiet.
Surface: grassy/metalled. 01/01-31/12.
Distance: 500m 1km on the spot on the spot on the spot.

S Pernis 9C2

Casa E Parking, Ring 156-158. **GPS**: n51,88581 e4,39008.

5 € 15 Ch WC € 2/2 included.
Surface: metalled. 01/01-31/12.
Distance: Rotterdam 11km 300m 300m 100m.

S Poeldijk 9B2

Booma Recreatie, Vredebestlaan 14b. **GPS**: n52,02464 e4,21242.

10 € 6 Ch included (10x)€ 2/day.
Location: Rural, simple, quiet. **Surface:** gravel. 01/01-31/12.
Distance: 800m 50m 800m 800m 800m on the spot on the spot.

S Sassenheim 9C2

Jachthaven Jonkman, Jonkman 1. **GPS**: n52,22074 e4,54476.

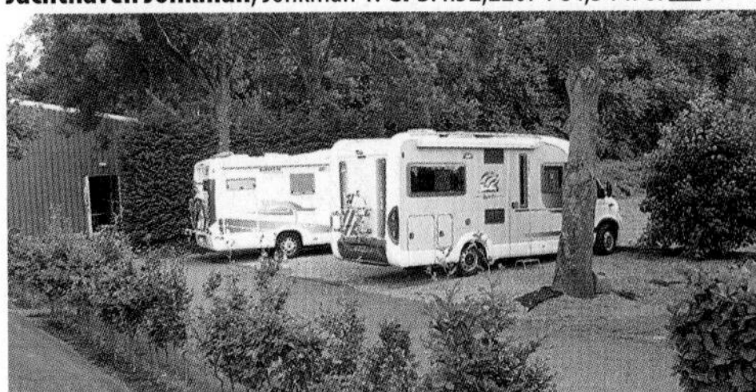

6 € 15 € 0,50 Ch € 1 WC € 0,50 € 5 included.
Location: Comfortable. **Surface:** grassy/gravel. 15/03-01/11.
Distance: 2km 1km on the spot on the spot on the spot 2km on the spot.
Remarks: Check in at harbourmaster.

Schiedam 9C2

Doeleplein 1. **GPS**: n51,91972 e4,40111.

NL

2 € 6,60. **Location:** Urban, simple, central, quiet. **Surface:** metalled. 01/01-31/12.
Distance: 500m 1,5km on the spot on the spot 500m 500m 500m.
Remarks: Max. 72h.

Schiedam 9C2

Noordvest 40. **GPS:** n51,91926 e4,39372.

6 € 7. **Location:** Urban, simple, central, quiet. **Surface:** metalled. 01/01-31/12.
Distance: city centre 100m.
Remarks: Max. 72h.

Tourist information Schiedam:
Het Jenever Museum, Lange Haven 74-76. Making distilled spirits. Tue-Su 12-17h.
Lange Kerkstraat. Fri 9-16h.

Streefkerk 9C2

Camperplaats Streefkerk, Middenpolderweg 2a.
GPS: n51,91266 e4,81287.
5 € 12,50 Ch WC included. **Location:** Rural.
Surface: metalled.

Strijensas 9C3

Jachthaven Strijensas, Sassendijk 6. **GPS:** n51,71472 e4,58735.

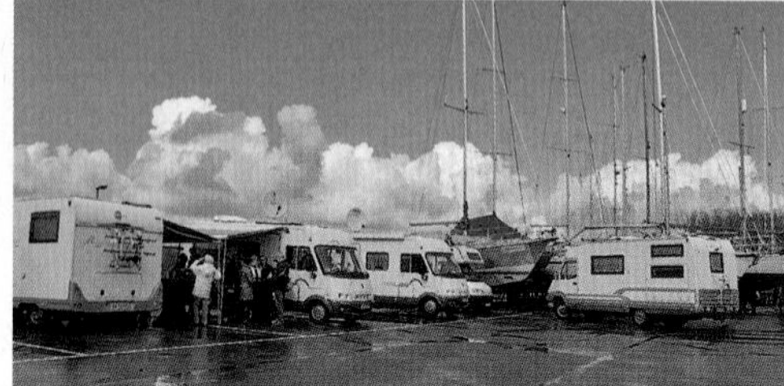

6 € 7 € 0,50/100liter Ch € 2,50 WC € 1 included.
Surface: asphalted. 01/01-31/12.
Distance: 500m on the spot on the spot on the spot.
Remarks: Max. 72h.

Vlaardingen 9C2

Parking Deltabrug, Oosthavenkade 81. **GPS:** n51,90364 e4,34769.

4 free. **Location:** Urban, noisy.
Surface: metalled. 01/01-31/12.
Distance: 1km on the spot 50m 100m 500m.
Remarks: Along railwayline, max. 48h.

Wijngaarden 9C3

't Koeiestalletje, Westeinde 26. **GPS:** n51,84378 e4,74631.

5 € 8 Ch service € 2 WC .
Location: Rural. **Surface:** metalled. 01/01-31/12 Su.
Distance: 5km 5km 5km on the spot on the spot.
Remarks: Charging point for electric bicycles, regional products.

Zevenhoven 9C2

Camperplaats Zevenhoven, Noordeinde 36.
GPS: n52,19475 e4,77305.

5 € 10 included. **Location:** Rural, comfortable.
Surface: grassy/metalled. 01/01-31/12.
Distance: 1km 1km on the spot on the spot.

Zealand

Axel 11B1

P Watertoren, Kinderdijk 4. **GPS:** n51,25972 e3,91028.

2 free. **Location:** Urban, simple, noisy. **Surface:** metalled. 01/01-31/12.
Distance: 800m on the spot on the spot 500m on the spot on the spot.
Remarks: Max. 24h.

Tourist information Axel:
Noordstraat. Sa 8-16h.

Breskens 9A3

Roompot Recreatie, Nieuwe Sluisweg. **GPS:** n51,40193 e3,54420.

10 € 14 Ch included WC . **Location:** Rural, comfortable, quiet. **Surface:** metalled. 01/01-31/12.
Distance: 500m 400m 100m 100m on the spot on the spot.
Remarks: Servicepoint at camping Zeebad, ferry to Vlissingen 500m (pedestrian/bicycles).

Graauw 11B1

Zandbergsestraat. **GPS:** n51,32519 e4,10420.

7 free. **Location:** Rural, simple, quiet. **Surface:** gravel/sand. 01/01-31/12.
Distance: 400m 400m on the spot.
Remarks: Max. 72h.

Groede 11A1

De Ploeg, Parking Zuid, Voorstraat 47. **GPS:** n51,38232 e3,51268.

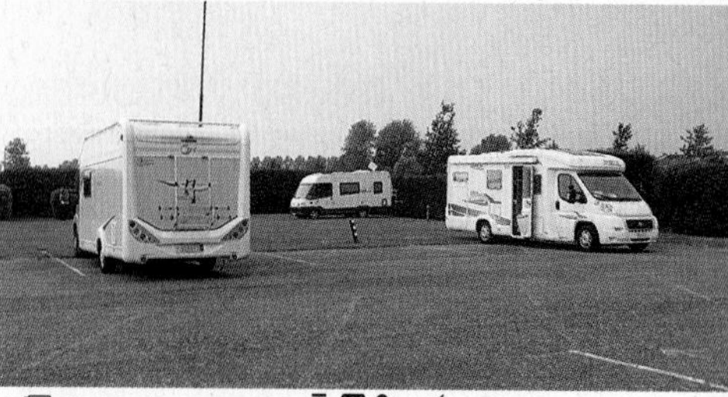

40 € 5 17-10h, € 12,50/24h Ch (35x) € 2,50/night WC . **Location:** Comfortable, central, quiet.
Surface: grasstiles/metalled. 01/04-01/10 22-7h.
Distance: 100m 3km 100m 100m 100m > Terneuzen on the spot on the spot.
Remarks: Caution € 10, sanitary/washing machine at campsite.

Groede 11A1

Strandcamping Groede, Zeeweg 1. **GPS:** n51,39632 e3,48719.

50 € 1/h. **Location:** Rural, simple, quiet. **Surface:** gravel. 01/01-31/12.
Distance: Groede 3km sandy beach 200m 60m on the spot on the spot on the spot.
Remarks: Max. 1 night.

Hansweert 9B3

Westhavendijk. **GPS:** n51,44483 e4,00629.

5 free. **Location:** Rural, simple, isolated, quiet. **Surface:** asphalted. 01/01-31/12.
Distance: 250m 4km on the spot 200m on the spot on the spot.

Hulst 11B1

Parkeerterrein Havenfort, Havenfort. **GPS:** n51,27700 e4,04912.

15 € 0,80/h, mo-sa 9-17h, su 12-18h.
Surface: metalled. 01/01-31/12.

NL

Distance: on the spot 25m 150m 150m 200m on the spot on the spot.
Remarks: Max. 72h, shops open on Sunday.

Tourist information Hulst:
VVV, Grote Markt 19, www.bezoekhulst.nl. Fortified city with city walls, shops open on Sunday.

S Kamperland 9B3

Camperpark Zeeland, Campensweg 5.
GPS: n51,57495 e3,65236.

102 € 14,50-19,50 € 0,20/min Ch (75x)€ 4/24h,16Amp WC € 0,25/min € 6/4 included **Location:** Rural, comfortable, luxurious, quiet. **Surface:** grassy/gravel. 01/01-31/12.
Distance: 3km 2km 50m 50m 100m 4km 2km on the spot on the spot.

S Kamperland 9B3

Roompot Beach Resort, Mariapolderseweg 1.
GPS: n51,58972 e3,71666.

20 € 6 10-17h, € 14 17-10h Ch WC € 4,50/1,20
Surface: asphalted. 01/01-31/12.
Distance: 3km 500m 500m 500m 500m 1km.

Kloosterzande 11B1

Hulsterweg. **GPS:** n51,36555 e4,02121.

2 free. **Location:** Rural, simple, central, quiet. **Surface:** metalled. 01/01-31/12.
Distance: 500m 80m 700m on the spot on the spot.

S Kruiningen 9B3

Landwinkel de Plantage, Kaasgat 4a. **GPS:** n51,46865 e4,04445.

15 € 12,50 Ch € 2,50/night,10Amp WC included.
Surface: grassy. 01/01-31/12.
Distance: 3km 3km 3km 3km on the spot 1km on the spot on the spot.

S Kruiningen 9B3

Den Inkel, Polderweg 12. **GPS:** n51,43485 e4,04448.
6 € 15-21 Ch WC included. 01/01-31/12.

S Middelburg 9A3

Hof van Tange, Hof van Tange. **GPS:** n51,49688 e3,60474.

6 € 9,50, Su/holidays free WC € 0,50.
Location: Simple, central, quiet. **Surface:** gravel/sand.
01/01-31/12 1st week Aug.
Distance: 500m 5km 500m 300m on the spot on the spot on the spot.
Remarks: Motorhome <6m, max. 48h.

S Middelburg 9A3

Oude Veerseweg. **GPS:** n51,50071 e3,62842.

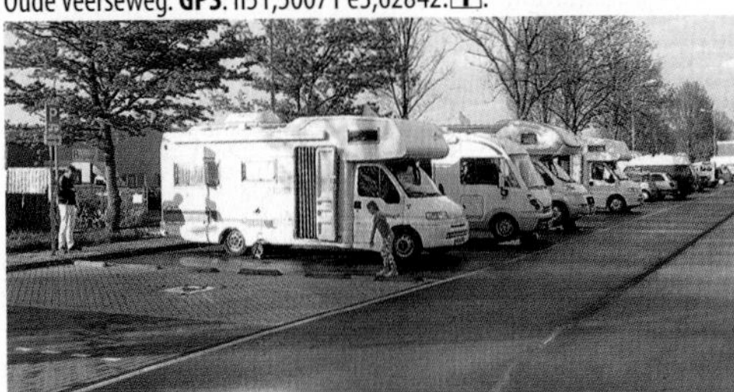

5 free € 1 Ch (4x)€ 4. **Location:** Comfortable, central, quiet. **Surface:** metalled. 01/01-31/12.
Distance: 1km 100m 500m 1km on the spot.

Middelburg 9A3

Kanaalweg. **GPS:** n51,49432 e3,61519.

3 € 9,50. **Location:** Urban, simple, central, noisy.
Surface: concrete. 01/01-31/12.
Distance: 500m on the spot on the spot 500m on the spot.
Remarks: Max. 48h.

Oosterland 9B3

Wok van Zeeland, Rijksweg 6. **GPS:** n51,65767 e4,05336.

3 free. **Location:** Simple, isolated, noisy. **Surface:** asphalted.
01/01-31/12.
Distance: 2km on the spot.
Remarks: Only overnight stays.

S Oostkapelle 9A3

De Pekelinge, Landmetersweg 1. **GPS:** n51,55725 e3,55139.
20 € 18,50-27,50 Ch included. **Location:** Simple, isolated, quiet. **Surface:** gravel/sand. 27/03-01/11.
Distance: nearby nearby on the spot on the spot.
Remarks: Arrival >20h departure <10h, max. 1 night.

Paal 11B1

Jachthaven, Zeedijk van de van Alsteinpolder.
GPS: n51,35331 e4,10937.

4 free. **Location:** Rural. **Surface:** asphalted/metalled.
01/01-31/12.
Distance: 100m on the spot on the spot on the spot on the spot on the spot.
Remarks: Max. 72h.

S Renesse 9B3

Camping International, Scharendijkseweg 8.
GPS: n51,74030 e3,78967.

20 € 20, 11/07-22/09 € 35 Ch (16x)WC included € 5/3,50 € 2.
Location: Rural. **Surface:** metalled. 04/03-01/11.
Distance: 1,5km 2,5km on the spot on the spot on the spot 1,5km on the spot on the spot.

Sas van Gent 11B1

Kanaaleiland, Oostkade. **GPS:** n51,22527 e3,80246.

2 free. **Surface:** metalled.
Distance: 100m 100m 100m.
Remarks: Max. 24h.

Tourist information Sas van Gent:
Keizer Karelplein. Tue 9-16h.

Terneuzen 11B1

Oostsluis, Binnenvaartweg. **GPS:** n51,33555 e3,82117.

4 free. **Location:** Rural, simple, isolated, quiet.
Surface: grassy/metalled. 01/01-31/12.
Distance: 500m on the spot 500m 200m on the spot on the spot.
Remarks: Max. 24h.

Tourist information Terneuzen:
Portaal van Vlaanderen, Zeevaartweg 11. Interactive Visitors Centre at the Terneuzen Locks, guided tour and boat excursions.
Markt. Sa 9-16h.

S Tholen 9B3

Jachthaven, Contre Escarpe 4. **GPS:** n51,53112 e4,22390.

NL

4 € 10,50 + € 1/pp tourist tax Ch € 1,50/24h WC € 5 included. **Surface:** metalled. 01/01-31/12.
Distance: 100m 100m 100m.
Remarks: Max. 72h.

Vogelwaarde 11B1

Populierenstraat. **GPS**: n51,32562 e3,97758.

2 free. **Location:** Urban, simple, quiet. **Surface:** metalled.
01/01-31/12.
Distance: 1km 400m on the spot on the spot.

Westdorpe 11B1

De Baeckermat, Bernhardstraat. **GPS**: n51,22917 e3,82167.

2 free. **Location:** Rural, simple, quiet. **Surface:** metalled.
01/01-31/12.
Distance: 500m on the spot 100m 500m on the spot on the spot on the spot.
Remarks: Max. 24h.

Wolphaartsdijk 9B3

Camping 't Veerse Meer, Veerweg. **GPS**: n51,54325 e3,81253.

7 € 15/22 Ch (5x) WC on camp site on camp site included. **Location:** Rural, comfortable, isolated, quiet.
Surface: metalled. 01/01-31/12 15/11-15/12.
Distance: 1,5km 100m 100m 100m on the spot on the spot on the spot.

Zierikzee 9B3

De Zandweg, Zandweg 30. **GPS**: n51,65691 e3,91210.

12 € 12,50 Ch (12x),10Amp included.
Location: Rural, comfortable, central, noisy. **Surface:** asphalted.
01/01-31/12.
Distance: 800m on the spot on the spot 350m 1km 350m on the spot.
Remarks: Service passerby € 3.

North Brabant

Asten 11E1

Camperpark Wetland, Tureluurweg 7. **GPS**: n51,36687 e5,84214.

50 € 9,60, 2 pers.incl Ch (37x) € 1,50 WC € 2/2 included. **Location:** Rural. **Surface:** grassy/metalled.
01/01-31/12.
Distance: 2km 4km 9km 5km 2km 1,5km on the spot on the spot.
Remarks: Located in nature reserve De Groote Peel.

Bakel 9D3

Sporthal de Beek, De Beekakker 13a. **GPS**: n51,50061 e5,74377.

2 free. **Location:** Urban, simple. **Surface:** metalled.
01/01-31/12.
Distance: 500m on the spot on the spot.
Remarks: At gymnasium.

Bergen op Zoom 9B3

De Boulevard. **GPS**: n51,48405 e4,27941.

8 free. 01/01-31/12.
Remarks: Max. 72h.

Bergen op Zoom 9B3

De Boulevard Noord. **GPS**: n51,48735 e4,27708.

5 free. **Surface:** metalled. 01/01-31/12.
Distance: 1km 3,8km on the spot on the spot.
Remarks: Max. 72h. On the level of restaurant 'La Playa'.

Tourist information Bergen op Zoom:
De Markiezenhof, Steenbergsestraat 8. Medieval palace built in the late 15th century. Tue-Su 11-17h.

Best 9D3

Carpoolplaats De Wilg. **GPS**: n51,52106 e5,39423.

3 free. **Location:** Motorway, isolated. **Surface:** metalled.
01/01-31/12.
Distance: 500m 150m on the spot on the spot.
Remarks: Max. 24h.

Boxtel 9D3

Dennenoord, Dennendreef 5. **GPS**: n51,59770 e5,28661.

4 € 12,50 + € 1/pp tourist tax Ch WC € 4 included. **Location:** Rural, simple, isolated. **Surface:** metalled.
01/01-31/12.
Distance: 4km 4km.
Remarks: Max. 3 nights.

Breda 9C3

Nijverheidssingel 391. **GPS**: n51,58793 e4,76366.
6 € 14.
Surface: metalled. 01/01-31/12.
Distance: 900m 800m 900m 200m.

Tourist information Breda:
VVV, Willemstraat 17-19, www.vvvbreda.nl. Many historical bldg. And castles.

Budel 11D1

Camperplaats Budel, Heikantstraat 16. **GPS**: n51,26163 e5,59007.

25 € 9,50 Ch € 2,50/day,4Amp included.
Location: Urban. **Surface:** grasstiles/grassy. 01/01-31/12.
Distance: 800m 2km 600m 800m 800m 600m on the spot on the spot.
Remarks: Max. 72h, video surveillance, barbecue place, charging point for electric bicycles.

De Heen 9B3

Akkermans leisure&golf, Heensemolenweg 23.
GPS: n51,60654 e4,24547.

5 € 12,50 Ch (16x) WC included.
Location: Rural, comfortable, isolated, quiet.
Surface: asphalted/metalled. 01/01-31/12.
Distance: on the spot on the spot on the spot.

NL

Drimmelen 9C3

Camperpark Jachthaven Biesbosch
Drimmelen
Located near marina
Ideal base for walking and cycling
Luxurious motorhome stopover
www.jachthavenbiesbosch.nl
info@jachthavenbiesbosch.nl

Camperpark Jachthaven Biesbosch, Nieuwe Jachthaven 5.
GPS: n51,70750 e4,81008.
18 € 13,50, 15/06-15/09 € 16,50 Ch € 3/24h WC € 5/1,50 included.
Surface: asphalted/grassy. 01/01-31/12.
Distance: 1km on the spot 200m on the spot on the spot on the spot.
Remarks: Barbecue place.

Eindhoven 9D3

P+R Meerhoven, Sliffertsestraat 304. **GPS**: n51,43507 e5,42444.

10 first 24h € 3, € 5/24h Ch WC free.
Location: Simple. **Surface:** metalled. 01/01-31/12.
Distance: 4km on the spot 200m 500m on the spot on the spot on the spot.
Remarks: Free bicycles available.

Escharen 9D3

Bar Bistro De Brouwketel, Hoogeweg 9.
GPS: n51,74152 e5,73376.

15 free. **Surface:** grassy. 01/01-31/12.

Etten-Leur 9C3

Jachthaven Turfvaart, Westpolderpad 6. **GPS**: n51,59512 e4,65102.

5 € 10, 01/04-01/10 € 15 € 0,50/100liter Ch WC € 1 included. **Surface:** grassy/metalled. 01/01-31/12.
Distance: 1,5km on the spot 500m.
Tourist information Etten-Leur:
Mo-morning.

Geertruidenberg 9C3

WSV Geertruidenberg, Statenlaan 15. **GPS**: n51,70362 e4,86311.

8 € 10 Ch WC included.
Location: Comfortable, quiet. **Surface:** gravel. 01/05-31/10.
Distance: 500m 3km on the spot on the spot 500m.
Remarks: Max. 3 days, max. 9m, only cash payment.

Geertruidenberg 9C3

Statenlaan 2. **GPS**: n51,70333 e4,86333.

10 free. **Surface:** metalled. 01/01-31/12.
Distance: 500m on the spot on the spot 500m.
Remarks: Max. 24h.

Gemert 9D3

St.Gerardusplein. **GPS**: n51,55354 e5,69109.

2 free. **Location:** Urban, simple.
Surface: gravel. 01/01-31/12.
Distance: on the spot 300m 200m 100m on the spot on the spot.

Gemert 9D3

Koksehoeve, Koksedijk 25. **GPS**: n51,57380 e5,65846.

10 free, use of a meal obligated. **Location:** Rural, simple, isolated, quiet. **Surface:** metalled. 01/01-31/12.
Distance: 2km.

Grave 9D3

Gemaal van Sasse/Kazematten, Mars en Wijthdijk.
GPS: n51,76859 e5,73085.
2 free. **Location:** Rural. **Surface:** metalled. 01/01-31/12.
Distance: 2,5km 2,5km 2,5km on the spot on the spot.

Grave 9D3

Het Arsenaal, Trompetterstraat. **GPS**: n51,75925 e5,73769.
1 free. **Surface:** metalled. 01/01-31/12.
Distance: 200m 200m 50m 200m.

Heeswijk-Dinther 9D3

Hotel-Restaurant de Leygraaf, Meerstraat 45A.
GPS: n51,66445 e5,47511.

4 € 11,20 WC included € 2,50.
Location: Rural, comfortable.
Surface: grassy. 01/01-31/12.
Distance: 1,5km 6km on the spot on the spot on the spot.
Remarks: Check in on arrival.

Helenaveen 9E3

Oude Hoeven, Soemeersingel 99. **GPS**: n51,40951 e5,90594.

5 € 7,50, 2 pers. incl Ch € 1,50. **Location:** Quiet.
Surface: grassy. 01/04-01/11.
Distance: on the spot on the spot.
Remarks: Max. 72h, money in envelope in mail box.

Helmond 9D3

Parking Beatrixlaan, Beatrixlaan. **GPS**: n51,48100 e5,64870.

6 € 3/24h. **Location:** Urban, simple, quiet. **Surface:** metalled. 01/01-31/12.
Distance: 300m 500m 300m 500m on the spot on the spot on the spot.
Remarks: Castle 500m.

Hoogerheide 9B3

METO parking, Huijbergseweg.
GPS: n51,42318 e4,33452.
5 free. **Location:** Simple. **Surface:** metalled. 01/01-31/12.
Distance: 800m 800m 800m.

Hoogerheide 9B3

Fa. Broos, Buitendreef 4, De Kooi. **GPS**: n51,42522 e4,34656.

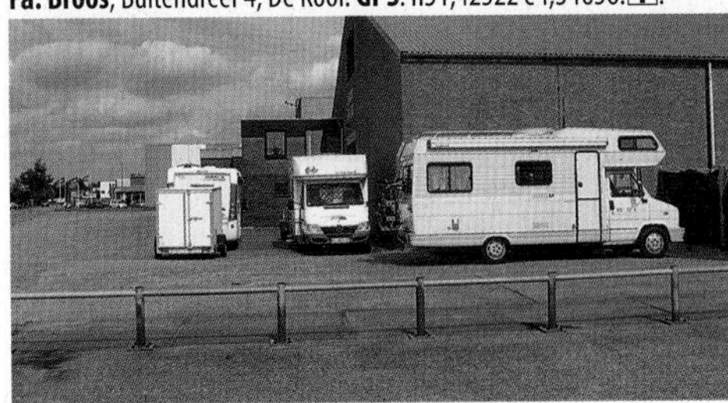

5 free (3x)free.
Location: Rural, simple, isolated.
Surface: metalled. 01/01-31/12.
Distance: 3km 3km 3km 3km on the spot on the spot.

Hulten 9C3

Restaurant Stad Parijs, Rijksweg 6. **GPS**: n51,56996 e4,96446.

NL

15 free € 0,75. **Location:** Rural, simple, quiet. **Surface:** asphalted. 01/01-31/12.
Distance: on the spot.
Remarks: Free, use of a meal obligated.

Linden 9E3

Jachthaven 't Loo, Hardweg 15. **GPS**: n51,75182 e5,82740.

11 € 12,50-15 Ch € 2,50/day WC € 1 €4/3 included.
Surface: grassy. 01/01-31/12.
Distance: on the spot on the spot on the spot on the spot on the spot on the spot.
Remarks: Check in at harbourmaster 9-12h, 15-18h, caution key sanitary building € 20.

Nuenen 9D3

Sportpark RKSV Nuenen, Pastoorsmast 14.
GPS: n51,46317 e5,56277.

5 free . **Location:** Rural, simple, isolated. **Surface:** grassy. 01/01-31/12 July.
Distance: 1,7km 800m 900m.
Remarks: Max. 5 days a month.

Oijen 9D3

Speciaalbierbrouwerij Oijen, Oijensebovendijk.
GPS: n51,81049 e5,53126.

3 € 10, free with a meal included. **Location:** Rural, simple, quiet. **Surface:** grassy/gravel. 01/01-31/12.
Distance: on the spot on the spot on the spot on the spot on the spot.

Oirschot 9D3

Camperplaats Oirschot, De Rijt. **GPS**: n51,50064 e5,32366.

28 € 13 Chincluded (28x)€ 2. **Surface:** gravel.
Distance: 1km on the spot 1km 900m.
Remarks: Max. 72h.

Tourist information Oirschot:
VVV, Sint Odulphusstraat 11, www.vvvoirschot.nl. City with 100 monumental buildings, hiking and biking routes.
01/01-31/12.
Museum de Vier Quartieren, Sint Odulphusstraat 11. Regional museum.
Tue-Su 13-16.30h.

Oosteind 9C3

Camperplaats Oosteind, Ter Horst 19. **GPS**: n51,64705 e4,88326.

4 € 8 Ch included. **Location:** Rural, comfortable, isolated.
Surface: grassy. 01/01-31/12.
Distance: 2km 1km 500m.

Oss 9D3

Van Venrooy Motorhomes, Galliërsweg 39.
GPS: n51,75981 e5,55642.

2 free free. **Surface:** metalled. 01/01-31/12.

Oss 9D3

Sportpark Rusheuvel. GPS: n51,77657 e5,52409.

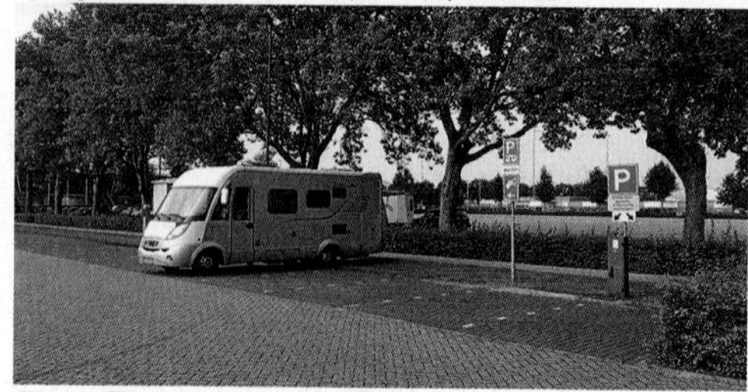

free. **Surface:** metalled. 01/01-31/12.
Distance: 750m 750m AH 500m.
Remarks: Max. 3 nights.

Oudenbosch 9C3

Het Oude Bossche veld, Moerdijksestraat 1. **GPS**: n51,59558 e4,54117.

15 € 15,20, tourist tax incl Ch included.
Surface: grassy/metalled. 01/04-01/11.
Distance: city centre 1km 600m 1km 1km on the spot on the spot.
Remarks: Max. 72h, possibility for reservation.

Overloon 9E3

Van Well, Roosendaalseweg 1. **GPS**: n51,56377 e5,91995.

15 voluntary contribution Ch € 2. **Location:** Quiet.
Surface: grassy. 01/01-31/12.
Distance: 2,5km 4km 2,5km 2,5km on the spot on the spot.

Raamsdonksveer 9C3

De Uilendonck, Lageweg 8, Raamsdonk. **GPS**: n51,68540 e4,91380.

3 free. **Location:** Rural, simple, isolated, quiet. **Surface:** metalled. 01/01-31/12.
Distance: 1km on the spot.

Raamsdonksveer 9C3

Kloosterweg 1. **GPS**: n51,68908 e4,87582.

4 free. **Surface:** metalled.
Distance: 800m on the spot 800m.
Remarks: Parking at sports park.

Reusel 11D1

De Wekker, Wilhelminalaan 97. **GPS**: n51,36187 e5,17339.

5 Free, use of a meal obligated .
Location: Simple, quiet. **Surface:** sand. 01/01-31/12 Tue.
Distance: on the spot.

Roosendaal 9C3

Mobildrôme, Argon 31-33, Oud Gastel. **GPS**: n51,56333 e4,46278.

8 free € 0,50 Ch € 0,50. **Surface:** metalled.
Distance: 2km 1,1km 2km.

Tourist information Roosendaal:
Rosada, A17, afrit 19. Factory outlet.

NL

Vessem 9D3

Eurocamping Vessem, Zwembadweg 1. **GPS:** n51,41197 e5,27490.
40 € 7, 19/03-31/10 € 10 € 1/80liter Ch € 0,60/kWh € 0,50 € 1/day. **Location:** Rural. **Surface:** grassy. 01/01-31/12.
Distance: 1,5km 7km 5km on the spot 1,5km on the spot 300m on the spot on the spot.

Vianen 9E3

Ons Plekske, Berkenkamp 59. **GPS:** n51,71602 e5,84489.
25 € 10 Ch WC included. **Location:** Comfortable, luxurious, quiet. **Surface:** grassy.
Distance: on the spot 3,5km 2,6km 2,6km on the spot on the spot.
Remarks: Monitored parking 24/24.

Wijk en Aalburg 9D3

Bakkerij Hardeman, Torenstraat 4. **GPS:** n51,75976 e5,13123.

5 € 3 Ch € 2 WC € 7,50 included. 01/01-31/12.
Distance: on the spot on the spot.

Zundert 9C3

Museum de Scooter, Heischoorstraat 4. **GPS:** n51,49025 e4,64532.

10 € 10 Ch WC included. 01/01-31/12.
Distance: 2,8km A1 7km on the spot on the spot.
Remarks: Reservation during flower parade: museum@lambretta-nl.net.

Limburg

Afferden 9E3

Roland, Rimpelt 17.
GPS: n51,63766 e6,03035.
40 € 8 Ch (20x)€ 2/day WC included € 0,50 € 4,50/2,50 € 5/day. **Location:** Rural. **Surface:** grassy. 15/03/2017-01/11.
Distance: 1,5km 1km 300m 1,5km 2km on the spot on the spot.
Remarks: Dog € 3, sanitary/washing machine at campsite.

Brunssum 11E1

Schutterspark P1, Heidestraat 20. **GPS:** n50,94582 e5,98385.

10 free. **Surface:** metalled. 01/01-31/12.
Distance: 1,5km 100m Schuttershuuske.
Remarks: Max. 72h, barefoot path.

Gennep 9E3

Martinusplein. **GPS:** n51,69985 e5,97206.

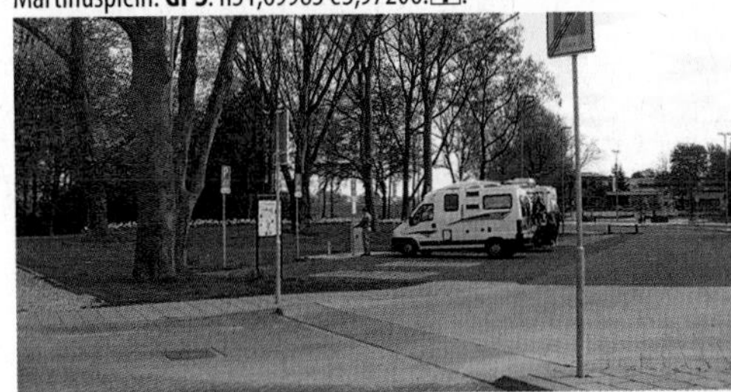

5 free. **Location:** Urban, simple, quiet. **Surface:** metalled. 01/01-31/12.
Distance: 100m 4,6km 200m 150m bakery 100m, supermarket 250m on the spot on the spot.
Remarks: Max. 72h.

Gronsveld 11D2

A2 Campeercentrum, Veilingweg 13. **GPS:** n50,80632 e5,72201.
4 free. 01/01-31/12.
Distance: 500m 1,1km.
Remarks: Industrial area, only overnight stays.

Grubbenvorst 9E3

Het Kompas, Meerlosebaan 7. **GPS:** n51,42861 e6,12889.

38 € 10 Ch (39x),4Amp included. **Location:** Rural. **Surface:** grassy/gravel. 01/03-30/11.
Distance: 2km 500m 2km 2km 1km on the spot on the spot.
Remarks: Money in envelope in mail box.

Heel 11E1

De Tump, Heelderweg 13. **GPS:** n51,17698 e5,88315.

5 € 7. **Surface:** grassy. 01/05-31/10.
Distance: 1km on the spot.
Remarks: Max. 48h.

Ittervoort 11E1

Camperplaats Ittervoort, Brigittastraat 31.
GPS: n51,17565 e5,82228.

15 € 10, 2 pers. incl., dog € 1,50 Ch included € 2,50 WC € 1/day. **Location:** Rural, simple. **Surface:** grassy. 01/01-31/12.
Distance: Ittervoort 500m, Thorn 2km 2,6km on the spot Jan Linders 750m. **Remarks:** Vineyard Thorn 600m.

Kessel 11E1

Hazenakkerweg 1. **GPS:** n51,29856 e6,05009.
18 € 12, tourist tax incl Ch (18x)€ 2,50/24h WC included.
Location: Rural. **Surface:** asphalted/grassy. 01/01-31/12.
Distance: city centre 200m 10km 100m 200m 500m 300m on the spot on the spot.
Remarks: Max. 8M.

Landgraaf 11E1

Camperplaats Landgraaf, Casinolaan 6. **GPS:** n50,87294 e6,02205.
28 € 15 € 0,50/50liter Ch (18x)€ 0,50/kWh.
Location: Rural. **Surface:** grassy/gravel.
01/04-31/12.
Distance: 300m 1,5km 300m 300m 300m 50m 50m 250m.

Landgraaf 11E1

De Watertoren, Kerkveldweg 1. **GPS:** n50,91016 e6,07300.

6 € 10, peak season € 15 + € 0,90/pp tourist tax € 1/90liter Ch included. **Location:** Simple, isolated, quiet.
Surface: grassy/gravel. 01/01-31/12.
Distance: 2km.

Maasbree 11E1

Camperplaats Rooth, Rooth. **GPS:** n51,36820 e6,08374.
15 € 12 Ch (18x) WC . **Location:** Rural, comfortable. **Surface:** grassy/sand. 01/04-01/11.
Distance: 3km 4km 2km 500m 3km 700m on the spot on the spot.
Remarks: Max. 72h.

Maasbree 11E1

Restaurant Boszicht, Provincialeweg 2. **GPS:** n51,36395 e6,07980.

3 Free, use of a meal obligated. **Location:** Simple, noisy.
Surface: gravel.
Distance: 2km 2km on the spot.

NL

S Maastricht 11D2

Camperplaats Maastricht, Bosscherweg 35. **GPS**: n50,87553 e5,68018.
100 € 15 € 0,50/50liter Ch (67x)€ 0,50/kWh,16Amp.
Surface: grassy/gravel. 01/01-31/12.
Distance: 2,9km 100m 800m 600m 50m on the spot on the spot.

S Maastricht 11D2

Maastricht Marina, Hoge Weerd 20. **GPS**: n50,82389 e5,69944.

20 € 18 Ch (20x),6Amp WC € 3,50/2,50 included.
Surface: gravel/metalled. 03/02-31/12.
Distance: 1,5km 2,8km 50m 50m 50m 1,5km 800m on the spot on the spot.
Remarks: Arrival < 19h.

S Meijel 11E1

Nieuwehof, Vieruitersten 25. **GPS**: n51,35410 e5,89717.
29 € 10 + € 1/pp tourist tax Ch WCincluded on demand. **Location:** Rural, comfortable, quiet.
Surface: grassy/sand. 01/01-31/12.
Distance: 1,8km 14km on the spot on the spot.

Milsbeek 9E3

Toeristisch knooppunt de Diepen, Zwarteweg 60.
GPS: n51,73788 e5,95510.

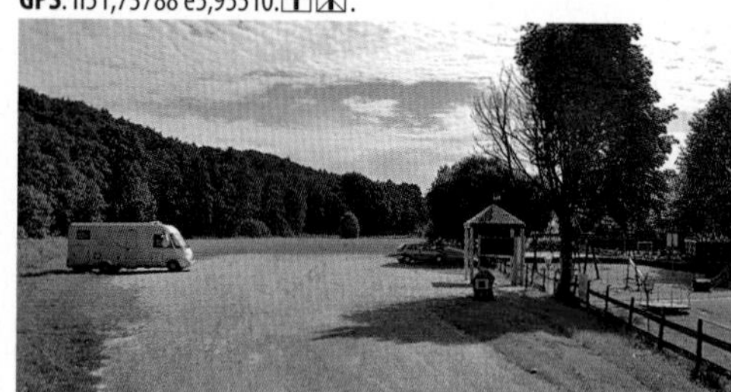

4 free. **Surface:** grassy/sand.
Distance: on the spot.
Remarks: Next to Eethuis de Diepen.

S Neer 11E1

Jachthaven Hanssum, Hanssum 40b. **GPS**: n51,25778 e6,00361.

12 € 12,50 Ch WC € 0,50. **Surface:** grassy/metalled.
Distance: 3km on the spot 200m.
Remarks: Max. 48h, service near marina.

S Neer 11E1

Café Restaurant Boothuis de Troost, Hanssum 47.
GPS: n51,25964 e6,00380.

4 € 7,50, guests free . **Surface:** metalled.

S Nieuw Bergen 9E3

Camperplaats Bos&Heide, Op de Paal 4. **GPS**: n51,59008 e6,07269.

25 € 6,50 + € 1/pp tourist tax included Ch (15x)€ 2 WC.
Surface: grassy. 01/03-31/10.
Distance: 1,5km 2km 1,5km 1,5km.
Remarks: Located in nature reserve Maasduinen.

Ottersum 9E3

Bier-Café Restaurant Old Inn, Siebengewaldseweg 13.
GPS: n51,68935 e6,00728.

20 free. **Surface:** metalled. 01/01-31/12.

S Plasmolen 9E3

Eldorado, Witteweg 18. **GPS**: n51,73284 e5,91639.

13 € 14,50-17 + € 1/pp tourist tax € 0,50/100liter Ch (13x)€ 0,50/kWh WCincluded € 1 € 3 € 5/24h.
Location: Rural, comfortable, quiet.
Surface: grassy.
01/01-31/12 Service: winter.

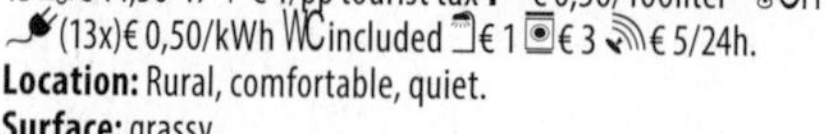

Distance: 200m 8km on the spot on the spot 200m 200m on the spot on the spot.
Remarks: Check in at Eldorado Boatshop Witteweg 9, max. 72h.

S Sittard 11E1

De Nieuwe Hateboer, Sportcentrumlaan. **GPS**: n51,00794 e5,88150.

10 free Ch WC use sanitary facilities at swimming pool .
Surface: asphalted. 01/01-31/12.
Distance: 2km 6,2km 2km 2km 100m on the spot.

Remarks: At swimming pool, register via SMS (licence plate number) +31 6 27 82 55 82, max. 48h.

Thorn 11E1

Waterstraat. **GPS**: n51,15860 e5,84403.

3 € 2,50/9-18h. **Surface:** gravel. 01/01-31/12.
Distance: 150m 150m.
Remarks: Max. 24h.

Tourist information Thorn:
VVV, Wijngaard 14, www.lekker-genieten.nl. The white village, with historical centre and Gothic collegiate church.

S Valkenburg 11E2

Camperplaats Valkenburg aan de Geul, Heunsbergerweg 1.
GPS: n50,86037 e5,83148.
40 € 15-25 € 1/100liter Ch (30x)€ 0,60/kWh,16Amp WCincluded € 0,70 € 4,75/2,25 € 2,50/24h.
Location: Rural, comfortable, quiet. **Surface:** grassy/metalled.
01/01-31/12.
Distance: 500m 2km 1,5km 1,5km on the spot 500m 500m on the spot on the spot.
Remarks: Maastricht 15km.

P Valkenburg 11E2

Burgemeester Henssingel. **GPS**: n50,86361 e5,83725.

6 € 1,70/h, max. € 7.
Surface: metalled.
01/01-31/12.
Distance: 300m.

Tourist information Valkenburg:
VVV, Th.Dorrenplein 5, www.vvvzuidlimburg.nl. Popular holiday resort.
Gemeentegrot, Cauberg 4. Marl caves.
Steenkolenmijn, Daalhemerweg 31. Visiting a gallery of a mine.
01/04-30/11 10-17, 01/11-07/01 + weekend, guided tour 12h, 13h, 14h and 15h.

S Venlo 9E3

De Boswesels, Weselseweg/Kikvorstraat.
GPS: n51,39270 e6,19990.

16 € 12 Ch (16x) included. **Location:** Simple. **Surface:** grassy. 01/04-01/11.
Distance: 1km 500m 1,8km.

S Venlo 9E3

WSV De Maas, Jachthavenweg 50. **GPS**: n51,39245 e6,14854.

20 € 13 € 2,10Amp WC € 3/2 included.
Surface: metalled. 01/03-30/11.
Distance: Venlo centre 4km 3,5km on the spot 500m.
Remarks: Max. 48h, check in at harbourmaster, free bicycles available, free ferry to city centre.

S Weert 11D1

Suffolkweg Zuid 30. **GPS**: n51,25435 e5,69283.

20 € 12 Ch included € 2. **Surface:** gravel/metalled.
Remarks: Max. 72h.

S Well 9E3

Camperplaats De Wellsche Hut, Wezerweg 13.
GPS: n51,58687 e6,12344.

18 € 10 Ch WC included . **Surface:** metalled.
01/01-31/12.
Distance: 4km 6km on the spot.
Remarks: At mountainbike trail, dog on leads, nature reserve Maasduinen.

S Well 9E3

Jachthaven 't Leuken, De Kamp 7a. **GPS**: n51,56361 e6,06360.

30 € 10 Ch WC included.
Location: Simple, quiet. **Surface:** grassy. 01/04-01/11.
Distance: Well 2km 11km on the spot on the spot on the spot on the spot on the spot.
Remarks: Walking and bicycle area, acquatic sports area.

NL

Norway

Capital: Oslo
Government: parliamentary constitutional monarchy
Official Language: Norwegian
Population: 5,166,000 (2014)
Area: 381,155 Km²

General information
Dialling code: 0047
General emergency: 112
Currency: Norwegian krone (NOK),
€ 1 = NOK 9,07, NOK 1 = € 0,11
£1 = NOK 10,54, NOK 1 = £0.09 (November 2016)
Credit cards are accepted almost everywhere.

Regulations for overnight stays
In general wild camping is allowed, you must hold at least 150 metres from the nearest house or cabin.

Camping Key Europe is obligatory when using campsites: the card can be purchased at any campsite for NOK 160 (± € 17,85/ £16), valid for one year.

Additional public holidays 2017
April 14 Good Friday
April 17 Easter Monday
May 17 Constitution Day
June 5 Pentecost Monday
July 29 St. Olaf's Day

Time Zone
Winter (Standard Time) GMT+1
Summer (DST) GMT+2

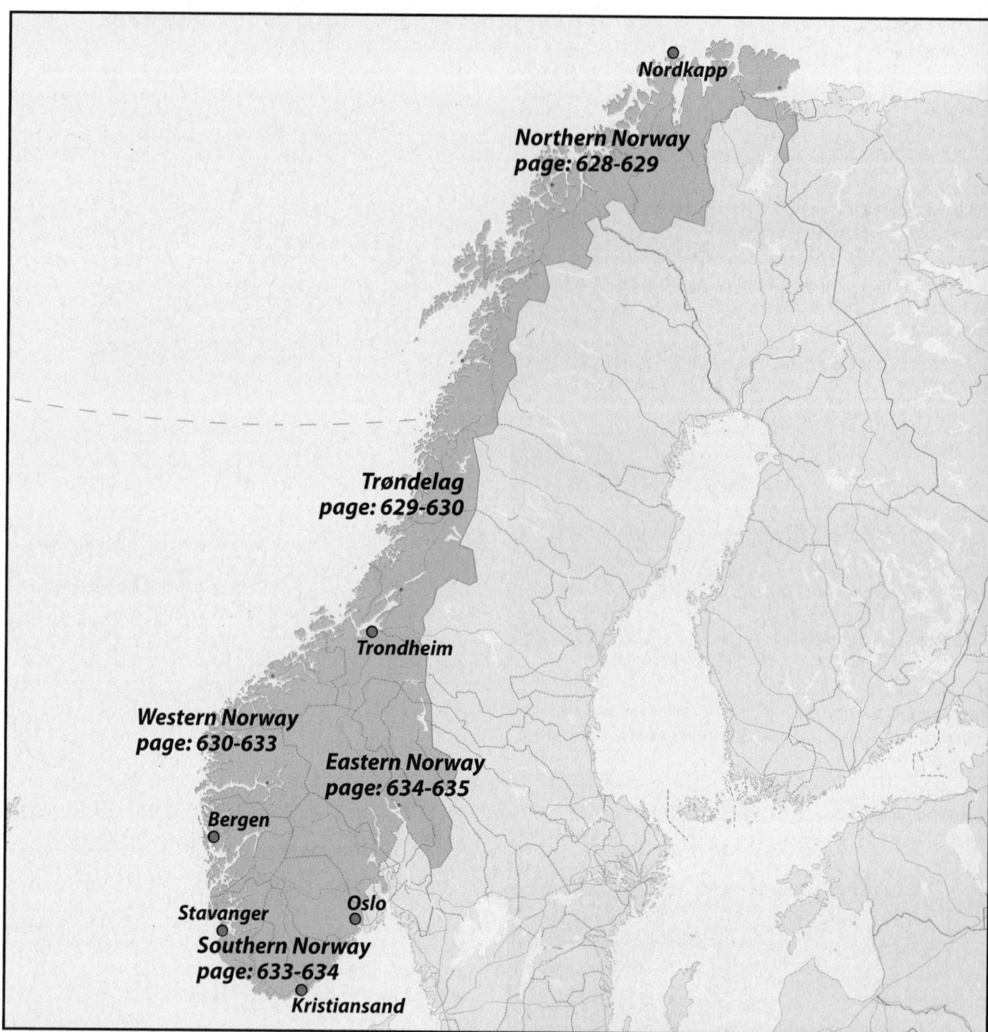

NO

Northern Norway

Båstad 3A2
Eggumsveien. **GPS**: n68,30729 e13,65160.
30 NOK 100 WC. **Location:** Rural, isolated, quiet.
Surface: asphalted.
Distance: on the spot on the spot.
Remarks: Check in at cafe.

Bodø 3A3
Bobilparkering Sentrum, Hålogalandsgata 11.
GPS: n67,27866 e14,41026.
4 NOK 10/h, overnight stay free Chfree.
01/01-31/12.
Distance: 500m.

Botnhamn 3A2
Sjark- Og Småbåtforening. GPS: n69,50743 e17,90753.
5 NOK 75 Ch NOK 50. **Surface:** concrete.
Distance: on the spot on the spot on the spot on the spot.

Brønnøysund 4B1
Brønnøy havn, Havnegata. **GPS**: n65,47271 e12,20725.
free. **Surface:** gravel. 01/01-31/12 snow.
Distance: on the spot on the spot on the spot.
Remarks: At shopping centre.

Brønnøysund 4B1
Statiol, Valveien 48. **GPS**: n65,47919 e12,21634.
NOK 130 Ch.
Distance: on the spot on the spot 200m.
Remarks: Behind petrol station.

Evenes 3A2
Evenes Lofoten, Nerveien 654. **GPS**: n68,45810 e16,70223.

10 NOK 170 Chincluded (10x)NOK 30/day WC.
Location: Rural, simple. **Surface:** gravel. 01/01-31/12.
Distance: on the spot on the spot on the spot. **Remarks:** Money in envelope in mail box, use of sauna against payment.

Fauske 3A3
Fauske Parkering AS. GPS: n67,25741 e15,38421.

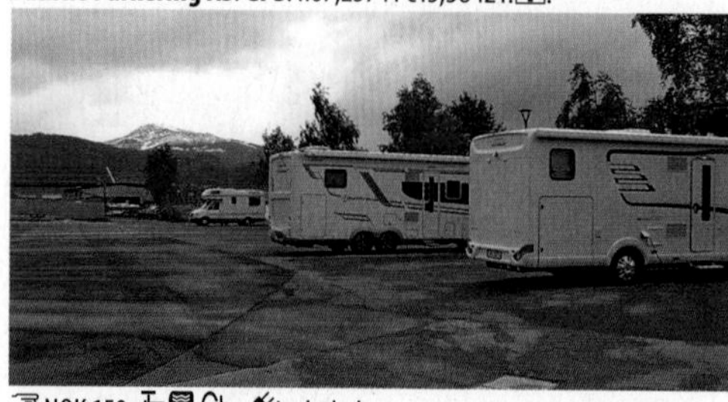

NOK 150 Ch included.
Surface: asphalted. water disconnected in winter.
Distance: 700m on the spot on the spot on the spot.
Remarks: Max. 24h, money in envelope in mail box.

Fiskåbygd 4A3
Statoil, Van ylven. **GPS**: n62,08607 e5,57917.

6 free Ch. **Location:** Rural, simple, simple.
Surface: asphalted. 01/01-31/12.
Distance: on the spot on the spot on the spot 300m 100m.
Remarks: At petrol station, max. 3 days.

Hammerfest 3B1
Jernbanetrasken. **GPS**: n70,66290 e23,67571.

Distance: 300m.
Remarks: Behind the hotel.

Hattfjelldal 4C1
RV 73. **GPS**: n65,59578 e13,99090.
60 free Chfree. **Surface:** asphalted.
Distance: 100m.

Hovden 3A3
Hovden-Halsa, E 17. **GPS**: n66,72466 e13,69884.

10 free ChWC free. **Location:** Rural, simple.

Surface: asphalted. 01/01-31/12.
Distance: 10km on the spot on the spot on the spot.

Husøy i Senja 3A2

Fylkesveg. **GPS:** n69,54522 e17,67056.
6 NOK 100.
Distance: on the spot on the spot.

Innhavet 3A2

Innhavet bobilparkering. **GPS:** n67,96367 e15,92576.

NOK 100 Ch NOK 30.
Surface: gravel. 01/01-31/12.
Distance: on the spot on the spot on the spot 150m.

Jøkelfjord 3B1

Jøkelfjord Bobilcamping. **GPS:** n70,06207 e21,92987.
10 NOK 100 Ch NOK 50.
Distance: on the spot on the spot.

Kabelvåg 3A2

Kabelvåg Feriehus & Camping, Mølnosveien.
GPS: n68,21747 e14,44541.
25 NOK 240 Ch NOK 40 NOK 50.
Surface: gravel/metalled. 01/01-31/12.
Distance: 2,5km on the spot on the spot.
Remarks: Canoe rental.

Kirkenes 3C1

Havneveien. **GPS:** n69,72754 e30,07291.

free Ch. **Surface:** asphalted.
Distance: 1km on the spot on the spot 100m.

Kleppstad 3A2

Lofoten Bobilcamping, Lyngvær. **GPS:** n68,22915 e14,21571.
NOK 125 NOK 40 WC. 01/05-15/09.
Distance: on the spot.

Lødingen 3A2

Båtforeningen. **GPS:** n68,41249 e16,00871.
NOK 120 (18x)NOK 30 WC NOK 20. **Surface:** grassy/gravel.
Distance: on the spot on the spot 1km 1km.
Remarks: Money in envelope in mail box.

Melbu 3A2

Melbu Båtforenings, Neptunveien. **GPS:** n68,49493 e14,81248.
NOK 100 included. **Surface:** gravel.
Distance: on the spot on the spot 900m.

Mo i Rana 3A3

E6. **GPS:** n66,30462 e14,12296.
Ch.

Narvik 3A2

Turist Parking, Brugata. **GPS:** n68,44172 e17,41705.
free. **Surface:** asphalted.

Oksfjordhamn 3B1

Oksfjord Båtforening. **GPS:** n69,90620 e21,32404.
NOK 100 Ch WC. **Surface:** gravel.

Skaland 3A2

Senjatrollet, Finnsæter. **GPS:** n69,41020 e17,26334.
20 free Ch. **Location:** Isolated.

Skutvik 3A3

Skutvik Båtforening. **GPS:** n68,01368 e15,33414.
NOK 100. **Surface:** grassy.
Distance: on the spot on the spot.

Sommarøy 3A2

Skipsholmvegen. **GPS:** n69,63335 e17,99490.
voluntary contribution Ch. **Surface:** gravel.

Distance: 1km on the spot on the spot 800m.
Remarks: At the beach.

Stokkvägen 3A3

Grønsvik Kystfort, Aldesundveien R 17. **GPS:** n66,34991 e13,00156.

8 free WC.
Location: Rural, simple. **Surface:** asphalted. 01/01-31/12.
Distance: on the spot 300m on the spot.

Storforshei 3A3

Polarsirkel-Senteret, Saltfjellet. **GPS:** n66,55175 e15,32134.
free. **Location:** Isolated, quiet. **Surface:** asphalted.

Stø 3A2

Stø Bobilcamp. **GPS:** n69,01984 e15,10762.
13 NOK 180 Ch WC. **Surface:** gravel. 01/05-15/09.
Distance: on the spot on the spot on the spot.

Svolvær 3A2

Bobilcamp Svolvær, Purkholmen. **GPS:** n68,22733 e14,56016.

30 NOK 250 Ch WC included. **Location:** Urban, simple. **Surface:** gravel/metalled. 01/01-31/12.
Distance: 200m on the spot 200m 200m 200m on the spot on the spot.

Svolvær 3A2

Vestfjord Hotell Lofoten, Fiskergata 46. **GPS:** n68,22949 e14,56492.

28 NOK 250 (34x) WC included NOK 5.
Distance: 200m on the spot on the spot 400m 250m 2km 2km.

Utskarpen 3A3

Flostrandveien. **GPS:** n66,31917 e13,31009.

7 free. **Location:** Rural. **Surface:** asphalted/grassy.
Distance: on the spot on the spot on the spot.

Utskarpen 3A3

Flostrandveien. **GPS:** n66,31387 e13,28420.

Vestpollen 3A2

Vestpollen, E10. **GPS:** n68,31583 e14,71576.

8 free.
Location: Rural, simple. **Surface:** asphalted. 01/01-31/12.
Distance: 3km on the spot on the spot.

Vevelstad 4B1

Steinmo Bobilparkering, Fv17. **GPS:** n65,60550 e12,36637.
NOK 100. **Location:** Isolated, quiet. **Surface:** grassy/gravel.
Distance: on the spot on the spot.

Øvergård 3B2

Hatteng, E 6. **GPS:** n69,27228 e19,93653.

12 free Ch WC. **Location:** Rural, simple. **Surface:** metalled. 01/01-31/12.
Distance: 4km on the spot on the spot 4km.

Trøndelag

Grong 4B1

Fv391. **GPS:** n64,46587 e12,31143.

5 free. **Surface:** asphalted.
Distance: 100m 100m 400m.
Remarks: Picnic area.

Heimdal 4B2

Sandmoen Bobilparkering, Sandmoflata 6.
GPS: n63,33155 e10,35678.

26 NOK 100-200 Ch (13x)NOK 100 WC free NOK 20 NOK 50/24h.
Location: Simple, noisy. **Surface:** asphalted. 01/01-31/12.
Distance: on the spot.
Remarks: Check in at reception, breakfast-service.

Inderøy 4B2

Inderøy Bobilcamp, Sakshangvegen. **GPS:** n63,87790 e11,26847.

NO

14 NOK 100 free. **Location:** Rural, simple, isolated, quiet. **Surface:** gravel. 01/01-31/12.
Distance: 1,5km 300m on the spot.
Remarks: Pay at restaurant.

S **Inderøy** 4B2
Kjerknesvågen Kai, Vågavegen 650. **GPS**: n63,91311 e11,19049.

10 NOK 200 Ch WCincluded NOK 20.
Location: Simple, quiet. **Surface:** gravel. 01/01-31/12 1st and 3rd weekend July.
Distance: on the spot on the spot on the spot.

S **Leksvik** 4B2
Hammerbergvegen. **GPS**: n63,66747 e10,61449.

14 NOK 150 included.
Location: Urban, simple. **Surface:** asphalted. 01/01-31/12.
Distance: 500m on the spot on the spot on the spot 1km.
Remarks: Pay at restaurant.

S **Oppdal** 4B2
Trollheimsporten Turistsenter, Festa. **GPS**: n62,61610 e9,47695.

8 NOK 150 Ch WCincluded NOK 10/4minutes.
Location: Rural, comfortable, quiet. **Surface:** asphalted.
Distance: 12km on the spot on the spot on the spot.
Remarks: Sauna incl..

S **Rennebu** 4B2
Berkåk Veikro, Mjukliveien 1. **GPS**: n62,83215 e10,01117.

8 NOK 200 Chfree WC NOK 50. **Location:** Urban, simple, noisy. **Surface:** gravel. 01/01-31/12.
Distance: on the spot on the spot 100m.

S **Rinnan** 4B2
Rinnleirets Bobilcamp, E 6. **GPS**: n63,76421 e11,43589.

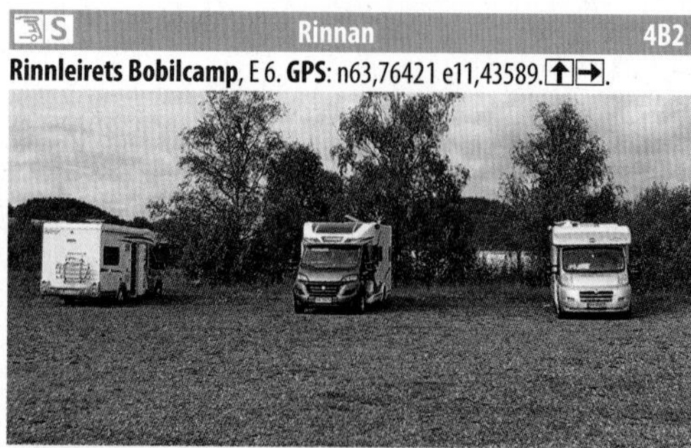

50 NOK 150 Ch (16x)included WC.
Location: Rural, simple. **Surface:** gravel. 01/01-31/12.
Distance: on the spot on the spot on the spot.
Remarks: Money in envelope in mail box.

Trofors 4B1
Store Svenningvatn. **GPS**: n65,32528 e13,37714.
NOK 80. **Location:** Rural, isolated, quiet. **Surface:** gravel.
Distance: Trofors 25km on the spot on the spot.
Remarks: Money in envelope in mail box.

Trondheim 4B2
Øya Stadion, Klostergata. **GPS**: n63,42565 e10,38172.

20 free. **Location:** Urban, simple. **Surface:** asphalted. 01/01-31/12.
Distance: 1km on the spot 1km 200m.
Remarks: At stadium, max. 24h.

Western Norway

S **Ålesund** 4A2
Hjelsetgaarden Motorhome, Sorenskriver Bullsgate. **GPS**: n62,47670 e6,16110.

45 NOK 160 (30x) WC included. **Location:** Urban, comfortable. **Surface:** asphalted. 01/01-31/12.
Distance: on the spot on the spot on the spot 50m 150m 200m.

S **Åndalsnes** 4A2
Rauma, Isfjordsvegen. **GPS**: n62,56659 e7,69109.

20 free . **Location:** Urban, simple. **Surface:** asphalted. 01/01-31/12.
Distance: 300m 100m 100m 200m 300m.
Remarks: Whale safari.

S **Askvoll** 4A3
Askvoll Småbåtlag, Rv608. **GPS**: n61,34679 e5,06360.

15 NOK 125 Ch NOK 35 WC NOK 10 NOK 50.
Location: Simple, quiet. **Surface:** gravel. 01/01-31/12.
Distance: 300m on the spot on the spot on the spot 300m.

S **Austrheim** 4A3
Mastrevikane. **GPS**: n60,78886 e4,93870.
. **Surface:** asphalted.
Distance: 1km on the spot on the spot.

S **Austrheim** 4A3
Kjelstraumen vertshus, Austrheimsvegen. **GPS**: n60,79825 e4,93908.
20 NOK 150 (15x) WC .
Distance: on the spot on the spot 300m.

S **Averøy** 4A2
Atlanterhavsveien. **GPS**: n63,01244 e7,42807.

15 NOK 210 NOK 20 Ch NOK 30 WC NOK 20/20.
Location: Rural, comfortable. **Surface:** gravel.
Distance: on the spot on the spot on the spot on the spot.
Remarks: Boat rental.

S **Bergen** 4A3
Bergenshallen, Vilhelm Bjerknes vei 24. **GPS**: n60,35421 e5,35876.

28 NOK 150/24h Chincluded .
Location: Urban, simple. **Surface:** asphalted. 01/05-31/08.
Distance: 5km 500m on the spot.
Remarks: Max. 48h.

Bokn 5A1
Langtid, Langtid. **GPS**: n59,16978 e5,45382.

25 free. **Location:** Rural, simple. **Surface:** metalled. 01/01-31/12.
Distance: 100m 100m.
Remarks: Parking at ferry-boat.

S **Bokn** 5A1
Føresvikvegen 580. **GPS**: n59,23255 e5,43919.
4 (2x)NOK 50. **Location:** Rural, simple. **Surface:** asphalted. 01/01-31/12.
Distance: on the spot on the spot on the spot on the spot.
Remarks: At supermarket.

S **Bremanger** 4A3
Iglandsvik Marina. **GPS**: n61,83631 e4,93487.

NO

20 NOK 200 included NOK30/40. **Location:** Simple, quiet. **Surface:** gravel. 01/01-31/12.
Distance: on the spot on the spot 500m 300m on the spot.

Bru — 5A1

Sokn Marina, Åmøyveien. **GPS**: n59,05210 e5,67691.
30 NOK 180 Ch WC . 01/01-31/12.
Distance: on the spot on the spot.

Bryne — 5A2

Abobil.no, Vesthagen 11. **GPS**: n58,72057 e5,64894.

25 free Ch (25x)free.
Surface: asphalted. 01/01-31/12.
Distance: 1km 800m 800m 1km.
Remarks: At motorhome dealer.

Egersund — 5A2

Nordre Eigerøy, Ytstebrødveien. **GPS**: n58,45522 e5,90852.
NOK 150 included.
Location: Isolated. **Surface:** grassy. 01/01-31/12.
Distance: 5,5km on the spot on the spot 5,5km on the spot.

Egersund — 5A2

Ved taxi-stasjon, Jernbaneveien. **GPS**: n58,45373 e6,00243.
10 free. **Surface:** asphalted.
Distance: 300m on the spot on the spot 300m.

Erfjord — 5A1

Hålandsosen, Riksveg. **GPS**: n59,34806 e6,23703.
free. **Location:** Isolated, quiet. **Surface:** gravel.
Distance: on the spot on the spot 200m.

Florø — 4A3

Bobilparkering Florø, Strandavegen 19. **GPS**: n61,60061 e5,02252.

NOK 60-150.
Location: Simple. **Surface:** asphalted. 01/01-31/12.
Distance: 600m on the spot 100m 100m.
Remarks: Pay at tourist office.

Fosnavåg — 4A2

Gerhard Voldnes veg. **GPS**: n62,33913 e5,63907.

free (10x)NOK50.
Distance: 800m on the spot on the spot 300m 800m.
Remarks: Coins at town hall.

Gurskøy — 4A2

Leikong bubilparkering, Riksveg. **GPS**: n62,25072 e5,78544.

6 NOK 100/24h Ch included. **Surface:** gravel.
Distance: on the spot on the spot on the spot.
Remarks: Money in envelope in mail box, beautiful view.

Haugesund — 5A1

Kvalsvik, Skjelavikvegen. **GPS**: n59,43541 e5,24054.

5 free. **Location:** Simple. **Surface:** gravel/metalled.
Distance: 4km on the spot on the spot on the spot.

Hebnes — 5A1

Joker Vatlandsvåg kai. **GPS**: n59,41009 e6,01843.
NOK 100 . 01/01-31/12.
Distance: on the spot on the spot takeaway restaurant on the spot.

Husnes — 5A1

Husnes Båtlag, Onarheimsvegen. **GPS**: n59,87187 e5,76195.

NOK 150 Ch included NOK50 WC NOK10 NOK40 free.
Location: Rural, simple. **Surface:** metalled. 01/01-31/12.
Distance: 1,5km on the spot on the spot 1,5km.
Remarks: Golf court 300m.

Isfjorden — 4A2

Gjerdset Turistsenter, Gjerdsetbygda. **GPS**: n62,57868 e7,56713.

5 NOK 100 WC .
Location: Rural, comfortable. **Surface:** gravel.
Distance: 13km 200m 200m 100m.

Jørpeland — 5A1

Jørpeland Bobilparkering. **GPS**: n59,01757 e6,04377.
NOK 150 NOK50 WC . **Surface:** asphalted.
Distance: 500m on the spot on the spot 450m.

Klokkarvik — 4A3

Kleppe Båtlag, Kleppholmen. **GPS**: n60,18462 e5,15163.

30 NOK 100 Ch (10x)NOK50 WC NOK10 included.
Location: Simple. **Surface:** asphalted. 01/01-31/12.
Distance: 6km on the spot on the spot.

Kristiansund — 4A2

Freiveien. **GPS**: n63,12188 e7,72856.

10 . **Location:** Simple. **Surface:** gravel.
Distance: on the spot on the spot on the spot on the spot.

Kristiansund — 4A2

Kristiansund Småbåtlag, Freiveien 50. **GPS**: n63,11713 e7,73168.

5 NOK 7-35, overnight stay free.
Location: Urban, simple. **Surface:** asphalted. 01/01-31/12.
Distance: 1km on the spot on the spot on the spot.

Kulleseid — 5A1

Kulleseidkanalen, Kulleseidkanalen.
GPS: n59,74194 o5,23481.
NOK 100 50 .
Distance: on the spot 300m.

Måløy — 4A3

Småbåthavn, Gate 1 vagsoy. **GPS**: n61,93236 e5,11212.

10 NOK 200 WC included . **Location:** Urban, central.
Surface: asphalted.
Distance: on the spot on the spot on the spot on the spot on the spot.
Remarks: Behind Aldi-süd.

Matre — 5A1

Matre Havn, Matre Havn. **GPS**: n59,84352 e5,98434.

6 NOK 100 included NOK50 WC. **Location:** Rural, isolated, quiet. **Surface:** asphalted. 01/01-31/12.
Distance: on the spot on the spot.

NO

Remarks: Money in envelope in mail box.

Nesflaten 5B1

Fylkesveg. **GPS:** n59,64471 e6,80223.
3 free. **Surface:** asphalted. 01/01-31/12.
Distance: on the spot on the spot.
Remarks: At the quay.

Norheimsund 4A3

Rosselandsvegen. **GPS:** n60,37007 e6,10616.

8 WC.
Location: Rural, simple. **Surface:** asphalted. 01/01-31/12.
Distance: 2,5km on the spot on the spot 100m.
Remarks: Nearby waterfalls.

Norheimsund 4A3

Norheimsund Badstrand, Sandvegen 36.
GPS: n60,36869 e6,14811.

20 free WC.
Location: Urban, simple. **Surface:** gravel. 01/01-31/12.
Distance: 200m on the spot on the spot 200m 200m on the spot on the spot.

Norheimsund 4A3

Norheimsund Badstrand, Sandvegen 36.
GPS: n60,36869 e6,14811.
20 free WC. **Location:** Urban, simple. **Surface:** gravel. 01/01-31/12.
Distance: 200m on the spot on the spot 200m 200m on the spot on the spot.

Odda 4A3

Odda bobilcamp, Røldalsvegen. **GPS:** n60,07144 e6,54865.
40 NOK 150 included. **Surface:** asphalted.
Distance: on the spot on the spot.
Remarks: Max. 3 days.

Rennesøy 5A1

GPS: n59,13787 e5,59161.
free. **Surface:** asphalted.
Distance: on the spot on the spot.

Rognaldsvåg 4A3

Rognaldsvåg Bobilparkering. GPS: n61,56494 e4,79580.
8 NOK 150 WC. **Surface:** gravel. 01/01-31/12.
Distance: 150m 150m on the spot.

Rosendal 5A1

Skåla Vika, Skålafjæro. **GPS:** n59,98528 e6,00708.

80 NOK 175 Ch NOK25 included.
Location: Rural, simple. **Surface:** gravel. 01/01-31/12.
Distance: 200m on the spot on the spot 200m.
Remarks: Money in envelope in mail box.

Sand 5A1

Hydrokaien, Nordenden. **GPS:** n59,48516 e6,24756.
6 free WC. **Surface:** asphalted.
Distance: 300m on the spot on the spot 800m 300m on the spot.
Remarks: At museum.

Sand 5A1

Stasjon XY. GPS: n59,47590 e6,28913.
Ch.
Remarks: At petrol station.

Sandeid 5A1

Kai. GPS: n59,54198 e5,86770.

5 NOK 100 NOK25 NOK10.
Location: Rural, simple. **Surface:** asphalted. 01/01-31/12.
Distance: on the spot on the spot on the spot.
Remarks: Money in envelope in mail box.

Sauda 5A1

Bobil Havn, Treaskjæret. **GPS:** n59,64480 e6,33716.
15 NOK 100 ChWC.
Distance: 1,2km on the spot on the spot 1,2km 1,2km 100m.
Remarks: At the quay.

Skånevik 5A1

Fylkesveg. **GPS:** n59,73385 e5,92672.

8 NOK 150 Ch included WC.
Location: Urban, simple. **Surface:** gravel. 01/01-31/12.
Distance: 500m on the spot on the spot 400m.

Skare 5B1

Skare Kommune Odda, Riksveg 13 144 langs E 134.
GPS: n59,88666 e6,65612.

50 NOK 100 Ch. **Location:** Motorway, simple.
Surface: gravel. 01/01-31/12.
Distance: 6km on the spot on the spot on the spot.
Remarks: Service 2km, money in envelope in mail box.

Sveio 5A1

Victors Bobil camping, Fylkesveg. **GPS:** n59,53016 e5,44353.

NOK 250-300 Ch WC included.
Location: Rural, isolated. **Surface:** grassy/gravel. 01/04-31/10.
Distance: 9km on the spot on the spot 9km.
Remarks: Small pitches.

Svelgen 4A3

Svelgen Hotell, Granden. **GPS:** n61,76978 e5,29393.

7 free. **Location:** Simple. **Surface:** asphalted. 01/01-31/12.
Distance: on the spot on the spot on the spot 200m on the spot.

Sykkylven 4A2

Sykkylven Småbåthamn, Ullavikvegen. **GPS:** n62,39679 e6,58192.
NOK 90 NOK30 WC. **Surface:** asphalted.
Distance: 500m on the spot on the spot 500m 500m.

Sæbøvik 5A1

Halsnøy Samfunnshus, Riksveg. **GPS:** n59,79431 e5,71196.

12 NOK 100 Chincluded NOK50 WC NOK30.
Location: Rural, simple. **Surface:** asphalted. 01/01-31/12
water disconnected in winter.
Distance: on the spot on the spot on the spot 200m.

Tau 5A1

Tau Båtforening, Kvernvegen. **GPS:** n59,06086 e5,91343.
8 NOK 150 ChWC included. 01/01-31/12.
Distance: on the spot on the spot 1km 1km.

Tjøvåg 4A2

Laternen Marina. GPS: n62,31388 e5,70805.

NOK 100 (4x)NOK25 NOK20 NOK30.
Location: Comfortable. **Surface:** gravel. 01/01-31/12.
Distance: 5km on the spot on the spot on the spot.
Remarks: Boat rental.

Tresfjord 4A2

Småbåthavn. GPS: n62,52520 e7,13085.

4 NOK 150 NOK30 NOK30 ChNOK30 WC.
Location: Rural, simple, quiet. **Surface:** gravel.
Distance: 100m on the spot on the spot 100m.
Remarks: At petrol station.

Urangsvåg 5A1

Fylkesveg. **GPS:** n59,84002 e5,15190.
6 NOK 180 ChWC. **Surface:** asphalted.
Distance: on the spot on the spot.

Vikedal 5A1

Vikedal Båthavn, Riksveg. **GPS:** n59,49632 e5,89837.

NO

30 NOK 100 Ch NOK50 WC included NOK30.
Location: Rural, simple. **Surface:** metalled.
01/01-31/12.
Distance: 200m on the spot on the spot 200m 200m.
Remarks: Money in envelope in mail box.

S Viksdalen 4A3

GPS: n61,39096 e6,26945.

6 NOK 150 Ch included. **Location:** Rural, simple, isolated, quiet. **Surface:** gravel. 01/01-31/12.
Distance: 12km on the spot on the spot 12km.
Remarks: Dead end street, narrow road, boat rental.

Ølen 5A1

Fjellstøl Skianlegg, Helgaland. **GPS:** n59,58853 e5,88857.

30 NOK 40. **Location:** Rural, simple. **Surface:** gravel.
01/01-31/12.
Distance: 6km on the spot on the spot.
Remarks: Money in envelope in mail box.

S Ølen 5A1

Båtlag, Fylkesveg. **GPS:** n59,60748 e5,81448.

10 NOK 140 included WC NOK30.
Location: Rural, simple. **Surface:** gravel. 01/01-31/12.
Distance: 150m on the spot on the spot 300m 600m.
Remarks: Money in envelope in mail box.

S Ølensvåg 5A1

Ask Bobilparkering, Gjerdevikvegen 46.
GPS: n59,59728 e5,75857.

30 NOK 100 Ch (12x)NOK30 included.
Location: Rural, luxurious. **Surface:** gravel. 01/01-31/12.
Distance: 1km on the spot on the spot.

Remarks: Money in envelope in mail box, barbecue place.

S Øydegard 4A2

Riksvei, E39 70. **GPS:** n62,98958 e7,88272.

10 free WC free. **Location:** Rural, simple, isolated, quiet.
Surface: asphalted.
Distance: on the spot on the spot.

Southern Norway

S Åmli 5B2

Dølemo. **GPS:** n58,71102 e8,34497.
NOK 150 Ch WC . **Location:** Isolated, quiet.
Surface: grassy. 01/01-31/12.
Distance: on the spot on the spot.

S Åmli 5B2

Pan Garden, Tveit 38. **GPS:** n58,74697 e8,50946.
10 NOK 100 NOK50 NOK30. **Location:** Isolated, quiet.
Distance: on the spot on the spot on the spot.

Borhaug 5B2

Lista Fyr, Toppveien 10. **GPS:** n58,10943 e6,56863.
free. 01/01-31/12.
Distance: 1,5km.
Remarks: At lighthouse, max. 2 nights.

S Borhaug 5B2

Borshavn. **GPS:** n58,10081 e6,58335.
NOK 200 Ch WC . **Surface:** asphalted.
Distance: on the spot on the spot.
Remarks: Max. 1 day.

S Eidstod 5B1

Eidstod Kommune Vrådal, Vråliosvegen.
GPS: n59,32570 e8,48630.

20 free Ch free. **Location:** Rural, simple.
Surface: gravel/sand. 01/01-31/12.
Distance: on the spot on the spot on the spot on the spot on the spot.

S Farsund 5B2

Farsund Bobil Camp, Ferjeveien. **GPS:** n58,09439 e6,81278.
NOK 175 . **Surface:** metalled. 01/01-31/12
Service: winter.
Distance: 500m on the spot on the spot 500m 1,5km.

S Flekkefjord 5B2

Tollbodbrygga. **GPS:** n58,29267 e6,66296.

25 NOK 200 Ch (16x)included WC . **Surface:** gravel.
Distance: 850m on the spot 850m 200m.
Remarks: Pay at shop.

S Grimstad 5B2

Sørlandets Caravansenter, Grøm Næringspark 2.
GPS: n58,34011 e8,56658.
3 free Ch free. **Location:** Simple.
Distance: 1km 200m 1km 1km.

Remarks: At motorhome dealer, max. 24h.

Hidrasund 5B2

Kirkehavn. **GPS:** n58,22896 e6,52919.
. **Location:** Isolated, quiet. **Surface:** asphalted.
Distance: 2km on the spot 2km 1km on the spot.

S Hornes 5B2

Mineralparken Bobilcamp, Mineralvegen 1.
GPS: n58,54993 e7,77542.
40 NOK 200 Ch NOK20 NOK40/40 included.
Surface: grassy.
Distance: 700m on the spot on the spot.
Remarks: Bread-service in summer period.

Kviteseid 5B1

Kviteseid, Garverivegen. **GPS:** n59,40275 e8,48675.

5 free. **Location:** Rural, simple. **Surface:** gravel.
01/01-31/12.
Distance: on the spot on the spot on the spot on the spot on the spot on the spot on the spot on the spot.

S Lillesand 5B2

Lillesand gjesthavn, Kokkenes. **GPS:** n58,24745 e8,38349.
25 NOK 200 Ch included WC . **Surface:** asphalted.
Service: winter.
Distance: 500m on the spot on the spot 200m 500m.

S Lindesnes 5B2

Spangereidveien. **GPS:** n58,03998 e7,15014.

2 NOK 150 WC NOK20 NOK45/45.
Distance: on the spot on the spot on the spot.
Remarks: Boat rental.

S Mandal 5B2

Mandal Havn, Havnegata. **GPS:** n58,02440 e7,45566.
10 NOK 180 . **Surface:** asphalted.
Distance: 400m on the spot 400m 1km.

S Risør 5C2

Tjenngata. **GPS:** n58,72093 e9,22567.

NOK 20/h, NOK 100/day NOK10 NOK30/30.
Surface: grassy. 01/01-31/12 Service: winter.
Distance: 600m 500m 500m 600m.

S Snig 5B2

Snig, Stegganskogen R460. **GPS:** n58,05313 e7,27103.

NO

6 free WC.
Location: Rural, simple. **Surface:** gravel. 01/01-31/12.
Distance: 4,5km on the spot on the spot on the spot on the spot.

S Valle 5B1
Sanden Såre. GPS: n59,27128 e7,46221.
NOK 150-200 Ch . **Location:** Rural, isolated, quiet.
Surface: grassy.
Distance: 10km on the spot on the spot.
Remarks: Nearby waterfalls.

Eastern Norway

S Bjørkelangen 4B3
Bjørkelangen bobilparkering, Stasjonsveien 25.
GPS: n59,88058 e11,57102.
10 free ChWC. 01/03-01/10.
Distance: 500m 600m.
Remarks: Next to sports fields.

S Brandbu 4B3
Tegneseriemuseet, Rosendalsvegen. **GPS:** n60,41719 e10,50940.
4 NOK 100 NOK 50 . **Surface:** asphalted. 01/03-01/10.
Distance: 500m 400m 300m.
Remarks: At museum.

S Bøverdalen 4A3
Leirvassbu. GPS: n61,54917 e8,24694.
NOK 200 WC . **Location:** Isolated, quiet. 20/06-30/09.
Remarks: Accessible via toll road (NOK 60).

S Dalen 5B1
Bobilparkering Dalen Bryggje. GPS: n59,44515 e8,02292.

NOK 200-280 Ch WC included.
Surface: metalled.
Distance: 900m on the spot on the spot on the spot.
Remarks: Money in envelope in mail box.

Dovre 4B2
Krymsdalhyte. **GPS:** n62,08557 e9,64947.

free. **Location:** Isolated. **Surface:** grassy.
01/01-31/12.
Distance: on the spot 300m on the spot.
Remarks: Accessible via toll road (NOK 80), national Park 'Rondane'.

Etnedal 4B3
Sebu Røssjøen, Lenningsvegen. **GPS:** n61,12502 e9,71475.
free.
Distance: on the spot.

S Flatdal 5B1
Kvåle Din gard, Kvålevegen. **GPS:** n59,56042 e8,56248.
5 NOK 200 Ch . **Surface:** grassy. 01/01-31/12.
Distance: on the spot on the spot.

S Fredrikstad 5C1
Gjestehavn. GPS: n59,21423 e10,92512.
60 NOK 250 WC . **Surface:** asphalted.
Distance: on the spot on the spot 150m.

S Gjøvik 4B3
Gjøvik Marina, Bryggevegen. **GPS:** n60,79555 e10,70116.
25 NOK 50 Ch. **Surface:** gravel. 15/06-13/09.
Distance: on the spot on the spot McDonalds 300m.
Remarks: To be paid at petrol station.

S Halden 5D1
Kiellands gate. **GPS:** n59,11539 e11,38128.
5 NOK 150 .
Distance: 800m on the spot on the spot 800m.

S Hamar 4B3
Hamar båtforening, Brygga. **GPS:** n60,78846 e11,07138.
20 NOK 120 Ch (6x). **Surface:** asphalted.
01/06-30/09.
Distance: 300m on the spot on the spot 1km 400m.

Holmestrand 5C1
Hagemannsveien. **GPS:** n59,48048 e10,32933.
free. **Surface:** asphalted.
Distance: on the spot on the spot.
Remarks: At harbour.

S Holmestrand 5C1
Weidemannsgate 13. **GPS:** n59,48921 e10,32294.
NOK 150 Ch NOK 2,80/kWh. 01/06-15/09.
Distance: on the spot on the spot on the spot.

S Horten 5C1
Horten Havn. GPS: n59,41302 e10,48695.
14 NOK 180 WC . **Surface:** asphalted.
Distance: on the spot on the spot on the spot 100m 600m.

S Hov 4B3
Fjordvegen 27. **GPS:** n60,69915 e10,33972.
2 NOK 100 Ch . **Surface:** grassy.
Distance: on the spot on the spot.

S Høvringen 4B3
Rondane Haukliseter Fjellhotell. GPS: n61,88853 e9,48745.
NOK 200 Ch WC . **Surface:** grassy.
Distance: 1km 1km.
Remarks: Use of sauna against payment.

Kongsberg 5C1
Glabak. **GPS:** n59,67205 e9,64166.
. **Surface:** asphalted.
Distance: on the spot 400m 550m.
Remarks: At swimming pool.

Kragerø 5C1
Allemannsveien. **GPS:** n58,87553 e9,41766.
NOK 150. **Surface:** unpaved.
Distance: on the spot 100m.

Kvelde 5C1
Roppestad. GPS: n59,15310 e9,90844.
free. **Location:** Isolated, quiet. **Surface:** grassy.
Distance: 50m 50m.
Remarks: Max. 2 days.

S Langesund 5C1
Skjærsgårdshallen, Stathelleveien 33. **GPS:** n59,01285 e9,74301.
8 NOK 150 Ch WC . **Surface:** asphalted. 13/04-11/10.
Distance: 2km 700m.
Remarks: At gymnasium.

S Larvik 5C1
Indre Havn, Strandpromenaden. **GPS:** n59,04892 e10,03361.
21 € 15 or NOK 120 Ch included.
Distance: on the spot on the spot 500m 500m.

Lillehammer 4B3
Lysgårdsbakkene, Lysgårdsvegen 55. **GPS:** n61,12431 e10,48914.
NOK 70/24h. **Surface:** metalled.
Distance: 250m.

S Lunde 5C1
Hogga Sluser, Gamle Strengenvegen. **GPS:** n59,30216 e9,04331.
12 NOK 150 Ch included NOK 10.
Distance: on the spot on the spot.

S Moss 5C1
Bobilhavn, Værftsgata. **GPS:** n59,43486 e10,65141.
14 NOK 150 included WC .
Distance: on the spot on the spot 300m 100m.
Remarks: Max. 3 days.

Mysusæter 4B3
Mysuseter Fjellstue. GPS: n61,81161 e9,68463.
NOK 40. **Surface:** metalled.

S Notodden 5C1
Bobilcamp Nesøya, Heddalsvegen. **GPS:** n59,55876 e9,24851.
13 (13x)included. **Surface:** unpaved.
Distance: 1km on the spot on the spot on the spot 250m.

S Notodden 5C1
Heddalsvegen. **GPS:** n59,55981 e9,24834.
NOK 2 ChWC NOK 1 NOK 2. 01/01-31/12.

Oslo 4B3
Øvreseterveien. **GPS:** n59,98130 e10,67166.

15 . **Location:** Rural. **Surface:** gravel.
Distance: 3km on the spot on the spot 3km 200m on the spot.

S Oslo 4B3
Sjølyst Marina, Drammensveien 164. **GPS:** n59,92026 e10,67506.
250 NOK 200 Ch WC included. **Surface:** asphalted.
01/06-20/09.
Distance: 6km on the spot on the spot.

S Oslo 4B3
Bogstad Camp, Ankerveien 117. **GPS:** n59,96293 e10,64203.
38 NOK 280, 4 pers.incl WC NOK 15. **Surface:** grassy/gravel.
01/01-31/12.
Distance: 700m on the spot.

Rauland 5B1
Raulandsfjell. GPS: n59,71963 e8,00084.
14 .
Distance: 5km on the spot on the spot.
Remarks: At ski-lift.

S Sandefjord 5C1
Sandefjord Bobil havn, Sandefjordsveien.
GPS: n59,12506 e10,22108.
16 NOK 200 included. **Surface:** asphalted.
Distance: 700m on the spot on the spot 700m 1km.
Remarks: Max. 24h.

Sarpsborg 5D1
Tindlund bobilparkering, Østre Greåkervei.
GPS: n59,27398 e11,04709.
NOK 100 (4x). **Surface:** gravel.
Distance: 1,3km.

S Sarpsborg 5D1
Stamsaas Fritid, Vogtsvei 40. **GPS:** n59,28532 e11,08414.
free .
Distance: 350m.
Remarks: Service during opening hours.

S Seljord 5B1
Flatin Gard, Flatingrendi 3. **GPS:** n59,50725 e8,63964.
40 NOK 100, NOK 200 service incl WC .
Distance: 100m 100m.

Siljan 5C1
Sporevann. GPS: n59,38476 e9,69584.
10 free. **Location:** Simple, isolated.
Distance: 11km on the spot on the spot.

S Skien 5C1
Fritidspark, Moflatveien 59. **GPS:** n59,18510 e9,59698.
14 NOK 200 Ch WC included NOK 20.
Surface: asphalted. 01/04-01/10.
Distance: on the spot.
Remarks: Pay at hotel.

Skien 5C1
Teg Seil, Bøleveien 4. **GPS:** n59,19634 e9,62039.
10 NOK 150. 01/05-30/09.
Distance: 700m on the spot on the spot 400m on the spot.
Remarks: At sailmaker.

Skreia 4B3
Hersjøen. GPS: n60,54498 e11,03309.
NOK 45. **Location:** Isolated, quiet. **Surface:** grassy.
Distance: on the spot on the spot 6,5km.

NO

Tyristrand 4B3

Stall Myhre, Holleiaveien 263. **GPS**: n60,11111 e10,07194.
NOK 100. **Location:** Isolated, quiet. **Surface:** grassy.
01/03-01/10.
Distance: 3,5km.
Remarks: At horse farm.

S Tønsberg 5C1

Storgaten. **GPS**: n59,26323 e10,41569.
8 NOK 150 . **Surface:** asphalted.
Distance: on the spot 100m.
Remarks: Max. 7 days.

Tønsberg 5C1

Fjordgaten. **GPS**: n59,27390 e10,40009.
23. **Surface:** asphalted.
Distance: 1km 50m 50m.

Tønsberg 5C1

Messeområdet. **GPS**: n59,28069 e10,41015.
12 free.
Remarks: At the skating rink.

S Tønsberg 5C1

Shell, Kjelleveien 28. **GPS**: n59,27879 e10,40092.
Ch.

Ulefoss 5C1

Norsjø Golfpark, Romnesvegen 98. **GPS**: n59,30248 e9,26511.
NOK 50.
Distance: 4km.
Remarks: At golf court.

Uvdal 4B3

Uvdal resort. **GPS**: n60,26515 e8,78849.
NOK 150. **Surface:** grassy.
Distance: on the spot on the spot.

Vågå 4B3

Steinhole fjellcamp. **GPS**: n61,62293 e8,99682.
NOK 50. **Location:** Isolated, quiet. **Surface:** grassy.

S Voll 5C1

Ole"s Kios og gatekjøkken, Svanvikveien 653.
GPS: n59,12797 e9,51008.
NOK 150 included.
Distance: on the spot.
Remarks: Regional products.

S Ytre Enebakk 5C1

Holtopp gård, Skiveien 127. **GPS**: n59,72795 e11,00472.
NOK 125 NOK30. **Location:** Isolated, quiet. 01/03-01/10.
Distance: 100m.

NO

Poland

Capital: Warsaw
Government: parliamentary republic
Official Language: Polish
Population: 38,562,100 (2015)
Area: 311,888 Km²

General information
Dialling code: 0048
General emergency: 112
Currency: Zloty (PLN)
€ 1 = 4,44 PLN, 1 PLN = € 0,23
£1 = 5,16PLN, 1PLN = £0.19 (November 2016)
Credit cards are accepted almost everywhere.

Regulations for overnight stays
Free overnight stay is not allowed. On private property with permission of the owner.

Additional public holidays 2017
January 6 Epiphany
May 3 Constitution Day
June 15 Corpus Christi
August 15 Assumption of Mary
November 1 All Saints' Day
November 11 Independence Day

Time Zone
Winter (Standard Time) GMT+1
Summer (DST) GMT+2

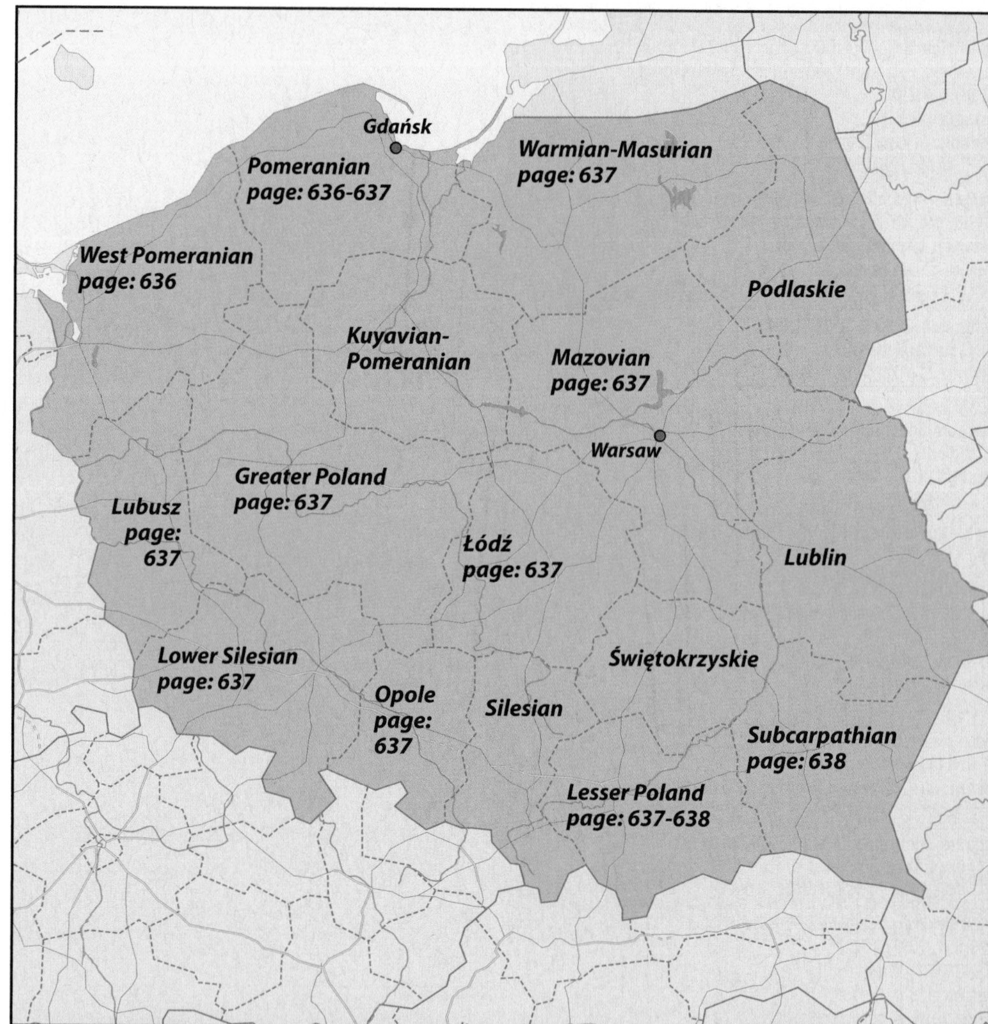

PL

West Pomeranian

Czaplinek 36A3
Drawtur, Ul. Pieciu Pomostów 1. **GPS**: n53,57671 e16,21984.

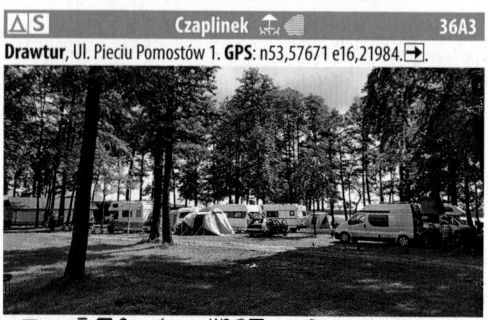

50 € 12 Ch €2,50 WC €3,50 included.
Location: Rural, noisy. **Surface:** grassy.
Distance: 2km 50m on the spot on the spot 2km.
Remarks: Dog € 2/day.

Miedzywodzie 6H3
Narcyz, Armii Krajowej 33. **GPS**: n54,00376 e14,69290.

8 € 20 Ch WC on demand included.
Location: Rural, central, noisy. **Surface:** grassy. 01/05-01/10.
Distance: 100m 800m 600m 100m 100m 50m.
Remarks: Breakfest-service.

Miroslawiec 36A3
Hotel Park Reduta Napoleona, Lowicz Walecki 60.
GPS: n53,33081 e16,02333.

30 € 8,50 €2,25 Ch €7,50 WC €2,50 included.
Location: Rural, isolated, quiet. **Surface:** grassy.
01/01-31/12.
Distance: 5km 100m 500m 50m 700m.

Szczecin 8H2
Hotel Panorama, Ul.Radosna 60. **GPS**: n53,36420 e14,61550.

10 € 17 on demand included WC .
Location: Urban, simple. **Surface:** metalled. 01/01-31/12.
Distance: 10km 1km on the spot 1km on the spot.

Wolin 8H1
Fam. Lafrentz, Gogolice 20, Gogolice. **GPS**: n53,83300 e14,62262.

13 € 12 Ch included. **Location:** Rural, quiet.
Surface: gravel. 01/01-31/12.
Distance: 1,4km 500m 50m 1,4km 1,4km 1,4km.

Pomeranian

Gdańsk 36B2
Akademia Muzycna, Lakowa 1-2. **GPS**: n54,34561 e18,66357.

15 € 1-1,50/h. **Location:** Urban, central.
Surface: grassy/metalled. 01/01-31/12.
Distance: 100m 100m 100m.

Malbork 36B2
Nad Stawem, Ul. Solskiego 10. **GPS**: n54,04285 e19,02536.

30 € 12 Ch €2,50 WC included.
Location: Urban, central. **Surface:** grassy. 01/03-01/11.
Distance: 200m 50m 200m.

S **Parchowo** 36A2

Kalex, Jamnowski Mlyn 15. **GPS**: n54,22644 e17,63750.

10 € 14 Ch WC €2 €2 included.
Location: Rural, isolated, quiet. **Surface:** grassy/sand.
01/04-01/11.
Distance: 5km on the spot on the spot 5km.

S **Wierzbna** 36A3

De Vuijle vaetdoek "carpe Diem", 66-340 Przytoczna.
GPS: n52,56639 e15,81722.

70 € 17,50 Ch WC included . **Location:** Rural, simple, isolated. **Surface:** grassy. 01/05-01/09.

S **Zagaje** 36A2

Gosciniec Zagaje, Zagaje 1. **GPS**: n54,00583 e17,12778.
6 € 20 WC included. **Location:** Rural.
Surface: grassy. 01/01-31/12.
Distance: 4km 200m on the spot 4km on the spot on the spot.

Warmian-Masurian

S **Dobre Miasto** 36B2

Garnizonowa 16. **GPS**: n53,98594 e20,41430.
3 free . **Location:** Simple. **Surface:** metalled.
01/01-31/12.
Distance: 1km.
Remarks: At swimming pool.

S **Mikolajki** 36C2

Parking Hotelik Caligula, Ul.Jana Pawla II. **GPS**: n53,80278 e21,57444.
20 € 14 Ch on demand included. **Surface:** gravel.
01/01-31/12.
Distance: 100m 200m 500m 200m 200m.

S **Milolyn** 36B2

Mazur, Ul Twarda 28a, Milomlyn. **GPS**: n53,76583 e19,84639.

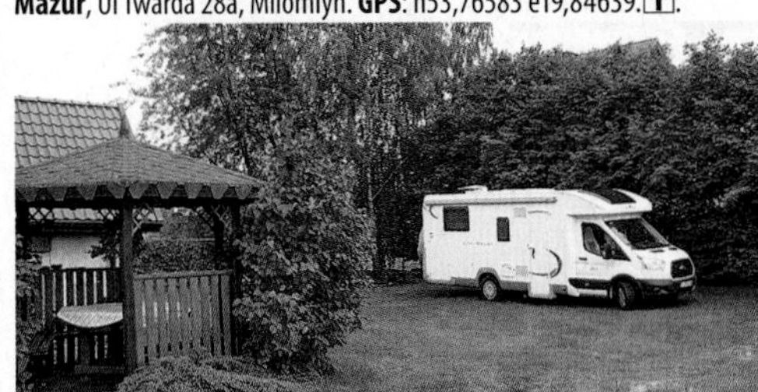

4 € 7,50 €1 €1 Ch€1 €1. **Location:** Rural, quiet.
Surface: grassy. 01/01-31/12.
Distance: 500m 500m 1km 1km 400m 200m 500m 100m 100m.

S **Osetno** 36B3

Osetno 16a. **GPS**: n53,41562 e19,31729.

20 € 7,50 Ch WC on demand included.
Location: Rural, simple, isolated. **Surface:** grassy.
01/01-31/12.
Distance: 12km 30km 800m 800m 1km 100m on the spot.
Remarks: Bread-service.

S **Paslek** 36B2

Kemping Bezplatny, 526. **GPS**: n53,98052 e19,62524.

100 € 12,50 free WC. **Location:** Rural, simple, isolated.
Surface: grassy. 01/01-31/12.
Distance: 10km 10km on the spot 10km on the spot on the spot.

S **Piecki** 36C2

Restaurant Krutynska, Krutyn 72. **GPS**: n53,68807 e21,43075.
20 € 13 Ch included. **Location:** Rural. **Surface:** grasstiles.
01/01-31/12.
Distance: 300m 300m.

S **Pieniezno** 36B2

Caravanparc Pieniezno, 14-520. **GPS**: n54,23454 e20,13697.

20 € 10 Ch WC included on demand.
Location: Rural, quiet. **Surface:** grassy. 01/01-31/12.
Distance: 1km 800m 800m 500m.

S **Sorkwity** 36C2

Haus am see, Janowo 1. **GPS**: n53,83495 e21,20284.
5 € 10-15 Ch included . **Location:** Rural.
Surface: grassy. 01/01-31/12.
Distance: 500m 50m 1km.

Tolkmicko 36B2

Swietokanska. **GPS**: n54,32367 e19,52264.

10 € 5 WC €0,50 €2. **Location:** Rural, noisy.
Surface: metalled. 01/01-31/12.
Distance: 100m 50m on the spot 100m 100m.

S **Łukta** 36B2

Plichta 9. **GPS**: n53,75989 e20,05300.
20 € 5 €1 .
Location: Rural. **Surface:** grassy. 01/04-01/11.

Lubusz

S **Owince** 8H3

Fisch Camp, Wolności 40. **GPS**: n52,53517 e14,89269.

30 € 12 Ch WC included €1/1day. **Location:** Rural.
Surface: grassy. 01/01-31/12.

Greater Poland

S **Biskupice** 36A3

WojciechSzczepanski, Jankowo-Mlyn 23. **GPS**: n52,44965 e17,16442.
20 € 20 Ch included. **Location:** Rural. **Surface:** grassy.
01/01-31/12.

Mazovian

S **Gierloz** 36C2

Wolf's Liar - Wilczy Szaniec, 11-400 Kętrzyn.
GPS: n54,07925 e21,49309.
10 € 12,50 included WC . **Location:** Rural, comfortable.
01/01-31/12.
Distance: on the spot.
Remarks: Former headquarters of Hitler.

S **Warszawa** 36C3

Parking, 1 Sierpinia, Warsaw (Warszawa). **GPS**: n52,19189 e20,98069.
10 € 10 €2 €2 Ch€3 €5. **Location:** Urban.
Surface: metalled. 01/01-31/12.
Distance: city centre 5,5km 2km 100m 500m 300m.

Warszawa 36C3

Parking, Wybrzeze Gdanskie, Warsaw (Warszawa).
GPS: n52,25133 e21,01469.
15 € 25. **Location:** Urban. **Surface:** metalled. 01/01-31/12.
Distance: city centre 3km 5km on the spot on the spot 250m.

Lower Silesian

S **Karpacz** 37A1

Rezydencja Holandia, Ul.Konstytucji 3-go Maja 67.
GPS: n50,77345 e15,74734.
15 € 5 €1 €1 Chfree €1. **Location:** Rural.
Surface: metalled. 01/01-31/12.
Distance: 1km 900m.

Opole

S **Gora Swietej Anny** 37B1

P Najem Pokoi, Ul.Strzelecka 2A. **GPS**: n50,45785 e18,16895.
20 € 10 Ch included. 01/01-31/12.
Distance: 600m 100m.

S **Naklo** 37B1

Fam Urban, Ul Strzelecka 91. **GPS**: n50,57790 e18,12715.
10 € 12 Ch WC included. **Location:** Rural.
Surface: grassy.
Distance: 400m 100m.

Łódź

S **Lipce Reymontowskie** 36B3

Bumerang, Chlebow 3. **GPS**: n51,92795 e19,92847.
8 € 10 Chincluded €3. **Location:** Rural. **Surface:** grassy.
01/01-31/12.

Lesser Poland

S **Kraków** 37C1

Guesthaus Apis, Ul.Podgorki 60. **GPS**: n49,98885 e19,96210.
5 € 15 Ch WC included.
Surface: metalled.
01/01-31/12.
Distance: 50m 400m.

S **Kraków** 37C1

Elcamp, Ul.Tyniecka 118e. **GPS**: n50,03418 e19,87658.
10 € 7 €1,20 Ch €1,20 . **Surface:** grassy/gravel.
01/01-31/12.

PL

Distance: Kraków 5km ⊗100m.

P S	Oswiecim	37B1

Auschwitz Parking, Stanislaw-Leszezynskiej 11.
GPS: n50,02867 e19,20111.
10 € 10 €2,50. **Surface:** metalled. 01/01-31/12.
Remarks: Near Auswitz-Birkenau memorial and museum.

☺	Wieliczka	37C1

Salt Mine, Edwarda Dembowskiego 22. **GPS**: n49,98542 e20,05338.
20 € 7,50. **Location:** Urban. **Surface:** gravel/sand.
01/01-31/12.
Distance: 1,5km ⊗400m 50m 500m.

Subcarpathian

△ S	Wetlina	37D2

Górna Wetlinka, 38-608. **GPS**: n49,14740 e22,52028.
15 € 15 included €3. **Location:** Rural. 01/04-01/10.
Distance: ⊗200m on the spot on the spot.

PL

Portugal

Capital: Lisbon
Government: Parliamentary democracy
Official Language: Portuguese
Population: 10.825.000 (2015)
Area: 91,642 km²

General information
Dialling code: 00351
General emergency: 112
Currency: Euro
Payments by credit card are accepted almost everywhere.

Regulations for overnight stays
If there is no local prohibition wild camping is allowed, max. 48h, exept in urban areas and drinking water protection areas.

Additional public holidays 2017
January 6 Epiphany
April 14 Good Friday
April 25 Liberationday
May 1 Labor Day
June 10 National Holiday
June 15 Corpus Christi
August 15 Assumption of the Virgin Mary
October 5 Republic day
November 1 All Saints' Day
December 8 Immaculate Conception

Time Zone
Winter (Standard Time) GMT+0
Summer (DST) GMT+1

PT

Portugal North

Aguçadoura 29B3

Aguaçadoura Futebol Clube. GPS: n41,44389 w8,77722.

5 free. **Location:** Rural, simple. **Surface:** gravel/sand.
01/01-31/12.
Distance: 500m 50m 500m 500m.
Remarks: Parking at the beach.

Amarante 29C3

Av. Alexandre Herculano. **GPS**: n41,27286 w8,07178.

Surface: metalled.
Distance: 800m on the spot on the spot 50m.
Remarks: Parking near sports centre.

Amarante 29C3

GPS: n41,27020 w8,07708.

Surface: metalled. Wed.
Distance: on the spot on the spot.
Remarks: Market square along the river.

Amarante 29C3

Penedo da Rainha, São Gonçalo. **GPS**: n41,28031 w8,06925.
€ 10,90-22 Ch. 04/01-30/11.
Distance: 1km on the spot on the spot 1km.

Tourist information Amarante:
Museu Municipal Amadeu de Souza Cardoso, Alameda Teixeira Pascoaes. Modern art.

Arcos de Valdevez 29C3

N202. **GPS**: n41,84749 w8,41524.

10 free. **Location:** Rural, simple. **Surface:** metalled.
01/01-31/12.
Distance: 300m.
Remarks: Along the Vez river.

Avintes 29B3

Parque Biológico de Gaia, Rue da Cunha.
GPS: n41,09730 w8,55414.

9 €4 + €4 /pp, entrance park incl Ch included WC free, at reception. **Location:** Luxurious, quiet.
Surface: grasstiles. 01/01-31/12.
Distance: 10km 800m 100m > Porto.
Remarks: Check in at reception.

Barcelos 29C3

R.Rosa Ramalho. **GPS**: n41,52829 w8,61547.

12 free. **Location:** Rural, simple. **Surface:** metalled.
01/01-31/12.
Distance: centre 800m 3,5km on the spot.
Remarks: Parking swimming pool.

Tourist information Barcelos:
Museu de Olaria de Barcelos, R. Cónego Joaquim Gaiolas. Ceramics and archeology. Tue-Su 10-12.30h, 14-18h, Thu 10-18h.

Bico 30B1
R. Vasco da Gama. **GPS**: n40,73016 w8,64747.

30 free. **Location:** Rural, simple, isolated, quiet.
Surface: metalled. 01/01-31/12.
Distance: 300m on the spot on the spot on the spot.
Remarks: In fishing port.

Braga 29C3
Bom Jesus do Monte. **GPS**: n41,55278 w8,38137.

25 free ChWCfree. **Location:** Urban, simple. **Surface:** concrete.
01/01-31/12.
Distance: 6km 20m 100m.
Remarks: Parking at funicular railway.

Braga 29C3
Sameiro. **GPS**: n41,53928 w8,36743.

10 free. **Location:** Simple.
Surface: gravel/sand.
Remarks: Parking at place of pilgrimage.

Tourist information Braga:
Semana Santa. Procession.
week before Easter.
Parque Nacional da Peneda-Gerês. Hiking routes.

Bragança 29D3
Parque de Merendas, Rue Miguel Torga. **GPS**: n41,80417 w6,74611.

30 free Chfree.
Location: Rural, comfortable, quiet.
Surface: metalled.
01/01-31/12.
Distance: 200m 200m 200m.
Remarks: P below the castle, 01/07-15/09, max. 24h, beautiful view.

Tourist information Bragança:
Medival upper city and castle.
Museu Militar.
9-11.45h, 14-18.15h.
Parque Natural de Montesinho. Nature reserve.

Caminha 29B3
Largo da Feira. **GPS**: n41,87490 w8,84113.

10 free. **Location:** Urban, simple. **Surface:** metalled.
01/01-31/12.
Distance: 500m 100m.

Carrazeda de Ansiães 29D3
Rua Engenheiro Camilo de Mendonça. **GPS**: n41,24498 w7,30386.
Ch. 01/01-31/12.
Remarks: Parking swimming pool.

Carregal do Sal 30C1
Quinta de Cabriz. **GPS**: n40,42465 w8,01856.
free. **Surface:** unpaved.
Distance: on the spot.
Remarks: Portugal Tradicional, max. 24h.

Carregal do Sal 30C1
Luzio, Arruamento Urbano a Sul da Vila. **GPS**: n40,43116 w7,99471.

3 free Chfree. **Location:** Simple. **Surface:** grassy.
01/01-31/12.
Distance: 1km.
Remarks: Behind petrol station.

Castelo do Neiva 29B3
Av, de Santoinho. **GPS**: n41,67501 w8,78243.

Chaves 29C3
Alameda do Trajano. **GPS**: n41,73694 w7,46917.

6 free. **Location:** Urban, simple. **Surface:** metalled.
01/01-31/12.
Distance: historical centre 300m 8,6km 100m 100m.
Remarks: Along the Tâmega river.

Chaves 29C3
Quinta do Rebentão, Vila Nova de Veiga. **GPS**: n41,70127 w7,50013.
100 € 16,40-20,40 Ch WC. 01/01-30/11.
Distance: 4km 400m 1km 800m.

Tourist information Chaves:
Torre de Mengem. Military museum.

Covas 29C3
Parque Campismo de Covas, Lugar de Pereiras.
GPS: n41,88758 w8,69497.
€ 5,30-8 Ch WC. 01/01-31/12.

Covas 29C3
Quinta do Retiro, Lugar Quinta do Retiro s/n. **GPS**: n40,35230 w7,91583.
5 01/09-30/06 € 17,50, 01/07-31/08 € 22 Ch (5x),10Amp
WC €1/1 included. **Surface:** grassy. 01/01-31/12.
Distance: 800m 3km 3km 3km 8km on the spot.

Entre-os-Rios 29C3
GPS: n41,08357 w8,29322.

4 WC Lunchroom&co.
Location: Simple, central, noisy. 01/01-31/12.
Distance: 100m on the spot on the spot 100m 100m.
Remarks: Parking along the Douro river.

Espinho 29B3
GPS: n40,98916 w8,6452.

+10 free free,beach. **Location:** Rural, simple, isolated, quiet.
Surface: gravel/sand. 01/01-31/12.
Distance: 1km 25m 1km 1km.
Remarks: Beach parking.

Espinho 29B3
Municipal de Espinho, Zona da Ribeira dos Mochos.
GPS: n41,01402 w8,63743.
€ 18,90-23,30 Ch WC. 01/01-31/12.

Esposende 29B3
Forte de S.João Baptiste, Rue do Farol. **GPS**: n41,54222 w8,79111.

5 free free.
Location: Urban, simple.
Surface: asphalted. 01/01-31/12.
Distance: 1,5km on the spot on the spot 1,5km.
Remarks: Parking at lighthouse, free wifi for clients restaurant.

Esposende 29B3
Parque de Campismo de Fão, Lírios - Fão. **GPS**: n41,50778 w8,77833.
Ch WC. 01/01-31/12.
Distance: 500m 500m on the spot 500m.

Freixo de Espada a Cinta 30D1
Espaço Multiusos, R. do Samiteiro de Cima.
GPS: n41,08826 w6,81751.
12 free Ch (12x)free.
Surface: metalled. 01/01-31/12.
Distance: 900m 900m.
Remarks: Arrival <18h.

Freixo de Numão 30D1
Area de autocaravanas Jean Pierre Rossi, Sebarigos.
GPS: n41,06000 w7,22111.

30 € 5/night Ch WC included. **Surface:** metalled.
Distance: 900m 500m 500m.

Gerês 29C3
Vila do Gerês. **GPS**: n41,73538 w8,15969.

PT

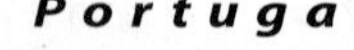

4 free. **Location:** Rural, simple. **Surface:** asphalted.
01/01-31/12.
Distance: 1km on the spot.

Gondomar 29C3

Medas, Gavinho - Medas. **GPS:** n41,03917 w8,42694.
€ 26-32 Ch WC. 01/01-31/12.

Gosende 30C1

Cooperativa Capuchinhas CRL, Campo Benfeito.
GPS: n40,99799 w7,9269.
free.
Surface: unpaved. 01/01-31/12.
Distance: 5,1km.
Remarks: Portugal Tradicional.

Guilhufe 29C3

EM594. **GPS:** n41,19541 w8,31605.

3 free Chfree. **Location:** Simple, noisy. **Surface:** metalled.
01/01-31/12.
Distance: 1km 1,6km 1km 1km.

Izeda 29D3

Largo do Toural. **GPS:** n41,56750 w6,72333.

30 free Chfree. **Location:** Rural, simple, central, quiet.
Surface: metalled. 01/01-31/12.
Distance: centre 200m 200m.

Lamego 30C1

Parque Lamego, N2, Lugar da Raposeira.
GPS: n41,09016 w7,82214.

40 € 5 + € 3/pp Ch €4/day WC. **Location:** Luxurious, isolated, quiet. **Surface:** unpaved. 01/01-31/12.
Distance: 1,2km 4,5km 500m 2km on the spot.
Remarks: Baker every morning, beautiful view, near Caves da Raposeira, sale of wines.

Lamego 30C1

GPS: n41,09501 w7,80372.

free. **Surface:** metalled. 01/01-31/12.
Distance: on the spot on the spot on the spot.
Remarks: At the foot of monumental stairs of the Santuari.

Tourist information Lamego:
Bodega Raposeira. T free.
Nossa Senhora dos Remédios. Pilgrimage in Portugal, most important festivity of the country. end Aug-beginning Sep.

Lordelo 29C3

R. da Igreja 350. **GPS:** n41,23472 w8,41139.

20 free Chfree. **Location:** Simple, quiet.
Surface: gravel/sand. 01/01-31/12.
Distance: 400m 400m 400m.

Macedo de Cavaleiros 29D3

Rua das Piscinas. **GPS:** n41,53756 w6,95715.

8 free €2/100liter Ch €2/1h.
Location: Urban, simple, central, quiet. **Surface:** asphalted.
01/01-31/12.
Distance: 200m 200m 300m on the spot.

Macedo de Cavaleiros 29D3

Barragem do Azibo, Frada da Pegada. **GPS:** n41,58333 w6,89944.

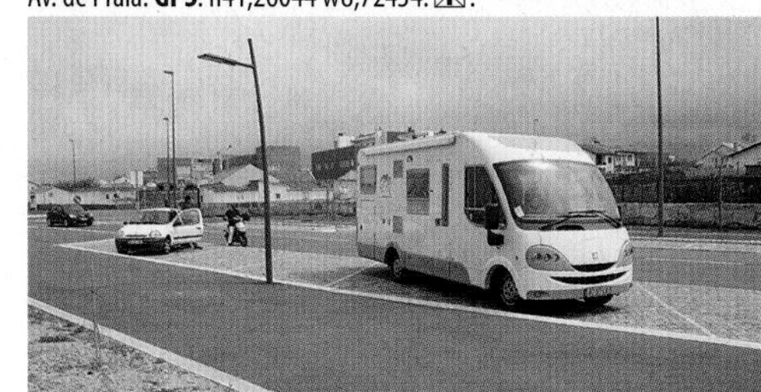

10 free. **Location:** Rural, simple, quiet. **Surface:** metalled.
01/01-31/12.
Distance: 2km Sandy beach on the spot.
Remarks: At barrage, guarded during summer period.

Matosinhos 29B3

Av. de Praia. **GPS:** n41,26044 w8,72434.

10 free. **Location:** Simple, noisy. **Surface:** metalled.
01/01-31/12.
Distance: 200m 200m 600m on the spot.

Remarks: Beach parking.

Matosinhos 29B3

Municipal de Angeiras. GPS: n41,26722 w8,71972.
€ 18,50-29 Ch. 01/01-31/12.
Remarks: Service only € 3,15-5,40.

Melgaço 29C2

Porta de Lamas de Mouro, Lamas de Mouro.
GPS: n42,05202 w8,19413.
free. **Surface:** metalled.

Melgaço 29C2

Rua do Mercado. **GPS:** n42,11549 w8,26095.

6 free. **Location:** Rural, simple. 01/01-31/12.
Distance: on the spot.

Miranda do Douro 29E3

Av. Eduardo Quero. **GPS:** n41,49167 w6,27333.

free. **Surface:** metalled.
Distance: 25m 200m.
Remarks: Near city wall.

Miranda do Douro 29E3

Largo do Cestelo. **GPS:** n41,49611 w6,275.

free. **Surface:** metalled.
Distance: on the spot 50m 50m.
Remarks: Parking near ruins of castle.

Mirandela 29D3

Largo Cardal. **GPS:** n41,48685 w7,18391.

15 free Fon. **Location:** Rural, simple, central, noisy.
Surface: metalled.
Distance: centre on the spot on the spot on the spot.
Remarks: Large parking along the river.

Mirandela 29D3

Três Rios-Maravilha.
GPS: n41,50683 w7,19716.
€ 16,50-21,50 Ch WC.
02/02-01/12.

Tourist information Mirandela:
Museu municipal. Modern Portuguese painting art. T free.
Villa Flôr. Village museum. T free.

PT

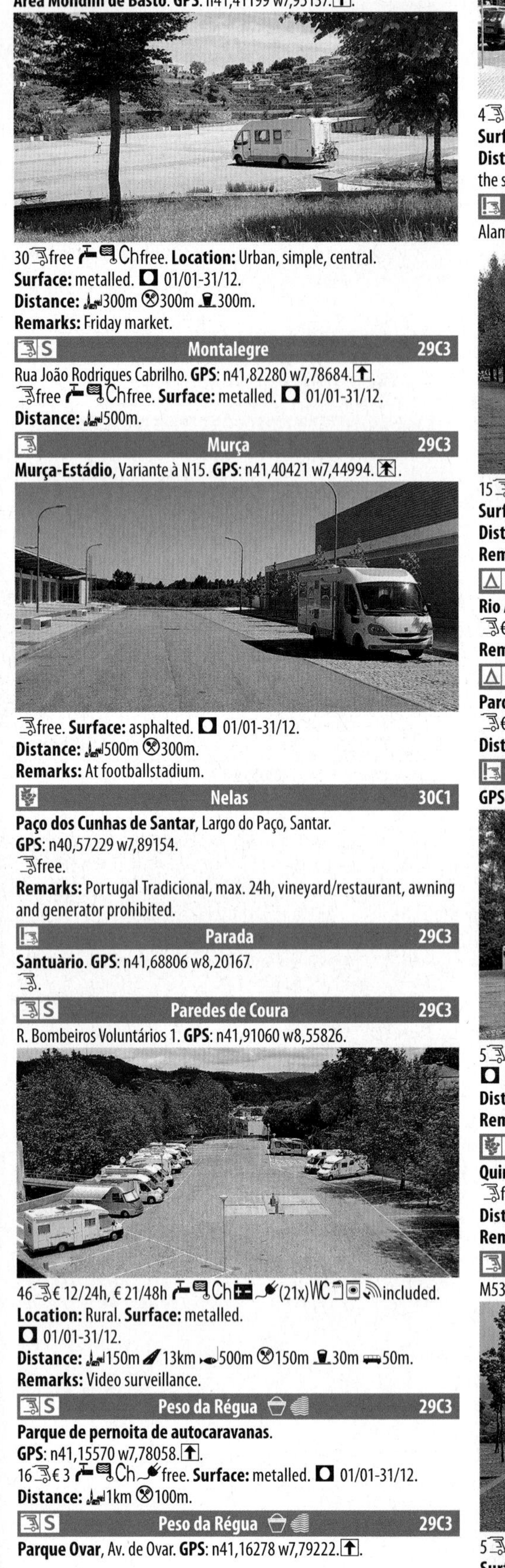

Mogadouro 29D3

Mogadouro, Complexo Desportivo Municipal. **GPS**: n41,33528 w6,71861.
€ 13-15 Ch WC. 01/04-30/09.
Distance: 500m on the spot 500m.

Mondim de Basto 29C3

Area Mondim de Basto. **GPS**: n41,41199 w7,95137.

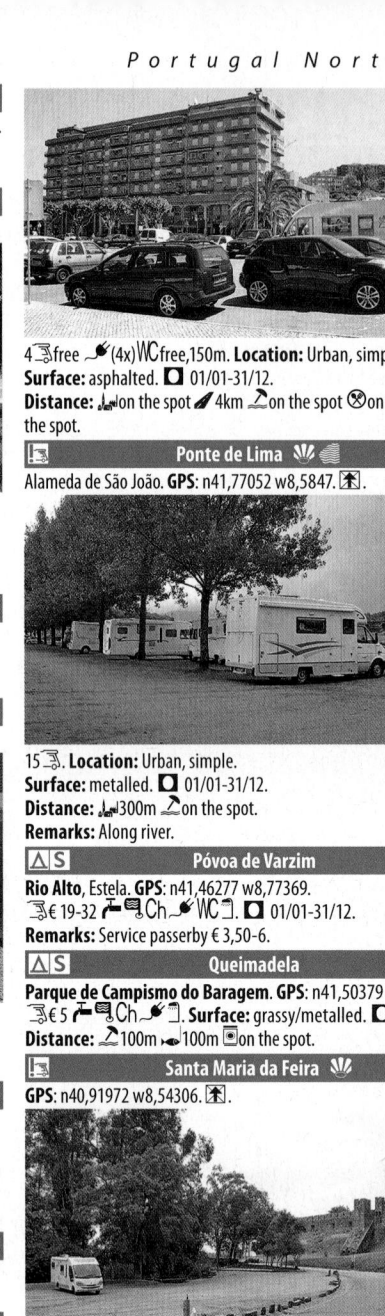

30 free Chfree. **Location:** Urban, simple, central.
Surface: metalled. 01/01-31/12.
Distance: 300m 300m 300m.
Remarks: Friday market.

Montalegre 29C3

Rua João Rodrigues Cabrilho. **GPS**: n41,82280 w7,78684.
free Chfree. **Surface:** metalled. 01/01-31/12.
Distance: 500m.

Murça 29C3

Murça-Estádio, Variante à N15. **GPS**: n41,40421 w7,44994.

free. **Surface:** asphalted. 01/01-31/12.
Distance: 500m 300m.
Remarks: At footballstadium.

Nelas 30C1

Paço dos Cunhas de Santar, Largo do Paço, Santar.
GPS: n40,57229 w7,89154.
free.
Remarks: Portugal Tradicional, max. 24h, vineyard/restaurant, awning and generator prohibited.

Parada 29C3

Santuàrio. **GPS**: n41,68806 w8,20167.

Paredes de Coura 29C3

R. Bombeiros Voluntários 1. **GPS**: n41,91060 w8,55826.

46 € 12/24h, € 21/48h Ch (21x)WC included.
Location: Rural. **Surface:** metalled.
01/01-31/12.
Distance: 150m 13km 500m 150m 30m 50m.
Remarks: Video surveillance.

Peso da Régua 29C3

Parque de pernoita de autocaravanas.
GPS: n41,15570 w7,78058.
16 € 3 Ch free. **Surface:** metalled. 01/01-31/12.
Distance: 1km 100m.

Peso da Régua 29C3

Parque Ovar, Av. de Ovar. **GPS**: n41,16278 w7,79222.

4 free (4x)WCfree,150m. **Location:** Urban, simple, central, noisy.
Surface: asphalted. 01/01-31/12.
Distance: on the spot 4km on the spot on the spot on the spot.

Ponte de Lima 29C3

Alameda de São João. **GPS**: n41,77052 w8,5847.

15. **Location:** Urban, simple.
Surface: metalled. 01/01-31/12.
Distance: 300m on the spot.
Remarks: Along river.

Póvoa de Varzim 29B3

Rio Alto, Estela. **GPS**: n41,46277 w8,77369.
€ 19-32 Ch WC. 01/01-31/12.
Remarks: Service passerby € 3,50-6.

Queimadela 29C3

Parque de Campismo do Baragem. **GPS**: n41,50379 w8,16216.
€ 5 Ch. **Surface:** grassy/metalled. 01/01-31/12.
Distance: 100m 100m on the spot.

Santa Maria da Feira 30B1

GPS: n40,91972 w8,54306.

5 free. **Location:** Rural, simple, quiet. **Surface:** gravel/sand.
01/01-31/12.
Distance: 600m 600m.
Remarks: Parking at castle.

São Romão do Corgo 29C3

Quinta de Bourça, Lugar de Vila Nova. **GPS**: n41,44348 w7,9932.
free €2,50 €2,50. **Location:** Rural.
Distance: 11km.
Remarks: Portugal Tradicional.

Soajo 29C3

M530. **GPS**: n41,87197 w8,2633.

5 free. **Location:** Rural, simple.
Surface: metalled. 01/01-31/12.
Distance: 100m 100m.
Remarks: Parking near school.

Torre de Moncorvo 30D1

GPS: n41,18083 w7,04167.
9 free Chfree. **Surface:** metalled. 01/01-31/12.
Distance: 1,5KM.

Remarks: At sports park.

Valadares-SP do Sul 30C1

Cooperativa Mimos, Largo do Cruzeiro 1. **GPS**: n40,75704 w8,19997.

3 free. **Location:** Simple.
Surface: grassy. 01/01-31/12.
Distance: on the spot.
Remarks: Portugal Tradicional.

Valpaços 29D3

Do Rabaçal, Rua Gago Coutinho. **GPS**: n41,63222 w7,24778.
€ 15-19 Ch WC. 01/01-31/12.

Viana do Castelo 29B3

Praia do Cabadelo, Av. do Cabedelo. **GPS**: n41,68388 w8,83333.
20 free Chfree. **Surface:** metalled. 01/01-31/12.
Distance: 400m on the spot 100m.

Viana do Castelo 29B3

Rua de Lima. **GPS**: n41,69534 w8,81875.

15 free. **Location:** Urban, simple.
Surface: metalled/sand.
Distance: centre 700m.
Remarks: Large parking along the Limia river.

Tourist information Viana do Castelo:
Campo do Costelo. Market. Fri.
Romaria da Nossa Senhora da Agonia. Procession with Gigantes (giants). 3rd week Aug.

Vila Chã 29B3

Sol de Vila Chã, Rua do Sol, Facho. **GPS**: n41,29825 w8,73263.
Ch. 01/01-31/12.
Distance: 300m 10m on the spot 100m.

Vila do Conde 29B3

Av. Júlio Graça. **GPS**: n41,34476 w8,74541.

20 free. **Location:** Urban, simple, central, noisy. **Surface:** metalled.
01/01-31/12.
Distance: 400m 150m 150m 200m 400m.
Remarks: Along the Este river.

Vila do Conde 29B3

Av. Marques de Sa Bandiera. **GPS**: n41,34270 w8,74587.

20 free. **Location:** Urban, simple, central. **Surface:** gravel/sand.
01/01-31/12.

PT

Distance: 500m on the spot 200m 400m.
Remarks: Parking at sea.

S Vila Nova de Cerveira 29B2
Av. dos Pescadores. **GPS**: n41,93823 w8,74685.

4 free Ch free. **Location:** Rural, simple.
Surface: asphalted. 01/01-31/12.
Distance: historical center 150m river-beach.
Remarks: Near Minho river and public pool park.

S Vila Nova de Foz Côa 30D1
Autocross, N102. **GPS**: n41,06727 w7,15496.
free Ch free. **Location:** Isolated, quiet.
Distance: 2km.

Vila Nova de Foz Côa 30D1
Rua Engenheiro Eugénio Nobre. **GPS**: n41,08028 w7,14806.
+50 free. **Location:** Rural. 01/01-31/12.
Distance: 500m 500m.

S Vila Nova de Gaia 29B3
Madalena, Rua de Cerro, Praia de Madalena.
GPS: n41,10750 w8,65556.
€ 18,30-28,80 Ch WC. 01/01-31/12.
Remarks: Service only € 3,15-5,40.

Tourist information Vila Nova de Gaia:
City of the port wine, at the left bank of the river Douro, Port houses can be visited daily.

S Vila Real 29C3
Municipal de Vila Real, Rua Dr. Manuel Cardona, Quinta da Carreira.
GPS: n41,30333 w7,73667.
€ 13,20-20,90 Ch WC.
01/01-31/12.

Tourist information Vila Real:
Solar de Mateus. Baroque country house, 18th century, known from label of the Matheus wine.

S Vinhais 29D3
GPS: n41,83381 w7,00271.

6 free Ch free.
Location: Urban, simple. **Surface:** gravel. 01/01-31/12.
Distance: 200m 100m.
Remarks: Nearby swimming pool.

Beira

S Aldeia da Ponte 30D1
Caminho do Freguil. **GPS**: n40,41092 w6,87159.

4 free Ch free.
Location: Rural, simple. **Surface:** metalled. 01/01-31/12.
Distance: 300m.
Remarks: Near old Roman bridge.

S Almeida 30D1
Rua da Guerreira. **GPS**: n40,72753 w6,90402.

free WC. **Surface:** metalled. 01/01-31/12.
Remarks: At fort-castle.

Anadia 30B1
Rua Seabras de Castro. **GPS**: n40,44056 w8,4375.

free. **Surface:** asphalted.
Distance: 100m 100m.

S Aveiro 30B1
Parque de S João, Canal São Roque. **GPS**: n40,64328 w8,65859.

10 free free. **Surface:** grasstiles. 01/01-31/12.
Distance: 200m 25m 200m 200m.
Remarks: Parking at the Canal and A25.

Tourist information Aveiro:
Ecomuseu da Troncalhada, Canal das Pirâmides. Salt-making.
summer.
Museu de Aveiro, Av. Sta. Joana Princesa. Collection baroque art.
Tue-Su 10-17.30h.

S Barril de Alva 30C1
EM517-1. **GPS**: n40,28611 w7,96167.

50 free Ch WC free. **Location:** Rural, simple, quiet.
Surface: unpaved. 01/01-31/12.
Distance: 500m river-beach on the spot.

Barriosa 30C1
Poço da Broca. **GPS**: n40,29366 w7,75376.

free. **Location:** Rural.
Distance: on the spot on the spot.
Remarks: Portugal Tradicional, restaurant and regional products for sale.

S Belmonte 30C2
Parque de Santiago, N345. **GPS**: n40,21835 w7,20459.

4 free Ch WC free. **Surface:** metalled. 01/01-31/12.
Distance: 500m on the spot 150m on the spot.

Castelo Bom 30D1
Avenida Santa Maria, N16. **GPS**: n40,61261 w6,83398.

3 free. **Location:** Rural, simple. **Surface:** metalled.
01/01-31/12.
Distance: on the spot.
Remarks: Less suitable for motorhomes >6,5m, typical village nearby spanish border.

S Castelo Branco 30C2
Municipal de Castel Branco, N18. **GPS**: n39,85815 w7,49351.
Ch WC. 02/01-15/11.

Tourist information Castelo Branco:
Castelo. Ruins of castle of the Templars.
Alameda da Liberdade. Mo.

S Castelo de Paiva 29C3
R. Emidio Navarro. **GPS**: n41,03955 w8,27406.

50 free Ch WC free. **Location:** Simple, central, quiet.
Surface: metalled. 01/01-31/12.
Distance: on the spot on the spot on the spot.
Remarks: Market square.

S Castelo Mendo 30D1
P5, N16. **GPS**: n40,59444 w6,94833.

3 free free. **Location:** Rural, simple. **Surface:** grassy/sand.
01/01-31/12.
Distance: on the spot 6,8km.

Castelo Rodrigo 30D1
GPS: n40,87778 w6,96611.

PT

free. **Surface:** sand.
Remarks: At the entrance of fort.

Celorico da Beira 30C1

GPS: n40,63389 w7,40472.

10. **Location:** Isolated. **Surface:** metalled.
Distance: 2km.
Remarks: Parking sports park.

Cinfães 29C3

GPS: n41,07167 w8,08719.

. **Surface:** metalled. 01/01-31/12.
Distance: 100m 100m 100m.

S Coimbra 30B1

Parque do Choupalinho, Av. Inês de Castro.
GPS: n40,19970 w8,42905.

20 free Ch free.
Surface: metalled. 01/01-31/12.
Remarks: Max. 24h.

Tourist information Coimbra:
Portugal dos Pequeninos. Miniature Portugal.
9-19h.

S Coimbrão 30B2

Praia do Pedrógão. **GPS**: n39,91500 w8,95.
€ 15,60-18,20 Ch WC 16/02-15/12.
Distance: 50m on the spot on the spot 10m.

S Condeixa 30B1

Av. Bombeiros Voluntarios de Condeixa. **GPS**: n40,11291 w8,49336.

6 free Chfree. **Surface:** asphalted. 01/01-31/12.
Distance: 500m on the spot 300m.

Remarks: Max. 48h, market Friday-morning.

Condeixa 30B1

Conímbriga, Praça da Republiça Condeixa.
GPS: n40,09895 w8,4894.

5 free. **Location:** Simple. **Surface:** grassy/metalled.
01/01-31/12.
Remarks: Parking next to archaeological site.

S Covas do Monte-SP do Sul 30C1

Covas do Monte.
GPS: n40,88873 w8,09823.
free free.
Distance: 250m.
Remarks: Portugal Tradicional.

S Escalos de Baixo 30C2

Hanmar, Estrada National 352. **GPS**: n39,89917 w7,40028.

20 € 8, May-Aug € 10 Ch WC included. **Surface:** grassy.
01/01-31/12.
Distance: 1km 1km.

S Estarreja 30B1

R. Dr. Antonio Madureira. **GPS**: n40,75417 w8,56611.

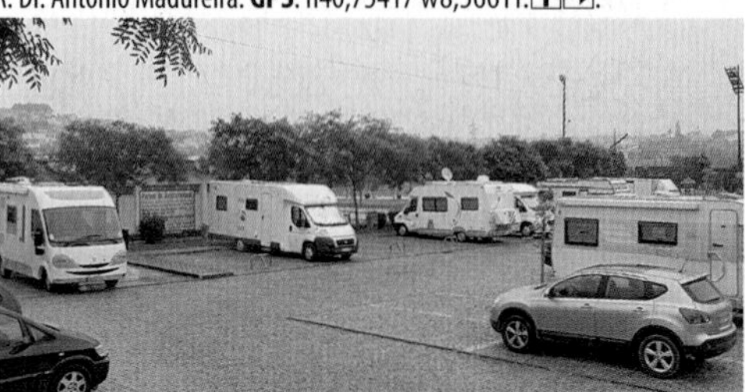

6 € 2/48h Ch included. **Location:** Urban, simple, central.
Surface: metalled. 01/01-31/12.
Distance: on the spot on the spot on the spot.
Remarks: Check in Cafe Piscina, Ag. Seguros Rebelo, tuesday market 100m.

S Estarreja 30B1

Ribeira do Maurão. **GPS**: n40,81328 w8,61588.

6 free €2 Ch. **Location:** Rural, simple, isolated, quiet.
Surface: metalled. 01/01-31/12.
Distance: on the spot on the spot.
Remarks: Nature reserve.

S Figueira da Foz 30B1

Av. de Espanha. **GPS**: n40,14856 w8,86791.

30 € 0,80/h, overnight stay free WC.
Surface: asphalted. 01/01-31/12.
Distance: on the spot on the spot 100m.

Figueira da Foz 30B1

R.do Cabedelo. **GPS**: n40,14403 w8,86395.

10. **Location:** Simple. **Surface:** sand. 01/01-31/12.
Distance: on the spot on the spot.
Remarks: Beach parking.

S Figueira da Foz 30B1

Jumbo, Av. Francisco de Sá Carneiro. **GPS**: n40,16413 w8,8413.
Chfree. 01/01-31/12.
Remarks: At petrol station.

S Fratel 30C2

Vila Velha de Ródão. **GPS**: n39,63250 w7,74694.

10 free Chfree. **Surface:** grassy. 01/01-31/12.
Distance: 200m 1km 300m 300m.

S Fundão 30C2

Quinta do Convento. **GPS**: n40,13276 w7,51205.
150 € 13-17 Ch WC . 01/01-31/12.

S Furadouro 30B1

Praia do Furadouro. **GPS**: n40,87645 w8,67381.

30 free WC50m. **Location:** Rural, simple, quiet. **Surface:** asphalted.
01/01-31/12.
Distance: on the spot 300m 300m.
Remarks: Beach parking.

S Guarda 30C1

Parque Pólis, Rua da Direcção Geral de Viação.
GPS: n40,54894 w7,24083.

PT

20 free Ch free. **Location:** Simple. **Surface:** metalled.
01/01-31/12.
Distance: historical centre 4km 2,4km 700m.
Remarks: Recreation park.

S Guarda 30C1

Rossio de Valhelhas. GPS: n40,40333 w7,40528.
 Ch . 01/05-30/09.
Distance: 50m 300m 150m 100m.

Tourist information Guarda:
Medieval city.

S Idanha-a-Nova 30C2

Municipal de Idanha-a-Nova, Albufeira da Barragem Marechel Carmona. **GPS:** n39,95056 w7,18722.
€ 11-14 Ch WC . 01/01-31/12.
Distance: 50m on the spot on the spot 8km.
Remarks: Service only € 2,60-4,40.

Idanha-a-Velha 30C2

N332. **GPS:** n39,99830 w7,1445.
.

Tourist information Idanha-a-Velha:
Archeological tour.

Ilhavo 30B1

Av. Infante Dom Henrique, Praia da Barra. **GPS:** n40,64375 w8,74456.

30 free. **Surface:** metalled. 01/01-31/12.
Distance: 300m 300m.

Ilhavo 30B1

Costa Nova do Prado. **GPS:** n40,61222 w8,74917.

7 free. **Surface:** metalled. 01/01-31/12.
Distance: on the spot on the spot on the spot on the spot.
Remarks: Beach parking.

S Ilhavo 30B1

Av Ns.da Saude. **GPS:** n40,61417 w8,75222.
Ch WC. 01/01-31/12.

Tourist information Ilhavo:
Museu Histórico da Vista Alegre, Fábrica de Porcelanas da Vista Alegre. Collection of porcelain. Tue-Fri 9-18h, Sa-Su 9-12.30h, 14-17h. Museu Marítimo de Ílhavo, Av. Dr. Rocha Madahil. Shipping museum. Tue-Fri 10-12.30h, 14.30-18h, Sa-Su 14.30-17.30h.

S Lorvão 30C1

Rua do Malhao. **GPS:** n40,25896 w8,31468.

10 free Ch free. **Surface:** metalled.
Distance: on the spot.

Luso 30B1

GPS: n40,38639 w8,38139.

10 free. **Surface:** metalled. 01/01-31/12.
Remarks: Parking next to Hotel de Terme.

Tourist information Luso:
Mata Nacional do Buçaco. Nature reserve.

S Melo-Gouveia 30C1

Quinta das Cegonhas, Nabainhos. **GPS:** n40,52057 w7,54169.
50 € 19,10-23 Ch WC . 01/01-31/12.

S Mira 30B1

Praia de Mira. GPS: n40,44472 w8,79806.
 Ch WC . 16/01-15/11.
Remarks: Service only € 3,15-5,40.

S Miranda do Corvo 30B2

Rua Porto Mourisco. **GPS:** n40,08803 w8,33232.

8 free Ch free. **Location:** Rural. **Surface:** asphalted.
01/01-31/12.
Distance: 700m.

S Oleiros 30C2

R. Dr. Barata Relvas. **GPS:** n39,92056 w7,91389.
free Ch free. **Surface:** metalled. 01/01-31/12.

S Pardilhó 30B1

Parque de Merendas, R. Joaquim Maria Resende.
GPS: n40,80111 w8,63472.

15 € 2/48h Ch included. **Location:** Rural, comfortable, isolated, quiet. **Surface:** metalled. 01/01-31/12.
Distance: 600m on the spot on the spot.
Remarks: Max. 48h, check in at bar (service).

S Penacova 30C1

Bairro de Carrazedos. **GPS:** n40,26722 w8,28306.

10 free Ch WC free.
Surface: metalled. 01/01-31/12.
Distance: 400m 3km 800m 400m.

S Penamacor 30C2

Lazer de Benquerença, Benquerença. **GPS:** n40,22938 w7,22136.

10 free Ch free. **Location:** Rural, simple, quiet.
Surface: gravel/sand. 01/01-31/12.
Distance: 2km on the spot.

Pinhel 30D1

GPS: n40,77389 w7,06194.

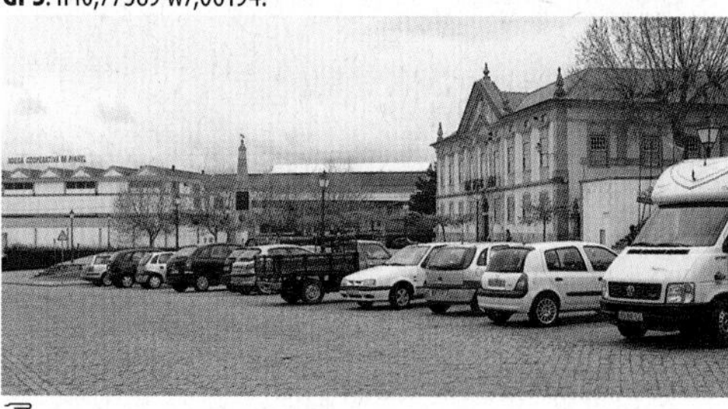

.
Distance: on the spot on the spot.
Remarks: At townhall.

S Praia de Mira 30B1

Praia da Mira. **GPS:** n40,45800 w8,8025.

6 free. **Location:** Simple.
Surface: metalled. 01/01-31/12.
Distance: on the spot.
Remarks: Beach parking.

Praia de Mira 30B1

GPS: n40,44620 w8,80447.

20 free. **Surface:** sand.
Distance: 500m.
Remarks: Beach parking.

S Praia de Quiaos 30B1

Praia de Quiaos. **GPS:** n40,22034 w8,89116.

15 free. **Location:** Simple.
Surface: metalled. 01/01-31/12.
Remarks: Beach parking.

S Sabugal 30D1

Rua do Cemitério. **GPS:** n40,34843 w7,08653.

PT

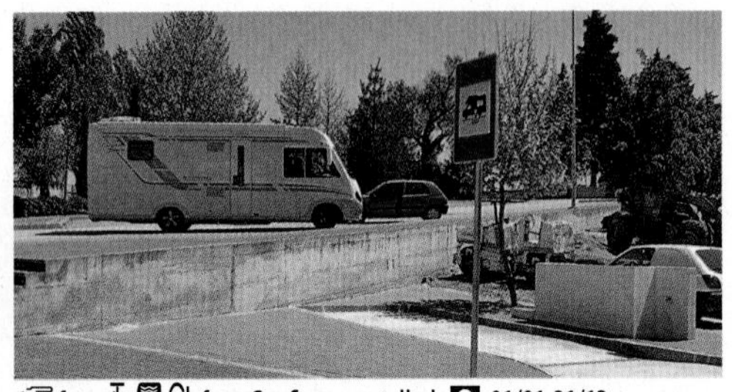

6 free Chfree. **Surface:** metalled. 01/01-31/12.
Distance: 500m 400m.

Sangalhos 30B1
R. Mercado 150. **GPS:** n40,48639 w8,47528.

20 free Chfree.
Location: Simple. **Surface:** metalled. 01/01-31/12.
Remarks: At sports centre.

Santa Ovaia 30C1
Ponte das Três Entradas, Avô.
GPS: n40,30667 w7,87139.
€ 13-14,50 WC. **Surface:** grassy.
01/01-31/12.
Distance: 10m on the spot on the spot on the spot 10m.

São João da Pesqueira 29C3
Rua General Ramalho Eanes. **GPS:** n41,14682 w7,40187.
10 € 10 Ch WC.
Distance: 400m.
Remarks: At fire-station.

São João da Pesqueira 29C3
Restaurant Carocha, N222. **GPS:** n41,15120 w7,42378.
50 free Chfree. 01/01-31/12.
Distance: 1km on the spot.
Remarks: Next to restaurant and Port wine cellar Cave Cadão.

Sao Joao de Areias 30C1
Terra de Iguanas, Estrada principal 76, Vila Dianteira.
GPS: n40,39045 w8,08574.

4 € 10 Ch WC included. **Location:** Rural, comfortable, quiet. **Surface:** sand. 01/01-31/12.
Distance: 2km 1km 1,2km 2km 400m 2km on the spot.
Remarks: Max. 3 nights, swimming pool incl., vegetables and fruit from the garden.

São Lourenço do Bairro 30B1
Quinta do Encontro, N334. **GPS:** n40,44136 w8,49014.
free. 01/01-31/12.
Remarks: Portugal Tradicional, max. 24h, vineyard/shop/restaurant, awning and generator prohibited.

São Pedro do Sul 30C1
Termas São Pedro do Sul, N46. **GPS:** n40,74056 w8,08639.

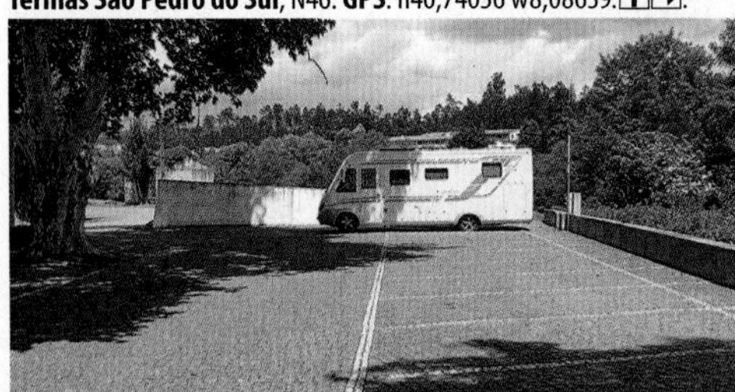

6 free Chfree. **Location:** Simple. **Surface:** asphalted.
01/01-31/12.
Distance: 1km.
Remarks: Max. 48h.

Sertã 30C2
R. Amaro Vicente Martins. **GPS:** n39,79729 w8,09588.

4 free Chfree.
Location: Simple. **Surface:** asphalted. 01/01-31/12.
Distance: 500m 3km 50m.
Remarks: At sports park.

Sertã 30C2
Palácio da Justiça, R. Baden Powell. **GPS:** n39,80028 w8,09944.

free. **Location:** Simple.
Surface: gravel/sand. 01/01-23/12.
Distance: 100m 3km 50m 100m.

Sertã 30C2
Albergue do Bonjardim, Nesperal, Sertã. **GPS:** n39,81306 w8,16278.

4 € 6 €4 WC. **Location:** Luxurious, isolated.
Surface: unpaved. 01/04-31/10.
Distance: 200m 2,5km 1km 50m.
Remarks: Sauna, steam bath and covered pool € 7,50, breakfast € 7,50.

Tabua 30C1
Piscina. GPS: n40,36306 w8,03.

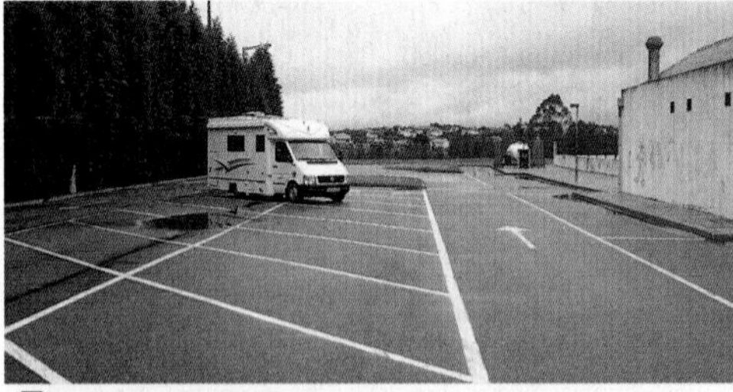

3 free. **Surface:** metalled.

Tabua 30C1
Rua Aurora Jesus Goncalves. **GPS:** n40,36306 w8,02278.

10 free. **Surface:** metalled.

Trancoso 30C1
Parque Sportivo. GPS: n40,77160 w7,35621.

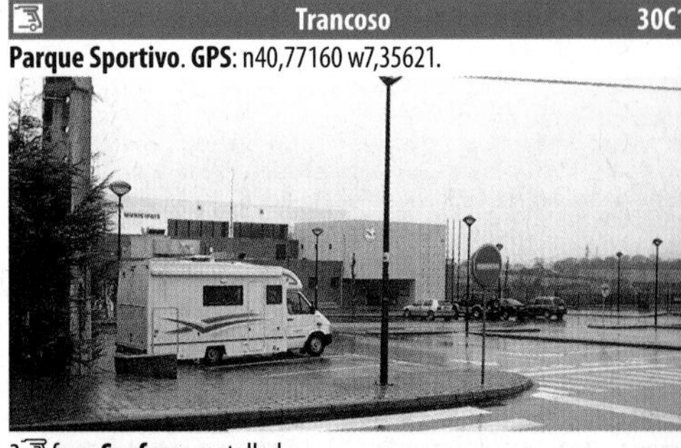

3 free. **Surface:** metalled.

Trancoso 30C1
Av. Heróis de São Marcos. **GPS:** n40,77583 w7,35056.

10. **Surface:** metalled.
Distance: 50m.
Remarks: Note: Friday market day.

Vagos 30B1
Praia da Vagueira. GPS: n40,54944 w8,77056.
20 € 7,50, 01/10-31/05 € 5 Ch €2 €0,50. **Surface:** sand.
01/01-31/12.
Remarks: Service passerby € 2,50.

Vagos 30B1
Vagueira, Gafanha da Boa Hora. **GPS:** n40,55806 w8,74528.
€ 16-25 Ch WC. 01/01-31/12.
Distance: 1km on the spot 1km 500m.
Remarks: Service only € 2,60-4,40.

Vagueira 30B1
Rua Arménio, Praia da Vagueira. **GPS:** n40,56506 w8,76697.

20 free. **Surface:** metalled.
Distance: 200m sandy beach 50m.
Remarks: Beach parking.

Vila Nova de Oliveirinha 30C1
Quinta do Tapadinho, Rua dos Brandões. **GPS:** n40,36520 w7,92195.

5 € 13,25 €2/100liter Ch (5x)€5/24h,10Amp WC €4 included. **Surface:** grassy/sand. 01/01-31/12.
Distance: 1km 6km 1km 8km 1km on the spot.

Vila Pouca da Beira 30C1
Despinheiro, Avenida Principal. **GPS:** n40,30159 w7,9257.

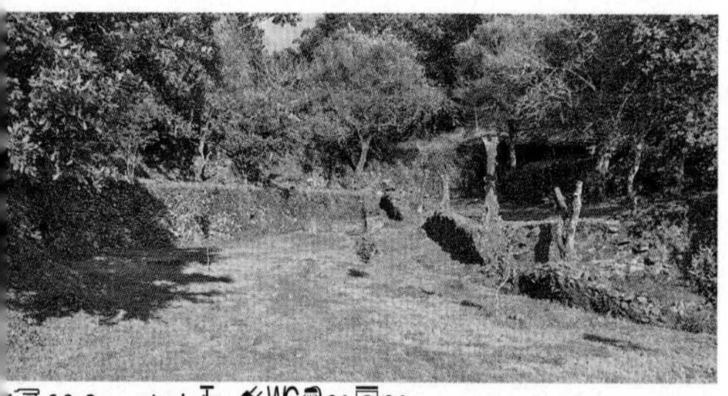

4 € 8, 2 pers.incl WC €1 €4.
Location: Rural, isolated, quiet. **Surface:** grassy. 01/01-31/12.
Distance: 500m 2km 2km 800m on the spot on the spot.

Vilar Formoso 30D1

Zaza, Avenida das Tilia's, N332. **GPS:** n40,61528 w6,83833.

12 € 5/24h €2 Ch (12x)€3/day.
Location: Simple. **Surface:** asphalted/gravel. 01/01-31/12.
Distance: 500m baker on site.

Viseu 30C1

Av. Europa. **GPS:** n40,66533 w7,91681.
free Chfree.
Surface: asphalted.
01/01-31/12.
Distance: on the spot 6km.

Tourist information Viseu:
Centre of Vinho do Dão.
Museu municipal, Castro Daire. Etnographical collection.

Portugal Central and Lisbon

A-dos-Cunhados 30A2

R. Monsenhor José Fialho. **GPS:** n39,15222 w9,30083.

0 free Chfree.
Location: Simple, quiet. **Surface:** asphalted. 01/01-31/12.
Distance: 100m 6km beach 7km 200m.

Abrantes 30B2

Aquapolis, São Joao. **GPS:** n39,45489 w8,18977.

0 free Chfree. **Location:** Rural, simple. **Surface:** metalled.
01/01-31/12.
Distance: 3km 4,7km on the spot 100m 6km.
Remarks: Service 100m.

Abrantes 30B2

Aquapolis, São Joao. **GPS:** n39,45347 w8,19072.

2 free Ch free. **Surface:** metalled.
Distance: 3km 4,8km Sandy beach.
Remarks: Along the Tagus river.

Abrantes 30B2

Largo do Pralvo. **GPS:** n39,44956 w8,18968.

10 free. **Location:** Urban, simple, quiet. **Surface:** metalled.
01/01-31/12.
Distance: 1km 6,5km on the spot 1km 1km.
Remarks: Along the Tagus river.

Abrantes 30B2

Parque Urbano de São Lourenço, São Vincente.
GPS: n39,47530 w8,21541.

10 free. **Location:** Rural, simple, quiet. **Surface:** grassy/gravel.
01/01-31/12.
Distance: centre 2,4km 4,4km 50m 1,8km.
Remarks: Max. 48h.

Tourist information Abrantes:
Posto de Turismo, Esplanada 1º de Maio, www.cm-abrantes.pt. City with historical centre.

Alenquer 30B3

Alenquer camping, Casal das Pedras. **GPS:** n39,05917 w9,02833.
4 € 15,50 €2,50 Ch. 01/01-31/12.
Distance: on the spot on the spot.

Almada 30A3

Costa de Caparicia, R. Eduardo Luis. **GPS:** n38,56691 w9,19308.

10 free. **Location:** Simple. **Surface:** sand.
Distance: on the spot on the spot on the spot.

Almourol 30B2

Castelo de Almourol, Praia do Ribatejo. **GPS:** n39,46295 w8,38297.

10 free. **Location:** Simple. **Surface:** metalled.
Distance: 2km 4km on the spot 2km.
Remarks: On the banks of the Tejo river, parking castle.

Arruda dos Vinhos 30B3

Casal da Pevide. GPS: n38,99861 w9,08417.

3 free. **Location:** Urban, simple, noisy. **Surface:** asphalted.
01/01-31/12.
Distance: 2km on the spot on the spot.
Remarks: Parking Intermarché.

Assafora 30A3

Pic-nic area, Estr. de São Julião. **GPS:** n38,91167 w9,41138.

4 free. **Location:** Rural, simple, quiet. **Surface:** metalled.
01/01-31/12.
Distance: 800m on the spot.

Baleal 30A2

Estrada do Baleal. **GPS:** n39,37240 w9,33702.

30 free free. **Location:** Rural, simple, quiet. **Surface:** asphalted.
01/01-31/12.
Distance: 2km on the spot on the spot on the spot 2km on the spot.
Remarks: Parking next to bar restaurant in village square, not recommended at the weekend.

Batalha 30B2

Parque Cónego M. Simões Inácio, Rua Cerca Conventual.
GPS: n39,66134 w8,82516.

15 free Ch free. **Location:** Urban, simple, quiet.
Surface: asphalted. 01/01-31/12 Mo.
Distance: 100m on the spot.
Remarks: At football ground/tennis, max. 48h.

PT

Cabo Espichel 30A3

P Cabo Espichel. **GPS**: n38,42031 w9,21353.

free. **Location:** Rural, isolated.
Surface: sand. 01/01-31/12.
Distance: Sesimbra 13km At the sea.
Remarks: Beautiful view.

Cascais 30A3

Cap Raso. **GPS**: n38,71134 w9,48498.

free. **Location:** Rural, simple, quiet. **Surface:** sand.
01/01-31/12.
Distance: 6km on the spot 6km on the spot on the spot.

Cascais 30A3

Ponta da Gate, Estrada do Guincho. **GPS**: n38,72769 w9,47555.

10 free. **Location:** Simple, quiet.
Surface: gravel. 01/01-31/12.
Distance: 8km on the spot on the spot on the spot 8km on the spot.

Cascais 30A3

Guincho, Areia, Guincho. **GPS**: n38,72167 w9,46639.
€ 19,50-42,30 Ch WC . 01/01-31/12.
Remarks: Service only € 3,15-5,40.

Cerradas 30A3

Estrada Á-dos-Serrados. **GPS**: n38,91798 w9,38292.

20 free Ch free. **Location:** Rural, simple, quiet.
Surface: gravel. 01/01-31/12.
Distance: on the spot 5km on the spot.
Remarks: At gymnasium, max. 48h.

Constância 30B2

Estrada National. **GPS**: n39,47670 w8,34365.

20 free Ch free. **Location:** Rural, comfortable, quiet.
Surface: metalled. 01/01-31/12.
Distance: 500m 2,3km on the spot on the spot 500m 300m.
Remarks: Along the Zêzere river.

Coruche 30B3

Area autocaravana, Rua 5 de Outubro. **GPS**: n38,96139 w8,51944.

100 free Ch free. **Surface:** metalled. 01/01-31/12 last Sa of the month.
Distance: on the spot on the spot.

Costa da Caparica 30A3

Caravanismo da Costa da Caparica, Santo António da Caparica.
GPS: n38,65389 w9,23833.
€ 18,89-36 Ch WC . 01/01-31/12.
Distance: 500m on the spot on the spot 100m.
Remarks: Service only € 3,15-5,40.

Dois Portos 30A3

R. da Azenha. **GPS**: n39,03689 w9,18098.

4 free free. **Location:** Simple, quiet. **Surface:** metalled.
01/01-31/12.
Distance: on the spot.

Ericeira 30A3

Municipal de Mil Regos, N247, Casal do Moinho Velho.
GPS: n38,97778 w9,41861.
€ 13-17 Ch WC . 01/01-31/12.
Remarks: Service in front of campsite.

Tourist information Ericeira:
Aldeia Museu de José Franco, Sobreiro. Miniature village. 9-19h. free.

Fátima 30B2

Rua de Sao Vicente de Paulo. **GPS**: n39,63389 w8,67111.

6 free WC free. **Location:** Urban, simple, quiet.
Surface: asphalted. 01/01-31/12.
Distance: 1km 3,2km 100m 1km.
Remarks: May 12-13 festivities.

Foz do Arelho 30B2

Av. do Mar. **GPS**: n39,42828 w9,22055.

120 € 3 Ch WC €1 included. **Location:** Rural, simple, quiet. **Surface:** unpaved. 01/01-31/12.
Distance: 1km 50m 50m 1,5km on the spot on the spot.
Remarks: Beach parking.

Lisbon 30A3

Municipal de Lisboa-Monsanto, Monsanto, Estrada da Circunvalação.
GPS: n38,72472 w9,20805.
€ 24-30 Ch WC .
01/01-31/12.
Distance: 3km on the spot on the spot 50m.

Tourist information Lisbon:
Lisboa Card. Card gives entrance to museums, public transport, available at: Rua Jardim do Regedor 50 (10-18), Mosteiros do Jeronimos, Museu dos Coches. € 18,50/24h, € 31,50/48h, € 39/72h.
Market. Tue, Sa.
32 Covered markets, most important market: Av. 24 de Julho.
6-14h Su.
Campo de Sta Clara. Flea market.
Rua de São Bento. Antiques market.
Arena near metro Campo Pequeno.
01/05-30/09 Thu.
Feira Popular. Fairground, opposite the Entrecampos metro.
01/05-30/09.
Oceanário, Parque das Nações. Aquarium. 10-19h. € 15,30.
Chiado. Elegant shopping district. elevator 7-24h.

Mação 30C2

Campo de Feiras, Av. Vicente Mirrado. **GPS**: n39,55723 w7,99303.

10 free Ch WC free. **Location:** Urban, simple.
Surface: metalled. 01/01-31/12.
Distance: 500m 6km 500m 500m.
Remarks: Max. 48h.

Mafra 30A3

R. Arieiro. **GPS**: n38,95451 w9,33555.

4 free €1/80liter Ch. **Location:** Urban, simple, central, quiet.
Surface: asphalted. 01/01-31/12.
Distance: 1,5km 2km on the spot.
Remarks: Max. 24h.

Tourist information Mafra:
Posto do turismo, Palácio Nacional de Mafra - Torreão Sul, Terreiro D. João V, www.cm-mafra.pt/turismo.
Parque Tapada Nacional, Portão do Codeçal. Safaripark. 10-19h.

Marinha Grande 30B2

Praia Velha, São Pedro de Moel. **GPS**: n39,76974 w9,02752.

PT

10 free. **Location:** Rural, simple, quiet. **Surface:** metalled.
01/01-31/12.
Distance: 5km 100m 100m 50m.
Remarks: Beach parking.

S Marinha Grande 30B2

Parque de Campismo Orbitur, São Pedro de Moel.
GPS: n39,75806 w9,02583.
Ch. 01/01-31/12.
Remarks: Service only € 3,15-5,40.

S Mira de Aire 30B2

Av. Mota Pinto. **GPS**: n39,54240 w8,70347.

12 free Ch free. **Location:** Simple, quiet.
Surface: asphalted. 01/01-31/12.
Distance: 500m 500m.
Remarks: Steep entrance road, caves 1,8km.

S Montalvo 30B2

Horta Do Casinha, Rua Circulação de Montalvinho.
GPS: n39,48550 w8,30765.
6 free Ch . **Location:** Rural, simple, quiet.
Surface: grassy. 16/12-01/01.
Distance: on the spot.
Remarks: Narrow entrance.

Montijo 30B3

GPS: n38,70286 w8,97665.

50 free. **Surface:** metalled.
Distance: 800m 200m 100m 200m 2km.
Remarks: Parking at ferry-boat to Lisbon.

S Nazaré 30B2

Rua Nossa Senhora da Vitória. **GPS**: n39,64696 w9,06936.

20 free Ch free. **Location:** Rural, isolated, quiet.
Surface: metalled. 01/01-31/12.
Distance: on the spot on the spot.
Remarks: Max. 24h.

Nazaré 30B2

Avenue do Municipio. **GPS**: n39,59741 w9,0696.

20 free. **Location:** Urban. **Surface:** asphalted. 01/01-31/12.
Distance: 200m 250m 250m 250m 750m.

S Obidos 30B2

Casa Azzurra, Rua do's Cumeiras 10. **GPS**: n39,39250 w9,16947.

10 € 8 €2/100liter Ch €2/night WC €1 €4/4 €1/day.
Location: Rural, comfortable, isolated. **Surface:** grassy/metalled.
01/01-31/12.
Distance: 4km on the spot 4km 4km on the spot on the spot.
Remarks: Service passerby € 5, barbecue place, swimming pool available.

S Obidos 30B2

Rue do Ginasio. **GPS**: n39,35628 w9,15672.

20 € 6/24h Ch included. **Location:** Rural, simple, quiet.
Surface: gravel/sand. 01/01-31/12.
Distance: 500m 1km 500m 500m.
Remarks: Service passerby € 2.

S Odrinhas 30A3

Parque Autocaravanas Odrinhas, R. do Castanhal.
GPS: n38,88312 w9,37491.

40 € 6 Ch €3,50/day WC €1 €4,50 included.
Location: Rural, comfortable, quiet. **Surface:** gravel/sand.
01/01-31/12.
Distance: on the spot on the spot on the spot.
Remarks: Repair possibilities motorhome, swimming pool available.

S Outeiro da Cabeça 30B2

Rua do Pavilhão Gimnodesportivo. **GPS**: n39,19306 w9,1825.

5 free Ch free. **Location:** Rural, simple, isolated.
Surface: gravel. 01/01-31/12.

Distance: 300m 2,5km 300m 300m.

Palmela 30B3

GPS: n38,56664 w8,90032.

6 free. **Location:** Urban, simple, quiet. **Surface:** sand.
01/01-31/12.
Remarks: Parking at castle.

S Pataias 30B2

Intermarché. **GPS**: n39,66041 w9,0151.

10 free Ch free . **Location:** Rural, simple, quiet.
Surface: asphalted. 01/01-31/12.
Distance: 200m on the spot on the spot on the spot.
Remarks: Parking Intermarché, max. 48h.

S Peniche 30A2

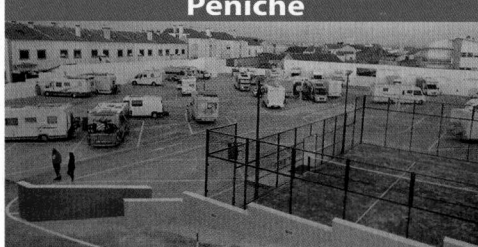

ASA Peniche - Motorhome Park, Rua da Liberdade 12.
GPS: n39,36622 w9,37917.
60 € 5 Ch €3 WC €1 included.
Location: Comfortable, luxurious, central. 01/01-31/12.
Distance: city centre 1km 300m 300m 400m 300m.
Remarks: Arrival <19.30h, bread-service, video surveillance, picnic and barbecue place.

Peniche 30A2

Av. Porto De Pesca. **GPS**: n39,35852 w9,37752.
50 free. **Location:** Urban, simple, central. **Surface:** asphalted.
01/01-31/12.
Distance: 500m 900m 1km 500m 500m 500m.
Remarks: At fire-station and marina.

Peniche 30A2

Farol do Cabo Cavoeiro, Caminho do Farol.
GPS: n39,35989 w9,4082.

5 . **Location:** Rural, simple, isolated. **Surface:** metalled.

PT

01/01-31/12.
Distance: 5km 300m on the spot 3km.
Remarks: At lighthouse.

Peniche 30A2

R. de Liberdade. **GPS**: n39,36577 w9,37417.

10. **Location:** Rural, simple. **Surface:** sand.
01/01-31/12.
Distance: 1,7km 50m 200m 200m.

Peniche 30A2

Peniche Praia, Estrada Marginal Norte. **GPS**: n39,36959 w9,392.

23 € 9, Jul/Aug € 15 Ch WC included €6,20/4,50 . **Location:** Rural, comfortable, quiet. **Surface:** grassy.
01/01-31/12.
Distance: 1,5km At the sea on the spot on the spot 1,5km on the spot 1,5km.

Tourist information Peniche:
Fortaleza de Peniche. Bathing resort.
Posto de Turismo, Rua Alexandre Herculano, www.cm-peniche.pt. Bathing resort.

PT

Póvoa e Meadas 30C2

Barragem de Nisa, M1007. **GPS**: n39,48394 w7,5476.

10 free ChWC free. **Location:** Rural, simple, isolated, quiet.
Surface: grasstiles/grassy. 01/01-31/12.
Distance: 4km 4km.

Póvoa e Meadas 30C2

Casa Carita, Rua de Santo Antonio. **GPS**: n39,50532 w7,53139.

4 € 5 included. **Location:** Rural, simple, isolated.
Surface: grassy/sand. 01/01-31/12.
Distance: 500m 500m.

Praia de Santa Cruz 30A2

GPS: n39,14418 w9,37482.

50 free WC free. **Location:** Rural, simple. **Surface:** asphalted.
01/01-31/12.
Distance: 300m 20m on the spot 300m.
Remarks: Parking at the beach or near the cliffs.

Ribamar 30A3

R. do Cacho Longo, São Lourençio. **GPS**: n39,01120 w9,42078.

10 free. **Location:** Rural, simple, isolated. **Surface:** gravel.
01/01-31/12.
Distance: 2km Sandy beach on the spot 6km.

São Mamede 30B2

Rua de São Martinho. **GPS**: n39,62238 w8,71536.

10 free Ch free. **Location:** Urban, simple, quiet.
Surface: metalled.
Distance: on the spot 200m 200m.

São Martinho do Porto 30B2

Av. Marigal. **GPS**: n39,50176 w9,14132.

15 free. **Location:** Rural, simple, noisy. **Surface:** metalled.
01/01-31/12.
Distance: 1,4km 5,5km sandy beach 50m 50m 850m on the spot.

Sintra 30A3

Avenida Conde Sucena, São Pedro de Penaferrim.
GPS: n38,78883 w9,37473.

10 € 5 Ch included. **Location:** Rural, simple, quiet.
Surface: asphalted. 01/01-31/12.
Distance: 2km on the spot.
Remarks: At footballstadium.

Tomar 30B2

Av. Gen. Bernardo Faria. **GPS**: n39,59972 w8,41306.

free WC. **Location:** Simple.
Surface: gravel/sand.
01/01-31/12.
Distance: 200m 200m 300m.
Remarks: Nearby railway station.

Tourist information Tomar:
Sinagoga de Tomar, Museu Luso-Hebraico, Rua Dr. Joaquim Jacinto, 75. Synagogue and Jewish Portuguese history.
free.
Convento de Cristo. Fortified monastery.
Festa dos Tabuleiros. Whitsuntide.
Barragem de Castelo de Bode. Artificial lake, 15km east of the city.

Torres Vedras 30A2

Municipal da Praia de Santa Cruz. **GPS**: n39,13444 w9,37472.
Ch WC . 01/01-31/12.

Turcifal 30A3

Largo Brigadeiro França Borges. **GPS**: n39,04288 w9,26581.

5 free Ch free. **Location:** Urban, central, quiet.
Surface: metalled. 01/01-31/12.
Distance: on the spot on the spot on the spot.

Vermoil 30B2

R. Vale de Fojo, Pombal. **GPS**: n39,85080 w8,66125.

5 free Ch free. **Surface:** gravel/sand. 01/01-31/12.
Distance: 200m 300m 300m.
Remarks: At cemetery.

Vila Nova da Barquinha 30B2

Parque De Pernoita, Largo do Primeiro de Dezembro.
GPS: n39,45763 w8,43297.

10 free ChWC free. **Location:** Rural, simple, quiet.
Surface: metalled.
Distance: 100m on the spot on the spot on the spot 150m on the spot on the spot on the spot.
Remarks: Along the Tagus river.

Alentejo

Alcácer do Sal 30B3

Barragem Pego do Altar, Alcácer do Sal > N253 > Montemoro o Novo > N380. **GPS**: n38,42055 w8,39384.

15 free Ch WC free. **Location:** Rural. **Surface:** sand.
01/01-31/12.
Distance: Alcácer do Sal 13km on the spot 100m.

Alcácer do Sal 30B3

Rua do Cabo da Vila.
GPS: n38,36903 w8,50276.
free. 01/01-31/12.
Distance: Old city 600m 5,6km 400m.
Remarks: Near arena.

Tourist information Alcácer do Sal:
Little town on the Rio Sado.

Almograve 31B1

Avenida da Praia. **GPS**: n37,65303 w8,80059.

30 free free. **Location:** Simple. **Surface:** grasstiles.
01/01-31/12.
Distance: on the spot.

Alvito 31B1

Rua de Tapadinha. **GPS**: n38,25917 w7,99222.
free.
Remarks: At swimming pool.

Avis 30C3

Municipal Albufeira do Maranhão, Barragam Albufeira do Maranhão.
GPS: n39,05682 w7,91145.
€ 8-12 Ch WC .
Distance: on the spot.
Remarks: Service only € 1,90.

Campo Maior 30C3

Barragem do Caia. **GPS**: n39,00308 w7,14219.

Castelo de Vide 30C2

Estr. de São Vincente. **GPS**: n39,41028 w7,44917.

. **Location:** Rural, quiet. **Surface:** metalled. 01/01-31/12.
Distance: 1km 300m.
Remarks: At stadium.

Castelo de Vide 30C2

Rua Luís de Camões. **GPS**: n39,41583 w7,45778.

free. **Location:** Urban, simple, central.
Surface: concrete.
01/01-31/12.
Remarks: Near city wall.

Tourist information Castelo de Vide:
www.cm-castelo-vide.pt. Historical centre with medieval citadel.

Cavaleiro 31B1

Cabo Sardano. **GPS**: n37,59810 w8,80608.

30 free. **Location:** Simple. **Surface:** sand. 01/01-31/12.
Distance: on the spot.
Remarks: At lighthouse.

Comporta 30B3

GPS: n38,37849 w8,78544.

40 free Ch free. **Location:** Urban, simple, quiet.
Surface: gravel/sand. 01/01-31/12.
Distance: 250m 1km 250m 250m.

Comporta 30B3

GPS: n38,38308 w8,78712.

± 6 free. **Location:** Urban, simple, quiet. **Surface:** gravel/sand.
01/01-31/12.
Distance: 250m 1km 300m 500m.
Remarks: Near church.

Elvas 30C3

Intermarché, Rue Paco Bandera. **GPS**: n38,87458 w7,18429.

15 free Ch free. **Surface:** asphalted. 01/01-31/12.
Distance: historical centre 1,7km on the spot.
Remarks: At petrol station and supermarket, max. 48h.

Elvas 30C3

GPS: n38,87766 w7,17763.

. **Surface:** metalled.
Remarks: Parking at aqueduct.

Tourist information Elvas:
Fortified city.

Estrela 31C1

Aldeia de Estrela, Cais. **GPS**: n38,26637 w7,38906.
5 free. **Location:** Rural, simple. **Surface:** gravel/sand.
Distance: on the spot.

Estremoz 30C3

Rossio Marquês de Pombal. **GPS**: n38,84320 w7,58672.

10 .
Location: Urban, simple, central. **Surface:** metalled. 01/01-31/12.
Distance: on the spot 50m 50m.

Tourist information Estremoz:
Market. Sa.

Evora 30C3

GPS: n38,57529 w7,90519.

free. **Location:** Urban, simple, noisy. **Surface:** gravel/metalled.
01/01-31/12.
Distance: 1km 500m 500m.
Remarks: Parking university, illuminated.

Evora 30C3

Avenida Condas De Vilalva. **GPS**: n38,57592 w7,91491.

. **Location:** Urban, noisy.
Surface: metalled. 01/01-31/12.
Distance: 1km.

Evora 30C3

Lago da Porta de Avis. **GPS**: n38,57672 w7,91096.

PT

free. **Location:** Urban, simple, noisy.
Surface: gravel/metalled.
01/01-31/12.
Distance: 1,5km.
Remarks: Parking at aqueduct.

Tourist information Evora:
Posto de Turismo, Praça do Geraldo, www.cm-evora.pt.
City with historical centre.
Igreja de S. Francisco, Capela dos Ossos.
Chapel of the bones.
8-18h 12-14h.
Tue.

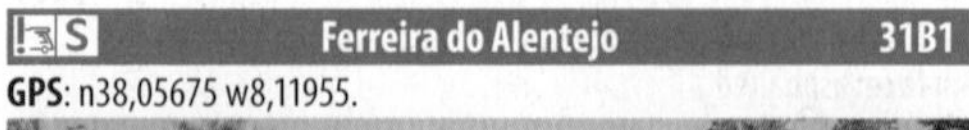

S Ferreira do Alentejo 31B1
GPS: n38,05675 w8,11955.

free. **Surface:** asphalted.
Distance: 500m 100m 1km 1,5km.
Remarks: Parking sports park.

S Grândola 31B1
Parque de Grândola. **GPS**: n38,18525 w8,564.

7 free Ch. **Location:** Simple. **Surface:** asphalted.
01/01-31/12.
Distance: 1km 7,4km 600m 500m 1,4km.
Remarks: At sports grounds.

S Lousal 31B1
Rua 25 Abril. **GPS**: n38,03591 w8,42908.

6 free Chfree. **Surface:** gravel. 01/01-31/12.
Distance: 15km 250m 400m bakery on the spot.
Remarks: At the site of the old mines of Lousal.

S Luz 31C1
R. de Mourão. **GPS**: n38,34278 w7,37389.

free Chfree. **Surface:** metalled.

S Marvão 30C2
N359-6. **GPS**: n39,39434 w7,3736.

12 free Chfree. **Location:** Rural, simple, quiet.
Surface: grassy/gravel. 01/01-31/12.
Distance: on the spot 500m.

Melides 31B1
Praia de Melides. **GPS**: n38,12897 w8,79262.

Surface: metalled. 01/01-31/12.
Distance: Melides 6,2km Sandy beach on the spot.

Mértola 31C1
N122/IC27. **GPS**: n37,64250 w7,65833.

Distance: 200m 200m.

Mértola 31C1
Rua dos Bombeiros Voluntários.
GPS: n37,64114 w7,66326.
10 free.
Surface: gravel/sand.
Remarks: At fire-station.

Tourist information Mértola:
Convento São Francisco. Former convent, exposition room and atelier. 10-17h.

S Messejana 31B1
GPS: n37,83167 w8,24694.

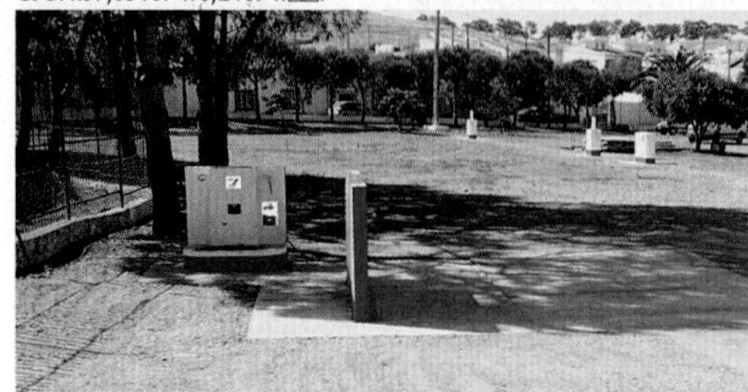

50 €7 Ch. **Location:** Rural. 01/01-31/12.
Distance: on the spot 10km.

S Mina de São Domingos 31C1
Rua Catarina Eufémia. **GPS**: n37,67052 w7,50194.
free €2 Ch.

Mina de São Domingos 31C1
Praia Fluvial, R265. **GPS**: n37,67228 w7,50418.

20 free. **Location:** Simple. **Surface:** metalled/sand.
Distance: 750m 50m.
Remarks: At recreation area, marked pitches.

Monsaraz 30C3
GPS: n38,44250 w7,38003.

±15 free. **Location:** Quiet. **Surface:** metalled. 01/01-31/12.
Distance: 100m 100m.
Remarks: Near city wall, beautiful view.

S Monsaraz 30C3
Rue da Fonte.
GPS: n38,45317 w7,38117.
€3,50 Ch.
Mo-Fr 8-21h, Sa-Su 8-12h.
Remarks: Call for the key.

Tourist information Monsaraz:
www.monsaraz.com.pt/. Small medieval town.

S Montargil 30B3
Ponte de Sôr. **GPS**: n39,09972 w8,145.
70 € 30-37 Ch. WC. 01/01-31/12.
Remarks: Service only € 3-5.

S Montemor-o-Novo 30B3
A6-IP7. **GPS**: n38,61856 w8,07924.

2 free. **Location:** Motorway, simple, quiet.
Surface: asphalted/metalled. 01/01-31/12.
Remarks: Note: toll ticket is valid for 12 hours!.

Odeceixe 31B1
GPS: n37,43750 w8,79833.

30 free. **Location:** Simple. **Surface:** sand. 01/01-31/12.
Distance: 6km on the spot.
Remarks: Beach parking.

Odemira 31B1
GPS: n37,59839 w8,64615.

PT

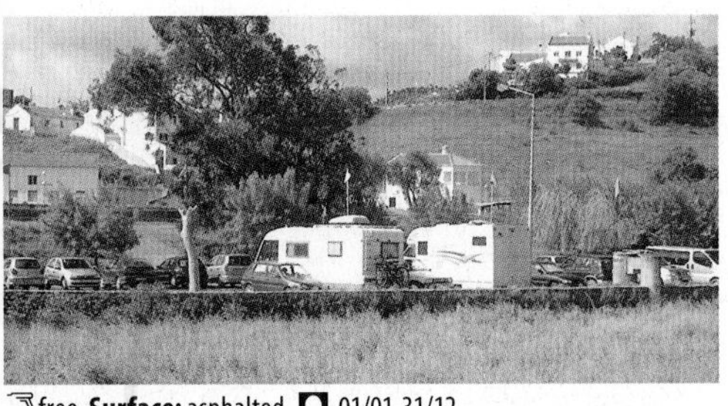

free. **Surface:** asphalted. 01/01-31/12.
Remarks: Along river.

Pedrogão do Alentejo 31C1

Alqueva Camping-Car Park, Estrada nacional 258, Km38,5.
GPS: n38,11705 w7,63571.

25 first night € 7,50, € 6 each additional night Ch.
Location: Rural. **Surface:** gravel. 01/01-31/12.
Distance: 1km 1km 1km 1km on the spot on the spot on the spot.

Ponte de Sôr 30C2

Avenida da Liberdade. **GPS**: n39,24996 w8,00824.

10 free. **Location:** Rural, simple, central, noisy. **Surface:** concrete.
01/01-31/12.
Distance: on the spot 100m 100m.

Porto Covo 31B1

Rua Francisco Albino. **GPS**: n37,85225 w8,78874.
30 free Chfree. **Surface:** metalled. 01/01-31/12.
Distance: centre 250m 750m.

Porto Covo 31B1

Forte do Pessegueiro, Praia da Ilha. **GPS**: n37,49389 w8,47268.

10. **Location:** Simple. **Surface:** sand. 01/01-31/12.
Distance: 4km on the spot.
Remarks: Parking at castle.

Porto Covo 31B1

Praia Grande, Rua do Mar. **GPS**: n37,85054 w8,79299.

15. **Location:** Simple. **Surface:** gravel.
Distance: 1km 100m 100m 1km.
Remarks: Beach parking.

Redondo 30C3

Zona Industrial. **GPS**: n38,64521 w7,54266.

50 free Chfree. **Location:** Urban, simple.
Surface: gravel/sand. 01/01-31/12.
Distance: 400m 400m 100m.

Reguengos de Monsaraz 30C3

N255. **GPS**: n38,43077 w7,53315.

free. **Surface:** asphalted.
Remarks: Parking at swimming pool.

Reguengos de Monsaraz 30C3

Campo 25 de Abril. **GPS**: n38,42150 w7,53534.
€3,50 Ch.
Remarks: Next to fire-station.

Santa Clara-e-Velha 31B1

Barragem de Santa Clara. **GPS**: n37,51303 w8,44024.

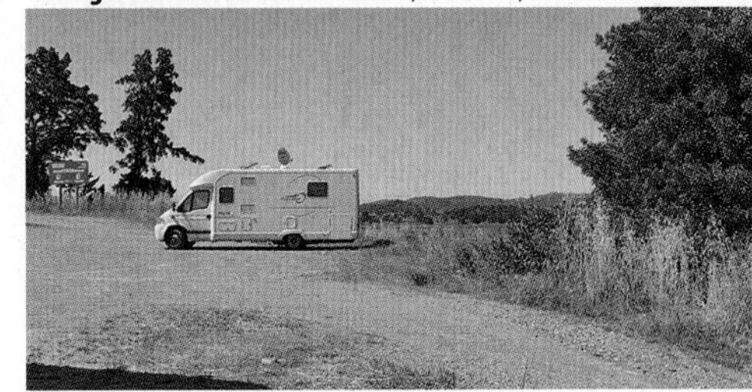

free. **Location:** Isolated. **Surface:** metalled/sand.
Distance: on the spot.
Remarks: Follow 'Pousada/Zona recreitiva balnear'.

Santiago do Cacém 31B1

Rua das Nogueiras. **GPS**: n38,01276 w8,69453.

7 free Chfree. **Surface:** grasstiles.
Distance: 600m 100m 600m.
Remarks: At swimming pool.

Santo António das Areias 30C2

Camping Asseiceira, Asseiceira. **GPS**: n39,41012 w7,34062.
10 € 16-20 Ch WC. **Surface:** grassy.
01/01-31/10.

São Martinho das Amoreiras 31B1

N503. **GPS**: n37,56250 w8,34139.

free. **Surface:** metalled.
Remarks: At barrage.

Terrugem 30C3

Largo Joaquim Codero Vinaigre. **GPS**: n38,84556 w7,34861.

10 free Chfree. **Location:** Rural, simple, quiet.
Surface: asphalted.
Distance: 300m.

Vila Nova de Santo André 31B1

Intermarché. **GPS**: n38,06521 w8,77951.
5 free Chfree €4/2.
Surface: metalled. 01/01-23/12.
Distance: on the spot.
Remarks: At petrol station.

Vila Nova de Santo André 31B1

Praia de Santo André, Lagoa de Santo Andre.
GPS: n38,11396 w8,79552.

±15 free. **Location:** Simple.
Surface: sand. 01/01-23/12.
Distance: 5km on the spot on the spot bakery 1km.
Remarks: Beach parking.

Vila Viçosa 30C3

Avenida do Alandroal. **GPS**: n38,76988 w7,4154.

10 € 3 €2 Ch. **Location:** Rural, simple, quiet.
Surface: asphalted. 01/01-31/12.
Distance: 1km 100m.
Remarks: At fire-station, monitored parking.

Vila Viçosa 30C3

Largo Gago Coutinho. **GPS**: n38,77661 w7,42034.

10 free. **Location:** Urban, simple, central. **Surface:** sand.

PT

01/01-31/12.
Distance: 250m 25m 100m.

Algarve

S Albufeira 31B2

Parque da Galé, Rua do Barranco Vale Rabelho.
GPS: n37,09347 w8,31125.

28 € 8 Ch (28x) included.
Location: Comfortable. **Surface:** unpaved. 01/01-31/12.
Distance: 600m 1,8km 200m 500m.

S Albufeira 31B2

Parque da Palmeira, Rua da Palmeira. **GPS**: n37,09829 w8,24339.

90 € 8 Ch WC €4,50 included.
Location: Urban. **Surface:** gravel. 01/01-31/12.
Distance: Old city 1,7km 7km 1,5km 800m Lidl bus terminal 300m.

S Albufeira 31B2

Park Falesia, Estrada do Alfarmar. **GPS**: n37,09036 w8,16044.

30 € 12 Ch included.
Surface: gravel. 01/01-31/12.
Distance: 4km 500m 1km 500m 200m.
Remarks: Video surveillance.

Tourist information Albufeira:
Posto de Turismo, R. 5 de Outubro 4, www.cm-albufeira.pt. 10-20h.
ZooMarine, N125. Attractions park, dolphinarium, aquarium. 10-20h.

S Alcoutim 31C2

Estrada da Pousada da Juventude. **GPS**: n37,47500 w7,47472.
free Chfree.
Surface: sand. 01/01-31/12.
Distance: 500m 200m.
Remarks: Next to 'Centro de Saude'.

Tourist information Alcoutim:
Fortified city. 9-17.30h.

S Aljezur 31A1

Largo do Mercado. **GPS**: n37,31611 w8,80278.

10 free WCfree. **Location:** Simple. **Surface:** metalled.
01/01-31/12.
Distance: 200m 500m.

Altura 31C2

Rua de Alagoa. **GPS**: n37,17138 w7,49952.

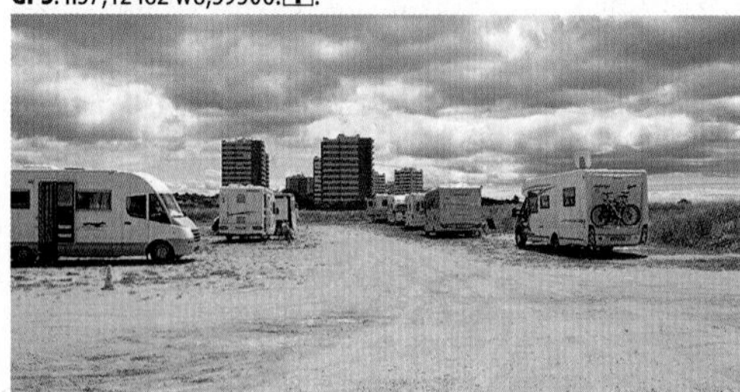

+10 free. **Surface:** unpaved. 01/01-31/12.
Distance: 100m on the spot 100m.
Remarks: Beach parking.

S Alvor 31B2

Zona para autocaravanas, Praia de Alvor.
GPS: n37,12482 w8,59506.

150 € 4 Ch included. **Location:** Central. **Surface:** sand.
01/01-31/12.
Distance: centre 400m 100m on the spot.

S Ameixial 31B2

Estacionamento de Autocaravannas. **GPS**: n37,36539 w7,97165.
10 free Chfree. **Location:** Rural, isolated, quiet.
Surface: unpaved. 01/01-31/12.

S Budens 31A2

Figueira Caravan Park, R. da Fonte.
GPS: n37,07300 w8,84519.
35 € 7,50-10 Ch 10Amp included. **Location:** Rural, comfortable. **Surface:** gravel. 01/01-23/12.
Distance: Budens 2,5km 1,8km 250m Intermarché Budens.
Remarks: Discount longer stays.

Budens 31A2

Praia Boca do Rio. **GPS**: n37,06563 w8,82434.

20 free. **Location:** Simple. **Surface:** sand. 01/01-31/12.
Distance: 2,2km 50m.
Remarks: Forbidden during Summer period.

Cabo de São Vicente 31A2

N268. **GPS**: n37,02361 w8,995.

8 free. **Surface:** metalled. 01/01-31/12.
Distance: Sagres 6km.
Remarks: Parking at lighthouse.

S Caldas de Monchique 31B2

Parque Rural Autocaravanas Vale da Carrasqueira, Barracão 190.
GPS: n37,27667 w8,54333.

14 € 12,50/24h Ch WC included .
Location: Rural, comfortable. **Surface:** gravel.
Distance: on the spot.

Carrapateira 31A2

Praia de Amado. **GPS**: n37,19623 w8,90156.

30 free. **Location:** Simple. **Surface:** gravel.
Distance: Carrapateira 2km 100m on the spot.
Remarks: Beach parking, no camping activities.

Carrapateira 31A2

Praia de Bordeira. **GPS**: n37,19735 w8,90726.

10 free. **Location:** Simple. **Surface:** metalled.
Distance: Carrapateira 2,5km.
Remarks: Parking near the cliffs.

Carvoeiro 31B2

Estr. do Farol. **GPS**: n37,08774 w8,44285.

8 . **Location:** Isolated. **Surface:** sand.
Distance: 500m on the spot.
Remarks: Parking at lighthouse.

Carvoeiro 31B2

Praia Marinha. **GPS**: n37,09026 w8,41254.

free. **Location:** Isolated.
Surface: unpaved. 04/01-31/12.
Distance: 4km on the spot.
Remarks: Beach parking, beautiful view.

S Castro Marim 31C2

Av. Dr. José Afonso Gomes. **GPS**: n37,21984 w7,44434.

PT

± 20 free €2 Ch. **Surface:** gravel. 01/01-31/12 2nd Sa of the month.
Distance: 1,3km 50m.
Remarks: Coins at the shops in the village.

S Falésia 31B2

Algarve Motorhome Park, Praia da Falésia.
GPS: n37,09015 w8,16015.
55 € 8/24h Ch €2 included. **Location:** Luxurious.
Surface: gravel. 01/01-31/12.
Distance: 850m on the spot 250m.

Faro 31B2

Avenida Calouste Gulbenkian.
GPS: n37,02599 w7,94692.
8 free. **Location:** Isolated. **Surface:** metalled. 01/01-31/12.
Distance: city centre 1,5km 600m 600m.
Remarks: Along railwayline.

Faro 31B2

Doca de Faro. **GPS:** n37,02551 w7,94657.

15 free. **Location:** Urban, simple. **Surface:** metalled.
01/01-31/12.
Distance: 600m.

Faro 31B2

Parking Largo de São Francisco. GPS: n37,01132 w7,93184.

±6 free. **Surface:** metalled.
Distance: centre 400m 300m.

S Lagos 31B2

Area de servico, Junto ao Estadio Municipal de Lagos.
GPS: n37,11563 w8,678.

20 € 3, from 4th night € 2,50 €2/100 Ch WC free.
Surface: gravel. 01/01-31/12.
Distance: city centre 2km 7,3km 2,3km McDonalds 450m.
Remarks: Check in and pay at reception stadio, market 1st Saturday each month.

Tourist information Lagos:
M Museu Municipal, Rua General Alberto da Silveira. Regional museum. 9.30-12.30h, 14-17h holiday.

S Manta Rota 31C2

Praia de Manta Rota, Quinta Manta Rota 15.
GPS: n37,16513 w7,52096.

80 € 4,50 Ch €2,50 included. **Surface:** metalled.
16/09-30/06.
Distance: on the spot 6,5km 100m 100m 500m.

S Moncarapacho 31B2

Route 66. GPS: n37,08313 w7,76494.
40 € 8 Ch WC €3 included. **Location:** Rural, comfortable, isolated. **Surface:** gravel/sand. 01/01-31/12.
Distance: 2,5km 3km on the spot.

S Moncarapacho 31B2

Caravanas Algarve. GPS: n37,09502 w7,77427.

20 € 8,50 Ch WC .
Surface: gravel.
01/01-31/12.
Distance: 1km beach 6km 1km on the spot on the spot.

S Odeleite 31C2

Almada D´Ouro Club-Algarve, M1063, Alcarias-Odeleite.
GPS: n37,33187 w7,46865.

10 + 20 € 4,50 €2,50 Ch €2,50 €5 included.
Location: Isolated, quiet. **Surface:** gravel. 01/01-31/12.
Distance: Odeleite 2,3km on the spot.
Remarks: At hunting club, discount longer stays.

S Paderne 31B2

Motorhome Friends. GPS: n37,15643 w8,20972.

16 € 4,50 Ch (9x)€3 WC €5 included.
Location: Rural. **Surface:** gravel. 01/01-31/12.
Distance: 1km 10km on the spot.
Remarks: Bicycle rental € 5, car rental € 15.

S Paderne 31B2

Cm 1177 920N. **GPS:** n37,16801 w8,20897.

12 free Ch free. **Surface:** metalled. 01/01-31/12.
Distance: 1km 1km.

S Pêra 31B2

Mikki's Place, Sitio das Arreias. **GPS:** n37,12781 w8,32305.

100 € 8-10,50 Ch €2,50/day WC on demand included. **Location:** Rural, comfortable, isolated, quiet.
Surface: gravel/metalled. 01/01-31/12.
Distance: 2km 3km on the spot 2km.

S Pêra 31B2

KM 64 Parque de Autocaravanas, ES125, km64.
GPS: n37,12420 w8,32607.
50 € 3 €2 Ch included €3.
Surface: asphalted. 01/06-01/10.
Distance: 1,5km 4km.

S Pereiro 31C2

Parque de autocaravanismo do Pereiro, Pereiro.
GPS: n37,44695 w7,5924.
16 free Ch free. **Surface:** unpaved. 01/01-31/12.
Distance: 500m.

S Portimão 31B2

Praia da Rocha, Avenida Rio Arade,. **GPS:** n37,11898 w8,53037.

200 € 2,50 €2/100liter Ch free.
Surface: metalled/sand.
Distance: on the spot 100m on the spot 200m on the spot.

Portimão 31B2

Rue Três Castelos. **GPS:** n37,11969 w8,54723.

25 free. **Surface:** asphalted.
Distance: Praia da Rocha 700m sandy beach 250m 1km.

S Quarteira 31B2

Estrada Fonte Santa, M527-2. **GPS:** n37,07322 w8,07716.

100 € 2/24h €2 Ch €2.
Surface: gravel.
01/01-31/12.
Distance: 2km 6,8km sandy beach 2,5km 50m 150m Lidl on the spot.
Remarks: Tue 17h-Wed 17h adjacent parking because of Gypsy Market.

S Sagres 31A2

Fortaleze de Sagres. GPS: n37,00523 w8,94545.

PT

50 free WC. **Surface:** asphalted. 01/01-31/12.
Distance: 500m.
Remarks: At fort-castle.

S São Bartolomeu de Messines 31B2

Camperstop Messines. GPS: n37,27979 w8,24133.

40 € 6, 01/07-31/08 € 7,50 Ch WC €4/4 included.
Location: Rural, quiet. **Surface:** gravel. 01/01-31/12.
Distance: 6,5km 6,4km 1,2km.
Remarks: Shopping service.

S São Bartolomeu de Messines 31B2

Rua António Aleixo. **GPS:** n37,25514 w8,2847.

4 free Ch free. **Location:** Rural. **Surface:** gravel.
01/01-31/12.
Distance: centre 150m 2,7km.
Remarks: Monday regional market.

S Silves 31B2

Algarve Motorhome Park Silves, N124. **GPS:** n37,18722 w8,45158.

50 € 5/24h Ch €2 included. 01/01-31/12.
Distance: 1km 800m.

S Silves 31B2

Club Autocaravana Vacaria, N124. **GPS:** n37,21834 w8,36924.

15 € 5 Ch €1/24h WC €1 included.
Location: Rural, comfortable, isolated. **Surface:** gravel/metalled.
01/01-31/12.
Distance: 9km 100m.

S Silves 31B2

Parque do Castelo, Rua do Encalhe. **GPS:** n37,19388 w8,43614.
40 first night € 5, € 4,50 each additional night, >10m + € 1
Ch €2,50/24h,6Amp WC €0,50 included. **Surface:** gravel.
01/09-31/05.
Distance: centre 500m 500m Lidl 550m on the spot.

S Silves 31B2

Estação de serviço para autocaravanas municipal.
GPS: n37,18527 w8,44551.
€ 3 Ch free. **Surface:** gravel. 01/01-31/12.
Distance: centre 650m 650m 450m.

Silves 31B2

Barregem do Arade, N124-3. **GPS:** n37,23960 w8,37699.

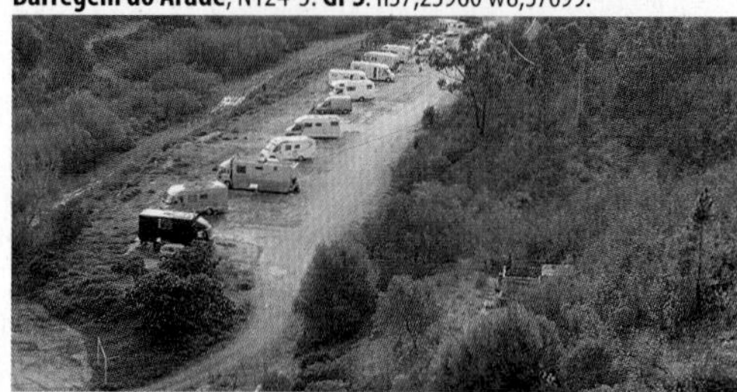

10 free. **Location:** Isolated.
Surface: sand.
Distance: Silves 10km.

Tourist information Silves:
Museu Municipal de Arqueologia. Archeological findings.
Castello. 9-18h.
Festival da cerveja. Beer festival. July.

S Tavira 31B2

Parque de Autocaravanes. GPS: n37,13637 w7,64013.

20 € 9,90 Ch WC €2 included.
Surface: grassy/gravel. 15/09-15/06 summer.
Distance: 1km.
Remarks: Swimming pool.

Tourist information Tavira:
Castello. Mo-Fri 8-17.30h.

Vila do Bispo 31A2

Praia da Barriga, N1265. **GPS:** n37,09970 w8,94445.

free. **Surface:** asphalted.
Distance: Vila do Bispo 3,8km on the spot.
Remarks: Beach parking.

S Vila do Bispo 31A2

Sagres, Cerro da Moita. **GPS:** n37,02278 w8,94583.
550 € 30-38 Ch WC . 01/01-31/12.
Distance: 2km on the spot on the spot 500m.

S Vila Real de Santo António 31C2

Avenida de República. **GPS:** n37,19955 w7,4153.

70 € 4,50 Ch €5/24h included. **Surface:** metalled/sand.
01/01-31/12.
Distance: 500m on the spot.

Romania

Capital: Bucharest
Government: semi presidential republic
Official Language: Romanian
Population: 21,666,000 (2015)
Area: 238,391 Km²

General information
Dialling code: 0040
General emergency: 112
Currency: Leu (RON)
€ 1 = 4,52 RON, 1 RON = € 0,22
£1 = 5,25 RON, 1 RON = £0.19 (November 2016)
Credit card are mostly accepted in the main cities.

Regulations for overnight stays
Wild camping is allowed with permission from land owner/manager or local government.

Additional public holidays 2017
January 6 Epiphany
May 1 Labour Day
August 15 Assumption of Mary
November 1 All Saints' Day
November 30 Saint Andrew's Day
December 1 National Holiday

Time Zone
Winter (Standard Time) GMT+2
Summer (DST) GMT+3

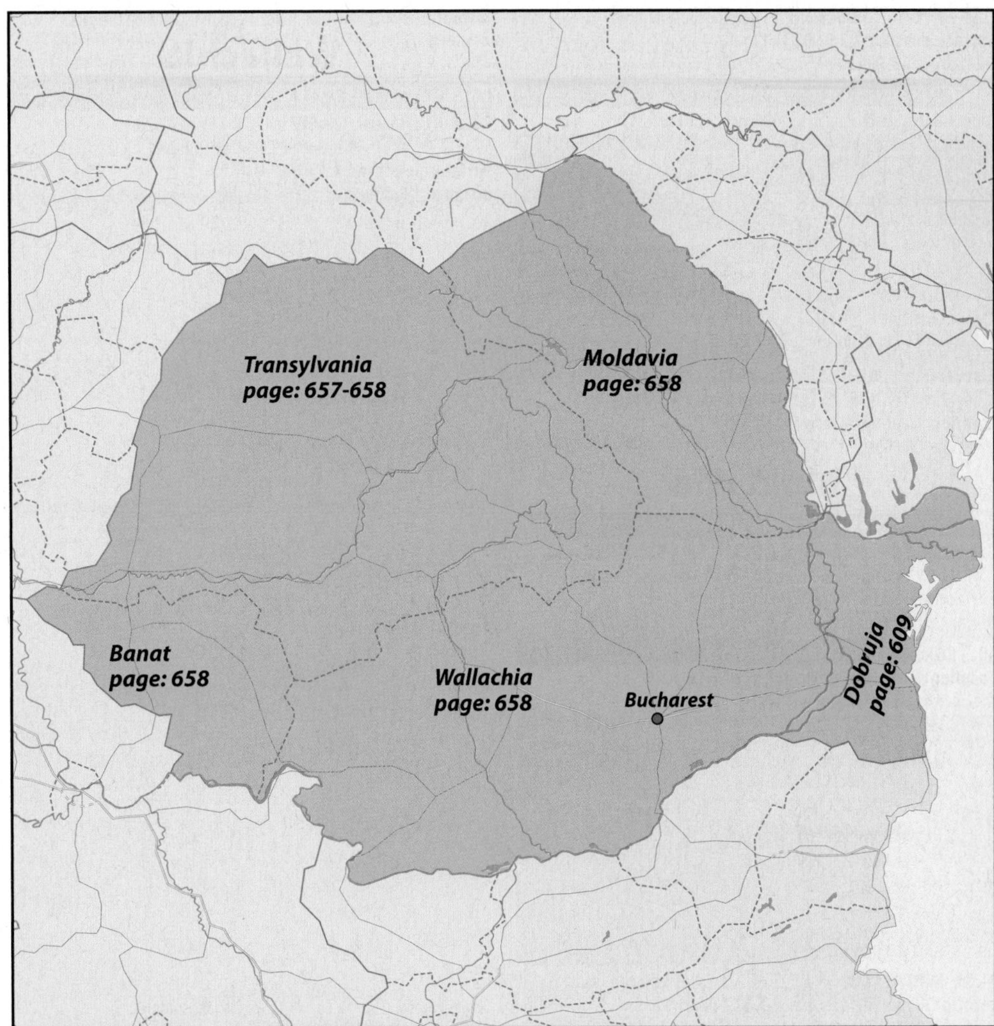

RO

Transylvania

Aurel Vlaicu 40B2

Camping Aurel Vlaicu, Str. Pricipala 155. **GPS**: n45,91424 e23,27938.
€ 12,50 Ch € 2,50 WC included. **Location:** Rural.
Surface: grassy. 15/04-30/09.
Distance: 250m 250m 100m 300m 250m.

Baile Felix 40A2

Camping Apollo. **GPS**: n46,99608 e21,98056.
€ 14 Ch WC included. 01/01-31/12.
Distance: 100m 400m 100m.

Blăjel 40B2

Camping Doua Lumi, Strada Tudor Vladimirescu 87-89.
GPS: n46,21032 e24,32478.

15 € 13 Ch € 3 WC included. **Surface:** grassy.
01/04-15/10.
Distance: 10km.

Borşa 40B1

Borşa Turism, Strada Pietroasa 9. **GPS**: n47,64914 e24,66801.
4 € 9 Ch WC € 3,50 included. **Location:** Urban.
Surface: gravel. 01/01-31/12.
Distance: 1km 1,5km 900m.

Bran 40C2

Vampire camping, Soholstr. **GPS**: n45,52787 e25,37183.
€ 15 Ch € 3,50 WC included. **Location:** Rural.
Surface: grassy. 01/04-01/11.
Distance: 650m.

Cârța 40B2

Camping de Oude Wilg, Str. Prundului 311. **GPS**: n45,78332 e24,56700.
€ 11 € 2,50 Ch € 2,50 WC included € 3,50.
Location: Rural. **Surface:** grassy.
Distance: 500m 500m on the spot on the spot.

Gârbova 40B2

Poarta Oilor, Str. Eminescu 573. **GPS**: n45,85933 e23,72019.
€ 15 Ch WC included. **Location:** Rural.
Surface: grassy. 01/05-30/09.

Gilău 40B2

Camping Eldorado. **GPS**: n46,76748 e23,35381.
€ 13 Ch € 2,50 WC included. **Surface:** grassy.
15/04-15/10.
Distance: 15km 50m 750m.

Miniş 40A2

Camping Route Roemenië, Minis 298. **GPS**: n46,13356 e21,59788.

from € 12,50 € 1,50 € 2,50 Ch € 2,75 WC included € 4.
Location: Rural. **Surface:** grassy. 15/04-15/09.
Distance: 1km.

Mureş 40B2

Camping Mustang, Câmpu Cetăţii 16/A. **GPS**: n46,66750 e25,00361.
€ 11,50 Ch WC € 2,50 included. **Location:** Rural.
Surface: grassy. 01/04-31/10.
Distance: 3km 500m 400m.

Nireş 40B2

Camping Zwaluwnest, Com. Mica 42A. **GPS**: n47,11918 e23,96788.

€ 11 Ch € 2,50 WC included € 4.
Location: Rural. **Surface:** grassy. 01/04-15/10.

Ocna Sibiului 40B2

Strada Mihai Viteazul 90. **GPS**: n45,88040 e24,04437.
20 € 5 € 1 € 2. **Surface:** grassy. 01/04-01/10.
Distance: 800m.

Remetea 40A2

Camping Turul, Bihor 8. **GPS**: n46,73443 e22,34436.
€ 10 Ch € 2,50 WC included. **Location:** Rural.
Surface: grassy.
Distance: 100m 700m 900m.

Richis 40B2

Camping La Curtea Richvini. **GPS**: n46,09797 e24,48066.
€ 10 Ch € 3 WC included € 4. **Location:** Rural.
Surface: grassy.

Vişeu de Sus 40B1

Gara CFF Mocanita, Strada Cerbului 5. **GPS**: n47,71461 e24,44282.

€ 9 Ch WCincluded according consumption.
Surface: metalled. 01/01-31/12.
Distance: 1,5km.

Zărnești 40C2

Alpin Ranch, Strada Pinului 13. **GPS**: n45,57861 e25,34389.

€ 12 Ch WC included.
Location: Rural. **Surface:** grassy.
Distance: 800m.

Moldavia

Dărmănești 40C2

Camperland, Calea Trotusului 272. **GPS**: n46,40150 e26,48267.
€ 15 Ch WC € 3,25 included.
Surface: grassy. 15/04-15/10.
Distance: 400m.

Fundu Moldovei 40B1

Camping de Vuurplaats, Strada Principale 130.
GPS: n47,53417 e25,41528.

24 € 14,75 Ch € 2,75 WC € 4 included.
Location: Rural. **Surface:** grassy. 01/04-01/10.
Distance: on the spot on the spot.
Remarks: Barbecue place.

Dobruja

Jupiter 40D3

Camping Popas Zodiac, Gala Galaction str 49.
GPS: n43,85860 e28,59960.
€ 16,50 - € 19,25 Ch included.
Surface: grassy. 01/05-31/10.
Distance: 200m 200m 100m.

Murighiol 40D2

La doi Sturioni, Str. Portului 2. **GPS**: n45,03632 e29,16677.

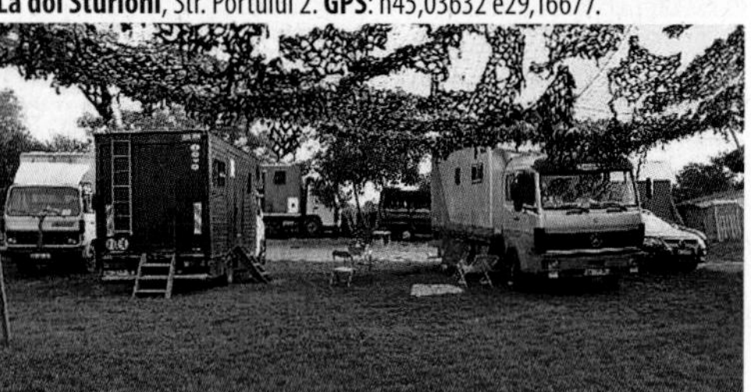

10 € 12 Ch included. **Location:** Simple.
Surface: unpaved. 01/05-01/10.
Distance: 200m 200m.

Murighiol 40D2

Pension Laguna Albastra. **GPS**: n45,03824 e29,18161.
25 € 12 Ch included. **Location:** Simple. **Surface:** grassy.
01/04-15/10.
Distance: on the spot on the spot on the spot.

Navodari 40D3

GPM Camping Holiday. **GPS**: n44,27467 e28,61774.
30 € 16 Chincluded . 25/04-30/09.
Distance: on the spot on the spot on the spot.

Banat

Mehadia 40B3

Camping Hercules, DN6. **GPS**: n44,86918 e22,38774.
5 € 15 Ch WC.

Distance: on the spot 500m on the spot on the spot.

Wallachia

Paclele Mici 40C2

Popasul La Hangar, 108. **GPS**: n45,34711 e26,70928.
5 € 7 Ch included. **Location:** Simple.
Surface: gravel/sand. 01/01-31/12.
Distance: on the spot.

RO

Sweden

Capital: Stockholm
Government: parliamentary constitutional monarchy
Official Language: Swedish
Population: 9,801,500 (2015)
Area: 450,295 Km^2

General information
Dialling code: 0046
General emergency: 112
Currency: Swedish Krona (SEK)
€ 1 = SEK 9,83, SEK 1 = € 0,10
£1 = SEK 11,42, SEK 1 = £0.09 (November 2016)
Credit cards are accepted almost everywhere.

Regulations for overnight stays
In general wild camping is allowed, not in private gardens and agricultural land.

Camping Key Europe is obligatory when using campsites: the card can be purchased at any campsite for SEK 160 (± € 16,50/ £14.50), valid for one year.

Additional public holidays 2017
April 14 Good Friday
April 17 Easter Monday
May 1 Labour Day
June 6 National day
June 23-24 Midsummer
November 1 All Saints' Day

Time Zone
Winter (Standard Time) GMT+1
Summer (DST) GMT+2

Norrbotten page: 659-660
Västerbotten page: 659
Västernorrland page: 666
Jämtland page: 666
Gävleborg page: 666
Dalarna page: 666
Uppsala page: 660
Västmanland page: 666
Stockholm page: 659
Värmland page: 665-666
Stockholm
Södermanland page: 6
Västra Götaland page: 665
Östergötland page: 660
Jönköping page: 660
Gotland page: 663
Kalmar page: 661-663
Halland page: 665
Blekinge page: 663
Skåne page: 663-664

Stockholm

S Norrtälje 4D3
Nässelgrundet 7. **GPS**: n59,68147 e18,81752.
3 SEK 200. **Surface:** grassy.
Distance: Norrtälje 19km on the spot on the spot.
Remarks: Canoe and boat rental.

S Skarpnäck 5G1
Ställplatsstockholm, Flatens Skogsväg 30.
GPS: n59,24822 e18,16159.
48 SEK 180 Ch.
Distance: Stockholm 15km.

S Stockholm 5G1
Långholmens Husbilscamping Stockholm, Skutskepparvägen 1.
GPS: n59,32021 e18,03200.
76 SEK 250, 19/06-30/08 SEK 280 Ch included WC SEK 5.
Location: Urban. **Surface:** metalled. 13/05-13/09.
Distance: 4km 200m 500m.

S Stockholm 5G1
Tantolundens Husbilscamping Stockholm, Ringvägen 24.
GPS: n59,31241 e18,05299.
14 SEK 250, 19/06-30/08 SEK 280 WC included.
Location: Urban. **Surface:** gravel. 01/01-31/12.
Distance: 5km 2km 350m.

Stockholm 5G1
Strandvägen. **GPS**: n59,33124 e18,08595.
SEK 15/h, overnight stay free. **Surface:** asphalted.
Distance: 1km on the spot 300m.
Remarks: At the quay.

Västerbotten

Byske 4D1
E45. **GPS**: n64,94809 e21,18009.
free. **Location:** Rural, simple, isolated, noisy.
Distance: 1,7km 1,5km 1,7km.

Klimpfjäll 4C1
Stekenjokk. **GPS**: n65,09030 e14,45897.
free. **Location:** Isolated, quiet. **Surface:** unpaved.
With snow.
Distance: on the spot on the spot on the spot.

Marsfjäll 4C1
Trappstegsforsen. **GPS**: n64,95526 e15,46639.
free. **Location:** Isolated, quiet. **Surface:** gravel.
Distance: 7km on the spot.

S Sävar 4D1
Sävar Rastplats, Skomakarvägen. **GPS**: n63,89191 e20,53027.

free Ch free. **Surface:** asphalted.
Distance: 2km 100m 1,7km.

S Skellefteå 4D1
Ställplats Campus, Laboratorgränd.
GPS: n64,74601 e20,95595.
10 SEK 100 WC included.
Location: Urban.
Surface: metalled.
20/06-14/08.
Distance: 1km on the spot on the spot 100m on the spot.

S Tärnaby 4C1
Joeström. **GPS**: n65,74384 e15,08882.
voluntary contribution. **Location:** Rural. **Surface:** grassy.
Distance: 10km on the spot on the spot.

S Vilhelmina 4C1
Meselefors Rastplats, E45. **GPS**: n64,43398 e16,78733.
2 free Ch free.
Distance: on the spot on the spot.
Remarks: Max. 12h.

Vormsele 4C1
Blåviksjöns, Blå vägen. **GPS**: n64,82994 e18,03335.
free. **Location:** Isolated, quiet. **Surface:** asphalted.
Distance: Vormsele 47km on the spot on the spot.

Norrbotten

S Gällivare 3B3
Lappeasuando. **GPS**: n67,49093 e21,12025.

free Ch WC free. **Location:** Isolated, quiet.
Surface: asphalted.
Distance: Gällivare 56km 200m 200m.

S Jävrebyn 4D1
Jävrefyrens väg. **GPS**: n65,14339 e21,50862.

SEK 50 Ch.
Location: Rural. **Surface:** grassy/gravel.
Distance: on the spot on the spot 500m.

Jokkmokk 3B3

Polcirkeln. GPS: n66,55058 e19,76375.
SEK 100 Ch. SEK 40 WC included. **Location:** Rural.
Surface: asphalted/grassy.
Distance: 2km on the spot.

Jokkmokk 3B3

Laponia Rastplats, E45. **GPS:** n66,64258 e19,82465.

free. **Surface:** grassy/gravel.
Distance: 5km 100m.

Moskosel 3B3

E45. **GPS:** n65,95231 e19,51979.
free Ch free.
Distance: 10km on the spot on the spot.
Remarks: Along river.

Nikkala 3C3

Båtklubben Bothnia, Haparandahamn 65.
GPS: n65,77154 e23,90442.
SEK 100 SEK 40. **Surface:** asphalted/grassy.
Distance: on the spot on the spot.
Remarks: Borrow cycles for free, use of sauna against payment.

Övre Soppero 3B2

Ryssäjoki Naturrastplats. GPS: n68,15435 e21,78256.
. **Location:** Rural, isolated. **Surface:** unpaved.
Distance: 8km on the spot on the spot.

Porjus 3B3

Strömgatan. **GPS:** n66,95671 e19,80798.
free. **Surface:** asphalted.
Distance: 500m.
Remarks: In front of fire-station.

Vittangi 3B2

Rastplats Suptallen. GPS: n67,66938 e21,40521.
free.
Distance: 15km.

Uppsala

Älvkarleby 4D3

Älvkarleby Turist & Konferenshotell, Västanåvägen 54.
GPS: n60,56518 e17,43796.
20 SEK 100 WC.
Distance: 100m on the spot.
Remarks: Pay at reception.

Öregrund 4D3

Kyrkogatan. **GPS:** n60,33958 e18,43672.
5. **Surface:** asphalted.
Distance: 200m on the spot on the spot 350m 200m.

Öregrund 4D3

GPS: n60,34091 e18,44107.
3 free free WC. **Surface:** asphalted.

Distance: on the spot on the spot on the spot 100m 200m.

Södermanland

Eskilstuna 5F1

Sundbyholms Gästhamn, Sundbyholm. **GPS:** n59,44749 e16,62593.
6 SEK 150 SEK 40.
Distance: on the spot on the spot on the spot on the spot.
Remarks: Next to castle.

Mariefred 5F1

Mariefreds gästhamnen, Gripsholmsvägen.
GPS: n59,25793 e17,22160.
4 SEK 260 WC. **Surface:** asphalted.
Distance: on the spot 200m 200m.

Mariefred 5F1

Statoil, Storgatan 18. **GPS:** n59,25944 e17,21805.
2. **Surface:** asphalted.

Nyköping 5F1

Nyköpings hamn, Spelhagsvägen. **GPS:** n58,74460 e17,01524.
10 free Ch.
Distance: 1km.
Remarks: Max. 2 days, service 100m.

Oxelösund 5F1

Femöre Marina, Fiskehamnsvägen 12. **GPS:** n58,65830 e17,11123.
15 SEK 150 Ch (10x)SEK 50. **Surface:** gravel.
Distance: 3km on the spot on the spot on the spot.

Strängnäs 5F1

Strängnäs Gästhamn, Storgatan 38. **GPS:** n59,37860 e17,02599.
8 SEK 260. 01/05-30/09.
Distance: on the spot on the spot on the spot 200m.
Remarks: Max. 48h.

Trosa 5G1

Trosa Gästhamn, Uddbergagatan 1. **GPS:** n58,89090 e17,55360.
8 SEK 160 Ch included WC.
Distance: on the spot on the spot 200m 1km.
Remarks: Use of sauna against payment.

Östergötland

Borensberg 5F1

Kaffeteriet, Magasinsgatan 7. **GPS:** n58,55885 e15,27995.
SEK 200 included.
Distance: 550m on the spot on the spot on the spot 550m.

Borensberg 5F1

Glasbruket, Kanalvägen. **GPS:** n58,55909 e15,30322.
8 SEK 185 (8x)SEK 30 WC. **Surface:** grassy. 01/05-30/09.
Distance: 1,5km 1,5km.
Remarks: At Göta Canal.

Linköping 5F2

Flygvapenmuseum. GPS: n58,41107 e15,52588.
20 free.
Distance: 1km 1km.
Remarks: Parking museum.

Motala 5E1

Södra Hamnen, Fabriksgatan 12 H. **GPS:** n58,52979 e15,03811.
SEK 180 Ch WC included. **Surface:** grassy.
01/01-31/12.
Distance: 1km on the spot on the spot 500m.

Motala 5E1

Berggrens Källare, Verkstadsvägen 91. **GPS:** n58,55550 e15,07820.
6 SEK 150 SEK 50. 01/05-31/08.
Distance: on the spot on the spot.
Remarks: Nearby sluices.

Motala 5E1

Café Mallboden, Varvsgatan 17. **GPS:** n58,54829 e15,06689.
5 SEK 200 included. **Surface:** grassy. 01/05-30/09.
Remarks: At Göta Canal.

Norrköping 5F1

Albrektsvägen. **GPS:** n58,58403 e16,20064.
SEK 60. **Surface:** asphalted.
Distance: 1km 300m 600m.
Remarks: At swimming pool.

Norsholm 5F1

Kapten Bille´s, Slussvägen. **GPS:** n58,50741 e15,97546.
14 SEK 185 WC. 01/04-30/09.
Distance: on the spot on the spot.
Remarks: At Göta Canal.

Ödeshög 5E2

Hästholmens hamn, Hamngatan. **GPS:** n58,27904 e14,63522.
5 SEK 120. **Surface:** asphalted.
Distance: on the spot on the spot on the spot.

Skänninge 5E2

Gripenbergs gårdsbutik, Gripenberg 1. **GPS:** n58,40659 e15,08026.
SEK 100 SEK 25 WC included. **Location:** Isolated.
Surface: grassy.
Distance: 1,5km 2km 1,5km.

Söderköping 5F1

Bergaskolan, Tingshusgatan. **GPS:** n58,48033 e16,32952.
10 SEK 120 Ch. **Surface:** gravel. 15/06-15/08.
Distance: 350m 350m.
Remarks: At former school, service on campsite.

Söderköping 5F1

Kanalmagasinet AB, Mem. **GPS:** n58,47923 e16,41422.
4 SEK 185. **Surface:** gravel.
Distance: on the spot on the spot.
Remarks: Pay at Kanalmagasinet.

Vadstena 5E2

Vadstena Slott, Järnvägsgatan. **GPS:** n58,44569 e14,88167.
SEK 100, May-Sep SEK 130 Ch SEK 30 WC.
Surface: grassy. Service: winter.

Vreta Kloster 5F1

Bergs Slussar Vandrarhem, Oscars Slussar 2.
GPS: n58,48524 e15,52970.
25 SEK 185 WC. **Surface:** grassy. 01/04-30/09.
Remarks: Nearby sluices, at Göta Canal.

Jönköping

Bredaryd 5E3

Pelles, Sunnaryd Solbacka. **GPS:** n57,01704 e13,69058.
2 SEK 200 WC SEK 50. **Surface:** grassy/gravel.
01/01-31/12.
Remarks: Breakfast-service.

Gränna 5E2

BauerGårdens, Bunn. **GPS:** n57,93629 e14,49227.
100 SEK 200 Ch (70x)WC included.
10/04-01/12.

Gränna 5E2

Gränna Hamn, Hamnvägen. **GPS:** n58,02728 e14,46070.
30 SEK 180 Ch (20x)included.
Distance: 800m 100m 100m 400m on the spot on the spot.
Remarks: Nights closed with barrier.

Gränna 5E2

Gränna Hamn, Amiralsvägen. **GPS:** n58,02868 e14,45960.
SEK 120. **Surface:** asphalted.
Distance: 100m 100m 100m on the spot on the spot.

Hult 5F2

Ställplats Lyckarps, Hultvägen. **GPS:** n57,63577 e15,09830.

19 € 10 Ch included (15x)SEK 3. **Location:** Rural, isolated.
Surface: grassy/gravel. 01/05-31/10.
Distance: 8km on the spot 200m.

Jönköping 5E2

Statoil Hyltena, Hyltena 50. **GPS:** n57,66554 e14,18237.
17 SEK 99 WC. **Surface:** asphalted.
Distance: Jönköping 15km 500m.

Rydaholm 5E3

Skeda Strand, Skeda gård 1. **GPS:** n57,03714 e14,18198.
10 SEK 100 (6x)SEK 30 WC included. **Surface:** gravel.
Distance: on the spot on the spot.
Remarks: Boat rental.

Rydaholm 5E3

Lady & Lufsen Ställplats Husbil, Krusebacken.
GPS: n56,98089 e14,22967.
10 SEK 100 Ch SEK 15. **Surface:** grassy.
15/05-15/09.
Distance: 5km on the spot.

SE

Remarks: Max. 2 nights.

Vrigstad 5E3

Timjan Café & Restaurang, Flahult 2. **GPS**: n57,31552 e14,29112.
6 SEK 100 SEK50.
Distance: on the spot on the spot.

Kronoberg

Växjö 5E3

Askelövsgatan. **GPS**: n56,87743 e14,79634.
5 SEK 5/h, overnight stay free. **Surface:** asphalted.
Distance: 500m 350m 300m.

Kalmar

Bläsinge 5F3

Bläsinge Hamn. **GPS**: n56,62015 e16,70076.

15 SEK 100 (14x) WC included .
Location: Rural, simple, isolated, quiet. **Surface:** grassy/gravel.
01/01-31/12.
Distance: on the spot on the spot on the spot 15km.
Remarks: Money in envelope in mail box.

Borgholm 5F3

Stug o Fiske, Verkstadsgatan 5. **GPS**: n56,86841 e16,66309.

29 SEK 150 free Ch (20x) WC included.
Location: Rural, comfortable, quiet. **Surface:** grassy/gravel.
24/03-10/10.
Distance: 2km on the spot on the spot 2km.
Remarks: Pay at restaurant.

Borgholm 5F3

Lindby Boden, Lindby Bygata 23. **GPS**: n56,81571 e16,70548.

50 SEK 70 included (5x). **Location:** Rural, simple, isolated, quiet. **Surface:** grassy. 01/01-31/12.
Distance: Borgholm 10km 10km 10km on the spot on the spot.
Remarks: Money in envelope in mail box.

Borgholm 5F3

Slot Borgholm, Sollidenvägen 5. **GPS**: n56,86975 e16,64785.

20 SEK 100. **Location:** Rural, simple, isolated, quiet.
Surface: gravel. 01/01-31/12.
Distance: 2km 2km 2km.

Remarks: Service 2,5km GPS N56,88224 E16,66190.

Borgholm 5F3

Hamnvägen. **GPS**: n56,88301 e16,64790.

40 SEK 140 Ch free WC included .
Location: Urban, simple, central, quiet. **Surface:** grassy.
01/01-31/12.
Distance: on the spot on the spot on the spot 200m 200m.
Remarks: Service 500m.

Byxelkrok 5F2

Byxelkrok, Neptunivägen. **GPS**: n57,34969 e17,03601.

15 SEK 100. **Location:** Rural, simple, isolated, quiet.
Surface: forest soil.
Distance: 4km 100m 100m 4km 4km.
Remarks: Money in envelope in mail box.

Byxelkrok 5F2

Oskarshamn, Neptunivägen. **GPS**: n57,32767 e17,00812.

8 SEK 140 Ch WC included.
Location: Rural, simple, noisy. **Surface:** gravel. 15/05-30/09.
Distance: 500m on the spot on the spot on the spot 500m.
Remarks: Check in at harbourmaster.

Degerhamn 5F3

Gräsgårds hamn. **GPS**: n56,31722 e16,53167.

25 SEK 80 included (20x). **Location:** Rural, simple, isolated, quiet. **Surface:** grassy. 01/01-31/12.
Distance: 15km on the spot 15km 15km.
Remarks: Pay in at kiosk.

Degerhamn 5F3

Degerhamns Ställplats & Hamn. **GPS**: n56,35723 e16,40734.

40 free. **Location:** Rural, simple, isolated, quiet. **Surface:** grassy.
15/04-18/10.
Distance: 1,5km on the spot on the spot 300m 1,5km.

Färjestaden 5F3

Köpsenter, Brovägen. **GPS**: n56,65293 e16,47138.

17 free. **Location:** Urban, simple, central, noisy. **Surface:** asphalted.
01/01-31/12.
Distance: 500m 50m 50m 50m on the spot.
Remarks: At shopping centre, max. 1 night.

Figeholm 5F2

Figeholms Båtklubb, Vasakajen. **GPS**: n57,37267 e16,55416.

8 SEK 150 Ch (8x) SEK 20/24h WC included.
Location: Rural, comfortable, central, quiet. **Surface:** asphalted.
01/01-31/12.
Distance: 100m on the spot 200m.
Remarks: Pay at harbourmaster.

Fliseryd 5F3

Ställplats Jungnerholmarna, Jungnerholmarna.
GPS: n57,13000 e16,25587.

10 SEK 90 Ch (6x) WC included.
Location: Rural, comfortable, central, quiet. **Surface:** grassy.
01/01-31/12.
Distance: 500m on the spot on the spot 1,5km on the spot.
Remarks: Check in and key electricity at supermarket.

Grönhögen 36A1

Ventlinge Stellplats, Ventlinge 118. **GPS**: n56,28372 e16,40681.

20 SEK 120 Ch (8x) WC included.
Location: Rural, comfortable, quiet.

SE

Surface: grassy. 01/04-01/11.
Distance: 1,5km 300m 300m 1,5km 1,5km.
Remarks: At golf court, farm products.

Grönhögen 36A1

Grönhögens hamn, Fiskaregränd. **GPS**: n56,26652 e16,39722.

30 SEK 150 Ch (28x) WC included SEK 15.
Location: Rural, comfortable, quiet. **Surface:** grassy.
01/01-31/12.
Distance: on the spot 50m on the spot 500m 500m on the spot on the spot.
Remarks: Golf court 1km.

Hjorted 5F2

Vattencafé "Vattenfronten", Blankaholm.
GPS: n57,59028 e16,52972.

8 SEK 140 included SEK 40/24h WC. **Location:** Rural.
Surface: grassy/gravel. 01/01-31/12.
Distance: 300m on the spot on the spot 300m.
Remarks: To be paid at bar.

Kalmar 5F3

Ölandskajen, ölandskajen 1. **GPS**: n56,66030 e16,36130.

18 SEK 160 SEK 40/24h WC included. **Location:** Urban, simple, central, noisy.
Surface: asphalted.
01/01-31/12 water disconnected in winter.
Distance: 200m 1km on the spot 200m 200m on the spot.
Remarks: Pay and coins at tourist office, historical centre.

Kalmar 5F3

Svinö. **GPS**: n56,68111 e16,38079.

20 free Ch WC free. **Location:** Rural, simple, isolated, noisy.
Surface: gravel. 01/01-31/12 Service: winter.
Distance: 4km 200m on the spot on the spot 4km 4km 5km on the spot.

Kalmar 5F3

Elevatorkajen, Skeppsbrogatan 49. **GPS**: n56,66360 e16,37060.

6 SEK 5/h, overnight stay free.
Location: Urban, simple, central, quiet.
Surface: asphalted.
01/01-31/12.
Distance: 100m 1km on the spot 200m 200m 400m.
Remarks: Service 4km GPS N56,68111 E16,38079, historical centre.

Köpingsvik 5F3

Kårehamns Fiskaffär. GPS: n56,95623 e16,88755.

40 SEK 140 Ch (25x) WC included. **Location:** Rural, comfortable, isolated, quiet. **Surface:** gravel.
01/01-31/12.
Distance: 15km 100m on the spot on the spot 15km.
Remarks: Service 200m.

Löttorp 5G2

Böda, Bödahamnsvägen. **GPS**: n57,24052 e17,07503.

50 SEK 140 Ch (10x) SEK 20/24h WC included.
Location: Rural, comfortable, quiet. **Surface:** grassy/gravel.
01/01-31/12.
Distance: 1km on the spot on the spot 1km.

Mönsterås 5F3

Hamnen Mönsterås, Hamngatan. **GPS**: n57,04151 e16,44874.

13 SEK 125 Ch (8x) WC included.
Location: Urban, comfortable, quiet. **Surface:** asphalted.
01/01-31/12.
Distance: 100m on the spot on the spot 100m.
Remarks: At the quay, code internet at tourist office.

Nabelund 5G2

Nabelundsvägen 1. **GPS**: n57,34882 e17,08904.

40 SEK 140 Ch (4x) WC included. **Location:** Rural, simple, isolated, quiet. **Surface:** grassy/gravel.
01/01-31/12.
Distance: 7km on the spot on the spot 7km 7km.
Remarks: Pay at harbourmaster.

Oskarshamn 5F2

Oskarshamns gästhamn, Norra Strandgatan.
GPS: n57,26768 e16,45516.

10 SEK 100-150 Ch WC included.
Location: Urban, simple, central, noisy.
Surface: asphalted.
01/01-31/12.
Distance: 500m on the spot on the spot 500m 500m 400m.
Remarks: Pay at harbourmaster, service 2km GPS N57,27830 E16,47543.

Sandvik 5F3

Gästhamnen Sandvik, Stenhuggarvägen.
GPS: n57,07143 e16,85335.

30 SEK 160 Ch (30x) WC included.
Location: Rural, comfortable, quiet. **Surface:** gravel.
01/01-31/12.
Distance: 100m on the spot on the spot on the spot 50m.

Stora Rör 5F3

Stora Rörs Hamn, Stora Rörsvägen. **GPS**: n56,75654 e16,52817.

8 SEK 160 (6x) WC included. **Location:** Rural, simple, quiet.
Surface: asphalted. 01/01-31/12.
Distance: on the spot on the spot on the spot on the spot 100m.
Remarks: Pay at shop.

Storebrö 5F2

Stellplats Storbro Sportclub, Ulvekarrsvägen.
GPS: n57,59367 e15,83992.

20 SEK 150 (4x) WC included free. **Location:** Rural, simple, quiet. **Surface:** gravel. 01/01-31/12.
Distance: 300m.
Remarks: Money in envelope in mail box.

Storebrö 5F2

Tobo Golgklubb camping, Fredensborg 133.
GPS: n57,57566 e15,81154.

10 SEK 100 free Ch (10x) WC included.
Location: Rural, simple, isolated, quiet. **Surface:** gravel.
01/01-31/12.
Distance: 7km 50m 7km.
Remarks: Payment and sanitary facilities at Golfclub.

Timmernabben 5F3

Festplatsen Timmernabben, Botsmansvägen.
GPS: n56,97350 e16,44028.

30 SEK 150 (20x) WC included. **Location:** Rural, simple, quiet. **Surface:** grassy/gravel. 01/01-31/12.
Distance: 100m on the spot on the spot 1km 1km.

Torngärd 36A1

Parkeerterrein Natuurreservaat, Fagelvägen.
GPS: n56,33169 e16,54289.

6 SEK 40 WC free. **Location:** Rural, simple, quiet. **Surface:** gravel.
01/01-31/12.
Distance: 15km on the spot 15km 15km 15km.
Remarks: Bird reserve, money in envelope in mail box.

Tuna 5F2

Ställplats Tuna, Lillgatan. **GPS**: n57,57716 e16,10351.

12 SEK 100 SEK 60 Ch (4x) WC SEK 10/time.
Location: Rural, simple, central, quiet. **Surface:** gravel.
01/01-31/12.
Distance: 2,5km 100m on the spot.
Remarks: Money in envelope in mail box, moose park 9km, tourist train.

Västervik 5F2

Ställplats Sågen, Värmeverksgatan. **GPS**: n57,75138 e16,65541.

45 SEK 100 Ch free (15x) SEK 40.
Location: Urban, simple, central, quiet. **Surface:** gravel.
01/01-31/12.
Distance: 1,5km on the spot on the spot 800m.
Remarks: Money in envelope in mail box, service 1,5km GPS N57.74120 E16.66293.

Vimmerby 5F2

Astrid Lindgrens Värld, Fabriksgatan 8.
GPS: n57,67514 e15,84151.

200 SEK 200. **Location:** Urban, simple, central.
Surface: asphalted. 01/01-31/12.
Distance: 1km 1km 1,3km.
Remarks: Quick-Stop: >19h - <8h.

Gotland

Burgsvik 5G2

Ställplats Sandkvie, Öja Sandkvie 173. **GPS**: n57,01533 e18,31373.
35 SEK 120 Ch SEK 30 WC. **Surface:** grassy.
01/01-31/12.
Distance: 4km 2km on the spot.

Fårö 5G2

Lauterhorns. **GPS**: n57,95249 e19,07995.
15 SEK 100, 01/06-31/08 SEK 120 SEK 10/20liter (8x) SEK 30.
Surface: gravel.
Distance: on the spot.

Gotlands Tofta 5G2

Tofta Beach, Malvavägen 17. **GPS**: n57,49233 e18,13133.
250 SEK 130. 15/04-18/10.

Visby 5G2

Park and Stay, Gutevägen. **GPS**: n57,62855 e18,28034.
35 SEK 169 Ch. **Surface:** gravel. 15/04-18/10.
Distance: 700m.

Blekinge

Hasslö 5F3

Garpahamnen Hasslö, Hamnvägen. **GPS**: n56,09990 e15,47368.
SEK 130 WC.
Distance: on the spot on the spot.

Hasslö 5F3

Hasslö Stugby, Fiskaregårdsvägen 2, Garpahamnen.
GPS: n56,10227 e15,47770.

Karlshamn 5F3

Ställplats Väggaviken, Saltsjöbadsvägen.
GPS: n56,15840 e14,88486.
SEK 180 included WC. **Surface:** gravel.
01/06-31/08.

Karlshamn 5F3

Hamngatan. **GPS**: n56,16504 e14,86546.
6 free. **Surface:** asphalted. 01/01-31/12 during event.
Distance: 500m on the spot on the spot.

Karlshamn 5F3

Saltsjöbadsvägen. **GPS**: n56,15835 e14,87974.
free. **Location:** Rural, isolated. **Surface:** gravel.
Distance: 2,5km.

Karlshamn 5F3

Stationsvägen. **GPS**: n56,17563 e14,86610.
free. **Surface:** asphalted. 01/01-31/12.
Distance: 800m 800m 800m on the spot.

Karlshamn 5F3

Svaneviks småbåtshamn. **GPS**: n56,15649 e14,88870.
SEK 180 WC included. 01/06-31/08.
Distance: 3km on the spot on the spot on the spot.
Remarks: Pay at harbourmaster.

Karlshamn 5F3

Kreativum Science Center, Strömmavägen 28.
GPS: n56,19288 e14,85211.
free.
Distance: 4km 800m.
Remarks: At museum, check in on arrival.

Karlskrona 5F3

Karlskrona Stadsmarina, Skeppsbrokajen.
GPS: n56,16723 e15,58893.
24 SEK 180 WC included. **Surface:** asphalted.
01/01-31/12.
Distance: 1km on the spot on the spot 200m 1km.
Remarks: Pay at harbourmaster, out of season less pitches.

Karlskrona 5F3

Argongatan. **GPS**: n56,16988 e15,59426.
Ch.

Ramdala 5F3

Brofästet Senoren gårdsbutik, Säby Gård.
GPS: n56,13755 e15,74195.
28 SEK 100 Ch included SEK 50. **Surface:** grassy.
01/04-30/09.
Distance: 7km on the spot on the spot 1,5km.

Ronneby 5F3

Ronneby Golfklubb, Reddvägen 14. **GPS**: n56,18962 e15,29355.
6 SEK 100 WC.

Ronneby 5F3

Ronneby Hamn, Östra Piren. **GPS**: n56,17527 e15,30177.
20 SEK 150. **Surface:** metalled.
Distance: on the spot on the spot.

Sölvesborg 6H1

Hörviks gästhamn, Kustvägen, Hörvik. **GPS**: n56,04139 e14,76556.
9 SEK 100.
Distance: 12km on the spot on the spot 300m.

Sölvesborg 6H1

Krokås gästhamn, Hörvik. **GPS**: n56,04893 e14,75663.
Distance: 15km on the spot on the spot 1,5km.

Sölvesborg 6H1

Nogersunds gästhamn, Östra Hamnvägen, Nogersunds.
GPS: n56,00509 e14,73863.
SEK 160 included.
Distance: on the spot on the spot.

Sölvesborg 6H1

Torsö gästhamn, Oastensvägen, Västra Torsö.
GPS: n55,99952 e14,64871.
6 SEK 130 WC included.
Distance: 7km on the spot on the spot.

Sölvesborg 6H1

Sölveborgs golfbana, Ljunganabbevägen. **GPS**: n56,04428 e14,59946.
10 SEK 150 WC included.
Distance: 7km on the spot.
Remarks: At golf court.

Sturkö 5F3

Ekenabben. **GPS**: n56,10142 e15,63803.
SEK 130 SEK 30. 01/04-27/09.
Distance: 7km on the spot on the spot.

Sturkö 5F3

Ställplats Sanda, Hamnvägen. **GPS**: n56,11966 e15,65123.
SEK 130 SEK 30. 01/04-27/09.
Distance: 1,5km on the spot.

Torhamn 5F3

Sandhamn Marine. **GPS**: n56,09351 e15,85479.
SEK 100, 01/05-30/09 SEK 150 Ch WC SEK 50 included. **Surface:** grassy/gravel. 01/01-31/12.
Distance: 1km on the spot on the spot on the spot.

Skåne

Åhus 6G1

Strandvillan, Kolonivägen 62. **GPS**: n55,94443 e14,32109.

SE

16 SEK 150 WC included.
Surface: grassy. 01/01-31/12.
Distance: 2km 700m.

Åhus 6G1

Åhus Gästhamn, Stavgatan 3. **GPS**: n55,92568 e14,30284.
SEK 50 WC.
Distance: on the spot on the spot.
Remarks: Check in on arrival.

Anderslöv 6G2

Sörbyvägen 99. **GPS**: n55,44370 e13,32866.
20 SEK 100. **Surface:** grassy.
Distance: 900m 1km 900m.

Ängelholm 5E3

Sibirienvägen. **GPS**: n56,23618 e12,81852.

8 WC free. **Surface:** grassy.
Distance: 4km 100m 4km on the spot on the spot.
Remarks: Nature reserve.

Ängelholm 5E3

Ängelholms Föreningshamn, Segelvägen 9.
GPS: n56,26704 e12,84138.
30 SEK 150 (16x)included.
01/06-06/12.
Distance: 5km on the spot on the spot on the spot 5km.
Remarks: Max. 48h, pay at harbourmaster.

Båstad 5E3

Italienska vägen. **GPS**: n56,43383 e12,83132.
SEK 50. **Surface:** grassy. 01/01-31/12.
Distance: 1km 400m 500m.

Borrby 6G1

Catrinegården. **GPS**: n55,46673 e14,21090.
SEK 100 SEK 20. **Location:** Rural. **Surface:** gravel.
01/01-31/12.
Distance: 2,5km 2,5km.

Bromölla 6H1

Skåneporten Bromölla, Kristianstadsvägen.
GPS: n56,06414 e14,49689.
free Ch WC. **Surface:** asphalted.
Distance: 200m on the spot 1km.
Remarks: Service to be paid at campsite.

Fjälkinge 6G1

Tosteberge Ångar. **GPS**: n56,01567 e14,45466.
. **Location:** Rural. **Surface:** forest soil. 01/01-31/12.

Höllviken 6F2

Ställplats Foteviken, Museivägen. **GPS**: n55,42810 e12,95237.
SEK 100 Ch against payment WC. **Surface:** grassy.
Distance: 1km on the spot 1km 1km.
Remarks: At museum.

Jonstorp 5E3

Bläsinge Gård, Gamla Södåkravägen 127. **GPS**: n56,23770 e12,65567.
20 SEK 150 SEK 50. **Surface:** gravel. 01/01-31/12.

Kristianstad 6G1

Sommarlust, Kanalgatan 100. **GPS**: n56,04442 e14,16646.

free. **Surface:** asphalted.
Distance: 2km 300m on the spot on the spot.
Remarks: Max. 24h.

Landskrona 6F1

Lundåkrahamnen, Stuverigatan 43. **GPS**: n55,86171 e12,85009.

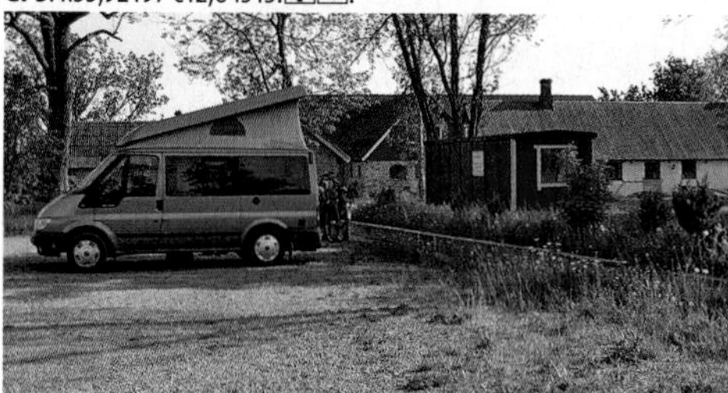

48 SEK 180 Ch WC included.
Location: Rural, simple, quiet.
Surface: grassy. 01/01-31/12.
Distance: 2km on the spot on the spot
300m on the spot on the spot.
Remarks: Arrival <22h, monitored parking.

Landskrona 6F1

Gammeleksgården, Rosenhällsvägen 40.
GPS: n55,92197 e12,84515.

6 SEK 150 Ch WC included on demand.
Location: Rural, simple, noisy. **Surface:** gravel. 01/01-31/12.
Distance: on the spot on the spot.
Remarks: Arrival >18h, departure <10h, check in at B&B <22h, breakfast € 6.

Limhamn 6F1

Lagunen, Vakgatan 9. **GPS**: n55,59593 e12,93305.

25 SEK 180 Ch WC included.
Location: Rural, simple, quiet. **Surface:** gravel.
01/01-31/12.
Distance: 5km on the spot 5km 5km on the spot on the spot.

Limhamn 6F1

Limhamns Småbåtshamn, Bryggövägen.
GPS: n55,58358 e12,91824.

40 SEK 220 Ch WC included.
Location: Rural, simple, quiet. **Surface:** grasstiles.
01/01-31/12 Service: winter.
Distance: 700m, Malmö 6km on the spot on the spot on the spot on the spot on the spot.

Örkelljunga 5E3

Bengt i Örkelljunga, Skåneporten 2. **GPS**: n56,28548 e13,33957.

20 SEK 50 SEK 15 Ch SEK 50.
Surface: grassy. 01/01-31/12.
Distance: 4km on the spot 1km.
Remarks: At motorhome dealer, max. 24h, pay at reception.

Osby 5E3

Spegeldammen, Hässleholmsvägen. **GPS**: n56,36871 e13,98441.
free.
Distance: 1,6km on the spot.
Remarks: Max. 2 nights.

Simrishamn 6G1

Camping car parking Hammarlunda, Gislövshammar.
GPS: n55,49015 e14,30745.
SEK 100 Ch. **Surface:** grassy.
Distance: 700m 700m 2,5km.

Simrishamn 6G1

Småbåtshamnen. **GPS**: n55,56035 e14,34906.
5 SEK 200 Ch (4x)SEK 2/kWh WC.
Surface: asphalted.
Distance: 500m on the spot on the spot on the spot on the spot.
Remarks: Tallycard.

Simrishamn 6G1

Tobisviks Camping, Tobisvik. **GPS**: n55,56693 e14,33750.

20 SEK 120-200. **Surface:** grassy. 01/01-31/12.
Distance: 3km on the spot on the spot.

Skanör 6F2

Skanör hamn, Hamnvägen. **GPS**: n55,41608 e12,83168.
10 SEK 120.
Distance: on the spot on the spot on the spot 1,2km.
Remarks: Max. 24h.

Smygehamn 6G2

Smyge strandväg. **GPS**: n55,33978 e13,36172.
SEK 150. **Surface:** grassy.
Distance: on the spot on the spot.

Trelleborg 6G2

Trelleborgs turist Parkering, Västra Trelleborg.
GPS: n55,37536 e13,12004.
free, night SEK 80. **Surface:** gravel.
Distance: 2km on the spot on the spot 1,5km 800m.

Yngsjö 6G1

Gamla skolan, Yngsjövägen 1065. **GPS**: n55,84441 e14,20019.
SEK 150 WC included. **Surface:** grassy.
Distance: 1,5km.
Remarks: Breakfast-service.

Ystad 6G2

Ystads Marina, Segelgatan 1. **GPS**: n55,42666 e13,81730.
free, night SEK 150 Ch (16x) WC. 01/06-15/09.
Distance: on the spot on the spot on the spot on the spot.
Remarks: Caution SEK 50.

Halland

Falkenberg 5D3

Lövstavikens Båtförening, Sanddynevägen 58.
GPS: n56,89329 e12,46795.
20 SEK 160 Ch WC included.
Surface: grassy/gravel.
Distance: 3km on the spot.

Fjärås 5D3

Tjolöholms Slott, Tjolöholms byväg. **GPS**: n57,40173 e12,10161.
SEK 100. **Surface:** grassy/gravel. 01/01-31/12.
Distance: on the spot.
Remarks: At castle, max. 2 days.

Fjärås 5D3

Skårs Gård, Förlandavägen. **GPS**: n57,40081 e12,26869.
6 SEK 140 WC included. **Location:** Rural.
Distance: 11km.

Frillesås 5D3

Espenäsvägen. **GPS**: n57,31674 e12,15298.
5 SEK 100. **Surface:** grassy. 01/04-01/10.
Distance: 1,5km on the spot.
Remarks: Money in envelope in mail box.

Gullbrandstorp 5E3

Strandgården, Skarviksvägen 2. **GPS**: n56,69518 e12,68550.
8 SEK 250 included.
Distance: on the spot on the spot.
Remarks: Max. 3 days, golf court 300m.

Halmstad 5E3

Citycamp Halmstad, Styrmansgatan. **GPS**: n56,66682 e12,86145.
50 SEK 120, 01/06-31/08 SEK 140.
Distance: on the spot.

Halmstad 5E3

Halmstad Segelsällskap, Grötviksvägen. **GPS**: n56,64191 e12,77782.
10 SEK 150 included.

Ullared 5D3

Ställplats Ullared, Värnamovägen. **GPS**: n57,13232 e12,73472.
100 free, night SEK 90. **Surface:** gravel.
Distance: 1km.
Remarks: Max. 48h.

Unnaryd 5E3

Tiraholms Fisk. **GPS**: n56,94263 e13,64560.
SEK 100 . **Surface:** grassy.
Distance: on the spot on the spot.
Remarks: At small lake, check in on arrival.

Varberg 5D3

Apelvik Strand, Tångkörarvägen, Apelviken.
GPS: n57,08157 e12,26156.

SEK 150 WC.
Distance: on the spot.
Remarks: Beach parking.

Varberg 5D3

Naturum Getterön, Lassavägen 1. **GPS**: n57,12627 e12,25332.

24 SEK 125, 01/06-31/08 SEK 200 included.
Surface: gravel.
Distance: on the spot.
Remarks: Nature reserve.

Varberg 5D3

Getterön Marina, Änggärdev. 1. **GPS**: n57,11399 e12,22588.
21 SEK 170-200 Ch included.
Surface: metalled. 01/01-31/12.
Distance: on the spot on the spot.
Remarks: Monitored parking.

Värobacka 5D3

Bua hamn, Hamnvägen. **GPS**: n57,23926 e12,11410.
SEK 180, 15/06-15/08 SEK 200 Ch WC.
Surface: asphalted. 01/01-31/12.
Distance: 1km on the spot on the spot 200m 500m.

Västra Götaland

Åmål 5D1

Måkebergsvägen. **GPS**: n59,05615 e12,70862.
SEK 100 SEK 40 Ch. **Surface:** asphalted. 01/04-15/10.
Distance: 600m on the spot on the spot 600m 600m.
Remarks: Pay at harbourmaster, servicepoint at Camping Örnäs.

Bohus-björkö 5D2

Björkö Hamn, Ljungblomsvägen 7. **GPS**: n57,72812 e11,67751.
SEK 250 included SEK 10 SEK 50. **Surface:** gravel.
01/01-31/12.
Distance: on the spot on the spot on the spot 500m.

Dals Långed 5D1

Ställplats Dals Långed, Christian Aarsruds väg 2.
GPS: n58,92272 e12,30742.
8 SEK 150.
Distance: 400m.

Fiskebäckskil 5D2

Skaftö Golfklubb, Stockeviksvägen 2. **GPS**: n58,23213 e11,45394.
5 SEK 200 included.
Distance: on the spot.
Remarks: At golf court.

Floda 5D2

Öijared Golf, Öjaredsvägen. **GPS**: n57,85467 e12,39777.
. **Surface:** asphalted.
Remarks: At golf court.

Forsvik 5E1

Ställplats Forsvik Göta kanal, Baltzar von Platens väg.
GPS: n58,57525 e14,43557.
15 SEK 150 WC included. 01/05-30/09.
Remarks: At Göta Canal.

Göteborg 5D2

Lisebergs ställplats Skatås, Skatåsvägen.
GPS: n57,70303 e12,03513.
37 SEK 240/24h Ch included. **Surface:** asphalted.
30/05-13/09.
Distance: 750m 750m 750m.

Hälsö 5D2

Tjolmenvägen. **GPS**: n57,73152 e11,65794.
15 SEK 180 WC included.
Distance: on the spot on the spot.

Karlsborg 5E1

Carlsborg Segelsällskap. **GPS**: n58,53998 e14,50208.
SEK 170 Ch WC included. 29/04-18/09.
Distance: 200m.

Kungshamn 5D2

Smögenbrons Rum, Dinglevägen 27. **GPS**: n58,36903 e11,24984.
SEK 100 Ch. 01/06-31/08.
Distance: 1km on the spot on the spot 1km.

Lidköping 5E1

Spikens Båtsällskap. **GPS**: n58,68952 e13,20174.
SEK 120 Ch SEK 30 SEK 5/3minutes. 01/05-30/09.
Distance: Lidköping 25km on the spot on the spot on the spot.

Lyrestad 5E1

Kanalvägen. **GPS**: n58,80324 e14,05721.
25 SEK 150, 15/06-09/08 SEK 175 Ch WC. **Surface:** grassy.
24/04-30/09.
Distance: on the spot 200m 200m.
Remarks: At Göta Canal, next to midget golf, caution SEK 100.

Lyrestad 5E1

Norrqvarn Hotell & Konferens, Norrqvarns Slussområde.
GPS: n58,78636 e14,08338.
15 SEK 150 (5x)SEK 25.
Distance: 3km on the spot.
Remarks: At Göta Canal, check in on arrival, canoe and bicycle rental, restaurant only in summer.

Lysekil 5D2

Valbodalens. **GPS**: n58,28905 e11,43849.
30 SEK 180 (20x) WC included. 25/04-30/09.
Distance: 2km on the spot on the spot.

Lysekil 5D2

Kolholmarnas, Bangårdsgatan. **GPS**: n58,27418 e11,43912.
36 SEK 180.
Distance: 600m 600m 600m.

Mariestad 5E1

Hamnmagasinet i Mariestad, Kajgatan 1. **GPS**: n58,71366 e13,81948.
40 SEK 140 Ch SEK 25 SEK 30. **Surface:** asphalted.
Distance: 500m on the spot 500m.
Remarks: Max. 3 days, pay at harbourmaster.

Öckerö 5D2

Hönö Röd, Rödvägen. **GPS**: n57,69933 e11,63954.
30 SEK 150 Ch WC included.
Distance: 300m 300m 500m.

Öckerö 5D2

Hönö Klåva Hamn, Öckerövägen. **GPS**: n57,68345 e11,65156.
SEK 170, 15/06-15/08 SEK 200 included. 01/01-31/12.
Distance: on the spot 500m.

Sjötorp 5E1

Ställplats Göta kanal, Stenbordsvägen. **GPS**: n58,83716 e13,97865.
28 SEK 185 WC included. **Surface:** grassy/gravel.
01/05-30/09.
Distance: on the spot on the spot on the spot.
Remarks: At Göta Canal, caution SEK 200.

Strömstad 5D1

Kebalvägen. **GPS**: n58,95115 e11,17330.

SEK 100/24h Ch free.
Location: Rural, simple, quiet. **Surface:** gravel. 01/01-31/12.
Distance: 3km 200m 300m.
Remarks: Free bus to centre.

Tidaholm 5E2

Södra Kungsvägen. **GPS**: n58,17838 e13,96083.
2 free.
Distance: 200m.
Remarks: Max. 48h.

Trollhättan 5D2

Ställplatser Trollhättan, Åkerssjövägen. **GPS**: n58,26531 e12,26549.
16 SEK 150 Ch .
Distance: 2,8km.

Värmland

Årjäng 5D1

Sandaholm Restaurang & Camping, Sanda Sjövik.
GPS: n59,36078 e12,27807.

12 SEK 100 Ch (8x)SEK 40/24h SEK 30/24h.
Surface: metalled. 01/04-01/10.
Distance: 6km on the spot on the spot on the spot 6km on the spot on the spot.

Filipstad 5E1

Asphyttans Slussar, Konsul Lundströms väg. **GPS**: n59,61839 e14,18147.
SEK 120 included.
Distance: 12km.
Remarks: Canoe and boat rental.

Karlstad 5E1

Sävegatan 2. **GPS**: n59,39329 e13,51467.
free. **Surface:** metalled.
Distance: 100m.

SE

Karlstad 5E1
Trädgårdsgatan. **GPS**: n59,37726 e13,50376.
4.
Distance: 500m 500m.
Remarks: Along railwayline.

Kil 5E1
Fryksta, Sjöleden. **GPS**: n59,52045 e13,32507.
6 free. **Surface:** gravel.
Distance: on the spot.
Remarks: Only overnight stays 18-10h.

Kristinehamn 5E1
Kristinehamns Gästhamn och Ställplats, Hamnvägen 9.
GPS: n59,31138 e14,09558.
36 SEK 165 Ch (20x)SEK30 WC included.
Surface: gravel.
Distance: 700m 300m.
Remarks: Next to midget golf.

Morokulien 4B3
Kungsvägen. **GPS**: n59,93089 e12,24181.
free ChWC. **Surface:** asphalted/metalled.
Distance: on the spot.
Remarks: Next to petrol station.

Nysäter 5D1
Högsäter. **GPS**: n59,34900 e12,80561.
5 SEK 80 SEK20 included. **Surface:** grassy.
Distance: Nysäter 8,5km.

Nysäter 5D1
Nysäters gästhamn, Marknadsvägen. **GPS**: n59,28417 e12,78242.
20 SEK 100 Ch SEK20 included. **Surface:** gravel.
Distance: 500m on the spot 500m.

Säffle 5D1
Karlsborgsgatan. **GPS**: n59,12405 e12,92426.
10 SEK 100 WC included. **Surface:** grasstiles.
Distance: 1km on the spot on the spot 1km.
Remarks: Check in at harbourmaster.

Säffle 5D1
Medborgarhusets, Magasinsgatan 2. **GPS**: n59,13499 e12,92178.
8 SEK 100, 01/06-31/08 SEK 150. 01/01-31/12.
Distance: 700m 500m on the spot.
Remarks: Pay at harbourmaster.

Örebro

Askersund 5E1
Askersund Citycamp & Gästhamn, Södra Infarten.
GPS: n58,87879 e14,89886.
20 SEK 160 Chincluded (20x)SEK40.
Surface: grassy/gravel. 01/04-01/11.
Distance: 350m 2km 350m 400m 150m.

Västmanland

Lindesberg 5E1
Fotbollsgatan. **GPS**: n59,60157 e15,18676.
10 free Chfree. **Surface:** asphalted. 01/01-31/12.
Distance: centre 2,5km 2,5km 2,5km.
Remarks: Max. 24h.

Västerås 4D3
Västerås Gästhamn. **GPS**: n59,60190 e16,54648.
15 SEK 200 WC included. 01/01-31/12.
Distance: 500m on the spot on the spot 500m.
Remarks: Pay at harbourmaster.

Dalarna

Ludvika 4C3
Eriksgatan. **GPS**: n60,15020 e15,18936.
. **Location:** Urban. **Surface:** asphalted.
Distance: on the spot 200m.
Remarks: Max. 24h.

Särna 4C3
Lägerplats, Byvägen. **GPS**: n61,80383 e12,90931.
6 SEK 60. **Location:** Rural. **Surface:** grassy.
Distance: on the spot on the spot.
Remarks: Along river.

Säter 4C3
Säterdalens Folkpark. **GPS**: n60,34854 e15,75439.
free.
Distance: 650m 650m 850m.

Smedjebacken 4C3
Smedjebackens. **GPS**: n60,13828 e15,41647.
5 SEK 100 Ch . **Surface:** gravel. 01/05-01/10.
Distance: 500m on the spot 200m 500m on the spot on the spot.

Sollerön 4C3
Sollerö camping, Levsnäs. **GPS**: n60,90048 e14,58318.
18 SEK 80-100 (8x)SEK30. **Surface:** asphalted.
Distance: on the spot on the spot.
Remarks: Quick-Stop: >18h - <9h.

Stjärnsund 4C3
Villa Solhem, Bruksallén 17. **GPS**: n60,43421 e16,20744.
11 SEK 200 (4x)SEK20 WC included.
Distance: on the spot 300m 300m.

Gävleborg

Axmar 4D3
Axmarbrygga Havskrog, Boskär. **GPS**: n61,04877 e17,15774.
30 SEK 90 Ch SEK40 WCincluded SEK10.
Surface: gravel. 03/04-01/11.
Distance: on the spot on the spot on the spot.
Remarks: Bread-service.

Gävle 4D3
Hemlingbystugan, Hemlingbyvägen 93. **GPS**: n60,65005 e17,16996.
free WC. **Surface:** asphalted.
Distance: 2km 2km 1,8km.
Remarks: Max. 3 days.

Gävle 4D3
Culinarparkeringen, Drottningsgatan 47, Anderholmen.
GPS: n60,67810 e17,15493.

12 SEK 2/h, overnight stay and weekend free. **Surface:** gravel.

Gävle 4D3
Södra Skeppsbron. **GPS**: n60,67670 e17,15985.

2 free. **Location:** Urban. **Surface:** asphalted. 01/01-31/12.
Distance: on the spot on the spot on the spot on the spot.
Remarks: Max. 48h.

Ockelbo 4C3
Wij Trädgårdar, Vigatan 4. **GPS**: n60,88722 e16,70139.
free. 23/05-06/09.
Distance: 1km.
Remarks: Near mill, max. 3 days.

Västernorrland

Kvissleby 4D2
Svartvik. **GPS**: n62,31935 e17,36955.

20 free. **Surface:** grassy/gravel.
Distance: on the spot on the spot 500m.

Sandöverken 4D2
Hotell Höga Kusten AB, Hornöberget. **GPS**: n62,80468 e17,95136.

free. **Surface:** asphalted.
Distance: on the spot on the spot.

Skatan 4D2
Galströmsvägen. **GPS**: n62,19896 e17,49645.
free ChWC. 01/01-31/12.
Distance: 500m 200m.

Jämtland

Bispgården 4C2
Rojo Zweden, Sörböle 230. **GPS**: n62,99040 e16,62163.
25 € 10,60 Ch WC included. **Location:** Isolated.
Surface: grassy. 01/05-01/09.
Distance: 8km.

Gällö 4C2
Alma Ångbåt. **GPS**: n62,82794 e15,30652.
SEK 150. **Surface:** grassy.
Distance: on the spot on the spot 300m.

Hammarstrand 4C2
Zorbcenter, Dödviken 145. **GPS**: n63,14690 e16,17890.

11 € 16 (5x)SEK2 WC included.
Surface: grassy. 01/05-31/09.
Distance: 15km on the spot 1km.
Remarks: Canoe and boat rental.

Mattmar 4C2
Ångaren Östersund, Södra Arvesund 516. **GPS**: n63,23573 e14,06810.
SEK 60 SEK60 SEK20.
Surface: grassy/metalled. 01/01-31/12.
Distance: on the spot on the spot on the spot.

Svenstavik 4C2
Centrumvägen. **GPS**: n62,76731 e14,43496.
SEK 100 Chfree WC.
Location: Urban. **Surface:** asphalted.
Distance: on the spot on the spot on the spot.

Slovakia

Capital: Bratislava
Government: parliamentary republic
Official Language: Slovak
Population: 5,445,000 (2015)
Area: 49,036 Km^2

General information
Dialling code: 0421
General emergency: 112
Currency: Euro
Credit cards are accepted almost everywhere.

Regulations for overnight stays
Wild camping is not allowed.

Additional public holidays 2017
January 1 Republic Day
January 6 Epiphany
May 1 Labour Day
May 8 End of World War II
July 5 St. Cyril & St. Methodius Day
August 29 National Uprising Day
September 1 Constitution Day
September 15 Day of Lady Sorrows
November 1 All Saints' Day
November 17 Freedom and Democracy Day

Time Zone
Winter (Standard Time) GMT+1
Summer (DST) GMT+2

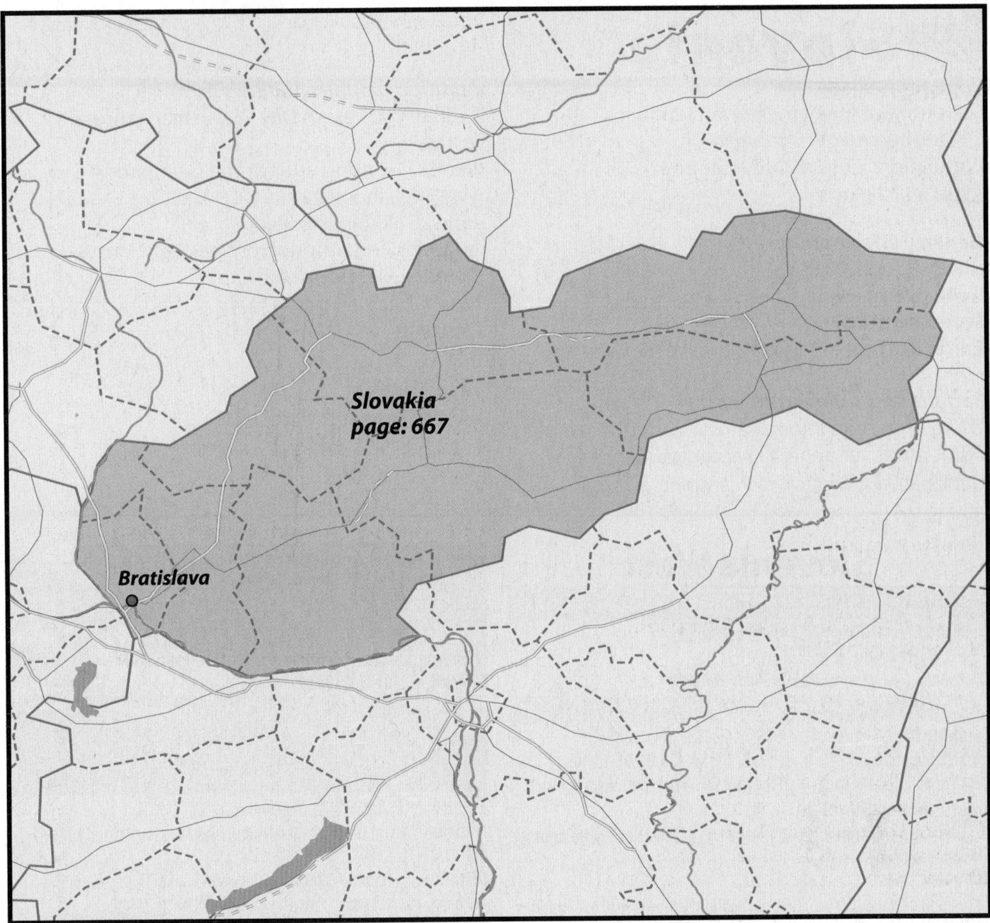

Bratislava

Bratislava 37B3

Camping Zlate Piesky, Senecká cesta 2. **GPS**: n48,18836 e17,18557.
€ 15,80, 2 pers.incl Ch €3,50 WC included. **Location**: Urban. **Surface**: grassy. 01/05-15/10.
Distance: 8km 100m on the spot 200m.

Trnava

Banka 37B2

Camping Pullmann Piestany, Cesta Janka Alexyho 921.
GPS: n48,57609 e17,83444.
€ 8 Ch WC included. **Surface**: grassy.
Distance: 2km on the spot.

Dunajská Streda 37B3

CaravanCamp DS, Kúpelná ulica 21. **GPS**: n47,98689 e17,61150.
15 € 12 Ch WC included. **Location**: Rural.
Surface: grassy. 01/04-01/11.
Distance: 1km 350m 900m.

Šamorín 37B3

Stellplatz Čilistov, Čilistov. **GPS**: n48,01364 e17,30850.

25 €7 Ch €3 WC included. **Location**: Rural, simple.
Surface: grassy/gravel. 01/04-31/10.
Distance: Bratislava 20km 50m 500m 200m.
Remarks: Dog € 3, golf court 2km.

Žilina

Liptovský Ján 37C2

Pension Horec, Starojanka. **GPS**: n49,03709 e19,67526.
15 free. **Location**: Rural. **Surface**: metalled. 01/01-31/12.

Varín 37B2

Autocamp Varin, Doktor Jozefa Tisu 13. **GPS**: n49,20833 e18,87861.
€ 12 Ch €3,30 WC included. **Location**: Rural.
Surface: grassy. 01/05-11/10.
Distance: on the spot.

Banská Bystric

Brezno 37C2

Sedliacky Dvor, Hliník 7, Rohozná. **GPS**: n48,79535 e19,72869.

20 € 17,25 Ch WC €3,25 included.
Location: Rural. **Surface**: grassy. 15/04-31/10.
Distance: 7km 1,2km 1,2km 700m on the spot on the spot.
Remarks: Bread-service.

Prešov

Haligovce 37C2

Camping Goralsky Dvor. **GPS**: n49,37984 e20,43972.
€ 10,50 Ch €3,50 WC included. **Location**: Rural.
Surface: grassy.
Distance: on the spot.

Snina 37D2

Camping Snina, Rybnícka 4483. **GPS**: n48,97384 e22,18919.
25 € 9 Ch included €2,50 €0,50 . 15/05-30/09.
Distance: 3km 50m 50m on the spot on the spot.

Vysoké Tatry 37C2

Pension Slnecny Dom, Tatranská Lomnica 287.
GPS: n49,16664 e20,28169.
4 € 10 Ch included. 01/01-31/12.
Distance: on the spot on the spot.

Košice

Vyšný Medzev 37C2

Camping Sokol, Hrdinov SNP 64 - 68. **GPS**: n48,71472 e20,90222.
€ 17,50 Ch €2,50 WC included. **Location**: Motorway.
Surface: grassy. 01/04-01/10.
Distance: on the spot.

SK

Slovenia

Capital: Ljubljana
Government: parliamentarian republic
Official Language: Slovenian
Population: 2,061,000 (2015)
Area: 20,273 km^2

General information

Dialling code: 00386
General emergency: 112
Currency: Euro
Credit card are accepted almost everywhere.

Regulations for overnight stays

There is no regulation against overnight camping, but it is not yet generally accepted. In the National Park Triglav wild camping is forbidden.

Additional public holidays 2017

February 8 Prešern Day - Slovenian cultural festival
April 27 Uprising against the Occupation Day
May 1-2 Labour Day
June 25 National Holiday
August 15 Assumption of the Virgin Mary
October 31 Reformation Day
November 1 All Saints' Day
December 26 Independence Day

Time Zone

Winter (Standard Time) GMT+1
Summer (DST) GMT+2

Slovenia West

Bled 38A1

Ljubljanska cesta. **GPS**: n46,36957 e14,11700.
€ 8. **Surface:** metalled. 01/01-31/12.
Distance: city centre 1km 300m 100m.

Bled 38A1

Camping Bled, Kidričeva 10 c. **GPS**: n46,36162 e14,08221.
€ 28,50-31,50 Ch WC. 01/04-15/10.
Distance: on the spot on the spot on the spot on the spot.

Tourist information Bled:
Bled Castle. Exhibition about the history of Bled, during the summer also open-air concerts.
8-17h.
Soteska Vintgar Gorge, TD Gorje, Podhom 0, Gorje. Trail over bridges and galleries along a river.

Bohinjsko jezero 38A1

Zlatorog. **GPS**: n46,27887 e13,83739.
200 € 20-30 Ch WC. 25/04-30/09.
Distance: on the spot on the spot 150m.

Tourist information Bohinjsko jezero:
Savica Falls. Water falls.

Bovec 23H1

Alpski turistični center Kanin Bovec, Dvor 43.
GPS: n46,33306 e13,53944.

14 € 20/24h, € 30/36h Ch included.
Location: Rural.
Surface: asphalted.
01/01-31/12
service 01/11-15/03.
Distance: 1km on the spot on the spot.
Remarks: Max. 36h, payment only with coins.

Tourist information Bovec:
Triglav National Park, Dom Trenta, Soča. Information centre.
Kluže Fortress, Trg golobarskih žrtev 8. Fort above gorge.
Soča Trail, Soča. Hiking trail along the Soca river.

Cerkno 38A1

Kmetija Želinc, Straža 8. **GPS**: n46,10259 e13,94670.
5 € 12. 01/01-31/12.
Distance: on the spot on the spot.

Domžale 38A1

ACG Autocenter Glavan, Češminova ulica 1a.
GPS: n46,14637 e14,60047.

2 free Ch (2x)free,16Amp.
Location: Urban, simple, central, noisy. **Surface:** asphalted/gravel.
01/01-31/12.
Distance: 100m 3km 500m 300m 150m 150m 500m on the spot on the spot 20km 20km.

Dornberk 38A2

Saksida, Zalošče 12a. **GPS**: n45,88963 e13,74751.

15 € 10/pp Ch (15x),16Amp WC included.
Location: Rural, comfortable, isolated. **Surface:** gravel/metalled.
01/01-31/12.
Distance: 1km 350m 350m on the spot 1km 300m on the spot on the spot.
Remarks: Covered picnic area, swimming pool available.

DovjeMojstrana 38A1

Kamne. **GPS**: n46,46444 e13,95778.
€ 15,20-21 Ch WC. 01/01-31/12.
Distance: 1km 1km.

Hruševje 38A2

Penzion & Camp Mirjam, Razdrto 19. **GPS**: n45,75690 e14,06126.

9 € 12 Ch included WC on demand € 1.
Location: Urban, simple, central, quiet. **Surface:** gravel.
01/05-31/10.
Distance: on the spot 1km 10km 10km 50m on the spot on the spot.

Idrija 38A2

Veri Krajnik, Carl Jakoba ulica 9. **GPS**: n45,99879 e14,02595.

3 € 5 Ch included. **Location:** Rural, simple, isolated, quiet. **Surface:** grassy/gravel. 01/01-31/12.
Distance: 1,5km 1,5km 1,5km 1,5km on the spot on the spot.
Remarks: Narrow entrance.

Ilirska Bistrica 38A2

Grill Danilo, Bazoviška cesta 46. **GPS**: n45,55846 e14,24340.

6 € 10 Ch (6x),16Amp WC included.
Location: Rural, comfortable, central, quiet.
Surface: asphalted.
01/01-31/12.
Distance: 500m 10km 20km 50m on the spot 200m 100m 500m on the spot on the spot 20km 20km.

Izola 38A2

Cankarjev Drevored. **GPS**: n45,53808 e13,66397.

5 € 15/24h Ch (4x)included,16Amp.
Location: Urban, simple, quiet. **Surface:** asphalted.
01/01-31/12.
Distance: 500m 500m on the spot 500m 500m on the spot on the spot on the spot.

Kamniška Bistrica 38A1

Kamp Alpe. **GPS**: n46,30543 e14,60794.
10 € 25 Ch WC. 01/05-01/10.

Kobarid 23H1

Koren, Drezneske Ravne 333. **GPS**: n46,25083 e13,58667.
Ch WC. 01/01-31/12.
Distance: 500m on the spot on the spot on the spot.

SL

Kobarid 23H1

Lazar, Gregorciceva 63. **GPS**: n46,25530 e13,58720.
€ 26 Ch WC. 01/04-31/10.
Distance: on the spot on the spot.

Tourist information Kobarid:
Kobariski muzej, Gregorciceva 1. Museum about the first World War. 01/04-30/09 9-18h, 01/10-31/03 10-17h.
Tolmin Chutes, LTO Sotočje, Petra Skalarja 4, Tolmin. Touristic route along the rapid to the thermal source of the river.

Koper 38A2

Ljubljanjanska cesta 13. **GPS**: n45,53790 e13,73780.
36 € 10/24h Ch WC included. **Surface:** asphalted.
01/01-31/12.
Distance: city centre 1,5km 2km.
Remarks: Nearby bus station.

Kranj 38A1

Stara Sava, Gregorčičeva ulica. **GPS**: n46,24307 e14,35771.
6 € 10/24h €0,50/40liter Ch €0,20/kWh. **Surface:** gravel.
01/01-31/12.
Distance: 200m 200m.

Kranjska Gora 38A1

Borovška cesta. **GPS**: n46,48746 e13,77510.
20 € 15 Ch included. **Location:** Rural.
Surface: gravel.

Ljubljana 38A1

Alo Camp, Peruzzijeva ulica 105.
GPS: n46,02151 e14,52303.

13 € 10 Ch (13x)€5 WC included.
Surface: asphalted. 01/01-31/12.
Distance: 3km on the spot 500m 50m on the spot on the spot.
Remarks: Check in at hotel, borrow cycles for free, free bus to centre.

Ljubljana 38A1

Pri Kovaču, Cesta II. grupe odredov 82, Dobrunje.
GPS: n46,03162 e14,60386.

10 € 8/night, guests free Ch (20x)€2/night,16Amp WC €0,80 included. **Location:** Rural, comfortable, central, quiet. **Surface:** gravel.
01/01-31/12 Restaurant: Tue.
Distance: 8km 2,5km 5km 4km on the spot 100m, bakery 200m 20m on the spot on the spot 400m.

Ljubljana 38A1

Sraka, Masarykova cesta 17.
GPS: n46,05740 e14,51870.

15 € 15, park € 10 Ch included.
Location: Urban.
Surface: gravel. 01/01-31/12.
Distance: 1km on the spot 100m on the spot on the spot on the spot.
Remarks: Motorhome washing place.

Tourist information Ljubljana:
Ljubljana Tourist Card. Card offers among other things free public transport, free access at museums and discount in restaurants, shops etc. Available at Tourist Office, railway station and several hotels. € 20,70/24h.
Ljubljana Tourist Information Center, Krekov trg 10, www.visitljubljana.com. Capital, historical city with a lot of annual events.
National museum, Muzjeska 1. Archeological and historical museum. 10-18h, Thu 10-20h Mo.
Plecnik museum, Kurunova 4. Architectonic museum in the house of Joze Plecnik. Tue, Thu 10-14h.
Slovene Natural History Museum, Muzjeska 1. Zoological and botanic museum. daily 10-18h, Thu 10-20h Mo.
Ljubljana Castle. Medieval fortress, tourist train at town centre. 01/10-30/04 10-21h, 01/05-30/09 9-22h.
Vodnikov trg. daily, summer 6-18h, winter 6-16h.
Zoo Ljubljana, Večna pot 70. Zoo.
summer 9-19h, winter 9-16h.

Logatec 38A2

Počivališče Lom. **GPS**: n45,89817 e14,25486.
6 free. **Location:** Motorway. **Surface:** asphalted.
Distance: on the spot on the spot on the spot.
Remarks: At petrol station.

Luče 38A1

Camp Smica, Luče 4. **GPS**: n46,36117 e14,73626.
€ 12-16 Ch WC. 01/05-30/10.
Distance: on the spot on the spot 900m.

Lukovica 38A1

Gostilna Furman, Stari trg 19. **GPS**: n46,17026 e14,69233.

10 € 10, € 15 service incl Ch (10x) WC.
Location: Urban, simple, central, quiet. **Surface:** gravel.
01/01-31/12.
Distance: on the spot 3km 3km on the spot 200m 100m on the spot on the spot.

Lukovica 38A1

OMV Istrabenz. **GPS**: n46,16690 e14,69380.
2 free. **Location:** Motorway, noisy.
Distance: on the spot on the spot.
Remarks: Parking petrol station OMV Istrabenz.

Portorož 38A2

Marina Portorož, Cesta solinarjev 8. **GPS**: n45,50505 e13,59847.

60 € 17, 15/04-20/09 € 26 + tourist tax € 0,63/pp Ch (64x),16Amp included.
Location: Urban, simple, quiet. **Surface:** gravel. 01/01-31/12.
Distance: 1km on the spot on the spot on the spot on the spot 500m on the spot on the spot.
Remarks: Monitored parking 24/24, swimming pool available.

Tourist information Portorož:
Turistična organizacija Koper, Verdijeva 10, Koper. City with a Venetian past and a lot of curiosities.
Pomorski muzej Sergej Mašera, Cankarjevo nabrežje 3, Piran. Maritime museum. 9-12h, 15-18h, 01/07-31/08 9-12h, 18-21h Mo.

Postojna 38A2

Park Postojnska Jama, Veliki Otok. **GPS**: n45,78066 e14,20322.

20 € 18/24h Ch (20x)included,16Amp.
Location: Rural, simple, quiet.
Surface: concrete. 01/04-30/09.
Distance: 1km 3km 100m 1km on the spot on the spot on the spot.
Remarks: Postojna caves 300m.

Tourist information Postojna:
Križna jama, Bloška polica 7, Grahovo. Largest water caves of Slovenia.
Perdjama Grad. Castle, 16th century and caves. 01/05-30/09 9-18, 01/10-30/04 10-16h.
Postojnska Jama, Jamska cesta 30. Postojna caves. 01/05-30/09 9-18, 01/10-30/04 10-16h.

Rateče 23H1

Nordijski center Planica. **GPS**: n46,47708 e13,72418.
€ 12 Ch WC included. 01/01-31/12.

Šenčur 38A1

Camper Stop Cubis, Poslovna cona A 2.
GPS: n46,23855 e14,40769.

14 € 10 Ch (12x) included.
Surface: gravel. 01/01-31/12.
Distance: 1km 150m 1km on the spot.
Remarks: Video surveillance.

Šmarje 38A2

Garni Mimosa, Srgaši 38a. **GPS**: n45,50843 e13,70560.

5 € 10 €8/100liter (1x)included,16Amp WC on demand .
Location: Urban, simple, central, quiet. **Surface:** gravel.
01/01-31/12.
Distance: 6km 50m 50m 100m on the spot on the spot.

Smlednik 38A1

Hotel Kanu, Valburga 7. **GPS**: n46,16927 e14,42228.

20 € 10 Ch (4x),16Amp WC €5 included.
Location: Rural, isolated, quiet. **Surface:** grasstiles.
01/01-31/12 water disconnected in winter.
Distance: 300m 5km on the spot on the spot on the spot 300m 300m on the spot on the spot 20km 7km.

SL

S Tolmin 38A1
Kamp Siber, Klanec 8. **GPS**: n46,18082 e13,73792.
50 € 8/pp Ch WC .
Location: Rural. **Surface:** grassy/gravel. 01/01-31/12.
Distance: 1km on the spot on the spot 1km.

Slovenia East

S Braslovče 38A1
Najem & Kamping, Preserje 16b. **GPS**: n46,28915 e15,05524.
20 € 5 Ch (2x)€5/day,16Amp included.
Location: Rural, comfortable, isolated, quiet. **Surface:** gravel.
01/01-31/12.
Distance: 1km on the spot on the spot 1km 1km 1km on the spot on the spot 10km 10km.
Remarks: Opening hours 7-22h.

S Brestanica 38B1
Bazen Brestanica, Jetrno selo 2. **GPS**: n46,00124 e15,47492.
4 free Ch . **Surface:** gravel.
Remarks: At swimming pool.

S Brestanica 38B1
Ribiška družina Brestanica, Raztez 1a. **GPS**: n46,00504 e15,49751.

5 free WC . **Location:** Isolated, quiet.
Surface: gravel.
Distance: on the spot on the spot on the spot.
Remarks: Fishpond, check in at restaurant.

S Celje 38B1
Parking Glazija, Ljubljanska cesta 20. **GPS**: n46,23319 e15,25904.
2 € 10 included. **Location:** Urban.
Surface: metalled.
Distance: on the spot.

S Celje 38B1
Glavan Center Karavaninga, Gaji 45. **GPS**: n46,24406 e15,30217.

6 € 5 €1/100liter Ch (2x)€0,50/kWh,16Amp .
Location: Rural, simple, isolated, quiet.
Surface: gravel.
01/01-31/12.
Distance: 3km 4km 4km 200m 2km on the spot on the spot on the spot.
Remarks: At motorhome dealer.

Tourist information Celje:
Jama Pekel, Šempeter. Caves.
Stari Grad Castle. Remainders of castle.
Rimska Nekropola, Šempeter. Roman Necropolis, archeological park.

S Cirkulane 38B1
Herman Lederhaus, Dolane 8. **GPS**: n46,37114 e15,99682.

10 € 10 Ch WC included.
Surface: grassy/gravel. 01/01-31/12.
Distance: on the spot on the spot on the spot 50m.
Remarks: Restaurant and leather factory.

S Dolenjske Toplice 38A2
Dolenjske Toplice, Meniška vas. **GPS**: n45,76739 e15,05151.

10 € 8, 20/06-24/08, € 12 + tourist tax Ch €3,50 included. **Location:** Rural, simple, isolated, quiet.
Surface: grassy/gravel. 01/01-31/12.
Distance: 800m on the spot on the spot 800m 800m on the spot on the spot.
Remarks: Along the Krka river, terme Dolenjske Toplice 800m.

Hinje 38A2
Domačija Krnc, Hrib pri Hinjah 9. **GPS**: n45,76729 e14,88887.
. **Surface:** grassy.
Distance: on the spot.

Ivanjkovci 38B1
Vinoteka Svetinjska Klet, Svetinje 5.
GPS: n46,46220 e16,16990.

10 free. **Surface:** metalled.
Remarks: Sale of wines.

S Jesenice na Dolenjskem 38B2
Gostinstvo Strnisa, Jesenice na Dolenjskem 7c.
GPS: n45,85869 e15,68979.

5 € 6 €2 Ch €2,50 WC . **Location:** Urban.
Surface: concrete.
Distance: on the spot.

Kamnica 38B1
Gostilna Koblarjev Zaliv, Na otok 20. **GPS**: n46,56560 e15,61908.

20 free, use of a meal desired free. **Surface:** grassy.
01/01-31/12.
Distance: Maribor 2km on the spot on the spot on the spot 2km 300m.
Remarks: Walking and bicycle area along the Drava river to Maribor centre.

Kocevje 38A2
Turistični Komplex Jezero, Trdnjava 3. **GPS**: n45,64421 e14,87140.

3 free. **Location:** Simple, isolated, quiet. **Surface:** asphalted.
01/01-31/12.
Distance: 1km 200m 200m 1km 1km on the spot on the spot.
Remarks: Nature reserve.

Kostanjevica na Krki 38B2
Krška cesta. **GPS**: n45,84891 e15,41795.
5 free. **Surface:** grassy/metalled. 01/01-31/12.
Distance: 300m on the spot on the spot 300m.
Remarks: Along river.

S Krško 38B1
Raceland, Pesje 30. **GPS**: n45,92977 e15,53500.
50 € 12 WC included. **Location:** Rural, isolated, noisy. **Surface:** asphalted.
Distance: on the spot.
Remarks: Parking at Karting.

Krško 38B1
Stadium Matija Gubec, Cesta krških žrtev 130a.
GPS: n45,94691 e15,48832.

30 free. **Surfac:** grassy/gravel. 01/01-31/12.

Krško 38B1

Gostilna Stanislava Pečnik, Gunte 8. **GPS**: n45,98645 e15,46572.

2 free. Su.
Distance: on the spot on the spot on the spot.

Laško 38A1

Thermana Park Laško, Zdraviliška cesta 6.
GPS: n46,16188 e15,23132.

16 € 7-10/pp, dog € 4 Ch included (16x)€ 4/day,16Amp WC **Location:** Urban, simple, central, noisy.
Surface: grasstiles/metalled. 01/01-31/12.
Distance: 700m on the spot 700m on the spot on the spot on the spot on the spot 10km 10km.
Remarks: Max. 24h, check in at reception.

Laško 38A1

Zdraviliške Laško, Zdraviliška cesta 4. **GPS**: n46,15761 e15,23224.

4 € 7-10/pp, dog € 4 Ch included (4x)€ 4/day,16Amp WC **Location:** Urban, simple, central, noisy.
Surface: asphalted. 01/01-31/12.
Distance: 500m on the spot 500m on the spot on the spot on the spot on the spot 10km 10km.

Lendava 38B1

Terme Lendava, Tomsiceve 21A. **GPS**: n46,55396 e16,45813.

90 € 12,50-13,50/pp, dog € 3 Ch € 4 WC € 1/30minutes. **Surface:** asphalted/grassy. 01/01-31/12.
Remarks: Including access spa resort.

Ljutomer 38B1

Gostilna Trnek, Mota 76. **GPS**: n46,55516 e16,21929.

25 guests free Ch included € 3 WC .
Location: Rural, isolated, quiet. **Surface:** grassy/gravel.
01/01-31/12.
Distance: on the spot on the spot on the spot 1km.
Remarks: Use sanitary only during opening hours.

Maribor 38B1

Avtobusna postaja Maribor, Mlinska ulica 1.
GPS: n46,55852 e15,65573.

4 € 10 Ch . **Location:** Noisy. **Surface:** asphalted.
Distance: on the spot fast food on the spot on the spot.
Remarks: Nearby bus station P4, check in at tourist office.

Maribor 38B1

Partizanska cesta 50. **GPS**: n46,56315 e15,65819.
8-17h € 0,50/h, overnight stay and weekend free.
01/01-31/12.
Distance: city centre 1km 200m.
Remarks: At station.

Metlika 38B2

Dependansa sobe Metlika, Cesta bratstra in enotnosti 77.
GPS: n45,64663 e15,31778.

3 € 15 + € 0,64/pp tourist tax Ch included.
Location: Urban, simple, central, quiet. **Surface:** asphalted.
01/01-31/12.
Distance: 100m 1km 1km 100m 100m 100m on the spot on the spot.

Moravske Toplice 38B1

Kamp Moravske Toplice, Kranjčeva ulica 12 .
GPS: n46,67862 e16,22151.

€ 3,20 2 pers. Incl., dog € 3 Ch € 4 .
Surface: grassy/gravel. 01/01-31/12.
Distance: 400m 100m 200m on the spot on the spot.
Remarks: Including access spa resort 3000.

Tourist information Moravske Toplice:
Goričko Regional Park, Ulica ob igrišču 3, www.park-goricko.org. Information centre.

Novo Mesto 38B2

Old Gardening, Skalickega 3. **GPS**: n45,79536 e15,17039.

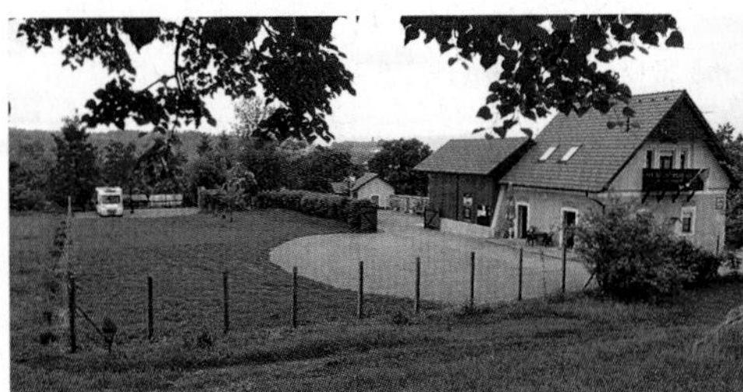

10 € 15 Ch (10x) WC included.
Location: Comfortable, quiet. **Surface:** grassy/gravel.
01/01-31/12 with mucht snowfall.
Distance: 400m 400m 300m 400m on the spot on the spot.

Novo Mesto 38B2

Pri Belokranjucu, Kandijska cesta 63. **GPS**: n45,79947 e15,17865.

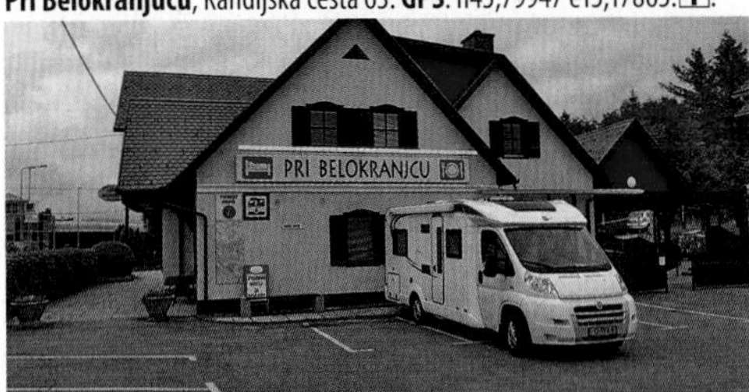

3 € 15 Ch ,16Amp included
Location: Urban, simple, central, noisy. **Surface:** asphalted.
01/01-31/12.
Distance: 400m 5km 400m on the spot 200m on the spot 200m on the spot on the spot.

Obrežje Jug 38B2

OMV Istrabenz. **GPS**: n45,85517 e15,68513.
2 free. **Location:** Motorway, noisy.
Distance: on the spot.
Remarks: Parking petrol station OMV Istrabenz.

Ormož 38B1

Bar Ribnik, Ob ribniku 1. **GPS**: n46,40588 e16,15963.

3 free included. **Location:** Rural. **Surface:** asphalted.
01/01-31/12.
Distance: on the spot on the spot.

Otočec 38B2

Otočec. **GPS**: n45,83794 e15,23821.
40 € 18, 20/06-24/08 € 22 Ch € 3,50 included.
Surface: grassy/gravel. 01/04-30/09.
Distance: 500m on the spot on the spot 500m 500m.
Remarks: Along river.

Pivka 38A2

Park of Military History Pivka, Kolodvorska cesta.
GPS: n45,66812 e14,18779.

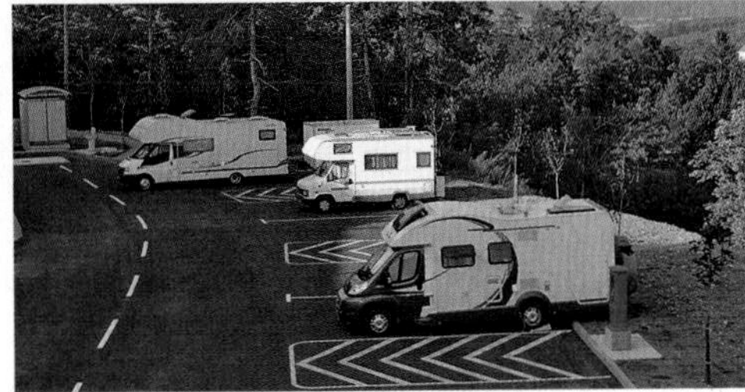

8 € 10 Ch included,at restaurant.
Surface: asphalted. 01/01-31/12.
Distance: 2km on the spot.
Remarks: At museum, video surveillance.

Podbočje 38B2

Turistična kmetija Hribar, Podbočje 36. **GPS**: n45,86190 e15,47110.

SL

5 free. **Surface:** gravel.
Distance: 400m on the spot on the spot on the spot on the spot.

Podčetrtek 38B1

Golf Klub a Podčetrtek Amon, Olimje 24. **GPS:** n46,14400 e15,56493.

20 € 10 + € 1,25/pp tourist tax WC included.
Location: Isolated, quiet. **Surface:** asphalted/gravel.
01/01-31/12 With snow.
Distance: on the spot on the spot on the spot.
Remarks: At golf court, bicycle rental.

Podčetrtek 38B1

Terme Olimia Kamp Natura, Zdravillška cesta 24.
GPS: n46,16529 e15,60522.

15 € 16,50-21,50/pp, dog € 3 Ch €4,20 WC €3.
Surface: metalled. 21/04-30/09.
Distance: on the spot on the spot.
Remarks: Including access spa resort.

Tourist information Podčetrtek:
Sedovška Homestead, Aškercev trg 24, Šmarje pri Jelšah. Traditional farmstead.
Rogatec Open-air Museum, Ptujska cesta 23, Rogatec. Open air museum, 18-20th century. 01/04-31/10 Mo.
Božjepotna Marijina cerkev, Sladka Gora, Šmarje pri Jelšah. Pilgrimage church.
Olimje Monastery and Pharmacy, Olimje 82. Monastery and one of the oldest pharmacies in the world.

Podsmreka 38A2

A2. **GPS:** n45,94805 e14,77065.
5 free free. **Location:** Motorway.
Distance: 100m.
Remarks: Guarded parking petrol station Petrol Podsmereka, highway Novo Mesto-Ljubljana.

Prebold 38A1

Dolina, Dolenja Vas 147. **GPS:** n46,24015 e15,08771.
€ 15,50 Ch WC. 01/01-31/12.
Distance: 200m 200m.

Ptuj 38B1

Terme Ptuj, Pot v toplice 9.
GPS: n46,42109 e15,85585.
20 € 20 + € 1,63/registration + tourist tax Ch (2x),16Amp WC €5/5 included.
Location: Simple. **Surface:** gravel. 01/01-31/12.
Distance: 800m 3km 500m 100m 1km on the spot 25km.

Tourist information Ptuj:
Maribor Tourist Board, Partizanska 47, Maribor, www.maribor-tourism.si. Old city with historical centre.
Mariborski Grad, Maribor. Castle, 15th century, regional museum.
01/04-31/12 Tue-Sa 9-17h, Su 9-14h Mo.
Ptujski Grad. Castle, 11th century with regional museum.
01/05-31/10 9-18h.

Rečica ob Savinji 38A1

Menina. GPS: n46,31167 e14,90917.
€ 18-22 Ch WC. 01/01-31/12.
Distance: on the spot on the spot 300m.

Tourist information Rečica ob Savinji:
Mozirski gaj, Hribernikova 1, Mozirje. Botanical garden. 01/04-31/10 9-19h.
Musej Premogovništva, Stari jašek - Koroška cesta, Velenje. Coal mining museum.

Rogla 38B1

Rogla. **GPS:** n46,45259 e15,33117.

€ 12 Ch included. **Surface:** gravel.
Distance: Zreče 10km 200m on the spot on the spot on the spot on the spot.
Remarks: Altitude 1517m.

Sevnica 38B1

Cesta na Grad. **GPS:** n46,00862 e15,31527.
free. **Surface:** gravel. 01/01-31/12.
Distance: 500m 500m.
Remarks: Next to castle.

Slovenj Gradec 38A1

Camperstop Slovenj Gradec, Ozare 18.
GPS: n46,51418 e15,07678.

6 € 5 Ch (4x) included. **Location:** Comfortable, quiet.
01/01-31/12.

Distance: 500m 500m 500m on the spot.
Remarks: At youth hostel.

Solcava 38A1

Park Logarska Dolina, Logarska Dolina 9.
GPS: n46,41999 e14,64555.

20 € 10. **Location:** Rural, simple, isolated, quiet.
Surface: grassy/gravel. 01/01-31/12.
Distance: 5km on the spot 5km 5km on the spot on the spot on the spot on the spot.
Remarks: Entrance park € 7/pp.

Stahovica 38A1

Pri Jurju, Kamniska Bistrica 5. **GPS:** n46,32685 e14,58706.

20 € 5 Ch (20x)€2/day,16Amp WC included €5/day.
Location: Rural, simple, isolated, quiet. **Surface:** grassy.
01/01-31/12.
Distance: 8km 6km on the spot 8km 300m on the spot on the spot 3km 3km.

Tepanje 38B1

A1. **GPS:** n46,34776 e15,48695.
5 free free. **Location:** Motorway, noisy.
Distance: on the spot.
Remarks: Guarded parking petrol station Petrol Tepanje I, on both sides of the highway Maribor-Ljubljana.

Visnja Gora 38A1

Mestno kopališče, Kopaliska Ulica 25.
GPS: n45,95268 e14,75097.

20 free (1x) WC free. **Location:** Rural, simple, isolated, quiet. **Surface:** asphalted/gravel. 01/01-31/12.
Distance: on the spot 1,7km 1km 200m on the spot on the spot 10km 10km.
Remarks: Check in at swimming pool, service during opening hours.

Visnja Gora 38A1

PrinceSport&Fun Center, Kopališka ulica 27.
GPS: n45,95207 e14,75201.
€ 10 WC included. **Surface:** grassy/gravel.
01/01-31/12.

Žalec 38A1

Camperstop Žalec, Mestni trg. **GPS:** n46,25418 e15,16274.

4 free Ch (4x)free,16Amp. **Location:** Urban, simple,

SL

central, quiet. **Surface:** metalled.
01/01-31/12.
Distance: 500m 100m 500m 500m on the spot on the spot.
Remarks: At sports park, caution key service € 20 at hotel.

S Zdole 38B1

Etnoart tourism Špiler, Kostanjek 18. **GPS**: n46,01018 e15,54409.

5 . **Surface:** grassy.
Distance: on the spot.

S Zdole 38B1

Gostilna pri Dularju, Kostanjek 20. **GPS**: n46,00975 e15,54155.

10 Ch (3x). **Location:** Rural, quiet.

S Zgornje Jezersko 38A1

Camperstop Stara Pošta, Zgornje Jezersko 124.
GPS: n46,40240 e14,50673.

9 € 12 Ch (16x)€3/24h WC €4 included.
Location: Rural, luxurious, quiet. **Surface:** grassy. 01/04-30/09.
Distance: 1km 1km 1km 1km 1km 100m on the spot on the spot.

S Zgornje Jezersko 38A1

Camperstop Šenkova Domačija, Zgornje Jezersko 12.
GPS: n46,40792 e14,51769.

5 € 10, Jul/Aug € 15 Ch (5x)€3/night WC €3 included.
Location: Rural, quiet. **Surface:** gravel/metalled. 01/01-31/12.
Distance: 2km 300m 300m 300m 2km 100m on the spot on the spot on the spot.

S Zreče 38B1

Thermal Spa, Cesta na Roglo 15. **GPS**: n46,37096 e15,39021.

4 € 10 + € 1,30/pp tourist tax included.
Surface: asphalted.
Distance: 300m 300m on the spot 300m.
Remarks: Check in at hotel, 20% reduction swimming pool.

SL

INDEX

INDEX

INDEX